ISBN 978-1-5277-9184-8
PIBN 10896494

THE

COUNTY FAMILIES

OF

THE UNITED KINGDOM

OR

ROYAL MANUAL OF THE TITLED AND UNTITLED ARISTOCRACY
OF GREAT BRITAIN AND IRELAND.

CONTAINING A BRIEF NOTICE OF

THE DESCENT, BIRTH, MARRIAGE, EDUCATION, AND APPOINTMENTS OF EACH PERSON, HIS
HEIR APPARENT OR PRESUMPTIVE, AS ALSO A RECORD OF THE OFFICES WHICH HE
HAS HITHERTO HELD; TOGETHER WITH HIS TOWN ADDRESS
AND COUNTRY RESIDENCE.

BY

EDWARD WALFORD, M.A.

LATE SCHOLAR OF BALLIOL COLLEGE, OXFORD, AND FELLOW OF THE GENEALOGICAL
AND HISTORICAL SOCIETY OF GREAT BRITAIN.

FOURTH EDITION, GREATLY ENLARGED.

LONDON:
ROBERT HARDWICKE, 192 PICCADILLY.
1868.

F 0845. 947

L   1800526

LABOUCHERE, Henry, Esq., late of Broome Hall, Surrey.

Elder son of the late John Labouchere, Esq., of Broome Hall (who was a J.P. and D.L. for Surrey), by Mary, dau. of James Du Pré, Esq., of Wilton Park, Bucks; *b.* 1831; *s.* 1863. Is Patron of 2 livings; was M.P. for Windsor 1865-6, elected M.P. for Middlesex 1867. —*Reform Club*, s.w.; *The Albany*, w.

LABOUCHERE. (See under *Taunton, Lord*.)

LACAITA, Sir James Philip, K.C.M.G. (cr. 1861).

Only son of the late Diego Lacaita.; *b.* 1814 ; *m.* 1852 Maria Clavering, eldest dau. of the late Sir Thomas Gibson-Carmichael, Bart. (she *d.* 1853). Educated at the University of Naples, and called to the Neapolitan Bar 1836 ; was formerly in civil employ in the Ionian Islands.—27, *Duke Street*, s.w.

LACON, Sir Edmund Henry Knowles, Bart., of Ormesby, Norfolk (cr. 1818).

Eldest son of the late Sir Edmund Knowles Lacon, Bart., by Eliza Dixon, dau. of Thomas Beecroft, Esq., of Saxethorpe Hall, Norfolk ; *b.* 1807 ; *s.* as 3rd Bart. 1839 ; *m.* 1839 Eliza Georgina, dau. of James Esdaile Hammet, Esq., of Battersea, Surrey. Educated at Eton and Emmanuel Coll., Cambridge (B.A. 1828); is a J.P. and D.L. for Norfolk, a Magistrate for Suffolk, Lieut.-Col. Commanding E. Norfolk Militia, and Major E. Norfolk Volunteer Artillery; was M.P. for Yarmouth 1852-7, and 1859-68.— *Ormesby, Gt. Yarmouth ; Union, Junior United Service, and Carlton Clubs,* s.w.

Heir, his son Edmund Broughton Knowles, a Magistrate for Norfolk, late of the 23rd Foot, *b.* 1842 ; *m.* 1868 Henrietta Julia, eldest dau. of Robert John Harvey Harvey, Esq., of Bracondale, Norfolk.

LACY, Henry Charles, Esq., of Withdeane, Sussex.

Second son of the late James Lacy, Esq., of Salisbury, by Mary, dau. of Charles Bemister, Esq., of Wimborne, Dorset; *b.* 1790; *m.* 1813 Susannah, dau. of John Jeboult, Esq., of Salisbury, and has surviving issue,

*Three daughters.

Mr. Lacy, who is a Magistrate for cos. Lancaster and Surrey, and a Director of the London and South-Western Railway, was M.P. for Bodmin 1847-52.—*Withdeane Hall, Brighton.*

LADE, John Pryce, Esq., of Nash Court and Brenley House, Kent.

Only son of the late John Holyday Lade, Esq., of Boughton House, by Eliza, dau. of David Evors, Esq., and niece of Sir John Powel Pryce, Bart.; *b.* 18—; Educated at St. John's Coll., Cambridge; is a J.P. and D.L. for Kent, and late Major East Kent Militia.—*Nash Court, Boughton-under-Blean, and Brenley House, Faversham ; Union Club,* s.w.

+LAFFAN, Capt. Robert.

Second son of John Laffan, Esq., of Limerick, Supervisor of Excise, and nephew of the late Sir Joseph De Courcy Laffan, Bart. (*ext.*) ; *b.* 1821 ; *m.* 1852 Emma, dau. of William Norsworthy, Esq., of Oxford Terrace, London. Educated at the Royal Military Academy, Woolwich ; is a Capt. Royal Engineers ; was Inspector of Railways, 1847-52; M.P. for St. Ives 1852-7.—*Army and Navy Club,* s.w.

LAIDLAY, John Watson, Esq., of Seacliff, Haddingtonshire, and Drumore, Argyllshire.

Son of the late J. Laidlay, Esq.; *b.* 18—; is a Magistrate for co. Haddington, and Lord of the Barony of Seacliff.—*Seacliff House, North Berwick, N.B.*

LAING, Samuel, Esq., of Hordle House, Hants.

Son of the late Samuel Laing, Esq., of Papdale, co. Orkney, by Agnes, youngest dau. of John Kelly, Esq., of Hythe ; *b.* 1810; *m.* 1841 Mary, dau. of Capt. Cowan, R.N. Educated at Harrow and St. John's Coll., Cambridge (B.A. 1832); was afterwards Fellow and Tutor of his College; is a J.P. and D.L. for the Isle of Orkney, and Lord of the Manor of Hordle ; has been a Railway Commissioner, Chairman of the Brighton Railway, &c.; was M.P. for Wick, &c., 1852-7, and 1859-61, re-elected 1865; was Chancellor of the Exchequer in India 1860-66.—*Hordle House, Lymington ; Reform Club,* s.w.

LAIRD, David, Esq., of Strathmartine, Forfarshire.

Eldest son of the late William Butler Laird, Esq., by Elizabeth, dau. of George Lloyd, Esq., of Manchester; *b.* 1809 ; *s.* his grandfather, Rear-Admiral D. Laird, 1812 ; *m.* 1833 Margaret, youngest dau. of John Corse Scott, Esq., of Sinton, co. Roxburgh, and by her, who *d.* 1865, has, with other issue,

* Catherine.

Mr. Laird, who was educated at the High School and Military Academy, Edinburgh, is a J.P. and D.L. for co. Forfar, Lord of the Barony of Strathmartine, and Lieut.-Col. Commandant Forfar and Kincardine Mil. Artillery ; formerly Lieut. 72nd Highlanders.—*Strathmartine, Dundee; Belmont Castle, Aleigle, Forfarshire, N.B.*

LAIRD, John, Esq., of Birkenhead, Cheshire.

Eldest son of the late William Laird, Esq., of Birkenhead, and brother of the late M'Gregor Laird, Esq., the African explorer and founder of steam navigation with Africa ; *b.* 1805 ; *m.* 1829 Elizabeth, 3rd dau. of Nicholas Hurry, Esq., of Liverpool, and has issue. Mr. Laird is a J.P. and D.L. for co. Chester. Was head of the firm of Laird and Sons, Iron-Shipbuilders, until 1861 ; has been an active promoter of the docks and other public works at Birkenhead, and is one of the four Government Nominees at the Mersey Dock and Harbour Board ; elected M.P. for Birkenhead 1861.—*Hamilton Square, Birkenhead ; Conservative and Carlton Clubs,* s.w.

LAKE, Sir Atwell King, Bart. (cr. 1711).

Eldest son of the late Sir James Samuel Lake, Bart., of Edmonton, Middlesex, by Anne Marla, dau. of the late Vice-Admiral Sir Richard King, Bart.; *b.* 1834 ; *s.* as 6th Bart. 1846. Late Lieut. 104th Foot; formerly Lieut. 2nd Bengal European Fusiliers, and Acting Adjutant 4th Irregular Cavalry, Delhi.

LAKEMAN, Sir Stephen Bartlett, Knt. (cr. 1853).

Son of the late Stephen Lakeman, Esq., of Grange-Wood Hall, by Mary, dau. of — Preston, Esq.; *b.* 1823; *m.* 1856 the Princess Marie de Philippesco. Educated at the Military Coll. of La Flèche, in France; is Lieut.-

General in the Turkish service; late in command of the Waterkloof Rangers; served with distinction in the Kaffir war 1852, and in the Danubian campaign 1854-5.

+ **LAKES**, ROBERT GOULD, Esq., of Trevarrick, Cornwall.
Son of the late Henry Lakes, Esq., of Trevarrick, by a dau. of — Gould, Esq.; *b.* 18—. Is; a Magistrate for Cornwall—*Trevarrick House, St. Austell, Cornwall.*

LAKIN, the Rev. JOHN MARSH, of Gilmorton, Leicestershire.
Younger son of the late John Lakin, Esq., of Twycross, co. Leicester, by Ann Cooper, dau. of Christopher Marsh, Esq., of Bath; *b.* 1816; *m.* 1844 Barbara Louisa, dau. of William Smallwood, Esq., of Sheldon House, co. Warwick, and has issue,
* Three daughters.

Mr. Lakin was educated at Worcester Coll., Oxford (B.A. 1839, M.A. 1842); is a Rural Dean in the Diocese of Peterborough, and a Magistrate for co. Leicester, and Patron of 1 living; he was formerly Incumbent of Ber-row, in the county of Worcester—*Gilmorton Rectory, Lutterworth.*

LALOR, RICHARD, Esq., Tenakill, Queen's Co.
Son of the late Patrick Lalor, Esq., J.P., of Tenakill (who was M.P. for Queen's Co. 1833-4); by Anne, dau. of Patrick Dillon, Esq., of Shane, Queen's Co.; *b.* 1823; *s.* 1856; *m.* 1852 Margaret, dau. of Mr. Michael Dunne, of Mountrath. Is a Magistrate for Queen's Co. This family were formerly known as the O'Lalors of Leix, Queen's Co.—*Tenakill, Abbeyleix, Queen's Co.*

+ **LALOR**, THOMAS, Esq., of Cregg, co. Tipperary.
Son of the late Thomas Edmund Lalor, Esq., J.P. and D.L., of Cregg, by Anne, dau. of Richard Power, Esq., of Carrick-on-Suir; *b.* 18—; *s.* 1847. Is a J.P. and D.L. for co. Tipperary (High Sheriff 1860), and a Magistrate for co. Kilkenny.—*Cregg, Carrick-on-Suir.*

LALOR. (See *Power Lalor*.)

LAMB, Sir ARCHIBALD, Bart., of Beauport, Sussex.
Elder son of the late Charles James Savile Montgomerie Lamb, Esq. (who *d.* 1856), by Anna Charlotte, dau. of Arthur Grey, Esq., of Bersted, Sussex; *b.* 1845; *s.* his grandfather as 3rd Bart. 1860. Educated at Eton and Trinity Coll. Cambridge; is Cornet 2nd Life Guards. Lord of the Manor of Beauport, &c., and Patron of 2 livings—*Beauport, Battle.*
Heir Pres., his brother Charles Anthony, *b.* (posthumous) 1857.

LAMB, RICHARD WESTBROOK, Esq., of West Denton, co. Northumberland.
Second, but eldest surviving son of the late Joseph Lamb, Esq., J.P. and D.L., of West Denton and Temon, by Amelia Mary. dau. of Joseph Michael, Esq., of Stamford, co. Lincoln; *b.* 1820; *s.* 1860; *m.* 1866 Georgiana Elizabeth, dau. of the late Stephen Eaton, Esq., of Ketton Hall, co. Rutland, and by her, who *d.* 1868, has, with other issue,
* Joseph John Talbot, *b.* 1857.

Mr. Lamb is a Dep. Lieut. for co. Durham.—*West Denton, Newcastle-upon-Tyne.*

LAMB, WILLIAM ANDREW, Esq., of Kilcoleman Park, co. Cork.
Eldest son of the late Vincent Lamb, Esq., of Kilcoleman Park, by Anna Maria, dau. of John Andrews, Esq., of Ratheny House, King's Co.; *b.* 1793; *s.* 1817; *m.*
558

1821 Eliza, dau. of Walter Atkin, Esq., of Leddington, co. Cork, and has, with other issue,
* Vincent, in Holy Orders, *b.* 1826.

Mr. Lamb, who is a Magistrate for co. Cork, was Sheriff and Mayor of Youghal 1832 and 1836.—*Kilcoleman Park, Bandon, co. Cork.*

LAMBARDE, MULTON, Esq., of Beechmont, Kent.
Eldest son of the late William Lambarde, Esq., J.P. and D.L. of Beechmont, by Harriet Elizabeth, 5th dau. of the late Sir James Naesmyth, Bart., of Posso, co. Peebles; *b.* 1821; *s.* 1866; *m.* 1848 Teresa Livesay, dau. of Edmund Turton, Esq., of Brasted Park, Kent, and has, with other issue,
* John Bell William Edmund, *b.* 1850.

Mr. Lambarde is a Magistrate for Kent, and Patron of 2 livings.—*Beechmont, Sevenoaks.*

LAMBART, GUSTAVUS WILLIAM, Esq., of Beau Parc, co. Meath.
Eldest son of the late Gustavus Lambart, Esq., of Beau Parc, by Anna Butler, dau. of the late Sir John Stevenson, of Dublin; *b.* 1814; *s.* 1849; *m.* 1847 Lady Frances Caroline Maria, 2nd dau. of Francis, 2nd Marquis of Conyngham, K.P., and has, with other issue,
* Gustavus William Francis, *b.* 1848.

Mr. Lambart, who was educated at Trinity Coll., Dublin (B.A. 1835), is a Magistrate for cos. Meath and Westmeath; he was formerly Major in the Royal Meath Militia, and was State Steward to the Lord-Lieutenant of Ireland 1858-9.—*Beau Parc, Slane, co. Meath; Kildare Street Club, Dublin.*

LAMBART. (See under *Cavan, Earl of*.)

LAMBERT, Sir HENRY EDWARD FRANCIS, Bart., of Malvern, Worcestershire (cr. 1710).
Eldest son of the late Sir Henry John Lambert, of Aston House, Oxon, by Anna Maria, youngest dau. of the late Hon. Edward Foley, of Stoke Edith Park co. Hereford; *b.* 1822; *s.* as 6th Bart. 1858; *m.* 1860 Eliza Catherine, dau. of Lionel Charles Hervey, Esq. Educated at Eton and Balliol Coll., Oxford (B.A. 1843, M.A. 1847); is a J.P. and D.L. for cos. Worcester and Oxon, and a Magistrate for cos. Hereford and Bucks.—*The Lodge, Great Malvern.*
Heir, his son Henry Foley, *b.* 1851.

LAMBERT, Sir GEORGE ROBERT, G.C.B. (cr. 1853).
Son of the late Capt. Robert Lambert, R.N., by Catherine, dau. of Matthew Byndlass, Esq.; *b.* 1795; *m.* 1st 1822 Katherine, dau. of the Rev. Thomas Cobb, Rector of Ightham and Vicar of Sittingbourne, Kent, and Prebendary of Chichester; 2nd 1864 Katharine, widow of Col. J. Roger Palmer, and has by the former, with other issue,
* Rowley, Capt. R.N., *b.* 1824; *m.* 1863 Helen Elizabeth, dau. of James Campbell, Esq.

Sir G. R. Lambert, who entered the Navy in 1809, is a Magistrate for Surrey, and an Admiral on the reserved list.—*Norbiton Place, Kingston-on-Thames, s.w.*

LAMBERT, ALEXANDER CLENDINING, Esq., of Brook Hill, co. Mayo.
Eldest surviving son of the late Joseph Lambert, Esq., of Brook Hill, by Mary, dau. of the Rev. Alexander Clendining, D.D., Rector of Westport, co. Mayo; *b.* 1808; *s.* 1855; *m.* 1848 Emma Mary, dau. of Guy Lenox Prendergast, Esq., and has, with other issue,
* Joseph Alexander, *b.* 1858.

Mr. Lambert, who is a Magistrate for co. Galway, and a Dep. Lieut. for co. Mayo, was appointed Treasurer

for co. Mayo in 1836.—*Brook Hill, Claremorris, co. Mayo ; Seafield House, Monkstown, co. Dublin ; Kildare Street and United Service Clubs, Dublin.*

LAMBERT, HENRY, Esq., of Carnagh, co. Wexford.
Eldest son of the late Henry Lambert, Esq., D.L., of Carnagh (who was M.P. for co. Wexford 1833–4), by Katherine, dau. of the late William Talbot, Esq., of Castle Talbot, co. Wexford ; *b.* 1836 ; *s.* 1861 ; *m.* 186—Miss ———, and has issue,
  • A son, *b.* 1866.
Mr. Lambert is a Magistrate for co. Wexford.—*Carnagh, New Cross, co. Wexford.*

⁴ **LAMBERT, HENRY**, Esq., of Tan y Graig, Anglesey.
Son of the late H. Lambert, Esq.; *b.* 18—. Was High Sheriff of Anglesey 1868.—*Tan y Graig, Anglesey.*

LAMBERT, WALTER MACCLELLAN, Esq., of Waterdale, co. Galway.
Eldest son of the late James Staunton Lambert, Esq., of Waterdale (who was M.P. for co. Galway 1826–33), by the Hon. Camden Elizabeth, only dau. and heir of Camden Gray, 9th and last Lord Kircudbright (*ext.*); *b.* 1833 ; *s.* 1867. Late Capt. 41st Regt. This family was formerly of Creg Clare, co. Galway.—*Waterdale, Galway ; Camden Place, Bath.*
  Heir Pres. his brother Thomas Camden, Capt. 29th Regt.; *b.* 1841.

LAMBERT, JOHN, Esq., of Garratt's Hall, Surrey.
Only surviving son of the late John Lambert, Esq., of Banstead (who *d.* 1850); *b.* 1813 ; *s.* his brother Daniel 1859 ; *m.* 1848 Harriet Melville, dau. of Richard Cooper, Esq., and has, with other issue,
  • John Wilmot, *b.* 1851.
Mr. Lambert is a Magistrate for Surrey. This family have been seated in Surrey since *temp.* Edward II.—*Garratt's Hall, Banstead, Epsom.*

+**LAMBERT, JOHN WALTER HENRY**, Esq., of Aggard, co. Galway.
Son of the late Thomas Lambert, Esq., of Aggard, by Lydia, dau. of — Fetherstonhaugh, Esq.; *b.* 1811 ; *m.* 1834 Anne, dau. of William Fetherstonhaugh, Esq., of Derrahing, co. Galway, and has, with other issue,
  • Thomas Walter, *b.* 1840.
Mr. Lambert is a Magistrate for co. Galway (High Sheriff 1850).—*Aggard, Craughwell, co. Galway.*

LAMBERT, NATHANIEL GRACE, Esq., of Denham Court, Bucks.
Second son of the late Richard Lambert, Esq., of Newcastle-on-Tyne, by Achsah, dau. of Nathaniel Grace, Esq.; *b.* 1811 ; *m.* 1843 Mary Ann, dau. of Thomas Wright Richards, Esq., of Rushden, co. Northampton, and has issue two daughters. Mr. Lambert is a Magistrate for Bucks (High Sheriff 1865), and Capt. Commandant Taplow Yeomanry.—*Denham Court, Uxbridge.*

LAMBERT, THOMAS EYRE, Esq., of Castle Lambert, co. Galway.
Eldest son of the late Walter Lambert, Esq., J.P., of Castle Lambert (who was High Sheriff of co. Galway 1827), by Anne, dau. of Giles Eyre, Esq.; *b.* 1820 ; *s.* 1867 ; *m.* 1850 Sarah, 3rd dau. of John Wilson Trousdell, Esq., of Fort House, co. Clare, and grand-dau. of William Blakeney Persse, Esq., of Athenry, co. Galway. Is a Magistrate for co. Galway, and a Capt. in the Army retired; was formerly Capt. 74th Highlanders.—*Castle Lambert, Athenry, co. Galway.*
  Heir Pres. his brother Giles Eyre, *b.* 1822 ; *m.* 1850 Mary, only child of Francis Rea, Esq., of Richview, co. Dublin.

LAMBERT, the Rev. WILLIAM, of Woodmansterne, Surrey.
Eldest son of the late William Lambert, Esq., J.P., of Woodmansterne (formerly of the H.E.I.C.'s Bengal Service), by Mary Anne, dau. of Col. Denniss ; *b.* 1814 ; *s.* 1860 ; *m.* 1846 Margaret, dau. of Major Fisher, of Aberdeen; and has, with other issue,
  • William, *b.* 1855.
Mr. Lambert, who was educated at Exeter Coll., Oxford (B.A. 1836, M.A. 1841), is Perpetual Curate of Pennington, Hants.—*Woodmansterne, Epsom ; Pennington Parsonage, Lymington, Hants.*

LAMBERT, WILLIAM CHARLES, Esq., of Knowle, Dorset.
Fourth and only surviving son of the late Robert Lambert, Esq., of Winterborne Stepleton, Dorset, by Sibella, dau. of James Green, Esq., of Denbury, Devon; *b.* 1797 ; *m.* 1st 1829 Georgiana Charlotte, 3rd dau. of the late General Sir Amos Norcot ; 2nd 1844 Agnes Grove, eldest dau. of William Helyar, Esq., of Coker Court, Somerset, and Sedghill, Wilts. Educated at Winchester and Trinity Coll., Cambridge (B.A. 1820, M.A. 1828); called to the Bar at the Middle Temple, 1824 ; is a J.P. and D.L. for Dorset and a Magistrate for Somerset.—*Knowle, Wimborne ; Misterton Manor, Crewkerne; Athenæum Club, s.w.*

LAMBTON, HEDWORTH, Esq., of Murton House, co. Durham.
Third son of the late William Henry Lambton, Esq., of Lambton, by Lady Anne Barbara Frances, dau. of George, 4th Earl of Jersey, and brother of John George, 1st Earl of Durham ; *b.* 1797 ; *m.* 1835 Anna, eldest dau. of the late Gervais Parker Bushe, Esq., of Kilfane, co. Kilkenny (she *d.* 1843). Is a Dep.-Lieut. for co. Durham; was M.P. for N. Durham 1832–47.—*Murton House, Durham ; 17, Chesham Place, s.w.*

+**LAMBTON, Lieut.-Col. FRANCIS**, of Biddick Hill, co. Durham.
Son of the late William Henry Lambton, Esq., of Biddick Hill, by Henrietta, 2nd dau. of the late Cuthbert Ellison, Esq., M.P., of Hepburn, co. Durham; *b.* 1826 ; *s.* 1866 ; *m.* 1866 Lady Victoria Alexandrina Elizabeth, eldest dau. of John Frederick, 2nd Earl of Cawdor. Educated at Eton; is Lord of the Manor of Biddick, and a Capt. and Lieut.-Col. Scots Fusilier Guards.—*Biddick Hall, Newbiggin, co. Durham.*

LAMBTON. (See under *Durham, Earl of.*)

LAMING, JAMES, Esq., of Birchington, Kent.
Second but eldest surviving son of the late James Laming, Esq., of Birchington Hall (who *d.* 1864), by Ann, dau. of Benjamin Noakes, Esq.; *b.* 1818 ; *s.* his brother 1866 ; *m.* 1851 Frances, 2nd dau. of R. M'Cabe, Esq., of Kensington Gardens, London. This family has been located for three centuries in the Isle of Thanet.—*Birchington Hall, Margate ; The Manor House, Richmond, s.w.*

LAMONT, JAMES, Esq., of Knockdow, Argyllshire.
Eldest son of the late Alexander Lamont, Esq., J.P. and D.L., of Knockdow (many years Lieut.-Col. Bute-shire Militia), by Jane, dau. of Alexander Chrystie, Esq., of Balchrystie, co. Fife ; *b.* 1830 ; *s.* 1861 ; *m.* 1868 Adelaide Eliza, elder surviving dau. of Sir George Wm. Denys, Bart. Educated at Rugby; is a Magistrate for co. Argyll, a Dep.-Lieut for co. Bute, F.G.S. and F.R.G.S., and author of 'Seasons with the Seahorses;' elected M.P. for co. Bute 1865.—*Knockdow, Innellan, N.B.; Brooks's and Arthur's Clubs, s.w.*
  Heir Pres. his cousin Humphrey Lamont Colquhoun, Capt. 77th Foot, *b.* 1836.

LAMONT, John Henry, Esq., of Lamont, Argyllshire.
Eldest son of the late Archibald James Lamont, Esq., J.P. and D.L., of Lamont, by his 2nd wife Harriet, dau. of the late Col. Alexander Campbell, of Possil (she remarried 1864 the Rev. Charles B. Coney); *b.* 1854; *s.* 1862. Is Lord of the Barony of Lamout and Patron of 1 living.—*Lamont, Greenock, N.B.*

Heir Pres., his brother Celestine Norman, *b.* 1859.

LAMPET, Edward, Esq., of Great Bardfield, Essex.
Only son of the late Rev. Barrett Edward Lampet, Vicar and Patron of Great Bardfield, and a Magistrate for Essex, by Rose, dau. of William Cade Key, Esq., of Hampstead; *b.* 1841; *s.* 1867. Is Lord of the Manor of Great Bardfield, and Patron of that living.—*Great Bardfield, Braintree, Essex.*

LAMPLUGH-RAPER, the late Henry Raper, Esq., of Lamplugh Hall, Cumberland.
Younger son of the late John Raper, Esq., of Aberford, co. York (who *d.* 1824), by Katharine, dau. of the late Rev. Godfrey Wolley; *b.* 1795; *s.* his brother 1867, and *d.* 1867. He assumed the additional name of Lamplugh, by Royal licence, in 1825, under the will of his relative.—*Lamplugh Hall, Cockermouth.*

LAMPSON, Sir Curtis Miranda, Bart., of Rowfant, Sussex (cr. 1866).
Fourth and youngest son of the late William Lampson, Esq., of New Haven, Vermont, U. S., by Rachel, dau. of George Powell, Esq., of Lainsborough, Massachusetts, U.S.; *b.* 1806; *m.* 1827 Jane Walter, dau. of Gibbs Sibley, Esq., of Sutton, Massachusetts, U.S. Is a Merchant in London; late Deputy Chairman of the Atlantic Telegraph Company; he became a naturalised British subject in 1848.—*Rowfant, Worth, Sussex; 80, Eaton Square, w.*

Heir, his son, George Curtis, *b.* 1833.

L'AMY, John Ramsay, Esq., of Dunkenny, Forfarshire.
Eldest son of the late James L'Amy, Esq., of Dunkenny, by Mary, dau. of Joseph Carson, Esq., M.D., of Philadelphia, U.S.; *b.* 1813; *s.* 1854; *m.* 1845 Mary Riche Macleod, only dau. of the late William Mitchell Innes, Esq., of Ayton, N.B., and has, with other surviving issue,

   • William, *b.* 1850.

Mr. L'Amy is a J.P. and D.L. for co. Forfar.—*Dunkenny, Forfar, N.B.; Netherbyres, Ayton, Berwickshire, N.B.; New Club, Edinburgh; Junior United Service Club, s.w.*

+LANCASTER-LUCAS, Samuel Lucas, Esq., of Wateringbury House, Kent.
Eldest son of the late — Lancaster, Esq., of Wateringbury House, by Mary, dau. and heir of the late Alderman Lucas, of Wateringbury Place; *b.* 181-; *m.* 1848 Mary, 3rd dau. of the late Hon. and Rev. William Eden, Canon of Canterbury, and the Baroness Grey de Ruthyn, and has issue. Mr. Lancaster-Lucas, who is a Magistrate for Kent, and Lord of the Manor of Wateringbury, assumed the additional name of Lucas after his maternal grandfather.—*Wateringbury Place, Maidstone.*

LANDOR, Arnold Savage, Esq., of Llanthony Abbey, Monmouthshire.
Eldest son of the late Walter Savage Landor, Esq., of Ipsley Court, co. Warwick (who *d.* 1864), by Julia, dau. of Mons. Thuilliero (Baron de Nieuveville in France); *b.* 1818. This family were formerly resident in Staf-

560

fordshire, where they held property for many generations.—*Llanthony Abbey, Abergavenny; Ipsley Court, Redditch, Residence: Florence, Italy.*

LANDOR, Miss, of Tachbrooke, Warwickshire.
Elizabeth Sophia, eldest dau. of the late Rev. Charles Savage Landor, Rector of Colton, co. Stafford (who *d.* 1849), by Catherine, only child of the late Joseph Wilson, Esq., of Marston, Montgomery, co. Derby; *s.* her uncle, H. E. Landor, Esq., of Tachbrooke, 1866; which was purchased *temp.* Edward IV. by Thomas Savage.—*Tachbrooke, Leamington.*

Heir Pres., her uncle the Rev. Robert Eyres Landor (whom see)

LANDOR, the Rev. Robert Eyres, of Whitnash, Warwickshire.
Only surviving son of the late Walter Landor, Esq., of Ipsley Court, co. Warwick, and of Rugeley, co. Stafford (who *d.* 1805), by his 2nd wife Elizabeth, eldest dau. of Charles Savage, Esq., of Tachbrooke, and brother of the late Walter Savage Landor, Esq.; *b.* 1781. Educated at Worcester Coll., Oxford (B A. 1801, M.A. 1804); is Rector and Patron of Birlingham, co. Worcester, and Lord of the Manor of Whitnash, which was purchased *temp.* Edward IV. by Thomas Savage.— *Whitnash, Leamington; Birlingham Rectory, Pershore.*

LANDSEER, Sir Edwin, Knt. (cr. 1850).
Youngest son of the late John Landseer, Esq., Associate Engraver to the Royal Academy; *b.* 1803. Elected an Associate of the Royal Academy 1827; became a Royal Academician in 1830; is a celebrated animal painter.—*1, St. John's Wood Road, N.W.*

LANE, Charles, Esq., of Badgemore, Oxfordshire.
Only son of the late Thomas Lane, Esq. (who *d.* 1822), by Sarah Charlotte, dau. of John Williams, Esq.; *b.* 1792; *m.* 1824 Emily Maria, dau. of the late John Thornhill, Esq., and has, with other issue,

   • Charles Powlett, a Major in the Army and Capt. 21st Hussars, V.C.: *b.* 1828; *m.* 1860 Caroline, dau. of the late G. Lucy, Esq., of Charlecote Park, co. Warwick (she *d.* 1864).

Mr. Lane, who was called to the Bar at the Inner Temple 1825, is a Magistrate for Oxon. This family are descended from the Lanes of Northamptonshire.—*Badgemore, Henley-on-Thames.*

LANE, Henry Charles, Esq., of Middleton, Sussex.
Eldest son of the late Henry Thomas Lane, Esq., of Middleton House, by Jane Rachel, dau. of Charles Lambert, Esq.; *b.* 1832; *s.* 1834; *m.* 1860 Catherine, youngest dau. of the Rev. Anthony L. Lambert, Rector of Chilbolton, Hants. Educated at Eton and Ch. Ch., Oxford; is a Magistrate for Sussex, Lord of the Manors of Newick, Streat, Middleton, and Westmeston, and Patron of one living; was formerly Lieut. 2nd Life Guards.—*Middleton House, Westmeston, Hurstpierpoint; Arthur's Club, s.w.*

LANE, John Newton, Esq., of King's Bromley Manor, Staffordshire.
Eldest son of the late John Lane, Esq., of King's Bromley, by Sarah, dau. of Thomas Lloyd, Esq., of Wyle Cop, Shrewsbury; *b.* 1800; *s.* 1824; *m.* 1828 the Hon. Agnes, 2nd dau. of William, 2nd Lord Bagot, and has, with other issue,

   • John Henry Bagot, Capt. Coldstream Guards; *b.* 1829; *m.* 1864 Susan Anne, dau. of Henry William Vincent, Esq., and has issue 2 daughters.

Mr. Lane, who was educated at St. John's Coll., Cambridge, is a J.P. and D.L. for co. Stafford, Lord of the Manor of King's Bromley, and Joint Patron of 3 livings.—*King's Bromley, Lichfield; 7, Grafton Street, w.*

LANE, ROBERT, Esq., of Ryelands, Hereford-shire.

Eldest son of the late Robert Lane, Esq., of Ryelands, by Anne, dau. of Peter Symons, Esq., of Plymouth ; *b.* 1785; *s.* 1816; *m.* 1813 Anne, dau. of John Livesey, Esq., of Coppul Hall, co. Lancaster, and has, with other issue,

* Theophilus William, J.P. and D.L. for co. Hereford ; *b.* 1817 ; *m.* 1848 Emily, dau. of Charles Bowen, Esq., of Kilna Court, Queen's Co., Ireland.

Mr. Lane, is a J.P. and D.L. for co. Hereford (High Sheriff 1811).—*Ryelands, Leominster.*

LANE, THOMAS, Esq., of Kingsnorton, Worcestershire.

Only son of Joseph Lane, Esq., of Birmingham, by Sarah, dau. of the late Richard Swinburn, Esq., of Yardley; *b.* 1820 ; *m.* 1843 Anne, 2nd dau. of Charles Shaw, Esq., of Birmingham, and has, with other issue,

* Charles Pelham, *b.* 1851.

Mr. Lane is a Magistrate for co. Worcester, and for Birmingham.—*Moundsley Hall, Kingsnorton.*

LANE-FOX, GEORGE, Esq., of Bramham Park, Yorkshire.

Only son of the late George Lane-Fox, Esq., M.P., of Bramham Park, by Georgiana Henrietta, dau. of Edmund P. Buckley, Esq., of Minestead, Hants ; *b.* 1816 *s.* 1848 ; *m.* 1837 Katharine, dau. of the late John Stein, Esq., M.P., and has, with other issue,

* George Sackville, educated at Ch. Ch., Oxford ; a Magistrate for the W. Riding of co. York; *b.* 1849.

Mr. Lane-Fox, who was educated at Eton and Ch. Ch., Oxford, is a J.P. and D.L. for the W. Riding of co. York, a Dep.-Lieut. for co. Leitrim (of which co. he has been High Sheriff), and Patron of 3 livings.—*Bramham Park, Tadcaster* ; 43, *Grosvenor Street*, w.

LANE-FOX. SACKVILLE WALTER, Esq., of Oran House, Yorkshire.

Third son of the late James Lane Fox, Esq., M.P., of Oran House, by the Hon. Maria Lucy, dau. of George, 1st Lord Rivers; *b.* 1800 ; *m.* 1826 Lady Charlotte Mary Anne Georgiana, only dau. of George, 6th Duke of Leeds, K.G., and by her, who *d.* 1836, has issue,

* Sackville George, Lord Conyers (whom see).

Mr. Lane-Fox, who was educated at Eton and Ch. Ch., Oxford, is a Dep.-Lieut. for the N. Riding of co. York, and Lord of the Manor of Stanley, co. York; he was M.P. for Helston 1833–4, for Beverley 1840–1, and for Ipswich 1842–7; was formerly in the Grenadier Guards.—*Oran House, Tadcaster* ; *Carlton Club*, s.w.

LANE-FOX. (See under *Conyers, Lord*.)

LANESBOROUGH, Earl of (JOHN VANSITTART DANVERS BUTLER-DANVERS).—Cr. 1756.

Elder son of the late Hon. Charles Augustus Danvers-Butler, of the Madras Army (who *d.* 1849), by Letitia, dau. of the late Col. Freese; *b.* 1839 ; *s.* his uncle as 6th Earl 1866 ; *m.* 1861 Anne Elizabeth, only child of the Rev. John Dixon Clark, of Belford Hall, Northumberland. Is a Commander R.N.—*Lanesborough Lodge, Belturbet, co. Cavan; Swithland Hall, Loughborough; Junior Carlton Club*, s.w.

Heir, his son Charles John Brinsley, Lord Newtown-Butler, *b.* 1865.

+LANGAN, RICHARD, Esq., of Bellewstown House, co. Meath.

Son of the late John Langan, Esq., of Bellewstown House, by Jane, dau. of Michael Flanagan, Esq., of Walterstown and Corballis, co. Meath ; *b.* 1816 ; *s.* 1858 ; *m.* 1860 Juliet, eldest dau. of the late Hugh Thomas Stafford, Esq., J.P., of Corrygrane Lodge, co. Longford, and has, with other issue,

* Richard Stephens Stafford, *b.* 1861.

Mr. Langan is a Magistrate for co. Meath, and Lord of the Manor of Bellewstown.—*Bellewstown House, Drogheda, co. Meath.*

LANGDALE, the Hon. CHARLES, of Houghton Park, Yorkshire.

Third son of Charles Philip, 16th Lord Stourton, by the Hon. Mary, 2nd dau. of Marmaduke, 5th Lord Langdale; *b.* 1787 ; *m.* 1st 1815 the Hon. Charlotte Mary, 5th dau. of Charles, 7th Lord Clifford (she *d.* 1819) ; 2nd 1821 Mary, dau. of Marmaduke Constable-Maxwell, Esq., and sister of Lord Herries, and by her, who *d.* 1857, has, with other issue,

* Charles, a J.P. and D.L. for the E. Riding of co. York; *b.* 1822; *m.* 1852 Henrietta, eldest dau. of the late Henry Grattan, Esq., M.P., of Celbridge Abbey, co. Meath, and has, with other issue, * Charles, *b.* 1861.

Mr. Langdale, who assumed that name in 1815, is a J.P. and D.L. for the E. Riding of co. York ; was M.P. for Beverley 1832–4, for Knaresborough 1837–41.—*Houghton Park, Brough ; Stafford Club*, w.

LANGDALE, Lady, of Eywood, Herefordshire.

Jane Elizabeth, eldest dau. of Edward, 5th Earl of Oxford (*ext.*), by Jane Elizabeth, dau. of the Rev. James Scott; *m.* 1835 Henry, Lord Langdale, some time Master of the Rolls, who *d.* 1851 (when the title became ext.), leaving issue an only child,

* Jane Frances, *m.* 1857 Alexander, Count Teleki de Szék.

Lady Langdale, who resumed her maiden name of Harley, by Royal licence, in 1853, is Lady of the Manor Titley.—*Eywood, Titley, Kington.*

+LANGDALE, MARMADUKE ROBERT, Esq., of Garston House, Surrey.

Elder son of the late Marmaduke Langdale, Esq. (who *d.* 1842), by Henrietta, dau. of George Chapman, Esq., of Madras; *b.* 1838 ; *s.* his grandfather 1861. This family is descended from a common ancestor with the ancient Roman Catholic family of Langdale, Lord Langdale, now extinct in the male line.—*Garston House, Godstone.*

Heir Pres., his brother Albert, *b.* 1842.

LANGDALE. (See *Kilham*.)

LANGFORD, Lord (HERCULES EDWARD ROWLEY).—Cr. 1800.

Elder son of Clotworthy, 3rd Lord, by Louisa Augusta, dau. of the late Col. Edward Michael Conolly, M.P., of Cliff House, co. Donegal; *b.* 1848 ; *s.* 1854. Educated at Eton ; is Ensign and Lieut. Grenadier Guards.—*Summerhill House, co. Meath, Ireland.*

Heir Pres., his brother William Chambré, *b.* 1849.

LANGHAM, Sir JAMES HAY, Bart., of Cottesbrooke, Northamptonshire (cr. 1660).

Eldest son of the late Sir James Langham, Bart., of Cottesbrooke, by Elizabeth, youngest sister of the late Sir Francis Burdett, Bart., M.P., of Foremark, co. Derby ; *b.* 1802 ; *s.* as 11th Bart. 1833 ; *m.* 1828 the Hon. Margaret Emma, dau. of George, 2nd Lord Kenyon (she *d.* 1829). Educated at Eton and Ch. Ch., Oxford ; is Lord of the Manor of Cottesbrooke, and Patron of 3 livings.—*Cottesbrooke Park, Northampton ; Teddington, Middlesex*; s.w.

Heir Pres., his brother Herbert, educated at Eton and St. John's Coll., Cambridge (B.A. 1826, M.A. 1899) ; Barrister-at-Law of Lincoln's Inn and a Magistrate for co. Northampton ; *b.* 1804 ; *m.* 1839 Laura Charlotte, dau. of the late Nathaniel Micklethwait, Esq., of Taverham Hall, Norfolk, and by her, who *d.* 1861, has, with other issue, * Herbert Hay, late Lieut. 1st Life Guards, *b.* 1840.

LANGLEY, HENRY, Esq., of Archerstown House, co. Tipperary.
Son of the late Henry Langley, Esq., of Archerstown, by Lydia, dau. of Richard Levinge, Esq., of Bellview, co. Kilkenny; *b.* 1820; *s.* 1859; *m.* 1860 Catherine Maria, dau. of Dr. Toler, and has, with other issue,
* Henry, *b.* 1862.
Mr. Langley is a Magistrate for co. Tipperary.—*Archerstown House, Thurles, co. Tipperary.*

LANGLEY, JOHN, Esq., of Knockanure, co. Tipperary.
Eldest son of the late Fergus Langley, Esq., J.P., of Knockanure, by Elizabeth, dau. of the late Charles Atkinson, Esq., of Rehins, co. Mayo; *b.* 1807; *s.* 1851; *m.* 1844 Sarah Geraldine, dau. of Robert Neville, Esq., of Borrismore, co. Kilkenny, and has, with other issue,
* John Neville, *b.* 1847.
Mr. Langley is a Magistrate for co. Tipperary.—*Knockanure, Killenaule, co. Tipperary.*

LANGRISHE, Sir JAMES, Bart., of Knocktopher Abbey, co. Kilkenny (cr. 1777).
Eldest son of the late Rev. Sir Hercules Richard Langrishe, Bart., of Knocktopher (who was formerly Rector of Killaloe), by Maria, dau. of James Cottingham, Esq., of Somerville, co. Cavan; *b.* 1823; *s.* as 4th Bart. 1862; *m.* 1857 Adela de Blois, only dau. of the late T. Blois Eccles, Esq., of Chairlemont, co. Stafford. Is a J.P. and D.L. for co. Kilkenny (High Sheriff 1866), and Major Kilkenny Fusiliers.—*Knocktopher Abbey, Thomastown, co. Kilkenny.*
Heir, his son Hercules Robert, *b.* 1859.

LANGSTON, of Sarsden House, Oxon.
(See *Ducie, Earl.*)

LANGTON, BENNET ROTHES, Esq., of Langton Hall, Lincolnshire.
Eldest son of the late George Bennet Langton, Esq., of Langton, by Marianne, youngest dau. of the late Langley Brackenbury, Esq., of Brighton; *b.* 1840; *s.* 1844; *m.* 1865 Lucy Katharine, only dau. of the Rev. Langhorn Burton Burton, Rector of Somersby, and has issue, two daughters. Mr. Langton is Lord of the Manor of Langton, Patron of that living, and Lieut. Royal N. Lincoln Militia.—*Langton Hall, Spilsby; Penlee Villas, Stoke, Devonport.*
Heir Pres., his brother John Stephen Algernon, *b.* 1842.

LANGTON, HENRY MICHAEL FAUSTINUS, Esq., of Danganmore, co. Kilkenny.
Eldest son of the late Michael Theobald Langton, Esq., of Danganmore, by Mary, eldest dau. of the late Jeremiah Ryan, Esq., of Danganmore and Newtown, (who succeeded to the property of Danganmore and Ballybur 1842); *b.* 1829; *s.* his mother 1864. Was formerly Capt. Louth Rifles. This family was resident in Cadiz for the last three generations, but settled in England on the French invasion of Cadiz.—*Danganmore, Thomastown, co. Kilkenny; 6, Southwick Place,* w.

LANGTON. (See *Gore-Langton.*)

LANGWORTHY, EDWARD RYLEY, Esq.
Son of the late E. Langworthy, Esq., of Salford; *b.* 1796; is married. Is a Magistrate for co. Lancaster, and an Alderman of and Merchant in the borough of Salford; was M.P. for Salford February—March, 1857. —*Victoria Park, Manchester.*

LANIGAN, JOHN, Esq., of Richmond, co. Tipperary.
Only surviving son of the late Stephen Lanigan, Esq., by Anne McMahon, dau. of M Sweeney, Esq., of

562

Farrenderra; *b.* 1810; *m.* 1839 Frances, dau. of Charles O'Keefe, Esq.; is a Magistrate for co. Tipperary; was M.P. for Cashel 1859–65.—*Richmond, Templemore; Reform Club,* s.w.

LANSDOWNE, Marquis of (HENRY CHARLES KEITH-PETTY-FITZMAURICE).—Cr. 1784.
Elder son of Henry, 4th Marquis, K.G. (who was called to the House of Peers in 1856, as Lord Wycombe), by his 2nd wife, the Hon. Emily Jane, eldest dau. of the Comte de Flahault (in her own right Baroness Nairne, *see that title*); *b.* 1845; *s.* 1866. Educated at Eton and Balliol Coll., Oxford; is Lord of the Manor of Bowood, Patron of 3 livings, and Capt. Royal Wilts Yeomanry Cavalry. The 1st Marquis, as Earl of Shelburne, was Premier 1782–3.—*Bowood Park, Calne, Wilts; Lansdowne House, Berkeley Square,* w.
Heir Pres., his brother Lord Edmond George, educated at Trinity Coll., Cambridge, *b.* 1846.

LANYON, Sir CHARLES, Knt., of White Abbey, co. Antrim (cr. 1868).
Son of the late John Lanyon, Esq., of East Bourne, by Catherine Anne, dau. of Charles Smith Mortimer, Esq., of East Bourne; *b.* 1813; *m.* 1837 Elizabeth Helen, dau. of J. Owen, Esq., of the Board of Public Works, Dublin. Is a Magistrate for co. Antrim, and President of the Royal Institute of Architects in Ireland; elected M.P. for Belfast 1866.—*White Abbey, Belfast; Carlton and Junior Carlton Clubs,* s.w.

LARCOM, Sir THOMAS AISKEW, K.C.B., F.R.S. (cr. 1860).
Eldest son of the late Capt. Joseph Larcom, R.N., by Anne, dau. of William Hollis, Esq., of Alverstoke, Hants; *b.* 1801; *m.* 1840 Georgina, dau. of the late Lieut.-General Sir George d'Aguilar, K.C.B. Educated at the Royal Mil. Academy, Woolwich; is a Major-General in the Army; served formerly in the Royal Engineers; was in charge of the Ordnance Survey Office 1828–46; Dep.-Chairman of Board of Works, Ireland, 1846–53; has been Under-Secretary for Ireland since that time.—*Phœnix Park, Dublin; Junior United Service and Athenæum Clubs,* s.w.

LARKING, JOHN WINGFIELD, Esq., of Lee, Kent.
Second son of the late John Larking, Esq., of Clare House, East Malling, Kent, by Dorothy, dau. of the late Sir T. Charles Style, Bart., of Wateringbury House, Kent; *b.* 1802; *m.* 1840 Rosina Teresa Elizabeth Tibaldi, and by her, who *d.* 1866, has, with other issue,
* Cuthbert, late of the 13th Hussars; *b.* 1842; *m.* 1864 Lady Adéla, dau. of William, 2nd Earl of Listowel.
Mr. Larking, who is a Magistrate for Kent, was formerly British Consul at Alexandria, in Egypt.—*The Firs, Lee, Blackheath,* s.e.; *Athenæum Club,* s.w.

LARPENT, Sir GEORGE ALBERT DE HOCHEPIED, Bart. (cr. 1841).
Only son of the late Sir Albert John Larpent, Bart., by Catherine Lydia, dau. of Capt. L. M. Shaw, of the Bengal Army; *b.* 1816; *s.* as 3rd Bart. 1861. Is Ensign 88th Regt.
Heir Pres., his half-uncle Seymour George, *b.* 1832.

LA SAUSSAYE. (See *De La Saussaye.*)

LASCELLES, the Hon. ARTHUR, of Norley Hall, Cheshire.
Fifth son of Henry, 2nd Earl of Harewood, by Henrietta, eldest dau. of the late Lieut.-General Sir John Saunders Sebright, Bart.; *b.* 1807; *m.* 1834 Caroline Frances,

4th dau. of Sir Richard Brooke, Bart., of Norton Priory, co. Chester, and has, with other issue,

* Walter Richard, Capt. Rifle Brigade; b. 1837.

Mr. Lascelles, who was educated at Eton and Ch. Ch., Oxford (B.A. 1828), is a J.P. and D.L. for the W. Riding of Yorkshire, and a Magistrate for co. Chester; late Capt. Cheshire Yeomanry.—*Norley Hall, Northwich; Travellers' Club, s.w.*

LASCELLES, the Hon. EGREMONT WILLIAM.
Second son of Henry, 3rd Earl of Harewood, by Lady Louisa Thynne, 2nd dau. of Thomas, 2nd Marquis of Bath; b. 1825; m. 1856 Jessie, dau. of the late Neil Malcolm, Esq., of Poltallock, and has issue. Educated at Eton; late Lieut. and Capt. Grenadier Guards; is a J.P. and D.L. for co. York, and Major 1st Royal York Militia; elected M.P. for Northallerton 1866.—*Harewood, Leeds; 13, Hanover Square, w.*

LASCELLES, the Hon. GEORGE EDWIN, of Sion Hill, Yorkshire.
Third son of Henry, 3rd Earl of Harewood, by Lady Louisa Thynne, 2nd dau. of Thomas, 2nd Marquis of Bath; b. 1826; m. 1851 Lady Louisa Nina Murray, only dau. of William David, 4th Earl of Mansfield, and has, with other issue,

* David Arthur George, b. 1852.

Mr. Lascelles is a Magistrate for the W. Riding of Yorkshire; late Capt. Yorkshire Yeomanry Hussars. —*Sion Hill, Thirsk, Yorkshire.*

LASCELLES. (See *Harewood, Earl of.*)

LASLETT, WILLIAM, Esq., of Abberton Hall, Worcestershire.
Son of the late Mr. Thomas Emerson Laslett by Sophia his wife; b. 1801; m. 1842 Maria, eldest dau. of the late Right Rev. Dr. Carr, Lord Bishop of Worcester (she d. 1863). Called to the Bar at the Inner Temple 1856; is Lord of the Manors of Abberton, &c., and Patron of 5 livings; was formerly a Solicitor; was M.P. for Worcester 1852-60.—*Abberton Hall, Pershore.*

LATHAM, GEORGE WILLIAM, Esq., of Bradwall Hall, Cheshire.
Second but eldest surviving son of the late John Latham, Esq., of Bradwall Hall, by Elizabeth Anne, dau. of the late Sir H. Dampier; b. 1827; s. 1853; m. 1856 Elizabeth Sarah, eldest dau. of the Rev. H. Luttman-Johnson, of Binderton House, Sussex, and has, with other issue,

* Alexander Mere, b. 1862.

Mr. Latham, who was educated at Brasenose Coll., Oxford (B.A. 1849, M.A. 1852), called to the Bar at the Inner Temple 1852, and went the North Wales and Chester Circuit, is a Magistrate for co. Chester.—*Bradwall Hall, Sandbach.*

LA TOUCHE, DAVID CHARLES, Esq., of Marlay, co. Dublin.
Eldest son of the late John David La Touche Esq., of Marlay, by Anne Caroline, dau. of the late Charles Tottenham, Esq., of New Ross; b. 1800. Educated at Trinity Coll., Dublin; is a J.P. and D.L. for co. Dublin, and a Magistrate for co. Wicklow, and has been High Sheriff for both counties.—*Marlay, Rathfarnham, co. Dublin; Luggelaw, co. Wicklow.*

LA TOUCHE, JOHN, Esq., of Harristown, co. Kildare.
Eldest son of the late Robert La Touche, Esq., of Harristown, by Emily, 7th dau. of William, 1st Earl of Clancarty; b. 1814; s. 1844; m. 1843 Maria, only

dau. of Robert Lambert Price, Esq., of Trengwainton, Cornwall, and has, with other issue,

* Robert Percy O'Connor, b. 1846.

Mr. La Touche, who was educated at Ch. Ch., Oxford, is a J.P. and D.L. for co. Kildare (High Sheriff 1846). —*Harristown, Newbridge, Kildare; Brooks's Club, s.w.*

LA TOUCHE, WILLIAM ROBERT, Esq., of Bellevue, co. Wicklow.
Third son of the late Peter La Touche, Esq., M.P., of Bellevue (who d. 1830), by the Hon. Charlotte, dau. of Cornwallis, 1st Viscount Hawarden; b. 1810; s. his brother 1856; m. 1867 Ellen, 4th dau. of the late William Henn, Esq., Master in Chancery, Dublin. Educated at Harrow and Exeter Coll., Oxford, is a Dep.-Lieut. for co. Leitrim, a Magistrate for Wicklow (High Sheriff 1860). This family, which is of French Huguenot extraction, settled in Ireland in 1690.—*Bellevue, Delgany, co. Wicklow.*

LAUDER, Sir THOMAS NORTH DICK-, Bart., of Fountain Hall, Haddingtonshire (cr. 1688).
Eldest son of the late Sir John Dick-Lauder, Bart., of Fountain Hall, by Lady Anne, dau. of North, 9th Earl of Stair; b. 1846; s. as 9th Bart. 1867. Is Lieut. 60th Rifles.—*Fountain Hall, Pencaitland, N.B.; The Grange House, Edinburgh.*

Heir Pres., his brother John Edward Arthur, b. 1848.

LAUDERDALE, Earl of (THOMAS MAITLAND, K.C.B., K.C.S.).—Cr. 1624.
Son of the late Hon. General William Mordaunt Maitland, by his 1st wife, Mary, dau. of the Rev. Richard Orpen, of Killowen, co. Kerry, and widow of John Travers, Esq., of Fir Grove, co. Cork; b. 1803; s. his cousin as 11th Earl 1863; m. 1828 Amelia, dau. of William Young, Esq. Is a Dep. Lieut. for co. Berwick, a Vice-Admiral, retired, and principal Naval A.D.C. to the Queen; elected a Representative Peer for Scotland, 1867.—*Thirlestune Castle, Lauder, N.B.; Madderstown, Berwick; United Service Club, s.w.*

Heir Pres., his cousin Charles (only son of the late Rev. Charles Maitland, who d. 1844, by Anne, dau. of Thomas Knott, Esq., of Stockland); b. 1822.

LAUGHARNE, the Rev. THOMAS ROBERT JOHN, of Laugharne, Carmarthenshire.
Only son of the late Thomas Lamb Polden Laugharne, Esq., of Laugharne, by Mary Amelia, eldest dau. of the late Sir Stowkeley Shuckbrugh, Bart.; b. 1821; s. 1863; m. 1859 Ellen Maria, eldest dau. of Joseph Wilks, Esq., and has, with other issue,

* Thomas, b. 1863.

Mr. Laugharne, who was educated at Jesus Coll., Oxford (B.A. 1843, M.A. 1845), is Lord of the Manor of Laugharne, and Curate of Calverton, Bucks. —*Laugharne Hall, Carmarthen; Calverton, Stony Stratford.*

LAURIE, JOHN WIMBURN, Esq., of Laurietown, Essex.
Eldest son of the late John Laurie, Esq., J.P. and D.L., of Laurietown, M.P. for Barnstaple (who assumed the name of Laurie in lieu of Snaddon), by Eliza Ellen, dau. of Kenrick Collett, Esq.; b. 1836; s. 1864; m. 1863 Frances Robie, dau. of the Hon. Enos Collins. Is a Lieut.-Col in the Army, and Inspector of Militia at Nova Scotia, Romford.—*Laurietown, Romford.*

LAURIE, JOHN MINET FECTOR-, Esq., of Maxwelton, Dumfries-shire.
Eldest son of the late John Minet Fector, Esq., of Kearsney Abbey and Updown House, Kent, by Anne

Wortley Montague, dau. of Lieut.-General Sir Robert Laurie, Bart., M.P., of Maxwelton, co. Dumfries, whose name he assumed in 1848 ; *b.* 1812 ; *s.* 1848 ; *m.* 1841 Isabella, dau. of Major-General Murray, C.B. Educated at Eton and Trinity Coll., Cambridge ; is a J.P. and D.L. for Kent ; was formerly M.P. for Dover and Maidstone.—*Maxwelton House, Thornhill, N.B. ; Carlton Club, s.w. ; 4, St. George's Place, w.*

LAURIE. (See *Craig-Laurie.*).

LAW, the Hon. HENRY SPENCER, late of Ellington House, Kent.
Fifth son of Edward, 1st Lord Ellenborough, by Anne, dau. of the late George P. Towry, Esq. ; *b.* 1802 ; *m.* 1839 Dorothea Anne, dau. of George Rochfort, Esq., of Clogrenane, co. Carlow, and has, with other issue,

   • Edward Downes, Lieut. R.N., *b.* 1841.

Mr. Law, who was educated at Eton and St. John's Coll., Cambridge (M.A. 1821), was called to the Bar at the Inner Temple 1833.—*Portland Terrace, Richmond, s.w.*

LAW, the Hon. WILLIAM TOWRY.
Fifth son of Edward, 1st Lord Ellenborough, by Anne, dau. of the late George P. Towry, Esq., Capt. R.N. ; *b.* 1809 ; *m.* 1st 1831 the Hon. Augusta, 4th dau. of Thomas North ; 2nd Lord Graves (*d.* 1844) ; 2nd 1846 Matilda, dau. of the late Sir Henry Montgomery, Bart., and has by the former, with other issue,

   • Augustus Henry, in Holy Orders of the Church of Rome ; *b.* 1832.

Mr. Law, who was educated at Eton and St. Peter's Coll., Cambridge (M.A. 1834), and served in the Army 1826–31, was formerly Chancellor of Bath and Wells —*Stafford Club, w. ; Hampton Court Palace, s.w.*

LAW, JAMES ADEANE, Esq., of Banwell, Somerset.
Second son of the Rev. James Thomas Law, Chancellor of Lichfield, by Lady Henrietta Charlotte, dau. of George, 6th Earl of Stamford ; *b.* 1824 ; *m.* 1857 Harriet Ellen, 3rd dau. of the Rev. William H. Turner, Vicar of Banwell, and has, with other issue,

   • James Henry Adeane, *b.* 1860.

Mr. Law, who was educated at St. John's Coll., Cambridge, is a Magistrate for Somerset, and a Major 3rd Battalion Somerset Rifle Volunteers ; was formerly Capt. Bengal Native Infantry. This family descend from the celebrated John Law, projector of the Mississippi scheme. — *The Caves, Banwell, Weston-super-Mare.*

LAW. (See under *Ellenborough, Earl of.*)

LAWDER, HORATIO NELSON, Esq., of Aughamore, co. Roscommon.
Sixth son of the late John Lawder, Esq., by Margaretta, dau. of Oliver Moore, Esq., of Dublin ; *b.* 1810 ; *m.* 1842 Judith Marcella, dau. of Arthur Auchmuty, Esq., and has, with other issue,

   • Arthur Auchmuty, *b.* 1846.

Mr. Lawder is a Magistrate and Grand Juror for cos. Roscommon and Leitrim.—*Aughamore, Drumsna, co. Roscommon ; Rathmines Road, Dublin.*

LAWES, JOHN BENNET, Esq., of Rothamsted, Herts.
Eldest son of the late John Bennet Lawes, Esq., of Rothamsted Manor, by Marianne, dau. of John Sherman, Esq., of Drayton, Oxon, and widow of the Rev. D. G. Knox ; *b.* 1815 ; *s.* 1822 ; *m.* 1842 Caroline, dau.

of the late Andrew Fountaine, Esq., of Narford Hall, Norfolk, and has, with other issue,

   • Charles Bennet, educated at Eton, *b.* 1843.

Mr. Lawes, who was educated at Eton and Brasenose Coll., Oxford, is a Magistrate for Herts.—*Rothamsted Manor House, St. Alban's.*

LAWES, ROBERT BARTHOLOMEW, Esq., of Kingston Hall, Surrey.
Eldest son of the late Robert Lawes, Esq., of Kingston Hall, Surrey, by Elizabeth Gilham, dau. of Bartholomew J. Bull, Esq. ; *b.* 1824 ; *s.* 1858 ; *m.* 1854 Emma Selina, dau. of the Rev. Edward Murray, and has, with other issue,

   • Robert Murray, *b.* 1857.

Mr. Lawes is a Magistrate for Surrey, and Commandant of the Battalion of 16th Middlesex Rifle Volunteers. — *Kingston Hall, Kingston-on-Thames ; Conservative Club, s.w. ; 2, Hyde Park Place, w.*

LAWLESS. (See under *Cloncurry, Lord.*)

LAWLEY, the Hon. ROBERT NEVILLE, of Hutton Hall, Yorkshire.
Second son of Paul Beilby, 1st Lord Wenlock, by the Hon. Caroline, 3rd dau. of Richard, 2nd Lord Braybrooke ; *b.* 1819 ; *m.* 1852 Georgiana Emily, dau. of the late Lord Edward Somerset. Educated at Eton ; entered the 2nd Life Guards 1839, became Capt. 1848, retired 1853 ; is Capt. Yorkshire Hussars.—*Hutton Hall, Marston, York ; White's Club, s.w.*

LAWLEY, the Hon. and Rev. STEPHEN WILLOUGHBY.
Third son of Paul Beilby, 1st Lord Wenlock, by the Hon. Caroline, 3rd dau. of Richard, 2nd Lord Braybrooke ; *b.* 1823. Educated at Rugby and Balliol Coll., Oxford (B.A. 1845, M.A. 1848) ; appointed Rector of Escrick 1848, Sub-Dean of York 1852.—*Escrick Rectory, York.*

LAWLEY, Lady.
Mary Anne, eldest dau. of the late George Talbot, Esq., of Temple Guiting, co. Gloucester, by Charlotte Elizabeth, 4th dau. of the late Rev. Thomas Drake, D.D., of Amersham, Bucks ; *m.* 1815 Sir Francis Lawley, Bart. who *d.* 1851, when his title passed to Paul Beilby, 1st Lord Wenlock.—18, *Grosvenor Square, w.*

LAWLEY. (See *Wenlock, Lord.*)

LAWLOR, DENIS SHYNE-, Esq., of Grenagh, co. Kerry.
Eldest son of the late Denis Shyne, Esq., of Killarney, by Ellen, dau. of Martin Lawlor, Esq., of Killarney, whose name he assumed ; *b.* 1808 ; *s.* 1812 ; *m.* 1840 Isabella, 2nd dau. of the late Edward Huddleston, Esq., of Sawston, co. Cambridge, and has, with other issue,

   • Denis Alexander, *b.* 1843.

Mr. Shyne-Lawlor, who was educated at Oscott Coll., is a Magistrate for co. Kerry (High Sheriff 1840). —*Grenagh House, Killarney, co. Kerry.*

LAWRENCE, Sir HENRY HAYES, Bart. (cr. 1858).
Only son of the late Sir Alexander Hutchinson Lawrence, Bart., by Alice Eacy, dau. of Every Kennedy, Esq., M.D. and J.P., of Belgard Castle, co. Dublin ; *b.* 1864 ; *s.* as 2nd Bart. 1864. The late Bart. was created a Baronet for his father's services during the Indian mutiny.

   Heir Pres. (under a special remainder), his uncle Rev. Henry Waldemar, of Trinity Coll., Cambridge, *b.* 1846.

LAWRENCE, the Right Hon. Sir JOHN LAIRD MAIR, Bart., G.C.B., G.C.S.I. (cr. 1858).
Younger son of the late Col. Alexander Lawrence, by Catherine, dau. of the late Rev. A. G. Knox, and brother of the late Col. Sir Henry Montgomery Lawrence, K.C.B.; *b.* 1811; *m.* 1842 Harriette Katharine, dau. of the late Rev. Richard Hamilton. Educated at Hailey-bury Coll.; entered the H.E.I.C.'s Civil Service 1829; was Chief Commissioner of the Punjaub 1849–58; ap-pointed one of the Indian Council 1858; Governor-General of India 1863.—*Government House, Calcutta.*

Heir, his son John Hamilton, b. 1846.

LAWRENCE, Sir JOHN JAMES TREVOR, Bart., of Ealing, Middlesex (cr. 1867).
Only son of the late Sir William Lawrence, Bart., of Ealing Park, by Catharine, dau. of James Trevor Senior, Esq., of Broughton House, Bucks; *b.* 1831; *s.* as 2nd Bart. 1867. Is a Medical Officer in the Indian Army. —*Ealing Park, Middlesex ; 18, Whitehall Place, s.w.*

LAWRENCE, Sir GEORGE ST. PATRICK, K.C.S.I., C.B. (cr. 1866).
Third son of the late Col. Alexander Lawrence, Governor of Upnor Castle, Kent, by Catharine, dau. of the late Rev. James Knox, and brother of the late Sir Henry and the Right Hon. Sir John Lawrence, Bart.; *b.* 1805; *m.* 1830 Charlotte, dau. of Dr. John Browne, Surgeon-General, and Medical Board, Bengal. Educated at Foyle Coll., Londonderry, and Addiscombe Military Coll.; is a Major-Gen. in the Bengal Army, late Poli-tical Agent Peshawur, Political Agent at Meywar, and Agent to the Governor-Gen. of India Rajpootana. —*Oriental Club, w.; 20, Kensington Park Gardens, s.w.*

LAWRENCE, HENRY, Esq., of Bank House, Carmarthenshire.
Seventh son of the late Richard Lawrence, Esq., of Duffryn Manor, co. Brecon, by Anne Texley, only dau. and heir of Arthur Sealy, Esq., of Wick and Moorlinch, Somerset; *b.* 1785; *m.* 1st 1824 Jane, only dau. and heiress of David W. Stephenson, Esq., of Sterling Park, co. Carmarthen (she *d. s. p.*); 2nd 1828 Frances Justina Maria Jane, 4th dau. of the late John William Hughes, Esq., J.P. and D.L., of Bwlch Gwynt, and has issue,
    * Henry John Hughes, Assistant Surgeon, Grenadier Guards, and a Magistrate for co. Carmarthen, b. 1832.

Mr. Lawrence, who graduated M.D. at Edinburgh, is a Magistrate for cos. Pembroke and Carmarthen, and for the borough of Carmarthen.—*Bank House, Carmarthen.*

LAWRENCE, WALTER, Esq., of Lisreaghan, co. Galway.
Eldest son of the late Walter Lawrence, Esq., of Lis-reaghan, by Catherine, dau. of John D'Arcy, Esq., of Ballykine, co. Mayo; *b.* 1794; *s.* 1796; *m.* 1820 Georgina, 2nd dau. of the late Charles Blake, Esq., of Merlin Park, co. Galway, and by her (who *d.* 1863) has, with other issue,
    * John, b. 1822.

Mr. Lawrence, who was educated at Winchester, is a Magistrate for co. Galway (High Sheriff 1820), Lord of the Manor of Lisreaghan, and a Governor of the Con-naught Lunatic Asylum.—*Lisreaghan, Laurencetown.*

LAWRENCE, WALTER LAWRENCE, Esq., of Sandywell Park, Gloucestershire.
Son of the late William Morris, Esq., of Sevenhampton, co. Gloucester, by Mary, only dau. of Walter Lawrence, Esq., of Sevenhampton; *b.* 1799; *m.* 1824 Mary, only child of the late Christian Splidt, Esq., of Stratford, Essex, and has, with other issue,
    * Christian William, b. 1836.

Mr. Lawrence, who was educated at Magdalen Coll.,

Oxford, is a J.P. and D.L. for co. Gloucester.—*Sandy-well Park, Andoversford.*

LAWRENCE, WILLIAM, Esq.
Eldest son of the late Alderman William Lawrence, by Jane, 4th dau. of the late J. Clarke, Esq.; *b.* 1818. Is a Magistrate for Middlesex and Westminster, a Dep. Lieut. and an Alderman of London; was Sheriff of London and Middlesex 1857-8, Lord Mayor 1863-4; elected M.P. for London 1865.—*Reform Club, s.w.; 94, Westbourne Terrace, w.*

LAWRIE, WILLIAM KENNEDY, Esq., of Wood-hall, Kirkcudbrightshire.
Eldest son of the late William B. Kennedy Lawrie, Esq., of Woodhall, by Antonia, dau. of Arthur Grant Robertson, Esq., M.D., of Antigua; *b.* 1820; *s.* 1835. Mr. Lawrie, who was educated at Edinburgh and Göt-tingen, is a J.P. and D.L. for co. Kirkcudbright, and formerly an Officer in the Galloway Rifle Volunteers, was formerly an Officer in the Black Brunswickers.—*Wood-hall, Lauriesfon, Castle Douglas, N.B.; Union and Arling-ton Clubs, 34, Duke Street, s.w.*

Heir Pres., his brother Walter Kennedy, b. 1833; is married and has issue.

LAWSON, Sir WILFRID, Bart., of Brayton, Cumberland (cr. 1831).
Eldest son of the late Sir Wilfrid Lawson, Bart., of Brayton, by Caroline, dau. of the late Rt. Hon. Sir James Graham, Bart., of Netherby; *b.* 1829; *s.* as 2nd Bart. 1867; *m.* 1860 Mary, 3rd dau. of Joseph Pock-lington-Senhouse, Esq., of Netherhall, Cumberland. Is a Magistrate for Cumberland; was M.P. for Carlisle 1859-65.—*Brayton Hall, Carlisle; Reform Club, s.w.*

Heir, his son Wilfrid, b. 1862.

LAWSON, Sir JOHN, Bart., of Brough Hall, Yorkshire (cr. 1841).
Eldest son of the late Sir William Lawson, Bart., of Brough Hall (who assumed the name of Lawson in lieu of Wright in 1834, on succeeding to the Lawson estates), by Clarinda Catherine, dau. of John Lawson, Esq., M.D.; *b.* 1829; *s.* as 2nd Bart. 1865; *m.* 1856 Mary Ann, elder dau. of Frederick Sewallis Gerard, Esq., of Aspull House, co. Lancaster. Educated at Stonyhurst; is a J.P. and D.L. for N. Riding of Yorkshire, and Patron of 1 living.—*Brough Hall, Catterick.*

Heir Pres., his brother William, b. 1834.

LAWSON, ANDREW SHERLOCK, Esq., of Ald-borough Manor, Yorkshire.
Eldest son of the late Andrew Lawson, Esq., M.P., of Aldborough Manor, by Marianne Anna Maria, dau. of the late Sir Thomas Sherlock Gooch, Bart., of Benacre Hall, Suffolk; *b.* 1824; *s.* 1853; *m.* 1852 Isabella, younger dau. of John Grant, Esq., of Nuttall Hall, co. Lancaster, and has, with other issue,
    * Andrew Sherlock, b. 1853.

Mr. Lawson, who was educated at Harrow and Merton Coll., Oxford, is a J.P. and D.L. for the W. Riding, a Magistrate for the N. Riding of Yorkshire, and Patron of 1 living.—*Aldborough Manor, and Boroughbridge Hall, York.*

LAWSON, CHARLES, Esq., of Halheriot, Mid-lothian, and Ballo, Perthshire.
Second son of the late Peter Lawson, Esq., Merchant, of Edinburgh, by Patricia, dau. of Lieut. Grant, R.N.; *b.* 1795; *m.* 1825 Graham, elder dau. of John Stoddart, Esq., of Dunse, and niece of John Balraird, Esq., of Ballo, and by her, who *d.* 1854, has, with other issue,
    * Charles, b. 1827; m. 1st 1853 Rebecca, younger dau. of Thomas Robertson, Esq., Surgeon R.N. (she d. 1859); 2nd 1864 Mary, eldest dau. of Robert Steuart, Esq., of Westwood, Linlithgowshire.

Mr. Lawson, who was educated at the High School and

University of Edinburgh, is a Magistrate for Midlothian, a Merchant in Edinburgh and London, and a Fellow of the Royal Society of Edinburgh; was formerly Chairman of the Chamber of Commerce and Master of the Merchant Company, and late Lord Provost of the City of Edinburgh.—*Borthwick Hall, Heriot, Gorebridge, N.B.; Ballomill, Abernethy, Perthshire; 35, George Square, Edinburgh; 12, Stanhope Gardens, s.w.*

+ LAWSON, the Rev. GEORGE ROBERT, of Pitminster, Somerset.
Son of the late G. Lawson, Esq.; *b.* 1805. Educated at Trinity Coll., Cambridge (B.A. 1828, M.A. 1835); appointed Vicar of Pitminster 1837; is Patron of that living.—*Pitminster Vicarage, Taunton.*

LAWSON, the Rt. Hon. JAMES ANTHONY, Q.C., of Clontra, co. Wicklow.
Eldest son of the late James Lawson, Esq., by Mary, dau. of J. Anthony, Esq., of Waterford; *b.* 1817; *m.* 1842 Jane, eldest dau. of S. Meyrick, Esq., of Cork. Educated at Trinity Coll., Dublin (B.A. 1839, LL.D. 1840); called to the Irish Bar 1840; became a Q.C. in 1857, when he was appointed Law Adviser of the Crown in Ireland; was Solicitor-General for Ireland 1861–5; Attorney-General 1865–6; elected M.P. for Portarlington 1865.—*Clontra, Bray, co. Wicklow; 27, Upper Fitzwilliam Street, Dublin; Reform Club, s.w.; 119, St. George's Road, s.w.*

LAWSON, the Rev. EDWARD, of Longhirst, Northumberland.
Eldest surviving son of the William Lawson, Esq., of Longhirst (who *d.* 1855); by Jane Hester, dau. of John Clarke, Esq., of Haddington; *b.* 1824; *s.* his brother William J. Lawson, Esq., 1859; *m.* 1853 Mary, dau. of George Maule, Esq., and has, with other issue,
* William Edward, *b.* 1855.
Mr. Lawson, who was educated at Trinity Coll., Cambridge (B.A. 1847, M.A. 1852), is a Magistrate for Northumberland.—*Longhirst, Morpeth; Oxford and Cambridge Club, s.w.*

LAWTON, CHRISTOPHER, Esq., of Cape View, co. Cork.
Son of the late Hugh Lawton. Esq., of Cape View, by Anna Maria, dau. of William Warren, Esq., of Lisgoold, co. Cork; *b.* 1800; *s.* 1859; *m.* 1822 Mary Anne, dau. of — Knowles, Esq. Is in the Commission of the Peace for co. Cork.—*Cape View, Ballydehob, co. Cork.*

LAWTON, WILLIAM JOHN PERCY, Esq., of Lawton Hall, Cheshire.
Eldest son of the late John Lawton, Esq., of Lawton Hall, by Emily Anne, youngest dau. of the late Thomas Legh, Esq., of Attlington Hall, co. Chester (she *m.* 2nd 1865 Frank Renaud, Esq., M.D., of Manchester); *b.* 1849; *s.* 1864. Is Lord of the Manor of Church Lawton, and Patron of 2 livings.—*Lawton Hall, Cheshire.*

LAYARD, AUSTEN HENRY, Esq., D.C.L.
Son of the late Henry P. J. Layard, Esq. (who *d.* 1834), by Marianne, dau. of —Austen, Esq., and grandson of the late Very Rev. D. Layard, Dean of Bristol; *b.* 1817. Formerly Attaché at Constantinople; was M.P. for Aylesbury 1852–7, Under-Secretary of State for Foreign Affairs January-February, 1852, and 1859-66; cr. Hon. D.C.L. of Oxford 1848; elected M.P. for Southwark 1860; appointed a Trustee of the National Gallery 1866; author of 'Nineveh and its Remains,' 'Monuments of Nineveh,' &c.—*Athenæum Club, s.w.; 130, Piccadilly, w.*
566

LAYARD, BROWNLOW VILLIERS, Esq., of Riversdale, co. Dublin.
Only son of the late Lieut.-Col. Brownlow Villiers Layard, M.P., of the 9th Regt., by Elizabeth, only dau. of the late J. D. Digby, Esq., late of the 5th Royal Irish Dragoons; *b.* 1838; *s.* 1853. Educated at St. Columba's Coll., Ireland; was formerly Lieut. 9th Regt. —*Riversdale, Palmerston, co. Dublin.*

LAYCOCK, JOSEPH, Esq., of Lintz Hall, co. Durham, and Gosforth, Northumberland.
Second son of the late Robert Laycock, Esq., by Mary, dau. of James Douglas, Esq.; *b.* 1798; *m.* 1832 Barbara, dau. of John Nicholson, Esq., and has issue;
* Robert, M.A. of Trinity Coll., Cambridge, *b.* 1833; *m.* 1866 Annie, 2nd dau. of Christian Allhusen, Esq., of Elswick Hall, Newcastle-on-Tyne, and has issue * Joseph Frederick, *b.* 1867.
Mr. Laycock, who is a Magistrate for cos. Durham and Northumberland, was Mayor of Newcastle 1858-9.—*Lintz Hall, Gateshead, Durham; Low Gosforth Hall, Newcastle, Northumberland; Winlaton, Newcastle-on-Tyne; Wiseton Hall, Notts.*

LEA, THOMAS SIMCOX, Esq., of Astley Hall, Worcestershire.
Eldest son of the late John Lea, Esq., of The Lakes, near Kidderminster, by Ann, dau. of Thomas Simcox, Esq., of West Bromwich; *b.* 1785; *m.* 1st 1818 Elizabeth Pratt, eldest dau. of George Simcox, Esq., of Harborne, co. Stafford; 2nd 1835 Lavinia Ann, dau. of W. B. Tarbutt, Esq., of London, and has, with other issue,
* Frederic Simcox, in Holy Orders, M.A. and late Fellow of Brasenose Coll., Oxford; *b.* 1823; *m.* 1855 Elizabeth Catherine, dau. of the Rev. Henry Clark, Vicar of Harmston, co. Lincoln.
Mr. Lea is a Magistrate for cos. Worcester, Stafford, and Salop, and a Dep. Lieut. for co. Worcester (High Sheriff 1845).—*Astley Hall, Stourport.*

LEACH, HENRY, Esq., of Corston, Pembrokeshire.
Eldest son of the late Henry Leach, Esq., J.P. and D.L., of Corston (who was High Sheriff of co. Pembroke 1852), by Elizabeth, youngest dau. of the late W. O. Brigstocke, Esq., of Blaenpant, co. Cardigan; *b.* 1824; *s.* 1864; *m.* 1867 Mary, 2nd dau. of the late Francis Edwardes Lloyd, Esq., of Plas-Cil-y-belyll, co. Glamorgan. Is a Magistrate for co. Pembroke; late Capt. 45th Regt. —*Corston, Pembroke; Junior United Service Club, s.w.*
Heir Pres., his brother William, Capt. 46th Regt., and A.D.C. to the Governor of Bombay; b. 1827.

LEACH, JOHN, Esq., of Ivy Tower, Pembrokeshire.
Only son of the late John Leach, Esq., of Pembroke, by Charlotte, dau. of G. Elliot, Esq.; *b.* 1826; *s.* 1857; *m.* 1851 Mary Anne Agnes, dau. of the late Henry Skrine, Esq., of Stubbings House, Berks, and Warleigh, Somerset. Educated at Harrow and University Coll., Oxford; is a Magistrate for co. Pembroke (High Sheriff 1855), and Lord of the Manor of St. Florence. —*Ivy Tower, Tenby; Windham Club, s.w.*

LEACH. (See *Lloyd*.)

+ LEACROFT, Col. RICHARD BECHER, of Matlock Bath, Derbyshire.
Son of the late R. Leacroft, Esq.; *b.* 18—; is a Dep. Lieut. for co. Derby, and a Col. in the Local Militia. —*Tor House, Matlock Bath, Derbyshire.*

+ LEADER, HENRY EUSTACE, Esq., of Mount Leader, co. Cork.
Eldest son of the late Henry Leader, Esq., J.P., of Mount Leader, by Elizabeth, only dau. of the late Rev.

Charles Eustace, of Robertstown, co. Kildare; *b.* 1833; *s.* 1868. Was formerly Capt. 16th Light Dragoons. —*Mount Leader, Millstreet, co. Cork.*

LEADER, NICHOLAS PHILPOT, Esq., of Dromagh, co. Cork.
Eldest son of the late Henry Leader, Esq., and nephew of the late Nicholas Philpot, Leader, Esq., some time M.P. for Kilkenny; *b.* 1808; *s.* 1836; *m.* 1847 Dorothea, dau. of the late Mac Gillicuddy, of The Reeks, and has, with other issue,

 • William, *b.* 1849.

Mr. Leader, who was educated at Trinity Coll., Dublin, is a Magistrate for co. Cork; he was elected M.P. for that county 1861.—*Dromagh Castle, Kanturk, co. Cork; Rosnalie, Banteer, co. Cork; Conservative Club, s.w.*

LEAHY, FRANCIS ROBERT, Esq., of Shanakiel, co. Cork.
Second son of the late Daniel Leahy, Esq., J.P. and D.L., of Shanakiel, by Margaret, dau. of the late Francis Arthur, Esq., of Limerick; *b.* 1825; *m.* 1850 Mary, 2nd dau. of Edmund Scully, Esq., of Bloomfield House, co. Tipperary. Is a Magistrate for co. Cork; was High Sheriff of the city of Cork, 1860.—*Shanakiel House, Cork; Windham Club, s.w.*

 Heir Pres., his brother Daniel Francis (of Woodlawn, near Cork), a Magistrate for the co. and city of Cork (High Sheriff 1867); *b.* 1832; *b.* 1855; *m.* 1856 Mary, only dau. of the late William Trant Fagan, Esq., M.P., of Feltrim, co. Cork.

LEAHY-ARTHUR, DAVID, Esq., of Hyde Park, co. Cork.
Eldest son of the late Daniel Leahy, Esq., of Shanakiel, co. Cork, by Margaret, dau. of the late Francis Arthur, Esq., of Limerick, whose name he has assumed; *b.* 1820; *s.* his maternal grandfather 1841; *m.* 1846 Amelia, dau. of Sir Joseph Radcliffe, Bart., of Rudding Park, co. York; is a Magistrate for co. Cork; has been High Sheriff of Cork and Limerick.—*Hyde Park, Cork.*

LEAKE. (See *Martin-Leake.*)

LEAN, JOHN STUCKEY, Esq., of Ridge, Somerset.
Eldest son of the late James Lean, Esq., of Clifton, co. Gloucester, by Lucy, dau. of the late Samuel Stuckey, Esq., of Langport, Somerset; *b.* 1802; *m.* 1831 Monique, dau. of the late Alan Bellingham, Esq., of Castle Bellingham, co. Louth. Is a Magistrate for Somerset. —*Ridge, Milverton; Corston Lodge, Bath.*

 Heir Pres., his brother James, late of the Bengal Civil Service; *b.* 1809.

LEARMONTH, ALEXANDER, Esq., of Dean, Midlothian.
Eldest surviving son of the late John Learmonth, J.P. and D.L., Esq. (who was some time Lord Provost of Edinburgh), by Margaret, dau. of the late Dr. James Cleghorn, of Dublin; *b.* 1829; *s.* 1858; *m.* 1858 Charlotte Salter, eldest dau. of Col. Humphrey Lyons, H.E.I.C.S., and has, with other issue,

 • Alexander, *b.* 1860.

Mr. Learmonth, who was educated at Eton and University Coll., Oxford, is a Magistrate for Midlothian, and a Lieut.-Col. in the Army; late Lieut.-Col. 17th Lancers. —*Murieston House, Midcalder, N.B.; Dean, Edinburgh; Army and Navy Club, s.w.; 93, Eaton Place, w.*

LEATHAM, EDWARD ALDAM, Esq., of Whitley Park, Yorkshire.
Son of the late William Leatham, Esq., of Heath, co. York, by Margaret, dau. and heir of Joshua Walker, Esq., M.D., of Leeds; *b.* 1828; *m.* 1851 Mary Jane,

only dau. of John Fowler, Esq., of Elm Grove, Melksham, Wilts, and has, with other issue,

 • Arthur William, *b.* 1852.

Mr. Leatham, who was educated at University Coll., London (B.A. 1848, M.A. 1851), is a Banker at Wakefield and Pontefract, and in the Commission of the Peace for the W. Riding of co. York; was M.P. for Huddersfield 1859-65, re-elected 1868.—*Whitley Park, Huddersfield; Reform Club, s.w.*

LEATHAM, WILLIAM HENRY, Esq., of Hemsworth Hall, Yorkshire.
Eldest surviving son of the late William Leatham, Esq., of Heath, near Wakefield, by Margaret, dau. of Joshua Walker, Esq., M.D., of Leeds; *b.* 1815; *m.* 1839 Priscilla, 4th dau. of Samuel Gurney, Esq., of West Ham, Essex, and has, with other issue,

 • Samuel Gurney, *b.* 1840; *m.* 1867 Annie Gertrude, 3rd dau. of John Frederick Bateman, Esq., of Moor Park, Surrey.

Mr. Leatham, who is a J.P. and D.L. for the W. Riding of Yorkshire, was formerly a Banker at Wakefield, Pontefract, and Doncaster; was elected M.P. for Wakefield 1859, but unseated on petition; re-elected 1865. —*Hemsworth Hall, Pontefract; 45, St. James's Place, s.w.*

LEATHER, JOHN TOWLERTON, Esq., of Middleton Hall, Northumberland, and Leventhorpe Hall, Yorkshire.
Eldest son of the late James Leather, Esq., of Beeston Park, near Leeds, by Mary, dau. of John Towlerton, Esq., of Kirkham Gate, co. York; *b.* 1804; *m.* 1st 1832 Maria, dau. of George Leather, Esq., of Leeds; 2nd 1852 Harriet Spencer, dau. of J. Spencer Page, Esq., and by her (who *d.* 1859) has, with other issue,

 • Frederick John, *b.* 1835; *m.* 1863 Gertrude Elizabeth Sophia, dau. of the Rev. Charles Walters, M.A., Wardington, Oxon.

Mr. Leather is a Magistrate for co. Northumberland, Capt. 2nd Dorset Artillery Volunteers, Lord of the Manor of Middleton and Detchant, and Patron of 2 livings.—*Middleton Hall, Belford; Leventhorpe Hall, Leeds; Conservative and Junior Carlton Clubs, s.w.; 19, Carlton House Terrace, s.w.*

LEATHES, EDWARD, Esq., of Normanstone, Suffolk.
Youngest son of the late George Leathes, Esq., of Bury St. Edmund's, Suffolk, formerly Major 1st Royal Dragoons, by Mary, dau. of J. Moore Esq., of Worcester; *b.* 1797; *m.* 1823 Eliza, dau. of John Galloway, Esq., and has, with other surviving issue,

 • William Charles Edwards, *b.* 1842.

Mr. Leathes is a J.P. and D.L. for Suffolk, Capt. Commandant of the 17th East Suffolk Rifles, and was formerly in the 1st Royal Dragoons.—*Normanstone, Lowestoft.*

LEATHES, HILL MUSSENDEN, Esq., of Herringfleet, Suffolk.
Eldest son of the late Henry Mussenden Leathes, Esq., of Herringfleet, by Charlotte, 2nd dau. of the late Thomas Fowler, Esq., of Gunton Hall, Suffolk; *b.* 1829; *s.* 1864; *m.* 1856 Mary Louisa, dau. of the late J. D Thomson, Esq., of Sunny Bank, co. Pembroke, and has issue. Mr. Leathes is a Magistrate for Suffolk, Lord of the Manors of Herringfleet and Reedham, and Patron of 4 livings, and Major of the East Suffolk Artillery Militia.—*Herringfleet Hall, Lowestoft.*

LEATHES, THOMAS LEATHES STANGER, Esq., of Dalehead Hall, Cumberland.
Eldest son of the late Thomas Stanger Leathes, Esq., of Dalehead Hall, by Charlotte, dau. of Edward Joanes, Esq., of Horsham, Sussex; *b.* 1790; *s.* 1838; *m.* 1816

Charlotte Ann, dau. of Bartholomew Browne, Esq., E.I.C.S., and has, with other issue,
* George, b. 1827; m. 1855 Emma Lee, dau. of — Woodhouse, Esq., and has issue, two daughters.

Mr. Leathes is Lord of the Manor of Legburthwaite, Cumberland. This family is descended from the De la Leathes of Leathes, Cumberland, who came over with William the Conqueror, settled in Cumberland, and became possessed of the Manor of Bowness, and much of the surrounding country, extending to Leathes and Wigton. In the 19th year of Elizabeth they sold most of that property and purchased Dalehead.—*Dalehead Hall, Keswick; Elm Bank, Lillington, Warwickshire.*

LEATON. (See Blenkinsopp.)

LE BLANC, Col. FRANCIS, of Blackbrook House, Hampshire.

Youngest son of the late Thomas Le Blanc, Esq., formerly of Cavenham, Suffolk, by Felicia, dau. of — Relhan, Esq., of London‡ b. 1790; m. 1828 Elizabeth Harriet, 2nd dau. of the late Thomas Porter, Esq., of Rockbeare House, Devon, but by her (who d. 1867) has no surviving issue. Col. Le Blanc, who was educated at Rugby, and entered the Army in 1807, is a Magistrate for Hants, and a Col. in the Army (retired 1842); was formerly in the Rifle Brigade, and 43rd Regt. This family is of French Huguenot extraction.—*Blackbrook House, Fareham.*

LECHE, JOHN HURLESTON, Esq., of Carden, Cheshire.

Eldest son of the late John Hurleston Leche, Esq., of Carden Park, by Elizabeth Antonia, dau. of Anthony Innys Stokes, Esq., of St. Botolph's, co. Pembroke; b. 1827; s. 1848; m. 1st 1850 Caroline, dau. of Edwin Corbett, Esq., of Tilstone Lodge; 2nd 1855 Eleanor Frances Stanhope, dau. of the late Charles Stanhope Jones, Esq., of Anglesea. Educated at Eton and Coblentz; is a Magistrate for co. Chester; Lord of the Manor of Carden, and Senior Capt. 1st Cheshire Militia.—*Carden Park, Chester.*

LECHMERE, Sir EDMUND ANTHONY HARLEY, Bart., of The Rhydd, Worcestershire (cr. 1811).

Eldest son of the late Sir Edmund Hungerford Lechmere, Bart., of Rhydd, by Maria Clara, dau. of the late Hon. David Murray; b. 1826; s. as 3rd Bart. 1856; m. 1858 Louisa Rosamond, dau. and heir of John Haigh, Esq., of Whitwell Hall, co. York. Educated at the Charterhouse and Ch. Ch., Oxford (B.A. 1849); is a J.P. and D.L. for co. Worcester (High Sheriff 1862), and Patron of 2 livings; elected M.P. for Tewkesbury 1866.—*The Rhydd, Worcester; Severn End, Upton-on-Severn; Whitwell Hall, York; Carlton Club, s.w.*
Heir, his son Edmund Arthur, b. 1865.

LECHMERE, Mrs., of Ludford, Shropshire.

Anna Maria, youngest dau. of the Hon. Andrew Foley (who d. 1818), by Elizabeth, dau. and heir of Boulter Tomlinson; m. 1823 John Lechmere, Esq., of Ludford, who was a J.P. and D.L. for Oxon, and formerly a Lieut. R.N., and who d. 1866.—*Ludford, Ludlow; Hill House, Steeple Aston, Oxon.*

LECHMERE, THOMAS, Esq., of Fownhope Court, Herefordshire.

Eldest son of the late Capel Lechmere, Esq., of Fownhope Court, formerly Capt. 15th Foot, by Mary, dau. of — Walker, Esq.; b. 1819; s. 1811; m. 1846 Elizabeth, only dau. of the Rev. John Eckley, of Credenhill Court, co. Hereford, and has, with other issue,
* John, b. 1850.

Mr. Lechmere is a Magistrate for co. Hereford.—*Fownhope Court, Hereford.*

568

LECKY, HUGH, Esq., of Bushmills, co. Antrim.

Eldest son of the late Hugh Lecky, Esq., of Bushmills, by Elizabeth, dau. of James Orr, Esq., of Keely, co. Londonderry; b. 1804; s. his uncle John Gage Lecky, Esq., 1819; m. 1837 Matilda, dau. of George Hutchinson, Esq., of Ballymoney, co. Antrim, and has, with other issue,
* Hugh, b. 1839.

Mr. Lecky, who was educated at Trinity Coll., Dublin, is a Magistrate for co. Antrim (High Sheriff 1836.)—*Beardiville, Bushmills, co. Antrim.*

LECKY, JOHN JAMES, Esq., of Ballykealey, co. Carlow.

Second son of the late John Lecky, Esq., of Ballykealey, by Elizabeth, dau. of Jacob Goff, Esq., of Horetown, co. Wexford; b. 1797; m. 1825 Sarah Lucia, only dau. of John Smith, Esq., of Baulby, co. York, and has, with other issue,
* John Frederick (of Lenham, Milford, co. Carlow), educated at Eton and Trinity Coll., Dublin; a Magistrate for co. Carlow (High Sheriff 1863); b.1826; m. 1853 Frances Margaret Featherstonhaugh, only dau. of John Beauchamp Brady, Esq., of Myshall, co. Carlow, and has, with other issue, * John Rupert Robert, b. 1855.

Mr. Lecky, who is a J.P. and D.L. for co. Carlow, represents a family of Scottish extraction.—*Ballykealey, Tullow, co. Carlow; Kildare Street Club, Dublin.*

LECONFIELD, Lord (GEORGE WYNDHAM).—Cr. 1859.

Eldest natural son of George, 3rd Earl of Egremont; b. 1787; m. 1815 Mary, only dau. of the late Rev. William Blunt, of Crabett, near Crawley, Sussex (she d. 1863). Is a Col. in the Army, a Magistrate for Sussex (High Sheriff 1842), Lord of the Manors of Petworth, &c., and Patron of 22 livings.—*Petworth House, Sussex; Boodle's Club, s.w.*
Heir, his son Henry, educated at Eton and Ch. Ch., Oxford, and M.P. for West Sussex; late Capt. 2nd Life Guards; b. 1830; m. 1867 the Hon. Constance Evelyn, 2nd dau. of Archibald, late Lord Dalmeny, and grand-dau. of Archibald John, 4th Earl of Rosebery.

LE DESPENCER, Baroness (MARY FRANCES ELIZABETH BOSCAWEN).—Cr. 1264.

Only child of the late Hon. Thomas Stapleton (who d. 1829), by Maria, dau. of the late Henry Bankes, M.P., of Kingston Hall, Dorset; b. 1822; s. her grandfather as 23rd Baroness 1831; m. 1845 Evelyn, 6th Viscount Falmouth (whom see). Is Hereditary Visitor of Emmanuel Coll., Cambridge, Lady of the Manors of Tregothnan and Mereworth, &c., and Patron of 2 livings.—*Mereworth Castle, Maidstone; Tregothnan, Truro; 2, St. James's Square, s.w.*
Heir, her son Evelyn Edward Thomas, b. 1847.

LEDSAM, JOSEPH, Esq., of Northfield, Worcestershire.

Eldest son of the late Joseph Frederick Ledsam, Esq., of Northfield and Edgbaston, co. Warwick, by Elizabeth Ann Ashton, only dau. of James Goddington, Esq., of Camp Hill, Birmingham; b. 1823; s. 1851; m. 1st 1850 Frances Barbara, dau. of George E. Jackson, Esq., of Harborne, co. Stafford; 2nd 1861 Anne Maria, dau. of Thomas Clutton Salt, Esq., and has issue. Is a Magistrate for co. Warwick.—*Northfield, Worcester; Hazlewood, Edgbaston, Birmingham.*

LEE, Sir GEORGE PHILIP, Knt., of Windlesham Court, Surrey (cr. 1844).

Son of the late Edward Lee, Esq., of London, by Charlotte, dau. of John Ede. Esq., of Bruce Castle and Harley Street; b. 180-; m. 1843 Charlotte, dau. of the late John Ede, Esq., of London. Late Lieut. of the Yeomen of the Guard.—*Windlesham Court, Bagshot; Windham Club, s.w.; 58, Brimstone Square, w.*

LEE, the Rev. ALFRED THEOPHILUS, LL.D., M.R.I.A., of Aghoghill, co. Antrim.

Son of the late Sir John Theophilus Lee, Knt., of Lauriston Hall, Torquay, by Sophia, dau. of Major Lawlor, of Greenwich; *b.* 1829; *m.* 1853 Euphemia, only dau. of Marriott Dalway, Esq., of Bella Hill, and has, with other issue,

* Robert McClellan Lauriston, *b.* 1855.

Dr. Lee, who was educated at Christ's Coll., Cambridge (B.A. 1853, M.A. 1856), Hon. LL.D. Trinity Coll., Dublin 1866, is Rector of Aghoghill, and Rural Dean in the diocese of Connor; appointed Chaplain to the Marquis of Abercorn, Lord Lieutenant of Ireland 1866. Is descended from the McClellans of Annan, Dumfries, and maternally from the celebrated John Law, of Lauriston.—*Aghoghill Rectory, Ballymena, co. Antrim; National Club,* s.w.

+ **LEE, EDWARD, Esq., of Ditton House, Berks.**

Son of the late E. Lee, Esq., of Ditton House, by a dau. of — Murrice, Esq.; *b.* 18—. This family descend from a common ancestor with the Lees, anciently Earls of Lichfield, of which title Mr. Lee is a claimant.—*Ditton House, Pinkneys Green, Maidenhead.*

LEE, EDWARD DYKE, Esq., of Hartwell, Bucks, and Totteridge Park, Herts.

Second but only surviving son of the late Rev. Nicholas Fiott, by Harriet Jenner, dau. of Sir Percyvall Hart Dyke, Bart., of Lullingstone Castle, Kent; *b.* 1843; *s.* his uncle, 1866; educated at Rugby and Ch. Ch., Oxford; is Lord of the Manors of Hartwell, Stone, Bishopstone, and Totteridge, and Patron of 2 livings. This family assumed the name of Lee by royal mandate, in 1853, as heirs of the entailed estates of Hartwell and Colworth. Coming originally from Cheshire, they settled in Buckinghamshire as early as the fourteenth century. Thomas Lee, of Hartwell, was created a Baronet by Charles II. in 1660, and the title descended from father to son until the year 1827, when, the Rev. Sir George Lee, Bart., dying unmarried, the estates devolved upon John Lee, Esq., LL.D., his nearest male kin, and uncle of the present owner.—*Hartwell House, Aylesbury; Totteridge Park, Barnet.*

Heirs Pres., his sisters.

LEE, the Rev. HARRY, of Kingsgate House, Hants, and Vowchurch, Herefordshire.

Eldest son of the late Rev. Harry Lee, of Kingsgate House, by Philippa, dau. of the late Sir William Blackstone, Knt., of the Priory, Wallingford; *b.* 1795; *s.* 1838; *m.* 1831 Julia, dau. of the late Gorges Lowther, Esq., of Kilrue, co. Meath. Educated at Winchester and New Coll., Oxford (B.A. 1816, M.A. 1820, B.D. 1827); appointed Fellow of Winchester Coll. 1827; is a Magistrate for co. Hereford, and Prebendary of Hereford. —*Kingsgate House, Winchester; Vowchurch, Hereford.*

Heir Pres., his brother William, *b.* 1796; *m.* 1836 Elizabeth, dau. of — Thomson, Esq., Master in Chancery, of Awbry, Sussex.

LEE, HENRY ALBERT, Esq., of Barna, co. Tipperary.

Eldest son of the late Henry Lee, Esq., of Barna, by Maria, dau. of Christopher Crofts, Esq., of Stream Hill, co. Cork; *b.* 1818; *s.* 1848; *m.* 1852 Susan Kate, eldest dau. of the late John Bonn, Esq., and has, with other issue,

* Albert Henry, *b.* 1853.

Mr. Lee, who was educated at Trinity Coll., Dublin, is descended from the ancient house of Lee of Oxfordshire. —*Barna, Newport, co. Tipperary.*

LEE, the Rev. HENRY THOMAS, of Dynas Powis, Glamorganshire.

Only son of the late Edward Herbert Lee, Esq., of The Mount, Dynas Powis, by Mary Anne, dau. of Thomas Thompson, Esq., of London; *b.* 1811; *s.* 1862; *m.* 1837 Catherine Frances, 5th dau. of James Broadwood, Esq., of Lyne, Surrey, and has, with other issue,

* Henry Herbert, Lieut. Royal Bombay Engineers, *b.* 1838.

Mr. Lee, who was educated at Eton and Trinity Coll., Cambridge (B.A. 1833, M.A. 1844), is a Magistrate for co. Glamorgan, Lord of the Manor of Dynas Powis, Glamorgan, Vicar of South Raynham, Norfolk, and Rural Dean.—*The Mount, Dynas Powis, Cardiff.*

LEE, JOHN HUTCHINSON, Esq., of Balsdon, Devon.

Second son of the late Sir John Theophilus Lee, Knt., of Balsdon, by Sophia, dau. of Major Lawler, of Greenwich, Kent; *b.* 1810; *s.* 1843; *m.* 1847 Caroline, youngest dau. of the late John Hives, Esq., of Gledhow Grove, Leeds, and has, with other issue,

* John Theophilus, *b.* 1850.

Mr. Lee, who was educated at Eton, is a Magistrate for Middlesex and Westminster.—*Balsdon, Torquay.*

LEE, JOHN LEE, Esq., of Dillington, Somerset, and Orleigh, Devon.

Eldest son of the late William Hanning, Esq., of Dillington, by Harriet, dau. of Edward Lee, Esq., of Pinhoe, near Exeter; *b.* 1802; *s.* 1834; *m.* 1st 1834 Jessy, dau. of John Edwards Vaughan, Esq., of Rheola, co. Glamorgan; 2nd 1841 the Hon. Sophia Mary, dau. of Samuel, 1st Lord Bridport, and has, by the former,

* Vaughan Hanning Lee, Capt. Glamorganshire Light Infantry; late Capt. 21st Fusiliers; *b.* 1836.

Mr. Lee, who was educated at Westminster and Ch. Ch., Oxford is a J.P. and D.L. for Somerset (High Sheriff 1845), a Magistrate for Devon, and Patron of 1 living: he was M.P. for Wells 1831–7; assumed the surname of Lee 1820, on succeeding to the property of his uncle, Edward Lee, Esq., of Orleigh.—*Dillington House, Ilminster; Orleigh Court, Bideford.*

LEE, RICHARD THOMAS, Esq., of Grove Hall, Yorkshire.

Second but eldest surviving son of the late William Lee, Esq., of Grove Hall, by Sophia, 2nd dau. of Sir Thomas Wentworth-Blackett, Bart., of Bretton Hall, co. York; *b.* 1808; *m.* 1853 Louisa, dau. and co-heir of the late Lieut.-General Sir Andrew Pilkington, K.C.B., of Catsfield Place, Sussex, and has, with other issue,

* Frederick William, *b.* 1857.

Mr. Lee is a Magistrate for the W. Riding of co. York. —*Grove Hall, Pontefract.*

LEE, THOMAS YATE, Esq., of Redcliffe Kinver, Staffordshire.

Eldest son of the late Thomas Eyre Lee, Esq., of Birmingham (who *d.* 1852), by Rebecca, dau. of Benjamin Hodgson, Esq., of London; *b.* 1819; *m.* 1817 Mary Joanna, dau. of the Rev. Charles Berry, of Leicester, and has, with other issue,

* Thomas Grosvenor, B.A., of University Coll., London; *b.* 1848.

Mr. Lee was educated at University Coll., London (B.A. 1839), and called to the Bar at Lincoln's Inn 1845, is a Magistrate for co. Stafford, and a manufacturer at the Hyde Iron Works, near Stourbridge; was formerly Capt. 35th Staffordshire Rifle Volunteers. This family was formerly of East Farndon, Northamptonshire, Abingdon, Berkshire, and Egginton, Derbyshire, and is derived through heiresses from the families of De Corona and Venables, Barons of Kinderton, in Cheshire. —*Redcliffe, Kinver, Stourbridge*

LEE, WILLIAM, Esq., of Holborough, Kent.
Son of the late Henry Lee, Esq., of Lewisham, Kent; *b.*
1801; *m.* 1820 Christiana, 2nd dau. of the late Samuel
Reynolds, Esq., of Theydon, Essex, and has issue. Is
a J.P. and D.L. for Kent, and a Merchant in London
and Rochester; was M.P. for Maidstone 1853–7, re-
elected 1859.—*Holborough Court, Snodland, Rochester;
Reform Club,* s.w.

LEE. (See under *Dillon, Viscount*.)

LEE. (See *Supplement*.)

LEE-HARVEY. (See *Harvey*.)

LEE-JORTIN, HENRY WILLIAM, Esq.
Only son of the late William Lee-Jortin, Esq., of Nibley House, co. Gloucester (who assumed in 1843 the additional name of Jortin on succeeding to Nibley), by
Charlotte Hardtman, dau. of Thomas Pemberton, Esq.,
of St. Christopher, West Indies, and widow of Alfred
Thrale Perkins, Esq.; *b.* 1833; *s.* 1861; *m.* 1865 Lucy
Gratiana, only dau. of Samborne Stucley Palmer-Samborne, Esq., of Timsbury House, Somerset; was formerly Lieut. 2nd Life Guards.—*Army and Navy and
Conservative Clubs,* s.w.; 38, *Curzon Street,* w.

+LEE-MAINWARING, CHARLES BENJAMIN,
Esq., of Knaresborough Abbey, Yorkshire.
Eldest son of the late John Lee, Esq., D.L., of Knares-
borough Abbey, by Miss Maria Mainwaring, of Goltho
Hall, co. Lincoln; *b.* 179–; *m.* 1839 the Hon. Mary
Stuart, dau. of James, 18th Lord Forbes, and had,
with other issue, an only son,
   Charles Walter, *b.* 1841; *d.* 1866.
Mr. Lee has assumed the additional name of Main-
waring.—*The Abbey, Knaresborough; The Old Palace,
Richmond,* s.w.

LEE-NORMAN, THOMAS, Esq., of Corbollis, co.
Louth.
Eldest son of the late Thomas Lee, Esq., of Corbollis,
by Sarah, dau. of the Rev. Thomas Norman, of Lagore,
whose name he has assumed; *b.* 1790; *s.* 1800. Edu-
cated at Trinity Coll., Cambridge; is a J.P. and D.L.
for co. Louth (High Sheriff 1820).—*Corbollis, Ardee.*
   * *Heir Pres.,* his nephew Cadwallader Blayney, son of the
   Rev. William Lee, by Florinda Frances, dau. of the late
   Thomas Lee, Esq.; *b.* 18—.

LEE-WARNER, HENRY JAMES, Esq., of Wal-
singham Abbey, Norfolk.
Eldest son of the late Rev. D. Henry Lee-Warner, of
Walsingham Abbey, by Anne, dau. of Francis William
Thomas Brydges, Esq., of Tibberton Court, co. Hereford;
b. 1809; *s.* 1858; *m.* 1846 Ellen Rosetta, youngest dau.
of the late Jonathan Bullock, Esq., of Faulkbourne Hall,
Essex, and has, with other issue,
   * Henry, *b.* 1847.
Mr. Lee-Warner, who was educated at Eton and Ch.
Ch., Oxford, is a J.P. and D.L. for cos. Norfolk and
Hereford (High Sheriff 186).— *Walsingham Abbey,
Fakenham; Athenæum Club,* s.w.

LEE-WARNER, ROBERT HENRY, Esq., of Tibberton Court, Herefordshire.
Seventh son of the late Rev. Daniel Henry Lee-Warner,
of Walsingham Abbey, Norfolk (who *d.* 1858), by Anne,
eldest dau. of the late Francis William Thomas Brydges,
Esq., of Tibberton Court; *b.* 1823; *s.* under the will of
his father, 1858; *m.* 1866 Isabella Margaret, third dau.
of the late Charles David Gordon, Esq., of Abergeldie
Castle, N.B., and widow of Antony Gibbs, Esq., of
Merry Hill, Herts. Is a J.P. and D.L. for co. Hereford (High Sheriff 1861); was formerly in the Navy,
and was present at the siege of Acre. The Brydges
570

family, whom he represents maternally, migrated from
Bosbury, and have been seated at Tibberton above two
centuries.—*Tibberton Court, Hereford.*

+LEECH, GEORGE WILLIAMS, Esq., of Rathkeale Abbey, co. Limerick.
Son of the late John Bourke Leech, Esq., of Rathkeale,
by Helena his wife; *b.* 1810; *m.* 1st 1835 Anna Maria,
dau. of General George Bellasis; 2nd 1846 Catherine,
dau. of Hunt Walshe Chambre, Esq., of Hawthorne
Hill, co. Armagh, and has, by the former,
   * Robert Stockholm Brydges, late Capt. 94th Foot, *b.* 1836.
Mr. Leech, who was called to the Bar at Lincoln's Inn
1849, is a Magistrate for co. Limerick.—*The Abbey,
Rathkeale, Limerick.*

LEEDS, Duke of (GEORGE GODOLPHIN OSBORNE).
—Cr. 1694.
Eldest son of the late Lord Francis Godolphin Osborne
(1st Lord Godolphin), by the Hon. Elizabeth Charlotte,
dau. of William, 1st Lord Auckland, and grandson of
Francis, 5th Duke of Leeds; *b.* 1802; *s.* his father as
2nd Lord 1850, and his cousin as 8th Duke 1859;
m. 1824 Miss Harriet Emma Arundel Stewart (she *d.*
1852). Educated at Westminster and Ch. Ch., Oxford;
is Patron of 4 livings.—*Gogmagog Hills, Cambridge;
Godolphin Park, Cornwall;* 15, *Portman Square,* w.
   Heir, his son George Godolphin, Marquis of Carmarthen,
   Capt. North York Militia Rifles; *b.* 1828; *m.* 1861 the Hon.
   Fanny Georgiana, Lady of the Bedchamber to the Princess
   of Wales, 2nd dau. of George, 4th Lord Rivers, and has,
   with other issue, * George Godolphin, Earl of Danby, *b.*
   1862.

LEEDS, Dowager Duchess of, of Hornby
Castle, Yorkshire.
Louisa Catherine, 3rd dau. and co-heir of the late
Richard Caton, Esq., of the United States; *m.* 1st 1817
Sir Felton Elwell Bathurst-Hervey, Bart., who *d.* 1819;
2nd 1828 Francis Godolphin, 7th Duke of Leeds, who
d. 1859.—*Hornby Castle, Catterick; Clarendon Hotel,* w.

LEEDS, Sir EDWARD, Bart. (cr. 1812).
Eldest son of the late Sir Joseph Edward Leeds, Bart.,
formerly of Croxton Park, by Marian, only dau. of the
late William Thomas Stretton, Esq., of London; *b.*
1825; *s.* 1862; *m.* 1st 1848 Emily Ann, only dau. of
Major Bolton (she *d.* 1849); 2nd 1854 Fanny, only dau.
of Col. Templer, H.E.I.C.'s Service. Educated at the
Military Coll., Addiscombe; is a Major in the Bengal
Staff Corps.—*Pitteville Parade, Cheltenham.*
   Heir, his son George Augustus, *b.* 1849.

LEEKE, Sir HENRY JOHN, K.C.B., K.H. (cr.
1835).
Eldest surviving son of the late Samuel Leeke, Esq., of
Havant, and of St. John's, Isle of Wight (who was a
J.P. and D.L. for Hants); *b.* 1794; *m.* 1st 1818 Augusta
Sophia, 2nd dau. of James Dashwood, Esq., of Park-
hurst, Surrey (she *d.* 1861); 2nd 1863 Georgiana Lucy
Cecilia, only dau. of the late Rev. Geoffrey Hornby, and
has by the former, with other issue,
   * Henry Edwin, *b.* 1823.
Sir Henry, who is a J.P. and D.L. for Hants, a Magis-
trate for Middlesex and Sussex, and an Admiral R.N.,
was Commander-in-Chief of the Indian Navy 1851–8;
commanded the fleet against Persia 1856–7; was M.P.
for Dover 1859–65, a Lord of the Admiralty in 1859.
—*Residence: Hill Hall, Epping; United Service Club,* s.w.

LEEKE, RALPH MEYRICK, Esq., of Longford
Hall, Shropshire.
Eldest son of the late Thomas Leeke, Esq., of Longford
Hall, by his 1st wife Louisa, dau. of Brig.-General R.
Shawe; *b.* 1813; *s.* 1813; *m.* 1817 Lady Hester Urania,

2nd dau. of Newton, 4th Earl of Portsmouth, and has, with other issue,

* Ralph, b. 1849.

Mr. Leeks, who was educated at Harrow and Ch. Ch., Oxford, is a J.P. and D.L. for co. Salop (High Sheriff 1850), a Magistrate for co. Stafford, Lord of the Manor of Longford, Patron of that living, and Capt. S. Salop Yeomanry Cavalry.—*Longford Hall, Newport, Salop; Boodle's and Carlton Clubs, s.w.*

LEES, Sir JOHN, Bart. (cr. 1804).
Eldest son of the late Rev. Sir Harcourt Lees, Bart., by Sophia, dau. of the late Col. Lyster, Esq., of Grange, co. Roscommon; b. 1816; s. as 3rd Bart. 1852; m. 1839 Maria Charlotte, dau. of Edward R. Sullivan, Esq., of the Madras Civil Service; is Capt. Hants Militia.—*Ryde, I. of Wight.*

> *Heir*, his son Harcourt James, Lieut. 60th Rifles and Ensign in the Warwick Militia; b. 1840; m. 1860 Charlotte, dau. of J. McTagart, Esq., and has, with other issue, * John Caldwell, b. 1861.

LEES, Sir JOHN CAMPBELL, Knt. (cr. 1865).
Eldest son of the late James Lees, Esq., by Rebecca, dau. of Archibald Esdaile, Esq.; b. 1796; m. 1st 1824 Mary, dau. of William Vesey Mannings, Esq.; 2nd 1849 Ellen, dau. of Francis Nivaz, Esq.; called to the Bar at the Inner Temple 1833; was formerly Chief Judge in Admiralty, and President of the Legislative Council of the Bahamas.—*Lesness Park, Belvedere, Kent, s.e.; Athenæum Club, s.w.*

LEES, JAMES, Esq., of Delph Lodge, Yorkshire.
Eldest son of the late James Lees, Esq., of Delph Lodge; b. 1797; s. 1810; m. 1830 Mary, dau. of J. Smith, Esq., and has issue an only surviving dau.,

> * Mary Adelaide, m. 1859 James Wood Baker, Esq., of Bury, co. Lancaster, son of James Earnshaw Baker, Esq., of Acomb, near York.

Mr. Lees is a Magistrate for the W. Riding of Yorkshire and for co. Lancaster.—*Delph Lodge, Saddleworth.*

LEESON, Sir WILLIAM EDWARD, Knt. (cr. 1888).
Youngest son of the late Hon. Robert Leeson, by his 1st wife Grace, dau. of the late Michael Head, Esq., and grandson of Joseph, 1st Earl of Milltown; b. 1801; m. 1st 1826 Louisa Araminta, dau. of Col. Sewell (she d. 1851); 2nd 1853 Julia, dau. of Capt. Edwin Roberts, R.N., of Rivington House, co. Cavan, and has by the former, with other issue,

> * Richard, b. 1829.

Sir William is Chamberlain of Dublin Castle, and Genealogist of the Order of St. Patrick; was formerly Usher of the Black Rod.—*Percy Place, Dublin.*

LEESON. (See under *Milltown, Earl of.*)

LEESON-MARSHALL. (See *Supplement.*)

LEFEVRE, Sir JOHN GEORGE SHAW-, K.C.B. (cr. 1857).
Second son of the late Charles Shaw-Lefevre, Esq., M.P., of Heckfield Place, Hants, by Helena, dau. of J. Lefevre, Esq., and brother of Viscount Eversley; b. 1797; m. 1824 Rachel Emily, 5th dau. of the late Ichabod Wright, Esq., of Mapperley, Notts, and has, with other issue,

> * George John, educated at Eton and Trinity Coll., Cambridge, M.P. for Reading, and late a Lord of the Admiralty; b. 1832.

Sir J. G. Shaw-Lefevre was educated at Eton and Trinity Coll., Cambridge (B.A. 1818. M.A. 1821); became Fellow of Trinity Coll. 1819; D.C.L. of the Universities of Ox-

ford and Dublin; F.R.S.; is Clerk of the Parliaments, an Ecclesiastical Commissioner, and a Member of the Senate of the University of London; called to the Bar at the Inner Temple 1824, and elected a Bencher of that Inn 1856; has been Under-Secretary of State for the Colonies, Poor-Law Commissioner, and Joint Assistant-Secretary of the Board of Trade; Emigration Commissioner, Church Estates Commissioner, Civil Service Commissioner, and Vice-Chancellor of the University of London; was M.P. for Petersfield 1832–4.—*Residence: Ascot Wood, Staines; Athenæum Club, s.w.; 18, Spring Gardens, s.w.; House of Lords, s.w.*

LEFEVRE. (See under *Eversley, Viscount.*)

LE-FLEMING, Sir MICHAEL, Bart. (cr. 1705).
Eldest son of the late Rev. Sir Richard Fleming, Bart., of Rydal, Westmoreland, by Sarah, dau. of the late W. B. Bradshaw, Esq., of Hulton Hall, co. Lancaster; b. 1828; s. as 7th Bart. 1857; m. 1853 Mary, dau. of Capt. Boddie. Is a Landowner in New Zealand.—*Canterbury, New Zealand.*

> *Heir*, his son Andrew, b. 1854.

LE-FLEMING, GEORGE CUMBERLAND HUGHES, Esq., of Rydal Hall, Westmoreland.
Eldest son of John Cumberland Hughes, Esq., by Elizabeth, dau. of George Edward Stanley, Esq., of Ponsonby Hall, Cumberland; a Major-General in Her Majesty's Indian Army; b. 18—; s. his cousin Lady Ann Frederica Elizabeth Fleming 1861, when he assumed the name of Le-Fleming in lieu of his patronymic; m. 1st 1848 Mary, dau. of John McPherson, Esq.; 2nd 1853 Anne Jane, dau. of Major Alexander Rennick, of the Bengal Army. This family descend from Sir Michael Le-Fleming, a relative of Baldwin, Earl of Flanders, father-in-law to William the Conqueror, who came over to England at the Conquest.—*Rydal Hall, Ambleside.*

LEFROY, Capt. BENJAMIN LANGLOIS, of Cardenton House, co. Kildare.
Third son of the late Lieut.-Col. Anthony Lefroy, of the 9th Dragoons, by Anne, dau. of — Gardiner, Esq., and brother of the Right Hon. Thomas Lefroy; b. 1782; m. 1807 Margaret, dau. of the late Philip Savage, Esq., of Kilgibbon, co. Wexford, and niece of the late Lord Callan (ext.), and has, with other issue,

> * Anthony George, b. 1809.

Mr. Lefroy, who was educated at the Royal Military Academy, Woolwich, and entered the Royal Artillery in 1800, is a Magistrate for co. Kildare, and Lord of the Manor of Cardenton.—*Cardenton House, Athy.*

LEFROY, CHARLES JAMES MAXWELL, Esq., of Itchel Manor, Hampshire.
Eldest son of the late Charles Edward Lefroy, Esq., of Itchel Manor, by Janet, dau. of James Walker, Esq., F.R.S.; b. 1848; s. 1861. Educated at Eton; is Lord of the Manors of Itchel and Ewshott, and Patron of 2 livings.—*Itchel Manor, Crondall, Farnham.*

> *Heir Pres.*, his brother Clement George, b. 1850.

LEFROY, the Right Hon. THOMAS, of Carrickglass, co. Longford.
Eldest son of the late Anthony Lefroy, Esq., of Carrickglass (some time Lieut.-Col. 9th Dragoons, who d. 1819), by Anne, dau. of — Gardiner, Esq.; b. 1776; m. 1799 Mary, only dau. and heir of Jeffry Paul, Esq., of Silver Spring, co. Wexford, and has, with other issue,

> * Anthony, educated at Trinity Coll. Dublin (B.A. 1821. LL.D. 1841); a Ser.-Lieut. for co. Longford, of which he has been High Sheriff; M.P. for co. Longford 1830-7, and 1841-7; elected M.P. for Dublin University 1858; b. 1800; m. 1824 the Hon. Jane, eldest dau. of Robert Edward, 1st Viscount Lorton, and has issue two daughters.

Mr. Lefroy was educated at Trinity Coll., Dublin (B.A.

1796, M.A. 1800); called to the Irish Bar 1797; appointed a Bencher of King's Inns 1819, a Baron of the Irish Exchequer 1841, was Chief Justice of Queen's Bench 1852–66; was M.P. for the University of Dublin 1830–41.—*Carrickglass, Longford; 18, Leeson Street, Dublin.*

LEGARD, Sir CHARLES, Bart., of Ganton Hall, Yorkshire (cr. 1660).

Only surviving son of the late Sir Thomas Digby Legard, Bart., of Ganton (who *d.* 1860), by the Hon. Frances, dau. of Charles, 1st Lord Feversham; *b.* 1846 ; *s.* his brother as 11th Bart. 1866. Is Lord of the Manor of Ganton, and Patron of that living.—*Ganton Hall, York.*

    Heir Pres., his cousin Algernon Willoughby (elder son of the late Henry Willoughby Legard, Esq., who *d.* 1845, by Charlotte Henrietta, eldest dau. of Henry Willoughby, Esq.. of Birdsall, co. York) ; *b.* 1842.

LEGARD, Capt. JAMES ANLABY, K.T.S., of Cowes, Isle of Wight.

Eldest son of the late Rev. William Legard, Vicar of Ganton, co. York (who *d.* 1825), by Cecilia Elizabeth, dau. of James Oldershaw, Esq., M.D., of Stamford ; *b.* 1805; *m.* 1845 Catharine, dau. of Sir George Cayley, Bart., and widow of Henry R. Beaumont, Esq., by whom he has, with other issue,

    * James Digby, *b.* 1846.

Capt. Legard, is a Magistrate for Hants, Notts, and the N. Riding of Yorkshire, and is a Capt. R.N. retired; represents a younger branch of the Legards, Barts., of Ganton.—*The Grove, Cowes, I. of Wight.*

LEGG. (See *Rowan-Legg.*)

LEGGE, Lady GEORGIANA CAROLINE, of Keston, Kent.

Seventh dau. of George, 3rd Earl of Dartmouth, by the Hon. Frances, dau. of Heneage, 3rd Earl of Aylesford. Was formerly a Lady of the Bedchamber to the late Duchess of Gloucester.—*Keston, Bromley.*

LEGGE, Ladies MARY and ANNE, of Holmwood Lodge, Surrey.

Daughters of George, 3rd Earl of Dartmouth, by the Lady Frances, 2nd dau. of Heneage, 3rd Earl of Aylesford.—*Holmwood Lodge, Dorking.*

LEGGE, the Hon. ARTHUR CHARLES, of Caynton, Shropshire.

Fifth son of George, 3rd Earl of Dartmouth, by the Hon. Frances, dau. of Heneage, 3rd Earl of Aylesford ; *b.* 1800 ; *m.* 1st 1827 Lady Anne Frederica, 3rd dau. of John, 1st Earl of Sheffield (she *d.* 1829) ; 2nd 1837 Caroline, dau. of the late James Charles Philip Bouwens, Esq., and has, with other issue,

    * Charles, *b.* 1829.

Mr. Legge, who was educated at Eton, and became a Magistrate for co. Salop, is a Dep.-Lieut. for Kent, and a Major-General in the Army.—*Caynton, Shiffnall.*

LEGGE, the Hon. and Rev. HENRY.

Sixth son of George, 3rd Earl of Dartmouth, by Lady Frances, dau. of Heneage, 3rd Earl of Aylesford ; *b.* 1803 ; *m.* 1842 Marian, dau. of Sir Frederick Leman Rogers, Bart. Educated at Eton and Ch. Ch., Oxford (B.A. 1824) ; was afterwards Fellow of All Souls Coll.; graduated B.C.L. 1835, D.C.L. 1840; appointed Vicar of Lewisham 1831.—*The Hollies, Blackheath, s.e.*

LEGGE, the Rev. WILLIAM, of Mareland and Bramdean, Hants.

Eldest surviving son of the late Hon. and Rev. Augustus George Legge, Prebendary of Winchester, Rector of Wonston, &c., by Honora, dau. of the late Rev. Walter Bagot, of Blithfield, co. Stafford, and niece of William,

1st Lord Bagot; *b.* 1802. Educated at Westminster and Ch. Ch., Oxford (B.A. 1824) ; is Rector of Ashtead, Surrey, and Lord of the Manors of Mareland, Weston, &c.—*Ashtead Rectory, Epsom ; Mareland, Farnham ; Bramdean House, Alresford.*

LEGGE, WILLIAM WALLACE-, Esq., of Malone House, co. Antrim.

Eldest son of the late William Wallace-Legge, Esq., of Malone House, by Eleanor Wilkie, 3rd dau. of Thomas Forster, Esq., of Adderstone, Northumberland; *b.* 1841 ; *s.* 1868. The late Mr. Wallace-Legge, was a J.P. and D.L. for co. Antrim (High Sheriff 1823); he assumed the additional arms and surname of his maternal uncle, the late William Legge, Esq., of Malone House.—*Malone House, Belfast.*

LEGGE. (See under *Dartmouth, Earl of.*)

+**LEGH**, CHARLES RICHARD BANASTRE, Esq., of Adlington Hall, Cheshire.

Eldest son of the late Thomas Legh. Esq., of Adlington Hall, by Louisa, dau. of George Newnham, Esq., of New-Timber Place, Sussex (she re-married 1830 Thomas, 3rd Lord Erskine); *b.* 1825; *s.* 1829. Is a J.P. and D.L. for co. Chester, Lord of the Manor and Patron of Prestbury.—*Adlington Hall, Macclesfield.*

LEGH, GEORGE CORNWALL, Esq., of High Legh, Cheshire.

Eldest son of the late George John Legh, Esq., of High Legh, by Mary, dau of the late John Blackburne, Esq., M.P., of Hale, co. Lancaster; *b.* 1804 ; *s.* 1832; *m.* 1828 Louisa Charlotte, dau. of Edward Taylor, Esq., of Bifrons, Kent. Educated at Ch. Ch., Oxford (B.A. 1826); is a J.P. and D.L. for co. Chester (High Sheriff 1838), and Major 2nd Cheshire Militia; was M.P. for N. Cheshire 1841–7, and has represented that division since 1848.—*High Legh, Knutsford ; Carlton and Travellers' Clubs, s.w. ; 93, Eaton Place, s.w.*

LEGH, JOHN PENNINGTON-, Esq., of Norbury Booths, Cheshire.

Eldest son of the late Rev. Edmund Dawson Legh, by Catherine, eldest dau. of the late Right Hon. Sir Christopher Robinson ; *b.* 1827 ; *s.* his uncle 1857 ; *m.* 1858 Emily Jane, 2nd dau. of the Rev. Robert Grant, of Bradford Abbas, Dorset, and has issue,

    * A dau., *b.* 1863.

Mr. Pennington-Legh, who was educated at the Charterhouse and Wadham Coll., Oxford (B.A. 1819). is a Magistrate for co. Chester. This family were formerly named Pennington, but they assumed the name of Legh on marriage with the heiress of that family.—*Norbury Booths Hall, Knutsford.*

LEGH, WILLIAM JOHN, Esq., of Lyme Park, Cheshire.

Eldest surviving son of the late William Legh, Esq., by Mary, dau. of — Wilkinson, Esq., of Brymbo, co. Denbigh; *b.* 1829; *s.* his uncle Thomas 1857 ; *m.* 1856 Emily Jane, dau. of the Ven. Archdeacon Wodehouse, and has, with other issue,

    * A son, *b.* 1859.

Mr. Legh is a J.P. and D.L. for cos. Chester and Lancaster. Patron of 1 living, and Capt. Lancashire Hussars; late Capt. 21st Fusiliers ; was M.P. for S. Lancashire 1859–65.—*Lyme Park, Stockport ; Golborne Park ; Warrington ; Carlton and Army and Navy Clubs, s.w.*

LE GRICE, DAY PERRY, Esq., of Trereife, Cornwall.

Only son of the late Rev. Charles Valentine Le Grice, by Mary, widow of William Nicholls, Esq., of Trereife. *b.* 1800; *s.* 1858; *m.* 1829 Arabella, dau. of the Rev.

Christopher Tuthill, of Webbville House, co. Cork, and has, with other issue, an only son,

* Charles Day Nicholls, a Magistrate for Cornwall, *b.* 1839 ; *m.* 1864 Laura, youngest dau. of George Elers, Esq., of Gloucester Terrace, Hyde Park.

Mr. Le Grice, who was educated at Eton and Oriel Coll., Oxford (B.A. 1822), is a J.P. and D.L. for Cornwall (High Sheriff 1864), and a Dep. Warden of the Stannaries.—*Trereife House, Penzance.*

LE HUNTE, George, Esq., of Artramont, co. Wexford.

Eldest son of the late William Augustus Le Hunte, Esq., of Artramont, by Henrietta, dau. of the Rev. John Miller ; *b.* 1815 ; *s.* 1820 ; *m.* 1845 Mary, 5th dau. of the late Right Hon. Edward Pennefather, and has, with other issue,

* George Ruthven, *b.* 1852.

Mr. Le Hunte, who was educated at Trinity Coll., Cambridge (B.A. 1836, M.A. 1840), is a Magistrate for co. Wexford.—*Artramont, Castle Bridge, co. Wexford ; Oxford and Cambridge Club, s.w.*

LE HUNTE, William Augustus, Esq., of Knocknalier, co. Wexford.

Second son of the late William Augustus Le Hunte, Esq., by Henrietta Eliza, dau. of the Rev. Joseph Miller ; *b.* 1819. Is a Magistrate for co. Wexford. —*Knocknalier, Enniscorthy, co. Wexford.*

LEICESTER, Earl of (Thomas William Coke). —Cr. 1837.

Eldest son of Thomas William, 1st Earl (who was M.P. for Norfolk during more than 50 years), by his 2nd wife Lady Anne Amelia, dau. of William Charles, 4th Earl of Albemarle ; *b.* 1822 ; *s.* 1842 ; *m.* 1843 Juliana, dau. of Samuel Charles Whitbread, Esq., of Cardington, Beds. Educated at Eton and Winchester ; is Lord-Lieut. and Custos Rotulorum of Norfolk, Lord of the Manors of Holkham, &c., and Patron of 8 livings. —*Holkham Hall, Lynn, Norfolk ; 131, Piccadilly, w.*

Heir, his son Thomas William, Viscount Coke, *b.* 1848.

LEIGH, Lord (William Henry Leigh, LL.D.). —Cr. 1839.

Eldest son of Chandos, 1st Lord, by Margaret, dau. of the late Rev. William Shippen Willes, of Astrop House, co. Northampton ; *b.* 1824 ; *s.* 1850 ; *m.* 1848 Lady Caroline Amelia, dau. of Richard, 2nd Marquis of Westminster, K.G. Educated at Harrow and Trinity Coll., Cambridge ; is Lord Lieutenant and Custos Rotulorum of co. Warwick, a Magistrate for co. Gloucester. Patron of 9 livings, Hon. Col. 1st Warwickshire Militia, and a Trustee of Rugby School ; late Capt. Warwickshire Yeomanry ; cr. Hon. LL.D. Cambridge 1864. —*Stoneleigh Abbey, Kenilworth, Warwick ; Adlestrop House, Chipping Norton, Oxon ; Brooks's and Travellers' Clubs, s.w. ; 37, Portman Square, w.*

Heir, his son Gilbert Henry Chandos, *b.* 1851.

LEIGH, the Rev. Charles Brian, of Goldhanger, Essex.

Eldest surviving son of the late Rev. Thomas Leigh, many years Vicar of Wickham Bishops (who *d.* 1847), by Emma Mason, dau. of William Morris, Esq., of Havering, Essex ; *b.* 1815 ; *m.* 1st 1847 Mary, younger dau. of the late Sir John Tyrell, Bart., and widow of John Wright, Esq., of Hatfield Priory, Essex ; 2nd 1852 Olympia Priscilla, dau. of the late Richard Hanbury, Esq., and has, with other issue,

* Charles Edward, *b.* 1856.

Mr. Leigh, who was educated at Christ's Coll., Cambridge (B.A. 1837), is a Magistrate for Essex, and Rector and Patron of Goldhanger.—*Goldhanger, Ma'don.*

LEIGH, Egerton, Esq., of High Leigh, Cheshire.

Eldest son of the late Egerton Leigh, Esq., J.P. and D.L., of High Leigh (who was High Sheriff of co. Chester 1836), by Wilhelmina Sarah, dau. of the late George Stratton, Esq., of Tew Park, Oxon ; *b.* 1815 ; *s.* 1865 ; *m.* 1842 Lydia, dau. and co-heir of the late John Smith Wright, Esq., of Bulcote Lodge, Notts, and has, with other issue,

* Egerton, *b.* 1843.

Mr. Leigh, who was educated at Eton, is a J.P. and D.L. for co. Chester, Lord of the Manor of High Leigh, Patron of 2 livings, and Major 1st Cheshire Militia ; late Capt. 2nd Dragoon Guards.—*West Hall, High Leigh, Knutzford ; Jodrell Hall, Congleton ; Bulcote Lodge, Nottingham.*

LEIGH, Francis, Esq., of Sion House, co. Wexford, and Thorn Hill, co. Dublin.

Youngest, but only surviving son of the late Francis Leigh, Esq., M.P., of Rosegarland, co. Wexford, by Grace, only dau. of Richard Baldwin, Esq., of King's Co. ; *b.* 1808 ; *m.* 1830 Mary Martin, youngest dau. of John Southcote Mansergh, Esq., of Greenane, co. Tipperary, and has, with other issue,

* Francis Charles William, *b.* 1831.

Mr. Leigh, who was educated at Trinity Coll., Dublin, is a Magistrate for co. Wexford.—*Sion House, Kyle, co. Wexford ; Thorn Hill, Bray, co. Dublin.*

+LEIGH, Francis Augustine, Esq., of Rosegarland, co. Wexford.

Eldest son of the late John Leigh, of Rosegarland, by a dau. of — FitzGerald, Esq. ; *b.* 18— ; *m.* 18— a foreign lady, and has issue,

* John, *b.* 18—.

Mr. Leigh, who is a Magistrate for co. Wexford (High Sheriff 1867), was formerly in the Army.—*Rosegarland, Foulksenhill, co. Wexford.*

LEIGH, John Shaw, Esq., of Luton Hoo, Beds.

Eldest son of the late John Leigh, Esq. (who *d.* 1823), by Elizabeth, dau. of Richard Gerard, Esq. ; *b.* 1791 ; *m.* 1818 Hannah, dau. of Henry B. Hollinshead, Esq. of Deysbrook, co. Lancaster, and has, with other issue,

* John Gerard, a Magistrate for Beds, *b.* 1821.

Mr. Leigh, who was educated at Rugby, is a Magistrate for Herts and Liberty of St. Albans, Cheshire, and Beds (High Sheriff 1856), and Lord of the Manors of Luton, Hyde, Leagrave, &c., and Patron of 1 living. —*Luton Hoo Park, Beds ; Carlton Club, s.w.*

+LEIGH, John Ward-Boughton-, Esq., of Brownsover Hall, Warwickshire.

A younger son of the late William Zouche Ward, Esq., of Guilsborough Park, co. Northampton ; *b.* 17— ; *m.* 1811 Theodosia Malsburgh, dau. and heir of the late Sir Egerton Leigh, Bart., of Brownsover Hall, and has, with other issue,

* Edward Allesley Boughton (of Newbold-on-Avon, near Rugby), a J.P. and D.L. for cos. Warwick and Northampton ; *b.* 1810, *m.* 18-? Ellen Caroline, dau. of the Hon. Charles Lennox Butler, of Coton House, &c. Warwick.

Mr. Leigh is a J.P. and D.L. for cos. Warwick and Northampton. Lord of the Manor of Guilsborough, and Patron of 2 livings.—*Brownsover Hall, Rugby ; Guilsborough Park, Northampton.*

LEIGH, Joseph, Esq., of Belmont, Cheshire.

Eldest son of the late James Heath Leigh, Esq., of Belmont, by Frances, dau. of Sir Oswald Moseley, Bart., of Rolleston Hall, co. Stafford ; *b.* 1830 ; *s.* 1848 ; *m.* 1852 Fanny Penelope, eldest dau. of the Rev. James Streynsham, Master, Rector of Chorley, co. Lancaster.

Educated at Eton; is Capt. in the Earl of Chester's Yeomanry Cavalry.—*Belmont, Northwich.*

Heir Pres., his brother Oswald Peter, of Marton House, Cheshire; late Lieut. 22nd Foot; *b.* 1833; *m.* 1863 Frances, only dau. of the Rev. George A. Whitaker (whom see), and has, with other issue, * a son, *b.* 1864.

LEIGH, WILLIAM, Esq., of Woodchester Park, Gloucestershire.

Only son of the late William Leigh, Esq., of Roby Hall, co. Lancaster, by Catherine, dau. of Richard Robinson, Esq., of Liverpool; *b.* 1802; *m.* 1828 Caroline, dau. of the late Sir John Geers Cotterell, Bart.,M.P., of Garnons, co. Hereford, and has, with other issue,

* William, *b.* 1829; *m.* 1859 Mary Victoria, dau. of the late Thomas Jarrett, Esq., of Madras, and has issue, * Francis William, *b.* 1860.

Mr. Leigh, who was educated at Eton and Brasenose Coll., Oxford, was formerly a Dep.-Lieut. for cos. Lancaster and Stafford, a Magistrate for co. Stafford, and Lord of the Manor of Stanley, co. Gloucester; he bears the cross of the order of St. Gregory the Great.—*Woodchester Park, Stonehouse, Gloucestershire.*

LEIGH. (See *Hanbury, of Pontypool.*)

LEIGH. (See *Pemberton-Leigh.*)

LEIGH-KECK. (See *Powys-Keck.*)

LEIGHTON, Sir BALDWIN, Bart., of Loton Park, Shropshire (cr. 1692).

Only son of the late Sir Baldwin Leighton, Bart., of Loton Park, by his 2nd wife Louisa Margaretta Anne, dau. of Sir John Thomas Stanley Bart., and sister of John Thomas, 1st Lord Stanley of Alderley; *b.* 1805; *s.* 1828; *m.* 1832 Mary, eldest dau. of Thomas Netherton Parker, Esq., of Sweeney, co. Salop (she *d.* 1864). Educated at Rugby and Magdalen Coll., Oxford; is a J.P. and D.L. for co. Salop (High Sheriff 1835), Chairman of the Shropshire Quarter Sessions, a Magistrate for co. Montgomery, and Patron of 1 living; was M.P. for South Salop 1859–65; late Chairman of Montgomery Quarter Sessions.—*Loton Park, Shrewsbury; Carlton, and Oxford and Cambridge Clubs, s.w.*

Heir, his son Baldwyn, a Magistrate for cos. Montgomery and Salop; *b.* 1836; *m.* 1864 the Hon. Eleanor Leicester, 3rd dau. of George, 2nd Lord de Tabley.

LEIGHTON, DAVID CLARANCE RUSSELL, Esq., of Bafford House, Gloucestershire.

Eldest son of the late General Sir David Leighton, K.C.B., of Bafford House (who was many years Adjutant-General of the Bombay Army, and Col. 7th Bombay Native Infantry), by Isabella Constantia, dau. of Henry Thomas Williams, Esq.; *b.* 1826; *s.* 1860; *m.* 1849, Jane, youngest dau. of Capt. Andrew Creagh, late of the 86th Foot, and has issue,

* David Edmund, *b.* 1851.

Mr. Leighton, who was educated at the East India College, Haileybury; was formerly in the Bombay Civil Service.—*Bafford House, Charlton Kings, Cheltenham.*

LEIGHTON, the Rev. FRANCIS KNYVETT, of Bauseley, Montgomeryshire.

Only surviving son of the late Col. Francis Knyvett Leighton, of Bauseley, by the Hon. Louisa Anne, 4th dau. of St. Leger, 1st Viscount Doneraile; *b.* 1806; *s.* 1834; *m.* 1843 Catherine, 2nd dau. of the Hon. and Rev. James St. Leger, and has, with other issue,

* Charles Arthur Baldwin Knyvett, *b.* 1854.;

Mr. Leighton was educated at Rugby and Magdalen Coll., and was afterwards Fellow of All Souls (B.A. 1828, M.A. 1831, B.D. and D.D. 1858), was appointed Vicar of St. Chad's, Shrewsbury, 1835, of Great Ilford, Essex, 1836. Rector of Harpsden, Oxon, 1841, Warden of All Souls Coll., Oxford, and Rector of Lock-

574

hinge, Berks, 1858.—*Bauseley, Welshpool, Montgomeryshire; All Souls' Coll., Oxford; Harpsden, Henley-on-Thames; University Club, s.w.*

LEINSTER, Duke of (AUGUSTUS FREDERICK FITZGERALD, P.C.).—Cr. 1766.

Eldest son of William Robert, 2nd Duke, by the Hon. Emilia Olivia, dau. of the last Lord St. George (*ext.*); *b.* 1791; *s.* 1804; *m.* 1818 Lady Charlotte Augusta, dau. of Charles, 3rd Earl of Harrington. Educated at Eton and Ch. Ch., Oxford; sits in the House of Lords as Viscount Leinster (cr. 1747); is Premier Duke, Marquis, and Earl in Ireland; Lord-Lieutenant and Custos Rotulorum of co. Kildare; a Visitor of St. Patrick's Coll., Maynooth; and G.M. of the Freemasons in Ireland.—*Carton, Maynooth, co. Kildare; 6, Carlton Terrace, s.w.*

Heir, his son Charles William, Marquis of Kildare, educated at Ch. Ch., Oxford (B.A. 1840, M.A. 1843); a J.P. and D.L. for co. Kildare, Col. of the Kildare Militia, and a Commissioner of Education in Ireland; M.P. for co. Kildare 1847–52; *b.* 1819; *m.* 1847 Lady Caroline, 3rd dau. of George Granville, 2nd Duke of Sutherland, and has, with other issue, * Gerald, Earl of Offaly, *b.* 1851.

LEIR, THOMAS MACIE, Esq., of Jaggard's, Wilts.

Eldest son of the late Thomas Leir, Esq., J.P., of Jaggard's House, by Jane, dau. of the Rev. John Jekyll, D.D., of Evercreech, Somerset; *b.* 1795; *s.* 1836; *m.* 1822 Anne, 2nd dau. of J. Collard, Esq., of Swansea, and has, with other issue,

* Thomas Main Kington, *b.* 1823; *m.* 1847 Maria Louisa, only dau. of Rear-Admiral William Jones Lye, of Bath.

Mr. Leir, who was educated at Rugby and Exeter Coll., Oxford, represents a family of German extraction.—*Jaggard's House, Chippenham; Uphill, Weston-super-Mare; Royal Thames Yacht Club, s.w.*

LEIR, the Rev. WILLIAM MARRIOTT, of Ditcheat, Somersetshire.

Eldest son of the late Rev. William Leir, Rector of Ditcheat (who was a Magistrate for Somerset), by Harriott, dau. of Randolph Marriott, Esq., of Leases Hall, co. York; *b.* 1805; *s.* 1861; *m.* 1840 Mary Anne, dau. of Edward Langford, Esq., of Trungle, St. Paul, Cornwall, and has, with other issue,

* Richard Langford, Lieut. 31st Regt., *b.* 1841.

Mr. Leir, who was educated at Wadham Coll., Oxford (B.A. 1828, M.A. 1836), is Rector and Patron of Ditcheat; he was Rector of West Bagborough, Somerset, 1855–61. This family, of German extraction, have held the Rectory of Ditcheat since 1699, and are descended from a common ancestor with the Leirs of Jaggards (whom see). A baronetcy was conferred upon the family in 1660.—*Ditcheat Rectory, Castle Cary.*

LEITH, Sir GEORGE HECTOR, Bart. (cr. 1775).

Eldest son of the late Sir Alexander Wellesley William Leith, Bart., of Burgh St. Peter's, Norfolk, by Jemima, dau. of Hector Macdonald Buchanan, Esq.; *b.* 1833; *s.* his uncle as 4th Bart. 1840; *m.* 1st 1856 Ella Maria, dau. of David Barclay Chapman, Esq., of Roehampton (she *d.* 1857); 2nd 1861 Eliza Caroline, only child of the late Thomas Tod, Esq., of Drygrange, co. Roxburgh. Is a Magistrate for co. Dumbarton, and Major Dumbartonshire Rifle Volunteers; late Capt. 17th Light Dragoons.—*Drygrange, Melrose, N.B.; Union Club, s.w.*

Heir Pres., his uncle George Gordon Browne (son of the late Sir George Alexander William Leith, Bart., by Albinia, dau. of Thomas Wright Vaughan, Esq., of Moulsey, Surrey), *b.* 1812.

LEITH, ALEXANDER, Esq., of Freefield and Glenkindic, Aberdeenshire.

Eldest son of the late General Sir Alexander Leith, K.C.B., of Freefield and Glenkindic, by his 1st wife Maria, eldest dau. of Dr. Thorp, of Headingley, near Leeds; *b.* 1817; *s.* 1839; *m.* 1843 Mary Anna, dau. of the late General Sir Alexander Halkett, K.H. Educated

at Trinity Coll., Cambridge, (B. A. 1840, M.A. 1843); is a J.P. and D.L. for co. Aberdeen, and Patron of the Church of Towie; formerly an Advocate at the Scottish Bar.—*Freefield, Old Rayne, N.B.; Glenkindie, Inverkindie, Aberdeenshire.*

Heir Pres., his brother Col. Robert William Disney, late Lieut.-Col. 106th Regt.; b. 1819; m. 1865 Mary Charlotte Julia, only child of Sir Henry Percy Gordon, Bart.

·LEITH. (See *Forbes-Leith*.)

LEITH-HAY, Col. ALEXANDER SEBASTIAN, C.B., of Leith Hall, Aberdeenshire.

Eldest son of the late Sir Andrew Leith-Hay, K.H., of Leith Hall and Rannes, by Mary Margaret, dau. of William Clark, Esq., of Buckland Manor, Devon; *b.* 1819; *s.* 1862; *m.* 1861 Christina Grace Agnes, dau. of William Charles Hamilton, Esq., of Craighlaw, co. Wigton. Is a J.P. and D.L., a Commissioner of Supply, for co. Aberdeen, late Capt. 93rd Highlanders—*Leith Hall, Kenethmount, Aberdeenshire; New Club, Edinburgh; Junior United Service and Arthur's Clubs, s.w.*

LEITRIM, Earl of (WILLIAM SYDNEY CLEMENTS).—Cr. 1795.

Second but eldest surviving son of Nathaniel, 2nd Earl, by Mary, dau. and co-heir of the late William Bermingham, Esq., of Ross Hill, co. Galway; *b.* 1806; *s.* 1854. Sits in the House of Peers as Lord Clements, U.K. (cr. 1831); is a Magistrate for cos. Donegal, Galway, and Leitrim; late Lieut.-Col. 51st Foot, and Col. Leitrim Militia; was M.P. for co. Leitrim 1839–47.—*Lough Rynn, Dromod, co. Leitrim; Killadoon, Celbridge, co. Kildare; Carlton and Junior United Service Clubs, s.w.*

Heir Pres., his brother Charles Skeffington, educated at Harrow; a Magistrate for co. Donegal and a Dep.-Lieut. for co. Leitrim; a Poor-Law Commiss·oner in Ireland 1838–46, and M.P. for co. Leitrim 1847–52; late Capt. 35th Foot; b. 1808.

LELY, WILLIAM GRINFIELD, Esq., of Framingham Hall, Norfolk.

Eldest son of the late John Lely Ostler, Esq., of Cawthorpe House, co. Lincoln, by Laura, dau. of Rev. Edward William Grinfield; *b.* 1838; *s.* 1859; *m.* 1867 Annette Jane, dau. of Edward Taylor Massy, Esq., of Cottesmore, co. Pembroke. Mr. Lely, who was educated at University Coll., Oxford (B.A. 1861), and was formerly Ensign 89th Regt., has assumed the name of Lely under the will of the late Frederic Lely, Esq. This family descend from Sir Peter Lely, court painter to Charles II.—*Framingham Hall, Norwich.*

Heir Pres., his brother John Mountney Lely, Esq., M.A. of Magdalen Coll., Oxford, and a Barrister-at-Law of the Inner Temple; b. 1839.

LELY. (See under *Ostler*.)

LEMAN, the Rev. ROBERT ORGILL, of Brampton Hall, Suffolk.

Eldest surviving son of the late Rev. Naunton Thomas Orgill, of Worlingham and Brampton Hall (who assumed the additional name of Leman by Royal licence in 1808, and *d.* 1837), by Henrietta Jane, dau. of the late Rev. Sir William Anderson, Bart., of Lea, co. Lincoln; *b.* 1799; *s.* his brother 1867; *m.* 1st 1824 Isabella Camilla, dau. of the late Sir William J. Twysden, Bart.; (she *d.* 1850); 2nd 1859 Ellen Maria, dau. of the Rev. John A. Ross, Vicar of Westwell, Kent, and has issue,

    * A son, *b.* 1862.

Mr. Orgill-Leman, who was educated at Trinity Coll., Oxford (B.A. 1822), is Rector and Lord of the Manor of Brampton, and Patron of Stoven and Brampton. —*Brampton Hall, Wangford.*

LE-MARCHANT, Sir DENIS, Bart., of Chobham Place, Surrey (cr. 1841).

Second but eldest surviving son of the late Major-General John G. Le-Marchant (formerly of Manor Le Marchant, Guernsey), by Mary, eldest dau. of John Carey, Esq., of the same island; *b.* 1795; *m.* 1835 Sarah Eliza. 4th dau. of Charles Smith, Esq., formerly M.P. for Westbury. Educated at Eton and Trinity Coll., Cambridge; called to the Bar at Lincoln's Inn 1823; is a Magistrate for Surrey, and Chief Clerk to the House of Commons; was formerly Clerk to the Crown in Chancery, Secretary to the Board of Trade 1836–41 and 1848–50; Secretary to Treasury 1841, Under-Secretary for the Home Department 1846–7, M.P. for Worcester 1846–7.—*Chobham Place, Bagshot, Surrey; Brooks's and Athenæum Clubs, s.w.; Speaker's Court, Westminster Hall, s.w.*

Heir, his son Henry Denis, b. 1839.

LE-MARCHANT, Sir JOHN GASPARD, Knt. (cr. 1838).

Younger son of the late Major-General Le-Marchant, by Mary, dau. of Major-General John Carey, and brother of Sir Denis Le-Marchant, Bart. (whom see); *b.* 1803; *m.* 1839 Margaret Ann, dau. of the Rev. Robert Taylor. Educated at Sandhurst; is a Lieut.-General in the Army, and Col. 11th Foot; formerly Lieut.-Col. 85th Foot; served in the Peninsula as Brigadier and Adjutant-General of the Anglo-Spanish Legion; was Governor of Newfoundland 1847–52; Lieut.-Governor of Nova Scotia 1852–7; Governor of Malta 1857–64; appointed Commander-in-Chief at Madras 1865.—*United Service and Junior United Service Clubs, s.w.; Government House, Madras.*

LE MARCHANT-THOMAS, LE MARCHANT, Esq., of Sea View, Isle of Wight.

Eldest son of the late John Thomas, Esq., of Upper Harley Street, by Ann, dau. of J. Le Marchant, Esq., of Haye du Puits, Guernsey; *b.* 1809; *m.* 1837 Margaret, dau. of the late Right Hon. Sir John Vaughan and the Hon. Augusta St. John, and has, with other issue,

    * Henry St. John Le Marchant, R.A., *b.* 1840; *m.* 1866 Agnes Maria, dau. of Sir J. H. Lethbridge, Bart., and widow of Capt. Peter Valentine Purcell, of Halverstown House, co. Kildare.

Mr. Le Marchant-Thomas, who is a Magistrate for Hants and Berks, assumed the name of Le Marchant by Royal licence 1865.—*Sea View, Ryde, I. of Wight; Haye du Puits, Guernsey; Royal Yacht Squadron, Cowes; Athenæum Club, s.w.*

LE-MARCHANT, Col. THOMAS, of New Lodge, Herts.

Third son of the late Major-General Le-Marchant, and brother of Sir Denis Le-Marchant. Bart. (whom see): *b.* 1812; *m.* 1846 Frances Mary Isabella, only dau. of James Smith, Esq., of Ashlyns Hall, Herts. Educated at Eton and has, with other issue,

    * St. John, R.H.A., *b.* 1847.

Col. Le-Marchant, who is a Magistrate for Hants and Herts, was appointed A.D.C. to Lord Sydenham, G.C.B., Governor-General of Canada in 1839, and in 1855 Military Secretary to the General Commanding the Troops in Nova Scotia and New Brunswick.—*New Lodge, Great Berkhamstead; Sea View, Ryde, I. of Wight; Haverstown House, Kilcullen, co. Kildare; Haye du Puits, Guernsey; Athenæum Club, s.w.*

LEMON, Sir CHARLES, Bart.,‡ of Carclew, Cornwall (cr. 1774).

Eldest son of the late Sir William Lemon. Bart., of Carclew, by Jane, dau. of the late James Buller, Esq.,

‡ Died whilst these sheets were at press.

of Morval, Cornwall; *b.* 1784; *s.* as 2nd Bart. 1824; *m.* 1810 Lady Charlotte, dau. of Henry Thomas, 2nd Earl of Ilchester (she *d.* 1826). Is a J.P. and D.L. for Cornwall, and a Special Deputy-Warden of the Stannaries; was M.P. for Penryn 1807–12 and 1830–1, and for W. Cornwall 1831–57.—*Carclew, Penryn; Athenæum Club,* s.w.; 46, *Charles Street,* w.

LEMPRIERE, ALGERNON THOMAS, Esq., of Newton Valence, Hants.
Only surviving son of the late Admiral George Oury Lempriere, Pelham (who was a J.P. for Hants, and Seigneur of Chesnel, Jersey), by Frances, only dau. and heir of William Dumaresq, Esq., of Pelham, Hants; *b.* 1835; *s.* 1864. Educated at Eton and Trinity Coll., Oxford (B.A. 1858, M.A. 1861); called to the Bar at the Inner Temple 1863.—*Pelham, Newton Valence, Alton; United University Club,* s.w.

LEMPRIERE, the Rev. WILLIAM, of Rozel, Jersey.
Eldest surviving son of the late Philip Raoul Lempriere, Seigneur of Rozel, and Col. in the Jersey Militia, by Elizabeth, dau. of John Poingdestre, Esq., of Jersey; *b.* 1819; *s.* 1859; *m.* 1850 Julia Anne, dau. of Thomas Moore Wayne, Esq., of South Warnborough, Hants, and has, with other issue,

  • Reginald Raoul, *b.* 1851.

Mr. Lempriere, who was educated at Rugby and Ch. Ch., Oxford (B.A. 1839, M.A. 1843), is Seigneur of Rozel and Dielament, in Jersey.—*Rozel Manor, Jersey.*

LENDRUM, JAMES, Esq., of Magheracross, co. Fermanagh.
Eldest son of the late George Lendrum, Esq., of Magheracross, by Mary Jane, dau. of the late Henry Coddington, Esq., of Old Bridge, co. Meath; *b.* 1806; *s.* 1855; *m.* 1843 Anne, eldest dau. of Samuel Vesey, Esq., of Derrabard, co. Tyrone, and has, with other issue,

  • George Cosby, *b.* 1846.

Mr. Lendrum, who was educated at Armagh and Trinity Coll., Cambridge (B.A. 1830), is a J.P. and D.L. for cos. Fermanagh and Tyrone (High Sheriff 1835 and 1837).—*Magheracross, Enniskillen, co. Fermanagh.*

LENIGAN, JAMES, Esq., M.R.I.A., of Castle Ffogerty, co. Tipperary.
Eldest son of the late Thomas Lenigan. Esq., of Castle Ffogerty, by Peniel, dau. of Edmund Armstrong, Esq., of Bnncraggy, co. Clare; *b.* 1797; *s.* 1825; *m.* 1825 Eleanor Frances, only dau. of John Evans, Esq., of Hertford Street, Mayfair, and has surviving issue,

  • Penelope Elizabeth Marie.

Mr. Lenigan, who was educated at Trinity Coll., Dublin (B.A. 1816, M.A. 1819), is a J.P. and D.L. for co. Tipperary (High Sheriff 1863).—*Castle Ffogerty, Thurles; Kildare Street Club, Dublin; Athenæum Club,* s.w.

LENNARD, Sir THOMAS BARRETT, Bart., of Belhus, Essex (CR. 1801).
Eldest son of the late Thomas Barrett Lennard, Esq. (who was many years M.P. for Maldon, and *d.* 1856), by Mary, dau. of Bartlet Bridges Shelden, Esq., of Aldham Hall; *b.* 1826; *s.* his grandfather as 2nd Bart. 1857; *m.* 1853 Emma, dau. of the late Rev. Sir John Page Wood, Bart. Educated at Eton and St. Peter's Coll., Cambridge (B.A. 1850, M.A. 1853); is a J.P. and D.L. for Essex (High Sheriff 1865), and Patron of 1 living—*Belhus, Romford, Essex; Manor St. Tierney, Clonts, co. Monaghan; University Club,* s.w.; 9, *Hyde Park Terrace,* w.

  *• his son Thomas Barrett, *b.* 1853.

LENNARD, Lieut.-Col., JOHN FARNABY, of Wickham Court, Kent.
Eldest son of the late Lieut.-General Sir William Cator, K.C.B., Col.-Commandant R.A. (who *d.* 1866), by Penelope Anne, only dau. of the late Sir John Farnaby, Bart., of Kippington, and Wickham Court, and grand-dau. and heir of Sir Samuel Lennard, Bart., of Wickham Court; *b.* 1816; *s.* his uncle, Sir Charles Farnaby, Bart., 1861; *m.* 1st 1847 Laura, youngest dau. of the late Edward Golding, Esq., of Maiden Erleigh, Berks. (she *d.* 1850, leaving issue, two daughters); 2ndly 1852 Julia Maria Frances, only surviving child of the late Henry Hallam, Esq., F.R.S., and has, with other issue,

  • Henry Arthur Hallam, *b.* 1859.

Lieut.-Col. Lennard, who was educated at the Royal Military Academy, Woolwich, is a J.P. and D.L. for Kent, Lord of the Manor and Patron of West Wickham, and Lord of the Manors of Baston and Keston, Kent; Lieut.-Col. Commandant Kent Militia Artillery; late Capt. R.A. He assumed the name and arms of Lennard by Royal licence under the will of the late Sir Charles F. Farnaby, Bart., in 1861.—*Wickham Court, West Wickham, Bromley; United Service and Carlton Clubs,* s.w.; 24, *Wilton Crescent,* s.w.

LENNOX, Lord ALEXANDER FRANCIS CHARLES GORDON-.
Third son of Charles, 5th Duke of Richmond, by Lady Caroline, eldest dau. of Henry William, 1st Marquis of Anglesey; *b.* 1825; *m.* 1863 Emily, dau. of Charles Towneley, Esq., of Towneley Hall, co. Lancaster. Is a Magistrate for co. Banff and for Sussex, and Capt. Royal Horse Guards; was M.P. for Shoreham 1849–59.—*Goodwood, Chichester;* 51, *Portland Place,* w.

LENNOX, Lord GEORGE CHARLES GORDON-.
Fifth son of Charles, 5th Duke of Richmond, by Lady Caroline, eldest dau. of Henry William, 1st Marquis of Anglesey; *b.* 1829. Educated at Eton; entered the Royal Horse Guards as Cornet 1846, retired 1853: is a J.P. and D.L. for Sussex, and a Magistrate for co. Banff; elected M.P. for Lymington 1860.—*Goodwood, Chichester; White's, Junior Athenæum, and Carlton Clubs,* s.w.; 51, *Portland Place,* w.

LENNOX, Lord HENRY CHARLES GEORGE GORDON-.
Third son of Charles, 5th Duke of Richmond, by Lady Caroline, eldest dau. of Henry William, 1st Marquis of Anglesey; *b.* 1821. Educated at Westminster and at Ch. Ch., Oxford (B.A. 1843, M.A. 1847); is a Dep.-Lieut. for Sussex, a Magistrate for co. Banff, and Secretary to the Admiralty; was a Lord of the Treasury in 1852; elected M.P. for Chichester 1846.—*Gordon Castle, Fochabers, N.B.; White's, Junior Athenæum, and Carlton Clubs,* s.w.; 13, *Albert Terrace, Knightsbridge,* s.w.

LENNOX, Lord JOHN GEORGE.
Second son of Charles, 4th Duke of Richmond, by Lady Charlotte, eldest dau. of Alexander, 4th Duke of Gordon; *b.* 1793; *m.* 1818 Louisa Frederica, dau. of the Hon. J. Rodney (she *d.* 1860). A Lieut.-Col. in the Army; was M.P. for W. Sussex 1832–41; formerly a Lord of the Bedchamber to H.R.H. the Prince Consort.—*Buckingham Palace,* s.w.

LENNOX, Lord WILLIAM PITT.
Fourth son of Charles, 4th Duke of Richmond, K.G., by Lady Charlotte, eldest dau. of Alexander, 4th Duke of Gordon; *b.* 1799; *m.* 1st 1824 Miss Paton; 2nd 1854 Ellen, dau. of Mr. Smith (she *d.* 1859); 3rd 1863 Maria Jane, eldest dau. of the Rev. Capel Molyneux; he has issue, by his 2nd wife,

  • William Robert, *b.* 1855.

Lord William, who was educated at Westminster; is a Magistrate for co. Banff; was formerly Capt. Royal

Horse Guards Blue; was A.D.C. to the late Sir Peregrine Maitland and the late Duke of Wellington in 1815–16; was M.P. for King's Lynn 1832–4.—8, *Prince of Wales' Terrace, Kensington, w.*

LENNOX. (See under *Richmond, Duke of.*)

LENNOX. (See *Hanbury-Kincaid-Lennox.*)

LENTAIGNE, JOHN, Esq., of Tallaght, co. Dublin.
Eldest son of the late Benjamin Lentaigne, Esq., by Mary Theresa, dau. of John O'Neill, Esq.; *b.* 1803; *m.* 1841 Mary, dau. of Francis Magan, Esq., of Emoe, co. Westmeath, and has, with other issue,

    • Francis Bagot, *b.* 1846.

Mr. Lentaigne, who was educated at Trinity Coll., Dublin (B.A. 1825, M.B. 1838), is a Magistrate for cos. Dublin and Monaghan (High Sheriff 1844); Inspector-General of Prisons, and Commissioner of National Education in Ireland; was appointed Government Commissioner of Loan Funds 1841; Director of Convict Prisons, Ireland, 1854.—*Tallaght, Dublin; Stephen's-Green Club, and 1, Great Denmark Street, Dublin.*

LENTHALL, KYFFIN JOHN WILLIAM, Esq., of Bessels Leigh, Berks.
Only son of the late William John Lenthall, Esq., of Broadwell, co. Gloucester, and of Bessels Leigh, by Elizabeth, eldest dau. and co.-heir of Sir Thomas Kyffin, of Maynan Hall, co. Carnarvon; *b.* 1789; *s.* 1835; *m.* 1818 Mary Anne, dau. of John Ashton, Esq., of The Grange, co. Chester, and by her, who *d.* 1866, has, with other issue,

    • Edmund Kyffin, a Magistrate for Berks, *b.* 1821.

Mr. Lenthall, who is a J.P. and D.L. for co. Carnarvon (High Sheriff 1828), a Magistrate for co. Denbigh, Lord of the Manor of Bessels Leigh, and Patron of 2 livings, was formerly a Capt. in the Royal Denbighshire Militia.—*Bessels Leigh, Abingdon; Maynan Hall, Llanrwst, Carnarvonshire; Long's Hotel, w.*

LENY. (See *Macalpine-Leny.*)

LE-POER-TRENCH, the Hon. Mrs. WILLIAM, of Mount Pleasant, co. Galway.
Margaret, dau. of the late Dawson Downing, Esq.; *m.* 1st 1817 the Hon. A. Handcock, who *d.* 1826; 2nd 1837 Admiral the Hon. William Le Poer Trench, who *d.* 1846.—*Mount Pleasant, Ballinasloe, co. Galway.*

LESCHER, JOSEPH SAMUEL, Esq., of Boyles, Essex.
Eldest son of the late Joseph Lescher, Esq., of Boyles Court, by Martha, dau. of J. Bond, Esq., of Somerset; *b.* 1796; *m.* 1829 Martha, dau. of John Hocy, Esq., of Stoke Nayland, Suffolk, and has, with other issue,

    • Joseph Francis, *b.* 1842.

Mr. Lescher, who was educated at Stonyhurst, is a Magistrate for Essex (High Sheriff 1862).—*Boyles Court, Brentwood.*

LESLIE, Sir CHARLES HENRY, Bart. (cr. 1625).
Only son of the late Sir Norman Robert Leslie, Bart. (who was killed in the Indian Mutiny), by Jessie, 3rd dau. of the late Major R. W. Smith, of the Bengal Cavalry; *b.* 1848; *s.* as 7th Bart. 1857. Educated at the Royal Military Coll., Sandhurst; is Ensign 103rd Foot, late Cornet W. Essex Yeomanry Cavalry.—*Chelmsford, Essex.*

    Heir Pres., his great-uncle Thomas, *b.* 1800; *m.* 1839 Penuel, dau. of John Grant, Esq., late of the 78th Regt., and has issue, • John, *b.* 1840.

LESLIE, Col. CHARLES, K.H., of Balquhain, Aberdeenshire.
Eldest surviving son of the late John Leslie, Esq., of Balquhain, by Violet, dau. of John Dalzell, Esq.; *b.* 1786; *m.* 1st 1826 Mary, dau. of Major-General Sir C. Holloway (she *d.* 1832); 2nd 1836 Lady Dorothy Eyre, dau. of Francis, 6th Earl of Newburgh ‡ (who *s.* her brother 1852, and *d.* 1853), and has by the former,

    • Charles Stephen, *b.* 1832; *m.* 1853 Jane, dau. of — Bounding, Esq., and has, with other issue, • Charles, *b.* 1859.

Col. Leslie, who is a J.P. and D.L. for cos. Aberdeen and Derby, and a Col. in the Army, late of the Grenadier Guards, is 26th possessor of the Barony of Balquhain.—*Hassop Hall, Bakewell; Fetternear House, by Kemnay, Aberdeenshire; Slindon Hall, Arundel; Brooks's Club, s.w.*

LESLIE, Col. CHARLES POWELL, of Glasslough, co. Monaghan.
Eldest son of the late Charles Powell Leslie, Esq., M.P., of Glasslough, by his 2nd wife Christiana, dau. of George Fosberry, Esq., of Clorane, co. Limerick; *b.* 1821; *s.* 1831. Is Lord-Lieutenant and Custos Rotulorum of co. Monaghan, and Col. of the Monaghan Militia; has been M.P. for co. Monaghan since 1842.—*Glasslough, Monaghan, Ireland; Carlton Club, s.w.; 48, Berkeley Square, w.*

    Heir Pres., his brother John, B.A. of Ch. Ch., Oxford; *b.* 1823.

LESLIE, FRANCIS CHARLES, Esq., of Ballyward, Downshire.
Eldest son of the late William Beers, Esq., J.P. of Ballyward, by Jane, dau. of the late Ven. Charles Leslie, D.D., of Kincraigie Castle, co. Donegal, some time Archdeacon of Raphoe; *b.* 1796; *s.* his father in 1829, and his uncle in 1850, when he assumed his name; *m.* 1837 Theodosia, dau. of Lieut.-Col. Thompson, and has, with other issue,

    • John, late Lieut. 5th Fusiliers, *b.* 1839.

Mr. Leslie is a Magistrate for co. Down (High Sheriff 1856).—*Ballyward, Castlewellan, Downshire.*

LESLIE, GEORGE, Esq., of Donaghadee, Downshire.
Second son of the late George Leslie, Esq., of Donaghadee, by Elizabeth, dau. and heir of the Rev. Francis Hutcheson, D.D., of Donaghadee; *b.* 1825; *s.* his brother Edmund Francis 1862; *m.* 1855 Albina Jane, dau. of the late James Shaw, Esq., a Judge of the Supreme Court, Calcutta, and has, with other issue,

    • George Francis, *b.* 1856.

Mr. Leslie, who was a educated at Woolwich, is a Capt. R.A.—*Donaghadee, Downshire; Army and Navy Club, s.w.*

LESLIE, GEORGE ABERCROMBY YOUNG, Esq., of Kininvie, Banffshire.
Eldest son of the late Archibald Young Leslie, Esq., of Kininvie, by Jane, dau. of the late James Donaldson, Esq., of Kinairdy; *b.* 1803; *s.* 1841; *m.* 1841 Barbara King, dau. of the late General William Stewart, C.B., and has, with other issue,

    • Archibald, Lieut. 13th Royal Welsh Fusiliers, *b.* 1843.

Mr. Leslie, who was educated at the University of Aberdeen, is a J.P. and D.L. for co. Banff, and proprietor of the estate of Kininvie; he was formerly a Solicitor in Banff.—*Kininvie House, Craigellachie, N.B.*

LESLIE, HENRY, Esq., of Seaport, co. Antrim.
Second son of the late James Leslie, Esq., of Leslie Hill, co. Antrim (who *d.* 1847), by Mary, dau. of Adam Cuppage, Esq., of Doniconey, co. Down; *b.* 1806; *m.*

‡ This nobleman was grandson of Charles Radcliff, last Earl of Derwentwater, beheaded A.D. 1746.

1849 Harriet Ann, dau. of Capt. Thos. Hanmer, R.N., of Holbrook Hall, Suffolk, and has, with other issue,
* Henry Hanmer, *b.* 1853.

Mr. Leslie is a Magistrate for co. Antrim.—*Seaport Lodge, Bushmills, co. Antrim.*

LESLIE, JAMES EDMUND, Esq., of Leslie Hill, co. Antrim.
Eldest son of the late James Leslie, Esq., of Leslie Hill (who was High Sheriff of co. Antrim 1797), by Mary, dau. of A. Cuppage, Esq.; *b.* 1800; *m.* 1847; *m.* 1823 Sarah, dau. of the late Right Rev. Bishop Sandford, of Edinburgh, and by her, who *d.* 1864, has, with other issue,
* Edmund Douglas, Capt. Antrim Rifles, *b.* 1828.

Mr. Leslie, who was educated at Armagh and Ch. Ch., Oxford, is a J.P. and D.L. for co. Antrim (High Sheriff 1854); descended from a common ancestor with the Leslies of Ballibay.—*Leslie Hill, Ballymoney, co. Antrim.*

LESLIE, Mrs., of Ballibay, co. Monaghan.
Emily Eleanora Wilhelmina, eldest dau. of the late Charles A. Leslie, Esq., by Ellen, dau. of Richard Magenis, Esq., of Waringstown, co. Down; *s.* 1838; *m.* 1st 1827 Arthur French, Esq., 2nd 18— the Rev. John Charles William Leslie, and has by the former, with other issue,
* Robert Charles French, Esq., *b.* 1828.

This family, a branch of the house of Rothes, settled in Ireland about 1630.—*Ballibay House, Monaghan.*

+LESLIE, ROBERT, Esq., of Tarbert, co. Kerry.
Son of the late R. Leslie, Esq.; *b.* 1800; is a Magistrate for co. Kerry (High Sheriff 1864).—*Tarbert House, Tarbert, co. Kerry.*

LESLIE, WILLIAM, Esq., of Warthill and Drumrossie, Aberdeenshire.
Eldest son of the late William Leslie, Esq., of Warthill, by Jane, dau. of the late Rev. Patrick Davidson, D.D., of Rayne; *b.* 1814; *s.* 1857; *m.* 1848 Matilda Rose, 2nd dau. of William Rose Robinson, Esq., of Clermiston, Midlothian, and has, with other issue,
* William Douglas, *b.* 1849.

Mr. Leslie, who was educated at Aberdeen University (M.A. 1832), is a J.P. and D.L. for co. Aberdeen; was M.P. for co. Aberdeen 1861-66. This family has been established at Warthill since 1518. Mr. Leslie is 11th possessor of Warthill, and 23rd lineal male descendant of the founder of the Leslie family in 1067.—*Warthill and Drumrossie, Aberdeen, N.B.; Carlton Club, s.w.*

LESLIE.
(See under *Rothes, Countess of;* and *Leven, Earl of.*)

LESLIE. (See *Forbes-Leslie.*)

LESLIE-FRENCH. (See *French.*)

LESLIE-MELVILLE, the Hon. ALEXANDER, of Branston Hall, Lincolnshire.
Fifth son of Alexander, 9th Earl of Leven and Melville, by Jane, dau. of the late John Thornton, Esq., of Clapham, Surrey; *b.* 1800; *m.* 1825 Charlotte, dau. of the late Samuel Smith, Esq., of Woodhall Park, Herts, and has, with other issue,
* Alexander Samuel, *b.* 1829; *m.* 1856 the Hon. Albinia Frances, 3rd dau. of Charles, 6th Viscount Midleton, and has issue.

Mr. Leslie-Melville, who was educated at Trinity Coll., Cambridge (M.A. 1821), and admitted an Advocate at the Scottish Bar 1826, is a J.P. and D.L. for co. Lincoln, and Lord of the Manor of Branston.—*Branston Hall, Lincoln.*
578

LESLIE-MELVILLE-CARTWRIGHT.
(See *Cartwright.*)

LESLIE [WALDEGRAVE-]. (See under *Rothes.*)

L'ESTRANGE, Sir GEORGE BURDETT, Knt. (cr. 1860).
Second son of the late Henry Peisley L'Estrange, Esq., of Moystown, King's Co., by Grace, dau. of George Burdett, Esq., M.P.; *b.* 1796; *m.* 1832 Louisa, dau. of Herbert Rawson Stepney, Esq. (she *d.* 1855). Educated at Westminster; appointed Gentleman Usher of the Black Rod to the Order of St. Patrick 1858; formerly an Officer in the Guards.—*The Castle, Dublin; Kildare Street Club, Dublin.*

L'ESTRANGE, EDMUND, Esq., of Tynte Lodge, co. Leitrim.
Fifth son of the late Henry Peisley L'Estrange, Esq., of Moystown, King's Co. (some time Col. of the King's Co. Militia), by Grace, dau. of George Burdett, Esq., M.P.; *b.* 1813; *m.* 1835 Lady Henrietta Susan, 2nd sister of Richard George, 9th Earl of Scarborough, and has, with other issue,
* Savile Richard William, *b.* 1849.

Mr. L'Estrange, who was educated at Trinity Coll., Dublin, represents a younger branch of the Styleman-L'Estranges of Hunstanton.—*Tynte Lodge, Leitrim.*

L'ESTRANGE, THOMAS, Esq., of Cartronganny, co. Westmeath.
Eldest son of the late Torriano Francis L'Estrange, Esq., of Cartronganny, by Jane Martha, dau. of Thomas Mulock, Esq., of Kilnagarna, King's Co.; *b.* 1822; *s.* 1867; *m.* 1850 Sarah, dau. of Thomas Garrett, Esq., of Belfast. The head of this family is Mr. Styleman-L'Estrange, of Hunstanton, Norfolk.—*Cartronganny, Mullingar, co. Westmeath.*

L'ESTRANGE-CARLETON, GEORGE, Esq., of Market Hill, co. Fermanagh.
Second son of the late Christopher L'Estrange, Esq., of Market Hill (who assumed the surname and arms of Carleton on the death of his mother in 1830), by Jane, dau. of Col. Jackson, of Enniscoe, co. Mayo; *b.* 18—; *s.* 1843. This family is descended from a common ancestor with the Styleman L'Estranges of Norfolk.—*Market Hill, Enniskillen, co. Fermanagh; Ballymote, co. Sligo; Carlton Club, s.w.*

L'ESTRANGE. (See *Styleman-L'Estrange.*)

LETHBRIDGE, Sir JOHN HESKETH, Bart., of Sandhill Park, Somerset (cr. 1804).
Eldest son of the late Sir Thomas Buckler Lethbridge, Bart., M.P., of Sandhill Park, by his 1st wife Jessy Catharine, sister of the late Sir T. D. Hesketh, Bart., of Rufford Hall; *b.* 1798; *s.* 1849; *m.* 1st 1817 Harriet Rebecca, only dau. of John Mytton, Esq., of Halston, co. Salop; 2nd 1827 Julia, dau. of the late Sir Henry Hugh Hoare, Bart.; 3rd 1855 Anna, eldest dau. of the late R. Wright, Esq., M.D., 1st Physician to Greenwich Hospital, &c. Educated at Eton; is a J.P. and D.L. for Somerset and Dorset, and Patron of 5 livings; formerly Lieut.-Col. 2nd Somerset Militia.—*Sandhill Park, Taunton; Woods Bradley, Tavistock; Residence: 6, Hillsborough Terrace, Ilfracombe: Long's Hotel, w..*
Heir, his son Wroth Acland, late of the Rifle Brigade; *b.* 1831; *m.* 1861 Anne William, dau. of Thomas Bengou, Esq., and has issue, * a son, *b.* 1867.

LETHBRIDGE, AMBROSE GODDARD, Esq., of Eastbrooke House, Somerset.
Second son of the late Sir Thomas Buckler Lethbridge, Bart., of Sandhill Park, Somerset (many years M.P. for Somerset), by his 2nd wife Anna, dau. of Ambrose

Goddard, Esq., of The Lawn, Swindon, Wilts, and half-brother of Sir John H. Lethbridge, Bart. (whom see); *b.* 1804; *m.* 1856 Fanny, dau. of the late Rev. Francis Follett. Educated at Winchester and Ch. Ch., Oxford (B.A. and elected Fellow of All Souls Coll. 1827); called to the Bar at the Middle Temple 1831; is a J.P. and D.L. for Somerset.—*Eastbrooke House, Taunton.*

Heir Pres., his nephew Charles (son of the late Rev. Thomas Prowse Lethbridge, by Isabella, dau. of the Rev. Thomas Sweet Escott, of Hartrow, Somerset), *b.* 1836; *m.* 1865 Susan Ann, younger dau. of G. J. Yarburgh, Esq., of Heslington Hall, co. York, and has issue, * two daus.

LETHBRIDGE, JOHN CHRISTOPHER BARON, Esq., of Tregeare House, Cornwall.
Eldest son of the late John King Lethbridge, Esq., of Tregeare, by Emma, dau. of the late Rev. Edward Palmer, Esq., of Mosely, co. Warwick; *b.* 1839; *s.* 1864; *m.* 1866 Millicent Galton, dau. of the late Rev. R. Shirley Bunbury, of Swansea. Educated at St. John's Coll., Oxford; is a Magistrate for Cornwall, and Patron of 1 living.—*Tregeare House, Launceston.*

LEVEN AND MELVILLE, Earl of (JOHN THORNTON LESLIE-MELVILLE).—Cr. 1641.
Second but eldest surviving son of Alexander, 7th Earl (who *d.* 1820), by Jane, dau. of John Thornton, Esq., of Clapham, Surrey; *b.* 1786; *s.* his brother as 9th Earl 1860; *m.* 1st 1812 Harriet, dau. of the late Samuel Thornton, Esq., of Albany Park, and M.P. for Surrey; 2nd 1834 Sophia, dau. of the late Henry Thornton, Esq., M.P.; is a Dep.-Lieut. for Surrey; elected a Representative Peer for Scotland 1865.—*Roehampton House, Surrey,* s.w.; *Carlton and Windham Clubs,* s.w.

Heir, his son Alexander, Viscount Kirkaldie, *b.* 1817; educated at Eton and Trinity Coll., Cambridge (M.A. 1839).

LEVER, JOHN ORRELL, Esq.
Eldest son of James Lever, Esq., of Manchester, and a descendant of the late Sir Ashton Lever; *b.* 1824; *m.* 1847 Elizabeth, dau. of Jonathan Dorning, Esq., of Swinton, co. Lancaster, and has, with other issue,

* Charles Lever, *b.* 1848.

Mr. Lever, who is a Merchant and Shipowner, a Magistrate for co. Galway, a Director of the South Wales Railway Company and of the Atlantic Royal Mail Steam Navigation Company (Lever Line), was M.P. for Galway 1859–65.—*Hyde, Manchester;* 40, *Cannon Street,* E.C.; 60, *Eccleston Square,* s.w.

LEVESON-GOWER, Lord RONALD CHARLES.
Youngest son of George Granville, 2nd Duke of Sutherland, K.G., by Lady Harriet Elizabeth Georgiana, 3rd dau. of George, 6th Earl of Carlisle; *b.* 1845; educated at Eton; elected M.P. for Sutherland 1867.—*Stafford House, St. James's,* s.w.

LEVESON-GOWER.
(See under *Sutherland, Duke of; Granville, Earl;* and *Cromartie, Countess of.*)

LEVESON-GOWER, JOHN, Esq., of Bill Hill, Berks, and Westwood, Essex.
Eldest son of the late General John Leveson-Gower, of Bill Hill, by Isabella Mary, 2nd dau. of Philip Bowes Broke, Esq., of Broke Hall, Suffolk; *b.* 1802; *s.* 1816; *m.* 1825 Charlotte Gertrude, dau. of Lieut.-Col. Mitchell and of Lady Harriet Isabella Somerset, and has, with other issue,

* John Edward, a Magistrate for Berks and Capt. 68th Foot; *b.* 1826; *m.* 1850 Harriet Jane, dau. of the late John Hunter, Esq.

Mr. Leveson-Gower, who was educated at Eton and Ch. Ch., Oxford, is a J.P. and D.L. for Berks and Essex.—*Bill Hill, Finchampstead, Wokingham, Berks; Westwood, Great Horkesley, Colchester; Travellers' Club,* s.w.

LEVESON - GOWER, GRANVILLE WILLIAM GRESHAM, Esq., of Titsey Park, Surrey.
Elder son of the late William Leveson-Gower, Esq., of Titsey Park (who was High Sheriff of Surrey in 1839), by Emily Josephine, dau. of Sir Francis Hastings Doyle, Bart.; *b.* 1838; *s.* 1860; *m.* 1861 the Hon. Sophia Leigh, youngest dau. of Chandos, 1st Lord Leigh, and has, with other issue,

* Ronald William Gresham, *b.* 1863.

Mr. Leveson-Gower, who was educated at Eton and Ch. Ch., Oxford, is a J.P. and D.L. for Surrey, Lord of the Manors of Titsey, Tatsfield, and Limpsfield, and Patron of 3 livings; was M.P. for Reigate 1863–66.—*Titsey Park and Hookwood, Godstone; Oxford and Cambridge and Travellers' Clubs;* 88, *Brook Street,* w.

LEVETT, RICHARD BYRD, Esq., of Milford Hall, Staffordshire.
Eldest son of the late Rev. Richard Levett, of Milford Hall, by Louisa, dau. of the Rev. Walter Bagot, of Blithfield; *b.* 1810; *s.* 1843; *m.* 1848 Elizabeth Mary, eldest dau. of the late John Mirehouse, Esq., Common Serjeant of London, and has, with other issue,

* Richard Walter Byrd, of Brownslade, co. Pembroke; *b.* 1849.

Mr. Levett, who was educated at Westminster and Ch. Ch., Oxford (B.A. 1830), is a J.P. and D.L. for co. Stafford, and Lieut.-Col. Commandant 3rd Staffordshire Rifles; he was formerly in the 60th Rifles.—*Milford Hall, Walton, Stafford; Army and Navy Club,* s.w.

LEVETT, ROBERT THOMAS KENNEDY, Esq., of Packington Hall, Staffordshire.
Second son of the late John Levett, Esq., of Wichnor Park (who *d.* 1853), by Sophia Eliza, dau. of the Hon. Robert Kennedy, and niece of Archibald, 1st Marquis of Ailsa; *b.* 1831; *s.* 1853; *m.* 1860 Margaret Catherine, only surviving dau. of the late Thomas Levett Prinsep, Esq., of Croxall Hall, and has, with other issue,

* Thomas Prinsep, *b.* 1862.

Mr. Levett is a J.P. and D.L. for co. Stafford, and Lord of the Manor of Packington.—*Packington Hall, Lichfield.*

LEVETT, Capt. THEOPHILUS JOHN, of Wichnor Park, Staffordshire.
Eldest son of the late John Levett, Esq., of Wichnor Park, by Sophia Eliza, dau. of the Hon. Robert Kennedy; *b.* 1829; *s.* 1854; *m.* 1856 Lady Jane Lissey Harriet, 3rd dau. of William, 7th Earl of Denbigh, and has with other issue,

* Theophilus Basil Percy, *b.* 1856.

Capt. Levett, who is a J.P. and D.L. for co. Stafford, Patron of 2 livings, and Lieut. Queen's Own Staffordshire Yeomanry, was formerly Capt. 1st Life Guards.—*Wichnor Park, Burton-on-Trent; Carlton Club,* s.w.; 13, *Chesham Street,* s.w.

LEVINGE, Sir RICHARD GEORGE AUGUSTUS, Bart., of Knockdrin Castle, co. Westmeath (cr. 1704).
Eldest son of the late Sir Richard Levinge, Bart., of Knockdrin Castle, by the Hon. Elizabeth Anne, dau. of the late Lord Rancliffe; *b.* 1811; *s.* as 7th Bart. 1848; *m.* 1849 Caroline Jane, dau. of the late Col. Lancelot Rolleston, of Watnall Hall, Notts (she *d.* 1858). Is a J.P. and D.L. for co. Westmeath (High Sheriff 1851) and Lieut.-Col. of Westmeath Militia; formerly Capt. 5th Dragoon Guards; was M.P. for co. Westmeath 1857–65.—*Knockdrin Castle, Mullingar, co. Westmeath; Army and Navy Club,* s.w.; 30, *Belgrave Square,* s.w.

Heir Pres., his brother Vere Henry, of the Madras Civil Service; *b.* 1819.

LEVINGE, Capt. RICHARD HUGH, of Levington Park, co. Westmeath.

Son of the late Sir Richard Levinge, 4th Bart., of Levington Park, by Mary, natural dau. of Sir Henry Tuite, 6th Bart., of Sonna; *b.* 1774; *s.* to the estate of Levington 1786; *m.* 1797 Jane, dau. of Thomas Child, Esq., of Brookfield, co. Cork, and had, with other issue,

Charles William, M.A. of Trinity Coll., Dublin, a Magistrate for cos. Westmeath and Longford; *b.* 1817; *m.* 1842 Annie, dau. of Robert Barlow, Esq., of Annebrook, and *d.* 1868, leaving, with other issue, ° Richard William Chaworth, *b.* 1843.

Capt. Levinge, who is a Magistrate for co. Westmeath, was appointed Deputy-Governor of co. Westmeath in 1809; he was formerly a Capt. in the Westmeath Regiment of Militia.—*Levington Park, Mullingar, co. Westmeath;* 78, *Lower Leeson Street, Dublin.*

+ **LEVY**, WILLIAM, Esq., of Woughton Green, Bucks.

Son of the late Wm. Levy of Newport Pagnell, Bucks; *b.* 1809; *m.* 1863 Mary, dau. of Mr. ———, of Gloucestershire, and has issue,

° A son, *b.* 1864.

Mr. Levy, who is a Magistrate for Bucks, and Capt. Bucks Yeomanry, is of Jewish extraction.—*Woughton Green, Fenny Stratford, Bucks.*

LEWEN, FREDERIC THOMAS, Esq., of Cloghans, co. Mayo.

Eldest son of Thomas Lewen, Esq., of Cloghans, by Anna, dau. of Westropp Ross-Lewin, Esq., of Cornfield, co. Clare, and grandson of Harrison Ross-Lewin, Esq., of Fortfergus; *b.* 1828; *m.* 1867 Lucy Emma, dau. of the late William Byrom Corrie, Esq., of Cheltenham. Mr. Lewen is a Magistrate for cos. Mayo and Galway. This family was formerly settled in co. Limerick, and came to Cloghans in 1678.—*Cloghans, Foxhall, co. Mayo.*

LEWES, Lieut.-Col. JOHN, of Llanllear, Cardiganshire.

Eldest son of the late John Lewes, Esq., of Llanllear, by Mary Anne, dau. of John Vaughan Lloyd, Esq., of Greengrove, co. Cardigan; *b.* 1829; *s.* 1860; *m.* 1858 Mary Jane, dau. of the Rev. Charles Griffith, and has, with other issue,

° John, *b.* 1860.

Lieut.-Col. Lewes, who entered the Army in 1847, and served with the Buffs in the Crimea, Central America (Honduras) and the West Indies, is a J.P. and D.L. for co. Cardigan (High Sheriff 1865).—*Llanllear, Cardigan; Junior United Service Club, s.w.*

LEWES, WILLIAM PRICE, Esq., of Llysnewydd, Carmarthenshire.

Eldest son of the late William Lewes, Esq., of Llysnewydd, by Williama Eliza Anne, dau. of William Lewis, Esq., of Llanayron, co. Cardigan; *b.* 1813; *s.* 1849; *m.* 1837 Anna, dau. of James Beatty, Esq., M.D., of Enniskillen, co. Fermanagh, and has, with other issue,

° William Price Llewellyn, *b.* 1874.

Mr. Lewes is a J.P. and D.L. for co. Carmarthen (High Sheriff 1859), a J.P. and D.L. for co. Cardigan (on the roll of High Sheriffs for 1864), a Dep.-Lieut. for co. Pembroke, and Major Carmarthen Militia Artillery; late Lieut. 96th Regt.—*Llysnewydd, Carmarthen.*

LEWIN, FREDERICK MORTIMER, Esq., of The Hollies, Bexley, Kent.

Fourth son of the late Thomas Lewin, Esq., of The Hollies, Bexley, by Mary, dau. of General Hale, of Plantation, Gisborough, co. York; *b.* 1798; *s.* 1843; *m.* 1839 Augusta Diana, dau. of Thomas G. Babington,

580

Esq., of Rothley Temple, co. Leicester, and has, with other issue,

° Frederick Chaloner, Lieut. 85th Foot, *b.* 1842.

Mr. Lewin, who was educated at Harrow, is a Magistrate for Kent and Hants.—*The Hollies, Bexley, Dartford; Windham Club, s.w.;* 69, *South Audley Street, w.*

LEWIN. (See *Ross-Lewin.*)

LEWIS, the Rev. Sir GILBERT FRANKLAND, Bart., of Harpton, Radnorshire (cr. 1846).

Second son of the late Right Hon. Sir Thomas Frankland Lewis, Bart., M.P., of Harpton Court (who *d.* 1855), by his 1st wife Harriet, 4th dau. of the late Sir George Cornewall, Bart., of Moccas Court, co. Hereford; *b.* 1808; *s.* his brother, the Right Hon. Sir George Cornewall Lewis (some time Chancellor of the Exchequer and Secretary of State for the Home and War Departments), as 3rd Bart. 1863; *m.* 1843 Jane, eldest dau. of Sir Edmund Antrobus, Bart. Educated at Eton and Magdalen Coll., Cambridge (B.A. 1830, M.A. 1833); is a Magistrate for co. Hereford, Rector of Monnington-on-Wye (1834); and a Canon of Worcester (1860).—*Harpton Court, Radnor; Monnington-on-Wye, Hereford.*

Heir, his son Herbert Edmund Frankland, *b.* 1846.

LEWIS, Lieut.-Col. ARTHUR GAMBELL, of Sea Town, co. Dublin, and Clanamully, co. Monaghan.

Son of the late Michael Lewis, Esq., of Spring Hill, co. Dublin, by Anne Elizabeth, only dau. of Richard Frizell, Esq., of Beaufort House, co. Dublin; *b.* 1790; *m.* 1st 1820 Hester, dau. of Richard Westenra, Esq., of Rutland Square, Dublin (uncle of Lord Rossmore); 2nd 1841 Henrietta, only child of Henry Owen Scott, Esq., late of Clanamully, co. Monaghan, and widow of the Hon. Richard Westenra (she *d.* 1860); he has issue, an only surviving child,

° Henry Owen, of Raconnell, co. Monaghan; *b.* 1842; *m.* 1866 Frances Sophia, only child of the late F. C. Elsegard, Esq., of Upper Brook Street, w.

Lieut.-Col. Lewis, who is a J.P. and D.L. for cos. Dublin and Monaghan (High Sheriff 1847), and late Lieut.-Col. Monaghan Militia, was High Sheriff of co. Longford 1854.—*Sea Town, co. Dublin; Clanamully, Scottstown, co. Monaghan;* 43, *Fitzwilliam Square, Dublin.*

LEWIS, CHARLES BASSETT, Esq., of Gwinfe, Carmarthenshire.

Eldest son of the late Lewis Lewis, Esq., of Gwinfe, by Sarah Simmons, dau. of William Colborne, Esq., of Clifton, co. Gloucester; *b.* 1831; *s.* 1839; *m.* 1863 Sarah Amelia, 2nd dau. of the late Samuel Brown, Esq., of Clifton, and has issue,

° A dau., *b.* 1865.

Mr. Lewis, who was educated at Jesus Coll., Oxford, is a Magistrate for co. Carmarthen, and Adjutant Royal Cardigan Militia; was formerly Lieut. 20th Foot, and 44th Foot.—*Gwinfe, Glangadock, Carmarthenshire.*

LEWIS, DAVID, Esq., of Stradey, Carmarthenshire.

Only surviving son of the late Thomas Lewis, Esq., of Stradey, by Catherine, dau. of William Lloyd, Esq., of Laques, co. Carmarthen; *b.* 1797; *m.* 1856 Ledith, youngest dau. of the late Benjamin Way, Esq., of Denham Place, Bucks, and has issue,

° Charles William Mansel, *b.* 1845.

Mr. Lewis, who was educated at Eton and Brasenose Coll., Oxford (B.A. 1818), and called to the Bar at Lincoln's Inn 1822, is a J.P. and D.L. for co. Carmarthen, and a Director of the South Wales, Vale of Neath, and Llanelly and Llandilo Railways; was M.P. for Carmarthen 1835-7.—*Stradey, Llanelly; Carlton and University Clubs, s.w.*

+ LEWIS, the Rev. FRANCIS, of St. Pierre, Monmouthshire.

Third son of the late Charles Lewis, Esq., of St. Pierre, by Susannah, dau. of Francis Davis, Esq., of Chepstow; b. 178—; m. 1st 182— Mary, dau. of the Rev. Edward Lewis, of Portskewet; 2nd 1853 Jane, only dau. of Vice-Admiral Charles Gordon, and has, with other issue,

* Rev. Charles Edward, educated at Rugby, a J.P. and D.L. for co. Monmouth; b. 1830; m. 1858 Sarah Elizabeth. dau. of the late James Staunton Lambert, Esq., of Waterdale House, co. Galway.

Mr. Lewis, who was educated at University Coll., Oxford (B.A. 1802, M.A. 1805, B.D. 1826), is a Magistrate for cos. Hereford and Monmouth, Patron of 2 livings, and Vicar of Holme Lacy, co. Hereford.—St. Pierre and Dennell Hill, Chepstow; Holme Lacy, Hereford.

LEWIS, HENRY, Esq., of Green Meadow, Glamorganshire.

Eldest son of the late Henry Lewis, Esq., of Green Meadow, by Mary, dau. of George Emerson, Esq.; b. 1815; s. 1838; m. 1st 1844 Anne, dau. of Walter Morgan, Esq., of Merthyr (she d. 1857); 2nd 1858 Sophia, dau. of the late Col. Gwynne, of Glanbrane, and has by the former, with other issue,

* Henry, b. 1847.

Mr. Lewis is a J.P. and D.L. for co. Glamorgan (High Sheriff 1858).—Green Meadow, Cardiff.

LEWIS, JOHN DELAWARE, Esq., of Membland, Devon, and Westbury House, Hants.

Only surviving son of the late John Delaware Lewis, Esq., Russia Merchant, by Emma, dau. of James Hamilton Clewlow, Esq., R.N.; b. 1828; m. 1868 Teresa, eldest dau. of Sir Jervois Clarke-Jervoise, Bart. Educated at Eton and Trinity Coll., Cambridge (B.A. 1850, M.A. 1853; is a Magistrate for Devon, Lord of the Manor of Revelstoke, and late 1st Lieut. Pembroke Artillery Militia. This family came originally from Glamorganshire, and were among the earliest settlers in Delaware (U.S.) at the close of the 17th century.—Membland Hall, Ivybridge; Westbury House, Petersfield; Reform and Union Clubs, s.w.; Garrick Club, s.w.

LEWIS, JOHN HARVEY, Esq., of Kilcullen, co. Kildare.

Son of the late William Lewis, Esq., of Harlech, co. Dublin, by Dora, dau. of the late John Cassidy, Esq., of Monasterevan, co. Kildare; b. 1814; m. 1st 1840 Emily, only child and heiress of the late George Ball, Esq., of Richmond Hill, Surrey (she d. 1850); 2nd 185— Jane Isabella, dau. of the late William Browne, Esq. Graduated at Trinity Coll., Dublin (B.A. 1835, M.A. 1838); called to the Irish Bar 1838, but relinquished practice in 1853; is a Magistrate for Westminster and Middlesex, and a Dep.-Lieut. for Middlesex and the Tower Hamlets; was High Sheriff of co. Kildare 1857; elected M.P. for Marylebone 1861. —Kilcullen, co. Kildare; Union and Reform Clubs, s w : 24, Grosvenor Street, w.

Heir Pres., his brother William (of Haddington House, co. Dublin), b. 1818; m. 1845 Jane, dau. of Michael Hackett, Esq., of Parsonstown, King's Co.

LEWIS, JOHN LENNOX GRIFFITH POYER, Esq., of Henllan, Pembrokeshire.

Eldest son of the late John Lewis, Esq., of Henllan, by Eliza, dau. of the late Charles Callen, Esq., of Grove, co. Pembroke; b. 1819; s. 1834; m. 1857 Katherine, youngest and only surviving child of the late Daniel Poyer Callen, Esq., of Molleston. Educated at Broomsgrove and St. John's Coll., Cambridge; called to the Bar at Lincoln's Inn 1848; is a Magistrate for co. Carmarthen (High Sheriff 1867), and a J.P. and D.L.

for co. Pembroke.—Henllan, Narberth, Pembrokeshire; Oxford and Cambridge Club, s.w.

Heir Pres., his brother Richard (in Holy Orders), Rector of Lampeter Velfrey; b. 1820; m. 1841 Georgiana, dau. of Capt. Lewis, and has issue, * Arthur Griffith Poyer, b. 1848.

+ LEWIS, Capt. JOHN LEWIS HAMPTON-, of Henllys, Anglesey.

Eldest son of the late John H. Hampton-Lewis, Esq., of Henllys and Bodjor, Anglesey, by Mary, dau. of Richard Chambers, Esq., of Whitbourne Court. co. Hereford; b. 1795; s. 1843; m. 1833 Frances Elizabeth, only child of Thomas Panson, Esq., of Prior House, Richmond, co. York, and has, with oth er issue,

* Thomas Lewis, late Capt. 5th Dragoons; b. 1834.

Mr. Hampton-Lewis, who is a J.P. and D.L. for co. Anglesey (High Sheriff 1847), was formerly an Officer in the Army.—Henllys, Beaumaris.

LEWIS, Mrs., of Yatton Court, Herefordshire.

Elizabeth, eldest dau. of Admiral Ferguson, of Pitfour, co. Aberdeen, by his 1st wife, Elizabeth Holcombe, only dau. and heir of John Woodhouse, Esq., of Aramstone and Yatton Court; s. her mother in this estate 1814; m. 1838 the Rev. Thomas Taylor Lewis, Incumbent of Bridstow, who d. 1858, leaving issue, three daughters.—Yatton Court, Aymestrey, Leominster.

+ LEWIS, PRICE, Esq., of Gwastod, Cardiganshire.

Son of the late P. Lewis, Esq., of Gwastod; b. 18—. Was High Sheriff of co. Cardigan 1863.—Gwastod, Lampeter, Cardiganshire.

LEWIS, WILLIAM HENRY, Esq., of Clynfiew, Pembrokeshire.

Eldest son of the late Thomas Lewis, J.P. and D.L. for co. Pembroke, by Elizabeth, dau. of William Lewis, Esq.; b. 1807; s. 1845; m. 1850 Mary, dau. of John Colby, Esq., of Fynone, co. Pembroke. Educated at Harrow and Trinity Coll., Oxford; is Lord of the Manor of Castellan, a Magistrate for cos. Cardigan and Carmarthen (High Sheriff 1847), a J.P. and D.L. for co. Pembroke, and Major Pembroke Artillery.—Clynfiew, Newcastle Emlyn; Oxford and Cambridge Club, s.w.

LEWIS, WILLIAM WYNDHAM, Esq., of The Heath, and Newhouse, Glamorganshire.

Second son of the late Henry Lewis, Esq., by Mary, dau. of George Emerson. Esq.; b. 1827; s. to the estates of his uncle, the late Rev. W. P. Lewis, 1849; m. 1st 1851 Annie, dau. of George Overton, Esq., of Llanthetty Hall, co. Brecon; 2nd 1867 Maud, youngest dau. of the late William Williams, Esq., of Aberpergwm, co. Glamorgan, and has issue,

* Annie Mary Price.

Mr. Lewis, who was educated at Worcester Coll., Oxford, is a J.P. and D.L. for co. Glamorgan (High Sheriff 1855).—The Heath, and Newhouse, Cardiff.

LEWIS, of Glyn Podr, Brecknockshire.

(See Jones.)

LEWIS-LLOYD, THOMAS, Esq., of Nantgwillt, Radnorshire.

Eldest son of the late John Lewis, Esq., of Cwintoyddwr, by Elizabeth Mary, dau. of Thomas Lewis Lloyd, Esq., of Nantgwillt, co. Radnor; b. 1799; m. 1825 Anna Elizabeth, dau. of Evan Davies, Esq., of Treforgan, co. Cardigan, and has, with other issue,

* Robert, b. 1836; m. 1866 Mary Anne Jane, eldest dau. of the late Capt. Lewes, of Llanleer, co. Cardigan.

Mr. Lewis-Lloyd, who was educated at Rugby, is a

J.P. and D.L. for cos. Radnor and Cardigan (High Sheriff 1822); assumed by Royal licence, in 1824, the surname of Lloyd.—*Nantgwillt, Rhayader.*

LEWTHWAITE, WILLIAM, Esq., of Broadgate, Cumberland.
Eldest son of the late John Lewthwaite, Esq., J.P. and D.L., of Broadgate, by Anne, dau. of William Kirkbank, Esq.; *b.* 1826; *s.* 1863; *m.* 1851 Mary, dau. of William Challinor, Esq., of Leek, co. Stafford, and has, with other issue,
* William, *b.* 1853.
Mr. Lewthwaite, who was educated at Trinity Coll., Cambridge (B.A. 1849, M.A. 1852), is a Magistrate for Cumberland.—*Broadgate, Broughton-in-Furness.*

LEY, HUGH HALSE, Esq., of Jetwells, Cornwall.
Eldest son of the late Edwin Ley, Esq., of Jetwells, by Cecilia, dau. of Henry Grantham, Esq., of Scawby, co. Lincoln; *b.* 1851; *s.* 1865. The late Mr. Ley was a Magistrate for Cornwall, a Deputy-Warden of the Stannaries, and Lord of the Manor of Alwarton, Penzance, and Mousehole.—*Jetwells, Camelford.*

LEY, JOHN HENRY, Esq., of Trehill, Devon.
Eldest son of the late John Henry Ley, Esq., of Trehill (many years Chief Clerk in the House of Commons), by Lady Dorothea Frances Hay, 2nd dau. of George, 7th Marquis of Tweeddale, K.T.; *b.* 1812; *s.* 1850; *m.* 1845 Henrietta, dau. of Henry Porter, Esq., of Winslade House, Devon, and has, with other issue,
* John Henry Francis, *b.* 1847.
Mr. Ley, who was educated at Westminster, is Patron of 1 living.—*Trehill, Exeter.*

LEY, Mrs., of Woodlands, Devon.
Rebecca Maria, dau. of the late Lewis George Dive, Esq., of Tavistock Street, London; *m.* 1853, as his 2nd wife, William Ley, Esq., of Woodlands, who was a Magistrate for Devon, and many years Assistant Clerk of the House of Commons, and who *d.* 1864, leaving, with other issue, * William Henry, *b.* 1860.—*Woodlands, Kennford, Exeter.*

LEYBORNE-POPHAM, ALEXANDER HUGH, Esq., of Kevinsfort, co. Sligo.
Eldest son of the late Alexander Hugh Leyborne-Popham, by Anne, dau. and heir of George Dodswell, Esq., of Kevinsfort, co. Sligo; *b.* 1855; *s.* 1866. —*Kevinsfort, Sligo; Northerwood House, Lyndhurst.*

LEYBORNE-POPHAM, EDWARD, Esq., of Littlecote, Wilts.
Eldest son of the late Lieut.-General Edward W. Leyborne-Popham, of Littlecote, J.P. and D.L., and formerly High Sheriff of Wilts (who assumed the additional name of Popham by Royal licence), by Elizabeth, dau. of the late Ven. Archdeacon Andrew, Rector of Powderham, Devon; *b.* 1807; *s.* 1853; is Lord of the Manor and Patron of Littlecote.—This family is descended from Sir John Popham, Lord Chief Justice of England *temp.* Elizabeth, who purchased the estate of Littlecote.—*Littlecote, Hungerford.*

Heir Pres., his brother Francis, educated at University Coll., Oxford (B.A. 1831, M.A. 1834), and subsequently Fellow of All Souls Coll.; J.P. and D.L. for Wilts; *b.* 1810; *m.* 1857 Elizabeth, 3rd dau. and co-heir of James Block, Esq., of Charlton, Wilts, and by her, who d. 1865, has, with other issue, * Francis, *b.* 1867.

LEYCESTER, Capt. EDMUND MORTIMER, R.N., of White Place, Berks.
Fifth but eldest surviving son of the late George Hanmer Leycester, Esq., of White Place (who *d.* 1838), by Charlotte Jemima, dau. of the late Hans Wintrop Mortimer, Esq., M.P., of Caldwell Hall, co. Derby; *b.*

1810; *s.* his brother 1862; *m.* 1842 Harriet, dau. of Capt. James Neville, R.N., of Stoke, Devon, and has, with other issue,
* Rafe Neville, *b.* 1843.
Capt. Leycester is a Capt. R.N., and Superintendent of H.M. Mail Packet and Transport Service at Liverpool.—*White Place, Cookham, Maidenhead; Admiralty Office, Liverpool.*

LEYCESTER, RAFE OSWALD, Esq., of Toft Hall, Cheshire.
Eldest son of the late Ralph Gerard Leycester, Esq., of Toft Hall, by Emily Elizabeth, dau. of Charles Tyrwhitt Jones, Esq.; *b.* 1844; *s.* 1851; *m.* 1867 Edith, dau. of Hubert de Burgh, Esq., of West Drayton Park, Middlesex. Educated at Eton; is Patron of 1 living. —*Toft Hall, Knutsford;* 101, *Eaton Place, s.w.*

LEYCESTER, WILLIAM WRIXON, Esq., of East View, co. Cork.
Only son of the late Joseph Leycester Esq., M.P., of East View, by Catharine, dau. and co-heir of Nicholas Wrixon, Esq., Solicitor, of Dublin; *b.* 1808; *s.* 1859; *m.* 1840 Barbara, dau. of Thomas McCall, Esq., of Craighead, co. Lanark, and has issue, * Joseph, *b.* 1855. —*East View, near Cork.*

LEYCESTER. (See *Penrhyn.*)

LEYLAND, THOMAS, Esq., of Haggerston Castle, Northumberland.
Son of the late Thomas Leyland, Esq., of Walton Hall, co. Lancaster; *b.* 1812; *m.* 1840 Miss Naylor, and has, with other issue,
* Tom Naylor, late of the 2nd Life Guards; *b.* 1841; *m.* 1862 Mary Ann, dau. of the late Charles Scarisbrick, Esq., of Scarisbrick Hall, and Wrightington, co. Lancaster, and has, with other issue, * Herbert Scarisbrick, *b.* 1864.
Mr. Leyland, who is Lord of the Manor of Islandshire, was formerly in the 15th Hussars, and Capt. 2nd Life Guards; purchased this property 1859.—*Haggerston Castle, Beal, Northumberland; Hyde Park House, Albert Gate, s.w.*

LICHFIELD, Bishop of (the Right Rev. GEORGE AUGUSTUS SELWYN, D.D.),
Second son of the late William Selwyn, Esq., Q.C., of Richmond, Surrey, by Lætitia Frances, dau. of Thomas Kynaston, Esq., of Witham, Essex; *b.* 1809; *m.* 1839 Sarah Harriet, dau. of the late Sir John Richardson, Knt., Judge of the Court of Common Pleas. Educated at Eton and St. John's Coll., Cambridge (B.A. 1831, M.A. 1834, D.D. 1841); was formerly Curate of Windsor; consecrated Bishop of New Zealand 1841; translated 1867: patron of 90 livings, partly alternate. —*The Palace, Lichfield.*

LICHFIELD, Earl of (THOMAS GEORGE ANSON). —Cr. 1832.
Eldest son of Thomas William, 1st Earl. by Louisa, Katharine, dau. of the late Nathaniel Philips, Esq., of Slebeck Hall, co. Pembroke; *b.* 1822; *s.* 1854; *m.* 1855 Lady Harriet Georgiana, eldest dau. of James, 2nd Marquis of Aberoorn, K.G. Is Lord Lieutenant and Chairman of the Quarter Sessions co. Stafford. Patron of 4 livings; late Major Staffordshire Yeomanry; was M.P. for Lichfield 1847-54.—*Shugborough Park, Stafford; Brooks's, Travellers', and Boodle's Clubs, s.w.*

Heir, his son Thomas Francis, Viscount Anson, *b.* 1856.

LIDDELL, the Hon. ADOLPHUS FREDERICK OCTAVIUS.
Eighth son of Thomas Henry, 1st Lord Ravensworth, by Maria Susannah, dau. of John Simpson, Esq., of Bradley, co. Durham; *b.* 1818; *m.* 1845 Frederica

Elizabeth, dau. of G. Lane Fox, Esq., of Bramham Park, co. York, and has, with other issue,

* Adolphus George Charles, b. 1846.

Mr. Liddell, who was educated at Eton and Ch. Ch., Oxford (B.A. 1838), Fellow of All Souls 1840, and called to the Bar at the Inner Temple 1844, Q.C. and Bencher of Inner Temple 1861; appointed Permanent Under-Secretary of State for the Home Department 1867. —*Park Cottage, East Sheen*, s.w.; *Home Office*, s.w.; *Twisden Buildings, Temple*, E.C.

LIDDELL, the Hon. GEORGE AUGUSTUS FREDERICK.

Sixth son of Thomas Henry, 1st Lord Ravensworth, by Maria Susannah, dau. of John Simpson, Esq., of Bradley, co. Durham; b. 1812; m. 1842 Cecil Elizabeth, dau. of the Hon. and Rev. Dr. Gerald V. Wellesley, and has, with other issue,

* Edward Thomas, b. 1845.

Mr. Liddell, who was educated at Eton, entered the Scots Fusilier Guards 1828, and became Lieut.-Col. 1846, and Col. 1854, is Dep. Ranger of Richmond Park, a Groom-in-Waiting to the Queen, and Treasurer to Prince Alfred; he was Comptroller to the Household, and Equerry to H.R.H. the late Duchess of Gloucester.—49, *Cadogan Place*, s.w.

LIDDELL, the Hon. and Rev. ROBERT.

Fifth son of Thomas Henry, 1st Lord Ravensworth, by Maria Susannah, dau. of John Simpson, Esq., of Bradley, co. Durham; b. 1808; m. 1836 Emily, dau. of the Hon. and Rev. Dr. Gerald V. Wellesley, and has, with other issue,

* Arthur Thomas, b. 1837; m. 1866 Sophia Harriett, 2nd dau. of Sir Thomas Waller, Bart.

Mr. Liddell, who was educated at the Charterhouse and Ch. Ch., Oxford (B.A. 1829, M.A. 1832), and was afterwards Fellow of All Souls Coll., was appointed Vicar of Barking 1836, Incumbent of St Paul's, Knightsbridge 1851.—16, *Wilton Crescent*, s.w.

LIDDELL, Sir JOHN, Knt., K.C.B., F.R.S. ‡ (cr. 1848).

Son of the late J. Liddell, Esq.; b. 1794; m. 1837 Fauny, dau. of Robert Clement Sconce, Esq., and has, with other issue,

* John, Commander, R.N., b. 1838; m. 1861 Sydney Elizabeth, eldest dau. of the late George Carew-Gibson, Esq., of Bradston Brook, Surrey.

Sir John, who graduated M.D. at Edinburgh, was formerly Inspector of Royal Hospitals at Malta, Haslar, and Greenwich; late Director-General of the Medical Department of the Navy.—*United Service Club.* s.w.; 72, *Chester Square*, s.w.; *The Admiralty, Somerset House*, w.c.

LIDDELL, the Rev. HENRY GEORGE.

Younger son of the late Sir Henry George Liddell, Bart., of Ravensworth Castle, co. Durham, by Elizabeth, dau. of Thomas Steele, Esq., of Hampnet, Sussex, and brother of Thomas Henry, 1st Lord Ravensworth; b. 1787; m. 1809 Charlotte, dau. of the Hon. Thomas Lyon, of Hetton House, co. Durham, and has, with other issue,

* Henry George, Dean of Ch. Ch., Oxford, educated at the Charterhouse and Ch. Ch., Oxford (B.A. 1833, M.A. 1855); b. 1811; m. 1849 Lorina, dau. of James Reeve, Esq., of Lowestoft, Suffolk, and has issue.

Mr. Liddell, who was educated at Westminster and Brasenose Coll., Oxford (B.A. 1809, M.A. 1812), ordained Deacon 1810, and Priest 1811, is a Magistrate for co. Durham; was Rector of Easington, co. Durham, 1820-62.—*Charlton Kings, Cheltenham.*

LIDDELL. (See under *Ravensworth*.)

‡ Died whilst these sheets were at press

LIDWILL, FREDERICK, Esq., of Dromard, co. Tipperary.

Only surviving son of the late George Lidwill, Esq., of Dromard, by Eleanor, dau. of Morgan Kavanagh, Esq., of Borriss Castle, co. Carlow, and of Lady Frances Butler, sister of John, Earl of Ormonde; b. 1809; s. 1826; m. 1826 Christiana, dau. of the late William Hutchinson, Esq., and has, with other issue,

* George, late Capt. 19th Foot, b. 1828; m. 1863 Edith Wheatley, eldest dau. of Henry Adams, Esq.

Mr. Lidwill, who was educated at Trinity Coll., Dublin, is a Magistrate for cos. Kilkenny and Tipperary, and for Queen's Co.—*Dromard, Templemore, co. Tipperary.*

LIFFORD, Viscount (JAMES HEWITT). — Cr. 1781.

Eldest son of James, 3rd Viscount, by the Hon. Mary Anne, 8th dau. of Cornwallis, 1st Viscount Hawarden; b. 1811; s. 1855; m. 1st 1835 Lady Mary, eldest dau. of Archibald, 2nd Earl of Gosford (she d. 1850); 2nd 1851 Lydia Lucy, eldest dau. of the Rev John Digby Wingfield Digby, Rector of Coleshill, co. Warwick, and widow of Charles Purdon-Coote, Esq. Educated at Ch. Ch., Oxford (B.A. 1833); is a J.P. and D.L. for cos. Warwick and Donegal; elected a Representative Peer for Ireland 1855.—*Meenglas, Stranorlar, co. Donegal ; Cecil House, Wimbledon, Surrey ; Carlton Club*, s.w.

Heir, his son James Wilfrid, late Lieut. 3rd Foot, b. 1837; m. 1867 Annie Frances, eldest dau. of Arthur Hodgson, Esq., of Queensland, Australia.

LIFFORD, Dowager Viscountess.

Mary Anne, 8th dau. of Cornwallis, 1st Viscount Hawarden, by his 3rd wife Anne Isabella, dau. of Thomas Monck, Esq.; m. 1809 James, 3rd Viscount Lifford, who d. 1855.—*Ashcldon, Torquay.*

LIGHT, Sir HENRY, K.C.B. (cr. 1848).

Son of the late William Light, Esq., of the H.E.I.C.'s Civil Service, by Lucretia, dau. of the Chevalier Alexander de Lüders; b. 1783; m. 1819 Charlotte, dau. of Richard Parry, Esq., of Warfield Hall, Berks, and has, with other issue,

* Alfred, Lieut.-Col, Royal Artillery, b. 1821.

Sir Henry was educated at Rugby and Woolwich; received his Commission in the Royal Artillery in 1799; retired from the service in 1824; he was subsequently Lieut.-Governor of Antigua and Dominica, and was Governor and Commander-in-Chief of British Guiana 1838-48.—*Hawthorn Hill, Bracknell.*

LIGHTON, the Rev. Sir CHRISTOPHER ROBERT, Bart., of Merville, co. Dublin (cr. 1791).

Second but eldest surviving son of the late Rev. Sir John Lighton, Bart., of Merville (who d. 1827), by Mary Hamilton, dau. of Christopher Robert Pemberton, Esq., M.D., of London; b. 1819; s. his brother 1844; m. 1843 Mary Anne Elizabeth, dau. of the Rev. Digby Joseph Stopford Ram, of Brookville, co. Cork. Educated at St. John's Coll., Cambridge (B.A. 1843, M.A. 1846); appointed Vicar of Ellastone 1848.—*Ellastone Vicarage, Ashbourne.*

Heir, his son Christopher Robert, b. 1848.

LILFORD, Lord (THOMAS LITTLETON POWYS). —Cr. 1797.

Eldest son of Thomas, 3rd Lord, by the Hon. Mary Elizabeth Fox, dau. of the 3rd Lord Holland (ext.); b. 1833; s. 1861; m. 1859 Emma Elizabeth, dau. of Robert W. Brandling, Esq., late of Low Gosforth Hall, Northumberland. Educated at Harrow and Ch. Ch., Oxford; is a J.P. and D.L. for co. Northampton, and Patron of 9 livings; late Lieut. Northamptonshire Militia.—*Lilford Hall, Oundle ; Bank Hall, Chorley ; Carlton, Travellers', and St. James's Clubs*, s.w.

Heir, his son, Thomas Atherton, b. 1861.

LILLIE, Sir JOHN SCOTT, Knt., C.B., K.T.S. (cr. 1817).

Eldest son of the late Philip Lillie, Esq., of Drimdoe Castle, co. Roscommon; *b.* 1790; *m.* 1st 1820 Louisa, dau. of Capt. Sutherland (she *d.* 1860); 2nd 1862 Elizabeth Hannah, only child of Thomas Reid Clarke, Esq., of Turnham House, Charl, Somerset, and widow of Thomas G. Warrington Carew, Esq., and has by the former, with other issue,

* John Edward Sutherland, of the Bengal Civil Service; *b.* 1822; *m.* 1859 Cecilia Mary, dau. of the late Major Justinian Nutt, of the Bombay Engineers.

Sir John is a J.P. and D.L. for Middlesex, a Lieut.-Col. in the Army (retired), and a Major-Gen. Portuguese service; late Lieut.-Col. Grenadier Guards.—*Reform and Union Clubs*, s.w.; 8, *Albert Terrace*, s.w.

LILLINGSTON, CHARLES ALFRED GORDON, Esq., of Southwold Lodge, Suffolk.

Son of the late Alfred Lillingston, Esq., J.P., of Southwold Lodge, by his 2nd wife Mary Grey. dau. of Capt. Monck Mason, R.N.; *b.* 1857; *s.* 1866. This family was formerly of Elmdon Hall, co. Warwick.—*Southwold Lodge, Wangford, Suffolk.*

LILLINGSTON, FREDERICK GEORGE INNES, Esq., of Childhay, Dorset.

Only son of the late Isaac William Lillingston, Esq., of Childhay, by Katharine Innes Lindsay, only child of Hugh Lindsay, Esq.; *b.* 1849; *s.* 1850; entered the Royal Navy 1862. His grandfather, Abraham Spooner-Lillingston, Esq., of Elmdon, co. Warwick, assumed the name of Lillingston on his marriage with Elizabeth Mary Agnes Lillingston, of Ferriby Grange, co. York. —*Childhay, Beaminster.*

LILLINGSTONE. (See *Johnson.*)

LIMERICK, ARDFERT, and AGHADOE, Bishop of (the Rt. Rev. CHARLES GRAVES, D.D.).

Youngest son of the late John Crosbie Graves, Esq., Barrister-at-law, of Dublin, by Helena, eldest dau. of the Rev. Charles Perceval, Rector of Churchtown. co. Cork; *b.* 1812; *m.* 1840 Selina, eldest surviving dau. of John Cheyne, Esq., M.D., Physician General to Her Majesty's Forces in Ireland. Educated at Trinity Coll., Dublin (B.A. 1835, M.A. 1838); became Fellow of his College 1836, and Erasmus Smith's Professor of Mathematics 1843; was appointed Dean of the Chapel Royal Ireland 1860, and Dean of Clonfert 1864; was President of the Royal Irish Academy 1861–6; consecrated 1866; Patron of 47 livings.—*The Palace, Limerick; Athenæum Club*, s.w.

LIMERICK, Earl of (WILLIAM HALE JOHN CHARLES PERY).—Cr. 1803.

Eldest son of William Henry Tennison. 2nd Earl, by his 1st wife Susannah, dau. of the late William Sheaffe. Esq.; *b.* 1840; *s.* 1866; *m.* 1862 his cousin Caroline Maria, dau. of the late Rev. Henry and Lady Emilie Caroline Gray. Sits in the House of Lords as Lord Foxford, U.K. (cr. 1815). Is a J.P. and D.L. for co. Limerick, Patron of 2 livings, Major 1st Gloucestershire Artillery Volunteers, and Capt. co. Limerick Militia. —*Carlton Club*, s.w.; 79, *Chester Square*, s.w.

Heir, his son William Edmond de Vere Sheaffe, Viscount Glentworth, *b.* 1863.

LINCOLN, Earl of. (See under *Newcastle.*)

LINCOLN, Bishop of (the Right Rev. JOHN JACKSON, D.D.).

Son of the late Henry Jackson, Esq., by Lucy, dau. of Robert Chipchase, Esq.; *b.* 1811; *m.* 1838 Mary, dau. of Henry Drowell, Esq. Educated at Reading and I'em

584

broke Coll., Oxford (B.A. 1833, M.A. 1836); gained the Theological Prize 1834; appointed Head Master of Islington School 1836, Rector of St. James's, Piccadilly, 1846, Chaplain to the Queen 1847, and Canon of Bristol 1852; consecrated 1853. Patron of 68 livings.—*Riseholme Palace, Lincoln.*

LINDESAY, FREDERICK, Esq., of Loughry, co. Tyrone.

Third but eldest surviving son of the late Robert Lindesay, Esq., of Loughry (who was High Sheriff of co. Tyrone 1788), by Jane, eldest dau. and co-heir of the late Thomas Mauleverer, Esq., of Arncliffe Hall, co. York; *b.* 1792; *s.* his nephew 1848; *m.* 1st 1823 Agnes Cornish, dau. and co-heir of Sir Edwin Bayntun Sandys, Bart., of Miserden Park, co. Gloucester, and Chadlington Hall, Oxon; 2nd 1856 Charlotte, dau. of H. C. B. Mac-Murrough Murphy, Esq., late of Hume Street, Dublin, and has by the former, with other issue,

* Robert Sandys, Capt. Tyrone Fusiliers, late Ensign 30th Foot; *b.* 1825.

Mr. Lindesay, who was educated at Armagh and Trinity Coll., Dublin (B.A. 1813, M.A. 1833), and called to the Irish Bar 1817, is a J.P. and D.L. for co. Tyrone (High Sheriff 1859), and Capt. Commandant of the Loughry Corps of Yeomanry Infantry.—*Loughry, Dungannon, co. Tyrone; Sackville-Street Club, Dublin; 67, Mountjoy Square, Dublin.*

LINDESAY-BETHUNE. (See *Bethune.*)

LINDESAY, WALTER, Esq., of Greenville, co. Dublin.

Only son of the late Robert Lindesay, Esq., of Cahoo, co. Tyrone, by Georgina, dau. of the Very Rev. J. Brocas. Dean of Killala; *b.* 1808; *m.* 1st 183–Thomasina Jane. only dau. of Robert Jephson. Esq., and niece of the late Sir Richard Mounteney Jephson, Bart.; 2nd 1838 Harriet Cole, 2nd dau. of Wm. Cornish, Esq., J.P. and D.L., of Marazion, Cornwall; and has, with other issue,

* Walter Brocas, *b.* 1848.

Mr. Lindesay, who was educated at Trinity Coll., Dublin (B.A. 1829), and called to the Irish Bar 1838, is a Magistrate for cos. Wicklow and Dublin.—*Greenville, Dublin; Glenview, Bray; University Club, Dublin.*

LINDOW, HENRY WILLIAM, Esq., of Gawcomb, Gloucestershire.

Eldest son of the late Henry Lindow Rawlinson, Esq. (who in 1792 assumed the name of Lindow on succeeding to the property of his uncle. William Lindow, Esq.). by Charlotte Elizabeth, dau. of the Rev. Robert Cary Barnard, of Withersfield. Suffolk; *b.* 1824; *s.* 1848. Educated at Rugby and Oriel Coll., Oxford; is a Magistrate for co. Gloucester; was formerly an Officer in the 17th Lancers.—*Gawcomb, Stow-on-the-Wold; Army and Navy Club*, s.w.; 37, *Bedford Place*, w.c.

+ LINDOW, SAMUEL, Esq., of Cleator, Cumberland.

Son of the late S. Lindow, Esq.; *b.* 18—; is married, and has issue,

* John, a Magistrate for Cumberland; *b.* 18—.

Mr. Lindow is a Magistrate for Cumberland (High Sheriff 1862).—*Cleator, Egremont, Cumberland.*

LINDSAY, the Hon. CHARLES HUGH.

Third son of James, 24th Earl of Crawford, by the Hon. Maria Margaret, dau. of John, 1st Lord Muncaster; *b.* 1816; *m.* 1851 Emilia, dau. of the Hon. and Very Rev. Henry Montague Browne, Dean of Lismore, and has. with other issue,

* Charles Ludovic, *b.* 1852.

Mr. Lindsay, who is a Col. in the Army and Groom in Waiting to Her Majesty, was formerly in the 43rd Regt.

and in the Grenadier Guards; he was elected M.P. for Abingdon 1865.—*Haigh Hall, Wigan; United Service, Guards', and Carlton Clubs, s.w.*

LINDSAY, the Hon. COLIN, of Deer Park, Devon.
Youngest son of James, 24th Earl of Crawford, by the Hon. Maria Margaret, dau. of John, 1st Lord Muncaster; *b.* 1819; *s.* his uncle, William Meade Smythe, Esq., of Deer Park, 1866; *m.* 1845 Lady Frances, 3rd dau. of William, 4th Earl of Wicklow, and has, with other issue,
  • William Alexander, *b.* 1846.
Mr. Lindsay is a Magistrate for cos. Devon and Lancaster.—*Deer Park, Honiton.*

LINDSAY, the Hon. Major-General JAMES.
Second son of James, 24th Earl of Crawford, by the Hon. Maria Margaret, dau. of John, 1st Lord Muncaster; *b.* 1815; *m.* 1845 Lady Sarah Elizabeth, dau. of John, 3rd Earl of Mexborough, and has issue. Educated at Eton; entered the Army 1832, became Lieut.-Col. Grenadier Guards 1860, Major-General in the Army 1861; is a Dep.-Lieut. for co. Lancaster; was M.P. for Wigan 1845-57 and 1859-66; commanded a district in Canada 1863 to 1867.—*Guards' and United Service Clubs, s.w.;* 25, *Portman Square, w.*

LINDSAY, Sir COUTTS, Bart. (cr. 1821).
Eldest son of the late Lieut.-General James Lindsay, of Balcarres, co. Fife (grandson of James, 5th Earl of Balcarres), by his 2nd wife Anne, dau. of the late Sir Coutts Trotter, Bart., of Westville, co. Lincoln; *b.* 1824; *s.* his grandfather as 2nd Bart. 1837; *m.* 1864 Caroline Blanche, only surviving child of the late Rt. Hon. Henry FitzRoy, M.P. Is a Dep.-Lieut. for co. Fife, a Lieut.-Col. in the Army, and a Trustee of the National Portrait Gallery; formerly Capt. Grenadier Guards.—11, *Grosvenor Square, w.*
  Heir Pres., his brother Robert James Loyd-Lindsay, Esq. (whom see).

LINDSAY, Sir ALEXANDER, K.C.B., of Early Bank, Perthshire (cr. 1862).
Third son of the late James Smyth Lindsay, Esq., by Anne, dau. of — Pillans, Esq.; *b.* 1785; *m.* 1820 Flora Loudoun, dau. of Donald Mackenzie, Esq., of Hartfield, Applecross, co. Ross (she *d.* 1862). Educated at the Royal Military Academy, Woolwich; entered the Bengal Artillery in 1804; is a General in the Indian Army, and Col. of the Bengal Artillery.—*Early Bank, Perth, N.B.; Senior United Service Club, s.w.*

LINDSAY, GEORGE HAYWARD, Esq., of Glasnevin, co. Dublin.
Fourth son of the late Hon. and Right Rev. Dr. Charles Lindsay, Lord Bishop of Kildare, by his 2nd wife Katherine, dau. of the late Evert George Coussmaker, Esq.; *b.* 1799; *m.* 1828 Lady Mary Catherine, eldest sister of Philip Yorke, 4th Earl of Arran, K.P., and has with other issue,
  • Henry Gore (of Woodlands, Cardiff), educated at Eton; Chief Constable of Glamorganshire, late Capt. Rifle Brigade; a J.P. and D.L. for cc. Brecknock and Lieut.-Col. Brecknock Volunteer Rifles; *b.* 1829; *m.* 1856 the Hon. Eliza Sarah, 4th dau. of Charles, 1st Lord Tredegar, and has, with other issue, • Henry Morgan, *b.* 1857.
Mr. Lindsay, who was educated at Eton, is a J.P. and D.L. for co. Dublin; was formerly a Capt. in the Army.—*Glasnevin House, Dublin; Junior United Service Club, s.w.*

LINDSAY, HUGH HAMILTON, Esq.
Only son of the late Hon. Hugh Lindsay, by Jane, dau. of the late Hon. Alexander Gordon; *b.* 1802; *m.* 1852 Anna, eldest dau. of Æneas Ranald Macdonnell, Esq., of the Madras Civil Service, and widow of Charles Bazil Lindsay, Esq.; was M.P. for Sandwich 1841-7.—22, *Berkeley Square, w.*

LINDSAY, Mrs., of Balcarras and Leuchars, Fifeshire.
Anne, dau. of the late Sir Coutts Trotter, Bart., *m.* 1823 Lieut.-General James Lindsay, of Balcarras and Leuchars, who *d.* 1855, leaving issue,
  • Sir Coutts Lindsay, Bart. (whom see).
This family is a branch of that of the Earl of Crawford.—*Balcarras, St. Andrew's, N.B.*

LINDSAY, ROBERT, Esq., of Straiton, Fifeshire.
Second son of the late Hon. Robert Lindsay, by Elizabeth, 3rd dau. of Sir Alexander Dick, Bart.; *b.* 1795; *m.* 1824 Frances, dau. of the late Sir Robert Henderson, Bart., and by her, who *d.* 1865, has issue,
  • Alexander William, *b.* 1832.
Mr. Lindsay is a Magistrate for co. Fife.—*Straiton, Cupar-Fife, N.B.*

LINDSAY, WILLIAM SCHAW, Esq., of Shepperton Manor, Middlesex.
Third son of the late Joseph Lindsay, Esq., of Ayr, by Mary, dau. of Peter Belch, Esq., of Stirling, N.B.; *b.* 1816; *m.* 1843 Helen, dau. of the late James Stewart, Esq., of Glasgow, and has, with other issue,
  • William Stewart, *b.* 1849.
Mr. Lindsay, who is a J.P. and D.L. for Middlesex, and a Merchant in the City, was M.P. for Tynemouth 1854-9; was M.P. for Sunderland 1859-65; formerly in the Merchant Service.—*The Manor House, Shepperton; Reform Club, s.w.; City Club, e.c.; Austin Friars, e.c.*

LINDSAY, Viscount.
  (See under *Crawford and Balcarres, Earl of.*)

LINDSAY. (See *Lloyd-Lindsay.*)

+LINDSAY-BUCKNALL, JOHN CHARLES, Esq., of Turin Castle, co. Mayo.
Eldest son of the late Samuel Lindsay-Bucknall. Esq., J.P., of Turin Castle, by Jane, dau. of Richard Holmes Esq., of Prospect, King's Co.; *b.* 181−; *m.* 183− Anne, only child of Charles Crawford, Esq., of Oatlands, co. Donegal, and has, with other issue,
  • Samuel, *b.* 184−.
Mr. Lindsay-Bucknall is a Magistrate for co. Mayo. The additional name of Bucknall was assumed by the grandfather of the present owner, after his maternal grandfather, the Right Hon. Col. Bucknall, M.P.—*Turin Castle, Hollymount, co. Mayo.*

LINDSAY-CARNEGIE, HENRY ALEXANDER, Esq., of Kinblethmont, Forfarshire.
Son of the late Lieut. William Fullarton Lindsay-Carnegie, R.A., of Kinblethmont (who was a Vice-Lieut. of co. Forfar), by Lady Jane Christian, dau. of William, 7th Earl of Northesk; *b.* 1836; *s.* 1860; *m.* 1862 Agnes, eldest dau. of Col. Rait, of Anniston, N.B. Is a Dep.-Lieut. for co. Forfar, late a Lieut. Bengal Engineers.—*Kinblethmont, Arbroath, N.B.*

LINDSELL, Col. ROBERT HENRY, of Fairfield, Beds.
Eldest son of the late Robert Lindsell, Esq., of Fairfield, by Frances, dau. of Samuel Wells, Esq., Banker, of Biggleswade; *b.* 1818; *s.* 1856; *m.* 1845 Emma, only dau. of the Rev. Martin Hogge, Rector of Southacre, Norfolk, and has, with other issue,
  • Henry Martin, *b.* 1846.
Lieut.-Col. Lindsell, who was educated at Rugby, served in India with the 25th Regt., and in the Crimea with the 28th Regt., and retired as Lieut.-Col. in 1857, is a Magistrate for Beds (High Sheriff 1864).—*Fairfield, Biggleswade; United Service Club s.w.*

LINDSEY, Earl of (GEORGE AUGUSTUS FREDE-RICK ALBEMARLE BERTIE).—Cr. 1626.
Eldest son of Albemarle, 9th Earl, by his 2nd wife, Charlotte Susannah, dau. of the late Very Rev. Charles Peter Layard, Dean of Bristol; *b.* 1814; *s.* 1818. Is a Dep.-Lieut. for co. Lincoln, and Patron of 2 livings; descended from a common ancestor with the Earl of Abingdon.—*Uffington House, Stamford.*

Heir Pres., his brother Montagu Peregrine, educated at Eton; a J.P. and D.L. for co. Lincoln; formerly Lieut. and Capt. Grenadier Guards; *b.* 1815; *m.* 1854 Felicia Elizabeth, dau. of the late Rev. John Earle Welby, and has, with other issue, * Montague Peregrine Albemarle, *b.* 1861.

+**LINDSEY, JOHN**, Esq., of Gortavale, co. Tyrone.
Only son of the late John Lindsey, Esq., of Killyleagh, co. Down; *b.* 18—; is married, and has, with other issue,
* Acheson, *b.* 18—.
Mr. Lindsey, who is a Magistrate for Hants, and Lord of the Manor of Gortavale, co. Tyrone, was formerly in the Life Guards.—*Gortavale, co. Tyrone; Residence: Burlyns, East Woodhay, Newbury, Hants; Army and Navy and Junior United Service Clubs, s.w.*

LINDSEY, THOMAS SPENCER, Esq., of Holly-mount, co. Mayo.
Eldest son of the late Thomas Spencer Lindsey, Esq., J.P., of Hollymount (who was High Sheriff of co. Mayo, 1822), by Margaret Hester, only dau. of the late Richard Alexander Oswald, Esq., of Auchincruive, co. Ayr; *b.* 1828; *s.* 1867; *m.* 1864 Mary Catherine, 2nd dau. of George Hayward Lindsay, Esq. (whom see). Is a J.P. and D.L. for co. Mayo, and Major South Mayo Militia.—*Hollymount House, co. Mayo.*

LINDSEY-BIRCHALL. (See *Birchall.*)

LINGEN, HENRY, Esq., of Penlanole, Radnor-shire.
Second son of the late William Lingen, Esq., formerly of Burghill Lodge, co. Hereford, by Anne, dau. of John Barrett, Esq., of Hollins Hill; *b.* 1803; *m.* 1837 Priscilla, dau. of Joseph Jones, Esq., of Aberystwith, and has, with other issue,
* Henry Jones, *b.* 1839.
Mr. Lingen was called to the Bar at the Middle Temple 1838, is a J.P. and D.L. for co. Radnor (High Sheriff 1839).—*Penlanole, Rhayader, Radnorshire.*

LINGWOOD, ROBERT MAULKIN, Esq., of Lyston House, Herefordshire.
Only son of the late Peter Lathbury Lingwood, Esq., of Honington, Suffolk (who *d.* 1826), by Maria, 2nd dau. of Robert Maulkin, Esq., of Bury St. Edmund's; *b.* 1814; *m.* 1836 his cousin Elizabeth Sole, dau. of Benjamin Lingwood, Esq., of Little Saxham, Suffolk. Educated at Christ's Coll., Cambridge (B.A. 1833, M.A. 1836); is a J.P. and D.L. for co. Hereford (High Sheriff 1848.—*Lyston House, Llanwarne, Ross.*

LINSKILL, WILLIAM, Esq., of Morwick Hall, Northumberland.
Eldest son of the late William Linskill, Esq., of Tynemouth, by Elizabeth Mary, dau. of R. W. Grey, Esq., of Backworth, Northumberland; *b.* 1807; *s.* 1845; *m.* 1853 the Hon. Frances A. Charlotte, 2nd dau. of Arthur, 10th Viscount Valentia, and has, with other issue,
* William Thomas, *b.* 1855.
Mr. Linskill, who was educated at Harrow, is a J.P. and D.L. for Northumberland, and was formerly in the Army.—*Morwick Hall, Aclington, Northumberland; Junior United Service Club, s.w.*

586

LINTON, Sir WILLIAM, K.C.B. (cr. 1865).
Eldest son of the late Jabez Linton, Esq., late of Hardrigg Lodge, co. Dumfries, by Jane, dau. of William Crocket, Esq., of Grahamshill, co. Dumfries; *b.* 180—. Educated at Edinburgh University; is Hon. Physician to the Queen; entered the Medical Department of the Army in 1826, was Inspector-General of Hospitals 1856–63; served in Canada, the Mediterranean, the W. Indies, Turkey, the Crimea, India, &c.—8, *Grosvenor Place, Cheltenham; Army and Navy Club, s.w.*

+**LINTON, Col. JOHN**, of Stirtloe, Hunting-donshire.
Son of the late J. Linton, Esq.; *b.* 1780; *m.* 18—. Entered the Army in 1799. Is a J.P. and D.L. for Hunts, and a Col. in the Army retired; was formerly in the Coldstream Guards, and served at Waterloo.—*Stirtloe, Doddington, Buckden, Hunts.*

LINZEE, ROBERT GEORGE, Esq., of Jermyns, Hants.
Younger son of the late Rev. Edward Linzee, Rector of West Tilbury, Essex (who *d.* 1842), by Caroline, dau. of Joseph Warner, Esq., of Hornsey, Middlesex; *b.* 1820; *m.* 1849 Maria Frederica, 2nd dau. of the late Alexander Gordon, Esq., of Cluny, co. Aberdeen, and has, with other issue,
* Edward Gordon, *b.* 1853.
Mr. Linzee, who was educated at Eton and Ch. Ch., Oxford (B.A. 1843), is a Magistrate for Hants.—*Jermyns, Romsey.*

LIPPINCOTT, ROBERT CANN-, Esq., of Over Court, Gloucestershire.
Natural son of the late Sir Henry Cann-Lippincott, Bart. (ext.), of Over Court, whose name he assumed by Royal licence in 1831, on succeeding to the property of Over Court; *b.* 181—; *m.* 1st 183— Margaret Agnes, dau. of Mr. Sergeant Ludlow (she *d.* 1845): 2nd 1854 Julia Sulivan, 2nd dau. of Sir John Francis Davis, Bart., and has, by the former, with other issue,
* Robert Charles, educated at Harrow, *b.* 1844.
Mr. Lippincott, who was educated at Eton and Ch. Ch., Oxford, is Lord of the Manors of Compton, Greenfield, Littleton-upon-Severn, and Aust, and Patron of 2 livings.—*Over Court, Almondsbury, Bristol.*

LIPSCOMB, HENRY, Esq., of Staindrop, co. Durham.
Youngest son of the late Rev. William Lipscomb, M.A., Rector of Welbury, co. York, by Margaret, dau. of Francis Cooke, Esq., of Gower Street. London; *b.* 1799; *m.* 1838 Frances Mary, eldest dau. of Charles Rattray, Esq., M.D., of Daventry, co. Northampton. Is a Dep.-Lieut. for co. Durham; formerly Registrar of the Diocese of Jamaica.—*Staindrop, Darlington.*

LISBURNE, Earl of (ERNEST AUGUSTUS VAUGHAN).—Cr. 1776.
Eldest son of John, 3rd Earl, by the Hon. Lucy, 5th dau. of William, 2nd Viscount Courtenay (ext.); *b.* 1800; *s.* 1831; *m.* 1st 1835 Mary, dau. of the late Sir Lawrence Palk, Bart.; 2nd 1853 Harriet Elizabeth, dau. of the late Col. Henry Hugh Mitchell. Is a J.P. and D.L. for co. Cardigan (High Sheriff 1851), and Patron of 7 livings; was M.P. for co. Cardigan 1854–9.—*Crosswood, Aberystwith; Carlton Club, s.w.*

Heir, his son Ernest Augustus Mallet, Viscount Vaughan (of Birch Grove, Cardican), educated at Eton and Ch. Ch., Oxford; a Magistrate for co. Cardigan; *b.* 1836; *m.* 1858 Gertrude, 3rd dau. of Edwin Burnaby, Esq., of Baggrave Hall, co. Leicester, and by her, who *d.* 1865, has, with other issue, * Henry Arthur, *b.* 1862.

LISLE, Lord (GEORGE LYSAGHT).—Cr. 1758.
Second son of John, 2nd Lord, by Marianne, dau. of George Conner, Esq., of Ballybricken, co. Cork; *b.* 1783;

s. 1834; *m.* 1st 1810 Elizabeth, dau. of Samuel Knight, Esq. (she *d.* 1815); 2nd 1816 Elizabeth, dau. of the late John Church, Esq. (she *d.* 1855). This family is of Norman extraction, and have been seated in Ireland since the 17th century.—*Kenton, Exeter.*

Heir, his son John Arthur, Lieut. South Devon Militia; *b.* 1811; *m.* 1837 Henrietta Jane, dau. of the late John Church, Esq., and has, with other issue, * John Arthur, *b.* 1838.

LISLE, HUGH, Esq., of Dalton, Northumberland.

Only son of the late Rev. William Bell Moises, Vicar of Felton, Northumberland, by Mary, eldest dau. of the late John Orde, Esq., of Weetwood, Northumberland; *b.* 1792; *m.* 1821 Isabella, dau. and heir of the late Robert Lisle, Esq., of Acton House, Northumberland, whose name he has assumed. Is a Magistrate for Northumberland; was formerly in the 7th Dragoon Guards.—*Acton House, Alnwick.*

Heir Pres., his wife's sister, Anna Maria; *m.* 1824 the Rev. Robert Brodie, of Mangotsfield, co. Gloucester, and has issue.

LISLE. (See *De Burgh.*)

LISMORE, Viscount (GEORGE PONSONBY O'CALLAGHAN, K.P., P.C.).—Cr. 1806.

Only surviving son of Cornelius, 1st Viscount, by Lady Eleanor, 2nd dau. of John, 17th Earl of Ormonde; *b.* 1815; *s.* 1857; *m.* 1839, Mary, dau. of the late John George Norbury, Esq. Educated at Oriel Coll., Oxford; sits in the House of Peers as Lord Lismore, U.K. (cr. 1838); is Lord-Lieutenant of co. Tipperary; formerly Lieut. 17th Light Dragoons.—*Shanbally, Clogheen, co. Tipperary; Travellers' and White's Clubs, s.w.; 34, Grosvenor Street, w.*

Heir, his son George Cornelius Gerald; *b.* 1846.

LISTER, GEORGE SPOFFORTH, Esq., of Hirst Priory, Lincolnshire.

Eldest son of the late James Lister, Esq., of Ousefleet, co. York (who *d.* 1866), by Alice, dau. of Robert Spofforth, Esq., of Howden, co. York, and brother of Robert C. Lister, Esq., of Ousefleet (whom see); *b.* 1811; *m.* 1848 Caroline, 3rd dau. of William Mostyn Owen, Esq., of Woodhouse, co. Salop. Is a Magistrate for co. Lincoln and a Dep.-Lieut. for the W. Riding of Yorkshire. —*Hirst Priory, Epworth.*

LISTER, JOHN SAMUEL, Esq., of Saleby Grange, Lincolnshire.

Second surviving son of the late Matthew Bancroft Lister, Esq., of Burwell Park, by Sophia, dau. of John Bolton, Esq., of London; *b.* 1812; *m.* 1842 Elizabeth, eldest dau. of William Wilcock, Esq., of Halifax, co. York, and has, with other issue,

* Matthew William, *b.* 1845.

Mr. Lister, who was educated at C. C. Coll., Cambridge (B.A. 1835), is a Magistrate for co. Lincoln.—*Saleby Grange, Alford.*

+LISTER, MATTHEW HENRY, Esq., of Burwell Park, Lincolnshire.

Eldest son of the late Matthew Bancroft Lister, Esq., of Burwell, by Sophia, dau. of John Bolton, Esq., of London; *b.* 1801; *s.* 1843; *m.* 1828 Arabella, dau. of the late John Cracroft, Esq., of Hackthorn, co. Lincoln, and by her, who is deceased, has, with other issue,

* Matthew Henry, *b.* 1829.

Mr. Lister is Lord of the Manor of Burwell, and Patron of that living.—*Burwell Park, Louth, Lincolnshire.*

LISTER, ROBERT CORNELIUS, Esq., of Ousefleet Grange, Yorkshire.

Second son of the late James Lister, Esq., of Ousefleet, by Alice, dau. of Robert Spofforth, Esq., of Howden,

co. York; *b.* 1818; *s.* 1866; *m.* 1842 Elizabeth Cornwell, dau. of Jarvis Empson, Esq., of Goole Hall, co. York, and has, with other issue,

* James Empson, *b.* 1851.

Mr. Lister, who was educated at Shrewsbury, is a Magistrate for the W. Riding of Yorkshire.—*Ousefleet Grange, Goole, Yorkshire.*

LISTER, SAMUEL CUNLIFFE-, Esq., of Manningham Hall, Yorkshire.

Second surviving son of the late Ellis Cunliffe-Lister-Kay, Esq., by Mary, only dau. of the late William Ewbank (afterwards Kay), Esq., of Cottingham, co. York, and brother of John Cunliffe Kay, Esq., of Fairfield Hall (whom see); *b.* 1815; *s.* 1852; *m.* 1854 Anne, dau. of Col. Dearden, of Hollings Hall, near Halifax, and has, with other issue,

* Samuel Cunliffe, *b.* 1857.

Mr. Lister is a Magistrate for the W. Riding of Yorkshire and for the borough of Bradford; late Col. of the W. Riding Militia.—*Manningham Hall, Bradford.*

+LISTER, the Rev. THOMAS HENRY, of Scremby Hall, Lincolnshire.

Youngest son of the late James Lister, Esq., of Ousefleet, co. York (who *d.* 1866), by Alice, dau. of Robert Spofforth, Esq.; *b.* 1824; *m.* 1853 Mary Charlotte, dau. of the Rev. Francis Swan, Rector of Bennington, co. Lincoln. Educated at St. Catherine Hall, Cambridge (B.A. 1847, M.A. 1851); is a Magistrate for co. Lincoln, and Vicar of Luddington.—*Scremby Hall, Spilsby.*

LISTER, THOMAS THOMPSON CUNLIFFE-, of Beamsley Hall, Yorkshire.

Fifth son of the late Ellis-Cunliffe-Lister, Esq., M.P., of Manningham Hall, co. York (who assumed the additional name of Kay), by his 2nd wife Mary, only child of William Kay, Esq., of Cottingham, co. York; *b.* 1821; *m.* 1857 Margaret, dau. of John Dearden, Esq., of The Hollins, Halifax. Mr. Lister, who was educated at Magdalen Coll., Cambridge, is a Magistrate for the W. Riding of Yorkshire.—*Beamsley Hall, Skipton.*

LISTER, THOMAS VILLIERS, Esq.

Son of the late Thomas H. Lister, Esq., of Armitage Park, co. Stafford, by Maria Theresa, dau. of the late Hon. G. Villiers (she *m.* 2nd the late Right Hon. Sir George Cornewall Lewis, Bart., and *d.* 1865); *b.* 1832; *s.* 1842; *m.* 1862 Fanny, dau. of the late Wm. Coryton, Esq., of Pentillie, Cornwall, and has, with other issue,

* George Coryton, *b.* 1863.

Mr. Lister, who was educated at Harrow and Trinity Coll., Cambridge (M.A. 1853), is a Dep.-Lieut. for co. Radnor.—61, *Eaton Square, s.w.*

LISTER. (See under *Ribblesdale, Lord.*)

LISTER. (See *Kay.*)

LISTER-KAYE, Sir JOHN LISTER, Bart., of Denby Grange, Yorkshire (cr. 1812).

Eldest son of the late Sir John Lister-Kaye, Bart., by Lady Amelia, dau. of George Harry, 6th Earl of Stamford and Warrington; *b.* 1801; *s.* as 2nd Bart. 1827; *m.* 1824 Matilda, only dau. and heiress of George Arbuthnot, Esq. (she *d.* 1867). Educated at Westminster; is a J.P. and D.L. for the W. Riding of co. York, a Magistrate for co. Chester, and Patron of 1 living. —*Denby Grange, Wakefield; Boodle's, Union, and Arthur's Clubs, s.w.; 17, Cromwell Road, s.w.*

Heir, his grandson John Pepys (eldest son of the late Lister Lister-Kaye, Esq., who *d.* 1855, by Lady Caroline, dau. of Charles Christopher, 1st Earl of Cottenham); *b.* 1853.

LISTOWEL, Earl of (WILLIAM HARE).—Cr. 1822.

Eldest son of William, 2nd Earl, by Maria Augusta, dau. of the late Vice-Admiral William Windham, of Fellbrigge Hall, Norfolk, and widow of George Thomas Wyndham, Esq., of Cromer Hall, Norfolk; *b.* 1833; *s.* 1856; *m.* 1865 Ernestine Mary, younger dau. of the Right Hon. Lord Ernest Bruce, M.P. Educated at Eton; is a Magistrate for co. Kerry, late Capt. Scots Fusilier Guards.— *Convamore, Mallow, co. Cork; Kingston House, Knightsbridge, s.w.*

Heir, his son Richard Granville, Viscount Ennismore, b. 1866.

LISTOWEL, Countess of.

Maria Augusta, 2nd dau. of the late Vice-Admiral William Windham, M.P., of Fellbrigge Hall, Norfolk, by Anne, dau. of Peter Thellusson, Esq., of Broadsworth, co. York; *m.* 1st 18— George Thomas Wyndham, Esq., of Cromer Hall, Norfolk; 2nd 1831 William, 2nd Earl of Listowel, who *d.* 1856.— *Cromer Hall, Norfolk.*

+LITCHFORD, JOHN, Esq., of Boothby Hall, Lincolnshire.

Eldest son of the late John Litchford, Esq., of Boothby Hall, by Louisa Elizabeth, dau. of the late Sir Charles E. Kent, Bart., of Little Penton House, co. Lincoln; *b.* 182-. Is Lord of the Manor of Boothby Pagnell, and Patron of that living.— *The Hall, Boothby Pagnell, Colsterworth, Lincolnshire.*

LITTLE, FRANCIS, Esq., of Salem House, Lancashire.

Second son of the late Francis Little, Esq., of Hulme, co. Lancaster, by Elizabeth his wife; *b.* 1812; *m.* 1st 1834 Ann, youngest dau. of William Hall, Esq., of Broughton, co. Lancaster (she *d.* 1841); 2nd 1843 Jane, relict of William Lees, Esq., of Clarkefield, co. Lancaster (she *d.* 1854), and has issue by the former, * Frederick William, *b.* 1835.— *Salem House, Lees, Lancashire; Conservative Club, s.w.; 7, Onslow Square, s.w.*

LITTLE, Capt. JAMES, of Cliff Castle, co. Dublin.

Only son of the late Rev. J. Little, D.D.; *b.* 18—; *m.* 1st 1863 the Hon. Anne Henrietta, dau. of the late Hon. Henry Butler, and sister of Henry Edmond, 13th Viscount Mountgarrett (she *d.* 1866); 2nd 1867 Mary Henrietta, dau. of William Gabbett, Esq., of Mount Minnet, co. Limerick, and widow of J. R. Curry, Esq. Is a Magistrate for cos. Down and Wicklow, and Capt. Royal Downshire Militia.— *Cliff Castle, Dalkey, co. Dublin; Bavennett, Downshire; Royal Agricultural Club, Dublin; Royal Thames Yacht Club, London.*

LITTLE, JOSEPH BENNETT, Esq., of Knockadoo, co. Cork.

Eldest son of the late John Little, Esq., of Ballinamore, by Eliza, dau. of the Rev. Joseph Bennett; *b.* 18—; *m.* 1857 Emily, dau. of the late William White, Esq., of Shrubs, and grand-dau. of the late Luke White, Esq., M.P., and has, with other issue,

* A son, *b.* 1859.

Mr. Little is a Magistrate for cos. Roscommon and Leitrim (High Sheriff 1860).— *Knockadoo, Boyle, co. Cork, Kilrush; Ballinamore, co. Leitrim.*

LITTLE, Mrs., of Llanvair, Monmouthshire.

Georgiana, dau. of Winchcombe H. Hartley, Esq., of Ashford, Kent; *m.* 1836 (as his 2nd wife) William Hunter Little, Esq., J.P. and D.L., of Llanvair Grange, who was High Sheriff of co. Monmouth 1852, and who *d.* 1864, leaving, with other issue,

* George Savile Lumley, in Holy Orders, educated at Rugby, B.A. of Trinity Coll., Cambridge, Perpetual Curate of Buildwas, co. Salop; *b.* 1837; *m.* 1st 1862 Sophia Louisa, only dau. of the Rev. Wm Corfield, Rector of Llangalton,

588

co. Monmouth (she *d.* 1862); 2nd 1864 Mary Sarah, eldest dau. of Henry Yates Whitehead, Esq., of Crake, co. York.

— *Llanvair Grange, Abergavenny.*

LITTLEDALE, CHARLES RICHARD, Esq.

Eldest son of the late Charles Littledale, Esq., of Portland Place (who *d.* 1849). by Louisa, dau. of the late Samuel Castell, Esq., of Wimbledon; *b.* 1807; *m.* 1835 Emily, dau. of Charles Hammersley, Esq., of 25, Park Crescent, London. Educated at Westminster and Ch. Ch., Oxford (B.A. 1830, M.A. 1831); called to the Bar at Lincoln's Inn 1833; is a Magistrate for Berks.—Residence: *Scarletts, Twyford, Berks; United University and Union Clubs, s.w.*

LITTLEDALE, the late HENRY, Esq., of Kempstone, Beds.

Youngest son of the late Thomas Littledale, Esq., by Anne Elizabeth, dau. of Charles Allan, Esq., of Beverley, co. York, and cousin of the late Mr. Justice Littledale; *b.* 1785; *d.* 1866. Educated at Westminster; was a J.P. and D.L. for Beds (High Sheriff 1853).— *Kempstone Grange, Bedford.*

LITTLEDALE, HENRY WILLIAM ASSHETON, Esq., late of Bolton Hall, Yorkshire.

Eldest son of the late Henry Anthony Littledale, Esq., J.P. and D.L., of Bolton Hall, by Mary Elizabeth, eldest sister of Sir George Armitage, Bart., of Kirklees; *b.* 1846; *s.* 1859. Educated at Eton.— *Bolton Hall, Craven.*

Heir Pres., his brother Godfrey, b. 1854.

LITTLEHALES, BENDALL, Esq., of Buckshaw House, Dorsetshire.

Eldest Son of the late Vice-Admiral, Bendall Robert Littlehales, (who *d.* 1847), by Mary Anne, dau. of Thos. Cleather, Esq., of Plymouth, and grandson of the late Baker John Littlehales, Esq., of Montsey House, Surrey; *b.* 1804; *m.* 1838 Nancy Kegan, dau. of John Home, Esq. Educated at Winchester and Oriel Coll., Oxford (B.A. 1825); is a Magistrate for Dorset. This family was formerly seated at Dawley, near Bridgnorth, co. Salop; the head of the family is Sir E. B. Baker, Bart., of Ranston (whom see). — *Buckshaw House, Holwell, Sherborne.*

LITTLETON. (See under *Hatherton, Lord.*)

LITTLEWOOD, BENJAMIN, Esq., of Clent House, Worcestershire.

Eldest son of the late Benjamin Littlewood. Esq., of Amblecote, by Esther, dau. of T. Badger, Esq., of Stourbridge; *b.* 1802; *s.* 1845; *m.* 1839 Mary, dau. of Thomas Bate, Esq., of Oldswinford, and has, with other issue,

* Henry Charles, *b.* 1850.

Mr. Littlewood, who was educated at Eton, is a J.P. and D.L. for co. Worcester, and a Magistrate for co. Stafford.— *Clent House, Stourbridge.*

LITTON, EDWARD, Esq., of Altmore, co. Tyrone.

Third son of the late Edward Litton, Esq., of Glasnevin House, co. Dublin, by Charlotte, dau. of the late Very Rev. Daniel Lorabbere, Dean of Tuam; *b.* 1789; *m.* 1813 Sophia, dau. of the Rev. Dr. Stewart, and niece of the late Right Hon. Sir John Stewart, Bart., M.P., and has, with other issue,

* Edward Arthur, in Holy Orders, educated at Winchester, M.A. of Balliol Coll., Oxford, and for some time Fellow of Oriel Coll.; Rector of Naunton, co. Gloucester; *b.* 1813; *m.* 1843 Anne, dau. of the Rev. W. Carus-Wilson, and has, with other issue, * Edward, *b.* 1845.

Mr. Litton, who was educated at Trinity Coll., Dublin (B.A. 1808, M.A. 1811), and called to the Irish Bar 1811. Is a Magistrate for co. Tyrone; he became a Queen's Counsel 1830, and a Master in Chancery 1842;

was M.P. for Coleraine 1837-42.—*Altmore, Dungannon, co. Tyrone ; Sackville Street Club, and Merrion Square, Dublin ; Carlton Club, s.w.*

LIVESEY, JOSEPH MONTAGUE, Esq., of Stourton Hall, Lincolnshire.

Eldest surviving son of the late Joseph Livesey, Esq., of Stourton Hall (who was High Sheriff of co. Lincoln 1854), by Sarah Maria, dau. of the Rev. John Earle Welby, Rector of Hareston, co. Leicester ; *b.* 1851 ; *s.* 1854. Is Lord of the Manors of Stourton and Baumber, and Patron of Farlesthorpe.—*Stourton Hall, Horncastle.*

Heir Pres., his brother Thomas, in Holy Orders, a Magistrate for the Parts of Lindsey, co. Lincoln, and M.A. of Trinity Coll., Cambridge ; b. 1812.

LIVINGSTONE, THOMAS LIVINGSTONE FENTON-, Esq., of Westquarter, Stirlingshire, and Bedlormie, Linlithgowshire.

Only son of John Thomas Fenton, Esq., by Selina, younger dau. of the late Sir John Edensor Heathcote, Knt., of Longton Hall, co. Stafford ; *b.* 1829 ; *s.* his great-uncle, Admiral Sir Thomas Livingstone, Bart., of that Ilk, 1853, when he assumed the additional name of Livingstone ; *m.* 1855 Christian Margaret, only dau. of William Waddell, Esq., D.L., of Moffat House, co. Lanark, and has, with other issue,

* Thomas, b. 1856.

Mr. Fenton-Livingstone is a Magistrate for co. Stirling, and Lord of the Barony of Bedlormie.—*Westquarter, Falkirk, N.B. ; Bedlormie, Bathgate, N.B.*

LLANDAFF, Bishop of (the Right Rev. ALFRED OLLIVANT, D.D.).

Son of the late William Ollivant, Esq., of Manchester, by Elizabeth, dau. of the late Sir Stephen Langston, of Great Horwood, Bucks ; *b.* 1798 ; *m.* 1828 Alicia Olivia, dau. of General William Spencer, of Bramley Grange, co. York. Educated at St. Paul's School and Trinity Coll., Cambridge ; graduated B.A. 1821 as 6th Wrangler and Senior Medallist ; was Fellow of Trinity Coll., Vice-Principal of St. David's Coll., Lampeter, Regius Professor of Divinity at Cambridge, and Prebendary of St. David's and Brecon ; consecrated 1849. Patron of 61 livings.—*Bishop's Court, Llandaff, Cardiff ; Athenæum Club, s.w.*

LLANOVER, Dowager Lady, of Llanover, Monmouthshire.

Augusta, dau. and co-heir of the late Benjamin Waddington, Esq., of Llanover, by Georgina Mary Ann, dau. of John Port, Esq., of Ilam, co. Derby ; *m.* 1823 the Rt. Hon. Benjamin Hall, Lord Lieutenant of co. Monmouth, who was created Lord Llanover 1859, and who *d.* 1867 (when his title became extinct), by whom she has surviving issue, * Augusta Charlotte Elizabeth, *m.* 1846 John Arthur Herbert, Esq., of Llanarth (whom see).—*Llanover, Abergavenny ; Abercarn, Newport, Monmouthshire.*

LLEWELLIN, EDWARD TURBERVILLE, Esq., of Hendrescythan, Glamorganshire.

Only son of the late Edward Llewellin, Esq., of Stockland, co. Glamorgan, by Elizabeth, dau. of Morgan Williams, Esq., J.P., of Pendoylan, in the same county ; *b.* 1809 ; *s.* his uncle the Rev. Henry Llewellin 1836 ; *m.* 1844 his cousin Elizabeth, only dau. of Richard Reece, Esq., F.S.A., of Cardiff, and widow of Capt. Henry Church, R.N. Is a J.P. and D.L. for co. Glamorgan.—*Hendrescythan, Cardiff ; Oakfield, Bath.*

LLEWELLIN, RICHARD, Esq., of Tregwynt, Pembrokeshire.

Eldest son of the late Richard Llewellin, Esq., of Holmwood, co. Gloucester, by Anna Maria, dau. of Levi Ames, Esq., of Clifton Wood, Bristol ; *b.* 1802 ; *s.* 1825.

Educated at University Coll., Oxford (B.A. 1823) ; entered as a Student at Lincoln's Inn, but was not called to the Bar ; is a J.P. and D.L. for co. Pembroke (High Sheriff 1840).—*Tregwynt, Haverfordwest ; University and Oxford and Cambridge Clubs, s.w.*

Heir Pres., his nephew Richard Llewellin Purcell (eldest son, of the Rev. William Purcell, by the late Anna Maria, eldest dau. of the late Richard Llewellin, Esq.) ; b. 1840. B.A. of Exeter Coll., Oxford, and of Lincoln's Inn.

LLEWELLYN, GRIFFITH, Esq., of Baglan Hall, Glamorganshire.

Eldest son of the late Griffith Llewellyn, Esq., by Catherine, dau. and heir of the late J. Jones, Esq., of Baglan Hall ; *b.* 1807 ; *s.* his mother 1840 ; *m.* 1850 Madeline, dau. of Pascoe St. L. Grenfell, Esq., of Maesteg House, Swansea. Mr. Llewellyn, who was educated at Rugby, is a J.P. and D.L. for co. Glamorgan (High Sheriff 1852), and Patron of 1 living.—*Baglan Hall, Briton Ferry, Glamorganshire ; Union Club, s.w.*

LLEWELLYN, Mrs., of Buckland Filleigh, Devon.

Eliza Williams, dau. of the late John Strick, Esq., of Swansea ; *m.* 1839 Llewellyn Llewellyn, Esq., of Ynispenllwch, co. Glamorgan, who purchased the estate of Buckland Filleigh from Lord Ashburton in 1853, and *d.* 1860.—*Buckland Filleigh, Hatherleigh.*

LLEWELLYN, WILLIAM, Esq., of Court Colman, Glamorganshire.

Only child of the late William Llewellyn, Esq., of Margam, co. Glamorgan, by Catherine, eldest dau. of the late John Place, Esq. ; *b.* 1820 ; *m.* 1844 Eleanor Emma, dau. of the late Rev. Robert Knight, of Tythegston Court, co. Glamorgan ; and has, with other issue,

* Robert William, b. 1848.

Mr. Llewellyn is J.P. and D.L. for co. Glamorgan (High Sheriff 1854), Lord of the Manor of Cwrt Colman, and Capt. 1st Glamorganshire Rifle Volunteers.—*Court Colman, Bridgend, Glamorganshire.*

LLEWELYN. (See *Dillwyn-Llewelyn.*)

LLOYD, Sir THOMAS DAVIES, Bart., of Bronwydd, Cardiganshire (cr. 1863).

Eldest son of the late Thomas Lloyd, Esq., of Bronwydd (who *d.* 1845), by Ann Davies, dau. of John Thomas, Esq., of Llwydcoed, co. Carmarthen ; *b.* 1820 ; *m.* 1846 Henrietta Mary, 4th dau. of the late George Rice, Esq., of Watlington Hall, Norfolk. Educated at Harrow and Ch. Ch., Oxford ; is a J.P. and D.L. for cos. Cardigan, Carmarthen, and Pembroke ; elected M.P. for co. Cardigan 1865 ; was formerly in the 13th Light Dragoons.—*Bronwydd, Carmarthen ; Kilrhue, Cardigan ; University and Junior United Service Clubs, s.w.*

Heir, his son Marteine Owen Mowbray, b. 1851.

LLOYD, the Hon. THOMAS PRYCE, of Nannau, Merionethshire.

Younger son of Edward Pryce, 1st Lord Mostyn, by Elizabeth, 3rd dau. of the late Sir Roger Mostyn, Bart. ; *b.* 1800 ; *s.* under the will of Sir Robert Williames-Vaughan, Bart., 1859. Is a J.P. and D.L. for co. Flint, and a Magistrate for co. Denbigh.—*Nannau, Rhug, Merionethshire.*

LLOYD, ARTHUR PHILIP, Esq., of Shawbury, Shropshire.

Eldest son of the late Rev. Henry James Lloyd, of Selattyn, co. Salop, by Elizabeth, dau. of the late Philip J. Miles, Esq., of Leigh Court, Somerset ; *b.* 1853 ; *m.* 1863 Katrine Selina, 5th dau. of the late Admiral the

589

Hon. Charles Orlando Bridgeman, of Knockyn Hall, co. Salop, and has, with other issue,

* Arthur Henry Orlando, b. 1864.

Mr. Lloyd, who was educated at Eton and Ch. Ch., Oxford, is a Magistrate for co. Salop, and Lieut. Yeomanry Cavalry.—*Shawbury, Shrewsbury; Arthur's Club, s.w.*

LLOYD, CHARLES, Esq., of Brunant, Carmarthenshire.
Third son of the late George Lloyd, Esq., of Brunant, by Margaret Jane Martha, youngest dau. of the late George Harries, Esq., of Priskilly, co. Pembroke; b. 1830; s. 1861; m. 1862 Emma Webb, eldest dau. of the Rev. W. W. Webb Bowen, Vicar of Camrose, co. Pembroke, and has, with other issue,

* George William D. Bowen, b. 1866.

Mr. Lloyd is a Magistrate for co. Carmarthen; late Ensign 4th Carmarthen Rifle Volunteers; formerly in the Carmarthen Militia.—*Brunant, Llandilo.*

LLOYD, the Rev. CHARLES.
Eldest son of the late Major Charles Lloyd, by Emma, dau. of General Hale, of Plantation, co. York; b. 1809; m. 1841 Caroline Alicia, dau. of the Rev. Charles Sheffield. Educated at Harrow and Ch. Ch., Oxford (B.A. 1831); appointed Rector of Hampden 1841, of Chalfont St. Giles 1859; is a Magistrate for Bucks. —*Chalfont St. Giles, Slough, Bucks.*

LLOYD, CHARLES HENRY, Esq., of Lisheen, co. Tipperary.
Eldest son of John Lloyd, Esq., of Lisheen, by Catherine, dau. of John Rotton, Esq., of Bath, who was formerly Capt. in the Rifles, and A.D.C. to Lord Dorchester; b. 1821; s. 1856; m. 1st 1846 Anna, dau. of Major George Jackson; 2nd 1849 Anne, dau. of Fergus Langley, Esq., and has, with other issue,

* Charles Edward, b. 1854.

Mr. Lloyd, who was educated at Shrewsbury and Trinity Coll., Dublin, is a Magistrate for co. Tipperary.—*Lisheen Castle, Templemore.*

LLOYD, CHARLES SPENCER, Esq., of Leaton Knolls, Shropshire.
Only surviving son of the late Francis LLoyd, Esq., of Dongay, co. Montgomery, and of Leaton, co. Salop (who d. 1799), by Elizabeth, dau. of Arthur Graham, Esq., of Hockley Lodge, co. Armagh; b. 1789; s. his brother 1864. Educated at Harrow; is a J.P. and D.L. for co. Salop (High Sheriff 1868), and Patron of 1 living. —*Leaton Knolls, Shrewsbury; Union and Junior Carlton Clubs, s.w.*

Heir Pres., his nephew Arthur Philip Lloyd, Esq., a Magistrate for co. Salop; b. 1834; m. 1861 Leila, dau. of Admiral the Hon. Charles Orlando Bridgeman, of Knockin Hall, co. Salop, and has issue, * Arthur, b. 1864.

+LLOYD, DAVID WATKINS, Esq., of Aberllech, Brecknockshire.
Son of the late David Lloyd, Esq., of Aberllech; b. 1800. Is a Magistrate for co. Brecon, of which he has been High Sheriff.—*Aberllech, Llandilo Vân, Brecon.*

LLOYD, EDWARD OWEN VAUGHAN, Esq., of Rhagatt, Merionethshire.
Son of the late Edward Lloyd, Esq., of Bryn Tysilio, co. Denbigh (who d. 1864), by Mary Eliza, dau. of the late John Madocks, Esq., of Glanywern, co. Denbigh; b. 1857; s. his uncle, John Lloyd, Esq., of Rhagatt, 1865. This family is descended from Tudor Trevor, Earl of Hereford.—*Rhagatt, Corwen.*

+LLOYD, EDWARD PRYSE, Esq., of Glansevin, Carmarthenshire.
Eldest son of the late Morgan Pryse Lloyd, Esq., of Glansevin, by Catherine, dau. of Price Jones, Esq., of

Glanhafren, co. Montgomery; b. 1785; m. 1819 Anne, dau. of Wm. Hughes, Esq., and has, with other issue,

* Morgan Pryse, a Magistrate for co. Carmarthen; b. 1823; m. 184- Georgiana Caroline, dau. of the late Col. Sackville Gwynne, of Glanbrane Park.

Mr. Lloyd, who is a J.P. and D.L. for co. Carmarthen, has been High Sheriff of co. Cardigan.—*Glansevin, Llangadock.*

LLOYD, EVAN GARNONS, Esq., of Blaenglyn, Merionethshire, and Plas Coedana, Anglesey.
Eldest son of the late Rev. William Lloyd, M.A., of Blaenglyn (Rector of Llanfaethlu, Anglesey), by Margaret, dau. and co-heir of John Jones, Esq., of Bodednyfed, Anglesey; b. 1806; s. 1844. Is in the Commission of the Peace for cos. Merioneth and Anglesey; was formerly Assistant-Surgeon and Surgeon of the 1st Battalion of the Rifle Brigade.—*Blaenglyn, Merioneth; Plas Coedana, Llanerchymedd, Anglesey; Junior United Service Club, s.w.*

Heir Pres., his nephew, Robert Owen Lloyd, b. 1846.

LLOYD, EYRE, Esq., of Prospect, co. Limerick.
Second son of the late Thomas Lloyd, Esq., of Beechmount (who was M.P. for co. Limerick 1810–30), by Catherine, youngest dau. of Eyre Evans, Esq., of Miltown Castle, co. Cork, nephew of George, 1st Lord Carbery; b. 1800; s. 1830; m. 1st 1828 Anne Hutchinson, only child and heir of Capt. Hugh Massy, of Glenville, co. Limerick; 2nd 1865 Sarah, 2nd dau. of the Rev. Samuel Paynter, of Stoke Hill, Surrey; he has by the former, with other issue,

* Thomas, of Huntingdon Court, co. Hereford, educated at Rugby, late Capt. 87th Fusiliers and 5th Middlesex Militia; b. 1829; m. 1853 Anne Cowper, only child and heir of the late James Cheese, Esq., of Huntingdon Court, and has issue, * Anne.

Mr. Lloyd, who was educated at Trinity Coll., Dublin, is a Magistrate for co. Limerick (High Sheriff 1850). —*Prospect, Castleconnell, co. Limerick.*

LLOYD, GEORGE WHITELOCKE, Esq., of Strancally Castle, co. Waterford.
Second but eldest surviving son of the late William H. Lloyd, Esq., of Calton, co. York, by Mary, dau. of George Whitelocke, Esq., of Fortoiseau, France; b. 1830; s. 1849; m. 1st 1854 Selina Jane, dau. of Arthur Henry, Esq., of Lodge Park, co. Kildare (she d. 1860); 2nd 1861 Lady Anne, dau. of Somerset Richard, 3rd Earl of Carrick, and has by the former, with other issue,

* William Whitelocke, b. 1856.

Mr. Lloyd, who was educated at Trinity Coll., Cambridge, is a Magistrate for co. Waterford (High Sheriff 1859).—*Strancally Castle, Villierstown, co. Waterford; Buttevant Castle, co. Cork; Kildare Street Club, Dublin; Union Club, s.w.*

LLOYD, GUY, Esq., of Croghan, co. Roscommon.
Eldest son of the late Guy Lloyd, Esq., of Croghan, by Susanna Martha, dau. of John Stephenson Cann, Esq., of Wramplingham, Norfolk; b. 1833; s. 1860; m. 1865 Elizabeth, dau. of Sir Gilbert King, Bart., of Charlestown, co. Roscommon. Is a J.P. and D.L. for co. Roscommon (High Sheriff 1867).—*Croghan House, Boyle, co. Roscommon.*

Heir Pres., his brother John Merrick, b. 1846.

LLOYD, HERBERT, Esq., of Plas Cil-y-bebyll, Glamorganshire.
Eldest son of the late Francis Edwardes Lloyd, Esq., of Plas Cil-y-bebyll (who assumed the name of Lloyd, in lieu of Leach, by Royal licence, on the death of his mother in 1849), by Harriet Goodwin, dau. of William Page, Esq., of Fitzroy Square, London; b. 1838; s. 1865; m. 1864 Frances Harriet, eldest dau. of the late

Simon G. Pardon, Esq., of Tinerara, co. Clare, and has issue,

* A dau.

Mr. Lloyd is Patron of 1 living.—*Plas Cil-y-bebyll, Swansea.*

+LLOYD, JAMES, Esq., of Showel Green, Worcestershire.
Son of the late J. Lloyd, Esq.; *b.* 18—; is a J.P. and D.L. for co. Worcester.—*Showel Green, Sparbrook, Birmingham.*

LLOYD, JOHN, Esq., of Dinas, Brecknockshire.
Eldest son of the late John Lloyd, Esq., of Dinas, by Elizabeth, dau. of Roger Williams, Esq., of Brecon; *b.* 1797; *s.* 1818; *m.* 1826 Mary Anne, dau. of Osborne Yeats, Esq., of Llangattock Court, co. Brecon; 2nd 1838 Frances, dau. of Thomas Maybery, Esq., of Brecon, and has, with other issue,

* Thomas Conway, a Magistrate for co. Brecon, *b.* 1830.

Mr. Lloyd, who was educated at Eton and Balliol Coll., Oxford, is a Magistrate for co. Brecon (High Sheriff 1846). This family is lineally descended from Thomas Lloyd, the first Lord-Lieutenant of Brecknockshire, *temp.* Henry VIII. A large portion of the sequestered estates of Strata Florida Abbey were granted by that king to the said Thomas Lloyd, in consideration of services rendered to the Earl of Richmond, on his march from Milford to Bosworth Field.—*Dinas, Brecon.*

+LLOYD, JOHN, Esq., of Gloster, King's Co.
Only son of the late Col. Hardress Lloyd, of Gloster (who was M.P. for King's Co. 1807–16, and many years Col. of the County Militia); *b.* 18—; *s.* 1860. Is a Magistrate for King's Co. This family is of Welsh extraction, and have been seated in King's Co. since the reign of Charles I.—*Gloster, Shinrone, King's Co.*

LLOYD, JOHN JESSE, Esq., of Lloydsborough, co. Tipperary.
Eldest son of the late John Lloyd, Esq., of Lloydsborough, by Deborah Ann, dau. of John Lloyd, Esq., of Cranagh, co. Tipperary; *b.* 1816; *s.* 1862; *m.* 1844 Mary, dau. of Edmund Fortescue, Esq., of Fallapit, Devon, and has, with other issue,

* John, *b.* 1845.

Mr. Lloyd, who was educated at Trinity Coll., Dublin, is a Magistrate for co. Tipperary.—*Lloydsborough and Cranagh, Templemore; Kildare Street Club, Dublin.*

LLOYD, JOHN HORATIO, Esq.
Eldest son of the late John Lloyd, Esq., of Stockport, afterwards of Chester, Prothonotary, and Clerk of the Crown, by Mary, dau. of James Watson, Esq., of Swinton; *b.* 1799; *m.* 182– Caroline, dau. of Holland Watson, Esq., and has issue. Educated at Queen's Coll., Oxford (B.A. 1822, M.A. 1824), and was some time Fellow of Brasenose Coll.; called to the Bar at the Inner Temple 1826; was M.P. for Stockport 1833–4. —1, *King's Bench Walk, Temple,* E.C.; *Athenæum Club,* s.w.; 30, *Dorset Square,* N.W.

LLOYD, JOHN WILLIAM, Esq., of Dan-yr-alt, Carmarthenshire.
Eldest surviving son of the late Major John Lloyd, 46th Foot (who *d.* 1801), by Corbetta, dau. of the late Ven. Archdeacon Holcombe; *b.* 1781; *s.* his brother Major William John Lloyd, R.A., 1815; *m.* 1807 Anna Maria, 5th dau. of the late John Longley, Esq., Recorder of Rochester, and sister of the Archbishop of Canterbury, and has, with other issue,

* Henry Robert, Vicar of Owersby, co. Lincoln, a Magistrate for co. Carmarthen; *b.* 1809; *m.* 1843 Harriet, dau. of the

late Hon. and Right Rev. Edward Grey, D.D., Lord Bishop of Hereford.

Mr. Lloyd is a Magistrate for co. Carmarthen.—*Dan-yr-alt, Llangadock.*

LLOYD, JOSEPH SKIP, Esq., of Flaxley Grange, Gloucestershire.
Eldest son of the late Joseph Lloyd, Esq., of Abenhall, and The Grange, co. Gloucester, by Penelope, dau. of George Skip, Esq., of the Grange; *b.* 1810; *s.* 1844. Educated at St. John's Coll., Oxford (B.C.L. 1835); called to the Bar at the Inner Temple 1836; appointed Clerk of the Cheque of the Royal Body Guard 1852. —*The Grange, Flaxley, Newnham-on-Severn; Windham Club,* s.w.

Heir Pres., his brother George, a Stipendiary Magistrate in New Zealand, *b.* 1820.

LLOYD, LLEWELYN FALKNER, Esq., of Cilcen Hall and Nannerch, Flintshire.
Eldest son of Llewelyn Lloyd, Esq., of Pontriffith, co. Flint, by Jane, dau. of Edward Falkner, Esq., of Fairfield, co. Lancaster; *b.* 1809; *s.* his cousin Miss Mostyn Edwards 1841; *m.* 1841 Mary Susan, dau. of the Rev. William Wickham Drake, Rector of Malpas, co. Chester, and has issue,

* Mary Frances.

Mr. Lloyd is a J.P. and D.L. for co. Flint (High Sheriff 1847), and a Magistrate for co. Denbigh. —*Cilcen Hall and Nannerch, Mold; Brooks's and Boodle's Clubs,* s.w.

+LLOYD, Miss, of Laques, Carmarthenshire.
Elizabeth, only dau. of the late William Lloyd, Esq., D.L., of Laques, formerly High Sheriff of co. Carmarthen (who *d.* 1840), by Maria Elenora, only child of John Colborne, Esq., of Swindon, co. Stafford; *s.* her brother William 1854.—*Laques, Llanstephen.*

LLOYD, RICHARD THOMAS, Esq., of Rolls Park, Essex.
Only son of the late William Lloyd, Esq., of Aston Hall, co. Salop (who *d.* 1843), by Louisa, eldest dau. and co-heiress of the late Admiral Sir Eliab Harvey, K.C.B., of Rolls Park; *b.* 1820; *s.* his mother 1866; *m.* 1852 Lady Frances, 3rd dau. of Thomas Robert, 10th Earl of Kinnoull, and has issue,

* A son, *b.* 1853.

Mr. Lloyd is a J.P. and D.L. for co. Salop; late Capt. North Salop Yeomanry, and formerly Lieut. and Capt. Grenadier Guards.—*Rolls Park, Chigwell, Essex; Aston Hall, Oswestry.*

+LLOYD, THOMAS, Esq., of Beechmount, co. Limerick.
Eldest son of the late Thomas Lloyd, Esq., K.C., of Beechmount (who was M.P. for co. Limerick 1826–30), by Katharine, dau. of Eyre Evans, Esq., of Miltown Castle; *b.* 18—; *s.* 1830; *m.* 1st 1827 Anne. only dau. and heiress of General Burke; 2nd 1838 Julia Palmer, eldest dau. of F. T. Hall, Esq., and has issue. Is a J.P. and D.L. for co. Limerick, of which he has been High Sheriff.—*Beechmount, Rathkeale, co. Limerick.*

LLOYD, THOMAS, Esq., of Castle Lloyd, co. Limerick.
Eldest son of the late Rev. William Edward Lloyd, by Anne, dau. of Thomas Peacocke, Esq., of Fort Etna, co. Limerick; *b.* 1814; *s.* 1853; *m.* 1838 Mary, eldest dau. of the Rev. Charles Philip Coote, Rector of Ibon, co. Limerick, and has, with other issue,

* William Thomas Llewelyn, *b.* 1839.

Mr. Lloyd, who was educated at Trinity Coll., Dublin is a Magistrate for co. Limerick.—*Castle Lloyd, Ulla, co. Limerick.*

LLOYD, THOMAS, Esq., late of Spark Hill, Warwickshire.
Youngest son of the late James Lloyd, Esq., of Bingley Hall, Birmingham; b. 1814; m. 1845 Emilia, dau. of the late John Travers, Esq. Is a J.P. and D.L. for co. Warwick; was M.P. for Barnstaple 1863–4; formerly a Banker at Birmingham.—Residence: *The Priory, Warwick; Reform Club,* s.w.

LLOYD, THOMAS EDWARD, Esq., of Coedmore, Cardiganshire.
Eldest son of the late Thomas Lloyd, Esq., of Coedmore (who was Lord-Lieut. of co. Cardigan, and High Sheriff 1857), by Charlotte, dau. of the late Charles Loncroft, Esq., R.N.; b. 1820; s. 1859; m. 1850 Clemena Frances, 2nd dau. of the late Rev. David Daniel, and has issue,
    * A daughter.
Mr. Lloyd, who was educated at Rugby, called to the Bar at the Middle Temple 1845, and practises at the Chancery Bar, is a Magistrate for co. Carmarthen. —*Coedmore, Cardigan; 5, New Square, Lincoln's Inn,* N.C.; *3, Victoria Street, Westminster,* s.w.

LLOYD, THOMAS WILLIAM, Esq., of Cowesby Hall, Yorkshire.
Eldest son of the late George Lloyd, Esq., of Cowesby Hall, by Elizabeth Henrietta, dau. of William Leedes Rookes Serjeantson, Esq., of Camp Hill, co. York; b. 1826; s. 1844; m. 1849 Elizabeth Ann, 3rd dau. of Francis Beynon Hacket, Esq., of Moor Hall, co. Warwick. Educated at Trinity Coll., Cambridge; is a J.P. and D.L. for the N. Riding of Yorkshire. —*Cowesby Hall, Northallerton.*

+LLOYD, WILLIAM BUTLER, Esq., of Monk-moor, Shropshire.
Son of the late W. Lloyd, Esq.; b. 18—. Is a J.P. and D.L. for co. Salop, and Capt. South Salop Yeomanry Cavalry.—*Monkmoor, Shrewsbury.*

LLOYD-GREAME, the Rev. YARBURGH, of Sewerby House, Yorkshire.
Second son of the late George Lloyd, Esq., of Stockton Hall, co. York (who d. 1863), by Alicia Maria, dau. of John Greame, Esq., of Sewerby House, whose name he has assumed in addition to that of Lloyd; b. 1813; s. his mother 1867; m. 1859 Editha Christiana, dau. of William Augustus Le Hunte, Esq., of Artramont, co. Wexford, and has, with other issue, an only son,
    * Yarburgh George, Capt. East and North Yorkshire Artillery Militia; b. 1840; m. 1867 Dora Letitia, 2nd dau. of the Rt. Rev. J. T. O'Brien, Lord Bishop of Ossory.
Mr. Lloyd-Greame, who was educated at Rugby and Trinity Coll., Cambridge (B.A. 1836, M.A. 1841), and ordained in 1836, is a Magistrate for the E. Riding of Yorkshire, Lord of the Manor of Sewerby-cum-Marton, and Patron of 1 living; he was formerly Vicar of Dunston, co. Lincoln.—*Sewerby House, Bridlington.*

LLOYD. (See under *Mostyn, Lord.*)

LLOYD, of Bluendyffryn. (See *Davies-Lloyd.*)

LLOYD, of Heslington. (See *Yarburgh.*)

LLOYD, of Lancing. (See *Carr-Lloyd.*)

LLOYD, of Nantgwilt. (See *Lewis-Lloyd.*)

LLOYD-APPJOHN. (See *Appjohn.*)

LLOYD-PHILIPPS. (See *Philipps.*)

592

LLOYD-PHILIPPS, JOHN PHILIPPS ALLEN, Esq., of Dole Castle, Pembrokeshire.
Eldest son of the late Capt. John Allen Lloyd, of Dale Castle (who d. 1805), by Elizabeth, dau. of Col. Harry Bisshopp, of Storrington, Sussex; b. 1802; s. his grandfather John Lloyd, Esq., 1820; m. 1st 1823 Charlotte Caroline, dau. of Capt. Bartlet, R.E.; 2nd 1865 Elizabeth Anne Bellairs, eldest dau. of James Peel Sterenson, Esq., of Uffington, co. Lincoln; he has by the former, with other issue,
    * John Allen, late Capt. 82nd Regt., b. 1824; m. 1845 Elizabeth, dau. of Richard Jones, Esq., of Plymouth.
Mr. Lloyd-Philipps, who is a J.P. and D.L. for cos. Pembroke and Cardigan (High Sheriff 1844), and a Magistrate for co. Carmarthen and for Haverfordwest, was formerly Major Royal Cardigan Militia; he assumed the additional name of Philipps, under the will of the late James Philipps, Esq., of Penty Park.—*Dale Castle, Milford; Mabwys, Aberystwith.*

LLOYD-VAUGHAN, WILLIAM PEISLEY HUTCHINSON, Esq., of Golden Grove and Mount Heaton, King's Co.
Only child of the late Samuel Dawson Hutchinson, Esq., J.P., of Mount Heaton, by Mary, only child and heir of John Lloyd, Esq., of Parsonstown, and of Martha, sister of William Peisley Vaughan, Esq., of Golden Grove (whose name he assumed by Royal licence, as well as that of his father-in-law); b. 1844; s. 1854. Educated at Trinity Coll., Dublin.—*Golden Grove, Roscrea, King's Co.*

LOCH, GEORGE, Esq., of Uppat, Sutherland-shire, and Tittensor, Staffordshire.
Eldest son of the late James Loch, Esq., M.P., of Uppat, by Anne, dau. of the late Patrick Orr, Esq., of Bridgeton; b. 1811; s. 1855; m. 1836 Catharine, eldest dau. of Joseph Pilkington Brandreth, Esq., of Liverpool, M.D. Educated at the Charterhouse; called to the Bar at the Middle Temple 1847; is a Magistrate for co. Lancaster, a J.P. and D.L. for co. Sutherland, and Capt. Staffordshire Yeomanry.—*Tittensor, Stone, Staffordshire, N.B.; Uppat, Golspie, N.B.; Athenæum and Brooke's Clubs,* s.w.; *12, Albemarle Street,* w.

LOCKE, FRANCIS ALEXANDER SYDENHAM, Esq., of Rowde Ford, Wilts.
Second son of the late Wadham Locke, Esq., M.P. of Rowde Ford, by Anna Maria Selina, only dau. of the late Alexander Powell, Esq., of Hurdcott House. Wilts; b. 1804; s. 1836; m. 1830 Katharine Harriet, dau. of the late Admiral Sir Thomas Fellowes, C.B., and has surviving issue,
    * Katharine Selina.
Mr. Locke is a J.P. and D.L. for Wilts (High Sheriff 1840).—*Rowde Ford, Devizes.*

LOCKE, JOHN, Esq., of Chicklade, Wilts.
Fourth son of the late Wadham Locke, Esq., M.P., of Rowde Forde, by Anna Maria Selina, only dau. of the late Alexander Powell, Esq., of Hurdcott. Wilts; b. 1808; m. 1839 Frances Augusta, dau. of Thomas Moore Wayne, Esq. Educated at Harrow; is a J.P. and D.L. for Wilts; was formerly in the Military Service of the H.E.I.C.—*Chicklade House, Hindon.*

LOCKE, JOHN, Esq., Q.C.
Son of the late John Locke, Esq., of Herne Hill, Surrey; b. 1805; m. 1847 Laura Rosalie, dau. of the late Col. Thomas A. Cobbe, E.I.C.S., and has issue,
    * John Henry, b. 1848.
Mr. Locke, who was educated at Trinity Coll., Cambridge (B.A. 1829, M.A. 1832), called to the Bar at the Inner Temple 1833, and is a Member of the Home Circuit, was a Common Pleader of the City of London,

which office he resigned in 1857, upon being appointed one of Her Majesty's Counsel; is a Bencher of the Inner Temple, and Recorder of Brighton; has been M.P. for Southwark since 1857.—*Reform, Garrick, and Oxford and Cambridge Clubs*, s.w. ; 2, *Harcourt Buildings, Temple*, e.c.; 63, *Eaton Place*, s.w.

+ LOCKE, John Arthur, Esq., of North Moor, Somerset.

Son of the late W. Locke, Esq.; *b.* 1820; *m.* 1858 Adèle Caroline, eldest dau. of Edward Simcoe Drewe, Esq., of The Grange, Devon, and has issue. Is a Magistrate for Devon and Somerset.—*North Moor House, Dulverton.*

LOCKE, Wadham, Esq., of Cleve House, Wilts.

Eldest son of the late Wadham Locke, Esq., M.P., of Rowde Ford, by Anna Maria Selina, only dau. of the late Alexander Powell, Esq., of Hurdcott House, Wilts ; *b.* 1803 ; *s.* 1836 ; *m.* 1st 1828 Caroline Mary, dau. of Henry Thompson, Esq., of Yorkshire; 2nd 1844 Albinia, dau. of John Dalton, Esq., of Sleningford Park, co. York, and has, with other issue,

• Wadham, *b.* 1845.

Mr. Locke, who was educated at Harrow and Merton Coll., Oxford, is a Magistrate for Wilts, of which co. he has been High Sheriff; was formerly in the King's 1st Dragoon Guards.—*Cleve House, Seend, Melksham.*

LOCKE-KING. (See *King.*)

LOCKHART, Sir Norman Macdonald-, Bart., of Lee and Carnwath, Lanarkshire (cr. 1806).

Eldest son of the late Sir Norman Macdonald-Lockhart, Bart., by Margaret, dau. of John McClean, Esq., of Cambeltown, co. Argyle ; *b.* 1844 ; *s.* us 4th Bart. 1849. Educated at Eton and Ch. Ch., Oxford ; is Lord of the Baronies of Lee and Carnwath. The additional name of Lockhart was assumed by the 1st Bart. in 1806, on inheriting the estates of his cousin Charles, Count Lockhart-Wishart.—*Lee Castle, and Carnwath House, Lanark, N.B.*

Heir Pres., his brother Simon, *b.* 1849.

LOCKHART, Allan Eliott-, Esq., of Borthwickbrae, Roxburghshire.

Eldest son of the late William Eliott-Lockhart, Esq., M.P., of Borthwickbrae, by Marianne, dau. of Allan Lockhart, Esq., of Cleghorn, N.B. ; *b.* 1803 ; *s.* 1832 ; *m.* 1830 Charlotte, dau. of the late Sir Robert Dundas, Bart., and has, with other issue,

• William, Capt. 74th Highlanders, *b.* 1833 ; *m.* 1866 Dorothea Helen, eldest dau. of Sir Walter Elliot, K.C.S.T., of Wolfelee, co. Roxburgh.

Mr. Lockhart, who was educated at Edinburgh University, and called to the Scottish Bar 1824, is Lord-Lieut. of co. Selkirk, and a J.P. and D.L. for cos. Lanark and Roxburgh; was M.P. for co. Selkirk 1846-61.—*Borthwickbrae, Hawick, N.B.; Cleghorn, Lanark, N.B.; Carlton Club*, s.w.

LOCKHART, James, Esq., of Sherfield English, Hampshire.

Eldest son of the late James Lockhart, Esq., of Lanhams, Essex (who *d.* 1852), by his 1st wife Mary, dau. of Leonard Coxe, Esq., of Philadelphia, U.S. ; *b.* 1796 ; *s.* his uncle 1836 ; *m.* 1830 Caroline, dau. of Signor Manzini, of Rome, and had, with other issue, an only surviving son,

Edgar Henry (M.A. and Fellow of University Coll., Oxford), *b.* 1836 ; *d.* 1868.

Mr. Lockhart was educated at the University Coll., Oxford (B.A. 1819, M.A. 1823, called to the Bar at Gray's

Inn 1824, and went the Oxford Circuit ; Lord of the Manor of Sherfield English, and also of Lanhams and Temple Cressing.—*Sherfield English, Romsey.*

+ LOCKHART, James Sinclair, Esq., of Castle Hill, Lanarkshire.

Eldest son of the late Robert Lockhart, Esq., of Castlehill, by Eliza Anne, dau. of Richard Tolle Newman, Esq., of Thornbury Park, co. Gloucester; *b.* 1809; *s.* 1852. Is a J.P. and D.L. for co. Lanark, Lord of the Barony of Castlehill, and Patron of 2 livings; was formerly an officer in the Lanark Militia.—*Cumnethan House and Castlehill, Motherwell, Lanarkshire.*

Heir Pres., his brother Graeme Alexander, late Col. 78th Regt. ; *b.* 1811.

LOCKHART, the Rev. Laurence, D.D., of Wicketshaw and Milton Lockhart, Lanarkshire.

Fifth but eldest surviving son of the late Rev. John Lockhart, D.D., by Violet, niece and heir of James Somerville, Esq., of Corehouse, N.B. ; *b.* 1796 ; *s.* his half-brother, William Lockhart, Esq., M.P., 1856 ; *m.* 1st 1825 Louisa. dau. of the late D. Blair, Esq.; 2nd 1849 Marion, dau. of the late William Maxwell, Esq., of Dargavel, co. Renfrew, and has, with other issue,

• David Blair, Capt. 107th Regt., *b.* 1829.

Dr. Lockhart, who was educated at Glasgow University (D.D. 1849), is a Magistrate for co. Lanark; was Incumbent of Inchinnan, co. Renfrew 1822-60.—*Milton Lockhart, Carluke, Lanarkshire, N.B.*

LOCKLEY, Thomas, Esq., M.D., of Baildon Lodge, Yorkshire.

Third son of the late George F. Lockley, Esq., of London, by Margaret, youngest dau. and co-heir of Thomas Holt, Esq., of Ruswarp, co. York ; *b.* 1811 ; *m.* 1852 Caroline Anne, 2nd dau. and co-heir of the late John Lambert, Esq., of Baildon, co. York, and has issue,

• Edward Holden, *b.* 1855.

Dr. Lockley, who was educated at Caius Coll., Cambridge (M.B. 1835, M.D. 1852), is a Magistrate for the W. Riding of Yorkshire, and Physician to the Bradford Infirmary.—*Baildon, Lodge, Leeds ; 18, Bootham, York.*

LOCKWOOD, Sir George Henry, K.C.B. (cr. 1867).

Son of the late Thomas Lockwood, Esq., of Dun-y-Greig. co. Glamorgan, by Charlotte, dau. of the late Lord George Manners-Sutton, and granddau. of John, 3rd Duke of Rutland; *b.* 1806. Educated at Eton and Trinity Coll., Cambridge ; is a Lieut.-Gen. in the Army, and Col. 12th Royal Lancers ; was formerly in the 3rd King's Own Dragoons.—*United Service Club*, s.w.; 18, *Wilton Street*, s.w.

LOCKWOOD, Lady Julia, of Barcombe, Devon.

Youngest dau. of Arthur Saunders. 2nd Earl of Arran. by his 3rd wife Elizabeth, dau. of Richard Underwood, Esq.; *m.* 1821 Robert Manners Lockwood, Esq., who *d.* 1865, leaving, with other issue,

• Henry John Arthur, *b.* 1823 ; *m.* 1853 Dorothea, only dau. of the Hon. W. Keith Falconer.

Lady J. Lockwood is Lady of the Manor of Barcombe. —*Barcombe, Paignton.*

LOCKWOOD. (See *Wood.*)

LOCKYER, the Rev. Edmund Leopold, M.A. Only son of the late Edmund Lockyer, Esq., M.D., F.S.L., of Plymouth (who *d.* 1816), by Eliza, dau. and co-heir of Capt. Thomas Braithwaite, R.N. ; *b.* 1816 ; *s.* his grandfather 1836 ; *m.* 1839 Julia Mary, 2nd dau.

of the Rev. Thomas Woodford, M.A., Rector of Ansford, Somerset, and has, with other issue,

* Edmund Stoughton Braithwaite, Lieut. R.A.; b. 1842.

Mr. Lockyer was educated at Eton and Emmanuel Coll., Cambridge (B.A. 1846. M.A. 1849), ordained 1846, and appointed Rector of Westcot Barton, 1852.—*Westcot Barton, Oxford.*

LOCOCK, Sir CHARLES, Bart., of Speldhurst, Kent (cr. 1857).
Third son of the late Henry Locock, Esq., M.D., of Northampton, by Susannah, dau. of the Rev. William Smyth, of Great Linford, Bucks; b. 1799; m. 1826 Amelia, dau. of John Lewis, Esq. (she d. 1867). Educated at the University of Edinburgh; graduated M.D. 1821; is a J.P. and D.L. for Kent, a Fellow of the Royal College of Physicians of London, and First Physician Accoucheur to Her Majesty.—*Holmewood, Speldhurst, Tunbridge Wells* ; 26, *Hertford Street,* w.

Heir, his son Charles Brodie. b. 1827 ; m. 1859 Fanny Bird, dau. of the Rev. Thomas Pitman, Vicar of Eastbourne, Sussex, and has issue a dau.

LOFFT, ROBERT EMLYN, Esq., of Troston Hall, Suffolk.
Eldest surviving son of the late Robert E. Lofft, Esq., of Troston, by Letitia Niel, dau. of Lieut.-Col. Richardson, and grandson of Capel Lofft, Esq., of Troston, who d. 1824 ; b. 1830 ; s. his brother 1866. Is Lord of the Manors of Troston and Stanton, and Patron of the living of Stanton.—*Troston Hall, Ixworth.*

LOFT. (See *Wallis.*)

LOFTUS, Lord AUGUSTUS WILLIAM FREDERICK, G.C.B. (cr. 1866).
Fourth son of John, 2nd Marquis of Ely, by Anna Maria, eldest dau. of Sir Henry Watkin Dashwood, Bart.; b. 1817 ; m. 1845 Emma, dau. of Capt. Henry Francis Greville, R.N., and has, with other issue,

* Henry John, who was educated at Trinity Coll., Cambridge, late Page of Honour to Her Majesty, b. 1849.

Lord Augustus became Attaché at Berlin 1837, at Stuttgardt 1844, Secretary of Legation at Stuttgardt 1848, at Berlin 1853-8, where he was for some time Chargé d'Affaires; appointed Ambassador at Vienna 1858 ; Minister at Munich 1862 ; Ambassador at Berlin 1865 ; Ambassador to the North German Confederation 1868.—Residence: *British Embassy, Berlin.*

LOFTUS, GEORGE WILLIAM FERRARS, Esq., of Bracon Lodge, Norfolk.
Only son of Arthur Loftus, Esq., M.A.. by Mary Anne, only dau. and heir of the late Rev. William Ray Clayton, of Churchman House, Norwich ; b. 1839 ; s. his maternal grandfather 1860 ; m. 1861 Barbara, dau. of Benjamin James, Esq., of Norwich. Educated at Trinity Hall, Cambridge; is a Magistrate for Norfolk, and Master of the Braconash Harriers. He purchased this estate in 1862.—*Bracon Lodge, Braconash, Wymondham.*

LOFTUS, Col. FERRARS.
Fourth son of the late General William Loftus. M.P., by his 2nd wife Lady Elizabeth, eldest dau. of George, 1st Marquis of Townshend, K.G.; b. 1798 ; m. 1832 Louisa, only child of the Rev. John Bastard, of West Lodge, co. Dorset, and has issue. Col. Loftus, who is a Dep.-Lieut. for the W. Riding of Yorkshire, and Col. 3rd W. Yorkshire Militia, was formerly Capt. and Lieut.-Col. Grenadier Guards.—Residence: *Sunderlandwick, Driffield, Yorkshire ; United Service Club,* s.w.

594

LOFTUS, Lieut.-Col. WILLIAM JAMES, of Balcummin, and of Oldtown, co. Dublin.
Eldest son of the late Lieut.-General William Francis Bentinck Loftus. of Kilbride, by Margaret Harriet, dau. of the Ven. Archdeacon Langrishe, 2nd son of Sir Hercules Langrishe, Bart.; b. 1822. Is Lieut.-Col. 36th Foot, and heir male of the family of Viscount Loftus of Ely (ext.).—Residence: *Westcott, Dorking.*

Heir Pres., his uncle Arthur, M.A. of Clare Hall, Cambridge (eldest surviving son of the late Gen. William Loftus, who d. 1831, by his second wife Lady Elizabeth, only surviving dau. of George, 1st Marquis Townshend) ; b. 1796 ; m. 1836 Mary Anne, only child of the late Rev. William Ray Clayton, and by her, who d. 1856, has issue, * George William Ferrars (whom see).

LOFTUS. (See under *Ely, Marquis of.*)

LOFTUS-TOTTENHAM. (See *Tottenham.*)

LOGAN, Sir WILLIAM EDMOND, Knt., F.R.S., F.G.S. (cr. 1856).
Son of the late William Logan, Esq., of Montreal, and nephew of the late Hart Logan, Esq., M.P. for E. Suffolk ; b. 1798. Educated at Montreal and the High School and University of Edinburgh ; is Director of the Geological Survey in Canada, and a Chevalier of the Legion of Honour in France.—*Montreal, Canada.*

LOGAN-HOME. (See *Home.*)

+**LOMAX,** JAMES, Esq., of Clayton Hall, Lancashire.
Eldest surviving son of the late Richard Grimshaw Lomax, Esq., of Clayton Hall (who d. 1837), by Catharine, dau. of Thomas Greaves Esq., of Preston ; b. 1820 ; s. his brother, 1849 ; m. 1845 Frances Cecilia. eldest dau. of Charles Walmesley, Esq. Is a Dep.-Lieut. for co. Lancaster.—*Clayton Hall, Blackburn.*

LOMAX, THOMAS OPENSHAW, Esq., of Bodfach, Montgomeryshire.
Eldest son of the late John Lomax. Esq., J.P. of Springfield, co. Lancaster, and Bodfach. co. Montgomery, by Anne, dau. of Thomas Openshaw, Esq., of High Bank, Bury, co. Lancaster ; b. 1836 ; s. 1862 ; m. 1863 Anne, 3rd dau. of the late Rev. R. Pughe. Rector of Llanfihangel, co. Montgomery. Educated at Rugby ; is Lieut. Montgomeryshire Yeomanry Cavalry. —*Bodfach, Llanfyllin, Oswestry.*

LOMBARD, JAMES FITZGERALD, Esq., of South Hill, co. Dublin.
Second son of the late Roger Lombard. Esq., of Woodville, co. Kerry, by Jane, dau. of the late James Fitzgerald, Esq., of the city of Limerick ; b. 1817 ; m. 1844 Margaret, relict of the late Charles Tuite, Esq., of Tralee, co. Kerry, and has, with other issue,

* James William, b. 1845.

Mr. Lombard is a Magistrate for co. Dublin.—*South Hill, Upper Rathmines, co. Dublin.*

LOMBE, the Rev. HENRY, of Bylaugh Hall. Norfolk.
Eldest son of the Rev. Henry Evans, Rector of Lynn, Norfolk, J.P., by Sophia, dau. of Thomas Cubitt, Esq. of Honing Hall, Norfolk ; b. 1821 ; s. his cousin, the Rev. Edward Lombe, 1852 (when he assumed, by Royal licence, the name and arms of Lombe only) ; m. 1849 his cousin Louisa, dau. of — Lombe, Esq., and has issue. Mr. Lombe, who was educated at Corpus Christi Coll., Cambridge (B.A. 1843), is a Magistrate for Norfolk and Suffolk, and Rector of Eriswell, Suffolk. Lord of the Manors of Alderford, Foxley, Bylaugh, and Bil-

lingford, Norfolk, and Patron of the livings of Foxley, Bawdeswell, and Bylaugh.—*Bylaugh Hall, E. Dereham; Eriswell Rectory, Mildenhall, Suffolk.*

LONDESBOROUGH, Lord (WILLIAM HENRY FORESTER DENISON).—Cr. 1850.

Eldest son of Albert Denison, 1st Lord, by his 1st wife the Hon. Henrietta Maria, dau. of Cecil Weld, 1st Lord Forester; b. 1834; s. 1860; m. 1863 Lady Edith Frances, youngest dau. of Henry, late Duke of Beaufort. Educated at Eton; is a J.P. and D.L. for the E. and N. Ridings of co. York, and Patron of 5 livings; Hon. Col. of the Hull Artillery Volunteers; was M.P. for Beverley 1857–9, and for Scarborough 1859–60. —*Grimston Park, Tadcaster ; 3, Grosvenor Square, s.w.*

Heir, his son William Francis Henry, b. 1864.

LONDON, Bishop of (the Right Rev. ARCHIBALD CAMPBELL TAIT, D.C.L., P.C.).

Son of Crauford Tait, Esq., of Harvieston, co. Clackmannan, by Susan, 4th dau. of the late Sir Islay Campbell, Bart. (Lord President of Scotland); b. 1811; m. 1843 Catharine, dau. of the late Ven. Archdeacon Spooner, and has issue, an only son,

* Crauford, b. 1849; educated at Eton.

The Bishop was educated at Glasgow and Balliol Coll., Oxford (B.A. 1833. M.A. 1836); was successively Scholar, Fellow, and Tutor of Balliol Coll., Head Master of Rugby 1842, Dean of Carlisle 1849; consecrated 1856; appointed Dean of the Chapel Royal 1857. Patron of 98 livings.—*The Palace, Fulham, s.w.; Athenæum, and Oxford and Cambridge Clubs, s.w.; 22, St. James's Square, s.w.*

LONDONDERRY, Marquis of (FREDERICK WILLIAM ROBERT STEWART, K.P., P.C.).— Cr. 1816.

Eldest son of Charles William, 3rd Marquis, by his 1st wife Lady Katharine, dau. of John, 3rd Earl of Darnley; b. 1805; s. 1854; m. 1846 Lady Elizabeth Frances, eldest dau. of Robert, 3rd Earl of Roden. the widow of Richard, 6th Viscount Powerscourt. Educated at Eton and Ch. Ch., Oxford; sits in the House of Lords as Lord Stewart, U.K. (cr. 1814); late Lord Lieutenant of co. Down; is Col. N. Down Militia; was M.P. for co. Down 1826–52.—*Powerscourt, Enniskerry, co, Wicklow; Mount Stuart, co. Down ; 35, Chesham Place, s.w.*

Heir Pres., his brother Earl Vane (whom see).

LONG, HENRY LAWES, Esq., ‡ of Hampton Lodge, Surrey, and East Barnet, Herts.

Eldest son of the late Edward Beeston Long, Esq., of Hampton Lodge, by Mary, dau. of John Tomlinson, Esq., M.P.; b. 1795; s. 1825; m. 1822 Lady Catharine, dau. of Horatio, 2nd Earl of Orford, and by her, who d. 1867, has, with other issue,

* Charles Dudley, b. 1839.

Mr. Long. who was educated at Harrow and Trinity Coll., Cambridge, is a Magistrate for Surrey.—*Hampton Lodge, Farnham.*

LONG, JOHN, Esq.

Third son of Walter Long, Esq., of Preshaw House, Hants, by Lady Mary, eldest dau. of William, 7th Earl of Northesk, G.C.B.; b. 1818; m. 1842 Georgiana Frances, eldest dau. of Sir Simeon H. Stuart, Bart., and has issue, a son, in the Navy. Mr. Long was formerly an Officer in the 10th Hussars.—*Hill Cottage, Walberton, Arundel; Army and Navy Club, s.w.*

LONG, ROBERT KELLETT, Esq., of Dunston, Norfolk.

Eldest son of the late Rev. Robert Churchman Long, of Dunston Hall, by Jane, only child of the late Rev. Nevill Walter, Rector of Denghapton, Norfolk; b. 1804;

‡ Died whilst these sheets were at press.

s. 1841 ; m. 1843 Maria Louisa, eldest dau. of William Fortescue, Esq., formerly of Writtle, Essex, and has, with other issue,

* Fortescue Walter Kellett, b. 1843.

Mr. Long who was educated at Harrow and Trinity Coll., Cambridge (B.A. 1825, M.A. 1832), is a J.P. and D.L. for Norfolk (High Sheriff 1856), Lord of the Manor of Dunston, and Patron of 2 livings.—*Dunston Hall, Norwich; Oxford and Cambridge Club, s.w.*

LONG, Lieut.-Col. SAMUEL, of Bromley Hill, Kent.

Eldest son of the late Samuel Long, Esq., of Carshalton, Surrey, by Lady Jane, 4th dau. of James, 7th Earl of Lauderdale, K.T.; b. 1799; m. 1st 1825 Lady Louisa Emily, 2nd dau. of Edward, 13th Earl of Derby, K.G. (she d. same year); 2nd 1827 Sidney, dau. of Arthur Atherley, Esq.; 3rd 1854 Emily, dau. of the late Charles John Herbert, Esq., of Muckross, Killarney (she d. 1864); 4th 1866 the Hon. Eleanor, eldest dau. of Edward Stanley, Esq., of Crosshall, co. Lancaster. Educated at Westminster; is a J.P. and D.L. for Kent (High Sheriff 1863); was formerly in the Grenadier Guards.—*Bromley Hill, Kent ; United Service Club, s.w.*

LONG, RICHARD PENRUDDOCKE, Esq., of Rood Ashton, Wilts, and Dolforgan, Montgomeryshire.

Eldest surviving son of the late Walter Long, Esq., of Rood Ashton (who was many years M.P. for N. Wilts), by his first wife Mary Anne, dau. of the late Right Hon. Archibald Colquhoun, Lord Registrar of Scotland; b. 1825; s. 1867; m. 1853 Charlotte Anna, only surviving dau. of W. W. Fitzwilliam Hume (now Dick), Esq., M.P., of Humewood, co. Wicklow, and has, with other issue,

* Walter Hume, b. 1854.

Mr. Long, who was educated at Harrow and Trinity Coll., Cambridge (B.A. 1848, M.A. 1852), is a Magistrate for Wilts, and a J.P. and D.L. for co. Montgomery (High Sheriff 1858), Lord of the Manor of Steeple Ashton, &c., and Patron of 4 livings; he was M.P. for Chippenham 1859–65, elected M.P. for N. Wilts 1865. —*Dolforgan, Newtown, Montgomeryshire ; Rood Ashton, Trowbridge; Carlton and National Clubs, s.w.; 20, Curzon Street, w.*

LONG, WALTER, Esq., of Preshaw, Hants.

Only son of the late John Long, Esq., of Preshaw House, by Ellen, dau. of R. H. Trenchard. Esq., of Stanton Fitzwarren, Wilts; b. 1788; s. 1797; m. 1810 Lady Mary, eldest dau. of William, 7th Earl of Northesk, G.C.B., and has, with other issue,

* Walter Jervis (of Belmore House, near Bishop's Waltham), educated at Oriel Coll., Oxford ; a Magistrate for Hants ; b. 1816 ; m. 1839 Emily Jane, eldest dau. of Edward Morant Gale, Esq., and has issue. * Walter, late Ensign 11th Foot, b. 1842 ; m. 1866 Fanny, 2nd dau. of Lieut.-Col. Vansittart, of Chuffs, Maidenhead, Berks, and has issue.

Mr. Long, who was educated at Oriel Coll., Oxford. (B.A. 1809, M.A. 1812). is a J.P. and D.L for Hants (High Sheriff 1824). Descended from the ancient family of the same name settled in Wilts.—*Preshaw House, Bishop's Waltham ; University Club. s.w.*

LONG, WILLIAM. Esq.

Second son of Walter Long. Esq., of Preshaw House. Hants (whom see). by Lady Mary. eldest dau. of William. 7th Earl of Northesk, G.C.B., Admiral of the Red, and Rear-Admiral of Great Britain ; b. 1817 ; m. 1841 Elizabeth Hare, only child of James Hare Jolliffe. Esq., and has, with other issue,

* William, educated at Eton ; Lieut. 46th Foot ; b. 1843 ; m. 1867 Anna Mary, dau. of the late Henry Hunter. Esq., Capt. 5th Dragoon Guards.

Mr. Long. who was educated at Balliol Coll., Oxford (B.A. 1839, M.A. 1843), is a Magistrate for Somerset. —16, Lansdown Place, Bath.

LONG, WILLIAM, Esq., of Hurts Hall, Suffolk.
Son of the late Beeston Long, Esq., of Coombe House, Surrey, by Frances Louisa, dau. of Sir Richard Neave, Bart.; *b.* 1802; *s.* 1833; *m.* 1830 Eleonore Charlotte, dau. of Edward Poore, Esq., of Rughall, Wilts, and has, with other issue,

  • William Beeston, a Magistrate for Suffolk; *b.* 1833; *m.* 1859 Arethusa Marianne, dau. of Sir Robert Charles Rowley, Bart.

Mr. Long, who was educated at Eton, is a J.P. and D.L. for Suffolk (High Sheriff 1843), Lord of the Manor of Hurts, &c., and Patron of 3 livings.—*Hurts Hall, Saxmundham; National Club*, s.w.; *28, Great Cumberland Place*, w.

LONGDEN. (See *Gregory.*)

LONGE, JOHN, Esq., of Spixworth, Norfolk.
Second son of the late Rev. John Longe, Vicar of Coddenham, Suffolk; by Charlotte, dau. of John Browne, Esq., of Ipswich; *b.* 1799; *s.* 1828; *m.* 1829 Caroline Elizabeth, eldest dau. and co-heir of the late Col. Francis Warneford, of Warneford Place, Wilts (she *d.* 1846). Educated at Jesus Coll., Cambridge; is a J.P. and D.L. for Norfolk, Lord of the Manor of Spixworth, and Patron of the living.—*Spixworth Park, Norwich.*

  Heir Pres., his brother Robert, B.A. of Caius Coll., Cambridge, Vicar and Patron of Coddenham, Suffolk, and Rural Dean; *b.* 1800; *m.* 1828 Margaret Douglas, dau. of the late Rev. Charles Davy, Rector of Barking, Suffolk, and has, with other issue, *Robert Bacon, b.* 1830; *m.* 1853 Caroline Elizabeth, dau. of the late Rev. Charles J. Orman, F.C. of Shouldham, Norfolk, and has issue.

LONGFIELD, Capt. JOHN POWELL, of Waterloo, co. Cork.
Eldest son of the late Henry Longfield, Esq., of Waterloo, by Mary, only dau. of John Powell, Esq., of Sea Court, co. Cork; *b.* 1817; *s.* 1851; *m.* 1848 Louisa, 6th dau. of the late Rev. Matthew Purcell, of Burton, co. Cork. Educated at Trinity Coll., Dublin (B.A. 1838); is a Magistrate for co. Cork, and Capt. R. Cork Artillery Militia.—*Waterloo House, Mallow, co. Cork.*

  Heir Pres., his brother Henry, *b.* 1828; *m.* 1857 Eliza Augusta, only dau. of the late William Purcell, Esq., of Atimira, co. Cork, by whom he has issue three sons and one daughter.

LONGFIELD, Mrs. of Castle Mary, co. Cork.
Caroline Augusta, only dau. of the late George Courtenay, Esq., of Ballyedmond, co. Cork (who was High Sheriff of that county in 1826, and who *d.* 1837), by Caroline Augusta, dau. of the late James Hugh Smith-Barry, Esq., of Marbury Hall, co. Chester; *m.* 1840 Mountifort Longfield, Esq., of Castle Mary, who was a J.P. and D.L. for co. Cork, High Sheriff in 1855, and who *d.* 1864, leaving, with other issue,

  • Mountifort, *b.* 1858.

This family is a branch of that of Viscount Longueville (*ext.*).—*Castle Mary, Cloyne, co. Cork.*

LONGFIELD, the Rt. Hon. MOUNTIFORT. LL.D.
Second son of the late Rev. Mountifort Longfield, Vicar of Desertserges. co. Cork, by Grace, dau. of William Lysaght, Esq., of Fort William and Mount North, co. Cork; *b.* 1806; *m.* 1852 Elizabeth, dau. of Andrew Armstrong, Esq., of Kilsharvan, co. Meath. Educated at Trinity Coll., Dublin (B.A. 1825, LL.D. 1831); is a Bencher of King's Inn, Dublin; was appointed Professor of Political Economy to the University 1832, Professor of Feudal and English Law 1834, one of the Commissioners of the Encumbered Estates Court 1847, a Commissioner of National Education 1853, and a Judge of the Landed Estates Court 1858; sworn a member of the Privy Council (Ireland) 1867.—47, *Fitzwilliam Square West, Dublin.*

596

LONGFIELD, RICHARD, Esq., of Longueville, co. Cork.
Eldest son of the late John Longfield, Esq., of Longueville, by Ellen, dau. of John Lucas, Esq., of Mount Lucas; *b.* 1802; *s.* 1842; *m.* 1st 1832 Harriett Elizabeth, dau. of the late John MacClintock, Esq., of Drumcar; 2nd 1841 Jemima, dau. of the late Wyrley Birch, Esq., of Wretham Hall, Norfolk, has issue,

  • Richard Edmund, *b.* 1842.

Mr. Longfield, who was educated at Trinity Coll., Dublin, is a J.P. and D.L. for co. Cork (High Sheriff 1833); he was M.P. for co. Cork 1835-7.—*Longueville, Mallow, co. Cork; Carlton Club*, s.w.

LONGFIELD, ROBERT, Esq., Q.C. ‡
Third son of the late Rev. M. Longfield, Vicar of Desertserges, co. Cork, by Grace, dau. of William Lysaght, Esq., and cousin of Richard Longfield, Esq., of Longueville (whom see); *b.* 1810; *m.* 1840 Charlotte, dau. of the late George Stawell, Esq., of Crobeg, co. Cork. Educated at Trinity Coll., Dublin (B.A. 1831, M.A. 1834); called to the Irish Bar in 1834; appointed a Queen's Counsel in 1852; was M.P. for Mallow 1859-65; appointed Law Adviser of the Crown for Ireland 1866.—33, *Merrion Square South, Dublin; Carlton Club*, s.w.

LONGFORD, Earl of (WILLIAM LYGON PAKENHAM, K.C.B.).—Cr. 1785.
Second son of Thomas, 2nd Earl of Longford (who *d.* 1835), by Lady Georgiana Emma Charlotte, dau. of William, 1st Earl Beauchamp; *b.* 1819; *s.* his brother 1860; *m.* 1862 the Hon. Selina, 3rd dau. of George, 3rd Lord Dynevor. Sits in the House of Lords as Lord Silchester, U.K. (cr. 1821). Educated at Winchester; is a J.P. and D.L. for cos. Westmeath and Longford, and a Col. in the Army; appointed Under Secretary of State for War 1867; was formerly Adjutant-General to the Forces in the Crimea and India.—*Pakenham Hall, Castle Pollard, co. Westmeath; Carlton, White's and United Service Clubs*, s.w.; *24, Burton Street*, w.

  Heir, his son William, Lord Pakenham, *b.* 1864.

LONGMAN, CHARLES, Esq., of Shendish, Herts.
Second son of the late Thomas Norton Longman. Esq., of Hampstead, Middlesex, by Mary, dau. of — Slater. Esq.; *b.* 1809; *m.* 1835 Anna Maria Surman, dau. of the late John H. Hampton-Lewis, Esq., of Henllys, co. Anglesea, and has issue,

  • Arthur Hampton, *b.* 1843; *m.* 1866 Alicia, 3rd dau. of John Forster, Esq., of Malverleys, Hants.

Mr. C. Longman, who was educated at Westminster School, is a Magistrate for Herts and the Liberty of St. Alban's.—*Shendish, Hemel Hempstead.*

LONGMAN, THOMAS, Esq., of Farnborough Hill, Surrey.
Eldest son of the late Thomas Norton Longman. of Hampstead, Middlesex. by Mary, dau. of — Slater, Esq.; *b.* 1804; *m.* 1838 Georgiana Townsend, eldest dau. of the late Major Bates, R.A. Mr. Longman, who is a Publisher in London, purchased this property from the Rev. J. Chandler in 1860.—*Farnborough Hill, Bagshot; Athenæum Club*, s.w.

LONGUEVILLE, THOMAS LONGUEVILLE, Esq., of Penylan, Shropshire.
Second but eldest surviving son of the late Thomas Longueville-Jones. Esq. (who assumed the name of Longueville), by Miss Anne Gibbons; *b.* 1803; *m.* 1838

Anne, 2nd dau. of Charles Thomas Jones, Esq., and has, with other issue,

• Thomas, *b.* 1844.

This family was formerly seated at Overton-Longueville, Hunts, and Wolverton, Bucks.—*Penylan, Oswestry.*

LONGWORTH, JOHN, Esq., of Glynwood, co. Westmeath.

Eldest son of the late Francis Longworth, Esq., of Glynwood, by Anne, dau. of James Whitaker, Esq., of Spark Brook, co. Warwick; *b.* 18—. Educated at Trinity Coll., Dublin; is a J.P. and D.L. for co. Westmeath (High Sheriff 1859), and for King's co. 1865.—*Glynwood, Athlone; Oatfield, Ballinasloe, co. Galway.*

LONSDALE, Earl of (WILLIAM LOWTHER, P.C., F.R.S.).—Cr. 1807.

Elder son of William, 1st Earl, by Lady Augusta, eldest dau. of John, 9th Earl of Westmoreland; *b.* 1787; *s.* 1844. Educated at Westminster and Trinity Coll., Cambridge; is Lord-Lieut. and Vice-Admiral of Westmoreland and Cumberland, Patron of 32 livings, and Lieut.-Col. Westmoreland Militia; was M.P. for Westmoreland 1818–31 and 1832–44; has been a Lord of the Admiralty and Treasurer, Chief Commissioner of Woods and Forests 1829–30; Treasurer of the Navy and Vice-President of the Board of Trade 1834–5; Postmaster-General 1841–6; President of the Council February–December, 1852; called to the Upper House in 1841 as Lord Lowther (cr. 1787).—*Lowther Castle, Penrith; The Castle, Whitehaven, Cumberland; St. Anne's, Barnes, s.w.; Athenæum, United Service, and Carlton Clubs, s.w.; 14, Carlton Terrace, s.w.*

Heir Pres., his nephew Henry (of Barley-Thorpe Hall, Oakham, co. Rutland), M.A. of Trinity Coll., Cambridge; a J.P. and D.L. for Cumberland, and a Magistrate for Westmoreland; M.P. for West Cumberland, Major of the Cumberland and Westmoreland Yeomanry Cavalry, and Hon. Col. Cumberland Volunteers; late Capt. 1st Life Guards (eldest son of the late Hon. Henry Cecil Lowther, M.P., who *d.* 1867, by Lady Lucy Eleanor, eldest dau. of Philip, 5th Earl of Harborough (ext.); *b.* 1818; *m.* 1852 Emily Susan, dau. of St. George Francis Caulfeild, Esq., and has, with other issue, • St. George Henry, *b.* 1855.

LONSDALE, JAMES JOHN, Esq., of Sandgate, Kent.

Second son of the late James Lonsdale, Esq. (the eminent artist), by Jane, dau. of Edward Thornton, Esq., of Lancaster; *b.* 1810; *m.* 1854 Jessica Matilda, only dau. of the late Samuel James Arnold, Esq., of Orchard House, Walton-on-Thames, Surrey, and widow of Dr. Herbert Mayo, F.R.S. (she *d.* 1866). Educated at University Coll., London; called to the Bar at Lincoln's Inn 1836; appointed Recorder of Folkestone 1847, and a Judge of County Courts on Circuit No. 11, 1855; was transferred to Circuit No. 48, 1867; is a Magistrate for the W. Riding of Yorkshire, and a J.P. and D.L. for Kent; was formerly Secretary to the Criminal Law Commissioners.—*The Cottage, Sandgate; Thorlcby House, Skipton, Yorkshire; Reform Club, s.w.*

LOPDELL, JOHN JOSEPH, Esq., of Raheen Park, co. Galway.

Eldest son of the late John Lopdell, Esq., J.P., of Raheen Park, by Jane, dau. of Peter Blake, Esq., of Corbally Castle, co. Galway; *b.* 1826; *s.* 1860. Educated at Trinity Coll., Dublin; is a Magistrate for co. Galway and Capt. Galway Militia.—*Raheen Park, Athenry.*

Heir Pres., his brother Thomas, *b.* 1832.

LOPES, Sir MASSEY, BART., of Maristow, Devon, (cr. 1805).

Eldest son of the late Sir Ralph Lopes, Bart., of Maristow (who was formerly M.P. for Westbury), by Susan Gibbs, dau. of Abraham Ludlow, Esq., of Heywood House, Wilts; *b.* 1818; *s.* as 3rd Bart. 1854; *m.* 1854 the Hon. Bertha, only dau. of John, 1st Lord Churston.

Educated at Winchester and Oriel Coll., Oxford (M.A. 1842); is a Magistrate for Wilts, a J.P. and D.L. for Devon (High Sheriff 1857), Lord of the Manor of West-bury, and Patron of 2 livings; formerly Capt. South Devon Militia; has been M.P. for Westbury since 1857.—*Maristow, Roborough, Plymouth; Manor House, Westbury, Wilts; Carlton and Conservative Clubs, s.w.*

Heir, his son Henry Yarde Buller, *b.* 1859.

LOPES, HENRY CHARLES, Esq., of East Hill, Somerset.

Third son of the late Sir Ralph Lopes, Bart., of Maristow, Devon, by Susan Gibbs, dau. of the late Abraham Ludlow, Esq., of Heywood House, Wilts; *b.* 1827; *m.* 1854 Cordelia Lucy, eldest dau. of the late Erving Clark, Esq., of Efford Manor, Devon, and has, with other surviving issue,

• Henry Ludlow, *b.* 186-.

Mr. Lopes, who was educated at Winchester and Balliol Coll., Oxford (B.A. 1849), and called to the Bar at the Inner Temple 1852, is a Magistrate for Wilts, a Member of the Western Circuit, and Recorder of Exeter; elected M.P. for Launceston 1868—*East Hill, Frome; 8, Cromwell Place, s.w.; Goldsmith Building, Temple, E.C.*

LOPES, RALPH LUDLOW, Esq., of Sandridge, Wilts.

Second son of the late Sir Ralph Lopes, Bart., of Maristow, by Susan Gibbs, dau. of Abraham Ludlow, Esq., of Heywood House, Westbury, Wilts; *b.* 1820; *m.* 1851 Elizabeth, 3rd dau. of Samuel T. Kekewich, Esq., M.P., of Peamore, and has, with other issue,

• Ralph Kekewich, *b.* 1852.

Mr. Lopes, who was educated at Winchester and Ch. Ch., Oxford (B.A. 1844, M.A. 1846), and called to the Bar at the Inner Temple 1847, is a J.P. and D.L. for Wilts, and a Magistrate for Devon and Somerset.—*Sandridge Park, Melksham.*

LORAINE, Sir LAMBTON, Bart. (cr. 1664).

Eldest son of the late Sir John Lambton Loraine, Bart., of Kirk Harle, by Caroline Isabella, eldest dau. of the Rev. Frederick Ekins, Rector of Morpeth and Ulgham; *b.* 1838; *s.* 1852. Is a Commander R.N.; has served on the Pacific and Mediterranean stations.

Heir Pres., his brother William Charles, late an Officer in the Indian Navy; served in Persia 1856–7; *b.* 1841.

LORD, JOHN PICKUP, Esq., of Elmley Park, Worcestershire.

Eldest son of the late John Lord, Esq., of Elmley Park, by Anne, dau. of Robert Pickup, Esq., of Blackburn, co. Lancaster; *b.* 1821; *s.* 1863; *m.* 1858 Constance Charlotte Hallet, 2nd dau. of Frederick Hale, Thomson, Esq., of Clarges Street, London, and has, with other issue,

• John Frederick, *b.* 1860.

Mr. Lord, who was educated at Rugby and Brasenose Coll., Oxford, was formerly Capt. 5th Royal Lancashire Militia and Lancashire Yeomanry Cavalry.—*Elmley Park, Pershore; Inglewood Bank, Penrith.*

✝LORD, FREDERICK BAYLY, Esq., of Farmborough, Somerset.

Only son of the late Rev. Samuel Curlewis Lord, D.D., Rector of Farmborough; *b.* 182-; *s.* 1867; *m.* 1865 Caroline Annie, elder dau. of the late Arthur Ley, Esq., of Bideford. Is Patron of the living of Farmborough.—*Farmborough, Bath.*

LORING, Lady.

Anna, dau. of the late Admiral Patton; *m.* 1804 Admiral Sir John Wentworth Loring, K.C.B., K.C.H., &c., who *d.* 1852.—*Ryde, Isle of Wight.*

597

LORING, the Rev. HENRY NELF, of Southwick and Boarhunt, Hants.
Eldest son of the late Admiral Sir John Wentworth Loring, K.C.B., K.C.H., of Peartree Green, near Southampton (who *d.* 1852), by Anna, dau. of the late Admiral Patton, of Fleetlands, near Fareham; *b.* 1811; *m.* 1863 Jean, 2nd dau. of the late Admiral Sir Charles Sullivan, Bart. (she *d.* 1865). Educated at Winchester and Exeter Coll., Oxford (B.A. 1832, M.A. 1837); appointed Incumbent of Southwick and Boarhunt 1860.—*Southwick, Fareham, Hants.*

LORNE, Marquis of. (See under *Argyll, Duke of.*)

LORTON, Viscount (ROBERT KING).—Cr. 1806.
Elder son of Robert Edward, 1st Viscount, G.C.B., by Lady Frances, eldest dau. of Edward, 1st Earl of Rosse; *b.* 1804; *s.* 1854; *m.* 1829 Anne, dau. of the late Sir Robert Gore-Booth, Bart. Is a Dep.-Lieut. for co. Sligo, and heir pres. to the Earldom of Kingston.—*Rockingham House, co. Roscommon.*

Heir, his son Robert Edward, J.P. and D.L. for co. Roscommon (of which he has been High Sheriff) ; *b.* 1831 ; *m.* 1854 the Hon. Augusta, dau. of Henry Spencer, 1st Lord Templemore, and has issue, *a dau.

LOTHIAN, Marquis of (WILLIAM SCHOMBERG ROBERT KERR).—Cr. 1701.
Eldest son of John, 7th Marquis, by Lady Cecil, dau. of Charles Chetwynd, 2nd Earl Talbot, and sister of Charles, 17th Earl of Shrewsbury ; *b.* 1832 ; *s.* 1841 ; *m.* 1857 Lady Constance Harriet, eldest surviving dau. of Henry, 18th Earl of Shrewsbury. Sits in the House of Lords as Lord Kerr, U.K. (cr. 1821). Educated at Eton and Ch. Ch., Oxford (B.A. 1854); is a J.P. and D.L. for Norfolk and Midlothian, and Capt. Edinburgh Militia.—*Blickling Hall, Aylsham; Newbattle Abbey, Dalkeith, co. Edinburgh; Mount Teviot, Jedburgh, N.B.; Carlton Club, s.w.*

Heir Pres., his brother Lord Schomberg Henry, 2nd Secretary of H.M.'s Legation at Frankfort, *b.* 1833 ; *m.* 1865 Lady Victoria Alexandrina, dau. of Walter, 5th Duke of Buccleuch, and has, with other issue, *William Walter Schomberg, *b.* 1867.

LOUGHBOROUGH, Lord.
(See under *Rosslyn, Earl of.*)

LOUIS, Sir JOHN, Bart., of Cadwell House, Devon (cr. 1806).
Eldest son of the late Thomas Louis, Esq. (who *d.* 1857), by Anne, dau. of the late Col. English; *b.* 1832; *s.* his grandfather as 3rd Bart. 1863 ; *m.* 1854 Fanny Anne, dau. of J. Bland, Esq. Is an officer in the Indian Civil Service.—*Cadwell House, Torquay.*

Heir Pres., his brother William Lumley, *b.* 1834.

LOUSADA, JOHN BARUH, Esq., of Peak House, Devon.
Second son of the late M. B. Lousada, Esq., of Finsbury Square, London, by Bella, dau. of J. Barrow, Esq., of Jamaica; *b.* 1809; *s.* his uncle in 1854 ; *m.* 1832 Tryphena, dau. of the late B. Barrow, Esq., J.P., of Bath, and has, with other issue,

* Mortimer John, *b.* 1841.

Mr. Lousada, who is a Magistrate for Devon, and Major Devon Artillery Volunteers, was formerly Capt. Hants Militia.—*Peak House, Sidmouth ; Portland Club, w.*

LOUTH, Lord (RANDALL PERCY OTTWAY PLUNKETT).—Cr. 1541.
Eldest son of Thomas Oliver, 12th Lord, by Anne Maria, dau. of the late Philip Roche, Esq., of Donore, co. Kildare; *b.* 1832 ; *s.* 1849 ; *m.* 1867 Anne Maria McGeough, 2nd dau. of the late Walton McGeough Bond, Esq. Educated at Eton ; formerly Lieut. 79th and
598

24th Foot. Descended from a common ancestor with Lord Dunsany.—*Louth Hall, Drogheda, co. Louth ; Junior United Service Club, s.w.*

Heir Pres., his brother Thomas Oliver Westenra, Capt. 1st Foot ; *b.* 1838 ; *m.* 1862 Clara Anne, only child of John Kirkby, Esq., of Fern Bank, co. York, and by her, who *d.* 1867, has issue, *a son, *b.* 1867.

LOVAINE, Lord. (See under *Beverley, Earl of.*)

LOVAT, Lord (THOMAS ALEXANDER FRASER, K.T.).—Cr. 1472.
Only son of the late Alexander Fraser, Esq., of Stricken co. Aberdeen (some time Capt. Dragoon Guards, who *d.* 1803), by his 1st wife Amelia, eldest dau. of John Leslie, Esq., of Balquhain, co. Aberdeen, and eldest representative of the Hon. Thomas, 2nd son of Alexander, 6th Lord Lovat; *b.* 1802; *m.* 1823 the Hon. Charlotte Georgiana, eldest dau. of George William, 8th Lord Stafford. Is Lord-Lieutenant of co. Inverness, and a Dep.-Lieut. for cos. Banff and Aberdeen; sits in the House of Peers as Lord Lovat, U.K. (cr. 1837). The Scotch Barony was forfeited in the Scottish Rebellion of 1745, but restored in 1857.—*Beaufort Castle, Beauly, N.B. ; Reform and Brooks's Clubs, s.w.*

Heir, his son Simon, Master of Lovat, a Dep.-Lieut. for co. Inverness, Lieut.-Col. Inverness Militia, and Capt. 7th Aberdeenshire Rifle Volunteers; *b.* 1828 ; *m.* 1866 Alice Mary, dau. of Thomas Weld-Blundell, Esq., of Ince Blundell Hall, co. Lancaster, and has issue, *Simon Thomas Joseph, *b.* 1867.

LOVEDEN. (See *Pryse.*)

LOVELACE, Earl of (WILLIAM KING-NOEL).—Cr. 1838.
Elder son of Peter, 7th Lord King, by Lady Hester, eldest dau. of Hugh, 1st Earl Fortescue, K.G.; *b.* 1805; *s.* as Lord King 1833 ; was raised to the Earldom in 1838 ; *m.* 1st 1835 the Hon. Augusta Ada, only child of George Gordon, 6th Lord Byron (she *d.* 1852) ; 2nd 1865 Jean Crawford, widow of Edward Jenkins, Esq., of the Bengal Civil Service. Educated at Eton and Trinity Coll., Cambridge; is Lord-Lieutenant and Custos Rotulorum of Surrey, a Magistrate for Somerset. Patron of 5 livings, and Col. 2nd Surrey Militia. Assumed the additional name of Noel by Royal licence in 1860.—*East Horseley, Ripley, Surrey; Ashley Combe, Minehead, Somerset; Athenæum Club, s.w.*

Heir, his son Ralph Gordon, Viscount Ockham (see *Wentworth, Lord*).

LOVELL, PETER AUDLEY, Esq., of Cole Park, Wilts.
Eldest son of the late Peter Harvey Lovell, Esq., of Cole Park, by Charlotte, dau. of the late Ven. Archdeacon Willes; *b.* 1808; *s.* 1841; *m.* 1857 Mary Jane, dau. of the late David Pugh, Esq., M.P., of Llanerchydol, co. Montgomery, and has, with other issue,

* Peter Audley David, *b.* 1857.

Mr. Lovell, who is a J.P. and D.L. for Wilts, was formerly in the 7th Dragoon Guards.—*Cole Park, Malmesbury; Carlton Club, s.w.*

+LOVERIDGE, CHARLES WARRE, Esq., of Paradise House, Dorsetshire.
Son of the late C. Loveridge, Esq., of Paradise House; *b.* 18—; is a Magistrate for Devon, Dorset, and Somerset, and a Banker at Chard.—*Paradise House, Chardstock, and Bank House, Chard.*

LOVESY, CONWAY WHITHORNE, Esq., of Charlton Kings, Gloucestershire.
Eldest surviving son of the late Conway Whithorne Lovesy, Esq., of Charlton Kings, by Margaret, dau. of James Bennett, Esq., of Elkstone and Tetbury, co. Gloucester; *b.* 1818 ; *s.* 1846 ; *m.* 1847 Colin Campbell.

dau. of Rear-Admiral Edward Lloyd, K.H., and has issue a daughter,

* Colin Campbell.

Mr. Lovesy, who was educated at Bridgenorth and Queen's Coll., Oxford (B.A. 1841), and called to the Bar at the Middle Temple 1845, is a Magistrate for co. Gloucester, and late Capt. R. S. Gloucester Militia. —*Charlton Kings, Cheltenham; Junior United Service Club, s.w.; 2, Plowden Buildings, Temple, E.C.*

LOVETT, JOHN HENNIKER, Esq., of Fernhill Hall, Shropshire.

Eldest son of the late Thomas Lovett, Esq., J.P. and D.L. of Fernhill Hall. by the Hon. Emily, 3rd dau. of John, 3rd Lord Henniker; *b.* 1836; *s.* 1863; *m.* 1859 Laura, dau. of the late Philip Morier, Esq., H.M. Minister at Dresden, and has, with other issue,

* Horace William Fitz Roy, b. 1862.

Mr. Lovett, who was educated at Eton, is a J.P. and D.L. for Shropshire; he was formerly Capt. 2nd Life Guards.—*Fernhill Hall, Oswestry; Arthur's Club, s.w.*

LOVETT, PHILIPS COSBY, Esq., of Liscombe House, Bucks.

Fourth son of the late Robert Lovett, Esq., of Limerick, Ireland, by Mary, dau. of — Howell, Esq.; *b.* 1814; *s.* 1855 under the will of his kinswoman Miss Elizabeth Lovett (only surviving child of the late Sir Jonathan Lovett, Bart., *ext.*); *m.* 1844 Katherine, dau. of — Gubbins, Esq., and has, with other issue, an only son,

* Philips, b. 1846.

Mr. Lovett, who is a J.P. and D.L. for Bucks (High Sheriff 1863), Lord of the Manors of Liscombe, Hollingdon, and Soulbury, and alternate Patron of the living of Soulbury, was formerly Capt. R.N.—*Liscombe House, Leighton Buzzard.*

LOVETT, Major THOMAS HEATON, of Belmont, Shropshire.

Eldest son of the late Joseph Venables Lovett, Esq., of Belmont (who was a J.P. and D.L. for county Salop), High Sheriff in 1847), by Margaret, 2nd dau. of the late Richard Heaton, Esq., of Plâs Heaton, co. Denbigh; *b.* 1817; *s.* 1866; *m.* 1851 Cecil Elizabeth, dau. of the late Wilson Jones, Esq., M.P., of Hartsheath Park, co. Flint, and has, with other issue,

* Hubert Richard, b. 1854.

Major Lovett, who was educated at the R. M. Coll., Sandhurst, is a Magistrate for co. Salop, Lieut.-Col. 2nd Salop Rifle Volunteers, and a Major in the Army retired; was formerly in the 98th Foot.—*Belmont and Ebnal Lodge, Oswestry.*

LOW, Sir JOHN, K.C.B., of Clattow, Fifeshire (cr. 1862).

Eldest son of the late Robert Low, Esq., of Clatto, by Susan, dau. of the late Dr. Robert Malcolm; *b.* 1788; *m.* 1829 Augusta, dau. of the late John Talbot Shakespear, Esq. Educated at St. Andrew's University; is a General in the Indian Army, which he entered in 1805. —*Clatto, Cupar-Fife, N.B.; United Service Club, s.w.; Oriental Club, w.*

LOW, JOHN, Esq., of Sunvale, co. Limerick.

Eldest son of the late Peter Low, Esq., D.L., of Lowtown, co. Limerick, by Louisa, dau. of the late Sir Richard Butler, Bart., of Garryhundon, co. Carlow; *b.* 1813; *s.* 1842; *m.* 1841 Sophia Georgiana, dau. of George Mahon, Esq., of Mount Pleasant, co. Mayo, and has, with other issue,

* George Peter, B.A. of Oriel Coll., Oxford, and Cornet 8th Hussars; b. 1843.

Mr. Low, who was educated at Trinity Coll., Dublin

(B.A. 1832, M.A. 1833), and called to the Irish Bar 1835, is a J.P. and D.L. for co. Limerick (High Sheriff 1852).—*Sunvale, Kilmallock, co. Limerick; Kildare Street Club, Dublin.*

LOWE, Col. ARTHUR CHARLES, of Court of Hill, Shropshire.

Younger son of the late Thomas Humphrey Lowe, Esq., by Lucy, dau. of Thomas Hill, Esq., of Court of Hill; *b.* 1796; *m.* 1st 1841 Mary, only dau. of Benjamin Flounders, Esq., of Calmington, co. Salop; 2nd 1846 Caroline Elizabeth, dau. of Thomas Baker, Esq., of Ashurst Lodge, Kent, and by her, who *d.* 1861, has, with other issue,

* Arthur Hill Lowe, b. 1847.

Mr. Lowe, who was educated at Westminster, is a Magistrate for co. Worcester, a J.P. and D.L. for co. Salop, and a Col. in the Army; was formerly in the 16th Lancers.—*Court of Hill, Tenbury.*

LOWE, EDWARD JOSEPH, Esq., of Highfield House, Notts.

Second son of the late Alfred Lowe, Esq., J.P., of Highfield House, by Charlotte Octavia, youngest dau. of Edward Swann, Esq., of Nottingham; *b.* 1825; *s.* 1865; *m.* 1848 Annie, eldest dau. of George Allcock, Esq., of Nottingham, and has, with other issue,

* Alfred Edward Lawson, Lieut. Royal Sherwood Foresters, b. 1849.

Mr. Lowe is a Fellow of the Royal Society; also a Fellow of the Royal Astronomical, Linnean, Geological, Zoological, and Meteorological Societies. This family is of long standing in co. Chester, but settled in Nottinghamshire about 1710.—*Highfield House, Nottingham.*

LOWE, the Rev. JOHN.

Eldest son of the late Rev. John Lowe, Rector of Tenkersley, Yorkshire, and Prebendary of York, by Elizabeth, dau. of John Jackson, Esq., of Fairburn, co. York; *b.* 1790; *m.* 1815 Susanna, eldest dau. of the Rev. Thomas Hind, M.A., Rector of Ardley, and has, with other issue,

* Thomas, M.A. of Oriel Coll., Oxford, Vicar of Willingdon, Sussex; b. 1818; m. 1847 Harriet De Saumarez, dau. of William Dalgairns, Esq., and has, with other issue, * Henry, b. 1851.

Mr. Lowe, who was educated at Lincoln Coll., Oxford (B.A. 1813, M.A. 1839), is a Magistrate for Oxon; he was appointed Rector of Ardley 1815, and was formerly Incumbent of Swinton, co. York.—*Ardley Rectory, Bicester.*

LOWE, the Right Hon. ROBERT, of Caterham, Surrey.

Son of the late Rev. Robert Lowe. Rector of Bingham, Notts, by Mary, dau. of the Rev. Reginald Pyndar, Rector of Madresfield, co. Worcester; *b.* 1811; *m.* 1836 Georgiana, dau. of the late George Orred. Esq., of Aigbirth House, co. Lancaster. Educated at Winchester and University Coll., Oxford (B.A. 1833), and was afterwards Fellow of Magdalen Coll.; called to the Bar at Lincoln's Inn 1842, and practised at the Australian Bar; is a Magistrate for Surrey, and a Trustee of the British Museum; was a Member of the Council at Sydney 1848-50, and M.P. for Sydney 1848-50; Joint Secretary to the Board of Control 1852-5; Paymaster of the Forces and Vice-President of the Board of Trade 1855-8; Vice-President of the Committee of Council on Education 1859-64; was M.P. for Kidderminster 1852-9; elected M.P. for Calne 1859. — *Caterham, Croydon; Reform Club, s.w.; 34, Lowndes Square, s.w*

LOWE, WILLIAM DRURY, Esq., of Locko, Derbyshire.

Eldest son of the late Robert Holden. Esq., by Mary Anne, dau. and heir of William Drury Lowe, Esq., of

Locko Park, co. Derby, whose name he has assumed; *b.* 1802; *s.* his maternal grandmother 1848; *m.* 1827 the Hon. Caroline Esther, dau. of Nathaniel, 2nd Lord Scarsdale, and has, with other issue,

* William Drury Nathaniel, late Lieut. 11th Hussars, *b.* 1828.

Mr. Lowe, who was educated at Ch. Ch., Oxford (B.A. 1826), is a J.P. and D.L. for co. Derby (High Sheriff 1854), Lord of the Manor of Denby, and Patron of 2 livings.—*Locko Park, Derby;* 10, *Green Street,* w.

LOWE. (See *Hill.*)

LOWE. (See *Sherbrooke.*)

LOWIS, JOHN, Esq., of Plean, Stirlingshire.
Only surviving son of the late Ninian Lowis, Esq., of Plean, (who *d.* 1825), by Isabella, dau. of John Monro, Esq., of Auchenbowie, co. Stirling; *b.* 1801; *s.* his brother Robert 1856; *m.* 1823 Louisa, dau. of John Fendall Esq., and has, with other issue,

* John Mangles, of the Indian Civil Service; *b.* 1827.; *m.* 1854 Ellen, dau. of R. D. Mangles, Esq.

Mr. Lowis, who was educated at the High School, Edinburgh, and East India Coll., Hayleybury, is a J.P. and D.L. for co. Stirling; he was formerly in the Bengal Civil Service, and a Member of the Supreme Council of India.—*Plean, Stirling, N.B.*

LOWNDES, the Rev. CHARLES WILLIAM SELBY-, B.A., of North Crawley, Bucks.
Youngest son of the late William Selby-Lowndes, Esq., of Whaddon Hall, by Ann Isabella, dau. of the Rev. Graham Hanmer; *b.* 1815; *m.* 1840 Laura Ann, dau. of Thomas Delves Broughton, Esq., and by her, who *d.* 1865, has, with other issue,

* Charles William, Lieut. 93rd Foot, *b.* 1845.

Mr. C. Selby-Lowndes, who was educated at Harrow and Christ's Coll., Cambridge (B.A. 1840), is a Magistrate for Bucks, and Rector of North Crawley.—*North Crawley, Newport Pagnell.*

LOWNDES, EDWARD CHADDOCK, Esq., of Palterton, Derbyshire, and Castle Combe, Wilts.
Eldest son of the late Edward Chaddock Lowndes, Esq. (formerly Gorst), by Elizabeth, dau. of J. D. Nesham, Esq., of Houghton-le-Spring, co. Durham; *b.* 1833; *s.* 1859. Educated at Rugby and Trinity Coll., Cambridge (B.A. 1856, M.A. 1859); is a Magistrate for co. Lancaster, Lord of the Manor for Castle Combe, and Patron of 1 living. He assumed the name of Lowndes in lieu of Gorst, by royal licence, in 1852, and purchased the property of Castle Combe in 1867 from Mr. Poulett Scrope, M.P.—*Castle Combe, Chippenham; Palterton Hall, Mansfield; Oxford and Cambridge Club,* s.w.; 84, *Eaton Place,* w.

Heir Pres., his brother J. E. Gorst, Esq., M.P. (whom see).

LOWNDES, EDWARD WILLIAM SELBY-, Esq., of Winslow House, Bucks.
Fifth son of the late William Selby-Lowndes, Esq., of Whaddon Hall, by Ann Isabella, dau. of the Rev. Graham Hanmer; *b.* 1813; *m.* 1834 Mary Elizabeth, dau. of Isaac R. Hartman, Esq., and has, with other issue,

* William Seymour, *b.* 1838.

Mr. E. Selby-Lowndes, who was educated at Harrow, is a Magistrate for Bucks.—*Winslow House, and Whaddon Hall, Winslow, Bucks; Conservative Club,* s.w.

LOWNDES, GEORGE ALAN, Esq., of Barrington Hall, Essex.
Eldest son of William Clayton, Esq., of Lostock Hall, co. Lancaster, by Mary, dau. of Edward Gorst, Esq., of Preston; *b.* 1829; *s.* 1840 under the will of his cousin Thomas Lowndes, Esq., of Barrington Hall (whose name he assumed by Royal licence); *m.* 1st 1856 Helen

600

Emma, dau. of the Rev. Arthur Johnson Daniell, of Rampisham Manor, Dorset (she *d.* 1863); 2nd 1864 Fanny, dau. of the late George Farley, Esq., of Henwick and Crowle, co. Worcester; he has by the former, with other issue,

* Alan Herbert Wattington, *b.* 1859.

Mr. Lowndes, who was educated at Trinity Coll., Cambridge (B.A. 1853, M.A. 1856), is a J.P. and D.L. for Essex (High Sheriff 1861), and a Magistrate for Herts, Lord of the Manors of Hatfield Broad Oak and Fouchers Heron, Essex, and was formerly Capt. West Essex Yeomanry Cavalry.—*Barrington Hall, Harlow; Carlton and Oxford and Cambridge Clubs,* s.w.

LOWNDES, JAMES, Esq., of Arthurlie, Renfrewshire.
Eldest son of the late William Lowndes, Esq., of Arthurlie, by Janet, dau. of Adam Keir, Esq., Banker, of Paisley, N.B.; *b.* 1822; *s.* 1849; *m.* 1859 Eleanor Jane, dau. of John Marston, Esq. Is a Magistrate for co. Renfrew, and Capt. Prince of Wales's Regt. Renfrew Militia; appointed to H.M.'s Royal Body-guard 1858.—*Arthurlie, Renfrew, N.B.; Junior United Service and Windham Clubs,* s.w.

LOWNDES, RICHARD WILLIAM SELBY-, Esq., of Bletchley, Bucks.
Third son of the late William Selby-Lowndes, Esq., of Whaddon Hall, Bucks, by Ann Isabella, dau. of the Rev. Graham Hanmer, of Sympson, Bucks; *b.* 1811; *m.* 1842 Mary Susan, dau. of the Rev. William Fletcher, of Harwell, Berks, and has, with other issue,

* Richard William, *b.* 1848.

Mr. R. W. Selby-Lowndes, who was educated at Harrow, and St. John's Coll., Cambridge, is a Magistrate for Bucks.—*The Elms, Bletchley, Bucks.*

LOWNDES, WILLIAM, Esq., of Chesham Bury, Bucks.
Eldest son of the late William Lowndes, Esq.,‡ of Chesham Bury (a J.P. and D.L. for Bucks, and High Sheriff 1848), by his 1st wife Mary Harriet, 3rd dau. of Kender Mason, Esq., of Beel House, Amersham; *b.* 1834; *s.* 1864. Is a Magistrate for Bucks. The petition of this family for the ancient Barony of Monthermer is now (1868) before the Committee of Privileges in the House of Lords.—*The Bury, Chesham, Bucks.*

LOWNDES, WILLIAM LAYTON, Esq., of Broughton, Bucks.
Only son of the late Henry Dalston Lowndes, Esq., by Sarah, dau. of William Lowe, Esq.; *b.* 1822; *m.* 1850 Jane Alexandrina, eldest dau. of Sir Alexander Young Spearman, Bart. Mr. Lowndes, who was educated at Winchester and Oriel Coll., Oxford (B.A. 1844, M.A. 1848), and called to the Bar at Lincoln's Inn 1848, is a J.P. and D.L. for co. Salop, and a J.P. for Wenlock and Bridgnorth.—*Linley Hall, Bridgnorth.*

+LOWNDES, WILLIAM SELBY-, Esq., of Whaddon Hall, Bucks.
Eldest son of the late William Selby-Lowndes, Esq., M.P., of Whaddon Hall (who assumed the additional name of Selby in 1813, in respect to the memory of Thomas Selby-Lowndes, Esq., of Warendon and Whaddon Hall), by Ann Isabella, dau. of the Rev. Graham Hanmer; *b.* 1807; *s.* 1849; *m.* 1st 1833 Lucy, dau. of the late Isaac Rawlings Hartman, Esq.; 2nd 1854

‡ His great-grandfather was the well-known financier in the reign of Queen Anne, to whom the nation is indebted for originating the funding system. He was for many years a member of the House of Commons and Chairman of Ways and Means. Mr. Lowndes is entitled to quarter the Royal Arms, as one of the co. representatives of Margaret Plantagenet, Countess of Salisbury —See 'The Patrician,' vol. v., p. 781.

Clara, 2nd dau. of the late I. R. Hartman, Esq. (she d. 1864). He has, with other issue,

* William, b. 1835 ; m. 1867 Jessie Mary, dau. of Lieut.-Gen. Lechmere Worrell, and widow of Eyre Coote, Esq., of West Park, Hants.

Mr. Selby-Lowndes is a Magistrate for Bucks, and Patron of 1 living.—*Whaddon Hall, Winslow.*

LOWNDES-NORTON, Mrs., of Brightwell Park, Oxon.

Catherine Isabella, eldest dau. of the late William Charles Lowndes, Esq. (who d. 1845), by Catherine, 2nd dau. of the Rev. Reginald Wynniatt; s. her grandfather William Francis Lowndes-Stone, Esq., of Brightwell Park, 1855; m. 1862 her cousin, Capt. Robert Thomas Norton, late of the Grenadier Guards (who assumed her name), and has, with other issue,

* Roger Fletcher Earle, b. 1863.

This lady is one of the representatives of the family of Lowndes, of Orton and Lee Hall, co. Chester, and this branch of the family assumed the additional name of Stone in 1740.—*Brightwell Park, Tetsworth.*

LOWRY, JAMES CORRY, Esq., of Rockdale House, co. Tyrone.

Eldest son of the late James Lowry, Esq., of Rockdale, by Henrietta, dau. of Thomas Pepper, of Gallygarth Castle, co. Meath; b. 1809; m. 1st 1832 Dorinda, dau. of the late Capt. Jones; 2nd 1847 Ellen, widow of Frederick Gamble, Esq.; 3rd 1850 Anne, dau. of Booth Jones Esq., and has by the former, with other issue,

* James Corry Jones, 2nd Capt. R.A.; b. 1835 ; m. 1863 Elizabeth Jackson, 2nd dau. of Thomas Greer, Esq., of Tullylagan, co. Tyrone, and widow of the Rev. Thomas F. Bushe, and has issue * a dau.

Mr. Lowry, who was called to the Irish Bar in 1837, is a Magistrate for co. Tyrone.—*Rockdale House, Dungannon, co. Tyrone;* 42, *Mountjoy Square South, Dublin.*

LOWRY, JOHN FETHERSTONHAUGH, Esq., of Pomeroy House, co. Tyrone.

Second son of Robert William Lowry, Esq., of Pomeroy (whom see), by Anna, only dau. of Admiral Graves, b. 1819; m. 1854 Dora Elizabeth, dau. of W. Moore, Esq., and relict of George Folliott, Esq., of Vicar's Cross, near Chester, and has issue,

* Anna Graves.

Mr. Lowry, who was educated at Rugby and Brasenose Coll., Oxford (B.A. 1840), and called to the Irish Bar in 1843, is a Magistrate for co. Tyrone.—*Kildare Street Club, Dublin ;* 11, *Fitzwilliam Place, Dublin.*

LOWRY, ROBERT WILLIAM, Esq., of Pomeroy House, co. Tyrone.

Second but eldest surviving son of the late Robert Lowry, Esq., of Pomeroy House, by Hester, dau. of Major William Tighe, of Ballyshannon; b. 1787; m. 1815 Anna, only dau. of Admiral Graves, and has, with other issue,

* Robert William, educated at Brasenose Coll., Oxford (B.A. 1840) ; a Magistrate for co. Tyrone (High Sheriff 1852) ; b. 1818 ; m. 1852 Fanny, dau. and heir of Benjamin Geale-Brady, Esq., of Mount Geale, co. Kilkenny, and has issue.

Mr. Lowry is a J.P. and D.L. for co. Tyrone (High Sheriff 1812).—*Pomeroy House, Dungannon ; Belmore Place, co. Westmeath ; United Service Club, Dublin.*

LOWRY, WILLIAM, Esq., of Drumreagh, co. Tyrone.

Fifth son of the late Robert Lowry, Esq., of Pomeroy House, co. Tyrone, by Hester, dau. of Major William Tighe, of Ballyshannon, b. 1793; m. 1819 Isabella,

dau. of the Rev. James Graham, Rector of Pomeroy, and has, with other issue,

* Robert William, b. 1824; m. 1852 Emily, dau. of the late Sir Henry G. Ward, G.C.M.G.

Mr. Lowry was formerly in the Royal Navy.—*Drumreagh, Dungannon, co. Tyrone.*

LOWRY-CORRY, the Hon. HENRY WILLIAM, of Edwardston Hall, Suffolk.

Youngest son of Armar, 3rd Earl of Belmore, by Emily Louise, younger dau. of the late William Shepherd, Esq., of Bradbourne, Kent; b. 1845; s. his grandmother, Mrs. Shepherd, 1864. Educated at Trinity Coll., Cambridge; is a Magistrate for Suffolk, Lord of the Manor and Patron of Edwardston ; and Ensign and Lieutenant Coldstream Guards.—*Edwardston Hall, Boxford.*

LOWRY-CORRY. (See under *Belmore, Earl of.*)

LOWRY-CORRY. (See *Corry.*)

LOWSON, WILLIAM, Esq., of Balthayock, Perthshire.

Eldest son of the late Alexander Lowson. Esq., W.S., of Arbroath, N.B., by Margaret, dau. of Capt. Andrew Small; b. 1814 ; m. 1851 Helen, dau. of William Flowerdew, Esq., Dundee, and has other issue,

* William, b. 1852.

Mr. Lowson is a Merchant at Dundee.—*Balthayock House ; Gray Bank, Dundee, N.B.*

LOWTHER, Sir JOHN HENRY, Bart.,+ of Swillington House, Yorkshire (cr. 1824).

Eldest son of the late Sir John Lowther, Bart., by Lady Elizabeth, dau. of John, 9th Earl of Westmoreland ; b. 1793 ; s. as 2nd Bart. 1844. Educated at Westminster; is a Dep.-Lieut. for the N. and W. Ridings of co. York (High Sheriff 1852), and Patron of 3 livings; was M.P. for Wigton 1831-2, and for York 1835-47. This family is a younger branch of that of the Earl of Lonsdale. —*Swillington House, Leeds ; Wilton Castle, Redcar, Yorkshire ;* 127, *Park Street, Grosvenor Square,* w.

Heir Pres., his brother Charles Hugh, b. 1803 ; m. 1524 Isabella, dau. of the late Rev. Robert Morehead, D.D., Rector of Easington, co. Durham, and has, with other issue, * George, b. 1837.

LOWTHER, the Rev. BERESFORD, of Turmastone, Herefordshire.

A younger son of the late Gorges Lowther, Esq., formerly of Kilrue, Westmeath (who was M.P. for Ratoath, Ireland, 1790-1800), by Julia, dau. of the late Rev. Thomas Huntingford; b. 1815; m. 1849 Laura Alice, 3rd dau. of the late Lieut.-General Horsford. Educated at Exeter Coll., Oxford (B.A. 1857): appointed Vicar of Vowchurch, co. Hereford, 1838 ; is Domestic Chaplain to the Earl of Lonsdale, and a Magistrate for co. Hereford.—*Turmastone, Hereford.*

LOWTHER, the Rev. BRABAZON, of Shrigley Hall, Cheshire.

A younger son of the late Gorges Lowther, Esq., formerly of Kilrue, co. Meath, by Julia, dau. of the Rev. T. Huntingford; b. 1813; m. 1847 Eden Jane, only child of the late Thomas Legh, Esq., M.P., of Lyme Park, co. Chester, and has, with other issue,

* Brabazon, b. 1847.

Mr. Lowther, who was educated at Lausanne and Merton Coll., Oxford (B.A. 1834), is a Magistrate for Cheshire, Lord of the Manor of Shrigley, and Patron of that living.—*Shrigley Hall, Macclesfield.*

LOWTHER, the Rev. GORGES PAULIN, of Orcheston St. George, Wilts.

Eldest son of the late Gorges Lowther, Esq., of Kilrue, co. Meath, by Catherine Pauline, dau. of M. Cayen de

‡ Died whilst these sheets were at press.

Montbrison, of Herault, France; *b.* 1792; *s.* 1854; *m.* 1815 Elizabeth, dau. of Edward Charles Windsor, Esq. (who was High Sheriff of Shropshire in 1807, and collaterally descended from the same ancestor now represented by the Baroness Windsor), and by her, who *d.* 1866, has, with other issue,

• Gorges, *b.* 1824 ; *m.* 1858 Lillie, dau. of P. W. Walsh, Esq.; she *d. s. p.* 1860.

Mr. Lowther, who was educated at Winchester and St. Mary's Hall, Oxford (B.A. 1815, M.A. 1819), is a Magistrate for Wilts, Rector of Orcheston St. George, Rural Dean, Prebendary of Sarum, and Proctor in Convocation for the Diocese of Sarum.—*Orcheston St. George, Devizes.*

LOWTHER, JAMES, Esq., of Bawtry Hall, Yorkshire.
Second son of Charles Hugh Lowther, Esq., by Isabella, dau. of the Rev. R. Morehead, D.D., and nephew of Sir J. H. Lowther, Bart.; *b.* 1840. Educated at Westminster and Trinity Coll., Cambridge (B.A. 1862); called to the Bar at Inner Temple 1864; elected M.P. for York 1865.—*Bawtry Hall, Doncaster*; 3, *Paper Buildings, Temple*, E.C.

LOWTHER, of Barleythorpe.
(See under *Lonsdale, Earl of*.)

LOXDALE, JAMES, Esq., of Castle Hill, Cardiganshire.
Third, but eldest surviving, son of the late Joseph Loxdale, Esq. (who was formerly High Steward and Deputy-Recorder of Shrewsbury), by Anna Maria, dau. of Mr. William Wood, of Bayston, co. Salop: *b.* 1797; *s.* 1846. Educated at Shrewsbury and St. John's Coll., Cambridge (B.A. 1820, M.A. 1823); called to the Bar at the Middle Temple 1825; is a J.P. and D.L. for cos. Salop, Stafford, and Cardigan (High Sheriff 1867). This family was formerly of Shrewsbury and Albrighton, co. Salop.—*Castle Hill, Aberystwith*; *University Club*, s.w.

Heir Pres., his brother John. *b.* 1799; *m.* 1st 1830 Anne, only child of the late Thomas Loxdale, Esq., J.P. and D.L. (she *d.* 1848); 2nd 1854 Anna Rice, dau. of the Rev. John Watson, D.D.

LOYD, EDWARD, Esq., of Lillesden, Kent.
Second son of the late Edward Loyd, Esq., of Coombe House, Croydon, Surrey (a Banker in London and Manchester, who *d.* 1863), by Sarah, dau. of Joseph Taylor, Esq., of Blackley, co. Lancaster: *b.* 1820; *m.* 1846 Caroline Louisa, dau. of John Frederick Foster, Esq., of Sale Priory, co. Lancaster, and has, with other issue,

• Frederick Edward, *b.* 1856.

Mr. Loyd, who was educated at Eton and Trinity Coll., Cambridge, is a Magistrate for Kent, a J.P. and D.L. for co. Lancaster, and Lieut.-Col. 1st Manchester Rifle Volunteers.—*Lillesden, Hawkhurst, Staplehurst*; *Oxford and Cambridge and Junior Carlton Clubs*, w.

LOYD, LEWIS Esq., of Monk's Orchard, Surrey.
Eldest son of the late Edward Loyd, Esq., of Coombe House (who was a Magistrate for co. Lancaster, and formerly a Banker at Manchester), by Sarah, dau. of Joseph Taylor, Esq., of Blackley, co. Lancaster; *b.* 1811; *s.* 1863; *m.* 1845 Frances Harriet, dau. of the late Admiral the Hon. Frederick Paul Irby, of Boyland Hall, Norfolk. Educated at Eton and Trinity Coll. Cambridge; was a Banker in London, and is a Commissioner of Lieutenancy for that city; he is a Magistrate for Surrey (High Sheriff 1863).—*Monk's Orchard, Bromley, Kent*; 20, *Hyde Park Gardens*, w.

Heir Pres., his brother Edward, of Lillesden, Kent (whom see).

602

LOYD, WILLIAM JONES, Esq., of Langleybury, Herts.
Third son of the late Edward Loyd, Esq., of Greenhill Manchester, by Sarah, dau. of Joseph Taylor, Esq., and cousin of Lord Overstone; *b.* 1821; *m.* 1848 Caroline Gertrude, 3rd dau. of the late John H. Vivian, Esq., M.P., of Singleton, co. Glamorgan, by whom he has, with other issue,

• Lewis Vivian, *b.* 1852.

Mr. Loyd is a Magistrate for Herts (High Sheriff 1861). —*Langleybury, Watford*; 77, *Eaton Square*, s.w.

LOYD-LINDSAY, ROBERT JAMES, Esq., of Lockinge Hall, Berks.
Second son of the late Lieut.-Gen. James Lindsay, of Balcarres, co. Fife (grandson of James, 5th Earl of Balcarres), by his 2nd wife Anne, dau. of the late Sir Coutts Trotter, Bart., of Westrille, co. Lincoln; *b.* 1832; *m.* 1858 the Hon. Harriet Sarah, only dau. of Lord Overstone, when he assumed, by Royal licence, the additional name of Loyd. Educated at Eton; is a Magistrate for Berks and co. Northampton, Lieut.-Col. in the Army, and Lieut.-Col. Hon. London Artillery Company; late of the Scots Fusilier Guards, and formerly Equerry to H.R.H. the Prince of Wales; elected M.P. for Berks 1865.—*Lockinge Hall, Wantage*; *Guards' Club*, s.w.; 2, *Carlton Gardens*, s.w.

LUARD, GEORGE AUGUSTUS, Esq., of Blyborough Hall, Lincolnshire.
Eldest son of the late Charles Bourryan Luard, Esq. of Blyborough Hall, by Henrietta, dau. of John Armytage, Esq., of Northampton; *b.* 1824; *s.* 1855; *m.* 1855 Maria Louisa Elizabeth, 4th dau. of the Rev Joseph Story, of Bingfield, co. Cavan, Ireland. Educated at Jesus Coll., Cambridge; is a Magistrate for co. Lincoln.—*Blyborough Ha'l, Kirton in Lindsey.*

Heir Pres., his nephew John Godfrey (son of the late John Godfrey Luard, Esq., who *d.* 1862), *b.* 1842.

LUARD-SELBY, Mrs., of Ightham Mote, Kent.
Lewis Marianne, eldest dau. and co-heir of the late Prideaux John Selby, Esq., of Twizell House, Northumberland, and of The Mote, Kent, by Lewis Tabitha, dau. of the late Bertram Mitford, Esq., of Mitford Castle, in the same co.; *m.* 1st 1832 Charles John Bigge, Esq., eldest son of the late Charles William Bigge, Esq., of Linden, Northumberland (he *d.* 1846); 2nd 1848 Major Robert Luard (7th son of the late Peter J. Luard, Esq., of Blyborough Hall, co. Lincoln), who, with his wife, assumed the additional surname of Selby in 1867. —*The Mote, Ightham, Tunbridge.*

LUARD, Capt. WILLIAM GARNHAM, C.B., of Witham Lodge, Essex.
Eldest son of the late William Wright Luard, Esq., J.P. and D.L., of Witham Lodge, by Charlotte, only child of Thomas Garnham, Esq., of Felsham Hall, Suffolk; *b.* 1820; *s.* 1857; *m.* 1858 Charlotte, 3rd dau. of the late Rev. Henry Du Cane, of The Grove, Witham, Essex, and has, with other issue,

• William Du Cane, *b.* 1861.

Capt. Luard is a Magistrate for Essex and a Capt. R.N.; late Lieut. Essex Rifle Volunteers.—*The Lodge, Witham, Essex*; *United Service Club*, s.w.

LUBBOCK, Sir JOHN, Bart., F.R.S., of High Elms, Kent (cr. 1806).
Eldest son of the late Sir John William Lubbock, Bart., of High Elms, by Harriet, dau. of Col. George Hotham; *b.* 1834; *s.* 4th 1865; *m.* 1856 Ellen Frances, dau. of the Rev. Peter Horslern. Educated at Eton and Trinity Coll., Cambridge; is a Magistrate for Kent, President of the Entomological Society, Vice-President

of the Linnæan and Ethnological Societies, and a Partner in the Bank of Messrs. Robarts, Lubbock, & Co. —*High Elms, Farnborough, Kent; Athenæum Club*, s.w.; 15, *Lombard Street*.

Heir, his son John Birkbeck, b. 1858.

LUCAN, Earl of (GEORGE CHARLES BINGHAM, K.C.B.).—Cr. 1795.

Elder son of Richard, 2nd Earl, by Lady Elizabeth, 3rd dau. of Henry, 2nd and last Earl of Fauconberg; *b.* 1800; *s.* 1839; *m.* 1829 Lady Anne, dau. of Robert, 6th Earl of Cardigan. Educated at Westminster; is a Magistrate for Middlesex, and Lord-Lieutenant, and Custos Rotulorum of co. Mayo, for which he was M.P. 1826–30; elected a Representative Peer for Ireland 1841; a General in the Army and Col. 1st Life Guards, late Col. 8th Hussars; commanded the Cavalry in the Crimea 1854–5; Patron of 1 living.—*Laleham House, Chertsey; Castlebar House, co. Mayo; Carlton Club*, s.w.; 20, *Hanover Square*, w.

Heir, his son George, Lord Bingham; educated at Rugby; M.P. for co. Mayo; Brevet-Major in the Army and Lieut.-Col. Coldstream Guards; b. 1830; *m.* 1859 *Lady Cecilia Catharine, 5th dau. of Charles, 5th Duke of Richmond, K.G., and has, with other issue, * Charles George, b.* 1860.

LUCAS, Baroness, of Wrest, Beds, and Panshanger, Herts (cr. 1663).

Anne Florence, eldest dau. and co-heir of Thomas Philip, 2nd Earl De Grey, K.G., by Henrietta Frances, 5th dau. of William Willoughby, 1st Earl of Enniskillen; *s.* her father in the Barony of Lucas 1859; *m.* 1833 George Augustus, 6th Earl Cowper, who *d.* 1856.—*Wrest Park, Ampthill, Beds; Panshanger House, Hertford*; 4, *St. James's Square*, s.w.

Heir, her son Earl Cowper (whom see).

LUCAS, the Right Hon. EDWARD, of Castle Shane, co. Monaghan.

Only child of the late Charles Lucas, Esq., of Castle Shane, by Sarah, eldest dau. of Sir James Hamilton, Knt., of Monaghan; *b.* 1787; *s.* 1796; *m.* 1812 Anne, 2nd dau. of William Ruxton, Esq., M.P. of Ardee House, co. Louth, and has, with other issue,

* Edward William, a Dep. Lieut. for co. Monaghan ; formerly Lieut. 88th Regt. *b.* 1819.

Mr. Lucas, who was educated at Harrow and Ch. Ch., Oxford, and the University of Edinburgh, is a Magistrate for cos. Monaghan and Armagh (High Sheriff 1817); he was M.P. for co. Monaghan 1834–41, Under-Secretary of State for Ireland 1841–6, and sworn a Privy Councillor in Ireland 1845.—*Castle Shane, Monaghan; Carlton Club*, s.w.

+LUCAS, Major ARTHUR HYDE, of Rathealy, co. Cork.

Eldest son of the late Arthur Hyde Lucas, Esq., of Rathealy, by Frances, dau. of Henry Adams, Esq., of Cregg, co. Cork; *b.* 1812; *s.* 183–. Is a Magistrate for co. Cork, and Major in the Cork Militia; late Capt. 45th Foot.—*Rathealy, Fermoy, co. Cork.*

LUCAS, the Rev. CHARLES, of Filby, Norfolk.

Son of the Rev. Gibson Lucas, Rector of Filby, by Mary, dau. of the late Rev. B. W. Salmon, Rector of Caistor, Norfolk; *b.* 1805; *m.* 1848 Frances, dau. of the Rev. William Belgrave, of Preston Hall, co. Rutland, and has, with other issue,

* Charles, *b.* 1851.

Mr. Lucas, who was educated at Trinity Hall, Cambridge (B.A. 1826), is a Magistrate for Norfolk, Rector of Filby, Lord of the Manor of Filby, and Patron of that living.—*Filby House, Gt. Yarmouth.*

LUCAS, HENRY, Esq., of Uplands, Glamorganshire.

Younger son of the late John Lucas, Esq., of Stout Hall, co. Glamorgan (who *d.* 1831), by Catherine, dau. of William Powell, Esq., of Glanraeth, co. Carmarthen; *b.* 1797; *m.* 1st 1819 Caroline, dau. and co-heir of Ponsonby Tottenham, Esq., M.P., of co. Wexford; 2nd 1837 Caroline, dau. of Robert James, Esq., of Wyke House, Dorset; and has by the former, with other issue,

* John Ponsonby (in Holy Orders), educated at New Inn Hall, Oxford (B.A. 1851); Rector of Rhosili and Vicar of Llangennith, co. Glamorgan; *b.* 1823; *m.* 1858 Hannah Rebecca Dolbeare, dau. of the late Rev. T. R. Matthews, B.A., and has issue, *Charles Gardener Tottenham, *b.* 1859.

Mr. Lucas, who is a Magistrate for co. Glamorgan (High Sheriff 1842), was formerly Capt. Royal Glamorgan Militia.—*Uplands, Swansea.*

LUCAS, JOHN, Esq., of Mt. Lucas, King's Co.

Eldest son of the late Benjamin Lucas, Esq., J.P. and D.L., of Mount Lucas, by Eliza, dau. of Capt. Ormsby; *b.* 1812; *s.* 1847; *m.* 1853 Elizabeth, dau. of James Wakely, Esq., of Dublin, and has issue two daughters. Mr. Lucas is a Magistrate for King's Co.—*Mount Lucas, Philipstown, King's Co.*

LUCAS, RICHARD, Esq., of Edithweston Hall, Rutlandshire, and Fenton, Lincolnshire.

Eldest son of the late Rev. Richard Lucas, Rector of Edithweston, by Mary Dorothy, dau. of the Rev. Jacob Costobadie, Rector of Wensley, co. York; *b.* 1820; *s.* 1846; *m.* 1847 Mary, dau. of J. E. Bennet, Esq. Is a Magistrate for co. Rutland (High Sheriff 1847), Lord of the Manors of Edithweston and Fenton, co. Lincoln, and Newton Lodge, in the parish of Lofthouse, co. York, and Patron of Edithweston Rectory; was formerly an Officer in the Army. This family acquired the estate of Edithweston by marriage with the coh-eiress of the Halfords in the 18th century; and Mr. Lucas inherited the Newton estate from his grandmother.—*Edithweston Hall, Stamford; Newton Lodge, Wakefield.*

LUCAS. (See *Braithwaite*.)

LUCAS. (See *Lancaster-Lucas*.)

LUCAS, of Stout Hall. (See *Wood*.)

LUCAS-CALCRAFT, EDMUND JAMES, Esq., of Ancaster Hall, Lincolnshire.

Eldest surviving son of the late Charles Yorke Lucas, Esq., J.P. and D.L., of Ancaster Hall (who *d.* 1855), by Mary Jane Elizabeth, dau. of James Lock Nixon, Esq.; *b.* 1845; *s.* his brother 1860. (The late owner assumed the additional name of Calcraft on succeeding to the estates of Ancaster, derived from his mother's family.—*Ancaster Hall, Grantham.*

Heir Pres., his brother Granby, b. 1846.

LUCAS-SHADWELL. (See *Shadwell*.)

LUCE, THOMAS, Esq., of Malmesbury, Wilts.

Son of the late Thomas Luce, Esq.; *b.* 1790; *m.* 1820 Susan, dau. of William Hollis, Esq., of Mount Town, co. Monmouth, and has, with other issue,

* William Hollis, *b.* 1821; educated at Eton.

Mr. Luce, who is a J.P. and D.L. for Wilts, and a Director of the Bank of London, was M.P. for Malmesbury 1852–9.—*Malmesbury, Wilts; Oriental Club*, w.

LUCY, HENRY SPENCER, Esq., of Charlecote Park, Warwickshire.

Second but eldest surviving son of the late George Lucy, Esq., of Charlecote, by Mary Elizabeth, dau. of

603

the late Sir John Williams, Bart., of Bodelwydden, St. Asaph; *b.* 1830; *s.* 1851; *m.* 1865 Christina Cameron, eldest dau. of Alexander Campbell, Esq., of Monzie, N. B. (whom see). Educated at Ch. Ch., Oxford; is Lord of the Manor of Charlecote, and Patron of 2 livings; was High Sheriff of co. Warwick 1857. —*Charlecote Park, Warwick; Arthur's Club,* s.w.

Heir Pres., his brother Edmund Berkeley, *b.* 1842.

LUCY, the Rev. JOHN.
Second son of the late Rev. John Lucy, by Maria, dau. of John Lane, Esq., of Leighton Grange, Middlesex; *b.* 1790. Educated at Winchester and Trinity Coll., Cambridge (B.A. 1814, M.A. 1817); appointed Rector of Hampton Lucy 1815, Vicar of Charlecote 1823; is a Magistrate for co. Warwick, and Patron of 2 livings. —*Hampton Lucy, Warwick; University and Arthur's Clubs,* s.w.

LUCY, WILLIAM CHARLES, Esq., of Claremont House, Gloucestershire.
Eldest son of the late Charles Lucy, Esq., of Stratford-on-Avon, by Sarah, dau. of W. Tasker, Esq., of Stratford-on-Avon; *b.* 1822; *m.* 1845 Elizabeth, dau. of Thomas Sowdon, Esq., of Woolhope, co. Hereford, and has, with other issue,

• William Charles, *b.* 1848.

Mr. Lucy is a Magistrate for co. Gloucester, and a Fellow of the Geological and Anthropological Societies. —*Claremont House, Gloucester.*

+LUDLOW, HENRY GAISFORD GIBBS, Esq., of Heywood House, Wilts.
Eldest son of the late Abraham Ludlow, Esq., of Heywood House, by Susannah, only dau. and heir of G. Gibbs, Esq.; *b.* 1810; *m.* 1833 Frances, dau. of R. Clarke, Esq. He is a J.P. and D.L. for Wilts (of which he has been High Sheriff), and a Magistrate for Somerset; Lord of the Manor of Heywood, and Patron of 2 livings.—*Heywood House, Westbury, Wilts.*

LUDLOW-BRUGES, WILLIAM PENRUDDOCKE, Esq., of Seend, Wilts.
Eldest son of the late William Heald Ludlow, Esq. (who assumed the name of Bruges in 1835, on succeeding to the property of his maternal great-uncle, Thomas Bruges, Esq., of Seend, and who was M.P. for Bath and Devizes, and Chairman of Quarter Sessions for North Wilts, and Recorder of Devizes), by his 2nd wife Agnes, dau. of Thomas Penruddocke, Esq., of Winkton, Hants; *b.* 1836; *s.* 1856; is Lord of the Manor of Seend.—*Seend, Melksham.*

Heir Pres., his brother Richard Heald, a Magistrate for Wilts, *b.* 1845.

LUGARD, Sir EDWARD, G.C.B. (cr. 1858).
Son of the late Capt. John Lugard, of the 6th Inniskilling Dragoons, by Jane Llewellyn, dau. of Robert Trewman, Esq., of Exeter; *b.* 1810; *m.* 1837 Isabella Mowbray, eldest dau. of Henry Hart, Esq., of Sligo. Educated at Sandhurst; entered the Army 1828, is a Lieut.-General in the Army, Col. 31st Foot, and permanent Under-Secretary of State for War; was formerly Adjutant-General to the Forces in the Punjab, and A.D.C. to the Queen.—*War Office,* s.w.; *United Service Club,* s.w.; 57, *Eaton Square,* s.w.

LUMLEY. (See under *Scarborough, Earl of.*)

LUMSDAINE, STAMFORD ROBERT, Esq., of Lathallan, Fifeshire.
Fourth but only surviving son of the late James Lumsdaine, Esq., of Lathallan (who *d.* 1857), by Sophia, dau. of A. Lindesay, Esq., of Balmungo, co. Fife; *b.*

604

1831; *s.* his brother 1860; *m.* 1864 Anna Maria, 2nd dau. of Capt. David Briggs, R.N., and has issue,

• A son, *b.* 1865.

Mr. Lumsdaine is a J.P. and D.L. for co. Fife, and Capt. Fifeshire Militia Artillery.—*Lathallan, Colinsburgh, N. B.*

LUMSDAINE. (See *Sandys-Lumsdaine.*)

LUMSDEN, HENRY, Esq., of Pitcaple, Aberdeenshire.
Eldest son of the late Hugh Lumsden, Esq., J.P. and D.L., of Pitcaple, by his 2nd wife Isabella, dau. of Walter Fergus, Esq., of Strathore; *b.* 1825; *s.* 186—; *m.* 1860 Edith Jane, dau. of the Rev. Robert S. Battiscombe, M.A., and has, with other issue,

• Henry, *b.* 1864.

Mr. Lumsden is a Magistrate for co. Aberdeen, and Lord of the Barony of Pitcaple.—*Pitcaple Castle, Aberdeen;* 20, *Onslow Square,* s.w.

LUMSDEN, the Rev. HENRY THOMAS,‡ of Cushnie, Aberdeenshire.
Only son of the late John Lumsden, Esq., of Cushnie, by Magdalene, dau. of P. Friell, Esq.; *b.* 1808; *s.* 1829; *m.* 1832 Susanna, 3rd dau. of Neil Benjamin Edmonstone, Esq., and niece of the late Sir Charles Edmonstone, Bart., of Duntreath. Educated at St. John's Coll., Cambridge (B.A. 1831); is a Magistrate for co. Aberdeen, and Lord of the Barony of Cushnie. This family was originally settled at Cushnie, between the years 1400 and 1450.—*Cushnie, Alford, Aberdeenshire;* 15, *Lower Berkeley Street, Portman Square,* w.

LUMSDEN, WILLIAM JAMES, Esq., of Balmedie, Aberdeenshire.
Sixth son of the late Harry Lumsden, Esq., of Belhelvie, by Catherine, dau. of Hugh McVeagh, Esq., of Huntly, N.B.; *b.* 1794; *m.* 1st 1837 the Hon. Margaret, dau. of John, 8th Viscount Arbuthnott (she *d.* 1845); 2nd 1846 Mary Elizabeth, eldest dau. of Matthew Thompson, Esq., of Maningham Lodge, co. York (she *d.* 1863); 3rd 1865 Williamina Stewart, eldest dau. of the late Col. James John Stewart-Forbes-Leith, of Whitehaugh, N.B.; he has, with other issue,

• William Harry, *b.* 1852.

Mr. Lumsden, who was educated at Aberdeen and Haileybury Coll., is a Magistrate and Commissioner of Income Tax for co. Aberdeen, and Lord of the Baronies of Balmedie, &c., and was formerly in the Bombay Civil Service. — *Balmedie House, Belhelvie, N.B.; Oriental Club,* w.; 19, *Queen's Gate,* w.

LUNDIN, Mrs., of Auchtermairnie, Fifeshire.
Elizabeth, 4th dau. of the late Christopher Lundin, Esq., of Auchtermairnie, by Rachel, dau. of Andrew Johnston, Esq., of Rennyhill; *s.* 1855; *m.* 1827 the Rev. Robert Brown, who has assumed the surname of Lundin, and has, with other issue, • James, *b.* 1828. —*Auchtermairnie, Kennoway, Fifeshire.*

LURGAN, Lord (CHARLES BROWNLOW, K.P.),— Cr. 1839.
Eldest son of Charles, 1st Lord, by his 2nd wife Jane, dau. of the late Roderick M'Neill, Esq., of Barra, co. Inverness; *b.* 1831; *s.* 1847; *m.* 1853 the Hon. Emily Anne, dau. of John Cavendish, 3rd Lord Kilmaine. Is Lord Lieutenant of co. Armagh, and a J.P. and D.L. for co. Down; was formerly Lieut. 43rd Light Infantry. The first Lord was M.P. for co. Armagh 1818–53. —*Brownlow House, Lurgan, co. Armagh; Boodle's Club,* s.w.; 17, *Park Lane,* w.

Heir, his son William, *b.* 1858.

‡ Died whilst these sheets were at press.

LUSCOMBE, JOHN, Esq., of Combe Royal, Devon.
Eldest son of the late John Luscombe Luscombe, Esq., of Combe Royal, by Sarah, dau. of James Hawker, Esq., of Plymouth; *b.* 1806; *s.* 1831. Is a J.P. and D.L. for Devon.—*Combe Royal, Kingsbridge.*

Heir Pres., his nephew John (eldest son of the late Rev. Edward Knighton Luscombe, who *d.* 1867, by Anna, eldest dau. of William M'Culloch, Esq., of Barholm, co. Kirkcudbright), *b.* 1848.

LUSH, Sir ROBERT, Knt. (cr. 1865).
Eldest son of the late Mr. Robert Lush, of Shaftesbury, by Lucy, dau. of Mr. Joseph Foot, of Tollard, Wilts; *b.* 1807; *m.* 1839 Elizabeth Ann, eldest dau. of the Rev. C. Woollacott; called to the Bar at Gray's Inn 1840; made a Q.C. 1857; Serjeant-at-Law 1865; appointed a Judge of the Queen's Bench 1865.—60, *Avenue Road, N.W.*

LUSHINGTON, Sir HENRY, Bart., of Aspenden Hall, Herts (cr. 1791).
Eldest son of the late Sir Henry Lushington, Bart., of Aspenden Hall, by Fanny Maria, dau. of Matthew Lewis, Esq., Under-Secretary at War; *b.* 1802; *s.* as 3rd Bart. 1863; *m.* 1st 1826 Eliza Louisa, dau. of William Trower, Esq. (she *d.* 1862); 2nd 1863 Eliza Hannah, dau. of John Shelley, Esq. Educated at Haileybury Coll.; was formerly in the Indian Civil Service.—*Aspenden Hall, Buntingford;* 32, *Montagu Square, W.*

Heir, his son Henry, *b.* 1826; *m.* 18—Miss Lisetta Cheape.

LUSHINGTON, Sir STEPHEN, G.C.B. (cr. 1855).
Second son of the late Sir Henry Lushington, Bart., of Aspenden Hall, Herts, by Fanny Maria. dau. of Matthew Lewis, Esq.; *b.* 1803; *m.* 1841 Henrietta, dau. of Admiral Sir Henry Prescott, K.C.B.; is an Admiral on the retired list, late Lieutenant-Governor of Greenwich Hospital; commanded the Naval Brigade at the capture of Sebastopol; has been Superintendent of the Indian Navy; served on the coast of Turkey and Greece in 1828; appointed to the command of the Brazilian station 1858.—*Oak Lodge, Thornton Heath, s.*

LUSHINGTON, the Right Hon. STEPHEN, D.C.L., of Merry Hill, Herts.
Second son of the late Sir Stephen Lushington, Bart., by Hester, dau. of John Boldero, Esq., of Aspenden Hall, Herts; *b.* 1782; *m.* 1821 Sarah Grace, dau. of the late Thomas William Carr, Esq., of Frognal, Middlesex, and has, with other issue,

*Vernon, a Barrister-at-Law of the Inner Temple, *b.* 182—; *m.* 1865 Jane, third dau. of Francis Mowatt, Esq. .

Dr. Lushington, who was educated at Eton and Ch. Ch., Oxford, and was Fellow of All Souls Coll. (B.A. 1802, M.A. 1806, B.C.L. 1807, D.C.L. 1808); was called to the Bar at the Inner Temple 1806, and was subsequently admitted an Advocate in Doctors' Commons; he was Judge of the Consistory Court 1828–38; Judge of the Admiralty 1838–67; late Chancellor of the Dioceses of London and Rochester; was M.P. for Ilchester 1820–6, for Tregony 1826–30, for the Tower Hamlets 1832–41.—*Merry Hill, Watford;* 18, *Eaton Place, s.w.*

LUSHINGTON, the Right Hon. STEPHEN RUMBOLD, D.C.L., of Norton Court, Kent.
Second son of the late Rev. J. S. Lushington, Prebendary of Carlisle, by his 2nd wife Mary, dau. of the Rev. H. Christian, of Docking, Norfolk; *b.* 1776; *m.* 1st 1798 Anne Elizabeth, dau. of 1st Lord Harris, G.C.B. (she *d.* 1856); 2nd 1858 Marianne, dau. of Mr. James Hearne, of London (she *d.* 1864). He had by the former, with other issue,

Charles Manners, late Capt. East Kent Rifles, and formerly M.P. for Canterbury; educated at Eton, M.A. of Oriel Coll.,

Oxford, and afterwards Fellow of All Souls Coll.; *b.* 1819; *d.* 1864, having *m.* 1846 Henrietta, sister of Sir S. H. Northcote, Bart., M.P.

Mr. Lushington, who was educated at Rugby, created Hon. D.C.L. Oxford 1839, is a Magistrate for Kent; was Private Secretary to Lord Harris 1795–9; M.P. for Rye 1807–12, for Canterbury 1812–30 and 1835–7, and for many years Chairman of Ways and Means in the House of Commons; Joint Secretary of the Treasury 1824–7; Governor of Madras 1827–32; sworn a member of the Privy Council 1827.—*Norton Court, Faversham; Travellers' Club, s.w.*

LUSHINGTON, EDMUND LAW, Esq., of Park House, Kent.
Eldest son of the late Edmund Henry Lushington, Esq., of Park House, by his 2nd wife, Sophia, dau. of Thomas Philips, Esq., of Sedgeley, co. Lancaster; *b.* 1811; *s.* 1839; *m.* 1842 Cecilia, dau. of the Rev. Dr. Tennyson, of Somersby, co. Lincoln, and has issue,

* Cecilia, Emily, and * Lucy.

Mr. Lushington was educated at the Charterhouse, and Trinity Coll., Cambridge (B.A. 1832, M.A. 1835). This family has been settled in Kent for several generations. —*Park House, Maidstone.*

LUSK, ANDREW, Esq., M.P.
Son of Mr. John Lusk, of Balbirnie, co. Ayr; *b.* 1813; is a Magistrate for Middlesex, an Alderman of London, and a Merchant in the City; was Sheriff of London and Middlesex 1861; elected M.P. for Finsbury 1865. —*Reform Club, s.w.;* 64, *Westbourne Terrace, w.*

LUTTLEY. (See *Barneby-Luttley*.)

LUTTRELL, the Rev. ALEXANDER FOWNES-, of East Quantoxhead, Somerset.
Fourth son of the late John Fownes-Luttrell, Esq., of Dunster Castle, Somerset, by Mary, eldest dau. of Francis Drewe, Esq., of Grange, Devon; *b.* 1793; *m.* 1824 Jane, dau. of William Leader, Esq., of Putney, Surrey. and has, with other issue,

* Henry Acland, *b.* 1826; *m.* 1857 Mary Anne, dau. of J. Ruscombe Poole, Esq., and has issue, * Eva.

Mr. A. Fownes-Luttrell, who was educated at Exeter Coll., Oxford (B.C.L. 1816), is a Magistrate for Somerset, and Rector of East Quantoxhead.—*East Quantoxhead, Bridgewater.*

LUTTRELL, GEORGE FOWNES-, Esq., of Dunster Castle, Somerset.
Eldest son of the late Lieut.-Col. Francis Fownes Luttrell, of Kilve Court (who *d.* 1862), by Emma Louisa. dau. of the late Samuel Drewe, Esq., of Kensington. Middlesex; *b.* 1828; *s.* his uncle 1867; *m.* 1852 Annie Elizabeth, dau. of the late Sir Alexander Hood, Bart., M.P., and has, with other issue,

* Alexander, *b.* 1853.

Mr. Fownes-Luttrell, who was educated at Eton and Ch. Ch., Oxford (B.A. 1850). is a Magistrate for Somerset. Lord of the Manor of Dunster. Patron of 4 livings, and Capt. 11th Somersetshire Rifle Volunteers.—*Dunster Castle, Minehead, Taunton; Woodlands, Bridgewater.*

LUTTRELL, HENRY ACLAND FOWNES-, Esq., of Badgworth Court, Somerset.
Eldest son of the Rev. Alexander Fownes-Luttrell, Rector of East Quantoxhead, Somerset, by Jane, dau. of William Leader, Esq., of Putney, Surrey; *b.* 1826; *m.* 1857 Mary Anne, dau. of Joseph Ruscombe Poole, Esq., of Bridgewater, and has issue,

* Eva, *b.* 1858.

Mr. Luttrell, who was educated at Eton and Trinity

Coll., Oxford (B.A. 1850, M.A. 1851), is a Magistrate for Somerset, and Lieut.-Col. 3rd Somerset Rifle Volunteers, and formerly served in the Rifle Brigade. —*Badgworth Court, Axbridge.*

LUTTRELL, Mrs., of Wootton Fitz Paine, Dorset.
Emma Louisa, 2nd dau. of the late Samuel Drewe, Esq., of London, by Selina, dau. of the late Rev. F. Thackeray, D.D., of Windsor; *s.* her brother, the late Frederick William Drewe, Esq., 1856; *m.* 1824 her cousin, the late Lieut.-Col. Francis Fownes-Luttrell, D.L., of Kilve Court, Somerset, some time Capt. Grenadier Guards, 3rd son of the late John Fownes-Luttrell, Esq., M.P., of Dunster Castle, Somerset, by whom (who *d.* 1862) she has, with other issue,
 * George, of Dunster Castle (whom see).
This family is a branch of the Drewes of the Grange, Devon.— *Wootton House, Charmouth, Dorset; Kilve Court, Bridgewater.*

LUTTRELL, the Rev. THOMAS FOWNES-, of Dunster, Somerset.
Youngest son of the late John Fownes-Luttrell. Esq., of Dunster Castle, by Mary, eldest dau. of Francis Drewe, Esq., of Grange, Devon; *b.* 1794. Educated at Eton and Exeter Coll., Oxford (B.A. 1817); is a Magistrate for Somerset, Vicar of Carhampton, and Incumbent of Dunster.—*Dunster, Taunton.*

LUXFORD, Rev. GEORGE CURTEIS, of Higham, Sussex.
Second son of the late John Luxford, Esq., of Higham House, by Catharine Sarah, dau. of the late Jeremiah Curteis, Esq., of Rye; *b.* 1810; *s.* under the will of his father 1862; *m.* 1839 Pauline, dau. of the late Sir Josias Henry Stracey, Bart., and has, with other issue,
 * George Bentinck. *b.* 1842; educated at Eton, and a Lieut. in the Royal Welsh Fusiliers.
Mr. Luxford, who was educated at the Charterhouse and Trinity Coll., Cambridge (B.A. 1833, M.A. 1837), is a Magistrate for Sussex; was formerly Rector of Middleton, Sussex.—*Higham House, Hurst Green.*

LUXMOORE, the Rev. JOHN, of Kerslake, Devon.
Second son of the late Thomas Bridgeman Luxmoore, Esq. (who *d.* 1844), by Mary, dau. of N. Cartwright, Esq.; *b.* 1802; *s.* his uncle, Charles Luxmoore, Esq., 1834; *m.* 1st 1828 Isabella, dau. of William Scott, Esq.; 2nd 1850 Anne, dau. of Jonathan Steele, Esq., of Poole, Dorset; 3rd 1857 Elizabeth, dau. of Felix Boylan, Esq., of Dublin. He has surviving issue,
 * Three daughters.
Mr. Luxmoore, who was educated at Bath and Pembroke Coll., Cambridge (B.A. 1825, M.A. 1829), is Rector of Llanymynech, Vicar of Berriew, co. Montgomery, and Lord of the Manors of Halstock and Meldon. —*Kerslake, Okehampton; Llanymynech, Oswestry.*

LUXMOORE, JOHN CHAVE, Esq.
Only son of the late Solon Luxmoore, Esq., of Okehampton, by Sarah, dau. of A. Chave, Esq., of Exeter; *b.* 1808; *m.* 1830 Maria, dau. of Lieut.-Col. South. Educated at St. Peter's Coll., Cambridge; is a Magistrate for Devon.—*Reform Club, s.w.; 16, Gloucester Square, w.*
 Heir Pres., his grandchild William Chave (son of William Nainby, Esq., of Barnoldby-le-Beck, co. Lincoln, by Sarah, dau. of J. C. Luxmoore, Esq.), *b.* 1850.

LUXMOORE, Mrs., of Witherdon, Devon.
Frances, eldest dau. of the late Thomas Brooke, Esq., of Church Minshull, co. Chester, by Mary, dau. of the late Sir Richard Brooke, of Norton Priory, co. Chester; *m.* 1823 the Rev. Charles Thomas Coryndon Luxmoore, of Witherdon, Devon (many years Vicar of Guilsfield,

606

---

co. Montgomery), who *d.* 1863, leaving, with other issue, * Charles, late Capt. 37th Foot, *b.* 1824.—*Witherdon, Okehampton.*

LYALL, GEORGE, Esq., of Hedley House, Surrey.
Eldest surviving son of the late George Lyall, Esq., M.P., of Findon, Sussex (Chairman of the H.E.I.C.), by Mary, dau. of John Edwards, Esq.; *b.* 1819; *m.* 1st 1845 Eleanor Harriet, dau. of the Rev. John Manley; 2nd 1855 Frances, dau. of Daniel Cave, Esq., of Cleve Hill, co. Gloucester, and has, with other issue,
 * George Arthur Cave, *b.* 1856.
Mr. Lyall, who was educated at Winchester, is a Magistrate for Surrey, a Commissioner of Lieutenancy for Middlesex, and a Director of the Bank of London; was M.P. for Whitehaven 1857-65.—*Hedley House, Epsom; Carlton and Union Clubs, s.w.*

LYBBE. (See *Powys-Lybbe.*)

LYCETT, Sir FRANCIS, Knt. (cr. 1867).
Eldest son of the late Philip Francis Lycett, Esq., of Worcester; *b.* 1803; *m.* 1836 Emily Sarah Amelia. dau. of the late John Vanderpunt, Esq., of the Bank of England; was Sheriff of Middlesex 1866-7; formerly a merchant in the City, and a partner in the firm of Dent, Allcroft, Lycett, & Co., wholesale glovers. —*City Club, e.c.; 18, Highbury Grove, N.*

LYDEKKER, GERARD WOLFE, Esq., of Harpenden Lodge, Herts.
Only son of the late Richard Lydekker, Esq., M.D., of Harpenden Lodge, by Elizabeth, dau. of Robert Wolfe, Esq., of Roxwell, Essex; *b.* 1811; *s.* 1844; *m.* 1848 Martha Margaret, dau. of the late Thos. Peake, Esq., Serjeant-at-Law, and has, with other issue,
 * Richard, of Trinity Coll., Cambridge, *b.* 1849.
Mr. Lydekker, who was educated at Eton and Trinity Coll., Cambridge (B.A. 1833, M.A. 1836). and called to the Bar at the Inner Temple 1841, is a Magistrate for Herts, Beds, and the Liberty of St. Alban's; was formerly a Member of the Home Circuit. and Classical Examiner in the Inner Temple.—*Harpenden Lodge, St. Alban's; 13, St. James's Square, s.w.*

LYELL, Sir CHARLES, Bart., D.C.L., of Kinnordy, Forfarshire (cr. 1864).
Eldest son of the late Charles Lyell, Esq., of Kinnordy. co. Forfar (who *d.* 1849), by Frances, dau. of Thomas Smith, Esq., of Maker Hall, Swaledale, co. York; *b.* 1797; *m.* 1832 Mary Elizabeth, eldest dau. of the late Leonard Horner, Esq. Educated at Exeter Coll., Oxford (B.A. 1819 as 2nd Class in Classical Honours, M.A. 1821, cr. Hon. D.C.L. 1855); is a J.P. and D.L. for Forfar; has been twice President of the Geological Society; Author of 'Principles and Manual of Geology,' and of 'Travels in North America;' received the honour of Knighthood 1848.— *Kinnordy, Kirriemuir, N.B.; 73, Harley Street, w.*

LYGON. (See under *Beauchamp, Earl.*)

LYLE, ACHESON, Esq., of The Oaks, co. Londonderry.
Second son of the late Samuel Lyle, Esq., of The Lodge, co. Londonderry, by Esther, only dau. of John Acheson, Esq., of the city of Londonderry; *b.* 1795; *m.* 1825 Eleanor, dau. of James Warre, Esq., of Randalls Park, Surrey, and has, with other issue.
 * James Acheson, of Portstewart House, co. Londonderry, Barrister-at-Law; *b.* 1827; *m.* 1851 Ida Elizabeth, dau. of the Rev. Francis Ruthdge, of Bloomfield, co. Mayo, and has, with other issue. * Francis Acheson, *b.* 1853.
Mr. Lyle, who was educated at Trinity Coll., Dublin (B.A. 1815), and called to the Irish Bar 1818, was ap

pointed Lieutenant of co. Londonderry 1860; he was formerly Second and afterwards Chief Remembrancer of the Court of Exchequer, and latterly a Master in Chancery, Ireland.—*The Oaks, Londonderry; Sackville Street Club, Dublin; Union Club,* s.w.

LYLE. (See *Supplement.*)

LYNCH, CHARLES, Esq., of Ballycurrin, co. Mayo.
Son of the late Capt. Peter Lynch, J.P., of Ballycurrin, by Julia Maria Lynch, grand-dau. of the late Sir Peter Lynch, of Petersburg; *b.* 1812. Is a J.P. and D.L. for co. Mayo (High Sheriff 1854-5).—*Ballycurrin Castle, Headfort, co. Mayo.*

LYNCH, Capt. HENRY BLOSSE-, C.B., of Partree House, co. Mayo.
Eldest surviving son of the late Major Henry Blosse-Lynch, of Partree, by Elizabeth, dau. of Robert Finnis, Esq., of Hythe, Kent; *b.* 1807; *s.* 1855; *m.* 1838 Caroline, dau. of Col. Taylor, of the Bombay Army, and has, with other issue,

* Quested Finnis, *b.* 1850.

Mr. Lynch is a Capt. in the Indian Navy, and a K.G.C. of the Order of the Lion and Sun of Persia.—*Partree House, Ballinrobe, co. Mayo; Athenæum Club,* s.w.

LYNCH, HENRY JAMES, of Rathtarmon, co. Sligo.
Eldest son of the late Patrick Lynch, Esq., J.P., of Rathtarmon, by Marcella, dau. of John Flanagan, Esq., of Clogher, co. Roscommon; *b.,* 1824; *s.* 1859; *m.* 1860 Jane Frances, dau. of James Joyes, Esq., of Belmont, co. Galway, and has issue,

* Patrick, *b.* 1862.

Mr. Lynch, who was educated at St. Mary's Coll., Oscott, is a Magistrate for co. Roscommon; appointed one of Her Majesty's Inspectors of Schools 1860.—*Rathtarmon, Sligo; Stafford Club,* w.

LYNCH, JAMES MATTHEW, Esq., of Whiteleas, co. Kildare.
Eldest son of the late James Lynch, Esq., of Whiteleas, by Elizabeth, dau. of Thomas Murray, Esq., of Sheepwalk, co. Wicklow; *b.* 1810; *s.* 1829; *m.* 1839 Eleanor, dau. of John McDonnell, Esq., of Merrion Square, Dublin, and has, with other issue,

* James Henry De Robeck, late Ensign 17th Foot, *b.* 1841.

Mr. Lynch, who was educated at Clongowes Coll, is a Magistrate for cos. Kildare and Dublin.—*Whiteleas, Ballymore Eustace, co. Kildare.*

LYNCH, JOHN BREEN, Esq., of Roebuck House, co. Cavan.
Eldest son of the late Joseph Lynch, Esq., J.P., of Roebuck House, by Belinda Jane, dau. of John Breen, Esq., M.D., of Dublin; *b.* 1839; *s.* 1858. Educated at Oscott Coll.; is a Magistrate for cos. Cavan and Meath, Capt. Cavan Militia, and a Grand Juror of that county.—*Roebuck House, Mount Nugent, Cavan; United Service Club, Dublin.*

LYNCH, JOHN WILSON, Esq., of Duras, co. Galway.
Eldest surviving son of the late Patrick Mark Lynch, Esq., of Duras, by Ellen, only dau. of John Wilson, Esq., of Belvoir, co. Clare; *b.* 1831; *s.* 1861; *m.* 1865 Fanny, 2nd dau. of the late Sir Thos. N. Redington, K.C.B., of Kilcornan, co. Galway.

* Mark, *b.* 1866.

Mr. Lynch, who was educated at Ushaw Coll., Durham, is a Dep.-Lieut. for co. Galway (High Sheriff 1858), a Magistrate for cos. Galway and Clare (High Sheriff 1866), and a Capt. co. Galway Militia.—*Duras, Kinvara, co. Galway; Renmore, Galway; Belvoir, Six Mile Bridge, co. Clare.*

+LYNCH, NICHOLAS, Esq., of Barna, co. Gal. way.
Only son of the late Marcus Blake Lynch, Esq., of Barna, by his 2nd wife Clarinda, dau. of the late J. Segrave, Esq., of Cabra, co. Dublin; *b.* 1805; *m.* 1825 Eliza, 2nd dau. of the late Stephen Grehan, Esq., of Dublin, and has issue,

* Marcus Nicholas, *b.* 1837; *m.* 1867 Blanche, dau. of M. de Marylski.

Mr. Lynch is a Dep.-Lieut. for co. Galway.—*Barna, Galway.*

LYNCH, MAJOR PATRICK CREAN-, of Clogher, co. Mayo.
Eldest son of the late Andrew Crean-Lynch, Esq., of Clogher, J.P. and D.L., by Elizabeth, eldest dau. of Patrick Lynch, Esq., of Clogher House; *b.* 1813; *s.* 1853; *m.* 1845 Marcella, dau. of the late Sir Michael Dillon Bellew, Bart., of Mount Bellew, co. Galway, and by her, who *d.* 1867, has issue,

* Four daughters.

Mr. Crean-Lynch is a J.P. and D.L. for co. Mayo, and a Magistrate for co. Galway (High Sheriff 1845), and Major in the Local Militia.—*Clogher, Ballyglass.*

LYNCH-BLOSSE, Sir ROBERT, Bart., of Castle Carra, co. Mayo (cr. 1662).
Eldest son of the late Rev. Sir Francis Lynch-Blosse, Bart., of Castle Carra, by the Hon. Elizabeth, 2nd dau. of William, 1st Lord Plunket; *b.* 1825; *s.* as 10th Bart. 1840; *m.* 1853 Lady Harriet, 4th dau. of Howe Peter, 2nd Marquis of Sligo. Educated at Rugby; is a Magistrate for co. Mayo, of which he has been High Sheriff.—*Athavallie, Balla, co. Mayo; Brooks's Club,* s.w.

Heir, his son Henry, *b.* 1857.

LYNCH-BLOSSE, the Ven. HENRY, M.A., of New Castle, Glamorganshire.
Second son of the late Sir Robert Lynch-Blosse, Bart., of Athavallie, co. Mayo, by Charlotte Diana, dau. of John Richards, Esq., of Cardiff; *b.* 1813; *m.* 1844 Charlotte Frances, dau. of the Rev. Robert Knight, of Tythegston, co. Glamorgan, and has, with other issue,

* Robert Charles, *b.* 1848.

Archdeacon Lynch-Blosse, who was educated at Trinity Coll., Dublin (B.A. 1835, M.A. 1860), is a Magistrate for co. Glamorgan, Archdeacon of Llandaff, and Vicar of New Castle.—*New Castle House, Bridgend.*

LYNCH-STAUNTON, GEORGE STAUNTON, Esq., of Clydagh, co. Galway.
Eldest son of the late Mark Lynch, Esq., of Duras, co. Galway, by Victoire, dau. of Richard W. Cormick, Esq., of Wolsley Park, Grenada; *b.* 1798; *s.* 1822; *m.* 1824 Sarah Jane, dau. of Capt. Francis Hardwick, 62nd Foot, and has, with other issue,

* Marcus Staunton, *b.* 1826; *m.* 1851 Horatia Anne, dau. of Charles Prescott Rushworth, Esq., Commissioner of Ireland Revenue (she *d.* 1859).

Mr. Lynch-Staunton, who was educated at Oscott Coll., is a J.P. and D.L. for co. Galway (High Sheriff 1867), and a Magistrate for co. Mayo. He assumed the additional name of Staunton by Royal sign-manual in 1859, under the will of his cousin the late Sir G. T. Staunton, Bart.—*Clydagh House, Headfort, co. Galway.*

LYNDHURST, Dowager Lady.
Georgiana, dau. of Lewis Goldsmith, Esq.; *m.* 1837 as his 2nd wife, John Singleton, Lord Lyndhurst, who *d.* 1863, when his title became ext. His Lordship was High Steward of Cambridge University, Chief Justice of Chester, Solicitor-General 1819, Attorney-General

1824, Master of the Rolls 1826, Lord Chancellor 1827–30, Chief Baron of the Exchequer 1831–4; Lord Chancellor 1831–5 and 1841–6. — *Hampton Court Palace*, s.w.

+LYNE, the Rev. CHARLES, M.A., of Tywardreath, Cornwall.
Son of the late C. Lyne, Esq.; *b.* 1802; *m.* 183- Mary, dau. of — De Castro, Esq., and has, with other issue,
• De Castro, Barrister-at-Law, *b.* 18—.
Mr. Lyne, who was educated at St. John's Coll., Cambridge (B.A. 1825, M.A. 1842), is a Magistrate for Cornwall, Vicar of Tywardreath, and Prebendary of Exeter; he was formerly Rector of Roach and Tywardreath.—*Tywardreath Parsonage, St. Austell.*

LYNE-STEPHENS, Mrs., of Lynford Hall, Norfolk.
Yolande Marie Louise, dau. of Monsieur Jean Louis Duvernay; *m.* 1845 Stephens Lyne-Stephens, Esq., of Lynford Hall, J.P. and D.L. for Norfolk (High Sheriff 1858–9) (only son of the late Charles Lyne, Esq., of Roehampton, who assumed by Royal Licence, in 1826, the name of Stephens, after his cousin John Stephens, Esq., formerly of Lisbon), who was M.P. for Barnstaple 1830–1.—*Lynford Hall, Brandon; Roehampton, Surrey*, s.w.

+LYNES, SAMUEL PARR, Esq., of Tooley Park, Leicestershire.
Only son of the late Rev. John Lynes, of Tooley Park, by Sarah Anne, only surviving dau. and heir of the late Rev. Dr. Samuel Parr, LL.D., of Hatton, Norfolk; *b.* 183–; *s.* 1843. This family is said to be of Saxon origin.—*Tooley Park, Peckleton, Hinckley.*
Heirs Pres., his sisters.

LYON, CHARLES WALTER, Esq., of Silver Hill, Staffordshire.
Eldest son of the late William Walter Lyon, Esq., of Silver Hill, by Elizabeth, dau. of W. Power, Esq., of Dublin; *b.* 1803; *m.* 1st 1829 Sarah, dau. of John Joule, Esq., of Oulton, co. Stafford; 2nd 1838 Mary Ann, dau. of John Webb, Esq., of Barton-under-Needwood, and has, with other issue,
• Walter John, *b.* 1841.
Mr. Lyon, who is a Magistrate for co. Stafford, was formerly a Merchant at Liverpool.—*Silver Hill, Barton-under-Needwood, Burton-upon-Trent.*

LYON, DAVID, Esq., of Goring, Sussex.
Third son of the late David Lyon, Esq., of Jamaica, and of Portland Place, London, by Isabella, dau. of J. Read, Esq., of Cairney, N.B., and of Ann, only dau of William Guthrie, Esq., of Cleppington, N.B.; *b.* 1794. Is a J.P. and D.L. for Sussex, and Patron of 1 living: was M.P. for Beeralston 1831–2.—*Goring Hall, Worthing; Balentore Castle, Leakethen, Forfarshire, N.B.; 31, South Street*, w.

LYON, HUGH, Esq., of Glenogil, Forfarshire.
Eldest son of the late George Lyon, Esq., of Glenogil, by Catherine Menzies, dau. of the Rev. Dr. Fleming, of Edinburgh; *b.* 1812; *s.* 1866. Educated at the University of Edinburgh: is Proprietor of the Barony of Wester Ogil, and Solicitor in the Supreme Courts at Edinburgh; descended from a common ancestor with the Earl of Strathmore.—*Glenogil House, Kirriemuir, N.B.*
Heir Pres., his brother Thomas, *b.* 1814.

LYON, THOMAS HENRY, Esq., of Appleton, Cheshire.
Second son of the late Thomas Lyon, Esq., J.P. and D.L., of Appleton Hall (who *d.* 1859), by Eliza, youngest dau. of George Clayton, Esq., of Lostock Hall, co. Lancaster.

b. 1825; *m.* 1860 Vanda, 3rd dau. of the Rt. Hon. John Wilson-Patten, M.P. of Bank Hall, co. Lancaster (she *d. s. p.* 1861). Mr. Lyon, who was formerly an Officer in the Royal Navy, is a Magistrate for co. Chester (High Sheriff 1867). Lord of the Manors of Stretton, co. Chester, and Burton Wood, co. Lancaster, and Patron of 1 Living.—*Appleton Hall, Warrington; Army and Navy Club*, s.w.
Heir Pres., his brother Francis, Capt. R.H.A., *b.* 1834; *m.* 1863 Flora, youngest dau. of the late Hon. Capt. Arthur Annesley, eldest son of Arthur, 10th Viscount Valentia.

+LYON, Major WILLIAM, of Woking, Surrey.
Fifth son of the late David Lyon, Esq., of Jamaica and of Portland Place, London, by Isabella, dau. of John Read, Esq., of Cairney, co. Forfar; *m.* 18— Mary, dau. of the late Dugald Gilchrist, Esq., of Opisdale, co. Sutherland. Is a Magistrate for Surrey and Middlesex; late Major 8th Hussars; was M.P. for Seaford 1831–2.—*The Hermitage, Woking, Surrey; 22, Park Lane*, w.

LYON. (See under *Strathmore, Earl of.*)

LYONS, Lord (RICHARD BICKERTON PEMELL LYONS, G.C.B. P.C.).—Cr. 1856.
Only surviving son of Edmund, 1st Lord, by Augusta Louisa, dau. of the late Capt. Josias Rogers, R.N.; *b.* 1817; *s.* 1858. Educated at Winchester and Ch. Ch., Oxford (B.A. 1838, M.A. 1845); was Secretary of Legation at Florence 1856–8; British Minister there Feb.—Dec. 1858, at Washington 1858–65, Ambassador at Constantinople, 1865–7; appointed Ambassador at Paris 1867. The 1st Lord was an Admiral and G.C.B., and chief in command in the Black Sea 1855–6.—*British Embassy, Paris; Travellers' Club*, s.w.

LYONS, FRANCIS, Esq., M.D., of Cork.
Eldest son of the late Thomas Lyons, Esq., of Cork, by Mary, dau. of the late William Hackett, Esq. *b.* 1797; *m.* 1833 Ellen, dau. of D. Cagney, Esq., of Park Garriffe, co. Cork, and has issue,
• Francis, *b.* 1834.
Mr. Lyons, who was educated at the University of Paris, graduated M.D. in 1822, but never practised; is a J.P. and D.L. for the city of Cork; was M.P. for Cork 1859–65.—32, *South Terrace, Cork; Marine Villa, Queenstown, co. Cork; Reform Club*, s.w.

LYONS, HENRY, Esq., of Croom, co. Limerick.
Eldest son of the late James Denis Lyons, Esq., of Croom House (a J.P. and D.L., and High Sheriff of co. Limerick 1838), by Bridgette, dau. of John Kennedy, Esq., of Limerick; *b.* 1828; *s.* 1853. Is a Magistrate for co. Limerick (High Sheriff 1860).—*Croom House, co. Limerick; County Club, Limerick; Stafford Club*, w.

LYONS, JOHN CHARLES, Esq., of Ledestown, co. Westmeath.
Eldest son of the late Charles John Lyons, Esq., by Mary Anne, dau. of Sir Richard Levinge, Bart.; *b.* 1792; *s.* his grandfather 1803; *m.* 1st 1820 Penelope Melesina, only dau. of the late Hugh Tuite, Esq., of Sonna (she *d.* 1855); 2nd 1856 Frances Ellen, dau. of Thomas Walsh, Esq., of Belleville, co. Westmeath. Educated at Pembroke Coll., Oxford: is a J.P. and D.L. for co. Westmeath (High Sheriff 1816); Capt. Westmeath Militia.—*Ledestown, Mullingar.*

LYONS, JOSEPH, Esq., of Moyanna, Queen's Co.
Second son of the late William Lyons, Esq., of Moyanna, by Catharine, dau. of Joseph Selby, Esq., of Dublin; *b.* 1797; *s.* 1840; *m.* 1828 Alicia, dau. of

the late William Dunne, Esq., of Ballymanus, Queen's Co., and has, with other issue,

* William Selby, b. 1830.

Mr. Lyons, who was educated at Carlow, is a Magistrate for Queen's Co.—*Moyanna, Stradbally.*

LYONS, WILLIAM THOMAS BIRSTOW, Esq., of Old Park, co. Antrim.
Eldest son of the late William Henry Holmes Lyons, Esq., of Old Park, by Anne, dau. of the Rev. W. Birstow, of Belfast; b. 1812; s. 1849; m. 1840 Julia Maria, 2nd dau. of Capt. Jones, of Mount Edward, co. Sligo, and has, with other issue,

* William Henry Holmes, b. 1843.

Mr. Lyons, who was educated at Eton and Trinity Coll., Dublin (B.A. 1831), and called to the Irish Bar 1835, is a J.P. and D.L. for co. Antrim and a Magistrate for co. Down.—*Old Park, Belfast.*

LYONS-MONTGOMERY.   (See *Montgomery.*)

LYSAGHT.   (See under *Lisle, Lord.*)

LYSLEY, WILLIAM JOHN, Esq., F.S.A., of Pewsham, Wilts.
Only son of William Lysley, Esq., of Warmfield, co. York (who d. 1792), by Ann, dau. of William Barker, Esq., of Wakefield; b. 1791; m. 1828 Caroline, dau. of John Marshall, Esq., of Ardwick House, co. Lancaster, and by her, who d. 1865, has, with other issue,

* William Gerard, educated at Eton, Barrister-at-Law, b. 1831.

Mr. Lysley, who was called to the Bar at the Inner Temple 1825, and went the Northern Circuit, is a J.P. and D.L. for Herts (High Sheriff 1851), and a Magistrate for St. Alban's; was M.P. for Chippenham 1859–65.—*Pewsham, Chippenham; Athenæum Club,* s.w.; 23, *Prince's Gardens,* w.

LYSONS, the Rev. SAMUEL, of Hempsted Court, Gloucestershire.
Eldest son of the late Rev. Daniel Lysons, M.A., of Hempsted Court, M.A., F.R.S., &c. &c. (Author of ' Magna Britannia,' &c.), by Sarah, eldest dau. of Col. Thomas Carteret Hardy; b. 1806; s. 1834; m. 1st 1834 Eliza Sophia Teresa, dau. of Major-General Sir Lorenzo Moore, K.C.H. and C.B.; 2nd 1847 Lucy, dau. of the Rev. John Adey Curtis (by Albinia Frances, his wife, who, after his decease, assumed the family name of Hayward in addition to that of Curtis), and has by the former, with other issue,

* Lorenzo George, late Capt. 23rd Royal Welsh Fusiliers, Adjutant of the Admin. Battalion Royal Aberdeenshire Volunteers; b. 1839; m. 1862 Victoria, dau. of the late General Sir William Richards, K.C.B., and has, with other issue, * William Lorenzo George, b. 1863.

Mr. Lysons, who was educated at Exeter Coll., Oxford (B.A. 1830, M.A. 1836), and appointed Rector of Rodmarton, co. Gloucester, 1833, resigned in 1866; appointed Rural Dean of the Deanery of Gloucester 1866; is a Magistrate for co. Gloucester, and Lord of the Manor of Hempsted. *Hempsted Court, Gloucester; Cavendish Club,* w.

LYSTER, Lady CHARLOTTE BARBARA, of Rowton Castle, Shropshire.
Third dau. of Cropley, 6th Earl of Shaftesbury, by Lady Anne, 4th dau. of George, 4th Duke of Marlborough, m. 1824 Henry Lyster, Esq., of Rowton Castle, who was formerly a Lieut. 7th Hussars, and who d. 1863.—*Rowton Castle, Shrewsbury.*

Heir Pres., her nephew Armar Henry, eldest son of the Right Hon. H. T. Lowry-Corry (whom see); b. 1836; m. 1867 Alice, only dau. of Thomas Creg, Esq., of Ballymenoch, co. Down, and has issue, * a son, b. 1907.

+LYSTER, ANTHONY LYSTER, Esq., of Stillorgan Park, co. Dublin.
Son of the late A. Lyster, Esq., of Stillorgan; b. 18—; is married, and has issue a daughter,

* Emily Sophia, m. 1845 Sir George S. Jenkinson, Bart., of Eastwood Park (whom see).

Mr. Lyster, who is Lord of the Manor of Stillorgan, descends from a common ancestor with the Lysters of Rowton and the Listers of Yorkshire.—*Stillorgan Park, co. Dublin.*

LYSTER, the Very Rev. JAMES, M.A., of Lysterfield, co. Roscommon.
Eldest son of the late Col. Anthony Lyster, of Lysterfield (formerly High Sheriff of co. Roscommon), by Jane, dau. of George Fosbery, Esq., of Cloran; b. 1810; s. 1841; m. 1837 Maria, dau. of the Rev. George Keating, M.A., Rector of Edgeworthstown co. Longford, and has, with other issue,

* Anthony, b. 1838.

Mr. Lyster, who was educated at Trinity Coll., Cambridge (B.A. 1835, M.A. 1840), is Dean of Leighlin and Rector of Wells; was formerly Rector of the Union of Tashinny.—*Lysterfield, Roscommon; The Deanery, Leighlin Bridge, co. Carlow.*

LYTTELTON, Lord (GEORGE WILLIAM LYTTELTON, F.R.S., LL.D.).—Cr. 1794.
Eldest son of William Henry, 3rd Lord, by Lady Sarah, eldest dau. of George John, 2nd Earl Spencer, K.G.; b. 1817; s. 1837; m. 1839 Mary, dau. of the late Sir Stephen Richard Glynne, Bart., of Hawarden Castle, co. Flint (she d. 1857). Educated at Eton, graduated M.A. at Trinity Coll., Cambridge, in 1838 as Joint Senior Classic; is Lord-Lieutenant and Custos Rotulorum of co. Worcester, a Magistrate for cos. Salop and Stafford, High Steward of Bewdley, Lord of the Manor of Clent and Hagley, and Patron of 4 livings; was formerly Under-Secretary for the Colonies; sits in the House of Lords as Lord Lyttelton, U.K. (cr. 1794).—*Hagley Hall, Stourbridge; Athenæum Club,* s.w.; 12, *Stratton Street,* w.

Heir, his son Charles George, educated at Eton, and M.A. of Trinity Coll., Cambridge; a Magistrate for co. Worcester, M.P. for E. Worcestershire, and Lieut. Queen's Own Worcestershire Yeomanry Cavalry, b. 1842.

LYTTELTON, Dowager Lady.
Sarah, eldest dau. of George John, 2nd Earl Spencer, K.G., by Lady Lavinia Bingham, eldest dau. of Charles, 1st Earl of Lucan; m. 1813 William Henry, 3rd Lord Lyttelton, who d. 1837. Was formerly Governess to the children of Her Majesty.—12, *Stratton Street,* w.

LYTTELTON, the Hon. SPENCER.
Second son of William Henry, 3rd Lord Lyttelton, by Lady Sarah, eldest dau. of George John, 2nd Earl Spencer, K.G.; b. 1818; m. 1848 Henrietta, dau. of the late Frederick Hamilton Cornewall, Esq., of Delbury Hall, co. Salop, and has issue.

* William Henry Cornewall, b. 1849.

Mr. Lyttelton, who served 7 years in the R.N. and afterwards in the Scots Fusilier Guards, is a Magistrate for co. Worcester; was appointed Marshal of the Ceremonies in the Royal Household 1847.—13, *Eaton Terrace,* s.w.

LYTTELTON, the Hon. and Rev. WILLIAM HENRY.
Third son of William Henry, 3rd Lord Lyttelton, by Lady Sarah, eldest dau. of George John, 2nd Earl Spencer, K.G.; b. 1820; m. 1854 Emily, dau. of the

M

MABERLY, Joseph James, Esq., of Hawkley Hurst, Hampshire.

Second son of the late Joseph Maberly, Esq., of Mytten, near Cuckfield, Sussex, and Harley Street, London (who *d.* 1860), by Henrietta, dau. of James Serle, Esq., of King's House, Hants; *b.* 1816; *m.* 1854 Rebecca Dennistoun, youngest dau. of Alexander Lang, Esq., of Overton, co. Dumbarton. Educated at Eton and Brasenose Coll., Oxford (B.A. 1836, M.A. 1845), is Patron of the Perpetual Curacy of Hawkley.—*Hawkley Hurst, Petersfield; Oxford and Cambridge Club, s.w.; 19, Upper Harley Street, w.*

MABERLY, the Rev. Thomas Astley, of Mytten, Sussex.

Eldest son of the late Joseph Maberly, Esq., of Mytten, by Henrietta, dau. of James Serle, Esq., of King's House, Hants; *b.* 1810; *s.* 1860; *m.* 1841 Caroline Emily, dau. of the late Rev. Samuel White, D.D., Vicar of Hampstead, and has, with other issue,

 * Thomas Astley, *b.* 1842; educated at Eton and Ch. Ch., Oxford; Lieut. 35th Foot.

Mr. Maberly, who was educated at Eton and Ch. Ch., Oxford (B.A. 1833, M.A. 1836), was appointed Vicar of Cuckfield 1841.—*Mytten, Cuckfield.*

MABERLY, Lieut.-Col. William Leader.

Son of the late John Maberly, Esq., of Shirley House, near Croydon, Surrey (who was M.P. for Abingdon 1820–31); *b.* 1798; *m.* 1830 the Hon. Catharine Charlotte, dau. of the Hon. Francis Aldborough Prittie, of Corvillie, co. Tipperary, and 2nd sister of Henry, 3rd Lord Dunalley. Is a Lieut.-Col. in the Army; formerly Col. 76th Foot; was M.P. for Westbury 1819–20, for Northampton 1820–30, for Shaftesbury 1831–2, for Chatham, 1832–4; formerly Clerk of the Ordnance, Joint Secretary of the General Post-Office, a Commissioner of Customs, and Commissioner of Audit.—15, *Manchester Square, w.*

M'ADAM, Christopher, Esq., of Ballochmorrie, Ayrshire.

Eldest surviving son of the late William M'Adam, Esq. (who *d.* 1836), by Jane, dau. of Capt. Pickard, of the 13th Light Dragoons; *b.* 1807; *s.* his brother William, as chief of that name, 1861; *m.* 1837 Eleanor, dau. of Edward Stephens Trelawny, Esq., of Coldrinnick, Cornwall, and by her, who *d.* 1852, had issue,

 * Ellen Jane; Agnes Henrietta, *d.* 1862; Emily Darell Louisa.

This family, a branch of the Clan Gregor, or M'Gregor, was formerly of Waterhead, in the Stewartry of Kirkcudbright.—*Ballochmorrie House, Girvan, Ayrshire, N.B.*

MACADAM, Thomas Stannard, Esq., of Blackwater, co. Clare, and Borde Hill, Sussex.

Eldest son of the late Philip Macadam, Esq., of Blackwater, by Elizabeth, dau. of J. L. Stannard, Esq., of The Grange, co. Kilkenny; *b.* 1827; *s.* 1855; *m.* 1st 1855 Eliza Chivers, dau. of the late J. S. Bower, Esq., of Broxholme House, co. York (she *d.* 1856); 2nd 1858 Ellen, eldest dau. of the late William D'Arcy Preston, Esq., Capt. R.N., of Borde Hill, Sussex, and has by the former, with other issue,

 * Philip Bower, *b.* 1856.

Mr. Macadam is a Magistrate for co. Clare, and Major 3rd W. York Militia.—*Blackwater, Limerick; Borde Hill, Cuckfield; County Club, Limerick.*

McADAM. (See *Cathcart.*)

M'ALESTER, Charles Archibald, Esq., K.H., of Loup Villa, Devon.

Son of the late Col. Archibald M'Alester, by Sarah, dau. of William Haigh, Esq., of Elmsal, co. York, and brother to the chieftain of the Scottish clan of that name; *b.* 1790; *m.* 1814 Adrienne, dau. of Christophe Didier, of Provence, in France. Is a J.P. and D.L. for Devon, a Magistrate for Dorset, and a retired Lieut.-Col. in the Army.—*Loup Villa, Axminster.*

M'ALESTER, Charles Somerville, of Kennox, Ayrshire (Chief of Clan Alester).

Eldest son of the late Col. Charles M'Alester, of Loup, co. Argyle, by Jessie, dau. and heir of William Somerville, Esq., of Kennox; *b.* 1799; *s.* 1847; *m.* 1828 Mary Adeline Brabazon, only dau. of Edward Lyon, Esq., of Dublin, and by her, who *d.* 1861, has, with other issue,

 Charles Somerville, Capt. 46th Foot; *b.* 1830; *m.* 1857 Williamina, youngest dau. of William Pollock Morris, Esq., of The Craig, co. Ayr.

Mr. M'Alester, who was educated at the Universities of Edinburgh and Glasgow, is a Magistrate for co. Ayr, and Major of the Royal Ayrshire Rifle Regiment of Militia.—*Kennox, Stewarton, Ayrshire, N.B.*

MACALISTER, Keith, Esq., of Glenbarr and Cour, Argyleshire.

Only son of the late Col. Matthew Macalister, by Charlotte, dau. of James Brodie, Esq., M.P., of Brodie, Lord Lieutenant of co. Nairn; *b.* 1803; *s.* 1830; *m.* 1st 1830 Mary Agatha, only dau. of Robert Campbell, Esq., of Skipness; 2nd 1858 Alexandrina Georgina Cuninghame, dau. and co-heir of W. Millar, Esq., of Monkcastle and Monkridden, co. Ayr, and has issue by the former,

 * Matthew Charles Brodie, late a Capt. in the Army, *b.* 1838.

Mr. Macalister is a J.P. and D.L. for co. Argyle.—*Glenbarr Abbey, Greenock, N.B.; New Club, Edinburgh; Union Club, s.w.*

MACALPINE-LENY, William, Esq., of Dalswinton, Dumfries-shire.

Son of the late James Macalpine-Leny, Esq., of Dalswinton (who was a Magistrate for her, and Convener of, co. Dumfries, and formerly in the 8th Royal Irish Dragoons), by Marion, 3rd dau. and co-heir of the late Robert Downie, Esq., M.P., of Appin, co. Argyle; *b.* 1839; *s.* 1867.—*Dalswinton, Dumfries, N.B.; 27, Abercromby Place, Edinburgh.*

MACARTHUR, Sir William, Knt. (cr. 1856).

Son of the late John Macarthur, Esq., of Camden Park, New South Wales, by Mary, dau. of John Vial, Esq., of Bridge Ride, Devon; *b.* 1800. Late Member of Legislative Council at Sydney; was Special Commissioner from that colony to the Great Exhibition of Paris in 1855.—*Camden Park, Sydney, N. S. Wales; Windham Club, s.w.*

MACARTHUR, Sir Edward, K.C.B. (cr. 1862).

Eldest son of the late John Macarthur, Esq., of Camden Park, New South Wales, by Mary, dau. of John Vial, Esq., of Bridge Ride, Devon; *b.* 1790; *m.* 1862 Sarah, 3rd dau. of the late Lieut.-Col. William Smith Neill, of

Barnwell and Swindrigemuir, co. Ayr. Is a Lieut.-General in the Army and Col. 100th Foot; served in the Peninsular war; has been on the Staff in Ireland, and Commander of the Forces in Australia.—*United Service Club*, s.w.; 27, *Prince's Gardens*, w.

MACARTNEY, Sir John, Bart., of Lish, co. Armagh (cr. 1799).
Eldest son of the late Rev. Sir William Macartney, Bart., Rector of Dysertegny, co. Londonderry, by Ellen, dau. of the late Sir John Barrington, Bart.; *b.* 1832; *s.* as 3rd Bart. 1867. This family is descended from a common ancestor with the Macartneys of Lissanoure. —*Lish, Armagh.*
Heir Pres., his brother William George, *b.* 1834.

MACARTNEY, George, Esq., of Lissanoure, co. Antrim.
Eldest son of the late Rev. Travers Hume, by Elizabeth, dau. of Major J. Ballyguier, of Dublin; *b.* 1793; *s.* his mother (who inherited, as niece, the late Earl Macartney's estates in Ireland and Scotland) 1825; *m.* 1828 Ellen, only dau. and heir of the late Townley Filgate, Esq., of Lowther Lodge, Dublin, and has, with other issue,
* George Travers,‡ late Capt. 15th Hussars; *b.* 1830; *m.* 1865 Henrietta Frances, youngest dau. of Robert Smyth, Esq.
Mr. Macartney, who was educated at Trinity Coll., Dublin (B.A. 1814), is a Magistrate for co. Dublin and a J.P. and D.L. for co. Antrim; was M.P. for co. Antrim 1852-9.—*Lissanoure, Ballymoney, co. Antrim; Lowther Lodge, Balbriggan, co. Dublin; Sackville Street Club, Dublin; Carlton and National Clubs*, s.w.

MACARTNEY, John William Ellison-, Esq., of The Palace, Clogher, co. Tyrone.
Only son of the late Rev. Thomas Ellison, by Catherine, 2nd dau. of Arthur Chichester Macartney, Esq., K.C., of Murlough, co. Down; *b.* 1818; *s.* his uncle 1858; *m.* 1851 Elizabeth Phœbe, eldest surviving dau. of the Rev. John Grey Porter, and has, with other issue,
* William Grey, *b.* 1852.
Mr. Ellison-Macartney, who was educated at the Universities of Bonn and Munich, called to the Bar at the Middle Temple 1846, and to the Irish Bar at King's Inns, Dublin, 1848, is a Magistrate for co. Tyrone; was formerly a Magistrate for co. Fermanagh: he assumed, by Royal licence, in 1859, the surname and arms of Macartney, after his maternal uncle, the late Rev. W. G. Macartney.—*The Palace, Clogher, co. Tyrone.*

MACAULAY, Lady.
Mary, dau. of John Gamble, Esq., M.D.; *m.* 18— the Hon. Sir James Buchanan Macaulay, C.B., Chief Justice of Canada (*d.* 1859), son of James Macaulay, Esq., M.B., Inspector-General of Hospitals.— *Wykeham Lodge, Toronto, Canada.*

MACAULAY, Mrs., of Ardingcaple House, Cambridgeshire.
Harriet, only dau. of W. Woollcombe, Esq., M.D.; *m.* 1813 Kenneth Macaulay, Esq., Q.C., who was M.P. for Cambridge 1857-65, and who *d.* 1867.—*Ardingcaple House, Cambridge;* 48, *Cadogan Place*, s.w.

MACAUSLAND, Oliver Plunket, Esq., of Woodbank, co. Londonderry.
Eldest son of the late Rev. Redmond Conyngham Macausland, Rector of Desartoghill, co. Derry, by Martha, dau. of Samuel Babington, Esq., and grand-dau. of the Rev. W. Babington, Rector of Cossington,

‡ The heir to his mother's estates is his youngest son, Townley Patten Hume Macartney Filgate, Capt. 18th Hussars, *b.* 1841.

co. Leicester; *b.* 1851; *s.* 1856. Educated at Hailey-bury Coll.; is head and representative of the Macausland family.—*Woodbank, Garvagh, co. Londonderry.*

M'CALL, Henry, Esq., of Daldowie, Lanark-shire.
Eldest son of the late James M'Call, Esq., J.P. and D.L. of Daldowie, by Anna C. I. Fehrszen-de-Wet, dau. of Henricus Fehrszen; *b.* 1818; *s.* 1866. Is a Magistrate for co. Lanark.—*Daldowie, Glasgow, N.B.*

McCALLUM, George Kellie-, Esq., of Braco, Perthshire, and Reddoch, Stirlingshire.
Only child of the late George McCallum, Esq., of Thornhill, by Margaret, dau. of James Dalgleish, Esq., of Reddoch (the younger branch of Dalgleish, of Scotscraig, co. Fife); *b.* 1804; *m.* 1841 Margaret Ann, only surviving child of George Kellie, Esq., M.D., and has, with other issue,
* George, Capt. 92nd Gordon Highlanders; *b.* 1842; *m.* 1866 Mary Catherine, only dau. of John Stirling, Esq., of Kippendavie, co. Perth.
Mr. McCallum, who was educated at the University of Edinburgh, is a J.P. and D.L. for co. Perth and a Magistrate for co. Stirling.—*Braco Castle, Perth, N.B.*

McCANN, James, Esq., of Staleen House, co. Meath.
Eldest son of the late John McCann, Esq., of Drogheda; *b.* 1789; *m.* 1st 18— Miss Catharine Coleman; 2nd 1863 Mary, dau. of — McKenna, Esq., and widow of William Campbell, Esq., Alderman of Drogheda, and has by the former, with other issue,
* John, a Magistrate for the borough of Drogheda, *b.* 1828.
Mr. McCann, who is a Merchant in Drogheda, of which borough he was Sheriff 1851, was M.P. for Drogheda 1852-65.—*Staleen House, Drogheda.*

McCANN, Albert, Esq., of Lismoy House, co. Longford.
Only son of the late Nicholas McCann, Esq., D.L., of Lismoy House, by Mary, 2nd dau. of the late Edward Black, Esq., of Bennington Hall, co. Lincoln; *b.* 1846; *s.* 1867. This family is of Scottish origin, whence they removed to Armagh, co. Tyrone, where they held large estates, *temp.* Edward IV.—*Quadring, Spalding, Lincolnshire; Lismoy House, Newtownforbes, co. Longford;* 50, *Parliament Street*, s.w.

MACCARTHY, Lady.
Sophia Brunel, eldest dau. of the late Sir Benjamin Hawes, K.C.B., by Sophia Macnamara, eldest dau. of the late Sir Marc Isambard Brunel, Knt.; *m.* 1848 Sir Charles Justin Maccarthy, Knt., who was Governor of Ceylon, and formerly Auditor-General of that island, who *d.* 1864.

McCARTHY, the late Alexander, Esq., of Currymount, co. Cork.
A member of the ancient sept of the Macarthys of co. Cork; *b.* 1800. Called to the Irish Bar 1826; was a Magistrate for co. Cork; M.P. for Cork city 1846-7, and for co. Cork 1857-9; he *d.* 1868.—*Currymount, Buttevant, co. Cork.*

M'CARTHY, John, Esq., of Rathduane, co. Cork.
Youngest son of the late Denis M'Carthy, Esq., of Rathree, and brother of the late Eugene M'Carthy, Esq., of Rathduane; *b.* 1814; *s.* his brother 1853; *m.* 1852 Anne, dau. of the late Philip Harding, Esq., of Firville, co. Cork, and has, with other issue,
* John Jeremiah Philip, *b.* 1853.
Mr. M'Carthy is a J.P. and D.L. for co. Cork, and Lord of the Manor of Rathduane.—*Rathduane, Millstreet, co. Cork; County Club, Cork.*

MacCAUSLAND, Sir RICHARD BOLTON, Knt. (Cr. 1856).
Son of the late William James MacCausland, Esq., of Dublin, and nephew of the late Marcus MacCausland, Esq., of Fruit Hill, co. Londonderry ; *b.* 1810. Educated at Trinity Coll., Dublin (B.A. 1831, M.A. 1834), called to the Irish Bar 1834 ; formerly Assistant Barrister for Galway ; appointed Clerk of the Custodies in Lunacy 1853, Recorder of Singapore 1856.—*Merville, Stillorgan, Dublin ; Kildare Street Club, Dublin ;* 36, *St. James's Place,* s.w.

+MACCAUSLAND, CONOLLY THOMAS, Esq., of Drenagh, co. Londonderry.
Only surviving son of the late Marcus MacCausland, Esq., of Fruit Hill (who was a J.P. and D.L. for co. Londonderry, and High Sheriff in 1826), by Marianne, dau. of the late Thomas Tyndal, Esq., of The Fort, Clifton, co. Gloucester ; *b.* 1828 ; *s.* 1862 ; *m.* 1867 the Hon. Laura, youngest dau. of St. Andrew Beauchamp, 14th Lord St. John of Bletsoe. Educated at Eton and Ch. Ch., Oxford ; is a J.P. and D.L. for co. Londonderry (High Sheriff 1866), late Capt. Derry Militia ; was formerly in the diplomatic service.—*Drenagh, Newton Limavady, co. Londonderry ; Carlton Club,* s.w.

MACCLESFIELD, Earl of (THOMAS AUGUSTUS WOLSTENHOLME PARKER).—Cr. 1721.
Eldest son of Thomas, 5th Earl, by his 2nd wife Eliza, dau. of the late William Breton Wolstenholme, Esq., of Hollyhill, Sussex ; *b.* 1811 ; *s.* 1850 ; *m.* 1st 1839 Henrietta, dau. of the late Edmund Turnor, Esq., of Stoke Rochford, co. Lincoln (she *d.* 1839) ; 2nd 1842 Lady Mary Frances, dau. of Richard, 2nd Marquis of Westminster. Educated at Eton ; is a J.P. and D.L. for Oxon, High-Steward of Henley-on-Thames, and Patron of 6 livings ; was M.P. for Oxfordshire 1837–41. —*Shirburn Castle, Tetsworth ; Carlton Club,* s.w. ; 94, *Eaton Square,* s.w.

Heir, his son George Angustus, Viscount Parker ; educated at Ch. Ch., Oxford ; late Lieut. 1st Life Guards ; b. 1843.

McCLINTOCK, Sir FRANCIS LEOPOLD, Knt. (cr. 1860.)
Second son of the late Henry McClintock, Esq., formerly in the 3rd Dragoon Guards, by Elizabeth Melesina, dau. of the late Venerable George Fleury, D.D., Archdeacon of Waterford ; *b.* 1819. Entered the Navy 1831, became Capt. 1854 ; knighted for his services in the Arctic regions in the search for Sir John Franklin. —*United Service Club,* s.w.

M'CLINTOCK, Lieut.-Col. GEORGE AUGUSTUS JOCELYN, of Fellow's Hall, co. Armagh.
Youngest son of the late John M'Clintock, Esq., of Drumcar, co. Louth, by Lady Elizabeth, dau. of William, 1st Earl of Clancarty ; *b.* 1822 ; *m.* 1850 Catherine Caroline, dau. of Sir James Matthew Stronge, Bart., and has, with other issue,

* Arthur, *b.* 1856.

Lieut.-Col. M'Clintock, who is a Magistrate for cos. Tyrone and Armagh, was Lieut.-Col. Sligo Rifle Militia, and formerly Capt. 52nd Foot.—*Fellow's Hall, Tynan, co. Armagh ; Kildare Street Club, Dublin.*

M'CLINTOCK, HENRY STANLEY, Esq., of Millmount, co. Antrim.
Son of the late John M'Clintock, Esq., M.P., of Drumcar, co. Louth, by his 2nd wife Lady Elizabeth, dau. of William, 1st Earl of Clancarty ; *b.* 1814 ; *s.* 1855 ; *m.* 1839 Gertrude, only dau. of the late Robert La Touche, Esq., and has, with other issue,

* Frederick Robert, *b.* 1842.

Mr. M'Clintock, who was educated at the Royal Military

Coll., Woolwich, is a Magistrate for cos. Antrim and Kildare, and a Major Antrim Artillery ; was formerly in the Royal Artillery.—*Millmount, Randalstown, co. Antrim ; Carlton Club,* s.w.

M'CLINTOCK, JOHN, Esq., of Drumcar, co. Louth.
Eldest son of the late John M'Clintock, Esq., of Drumcar (formerly M.P. for co. Louth), by his 1st wife Jane, dau. of William Bunbury, Esq., M.P., of Lisnavagh, co Carlow ; *b.* 1798 ; *s.* 1855 ; *m.* 1829 Anne, eldest dau. of the late Rev. John Henry G. Lefroy, of Ewshot House, Hants. Educated at Sandhurst Coll. ; was formerly in the Army ; is Lord-Lieut. of co. Louth (High Sheriff 1840), Dep.-Lieut. for co. Fermanagh, and Col. Louth Militia ; was M.P. for co. Louth 1857-9. —*Drumcar, Dunleer, co. Louth ; Carlton Club,* s.w.

+M'CLINTOCK, THOMPSON MACKAY, Esq., of Hampstead Hall, co. Londonderry.
Eldest surviving son of the late William Kerr M'Clintock, Esq., J.P., of Hampstead Hall, by Sarah, eldest dau. of William Mackay, Esq., of Londonderry ; *b.* 182–; *m.* 1856 Sarah, dau. of the Rev. J. Conyngham M'Causland, and has issue,

* William Kerr, *b.* 1859.

Mr. M'Clintock is a Magistrate for co. Donegal, and late Capt. 87th Foot.—*Hampstead Hall and Muff Lodge, Londonderry.*

M'CLINTOCK, ROBERT, Esq., of Dunmore, co. Donegal.
Eldest son of the late William M'Clintock, Esq., of Dunmore, by Catharine, dau. of J. Ramage, Esq., of Londonderry ; *b.* 1804 ; *m.* 1833 Margaret, dau. of Robert Macan, Esq., of Ballinahone, and has, with other issue,

* Robert, *b.* 1838.

Mr. M'Clintock, who was educated at Rugby and Trinity Coll., Dublin, is a J.P. and D.L. for cos. Donegal and Londonderry ; was High Sheriff of co. Donegal 1833. —*Dunmore, Londonderry.*

M'CLINTOCK-BUNBURY, THOMAS KANE, Esq., of Lisnavagh, co. Carlow.
Elder son of the late Captain William Bunbury M'Clintock-Bunbury, R.N., of Lisnavagh (who was many years M.P. for co. Carlow) by Pauline Caroline Diana Mary, 2nd dau. of Sir J. M. Stronge, Bart., of Tynan Abbey, co. Armagh ; *b.* 1848 ; *s.* 1866.—*Lisnavagh, Rathvilly, co. Carlow.*

Heir Pres., his brother John William, b. 1851.

McCLURE, Sir ROBERT JOHN LE MESURIER, K.t., C.B., of Ballylech, co. Monaghan (cr. 1855).
Son of Capt. McClure, of the 89th Foot, by Jane, dau. of the Ven. Archdeacon Elgar ; *b.* 1807. Educated at Winchester and the Royal Military Coll., Sandhurst, but subsequently entered the Navy ; is a Rear-Admiral R.N., distinguished for his services in the Arctic expedition, in command of H.M.'s ship *Enterprise* ; served on the Canadian and American coasts 1857–46, and in the Coast Guard 1846–8.—*Ballylech House, co. Monaghan ; Athenæum and United Service Clubs,* s.w.

McCLURE, THOMAS, of Belmont, co. Down.
Second son of the late William McClure, Esq., of Belfast, by Elizabeth Thomson, dau. of the Rev. John Thomson, of Carmoney ; *b.* 1806. Is a J.P. and D.L. for co. Down, and a Magistrate for co. Antrim (High Sheriff of co. Down for 1861).—*Belmont, Belfast.*

McCONNEL, Frederic, Esq., of Robgill Tower, Dumfries-shire.

Youngest son of the late James McConnel, Esq., of Carsriggan and Urral, co. Wigtown, by Margaret, dau. of Henry Houldsworth, Esq., of Gonalston, Notts; b. 1821; m. 1845 John Anne, dau. of the late George Whigham, of Halliday Hill, co. Dumfries, and has, with other issue,

* Frederic Robert, b. 1857.

This family is of ancient Irish extraction.—*Robgill Tower, Ecclefechan, N.B.*

McCORMICK, WILLIAM, Esq., of Lisahawley House, co. Londonderry.

Son of the late Mr. William McCormick; b. 1800; m. 1st Miss Smith; 2nd 1865 Ellen Mary, widow of Edward Coote, Esq., of Bellamont Forest, co. Cavan, and has issue. Is a Magistrate for co. Londonderry, and a Contractor for Public Works; was M.P. for Londonderry, 1860-5.—*Lisahawley House, Londonderry; Conservative Club, s.w.; 10, Cambridge Terrace, N.W.*

McCULLAGH. (See *Torrens.*)

+McCULLOCH, WALTER, Esq., of Ardwall, Kirkcudbrightshire.

Eldest son of the late John M. McCulloch, Esq., J.P. and D.L. of Ardwall, by Christian, dau. of Walter Robinson, Esq.; b. 1807; s. 1858. Is Lord of the Barony of Ardwall.—*Ardwall House, Gatehouse, Castle Douglas, N.B.*

Heir Pres., his brother James Robinson, b. 1809.

MAC DERMOT, CHARLES JOSEPH, Esq., of Coolavin, co. Sligo.

Eldest son of the late Hugh Mac Dermot, Esq., of Coolavin; b. 18—; is married, and has issue. Is called a Prince of Coolavin. This family is of ancient Celtic extraction.—*Coolavin, Ballaghadereen, co. Sligo.*

MACDONALD, Lord (SOMERLED JAMES BRUDENELL-MACDONALD).—Cr. 1776.

Eldest son of Godfrey, 4th Lord, by Maria. dau. of George Thomas Wyndham, Esq., of Cromer Hall, Norfolk; b. 1849; s. 1863. Educated at Eton; is Patron of 2 livings. This family is the head of the Clan MacDonald, which claims descent from the Lords of the Isles.—*Seltrington, Malton; Armadale, Isle of Skye, Inverness-shire, N.B.*

Heir Pres., his brother Ronald Archibald, b. 1853.

MACDONALD, Sir ARCHIBALD KEPPEL, Bart., of Woolmer Lodge, Hants (cr. 1813).

Eldest son of the late Sir James Macdonald, Bart., M.P., by Lady Sophia Keppel, dau. of William Charles, 4th Earl of Albemarle; b. 1820; s. as 3rd Bart. 1832; m. 1849 Lady Margaret Sophia, dau. of Thomas William, 1st Earl of Leicester. Educated at Harrow; is a J.P. and D.L. for Hants (High Sheriff 1865), a Magistrate for Surrey, and Lord of the Manor of Bramshott, Hants. Was formerly Capt. Scots Fusilier Guards, and Equerry to H.R.H. the Duke of Sussex.—*Woolmer Lodge, Liphook; Travellers' Club, s.w.*

MACDONALD, Sir JOHN ALEXANDER, K.C.B. (cr. 1867).

Son of the late J. Macdonald, Esq., b. 18—; is Minister of Justice at Canada; was Chairman of the Conference of Delegates from British North America on the measure of Confederation, 1867.—*Toronto, Canada.*

McDONALD, Lieut.-Col. ALASTAIR MacIAN, of Dun Alastair, Perthshire.

Eldest son of the late Sir John McDonald, K.C.B., of Dun Alastair, by Adriana, eldest dau. of the late

611

James M'Inroy, Esq., of Lude, co. Perth; b. 1830; s. 1866. Entered the army in 1846; is a Col. in the army, and Lieut.-Col. Depot Battalion; was formerly Capt. 92nd Foot. Is Chief of the McDonalds of Keppoch.—*Dun Alastair, Dalchosnie, Pitochry, N.B.*

MACDONALD, Capt. DONALD, of Sandside, Caithness-shire.

Only son of the late Col. John Macdonald, by Mary eldest dau. of William Innes, Esq., of Sandside; b. 1791; s. his uncle William Innes, Esq., of Sandside, 1842; m. 1826 Lady Ramsay, 5th dau of William, 1st Lord Panmure, and sister of Fox, 11th Earl of Dalhousie, and has, with other issue,

* William Donald, late Major 93rd Highlanders; b. 1828; m. 1860 Emma Anne Elizabeth, dau. of the late Colin Lindsay, Esq.

Capt. Macdonald is a retired Capt. R.E., and a Dep. Lieut. for co. Caithness.—*Sandside House, Thurso, N.B.*

MACDONALD, DOUGLAS JOHN KINNEIR, Esq., of Sanda, Argyllshire.

Eldest son of the late Rev. Douglas Macdonald, of Sanda, (sometime Vicar of West Alvington, Devon), by Flora Georgiana, dau. of Patrick Hadow, Esq.; b. 1839; s. 1865; m. 1866 Jane Martha MacNeill, eldest dau. of John Alexander Mackay, Esq., of Blackcastle, Midlothian, N.B. Educated at Marlborough Coll. and Jesus Coll., Cambridge (B.A. 1860); is Lord of the Barony of Sanda. This family descend in a direct line from John, Lord of Kintyre, 2nd son of John the 7th and last King of the Isles, and were once as powerful as the Lords of the Isles were in the northern part of the west of Scotland, though they were deprived of much of their possessions *temp.* James I.—*Sanda, Camphelton, N.B.; New University Club, s.w.*

Heir Pres., his brother, Maurice Patrick, b. 1850.

MACDONALD, REGINALD GEORGE, Capt. and Chief of Clanranald.

Eldest son of the late Chief of Clanranald; b. 1789; m. 1st 1812 Lady Caroline Anne, younger dau. of Richard, 2nd Earl of Mount Edgecumbe (she d. 1824); 2nd 182- Anne, dau. of William Cunningham. Esq., and widow of Richard, Lord Ashburton (she d. 1855); 3rd 185- Miss Elizabeth Rebecca Newman. Is a J.P. and D.L. for co. Inverness; was M.P. for Plympton 1812-24. This family is lineally descended from Reginald, eldest son of John, last Lord of the Isles.—*Residence: Scarsdale Villas, Kensington, w.*

Heir, his only son Reginald John James George, Capt. R N.; b. 181-; m. 1854 the Hon. Adelaide Louisa Warren, 2nd dau. of George John, 5th Lord Vernon.

+MACDONALD, ROBERT DOUGLAS, Esq., of Inchkenneth, Argyllshire.

Eldest son of the late Col. Robert Macdonald, C.B., of Inchkenneth, formerly of the Royal Horse Artillery; b. 18—; s. 1855. Was formerly Capt. 42nd Foot; is Barrack-master at Brecon.—*Inchkenneth, Aros, Argyllshire, N.B.*

MACDONALD, WILLIAM BELL, Esq., of Rammerscales, Dumfries-shire.

Eldest son of the late William Bell Macdonald. Esq., of Rammerscales (who was a Magistrate for co. Dumfries), by Helen, 3rd dau. of Thomas Johnstone, Esq., of Underwood, co. Dumfries; b. 1845; s. 1862. Educated at Cheltenham Coll. and the University of Glasgow; is Lord of the Manor and Barony of Rammerscales.—*Rammerscales, Lockerby, N.B.*

Heir Pres., his brother Donald, b. 1846.

MACDONALD, WILLIAM MACDONALD, Esq., of St. Martin's Abbey, Perthshire.

Only son of the late General Farquharson, of Oakley, co. Fife, by Rebecca, dau. and co-heir of Sir G. Col-

quhoun, Bart.; *b.* 1822; *s.* his father 1834; *s.* his cousin, William Macdonald, Esq., of Runathan and St. Martin's, 1841, when he took the name and arms of Macdonald; *m.* 1849 the Hon. Clara Ann Jane, dau. of Charles, 1st Lord Lurgan, and has, with other issue,

* Montagu William Colquhoun Farquharson, *b.* 1851.

Mr. Macdonald, who was educated at the Royal Military Coll., Sandhurst, is a J.P. and D.L. for cos. Forfar and Perth; was formerly an Officer in the Army.—*St. Martin's Abbey, Perth; Garth House, Aberfeldy; Crossmount Lodge, Pitlochrie; Glenshee Lodge, Blairgowrie, Perthshire; Rossie Castle, Montrose, Forfarshire; Carlton Club,* s.w.; 1, *Whitehall Gardens,* s.w.

MACDONALD. (See *Steuart.*)

MACDONALD-HUME. (See *Hume, of Ninewalls.*)

MACDONALD-LOCKHART. (See *Lockhart.*)

MACDONALD-MORETON, CHARLES, Esq., of Largie Castle, Argyleshire.

Eldest son of the late Hon. Augustus Moreton, who assumed the additional name of Macdonald on his marriage with Mary Jane, dau. of the late Sir Charles Macdonald Lockhart, Bart., of Lee, N.B.; *b.* 1840; *s.* 1862. Educated at Eton; is a J.P. and D.L. for co. Argyle, Lord of the Manor and Barony of Largie, and an Officer in the Argyleshire Artillery.—*Largie Castle, Tainloan, Argyleshire; Kildare Street Club, Dublin; St. James's Club,* s.w.

Heir Pres., his brother Augustus Henry, *b.* 1848.

MACDONELL, CHARLES RONALDSON, Esq., of Glengarry and Clanranald.

Only surviving son of the late Æneas Ronaldson Macdonell, Esq., of Glengarry and Clanranald (who *d.* 1852), by Josephine, dau. of the late W. Bennet, Esq., of the 32nd Regt. of Foot, and niece of the late Bishop of Cloyne; *b.* 1838; *s.* his brother 1862; *m.* 1866 Agnes Campbell, eldest dau. of Alexander Cassels, Esq. Is a Lieut. R.N. The Macdonells of Glengarry trace back their descent to Somerled, Lord of the Isles, Thane of Argyle, and Lord of the Province of Kintyre. —*29, Northumberland Street, Edinburgh.*

MACDONELL, ENEAS RONALD, Esq., of Morar, Inverness-shire.

Eldest son of the late Col. D. Macdonell, of Morar, by Ann Isabella, dau. of Archibald Macdonald, Esq., of Lochsheil; *b.* 1822; *s.* 1856; *m.* 1859 Catharine, only dau. of the late James Sidgreaves, Esq., of Inglewhite Lodge, co. Lancaster, and has, with other issue,

* Ronald Talbot, *b.* 1861.

Mr. Macdonell, who was educated at Stonyhurst and the Edinburgh University, and called to the Scottish Bar 1845, is a J.P. and D.L. for co. Inverness.—*Morar, Fortwilliam, N.B.; 7, Coates Crescent, Edinburgh; Reform Club,* s.w.

MACDONNELL, Sir RICHARD GRAVES, Knt., C.B., LL.D. (cr. 1855).

Eldest surviving son of the late Rev. Dr. Richard Macdonnell, Provost of Trinity Coll., Dublin (who *d.* 1867), by Jane, dau. of the late Very Rev. Richard Graves, Dean of Ardagh; *b.* 1815; *m.* Blanche Ann, dau. of Francis Skurray, Esq., of Brunswick Square, Brighton. Educated at Trinity Coll., Dublin (B.A. 1835, M.A. 1838, Hon. LL.D. 1844); called to the Bar of Ireland 1838, and at Lincoln's Inn 1840; late Governor of the Gambia and St. Vincent; was Capt.-General and Governor-in-Chief of South Australia 1855–63; appointed Lieut.-Governor of Nova Scotia 1864, and Governor of Hong Kong 1865.—*Sorrento, co. Dublin; Government House, Hong Kong, China.*

MACDONNELL, the Right Hon. ALEXANDER.

Son of the late Dr. James Macdonnell, of Belfast, and cousin of the late Randal Macdonnell, Esq., of Glengariff, co. Antrim; *b.* 1794; *m.* 1826 Barbara, eldest dau. of the late Hugh Montgomery, Esq., of Glenarm, co. Antrim, and widow of Richard Staples, Esq. (she *d.* 1865). Educated at Westminster and Ch. Ch., Oxford; called to the Bar at Lincoln's Inn 1824; is a Privy Councillor for Ireland, and Resident Commissioner of the Board of National Education in Ireland.—*Marlborough Street, Dublin.*

McDONNELL, FRANCIS, Esq., of Plas Newydd, Monmouthshire.

Eldest son of the late Francis McDonnell, Esq., of Plas Newydd (who was a Magistrate for co. Monmouth), by Ann, dau. of the late Thomas Prothero, Esq., of Usk; *b.* 1828; *s.* 1860. Educated at Oscott and Trinity Coll., Dublin (B.A. 1850); is a Magistrate for co. Monmouth, and Major Royal Monmouth Militia; was formerly in the 71st Highlanders.—*Plas Newydd, Usk; Army and Navy Club,* s.w.

MAC DONNELL, FRANCIS EDMUND JOSEPH, Esq., of Donforth, co. Kildare.

Eldest surviving son of the late Sir Francis Mac Donnell, of Donforth, by Bridget Mary, dau. of James O'Connor, Esq., of Madrid; *b.* 1823; *s.* 1840; *m.* 1st 1859 Ellen, only child of the late Henry McNamara, Esq., of Barbados; 2nd 1865 Georgina, only surviving dau. of James Gernon, Esq., of Athcarne Castle, co. Meath. Educated at Clongowes Coll.; is a Magistrate for cos. Meath and Kildare (High Sheriff 1866).—*Donforth, Enfield, Ireland; Stephen's-Green Club, Dublin.*

McDONNELL, Lieut.-Col. JOHN, of Kilmore, co. Antrim.

Only surviving son of the late Randall McDonnell, Esq of Kilmore, by Mary, dau. of Archibald M'Elheran, Esq., of Glassmullin; *b.* 1823; *s.* his brother Alexander 1862. Is a Magistrate for co. Antrim, and served at the Cape and Natal (including the Kaffir Wars of 1846–7 and 1851–2–3, and the Dutch Boer Rebellion 1849. Lieut.-Col. (unattached) McDonnell, who is descended from a common ancestor with the Earl of Antrim, is 5th in descent on the male and female side from Sir Alister Mac Coll Kittagh McDonnell, Montrose's celebrated Major-General, who was 9th in direct male descent from John, Lord of the Isles, and Margaret, dau. of Robert II., of Scotland.—*Glengariff, Glenarm, co. Antrim; Army and Navy Club,* s.w.

Heir Pres., his niece Mary Rachel Josephine, dau. of the late Alexander McDonnell, Esq., by Margaret Anne, dau. of the late Alexander McMullan, Esq., of Cabra House, co. Down.

MACDONNELL, JOSEPH MYLES, Esq., of Doo Castle, co. Mayo.

Eldest son of Myles Macdonnell, Esq., of Doo Castle, by Mary Anne, dau. of James Hughes, Esq., J.P. for cos. Mayo and Roscommon; *b.* 1796; *m.* 1828 Eleanor, dau. of Mark Lynch, Esq., of Ballinasloe, co. Galway, and has issue,

* Three daughters

Mr. Macdonnell, who is a Magistrate for cos. Sligo, Galway, Roscommon, and Mayo, was M.P. for co. Mayo 1846–7.—*Doo Castle, Ballaghaderreen, co. Mayo.*

MACDONNELL, WILLIAM EDWARD ARMSTRONG-, Esq., F.G. and H.S., M.R.I.A., of New Hall, co. Clare.

Second surviving son of the late William Henry Armstrong, Esq., M.P., of Mount Heaton, King's Co., by Bridget, only dau. of the late Col. C. Mac-Donnell, M.P., of New Hall and Kilkee, co. Clare; *b.* 1826; *s.*

1850 ; *m.* 1858 the Hon. Juliana Cecilia, eldest dau. of Lucius, 13th Lord Inchiquin, and has, with other issue,

    * Charles Randal, *b.* 1862.

Mr. Armstrong-Macdonnell, who assumed by Royal licence, 1858, the additional name of Macdonnell, after his maternal uncle, is a J.P. and D.L. for, and Vice-Lieut. of, co. Clare (High Sheriff 1853), and Major co. Clare Militia.—*New Hall, Ennis, co. Clare ; Liscrona House, Kilkee, co. Clare ; Kildare Street Club, Dublin.*

McDONNELL.   (See under *Antrim, Earl of.*)

MACDONOGH, Francis, Q.C.

Son of the late Morgan Macdonogh, Esq., of Sligo, by Catharine, dau. of Patrick Tondray, Esq.; *b.* 1806; *m.* 1st 1830 Anne Maria, dau. of Thomas Shore, Esq., M.D. (she *d.* 1857); 2nd 1865 Anne, dau. of Alexander Cross, Esq., of Armagh, widow of the late Arthure Dillon, Esq., of Ballyguin House, co. Kilkenny. Educated at Trinity Coll., Dublin (B.A. 1825, M.A. 1865); called to the Irish Bar 1829 ; became a Q.C. 1842 ; is a Magistrate for co. Sligo and Counsel to Inland Revenue of Ireland; was M.P. for Sligo 1860–65.—*Ballyguin House, Mullinavat, co. Kilkenny ;* 41, *Rutland Square, Dublin ; Carlton Club, s.w.*

M'DOUALL, Col. James, of Logan, Wigtonshire.

Eldest son of the late Col. Andrew M'Douall, M.P., of Logan, by Mary, dau. of James Russell, Esq., of Shottsburn; *b.* 1796; *s.* 1834; *m.* 1836 Jane, dau. of William Barnet, Esq., of Barbie, and has, with other issue,

    * James, educated at Eton, *b.* 1840.

Col. M'Douall, who was educated at Trinity Coll., Cambridge, entered the 2nd Life Guards 1819, became Col. 1845, and retired 1854, is a J.P. and D.L. for co. Wigton.—*Logan, Stranraer, N.B. ; Carlton Club, s.w.*

McDOUGALL, Major John, of Gallanach, Argyleshire.

Second but eldest surviving son of the late Dugald McDougall, Esq., of Gallanach, by Margaret, dau. of Murdoch McLaine, Esq., of Lochbury ; *b.* 1822 ; *s.* 1866. Is a Major in the Indian Army, was formerly Capt. 17th Madras N. Infantry.—*Gallanach, Oban, N.B.*

    Heir Pres., his brother Murdoch, *b.* 182–.

McDOUGALL, Patrick Charles Campbell, Esq., of Mac Dougall and Dunolly, Argyleshire.

Second but eldest surviving son of the late Admiral Sir John McDougall, K.C.B., of MacDougall and Dunolly (who *d.* 1865), by Elizabeth Sophia, only child of Charles S. Timins, Esq., of Oriel Lodge, Cheltenham : *b.* 1830 ; *s.* his brother 1867 ; formerly a Commander R.N. This family descend from Somerled, Thane of Argyle and the Isles.—*Dunolly Castle, Oban, N.B.*

MACDOWALL, Lieut.-General Day Hort, of Garthland, Renfrewshire.

Third son of the late Day Hort Macdowall, Esq., of Walkenshaw, by Wilhelmina, dau. of William Graham, Esq., of Airth, co. Stirling ; *b.* 1795 ; *s.* his cousin Lawrence Macdowall, Esq., 1812 , *m.* 1838 Eleanor Frances, dau. of David Macdowall Grant, Esq., of Arndilly, N.B. Is a Lieut.-General in the Army, a J.P. and D.L. for co. Renfrew, Col. 3rd Foot, and Lord of the Barony of Garthland and Carruth, co. Renfrew.—*Garthland, Lochwinnoch, N.B. ; United Service Club, s.w.*

    Heir Pres., his brother Henry Macdowall, a Magistrate for co. Renfrew, *b.* 1796 ; *m.* 1839 Isabella, dau. of A. Dennistoun, Esq., of Golfhill, near Glasgow, and has, with other surviving issue, Henry, *b.* 1846.

McDOWELL-JOHNSTON.   (See *Johnston.*)

MAC EVOY, Edward Francis, Esq., of Tobertinan, co. Meath.

Eldest son of the late James Mac Evoy, Esq., of Tobertinan, by Teresa Maria, dau. of the late Sir Joshua Colles Meredyth, Bart.; *b.* 1826 ; *s.* 1840; *m.* 1850 Eliza Teresa, only child of Andrew Browne, Esq., of Mount Hazel, co. Galway. Educated at Magdalen Coll., Cambridge; is a Magistrate for co. Meath ; was formerly Lieut. 6th Dragoon Guards (Carabineers) ; has been M.P. for co. Meath since 1855.—*Tobertinan, Rathmolyon, co. Meath ; Army and Navy Club, s.w.*

M'EVOY, Thomas, Esq., of Balmarino, co. Meath.

Eldest son of the late Peter M'Evoy, Esq., of Balmarino, by Anne, dau. of the late B. Ennis, Esq. ; *b.* 1845; *s.* 1866. This family is maternally descended from Henry Dowall, Recorder of and M.P. for Drogheda in 1689.—*Balmarino, Drogheda, co. Meath.*

MACFARLANE, Alexander, Esq., of Thornhill, Stirlingshire.

Eldest son of the late Robert Macfarlane, Esq., of Alloa, co.-Clackmannan, by Elizabeth, dau. of James Morrison, Esq., of Hawkhill ; *b.* 1790 ; *s.* 1819 ; *m.* 1814 Helen, dau. of John Mitchell, Esq., of Tullybody, co. Clackmannan, and has, with other issue,

    * Alexander, a Magistrate for co. Stirling ; *b.* 1828 ; *m.* 1852 Marion Clark, dau. of John Scott, Esq., of Finnart House, near Greenock, Renfrewshire.

Mr. Macfarlane, who was educated at the University of St. Andrew's, is a J.P. and D.L. for co. Stirling.—*Thornhill, Falkirk, N.B.*

MACFARLANE, Henry James, Esq., D.C.L., of Hunstown House, co. Dublin.

Eldest son of the late Henry MacFarlane. Esq., of Stirling, co. Meath, and of Hunstown House, by Mary, dau. of Ross Maguire, Esq., of Oak Park, Castleknock ; *b.* 1817 ; *s.* 1851 ; *m.* 1840 Jane, dau. of Hamilton Wallace, Esq., of co. Tyrone, and has, with other issue,

    * James Francis Lenox, Cornet 3rd Dragoon Guards, *b.* 1845.

Mr. MacFarlane, who was educated at Trinity Coll., Dublin, of which he is a D.C.L., is a Magistrate for cos. Tyrone and Dublin, and Chairman of North Dublin Union.—*Hunstown House, Mulhuddart, co. Dublin ; Fallagh Erin, Ballygawley, co. Tyrone.*

M'FARLAN, John Warden, Esq., of Ballencleroch, Stirlingshire.

Eldest son of the late John M'Farlan, Esq., of Ballencleroch, by Janet Buchanan. dau. of Robert Ewing. Esq., of Glasgow ; *b.* 1824 ; *s.* 1852 ; *m.* 1857 Elizabeth, dau. of Duncan Gibb. Esq., of Liverpool. Educated at Edinburgh ; is a Capt. 5th Lancers, and Superior of Ballencleroch. This family claims descent from the Chiefs, the first of whom was a son of an Earl of Lennox (*ext.*).—*Ballencleroch House, Campsie, Glasgow, N.B. ; Army and Navy Club, s.w.*

    Heir Pres., his brother William Leckie, Minister of Cupar, co. Fife ; *b.* 1832 ; *m.* 1860 Isabella Leckie, dau. of William Leckie Ewing, Esq., of Arngomery, co. Stirling.

MACFIE, Robert, Esq., of Airds, Argyleshire.

Eldest son of the late William Macfie, Esq., of Langhouse, co. Renfrew, by Jessie, dau. of David Johnstone, Esq., of Port Glasgow; *b.* 1812 ; *s.* 1854 ; *m.* 1838 Agnes, dau. of James Fairrie, Esq., of Greenock, N.B., and has, with other issue,

    * William, *b.* 1840 ; *m.* 1864 Agnes Hamilton, eldest dau. of the Rev. James Towers.

Mr. Macfie is a J.P. and D.L. for co. Argyle, and a Magistrate for co. Renfrew.—*Airds House, Appin, Argyleshire ; Langhouse, Greenock, N.B.*

MACFIE, ROBERT ANDREW, Esq., of Dreghorn, Midlothian, and New-ferry, Cheshire.

Eldest son of the late John Macfie, Esq., of Edinburgh (a. Dep. Lieut. of the city of Edinburgh), by Alison, dau. of William Thorburn, Esq., of Leith; *b.* 1811; *m.* 1840 Caroline Eliza, dau. of John Easton, Esq., M.D. (of the 15th Hussars), of Courance Hill, Dumfriesshire, by whom he has issue. Mr. Macfie, who was educated at the High School and University of Edinburgh, is a Magistrate for co. Edinburgh.—*Dreghorn, Edinburgh.* Residence: *Ashfield Hall, Neston, Chester.*

MACFIE. (See *Shaw*.)

+McGAREL, CHARLES, Esq., of Magheramorne House, co. Antrim.

Son of the late — McGarel, Esq., of Magheramorne House; *b.* 18—; *m.* 1855 Mary Rosina, 2nd dau. of Sir James W. Hogg, Bart. Is a Magistrate for co. Antrim (of which county he has been High Sheriff), and Lord of the Manor of Magheramorne.—*Magheramorne House, Larne, co. Antrim.*

M'GEACHY, FORSTER ALLEYNE, Esq., of Shenley Hill, Herts.

Only son of the late Major M'Geachy, by Sarah Gibbes, eldest dau. of John Forster Alleyne, Esq., of Porters, in the island of Barbados; *b.* 1809; *m.* 1st 1834 Anna Maria Letitia, eldest dau. of the late Charles Clement Adderley, Esq., of Hams Hall, Warwick (she *d.* 1841); 2nd 1848 Clara, dau. of the Rev. Thomas Newcome, Rector of Shenley, and widow of the Rev. W. R. Hall. Educated at Balliol Coll., Oxford (B.A. 1831); is a J.P. and D.L. for Herts (High Sheriff 1865), and a Magistrate for Middlesex and for the Liberty of St. Alban's, and one of the Council of Marlborough College; was M.P. for Honiton 1841–7.—*Shenley Hill, Barnet; Carlton and Athenæum Clubs, s.w.*

McGILDOWNY, ROMALDO KING, Esq., of Ollerton Hall, Cheshire.

Son of Edmund McGildowny, Esq., of Culmore, co. Londonderry; *b.* 18—; *m.* 1863 Sarah Frances Elizabeth, dau. of the late Capt. W. Fowden Hindle. of the 6th Dragoon Guards (she *d.* 1864). This family was formerly seated in the North of Ireland.—*Ollerton Hall, Knutsford.*

+McGILLDOWNY, Capt. JOHN, of Clare Park, co. Antrim.

Only son of the late Charles McGilldowny, Esq., by Rosetta, dau. of — Boyd, Esq.; *b.* 1820; *s.* 1842; is married, and has issue. Is a J.P. and D.L. for co. Antrim (High Sheriff 1843), and Capt. in the local Militia.—*Clare Park, Ballycastle, co. Antrim; Carlton Club, s.w.*

M'GILLICUDDY, DANIEL DE COURCY, Esq., of Tralee, co. Kerry.

Eldest son of the late Daniel M'Gillicuddy, Esq., of Tralee, by Sophia, dau. of the late Sir Rory Denny, Bart., of Tralee Castle; *b.* 1816; *s.* 1826; *m.* 1839 Lucinda Margaret, dau. of the late Richard Murphy, Esq., and Sarah, dau. of Edward Orpen, Esq., and has, with other issue,

* Daniel De Courcy, *b.* 1840.

Mr. M'Gillicuddy is a Magistrate for co. Kerry.—*Day Place, Tralee, co. Kerry.*

McGILLYCUDDY, RICHARD PATRICK, Esq., of The Reeks, co. Kerry.

Eldest son of the late Richard MacGillycuddy, Esq., of The Reeks, by Anna, dau. of John Johnstone, Esq., of Mainstone Court, co. Hereford; *b.* 1850; *s.* 1866. Educated at St. John's Coll., Cambridge; is Patron of

2 livings, and a Ward in Chancery.—*The Reeks, Killarney, Ireland.*

Heir Pres., his brother Donough Charles, a Midshipman R.N.; *b.* 1852.

MAC GREGOR, Sir MALCOLM, Bart., of Edinchip, Perthshire (cr. 1795).

Eldest son of the late Sir John Atholl Bannatyne Murray-Mac Gregor, Bart., by Mary Charlotte, dau. of the late Admiral Sir Thomas Masterman Hardy, Bart., G.C.B.; *b.* 1834; *s.* as 4th Bart. 1851; *m.* 1864 Lady Helen Laura, only dau. of Hugh Seymour, 7th Earl of Antrim; is a Magistrate for co. Perth, and a Capt. R.N.; was formerly Flag-Lieutenant at Constantinople. —*Edinchip House, Loch Earn Head, Perthshire, N.B.; United Service Club, s.w.*

Heir Pres., his brother Atholl, of the Indian Civil Service, *b.* 1836.

MACGREGOR, the Rev. Sir CHARLES, Bart. (cr. 1828).

Only surviving son of the late Sir Patrick Macgregor, Bart., by Bridget, dau. of James Glenny, Esq., of Quebec; *b.* 1819; *s.* as 3rd Bart. 1846; *m.* 1845 Eliza Catherine, dau. of John Jeffreys, Esq., of Fynone, co. Glamorgan. Educated at St. Catharine's Hall, Cambridge (B.A. 1842, M.A. 1851); is Rector of Swallow, and Rural Dean; was formerly Minor Canon of Bristol. —*Swallow Rectory, Caistor, Lincolnshire.*

Heir, his son William Gordon, *b.* 1846.

M'GREGOR, Sir DUNCAN, K.C.B. (cr. 1848).

Son of the late D. M'Gregor, Esq.; *b.* 1787; *m.* 18— Elizabeth, dau. of the late Sir William Dick, Bart. (she *d.* 1858). Educated at the Royal Military Coll., Wycombe; is a General in the Army, and Inspector-General of the Constabulary Force in Ireland; served in Egypt, Italy, Holland, West Indies, America, and the Peninsula. —*The Castle, Dublin; Belvedere, Drumcondra, Dublin; United Service Club, s.w.*

MACGREGOR, Lady.

Ellen Grace, youngest dau. of the late Nathaniel Brassey, Esq., Banker, of Lombard Street, London; *m.* 1846 Sir John MacGregor, K.C.B., Inspector-General of Hospitals, who *d.* 1864, leaving, with other issue,

* John Lennox, *b.* 1822; *m.* 1834 Emily Philippa, eldest dau. of James Whelan, Esq., of London.

This family is descended from the MacGregors of Rora; the name was changed to McAndrew after the rebellion in Scotland 1745, but resumed by the late Sir J. Mac-Gregor, by Royal licence, in 1853.—*Curatorphine Lodge, Ryde, I. of Wight.*

MACGREGOR, Sir GEORGE HALL, K.C.B. (cr. 1861).

Eldest son of General John Alexander Paul MacGregor, of Sussex Place, Hyde Park, by Jane, dau. of the late James Burdett Ness, Esq., of Osterly Hall. co. York; *b.* 1810; *m.* 1845 Harriett, dau. of the late Lieut.-General Sir Thomas Whitehead. K.C.B., of Uplands Hall, co. Lancaster. Educated at Addiscombe; entered the Bengal Artillery 1826; retired as Major-General 1859; was formerly employed in high political and civil appointments in India.—*Glencarnock, Torquay.*

McGRIGOR, Sir CHARLES RODERICK, Bart. (cr. 1831).

Eldest son of the late Sir James McGrigor, Bart., K.C.B., M.D. (who was many years Director-General of the Army Medical Department), by Mary, dau. of Duncan Grant, Esq., of Lingeistone, co. Moray; *b.* 1811; *s.* as 2nd Bart. 1858; *m.* 1850 Elizabeth Anne, dau. of the late Major-General Sir Robert Nickle, K.H. Educated at Eton.—6, *Hyde Park Street, w.*

Heir, his son James Roderick Duff, *b.* 1847.

617

M'GRIGOR, ALEXANDER BENNETT, Esq., of Cairnoch, Stirlingshire.

Only son of the late Alexander M'Grigor, Esq., of Cairnoch, by his 1st wife Janet Stevenson, dau. of William Bennet, Esq., of Moore Place, Glasgow ; b. 1827 ; s. 1853 ; m. 1848 Elizabeth, youngest dau. of the late John Robertson, Esq., Merchant, of Hamburgh, by whom he has, with other issue,
* Alexander, b. 1858.

Mr. M'Grigor is a Magistrate for co. Stirling, and a Member of the Faculty of Procurators, Glasgow.—*Cairnoch, near Denny, N.B.* ; 19, *Woodside Terrace, Glasgow.*

MACHELL, JOHN PENNY, Esq., of Hollow Oak, Lancashire.

Eldest son of the late James Penny Machell, Esq., of Penny Bridge, co. Lancaster, by Anne, dau. of the late James Penny, Esq., of Arrad, in the same co. ; b. 1800 ; s. 1854 ; m. 1837 Eliza, 4th dau. of the late Right Hon. Lord Chief Justice Dallas, and has issue.
* Justina Madeline.

Mr. Machell, who was educated at Rugby and Ch. Ch., Oxford, is a J.P. and D.L. for co. Lancaster, and Patron of 1 living.—*The Hall, Pennybridge ; Hollow Oak, Ulverstone.*

MACHELL, the Rev. RICHARD BEVERLEY, Rector of Roos, Yorkshire.

Eldest son of the late Rev. Robert Machell, Vicar of Marton-in-Cleveland ; b. 1823 ; m. 1850 Hon. Emma, dau. of Henry Willoughby, Esq., of Birdsall and Settrington, sister of Henry, 8th Lord Middleton, and raised to the rank of a Baron's dau. by Royal warrant, and has, with other issue,
* Hugh Lancelot, b. 1851.

Mr. Machell, who was educated at Shrewsbury and Magdalen Coll., Cambridge (B.A. 1846), is a Magistrate for The Parts of Lindsey, Lincolnshire, and Rector of Roos ; was formerly Vicar of Barrow-on-Humber, co. Lincoln. This family was formerly of Crakenthorpe Hall, Westmoreland.—*Roos Rectory, Holderness, Hull.*

MACHEN, the Rev. EDWARD, of Eastbach Court, Gloucestershire.

Eldest son of the late Edward Tomkins Machen, Esq., of Eastbach Court, by Sophia, dau. of Richard Dighton, Esq., of The Wilderness, co. Gloucester ; b. 1817 ; m. 1847 Sophia, dau. of the Rev. James L. Dighton, Vicar of Dixton, co. Monmouth, and has, with other issue,
* Charles Edward, b. 1819.

Mr. Machen, who was educated at Rugby and Exeter Coll., Oxford (B.A. 1840), is Rector and Patron of Staunton, co. Gloucester.—*Eastbach Court, Coleford.*

MACHIN, JOHN VESSEY, Esq., of Gateford Hill, Notts.

Son of the late Henry Machin, Esq., of Gateford Hill, by Mary, dau. of Henry Swan, Esq., of Lincoln ; b. 1826 ; s. 1815 ; m. 1852 Delia, dau. of J. K. Watson, Esq., and has, with other issue,
* John Vessey, b. 1857.

Mr. Machin, who was educated at Emmanuel Coll., Cambridge (B.A. 1849, M.A. 1852), is a Magistrate for Notts, late a Capt. in the Sherwood Rangers.—*Gateford Hill, Worksop.*

M'INROY, Col. WILLIAM, of The Burn, Kincardineshire.

Second son of the late James M'Inroy, Esq., of Lude, co. Perth, by Elizabeth, dau. of William Moore, Esq., of St. Eustatia ; b. 1804 ; m. 1839 Harriet Barbara, dau. of Elias Jones, Esq., of Boughton, co. Worcester. Educated at Glasgow and Edinburgh Coll., is a J.P.

618

and D.L. for co. Kincardine, and Lieut.-Col. Kincardineshire Rifle Volunteers ; was formerly a Major in the Army.—*The Burn, Edzell, Brechin, N.B. ; Junior United Service Club, s.w.*

Heir Pres., his brother James Patrick, of Lude, a Magistrate for co. Perth ; b. 1799 ; m. 1822 Margaret Seton, dau. of David Lillie, Esq., of Glasgow, N.B.

+McIVER, DUNCAN CAMPBELL, Esq., of Asknish, Argyllshire.

Eldest son of the late Duncan McIver, Esq., of Asknish ; b. 18—. Is a Magistrate for co. Argyll and Lord of the Barony of Asknish.—*Lochgair House, Inverary, N.B.*

MACKAY, GEORGE, Esq., of Bighouse, Argyleshire.

Eldest son of the late Col. Colin Campbell Mackay, of Bighouse, by Marjory Gerard, 5th dau. of the late P. Cruikshank, Esq., of Stracathro', N.B. ; b. 1817 ; s. 1841 ; m. 1861 Annie Moore, only dau. of the late Capt. F. Campbell, 2nd son of the late A. Campbell, Esq., of Melfort, co. Argyle. Is a Magistrate for co. Argyle ; was formerly an officer in the 62nd Regt. and 7th Fusiliers.—*Bighouse, Morinish, Isle of Mull, N.B.*

MACKAY, HENRY RAMSAY, Esq., of Petham, Kent.

Eldest son of the late Thomas Henry Mackay, Esq., J.P. and D.L., of Petham House, by Elizabeth, eldest dau. of the late Hon. Andrew Ramsay ; b. 1843 ; s. 1865.—*Petham House, Canterbury.*

MACKAY. (See under *Reay, Lord.*)

M'KENNA, Sir JOSEPH NEALE, Knt. of Admore, co. Cork (cr. 1867).

Eldest son of the late Michael McKenna, Esq., by Mary, eldest dau. of the late Oliver Grogan, Esq., of Dublin ; b. 1819 ; m. 1843 Esther Louisa, youngest dau. of the late Edmund Howe, Esq., of Dublin. Educated at Trinity Coll., Dublin ; called to the Irish Bar 1848 ; is a Dep. Lieut. for co. Cork ; elected M.P. for Youghal 1865.—*Ardo House, Ardmore, Youghal ; 84, Lancaster Gate, w.*

MACKENZIE, Sir KENNETH SMITH, Bart., of Gairloch, Ross-shire (cr. 1629).

Eldest son of the late Sir Francis Alexander Mackenzie, Bart., of Gairloch, by his 1st wife Kythe Caroline, dau. of John Smith Wright, Esq., of Kempstone Hall, Notts ; b. 1832 ; s. 1843 ; m. 1860 Eila Frederica, dau. of the late W. F. Campbell, Esq., of Islay, co. Argyle. Is a J.P. and D.L. for Ross-shire, and Convener of that county ; Capt. Ross Militia.—*Conan House and Gairloch, Dingwall, N.B. ; Arthur's Club, s.w.*

Heir, his son Kenneth John, b. 1861.

MACKENZIE, Sir WILLIAM, Bart., of Coul, Ross-shire (cr. 1673).

Second but eldest surviving son of the late Sir George Stewart Mackenzie, Bart., co. Ross., by Mary, dau. of Donald Macleod, Esq., of Geanies, co. Ross ; b. 1806 ; s. as 9th Bart. 1856 ; m. 1858 Agnes, 2nd dau. of Ross T. Smyth, Esq., of Ardmore, co. Londonderry. Educated at Edinburgh High School and University ; a J.P. and D.L. for co. Ross ; formerly in H.E.I.C.'s Maritime Service.—*Coul House, Dingwall, N.B.*

Heir, his brother Robert Ramsay, b. 1811 ; m. 1846 Louisa Alexandrina, dau. of the late Richard Jones, Esq., M.L.C., of Sydney, N.S. Wales.

MACKENZIE, Sir JAMES JOHN RANDOLL, Bart., of Scatwell, Ross-shire (cr. 1703).

Eldest son of the late Sir James Wemyss Mackenzie, Bart., of Scatwell, by Henrietta Wharton, sister and

sole heir of Major-General John Randoll Mackenzie, of Suddy; *b.* 1814; *s.* as 7th Bart. 1843; *m.* 1838 Lady Anne, dau. of Charles William, 5th Earl Fitzwilliam, K.G. Educated at Westminster and Trinity Coll., Cambridge; is a J.P. and D.L. for cos. Ross and Cromarty, and Capt. in the 3rd Ross-shire Rifle Volunteers. —*Carlton and Travellers' Clubs*, s.w.

Heir Pres., his cousin James Dixon Mackenzie, Esq., of Findon (whom see).

MACKENZIE, Sir ALEXANDER MUIR-, Bart., of Delvine, Perthshire (cr. 1805).
Eldest son of the late Sir John William Pitt Muir-Mackenzie, Bart., of Delvine (whose father, the 1st Bart., assumed the additional name of Mackenzie), by Sophia Matilda, dau. of James Raymond Johnstone, Esq., of Alva, co. Clackmannan; *b.* 1840; *s.* as 3rd Bart. 1855. Educated at Harrow; is a Capt. in the 78th Highlanders. —*Delvine, Dunkeld, N.B.*

Heir Pres., his brother Robert Smyth, *b.* 1841.

MACKENZIE, Sir EVAN, Bart., of Kilcoy, Ross-shire (cr. 1836).
Second but eldest surviving son of the late Sir Colin Mackenzie, Bart., of Kilcoy, by Isabella, dau. of Ewen Cameron, Esq., of Glenevis, co. Inverness; *b.* 1816; *s.* as 2nd Bart. 1845; *m.* 1844 Sarah Anne Philomena, dau. of J. Parks, Esq.; is a J.P. and D.L. for co. Ross. —*Belmaduthie House, Munlochy, Ross-shire, N.B.*

Heir, his son Colin Charles, *b.* 1848.

MACKENZIE, Dowager Lady, of Kilcoy, Ross-shire.
Isabella, 2nd dau. of Ewen Cameron, Esq., of Glenevis, co. Inverness, N.B., by Helen, dau. of Patrick Grant, Esq., of Glenmoriston, N.B.; *m.* 1805 Sir Colin Mackenzie, Bart., of Kilcoy, who *d.* 1845, leaving, with other issue, * Charles. *b.* 1811.— *Belmaduthy House, Munlochy, Ross-shire, N.B.*

MACKENZIE, the Hon. Mrs., late of Belmont, Midlothian.
Helen Anne, youngest but only surviving dau. of Francis, last Lord Seaforth, by Mary, dau. of the late Very Rev. Baptist Proby, D.D., Dean of Lichfield; *m.* 1821 Joshua Henry, Lord Mackenzie, of Belmont, Midlothian, a Judge in the Supreme Courts of Scotland, who *d.* 1851, leaving issue, * Frances Mary and Penuel Augusta. —16, *Moray Place, Edinburgh.*

MACKENZIE, COLIN JAMES, Esq., of Portmore Peeblesshire.
Only son of the late William Forbes Mackenzie, Esq., of Portmore (who was J.P. and D.L. for co. Peebles, Convener of that co. and formerly M.P.), by Helen Anne, dau. of the late Sir James Montgomery, Bart., of Stanhope, N.B.; *b.* 1835; *s.* 1862. Educated at Trinity Coll., Glenalmond, and Haileybury Coll.; is a Member of the Bengal Civil Service.—*Portmore, Eddleston, N.B.*

MACKENZIE, EDWARD, Esq., of Fawley Court, Bucks.
Youngest son of the late Alexander Mackenzie, Esq., C.E., of Fairburn, co. Ross, by Mary, dau. of W. Roberts, Esq.; *b.* 1811; *s.* his brother William, C.E., of Newbie, co. Dumfries, 1851; *m.* 1st 1839 Mary, eldest dau. of William Dalziel, Esq., of The Craigs, co. Dumfries; 2nd 1864 Ellen, dau. of A. Mullett, Esq.; he has by the former, with other issue,

* William Dalziel, educated at Harrow, M.A. of Magdalen Coll., Oxford, Barrister-at-Law of the Inner Temple, and a Magistrate for cos. Oxford, Dumfries, and Kirkcudbright; *b.* 1840; *m.* 1863 Mary Anna, eldest dau. of Henry Baskerville, Esq., of Crowsley Park, Oxon, and has, with other issue, * William Roderick Dalziel, *b.* 1864.

Mr. Mackenzie, who was formerly a Civil Engineer,

purchased the estate and manor of Fawley from W. Peere Williams Freeman, Esq., in 1853; he is a Magistrate for cos. Dumfries, Kirkcudbright, Bucks, and Oxon (High Sheriff 1862).—*Fawley Court, Henley-on-Thames*; 9, *Portman Square*, w.

+**MACKENZIE, GEORGE, Esq., of Alyth, Ross-shire.**
Son of the late G. Mackenzie, Esq., of Alyth; *b.* 18—; is married, and has issue,

* George, a J.P. and D.L. for co. Ross, *b.* 18—.

Mr. Mackenzie is a Magistrate for co. Ross, and Lord of the Barony of Alyth.—*Alyth Park, Meigle, N.B.*

MACKENZIE, the Right Hon. HOLT.
Son of the late Henry Mackenzie, Esq., by Penuel, dau. of the late Sir Ludovic Grant, Bart., of Grant; *b.* 1777; *m.* 1853 Frances Isabella, only dau. of J. Smith, Esq., and widow of Major Thomas Le Marchant, Esq., of Aspeden Lodge, Herts. Educated at Haileybury Coll.; appointed to the H.E.I.C.'s Civil Service 1807, retired 1833; was formerly a Judge in India, Secretary to the Governor-General of India, &c.; a Commissioner of the Board of Control 1833-4; sworn a Member of the Privy Council 1833.—Residence: *Aspeden, Buntingford, Herts; Oriental and Travellers' Clubs*, s.w.; 28, *Wimpole Street*, w.

MACKENZIE, JAMES DIXON, Esq., of Findon, Ross-shire.
Third son of the late Major Lewis Mackenzie, 2nd Royal N.B. Dragoons (who *d.* 1853), by Nancy, only dau. and heir of S. Forester Bancroft, Esq.; *b.* 1830; *s.* his brother 1865; *m.* 1858 Julia Stanley, dau. of Samuel Letsam, Esq., of New Providence, W. Indies, and has, with other issue,

.* James Kenneth Douglas, *b.* 1859.

Capt. Mackenzie, who was educated at Rugby, is Lord of the Barony of Findon and manor of Mountgerald, and Capt. in the 14th Foot. This family is that of the Mackenzies, Barts., of Scatwell, to which Baronetcy Capt. J. D. Mackenzie is heir presumptive.—*Mountgerald House, and Findon, Dingwall, Ross-shire; Army and Navy Club*, s.w.; 12, *Southwick Crescent*, w.

MACKENZIE, JAMES FOWLER, Esq., of Allangrange, Ross-shire.
Second son of the late George Falconer Mackenzie, Esq., of Allangrange, by Isabella Reid, dau. of James Fowler, Esq., of Raddery and Fairburn; *b.* 1833; *s.* his brother, John Falconer Mackenzie, Esq., 1849; is a J.P. and D.L. for co. Ross, Lieut. 4th Ross-shire Rifle Volunteers, and reputed heir male of the Earls of Seaforth.—*Allangrange, by Munlochy, Inverness, N.B.*

Heir Pres., his brother George Thomas, *b.* 1834.

+**MACKENZIE, JOHN, Esq., of Glack, Aberdeenshire.**
Eldest son of the late Roderick Mackenzie, Esq., of Glack, by his 2nd wife Christina dau. of John Niven, Esq.; *b.* 1810; *s.* 1812. Is a J.P. and D.L. for co. Aberdeen.—*Glack, Aberdeen, N.B.*

Heir Pres., his brother Roderick, *b.* 1814.

†**MACKENZIE, JOHN ANDREW SHAW, Esq., of Newhall, Cromartyshire.**
Son of the late A. Mackenzie, Esq., of Newhall; *b.* 18—. Is a J.P. and D.L. for co. Cromarty.—*Newhall House, Poyntzfield, via Inverness, N.B.*

MACKENZIE, JOHN ORD, Esq., of Dolphinton, Lanarkshire.
Eldest son of the late Richard Mackenzie, Esq., of Dolphinton, by Jane, dau. of Capt. Hamilton, of 73rd

619

(afterwards 71st) Regt. of Foot; b. 1811; s. 1850; m. 1833 Margaret Hope, dau. of the late Sir Thos. Kirkpatrick, Bart., of Closeburn, and has, with other issue,

* Thomas Kirkpatrick, Commander R.N., b. 1836.

Mr. Mackenzie, who was educated at the High School and University of Edinburgh, and became Writer to the Signet in 1832, is a Magistrate for cos. Lanark and Peebles, and proprietor of Dolphinton. —Dolphinton House, Edinburgh; 7, Royal Circus, Edinburgh.

MACKENZIE, KEITH WILLIAM STEWART., Esq., of Seaforth, Ross-shire.
Eldest son of the late Right Hon. James Alexander Stewart-Mackenzie, M.P., of Seaforth (who was grandson of John, 7th Earl of Galloway), by the Hon. Mary Elizabeth Mackenzie, dau. of the last Lord Seaforth, and widow of Sir Samuel Hood; b. 1818; s. his mother 1862; m. 1844 Hannah Charlotte, dau. of J. J. Hope-Vere, Esq., of Craigie Hall (she d. 1868). Is a J.P. and D.L. for co. Ross, and Major Commandant 1st Ross-shire R.V. This family on the maternal side is the chief of the Mackenzies, and represents the Earl of Seaforth (ext.).—Brahan Castle, Dingwall, N.B.

+MACKENZIE, KENNETH, Esq., late of Applecross, Ross-shire.
Eldest son of the late Thomas Mackenzie, Esq., of Applecross (who was M.P. for cos. Ross and Cromarty 1837-47), by Mary, dau. of the late G. Mackenzie, Esq.; b. 1819; s. 1856. Educated at Edinburgh; is a Magistrate for co. Ross.—10, Heriot Row, Edinburgh.

MACKENZIE, RODERICK GROGAN, Esq., of Flowerburn, Ross-shire.
Only son of the late Roderick Mackenzie. Esq., of Flowerburn, by Harriet, dau. of Col. Grogan; b. 1844; s. 1848. Is a Dep.-Lieut. for co. Ross, Lord of the Barony of Flowerburn, and Cornet 16th Lancers. —Flowerburn, Fortrose, N.B.; Junior Carlton Club, s.w.

Heirs Pres., his sisters Georgina Adelaide (m. 1867 Roderick Mackenzie, Esq., of Kincraig, N.B.), and Elma.

MACKENZIE, THOMAS, Esq., of Corryvoulzie, and Ord, Ross-shire.
Eldest son of the late Alexander Mackenzie, Esq., of Ord, by Helen, dau. of Niel McInnes, Esq., of Aberdeen; b. 1797; s. 1821; m. 1825 Anna Watson, 4th dau. of James Fowler, Esq., of Raddery, and has issue,

* Alexander Watson-late Capt. 91st Foot ; b. 1827 ; m. 1857 Angela Babington, dau. of the late Rev. Benjamin W. Pole, of Bishop's Hatfield, Herts, and has issue.

Mr. Mackenzie, who was educated at the University of Aberdeen, is a J.P. and D.L. for co. Ross.—Corryvoulzie, by Gave, Ross-shire; Ord House, Beauly, N.B.

MACKENZIE-DOUGLAS. (See Douglas.)

McKERRELL, WILLIAM, Esq., of Hill House, Ayrshire.
Third son of the late John McKerrell, Esq., of Hill House, by Cecilia, dau. of J. Harvey, Esq., M.D., of London; b. 1800; m. 1835 Charlotte, dau. of J. E. Wright, Esq., of Bolton-Hall-on-Swale. Is a Magistrate for cos. Ayr and Renfrew.—Hill House, Irvine, N.B.; Barrassie House, Great Malvern.

MACKIE, IVIE, Esq., of Auchencairn, Kirkcudbrightshire.
Son of the late James Mackie, Esq., Merchant, of Girvan, N.B.; b. 1805; m. 1839 Agnew, 2nd dau. of

620

the late John Gladstone, Esq., C.E., of Castle Douglas, and has, with other issue,

* James Todd, b. 1843 ; m. 1864 Constantia Mary, only dau. of the late Thornton Raleigh Trevelyan, Esq., of Netherwitton Hall, Northumberland (see that family).

Mr. Mackie is a Magistrate for co. Kirkcudbright, and an Alderman and Magistrate for Manchester, of which he has been thrice Mayor, Lord of the Manor or 'Superior' of Auchencairn, and a Merchant and Banker at Manchester.—Auchencairn House, Castle Douglas, N.B.; Ivy House, Plymouth Grove, Manchester.

MACKIE, Mrs., of Ernespie, Kirkcudbrightshire.
Jane, dau. of Archibald Horne, Esq., of Edinburgh; m. 1853 James Mackie, Esq., M.P., of Ernespie, who was a Dep.-Lieut. for co. Kirkcudbright, and who d. 1867, leaving issue,

* Twin sons, b. 1866.

—Bargraly and Ernespie, Kirkcudbrightshire, N.B.

+MACKINNON, ALEXANDER KENNETH, of Corry House, Inverness-shire.
Son of the late — Mackinnon, Esq.; b. 18—. Is a J.P. and D.L. for co. Inverness.—Corry House, Broadford, N.B.

MACKINNON, LAUCHLAN, Esq., of Bittacy House, Middlesex.
Second son of the late Rev. John Mackinnon. of Strath. Isle of Skye (who d. 1856), by Ann. dau. of Lauchlan Mackinnon, Esq., of Corry, Isle of Skye; b. 1817; m. 1st 1841 Jane, dau. of Robert Montgomery, Esq.; 2nd 1850 Emily, dau. of John Bundoch, Esq.; is a Magistrate for Middlesex.—Residence: Menabilly, Par, Cornwall; Reform Club, s.w.

MACKINNON, Capt. LAUCHLAN BELLINGHAM, of Ormely Lodge, Surrey.
Second son of William Alexander Mackinnon. Esq. (whom see); b. 1815; m. 1842 Augusta, dau. of the late John Entwisle, Esq., M.P., of Foxholes, co. Lancaster, and has, with other issue,

* Lauchlan, b. 1843.

Mr. Mackinnon, who is a Magistrate for Surrey, and a Capt. R.N., retired, was elected M.P. for Rye. 1865. —Ormely Lodge, Ham. Richmond, Surrey; 93, Belgrave Road, s.w.

MACKINNON, WILLIAM ALEXANDER, Esq., of Mackinnon, and of Acrise Park, Kent.
Son of the late William Mackinnon, Esq., of Mackinnon. by Mary, dau. of R. Palmer, Esq.; b. 1789; s. 1809; m. 1812 Emma, dau. of Joseph Palmer, Esq., of Dublin, and has, with other issue,

* William Alexander, M.P. for Lymington, a Magistrate for Hants and Middlesex, and a J.P. and D.L. for Kent ; b. 1813 ; m. 1846 Margaret Sophia, only dau. of P. Willes, Esq.

Mr. Mackinnon, who was educated at St. John's Coll., Cambridge (LL.A. 1804, M.A. 1807), kept terms at Lincoln's Inn, but was not called to the Bar; is a Magistrate for Middlesex, Kent, and Hants, and a Dep.-Lieut. for Middlesex; was M.P. for Lymington 1831-2 and 1835-52, and for Rye 1853-65; formerly a Commissioner for Colonization of South Australia. — Acrise Park, Canterbury; Belvedere, Broadstairs; Alfred, Oriental, and Brooks's Clubs, s.w.; 4, Hyde-Park Place, w.

MACKINTOSH, ÆNEAS, Esq., of Balnespick, Inverness-shire.
Eldest son of the late William Mackintosh, Esq., of Balnespick, by Emily, dau. of William Chisholm, Esq.,

of Chisholm; b. 1810; m. 1858 Isabella. dau. of J. Barker, Esq., and has, with other issue,

* William, b. 1859.

Mr. Mackintosh, who was educated at Eton, is a J.P. and D.L. for co. Inverness.—*Corrobrymore Lodge, Balnespick, Inverness, N.B.; New Club, Edinburgh; Oriental Club, w.*

+ MACKINTOSH, ÆNEAS, Esq., of Daviot, Inverness-shire.

Third son of the late Hon. Angus Mackintosh (a member of the Legislative Council of Upper Canada, who d. 1833), by Archange St. Martin; b. 1813; m. 1st 184–Mary, dau. of the late Alexander McLeod, Esq., of Dalvey, N.B. (she d. 1848); 2nd 1851 Louisa Fanny, 3rd dau. of the late Major Alexander McLeod, of the B.N.I., and has issue. Is a J.P. and D.L. for co. Inverness.—*Daviot House, Inverness, N.B.*

+ MACKINTOSH, ÆNEAS WILLIAM, Esq., of Raigmore, Inverness-shire.

Son of the late Lauchlan Mackintosh, Esq., of Raigmore, by Margaret, dau. of the late Sir Archibald Dunbar, Bart.; b. 1819; m. 1856 Grace Ellen Augusta, dau. of the late Sir Neil Menzies, Bart., and has, with other issue,

* A son, b. 1863.

Mr. Mackintosh is J.P. and D.L. for co. Inverness, and Capt. Inverness-shire Volunteer Artillery.—*Raigmore, Inverness, N.B.*

MACKINTOSH, ALEXANDER ÆNEAS, Esq., of Mackintosh, Inverness-shire.

Eldest son of the late Alexander Mackintosh, Esq., of Mackintosh, by Charlotte, dau. of the late Alexander Macleod, Esq., of Dalvey, Morayshire; b. 1847; s. 1861. Educated at Harrow; is Chief of the Clan Chattan. —*Moy Hall and Dunachton House, Inverness, N.B.*

Heir Pres., his brother Alfred Norman, b. 1851.

MACKINTOSH, ANGUS, Esq., of Holme, Inverness-shire.

Only surviving son of the late John Mackintosh, Esq., of Holme, by Janet, dau. of Donald Macpherson, Esq., J.P., of Inverness, N.B.; b. 1826; s. 1847. Educated at the Edinburgh Academy and University Coll., Oxford; is a Magistrate for co. Inverness.—*Ness Side House, Inverness, N.B.*

Heir Pres., his sister Jessie, m. 1848 Major T. T. Bolleau, 20th Hussars.

+ MACKINTOSH, DAVID, Esq., of Marshalls, Essex.

Son of the late D. Mackintosh. of ——, co. Inverness; b. 180–; s. his cousin 1856. Is Lord of the Manors of Havering, Hornchurch, and Romford. This family is of Scottish extraction.—*Marshalls, Romford, Essex.*

+ MACKINTOSH, GEORGE, Esq., of Geddes, Nairnshire.

Son of the late G. Mackintosh, Esq., of Geddes; b. 18—; is married, and had issue an only son, William Alfred Bruce, b. 1857; d 1868. Mr. Mackintosh is a J.P. and D.L. for, and Convener of, co. Nairn, and a Magistrate for co. Inverness.—*Geddes House, Nairn, N.B.*

MACKINTOSH, GEORGE GORDON, Esq., of Twickenham, Middlesex.

Second son of the late William Mackintosh, Esq., of Balnsfield, co. Inverness, by Emily, dau. of William Chisholm,-Esq., of Chisholm; b. 1812; m. 1846 Jane, dau. of Thomas George Gardiner, Esq., of the Bombay Civil Service. Educated at Haileybury Coll.; is a Magistrate for cos. Hereford and Inverness, and was formerly in the Bengal Civil Service.—*Richmond House, Twickenham, Middlesex; Oriental Club, w.*

MACKINTOSH, JAMES, Esq., of Lamancha, Peeblesshire.

Only son of Donald Mackintosh. the younger. of Aberairder, by Elespath Forbes, dau. of Mr. Forbes Buchan; b. 1789; m. 1823 Sarah, dau. of Robert Airey, Esq., of Kendal, and has, with other issue,

* James, b. 1825; m. 1853 Ellen Louisa, dau. of James Powell Parker, Esq., of Calcutta, and has issue, * James, b. 1858.

Mr. Mackintosh is a Magistrate for cos. Banff and Peebles, and Lord of the Lamancha Estate, which he acquired in 1831, from Thomas, 8th Earl of Dundonald. —*Lamancha House, by Leadburn, Edinburgh, N.B.; 38, Charlotte Square, Edinburgh.*

MACKINTOSH, JAMES EATON ANGUS, Esq., of Farr, Inverness-shire.

Eldest son of the late Lieut.-Col. Alexander Mackintosh, of Farr, late of the Madras Infantry, by Fanny, dau. of the late Capt. Thomas Eaton, R.N.; b. 1835; s. 1867; is a Capt. 109th Regt. This family belongs to the Kylachie Mackintoshes, who under Allan. 3rd son of Malcolm, 10th chief of the Mackintoshes and Capt. of the Clan Chattan, branched off and settled at Kylachie, in Strathdearn. about the year 1440.—*Farr House, Inverness, N.B.; Naval and Military Club, s.w.*

McKIRDY, JOHN GREGORY, Esq., of Birkwood, Lanarkshire.

Eldest son of the late John McKirdy, Esq., of Birkwood. by Mary, eldest dau. of David Elliott, Esq. of Liddlesdale; b. 1806; s. 1835; m. 1841 Augusta, eldest dau. of the late Capt. James Bradshaw, R.N., M.P. (she d. 1865). Educated at Edinburgh and Glasgow; is a J.P. and D.L. for co. Lanark.—*Birkwood, Lesmahago, N.B.*

Heir Pres., his brother Charles Clark, b. 1811.

MACKWORTH, Sir ARTHUR WILLIAM, Bart., of Glen Uske, Monmouthshire (cr. 1776).

Eldest son of the late Sir Digby Francis Mackworth. Bart., of Glen Uske, by Mathilde, dau. of the late Lieut.-Col. Peldie K.H.; b. 1842; s. as 6th Bart. 1857; m. 1865 Alice, dau. of Joseph Cubitt, Esq.; is a Lieut. R.E. This family is of great antiquity in Derbyshire. —*Glen Uske, Caerleon; Cefn-Idfa, Bridgend,*

Heir, his son, b. 1868.

MACKWORTH-DOLBEN. (See *Dolben.*)

+ MACKY, JAMES THOMPSON, Esq., of Belmont, co. Londonderry.

Son of the late J. Macky. Esq., of Belmont; b. 1810. Is a Magistrate for cos. Londonderry and Donegal (High Sheriff 1860).—*Belmont, Londonderry.*

MACLACHLAN, the Rev. ARCHIBALD NEIL CAMPBELL, of Earl's Island, and Knocknakerna, co. Galway.

Only son of the late Lieut.-General Archibald Maclachlan (who d. 1854), by Jane, dau. of Neil Campbell, Esq., of Duntroon Castle ... Argyll: b. 1819; e his uncle, Lachlan Maclachlan, Esq., M.P., 1849; m. 1855 Mary Elizabeth, dau. of Charles Sidebottom, Esq., of Ham Bank, co. Worcester, and has, with other issue,

* Archibald Campbell, b. 1874.

Mr. Maclachlan, who was educated at Winchester and Exeter Coll., Oxford (B.A. 1841, M.A. 1844), is Vicar and Patron of Newton Valence.—*Newton Valence Vicarage, Alton, Hants; University Club, s.w.*

+ MACLACHLAN, ROBERT, Esq., of Maclachlan, Argyleshire.

Son of the late Donald Maclachlan, Esq., of that Ilk, by Susannah, dau. of Colin Campbell, of Park; b. 18—;

621

m. 18— Helen, dau. of William A. Carruthers, Esq., of Dormont, co. Dumfries. Is a J.P. and D.L. for, and Convener of, co. Argyle.—*Maclachlan, Strachur, N.B.*

MACLAE, ALEXANDER CRUM-, Esq., of Caithkin, Lanarkshire.

Eldest son of the late John Crum, Esq., of Thornliebank. co. Renfrew, by the late Agnes Dunlop, dau. of the late Hugh Brown, Esq., of Broadstone, co. Ayr; *b.* 1838; *s.* his grand-uncle 1860. Educated at the University of Glasgow; is a Magistrate for co. Lanark, and a Solicitor in Glasgow.—*Hazelwood, near Row, Dumbartonshire; Western Club, Glasgow.*

Heir Pres., his brother Hugh Brown, *b.* 1840.

McLAGAN, PETER, Esq., of Pumpherston, Linlithgowshire.

Only surviving son of the late Peter MacLagan, Esq., of Pumpherston; *b.* 1815. Educated at Edinburgh University; is a Magistrate for co. Edinburgh, J.P. and D.L. for co. Linlithgow, and a Member of the Council of the University of Edinburgh; elected M.P. for co. Linlithgow 1865.—*Pumpherston, Midcalder, N.B.; University Club, Edinburgh; Junior Athenæum Club, s.w.*

MACLAINE, MURDOCH GILLIAN, Esq., of Lochbuy, Argyleshire.

Eldest son of the late Donald Maclaine, Esq., J.P. and D.L., of Lochbuy, by Emilie Guillamaine, 3rd dau. of Charles Anthony Vincent, Esq.; *b.* 1845; *s.* 1863. Educated at Edinburgh Academy; is Lord of the Barony of Lochbuy.—*Lochbuy House, Oban, N.B.*

MACLAINE, WILLIAM OSBORNE, Esq., of Kingston House, Gloucestershire.

Only son of the late Col. Hector Maclaine, of Kington House, by Martha, only dau. of William Osborne, Esq., of Kington, co. Gloucester; *b.* 1818; *s.* 1847; *m.* 1849 Anna, eldest dau. of John Thurburn, Esq., of Murtle, co. Aberdeen, and has, with other issue,

* Hector, *b.* 1851.

Mr. Maclaine, who was educated at Wadham Coll., Oxford (B.A. 1841, M.A. 1844), and called to the Bar at Lincoln's Inn 1844, is a J.P. and D.L. for co. Gloucester, and Lieut. Gloucestershire Yeomanry.—*Kington House, Thornbury; Arthur's Club, s.w.*

McLAREN, DUNCAN, Esq., of Newington House, Midlothian.

, Son of the late Mr. John McLaren; *b.* 1800; *m.* 1849 Priscilla, dau. of the late Jacob Bright, Esq., of Rochdale. Is a J.P. and D.L. for Edinburgh, and President of the Chamber of Commerce in that city; was Lord Provost of that city 1851–4; elected M.P. for Edinburgh 1865.—*Newington House, Edinburgh, N.B.; Reform Club, s.w.*

McLAUGHLIN, the Rev. HUBERT.

Youngest son of the late Thomas McLaughlin, Esq., of Ballythomas, Queen's Co., by Elizabeth, dau. of Theobald Butler, Esq., of Wilford, co. Tipperary; *b.* 1805; *m.* 1835 the Hon. Frederica Cecilia, sister of Edward, 2nd Lord Crofton, and has, with other issue,

* Edward, Capt. R.A., *b.* 1838; *m.* 1867 Annie, only child of the late James Bromilaw, Esq., of Green and Hume, &c. Helen's, Lancashire.

Mr. McLaughlin, who was educated at Trinity Coll., Dublin (B.A. 1828, M.A. 1831), is Prebendary of Herrford and Rector of Burford (first portion).—*Boraston Rectory, Tenbury.*

+MACLAVERTY, JOHN FREEMAN, Esq., of Keill, Argyleshire.

Son of the late J. Maclaverty, Esq.; *b.* 18—. Is a Magistrate for co. Argyle.—*Keill House, Southend, Campbeltown, N.B.*

MACLEAN, Sir CHARLES FITZROY, Bart. (cr. 1632).

Eldest son of the late General Sir Fitzroy Grafton Maclean, Bart., by Mary, only child of Charles Kyd, Esq., of Barbados, and widow of John Bishop, Esq.; *b.* 1798; *s.* 1847; *m.* 1831 Emily Eleanor, dau. of the Hon. and Rev. Jacob Marsham, D.D. Educated at Eton and the Royal Military Coll., Sandhurst; is a Col. in the Army, unattached; formerly Lieut.-Col. 81st Foot; late Military Secretary at Gibraltar.—*United Service Club, s.w.*

Heir, his son FitzRoy Donald, Major 13th Hussars, *b.* 1835.

MACLEAN, ALEXANDER, Esq., of Ardgour, Argyleshire.

Fourth and eldest surviving son of the late Alexander Maclean, Esq., of Ardgour, by Lady Margaret, dau. of John, 2nd Earl of Hopetoun, K.T.; *b.* 1799; *s.* 1855; *m.* 1833 Helen Jane Hamilton, eldest dau. of Sir John Dalrymple, Bart., of North Berwick, co. Haddington, and has, with other issue,

* Alexander Thomas, *b.* 1835.

Mr. Maclean, who was educated at Harrow and the East India Coll., Haileybury, is a J.P. and D.L. for cos. Argyle and Inverness; was formerly in the H.E.I.C.'s Civil Service. — *Ardgour House, Ardgour, N.B.; New Club, Edinburgh, N.B.*

MACLEAN, ALEXANDER, Esq., of Pennycross, Argyleshire.

Eldest son of the late Archibald Maclean, Esq., of Pennycross, by Alicia, dau. of Hector Maclean, Esq., of Torran, co. Argyle; *b.* 1790; *s.* 1830; *m.* 1840 Charlotte Brodie, dau. of John M'Lean, Esq., of Campbeltown, co. Argyle, and has, with other issue,

* Archibald John, *b.* 1842.

Mr. Maclean, who was educated at the Universities of Edinburgh and Glasgow, is a Commissioner and J.P. and D.L. for co. Argyle.—*Pennycross, by Auchnacraig, Oban, N.B.; United Service Club, Edinburgh.*

MACLEAN, Mrs., of Lazonby, Cumberland.

Eleanor, dau. of the Rev. Joseph Dacre Carlyle, Chancellor of Carlisle; *m.* 1840 Col. Henry Dundas Maclean, of Lazonby Hall, who was a J.P. and D.L. for Cumberland (High Sheriff 1848), formerly a Lieut.-Col. in the Army, and who *d.* 1863.—*Lazonby Hall, Penrith.*

MACLEAR, Sir THOMAS, F.R.S. (cr. 1860).

Son of the late James Maclear, Esq., of Tyrone, Ireland, by Mary, dau. of John Magrath, Esq.; *b.* 1795; *m.* 1825 Mary, dau. of Theod Pearse, Esq., of Bedford (she *d.* 1861); is Astronomer Royal at the Cape of Good Hope, a corresponding member of the Imperial Institute of France, and a member of the Academy of Sciences at Palermo; was formerly a surgeon at Biggleswade.—*Cape Town, South Africa.*

MACLEAY, KENNETH, Esq., of Keiss, Caithness-shire.

Eldest son of the late Kenneth Macleay, Esq., of Keiss, and of Newmore, co. Ross, by Isabella, dau. of the late John Horne, Esq., of St. Kilda, co. Caithness; *b.* 1817; *s.* 1826; *m.* 1852 Jane, dau. of Joseph Coote, Esq., (she *d.* 1858). Educated at the Academy and University of Edinburgh; is a J.P. and D.L. for co. Caithness, and a Major in the Ross, Caithness. Sutherland, and Cromarty Militia.—*Keiss Castle, Wick, N.B.; Carlton and Junior United Service Clubs, s.w.*

Heir Pres. his brother William John, *b.* 1820; *m.* 1857 Susan Emmeline, dau. of E. Deas Thomson, Esq., C.B.

MACLEOD, Sir JOHN MACPHERSON, K.C.S.I. (cr. 1866).

Eldest son of the late Colonel Donald Macleod, of St. Kilda, by Diana, dau. of Donald Macdonald, Esq., of Tormore, co. Inverness; *b.* 1792; *m.* 1822 Catharine,

dau. of William Greig, Esq., of Thornbill, co. Stirling. Educated at the University of Edinburgh and Hailey-bury Coll.; is a Dep.-Lieut. for co. Inverness, and a Member of the Indian Law Commission; was formerly in the Madras Civil Service, and held in succession, from 1823 to 1838, the Offices of Secretary to Government at Madras, Commissioner for the Government of Mysore, and Member of the Indian Law Commission, which sat at Calcutta.—*Glendale, Isle of Skye, Inverness-shire; Athenæum Club, s.w.; 1, Stanhope Street, w.*

MACLEOD, NORMAN, Esq., of Macleod, Inver-ness-shire.

Eldest son of the late John Norman Macleod, M.P., of Macleod, by Anne, dau. of John Stephenson, Esq., of Mersham, Kent; *b.* 1812; *s.* 1835; *m.* 1837 the Hon. Louisa Barbara, only dau. of St. Andrew, 13th Lord St. John, and has, with other issue,

* Norman Magnus, Capt. 74th Highlanders, *b.* 1839.

Mr. Macleod, who was educated at Harrow, is a J.P. and D.L. for co. Inverness, Lieut.-Col. 1st Middlesex Volunteer Artillery, and chief of his clan.—*Dunvegan Castle, Isle of Skye, N.B.; Spratton House, Northampton; 9, Cambridge Square, w.*

+MACLEOD, NORMAN, Esq., of Dalvey, Elgin-shire.

Eldest son of the late — Macleod, Esq., of Dalvey; *b.* 18—. Is a J.P. and D.L. for co. Elgin.—*Dalvey, Forres, N.B.*

Heir Pres., his brother Donald, *b.* 18 —.

MACLEOD, ROBERT BRUCE ÆNEAS, Esq., of Cadboll, Cromartyshire.

Eldest son of the late Roderick Macleod, Esq., M.P., of Cadboll (who was Lord-Lieutenant of co. Cromarty,) by Isabella, dau. of William Cuninghame, Esq., of Lainshaw, co. Ayr; *b.* 1818; *s.* 1853; *m.* 1857 Ellen Augusta, dau. of the late Sir J. Pollard Willoughby, Bart., and has, with other issue,

* Roderick Willoughby, *b.* 1858.

Mr. Macleod, who was educated at the R. Naval Coll., Portsmouth, is a J.P. and D.L. for cos. Ross and Cromarty, and a Lieut. R.N.—*Cadboll, Cromarty, N.B.; Invergordon Castle, Ross-shire; Army and Navy Club, s.w.*

MACLEOD. (See Annesley.)

MACLURE, JOHN WILLIAM, Esq., of Fallow-field, Lancashire.

Second son of the late John Maclure, Esq., of Manchester, by Elizabeth, dau. of William Kearsley, Esq., of Manchester; *b.* 1835; *m.* 1859 Eleanor, dau. of Thomas Nettleship, Esq., of East Sheen, Surrey. Mr. Maclure was educated at the Manchester Grammar School; is a Magistrate for co. Lancaster and City of Manchester, and a Merchant at Manchester, a F.R.G.S., &c., and Capt. 40th Lancashire Rifle Volunteers. —*Fallowfield, Manchester; Princes Club, Manchester; Conservative Club, s.w.*

McMAHON, Sir BERESFORD BURSTON, Bart., of Fecarry, co. Tyrone (cr. 1815).

Eldest son of the late Right Hon. Sir William McMahon, Bart., of Fecarry (formerly Master of the Rolls in Ireland), by Frances, dau. of Beresford Burston, Esq.; *b.* 1808; *s.* as 2nd Bart. 1837; *m.* 1838 Maria Catherine, dau. of the late Sir Robert Bateson, Bart., M.P., of Belvoir Park, co. Down. Educated at Trinity Coll., Dublin (B.A. 1829); is a J.P. and D.L. for co. Tyrone; formerly Capt. Scots Fusilier Guards.—*Fecarry House, Mountfield, co. Tyrone.*

Heir, his son William Samuel, *b.* 1839.

M'MAHON, Sir THOMAS WESTROPP, Bart., C.B. (cr. 1817).

Eldest son of the late General Sir Thomas M'Mahon, Bart., G.C.B., by Emily Anne, dau. of Michael Roberts Westropp, Esq.; *b.* 1813; *s.* 1860; *m.* 1st 1851 Dora Paulina, dau. of Evan Hamilton Baillie, Esq. (she *d.* 1852); 2nd 1859 Frances Mary, dau. of the late J. Holford, Esq. (she *d.* 1867). Is Col. 5th Dragoon Guards. —*United Service Club, s.w.; 41, Grosvenor Place, s.w.*

Heir, his son Aubrey, *b.* 1862.

McMAHON, PATRICK, Esq.

Son of the late James McMahon, Esq., of Lakeview, co. Limerick, by Catherine, dau. of James Bourke, Esq., of Arlemont, co. Limerick; *b.* 1815. Educated at Trinity Coll., Dublin (B.A. 1836); called to the Bar at Gray's Inn 1842, and goes the Oxford Circuit; was M.P. for co. Wexford 1852-65.—3, *Johnson's Buildings, Temple,* E.C.

MACMAHON, THOMAS, Esq., of Knockane, co. Clare.

Eldest son of the late John MacMahon, Esq., of Knockane, by Margaret, dau. of John Ryan, Esq., of Limerick; *b.* 1825. Educated at Trinity Coll., Dublin (B.A. 1845); called to the Irish Bar 1847; is a Magistrate for co. Clare.—*Knockane, Newmarket-on-Fergus, co. Clare; 24, Lower Pembroke Street, Dublin.*

Heir Pres., his brother Patrick, *b.* 1827.

McMICKING, THOMAS, Esq., of Miltonise, Wigtownshire.

Eldest son of the late Thomas McMicking, Esq., of Miltonise, by Jane, dau. of John Morin, Esq., of Lagan, co. Dumfries; *b.* 1812; *s.* 1866; *m.* 1847 Agnes, only dau. of the late James Andrew, Esq., of Craigend, co. Stirling, and by her, who *d.* 1867, has, with other issue,

* Thomas, *b.* 1848.

Mr. McMicking is a Magistrate for cos. Wigtown and Dumbarton, and representative of an old Covenanter family on the borders of Wigtown and Ayrshire.—*Burnbrae, Helensburgh, N.B.; Miltonise, Wigtownshire.*

McMURRAY, ROBERT, Esq., of Roxborough House, co. Limerick.

Only son of the late John McMurray, Esq., of Marlmount, co. Down, by Margaret, dau. of Robert Allen, Esq., of Ballygrote, co. Down; *b.* 1806; *m.* 1st 1838 Sarah Anne, dau. of the late T. Knox Hannyngton, Esq., J.P., of Dungannon Castle, co. Tyrone; 2nd 1844 Elizabeth Anne, eldest dau. of the late Capt. John W. Hayton, of Greenfield Abbey, co. Flint, and has, with other issue,

* John Ripley, *b.* 1852.

Mr. McMurray, who is a Magistrate for co. Limerick, descends from a common ancestor with the family of Murrays of Blackbarony.—*Roxborough House, Limerick; Patrickswell, co. Limerick.*

+McNABB, JAMES WILLIAM, Esq., of Highfield, Hampshire.

Eldest son of the late James Munro McNabb, Esq., of Highfield; *b.* 18—; *m.* 1860 Amy, 4th dau. of Sir James W. Hogg, Bart. Was formerly in the H.E.I.C.'s Service. This family is of Highland extraction.—*Highfield Park, Southampton.*

MACNAGHTEN, Sir EDMUND CHARLES WORK-MAN-, Bart., of Dundarave, co. Antrim (cr. 1836).

Eldest son of the late Sir Francis Workman-Macnaghten, Bart., of Dundarave, by Letitia, dau. of Sir William Dunkin, of Clogher; *b.* 1790; *s.* as 2nd Bart. 1843; *m.* 1827 Mary, dau. of P. Wall Gwatkin, Esq. Educated at the Charterhouse and Trinity Coll., Dublin (B.A.

623

1811); called to the Irish Bar 1813; is a J.P. and D.L. for cos. Antrim and Londonderry; formerly held a post in the Supreme Court at Calcutta; was M.P. for co. Antrim 1847–52.—*Dundarave, Bushmills, co. Antrim; Carlton Club*, s.w.; 18, *Eaton Square*, s.w.

Heir, his son Francis Edmund, Lieut.-Col. 8th Hussars, *b.* 1828; *m.* 1866 Alice Mary, eldest dau. of William Howard Russell, Esq., LL.D.

MACNAGHTEN, STEUART, Esq., of Invertro-sachs, Perthshire, and Bittern, Hants.

Youngest son of the late Sir Francis Workman-Macnaghten, Bart. (see that title); *b.* 1815; *m.* 1848 Agnes, only surviving child of James Eastmont, Esq., of St. Berner's, near Edinburgh, and widow of Capt. Shedden (she *d.* 1863). Educated at Edinburgh and Trinity Coll., Dublin (B.A. 1835); called to the Bar at the Middle Temple 1839; is a Magistrate for Hants.—*Bittern Manor, Southampton; Invertrosachs, Callander, N.B.; Carlton Club*, s.w.; 3, *Portman Square*, w.

MAC NAMARA, Sir BURTON, Knt. (cr. 1839).

Younger son of the late Francis Mac Namara, Esq., of Doolin, co. Clare, by Jane, dau. of George Stamer, Esq., of Carnelly, co. Clare; *b.* 1794; *m.* 1832 Catharine, dau. of Daniel Galbett, Esq. Is a Magistrate for co. Clare, and an Admiral on reserved list; late Inspector of Coast Guard in Ireland; served in Canada.—*Tromera, Miltownmalbay, co. Clare; The Strand, Limerick; United Service and Junior United Service Clubs*, s.w.

MACNAMARA, ARTHUR, Esq., of Caddington, Herts.

Eldest son of the late Arthur Macnamara, Esq., of Langoed Castle, co. Brecon, by Anne. dau. of William Lee, Esq; *b.* 1829; *s.* 1851; *m.* 1854 Lady Sophia Eliza, dau. of William, 3rd Earl of Listowel. Is a Magistrate for Beds, Herts, and co. Radnor; formerly Capt. Beds Militia.—*Caddington Hall, Market-street; Cheverells, Dunstable; White's and Boodle's Clubs*, s.w.

Heir Pres., his twin brother John, *b.* 1829; *m.* 1860 Sarah Anne, eldest dau. of Edward Vicars, Esq., of Tapton Hall, Sheffield, co. York, and has issue * a daughter.

MACNAMARA, FRANCIS, Esq., of Ennistymon, co. Clare.

Only son of the late Major William Nugent MacNamara, M.P., of Doolin, co. Clare, by Susanna, dau. and co-heir of the Hon. Mathias Finucane, a Judge of the Common Pleas in Ireland; *b.* 1802; *s.* 1856; *m.* 18-- Helena, dau. of William Mac Dermott, Esq., Solicitor, of Dublin, and has, with other issue,

* Henry Valentine, *b.* 18—.

Mr. MacNamara, who is a J.P. and D.L. for co. Clare (High Sheriff 1849), and Lieut.-Col.Clare Militia, and late Officer in the 8th Hussars, was M.P. for Ennis 1832–5.—*Ennistymon, Ennis, co. Clare.*

MACNAMARA. PATRICK JAMES DILLON, Esq., of Ayle, co. Clare.

Second son of the late Dillon Magnamara Esq of Keilty, co. Clare, and of Birchfield, co. Dublin (who *d.* 1838), by Charlotte, dau. of Alexander Campbell, Esq., of Invarock, co. Argyle, *b.* 1822; *s.* his cousin, James Macnamara, Esq. 1838; *m.* 1842 Jane Louise Mary Anne, only child of John Grant, Esq., Capt. R.N., of Stoke, Devon (she *d.* 1851), and has issue,

* Dillon Temple John Macnamara, Lieut. R.N., *b.* 1843.

Mr. Macnamara, who was educated at Trinity Coll., Dublin (B.A. 1845), is a Magistrate for co. Clare; late Lieut. 59th Regt.—*Ayle, Tulla, co. Clare; Royal Western Yacht Club, Kingston, Dublin.*

021

MACNEAL, HECTOR, Esq., of Ugadale, Argyleshire.

Eldest son of the late George Macneal, Esq., of Ugadale and Losset, by Mary Eliza, dau. of Capt. Loring, R.N.; *b.* 1822; *s.* 1861; *m.* 1862 Constance, eldest dau. of Col. Campbell, of Skipness, co. Argyle, and has, with other issue,

* Hector, *b.* 1862.

Mr. Macneal, who is a J.P. and D.L. for co. Argyle, was formerly Capt. 79th Highlanders.—*Losset Park and Ugadale, Campbelton, Argyleshire.*

+McNEILE, HENRY HUGH Esq., of Parkmount, co. Antrim.

Son of the late John McNeile, Esq.; *b.* 1820; *m.* 1859 Sophia, dau. of the late James Munro Macnabb, Esq., of Highfield Park, Hants, and has issue,

* A son, *b.* 1864.

Mr. McNeile is a Magistrate for co. Antrim (High Sheriff 1860).—*Parkmount, Belfast, co. Antrim.*

M'NEILL, the Right Hon. Sir JOHN, G.C.B., F.R.S.E., D.C.L., of Granton, Midlothian (cr. 1839).

Third son of the late John M'Neill, Esq., of Colonsay, N.B., by Hester, dau. of Duncan M'Neill, Esq., of Dunmore, co. Argyle; *b.* 1795; *m.* 1823 Mary, 4th dau. of John Wilson, Esq. Educated at Edinburgh University; is a Dep.-Lieut. for Edinburgh; formerly Envoy and Minister Plenipotentiary at the Court of Persia; was previously in the H.E.I.C.'s Military Service at Bombay; is Chairman of the Poor Law Board (Scotland); was Commissioner in the Crimea 1855; elected Hon. President of the Associated Societies of Edinburgh University, and sworn a Member of the Privy Council, 1857.—*Granton House, Edinburgh.*

MAC NEILL, Sir JOHN Knt., LL.D., F.R.S., &c (cr. 1844).

Son of the late Capt. Torquil P. Mac Neill, of Mount Pleasant, Dundalk; *b.* 1794. Is Professor of Civil Engineering in Trinity Coll., Dublin; Knighted for his services in constructing the Dublin and Drogheda Railway.—*Mount Pleasant, Dundalk, Ireland; 23, Cockspur Street*, s.w.

+MACNEILL, DONALD, Esq., of Canna, Argyleshire.

Son of the late D. MacNeill. Esq., of Canna; *b.* 1800. Is a Magistrate for co. Argyle, and Lord of the Barony of Canna.—*Canna, Tobermory, Oban, N.B.*

MAC NEILL, NEIL, Esq., of Bordlands, Peebles-shire.

Eldest son of the late Alexander Mac Neill. Esq., J.P., of Bordlands (formerly a Merchant and British Consular Agent at Samarang, Java), by Isabella Maria, dau. of Capt. Wm. London, R.N., of Musselburgh, N.B.; *b.* 1853; *s.* 1867.—*Bordlands, Noblehouse, Edinburgh, N.B.*

+M'NEILL, MALCOLM McMILLAN, Esq., of Carskey Argyleshire.

Son of the late — McNeill. Esq., of Carskey; *b.* 18—. Is a Magistrate for co. Argyll, and Lord of the Barony of Carskey.—*Carskey, Southend, Campbeltown, N.B.*

McNEILL. (See under *Colonsay, Lord.*)

MACNEILL-HAMILTON. (See *Hamilton.*)

MACONCHY, GEORGE, Esq., of Rathmore, co. Longford.

Eldest son of the late John Maconchy, Esq., of Rathmore, by Deborah, dau. of the late Stewart King, Esq. Master in Chancery, Dublin; *b.* 1818; *s.* 1843; *m.* 1843

Louisa Elizabeth, dau. of John Goddard Richards, Esq., of Ardemine, Wexford, and by her, who d. 1864, has, with other issue,

• John Arthur, b. 1852.

Mr. Maconchy, who was educated at Trinity Coll., Dublin (B.A. 1838), is a Magistrate for cos. Wexford and Longford (High Sheriff 1845).—*Rathmore, co. Longford ; Sackville Street Club, Dublin ; Cadwell House, Torquay.*

MACONOCHIE-WELWOOD, ALLAN ALEXANDER, Esq., LL.D., of Garvock, Fifeshire, and Meadowbank, Midlothian.
Eldest son of the late Alexander Maconochie-Welwood, Esq., of Garvock and Meadowbank (a Judge of the Court of Session, with the title of Lord Meadowbank), by Anne, dau. of the Right Hon. Robert Blair, of Avontoun, Lord President of the Court of Session ; b. 1806 ; s. 1861 ; m. 1st Ellen, dau. of T. Wiggin, Esq., of Boston, U.S. ; 2nd 1859 Lady Margaret, dau. of North, 9th Earl of Stair. Is a Magistrate for Midlothian, and a J.P. and D.L. for co. Fife ; was formerly Regius Professor of Roman and Scotch Law in the University of Glasgow.—*Meadowbank House, Kirknewton, Edinburgh ; Pitliver, Dunfermline ; New Club, Edinburgh ; Union Club, s.w.*

Heir Pres., his brother Robert Blair-Maconochie, Esq., of Gattonside, co. Roxburgh, a Magistrate for Midlothian and Roxburgh ; b. 1814 ; m. 1847 Charlotte Joanna, dau. of John Tod, Esq., of Kirkhill, and has issue three sons and one daughter.

MACPHERSON, ALLAN, Esq., of Blairgowrie, Perthshire.
Only son of the late William Macpherson, Esq., of Blairgowrie (Chief Clerk of the Legislative Assembly of New South Wales), by Jessie, 3rd dau. of William Chalmers, Esq., of Glenericht, co. Perth ; b. 1818 ; s. 1866 ; m. 1853 Emma, youngest dau. of Charles Henry Blake, Esq., of London, and has issue. Mr. Macpherson is a Magistrate for co. Perth and a Member of the Legislative Assembly of New South Wales.—*Blairgowrie House, Perthshire ; Bernera, near Liverpool, New South Wales.*

MACPHERSON, DAVID EDWARD, Esq., of Belleville, Inverness-shire.
Eldest surviving son of the late Sir David Brewster, K.H. (who d. 1868), by his 1st wife Juliet, youngest dau. and co-heir of the late James Macpherson, Esq., of Belleville (the translator of ' Ossian ') ; b. 1815 ; s. his aunt, the late Miss Ann Macpherson, 1862 ; m. 1849 Lydia Julia, dau. of the late Henry James Blunt, Esq., of the Indian Army, and has, with other issue,

• Charles Julian Brewster, b. 1855.

Mr. Macpherson, who was educated at the University of Edinburgh, is a Dep.-Lieut. for co. Inverness, and a Lieut.-Col. on the retired list of Her Majesty's Indian Army.—*Belleville House, Kingussie, Inverness-shire.*

MACPHERSON, EWEN, of Cluny, Inverness-shire.
Eldest son of the late Lieut.-Col. Duncan Macpherson, of Cluny, by Catherine, dau. of the late Sir Ewen Cameron, Bart., of Fassiferne ; b. 1804 ; s. 1855 ; m. 1832 Sarah Justina, youngest dau. of the late Henry Davidson, Esq., of Tulloch, co. Ross, and has, with other issue,

• Duncan, Major 42nd Royal Highlanders ; b. 1833.

Mr. Macpherson, who was educated at Edinburgh University, is a J.P. and D.L. for co. Inverness ; formerly Capt. 42nd Highlanders ; is chief of the Clan Macpherson and Clan Chattan.—*Cluny Castle, Kingussie, Inverness-shire ; New Club, Edinburgh ; Junior United Service Club, s.w.*

MACPHERSON-CAMPBELL.
(See *Campbell of Ballimore.*)

MACPHERSON-GRANT.
(See *Grant of Ballindalloch.*)

+**MACQUARIE,** Mrs., of Jarvisfield, Argyle-shire.
Isabella Hamilton Dundas, 3rd dau. of the late Colin Campbell, Esq., of Jura and Craignish, co. Argyle ; m. 1836 Lachlan Maclachlan, only son of the late General Macquarie, formerly Governor of New South Wales ; a J.P. and D.L. for co. Argyle, and a Capt. in the Scots Greys (who d. 1845).—*Jarvisfield, Oban, N.B.*

MACQUEEN, JOHN FRASER, Esq., Q.C., of Airds, Inverness-shire.
Eighth son of the late Donald Macqueen, Esq., of Corrybrough, co. Inverness (who d. 1813), by Elizabeth, dau. of Hugh Fraser, Esq., of Brightmony, co. Inverness ; b. 1810 ; m. 1840 Georgiana, dau. of the Rev. George Dealtry, Vicar of Hinckley, co. Leicester. Called to the Bar at Lincoln's Inn 1838 ; is a J.P. and D.L. for co. Inverness, a Queen's Counsel, and a Bencher of Lincoln's Inn. — *Airds, Bonaw, Inverness-shire ; Athenæum Club,* s.w. ; 4, *Upper Westbourne Terrace,* w.

MACQUEEN, the late ROBERT, Esq., of Hardington House, Lanarkshire.
Eldest son of the late John Macqueen, Esq., of Hardington House, by Anne, dau. of Thomas Mecan, Esq., of Cariff, co. Armagh ; b. 1789 ; s. 1837 ; m. 1st 1819 Zepherina, dau. of Henry Veitch, Esq., of Eliock House, co. Dumfries (she d. 1863) ; 2nd 1864 Elizabeth Anne, dau. of Hugh Veitch, Esq., Stuartfield, and widow of Dr. Ogilvie, C.B. Educated at Edinburgh University ; called to the Scottish Bar 1810 ; was a J.P. and D.L. for co. Peebles, and a Magistrate for co. Lanark. He d. s. p. 1867, and is s. in his estates by nephew, Arthur J. Macqueen, Esq. ; b. 18— ; m. 1868 Emma, 5th dau. of the late C. S. Kennedy, Esq., of Fair View, co. Lancaster.—*Hardington House, Biggar, N.B.*

MACRAE, JAMES CHARLES, Esq., late of Holmains, Dumfries-shire.
Only son of the late James Macrae, Esq., of Holmains, by Maria, dau. of Judge Le Maistre, who d. in India ; b. 1791 ; m. 1820 Margaret Elizabeth, dau. of the late Sir Alexander Grierson, Bart., of Lag (she d. 1867). Educated at the Royal Military Coll., Great M rlow ; is a J.P. and D.L. for co. Dumfries ; was formerly an Officer in the Army.—*Erleigh Lodge, Reading.*

MACREDIE, Mrs. MURE-, of Perceton, Ayrshire.
Rachel Ann, only child of the late John Macredie, Esq., of Perceton, by Mary Rachel, dau. of Major David Morrieson, late H.E.I.C.S. ; s. 1834 ; m. 1836 Patrick Boyle Mure, Esq., son of the late Thomas Mure, Esq., of Warriston, Midlothian ; a member of the Scottish bar, who assumed the surname of Macredie, and d. 1850, leaving, with other issue,

• Thomas Mure Mure, Advocate at the Scottish Bar ; b. 1840.

—*Perceton, Irvine, Ayrshire, N.B.*

McTAGGART, of Ardwell. (See *Ommanney.*)

+**McTAVISH,** CHARLES CARROLL, Esq.
Son of the late C. McTavish, Esq., of the United States, but descended from an old Irish family ; was M.P. for Dundalk 1817-8.

625

M'TIER, Alexander Walker, Esq., of Durris, Aberdeenshire.

Eldest son of the late Anthony M'Tier, Esq., of Durris, by Maria, dau. of Alexander Binny, Esq., of St. Andrews, N.B.; b. 1819; s. 1854. Educated at Edinburgh and Trinity Coll., Cambridge (B.A. 1842, M.A. 1845); called to the Bar at the Inner Temple 1846; is a J.P. and D.L. for co. Kincardine, and Lord of the Barony of Durris. — Durris House, Aberdeen, N.B.; Reform Club, s.w.

M'VEAGH, Ferdinand, Esq., of Drewstown, co. Meath.

Only son of the late Ferdinand Meath M'Veagh, Esq., of Drewstown, by Charlotte, dau. of Henry Brooke, Esq., of Rathcoffy, co. Kildare; b. 1813; s. 1866; m. 1835 Maria, only surviving dau. of Thomas Rotherham, Esq., Triermore, co. Meath, and has, with other issue,

    • George Joseph Brooke, b. 1866.

Mr. M'Veagh was educated at Trinity Coll., Dublin. —Drewstown, Athboy, co. Meath.

MADDEN, Sir Frederic, K.H., F.R.S. (cr. 1833).

Seventh son of the late Capt. William John Madden, R.M., by Sarah, dau. of the Rev. Arnold Carter, Minor Canon of Rochester; b. 1801; m. 1st 1829 Mary, dau. of Robert Hayton, Esq., of Sunderland (she d. 1830); 2nd 1837 Emily Sarah, dau. of William Robinson, Esq., LL.D., of Tottenham, Middlesex. Is a Gentleman of Her Majesty's Privy Chamber; late Head Keeper of the MSS. at the British Museum.—Athenæum Club, s.w.; 25, St. Stephen's Square, w.

MADDEN, John, Esq., of Hilton, co. Monaghan, and Manor Waterhouse, co. Fermanagh.

Eldest son of the late John Madden, Esq., J.P. and D.L. of Hilton Park and of Manor Waterhouse (Col. of the Monaghan Militia), by Sydney Anne, 2nd dau. of Admiral William Wolseley, of Rostrevor, co. Down; b. 1836; s. 1844; m. 1864 Caroline, 2nd dau. of the Hon. and Rev. Francis Clements, and has issue,

    • Caroline Sydney Anne, b. 1866.

Mr. Madden, who was educated at Eton, is a Magistrate for cos. Monaghan, Fermanagh, Cavan, and Leitrim (High Sheriff for Fermanagh, 1859, and for Monaghan 1863), and a Dep.-Lieut. for cos. Monaghan and Fermanagh, Lords of the Manors of Hilton and Manor Waterhouse.—Hilton Park, Clones, co. Monaghan; Kildare Street and Sackville Street Clubs, Dublin; Junior Carlton Club, s.w.

    Heir Pres., his brother Charles Dudley Ryder, Capt. 8th Foot; b. 1839.

MADDEN, John, Esq., of Roslea Manor, co. Fermanagh.

Second son of the late Charles Dudley Madden, Esq., of Roslea Manor, by Harriet, dau. of the Rev. Michael Baxter; b. 1819; s. 1840; m. 1847 Clara Elizabeth, 2nd dau. of the Rev. Spencer Knox, and has issue,

    • Charles Dudley, b. 1851.

Mr. Madden, who was educated at Harrow and St. Peter's Coll., Cambridge, is a J.P. and D.L. for co. Fermanagh (High Sheriff 1848), and a Magistrate for co. Monaghan; formerly in the 41st Foot. — Roslea Manor, co. Fermanagh; Kildare Street Club, Dublin.

MADDEN, John Travers, Esq., of Inch, co. Dublin.

Only son of the late John Madden, Esq., of Inch, by Lucretia, dau. of the Rev. Samuel Madden, Vicar-General of the Diocese of Ossory; b. 1810; s. 1833;

626

m. 1834 Margaret, eldest dau. of the late Owen Armstrong, Esq., and has, with other issue,

    • John Eeles, b. 1838.

Mr. Madden is a Magistrate for co. Dublin.—Inch House, Balbriggan; co. Dublin; 47, Upper Sackville Street, Dublin.

MADDISON, George Wilson, Esq., of Partney Hall, Lincolnshire.

Only son of the late Lieut.-Col. Maddison, of Partney, by Mary, dau. of the Rev. Henry Alington. of Swinhope, co. Lincoln; b. 1797; s. 1816; m. 1825 Frances Elizabeth, 2nd dau. of the late Sir Alan Bellingham, Bart., and has, with other issue,

    • Henry, b. 1829.

Mr. Maddison, who was educated at Rugby and Christ's Coll., Cambridge, is a Magistrate for co. Lincoln.—Partney Hall, Spilsby.

MADDOCK, Sir Thomas Herbert, Knt. (cr. 1844).

Son of the late Rev. Thomas Maddock, by Mary, dau. of Rokeby Scott, Esq.; b. 1792. Was formerly in the Bengal Civil Service of H.E.I.C.; was successively Secretary to the Indian Government, Deputy-Governor of Bengal, and President of the Council of India 1845–49; was M.P. for Rochester 1852–7.—Union Club, s.w.; 4, Park Place Villas, Maida Hill, w.

MADDOCK, of Naseby. (See Ashby.)

MADDOCKS, John Edward, Esq., of Glanywern and Vron Iw, Denbighshire.

Eldest son of the late John Madocks. Esq., M.P., of Glanywern and Vron Iw, by Sidney, dau. of the late Abraham Wildey Robarts, Esq., M.P., of Putney Heath, Surrey; b. 1820; s. 1837. Educated at Harrow and Royal Military Coll., Sandhurst; is a J.P. and D.L. for co. Denbigh (High Sheriff 1856), and Lieut.-Col. of the 7th Lancashire Rifles Militia; was formerly Capt. 13th Light Dragoons.—Glanywern, Denbigh; Army and Navy and Boodl-'s Clubs, s.w.

    Heir Pres., his brother Henry Robarts, b. 1825.

MADOX-BLACKWOOD, Miss, of Pitreavie, Fifeshire.

Caroline Augusta, elder dau. of the late William Madox. Esq., who assumed the name of Blackwood on succeeding his mother at Pitreavie. by Caroline, dau. of Robert Porrett, Esq.; s. 1863. The estate of Pitreavie formerly belonged to the Wardlaws.—Pitreavie, near Dunfermline, N.B.; Residence: 1, Queen's Villas, Windsor.

    Heir Pres., her sister Sarah Jane, m. 1866 the Rev. Erasmus Valentine Mason; M.A. of Trinity College, Cambridge, Vicar of Denney, Bucks.

MAGAN, Mrs., of Cloncarl. King's Co.

Elizabeth Georgiana, 2nd dau. and co-heir of the late Dudley Loftus, Esq., of Killyan, co. Meath (who d. 1807); m. 1st 1814 Col. Thomas Lowther Allen; 2nd 1817 William Henry Magan, Esq., of Clonearl (formerly High Sheriff of co. Westmeath), by whom, who d. 1860, she has surviving issue, an only daughter,

    • Augusta-Elizabeth.

The late Mr. Dudley Loftus was head of the ancient and distinguished house of Loftus.—Clonearl, King's Co.; Killyan, co. Meath; Eagle Hill, co. Kildare; Wind Lawn, Bray, co. Dublin; 77, Stephen's Green, Dublin.

MAGAN, Percy, Esq., of Marlfield, co. Wexford.

Second son of the late Percy Magan, Esq., of Doninga (who d. 1857), by Ellen, dau. of the late Valentine O'Connor, Esq., of Dublin; b. 1820, m. 1866 Anne Catherine, only dau. of the Rev. Edward Richards.

Rector of Cloonllon, and Chancellor of Dromore. Is a Magistrate for cos. Wexford and Roscommon, and Lord of the Manor of Cloonlaughlin, co. Roscommon.—*Marlfield, Gorey, co. Wexford.*

MAGENS, John Dorrien-, Esq., of Hammerwood Lodge, Sussex.

Eldest son of the late Magens Dorrien-Magens, Esq., of Hammerwood, and of Brightlingsea Hall, Essex, by the Hon. Henrietta Cecilia, eldest sister of George, 3rd Lord Dynevor; *b.* 1796; *s.* 1849; *m.* 1830 Mary Stephana, dau. of Lieut.-Col. Rudsdell, and has, with other issue,

* Frederick (of Ashdean House, Sussex, which he inherited from his uncle, Charles Dorrien, Esq., 1866), educated at Eton, late Capt. 1st Life Guards; *b.* 1834.

Mr. Magens, who was educated at Westminster and Ch. Ch., Oxford, is a J.P. and D.L. for Sussex, and Lord of the Manor of Brightlingsea. — *Hammerwood Lodge, East Grinstead; Brightlingsea Hall, Colchester; Carlton Club, s.w.*

MAGILL, William, Esq., of Lyttleton, co. Westmeath.

Eldest son of the late George Magill, Esq., of Lyttleton, by Hester, 5th dau. of John Nugent, Esq., of Clonlost, co. Westmeath; *b.* 1797; *s.* 1808; *m.* 1833 Harriette, dau. of Thomas Stannus, Esq., and has, with other issue, an only son,

* William James Napier, a Magistrate for co. Westmeath, and Capt. Dublin Artillery Militia, *b.* 1834; *m.* 1867 Eliza Isabel, eldest dau. of James Stirling, Esq., of Ballawley Park, co. Dublin.

Mr. Magill, who was educated at Trinity Coll., Dublin, is a Magistrate for co. Westmeath.—*Lyttleton, Ballymahon, co. Westmeath.*

MAGNAY, Sir William, Bart., of Postford House, Surrey (cr. 1844).

Eldest son of the late Christopher Magnay, Esq., of Wandsworth, by Jane, dau. of the Rev. James Smith, Rector of Bellingham; *b.* 1797; *m.* 1854 Amelia, dau. of Thomas Clarke, Esq., of St. John's Wood (she *d.* 1863). Is a Commissioner of the Lieutenancy for London, and an Alderman and wholesale Stationer in the City; formerly Sheriff and Lord Mayor of London.

Heir, his son William, *b.* 1855.

MAGOR, John Penberthy, Esq., of Penventon, Cornwall.

Eldest son of the late Reuben Magor, Esq., of Redruth, Cornwall, by Mary, dau. of John Penberthy, Esq., of St. Just; *b.* 1796; *m.* 1825 Elizabeth Ann Moyle, only child of John Furniss, Esq., of Lamellen, Cornwall, and has, with other issue,

* Reuben Frederick, late Lieut. 12th Foot; *b.* 1831.

Mr. Magor is a J.P. and D.L. for Cornwall.—*Penventon, Redruth; Lamellen, Bodmin.*

MAGUIRE, Edward, Esq., of Gortoral, co. Fermanagh.

Son of the late Alexander Maguire, Esq., D.L., of Gortoral, by Mary, dau. of John Nicholls, Esq., of Dring, co. Longford; *b.* 1827; *s.* 1850; *m.* 1866 Cecilia Mary, only dau. of John H. O'Rorke, Esq., of Jamestown House, Golden Ball, co. Dublin. Educated at Trinity Coll., Dublin (B.A. 1848): called to the Irish Bar 1851; is a J.P. and D.L. for co. Leitrim, and a Magistrate for cos. Cavan and Fermanagh; was High Sheriff for Leitrim 1858-9, and of co. Fermanagh 1860-1.—*Gortoral House, Swanlinbar, co. Fermanagh.*

MAGUIRE, John Francis, Esq., of Ardmanagh, co. Cork.

Eldest son of the late John Maguire, Esq., Merchant, of Cork; *b.* 1815; *m.* 1843 Margaret, dau. of R. Daily,

Esq., of Cork. Called to the Irish Bar 1843; was Mayor of Cork 1853, also in 1862-3-4; is principal Editor and Proprietor of the 'Cork Examiner;' is a Magistrate for, and Alderman of, Cork city; was M.P. for Dungarvan 1852-65, when he was returned for Cork. Author of 'Rome and its Ruler,' 'Father Mathew, a Biography,' and 'The Irish in America.'—*Ardmanagh, Passage West, Cork; Reform Club, s.w.; 21, Besborough Gardens, Pimlico, s.w.*

MAHER, Matthias A., Esq., of Ballinkeele, co. Wexford.

Eldest son of the late John Maher, Esq., J.P. and D.L., of Ballinkeele (who was High Sheriff 1853, and formerly M.P. for co. Wexford), by Louisa Katharine, dau. of George Bourke O'Kelly, Esq., of Acton House, Middlesex; *b.* 1846; *s.* 1860. Is a Magistrate for co. Wexford.—*Ballinkeele, Enniscorthy, co. Wexford.*

Heir Pres., his brother George Maurice, *b.* 1848.

+**MAHER, Mrs.**, of Tullemaine, co. Tipperary.

Catharine, dau. of W. Prendergast, Esq.; *m.* 18— John Maher, Esq., J.P., of Tullemaine Castle, who *d.* 1850. —*Tullemaine Castle, Fethard, co. Tipperary.*

+**MAHER, Nicholas Valentine**, Esq., of Turtulla, co. Tipperary.

Eldest son of the late Thomas Maher, Esq., M.D., of Cashel, co. Tipperary, by Margaret, dau. of — Maher, Esq.; *b.* 18—; *s.* his cousin, Valentine Maher. Esq., M.P., 1844; *m.* 1845 Margaret Jane. elder dau. of Walter Otway Herbert, Esq., of Pill House, co. Tipperary. Educated at Trinity Coll. Cambridge; is a Magistrate for co. Tipperary; was M.P. for co. Tipperary, 1844-52.—*Turtulla, Thurles, co. Tipperary; Reform Club, s.w.*

MAHON, the Rev. Sir William Veset Ross, Bart., of Castlegar, co. Galway (cr. 1810).

Third son of the late Sir Ross Mahon, Bart., of Castlegar, by the Hon. Mary Geraldine, dau. of the late Right Hon. James Fitzgerald and the Baroness Fitzgerald and Vesey; *b.* 1813; *s.* as 4th Bart. 1852; *m.* 1853 Jane, dau. of the Rev. H. King, of Ballylin, King's Co. Educated at Trinity Coll. Dublin (B.A. 1835, M.A. 1838): is Rector of Rawmarsh.—*Rawmarsh Rectory, Rotherham; Castlegar, Ahascragh, co. Galway; Kildare Street Club, Dublin.*

Heir, his son Ross, *b.* 1856.

MAHON, Henry Sandford Pakenham-, Esq., of Strokestown, co. Roscommon.

Eldest son of the late Hon. and Very Rev. Henry Pakenham, Dean of St. Patrick's. (who *d.* 1863), by Eliza Catherine Sandford, sister of the late Henry, 2nd Lord Mount Sandford; *b.* 1823; *m.* 1847 Grace. only dau. and heiress of Major Denis Mahon (who succeeded to the estates of Maurice, last Lord Hartland, in 1845), and has, with other issue,

* Henry, *b.* 1851.

Mr. Mahon, who assumed that name, by Royal licence, in addition to his patronymic, in 1847, is a J.P. and D.L. for co. Roscommon, and was formerly in the 8th Hussars.—*Strokestown House, co. Roscommon.*

MAHON, Col. Magntainna James Patrick O'Gorman (The O'Gorman Mahon), late of Mahonburgh, co. Clare.

Son of the late Patruic Mòr Mhaghthamhna. by Barbara, dau. of the late O'Gorman Mahon: *b.* 1803; *m.* 1828 Christina, dau. of M. O'Brien, Esq., of Fitzwilliam Square, Dublin, and has, surviving issue an only son,

* James, *b.* 183—

The O'Gorman, who was educated at Trinity Coll., Dublin, and called to the Irish Bar 1834, is a J.P. and

s s 2   627

D.L. for co. Clare, late Capt. in the Clare Militia; was M.P. for co. Clare 1830–1; for Ennis 1847–52.—*Ennis, co. Clare;* Residence: 38, *Rue de Berri, Paris.*

MAHON, Viscount. (See under *Stanhope, Earl.*)

MAHONY, DANIEL, Esq., of Dunloe, co. Kerry.
Eldest surviving son of the late Daniel Mahony, Esq., of Dunloe, by Elizabeth, dau. of Patrick Creagh, Esq., of Cork; *b.* 1793; *s.* 1832; *m.* 1836 Frances, 5th dau. of John Mahony, Esq., of Point House, Killarney, and has, with other issue,
* John, a Magistrate for co. Kerry; *b.* 1841.
Mr. Mahony, who was educated at Stonyhurst and Trinity Coll., Dublin, is a Magistrate for co. Kerry (High Sheriff 1841).—*Dunloe Castle, Beaufort, co. Kerry.*

MAHONY, MYLES, Esq., of Castlequin, co. Kerry.
Eldest son of the late Kean Mahony, Esq., of Castlequin, by Mary Anne, dau. of the late Daniel Cronin, Esq., of Park, Killarney; *b.* 1841; *s.* 1846. Educated at Eton.—*Castlequin, Cahirciveen, co. Kerry.*

+MAHONY, PIERCE, Esq., of Gunsborough, co. Kerry.
Eldest son of the late Pierce Mahony, Esq., of Woodlawn, co. Kerry, by Anna Maria. dau. of John Maunsell, Esq., of Ballybroad House, co. Limerick; *b.* 1792; *m.* 1815 Jane, only dau. of Edmund Kenfeg, Esq., of Ballindeasig House, Kinsale, co. Kerry. Educated at Trinity Coll. Dublin; is a M.R.I.A., and a Solicitor in Dublin; was M.P. for Kinsale 1837–8.—*Gunsborough, Ballylongford, co. Kerry; Reform Club, s.w.*

MAHONY, RICHARD JOHN, Esq., of Dromore, co. Kerry.
Eldest son of the late Rev. Denis Mahony, of Dromore, by Lucinda Catherine, dau. of John Segerson, Esq., of West Cove, co. Kerry; *b.* 1828; *s.* 1851; *m.* 1856 Mary Harriette, dau. of John Waller, Esq., of Shannon Grove, co. Limerick, and has, with other issue,
* Harald Segerson, *b.* 1867.
Mr. Mahony, who was educated at Worcester Coll., Oxford (B.A. 1851), is a J.P. and D.L. for co. Kerry (High Sheriff 1853).—*Dromore Castle, Kenmare, co. Kerry.*

MAHONY, THOMAS M'DONOGH, Esq., of Cullina, co. Kerry.
Eldest son of the late Francis M'Donogh. Esq., M.D., of Killarney, by Mary, eldest dau. of Kean Mahony, Esq., of Cullina; *b.* 1825; *s.* his uncle, Kean Mahony, Esq., 1862; *m.* 1859 his cousin, Mary Anne, only dau. of the late Kean Mahony, Esq., of Castlequin, and has issue,
* Thomas, *b.* 1863.
Mr. Mahony, who was educated at Carlow Coll., represents a family who were formerly powerful in co. Cork.—*Cullina, Beaufort, Killarney, co. Kerry; Casilequin, Cahirciveen, co. Kerry.*

MAILLARD, PARNELL ROBERT. Esq., of Huntington, Queen's Co.
Third son of the late Major James N. Maillard, 18th Royal Irish, by Catherine, dau. of the Rev. Sewell Stubber, of Moyne, Queen's Co.; *b.* 1808; *m.* 1836 Mary Ann, eldest dau. of Francis Thirkill, Esq., of Boston, co. Lincoln, and has, with other issue,
* Robert Thirkill, *b.* 1836.
Mr. Maillard is a Magistrate for Queen's Co.—*Huntington, Portarlington, Queen's Co.*

+MAINE, the Rev. JOHN THOMAS, of Bighton Wood, Hampshire.
Son of the late J. Maine, Esq.; *b.* 1803. Educated at Trinity Coll., Cambridge (B.A. 1826, M.A. 1836); is a

Magistrate for Hants, Lord of the Manor and Patron of Bighton; formerly Rector of Brinkhill and Harrington, co. Lincoln.—*Bighton Wood, Alresford.*

MAINWARING, Sir HARRY, Bart., of Peover, Cheshire (cr. 1804).
Eldest son of the late Sir Henry Mainwaring Mainwaring, Bart., of Peover, by Sophia. dau. of the late Sir R. S. Cotton, Bart., and sister of F. M. Viscount Combermere. G.C.B.; *b.* 1801; *s.* 1860; *m.* 1832 Emma, dau. of Thomas William Tatton, Esq., of Wythenshawe, co. Chester. Educated at Rugby and C.C.C., Oxford; is a J.P. and D.L. for co. Chester, and Dep.-Chairman of Cheshire Quarter Sessions; Lord of the Manors of Over-Peover, Goostrey, and Snelson, and Patron of 1 living.—*Peover Hall, Knutsford; St. James's Club, s.w.*
Heir. his son Stapleton Thomas, *b.* 1838; *m.* 1867 Elizabeth, 3rd dau. of Michael Kinneen, Esq., of Athenry, co. Galway.

MAINWARING, the Rev. CHARLES HENRY, of Whitmore Hall, Staffordshire.
Son of the late Admiral Rowland Mainwaring. J.P. and D.L., of Whitmore Hall, by his first wife Sophia Henrietta, only child of the late Major Duff; *b.* 1821; *s.* 1862; *m.* 184– Jane, dau. of the late Sir Henry Broughton. Bart., of Doddington, co. Chester. Educated at Oriel Coll., Oxford (B.A. 1813, M.A. 1844); is a Magistrate for co. Stafford, and Lord of the Manor, Patron, and Rector of Whitmore.—*Whitmore Hall, Newcastle-under-Lyne.*

MAINWARING, SALUSBURY KYNASTON, Esq., of Oteley Park, Shropshire.
Eldest son of the late Charles Kynaston Mainwaring, Esq., J.P. and D.L., of Oteley Park (who was High Sheriff of co. Salop 1829). by Frances, dau. of Col. John Lloyd Salusbury, of Galltfaenan, co. Denbigh: *b.* 1844; *s.* 1862. Educated at Eton and Ch. Ch., Oxford; is a Magistrate for co. Salop, Lord of the Manor of Oteley, and Patron of 2 livings, and an Officer in the North Shropshire Yeomanry.—*Oteley Park, Ellesmere; Carlton Club, s.w.; 83, Eaton Square, s.w.*
Heir Pres., his uncle Townshend Mainwaring. Esq., M.P., of Galltfaenan, near Denbigh, a Magistrate for co. Denbigh (younger son of the late Rev. Charles Mainwaring, by Sarah, dau. of John Townshend, Esq.); *b.* 1807; *m.* 1837 Anna Maria, dau. of Col. John Lloyd Salusbury, of Galltfaenan, co. Denbigh. and has, with other issue,
* Charles Salusbury, *b.* 1845.

MAINWARING. (See *Lee-Mainwaring.*)

MAINWARING-ELLERKER-ONSLOW. (See *Onslow.*)

MAISTER, the Rev. HENRY, of Skeffling, Yorkshire.
Eldest son of the late Arthur Maister. Esq., J.P., formerly of Winestead and Wood Hall. co. York, by Ann, dau. of Joseph Robinson Pease, Esq., of Hesslewood, near Hull; *b.* 1813; *m.* Grace. dau. of George William Sutton. Esq., of Elton Hall. co. Durham, and has, with other issue,
* Reginald Henry, *b.* 1851.
Mr. Maister, who was educated at Winchester and New Inn Hall, Oxford (B.A. 1838. M.A. 1850). is Vicar of Kilnsea, and Perpetual Curate of Easington-in-Holderness, co. York.—*Skeffling, Patrington, Yorkshire.*

MAITLAND, Sir ALEXANDER CHARLES RAMSAY-GIBSON-, Bart., of Clifton Hall, Midlothian (cr. 1818).
Eldest son of the late Alexander Maitland. Gibson. Esq., of Clifton Hall, by Susan, eldest dau. of George Ramsay, Esq., of Barnton (whose name he has assumed); *b.* 1820; *s.* his grandfather as 3rd Bart. 1848; *m.* 1841

628

Thomasina Agnes, elder dau. of James Hunt, Esq., of Pittencrieff. Educated at Edinburgh; is a J.P. and D.L. for Midlothian and co. Stirling, and formerly Capt. Midlothian Yeomanry, Col. Stirling Militia, and Lieut. 79th Highlanders.—*Clifton Hall, and Barnton, Edinburgh; Sauchie, Stirling, N.B.; New Club, Edinburgh; 13, Moray Place, Edinburgh; Garrick Club, w.c.*

Heir, his son James, b. 1848.

MAITLAND, HENRY, Esq., of Whirfield, Kinross-shire.
Youngest son of the late Charles Maitland, Esq., of Rankeilour, Fifeshire, by Mary, dau. of David Johnston, Esq., of Lathrisk; b. 1813; m. 1838 Anna, dau. of John Stirling, Esq., of St. Andrews, N.B.; is a Magistrate for co. Kinross.—*Whirfield, Kinross, N.B.*

MAITLAND, the Rev. JAMES, D.D.
Eldest son of the late Rev. John Garlies Maitland, M.A., of Fairgirth, co. Kirkcudbright, by Margaret, dau. of the Rev. John Scott, D.D., of Foulshields, co. Linlithgow; b. 1797; s. 1835; m. 1st 1826 Jessie Tennant, dau. of Cosby Swindell Norvell, Esq., of Boghall, co. Linlithgow; 2nd 1837 Louisa, eldest dau. and heir of the Hon. Mrs. Bellamy-Gordon (whom see under *Gordon*), and has issue by the former,

Garlies Cosby, b. 1830; m. 1852 Jane, dau. of the late Major Francis Smalpage, H.E.I.C.'s Service; and d. 1863, leaving issue. * Francis James Norvell, b. 1857.

Dr. Maitland was educated at the University of Edinburgh, and ordained Minister of Kells 1826, had title of D.D. conferred by the University of Glasgow 1852, was chosen Moderator of the General Assembly of the Church of Scotland 1860, is a J.P. and D.L. for co. Kirkcudbright.—*Kells Manse, New Galloway, co. Kirkcudbright.*

MAITLAND, JAMES, Esq., of Rossie House, Fifeshire.
Third son of the late Charles Maitland, Esq. of Rankeilour and Lindores, by Mary, dau. of David Johnston, Esq., of Lathrisk; b. 1806; m. 1st 1836 Emma, dau. of Thomas M. Willing, Esq.; 2nd 1840 Frances Harriet, dau. of R. S. Short, Esq., of Edlington Grove, co. Lincoln. Entered the Navy 1819, became Commander R.N. 1836; is a Magistrate for co. Fife, and a Capt. on the retired list.—*Rossie House, Auchtermuchty, N.B.*

MAITLAND, JOHN, Esq., of Freugh, Wigtownshire.
Eldest son of the late Patrick Maitland, Esq., of Freugh, by Matilda Frances Harriet, dau. of James Buchanan, Esq., of Craigend Castle, co. Stirling; b. 1845; s. 1859. Educated at Eton. His great-grandfather, a son of Charles, 6th Earl of Lauderdale, purchased the estate of Freugh in 1775.—*Balgreggan House, Freugh, Wigtown, N.B.*

Heir Pres., his brother William, b. 1846.

MAITLAND, the Rev. JOHN WHITAKER, of Loughton, Essex.
Third son of the late William Whitaker Maitland, Esq., D.L., of Loughton Hall and Woodford Hall, Essex, by Anne, dau. of the late Benjamin Gott, Esq., of Armley House, near Leeds; b. 1831; s 1861; m. 1860 Venetia, 3rd dau. of the late Sir Richard D. Neave, Bart., and has, with other issue,

* William Whitaker, b. 1864.

Mr. Maitland, who was educated at Harrow and Trinity Hall, Cambridge (B.A. 1854, M.A. 1858), is Rector and Lord of the Manor of Loughton, and Patron of that living.—*Loughton Rectory, Loughton, Essex.*

MAITLAND, LAUDERDALE, Esq., of Eccles, Dumfriesshire.
Eldest son of the late John Maitland, Esq., of Eccles; b. 1809; s. 1822; m. 1843 Mary Catharine, dau. of

Alexander Gillespie, Esq., and by her, who d. 1857, has issue,

* Lina Mary.

Mr. Maitland, who is a Magistrate for co. Dumfries, represents a younger branch of the family of the Earl of Lauderdale.—*Eccles, Thornhill, N.B.*

MAITLAND, STUART CAIRNS, Esq., of Dundrennan, Kirkcudbrightshire.
Eldest son of the late Thomas Maitland, Esq., of Dundrennan (who was M.P. for co. Kirkcudbright 1845–51, Solicitor-General for Scotland 1840–1 and 1846–52, and afterwards a Scottish Judge as Lord Dundrennan), by Isabella, dau. of James McDowall, Esq.; b. 1816; s. 1854; m. 1841 Margaret, dau. of the late Dominick Lynch, Esq., of New York, and has, with other issue,

* David, b. 1848.

This family is a cadet branch of that of the Earl of Lauderdale. — *Dundrennan and Compstone, Kirkcudbrightshire, N.B.*

MAITLAND. (See under *Lauderdale, Earl of*.)

MAITLAND. (See *Fuller-Maitland*.)

MAITLAND. (See *Gammie-Maitland*.)

MAITLAND-DOUGALL. (See *Dougall*.)

MAITLAND-HERIOT. (See *Heriot*.)

MAITLAND-KIRWAN, CHARLES, Esq., of Gelston Castle, Kirkcudbrightshire.
Eldest son of the late Charles Lionel Kirwan, Esq. (who was a J.P. and D.L. for co. Mayo, and High Sheriff in 1846), who assumed the additional name of Maitland on his marriage with Matilda Elizabeth, dau. of the late William Maitland, Esq., of Gelston Castle, and Auchlane, co. Kirkcudbright; b. 1843; s. 1862. Is Lord of the Barony of Gelston.— *Gelston Castle, Castle Douglas, N.B.*

Heir Pres., his brother William Francis, Lieut. 78th Foot, late of the 15th Foot; b. 1844.

MAITLAND-MAKGILL-CRICHTON, DAVID, Esq., of Rankeilour-Makgill, Fifeshire.
Eldest son of the late Charles Julian Maitland-Makgill-Crichton, Esq., of Rankeilour-Makgill, by Anna Campbell, dau. of the late James Nibbs Jarvis, Esq.; b. 1854; s. 1858. Is Lord of the Barony of Rankeilour-Makgill, and is descended from Charles, 6th Earl of Lauderdale. —*Rankeilour and Barham Cottage, Springfield, Cupar-Fife, N.B.*

Heir Pres., his brother James Bertie, b. 1856.

MAJENDIE, LEWIS ASHHURST, Esq., of Hedingham Castle, Essex.
Eldest son of the late Rev. Henry Lewis Majendie, M.A., Vicar of Great Dunmow (who d. 1862), by Emma Sophia, dau. of T. F. Gepp, Esq.; b. 1835; s. his uncle Ashhurst Majendie, Esq. 1867. Educated at Marlborough Coll., and Ch Ch Oxford. Is a Magistrate for Essex, and Patron of 1 living. This family is of foreign extraction, and settled in England after the Revocation of the Edict of Nantes.—*Hedingham Castle, Halstead, Essex; Carlton Club, s.w.*

Heir Pres., his brother Arnold Henry, b. 1838.

MAJOR. (See under *Henniker, Lord*.)

MAKDOUGALL. (See *Scott-Makdougall*.)

MALCOLM, JOHN, Esq., of Poltalloch, Argyleshire.
Second son of the late Neill Malcolm, Esq., of Poltalloch, by Mary Anne, dau. of David Orme, Esq., M.D.,

of Lamorbey, Kent; *b.* 1805; *s.* his brother Neill Malcolm, Esq., 1837; *m.* 1832 Isabella Harriett, 2nd dau. of the Hon. John Wingfield-Stratford, of Addington Kent, and by her, who *d.* 1858, has, with other issue,

* John Wingfield, educated at Eton and Ch. Ch., Oxford, a Magistrate for Kent, and M.P. for Boston; *b.* 1853; *m.* 1861 the Hon. Alice Frederica, younger dau. of George Ives, 4th Lord Boston.

Mr. Malcolm, who was educated at Harrow and Ch. Ch., Oxford (B.A. 1827, M.A. 1830), is a J.P. and D.L. for Kent and co. Argyle.—*Calltonnor,Lochgilphead, Argyleshire; Carlton and University Clubs,* s.w.; *7, Great Stanhope Street,* w.

MALCOLM, Mrs., of Beechwood, Hants.

Louisa, younger dau. of the late Evelyn John Shirley, Esq., of Eatington, co. Warwick, by Eliza, dau. of Arthur Stanhope, Esq.; *m.* 1843 Neill Malcolm, Esq., of Poltalloch and Calton Moor, co. Argyll (who *d.* 1857); is Lady of the Manors of Beechwood and Bartley.—*Beechwood, Southampton.*

MALCOLM, William Elphinstone, Esq., of Burnfoot, Dumfriesshire.

Only surviving son of the late Admiral Sir Pulteney Malcolm, G.C.B., of Burnfoot, by Cl~mentina, dau. of the late Hon. W. Elphinstone; *b.* 1817; *s.* 1838; *m.* 1st 1857 Mary, 2nd dau. of the late James Douglas, Esq., of Cavers, co. Roxburgh (she *d.* 1859); 2nd 1866 Charlotte Elizabeth, eldest dau. of the Hon. Alexander Leslie Melville, of Branston Hall, co. Lincoln; he has issue by the former, an only dau.,

* Mary Douglas.

Mr. Malcolm, who was educated at Trinity Coll., Cambridge (B.A. 1840, M.A. 1843), is a J.P. and D.L. for co. Dumfries. — *Burnfoot, near Langholm, Dumfriesshire; Oxford and Cambridge Club,* s.w.

MALDEN, Viscount. (See under *Essex, Earl of.*)

MALET, Sir Alexander, Bart., K.C.B., of Wilbury, Wilts (cr. 1791).

Eldest son of the late Sir Charles Ware Malet, Bart., of Wilbury House, by Susannah, dau. of James Wales, Esq.; *b.* 1800; *s.* as 2nd Bart. 1815; *m.* 1834 Mary Anne Dora, dau. of the late John Spalding, Esq., of The Holme, and step-dau. of Henry, 1st Lord Brougham. Educated at Winchester and Ch. Ch., Oxford (B.A. 1822); is a J.P. and D.L. for Wilts, Lord of the Manor of Newton Tony, and Envoy Extraordinary and Minister Plenipotentiary to the Germanic Confederation; was formerly Attaché to the Embassy at Paris, Lisbon, and St. Petersburg; Secretary of Legation at Turin and the Hague, Secretary of Embassy at Vienna, and Minister at Wartemburg.—*Wilbury House, Newton Tony, Salisbury; Residence: British Embassy, Frankfort; Brooks's and Travellers' Clubs,* s.w.

Heir, his son Henry Charles Eden, Lieut.-Col. Grenadier Guards; *b.* 1835.

MALET, Charles St. Lo, Esq., of Fontmell Parva, Dorsetshire.

Second son of the late Sir Charles Warre Malet, Bart., of Wilbury, Wilts, by Susanna, dau. of James Wales, Esq.; *b.* 1802; *m.* 1837 James St. Lo, only dau. of I. Clarke, Esq., and has, with other issue,

* William St. Lo, *b.* 1843.

Mr. Malet, who was educated at Sandhurst Coll., is a Magistrate for Dorset, and a Lieut.-Col. in the Army, retired.—*Fontmell Parva, Child Okeford, Blandford; United Service Club,* s.w.

MALINS, Sir Richard, Knt. (cr. 1867).

Third, but only surviving, son of the late William Malins, Esq., of Ailston, co. Warwick, by Mary, eldest

630

dau. of Thomas Hunter. Esq., of Pershore, co. Worcester; *b.* 1805; *m.* 1831 Susanna, eldest dau. of the late Rev. Arthur Farwell, Rector of St. Martin's, Cornwall. Educated at Caius Coll., Cambridge (B.A. 1827); called to the Bar at Lincoln's Inn 1830, and is a Bencher of Lincoln's Inn; was M.P. for Wallingford 1852-65; appointed a Vice-Chancellor 1866.—*Carlton, and Oxford and Cambridge Clubs,* s.w.; *9, Old Square, Lincoln's Inn,* e.c.; *57, Lowndes Square,* s.w.

MALKIN, Arthur Thomas, Esq., of Corrybrough, Inverness-shire.

Son of the late Benjamin H. Malkin, Esq., D.C.L. Head Master of the Royal Grammar School, Bury St. Edmunds, by Charlotte, dau. of the Rev. I. Williams. of Cowbridge, co. Glamorgan; *b.* 1803; *m.* 1833 Mary Anne, dau. of the Rev. J. A. Carr, Rector of Hadstock, Essex. Educated at Bury St. Edmunds and Trinity Coll., Cambridge (B.A. 1825, M.A. 1828); is a Dep. Lieut. for co. Inverness.—*Corrybrough, Inverness, N.B.; University Club,* s.w.; *21, Wimpole Street,* w.

MALLET, Hugh, Esq., of Ash, Devon.

Eldest son of the late Hugh Mallet, Esq., of Ash, by Caroline, eldest dau. of the late Hon. John Coventry, of Burgate House, Hants; *b.* 1827; *s.* 1865; *m.* 1853 Georgiana. dau. of the late Ven. Archdeacon Bathurst, of Norwich, and has, with other issue,

* Hugh, *b.* 1855.

Mr. Mallet was formerly Lieut. 4th Light Dragoons, late Lieut. N. Devon Yeomanry Cavalry.—*Ash, Hatherleigh, Crediton; Penrose Villa, Heavitree, Exeter.*

MALLOCK, Charles Herbert, Esq., of Cockington Court, Devon.

Fourth son of the late Rev. Roger Mallock. of Cockington Court, by Mary. dau. of Thomas Mudge, M.D.; *b.* 1802; *s.* 1846; *m.* 1836 Maria, youngest dau. of the late Arthur Champernowne, Esq., of Dartington House, Devon, and has, with other issue.

* Charles Herbert, Barrister-at-Law of the Inner Temple, *b.* 1840.

Mr. Mallock, who was educated at Harrow, is a Magistrate for Devon, and Patron of the living of Tormoham and Cockington.—*Cockington Court, Torquay.*

MALLOCK, Thomas, Esq., of Mount Hill, Devon.

Second son of the late Rawlin Mallock. Esq., of Axminster. Devon, by Charlotte, dau. of James Sibey. Esq.; *b.* 1799; *m.* 1st 1858 Edith Styles Peterson, dau. of Daniel Goddard. Esq., of Lyme Regis; 2nd 1860 Henrietta, dau. of the late J. W. Clough, Esq. of Oxton House. and Newbald Hall, Yorkshire, and has by the former, with other issue,

* Thomas John Raymond, 7th Royal Fusiliers; *b.* 1845.

Mr. Mallock, who is a Comm. R.N., on retired half-pay, represents a younger branch of the Mallocks of Cockington.—*Mount Hill, Axminster.*

MALLORY, the Rev. George, of Mobberley Old Hall, Cheshire.

Youngest son of the late Rev. George E. Leigh, by Elizabeth, dau. of John Philips, Esq., of Bank Hall; *b.* 1806; *m.* 1st 1832 Julia, only child and heir of the Rev. John Holdsworth Mallory, Rector of Mobberley; 2nd Henrietta, dau. of Trafford Trafford, Esq., of Oughtrington, co. Chester, and has, with other issue,

* Edward Leigh, *b.* 1837.

Mr. Mallory, who was educated at Macclesfield, and Brasenose Coll., Oxford (B.A. 1828), is Rector of Mobberley.—*Old Hall, Mobberley, Knutsford.*

MALMESBURY, Earl of (JAMES HOWARD HARRIS, P.C., D.C.L., G.C.B).—Cr. 1800.

Eldest son of James Edward, 2nd Earl, by Harriett Susan, dau. of the late Francis Bateman Dashwood, Esq., of Well Vale, co. Lincoln; *b.* 1807; *s.* 1841; *m.* 1830 Lady Emma, dau. of Charles Augustus, 5th Earl of Tankerville. Educated at Eton and Oriel Coll., Oxford (B.A. 1828); is a Magistrate for Hants, and Col. Hants Artillery, an official Trustee of the British Museum, and High Steward of Wallingford; was M.P. for Wilton July–Sept. 1841; Secretary for Foreign Affairs Feb.–Dec. 1852 and 1858–9; appointed Lord Privy Seal 1866.—*Heron Court, Christchurch, Hants; Dunford, Salisbury; Carlton Club, s.w.; 19, Stratford Place.*

Heir Pres., his brother Edward Alfred John, C.B., educated at Eton and the Royal Naval Coll., a J.P. and D.L. for Hants, a Vice-Admiral, reserved; was M.P. for Christchurch 1844–52; appointed British Consul at Elsinore 1852; Chargé d'Affaires and Consul-General in Peru 1852, and in Chili 1853, and Minister Plenipotentiary at Berne in 1858; Envoy Extraordinary at the Netherlands 1867; *b.* 1808; *m.* 1841 Emma Wylie, dau. of Capt. Samuel Chambers, R.N., and has, with other issue, * Edward James, Lieut. 56th Foot, *b.* 1842.

MALPAS, ALEXANDER EUSTACE-, Esq., of Rochestown, co. Dublin.

Only son of the late General Sir William Cornwallis Eustace, C.B., K.C.H. (who *d-* 1855), by his first wife Catherine Frances, only dau. of Richard Wogan, 2nd Lord Talbot de Malahide; *b.* 1810; *m.* 18— a dau. of J. Drummond, Esq., and has issue. Assumed the name of Malpas on succeeding to the estates of his maternal grandmother. Was formerly an Officer in the Army and City of Dublin Militia.—*Rochestown, co. Dublin.*

MALTHUS, SYDENHAM, Esq., of Hadstock, Essex.

Eldest son of the late Sydenham Malthus, Esq., of Hadstock, by Mary Anne, dau. of the late Rev. Samuel White, D.D., Incumbent of Hampstead, Middlesex, and Rector of Brightwell, Baldwin, Oxon; *b.* 1831; *s.* 1868; *m.* 1867 Henrietta, eldest dau. of the Rev. T. A. Maberly, of Cuckfield, Sussex. Is Lord of the Manor of Hadstock, and Capt. 94th Regt.—*Hadstock, Linton, Essex.*

Heir Pres., his brother Charles, *b.* 1838.

MANCHESTER, Duke of (WILLIAM DROGO MONTAGU, LL.D.).—Cr. 1719.

Eldest son of George, 6th Duke, by his 1st wife Millicent, dau. of the late General Robert Bernard and Lady Olivia Sparrow; *b.* 1823; *s.* 1855; *m.* 1852 the Countess Louise Frederice Auguste von Alten, of Hanover. Educated at Sandhurst; is a J.P. and D.L. for Hunts, Patron of 3 livings, and Major Hunts Militia; Lieut.-Colonel Commanding 1st Light Horse Volunteers; late Capt. Grenadier Guards; was M.P. for Bewdley 1848–52, for Hunts 1852–5.—*Kimbolton Castle, St. Neots; The Castle, Tandragee, co. Armagh; Carlton Club, s.w.; 1, Great Stanhope Street, w.*

Heir, his son George Victor Drogo, Viscount Mandeville, *b.* 1853.

MANCHESTER, Bishop of (the Right Rev. JAMES PRINCE LEE, D.D.).

Eldest son of the late Stephen Lee, Esq. (sometime Secretary and Librarian to the Royal Society), by Sarah, dau. of — Challey, Esq.; *b.* 1804; *m.* 1830 Susan, dau. of the late George Penrice, Esq. Educated at St. Paul's School; graduated B.A. 1828, at Trinity Coll., Cambridge, of which he became Fellow; was Assistant Master of Rugby, and Head Master of King Edward's School, Birmingham; consecrated 1848. Patron of 2 livings, and 70 alternate.—*Mauldeth Hall, Manchester; Athenæum Club, s.w.; 55, Jermyn Street, s.w.*

MANGLES, Capt. CHARLES EDWARD.

Son of the late James Mangles, Esq., formerly M.P. for Guildford, by Mary, dau. of John Hughes, Esq.; *b.* 1798; *m.* 1831 Rose, dau. of George Newcome, Esq., of Upper Wimpole Street, London. Is a Magistrate for Surrey; formerly Capt. in the Maritime Service of the H.E.I.C.; was M.P. for Newport 1857–9.—Residence: *Poyle Park, Farnham, Surrey; Oriental Club, w.*

MANGLES, FREDERICK, Esq., of Pendell Court, Surrey.

Eldest son of the late James Mangles, Esq. (who was M.P. for Guildford 1831–7), by Mary, dau. of John Hughes, Esq.; *b.* 1794; *m.* 1832 Marian, dau. of George Scott, Esq., of Ravenscourt, Middlesex, and co-heir of Harry Stoe, Esq., and has, with other issue, * Frederick Scott; *b.* 1833.—*Pendell Court, Bletchinley, Surrey.*

MANGLES, ROSS DONNELLY, Esq., late of Woodbridge House, Surrey.

Third surviving son of the late James Mangles, Esq. (who was M.P. for Guildford 1831–7), by Mary, dau. of John Hughes, Esq.; *b.* 1801; *m.* 1830 Harriet, dau. of the late George Newcome, Esq., of Upper Wimpole Street, London, and has issue. Educated at Eton and Haileybury Coll.; appointed 1820 to the Civil Service, Bengal, where he held several high posts in the Revenue and Judicial Departments; was M.P. for Guildford 1841–58, a Director of the East-India Company 1847–58, and Chairman 1857–8; appointed one of the Council for India 1858.—*Stoke, Guildford; Athenæum Club, s.w.*

MANLEY, AUGUSTUS EAST, Esq., of Manley Hall, Staffordshire.

Eldest surviving son of the late John Shawe Manley, Esq., of Manley Hall, by Catherina Emilia, dau. of the late Sir William R. Clayton, Bart., of Harleyford, Bucks; *b.* 1824; *s.* 1857; *m.* 1849 Margaret Christabelle, dau. of John Burton Philips, Esq., of Heath House, Cheadle, co. Stafford, and has, with other issue,

* Francis Capel, *b.* 1850.

Mr. Manley is a J.P. and D.L. for co. Stafford.—*Manley Hall, Lichfield; Union Club, s.w.*

MANLEY, GEORGE, Esq., of Caley Hall, Yorkshire.

Only son of Count George Manley, of Buckland, Somerset, by his 2nd wife Sara, only child of William Stuckey, Esq., of Swaffham, Norfolk; *b.* 1825; *m.* 1st 1849 Isabel, dau. of J. W. Russell, Esq., of Ham Hall, co. Stafford; 2nd 1853 Charlotte, dau. of P. Middleton, Esq., of Stockeld Park, co. York, and niece of William, 17th Lord Stourton, and has, with other issue,

* George, *b.* 1856.

Mr. Manley is a Count Palatine by inheritance; was formerly Captain 2nd W. York Militia.—*Caley Hall, Otley; Arthur's Club, s.w.*

MANN, DEANE, Esq., of Dunmoyle, co. Tyrone.

Only surviving son of the late Deane Mann, Esq., of Corvey Lodge, co. Tyrone, by Sarah, dau. of Arthur Mulholland, Esq., of Pomeroy, co. Tyrone; *b.* 1821; *s.* 1844; *m.* 1856 Mary Stewart, only surviving dau. of William Jeffcock, Esq., of High Hazles, co. York, and has surviving issue.

* Catherine Mary Jeffcock.

Mr. Mann, who was educated at Dungannon and Trinity Coll., Dublin, is a Magistrate for co. Tyrone, and Capt. R. Tyrone Fusiliers.—*Dunmoyle, Sixmilecross, and Corvey Lodge, Carrickmore, co. Tyrone.*

MANNERS, Lord (JOHN THOMAS MANNERS).— Cr. 1807.

Eldest son of John Thomas, 2nd Lord, by Lydia Sophia, 3rd dau. of Vice-Admiral William Bateman Dashwood; *b.* 1852; *s.* 1864. Educated at Eton. The 1st Peer, a grandson of John, 3rd Duke of Rutland, was many years Lord Chancellor of Ireland.—43, *Prince's Gate*, w.

Heir Pres., his brother Arthur, *b.* 1855.

MANNERS, Lord GEORGE JOHN, of Cheveley Park, Cambridgeshire.

Third son of John Henry. 5th Duke of Rutland, K.G., by Lady Elizabeth, 5th dau. of Frederick, 5th Earl of Carlisle, K.G.; *b.* 1820; *m.* 1855 Lady Adeliza Matilda, 2nd dau. of Henry Charles, 16th Duke of Norfolk, and has, with other issue,

* Charles George Edmund John, *b.* 1858. .

Lord G. Manners, who was educated at Eton and Trinity Coll., Cambridge (M.A. 1841), is a Magistrate for co. Cambridge, a Col. in the Army; late Lieut.-Col. Royal Horse Guards; was M.P. for Cambridgeshire 1847–57, re-chosen 1863.—*Cheveley Park, Newmarket; Carlton Club*, s.w.; 3, *Hamilton Place*, w.

MANNERS. (See under *Rutland, Duke of,* and *Canterbury, Viscount.*)

MANNERS-SUTTON, the Hon. Sir JOHN HENRY THOMAS, K.C.B.—Cr. 1866.

(See under *Canterbury, Viscount.*)

MANNERS-SUTTON, JOHN HENRY, Esq., of Kelham Hall, Notts.

Eldest son of the late Rev. Frederick Manners-Sutton, of Kelham Hall (who was a great-grandson of John, 3rd Duke of Rutland), by Henrietta Barbara, 3rd dau. of John, 7th Earl of Scarborough; *b.* 1822; *s.* 1826; *m.* 1853 Mary, eldest dau. of the Rev. Gustavus A. Burnaby, Canon of Middleham, and has, with other issue,

* John Henry Evelyn, *b.* 1854.

Mr. Manners-Sutton, who was educated at Eton, is a J.P. and D.L. for Notts (High Sheriff 1863), was M.P. for Newark 1852–7.—*Kelham Hall, Newark; Carlton, Arthur's,* and *Boodle's Clubs*, s.w.

MANNING, Sir WILLIAM MONTAGU, LL.D. (cr. 1858).

Second son of John E. Manning, Esq., of Clifton, co. Gloucester, and nephew of Mr. Serjeant Manning; *b.* 1811; *m.* 1st 1836 Emily Anne, dau. of Edward Wise, Esq., of Bembridge, Isle of Wight; 2nd 1849 Eliza Anne, dau. of the Rev. William Sowerby, of Goulburn, N. S. Wales, and has, with other issue,

* Edward Montagu, Lieut. 47th Regt.; *b.* 1841; *m.* 1868 Anne Esther, only dau. of the late William Powell, Esq., of Kensington Palace Gardens.

Sir William, who was educated at University Coll., London, and called to the Bar at Lincoln's Inn 1832, is a Member of the Executive Council of New South Wales, and a Queen's Counsel and Magistrate of that colony; was for twenty years a Law Officer of that colony; was for twenty years a Law Officer of the Government of New South Wales, and resigned the office of Attorney-General in 1857.—*Wallaroy, Sydney, N. S. Wales.*

MANNING, CHARLES AUGUSTUS, Esq., of Portland Castle, Dorset.

Second son of the late Rev. John Manning (who *d.* 1826), by Catherine, dau. of William Spencer, Esq., of Huntingdon; *m.* 1830 Margaret Elizabeth, eldest dau. of the late Peter Davis Sherston, Esq., of Stoberry Park, Somerset. Is a J.P. and D.L. for Dorset, Lord of the Manor of Church Clent, co. Worcester, and Capt. of Portland Castle.—*Portland Castle, Weymouth; Junior United Service Club*, s.w.; 15, *Regent Street*, s.w.

MANNING, the Rev. CHARLES ROBERTSON.

Second son of the late Rev. William Manning, J.P., Rector of Diss (who *d.* 1857), by Elizabeth, dau. of the Rev. W. S. Donne, of Mattishall, Norfolk; *b.* 1825; *m.* 1855 Emilia, dau. of the late Rev. Thomas T. Upwood, M.A., of Lovell's Hall, Norfolk, and has, with other issue,

* Charles Upwood, *b.* 1857.

Mr. Manning, who was educated at Corpus Christi Coll., Cambridge (B.A. 1847. M.A. 1850), is a Magistrate for Norfolk, Rector of Diss, and Patron of that living.—*The Rectory, Diss, Norfolk.*

MANNING, THOMAS ELLIS, Esq., of Bratton Clovelly, Devon.

Son of the late John Glanville Manning, Esq., by Eleanor, dau. of the Rev. John Eversfield, by Elizabeth, dau. and co-heiress of Robert Maunder, Esq., of Bicknoller, Somerset; *b.* 1802; *m.* 1854 Elizabeth, dau. of David Jones, Esq., of Plymstock. Is a Magistrate for Devon, and Lord of the Manor of Bratton Clovelly. —*Eversfield, Bratton Clovelly, Lewdown, North Devon.*

MANNING, WILLIAM WOODWARD, Esq., of Coldbrook Park, Monmouthshire.

Eldest son of the late Rev. William Manning, Rector of Diss and Weeting, Norfolk, by Elizabeth, dau. and co-heir of the Rev. William Sayer Donne; *b.* 1822; *m.* 1849 Emily Octavia, dau. of Thomas Batt, Esq., and has, with other issue,

* William Edward, *b.* 1853.

Mr. Manning, who was called to the Bar at the Middle Temple in 1849, is a Magistrate for co. Monmouth. —*Coldbrook Park, Abergavenny.*

MANNINGHAM-BULLER. (See *Buller.*)

MANNOCK, PATRICK NICHOLAS PLACIDE, Esq., of Gifford's Hall, Suffolk.

Son of the late — Power, Esq., by Mary, dau. of the late Mr. White; *b.* 1793; *m.* 1820 his cousin Miss Catherine Power, and has, with other issue,

* Walter Strickland, *b.* 1826.

Mr. Mannock, who is Lord of the Manors of Stoke-by-Nayland, &c., assumed the name of Mannock in lieu of his patronymic by royal licence 1830, under the will of his cousin William Mannock, Esq., of Gifford's Hall. —*Gifford's Hall, Stoke-by-Nayland, East Bergholt.*

MANSEL, Sir JOHN BELL WILLIAM, Bart., of Ischoed, Carmarthenshire (cr. 1621).

Eldest son of the late Sir William Mansel, Bart., of Muddlescombe, co. Carmarthen, by Elizabeth, dau. of John Bell, Esq., of Harefield, Middlesex; *b.* 1866; *s.* as 9th Bart. 1829; *m.* 1832 Mary Georgiana, dau. of the Rev. John Dymoke, of Scrivelsby, co. Lincoln. Is a J.P. and D.L. for co. Carmarthen (High Sheriff 1846). —*Ischoed, Llandilo; Carlton Club*, s.w.

Heir Pres., his cousin Courtenay Mansel, Esq. (whom see).

+MANSEL, GODFREY, Esq., of Coedgain, Carmarthenshire.

Eldest son of the late Richard Mansel-Philips, Esq., M.P., of Coedgain who *d.* 1844), by Caroline, only dau. and heir of the late B. Bond Hopkins, Esq.; *b.* 1804; *m.* 18— Eliza, dau. of the Rev. John Sidney, and has issue. Is a Magistrate for co. Carmarthen, late Major 15th Hussars; resumed the ancient family name of Mansel only by Royal licence 1866.—*Coedgain, Carmarthen.*

MANSEL, Mrs., of Puncknoll, Dorsetshire.

Elizabetha Arundell, 2nd dau. of the late Rev. George Clutterbuck Frome, of Puncknoll (who *d.* 1845), by Mary Sophia, 3rd dau. of Edmund Morton Pleydell, Esq., of Whatcombe House; *m.* 1848 Morton Grove

Mansel, Esq., late H. M. 10th Foot, 3rd son of Col. Mansel, C.B., of Smedmore, Dorset, who d. 1859, leaving, with other issue,

   • George Morton, R.N. ; b. 1849.

Mrs. Mansel is Lady of the Manor and joint Patron of Puncknoll.—*Puncknoll Manor, Bridport.*

+ MANSEL, GEORGE PLEYDELL, Esq., of Langton Lodge, Dorsetshire.

Third son of the late Lieut.-Col. John Mansel, C.B., of Smedmore, Dorset, by his 2nd wife Louisa, dau. of Edmund Morton Pleydell, Esq., of Whatcombe House, Dorset; b. 1824 ; m. 1848 Jemima Henrietta, dau. of William Gambier, Esq., and of the late Countess of Athlone. Is a J.P. and D.L. for Dorset ; was formerly Capt. 60th Rifles.—*Langton Lodge, Blandford:*

MANSEL, JOHN CHRISTOPHER, Esq., of Cosgrove Hall, Northamptonshire.

Eldest son of the late Rear-Admiral Robert Mansel, of Cosgrove Hall, by Frances Charlotta, dau. of the late Rev. William Thorold, of Weelsby House, co. Lincoln ; b. 1813 ; s. 1843 ; m. 1853 Katherine Margaret, dau. of the late Rev. Henry Longueville Mansel. Educated at Harrow; is a Magistrate for co. Northampton and Bucks (High Sheriff 1858) ; is Lord of the Manor and Patron of Cosgrove.—*Cosgrove Hall, Stony Stratford.*

MANSEL, JOHN CLAVELL, Esq., of Smedmore, Dorset. ·

Eldest son of the late Lieut.-Col. John Mansel, C.B., of Smedmore, by his 2nd wife, Louisa, dau. of the late Edmund Morton Pleydell, Esq., of Whatcombe, Dorset; b. 1817 ; s. 1863 ; m. 1st 1844 Emily, dau. of Capt. A. Bingham (she d. 1845) ; 2nd 1849 Isabel, dau. of Frederick C. A. Colvile, Esq., and has, with other issue,

   • Edmund Morton, b. 1850.

Mr. Mansel, who was educated at St. John's Coll., Cambridge (B.A. 1839), is a J.P. and D.L. for Dorset, Lord of the Manor of Smedmore, Patron of 2 livings, and Capt. Q.O. Dorsetshire Yeomanry Cavalry. Is also heir presumptive to the estates of Mrs. Michel of Whatcombe (whom see).—*Smedmore, Wareham ; Longthorns, Blandford ; Boodle's and Athenæum Clubs, s.w.*

MANSELL, Lady.

Charlotte, dau. of John Wood, Esq. ; m. 1845 (as 2nd wife) Rear-Admiral Sir Thomas Mansell, K.C.H., K.S., who d. 1858.—*Guernsey.*

MANSERGH, CHARLES CARDEN, Esq., of Lisnegar, co. Cork.

Third, but second surviving, son of the late John Southcote Mansergh, Esq., of Greenane, co. Tipperary, by his first wife Mary, only dau. of the late Richard Martin, Esq., of Clifford, co. Cork ; b. 1802 ; s. to his maternal estate, Bridgetown, co. Cork, 1817 ; m. 1833 Elizabeth, dau. of the late Capt. Loftus Otway Bland, R.N., and has, with other issue,

   • Charles Stepney, b. 1835.

Mr. Mansergh, who was educated at Trinity Coll., Dublin (B.A. 1824, M.A. 1832), is a Magistrate for co. Cork; was formerly Lieut. 3rd Dragoon Guards.—*Lisnegar, Rathcormack, co. Cork ; Hibernian United Service Club, Dublin.*

MANSERGH, JOHN CRAVEN, Esq., of Rocksavage, co. Cork.

Fourth son of the late John Southcote Mansergh, Esq., of Greenane, co. Tipperary, by his first wife, Mary, only dau. and heir of Richard Martin, Esq., of Clifford, co. Cork, and brother of R.M.S. Mansergh, Esq. (whom see); b. 1810; m. 1st 1832 Anna, eldest dau. of Thomas Van Wilmsdorff Richards, of Rathaspeck, co. Wexford (she d. 1844); 2nd 1855 Jane Annie, only dau. of John

Campbell, late Major 74th Regt. ; he has, by the former, with other issue,

   • Henry Charles, Capt. 4th West India Regt., b. 1833 ; m. 1865 Emily, dau. of the Right Hon. William Yates Peel.

Mr. Mansergh, who was educated at Trinity Coll., Dublin; is a Magistrate for cos. Cork and Tipperary, and Paymaster of the Royal Artillery.—*Rocksavage, co. Cork.*

MANSERGH, NICHOLAS, Esq., of Macroney, co. Cork.

Eldest son of the late Daniel Mansergh, Esq., of Cashel, co. Tipperary, by Catherine, dau. of Kingsmill Pennefather, Esq., M.P.; b. 1789; s. 1823. Educated at Trinity Coll., Dublin (B.A. 1811, M.A. 1815) ; called to the Irish Bar 1813 ; appointed Recorder of Cashel 1836; is a Magistrate for cos. Cork and Tipperary. —*Macroney Castle, Kilworth, co. Cork ; University Club, Dublin.*

   Heir Pres., his nephew Nicholas.

MANSERGH, RICHARD MARTIN SOUTHCOTE, Esq., of Greenane House, co. Tipperary.

Eldest son of the late John Southcote Mansergh, Esq., of Greenane, by his first wife, Mary, only dau. of Richard Martin, Esq., of Clifford, co. Cork ; b. 1800 ; s. 1817 ; m. 1st 1822 Jane Rosetta, dau. of Robert Bomford, Esq.; 2nd 1843 Christiana, dau. of the Rev. Richard Mauleverer. Educated at Glasgow; is a Magistrate for co. Tipperary.—*Greenane House, Tipperary.*

MANSERGH, SOUTHCOTE, Esq., of Grallagh Castle, co. Tipperary.

Fifth son of the late John Southcote Mansergh, Esq., of Greenane, co. Tipperary, by his first wife, Mary, only dau. and heir of Richard Martin, Esq., of Clifford, co. Cork; b. 1807; m. 1841 Anna Matilda, dau. of the late Stepney St. George, Esq., of Headford, co. Galway, and widow of William Nicholson, Esq., of Turtola. Is a Magistrate for co. Tipperary.—*Grallagh Castle, Thurles, co. Tipperary.*

MANSERGH-ST. GEORGE, RICHARD JAMES, Esq., of Headford Castle, co. Galway.

Eldest son of the late Capt. Stepney St. George, of Headford, by Frances, dau. of General L'Estrange, of Moystown ; b. 1838 ; s. 1858. Educated at Eton ; was formerly a Lieut. 3rd Light Dragoons.—*Headford Castle, co. Galway ; Kildare Street Club, Dublin.*

   Heir Pres., his brother Henry P. L'Estrange, b. 1839.

MANSFIELD, Earl of (WILLIAM DAVID MURRAY, K.T.).—CR 1776.

Eldest son of William, 3rd Earl, by Frederica, dau. of the late Most Rev. William Markham, D.D., Lord Archbishop of York ; b. 1806 ; s. 1840 ; m. 1829 Louisa, dau. of the late Cuthbert Ellison, Esq., of Hebburn, co. Durham (she d. 1857). Educated at Westminster; is Lord Lieutenant and Sheriff Principal of co. Clackmannan, a Dep.-Lieut. for co. Perth, and Patron of 2 livings ; Lieut.-Col. Perth Militia, and Keeper of Scone Palace: was M.P. for Norwich 1832-7, for Perthshire 1837-40 ; a Lord of the Treasury 1834-5; Lord High Commissioner to the Church of Scotland 1858-9.—*Scone Palace, Perth, N.B. ; Schaw Park, Clackmannan ; Carlton Club, s.w. ; Caen Wood, Hampstead, n.w.*

   Heir, his son William David, Viscount Stormont, late Lieut. and Capt. Grenadier Guards ; b. 1835 ; m. 1857 Emily Louisa, dau. of the late Sir John Athell McGregor, Bart., and has, with other issue, • William David, b. 1860.

MANSFIELD, Sir WILLIAM ROSE, K.C.B., K.C.S.I. (cr. 1858).

Son of the late John Mansfield, Esq., of Diggeswell House, Herts; b. 1818 ; m. 1854 Mary, dau. of Robert

Fellowes, Esq., of Shotesham, Norfolk. Is a General in the Army, Commander-in-Chief in India, and Col. 38th Foot; was Chief of the Staff in India; appointed Commander-in-Chief of the Bombay Army, 1860.—*Residence: Calcutta ; United Service Club*, s.w.

MANSFIELD, FRANCIS, Esq., of Ardrummon House, co. Donegal.
Third but eldest surviving son of the late Francis Mansfield, Esq., J.P., by Margaret West, grand-dau. of John Leonard, Esq., of co. Fermanagh; *b.* 1796; *s.* 1854; *m.* 1832 Mary, 3rd dau. of the late Sir Samuel Hayes, Bart., of Drnnboe Castle, and has, with other issue,

* Francis Stewart, B.A. of Trinity Coll., Dublin, a Magistrate for co. Donegal (High Sheriff 1859), and Capt. Donegal Militia: *b.* 1833 ; *m.* 1861 Anna Phillppa, eldest surviving dau. of George Simon Harcourt, of Ankerwyke House, Bucks.

Mr. Mansfield, who is a J.P. and D.L. for co. Donegal, was elected Treasurer for co. Donegal 1836.—*Ardrummon House, Ballynnleel, co. Donegal ; Castle Wray, Strabane, co. Donegal.*

MANSFIELD, GEORGE PATRICK LATTIN, Esq., of Morristown Lattin, co. Kildare.
Eldest son of the late Alexander Mansfield, Esq., of Yeomanston House, co. Kildare, and Ballinamultina, co. Waterford, by Pauline, only dau. and heir of Patrick Lattin, Esq., of Morristown Lattin ; *b.* 1820 ; *s.* 1842 ; *m.* 1843 Mary Frances Constantia, youngest dau. of the late George Bourke O'Kelly, Esq., of Acton House, Middlesex, and has, with other issue,

* George, *b.* 1845.

Mr. Mansfield, who was educated at Oscott Coll., is a Magistrate for co. Kildare (High Sheriff 1851).—*Morristown Lattin, Naas, co. Kildare ; Kildare Street Club, Dublin.*

MANTELL, Sir JOHN ILES, Knt. (cr. 1867).
Son of the late J. Mantell, Esq., *b.* 182–; called to the Bar at the Middle Temple, 1847 ; late Chief Justice at the Gambia.

MANVERS, Earl (SYDNEY WILLIAM HERBERT PIERREPONT).—Cr. 1806.
Only surviving son of Charles Herbert, 2nd Earl, by Mary Letitia, eldest dau. of the late Anthony Hardolph Eyre, Esq., of Grove Park, Notts; *b.* 1825 ; *s.* 1861 ; *m.* 1852 Georgiana Jane, dau. of the late Duc de Coigny. Educated at Ch. Ch., Oxford (B.A. 1846); is a J.P. and D.L. for Notts, Capt. South Notts Yeomanry Cavalry and Patron of 13 livings; was M.P. for South Notts 1852–61.—*Thoresby Park, Ollerton ; Holme Pierrepont, Nottingham ; Carlton Club*, s.w.; 6, *Tilney Street*, w.

Heir, his son Charles William Sydney, Viscount Newark, *b.* 1854.

MAR, Earl of (JOHN FRANCIS ERSKINE GOODEYE-ERSKINE).—Cr. 1457.
Only son of the late William James Goodeve, Esq., of Clifton, by the late Lady Frances Jemima, elder dau. of John Thomas, 32nd Earl of Mar ; *b.* 1836 ; *s.* his uncle as 34th Earl 1866, when he assumed the additional surname of Erskine; *m.* 1866 Alice Mary Sinclair, elder dau. and heir of John Hamilton, Esq., of Hilston Park, co. Monmouth. Educated at King's Coll., London, and Queens' Coll., Cambridge (M.A. 1860, and M.A. Oxon 1862); is in deacon's orders.—*Hilston Park, Monmouth ; Junior Athenæum Club*, s.w.

Heir, his son, *b.* 1868.

MARCH, Earl of. (See under *Richmond, Duke of.*)

MARCH-PHILLIPPS. (See *Phillipps de Lisle.*)

634

MARCON, Major JOHN, of Wallington, Norfolk.
Eldest son of the late John Marcon, Esq., of Swaffham, Norfolk, by Jane, dau. of the Rev. Andrew Edwards, of Great Cressingham, Norfolk ; *b.* 1818 ; *s.* 1833 ; *m.* 1850 Ellen, 2nd dau. of J. T. Anstey, Esq., of Bath, and has, with other issue,

* John, *b.* 1855.

Major Marcon, who was educated at Rugby, appointed Capt. East Norfolk Militia 1852, and Major 1859, is a Magistrate for Norfolk, Lord of the Manor and Patron of Edgefield; was formerly Capt. 12th Regt. This family was formerly of Swaffham, Norfolk.—*Wallington Hall, Downham ; Union Club*, s.w.

MARCORAN, Sir GEORGE, G.C.M.G. (cr. 1867).
Son of the late G. Marcoran, Esq.; was formerly Chief Justice of the Ionian Islands.—*Corfu.*

MARGITSON, Capt. JOHN, of Ditchingham, Norfolk.
Only son of the late James Taylor Margitson, Esq., of Bungay, Suffolk, by Louisa Sophia, dau. of the Rev. Thomas Beckwith, of St. Martin's, Norwich; *b.* 1821 ; *m.* 1858 Elizabeth Mary Anna Agnes, 5th dau. of John William Hamilton, Esq., and has issue,

* One daughter.

Mr. Margitson, who was educated at St. John's Coll., Cambridge (B.A. 1859), is a Magistrate for Suffolk, and Capt. in the Suffolk Rifle Volunteers ; he was formerly Capt. 19th Foot.—*Ditchingham House, Bungay.*

MARJORIBANKS, Sir JOHN, Bart., of Lees, Berwickshire (cr. 1815).
Elder son of the late Sir William Marjoribanks, Bart., of Lees, by Mary, dau. of Henry Stone, Esq., of London; *b.* 1830 ; *s.* as 3rd Bart. 1834 ; *m.* 1858 Charlotte Athol Mary, dau. of Richard Trotter, Esq., of Morton Hall. Educated at Eton and Ch. Ch., Oxford (B.A. 1851); is a Magistrate for cos. Berwick and Northumberland. —*Lees, Coldstream, N.B.; Carlton Club*, s.w.

Heir Pres., his brother William, *b.* 1832 ; *m.* 1860 Frances Anne, dau. of the late Baldwin D. Duppa, Esq., of Hollingbourne House, Kent.

MARJORIBANKS, Sir DUDLEY COUTTS, Bart., of Guisachan, Inverness-shire (cr. 1866).
Second surviving son of Edward Marjoribanks, Esq., of Greenlands, Bucks (whom see), by Georgiana, 3rd dau. of Joseph Francis Louis Latour, Esq., of Hexton House, Herts ; *b.* 1820 ; *m.* 1848 Isabella, eldest dau. of Sir John Weir Hogg, Bart. Educated at Harrow and Ch. Ch., Oxford; is a Dep.-Lieut. for London and co. Inverness, and a Magistrate for Middlesex ; elected M.P. for Berwick 1853.—*Guisachan, Beauly, N.B.; Arthur's and Travellers' Clubs*, s.w.; *29- Upper Brook Street*, w.

Heir, his son Edward, *b.* 1849.

MARJORIBANKS, ALEXANDER, Esq., of Marjoribanks, Linlithgowshire.
Eldest son of the late Alexander Marjoribanks, Esq., of Marjoribanks, by Katharine, dau. of Gilbert Laurie, Esq., of Pelmont ; *b.* 1792 ; *s.* 1830. Educated at the High School and University of Edinburgh; is a Magistrate for co. Linlithgow.—*Balbardie, Bathgate, Linlithgowshire, N.B.*

Heir Pres., his brother Thomas, in Holy Orders ; *b.* 1809 ; *m.* 1855 Mary, dau. of the late Rev. George Cook, D.D.

MARJORIBANKS, EDWARD, Esq., of Greenlands, Bucks.
Fourth son of the late Edward Marjoribanks, Esq., of Lees, co. Berwick, by Grizel, dau. of Archibald Stewart, Esq., of Allanbank ; *b.* 1776 ; *m.* 1810 Georgiana, dau.

of Joseph Francis Louis Lautour, Esq., of Hexton House, Herts, and has, with other surviving issue,

* Edward (of Bushey Grove, Watford), a Magistrate for Herts; b. 1814; m. 1843 Marion Fenella, dau. of the late John Loch, Esq., and has, with other issue, * Edward Coutts, b. 1844.

Mr. Marjoribanks, who was educated at Edinburgh, is a Banker in London; he was formerly M.P. for Berwick. —*Greenlands, Hambleden, Henley-on-Thames; Travellers' and Arthur's Clubs*, s.w.; 34, *Wimpole Street*, w.

MARKER, GEORGE MARKER, Esq., of Grant-lands, Devon.

Only surviving child of the Rev. George Townsend Marker, Vicar of Uffculme, Devon, by Margaret Frances, dau. of the Rev. Henry Marker, Vicar of Aylesbeare, Devon; b. 1840; m. 1866 Alice Maria, 2nd dau. of the Rev. J. Forster Alleyne, Rector of Kentisbeare, Devon. Educated at Harrow; is a Magistrate for Devon. —*Grantlands, Uffculme, Collumpton.*

MARKHAM, WILLIAM THOMAS, Esq., of Becca (or Cufforth) Hall, Yorkshire.

Eldest son of the late William Markham, Esq., of Becca Hall, by Lucy Anne, dau. of William Holberch, Esq., of Farnborough, co. Warwick; b. 1830; s. 1852; m. 1857 Anne Emily Sophia, dau. of Sir Francis Grant, P.R.A., of The Lodge, Melton Mowbray, and has, with other issue,

* William Hope, b. 1859.

Mr. Markham, who was educated at Eton, is a Magistrate for the W. Riding of Yorkshire, Capt. in the Yorkshire Hussars, and Lieut.-Col. of the Leeds Volunteer Rifles; late Capt. Coldstream Guards; was formerly in the Rifle Brigade.—*Becca Hall, Aberford, Tadcaster; Boodle's and Guards' Clubs*, s.w.

MARKLOVE, MAURICE WILLIAM CARRINGTON, Esq., of Lullingworth, Gloucestershire.

Eldest son of the late John Marklove, Esq., formerly Lieut. 56th Foot, by Mary, only dau. of the late Rev. Caleb Carrington, and sister and heir of the late F. A. Carrington, Esq., of Ogbourne St. George, Wilts; b. 1847; s. 1849. This family was formerly of Berkeley. —*Lullingworth House, Painswick, Gloucestershire; Woburn Hall, Cheltenham.*

MARKLOVE, Mrs., of Ogbourne St. George, Wilts.

Mary, dau. of the late Rev. Caleb Carrington, Vicar of Berkeley, by Elizabeth, dau. of Mr. Edward Rawlins, of Enford, Wilts; s. her brother Frederick Augustus Carrington, Esq., J.P. and D.L. for Berks 18—; m. 1826 John Marklove, Esq., of Lullingworth House, co. Gloucester (who d. 1849). This family was formerly of Cheshire.—*Ogbourne St. George, Marlborough.*

MARLAY, CHARLES BRINSLEY, Esq., of Belve-dere, co. Westmeath.

Eldest son of the late Lieut.-Col. George Marlay, C.B., by Catherine Louisa Augusta, dau. of James Tisdall, Esq., of Bawn, and Catharine Maria, afterwards Countess of Charleville; b. 1830. Educated at Eton and Trinity Coll., Cambridge (B.A. 1855); is a Dep.-Lieut. for co. Westmeath (High Sheriff 1855); inherited the entailed portion of the estates of George, last Earl of Belvedere (ext.) 1847.—*Belvedere, Mullingar, co. Westmeath; Bawn, co. Louth; Travellers' Club*, s.w.; *St. Katharine's Lodge, Regent's Park*, N.W.

MARLBOROUGH, Duke of (JOHN WINSTON SPENCER-CHURCHILL, K.G., D.C.L., P.C.). —Cr. 1702.

Eldest son of George, 6th Duke, by his 1st wife, Lady Jane, eldest dau. of George, 8th Earl of Galloway; b. 1822; s. 1857; m. 1843 Lady Frances Anne Emily,

eldest dau. of Charles William, 3rd Marquis of London-derry, K.G. Educated at Eton and Oriel Coll., Oxford; is a Prince of the Holy Roman Empire, Lord Lieutenant of Oxfordshire, and Patron of 9 livings; President of the Privy Council, late Lord Steward of the Household; formerly Capt. 1st Oxfordshire Yeomanry; was M.P. for Woodstock 1844–5 and 1847–57. The 1st Duke was an eminent Military Commander in the reign of Queen Anne.—*Blenheim Palace, Woodstock; Athenæum Club*, s.w.; 10, *St. James's Square*, s.w.

Heir, his son George Francis, Marquis of Blandford, educated at Eton, Lieut. Royal Horse Guards; b. 1844.

MARLING, HARRY HOTSPUR, Esq., of Stone-house Court, Gloucestershire.

Eldest son of the late Henry Hotspur Marling, Esq., of Stonehouse Court, by Ada, eldest dau. of James W. McLeod, Esq., of Perdiswell Hall, co. Worcester; b. 1864; s. 1865. Is Lord of the Manor of Stonehouse, and represents the elder branch of the Marlings of Stanley Park (whom see).—*Stonehouse Court, Gloucester.*

MARLING, SAMUEL STEPHENS, Esq., of Stanley Park, Gloucestershire.

Sixth son of William Marling, Esq., by Sarah, dau. of Nathaniel Hillman, Esq., of Woodchester, co. Gloucester; b. 1810; m. 1834 Margaret Williams, eldest dau. of William Bentley Cartwright, Esq., and has, with other issue,

* William Henry, b. 1835; m. 1860 Mary Emily, dau. of John Abraham, Esq., and has issue, * Percival Scrope, b. 1861.

Mr. Marling is a Magistrate for co. Gloucester, Lord of the Borough Manor of Stanley, and Patron of 1 living. —*Stanley Park, Stroud.*

MARLING, THOMAS, Esq., of Norton Court, Gloucestershire.

Fourth son of the late William Marling, Esq., of Stroud, co. Gloucester, by Sarah, dau. of Nathaniel Hillman, Esq., of Rodborough, co. Gloucester; b. 1803; m. 1st 1839 Maria Louisa, dau. of Joseph Overbury, Esq.; 2nd 1862 Catharine Anne, dau. of Wm. Playne, Esq., of Longford House, co. Gloucester, and by her, who d. 1863, has issue,

* William Payne, b. 1863.

Mr. Marling is a Magistrate for co. Gloucester and Lord of the Manor of Norton; he purchased Norton Court from Miss Webb, dau. of the late Edward Webb, Esq., M.P.—*Norton Court, Gloucester.*

MARRIOTT, EDWARD JOHN BECKETT, Esq., of Avonbank, Worcestershire.

Second son of the late General Thomas Marriott, J.P. and D.L., of Avonbank, by Anne, 3rd dau. of the late Sir John Beckett, Bart., of Meanwood Park; b. 18—; m. 18— Mary Georgiana, dau. of Harry Edmund Waller, Esq., of Farmington Lodge. Is a J.P. and D.L. for cos. Worcester and Gloucester, a Magistrate for Oxon, and Lord of the Manor of Avonbank.—*Avonbank, Pershore; Arthur's Club*, s.w.

MARRIOTT, of Cotesbach.
(See *Gouldon-Constable.*)

MARRIOTT. (See *Smith-Marriott.*)

MARRIOTT-DODINGTON. (See *Padington.*)

MARRYAT, JOSEPH, Esq., of Macsydderwen, Brecon.

Son of the late Joseph Marryat, Esq.; b. 1790. Is a Magistrate for co. Brecon, and a Dep.-Lieut. for Middlesex.—*Macsydderwen, Ystradgynlais, Brecknockshire; Athenæum Club*, s.w.

635

MARSDEN, Lieut.-Col. FREDERICK CARLETON, C.B., of Colne House, Essex.
Eldest son of the late Captain James Marsden, formerly of 7th Dragoon Guards (who *d.* 1841). by Harriette, dau. of Wakeman Long, Esq., of Pershore; *b.* 1803; *m.* 1838 Sidney Jane, youngest dau. of Sir William Bulkley Hughes, Knt., of Plas Coch, Anglesea, and by her (who *d.* 1866) has, with other issue,
* Frederick John, educated at Rugby ; a student at the Bar ; *b.* 1844.
Col. Marsden, who is a Magistrate for Essex, was formerly in H. M. Indian Army, holding civil situations; he purchased the above estate from the legatee of Mrs. Gee, his late sister-in-law.—*Colne House, Earl's Colne, Halstead, Essex.*

MARSDEN, the Rev. JOHN HOWARD, B.D., F.R.S.L., of Great Oakley, Essex.
Eldest son of the Rev. William Marsden, B.D., Vicar of Eccles, co. Lancaster, by Sarah, dau. of John Howard, Esq., of Manchester ; *b.* 1803 ; *s.* his cousin, William Marsden, Esq., 1839 ; *m.* 1840 Caroline, dau. of the Rev. W. Moore, D.D., of Spalding, and has issue,
* William, M.A. of St. John's Coll., Cambridge, Lieut. 87th Royal Irish Fusiliers, *b.* 1841.
Mr. Marsden, who was educated at St. John's Coll., Cambridge (B.A. 1826, M.A. 1829, B.D. 1836), and was formerly Fellow of St. John's Coll., formerly held the offices of Hulsean Lecturer and Disney Professor of Archæology in that University ; he is a Canon of Manchester, Rector of Great Oakly, Rural Dean, and a Magistrate for Essex.—*Great Oakley, Harwich ; Cliff Grange, Manchester ; Oxford and Cambridge Club, s.w.*

MARSH, Sir HENRY, Bart.,‡ of Dublin (cr. 1839).
Only son of the late Sir Henry Marsh, Bart. (who was Physician to the Queen in Ireland), by his 1st wife Anna, dau. of Thomas Crowe, Esq., of Ennis, co. Clare, and widow of William Arthur, Esq. ; *b.* 1821 ; *s.* 1860; late Major in the 3rd Dragoon Guards.—*Kerrahull, Kilkenny ; De Marisco, Donnybrook, co. Dublin.*

MARSH, EDWARD, Esq., of Nethersole, Somerset.
Only surviving son of the late John Marsh, Esq., of Snave Manor and Ivychurch, Kent, by Sophia, dau. of John Henry Pakenham, Esq. ; *b.* 1806 ; *s.* 1838 ; *m.* 1827 Jane Inglis, dau. of William Forlong, Esq., of Wellshot, co. Lanark, N.B., and has, with other issue,
* Edward, a Capt. in the Indian Army, *b.* 1830 ; *m.* 1864 Louisa Sarah Elizabeth, dau. of Major Caldecot, of Holton Hall, co. Lincoln.
Mr. Marsh, who is a Magistrate for Bath, was formerly on the Staff of the Bombay Army.—*Nethersole, Bath.*

MARSH, FRANCIS, Esq., of Springmount, Queen's Co.
Eldest son of the late Rev. Jeremy Marsh, of Ballyadams, Queen's Co., by Sarah, dau. of Richard Connell, Esq., of Stradbally ; *b.* 1817 ; *s.* 1830 ; *m.* 1838 Anna Maria, dau. of the late Arthur Maxwell, Esq., of Gardiner Street, Dublin, and has, with other issue,
* Jeremy Taylor, Lieut. R.E., *b.* 1841 ; *m.* 1864 Rachel Gertrude, only child of the late Charles Ferdinand Smyth, Esq., of Endsleigh, Streatham, Surrey, and has issue,
* Francis Charles, *b.* 1846.
Mr. Marsh, who was educated at Trinity Coll., Dublin (B.A. 1839), is a Magistrate for Queen's Co.—*Springmount, Mountrath, Queen's Co.*

MARSH, the Rev. HENRY AUGUSTUS.
Youngest son of the late William C. Marsh, Esq., of Gaynes Park, Essex, by Sophia, dau. of the late Rev. J. Swaine, of Leverington, co. Cambridge; *b.* 1817 ;

‡ Died whilst these sheets were at press.
636

m. 1850 Eliza, eldest dau. of the late Very Rev. J. Lamb, Dean of Bristol. Educated at Shrewsbury and Trinity Coll., Cambridge (B.A. 1840, M.A. 1842); appointed Vicar of Tuxford 1849 ; is a Magistrate for Notts, a Rural Dean and a Surrogate; was formerly Fellow of Trinity Coll., Cambridge.— *The Vicarage, Tuxford, Notts.*

MARSH, Capt. HENRY GODFREY.
Eldest son of the late Major Henry Marsh, of Bath, by Sarah Matilda, dau. of Major John Godfrey, of Bath, and grand-dau. of the late General William Earle Bulwer, of Heydon Hall, Norfolk ; *b.* 1811 ; *m.* 1832 Josephine, dau. of Wienand Wassermeyer, of Bonn, and has, with other issue,
* Henry William, *b.* 1837.
Capt. Marsh, who was educated at Berlin and Bonn, and appointed Capt. 1st Somerset Militia 1831, is a Magistrate for co. Monmouth.—Residence: *Winterbourne, Gloucester ; Blackwood, Newport, Monmouthshire.*

MARSH, MATTHEW HENRY, Esq., of Ramridge, Hants.
Son of the Rev. Matthew Marsh, Chancellor and Canon of Salisbury, by Margaret, dau. of the late Rev. Peter B. Brodie; *b.* 1810 ; *m.* 1844 Eliza Mary Anne, dau. of the late Mr. Serjeant Merewether. Educated at Westminster and Ch. Ch., Oxford (B.A. 1833, M.A. 1835); called to the Bar at the Inner Temple 1836 ; is a J.P. and D.L. for Wilts ; has been M P. for Salisbury since 1857 ; was formerly a Member of the Legislative Council of New South Wales.—*Ramridge House. Andover.; Athenæum, Oxford and Cambridge, and Reform Clubs, s.w. ; 47, Dover Street, w.*

+MARSH, THOMAS COXHEAD CHISENHALE-, Esq., of Gaynes and Marden Ash, Essex.
Eldest son of the late William Coxhead Marsh, Esq., J.P. and D.L., of Gaynes Park, by Sophia, dau. of the late Rev. — Swaine ; *b.* 1811 ; *s.* 1867 ; *m.* 1846 Eliza Anne Chisenhale, dau. of John Chisenhale Chisenhale, Esq., of Arley, co. Lancaster, whose name he has assumed, and by whom he has issue,
* William, *b.* 1865.
Mr. Coxhead-Marsh, who was educated at Eton and Trinity Coll., Cambridge (B.A. 1834, M.A. 1837), and called to the Bar at the Inner Temple 1837, is a J.P. and D.L. for Essex, a Magistrate for co. Lancaster, and Chairman of the Essex Quarter Sessions.—*Gaynes Park, Epping ; Marden Ash, Ongar, Essex.*

MARSH. (See *Tilson-Marsh.*)

MARSH-CALDWELL, Mrs., of Linley Wood, Staffordshire.
Anne, 4th dau. of the late James Caldwell, Esq., D.L., of Linley Wood (Recorder of Newcastle-under-Lyme) by Elizabeth, dau. and co-heir of Thomas Stamford, Esq., of Derby ; *s.* her brother, the late James S. Caldwell, Esq., of Linley Wood, and assumed his name in 1860 ; *m.* 1830 Arthur Cuthbert Marsh, Esq., of Eastbury, Herts (who *d.* 1849, leaving issue six daughters).—*Linley Wood, Lawton ; Deacons, Dorking ; 3, Lowndes Street, s.w.*

MARSHALL, Sir CHARLES, Knt. (cr. 1832).
Only son of the late Mr. Serjeant Marshall ; *b.* 1788. *m.* 1851 Mary, widow of John Cox, Esq. Educated at Westminster and Jesus Coll., Cambridge (B.A. 1810); was called to the Bar at the Inner Temple 1815 ; has been Chief Justice in Ceylon.—*5, Kensington Garden Terrace, w.*

MARSHALL, Lady, late of Pen-y-Gardden, Denbighshire.
Augusta Eliza, dau. of John Wynne, Esq., of Garthmeilis, co. Denbigh. by Sarah Ann, only child of the Rev. Dr. Samuel Parr. Prebendary of St. Paul's; *m.* 1828 Admiral Sir John William Phillips Marshall, C.B., who *d.* 1850.

MARSHALL, Bouchier Mervyn, Esq., of Blagdon, Devon.
Eldest son of the late Rev. Bouchier Marshall, Rector of Nymet-Tracey, Devon, by Elizabeth, dau. of the late John Norris, Esq., of Nonsuch, Wilts, and nephew of John Marshall, Esq., of Barnstaple (whom see); *b.* 1821; *m.* 1858 Elizabeth Georgiana, eldest dau. of the Rev. J. D. Baker, Vicar of Bishop's Tawton, Devon. Educated at Ch. Ch., Oxford; is a Magistrate for Devon.—*Blagdon, Launceston.*

MARSHALL, Frederick Earnshaw, Esq., of Penwortham Hall, Lancashire.
Eldest son of the late William Marshall, Esq., J.P. and D.L., of Penwortham Hall, by Anne, dau. of Thomas Miller, Esq., of Preston; *b.* 1820; *s.* 1863. Educated at Rugby and Brasenose Coll., Oxford (B.A. 1843, M.A. 1848); called to the Bar at the Inner Temple 1847; is a J.P. and D.L. for co. Lancaster.—*Penwortham Hall, Preston; Athenæum, and Oxford and Cambridge Clubs, s.w.; 4, Paper Buildings, Temple, E.C.*
Heir Pres., his brother John, M.A. of Downing Coll., Cambridge, *b.* 1822.

MARSHALL, George, Esq., of Broadwater, Surrey.
Eldest son of the late Robert Marshall, Esq., of Broadwater; *b.* 18—; is married, and has, with other issue,
• Alexander, late Capt. Surrey Militia; *b.* 1830.
Mr. Marshall, who is a Magistrate for Surrey, was formerly a Merchant in London.—*Broadwater, Godalming.*

MARSHALL, Henry Cowper, Esq., of Weetwood Hall, Yorkshire.
Fourth son of the late John Marshall, Esq., M.P., of Headingley, co. York, by Jane, dau. of the late William Pollard, Esq., of Halifax; *b.* 1808; *m.* 1837 the Hon. Catherine Anne Lucy, 2nd dau. of Thomas, 1st Lord Monteagle, and has, with other issue,
• Edmond Henry, *b.* 1838.
Mr. Marshall, who is a J.P. and D.L. for the W. Riding of Yorkshire, was formerly Mayor of Leeds.—*Weetwood Hall, Leeds.*

MARSHALL, Major Henry Octavius, of St. John's, co. Londonderry.
Son of the late Rev. George Marshall, Rector of Carndonagh, by Elizabeth Sophia, dau. of T. Wilson, Esq., of Carrickfergus; *b.* 1810; *m.* 1848 Ellen, dau. of the Rev. T. Robyns, Rector of Maristow, Devon. Is a retired Major in the Indian Army, and a Magistrate for co. Donegal.—*St. John's, Fahan, Londonderry.*

MARSHALL, James Garth, Esq., of Monk-Coniston, Lancashire, and Headingley, Yorkshire.
Third son of the late John Marshall, Esq., of Headingley, co. York. by Jane, dau. of the late William Pollard, Esq., of Halifax; *b.* 1802; *m.* 1841 the Hon. Mary Alicia Pery, eldest dau. of Thomas, 1st Lord Monteagle, and has, with other issue,
• Victor Alexander, *b.* 1841.
Mr. Marshall, who is a J.P. and D.L. for co. Lancaster and the West Riding of Yorkshire (High Sheriff 1860), was M.P. for Leeds 1847-52.—*Monk Coniston Hall, Ambleside; Headingley House, Leeds; Reform Club, s.w.*

MARSHALL, John Philip Sydenham, Esq., of Barnstaple, Devon.
Eldest son of the late John Marshall, Esq., J.P. and D.L., of Barnstaple, by Mary, eldest dau. of Thomas Docker, Esq.; *b.* 1830; *s.* 1866. Is a Banker at Barnstaple.—*Barnstaple, Devon.*

MARSHALL, John Rowlandson, Esq.
Only son of the late Richard Marshall, Esq. (formerly Leeming), of Wray House, near Lancaster, by Eleanor dau. of the late Edmund Bainbridge, Esq., of Carnforth; *b.* 1828; *m.* 1860 Jane, dau. of Thomas Bainbridge, Esq., and has surviving issue,
• Edith Jane.
Mr. Marshall is a J.P. and D.L. for co. Lancaster.—*Hollington House, St. Leonard's-on-Sea, Sussex.*

MARSHALL, the Rev. Joseph, of Baronnecourt, co. Tipperary.
Eldest surviving son of the late Rev. Cornelius Marshall, by Margaret, dau. of the late Rev. John Brydge; *b.* 1801; *s.* 1849 his paternal cousin Sarah, Baroness de Prigny, de Querieux; *m.* 1853 Sophia Jane, dau. of the late Hugh Kennedy, Esq., of Cultra, co. Down, and has, with other issue,
• William Kennedy, *b.* 1858.
Mr. Marshall, who was educated at Trinity Coll., Dublin (B.A. 1823), is a Magistrate for co. Tipperary and King's Co.; was formerly Chaplain in the Royal Navy.—*Baronnecourt, Riverstown, co. Tipperary; University Club, Dublin.*

+**MARSHALL, Joseph,** Esq., of Heslerton Hall, Yorkshire.
Eldest son of the late J. Marshall, Esq.; *b.* 18—. Is a J.P. and D.L. for the E. N., and W. Ridings of Yorkshire; was formerly a Merchant and Manufacturer at Leeds.—*Heslerton Hall, Malton.*

MARSHALL, Reginald Dykes, Esq., of Cookridge, Yorkshire, and Keswick, Cumberland.
Eldest son of the late John Marshall. Esq., M.P., of Headingley, co. York, and Keswick, Cumberland. by Mary, eldest dau. of the late Joseph Daliantine-Dykes, Esq., of Dovenby Hall, Cumberland; *b.* 1832; *s.* 1836; *m.* 1st 1858 Margaret Louisa, 3rd dau. of Sir J. F. W. Herschel, Bart., K.H. (she *d.* 1861); 2nd 1864 Mary Jane, eldest dau. of Rear-Admiral the Hon. Keith Stewart, C.B., and has issue by the former,
• Mary Adelina Louisa, and Margaret Alice Edith.
Mr. Marshall, who was educated at Trinity Coll., Cambridge, is a Magistrate for the W. Riding of co. York. Lord of the Manors of Derwentwater and Thornthwaite, Patron of 1 living, and Lieut. Yorkshire (Princess of Wales' Own) Hussars.—*Cookridge Hall, Leeds; Oxford and Cambridge Club, s.w.*

MARSHALL, Thomas Horatio, Esq., of Hartford Beach, Cheshire.
Eldest son of the late Thomas Marshall, Esq., of Hartford Beach, Barrister-at-Law, by Phœbe, dau. of Digby Legard, Esq., of Wetton Abbey, co. York; *b.* 1833; *s.* 1854; *m.* 1st 1857 Laura Anne, dau. of the Rev. Martin Stapylton, Rector of Barlborough, co. Derby (she *d.* 1858); 2nd 1862 Lucy Martena, dau. of the Rev. Edward N. Bree, and has issue by the former,
• Henry Stapylton, *b.* 1858.
Mr. Marshall, who was educated at Eton and Exeter Coll., Oxford (B.A. 1856, M.A. 1859), is a Magistrate for co. Chester; Capt. 1st Royal Cheshire Militia, and Lieut.-Col. 2nd Battalion Cheshire Rifle Volunteers.—*Hartford Beach, Northwich.*

MARSHALL, WILLIAM, Esq., of Patterdale Hall, Westmoreland.

Eldest son of the late John Marshall, Esq., M.P., of Headingley, co. York, by Jane, dau. of William Pollard, Esq., of Halifax; *b.* 1796; *m.* 1828 Georgiana Christiana, youngest dau. of George Hibbert, Esq , of Munden Park, Herts, and .by her, who *d.* 1866, has, with other issue,

 • John William. educated at Eton and Trinity Coll., Cambridge ; a Magistrate for Cumberland ; *b.* 1829.

Mr. Marshall, who was educated at St. John's Coll., Cambridge, and called to the Bar at the Inner Temple 1823, is a J.P. and D.L. for Cumberland and a Magistrate for Westmoreland ; was M.P. for Petersfield 1826–30, for Beverley 1831, and for Carlisle 1835–47 ; has been M.P. for E. Cumberland since 1847.—*Patterdale Hall, and Hollstead, Penrith ; Brooks's, Reform, and Athenæum Clubs, s.w. ; 32, St George's Road, s.w.*

MARSHALL, WILLIAM, Esq., of Treworgy, Cornwall.

Eldest son of the late Rev. Lewis Marshall, Vicar of Davidstowe and Lesnewth, Cornwall, by Armenell, dau. of John Inch, Esq., of Camelford; *b.* 1798; *s.* 1826; *m.* 1840 Everilda, dau. of the late Rev. Robert Palk Carrington, and has, with other issue,

 • William Nicholas Connock, *b.* 1846 ; *m.* 1867 Alice Ann Grey, only child of the late Rev. John Glanville, Vicar of Jacobstow, Cornwall.

Mr. Marshall was High Sheriff of Cornwall in 1843. —*Treworgy, Liskeard.*

MARSHALL, the Rev. WILLIAM;KNOX, B.D., of Wragby, Lincolnshire.

Eldest surviving son of the late Rev. George Marshall, M.A., Rector of Carndonagh, co. Donegal, by Elizabeth Sophia, dau. of James Willson, Esq., M.P., of Purdysburn, co. Antrim ; *b.* 1807 ; *m.* 1st 1834 Louisa Sophia, 3rd dau. of the late Rev'. W. Marsh, D.D., Rector of Beddington, Surrey ; 2nd 1859 Elizabeth, eldest dau. of the late Rev. John Storer, M.A., Rector of Hawkesworth, Notts, by Elizabeth, dau. of Thomas Whitmore, Esq., of Apley Park, co. Salop, and has, with other issue,

 • Charles Henry Tilson. Bengal Staff Corps, Assistant Commissioner at Lahore ; *b.* 1841 ; *m.* 1865 Laura Frances, dau. of the Right Hon. Sir Frederick Pollock, Bart., late Lord Chief Baron.

Mr. Marshall, who was educated at Trinity Coll., Dublin (B.A. 1832, M.A. and B.D. 1855), is a Magistrate for co. Lincoln, Prebendary of Hereford, and Rector of Panton with Wragby; was formerly Rector of St. Mary's, Bridgnorth, and Official of the Royal Peculiar of the Deanery of Bridgnorth. This family settled in the north of Ireland early in the 17th century.—*Wragby Vicarage, Lincolnshire.*

MARSHALL. (See *Leeson-Marshall.*)

MARSHALL-HALL. (See *Hall.*)

MARSHAM, CHARLES ROBERT, Esq., of Stratton-Strawless Hall, Norfolk.

Only son of the late Charles Marsham, Esq. (who *d.* 1852), by Emily Louisa. dau. of the Chief of Clanronald (she re-married in 1846 Lieut.-Col. Hugh Fitz-Roy, late of the Grenadier Guards, whom see); *b.* 1853 ; *s.* his grandfather 1855. Is Lord of the Manors of Stratton-Strawless and Haynford. Norfolk.—*Stratton-Strawless Hall. Norwich.*

 Heir Pres., his uncle Henry Philip, *b.* 1817.

MARSHAM, GEORGE AUGUSTUS, Esq., of Haynford, Norfolk.

Fifth son of the late Robert Marsham, Esq., of Stratton-Strawless, Norfolk, by Frances Anne, dau. of John

638

Custance, Esq., of Weston House, Norfolk; *b.* 1824. Educated at Eton and Trinity Hall Coll., Cambridge ; is a Magistrate for Norfolk, and a Major in the West Norfolk Militia. –*Haynford, Norwich.*

MARSHAM, the Rev. HENRY PHILIP, of Rippon Hall, Norfolk.

Eldest surviving son of the late Robert Marsham, Esq., of Stratton-Strawless, Norfolk, by Frances Anne, dau. of John Custance, Esq., of Weston House, Norfolk ; *b.* 1817 ; *s.* 1855; *m.* 1843 Caroline Savill, eldest dau. of Onley Savill Onley, Esq., of Stisted Hall, Essex, and has issue,

 • Henry Savill, *b.* 1844.

Mr. Marsham, who was educated at Trinity Hall, Cambridge (B.C.L. 1846), is a Magistrate for Norfolk. —*Rippon Hall, Hevingham ; University Club, s.w.*

MARSHAM, Admiral HENRY SHOVELL.JONES-, of Hayle, Kent.

Third son of the late Hon. and Rev. Jacob Marsham. D.D., Esq., of Caversfield. Oxon; *b.* 1794 ; *m.* 1838 Maria Sophia, dau. of the late Col. Walter Jones. many years M.P. for co. Leitrim, whose name he assumed (she *d.* 1861). Is a Magistrate for Kent, and a Vice-Admiral on the retired list.—*Hayle Cottage, Maidstone ; United Service Club, s.w.*

MARSHAM, the Rev. JACOB JOSEPH.

Fourth son of the late Hon. and Rev. Jacob Marsham. D.D., Canon of Windsor, by Amelia Frances, only dau. and heir of the late Joseph Bullock, Esq. of Caversfield, Oxon, and grandson of Robert, 1st Earl of Romney ; *b.* 1804. Educated at Eton and Ch. Ch., Oxford (B.A. 1826, M.A. 1830) ; is a Magistrate for co. Kent, and Vicar of Shorne.—*Shorne Vicarage, Gravesend.*

MARSHAM, ROBERT BULLOCK, Esq., of Caversfield, Oxon.

Eldest son of the late Hon. and Rev. Jacob Marsham, D.D., Canon of Windsor, by Amelia Frances, only dau. and heir of the late Joseph Bullock, Esq., of Caversfield, Oxon, and grandson of 1st Earl of Romney ; *b.* 1786 ; *m.* 1828 Jessie, dau. of the late General D. Dewar, of Gilston House, co. Fife, and widow of Sir John Carmichael Anstruther, Bart., and has, with other issue,

 • Charles Jacob, a Magistrate for Oxon, and Lieut. 7th Oxfordshire Rifle Volunteers, *b.* 1829.

Mr. Marsham, who was educated at Eton and Ch. Ch., Oxford, and was afterwards Fellow of Merton Coll. (B.A. 1807. M.A. 1814, D.C.L. 1826), and elected Warden of Merton Coll. 1826, is a J.P. and D.L. for Oxon, Lord of the Manor of Caversfield, and Patron of that living.—*Merton Coll. Oxford; Caversfield, Bicester ; University Club, s.w.*

MARSHAM, the Rev. THOMAS JOHN GORDON, of Saxlingham, Norfolk.

Fourth son of Robert Marsham, Esq., of Stratton Strawless, Norfolk, by Frances Anne, dau. of John Custance. Esq., of Weston. Norfolk. 1821. Educated Magdalen Coll., Cambridge (B.A. 1841. M.A. 1841,); is a Magistrate for Norfolk, and Rector of Saxlingham, was formerly Rector of Wramplingham, near Norwich. —*Saxlingham, Hall, Norfolk.*

MARSHAM, Viscount. (See under *Romney, Earl of.*)

MARSLAND, Mrs., of Henbury Hall, Cheshire.

Jane, dau. of — Haigh, Esq., of West Field, Huddersfield, co. York ; *m.* 1843 Edward Marsland, Esq., of Henbury Hall, who was a Magistrate for cos. Chester, Lancaster, and Derby, and Capt. of the Stockport Troop of Yeomanry, and who *d.* 1867, leaving issue an only child, • Ellen.—*Henbury Hall, Macclesfield.*

MARSLAND, Rev. GEORGE, of Beckingham, Notts.

Fourth son of the late Major Thomas Marsland, of Henbury Hall, co. Chester, by Frances Ann, dau. of — Thompson, Esq.; b. 1811; m. 1835 Anne, dau. of the late Samuel Hole, Esq., of Caunton Manor, Notts, and has issue,

* Edward Ashhurst, Lieut. 18th Royal Irish Regt., b. 1839; m. 1863 Elizabeth Mary, dau. of Col. Cranfurd Kennedy.

Mr. Marsland, who was educated at Macclesfield and Brasenose Coll., Oxford (B.A. 1834, M.A. 1837), is Patron, Rector, and Lord of the Manor of Beckingham. —Beckingham Rectory, Newark.

+MARSLAND, HENRY, Esq., of Woodbank, Cheshire.

Younger son of the late Peter Marsland, Esq., of Woodbank, and brother of the late Major Thomas Marsland, of Henbury Hall; b. 179—; is married, and has issue. Is a Magistrate for cos. Chester and Lancaster and for the borough of Stockport, and a Manufacturer at Stockport; was M.P. for Stockport 1835-47.—Woodbank, Stockport.

+MARSLAND, PETER EDWARD, Esq., of Stockport, Cheshire.

Eldest son of the late Peter Marsland, Esq., of Woodbank, Stockport, and brother of the late Major T. Marsland, of Henbury Hall; b. 179–. Is a Magistrate for cos. Chester and Lancaster and a Manufacturer at Stockport.—Residence: Stockport.

MARTEN, GEORGE ROBERT, Esq., of Marshall's Wick, Herts.

Eldest son of the late George Sulivan Marten, Esq., of Radford, by Jane, dau. of the late Charles Nevinson, Esq., of London; b. 1801; s. 1826. Educated at Westminster and Trinity Coll., Cambridge (B.A. 1822); is a J.P. and D.L. for Herts, and a Magistrate for the Liberty of St. Albans.—Marshall's Wick, St. Alban's; Brooks's Club, s.w.

Heir Pres., his brother Thomas Powney, a Magistrate for Herts; b. 1807; m. 1836 Clara Elizabeth, dau. of Robert Parry Nisbet, Esq., of Southbroome House, Wilts, and has, with other issue, * George Nisbet, b. 1840.

MARTEN, Lieut.-General THOMAS, K.H., of Beverley, Yorkshire.

Eldest son of the late Thomas Marten, Esq., of Winchilsea, Sussex; b. 1797; m. 1500; s. his cousin Sir Henry, youngest dau. of the late Henry Ellison, Esq., of Sudbrooke Holme, co. Lincoln and of Beverley, co. York. Is a J.P. and D.L. for the E. Riding of co. York, a Lieut.-General in the Army, and Col. of the 6th Inniskilling Dragoons.—Beverly, Yorkshire.

MARTIN, Sir WILLIAM FANSHAWE, Bart., K.C.B., of Lockinge, Berks (cr. 1791).

Eldest son of the late Admiral Sir Thomas Byam Martin, G.C.B., by Catharine, dau. of Capt. Robert Fanshawe, R.N.; b. 1500; s. his cousin Sir Henry Martin as 4th Bart. 1863; m. 1st 1826 the Hon. Anne, dau. of William, 1st Lord Wynford; 2nd 1848 Sophia Elizabeth, dau. of Richard Hurt Esq., of Wirksworth, co. Derby. Is an Admiral R.N., 1863; late in command of Mediterranean Fleet; was made a K.C.B. 1861. —Lockinge, Wantage; United Service Club, s.w.

Heir, his son William Best, b. 1830.

MARTIN, Sir SAMUEL, Knt. (cr. 1850).

Son of the late Samuel Martin, Esq., of co. Londonderry; b. 1802; m. 1838 Frances, dau. of the Right Hon. Sir Frederick Pollock, Bart. Educated at Trinity Coll., Dublin (B.A. 1820); called to the Bar at the Middle Temple 1830; was M.P. for Pontefract 1847-51; appointed a Baron of the Exchequer 1850.—75, Eaton Square, s.w.

MARTIN, Sir JAMES RANALD, C.B., F.R.S. (cr. 1860).

Son of the late Rev. Donald Martin, of Kilmuir, Isle of Skye, by Mary, elder dau. of Norman Macdonald, Esq., of Scalps; b. 179–; m. 1826 Jane Maria, 3rd dau. of Col. Paton, C.B.; is Physician to the Council of India; was formerly in the Medical Staff of the Bengal Army; served in the first Burmese war.—37, Upper Brook Street, w.

MARTIN, Sir WILLIAM (cr. 1860).

Son of the late Mr. W. Martin; b. 181–; m. 1841 Mary Anne, youngest dau. of the late Rev. William Parker, Rector of St. Ethelburgha, London, and Prebendary of St. Paul's; called to the Bar at Lincoln's Inn 1836; late Chief Justice of New Zealand.

MARTIN, Capt. ABRAHAM, of Bloomfield, co. Sligo.

Eldest and only surviving son of the late Gregory Cuffe Martin, Esq., of Sligo, by Louisa, dau. of Major Thomas Jones, of Ardinglasse, co. Sligo; b. 1838; s. his uncle, the late James Martin, Esq., 1860. Is a J.P. and D.L. for co. Sligo (High Sheriff 1862); was formerly Capt. 11th Foot.—Clevragh and Bloomfield, Sligo; Esker, co. Galway; Junior United Service Club, s.w.

Heir Pres., his cousin Gregory Wood (son of James Wood, Esq., of Woodville, co. Sli o. by Anne, dau. of the late Abraham Martin, Esq.); b. 1848.

MARTIN, CHARLES WYKEHAM., Esq., of Leeds Castle, Kent, and Chacombe, Northamptonshire.

Eldest son of the late Fiennes Wykeham-Martin, Esq., of Leeds Castle (who assumed the additional surname of Martin, by Royal licence in 1821), by Eliza, dau. of Richard Bignell, Esq.; b. 1801; s. 1840; m. 1st 1828 Lady Jemima Isabella, dau. of James, 5th and last Earl Cornwallis (ext.); 2nd 1838 Matilda, dau. of the late Sir John Trollope, Bart., and has by the former, with other issue,

* Philip, of Leamington Priors, educated at Eton and Balliol Coll., Oxford, a Magistrate for co. Warwick, and M.P. for Rochester; b. 1829; m. 1850 Elizabeth, dau. of J. Ward, Esq., and has issue, * Cornwallis, b. 1856.

Mr. Wykeham-Martin, who was educated at Eton and Balliol Coll., Oxford, is a Magistrate for Kent and Hants, and a Dep.-Lieut. for Kent: Lord of the Manor of Chacombe, and Patron of that living; was M.P. for Newport, Isle of Wight, 1841-52, and for West Kent 1857-9; re-elected for Newport, 1865.—Leeds Castle; Maidstone; Chacombe Priory, Banbury; University Club, s.w.; 25, Great Cumberland Place, w.

MARTIN, FRANCIS OFFLEY, Esq., of Rose Hill, Middlesex.

Fourth son of the late Henry Martin, Esq., M.P., of Colston Basset, Notts (who d. 1839), by Maria Elizabeth, eldest dau. and co-heir of Francis Edmunds, Esq., of Worsbrough, co. York; b. 1805; m. 1841 Mary, dau. of the late Very Rev. Samuel Smith, D.D., Dean of Ch. Ch., Oxford, and has, with other issue,

* William Henry, b. 1851.

Mr. Martin, who was educated at the Charterhouse and at Caius Coll., Cambridge (B.A. 1826, M.A. 1829, and called to the Bar at Lincoln's Inn 1829, is an Inspector of Charities, and was formerly an Assistant Tithe Commissioner.—Rose Hill, Hampton, Middlesex.

+MARTIN, HENRY, Esq., of Littleport Cambridgeshire.

Eldest son of the late — Martin, Esq.; b. 18—. Is a Dep.-Lieut. for co. Cambridge (on the roll for High

Sheriff 1869), and a Magistrate for the Isle of Ely.—*Littleport, Isle of Ely.*

MARTIN, HENRY BURGES, Esq., of Colston Basset, Notts.
Second son of the late Henry Martin, Esq., M.P., of Colston Basset, by Maria Elizabeth, eldest dau. of Francis Edmunds, Esq., of Worsborough, co. York; *b.* 1797; *s.* 1839. Educated at Westminster and Trinity Hall, Cambridge (LL.B. 1820); is a Magistrate for Notts.—*Colston Basset, Bingham.*

Heir Pres., his nephew Thomas Wentworth Martin-Edmunds. Esq., of Worsborough Hall (whom see).

MARTIN, JAMES, Esq., of Old Colwall, Herefordshire, and Chiselhurst, Kent.
Third son of the late John Martin, Esq., of Overbury, co. Worcester (M.P. for Tewkesbury 1812-32), by Frances, dau. of Richard Stone, Esq., of Chiselhurst, Kent; *b.* 1807. Educated at the Charterhouse; is a J.P. and D.L. for co. Hereford, and a Banker in London; was M.P. for Tewkesbury 1859-65.—*Old Colwall, Ledbury; Chiselhurst, Kent; Windham Club, s.w.; 68, Lombard Street, E.C.*

MARTIN, JAMES, Esq., of Ross, co. Galway.
Eldest son of Robert Martin, Esq., of Ross, by Marian, dau. of John Blackney, Esq., of Waterford; *b.* 1804; *m.* 1844 Anna Selina, eldest dau. of Charles Fox, Esq., of New Park, co. Longford, and has, with other issue,
* Robert Jasper, *b.* 1846.
Mr. Martin, who was educated at Trinity Coll., Dublin (B.A. 1824; M.A. 1832), called to the Bar at Dublin 1830, and appointed Government Auditor of Poor-Law Accounts 1852, is a J.P. and D.L. for co. Galway (High Sheriff 1826).—*Ross, Moycullen, co. Galway; Kildare Street Club, Dublin.*

MARTIN, JOHN, Esq., of The Upper Hall, Ledbury, Herefordshire.
Eldest son of the late John Martin, Esq., M.P., of Overbury, co. Worcester, by Frances, dau. of Richard Stone, Esq., of Chiselhurst, Kent; *b.* 1805; *m.* 1st 1837 Mary, dau. of Capt. T. A. Morse; 2nd 1847 Maria Henrietta, dau. of Evan H. Baillie, Esq., and by her, who *d.* 1865, has, with other issue,
* Waldyve Alexander Hamilton, *b.* 1854.
Mr. Martin, who is a Magistrate for co. Hereford, and a Banker in London; was M.P. for Tewkesbury 1832-5 and 1837-59.—*The Upper Hall, Ledbury; Reform Club, s.w.; 14, Berkeley Square, w.*

MARTIN, the Ven. JOHN CHARLES, D.D.
Second son of the late John Martin, Esq., of Blackrock, Cork, by Mary, dau. of Aylmer Allen, Esq., of Woodview; *b.* 1797; *s.* 1821; *m.* 1829 Agatha, only dau. of the late Right Rev. Richard Mant, D.D., Bishop of Down and Connor, and has, with other issue,
* John Charles (in Holy Orders), B.A. of Trinity Coll., Dublin. Curate of Killeshandra; *b.* 1831.
Dr. Martin was educated at Trinity Coll., Dublin (B.A. 1816, M.A. 1819, F.T.C.D. 1821, D.D. 1854); ordained 1825; appointed Rector of Killeshandra 1834, Archdeacon of Ardagh 1854, Archdeacon of Kilmore 1866.—*Rectory House, Killeshandra, co. Cavan; University Club, Dublin; National Club, s.w.*

MARTIN, JOSEPH JOHN, Esq., of Ham Court, Worcester.
Eldest son of the late Rev. Joseph Martin, of Ham Court, Rector of Bourton on-the-Hill, co. Gloucester, and Canon of Exeter, by Isabella Margaret, dau. of the Rev. John Sturges, D.D., Prebendary and Chancellor of Winchester; *b.* 1790. Educated at Winchester Coll. and Ch. Ch. Oxford (B.A. 1811, M.A. 1815), was Fellow of All Souls Coll.; is a J.P. and D.L. for co.

Worcester (High Sheriff 1832), Lord of the Manor of Upton-on-Severn; late Major of Queen's Own Worcestershire Yeomanry.—*Ham Court, Upton-on-Severn; Athenæum and United University Clubs, s.w.*

Heir Pres., his nephew George Edward, of St. Cloud, near Worcester, a J.P. and D.L. for co. Worcester (eldest son of the late Rev. George Martin, Canon Residentiary, and Chancellor of the diocese of Exeter, and Vicar of Harberton, by Lady Charlotte Sophia, dau. of William, 2nd Earl of St. Germans), *b.* 1829; *m.* 1862 Maria Henrietta, eldest dau. of Benjamin Cherry, Esq., of Brikendon Grange, Herts.

MARTIN, Mrs., of East Bridgeford, Notts.
Isabella Harriet, dau. of the late Rear-Admiral Sir Thomas Briggs, of Burnside, co. Dumfries, by Isabella, dau. of the late Lieut.-General Trapaud; *m.* 1835 Capt. George Bohun Martin, C.B., who was a Magistrate for Notts, a Capt. R.N., and *d.* 1854, leaving, with other issue,
* Henry, Lieut. Scinde Cavalry, *b.* 1840; *m.* 1864 Fanny Georgina, only dau. of the late Selby Hutton, Esq., of Carlton-on-Trent, and has issue, * a son, *b.* 1864.
Mrs. Martin is joint Lady of the Manor of East Bridgeford.—*East Bridgeford, Radcliffe, Notts; Crabb's Abbey, Wiggenhall, St. Mary Lynn, Norfolk.*

MARTIN, Mrs., of Whatton, Leicestershire.
Augusta Louisa, dau. of William Hopkins, Esq., M.A. of St. Peter's Coll., Cambridge; *m.* 1852 John Martin, Esq., of Whatton House, who *d.* 1864, leaving, with other issue,
* William John, *b.* 1853.
The late Mr. Martin was a J.P. and D.L. for co. Leicester (High Sheriff 1863).—*Whatton House, Loughborough.*

MARTIN, the Rev. ROBERT, of Anstey Pastures, Leicestershire.
Eldest surviving son of the late William Martin, Esq., of Stewardshey, co. Leicester, by Ann Wood, only child of John Richards, Esq., of Normanton-on-Soar. Notts; *b.* 1809; *s.* 1850; *m.* 1st 1839 Selina, dau. of John Frewen Turner, Esq., of Cold Overton Hall, co. Leicester; 2nd 1860 Marian Cecil, only child of R. W. Wood, Esq., of Stoneygate, and has by the former, with other issue,
* Robert Frewen, *b.* 1842.
Mr. Martin, who was educated at Queen's Coll., Cambridge (B.A. 1832, M.A. 1835), appointed Vicar of Ratby and Breedon, 1833, is in the Commission of the Peace for co. Leicester.—*Anstey Pastures, Leicester.*

MARTIN, ROBERT, Esq., of Overbury Court, Worcestershire.
Fourth son of the late John Martin, Esq., M.P., of Overbury Court, by Frances, dau. of Richard Stone, Esq., of Chiselhurst, Kent; *b.* 1808; *m.* 1837 Mary Anne, dau. of the late John Biddulph, Esq., of Ledbury, and has, with other issue,
* Richard Biddulph, *b.* 1838; *m.* 1864 Mary Frances, only dau. of Admiral Richard Crozier, of West Hill, I. of Wight.
Mr. Martin, who was educated at the Charterhouse and Exeter Coll., Oxford, is a Banker in London.—*Overbury Court, Tewkesbury; Windham Club, s.w.; 21, Eaton Square, s.w.*

MARTIN, Admiral THOMAS, of Bittern, Hants.
Only surviving son of the late Captain John N. Martin, of Wollaton, Notts, by Elizabeth, dau. and heir of John Hutchinson, Esq., of Crossfield House, Cumberland; *b.* 1787; *m.* 1828 Anne, dau. of John Miles, Esq., of London, and has, with other issue,
* Thomas Hutchinson Mangles, Capt. R.N., *b.* 1828; *m.* 1858 Charlotte Beatley, eldest dau. of the late S. H. Egginton, Esq., of North Ferriby, co. York.
Admiral Martin, who entered the Navy in 1799, and

served on the North-American and West-Indian Stations, &c., became Vice-Admiral in 1860.—*Bittern Lodge, Southampton.*

MARTIN, Capt. WILLIAM GEORGE, R.H.A., of Hemingstone Hall, Suffolk.
Eldest son of the late Richard Bartholomew Martin, Esq., of Hemingstone Hall (who was a Lieut. 5th Dragoon Guards), by Juliana, dau. of John Donovan Verner, Esq., of Dublin; *b.* 1835 ; *s.* 1855 ; *m.* 1863 Margaret, 2nd dau. of William Strahan, Esq., of Sidmouth, Devon, and has issue,

* A dau., *b.* 1866.

Capt. Martin, who was educated at the Royal M. Academy, Woolwich, was appointed to the Royal Artillery, 1854.—*Hemingstone Hall, Ipswich ; Junior United Service Club, s.w.*

MARTIN-ATKINS, EDWIN, Esq., of Kingston Lisle, Berks.
Eldest son of the late Edwin Martin-Atkins, Esq., of Kingston Lisle, by Caroline, dau. of the late Thomas Duffield, Esq., of Marcham Park, Berks; *b.* 1838 ; *s.* 1859 ; *m.* 1st 1862 Mary Georgina Louisa, 2nd dau. of the Lieut.-General Wm. A. Johnson, of Wytham-on-the-Hill, co. Lincoln (she *d.* 1863); 2nd 1865 Amy, youngest dau. of Charles Hutton, Esq., of Bath. Is a Magistrate for Berks, and Lieut. Berks Yeomanry.—*Kings on Lisle, Wantage.*

MARTIN-ATKINS, WILLIAM HASTINGS, Esq., of Farley Castle, Berks.
Second son of the late Atkins Edwin Martin-Atkins, Esq., of Kingston Lisle, Berks, by Anne, 2nd dau. of Major William Cook, of Hothorpe, co. Northampton, and grandson of Edwin Martin, Esq., who assumed the name of Atkins in conformity with the will of his maternal uncle, Abraham Atkins, of Kingston Lisle, about the year 1780 ; *b.* 1811 ; *m.* 1st 1844 Diana Mary, 2nd dau. of the Rev. James Wyld, of Blunsdon St. Andrews, Wilts (she *d.* 1862); 2nd 1865 Georgiana, eldest dau. of George Edward Beauchamp, Esq., of Thetford, Norfolk, and widow of Edward Lloyd Edwards, Esq., of Cerrig-Llwydion, co. Denbigh. Educated at Rugby and University Coll., Oxford (B.A. 1834); is a Magistrate for Berks, and Capt. Royal Berks Militia, and Berks Volunteer Rifles. The family descend from an ancient Huguenot family (named Martin), who quitted France on the revocation of the Edict of Nantes.—*Farley Castle, Reading ; Union Club. s.w.*

MARTIN-EDMUNDS, WILLIAM HENRY MORTIMER, Esq., of Worsborough, Yorkshire.
Only surviving son of the late William Bennet Martin, Esq., J.P. and D.L., of Worsborough Hall (who assumed the additional name of Edmunds, and who *d.* 1847), by Augusta Marcia, dau. of the Rev. John Chaloner, of Newton Kyme; *b.* 1844 ; *s.* his brother 1866. Educated at Trinity Coll., Cambridge ; is Lord of the Manor of Worsborough.—*Worsborough Hall, Barnsley.*

MARTIN-LEAKE, STEPHEN, Esq., of Thorpe Hall, Essex.
Eldest son of the late Stephen Ralph Martin-Leake, Esq., of Thorpe Hall, by Georgiana, dau. of Capt. George Stevens, H.E.I.C.'s Service, of Old Windsor Lodge, Berks; *b.* 1826 ; *s.* 1865 ; *m.* 1859 Isabel, dau. of the late William Plunkett, Esq., Barrister-at-Law, and has, with other issue,

* Stephen, *b.* 1861.

Mr. Martin-Leake, who was educated at St. John's Coll., Cambridge (B.A. 1848), and called to the Bar at the Middle Temple 1853, is Lord of the Manor of Thorpe. The surname of Leake was assumed by an

ancestor of the present owner in 1721.—*Thorpe H.l', Colchester ; Residence : Marshalls, Ware, Herts ; 1, Elm Court, Temple, E.C.*

MARTINS, Sir WILLIAM, Knt., of Westmont, Isle of Wight (cr. 1840).
Son of the late Mr. W. Martins ; *b.* 18— ; *m.* 1837 Harriet, dau. of the late Sir Thomas B. Mash. Is Gentleman Usher to the Queen, and Usher of the Sword of State.—*Westmont, Ryde, I. of Wight ; Union Club, s.w. ; 3, Hyde Park Gardens, w.*

MARTON, GEORGE BLUCHER HENEAGE, Esq., of Capernwray Hall, Lancashire.
Only son of the late George Marton, Esq., J.P. and D.L., of Capernwray Hall (who was High Sheriff of co. Lancaster 1858), by Lucy Sarah, dau. of the Right Hon. Lord Chief Justice Dallas; *b.* 1839 ; *s.* 1867 ; *m.* 1866 the Hon. Caroline Gertrude, youngest dau. of Henry, 5th Viscount Ashbrook. Is a Magistrate for co. Lancaster, Lord of the Manor of Capernwray, Patron of 2 livings, and a Capt. 1st Royal Lancashire Militia.—*Capernwray Hall, Lancaster.*

MARTYN, the Rev. THOMAS, of Ludgershall, Buckinghamshire.
Eldest son of the late Claudius Martyn, Rector of Ludgershall, by Mary, dau. of — Stalley, Esq.; *b.* 1792; *s.* 1821 ; *m.* 1814 Catherine Horner Strangeways, dau. of the Rev. John Pearson, M.A., and has, with other issue,

* Claudius Robert, M.A., of Lincoln Coll., Oxford (in Holy Orders), a Magistrate for Bucks, and a Surrogate for the Archdeaconry of Buckingham ; *b.* 1816.

Mr. Martyn, who was educated at Eton and Queen's Coll., Oxford (B.A. 1823, M.A. 1828), is a Magistrate for Bucks, Rector, Patron, and Lord of the Manor of Ludgershall.—*Ludgershall, Aylesbury.*

MARUM, EDWARD PURCELL MULHALLEN, Esq., of Aharney, Queen's Co.
Only son of the late Richard C. Marum, Esq., of Aharney, by Elizabeth Mary Anne, dau. of John Purcell Mulhallen, Esq., Capt. 86th Regt. and of the city of Kilkenny ; *b.* 1827. Educated at the London University (B.A. 1844, M.A. 1846. LL.B. 1848) ; called to the Irish Bar 1849, and goes the Leinster Circuit ; is a Magistrate for Queen's Co.—*Aharney House, Durrow.*

+**MARWOOD**, GEORGE, Esq., of Bushby Hall, Yorkshire.
Eldest son of the Rev. George Metcalfe, of Bushby Hall, Canon of Chichester (who assumed the name of Marwood in 1809); *b.* 18— ; *m.* 18— Miss Peel, and has issue. Mr. Marwood is a J.P. and D.L. for the N. Riding of Yorkshire. A Baronetcy in this family became extinct in 1740.—*Bushy Hall, Northallerton.*

MARWOOD-ELTON. (See Elton.)

MARX, FRANCIS JOSEPH PETER, Esq., of Arlebury, Hants.
Only son of the late George Marx, Esq., of Eaton Square, London, by Selina, dau. of Francis Chambers, Esq.; *b.* 1816 ; *s.* 1855 ; *m.* 1848 Anna Maria Selina, eldest dau. of the late Wadham Locke, Esq., M.P. of Rowdeford House, Wilts, and has, with other issue,

* George Francis, *b.* 1849

Mr. Marx, who was educated at Eton and Ch. Ch., Oxford (B.A. 1839), is a Magistrate for Hants, and Major of the 1st Hants Rifle Volunteers.—*Arle-Bu y, Alresford ; Oxford and Cambridge Club, s.w.*

MASEFIELD, WILLIAM, Esq., of Stone, Staffordshire.

Second but eldest surviving son of the late John Masefield, Esq., by Elizabeth, eldest dau. of William Taylor, Esq., of the Day House, Salop; b. 1799; s. 1822; m. 1831 Mary Elizabeth, only child of Richard Beech, Esq., J.P., of Wootton Lodge, Eccleshall, co. Stafford, and has, with other issue,

   * William Beech, b. 1843.

Mr. Masefield is a Magistrate for co. Stafford.—*Stone, Staffordshire.*

MASHITER, OCTAVIUS, Esq., of Priests, Essex.

Third son of the late William Mashiter, Esq., of Cottons, Romford, Essex (who d. 1811), by his cousin Blandina, dau. of Thomas Mashiter, Esq.; b. 1783; m. 1815 Maria, dau. of Christopher Tyler, Esq., of Essex, and has, with other issue,

   * Thomas, b. 1816.

Mr. O. Mashiter is a Magistrate for Essex and the Liberty of Havering-atte-Bower, and a J.P. and D.L. for the Tower Hamlets.—*Priests, Romford.*

+MASKELL, WILLIAM, Esq., of Bude Castle, Cornwall.

Eldest son of the late William Maskell, Esq., of Shepton Mallet, Somerset; b. 1814; m. 1st 1843 Mary, dau. of — Scott, Esq., of Bath (she d. 1847); 2nd 1853 Monique, only dau. of the late John Stein, Esq.; he has by the former, with other issue,

   * William, late an Officer in the Army; b. 1846.

Mr. Maskell, who was educated at University Coll., Oxford (B.A. 1836, M.A. 1838), is a Magistrate for Cornwall and was formerly Vicar of St. Mary Church, Devon.—*Bude Castle, Stratton, Cornwall; Reform Club, s. w.*

MASON, GEORGE WILLIAM, Esq., of Morton Hall, Notts.

Eldest son of the late Rev. George Mason, of Cuckney, Notts, by Harriet, dau. of James Coldham, Esq., of Anmer Hall, Norfolk; b. 1819; m. 1844 Marianne, dau. of Capt. J. G. Mitford, of Langharne, co. Carmarthen, and has, with other issue,

   * William Henry, b. 1846.

Mr. Mason was educated at Trinity Coll., Cambridge (B.A. 1841, M.A. 1846); is a Magistrate for Notts. This family was seated at Egmanton, Notts, in the reign of Elizabeth, and is believed to be sprung from the same family as the poet Mason.—*Morton Hall, Babworth, Retford.*

MASON, the Rev. JOHN, M.A., of Aldenham Lodge, Herts.

Only son of the late John Finch Mason, Esq., of Aldenham Lodge, by Mary, dau. of Col. Samuel Cox, of Sandford Park, Oxon; b. 1819; s. 1853; m. 1841 Charlotte Frances, dau. of the Rev. Charles Yonge, of Eton Coll., and by her, who d. 1860, has, with other issue,

   * George Finch, b. 1847.

Mr. Mason was educated at Eton and Ch. Ch., Oxford (B.A. 1849, M.A. 1815). *Aldenham Lodge, Watford; Oxford and Cambridge Club, s.w.*

MASON, the Rev. JOHN MASON, of Whitfield, Northumberland.

Eldest son of the late Thomas Mason, Esq., of Kirkby Stephen, Westmoreland; b. 1820; m. 1853 Ellen, dau. of Thomas Benn, Esq., Commander R.N., of Dean Scales, Cumberland. Educated at Sedbergh, and St. John's Coll., Cambridge (B.A. 1844); is a Magistrate for Northumberland; formerly Perpetual Curate of Jarrow-on-Tyne.—*Whitfield Rectory, Carlisle.*

612

MASON, of Necton, Norfolk. (See *Elomefield.*)

MASSAREENE AND FERRARD, Viscount (CLOTWORTHY JOHN EYRE FOSTER-SKEFFINGTON, K.P.).—Cr. 1660.

Eldest son of John, 3rd Viscount Ferrard and Massareene, by Olivia, dau. of the late Henry Deane O'Grady, Esq., of Lodge, co. Limerick; b. 1842; s. 1863. Sits in the House of Lords as Lord Oriel, U.K. (cr. 1821); is Capt. Antrim Militia; his great-grandfather, the 1st Lord Ferrard, was the last Speaker of the Irish House of Commons.—*Antrim Castle, co. Antrim; Oriel Temple, co. Louth.*

   Heir Pres., his brother Hungerford Henry, late Lieut. Antrim Militia, b. 1845.

+MASSEY, WILLIAM, Esq., of Cornelyn, Anglesey.

Son of the late W. Massey, Esq.; b. 18—. Was High Sheriff of Anglesey 1864.—*Cornelyn, Anglesey.*

MASSEY, the Right Hon. WILLIAM NATHANIEL, P.C.

Son of William Massey, Esq.; b. 1809; m. 1833 Frances Carleton, dau. of the Rev. John Orde. Called to the Bar at the Inner Temple 1844; was formerly of the Western Circuit; late Recorder of Portsmouth; was Under-Secretary of State for the Home Department 1855-8; M.P. for Newport 1852-7; was M.P. for Salford 1857-65; he was nominated Finance Minister of India, and sworn a Member of the Privy Council 1865.—*Athenæum Club, s.w.; 4, Upper Wimpole Street, w.*

MASSEY. (See under *Clarina, Lord.*)

MASSINGBERD, CHARLES LANGTON-, Esq., of Gunby Hall, Lincolnshire.

Fifth but eldest surviving son of the late Peregrine Langton, Esq., of Langton, by Elizabeth Mary Anne, only child and heir of the late Henry Massingberd, Esq., of Gunby, whose name he assumed; b. 1815; m. 1st 1843 Harriet Ann, dau. of the late Richard Langford, Esq.; 2nd 1863 Harriet, youngest dau. of the late Sir Robert W. Newman, Bart., and has issue by the former,

   * Emily Caroline and Alice Langton.

Mr. Massingberd, who is Lord of the Manor of Gunby, was formerly in the Austrian service.—*Gunby Hall, Spilsby; Conservative Club, s.w.*

MASSINGBERD, the Rev. FRANCIS CHARLES.

Only son of the late Rev. F. Massingberd, Prebendary of Lincoln, by Eliza, dau. of the late W. B. Massingberd, Esq., of Ormsby; b. 1800; m. 1839 Fanny, eldest dau. of the late William Baring, Esq., and grand-dau. of the late Sir Francis Baring, Bart., and has, with other issue,

   * Francis Burrell, Capt. 5th Lancers; b. 1843.

Mr. Massingberd, who was educated at Rugby and Magdalen Coll., Oxford (B.A. 1822, M.A. 1825), appointed Rector of South Ormsby 1825, and Chancellor of Lincoln Cathedral 1862, is male representative of the Massingberd family, through his grandfather, Francis B. Massingberd, only brother of the above W. B. Massingberd, Esq., of Ormsby.—*The Chantery, Lincoln.*

MASSINGBERD. (See *Mundy-Massingberd.*)

MASSY, Lord (HUGH HAMMOND INGOLDSBY MASSY).—Cr. 1776.

Elder son of Hugh Hammond, 4th Lord, by Matilda, dau. of the late Luke White, Esq., of Woodlands, co. Dublin; b. 1827; s. 1836; m. 1855 Isabella, eldest dau. of the late George More Nisbett, Esq., of Cairnhill, co. Lanark. Is a Magistrate for co. Limerick,

—*Duntryleague, and Hermitage, Castle-Connell, co. Limerick.*

*Heir Pres., his brother John Thomas William, b. 1835 ; m 1863 Lady Lucy Maria, dau. of Somerset, 3rd Earl of Carrick, and has, with other issue, * Hugh Somerset John, b. 1864.*

MASSY, Sir HUGH DILLON, Bart., of Doonas, co. Clare (cr. 1781).

Only son of the late Rev. Charles Massy, Prebendary of Lakeen and Rector of Doonas, by Mary Anne, dau. of J. Ross Lwin, Esq., of Fortfergus, co. Clare; *b.* 1797; *s.* his uncle as 3rd Bart. 1842 ; *m.* 1818 Mary Johnson, dau. of John Westropp, Esq., of Attyflin Park, co. Limerick. Is a J.P. and D.L. for co. Clare (High Sheriff 1833), and Capt. Limerick City Militia; was formerly in the Irish Militia.—*Doonas House, Clonlara, Ireland.*

MASSY, EDWARD TAYLOR, Esq., of Cottesmore, co. Pembroke, and Dirreens, co. Limerick.

Only son of the late Hon. Edward Massy (who *d.* 1836), by Catharine, only dau. of John Villiers Tuthill, Esq., of Kilmore, co. Limerick; *b.* 1807 ; *m.* 1835 Helen, only dau. of Jonathan Haworth Peel, Esq., of Denant, co. Pembroke, and has, with other issue,

* Edward Hugh Hamon; b. 1836.

Mr. Massy, who was educated at Brasenose Coll., Oxford (B.A. 1830), is a J.P. and D.L. for co. Pembroke. —*Cottesmore, Haverfordwest.*

MASSY, HUGH HAMON GEORGE WILLIAM CARRUTHERS, Esq., of Hazelhurst, Hants.

Elder son of the late Hugh Hamon John Massy, Esq., of Hazelhurst (who was formerly Capt. 44th Foot), by Annie Margaret, 2nd dau. of the late Morgan John Evans, Esq., of Llwynbarried, co. Radnor ; *b.* 1851 ; *s.* 1867 ; is descended from a common ancestor with Lord Massy and the Baronets of that name. —*Hazelhurst, Lymington.*

Heir Pres., his brother Rollo Dillon Dunham, b. 1856.

MASSY, JOHN, Esq., of Kingswell House, co. Tipperary.

Son of the late Charles Massy, Esq., by Margaret, granddau. of Charles Spread, Esq. ; *b.* 1810 ; *m.* 1832 Alicia, dau. of the late Capt. Chadwick, of Chadville, co. Tipperary, and has, with other issue, one only surviving son,

* Richard Albert, a Resident Magistrate for co. Leitrim, late Lieut. 60th Rifles ; b. 1840.

Mr. Massy is a Magistrate for cos. Tipperary and Limerick.—*Kingswell House, Tipperary.*

MASSY, JOHN BOLTON-, Esq., of Clareville, co. Dublin.

Eldest surviving son of the late Robert Bolton, Esq., of Brazille, co. Dublin, by Elizabeth, eldest dau. of the late Hon. James Massy Dawson, of Ballynacourty, co. Tipperary ; *b.* 1785 ; *m.* 1815 his cousin Jane, dau. of Major Greene, M.P., and has, with other issue,

* Robert Dawson, a Magistrate for co. Limerick ; b. 1817.

Mr. Massy, who was educated at Trinity Coll., Dublin (B.A. 1805, M.A. 1852), and called to the Irish Bar 1809, retired 1815, on succeeding to the estates in cos. Tipperary and Limerick, by the will of his maternal grand-uncle, the Hon. John Massy, whose name he assumed by Royal licence, is a Grand Juror of cos. Dublin and Limerick (High Sheriff 1826), and a Magistrate for co. Dublin.—*Clareville, Booterstown, Black Rock, co. Dublin ; Ballywire (co. Tipperary), Galbally, Ireland ; Kildare Street Club, Dublin.*

MASSY, WILLIAM HUGH MASSY HUTCHINSON, Esq., of Mount-Massy, co. Cork.

Eldest son of the late Massy Hutchinson Massy, Esq., of Mount-Massy, by Sarah, dau. of the Rev. Simon Davies, of Macroom; *b.* 1828 ; *s.* 1852 ; *m.* 1868 Eliza-

beth, dau. of the late Sir John Borlase Warren, Bart. ; is a Magistrate for co. Cork ; descended from a common ancestor with Lord Massy.—*Mount-Massy, Macroom, co. Cork.*

MASSY-DAWSON, GEORGE STAUNTON KING, Esq., of New Forest and Ballynacourty, co. Tipperary.

Sixth son of the late James Hewitt Massy-Dawson, Esq., of New Forest (who *d.* 1834), by Eliza Jane, dau. of Francis Dennis, Esq.; *b.* 1816 ; *s.* his brother 1850 ; *m.* 1854 Grace Elizabeth, 2nd dau. of Sir William Leeson, of Kingstown, near Dublin, and by her, who *d.* 1865, has, with other issue,

* James, b. 1857.

Mr. Dawson is a J.P. and D.L. for co. Tipperary (High Sheriff 1854), and a Magistrate for co. Limerick; was formerly in the 14th Light Dragoons.—*New Forest, and Ballynacourty, Tipperary ; Kildare Street Club, Dublin, Naval and Military Club, w.*

MASTER, CHARLES HOSKINS, Esq., of Barrow Green, Surrey.

Only son of the late Charles Legh Hoskins Master, Esq., J.P. and D.L., of Barrow Green, by Louisa, dau. of the Rev. John Williamson, Rector of Thakeham, Sussex ; *b.* 1816 ; *s.* 1861 ; *m.* 1844 Emily, dau. of Nathaniel Borrer, Esq., of Pakyns Manor, Sussex, and has, with other issue,

* Charls Hoskins, b. 1846.

Mr. Master, who was educated at Eton and St. John's Coll., Cambridge (B.A. 1838), is Lord of the Manor and Patron of Oxted.—*Barrow Green, Godstone.*

MASTER, Col. WILLIAM CHESTER, of Knole and of Cirencester Abbey, Gloucestershire.

Eldest son of the late Richard Thomas Master. Esq., of Knole Park, by Isabella, 3rd dau. of Col. W. Egerton. of Windsor Castle ; *b.* 1785; *s.* his uncle in the Knole Park estate 1823, and Lady Cartaret in the Abbey property 1863 ; *m.* 1814 Isabella Margaret, dau. of the late Col. the Hon. Stephen Thomas Digby, and by her, who *d.* 1860, has, with other issue,

* Thomas William Chester, a Magistrate for co. Gloucester and late M.P. for Cirencester ; b. 1815 ; m. 1840 Catherine Elizabeth, dau. of the late Sir George Cornewall, Bart., and has, with other issue, * Thomas William Chester, a Magistrate for co. Gloucester, b. 1841 ; m. 1866 Georgina Emily, 5th dau. of John Etherington Welch Rolls, Esq., of The Hendre, co. Monmouth (whom see), and has issue, Thomas, b. 1867.

Col. Master, who was educated at Westminster, and entered the Army 1801, is a Magistrate for co. Gloucester, Patron of 3 livings, late Lieut.-Col. 3rd Foot Guards; was Gentleman-Usher of the Privy Chamber to H.M. George III., George IV., and William IV., and holds the same office to Her Majesty.—*Knole Park, Almondsbury, Bristol; The Abbey, Cirencester; United Service Club, s.w.*

MASTERS-SMITH, of Camer.

(See *Smith-Masters.*)

MATCHAM, GEORGE, Esq., LL.D., of New House, Wilts.

Eldest son of the late George Matcham, Esq., of Ashfold Lodge, Sussex, by Catherine, dau. of the Rev. Edmund Nelson, Rector of Burnham Thorpe, co. Norfolk, and sister of Horatio, Viscount Nelson; *b.* 1789 ; *s.* 1833 ; *m.* 1817 Harriet, dau. and heiress of William Purvis (afterwards Eyre), Esq., of Newhouse, and has, with other issue,

* William Eyre, a J.P. and D.L. for Wilts, b. 1824 ; m. 1851 Mary Elizabeth, 4th dau. of Henry Lawes Long, Esq., of Hampton Lodge, Surrey.

Mr. Matcham, who was educated at St. John's Coll., Cambridge (LL.B. 1814, LL.D. 1820), and admitted an

Advocate in Doctors' Commons 1820, is a J.P. and D.L. for Wilts, and late a Chairman of the Wilts Quarter Sessions. This family are in remainder to the Earldom of Nelson.—*New House, near Downton, Wilts.*

MATHESON, Sir JAMES, Bart., of Achany, Sutherlandshire, and Lews, Ross-shire (cr. 1851).

Second son of the late Donald Matheson, Esq., chief of the Clan Matheson, in Sutherland, by Katherine, dau. of the Rev. Thomas Mackay, of Lairg, N.B.; *b.* 1796; *m.* 1843 Mary Jane, dau. of M. H. Perceval, Esq. Educated at the High School and University of Edinburgh; is Lord Lieut. of co. Ross, and a J.P. and D.L. for co. Sutherland, and formerly a partner in the house of Jardine, Matheson, & Co., China; was M.P. for Ashburton 1843–7; has been M.P. for Ross and Cromarty since 1847.—*Achany, Bonar Bridge, N.B.; Stornoway Castle, Ross-shire; Brooks's Club,* s.w.; 13, *Cleveland Row,* s.w.

MATHESON, ALEXANDER, Esq., of Ardross Castle, Ross-shire.

Eldest son of the late John Matheson, Esq., of Attadale, co. Ross, by Margaret, dau. of Donald Matheson, Esq., and nephew of Sir J. Matheson, Bart.; *b.* 1805; *m.* 1st 1840 Mary, only dau. of James Crawford Macleod, Esq., of Granies, N.B. (she *d.* 1841); 2nd 1853 Lavinia Mary, sister of the late Lord Beaumont (she *d.* 1855); 3rd 1860 Eleanor Irving, 5th dau. of the late Spencer Perceval, Esq., of Portman Square, London, and has by his 2nd wife, with other issue,

• Kenneth James, *b.* 1854.

Mr. Matheson is a Merchant in London, and a Director of the Bank of England; a J.P. and D.L. for cos. Ross, Cromarty, and Inverness, and also for London; has been M.P. for the Inverness Burghs since 1847; was formerly a Merchant at Canton, in China. Mr. Matheson acquired by purchase in 1851 the estate of Lochalsh, forfeited by his ancestors in 1427.—*Ardross Castle, Alness, N.B.; 58, South Street,* w.

MATHESON, Major-General THOMAS, of Achany, Sutherlandshire.

Third son of the late Donald Matheson, Esq., and brother of Sir James Matheson. Bart. (whom see); *b.* 1798. Educated at Edinburgh; entered the Army 1815; became Lieut.-Col. 1843, when he went on half-pay; promoted to the rank of Major-General 1859; is a Magistrate for co. Sutherland; was M.P. for Ashburton 1847–52. —*Achany, Lairg, N.B.; United Service Club,* s.w,

MATHEW, EDWARD WINDUS, Esq.

Only son of the late Nathaniel Mathew, Esq., of Wern (who was a J.P. and D.L. for cos. Carnarvon and Merioneth), by Mary, only dau. of Edward William Windus, Esq., of Tottenham, Middlesex; *b.* 1812; *s.* 1867; *m.* 1st 1848 Charlotte Isabella, dau. of the late Abraham Thompson, Esq., of Bewdley, co. Worcester (she *d.* 1863); 2nd 1867 Charlotte Anne, youngest dau. of the late Arthur Edward Burtonshaw Windus, Esq., of Lewes, Sussex, and has issue,

• A son, *b.* 1868.

Mr. Mathew is a J.P. and D.L. for co. Carnarvon (on the roll for High Sheriff 1869), and Capt. 4th Carnarvonshire Rifle Volunteers.—*Residence: Wern, Carnarvon; Farmers' Club,* E.C.

MATHEW, GEORGE BENVENUTO BUCKLEY, Esq., C.B., of Pennytenny, Cornwall.

Eldest son of the late George Mathew, Esq., of the Coldstream Guards (who *d.* 1846), by Euphemia, eldest dau. of John Hamilton, Esq., of Rocklands; *b.* 1807; *m.* 1st 1833 Anne, dau. and heir of Henry Hoare, Esq., of Stourhead, Wilts (from whom he was divorced in 1817);

644

2nd 1850 Rosina Adelaide, dau. of J. C. Handley, Esq., and has by the former, with other issue,
• Brownlow Hugh, Capt. R.E.; *b.* 1835.

Mr. Buckley-Mathew, who was formerly Lieut. and Capt. Coldstream Guards, and Governor of the Bahama Isles, Secretary to the Legation at Mexico, &c., was appointed Chargé d'Affaires and Consul-General at Guatemala, &c., 1861, and in the same year Minister Plenipotentiary to the Republics of Central America; appointed Envoy Extraordinary to Brazil, 1867; he was M.P. for Athlone 1835–7, and for Shaftesbury 1837–41, and assumed the additional surname of Buckley by Royal licence 1865.—*Junior United Service Club,* s.w.

MATHEW, HENRY COLDHAM, Esq., of Pentloe Hall, Essex, and Lanyer House, Suffolk.

Second son of the late Rev. Edward Mathew, Vicar of Coggeshall, Essex, and grandson of the late Col. Mathew, of Pentloe Hall; *b.* 1825; *m.* 1854 Emily de Vere, dau. of the Rev. A. G. H. Hollingsworth, Vicar of Stowmarket, Suffolk, and has, with other issue,
• William Edward, *b.* 1855.

Mr. Mathew is a Magistrate for Essex, and a Capt. East Norfolk Militia.—*Pentloe Hall, Clare; Lanyer House, Ipswich.*

MATHIAS, LEWIS, Esq., of Lamphey Court, Pembrokeshire.

Eldest son of the late Charles Mathias, Esq., of Lamphey Court, by Mary, dau. of John Bethel, Esq., of Hassage, Somerset; *b.* 1813; *s.* 1851; *m.* 1845 Emily Catherine, dau. of the late John Bennet Lawes, Esq., of Rothamsted, Herts, and has, with other issue,
• Charles, *b.* 1849.

Mr. Mathias, who was educated at Brasenose Coll., Oxford, is a J.P. and D.L. for co. Pembroke (High Sheriff 1856), and Lord of the Manor of Lamphey.—*Lamphey Court, Pembroke.*

MATHEWS, BENJAMIN ST. JOHN, Esq., of Kingswinford, Staffordshire.

Only son of William Mathews, Esq., of Great Malvern. by Rachel Maria, dau. of Matthias Attwood. Esq., of Hawne House, Halesowen. co. Stafford; *b.* 1830; *m.* 1860 Florence, dau. of J. J. Garth Wilkinson, Esq., of London. Mr. Mathews, who was educated at Trinity Coll., Cambridge (B.A. 1852, M.A. 1855) is a Magistrate for co. Stafford. This family was formerly of the Leasowes, Halesowen.—*Kingswinford, Stourbridge.*

+**MATTHEWS,** JOHN, Esq., of Donnington, Berks.

Son of the late J. Matthews, Esq.; *b.* 18—. Is a Magistrate for Berks, and a Banker at Newbury.—*Donnington House, Newbury.*

MATTHEWS, WILLIAM EDWIN, Esq., of Lukesland, and Coombe. Devonshire.

Only son of the late William Matthews. Esq., of Coombe, Devon, and Sydney, N. S. Wales, by Sarah, dau. of William Widdicombe, Esq., of Devon; *b.* 18—; *s.* 1854; *m.* 1853 Elizabeth Allen dau. of Jonathan Cundy Page, Esq., and has issue two daughters,
• Sarah Elizabeth and Emily

Mr. Matthews, who was educated at Magdalen Hall, Oxford, is a Magistrate for Devon. He purchased this estate from the executors of the Rev. Christopher Savage in 1862.—*Lukesland, Ivybridge.*

+**MATTOCK,** ROBERT, Esq., of Angersleigh, Somerset.

Son of the late Mr. Mattock, of Angersleigh (who *s.* under the will of Thomas Southwood. Esq., in 1850); *b.* 18—. Is Lord of the Manors of Taunton Deane and Angersleigh.—*Angersleigh, Wellington.*

MAUDE, the Hon. FRANCIS.

Fifth son of Cornwallis, 1st Viscount Hawarden, by his 3rd wife Anne Isabella, dau. of Thomas Monck, Esq.; *b.* 1798; *m.* 1st 1827 Frances, dau. of A. H. Brooking, Esq., of St. John's, Newfoundland (*d.* 1832); 2nd 1849 Georgiana, dau. of the late Gervaise Parker Bushe, Esq., Barrister-at-Law, and has by the former, with other issue,

* Francis Cornwallis, C.B., Lieut.-Col. in the Army, and Capt. R.A.; *b.* 1828; *m.* 1860 Pauline, dau. of the Hon. Paul Sterling, Chief Justice of Ceylon.

Mr. Maude, who was educated at the Royal Naval Coll., is a Captain, R.N., retired.—*75, Onslow Square, s.w.*

MAUDE, Mrs., of Knowsthorpe, Yorkshire.

Georgianna Catharine, dau. of F. B. Natusch, Esq., of London; *m.* 1850 Edward James Maude, Esq., of Knowsthorpe (eldest son of William Milthorp Maude, Esq., of Knowsthorpe, J.P. and D.L.), who *d.* 1865. —*Knowsthorpe House, Leeds.*

MAUDE. (See under *Hawarden, Viscount.*)

MAULE, the Hon. Mrs., of Maulesden, Forfar-shire.

Elizabeth, dau. of Thomas Binney, Esq.; *m.* 1844 the Hon. William Maule, youngest son of William 1st Lord Panmure, and brother of Fox, 11th Earl of Dalhousie, who *d.* 1859.—*Maulesden, Brechin, N.B.*

MAULE. (See under *Dalhousie, Earl of.*)

MAULEVERER. (See *Brown, of Arncliffe.*)

MAUND, JOHN, Esq., of Tymawr, Brecknock-shire.

Only son of the late John Maund, Esq., of Tymawr, by Mary, eldest dau. of the Rev. Matthew Monkhouse, of Sirhowy, co. Monmouth; *b.* 1835; *m.* 1860 Louisa Clifford, 4th dau. of Michael Hansby, Esq., of Aber-gavenny, and has, with other issue,

* John, *b.* 186-.

Mr. Maund, who was educated at Winchester and Brase-nose Coll., Oxford, is a J.P. and D.L. for co. Brecon (High Sheriff 1859)—*Tymawr, Abergavenny; Wind-ham Club, s.w.*

MAUNSELL, CHARLES CULLEN, Esq., of Roth-well, Northamptonshire.

Youngest son of the late Col. Thomas Philip Maunsell, of Thorpe Malsor, co. Northampton (who *d.* 1866), by the Hon. Caroline Elizabeth, dau. of the late Hon. Wil-liam Cockayne, and grandaughter of the 6th and last Viscount Cullen (ext.); *b.* 1833. Educated at St. John's Coll., Cambridge, (B.A. 1856); was formerly Capt. 54th Regt.—*Rothwell Manor House, Kettering; Army and Navy Club, s.w.*

MAUNSELL, EDWARD EYRE, Esq., of Fort Eyre, co. Galway.

Eldest son of the late Rev. Edward Eyre Maunsell, M.A., Vicar of Galway, by Eliza Maria, 2nd dau. of Thomas Studdert, Esq., of Bunratty Castle, co. Clare; *b.* 1823. Educated at Trinity Coll., Dublin (B.A. 1846); called to the Irish Bar 1819; is a Magistrate for the co. and borough of Galway; was High Sheriff of Galway 1854.—*Fort Eyre, Galway.*

MAUNSELL, Lieut.-General FREDERICK, of Gortbwee and Clonan, co. Limerick.

Sixth but second surviving son of the late Robert Maun-sell, Esq., of co. Limerick, by Anne, dau. of John Maxwell Stone, Esq., of the Madras Presidency; *b.*

1794; *m.* 1834 Alicia, dau. of Thomas Studdert, Esq., D.L., of Bunratty Castle, co. Clare, and has issue,

* Robert George, *b.* 1842.

Lieut.-General Maunsell, who entered the Army 1812, and served in the Peninsula and America, is a Lieut.-General, late Col. 53rd Regt.—*Gortbwee and Clonan, Limerick; Hibernian U.S. Club, and 26, Herbert Place, Dublin; United Service Club, s.w.*

MAUNSELL, GEORGE MEARES, Esq., of Bally-william, co. Limerick.

Eldest son of the late Daniel Maunsell, Esq., of Bally-william, by Sarah, dau. of George Meares, Esq., of Hume Street, Dublin; *b.* 1785; *s.* 1824; *m.* 1st 1817 Cathe-rine, dau. of Thomas Lloyd, Esq., M.P. for co. Limerick; 2nd 1833 Mary, dau. of the Rev. W. Stopford, and has by the former, with other issue,

* Daniel Meares, educated at Trinity Coll., Dublin, a Magis-trate for co. Limerick; *b.* 1819; *m.* 1859 Eliza, dau. of Christopher Delmege, Esq.

Mr. Maunsell, who was educated at Oriel Coll., Oxford (B.A. 1807), was a Magistrate for co. Limerick (High Sheriff 1833).—*Ballywilliam, Rathkeale.*

MAUNSELL, HENRY, Esq., of Fanstown, co. Limerick.

Third but eldest surviving son of the late Robert Maunsell, Esq., of Limerick, by Anne, dau. of John Maxwell Stone, Esq., of Madras; *b.* 1790; *m.* 1821 Eliza, dau. of Pryce Peacock, Esq., of Limerick, and has, with other issue,

* Robert, Major 85th Foot, *b.* 1826.

Mr. Maunsell, who was educated at Trinity Coll., Dublin (B.A. 1812, M A. 1832), called to the Irish Bar 1813, is a Magistrate for co. Limerick; was High Sheriff of the city of Limerick 1848, and of co. Lime-rick 1851.—*Fanstown, Kilmallock. co. Limerick; County Club, Limerick; 78, George Street, Limerick.*

+**MAUNSELL**, JOHN, Esq., of Oakley Park, co. Kildare.

Eldest son of the late Richard Maunsell, Esq., of Oak-ley Park (who was High Sheriff of co. Kildare 1850), by Maria, dau. of John Woods. Esq., of Winter Lodge, co. Dublin; *b.* 1810; *s.* 1866. Educated at Trinity Coll., Dublin; and called to the Irish Bar 1837.—*Oak-ley Park, Celbridge, co. Kildare.*

Heir Pres., his brother George Woods, a Barrister-at-Law, *b.* 181-; *m.* 1843 Maria, dau. of the late Mark Synnot, Esq., of Monasterevin, King's Co., and has issue.

MAUNSELL, the Rev. GEORGE EDMUND.

Eldest son of the late Col. Thomas Philip Maunsell, J.P. and D.L., of Thorpe Malsor (who was High Sheriff of co. Northampton 1821), by the Hon. Caroline Eliza-beth Cockayne, dau. of the late Hon. William Cockayne, and sister of the late Viscount Cullen (ext.); *b.* 1816; *s.* 1866; *m.* 1846 Theodosia Mary, dau. of the late Sir John Palmer, Bart., of Carlton, co. Northampton. and has issue,

* Cecil Henry, *b.* 1847.

Mr. Maunsell, who was educated at Eton and Ch. Ch., Oxford (B.A. 183?) is Rector of Thorpe Malsor, and Rural Dean.—*Thorpe Malsor, Kettering.*

MAUNSELL, THOMAS COCKAYNE, Esq., of Thorpe Malsor, Northamptonshire.

Son of the late Col. Thomas Philip Maunsell, of Thorpe Malsor (who was High Sheriff of co. Northampton 1821), by the Hon. Caroline Elizabeth, dau. of the late Hon. William Cockayne, and niece of the last Viscount Cullen (ext.); *b.* 1820; *s.* 1866; *m.* 1867 Catherine Eliza-beth, 2nd dau. of the Hon. Richard Cavendish (see Waterpark), of Thornton Hall, Bucks. Educated at Eton and Ch. Ch., Oxford; is a Magistrate for co. Northamp-ton, Lord of the Manor of Thorpe Malsor. Patron

of 1 living, and Capt.-Commandant Royal Kettering Yeomanry Cavalry; he was formerly Capt. 12th Royal Lancers.—*Thorpe Malsor Hall, Kettering; Army and Navy Club, s.w.*

MAUNSELL. (See *Tibbits*.)

MAURICE, JAMES, Esq., of Ruthin, Denbighshire.

Youngest son of the late Thelwall Maurice, Esq., M.D., of Marlborough, Wilts (who *d.* 1830); *b.* 1809; called to the Bar at the Middle Temple 1853; is a J.P. and D.L. for co. Denbigh.—*Ruthin, Denbighshire.*

MAURICE, the Rev. JOHN PIERCE.

Son of the late Thelwall Maurice, Esq., M.D., of Marlborough, Wilts; *b.* 1799; *m.* 1836 the Hon. Jane Lucy, 6th dau. of Thomas, 2nd Lord Lilford, and has, with other issue,

* Littleton Henry Powys (in Holy Orders), *b.* 1837; *m.* 1864 Georgiana Elizabeth, eldest dau. of Frank Heathcote, Esq., of Mountfield, Hants.

Mr. Maurice, who was educated at Brasenose Coll., Oxford (B.A. 1818, M.A. 1821), and appointed Rector of Michelmersh 1840, descends from the Royal (Welsh) line of Powys.—*Michilmersh Rectory, Romsey.*

MAURICE, ROBERT MAURICE BONNOR-, Esq., of Boydnfoel, Montgomeryshire.

Second son of the late John Bonnor, Esq., of Bryn-y-Gwalie, by Jane, only child and heir of the Rev. Richard Maurice, of Bryn-y-Gwalie, co. Denbigh; *b.* 1805; *s.* 1828 to the estates of his maternal uncle, the Rev. Robert Maurice, of Lazarton, Dorset, whose name he assumed; *m.* 1834 Judith, dau. of the late Rev. Henry Cripps, of Preston and Stonehouse, co. Gloucester, and has issue. Mr. Maurice, who was educated at Westminster and Ch. Ch., Oxford (B.A. 1827), is a Magistrate for co. Denbigh, and a J.P. and D.L. for co. Montgomery (High Sheriff 1831).—*Bodynfoel, Oswestry.*

MAXTONE-GRAHAM, JAMES, Esq., of Cultoquhey, Perthshire.

Eldest son of the late Anthony Maxtone, Esq., of Cultoquhey, by Alexina, dau. of John Græme, Esq.; *b.* 1819; *s.* 1846; *m.* 1851 Caroline Mary Anne, dau. of George E. Russell, Esq., H.E.I.C.'s Civil Service, and has, with other issue,

* Anthony George, *b.* 1854.

Mr. Maxtone-Graham, who was educated at Edinburgh Academy and University, is a J.P. and D.L. for co. Perth; he assumed the name of Graham on succeeding to the estate of his uncle, Robert Graham, Esq., of Redgorton, co. Perth, 1859 (see *Murray-Graham*).—*Cultoquhey, Crieff, N.B.; Battleby, Redgorton, N.B.*

MAXWELL, Sir HUGH BATES, Bart., of Calderwood Castle, Lanarkshire (cr. 1627).

Only surviving son of the late General Sir William Maxwell, Bart., of Calderwood Castle (who *d.* 1837), by Isabella, dau. of Henry Wilson, Esq., of Newcastle, co. Durham, *b.* 1797; a his brother a 9th Bart. 1865; *m.* 1827 Marianne Barbara, dau. of John Hunter, Esq., of Lisburn, Coleburn. Is a J.P. and D.L. for co. Lanark.—*Calderwood Castle, Blantyre, Glasgow.*

Heir, his son William, b. 1828.

MAXWELL, Sir WILLIAM, Bart., of Monreith, Wigtonshire (cr. 1681).

Eldest son of the late Lieut.-Col. Sir William Maxwell, Bart., of Monreith, by Catharine, dau. of John Fordyce, Esq., of Ayton, co. Berwick; *b.* 1805; *s.* 1838; *m.* 1833 Helenora, dau. of the late Sir Michael Shaw Stewart, Bart. Educated at Harrow; is a J.P. and D.L. for co.

646

Wigton and Lieut.-Col. Galloway Rifles; was formerly Capt. in the Army.—*Monreith, Newton Stewart, N.B.*

Heir, his son Herbert Eustace, b. 1845.

MAXWELL, Sir JOHN HERON-, Bart., of Springkell, Dumfries-shire (cr. 1683).

Eldest son of the late Lieut.-General Sir John Maxwell, 4th Bart., of Springkell, by Stuart Mary, eldest dau. of Patrick Heron, Esq., of Heron, co. Galloway (whose name he assumed); *b.* 1808; *s.* his brother as 6th Bart. 1844; *m.* 1833 Caroline, dau. of the Hon. Montgomery Granville John Stewart, and niece of George, 8th Earl of Galloway. Is a J.P. and D.L. for co. Dumfries, a Magistrate for co. Kirkcudbright, and a Commander R.N. retired.—*Springkell, Ecclefechan, N.B.; Carlton Club, s.w.*

Heir, his son John Robert H., late Capt. 15th Hussars, and formerly of the Royal Horse Guards, b. 1836; m. 1866 Caroline Harriette, 3rd dau. of Richard Howard-Brooke, Esq., of Castle Howard, co. Wicklow.

MAXWELL, Sir WILLIAM, Bart., of Cardoness, Kirkcudbrightshire (cr. 1804).

Only surviving son of the late Sir David Maxwell, Bart., of Cardoness, by Georgina, dau. of Samuel Martin, Esq., *b.* 1809; *s.* as 3rd Bart. 1860; *m.* 1841 Mary, dau. of John Sprot, Esq.; 2nd 1851 Louisa Maria, dau. of Geoffrey J. Shakerley, Esq. Is a J.P. and D.L. for Kirkcudbright.—*Cardoness, Gatehouse, Kirkcudbrightshire, N.B.*

Heir, his son David, b. 1842.

MAXWELL, Sir PETER BENSON, Knt. (cr. 1856).

Fourth son of the Rev. Peter Benson Maxwell, of Birdstown, co. Donegal, by Mary, dau. of — O'Hara, Esq., of Raheen, co. Galway; *b.* 1817; *m.* 1842 Frances Dorothea, dau. of Francis Synge, of Glenmore Castle, co. Wicklow, and has issue,

* Peter Benson, *b.* 1843.

Sir Peter, who was educated at Trinity Coll., Dublin (B.A. 1838), and called to the Bar at the Middle Temple 1841, was appointed Commissioner of Hospitals 1854. Recorder of Penang 1856; Recorder of Singapore 1866. This family is in possession of Birdstown, near Londonderry.—*Penang, Singapore.*

MAXWELL, the Hon. HENRY CONSTABLE-, of Milnhead, Dumfries-shire.

Fourth son of the late Marmaduke Constable-Maxwell, Esq., of Everingham, co. York, by Teresa, dau. of Edmund Wakeman, Esq., of Beckford, and brother of Lord Herries (whom see); *b.* 1810; *m.* 1840 Juliana, dau. of Peter Middleton Esq., of Stockheld Park, co. York, and has, with other issue,

* Herbert Constable, *b.* 1842.

Mr. Maxwell, who was educated at Stonyhurst Coll., Lancashire, is a J.P. and D.L. for co. Dumfries, a Magistrate for the W. Riding of Yorkshire, and Lord of the Barony of Milnhead.—*Scarthingwell Hall, Tadcast r; Milnhead, Kirkmahoe, N.B.*

MAXWELL, the Hon. MARMADUKE CONSTABLE-, of Terregles, Kirkcudbrightshire.

Second son of the late Marmaduke William Constable Maxwell, Esq., by Theresa Apollonia, dau. of Edmund Wakeman, Esq., of Beckford, co. Worcester, and brother of William, 13th Lord Herries; *b.* 1806; *m.* 1836 Mary, only dau. of the late Rev. Anthony Marsden, of Gargrave, co. York. Is a J.P. and D.L. for co. Dumfries and the Stewartry of co. Kirkcudbright, and a Lieut. Yorkshire Hussars.—*Terregles, Dumfries, N.B.*

MAXWELL, the Hon. JAMES PIERCE.

Sixth son of Henry, 6th Lord Farnham, by Lady Anne Butler, eldest dau. of Henry Thomas, 2nd Earl of Car-

rick; *b.* 1813. Is Lieut.-Col. in the Army unattached; formerly Capt. 59th Foot; served as Brevet-Major 50th Foot in the Crimea 1854-5; was M.P. for co. Cavan 1843-65.—*Farnham Castle, co. Cavan; Carlton Club, s.w.*; 45, *Curzon Street, w.*

MAXWELL, the Hon. RICHARD THOMAS, of Fortland, co. Cavan.
Seventh son of Henry, 6th Lord Farnham, by Lady Anne Butler, eldest dau. of Henry Thomas, 2nd Earl of Carrick; *b.* 1815; *m.* 1848 Charlotte Anne, 2nd dau. of the Rev. Henry P. Elrington, D.D., Precentor of Ferns Cathedral, and has, with other issue,

* Somerset Henry, *b.* 1849.

Mr. Maxwell is a J.P. and D.L. for co. Cavan, and a Magistrate for co. Wexford.—*Fortland, Mount Nugent, co. Cavan.*

MAXWELL, EDWARD HERON-, Esq., of Teviotbank, Roxburghshire.
Seventh son of the late Sir John Shaw Heron-Maxwell, Bart., of Springkell, co. Dumfries, by Stuart Mary, only dau. and heir of Patrick Heron, Esq., of Heron and Kirroughtrie, co. Kirkcudbright; *b.* 1821; *m.* 1847 Elizabeth Ellen, only dau. of Col. Stopford-Blair, of Penninghame, co. Wigtown, and has, with other issue,

* John Shaw, *b.* 1850.

Mr. Maxwell was educated at Harrow, is a Magistrate for co. Roxburgh, and a Dep.-Lieut. for co. Dumfries; he purchased Teviotbank in 1850.—*Teviotbank, Hawick, N.B.*

MAXWELL, GEORGE, Esq., of Broomholme, Dumfries-shire.
Eldest son of the late David Maxwell, Esq., Jun., of Westwater, by Elizabeth, dau. of the late Rev. John Laurie, of Ewes, co. Dumfries; *b.* 1819; *s.* his grandfather 1834; *m.* 1846 Charlotte, only child of the late John William Ardill, Esq., LL.D. of the Irish Bar, and has, with other issue,

* David Ardill, *b.* 1845.

Mr. Maxwell is a Magistrate for co. Dumfries.—*Broomholme, Langholm, N.B.; Tarras Lodge, Beckenham, s.e.*

MAXWELL, GEORGE, Esq., of Glenlee, Kirkcudbrightshire.
Elder son of the late Wellwood Maxwell, Esq., of Glenlee, by Elizabeth, dau. of Mark Dewsnap, Esq., *b.* 1856; *s.* 1866.—*Glenlee, New Galloway, N.B.*

Heir Pres., his brother Alexander, *b.* 1861.

+MAXWELL, JOHN CLERK, Esq., of Middlebie and Glenair, Midlothian.
Son of the late J.Maxwell, Esq., of Middlebie; *b.* 18—; *m.* 18— Frances, only dau. of the late Robert H. Cay, Esq., of North Charlton Hall, co. Northumberland. Is a Magistrate for Midlothian.—*Middlebie and Glenair, Edinburgh, N.B.*

MAXWELL, Col. JOHN HARLEY-, R.E., of Portrack, Dumfries-shire.
Eldest son of the late Alexander Harley-Maxwell, Esq., of Portrack (who assumed the surname of Maxwell on succeeding to this part of the estates of his uncle, A. H. Maxwell, Esq., of Munches and Terraughtie), by Sarah, dau. of the late John Hyslop, Esq., of Lochend; *b.* 1822; *m.* 1851 Catherine Anne, dau. of the late Admiral Johnston, of Cowhill, co. Dumfries. Educated at Addiscombe; entered the Bengal Engineers 1840; is a Brevet-Major in H.M.'s Indian Army.—*Portrack, near Dumfries, N.B.*

Heir Pres. his brother Alexander Harley, Esq., *b.* 1821; *m.* 1855 Catherine, dau. of Edward Potter, Esq., of Cramlington, near Newcastle.

+MAXWELL, JOHN WARING-, Esq., of Finnebrogue, Downshire.
Eldest son of the late John Waring, Esq., by Dorothea, dau. and heir of the late Robert Maxwell, Esq., of Finnebrogue (whose name he assumed); *b.* 18—; *m.* 18— Madeline Martha, dau. of the late David Ker, Esq., of Portavo, co. Down. Is a J.P. and D.L. for co. Down; was formerly M.P. for Downpatrick.—*Finnebrogue, Downpatrick.*

MAXWELL, ROBERT, Esq., of Islanmore, co. Limerick.
Eldest son of the late Robert Maxwell, Esq., of Islanmore, by Catherine, dau. of Sir Richard Harte, of Coolrus; *b.* 1804; *s.* 1834; *m.* 1st 1835 Lady Lucy, dau. of Richard, 2nd Earl of Clancarty (she *d.* 1839); 2nd 1842 Elizabeth Catherine, dau. of Hugh Lyons Montgomery, Esq., of Belhavil, co. Leitrim, and widow of Joseph May, Esq., of Hale Park, Hants, and has by the former, with other issue,

* Robert James, Capt. 80th Regt.; *b.* 1837.

Mr. Maxwell, who was educated at Trinity Coll., Dublin (B.A. 1823, M.A. 1827), is a Magistrate for co. Cork, and a J.P. and D.L. for co. Limerick (High Sheriff 1843).—*Islanmore, Croom, co. Limerick; Kildare Street Club, Dublin; Carlton Club, s.w.*

MAXWELL, WELLWOOD HERRIES, Esq., of Munches, Stewartry of Kirkcudbright.
Eldest son of the late John Herries Maxwell, Esq., of Munches, by Clementina, dau. of William Maxwell, Esq. (who was 2nd son of John Maxwell, of Terraughtie); *b.* 1817; *s.* his mother 1858; *m.* 1844 Jane Home, eldest dau. of Sir William Jardine, Bart., of Applegarth, and has, with other issue,

* William Jardine, *b.* 1852.

Mr. Maxwell, who was educated at Edinburgh Academy and University, and Exeter Coll., Oxford, called to the Scottish Bar 1839, and appointed Convener of Commissioners of Supply of Stewartry of Kirkcudbright 1850, is a J.P. and D.L. for the Stewartry of Kirkcudbright; was elected M.P. for co. Kirkcudbright 1868.—*Munches, Dalbeattie, N.B.; Terraughtie, Dumfries, N.B.*

MAXWELL, Mrs., of Carruchan, Kirkcudbrightshire.
Mary, dau. of John Clark, Esq., of Speddoch, N.B., *m.* 1847 William Maxwell, Esq., of Carruchan, who was a J.P. and D.L. for the Stewartry of Kirkcudbright, a Magistrate for co. Dumfries, and representative of the Earls of Nithsdale (forfeited 1716), to whom he was served heir male in 1829. Mr. Maxwell *d.s.p.* 1863.—*Carruchan, Dumfries, N.B.*

MAXWELL, WILLIAM HALL-, Esq., of Dargavel, Renfrewshire.
Elder son of the late John Hall-Maxwell, Esq., C.B., J.P. and D.L., of Dargavel, by Anne, dau. of Thomas Williams, Esq., of Fairwood House, *b.* 1847; *s.* 1866. Represents two very old Renfrewshire families. Mr. Maxwell, of Dargavel, and H.H. of Pollur.—*Dargavel House, Bishopton, N.B.; Torr Hall, Weirbridge, Paisley.*

Heir Pres. his brother Edward, *b.* 1849.

MAXWELL.
(See under *Farnham, Lord.* and *Herries, Lord.*)

MAXWELL.   (See *Graham-Maxwell.*)

MAXWELL.   (See *Perceval-Maxwell.*)

MAXWELL.   (See *Stirling-Maxwell.*)

MAY, Sir THOMAS ERSKINE, K.C.B. (cr. 1866)
b. 1815; *m.* 1849 Louisa Johanna, only dau. of George
Laughton, Esq., of Fareham, Hants; called to the Bar
at the Middle Temple 1848. Is Clerk Assistant of the
House of Commons; author of 'A Treatise on the Law,
Privileges, Proceedings, and Usage of Parliament,' of
'The Constitutional History of England since the Ac-
cession of George III., 1760-1860,' and other works;
was formerly Examiner of Standing Orders to both
Houses of Parliament, and Taxing-Master of the House
of Commons.—*Athenæum and Union Clubs*, s.w.; 60,
Chester Square, s.w.

MAYBERRY, GEORGE, Esq., M.D., of Rivers-
dale, co. Kerry.
Fourth son of the late John Mayberry, Esq., J.P., of
Green Lane, co. Kerry, by Honora, dau. of Daniel
Mahony, Esq., of Emelickmore, co. Kerry; *b.* 1814; *m.*
1840 Ursula, dau. of Francis Chute McGillycuddy,
Esq., of Tralee, and has, with other issue,

   * Francis, *b.* 1847.

Mr. Mayberry, who was educated at Dublin and in Scotland (M.D. 1838), is a Magistrate for co. Kerry.—*Riversdale, Kenmare, co. Kerry.*

MAYBERRY, WALTER, Esq., of Brecon.
Eldest son of the late Thomas Maybery, Esq., of Brecon, by Elizabeth, dau. of the Rev. Richard Davies,
Vicar of Brecon; *b.* 1800; *s.* 1829; *m.* 1858 Diana
Middleton, eldest dau. of the late Rev. Samuel Phillips,
Rector of Pickwell, co. Leicester. Educated at Rugby;
appointed Prothonotary of the Brecon Circuit 1822; is
a Magistrate for co. Brecon (High Sheriff 1842).—*Brecon, South Wales.*

MAYD, the Rev. WILLIAM, of Withersfield,
Suffolk.
Only son of the late John Winslow Mayd, Esq., D.D.
(who *d.* 1848), by Harriet, dau. of Christopher Raven,
Esq., of Epsom, Surrey; *b.* 1797; *m.* 1827 Emily
Matilda, dau. of John Kemp Jardine, Esq., of Wixoe,
Suffolk, and has, with other issue,

   * John George Duffield, *b.* 1828.

Mr. Mayd, who was educated at Eton and Exeter
Coll., Oxford (B.A. 1821, M.A. 1822), was appointed
Vicar of Ewell, Surrey, 1824, and Rector of Withersfield 1827, is a Magistrate for Suffolk, a Surrogate for
the Archdeaconry of Sudbury, and Rural Dean of Clare;
is also Lord of the Manor and Patron of Withersfield.
—*Withersfield Rectory, Haverhill.*

MAYNARD, EDMUND GILLING, Esq., of Chesterfield, Derbyshire.
Fourth son of the late John Maynard, Esq., of Eyre-
holme, co. York, by Elizabeth, dau. and co.-heir of
Edmund Gilling, Esq., of Marton-le-Moor, co. York;
b. 1793; *m.* 1st 1826 Elizabeth, eldest dau. of the late
Robert Waller, Esq., of Chesterfield, but has no surviving issue; 2nd 1848 Ann, eldest dau. of John Jell,
Esq., of Dover, and has, with other issue,

   * Edmund, *b.* 1851.

Mr. Maynard, who is a J.P. and D.L. for co. Derby,
represents a younger branch of the Maynards of Harlsey
Hall, co. York.—*Chesterfield, Derbyshire.*

+**MAYNARD**, JOHN CHARLES, Esq., of Harlsey
Hall, Yorkshire.
Eldest son of the late John Lax, Esq., by Elizabeth,
dau. of Edmund Gilling, Esq.; *b.* 1788; *s.* his uncle,
Anthony Lax Maynard, Esq. (whose name he has as-
sumed), in 1825; *m.* 1815 Catherine Grace, dau. of

648

John Easterby, Esq., of Skiningrove, co. York, and by
her, who *d.* 1858, has, with other issue,

   * Anthony Lax, *b.* 1814.

Mr. Maynard is Lord of the Manor and Patron of
Harlsey.—*Harlsey Hall, Northallerton.*

MAYNARD, Miss, of Easton Lodge, Essex.
Frances Evelyn, elder dau. of the late Hon. Charles
Henry Maynard (who *d.* 1865), by his 2nd wife Blanche
Adeliza, 2nd dau. of Henry Fitz-Roy, Esq., of Salcey
Lawn, co. Northampton, and grand-dau. of Charles, 3rd
and last Viscount Maynard (ext.); *s.* her grandfather
1865. Is Lady of the Manor of Easton, &c., and
Patron of 6 livings. The estate of Easton was inherited
by William Maynard, Esq., who was created a Baronet
in 1611, and Lord Maynard of the United Kingdom
1628.—*Easton Lodge, Dunmow, Essex.*

   Heir Pres., her sister Blanche.

MAYNE, Sir RICHARD, K.C.B. (cr. 1851).
Son of the late Hon. Edward Mayne, a Judge of the
King's Bench in Ireland; *b.* 1796; *m.* 1831 Georgina,
dau. of Thomas Carrick, Esq., of Wyke, co. York, and
has, with other issue,

   * Richard Charles, Commander R.N., *b.* 1835.

Sir Richard, who was educated at Trinity Coll., Dublin,
and at Trinity Coll., Cambridge (B.A. 1817, M.A.
1821), and called to the Bar at Lincoln's Inn 1822,
was appointed Chief Commissioner of the Metropolitan
Police 1829.—4, *Whitehall Place*, s.w.; 80, *Chester
Square*, s.w.

MAYNE, Mrs., of Teffont, Wiltshire.
Sarah Frances, eldest dau. of the late John Start, Esq.,
of Halsted, Essex; *m.* 1819 John Thomas Mayne, Esq.,
J.P. and D.L., of Teffont Manor, who *d.* 1843, leaving
issue three daughters, Emily Harriette, *m.* 1859 to
Count Fane De Salis, of Dawley Court (whom see);
Margaret Hele, and Ellen Flora, *m.* to Maurice, eldest
son of the Right Hon. Richard Keatinge, Judge of the
Court of Probate, Ireland. Mrs. Mayne is Lady of the
Manor and Patron of Teffont Ewyas.—*Teffont, Salisbury.*

MAYNE, RICHARD, Esq., of Glynch House, co.
Monaghan.
Eldest son of the late William Mayne, Esq., of Freame
Mount, co. Monaghan, by Harriet, dau. of Rowland
Rochfort, Esq., of Westmeath; *b.* 1800; *m.* 1835 Louisa,
dau. of Charles Coote, Esq., of Bellamont Forest, and
has, with other issue,

   * William Dawson, *b.* 1840.

Mr. Mayne, who is a Magistrate for cos. Monaghan
and Cavan, represents an old Kentish family.—*Glynch
House, Newbliss, co. Monaghan; Martello Terrace,
Kingstown, Dublin.*

MAYNE, WILLIAM, Esq., of Rahaghey, co.
Tyrone.
Eldest son of the late Nathaniel Mayne Esq., of
Rahaghey, by Elizabeth, 2nd dau. of James Newell,
Esq., of Castle Hill, co. Down; *b.* 1832; *s.* 1865; *m.*
1858 Edith Caroline, only child of Henry Talbot, Esq.,
of Oakland, co. Worcester, and has issue.

   * William Henry Talbot, *b.* 1861.

Mr. Mayne, who was educated at Trinity Coll., Dublin,
is a Magistrate for co. Tyrone, and late Capt. 10th
Hussars. This family came from Scotland, and have
been settled at Rahaghey since 1673.—*Rahaghey,
Aughnacloy, co. Tyrone.*

MAYNE, WILLIAM HENN, Esq., of Killaloe, co.
Clare.
Eldest son of the Rev. Charles Mayne, Vicar-General
of the Diocese of Cashel, by Susan, dau. of the late
William Henn, Esq., Master in Chancery in Ireland;
b. 1816; *m.* 1851 Elizabeth Amelia, dau. of the late

Thomas Murray, Esq., of Edenderry, King's Co., and has issue,

* Margaret Caroline and Susan Edith.

Mr. Mayne, who was educated at Trinity Coll., Dublin (B.A. 1838), is a Magistrate for co. Clare.—*Killaloe, co. Clare.*

MAYO, Earl of (RICHARD SOUTHWELL BOURKE). —Cr. 1785.

Eldest son of Robert, 5th Earl, by Anne Charlotte, dau. of the late Hon. John Jocelyn, of Fairhill, co. Louth; *b.* 1822; *s.* 1847; *m.* 1848 Blanche Julia, 3rd dau. of George, 1st Lord Leconfield. Educated at Trinity Coll., Dublin (M.A. 1844); is a J.P. and D.L. for co. Kildare; was Chief Secretary for Ireland March–Dec. 1852, and 1858-9; re-appointed 1866; M.P. for co. Kildare 1847-52, for Coleraine 1852-7; has been M.P. for Cockermouth since that time.—*Palmerston Lodge, Naas, co. Mayo ; Carlton, Travellers', and White's Clubs, s.w. ; 8, Queen Street, w.*

Heir, his son Dermot Robert Wyndham, Lord Naas, *b.* 1851.

MAYO, WILLIAM HERBERT, Esq., of Cheshunt, Herts.

Eldest son of the late Pagger William Mayo, M.D., of Bridlington, co. York, by Charlotte, dau. of the Rev. Stephen Buckle, LL.D., Rector of St. Mary Coslany, and St. Peter's, Norwich; *b.* 1799; *s.* his uncle; the Rev. Charles Mayo, of Cheshunt Park, 1859. Is Lord of the Manor of Andrew Le Mote, Cheshunt.—*Cheshunt Park, Herts.*

Heir Pres., his brother Herbert Mayo, Esq., *b.* 1802; *m.* 1830 Sarah, dau. of Ezekiel Harman, Esq., of Theobald's, Cheshunt, and has, with other issue, * Herbert Harman, *b.* 1831.

MAYOW, Col. GEORGE WYNELL, of Bray, Cornwall.

Eldest son of the late Philip Wynell Mayow, Esq., of Bray, Cornwall, and Hanworth Hall, Norfolk, by Elizabeth, dau. of Col. Charles Doare; *b.* 1808; *s.* 1844; *m.* 1842 Jane Elizabeth, dau. of the late Right Rev. Samuel Kyle, D.D., Lord Bishop of Cork (she *d. s. p.* 1848). Entered the Army 1825, and is a Col. in the Army ; was formerly a Capt. in the Dragoons ; served in the Crimea 1854-6 as Brigade-Major to the Light Cavalry Brigade, and appointed Quartermaster-General of the Cavalry Division.—*Bray, Morval, Liskeard.*

MAYSON, JOHN SCHOFIELD, Esq., of Fallowfield, Manchester, Lancashire.

Only son of the late John Mayson, Esq., J.P., of Manchester, by Alice, dau. of John Schofield, Esq., sometime of Manchester; *b.* 1824; *m.* 1849 Elizabeth, dau. of Charles Simpson, Esq., of Motley Bank, Bowdon, co. Chester. Mr. Mayson was educated at Manchester, is a Magistrate for co. Lancaster, and a Merchant at Manchester, was formerly Capt. 40th Lancashire Rifle Volunteers. — *Oakhill, Fallowfield, Manchester ; Union Club, Manchester.*

MAZE, PETER, Esq.

Only surviving son of the late Peter Maze, Esq.; *m.* 1828 Charlotte Anne, dau. of James Gordon, Esq., of London, and has issue,

* Charlotte Emma, *m.* 1855 W. J. Blackburne-Maze, Esq. (whom see).

Mr. Maze, who was one of the Sheriffs for the city and co. of Bristol 1833-4, and High Sheriff 1848-9, was formerly Capt. N. Somerset Yeomanry, and Master of the Guild of Merchant Venturers.—Residence : *Clifton ; Carlton Club,* s.w.; 12, *Portland Place,* w.

MAZE. (See *Blackburne-Maze.*)

MEADE, the Rev. JOHN, of Ballintober, co. Cork.

Eldest son of the late John Meade, Esq., of Ballintober, by Alice, dau. of the Ven. Archdeacon Corker, of Ballymaloe and Glanmire, co. Cork ; *b.* 1792; *s.* 1817 ; *m.* 1831 Sarah, dau. of G. P. Wood, Esq., and has issue,

* John, *b.* 1833.

Mr. Meade, who was educated at Trinity Coll., Dublin (B.A. 1813), is a Magistrate for co. Cork.—*Ballintober, Kinsale, co. Cork ; Kildare Street Club, Dublin.*

+**MEADE, JOHN,** Esq., of Burrenwood, Downshire.

Son of the late J. Meade, Esq., of Burrenwood; *b.* 18—. Is a J.P. and D.L. for co. Down.—*Burrenwood, Castlewellan, Downshire.*

MEADE. (See under *Clanwilliam, Earl of.*)

MEADE-KING, RICHARD KING, Esq., of Walford House, Somerset.

Eldest son of the late Richard Meade-King, Esq., J.P. and D.L., of Pyrland Hall, Somerset (who was High Sheriff of Somerset in 1846), by Elizabella, only dau. of John Warren, Esq., M.D., of Taunton ; *b.* 1846 ; *s.* 1866; *m.* 1831 Catherine, dau. of the late William Oliver, Esq., and has, with other issue,

* Richard, a Magistrate for Somerset, *b.* 1831 ; *m.* 1862 Flora Evelyn, eldest dau. of the Rev. William C. Kinglake, of West Monckton, Somerset.

Mr. Meade-King is a J.P. and D.L. for Somerset, and Patron of 1 living.—*Walford House, Taunton.*

MEAGHER, FRANCIS O'CARROLL, Esq., of Ballinderry House, co. Tipperary.

Only son of the late Francis Meagher, Esq., of Dublin, Barrister-at-Law, by Kate, dau. of Thomas Neville Bagot, Esq., of Ballymoe, co. Galway; *b.* 1853 ; *s.* 1853. Is a lineal descendant of the Lords of Ikerrin.—*Ballinderry House, Borrisokane, co. Tipperary.*

Heir Pres., his sister Ellen.

MEAGHER, THOMAS, Esq., of Waterford.

Son of the late Thomas Meagher, Esq., of Waterford ; *b.* 1796; *m.* 182- Alice Mary, dau. of Thomas Quair, Esq., Merchant, of Waterford, and has, with other surviving issue,

* Henry, a Magistrate for co. Waterford (High Sheriff 1867), and Capt. Waterford Militia ; *b.* 182- ; *m.* 1857 Marian Olivia, 2nd dau. of Francis Murphy, Esq., of Kilcairne House, co. Meath (whom see).

Mr. Meagher, who is a Magistrate for the City of Waterford, was Mayor of Waterford 1813-4, and M.P. for that City 1847-57.—*The Mall, Waterford.*

MEALY, the Rev. RICHARD RIDGEWAY PARRY-, of Perfeddgoed, Carnarvonshire.

Only child of the late Rev. Pierce Owen Mealy, of Perfeddgoed, by Susannah, dau. of Richard Burnett, Esq., of Dublin; *b.* 1801; *s.* 1801. Educated at St. John's Coll., Oxford (B.A. 1846, M.A. 1877); is a J.P. and D.L. for co. Carnarvon ; was formerly Curate of Windsor.—*Perfeddgoed, Bangor ; Residence : Tanycoed, Menai Bridge, Bangor.*

MEARES. (See *Devenish-Meares.*)

+**MEASON, MAGNUS GEORGE LAING,** Esq., of Lindertis, co. Forfar.

Son of the late Magnus Meason, Esq., of Lindertis ; *b.* 18—; *m.* 1846 Eliza, widow of the Hon. Lieut.-Col. George B. Molyneux, of Seafield Lodge, Hove, Sussex. —*Lindertis, Kirriemuir, Forfarshire.*

619

MEATH, Earl of (WILLIAM BRABAZON).—Cr. 1627.

Eldest surviving son of John Chambré, 10th Earl, by Lady Melosina Adelaide, 4th dau. of John, 1st Earl of Clanwilliam: b. 1803; s. 1851; m. 1837 Harriet, 2nd dau. of Sir Richard Brooke, Bart. Educated at Eton; sits in the House of Lords as Lord Chaworth, U.K. (cr. 1831); is a J.P. and D.L. for co. Dublin, Lord Lieut. of co. Wicklow (High Sheriff 1848), and Col. of the Dublin Militia; was M.P. for co. Dublin 1837–41.—*Kilruddery House, Bray, co. Wicklow; Eaton Court, Ledbury; 43, Brook Street, w.*

Heir, his son Reginald, Lord Brabazon, a Third Sec. in H.M.'s Diplomatic Service; b 1841; m. 1868 Lady Mary Jane, only dau. of Thomas, 11th Earl of Lauderdale.

MEATH, Bishop of (the Rt. Hon. and Most Rev. SAMUEL BUTCHER, D.D., P.C.)

Second son of the late Vice-Admiral Butcher, R.N., by Elizabeth Anne, dau. of Richard T. Herbert, Esq., of Killarney; b. 1811; m. 1847 Mary, 2nd dau. of John Leahy, Esq., of Killarney, co. Kerry. Educated at Trinity Coll., Dublin; became Scholar 1832, Fellow 1837, Professor of Ecclesiastical History 1850, Regius Professor of Divinity 1852; consecrated 1866. Is a P.C. in Ireland, and Premier Bishop. Patron of 24 livings.—*Ardbraccan House, Navan, co. Meath; 40, Fitzwilliam Square, Dublin.*

MECHI, JOHN JOSEPH, Esq., of Tiptree Hall, Essex.

Eldest son of the late James Mechi, of Bologna, Italy, by Elizabeth, dau. of J. Beyor, of Poland Street, London; b. 1802; m. 1st 1823 Fanny, dau. of Mr. Frost; 2nd 1846 Charlotte, dau. of Mr. Francis Ward, of Chillesford, Suffolk, and has, with other issue,

* Joseph, b. 1853.

Mr. Mechi is a Magistrate for Middlesex, and a Dep.-Lieut. for London; elected Sheriff of the City of London 1856; was an Alderman of London 1858–66.—*Tiptree Hall, Kelvedon, Essex; 112, Regent Street, w.*

MEDHURST, FRANCIS WILLIAM HASTINGS, Esq., of Kippax Hall, co. York.

Eldest son of the late Francis Hastings Medhurst, Esq., of Kippax Hall, by Mary Anne, dau. of C. O. Bushman, Esq., of London; b. 1844; s. 1852; educated at the Charterhouse and the Royal Military Coll., Woolwich; is a Capt. R.A. and Lord of the Manor of Kippax.—*Kippax Hall, Leeds.*

Heir Pres., his brother Arthur, b. 1853.

MEDHURST (See *Wheeler*.)

MEDLICOTT, EDWARD JAMES, Esq., of Dunmurry, co. Kildare.

Eldest son of the late James Medlicott, Esq., of Dunmurry, by Mary, dau. of Thomas Graydon, Esq., of Greenhills, co. Kildare; b. 1791; s. 1827; m. 1827 Anne, dau. of Solomon Speer, Esq., of Granitefield, co. Dublin, and by her, who d. 1866, has, with other issue,

* James Edward, a Magistrate for co. Kildare; b. 1827; m. 1858 Margaret, dau. of Joshua Henry Peckson, Sc t. M.D., of Edinburgh, and has, with other issue, • Henry Edward, b. 1853.

Mr. Medlicott is a Magistrate for co. Kildare.—*Dunmurry, Kildare; Royal Terrace, Kingstown, Dublin.*

MEDLYCOTT, Sir WILLIAM COLES, Bart., D.C.L., of Ven House, Somerset (cr. 1808).

Eldest son of the late Sir William Coles Medlycott, Bart., of Ven House, by Elizabeth, dau. of William Tugwell, Esq., of Bradford, Wilts; b. 1806; s. as 2nd Bart. 1835; m. 1830 Sarah Jeffrey, dau. of the Rev. Edward Bradford, Rector of Stalbridge, Dorset. Educated at Trinity Coll., Oxford; created D.C.L., Oxon. 1810; is a J.P. and D.L. for Dorset (High Sheriff 1839), (610)

a Magistrate for Somerset, and Patron of 1 living.—*Ven House, Milborne Port.*

Heir, his son William Coles Paget, b. 1831.

MEDLYCOTT, the Rev. JOHN THOMAS, of Rocket's Castle, co. Waterford.

Son of the late John Thomas Medlycott, Esq.: b. 17—; m. 1820 Mary, eldest dau. of the late Ambrose Usher Congreve, Esq., of Mount Congreve, co. Waterford, and has, with other issue, an only son,

* John Thomas, a Magistrate for co. Waterford; b. 1822; m. 1867 Florence Caroline, youngest dau. of Sir William Coles Medlycott, Bart., and by her, who d. 1868, has issue, • a son, b. 1868.

Mr. Medlycott, who was educated at Trinity Coll., Dublin, is a Magistrate for co. Waterford.—*Rocket's Castle, Portlaw, co. Waterford.*

MEEK, GEORGE, Esq., of Brantridge, Sussex.

Only son of the late George Meek, Esq., of Brantridge Park, by Amelia, dau. of the late Samuel Weston, Esq., of Weymouth, Dorset; b. 1827; s. 1852; m. 1858 Fanny Amelia, only dau. of the late Josiah Wilson, Esq., of Stamford Hill, Middlesex, by whom he has issue,

* Two daughters.

Mr. Meek, who was educated at Trinity Coll., Cambridge (B.A. 1850, M.A. 1854), and called to the Bar at the Inner Temple 1853, is a J.P. and D.L. for Sussex, and Capt. Commandant of the 2nd Sussex Volunteers, Esq., was formerly Capt. Sussex Militia.—*Brantridge Park, Balcombe, Sussex; Oxford and Cambridge Clubs, s.w.*

+**MEEKING**, CHARLES, Esq., of Richings Park, Bucks.

Son of the late C. Meeking, Esq., of London; b. 180-; m. 1830 Charlotte, dau. of the Rev. — Williams, and has, with other issue, an only son,

* Charles, educated at Trinity Coll., Cambridge; b. 1832; m. 1861 Adelaide Caroline, 4th dau. of Christopher Tower, Esq., of Huntsmore Park, Bucks, and has, with other issue, • Charles, b. 1865.

Mr. Meeking is a Magistrate for Bucks, Lord of the Manor of Richings, and Patron of 2 livings. He purchased the estate and Manor of Richings in 1855, from John Sullivan, Esq.—*Richings Park, Colnbrook; 56, Chester Square, s.w.*

MEEKINS, ROBERT, Esq., of Glasthule, co. Dublin.

Only son of the late Richard Meekins, Esq., by Maria, only child and heir of Thomas Mossom, Esq., M.A. of the Middle Temple Barrister-at-Law; b. posthumous 1790; m. 1820 Elizabeth, only dau. and eventually heir of R. Christmas, Esq., of the 14th Light Dragoons, and has, with other issue,

* Thomas, D.C.L., LL.B., F.S.A., of the Inner Temple, Barrister-at-Law (who has assumed the ancient spelling of the family surname De Meschin); b. 1822.

This family descend from the De Meschines, who were Earls of Chester, Cambridge, Carlisle, and Lincoln, in the 11th–13th centuries.— *Glasthule House, co. Dublin.*

MEETKERKE, ADOLPHUS, Esq., of Julians, Herts.

Eldest son of the late Adolphus Meetkerke, Esq., of Julians, by Matilda, dau. of Robert Wilkinson, Esq.; b. 1819; s. 1840; m. 1st 1811 Maria Henrietta, dau. of Geneva, Hare (she d. 1817); 2nd 1848 Cecilia Elizabeth, dau. of the Hon. Edward Gore, and has issue by the former, two daughters.

* Mary Florence and Cecilia Laura.

Mr. Meetkerke, who was educated at Eton and Trinity Coll., Cambridge, is a Magistrate for Herts, and Lord of the Manor of Baldock; he was formerly Capt. Herts Militia.—*Julians, Buntingford.*

+ MEIGH, WILLIAM MELLOR, Esq., of Ash Hall, Staffordshire.

Eldest son of the late Job Meigh, Esq., of Ash Hall (who was a J.P. and D.L. for co. Stafford), by Mary, dau. of — Mellor, Esq.; *b.* 180—; *s.* 1862; *m.* 1837 Eliza, dau. of S. Goodman, Esq. Is a Magistrate for co. Stafford.—*Ash Hall, Hanley.*

+ MELDRUM, DAVID, Esq., of Kincaple, Fife-shire.

Eldest son of the late Alexander Meldrum, Esq., of Kincaple, by Elizabeth, youngest dau. of the late Charles Maitland, Esq., of Rankeilour, N.B.; *b.* 18—; *s.* 1866. Is a Magistrate for co. Fife and Lord of the Barony of Kincaple.—*Kincaple House, St. Andrew's.*

MELGUND. (See under *Minto, Earl of.*)

MELHUISH, JOHN JAMES, Esq., of Green Mount, Devonshire.

Eldest son of the late William Melhuish, Esq., of St. Austell, Cornwall, by Elizabeth, dau. of William Webb, Esq., of Lonnon, co. Glamorgan; *b.* 1810; *m.* 1837 Anne Willet, dau. of Hill Cox, Esq., of Great Barr, co. Stafford. Is a Magistrate for Devon. This family descended from a common ancestor with the Melhuishes of Court Barn (whom see).—*Green Mount, Salcombe Regis, Sidmouth.*

MELHUISH, WALTER WILLIAM, Esq., of Court Barn, Devon.

Younger and only surviving son of the late Rev. Thomas Melhuish, Rector of Ashwater, Devon, by Elizabeth, dau. of the late Rev. Richard Walter, Rector of Parkham, Devon; *b.* 1820; *m.* 1849 Mary, eldest dau. of John Vowler, Esq., of Parnacott, Devon, and has, with other issue,

　　* George Douglas, *b.* 1856.

Mr. Melhuish, who was educated at Tiverton and Magdalen Hall, Oxford (B.A. 1842), is a Magistrate for Devon and Patron of 2 livings.—*Court Barn, Clawton, Holsworthy.*

MELLIAR. (See *Foster-Melliar.*)

MELLIS-NAIRNE. (See *Nairne.*)

MELLER, WALTER, Esq., of Broadlands, Surrey.

Youngest son of the late Thomas William Meller, Esq., D.L., of Denmark Hill, Surrey, by Sarah, dau. of John Thomas, Esq., of Sydenham, Kent; *b.* 1818; *m.* 1845 Elizabeth, youngest dau. of Thomas Peters, Esq., of Kilburn Grange; is a J.P. and D.L. for the Tower Hamlets; late Captain-Commandant 1st Surrey Light Horse Volunteers; elected M.P. for Stafford 1865. —*Broadlands, Clapham, s.; Junior Carlton, Royal Thames Yacht, and British Service Clubs, s.w.*

MELLISH, Miss, of Hamels Park, Herts.

Catherine, only child of the late John Mellish, Esq., of Hamels Park, by Charlotte, dau. of the late — Pinfold, Esq.; *s.* 1866. This family was formerly of Blyth, Notts.—*Hamels Park, Puckeridge, Ware; 1, Great Stanhope Street, w.*

MELLISH, Mrs., of Hodsock Priory, Notts.

Margaret, 2nd dau. of the late Sir Samuel Canaad, Bart., by Susan, dau. of William Duffus, Esq., of Halifax, N. Scotia; *m.* 1843 William Leigh Mellish, Esq., of Hodsock Priory, who *d.* 1864, leaving, with other issue,

　　* Henry, *b.* 1856.

The late Mr. Mellish was a Magistrate for Notts and Lieut.-Col. Notts Militia. This family was formerly of Blyth, Notts.—*Hodsock Priory, Worksop.*

MELLOR, Sir JOHN, of Otterhead, Devon (cr. 1862).

Son of the late John Mellor, Esq., of Leicester (who *d.* 1861); *b.* 1809; *m.* 1833 Elizabeth, dau. of the late William Moseley, Esq., and has, with other issue,

　　* John William, Barrister-at-Law, of the Inner Temple; *b.* 1835; *m.* 1860 Caroline, 4th dau. of Charles Paget, Esq., of Ruddington Grange, co. Leicester.

Sir John, who was educated at Leicester. and called to the Bar of the Inner Temple 1833, was a Barrister of the Midland Circuit, a Bencher of the Inner Temple, and Recorder of Leicester; became a Q.C. 1851; was M.P. for Yarmouth 1857, and for Nottingham 1859–61; appointed a Judge of the Queen's Bench 1861.—*Otterhead House, Church Stanton, Devon; Athenæum Club, s.w.; 16, Sussex Square, w.*

MELLY, GEORGE, Esq., of Liverpool, Lancashire.

Second son of the late Andrew Melly, Esq., of Liverpool, by Ellen, dau. of Samuel Greg, Esq., of Manchester; *b.* 1830; *m.* 1852 Sarah Elizabeth Mesnard, dau. of Samuel Bright, Esq., of Liverpool; educated at Rugby; is a Merchant at Liverpool; elected M.P. for Stoke-upon-Trent 1868.—*Abercromby Square, Liverpool; Reform Club, s.w.; 1, Queen's Gate Place, w.*

MELVILL, Sir PETER MELVILL, K.C.B. (cr. 1860).

Fourth and youngest son of the late Capt. Philip Melvill, of the 73rd Foot, Lieut.-Governor of Pendennis Castle, Falmouth, by Elizabeth Carey, 3rd and youngest dau. of Peter Dobree, Esq., of Beauregard, Guernsey; *b.* 1803; *m.* 1836 Catherine Mary, dau. of John Robertson, Esq., of Tweedmouth, Berwick-on-Tweed. Late Military and Naval Secretary to the Government of Bombay; is a Major-General in the Bombay Army, retired.—*United Service Club, s.w.*

MELVILLE, Viscount (HENRY DUNDAS, G.C.B.). —Cr. 1802.

Eldest son of Robert, 2nd Viscount, by Anne, dau. of the late Richard Huck-Saunders, Esq., M.D.; *b.* 1801; *s.* 1851. Is a J.P. and D.L. for Midlothian, a Magistrate for co. Perth, and Patron of 1 living; a General in the Army, General in command in Scotland. Col. 32nd Foot, and Governor of Edinburgh Castle; was appointed Col.-Commandant 60th Rifles 1863; late Lieut.-Col. 60th Rifles; was formerly of the 83rd Foot; has been A.D.C. to the Queen; served in Canada and India.—*Melville Castle, Edinburgh; Travellers' and United Service Clubs, s.w.; New Club, Edinburgh; 7, Portugal Street, w.*

Heir Pres., his brother Robert, Storekeeper-General of the Navy; *b.* 1803.

MELVILLE, JAMES MONCRIEFF, Esq., of Hanley, Midlothian.

Son of the late Dr. Melville (who *d.* 1825), by Janet, dau. of William Lindesay, Esq., of Feddinch; *b.* 1793; *m.* 1st 1832 Augusta, dau. of the late Vice-Admiral Lechmere of Steeple Aston, Oxon (she *d.* 1837); 2nd 1839 Margaret, dau. of [...]; is a Magistrate for Midlothian, and a Writer to the Signet.—*Hanley, Corstorphine, Edinburgh, N.B.; 116, George Street, Edinburgh.*

MELVILLE. (See *Leslie-Melville.*)

MELVILLE. (See *Whyte-Melville.*)

MENTETH, Sir JAMES STUART-, Bart., of Closeburn and Mansfield, Ayrshire (cr. 1838).

Eldest son of the late Sir Charles Granville Stuart-Menteth, Bart., by Ludivina, dau. of Thomas Loughnan,

Esq., of Madeira; *b.* 1792 ; *s.* as 2nd Bart. 1847 ; *m.* 1846 Jane, dau. of the late Sir Joseph Bailey, Bart., M.P. Educated at Rugby and Brasenose Coll., Oxford ; is a J.P. and D.L. for co. Dumfries, and representative of the Stuarts, Earls of Menteth, which title was forfeited by James I. of Scotland.—*Mansfield House, Cumnock, N.B.*

Heir Pres., his nephew James Stuart (son of his late brother Thomas Loughnan, who *d.* 1854, by a dau. of — Tobin, Esq.), late of the 17th Lancers.

MENZIES, Sir ROBERT, Bart., of Menzies, Perthshire (cr. 1666).
Eldest son of the late Lieut.-Col. Sir Neil Menzies, Bart., of Menzies, by the Hon. Grace Charlotte Conyers, dau. of the late Hon. Fletcher Norton, Baron of the Court of Exchequer in Scotland, and sister of Fletcher, 3rd Lord Grantley ; *b.* 1817 ; *s.* as 7th Bart 1844 ; *m.* 1846 Annie Balcarres, dau. of Major James Alston-Stewart, of Urrard. Educated at University Coll., Oxford (S.C.L. 1842) ; is a J.P. and D.L. for co. Perth, Capt. Perthshire Rifles, and chief of the Clan Menzies. —*Castle Menzies, Dunkeld, N.B* ; 10, *Wilton Place*, s.w.

Heir, his son Neil James, *b.* 1856.

MENZIES, Sir CHARLES, K.C.B., K.H. (cr. 1865).
Son of the late Capt. Menzies, 71st Highlanders, by Sarah, dau. of Dr. Walker ; *b.* 1783 ; *m.* 1820 Maria, dau. of Dr. Bryant. Educated at Stirling, N.B.; entered the Army 1793, and became a General 1857 ; is in command of the Royal Marine Artillery.—*Hastings.*

MENZIES, the Hon. Lady, of Rannoch, Perthshire.
Grace Conyers Charlotte, eldest dau. of the late Hon. Fletcher Norton, by Caroline Elizabeth, only dau. of James Balmain, Esq., and sister of Fletcher, 3rd Lord Grantley ; *m.* 1816 Sir Neil Menzies, Bart., who *d.* 1844.—*Rannoch Lodge, Pitlochry, N.B. ; Abbey Hill, Edinburgh.*

MENZIES, RANALD STEUART-, Esq., of Culdares and Cardney, Perthshire.
Eldest son of the late Ranald Steuart-Menzies, Esq., by Mary, dau. of the late John Steuart-Menzies, Esq., of Culdares ; *b.* 1824 ; *s.* 1828 ; *m.* 1849 Margery, dau. of the late William Macdowall Grant, Esq., of Arndilly, and has, with other issue,

* Ranald, *b.* 1858.

Mr. Steuart-Menzies, who was educated at Ch. Ch., Oxford, is a Magistrate for co. Perth.—*Meggernie Castle, Culdares, Glenlyon, N.B.*

MERCER-HENDERSON, GEORGE WILLIAM, Esq., of Fordell House, Fifeshire.
Eldest son of the late Lieut.-General Douglas Mercer, of Fordell (who assumed the additional name of Henderson), by Susan Arabella, dau. of the late Sir William Rowley, Bart., of Tendring Hall, Suffolk ; *b.* 1823 ; *s.* 1854 ; *m.* 1868 Alice Jane, eldest surviving dau. of the Hon. Bouverie Francis Primrose. Is a J.P. and D.L. for co. Fife ; was formerly Capt. Scots Fusilier Guards. — *Fordell House, Inverkeithing, N.B.* ; 103, *Eaton Square*, s.w.

Heir Pres., his sister Jane, *m.* 1851 Sir James Clerk, Bart., of Penicuik, Midlothian (whom see).

MEREDITH, Lord. (See *Athlumney.*)

+**MEREDITH, HENRY WARTER-, Esq., of Pentrebychan Hall, Denbighshire.**
Son of the late Joseph Warter, Esq., of Sibberscot, co. Salop, by Margaret, sister of the late Thomas Meredith, Esq., M.D., of Pentrebychan, whose name he assumed, by Royal licence, in 1821 ; *b.* 17— ; *m.* 1821 Elizabeth,

652

only dau. of Mungo Park. Is a Magistrate for cos. Denbigh and Sutherland.—*Pentrebychan Hall, Wrexham ; Torrance, Wick, Sutherlandshire.*

MEREDITH, HERBERT WILLOUGHBY, Esq., of Cloonamahon, co. Sligo.
Only son of the late Thomas James Meredith, Esq., of Cloonamahon, by Sidney, only dau. of Willoughby Bond, Esq., of Farragh, co. Longford ; *b.* 1830 ; *s.* 1860. This family is of Welsh extraction.—*Cloonamahon, Collooney, co. Sligo.*

Heirs Pres., his sisters.

MEREDYTH, Sir EDWARD HENRY JOHN, Bart., of Madaleen House, co. Kilkenny (cr. 1660).
Only son of the late Sir Edward Newenham Meredyth, Bart., of Madaleen, by his 1st wife, Lucretia, dau. of Samuel Holmes, Esq., of Keady, co. Armagh ; *b.* 1828 ; *s.* as 10th Bart. 1865 ; *m.* 1861 Agnes Margaret, dau. of the Rev. Pierce William Drew, Rector of Youghall, co. Cork. Is a Magistrate for co. Kilkenny, late Capt. 87th Foot.—*Madaleen House, Jenkinstown, co. Kilkenny.*

Heir, his son Edward Paul, *b.* 1865.

MEREDYTH, Sir HENRY, Bart., of Carlanstown, co. Meath (cr. 1795).
Only son of the late Sir Henry Meredyth, Bart., Q.C. (sometime Judge of the Admiralty in Ireland), by Edith, dau. of George Le Hunte, Esq., of Artramont, co. Wexford ; *b.* 1801 ; *s.* as 4th Bart. 1859 ; *m.* 1828 Mary Anne, dau. of William E. M. Bayly, Esq., of Norelands, co. Kilkenny. Educated at Trinity Coll., Cambridge ; is a J.P. and D.L. for cos. Kilkenny and Meath (High Sheriff 1835).—*Thomastown, co. Kilkenny ; Kildare Street Club, Dublin ; Brooks's and University Clubs,* s.w.

Heir, his son Henry William (of Hollymount, co. Down, and Norelands, co. Kilkenny), late Lieut. 7th Hussars ; *b.* 1829 ; *m.* 1862 Harriet Anne, dau. of the late Rev. William and Lady Louisa Le Poer Trench, and has, with other issue, * Henry Bayly, *b.* 1863.

+**MEREWETHER, HENRY ALDWORTH, Esq., of Bowden Hill, Wiltshire.**
Eldest son of the late Henry Aldworth Merewether, Esq., D.C.L., Q.C., Serjeant-at-Law (who *d.* 1864) ; *b.* 1812 ; *m.* 1840 Maria, eldest dau. of the late Sir James Fellowes, of Adbury House, Hants, and has issue. Mr. Merewether, who was called to the Bar at the Inner Temple 1837, is a J.P. and D.L. for Wilts and Recorder of Devizes.—*Bowden Hill, Chippenham ; Carlton Club,* s.w. ; 1, *Johnson's Buildings, Temple,* E.C.

MERIVALE, the Rev. CHARLES.
Second son of the late John Herman Merivale, Esq., of Barton Place, Devon, by Louisa Heath, dau. of the Rev. Joseph Drury, D.D., of Cockwood House, Devon : *b.* 1808 ; *m.* 1850 Judith Mary Sophia, dau. of George Frere, Esq., of Twyford House, Herts. Educated at Harrow and St. John's Coll., Cambridge (B.A. 1830, M.A. 1833, B.D. 1840) ; is a Magistrate for Essex, and Rector of Lawford, Essex ; was formerly Fellow and Tutor of St. John's Coll., Cambridge.—*Lawford Rectory, Manningtree.*

MERIVALE, HERMAN, Esq., C.B.
Eldest son of the late John Herman Merivale, Esq., of Barton Place, Devon, by Louisa Heath, dau. of the Rev. Joseph Drury, D.D., of Cockwood House, Devon ; *b.* 1806 ; *m.* 1831 Caroline Penelope, dau. of the Rev. William Villiers Robinson, and has, with other issue,

* Herman Charles, *b.* 1839.

Mr. Merivale, who was educated at Harrow and Trinity Coll., Oxford (B.A. 1827, M.A. 1833), and was sometime Fellow of Balliol Coll., is Under-Secretary of State for India.—26, *Westbourne Terrace,* w.

MERRY, JAMES, Esq., of Belladrum, Inverness-shire.

Son of James Merry, Esq., of Glasgow, by Janet, dau. of William Crealman, Esq.; *b.* 1805; *m.* 1847 Ann, dau. of J. McHardy, Esq., of Glenboig, co. Lanark, and has, with other issue,

    ● Archibald William, *b.* 1851.

Mr. Merry, who was educated at Glasgow, is a J.P. and D.L. for co. Inverness, and Magistrate for co. Lanark; is an Ironmaster in Lanark and Ayrshire; was M.P. for Falkirk, &c., March–July 1857, re-elected 1859. —*Belladrum, Beauly, N.B.; Brooks's and Reform Clubs, s.w.; New Club, Edinburgh.*

MERRY, WILLIAM, Esq., of Highlands, Berks.

Only son of the late William Merry, Esq., of Highlands (who was many years Under-Secretary of State for the War Department), by Elizabeth, dau. of Charles Walker, Esq., of Huntingdon; *b.* 1792 ; *s.* 1855; *m.* 1820 Anne, 2nd dau. of the late Kender Mason, Esq., of Beel House, Bucks. Educated at Winchester; entered the War Office 1810; was Private Secretary to Viscount Palmerston 1812–28; is a Magistrate for Berks.—*Highlands, Reading.*

MERVYN-D'ARCY-IRVINE.
  (See *D'Arcy, of Necarn Castle.*)

+MESSENGER, JAMES BRYANT, Esq., of Heath House, Cornwall.

Son of the late James Messenger, Esq., of Heath House; *b.* 18—; is married, and has, with other issue,

    ● James Bryant (in Holy Orders). *b.* 18—; *m.* 1849 Susan Christiana, eldest dau. of Major Milles, of Filleigh House, near Chudleigh, Devon.

—*Heath House, Calstock, Cornwall.*

+MESSITER, THOMAS, Esq., of Barwick, Somerset.

Son of the late Geo. Messiter, Esq., of Barwick House; *b.* 1804. Educated at Eton; is a Magistrate for Somerset. Lord of the Manor of Barwick, and Patron of that living.—*Barwick House, Yeovil.*

METCALFE, Sir THEOPHILUS JOHN, Bart. (cr. 1802).

Eldest son of the late Sir Thomas Theophilus Metcalfe, Bart., of Fern Hill, Berks, by Félicité Anne, dau. of John Browne, Esq., of the Bengal Medical Board, and nephew of the late Charles, Lord Metcalfe; *b.* 1828 ; *s.* as 5th Bart. 1853; *m.* 1851 Charlotte, dau. of Col. John Lowe, C.B., of Chatto, co. Fife. Was formerly in the East-Indian Civil Service.

  Heir, his son Charles Herbert Theophilus, *b.* 1853.

METCALFE, CHARLES, Esq., of Inglethorpe Hall, Norfolk.

Eldest son of the late Charles Metcalfe, Esq., J.P., of Wisbech, by Elizabeth, dau. of William Skrimshire, Esq., D.L., of Wisbech; *b.* 1796; *s.* 1853; *m.* 1826 Mary, dau. of Morehouse Metcalfe, Esq., of Gainsborough, and has, with other issue,

    ● Frederic Morehouse, a Solicitor at Wisbech, and Clerk to the Magistrates for the Isle of Ely; *b.* 1828.

Mr. Metcalfe is a Magistrate for the Isle of Ely, and Lord of the Manors of Walsoken Metcalfe and Hagbech and Inglethorpe in Emneth, and Patron of 1 living; was formerly a Solicitor at Wisbech.—*Inglethorpe Hall, Emneth, Wisbech.*

METCALFE, HENRY CHRISTOPHER, Esq., of Hawstead House, Suffolk.

Eldest son of the late Henry Metcalfe, Esq., of Hawstead, by Frances Jane, dau. of the late Martin Whish, Esq., of Mortimer House, Reading; *b.* 1822; *s.* 1849 :

m. 1845 Mary, dau. of George Price, Esq., late 21st Light Dragoons, and has, with other issue,

    ● Henry George Price, *b.* 1846.

Mr. Metcalfe, who was educated at Versailles, and was formerly in the 91st Regt., was Commandant and Superintendent of Kat River Settlement, Cape of Good Hope, in 1847.—*Hawstead House, Bury St. Edmund's; Conservative Club, s.w.*

METCALFE.   (See *Marwood.*)

METFORD, WILLIAM, Esq.,‡ of Flook House, Somerset.

Eldest son of the late Ellis Button Metford, Esq., M.D., of Flook House, by Anne, dau. of Thomas Nickleson, Esq., of Poole, Dorset; *b.* 1789 ; *s.* 1820 ; *m.* 1st 1821 Mary Eliza, dau. of Hobart Proctor Anderdon, Esq., of Mount Pleasant, Jamaica ; 2nd 1841 Fanny Isabella, dau. of John Bunter Liddon, Esq., of Axminster, Devon, and has, by the former, with other issue,

    ● William Ellis. *b.* 1824 ; *m.* 1857 Caroline, dau. of George Wallis, Esq., M.D., of Clifton.

Dr. Metford was educated at the University of Edinburgh (M.D. 1812.).—*Flook House, Taunton.*

METGE, PETER PONSONBY, Esq., of Athlumley, co. Meath.

Eldest son of the late John Metge, Esq. (sometime M.P. for Dundalk), by his 2nd wife Mary, dau. of Henry Cole Bowen, Esq., of Bowen's Court, co. Cork ; *b.* 18—. Educated at Trinity Coll., Dublin (M.A. 18—); is a Magistrate for co. Meath, and Patron of 1 living. This family is of French Huguenot extraction.—*Athlumley, Navan, co. Meath.*

METHUEN, Lord (FREDERICK HENRY PAUL METHUEN).—Cr. 1838.

Eldest son of Paul, 1st Lord (who was many years M.P. for Wilts), by Jane Dorothea, dau. of the late Sir Henry St. John Mildmay, Bart. ; *b.* 1818 ; *s.* 1849; *m.* 1844 Anna Horatia, only dau. of the Rev. John Sanford, of Nynehead, Somerset ; is an Aide-de-Camp to the Queen, and a J.P. and D.L. for Wilts, Patron of 1 living, and Lieut.-Col. Wilts Militia ; was a Lord in Waiting 1859–66 ; late Lieut. 71st Foot ; is a co-heir to the Earldom of Scarsdale and Barony of Deincourt.—*Corsham House, Chippenham; 4, Connaught Place, w.*

  Heir, his son Paul Sanford, Ensign and Lieut. Scots Fusilier Guards ; *b.* 1845.

MEUX, Sir HENRY, Bart., of Theobald's, Herts (cr. 1831).

Eldest son of the late Sir Henry Meux, Bart., of Theobald's, by Elizabeth Mary, dau. of Thomas Smith, Esq., of Castlebar House, Middlesex; *b.* 1817 ; *s.* as 2nd Bart. 1841 ; *m.* 1856 Louisa Caroline, dau. of Lord Ernest Bruce. Educated at Eton and Ch. Ch., Oxford (B.A. 1838); a Magistrate for Middlesex and Essex, and a J.P. and D.L. for Herts ; was M.P. for Herts 1847–59. —*Theobald's Park, Cheshunt ; Wrexham Club, s.w.*

  Heir, his son Henry Bruce, *b.* 1856.

MEXBOROUGH, Earl of (JOHN CHARLES GEORGE SAVILE).—Cr. 1766.

Eldest son of John, 3rd Earl, by Lady Anne, dau. of Philip, 3rd Earl of Hardwicke; *b.* 1810; *s.* 1860; *m.* 1842 Lady Rachel Catharine, eldest dau. of Horatio, 3rd Earl of Orford (she *d.* 1854); 2nd 1861 Agnes Louisa, youngest dau. of the late John Raphael, Esq. Educated at Eton and Trinity Coll., Cambridge (M.A. 1830); is a J.P. and D.L. for the W. Riding of co. York; was M.P. for Gatton 1831–2, for Pontefract 1835–7 and 1841–7.

  ‡ Died whilst these sheets were at press.

—Methley Park, Leeds; Carlton and Travellers' Clubs, s.w.; 33, *Dover Street,* w.

Heir, his son John Horace, Viscount Pollington, b. 1843; m. 1867 Venetia, younger dau. of Sir Rowland Stanley-Errington, Bart.

MEYER, JAMES, Esq., of Forty Hall, Middlesex.

Eldest son of the late Christian Paul Meyer, Esq., of Forty Hall, by Louisa, dau. of Rawson Hart Boddam, Esq., of Capel House, Enfield; *b.* 1815; *s.* 1836; *m.* 1861 Frances Sarah, dau. of the late Samuel Reynolds Solley, Esq., of Serge Hill, Herts. Mr. Meyer, who was educated at Eton and Trinity Coll., Cambridge, is a Magistrate for Middlesex and Herts, and Lord of the Manors of Worcesters and Capels, Middlesex. This family came from Hamburgh in about 1750, and settled in London as merchants.—*Forty Hall, Enfield, Middlesex.*

Heir Pres., his brother Philip Herman, a Magistrate for Essex; b. 1820.

+**MEYER,** PHILIP HERMAN, Esq., of Stondon House, Essex.

Eldest son of the late James Meyer, Esq., of Enfield, Middlesex; *b.* 1822; is married; is a Magistrate for Essex. This family were formerly Merchants in London.—*Stondon House, Ongar, Essex.*

Heir Pres., his brother Herman, of Little Laver, near Ongar; b. 1836; m. 1864 Mary, dau. of — Martin, Esq.

MEYNELL, EDWARD THOMAS, Esq., of The Fryerage, and Kilvington Hall, Yorkshire.

Only son of the late Edward Meynel, Esq., Barrister-at-Law (who *d.* 1856), by Katharine, dau. of Joseph Michael, Esq., M.D., of Stamford; *b.* 1841; *s.* his uncle Thomas Meynell, Esq., 1863. Educated at Stonyehurst; is Lord of the Manors of Kilvington, Yarm, and Sowerby.—*The Fryerage, near Yarm, and Kilvington Hall, near Thirsk; Union Club,* s.w.

Heir Pres., his uncle Edgar John Meynell, Esq., Barrister-at-Law, b. 1825; m. 185- Louisa, dau. of R. S. Short, Esq., of Ellington Grove, co. Lincoln, and has, with other issue, * Edgar, b. 1857.

MEYNELL, FRANCIS, Esq., of Brent Moor, Devon.

Fourth son of the late Godfrey Meynell, Esq., of Meynell Langley, co. Derby, by his 2nd wife Mary, only dau. of David Balfour, Esq., and grand-dau. of the late William Balfour, Esq., of Trenaby, N.B.; *b.* 1821; *m.* 1857 Miss Caroline Strachan Brown, of Glazebrook House, Devon, and dau. of the late Rev. Charles Brown, Rector of Whitestone, Devon, and has, with other surviving issue, * Edward, b. 1864.

Mr. Meynell, who was educated at the Royal Naval Academy at Gosport, was formerly Lieut. R.N.—*Brent Moor, Ivybridge.*

MEYNELL, GODFREY FRANCEYS, Esq., of Meynell Langley, Derbyshire.

Eldest son of the late John Meynell, Esq., of Meynell Langley, by Sarah Brooks, dau. of William Brooks Johnson, Esq., of Coxbench Hall, co. Derby; *b.* 1844; *s.* 1854; *m.* 1866 Emma Maria, eldest dau. of the late E. Wollat Wilmot, Esq., of Buxton, and has issue, * A son, b. 1867.

Mr. Meynell, who was educated at Harrow, is Lord of the Manor of Meynell Langley, and Patron of 1 living.—*Meynell Langley, Derby.*

MEYNELL-INGRAM, HUGO CHARLES, Esq., of Temple Newsam, Yorkshire, and Hoar Cross, Staffordshire.

Eldest son of the late Hugo Meynell, Esq., of Hoar Cross, by Elizabeth dau. and co-heir of the late Viscount Irvine, after whom he assumed the additional

654

name of Ingram; *b.* 1789; *s.* 1801; *m.* 1819 Georgina, dau. of Francis Pigou, Esq., of London, by whom he has issue,

* Hugo Francis, a J.P. and D.L. for cos. Stafford and Derby, and a Dep.-Lieut. for the W. Riding of Yorkshire; b. 1820; m. 18-3 the Hon. Emily Charlotte, dau. of Charles, 1st Viscount Halifax.

Mr. Meynell-Ingram is a J.P. and D.L. for co. Stafford (High Sheriff 1826), and a Dep.-Lieut for the W. Riding of Yorkshire.—*Temple Newsam, Leeds; Hoar Cross; Abbots Bromley, Staffordshire.*

MEYRICK, OWEN JOHN AUGUSTUS FULLER-, Esq., of Bodorgan, Anglesey, and Rosehill, Sussex.

Eldest son of the late Augustus Elliott Fuller, Esq., J.P. and D.L., of Rosehill (who was M.P. for E. Sussex 1841–57), by Clara, dau. of the late Owen Putland Meyrick, Esq., of Bodorgan; *b.* 1804; *s.* 1858. Educated at Harrow and Brasenose Coll., Oxford; is a J.P. and D.L. for Anglesey and Sussex, and Patron of 2 livings.—*Bodorgan, Anglesey; Rosehill, Hurst Green; Ashdown, Forest Row, Sussex;* 16, *Clifford Street,* w.

MEYRICK, Lieut.-Col. AUGUSTUS WILLIAM HENRY, of Goderich Court, Herefordshire.

Eldest son of the late Col. William Henry Meyrick, of Goderich Court, by Lady Laura, 4th dau. of William Henry, 1st Duke of Cleveland, K.G.; *b.* 1827; *s.* 1865. Educated at Eton; is a J.P. and D.L. for co. Hereford, and Lieut.-Col. Scots Fusilier Guards. This family descend from Rowland Meyrick, Esq., of the Body-guard to Henry VII. and VIII.—*Goderich Court, Ross; The Cove, Torquay, Devon;* 43, *Grosvenor Street,* w.

MEYRICK. (See *Charlton-Meyrick.*)

MIALL, EDWARD, Esq.

Son of the late Mr. Moses Miall, of Portsmouth. Hants; *b.* 1809; *m.* 1831 Louisa, dau. of the late E. Holmes, Esq. Is Proprietor and Editor of the 'Nonconformist' newspaper; formerly a Minister of the Congregational Dissenters; was M.P. for Rochdale 1852–7, and a Member of the Royal Commission on Education 1858–9–60.—*The Firs, Upper Norwood, S.;* 18, *Bouverie Street,* E.C.

MICHEL, Sir JOHN, K.C.B., of Dewlish, Dorset (cr. 1859).

Eldest son of the late Lieut.-General John Michel, of Dewlish, and Kingston Russell, Dorset, by his 2nd wife Anne, dau. of the late Hon. Henry Fane, of Fulbeck, co. Lincoln; *b.* 1805; *m.* 1838 Louisa Anne, only dau. of Major-General Churchill, and has, with other issue, * John Horace Charles, b. 1843.

Sir John Michel, who is a Lieut.-General in the Army, and Col. 86th Foot, was formerly Lieut.-Col. 6th Foot.—*Dewlish, Blandford; United Service Club,* s.w.

MICHEL, Major-Gen. CHARLES EDWARD, of St. Ives House, Hampshire.

Second son of the late Lieut.-Gen. John Michel, of Dewlish, Dorset, by his 2nd wife Anne, dau. of the late Hon. Henry Fane, of Fulbeck, co. Lincoln; *b.* 1810; *m.* 1850 Emily, dau. of Sir R. B. Clarke, Knt., C.B., Chief Justice of Barbadoes, and has, with other issue, * Cecil Bowcher Duff, b. 1854.

Major-Gen. Michel, who was educated at Sandhurst, is a Magistrate for Dorset and Hants, and a Major-Gen. in the Army; was formerly in the 66th Foot.—*St. Ives' House, Ringwood; Army and Navy Club,* s.w.

MICHEL, Mrs., of Whatcombe, Dorset.

Margaretta, eldest dau. of the late Edmund Morton Pleydell, Esq., of Whatcombe House, by Elizabetha Margaretta, dau. of William Richards, Esq., of Warmwell, Dorset; *s.* 1835; *m.* 1831 the Rev. James Michel,

Vicar of Sturminster Newton, Dorset; is Lady of the Manor of Whatcombe, and Patron of 3 livings.—*Whatcombe House, Blandford.*

Heir Pres., her nephew John Clavell Mansel, Esq. (whom see).

MICHELL, Sir FREDERICK THOMAS, K.C.B. (cr. 1867).

Eldest son of the late Admiral Sampson Michell, of the Portuguese Navy (who *d.* 1809), by Ann, dau. of Samuel Shears, Esq., M.D., of Bedminster, Somerset; *b.* 1788; *m.* 1826 Caroline, youngest dau. of the late Thomas Prideaux, Esq. of Pengelly House, Cornwall (she *d.* 1856). Educated at Lisbon and at the Royal Naval Academy, Portsmouth; is an Admiral R.N.—*Northgate House, Totnes.*

MICHELL, JOHN, Esq., of Forcett, Yorkshire.

Eldest son of the late John Michell, Esq., of Forcett (who *d.* 1822), by Katherine, only dau. (by his 2nd marriage) of John Niven, Esq., of Thornton, co. Aberdeen; *b.* 1818; *s.* his grandfather 1841; *m.* 1st 1842 June Young, only dau. of Admiral Sir Arthur Farquhar, K.C.B., and G.C.H.; 2nd 1845 Sophia Janet Ogilvie, youngest dau. of John Farquharson, Esq., of Haughton, co. Aberdeen, and has, with other issue,

* John, *b.* 1857.

Mr. Michell, who was educated at Trinity Coll., Cambridge, is a J.P. and D.L. for the N. Riding of Yorkshire, and a Magistrate for cos. Durham, Kincardine, and Aberdeen.—*Forcett Park, Darlington; Glassd, Banchory, Kincardineshire, N.B.*

MICHELL, WILLIAM, Esq., of Bodmin, Cornwall.

Eldest son of the late Bennet Michell, Esq.; *b.* 1794; *m.* 1832 Jane Millicent, dau. of the late Col. Adair, of Stonehouse, Devon. Educated at Emmanuel Coll., Cambridge (M.B. 1834, M.D. 1838); is a Magistrate for Cornwall, and a Member of the College of Surgeons, London; was formerly a Physician in practice at Bodmin; was M.P. for Bodmin 1852–7, and April–June, 1859.—*Bodmin, Cornwall.*

MICHELL, WILLIAM PEYCE, Esq., of Holwell, Devon.

Eldest son of the late Tobias Michell, Esq., M.D., F.R.G.S., of Redruth, Cornwall, by Ann, dau. of S. V. Pryce, Esq.; *b.* 1811; *s.* 1858; *m.* 1839 Louisa Catherine, dau. of John Scobell, Esq., of Holwell, but has no surviving issue. Is a J.P. and D.L. for Cornwall, and a Magistrate for Devon.—*Holwell, Whitchurch, Tavistock; Royal Western Yacht Club, Plymouth.*

Heir Pres., his brother George Aunger, *b.* 1813.

MICKLETHWAIT, the Rev. JOHN NATHANIEL, of Taverham Hall, Norfolk.

Eldest surviving son of the late Nathaniel Micklethwait, Esq., of Beeston Hall, Norfolk, by his 2nd wife Lady Charlotte Rous, 2nd dau. of John, 1st Earl of Stradbroke; *b.* 1812; *s.* 1856; *m.* 1849 Emily Elizabeth, eldest dau. of Charles Mills. Esq , of Hillingdon Court, Middlesex. Educated at Eton and Magdalen Coll., Cambridge (B.A. 1833, M.A. 1835); is a Magistrate for Norfolk and Sussex, Lord of the Manor of Taverham, and joint Patron of that living; was formerly Fellow of Magdalen Coll., Cambridge.—*Taverham Hall, Norwich; Arthur's Club, s.w.; 13, Hertford Street, w.*

Heir Pres., his brother Henry Sharnborne Nathaniel (of Iridge Place, Battle, Sussex), *b.* 1814.

MICKLETHWAIT, RICHARD, Esq., of Ardsley House, Yorkshire.

Eldest son of the late John Micklethwait. Esq., of Ardsley, by Mary Anne, dau. of Miles Atkinson, Esq., of Skipwith Hall; *b.* 1830; *s.* 1862; *m.* 1866 Frances Eleanor, eldest dau. of the late Rev. Samuel Key, of Fulford

Hale, co. York. Is a Dep.-Lieut. for the W. Riding of Yorkshire, Lord of the Manor of Ardsley, late Capt. W. York Rifles. This family have been seated in the neighbourhood of Barnsley since the time of Edward I. —*Ardsley House, Barnsley.*

Heir Pres., his brother John Pollard, of Thornhill Hall, co. York. Barrister-at-Law of the Middle Temple, *b.* 1850; *m.* 1865 Mary, only child of the late Frederick Gore, Esq.

MIDDLETON, CHARLES MARMADUKE, Esq., late of Linton Spring, Yorkshire.

Second son of the late Peter Middleton, Esq., of Stockeld Park (who *d.* 1866), by the Hon. Juliana, dau. of Charles Philip, 16th Lord Stourton; (he *d.* 1817; *m.* 1859 Helen, dau. of — Fraser, Esq. Is a J.P. and D.L. for the W. Riding of Yorkshire.—*Stoberry Wells, Somerset.*

Heir Pres., his brother John, *b.* 1830.

MIDDLETON, WILLIAM, Esq., of Stockeld Park and Myddelton Lodge, Yorkshire.

Eldest son of the late Peter Middleton, Esq., of Stockeld Park, by the Hon. Juliana, dau. of Charles Philip, 16th Lord Stourton; *b.* 1815; *s.* 1866. Educated at Stonyhurst; is Lord of the Manors of Ilkley Myddelton, and Stockeld. This family have held the estates of Stockeld and of Middleton since the reign of Henry II. —*Myddelton Lodge, Ilkley, Leeds; Stockeld Park, Wetherby; 2, Queen Street, Mayfair.*

MIDDLETON, Lord (HENRY WILLOUGHBY).— Cr. 1711.

Eldest son of the late Henry Willoughby, Esq., of Birdsall House, co. York, by Charlotte, dau. of the Ven. Archdeacon Eyre; *b.* 1817; *s.* his cousin as 8th Lord 1856; *m.* 1843 Julia Louisa, dau. of Alexander William Robert Bosville, Esq., of Thorpe Hall, near Bridlington, Yorkshire. Educated at Eton and Trinity Coll., Cambridge; is a Magistrate for the N. Riding of Yorkshire, is a Dep.-Lieut. for Notts, and for the E. Riding of Yorkshire (High Sheriff 1854), Patron of 13 livings, Capt. S. Nottinghamshire Yeomanry Cavalry, and Honorary Col. 1st Brigade of the East York Artillery Volunteers; was formerly in the Yorkshire Hussars.—*Wollaton Hall, Nottingham; Birdsall and Settrington, Malton, Yorkshire; Applecross, Dingwall, N.B.; Carlton and Boodle's Clubs, s.w.; St. George's Club, Albemarle Street, w.*

Heir, his son Digby Wentworth Bayard, Lieut. and Capt. Scots Fusilier Guards; *b.* 1844.

MIDDLETON, EDWARD CHATTERTON, Esq., of Loughborough, Leicestershire.

Third son of the late William Middleton. Esq., of Loughborough, by Anne, dau. of John Alleyne, Esq., of Derby; *b.* 1819 ; *s.* 1843; *m.* 1834 Anna Maria, dau. of the late James Stanborough, Esq., of Isleworth, Middlesex, and has, with other issue, an only son,

* Edward William Cradock, *b.* 1858 ; *m.* 1864 Augusta Sophia, youngest dau. of the Rev. Marmaduke Vavasour, Vicar of Ashby-de-la-Zouche, co. Leicester.

Mr. Middleton is a J.P. and D.L. for co. Leicester (High Sheriff 1857).—*The Grove, Loughborough.*

MIDDLETON, HASTINGS NATHANIEL, Esq., of Bradford Peverell, Dorset.

Eldest son of the late Hastings Nathaniel Middleton. Esq., of Townhill, Hants (who *d.* 1821), by Emilia, dau. of the late Charles Purling, Esq., of the H.E.I.C.'s Service; *b.* 1809; *m.* 1834 Mary Ann, dau. of the late Rev. Charles Berton, Rector of St. Andrew's, Holborn, and by her, who *d.* 1866, has, with other issue,

* Hastings Burton, *b.* 1838.

Mr. Middleton, who was called to the Bar at the Inner Temple 1834, is a J.P. and D.L. for Dorset (High Sheriff 1857), and Lord of the Manors of Bradford Peverell and Muckleford.—*Bradford Peverell, Dorchester; Athenæum Club, s.w.*

MIDDLETON. (See *Broke-Middleton.*)

MIDDLETON. (See *Monck.*)

MIDGLEY-MUNRO, CHARLES MUNRO, Esq., of Edge Hill, Lancashire.
Natural son of Sir Charles Munro, Bart., of Fowlis Castle, N.B., by Harriet, dau. of Robert Midgley, Esq., of Eastington, co. York; *b.* 1826; *m.* 1848 Eliza, dau. of James Hill, Esq., of Manchester, and has issue,
* Charles Edward, *b.* 1858.
Mr. Midgley-Munro, who assumed the latter name by Royal licence 1859, is a Merchant at Liverpool.—*Edge Hill, Liverpool.*

MIDLETON, Viscount (WILLIAM JOHN BRODRICK).—Cr. 1717.
Third and only surviving son of the Hon. and Most Rev. Charles Brodrick, D.D., Archbishop of Cashel (who *d.* 1822), by Mary, dau. of the Right Rev. Richard Woodward, Lord Bishop of Cloyne; *b.* 1798; *s.* his brother 1863; *m.* 1st 1824 Lady Elizabeth Anne, eldest dau. of Robert, 6th Earl of Cardigan, and widow of the Hon. John Perceval (she *d.* 1824); 2nd 1829 the Hon. Harriet, 3rd dau. of George, 4th Viscount Midleton. Educated at Eton and Balliol Coll., Oxford (B.A. 1820, M.A. 1823), appointed Chaplain to Her Majesty 1847, and Canon of Wells 1855; was Rector of Bath 1839-54, and Dean of Exeter 1862-67.—*P.per Harrow, Godalming, Surrey; Cahirmone, Midleton, co. Cork; 4, Upper Grosvenor Street,* w.
Heir, his son William, educated at Eton, and M.A. of Balliol Coll., Oxford, a Barrister-at-Law of Lincoln's Inn, and a Dep.-Lieut. for Surrey; *b.* 1830; *m.* 1853 Augusta Mary, 3rd dau. of the Right Hon. Sir T. F. Fremantle, Bart., and has, with other issue, * William St. John Fremantle, *b.* 1856.

MILBANK, AUGUSTUS SUSSEX, Esq., of Carlbury House, co. Durham.
Fourth son of Mark Milbank, Esq., of Thorp Perrow and Barningham, by Lady Augusta Henrietta, dau. of William Henry, 1st Duke of Cleveland, K.G.; *b.* 1827; *s.* 1850. Is a J.P. and D.L. for co. Durham.—*Carlbury House, Durham; Arthur's Club,* s.w.; 2, *Cleveland Row,* s.w.

MILBANK, FREDERICK ACCLOM, Esq., of Thorp Perrow, Yorkshire.
Second son of Mark Milbank, Esq., of Barningham Park (whom see), by Lady Augusta Henrietta, dau. of William Henry, 1st Duke of Cleveland; *b.* 1820; *m.* 1844 Alexina Harriet, dau. of the late Sir Alexander Don, Bart., of Newton Don, co. Roxburgh, and has, with other issue,
* Frederick, *b.* 184—.
Mr. Milbank, who was educated at Harrow, is a D.L. for co. Durham (High Sheriff 1852) and a Magistrate for the N. Riding of co. York; elected M.P. for N. Yorkshire 1865, late in the 70th Highlanders — *Thorp Perrow, Bedale; Brooks's Club,* s.w.; 9, *Clarges Street,* w.

MILBANK, HENRY JOHN, Esq., of Newsham, Yorkshire.
Third son of Mark Milbank, Esq., of Thorp Perrow and Barningham (whom see), by Lady Augusta Henrietta, dau. of William Henry, 1st Duke of Cleveland; *b.* 1824; *m.* 1846 Lady Margaret Henrietta Maria, dau. of Lord and Lady Grey of Groby, and sister of George Harry, 7th Earl of Stamford and Warrington, and has issue, two daughters. Educated at Rugby and Trinity Coll., Cambridge; is a Dep.-Lieut. for the N. Riding of Yorkshire.—*Newsham, Richmond, Yorkshire.*
656

MILBANK, MARK, Esq., of Barningham and Thorp Perrow, Yorkshire.
Eldest son of the late William Milbank, Esq., of Thorp Perrow, by Dorothy, dau. of John Wise, Esq., of Woolston, co. Devon; *b.* 1795; *s.* 1802; *m.* 1817 Lady Augusta Henrietta, 2nd dau. of William Henry, 1st Duke of Cleveland, K.G., and has, with other issue,
* Mark William Vane, a Magistrate for the N. Riding of Yorkshire; *b.* 1819; *m.* 1845 Barberina Sophia, dau. of the late Sir Thomas Farquhar, Bart., and has issue, * two daughters.
Mr. Milbank, who was educated at Harrow and Oriel Coll., Oxford, is a J.P. and D.L. for the N. Riding of Yorkshire (High Sheriff 1837), a Magistrate for co. Durham, Lord of the Manor of Snape, and Patron of 1 living; was M.P. for Camelford 1820-31.—*Thorp Perrow, Bedale; Barningham Park, Greta Bridge, Yorkshire.*

MILBANKE HUSKISSON-, Sir JOHN RALPH, Bart., of Halnaby, Yorkshire (cr. 1661).
Eldest son of the late Sir John Peniston Milbanke, Bart., of Halnaby, by Eleanor, dau. of Julines Herring, Esq., of Jamaica; *b.* 1800; *s.* as 8th Bart. 1850; *m.* 1843 Emily, dau. of John Mansfield, Esq., of Digwell House, Herts. Assumed the additional name of Huskisson by Royal licence 1866, under the will of Mrs. Eliza Emily Huskisson, of Eartham, widow of the Right Hon. William Huskisson; is Lord of the Manor of Eartham; late Envoy Extraordinary and Minister Plenipotentiary at the Hague.—*Low Gatherley, Middleton Tyas, Yorkshire; Eartham House, Chichester.*
Heir, his son John Ralph, *b.* 1847.

MILDMAY, Sir HENRY BOUVERIE PAULET ST. JOHN, Bart., of Dogmersfield, Hants (cr. 1772).
Eldest son of the late Sir Henry Carew Mildmay, Bart., of Dogmersfield, by Charlotte, eldest dau. of the late Hon. Bartholomew Bouverie, M.P., and grand-dau. of William, 1st Earl of Radnor; *b.* 1810; *s.* as 5th Bart. 1848; *m.* 1851 the Hon. Helena, 2nd dau. of Charles, Viscount Eversley. Is a J.P. and D.L. for Hants (High Sheriff 1862), and Lieut.-Col. Hants Yeomanry; was formerly Capt. 2nd Dragoon Guards.—*Dogmersfield Park, Winchfield; White's and Travellers' Clubs,* s.w.
Heir, his son Henry Paulet St. John, *b.* 1853.

MILDMAY, the Ven. CAREW ANTHONY ST. JOHN.
Seventh son of the late Sir Henry Paulet, Bart. (who assumed the additional name of Mildmay), by Jane, eldest dau. and co-heir of Carew Mildmay, Esq. of Shawford House, Hants; *b.* 1799; *m.* 1830 the Hon. Caroline, dau. of William, 1st Lord Radstock. Educated at Eton and Oriel Coll., Oxford (B.A. 1822, M.A. 1825); is a Magistrate for Essex; appointed Rector of Chelmsford 1826, Archdeacon of Essex 1860; was Vicar of Burnham 1827-58.—*The Rectory, Chelmsford; University Club,* s.w.

MILDMAY, EDWARD ST. JOHN, Esq., ‡ of Bishop's Hall, Essex.
Seventh son of the late Sir Henry P. St. John Mildmay, Bart. by Jane, eldest dau. and co-heir of Carew Mildmay, Esq., of Shawford House, Hants, whose name he assumed; *b.* 1797; *m.* 1818 1st Marianne, dau. of R. Sherson, Esq.; 2nd 1835 Frances Lucy Penelope, dau. of Edward Lockwood Percival, Esq., and has by the former, with other issue,
* Arthur George, *b.* 1819; *m.* 1848 Louisa Latham, dau. of the late Capt. Henry Gough Ord, R.A.
Mr. Mildmay is a Magistrate for Essex, and a J.P. and D.L. for Hants.—*Bishop's Hall, La Bourne, Romford; Travellers' Club,* s.w.; 2, *Wilton Crescent,* s.w.

‡ Died whilst these sheets were at press.

+MILDMAY, HENRY BINGHAM ST. JOHN, Esq., of Otford House, Kent.
Second son of the late Humphrey St. John Mildmay, Esq., of Shoreham Place, Kent, by his 1st wife Anne, eldest dau. of Alexander, 1st Lord Ashburton; *b.* 1827. Educated at Ch. Ch., Oxford; was formerly an Officer in the Army. This family is a younger branch of that of the Mildmays, Barts., of Dogmersfield.—*Otford House, Sevenoaks.*

MILDMAY, Capt. HERVEY GEORGE ST. JOHN, of Hazlegrove House, Somerset.
Eldest surviving son of the late Paulet St. John Mildmay, Esq., M.P. (who *d.* 1845), by Wyndham Anna Maria, youngest dau. of the late Hon. Bartholomew Bouverie, and grandson of the late Sir Henry Mildmay, Bart.; *b.* 1817; *s.* his brother, Paulet Henry, 1858; *m.* 1859 the Hon. Elizabeth, 3rd dau. of Charles, Viscount Eversley (she *d.* 1867). Is a Capt. R.N., retired. This family is an offshoot of that of Sir H. St. John Mildmay, Bart.—*Hazlegrove House, Taunton.*

Heir Pres., his brother Arundell Charles, B.A. of Merton Coll., Oxford; Rector of Lapworth, co. Warwick; *b.* 1819.

MILDMAY, Mrs., of Shoreham, Kent, and Gayton, Herefordshire.
Sybella Harriet, dau. of George Clive, Esq., M.P., of Perristone, co. Hereford; *m.* 1861 Humphrey Francis Mildmay. Esq., J.P. and D.L., of Shoreham Place, M.P. for co. Hereford 1859-65, who *d.* 1866.—*Shoreham Place, Sevenoaks; Gayton Hall, Ross; 46, Berkeley Square, W.*

MILES, Sir WILLIAM, Bart., of Leigh Court, Somerset (cr. 1859).
Eldest son of the late Philip John Miles, Esq., M.P., of Leigh Court (who *d.* 1845), by his 1st wife Maria, dau. of the Very Rev. Arthur Whetham, D.D., Dean of Lismore; *b.* 1797; *m.* 1823 Catharine, dau. of John Gordon, Esq. Educated at Eton and Ch. Ch., Oxford; is a J.P. and D.L. for Somerset, a Magistrate for co. Gloucester, and Patron of 1 living; was M.P. for Chippenham 1818-20, for Romney 1830-2, and for E. Somerset 1834-65.—*Leigh Court, Bristol; Arthur's and Boodle's Clubs, S.W.*

Heir, his son Philip John William, educated at Eton, a J.P. and D.L. for Somerset, late High Sheriff of Bristol, and formerly Lieut. 17th Lancers; *b.* 1825; *m.* 1847 Francis Elizabeth, dau. of the late Sir D. Roche, Bart., and has issue, *three daus.*

MILES, CHARLES WILLIAM, Esq., of Burton and Dauntsey, Wilts.
Sixth son of the late Philip John Miles, Esq., M.P., of Kingsweston, co. Gloucester, and Leigh Court, Somerset, by his 2nd wife Clarissa, dau. of Samuel P. Peach, Esq., and half-brother of Sir William Miles, Bart.; *b.* 1823; *m.* 1853 Maria, dau. of Jere Hill, Esq., and has issue,
* Charles Napier, *b.* 1854.

Mr. Miles, who was educated at Eton, is a Magistrate for Wilts (of which county he has been High Sheriff); Lieut.-Col. in the Royal Gloucestershire Hussars, and High Steward of Malmesbury; was formerly Capt. 17th Lancers.—*Burton Hill, Malmesbury.*

MILES, EDWARD PEACH WILLIAM, Esq., of Dauntsey House, Wiltshire.
Seventh son of the late Philip John Miles, Esq., of Kingsweston, co. Gloucester, and of Leigh Court, Somerset, by his 2nd wife Clarissa, dau. of Samuel Peach Peach, Esq.; *b.* 1829. Educated at Eton; is a Magistrate for co. Gloucester.—*Dauntsey House, Chippenham; Shirehampton, Bristol.*

MILES, GEORGE FREDERICK WILLIAM, Esq., of Llangattock Park, Brecknockshire.
Fifth son of the late Philip John Miles, Esq., M.P., of Kingsweston House, co. Gloucester, and Leigh Court, Somerset, by his 2nd wife Clarissa, dau. of Samuel Peach Peach, Esq., and half-brother of Sir William Miles, Bart.; *b.* 1820; *m.* 1851 Anne Augusta, dau. of the late Albany Savile, Esq. Educated at Eton; is a Magistrate for Somerset and Dorset (High Sheriff 1858).—*Llangattock Park, Crickhowell.*

MILES, JOHN WILLIAM, Esq., of Underdown, Herefordshire.
Third son of the late Philip John Miles, Esq., M.P., of Leigh Court, Somerset, and Kingsweston House, co. Gloucester, by his 2nd wife Clarissa, dau. of Samuel Peach Peach, Esq., and half-brother of Sir William Miles, Bart.; *b.* 1816. Educated at Eton and Ch. Ch., Oxford (B.A. 1839); is a J.P. and D.L. for co. Hereford, and a Banker at Bristol; elected M.P. for Bristol 1868, but unseated on petition.—*Underdown, Ledbury; Carlton Club, S.W.*

Heir Pres., his brother Philip William Skinner.

MILES, Mrs., of Firbeck Hall, Yorkshire.
Frances Harriett, second dau. of the late Col. Jebb, of Walton Hall, co. Derby, and sister of the late Major-General Sir John Jebb, K.C.B., by Dorothy, dau. of General Gladwyn, of Stubbing Court, co. Derby; *m.* 1829 William Miles, Esq., of Clifton House, co. Gloucester (who *d. s. p.* 1844). Mrs. Miles, who purchased this property in 1852, is one of an old family who allied themselves with the De Witts of Holland two centuries ago. It has produced many learned and literary men, as well as bishops and judges. She is also descended on her mother's side from the De Akenys, whose name is on the Battle Roll, and one of whom saved the life of King William at the Battle of the Boyne.—*Firbeck Hall, Rotherham.*

MILES, PHILIP WILLIAM SKINNER, Esq., of Kings-Weston House, Gloucestershire.
Second son of the late Philip John Miles, Esq., M.P., of Kings-Weston and Leigh Court, by his 2nd wife Clarissa, dau. of Samuel Peach Peach, Esq., and half-brother of Sir William Miles, Bart.; *m.* 1846 Pamela Adelaide, 5th dau. of the late Lieut.-General Sir William P. Napier, K.C.B., and has issue,
* Philip Napier, *b.* 1865.

Mr. Miles, who was educated at Eton and Ch. Ch., Oxford, is a J.P. and D.L. for cos. Gloucester and Somerset (High Sheriff of co. Gloucester 1863); was M.P. for Bristol 1837-52.—*Kings-Weston House, Bristol.*

MILES, WILLIAM, Esq., of Dixfield, Devon.
Only son of the late Richard Miles, Esq., of Exeter, by Elizabeth, dau. of Thomas Allden, Esq., of London; *b.* 1799; *m.* 1831 Dorothy Rose, only child of the late John Rose Drewe, Esq., of the Grange, Devon. Is a Magistrate for Devon; was formerly in the Life Guards.—*Dixfield, Exeter.*

MILES, WILLIAM HENRY, Esq., of Ham Green, Somerset.
Second son of Sir William Miles, Bart., of Leigh Court, Somerset, by Catherine, dau. of John Gordon, Esq.; *b.* 1830; *m.* 1862 Mary Frances, only dau. of the Rev. John Kynaston Charleton, Vicar of Ellerton, co. Gloucester. Educated at Eton and Balliol Coll., Oxford (B.A. 1851); is a Magistrate for Somerset and a Banker at Bristol.—*Ham Green, Bristol.*

MILFORD, Lady, of Upper Court, co. Kilkenny.
Ann June, 4th dau. of William, 4th Earl of Wicklow, by Lady Cecil Frances, 4th dau. of John James, 1st Marquis of Abercorn; *m.* 1st 1854 (as 2nd wife)

v v 657

Richard Bulkeley Philipps, Lord Milford (ext.), who d. 1857; 2nd 1861 Thomas Joseph Eyre, Esq., of Uppercourt, co. Kilkenny (whom see).—*Uppercourt, Freshford, co. Kilkenny; 27, Brook Street, w.*

MILFORD, JOHN, Esq., of Coaver, Devon.
Son of the late John Milford, Esq., of Exeter (who d. 1829), by Louisa, dau. of Lewis Duval, Esq., of London; b. 1792; m. 1817 Eliza, youngest dau. of John Neave, Esq., and grand-dau. of the late Sir Richard Neave, Bart., and by her, who d. 1865, has, with other issue,
  • John Calverley, educated at Rugby ; b. 1819.
Mr. Milford, who is a J.P. and D.L. for Devon, and a Banker at Exeter, represents a family settled at Wickington in S. Tawton in 1620.—*Coaver, Exeter.*

MILL, Lady BARKER-, of Mottisfont Abbey, Hants
Jane, dau. of the late Col. Swinburne, of Keynsham, Somerset; m. 1828 the Rev. Sir John Barker-Mill, Bart., who d. 1860, when his title became extinct. Is Lady of the Manor of Mottisfont, and Patron of 1 living.—*Mottisfont Abbey, King's Somborne, Romsey.*

MILL, JOHN STUART, Esq., LL.D.
Eldest son of the late James Mill, Esq. (Examiner of Indian Correspondence in the India House), by Harriet, dau. of George Burrow, Esq., of Hoxton; b. 1806; m. 1851 Harriet, widow of John Taylor, Esq. (she d. 1858); elected Rector of St. Andrew's University 1865; elected M.P. for Westminster 1865; Lord Rector of St. Andrew's University 1867; was Examiner of Indian Correspondence in the East India House 1856-8; author of a 'System of Logic,' 'Essays on Political Economy,' 'Principles of Political Economy,' 'On Liberty,' &c.—*Blackheath Park, s.e.*

MILLAR, CHARLES, Esq., M.D., of Penrhos, Carnarvonshire.
Eldest son of the late Matthew Millar, Esq., of Knutsford, by Hannah, dau. of John Holburt, Esq., of Knutsford, co. Chester; b. 1811; s. 1840; m. 1854 Harriet, dau. of Charles Cook, Esq., of Tetbury, co. Gloucester, and has, with other issue,
  • Charles John, b. 1855.
Mr. Millar, who was educated at University Coll., London, is a J.P. and D.L. for co. Carnarvon (High Sheriff 1865), and Lord of the Manor of Inglesham, Wilts.—*Penrhos, Carnarvon, N. Wales; Cator Court, Ashburton, Devon.*

MILLER, Sir CHARLES JOHN HUBERT, Bart., of Froyle, Hants (cr. 1705).
Elder son of the late Sir Charles Hayes Miller, Bart., of Froyle, by Katherine Maria, dau. of James Winter Scott, Esq., of Rotherfield Park, Hants; b. 1858; s. as 8th Bart. 1868. Is Lord of the Manor of Froyle, and Patron of that living.—*Froyle, Alton.*
Heir Pres., his brother Cecil Walter, b. 1860.

MILLER, Sir THOMAS McDONALD, Bart., of Glenlee, Kirkcudbrightshire (cr. 1788).
Eldest son of the late Sir William Miller, Bart., J.P. and D.L., by Emily, dau. of the late General Sir Thomas McMahon, Bart., G.C.B.; b. 1816; s. as 4th Bart. 1861; m. 1863 Isabella Freeman Seton, dau. of the late William Anderson, Esq., of Calcutta. The 1st Bart. was Lord President of the College of Justice; the 2nd Bart. was a Senator of the same, with the title of Lord Glenlee.—*Barskimming, Mauch'line, Ayrshire, N.B.*
Heir, his son Frederic, b. 1863.

MILLER, GEORGE, Esq., of Wadsley, Yorkshire.
Second son of the late Thomas Miller, Esq., of Ayton, co. Berwick, by Ann, dau. of John Forrester, Esq., of

Ayton; b. 1802; m. 1824 Mary, dau. of James Jones, Esq., of Milford Haven, and has, with other issue,
  • Henry, b. 1827.
This family is of Scottish extraction.—*Wadsley House, Ecclesfield, Yorkshire.*

MILLER, HENRY JOHN, Esq., of Anstey, Hants.
Second son of the late Sir Thomas Combe Miller, Bart., of Froyle, Hants, by Martha, dau. of the Rev. John Holmes, of Bungay, Suffolk; b. 1830; m. 1865 Jessie youngest dau. of John Orbell, Esq., of Hawkesbury, New Zealand. Educated at Eton; is Lord of the Manor of Anstey.—*Anstey Manor, Alton.*

MILLER, JAMES, Esq., of Millburn, Buteshire.
Youngest son of the late William Miller, Esq., of Port Glasgow; b. 1780; m. 1808 Catherine, dau. of Robert Angus, Esq., of Port Glasgow, and has, with other issue,
  • James, a Magistrate for co. Bute ; b. 1820.
Mr. Miller is a J.P. and D.L. for co. Bute, and a retired Commander in the Revenue Service.—*Millburn, Island of Cumbrae, N.B.*

+MILLER, Lieut.-Col. JAMES, of Mariemont, Middlesex.
Son of the late — Miller, Esq.; b. 1830. Is a J.P. and D.L. for Middlesex, and Lieut.-Col. 11th Hussars, retired.—*Mariemont, Eagleston, Middlesex.*

+MILLER, JAMES BOYD, Esq., of Collier's Wood, Surrey.
Elder son of the late Boyd Miller, Esq., of Collier's Wood (who assumed the name of Miller by royal licence in lieu of his patronymic Darby), by Margaret, dau. of — Montgomery, Esq.; b. 1823; s. 1865; m. 1848 Sophia, only dau. of William Harrington, Esq., of the Madras Civil Service. Was formerly Capt. 15th Light Dragoons.—*Collier's Wood, Mitcham, Surrey.*
Heir Pres., his brother Robert Montgomery, b. 1826 ; m. 1858 Mary Jane, dau. of Robert Ranking, Esq., of Ramsgate.

MILLER, JOHN ROWLEY, Esq., of Moneymore, co. Londonderry.
Eldest son of the late Rowley Miller, Esq., J.P. and D.L., of Moneymore, by Margaret, dau. of the Rev. Thomas Torrens; b. 1808; s. 1866; m. 1850 Emily Charlotte, dau. of the late Rev. Henry Stewart, D.D., and niece of the late Sir J. Stewart, Bart., of Ballygawly, co. Tyrone. Is a Magistrate for cos. Londonderry and Tyrone.—*Moneymore, co. Londonderry.*

MILLER, SAMUEL CHRISTIE-, Esq., of Britwell House, Bucks.
Second son of the late Thomas Christie, Esq., of Broomfield, Essex, by Rebecca, dau. of S. Howling, Esq.; b. 1811; m. 1842 Mary, dau. of Thomas Hardcastle, Esq., and has issue,
  • William Henry, b. 1850.
Mr. Christie-Miller, who is a Commissioner of Lieutenancy for London, was M.P. for Newcastle-under-Lyne 1847-59; he took the name of Miller by Royal licence in 1862, upon succeeding to the estates of W. H. Miller, Esq., M.P., of Craigentinny.—*Britwell House, Maidenhead; Craigentinny, Midlothian, N.B.; Carlton Club, s.w.; 21, St. James's Place, s.w.*

MILLER, STEARNE BALL, Esq., Q.C.
Son of the late Rev. George Miller, D.D., of Armagh, by Elizabeth, dau. of Robert Ball, Esq., of Ballyheury, co. Wicklow; b. 1813; m. 1856 Sarah, dau. of M. B. Rutherford, Esq., of Dublin. Called to the Irish Bar 1835, became a Q.C. 1852; was M.P. for Armagh 1857-9 and 1865-7; appointed a Judge of Bankruptcy in Ireland 1867.—6, *Rutland Square, Dublin.*

MILLER, WILLIAM, Esq., of Manderston, Berwickshire.
Second son of the late James Miller, Esq., of Leith, N.B, by Elizabeth, dau. of the Rev. William Sutherland, of Wick, co. Caithness; *b.* 1809; *m.* 1858 Mary Anne, dau. of John Farley Leith, Esq., Barrister-at-Law, and has, with other issue,
 * William Leith, *b.* 1863.
Mr. Miller, who was educated at the University of Edinburgh, is a J.P. and D.L. for co. Berwick; was formerly a Merchant and Honorary British Vice-Consul at St. Petersburg; he was elected M.P. for the Leith Burghs 1859.—*Manderston, Dunse, N.B.*; *Union Club,* s.w.; 135, *Piccadilly,* w.

MILLER, the Rev. WILLIAM SANDERSON, of Radway Grange, Warwickshire.
Eldest surviving son of Lieut.-Col. Fiennes Sanderson Miller, C.B., of Radway Grange, by Georgiana Sibella, 5th dau. of the Rev. Philip Story, of Lockington, co. Leicester; *b.* 1822; *s.* 1862; *m.* 1848 Henrietta Mary, only dau. of the Rev. Thomas Lea, Rector of Tadmarton, Oxon, and Vicar of Bishops Itchington, co. Warwick.   Educated at Winchester and New Coll., Oxford (B.A. 1853, M.A. 1854); is a Magistrate for co. Warwick.—*Radway Grange, Kineton.*
Heir Pres., his brother Frederick, Capt. R.A.; b. 1831.

MILLES. (See under *Sondes, Lord.*)

MILLIGAN, Mrs., of Acacia House, Yorkshire.
Phœbe, eldest dau. of the late Nathaniel Briggs, Esq., of Rawden, co. York; *m.* 1818 Robert Milligan, Esq., who was a Magistrate for the W. Riding of co. York, and for many years M.P. for Bradford, and *d.* 1862. —*Acacia House, Leeds.*

MILLS, ARTHUR, Esq.
Youngest son of the late Rev. Francis Mills, of Barford, co. Warwick, by Catharine, dau. of the late Sir John Mordaunt, Bart., of Walton, co. Warwick; *b.* 1816; *m.* 1848 Agnes Lucy, youngest dau. of Sir Thos. Dyke Acland, Bart., and has, with other issue,
 * Barton Reginald Vaughan, *b.* 1857.
Mr. Mills, who was educated at Rugby and Balliol Coll., Oxford (B.A. 1835, M.A. 1838), and called to the Bar at the Inner Temple 1842, was M.P. for Taunton, 1857-65.—*St. James's and Oxford and Cambridge Clubs,* s.w.; 34, *Hyde-Park Gardens,* w.

MILLS, CHARLES, Esq., of Hillingdon Court Middlesex.
Son of the late William Mills. Esq., of Bisterne, Hants (who was many years a Director of the H.E.I. Company), by Elizabeth, dau. of the Hon. Wriothesley Digby, of Mereden, co. Warwick; *b.* 1792; *m.* 1825 Emily, dau. of the late Richard Henry Cox, Esq., of Hillingdon, and has, with other issue,
 * Charles Henry, educated at Eton; a J.P. and D.L. for Middlesex, late M.P. for Northallerton, and Cornet Middlesex Yeomanry Cavalry; *b.* 1839; *m.* 1855 Lady Louisa Lascelles, eldest dau. of Henry, 3rd Earl of Harewood, and has issue.
Mr. Mills is a J.P. and D.L. for Middlesex, and a Member of the Council of India.—*Hillingdon Court, Uxbridge; Camelford House, Park Lane,* w.

MILLS, the Rev. HENRY.
Eldest son of the late Rev. Francis Mills, by Catharine, dau. of the late Sir John Mordaunt, Bart.; *b.* 1815; *m.* 1841 Mary, 3rd dau. of the Rev. H. Hippisley. Educated at Rugby and Balliol Coll., Oxford (B.A. 1837); is a Magistrate for co. Warwick, and Patron of 1 living; late Vicar of Pillerton.—*Pillerton, Kineton.*

MILLS, JOHN, Esq., of Bisterne, Hants.
Eldest son of the late William Mills, Esq., of Bisterne, by Elizabeth, dau. of the Hon. Wriothesley Digby, of

Mereden, co. Warwick; *b.* 1789; *s.* 1820; *m.* 1835 Sarah Charlotte, dau. of the late Nathaniel Micklethwait, Esq., of Taverham Hall, Norfolk, and has, with other issue,
 * John, a Magistrate for Hants; *b.* 1836.
Mr. Mills, who was educated at Harrow and Cb. Ch., Oxford, is a J.P. and D.L. for Hants, and a Verderer of the New Forest; late in the Coldstream Guards; was M.P. for Rochester 1831–4.—*Bisterne, Ringwood.*

MILLS, JOHN REMINGTON, Esq., of Tolmers, Herts.
Third son of the late Samuel Mills, Esq., of Russell Square, London, by Mary, dau. of Thomas Wilson, Esq.; *b.* 1798; *m.* 1831 Louisa Matilda, dau. of Joseph Trueman, Esq., of Walthamstow, Essex, and has, with other issue,
 * John Remington, *b.* 1833; *m.* 1863 Mary Ann, only dau. of the late Charles Gilmour, Esq., of Salisbury, and has issue.
 * Mary-Jane.
Mr. Mills is a Magistrate for Middlesex and Herts; elected M.P. for Wycombe 1862.—*Tolmers, Hertford;* Residence: *Tunbridge Wells, Kent; Reform Club,* s.w.

MILLS, JOSEPH TRUEMAN, Esq., of Clermont, Norfolk.
Second son of John Remington Mills, Esq., M.P., of Tolmers, Herts, Kent, by Matilda Louisa, dau. of the late Joseph Trueman, Esq., of Walthamstow, Essex; *b.* 1836; *s.* his uncle, Thomas Mills, Esq., M.P., 1862; *m.* 1858 Eliza Anna, 4th dau. of James Layton, Esq., of Mincing Lane, London, and has, with other issue,
 * Henry Trueman, *b.* 1860.
Mr. Mills is a Magistrate for Herts. Norfolk, and co. Leicester.—*Clermont, Thetford; Highfield, Husband's Bosworth, Rugby.*

MILLS, the Rev. THOMAS, of Stutton, Suffolk.
Youngest son of the late Thomas Mills, Esq., of Great Saxham Hall, Suffolk, by Susanna, dau. of Christopher Harris, E-q., of Plymstock, Devon; *b.* 1793; *m.* 1st 1815 Anne, dau. of Nathaniel Barnardiston, Esq.; 2nd 1836 the Hon. Elizabeth Frances, dau. of George, 5th Viscount Barrington, and has issue,
 * Barrington Stopford Thomas, M.A. of Ch. Ch., Oxford, and Rector of Lawshall, Suffolk; *b.* 1822; *m.* 1850 Georgiana Penelope, dau. of the late Henry C. Sturt, Esq., and Lady Charlotte Sturt, of Critchill House, Dorset, and has surviving issue Isabel Mary.
Mr. Mills, who was educated at Eton and Ch. Ch., Oxford (B.A. 1814), is a Magistrate for Suffolk, a Chaplain in Ordinary to Her Majesty, Rector of Stutton and Great Saxham, Proctor in Convocation for the Archdeaconry of Suffolk, Hon. Canon of Norwich, and Patron of 1 living.—*Stutton, Ipswich; University Club,* s.w.

MILLS, THOMAS RICHARD, Esq., of Saxham, Suffolk.
Eldest son of the late William Mills, Esq., J.P. and D.L., of Saxham Hall, by Clara Jane, dau. of the late Rev. Richard W. Huntley or Boswell Court, co. Gloucester; *b.* 1818; *s.* 1860; *m.* 1843 Emily, dau. of the Hon. Samuel Hatt, of Chambly, Canada East, and has with other issue,
 * William, *b.* 1844.
Mr. Mills, who was educated at Eton and Ch. Ch., Oxford, is Lord of the Manor of Great Saxham, and Patron of that living; was formerly in the King's Dragoon Guards.—*Saxham Hall, Bury St. Edmund's; United Service Club,* s.w.

MILLS, the Rev. WILLIAM YARNTON, of Miserdine, Gloucestershire.
Eldest son of the late William Y. Mills, Esq., of Shellyford Berks (who *d.* 1821); *b.* 1803; *m.* 18— Maria,

dau. of the late Robert Henry Hurst, Esq., of Horsham Park, Sussex, and has, with other issue,

* William, b. 18—.

Mr. Mills, who was educated at Westminster and Trinity Coll., Oxford (B.A. 1826, M.A. 1827); is a Magistrate for co. Gloucester, and Rector and Patron, and Lord of the Manor of Miserdine.—*Miserdine, Cirencester.*

MILLTOWN, Earl of (JOSEPH HENRY LEESON).—Cr. 1763.

Eldest son of the late Joseph, 4th Earl. K.P., by Barbara, dau. of the late Sir Joshua Colles Meredyth, Bart., and widow of the last Lord Castlecoote; b. 1829; s. 1866. Educated at Eton; late Capt. Royal Dublin Militia; formerly Ensign 68th Foot; was A.D.C. to the Lord Lieut. of Ireland, 1864—6.—*Russborough House, co. Wicklow.*

Heir Pres., his brother Edward Nugent, B.A. of Trinity Coll., Dublin, and a Barrister-at-Law of the Inner Temple; b. 1835.

MILMAN, Sir WILLIAM, Bart., of Moor Park, Shropshire (cr. 1800).

Eldest son of the late Sir William George Milman, Bart., of Levaton, Woodlands, Devon, by Elizabeth Hurry, dau. of the late Robert Alderson, Esq., of Norwich; b. 1813; s. as 3rd Bart. 1857; m. 1841 Matilda Frances, dau. of the late Rev. John Pretyman, of Sherington, Bucks. Educated at Westminster and Brasenose Coll., Oxford (B.A. 1837); called to the Bar at the Inner Temple 1841, and goes the Oxford Circuit.—*Moor Park, Ludlow; Oxford and Cambridge Club, s.w.*

Heir, his son Francis John, b. 1842.

MILN, ALEXANDER HAY, Esq., of Woodhill, Forfarshire.

Eldest son of the late James Yeaman Miln, Esq., of Murie and Woodhill, by Mary, dau. of Alexander Hay, Esq., of Letham; b. 1817; s. 1857; m. 1859 Sarah Isabella, eldest dau. of James Mackintosh, Esq., of Lamancha, co. Peebles, and has issue,

* John Alexander Hay, b. 1860.

Mr. Miln is a Magistrate for cos. Forfar and Perth.—*Woodhill, Carnoustie, N.B.*

MILN, JAMES, Esq., of Murie, Perthshire.

Second son of the late James Yeaman Miln, Esq., of Murie, and of Woodhill, co. Forfar, by Mary, dau. of Alexander Hay, Esq., of Letham; b. 1818; s. 1857. Is a J.P. and D.L. for co. Perth, and a Magistrate for co. Forfar; Fellow of the Society of Antiquaries of Scotland, and of the Royal Scottish Society of Arts.—*Murie House, Errol, N.B.; University Club, Edinburgh; Royal London Yacht Club, s.w.*

MILNE, HENRY TRAVIS, Esq., of Crompton Hall, Lancashire.

Younger son of the late James Milne, Esq., of Park House, co. Lancaster, by Alice, only dau. of Abram Crompton, Esq., of High Crompton, co. Lancaster; b. 1825. Mr. Milne, who is a Magistrate for co. Lancaster, represents a branch of an ancient family seated in the parish of Prestwich-cum-Oldham, co. Lancaster.—*Crompton Hall and Park House, near Oldham.*

MILNE, Sir ALEXANDER, K.C.B., of Inveresk, Midlothian (cr. 1858).

Second son of the late Admiral Sir David Milne, G.C.B., by Grace, dau. of Sir Alexander Purves, Bart.; b. 1806; m. 1850 Euphemia, dau. of the late Archibald Cochran, Esq., of Askirk, co. Roxburgh, and has, with other issue,

* A son, b. 185—.

Sir Alexander is a Magistrate for co. Berwick, a Vice-660

Admiral; served on Pacific, Brazil, W. Indian, N. American, Lisbon, and Home Stations; was a Lord of the Admiralty 1847–59; re-appointed 1866; was Commander in Chief on the N. American and W. India Station from 1860 to 1864.—*Inveresk, Musselburgh, Edinburgh; United Service Club, s.w.*

MILNE-HOME, DAVID, Esq., of Milne Graden, Berwickshire.

Eldest son of the late Admiral Sir David Milne, G.C.B., of Milne Graden, by Grace, dau. of Sir Alexander Purves, Bart., of Purveshall, N.B.; b. 1805; s. 1845; m. 1832 Jean, eldest dau. of the late William Foreman Home, Esq., of Paxton House, co. Berwick, and has, with other issue, an only son,

* David, Lieut. R. Horse Guards (Blue); b. 1834; m. 1867 Jane, dau. of Sir Thomas Buchan Hepburn, Bart, of Smeaston, co. Haddington.

Mr. Milne-Home, who was educated at Edinburgh University (B.A. 1824), was called to the Scottish Bar 1826, and appointed Advocate Depute 1838, is a J.P. and D.L. for co. Berwick, author of several treatises on Astronomy, Geology, Meteorology, and Social Reforms, Is proprietor, in right of his wife, also of the estates of Wedderburn, Billie, and Paxton, in Berwickshire. This family came originally from Inverness-shire.—Residence: *Paxton House, Berwick-on-Tweed, N.B.; 10, York Place, Edinburgh; Carlton Club, s.w.*

MILNER, Sir WILLIAM MORDAUNT, Bart., of Nun Appleton, Yorkshire (cr. 1717).

Eldest son of the late Sir William Mordaunt Edward Milner, Bart., of Nun Appleton, by Lady Anne Georgiana, 3rd dau. of Frederick Lumley, Esq., and sister of John, 7th Earl of Scarborough; b. 1848; s. as 6th Bart. 1867. Educated at Ch. Ch., Oxford; is Patron of 1 living.—*Nun Appleton, Tadcaster; 75, Eaton Place, s.w.*

Heir Pres., his brother Frederick George, b. 1850.

MILNER, Dowager Lady, of Aldwarke, Yorkshire.

Harriet Elizabeth, dau. of the late Lord Edward Charles Cavendish-Bentinck, by Elizabeth, dau. of Richard Cumberland, Esq.; m. 1809 (as 2nd wife) Sir William Mordaunt Sturt Milner, Bart. (sometime M.P. for York), who d. 1855.—*Aldwarke Hall, Rotherham.*

MILNER, HENRY BEILBY WILLIAM, Esq., of West Retford, Notts.

Second son of the late Sir William M. S. Milner, Bart., of Nun Appleton, by his 2nd wife, Harriet Elizabeth, dau. of Lord Edward Charles C. Bentinck; b. 1823; m. 1853 Charlotte, dau. of the Most Rev. Marcus Beresford, D.D., Lord Archbishop of Armagh. Educated at Eton and Merton Coll., Oxford (B.A. 1845, M.A. 1850); late Fellow of All Souls Coll.; is a Magistrate for Notts.—*West Retford House, Retford.*

MILNER-GIBSON, the Right Hon. THOMAS, of Theberton House, Suffolk.

Only son of the late Major Thomas Milner-Gibson, of the 37th Foot, by Isabella, one of Lt.-Gover. Esq., of Chester; b. 1806; m. 1832 Arethusa Susanna, only dau. of the late Sir Thomas Gery Cullum, Bart., and has, with other surviving issue,

* Jasper, b. 1832.

Mr. Milner-Gibson, who was educated at the Charterhouse, and Trinity Coll., Cambridge, (B.A. 1830), is a J.P. and D.L. for Suffolk; was Vice-President of the Board of Trade 1846–8; M.P. for Ipswich 1837–9, for Manchester, 1841–57; has been M.P. for Ashton-under-Lyne since 1857; was President of the Board of Trade 1859–66.—*Theberton House, Saxmundham; Brooks's, Athenæum, and Reform Clubs, s.w.; 3, Hyde Park Place, w.*

MILNES, the Rev. NICHOLAS BOURNE, of Stubbin Edge, Derbyshire.

Only surviving son of the late William Milnes, Esq., of Stubbin Edge (who was a J.P. and D.L. for co. Derby), by his 2nd wife Mary, dau. of Paul Bright, Esq.; *b.* 1826; *s.* 1866. Educated at Rugby and Trinity Coll., Oxford (B.A. 1849, M.A. 1853); is Lord of the Manor of Ashover, and Rector of Collyweston, co. Northampton.—*Stubbin Edge, Chesterfield ; Collyweston Rectory, Stamford.*

MILNES. (See *Houghton, Lord.*)

MILTON, Viscount. (See under *Fitz William, Earl.*)

MILTON, Viscountess.

Selina, 2nd dau. of Charles Cecil Cope, 3rd Earl of Liverpool, by Julia Evelyn Medley, only dau. and heir of the late Sir George Augustus William Shuckburgh-Evelyn, Bart.; *m.* 1st 1833 Charles, Viscount Milton (who *d* 1835); 2nd 1845 George Savile Foljambe, Esq. —*Osberton Hall, East Retford ; Highbeech, Northampton ; 2, Carlton House Terrace, s.w.*

MILWARD, GEORGE, Esq., of Lechlade Manor, Gloucestershire.

Only son of the late George Milward, Esq., of Lechlade Manor, by Mary Anne, dau. of the late John Atkins, Esq., M.P., who was Lord Mayor of London ; *b.* 1807 ; *s.* 1839 ; *m.* 1835 Sarah, dau. of Henry Grace, Esq., of Stockwell, Surrey, J.P., and has, with other issue,

* George, of Magdalen Coll., Oxford, *b.* 1843 ; *m.* 1866 Augusta Susannah Shaen, eldest dau. of Thomas Shaen Carter, Esq., of Watlington Park, Oxon, and has issue, * George Harold Shaen, *b.* 1867.

Mr. Milward (who was called to the Bar at Lincoln's Inn 1838) is a Magistrate for co. Gloucester.—*Lechlade Manor, Gloucestershire ; Cavendish Club, w.*

MILWARD, HENRY, Esq., of Redditch, Worcestershire.

Eldest son of the late Henry Milward, Esq., of Redditch, by Sarah, dau. of Thomas Smith, Esq. ; *b.* 1802 ; *s.* 1829 ; *m.* 1831 Catherine, dau. of John Gosling, Esq., and by her, who *d.* 1867, has, with other issue,

* Henry Charles (in Holy Orders), M.A. of Christ's Coll., Cambridge; *b.* 1831 ; *m.* 1856 Margaret Aston, dau. of the late W. A. Wilkinson, Esq.

Mr. Milward is a Magistrate for cos. Worcester and Warwick.—*Redditch, Worcester.*

MILWARD, RICHARD, Esq., of Thurgarton, Notts.

Eldest son of John Parkinson, Esq., of Ley Fields, Notts, by Ann, dau. of Richard Milward, Esq., of Hexgreave Park ; *b.* 1810 ; *s.* 1844 his uncle, the late Richard Milward, Esq., when he assumed his name ; *m.* 1840 Marianne, 3rd dau. of Charles Martin, Esq. Appointed Lieut. South Notts Yeomanry Cavalry 1847 ; is a Magistrate for Notts (High Sheriff 1857)—*Thurgarton Priory, and Hexgreave Park, Southwell ; Carlton Club, s.w.*

MINCHIN, CHARLES, Esq., of Rathclough, co. Tipperary.

Eldest son of the late Humphrey Minchin, Esq., of Rathclough, by Mary, dau. of the late Thomas Lockwood, Esq., of Cashel ; *b.* 1805 ; *s.* 1822 ; *m.* 1848 Charlotte Bingham, dau. of the late Henry M. Kelly, Esq., of Carrarce, co. Galway. Educated at Trinity Coll., Dublin ; is a Magistrate for co. Tipperary.—*Rathclough, Cashel, co. Tipperary.*

Heir Pres., his brother Stephen, b. 1807.

MINNITT, JOSHUA ROBERT, Esq., of Anaghbeg, co. Tipperary.

Eldest son of the late Joshua Minnitt. Esq., of Anaghbeg, by Mary, dau. of Capt. N. Kingsley, of H.M.'s 8th Regt. ; *b.* 1806 ; *s.* 1830 ; *m.* 1834 Elizabeth, dau. of Sir Charles Forster Goring, Bart., of Highden, Sussex, and has, with other issue,

* Charles Goring, Lieut. 18th Royal Irish Regt. ; *b.* 1836 ; *m.* 1866 Lizzie, dau. of F. Whittaker, Esq., of Auckland, New Zealand.

Mr. Minnitt, who was educated at Trinity Coll., Dublin, is a Magistrate for co. Tipperary.—*Anaghbeg, Nenagh, co. Tipperary.*

MINTO, Earl of (WILLIAM HUGH ELLIOT-MURRAY-KYNYNMOUND).—Cr. 1813.

Eldest surviving son of Gilbert, 2nd Earl, by Mary, eldest dau. of the late Patrick Brydone, Esq. ; *b.* 1814 ; *s.* 1859 ; *m.* 1844 Emma Eleanor, dau. of the late General Sir Thomas Hislop, Bart. Educated at Eton and Trinity Coll., Cambridge ; is a Dep.-Lieut. for co. Roxburgh ; was M.P. for Hythe 1837-41, for Greenock 1847-52, and for co. Clackmannan 1857-9.—*Minto House, Hawick, N.B. ; Melgund, Jedburgh, N.B. ; Brooks's and Travellers' Clubs,* s.w.; 24, *Chester Square,* s.w.

Heir, his son Gilbert John, Viscount Melgund, educated at Trinity Coll., Cambridge, Ensign and Lieut., Scots Fusilier Guards; *b.* 1845.

MIREHOUSE, the Rev. JOHN, of Hambrook Grove, Gloucestershire.

Eldest son of the late Rev. William Squire Mirehouse, of Hambrook Grove (who was Chaplain to H.R.H. the Princess Sophia), by Eliza Brunetta, only dau. of the late George Arthur Herbert, Esq., of Glan-Hasren and Llanllugan, co. Montgomery ; *b.* 1839 ; educated at Harrow and Clare Coll., Cambridge (B.A. 1861, M.A. 1865) ; is Rector of Colsterworth, Lincoln. This is one of the few existing Saxon families.—*Colsterworth Rectory, Grantham ; Hambrook, Bristol.*

Heir Pres., his brother William Edward ; educated at Harrow, B.A. of Clare Coll., Cambridge, and a member of Lincoln's Inn ; *b.* 1844.

MIREHOUSE, HENRY JOHN, Esq., of St. George's Hill, Somersetshire.

Eldest son of the late Rev. Thomas Henry Mirehouse, of St. George's Hill, by Milly, dau. of the late Philip John Miles, Esq., M.P., of Leigh Court, and sister of Sir William Miles. Bart.: *b.* 1835 ; *s.* 1866 ; *m.* 1861 Anna, dau. of the Rev. George Tierney Roche. Is a Magistrate for Somerset, and Patron of 1 living.—*St. George's Hill, Bristol.*

MITCHELL, Sir WILLIAM, Knt., F.R.G.S. (cr. 1867).

Son of the late Mr. John Mitchell, of Modbury, Devon ; *b.* 1811 ; *m.* 1835 Caroline, eldest dau. of Mr. Richard Andrews, of Modbury ; is a Magistrate for Devon, and Editor and Proprietor of the *Shipping and Mercantile Gazette*, London. He received the honour of Knighthood as a recognition of his services rendered to maritime commerce, extending over a period of 30 years, and attended with important National benefits.—*Street, Ivybridge, Devon ; Gresham Club,* E.C.; 6, *Hyde Park Gate,* w.

MITCHELL, ALEXANDER, Esq., of. Stow, co. Midlothian.

Eldest son of the late Alexander Mitchell. Esq., by Jane, dau. of John Gardiner, Esq., of Smithston ; *b.* 1831 ; *s.* 1839 ; *m.* 1856 Fanny Georgiana, dau. of Richard Hasler, Esq., of Aldingbourne, Sussex. Educated at Eton and Ch. Ch., Oxford ; is J.P. and D.L. for co. Berwick, a Magistrate for cos. Midlothian and Selkirk, and Provincial G.M. of the Freemasons of Berwick

wickshire; was formerly Capt. Grenadier Guards; elected M.P. Berwick-on-Tweed 1865.—*Carolside, Earlston, co. Berwick; Guards', Brooks's, R-form, and Garrick Clubs*, s.w.; 6, *Great Stanhope Street*, w.

MITCHELL, FRANK JOHNSTONE, Esq., F.G.S., of Llanfrechfa Grange, Monmouthshire.
Eldest son of Francis Henry Mitchell, Esq., of Upper Wimpole Street, London, by Frances Elizabeth, dau. of Robert Johnstone, Esq.; *b.* 1824; *m.* 1860 Elizabeth, dau. of John Etherington Welch-Rolls, Esq., of The Hendre, co. Monmouth, and has issue,
  • Gladys Elizabeth, and Hilda Mary.
Mr. Mitchell, who was educated at St. John's Coll., Cambridge, is a Magistrate for co. Monmouth (High Sheriff 1868).—*Llanfrechfa Grange, Ca.rleon, Usk.*

MITCHELL, JOHN WRAY, Esq., of Castlestrange, co. Roscommon.
Second but elde-t surviving son of the late Edward Mitchell, Es;., of Castlestrange, by Mary Ann, dau. of the late John Wray, Esq., of Park Place, London; *b.* 1808; *s.* 1858; *m.* 1838 his cousin, Anne Sarah, dau. of John Wray, Esq., of Suffolk Place, London, and has, with other issue,
  • Edward, Lieut. R.E.; *b.* 1839.
Mr. Mitchell, who was educated at the Royal Military Academy, Woolwich, is a Colonel R.A., and was formerly Commandant of the School of Gunnery at Shoeburyness.— *Castlestrange, Athl:ague, co. Roscommon; United Service Club*, s.w.

MITCHELL, THOMAS ALEXANDER, Esq.
A native of Montrose; *b.* 1812; is a Merchant in London, and Partner in the house of Sampson, Mitchell, and Co., New Broad Street; has been M.P. for Bridport since 1841.—*Brooks's, Union, and Reform Clubs*, s.w.; 50, *Charles Street*, w.

MITCHELL, WILLIAM GILLESPIE, Esq., of Carwood, Lanarkshire.
Second son of the late Rev. John Mitchell, D.D., by Anne, eldest dau. of William Gillespie, Esq., of Bishopton, co. Renfrew; *b.* 1801; *m.* 1846 Janet, youngest dau. of the late James Dennistoun, Esq., of Dennistoun, and has, with other issue,
  • John William, *b.* 1849.
Mr. Mitchell, who was educated at Glasgow, is a Magistrate for co. Lanark.—*Carwood House, Biggar, N.B.*

MITCHELL. (See *Forbes-Mitche'l.*)

MITCHELSON. (See *Hepburn-Mitch:lson.*)

+MITCHISON, WILLIAM ANTHONY, Esq., of Sunbury Manor, Middlesex.
Son of the late — Mitchison, Esq.; *b.* 181-; *m.* 18— Mary, dau. of General Shaw. Is a Magistrate for Middlesex.—*The Manor House, Sunbury, Middlesex.*

+MITFORD, HENRY REVELY, Esq., of Exbury Park, Hants.
Eldest son of the late Capt. Henry Mitford, R.N. (who was lost at sea in H.M.'s ship York), by his 2nd wife Mary, dau. of the Hon. David Anstruther; *b.* 1800; *s.*; his grandfather, the late William Mitford, Esq. (the Historian of Greece), 1827; *m.* 1828 Lady Georgina Jemima, dau. of George, 3rd Earl of Ashburnham (divorced 1837), and has, with other issue,
  • Percy, educated at Eton; 2nd Sec. of Legation at Berlin; *b.* 1829; *m.* 1863 the Hon. Emily Marion, 3rd dau. of William, 1st Lord Egerton of Tatton.
Mr. Mitford, who was educated at Eton, is a J.P. and D.L. for Hants, and Lord of the Manor of Exbury.—*Exbury Park, Fawley, Beaulhampton, 25, Grosvenor Street West*, s.w.
662

MITFORD, Admiral ROBERT, of Mitford, Northumberland, and Hunmanby, Yorkshire.
Second son of the late Bertram Mitford, Esq., of Mitford Castle (who *d.* 1842), by Tabitha, dau. of Francis Johnson, Esq., M.D., of Newcastle-on-Tyne; *b.* 1781; *s.* his brother 1842; *m.* 1830 Margaret, dau. of James Dunsmure, Esq., of Edinburgh, and has issue,
  • Margaret, *m.* 1856 W. A. Tyssen Amhurst, Esq., of Didlington Park, Norfolk (whom see).

Admiral Mitford, who entered the Navy in 1794, and attained Flag Rank 1846, is Lord of the Manors of Mitford and Hunmanby, and Patron of 4 livings.—*Hunmanby Hall, Scarborough; Mitford Hall, Morpeth; 1, Regent Street*, s.w.

Heir Pres., his cousin Major John Philip Mitford, a Magistrate for Northumberland; b. 1808; m. 1843 Fanny, dau. of the late Charles Mitford, Esq., of Pitshill, Sussex.

MITFORD, WILLIAM TOWNLEY, Esq., of Pitshill, Sussex.
Only son of the late Charles Mitford, Esq., of Pitshill, by Margaret, dau. of the late Richard Greaves Townley, Esq., M.P., of Fulbourn, co. Cambridge; *b.* 1817; *s.* 1831; *m.* 1855 the Hon. Margaret Emma, dau. of Lloyd, 3rd Lord Kenyon, and has, with other issue,
  • William Kenyon, *b.* 1857.
Mr. Mitford, who was educated at Eton and Oriel Coll., Oxford (B.A. 1839), is a J.P. and D.L. for Sussex (High Sheriff 1847); elected M.P. for Midhurst 1859.—*Pitshill, Petworth; Carlton Club*, s.w.; 12, *Cavendish Square*, w.

MITFORD. (See under *Redesdale, Lord.*)

MOFFATT, GEORGE, Esq.
Son of the late William Moffatt, Esq., of London (who *d.* 1850); *b.* 1810; *m.* 1856 Lucy, dau. of the late James Morrison, Esq., M.P., of Basildon Park, Berks. Is a Magistrate for Berks, and a Merchant in London; was M.P. for Dartmouth 1845-52, for Ashburton 1852-7, for Honiton 1858-65, elected for Southampton 1866. —*Residence: St. Leonard's Hill, Windsor; Reform Club*, s.w.; 103, *Eaton Square*, s.w.

MOGG, JOHN GEORGE, Esq., of Farrington Gurney, Somerset.
Eldest son of the late George Mogg, Esq., of Farrington Manor, by Martha, dau. of Francis Morgan, Esq., of Cornhill House, Somerset; *b.* 1813; *s.* 1818; *m.* 1842 Marianna, only child of Capt. Kearney White, R.N. Educated at the Charterhouse and Oriel Coll., Oxford; is a Magistrate for Somerset, and Major N. Somerset Yeomanry Cavalry.—*The Manor House, Farrington Gurney, Bristol; Victoria Terrace, Weymouth; Conservative Club*, s.w.

MOGGRIDGE, MATTHEW, Esq., F.G.S., of Woodfield, Monmouthshire.
Second son of the late John Holder Moggridge, Esq., of Woodfield, by Sarah, dau. of M. Jeffrys, Esq., of Bilkelbrook, co. Worcester; *b.* 1803; *s.* 1834; *m.* 1836 Fanny Llewelyn, eldest dau. of the late Lewis Weston Dillwyn, Esq., M.P., and has, with other issue,
  • Matthew Weston (in Holy Orders), *b.* 1838.
Mr. Moggridge, who is a Magistrate for cos. Glamorgan and Monmouth, was formerly Capt. Glamorganshire Yeomanry.—*Woodfield, Newport, Monmouthshire.*

MOGRIDGE, Mrs., of Arcot House, Devon.
Amelia, dau. of the late Major-General Rumley, by Mary, dau. of Richard Beough, Esq., of Dublin; *m.* 1815 Theodore B. Mogridge, Esq., M.D., of Ashted, Birmingham (who *d.* 1858).—*Arcot House, Sidmouth.*

MOILLIET, JAMES, Esq., of Abberley Hall, Worcestershire.

Third but eldest surviving son of the late John Lewis Moilliet, Esq., of Abberley Hall, by Amelia, dau. of James Keir, Esq., F.R.S.; *b.* 1806; *s.* 1845; *m.* 1st 1832 Lucy Harriot, dau. of Samuel T. Galton, Esq. (she *d.* 1848); 2nd 1853 Lisy, dau. of M. André Sayous, of Paris, and has by the former, with other issue,

   • James Keir, *b.* 1832.

Mr. Moilliet is a Magistrate for co. Worcester (High Sheriff 1861), Lord of the Manor and Patron of Abberley.—*Abberley Hall, Worcester.*

MOIR, JOHN McARTHUR, Esq., of Milton, Argyllshire, and Hillfoot, Clackmannanshire.

Only son of John Moir, Esq., W.S., of Hillfoot, by Mary Bell, dau. of John Gray, Esq., of Loss, N.B.; *b.* 1798; *m.* 1st 1833 Agnes, dau. of James McKell, Esq.; 2nd 1840 Catherine, dau. of Edward Alexander, Esq., of Powis, and has, with other issue,

   • John, *b.* 1842.

Mr. McArthur Moir, who was educated at the University of Edinburgh, is a Magistrate for cos. Argyll and Clackmannan.—*Milton House, Dunoon, N.B.; Hillfoot House, Dollar, N.B.*

MOIR, Mrs., of Leckie, Stirlingshire.

Anne Elizabeth, 2nd dau. of William Hay, Esq., of Dunse Castle, co. Berwick, by Mary, dau. of John Bradstreet Garstin, Esq., of Harrold House, Beds; *m.* 1855 Robert Graham Moir, Esq., of Leckie, who *d.* 1864, leaving, with other issue,

   • Charles William Graham Graham, *b.* 1858.

The late Mr. Moir was a J.P. and D.L. for co. Stirling, and a Magistrate for co. Perth.—*Leckie House, Gargunnock, Stirling, N.B.*

MOLECEY, JOHN MOLECEY TWIGGE, Esq., of West Deeping, Lincolnshire.

Eldest son of the late John Molecey Twigge, Esq., of West Deeping (who assumed the additional name of Molecey), by Eliza, dau. of the late Francis Simpson, Esq., of Stamford; *b.* 1838; *s.* 1864.—*Mill House, West Deeping.*

MOLESWORTH, Viscount (RICHARD PIGOT MOLESWORTH).—Cr. 1716.

Eldest son of the late Richard Molesworth, Esq. (who *d.* 1799), grandson of Robert, 1st Viscount, by Catharine, dau. of Thomas Cobb, Esq., of Twickenham, Middlesex; *b.* 1786; *s.* his cousin as 7th Viscount 1815.—43, Grand Parade, Brighton.

Heir Pres., his nephew Samuel, M.A. of St. John's Coll., Cambridge, Curate of Addlestone, Surrey (only son of the late Capt. John Molesworth, R.N., who *d.* 1858, by Louisa, dau. of the late Rev. Dr. Tomkyns); *b.* 1829; *m.* 1862 Georgina Charlotte, 4th dau. of the late Capt. George Bagot Gosset, 4th Dragoon Guards, and has, with other issue,
   • George Bagot, *b.* 1867.

MOLESWORTH, Sir PAUL WILLIAM, Bart. (cr. 1689).

Eldest surviving son of the late Rev. William Molesworth, of St. Breoke, Cornwall, by Katherine, eldest dau. of Paul Troby Treby, Esq., of Goodamoor, Devon; *b.* 1821; *s.* his brother as 10th Bart. 1862; *m.* 1849 Jane Frances, dau. of the late Gordon William Francis Gregor, Esq., of Trewarthenick, Cornwall. Educated at Eton and St. John's Coll., Cambridge (B.A. 1843, M.A. 1846); is descended from a common ancestor with Viscount Molesworth.—*Park Hill, Clapham, Surrey, s.*

Heir, his son Lewis William, b. 1853.

MOLESWORTH, Dowager Lady, of Tetcott, Devon.

Andalusia, dau. of the late Bruce Carstairs, Esq.; *m.* 1st Temple West, Esq., of Mathon Lodge, co. Worcester; 2nd 1844 the Right Hon. Sir William Molesworth, Bart., who *d.* 1855. Is joint Patron of 1 living.—*Tetcott, Holsworthy, Devon; Pencarrow, Bodmin; 87, Eaton Place, s.w.*

MOLESWORTH, ARTHUR NEPEAN, Esq., of Fairlawn, co. Armagh.

Eldest son of the late Major Arthur Molesworth, of Fairlawn, by his 3rd wife Elizabeth, dau. of E. Leggington, Esq.; *b.* 1799; *s.* 1803; *m.* 1820 Harriette, dau. of Capt. Hawkins, and has, with other issue,

   • Arthur, *b.* 1821; *m.* 1855 Elizabeth, dau. of the late Dr. King, R.N., and has, with other issue, • Arthur, *b.* 1856.

Mr. Molesworth represents a collateral branch of the family of Viscount Molesworth.—*Fairlawn, Moy, Ireland.*

MOLESWORTH, GEORGE MILL FREDERICK, Esq., of Northdown, Devonshire.

Fourth son of the Rev. John Edward Nassau Molesworth, D.D., Vicar of Rochdale, by his 1st wife Harriet, dau. of the late William Mackinnon, Esq., of Portswood, Hants; *b.* 1825; *m.* 1851 Sarah, dau. of the late Lawrence Newall, Esq., of Townhouse, Littleborough, co. Lancaster, and has, with other issue,

   • Reginald Balfour, *b.* 1852.

Mr. Molesworth, who is a Magistrate for co. Lancaster and for Devon, and a Lieut. R.N., is of a junior branch of the family of Viscount Molesworth.—*Northdown, Bideford; Townhouse, Littleborough, Lancashire.*

MOLESWORTH, the Rev. JOHN EDWARD NASSAU, D.D.

Only child of the late John Molesworth, Esq. (who *d.* 1791), by Frances, eldest dau. of Matthew Hill. Esq., and great-grandson of Robert, 1st Viscount Molesworth; *b.* 1790; *m.* 1st 1815 Harriet, dau. of the late William Mackinnon, Esq. (she *d.* 1850); 2ndly 1854 Harriett Elizabeth, 3rd dau. of the late Rev. Sir Robert Affleck, Bart., and widow of John T. Bridges, Esq., and has, by the former, with other issue,

   • William Nassau, of Spotland, co. Lancaster, in Holy Orders; *b.* 1816; *m.* 1844 Margaret, youngest dau. of George Murray, Esq., of Ancoats Hall, and has issue.
   • James Murray, *b.* 1849.

Dr. Molesworth, who was educated at Trinity Coll., Oxford (B.A. 1812, M.A. 1817, D.D 1838), is Vicar of Rochdale, and a Magistrate for the W. Riding of Yorkshire.—*The Vicarage, Rochdale.*

MOLESWORTH, Miss, of Cobham, Surrey.

Caroline, dau. of the late Sir William Molesworth, of Pencarrow, Cornwall, by Caroline Treby, dau. of Paul Henry Ourry, Esq., of Goodamoor, Plympton, Devon; *s.* her mother 1842, as tenant for life of this property, under the will of General Felix Buckley.—*Cobham Lodge, Esher.*

MOLESWORTH-ST. AUBYN. (See *St. Aubyn.*)

MOLONY, JAMES, Esq., of Kiltanon, co. Clare.

Eldest son of the late James Molony, Esq., of Kiltanon, by Selina, dau. of the Rev. John Mills, of Harford, co. Warwick; *b.* 1785; *s.* 1823; *m.* 1st 1820 Harriet, dau. of William Harding, Esq.; 2nd 1828 Lucy, 2nd dau. of Sir Trevor Wheler, Bart., and has, by the former, with other issue,

   • William Mills, a Magistrate for co. Clare (High Sheriff,

1865), late Major 22nd Regt.; *b.* 1825; *m.* 1865 Mariane eldest dau. of the late Robert Fannin, Esq.

Mr. Molony, who was formerly in the H.E.I.C.'s Service in China, is a J.P. and D.L. for co. Clare (High Sheriff 1828).—*Kiltanon, Tulla, Ireland.*

MOLYNEUX, Sir CAPEL, Bart., of Castle Dillon, co. Armagh (cr. 1730).

Only surviving son of the late Sir George King Adlercron Molyneux, Bart., of Castle Dillon, by Emma, dau. of — Green, Esq.; *b.* 1841; *s.* as 7th Bart. 1848; *m.* 1863 Mary Emily Frances, eldest dau. of Peter Fitzgerald, Knight of Kerry. Represents a younger branch of the family of the Earl of Sefton.—*Castle Dillon, co. Armagh.*

Heir Pres., his cousin Capel, in Holy Orders. B.A. of Christ's Coll., Cambridge. Incumbent of St. Paul's, Brompton; *b.* 1804; *m.* 1852 Maria, dau. of Admiral Carpenter, and has issue, *five daughters.

MOLYNEUX, the Hon. FRANCIS GEORGE, of Earl's Court, Kent.

Youngest son of William Philip, 2nd Earl of Sefton, by the Hon. Maria, dau. of William, 6th Lord Craven; *b.* 1805; *m.* 1842 Lady Georgiana Jemima Ashburnham (whose marriage with Henry Reveley Mitford, Esq., was dissolved in 1842), and has issue,
* Constance.

Mr. Molyneux, who was educated at Eton and Trinity Coll., Cambridge, is a Magistrate for Kent, was formerly Secretary of Legation to the Germanic Confederation, and a Clerk in the Foreign Office.—*Earl's Court, Tunbridge Wells.*

MOLYNEUX. (See under *Sefton, Earl of.*)

MOLYNEUX. (See *More-Molyneux.*)

MOLYNEUX-MONTGOMERIE, CECIL THOMAS, Esq., of Garboldisham Hall, Norfolk.

Son of the late Thomas Molyneux-Montgomerie, Esq., of Garboldisham Hall, Norfolk (who *d.* 1855), by Georgina Louisa, dau. of Thomas, 3rd Lord Foley, and Lady Cecilia FitzGerald, dau. of William Robert, 2nd Duke of Leinster; *b* 1846; *s.* his mother 1864. Educated at Eton; is Lord of the Manor and Patron of Garboldisham.—*Garboldisham Hall, East Harling.*

MOLYNEUX-SEEL, THOMAS, Esq., of Huyton Hey, Lancashire.

Eldest son of the late Thomas Unsworth, Esq., of Maghull, by Frances, dau. of Thomas Seel, Esq., of Huyton Hey; *b.* 1792; *s.* 1816; *m.* 1823 Agnes Mary, dau. of the late Sir Richard Bedingfeld, Bart., of Oxburgh, Norfolk, and has, with other issue,
* Edmund, *b.* 1824; *m.* 1847 Anna, dau. of M. de Lousada, Duke and Grandee of Spain.

Mr. Molyneux-Seel, who was educated at Stonyhurst Coll., is a Magistrate for Norfolk, J.P. and D.L. for co. Lancaster, and Lord of the Manor of Huyton; late Major R. Lancashire Militia.—*Hayton Hey, Prescot.*

MONAHAN, the Right Hon. JAMES HENRY.

Eldest son of the late Michael Monahan, Esq., of Heathlawn, co. Galway; *b.* 1804. Educated at Trinity Coll., Dublin (B.A. 1893); called to the Irish Bar 1828; appointed Queen's Counsel 1840; was Solicitor-General for Ireland 1846–7; Attorney-General 1817–50; appointed Chief Justice of Court of Common Pleas, Ireland, 1850; sworn a Member of the Privy Council in Ireland 1848; was M.P. for Galway, Feb.—July, 1847.—*5, Fitzwilliam Square, Dublin.*

MONCK, Viscount (CHARLES STANLEY MONCK). —Cr. 1800.

Eldest son of Charles Joseph Kelly, 3rd Viscount, by Bridget, dau. of John Willington, Esq., of Killoskehane,

co. Tipperary; *b.* 1819; *s.* 1849; *m.* 1844 Lady Elizabeth, 4th dau. of Henry Stanley, 1st Earl of Rathdown (*ext.*) Is a Magistrate for co. Dublin, and a J.P. and D.L. for co. Wicklow; was M.P. for Portsmouth 1852–7, a Lord of the Treasury 1854–5, Lord Privy Seal to the Prince of Wales 1855–8, appointed Governor-General of Canada 1861; created Lord Monck, U.K. 1866. —*Charleville, Enniskerry, co. Wicklow; Government House, Quebec, Canada; Brooks's, Athenæum, and Arthur's Clubs,* s.w.

Heir, his son Henry Power Charles Stanley, *b.* 1849; educated at Eton.

MONCK, Sir ARTHUR EDWARD, Bart., of Belsay Castle, Northumberland (cr. 1662).

Elder son of the late Charles Atticus Monck, Esq. (who *d.* 1856), by Laura, dau. of Sir Matthew White Ridley, Bart.; *b.* 1838; *s.* his grandfather as 7th Bart. 1867. Is a Magistrate for Northumberland, Lord of the Manor of Belsay, and Patron of 1 living.—*Belsay Castle, Newcastle-on-Tyne.*

Heir Pres., his brother Henry, *b.* 1840.

MONCK, JOHN BLIGH, Esq., of Coley Park, Berks.

Eldest son of the late John Berkeley Monck, Esq., of Coley Park, by Mary, dau. of William Stephens, Esq., of Aldermaston, Berks; *b.* 1811; *s.* 1834; *m.* 1841 Elizabeth Margaret, dau. of the Rev. S. Wildman Yates, and has, with other issue,
* William Berkeley, B.A. of Magdalen Coll., Oxford, *b.* 1842.

Mr. Monck, who was educated at Eton and Brasenose Coll., Oxford (B.A. 1833), is a Magistrate for Berks (High Sheriff 1845).—*Coley Park, Reading.*

MONCKTON, the Hon. EDMUND GAMBIER, of Southwell Manor, Notts.

Fourth son of William George, 5th Viscount Galway, by Catharine Elizabeth, only dau. of the late Capt. G. Handfield; *b.* 1809; *m.* 1845 Arabella Martha, dau. of the Rev. John Robinson, and has, with other issue,
* William Henry, *b.* 1846.

Mr. Monckton, who was educated at the Charterhouse and Ch. Ch., Oxford, is a Magistrate for Notts, a J.P. and D.L. for the W. Riding of Yorkshire, and Lieut.-Col. Commanding 1st West York Rifle Militia; he was formerly in the 50th Foot, and Capt. in the Rifle Brigade.—*The Manor House, Southwell.*

MONCKTON, EDWARD HENRY CRADOCK, Esq., of Fineshade Abbey, Northamptonshire.

Eldest son of the late Philip Monckton, Esq., of the Bengal Civil Service (who *d.* 1820), by Harriette, dau. of Michael Carter, Esq., of Inch, N.B.; *b.* 1812; *s.* his uncle, George Monckton, Esq., of Somerford Hall and Fineshade Abbey, 1858; *m.* 1st 1835 Caroline Rosa, youngest dau. of Charles Woodcock, Esq., of the Madras Civil Service (she *d.* 1838); 2nd 1839 Maria Catherine, youngest dau. of Henry W. Tydd, Esq., by whom he has, with other issue,
* Edward Philip, Lieut. Northampton-shire Militia, *b.* 1846; *m.* 1866 Christabel, 2nd dau. of the Rev. C. D. Francis, Vicar of Tysoe, co. Warwick.

Mr. Monckton, who was educated at Westminster and Haileybury Coll., was formerly in the Bengal Civil Service, and was High Sheriff of co. Rutland 1859, is Lord of the Manors of Fineshade and Duddington.—*Fineshade Abbey, Wansford; Cavendish Club,* w.

MONCKTON, FRANCIS, Esq., of Somerford Hall, Staffordshire.

Eldest son of the late General Henry Monckton, of Stretton Hall, by Anne, only dau. of John G. Smythe, Esq., of Hilton, co. Salop; *b.* 1844; *s.* his uncle George Monckton, Esq., 1858; educated at Eton and at Ch.

Ch., Oxford; is Lord of the Manor of Somerford. —*Somerford Hall, near Brewood.*

Heir Pres., his brother Arthur, *b.* 1845.

MONCKTON, Mrs. HENRY, of Stretton Hall, Staffordshire.
Anne, only dau. of the late John G. Smythe. Esq., of Hilton, co. Salop; *m.* 1839 General Henry Monckton, of Stretton Hall (4th son of the Hon. Edward Monckton, of Somerford, by Sophia, dau. of George, Lord Pigot), who *d.* 1854. leaving, with other issue,

▪ Francis, of Somerford Hall (whom see), *b.* 1844.

Mrs. Monckton is Lady of the Manor of Stretton. —*Stretton Hall, Penkridge, Staffordshire.*

MONCKTON. (See under *Galway, Viscount.*)

MONCREIFF, Sir HENRY WELLWOOD-, Bart., of Tulliebole, Kinross-shire (cr. 1626).
Eldest son of the late Sir James Wellwood-Moncreiff, Bart., of Tulliebole, by Anne, dau. of George Robertson, Esq., R.N.; *b.* 1809; *s.* as 10th Bart. 1851; *m.* 1838 Alexina Mary, dau. of George Bell, Esq., of Edinburgh. Educated at the High School, Edinburgh, and New Coll., Oxford (B.A. 1831; M.A. 1843); is a J.P. and D.L. for co. Kinross; was formerly a Clergyman of the established Church of Scotland; graduated D.D. at the University of Edinburgh 1860, and has been since that time a Clergyman of the Free Church.—*Tulliebole Castle, Kinross, N.B.; 2, Bruntsfield Place, Edinburgh.*

Heir Pres., his brother the Right Hon. James, educated at the High School and University of Edinburgh; an Advocate at the Scottish Bar (called 1833); a Dep.-Lieut. for co. Edinburgh, and Lieut.-Col Edinburgh Volunteers; was Solicitor-General for Scotland 1850–1, Lord Advocate 1851–2 and 1852–7, and 1859–66; was M.P. for Leith 1851–9: elected M.P. for Edinburgh 1859; *b.* 1811; *m.* 1834 Isabella, dau. of Robert Bell, Esq., of Edinburgh, and has, with other issue, ▪ Henry James, *b.* 1835; *m.* 1866 Susan Wilhelmina, 3rd dau. of Sir W. H. Dick Cunyngham, Bart.

MONCREIFFE, Sir THOMAS, Bart., of Moncreiffe, Perthshire (cr. 1685).
Elder son of the late Sir David Moncreiffe, Bart., of Moncreiffe, by Helen, dau. of the late Æneas Mackay, Esq., of Scotston, N.B.; *b.* 1822; *s.* 1830; *m.* 1843 Lady Louisa, dau. of Thomas Robert, 10th Earl of Kinnoull. Educated at Harrow; is a J.P. and D.L. for Perthshire, and Hon. Col. Royal Perth Rifles; was formerly Lieut. Grenadier Guards.—*Moncrieffe House, Bridge of Earn, N.B.; 3, Prince's Terrace, s.w.*

Heir, his son Robert Drummond, *b.* 1856.

MONCRIEFF. (See *Scott-Moncrieff.*)

MONEY, GEORGE HENRY, Esq.
Son of the late George Money, Esq., of Hill House, Berks, by Pulcherie, only dau. of Raoul, 16th Marquess de Bourbel-Montpinçon, of Montpinçon, in Normandy; *b.* 182–. Educated at Eton and Trinity Coll,. Cambridge (B.A. 1843, M.A. 1846); called to the Bar at the Inner Temple in 1846; is a Dep.-Lieut. for Middlesex.—*Carlton Club*, s.w.; 9. *Berkeley Street, Berkeley Square*, w.; 15, *Old Square, Lincoln's Inn*, w.c.

MONEY-KYRLE, WILLIAM KYRLE, Esq., of Homme House, Herefordshire.
Eldest son of the late Rev. William Money (who assumed the additional name of Kyrle). by Emma, dau. of Richard Down, Esq., of Halliwick Manor, Middlesex; *b.* 1808; *s.* 1848. Educated at Oriel Coll., Oxford (B.A. 1831, M.A. 1848; is a J.P. and D.L. for co. Hereford (High Sheriff 1853), Patron of 1 living, and Major in the Hereford Militia.—*Homme House, Much Marcle, Ledbury; Whetham, Wilts; Pitsford, Northampton.*

Heir Pres., his brother John Fardo, a Dep.-Lieut. for co. Hereford, and Adjutant of Hereford Militia; late Capt.

32nd Foot; *b.* 1812; *m.* 1842 Harriet Louisa, eldest dau. of William Sutton, Esq., of Hertingfordbury, Herts, and has issue.

MONINGTON-WESTON, Mrs., of Sarnesfield, Herefordshire.
Mary Ann, youngest dau. of the late John Wright, Esq., of Kelvedon Hall, Essex; *m.* 1822 Thomas Webb-Weston, Esq., J.P. (who assumed the name of Monington 1824, on succeeding to the estate of Sarnesfield). He was High Sheriff of co. Hereford 1837, and *d.* 1857. Mrs. Monington-Weston is Patron of 1 living.—*Sarnesfield Court, Hereford.*

+**MONINS, JOHN EATON, Esq., of Ringwould, Kent.**
Only son of the late Rev. Richard Eaton Monins (who *d.* 1852), by Emily, dau. of the late Rev. John Chevallier, of Aspall Hall, Suffolk, and grandson of the late Rev. John Monins, of Ringwould; *b.* 1851; *s.* his grandfather 1855: Is Patron of 2 livings, and represents a branch of the ancient family of Monins, of Waldershare.—*Ringwould, Walmer.*

Heir Pres., his only sister Mary.

MONK, CHARLES JAMES, Esq.
Only son of the late Right Rev. James H. Monk, D.D., Lord Bishop of Gloucester and Bristol (who *d.* 1856), by Jane Smart, only dau. of the Rev. H. Hughes, of Nuneaton; *b.* 1824; *m.* 1853 Julia, only dau. of the late P. Ralli, Esq., and has, with other issue,

▪ James Henry, *b.* 1865.

Mr. Monk, who was educated at Eton and Trinity Coll., Cambridge (B.A. 1847, M.A. 1850). and called to the Bar at Lincoln's Inn 1850, is a Dep.-Lieut. for co. Gloucester; he was appointed Chancellor of Bristol 1855, and Chancellor of Gloucester 1859; was M.P. for Gloucester April–July, 1859; re-elected 1865.—*Travellers' and Reform Clubs*, s.w.; 93, *Eaton Square*, s.w.

MONRO, Sir DAVID, Knt. (cr. 1866).
Younger son of the late Alexander Monro, Esq., of Craiglockhart, by his 1st wife Maria, dau. of the late James Carmichael Smyth, Esq.; *b.* 1813; *m.* 1845 Dinah, dau. of John Secker, Esq., of Widford, Oxon. Educated at Edinburgh University; is Speaker of the House of Assembly at New Zealand.—*Newstead, Nelson, New Zealand.*

MONRO, ALEXANDER BINNING, Esq., of Auchenbowie, Stirlingshire.
Second son of the late David Monro Binning. Esq., of Softlaw, N.B. (who *d.* 1843), by Sophia, only child and heiress of George Home. Esq., of Argaty. co. Perth; *b.* 1805; *s.* his grandmother, Mrs. Home, eldest dau. and heir of John Monro, of Auchenbowie. 1836; *m.* 1835 Harriet, dau. of the late Alexander Monro, Esq., of Craiglockhart, M.D., and has, with other issue,

▪ David Binning, M.A. Fellow of Oriel Coll., Oxon; *b.* 1836.

Mr. Monro, who was educated at Edinburgh, descends from the Monros of Fowlis.—*Auchenbowie, Stirling; Wedwood Lodge, Edinburgh, N.B.*

MONRO, CHARLES JAMES HALE, Esq., of Ingsdon, Devon.
Eldest son of the late Charles Hale Monro. Esq.. J.P. and D.L., of Ingsdon. by his 1st wife Mary Jane. dau. of the late Patrick MacDougall. Esq.. of MacDougall. co. Argyle; *b.* 1828; *s.* 1867; *m.* 1855 Marion, dau. of George Withington, Esq., of Parkfield, co. Lancaster: is a Magistrate for Devon, and Lord of the Manor of Ingsdon; late Capt. 36th Foot. — *Ingsdon, Newton Abbotts.*

MONRO, DAVID, Esq., of Allan, Ross-shire.
Eldest son of the late Charles Monro, Esq., of Allan, Ross-shire, by Catherine, eldest dau. of Hugh Houston,

Esq., late of Creich, co. Sutherland; *b.* 1809; *s.* 1817; *m.* 1831 Elizabeth, only child of the late William Bennet, Esq., and has, with other issue,

* William, late Ensign 76th Foot; *b.* 1836.

Mr. Monro, who was educated at the University of Edinburgh, is a J.P. and D.L. for cos. Cromarty and Ross; formerly in the 76th Regt.—*Allan, Tain, N.B.*

MONRO, HECTOR, Esq., of Edmondsham, Dorset. Only son of the late Hector William Bower Monro, Esq., of Edmondsham, and of Ewell Castle, Surrey, by Henrietta Lewina, dau. of Lewis Dimoke Grosvenor Tregonwell, Esq., of Cranbourne Lodge and Anderson, Dorset, and of Ashington, Somerset; *b.* 1827; *s.* 1842; *m.* 1854 Ada, dau. of Sebastian Smith, Esq., and has, with other issue,

* Hector Edmond, *b.* 1855.

Mr. Monro, who was educated at the Royal Military Coll., Sandhurst, is a Magistrate for Dorset; late Capt. 57th Foot.—*Edmondsham, Cranbourne; Army and Navy Club, s.w.*

MONRO, Mrs., of Craiglockhart, Midlothian. Elizabeth, dau. of the late Charles Balfour Scott, Esq. (of the family of Woll), and sister of Charles Plummer, Esq., of Sunderland Hall, co. Selkirk; *m.* 1846 Alexander Monro, Esq., of Craiglockhart, who was a Magistrate for cos. Berwick and Midlothian, and formerly Capt. in the Rifle Brigade, and who *d.* 1867.—*Craiglockhart, Slateford, Edinburgh; Cockburn, Dunse, Berwickshire.*

MONSELL, the Rt. Hon. WILLIAM, of Tervoe, co. Limerick. Eldest son of the late William Monsell, Esq., of Tervoe, by Olivia, elder dau. of the late Sir John Allen Walsh, Bart.; *b.* 1812; *s.* 1822; *m.* 1st 1836 Lady Anna Maria, dau. of Windham Henry, 2nd Earl of Dunraven (she *d.* 1855); 2nd 1857 Berthe, dau. of Le Comte de Montigny Boutainvilliers, and has by the latter, with other issue,

* Gaston William Thomas, *b.* 1858.

Mr. Monsell, who was educated at Winchester and Oriel Coll., Oxford, is a J.P. and D.L. for co. Limerick (High Sheriff 1835), and a Magistrate for co. Clare; Clerk to the Ordnance 1852–7; President of the Board of Health 1857–8, Vice-President of the Board of Trade in 1866; has been M.P. for co. Limerick since 1847.—*Tervoe, Limerick; Athenæum Club, s.w.; Stafford Club, w.*

MONSON, Lord (WILLIAM JOHN MONSON).— Cr. 1728. Eldest son of William John, 6th Lord, by Eliza, youngest dau. of Edmund Larken. Esq.; *b.* 1829; *s.* as 7th Lord 1862. Educated at Ch. Ch., Oxford (B.A. 1848); is a J.P. and D.L. for co. Lincoln and for Surrey, and Patron of 7 livings; Major North Lincoln Militia, and Lieut.-Col. 3rd Administrative Battalion, Surrey Rifle Volunteers; was M.P. for Reigate 1859–62.—*Burton Hall, Lincoln; Chart Lodge, Sevenoaks; Gatton Park, Reigate; Brooks's Club. s.w.*

Heir Pres., his brother Debonnaire John, a Magistrate for Kent, and Capt. 52nd Foot; *b.* 1830; *m.* 1861 Augusta Louisa Caroline, dau. of the late Hon. Lieut.-Col. Augustus F. Ellis, and has issue, * two daughters.

MONSON, the Rev. THOMAS JOHN, of Kirbyunder-Dale, Yorkshire. Only surviving son of the late Hon. and Rev. Thomas Monson, Rector of Bedale, by his 2nd wife Sarah, dau. of the late Rev. Christopher Wyvill; *b.* 1825; *m.* 1856 the Hon. Caroline Isabella, youngest dau. of William 5th Viscount Galway, and has, with other issue,

* George John, *b.* 1857.

Mr. Monson, who was educated at Rugby and Uni-
666

versity Coll., Durham (B.A. 1847, M.A. 1850), is a Magistrate for the E. Riding of Yorkshire and Rector of Kirby-under-Dale.—*Kirby-under-Dale, York.*

MONTAGU, the Rt. Hon. Lord ROBERT, P.C. Second son of George, 6th Duke of Manchester, by Millicent, dau. of the late General Robert Bernard and Lady Olivia Sparrow; *b.* 1825; *m.* 1st 1850 Ellen Mary, dau. of John Cromie, Esq., of Cromore, Coleraine (she *d.* 1857); 2nd 1862 Miss Elizabeth Catharine Wade, and has by the former, with other issue,

* Robert Acheson Cromie, *b.* 1854.

Lord R. Montagu, who was educated at Trinity Coll., Cambridge (M.A. 1848), is a J.P. and D.L. for cos. Londonderry and Antrim (High Sheriff 1856); elected M.P. for Hunts 1859; appointed Vice-President of the Council and sworn a Privy Councillor 1867.—*Carlton and Athenæum Clubs, s.w.; 72, Inverness Terrace, w.*

MONTAGU, ANDREW, Esq., of Melton, Yorkshire. Eldest son of the late Richard Fountayne-Wilson. Esq., M.P., of Melton Park (who assumed the name of Fountayne on succeeding to the estates of the Right Hon. Frederick Montagu, of Papplewick), by Sophia, dau. of the late George Osbaldeston, Esq., M.P., of Hutton Bushel, co. York; *b.* 180–; *s.* 1847. Is a Dep.-Lieut. for the W. Riding of Yorkshire (High Sheriff 1853), Lord of the Manors of High Melton, Ingmanthorpe and Wighill, and Patron of 1 living.—*Melton Park, Doncaster; Papplewick, Nottingham.*

Heir Pres., his brother James, *b.* 18—.

+MONTAGU, the late George HERVEY, Esq., of Caversham Hill, Oxon. Eldest son of the late William Hervey Montagu, Esq., of Caversham Hill; *b.* 1805; *d.* 1866. Educated at Worcester Coll., Oxford (B.A. 1843); was Lord of the Manors of Beadloe and Hawnes, Beds.—*Caversham Hill, Reading.*

MONTAGU, Capt. HORACE, of Bath, Somerset. Son of the late Rev. Horatio Montagu, M.A., by Frances Mary, dau. of the late Major-General Sir George Wood, K.C.B., of Gatton and Ottershaw, Surrey, and niece of the late Sir Mark Wood, Bart., of Gatton, Surrey; *b.* 1837; *s.* his uncle, Capt. Montagu Montagu, R.N., 1863. Is Capt. 8th Hussars, late of the 11th Hussars. —*Bath, Somerset.*

MONTAGU. (See under *Manchester, Duke of; Sandwich, Earl of;* and *Rokeby, Lord.*)

MONTEAGLE, Lord (THOMAS SPRING RICE).— Cr. 1839. Elder son of the late Hon. Stephen Edmond Spring Rice (who *d.* 1865), by Ellen Mary, eldest dau. of the late William Frere. Esq., Serjeant-at-Law, and grandson of Thomas Spring, 1st Lord; *b.* 1849; *s.* his grandfather 1866. Educated at Harrow. The late Lord was some years Colonial Secretary and Chancellor of the Exchequer.—*Mount Trenchard, Limerick.*

Heir Pres., his brother Francis Spring, R.N., *b.* 1852.

+MONTEATH, ALEXANDER, Esq., of Broich, Perthshire. Son of the late Alexander Monteath, Esq., of Broich; *b.* 1800. Is a Magistrate for co. Perth, and Lord of the Barony of Broich.—*Broich, Crieff, N.B.*

MONTEATH-DOUGLAS. (See *Douglas.*)

MONTEFIORE, Sir Moses, Bart., F.R.S., of East Cliffe Lodge, Kent (cr. 1846).
Eldest son of the late Joseph Montefiore, Esq., of London, by Rachel, dau. of Abraham Mocatta, Esq.; b. 1784; m. 1812 Judith, dau. of Levi Barent Cohen, Esq. (she d. 1862). Is J.P. and D.L. for Kent (High Sheriff 1847), and a Magistrate for Middlesex; was Sheriff of London and Middlesex 1837.—East Cliffe Lodge, Ramsgate; Athenæum Club, s.w.; 7, Grosvenor Gate, w.

MONTEFIORE, Joseph Meyer, Esq., of Worth Park, Sussex.
Only son of the late Abraham Montefiore, Esq., of Stamford Hill, Middlesex, by his 2nd wife Henrietta, dau. of Meyer A. Rothschild, of Frankfort-on-the-Maine, and nephew of Sir Moses Montefiore, Bart.; b. 1816. Is a Magistrate for Sussex.— Worth Park, Crawley; 4, Great Stanhope Street, w.

MONTEITH, Robert, Esq., of Carstairs, Lanarkshire.
Eldest son of the late Henry Monteith, Esq., M.P., of Carstairs (Lord Provost of Glasgow), by Christina, dau. of J. Cameron, Esq., of Over Carntyne, co. Lanark; b. 1812; s. 1848; m. 1844 Wilhelmina Anne, dau. of C. Mellish, Esq., of Blythe, Notts, and has, with other issue,
* Henry Aloysius, b. 1851.
Mr. Monteith, who was educated at Trinity Coll., Cambridge (B.A. 1834, M.A. 1837), is a J.P. and D.L. for co. Lanark, and one of H.M.'s Scottish Body Guard. —Carstairs House, Lanark, N.B.; Oxford and Cambridge Club, s.w.

MONTFORT, Lady.
Ann, dau. of the late William Burgham, Esq., of Upton-Bishop, co. Hereford; m. 1847 Henry, 3rd Lord Montfort, who d. 1851, when his title became extinct.—6, Milton Street, n.w.

MONTGOMERIE, Sir Patrick, K.C.B. (cr. 1865).
Son of the late Robert Montgomerie, Esq., by Jean, dau. of Robert Montgomerie, Esq., of Beith, co. Ayr, N.B.; b. 1793; m. 1847 Henrietta, third dau. of the late James Haldane, Esq., of Auchans, co. Ayr. Educated at the Academy, Woolwich; is a Lieut.-General in the Army, and Col. Commandant Royal (late Madras) Artillery; served in the Indian Army 1810–15.— United Service Club, s.w.; Oriental Club, w.

MONTGOMERIE. (See under Eglinton, Earl of.)

MONTGOMERIE. (See Molyneux-Montgomerie.)

MONTGOMERY, Sir Graham Graham, Bart., of Stobo Castle, Peeblesshire (cr. 1801).
Eldest surviving son of the late Sir James Montgomery, Bart., M.P., of Stanhope and Whim, co. Peebles, by his 2nd wife Helen, dau. of the late Thomas Graham, Esq., of Kinross, N.B.; b. 1823; s. 1839; m. 1845 Alice, dau. of John James Hope-Johnstone, Esq., of Annandale, co. Dumfries. Educated at Ch. Ch., Oxford (B.A. 1845, M.A. 1864); is Lord-Lieutenant of co. Kinross, a J.P. and Vice-Lieutenant for co. Peebles, and Patron of 1 living; has been M.P. for co. Peebles since 1852; appointed a Lord of the Treasury, 1866.—Stobo Castle, Peebles, N.B.; Carlton Club, s.w.; 54, Grosvenor Place, s.w.
Heir, his son James Gordon Henry, b. 1850.

MONTGOMERY, Sir Henry Conyngham, Bart., of The Hall, co. Donegal (cr. 1808).
Eldest son of the late Sir Henry Conyngham Montgomery, Bart., of the Hall, co. Donegal, by Sarah Mercer, dau. of Leslie Grove, Esq., of Castle Grove, co.

Donegal; b. 1803; s. as 2nd Bart. 1830; m. 1827 Leonora, dau. of General Pigot. Educated at Eton; is a Member of the Council for India; formerly a Member of Council, and Chief Secretary to the Government at Madras, and on the Lord-Lieutenant's Staff in Ireland. —Burnham, Grove, Bucks; Athenæum Club, s.w.
Heir Pres., his brother Alexander Leslie, a Rear-Admiral reserved; b. 1807; m. 1840 Caroline Rose, dau. of James Campbell, Esq., of Hampton Court, and has, with other issue, * Hugh Conyngham, b. 1847.

MONTGOMERY, Sir Robert, K.C.B., G.C.S.I., (cr. 1859).
Son of the late Rev. Samuel Law Montgomery, by Mary, dau. of James M'Clintock, Esq., of Trintaugh; b. 1810; m. 1st 1834 Mary, dau. of — Thomason, Esq. (she d. 1842); 2nd 1845 Ellen Jane, 2nd dau. of William Lambert, Esq., of Woodmansterne, Surrey. Educated at Haileybury Coll.; was Judicial Commissioner in the Punjaub 1853–7, Chief Commissioner in Oude 1857–9; Lieutenant-Governor of the Punjaub 1859–64.—Oriental Club, w.

MONTGOMERY, Alexander Shirley, Esq., of Ballykeel House, Downshire.
Eldest son of the late Rev. Thomas Hassard Montgomery, of Ballykeel House, by Emily Jane Saunders, 2nd dau. of the Rev. Boughey William Dolling, of Magherolin, co. Down; b. 1843; s. 1865. This family is a branch of the Montgomeries, who, temp. James 1., obtained large grants of land in Monaghan, Tyrone, Cavan, Leitrim, and Donegal.—Ballykeel House, Dromore, co. Down; Ulster Club, Belfast.
Heir Pres., his brother Boughey William Dolling, b. 1853.

MONTGOMERY, Hugh, Esq., of Grey Abbey, Downshire.
Eldest son of the late William Montgomery, Esq., of Grey Abbey, by Lady Amelia Elizabeth, dau. of Thomas, 5th Earl of Macclesfield; b. 1821; s. 1831; m. 1846 Lady Charlotte Elizabeth, 2nd dau. of Edward, 2nd Earl of Powis, and has, with other issue,
* William Edward, b. 1847.
Mr. Montgomery, who was educated at Eton and Ch. Ch., Oxford; is a J.P. and D.L. for co. Down (High Sheriff 1845). This family is the only branch of the Montgomerys descended uninterruptedly in the male line from Roger de Montgomery, who came from Normandy with William the Conqueror.— Grey Abbey, Newtonards, Downshire; Carlton Club, s.w.

MONTGOMERY, Hugh Parker, Esq., of Tyrella, Downshire.
Elder son of the late Arthur Hill Montgomery, Esq., J.P. and D.L., of Tyrella, by Lady Matilda Anne, 3rd dau. of Thomas, 5th Earl of Macclesfield; b. 1829; s. 1867. Educated at Eton; is Capt. 60th Royal Rifles. —Tyrella House, Clough, Downshire.
Heir Pres., his brother Arthur Hill Sandys, b. 1841.

MONTGOMERY, Hugh Lyons-, Esq., of Bellavel, co. Leitrim.
Eldest son of the late Hugh Lyons-Montgomery, Esq., of Bellavel, by Eliza, dau. of the Very Rev. Stewart Blacker, Dean of Leighlin; b. 1816; s. 1826; m. 1840 Elizabeth, dau. of Henry Smith, Esq., of Annesbrook, co. Meath. Educated at Trinity Coll., Dublin; is a J.P. and D.L. for co. Leitrim; was M.P. for co. Leitrim 1852–9.—Bellavel, Carrick-on-Shannon; Carlton Club, s.w.

MONTGOMERY, John, Esq., of Benvarden, co. Antrim.
Eldest son of the late Hugh Montgomery, Esq., of Benvarden, by Margaret, dau. of — Allen, Esq., of Kilmandle, co. Antrim; b. 1790; s. 1822; m. 1819

Jane, 3rd dau. of the late Sir Andrew Ferguson, Bart., (ext.) and has, with other issue,

* Robert James, a Dep.-Lieut. for co. Londonderry (High Sheriff 1867); Capt. 5th Dragoon Guards; b. 1828; m. 1864 Elizabeth, dau. of James Robert White, Esq., and has issue,
* John Alexander, b. 1866.

Mr. Montgomery, who was educated at Belfast and Trinity Coll., Dublin (B.A. 1811, M.A. 1831), and called to the Irish Bar 1815, is a J.P. and D.L. for co. Antrim (High Sheriff 1819).—Benvarden, Ballymoney; Ulster Club, Belfast; Conservative Club, s.w.

+MONTGOMERY, NATHANIEL, Esq., of Cullies House, co. Cavan.
Son of the late N. Montgomery, Esq., of Cullies House; b. 18—; is married and has issue. Is a Magistrate for co. Cavan (High Sheriff 1863).—Cullies House, Cavan.

MONTGOMERY, RICHARD THOMAS, Esq., of Beaulieu, co. Louth.
Eldest son of the late Rev. Alexander Johnston Montgomery, of Beaulieu. by Margaret, dan. of Andrew Johnston, Esq., of Littlemount, co. Fermanagh; b. 1813; s. 1856; m. 1845 Frances Barbara, dau. of St. George Smith, Esq., of Green Hills, co. Louth, and has, with other issue,

* Richard Johnston, b. 1855.

Mr. Montgomery, who was educated at the Charterhouse and Trinity Coll., Dublin, is a Magistrate for co. Louth (High Sheriff 1855); was formerly Lieut. 3rd Light Dragoons.—Beaulieu, Drogheda, co. Louth.

MONTGOMERY, ROBERT GEORGE, Esq., of Convoy, co. Donegal.
Only son of the late Robert Montgomery, Esq., of Convoy, by Maria Frances, dau. of Alexander Stewart, Esq., of Ard's House, co. Donegal; b. 1814; s. 1846. Is a J.P. and D.L. for co. Donegal (High Sheriff 1840). —Convoy House, Raphoe, co. Donegal.

+MONTGOMERY, THOMAS, Esq., of Birch Hall, co. Antrim.
Fourth son of the late Hugh Montgomery, Esq., of Benvarden, by Margaret, dau. of — Allen, Esq., of Kilmandle, and brother of John Montgomery, Esq., of Benvarden (whom see); b. 1810. Is a Magistrate for co. Antrim; was formerly an Officer in the 9th and 16th Lancers.—Birch Hall, Antrim.

MONTGOMERY, VAUGHAN, Esq., of Crilly House, co. Tyrone.
Second son of the late George Montgomery, Esq., of Belfast, by Margaret, dau. of John Campbell, Esq., M.D., of Belfast; b. 1819; m. 1851 Margaret, eldest dau. of the late George Pettigrew, Esq., of Crilly House, and has, with other issue,

* George Pettigrew, b. 1852.

Mr. Montgomery, who is a Magistrate for co. Tyrone, was formerly a Merchant at Belfast.—Crilly House, Aughnacloy, co. Tyrone.

MONTGOMERY, WILLIAM, Esq., of Milton House, Northamptonshire.
Eldest son of the late Rev. Francis Montgomery, who was some time Rector of Harleston, by Mary, dau. of the late Robert Andrew, Esq., of Harleston Park, co. Northampton; b. 1797; s. 1831. Is descended from a common ancestor with the noble families of the same name.—Milton House, Northampton.

Heir Pres., his brother Robert (in Holy Orders), M.A., of St. Peter's Coll., Cambridge; Rector and Patron of Holcott, Northampton; b. 1800; m. 1825 Jane, eldest dau. of the late Thomas Walker Esq., Senior Registrar in the Court of Chancery, who d. 1855.

668

MONTGOMERY-MOORE, ALEXANDER GEORGE, of Garvey, co. Tyrone.
Only surviving son of the late Alexander James Montgomery-Moore, Esq., of Garvey, by Susannah, youngest dau. of George Mateham, Esq., of Ashfold Lodge, Sussex; b. 1833; m. 1857 Jane, youngest dau. of James, 1st Lord Seaton, G.C.B., &c. Educated at Eton; late Capt. 4th Light Dragoons.—Garvey House, Aughnacloy, co. Tyrone; Royal Hospital, Dublin; Carlton and Army and Navy Clubs, s.w.

MONTRESOR, HENRY EDWARD, Esq., of Denne Hill, Kent.
Eldest son of the late General Sir Henry Montresor, of Denne Hill, by Annetta, dau. of the Rev. E. Cage, of Eastling, Kent; b. 1823; s. 1837; m. 1856, Laura, dau. of the late Rev. William Dickins, Rector of Adisham, Kent, and has issue. Educated at Sandhurst; was formerly Capt. and Lieut.-Col. in the Grenadier Guards. —Denne Hill, Canterbury.

MONTROSE, Duke of (JAMES GRAHAM, P.C., K.T., D.C.L.).—Cr. 1707.
Eldest son of James, 3rd Duke, by his 2nd wife Lady Caroline Maria, eldest dau. of George, 4th Duke of Manchester; b. 1799; s. 1836; m. 1836 the Hon. Caroline Agnes, dau. of John, 2nd Lord Decies. Educated at Eton; sits in the House of Lords as Earl Graham, G.B. (cr. 1722); is Lord-Lieutenant of co. Stirling; Hereditary Sheriff of co. Dumbarton; General of the Royal Archers of Scotland, and Col of the Stirling, Dumbarton, Clackmannan, and Kinross Militia; Chancellor of the University of Glasgow; was M.P. for Cambridge 1826-30; Lord Steward of the Household Feb. —Dec. 1852; Chancellor of the Duchy of Lancaster 1858-9; appointed Postmaster-General 1866.—Buchanan House, Glasgow; Carlton Club, s.w.; 45, Belgrave Square, s.w.

Heir, his son James, Marquis of Graham, b. 1847; educated at Eton; Lieut. 1st Life Guards.

MONYPENNY, the Rev. JAMES ISAAC, of Hadlow, Kent.
Second son of the late Thomas Monypenny, Esq., of Rye, Sussex, by Catherine, dau. of Isaac Rutton, Esq., of Ospringe, Kent; b. 1799; m. 1828 Mary Blackwell, dau. of Robert Monypenny, Esq., of Merrington Place, Rolvenden, Kent, and has, with other issue,

* James Robert Blackwell, Capt. E. Kent Militia; b. 1833; m. 1866 Mary Elizabeth, younger dau. of the Rev. Charlton Lane, Incumbent of Hampstead, and has issue.

Mr. Monypenny, who was educated at Wadham Coll., Oxford (B.A. 1820, M.A. 1825), is a Magistrate for Kent, Vicar of Hadlow, and Patron of 1 living. This family is descended from an ancient family established at Pitmilly, Fife, N.B. The Kentish branch have been settled at Rolvenden from the early part of the 18th century.—Hadlow, Tunbridge; National Club, s.w.

MONYPENNY, PHILIPS, Esq., of Hythe, Kent, Third son of the late Thomas Monypenny, Esq., of Rolvenden, Kent, by Catherine, dau. of Isaac Rutton, Esq., of Ospringe, and brother of the late T. G. Monypenny, M.P.; b. 1800; m. 183- Jane, dau. of Thomas Castle, Esq., of Ingles, Kent, and by her, who is deceased, has no issue. Mr. Monypenny is a J.P. and D.L. for Kent.—Hythe, Kent.

MONYPENNY, ROBERT THOMAS GYBBON GYBBON, Esq., of Maytham Hall, Kent.
Eldest son of the late Thomas Gybbon Monypenny. Esq., of Hole House, Kent, by Sylvestra Rose, dau. of Robert Monypenny, Esq., of Merrington, Kent; b. 1823; m. 1817 Janet Phillips, eldest dau. of Lieut. Col. Henry

Burney, H.E.I.C.'s Service, and by her, who d. 1863, has, with other issue,

* Henry Thomas, b. 1850.

Mr. Monypenny, who is a J.P. and D.L. for Kent, and Major West Kent Militia, was formerly in the 86th Foot.—*Maytham Hall, Rolvenden, Staplehurst ; Royal Thames Yacht Club.*

+MONYPENNY, WILLIAM TANKERVILLE, Esq., of Pitmilly, Fifeshire.
Son of the late Alexander Monypenny, Esq., of Pitmilly, and brother of David Monypenny, Esq. (one of the Scottish Judges); b. 1783 ; m. 1844 Hannah, dau. of Col. Spens. Is a Magistrate for co. Fife, and Lord of the Barony of Pitmilly.—*Pitmilly, St. Andrew's, N.B.*

MOODY, the Rev. HENRY RIDDELL.
Only surviving son of the late Robert Sadleir Moody, Esq., of Aspley, Beds, by Jane, dau. of Capt. Andrew Riddell, of Enfield ; b. 1792; s. 1825 ; m. 1819 Althea Jane, dau. of the Ven. Archdeacon Wollaston, and has, with other issue, .

* Robert Sadleir, M.A., educated at Eton and Ch. Ch., Oxford ; b. 1822; m. 1846 Ellen, dau. of John Sedgwick, Esq.

Mr. Moody, who was educated at Oriel Coll., Oxford (B.A. 1815, M.A. 1817), and appointed Rector of Chartham 1822, and Hon. Canon of Canterbury 1866, is representative of the Sadleirs of Temple Dinsley Herts, and of Aspley, Beds.—*Chartham Rectory, Canterbury ; University Club, s.w.*

MOODY, JOHN SADLEIR, Esq., of Stoneham, Hants.
Eldest son of the late Richard Vernon Moody, Esq., of Southampton, by Mary Annabella, dau. and co-heir of William Nicholas, Esq., of Froyle Park, Hants ; b. 1788; s. 1792; m. 1811 Mary, elder dau. of Samuel Silver Taylor, Esq., of Hockley House, Hants, and had issue, John Sadleir, b. 1813; d. 1823. Mr. Moody, who was educated at Winchester Coll., is a J.P. and D.L. for Hants.—*Park Cottage, Stoneham Park, Southampton.*

Heir Pres., his brother Thomas Sloan, a Dep.-Lieut for Hants ; b. 1789 ; m. 1813 Sarah, dau. of Samuel Silver Taylor, Esq., of Hockley House, Hants.

MOODY, WILLIAM, Esq., of Kingsdon, Somerset.
Eldest surviving son of the late Aaron Moody, Esq., of Kingsdon (who d. 1820), by Catharine, his wife ; b. 1800; s. his brother 1867. Is a Magistrate for Somerset, and Lord of the Manor of Kingsdon.—*Kingsdon, Taunton.*

MOON, Sir FRANCIS GRAHAM, Bart., F.S.A. (cr. 1855).
Youngest son of the late Christopher Moon, Esq., of London, by Ann, dau. of T. Withny, Esq.; b. 1796 ; m. 1818 Ann, dau. of John Chancellor, Esq., of Kensington. Middlesex ; is a J.P. and D.L. for Westminster and Middlesex, and an Alderman of London, of which he was Sheriff 1843, Lord Mayor 1855.—*Western House, Brighton ; 35, Portman Square, w.*

Heir, his son Edward Graham, M.A., of Magdalen Coll., Oxford, Rector of Fetcham, Surrey ; b. 1825; m. 1851 Ellen, eldest dau. of Alderman Thomas Sidney, M.P., of Bowes Manor, Middlesex, and I has, with other issue,
* *Francis Sidney Graham, b. 1855.*

MOOR, Major FREDERICK, of Pixton Hill, Sussex.
Youngest son of the late Henry I. Moor, Esq., of Kirby Hall, Kent, and Lord of the Manor of Otterham, in the same county, by Elizabeth, eldest dau. of the late John Remmington, Esq., D.L., of Barton-End House, Horsley, co. Gloucester ; b. 1816; m. 1841 Margaret, only surviving dau. of Col. Thomas Wood, C.B., and has, with other issue,

* Frederick, B.A. New Coll., Oxford ; b. 1846.

Major Moor, who was educated at the Royal Military Coll., Sandhurst, is a J.P. and D.L. for Sussex.—*Pixton House, East Grinstead ; Army and Navy Club, s.w.*

MOOR, HENRY, Esq.
Eldest son of the late Henry I. Moor, Esq., of Kirby Hall, Kent, by Elizabeth, eldest dau. of the late John Remmington, Esq., of Barton-End House, Horsley, co. Gloucester ; b. 1809; m. 1835 Mary, dau. of Thomas Ennis, Esq.; is a Dep.-Lieut. for Sussex; was M.P. for Brighton 1864–6.—4, *Sussex Square, Kemp Town, Brighton ; Oriental Club, w.*

MOORAT, JOHN SAMUEL, Esq., of Bush-Hill Park, Middlesex.
Younger son of the late Samuel Moorat, Esq., of Madras by Anne, dau. of Edward Raphael, Esq., of Madras ; b. 1795 ; m. 1813 Marie Delphine, dau. of Joseph White, Esq., of Pondicherry, and has, with other issue,

* Samuel, b. 1815 ; m. 1st 1840 Frances, dau. of Edward Hebden, Esq. (she d. 1857) ; 2nd 1858 Constance, dau. of the late R. T. Bateman, Esq., of Hartington Hall, co. Derby, and has issue by both marriages.

Mr. Moorat, who was educated at the Coll. of the Jesuits at Pondicherry, represents a family of Armenian extraction.—*Bush-Hill Park, Edmonton, N.E. ; 21, Gloucester Square, w.*

MOORE, Sir RICHARD EMANUEL, Bart. (cr. 1681).
Eldest son of the late Sir Emanuel Moore, Bart., by a dau. of the late Mr. Gillman ; b. 1810; s. as 10th Bart. 1849 ; m. 1st 1839 Mary Anne, dau. of A. Ryan O'Connor, Esq., of Kilboggin House, co. Cork; 2nd 1851 Margaret Matilda, sister of Roger O'Connor, Esq.—Residence : *Cork.*

Heir, his son Thomas O'Connor, b. 1843.

MOORE, Lady, of Brook Farm, Surrey.
Dora, younger dau. of the late Thomas Eden, Esq., of Wimbledon, Deputy-Auditor of Greenwich Hospital, by Mariana, dau. of Arthur Jones, Esq., and niece of William, 1st Lord Auckland; m. 1812 Vice-Admiral Sir Graham Moore, K.C.B., who d. 1843, leaving issue,
* John, Capt. R.N.. b. 1816 ; entered the Navy 1834, and served in the Black Sea 1854–6.—*Brook Farm, Esher.*

MOORE, the Hon. and Rev. EDWARD GEORGE.
Third son of Stephen, 2nd Earl of Mount Cashell, by Lady Margaret, eldest dau. of Robert 2nd Earl of Kingston; b. 1798 ; m. 1827 the Hon. Ann Matilda, 2nd dau. of Robert, 16th Lord Clinton, and has, with other issue,

* Edward George Augusta Harcourt, b. 1829.

Mr. Moore was educated at St. John's Coll., Cambridge (M. A. 1822), appointed Canon of Windsor 1851, Rector of West Ilsley 1840.—*The Cloisters, Windsor; West Ilsley Rectory, Newbury.*

MOORE, CHARLES, Esq., of Mooresfort, co. Tipperary.
Eldest son of the late Arthur Moore, Esq. (who d. 1850), by Mary, dau. of Henry O'Hara, Esq.; b. 1801 ; m. 1835 Marian Elizabeth, dau. of John Story, Esq., of Dublin, and has issue, an only surviving son.

* Arthur John, b. 1851.

Mr. Moore, who is a Magistrate for co. Tipperary, and Lord of the Manors of Mooresfort and Bansha, was elected M.P. for Tipperary. 1865 ; he purchased this property in 1850.—*Mooresfort, Tipperary ; Reform Club, s.w. ; 16, Berkeley Square, w.*

MOORE, Capt. CHARLES, of Maulden Cottage, Beds.

Son of the late Rev. Robert Moore, D.D., Vicar of Thurleigh, Beds, by Anne his wife; b. 1793; m. 1819 Elizabeth Anne, dau. of the late Richard Palmer, Esq., and grandson of the late Sir Gillies Payne, Bart., of Tempsford Hall, Beds., and by her, who d. 1857, has surviving issue,

* Four daughters.

Capt. Moore, who is a Post-Capt., retired, and served in the Coast Guard 1834–7, is a J.P. and D.L. for Beds. —*Maulden Cottage, Ampthill.*

MOORE, the Rev. CHARLES, of Wyberton, Lincolnshire.

Son of the late Edward Moore, Esq., of Stockwell House, Surrey, by Sarah Gray, dau. of Joseph Saunders, Esq., of Ealing; b. 1786; m. 1st 1824 Elizabeth Anna, dau. and heir of Thomas Tunnard, Esq., of Frampton Hall, co. Lincoln; 2nd 1842 Lucy, dau. of Edward Deakin, Esq., and has by the former, with other issue,

* Charles Thomas John, F.S.A. (of Frampton Hall, co. Lincoln, J.P. and D.L., High Sheriff 1856, and Major of the County Militia); b. 1827; m. 1849 Frances Mary Vassall, dau. of Henry Richard Roe, Esq., of Gnaton Hall, Devon, and has, with other issue, * Thomas Coney Tunnard, b. 1854.

Mr. Moore, who was educated for the Bar, and was for some years a member of the Inner Temple, is a Magistrate for co. Lincoln, Rector of Wyberton. and Domestic Chaplain to the Earl of Northesk.—*Wyberton Rectory, Boston.*

MOORE, the Rev. CHARLES AVERY.

Third son of the late Rev. William Moore, D.D., of Park Hill, Woodchester, co. Gloucester, by Elizabeth, dau. of Thomas Warner, Esq., of Marlborough, Wilts ; b. 1801; m. 1836 Mary Nankivell, youngest dau. of John Tripp, Esq., of Iwood House, Congresbury, Somerset, and widow of Thomas Townshend, and has an only surviving child,

* Henrietta Wolcot.

Mr. Moore, who was educated at Trinity Hall, Cambrige (LL.B. 1840), is a Magistrate for cos. Wilts and Lincoln, was appointed Vicar of Sutterton, 1860.—*The Vicarage, Sutterton, Boston.*

MOORE, the Rev. EDWARD, of Frittenden, Kent.

Son of the late Rev. George Moore. Prebendary of Canterbury, by Harriet Mary, dau. of the late Sir Brook Bridges, Bart. ; b. 1814 ; m. 1842 Lady Harriet Janet Sarah, youngest dau. of Charles William, 4th Duke of Buccleuch, K.G. Educated at Eton and Ch. Ch., Oxford (B.A. 1836, M.A. 1840); appointed Rector of Frittenden 1848.—*Frittenden House, Staplehurst; Oxford and Cambridge Club, s.w.*

MOORE, the Rev. EDWARD, F.S.A., of Spalding, Lincolnshire.

Third and only surviving son of the late Prebendary William Moore, D.D., of Spalding, by Ann Elizabeth, dau. of Prebendary Maurice Johnson, D.D., of Spalding; b. 1811 ; m. 1838 Elizabeth Sarah, dau. of Mr. Richard M. Stephenson, of Swineshead. Educated at Shrewsbury and St. John's Coll., Cambridge (B.A. 1835, M.A. 1838), is a Magistrate for co. Lincoln. Chairman of Quarter Sessions at Spalding, and Perpetual Curate of Spalding; was formerly Head Master of Spalding Grammar School, and Vicar of Weston St. Mary, &c. This family was formerly of Stockwell, Middlesex, and of Over, co. Chester.—*The Parsonage, Spalding.*

+ **MOORE, EDWARD, Esq., of Townend House, Worcestershire.**

Son of the late E. Moore, Esq., of Townend House; b.

18—. Is a J.P. and D.L. for co. Worcester, and a Magistrate for co. Stafford.—*Townend House, Halesowen, Worcestershire.*

MOORE, FRANK JOHN, Esq., of Woodcock Hill, Herts.

Eldest son of the late Frank Moore, Esq., of North Church, by Hannah, dau. of John Platt, Esq., Merchant, of London ; b. 1803. Educated at Rugby and Exeter Coll., Oxford (B.A. 1826, M.A. 1829) ; is a Magistrate for Herts and Bucks.—*Woodcock Hill, Berkhamstead.*

MOORE, GEORGE, Esq., of Appleby, Leicestershire.

Only son of the late George Moore, Esq., of Appleby, by Susan, dau. of John Drummond, Esq., of Megginch Castle, co. Perth; b. 1811 ; s. 1827; m. 1st 1833 Susan, youngest dau. of William Phillipps Inge, Esq., of Thorpe Constantine, co. Stafford (she d. 1836); 2nd 1839 Isabel Clara, dau. of the Rev. Charles Holden, of Aston, co. Derby, and by her, who d. 1867, has, with other issue,

* George John, b. 1842.

Mr. Moore, who was educated at Eton and Ch.-Ch., Oxford, is a J.P. and D.L. for cos. Leicester and Derby (High Sheriff 1837), a Magistrate for co. Warwick, Lord of the Manor and Patron of Little Appleby.—*Appleby Hall, Atherstone ; Boodle's and Carlton Clubs, s.w.*

MOORE, GEORGE, Esq., of Whitehall, Cumberland.

Second son of the late Mr. John Moore, of Mealsgate, Cumberland, by Margaret, dau. of William Lowes, of Crookdake ; b. 1806 ; m. 1st 1840 Eliza, dau. of John Ray, Esq., J.P., of Finchley, Middlesex (she d. 1858) ; 2nd 1861 Agnes Jane, 2nd dau. of the late Richard Breeks, Esq., of Warcop, Westmoreland. Mr. Moore, who was appointed a Commissioner of Lieutenancy for London 1853, is a Magistrate for Cumberland. Middlesex, and Westminster, Lord of the Manor of Whitehall, and a Merchant in the city of London ; elected 1852 Sheriff of London and Middlesex, but paid the fine for refusing to serve.—*Whitehall, Wigton, Cumberland ; Brooks's Club, s.w. ; 15, Palace Gardens, Kensington, w.*

MOORE, the Rev. GEORGE BRIDGES, of Tunstall, Kent.

Eldest son of the late Rev. George Moore, Rector of Wrotham, Canon of Canterbury, by Harriet Mary, dau. of Sir Brook William Bridges, Bart. ; b. 1808 ; m. 1835 Mary Elizabeth, dau. of the Ven. Archdeacon Croft ; 2nd 1838 Charlotte, dau. of the Hon. and Rev. J. E. Boscawen (she d. 1851); 3rd 1853 Augusta, dau. of the late Rev. Dr. Russell, and has by the former,

* John Croft, Capt. in P.C.O. Rifle Brigade ; b. 1836 ; m. 1862 Amy Sophia, eldest dau. of Thomas Chamberlayne, Esq., of Cranbury Park, Hants.

Mr. Moore, who was educated at Westminster and Ch. Ch., Oxford (B.A. 1831, M.A. 1836), is a Magistrate for Kent and Rector of Tunstall.—*Tunstall Rectory, Sittingbourne ; Arthur's, and Oxford and Cambridge Clubs, s.w.*

MOORE, GEORGE HENRY, Esq., of Moore Hall, co. Mayo.

Eldest son of the late George Moore, Esq., of Moore Hall, by Louisa, dau. of the Hon. John Browne ; b. 1811 ; s. 1801; m. 1851 Mary, dau. of Maurice Blake, Esq., of Ballinafad, and has, with other issue,

* George Augustus, b. 1852.

Mr. Moore, who was educated at Oscott and Christ's Coll., Cambridge, is a J.P. and D.L. for co. Mayo (High Sheriff 1867); was M.P. for co. Mayo 1847–57.—*Moore Hall, Ballyglass, co. Mayo.*

MOORE, HUBERT BUTLER, Esq., of Shannon Grove, co. Galway.

Second but eldest surviving son of the late John Hubert Moore, Esq., of Shannon Grove, by Maria, dau. of Theobald Butler, Esq., of Drum, co. Tipperary, and widow of John, 12th Lord Dunboyne; *b.* 1804; *m.* 1824 Mary, eldest dau. of Valentine Blake, Esq., of Tully, co. Galway, and has, with other issue,

* Butler Dunboyne, late Capt. 89th Regt.; *b.* 1827; *m.* 1854 Nannie, dau. of John Eyre, Esq., of Eyrecourt Castle, co. Galway.

Mr. Moore, who was educated at Trinity Coll., Dublin, is a Magistrate for co. Galway.—*Shannon Grove, Banagher, co. Galway.*

MOORE, HUGH, Esq., of Nootka, co. Louth.

Second and elder surviving son of the late Hugh Moore, Esq., J.P., of Nootka, by Mary, dau. of the Rev. John Wilton, of Bristol; *b.* 1818; *s.* his brother Ross S. Moore, Esq., Q.C., M.P., 1855; *m.* 1861 Mary, 3rd dau. of the late William Steele Nicholson, Esq., J.P., of Ballow, co. Down, and has issue. The Moores of Carlingford are lineal descendants of the O'Mores of Queen's Co., Lords of Dynasts or Leix.—*Nootka Lodge, Carlingford, co. Louth.*

MOORE, JAMES CLEGHORN, Esq., of Ballinrobe, co. Mayo.

Only surviving son of the late Rev. Charles Moore, of Monasterevan, co. Kildare, by Agnes, dau. and co-heir of the late James Cleghorn, Esq., M.D., of Kilcarty, co. Meath; *b.* 1820; *m.* 1847 Emily Jean, 2nd dau. of the late Rev. Henry Moore, of Ballyhale. Educated at Trinity Coll., Dublin (B.A. 1842); is a Magistrate for co. Wexford; appointed Resident Magistrate co. Mayo 1859.—*Ballinrobe, co. Mayo.*

MOORE, JAMES STEWART, Esq., of Ballidivity, co. Antrim.

Eldest son of the late James Stewart Moore, Esq., of Ballidivity, by Margaret, dau. of the Ven: William Sturrock, Archdeacon of Armagh; *b.* 1793; *s.* 1843; *m.* 1844 Frances, dau. of the Rev. Thomas Richardson, of Somerset, co. Derry, and has, with other issue,

* James, *b.* 1847.

Mr. Moore, who is a Magistrate and Dep.-Lieut. for co. Antrim (High Sheriff 1849), was formerly Capt. 11th Hussars.—*Ballidivity, Dervock, co. Antrim.*

+MOORE, Capt. JOHN ARTHUR HENRY, of Tara House, co. Meath.

Eldest son of the late Major John Arthur Moore, by Sophia, dau. of Col. Yates; *b.* 1828; *s.* his uncle, the Rev. W. J. Brabazon Moore, 1866. Educated at Addiscombe Coll.; is Capt. Bengal Staff Corps.—*Tara House and Tallyallen, co. Meath.*

MOORE, the Ven. JOSEPH CHRISTIAN.

Eldest son of the late James Moore, Esq., of Cronkbourne, Merchant, by Elizabeth, dau. of G. Jeale, Esq., of Kent; *b.* 1805. Educated at St. Edmund's Hall, Oxford (B.A. 1827, M.A. 1844), is a Magistrate for the Isle of Man, Archdeacon of the Isle of Man, and Rector of Kirk Andreas; was formerly Perpetual Curate of Measham, co. Derby.—*Kirk Andreas Rectory, Douglas, Isle of Man.*

MOORE, JOSEPH SCOTT, Esq., of Kilbride Manor, co. Wicklow.

Eldest son of the late Joseph Moore, Esq., of Bond's Glen, co. Londonderry (who *d.* 1852), by Anne, dau. of the late George Fletcher, Esq., of Tottenham, Middlesex; *b.* 1796; *m.* 1832 Elizabeth, dau. of the late

Thomas Browne, Esq., of Ardwick, near Manchester, and has, with other issue,

* Joseph Fletcher, *b.* 1835.

Mr. Moore, who is a Magistrate for co. Wicklow, represents a family of Scottish origin.—*Kilbride Manor, Blessinton, co. Wicklow;* 12, *Hume Street, Dublin.*

MOORE, PONSONBY, Esq., ‡ of Moorefield, co. Kildare.

Second son of the late Hon. Ponsonby Moore, of Ballyhale, co. Kilkenny, and Moorefield, co. Kildare, by Catherine, dau. of Frederic Trench, Esq., of Woodlawn, co. Galway; *b.* 1786; *m.* 1813 Barbara dau. of John Maconchie, Esq., of Edenmore, co. Longford, and by her, who *d.* 1866, has, with other issue,

* Henry Edward, late Capt. 95th Foot; *b.* 1826; *m.* 1865 Hannah Elizabeth, eldest dau. of Jasper Pratt Tynte, Esq., of Tynte Park, co. Wicklow (whom see).

Mr. Moore, who was educated at Eton, is a J.P. and D.L. for co. Kildare (High Sheriff 1820).—*Moorefield House, Newbridge, co. Kildare.*

MOORE, SAMUEL, Esq., of Moyne Hall, co. Cavan.

Only surviving son of the late Samuel Moore, Esq., of Moyne Hall, by Frances, dau. of Col. Thomas Nesbitt, of Lismore; *b.* 1814; *s.* 1848; *m.* 1849 his cousin Louisa, dau. of Thos. Nesbitt, Esq., R.N., and has issue,

* Frances.

Mr. Moore is Treasurer of co. Cavan, and Major of the Cavan Militia.—*The Rocks, Crossdoney, co. Cavan; Windham Club, s.w.*

MOORE, STEPHEN, Esq., of Barne, co. Tipperary.

Eldest son of the late Stephen Moore, of Barne, by his cousin Salusbury, dau. of Richard Moore, Esq., of Barne; *b.* 1782; *s.* 1829; *s.* 1829; *m.* 1805 Eleanor Anne, dau. of Henry Westrey, Esq., of Dublin, and has, with other issue,

* Stephen, *b.* 1808; *m.* 1833 Anna, eldest dau. of the late Lieut.-Col. Pennefather, of New Park, co. Tipperary.

Mr. Moore, who is a J.P. and D.L. for co. Tipperary (High Sheriff 1832), was formerly in the 5th Dragoon Guards, and Major of the Meath Militia.—*Barne, Clonmel, co. Tipperary; Kildare Street Club, Dublin.*

MOORE, the Rev. WILLIAM.

Eldest son of the late Rev. William Moore, D.D., of Woodchester, co. Gloucester, by Elizabeth, dau. of Thomas Warner, Esq., of Marlborough, Wilts; *b.* 1796; *m.* 1823 Sarah Eliza Emily, youngest dau. of the Rev. R. Worthington, M.D., late of Ashton-Hayes, co. Chester, and has, with other issue,

* Charles Caulfeild, *b.* 1825; *m.* 1851 Elizabeth Maria, dau. of the Rev. George Bonner, late Incumbent of St. James's, Cheltenham.

Mr. Moore was educated at Pembroke Coll., Oxford (B.A. 1815, M.A. 1818), was appointed Rector of Brimpsfield and Cranham 1829; Rural Dean of North Stonehouse 1864.—*Brimpsfield Rectory, Gloucester.*

MOORE, WILLIAM, Esq., of Moore Fort, co. Antrim.

Eldest son of the late James Moore, Esq., of Moor Fort, by Mary, dau. of the Rev. Lindsay Hall, Rector of Dunegore, co. Antrim; *b.* 1818; *s.* 1847; *m.* 1846 Mary, dau. of John Hill, Esq., J.P., of Ballaghy, co. Derry, and has, with other issue,

* William, *b.* 1852.

Mr. Moore, who was educated at Dungannon and Trinity Coll., Dublin (M.A. and LL.D.), and called to the Irish Bar 1842, was High Sheriff of co. Antrim 1847.—*Moore Fort, Ballymony, co. Antrim.*

MOORE, WILLIAM, Esq., of Wierton, Kent.
Third son of the late Rev. George Moore, by Harriet,
dau. of Sir Brook William Bridges, Bart.; b. 1815;
m. 1843 Anne, youngest dau. and co-heir of the late
Walter Jones, Esq., M.P., of Ballinamore, co. Londonderry. Is a Magistrate for Kent (High Sheriff 1867);
was formerly in the H.E.I.C.'s Maritime Service.
—Wierton, Staplehurst; Arthur's Club, s.w.; Royal
Yacht Squadron, Cowes.

MOORE, WILLIAM MIDDLETON, Esq., of Grimes-
hill, Westmoreland.
Eldest son of the late William Moore, Esq., J.P. and D.L.,
of Grimeshill (formerly High Sheriff of Westmoreland),
by Elizabeth, 2nd dau. of Thomas Fawcett, Esq., of
Gate House, co. York; b. 1834; s. 1862; m. 1863
Margaret Elizabeth, youngest dau. of the Rev. John M.
Wright, Rector of Tatham. Mr. Moore, who was edu-
cated at the Royal Military Coll., Sandhurst, is Lord
of the Manor of Middleton, and Capt. Lancashire
Militia; was formerly in the 15th Foot.—Grimeshill,
Kirkby Lonsdale.

MOORE. (See under Drogheda, Marquis of, and Mount
Cashell, Earl of.)

MOORE. (See Bramley-Moore.)

MOORE. (See Carrick-Moore.)

MOORE. (See Montgomery-Moore.)

MOORE. (See Smyth, of Ballynatray.)

MOORE-HALSEY, Mrs., of Great Gaddesden
Park, Herts.
Sarah, only child and heir of the late Thomas Halsey,
Esq., M.P., of Great Gaddesden Park (who d. 1788),
by Sarah, dau. of John Crawley, Esq., of Stockwood
Park, Beds; m. 1st 1804 Joseph Thomson Whately,
Esq. (who assumed the name of Halsey only, and d.
1818); 2nd 1821 the Rev. John Fitz Moore (who as-
sumed the additional name of Halsey, and who d. 1864).
By her first husband she had, with other issue,
Thomas Plumer, M.P. for Herts, b. 1815; m. 1839 Frederica,
dau. of Lieut.-Col. Frederick Johnston, of Hilton, and d.
1854, leaving issue. * Thomas Frederick, educated at Eton
and M.A. of Ch. Ch., Oxford; a Magistrate for Herts, and
Capt. Herts Yeomanry Cavalry; b. 1839; m. 1863 Mary
Julia, youngest dau. of the late F. O. Wells, Esq., L.C.S.,
and has issue * Florence, b. 1867.
Mrs. Moore-Halsey is Lady of the Manor of Hemel
Hempstead, and Patron of 2 livings.—Great Gaddesden
Park, Hemel Hempstead.

MOORE-HODDER, WILLIAM HENRY JOHN, Esq.,
of Hoddersfield, co. Cork.
Only son of the late William Henry Moore-Hodder,
Esq., J.P. and D.L., of Hoddersfield (Col. of the North
Cork Rifles), by his 2nd wife Lucy Eliza. eldest dau. of
Col. Need, of Mansfield Woodhouse, Notts; b. 1836;
s. 1859. Educated at Eton and the Royal Military
Coll., Sandhurst: is Ensign 10th Foot. His grand-
father assumed the additional name of Hodder on in-
heriting the estates of his maternal uncle William
Holder, Esq.—Hoddersfield, Crosshaven, co. Cork.

MOORE-SMYTH, the Hon. CHARLES WILLIAM,
of Ballynatray, co. Waterford.
Second son of Stephen, 3rd Earl of Mount Cashell, by
Anne Maria, dau. of Samuel Wyss, Esq., of Berne,
Switzerland; b. 1826; m. 1848 Charlotte Mary, only
child and heir of the late Richard Smyth, Esq., of
Ballynatray (whose name he assumed by Royal licence),
672

and grand-dau. of Hayes, 2nd Viscount Doneraile, and
has, with other issue,
* Richard Charles Moore, b. 1859.
Mr. Moore-Smyth, who was educated at Eton, is a
Magistrate for co. Cork, a J.P. and D.L. for co. Water-
ford (High Sheriff 1862), and Lord of the Manor of
Ballynatray (see also Smyth of Ballynatray).—Bally-
natray, Youghal; Royal Thames Yacht Club, w.

MOORHOUSE, JOSHUA, Esq., of Carr House,
Yorkshire.
Eldest son of the late Matthew Moorhouse, Esq., of
Holmfirth, co. York, by Mary, dau. of Capt. Wood, of
Denby Dale; b. 1806; s. 1825; m. 1st 1830 Sarah,
dau. of Jonathan Butterworth, Esq., of Hill House,
Holmfirth; 2nd 1837 Sarah Ann, dau. of B. Butter-
worth, Esq., of Holmfirth, and has, with other issue,
* Matthew, educated at Queen's Coll., Oxford (B.A. 1862);
b. 1840.
Mr. Moorhouse is a Magistrate for the W. Riding of
Yorkshire.—Carr House, Holmfirth, Yorkshire.

MORANT, GEORGE, Esq., of Shirley House, co.
Monaghan.
Eldest son of George Morant, Esq., late of Farnborough
Place, Hants, by Mary, dau. of the late Evelyn Shirley,
Esq., of Eatington co. Warwick; b. 1814; m. 1835
Lydia, youngest dau. of the late John Hemphill, Esq.,
of Rathkeany, co. Tipperary, and has, with other issue,
* George Digby, Commander, R.N.; b. 1837.
Mr. Morant, who was educated at Eton, is a Magis-
trate for co. Monaghan, late in the Grenadier Guards.
—Shirley House, Carrickmacross, co. Monaghan; Royal
St. George's Yacht Club, Kingstown, Dublin.

MORANT, HAY RICHARD, Esq., of Ringwood,
Hants.
Second son of the late John Morant, Esq., J.P. and
D.L., of Brockenhurst, Hants (who d. 1857), by Lady
Caroline Augusta, 3rd dau. of William, 16th Earl of
Erroll; b. 1828; m. 1861 Elizabeth Anne, eldest dau.
of the late Charles Fludyer, Esq., of Lymington, Hants,
and has issue.—Manor House, Ringwood.

MORANT, JOHN, Esq., of Brockenhurst, Hants.
Eldest son of the late John Morant, Esq., J.P. and D.L.,
of Brockenhurst House (who was High Sheriff of Hants
1820), by Lady Caroline Augusta, 3rd dau. of William,
16th Earl of Erroll; b. 1825; s. 1857; m. 1st 1855
Lady Henrietta Louisa, 3rd dau. of Henry, 7th Duke
of Beaufort (she d. 1863); 2nd 1866 Flora Jane,
youngest dau. of the late Hon. and Rev. William Eden,
and has issue,
* Edward John Harry Eden, b. 1868.
Mr. Morant, who was educated at Ch. Ch., Oxford, is a
J.P. and D.L. for Hants, and Lord of the Manor of
Ringwood.—Brockenhurst House, Lymington; Boodle's
Club, s.w.; 16, Park Lane, w.

MORAY, Earl of (ARCHIBALD GEORGE STUART).
—Cr. 1561.
Fourth but eldest surviving son of Francis, 10th Earl.
K.T. (who d. 1848), by his 2nd wife Margaret Jane,
2nd dau. of Sir Philip Ainslie, Knt., of Pilton, N.B.;
b. 1810; s. his brother as 13th Earl 1867. Is a Lieut.-
Col. in the Army, retired; was formerly Capt. 6th West
India Regt.—Doune Lodge, Perth; Darnaway Castle,
Forres, N.B.; Donibristle, Burntisland, Fifeshire;
Castle Stuart, Inverness, N.B.
Heir Pres., his brother George, b. 1814.

MORAY.　(See *Drummond-Moray*.)

MORDAUNT, Sir CHARLES, Bart., of Walton,
Warwickshire (cr. 1611).
Eldest son of the late Sir John Mordaunt, Bart., M.P.,
of Walton D'Eville, by Caroline Sophia, dau. of the
late Right Rev. George Murray, D.D., Lord Bishop of
Rochester; *b.* 1836; *s.* as 10th Bart. 1845; *m.* 1866
Harriet Sarah, 4th dau. of Sir Thomas Moncreiffe,
Bart. Educated at Eton and Ch. Ch., Oxford; is a
J.P. and D.L. for co. Warwick, Lord of the Manor of
Walton and Patron of 4 livings; elected M.P. for
South Warwickshire 1859.—*Walton, Warwick; Carlton
and Arthur's Clubs*; s.w.

Heir Pres., his brother John Murray, *b.* 1837; *m.* 1866 Elizabeth Evelyn, 3rd dau. of John Cotes, Esq., of Woodcot Hall,
co. Stafford.

MORDAUNT, Lady, of Goldicote House, War-
wickshire.
Caroline Sophia, dau. of the late Right Rev. George
Murray, D.D., Lord Bishop of Rochester, by Lady
Sarah Maria, younger dau. of Robert, 9th Earl of
Kinnoull; *m.* 1st 1834 Sir John Mordaunt, Bart., who
d. 1845; 2nd 1853 Gustavus T. Smith, Esq.—*Goldicote
House, Stratford-on-Avon.*

MORDAUNT, JOHN, Esq., of Flax Bourton,
Somerset.
Only surviving son of the late Rev. Charles Mordaunt,
of Massingham, Norfolk, and Badgworth, Somerset, by
Frances Harriet, youngest dau. of the late James Sparrow, Esq., of Flax Bourton; *b.* 1815; *m.* 1st 1848
Harriet Maria, youngest dau. of Capt. Cumberlage; 2nd
185- Isabel, 2nd dau. of Fletcher Norton Balmain, Esq.,
late Madras Cavalry, and has issue. Mr. Mordaunt,
who was educated at Rugby, and afterwards entered the
17th Light Dragoons, is a Magistrate for Somerset.
Descended from a common ancestor with the baronet of
the same name.—*Flax Bourton, Bristol.*

MORE, the Rev. THOMAS FREDERICK, of Linley
Hall, Shropshire.
Only surviving son of the late Robert More, Esq., of
Linley Hall (who *d.* 1818), by Eliza, dau. of James
Taylor, Esq., of Much Hadham, Herts; *b.* 1790; *s.*
his brother, Robert Bridgeman, 1851; *m.* 1831 his
cousin, Harriet Mary, dau. of Thomas More, Esq., of
Larden Hall, co. Salop, and has issue an only son,

* Robert Jasper, Barrister-at-Law, educated at Shrewsbury,
and M.A. of Balliol Coll., Oxford; a J.P. and D.L. for co.
Salop; and M.P. for S. Salop; *b.* 1836.

Mr. More, who was educated at Pembroke Coll., Cam-
bridge (B.A. 1815), is a Magistrate for co. Salop, and
Rector, Lord of the Manor and Patron of More.—*Linley
Hall, Bishops Castle, Shropshire.*

MORE-MOLYNEUX, JAMES, Esq., of Loseley
Park, Surrey.
Eldest son of the late James More-Molyneux, Esq., of
Loseley Park, by Ann, dau. of Mr. John Merriott, of
Farnham, Surrey; *b.* 1805; *s.* 1826; *m.* 1832 Caroline
Isabella, eldest dau. of the late William F. Lowndes-
Stone, Esq., of Brightwell Park, Oxon, and has, with
other issue,

* Christopher, *b.* 1833.

Mr. More-Molyneux, who was educated at Trinity Coll.,
Oxford, is a J.P. and D.L. for Surrey (High Sheriff
1867).—*Loseley Park, Guildford; Oxford and Cambridge Club, s.w.*

MORE-O'FERRALL.　(See *O'Ferrall*.)

MORESBY, Sir FAIRFAX, G.C.B. (cr. 1855).
Son of the late Fairfax Moresby, Esq., of Stow House,
Lichfield, by Mary, dau. of Joseph Rotton, Esq., of

Duffield, co. Derby; *b.* 1787; *m.* 1814 Eliza Louisa,
dau. of John Williams, Esq., of Bakewell, co. Derby,
and has, with other issue,

* Matthew Fortescue, Commander R.N.; *b.* 1820; *m.* 1850
Caroline, dau. of General Gold, and has issue, * Fairfax, *b.*
1861.

Sir Fairfax is an Admiral of the White, and Rear-
Admiral of the United Kingdom; late Commander-in-
Chief in the Pacific; created D.C.L. Oxon 1854.—*Bron-
wylfa, Exmouth; United Service Club, s.w.*

MORETON, the Hon. ALGERNON THOMAS, of
Eastwood, co. Carlow.
Second surviving son of Henry George, 2nd Earl of
Ducie, by the Hon. Elizabeth, dau. of John, 2nd Lord
Sherborne: *b.* 1829; *m.* 1857 Anna Jane, only dau. of
Thomas Paget, Esq., of Knockglass. Educated at
Trinity Coll., Cambridge, late Capt. 3rd Light Dragoons.
—*Eastwood, Bagenalstown, co. Carlow; Kildare Street
Club, Dublin; Pratt's and Army and Navy Clubs, s.w.*

MORETON, the Hon. PERCY, of Tortworth Old
Court, Gloucestershire.
Second son of Thomas, 1st Earl of Ducie, by Frances,
only dau. of Henry, 1st Earl of Carnarvon; *b.* 1808;
m. 1846 Jane Frances, 8th dau. of the late Sir Rose
Price, Bart., and has, with other issue,

* Francis, *b.* 1847.

Mr. Moreton was formerly Capt. 10th Hussars.—*Tortworth Old Court, Wootton-under-Edge.*

MORETON, the Hon. REYNOLDS, of Lindridge
House, Leicestershire.
Fifth son of Henry George, 2nd Earl of Ducie, by the
Hon. Elizabeth Dutton, eldest dau. of John, late Lord
Sherborne; *b.* 1835; *m.* 1860 Charlotte Constance,
only dau. of the late Sir John Dunlop, Bart., of Dunlop
(she *d.* 1865); 2nd 1866 Margaret Mahony, 2nd dau.
of the late Rev. D. Mahony, of Dromore Castle, co.
Kerry, and has, by the former, with other issue,

* Basil Hugh Reynolds, *b.* 1861.

Mr. Moreton is J.P. and D.L. for co. Leicester, a Capt.
R.N., and Major Leicestershire Rifle Volunteers.—*Lindridge House, Desford, Leicester.*

MORETON.　(See under *Ducie, Earl of*.)

MORETON.　(See *Macdonald-Moreton*.)

MORETON-CRAIGIE, Mrs., of Little Moreton
Hall, Cheshire.
Frances Annabella, elder dau. of the late Rev. William
Moreton Moreton, M.A., of Moreton Hall, by his 2nd
wife Elizabeth, eldest dau. of the late Rev. Henry
Hutton, M.A., Rector of Beaumont, Essex, and grand-
dau. of the late Sir William Pepperell, Bart.; *m.* 1852
John Craigie, Esq., of Jedbank, co. Roxburgh, and
Sheriff-Substitute of that county, who has assumed the
name of Moreton. The Moreton family have been
settled at Little Moreton since the reign of King John.
—*Little Moreton Hall, Congleton.*

Heir Pres., her sister Elizabeth.

MOREWOOD.　(See *Palmer-Morewood*.)

MORGAN, Sir WALTER, Knt. (cr. 1866.)
Son of the late W. Morgan, Esq.; *b.* 1818; is married
and has issue; called to the Bar at the Middle Temple
1844; is Chief Justice of the High Court of Judicature
of the N.W. Provinces of Bengal.—*Calcutta.*

MORGAN, the Hon. FREDERIC COURTENAY, of
Ruperra Castle, Monmouthshire.
Third son of Charles, 1st Lord Tredegar, by Rosamond,
dau. of the late General Godfrey Basil Mundy, of
Ruperra Castle; *b.* 1834; *m.* 1858 Charlotte, dau. of

the late Charles Williamson, Esq., of Lamers, co. Perth, N.B., and has issue,
  * Blanche and Violet.
Mr. Morgan, who was educated at Winchester, is a Magistrate for co. Monmouth and Lieut.-Col. 1st Battalion Monmouthshire Rifle Volunteers; formerly Capt. Rifle Brigade.—*Ruperra Castle, Newport, Monmouthshire ; 32, Portman Square, w.*

MORGAN, the Hon. Mrs. DEANE-, of Ardcandrisk, co. Wexford.
Elizabeth Geraldine, eldest dau and heir of the late Hamilton Knox Grogan-Morgac, Esq., by Sophia Maria, dau. of Ebenezer Radford Row, Esq., of Ballyharty; *b.* 1830 ; *s.* 1854 ; *m.* 1847 the Hon. Robert Tilson Fitz-Maurice-Deane (who assumed the name and arms of Morgan on the death of his father-in-law, and *d.* 1856), eldest son of Matthew, 3rd Lord Muskerry, and has issue,
  * Hamilton Matthew Fitz-Maurice-Deane.
This family was formerly Grogan, and the late Mr. Grogan-Morgan took the name of Morgan on inheriting the property of his father's cousin Samuel Morgan, Esq., of Waterford.—*Arcandrisk, Wexford.*

MORGAN, CHARLES OCTAVIUS SWINNERTON, Esq., F.R.S., F.S.A., of The Friars, Monmouthshire.
Fourth son of the late Sir Charles Morgan, Bart., of Tredegar, co. Monmouth, by Mary Margaret, dau. of George Stoney, Esq., and brother of Charles, 1st Lord Tredegar; *b.* 1803. Educated at Westminster and Ch. Ch., Oxford (B.A. 1825) ; is a J.P. and D.L. for co. Monmouth ; has been M.P. for co. Monmouth since 1840.—*The Friars, Newport, Monmouthshire ; University Club, s.w. ; 9, Pall Mall, s.w.*

MORGAN, EDWARD, Esq., of Bridestown, co. Cork.
Son of the late Edward Morgan, Esq., of Bridestown ; *b.* 18— ; *m.* 182- Maria Amelia, dau. of Richard Spread, Esq., of Ballycanon, and has, with other issue,
  * Richard Spread, Capt. in the City of Cork Militia ; *b.* 182-; *m.* 1858 Lady Catharine Louisa Moore, youngest dau. of Stephen, 3rd Earl of Mount Cashell, and has issue.
Mr. Morgan, who was educated at Trinity Coll., Dublin, is a Magistrate for co. Cork, and Lord of the Manor of Bridestown.—*Bridestown House, Rathcormac, co. Cork.*

MORGAN, Col. EDWARD, of Golden Grove, Flintshire.
Eldest son of the late Edward Morgan, Esq., J.P. and D.L., of Golden Grove, by Louisa, dau. of — Griffiths, Esq. ; *b.* 1790 ; *m.* 1827 Charlotte, dau. of Col. Warde, of Hartsheath. Is a J.P. and D.L. for co. Flint ; a Col. in the Army, unattached ; was formerly in the 75th Foot, and Lieut.-Col. Commandant Merioneth Militia. —*Golden Grove, Holywell.*

+MORGAN, Col. EVAN, of St. Helen's, Glamorganshire.
Son of the late E. Morgan, Esq., of St. Helen's ; *b.* 18—. Is a J.P. and D.L. for co. Glamorgan, and Lieut.-Col. Glamorganshire Artillery Militia.—*St. Helen's, Swansea.*

MORGAN, GEORGE MANNERS, Esq., of Biddlesden, Bucks.
Eldest son of the late George Morgan Esq., of Biddlesden Park, by Anna Eliza, dau. of the late Lavor Oliver, Esq., of Brill House, Bucks; *b.* 1833 ; *s.* 1847 ; *m.* 1858 Elizabeth, dau. of Thomas Robert Brigstocke, and has, with other issue,
  * Inis Ferdinand, *b.* 1860.
Mr. Morgan, who is in the Commission of the Peace for cos. Bucks and Northampton, Lord of the Manor

of Biddlesden, and of Brechfa, Patron of 2 livings, and a Capt. in the Bucks Yeomanry Hussars; was formerly Capt. 4th Dragoon Guards.—*Biddlesden Park, Brackley ; Army and Navy Club, s.w.*

+MORGAN, HOWELL, Esq., of Hengwrtucha, Carnarvonshire.
Second son of the late Phillip Morgan, Esq., of Derynock, co. Brecon; *b.* 18— ; *m.* 18— Mary, dau. and heir of —— Jones, Esq., of Hengwrtucha. Is a Dep. Lieut. for co. Brecon ; was High Sheriff of co. Merioneth 1863. — *Hengwrtucha, Carnarvon ; Gilvach-yr-haidd, Brecon.*

MORGAN, JOHN WILLIAMS, Esq., of Bolgoed, Brecknockshire.
Fourth son of the late William Morgan, Esq., of Bolgoed, by Mary, dau. of Jonathan Dixon, Esq., of Ashford ; *b.* 1834 ; *s.* his brother 1858 ; *m.* 1863 Ellen, dau. of Wilton Lee, Esq., of Egbaston, and has, with other issue,
  * William Lee, *b.* 1863.
Mr. Morgan is a J.P. and D.L. for co. Brecon (High Sheriff 1867), and Capt. Brecknock Militia.—*Bolgoed, Brecon.*

MORGAN, WILLIAM STEPHEN SULLIVAN, Esq., of Old Abbey, co. Limerick.
Second but eldest surviving son of the late George Morgan, Esq. (who *d.* 1816), by Melian, dau. of William Sullivan, Esq., of Tullilease, co. Cork ; *b.* 1796 ; *m.* 1833 Georgina, eldest dau. of Major Henry Ross-Lewin, of Ross Hill, co. Clare, and has, with other issue,
  * George Burdett, in Holy Orders; *b.* 1835.
Mr. Morgan, who was educated at Trinity Coll., Dublin (B.A. 1817, M.A. 1833), is a Magistrate for co. Limerick.—*Old Abbey, Shanagolden, co. Limerick.*

MORGAN. (See under *Tredegar, Lord.*)

MORGAN-CLIFFORD. (See *Clifford.*)

MORICE, FRANCIS, Esq., of Springfield, co. Clare.
Only son of the late Francis Morice, Esq., of Springfield, by Maria, dau. of Capt. William Spaight, of Corbally, co. Clare ; *b.* 1827 ; *s.* 1858. This family is of ancient Welsh extraction, and possessed estates in Essex, where they were seated from the time of Edward III. —*Springfield, Six-Mile Bridge, co. Clare.*

MORISON, Lady, of Johnsburn, Midlothian.
Grace, dau. of James Young, Esq., of Herstmonceux, Sussex : *m.* 1851 (as 2nd wife), Sir Alexander Morison, Knt., M.D., late President of the Royal College of Physicians of Edinburgh, who *d.* 1866.—*Johnsburn, Balerno, Midlothian. N.B. ; 26, Cavendish Square, w.*

+MORISON, ALEXANDER, Esq., of Bognie, Aberdeenshire.
Son of the late A. Morison, Esq., of Mountblarie ; *b.* 18—. Is a J.P. and D.L. for co. Aberdeen, Vice-Lieutenant of and a Magistrate for co. Banff, and Lord of the Barony of Bognie.—*Mountblarie House, Turriff, N.B.*

MORISON, Mrs. DUNCAN-, of Naughton, Fifeshire.
Catherine Eunice, dau. of Major Mackenzie, of Fodderty, N.B. ; *m.* 1853 Adam Alexander Duncan, Esq., of Naughton (only son of the late Capt. the Hon. Sir Henry Duncan, R.N., C.B., and K.C.H.), who assume the additional name of Morison, and *d.* 1855.—*Naughton, Newport, Fifeshire, N.B.*

MORLAND, Sir Francis BERNARD-, Bart., of Askett Lodge, Bucks (cr. 1769).
Eldest son of the late Sir Scrope Bernard-Morland, Bart., M.P., of Nettleham, co. Lincoln (who assumed the additional name of Morland in 1811), by Harriett, dau. of William Morland, Esq., of Lee, Kent; b. 1790; s. as 5th Bart. 1830. Is a J.P. and D.L. for Bucks. —*Askett Lodge, Great Kimble, Tring.*
Heir Pres., his brother Thomas Tyringham Bernard, Esq. (whom see).

MORLAND, the Rev. BENJAMIN, of Sheepstead House, Berkshire.
Second son of the late Benjamin Morland, Esq., of Sheepstead House (who d. 1833), by Elizabeth Rose, dau. of Edward Thornhill, Esq., of Kingston Lisle, Berks; b. 1805; s. his brother 1848; m. 1834 Anna Maria, dau. of the Rev. John F. Collins, of Betterton, Berks, and by her, who d. 1863, has, with other issue,
* Benjamin Henry, b. 1842.
Mr. Morland, who was educated at Pembroke Coll., Oxford, is Vicar of Shabbington, Bucks.—*Sheepstead House, Abingdon.*

MORLAND, EDWARD HENRY, Esq., of West Ilsley, Berks.
Fourth son of the late Benjamin Morland, Esq., of Sheepstead House, Berks, by Elizabeth Rose, dau. of Thomas Thornhill, Esq., of Kingstone Lisle, Berks; b. 1809; m. 1839 Caroline Matilda, eldest dau. of Bannatyne Macleod, Esq., M.D. Educated at Winchester and Haileybury Coll., Herts; appointed to the Bengal Civil Service 1827; retired 1857; is a Magistrate for Berks. —*West Ilsley, Newbury; Oriental Club, w.*

MORLAND, WILLIAM COURTENAY, Esq., of The Court Lodge, Kent.
Only son of the late Charles Morland, Esq., Col. of the 9th Lancers, by Lady Caroline Eustatia, dau. of William, 9th Earl of Devon; b. 1818; s. his uncle William Alexander Morland, Esq., 1846; m. 1843 Margaretta Eliza, 3rd dau. of General William Cator, C.B., R.A., and has, with other issue,
* Charles William, b. 1849.
Mr. Morland, who was educated at Eton and Ch. Ch., Oxford (B.A. 1839, M.A. 1842); called to the Bar at Lincoln's Inn 1843; is a J.P. and D.L. for Kent, a Magistrate for Sussex, and Lord of the Manor of Lamberhurst.—*The Court Lodge, Lamberhurst; Oxford and Cambridge Club, s.w.*

MORLEY, Earl of (ALBERT EDMUND PARKER). —Cr. 1815.
Only son of Edmund, 2nd Earl, by Harriet Sophia, dau. of the late Montagu Edmund N. Parker, Esq., M.P., of Whiteway, Devon, and widow of William Coryton, Esq., of Pentillie Castle, Cornwall; b. 1843; s. 1864. Educated at Eton and Balliol Coll., Oxford (B.A. 1863); is a Dep.-Lieut. for Devon, Lord of the Manor of Plympton St. Mary's, Patron of 2 livings, and Lieut. South Devon Militia.—*Saltram House, Plympton; Brooks's Club, s.w.; 2, Wilton Terrace, s.w.*

MORLEY, Sir ISAAC, Knt. (cr. 1841).
Son of Mr. William Morley, of Doncaster, by his wife Margaret; b. 1801; m. 1831 Sarah Elizabeth, dau. of Thomas Hall, Esq., of Barnby Dun, co. York. Educated at Doncaster and Hull; is a Magistrate for the W. Riding of Yorkshire and Borough of Doncaster; was formerly a Merchant at Doncaster, of which he was Mayor in 1840-1.—*South Parade, Doncaster.*

MORLEY, FRANCIS, Esq., of Marrick, Yorkshire.
Eldest son of the late Francis Morley, Esq., J.P., of Marrick Park and Hurst, Capt. N. York Militia, by Char-

lotte, eldest dau. of John Clervaux Chaytor, Esq., of Spennithorne Hall, co. York; b. 1836; s. 1854. Is Lord of the Manor and Patron of Marrick and Hurst, and Major 3rd Buffs; formerly in the 2nd W. York Infantry Militia.—*Marrick Park, Richmond.*
Heir Pres., his brother Clervaux, educated at the R. M. Coll., Woolwich; a Lieut. R.A.; b. 1841.

MORLEY, SAMUEL, Esq., of Stamford Hill, Middlesex.
Youngest son of the late John Morley, Esq., by Sarah, dau. of — Poulton, Esq., of Maidenhead, Berks; b. 1809; m. 1841 Rebekah Maria, dau. of Samuel Hope, Esq., of Liverpool. Is a Magistrate for Middlesex; was M.P. for Nottingham 1865-6.—*Craven Lodge, Stamford Hill, N.; 18, Wood Street, E.C.*

MORNINGTON. (See *Wellington, Duke of.*)

MORRALL, the Rev. CYRUS, of Plas Yolyn and Plas Warren, Shropshire.
Eldest son of the late Cyrus Morrall, Esq., of Liverpool, by Margaret, dau. of the Rev. Richard Owen, of Bodsilyn, co. Carnarvon; b. 1803; m. 1st 1833 Emily Jane, dau. of the Rev. Francis Blackburne, M.A., late Rector of Weston-super-Mare, Somerset (d.); 2nd 1860 E. Georgiana Fleming, dau. of Robert Fisher, Esq., and widow of Henry Urquhart, Esq., of Cheltenham, and has; by the former, with other issue,
* Cyrus, b. 1854.
Mr. Morrall, who was educated at Brasenose Coll., Oxford (B.A. 1825, M.A. 1828), is Lord of the Manor of Trayan, co. Salop; late Vicar of North Leigh, Oxon; was formerly P.C. of St. Michael's, Liverpool.—*Plas Yolyn, Ellesmere.*

MORRELL, Miss, of Headington House, Oxon.
Emily Alicia, only child and heir of the late James Morrell, Esq., J.P. and D.L., of Headington House, by Alicia Harriet, dau. of the late Rev. William Everett, B.D.; s. her mother 1864. Is Lady of the Manor of Headington.—*Headington House, Oxford.*

+MORRICE, FREDERICK EDWARD, Esq., of Bettshanger, Kent.
Eldest son of the late Rev. James Morrice, Rector of Bettshanger, by Maria, dau. of Adrian Charles Ducarel, Esq.; b. 1777; s. 1815; m. 1816 Elizabeth, youngest dau. of the late Henry Ellison, Esq., of Hebburn Hall, co. Durham, and has, with other issue,
* Frederick Francis James, b. 1820.
Mr. Morrice is a Dep.-Lieut. for Kent, and Patron and Lord of the Manor of Bettshanger.—*Bettshanger, Sandwich.*

MORRICE, JOHN WALTER, Esq., of Catthorpe Towers, Leicestershire.
Second son of the late John Morrice, Esq., Merchant, of London, by Mary, dau. of David Morice, Esq., of Tulloe, co. Aberdeen; b. 1821; purchased this property in 1853; m. 1848 Mary, dau. of the late John S. Donaldson-Selby, Esq., of Cheswick House, Northumberland, and has, with other issue,
* John George Selby, b. 1849.
Mr. Morrice, who was educated at Exeter Coll., Oxford (B.A. 1843, M.A. 1844), called to the Bar at Lincoln's Inn 1846, is a J.P. and D.L. for co. Leicester, and Lord of the Manor of Catthorpe.—*Catthorpe Towers, Rugby.*

MORRIS, Sir JOHN ARMINE, Bart., of Sketty Park, Glamorganshire (cr. 1806).
Eldest son of the late Sir John Morris, Bart., of Sketty Park, by the Hon. Lucy Juliana, dau. of John, 5th

Viscount Torrington; *b.* 1813; *s.* as 3rd Bart. 1855; *m.* 1847 Catherine, dau. of R. Macdonald, Esq. Educated at Westminster; is Patron of 1 living; was formerly Lieut. 60th Foot.—*Sketty Park, Swansea; Carlton Club, s.w.*

Heir, his son Robert Armine, b. 1848.

MORRIS, Sir BENJAMIN, Knt. (cr. 1836).

Eldest surviving son of the late George Morris Wall, Esq., of Waterford, by Jane, eldest dau. and heir of James Wall, Esq., of Clonea Castle, co. Waterford; *b.* 1798; *m.* 1824 Anna, dau. of Thomas Armstrong, Esq. Was formerly Capt. 25th Foot; is a J.P. and D.L. for Waterford, of which city he is an Alderman, and served as Mayor 1845–6 and 1867–8; High Sheriff 1855.—*The Mall, Waterford.*

MORRIS, Sir JOHN, Knt. (cr. 1866).

Eldest son of the late Edward Morris, Esq., of Wolverhampton; *b.* 1821; *m.* 1844 Elizabeth Mary, dau. of Edward Griffin, Esq., of Towersey Manor, Bucks. Is a Manufacturer and Alderman of Wolverhampton, (Mayor 1866–7).—*Elmsdale, Wolverhampton.*

MORRIS, Sir EDMUND FINUCANE, K.C.B. (cr. 1867).

Son of the late E. Morris, Esq.; *b.* 1792; is a General in the Army, and Col. 49th Regt.—*Ryde, I. of Wight.*

MORRIS, CHARLES JOHN, Esq., of Wood-Eaton, Staffordshire.

Eldest son of the late John Morris, Esq., J.P. and D.L., of Wood-Eaton, by Julia, youngest dau. of Samuel Amy Severne, Esq., of Thenford, co. Northampton, and Wallop Hall, co. Salop; *b.* 1831; *s.* 1866; *m.* 1862 Constance Lingen, only surviving dau. of the late Robert Burton, Esq., of Longner Hall, co. Salop, and has, with other issue,

* Charles Edward, *b.* 1863.

Mr. Morris, who was educated at Eton and Ch. Ch., Oxford (B.A. 1854), is a Magistrate for co. Stafford, and Lord of the Manor of Wood-Eaton.—*Wood-Eaton Manor, Stafford.*

MORRIS, CHOLMELEY, Esq., of Fishleigh, Devon.

Second but eldest surviving son of the late William Cholmeley Morris, Esq., of Fishleigh, by Jane, dau. of James Veale, Esq., of Passaford, Devon; *b.* 1822; *s.* his brother, the late Lieut.-Col. William Morris, C.B., 1858; *m.* 1853 Caroline, 2nd dau. of Hugh Mallet, Esq., of Ash, Devon, and has issue.— * William Cholmley, *b.* 1856.—*Fishleigh, Hatherleigh.*

MORRIS, EDWARD, Esq., of Oxon, Shropshire, and Berth-Lloyd, Montgomeryshire.

Younger son of the late Thomas Morris, Esq., of Newport, co. Salop (who *d.* 1817), by Margaret, dau. of the late William Spearman, Esq., and grand-dau. of William Marigold, Esq., of Aston, co. Salop; *b.* 1800. Is a Magistrate for co. Salop and Montgomery (High Sheriff 1859).—*Oxon, Shrewsbury; Berth-Lloyd, Montgomery.*

MORRIS, the Rev. FRANCIS ORPEN.

Eldest son of the late Rear-Admiral Henry Gage Morris, R.N., of Beverley, co. York, by Rebecca Newenham, 3rd dau. of the late Rev. Francis Orpen, B.A., Vicar of Kilgarvon, co. Kerry, and Rector of Dungorney and Douglas, co. Cork; *b.* 1810; *s.* 1852; *m.* 1835 Anne, 2nd dau. and co-heir of the late Charles Sanders, Esq., of Bromsgrove, co. Worcester, and has, with other issue,

* Amherst Henry Gage, of Magdalen Coll., Oxford, Lieutenant in the East York Militia; *b.* 1836.

Mr. Morris, who was educated at Bromsgrove and Wor-

676

cester Coll., Oxford (B.A. 1834), is a Magistrate for the E. Riding of Yorkshire and Rector of Nunburnholme. —*Nunburnholme Rectory, Hayton, York.*

MORRIS, GEORGE BYNG, Esq., of Sketty, Glamorganshire.

Second son of the late Sir John Morris, Bart., of Sketty Park, by the Hon. Lucy Juliana, youngest dau. of John, 5th Viscount Torrington; *b.* 1816; *m.* 1852 Emily Matilda, dau. of C. H. Smith, Esq., of Derwen Fawr, co. Glamorgan, and has, with other issue,

* Robert, *b.* 1853.

Mr. Morris is a J.P. and D.L. for co. Glamorgan. —*Sketty, Swansea.*

MORRIS, JONAS OLIVER, Esq., of Dunkathal, co. Cork.

Eldest son of the late Jonas Morris, Esq., of Dunkathal (formerly Capt. 1st Dragoons), by Ellen, dau. of Silver Charles Oliver, Esq., of Innishera, co. Cork (she *m.* 2nd 1865 Lieut.-Col. Grant); *b.* 1853; *s.* 1862. Is Lord of the Manor of Dunkathal.—*Dunkathal, Glanmire, co. Cork.*

MORRIS, the Right Hon. MICHAEL, P.C., of Well Park, co. Galway.

Eldest son of the late Martin Morris, Esq., J.P., Galway, by Julia, dau. of Dr. Charles Blake, of Galway; *b.* 1827; *m.* 1860 Anna, dau. of the Right Hon. H. G. Hughes, Baron of the Irish Exchequer Educated at Galway College and Trinity Coll., Dublin (B.A. 1847); called to the Irish Bar 1849; appointed a Q.C. 1853; is a Magistrate for co. Galway (High Sheriff 1850); formerly Recorder of Galway; was M.P. for Galway 1865–7; appointed Attorney-General for Ireland 1866; Justice of the Court of Common Pleas 1867.—*Well Park, Galway; University Club, Dublin; 22, Lower Fitzwilliam Street, Dublin.*

Heir Pres., his brother George, a Magistrate for co. Galway (High Sheriff 1860), and for the borough of Galway; Vice-Chairman of the Board of Guardians, and M.P. for Galway; b. 1829.

MORRIS, PHILIP, Esq., of The Hurst, Shropshire.

Eldest son of the late Rev. Philip Morris, of The Hurst, by Charlotte Margretta, dau. of the Rev. D'Elbœuf Edwards, of Pentre Hall, co. Montgomery; *b.* 1786; *s.* 1801; *m.* 1819 Elizabeth, dau. of George Field, Esq., and has, with other issue,

* Philip, Barrister-at-Law, of the Inner Temple, *b.* 1821.

Mr. Morris, who was educated at Eton and Worcester Coll., Oxford (M.A. 1809), and called to the Bar at Lincoln's Inn 1810, is a J.P. and D.L. for co. Salop; was High Sheriff of co. Montgomery 1827.—*The Hurst, Ludlow; Windham Club, s.w.*

MORRIS, RICHARD WALL, Esq., of Rockenham, co. Waterford.

Son of the late George Morris Wall, Esq. (late Governor of co. Waterford, who assumed the additional surname of Wall on succeeding to the estates of his father-in-law), by Jane, eldest dau. and heir of the late James Wall, Esq., of Clonea Castle, co. Waterford; *m.* 1st 1827 Eliza, dau. of Jesse Lloyd, Esq., of Lloydsborough, co. Tipperary; 2nd 1840 Eliza, only dau. of Edward Roberts, Esq., of Killoteran, co. Waterford, and has by the latter, with other issue,

* George William, *b.* 1844.

Mr. Morris, who was educated at Trinity Coll., Dublin (B.A. 1821, M.A. 1834), is a Magistrate for co. Waterford, and was High Sheriff for the city of Waterford 1843–4. The family of Morris possessed estates in Staffordshire, a remnant whereof still remains in their

possession at Marchington, in that county; but they removed thence and settled in Ireland *temp.* Charles I. —*Rockenham, Waterford.*

+ MORRIS, WILLIAM, Esq., of Carmarthen.
Son of the late William Morris, Esq., and brother of the late David Morris, Esq., many years M.P. for Carmarthen; *b.* 1800. Is a Magistrate for co. Carmarthen, and a Banker at Carmarthen; elected M.P. for that borough 1864.—*The Bank, Carmarthen.*

MORRIS, WILLIAM O'CONNOR, Esq., of Gartnamona (or Mount Pleasant), King's Co.
Eldest son of the late Rev. Benjamin Morris, of Gartnamona, by Elizabeth, 4th dau. of Maurice Nugent O'Connor, E-q., of Mount Pleasant; *b.* 1824; *s.* 1846; *m.* 1858 Georgiana Kathleen, eldest dau. of George H. Lindsay, Esq., of Glasnevin, co. Dublin, and has, with other surviving issue,

* Maurice Lindsay O'Connor, *b.* 186-.

Mr. Morris, who was educated at Oriel Coll., Oxford (B.A. 1853). and called to the Bar of Ireland 1854. is a Magistrate for King's Co.—*Mount Pleasant, Tullamore, King's Co.; Kildare Street Club, Dublin.*

MORRIS. (See *Pollok-Morris.*)

MORRIS-READE, FREDERICK RICHARD, Esq., of Rossenarra, co. Kilkenny.
Second and youngest son of the late William Morris-Reade, Esq., M.P.. of Rossenarra, (who *d.* 1847), by Eliza, only dau. of the late Patrick Maitland, Esq., of Kilmaron Castle, co. Fife, N.B.; *b.* 1833; *s.* to the property of Rossenarra by purchase of his father's Estates in the Encumbered Estates' Court, Ireland, in 1854. Is a Magistrate for co. Kilkenny.—*Rossenarra, Callan, co. Kilkenny.*

MORRISON, CHARLES, Esq., of Basildon, Berks.
Eldest son of the late James Morrison, Esq., M.P., of Basildon Park, by Mary Anne, dau. of the late Joseph Todd, Esq., of London; *b.* 1817; *s.* 1857. Is a J.P. and D.L. for Berks and for co. Argyle.—*Basildon Park, Reading; Islay, Argyleshire, N.B.; 57, Upper Harley Street, W.*

Heir Pres., his brother Alfred (of Fonthill House, near Hindon, Wilts); educated at Edinburgh, and Trinity Coll., Cambridge; is a J.P. and D.L. for Wilts (High Sheriff 1857); b. 1821; m. 1866 Mabel, eldest dau. of the late Rev. R. S. C. Chermside, Rector of Wilton, Wilts.

MORRISON, WALTER, Esq., of Malham Tarn, Yorkshire.
Fifth son of the late James Morrison, Esq., of Basildon Park, Berks (who *d.* 1857), by Mary Anne, dau. of the late John Todd, Esq., of London; *b.* 1836. Educated at Eton and Balliol Coll., Oxford (B.A. 1857, M.A. 1862); is a Magistrate for the W. Riding of Yorkshire, Lord of the Manor of Malham Moor, and Patron of 1 living; elected -Col. of 2nd Administrative West Riding Rifle Volunteers; elected M.P. for Plymouth 1861.—*Malham Turn, Settle; Reform Club, S.W.*

MORRITT, WILLIAM JOHN SAWREY, Esq., of Rokeby Park, Yorkshire.
Son of the late Rev. Robert Morritt; *b.* 1813; *s.* his uncle, the late John Bacon Sawrey Morritt, Esq., 1813; *m.* 1837 Ellen Frances, dau. of Sir Robert Wilmot, Bart., of Chaddesden, co. Derby. Is a J.P. and D.L. for the N. Riding of Yorkshire, and a Magistrate for co. Durham; was M.P. for the N. Riding of Yorkshire 1862-5, and formerly an Officer in the 77th Foot, the Yorkshire Hussars, and Yorkshire Rifles.—*Rokeby*

Park, Greta Bridge, Barnard Castle; Carlton Club, S.W.
Heir Pres., his brother Robert, b. 181-.

MORROGH, JAMES, Esq., of Old Court, co. Cork.
Eldest son of the late Edward Morrogh, Esq., of Glanmire House, co. Cork, by Christian, dau. of Robert J. Ffrench, Esq., of Rahasane, co. Galway; *b.* 1810; *s.* 1850; *m.* 1844 Christine, 2nd dau. of James D. Lyons, Esq., D.L., of Croome House, co. Limerick. Is a Magistrate for co. Cork (High Sheriff 1864).—*Old Court, Doneraile, co. Cork; County Club, Cork.*

MORSE, THOMAS, Esq., of Ashmead House, Gloucestershire.
Only son of the late Nicholas Morse, Esq., of Ashmead House; *b.* 1784; *s.* 1819 his cousin, the late Thomas Morse, Esq., J.P. and D.L., of Dursley; *m.* 1833 Maria, dau. of the late William Witchell, Esq., and has, with other issue,

* Thomas, educated at Eton and Queen's Coll., Oxford, a Magistrate for co Gloucester, and Capt. Royal Son h Gloucester Militia; *b.* 1833; *m.* 1858 Sarah Jane, eldest dau. of Arthur John Goldney, Esq.

—*Ashmead House, Cam, Dursley.*

+MORSE-BOYCOTT, JOHN HALL, Esq., of Sennow, Norfolk.
Eldest son of the late John Morse, Esq., of Sprowston Hall, Norfolk (formerly High Sheriff of Norfolk), by Elizabeth Anne, dau. of General Hall, of Weatting Park, co. Cambridge; *b.* 1800; *s.* his father in 1844, when he assumed, by Royal licence, the additional name of Boycott after his maternal grandfather; is married. —*Snnowvill, Bushey, Watford, Herts; Sennow Lodge, Great Ryburgh, Norfolk;* Residence: *White House, Harleston, Norfolk.*

MORSHEAD, Sir WARWICK CHARLES, Bart., of Forest Lodge, Berks (cr. 1783).
Eldest son of the late Sir Frederick T. Morshead, Bart., of Trenant Park, by Jane, dau. of Robert Warwick, Esq., of Warwick Hall, Cumberland; *b.* 1824; *s.* as 3rd Bart. 1828; *m.* 1854 Selina, dau. of the Rev. William Vernon Harcourt, of Nuneham Park, Oxon. Is a Magistrate for Berks; was formerly Capt. 6th Dragoons.—*Forest Lodge, Binfield, Berks; Army and Navy Club, S.W.*

MORSHEAD, the Rev. HENRY JOHN.
Third son of the late Rev. Edward Morshead, of Calstock, Cornwall, by Mary, eldest dau. of Arthur Kelly, Esq., of Kelly, Devon; *b.* 1807; *m.* 1834 Elizabeth, eldest dau. of the late Sir William Lewis Salusbury-Trelawny, Bart., of Trelawne, Cornwall, and has, with other issue,

* Walter, *b.* 1834; educated at Brasenose Coll., Oxford (B.A. 1857, B.C.L. and M.A. 1859); called to the Bar at Lincoln's Inn 1862.

Mr. Morshead, who was educated at Exeter Coll., Oxford (B.A. 1829, M.A. 1832), is a Magistrate for Devon and Cornwall, Rector of Kelly, Devon, and Vicar of St. Clether, Cornwall. This family is descended from a common ancestor with Sir W. C. Morshead, Bart. (whom see).—*Residence: Kelly Rectory, Tavistock.*

+MORSHEAD, the Rev. JOHN PHILIP ANDERSON, of Widey Court, Devon.
Eldest son of the late Col. Anderson, R.E., of Widey Court, by Elizabeth, dau. and heir of Philip Morshead, Esq., of Widey Court; *b.* 1810; *s.* 1846; *m.* 1845 Alethea, dau. of the Rev. John Yonge, of Puslinch, Devon, and has, with other issue,

* John Yonge Anderson, *b.* 1846.

Mr. Morshead was educated at Winchester and Exeter

Coll., Oxford (B.A. 1831, M.A. 1845), and appointed Vicar of Salcombe 1854.—*Salcombe Regis, Sidmouth.*

MORTIMER, CHARLES SMITH, Esq., of Wigmore House, Surrey.

Eldest son of the late Charles Mortimer, Esq., of Streatham, Surrey, by Maria, dau. of William Sims, Esq., of Norfolk; *b.* 1808; *s.* 1840; *m.* 1836 Harriet, dau. of John Fuller, Esq., of Coulsdon Court, Surrey, and has, with other issue,

* Charles Mortimer, *b.* 1837; *m.* 1867 Elizabeth, dau. of Beriah Drew, Esq., of Streatham, Surrey.

Mr. Mortimer, who is a Director of the London and South-Western Railway, is descended from the Mortimers of Wigmore, and of Rickards Castle in Wales. —*Wigmore House, Capel, Dorking.*

MORTLOCK, EDMUND JOHN, Esq., of Abington, Cambridgeshire.

Son of the late Rev. Henry Mortlock, of Morcott, and nephew of the late Sir John Mortlock; *b.* 1833 ; *m.* 1859 Mary Jane, 2nd dau. of Charles Hall, Esq. Is a Banker at Cambridge, Lord of the Manor of Great Abington, and Patron of 3 livings.—*Abington Lodge, Cambridge.*

MORTON, Earl of (SHOLTO JOHN WATSON-DOUGLAS).—Cr. 1458.

Eldest son of George Sholto, 17th Earl, by Frances Theodora, eldest dau. of the late Right Hon. Sir George Henry Rose, of Sandhills, Hants; *b.* 1818 ; *s.* 1858 ; *m.* 1st 1844 Helen, dau. of the late James Watson, Esq., of Saughton, Midlothian; 2nd 1853 Lady Alice Ann Caroline, dau. of John George, 1st Earl of Durham. Is a Dep.-Lieut. for Midlothian and co. Argyle, a Magistrate for co. Fife, and Lieut.-Col. Midlothian Yeomanry; was formerly Lieut. 11th Hussars.—*Dalmahoy, Edinburgh; Aberdour Castle, Fifeshire; Conaglen, Ardgour, Argyllshire; 47, Brook Street, w.*

Heir, his son Sholto George Watson, Lord Aberdour, educated at Trinity Coll., Cambridge; Lieut. Midlothian Yeomanry Cavalry, b. 1844.

MOSELEY, JOHN, Esq., of Glemham, Suffolk.

Only surviving son of the late William Moseley, Esq., of Owsden, and Fornham All Saints, by Elizabeth, dau. of Abraham Cocksedge, Esq., of Drinkstone, Suffolk; *b.* 1772 ; *s.* 1785 ; *m.* 1797 Charlotte, only dau. and heir of Stephen Payne-Gallwey, Esq., of West Tofts, Norfolk. Is Magistrate for Suffolk and Norfolk (High Sheriff 1805), and Lord of the Manor of Drinkstone, and other Manors in Suffolk and Norfolk; he purchased this property in 1829. — *Great Glemham House, Wickham Market.*

MOSELEY, WALTER, Esq., of Buildwas, Shropshire.

Eldest son of the late Walter Moseley, Esq., of Buildwas, by Elizabeth, dau. of S. E. Steward, Esq., of Myton, co. Warwick; *b.* 1832 ; *s.* 1849 ; *m.* 1864 Maria Catharine, 2nd dau. of the Rev. R. Anderson, of Bedale, co. York. Educated at Eton and Trinity Coll., Oxford; is Lord of the Manor, and Patron of Buildwas.—*Buildwas Park, Wenlock.*

Heir Pres., his brother Edwyn Samuel, b. 1838.

MOSLEY, Sir OSWALD, Bart., of Rolleston Hall, Staffordshire (cr. 1781).

Eldest son of the late Oswald Mosley, Esq., of Bolesworth Castle, co. Chester, by Elizabeth, only dau. and heir of the Rev. Thomas Tonman; *b.* 1785 ; *s.* his grandfather as 2nd Bart. 1798 ; *m.* 1804 Sophia Anne, dau. of the late Sir Edward Every, Bart. (she *d.* 1859). Educated at Rugby and B. N. C., Oxford (M.A. 1806) ; is D.C.L. Oxon ; a J.P. and D.L. for cos. Stafford and

678

Derby, and Patron of 3 livings; was M.P. for N. Staffordshire 1832-7.—*Rolleston Hall, Burton-on-Trent.*

*Heir, his son Tonman, of East Lodge, Burton-on-Trent, a J.P. and D.L. for co. Stafford, and a Magistrate for co. Derby; late Lieut. Inniskilling Dragoons; b. 1813; m. 1847 Catharine, dau. of the late Rev. J. Wood, of Swanwick, co. Derby, and has, with other issue, * Oswald, b. 185-.*

MOSLEY, ASHTON NICHOLAS EVERY, Esq., of Burnaston House, Derbyshire.

Only son of the late Ashton Nicholas Mosley, Esq., of Park Hill, co. Derby, by Mary, dau. of Edward Morley, Esq., of Horsely, and widow of Sir E. Every, Bart.; *b.* 1792 ; *s.* 1830 ; *m.* 1820 Mary Theresa, only child of W. Stables, Esq., and has, with other issue,

* Ashton, a J.P. and D.L. for co. Derby; late Capt. 60th Rifles; b. 1821.

Mr. Mosley is a J.P. and D.L. for co. Derby (High Sheriff 1835), and a Magistrate for co. Stafford.—*Burnaston House, Derby.*

MOSS. (See *Edwards-Moss.*)

MOSTYN, Lord EDWARD MOSTYN LLOYD-MOSTYN).—Cr. 1831.

Elder son of Edward Pryce, 1st Lord, by Elizabeth, dau. of the late Sir Roger Mostyn, Bart.; *b.* 1795; *s.* 1854; *m.* 1827 Lady Harriet Margaret. dau. of Thomas, 2nd Earl of Clonmell. Educated at Westminster; is Lord-Lieutenant of co. Merioneth, a Magistrate for cos. Carnarvon, Denbigh, and Flint, and a Dep.-Lieut. for co. Montgomery ; was M.P. for Flintshire 1831-7, 1841-2, and 1847-54, for Lichfield 1846-7 ; Patron of 1 living. Assumed the name of Mostyn in addition to that of Lloyd 1831.—*Pengwern, Rhyl ; Gloddeth, Conway ; Mostyn Hall, Holywell ; 9, Lower Seymour Street, w.*

Heir, his grandson Llewelyn Nevill Vaughan (elder son of the late Hon. Thomas Edward Mostyn Lloyd-Mostyn, M.P., who d. 1861, by Lady Henrietta Augusta, dau. of William, 4th Earl of Abergavenny), b. 1856.

MOSTYN, Sir PYERS, Bart., of Talacre, Flintshire (cr. 1670).

Eldest son of the late Sir Edward Mostyn, Bart., of Talacre, by his 1st wife Frances, dau. of William Blundell, Esq., of Crosby Hall, co. Lancaster; *b.* 1811 ; *s.* as 8th Bart. 1841 ; *m.* 1844 the Hon. Georgiana Frances Georgina, 2nd dau. of Thomas Alexander, 14th Lord Lovat. Is a J.P. and D.L. for co. Flint (High Sheriff 1843).—*Talacre, Rhyl; Brooks's and Reform Clubs, s.w.*

Heir, his son Pyers William, b. 1846.

MOSTYN, Dowager Lady, of Red Hill, Surrey.

Constantia, dau. of the late Henry Slaughter, Esq., of Ingatestone, Essex, and Frances Viscountess Montague; *m.* 1826 (as 2nd wife) Sir Edward Mostyn, Bart., of Talacre, co. Flint, who *d.* 1841, leaving issue.—*Red Hill, Reigate, Surrey.*

MOSTYN, EDWARD HENRY, Esq.

Second son of the late Sir Edward Mostyn, Bart., of Talacre, by his 1st wife Frances, dau. of Nicholas Blundell, Esq., of Crosby Hall, co. Lancaster; *b.* 1813 ; *m.* 1818 Anastasia Elizabeth, dau. of the late Sir John F. Fletcher Boughey, Bart., and widow of Edward J. Smythe, Esq., and has, with other issue,

* Edward Henry, b. 1857.

Mr. Mostyn, who was formerly Capt. 8th Hussars, is a J.P. and D.L. for co. Flint.—*Residence : Arundel, Sussex.*

MOSTYN, THOMAS ARTHUR BERTIE, Esq., of Llewesog, Denbighshire.

Youngest and only surviving son of the late John Meredith Mostyn, of Segroit, co. Denbigh, by Cecilia Margaretta, dau. of the late Henry Thrale, Esq., of Streatham

Park, Surrey ; *b.* 1801 ; *s.* 1841 ; educated at West-minster; was High Sheriff of co. Merioneth 1852.—*Lle-wesog, Denb'gh ;* 41, *St. James's Place,* s.w.

MOSTYN. (See under *Vaux, Lord.*)

MOTT, JOHN THOMAS, Esq., of Barningham, Norfolk.
Eldest son of the late John Thruston Mott, Esq., of Barningham Hall, by Sophia, 3rd dau. of the late Henry Partridge, Esq., of Cromer, Norfolk ; *b.* 1809 ; *m.* 1833 Caroline, 3rd dau. of the late William Sloane-Stanley, Esq., of Paultons, Hants, and has, with other issue,
  • John Stanley, *b.* 1838 ; *m.* 1867 Cordelia Euphemia, 3rd dau. of the late Sir Norman Macdonald Lockhart, Bart.
Mr. Mott, who was educated at Harrow and Ch. Ch., Oxford, is a J.P. and D.L. for Norfolk (High Sheriff 1861), Lord of the Manor of Barningham, and Patron of 3 livings.—*Barningham Hall, Hanworth.*

MOTT, WILLIAM, Esq., of Wall, Staffordshire.
Eldest son of John Mott, Esq., of Lichfield, by Henrietta dau. of the late Sir Charles Oakeley, Bart. ; *b.* 1815 ; *m.* 1st 1837 Louisa Ann, dau. of Roger Kynaston, Esq. of Dover Street, London (she *d.* 1863) ; 2nd 1867 Anna Maria, youngest surviving dau. of the late James Ward, Esq., of Willey Place, Farnham, and widow of Arthur Stephens, Esq., of Foston Hall, co. York, and has by the former, with other issue,
  • William Kynaston, *b.* 1840.
Mr. Mott, who was educated at Eton and Ch. Ch., Oxford (B.A. 1836), is a J.P. and D.L. for co. Stafford. —*Wall, Lichfield ; Arthur's Club,* s.w.

MOUBRAY, ROBERT FREDERICK NORTH BICKER-TON, Esq., of Cockairny, Fifeshire.
Eldest son of the late Lieut.-Col. Sir Robert Moubray, K.H., of Cockairny, by Laura, dau. of the late William Hobson, Esq., of Markfield, Middlesex ; *b.* 1808 ; *s.* 1848. Is a Magistrate for co. Fife.—*Cockairny House, Aberdour, N.B.*
  Heir Pres., his brother William Hobson (of Otterston, near Aberdour, co. Fife), a J.P. and D.L. for co. Fife, and a Commander R.N. retired; *b.* 1818; *m.* 1st 1847 Selina Mary Anna, 4th dau. of the late John Bonfoy Rooper, Esq., M.P., of Abbot's Ripton, Hunts; 2nd 1857 Adeline Hannah, only dau. of the late Capt. Babington, of the Madras Cavalry, and has, by the former, with other issue, • William Henry Hallowell Carew, *b.* 1852.

MOUBRAY. (See *Hussey.*)

MOULTRIE, JOHN AUSTIN, Esq., of St. Austin's, Surrey.
Eldest son of the late George Austin Moultrie, Esq., J.P. and D.L., of Aston Hall, co. Salop, by Jane, 4th dau. of the late Crawford Davison, Esq., of Pierrepoint Lodge, Farnham, Surrey ; *b.* 1829 ; *s.* 1866. Several branches of this family are settled in Carolina.—*St. Austin's, Farnham, Surrey.*

MOUNSEY, GEORGE GILL, Esq., of Castletown, Cumberland.
Eldest son of the late Robert Mounsey, Esq., of Castle-town, by Mary, dau. of Capt. Joseph Gill, of Carlisle ; *b.* 1797 ; *s.* 1842 ; *m.* 1827 Isabella, 2nd dau. of John Heyshanı, Esq., M.D., of Carlisle ; and by her, who *d.* 1848, has, with other issue,
  • Robert Heysham, *b.* 1828.
Mr. Mounsey, who was educated at Westminster, is Patron of 1 living.—*Castletown, Carlisle.*

MOUNT, the Rev. FRANCIS JOHN, of Poynters, Surrey.
Youngest son of William Mount, Esq., of Wasing, Berks (whom see), by Charlotte, dau. of George Talbot, Esq., of Temple Guiting, co. Gloucester; *b.* 1831 ; *s.* his

cousin, Miss Sophia Catharine Page, 1860. Educated at Eton and Oriel Coll., Oxford (B.A. 1854, M.A. 1857). —*Poynters, Cobham.*

MOUNT, WILLIAM, Esq., of Wasing, Berks.
Only son of the late William Mount, Esq., of Wasing Place, by Jane, dau. of Thomas Page, Esq., of Poyn-ters, co. Surrey ; *b.* 1787 ; *s.* 1815 ; *m.* 1818 Charlotte, dau. of the late George Talbot, Esq., of Temple Guiting, co. Gloucester, and has, with other issue,
  • William George, M.A. of Balliol Coll., Oxford, and a J.P. and D.L. for Berks; *b.* 1824.
Mr. Mount, who was educated at Eton and Oriel Coll., Oxford, is a J.P. and D.L. for Berks (High Sheriff 1826), a Magistrate for Hants, and Lord of the Manor and Patron of Wasing.—*Wasing Place, Reading.*

MOUNT, WILLIAM, Esq., of Canterbury, Kent.
Son of the late William Mount, Esq., of Howfield, by Mary, dau. of the late John Sankey, Esq., of Milton Chapel ; *b.* 1789 ; *s.* 1804; *m.* 1816 Sydney, dau. of William Chalk, Esq., of Milton Chapel, and has, with other issue,
  • Francis William, *b.* 1818 ; *m.* 1841 Martha, dau. of John James Peele, Esq., of Cockermouth Castle.
Mr. Mount, who is a J.P. and D.L. for Kent, has been for many years the Treasurer of the City of Canterbury and is a Lieut. East Kent Militia, retired.—*Canter-bury.*

MOUNTAIN, the Rev. HENRY JACOB HENRY BROOKE, D.D., of Blunham, Beds.
Eldest son of the late Right Rev. Jacob Mountain, D.D., of The Heath House, Hemel Hempstead (some time Bishop of Quebec), by Elizabeth, dau. and heir of the late — Kentish, Esq., of Great Bardfield Hall, Essex ; *b.* 1787; *s.* 1825 ; *m.* 1st 1812 Frances, dau. of W. Brooke, Esq. (she *d.* 1837); 2nd 1850 Frances Mar-garetta, widow of Frederick Polhill, Esq., M.P., and has issue. Mr. Mountain, who was educated at Trinity Coll., Cambridge (B.A. 1810, M.A. 1814, B.D. 1837, D.D. 1844), is a Magistrate for Herts and Beds : ap-pointed Rector of Blunham 1831. Prebendary of Lin-coln 1812.—*Blunham Rectory, St. Neots; Woodland Terrace, Blackheath, s.e.*

MOUNTCASHELL, Earl of (STEPHEN MOORE, F.R.S.).—Cr. 1781.
Eldest son of Stephen, 2nd Earl, by Lady Margaret, eldest dau. of Robert. 2nd Earl of Kingston ; *b.* 1792 ; *s.* 1822; *m.* 1819 Anna Maria, dau. of Samuel Wyss, Esq., of Switzerland. Educated at Trinity Coll., Cam-bridge (M.A. 1812) ; is a Magistrate for cos. Cork, Tip-perary, and Waterford : elected a Representative Peer for Ireland 1826.—*Moor Park, Kilworth, co. Cork ; National Club,* s.w.
  Heir, his son Stephen, Lord Kilworth, educated at Eton; Lieut. Rifle Brigade, a J.P. and D.L., and late High Sheriff of co. Cork; *b.* 1825.

MOUNTCHARLES.
(See under *Conyngham, Marquis.*)

MOUNT-EDGCUMBE, Earl of (WILLIAM HENRY EDGCUMBE).—Cr. 1789.
Eldest son of Ernest Augustus, 3rd Earl, by Caroline, dau. of the late Admiral Fielding ; *b.* 1832 ; *s.* 1861 . *m.* 1858 Lady Katharine Elizabeth, dau. of James, 2nd Marquis of Abercorn, K.G. Educated at Harrow and Ch. Ch., Oxford ; is a J.P. and D.L. for Cornwall, a Dep.-Lieut. for Devon, Patron of 4 livings, and an extra Lord in Waiting to the Prince of Wales : was M.P. for Plymouth 1859-61. — *Mount Edgcumbe, Devonport ; Cotehele House, Callington, Cornwall ; Carlton Club,* s.w.
  Heir, his son Piers Alexander Hamilton, Viscount Valletort, *b.* 1865.

MOUNTGARRET, Viscount (HENRY EDMUND BUTLER).—Cr. 1550.

Only surviving son of the late Hon. Henry Butler (who d. 1842), by Ann, youngest dau. and co-heir of John Harrison, Esq., of Newtown House, co. York; b. 1816; s. his uncle, the 12th Viscount (who was also Earl of Kilkenny), 1846; m. 1844 Frances Penelope, only dau. of Thomas Rawson, Esq., of Nidd Hall, co. York. Educated at Worcester Coll., Oxford; is a J.P. and D.L. for co. Kilkenny.—*Ballyconra. Kilkenny.*

Heir, his son Henry Edmund, b. 1844.

MOUNTMORRES, VISCOUNT (HERVEY DE MONTMORENCY).—Cr. 1763.

Eldest son of Francis Hervey, 3rd Viscount, by Anne, dau. of Joseph Reade, Esq., of Castlehoyle, co. Kilkenny; b. 1796; s. 1833; m. 1831 Sarah, dau. of William Shaw, Esq., of Temple Hill. Educated at Trinity Coll., Dublin (B.A. 1826, LL.D. 1849); appointed Dean of Cloyne 1844, Dean of Achonry 1850; is a Magistrate for co. Sligo, and Chaplain to the Lord-Lieutenant of Ireland.—*The Deanery, Achonry, Bally-mote, Ireland ; University Club, Dublin.*

Heir, his son William Browne, of Ebor Hall, co. Galway ; B.A. of Trinity Coll., Oxford ; a Magistrate for co. Galway ; b. 1832 ; m. 1862 Harriet, dau. of George Broadrick, Esq., of Hamphall. co. York, and grand-dau. of Sir Richard Fletcher, Bart.

MOUTRAY, ANKETELL, Esq., of Favour Royal, co. Tyrone.

Eldest son of the late John Corry Moutray, Esq., of Favour Royal (J.P. and D.L. for co. Tyrone), by Mary Anne Catherine, dau. of Ambrose Upton, Esq., of Dublin; b. 1797; s. 1859. Educated at Trinity Coll., Dublin; was High Sheriff of co. Tyrone 1855.—*Favour Royal, Aughnacloy, co. Tyrone.*

Heir Pres., his brother John James, in Holy Orders, b. 1802 ; m. 1836 Maria, dau. of the Rev. William Perceval, and has, with other issue, * John Maxwell, in Holy orders, b. 1837 ; m. 1864 Jane, dau. of the late David Harrel, Esq., of Mountpleasant, Downpatrick, and has issue, * John Corry Anketell, b. 1866.

MOWATT, FRANCIS, Esq., late of Trotton Park, Sussex.

Son of the late Capt. James R. Mowatt, of Eastbourne, Sussex; b. 1803; m. 1828, Sarah Sophia, dau. of Capt. G. Barnes, and has issue,

* Frank, b. 1837 ; m. 1864 Lucy Sophia, dau. of I. A. Frerichs, Esq., of Torkstaine Hall, Cheltenham.

Mr. Mowatt was M.P. for Penryn and Falmouth 1847-52, for Cambridge 1854-7.—*Athenæum Club, s.w.; 84. Eccleston Square, s.w.*

MOWBRAY, GEORGE THOMAS, Esq., of Grangewood House, Leicestershire.

Son of the late Capt. Thomas Mowbray, R.N., of Grangewood House, by Anne, elder dau. of Richard Thomas Streatfield, Esq., of the Rocks, Sussex ; b. 1824 ; s. 1864. Educated at Harrow and Trinity Coll., Cambridge (B.A. 1846); is a J.P. and D.L. for co. Leicester. Lord of the Manor of Overseale, and Capt. Leicestershire Militia. This branch of the family was formerly of Allandale, Northumberland.—*Grangewood House, Ashby-de-la-Zouch ; United University Club, s.w.*

Heir Pres., his sister Georgiana Anne, m. 1858 Monsieur Richard de Préville, of the Chateau des Mendrans, Basses Pyrénées, France, and has, with other issue, * André George, b. 1859.

MOWBRAY, the Right Hon. JOHN ROBERT, of Warrennes Wood, Berks.

Only son of Robert Stribling Cornish. Esq., of Exeter, Devon, by Marianne, dau. of John Powning, Esq., of Hill's Court, Exeter ; b. 1815 ; m. 1847 Elizabeth Gray, only child of George Isaac Mowbray, Esq., of Bishop-

wearmouth, whose name he assumed by Royal licence, and has, with other issue,

* Robert Gray Cornish, b. 1850.

Mr. Mowbray, who was educated at Westminster and Ch. Ch., Oxford (B.A. 1837, M.A. 1839), and called to the Bar at the Inner Temple 1841, is a J.P. and D.L. for co. Durham, and a Magistrate for Berks; was Judge-Advocate General 1858-9, sworn a Privy Councillor 1858; has been M.P. for Durham since 1853; appointed Judge-Advocate General 1866. — *Warrennes Wood, Mortimer, Reading ; Carlton, and Oxford and Cambridge Clubs, s.w.*

MOXON, WILLIAM, Esq., of Farncombe, Worcestershire.

Third son of the late Michael Moxon, Esq.; b. 1808; m. 184— Anne, youngest dau. of Timothy Horsfall, Esq., of Goitstock, co. York, and sister of Timothy Horsfall, Esq., J.P., of Hawksworth Hall, Co. York. Called to the Bar at the Middle Temple 1843, and practised at the Equity Bar. Is a Magistrate for co. Worcester. —*Farncombe House, Broadway ; Junior Carlton Club, s.w.*

MOYSEY, HENRY GORGES, Esq., of Bathealton Court, Somerset.

Eldest son of the late Ven. Archdeacon Moysey, of Bathealton Court, by his 1st wife Charlotte, dau. of the late Francis Fownes-Luttrell, Esq., of Dunster Castle, Somerset; b. 1813; s. 1859; m. 1841 Emily Faithful, dau. of the Rev. Charles R. Fanshawe, of Fanshawe Gate, Dronfield. Educated at Westminster and St. Mary Hall, Oxford ; is a Magistrate for Devon, and J.P. and D.L. for Somerset; late Lieut. 11th Hussars. —*Bathealton Court, Wellington ; Army and Navy Club, s.w.*

Heir Pres., his brother the Rev. Frederick Luttrell, b. 1815 ; m. 1859 Arabella, dau. of the Hon. John Petty Ward, and has, with other issue, * Charles John, Lieut. R.E., b. 1840.

MUDGE, ARTHUR, Esq., of Sydney House, Devon.

Only son of the late Zachary Mudge, Esq., Barrister-at-Law, of Sydney House, by Jane, dau. of George Frederick Dickson, Esq., Consul-General for Buenos Ayres ; b. 1847 ; s. 1867. Is a Lieut. 97th Regt., and represents an ancient Devonshire family.—*Sydney House, Plympton : South Pill, Saltash, Cornwall; Glentossera Lodge, Killala, co. Mayo.*

MUDIE, JOHN, Esq., of Pitmuies, Forfarshire.

Only surviving son of the late James Mudie, Esq., of Pitmuies, by Jane, dau. of Charles Aitkin, Esq., of Belvidere, Isle St. Croix, West Indies : b. 1812 ; s. 1850. Educated at Edinburgh University, and Trinity Coll., Cambridge; called to the Scottish Bar 1838 ; is a Magistrate for co. Forfar.—*Pitmuies. Arbroath, N.B.*

MUIR, Sir WILLIAM, K.C.S.I. (cr. 1867).

Son of the late William Muir, Esq., of Kilgarnock, by Helen, dau. of John Mactie, Esq.; b. 1819 ; m. 1840 Elizabeth Huntly, dau. of James Wemyss, Esq. Educated at the Edinburgh and Glasgow Universities (LL.D. of Glasgow) ; is in the Bengal Civil Service, and Foreign Secretary to the Government of India.—*Calcutta.*

+**MUIR**, JOHN, Esq., of Foley House, Buteshire.

Son of the late W. Muir, Esq., of Foley House ; b. 1800 ; Is a J.P. and D.L. for co. Bute.—*Foley House, Rothesay.*

MUIR-MACKENZIE. (See *Mackenzie.*)

+ MUIRHEAD, JAMES PATRICK, Esq., of Haseley Court, OXON.

Son of the late P. Muirhead, Esq., of Haseley Court ; *b.* 18 —. Is a Dep.-Lieut. for Oxon.—*Haseley Court, Tetsworth.*

MUIRHEAD.   (See *Steuart-Grosett-Muirhead.*)

MULCAHY, EDMUND, Esq., of Ballymakee, co. Waterford.

Second son of the late Edmund Mulcahy, Esq., of Tipperary, by Barbara, dau. of Roger Moore, Esq., of Ashgrove ; *b.* 1791 ; *s.* 1823 ; *m.* 1819 Maria, dau. of John Russell, Esq., of Ballycallam, co. Waterford, and has, with other issue,

* Edmund Moore, a Magistrate for co. Waterford, and Capt. South Tipperary Artillery ; *b.* 1821 ; *m.* 1849 Susan, eldest dau. of the late Nicholas P. O'Gorman, Esq., Q.C.

Mr. Mulcahy, who is a Magistrate for cos. Waterford and Tipperary, and a Grand Juror for co. Waterford, was formerly an Officer in the Tipperary Militia. —*Ballymakee, Clonmel, co. Waterford.*

MULCASTER, JOHN PETER, Esq., of Benwell Park, Northumberland.

Only son of the late John Mulcaster, Esq., of Blaydon, Durham ; *b.* 1818 ; *m.* 1850 Annie, dau. of Stephen Reed, Esq., of Newcastle-upon-Tyne, and has, with other issue,

* Henry John Percival, *b.* 1851.

Mr. Mulcaster, who was called to the Bar at the Middle Temple in 1843, and goes the Northern Circuit, is a Magistrate for Northumberland.—*Benwell Park, Newcastle-on-Tyne.*

MULCASTER, the Rev. RICHARD, of Laversdale, Cumberland.

Eldest son of the late Richard Mulcaster, Esq., of Laversdale, by Margaret, dau. of Thomas Calvert, Esq., of Clarke's Hill ; *b.* 1830 ; *s.* 1851. Educated at the University of Durham (B.A. 1854) ; is Curate of Ulverston. The first ancestor of this family was warder of Carlisle Castle *temp.* William II.—*Bothal, Morpeth, Northumberland ; Laversdale, Cumberland.*

MULGRAVE.   (See under *Normanby, Marquis of.*)

+ MULHOLLAND, ANDREW, Esq., of Spring Vale, Downshire.

Eldest son of the late Thomas Mulholland, Esq., of Spring Vale ; *b.* 1793 ; *m.* 1819 Elizabeth, dau. of T. MacDonnell, Esq., and has, with other issue,

* John, of Craigavad, near Holywood, co. Down, a J.P. and D.L. for cos. Antrim and Down ; *b.* 1820 ; *m.* 1851 Fanny, dau. of the late Hugh Lyle, Esq., of Knocktorna, co. Londonderry, and has, with other issue, * Andrew, *b.* 1852.

Mr. Mulholland, who is a J.P. and D.L. for cos. Down and Antrim, was formerly an Officer 18th Foot.—*Spring Vale, Ballywater, Downshire.*

MULLINGS, ARTHUR RANDOLPH, Esq., of Eastcourt, Wiltshire.

Younger son of the late Joseph R. Mullings, Esq., of Eastcourt (who was M.P. for Cirencester 1848-59), by Margarette, dau. of Richard Gregory, Esq., of Cirencester ; *b.* 1839 ; *s.* his brother Joseph 1860 ; *m.* 1864 Bellamira Emma, youngest dau. of the late Hon. Francis Ward Primrose, and grand-dau. of Neil, 3rd Earl of Roseberry, and has, with other issue,

* Joseph Randolph, *b.* 1867.

Mr. Mullings, who was educated at Eton, is Lord of the Manor of Minety, and Patron of 1 living ; late Capt. 15th Hussars.—*Eastcourt, Malmesbury ; Windham Club, s.w.*

MULLOY, the Rev. COOTE CHARLES, of Hughstown, co. Roscommon.

Eldest son of the late Coote Mulloy, Esq., of Hughstown, by Mary, dau. of William Lloyd, Esq., of Rockville, co. Roscommon ; *b.* 1803 ; *s.* 1842 ; *m.* 1st 1831 Alice, eldest dau. of Robert King Duke, Esq., of Newpark, Sligo ; 2nd 1857 Catherine Reddish, eldest dau. of the late Most Rev. Edward Stopford, D.D., Lord Bishop of Meath, and has, with other issue,

* William Hutchinson, R.E. ; *b.* 1829.

Mr. Mulloy, who was educated at Trinity Coll., Dublin (B.A. 1823), is in Holy Orders ; he claims the hereditary honour of Standard-bearer to the crown of England in Ireland.—*Hughstown, Carrick-on-Shannon, Ireland.*

MUNBEE, GORE BOLAND, Esq., of Weston-super-Mare, Somerset.

Youngest son of the late Major Valentine Munbee, of Horringer Hall, Suffolk, by Letitia, dau. of Major Richard Young, of Coolkeimagh House, co. Londonderry ; *b.* 1815. Educated at the Royal Military Coll., is a Magistrate for Somerset, and a Major-Gen. on the retired list of the Royal Engineers. This family is descended in the female line from Christopher Columbus, by a marriage with a noble Spaniard. It held land in Cuba and Jamaica on military tenure, and became British subjects when Jamaica was captured in 1655. Soon after that event the family settled near Bury St. Edmund's, and became possessed of estates in Suffolk and Cambridgeshire.—*Highbury Villa, Weston-super-Mare ; East India United Service Club, s.w.*

MUNCASTER, Lord (JOSSELYN FRANCIS PENNINGTON).—Cr. 1783.

Third but eldest surviving son of Lowther, 3rd Lord (who *d.* 1838), by Frances, dau. of the late Sir John Ramsden, Bart., and brother of Gamel, 4th Lord ; *b.* 1834 ; *s.* 1862 ; *m.* 1863 Constance, 2nd dau. of Edmund and Lady Harriet L'Estrange, of Tynte Lodge, co. Leitrim. Is a Magistrate for Cumberland, a J.P. and D.L. for the E. Riding of Yorkshire. Patron of 3 livings, and Capt. Cumberland Militia; late Capt. in the Rifle Brigade. — *Muncaster Castle, Whitehaven ; Warter Priory, Pocklington ; Boodle's, Army and Navy, and Carlton Clubs, s.w.*

Heir Pres., his brother Alan Joseph, *b.* 1837.

MUNDY, Vice-Admiral Sir GEORGE RODNEY, K.C.B. (Cr. 1862).

Second son of the late General Godfrey Basil Mundy, by the Hon. Sarah Brydges, youngest dau. of George, 1st Lord Rodney, and nephew of the late Admiral Sir G. Mundy, K.C.B. ; *b.* 1805. Educated at the Royal Naval Coll., Portsmouth ; is a Vice-Admiral R.N. ; was second in command in the Mediterranean 1859-62. —*United Service, and Army and Navy Clubs, s.w. ; 42, Bryanston Street, w.*

MUNDY, ALFRED MILLER, Esq., of Shipley Hall, Derbyshire.

Fourth son of the late Edward Miller Mundy, Esq. (who *d.* 1834), by Nelly, dau. of F. Burton, Esq., of Penwortham, Lancashire ; *b.* 1809 ; *s.* his brother, the late Edward M. Mundy, Esq., M.P. ; *m.* 1841 Jane, 2nd dau. of the late Rear-Admiral Sir John Hindmarsh, K.H., and has, with other issue,

* Alfred Edward Miller, *b.* 1848.

Mr. Mundy, who is a J.P. and D.L. for co. Derby (High Sheriff 1855), and a Magistrate for Notts, was formerly Lieut. 60th Rifles.—*Shipley Hall, Derby ; Arthur's Club, s.w.*

681

MUNDY, CHARLES JOHN HENRY MASSING-BERD-, Esq., of Ormsby, Lincolnshire.
Only son of the late Charles Godfrey Mundy, Esq., of Barton, co. Leicester, by Harriet, only dau. and heir of Charles Burrell Massingberd, Esq., of Ormsby Hall (who d. 1835); b. 1808 ; s. his step-grandmother 1863, when he assumed the additional name of Massingberd; m. 1838 Elizabeth Susan, 5th dau. of the late John Young, Esq., of Westridge, I. of Wight, and has, with other issue,

* Charles Francis, a Magistrate for co. Lincoln, late Lieut. 53rd Foot, b. 1839 ; m. 1865 Louisa Charlotte, dau. of the late Charles John Bigg, Esq., of Linden, Northumberland, and has issue, * Charles Draner, b. 1867.

Mr. Mundy, who was educated at Eton and Ch. Ch., Oxford, is a J.P. and D.L. for the Lindsey Division of co. Lincoln, and Lord of the Manors of S. Ormsby, Calceby, Driby, and Ingoldmells, and Patron of 2 livings.—South Ormsby Hall, Alford ; Carlton Club, s.w.

+MUNDY, MEYNELL HORTON MILLER, Esq., of Shipley Cottage, Derbyshire.
Youngest son of the late Edward Miller Mundy, Esq., of Shipley (who d. 1834). by Nelly, dau. of F. Barton, Esq.; b. 1828 ; entered the Navy in 1843, became a Lieut. in 1846 ; is a J.P. and D.L. for co. Derby.—Shipley Cottage, Derby.

MUNDY, Mrs., of Plâs Newydd, Glamorganshire.
Georgina, eldest dau. of the late Vice-Admiral Sir G. Tyler, K.H., of Cottrell, co. Glamorgan (who d. 1862), by Harriet Margaret, dau. of the Right Hon. John Sullivan, of Ritchings Park, Bucks; m. 1st 18— E. P. Richards, Esq., of Plâs Newydd, co. Glamorgan; 2nd 1859 Col. Pierrepont Henry Mundy, R.A., who d. 1866.—Plâs Newydd, Glamorganshire ; 5, Eaton Place, s.w.

MUNDY, Major ROBERT MILLER, of Holly Bank, Hants.
Youngest son of the late Edward Miller Mundy, Esq., M.P., of Shipley Hall, co. Derby, by Catherine, widow of Richard Barwell, Esq., of Stansted Park, Sussex; b. 1813 ; m. 1841 Isabella, youngest dau. of the late General Leyborne-Popham, of Littlecote, Wilts, and has, with other issue,

* Robert Leyborne, b. 1852.

Major Mundy, who was educated at the Royal Military Academy, Woolwich, is a Magistrate for Hants, and a Half-pay Major R. A.—Holly Bank, Emsworth ; Army and Navy Club, s.w.

MUNDY, WILLIAM, Esq., of Markeaton, Derbyshire.
Eldest son of the late Francis Mundy, Esq., of Markeaton Hall (who was many years M.P. for co. Derby), by Sarah, dau. of John Leaper Newton, Esq. ; b. 1801 ; s. 1837 ; m. 1830 Harriet Georgiana, dau. of James Frampton, Esq., of Moreton, Dorset, and grand-dau. of Henry Thomas, 2nd Earl of Ilchester, and has issue,

* Francis Noel, a Dep.-Lieut. for co. Derby, b. 1833 ; m. 1864 Emily Georgiana, 3rd dau. of the Hon. Richard Cavendish, of Thornton Hall, Bucks.

Mr. Mundy, who was educated at Eton and Ch. Ch., Oxford, is a J.P. and D.L. for co. Derby (High Sheriff 1843); was M.P. for S. Derbyshire 1849–57, and 1859–65.—Markeaton Hall, Derby ; Travellers', Boodle's, and Carlton Clubs, s.w.

MUNN, ROBERT, Esq., of Heath Hill, Lancashire.
Eldest son of the late John Munn, Esq., of Hilton House, Prestwich, co. Lancaster; b. 1800 ; m. 1833

682

Margaret, dau. of John Howorth, Esq., of Hempsteads, Rossendale, co. Lancaster, and has issue,

* James, a Magistrate for co. Lancaster, b. 1836 ; m. 1862 Mary Elizabeth, dau. of John Clegg, Esq., of Butt Hill, Prestwich, and has issue.

Is a Magistrate for cos. Lancaster and Dumfries, and Chairman of the Bacup and Rawtenstall Petty Sessional Division, and a Merchant and Manufacturer. This family is of Scottish extraction, the grandfather of the above having settled in Lancashire A.D. 1745.—Heath Hill, Stacksteads, near Manchester ; Whitecroft, Lockerbie, Dumfriesshire.

MUNN, ROBERT, Esq., of Newchurch, Lancashire.
Eldest son of John Munn, Esq., of Hilton Park, co. Lancaster, by Alice, dau. of James Clegg, Esq., of Prestwich ; b. 1832 ; m. 1854 Margaret Alice. dau. and co-heir of the late William Turner, Esq., of Flax Moss, co. Lancaster, and has, with other issue,

* Dugald, b. 1857.

Mr. Munn is a Magistrate for co. Lancaster, and Lieut.-Col. Commanding Lancashire Volunteer Rifles.—Newchurch, Manchester ; New United Service Club, s.w.

MUNN, Major WILLIAM AUGUSTUS, of Throwley, Kent.
Only son of the late Col. Henry Munn, by Harriet Comber, dau. of William Hood, Esq., of Blackheath, Kent ; b. 1814 ; m. 1st 1834 Elizabeth, eldest dau. of H. Hilton, Esq., of Sole Street, Kent; 2nd 1852 Marianne, eldest dau. of the late James Beckford Wildman, Esq., of Chilham Castle, Kent, and has, with other issue,

* Henry Oldman, educated at Eton, Capt. 13th Light Dragoons ; b. 1835.

Major Munn is a J.P. and D.L. for Kent, and a retired Major East Kent Militia.—Throwley House, Faversham.

MUNRO, Sir CHARLES, Bart., of Foulis, Rossshire (cr. 1634).
Eldest son of the late George Munro, Esq., of Culrain, co. Ross (who d. 1846), by Margaret, youngest dau. of J. Montgomery, Esq., of Milton, co. Ross; b. 1795 ; s. his kinsman as 9th Bart. 1848 ; m. 1st 1817 Amelia. dau. of F. Browne, Esq. (she d. 1849) ; 2nd 1853 Harriet, dau. of Robert Midgley. Esq. Educated at Edinburgh ; is a J.P. and D.L. for co. Ross.—Ardullie House and Foulis Castle, Evanton, Ross-shire, N.B. ; 30, Ann Street, Edinburgh.

Heir, his son Charles, J.P. and D.L. for co. Ross, b. 1821 ; m. 1847 Mary Anne, dau. of John Nicholson, Esq., of Camberwell, and has, with other issue, * Hector, b. 1848.

MUNRO, Sir THOMAS, Bart., of Lindertis, Forfarshire (cr. 1825).
Elder son of the late Major-General Sir Thomas Munro, Bart., K.C.B. (who was some time Governor of Madras), by Jane, dau. of Richard Campbell, Esq., of Craigie, co. Ayr ; b. 1819 ; s. as 2nd Bart. 1827. Educated at Eton and Ch. Ch., Oxford ; is a J.P. and D.L. for co. Forfar; late Captain Forfarshire Yeomanry; was formerly Capt. 10th Hussars.—Lindertis, Kirriemuir, N.B.

Heir Pres., his brother Campbell, late Lieut. and Capt. Grenadier Guards, b. 1823 ; m. 1853 Henrietta, dau. of John Drummond, Esq., and has, with other issue, * Hugh Thomas, b. 1856.

MUNRO, INNES COLIN, Esq., of Poyntzfield, Cromartyshire.
Youngest son of the late Major Sir George Gun Munro, Knt., of Poyntzfield (who d. 1852), by Jemima Charlotte, dau. of Lieut.-Col. Graham; b. 1831 ; s. his

brother 1860; *m.* 1856 Emily, dau. of Thomas Mason, Esq., of Tasmania, and has, with other issue,
* George Mackenzie Gun, *b.* 1862.

Mr. Munro, who is a Magistrate for co. Cromarty, was formerly a Capt. in the Army.—*Poyntzfield House, Fortrose, N.B.*

MUNRO, James St. John, Esq., of Teaninich, Ross-shire.
Eldest son of the late General John Munro, E.I.C., of Teaninich, by Charlotte, youngest dau. of the late Rev. Dr. St. John Blacker; *b.* 1810; *s.* 1858. Is a J.P. and D.L. for co. Ross; was formerly Major 31st Foot.—*Teaninich, Ross-shire, N.B.*

+**MUNRO, Matthew,** Esq., of Fritham, Hants.
Eldest son of the late M. Munro, Esq.; *b.* 18—; *m.* 18— Philadelphia Jane Caroline, eldest dau. of the late Wm. Hector Munro, Esq., of Ewell Castle, Surrey. Is a Magistrate for Hants.—*Fritham, Lyndhurst.*

MUNRO. (See *Midgley-Munro.*)

MUNSTER, Earl of (William George Fitz-Clarence).—Cr. 1831.
Eldest son of George, 1st Earl (who was a natural son of King William IV.), by Mary, dau. of George, 3rd Earl of Egremont; *b.* 1824; *s.* 1842; *m.* 1855 Wilhelmina, dau. of the Hon. John Kennedy-Erskine. Educated at Harrow; is a Dep.-Lieut. for Middlesex; was formerly Capt. 1st Life Guards.—23, *Palmyra Square, Brighton.*
Heir, his son Edward, Viscount FitzClarence, *b.* 1856.

MUNTZ, George Frederick, Esq., of Umberslade Hall, Warwickshire.
Eldest son of the late George Frederick Muntz, Esq., M.P., of Umberslade, by Eliza, dau. of the late John Pryce, Esq., of co. Montgomery; *b.* 1822; *s.* 1857; *m.* 1st 1844 Marianne Lydia, dau. of William Richardson, Esq., of Calcutta; 2nd 1866 Sarah Matilda, dau. of Charles Aylett, Kell, Esq., of Aylesbury House, co. Warwick, and has by the former, with other issue,
* Frederick Ernest, *b.* 1845.

Mr. Muntz is a Magistrate for co. Warwick, and a Manufacturer at Birmingham.—*Umberslade Hall, Hockly Heath, Warwickshire.*

MUNTZ, Philip Henry, Esq., of Edstone Hall, Warwickshire.
Second son of the late Philip Frederick Muntz, Esq., of Selly Hall, co. Worcester, by Catherine, dau. of the late Robert Purden, Esq., of Radford, co. Warwick; *b.* 1811; *m.* 1831 Wilhelmine, dau. of the late Conseiller de Finance D'Olhofen, of Carlsruhe, and has issue. Mr. Muntz, who was educated at Shrewsbury, is a Magistrate for co. Warwick and a Merchant at Birmingham.—*Edstone Hall, Stratford-on-Avon.*

MURCH, Jerom, Esq., of Cranwells, Somerset.
Son of the late William Murch, Esq., of Honiton, Devon, by Ann, dau. of R. Burnard, Esq., of Colyton, Devon; *b.* 1807; *m.* 1830 Anne, dau. of Meadows Taylor, Esq., of Diss, Norfolk, and has, with other issue,
* Charles Jerom, *b.* 1832; called to the Bar at the Inner Temple 1855, appointed Recorder of Barnstaple and Bideford 1864.

Mr. Murch, who was educated at University Coll., London, is a J.P. and D.L. for Somerset.—*Cranwell Bath.*

MURCHISON, Sir Roderick Impey, Bart., K.C.B., F.R.S. (cr. 1865).
Eldest son of the late Kenneth Murchison, Esq., of Tarndale, co. Ross, by Barbara, eldest sister of the late General Sir Alexander Mackenzie, Bart., G.C.H., of Fair-

burn and Strathconnan, co. Ross; *b.* 1792; *m.* 1815 Charlotte, dau. of the late General Hugonin, 4th Dragoons, of Nursted House, Hants. Educated at Durham and Marlow; formerly Capt. 36th Foot and 6th Dragoons; served in the Peninsula, Sicily, and elsewhere 1807-16; is Director-General of the Geological Survey, and a Trustee of the British Museum; late President of the Geological and Actual President of the Royal Geographical Society; nominated a K.C.B. (civil) 1863.—*Athenæum and Travellers' Clubs, s.w.; 16, Belgrave Square, s.w.*

+**MURCHISON, Kenneth Robert,** Esq., of Bathford, Somerset.
Elder son of the late Kenneth Murchison, Esq., formerly Governor of Singapore (who *d.* 1854), by his 2nd wife Anne, dau. of John D. Nesham, Esq., of Houghton-le-Spring, co. Durham, and nephew of Sir R. Murchison, Bart; *b.* 1830. Educated at Eton; is a Magistrate for Somerset.—*Bathford, Bath.*

MURDOCH, Mrs. BURN-, of Gartincaber, Perthshire.
Anne Maule, only child and heir of the late William Murdoch, Esq., of Gartincaber (who *d.* 1806); *m.* 1820 John Burn, Esq., J.P. and D.L. of Newick, who assumed the additional name of Murdoch, and who *d.* 1862, leaving, with other issue,
* John, an Advocate at the Scottish Bar; *b.* 1821; *m.* 1851 Dora, dau. of the late Capt. Monck Mason, R.N.

Mrs. Burn-Murdoch is Lady of the Barony of Gartincaber.—*Gartincaber, by Stirling, N.B.*

MURE, David, Esq.
Third son of the late Col. William Mure, of Caldwell, co. Ayr, by Anne, eldest dau. of the late Sir J. Hunter-Blair, Bart.; *b.* 1810; *m.* 1841 Helen. dau. of John Tod, Esq., of Kirkhill, Midlothian (*d.*). Educated at Westminster and the University of Edinburgh; called to the Scottish Bar 1831; is a Dep.-Lieut. for co. Bute; was Sheriff of co. Perth 1853-8; appointed Solicitor-General for Scotland 1858, Lord Advocate April 1859; M.P. for co. Bute 1859-65; appointed a Judge in the Supreme Courts of Scotland 1865.—12, *Ainslie Place, Edinburgh; Carlton Club, s.w.; 90, Jermyn Street, s.w.*

MURE, Mrs., of Herringswell, Suffolk.
Fanny Eliza, only dau. of Wright Thomas Squire, Esq.; *m.* 1835 George Mure, Esq., of Herringswell, formerly Lieut. Grenadier Guards, who *d. s. p.* 1868.—*Herringswell House, Mildenhall.*
Heir Pres., her husband's nephew Thomas Macredie (eldest son of the late Patrick Boyle Mure, Esq., who *d.* 18—, by Rachel Anne, only child of the late John Macredie, Esq.), *b.* 1840.

MURE, Lieut.-Col. William, of Caldwell, Ayrshire.
Eldest son of the late Col. William Mure, M.P., of Caldwell (who was a J.P. and D.L. for co. Ayr and Vice-Lieutenant for co. Renfrew, Col. of the Renfrew Militia), by Laura, dau. of William Markham, Esq., of Becca Hall, co. York; *b.* 1830; *s.* 1860; *m.* 1859 Constance Elizabeth, 3rd dau. of the 1st Lord Leconfield. Is a J.P. and D.L. for co. Renfrew; was formerly Lieut. Col. Scots Fusilier Guards.—*Caldwell House, Beith, N.B.; 55, Rutland Gate, s.w.*

MURE-MACREDIE. (See *Macredie.*)

MURGATROYD, Mrs., of Bankfield, Yorkshire.
Sarah, dau. of the late Joseph Croft, Esq., of Bradford, Yorkshire; *m.* 1825 William Murgatroyd, Esq., of Bankfield, who was a Magistrate for the W. Riding of

683

Yorkshire, and who *d.* 1865, leaving, with other issue,
* Ann, *m.* 1866 Walter B. Cheadle, Esq., M.D., of
Hyde Park Place, London.—*Bankfield, Bingley.*

MURPHY, Sir FRANCIS, Knt. (cr. 1860).
Son of the late — Murphy, Esq.; *b.* 18—; married, and
has issue. Educated at Trinity Coll., Dublin ; is Speaker
of the House of Assembly, Victoria; was Member for co.
Murray in the Parliament of Victoria, 1851–65.—*Melbourne, Victoria.*

MURPHY, EDWARD, Esq.
Son of the late Patrick Murphy, Esq., *b.* 1804 ; *m.* 1841
Elizabeth Mary Jane, dau. of the late William White,
Esq., of Limerick, and has, with other issue,
* Patrick William, *b.* 1842.
Mr. Murphy was High Sheriff of Limerick 1860.—*The
Crescent, Limerick..*

MURPHY, FRANCIS, Esq., of Kilcairne, co.
Meath.
Eldest son of the late Patrick Murphy, Esq., of Bayne-
ville, co. Meath, by Margaret, dau. of John M'Donnell,
Esq., of Dublin ; *b.* 1798 ; *s.* 1828 ; *m.* 1836 Eleanor
Honoria, eldest dau. of Luke Harkan, Esq., of Raheen,
co. Roscommon, and has, with other issue,
* Francis O'Donnell, Lieut. Royal Meath Militia ; *b.* 1845.
Mr. Murphy, who was educated at Trinity Coll., Dublin,
is a Magistrate for co. Meath.—*Kilcairne House, Navan ;
Upper Fitzwilliam Street, Dublin.*

MURPHY, JAMES, Esq., of Ring, Mahon, co.
Cork.
Son of the late James Murphy, Esq., of Ring Mahon,
by Mary, dau. of James Gallwey, Esq., of Cork ; *b.* 1797;
s. 1855 ; *m.* 1836 Anne, only dau. of John Macna-
mara, Esq., of Limerick, and has, with other issue,
* James, *b.* 1839.
Mr. Murphy, who was educated at St. Mary's, Oscott,
is a Magistrate for co. Cork (High Sheriff 1863), and a
D.L. for the city of Cork.—*Ring Mahon Castle, Cork.*

MURPHY, JOHN NICHOLAS, Esq., of Clifton, co.
Cork.
Eldest son of the late Nicholas Murphy, Esq., of
Clifton, by Susan, dau. of the late John Donegan,
Esq., of Cork; *b.* 1815 ; *s.* 1852 ; *m.* 1855 Alice Mary,
only dau. of the late Daniel Leahy, Esq., D.L., of Sha-
nakiel House, Cork, and has issue,
* Mary Margaret.
Mr. Murphy is a J.P. and D.L. for Cork, (High Sheriff
1857, and Mayor of Cork 1854).—*Clifton, Cork.*

MURPHY, NICHOLAS DANIEL, Esq., of Lauriston, co. Cork.
Fourth son of the late Daniel Murphy, Esq., of Belleville, Cork, by Frances, dau. of — Donegan, Esq.; *b.*
1811 ; *m.* 1838 Anne, dau. of Patrick Waldron, Esq.,
late of Rathgar House, co. Dublin ; is a Solicitor ; was
elected M.P. for Cork 1865.—*Lauriston, Glanmire, co.
Cork ; Reform Club, s.w.*

MURRAY, Sir ROBERT, Bart., of Clermont,
Fifeshire (cr. 1625).
Eldest surviving son of the late Rev. Sir William
Murray, 9th Bart. (who *d.* 1842), by Esther Jane,
dau. of — Gayton, Esq.: *b.* 1815 ; *s.* his brother as
11th Bart. 1843 ; *m.* 1839 Susan Katharine Saunders,
dau. of John Murray, Esq., of Ardeley-Bury, Herts.
and widow of Adolphus Cottin Murray, Esq. Is a
J.P. and D.L. for Herts.—49. *Devonshire Street*, w.
Heir, his son William Robert, *b.* 1840.

684

MURRAY, Sir JOHN DIGBY, Bart., of Black-
barony, Peeblesshire (cr. 1628).
Eldest surviving son of the late Sir John Murray,
Bart., of Blackbarony, by Anne, dau. of John Digby,
Esq.; *b.* 1798; *s.* his brother as 5th Bart. 1860; *m.*
1st 1823 Susannah, dau. of Frederick Cuthbert, Esq.;
2nd 1827 Frances, dau. of Peter Patten Bold, Esq.
Heir, his son Digby, *b.* 1831.

MURRAY, Sir PATRICK KEITH, Bart., of Och-
tertyre, Perthshire (cr. 1673).
Eldest son of the late Sir William Keith Murray,
Bart., of Ochtertyre, by his 1st wife Helen Margaret,
only surviving child and heir of the late Sir Alexander
Keith, of Dunnottar, Knight Marischal of Scotland ;
b. 1835 ; *s.* 1861. Is a Magistrate for cos. Perth, Kin-
cardine, and Midlothian ; late Capt. Grenadier Guards.
—*Ochtertyre, Crieff, N.B. ; Ravelston, Midlothian.*
Heir Pres., his brother Alexander, *b.* 1843.

MURRAY, Sir JOHN, Bart., of Philiphaugh,
Selkirkshire (cr. 1704).
Eldest son of the late James Murray, Esq., of Philiphaugh (who *d.* 1854), by Mary Dale, dau. of Henry
Hughes, Esq., and kinsman of the late Sir Albert
Joseph Murray, 5th Bart., to whose title he was served
heir male in 1863 ; *b.* 1817 ; *m.* 1840 Rosemary, only
dau. and sole heir of William Andrew Nesbitt, Esq.,
of Bombay. Is a J.P. and D.L. for co. Selkirk, and a
Magistrate for co. Roxburgh. This family held large
possessions in Scotland in the 13th century, and was
then designated 'of Falahill.'‡—*Philiphaugh and Hare-
head, Ettrick Forest, Selkirk, N.B. ; Reform Club, s.w.;
33, Queen's Gate Terrace, s.w.*
Heir, his son John, *b.* 1842.

MURRAY, Sir JAMES, Knt., M.D. (cr. 1833).
Eldest son of the late Edward Murray, Esq., by
Belinda, dau. of J. Towell, Esq., of co. Londonderry ;
b. 1788 ; *m.* 1st 1809 Mary, dau. of G. Sharrock, Esq.;
2nd 1848 Mary, dau. of Samuel Allen, Esq., of Antrim,
and has issue,
* Edward Francis, *b.* 18—; *m.* 1863 Emily Jane, eldest dau.
  of Henry Smith Boulderson, Esq., of Gloucester Square,
  and widow of Henry Breret-.n, Esq., E.I.C.S.
Sir J. Murray, who was appointed Physician to the
Viceroy of Ireland 1831, is M.D. of Edinburgh and
Dublin, and Inspector of Anatomy.—*Murray Terrace,
Belfast ; Temple House, Dublin.*

MURRAY, the Hon. Sir CHARLES AUGUSTUS,
K.C.B.
(See under *Dunmore, Earl of.*)

MURRAY, ALEXANDER, Esq., of Eriswell,
Suffolk.
Only son of the late Alexander Murray, Esq., of Eriswell, by Mary Barbara, dau. of Capt. Vincent, R.N.;
b. 1805; *s.* 1866; *m.* 1828 Eliza, dau. of Evans Ga-
thercole, Esq. Educated at Eton and Edinburgh.
—*Eriswell Lodge, Mildenhall ; Bedford Square, Brighton.*

MURRAY, the Rev. DAVID RODNEY.
Eldest son of the late Hon. David Murray (brother
of Alexander, 7th Lord Elibank), by Elizabeth, dau.
of the Right Hon. Thomas Harley, brother of the 4th
Earl of Oxford ; *b.* 1791 ; *s.* 1791 ; *m.* 1828 Frances,
3rd dau. of John Portal, Esq., of Freefolk, Hants, and
has, with other issue,
* David Mortimer, late Major 64th Regt.; served on the late
  Lord Clyde's Staff in India 1857-9; *b.* 1832 ; *m.* 1861 Eliza
  Ida, 2nd dau. and co-heiress of the late Lewis Fenton, Esq.,
  of Spring Grove, Yorkshire.
Mr. Murray, who was educated at Westminster and Ch.

‡ 'The outlaw Murray,' *temp.* James IV. of Scotland, was an
ancestor of the present representative of this family.

Ch., Oxford (B.A. 1813, M.A. 1816); is a J.P. and D.L. for co. Radnor, and a Magistrate for co. Hereford; appointed Rector of Brampton Brian 1826.—*Brampton Brian, Herefordshire.*

+MURRAY, FRANCIS, Esq.
Eldest son of the late William Murray, Esq., of Monkland House; *b.* 18—; *s.* 1858. Is a Magistrate for co. Lanark.—Residence: *Monkland House, Calderbank, Airdrie, Lanarkshire.*

MURRAY, HUGH ROBERTSON, Esq., of Househill, Nairnshire.
Eldest son of the late Robert Murray, Esq., of Hartfield, co. Ross, by Sarah, 2nd dau. of Hugh Robertson, Esq., of Househill; *b.* 1795; *s.* his uncle 1852; is a J.P. and D.L. for co. Nairn, and a Col. Bengal Infantry, retired.—*Househill, Nairn, N.B.*

MURRAY, Capt. JACK HENRY, R.N., of Croftinloan, Perthshire.
Eldest son of the late Hon. Leveson Granville Keith Murray, Madras Civil Service, by his 2nd wife Virginie, dau. of A. Malet, Esq., and widow of John Thursby, Esq. ; *b.* 1810 ; *m.* 1845 Catherine, dau. of the late Sir Neil Menzies, Bart., and has, with other issue,
  * Jack George, *b.* 1853.
Capt. Murray is a Magistrate for co. Perth, and a Capt. R.N., retired.—*Croftinloan, Pitlochry, N.B.*

+MURRAY, JAMES, Esq., of Callands, Peeblesshire.
Eldest son of the late — Murray, Esq., of Callands; *b.* 18—. Is Lord of the Barony of Callands, which was acquired by the late Mr. Murray by purchase in 185— from the family of the McArthurs.—*Callands, Noblehouse, Edinburgh, N.B.*

MURRAY, JAMES, Esq., of Caw, co. Londonderry.
Third son of the late Thomas Murray, Esq., Major 18th Royal Irish Regt., by Rose, dau. of the late Andrew Bond, Esq., of Clooney; *b.* 1802; *m.* 1st 1827 Anne, 2nd dau. of the late John Blair, Esq., of Newry, and widow of the Rev. J. Johnstone, of Coal Island, co. Tyrone (who *d.* 1836); 2nd 1839 Hannah, eldest dau. of the late John Alexander, Esq., of Caw House, co. Londonderry. Is a Magistrate for the city and co. of Londonderry (High Sheriff 1853).—*Caw House, Londonderry.*

MURRAY, JAMES WOLFE, Esq., of Cringletie, Peeblesshire.
Eldest son of the late James Wolfe Murray, Esq., of Cringletie (a Scottish Judge of Session as Lord Cringeletie), by Isabella Katharine, dau. of James Charles Edward Stuart Strange, Esq. (godson of Prince Charles Edward); *b.* 1814; *s.* 1836; *m.* 1st 1852 Elizabeth Charlotte, youngest dau. of John Whyte-Melville, Esq. (she *d.* 1857); 2nd 1862 Louisa Grace, 3rd dau. of the late Sir Adam Hay, Bart., of Haystoun, and has issue by the former,
  * James Wolfe, *b.* 1853.
Mr. Murray, who was appointed to the 42nd Royal Highlanders 1833, is a J.P. and D.L. for co. Peebles, and Capt. Peeblesshire Rifle Volunteers.—*Cringletie, Eddlestone, Peeblesshire, N.B.; West Shield, Lanark; New Club, Edinburgh.*

MURRAY, JOHN, Esq., of Murraythwaite, Dumfriesshire.
Only son of the late John Dalrymple Murray, Esq., of Murraythwaite, by his 1st wife Marion, dau. of William Hagart, Esq., of Edinburgh; *b.* 1828; *s.* 1863; *m.*

1864 Grace Harriett, 2nd dau. of Col. William Graham, of Mossknow, co. Dumfries, and has issue,
  * William, *b.* 1865.
Mr. Murray is a Magistrate and a Commissioner of Supply for co. Dumfries, and a Commander R.N. —*Murraythwaite, Ecclefechan, N.B.; Junior United Service Club, s.w.*

MURRAY, Lieut.-Col. JOHN, of Touchadam and Polmaise, Stirlingshire.
Eldest son of the late John Murray, Esq., of Polmaise, Vice-Lieutenant and Convener of co. Stirling, by Elizabeth, dau. of James Bryce, Esq., of Edinburgh; *b.* 1831; *s.* 1862; *m.* 1859 Lady Agnes Caroline Graham, dau. of James, 4th Duke of Montrose. Is a Magistrate and Vice-Lieutenant of co. Stirling, and Lord of the Baronies of Touchadam and Polmaise; late Lieut.-Col. Grenadier Guards.—*Polmaise, Stirling, N.B.; Guards' and White's Clubs, s.w.*
Heir Pres., his brother James, *b.* 1834.

MURRAY, JOHN, Esq., of Wooplaw, Roxburghshire.
Eldest son of the late Andrew Murray, Esq., of Wooplaw, by Mary, dau. of Capt. Charles Stewart, of the H.E.I.C.S.; *b.* 1829; *s.* 1844. Educated at the Edinburgh Academy and University; is a Magistrate for co. Roxburgh. This family was formerly connected with Perthshire, but settled in co. Roxburgh A.D. 1685.—*Wooplaw, Galashiels, N.B.*

MURRAY, JOSEPH, Esq., of Ayton, Fifeshire.
Eldest son of the late Alexander Murray, Esq., J.P. and D.L., of Ayton, by the Hon. Mary, dau. of the 7th Lord Banff; *b.* 1786; *s.* 1829; *m.* 1823 Grace, youngest dau. of the late Sir George Abercromby, Bart., of Birkenbog and Forglen, co. Banff, and has, with other issue,
  * Alexander, *b.* 1827 ; *m.* 1860 Elizabeth, dau. of the late Rev. J. Spencer, Incumbent of Crimplesham, Norfolk.
Mr. Murray, who was educated at Edinburgh, and was called to the Scottish Bar in 1808, is a Magistrate for cos. Fife and Perth, and Lord of the Barony of Ayton. —*Ayton, Newburgh, Fifeshire; Broomfield House, Cosham, Hants.*

MURRAY, MUNGO, Esq., of Lintrose, Perthshire.
Eldest son of the late John Murray, Esq., of Lintrose, by Anne, dau. of John Gray, Esq., of Balcolgarno, co. Perth; *b.* 1802; *s.* 1828; *m.* 1831 Mary, dau. of Thomas Willing, Esq.; is a J.P. and D.L. for cos. Forfar and Perth, and Lord of the Barony of Lintrose.—*Lintrose, Cupar-Angus, N.B.*
Heir Pres., his brother John, *b.* 1802.

+MURRAY, SUTHERLAND, Esq., of Kirkton, Sutherlandshire.
Son of the late S. Murray, Esq., of Kirkton; *b.* 18—; is a J.P. and D.L. for co. Sutherland.—*Kirkton, Golspie, N.B.*

MURRAY, THOMAS DOUGLAS, Esq., of Hoopern House, Devonshire.
Eldest son of the late Rev. Thomas B. Murray, M.A., of Hoopern House (some time Rector of St. Dunstan's-in-the-East, London), by Helen, eldest dau. of the late Major-General Sir William Douglas, K.C.B.; *b.* 1841; *s.* 1862; educated at Rugby and Exeter Coll., Oxford (B.A. 1864); is a student of Lincoln's Inn.—*Hoopern House, Exeter; New University Club, s.w.; 11, Cleveland Gardens, Hyde Park, w.*

MURRAY, WILLIAM, Esq.
Son of the late Mr. William Murray, of Portsea, Hants; *b.* 1796; *m.* 1824 Miss Maria Jane Blundell Guppey. Educated at Dr. Burney's, Gosport; admitted a Solicitor

685

1818; is a Solicitor in practice in London; was M.P for Newcastle-under-Lyne 1859-65.— 11, *Cambridge Square*, w.; 11, *Birchin Lane*, E.C.

MURRAY, the late WILLIAM HUGH, Esq., of Geanies, Ross-shire.

Eldest son of the late William Murray, Esq., of Tain, N.B., by Jane, dau. of Capt. Kenneth Mackay, of Torboll, co. Sutherland; *b.* 1824; *s.* his cousin, Miss Janet Murray, 1845; educated at the University of Edinburgh; called to the Scottish Bar 1846; was a J.P. and D.L. for co. Ross, and Sheriff-Substitute of E. Division of that county. He *d.* 1867.—*Geanies, Tain, N.B.*

MURRAY. (See under *Athole, Duke of; Dunmore* and *Mansfield, Earls of;* and *Elibank, Lord.*)

MURRAY. (See *Scott-Murray.*)

MURRAY-AYNSLEY. (See *Aynsley.*)

MURRAY-DUNLOP. (See *Dunlop.*)

MURRAY-GARTSHORE, JOHN, Esq., of Gart- shore, Dumbartonshire.

Second son of the late Sir Patrick Murray, Bart., of Ochtertyre, by Lady Mary, youngest dau. of John, 2nd Earl of Hopetoun; *b.* 1804; *s.* Miss Mary Gartshore in her name and estates 1814; *m.* 1st 1836 Mary, dau. of General Sir Howard Douglas (she *d.* 1851); 2nd 1852 Augusta Louisa, only child of the late Rev. George F. Tavel, and widow of the Rev. W. Casaubon Purdon, of Tinerana, co. Clare, and has issue by the former,
* Mary.
Mr. Murray-Gartshore, who is a Dep.-Lieut. for co. Dumbarton, was formerly in the Army.—*Gartshore, Kirkintilloch, N.B.*

MURRAY GRAHAM, JOHN, Esq., of Murrays- hall and Bertha Park, Perthshire.

Eldest son of the late Andrew Murray, Esq., of Murrayshall, by Janet; only child of Oliver Thomson, Esq., of Leckiebank, co. Fife; *b.* 1809; *s.* to Murrayshall 1847, and to Bertha Park in 1859, on the death of his cousin Robert Graham, Esq., of Redgorton; *m.* 1853 Robina, youngest dau. of Thomas Hamilton, Esq., and granddau. of Sir George L. A. Colquhoun, Bart. Educated at Edinburgh University (M.A. 1828); called to the Bar at Edinburgh 1831; is a Magistrate for co. Perth. —*Murrayshall, Perth ; New Club, Edinburgh.*
Heir Pres., his brother Andrew, *b.* 1812; *m.* 1842 Marianne, dau. of Henry Francis, Esq.

MURRAY-KER, ANDRE ALLEN, Esq., of New- bliss House, co. Monaghan.

Eldest son of the late Andre Allen Murray, Esq., Barrister-at-Law, of Loughoona, co. Monaghan, by Rebecca, dau. of the Rev. William Moffatt, of Cara House; *b.* 1818; *s.* 1827; *m.* 1854 Maryanne, only surviving dau. of the Rev. Richard Foster, and heir of the late Andrew Ker, Esq., M.D., of Newbliss, whose name he assumed, and by whom he has issue two daughters. Mr. Murray-Ker, who was educated at Trinity Coll., Dublin, is a J.P. and D.L. for co. Monaghan (High Sheriff, 1844), and a Magistrate for co. Cavan.—*Newbliss House, co. Monaghan; Sackville Street Club, Dublin.*

MURRAY-MACGREGOR. (See *Macgregor.*)

MURRAY-THREIPLAND. (See *Threipland.*)

MURRAY-STEWART, HORATIO GRANVILLE, Esq., of Broughton, Kirkcudbrightshire.

Only son of the late Capt. Horatio Stewart, of Broughton, by Sophia, dau. of the Hon. Montgomery Stewart; *b.* 1834; *s.* 1845; *m.* 1859 Ann Eliza, 3rd dau. of the

Rev. J. D. Wingfield-Digby, Vicar of Coleshill, co. Warwick. Educated at Harrow and Ch. Ch., Oxford; is a J.P. and D.L. for cos. Wigton and Donegal (High Sheriff 18.8), and a Magistrate for the Stewartry of Kirkcudbright,—*Cully and Castramont, Gatehouse, Kirkcudbrightshire, N.B. ; Whitehouse, Killybegs, co. Donegal ; Carlton Club, s.w.*

MURROUGH, JOHN PATRICK, Esq., of Shrub- lands, Sussex.

Son of John Murrough, Esq., Merchant, of Chichester, Sussex, by Lucy, dau. of Edward Patrick, Esq., of Heath House, Petersfield, a J.P. and D.L. for Hants; *b.* 1822 ; *m.* 1848 Isabella Maria, dau. of John Beart, Esq., of London, and has, with other issue,
* Patrick O'Donnell, *b.* 1851.
Mr. Murrough, who was admitted a Solicitor 1844, was M.P. for Bridport 1852-7.—*Shrublands, Graffham, Petworth ; 11, Great James Street, Bedford Row, w.c.*

MUSGRAVE, Sir GEORGE, Bart., of Eden Hall, Cumberland (cr. 1611).

Third but eldest surviving son of the late Sir John Chardin Musgrave, 7th Bart., of Eden Hall (who *d.* 1806), by Mary, dau. of the late Rev. Sir Edmund Filmer, Bart., of East Sutton Place, Kent ; *b.* 1799 ; *s.* his brother as 10th Bart. 1834 ; *m.* 1828 Charlotte, dau. of the late Sir James Graham, Bart., of Netherby. Is a J.P. and D.L. for Westmoreland, a Magistrate for Cumberland (High Sheriff 1840), and Patron of 1 living; was formerly an Officer in the 15th King's Hussars. —*Eden Hall, Penrith ; 43, Albemarle Street, w.*
Heir, his son Richard Courtenay, a Magistrate for Cumberland ; *b.* 1838 ; *m.* 1867 Adora Frances Olga, only dau. of Peter Wells, Esq.

MUSGRAVE, the Rev. Sir WILLIAM AUGUSTUS, Bart., of Barnsley Park, Gloucestershire (cr. 1638).

Second son of the late Sir James Musgrave, Bart., of Barnsley Park (who *d.* 1814), by Clarissa, dau. of Thomas Blackall, Esq., of Great Hasely, Oxon; *b.* 1791; *s.* his brother as 10th Bart., 1858. Educated at Westminster and Ch. Ch., Oxford (B.A. 1813, M.A. 1815); is a Magistrate for Oxon. Rector of Chinnor, and Patron of 2 livings.—*Barnsley Park, Cirencester ; Chinnor Rectory, Tetsworth, Oxon.*

MUSGRAVE, Sir RICHARD, Bart., of Tourin, co. Waterford (cr. 1782).

Eldest son of the late Sir Richard Musgrave, Bart., of Mount Rivers, co. Waterford, by Frances, dau. of the late Most Rev. Dr. Newcome, Lord Archbishop of Armagh; *b.* 1820; *s.* as 4th Bart. 1859; *m.* 1845 Frances Mary, eldest dau. of John Ashton Yates, Esq., formerly M.P. for Carlow. Educated at Caius Coll., Cambridge (B.A. 1842); is Vice-Lieutenant of co. Waterford (High Sheriff 1851).—*Tourin and Mount Rivers, Cappoquin, co. Waterford; 33, Bryanston Square, w.*
Heir, his son Richard John, *b.* 1850.

MUSGRAVE, CHRISTOPHER, Esq., of Claverdon, Warwickshire.

Elder son of the late Christopher Musgrave, Esq., by the Hon. Elizabeth Ann, dau. and co-heir of Andrew, late Lord Archer (ext.), of Umberslade, co. Warwick; *b.* 1799; *m.* 1832 Charlotte Mary, youngest dau. of the late Wm. Lushington, Esq., and has, with other issue,
* Christopher Edward, Capt. Rifle Brigade; *b.* 1857.
Mr. Musgrave is a Magistrate for co. Warwick.—*Malverton Hall, Claverdon, Leamington.*

MUSGRAVE, EDGAR, Esq., of Shillington, Beds.

Only surviving son of the Rev. George Musgrave, of Borden Hall, Kent, by Charlotte Emily, youngest dau-

of the late Thomas Oakes, Esq., formerly senior Member of Council, and President of the Board of Trade at Madras, and grandson of the late George Musgrave, Esq., by Margaret, only dau. of Edward Kennedy, Esq., of Grafton, co. York; *b.* 1535; *m.* 1860 Henrietta Maria, youngest dau. of the late John Teschemaker, Esq., D.C.L., of Exmouth, Devon, and has, with other issue,
* Horace Edgar, *b.* 1861.—*Skillington Manor, Hitchin.*

MUSGRAVE, HENRY MUSGRAVE, Esq.
Second son of the late George Musgrave, Esq., of Shillington Manor, Beds, and Borden Hill, Kent, by Margaret, dau. of E. Kennedy, Esq. ; *b.* 1800; *m.* 1841 Sarah Popplewell, youngest dau. of the late Richard Pullan, Esq., of Harewood, co. York, and by her (who *d.* 1861) has issue an only son,
* George Arthur, *b.* 1843 ; *m.* 1867 Theresa, only dau. of Josiah Jaques Jones, Esq., of Horton, co. Gloucester.
Mr. Musgrave, who was called to the Bar at Lincoln's Inn 1834, is a J.P. and D.L. for Bucks and Beds. —31, *Sussex Gardens, Hyde Park, w.; Union Club,* s.w.

+MUSGRAVE, JOHN, Esq., of Wasdale Hall, Cumberland.
Son of the late Mr. John Musgrave, of Whitehaven ; *b.* 18—; is married and has, with other issue,
* John, *b.* 18—.
Mr. Musgrave, who is a solicitor at Whitehaven, purchased this property from the trustees of the late C. S. Rawson, Esq., in 1865.—*Wasdale Hall, Whitehaven; Lonsdale Place, Moresby, Whitehaven.*

MUSGRAVE. (See *Sagar-Musgrave.*)

MUSGROVE, Sir JOHN, Bart., of Rusthall, Kent (cr. 1851).
Only son of the late John Musgrove, Esq., Merchant, of London, by Rebecca, dau. of Mr. Raworth, of Hackney, Middlesex ; *b.* 1793; *m.* 1814 Emma, dau. of Robert Brembridge, Esq. Is a J.P. and D.L. for Middlesex, a Magistrate for Kent and Sussex, and a Commissioner of the Lieutenancy of London; has been Sheriff of London and Middlesex, and was Lord Mayor of London in 1851.—*Rusthall, Speldhurst, Tunbridge Wells; 32, Russell Square, w.c.*

MUSGROVE, EDGAR, Esq., of West Tower, Lancashire.
Fourth son of the late Robert Musgrove, Esq., of Liverpool (who *d.* 1835), by Amelia, dau. of John Woodman, Esq., of Dunham ; *b.* 1817 ; *m.* 1838 Mary Anne, dau. of William Musgrove, Esq., of Altringham, co. Chester, and has issue.
* Viola Woodman. Fanny McBride, and Loraine Aughton.
Mr. Musgrove is a Magistrate for co. Lancaster.—*West Tower, Aughton, Ormskirk.*

MUSKERRY, Lord ‡ (MATTHEW FITZMAURICE DEANE).—Cr. 1781.
Younger son of Robert Tilson, 1st Lord, by Ann, dau. of Capt. John Fitzmaurice, of Springfield Castle, co. Limerick; *b.* 1795; *s.* his brother as 3rd Lord 1824 ; *m.* 1825 Louisa, dau. of the late Henry Deane O'Grady, Esq., of Lodge, co. Limerick (she *d.* 1846); 2nd 1864 Lucy, widow of Col. Aldridge, R.E. (she *d.* 1867). Is a J.P. and D.L. for co. Limerick.—*Springfield Castle, Dromcolloher, co. Limerick; Deane's Fort, Somerset; Carlton Club,* s.w.; 3, *Upper Wimpole Street, w.*
Heir. his grandson Hamilton Matthew Fitzmaurice (only son of the late Hon. Robert Tilson Fitzmaurice-Deane-Grogan-Morgan, who *d.* 1852, by Elizabeth Geraldine, eldest dau. of the late Hamilton Knox Grogan-Morgan, Esq., of Johns-town Castle, co. Wexford), *b.* 1854.

‡ Died whilst these sheets were at press.

MUSKETT, the Rev. HENRY JOSEPH, of Clippesby House, Norfolk.
Eldest son of the late Henry Muskett, Esq., of Clippesby House, by Emily, dau. of William Grant, Esq., of Norwich; *b.* 1820; *s.* 1851 ; *m.* 1847 Charlotte Heath, 2nd dau. of the late William Heath Jary, Esq. (she *d.* 1864). Educated at St. Peter's Coll., Cambridge (B.A. 1843, M.A. 1846); is Lord of the Manor and Patron of Clippesby.—*Clippesby House, Norwich.*

MUSSENDEN, WILLIAM, Esq., of Larchfield, co. Down.
Only son of the late William Mussenden, Esq., J.P. and D.L., of Larchfield (who was High Sheriff of co. Down 1830), by Sarah, dau. of Peter Low, Esq., of co. Limerick; *b.* 1835; *s.* 1861; *m.* 1866 Katharine Maud, only dau. of Sir Henry Boynton, Bart. Is Capt. 8th Light Dragoons.—*Larchfield, Hillsborough, co. Down; Army and Navy Club,* s.w.

MUSTERS, JOHN CHAWORTH, Esq., of Annersley Park and Colwick Hall, Notts.
Eldest son of the late John G. Musters, Esq., of Wiverton, Notts, by Emily, dau. of Philip Hamond, Esq., of Westacre, Norfolk; *b.* 1838 ; *s.* his grandfather 1849 ; *m.* 1859 Caroline Anne, eldest dau. of Henry Sherbrooke, Esq., of Oxton, Notts, and has issue,
* John Patricius, *b.* 1860.
Mr. Musters, who was educated at Eton and Ch. Ch., Oxford, is a J.P. and D.L. for Notts (High Sheriff 1864), and Patron of 4 livings.—*Annesley Park, Nottingham; Colwick Hall and Wiverton Hall, Bingham, Notts.*

MYDDELTON, the Rev. ROBERT, of Gwaenynog, Denbighshire.
Son of the late Rev. Robert Myddelton, D.D., of Gwaenynog, sometime Rector of Rotherhithe, by Mary, dau. of Capt. James Ogilvie, of Green Hall, co. Aberdeen ; *b.* 1795; *m.* 1823 Louisa, dau. of the late Sir George R. Farmer, Bart. Educated at Harrow and Clare Coll., Cambridge (B.A. 1818, M.A. 1821), entered Holy Orders 1821; is a Magistrate for co. Denbigh.—*Gwaenynog, Denbigh.*

MYDDELTON-BIDDULPH, Sir THOMAS, K.C.B. (cr. 1863).
Second son of the late Robert Myddelton-Biddulph, Esq., of Ledbury, co. Hereford, by Charlotte, eldest dau. of Richard Myddelton, Esq., of Chirk Castle, co. Denbigh ; *b.* 1809; *m.* 1857 the Hon. Mary Frederica (late Maid of Honour to the Queen), eldest dau. of the late Frederick Charles William Seymour, Esq. Educated at Eton; is a Magistrate for co. Denbigh, a Major-General in the Army, and Keeper of the Privy Purse, late Master of the Household, and formerly Extra-Equerry to the Queen; appointed Receiver-General of the Duchy of Cornwall 1866.—*Garter House, Windsor Castle; United Service Club,* s.w.; 22, *Chester Square,* s.w.

MYDDELTON-BIDDULPH, Col. ROBERT, of Chirk Castle, Denbighshire.
Eldest son of the late Robert Myddelton-Biddulph, Esq., of Ledbury co. Hereford, by Charlotte, eldest dau. and co-heir of Richard Myddelton. Esq., of Chirk Castle, whose name he assumed ; *b.* 1805 ; *s.* 1845 ; *m.* 1832 Fanny, 2nd dau. of William Mostyn Owen, Esq., of Woodhouse, co. Salop, and has, with other issue,
* Richard, educated at Eton; late Lieut. 1st Life Guards ; *b.* 1837 ; *m.* 1862 Catharine Arabella, 3rd dau. of the late Edward Howard, Esq., and has issue two daughters.
Mr. Myddelton-Biddulph, who was educated at Eton and Ch. Ch., Oxford, is Lord-Lieut. of co. Denbigh, a Magistrate for co. Hereford and Col. of the Denbigh Militia; was M.P. for Denbigh 1830-2, for co. Denbigh

1832-4, and since 1852.—*Chirk Castle, Denbighshire ;
Burghill House, Hereford ; Brooks's and Arthur's Clubs,
and 35, Grosvenor Place*, s.w.

MYERS, THOMAS BORRON, Esq., of Porters, Herts.
Eldest son of the late William J. Myers, Esq., of
Porters (who was High Sheriff of Herts 1856), by
Margaret, dau of Nicholas Crooke, Esq. ; *b.* 1826 ; *s.*
1858; *m.* 1856 Margaret, dau. of the Rev. Henry Mel-
vill, B.D., and has, with other issue,
* William Joseph, *b.* 1858.
Mr. Myers, who was educated at Eton and Ch. Ch.,
Oxford, is a Magistrate for Herts, Middlesex, and the
Liberty of St. Alban's.—*Porters, Shenley, St. Alban's;
Carlton Club*, s.w.

MYNORS, the Rev. EDMUND BASKERVILLE.
Second son of Peter Rickards Mynors, Esq., of Treago,
co. Hereford, by Mary Elizabeth, only dau. of Edmund
Trowbridge Halliday, Esq., of Chapel Cleeve, Somerset;
b. 1823 ; *m.* 1855 Horatia Charlotte Campbell, dau. of
John Crawfurd. Esq., of Blackbrook, co. Monmouth,
and has surviving issue,
* Four daughters.
Mr. Mynors, who was educated at Eton and Balliol
Coll., Oxford (B.A. 1845, M.A. 1848), is Rector of
Ashley, late Rector of Thelveton, Norfolk. — *Ashley
Rectory, Tetbury.*

+**MYNORS, HENRY EDEN, Esq., of Keynsham, Somerset.**
Only son of the late Henry Eden Mynors, Esq., of
Keynsham (who was a Magistrate for Somerset), by
Eliza Clara, only dau. of John Partridge, Esq., of
Stroud, co. Gloucester; *b.* 1826 ; *s.* 1860. Is a Magis-
trate for Somerset.—*Chewton Place, Keynsham, Bristol.*

Heirs Pres., his sisters Clara and Agnes.

**MYNORS, ROBERT BASKERVILLE, Esq., of Trea-
go, Herefordshire, and Evancoyd, Radnor-
shire.**
Eldest son of the late Peter Rickards Mynors, Esq.,
J.P. and D.L., of Treago (who was High Sheriff of co.
Rutland 1825), by Mary Elizabeth, only dau. of Edmund
Trowbridge Halliday, Esq., of Chapel Cleeve, Somerset;
b. 1819 ; *s.* 1866; *m.* 1852 Ellen Gray, only child of
the Rev. Edward Higgins, of Bosbury House, co. Here-
ford (whom see), and has, with other issue,
* Willoughby Baskerville, *b.* 1854.
Mr. Mynors, who was educated at Eton and Ch. Ch.,
Oxford (B.A. 1841, M.A. 1817), is a J.P. and D.L. for
cos. Hereford and Radnor (High Sheriff 1856), and
formerly Capt. Herefordshire Militia.—*Treago, Ross ;
Evancoyd, Radnor.*

**MYNORS, ROBERT, Esq., of Weatheroak, Wor-
cestershire.**
Eldest son of the late Robert Edward Eden Mynors,
Esq., of Weatheroak, by Mary, dau. of Thomas Has-
sall, Esq., of Hartshorne, co. Derby ; *b.* 1817 ; *s.* 1842.
Educated at Rugby and University Coll., Oxford (B.A.
1839, M.A. 1842); called to the Bar at the Inner
Temple 1842 ; is a J.P. and D.L. for co. Worcester, and

a Magistrate for co. Warwick.—*Weatheroak, Alve-
church ; Oxford and Cambridge Club*, s w.

Heir Pres., his brother Thomas Hassall, in Holy Orders, B.A.
of Wadham Coll., Oxford ; Incumbent of St. Patrick's, Tan-
worth, co. Warwick; *b.* 1819 ; *m.* 1854 Emily Anne, only
child of Thomas Worthington, Esq., of Hartshorne, co.
Derby, and has issue two daughters.

**MYNORS, THOMAS BASKERVILLE, Esq., of Bar-
land, Radnorshire.**
Fourth and youngest son of Peter Rickards Mynors,
Esq., of Treago, co. Hereford, by Mary Elizabeth, only
dau. of Edmund Trowbridge Halliday, Esq., of Chapel
Cleeve, Somerset ; *b.* 1834. Educated at Eton and Ch.
Ch , Oxford ; is a Magistrate for co. Radnor and Lord
of the Manor of Barland.—*Barland, Walton, Radnor.*

**MYNORS, the Rev. WALTER BASKERVILLE,
Rector of Llanwarne, Herefordshire.**
Third son of Peter Rickards Mynors, Esq., of Treago,
co. Hereford, by Mary Elizabeth, only dau. of Edmund
T. Halliday, Esq., of Chapel Cleeve, Somerset : *b.* 1826 ;
m. 1856 Caroline Elizabeth, dau. of Henry Clay, Esq.,
of Piercefield, co. Monmouth, and has, with other issue,
* Harry Walter Baskerville, *b.* 1857.
Mr. Mynors, who was educated at Eton and Oriel Coll.,
Oxford (B.A. 1850), is a Magistrate for co. Hereford,
Rector of Llanwarne, and Patron of 2 livings.—*Llan-
warne Rectory, Ross.*

MYNORS. (See *Baskerville*.)

+**MYTTON, HENRY GEORGE, Esq., of Cleobury
North, Shropshire.**
Younger and only surviving son of the late Thomas
Mytton, Esq., of Cleobury North, by Mary, dau. of —
Goodin, Esq.; *b.* 1795 ; *s.* 1830. Is a Magistrate for
cos. Hereford and Salop.—*Cleobury North, Bridgenorth.*

**MYTTON, RICHARD HERBERT, Esq., of Garth,
Montgomeryshire.**
Only son of the late Rev. Richard Mytton, of Garth,
by Charlotte, dau. of John Herbert, Esq., of Dolforgan;
b. 1808 ; *s.* 1828 ; *m.* 1830 Charlotte, 3rd dau. of Col.
Paul Macgregor, Military Auditor-General of Bengal,
and by her (who *d.* 1861) has, with other issue,
Devereux Herbert, Capt. 58th Foot ; *b.* 1832.
Mr. Mytton, who was educated at Eton and Haileybury Coll., was formerly in the Bengal Civil Service,
retired 1853, is a Magistrate and a Chairman of Quarter
Sessions for co. Montgomery (High Sheriff 1856). This
family, a branch of the Myttons of Halston, were
seated at Pontyscowryd, co. Montgomery, in the 16th
century ; Richard Mytton, of that place, early in the
15th century, married Dorothy, heiress of Brochwell
Wynne, Esq., of Garth.—*Garth, Welshpool.*

**MYTTON, THOMAS, Esq., of Shipton, co. Shrop-
shire.**
Only son of the late Benjamin Mytton, Esq., and grand-
son of Thomas Mytton, Esq., of Shipton Hall, by Mary,
grandmother 1830 ; *m.* 1910 Harriet, dau. of W.
Downes, Esq., of Newhouse, Shipton. Is a J.P. and
D.L. for co. Salop. Lord of the Manor of Shipton, and
Patron of that Living.—*Shipton Hall, Wenlock.*

N

NAAS. (See under *Mayo, Earl of.*)

NAESMYTH. (See *Nasmyth.*)

NAGHTEN, Arthur Robert, Esq., of Blighmont, Hampshire.
Son of the late Thomas Naghten, Esq., of Crofton House, Titchfield, Hants, by Maria, dau. of the late Robert Lang, Esq., of Moor Park, Surrey; *b.* 1829; *m.* 1859 Dora, dau. of St. John C. Charlton, Esq., of Apley Castle, co. Salop. Educated at Eton and Worcester Coll., Oxford (B.A. 1852, M.A. 1853); is a Magistrate for Hampshire, and Capt. Hants Artillery Militia. — *Blighmont, Millbrook, Southampton; United University Club*, s.w.

+**NAGLE**, Garrett, Esq., of Clogher House, co. Cork.
Son of the late Garrett Nagle, Esq., of Ballinamona (who *d.* 1853), by Mary, dau. of Richard Harrold, Esq.; *b.* 1810; *m.* 1839 Margaret, only dau. of John Neligan, Esq., of Tralee, and has. with other issue,

    * Garrett Thomas, *b.* 1853.

Mr. Nagle is a Magistrate for co. Cork.—*Clogher House, Doneraile, co. Cork.*

NAGLE. (See *Chichester-Nagle.*)

NAIRNE, Baroness (Emily Jane Petty-Fitz-Maurice).—Cr. 1681.
Elder dau. of Margaret, 2nd Baroness Keith and 7th Baroness Nairne, by the Count de Flahault; *b.* 1819; *s.* 1867; *m.* 1843 (as 2nd wife) Henry, 4th Marquis of Lansdowne (who *d.* 1866).—*Tulliallan Castle, Kincardine, N.B.; Meiklour House, Perth, N.B.;* 106, *Piccadilly*, w.

    Heir, her son Henry Charles, 5th Marquis of Lansdowne (whom see).

NAIRNE, William, Esq., of Dunsinane, Perthshire.
Eldest son of the late John Mellis Nairne, Esq., J.P. and D.L., of Dunsinane, by Jessie Isabella, dau. of James Featherstone, Esq., of Newbns Grange, co. Durham, and Blackhall, Northumberland; *b.* 1852; *s.* 1866. Is Lord of the Barony of Dunsinane, and sole heritor of the parish of Collace. This family represent the Nairnes, formerly of St. Fort or Sandford, co. Fife, who settled in Scotland *temp.* Robert III. (See Douglas's 'Peerage,' ii. 279).—*Dunsinane, Ballaggie, Perthshire.*

NAISH, Carrol John, Esq., of Ballycullen, co. Limerick.
Eldest son of Carrol Patrick Naish, Esq., of Limerick, by Mary, eldest dau. of Denis Sampson, Esq., of St. Catherine's, co. Clare; *b.* 1825; *m.* 1855 Eleanor Mary, only dau. of Michael J. Staunton, Esq., of Ballysimon, co. Limerick, and has, with other issue,

    * Carrol Joseph, *b.* 1856.

Mr. Naish, who was educated at Trinity Coll., Dublin, is a Magistrate for co. Limerick.—*Ballycullen, Askeaton, co. Limerick.*

NAISH, William Benjamin, Esq., of Ston Easton, Somerset, and Hardington Park, Somerset.
Only surviving son of the late Francis Naish, Esq., D.L., of Nonsuch House, Wilts (who *d.* 1833), by Ann, eldest dau. of the late Benjamin Greenhill, Esq., of Ston Easton; *b.* 1804; *m.* 1st 1838 Marianne, only dau. of the Rev. Thomas Parfitt, D.D., of Glastonbury, Somerset (she *d.* 1862); 2nd 1864 Emma, widow of the late Walker Busfeild, Esq., of Cottingley-bridge, co. York, and has issue by the former,

    * Marianne.

Mr. Naish is a Magistrate for Somerset.—*Ston Easton, Bath; Hardington Park, Frome; National Club*, s.w.

NANGLE, George, Esq., of Kildalkey, co. Meath.
Eldest son of the late Capt. Walton Nangle, of Kildalkey, by his 2nd wife Catharine, dau. of George Sall, Esq., of Dublin; *b.* 1791; *s.* his half-brother. Charles, 1847; *m.* 1st 1816 Elizabeth Caroline, dau. of the late Henry Halsey, Esq., of Henley Park, Surrey; 2nd 1823 Lucy Mary, only dau. of the late Sir Henry Tichborne, Bart., and has, with other issue,

    * George Courtenay Drummond, formerly Lieut. 47th Foot, *b.* 1826; *m.* 1853 Eleanor, dau. of H. Major, Esq.

Mr. Nangle, who is chief of his name, represents a family who were formerly Barons of Navan.—*Kildalkey, Kells, co. Meath.*

+**NANNEY**, the late John, Esq., F.R.S., of Maes-y-Neuadd, Merionethshire.
Only son of the late Rev. John Nanney, of Maes-y-Neuadd (who assumed that name in lieu of his patronymic Wynn), by Anne, dau. of John Fisher, Esq., of Chetwynd, co. Salop; *b.* 1853; *s.* 1838; *m.* 1839 Lucy Victoria, 3rd dau. of the late Rev. Edmund Williams, of Pentre Mawr. Llandyrnog, co. Denbigh. Mr. J. Nanney, who was a Magistrate for co. Merioneth, *d.* 1865, and was *s.* by the Rev. Simon Hart Wynn-Nanney, who *d.* the same year.—*Maes-y-Neuadd, Tulsarnau, Merionethshire.*

+**NANNEY**, Owen Jones-Ellis-, Esq., of Gwynfryn, Carnarvonshire.
Only surviving son of the late John Jones, Esq., of Brynhir, co. Carnarvon, by Elizabeth, dau. and heir of the late Rev. Richard Ellis, Canon of Bangor; *b.* 1790; *m.* 1813 Mary, dau. of Hugh Jones, Esq., and by her, who *d.* 1849, has issue,

    * Hugh John, *b.* 1814.

Mr. Jones-Ellis-Nanney, who is a J.P. and D.L. for co. Carnarvon (High Sheriff 1861), was M.P. for Carnarvon, &c., March–May, 1833; he assumed the additional surnames of Ellis and Nanney under the will of his uncle, the late David Ellis-Nanney, Esq.—*Gwynfryn, Pwllheli.*

NAPER, James Lennox William, Esq., of Loughcrew, co. Meath.
Eldest son of the late William Naper, Esq., of Loughcrew, by Jane, dau. of the Rev. F. T. Travell; *b.* 1791;

s. 1792; *m*. 1824 Selina, dau. of Sir Gray Skipwith, Bart., and has, with other issue,

• James Lennox, a Magistrate for co. Meath ; *b*. 1825.

Mr. Naper, who was educated at Eton and Ch. Ch., Oxford, is a J.P. and D.L. for co. Meath (High Sheriff 1814).—*Loughcrew, Old Castle, co. Meath; Brooks's Club, s.w.*

NAPIER Lord (FRANCIS NAPIER, K.T., P.C.). —Cr. 1627.
Eldest son of William John, 9th Lord, by Elizabeth, only dau. of the late Hon. Andrew James Cochrane Johnston; *b*. 1810; *s*. 1834; *m*. 1845 Anne Jane, dau. of Robert Manners Lockwood, Esq. Is a J.P. and D.L. for co. Selkirk; has been Secretary of Legation at Naples, Petersburg, and Constantinople, appointed Minister at Washington 1857, at the Hague 1858; Ambassador Extraordinary at St. Petersburg 1860, and at Berlin 1864; Governor of Madras 1866.—*Thirlestane, Selkirk, N.B.; Government House, Madras.*

Heir, his son William John George, *b*. 1846.

NAPIER, Sir ROBERT JOHN MILLIKEN, Bart., of Milliken House, Renfrewshire (cr. 1627).
Elder son of the late Sir William Milliken Napier, Bart., of Milliken House, by Elizabeth Christian, dau. of the late John Stirling, Esq., of Kippendavie, co. Perth; *b*. 1818; *s*. as 9th Bart. 1852; *m*. 1850 Anne Salisbury Meliora, dau. of John Ladeveze Adlercorn, Esq., of Moyglare, co. Meath. Is a J.P. and D.L. for co. Renfrew, and Col. Renfrew Militia; formerly Capt. 79th Foot. Is chief of the Napier family.—*Milliken House, Johnstone, N.B.; 32, Moray Place, Edinburgh.*

Heir, his son, Archibald Lennox, *b*. 1855.

NAPIER, the Right Hon. Sir JOSEPH, Bart. (cr. 1867).
Fourth son of the late William Napier, Esq., of Belfast, by Rose, dau. of Samuel MacNaghten, Esq., of co. Antrim; *b*. 1804; *m*. 1830 Cherry, dau. of John Grace, Esq. Educated at Belfast and Trinity Coll., Dublin (B.A. 1825, M.A. 1828, cr. Hon. D.C.L. 1853, and LL.D. 1850), and called to the Irish Bar 1831; became Q.C. 1844; appointed Attorney-General for Ireland in 1852, and Lord-Chancellor in 1858; was M.P. for Dublin University 1848–58; appointed Vice-Chancellor of the University 1867.—4, *Merrion Square, Dublin; Carlton and National Clubs, s.w.*

Heir, his son William John, *b*. 1837.

NAPIER, Sir ROBERT, G.C.B., G.C.S.I. (cr. 1858).
Second but only surviving son of the late Major Charles Frederick Napier, R.A., by Catherine Anne, dau. of the late Codrington Carrington, Esq., of The Chapel and Carrington's, Barbados; *b*. 1810; *m*. 1st 184– Anne, youngest dau. of James Pearse, M.D., H.E.I.C.S.; 2nd 18— Mary, dau. of Major-Gen. Scott, of the Bengal Artillery; he has by the former, with other issue,

• Robert William, *b*. 1845.

Sir Robert Napier, who was educated at Addiscombe, entered the Indian Army 1826; is a Lieut.-General in the Army, late Col. R.E. ; served in the Sutlej campaigns, and was present at Goojerat ; commanded the Engineers at the capture of Lucknow 1858 ; appointed a Member of the Supreme Council of India 1861 ; commanded-in-Chief at Bombay 1865 ; commanded the Abyssinian Expedition 1867-8. —*United Service Club, s.w.*

NAPIER, Lady, of Oaklands, Hants.
Frances Maria, dau. of William Phil'pps, Esq., of Court Henry, co. Carmarthen; *m*. 1st Richard Alcock, Esq. ; 2nd 1835; Lieut.-General Sir Charles James Napier, G.C.B., who *d*. 1853.—*Oaklands, Portsmouth.*

NAPIER, the Hon. CHARLES, of Woodlands, Somerset.
Second son of Francis, 8th Lord Napier, by Maria Margaret, dau. of Lieut.-General Sir John Clavering, K.B.; *b*. 1794; *m*. 1st 1824 Alice Emma, dau. of Roger Barnston, Esq. (she *d*. 1834); 2nd 1840 Annabella Jane, dau. of Col. Gatacre, and has, by the former, with other issue,

• John Warren, in Holy Orders. *b*. 1832 ; *m*. 1857 Anna Maria Margaret Helen, youngest dau. of Lieut.-Col. Francis Hunter, of Wheatleigh Lodge, near Taunton, late of the Madras Cavalry, and has issue, • Charles Warren, *b*. 1858.

Mr. Napier, who entered the Army 1812, is a Major retired.—*Woodlands, Taunton.*

NAPIER, the Hon. and Rev. HENRY ALFRED.
Fourth son of Francis, 8th Lord Napier, by Maria Margaret, eldest dau. of Lieut.-General Sir John Clavering, K.B., *b*. 1797. Educated at Ch. Ch., Oxford (B.A. 1820, M.A. 1822); was appointed Rector of Swyncombe 1826.—*Swyncombe Rectory, Henley-on-Thames.*

NAPIER, the Hon. WILLIAM, of Broadmeadows, Selkirkshire.
Second son of William John, 9th Lord Napier, by Eliza, only dau. of the late Hon. Andrew James Cochrane-Johnstone; *b*. 1821; *m*. 1854 Louisa Mary, dau. of John H. Lloyd, Esq., Q.C., and has, with other issue,

• Francis Horatio, *b*. 1861.

Mr. Napier, who was formerly Clerk of Public Works at Hong-Kong, is Managing Director of Lands' Improvement Company.—*Broadmeadows, Selkirk, N B.; 1, Old Palace Yard, Westminster, s.w.; 54, Green Street, w.*

NAPIER, EDWARD BERKELEY, Esq., of Pennard House, Somersetshire.
Eldest son of the late Gerard Martin Berkeley Napier, Esq., of Pennard House, by Mary, dau. of John Paul Paul, Esq., of High Grove, Gloucester; *b*. 1816; *b*. 1820 *m*. 1849 Emily Houlton, 2nd dau. of Col. Sir John Wilson, C.B., K.H., and has, with other issue,

• Gerard Berkeley, *b*. 1857.

Mr. Napier, who was educated at Harrow, is a J.P. and D.L. for Somerset (High Sheriff 1859), and a Lieut.-Col. North Somerset Yeomanry; formerly an Officer in the Army.—*Pennard House, Shepton Mallet; Army and Navy and Carlton Clubs, s.w.*

NAPIER, GERARD JOHN, Esq., of Pennard Cottage, Somersetshire.
Youngest son of the late Gerard Martin Berkeley Napier, Esq., by Mary, dau. of John Paul Paul. Esq., of High Grove, co. Gloucester, and brother of E. B. Napier, Esq. (whom see); *b*. 1818: *m*. 1859 Ella Louisa, 3rd dau. of Col. Sir J. Wilson Kelt, C.B., and has, with other issue,

• Gerard, *b*. 1860.

Mr. Napier, who was educated at the Royal Naval Coll., is a Dep.-Lieut. for Somerset, and a Capt. R.N.—*Pennard Cottage, Shepton Mallet; United Service Club, s.w.*

NAPIER, JOHN MOORE, Esq., of Holly Bank, Sussex.
Only son of the late General Sir William Francis Patrick Napier, K.C.B., of Scinde House, who *d*. 1860, by Caroline, dau. of the late General the Hon. Henry Edward Fox; *b*. 1816; *m*. 1847 Elizabeth Amelia, dau. of the late Col. Charles C. Alexander, C.B., R.E., and has, with other issue,

• William Charles Fox, *b*. 1854.

Mr. Napier, who was educated at Exeter, represents a younger branch of the family of Lord Napier.—*Holly Bank, St. Leonard's-on-Sea.*

NAPIER, JOHN STIRLING, Esq., of Merchiston House, Renfrewshire.
Younger son of the late Sir William Milliken Napier, Bart., of Milliken House, co. Renfrew (who d. 1852), by Elizabeth Christian, 5th dau. of the late John Stirling, Esq., of Kippendavie, co. Perth ; b. 1820 ; m. 1845 Janet, only child and heir of Andrew Brown, Esq., of Auchintorlie, co. Renfrew, and has, with other issue,

* William, b. 1850.

Mr. Napier, who was educated at the University of Edinburgh, is a J.P. and D.L. for co. Renfrew.—*Merchiston House, Johnstone, N.B.*

NAPIER. (See *Elers-Napier*.)

NAPIER, of Merchistoun Hall. (See *Jodrell*.)

+NAPPER, JOHN, Esq., of Ifold, Sussex.
Son of the late N. Napper, Esq., of Ifold House ; b. 18—. Is a J.P. and D.L. for Sussex.—*Ifold House, Petworth.*

NASH, JAMES, Esq., of Martley, Worcestershire.
Son of the late James Nash, Esq., of Hartlebury, co. Worcester, by Elizabeth, his wife ; b. 1801 ; m. 1826 Sarah, 2nd dau. of William Hurst, Esq., of Hartlebury, and has, with other issue,

* Richard, b. 1827 ; m. 1856 Sarah, only dau. of Joseph Rogers, Esq.

Dr. Nash, who graduated M.D. at Edinburgh, is a Magistrate for co. Worcester.—*Martley, Worcester.*

NASH, the Rev. ROBERT SEYMOUR, of Old Sodbury, Gloucestershire.
Eldest son of the late Rev. Thomas Nash, Vicar of Lancing, Sussex, by Dorinda Estella Maria, dau. of William Brander, Esq., of Morden Hall, Sussex ; b. 1822 ; m. 1848 Elizabeth, dau. of the late Right Hon. William Yates Peel, and has, with other issue,

* Robert George Frederick, b. 1852.

Mr. Nash, who was educated at Eton and Trinity Coll., Cambridge (B.A. 1844; M.A. 1847), is a Magistrate for co. Gloucester, and Vicar of Old Sodbury.—*Old Sodbury, Chipping Sodbury.*

NASMYTH, Sir JOHN MURRAY, Bart., of Dalwick, Peeblesshire (cr. 1706).
Only son of the late Sir James Nasmyth, Bart., of Dalwick, by Eleanor, dau. of the late John Murray, Esq., of Philiphaugh, co. Selkirk ; b. 1803 ; s. as 8th Bart. 1828 ; m. 1st 1826 Mary, dau. of Sir John Majoribanks, Bart., of Lees ; 2nd 1839 the Hon. Eleanor, dau. of Thomas, 2nd Lord Lilford. Is a J.P. and D.L. for co. Peebles.—*Dalwick, Peebles, N.B.*

Heir, his son James, H.E.I.C.'s Service, b. 1827 ; m. 1850 Eliza Gordon Brodie, dau. of F. Whitworth Russell, Esq., of the Bengal Civil Service.

NASON, the Rev. WILLIAM HENRY, of Newtown, co. Cork.
Fourth but only surviving son of the late John Nason, Esq., of Newtown, by Elizabeth, dau. of Richard Nason, Esq., of Dettyville; b. 1815 ; s. 1857 ; m. 1st. 1840 Catherine Elizabeth, dau. of John Gaggin, Esq., of Middleton, co. Cork ; 2nd 1864 Jane, dau. of the late Thomas Charles Haines, Esq., of Passage, co. Cork, and has, by the former, with other issue,

* John William Washington. b. 1846.

Mr. Nason, who was educated at Trinity Coll., Dublin (B.A. 1838, M.A. 1841), is Rector of Rathcormac, and was formerly Rector of Clontuskert, co. Galway.—*Newtown and Rathcormac Glebe, co. Cork.*

NATION, WILLIAM HAMILTON CODRINGTON, Esq., of Rockbeare House, Devon.
Only son of the late William Nation, Esq., J.P. and D.L., of Southernhay, Exeter, by his 1st wife Harriet, dau. of Alexander Hamilton, Esq., of The Retreat, Topsham, Devon; b. 1843; s. 1861. Educated at Eton and Oriel Coll., Oxford. This family is of Norman-French extraction.—*Rockbeare House, Exeter.*

Heir Pres., his half-brother Charles Codrington, b. 1853.

NAYLOR, RICHARD CHRISTOPHER, Esq., of Hooton Hall, Cheshire.
Youngest son of the late John Naylor, Esq., of Hartford Hill, co. Chester, by Dorothy, only dau. of Richard Bullin, Esq.; b. 1814 ; s. (as co-heir with his brother) to his maternal uncle, Christopher Leyland, Esq., of Walton Hall, co. Lancaster, 1849 ; m. 1st 1854 Caroline, dau. of the late Rev. Robert Tredcroft, of Tangmere, Sussex (she d. 1855); 2nd 1856 Mary Sophia, only dau. of Henry Thorold, Esq., of Cuxwold, co. Lincoln, and has issue,

* Two daughters.

Mr. Naylor, who was educated at Eton, is a J.P. and D.L. for co. Denbigh, a Magistrate for cos. Northampton and Chester (High Sheriff 1856), and Patron of 3 livings.—*Hooton Hall, Chester ; Kilmarsh Hall, Northampton ; Nantrhwyd Hall, Ruthyn ; Carlton Club, s.w. Hurlingham House, Fulham, s.w.*

NAYLOR, JOHN, Esq., of Leighton Hall, Montgomeryshire.
Second son of the late John Naylor, Esq., of Hartford Hill, co. Chester, by Dorothy, dau. of R. Bullen, Esq.; b. 1813 ; s. his maternal uncle, as joint heir with his younger brother, R. C. Naylor, Esq., 1849 ; m. 1846 Georgiana, 3rd surviving dau. of John Edwards, Esq., of Ness Strange, co. Salop, and has, with other issue,

* Christopher John, b. 1849.

Mr. Naylor, who was educated at Eton and Trinity Coll., Cambridge. is a J.P. and D.L. for co. Montgomery (High Sheriff 1853), Lord of the Manor of Leighton, and Patron of 2 livings.—*Leighton Hall, Welshpool ; Brynllywarch Hall, Newtown, Montgomeryshire.*

NEALE, EDWARD VANSITTART, Esq., of Allesley Park, Warwickshire.
Only son of the late Rev. Edward Vansittart-Neale (who assumed the additional name of Neale in 1805, on succeeding to the Neale property), of Allesley Park, by Ann, dau. of Isaac Spooner. Esq. late of Elmdon, co. Warwick ; b. 1810 ; s. 1850 ; m. 1837 Frances Sarah, dau. of James William Farrer, Esq., of Ingleborough, co. York, and has, with other issue,

* Henry James Vansittart. b. 1842.

Mr. Vansittart-Neale was educated at Oriel Coll., Oxford (B.A. 1832, M.A. 1836), and called to the Bar at Lincoln's Inn 1858. This family is a branch of the Vansittarts of Bisham.—*Allesl y Park, Coventry.*

+NEAME, GEORGE, Esq., of Harbledown, Kent.
Son of the late G. Neame, Esq.; b. 18—. Is a J.P. and D.L. for Kent.—*Tower House, Harbledown, Canterbury.*

+NEATE, the Rev. ARTHUR, of Alvescote, Oxfordshire.
Son of the late — Neate. Esq.; b. 1804; m. 1844 Eleanor, eldest dau. of the late Richard Burnaby, Esq., and niece of the late Sir W. Burnaby, Bart. Educated at Trinity Coll., Cambridge (B.A. 1827), and graduated at Trinity Coll. Oxford (M.A. 1829); is a Magistrate for Oxon and Rector of Alvescote.—*Alvescote, Lechlade.*

NEATE, CHARLES, Esq.
Son of the late Rev. Thomas Neate, of Adstock, Bucks,
by Catherine, dau. of the Rev. William Church; b.
1807. Educated at Lincoln Coll., Oxford, and was
afterwards Fellow of Oriel Coll. (B.A. 1828); called to
the Bar at Lincoln's Inn 1832. Elected Professor of
Political Economy at Oxford 1857; was M.P. for Oxford
in 1857; re-elected 1863.—Oriel Coll., Oxford; Oxford
and Cambridge Club, s.w.

NEAVE, Sir ARUNDELL, Bart., of Dagnam
Park, Essex (cr. 1795).
Eldest of the late Sir Richard Digby Neave, Bart.,
of Dagnam Park, by the Hon. Mary, dau. of James
Everard, 9th Lord Arundell of Wardour; b. 1828; s.
as 4th Bart. 1868. Was formerly Lieut. 3rd Dragoon
Guards. Educated at Eton; is a Magistrate for Essex.
—Dagnam Park, Romford; Pitt House, Epsom; 6, Albe-
marle Street, w.
Heir Pres. his brother Ednowain Reginald, b. 1842.

NEAVE, SHEFFIELD, Esq., of Oak Hill, Mid-
dlesex..
Third son of the late Sir Thomas Neave, Bart., of
Dagnam Park, Essex, by Frances Caroline, dau. of the
Hon. and Very Rev. William Digby, Dean of Durham;
b. 1799; m. 1851 Mary Henrica, dau. of D. R. Morier,
Esq., and has, with other issue,
    * Sheffield, b. 1853.
Mr. Neave, who was educated at Eton and Ch. Ch.,
Oxford (B.A. 1820), is a Magistrate for Essex, a Dep.-
Lieut. for London, and a Merchant in the City; was
Governor of the Bank of England 1857–8.—Oak Hill
House, Hampstead, N.W.; Carlton Club, s.w.

+NEED, SAMUEL WILLIAM, Esq., of Blidworth, Notts.
Second but eldest surviving son of the late John Need,
Esq. (who was many years Col. of the Notts Militia),
by Mary, 2nd dau. of the late Rev. Dr. Welfitt, Prebendary of Canterbury; b. 1805; m. 18— Letitia, only
dau. of the late Lieut.-General Hall, of Park Hall,
Notts. Is Lord of the Manor of Blidworth.—Foun-
taindale, Blidworth, Mansfield.

NEED, Capt. WALTER, of Mansfield Woodhouse, Notts.
Youngest son of the late John Need, Esq., of Blidworth
Hall, Notts (Col. Notts Militia), by Mary, 2nd dau. of
the late Rev. Dr. Welfitt, Prebendary of Canterbury;
b. 1810; m. 1857 Emily McMahon, dau. of Col. Lionel
Westropp, of Cork, and has, with other issue,
    * A son, b. 1864.
Mr. Need is a Magistrate for Notts, and a Capt. R.N.,
retired.—Mansfield Woodhouse, Mansfield; United Service Club, s.w.

NEED. (See Welfitt.)

NEEDHAM, Lady GEORGIANA, of Datchet
House, Bucks.
Sixth dau. of Francis, 1st Earl of Kilmorey, by Anne,
2nd dau. of Thomas Fisher, Esq.— Datchet House,
Windsor.

NEEDHAM, WILLIAM, Esq., late of Lenton
House, Notts.
Eldest son of the late Matthew Needham, Esq., of
Lenton House, by Mary, dau. of William Manning,
Esq., of Ormesby, Norfolk; b. 1799; s. 1810; m. 1836
Camilla, dau. of Samuel Bosanquet, Esq. (she d. 1862).
Is a Magistrate for cos. Monmouth, Notts, and Derby.
—Residence: 31, Montpelier Square, s.w.
Heir Pres. his brother John Manning, b. 1807; m. 1831 Jane,
dau. of John Fordham, Esq.
692

NEEDHAM. (See under Kilmorey, Earl of.)

NEELD, Sir JOHN, Bart., of Grittleton, Wilts,
(cr. 1859).
Second son of the late Joseph Neeld, Esq., of Fulham,
Middlesex (who d. 1829), by Mary, dau. of John Bond,
Esq., of Hendon, Middlesex; b. 1806; m. 1845 Harriet
Eliza, 2nd dau. of Major-General Dickson, C.B., of
Beenham House, Berks. Educated at Harrow, and
Trinity Coll., Cambridge (B.A. 1827, M.A. 1830);
is a J.P. and D.L. for Wilts and Lord of the Manor
of Grittleton, and Patron of 8 livings; was M.P. for
Cricklade 1835–59; elected M.P. for Chippenham 1865.
—Grittleton, Chippenham; R d Lodge, Braydon, Wilts;
Carlton and Boodle's Clubs, s.w.; 92, Eaton Square, s.w.
Heir, his son Algernon William, b. 1846.

NEILL, WILLIAM JAMES SMITH-, Esq., of
Barnweill, and Swindrigemuir, Ayrshire.
Eldest son of the late Brigadier-General James George
Smith-Neill, of Barnweill and Swindrigemuir, by Isa-
bella, dau. of Col. William Warde, of the 5th Bengal
Native Cavalry (who was raised to the rank of a Knight's
widow on the death of her husband in India); b. 1837;
s. 1857; m. 1863 Jessie Gideon, dau. of George L.
Wood, Esq., and has, with other issue,
    * James William, b. 1865.
Mr. Smith-Neill was educated at Woolwich, and became
Capt. Royal Artillery 1862.—Barnweill, Kilmarnock;
Swindrigemuir, Dalry, N.B.

NELSON, Earl (HORATIO NELSON).—Cr. 1805.
Eldest son of Thomas, 2nd Earl, by Frances Elizabeth,
dau. of the late John Maurice Eyre, Esq., of Landford
House, Wilts; b. 1823; s. 1835; m. 1845 Lady Mary,
dau. of Welbore Ellis, 2nd Earl of Normanton. Edu-
cated at Eton and Trinity Coll., Cambridge (M.A. 1849);
is a J.P. and D.L. for Wilts, Patron of 1 living, and
Capt. Wilts Yeomanry Cavalry. The 1st Earl was bro-
ther to the gallant Admiral Horatio Viscount Nelson.
—Trafalgar, Salisbury; Carlton Club, s.w.; 3, Seamore
Place, w.
Heir, his son Herbert Horatio, Viscount Trafalgar, b. 1854.

NELSON, Countess Dowager, of Landford
House, Wilts.
Frances Elizabeth, dau. and heir of John Maurice Eyre,
Esq., of Landford House, by Frances, dau. of the late
Rev. Edward Foyle; m. 1821 Thomas, 2nd Earl Nel-
son, who d. 1835. — Landford House, Salisbury; 28,
Cavendish Square, w.

NELSON, the Hon. and Rev. JOHN HORATIO.
Second son of Thomas, 2nd Earl Nelson, by Frances
Elizabeth, dau. of John Maurice Eyre, Esq., of Landford
House, Wilts; b. 1825; m. 1857 Susan, dau. of the late
Lord Chas. Spencer Churchill, and has, with other issue,
    * John Eyre, b. 1859.
Mr. Nelson was educated at Eton and Harrow, and
Trinity Coll., Cambridge (M.A. 1846), and appointed
Rector of Trinity Mary 1853, of Delaugh-cum-Sof-
towe 1857.—Southcote Vicarage, Norwich.

NELTHORPE, of Scawby Hall. (See Sutton.)

NEPEAN, Sir MOLYNEUX HYDE, Bart., of Bo-
thenhampton, Dorset (cr. 1802).
Eldest son of the late Sir Molyneux Hyde Nepean,
Bart., of Bothenhampton, by Charlotte, dau. of Philip
Tilghman, Esq., R.N.; b. 1811; s. 1856; m. 1841 Isabel,
dau. of Col. Geils, of Dumbuck House, co. Dumbarton.
Educated at Eton: is a Dep.-Lieut. for Dorset, and
Patron of 1 living; was formerly an Officer in the 77th
Regt.—Loder's Court, Bridport.
Heir Pres. his cousin Evan Yorke (in Ho'y Or krs), M.A. of
Queen's Coll. Oxford; Rector of Bucknall, co. Lincoln, & c.

of the late Major-Gen. William Nepean, who d. 1864, by Emilia, dau. of Col. Yorke); b. 1825; m. 1865 Maria Theresa, 2nd dau. of the Rev. F. Morgan-Payler, Rector of Willey, co. Warwick, and has issue, * a son, b. 1867.

NESBITT, ALEXANDER, Esq., of Lismore, co. Cavan.

Second son of the late John Nesbitt, Esq., of Lismore, by Elizabeth, dau. of John Tatam, Esq., of Moulton, co. Lincoln; b. 1817; s. his brother 1856; m. 1856 Cecilia, dau. of Capt. Frederick Franks, R.N. Was High Sheriff of co. Cavan in 1862.—*Lismore, Crossdoney, co. Cavan.*

+NESFIELD, ROBERT WILLIAM MILLS, Esq., of Castle Hill, Derbyshire.

Eldest son of the late William Nesfield, Rector of Brancepeth, co. Durham (M.A. of Caius Coll., Cambridge); b. 1816; m. 1844 Lucy Elizabeth, 2nd dau. of W. Underwood, Esq., of Castle Hill, co. Derby. Educated at University Coll., Oxford (B.A. 1838, M.A. 1840); called to the Bar at Lincoln's Inn 1841. Is a J.P. and D.L. for co. Derby.—*Castle Hill, Bakewell.*

NETHERCOTE, HENRY OSMOND, Esq., of Moulton Grange, Northamptonshire.

Eldest son of the late John Nethercote, Esq., J.P. and D.L., of Moulton Grange, by Charlotte Eliza Frances, dau. of the late William. O. Hammond, Esq., of St. Alban Court, Kent; b. 1819; s. 1867; m. 1st 1847 Anne, dau. of R. Garnett, Esq., of Wyreside, co. Lancaster; 2nd 1857 Charlotte Frances, dau. of Charles Allix, Esq., of Willoughby Hall, co. Lincoln. Is a Magistrate for co. Northampton. — *Moulton Grange, Northampton.*

NETTERVILLE, Viscount (ARTHUR JAMES NETTERVILLE).—Cr. 1622.

Only son of the late Robert William Netterville, Esq., of Cruicerath, co. Meath (who d. 1834), by Mary, dau. of John Bernard, Esq., of Ballynegar, co. Kerry; b. 18—; m. 1841 Constantia Frances, 2nd dau. of the late Sir Edward Joseph Smythe, Bart., of Acton Burnel. Is a Magistrate for co. Meath; established his claim to the Viscountcy (dormant since 1854) in 1867. —*Cruicerath, co. Meath.*

NETTERVILLE, Viscountess, of Dowth Castle, co. Louth.

Eliza, dau. of Joseph Kirwan. Esq., of Hillsbrook; m. 1834 James, 7th Viscount Netterville, who d. 1854, leaving issue, Elizabeth Gwendoline, and Mary, m. 1860 Joshua M'Evoy, Esq. This title was dormant 1854-67. —*Dowth Castle, Drogheda; Pembroke Place, Dublin.*

NETTLES, ROBERT, Esq., of Nettleville, co. Cork.

Son of the late Richard Nettles, Esq., of Nettleville. J.P., by Anne, dau. of Daniel Gibbs, Esq., of Derry, co. Cork; b. 1810; m. 1836 Elizabeth, dau. of T. Knowles, Esq., of Oatlands, co. Cork. Is a Magistrate for co. Cork.—*Nettleville, Killenardrish, co. Cork.*

NEVILE, the Rev. CHRISTOPHER, of Thorney, Notts.

Eldest son of the late Christopher Nevile, Esq., of Thorney, by Ann Elizabeth, dau. of Jonathan Acklom, Esq., of Wiseton Hall, Notts; b. 1000, s. 1814; m. 1830 Gertrude, dau. of Col. Hotham (she d. 1862); 2nd 1865 Mary Ann, eldest dau. of Robert Tooth, Esq., of Swift's Park, Kent, and has, with other issue,
* George, educated at Eton; a Magistrate for Notts; b. 1833.
Mr. Nevile, who was educated at Rugby and Trinity Coll., Cambridge (B.A. 1830), is a Magistrate for Notts and co. Lincoln, and Patron of 2 livings.—*Thorney Hall, Newark; Wiseton Hall, Clayworth, Notts; Athenæum Club, s.w.*

NEVILE, GEORGE, Esq., of Stubton, Notts.

Youngest son of the late Rev. Henry W. Nevile, Rector of Cottesmore, co. Rutland by Amelia, dau. of James Mann, Esq., of Hallow Park, near Worcester; b. 1822; m. 1846 Madeline, dau. of George M. Glasgow, Esq., Capt. R.A. Is a J.P. and D.L. for co. Lincoln (High Sheriff 1858); late Lieut. R.A.; inherits the estates of the late Sir R. Heron, Bart., whose wife, dau. of Sir Horace Mann, was his great-aunt.—*Stubton, Newark.*

NEVILE, HENRY, Esq., of Walcot, Northamptonshire.

Eldest son of the late Rev. Henry W. Nevile, of Walcot, by Amelia, dau. of James Mann, Esq., of Hallow Park, near Worcester, and brother of George Nevile, Esq., of Stubton (whom see); b. 1808; s. 1843; m. 1847 Ellen, eldest dau. of the Rev. C. Bryan, Rector of Woolastone, co. Gloucester, and has, with other issue,
* Ralph Henry Christopher, b. 1850.
Mr. Nevile, who was educated at Harrow, is a J.P. and D.L. for cos. Lincoln and Northampton (High Sheriff 1849); was formerly in the 1st Dragoon Guards. —*Walcot Hall, Barnack, Stamford.*

NEVILE, PERCY SANDFORD, Esq., of Shelbrooke Park, Yorkshire.

Eldest son of the late John Pate Nevile, Esq., of Shelbrooke Park, an Officer in the 76th Foot, by Louisa Mary, dau. of R. F. Grant Dalton, Esq., of Ingoldisthorpe Hall, Norfolk, and Shanks House, Somerset; b. 1840; s. 1847; m. 1865 Rhoda Marwood, eldest dau. of the late Harry Farr Yeatman, Esq., of Manston, Dorset, and by her, who d. 1866, has issue,
* A son, b. 1866.
Mr. Nevile, who is Lord of the Manors of Shelbrooke and Smeaton, was formerly Lieut. 22nd Regt.—*Shelbrooke Park, Doncaster.*

NEVILL, CHARLES WILLIAM, Esq., of Westfa, Carmarthenshire.

Eldest son of the late Richard J. Nevill, Esq., of Llanlliedi (High Sheriff of co. Carmarthen 1850), by Anne, eldest dau. of William Yalden, Esq., of Lovington, Hants; b. 1816; s. 1856; m. 1841 Jane, dau. and co-heir of David Davies, Esq., of Swansea, and has, with other issue,
* Hugh, b. 1853.
Mr. Nevill, who was educated at Rugby, is a Magistrate for co. Carmarthen (High Sheriff 1868).—*Westfa, Llanelly.*

+NEVILL, COSMO GEORGE, Esq., of Nevill Holt, Leicestershire.

Eldest son of the late Charles Nevill, Esq., of Nevill Holt, by Lady Georgiana, youngest dau. of Richard, 2nd Earl of Lucan; b. 1822; s. 1848. Is Lord of the Manor of Nevill Holt.—*Nevil Holt, Uppingham.*
Heir Pres., his brother George Henry, educated at Trior Park, late Capt. 7th Fusiliers; b. 1841; m. 1858 Matilda, eldest dau. of the late Sir Henry Paston Bedingfeld, Bart., of Oxburgh, Norfolk.

NEVILL, REGINALD HENRY, Esq., of Dangstein, Sussex.

Third and youngest son of the late Hon. George Henry Nevill, of Flower Place, Surrey, by Caroline, dau. of the late Hon. L. Walpole; b. 1807; m. 1847 Lady Dorothy Fanny, 2nd dau. of Horatio, 3rd Earl of Orford, and has, with other issue,
* Edward Augustus, b. 1854.
Mr. Nevill is a J.P. and D.L. for Sussex.—*Dangstein, Petersfield.*

NEVILL, Admiral WILLIAM.

Eldest son of the late William Nevill, Esq., of Easton, Hants; b. 179-; m. 184- Mary, dau. of John Griffith,

Esq., of King's Worthy, Hants, and has issue. Educated at the Royal Naval Coll.; is a J.P. and D.L. for Hants, and a Magistrate for Winchester Petty Sessions, and a Rear-Admiral (retired).—*Parchment Street, Winchester.*

NEVILL. (See under *Abergavenny, Earl of.*)

NEVILLE, JOHN, Esq., of Haselour, Staffordshire.
Eldest son of the late Thomas Neville, Esq., of Haselour Hall, by Mary, only dau. and heir of the late Michael Wilson, Esq., of Bromley Regis, co. Stafford; *b.* 1814; *s.* 1859. Is a Magistrate for cos. Stafford and Warwick, Lord of the Manor of Haselour, and Patron of 1 living. This family has been located in the vicinity of Tamworth for many generations.—*Haselour Hall, Tamworth.*

Heir Pres, his brother Thomas, of Shenstone House, near Lichfield, *b.* 1816.

NEVILLE, THOMAS, Esq., of Borrismore House.
Eldest son of the late Robert Neville, Esq., of Borrismore, by Catherine, dau. of John Langley, Esq., of Lekfin, co. Tipperary; *b.* 1818; *m.* 1846 Anne, dau. of Thomas Villiers Tuthill, Esq., of Rathgar Mansion, co. Dublin, and has issue,

* Anne.

Mr. Neville, who was educated at Trinity Coll., Dublin, is a J.P. and D.L. for co. Kilkenny.—*Borrismore House, Johnstown, co. Kilkenny.*

NEVILLE. (See under *Braybrooke, Lord.*)

NEVILLE-GRENVILLE, RALPH, Esq., of Butleigh Court, Somerset.
Eldest son of the late Hon. and Very Rev. George Neville-Grenville, of Butleigh Court (some time Dean of Windsor), by Charlotte, 2nd dau. of George 3rd Earl of Dartmouth, K.G.; *b.* 1817; *s.* 1854; *m.* 1845 Julia Roberta, 4th dau. of the late Sir Robert Frankland-Russell, Bart., and has, with other issue,

* Robert, *b.* 1846.

Mr. Neville-Grenville, who was educated at Eton and Magdalen Coll., Cambridge (M.A. 1837), is Lieut.-Col. of the West Somerset Regt. of Yeomanry Cavalry, a J.P. and D.L. for Somerset (High Sheriff 1862), and Patron of 1 living; was M.P. for Windsor 1841-7; elected M.P. for E. Somerset 1865; was a Lord of the Treasury 1846-7.—*Butleigh Court, Glastonbury; Carlton Club,* s.w.; *6, Grosvenor Gardens,* s.w.

NEVILLE-ROLFE' CHARLES FAWCETT, Esq., of Heacham Hall, Norfolk.
Eldest son of the late Rev. Strickland Charles Howard Neville-Rolfe, of Heacham Hall (who assumed the latter name in 1837, on succeeding to the estates of Edmund Rolfe, Esq., of Heacham Hall), by his 1st wife Agnes, only dau. of Henry Fawcett, Esq., M.P., of Carlisle; *b.* 1815; *s.* 1852; *m.* 1st 1841 Martha Holt, eldest dau. of William Chapman, Esq., of Newcastle-upon-Tyne (she *d* 1864); 2nd 1868 Maria Bolton, 2nd dau. of the Rev. Mordaunt Bernard, Rector of Preston Bagot, co. Warwick; he has by the former, with other issue,

* Eustace, *b.* 1845; *m.* 1867 Emily Amber Frances, youngest dau. of the late Robert Thornhill, Esq.

Mr. Neville-Rolfe, who was educated at Magdalen Hall, Oxford (B.A. 1840), is a Magistrate for Norfolk, and Patron of 1 living.—*Heacham Hall, Lynn.*

NEW, JOHN CAVE, Esq., of Craddock House, Devon.
Eldest son of the late John New, Esq., of Craddock House, by Harriet, only dau. of Stephen Cave, Esq., of Cleve Hill, co. Gloucester; *b.* 1828; *s.* 1862; *m.* 1864

Caroline Sophia, only dau. of the Rev. H. R. Somers-Smith, Rector of Little Bentley, Essex, and has issue,

* Caroline Harriet Lucy.

Mr. New, who was educated at St. John's Coll., Oxford (B.A. 1851, M.A. 1864), is a Magistrate for Devon, and Capt. in the Devon Militia Artillery. This family were formerly of Bristol.—*Craddock House, Uffculme, Collumpton.*

NEWALL, JOHN LIGHTFOOT, Esq., of Forest Hall, Essex.
Eldest son of the late John Newall, Esq., of Cheshire, by Martha, dau. of Wm. Lightfoot, Esq., of Cumberland; *b.* 1826; *m.* 1849 Mary, dau. of John Walker, Esq., of Liverpool, and has, with other issue, an only son,

* John Walker, educated at Harrow; *b.* 1851.

Mr. Newall, who is a Magistrate for Essex, and a Merchant at Liverpool, purchased this property in 1852.—*Forest Hall, Ongar, Essex; Reform Club,* s.w.

NEWBOROUGH, Lord (SPENCER BULKELEY WYNN).—Cr. 1776.
Third son of Thomas, 1st Lord (who *d.* 1807), by his 2nd wife Maria Stella Petronilla, dau. of Lorenzo Chiappini; *b.* 1803; *s.* his brother 1832; *m.* 1834 Frances, dau. of the Rev. Walter de Winton, of Hay Castle, co. Brecon (she *d.* 1857). Educated at Rugby and Ch. Ch., Oxford (B.A. 1824); is a J.P. and D.L. for co. Carnarvon (High Sheriff 1859); was High Sheriff of co. Anglesey 1847.—*Glynnllivon Park, Carnarvon; Athenæum Club,* s.w.

Heir, his son Thomas John late Ensign Rifle Brigade; *b.* 1840.

NEWBURGH, Countess of (CECILIA GIUSTIANI).—Cr. 1660.
Only dau. of the late Vincent Prince Giustiani, by Nicoletta, dau. of the Duke de Mondragone; *b.* 1796; *m.* 1815 Charles Marquis Bandini (who *d.* 1850); 2nd title Viscount Kynnayrd; established her claim to this title 1858. Is descended maternally from the Lords Clifford of Chudleigh.—*Residence: Rome.*

Heir, her son Sigismund, Viscount Kynnayrd, Marquis Bandini in Italy; *b.* 1818; *m.* 1844 Angelica, dau. of Signor Massani, and has, with other issue, *Charles, b.* 1862.

NEWBURGH, Dowager Countess of.
Margaret, 3rd dau. of Archibald, 1st Marquis of Ailsa, by Margaret, dau. of John Erskine. Esq., of Dun, co. Forfar, N.B.; *m.* 1817 Thomas, 7th Earl of Newburgh (who *d.* 1853).—*35, Wilton Crescent,* s.w.

NEWCASTLE, Duke of (HENRY PELHAM ALEXANDER PELHAM-CLINTON).—Cr. 1756.
Eldest son of Henry Pelham, 5th Duke, by Lady Susan Harriet, only dau. of Alexander, 10th Duke of Hamilton; *b.* 1834; *s.* 1864; *m.* 1861 Henrietta Adela, only dau. and heir of the late Henry Thomas Hope, Esq., of Deepdene, Surrey. Educated at Eton and Ch. Ch., Oxford; is Keeper of St. Briavel's Castle, a Dep.-Lieut. for Notts, Lord High Steward of Retford, and Patron of 10 livings; late Lieut. in the Sherwood Rangers; was M.P. for Newark 1857-9.—*Clumber Park, Worksop, Notts; White's and Arlington Clubs,* s.w.; *18, Carlton House Terrace,* s.w.

Heir, his son Henry Pelham Archibald Douglas, Earl of Lincoln, *b.* 1864.

NEWCOMB, the late Mrs., of Rock House, Lincolnshire.
Sarah, dau. of the late Rev. Nicholas Todd, of Corby, Vicar of Ritchfield, co. Lincoln, by Mary, dau. of Wm. Singleton, Esq., of Sylecroft, Cumberland; *s.* her son, Robert Nicholas Newcomb, Esq., 1863; *m.* 1816 Robert Edmund Newcomb, Esq., of Stamford, who *d.* 1831. Mrs. Newcomb *d.* 1866, and was *s.* by John Todd-

Newcomb, Esq., of Ulverstone, who d. 1867, leaving issue,
* Robert Nicholas, b. 186-.
This family were seated at Saltfleetby *temp.* Richard I.
—*Rock House, Stamford.*

+ NEWCOMBE, Capt. GEORGE, of Aldershott, Hants.
Son of the late W. Newcombe, Esq.; b. 1806. Is a Magistrate for Hants and Surrey; Lord of the Manor of Aldershott: was formerly Capt. in the Army. —*Aldershott Manor, Hants.*

+NEWCOME, EDWARD CLOUGH, Esq., of Hockwold, Norfolk.
Son of the late Rev. William Newcome, J.P., of Hockwold; b. 1812; m. 1846 Amelia, youngest dau. of the late Very Rev. Peter S. Wood, Dean of Middleham, co. York, and Rector of Littleton, Middlesex. Educated at Eton; is a J.P. and D.L. for Norfolk, and Lord of the Manor of Hockwold; was formerly Capt. E. Norfolk Artillery Militia.—*Hockwold Hall, Brandon.*

NEWCOME, the Rev. HENRY JUSTINIAN, of Shenley, Herts.
Eldest son of the late Rev. Thomas Newcome, by Charlotte, dau. of Thomas B. Winter, Esq., of Shenley Hill; b. 1815; m. 1846 Charlotte, dau. of John Winter, Esq. Educated at Eton and Trinity Coll. Oxford (B.A. 1837), and Patron of 1 living.—*Shenley, Barnet, Herts.*
Heir Pres., his brother Edward William, B.A., of Balliol Coll., Oxford, b. 1821.

+ NEWCOMEN, CHARLES, Esq., of Clonahard, co. Longford.
Son of the late C. Newcomen, Esq., of Clonahard; b. 178—; m. 1816 the Hon. Catharine, youngest sister of the last Viscount Newcomen, of Mostown, co. Longford, and has, with other issue,
* Charles, b. 181-.
Mr. Newcomen is a Grand Juror for co. Longford, and Lord of the Manor of Clonahard.—*Clonahard, co. Longford.*

NEWCOMEN, Mrs., of Kirkleatham, Yorkshire.
Teresa, only dau. of the late Henry Vansittart, Esq., of Foxley, Berks (who d. 1848), by the Hon. Teresa, 2nd dau. of the late Sir William Gleadowe, Bart., and Viscountess Newcomen (*ext.*), and widow of Sir C. Turner, Bart.; s. her mother 1860; m. 1811 her cousin Arthur Newcomen, Esq., R.H.A. (who d. 1848), leaving issue,
* Arthur Henry Turner, b. 1842; m. 1862 Rachel, 3rd dau. of Sir Jervoise Clarke Jervoise, Bart., of Idsworth, Hants, and has issue.
Mrs. Newcomen is Lady of the Manor, and Patron of the livings of Kirkleatham and Coatham.—*Kirkleatham Hall, Redcar.*

NEWDEGATE, CHARLES NEWDIGATE, Esq., D.C.L., of Arbury, Warwickshire.
Eldest son of the late C. Newdigate Newdegate, Esq., of Harefield Place, by Maria dau. of Ayscough Boucherett, Esq., of N. Willingham and Stallingborough, co. Lincoln; b. 1816; s. 1833. Educated at Eton and King's Coll., London, and Ch. Ch., Oxford (B.A. 1837, M.A. and D.C.L. 1852); is a J.P. and D.L. for Warwickshire, a Magistrate for Middlesex, and Patron of 3 livings; has been M.P. for N. Warwickshire since 1843. —*Arbury, Nuneaton; Harefield Place, Uxbridge; Carlton, White's, and Travellers' Clubs, s.w.; 3, Arlington Street, w.*

NEWDIGATE, Lieut.-Col. FRANCIS WILLIAM, of Byrkley Lodge, Staffordshire.
Eldest son of the late Francis Newdigate, Esq., J.P. and D.L., of Byrkley Lodge (formerly Lieut.-Col. of

Staffordshire Militia), by Lady Barbara Maria, dau. of George, 3rd Earl of Dartmouth; b. 1822; s. 1862; m. 1859 Charlotte Elizabeth Agnes Sophia, dau. of F. M. Sir Alexander Woodford, G.C.B., G.C.M.G., and by her, who d. 1866, has issue,
* Francis Alexander, b. 1862.
Lieut.-Col. Newdigate, who was educated at the Royal Military Coll., Sandhurst, is a J.P. and D.L. for co. Stafford, a Magistrate for co. Derby, and Patron of 2 livings; he was formerly Lieut.-Col. in the Coldstream Guards.—*Byrkley Lodge, Burton-upon-Trent; Guards' and Carlton Clubs, s.w.*

NEWDIGATE, GEORGE, Esq., of Derwent Hall, Derbyshire.
Fifth son of the late Francis Newdigate, Esq., J.P. and D.L., of Byrk ey Lodge, co. Stafford, by Lady Barbara Maria, dau. of George, 3rd Earl of Dartmouth; b. 1826. Is a Magistrate for co. Derby, Patron of 1 living, and Capt. 1st Derby Militia.—*Derwent Hall, Sheffield; Normanton Hall, Derby.*

+NEWELL-BIRCH, the late Mrs., of Henley Park, Oxfordshire.
Diana Eliza, dau. of the late James Bourchier, Esq., of Little Berkhampstead, Herts; d. 1864, having m. 1821 John William Newell-Birch, Esq., of Henley Park, who d. 1867. The late Mr. Newell-Birch, who was formerly High Sheriff of Oxon, assumed the name of Newell on inheriting the estate of Ardwell. Oxon.—*Henley Park, Henley-on-Thames, Oxon; 66, Wimpole Street, w.*

NEWENHAM, EDWARD EYRE, Esq., of Maryborough Park, co. Cork.
Fourth son of the late Richard Devonsher Newenham, Esq., by Helena, sister of Richard, 1st Earl of Bantry; b. 18—. Inherited by the will of his father estates in cos. Limerick, Tipperary. and Cork; m. 1853 Jessie, only dau. of Alexander Glasgow, Esq., of Old Court, co. Cork. Is a Magistrate for co. Cork.—*Maryborough Park, co. Cork.*

NEWENHAM, the Rev. EDWARD HENRY, of Coolmore, co. Cork.
Second son of the late Robert Newenham, Esq., of Sandford. co. Dublin, by Jane, dau. of Edward Hoare, Esq., of Factory Hill, co. Cork; b. 1817; s. his uncle the Rev. Thomas Newenham, in the Coolmore and Lehenagh estates, 1849; m. 1849 Lady Helena Adelaide, 2nd dau. of Stephen, 3rd Earl of Mount Cashell, and has, with other issue.
* William Thomas Worth, b. 1853.
Mr. Newenham, who was educated at Trinity Coll., Dublin (B.A. 1845, M.A. 1819), is a Magistrate for co. Cork.—*Coolmore, Carrigaline, co. Cork; Kildare Street Club, Dublin.*

NEWMAN, Sir LYDSTON, Bart., of Mamhead Park, Devon (cr. 1806).
Second son of the late Sir Robert William Newman, Bart., M.P., of Mamhead (who d. 1848, by Mary Jane, dau. of Richard Deane, Esq.; b. 1823; s. his brother as 3rd Bart. 1854. Is a Dep.-Lieut. for Devon, Lord of the Manors of Mamhead, &c., and Patron of 2 livings; was formerly Capt. 7th Hussars.—*Mamhead Park, Exeter; Stokeley, Crediton; Albany, w.*
Heir Pres., his brother Thomas Holdsworth, b. 1825; m. 1864 Elizabeth Laura, dau. of Martin Tucker Smith, Esq.

NEWMAN, ADAM, Esq., of Monkstown, Cork.
Eldest son of the late Richard Newman, Esq., of Dromineen Mallow, by Jane Harriet, dau. of James Langton, Esq., of Bruree House, co. Limerick; b. 1808; s.

1830; *m.* 1834 Mary, dau. of Adam Perry, Esq., of Cork, and has, with other issue,

  * Richard, *b.* 1836.

Mr. Newman, who was educated at Trinity Coll., Dublin, is a Magistrate for Cork.—*Monkstown, Cork.*

NEWMAN, HENRY ASHBURNHAM TOLL, Esq., of Thornbury Park, Gloucestershire.
Eldest son of the late Henry Wenman Newman, Esq., J.P. and D.L., of Thornbury Park (who was High Sheriff of co. Gloucester 1835), by Frances Margaret, eldest dau. of the late Rev. J. J. Goodenough, D.D.; *b.* 1847; *s.* 1865. Mr. Newman's grandfather assumed the name of Newman in lieu of his patronymic Toll; and he has a royal descent from King Edward I.—*Thornbury Park, Gloucestershire; Hillside, Cheltenham.*

NEWMAN, JOHN, Esq., of Brand's House, Bucks.
Eldest son of the late John Newman, Esq., of Brand's House, by Elizabeth, dau. of John Love, Esq., of London; *b.* 1792; *s.* 1845; *m.* 1819 Anna Harper, dau. of John Turner, Esq., and has, with other issue,

  * William Henry, *b.* 1821.

Mr. Newman is a J.P. and D.L. for Bucks.—*Brand's House, High Wycombe; Conservative Club, s.w.*

NEWMAN, JOHN ADAM RICHARD, Esq., of Dromore House, co. Cork.
Only son of the late John Newman, Esq., of Dromore, by Margaret, dau. of Nicholas Philpot Leader, Esq., of Dromagh Castle, co. Cork; *b.* 1844; *s.* his grandfather, the late Adam Newman, Esq., of Dromore. 1859. Educated at Eton and Magdalen Coll., Cambridge (B.A. 1866); is Lord of the Manors of Newberry and Dromore.—*Dromore House, Mallow, co. Cork.*

  Heir Pres., his uncle Robert, *b.* 1822.

NEWMAN, the Rev. THOMAS HARDING-, of Nelmes, Essex.
Eldest son of the late Thomas Harding-Newman, Esq., of Nelmes (who assumed the latter name by Royal licence), by his 1st wife Harriet, youngest dau. of the late John Cartwright, Esq., of Ixworth Abbey, Suffolk; *b.* 1811; *s.* 1847. Educated at Balliol and Magdalen Colls., Oxford (B.A. 1833, M.A. 1836, B.D. 1846, D.D. 1848); is a Fellow of Magdalen Coll.—*Nelmes, Hornchurch, Romford.*

  Heir Pres., his brother.

NEWPORT, the Rev. FRANCIS.
Eldest son of the late Rev. Francis Newport, Vicar of Polroane, co. Kilkenny, by Eleanor, dau. and co-heir of Charles Backas, Esq., M.D., of Waterford; *b.* 1805; *s.* 1815; *m.* 1838 Catherine, 4th dau. of the late Sir J. N. Humble, Bart., of Clonkoskoran, co. Waterford. Educated at Trinity Coll., Dublin (B.A. 1828, M.A. 1832); is Rector and Vicar of Rostellan, diocese of Cloyne; was formerly Chaplain to the Russia Company at Archangel.—*Kilbey, Cloyne, co. Cork.*

NEWPORT. (See under *Bradford, Earl of.*)

NEWRY, Viscount. (See under *Kilmorey, Earl of.*)

NEWRY AND MORNE, Viscountess.
Anne Amelia, eldest dau. of the late Hon. Sir Charles Colville, G.C.B., by Jane, eldest dau. of the late William Mure, Esq., of Caldwell, N.B., and sister of Charles John, 11th Lord Colville; *m.* 1859 Francis Jack, Viscount Newry and Morne, who *d.* 1851, leaving issue.—98, *Eaton Place, s.w.*

696

NEWSHAM, RICHARD, Esq., of Preston, Lancashire.
Younger but only surviving son of the late Richard Newsham, Esq., Alderman, and four times Mayor of Preston, by Margaret, dau. of Peter Hopwood, Gentleman, of Preston; *b.* 1798; *s.* 1843; *m.* 1829 Agnes, eldest dau. and co-heir of Thomas Bowes, Esq., of Lancaster.—*Winckley Square, Preston.*

NEWTON, Sir WILLIAM JOHN, Knt. (cr. 1837).
Son of the late Mr. James Newton, by Abigail, dau. of — Peet, Esq.; *b.* 1785; *m.* 1822 Anne, dau. of Robert Faulder, Esq., and by her, who *d.* 1856; has issue,

  * Harry Robert, *b.* 1828; *m.* 1860 Edith Nicola, youngest dau. of A. Billing, Esq., M.D., of Grosvenor Gate.

Sir William is a Miniature Painter of eminence.—6, *Argyll Street, w.*

NEWTON, CHARLES EDMUND, Esq., of Mickleover Manor, Derbyshire. -
Eldest surviving son of the late Wm. Leaper Newton, Esq., J.P. and D.L., of Leylands, co. Derby (who *d.* 1851), by Henrietta, dau. of John White, Esq., of The Lawn, Herts; *b.* 1831; *s.* his brother 1854; *m.* 1st 1855 Anne Rosamond, only dau. of John Curzon, Esq., of Breedon, co. Leicester (she *d.* 1864); 2nd 1866 Mary Henrietta, only dau. of the late Capt. Moore, of the 17th Regt.; he has by the former, with other issue,

  * Robert Curzon, *b.* 1857.

Mr. Newton, who was educated at Rugby and Trinity Coll., Cambridge, is a Magistrate for co. Derby. His grandfather, John Leaper, Esq., of Derby, assumed the name of Newton in 1789.—*Mickleover Manor, Derby.*

NEWTON, FRANCIS WHEAT, Esq., of Barton Grange, Somerset.
Second son of the late John Newton, Esq., of Walton-on-Thames, Surrey, by Fanny Margaret, dau. of William Skinner, Esq.; *b.* 1814; *s.* in 1848 his cousin Josepha Sophia, only child of Francis Milner Newton, Esq., of Harton Grange, and widow of Sir F. G. Cooper, Bart.; *m.* 1849 Catharine Bailey, only dau. of William Ainslie, Esq., of Woodhill, Guildford, and has, with other issue,

  * Francis Murray, *b.* 1852.

Mr. Newton, who was educated at Pembroke Coll., Oxford (B.A. 1835), is a J.P. and D.L. for Somerset (High Sheriff 1861), and Patron of 2 livings.—*Barton Grange, Taunton.*

NEWTON, GEORGE ONSLOW, Esq., of Croxton Park, Cambridgeshire.
Eldest son of the late George Newton, Esq., of Croxton Park, by Charlotte, dau. of General Onslow, of Stanchton; *b.* 1830; *s.* 1851; *m.* 1852 Mary, eldest dau. of Wyndham Berkeley Portman, Esq. (she *d.* 1855); 2nd 1858 Cecilia Florence, 2nd dau. of the late Edwyn Burnaby, Esq., of Baggrave Hall, co. Leicester, and has issue.

  * A son, *b.* 1860.

Mr. Newton, who was educated at Eton and Trinity Coll., Cambridge (B.A. 1850), is a J.P. and D.L. for co. Cambridge (High Sheriff 1861), and Patron of 2 livings.—*Croxton Park, St. Neots; Brooks's and Boodle's Clubs, s.w.*

NEWTON, GEORGE WILLIAM, Esq., of Ollersett Hall, Derbyshire.
Youngest surviving son of the late Robert Newton, Esq., of Heaton-Norris, co. Lancaster, by Lucy, younger dau. and co-heir of the late Buckley Bower, Esq., of Ollersett Hall; *b.* 1788; *m.* 1810 Louisa Maria Thomasine, eldest dau. of the late Rev. Charles Warre, Rector of Hillmorton, co. Warwick (she *d. s. p.* 1838). Mr. Newton,

who was educated at Rugby and Brasenose Coll., Oxford (B.A. 1809, M.A. 1814), is a J.P. and D.L. for cos. Chester, Derby, and Lancaster.—*Ollersett Hall, Glossop.*

NEWTON, the late Mrs., of Cheadle Heath, Cheshire.
Mary Anne, only dau. of the late John Done, Esq., of Saltershill House, Tarporley, co. Chester; *d.* 1866, having *m.* 1837 James Newton, Esq., who was a J.P. and D.L. for cos. Chester, Lancaster, and Derby (who *d.* 1862).—*Cheadle Heath, Stockport.*

NEWTON, PHILIP JOCELYN, Esq., of Dunleckney, co. Carlow.
Only son of the late Walter Newton, Esq., of Dunleckney, by Anne, dau. of the Hon. George Jocelyn; *b.* 1818; *s.* 1853; *m.* 1st 1841 Henrietta Maria, dau. of John Kennedy, Esq., of Cultra; 2nd 1851 Emily, dau. of Sir D. Toler Osborne, Bart. Educated at Eton and Ch. Ch., Oxford; is a J.P. and D.L. for co. Carlow (High Sheriff 1846).—*Dunlckney, Bagenalstown, co. Carlow; Kildare Street Club, Dublin.*

NEWTON, SAMUEL, Esq., of The Downs, Cambridgeshire.
Second son of the late Samuel Newton, Esq., of Croxton Park, co. Cambridge, and Pickhill Hall, co. Denbigh; *b.* 1803; *m.* 1838 Elizabeth, dau. of Thomas St. Quintin, Esq., of Hatley Park, co. Cambridge, and has, with other issue,
* Samuel Charles, Lieut. Royal Horse Guards; *b.* 1840.
Mr. Newton is a Magistrate for cos. Cambridge and Hunts.—*The Downs, Croxton, St. Neots.*

NEWTON, THOMAS HENRY GOODWIN, Esq., of Barrells Park, Warwickshire.
Eldest son of the late William Newton, Esq., of Whateley Hall and Barrells Park, by Mary, dau. of William Whincopp, Esq.; *b.* 1836; *s.* 1862; *m.* 1st 1861 Mary Jane, dau. of William Berrow, Esq. (who *d. s. p.* 1862); 2nd 1865 Matilda, dau. of the late William Thomas Mackrell, Esq., and has issue,
* A daughter.
Mr. Newton was educated at St. John's Coll., Cambridge (B.A. 1858, M.A. 1861), and called to the Bar at the Middle Temple 1861; is Lord of the Manors of Ullenhall and Oldborrow.—*Barrells Park, Hockley Heath, Warwickshire; National Club, s.w.*
Heir Pres., his brother William, in Holy Orders, *b.* 1837.

+NEWTON, WILLIAM SAMUEL, Esq., late of Elveden Hall, Suffolk.
Eldest son of the late William Newton, Esq., J.P. and D.L., of Elveden (who was formerly M.P. for Ipswich, and *d.* 1863), by Eliza, 3rd dau. of the late Richard S. Milnes, Esq., M.P., of Fryston Hall, co. York; *b.* 1816; *m.* 1856 Elizabeth Louisa, youngest dau. of the late Major-Gen. Sir Thos. Steele, and has, with other issue,
* A son, *b.* 1863.
Mr. Newton, who is a Magistrate for Suffolk, and a Major-General in the Army (retired), was Lord of the Manor and Patron of Elveden, and formerly Lieut.-Col. Coldstream Guards The estate of Elveden was sold in 1863 to Maharajah Dhuleep Singh.—13, *Lowndes Street, s.w.*

NEWTON, WILLIAM DRUMMOND OGILVY-HAY-, Esq., of Newton Hall, Haddingtonshire.
Eldest son of the late John Stuart Hay-Newton, Esq., of Newton Hall, by Margaret Eliza, youngest dau. of the late William Fairlie, Esq. (she *m.* 2ndly 1866 Major Robert Duncan Ferguson); *b.* 1832; *s.* 1863. Is Lord of the Barony of Newton: late Capt. 72nd Highlanders. This family is descended from John, 2nd Marquis of

Tweeddale.—*Newton Hall, Gifford, N.B.; 36, George Square, Edinburgh.*
Heir Pres., his brother Ernestine Eglinton, *b.* 183-.

NIAS, Sir JOSEPH, K.C.B. (cr. 1867).
Son of the late Joseph Nias, Esq., by Ann, dau. of — Cropper, Esq.; *b.* 1794; *m.* 1855 Isabella, only child of John Laing, Esq., of Montague Square, London. Is a Vice-Admiral R.N.—*Surbiton, s.w.; United Service Club, s.w.*

NIBLETT, JOHN DANIEL THOMAS, Esq., of Haresfield Court, Gloucestershire.
Eldest son of the late Daniel John Niblett, Esq., J.P. and D.L., of Haresfield Court, formerly High Sheriff of co. Gloucester, by Emma Catherine, eldest dau. and coheir of the Rev. Thomas Drake, D.D., Vicar of Rochdale; *b.* 1809; *m.* 1849 Caroline Anne, youngest dau. of David Arthur Saunders, Esq., J.P. Educated at Eton and Exeter Coll., Oxford (B.A. 1833, M.A. 1835); is a Magistrate for cos. Gloucester and Worcester.—*Haresfield Court, Stonehouse; Tuffley, Gloucester.*
Heir Pres., his brother Edward Henry, in Holy Orders, Rector of Redmarley, co. Worcester; *b.* 1810; *m.* 1848 Mary Anne, dau. of James Law Stewart, Esq., of Jamaica, and has, with other issue, * Arthur Edward, *b.* 1852.

NICHOLL, GEORGE WHITLOCK, Esq., of Court Blethin, Monmouthshire.
Second son of Iltyd Nicholl, Esq., J.P., of The Ham, co. Glamorgan, and Usk, co. Monmouth, by Eleanor, only child of George Bond, Esq., of Court Blethin, co. Monmouth, and Newland, co. Gloucester; *b.* 1816; *m.* 1853 Mary Lewisa, youngest dau. of the late William Nicholl, Esq., M.D., of Ryde, I. of Wight, and has, with other issue,
* Iltyd Bond, *b.* 1862.
Mr. Nicholl, who was called to the Bar at the Middle Temple 1840, is Recorder of Usk, and a Magistrate for cos. Monmouth and Glamorgan.—*Court Blethin, Usk; Athenæum Club, s.w.*

NICHOLL, ILTYD, Esq., of The Ham, Glamorganshire.
Eldest son of the late Rev. Iltyd Nicholl, D.D., of The Ham, by Anne, dau. of George Hatch, Esq., of Windsor; *b.* 1785; *s.* his father 1787; *m.* 1807 Eleanor, only child and heir of George Bond, Esq., of Newland, co. Gloucester, and Court Blethin, co. Monmouth, and by her, who *d.* 1850, has, with other surviving issue,
* George Whitlock, a Barrister-at-Law of the Middle Temple, Recorder of Usk, and a Magistrate for cos. Monmouth and Glamorgan; *b.* 1816, *m.* 1853 Mary Lewisa, youngest dau. and co-heir of William Nicholl, Esq., M.D., of Ryde, and has, with other issue, * Iltyd Bond, *b.* 1862.
Mr. Nicholl is a Magistrate for cos. Glamorgan and Monmouth.—*The Ham, Cowbridge; Usk, Monmouthshire.*

NICHOLL, JOHN COLE, Esq., of Merthyr Mawr, Glamorganshire.
Eldest son of the late Right Hon. John Nicholl, M.P., of Merthyr Mawr, by John H., 3rd dau. of the late Thomas Mansel Talbot, Esq., of Margam Abbey, co. Glamorgan; *b.* 1823, *s.* 1853, *m.* 1860 Mary De la Beche, dau. of L. Dillwyn, Esq., and has issue,
* John, *b.* 1861.
Mr. Nicholl, who was educated at Eton and Ch. Ch. Oxford, is a Magistrate for co. Glamorgan and Patron of 1 living: he was formerly Lieut. in the Rifle Brigade —*Merthyr Mawr, Bridgend; Carlton and Junior United Service Clubs, s.w.*

NICHOLL-CARNE, ROBERT CHARLES, Esq., of Nash Manor, Glamorganshire.
Eldest son of the late Rev. Robert Nicholl, M.A., of Dimlands Castle, co. Glamorgan (who assumed the

name of Carne in 1842), by Elizabeth, dau. and heir of Capt. Charles Loader Carne, R.N., of Nash Manor; b. 1806; s. 1849; m. 1838 Sarah Jane, dau. and co-heir of the Rev. Nathaniel Poyntz, M.A., of Alvescot House, Oxon (she d. s. p. 1861). Called to the Bar at the Middle Temple 1830, and went the Oxford and South Wales Circuits; is a J.P. and D.L. for co. Glamorgan, and Constable of the Castle of St. Quentin.—*Nash Manor, Cowbridge, Glamorganshire; Athenæum Club, s.w.*

<small>Heir Pres., his brother John Whitlock, of Diedlands and St. Donat's Castles. Glamorganshire. · ducated at Eton and Jesus Coll., oxford (B.A. 18:7, M.A. 1859, B.C.L. 1840, D.C.L. 1848); calle t to the Bar at the Inner Temple 1840; a J.P. and D.L. for co Glamorgan ; la:e Commi-sioner in Bankruptcy; b. 816; m. 1844 Mary Jane, only dau. of Peter W. Braecker Esq., of Field House, Waverfree, Lancashire, and has, with other issue, *John Deveraux Vaux Loder, b. 1854.</small>

NICHOLS, Francis Morgan, Esq., of Lawford Hall, Essex.
Third surviving son of the late John Bowyer Nichols, Esq., F.S.A., of London, by Eliza, dau. of John Baker, Esq., and grandson of the late John Nichols, Esq., F.S.A., Author of the 'Literary Anecdotes,' and of the 'History of Leicestershire;' b. 1826; m. 1857 Mary, elder dau. and co-heir of the late Walter Buchanan, Esq., of Penrith, and has, with other issue,

<small>• Bowyer Buchanan, b. 1859.</small>

Mr. Nichols, who was educated at Wadham Coll., Oxford (B.A. 1847, M A. 1853), and called to the Bar at Lincoln's Inn in 1852, is a Magistrate for Essex, and Lord of the Manor of Lawford.—*Lawford Hall, Manningtree, Essex ; Athenæum Club, s.w.*

NICHOLSON, Sir Charles, Bart., D.C.L., LL.D. (cr. 1859).
Only surviving son of the late Charles Nicholson, Esq., of London (who d. 1824), by Barbara, dau. of J. Ascough, Esq., of Bedale, co. York (she d. 1811), and grandson of the late Charles Nicholson, Esq., of Cockermouth, Cumberland; b. 1808; m. 1855 Sarah Elizabeth, eldest dau. of Archibald Keightley, Esq., of the Charterhouse, London. Educated at Edinburgh; was Chancellor of the University of Sydney, and three times elected Speaker of the Legislative Assembly of New South Wales.—*Hadleigh, Rayleigh, Essex ; Conservative Club, s.w.; 26, Devonshire Place, w.*

<small>Heir, his son Charles Archibald, b. 1867.</small>

NICHOLSON, Harvey, Esq., of Roe Park, co. Londonderry.
Second but only surviving son of the late John Nicholson, Esq., of Londonderry, by Everina, 2nd dau. of Alexander Scott, Esq.; b. 1795; s. 1818; m. 1824 Isabella Maria, dau. of John Harvey, Esq., of Londonderry. Is a Magistrate for the city and co. of Londonderry (High Sheriff 1856).—*Roe Park, Newtonlimavady, co. Londonderry.*

NICHOLSON, James, Esq., F.S.A., of Thelwall Hall, Cheshire.
Son of the late P. Nicholson, Esq., of Thelwall Hall, by Lucy, only dau. of W. Eyres, Esq.; b. 1818 ; m. 1852 Elizabeth, eldest surviving dau. of the Rev. J. P. Jones-Parry, M.A., Rector of Ederu, co. Carnarvon, and of Llangelynin, co. Merioneth. Is Patron of 1 living, and Capt. in the Earl of Chester's Yeomanry Cavalry. —*Thelwall Hall, Warrington; Cringlemire, Troutbeck, Westmoreland.*

NICHOLSON, John Armitage, Esq., of Balrath Burry, co. Meath.
Eldest son of the late Christopher Armitage Nicholson, Esq., of Balrath, by Katharine, dau. of the late Most Rev. William Newcome, D.D., Lord Archbishop of Armagh; b. 1798; m. 1824 Elizabeth Rebecca, dau. of

608

the late Most Rev. Nathaniel Alexander, D.D., Lord Bishop of Meath, and by her, who d. 1861, has, with other issue.

<small>• Christopher Armitage (High Sheriff of co. Meath 1850). b. 1825; m. 1858 Frances Augusta, dau. of the late Hon. A. H. Macdonald-Moreton.</small>

Mr. Nicholson, who was educated at Harrow and Trinity Coll., Cambridge (B.A. 1819, M.A. 1823), is a J.P. and D.L. for co. Meath (High Sheriff 1827).—*Balrath Burry, Kells, co. Meath.*

NICHOLSON, Robert, Esq., of Ballow, Down-shire.
Eldest son of the late William Steele-Nicholson, Esq., J.P., of Ballow (who assumed the name of Nicholson on succeeding to the property of his uncle, William Nicholson, Esq., in 1803), by Isabella, dau. of Jacob Hancock, Esq., of Lisburn, co. Antrim; b. 1809; s. 1840; m. 1841 Elizabeth Jane, youngest dau. of Walter Nangle, Esq., of Kildalkey, co. Meath, and has, with other issue,

<small>• Walter. b. 1843.</small>

Mr. Nicholson, who was educated at Trinity Coll., Dublin (B.A. 1830, M.A. 1868), and called to the Irish Bar 1836, is a Magistrate for co. Down.—*Ballow, Bangor.*

+NICHOLSON, Capt. Samuel, of Waverley Abbey, Surrey.
Eldest son of the late George Thomas Nicholson, Esq., of Waverley Abbey, by Anne Elizabeth, dau. of the late William Smith, Esq., M.P.; b. 1816 ; s. 1852. Educated at Eton; is a J.P. and D.L. for Surrey, and Capt. Surrey Militia.—*Waverley Abbey, Farnham.*

<small>Heir Pres., his brother William Smith, late Capt. 26th Foot ; b. 1818 ; m. 1849 Charlotte Elizabeth, dau. of the late Sir Thomas Miller, Bart.</small>

NICHOLSON, William, Esq.
Eldest son of the late Peter Nicholson, Esq., of Thelwall Hall, co. Lancaster, by Lucy, only dau. of William Eyres, Esq., of Warrington; b. 1816; m. 1850 Constance Ferrers, 2nd dau. of George Pickering, Esq., of Chester, and has, with other issue,

<small>• Edward Joseph, b. 1851.</small>

Mr. Nicholson is a Capt. in the 3rd Royal Lancashire Militia.—Residence: *Thelwall Lea, Warrington.*

NICHOLSON, William, Esq., of Basing Park, Hants.
Youngest son of the late John Nicholson, Esq., of Upper Clapton, Middlesex, by Ellen, dau. of Richard Payne, Esq.; b. 1824; m. 1858 Isabella Sarah, dau. of John Meek, Esq., and has, with other issue,

<small>• William Graham, b. 1862.</small>

Mr. Nicholson, who was educated at Harrow and Trinity Coll., Cambridge, is a Magistrate for Hants; was elected M.P. for Petersfield 1866.—*Basing Park, Alton, Hants ; Union Club, s.w.; 4, Sussex Square, w.*

NICHOLSON, William Nicholson, Esq., of Roundhay Park, Yorkshire.
Eldest son of the late Thomas Phillips, Esq., of Leeds, and nephew of the late Stephen Nicholson, Esq., whose name he assumed in 1827 ; b. 1803; s. 1858; m. 1827 Martha, dau. of Abram Rhodes, Esq., and has, with other surviving issue,

<small>• Rhodes, b. 1830.</small>

Mr. Nicholson, who was educated at Queen's Coll., Cambridge (M.A. 1832), is a J.P. and D.L. for the W. Riding of Yorkshire. Lord of the Manor of Roundhay, and Patron of 1 living.—*Roundhay Park, Leeds.*

NICHOLSON. (See *Shaw, of Arrowe Hall.*)

NICOL, JAMES DYCE, Esq., of Ballogie, Aberdeenshire.
Only son of the late W. Nicol, Esq., M.D., of Badentoy, co. Kincardine, by Margaret, dau. of J. Dyce, Esq., of Aberdeen, N.B.; b. 1805; s. 1841; m. 1844 Catherine, dau. of Edward Lloyd Esq., of Manchester, and has, with other issue,

* William, b. 1846.

Mr. Nicol is a J.P. and D.L. for cos. Aberdeen and Kincardine, elected M.P. for co. Kincardine 1865.—Ballogie, Aberdeen; Badentoy, Hillside, Kincardineshire, N.B.; Athenæum Club, s.w.; 13, Hyde-Park Terrace, w.

NICOL, WILLIAM, Esq., of Fawsyde, Kincardineshire.
Eldest son of the late James Nicol, Esq., of Banff, N.B.; b. 1790; m. 1820 Margaret Dyce, 3rd dau. of the late William Nicol, Esq., of Badentoy, co. Kincardine, N.B. (she d. 1869). Educated at Aberdeen; is a J.P. and D.L. for co. Kincardine; was an East India Merchant, long connected with Bombay; was M.P. for Dover, 1859–65.—Fawsyde, Bervie, N.B.; Carlton Club, s.w.; 41, Victoria Street, s.w.

NICOLL, DONALD, Esq.
Son of Mr. Nicoll, of Edinburgh; b. 1820; m. 1855 Melina, dau. of L. Jones, Esq., of Heath House, Essex. Is a Magistrate for Middlesex and Westminster, a Commissioner of Lieutenancy and late Sheriff of London and Middlesex; was M.P. for Frome 1857–9.—Oaklands Hall, West-End Park, Kilburn, N.W.

NICOLSON, Sir FREDERICK WILLIAM ERSKINE, Bart., C.B., of Tillicoultrie, Clackmannanshire (cr. 1686).
Eldest son of the late Major-General Sir William Nicolson, Bart., of Tillicoultrie, by Mary, dau. of J. Russell, Esq.; b. 1815; s. 1820; m. 1st 1847 Mary Clementina, dau. of the late J. Loch, Esq., M.P.; 2nd 1854 Augusta Sarah, dau. of R. Cullington, Esq., widow of Captain Hay (she d. 1861); 3rd 1867 Anne, only child of the late R. Crosse, Esq. Is a Rear-Admiral R.N.; served in China 1857–8; was Superintendent of Royal Dockyard, Woolwich, 1861–3.—15, William Street, s.w.

Heir, his son Frederick, b. 1848.

NICOLSON, Sir ARTHUR BOLT, Bart., of Lasswade, Midlothian (cr. 1629).
Eldest surviving son of the late Capt. James Nicolson, R.N.; b. 18—; is said to have s. his cousin 1863.—Fitzroy, Melbourne, Australia.

+NICOLSON, JAMES BADENOCH, Esq., of Glenbervie, Kincardineshire.
Son of the late J. Nicolson, Esq., of Glenbervie; b. 18—; is married, and has, with other issue,

* James Badenoch, an Advocate at the Scottish Bar; b. 18—; m. 18—! Eliza Jane, eldest dau. of the late James Burnett, Burnett, Esq., of Monbudio, co. Kincardine, and has issue, * a son, b. 1865.

Mr. Nicholson is a J.P. and D.L. for co. Kincardine, and Lord of the Barony of Glenbervie.—Glenbervie, Drumlithie, Fordoun, N.B.

NICOLSON. (See Stewart-Nicolson.)

NIGHTINGALE, Sir CHARLES, Bart. (cr. 1628).
Eldest son of the late Sir Charles Ethelston Nightingale, Bart., of Kneesworth Hall, co. Cambridge, by Maria, dau. of T. L. Dickenson, Esq.; b. 1809; s. 1813 m. 1829 Harriet Maria, dau. of E. B. Foster, Esq.

Was formerly an Officer in the Royal Navy.—The Lodge, Wimbledon, s.w.

Heir, his son Henry Dickenson. Capt. 45th Regt., late Capt. Royal Marines; b. 1830; m. 1854 Mary, dau. of Capt. Slaney J. Spark, R.N., and has, with other issue, * Edward Henry, b. 1856.

NIGHTINGALE, WILLIAM EDWARD, Esq., of Lea Hurst, Derbyshire, and Embley Hants.
Only son of the late William Shore, Esq., of Tapton, by Mary, dau. of George Evans, Esq., of Cromford, co. Derby; b. 1794; m. 1818 Frances, dau. of the late William Smith, Esq., M.P., of Parndon, Essex, and has issue,

* Frances Parthenope. m. 1858 Sir H. Verney, Bart.; and
* Florence, ‡ unmarried.

Mr. Nightingale, who was educated at Edinburgh and Trinity Coll., Cambridge, assumed the name of Nightingale under the will of his maternal granduncle, Peter Nightingale, Esq., to whose estates he succeeded in 1815. He is a J.P. and D.L. for Hants, a Magistrate for cos. Derby and Wilts, and Patron of 1 living.—Embley Park, Romsey; Lea Hurst, Matlock.

NISBET, ROBERT PARRY, Esq., of Southbroome House, Wilts.
Son of the late Walter Nisbet, Esq., of Grafton Street, and Nevis, and grandson of Archibald Nisbet, Esq., of Carfine, co. Lanark; b. 1793; m. 1st 1817 Clara Amelia, only dau. of Major T. Harriott, West Hall, Surrey; 2nd 1846 Elizabeth, only dau. of E. Green, Esq., of Hinxton Hall, co. Cambridge, and widow of the Rev. H. Curtis Smith; and has issue by the former,

* Five daughters.

Mr. Nisbet, who was educated at Haileybury Coll., is a J.P. and D.L. for Wilts (High Sheriff 1849); was formerly in the Bengal Civil Service, and for some time a Judge in that Presidency; was M.P. for Chippenham 1856–9.—Southbroome House, Devizes; Carlton Club, s.w.; Oriental Club, w.

NISBETT-HAMILTON. (See Hamilton.)

+NISBETT, JOHN MORE, Esq., of Cairnhill, Lanarkshire.
Eldest son of the late George More Nisbett, Esq., of Cairnhill, by Isabella Frances, dau. of the late Francis Cartaret Scott, Esq.; b. 1826; s. 1843; m. 1848 Lady Agnes, grand-dau. of North, 9th Earl of Stair, K.T., and has issue. Mr. Nisbett is a Magistrate for co. Lanark, and Lord of the Barony of Cairnhill.—Cairnhill, Airdrie, N.B.

NOBLE, JOHN, Esq., of Berry Hill, Bucks.
Only surviving son of the late John Noble, Esq., F.S.A., Merchant, of London (who d. 1849); b. 1812; m. 1852 Eliza Anne, dau. of Capt. Ellis, of the Bombay Artillery, and has, with other issue,

* Wilson, b. 1855.

Mr. Noble, who is a Merchant in London, represents a family formerly seated at Coldstream, co. Berwick.—Berry Hill, Taplow, Maidenhead; 50, Westbourne Terrace, w.

NOBLE, Mrs., of Danett's Hall, Leicestershire.
Mary Joanna, dau. of the late John Kershaw, Esq., of Halifax, co. York; m. 1824 Joseph William Noble, Esq., M.P., who was a Magistrate for co. Leicester, and d. 1861.—Danett's Hall, Leicester.

‡ This is the lady whose exertions in the cause of the sanitary condition of the British Army have earned for her a world-wide fame.

NOBLE, Capt. WILLIAM, of Forest Lodge, Sussex.

Eldest son of the late William Noble, Esq., of Berwick, by Mary, elder dau. of John Gould, Esq.; *b.* 1828; *m.* 1851 Emily Charlotte, only child of Edward Irving, Esq., of H.M.'s 61st Regt., and has, with other issue,
* William Edward van Lijnden Irving, *b.* 1852.

Capt. Noble, who is a Magistrate for Sussex and Patron of the living of Donoughmore, co. Donegal, and a Fellow of the Royal Astronomical Society, was formerly Capt. in the Queen's Own Light Infantry Militia. —*Forest Lodge, Maresfield, Uckfield.*

NOEL, the Hon. and Rev. Baptist WRIOTHESLEY.

Eleventh son of Diana, late Baroness Barham, and brother of Charles Noel, 1st Earl of Gainsborough; *b.* 1799; *m.* 1826 Jane, dau. of Peter Baillie, Esq., of Dochfour, co. Inverness, and has, with other issue,
* Wriothesley, *b.* 1827.

Mr. Noel, who was educated at Trinity Coll., Cambridge (M.A. 1821), was formerly Minister of St. John's, Bedford Row.—36, *Westbourne Terrace, w.*

NOEL, the Hon. GERARD JAMES, of Exton, Rutland.

Second son of Charles Noel, 1st Earl of Gainsborough, by his 3rd wife Arabella, 2nd dau. of the late Sir James Hamlyn-Williams, Bart.; *b.* 1823; *m.* 1863 Augusta Mary, 2nd dau. of Col. the Hon. Henry Cecil Lowther, M.P., and has issue,
* Gerard Cecil, *b.* 1864.

Mr. Noel, who is a J.P. and D.L. for Rutland, was formerly Capt. 11th Hussars, has been M.P. for co. Rutland since 1847; was appointed a Lord of the Treasury, 1866.—*Exton, Oakham ; Carlton Club, s.w. ;* 11, *Chandos Street, w.*

NOEL, the Hon. HENRY LOUIS, of Exton, Rutland.

Third son of Charles Noel, 1st Earl of Gainsborough, by his 3rd wife Arabella, 2nd dau. of the late Sir James Hamlyn-Williams, Bart.; *b.* 1824 ; *m.* 1852 his cousin, Emily Elizabeth, 2nd dau. of the Hon. and Rev. Baptist Wriothesley Noel, and has, with other issue,
* Gerard Thomas, *b.* 1856.

Mr. Noel is a Magistrate for co. Leicester and Rutland (High Sheriff 1863) ; late Capt. Commandant Rutland Militia.—*Exton, Oakham.*

NOEL, the Hon. and Rev. LELAND.

Ninth son of Diana, late Baroness Barham, and brother of Charles Noel, 1st Earl of Gainsborough ; *b.* 1797 ; *m.* 1824 Mary Arabella, dau. of John Savile Foljambe, Esq., of Osberton Hall, Notts, and by her, who *d.* 1859, has, with other issue,
* Horace George Wriothesley, in Holy Orders ; *b.* 1825.

Mr. Noel was educated at Trinity Coll., Cambridge (M.A. 1821), appointed Vicar of Exton 1832, and Honorary Canon of Peterborough 1850.—*Exton Vicarage, Oakham.*

NOEL, BERKELEY PLANTAGENET, Esq., of Moxhull Park, Warwickshire.

Eldest son of the late Hon. Berkeley O. Noel (who *d.* 1841), by Letitia Penelope, only dau. of the late Ralph Adderley, Esq., of Elmley Castle, co. Worcester, and widow of Andrew Hulkett, Esq., of Moxhull Park ; *b.* 1821 ; *s.* his mother 1860 ; *m.* 1852 Millicent Mary, 2nd dau. of the late Hon. and Rev. Francis James Noel, and has, with other issue,
* Charles Francis Adderley, *b.* 1854.

Mr. Noel, who was educated at Eton and Trinity Coll., Cambridge, is a J.P. and D.L. for co. Warwick, Lord of
700

the Manors of Moxhull, Wishaw, Curdworth, and Minworth, and Patron of the living of Moxhull.—*Moxhull Park, Birmingham.*

NOEL, CHARLES, Esq., of Bell Hall, Worcestershire.

Fourth son of the late John Perrott, Noel, Esq., of Bell Hall, by Margaret, dau. of the late John Amphlett, Esq., of Clent House, co. Stafford ; *b.* 1802 ; *m.* 1828 Mary, dau. of the Rev. John Wylde, Rector of Aldridge and Great Barr, co. Stafford, and by her, who *d.* 1861, has, with other issue,
* Charles Perrott, of Bradford House, near Stourbridge ; educated at Winchester, a J.P. and D.L. for cos. Worcester and Stafford, Capt. Worcester-shire Yeomanry Cavalry, and formerly an Officer in the 48th Regt. ; *b.* 1839 ; *m.* 1856 Henrietta Margaret, only dau. of the Rev. James Nelson Palmer.

Mr. Noel, who was educated at St. John's Coll., Oxford, is a Magistrate for co. Stafford and a J.P. and D.L. for co. Worcester (High Sheriff 1853).—*Bell Hall, Belbroughton, Stourbridge.*

NOEL, EDWARD ANDREW, Esq., of Clanna Falls, Gloucestershire.

Eldest son of the late Hon. and Rev. Francis J. Noel (brother of Charles Noel, 1st Earl of Gainsborough), by Cecilia Penelope, sister of Paul, 1st Lord Methuen ; *b.* 1824 ; *s.* his uncle, the late Hon. William M. Noel, 1859 ; *m.* 1849 Sarah, dau. of William B. Darwin, Esq., of Elston Hall, Notts, and has, with other issue,
* William Frederick Noel, *b.* 1850.

Mr. Noel, who is a J.P. and D.L. for co. Gloucester, and Lieut.-Col. Commandant Gloucestershire Rifle Volunteers, was Capt. 31st Foot.—*Clanna Falls, Lydney.*

NOEL.

(See under *Gainsborough, Earl of ; Berwick, Lord ; Lovelace, Earl of ;* and *Wentworth, Lord.*)

NORBURY, Earl of (HECTOR GRAHAM TOLER). —Cr. 1827.

Second son of Hector John, 2nd Earl, by Elizabeth, dau. of William Brabazon, Esq., of Ballinasloe Castle ; *b.* 1810 ; *s.* 1839 ; *m.* 1848 Stewart Lindesay, dau. of Major-General Sir Henry Lindesay Bethune, Bart. Educated at Eton and Ch. Ch., Oxford ; is a Magistrate for co. Cork.—*Valence, Westerham, Kent ; Carlton Club,* s.w. ; 54, *Belgrave Square, w.*

Heir Pres., his brother Otway Fortescue, late Cornet 8th Dragoon Guards, *b.* 1824 ; *m.* 1848 the Hon. Henrietta Eliza, elder dau. of Robert Campbell, 2nd Lord Abinger, and has, with other issue, * Hector Robert, *b.* 1847.

NORBURY, THOMAS CONINGSBY NORBURY, Esq., of Sherridge, Worcestershire.

Eldest son of the late Thomas Norbury, Esq., of Sherridge (who assumed that name in lieu of his patronymic Jones), by Mary Anne, only child and heir of the late Coningsby Norbury, Esq. ; *b.* 1829 ; *s.* 1866 ; *m.* 1855 the Hon. Gertrude O'Grady, dau. of Standish Darly, 2nd Viscount Guillamore, and has, with other issue,
* Thomas, *b.* 1865.

Mr. Norbury is a J.P. and D.L. for co. Worcester and a Magistrate for co. Hereford ; a Major Worcestershire Militia ; late Capt. 6th Dragoon Guards.—*Sherridge and The Norrest, Great Malvern.*

NORCLIFFE, Mrs., of Langton, Yorkshire.

Rosamond, elder dau. of Charles Best, Esq., M.D. of York, by Mary, dau. and heir of Thomas Norcliffe, Esq., of Langton Hall ; assumed the name and arms of Norcliffe in 1802 on succeeding to the estates of Major-General Norcliffe Norcliffe, K.H. ; *m.* 1850 Henry Robinson, Esq. (son of Rear-Admiral Hugh Robinson, of Ap-

pleby, co. Westmoreland), who *d.* 1858, leaving, with other issue,

 • Hugh, *b.* 1831, late a Capt. in the Army.

This family have held the estates and manors of Langton, Howsham, and Eddlethorpe for above 250 years.—*Langton Hall, Malton; Petergate House, York.*

NORFOLK, Duke of (HENRY FITZALAN-HOWARD). —Cr. 1483.

Eldest son of Henry Granville, 17th Duke, by Augusta, Mary Minna Catherine, dau. of Edmund, 1st Lord Lyons, G.C.B.; *b.* 1847; *s.* 1860. Is Premier Duke and Earl in the Peerage of England, Hereditary Earl Marshal of England, and Patron of 24 livings. Is descended from Sir Robert Howard, *temp.* Henry IV., who married the elder dau. of Thomas Mowbray, Duke of Norfolk, and his descendant, Thomas, 4th Duke, married the heiress of the Fitzalans, Earls of Arundel.—*Arundel Castle, Sussex; 21, St. James's Square, s.w.*

 Heir Pres., his brother Lord Edmund Bernard, *b.* 1855.

NORMAN, the Rev. CHARLES FREDERICK, of Mistley Place, Essex.

Eldest son of the Rev. Charles Norman, Vicar of Boxted, Essex; *b.* 1829; *s.* his uncle, Edward Norman, Esq., 1862; *m.* 1854 Janet, dau. of T. G. Kensit, Esq., of Bruton Street, London, and has, with other issue,

 • Edward Kensit, *b.* 1855.

Mr. Norman, who was educated at St. Catherine's Coll., Cambridge (B.A. 1852, M.A. 1855), was Rector of Portishead, Somerset 1854–67, and is Patron of that living.—*Mistley Place, Manningtree, Colchester; 35, Prince's Gardens, Kensington, w.*

NORMAN, the Rev. FREDERIC JOHN.

Fifth son of the late Richard Norman, Esq., of Melton Mowbray, by Lady Elizabeth Isabella, elder dau. of Charles, 4th Duke of Rutland, K.G.; *b.* 1814; *m.* 1848 his cousin Lady Adeliza Elizabeth Gertrude, 4th dau. of John Henry, 5th Duke of Rutland, K.G., and has, with other issue,

 • John Frederic Charles, *b.* 1850.

Mr. Norman, who was educated at Caius Coll., Cambridge (B.A. 1838), and appointed Rector of Bottesford 1846, is a Magistrate for co. Leicester.—*Bottesford Rectory, Nottingham.*

+NORMAN, GEORGE, Esq., of Goadby Marwood, Leicestershire.

Eldest son of the late Richard Norman, Esq., of Goadby Marwood, by Lady Elizabeth Isabella, elder dau. of Charles, 4th Duke of Rutland, K.G., and cousin of G. W. Norman, Esq., of Bromley (whom see); *b.* 1800; *s.* 1847. Educated at St. Peter's Coll., Cambridge (B.A. 1822, M.A. 1826); is a Magistrate for co. Leicester. —*Goadby Marwood Hall, Melton Mowbray.*

NORMAN, GEORGE WARDE, Esq., of Bromley, Kent.

Eldest son of the late George Norman, Esq., of Bromley (High Sheriff of Kent in 1735) by Charlotte, dau. of the Rev. Edwards Beadon, of North Stoneham, Hants; *b.* 1793; *m.* 1830 Sibella, dau. of Henry Stone, Esq., of Stanmore, and has, with other issue,

 • Charles Loyd, *b.* 1833 ; *m.* 1858 Julia, dau. of Charles Hay Cameron, Esq., of Freshwater, I. of Wight, and has issue.

Mr. Norman, who was educated at Eton, is a J.P. and D.L. for Kent.—*Bromley Common, s.e.; Athenæum Club, s.w.*

NORMAN, JOHN MANSHIP, Esq., of Dencombe, Sussex.

Eldest son of the late Robert Norman, Esq., of Dencombe, by Elizabeth, dau. of Simon Goodman Ewart, Esq., of Calcutta; *b.* 1799; *s.* 1813; *m.* 1830 Catha-

rine Eliza, eldest dau. of the late Rev. George Maximilian Bethune, LL.D., Rector of Worth, Sussex. Educated at Winchester and Trinity Coll., Cambridge (B.A. 1822, M.A. 1825); called to the Bar at Lincoln's Inn 1825, and went the Northern Circuit; is a J.P. and D.L. for Sussex, late Chairman of the Cuckfield Union.—*Dencombe, Slaugham, Crawley; University Club, s.w.*

 Heir Pres., his brother Robert Ewart, *b.* 1800.

+NORMAN, JOHN PAXTON, Esq., of Claverham House, Somersetshire.

Eldest son of the late John Norman, Esq., J.P. and D.L., of Claverham House, by his 2nd wife Sarah Elizabeth, eldest dau. of the Rev. Henry Paxton, of Baythorne, Essex; *b.* 1819; *s.* 1837. Educated at Exeter Coll., Oxford (B.A. 1841, M.A. 1844); called to the Bar at the Inner Temple 1852, and goes the Home Circuit; is Lord of the Manor of Claverham.—*Claverham House, Yatton, Bristol.*

 Heir Pres., his brother Henry Wilkins (Rev.), M.A., Fellow of New Coll., Oxford; *b.* 1820.

NORMAN, THOMAS, Esq., of Glengollan, co. Londonderry.

Only son of the late Charles Norman, Esq., of Glengollan, by Anne Eliza, dau. of Edward Kough, Esq., of New Ross, co. Wexford; *b.* 1831; *s.* 1843. Is a Magistrate for co. Donegal (High Sheriff 1864), and a Capt. Donegal Militia (retired).—*Glengollan House, Fahan, co. Londonderry.*

NORMAN. (See Lee-Norman.)

NORMANBY, Marquis of (GEORGE AUGUSTUS CONSTANTINE PHIPPS, P.C.).—Cr. 1838.

Eldest son of Constantine Henry, 1st Marquis, by the Hon. Maria, dau. of Henry, 1st Lord Ravensworth; *b.* 1819; *s.* 1863; *m.* 1844 Laura, dau. of the late Capt. Robert Russell, R.N. Is a J.P. and D.L. for the N. Riding of Yorkshire, and Major N. York Militia; formerly Lieut. Scots Fusilier Guards; was Comptroller of the Household 1851–2, Treasurer of the Household 1853–7, M.P. for Scarborough 1847–51 and 1852–8; Governor of Nova Scotia 1858–63; was a Lord-in-Waiting on the Queen in 1866.—*Mulgrave Castle, Whitby; Travellers' Club, s.w.*

 Heir, his son Constantine Charles Henry, Earl of Mulgrave, *b.* 1846.

NORMANTON, Earl of (WELBORE ELLIS-Agar). —Cr. 1806.

Eldest son of Charles, 1st Earl, by June, dau. of William Benson, Esq.; *b.* 1778; *s.* 1809; *m.* 1816 Lady Diana, dau. of George Augustus, 11th Earl of Pembroke (she *d.* 1841).—*Somerley. Ringwood. Hants; Athenæum, Carlton, Arthur's, and Boodle's Clubs, s.w.; 3, Seamore Place, w.*

 Heir, his son James Charles Herbert Welbore Ellis, Viscount Somerton, educated at Westminster, a J.P. and D.L. for Wilts and Hants late Lieut. Wilts Yeoman Cavalry; was M.P. for Wilton 1852-7, *b.* 1818; *m.* 1852 Susannah Augusta, 3rd dau. of William Keppel, 6th Viscount Barrington, and has with other issue, • Charles George Welbore Ellis, *b.* 1858.

NORREYS, Sir CHARLES DENHAM ORLANDO JEPHSON-, Bart., of Mallow, co. Cork (cr. 1838).

Son of the late Col. William Jephson, of Mallow Castle, by his 3rd wife Louisa, dau. of C. Kensington, Esq., of Blackheath, Kent; *b.* 1799; *m.* 1821 Katharine Cecilia Jane, dau. of William Franks, Esq., of Carrig, co. Cork (she *d.* 1853). Assumed the additional name of Norreys in 1838. Educated at Brasenose Coll., Oxford (B.A. 1820, M.A. 1828); is a J.P. and D.L. for co. Cork; was

M.P. for Mallow 1826–59.—*The Castle, Mallow, co. Cork ; Athenæum Club.* s.w.

Heir, his son Denham William, B.A. of New Inn Hall, Oxford ; a Magistrate for co. Cork ; b. 1821.

+NORREYS, Robert Henry, Esq., of Davyhulme Hall, Lancashire.

Only son of the late Robert Josias Jackson, Esq., who assumed the name of Norreys on his marriage with Mary, only child of Henry Norreys, Esq., of Davyhulme Hall ; *b.* 1812 ; *s.* 1851. Is a J.P. and D.L. for co. Lancaster.—*Davyhulme Hall, Manchester.*

Heirs Pres., his sisters.

+NORRIS, Henry, Esq., of Swalcliffe Park, Oxon.

Son of the late H. Norris, Esq. ; *b.* 1808. Educated at Balliol Coll., Oxford (B.A. 1831, M.A. 1834) ; is a J.P. and D.L. for Oxon, and a Magistrate for co. Warwick. —*Swalcliffe Park, Banbury.*

NORRIS, John Thomas, Esq., of Sutton Courtney, Berks.

Youngest son of the late Edmund Norris, Esq., of Sutton Courtney, by Sally Maria, only dau. of William Henly, Esq. ; *b.* 1808 ; *m.* 1st 1840 Emily Frances, only dau. of the late Francis Hume Choppin, Esq. ; 2nd 1858 Selina, dau. of Lieut. Mackenzie, R.N. Is a Magistrate for Berks, a Dep.-Lieut. for London, and a Member of the Common Council of London ; was M.P. for Abingdon 1857–65.—*Sutton Courtney, Abingdon ; Reform Club,* s.w.

+NORRIS, William, Esq., of Woodnorton, Norfolk.

Son of the late Rev. W. Norris, Rector of Guist and Woodnorton ; *b.* 1799. Is a J.P. and D.L. for Norfolk. —*Woodnorton, Thetford.*

NORTH, Baroness (Susan North).—Cr. 1554.

Dau. of George Augustus, 3rd Earl of Guilford, by his 2nd wife Susan, dau. of the late Thomas Coutts, Esq., Banker ; *b.* 1797 ; *m.* 1835 Capt. John Sidney Doyle (who has assumed the name of North ; *see below*). Is Patron of 1 living.—This title was in abeyance 1802–41.—*Wroxton Abbey, Banbury ; Putney Hill, Surrey,* s.w. ; 16, *Arlington Street,* s.w.

Heir, her son William Henry John, educated at Eton and Ch. Ch., Oxford, a Magistrate for Oxon and Lieut. of the Queen's Own Staffordshire Yeomanry Cavalry, late Lieut. 1st Life Guards, and formerly A.D.C. to the Lord-Lieut. of Ireland ; b. 1836 ; m. 1858 Frederica, dau. of the late R H Cockrell, Esq., R.N., and has issue, * William Frederick John, b. 1860.

NORTH, Frederick, Esq., of Rougham, Norfolk.

Eldest son of the late Frederick F. North, Esq., by Elizabeth, dau. of the late Rev. M. Whitear, of Hastings, Sussex ; *b.* 1800 ; *m.* 1824 Janet, dau. of the late Sir J. Marjoribanks, Bart., and widow of R. Shuttleworth, Esq., of Gawthorp Hall, co. Lancaster, and by her, who *d.* 1855, has, with other issue,

* Charles, educated at Eton and Trinity Coll., Cambridge (B.A. 1851, M.A. 1854), and called to the Bar at the Inner Temple 1854, a Magistrate for Norfolk, and formerly Capt. East Norfolk Artillery Militia ; b. 1828 ; m. 1859 Angus a.; el est dau. of the late Hon. and Rev. Thomas R. Keppel, of North Creake, Norfolk, Canon of Norwich, and has, with other issue, * Frederick Keppel, b. 1860.

Mr. North, who was educated at Harrow and St. John's Coll., Cambridge (B.A. 1822, M.A. 1825), and admitted a Student of the Inner Temple (but not called to the Bar), is a J.P. and D.L. for Norfolk and Sussex, and Lord of the Manor of Rougham ; he was M.P. for Hastings 1831–7 and 1854–65.—*Rougham Hall, Norfolk ; University and Athenæum Clubs,* s.w. ; 3, *Victoria Street,* s.w.

NORTH, Col. John Sidney, D.C.L., of Wroxton Abbey, Oxfordshire.

Son of the late Lieut.-General Sir Charles William Doyle, G.C.H., by his 1st wife Sophia, dau. of the late Sir John Coghill, Bart. ; *b.* 1804 ; *m.* 1835 Susan, Baroness North (whom see), whose name he assumed in lieu of Doyle 1838, and has, with other issue,

* William Henry John (whom see, under North, Baroness).

Col. North, who was educated at Sandhurst, is a J.P. and D.L. for Oxon and co. Northampton, a Dep.-Lieut. for co. Cambridge, a Magistrate for Middlesex and co. Warwick, and Lieut.-Col. Oxfordshire Rifle Volunteers ; late Lieut.-Col. Irish Fusiliers ; has been M.P. for Oxon since 1852.—*Wroxton Abbey, Banbury ; Kirtling Tower, Newmarket ; Putney Hill, Surrey ; Carlton, White's, Travellers', and United Service Clubs,* s.w. ; 16, *Arlington Street,* w.

+NORTH, North, Esq., of Thurland Castle, Lancashire.

Eldest son of the late John S. Burton, Esq., by Mary Anna, only dau. of David Morgan, Esq., and grandnephew of the late Richard Toulmin North, Esq., of Newton and Thurland Castle (whose name he has assumed) ; *b.* 1823 ; *s.* his grand-uncle 1865 ; *m.* 1856 Alicia Gertrude, only dau. of Capt. Versturme, and has, with other issue,

* A son, b. 1862.

Mr. Burton, who is a Magistrate for co. Lancaster, was formerly in the Army.—*Thurland Castle, Tunstall.*

NORTH. (See under *Guilford, Earl of.*)

NORTH-BOMFORD. (See *Bomford.*)

NORTHAMPTON, Marquis of (Charles Douglas-Compton).—Cr. 1812.

Eldest son of Spencer, 2nd Marquis, by Margaret, eldest dau. of the late General Douglas Maclean Clephane ; *b.* 1816 ; *s.* 1851 ; *m.* 1859 Theodosia, dau. of the late Henry Vyner, Esq., of Newby Hall, co. York (she *d.* 1864). Is a J.P. and D.L. for cos. Northampton and Argyle, Patron of 4 livings, and a Trustee of the National Gallery. — *Castle Ashby, Northampton ; Compton Winyates, Kineton, Warwickshire ;* 145, *Piccadilly,* w.

Heir Pres., his brother Lord William. Capt. R.N., retired ; b. 1818 ; m. 1844 Eliza, dau. of the late Admiral the Hon. Sir George Elliot, K C B., and has, with other issue, * William George Spencer Scott, b. 1851.

NORTHBROOK, Lord (Thomas George Baring).—Cr. 1865.

Eldest son of Francis Thornhill, 1st Lord, by his 1st wife, Jane, dau. of the late Sir George Grey, Bart. ; *b.* 1826 ; *s.* 1866 ; *m.* 1848 Elizabeth Harriet, dau. of the late Henry Charles Sturt, Esq., of Critchill, Dorset. Educated at Ch. Ch., Oxford (B.A. 1846) ; is a Magistrate for Hants, and Capt. Hants Yeomanry Cavalry ; was a Lord of the Admiralty 1857–8 ; Under-Secretary of State for War in 1861 ; Under-Secretary for India 1861–4 ; Under-Secretary for the Home Department 1861–6 ; Secretary to the Admiralty 1866 ; was M.P. for Falmouth 1857–66.—*Stratton Park, Winchester ; Brooks's and Travellers' Clubs,* s.w. ; 21 *Lowndes Square,* s.w.

Heir, his son Francis George, b. 1850.

NORTHCOTE, the Rt. Hon. Sir Stafford Henry, Bart., P.C., C.B., D.C.L., of Pynes, Devon (cr. 1641).

Eldest son of the late Henry Stafford Northcote, Esq. (who *d.* 1850), by Agnes, dau. of Thomas Cockburn, Esq. ; *b.* 1818 ; *s.* his grandfather 1851 ; *m.* 1843 Cecilia Frances, dau. of Thomas Farrer, Esq. Educated at Eton and Balliol Coll., Oxford (B.A. 1839, M.A. 1842) ; called to the Bar at the Inner Temple 1847 ; a J.P. and D.L. for Devon, and Patron of 3 livings ; was formerly

Legal Secretary to the Board of Trade ; Financial Secretary to the Treasury, and Capt. 1st Devon Yeomanry Cavalry ; was M.P. for Dudley 1855–7 ; for Stamford 1858–66; elected M.P. for N. Devon 1866; was President of the Board of Trade 1866–7 ; appointed Secretary of State for India 1867 ; cr. Hon. D.C.L. Oxon 1863.—*Pynes, Exeter ; Athenæum Club*, s.w. ; *16, Devonshire Place*, w.

Heir, his son Walter Stafford, b. 1845.

NORTHCOTE, GEORGE BARONS, Esq., of Somerset Court, Somerset.
Only surviving son of the late Robert Northcote, Esq., of Buckerell, by Sarah, dau. of James Cogan, Esq.; *b.* 1796; *s.* his brother 1833 ; *m.* 1818 Maria, 2nd dau. and co-heir of Gabriel Stone, Esq., of Somerset Court, and has, with other issue,
- • George Barons, *b.* 1820 ; *m.* 1st 1844 Eleanor, eldest dau. of Hector William Bower Monro, Esq., of Edmondsham, Dorset, and Ewell Castle, Surrey ; 2nd 1856 Catharine Bayard, dau. of Charles Alexander Williamson, Esq., of Balgray, co. Dumfries.

Mr. Northcote, who was educated at Eton and Corpus Christi Coll., Oxford, is a J.P. and D.L. for Devon and Somerset (High Sheriff 1855), and Patron of 1 living. —*Somerset Court, Bridgewater ; Buckerell, Honiton.*

+**NORTHCOTE**, Mrs., of Oakfield, Devon.
Elizabeth, eldest dau. of the late J. Smith, Esq., of Crediton, Devon ; *m.* 1842 Henry Northcote, Esq., of Oakfield House, Barrister-at-law, who *d.* 1867, leaving issue an only child,
- • Fanny Hinton, *b.* 1860 Herbert E. G. Crosse, late Lieut. 59th Foot.

This family are descended from a common ancestor with Sir S. Northcote, Bart.—*Oakfield House, Crediton.*

NORTHESK, Earl of (WILLIAM HOPETOUN CARNEGIE).—Cr. 1647.
Eldest surviving son of William, 7th Earl, by Mary, dau. of William Henry Ricketts, Esq.; *b.* 1794; *s.* 1831 ; *m.* 1843 Georgiana Maria, dau. of the late Admiral the Hon. Sir George Elliot, K.C.B. Educated at Winchester. Descended from a common ancestor with the Earl of Southesk. — *Longwood, Winchester ; Ethie House, Arbroath, Forfarshire, N.B. ; Athenæum Club*, s.w
Heir, his son George John, Lord Rosehill, Cant. Scots Fusilier Guards, b. 1843 ; m. 1865 Elizabeth, eldest dau. of Rear-Admiral George Elliot, and has, with other issue, • David, b. 1865.

NORTHEY, EDWARD RICHARD, Esq., of Woodcote House, Surrey.
Eldest son of the late Rev. Edward Northey, M.A., Canon of Windsor (who *d.* 1828), by Charlotte, dau. of the Rev. Edward Taylor, of Bifrons, Kent, *b.* 1795 ; *m.* 1st 1828 Charlotte Isabella, 2nd dau. of the late General Sir George Anson, G.C.B. (she *d.* 1842) ; 2nd 1814 Louisa Mary Anne, dau. of the Rev. Robert Hesketh, M.A., and has, with other issue,
- • Edward William, in Holy Orders, educated at Eton, M.A. of C. C. C., Oxford, late Incumbent of Atlow, co. Derby ; *b.* 1832 ; *m.* 1867 Florence Elizabeth, dau. of the late Sir John Honywood, Bart.

Mr. Northey, who was educated at Eton and the Royal Military Coll., is a J.P. and D.L. for Surrey (High Sheriff 1856) ; was formerly in the 52nd Regt. and in the 3rd Foot Guards.—*Woodcote House, Epsom.*

NORTHMORE, JOHN, Esq., of Cleve, Devon.
Second son of the late Rev. Thomas Welby Northmore, of Cleve (who *d.* 1829), by Katherine, 3rd dau. of the late Sir William Earle Welby, Bart., of Denton Hall, co. Lincoln ; *b.* 1826 ; *m.* 1863 Jemima Hayter, only dau. of the late Rev. William Hames, Rector of Chagford, Devon. Educated at Eton and Brasenose Coll., Oxford. Is a Magistrate for Devon, and an Officer 1st Devon Yeomanry Cavalry ; was formerly in the Ceylon Civil Service.—*Cleve House, Exeter.*

NORTHUMBERLAND, Duke of (ALGERNON GEORGE PERCY).—Cr. 1776.
Elder surviving son of George, 5th Duke, and 3rd Earl of Beverley, by Louisa Harcourt, 3rd dau. of the late Hon. James A. Stuart-Wortley-Mackenzie, and sister of John, 1st Lord Wharncliffe; *b.* 1810; *s.* 1867; *m.* 1845 Louisa, dau. of the late Henry Drummond, Esq., M.P., of Albury Park, Surrey. Educated at Eton and St. John's Coll., Cambridge (LL.D. 1842) ; is a J.P. and D.L. for Northumberland, a Magistrate and Chairman of Quarter Sessions for Surrey ; Lord of the Manor of Albury, Patron of 16 livings, and Lieut.-Col. Northumberland Militia ; formerly Capt. Grenadier Guards; was M.P. for Beeralston 1831–2 ; for N. Northumberland 1852–65 ; a Lord of the Admiralty 1858–9, and Vice-President of the Board of Trade February–June, 1859. —*Alnwick Castle, Northumberland ; Stanwick, Darlington ; Albury Park, Guildford ; Sion House, Isleworth,* s.w. ; *Travellers'· Club,* s.w. ; *11, Portman Square,* w. ; *Northumberland House, Charing Cross,* s.w.
Heir, his son Henry George, Earl Percy, b. 1846.

NORTHWICK, Lord (GEORGE RUSHOUT).—Cr. 1797.
Only son of the Hon. and Rev. George Rushout (who *d.* 1842), by Lady Caroline, dau. of John, 7th Earl of Galloway, and nephew of John, 2nd Lord ; *b.* 1811 ; *s.* his uncle as 3rd Lord 1859. Educated at Harrow and Ch. Ch., Oxford (B.A. 1833, M.A. 1836) ; is a Magistrate for cos. Hereford, Worcester, Gloucester, and Salop, and a Dep.-Lieut. for co. Salop ; Lord of the Manor of Harrow-on-the-Hill, and of Ketton, co. Rutland, and Patron of 2 livings; late Capt. 1st Life Guards, and Lieut.-Col. commanding the Herefordshire Militia ; was M.P. for Evesham 1837–41, for E. Worcestershire 1847–49.— *Northwick Park, Moreton-in-Marsh ; Burford, Tenbury ; Carlton Club,* s.w.

NORTON, JOSEPH, Esq., of Nortonthorpe, Yorkshire.
Son of the late Benjamin Norton, Esq., of Clayton West, co. York, by Elizabeth, dau. of Thomas Naylor, Esq., of Clayton West ; *b.* 1800 ; *s.* 1839 ; *m.* 1st 1822 Jane, dau. of George Lee, Esq., late of Clayton West ; 2nd 1864 Emmeline, dau. of the late Charles H. Graham, Esq., of Huddersfield, and has issue,
- • James Lee, *b.* 1823.

Mr. Norton, who holds lands at Nortonthorpe, Clayton West, High Hoyland, Skelmanthorpe, Denby, and Emley, co. York, and at Southport, Lancashire, was formerly a Manufacturer at Clayton. — *Nortonthorpe Hall, Huddersfield.*

+**NORTON**, the late WILLIAM FLETCHER NORTON, Esq., of Elton Manor, Notts.
Natural son of the late Lord Grantley ; *b.* 1790 ; *m.* 1845 Sarah, dau. of the late — Briscoe, Esq., of Cross Deep, Twickenham, and widow, successively, of — Carnac, Esq., of the Hon. East-India Company's Service, and of C. A. Lushington, Esq., of Hastings (she *d.* 1857). Was a Magistrate for cos. Derby, Leicester, Notts, and Sussex, Lord of the Manor of Elton, and Patron of that living. He died 1865, and was *s.* by his nephew.—*Elton Manor, Bingham.*

NORTON. (See under *Grantley, Lord.*)

NORTON. (See *Lowndes-Norton.*)

NORWAY, NEVIL, Esq., of Lawn Cliff, Cornwall.
Only surviving son of the late Capt. John Arthur Norway, R.N., of Flushing, by Amy, dau. of the late William Moorman, Esq.; *b.* 1807 ; *m.* 1st 1843 Judith Catharine, only child of Nicholas Cole, Esq., of Tre-

bvan; 2nd 1866 Catherine Letitia, eldest dau. of the
late Capt. Cary, R.N., and widow of Capt. G. Symons,
28th Regt. Is a Magistrate for Cornwall, and a Commander R.N., retired.—*Lawn Cliff, Flushing, Cornwall.*

NORWICH, Bishop of (the Hon. and Right
Rev. JOHN THOMAS PELHAM, D.D.).
Second surviving son of Thomas, 2nd Earl of Chiches-
ter, by Lady Mary, eldest dau. of Francis, 5th Duke of
Leeds, and brother of Henry Thomas, 3rd Earl of Chi-
chester; *b.* 1811; *m.* 1845 Henrietta, dau. of the late
Thomas William Tatton, Esq., of Wiltenshaw, co.
Chester, and has, with other issue,

* Henry Francis, *b.* 1846.

The Bishop, who was educated at Westminster and Ch.
Ch., Oxford (B.A. 1832, M.A. 1836, D.D. 1857), was
Rector of Burgh Apton 1837–52, Incumbent of Christ
Church, Hampstead, 1852–5, Rector of Marylebone
1855–7; appointed Chaplain to her Majesty 1847; con-
secrated 1857. Patron of 84 livings.—*The Palace,
Norwich.*

NORWOOD, CHARLES MORGAN, Esq.
Eldest son of the late Charles Norwood, Esq., of Ashford, Kent., by Catherine, 2nd dau. of the late C. Morgan, Esq., of Archangel, Russia; *b.* 1825; *m.* 1855
Anna, dau. of late John Henry Blakeney, Esq.; is
a Merchant and Steamship owner of London and Hull;
was twice President of the Hull Chamber of Commerce
and Shipping, and the first Chairman of the Association of Chambers of Commerce of the United Kingdom;
elected M.P. for Hull 1865.—*City Club, E.C.; 23,
Queen's Gate-gardens, w.*

NORWOOD, JOHN DOBREE, Esq., of Ashford,
Kent.
Only son of the late Edward Norwood, Esq., of Guil-
ford Lawn, Dover (who *d.* 1833), by Elizabeth, eldest
dau. of the late Peter Dobrée, Esq., of Beauregard,
Guernsey (she *d.* 1857); *b.* 1827. Editor of the last
edition of Robinson's work on the 'Customs of Kent.'
This family, whose name was originally written North-
wood and Northwode, was resident in Kent *temp.*
Henry II.—*Ashford, Kent.*

+**NOTLEY, JAMES THOMAS BENEDICTUS, Esq.,**
of Combe Sydenham, Somerset.
Second son of the late James Thomas Benedictus Not-
ley, Esq., J.P. and D.L., of Combe Sydenham, by his
second wife Elizabeth, dau. of — Palmer, Esq., of
Stanley, Somerset; *b.* 1830; *s.* 1851. Is Lord of the
Manor of Chillington.—*Combe Sydenham Hall, and
Chillington House, Taunton.*

Heir Pres., his brother Marwood, b. 1832.

NOTT. (See Pyke-Nott.)

NOTTER, RICHARD HENRY, Esq., of Lissacaha,
co. Cork.
Second son of the late Richard Notter, Esq., J.P., of
Carrigdave, co. Cork, and Rock Island Cottage, Baltie-
more, by Mary, dau. of the late Alexander Deane,
Esq., of Cork; *b.* 1822. Is a Magistrate for co. Cork,
and an Architect and Member of the Arcadian Coll.,
Rome.—*Lissacaha Cottage, Schull, co. Cork.*

NOWELL-USTICKE, STEPHEN USTICKE, Esq.,
of Ford Park, Devon.
Eldest son of the late Theophilus Samuel Beauchant,
Esq., Lieut. R.M.A., by Georgiana Ann, only dau. of the
Rev. George Allen, of Sevcock, Cornwall; *b.* 1818; *s.*
1851; *m.* 1838 Lucy Eliza Marianne, 2nd dau. of the late
Rev. R. Stapylton Bree, Vicar of Tintagel, Cornwall,
and has, with other issue,

* Robert Michael, *b.* 1839.
791

Mr. Nowell-Usticke, who assumed by Royal licence in
1852 the surnames of Sir Michael Nowell and the Rev.
R. M. Nowell-Usticke, his maternal uncles, is a Magistrate for Cornwall; late Lieut. Cornwall Rangers Militia.—*Ford Park, Plymouth.*

NOYES, THOMAS HERBERT, Esq., F.G.S.,
F.R.S.L., of Paxhill Park, Sussex.
Eldest son of the late Rev. Thomas Herbert Noyes,
B.A., of East Mascalls, Vicar of Batheaston, Somerset,
by Maria, dau. of Baker John Littlehales, Esq., of
Moulsey Park, Surrey, and sister of Sir Edward B.
Baker, Bart.; *b.* 1800; *s.* 1812; *m.* 1826 Mary Eliza-
beth Halsey, eldest dau. of Joseph Thompson Whately,
Esq., M.P. (who assumed the name of Halsey on his
marriage with the heiress of that family), and has,
with other issue,

* Thomas Herbert, B.A. of Ch. Ch., Oxford, a Magistrate for
Sussex; *b.* 1827.

Mr. Noyes, who was educated at Harrow and Ch. Ch.,
Oxford (B.A. 1822), and called to the Bar at Lincoln's
Inn 1826, is a Magistrate for Sussex.—*Paxhill Park,
Lindfield, Sussex; University Club, s.w.; 32, Dover
Street, w.*

NUGENT, Sir CHARLES, Bart., of Ballinlough
Castle, co. Westmeath (cr. 1795).
Elder surviving son of the late Sir John Nugent, Bart.,
of Ballinlough (who *d.* 1859), by Letitia Maria, dau. of
Charles Whyte Roche, Esq., of Ballygran, co. Limerick;
b. 1847; *s.* his brother as 5th Bart., 1863. Is a Count
of the Holy Roman Empire, and Cornet 17th Lancers.
The first Bart. exchanged the name of O'Reilly for
that of Nugent in 1811.—*Ballinlough Castle, Delvin, co.
Westmeath.*

Heir Pres., his brother John Nicholas, b. 1848.

NUGENT, Sir GEORGE EDMUND, Bart., of West
Harling, Norfolk (cr. 1806).
Eldest son of the late Field-Marshal Sir George Nu-
gent, Bart., G.C.B., of Westhorpe, Bucks, by Maria,
youngest dau. of Major-General Cortlandt Skinner, of
New York; *b.* 1802; *s.* 1849; *m.* 1830 the Hon. Maria
Charlotte, 2nd dau. and heir of Nicholas, 1st Lord Col-
borne (ext.). Educated at Ch. Ch., Oxford (B.A. 1823);
is a J.P. and D.L. for Bucks, and a Magistrate for Nor-
folk; was formerly Capt. and Lieut.-Col. Grenadier
Guards.—*West Harling Hall, East Harling; Travellers'
Club, s.w.; 32, Curzon Street, w.*

*Heir, his son Edmund Charles, a J.P. and D.L. for Norfolk,
late Capt. Grenadier Guards; b. 1829; m. 1863 Evelyn Henrietta, youngest dau. of Lieut.-General Gascoigne, and has
issue, * George Colborne, b. 1864.*

NUGENT, Sir PERCY, Bart., of Donore, co.
Westmeath (cr. 1831).
Eldest son of the late Thomas Fitzgerald, Esq., Commander R.N. (who *d.* 1810), by Mary, dau. of C. Dar-
dis, Esq., of Giggenstown, co. Westmeath; *b.* 1799; *s.*
1831 to the estates of his great-uncle, Sir Percy Nugent,
Bart., whose name he assumed; *m.* 1823 Elizabeth,
onr'dau of Walter Sweetman Esq., of Dublin. Educated at St. Edmund's Coll., Ware, Herts; is a J.P. and
D.L. for co. Westmeath (High Sheriff 1855); was M.P.
for co. Westmeath 1847–52.—*Donore, Mullingar; Stephen's Green Club, Dublin.*

*Heir Pres., his son Walter George, late Capt. 33rd Regt.; b.
1828; m. 1860 Maria, only dau. of the Right Hon. Richard
More O'Ferrall, M.P.*

NUGENT, ANDREW, Esq., of Portaferry, Down-
shire.
Eldest son of the late Col. Patrick John Nugent, of
Portaferry (High Sheriff of co. Down in 1845), by the
Hon. Catherine, dau. of John, 2nd Viscount de Vesci;
b. 1834; *s.* 1857. Educated at Eton and Trinity Coll.,
Cambridge; is a J.P. and D.L. for co. Down, and Mayor

Royal Scots Greys.—*Portaferry, Downshire; Army and Navy Club, s.w.*

Heir Pres., his brother John Vesey, b. 1837.

NUGENT, ANDREW, Esq., of Strangford, Downshire.

Third son of the late Andrew Savage Nugent, Esq., of Portaferry, co. Down, by the Hon. Selina, dau. of Viscount de Vesci; *b.* 1809; *m.* 1841 the Hon. Harriet Margaret, 2nd dau. of Henry, 6th Lord Farnham, and widow of Edward, 3rd Viscount Bangor, and has, with other issue,

  * Walter Andrew, *b.* 1846.

Mr. Nugent, who was educated at the Royal Military Coll., Sandhurst, is a J.P. and D.L. for co. Down (High Sheriff 1867), was formerly a Major in the army. —*Strangford, co. Down ; United Service Club, s.w.*

NUGENT, ANTHONY FRANCIS, Esq., of Pallas, co. Galway.

Eldest son of the late William Thomas Nugent, Esq., of Pallas, by Mary Catharine, only dau. of the late Michael Bellew, Esq., of Mount Bellew, co. Galway; *b.* 1805; *s.* 1851 ; *m.* 1829 Ann, dau. of the late Malachy Daly, Esq., of Raford, co. Galway, and has, with other issue,

  * William, Capt. 9th Foot; *b.* 1832 ; *m.* 1866 Emily Margaret, dau. of Andrew William Blake, Esq., of Furlough, co. Galway.

Mr. Nugent, who was educated at Trinity Coll., Dublin, is heir presumptive to the Earldom of Westmeath ; his direct ancestor was created Lord Riverston by James II., but the title has not been acknowledged.—*Pallas, Tynagh, co. Galway ; Kildare Street Club, Dublin.*

NUGENT, ARTHUR, Esq., of Cranna, co. Galway.

Eldest son of the late Hon. Arthur Anthony Nugent, of Cranna (2nd son of Arthur, 4th Lord Riverston), by Maria, dau. of Richard Gore, Esq., and cousin of A. F. Nugent, Esq., of Pallas (whom see); *b.* 1805; *s.* 1858; *m.* 1847 Ella, only dau. of Thomas Lalor Cooke, Esq., of Parsonstown, co. Galway, and has, with other issue,

  * William Arthur Antisel, *b.* 1859.

Mr. Nugent is descended from Richard, 2nd Earl of Westmeath, and 12th Baron of Delvin.—*Cranna, Portumna, co. Galway ; Hibernian Hotel, Dublin ; Volunteer Service Club, s.w.*

NUGENT, CHRISTOPHER JAMES, Esq., of Killasowna, co. Longford, and Lattoon, co. Cavan.

Eldest son of the late John Christopher Nugent, Esq., of Killasowna, by Rose, youngest dau. of Richard O'Ferrall, Esq., of Balyna, co. Kildare ; *b.* 1812 ; *s.* 1830 ; is a Grand Juror of co. Longford.—*Killasowna, Granard, co. Longford ; 40, Belvedere Place, Dublin.*

Heir Pres., his brother Ambrose, b. 1814.

NUGENT, EDMOND ROBERT, Esq., of Bobsgrove, co. Cavan.

Only son of the late Oliver Nugent, Esq., of Farrenconnell, co. Cavan, by Sophia Anna Maria, 2nd dau. of the late Robert Johnston, Esq., of Kinlough House, co. Leitrim, and grandson of the late Christopher Edmond John Nugent, Esq.; *b.* 1839 ; *s.* his grandfather 1853. Educated at Eton and Trinity Coll., Dublin. Is a Magistrate for cos. Cavan and Meath.—*Bobsgrove, Mount Nugent, co. Cavan.*

Heir Pres., his uncle Richard Nugent, Esq., late of Farrenconnell House, co. Cavan, a Magistrate for cos. Cavan and

Meath (fifth son of the late Christopher Edmond John Nugent, of Farrenconnell, by Sophia Maria, dau. of William Rathbone, Esq.) ; *b.* 1822 ; *m.* 1848 Amelia St. George, dau. of the late Most Rev. Edward Stopford, D.D., Lord Bishop of Meath, and has, with other issue, * Edward Stopford, *b.* 1851.

NUGENT, JOHN JAMES, Esq., of Clonlost, co. Westmeath.

Eldest son of the late Lieut.-Col. James Nugent, by Isabella, dau. of Andrew Parke, Esq., of Dunnally, co. Sligo; *b.* 1812; *s.* 1832; *m.* 1st 1844 Anne Grahame, dau. of Sir John Robison, K.H. ; 2nd 1851 Helen, dau. of Thomas Grahame, Esq., of Loudwater, Herts, and has issue,

  * Isabella Euphemia Anne.

Mr. Nugent, who was educated at Shrewsbury, is a J.P. and D.L. for co. Westmeath (High Sheriff 1855), and Major Westmeath Rifles; was formerly Capt. 3rd Dragoon Guards.—*Clonlost, Killucan, co. Westmeath ; Junior United Service Club, s.w.*

NUGENT. (See under *Westmeath, Marquis of.*)

NUGENT. (See *Greville-Nugent*, under *Greville, of Clonyn.*)

NUNN, EDWARD WESTBY, Esq., of St. Margaret's, co. Wexford.

Eldest son of the late Joshua Nunn, Esq., of St. Margaret's and of Hill Castle, co. Wexford, by Mary, dau. of the late Edward Westby, Esq., of High Park, co. Wicklow; *b.* 1818 ; *m.* 1852 Emily, dau. of the Rev. Hugh Stewart, and has, with other issue,

  * Joshua Arthur, *b.* 1853.

Mr. Nunn, who was educated at Eton and Christ's Coll., Cambridge, is a Magistrate for co. Wexford (High Sheriff 1849).—*St. Margaret's, co. Wexford ; Conservative Club, s.w.*

NUNN, JOHN, Esq., of Silverspring, co. Wexford.

Fifth son of the late Joshua Nunn, Esq., of St. Margaret's, by Frances, dau. and co-heir of Joseph Nunn, Esq., of Hill Castle; *b.* 1801; *m.* 1824 Harriett, dau. of Ebenezer Radford Rowe, Esq., of Ballyharty, co. Wexford, and has, with other issue,

  * John Joshua, *b.* 1825.

Mr. Nunn, who was educated at Trinity Coll., Dublin, is a Magistrate for co. Wexford.—*Silverspring, Bullycayly, co. Wexford.*

NUNN, THOMAS WILLIAM, Esq., of Bromley Hall, Essex.

Only son of the late Thomas Nunn, Esq., of Lawford House, Essex, by Maria, dau. of William Newman, Esq., of Nether Hall, Bradfield ; *b.* 1832 ; *s.* his cousin 1863 ; *m.* 1858 Annie, dau. of the Rev. H. G. Evans, Rector of Stradishall, Suffolk. Educated at Rugby ; is a Magistrate for Essex.—*Bromley Hall, Colchester.*

NUTTALL, JOHN FREEMAN, Esq., of Titlour, co. Wicklow.

Eldest son of the late John Nuttall, Esq., of Titlour, by Dorothea, dau. of the late Daniel Falkiner, Esq., of Abbotstown, co. Dublin ; *b.* 1810 ; *s.* 1849 ; *m.* 1838 Lucinda Helena, dau. of William Mackintosh, Esq., of Dublin, and has, with other issue,

  * John, *b.* 184-.

Mr. Nuttall is a Magistrate for co. Wicklow.—*Titlour, Newtown Mt. Kennedy, co. Wicklow.*

O

OAKDEN, RALPH, Esq., of Ladham House, Kent.
Eldest son of the late William Oakden, Esq., of Lee House, co. Stafford, by Elizabeth, dau. of Isaac Mather, Esq., of Hackney, Middlesex; b. 1806; m. 1838 Anne, dau. of Wm. Rollisson, Esq., and has, with other issue,
* Ralph, b. 1840.
Mr. Oakden is a Dep.-Lieut. for Kent.—Ladham House, Goudhurst, Staplehurst.

OAKELEY, Sir CHARLES WILLIAM ATHOLL, Bart. (cr. 1790).
Eldest son of the late Very Rev. Sir Herbert Oakeley, Bart., formerly Dean of Bocking, by Atholl Keturah, dau. of the Rev. Lord Charles Murray-Aynsley (youngest son of John, 3rd Duke of Athole); b. 1828; s. 1845; m. 1860 Ellen, dau. of John Meeson Parsons, Esq., of Angley Park, near Cranbrook, Kent. Educated at Eton and Ch. Ch., Oxford; late Capt. Bengal Cavalry.—Angley Park, Cranbrook, Kent; East India Club, s.w.
Heir, his son Charles John, b. 1862.

OAKELEY, the Rev. ARTHUR, of Oakeley, Salop.
Fourth but eldest surviving son of the late Rev. Herbert Oakeley, D.D., of Oakeley, Prebendary of Worcester, by Catherine, dau. of John Bolland, Esq., of Clapham; b. 1815; s. his brother 1851. Educated at Eton and New Inn Hall, Oxford (B.A. 1840, M.A. 1842); appointed Rector of Lydham 1843; is a Magistrate for co. Salop; is head of the Oakeley family, a branch of which is represented by the Baronet of the same name.—Oakeley, Bishop's Castle.
Heir Pres., his brother, Henry (of Roveries Hall. Bishop's Castle), a Magistrate for co. Salop, and a Commander R.N.; b. 1816; m. 1847 Emily Letitia, dau. of Col. Trelawny, R.A., and has, with other issue, * Arthur Henry, b. 1853.

OAKELEY, WILLIAM EDWARD, Esq.
Eldest son of the late William Oakeley, Esq., of Glen William, co. Carnarvon, by Mary Maria, only dau. of the late Sir Edward Miles. K.C.B., and grandson of the late Sir Charles Oakeley, Bart.; b. 1828; m. 1860 the Hon. Mary, 2nd dau. of Sophia (in her own right), Baroness de Clifford, and has issue,
* A son, b. 1864.
Educated at Eton and C.C.C., Oxford; is Capt. Staffordshire Yeomanry.—Residence: Cliff House, Alcerstone, Leicestershire; Arthur's and Boodle's Clubs, s.w.

OAKES, Sir REGINALD LOUIS, Bart. (cr. 1815).
Eldest son of the late Henry Frederick Oakes, Esq., of Louvain. by Mary Donety, dau. of John Ward, Esq., of Huntingdonshire; b. 1847; s. his grandfather as 4th Bart. 1830.—Louvain, Belgium.
Heir Pres., his uncle. Hildebrand Henry; b. 1829; m. 1852 Sophia, dau. of J. C. Crump, Esq., and widow of J. Bond, Esq.

OAKES, HENRY JAMES, Esq., of Nowton, Suffolk.
Eldest son of the late Orbell Ray Oakes, Esq., of Nowton Court, by Elizabeth Frances, dau. of John Plampin, Esq., of Chadacre Hall; b. 1796; s. 1837; m. 1820 Mary Anne, dau. of the Rev. Robert Porteus, and has, with other issue,
* James Henry Porteus, J.P. and D.L. for Suffolk; late M.P. for Bury St. Edmund's; b. 1821.
Mr. Oakes, who was educated at Reading and Em-
706

manuel Coll., Cambridge (B.A. 1817, M.A. 1820) is a J.P. and D.L. for Suffolk (High Sheriff 1847), and Patron of 1 living.—Nowton Court, Bury St. Edmund's; Conservative Club, s.w.

+OAKLEY, RICHARD BANNER, Esq., of Oswaldkirk Hall, Yorkshire.
Son of the late R. Oakley, Esq., of Oswaldkirk Hall; b. 1833; m. 1859 Mary Anne, only dau. of William Field, Esq., of Quarry House, Shrewsbury. Is Lord of the Manor of Oswaldkirk.—Oswaldkirk Hall, Helmsley; 41, Norfolk Square, w.

+O'BEIRNE, HUGH, Esq., of Jamestown Lodge, co. Leitrim.
Son of the late H. O'Beirne, Esq., of Jamestown; b. 18—. Is a J.P. and D.L. for co. Leitrim.—Jamestown Lodge, Drumsna, co. Leitrim.

O'BEIRNE, JAMES LYSTER, Esq.
Eldest son of the late Edmund O'Beirne, Esq., by Mary, dau. of James Lyster, Esq., of Lysterfield, co. Roscommon; b. 1820; educated at Trinity Coll., Dublin; elected M.P. for Cashel 1865.—Reform and Garrick Clubs, s.w.; Stafford Club, w.; 36, Sackville Street, w.

OBRÉ, RALPH SMITH, Esq., of Clantilew, co. Armagh.
Third but only surviving son of the late Edward Obré, Esq., of Clantilew, and grandson of Francis Obré, Esq.; b. 1808; m. 1844 Jane Caroline, 2nd dau. of the late Henry Bond, Esq., of Bondville, and has, with other issue,
* Edward, b. 1845.
Mr. Obré, who is a Magistrate for co. Armagh, represents a family of French extraction.—Clantilew, Loughgall, co. Armagh.

O'BRIEN, Sir PATRICK, Bart., of Borris-in-Ossory, Queen's Co.
Eldest son of the late Sir Timothy O'Brien. Bart.. J.P. and D.L. (who was M.P. for Cashel 1846-59), by Catherine, dau. of Edward Murphy, Esq., of Flemingtown, co. Dublin; b. 1823; s. 1862; m. 1866 Ida Sophia, widow of Lieut.-General Perry, and dau. of the late Commander Parlby, R.N. Educated at Trinity Coll.. Dublin (M.A. 1845); called to the Irish Bar 1844; is a Dep. Lieut. for Dublin, and a Magistrate for King's Co., for which he has been M.P. since 1852.—Borris-in-Ossory. Queen's Co.; University Club, Dublin; Reform Club, s.w.; 21, Bryanston Square, w.
Heir Pres. his brother Timothy b. 1827; m. 1860 Mary, only dau. of Andrew C. O'Dwyer, Esq.

O'BRIEN, the Hon. ROBERT, of Old Church, co. Limerick.
Fourth son of the late Sir Edward O'Brien. Bart.. of Dromoland, co. Clare, by Charlotte, eldest dau. and co-heir of the late Wm. Smith, Esq., of Cahirmoyle, and brother of the late Wm. Smith, Esq., of Cahirmoyle, and brother of Lord Inchiquin; b. 1809; m. 1835 Ellinor, dau. of the late Sir Aubrey de Vere, Bart., of Curragh Chase, co. Limerick, and has, with other issue,
* Aubrey Vere, Lieut. 60th Royal Rifles; b. 1837.
Mr. O'Brien is a Magistrate for cos. Clare and Limerick.—Old Church, Limerick.

+ O'BRIEN, ACHESON, Esq., of Rockfield, co.
Leitrim.

Son of the late A. O'Brien, Esq., of Rockfield; *b.* 18—.
Is a J.P. and D.L. for co. Leitrim.—*Rockfield, Killeshandra, co. Leitrim.*

O'BRIEN, DONAT JOHN HOSTE, Esq., of Butler's
Green, Herts.

Eldest son of the late Admiral O'Brien, of Yew House,
Hoddesdon, Herts, by Hannah, youngest dau. of the
late John Walmsley, Esq., of Castlemeer, co. Lancaster;
b. 1826; *s.* 1857; *m.* 1861 Martha Shepherd, dau. of
the Rev. R. W. Morice, Incumbent of Hoddesdon. Educated at Eton and St. John's Coll., Cambridge (B.A.
1848); called to the Bar at the Inner Temple 1852, and
went the Home Circuit; is a Magistrate for Herts and
Lord of the Manor of Aston, Herts.— *Aston House,
Stevenage, Herts ; Butler's Green Hall, Ware, Herts.*

Heir Pres., his brother William Edward Freeman, late Capt.
54th Regt.; *b.* 1827.

O'BRIEN, GEORGE, Esq., of Birchfield, co.
Clare.

Eldest surviving son of the late Cornelius O'Brien, Esq.,
M.P., of Birchfield (who was a Magistrate for co. Clare),
by Margaret, dau. of Peter Long, Esq., of Waterford,
and widow of James O'Brien, Esq.; *b.* 1810 ; *s.* 1860.
Educated at Trinity Coll., Dublin; is a Magistrate for
co. Clare.—*Birchfield, Ennistymon, co. Clare ; 20, Summer Hill, Dublin.*

O'BRIEN, EDWARD WILLIAM, Esq., of Cahirmoyle, co. Limerick.

Eldest son of the late William Smith O'Brien, Esq.,
M.P., of Cahirmoyle, by Lucy Caroline, eldest dau. of
Joseph Gabbett, Esq., of High Park, co. Limerick ; *b.*
1837 ; *s.* 1864 ; *m.* 1863 Mary, 2nd dau. of the Hon.
Stephen E. Spring-Rice, of Mount Trenchard, co. Limerick, and has, by her, who *d.* 1868, with other issue,

*   William Dermot, *b.* 1865.

Mr. O'Brien, who was educated at Trinity Coll., Dublin
(B.A. 1859), is a Magistrate for co. Limerick.—*Cahirmoyle, Newcastle West, co. Limerick.*

O'BRIEN, HENRY DE STAFFORD, Esq., of Blatherwycke, Northamptonshire, Tixover,
Rutlandshire, and Crathoe Woods, co.
Clare.

Eldest son of the late Stafford O'Brien, Esq., J.P., of
Blatherwycke Park (who was High Sheriff of Rutland
1809), by the Hon. Emma, sister of Charles, 1st Earl
of Gainsborough ; *b.* 1813 ; *s.* 1864 ; *m.* 1841 Lucy, 3rd
dau. of the late Rev. Henry William Nevile, of Walcot
Park, co. Lincoln, and has, with other issue,

*   Horace, Lieut. 2nd Dragoons ; *b.* 1842.

Mr. O'Brien, who was educated at Harrow and Trinity
Coll., Cambridge (B.A. 1835, M.A. 1838), is a Magistrate for co. Northampton (High Sheriff 1868), Lord of
the Manors of Blatherwycke and Tixover, and Patron
of 1 living.—*Blatherwycke Park, Wansford ; Tixover,
Stamford ; Crathoe Woods, near Limerick.*

+ O'BRIEN, JAMES, Esq., of Ballinalackin, co.
Clare.

Eldest son of the late John O'Brien, Esq., M.P., of Ballinalackin, by Mary, dau. of the late Jeremiah Murphy,
Esq.; *b.* 1833 ; *s.* 1855. Is a J.P. and D.L. for co.
Clare (High Sheriff 1858).—*Ballinalackin, Ennistymon,
co. Clare.*

O'BRIEN, JAMES, Esq.

Third son of the late James O'Brien, Esq., of Limerick,
by Margaret, dau. of Peter Long, Esq.; *b.* 1806; *m.*
1836 Margaret, dau. of the late Thomas Segrave, Esq.,
of Cabra. Educated at Trinity Coll., Dublin (B.A.
1827); called to the Irish Bar 1830; became Serjeant-

at-Law 1848, and a Bencher of King's Inn, Dublin,
1849; was M.P. for Limerick 1854–8; appointed a
Judge of the Queen's Bench, Ireland, 1858.—*Beulah
House, Dalkey, Dublin ; 92, Stephen's Green, Dublin.*

O'BRIEN. (See under *Inchiquin, Lord.*)

O'BRIEN. (See *Stafford.*)

+ O'BYRNE, WILLIAM RICHARD, Esq., F.R.G.S.,
of Cabinteely, co. Dublin.

Elder son of the late Robert O'Byrne, Esq. (who *d.*
1861), by Martha, dau. of Joseph Clarke, Esq., of Norwich ; *b.* 1823 ; *s.* his aunt, Miss Georgiana Byrne,
1864 ; *m.* 1851 Emily, dau. of John Handy, Esq., of
Malmesbury, Wilts, and has issue,

*   Five daughters.

Mr. O'Byrne, who was educated at Trinity Coll., Dublin,
is the author of the 'Naval Biography.'—*Cabinteely,
Loughlinstown, co. Dublin ; Cranford, Hounslow, Middlesex.*

O'CALLAGHAN, CHARLES GEORGE, Esq., of
Ballinahinch, co. Clare.

Eldest son of the late Cornelius O'Callaghan, Esq., of
Ballinahinch, by Frances, dau. of Henry Brady, Esq.,
of Raheens, co. Clare (who *m.* 2nd the Rev. Lord William Somerset, son of Henry Charles, 6th Duke of Beaufort); *b.* 1821 ; *m.* 1856 Marian, dau. of J. Kelly, Esq.,
of Dublin, and has, with other issue,

*   Frances Mary, *b.* 1856.

Mr. O'Callaghan, who was educated at Trinity Coll., Oxford, is a J.P. and D.L. for co. Clare (High Sheriff
1855); was formerly Capt. 1st Dragoon Guards.—*Ballinahinch, Tulla, co. Clare ; Army and Navy Club, s.w.*

Heir Pres., his brother Henry, *b.* 1825 ; *m.* 1852 Laura, dau. of
the Rev. J. Parsons.

O'CALLAGHAN, Capt. JOHN, of Maryfort, co.
Clare.

Eldest son of the late George O'Callaghan, Esq., of
Maryfort, by Mary, dau. of John Westropp, Esq., of
Fort Ann, co. Clare ; *b.* 1829 ; *s.* 1849 ; *m.* 1859 Mary
Johnson, dau. of John Westropp, Esq., of Attyflin, co.
Limerick. Is a Magistrate for co. Clare ; late Capt.
62nd Regt.—*Maryfort, Tulla, co. Clare ; Army and
Navy Club s.w.*

O'CALLAGHAN, PATRICK, Esq., of Cookridge,
Yorkshire.

Eldest surviving son of the late Edward O'Callaghan,
Esq., of Coolnaleen House, co. Clare (of the ancient
branch of the O'Callaghans at Bantire, co. Cork); *b.*
1804 ; *m.* 1st 1826 Marcella, dau. of the late George
Russell, Esq., of Limerick ; 2nd 1841 Mary, eldest dau.
of the late John Ballantyne Dykes, Esq., of Dovenby Hall,
Cumberland, and widow of John Marshall, Esq., Jun.,
M.P., of Headingley, co. York. and has by the former,

*   Edward, late Capt. 16th Regt.; *b.* 1827.

Mr. O'Callaghan was formerly an Officer in Prince Albert's Own Hussars.—*Cookridge Hall, Leeds.*

O'CALLAGHAN. (See under *Lismore, Viscount.*)

OCHTERLONY, Sir CHARLES METCALFE, Bart.,
of Ochterlony, Forfarshire (cr. 1823).

Eldest son of the late Roderick Peregrine Ochterlony,
Esq., of Delhi, by Sarah, dau. of Lieut.-Col. J. Nelley,
Bengal Engineers, H.E.I. Co.'s Service ; *b.* 1817 ; *s.* his
kinsman as 2nd Bart. 1825 ; *m.* 1844 Sarah, elder dau.
of William P. Tribe, Esq. Educated at Edinburgh and
Haileybury Coll.; is a Magistrate for co. Forfar; was
formerly in the Indian Civil Service.—*Ochterlony House,
Arbroath, N.B. ; Residence : St. Andrew's, Fife, N.B.*

Heir, his son David Ferguson, *b.* 1848.

OCKHAM. (See under *Lovelace, Earl of*.)

O'CONNELL, CHARLES, Esq., of Ballynabloun, co. Kerry.

Son of the late Daniel O'Connell, Esq., of Portmagee, co. Kerry, by Teresa, youngest dau. of George Lombard, Esq., of Cork; *b.* 1805; *m.* 1832 his cousin Catharine, 2nd dau. of the late Daniel O'Connell, Esq., of Darrynane Abbey, and has, with other issue,

    • Daniel, *b.* 1842.

Mr. O'Connell, who is a Magistrate for co. Kerry, and Resident Magistrate in Bantry, was M.P. for co. Kerry 1833–4.—*Ballynabloun, Cahirciveen, co. Kerry.*

O'CONNELL, DANIEL, Esq., of Darrynane Abbey, co. Kerry.

Eldest son of the late Maurice O'Connell, Esq., M.P., of Darrynane, by Mary Frances, dau. of the late J. Bindon Scott, Esq., of Cahiracon, co. Clare, and grandson of the late Daniel O'Connell, Esq., M.P.; *b.* 1836; *s.* 1853; *m.* 1861 Isabella Ellen, eldest dau. of Denis Shyne Lawlor, Esq., and has issue. Mr. O'Connell, who is a J.P. and D.L. for Kerry (High Sheriff, 1860), was a Midshipman R.N. 1850–3.—*Darrynane Abbey, Cahirciveen, co. Kerry.*

    Heir Pres., his brother John, *b.* 1839.

O'CONNELL, Capt. DANIEL.

Fourth son of the late Daniel O'Connell, Esq., M.P., of Darrynane, co. Kerry, by Mary, dau. of T. O'Connell, Esq.; *b.* 1820 ; *m.* 1866 Ellen, only dau. of E. Foster, Esq., of the Elms, Cambridge, and has issue a dau.,

    • Elly Mary Foster.

Mr. O'Connell was M.P. for Dundalk, 1846–7, for Waterford 1847–8, and for Tralee 1853–63; appointed a Commissioner of Income Tax 1863; late Capt. Kerry Militia.—*Reform Club*, s.w.; *Garrick Club*, w.c.; 5, *Onslow Square, s.w.*

O'CONNELL, JAMES, Esq., of Lakeview, co. Kerry.

Only surviving son of the late Morgan O'Connell, Esq., of Carhen, co. Kerry, by Catharine, dau. of John O'Mullan, Esq., of White Church, co. Cork; *b.* 1786; *m.* 1818 Jane, dau. of the late Charles O'Donoghue, Esq., of The Glens, co. Kerry, and has, with other issue,

    • Maurice James, J.P. and D.L. for co. Kerry (High Sheriff 1850) ; *b.* 1822 ; *m.* 1854 Emily, dau. of the late Rear-Admiral Sir R. O'Conor, and has issue.

Mr. O'Connell, who is a Magistrate for co. Kerry, represents a younger branch of the O'Connells of Darrynane (whom see).—*Lakeview House, Killarney.*

O'CONNELL, MORGAN JOHN, Esq., of Grena, co. Kerry.

Elder son of the late John O'Connell, Esq., of Grena, by Mary, dau. of William Coppinger, Esq., and nephew of the late Daniel O'Connell, Esq., M.P.; *b.* 1811 ; *m.* 1865 Mary, dau. of Charles Bianconi, Esq., of Longfield, Cashel, co. Tipperary. Educated at Trinity Coll., Dublin ; is a Magistrate for co. Kerry; was M.P. for co. Kerry 1835–52.—*Grena, Killarney, co. Kerry; Garrick Club, s.w.; 4, Pump Court, Temple, e.c.*

O'CONNOR, FRANCIS MACNAMARA, Esq., of Ballyclamesil, co. Kerry.

Only son of the late Gerald Fitzgerald O'Connor, Esq., of Ballyclamesil, by Matilda Mary, 4th dau. of the late Major William Nugent Macnamara, M.P., of Doolen, co. Clare; *b.* 1819 ; *s.* 1861. This family were formerly Princes of Munster. — *Ballyclamesil, Causeway, co. Kerry; Day Place, Tralee.*

O'CONNOR, PETER, Esq., of Cairnsfoot, co. Sligo.

Youngest son of the late Denis O'Connor, Esq., of Edenburne, by Bridget Ellen, dau. of Mr. Timothy

Ronyane, of Kilmacowen ; *b.* 1803; *m.* 1848 Ellen, youngest dau. of Timothy O'Connor, Esq., of Sligo. Is a Magistrate for co. Sligo (High Sheriff 1866).—*Cairnsfoot, Sligo.*

O'CONNOR, VALENTINE O'BRIEN, Esq., of Rockfield House, co. Dublin.

Third son of the late Valentine O'Connor, Esq., of Rockfield House, by Margaret, only dau. and heir of David Henchy, Esq., of Rockfield, co. Dublin, and Cloughlineigh and Garrane, co. Tipperary ; *b.* 1811 ; *m.* 1838 Monica, dau. of William Errington, Esq., of High Warden, and has, with other issue, an only son,

    • William, *b.* 1850.

Mr. O'Connor, who was educated at Stonyhurst Coll., is a J.P. and D.L. for the city of Dublin (High Sheriff 1853).—*Rockfield House, Blackrock, co. Dublin ; Royal Irish Yacht Club and Stephen's-Green Club, Dublin ; Beresford Place, Dublin.*

O'CONNOR-HENCHY. (See *Henchy*.)

O'CONOR, ARTHUR, Esq., of Elphin, co. Roscommon.

Second son of the late Matthew O'Conor, Esq., of Mount Druid, co. Roscommon, by Priscilla, dau. of — Forbes, Esq.; *b.* 181–; *m.* 1853 Katharine, dau. of the late Maurice Blake, Esq., of Ballinafad, co. Mayo, and has issue,

    • Arthur Matthew, *b.* 1855.

Mr. O'Conor is a Magistrate for co. Roscommon (High Sheriff 1857).—*Elphin House, co. Roscommon.*

O'CONOR, DENIS, Esq., of Mount Druid, co. Roscommon.

Eldest son of the late Matthew O'Conor, Esq., of Mount Druid, by Priscilla, dau. of — Forbes, Esq., and cousin of the late O'Conor Don, M.P.; *b.* 1808 ; *m.* 1841 Margaret Emily, dau. of Nicholas Mahon Power, Esq., of Faithlegg House, co. Waterford, and has issue,

    • Charles, *b.* 1847.

Mr. O'Conor, who was educated at Stonyhurst Coll., is a J.P. and D.L. for co. Roscommon (High Sheriff 1836–7), and a Magistrate for cos. Sligo and Mayo.—*Mount Druid, French Park, co. Roscommon.*

O'CONOR, PATRICK HUGH, Esq., of Dundermot, co. Roscommon.

Eldest son of the late Patrick O'Conor, Esq., J.P., of Dundermot (who was High Sheriff of co. Cork 1854–5), by June, dau. of Christopher French, Esq., J.P., of Frenchtown ; *b.* 1838 ; *s.* 1859. Educated at Stonyhurst Coll. Is a Magistrate for co. Roscommon (High Sheriff 1860).—*Dundermot, Ballymoe, co. Roscommon.*

O'CONOR, RODERIC, Esq., of Milton, co. Roscommon.

Eldest son of the late Roderic O'Conor, Esq., of Milton, by his 2nd wife Bridget, dau. of James Brown, Esq., of Brownville, co. Galway ; *b.* 1794 ; *m.* 1824 Cecilia, dau. of John McDonnell, Esq., of Carnason, and has, with other issue,

    • Roderic, a Magistrate for co. Roscommon (High Sheriff 1867) ; *b.* 1825 ; *m.* 1854 Ellen, dau. of Joseph Browne, Esq., J.P., of Elm Grove, co. Meath, and has issue, • Roderic, *b.* 1860.

Mr. O'Conor, who was educated at Trinity Coll., Dublin, and called to the Irish Bar 1828, is a Magistrate for co. Roscommon (High Sheriff 1859.)—*Milton, Castle Plunket, co. Roscommon ; 48, Leeson Park, Dublin.*

O'CONOR-DON, CHARLES OWEN (The O'Conor-Don), of Belanagre, co. Roscommon.

Eldest son of the late Denis O'Conor-Don, M.P., of Belanagre, by Mary, dau. of Maurice Blake, of Tower Hill, co. Mayo; *b.* 1838 ; *s.* 1847 ; *m.* 1868 Georgiana

Mary, 3rd dau. of Thos. A. Perry, Esq., of Bitham House, co. Warwick. Is a Magistrate for co. Roscommon; elected M.P. for co. Roscommon 1860.—*Bclanagre, French-park, co. Roscommon ; Clonalis, Castlerea, co. Roscommon ; Reform Club*, s.w.; 29, *Half-moon Street*, w.

Heir Pres., his brother Denis Maurice, *b.* 1840.

ODDIE, HENRY HOYLE, Esq., of. Colney Herts.
Eldest son of the late Henry Hoyle Oddie, Esq., J.P., of Colney House, by Georgiana, second dau. of George Woodford Thellusson, Esq., of Aldenham, Herts; *b.* 1816; *s.* 1844 Caroline Dorcas, dau. of the Rev. Robert Gream, Rector of Rotherfield, Sussex, and has, with other issue,

    • Henry Hoyle, late Ensign 15th Regt.; *b.* 1846.

Mr. Oddie, who was educated at Eton and Trinity Coll. Cambridge (B.A. 1837, M.A. 1840), is a Magistrate for Herts.—*Colney House, St. Alban's.*

+**ODELL**, EDWARD, Esq., of Carriglea, co. Waterford.
Second son of the late John Odell, Esq., of Carriglea; *b.* 1808; *s.* his brother John 1847; *m.* 1838 Harriet, dau. of the late Sir John Nugent Humble, Bart. Educated at Ch. Ch., Oxford (D.A. 1830, M.A. 1834). Is a Magistrate for co. Waterford.—*Carriglea, Dungarvan.*

O'DONELL, Sir RICHARD ANNESLEY, Bart., of Newport House, co. Mayo (cr. 1780).
Second son of the late Sir Neale O'Donell, Bart., of Newport House, by Lady Catharine, dau. of Richard, 2nd Earl Annesley; *b.* 1808; *s.* as 4th Bart. 1828; *m.* 1831 Mary, dau. of George Clendining, Esq. Is a J.P. and D.L. for co. Mayo (High Sheriff 1834); was Vice-Lieut. of co. Mayo 1854-6.—*Newport House, co. Mayo.*

Heir, his son George Clendining, *b.* 1832 ; *m.* 1865 Mary Stratford, eldest dau. of the late Euseby Stratford Kirwan, Esq., of Browne House, co. Longford.

O'DONNELL, Sir CHARLES ROUTLEGE, Knt., of Trugh, co. Clare (cr. 1835).
Son of the late Col. Henry A. O'Donnell, C.B., of the H.E.I.Co.'s Service ; *b.* 1794 ; *m.* 1826 Catherine Anne, dau. of the late Major-General James Patrick Murray, C.B., and cousin of Lord Elibank. Is a General in the Army, and Col. 18th Hussars ; late Secretary to the Commander-in-Chief in Canada ; is a Knight of St. John of Jerusalem, and a Member of the Royal Irish Academy.—*Trugh, Limerick ; United Service Club*, s.w.

O'DONOGHUE, DANIEL (the O'Donoghue of the Glens), co. Kerry.
Only son of the late O'Donoghue, of the Glens, by Jane, eldest dau. of John O'Connell, Esq., of Grena, co. Kerry, niece of the late Daniel O'Connell : *b.* 1833 ; *s.* 1833 ; *m.* 1858 Mary Sophie, dau. of Sir John Ennis, Bart., by whom he has issue,

    • A son, *b.* 1859.

The O'Donoghue, who was educated at Stonyhurst Coll., was formerly a Magistrate for cos. Cork and Kerry, and Major Kerry Militia; was M.P. for co. Tipperary 1857-65 ; elected M.P. for Tralee 1865.—*The Glens, Flesk, co. Kerry ; Stafford Club*, w.

O'DONOVAN, MORGAN WILLIAM, Esq., of Montpelier, co. Cork.
Eldest son of the late Rev. Morgan O'Donovan, by Alicia, eldest dau. of William Jones, Esq., of Cork ; *b.* 1796 ; *s.* 1839 ; *m.* 1844 Susanna, 2nd dau. of William Armstrong Creed, Esq. Educated at Trinity Coll., Dublin (B.A. 1817), called to the Irish Bar 1819. This family was formerly of Rahine Castle and Ballincolleh, in West Carbery, co. Cork.—*Montpelier, Cork.*

Heir, his brother Henry Winthrop (of Lisnard, Skibbereen, co. Cork), M.A. of Trinity Coll., Dublin ; a Magistrate for co. Cork ; *b.* 1811 ; *m.* 1848 Amelia, 5th dau. of Gerald De Courcy O'Grady, Esq., of Kilballyowen.

O'DWYER, ANDREW CAREW, Esq., of Orlagh, co. Dublin.
Son of the late Joseph O'Dwyer, Esq., Merchant of Waterford ; *b.* 1800 ; *m.* 1828 Selina, dau. of the late Sir R. Gillespie, K.C.B. Called to the Irish Bar 1830 ; is a Magistrate for co. Dublin ; was M.P. for Drogheda 1833-5 ; formerly held the patent office of Secondary of the Exchequer of Ireland until its abolition.—*Orlagh, Templeogue, co. Dublin ; Reform Club*, s.w.

O'FARRELL, CHARLES, Esq., of Dalyston, co. Galway.
Only son of the late James Carroll, Esq., of Edgeworthstown, co. Longford, by Margaret, dau. of James Farrell, Esq., of Minard, and nephew of the late Charles Farrell, Esq., M.D., of Dalyston; *b.* 1825 ; *s.* 1855. Assumed the name of Farrell in 1855 on succeeding to his uncle's property, and subsequently resumed, by Royal licence, the ancient orthography of that name. Is a Magistrate for co. Galway.—*Dalyston, Loughrea, co. Galway.*

Heir Pres., his sister Eliza.

O'FERRALL, the Right Hon. RICHARD MORE-, of Balyna, co. Kildare.
Eldest son of the late Ambrose More-O'Ferrall, Esq., of Balyna, by Anne, dau. of the late John Bagot, Esq., of Castle Bagot ; *b.* 1797 ; *m.* 1839 the Hon. Matilda, dau. of Thomas Anthony, 3rd Viscount Southwell, and has, with other issue,

    • Ambrose, *b.* 1846.

Mr. O'Ferrall, who is a J.P. and D.L. for co. Kildare and a Magistrate for co. Meath, was M.P. for co. Kildare 1830-47, for co. Longford 1851-2 ; and again for co. Kildare 1859-65 ; a Lord of the Treasury 1835-9 ; Secretary of the Admiralty 1839-41, of the Treasury 1841, and Governor of Malta 1847-51.—*Balyna House, Enfield, co. Kildare ; Brooks's and Reform Clubs*, s.w.

O'FERRALL, EDWARD MORE-, Esq., of Kildangan, co. Kildare.
Fifth son of the late Ambrose More-O'Ferrall, Esq., of Balyna, co. Kildare, by Anne, dau. of the late John Bagot, Esq., of Castle Bagot ; *b.* 1805 ; *m.* 1849 Susan, only dau. and heir of the late Dominick O'Reilly, Esq., of Kildangan, and by her, who *d.* 1854, has issue,

    • Dominick, *b.* 1854.

Mr. O'Ferrall is a Grand Juror of co. Kildare.—*Kildangan, Monastrevan, co. Kildare.*

O'FERRALL, JOHN LEWIS MORE-, Esq., of Lizard, co. Longford.
Second son of the late Ambrose More-O'Ferrall, Esq., of Balyna, co. Kildare, by Anne, dau. of the late John Bagot, Esq., of Castle Bagot ; *b.* 1800 ; *s.* under the will of his relative Gerald O'Ferrall, Esq., 1832 ; *m.* 1836 Clara, dau. of the late Thomas Segrave, Esq., of Cabra, and has, with other issue,

    • Edward More, *b.* 1846.

Mr. O'Ferrall, who was educated at Trinity Coll. Dublin (B.A. 1823, M.A. 1827), and called to the Irish Bar 1827, is a J.P. and D.L for and Grand Juror of co. Longford.—*Lizard, Edgeworthstown, co. Longford.*

O'FFLAHERTIE, GEORGE FORTESCUE, Esq., of Lemonfield, co. Galway.
Son of the late Theobald Richard O'Fflahertie, Esq.; *b.* 1810 ; *s.* his cousin and brother-in-law, the late Thomas Henry O'Fflahertie, Esq., J.P., 1848 ; *m.* 1844 Rebekah, dau. of John Fynn, Esq., J.P., co. Mayo. Is a Magistrate for co. Galway, and Chairman of Oughterard Union. — *Lemonfield, Oughterard, co. Galway ; County Club, Galway.*

Heir Pres., his nephew Theobald Richard O'Fflahertie, in Holy Orders, B.A. of St. John's Coll., Cambridge ; Perpetual Curate of Capel, Dorking, Surrey ; *b.* 1818.

O'FLAHERTY, ANTHONY, Esq., of Knockbane, co. Galway.
Eldest son of the late Anthony O'Flaherty, Esq., of Knockbane, a member of that ancient and once powerful Irish sept; b. 1800; m. 1819 Harriet, only dau. of the late Major-General Archer, of the Grenadier Guards. Educated at Trinity Coll., Dublin; is a Magistrate for co. Galway and a Dep.-Lieut. for Galway; was M.P. for Galway 1847–59.—Knockbane, Moycullen, co. Galway; Reform Club, s.w.

+ OGILBY, JAMES, Esq., of Pellipar House, co. Londonderry.
Eldest son of the late Alexander Ogilby, Esq., of Pellipar House, by Isabella, his wife (she re-married 1864 Eustace Meredith Martin, Esq.); b. 18—. Is a J.P. and D.L. for co. Londonderry, and Lord of the Manor of Pellipar.—Pellipar House, Dungiven, co. Londonderry.

OGILBY, ROBERT LESLIE, Esq., of Ardnargle, co. Londonderry.
Son of the late John Ogilby, Esq., by Jane, dau. of the late James Simpson, Esq., of Armagh; b. 1798; m. 1844 Elizabeth Matilda, dau. of Major William Henry Rainey, H.E.I.Co.'s Service, and has, with other issue,
* Robert Alexander, b. 1850.
Mr. Ogilby, who was educated at Trinity Coll., Dublin (B.A. 1820), is a J.P. and D.L. for co. Londonderry (High Sheriff 1854).—Ardnargle, Newtown-Limavady, co. Londonderry.

OGILBY, WILLIAM, Esq., of Altnachree, co. Tyrone.
Only son of the late Leslie Ogilby, Esq., of Liseleen; b. 1808; s. 1845; m. 1851 Adelaide Charlotte, dau. of the Hon. and Rev. Charles Douglas, and niece of George Sholto, 17th Earl of Morton, and has, with other issue,
* Claud William Leslie, b. 1851.
Mr. Ogilby, who was educated at Trinity Coll., Cambridge (B.A. 1832), and called to the Bar at Lincoln's Inn 1832, is a J.P. and D.L. for co. Tyrone (High Sheriff 1852).—Altnachree Castle, Dunamanagh, co. Tyrone.

OGILBY, Mrs., of Kilcatten, co. Londonderry.
Harriet, 4th dau. of the late Matthew Canny, Esq., of Castle Fergus, co. Clare; m. 1850 William Ogilby, Esq., of Kilcatten, a Magistrate for co. Londonderry; formerly H.M.'s Consul at Caen, in France, and Charleston, South Carolina, who is dec.—Kilcatten, Londonderry.

OGILVIE, WILLIAM, Esq., of Chesters, Roxburghshire.
Eldest son of the late Thomas Elliot Ogilvie, Esq., of Chesters, by Hannah, dau. of Francis Dashwood, Esq., b. 1785; s. 1831; m. 1818 Alexina, dau. of Alexander Falconer, Esq., of Woodcot Park, East Lothian, and has, with other issue,
* Thomas Elliot, a Magistrate for co. Roxburgh; b. 1824.
Mr. Ogilvie, who was educated at the High School of Edinburgh, and was called to the Scottish Bar 1808, is a J.P. and D.L. for co. Roxburgh, Lord of the Barony of Chesters, and Chamberlain to the Duke of Buccleuch at Branxholm; was formerly Major of the Dumfries, &c., Militia.—Chesters, Jedburgh, N.B.

OGILVIE [GRANT-]. (See under Seafield, Earl of.)

OGILVIE-FORBES, Mrs., of Boyndlie, Aberdeenshire.
Jane, dau. of the late John Forbes, Esq., of Boyndlie, by Katharine, dau. of Alexander Morison, Esq., of Bog-
710

nie; s. her brother 1862; m. 1818 John Charles Ogilvie, Esq., M.D., who d. 1839, leaving, with other issue,
* George, b. 1820; m. 1849 Jane, dau. of Robert Cordiner, Esq.
This family is a younger branch of that of Sir William Forbes, of Monymusk, co. Aberdeen.—Boyndlie House, Fraserburgh, Aberdeenshire.

OGILVY, Sir JOHN, Bart., of Baldovan, Forfarshire (cr. 1625).
Eldest son of the late Rear-Admiral Sir William Ogilvy, Bart., of Baldovan, by Sarah, dau. of James Morley, Esq.; b. 1803; s. as 9th Bart. 1823; m. 1st 1831 Juliana Barbara, youngest dau. of the late Lord Henry Howard; 2nd 1836 Lady Jane Elizabeth, dau. of Thomas, 16th Earl of Suffolk and Berkshire. Educated at Harrow and Ch. Ch., Oxford; is Vice-Lieutenant and Convener of co. Forfar; Lieut.-Col. 1st Forfarshire Rifle Volunteers; has been M.P. for Dundee since 1857. —Baldovan House, Dundee, N.B.; Travellers' and Brooks's Clubs, s.w.
Heir, his son Reginald Howard Alexander, B.A., of Oriel Coll., Oxford, J.P. and D.L. for co. Forfar, and Major Forfar and Kincardine Militia Artillery; b. 1832; m. 1859 the Hon. Olivia Barbara, dau. of George, 9th Lord Kinnaird, and has, with other issue, * Angus Howard Reginald, b. 1860.

OGILVY, the Hon. WILLIAM, of Logal, Perthshire.
Fourth son of Walter, 7th Earl of Airlie, by Jane, dau. of John Ogilvy, Esq., of Murkle; b. 1793. Is a Magistrate for cos. Aberdeen and Perth, a Dep.-Lieut. for co. Forfar, and was formerly Capt. 52nd Foot.—Logal, Alyth, N.B.

OGILVY, DONALD, Esq., of Clova, Forfarshire.
Second son of the late Hon. Donald Ogilvy, D.L., of Clova, by Maria, dau. of the late James Morley, Esq.; b. 1824; s. 1863; m. 1867 Anne Sarah, 2nd dau. of John Ogilvy, Esq., of Inshewan, co. Forfar. Educated at Haileybury Coll.; is Lord of the Baronies of Clova and Glenprosen, and represents a younger branch of the family of the Earl of Airlie; was formerly in the Bengal Civil Service.—Clova and Balnaboth House, Kirriemuir, N.B.; Junior Carlton Club, s.w.

OGILVY, GEORGE, Esq., of The Cove, Dumfriesshire.
Eldest son of the late Rev. Skene Ogilvy, D.D., by Isabella Seton, grand-dau. of Sir Alexander Seton, Bart., Lord Pittendden; b. 1786; m. 1st 1822 Maria Augusta, dau. of the late Dr. Grieve, Physician to the Emperor of Russia; 2nd 184– Margaret, dau. of the late James Inverarity, Esq., of Rosemount, co. Forfar, and has, with other issue,
* Augustus George, b. 1826; m. 1858 Mary Harriette, dau. and heiress of the late Capt. Crowyn, of the 7th Dragoon Guards, and of Huntstown and Newtown, co. Kilkenny, and by her, who d. 1865, has one daughter.
Mr. Ogilvy, who was educated at the University of Aberdeen, Edinburgh, and London, was formerly a Medical Officer in the H.E.I.C.'s Service.—The Cove, Ecclefechan, N.B.

OGILVY, JOHN, Esq., of Inshewan, Forfarshire.
Only son of the late William Ogilvy, Esq., by Elizabeth, dau. of John Ogilvy, Esq., of Inshewan; b. 1791; m. 1829 Anne Sarah, dau. of Charles Ogilvy, Esq., of Tannadice, co. Forfar, and has, with other issue,
* John, a Magistrate for co. Forfar, b. 1830; m. 1863 Agnes Gardyne, eldest dau. of William Rennie, Esq., of Hyde Park Square, London (she d. 1868).
Mr. Ogilvy, who was educated at Edinburgh, is a J.P. and D.L. for co. Forfar.—Inshewan, Forfar, N.B.

+ OGILVY, PETER WEDDERBURN, Esq., of Ruthven House, Forfarshire.

Son of the late P. Ogilvy, Esq., of Ruthven; *b.* 18—; is married, and has, with other issue,

* Thomas, a Magistrate for co. Forfar, and a Col. in the Army (retir-d); *b.* 1810; *m.* 1856 Lady Henrietta Louisa, younger dau. of Thomas William, 2nd Earl of Pomfret.

Mr. Ogilvy is a J.P. and D.L. for co. Forfar and Lord of the Barony of Ruthven.—*Ruthven House, Meigle, N.B.*

OGILVY, THOMAS, Esq., of Corrimony, Inverness-shire.

Only son of the late David Ogilvy, Esq., of Seacot, Leith, N.B., by Janet, dau. of Thomas Gladstone, Esq., of Leith, and sister of the late Sir John Gladstone, Bart.; *b.* 1796; *m.* 1st 1827 Elizabeth, dau. of the late John Wilson, Esq., of Liverpool; 2nd 1847 Margaret, dau. of the late William Fraser Tytler, Esq., of Balnain, co. Inverness; 3rd 1855 Jemima, dau. of the late James Hay, Esq., of Drum, Mid-Lothian; he has, by his 1st wife, with other issue,

* David Stewart. *b.* 1831; *m.* 1866 Eveline, 2nd dau. of Charles Van Lennep, Esq.

Mr. Ogilvy, who was educated at Old Aberdeen, is a J.P. and D.L. for co. Inverness, and was formerly Joint-Convener of that county.—*Corrimony, Inverness; New Club, Edinburgh, N.B.*

OGILVY. (See under *Airlie, Earl of.*)

OGILVY. (See *Balfour-Ogilvy.*)

OGLANDER, Sir HENRY, Bart., of Parnham, Dorset (cr. 1665).

Eldest son of the late Sir William Oglander, Bart., of Parnham, by Lady Maria Anne, dau. of George Henry, 4th Duke of Grafton, K.G.; *b.* 1811; *s.* as 7th Bart. 1852; *m.* 1845 Louisa, dau. of the late Sir George William Leeds, Bart. Educated at Winchester and Ch. Ch., Oxford; is a J.P. and D.L. for Dorset, Patron of 1 living, and Capt. 4th I. of Wight Rifles.—*Parnham, Beaminster; Nunwell, Brading, I. of Wight.*

OGLE, Sir WILLIAM, Bart. (cr. 1816).

Only surviving son of the late Admiral Sir Charles Ogle, of Worthy House, Hants (who *d.* 1858), by his 2nd wife Letitia, dau. of Sir William Burroughes, Bart.; *b.* 1823; *s.* his nephew, the late Sir Chaloner R. M. Ogle, Bart., 1861. Was formerly a Capt. in the Army.

Heir Pres., his cousin Graham, Capt. R.N. retired; *b.* 1814.

OGLE, Lady, of Withdeane Court, Sussex.

Eliza Sophia Frances, only dau. and heir of the late William Thomas Roe, Esq., of Withdeane Court, by Mary Elizabeth, only dau. of Daniel Byam Mathew, Esq., of Pennytenny and Cayenne, St. Christopher's, W. Indies; *s.* her mother 1842; *m.* 1842 Capt. Sir Chaloner Ogle, Bart., who *d.* 1859, leaving issue a son,

Sir Chaloner Roe Majendie Ogle, Bart., *b.* 1843; *d.* 1861; and a dau., * Hebe Emily Maritsma, *m.* 1865 Eldred, 3rd son of Edward Stanley Curwen, Esq., of Workington (whom see).

Lady Ogle is Lady of the Manor of Withdeane.—*Withdeane Court, Brighton.*

OGLE, the Rev. EDWARD CHALONER, of Kirkley Hall, Northumberland.

Third son of the late Rev. John Savile Ogle, of Kirkley Hall, Canon of Durham, by Catharine Hannah, dau. of Edward Sneyd, Esq., of Bishton; *b.* 1798; *s.* 1853; *m.* 1830 Sophia, youngest dau. of the late Admiral Sir Charles Ogle, Bart., and has, with other issue,

* John Savile, a Magistrate for Northumberland; *b.* 1836.

Mr. Ogle, who was educated at Eton and Merton Coll., Oxford (B.A. 1820, M.A. 1823), is a Magistrate for Northumberland and Prebendary of Salisbury Cathedral.—*Kirkley Hall, Newcastle-on-Tyne.*

OGLE, ROBERT, Esq., of Eglingham Hall, Northumberland.

Son of the late Robert Ogle, Esq., of Eglingham Hall, by Jane, dau. of John Burgess, Esq.; *b.* 1817; *s.* 1857; *m.* 1846 Mary, youngest dau. of the late Admiral Sir Edward Harvey, G.C.B., and has, with other issue,

* Robert Bertram Edward, R.N.; *b.* 1850.

Mr. Ogle, who was educated at Marlborough and Brasenose Coll., Oxford (B.A. 1841), and called to the Bar at the Inner Temple 1846, is a Magistrate for Northumberland. This family is of great antiquity in the county, the name occurring in old records *temp.* William the Conqueror.—*Eglingham Hall, Alnwick.*

O'GORMAN, NICHOLAS SMITH, Esq., of Bellevue, co. Clare.

Eldest son of the late Nicholas Purcell O'Gorman, Esq., Q.C., of Bellevue, by Frances Anne, dau. of Charles Smith, Esq., of Castle Park, Limerick; *b.* 1814; *s.* 1857; *m.* 1843 Margaret, dau. of Michael Kenny, Esq., and has, with other issue,

* Nicholas Purcell, *b.* 1845.

Mr. O'Gorman, who was educated at Clongowes and Trinity Coll., Dublin (B.A. 1834), and called to the Irish Bar 1838, is a Magistrate for co. Clare.—*Bellevue, Kilrush, co. Clare.*

O'GRADY, the Hon. RICHARD, of Monkstown House, co. Dublin.

Fifth son of Standish, 1st Viscount Guillamore, by Katharine, dau. of the late John Thomas Waller, Esq., of Castletown, co. Limerick; *b.* 179–. Educated at Trinity Coll., Dublin; called to the Irish Bar, 1822; appointed Chief Examiner of Exchequer in Ireland 1829.—*Monkstown House, co. Dublin.*

O'GRADY, STANDISH DARBY, Esq., of Aghamarta Castle, co. Cork.

Eldest son of the late Darby O'Grady, Esq., of Aghamarta, by Ellen, eldest dau. of the late Baron George, of Dublin; *b.* 1813; *s.* 1857; *m.* 1856 Fanny Selina, dau. of the Rev. Edward Groome, and by her, who *d.* 1861, has issue. Mr. O'Grady, who was educated at Trinity Coll., Dublin, is a Magistrate for co. Cork. The father of the present owner was brother to Standish, 1st Viscount Guillamore.—*Aghamarta Castle, near Carrigaline, co. Cork.*

Heir Pres., his brother George O'Grady, Esq., of Plattenstown, Arklow, co. Wicklow; a Magistrate for co. Wexford; *b.* 1815; *s.* to his grandfather's estates in Wexford 1846; *m.* 1858 the Hon. Jane Hare-Ruthven, dau. of the late Baroness Ruthven.

O'GRADY, WALTER, Esq., of Castle Garde, co. Limerick.

Eldest son of the late Hugh Hamon Massy O'Grady, Esq., J.P. and D.L. of Castle Garde (who was High Sheriff of co. Limerick 1809), by Eliza Selina Maria, eldest dau. of the late William Henry Hutchinson, Esq., of Rockforest, co. Tipperary (she *m.* 2nd 1862 William Bredin, Esq.); *b.* 1858; *s.* 1859. Represents a younger branch of the family of Viscount Guillamore.—*Castle Garde, Pallasgreen, co. Limerick.*

Heir Pres., his brother Hugh Hamon Massy, *b.* 1860.

O'GRADY, WILLIAM DE COURCY, Esq. (The O'Grady), of Kilballyowen, co. Limerick.

Eldest son of the late O'Grady, of Kilballyowen, J.P. and D.L. High Sheriff of co. Limerick, by Anne, only dau. of William Wise, Esq., of Cork; *b.* 1816; *s.* 1862; *m.* 1841 Anne Grogan, dau. of Thomas de Renzey, Esq., of Clobemon, co. Wexford, and has, with other issue,

* Thomas de Courcy, *b.* 1844.

The O'Grady, who was educated at Winchester and at

Trinity Coll., Dublin (B.A. 1837, M.A. 1840), is a Magistrate for co. Limerick and Lord of the Manor of Kilballyowen.—*Kilballyowen, Bruff, co. Limerick.*

O'GRADY. (See under *Guillamore, Viscount.*)

O'HARA, CHARLES, Esq., of O'Hara Brook, co. Antrim.

Eldest son of the late Henry O'Hara, Esq., of O'Hara Brook, by Eleanor, dau. of William Dunne, Esq., of the city of Dublin; *b.* 1797; *s.* 1823; *m.* 1823 Margaret, dau. of Arthur Innes, Esq., of Dromantine, co. Down, and has issue,

    • Charles, m. and has issue, • a son, b. 1863.

Mr. O'Hara is a Magistrate for co. Antrim (High Sheriff 1833).—*O'Hara Brook, Ballymoney, co. Antrim.*

O'HARA, CHARLES WILLIAM, Esq., of Cooper's Hill, Annaghmore, co. Sligo.

Second and only surviving son of the late Arthur Brooke Cooper, Esq., of Cooper's Hill, by Jane Frances, dau. of Charles O'Hara, Esq., M.P., of Annaghmore; *b.* 1817; assumed the name of O'Hara in 1860, on *s.* to the estates of his maternal uncle, Charles King O'Hara, Esq.; *m.* 1858 Annie Charlotte, eldest dau. of the late Richard Streatfeild, Esq., of The Rocks, Uckfield, Sussex, and has, with other issue,

    • Charles, b. 1860.

Mr. O'Hara, who was educated at Trinity Coll., Dublin (B.A. 1838), is J.P. and D.L. for co. Sligo (High Sheriff 1849); was M.P. for co. Sligo 1859–65.—*Annaghmore, Collooney, co. Sligo; Cooper's Hill, Ballymote, co. Sligo; Carlton Club, s.w.*

O'HARA, HENRY HUTCHINSON HAMILTON-, Esq., of Crebilly, co. Antrim.

Eldest son of the late John Hamilton, Esq., of Crebilly, who assumed the additional name of O'Hara; *b.* 1820; *m.* 1841 Alicia Isabella, youngest dau. of the late Lieut.-General the Hon. Sir Henry King, K.C.B. Is a Magistrate for co. Antrim.—*Crebilly House, Ballymena.*

OKEDEN, UVEDALE EDWARD PARRY, Esq., of Turnworth, Dorset.

Eldest son of the late William Parry Okeden, Esq., J.P. and D.L., of Turnworth (who was High Sheriff of Dorset 1849, and formerly in the Bengal Civil Service), by Julia Henrietta, dau. of the late Edward Harris-Greathed. Esq., of Uddens House, Dorset; *b.* 1845; *s.* 1868. Educated at Eton; is Lord of the Manor of Turnworth, and Lieut. 10th Royal Hussars. This family was formerly of Moro Crichel, Dorset.—*Turnworth House, Blandford.*

O'KEEFE, JOHN, Esq., of Ballinacourty, co. Waterford.

Eldest son of the late Patrick O'Keefe, Esq., of Mountain Castle, co. Waterford, by Margaret, dau. of Thomas Sargent, Esq., of Roanmore, co. Waterford; *b.* 1829; *s.* 1841. Educated at Clongowes Coll.; is a Magistrate for co. Waterford.—*Ballinacourty, Dungarvan; Stephen's Green Club, Dublin.*

O'KELLY, CORNELIUS JOSEPH, Esq., of Gallagh Castle, co. Galway.

Elder son of the late Festus O'Kelly, Esq., of Tycooley, co. Galway, by Mary Anne, dau. of Ambrose O'Madden, Esq.; *b.* 1806; *s.* 1834; *m.* 1831 Eliza, dau. of the late Walter Joyce, Esq., of Merview, co. Galway, and has, with other issue,

    • Festus Ignatius, b. 1833.

Mr. O'Kelly, who was educated at Trinity Coll., Dublin, is a Magistrate for co. Galway (High Sheriff 1861), Lord of the Manor of Gallagh, and a Count of the Holy Roman Empire.—*Gallagh Castle, Tuam, co. Galway.*

O'KELLY, PETER DE PENTHENY, Esq., of Barrettstown, co. Kildare.

Eldest surviving son of the late George Bourke O'Kelly, Esq., of Acton, by Maria, dau. of Peter de Pentheny, Esq., of St. Croix; *b.* 1807; *s.* 1857; *m.* 1830 Mary Anne, dau. of Matthias Maher, Esq., of Ballymullen, and has, with other issue,

    • George Lionel, b. 1831.

Mr. O'Kelly is a Magistrate for co. Kildare (High Sheriff 1858).—*Barrettstown, Newbridge, co. Kildare.*

OKEOVER, HAUGHTON CHARLES, Esq., of Okeover Hall, Staffordshire.

Only son of the late Rev. Charles Gregory Okeover, by Mary Anne, dau. of the late General Sir George Anson, G.C.B. (she re-m. 1833 R. Plumer Ward, Esq.); *b.* 1825; *s.* his uncle 1836; *m.* 1859 the Hon. Eliza Anne, eldest dau. of Henry, 3rd Lord Waterpark, and has surviving issue,

    • Four daughters.

Mr. Okeover is a Dep. Lieut. for co. Warwick, and a Magistrate for co. Stafford (High Sheriff of co. Derby 1862), Lord of the Manor of Okeover, Patron of 2 livings, and Major 8th Derbyshire Rifle Volunteers.—*Okeover Hall, Ashbourne; Oldbury Hall, Atherstone, Warwickshire.*

OLDFIELD, JOHN RAWDON, Esq., of Oldfield Lawn, Sussex.

Eldest son of the late General John Oldfield, K.H., of Oldfield Lawn, by his 1st wife Mary, dau. of Christopher Arden, Esq., of Dorchester; *b.* 1812; *s.* 1863; *m.* 1846 his cousin Jane, dau. of the late Christopher Arden, Esq. Educated at Addiscombe Coll., is a Magistrate for Sussex, and Col. of Bengal Engineers (on the retired list); he was formerly an Inspector of Schools in India. —*Oldfield Lawn, Westbourne, Emsworth; Athenæum Club, s.w.*

    Heir Pres., his nephew Anthony, son of the late Capt. Anthony Oldfield, R.A. (who was killed before Sebastopol in 1855), by Sophia, dau. of Capt. Buchan, R.N.; *b.* 1843.

OLDHAM, JOSEPH, Esq., of Strawbridge, Devon.

Eldest son of the late George Laing, Esq., of St. Alban's, Herts, by Mary, eldest dau. of E. Brooke, Esq., of Wargrave, Berks; *b.* 1806; *s.* 1863; *m.* 1830 Elizabeth, only dau. of the late Rev. Philip Traut Nind, Vicar of Wargrave, Berks. Educated at University Coll., Oxford (B.A. 1828); is a Magistrate for Devon, and Lord of the Manors of Hatherleigh and Twyford. He assumed the name of Oldham in lieu of his patronymic Laing, by Royal licence in 1830, as maternal descendant of the Oldhams, of Cainham Court, co. Salop. —*Strawbridge, Hatherleigh.*

OLDNALL-RUSSELL, Lady, of Sion House, Worcestershire.

Louisa Maria, eldest dau. of the late John Lloyd Williams, Esq., of Gwernant Park, co. Cardigan, by Martha Louisa, eldest dau. of Morley Saunders, Esq., of Saunders Grove, co. Wicklow, and of Lady Martha Saunders; *m.* 1814 Sir William Oldnall Russell, Chief Justice of Bengal, who *d.* 1832, leaving, with other issue, an only son, • Henry Steward, of the Civil Service, Ceylon; *b.* 1816; *m.* 1866 Frances Mary, only dau. of the late Henry Barry Domvile, Esq.—*Sion House, Kidderminster; Shelburne House, Cheltenham.*

O'LEARY, CORNELIUS, Esq., of Newtown House, co. Cork.

Son of the late C. O'Leary, Esq., of Newtown House; *b.* 1800; is married, and has issue an only son.

    • Denis Charles, b. 18—; m. 1863 Kate Maria, 3rd dau. of Michael Lyons, Esq., of Spancie Hill, co. Cork.

Mr. O'Leary is Lord of the Manor of Newtown. —*Newtown House, Bantry, co. Cork.*

O'LEARY, JOHN M'CARTHY, Esq., of Coomlagane, co. Cork.

Eldest son of the late Denis M'Carthy O'Leary, Esq., of Coomlagane, by Leonora, dau. of John Howley, Esq., of Limerick; *s.* 1829; *m.* 1839 Jane, eldest dau. of John O'Connell, Esq., of Grena, and has, with other issue,

   * John, *b.* 1840.

Mr. O'Leary, who was educated at Stonyhurst Coll., is a J.P. and D.L. for co. Cork (High Sheriff 1854), and a Magistrate for co. Kerry.—*Coomlagane, Mill Street, co. Cork.*

OLIPHANT, LAURENCE, Esq.

Only son of the late Sir Anthony Oliphant, C.B., by Catherine Maria, dau. of the late Col. Ronald Campbell; *b.* 1829; called to the Bar at Lincoln's Inn 1855; is also a Member of the Scotch Bar (called 1855); was M.P. for Stirling 1859–60; Secretary of Embassy in China 1859–60, and Secretary of Legation in Japan, 1861–2; was formerly Superintendent General of Indian affairs in Canada.—*Athenæum Club*, s.w.; 35, *Halfmoon Street*, w.

OLIPHANT, LAWRENCE JAMES, Esq., of Condie and Newtown, Perthshire.

Only son of the late Lawrence Oliphant, Esq., J.P. and D.L., of Condie and Newtown (who was M.P. for Perth 1835–7), by his 3rd wife Marianne, eldest dau. of Stuart Oliphant, Esq., of Rossie, in the same co.; *b.* 1846; *s.* 1862. Educated at Harrow; is Lord of the Manor of Condie.—*Condie House, Bridge of Earn, N.B.*

Heir Pres., his sister Mary Anna.

OLIPHANT. (See *Græme-Oliphant*.)

OLIPHANT-FERGUSON, GEORGE HENRY HEWITT, Esq., of Broadfield and Burgh, Cumberland.

Only son of the late George Henry Hewitt-Oliphant, Esq., of Broadfield (who assumed the additional name of Oliphant, on succeeding to the property of his cousin), by Sarah, dau. of the late Robert Ferguson, Esq., of Harker, Cumberland; *b.* 1817; *s.* 1861; *m.* 1867 Cecilia, fourth dau. of the late John Labouchere, Esq., of Broome Hall, Surrey. Educated at Trinity Coll., Cambridge (B.A. 1842); called to the Bar at the Inner Temple 1843; is a Magistrate for Cumberland. Mr. Oliphant assumed in 1861 the name of Oliphant-Ferguson under the will of his maternal uncle, Richard Ferguson, Esq., of Harker.—*Broadfield House, Carlisle; National Club*, s.w.

OLIVER, JOHN, Esq., of Circourt, Berks.

Eldest surviving son of the late Admiral Robert Dudley Oliver, by Mary, dau. of Sir Charles Saxton, Bart., of Circourt, Berks; *b.* 1809; *s.* 1838 to the Berkshire estates of his maternal uncle, Sir Charles Saxton, Bart.; *m.* 1st 1837 Matilda, only dau. of Col. Morgan, of Llandough Castle, co. Glamorgan (she *d.* 1838); 2nd 1849 Lucy Diana, dau. of the late Col. Thomas P. Maunsell, of Thorpe Malsor, co. and has, with other issue,

   * Robert Dudley Maunsell, *b.* 1853.

Mr. Oliver is a J.P. and D.L. for Berks, and was formerly an Officer in the Army.—*Circourt, Abingdon; Pitsford Hall, Northampton; Carlton Club*, s.w.

OLIVER, JOHN DUDLEY, Esq., of Cherrymount, co. Wicklow.

Eldest son of the late Rev. John Oliver, Rector of Swepstone, co. Leicester, by Sarah Catherine, dau. of Dudley Baxter, Esq., of Atherstone; *b.* 1809; *s.* 1832; *m.* 1st 1834 Mary Susanna, dau. of Valentine Green, Esq. (she *d.* 1853); 2nd 1857 Elizabeth, dau. of the Rev. Wyndham C. Madden (she *d.* 1860); 3rd 1866

Sydney, dau. of William Tongue, Esq., and has, by the first, with other issue,

   * John Byrne, Capt. R.A.; *b.* 1834.

Mr. Oliver, who was educated at Queen's Coll., Cambridge (B.A. 1832), is a Magistrate for co. Wicklow.—*Cherrymount, Ovoca, co. Wicklow.*

OLIVER. (See under *Rutherfurd, of Edgerston*.)

OLIVIER, HENRY ARNOLD, Esq., of Potterne, Wilts.

Eldest son of the late Henry Stephen Olivier, Esq., J.P. and D.L., of Potterne Manor, by Mary, 2nd dau. of Vice-Admiral Sir Richard Dacres, K.C.B.; *b.* 1826; *s.* 1864; *m.* 1850 Annie, dau. of the late Joseph Arnould, Esq., M.D., of Whitecross, Berks. Educated at Balliol Coll., Oxford (B.A. 1849). This family, which was formerly seated at Clifton, Bedfordshire, came to England from France at the revocation of the Edict of Nantes.—*Potterne Manor, Devizes; 19, Circus, Bath.*

OLLIFFE, Sir JOSEPH FRANCIS, Knt. (cr. 1853).

Son of the late Joseph Olliffe, Esq., Merchant, of Cork, by Elizabeth, dau. of Charles McCarthy, Esq., of Sunville, co. Cork; *b.* 1808; *m.* 1841 Laura, dau. of the late William Cubitt, Esq., M.P., and has issue. Is Physician to the British Embassy at Paris, at which University he graduated M.D.; is a Fellow of the Royal College of Physicians, London; is an Officer of the Legion of Honour.—*2, Rue St. Florentine, Paris; Trouville, Normandy.*

O'LOGHLEN, Sir COLMAN MICHAEL, Bart., of Drumconora, co. Clare (cr. 1838).

Eldest son of the late Right Hon. Sir Michael O'Loghlen, Bart. (Master of the Rolls in Ireland), by Bidelia, dau. of Daniel Kelly, Esq., of Dublin; *b.* 1819; *s.* as 2nd Bart. 1842. Educated at London University Coll. (B.A. 1840); called to the Irish Bar 1840; appointed Chairman of the Quarter Sessions co. Carlow 1856. and of co. Mayo 1859, a Queen's Counsel 1853; is a Magistrate for co. Clare; elected M.P. for that county 1863.—*Drumconora, Ennis, co. Clare.*

Heir Pres., his brother Bryan, b. 1828; m. 1863 Ella, dau. of J. M. Seward, Esq.

OLPHERT, WYBRANTS, Esq., of Ballyconnell, co. Donegal.

Eldest son of the late Rev. John Olphert, of Newtown-Limavady, by Anna Benjamina, dau. of Dominick Mac-Ausland, Esq., of Row Park, co. Londonderry; *b.* 1811; *s.* 1851; *m.* 1843 Marianne, 3rd dau. and co-heir of the late Robert Fannin, Esq., of Leeson Street, Dublin, and has, with other issue,

   * John, a Magistrate for co. Donegal; *b.* 1844.

Mr. Olphert, who was educated at Trinity Coll., Dublin (B.A. 1832), is a J.P. and D.L. for co. Donegal (High Sheriff 1842).—*Ballyconnell, Falcaragh, Letterkenny.*

OLPHERTS, FRANCIS MONTGOMERY, Esq., of Mountshannon, co. Sligo.

Third son of the late Rev. Richard Olpherts, of Charlestown Glebe, co. Louth, and Milburn, co. Derry, by Anne, eldest dau. of Sir Francis Workman Macnaghten, Bart., of Bushmills, co. Antrim; *b.* 1822; *m.* 1858 Marianna, eldest dau. of Owen Wynne, Esq., of Ardachowen, co. Sligo. Educated at Trinity Coll., Dublin (B.A. 1844, M.A. 1863); is a Magistrate for co. Sligo.—*Mountshannon, Sligo.*

OLPHERTS, RICHARD, Esq., of Carrowmore, co. Sligo, and Milburn, co. Derry.

Eldest son of the late Rev. Richard Olpherts, of Charlestown Glebe, co. Louth, and Milburn, co. Derry, by Anne, eldest dau. of Sir Francis Workman-Macnaghten, Bart.; *b.* 1818; *m.* 1849 Elizabeth, youngest dau. of

FitzHerbert Ruxton, Esq., of Ardee House. Educated at Trinity Coll., Dublin ; is a Magistrate for co. Sligo ; was formerly in the 40th Regt.—*Carrowmore, Ballisodare, co. Sligo ; Milburn, Coleraine, co. Londonderry.*

O'MALLEY, Sir WILLIAM, Bart., of Kilboyne, co. Mayo (cr. 1804).
Eldest son of the late Sir Samuel O'Malley, Bart., of Kilboyne, by Jane, dau. of the late J. Reilly, Esq., of Newark ; *b.* 1816 ; *s.* as 2nd Bart. 1864 ; *m.* 1860 Louisa Mary, 2nd dau. of the late Rev. Henry Du Cane, of The Grove, Witham, Essex ; was formerly Lieut.-Col. North Mayo Militia, and Capt. 7th Fusiliers ; High Sheriff of co. Mayo 1838.—*Kilboyne House, Castlebar, co. Mayo ; Summer Hill, Colchester.*

O'MALLEY, GEORGE JAMES, Esq., of Newcastle, co. Mayo.
Eldest son of the late Capt. Andrew Clark O'Malley, Esq., J.P., of Newcastle, by Maria, dau. of Capt. John Gardiner, of Farm Hill, co. Mayo ; *b.* 1810 ; *s.* 1815. Is a Magistrate for co. Mayo; appointed High Sheriff 1851, but did not act ; was formerly Capt. South Mayo Militia. This family is descended from a common ancestor with Sir S. O'Malley, Bart.—*Newcastle, Swineford, co. Mayo.*

Heir Pres., his brother Owen Bingham Manners, *b.* 1812.

OMMANNEY-McTAGGART, Mrs., of Ardwell, Wigtownshire.
Susanna, eldest surviving child of the late Sir John McTaggart, Bart., of Ardwell (*ext.*), by Susanna, dau. of John Kymer, Esq., of Streatham, Surrey ; *s.* 1867 ; *m.* 1839 John Orde Ommanney, Esq., who *d.* 1866, leaving issue,

* Marianne Susanna, *m.* 1866 Mark John, eldest son of Mark S. Stewart, Esq., of Southwick, co. Kirkcudbright (whom see).

Mrs. Ommanney-McTaggart is Lady of the Rectory of Ardwell.—*Ardwell House, Stranraer, N.B.*

O'NEILL, Lord (WILLIAM O'NEILL).—Cr. 1868.
Eldest son of the late Rev. Edward Chichester, Rector of Kilmore, co. Armagh (who *d.* 1855), by Catharine, dau. of the late Robert Young, Esq., of Culdaff House, co. Donegal ; *b.* 1813 ; *m.* 1st 1839 Henrietta, only dau. of the late Judge Torrens, who *d.* 1857 ; 2nd 1858 Elizabeth Grace, dau. of the Ven. Archdeacon Torrens. Educated at Trinity Coll., Dublin (B.A. 1835) ; was formerly Prebendary of St. Michael's, Dublin ; he assumed, by Royal licence 1855, the surname of O'Neill, on succeeding to the estates of the late Earl O'Neill. This family descend from the Chichesters, Baronets, who are a younger branch of the family of the Marquis of Donegall.—*Shane's Castle, Antrim ; 19, Belgrave Square, s.w.*

Heir his son Edward, *b.* 1839 ; educated at Eton ; a J.P. and D.L. for co. Antrim ; elected M.P. for co. Antrim 1863.

ONGLEY, Lord (ROBERT HENLEY-ONGLEY).— Cr. 1776.
Eldest son of Robert, 2nd Lord, by Frances, dau. of the late Sir John Burgoyne, Bart., of Sutton Park, Beds ; *b.* 1803 ; *s.* 1814. Is a Dep.-Lieut. for Beds, and Patron of 1 living.—*Old Warden, Biggleswade.*

Heir Pres., his brother George, a J.P. and D.L. for Beds, and formerly Capt. Coldstream Guards ; *b.* 1809.

ONLEY. (See *Savill-Onley.*)

ONSLOW, Earl of (ARTHUR GEORGE ONSLOW). —Cr. 1801.
Eldest son of Thomas, 2nd Earl, by Arabella, dau. of the late Eaton Mainwaring Ellerker, Esq., of Risby Park, co. York ; *b* 1777 ; *s.* 1827 ; *m.* 1818 Mary, dau. of the late George Fludyer, Esq. Educated at Harrow ;
714

is a J.P. and D.L. for Surrey, and Patron of 5 livings. —*Clandon Park, Guildford ; Richmond, Surrey, s.w.*

Heir Pres., his nephew William Hillier Onslow, Esq., of Stoke Park (whom see).

ONSLOW, Sir HENRY, Bart., of Hengar House, Cornwall (cr. 1797).
Eldest son of the late Sir Henry Onslow, Bart., of Hengar House, by Caroline, dau. of John Bond, Esq., of Mitcham, Surrey ; *b.* 1809 ; *s.* as 3rd Bart. 1853 ; *m.* 1848 Ellen, dau. of Samuel Peter, Esq., of Porthcothan, Cornwall. Is a Dep.-Lieut. for Cornwall (High Sheriff 1857).—*Chillterne All Saints, Southampton ; Hengar House, Bodmin.*

Heir Pres., his brother Matthew Richard, late Major Bengal Cavalry ; *b.* 1810 ; *m.* 1st 1847 Eliza Antonia, dau. of the late Col. Newton Wallace (she *d.* 1854); 2nd 1855 Mary, eldest dau. of the late J. Salter, Esq., and has, by the former, with other issue, * William Wallace Rhode, *b.* 1848.

+**ONSLOW, ARTHUR POOLEY, Esq., of Send Grove House, Surrey.**
Eldest son of the late Rev. Arthur Onslow, Rector of Crayford, Kent, by his 1st wife Marianna, dau. of Wm.-Campbell, Esq. ; *b.* 1804 ; *m.* 1832 Rosa Roberta, dau. of Alexander Macleay, Esq., and by her, who *d.* 1854, has, with other issue, a son,

Arthur Alexander Walter, Comm. R.N. ; *b.* 1853 ; *m.* 1866 Elizabeth, only dau. of James Mac Arthur, Esq., of Camden Park, N. S. Wales.

Mr. Onslow, who was educated at Haileybury Coll., was formerly in the Madras Civil Service.—*Send Grove House, Woking, Surrey.*

+**ONSLOW, DENZIL, Esq., of Staughton, Hunts.**
Eldest son of the late General Denzil Onslow, of Staughton House, by his 2nd wife Sophia, dau. of the late Sir Stephen Lushington, Bart., of South Hill Park, Berks ; *b.* 1802 ; *s.* 1838. Educated at Eton and Trinity Coll., Cambridge ; is a Magistrate for Hunts (High Sheriff 1863), and Lord of the Manor of Great Staughton.—*Staughton House, St. Neot's.*

Heir Pres., his brother Henry Cope, a Magistrate for Hunts; *b.* 1808.

ONSLOW, GUILDFORD JAMES HILLIER MAINWARING-ELLERKER-, Esq., of Risby Park, Yorkshire, and Ropley, Hants.
Second but eldest surviving son of the late Hon. Thomas Cranley Onslow, of Upton House, Hants (who *d.* 1861), by Susannah Eliza, dau. and co-heir of Nathaniel Hillier, Esq., of Stoke Park, Surrey, and nephew of Arthur, 3rd Earl of Onslow ; *b.* 1814 ; *m.* 1838 Rosa Anne, dau. of the late General Denzil Onslow, of Staughton House, Hunts. Is a Dep.-Lieut. for the E. Riding of co. York, and for co. Lincoln, and M.P. for Guildford ; late Capt. Scots Fusilier Guards. He assumed the additional names of Mainwaring and Ellerker, in 1861, on inheriting the estates of his uncle, the late Hon. Edward Mainwaring-Ellerker-Onslow. —*Risby Park, Beverley ; The Grove, Ropley, Alresford ; Reform Club, s.w. ; 33, St. James's Square, s.w.*

ONSLOW, PITCAIRN, Esq., of Dunsborough, Surrey.
Third son of the late Rev. George Walton Onslow (who *d.* 1844), by Elizabeth, dau. of William Campbell, Esq. ; *b.* 1813 ; *m.* 1843 Adelaide, only dau. of Capt. Saltren Willett, and has, with other issue,

* Arthur Foot, *b.* 1846.

Mr. Onslow, a Magistrate for Surrey and a Major in the Army, represents a younger branch of the family of the Earl of Onslow.—*Dunsborough House, Ripley.*

ONSLOW, RICHARD FOLEY, Esq., of Oxenhall, Gloucestershire.

Elder son of the late Ven. Richard Francis Onslow, Archdeacon of Worcester (who *d.* 1849), by Harriett Mary, 3rd dau. of the late Hon. Andrew Foley ; *b.* 1801 ; *m.* 1826 Catherine, 2nd dau. of the late Latham Blacker, Esq., of Newent, co. Gloucester, and by her, who *d.* 1865, has, with other issue,

　• Andrew George, Capt. 97th Foot ; *b.* 1830 ; *m.* 1861 Mary, 5th dau. of the late Sir John Owen, Bart.

Mr. Onslow, who was educated at Westminster and Ch. Ch., Oxford (B.A. 1825), is a J.P. and D.L. for cos. Gloucester and Hereford, and a Magistrate for co. Worcester, and represents a younger branch of the family of the Earl of Onslow.—*Oxenhall, Newent.*

ONSLOW, WILLIAM HILLIER, Esq., of Stoke Park, Surrey.

Only surviving child of the late George Augustus Cranley Onslow, Esq., of Stoke Park, by Mary Harriet Anne, eldest dau. of Lieut.-General Loftus, of Kilbride ; *b.* 1853 ; *s.* 1855. Inherited in 1859 the estates of the Hillier family, under the will of his great-grandfather, Nathaniel Hillier, Esq., of Stoke Park. Is Heir Pres. to the Earldom of Onslow.—*Stoke Park, Guildford ;* Residence : *Stapleton House, Dorking.*

　Heir Pres., his uncle Guildford James Hillier Mainwaring-Ellerker-Onslow, Esq. (whom see).

ONSLOW. (See *Hughes-Onslow.*)

OPENSHAW, THOMAS LOMAX, Esq., of Heaton Grove, Lancashire.

Eldest son of Jonathan Openshaw, Esq., of Bank House, by Eliza, dau. of Joseph Holt, Esq., of Heaton Grove ; *b.* 1828 ; *m.* 1849 Adelaide, dau. of William Turner, Esq., of Flax Moss House, Haslingden, co. Lancaster, and has, with other issue,

　• William Turner, *b.* 1851.

Mr. Openshaw is a J.P. and D.L. for co. Lancaster, and a Merchant and Manufacturer at Manchester and Bury. —*Heaton Grove, Bury.*

ORANMORE and BROWNE, Lord (GEOFFREY DOMINIC AUGUSTUS FREDERICK BROWNE-GUTHRIE).—Cr. 1836.

Only surviving son of Dominic, 1st Lord Oranmore and Browne, by Catherine Anne Isabella, dau. of the late Henry Monck, Esq. ; *b.* 1819 ; *s.* 1860 ; *m.* 1859 Christina, only surviving child and heir of the late Alexander Guthrie, Esq., of the Mount, co. Ayr, whose name he consequently assumed. Educated at Harrow and Trinity Coll., Cambridge ; is a J.P. and D.L. for co. Mayo (High Sheriff 1841), and a Magistrate for co. Galway.—*The Cottage, Troon, Ayrshire ; Castle Macgarret, Ballindine, co. Mayo ; Brooks's Club,* s.w.

　Heir, his son Geoffrey Henry Browne, *b.* 1861.

ORD, Sir HARRY ST. GEORGE, Knt., C.B. (cr. 1867).

Son of the late — Ord, Esq. ; *b.* 1819. Is a Col. in the Army, Lieut.-Col. R.E., and Governor of the Straits Settlements.

ORD, Miss, of Langton Hall, Leicestershire.

Jemima Elizabeth, only surviving child of the late Rev. James Ord, M.A., of Langton Hall, by Barbara, sister of the late Charles John Brandling, Esq., of Gosforth House, Northumberland (who *d.* 1836) ; *s.* her brother, James Pickering Ord, Esq., 1863 ; is Lady of the Manors of East and West Langton, and represents a younger branch of the Ords of Whitfield, Northumberland.—*Langton Hall, Market-Harborough.*

ORD, JOHN THOMAS, Esq., of Fornham, Suffolk.

Eldest son of the late Rev. John Norman Ord, by Anne, dau. of Thomas Cocksedge, Esq., of Bury St. Edmund's ; *b.* 1807 ; *m.* 1st 1833 Susanna Agnes, 3rd dau. of M. T. Cocksedge, Esq., of St. Edmund's Hill, Bury St. Edmund's (she *d.* 1860) ; 2nd 1863 Ellen Sophia, 3rd dau. of the late Harry Gough Ord, Esq., of Bexley, Kent, and had issue by the former,

　John Harry, *b.* 1840 ; *d.* 1858.

Mr. Ord, who was educated at Winchester and Exeter Coll., Oxford (B.A. 1830), is a Magistrate for Suffolk, and Capt. in the Long Melford Troop of Yeomanry Cavalry.—*Fornham House, Bury St. Edmund's ; University Club,* s.w.

ORD, of Whitfield. (See *Blackett-Ord.*)

ORDE, Sir JOHN POWLETT, Bart., of Kilmory, Argyleshire (cr. 1790).

Only surviving son of the late Admiral Sir John Orde, Bart., by his 2nd wife Jane, dau. of John Frere, Esq., of Roydon, Norfolk ; *b.* 1803 ; *s.* as 2nd Bart. 1824 ; *m.* 1st 1826 Eliza, dau. and co-heir of Peter Campbell, Esq., of Kilmory ; 2nd 1832 Beatrice, youngest dau. of James Edwards, Esq., of Harrow. Educated at Eton and Ch. Ch., Oxford (B.A. 1826) ; is a J.P. and D.L. for co. Argyle, and a Dep. Lieut. for co. Inverness ; formerly Capt. Argyle and Bute Militia.—*Kilmory, Loch Gilp Head, N.B. ; Loch Maddy, North Uist, Invernessshire, N.B ; Oriental Club,* w.

　Heir, his son John William Powlett, a Magistrate for co. Argyll, and late Capt. 42nd Highlanders ; *b.* 1827 ; *m.* 1862 Alice Louisa, dau. of the late Charles Atticus Monck, Esq., eldest son of the late Sir C. Monck, Bart., of Belsay, Northumberland, and has, with other issue, • a son, *b.* 1865.

ORDE, CHARLES WILLIAM, Esq., of Nunnykirk, Northumberland.

Son of the late Charles Orde, Esq., and nephew of the late William Orde, Esq., of Nunnykirk ; *b.* 1810 ; *s.* 1842 ; *m.* 1853 Frances Isabel, youngest dau. of the late Shallcross Jacson, Esq., and has, with other issue,

　• William, *b.* 1854.

Mr. Orde, who was educated at the University Coll., Oxford (B.A. 1831, M.A. 1836), and called to the Bar at Lincoln's Inn 1842, is a J.P. and D.L. for Northumberland (High Sheriff 1846), and Chairman of Quarter Sessions for Northumberland.—*Nunnykirk, Morpeth ; Union Club,* s.w.

ORDE, JAMES HENRY, Esq., of Hopton House, Suffolk.

Only son of the late General James Orde (who *d.* 1850), by Lady Elizabeth Susan Somerset, 2nd dau. of Henry Charles, 6th Duke of Beaufort ; *b.* 1830 ; *m.* 1856 Margaret Barclay, youngest dau. of Daniel Gurney, Esq., of North Runcton, and has, with other issue,

　• Charles Somerville, *b.* 1858.

Mr. Orde, who was educated at Oriel Coll., Oxford, is Major 2nd Norfolk Rifle Volunteers.—*Hopton House, Gt. Yarmouth.*

ORDE, the Rev. LEONARD SHAFTO, of Weetwood and Shoreston, Northumberland.

Second son of the late Lieut.-General Leonard Shafto Orde, of Weetwood Hall, by his 2nd wife Lady Louisa Jocelyn, dau. of Robert, 2nd Earl of Roden ; *b.* 1807 ; *m.* 1833 Anna Maria Charlotte, eldest dau. of the late Sir Horace St. Paul, Bart., and has, with other issue,

　• William Jocelyn, an Officer in the Army ; *b.* 1837.

Mr. Orde, who was educated at Queen's Coll., Cambridge (B.A. 1830, M.A. 1842), is a Magistrate for Northumberland and Incumbent of Alnwick.—*Shoreston House, Belford.*

ORDE-POWLETT. (See under *Bolton, Lord.*)

ORDE-POWLETT, the Hon. AMIAS CHARLES.
Youngest son of the late Hon. Thomas Powlett Orde-Powlett (who *d.* 1843), by Letitia, dau. of the late Henry O'Brien, Esq., and brother of William Henry, 3rd Lord Bolton; *b.* 1828; *m.* 1852 Annie Martha, dau. of Christopher Topham, Esq., of. Middleham Hall, co. York, and has, with other issue,

  * Amias Christopher Thomas, *b.* 1862.

Mr. Orde-Powlett is a J.P. and D.L. for the N. Riding of Yorkshire.—*Thorney Hall, Spennithorne, Bedale.*

O'REILLY, ANTHONY, Esq., of Baltrasna, co. Meath.
Third son of the late James O'Reilly, Esq., of Baltrasna, by Henrietta Catherine Blanche, youngest dau. of Oliver Nugent, Esq., of Bobsgrove; *b.* 1812; *s.* 1853; *m.* 1836 Alicia Maria, dau. of Capt. John Fortescue (she *d.* 1858), and has issue. Educated at Trinity Coll., Dublin; is a J.P. and D.L. for co. Cavan (High Sheriff 183–), and a Magistrate for co. Meath (High Sheriff 1845).—*Baltrasna, Oldcastle, co. Meath.*

O'REILLY, FRANCIS GAMMEL, Esq., of Scarborough, Yorkshire.
Son of the late Edward O'Reilly, Esq., Capt. Warwick Militia, by Elizabeth, youngest dau. of Capt. Charles Wood, R.N., of Bowling Hall, co. York, and sister of the late Sir Francis Lindley Wood, Esq., of Hickleton Hall, co. York, and sister of Charles, 1st Viscount Halifax; *b.* 1810; *m.* 1st 1852 Barbara Elizabeth, eldest dau. of the late John Balguy, Esq., Q.C., Commissioner of Bankruptcy, of Duffield, co. Derby (she *d.* 1854); 2nd 1856 Caroline Rachel, youngest dau. of the late Joshua Crompton, Esq., of Esholt Hall, co. York, and has issue by the former,

  * Barbara Louisa St. John.

Mr. O'Reilly, who was educated at Repton School, Derbyshire, and Giggleswick in Craven, was formerly in H.M.'s Customs, Bermuda.—*Scarborough, Yorkshire.*

O'REILLY, MYLES GEORGE, Esq., of The Heath House, co. Leitrim.
Eldest son of the late Myles John O'Reilly, Esq., M.P., of The Heath House, by Elizabeth Ann, dau. of the Hon. and Rev. George de la Poer Beresford, of Inniscara, co. Cork; *b.* 1830; *s.* 1857; *m.* 1857 Elizabeth, dau. of George Brunskill, Esq., of The Lodge, Turnham Green. Late Capt. North Cork Rifles. Is the senior representative of the eldest branch of the house of O'Reilly.—*Heath House, Carrick-on-Shannon.*

O'REILLY, MYLES WILLIAM PATRICK, Esq., of Knock Abbey, co. Louth.
Eldest son of the late William O'Reilly, Esq., M.P., of Knock Abbey, by Margaret, dau. of the late Dowell O'Reilly, Esq., of Heath House; *b.* 1825; *s.* 1844; *m.* 1859 Ida, dau. of the late Edmund Jerningham, Esq., of Rutland Gate, and has, with other issue,

  * William, *b.* 1861.

Mr. O'Reilly, who was educated at St. Cuthbert's Coll., Ushaw, and the London University (B.A. 1845), and became LL.D. of the Roman University 1847, is a J.P. and D.L. for co. Louth (High Sheriff 1848), and late Capt. Louth Militia; elected M.P. for co. Longford 1862.—*Knock Abbey, Dundalk; Stafford Club, w.*

+O'REILLY, PHILIP, of Clonamber, co. Longford.
Son of the late P. O'Reilly, Esq., of Clonamber; *b.* 1800. Is a J.P. and D.L. for co. Longford, and a Magistrate for co. Westmeath.—*Clonamber, Rathowen, co. Longford.*
716

O'REILLY-DEASE, Mrs., of Dee Farm, co. Louth.
Anna Maria, only surviving child and heir of the late Matthew O'Reilly, Esq., of Thomastown, co. Louth, by Anna Maria, dau. of the late John O'Conor, Esq.; *m.* 1814 Richard Dease, Esq., M.D., of Lisner, co. Cavan, who assumed the name of O'Reilly, and *d.* 1819, leaving issue, * Matthew, educated at the University of Paris, a J.P. and D.L. for cos. Cavan and Louth (High Sheriff 1857), and a Magistrate for co. Dublin; *b.* 1819.—*Dee Farm, Dunleer, co. Louth; Ravenswell, Bray, co. Wicklow.*

ORFORD, Earl of (HORATIO WILLIAM WALPOLE).—Cr. 1806.
Eldest son of Horatio, 3rd Earl, by Mary, dau. of the late William Augustus Fawkener, Esq.; *b.* 1813; *s.* 1858; *m.* 1841 Harriet Bettina Frances, dau. of the late Hon. Sir Fleetwood Broughton Reynolds Pellew. Educated at Eton and Trinity Coll., Cambridge; is a J.P. and D.L. for Norfolk, and Patron of 7 livings; was M.P. for E. Norfolk 1835–7.—*Wolterton Park and Mannington Hall, Aylsham; Travellers' Club, s.w.*
  Heir Pres., his brother Henry, *b.* 1818; *m.* 1845 Cecilia Eliza. beth, dau. of the late John McAlister, Esq., of Strathaird, N.B.

ORGILL-LEMAN. (See *Leman.*)

ORKNEY, Earl of (THOMAS JOHN HAMILTON FITZ-MAURICE).—Cr. 1696.
Eldest son of John O'Bryen, late Viscount Kirkwall (who *d.* 1820), by the Hon. Anna Maria, eldest dau. of John, 1st Lord De Blaquiere, and grandson of Mary, late Countess; *b.* 1803; *s.* his grandmother as 5th Earl 1831; *m.* 1826 the Hon. Charlotte Isabella, 2nd dau. of George, 2nd Lord Boston. Is a Magistrate for Bucks and Middlesex, a J.P. and D.L. for Berks, late Capt. Bucks Yeomanry Cavalry; late Cornet 9th Lancers; is a Scotch Representative Peer.—*Glen App, Ballintray, Ayrshire, N.B.; Carlton and Junior United Service Clubs, s.w.; Ennismore Place, Hyde Park, s.w.*
  Heir, his son George William Hamilton, Viscount Kirkwall, late Capt. Royal Bucks Yeomanry Cavalry; served in the 71st Highlanders in the Crimea; *b.* 1827.

ORLEBAR, RICHARD LONGUET, Esq., of Hinwick, Beds.
Eldest son of the late Richard Orlebar, Esq., of Hinwick House, by Maria, dau. of the late Benjamin Longuet, Esq., of Bath; *b.* 1806; *s.* 1833; *m.* 1831 Sophia, dau. of the late Jasper Parrott, Esq., M.P., of Dundridge, Devon, and has, with other issue,
  * Richard, a Magistrate for Beds and co. Northampton; *b.* 1833; *m.* 1861 Frederica St. John, youngest dau. of the late Sir W. E. Rouse Boughton, Bart., and has, with other issue, * Richard Rouse, *b.* 1862.
Mr. Orlebar, who was educated at Rugby, is a Magistrate for Beds and co. Northampton (High Sheriff 1859), a Dep. Lieut. for Beds and Patron of 1 living; was formerly in the 60th Rifles.—*Hinwick House, Willingborough.*

ORLEBAR, ROBERT SHIPTON, Esq., of Crawley House, Beds.
Eldest son of the late Robert Charles Orlebar, Esq., of Crawley House, by Charlotte, dau. and heiress of the Rev. Daniel Shipton, of Husborne-Crawley; *b.* 1808; *s.* 1812; *m.* 1834 Charlotte Elizabeth, dau. of the Rev. Valentine Ellis, Rector of Walton, Bucks, and of Barnardistone, Suffolk, by whom he has, with other issue,
  * Arabella Emily, *m.* 1858 her cousin Orlando Robert Hamond, late Capt. 28th Foot, who *d.* 1862, leaving, with other issue, * Orlando, *b.* 1859.
This family is a younger branch of the Orlebars of Hinwick (whom see).—*Crawley House, Husborne-Crawley, Woburn.*

ORMATHWAITE, Lord (JOHN BENN-WALSH). Cr. 1868.

Eldest son of the late Sir John Benn-Walsh, Bart., by Margaret, dau. of Joseph Fowke, Esq., of Bexley, Kent, and niece and heir of John Walsh, Esq., of Warfield Park, Berks ; *b.* 1798 ; *s.* as 2nd Bart. 1825 ; *m.* 1825 the Lady Jane, youngest dau. of George, 6th Earl of Stamford. Educated at Eton and Ch. Ch. Oxford; is a J.P. and D.L. for Berks, and Lord-Lieutenant of co.Radnor; was M.P. for Sudbury 1830-1 and 1838-40, and for co. Radnor 1840-68.—*Ormathwaite, Keswick ; Newcastle Court, Walton, Radnorshire ; Warfield Park, Bracknell ; Carlton, White's, and Travellers' Clubs, s.w.; 28, Berkeley Square, w.*

Heir, his son Arthur, educated at Eton and Trinity Coll., Cambridge ; M.P. for co. Radnor, a J.P. and D.L. for co. Radnor, a Magistrate for Berks and co. Hereford ; formerly Capt. 1st Life Guards, and late M.P. for Leominster ; *b.* 1827 ; *m.* 1858 Lady Katharine Emily Mary, dau. of Henry, 7th Duke of Beaufort, and has, with other issue, * Arthur Henry John, *b.* 1859.

ORME, ROBERT, Esq., of Enniscrone, co. Sligo.

Second son of the late William Orme, Esq., of Bellville, co. Mayo, by Isabella Maria, dau. of the late John Ormsby, Esq., of Gortner Abbey; *b.* 1815 ; *s.* 1837 ; *m.* 1843 Sidney Frances, dau. of Christopher L'Estrange Carlton, Esq., and has, with other issue,

* Robert William, *b.* 1856.

Mr. Orme, who was educated at Bath, is a J.P. and D.L. for co. Sligo, and a Magistrate for co. Mayo.—*Enniscrone, Ballina, co. Sligo ; Kildare Street Club, Dublin ; Merrion Square South, Dublin.*

ORME, WILLIAM, Esq., of Owenmore, co. Mayo.

Eldest son of the late William Orme, Esq., of Bellville, co. Mayo, by Isabella, dau. of John Ormsby, Esq., of Gortner Abbey; *b.* 1810 ; *s.* 1842 ; *m.* 1837 Janette, dau. of Christopher L'Estrange Carlton, Esq. Educated at Trinity Coll., Dublin ; is a Magistrate for cos. Mayo and Sligo.—*Owenmore, Crossmolina, co. Mayo.*

ORMEROD, GEORGE, Esq., D.C.L., F.R.S., F.S.A., &c., of Tyldesley House, Lancashire, and Sedbury Park, Gloucestershire.

Only child of the late George Ormerod, Esq., of Bury, co. Lancaster, by Elizabeth, dau. of Thomas Johnson, Esq., of Tyldesley House; *b.* 1785; *s.* his grandfather 1789 ; *m.* 1808 Sarah, dau. of John Latham, Esq., M.D., F.R.S., of Bradwall Hall, co. Chester, and has, with other issue,

* Thomas Johnson M.A., of Brasenose Coll., Oxford, a Magistrate for Norfolk, Rector of Redenhall, and Archdeacon of Suffolk; formerly Fellow of Brasenose Coll., and Examining Chaplain to the two late Bishops of Norwich ; *b.* 1809 ; *m.* 1838 Maria Susan, dau. of the late Sir Joseph Bailey, Bart., M.P., and has, with other issue, * George Thomas Bailey, *b.* 1846.

Mr. Ormerod, who was educated at Brasenose Coll., Oxford (Hon. M.A. 1807, Hon. D.C.L. 1818), is a Magistrate for cos. Chester and Monmouth, a J.P. and D.L. for co. Gloucester, and Author of 'The History of Cheshire.' This family is a collateral male line of Ormerod of Ormerod, co. Lancaster.—*Sedbury Park, Chepstow ; Athenæum Club, s.w.*

ORMEROD, GEORGE HENRY, Esq., of Edgeside, Lancashire.

Second son of the late George Ormerod, Esq., of Fern Hill, by Dorothy Ann, only dau. of the late John Whitaker, Esq., of Broadclough ; *b.* 1825 ; *m.* 1850 Ellen, dau. of William Turner, Esq., of Flax Moss House, Haslingden, co. Lancaster, and has with other issue,

* George William, *b.* 1851.

Mr. Omerod, who is a Magistrate for co. Lancaster, represents a junior branch of the Ormerods of Ormerod. —*Edgeside, Newchurch, in Rossendale, Lancashire.*

ORMONDE, Marquis of (JAMES EDWARD WILLIAM THEOBALD BUTLER).—Cr. 1825.

Eldest son of John, 2nd Marquis, by Frances Jane, dau. of the late General the Hon. Sir Edward Paget, and grand-dau. of George, 3rd Earl of Dartmouth ; *b.* 1844 ; *s.* 1854. Educated at Harrow; sits in the House of Lords as Lord Ormonde, U.K. (cr. 1821); is Hereditary Chief Butler of Ireland, and Lieut. 1st Life Guards. —*The Castle, Kilkenny, Ireland ; 17, Park Lane, w.*

Heir Pres., his brother Lord James Arthur Wellington Foley, *b.* 1849.

ORMROD, PETER, Esq., of Halliwell Hall, Lancashire.

Eldest son of the late James Ormrod, Esq., of Chamber Hall, co. Lancaster (who *d.* 1825), by Ann, dau. of — Woods, Esq.; *b.* 1795; *m.* 1838 Eliza, dau. of Thomas Hardcastle, Esq., of Firwood, Bolton. Is a Magistrate for co. Lancaster, Lord of the Manor of Nether Wyersdale, and a Banker, Merchant, and Manufacturer. This family is descended from a common ancestor with the Ormerods of Tyldesley (whom see). —*Halliwell Hall, Bolton ; Wyersdale Park, Garstang.*

ORMSBY, ANTHONY, Esq., of Ballinamore, co. Mayo.

Son of the late Lieut.-Col. Anthony Ormsby, of Ballinamore, by his 2nd wife Anne, dau. of John Lloyd, Esq., of Lisadurn, co. Roscommon ; *b.* 1820 ; *s.* his brother 1836. Educated at Trinity Coll., Dublin (B.A. 1842); is a Magistrate for co. Mayo (High Sheriff 1849).—*Ballinamore House, Keltimagh, Swinford, co. Mayo ; Sackville Street Club, Dublin.*

Heir Pres., his brother John Yeaden, *b.* 1822.

ORMSBY-GORE. (See *Gore.*)

O'RORKE, AMBROSE, Esq., of Ballybollan, co. Antrim.

Eldest son of the late Daniel O'Rorke, Esq., of Ballybollan, by Catherine, dau. of the Rev. Edward Hudson, late of Portglenone Castle ; *b.* 1808; *s.* 1835 ; *m.* 1852 Jane, dau. of Walter Molony, Esq., late of Belfast, co. Antrim. Is a J.P. and D.L. for co. Antrim (High Sheriff 1856). This family, formerly resident at Dromohaire, co. Leitrim, possessed a large territory there, and were Princes of Breffne. — *Ballybollan, Ahoghill, co. Antrim.*

+**O'RORKE, CHARLES DENNIS, Esq., of Clonbern, co. Galway.**

Son of the late C. O'Rorke, Esq.; *b.* 1810 ; *m.* 1854 Harriette Mary, dau. of the late Admiral the Hon. William Le Poer Trench. son of William, 1st Earl of Clancarty. Is a Magistrate for co. Galway.—*Clonbern and Moylough House, Moylough, co. Galway.*

ORPEN, Sir RICHARD JOHN THEODORE, Knt., of Ardtully, co. Kerry (cr. 1868).

Only surviving son of the late Rev. Francis Orpen, Rector of Dungourney, co. Cork, and Vicar of Kilgarvan, co. Kerry, &c., by Susanna, dau. and co-heir of Hugh Millerd, Esq., of Monard, co. Cork; *b.* 1788; *s.* 1805 ; *m.* 1819 Elizabeth, dau. of the Rev. Richard Stack, D.D., late Fellow of Trinity Coll., Dublin, and has, with other surviving issue,

* Richard Hugh Millerd, *b.* 1829.

Sir R. Orpen, who is Vice-Chairman of the Poor-Law Board of Guardians of the Kenmare Union, and a Solicitor in practice, was one of the Commissioners appointed by Her Majesty to inquire into the Courts of Law and Chancery.—*Ardtully, Kenmare, co. Kerry; 41, North Great George Street, Dublin.*

717

ORPEN, the Rev. EDWARD CHATTERTON.
Only son of the late Abram Edward Orpen, Esq., of
Killowen, co. Kerry, by Martha, 2nd dau. of Sir James
Chatterton, Bart., of Castlemahon, co. Cork ; *b.* 1831 ;
s. 1857; *m.* 1856 Marcella Carew, dau. of Octavius
Palmer, Esq., H.E.I.C.S., and has, with other issue,
   • Edward Chatterton Lewis, *b.* 1857.
Mr. Orpen, who was educated at Trinity Hall, Cam-
bridge (B.A. 1854, M.A. 1857), was appointed Vicar of
Dean Prior 1866.—*Dean Prior Vicarage, Ashburton.*

ORPEN, RICHARD HUNGERFORD, Esq., of Kil-
laha Castle, co. Kerry.
Eldest son of the late Samuel Orpen, Esq., of Woodville,
co. Kerry, by Bridget Sophia, dau. of the late Thomas
Hungerford, Esq., of The Island, co. Cork ; *b.* 1807 ; *s.*
1826 ; *m.* 1832 Frances Diana, dau. of the Rev. Basta-
ble Herbert, of Brewsterfield, co. Kerry, and has, with
other issue,
   • Arthur Herbert, *b.* 1833 ; *m.* 1862 Jane, dau. of the late Col.
Spenser.
Mr. Orpen, who was educated at Trinity Coll., Dublin
(B.A. 1830), is a Magistrate for co. Kerry.—*Killaha
Castle, Killarney ; Woodville, Kilgarvan, co. Kerry.*

ORR, Sir ANDREW, Knt., of Harviestoun, Clackmannanshire (cr. 1858).
Eldest son of the late Francis Orr, Esq., of Glasgow, by
Mary, dau. of the late John Glen, Esq., of Lumloch, co. Lanark ;
b. 1802. Educated at Glasgow University ; is a Magistrate for co. Lanark ; was formerly Lord Provost of
Glasgow.—*Harviestoun Castle, Dollar, N.B.*

ORR, Colonel WILLIAM ADAM, C.B., of Bridgeton, Kincardineshire.
Eldest son of the late William Orr, Esq. (who *d.* 1816),
by Margaret, dau. of the late A. Mackay, Esq., and
grandson of the late Patrick Orr, Esq., of Bridgeton ;
b. 1810 ; *s.* 1828 ; *m.* 1843 Elizabeth Anastasia, only
dau. of the late Capt. Hugh Robison, and niece of the
late Sir John Robison, of Edinburgh, and has, with
other issue,
   • John Elphinstone Hugh, *b.* 1855.
Col. Orr, who was educated at Addiscombe Coll., is an
Officer in the Royal Artillery, and A.D.C. to the Queen.
—*Bridgeton, Montrose, N.B. ; Oriental Club, w.*

OSBORN, Sir GEORGE ROBERT, Bart., of Chick-
sands, Beds (cr. 1661).
Eldest son of the late Sir John Osborn, Bart., M.P., of
Chicksands, by Frederica, dau. of Sir Charles Davers,
Bart., of Rushbrooke, Suffolk ; *b.* 1813 ; *s.* as 6th Bart.
1848 ; *m.* 1835 Lady Charlotte Elizabeth, dau. of Lord
Mark Kerr and Charlotte (in her own right), Countess
of Antrim (she *d.* 1866). Educated at Westminster and
Ch. Ch., Oxford ; is a J.P. and D.L. for Beds (High
Sheriff 1857), and Patron of 2 livings ; was formerly
Lieut. in the Army.—*Chicksands Priory, Biggleswade ;
Travellers' Club, s.w.*

*Heir, his son Henry John Robert, late Lieut. 1st Life Guards ;
b. 1839 ; m. 1861 Emily, dau. of Thomas St. Quintin, Esq.,
of Hatley Park, co. Cambridge.*

OSBORN, Dowager Lady, of Campton, Beds.
Frederica Louisa, dau. of the late Sir Charles Davers,
Bart. (*ext.*) ; *m.* 1809 Sir John Osborn, Bart., of Chicksands
(many years M.P. for Beds), who *d.* 1848, leaving issue
(see above).—*Campton Manor, Biggleswade.*

OSBORNE, the Rev. Lord SIDNEY GODOLPHIN.
Third son of Francis Godolphin, 1st Lord Godolphin, by
the Hon. Elizabeth Charlotte, 3rd dau. of William, 1st
Lord Auckland, and brother of George, 8th Duke of
Leeds ; *b.* 1804 ; *m.* 1834 Emily, dau. of the late Pascoe
718

Grenfell, Esq., of Taplow House, Bucks, and has, with
other issue,
   • Sidney Francis Godolphin, a Clerk in the War Office ; *b.*
   1835.
Lord Sidney Osborne was educated at Rugby and Brase-
nose Coll., Oxford (B.A. 1830), and appointed Rector of
Derweston 1841 ; is a Dep. Lieut. for Bucks ; he was
Rector of Stoke Pogis, Bucks. — *Derweston Rectory,
Blandford.*

OSBORNE, Sir WILLIAM TOLER, Bart., of
Beechwood, co. Tipperary (cr. 1629).
Eldest son of the late Sir Daniel Toler Osborne, Bart.,
of Beechwood, by Lady Harriette le Poer Trench, dau.
of William, 1st Earl of Clancarty ; *b.* 1805 ; *s.* as 12th
Bart. 1853 ; *m.* 1842 Mary, dau. of William Thompson,
Esq., of Clonfin, co. Longford. Educated at Trinity
Coll., Dublin ; is a J.P. and D.L. for co. Tipperary.
—*Beechwood, Tipperary ;* 41, *Fitzwilliam Place, Dublin.*

Heir Pres., his brother, Charles Stanley, b. 1810 ; *m.* 1846
Emelie Geantry de Reuilly.

OSBORNE, CHARLES WILLIAM, Esq., of Rosna-
ree, co. Meath.
Eldest son of the late Rev. Charles Osborne, of Bally-
magarvy, co. Meath, by Jane, dau. of the late Capt. N.
Maingay, 62nd Regt. ; *b.* 1831 ; *s.* 1853 ; *m.* 1855 Eliza-
beth Margaret, eldest dau. of John Edwards, Esq., of
Knockrobin, co. Wicklow, and has, with other issue,
   • Charles John, *b.* 1856.
Mr. Osborne is a Magistrate for co. Meath.—*Rosnaree,
Slane, co. Meath.*

+**OSBORNE**, FRANCIS NICHOLAS, Esq., of
Smithstown, co. Meath.
Third son of the late F. Osborne, Esq., of Dardastown
Castle ; *b.* 1819 ; is married, and has issue. Is a Ma-
gistrate for co. Meath.—*Smithstown, Julianstown,
Drogheda.*

OSBORNE, RALPH BERNAL, Esq., of Newtown Anner, co. Tipperary.
Eldest son of the late Ralph Bernal, Esq., M.P., by his
1st wife Mary, dau. of Henry White, Esq. ; *b.* 1814 ; *s.*
1854 ; *m.* 1844 Catharine Isabella, only dau. of the late
Sir T. Osborne, Bart., of Newtown-Anner, whose name
he assumed. Educated at the Charterhouse and Trinity
Coll., Cambridge ; entered the Army 1838, and served
in the 7th Fusiliers ; is a J.P. and D.L. for cos. Tipperary and Waterford ; was M.P. for Wycombe 1841-7,
for Middlesex, 1852-7, for Dover 1857-9, and for Liskeard 1859-65 ; elected M.P. for Nottingham 1866 ;
was Secretary to the Admiralty 1852-5.—*Newtown-Anner, Clonmel, co. Tipperary ; Reform Club, s.w.*

OSBORNE. (See under *Leeds, Duke of.*)

O'SHAUGHNESSY, Sir WILLIAM BROOKE,
Knt., F.R.S. (cr. 1856).
Son of the late Daniel O'Shaughnessy, Esq., of Lime-
rick ; *b.* 1809 ; *m.* 1855 Margaret, dau. of Francis
O'Shaughnessy, Esq. Educated at the University of
Edinburgh ; is Superintendent-General of Telegraphs in
British India ; appointed Assistant-Surgeon in the
H.E.I.C.'s Service 1830 ; was Physician to Lord Met-
calfe when Governor of Agra, and Professor of Chemis-
try in the Medical Coll. at Calcutta ; knighted for his
services in laying down the electric telegraph in India.

O'SHEE, NICHOLAS POWER, Esq., of Gardenmorris, co. Waterford.
Younger but only surviving son of the late Richard
Power O'Shee, Esq. (who *d.* 1829), by Margaret, dau.
of Nicholas Power, Esq., of Snow Hill, co. Kilkenny ;
b. 1821 ; *s.* his brother 1859 ; *m.* 1865 Lady Gwendo-

lena Isabella, youngest dau. of Thomas William; 1st Earl of Lichfield, and has issue,

* A son, b. 1867.

Mr. O'Shee is a J.P. and D.L. for co. Waterford (High Sheriff 1861).—*Gardenmorris, Kilmacthomas, co. Waterford ; Shee's-town, co. Kilkenny.*

+OSSALINSKY, the Countess, of Musgrave Hall, Cumberland.

Mary, dau. of the late ——, Esq. ; *m.* 18—; John, Count Ossalinsky, of the kingdom of Poland, and has issue, an only daughter, * Nathalie, *m.* 1862 William Harrison, Esq., of Bishop-yards, Westmoreland.—*Musgrave Hall, Penrith.*

OSSORY, FERNS, AND LEIGHLIN, Bishop of, JAMES THOMAS O'BRIEN, D.D.

Eldest son of the late Michael Burke O'Brien, Esq., by Mary, dau. of Thomas Kough. Esq. ; *b.* 1794 ; *m.* 1836 Ellen, dau. of the late Chief Justice Pennefather, and has issue. Educated at Trinity Coll., Dublin (B.A. 1815, M.A. 1820, D.D. 1831) ; became Fellow and Divinity Lecturer in the same year; appointed Dean of Cork 1842 ; consecrated 1842. Patronage 90 livings. —*The Palace, Kilkenny ; Athenæum Club, s.w.*

OSSULSTON.   (See under *Tankerville, Earl of.*)

OSTLER, WILLIAM, Esq., of Arnold Field, Grantham, Lincolnshire.

Eldest son of the late William Ostler, Esq., of Grantham (who *d.* 1853), by Lydia Ann, dau. of David Lely. Esq., and brother of the late John Lely Ostler, Esq., of Cawthorpe House, Bourne ; *b.* 1800 ; *m.* 1835 Emma Elizabeth, dau. of William King. Esq., of Spittlegate, co. Lincoln ; is a Magistrate for co. Lincoln (parts of Kesteven). This family has been settled in Lincolnshire for several generations.—*Arnold Field, Grantham.*

Heir Pres., his nephew William Grinfield, who has assumed the name of Lely instead of Ostler ; *b.* 1838 ; *m.* 1867 Annie, dau. of T. E. Massey, Esq., of Cottesmore, near Haverfordwest, and has issue, * one son.

OSWALD, Lady, of Dunnikier, Fifeshire.

Amelia June, dau. of the late Lord Henry Murray, by Eliza, dau. of Richard Kent, Esq. ; *m.* 1829 General Sir John Oswald. G.C.B., of Dunnikier, co. Fife, who *d.* 1840.—*Southbank, near Edinburgh, N.B.*

OSWALD, ALEXANDER, Esq., of Auchincruive, Ayrshire.

Eldest surviving son of the late Richard Alexander Oswald, Esq. (who *d.* 1822), by Elizabeth, dau. of John Anderson, Esq., of London ; *b.* 1811 ; *s.* his uncle 1853 ; *m.* 1844 Lady Louisa Elizabeth Frederica, dau. of William, 1st Earl Craven, and by her, who *d.* 1858, has surviving issue,

* Two daughters.

Mr. Oswald, who was educated at Ch. Ch., Oxford (B.A. 1834), is a J.P. and D.L. for cos. Ayr. Kirkcudbright, and Lanark ; was M.P. for co. Ayr 1843–52.—*Auchincruive, Ayr, N.B.; White's, Brooks's and Travellers' Clubs, s.w.; 58, Green Street, w.*

OSWALD, JAMES TOWNSEND, Esq., of Dunnikier, Fifeshire.

Eldest son of the late General Sir John Oswald, G.C.B., of Dunnikier, by his 1st wife, Charlotte, dau. of the late Rev. Lord Charles Murray-Aynsley, of Little Harle Tower, Northumberland ; *b.* 1820 ; *s.* 1840 ; *m.* 1848 Ellen Octavia, dau. of the late Philip John Miles, Esq., of Leigh Court, Somerset, and has, with other issue,

* John, *b.* 1856.

Mr. Oswald, who is a J.P. and D.L. for co. Fife, and Lord of the Barony of Dunnikier, was formerly Capt. Grenadier Guards.—*Dunnikier, Kirkcaldy, N.B.*

O'TOOLE.   (See *Hall.*)

+OTTLEY, WARNER, Esq., of Landmore, co. Antrim.

Eldest son of the late Herbert Taylor Ottley, Esq., of Landmore House, by Catharine, eldest dau. of James Bell, Esq., of Newton Forbes, co. Longford ; *b.* 185— ; *s.* 1863.—*Landmore House, Coleraine, Ireland; Moyola Lodge, co. Londonderry.*

OTWAY, Sir GEORGE GRAHAM, Bart. (cr. 1831).

Eldest son of the late Admiral Sir Robert Otway, Bart., G.C.B., of Hyde Park Gardens, Middlesex, by Clementina, dau. of Admiral Holloway, of Wells, co. Somerset ; *b.* 1816 ; *s.* as 2nd Bart. 1846 ; *m.* 1851 Eliza, youngest dau. and co-heir of the late John Campbell, Esq. Is a Rear-Admiral on the reserved list.—*United Service Club,* s.w.; 7, *Portman Square,* w.

Heir Pres., his brother Arthur John, of Teddington Place, Middlesex ; educated at Sandhurst Coll. ; called to the Bar at the Middle Temple 1850 ; a Magistrate for Middlesex, M.P. for Chatham, late M.P. for Stafford ; *b.* 1822 ; *m.* 1851 Henrietta, dau. of Sir James Langham, Bart.

OTWAY, Lady, of Cwm Elan, Radnorshire.

Frances, dau. of the late Sir Charles Blicke, of Caroon Park, Surrey, by Jane, dau. of Col. Phelp ; *m.* 1812 Sir Loftus William Otway. C.B., of Cwm Elan, who was a General in the Army, and who *d.* 1854. Lady Otway, who is Lady of the Manor of Cwmtawddwr, is maternally descended from the 3rd Earl of Thanet.—*Cwm Elan, Rhayader.*

OTWAY, Capt. ROBERT JOCELYN, R.N., of Castle Otway, co. Tipperary.

Second son of the late Rev. Samuel Jocelyn Otway, of Castle Otway, by Margaret, dau. of General Hart, H.E.I.C.S. ; *b.* 1808 ; *s.* 1850 ; *m.* 1836 Anne Digby, 4th dau. of the late Sir Hugh Crofton, Bart., and has issue, an only child,

* Frances Margaret, *m.* 1865 William Clifford Bermingham-Ruthven, Esq. (whom see).

Capt. Otway, who was educated at the Royal Naval Coll., is a J.P. and D.L. for co. Tipperary, and a Capt. R.N. retired.—*Castle Otway, Templederry, Ireland; United Service Club,* s.w.

OUSELEY, the Rev. Sir FREDERICK ARTHUR GORE, Bart. (cr. 1808).

Eldest son of the late Right Hon. Sir Gore Ouseley, Bart., by Harriott Georgiana, dau. of John Whitelocke, Esq. ; *b.* 1825 ; *s.* as 2nd Bart. 1844. Educated at Eton and Ch. Ch., Oxford (B.A. 1846, M.A. 1849); graduated in Music 1854 ; is in Holy Orders : Precentor of Hereford, Professor of Music in University of Oxford, and Patron of 1 living.—*The Cloisters, Hereford ; St. Michael's Coll., Tenbury.*

OUTRAM, Sir FRANCIS BOYD, Bart. (cr. 1858).

Only son of the late Lieut.-General Sir James Outram, Bart., G.C.B. &c., by Margaret Clementina, dau. of James Anderson, Esq., of Bridgend, Brechin. N.B. ; *b.* 1836 ; *s.* as 2nd Bart. 1863 ; *m.* 1860 June Anne, dau. of Frederick Davidson, Esq., of Inchmarlo, co. Kincardine, and has issue a daughter. Educated at Haileybury Coll. ; was formerly in the Bengal Civil Service, and Under-Secretary to the Government of the N.W. Provinces. —10, *Queen's Gate Gardens,* w.

Heir, his son James, *b.* 1864.

OUVRY, the Rev. PETER THOMAS.

Eldest son of the late Peter Aimé Ouvry, Esq., of East Acton. Middlesex ; *b.* 1811 ; *m.* 1st 1846 Jane, dau. of Sir George Nicholls, K.C.B. ; 2nd 1858 Anne Louisa youngest dau. of the late John Grubb, Esq., of Horsendon House, Bucks. Educated at Trinity Coll., Cam-

719

bridge (B.A. 1834, M.A. 1837); appointed Vicar of Wing 1850; is a Magistrate for Bucks.—*Wing Vicarage, Leighton Buzzard.*

OVENS, EDWARD, Esq., of Bowdon, Cheshire.
Eldest surviving son of the late Hugh Ovens, Esq., of St. Catharine's, co. Fermanagh, by Elizabeth, dau. of the late Hugh Lyle, Esq., of Coleraine; *b.* 1817; *m.* 1854 Sophia, youngest dau. of General de Gaja, and grand-dau. of Lord Robert Fitz-Gerald. Educated at Trinity Coll., Dublin, called to the Bar at the Middle Temple 1845, is a Magistrate for cos. Lancaster and Chester, was Chairman of the Salford Quarter Sessions 1858–62, appointed Judge of the Manchester County Courts 1862.—*Enville House, Bowdon, Cheshire.*

OVEREND, WILLIAM, Esq., Q.C.
Youngest son of the late Hall Overend, Esq., of Sheffield, by Ruth, dau. of James Wilson, Esq., of Rawdon, co. York; *b.* 1809. Educated at Sheffield; called to the Bar at Lincoln's Inn 1837; is a Bencher of Lincoln's Inn; was M.P. for Pontefract 1859–60.—*Conservative Club, s.w.; 6, Queen's Gardens, w.*

+ OVEREND, Mrs.,‡ of Sharrow Head, Yorkshire.
Mary, widow of Wilson Overend, Esq., of Sharrow Head, who was a J.P. and D.L. for the W. Riding of co. York, and who d. 1865.—*Sharrow Head, near Sheffield.*

OVERSTONE, Lord (SAMUEL JONES LOYD).—Cr. 1850.
Only son of the late Lewis Loyd, Esq. (who d. 1859), by Sarah, dau. of John Jones, Esq.; *b.* 1796; *m.* 1829 Harriet, dau. of the late Ichabod Wright, Esq., of Mapperley Hall, Notts (she d. 1864). Educated at Eton and Trinity Coll., Cambridge (B.A. 1815); a Magistrate for Berks and co. Carmarthen, and a J.P. and D.L. for co. Northampton, and Patron of 2 livings; was formerly a Banker in London; High Sheriff of co. Warwick 1838; was M.P. for Hythe 1819–26.—*Overstone Park, Northampton; University, Athenæum, and Reform Clubs, s.w.; 2, Carlton Gardens, w.*

OVERTON, GEORGE, Esq., of Ty Mawr, Monmouthshire.
Eldest son of the late George Overton, Esq., of Ty Mawr, by Mary, dau. of Daniel Francis, Esq., of Llanthetty Hall, co. Brecon; *b.* 1813; *s.* 1827; *m.* 1839 Eliza Ann, dau. of Michael Hansby, Esq. Is a J.P. and D.L. for Brecon; was formerly a Solicitor.—*Ty Mawr, Abergavenny; Windham Club, s.w.*

OWEN, Sir HUGH OWEN, Bart., of Taynton House, Gloucestershire (cr. 1813).
Eldest son of the late Sir John Owen, Bart., M.P., of Orielton House, co. Pembroke (who was Lord-Lieutenant of co. Pembroke), by his 1st wife Charlotte, dau. of the Rev. John Lort Phillips; *b.* 1803; *s.* as 2nd Bart. 1861; *m.* 1st 1825 Angelina Cecilia, dau. of the late Sir Charles Gould Morgan, Bart., and sister of Charles, 1st Lord Tredegar (she d. 1844); 2nd 1845 Henrietta Frances, dau. of the Hon. Capt. Edward Rodney, R.N. Is a J.P. and D.L. for co. Pembroke, and Patron of 4 livings; elected M.P. for Pembroke, 1861.—*Taynton House, Newent; Landshipping, Pembroke; University Club, s.w.*

Heir, his son Hugh Charles Owen, a Dep.-Lieut. for co. Pembroke, *b.* 1826.

OWEN, the Rev. FRANCIS, of Efenechtyd, Denbighshire.
Second son of the late Thomas Owen, Rector of Celynin, co. Merioneth, by Jane, dau. of Daniel Giles, Esq.,

of London; *b.* 1786; *m.* 1815 Jane, youngest dau. of John Phillips, Esq., Solicitor, of Ruthin, co. Denbigh. Educated at Ch. Ch., Oxford (B.A. 1807); appointed Rector of Efenechtyd, 1834; is a Magistrate for co. Denbigh.—*Efenechtyd, Ruthin, N. Wales.*

OWEN, the Rev. HENRY.
Eldest surviving son of the late Rev. Thomas Ellis Owen, Rector of Llandyfrydog, co. Anglesey, by Harriott, dau. of Robert Chester, Esq., of the Middle Temple; *b.* 1796; *m.* 1847 Jane, dau. of the Rev. Charles Chester, Rector of Ayot St. Peter's, Herts. Educated at Jesus Coll., Cambridge (B.A. 1822, M.A. 1853); is a Dep. Lieut. for co. Anglesey, and Rector of Llangefni; Proctor for the clergy of the Diocese of Bangor, and Rural Dean.—*The Rectory, Llangefni, Anglesey.*

OWEN, GRITFITH HUMPHREYS, Esq., of Ymwlch, Carnarvonshire.
Eldest son of the late Rev. Gritfith Owen, of Ymwlch, by Ann, dau. of Humphrey Jones, Esq., of Brithdir Mawr, co. Carnarvon; *b.* 1833; *s.* 1853; *m.* 1865 Marian, 2nd dau. of Josiah Radcliffe, Esq., of Werneth Park, co. Lancaster, and has issue,

* Gritfith Radcliffe, *b.* 1866.

Mr. Owen is a J.P. and D.L. for co. Carnarvon (High Sheriff 1864); late Capt. Royal Carnarvon and Anglesey Militia.—*Ymwlch, Tremadoc.*

OWEN, the Rev. HENRY, of Heveningham, Suffolk.
Eldest son of the late Rev. Hugh Owen, LL.D., Rector of Beccles and a Magistrate for Suffolk, by Elizabeth, dau. of the late Peter Williams, Esq.; *b.* 1806; *m.* 1st 1829 Louisa Long, only surviving child of the late John Stütter, Esq., of Haughley and Stowmarket, Suffolk, Barrister-at-Law; 2nd 1851 Annie, 2nd dau. of the late Davies Gilbert, Esq., M.P., D.C.L., of Tredrea and Trelissick, Cornwall, and of Gilbert House, Eastbourne, Sussex, President of the Royal Society. Educated at Magdalen Coll., Cambridge (B.A. 1828, M.A. 1831); is a Magistrate for Suffolk and Norfolk, Rector of Heveningham, and Rural Dean; was formerly Rector of Wilby, Suffolk. This family is of Welsh extraction, but has been resident in Suffolk since the year 1800.—*Heveningham Rectory, Yoxford; Clergy Club, s.w.*

OWEN, HUGH DARBY, Esq., of Bettws Hall, Montgomeryshire.
Eldest son of the late Rev. Edward Pryce Owen, of Bettws Hall (who was Rector of Eyton and Vicar of Wellington), by Mary, dau. of Samuel Darby, Esq., of Colebrook Dale; *b.* 1827; *s.* 1863; *m.* 1851 Harriet Eliza, dau. of the late Samuel Smith, Esq., Judge at Calcutta, and has issue,

* Hugh Darby Annesley, *b.* 1852.

Mr. Owen, who is a Lieut. Royal Gloucestershire Hussars, is thirtieth in descent from the Princes of Powys.—*Bettws Hall, Newtown, Montgomeryshire; Fretherne Lodge, Cheltenham; Windham Club, s.w.*

OWEN, the Rev. HUGH DAVIES, D.D., of Glynafon, Anglesey.
Eldest son of the late Owen Owen, Esq., by Anne, dau. of E. Owen, Esq., of Ty Obry and Fodsilin; *b.* 1796; *s.* 1833; *m.* 1st 1822 his cousin Sarah Elizabeth, dau. of Richard Owen, Esq.; 2nd 1856 Lucretia Ann, dau. of Samuel Newbould, Esq., of Broomhill, co. York, and has by the former, with other issue,

* Edward, *b.* 1826; B.D. and Fellow of Jesus Coll., Oxford.

Mr. Owen, who was educated at Beaumaris and Jesus Coll., Oxford (B.A. 1817, M.A. 1819, D.D. 1834), is a

Magistrate for Anglesey, and Rector of Trevdraeth; was formerly Incumbent of Penmon, co. Anglesey.—*Glynafon, and Trevdraeth Rectory, Anglesey.*

+OWEN, JOHN, Esq., of Broadway, Montgomeryshire.

Eldest son of the late John Dorset Owen, Esq., J.P., of Broadway (who was High Sheriff of co. Montgomery 1844), by his 1st wife Mary, dau. of C, Fleetwood, Esq., of Liverpool; *b.* 182-; *s.* 1866. Is J.P. and D.L. for cos. Salop and Montgomery.—*Broadway, Churchstoke, Montgomeryshire.*

+OWEN, the Rev. JOHN, of Llaniestyn, Carnarvonshire.

Son of the late — Owen, Esq.; *b.* 1790. Educated at Jesus Coll., Oxford (B.A. 1812, M.A. 1815); is a J.P. and D.L. for co. Carnarvon, and Rector of Llaniestyn, and Rural Dean.—*Llaniestyn, Pwllheli.*

OWEN, OWEN, Esq., of Gadlys, co. Anglesey.

Eldest son of the late Owen Owen, Esq., D.L., of Gadlys, by Mary Knight, dau. of the late Rev. Richard Prichard, of Dinam Hall, Anglesey; *b.* 1834; *s.* 1866; *m.* 1861 Mary Sophia, eldest dau. of Charles Prothero, Esq., of Llanvrechva Grange, co. Monmouth.—*Gadlys, Menai Bridge, Anglesey.*

Heir Pres., his brother Richard, *b.* 1836; *m.* 1867 Mary Jane, youngest dau. of the late Rev. William Birley.

+OWEN, WILLIAM, Esq., of Hermon's Hill, Pembrokeshire.

Son of the late Mr. Owen; *b.* 18—. Is a J.P. and D.L. for co. Pembroke, and late High Sheriff of that co.; was formerly a Merchant in Haverfordwest. He purchased this property in 1862.—*Hermon's Hill, Withybush, and Polygon, Haverfordwest.*

OWEN, WILLIAM MOSTYN, Esq., of Woodhouse, Salop.

Eldest son of the late William Mostyn-Owen, Esq., of Woodhouse, by Harriet Elizabeth, his wife; *b.* 18—. This family was formerly named Mostyn.—*Woodhouse, Shrewsbury.*

OWEN, of Condover Park. (See *Cholmondeley.*)

OWENS, JOHN, Esq., of Holestone, co. Antrim.

Eldest son of the late James Owens, Esq., of Holestone, by Mary, dau. of John Forsyth, Esq., of Ballynure; *b.* 1801; *s.* 1848; *m.* 1828 Jane, dau. of James Stewart-Moore, Esq., of Balladivity, co. Antrim, and by her, who *d.* 1860, has, with other issue,

* James, *b.* 1836 ; *m.* 1861 Evelyn Margaret, dau. of R. J. Tennant, Esq., J.P. and D.L. of Rushpark, co. Antrim.

Mr. Owens, who was educated at Worcester Coll., Oxford, is a Magistrate for co. Antrim.—*Holestone, Doagh, co. Antrim.*

OWSLEY, WILLIAM POYNTZ MASON, Esq., of Blaston, Leicestershire.

Only son of the late Rev. John Owsley, B.A., Rector of St. Giles's, Blaston, by Catharine Mason, dau. of Maydwell Mason Reed, Esq., of Market Deeping, co. Lincoln; *b.* 1812; *s.* 1835; *m.* 1832 Henrietta Jane,

eldest dau. of the Rev. Richard Farrer, Rector of Ashley, co. Northampton, and has, with other issue,

* Richard Farrer, *b.* 1839.

Mr. Owsley represents a family formerly settled in Northamptonshire.—*Blaston, Uppingham.*

OXENDEN, Sir HENRY CHUDLEIGH, Bart., of Broome Park, Kent (cr. 1678).

Eldest son of the late Sir Henry Oxenden, Bart., by Mary, dau. of Col. Graham, of Canterbury; *b.* 1795; *s.* 1838; *m.* 1st 1830 Charlotte, dau. of Capt. Browne, R.N.; 2nd 1818 Elizabeth Phœbe, dau. of J. King, Esq., of Brighton. Educated at Eton and St. John's Coll., Cambridge; is a J.P. and D.L. for Kent.—*Broome Park, Canterbury; University Club, s.w.*

Heir Pres., his brother George Chichester, *b.* 1797.

OXENDEN, PERCY DIXWELL NOWELL, Esq., of Eastwell, Kent.

Second son of the Rev. Montagu Oxenden, Rector of Eastwell and Luddenham, Kent, by Elizabeth, dau. of Richard Wilson, Esq., of Bildestone, Suffolk; *b.* 1838. Educated at Harrow and Ch. Ch., Oxford; is a Magistrate for Kent, and Capt. in East Kent Yeomanry.—*Eastwell, Ashford, Kent; St. James's and Grafton Clubs, s.w.*

OXFORD, Bishop of (the Right Rev. SAMUEL WILBERFORCE, D.D., F.R.S., &c.).

Third son of the late William Wilberforce, Esq., M.P., by Barbara Anne, dau. of Isaac Spooner, Esq., of Elmdon Hall, co. Warwick; *b.* 1805; *m.* 1828 Emily, dau. of the late Rev. J. Sargent, of Lavington House, Sussex (she *d.* 1841). Educated at Oriel Coll. Oxford (B.A. 1826, M.A. 1829, D.D. 1845); is Lord High Almoner and Chancellor of the Order of the Garter; appointed Select Preacher at Oxford 1837, Canon of Winchester 1840, Bampton Lecturer 1841, Rector of Brightstone, Isle of Wight, 1830, and of Alverstoke 1811; Archdeacon of Surrey 1839, Chaplain to Prince Albert 1843, Dean of Westminster 1845: Consecrated 1845. Patronage, 65 livings, 3 archdeaconries, and 1 canonry.—*Cuddesden Palace, Wheatley, Oxon; Lavington House, Petworth; Athenæum Club, s.w.; 26, Pall Mall, s.w.*

OXFORD AND MORTIMER, Countess of, of Brampton Brian, Herefordshire.

Eliza, natural dau. of George, 1st Marquis of Westmeath; *m.* 1831 Alfred, 6th Earl of Oxford and Mortimer (ext.), who *d.* 1853.—*Brampton Brian, Ludlow.*

OXLEY, CHARLES, Esq., of Ripon, Yorkshire.

Only son of the late Christopher Oxley, Esq., of Ripon, by Dorothy, dau. of William Beckwith, Esq., J.P. of Lamb Hill, co. York; *b.* 1775; *s.* 1803; *m.* 1800 Margaret, dau. of Edmund Lodge, Esq., of Willow Hall, co. York; 2nd 1820 Anne Margaret, dau. of the Very Rev. R. D. Waddilove, D.D., and has issue by the former.

* Charles Christopher, J.P. for the N. Riding of Yorkshire; *b.* 1810; *m.* 1838 Maria, dau. of the Rev. W. J. D. Waddilove.

Mr. Oxley is a Magistrate for the W. Riding of Yorkshire.—*The Hall, Ripon.*

P

PACK. (See *Reynell-Pack*.)

PACK-BERESFORD, DENIS WILLIAM, Esq., of Fenagh, co. Carlow.
Second son of the late Major-General Sir Denis Pack, K.C.B., by Elizabeth Louisa, youngest dau. of George, 1st Marquis of Waterford; *b.* 1818; *s.* to this property 1854 on the death of Viscount Beresford; *m.* 1863 Annette Caroline, only dau. of Robert Clayton Browne, of Browne's Hill, co. Carlow, and has issue,

   • A dau., *b.* 1865.

Mr. Pack-Beresford, who was educated at the Royal Military Academy, Woolwich, is a J.P. and D.L. for co. Carlow (High Sheriff 1856); late Capt. R.A.; elected M.P. for co. Carlow 1862.—*Fenagh, Carlow; Army and Navy and Carlton Clubs, s.w.;* 32, *Devonshire Place,* w.

PACKE, GEORGE HUSSEY, Esq., of Prestwold, Leicestershire, and Caythorpe, Lincolnshire.
Eldest surviving son of the late Charles James Packe, Esq., of Prestwold (Lieut.-Col. Leicestershire Militia), (who *d.* 1816,) by Penelope, dau. of R. Dugdale, Esq.; *b.* 1796; *s.* his brother 1867; *m.,* 1824 Mary Anne Lydia, eldest dau. of the late John Heathcote, Esq., of Connington Castle, Hunts, and has, with other issue,

   • Hussey, *b.* 1846.

Mr. Packe, who was educated at Eton, is a J.P. and D.L. for co. Lincoln (High Sheriff 1843); a Magistrate for Hunts, Vice-Chairman of the Great Northern Railway Company, and a Lieut.-Col. in the Army, retired; elected M.P. for S. Lincolnshire 1859; Lord of the Manor of Prestwold, Patron of 1 living.—*Prestwold Hall, Loughborough; Caythorpe Hall, Grantham; Brooksome Tower, Poole; Arthur's and Brooks's Clubs, s.w.;* 41, *Charles Street, Berkeley Square,* w.

PACKE, JAMES, Esq., of Melton Lodge, Suffolk.
Fourth son of the late Charles James Packe, Esq., of Prestwold Hall, co. Leicester, by Penelope, dau. of Richard Dugdale, Esq., of Blyth Hall, co. Warwick; *b.* 1801; *m.* 1848 Sarah Martha, dau. of the late Rev. Charles Chapman. Educated at Eton and King's Coll., Cambridge (B.A. 1824, M.A. 1828); was formerly Fellow and Vice-Provost of King's Coll., Cambridge; is a Magistrate for Suffolk.—*Melton Lodge, Woodbridge.*

PADDON, WILLIAM HUSBAND, Esq., of Thralcsend, Beds.
Eldest son of John Paddon, Esq., J.P., of Truro, Cornwall, by Mary Anne, only child of William Husband, Esq., of Devonport; *b.* 1813; *s.* 1852; *m.* 1852 Susan Johanna, *b.* 1820, dau. of R. B. Penwarden, Esq., and relict of S. Bacon, Esq., and has issue,

   • William Penwarden, *b.* 1853.

This family were formerly Merchants and Shipowners at Truro.—*Thralcsend, Harpenden, Beds; Norton Lodge, Swansea, Glamorganshire.*

+**PADLEY,** ALFRED, Esq., of Bulwell, Notts.
Eldest son of the late Rev. Alfred Padley, of Bulwell; *b.* 1816; *s.* 185-; *m.* 1868 Annis Capper, 2nd dau. of Thomas John Watson, Esq., of Fulham, Middlesex. Is Lord of the Manor and Patron of Bulwell.—*Bulwell Hall, Nottingham.*

   Heir Pres., his brother Charles John Allen Newton (in Holy Orders), B.A. of Exeter Coll., Oxford, and Curate of Bulwell; *b.* 1818.

PADMORE, RICHARD, Esq., of Henwick Hall, Worcestershire.
Eldest son of the late Thomas Padmore, Esq., of Ketley, co. Salop, by his 2nd wife Sarah: *b.* 1789; *m.* 1823 Emma, only dau. of John Jones, Esq., of Worcester. Is a Magistrate for co. Worcester (High Sheriff 18—), and Alderman of the city of Worcester (of which he has been twice Mayor), and an Ironfounder; elected M.P. for Worcester 1860.—*Henwick Hall, Worcester; Westminster Palace Hotel, s.w.*

+**PADWICK,** HENRY, Esq., of Horsham, Sussex.
Eldest son of the late H. Padwick, Esq., of Horsham; *b.* 18—; is married, and has issue an only son,

   • Henry, *b.* 18—; *m.* 1861 Eleanor, only child of Charles Chevall Tooke, Esq., of Hurston Clays, Sussex.

Is a Magistrate for Middlesex, and a Dep.-Lieut. for Sussex.—*The Manor House, Horsham.*

PAGAN, WILLIAM, Esq., of Clayton, Fifeshire, and Curriestanes, Kirkcudbrightshire.
Eldest son of the late William Pagan, Esq., of Curriestanes, by Mary, dau. of — Cunningham, Esq.; *b.* 1803; *m.* 1826 Janet, eldest dau. of the late George Hair, Esq., of Bankhouse, and by her (who *d.* 1866) has, with other issue, an only son,

   • George Hair, *b.* 1828.

Mr. Pagan is a Banker and Writer in Cupar-Fife, and Provost of the town.— *Clayton, Cupar-Fife; Curriestanes, Dumfries.*

+**PAGE,** ROBERT, Esq., late of Holebrook, Somerset.
Second son of the late Sir Thomas Hyde Page, Knt., R.E.; *b.* 17—; *m.* 1815 Eliza, youngest dau. of the late William Bowles, Esq., of Fitzharris House, near Abingdon, Berks. Is a Magistrate for Somerset; formerly Capt. 9th Foot.—*Pulteney Street, Bath.*

+**PAGE,** THOMAS, Esq., of Ely, Cambridgeshire.
Son of the late T. Page, Esq.; *b.* 18—; is a J.P. and D.L. for co. Cambridge.—*Ely, Cambridgeshire; Carlton Club, s.w.;* 38, *Hyde Park Gardens,* w.

PAGE-TURNER. (See *Turner*.)

PAGET, Lord ALFRED HENRY.
Fifth son of Henry William, 1st Marquis of Anglesey, (by his 2nd wife Lady Caroline, dau. of George, 4th Earl of Jersey); *b.* 1816; *m.* 1847 Cecilia, dau. of the late George Thomas Wyndham, Esq., of Cromer Hall, Norfolk, and has, with other issue,

   • Arthur Henry, a Page of Honour to the Queen; *b.* 1851.

Lord A. Paget, who is a Col. in the Army, on half-pay, was Chief Equerry and Clerk Marshal to the Queen 1846–52 and 1853–8; was M.P. for Lichfield 1837–65.—*Melford Hall, Sudbury; United Service Club, s.w.;* 42, *Grosvenor Place, s.w.*

PAGET, Lord CLARENCE EDWARD, C.B., P.C., of Plâs Llanfair, Anglesey.
Third son of Field-Marshal Henry William, 1st Marquis of Anglesey, K.G., by his 2nd wife Lady Charlotte, dau. of Charles, 1st Earl Cadogan; *b.* 1811; *m.* 1852

Martha Stuart, youngest dau. of Admiral Sir Robert Waller Otway, Bart., G.C.B., and has, with other issue,

* Fitzroy Richard Clarence, b. 1853.

Lord C. Paget, who was educated at Westminster, is a Magistrate for Anglesey, and a Vice-Admiral, R.N.; was M.P. for Sandwich 1847–52, and 1857–66; Secretary of the Ordnance 1847–52; appointed Secretary to the Admiralty 1859; Commander-in-Chief in the Mediterranean 1866.—*Plâs Llanfair, Anglesey; United Service Club*, s.w.

PAGET, Lord GEORGE AUG. FREDERICK, C.B.
Sixth son of 1st Henry William, Marquis of Anglesey, K.G., by his 2nd wife Lady Charlotte, 2nd dau. of Charles, 1st Earl Cadogan; b. 1818; m. 1st 1854 Agnes Charlotte, dau. of the late Right Hon. Sir Arthur Paget, G.C.B. (she d. 1858); 2nd 1861 Louisa, youngest dau. of Charles Heneage, Esq., and has by the former, with other issue,

* Cecil Stratford, b. 1856.

Lord G. Paget, who entered the Army 1834, is a Major-General in the Army and Col. 7th Dragoon Guards, late Lieut.-Col. 4th Light Dragoons; appointed to command of Cavalry in India 1857, Inspector-General of Cavalry 1865; was M.P. for Beaumaris 1847–57.—*Plasnewydd, Beaumaris, N. Wales; United Service Club*, s.w.

PAGET, Sir AUGUSTUS BERKELEY, K.C.B. (cr. 1863).
Second son of the late Right Hon. Sir Arthur Paget, G.C.B., by Lady Augusta, dau. of John, 10th Earl of Westmoreland, and nephew of Henry William, 1st Marquis of Anglesey, K.G.; b. 1823; m. 1860 Walpurga Ehrengarde Helena, eldest dau. of the late Charles Frederick Anthony, Count of Hohenthal, and has, with other issue,

* Victor Frederic William, b. 1861.

Sir A. B. Paget, who was educated at the Charterhouse, entered the Diplomatic Service 1843, was successively Secretary of Legation at Athens, the Hague, Lisbon, and Berlin; Envoy Extraordinary at Dresden, Stockholm, and Copenhagen; appointed Min. Plenipotentiary in Portugal 1866, at Florence 1867.—*British Legation, Florence; Travellers' Club*, s.w.

PAGET, CHARLES, Esq., of Ruddington, Notts.
Elder son of the late Joseph Paget, Esq., by Ann, 3rd dau. of the Rev. J. Byng, of Tamworth; b. 1799; m. 1st 1823 Eliza, 4th dau. of William Paget, Esq., of Southfield, Loughborough; 2nd 1835 Ellen, dau. of W. Tebbutt, Esq., and has by the former, with other issue,

* Joseph, b. 1825; m. 1858 Helen Elizabeth, eldest dau. of the Rev. H. Abney.

Mr. Paget, who is a J.P. and D.L. for Notts (High Sheriff 1814), was M.P. for Nottingham 1856–65.—*Ruddington Grange, Nottingham; Reform Club*, s.w.; 113, *Eaton Square*, s.w.

PAGET, EDMUND ARTHUR, Esq., of Thorpe Satchville, Leicestershire.
Second son of the late John Paget, Esq., of Thorpe Satchville, by Ann Paget, dau. of John Hunt, Esq., of Loughborough; b. 1810; s. 1833; m. 1858 Martha, dau. of Otho Manners, Esq., formerly of Goodby Marwood Hall, co. Leicester, and has, with other issue,

* Claude Arthur, b. 1859.

Mr. Paget, who is a Magistrate for co. Leicester, and Lord of the Manor of Thorpe Satchville, was formerly Capt. in the Leicestershire Regt. of Militia.—*Thorpe Satchville Hall, Melton Mowbray.*

PAGET, the Rev. FRANCIS EDWARD.
Only son of General the late Hon. Sir Edward Paget, G.C.B. (who was brother of Henry William, 1st Marquis of Anglesey, K.G.), by his 1st wife the Hon. Frances, dau. of William, 1st Lord Bagot, b. 1806; m. 1840

Fanny, dau. of the Rev. William Chester, and has issue. Educated at Westminster and Ch. Ch., Oxford (B.A. 1827, M.A. 1830); appointed Rector of Elford 1835.—*Elford Rectory, Tamworth.*

PAGET, Mrs., of Plasnewydd, Anglesey.
Maria Georgiana, eldest dau. of the late Charles Pascoe Grenfell, Esq., by Lady Georgiana Isabella, eldest dau. of William, 2nd Earl of Sefton; m. 1856 Col. Frederick Paget, who was M.P. for Beaumaris 1832–47, and who d. 1866.—*Plasnewydd, Beaumaris.*

PAGET, RICHARD HORNER, Esq., of Cranmore and Newberry, Somerset.
Only surviving son of the late John Moore Paget, Esq., J.P. and D.L., of Cranmore and Newberry, by Elizabeth Jane, eldest dau. of the Rev. J. F. Doveton, Rector of Mells, Somerset; b. 1832; s. 1866; m. 1866 Caroline Isabel, 2nd dau. of Henry Edward Surtees, Esq., M.P., of Redworth, co. Durham, and Dane End. Herts. Educated at Sandhurst, is a Magistrate for Somerset, Lord of the Manors of E. Cranmore, Clipsham, &c., and Patron of 1 living, and Capt. N. Somerset Yeomanry Cavalry; late Capt. 66th Foot; elected M.P. for E. Somerset 1865.—*Cranmore Hall, Shepton Mallet; Army and Navy and Carlton Clubs*, s.w.; 13, *Stratton Street*, w.

PAGET, THOMAS, Esq., of Knockglass, co. Mayo.
Eldest son of the late Robert Paget, Esq., of Faby (who d. 1826), by Catherine, dau. of the late William Orme, Esq., of Millbrook; b. 1796; m. 1st 1816 Margaret, dau. of the late James Paget, Esq., of Knockglass; 2nd 1829 Anne Emily, eldest dau. of the late Samuel Handy, Esq., of Bracca Castle, co. Westmeath, and has by the former, with other issue,

* James, educated at Trinity Coll., Dublin; Capt. N. Mayo Militia; b. 1820; m. 1857 Caroline, dau. of the late Major Knox, of Greenwood Park.

Mr. Paget, who is a Magistrate for cos. Mayo and Sligo, was formerly Capt. N. Mayo Regt. of Militia.—*Knockglass, Ballina, co. Mayo.*

PAGET, the Rev. THOMAS BEADLEY, of Welton, Yorkshire.
Son of the late Thomas B. Paget, Esq., of Cumberford Hall, Staffordshire, by his 1st wife Elizabeth, dau. of the Rev. John Watkins, of Clifton Campville Park, Staffordshire; b. 1812; m. 1847 Sophia Beckett, 3rd dau. of Edmund Denison, Esq., of Doncaster, and has issue. Educated at Trinity Coll., Cambridge (B.A. 1834, M.A. 1839); appointed Vicar of Welton-with-Melton, co. York, 1846, and Prebendary of York 1865.—*Welton Vicarage, Brough, East Yorkshire.*

PAGET, THOMAS TERTIUS, Esq., of Humberstone, Leicestershire.
Eldest son of the late Thomas Paget, Esq., M.P., of Humberstone, by Anne, 2nd dau. of the late John Pares, Esq., of Hopwell Hall, co. Derby, and of the Newarke, Leicester; b. 1807; m. 1850 Katherine Geraldine, 4th dau. of the late Marcus M'Causland, Esq., of Fruit Hill, co. Londonderry. Is a J.P. and D.L. for co. Leicester, Lord of the Manor and Patron of Lubbenham; elected M.P. for W. Leicestershire 1867.—*Humberstone, Leicester; Bostock, Ashby de la Zouch; Lubbenham Manor, Market Harborough; Oxendon Lodge, Northampton; Reform Club*, s.w.

PAGET. (See under *Anglesey, Marquis of.*)

PAINE, Lieut.-Col. JOHN, of Patcham, Sussex.
Son of the late John Paine, Esq., of Patcham, by Grace, dau. of George Kemp, Esq.; b. 1789; m. 1813 Sarah, dau. of the late Sir Robert Harvey, Bart. (she d. 1865). Is J.P. and D.L. for Sussex, and Col. Sussex Militia, retired.—*Patcham Place, Brighton; United Service Club*, s.w.

PAKENHAM, the Right Hon. Sir RICHARD, K.C.B., P.C. (cr. 1848).

Fifth son of the late Admiral the Hon. Sir Thomas Pakenham, G.C.B., by Louisa, dau. of the Right Hon. J. Staples, and cousin of Thomas, 2nd Earl of Longford; *b.* 1797. Educated for the Diplomatic Service; is a Magistrate for co. Westmeath; has been Attaché at the Hague, Secretary of Legation in Switzerland, Minister at Mexico, and Envoy Extraordinary and Minister Plenipotentiary at Washington and Lisbon. —*Coolure, Castlepollard, co. Westmeath ; Travellers' Club, s.w.*

+**PAKENHAM**, the Rev. ARTHUR HERCULES, of Langford Lodge, co. Antrim.

Eldest surviving son of the late Lieut.-General the Hon. Sir Hercules Pakenham, K.C.B. (who *d.* 1850), by the Hon. Emily Stapleton, 4th dau. of Thomas, 22nd Lord Despenser ; *b.* 1824 ; *s.* his brother 1854. Educated at Caius Coll., Cambridge (B.A. 1846, M.A. 1850); is a Magistrate for co. Antrim.—*Langford Lodge, Crumlin, co. Antrim ; 11, Hertford Street, w.*

Heir Pres., his brother Thomas Henry, a Col. in the Army and Lieut.-Col. 30th Foot ; Knight of the Medjidie, &c.; late M.P. for co. Antrim ; b. 1826,

PAKENHAM. (See under *Longford, Earl of.*)

PAKENHAM-MAHON. (See *Mahon.*)

PAKINGTON, the Right Hon. Sir JOHN SOMERSET, Bart., G.C.B., of Westwood, Worcestershire (cr. 1846).

Eldest surviving son of the late William Russell, Esq., of Powick, by Elizabeth, eldest dau. of the late Sir Herbert Perrott Pakington, Bart. (*ext.*), of Westwood; *b.* 1799; *m.* 1st 1822 Mary, only child of Moreton Aglionby Slaney, Esq., of Shiffnal, co. Salop ; 2nd 1844 Augusta, dau. of the late Right Rev. Dr. G. Murray, Lord Bishop of Rochester; 3rd 1851 Augusta, dau. of Thomas Champion de Crespigny, Esq., and widow of Col. H. Davies, M.P.; assumed the name of Pakington on his uncle's death, 1830, when he succeeded to his estates. Educated at Eton and Oriel Coll., Oxford ; is a J.P. and D.L. for co. Worcester, a Magistrate for co. Hereford, Chairman of Quarter Sessions in that county 1834–58, Patron of 1 living, and Lieut.-Col. Worcestershire Yeomanry Cavalry ; has been M.P. for Droitwich since 1837 ; was Secretary of State for the Colonies Feb.–Dec. 1852 ; First Lord of the Admiralty 1858-9 and 1866-7 ; appointed Secretary of State for War 1867. — *Westwood, Droitwich ; Carlton and Boodle's Clubs, s.w.; 41, Eaton Square, s.w.*

Heir, his son John Slaney, of Kent's Green, co. Worcester, educated at Eton and Ch. Ch., Oxford (B.A. 1847) ; a J.P. and D.L. for the co. and city of Worcester, Capt. Worcester Yeomanry Cavalry, Major Worcestershire Volunteers, Private Sec. at the War Office, and President of the Worcestershire Union of Educational Institutes; b. 1826 ; m. 1849 Diana, youngest dau. of the 4th Earl of Glasgow.

PALEY, the Rev. GEORGE BARROW, of Langcliffe, Yorkshire.

Eldest son of the late John Green Paley, Esq., J.P. and D.L. of Langcliffe and Oatlands, co. York, by Anne, dau. and co-heir of George Barber, Esq., of Cheek-House, Bradford, co. York ; *b.* 1799 ; *s.* 1860 ; *m.* 1837 Catherine Anne, dau. of Wm. Robertson, Esq., M.D., of Bath, and has, with other issue,

* John Paley, b. 1839.

Mr. Paley, who was educated at St. Peter's Coll., Cambridge (B.A. 1822; M.A. 1825, B.D. 1833), is a Magistrate for Suffolk, Rector of Freckenham, Suffolk, and Rural Dean, and Patron of 1 living. *Freckenham, So h ton, Suffolk ; Langcliffe, Settle ; Conservative Club, s.w.*

721

PALEY, Mrs., of Bishopton Grange, Yorkshire.

Mary, 3rd dau. of the late Ven. Archdeacon Paley ; *m.* 1807 Robert Paley, Esq., M.D., who was a Magistrate for the W. Riding of Yorkshire and for the Liberty of Ripon, and *d.* 1859.—*Bishopton Grange, Ripon.*

PALK, Sir LAWRENCE, Bart., of Haldon House, Devonshire (cr. 1782).

Eldest son of the late Sir Lawrence Vaughan Palk, Bart., of Haldon House (some time M.P. for Devon), by his 1st wife Eleanora, dau. of the late Sir Bourchier Wrey, Bart., of Tawstock Court, and widow of Edward Hartopp, Esq., of Dalby House, co. Leicester; *b.* 1818 ; *s.* 1860 ; *m.* 1845 Maria Harriet, dau. of the late Sir Thomas H. Hesketh, Bart., of Rufford Park, co. Lancaster. Educated at Eton, and formerly served in the 1st Dragoons ; is a J.P. and D.L. for Devon, Lord of the Manors of Haldon, Tor Moham, Kenn, &c., and Patron of 5 livings ; he has been M.P. for South Devon since 1859 ; Lieut.-Col. Devon co. Volunteers. —*Haldon House, near Exeter ; The Manor House, Torquay ; Carlton Club, s.w. ; 1, Grosvenor Gardens, w.*

Heir, his son Lawrence Hesketh, Ensign Scots Fusilier Guards; b. 1846.

PALLES, ANDREW CHRISTOPHER, Esq., of Little Mount Palles, co. Cavan.

Only son of the late Andrew Palles, Esq., by Elizabeth, dau. of Richard O'Ferrall, Esq., of Balyna, co. Kildare : *b.* 1801 ; *s.* 1812 ; *m.* 1828 Eleanor, eldest dau. of Matthew James Plunkett, of St. Margaret's, co. Dublin, and has, with other issue,

* Andrew, B.A. of Trinity Coll., Dublin ; *b.* 1829 ; *m.* 1853 Jane, dau. of Joseph Bruce, Esq., of Kingston, Canada West, and has, with other issue, * Andrew Christopher, *b.* 1860.

Mr. Palles, who was educated at Oscott Coll., is a Solicitor in Dublin. This family is of the De Palatios, of Lombardy, and have been settled in Ireland since the 15th century.—*Little Mount Palles, Mount Nugent, co. Cavan ; 12, Belvedere Place, Dublin.*

PALLISER, Sir HUGH PALLISER, Bart., of Castletown House, co. Wexford.

Eldest son of the late Sir Hugh Palliser Palliser, Bart., of Castletown House, by Mary, dau. of John Yates, Esq., of Dedham, Essex; *b.* 1796 ; *s.* as 3rd Bart. 1813. Is a Magistrate for co. Wexford. The family name was originally Walters, but the present name was assumed in 1798.—*Castletown House, Portobello, co. Wexford.*

PALLISER, Mrs. BURY-, of Wimbledon, Surrey.

Fanny, dau. of the late Joseph Marryat, Esq., M.P., of Wimbledon House, Surrey, by Charlotte, dau. of Frederick Geyer, Esq., of Boston, U.S. ; *m.* 1832 Richard Bury-Palliser, Esq., of Castlewarden, co. Dublin, J.P. for Sussex, who *d.* 1852, leaving, with other issue,

John Augustine, Capt, 76th Foot ; b. 1834 ; d. 1864.

This family is of Irish extraction. John Bury, of Shannon Grove, took the name and arms of Palliser on marrying Jane, dau. and heir of William Palliser, Archbp. of Cashel.—*Homestead House, Surrey, s.w.; 13a, Upper Brook Street, w.*

PALLISER, JOHN, Esq., of Comragh, co. Waterford.

Eldest son of the late Wray Palliser, Esq., J.P. of Comragh, Lieut.-Col. Waterford Artillery Militia, by Anne, dau. of John Gladstone, Esq., of Annes Gift, co. Tipperary ; *b.* 1817 ; *s.* 1862. Is a Magistrate for co. Waterford, and a Capt. in the Waterford Artillery Militia. This family, formerly named Bury, is a branch of the house of Charleville.—*Comragh House, Kilmacthomas, co. Waterford ; Deerpackban, Richard, co. Tipperary ; National Club, s.w.*

PALMER, Sir CHARLES JAMES, Bart., of Dorney, Bucks (cr. 1621).

Only son of the late Rev. Sir Henry Palmer, Bart., of Dorney, by Sarah, dau. of George Gerrard, Esq. (she m. 2nd 1866 T. M. Willson, Esq., of Darkes. Herts); b. 1828; s. as 9th Bart. 1865; m. 1862 Katharine Millicent, dau. of Peter Hood, Esq., M.D., of Windmill Hills, Gateshead, co. Durham, and has issue,

 • Edith Gerard Hood and Mabel.

Sir C. Palmer, who was called to the Bar at the Inner Temple 1863, is a J.P. and D.L. for Bucks, and a Magistrate for Berks, Lord of the Manor of Dorney-cum-Boveney and Burnham (alias Rokeby), Lay Rector of Dorney-cum-Boveney, and Patron of 1 living; late Capt. Bucks Militia. This family, formerly of Steyning, Angmering, and Parham, in Sussex, Wingham in Kent, and Fairfield in Somerset, is of Danish origin, and was reputed of note in Sussex before the Conquest.—*Dorney Court, Windsor; Junior United Service Club, s.w.*; 1, *Dr. Johnson's Buildings, Temple*, E.C.

 Heir Pres., his cousin John (of Oakley Place, Windsor, Berks, only son of the late Philip Palmer, Esq., of Oakley Place, who d. 1865, by his 1st wife Anne, dau. of — Woolhouse, Esq.); b. 1832.

PALMER, Sir GEOFFREY, Bart., of Carlton Park, Northamptonshire (cr. 1660).

Eldest son of the late Sir John Henry Palmer, Bart., of Carlton Park, by the Hon. Mary Grace, dau. of Lewis Thomas, 2nd Lord Sondes; b. 1809; s. as 8th Bart. 1865. Educated at Eton and Ch. Ch., Oxford (B.A. 1830); called to the Bar at the Inner Temple 1835; a Magistrate for cos. Leicester and Northampton, Lord of the Manor of Carlton, and Patron of 2 livings; late Capt. Leicestershire Yeomanry.—*Carlton Park, Rockingham.*

 Heir Pres., his brother Lewis Henry (Rev.), M.A. of Ch. Ch., Oxford; Rector of Carlton; b. 1818.

PALMER, Sir WILLIAM HENRY ROGER, Bart., of Keenagh, co. Mayo (cr. 1777).

Eldest son of the late Sir William Henry Palmer, Bart., of Castle Lachin, co. Mayo, by Alice, dau. of — Franklin, Esq.; b. 1802; s. as 4th Bart. 1810; m. 1826 Elenora, dau. of John Matthews, Esq., of Eyarth and Plas Bostock, co. Denbigh. Is a J.P. and D.L. for cos. Mayo and Sligo, and a Magistrate for co. Dublin.—*Kenure Park, Rush, co. Dublin; Keenagh, Crossmolina, co. Mayo; Osfu Park, Wrexham*; 56, *Portland Place*, w.

 Heir, his son Roger William Henry, educated at Eton; J.P. and D.L. for co. Sligo, a Magistrate for cos. Dublin and Mayo, and Capt. 2nd Life Guards; late M.P. for co. Mayo; b. 1832.

PALMER, Sir ARCHDALE ROBERT, Bart., of Wanlip Hall, Leicestershire (cr. 1791).

Elder son of the late Sir George Joseph Palmer, Bart., of Wanlip Hall, by Emily Elizabeth, 3rd dau. of George Peter Holford, Esq., of Westonbirt, co. Gloucester; b. 1838; s. as 4th Bart. 1866. Is Lord of the Manor and Patron of Wanlip; Lieut. and Adjutant Rifle Brigade, and Patron of 1 living.—*Wanlip Hall, Leicester; Carlton Club*, s.w.

 Heir Pres., his brother George Hudson, B.A. of Balliol Coll., Oxford; b. 1841.

PALMER, Sir JAMES FREDERICK, Knt. (cr. 1857).

Fourth son of the late Rev. John Palmer, of Torrington, Devon, by Jane, 2nd dau. of William Johnson, Esq.; b. 1804; m. 1832 Isabella, dau. of John Gunning, Esq. Was chosen first Speaker of the Legislative Council of Victoria 1851, first President of the Legislative Council 1856.—*Burwood Hill, Hawthorn, Melbourne, Australia.*

PALMER, the Rt. Hon. Sir ROUNDELL, Q.C., of Selborne, Hants (cr. 1861).

Second son of the late Rev. William Jocelyn Palmer, Rector of Mixbury, Oxon, by Dorothea Richardson, youngest dau. of the late Rev. William Roundell, of Gledstone, co. York, and grandson of William Palmer, Esq., of Nazing Park, co. Essex; b. 1812; m. 1848 Lady Laura, 2nd dau. of William, 8th Earl Waldegrave, and has issue. Educated at Rugby, Winchester, and Trinity Coll., Oxford, and was afterwards Fellow of Magdalen Coll. (B.A. 1834, M.A. 1836); called to the Bar at Lincoln's Inn 1837; became a Queen's Counsel 1849; Solicitor-General 1861, Attorney-General 1863–6; was M.P. for Plymouth 1847–52 and 1853–7; elected M.P. for Richmond 1861.—*Selborne, Alton; Athenæum and Oxford and Cambridge Clubs*, s.w.; 6, *Portland Place*, w.

PALMER, the Rev. CHARLES.

Second son of the late Charles Palmer, Esq., of Ladbroke, co. Warwick; b. 1782; m. 1823 Lady Charlotte, eldest dau. of Heneage, 4th Earl of Aylesford, and has with other issue,

 • Henry Charles, b. 1826; m. 1865 Frances, eldest dau. of the Rev. James Hughes Hallett, of Higham, Kent.

Mr. Palmer, who was educated at Ch. Ch., Oxford (B.A. 1805, M.A. 1808), and appointed Rector of Lighthorne 1834, is a Magistrate for co. Warwick.—*Lighthorne Rectory, Warwick.*

PALMER, CHARLES COLLEY, Esq., of Rahan, co. Kildare.

Son of the late William Lamb Palmer, Esq., J.P., of Rahan, by Elizabeth Emily Anne, 3rd dau. of the late James Nugent, Esq., of Clonlost, co. Westmeath; b. 1845; s. 1849; m. 1866 Mary Jane, only dau. of the late Francis L. Darnes, Esq., of Greenhill, King's Co., and has issue,

 • William Francis, b. 1867.

Mr. Palmer is a Magistrate for co. Kildare.—*Rahan House, Enfield, co. Kildare.*

PALMER, EDWARD HOWLEY, Esq., of Canon Hill, Berkshire.

Eldest son of the late John Horsley Palmer, Esq., Merchant, of London, by Elizabeth, dau. of John Delli, Esq., of Southampton; b. 1811; m. 1844 Jessie Fanny, dau. of Vice-Admiral Henry F. Greville, C.B., and has with other issue,

 • Greville Horsley, b. 1845.

Mr. Palmer, who was educated at the Charterhouse, is a Merchant in London.—*Canon Hill, Bray, Maidenhead; Travellers' Club*, s.w.

PALMER, FREDERICK, Esq., of Withcote Hall, Leicestershire.

Second surviving son of the late Rev. Henry Palmer, by Elizabeth, dau. of the Rev. Samuel Heyrick, Rector of Braunston, co. Northampton; b. 1825; m. 1850 Mary, only dau. of the late W. H. Harrison, Esq., of Conyngham Hall, co. York, and has with other issue,

 • Edward Geoffrey Bromley, b. 1864.

Mr. Palmer, who was educated at Eton, is a J.P. and D.L. for co. Leicester (High Sheriff 1865), a Magistrate for co. Rutland, Patron of 2 livings, and Capt. Prince Albert's Own Leicestershire Yeomanry Cavalry; late Capt. 27th Inniskilling Regt.—*Withcote Hall, Oakham; Conservative Club*, s.w.; 30, *Beaufort Gardens*, s.w.

PALMER, the Rev. FREDERICK RICHARD, of Caston, Norfolk.

Only son of the late Richard Palmer, Esq., J.P. of Caston, by Lucy, dau. of Richard Sappe, Esq.; b. 1841; s. 1855; m. 1862 Julia Jane, dau. of the Rev. William Frost, M.A., of the Oaks, Thorpe-next-Norwich, and

grand-dau. of the late Richard Crawshay, Esq., J.P. of Ottershaw Park, Surrey. Educated at Exeter Coll., Oxford (B.A. 1865, M.A. 1866); is a Magistrate for Norfolk.— *Caston, Attleborough ; Chalfont St. Giles, Slough ; University and Phœnix Clubs, s.w.* .

PALMER, George, Esq., of Nazing, Essex.
Eldest son of the late George Palmer, Esq., of Nazing Park (who was M.P. for South Essex 1836–47), by Anna Maria, dau. of W. Bund, Esq., of Wick, co. Worcester ; *b.* 1799 ; *m.* 1827 Elizabeth Charlotte, 2nd dau. of J. Surtees, Esq., of Newcastle-on-Tyne, and has, with other issue,

* George, of the Bengal Civil Service, educated at the Charterhouse ; served in India during the Mutiny ; *b.* 1828 ; *m.* 1861 Emily Eden, dau. of William Vansittart, Esq.

Mr. Palmer, who was educated at Harrow, is a Magistrate for Essex (High Sheriff 1863), a Verderer of Waltham Forest, and Lieut.-Col. Commandant of the Essex Yeomanry Cavalry.— *Nazing Park, Waltham Abbey ; Carlton Club, s.w.*

PALMER, the Rev. Henry, of Sullington, Sussex.
Second son of the late Rev. George Palmer, of Sullington, by Charlotte Elizabeth. dau. of Thomas Bonnor, Esq., of Lindsay House, Chelsea ; *b.* 1835 ; *s.* 1859. Educated at Marlborough and Trinity Coll., Cambridge (B.A. 1858, M.A. 1860) ; is Rector and Patron of Sullington.— *Sullington Rectory, Storrington, Sussex.*

PALMER, Henry, Esq., of Clifton, Beds.
Fourth son of the late Rev. Richard P. Palmer, by Elizabeth, 3rd dau. of the late Sir Gillies Payne, Bart., of Blunham House, Beds ; *b.* 1799 ; *m.* 1822 Mariana, youngest dau. of the late Hugh Perry Keane, Esq. ; is a Magistrate for Beds.— *Clifton Lodge, Biggleswade.*

PALMER, Henry Manley, Esq., of Shriff, co. Leitrim.
Only son of Henry Palmer, Esq., by Catherine, eldest dau. of the late Rev. C. Cullen, J.P., Rector of Manor Hamilton ; *b.* 1806 ; *m.* 1837 Mary Emma, 6th dau. of the late John Hawks, Esq., J.P. and D.L., of Gateshead, co. Durham, and has, with other issue,

* Manley Montgomery, a Magistrate for co. Leitrim, and Lient. Royal Limerick Regt. of Militia ; *b.* 1837 ; *m.* 1860 Ellen Elizabeth Westcar, youngest dau. of the late Jonathan Peel, Esq., of Culham House, Oxon.

Mr. Palmer was formerly a Magistrate for co. Leitrim. — *Shriff, Dromahair, co. Leitrim.*

PALMER, John Hinde, Esq., Q.C.
Only son of the late Samuel Palmer, Esq., of Dulwich, Surrey, and Loughworthy, Devon, by Mary. dau. and heiress of the late L. Hinde, Esq. ; *b.* 1808 ; *m.* 1849 Clara Maria. 2nd dau. of the late Right Hon. Charles Tennyson-d'Eyncourt, of Bayons Manor, co. Lincoln ; called to the Bar at Lincoln's Inn 1832, made a Queen's Counsel in 1859 ; is a J.P. and D.L. for Surrey.— *Reform Club, s.w. ; 8a, Gloucester Place, Portman Square, w.*

PALMER, John Whittuck, Esq., of Hanham. Gloucestershire.
Only son of the late Thomas Leach Palmer. Esq., of Keynsham (who *d.* 1827), by Martha, dau. of Abraham Whittuck, Esq., of Bitton, co. Gloucester ; *b.* 1809 ; *m.* 1836 Sarah Amy. fourth dau. of the late Samuel Whittuck, Esq., of Hanham, and has, with other issue,

* Alfred John, *b.* 1846.

Mr. Palmer is a Magistrate for co. Gloucester.— *Hanham, Bristol.*

PALMER, Robert, Esq., of Holme Park Berks.
Eldest son of the late Richard Palmer. Esq., of Hurst and Sonning, Berks, by Jane, eldest dau. of

726

Oldfield Bowles, Esq., of North Aston, Oxon ; *b.* 1793 ; *s.* 1806. Educated at Eton and Trinity Coll., Cambridge ; is a J.P. and D.L. for Berks (High Sheriff 1818), a Magistrate for Wilts and Lord of the Manor of Sunning ; was M.P. for Berks 1825–59.— *Holme Park. Sunning, Reading ; Boodle's, Arthur's, Carlton, and University Clubs, s.w.*

Heir Pres., his brother Richard. M.A. of Ch. Ch., Oxford, Rector of Purley, Berks ; *b.* 1796.

PALMER, Sandford, Esq., of Ballinlough, King's Co.
Eldest son of the late Robert Sandford Palmer, Esq., of Ballinlough (who was High Sheriff of King's Co. 1795, and formerly Capt. King's Co. Militia). by Mary Anne, dau. of Simon Farthing Davies, Esq., of Farthing Ville, co. Cork, Capt. 5th Dragoon Guards ; *b.* 1803 ; *s.* 1835 ; *m.* 1826 Mary Catherine, dau. of Edward Hoare Reeves, Esq., J.P., of Ballyglissane, co. Cork, and has, with other issue,

* Sandford Robert, Capt. King's co. Royal Rifles ; *b.* 1827.

Mr. Palmer, who was educated at Trinity Coll. Dublin (B.A. 1826), is a Magistrate for co. Tipperary and King's Co. (High Sheriff 1840).— *Ballinlough, Roscrea.*

+ PALMER, Thomas, Esq., of Summerhill, co. Mayo.
Elder son of the late Thomas Palmer, Esq., of Summerhill ; *b.* 1790 ; *m.* 1812 Miss Ormsby, and has issue,

* Thomas, a Magistrate for co. Mayo ; *b.* 1813 ; *m.* 1837 Emily, dau. of the late Major Perceval.

Mr. Palmer was formerly a Magistrate for co. Mayo (High Sheriff 1820).— *Summerhill, Killala, co. Mayo.*

PALMER, the Rev. William, of Streamstown, co. Westmeath, and Invermore, co. Mayo.
Eldest son of the late William Palmer, Esq. of Streamstown (who *d.* 1865), by his 1st wife Helen, dau. of J. G. Hill, Esq., of Fieldtown, co. Westmeath ; *b.* 1803 ; *m.* 1838 Sophia Mary Bonne. dau. of the late Admiral Sir Francis Beaufort, K.C.B. Educated at Trinity Coll., Dublin, and Worcester Coll., Oxford ; is Vicar of Whitchurch Canonicorum. Dorset.— *Streamstown, Mullingar, co. Westmeath ; Invermore, co. Mayo; Whitchurch Rectory, Bridport.*

PALMER-ACLAND. (See *Acland.*)

PALMER-MOREWOOD, Charles Rowland, Esq., of Alfreton, Derbyshire.
Eldest son of the late William Frederick Palmer-Morewood, Esq., J.P. and D.L., of Alfreton (High Sheriff 1835, and formerly Lieut.-Col. Stafford Militia), by Clara. 2nd dau. of Sir Charles Blois. Bart. ; *b.* 1817 ; *s.* 1863 ; *m.* 1842 the Hon. Georgiana. 2nd dau. of George Anson, 7th Lord Byron. Is a J.P. and D.L. for co. Derby. Lord of the Manor and Patron of Alfreton.— *Alfreton Park, Derby ; Ladbroke, Southam, Warwickshire.*

PALMERSTON, Viscountess, of Broadlands, Hants, and Brocket Hall, Herts.
The Hon. Emily, only surviving child of Peniston, 1st Viscount Melbourne (who *d.* 1828), by Elizabeth, dau. of Sir Ralph Milbanke, Bart. ; *m.* 1st Peter, 5th Earl Cowper, who *d.* 1837 ; 2nd 1839, Henry John. 3rd and last Viscount Palmerston, K.G., who was Prime Minister 1855–8 and 1859–65, and who *d.* 1865, when his title became extinct. Is Lady of the Manor of Romsey. — *Broadlands, Romsey ; Brocket Hall, Hatfield ; 21. Park Lane, w.*

PALMES, the Rev. William Lindsay, of Naburn, Yorkshire.
Eldest son of the late George Palmes. Esq., of Naburn Hall, by Margaret Isabella. dau. of William Lindsay. Esq., of Oaklands. co. Lanark ; *b.* 1813 ; *s.* 1851 ; *m.*

1849 Marion, eldest dau. of A. Empson, Esq., of Spellow Hill, and has, with other issue,

 * George, b. 1851.

Mr. Palmes, who was educated at Trinity Coll., Cambridge (B.A. 1836, M.A. 1839), ordained 1845, and appointed Vicar of Hornsea-cum-Riston 1849, is a Magistrate for the E. Riding of Yorkshire, Rural Dean of North Holderness, a Proctor in Convocation for the E. Riding, and Patron of 1 living.—*Naburn Hall, York.*

PANMURE. (See *Dalhousie*.)

PANTON, PAUL GRIFFITH, Esq., of Plas Fron, Denbighshire.
Second son of the late Jones Panton, Esq., of Plas Gwyn, Anglesey, by Ann Elizabeth, dau. of Thomas Whittaker, Esq.; b. 1795; m. 1826 Anne Barton, dau. of David Russell, Esq.; and by her, who d. 1856, has, with other issue,

 * Paul, b. 1836.

Mr. Panton is a Commander R.N., and a Magistrate for cos. Denbigh and Flint.—*Plas Fron, Wrexham.*

PAPILLON, THOMAS, Esq., of Crowhurst Park, Sussex.
Eldest son of the late Thomas Papillon, Esq., of Acrise Place, Kent, by Anne, dau. and co-heir of Henry Cressett Pelham, Esq., of Crowhurst, Sussex; b. 1803; s. 1838; m. 1825 Frances Margaret, 2nd dau. of Sir Henry Oxenden, Bart., and has, with other issue,

 * Philip Oxenden, educated at Rugby; M.A. of University Coll., Oxford; a Barrister-at-Law of the Inner Temple, a J.P. and D.L. for Essex, a Magistrate for Sussex, Major Royal East Kent Mounted Rifles, late M.P. for Colchester, Lord of the Manor of Lexden and Patron of 1 living; b. 1826 ; m. 1862 Emily Caroline, 3rd dau. of the Very Rev. Thomas Garnier, B.C.L., Dean of Lincoln, and has, with other issue, * Pelham-Rawstorne, b. 1864.

Mr. Papillon, who was educated at Winchester and Ch. Ch., Oxford, is a J.P. and D.L. for Kent and Sussex, and Patron of 3 livings. This family is of French extraction, and finally settled in England after the massacre of St. Bartholomew 1572, in which a direct lineal progenitor fell a victim.—*Crowhurst Park, Battle ; Lexden Manor, Colchester.*

PARBURY, GEORGE, Esq., of Caterham, Surrey.
Eldest son of the late Charles Parbury, Esq., by Hannah, his wife, and grandson of the late George Parbury, Esq.; b. 1807 ; m. 1st 1833 Mary Anne Jeanna, only child of Edward Ellis, Esq., of The Priory, Hertford (she d. 1815) ; 2nd 1819 Lucy Anne, dau. of the late Sir John Key, Bart., and has, with other issue,

 * Edward Fraser, b. 1843.

Mr. Parbury is a Magistrate for Surrey, for Middlesex, and for the City of Westminster, and a Dep.-Lieut. for the Tower Hamlets.—*Caterham Manor, Surrey ; 12, Hyde Park Place, s.w.*

PARDOE, the Rev. ARTHUR, of Stanton-Lacy House, Shropshire, and Witherstone, Dorset.
Youngest son of the late Rev. George Dansey Pardoe, of Nash Court, co. Salop, by Eleanor, dau. of the Rev. Samuel Sneade, of Bedstone and Ludlow; b. 1821 ; m. 1817 Mary Jane, dau. of the late Rev. William Jenkins, of Sidmouth, Devon, and Witherstone, Dorset, by whom he has issue,

 * Arthur John, b. 1851.

Mr. Pardoe, who was educated at Jesus Coll., Cambridge (B.A. 1843), is a Magistrate for Dorset and co. Salop.—*Stanton-Lacy House, Ludlow ; Witherstone, Bridport.*

PARDOE, GEORGE, Esq., of Nash Court, Shropshire.
Eldest son of the late Rev. George Dansey Pardoe, of Nash Court, by Eleanor, dau. of the Rev. S. Sneade, Rector of Bedstone, Salop; b. 1811 ; s. 1856; m. 1st 1843 Laura, dau. of the late Thomas White, Esq., of Bognor, Sussex; 2nd 185- Elizabeth Mary, dau. of the late J. F. Croome, Esq. Educated at St. John's Coll., Cambridge (B.A. 1833–4) ; is a J.P. and D.L. for co. Salop, and a Magistrate for Worcestershire.—*Nash Court, Tenbury.*

Heir Pres., his brother Henry, b. 1817.

PARDOE, JOHN, Esq., of Leyton, Essex.
Eldest son of the late John Pardoe, Esq., of Leyton (who d. 1790), by Jane, dau. of Thomas Oliver, Esq., of Leyton ; b. 1787; s. his grandfather 1796 ; m. 1808 Charlotte Jane, dau. of John P. Allix, Esq., of Swaffham, co. Cambridge, and has, with other issue,

 * John, in Holy Orders, M.A. of St. John's Coll., Cambridge, Vicar of Leyton ; b. 1813 ; m. 1838 Frances, dau. of the late George Thornhill, Esq., M.P., of Diddington Park, Hunts, and has issue, * John, b. 1839.

Mr. Pardoe, who was educated at Emmanuel Coll., Cambridge (B.A. 1810), is a Magistrate for Essex, a J.P. and D.L. for Herts, Lord of the Manor of Leyton, and Patron of 2 livings.—*Manor House, Leyton ; Arthur's Club, s.w.*

PARES, THOMAS HENRY, Esq., of Hopwell, Derbyshire.
Eldest son of the late Thomas Pares, Esq., J.P and D.L., of Hopwell (who was formerly M.P. for Leicester, and High Sheriff of co. Derby 1845), by Octavia, dau. of Edward Longdon Macmurdo, Esq. ; b. 1830 : s. 1866 ; m. 1852 Mary Louisa, dau. of the Rev. Richard Stephens, B.D., Vicar of Belgrave, co. Leicester, and has, with other issue, an only son,

 * Edward Henry, b. 1854.

Mr. Pares, who was educated at Eton, is Lord of the Manor of Hopwell, and Patron of 3 livings.—*Hopwell Hall, Derby ; Ulverscroft, Leicester.*

PARISH, Sir WOODBINE, K.C.H., F.R.S., F.G.S., &c. (cr. 1837).
Eldest son of the late Woodbine Parish, Esq. (Chairman of the Board of Excise, N.B.), by Eliza, dau. of the Rev. Henry Headley, of N. Walsham, Norfolk : m. 1st 1819 Emily, dau. of Leonard Becher Morse, Esq., of Norwood (she d. 1835) ; 2nd 1844 Louisa, dau. of John Hubbard, Esq., of Forest House, Essex, and has, by the former, with other issue,

 * Henry Woodbine, educated at Eton, Lieut.-Col. 48th Foot ; b. 1821 ; m. 1849 Charlotte, dau. of Judge Cloete, of the Cape of Good Hope.

Sir Woodbine, who was educated at Eton, is a Magistrate for Norfolk; he was formerly in the Diplomatic Service.—*St. Leonard's-on-Sea ; Athenæum Club, s.w.*

+PARK, the Rev. JAMES ALLAN, of Elwick Hall, co. Durham.
Elder son of the late Right Hon. Sir James Allan Park, Judge of the Common Pleas (who d. 1838) ; b. 1828. Educated at Oriel Coll., Oxford (B.A. 1851); is a J.P. and D.L. for co. Durham, a Magistrate for Norfolk, Rector of Elwick, Hon. Canon of Durham, and Vicar of Methwold.—*Elwick Hall, Stockton-on-Tees ; Methwold Vicarage, Brandon.*

PARK, JOHN, Esq., of Ollerton Hall, Lancashire.
Eldest son of the late John Park, Esq., of Ollerton Hall, by Ellen, dau. of the late William Rashall, Esq., of Camden Town; b. 1828 ; s. 1851. Is a Magistrate for co. Lancaster, and Lord of the Manor of Withnell.—*Ollerton Hall, Withnell, Chorley.*

PARKE, CHARLES JOSEPH, Esq., of Henbury, Dorset.

Eldest son of the late Charles Parke, Esq., J.P. and D.L., of Henbury House, by Letitia, eldest dau. of the late Joseph Alcock, Esq., of Tredelthorpe, co. Lincoln ; b. 1820 ; s. 1860 ; m. 1847 Ellen Mary, 2nd dau. of the Rev. Charles Wicksted Ethelston, of Wicksted Hall (whom see), and has, with other issue,

   * Charles Ethelston, b. 1850.

Mr. Parke, who was educated at Eton and Oriel Coll., Oxford (B.A. 1844, M.A. 1846), and called to the Bar at the Inner Temple 1847, is a Magistrate for Dorset (High Sheriff 1868). — Henbury House, Wimborne ; Oxford and Cambridge Club, s.w.

PARKE, ROGER CHARLES, Esq., of Dunally, co. Sligo.

Eldest son of the late Lieut.-Col. Sir William Parke, of Dunally (an Officer of the 66th Regt.), by Louisa El'zabeth, dau. of Charles Johnstone, Esq., of Ludlow ; b. 1816 ; s. 1851, Educated at Trinity Coll., Dublin (B.A. 1839) ; is a Magistrate for co. Sligo (High Sheriff 1858).—Dunally, Sligo.

Heir Pres., his brother Johnstone William, b. 1822.

PARKE. (See under Wensleydale, Lord.)

PARKER, Sir WILLIAM, Bart., of Melford Hall, Suffolk (cr. 1681).

Second son of the late Vice-Admiral Hyde-Parker, C.B., by Caroline, dau. of Sir Frederick Mostoп Eden, Bart. ; b. 1826 ; s. his cousin as 9th Bart. 1856 ; m. 1855 Sophia Mary, dau. of Nathaniel Clarke Barnardiston, Esq., of The Ryes, co. Suffolk. Is a Magistrate for Suffolk, Lord of the Manor of Melford, and a Capt. in the Army.—Melford Hall, Long Melford ; Junior United Service Club, s.w.

Heir, his son Hyde, b. 1861.

PARKER, Sir CHARLES CHRISTOPHER, Bart. (cr. 1782).

Third son of the late Vice-Admiral Christopher Parker, of Basingbourne, co. Cambridge (who d. 1804) by Augusta Barbara Charlotte, dau. of Admiral the Hon. John Byron ; b. 1792 ; s. his brother as 5th Bart. 1835 ; m. 1815 Georgina Ellis, dau. of — Palmer, Esq. Entered the Navy 1804 ; is an Admiral reserved.—Abbeville House. Exeter ; United Service Club, s.w.

PARKER, Sir HENRY, Bart., of Harburn, War-wickshire (cr. 1797.)

Fourth but eldest surviving son of the late Vice-Admiral Sir William George Parker (who d. 1848), by Elizabeth, dau. of James Charles Still, Esq., of East Knoyle, Wilts ; b. 1822 ; s. his nephew as 5th Bart. 1866.

Heir Pres., his brother Melville, b. 1824.

PARKER, Sir WILLIAM BIDDULPH, Bart., of Shenstone Lodge, Staffordshire (cr. 1844.)

Eldest son of the late Admiral Sir William Parker, Bart., by Frances Anne, youngest dau. of the late Sir Theophilus Biddulph, Bart., b. 1828 ; s. as 2nd Bart. 1866 ; m. 1855 Jane Constance, only dau. of Sir Theophilus Biddulph. Bart. Educated at Rugby; is a Dep.-Lieut. for co. Stafford, late Lieut. Scots Fusilier Guards. —Shenstone Lodge, Lichfield ; United Service Club, s.w.

Heir Pres., his brother George, Capt. R.N. ; b. 1837 ; m. 1857 Annie Elizabeth, dau. of the late William Mackworth Praed, Esq., of Delamore, Devon, and has issue.

PARKER, HENRY WATSON, Knt. (cr. 1858).

Son of the late Thomas Watson Parker, Esq., of Lee, Kent ; b. 1808 ; m. 1833 Mary, dau. of John McWithers, Esq., of Camden Park, New South Wales. Is a Member of the Executive Council of New South Wales, and late Colonial Secretary there.—Sydney.

PARKER, CHRISTOPHER, Esq., of Skirwith Abbey, Cumberland.

Eldest son of the late Rev. Christopher Parker, of Skirwith Abbey (formerly Rector of Ormside, Westmoreland), by Sarah, 2nd dau. of Edward Railton, Esq., of Unthank, Cumberland ; b. 1843 ; s. 1856. Educated at Harrow ; is Lord of the Manors of Skirwith Abbey, Culgaith. Patron of Skirwith, and Lieut. Royal Cumberland Militia.—Skirwith Abbey, Penrith ; British Service Club, s.w.

Heir Pres., his brother William, b. 1850.

+PARKER, CORNELIUS, Esq., of Louth, Lincolnshire.

Son of the late C. Parker, Esq. ; b. 18—. Is a Magistrate for co. Lincoln ; descended from a common ancestor with the Parkers of Hanthorpe.—Louth, Lincolnshire.

PARKER, the Rev. EDWIN JAMES, B.D., of Brunchetts, Berks.

Fourth son of the late Rev. Thomas Parker, M.A., by Susanna Frances, dau. of Henry Wintle, Esq., of Gloucester ; b. 1796 ; m. 1853 Anna Rosetta, 4th dau. of the late William Thoyts, Esq., of Sulhamstead, Berks, and widow of Major-General Sir H. Watson, C.B. Educated at Pembroke Coll. Oxford (B.A. 1814, M.A. 1817, B.D. 1837) ; appointed Vicar of Waltham St. Lawrence 1834.—Brunchetts, Waltham St. Lawrence, Reading.

PARKER, Capt. GEORGE, of Delamore, Devon.

Second son of Admiral Sir William Parker, Bart., G.C.B., of Shenstone Lodge (whom see) ; b. 1827 ; m. 1857 Anne Elizabeth, only child of the late William Mackworth Praed, Esq., of Delamore, and of Bitton House, Teignmouth, and has, with other surviving issue,

   * William Frederic, b. 1860.

Mr. Parker is a Capt. R.N.—Delamore, Ivybridge.

PARKER, HENRY HARDING, Esq., of Bellevue, co. Cork.

Eldest son of the late Nicholas Skottowe Parker, Esq., of Bellevue, by Dorcas Bonsfield, dau. of the late George Staveley, Esq. ; b. 1824 ; s. 1863 ; m. 1860 Anna Lucia, dau. of the late Henry Bennett, Esq. Is descended from a common ancestor with the Earl of Morley.—Bellevue and Glanbrook, Passage West. co. Cork.

PARKER, HENRY YARBOROUGH, Esq., of Streetthorpe, Yorkshire·

Second son of the late George Parker. Esq., by Diana Elizabeth, dau. of George Cooke, Esq. (afterwards George Cooke-Yarborough), of Streetthorpe ; b. 1814 ; s. 1854 ; m. 1842 Maria Margaret, only dau. of the late Rev. Orfeur Wm. Kilvington, and has, with other issue.

   * Yarborough Francis Henry, b. 1844.

For an account of this family, see Hunter's 'History of Doncaster.'—Streetthorpe, Doncaster.

PARKER, the Right Hon. John, of Darrington Hall, Yorkshire.

Eldest son of the late Hugh Parker, Esq., J.P., of Tickhill, co. York (who d. 1861), by Mary, dau. of Samuel Walker, Esq., of Masborough, co. York; b. 1799 ; m. 1853 Charlotte Eliza, dau. of George Vernon, Esq. of Clontarf Castle, co. Dublin. Educated at Repton and Brasenose Coll., Oxford (B.A. 1820, M.A. 1823), called to the Bar at Lincoln's Inn 1824, and went the Northern Circuit ; is a Magistrate for the W. Riding of Yorkshire; was formerly a Lord of the Treasury 1836–41, Secretary to the Admiralty May–Sept. 1841, and 1849–52, and Secretary to the Treasury 1846–9 ; M.P. for Sheffield 1832–52.—Darrington Hall, Pontefract ; Brooks's and Athenæum Clubs, s.w.

PARKER, John Bartholomew, Esq., of Little Cawthorpe, Lincolnshire.

Eldest son of the late Lysimachus Parker, Esq., of Little Cawthorpe, by Sarah, eldest dau. of John Green, Esq., of Dowsby Hall; b. 1824; s. 1860; m. 1862 Catherine Georgiana, dau. of Frederick Henry Alexander Forth, Esq., late Capt. 21st Fusiliers, and has issue, a daughter. Mr. Parker, who was educated at Harrow and Queen's Coll., Oxford, is Lord of the Manor of Little Cawthorpe, and was formerly Major Royal Bucks Hussars.—Little Cawthorpe Manor, Louth.

PARKER, John Oxley, Esq., of Woodham-Mortimer, Essex.

Only son of the late Christopher Comyns Parker, Esq., of Woodham-Mortimer, by Emma Elizabeth, dau. of Edward Gepp, Esq., of Chelmsford; b. 1812; s. 1843; m. 1847 Louisa, dau. of Richard Durant, Esq., of Sharpham, Devon, and High Canons, Herts, and has with other surviving issue,

* Christopher William, b. 1853.

Mr. Parker, who was educated at Eton and Oriel Coll., Oxford (B.A. 1833), is a J.P. and D.L. for Essex, and a Banker at Chelmsford.—Woodham-Mortimer Place, Maldon ; Oxford and Cambridge Club, s.w.

PARKER, John Robert Theophilus Hastings, Esq., of Swannington Hall, Norfolk.

Eldest son of Capt. Henry Parker, R.N., of Green Park, Youghall, co. Cork, by Lady Frances Theophila Anne, dau. of Hans Francis, 11th Earl of Huntingdon; b. 1823; m. 1858 Elizabeth Rachel Rosalie Dorothea, only child and heir of the late Major Charles Randall, of the 1st Dragoon Guards, and of Swannington Manor, by Rachel, dau. of the Rev. Christopher Harvey, D.D., of Temple Hill, co. Wexford. Mr. Hastings Parker, who was educated at the Charterhouse and Trinity Coll., Dublin, is a Magistrate for Norfolk, and Capt. W. Norfolk Militia. The ancient Manor of Swannington has descended to Mrs. Hastings Parker in direct line from the Bladwells, who held it in 1547 (temp. Edward VI.)—Swannington Hall, Norwich.

PARKER, Mrs., of Whiteway, Devonshire.

Harriet, dau. of the late John Newcombe, Esq., of Starcross, Devon, by Harriet, dau. of Jonathan Pleydell, Esq., of co. Cavan Ireland; m. 1806 Montague Edmund Parker, Esq., of Whiteway, by whom (who d. 1831) she has surviving issue an only child,

* Harriet Sophia, m. 1st 1834 William Coryton, Esq., of Pentillie, Cornwall; 2nd 1842 Edmund, 2nd Earl of Morley.

Mrs. Parker is Lady of the Manor of Whiteway.—Whiteway, Chudleigh.

PARKER, Mrs., of Edge Hall, Cheshire.

Frances Rosamond, younger dau. of the late Thomas Crewe Dod, Esq., of Edge Hall (who d. 1827) by Anne, 4th dau. of Ralph Sneyd, Esq., of Keele, co. Stafford; s. her sister 1867; m. 1823 the Rev. Pelly Parker, Rector of Houghton, Notts, who d. 1865, leaving issue,

* Frances Lucy, m. 1850 the Rev. Charles Wolley, only son of the Rev. John Wolley, of Beauston, Notts.

The ancient British family of Dod formerly possessed large estates, of which it was in part deprived by William the Conqueror.—Edge Hall, Malpas.

PARKER, Robert Townley, Esq., of Cuerden, Lancashire.

Only son of the late Thomas Townley Parker, Esq., of Cuerden, by Susanna, only dau. and heir of Peter Brooke, Esq., of Astley Hall, co, Lancaster; b. 1793;

s. 1794; m. 1816 Harriet, youngest dau. of Thomas Brooke, Esq., and has, with other issue,

* Thomas Townley, of Charnock Hall, Chorler, a J.P. and D.L. for co. Lancaster ; b. 1822 ; m. 1846 Katherine Margaret, dau. of the Rev. T. Blackburne, Rector of Prestwich.

Mr. Parker, who was educated at Eton and Ch. Ch., Oxford, is a J.P. and D.L. for co. Lancaster (High Sheriff 1817), and Patron of 1 living; he was M.P. for Preston 1837-57; Guild Mayor of Preston 1862.—Cuerden Hall, Preston.

PARKER, Thomas Goulbourne, Esq., of Alkincoats, Lancashire, and Brownsholme, Yorkshire.

Eldest son of the late Edward Parker, Esq., J.P. and D.L., of Alkincoats, by Ellen, only child of Ambrose W. Barcroft, Esq. ; b. 1818 ; m. 1845 Mary Anne, dau. and co-heiress of John Francis Carr, Esq., of Carr Lodge, Horbury, and has, with other issue,

* A son, b. 1846.

Mr. Parker, who was educated at Trinity Coll., Cambridge (B.A. 1841, M.A. 1844), is a Magistrate for co. Lancaster, and a J.P. and D.L. for the W. Riding of Yorkshire.—Alkincoats, Colne, Lancashire ; Brownsholme Hall, Clitheroe.

PARKER, William, Esq., of Hanthorpe House, Lincolnshire.

Son of the late William Thorpe, Gentleman, of London : b. 1791 ; s. his cousin, George Parker, Esq., D.L., of Edenham, co. Lincoln, 1831 ; m. 1817 Anne, dau. of John Bullivant, Gentleman, of London, and has, with other issue,

* William, educated at Eton and B.A. of Exeter Coll., Oxford, a J.P. and D.L. for co. Lincoln, and Major R. S. Lincoln Militia ; b. 1824 ; m. 1855 Anensta Milet Harriet, 2nd dau. of the late Lieut.-Col. C. W. Short, of the Coldstream Guards, and has issue.

Mr. Parker, who is a J.P. and D.L. for co. Lincoln (High Sheriff 1864), assumed his present name by Royal licence in 1831.—Hanthorpe House, Bourne.

PARKER, William, Esq., of Ware Park, Herts.

Second son of the late William Parker, Esq., of Hardwicke Court, co. Gloucester, and Clopton Hall, Suffolk, by Anne, dau. of William Windsor, Esq. ; b. 1803 ; m. 1842 Sarah, 2nd dau. of the late John Jackson, Esq., King's Proctor at Malta, and has, with other issue,

* John Harry Eyres, R.N.; b. 1845.

Mr. Parker, who was called to the Bar at Lincoln's Inn 1846, is a Magistrate for Middlesex and Herts (High Sheriff 1848) ; a Chairman of Quarter Sessions, and Lord of the Manor of Bengeo, Herts, and was formerly Capt. South Herts Yeomanry Cavalry.—Ware Park, Herts ; Carlton Club, s.w.

PARKER, Major Windsor, of Clopton Hall, Suffolk.

Eldest son of the late William Parker, Esq., of Hardwicke, co. Gloucester and Clopton Hall, Suffolk, by Anne, dau. of William Windsor, Esq. ; b. 1802 ; m. 1830 Elizabeth Mary, dau. of the late General Duncan. Is a J.P. and D.L. for Suffolk (High Sheriff 1854); Lord of the Manor of Clopton, and Major West Suffolk Militia ; elected M.P. for West Suffolk 1859.—Clopton Hall, Rattlesden, Stowmarket ; Carlton Club, s.w.

PARKER. (See Macclesfield, Earl of; Morley, Earl of.)

PARKER-JERVIS, the Hon. Edward Swynfen, of Aston Hall, Warwickshire.

Third son of Edward Jervis, 2nd Viscount St. Vincent, by his 2nd wife Mary Anne, dau. of the late Thomas

729

Parker, Esq., of Park Hall, co. Stafford (whose name he assumed by Royal licence in 1861); *b.* 1815; *m.* 1838 Mary, dau. of J. Barker, Esq., and has, with other issue,

* Edward John, a Magistrate for co. Stafford, and Lieut. 3rd Staffordshire Militia, *b.* 1839 ; *m.* 1861 Grace Catherine, youngest dau. of the late Right Hon. Sir John Jervis, Chief Justice of the Common Pleas, and has, with other issue, * a son, *b.* 1863.

Mr. Jervis was formerly Capt. Staffordshire Militia, and High Sheriff of co. Stafford 1857.—*Aston Hall, Sutton Coldfield, Birmingham ; Park Hall, Caverswall, Cheadle, Staffordshire ;* 25, *St. James's Place,* s.w.

PARKES, Sir HARRY SMITH, K.C.B. (cr. 1862).

Only son of the late Harry Parkes, Esq., of Birchill's Hall, co. Stafford, by Mary Anne, dau. of George Gitton, Esq., of Bridgnorth, co. Salop; *b.* 1828; *m.* 1856 Fanny Hannah, dau. of the late Thomas Plumer, Esq., of Canons Park, Middlesex, and has, with other issue,

* Harry Rutherford, *b.* 1862.

Sir H. S. Parkes entered the Civil Service in 1842, and held several Civil posts in China 1842–60 ; is H.B.M.'s Minister at Japan; late Consul at Shanghai.—*Yokohama, Japan ; Athenæum Club,* s.w. ; *Oriental Club,* w.

PARKHOUSE, Mrs., of Eastfield Lodge, Hants.

Frances, dau. of the late Edmund Armstrong, Esq., of Gallen Priory, King's Co., sister of the late Sir Andrew Armstrong, Bart., and niece of Frederic, 1st Lord Ashtown ; *m.* 1830 George Parkhouse, Esq., of Eastfield Lodge, who *d.* 1865, leaving issue,

* Elizabeth Mary Armstrong.

—*Eastfield Lodge, Bittern, Southampton.*

PARKINSON, JAMES BENNERS, Esq., of Cholesbury, Bucks.

Son of the late James Parkinson, Esq. ; *b.* 1809. Educated at Harrow ; is a Magistrate for Bucks ; was formerly Capt. 68th Foot.—*Cholesbury, Tring ; Junior United Service Club,* s.w.

PARKINSON, the Rev. JOHN POSTHUMUS, LL.D., of Ravendale, Lincolnshire.

Only son of the late John Wilson, Esq., M.D., of Spalding, co. Lincoln ; *b.* 1809 ; *m.* 1842 Mary, only dau. and heir of the Rev. Dr. Parkinson, of Ravendale, whose name he assumed, and has, with other issue,

* Robert John Hinman, *b.* 1844.

Mr. Parkinson, who was educated at Magdalen Coll., Oxford (B.A. 1831, M.A. 1834, D.C.L. 1845), is a Magistrate for co. Lincoln, and Rural Dean ; was formerly Fellow of Magdalen Coll., Oxford, and P.C. of Marsh Chapel, co. Lincoln.—*Ravendale, Grimsby.*

PARKYNS, Sir THOMAS GEORGE AUGUSTUS, Bart., of Ruddington, Notts (cr. 1681).

Eldest son of the late Thomas Boultbee Parkyns, Esq., by Charlotte Mary, dau. of the late George Smith, Esq., of Edwalton, Notts ; *b.* 1820 ; *s.* his cousin George, late Lord Rancliffe, as 9th Bart. 1850 ; *m.* 1817 Annie, dau. of W. Jennings, Esq. Is a J.P. and D.L. for Notts, and Lord of the Manor of Ruddington. The 4th Bart. was created Lord Rancliffe, but the title expired with the 5th Bart. in 1850.—*Ruddington Manor, Nottingham ;* 9, *Gloucester Square, Hyde Park,* w.

Heir, his son Thomas Mansfield Forbes, *b.* 1853.

PARKYNS, MANSFIELD, Esq., of Woodborough, Notts.

Younger son of the late Thomas Boultbee Parkyns, Esq., by Charlotte Mary, dau. of the late George Smith, Esq., of Edwalton, Notts, and Foëllallt, co. Cardigan, and brother of Sir Thomas G. A. Parkyns, Bart. (whom
730

see); *b.* 1823 ; *m.* 1854 the Hon. Emma Louisa, 3rd dau. of Richard, 1st Lord Westbury, and has issue,

* Seven daughters.

Mr. Parkyns, who was educated at Trinity Coll., Cambridge, is Lieut.-Col. Nottinghamshire Rifle Volunteers ; late Capt. Royal Sherwood Foresters ; was formerly attaché at Constantinople.—*Woodborough Hall, Nottingham ; Arthur's Club,* s.w.

PARLBY, the Rev. JOHN HALL, of Manadon, Devon.

Only son of the late John A. Parlby, Esq., of Stone Hall and Manadon, by Letitia, dau. and co-heir of Humphrey Hall, Esq., of Manadon ; *b.* 1805 ; *s.* 1849; *m.* 1st 1835 Emily Janetta, dau. of the late J. Hooper Holder, Esq., of Stanton Lacey House, co. Salop ; 2nd 1845 Emma Admonition. 3rd dau. of the late Rev. Walter Radcliffe, of Warleigh, Devon, and has issue, by the former,

* Gerard Charles Hall, Lieut. R.A. ; *b.* 1872.

Mr. Parlby, who was educated at University Coll., Oxford (B.A. 1827, M.A. 1830) ; ordained Deacon 1828, Priest 1829 ; is a Magistrate for Devon.—*Manadon, Plymouth.*

PARNELL, the Hon. and Rev. GEORGE DAMER.

Third son of Henry Brooke, 1st Lord Congleton, by Caroline, dau. of John, 1st Earl of Portarlington ; *b.* 1810 ; *m.* 1832 Catharine, dau. of the late Sir John St. Aubyn, Bart. Educated at Downing Coll., Cambridge (M.A. 1842) ; is Perpetual Curate of Long Cross. —*Long Cross, Chertsey, Surrey.*

PARNELL, JOHN HENRY, Esq., of Avondale, co. Wicklow.

Son of the late William Parnell-Hayes, Esq., of Avondale, by Frances, dau. of the late Hon. Hugh Howard, and grand-dau. of Ralph, 1st Viscount Wicklow: *b.* 1811 ; *s.* 1821 ; *m.* 1834 Delia, dau. of Commodore Charles Stewart, of the United States Navy, and has, with other issue,

* John Howard, *b.* 1842.

Mr. Parnell, who was educated at Eton, is a J.P. and D.L. for co. Wicklow.—*Avondale, Rathdrum.*

PARNELL. (See under *Congleton, Lord.*)

+PARR, CODRINGTON THOMAS, Esq., of Stonelands, Devon.

Eldest son of the late Codrington Parr, Esq., of Stonelands (who was formerly J.P. and D.L. and High Sheriff of Devon), by Harriet Lydia, dau. of H. Hannings, Esq., of Sidmouth, and niece of Admiral Sir R. Barlow, K.C.B.; *b.* 1828 ; *s.* 1854 ; *m.* 1852 Louisa Anne, only dau. of the Rev. H. Dashwood, of Halton, Bucks. Educated at Eton ; represents a branch of the Parrs of Lancashire.—*Stonelands, Dawlish.*

Heir Pres., his brother Henry Dimsdale, educated at Eton and Exeter Coll.. Oxford, late Capt. S. Devon Militia ; *b.* 1830.

PARR, the Rev. HENRY, of Bredon Old Hall, Gloucestershire.

Fourth son of the late Thomas Parr, Esq., of Lythwood Hall, co. Salop, by Katherine, dau. and co-heir of Robert Walter, Esq., Capt. R.N.; *b.* 1815 ; *m.* 1859 Susanna Hamilton, dau. of Thomas Dutton, Esq., and has, with other issue,

* Henry William FitzHugh, *b.* 1846.

Mr. Parr, who was some time Vicar of Taunton, Somerset, and late Incumbent of Ashchurch, Gloucestershire, is a member of a family seated at Parr, Lancashire, from the 13th to the 17th century.—*Bredon Old Hall, Tewkesbury.*

PARR, the Rev. JOHN OWEN.
Eldest son of the late John Owen Parr, Esq., Merchant, of London, by Elizabeth Mary, dau. of Thomas Patrick, Esq.; *b.* 1798; *m.* 1821 Maria Elizabeth, dau. of W. Wright, Esq., of Mattishall, Norfolk, and has, with other issue,

* John Owen, B.A. of Exeter Coll., Oxford, in Holy Orders; *b.* 1823; *m.* 1857 Mary Emily, youngest surviving dau. of Charles Pott, Esq., of Freelands, Kent.

Mr. Parr, who was educated at Charterhouse and Brasenose Coll., Oxford (B.A. 1818, M.A. 1830), ordained 1823, appointed Vicar of Preston 1840, and Hon. Canon of Manchester 1853, is a Magistrate for co. Lancaster. This family is a younger branch of the Parrs of Grappenhall Heyes (whom see).—*The Vicarage, Preston ; University Club, s.w.*

PARR, THOMAS, Esq., of Grappenhall, Cheshire.
Eldest surviving son of the late Joseph Parr, Esq., of Grappenhall Heyes (who *d.* 1820), by Ellen, dau. of Mathew Lyon, Esq.; *b.* 1792; *s.* his brother 1824; *m.* 1st 1825 Clare, dau. of the Rev. Croxton Johnson, LL.B., Rector of Wilmslow, co. Chester (she *d.* 1827); 2nd 1833 Alice, dau. of Philip Charlton, Esq., of Wytheford Hall, Salop, and has, with other issue,

* Thomas Philip, late Capt. Rl. Scots Greys ; *b.* 1834 ; *m.* 1866 Agnes Darby, only dau. of the late Major George Darby-Griffith.

Mr. Parr is a J.P. and D.L. for co. Chester, and a Magistrate for co. Lancaster.—*Grappenhall Heyes, Warrington.*

PARRATT, Lieut.-Col. HILLEBRAND MEREDITH,‡ of Effingham House, Surrey.
Son of the late James Meredith Parratt, Esq., M.D., of London, by Maria, dau. of Henry Cowper, Esq.; *b.* 1791; *m.* 1817 Lucy, dau. and co-heir of the late Sir Thomas Hussey Apreece, Bart., (ext.) of Effingham House, and has, with other issue,

* Hillebrand, *b.* 1818.

Lieut.-Col. Parratt, who was educated at the Royal Military Coll., Woolwich, and served in the Artillery 1808–17, is a J.P. and D.L. for Surrey, and Lieut.-Col. Royal Surrey Militia.—*Effingham House, Leatherhead ; 27, Victoria Street, s.w.*

PARRY, JOHN BILLINGSLEY, Esq., Q.C.
Second son of the late James Parry, Esq., of Preston, co. Salop, by Margaret, only dau. and heir of John Billingsley, Esq., of Yeaton, and of the Lea; *b.* 1798; *m.* 1st 1824 Ann, dau. of the late John Fane, Esq., M.P., of Wormsley, Oxon ; 2nd 1817 Mary, eldest dau. of the late Sir William Rawson, and has by the former, with other issue,

* Neville, *b.* 1826 ; *m.* 1853 Caroline, youngest dau. of the late Rear-Admiral Sir Thomas Ussher.

Mr. Parry, who was educated at Shrewsbury, called to the Bar at Lincoln's Inn 1824, and became Q.C. 1844, is a Magistrate for Berks and Oxon, a Bencher of Lincoln's Inn, and Judge of the County Courts for Oxfordshire.—*14, Great Cumberland Street, w.*

+PARRY, ROBERT SORTON, Esq., of Tan-y-Graig, Carnarvonshire.
Son of the late — Parry, Esq. ; *b.* 18 —; is a Magistrate for co. Carnarvon (High Sheriff 1868).—*Tan-y-Graig, Carnarvon.*

PARRY, THOMAS, Esq., of Sleaford, Lincolnshire.
Son of Mr. William Parry, of Lincoln, by Mary, dau. of Mr. H. Stanley; *b.* 1818 ; *m.* 1842 Henrietta, dau. of the late C. Kirk, Esq., of Sleaford; was M.P. for Boston 1865–6; re-elected 1867.—*Sleaford, Lincolnshire ; Reform Club, s.w. ; 4, Park Prospect, s.w.*

‡ Died whilst these sheets were at press.

PARRY, THOMAS GAMBIER, Esq., of Highnam Court, Gloucestershire.
Only son of the late Richard Parry, Esq., of Banstead, Surrey, by Mary Gambier, niece of the late Admiral Lord Gambier; *b.* 1816 ; *m.* 1st 1839 Anna Maria Isabella, 2nd dau. of the late Henry Fynes-Clinton, Esq., of Welwyn, Herts; 2nd 1851 Ethelinda, dau. of the Very Rev. Francis Lear, Dean of Salisbury, and has, by the former, with other issue,

* Charles Clinton, *b.* 1840.

Mr. Parry, who was educated at Eton and Trinity Coll., Cambridge (B.A. 1837, M.A. 1848), is a J.P. and D.L. for co. Gloucester (High Sheriff 1859), and Patron of 1 living.—*Highnam Court, Gloucester ; Athenæum and University Clubs, s.w.*

PARRY.　　(See *Jones-Parry*.)

PARRY.　　(See *Webley-Parry*.)

PARRY-MEALY.　　(See *Mealy*.) ―

PARRY-YALE.　　(See under *Yale*.)

PARSONS, the Hon. LAWRENCE.
Third son of Lawrence, 2nd Earl of Rosse, by Alice, dau. of John Lloyd, Esq., of Gloster, King's Co. ; *b.* 1805 ; *m.* 1st 1836 Lady Elizabeth, dau. of Hector, 2nd Earl of Norbury (she *d.* 1844, ; 2nd 1849 the Hon. Jane, eldest dau. of William, 2nd Lord Feversham, and has by the former, with other issue,

* Lawrence Hardress Hector. Lieut. R.A. ; *b.* 1839.

Mr. Parsons, who was educated at Trinity Coll., Dublin, is a Magistrate for King's Co. ; late Lieut.-Col. King's Co. Militia.—*Birr, Parsonstown, King's Co.*

PARSONS.　　(See under *Rosse, Earl of*.)

PARTINGTON, the Rev. HENRY.
Second surviving son of the late Thomas Partington, Esq., of Offham, Hamsey, Sussex, by Penelope Anne, dau. of the Rev. Thomas Anthony Trollope, Rector of Cottered, Herts ; *b.* 1808 ; *m.* 1848 Sarah, youngest dau. of the Rev. J. Roby, Rector of Congerston, co. Leicester, and has issue,

* Henrietta Catharine.

Mr. Partington, who was educated at Westminster and Ch. Ch., Oxford (B.A. 1830, M.A. 1832), and appointed Vicar of Wath-upon-Dearne 1853, is a Magistrate for the W. Riding.—*Wath-upon-Dearne, Rotherham.*

PARTRIDGE, EDWARD OTTO, Esq., of Hazelhurst, Herefordshire.
Second son of John Partridge, Esq., of Bishop's Wood, co. Hereford, by Eliza, dau. of Edward Ives, Esq.; *b.* 1819; *m.* 18— Catharine Maria, dau. of the Rev. George Bevan, of Crickhowell, co. Brecon, and has, with other issue,

* Charles Edward, *b.* 18—.

Mr. Partridge is a Magistrate for co. Hereford.—*Hazelhurst, Ross.*

PARTRIDGE, HENRY THOMAS, Esq., of Hockham Hall, Norfolk.
Eldest son of the late Henry Champion Partridge, Esq., Chairman of the Norfolk Quarter Sessions (who *d.* 1849), by Ethaldred Frances, eldest dau. of General Birch Reynardson, of Holywell Hall, co. Lincoln ; *b.* 1838 ; *s.* his grandfather 1858. Educated at Trinity and Magdalen Colls., Cambridge; is Lord of the Manors of Hockham and Northwold, and Patron of 1 living.—*Hockham Hall, Thetford ; University Club, s.w.*

Heir Pres., his brother Arthur William, b. 1849 ; m. 1867 Blanche Emily, youngest dau. of the late Rev. John A. Partridge, M.A.

PARTRIDGE, JOHN, Esq., of Bishop's Wood, Herefordshire.

Only son of the late William Partridge, Esq., of Bishop's Wood, by Ann Biby, dau. and co-heir of John Biby Hawker, Esq., of The Viney, Chepstow ; b. 1795 ; s. 1819 ; m. 1817 Eliza, eldest dau. of Edward Ives, Esq., of Collards, Hants, some time Resident at Lucknow, and has, with other issue,

* William, of Wyelands, Bishop's Wood, Herefordshire, educated at Winchester and Ch. Ch., Oxford (B.A. 1840, M.A. 1860) ; called to the Bar at the Middle Temple 1843 ; appointed Stipendiary Magistrate for the Wolverhampton District 1860 ; a J.P. and D.L. for co. Hereford, and a Magistrate for cos. Gloucester, Monmouth, Sussex, and Stafford ; b. 1818 ; m. 1841 Elizabeth Emily, dau. of Richard Webb, Esq., of Donnington Hall, co. Hereford, and has issue.

Mr. Partridge, who was educated at Queen's Coll., Oxford, is a Magistrate for cos. Gloucester and Monmouth, a J.P. and D.L. for co. Hereford (High Sheriff of co. Monmouth, 1824), and Patron of 1 living.—*Bishop's Wood, Ross.*

PARTRIDGE, the Rev. WALTER JOHN, M.A., of Caston Rectory, Norfolk.

Fourth son of the late Henry S. Partridge, Esq., of Hockham Hall, Norfolk, by Mary Frances, dau. of the late Ven. Luke Heslop, Archdeacon of Bucks and Rector of Marylebone ; b. 1813 ; m. 1st 1842 Maria Agnes, dau. of the late Sir Charles M. Clarke, Bart. ; 2nd 1858 Elizabeth Mary, dau. of George Gataker, Esq., of Mildenhall, Suffolk, and has, by his 1st wife, two sons. Mr. Partridge, who was educated at C. C. C., Cambridge (B.A. 1837, M.A. 1840), is a Magistrate for Norfolk, and Rector and Patron of Caston.—*Caston Rectory, Attleborough.*

PARTRIDGE, the Rev. WILLIAM EDWARDS, of Horsenden House, Bucks.

Only surviving son of the late Charles Anthony Partridge, Esq., of Cotham Lodge, co. Gloucester, by Mary, dau. of Thomas Oliver, Esq. ; b. 1809 ; m. 1842 Lucy Olivia Hobart, only dau. of T. O. Anderdon, Esq., Q.C., and has issue,

* Three daughters.

Mr. Partridge was educated at Rugby and Brasenose Coll., Oxford (B.A. 1832) ; is a Magistrate for Bucks, Rector and Lord of the Manor of Horsenden, and Patron of 2 livings.—*Horsenden House, Prince's Risborough ; Conservative Club, s.w.*

PASLEY, Sir THOMAS SABINE, Bart., of The Craig, Dumfriesshire (cr. 1794).

Eldest son of the late Major John Sabine, by Maria, eldest dau. of Admiral Sir Thomas Pasley, of Craig, co. Dumfries ; b. 1804 ; s. his maternal grandfather under a special remainder 1808 ; m. 1826 Jane Matilda Lilley, eldest dau. of the Rev. Montague John Wynyard ; is an Admiral R.N. and Naval Commander at Portsmouth ; late Superintendent of H.M.'s Dockyard, Devonport. —*Admiralty, Portsmouth . United Service Club, s.w.*

Heir, his son Thomas Malcolm, b. 1829 ; m. 1868 Emma Louisa, eldest dau. of the late W. Losh, Esq., of Trinidad, and has issue.

PASTON. (See *Bedingfeld, Bart.*)

PATERSON, EDMUND DE HAYA, Esq., of Carpow, Perthshire.

Eldest son of the late Peter Hay Paterson, Esq., J.P. of Carpow, by the Hon. Marianne, youngest dau. of Alexander, 8th Lord Elibank ; b. 1819 ; s. 1865. This family was formerly styled Paterson of Dinmore, co. Fife.—*Carpow, Newburgh, Perthshire, N.B.*
732

PATERSON, GEORGE FREDERICK, Esq., of Castle Huntly, Perthshire.

Eldest son of the late George Paterson, Esq., J.P., of Castle Huntly, by Catherine Jemima Jane, only dau. of the late Joseph Robertson, Esq. ; b. 1857 ; s. 1867. —*Castle Huntly, Longforgan, Dundee, N.B.*

PATERSON, Mrs., of Poyle House, Middlesex.

Frances, dau. of the late Thomas Barnard, Esq., of the Madras Civil Service, and aunt of Lady Bonham ; m. 1835 George Paterson, Esq., of Poyle House, a Magistrate for Middlesex, who d. 1866, leaving issue, * two daughters.—*Poyle House, Stanwell, Staines.*

PATERSON, Mrs., of Leesons, Kent.

Caroline Frances, youngest dau. of Robert Cattley, Esq., Merchant, of London ; m. 1819 Richard Paterson, Esq., J.P. of Leesons, who was High Sheriff of Kent 1856, and who d. 1865, leaving issue, * two daughters.—*Leesons, Chislehurst, Bromley.*

PATERSON, ROBERT, Esq., of Nunfield and Brockelhurst, Dumfriesshire.

Eldest son of the late James Paterson, Esq., of Nunfield, by Margaret, dau. of Robert Moore, Esq. ; b. 18— ; m. 18— Margaret, dau. of Richard Rimmer, Merchant, of Liverpool, and has, with other issue,

* William, b. 18—.

Mr. Paterson is a Magistrate for co. Dumfries, and Lord of the Barony of Nunfield.—*Nunfield, Dumfries, N.B.*

PATESHALL, EVAN, Esq.

Youngest son of the late David Thomas, Esq., of Welfield, co. Radnor, by Catharine, dau. of William Jones, Esq., of Henllys, co. Carmarthen ; b. 1817 ; m. 1842 Anne Elizabeth, only child of the late W. Pateshall, Esq., of Hereford, whose name he assumed in 1855. Educated at Shrewsbury School and King's Coll., London ; is a J.P. and D.L. for co. Hereford, and a Magistrate for cos. Brecon and Radnor.—*Residence : Hereford.*

PATON, Sir JOSEPH NOËL, Knt., R.S.A. (cr. 1867).

Eldest son of Joseph Neil Paton, Esq., F.S.A.S., of Dunfermline, N.B., by Catherine, 3rd dau. of Archibald McDiarmid, Esq., of Kuldaloskin, co. Perth, and Emilia, dau. of Robert Robertson of Drumachune, co. Perth : b. 1821 ; m. 1858 Margaret, 2nd dau. of the late Alexander Ferrier, Esq., of Bloomhill, co. Dunbarton.' Educated at Dunfermline ; is her Majesty's Limner for Scotland.—33, *George Square, Edinburgh.*

PATON, JOHN, Esq., of Crailing, Roxburghshire.

Eldest son of the late James Paton, Esq., of Crailing, by Christian Mary, dau. of John Cadell, Esq., of Tranent, Midlothian ; b. 1805 ; s. 1826 ; m. 1830 Ellen, dau. of William Elliot, Esq., of Harwood, co. Roxburgh, and has, with other issue.

* James, Major 4th Regt. ; b. 18—; m. 1868 Agnes Alice, eldest dau. of Joseph Charles Lamb, Esq., of Ryton House, co. Durham.

Mr. Paton, who was educated at Edinburgh, is a J.P. and D.L. for co. Roxburgh, and Lord of the Barony of Crailing.—*Crailing House, Kelso, N.B.*

PATON, JOHN, Esq., of Grandholme, Aberdeenshire.

Eldest son of the late William Paton, Esq., of Grandholme, by Louisa, dau. of S. Bird, Esq., of the H.E.I. Co.'s Service ; b. 1818 ; m. 1st 1844 Eliza Deborah, dau. of T. Burnett, Esq., of Kepplestone (she d. 1860) ; 2nd 1862 Catherine Margaret, dau. of Col. Lumsden, C.B.,

of Belhelvie Lodge, co. Aberdeen, and has by the former, with other issue,

* William Roger, *b.* 1857.

Mr. Paton, who was educated at Eton, is a J.P. and D.L. for co. Aberdeen, and Major Aberdeenshire Militia; late Lieut. 91st Foot.—*Grandholme, Aberdeen, N.B.; Army and Navy Club, s.w.*

PATRICK, John, Esq., of Dunminning, co. Antrim.

Eldest son of the late John Patrick, Esq., of Ballymena, by Anne, dau. of Barnett McKean, Esq., of Ballymena; *b.* 1802; *s.* 1858; *m.* 1835 Grace, 4th dau. of William Gihon, Esq., J.P., of Hillhead, co. Antrim, and has, with other issue,

* John. *b.* 1844.

Mr. Patrick is a Magistrate for co. Antrim. This family is of Scotch extraction, being a branch of the Patricks of Ayrshire.—*Dunminning, Ballymena, co. Antrim.*

PATRICK, Robert William Cochran-, Esq., of Woodside and Ladyland, Ayrshire.

Only son of the late William Cochran-Patrick, Esq., of Ladyland (who *d.* 1858), by Agnes, eldest dau. and heiress of William Cochran, Esq., of Ladyland, whose name his father and he assumed in terms of the entail of that estate; *b.* 1842; *s.* in 1861, on the death of his grand-uncle, William Patrick, Esq., of Woodside, to the estates of Woodside, in the counties of Ayr and Renfrew; *m.* 1866 Eleanora, younger dau. of Robert Hunter, Esq., of Hunter, co. Ayr. Educated at the Universities of Edinburgh and Cambridge (B.A. 1861, M.A. 1864); is a Magistrate for cos. Ayr and Renfrew. This family claim descent from Mary, dau. of Robert II. of Scotland.‡ —*Woodside, Beith; Ladyland, Kilbirnie, Ayrshire.*

PATTEN. (See *Wilson-Patten.*)

PATTENSON. (See *Tylden-Pattenson.*)

PATTESON, Henry Staniforth, Esq., of Thorpe, Norfolk.

Second son of the late John Staniforth Patteson, Esq., J.P. and D.L., of Norwich (formerly Lieut.-Col. E. Norfolk Militia), by Anne Elizabeth, dau. of the late William Tasker, Esq., of London; *b.* 1816; *m.* 1850 Isabella Katharine, eldest dau. of the Rev. John Anthony Partridge. Is a Dep.-Lieut. for Norfolk and Capt. Norfolk Rifle Volunteers.—*Thorpe, Norwich.*

PATTESON, James Henry, Esq., of Feniton, Devon.

Younger son of the late Right Hon. Sir John Patteson, of Feniton Court (many years a Judge of the King's Bench), by Frances Duke, dau. of the late James Coleridge, Esq., of Ottery St. Mary, Devon; *b.* 1828; *s.* 1861; *m.* 1860 Elizabeth Anne, dau. of the late Rev, T. H. Walker, Vicar of Bickleigh, Devon, and has issue,

* John Henry, *b.* 1862.

Mr. Patteson, who was educated at Eton and Balliol Coll., Oxford (B.A. 1850, M.A. 1854), was called to the Bar at the Middle Temple 1855, and goes the Northern Circuit, is Lord of the Manor of Feniton. —*Feniton Court, Honiton; University Club, s.w.; 3, Hyde Park Gate South, s.w.*

PATTON, the Right Hon. George, of The Cairnies, Perthshire.

Third son of the late James Patton, Esq., of Glenalmond, N.B., by Ann. dau. of Thomas Marshall, Esq.; *b.* 1803; *m.* 1857 Margaret, dau. of the late Lieut.- General Bethune, of Blebo, co. Fife. Educated at the University of Edinburgh, and Trinity Coll., Cambridge; is a Magistrate for co. Perth; was Solicitor-General for Scotland in 1859; Lord Advocate for Scotland 1866-7; appointed Lord Justice Clerk of Scotland, and sworn a member of the Privy Council 1867; was M.P. for Bridgewater, June–July 1866.—*The Cairnies House, Glenalmond, Perth, N.B.; 30, Heriot Row, Edinburgh; Oxford and Cambridge and Carlton Clubs, s.w.*

PATTON, Henry Bethune, Esq., of Bishop's Hull, Somerset.

Third son of Thomas Patton, Esq., of Bishop's Hull House, and Stoke Court (a retired Commander R.N.), by Matilda, dau. of the Rev. R. Winsloe, and grand-dau. of the late John Walter, Esq., of Bearwood, Berks; *b.* 1835; *m.* 1861 Clara, dau. of William Fripp, Esq. (Magistrate and Dep.-Lieut. of Gloucester), of The Grove, Teignmouth, and has, with other issue,

* Clara.

Mr. H. B. Patton, who was educated at Sandhurst, Coll., is a Magistrate for Somerset, and Capt. Somerset Yeomanry; was formerly Capt. 27th Inniskillings. This family descend from the elder branch of the Bethunes of Fifeshire, and from the Pattons of Springfield.—*Bishop's Hull House, Taunton; Boodle's, and Army and Navy Clubs, s.w.*

PATTON, Capt. Thomas, R.N., of Bishop's Hull House, and Stoke Court, Somerset.

Eldest son of the late Col. Thomas Patton, of Lichfield, by Merriell, only child of Thomas Docksey, Esq., of Snetstone, co. Derby, and co-heiress of the Garrick family; *b.* 1791; *m.* 1819 Matilda, dau. of the Rev. R. Winsloe, M.A., and grand-dau. of the late John Walter, Esq., of Bearwood, Berks, and has, with other issue,

* Walter Douglas Phillipps, a Major-General in the Army, late Col. 74th Highlanders; *b.* 1820; *m.* 1855 Julia. only dau. of Sir Howard Elphinstone, Bart., and has issue.

Capt. Patton, who entered the Royal Navy in 1805, is a Magistrate for Somerset. This family is of Scotch origin, lineally descended from Maximilian Bethune, Duc de Sully, 1560.—*Bishop's Hull House and Stoke Court, Taunton.*

PATY, Sir George William, K.C.B., K.H. ‡ (cr. 1861).

Son of the late William Paty, Esq., of Bristol, by Sarah, dau. of Thomas Hicks, Esq., of Berkeley, co. Gloucester; *b.* 1788. Entered the Army 1804, and served at Copenhagen and in the Peninsula; is a Lieut.-General, and Col. 70th Foot.

PAUL, Sir Robert Joshua, Bart., of Paulville, co. Carlow (cr. 1794).

Eldest son of the late William Gun Paul, Esq., by Marianne. dau. of the late Edward Moore. Esq., of Mooresfort, co. Tipperary; *b.* 1820; *s.* his uncle as William Blacker, Esq., of Woodlurock, co. Wexford. Is a J.P. and D.L. for co. Wexford; was High Sheriff of co. Carlow 1844.—*Paulville, Carlow; Ballinglass, co. Waterford.*

Heir, his son William Joshua, *b.* 1851.

PAUL, Sir John Dean, Bart. (cr. 1821).

Eldest son of the late Sir John Dean Paul, by Frances Eleanor, dau. of John Simpson, Esq., of Bradley Hall, co. Durham; *b.* 1802; *s.* as 2nd Bart. 1852; *m.* 1st 1826 Georgiana, dau. of Charles George Beauclerk, Esq., of St. Leonard's Lodge, Sussex; 2nd 1849 Susan. dau. of the late John Ewers, Esq., of Brighton; 3rd 1861 Jane Constance. dau. of the late Thomas Bagden.

‡ See Burke's 'Royal Families of England and Scotland,' Pedigree 50.

‡ Died whilst these sheets were at press.

PAUL, WALTER MATTHEWS, Esq., of High Grove, Gloucestershire.

Second son of the late John Paul Paul, Esq., of High Grove, by Mary, only child of W. Matthews, Esq., of Clapham, Surrey; *b.* 1797; *s.* 1828; *m.* 1819 Elizabeth, youngest dau. of John Hawker, Esq., of Dudbridge, and has, with other issue,

* Walter John, formerly Lieut. 43rd Foot; *b.* 1823.

Mr. Paul, who was educated at Winchester and Balliol Coll., Oxford (B.A. 1818), is a J.P. and D.L. for co. Gloucester, and a Magistrate for Wilts; was formerly Major R. N. Gloucester Militia, and Capt. R. Gloucestershire Hussars.—*High Grove, Tetbury.*

PAULET, the Rev. Lord CHARLES.

Second son of Charles Ingoldsby, 13th Marquis of Winchester, by Anne, dau. of John Andrews, Esq., of Shotney Hall, co. Northumberland; *b.* 1802; *m.* 1st 1831 Caroline Margaret, dau. of the late Sir John Ramsden, Bart.; 2nd 1850 Joan Frederica Mathewana, dau. of Bernard Granville, Esq., and has by the former, with other issue,

* Charles William, late Capt. 7th Hussars; *b.* 1832; *m.* 1863 Susan Amelia, 2nd surviving dau. of the late William Standish Standish, Esq., of Duxbury Hall, co. Lancaster.

Lord C. Paulet was educated at Clare Hall, Cambridge (M.A. 1824); was appointed Vicar of Wellesbourne 1830, Prebendary of Salisbury 1833—*Wellesbourne Vicarage, Warwick.*

PAULET, Lord FREDERICK, C.B.

Fifth son of Charles Ingoldsby, 13th Marquis of Winchester, by Anne, dau. of John Andrews, Esq., of Shotney Hall, co. Northumberland; *b.* 1810. Educated at Eton; entered the Army 1828 as Ensign and Lieut. Coldstream Guards; is a Major-General in the Army and Commander of the Brigade of Guards; also an Officer of the Legion of Honour; bears the Order of the Medjidie; served in Canada, and in the Crimea 1854–5.—*Guards' and United Service Clubs, s.w.; D 1, Albany.*

PAULET, Lord GEORGE, C.B.

Third son of Charles Ingoldsby, 13th Marquis of Winchester, by Anne, dau. of John Andrews, Esq., of Shotney Hall, Northumberland; *b.* 1803; *m.* 1855 Georgina, dau. of the late Major-General Sir G. Wood, K.C.B., of Ottershaw, Surrey, and has, with other issue,

* George, *b.* 1856.

Lord G. Paulet, who was educated at the Royal Naval Coll., is an Admiral retired; has served on the Channel, Mediterranean, and South American stations, and on the coast of Spain.—*United Service Club, s.w.; 11, Victoria Road, w.*

PAULET, Lord WILLIAM, K.C.B. (cr. 1865).

Fourth son of Charles Ingoldsby, 13th Marquis of Winchester, by Anne, dau. of John Andrews, Esq., of Shotney Hall, Northumberland; *b.* 1804. Educated at Eton; is a Major-Gen. in the Army and Col. 68th Regt., late Col. 87th Fusiliers; was formerly Lieut.-Governor of Portsmouth; appointed Adjutant-General to the Forces 1865; is an Officer of the Legion of Honour, and bears the Orders of St. Maurice, St. Lazare, and Medjidie.—16, *St. James's Square, s.w.*

PAULET, Sir HENRY CHARLES, Bart., of Little Testwood, Hants (cr. 1836).

Eldest son of the late Vice-Admiral Lord Henry Paulet, K.C.B. (who *d.* 1832), by Anna Maria, dau. of Edward Ravenscroft, Esq., of Portland Place, London.

734

PAULET. (See under *Winchester, Marquis of.*)

PAULL, HENRY, Esq.

Son of Archibald Paull, Esq.; *b.* 1822; *m.* 1862 Marianne, 2nd dau. of Henry Willis, Esq., of Hill Street, and Horton Lodge, Epsom, and has, with other issue,

* Herbert, *b.* 1863.

Mr. Paull, who was called to the Bar at the Middle Temple 1845, is a Dep.-Lieut. for Middlesex; he has been M.P. for St. Ives since 1857.—*Carlton and Athenæum Clubs, s.w.; 33, Devonshire Place, w.*

PAVIER. (See *Jackson*.)

PAXTON, Lady, of Sydenham, Kent.

Sarah, dau. of Thomas Bown, Esq., of Huntbridge House, Matlock, co. Derby; *m.* 1827 Sir Joseph Paxton, Knt., sometime M.P. for Coventry, who was the designer of the Crystal Palace in Hyde Park, and knighted for his services in that capacity, and who *d.* 1862.—*Rock Hills, Sydenham, s.e.*

PAXTON, ARCHIBALD FREDERIC, Esq., of Cholderton, Wilts.

Eldest son of the late Sir William Paxton, Knt., of Middleton Hall, co. Carmarthen, by Anne, dau. of T. Dawney, Esq., of Aylesbury, Bucks; *b.* 1793; *s.* 1824; *m.* 1838 Elizabeth, dau. of John Wyatt, Esq. Educated at Harrow; is a Magistrate for Wilts, and a Lieut. in the Army on reserved half-pay; served in the Peninsula.—*Cholderton, Salisbury; Reform and Junior United Service Clubs, s.w.*

PAYNE, Sir COVENTRY, Bart.,‡ of Wootton House, Beds (cr. 1737).

Eldest and only surviving son of the late Rev. Sir Coventry Payne, Bart., Vicar of Hatfield Peverel, Essex (who *d.* 1849), by Henrietta, 3rd dau. of the late Peter Wright, Esq., of Hatfield Priory, Essex, and grandson of the late Sir John Payne, Bart., of Tempsford Hall, Beds, by Mary, eldest surviving dau. and ultimately heir of Sir Philip Monoux, Bart., of Wootton House and Sandy Place; *b.* 1821; *s.* as 4th Bart. 1849; *s.* his grandmother, Lady Payne, in the Wootton estate 1850; *m.* 1852 his cousin Harriet, eldest dau. of the late John Wright, Esq., of Wickham Place, Essex, and niece of Sir J. T. Tyrell, Bart. Is Lord of the Manors of Wootton and Sandy, Beds, and, in right of his grandmother, representative of the ancient family of Monoux of Wootton, who were formerly seated at Walthamstow, in Essex. He has resumed the Baronetcy of Payne, as grandson of Sir John Payne, who *d.* 1803.—*Wootton House, Bedford; 14, Marine Parade, Hastings.*

Heir, his son Philip Monoux, *b.* 1858.

PAYNE, Sir CHARLES GILLIES, Bart.,‡ of Blunham House, Beds (cr. 1737).

Eldest son of the late Sir Peter Payne, Bart., of Blunham House (who was M.P. for Beds 1831–2), by Eliza Sarah, dau. of Samuel [....] co. Stafford; *b.* 1793; *s.* as 4th Bart. 1843; *m.* 1822 Mary Elizabeth, dau. of the Rev. Tadwall Salusbury, and niece of the late Sir Robert Salusbury, Bart. (she *d.* 1855). Educated at Merton Coll., Oxford (B.A. 1815, M.A. 1817); called to the Bar at the Middle Temple 1822; is a Magistrate for Herts and a J.P. and D.L. for Beds (High Sheriff 1851), was formerly one of the Council of the Island of St. Christopher.—*Blunham House, St. Neot's; University Club, s.w.*

Heir, his son Salusbury Gillies (of The Toft, Sharnbrook), a Magistrate for Beds; *b.* 1829; *m.* 1858 Catharine Ann, dau. of R. Chadwick, Esq., of High Bank, near Manchester, and has issue, * a son, *b.* 1861.

‡ This title is disputed by the other Baronet of the same name.

PAYNE, GEORGE, Esq., of Pitsford, North-amptonshire.

Only son of the late George Payne, Esq., of Sulby Hall, co. Northampton (who d. 1810), by Mary Eleanor, dau. of R. W. Grey, Esq., of Backworth House, Northumberland ; b. 1804 ; is a Dep.-Lieut. for co. Northampton (High Sheriff 1826). This family was formerly of Sulby Hall, in the same county.—*Pitsford, Northampton ; 4, John Street, Berkeley Square, w.*

PAYNE, ROBERT HENLEY, Esq., of Bordean, Hants.

Second son of the late Sir Peter Payne, Bart., M.P., of Blunham House, Beds (who d. 1843), by Eliza Sarah, dau. of Samuel Steward, Esq., of Stourton Castle, co. Stafford ; b. 1795 ; m. 1832 Louisa, dau. of the late Henry Chawner, Esq., of Newton Manor, Hants. and has, with other issue, * Henry Lavington, late 2nd Dragoon Guards, b. 1833.—*Bordean House, Petersfield.*

PAYNE, WILLIAM, Serjeant-at-Law.

Youngest son of the late William Payne, Esq., by Jane, dau. of Lucy Berry, a descendant of the Lord Protector; b. 1799 ; m. 1821 Kezia, dau. of Mr. Temple, of Dulwich Grove, and by her (who d. 1851), has issue.

  * William John, Recorder of Buckingham, and a Barrister-at-Law on the Norfolk Circuit.

Mr. Payne, who was called to the Bar at Gray's Inn 1843, appointed Coroner of London 1829, High Steward of Southwark and Judge of the Borough Court 1850, and created Serjeant-at-Law 1858, is a Magistrate for London, Southwark, Westminster, and Middlesex ; a Commissioner of Taxes for London, Middlesex, and Surrey, and a Governor of St. Bartholomew's Hospital. This family was resident at Bexley, Kent, as early as the year 1597. One of the paternal ancestors accompanied William III. from Holland to this country.—26, *Brunswick Square, w.c. ; 2, Serjeants' Inn, w.c.*

PAYNE-GALLWEY. (See *Gallwey.*)

PAYNE-TOWNSEND. (See *Townsend.*)

PAYNTER, REGINALD HEARLE, Esq., of Boskenna, Cornwall.

Only son of the late Thomas Paynter, Esq., J.P., of St. Buryan, by Ann, dau. of Aaron Moody, Esq., of Kingsdon, Somerset ; b. 1831 ; s. 1863 ; m. 1858 Mary Davies, eldest dau. of the Rev. John Oliver Willyams Hawels, of Brunswick Square, Brighton. Represents an ancient Cornish family.—*Boskenna, St. Buryan, Penzance.*

PAYNTER, WILLIAM, Esq., of Richmond, Surrey.

Eldest son of the late Samuel Paynter, Esq., of Camborne House, by Anne, dau. of W. Butler, Esq. ; b. 1799 ; s. 1844 ; m. 1825 Ann Berdmore, dau. of T. Best, Esq., of Stoke-on-Trent; and has, with other issue,

  * Samuel, b. 1826.

Mr. Paynter, who was educated at Harrow and Trinity Coll., Cambridge (B.A. 1820, M.A. 1823), and called to the Bar at Lincoln's Inn 1823, is a Magistrate for Surrey and D.L. and D.L. for Middlesex.—*Camborne House, Richmond, Surrey ; Carlton Club, s.w. ; 21, Belgrave Square, s.w.*

PEACH, the Rev. CHARLES PIERREPONT, of Tockington, Gloucestershire.

Eldest surviving son of the late Rev. James Jarvis Cleaver-Peach, of Tockington (who d. 1861), by Ellen Sybilla, dau. of Samuel Peach-Peach, Esq., of Tockington ; b. 1829 ; s. his brother 1867 ; m. 1860 Agnes

Lucy, dau. of George Legard, Esq., of Easthorpe Malton, co. York, and has, with other issue,

  * James Legard, b. 1861.

Mr. Peach, who was educated at Magdalen Coll., Cambridge (B.A. 1852), is Vicar of Appleton-le-Street, co. York, Lord of the Manor of Rockhampton and Alveston, and Patron of 1 living ; he assumed the name of Peach by Royal license 1868, under the will of his maternal grandfather.—*Tockington, Almondsbury, Bristol ; Appleton-le-Street, Malton ; Yorkshire Club, York.*

+PEACH, THOMAS, Esq., M.D., of Langley, Derbyshire.

Son of the late T. Peach, Esq., of Langley ; b. 18—. Is a J.P. and D.L. for co. Derby.—*Langley, Derby.*

PEACH. (See *Keighley-Peach.*)

PEACHEY, WILLIAM, Esq., of Ebernoe, Sussex.

Eldest son of the late Rev. John Peachey, of Ebernoe ; b. 1817 ; m. 1841 Rowena, dau. of the late George Barrett, Esq., of Wintershall, near Guildford. Is a Magistrate for Sussex, and descended from a common ancestor with the family of Lord Selsey (ext. 1838). —*Ebernoe, Petworth.*

PEACOCK, EDWARD, Esq., F.S.A., F.A.S.L., of Bottesford Manor, Lincolnshire.

Eldest son of the late Edward Shaw Peacock, Esq., of Bottesford Manor, by Catherine, dau. of Michael Woodcock, Esq., of Hemsworth, co. York ; b. 1831 ; s. 1861 ; m. 1853 Lucy Ann, dau. of John Swift Wetherell, Esq., of New York, and has, with other issue,

  * Edward Adrian Woodruffe, b. 1858.

Mr. Peacock is Lord of the Manor of Bottesford. This family has been settled near Bottesford for four centuries and a half; their present residence came into the possession of Mr. Peacock's ancestor, William Shaw, by purchase from the Tyrwhitts, A.D. 1595.—*Bottesford Manor, Brigg ; Junior Athenæum Club, s.w.*

+PEACOCK, JOSEPH, Esq., of Rhives, Sutherlandshire.

Son of the late J. Peacock. Esq., of Rhives ; b. 18—. Is a J.P. and D.L. for co. Sutherland.—*Rhives, Golspie.*

PEACOCK, WILKINSON, Esq., of Greatford Hall, Lincolnshire.

Youngest son of the late Anthony Peacock, Esq., of Kyme, co. Lincoln, by Mary, only dau. of the late Sir John Wilkinson, Esq. ; b. 1788 ; m. 1811 Mary, eldest dau. of the late Col. Gilbert Affleck, of Cavendish Hall, Suffolk, and by her, who d. 1847, has, with other issue,

  * Wilkinson Affleck, M.A., of C.C.C., Cambridge ; Rector and Patron of Ulceby, co. Lincoln, b. 1814.

Mr. Peacock, who is a J.P. and D.L. for co. Lincoln, was formerly Capt. 9th Lancers.—*Greatford Hall, Stamford.*

PEACOCK. (See *Willson.*)

PEACOCKE, Sir JOSEPH FRANCIS, Bart. (cr. 1802).

Only son of the late Lieut.-Col. Sir Nicholas Levett Peacocke, Bart., by Henrietta, dau. of the late Sir John Morris, Bart., of Clasemont, co. Glamorgan ; b. 1805 ; s. 1847. Was formerly an Officer in the 24th Foot.

PEACOCKE, Sir BARNES, Knt. (cr. 1859).

Son of the late B. Peacocke, Esq ; b. 1810 ; m. 1835 Elizabeth, dau. of William Fanning, Esq., and by her, who d. 1865, has issue.

  * Frederick Barnes, educated at Eton ; in the Bengal Civil Service ; b. 1856.

Sir Barnes, who was called to the Bar at the Inner Temple 1836, is Chief Justice of the Supreme Court of Judicature at Calcutta.—*Calcutta.*

PEACOCKE. (See *Sandford*.)

PEARCE, EDWARD, Esq., of Dorchester, Dorset.
Eldest son of the late Edward Pearce, Esq., of Bodmin, Cornwall, by Mary, dau. of the Rev. Richard Eliot, some time Vicar of Maker, Cornwall; *b.* 1817; *m.* 1848 Clara Jane, dau. of the Rev. John Palmer, some time of Torrington, Devon, Prebendary of Lincoln, and Rector of Clanaborough, Devon, and has, with other issue,
    * Edward Robert, *b.* 1851.
Mr. Pearce is a Magistrate for Dorset.—*Somerleigh, Dorchester.*

+ PEARCE, JOSEPH, Esq., of Llangarron Court, Herefordshire.
Son of the late J. Pearce, Esq., of Llangarron Court; *b.* 18—; is married. Is Lord of the Manor of Llangarron.—*Llangarron Court, Ross.*

PEARCE, Col. WILLIAM, K.H., of Ffrwdgrech, Brecknockshire.
Only son of the late Joseph Pearce, Esq., of Ffrwdgrech, by Elizabeth, dau. of Philip Lewis, of Llanrumney, co. Monmouth; *b.* 1789; *s.* 1807; *m.* 1838 Mary Church, only child of William Morrice, Esq., of Cardiff, widow of W. R. Ellis, Esq., of Arundel, and heir to her uncle Samuel Church, Esq., of Ffrwdgrech, and by her, who *d.* 1856, had issue an only child,
    * John Church Pearce-Church, Esq., of Staverton House, Gloucestershire, *b.* 1839; assumed the additional name of Church by Royal licence in 1847, and *d.* 1856,
Col. Pearce is a Magistrate for co. Gloucester, a J.P. and D.L. for co. Brecon (High Sheriff 1849), a Lieut.-Col. in the Army, and a Knight of the Guelphic Order.—*Ffrwdgrech, Brecon; Staverton House, Cheltenham; Fauconberg House, Cheltenham.*

PEARCE-SEROCOLD, WALTER SEROCOLD, Esq., of Cherryhinton, Cambridgeshire.
Eldest son of the late Rev. Edward Serocold Pearce-Serocold, of Cherryhinton, by Georgina, dau. of George Smith, Esq., of Selsdon, Surrey; *b.* 1825; *s.* 1849; *m.* 1853 Amelia, dau. of the Hon. Judge Duval, of Quebec, and has issue, a dau. Mr. Pearce-Serocold, who was educated at Eton, was formerly Capt. 66th Regt. This family assumed the name of Serocold by Royal licence in 1842.—*Cherryhinton, Cambridge.*

  Heir Pres., his brother Charles, of Prospect Lodge, Taplow, Bucks, educated at Eton; *b.* 1827; *m.* 1860 Maria Emilie, 2nd dau. of George St. Leger Grenfell, Esq., and has issue,
  * a son, *b.* 1865.

PEARD, JOHN WHITEHEAD, Esq., of Penquite, Cornwall.
Second son of the late Vice-Admiral Shuldham Peard, by Matilda, dau., of William Fortescue, Esq., of Penwarn, co. Cornwall; *b.* 1811; *m.* 1838 Catharine, dau. of the late Rev. Dr. Richards, of Teignmouth. Educated at Exeter Coll., Oxford (B.A. 1833, M.A. 1836); called to the Bar at the Inner Temple 1837. Is a J.P. and D.L. for Cornwall, and Capt. in the Duke of Cornwall's Rangers.—*Penquite, Lostwithiel; Carlton Club,* s.w.

PEARETH, WILLIAM, Esq., of Usworth, co. Durham.
Eldest son of the late William Peareth, Esq., of Usworth by Katharine, 5th dau. of the late Thos. Law Hodges, Esq., M.P., of Hemsted Park, Kent; *b.* 1831; *s.* 1854; *m.* 1856 Cecilia, 2nd dau. of John Lennox Kincaid-Lennox, Esq., of Lennox Castle, N.B., and has issue,
    * Christobbina Frances Catherine.
Mr. Peareth, who was educated at Eton, is a Magistrate for co. Durham (High Sheriff 1865), and Capt. 4th Stirlingshire Volunteers; was formerly Capt. 4th Light Dragoons.—*Usworth House, Gateshead; R.Y. Squadron, Cowes; Army and Navy Club,* s.w.
:56

PEARSE, EDWARD OCTAVIUS, Esq., of Bryncelyn, Anglesey.
Son of the late Rev. W. Pearse, of The Grove, Godmanchester, by Sarah, dau. of the late Rev. L. Shelford, B.D., Rector of Tuddenham, Norfolk; *b.* 1830; *m.* 1860 Jane, dau. of the late H. Williams, Esq., of Tre-y-ddyr and Trecastell, co. Anglesey, and has, with other issue,
    * Edward Vernon Dacres, *b.* 1861.
Major Pearse was educated at Marlborough Coll.; is a J.P. and D.L. for Anglesey; was Capt. and Adjutant Royal Anglesey Militia, Paymaster 5th Dragoon Guards, and Capt. in the Artillery, Turkish Contingent.—*Bryncelyn, Beaumaris; Royal Welsh Yacht Club.*

PEARSE, GEORGE, Esq., of Harlington, Beds.
Second son of the late Theed Pearse, Esq., of Bedford, by Susanna Rebecca, dau. of James Dickins, Esq.; *b.* 1795; *m.* 1819 Elizabeth, only child of the late John W. Jennings, Esq., of Harlington, and has issue,
    * George Wingate, in Holy Orders, M.A. of Corpus Christi Coll., Oxford, Rector of Walton; *b.* 1824; *m.* 1851 the eldest dau. of the Rev. Boteler Smith, of Aspley Guise, Beds.
Mr. Pearse is a J.P. and D L. for Beds (High Sheriff 1832),—*Harlington, Dunstable.*

PEARSON, Sir EDWIN, Knt., F.R S. (cr. 1836).
Son of the late John Pearson, Esq., F.R.S., of co. York, by Sarah, dau. of the late Hon. Alicia Anne, Esq.; *b.* 1802; *m.* 1841 the Hon. Alicia Anne, dau. of James, 3rd Viscount Lifford, and has issue,
    * Edwin James, *b.* 1842; *m.* 1868 Emily Margaret, eldest dau. of Richard Valpy, Esq., of Wimbledon.
Sir Edwin, who was educated at Trinity Coll., Cambridge (B.A. 1825), was formerly Lieut. of the Yeomen of the Guard.—*Wimbledon,* s.w.; *Athenæum Club,* s.w.

PEARSON, CHARLES, Esq., of Tempsford, Beds.
Youngest son of the late William Pearson, Esq., of Louth, co. Lincoln, by Mary, dau. of William Hyde, Esq.; *b.* 1790; *m.* 1830 Margaret, widow of William Graburn, Esq., and dau. of Joseph Brown, Esq., of Barton-upon-Humber, and has, with other issue,
    * Charles, *b.* 1833; *m.* 1856 Juliet, dau. of Kennet Dixon, Esq., and grand-dau. of Edward, 1st Lord St. Leonards.
Mr. Pearson is a Magistrate for Herts.—*Tempsford Hall, St. Neot's.*

PEARSON, GEORGE, Esq., of Southside, Cheshire.
Eldest son of the late Benjamin Pearson, Esq., of Southside, by Charlotte Elizabeth, dau. of Mark de Gilerne, Esq., of Wanstead, Essex; *b.* 1835; *s.* 1857. This family was formerly possessed of extensive estates in Yorkshire; one of its members, Sir Matthew Pearson, was High Sheriff of that county in 1702.—*Southside, Winslow.*

  Heir Pres., his brother Edward, *b.* 1846.

PEARSON, of Bodfari. (See *Pennant*.)

PEASE, HENRY, Esq., of Pierremont, and Stanhope Castle, co. Durham.
Third son of the late Edward Pease, Esq., of Darlington, by Rachel, dau. of John Whitwell, Esq., of Kendal; *b.* 1807; *m.* 1st 1835 Anna, dau. of Richard Fell, Esq.; 2nd 1859 Mary, dau. of S. Lloyd, Esq., of Wednesbury, and has, with other issue, by the former,
    * Henry Fell (of Brinkburn, Darlington), a Magistrate for co. Durham, *b.* 1838; *m.* 1862 Elizabeth, eldest dau. of John Beaumont Pease, Esq., of North Lodge, Darlington, and has, with other issue, by the former,—Norman Henry, *b.* 1865.
Mr. Pease, who is a Coalowner and Merchant, was M.P. for S. Durham 1857–65.—*Pierre mont, Darlington; Stanhope Castle, Weardale, co. Durham;* 13, *Park Place,* s.w.

PEASE, JOSEPH, Esq., of Southend, co. Durham.
Son of the late Edward Pease, Esq., of Darlington, by Rachel, dau. of John Whitwell, Esq., of Kendal; *b.* 1799; *m.* 1826 Emma, dau. of Joseph Gurney, Esq., of Lakenham Grove, Norwich, and by her, who *d.* 1860, has, with other issue,

* Joseph Whitwell (of Woodlands, Darlington, and Hutton Low Cross, Guisborough), a Magistrate for co. Durham and the N. Riding of Yorkshire; M.P. for S. Durham; *b.* 1828; *m.* 1854 Mary, dau. of Alfred Fox, Esq., of Falmouth, and has, with other issue, * Edward, *b.* 1857.

Mr. Pease was M.P. for South Durham 1832–41. —*Southend, Darlington; Cliff House, Marske, Redcar.*

PEASE, JOSEPH WALKER, Esq., of Hesslewood, Yorkshire.
Eldest son of the late Joseph Robinson Pease, Esq., J.P. and D.L., of Hesslewood, by Harriet, dau. of James Walker, Esq., of Beverley; *b.* 1820; *s.* 1866; *m.* 1843 Barbara, dau. of the Rev. Henry Palmer, of Withcote Hall, co. Leicester, and has, with other issue,

* Henry Joseph Robinson, *b.* 1843.

Mr. Pease is a J.P. and D.L. for the E. Riding of Yorkshire.—*Hesslewood House, Hull.*

PECHELL, Sir GEORGE SAMUEL BROOKE-, Bart., of Hazeleigh Hall, Essex (cr. 1797).
Eldest son of the late Capt. Samuel George Pechell, R.N., of Beroly, Hants (who *d.* 1840), by Caroline, dau. of the late William Thoyts, Esq., of Sulhamstead House, Berks; *b.* 1819; *s.* his cousin, Admiral Sir Geo. R. Brooke-Pechell, Bart., as 5th Bart. 1860; *m.* 1842 May Robertson, dau. of the late Lieut.-Col. Bremner. Appointed Ensign in the 47th Regt. Madras Native Infantry 1840; Major Shropshire Militia 1863; Lieut.-Col. 4th Hants Volunteers 1863; is Lord of the Manors of Hazeleigh and Ulting, Essex. Sir G. Pechell has assumed the surname of Brooke, after his great-grandmother, in conformity with the custom of the previous Baronets.—Residence: *Alton, Hants.*

Heir, his son Samuel George, *b.* 1852.

PECHELL. (See *Brooke-Pechell.*)

PECHELL, the Rev. HORACE ROBERT.
Fourth son of the late Augustus Pechell, Esq., of Bartleets, Herts, by Sarah, dau. and co-heir of the Rev. Thomas Drake, D.D., of Amersham, Bucks, and uncle to Sir G. S. Brooke-Pechell, Bart.; *b.* 1792; *m.* 1826 Lady Caroline Mary, dau. of the late Admiral Lord Mark Ker, and of Charlotte (in her own right) Countess of Antrim. Educated at Ch. Ch., Oxford (B.A. 1813, M.A. 1814), afterwards Fellow of All Souls' Coll.; appointed Rector of Bix 1822, and Chancellor and Canon of Brecon 1829.—*Bix Rectory, Henley-on-Thames.*

PECK, PHILIP WILLIAM RICHARDSON, Esq., of Cornish Hall, Denbighshire.
Only son of the late Philip Richardson Peck, Esq., of Cornish Hall, and of Temple Combe, Somerset, by Georgina, 3rd dau. of the late James Ford, Esq., of Finhaven Castle and Bromley House, co. Forfar, N.B.; *b.* 1849; *s.* 1858.—*Cornish Hall, Holt; Temple Combe, Wincanton, Somerset.*

PECK. (See under *Buckley of Ardwick.*)

PECKHAM, CHARLES PECKHAM, Esq., of Nyton, Sussex.
Eldest son of the late Charles Hewitt Smith, Esq., of Nyton and of Aldling Meadows, by Mary, dau. and heir of John Peckham, Esq., of Nyton, whose name he assumed; *b.* 1801; *s.* 1834; *m.* 1826 Sybella Jane,

dau. of the late Right Rev. Robert Carr, D.D., Lord Bishop of Worcester, and has, with other issue,

* Harry John Peckham, B.A. of Balliol Coll., Oxford; *b.* 1841.

Mr. Peckham, who was educated at Trinity Coll., Cambridge, is a Magistrate for Sussex. This family is of Saxon extraction, and has been settled in Kent and Sussex since the 13th century.—*Nyton, Chichester.*

PEDDER, HENRY NEWSHAM, Esq., late of Whinfield, Lancashire.
Fifth son of the late James Pedder, Esq., of Ashton Park, co. Lancaster, by June, only dau. of R. Newsham, Esq., of Preston; *b.* 1822. Is a Magistrate for co. Lancaster, and a Banker at Preston; late Capt. Lancashire Militia—Residence: 9, *Queen's Gate, w.*

PEDDER, RICHARD NEWSHAM, Esq.
Eldest son of the late Edward Pedder, Esq., of Ashton Park, J.P. and D.L. for co. Lancaster, by Amelia, dau. of Edward Gawne, Esq., of Kentraugh, Isle of Man; *b.* 1837; *s.* 1861; *m.* 1860 Mary Elizabeth, dau. of Sir William H. Ffeilden, Bart., and has, with other issue,

* Ernest William, *b.* 1862.

Mr. Pedder, who was educated at Eton, entered the Army in 1855, and is Capt. 8th Hussars. This family have been Bankers at Preston for upwards of a century, and were formerly owners of Ashton Park, near that town.—*Junior United Service Club,* s.w.

PEEK, the late RICHARD, Esq., of Hazelwood Park, Devon.
Son of the late John Peek, Esq., of Hazelwood Park, by Susan, dau. of John Foxworthy, Esq., of Loddiswell, Devon; *b.* 1782; *s.* 1847; *d.* 1867. He was a Magistrate for Devon; served as Sheriff for London and Middlesex in 1832–3.—*Hazlwood Park, Kingsbridge.*

PEEL, the Right Hon. Sir ROBERT, Bart., G.C.B., of Drayton, Staffordshire (cr. 1800).
Eldest son of the late Right Hon. Sir Robert Peel, Bart., M.P., of Drayton Manor (who was Premier 1834–5 and 1841–6), by Julia, dau. of the late General Sir John Floyd, Bart.; *b.* 1822; *s.* as 3rd Bart. 1850; *m.* 1856 Lady Emily, dau. of George, 8th Marquis of Tweeddale, K.T. Educated at Harrow and Ch. Ch., Oxford (B.A. 1843); is a J.P. and D.L. for co. Stafford, and Patron of 1 living; late Capt. Staffordshire Yeomanry; has been M.P. for Tamworth since 1850; was Chief Secretary for Ireland 1861–5; was formerly Attaché to the Legation at Madrid, and Secretary of British Embassy in Switzerland.—*Drayton Manor, Tamworth: Brooks's and Boodle's Clubs,* s.w.; 5, *Whitehall Gardens,* s.w.

Heir, his son Robert, *b.* 1857.

PEEL, the Right Hon. Sir LAWRENCE, Knt. (cr. 1842).
Son of the late Joseph Peel, Esq., of Bowes Farm, Southgate, Middlesex, by Anne, dau. of R. Haworth, Esq., and cousin of the late Right Hon. Sir R. Peel, Bart., M.P.; *b.* 1799. Educated at St. John's Coll., Cambridge (B.A. 1821); is a Bencher of the Middle Temple (where he was called 1824); Bar 1824); was Governor of Guy's Hospital; was successively a Barrister on the Northern Circuit, Advocate-General later on the Northern Circuit, Advocate-General in Bengal 1840–2, Chief-Justice at Calcutta 1842–55, Vice-President of the Legislative Council at Calcutta 1854–5; appointed a Director of the Hon. East India Company 1857.—*Under Rock, Bonchurch, I. of Wight: Athenæum and Windham Clubs,* s.w.; 4, *Durham Villas, Campden Hill,* w.

PEEL, ARTHUR WELLESLEY, Esq., of Sandy Lodge, Beds.
Youngest son of the late Right Hon. Sir Robert Peel, Bart., M.P., of Drayton Manor, co. Stafford, by Julia,

dau. of the late Gen. Sir John Lloyd, Bart.; *b.* 1829; *m.* 1862 Adelaide, dau. of William Stratford Dugdale, Esq., of Merevale Hall and Blyth Hall, co. Warwick, and has issue. Mr. Peel, who was educated at Eton and Balliol Coll., Oxford·(B.A. 1852), is a Magistrate for Beds, and Patron of 1 living; elected M.P. for Warwick 1865.—*Sandy Lodge, St. Neot's; University Club, s.w.; 70, Eaton Place, s.w.*

PEEL, the Right Hon. FREDERICK, P.C., of Hampton-in-Arden, Warwickshire.

Second son of the late Right Hon. Sir Robert Peel, Bart., M.P. (who *d.* 1850), by Julia, dau. of the late Gen. Sir John Floyd, Bart.; *b.* 1823; *m.* 1857 Elizabeth Emily, dau. of the late John Shelley, Esq., of Avington House, Hants (she *d.s.p.* 1855). Educated at Trinity Coll., Cambridge (B.A. 1845, M.A. 1849); called to the Bar at the Inner Temple 1849; is a Dep. Lieut. for co. Warwick; was M.P. for Bury 1852–7, and 1859–65; Under-Secretary of State for the Colonies 1851–2, and again in 1855; Under-Secretary for War 1855–7; Secretary to the Treasury 1859–65.—*Hampton-in-Arden, Birmingham; 3, Paper Buildings, Temple, e.c.*

PEEL, the Rev. FREDERICK.

Son of the late Right Hon. William Yates and Lady Jane Peel, and nephew of the Earl of Mount Cashell, and of the late Right Hon. Sir Robert Peel, Bart.; *b.* 1833; *m.* 1859 the Hon. Adelaide Frances Isabella, 3rd dau. of Thomas Charles, 2nd Lord Sudeley, and has, with other issue,

* A son, *b.* 1863.

Mr. Peel was educated at Oriel Coll., Oxford (B.A. 1858, M.A. 1859).—Residence: *Barassie House, Malvern Link, Worcestershire.*

+PEEL, GEORGE HENRY, Esq., of Swinton Park, Lancashire.

Eldest son of the late William Peel, Esq., of Swinton Park; *b.* 18—; *m.* 1867 Elizabeth, youngest dau. of William Harter, Esq., of Hope, Eccles, near Manchester. Is a Magistrate for co. Lancaster.—*Swinton Park, Manchester.*

PEEL, JOHN, Esq.

Youngest son of the late Thomas Peel, Esq., of Peelford, co. Lancaster, and Peel Park, Cornwall, by Dorothy, dau. of Robert Bolton, Esq.; *b.* 1804; *m.* 1830 Esther, dau. of Edmund Peel, Esq., and has issue. Mr. Peel, who is a Magistrate for cos. Stafford and Warwick, was elected M.P. for Tamworth 1863.—Residence: *Middleton Hall, Tamworth.*

PEEL, the Very Rev. JOHN, Dean of Worcester.

Fourth son of the late Sir Robert Peel, 1st Bart., of Drayton Manor, co. Stafford, by Ellen, dau. of William Yates, Esq., of Spring Side, co. Lancaster; *b.* 1798; *m.* 1824 Augusta, dau. of the late John Swynfen, Esq., of Swynfen, co. Stafford, and has, with other issue,

* Augustus Robert Laurence, *b.* 1825.

Dean Peel was educated at Rugby and Ch. Ch., Oxford (B.A. 1822, M.A. 1825, B.D. and D.D. 1845), appointed Vicar of Stone, co. Worcester, 1828 and Dean of Worcester 1845; is Patron of 3 livings.—*The Deanery, Worcester; University Club, s.w.*

PEEL, JOHN ENTWISLE, Esq., of Stone Hall, Pembrokeshire.

Younger son of the late Robert Peel, Esq., of Bath, by Elizabeth, dau. of the late John Entwisle, Esq., of Foxholes, co. Lancaster; *b.* 1800; *m.* 1842 Anne Maria Cordelia, only child of James James, Esq., and niece of

738

the late Sir William Philipps Laugharne-Philipps, Bart., and has issue,

* Ellen Louisa, *m.* 1863 Capt. Lloyd Still, R.A.; and Anne-Elizabeth-Margaret.

Mr. Peel, who is in the Commission of the Peace for co. Pembroke, represents a younger branch of the family of Sir R. Peel, Bart.—*Stone Hall, Haverfordwest.*

PEEL, the Right Hon. JONATHAN, of Marble Hill, Middlesex.

Fifth son of Sir Robert Peel, 1st Bart., of Drayton Manor, co. Stafford, by Ellen, dau. of William Yates, Esq., of Spring Side, near Bury, co. Lancaster; *b.* 1799; *m.* 1824 Lady Alicia Jane, dau. of Archibald, 1st Marquis of Ailsa, and has, with other issue,

* Edmund Yates, 85th Foot, *b.* 18—; *m.* 1848 Maria Frances Knighton, youngest dau. of the late Richard Chadwick, Esq., and grand-dau. of the late John Moore Knighton, Esq., of Greenofen, Devon.

Mr. Peel, who was educated at Rugby and Sandhurst, is a Lieut.-General in the Army, was Surveyor-General of the Ordnance 1841–6, Secretary of State for the War Department 1858–9 and 1866–7, has been M.P. for Norwich 1826–30, for Huntingdon since 1831.—*Marble Hill, Twickenham, s.w.; Carlton Club, s.w.; 8, Park Place, St. James's, s.w.*

PEEL, JONATHAN, Esq., of Accrington House, Lancashire, and Knowlmere, Yorkshire.

Eldest son of the late Robert Peel, Esq., of Accrington House, by Anne, dau. of William Peel, Esq., of Peel Fold and Church Bank; *b.* 1806; *s.* 1839; *m.* 1st 1833 Ann, youngest dau. of T. Peel, Esq., of Peel Fold, Lancashire, and Trenant Park, Cornwall; 2nd 1838 Mary, dau. of the Rev. J. Wilde, of Harnage, co. Salop, and has, with other surviving issue,

* William, *b.* 1844.

Mr. Peel, who was educated at St. John's Coll., Cambridge (B.A. 1828), called to the Bar at the Middle Temple 1833, and went the Northern Circuit; is a J.P. and D.L. for co. Lancaster, and a Magistrate for the W. Riding of Yorkshire.—*Knowlmere Manor, Clitheroe; Oxford and Cambridge Club, s.w.*

PEEL, GEORGE, Esq., of Singleton, Lancashire.

Eldest son of the late Joseph Peel, Esq., J.P. and D.L., of Singleton Brook, by Anne Frances, dau. of Thomas Voile, Esq., of Rugby; *b.* 1828; *s.* 1866. Represents a younger branch of the family of Sir R. Peel, Bart. —*Singleton Brook, Broughton, Manchester.*

PEEL, LAURENCE, Esq., of Kemp Town, Sussex.

Youngest son of the 1st Sir Robert Peel, Bart., M.P., by Ellen, dau. of William Yates, Esq., of Spring Side, Bury, co. Lancaster; *b.* 1801; *m.* 1822 Lady Jane Lennox, dau. of Charles, 4th Duke of Richmond, K.G., and by her, who *d.* 1861, has, with other issue,

* Laurence Charles Lennox, a Magistrate for Sussex, and late Capt. 7th Hussars; *b.* 1823; *m.* 1848 the Hon. Caroline Georgiana, eldest dau. of Arthur, 1st Lord Templemore.

Mr. Peel, who was educated at Ch. Ch., Oxford, is Patron of 1 living; he was M.P. for Cockermouth 1827–30, and formerly Secretary of the India Board.—*32, Sussex Square, Brighton; White's Club, s.w.*

PEEL, WILLIAM, Esq., of Ackworth Park, Yorkshire.

Only son of Samuel Peel, Esq., of Carrwood House, co. York, by Hannah, dau. of James Bottomley, Esq.; *b.* 1811; *m.* 1834 Lucy, dau. of Joseph Woodhead, Esq., of Wade House, co. York, and has, with other issue.

* George Frederick, *b.* 1834; *m.* 1859 Sarah Hannah, eldest dau. of the late G. A. Stanfield, Esq., of Brotherton House, co. York.

Mr. Peel is a Magistrate for the W. Riding of York-

shire, and a Merchant at Bradford.—*Ackworth Park, Pontefract ; Bradford, Yorkshire.*

+ PEEL, WILLIAM, Esq., of Peel Fold, Lancashire, and Trenant Park, Cornwall.
Third but eldest surviving son of the late Thomas Peel, Esq., of Peel Fold and Trenant Park, by Dorothy, dau. of — Bolton, Esq. ; b. 1796; m. 1827 Mary, dau. of Edmund Peel, Esq., of Church Bank, co. Lancaster, and has, with other issue,

* William Henry, J.P. for Cornwall ; b. 1828.

Mr. Peel is a Manufacturer in Lancashire. This family is the head of that of which Sir Robert Peel is a member. — *Trenant Park, Liskeard, Cornwall ; Peel Fold, Blackburn.*

PEEL, WILLIAM, Esq., of Taliaris Park, Carmarthenshire.
Only son of the late Robert Peel, Esq., of Taliaris Park, by his 1st wife Anne, dau. of Jonathan Peel, Esq., of Accrington House, co. Lancaster ; b. 1803 ; s. 1838 ; m. 1836 Anna Maria, eldest dau. of John William Lloyd, Esq., of Dan-y-ralt, co. Carmarthen, and has, with other issue,

* Herbert, B.A. of Christ's Coll., Cambridge, a Magistrate for co. Carmarthen ; b. 1840.

Mr. Peel is a J.P. and D.L. for co. Carmarthen (High Sheriff 1843), and Patron of the Donative of Taliaris. This family is an elder branch of that of Sir Robert Peel, Bart.—*Taliaris Park, Llandilo.*

+ PEEL, WILLIAM HENRY, Esq., of Aylesmore House, Gloucestershire.
Fourth son of the late Laurence Peel, Esq., of Ardwick, co. Lancaster, by his 1st wife Alice, dau. of Jonathan Haworth, Esq. ; b. 1795 ; m. 1st 1821 Elizabeth, eldest dau. of Col. Clutton, of Pensax Court, co. Worcester ; 2nd 1836 Rebecca Mary, dau. of the late William Curro, Esq., of Itton Court, co. Monmouth, and has by the former, with other issue,

* Laurence Henry, a Magistrate for co. Radnor, and Major Commanding Radnor Militia ; b. 1823 ; m. 1846 Catharine Maria, 2nd dau. of the late Rev. Walter de Winton, of Wallswork Hall, co. Gloucester, some time Rector of Llanstephan, co. Brecon.

Mr. Peel, who was formerly a Manufacturer in Lancashire, represents a younger branch of that of Sir R. Peel, Bart.—*Aylesmore House, St. Briavell's, Lydney.*

PEEL, XAVIER DE CASTANOS ROYDS, Esq., of Denant, Pembrokeshire.
Elder son of the late Jonathan Haworth Peel, Esq., of Cottsmore, co. Pembroke, by Ellen, dau. of Thomas Royds, Esq., of Greenhill, co. Lancaster ; b. 1808 ; s. 1853 ; m. 1838 Mary, dau. of Roger Eaton, Esq., of Parkglas. Mr. Peel, who entered the Army 1827, is a Magistrate for co. Pembroke and Lieut.-Col. Pembrokeshire Rifle Volunteers.—*Denant, Haverfordwest.*

PEEL, of Bryn-y-Pys. (See under *Ethelston.*)

PEGGE-BURNELL, EDWARD VALENTINE, Esq., of Beauchieff Abbey, Derbyshire,
Only son of the late Broughton Benjamin Pegge-Burnell, Esq., of Beauchieff Abbey ; b. 1805 ; s. 1850 ; m. 1832 Harriet, 2nd dau. of the late Hugh Parker, Esq., of Woodthorpe, co. York, and has, with other issue,

* Edward Strelley, Capt. Coldstream Guards ; b. 1835.

Mr. Pegge-Burnell was educated at Eton and Magdalen Coll., Oxford (B.A. 1827, M.A. 1828), is a Magistrate for co. Derby, a J.P. and D.L. for Notts (High Sheriff 1860), and Lord of the Manor and Patron of Winkburn.—*Beauchieff Abbey, Sheffield ; Winkburn Hall, Southwell, Notts ; Carlton and Oxford and Cambridge Clubs, s.w.*

PEIRSE. (See *Beresford-Peirse.*)

PELHAM, the Hon. Mrs.
Madeline, 2nd dau. of Sir John Gordon Sinclair, Bart., by Anne, only dau. of Admiral the Hon. M. de Courcy ; m. 1839 the Hon. Capt. Dudley Worsley Pelham, M.P. (uncle of Charles, 3rd Earl of Yarborough), who d. 1851, leaving issue, * Edith Charlotte.—*St. Lawrence, Ventnor, Isle of Wight.*

PELHAM.
(See under *Newcastle, Duke of ; Chichester, Earl of ; and Yarborough, Earl of.*)

PELHAM. (See *Thursby-Pelham.*)

PELHAM-CLINTON, the Ladies, of Ranby Hall, Notts.
Georgiana and Charlotte, daus. of Henry Pelham, 4th Duke of Newcastle, by Georgiana Elizabeth, dau. of Edward Miller-Mundy, Esq., M.P., of Shipley, co. Derby, and sisters of Henry Pelham, 5th Duke. Are Ladies of the Manor of Ranby.—*Ranby Hall, Balworth, East Retford.*

PELL, Sir WATKIN OWEN, Knt. (cr. 1837).
Son of the late Samuel Pell, Esq., of co. Northampton, by Mary, dau. of Owen Owen, Esq., of Llanrhiader ; b. 1788 ; m. 1847 Sarah Dorothea, dau. of Edward Owen, Esq., of Maesmynan. Is an Admiral R.N., and a Commissioner of Greenwich Hospital ; has served in the Mediterranean, and also (as Commodore) in the West Indies.—*Royal Hospital, Greenwich, s.E. ; United Service Club, s.w.*

PELL, ALBERT, Esq., of Haslebeech, Northamptonshire, and Wilburton, Cambridgeshire.
Eldest son of the late Sir Albert Pell. Knt., Judge of the Court of Bankruptcy (who d. 1832), by the Hon. Margaret Letitia Matilda. 3rd dau. of Henry, 12th Lord St. John of Bletsoe ; b. 1820 ; s. his mother 1863 ; m. 1846 Elizabeth Barbara, dau. of Sir Henry Halford, Bart., of Wistow, but has no issue. Educated at Rugby and Trinity Coll., Cambridge (B.A. 1842, Hon. M.A. 1842) ; is a Dep.-Lieut. for co. Cambridge, a Magistrate for the Isle of Ely, and co. Leicester, and Lord of the Manor of Wilburton.—*Haslebeech, Northampton ; Wilburton Manor, Ely.*

PELLEW, the Hon. and Rev. EDWARD.
Fourth son of Edward, 1st Viscount Exmouth, by Susannah, youngest dau. of James Frowde, Esq., of Sedgehill, Wilts ; b. 1799 ; m. 1826 Marianne, dau. of Stephen Winthrop, Esq., M.D., and by her, who d. 1867, has, with other issue,

* Edward Winthrop, b. 1830.

Mr. Pellew was educated at Oriel Coll., Oxford (B.A. 1823, M.A. 1824) and appointed Incumbent of St. James's, Bury St. Edmund's, 1845.—*St. James's, Bury St. Edmund's.*

PELLEW. (See under *Exmouth, Viscount.*)

PELLY, Sir HENRY CARSTAIRS, Bart., of Upton, Essex (cr. 1840).
Eldest son of the late Sir John Henry Pelly, Bart., of Upton, by his 1st wife, Johannah Jane, youngest dau. of John Carstairs, Esq., of Woodhurst, co. Hunts, and Stratford Green, Essex ; b. 1814 ; s. as 3rd Bart. 1864. Is a Lieut. 2nd Life Guards, late Lieut. 2nd Dragoons, A.D.C. to the Lord Lieutenant of Ireland.—*Upton House, West Ham ; Naval and Military Club, w.*

Heir Prea., his half-brother Alwyne Vincent, b. 1852.

PELLY, RAYMOND, Esq., of Plashet, Essex.
Second son of the late Sir John H. Pelly, Bart., of Upton, Essex, by Emma, dau. of Henry Boulton, Esq., of Thorncroft, Surrey; b. 1810; m. 1835 Louisa, dau. of J. Fry, Esq., and has, with other issue,

* Charles Raymond, a Magistrate for Essex, b. 1837; m. 1864 Louisa Catharine, dau. of Sir Robert N. C. Hamilton, Bart., K.C.B.

Mr. Pelly is a J.P. and D.L. for Essex.—Plashet House, East Ham, Essex.

PELLY, RICHARD WILSON, Esq., of Upminster, Essex.
Fifth son of Sir John H. Pelly, Bart. (who d. 1852), by Emma, dau. of Henry Boulton, Esq., of Thorncroft, Surrey; b. 1814; m. 1851 Katharine Jane, youngest dau. of John Gurney Fry, Esq.; of Hale End, Woodford, Essex Is a J.P. and D.L. for Essex, and a Capt. R.N. —The Cedars, Upminster.

PEMBERTON, Major CHRISTOPHER ROBERT, of Newton, Cambridgeshire.
Eldest son of the late Christopher Robert Pemberton, Esq., of Trumpington, by Eleanor, dau. of James Hamilton, Esq., of Strabane, Ireland; b. 1801; s. 1822; m. 1829 Henrietta, dau. of the late Nathaniel William Peach, Esq., M.P., of Ketteringham Hall, Norfolk, and has, with other issue,

* Christopher Peach, Capt. Scots Fusilier Guards; b. 1838.

Major Pemberton, who was educated at Westminster and Ch. Ch., Oxford (B.A. 1824, M.A. 1828), is a J.P. and D.L. for co. Cambridge (High Sheriff 1859), and a Major in the county Militia.—Newton, Cambridge; Carlton and White's Clubs, s.w.; Eaton Place, s.w.

PEMBERTON, EDWARD LEIGH, Esq., of Torry Hill, Kent.
Younger son of the late Robert Pemberton, Esq., Barrister-at-law, by Margaret, eldest dau. and co-heir of Edward Leigh, Esq., of Bispham Hall, co. Lancaster, and brother of the late Lord Kingsdown (ext.); b. 1795; m. 1820 Charlotte, dau. of the late Samuel Compton Cox, Esq., Master in Chancery, and has, with other issue,

* Edward Leigh (of Wrinsted Court, Sittingbourne); educated at Eton; B.A. of St. John's Coll., Oxford; a Barrister-at-Law of Lincoln's Inn; M.P. for E. Kent, and Major E. Kent Yeomanry Cavalry; b. 1823; m. 1849 Matilda Catharine Emma, dau. of the late Hon. and Rev. Francis J. Noel, and has, with other issue, * Robert Leigh, b. 1851.

Mr. Pemberton, who was educated at B.N.C., Oxford (B.A. 1814, M.A. 1817) and s. in 1867 to the estates of his brother, is Lord of the Manor and Patron of Frinsted, Kent.—Torry Hill, Sittingbourne; Hindley Hall, Wigan.

PEMBERTON, the Rev. EDWARD ROBERT, D.C.L., late of Milton, Northamptonshire.
Eldest son of the late Thomas Butcher, Esq., of Northampton, by Judith, dau. and heir of the Rev. John Pemberton, Vicar of Carlington, Beds, whose name he has assumed; b. 1792; s. 1812; m. 1st 1823 Caroline, dau. of John Jackson, Esq. (who d. in 1814); 2nd 1851 Susan, dau. of Christopher Bassett, Esq., of Boverton House, co. Glamorgan. Educated at Rugby and University Coll., Oxford (B.A. 1814, M.A. 1817. D.C.L. 1823), is a Magistrate for co. Northampton; and formerly Rector and Patron of Milton and of West Haddon Manor, and Vicar of Wandsworth, Surrey.

PEMBERTON, HENRY WILLIAMS, Esq., of Trumpington, Cambridgeshire.
Eldest son of the late Rev. Edward Hodgson, by Charlotte, dau. of Francis Pemberton, Esq., of Trumpington; b. 1819; m. 1855 Frances Maria Sophia, widow of the

late Huntly Campbell, Capt. 20th Foot, and only child of the late Francis Charles James Pemberton, Esq., whose name he assumed. Educated at Eton and Trinity Coll., Cambridge (B.A. 1841, M.A. 1844), and was called to the Bar at the Inner Temple 1844, is a Magistrate for co. Cambridge.—Trumpington, Cambridge; Arthur's, and Oxford and Cambridge Clubs, s.w.

Heir Pres. to the Property (his wife's son by her first marriage), Francis Pemberton Campbell, Esq., Capt. 14th Hussars, b. 1837.

PEMBERTON, RICHARD LAURENCE, Esq., of Barnes, co. Durham.
Only son of the late Richard Pemberton, Esq., of Barnes, by Ellen, dau. of the late Capt. Robert Junju. R.N., of Bath; b. 1831; s. 1843; m. 1st 1854 Jan.; Emma, 2nd dau. of the Rev. Martin Stapylton (she d. 1865); 2nd 1867 Elizabeth Jane, elder dau. of the Rev. J. S. W. Donnison, M.A., of Mendham, Norfolk; he has, by the former,

* John Stapylton Grey, b. 1856.

Mr. Pemberton, who was educated at Eton and Pembroke Coll., Oxford, is a J.P. and D.L. for Durham (High Sheriff 1861), Lord of the Manors of Cold-Heselden and Hawthorn, and a moiety of that of Barnes, and Patron of 1 living; he was formerly Capt. N. Durham Militia.—Barnes and Bainbridge Holme, Sunderland; Hawthorn Tower, Seaham, co. Durham; Athenæum and Windham Clubs, s.w.

PEMBERTON. (See Childe-Pemberton.)

+**PEMBERTON-BARNES**, WILLIAM, Esq., of Havering-atte-Bower, Essex.
Son of the late Joseph Pemberton, Esq., of Beauchamp Roding, Essex; b. 18—; m. 18— Ann. dau. of the late John Barnes, Esq., of The Round House. Havering-atte-Bower, and has issue. Is Patron of the living of Havering. He assumed, by Royal licence, the name of Barnes on inheriting the property of the late John Barnes, Esq., in Middlesex, Surrey, and Essex. The family were originally seated in co. Durham.—The Hall, Havering-atte-Bower, Romford.

PEMBROKE, Earl of (GEORGE ROBERT CHARLES HERBERT).—Cr. 1551.
Eldest son of the late Right Hon. Sidney Herbert, 1st Lord Herbert of Lea (who d. 1861), by Elizabeth, only dau. of the late General Charles Ashe A'Court. of Amington Hall (brother of the 1st Lord Heytesbury); b. 1850; s. his father 1861 in the Barony of Herbert, and his uncle, in the Earldom, 1862. Educated at Eton; is Hereditary High Steward of Wilton: Visitor of Jesus Coll., Oxford; Lord of the Manors of Wilton, &c., and Patron of 10 livings.—Wilton House, Salisbury; 38, Chesham Place, s.w.

Heir Pres., his brother Sidney, b. 1853.

PENDER, JOHN, Esq., of Crumpsall House, Lancashire, and Minard, Argyllshire.
Second son of the late James Pender, Esq., of Vale of Leven, co. Dumbarton; b. 1816; m. 1st 1840 Marion, dau. of James Cearns, Esq.; 2nd 1851 Emma, dau. of the late Henry Denison, Esq., of Daybrook, Notts, and has by the former, with other issue,

* James, Lieut. 25th Regt.; b. 1842; m. 1867 Mary Rose, 3rd dau. of Edward Greye Hopwood, Esq., of Hopwood Hall, co. Lancaster.

Mr. Pender, who was educated at the High School, Glasgow, is a Dep. Lieut. for co. Lancaster, and a Merchant in London, Manchester, and Glasgow; late M.P. for Totnes.—Crumpsall House, Manchester; Minard Hall, Linlithgow; Minard Castle, Inverary, Argyllshire; Reform Club, s.w.; 18, Arlington Street, w.

74

PENDLEBURY, Lady.
Mary Ann, only dau. of the late John Stringer, Esq., of Stockport. and widow of Henry Brownhill, Esq.; *m.* 1834 Sir Ralph Pendlebury, Knt. (who *d.* 1861).—*Mersey Bank House, Heaton Mersey, Manchester.*

PENFOLD. (See *Wyatt.*)

+PENGELLEY, the Rev. WILLIAM HENRY, of Cawthorpe House, Lincolnshire.
Son of the late W. Pengelley. Esq.; *b.* 1829; *m.* 1859 Letitia Lely, only dau. and heir of the late John Lely Ostler, Esq., of Cawthorpe House (to whose property she succeeded at her father's decease, 1860). Educated at C.C.C., Cambridge (B.A. 1851, M.A. 1856); is Rector of Gt. Gonerby, co. Lincoln; was formerly curate of Bourne, and of Grantham. · This family is of Cornish extraction.—*Cawthorpe House, Bourne; Gt. Gonerby Rectory, Grantham.*

PENNANT, PHILIP PENNANT, Esq., of Bodfari, Flintshire.
Fourth son of the late Rev. George Pearson, Rector of Castle Camps, co. Cambridge, by Catherine, dau. of the late Philip Humberston, Esq., of Chester; *b.* 1834; *s.* 1853 to the Bodfari estates of the late David Pennant, Esq., of Downing, co. Flint; *m.* 1862 Mary, dau. of the Rev. Edward Bankes, of Soughton Hall, co. Flint, and has, with other issue,
    * David Falconer, *b.* 1867.
Mr. Pennant, who was educated at the Charterhouse and St. John's Coll., Cambridge (B.A. 1857, M.A. 1860), is a Magistrate for co. Flint (High Sheriff 1859 and 1862); he assumed the name of Pennant; by Royal licence, in 1860.—*Bodfari, Flint; Brynbella, St. Asaph, N. Wales; Oxford and Cambridge Club, s.w.*

PENNANT. (See *Douglas-Pennant.*)

PENNEFATHER, Sir JOHN LYSAGHT, K.C.B. (cr. 1855).
Third son of the late Rev. John Pennefather, by Mary, dau. of Major Perceval; *b.* 1800; *m.* 1834 Catharine, dau. of John Carr, Esq. Is a Magistrate for co. Tipperary, a Lieut.-General in the Army, and Col. 22nd Foot; served in India 1830–43, and as Deputy Quartermaster-General in Ireland; commanded a Division in the Crimea 1854–5; appointed to Chief Command of the Camp at Aldershott, 1860.—*South Camp, Aldershott; United Service Club, s.w.*

PENNEFATHER, EDWARD, Esq., of Rathsalla, co. Wicklow.
Eldest son of the late Right Hon. Edward Pennefather, Lord Chief Justice of the Court of Queen's Bench, Ireland (who *d.* 1847), by Susan, eldest dau. of the late John Darby, Esq., of Markly, Sussex, and of Leap Castle, King's Co.; *b.* 1809; *m.* 1841 Harriet, dau. of the late Richard Hall, Esq., of Copped Hall, Herts, and has, with other issue,
    * Charles Edward, *b.* 1849.
Mr. Pennefather, who was educated at Balliol Coll., Oxford (B.A. 1830), and called to the Irish Bar in 1874, was appointed a Queen's Counsel 1859, and a Bencher of the Hon. Society of King's Inns, Dublin, 1862; he is a Governor of the Board of Erasmus Smith's Schools, and of the King's Hospital and Free School, Dublin.—*Rathsalla, Dunlavin, co. Wicklow; Kildare Street Club, Dublin; 6, Fitzwilliam Place, Dublin.*

PENNEFATHER, WILLIAM, Esq., of Lakefield, co. Tipperary.
Eldest surviving son of the late Richard Pennefather, Esq., M.P., of New Park, co. Tipperary (who *d.* 1831),

by his 1st wife Anna, only dau. and heir of the late Matthew Jacob, Esq., of St. Johnstown, co. Tipperary; *b.* 1793; *m.* 1823 Charity Maria, dau. of Richard Long, Esq., of Longfield, and has, with other issue,
    * Richard, a Magistrate for co. Tipperary, and Lord of the Manor of Lakefield; *b.* 1827; *m.* 1857 Emma Elizabeth, dau. of the late Robert Darwin Vaughton, Esq., of Ashfor. long House, co. Warwick, and has, with other issue,
    * William Vaughton, *b.* 1862.
Mr. Pennefather is a Magistrate for co. Tipperary.—*Lakefield, Clonmel, co. Tipperary; Royal St. George Yacht Club, Kingstown, co. Dublin.*

PENNEFATHER, WILLIAM, Esq., of Ballylanigan, co. Tipperary.
Only son of the late William Pennefather, Esq., of Ballylanigan, late Capt. 30th Regt., by Susanna, dau. of Anthony Dwyer, Esq., of Cashel; *b.* 1823; *s.* 1829; *m.* 1852 Kate, younger dau. of Richard Scott, Esq., and has, with other issue,
    * William, *b.* 1853.
Mr. Pennefather, who was educated at Trinity Coll., Dublin (B.A. 1848), and called to the Irish Bar 1849, is a Magistrate for co. Tipperary.—*Ballylanigan Hall, Mullinahone, co. Tipperary.*

PENNELL, Sir CHARLES HENRY, Knt. (cr. 1867).
Son of the late William Pennell, Esq., Her Majesty's Consul-Gen. for the Brazils, by Elizabeth, dau. of the Rev. J. Carrington, Prebendary of Exeter; *b.* 1805; *m.* 1836 Harriet Emily, dau. of Philip Francis, Esq., and grand-dau. of Sir Philip Francis, K.B. Was formerly Chief Clerk of the Admiralty, Whitehall. —*Woodlands, Weybridge.*

+PENNINGTON, RICHARD, Esq., of Hindley Lodge, Lancashire.
Eldest son of the late Capt. Rowland Pennington; is a Magistrate for co. Lancaster, and a Merchant at Wigan. This family is of Cumberland extraction.—*Hindley Lodge, Wigan.*

PENNINGTON, WILLIAM, Esq., of Thickthorn, Warwickshire.
Youngest son of the late Rev. Thomas Pennington, of Alford, co. Lincoln, by Elizabeth, dau. of C. Riggally. Esq., of Nocton, co. Lincoln; *b.* 1807; *m.* 1844 Mary Elizabeth, dau. of Charles James, Capt. Scots Greys, by whom he has, with other issue,
    * William Alexander, *b.* 1848.
Mr. Pennington is a J.P. and D.L. for Bucks (High Sheriff 1862).--*Thickthorn, Kenilworth; Conservative Club, s.w.; 18, Portman Square, w.*

PENNINGTON. (See under *Muncaster, Lord.*)

PENNINGTON-LEGH. (See *Legh.*)

PENNYMAN, JAMES WHITE, Esq., of Ormesby Hall, Yorkshire.
Eldest son of the late Col. Worsley, of Ormesby Hall, by Lydia, dau. of Taylor White, Esq., of Walling Wells. co. Notts; *b.* 1792; *s.* 1853; *m.* 1828 Frances, dau. of the Rev. James Stovin, D.D., of Rossington, co. York, and has, with other issue,
    * James Stovin, a Magistrate for the N. Riding of Yorkshire; *b.* 1830; *m.* 1855 Mary Mackenzie, youngest dau. of William Joseph Coltman. Esq., of Saburn Hall, co. York.
Mr. Pennyman, who was educated at Woolwich, is a Magistrate for the N. Riding of Yorkshire, and was formerly Capt. in the Royal Engineers; he assumed by Royal licence, in 1853, the name of Pennyman, after his cousin, the late Sir William H. Pennyman, Bart. (ext.).—*Ormesby Hall, Middlesbrough.*

741

PENRHYN, Lord (EDWARD GORDON DOUGLAS-PENNANT).—Cr. 1866.
Third son of the late Hon. John Douglas, by Lady Frances, dau. of Edward, 1st Earl of Harewood, and brother of George, 18th Earl of Morton; *b.* 1800; *m.* 1st 1833 Juliana Isabella Mary, dau. of the late George Hay Dawkins-Pennant, Esq., whose name he assumed, and who *d.* 1842; 2nd 1846 Lady Maria Louisa, youngest dau. of Henry, 5th Duke of Grafton. Entered the Army as Ensign Grenadier Guards 1815; became Col. 1846, retired 1847; is Lord Lieut. for co. Carnarvon, a Magistrate for Bucks and co. Northampton, and Col. Carnarvon Militia; was M.P. for co. Carnarvon 1841-66.—*Penrhyn Castle, Carnarvon; Wicken Park, Stoney Stratford, Northamptonshire; Arthur's, Travellers', and Carlton Clubs, s.w.; Mortimer House, Halkin Street, s.w.*

Heir, his son George Sholto, educated at Eton and Ch. Ch., Oxford; a Magistrate for co. Carnarvon, Major Commandant Royal Carnarvonshire Militia Rifles, and M.P. for co. Carnarvon; *b.* 1836; *m.* 1860 Pamela Blanche Rushout, 2nd dau. of Sir Charles Rushout Rushout, Bart., and has issue.

PENRHYN, EDWARD HUGH LEYCESTER, Esq., of East Sheen, Surrey.
Eldest son of the late Edward Leycester, Esq., J.P. and D.L., of East Sheen (who assumed the name of Penrhyn only, under the will of Anne Susannah Baroness Penrhyn), by Lady Charlotte, eldest dau. of Edward, 13th Earl of Derby, K.G.; *b.* 1827; *s.* 1861; *m.* 1853 Vere, dau. of Robert Gosling, Esq., of Botleys Park, Surrey, and has, with other surviving issue,

* Arthur Leycester, *b.* 1866.

Mr. Penrhyn, who was educated at Eton and Balliol Coll., Oxford (B.A. 1849, M.A. 1851), is a J.P. and D.L. and Chairman of the Quarter Sessions for Surrey, and was formerly a Major 1st Surrey Militia.—*East Sheen, Surrey, s.w.*

PENRICE, JOHN, Esq., of Yarmouth, Norfolk.
Eldest son of the late John Penrice, Esq., of Great Yarmouth, by Maria Catherine, dau. of Herbert Newton Jarrett, Esq., of Orange Valley, Jamaica; *b.* 1818; *s.* 1844. Educated at Eton and Brasenose Coll., Oxford (B.A. 1821); is a J.P. and D.L. for Norfolk, and a Major in the Norfolk Artillery.—*Gt. Yarmouth, Norfolk; Oxford and Cambridge Club, s.w.*

PENRICE, THOMAS, Esq., of Kilvrough, Glamorganshire.
Second son of the late John Penrice, Esq., of Gt. Yarmouth, Norfolk, by Maria Catherine, dau. of Herbert Newton Jarrett, Esq., of Orange Valley, Jamaica, and nephew of the late Thomas Penrice, Esq., of Kilvrough; *b.* 1820; *s.* 1846; *m.* 1852 Louisa, 2nd dau. of the Rev. George Ernest Howman, Rector of Barnsley, co. Gloucester, and has issue. Educated at Eton; is a Magistrate for co. Glamorgan (High Sheriff 1867).—*Kilvrough, Swansea.*

PENROSE, the Rev. JOHN DENNIS, of Wood Hill, co. Cork.
Third but eldest surviving son of the late James Penrose, Esq., of Wood Hill, by Louisa Petitot, eldest dau. of Robert Uniacke Fitzgerald, Esq., M.P., of Corkbeg, co. Cork; *b.* 1804; *s.* his brother 1862; *m.* 1849 Harriet Susan, dau. of the Rev. John Hardy, of Kilcullen, co. Kildare, and has, with other issue,

* James Edward, *b.* 1850.

Mr. Penrose, who was educated at Trinity Coll., Dublin (B.A. 1827) is Rector of Magourney, co. Cork.—*Glebe House, Magourney, Coachford, co. Cork; Wood Hill, Cork.*

742

PENROSE, SAMUEL, Esq., of Shandangan, co. Cork.
Eldest son of the late Samuel Penrose, Esq., of Farren, co. Cork, by Mary, dau. of George Randall, Esq., of Barnhill and Red Abbey, in the same county, and niece of Abraham Devonsher, Esq., of Kilbanick; *b.* 1776; *s.* 1815; *m.* 1800 Mary, dau. of John Hawkes, Esq., of Sirmount, and has, with other issue,

* Samuel, in Holy Orders; *b.* 1801; *m.* 1851 Mary, dau. of Henry O'Callaghan, Esq., of Nodrid, co. Cork.

Mr. Penrose, who was educated at Glasgow University, is a Magistrate for co. Cork.—*Shandangan, Port Killinardrish, Macroom, co. Cork.*

+PENROSE, WILLIAM HENRY, Esq., of Dedham, Essex.
Son of the late W. Penrose, Esq., of Dedham; *b.* 1813; *m.* 1st 1858 Anne Agnes, eldest dau. of the late Charles Lillingston, Esq., of The Chauntry, Suffolk (she *d.* 1860); 2nd 186- Miss ——. Is a Magistrate for Essex (High Sheriff 18—).—*Lower Park, Dedham, Colchester.*

PENROSE-FITZGERALD, ROBERT UNIACKE, Esq., of Corkbeg Castle, co. Cork.
Eldest son of the late Robert Uniacke Penrose-Fitzgerald, Esq., of Corkbeg Castle, by Frances Matilda, eldest dau. of the late Rev. Robert Austen, D.D., Rector of Midleton, co. Cork; *b.* 1839; *s.* 1847. Educated at Westminster and Trinity Hall, Cambridge; is Lord of the Manor of Corkbeg.—*Corkbeg Castle, Whitegate, Cloyne, co. Cork.*

Heir, his brother Charles Cooper, *b.* 1842.

PENRUDDOCKE, CHARLES, Esq., F.G.H.S., of Compton Park, Wilts.
Son of the late Charles Penruddocke, Esq., of Bath, co. Somerset, by Juliana Laetitia, dau. of Capt. Thomas Penruddocke; *b.* 1828; *s.* his great-uncle 1849; *m.* 1853 Flora Henrietta, 2nd dau. of the late Walter Long, Esq., M.P., of Rood Ashton, Wilts, and has, with other issue,

* Charles, *b.* 1858.

Mr. Penruddocke, who was educated at Eton, and called to the Bar at the Inner Temple 1853, is a J.P. and D.L. for Wilts (High Sheriff 1861). Patron of 1 living, and Capt. Commandant 14th Wilts Rifle Volunteers (Wilton), and Royal Wilts Yeomanry Cavalry.—*Compton Park, Salisbury; 17, Hereford Street, w.*

PENTLAND, GEORGE HENRY, Esq., of Black Hall, co. Louth.
Eldest son of the late George Pentland, of Black Hall, by Mary Murray, dau. of James Murray, Esq., of Dublin; *b.* 1800; *s.* 1834; *m.* 1st 1827 Rebecca, eldest dau. of the late Wallop Brabazon, Esq., of Rath House, co. Louth; 2nd 1846 Sophia Mabella, 2nd dau. of the late Rev. Alexander Johnstone Montgomery, of Beaulieu, co. Louth, by whom he has, with other issue,

* George Henry, *b.* 1849.

Mr. Pentland is a Magistrate for cos. Louth and Meath.—*Black Hall, Drogheda, co. Louth.*

PENTON, Colonel HENRY, of Pentonville, Middlesex.
Eldest son of the late Henry Penton, Esq., by Mary, dau. of Charles Prichard, Esq., of The Graigue, co. Monmouth, and grandson of Henry Penton, Esq., M.P. for Windsor etc. late 2nd Life Guards; *b.* 1817; *s.* 1855; *m.* 1839 Eliza Maria, eldest dau. of Major Henry Langley, of Brittas Castle, co. Tipperary, and has, with other surviving issue,

* Frederick Thomas, *b.* 1851.

Col. Penton, who was educated at St. John's Coll., Cambridge, is a J.P. and D.L. for Middlesex, a Major and Royal Middlesex Militia, and Honorary Col. 39th

Middlesex Rifle Volunteers, and Lieut.-Col. 1st Sussex Rifle Volunteers.—100, *Lansdowne Place, Brighton ; Carlton and Junior United Service Clubs*, s.w.

PEPLOE, the Rev. JOHN BIRCH, of Garnstone Castle, Herefordshire.

Second but eldest surviving son of the late Daniel Webb, Esq., of Audley Square, London (who *d.* 1828), by Anne, dau. of the late John Peploe Birch, Esq., of Garnstone ; *b.* 1801 ; *s.* his brother, Daniel Peploe Peploe, Esq., 1866, when he assumed the name of Peploe ; *m.* 1828 Annie, dau. of John Molyneux, Esq., and grand-dau. of Sir Capel Molyneux, Bart., of Castle Dillon, co. Armagh, and has, with other issue,

* Daniel Peploe, *b.* 1839.

Mr. Webb, who was educated at Eton and Brasenose Coll., Oxford (B.A. 1822, M.A. 1825), is a Magistrate for co. Hereford, Vicar of King's Pyon and Vicar of Weobly ; Lord of the Manor of Garnstone, and Patron of the Vicarage of King's Pyon cum-Birley ; was formerly Prebendary of Preston Wynne in Hereford Cathedral.— *King's Pyon House, Weobly ; Garnstone Castle, Hereford.*

PEPPARD, ROBERT STANDISH, Esq., of Cappagh House, co. Limerick.

Eldest son of the late Robert Peppard, Esq., of Cappagh House, by Anne, dau. of the late John Brown, Esq., of Mount Brown, co. Limerick ; *b.* 1790 ; *s.* 1845. Educated at Trinity Coll., Dublin ; was formerly an Officer in the 3rd West York Rifle Corps. This family were Barons of England down to the reign of Henry VII.—*Cappagh House, Rathkeale, co. Limerick.*

Heir Pres., his brother John Southwell, *b.* 1796 ; *m.* 1830 a dau. of Herbert Park, Esq., M.D., late of Canterbury.

+**PEPPER**, THOMAS ST. GEORGE, .Esq., of Ballygarth Castle, co. Meath.

Eldest son of the late Col. Charles Pepper, by Matilda Mary, dau. of Arthur St. George, Esq., of Tyrone House, co. Galway ; *b.* 1837 ; *s.* his uncle, George Pepper, Esq., 1861. Is a Magistrate for co. Meath. —*Ballygarth Castle, Julianstown, co. Meath.*

PEPYS, PHILIP HENRY, Esq., Chancellor of Worcester.

Eldest son of the late Right Rev. Henry Pepys, D.D., some time Lord Bishop of Worcester (who *d.* 1861), by Maria, dau. of the late Right Hon. John and Lady Harriet Sullivan, of Richings Lodge, Bucks ; *b.* 1824 ; *m.* 1848 Louisa Eleanor, dau. of Col. Bishowe, and niece of Lord Kilmaine. Educated at Trinity Coll., Cambridge (B.A. 1846, M.A. 1849), and called to the Bar at Lincoln's Inn 1849 ; is Chancellor of Worcester ; he was formerly Secretary of Presentations to Lord Chancellors Cottenham, Truro, Cranworth, Chelmsford, Campbell, Westbury, &c.— *Oxford and Cambridge Club*, s.w. ; 44, *Lowndes Street*, s.w.

PEPYS. (See under *Cottenham, Earl of*.)

PERCEVAL, the late ALEXANDER, Esq., of Temple House, co. Sligo.

Third son of the late Col. Alexander Perceval, M.P., of Temple House (Serjeant-at-Arms to the House of Lords), by Jane Anne, dau. of the late John L'Estrange, of Moystown, King's Co.; *b.* 1821 ; *d.* 1866, having married, and left issue. Mr. Perceval, who was a Merchant in China, and a Member of the Legislative Council of the Colony of Hong Kong, purchased the Temple House Estate in 1860, from R. W. Hall-Dare, Esq., of Newtownbarry, co. Wexford, to whom it had been sold by Philip Perceval, Esq., in 1857.—*Temple House, Ballymote, co. Sligo.*

PERCEVAL, PHILIP, Esq.

Eldest son of the late Col. Alexander Perceval, M.P., (Serjeant-at-Arms to the House of Lords), by Jane Anne, dau. of Col. L'Estrange, of Moystown, King's Co.; *b.* 1813 ; *s.* 1858 ; *m.* 1843 Frederica Penelope, youngest dau. of the late Col. H. D. Baillie, of Redcastle, N.B., and by her (who *d.* 1861) has, with other issue,

* Alexander Clifton, *b.* 1847.

Mr. Perceval, who was educated at Winchester and Corpus Christi Coll., Oxford, is a Dep. Lieut. for co. Fermanagh, and was formerly Lieut. Royal Horse Guards.—*White's and Boodle's Clubs*, s.w. ; 15, *South Audley Street*, w.

PERCEVAL. (See under *Egmont, Earl of*.)

PERCEVAL-MAXWELL, ROBERT, Esq., of Groomsport House, Downshire, and of Moore Hill, co. Waterford.

Eldest son of the Rev. William Perceval, by Anne, dau. of the late John Waring Maxwell, Esq., of Finnebrogue, co. Down ; *b.* 1813 ; *s.* to the Moore Hill estate on the decease of his brother-in-law, 1856 ; *m.* 1839 Helena Anne, only dau. of Wm Moore, Esq., of Moore Hill, co. Waterford, and has, with other issue,

* John William, *b.* 1840.

Mr. Perceval-Maxwell, who was educated at Brasenose Coll., Oxford (B.A. 1834), is a Magistrate for co. Waterford (High Sheriff 1864), and a J.P. and D.L. for co. Down (High Sheriff 1841) ; was formerly Major Royal N. D. R. M.— *Groomsport House, Bangor, co. Down ; Moore Hill, Tallow, co. Waterford ; Sackville Street Club, Dublin ; Union Club*, s.w.

PERCEVAL-WESTBY. (See *Westby*.)

PERCIVAL, STANLEY ORRED, Esq., of Bridgefoot House, Middlesex.

Son of the late Thomas Percival, Esq., M.D., F.R.S., &c., of Hart Hill, co. Lancaster, by Elizabeth, only dau. of the late Nathaniel Bassnett, Esq., of London ; *b.* 1789 ; *m.* 1815 Elizabeth, dau. of Thomas Hayhurst France, Esq., of Bostock Hall, co. Chester, and has, with other issue,

* Stanley, *b.* 1820 ; *m.* 1853 Charlotte, dau. of Archibald Paris, Esq., of Abdale, Herts.

Mr. Percival is a Magistrate for Herts and Middlesex. —*Bridgefoot House, South Mimms, Middlesex.*

PERCY, Lord HENRY HUGH MANNERS.

Youngest son of George, 5th Duke of Northumberland, by Louisa Harcourt, 3rd dau. of the late Hon. James Archibald Stuart Wortley, and sister of James, 1st Lord Wharncliffe ; *b.* 1817. Educated at Eton. Is a Major-Gen. in the Army (V.C.); formerly of the Grenadier Guards, and A.D.C. to the Queen ; elected M.P. for N. Northumberland, 1865.— *Travellers', United Service, and White's Clubs*, s.w.; *Northumberland House*, s.w.

PERCY, Lord JOSCELINE WILLIAM.

Second son of George, 5th Duke of Northumberland, by Louisa Harcourt, 3rd dau. of the late Hon. James Archibald Stuart Wortley, and sister of James, 1st Lord Wharncliffe ; *b.* 1811 ; *m.* 1848 Margaret, dau. of Sir David Davidson (widow of Sir Robert Grant), and has issue,

* George Algernon, *b.* 1849.

Lord Percy, who was educated at Eton and St. John's Coll., Cambridge (M.A. 1833), is a Dep.-Lieut. for the W. Riding of Yorkshire; was M.P. for Launceston 1852-9.—*Travellers' Club*, s.w., 24, *Prince's Terrace, Prince's Gate*, s.w.

PERCY, ALGERNON CHARLES HEBER-, Esq., of Hodnet Hall, Shropshire.
Eldest son of the late Hon. and Right Rev. Dr. Hugh Percy, Lord Bishop of Carlisle (who was 3rd son of Hugh, 1st Earl of Beverley), by his 1st wife Mary, eldest dau. of the late Archbishop (Manners-Sutton) of Canterbury; b. 1812; m. 1839 Emily, eldest dau. of the late Right Rev. Reginald Heber, Bishop of Calcutta, and niece of the late Richard Heber, Esq., M.P., of Hodnet Hall (whose name he assumed in 1848), and, has, with other issue,
 * Algernon, Lieut. R.N.; b. 1845.
Mr. Heber-Percy, who was educated at Eton and St. John's Coll., Cambridge, is a Magistrate for co. Salop (High Sheriff 1853), Patron of 2 livings, and Capt. of the Hodnet Rifle Volunteers, and was formerly in the Rifle Brigade. He is in remainder to the Dukedom of Northumberland.—Hodnet Hall, Market-Drayton.

PERCY. (See under Northumberland, Duke of, and Beverley, Earl of.)

PERCY, HUGH JOCELINE, Esq., of Eskrigg, Cumberland.
Youngest son of the late Rt. Rev. Hugh Percy, Lord Bishop of Carlisle (who d. 1856), by his 1st wife Mary, eldest dau. of the late Most Rev. C. Manners-Sutton, D.D., Archbishop of Canterbury; b. 1817. Is a J.P. and D.L. for Cumberland; was formerly in the 7th Hussars. This family is a junior branch of the Ducal House of Northumberland.—Eskrigg, Wigton.

PERCY-BERTIE, Lord CHARLES, of Guy's Cliffe, Warwickshire.
Youngest son of Algernon, 1st Earl of Beverley, by Isabella Susannah, sister of 1st Lord Gwydir, and brother of George, 5th Duke of Northumberland; b. 1794; m. 1822 Ann Caroline Greatheed, grand-dau. and heir of the late B. Bertie-Greatheed, Esq. of Guy's Cliffe, and has issue,
 * Ann Barbara Isabel.
Lieut.-Col. Bertie-Percy, who was educated at Eton and Ch. Ch., Oxford (B.A. 1818), is a J.P. and D.L. for co. Warwick, and was M.P. for Newport, Cornwall, 1826–30; assumed the additional name of Bertie in 1826.—Guy's Cliffe, Warwick.

PERFECT, ROBERT, Esq., of Woolstone, Somerset.
Only son of the late William Perfect, Esq., M.D., of Wincanton, and Bath, Somerset, by Mellier, dau. of Wm. Cornish, Esq.; b. 1799; m. 1825 Eliza Harriet, dau. of the late J. Strode Butt, Esq. (she d. 1859). Mr. Perfect, who was educated at Queen's Coll., Oxford (B.A. 1822), is a J.P. and D.L. for Somerset, and a Magistrate for Sussex; was M.P. for Lewes 1847–52.—Woolstone House, Castle Cary; Reform Club, s.w.

† PERKINS, ALGERNON, Esq., of Hanworth Park, Middlesex.
Son of the late Henry Perkins, Esq. of Hanworth Park, b. 18—; is married, but has no issue. Is a J.P. and D.L. for Surrey, and a Brewer in London.—Hanworth Park, Hounslow; 81, Harley Street, w.
Heir Pres., his nephew.

PERKINS, CHARLES FREDERICK, Esq., of Kingston Grange, Somerset.
Eldest son of the late Charles Perkins, Esq., of Bewley, co. Durham, by Jane Hornby, dau. of Charles William Barkley, Esq., of Bath, and Upper Halliford, Middlesex; b. 1820; m. 1847 Mary, dau. of Philip Griffith, Esq. of Pall Mall, London. Is a Magistrate for cos. Durham and Somerset.—The Grange, Kingston, Taunton; Civil Service Club, s.w.
744

PERKINS, the Rev. DUNCOMBE STEELE, of Orton Hall, Leicestershire.
Eldest son of the late Shirley-Farmer Steele Perkins, Esq., of Orton Hall, by Elizabeth, dau. of Jos. Duncombe, Esq., of Sutton Coldfield; b. 1798; s. 1852; m. 1827 Ann, dau. of Josiah Gist, Esq., of Wormington Grange, co. Gloucester, and has, with other issue,
 * Duncombe Steele, educated at Ch. Ch. Oxford; b. 1836.
Mr. Perkins, who was educated at Rugby and Trinity Coll., Oxford (B.A. 1820), is Lord of the Manor of Orton. This family was settled at Hilmorton, co. Warwick in the 15th century—Orton Hall, Atherstone.

PERKINS, GEORGE, Esq., of Chipstead, Kent.
Eldest son of the late Frederick Perkins, Esq., J.P., of Chipstead Place, by Susan, dau. of Samuel Saunders, Esq., of Denmark Hill, Surrey; b. 1805; s. 1861; m. 1840 Mdlle. Louisa, dau. of Mons. Beër, of Frankfort, and has, with other issue,
 * George, b. 1843; m. 1866 Miss —, of — Theatre.
Mr. Perkins, who is a Magistrate for Kent, was formerly Capt. W. Kent Light Infantry Regt.—Chipstead Place, Sevenoaks; Royal Thames Yacht Club, 7, Albemarle Street, w.

PERKINS, HENRY, Esq., of Thriplow, Cambridgeshire.
Eldest son of the late Rev. Henry Perkins, M.A., of Arkesden, Essex, by Jane, dau. of George Barnes, Esq., of Sawston, co. Cambridge; b. 1832; s. his uncle 1842; m. 1855 Blanche, dau. of Charles Fiddey, Esq., of London, and has, with other issue,
 * Robert Baring, b. 1857.
Mr. Perkins, who was educated at Bury St. Edmund's and Trinity Coll., Cambridge (B.A. 1852, M.A. 1857), and called to the Bar at the Inner Temple 1858, is Lord of the Manor of Thriplow.—Thriplow Place, Royston.

PERKINS, GEORGE DUNCOMBE PERKINS, Esq., of Sutton Coldfield, Warwickshire.
Eldest son of the late William Steele Perkins, Esq., of Sutton Coldfield, by Sarah Penelope, dau. of R. Chawner, Esq.; b. 1827; s. 1864. Is Capt. 2nd Warwickshire Militia.—Sutton Coldfield, Warwickshire; Residence: Hints, Tamworth.
Heir Pres., his brother Edmund Steele, b. 1830.

PERRIER, ANTHONY, Esq., of Lota, co. Cork.
Third son of the late Sir Anthony Perrier, of Carrignore, co. Cork, by Jane Moore, dau. of George Black, Esq., of Limerick; b. 1815; m. 1853 Charlotte, only child of the late Major-General Henry Roome, Bombay Army. Is a Magistrate for co. Cork.—Lota, co. Cork; Conservative Club, s.w.

PERRIN, Mrs., of Sea Park, co. Dublin.
Penelope, eldest dau. of the Right Hon. John Hatchell, of Fortfield House, co. Dublin, by Mary Anne, dau. of R. Waddy, Esq., of Clonghurst Castle, co. Wexford; m. 18— John Perrin, Esq., barrister-at-Law, who d. 1860. Mr. Perrin was the eldest son of the late Right Hon. Louis Perrin, of Sea Park, formerly Attorney-General for Ireland, and a Judge of the King's Bench in Ireland, who d. 1864.—Sea Park, Clontarf, Dublin; 42, Rutland Square, Dublin.

PERRING, the Rev. Sir PHILIP, Bart. (cr. 1808).
Only surviving son of the late Rev. Sir Philip Perring, Bart., by Frances Mary, dau. of the late Henry Ley, Esq., of Guaton, co. Devon; b. 1828; s. as 4th Bart. 1866. Educated at Trinity Coll., Cambridge (B.A. 1852, M.A. 1855); is in Holy Orders; late Curate of St. James's, Westminster.—Residence: Exmouth, Devon.

PERROTT, Sir EDWARD GEORGE LAMBERT, Bart. (cr. 1716).

Eldest son of the late Sir Edward Bindloss Perrott, Bart., by Louisa Augusta, dau. of Col. Nicholas Bayly, M.P., 1st Foot Guards; *b.* 1811; *s.* 1859; *m.* 1847 Emma Maria, dau. of Charles Evelyn Houghton, Esq., Commander R.N. Was formerly Capt. E. Kent Militia, which rank he still retains.—*Plumstead, Kent, s.e.*

Heir, his son Herbert Charles, b. 1849.

+PERROTT, ROBERT SIMCOCKS, Esq., of Bronhyddon, Montgomeryshire.

Eldest son of the late — Perrott, Esq.; *b.* 18—. Is a Magistrate for co. Montgomery (High Sheriff 1865). —*Bronhyddon, Llansaintffraid.*

PERRY, Sir THOMAS ERSKINE, Knt. (cr. 1841).

Son of the late John Perry, Esq., Proprietor of the *Morning Chronicle,* by Mary, dau. of John Hull, Esq.; *b.* 1806; *m.* 1st 1833 Louisa, only child of James Mc-Elkiney, Esq. (she *d.* 1841); 2nd 1855 Elizabeth Margaret, dau. of Sir John Vanden Bempde Johnstone, Bart., M.P. Educated at the Charterhouse and Trinity Coll., Cambridge (B.A. 1829); called to the Bar at the Inner Temple 1841; was Chief Justice of Bombay 1847–52; appointed a Member of the India Council 1859, and Chairman of the Judicial and Legislative Committee of the same 1860; was M.P. for Devonport 1854–9. — *Brooks's and Athenæum Clubs, s.w.; 36, Eaton Place, s.w.*

PERRY, the Rev. JOHN, of Perranporth, Cornwall.

Eldest son of the late William Perry, Esq., of Churchill, Somerset, by Mary Anne, dau. of Samuel Whitchurch, Esq., of Bristol; *b.* 1804; *m.* 1835 Sophia, dau. of the Rev. Thomas Stabback, of Helston, Cornwall, and has, with other issue,

    * William, *b.* 1840.

Mr. Perry, who was educated at Balliol Coll., Oxford (B.A. 1826, M.A. 1832), is a Magistrate for Cornwall, and Vicar of Perranzabuloe.—*Perranporth, Truro.*

PERRY, THOMAS ALOYSIUS, Esq., of Bitham House, Warwickshire.

Eldest son of Thomas Perry, Esq., of Banbury, Oxon, by Mary Anne, dau. of Robert Budd, Esq.; *b.* 1820; *m.* 1840 Helen, dau. of William Knight, Esq., of Houghton, niece and heir of the late Joseph Knight, Esq., of Chelsea, and has surviving issue six daughters. This family is of Welsh extraction.—*Bitham House, Avon Dasset, Banbury; Stafford Club, w.*

PERRY, THOMAS JOSEPH, Esq., of Tettenhall, Staffordshire.

Youngest son of the late Thomas Perry, Esq., of Bilston, by Mary, dau. of Charles Keeling, Esq., of Cougreve, co. Stafford; *b.* 1824. Is a Magistrate for co. Stafford, and Captain Staffordshire Yeomanry Cavalry.—*Manor House, Tettenhall, Wolverhampton.*

PERRY, WILLIAM, Esq., of Woodroof, co. Tipperary.

Eldest son of the late Samuel Perry, Esq., of Woodroof, by the Hon. Deborah, 2nd dau. of Henry, 1st Lord Dunalley; *b.* 1793; *s.* 1829; is married, and has issue an only son,

    * Samuel, *b.* 18—; *m.* 1867 Mary, 2nd dau. of the late John Power, Esq., of Gurteen, co. Waterford.

Is a J.P. and D.L. for co. Tipperary (High Sheriff 1827–8).—*Woodroof, Clonmel, cc. Tipperary.*

PERRY-HERRICK. (See *Herrick.*)

PERRY-KEENE, WILLIAM THOMAS KEENE, Esq., of Minety House, Wilts.

Eldest son of the late John Perry, Esq., of Purton. Wilts, by Frances, dau. of the Rev. Thomas Jones, M.A., of Hullavington, Wilts; *b.* 1814; *s.* his uncle 1829; *m.* 1836 Elizabeth, dau. of William Page Stevens, Esq., of Yanworth, co. Gloucester, and has, with other issue,

    * Henry, *b.* 1842.

Mr. Keene, who is a J.P. and D.L. for Wilts, and Major 2nd Batt. Wiltshire Volunteers, was formerly Capt. Royal North Gloucester Militia; he assumed the additional name of Keene, by Royal licence, in 1839, under the will of his uncle, William Keene, Esq., of Minety. —*Minety House, Malmesbury.*

PERRY-WATLINGTON. (See *Watlington.*)

+PERRYN, the Rev. GERARD ALEXANDER, of Trafford Hall, Cheshire.

Son of the late R. G. Perryn, Esq., of Trafford Hall; *b.* 1823; *s.* 185–; *m.* 1860 Elizabeth Massey, eldest dau. of Vice-Admiral Sir Provo W. P. Wallis, K.C.B., of Funtington House, Sussex, and has issue. Educated at Brasenose Coll., Oxford (B.A. 1845, M.A. 1849); is Incumbent of Guilden Sutton.—*Trafford Hall, Chester.*

PERSSE, BURTON ROBERT PARSONS, Esq., of Moyode Castle, co. Galway.

Eldest son of the late Burton Persse, Esq., of Moyode Castle, by Matilda, dau. of the late Henry S. Persse, Esq., of Galway; *b.* 1828; *s.* 1859; *m.* 1852 Madeline, dau. of Col. William Persse, C.B., of the 16th Lancers, and has, with other issue,

    * Burton Walter, *b.* 1854.

Mr. Persse is a J.P. and D.L. for co. Galway (High Sheriff 1862). and Master of the co. Galway Hunt. —*Moyode Castle, Craughwell, co. Galway; Kildare Street Club, Dublin.*

+PERSSE, DUDLEY, Esq., of Roxborough, co. Galway.

Eldest son of the late Dudley Persse. Esq., of Roxborough; *m.* 1826 the Hon. Katharine, dau. of Standish, 1st Viscount Gallimore, and by her, who *d.* 1829, has issue,

    * Dudley, late Capt. 7th Foot; *b.* 1827.

Mr. Persse is a J.P. and D.L. for co. Galway.—*Roxborough, Loughrea, co. Galway.*

PERTH AND MELFORT, Earl of (GEORGE DRUMMOND).—Cr. 1605.

Eldest son of Leon Maurice Drummond. Esq., by Maria Elizabeth Lucy de Longuemare; *b.* 1807; *m.* 1st 1831 Albertina, Baroness de Rotberg (widow of Count Rapp); 2nd 1847 Susan Harriet, dau. of Col. Thomas Henry Bermingham Daly Sewell (widow of Col. Burrowes). Is Duke de Melfort in France; Major in the Victoria Rifle Corps of Middlesex Volunteers, and was formerly Capt. 93rd Highlanders. This Earldom, attained in 1745, was restored in 1853.— *U.U.'s Club, s.w.*

Heir, his grandson George Essex Montifex, Lord Drummond, (only son of the late George Henry Charles Francis Malcolm, Viscount Forth, who d. 1861, by Harriet Mary, eldest dau. of the Hon. Adolphus Capel), b. 1856.

PERY, the Hon. Mrs. of Cottingham House, Northamptonshire.

Elizabeth Charlotte, 10th dau. of the late Hon. William Cockayne, by Barbara, dau. of George Hill, Esq., Serjeant-at-Law, and grand-dau. of Charles, 5th Viscount Cullen (*ext.*); *s.* her mother 1858; *m.* 1825 the Hon. Edmund Sexten Pery, 3rd son of Edmond, 1st Earl of Limerick, who *d.* 1860, leaving, with other issue, * Edmund Henry Cockayne, *b.* 1826; *m.* 1860

Sarah Jane, dau. of Col. Arthur Knox-Gore, of Bellick Manor, co. Mayo.—*The Bury House, Cottingham, Rockingham.*

PERY. (See under *Limerick, Earl of.*)

PETER, JOHN THOMAS HENRY, Esq., of Chyverton, Cornwall.

Eldest son of the late William Peter, Esq., of Harlyn. and Chyverton (who was M.P. for W. Cornwall 1833–4, and who d. 1839), by Frances, dau. of John Thomas, Esq., of Chyverton, Vice-Warden of the Stannaries of Devon and Cornwall; *b.* 1812; *m.* 1861 Mary Ann, eldest dau. of the late J. P. Major, Esq., of Lamellyn, Cornwall. Educated at Westminster and Ch. Ch., Oxford, and was afterwards Fellow of Merton Coll. (B.A. 1833); called to the Bar at the Inner Temple 1843; is a J.P. and D.L. for Cornwall (High Sheriff 1866). This family were formerly of Harlyn, which they obtained in 1632, by marriage with the heiress of the Michells.—*Chyverton, Truro ; Athenæum Club,* s.w

· *Heir Pres.,* his brother Robert Godolphin, in Holy Orders, B.A., and late Fellow of Jesus Coll., Cambridge, Rector of Cavendish, Suffolk ; *b.* 1819 ; *m.* 1861 Catherine Stewart, dau. of the Rev. Alfred Lyall, Rector of Harbledown, Kent.

+PETER, the Rev. LEWIS MORGAN, M.A., of Ruanlanyhorn, Cornwall.

Eldest son of the late Rev. John Peter, Rector of Grade and Ruan Minor, by Mary, dau. of the late Rev. Lewis Morgan; *b.* 181–. Educated at Exeter Coll., Oxford (B.A. 1840, M.A. 1843); is a Magistrate for Cornwall, and Perpetual Curate of Comelly.–*Ruanlanyhorn, Grampound.*

PETER-HOBLYN, DEEBLE, Esq., of Colquite, Cornwall.

Seventh son of the late Hoblyn Peter, Esq., of Porthcothan, Cornwall, by Elizabeth, dau. of John Pomeroy, Esq.; *b.* 178–; *s.* 1836 his uncle Deeble Peter, Esq. (under whose will he assumed the name of Hoblyn). Is a Magistrate for Cornwall (High Sheriff 1830). —*Colquite, Bodmin.*

Heir Pres., his nephew John Harris Peter, *b.* 18—.

PETERBOROUGH, Bishop of (the Right Rev. FRANCIS JEUNE, D.C.L.).

Eldest son of the late Francis Jeune, Esq., of Jersey, by Elizabeth, dau. of Ji. Le Capetain, Esq., of Jersey ; *b.* 1806 ; *m.* 1836 Margaret Dyne, dau. of Henry Symons, Esq., of Axbridge, Somerset, and has, with other issue,

* Francis Henry, B.A. of Balliol Coll., Oxford ; *b.* 1843.

The Bishop, who was educated at Pembroke Coll. Oxford (B.A. 1827, M.A. 1830, B.C.L. 1834, D.C.L. 1834), was Head Master of King Edward's School, Birmingham, 1834–8 ; Master of Pembroke Coll., Oxford, 1843–64 ; Vice-Chancellor of the University of Oxford, 1858–62 ; he was formerly Dean of Jersey, and Rector of St. Helier's, and subsequently a Canon of Gloucester and Rector of Taynton ; consecrated 1864 ; Patron of 11 livings.—*The Palace, Peterborough ; University Club,* s.w.

PETERKIN. (See *Grant-Peterkin.*)

PETERS, the Rev. THOMAS, of Eastington, Gloucestershire.

Eldest son of the late Ralph Peters, Esq., of Platbridge, co. Lancaster, by Frances, eldest dau. and co-heir of the Rev. Thomas Blackburne, of Thelwall Hall, co. Chester ; *b.* 1813 ; *m.* 1840 Frances, dau. of John Curtis-Hayward, Esq., of Quedgeley House, co. Gloucester, and has, with other issue,

* Ralph Entwistle, *b.* 1843.

Mr. Peters, who was educated at Rugby and St. Alban's

746

Hall, Oxford (B.A. 1834), is a Magistrate for co. Gloucester, and Rector and Patron of Eastington. —*Eastington, Stonehouse, Gloucestershire.*

PETERS, WILLIAM HENRY, Esq., of Harefield, Devon.

Son of the late Ralph Peters, Esq., of Platbridge House, co. Lancaster, by Frances, eldest dau. and co-heir of the Rev. Thomas Blackburne, LL.D., of Thelwall Hall, co. Chester; *b.* 1814 ; *m.* 1840 Mary Jane, dau. of A. Levy, Esq., of Hutton Hall, Cumberland, and has, with other issue,

* William Henry Brooke, *b.* 1842.

Mr. Peters, who was educated at Rugby, is a Magistrate for Devon; was a Lieut. 7th Dragoon Guards. —*Harefield House, Lympstone, Devon ; Park Poslyn, Denbigh ; National and Junior Carlton Clubs,* s.w.

PETERS. (See *Burton-Peters.*)

PETLEY, CHARLES ROBERT CARTER, Esq., of Riverhead, Kent.

Eldest son of the late Charles Carter Petley, Esq., of Riverhead, by Annabella, dau. of Donald Macleod, Esq., of Geanies, Ross-shire, N.B.; *b.* 1807 ; *s.* 1830 ; *m.* 1843 Martha, dau. of Francis Woodgate. Esq., of Ferox Hall, Tunbridge, and has, with other issue,

* Charles Carter, *b.* 1844.

Mr. Petley, who was educated at the Charterhouse and St. John's Coll., Oxford, is a Magistrate for Kent. —*Riverhead, Sevenoaks ; Oxford and Cambridge Club,* s.w.

PETO, Sir SAMUEL MORTON, Bart. (cr. 1855).

Eldest son of the late William Peto, Esq., of Cookham. Berks, by Sophia, dau. of R. Alloway, Esq., of Dorking. Surrey; *b.* 1809 ; *m.* 1st 1831 Mary, dau. of T. De la Garde Grissell. Esq.; 2nd 1843 Sarah Ainsworth. dau. of H. Kelsall, Esq. Is an eminent contractor for Public Works, a Magistrate for Norfolk and Suffolk, and a Dep. Lieut. for Suffolk and Middlesex ; was M.P. for Norwich 1847–54, for Finsbury 1859–65, and for Bristol 1865–8.— Residence : *Chipstead, Sevenoaks ; Reform Club,* s.w.; 9, *Great George Street,* s.w.

Heir, his son Henry, *b.* 1840.

PETRE, Lord (WILLIAM BERNARD PETRE).— Cr. 1603.

Eldest son of William, 11th Lord, by his 1st wife Frances Charlotte. dau. of the late Sir Richard Bedingfeld, Bart., of Oxburgh. Norfolk : *b.* 1817 ; *s.* 1850 ; *m.* 1843 Mary Teresa. dau. of the Hon. Charles Howard Clifford. Is a J.P. and D.L. for Essex, and Patron of 4 livings. — *Thorndon Hall, Brentwood ; Travellers' Club,* s.w. ; 57, *Portland Place,* w.

Heir, his son William Joseph, *b.* 1847.

PETRE, the Hon. ARTHUR CHARLES AUGUSTUS.

Fourth son of William, 11th Lord Petre, by his 2nd wife Emily Agnes. dau. of the late Henry Howard, Esq.; *b.* 1827 ; *m.* 1855 Lady Catharine, 6th dau. of William, 4th Earl of Wicklow, and has, with other issue,

* Ralph William, *b.* 1856.

Mr. Petre is a Magistrate for Essex.—*Coptfold Hall, Ingatestone, Essex ; 2, Cavendish Square,* w.

PETRE, the Hon. FREDERIC CHARLES EDMUND.

Third son of William, 11th Lord Petre, by his 2nd wife Emily Agnes. dau. of the late Henry Howard, Esq.; *b.* 1824 ; *m.* 1847 Georgiana, eldest dau. of the late Sir Christopher Musgrave, Bart., and by her, who d. 1868, has, with other issue,

* Augusta, *b.* 1848.

M. Petre is a Magistrate for Essex and Capt. W. Essex Yeomanry Cavalry.—*Bowe Hatch, Brentwood, Essex.*

PETRE, the Hon. HENRY WILLIAM, of Spring-field Place, Essex.

Second son of William, 11th Lord Petre, by his 1st wife Frances Charlotte, eldest dau. of Sir Richard Beding-field, Bart.; *b.* 1823 ; *m.* 1842 Ellen, dau. of R. Wal-mesley, Esq. Is a Dep.-Lieut. for Essex.—*Springfield Place, Chelmsford.*

PETRE, CHARLES EDWARD, Esq., of Shenfield, Essex.

Only son of the late Hon. Charles Berney Petre, of Shenfield Place (who was 2nd son of Robert Edward, 10th Lord Petre), by Eliza, dau. of Edward C. Howard, Esq.; *b.* 1823 ; *s.* 1854 ; *m.* 1842 his cousin the Hon. Charlotte Eliza Petre, younger dau. of William, 11th Lord Petre, by whom he has, with other issue,

* Augustus William Berney, *b.* 1850.

Mr. Petre, who is a Dep. Lieut. for Essex, was formerly Capt. Dragoon Guards.—*Shenfield Place, Brentwood.*

PETRE, EDWARD HENRY, Esq., of Whitley. Warwickshire, and Samlesbury, Lancashire.

Third son of the late Henry William Petre, Esq., of Dunkenhalgh, co. Lancaster (who *d.* 1852), by his 2nd wife Adeliza Maria, 3rd dau. of the late Henry Howard, Esq., of Corby Castle, Cumberland; *b.* 1831 ; *m.* 1857 Lady Gwendeline Elizabeth Talbot, sister of Bertram, 17th Earl of Shrewsbury, and has, with other issue,

* Oswald Henry, *b.* 1862.

Mr. Petre, who is Lieut. Lancashire Yeomanry Hussars, purchased this property in 1867 from Viscount Hood.—*Whitley Abbey, Coventry* ; 38, *Brook Street, w.*

PETRE, HENRY, Esq., of Dukenhalgh, Lanca-shire.

Elder son of the late Henry William Petre, Esq., of Dunkenhalgh, by his 1st wife Elizabeth Anne, eldest dau. of Edmund John Glynn, Esq., of Glynn, Cornwall ; *b.* 1821 ; *s.* 1852 ; *m.* 1846 Mary, dau. of the late Ed-mond Power, Esq., of Gurteen, co. Waterford. Edu-cated at Stonyhurst Coll. ; is a J.P. and D.L. for Lan-cashire. Represents a younger branch of the family of Lord Petre.—*Dunkenhalgh, Accrington* ; *Carlton and Travellers' Clubs, s.w.*

Heir Pres., his brother George Glynn, Secretary of Legation at Brussels; *b.* 1822 ; *m.* 1858 Katherine, youngest dau. of the late Major Henry Ralph Sneyd, and has, with other issue, *George Ernest Augustus Henry, b.* 1860.

PETRE, JOHN BERNEY, Esq., of Westwick Hall, Norfolk.

Only son of the late Col. Jack Petre, of Westwick Hall by the Hon. Maria Harbord, 2nd dau. of Harbord, 2nd Lord Suffield ; *b.* 1805 ; *s.* 1855 ; *m.* 1844 Caroline Susan, 2nd dau. of the late Right Hon. J. A. Stewart-Mackenzie. Educated at Eton ; is a J.P. and D.L. for Norfolk, and Lord of the Manor of Westwick ; represents a branch of the family of Lord Petre.—*Westwick Hall, Norwich.*

PETTIWARD, ROBERT JOHN, Esq., of Fin-borough Park, Suffolk.

Only son of the late Robert Bussell, Esq., of Bath, by Frances, dau. of the Rev. Henry Eyre, of Landford, Wilts ; *b.* 1819 ; *m.* 1855 Lady Frances Catherine, dau. of Thomas, 2nd Earl Nelson, and has issue nine daus. Mr. Petti-ward, who was educated at Trinity Coll., Cambridge (B.A. 1841, M.A. 1844), is a Magistrate for Suffolk (High Sheriff 1867), Lord of the Manors of Finborough, Onehouse, and Harleston, Patron of 2 livings, and Capt. W. Suffolk Militia. He assumed the name of Petti-ward by Royal licence, in 1856, on succeeding to the

estates of the late Roger Pettiward, Esq.—*Finborough Park, Stowmarket.*

Heir Pres., his cousin the Rev. C. Terry, *b.* 1824 ; *m.* 1855 Isabella, dau. of the late Professor Ogle, of Oxford, and has issue, *four sons and six daus.

PETTY. (See under *Lansdowne, Marquis of.*)

PEVENSEY. (See under *Sheffield, Earl of.*)

PEYTON, Sir ALGERNON WILLIAM, Bart., of Doddington, Cambridgeshire (cr. 1776).

Only surviving son of the late Sir Henry Peyton, Bart., by Georgina Elizabeth, dau. of Sir Christopher Bethell Codrington, Bart., of Dodington Park, co. Gloucester ; *b.* 1833 ; *s.* as 4th Bart. 1866 ; *m.* 1864 Mary, dau. of J. Sherwood, Esq. (she *d.* 1866). Educated at Eton ; is a Magistrate for Oxon, Patron of 1 living, and Capt. 1st Life Guards.—*Swift's House, Bicester, Oxon* ; *Doddington, March, Cambridgeshire ; Guards' Club, s.w.*

PEYTON, the Rev. ALGERNON.

Youngest son of the late Sir Henry Peyton, 1st Bart., by Frances, sister of John, 1st Earl of Stradbroke ; *b.* 1786 ; *m.* 1811 Isabella Anne, dau. of Thomas Hussey, Esq. (she *d.* 1827). Educated at Westminster and Emmanuel Coll., Cambridge (B.A. 1809, M.A. 1812) ; is a Magistrate for the Isle of Ely, and Rector of Doddington.—*Doddington, March, Cambridgeshire ; Clarendon Hotel, w.*

PEYTON, CHARLES ROBERT, Esq., of Castle Carrow, co. Leitrim.

Eldest son of the late William Peyton, Esq., of Annagh, by Mary Donathea, dau. of Charles Moreton, Esq., of Liscarlon ; *b.* 1795 ; *s.* 1840 ; *m.* 1819 Mary, dau. of John O'Beirne, Esq., of Carrick-on-Shannon, and has issue,

* William, a Magistrate for co. Leitrim, *b.* 1821 ; *m.* 1842 Elizabeth, dau. of the late Major-General Thomas L. Yates, of Brockhurst Lodge, Hants.

Mr. Peyton is Lord of the Manor of Castle Carrow. This family is descended from a common ancestor with the Peytons of Driney House (whom see).—*Castle Car-row, Carrick-on-Shannon, co. Leitrim.*

PEYTON, GEORGE RICHARD, Esq.

Third son of the late George Hamilton Cunningham Peyton, Esq., J.P. and D.L., of Driney House (who *d.* 1855), by Eliza, only dau. of James Duncan, Esq., of Dublin ; *b.* 1824. Is a Magistrate for co. Leitrim.—*Residence: Driney, Drumcong, co. Leitrim.*

PEYTON, JOHN EAST HUNTER, Esq., of Wake-hurst Place, Sussex.

Eldest son of the late Joseph John Wakehurst Peyton, Esq., of Wakehurst Place, by Marianne Gilberta, eldest dau. of the late Sir East George Clayton-East, Bart., of Hall Place, Berks ; *b.* 1811 ; *s.* 1844 ; *m.* 1866 Sophia Henrietta, eldest dau. of the late Frederick H. Lindsay, Esq., and has issue, a dau. Mr. Peyton, who was edu-cated at the Royal Military Coll., Sandhurst, and was formerly Lieut. 60th Royal Rifles, is Patron of 1 living.—*Wakehurst Place, Cuckfield.*

Heir Pres., his brother Edward Gilbert, Lieut. 106th Regt. (Bombay Light Infantry), *b.* 1842 ; *m.* 1862 Martha, youngest dau. of Capt. Weir, 6th (Inniskilling) Dragoons.

PEYTON, RICHARD REYNOLDS, Esq., of Lough-scur, co. Leitrim.

Eldest son of the late John Reynolds Peyton, Esq., J.P. and D.L., of Loughscur, by Alicia, youngest dau. of the late Andrew Ennis, Esq., of Ballinahowe, co. Westmeath ; *b.* 1838 ; *s.* 1850. Is a J.P. and D.L. for co. Leitrim (High Sheriff 1865-6), and Lord of the Manors of Loughscur, &c. ; was formerly an Officer in the 1st Dragoons.—*Loughscur, Keshcarrigan, co. Leitrim.*

Heir Pres., his brother James, *b.* 1842.

+PEYTON, Thomas Griffith, Esq., of Barton Colwall, Herefordshire.
Eldest son of the late T. Peyton, Esq.; *b.* 1820. Educated at St. Mary Hall, Oxford (B.A. 1843, M.A. 1844); is a Magistrate for co. Hereford.—*Barton Colwall, Ledbury.*

PEYTON, the Rev. Walter Cunningham, of Driney House, co. Leitrim.
Eldest son of the late George Hamilton Cunningham Peyton, Esq., J.P. and D.L., of Driney House (High Sheriff of co. Leitrim 1817), by Eliza, only dau. of James Duncan, Esq., of Dublin, and grandson of the late Walter Peyton, Esq., Dep.-Governor of co. Leitrim; *b.* 1821; *s.* 1855; *m.* 1856 Margaret, dau. of the Rev. James McCreight, Rector of Keady. Educated at Trinity Coll., Dublin (B.A. 1847); is Incumbent of Billis, co. Cavan. This family is descended from a common ancestor with the Peytons of Loughscur Castle (whom see).— *Driney House, Drumcong, co. Leitrim; Billis Glebe, Virginia, co. Cavan.*

PHAIRE, Frederick Robert, Esq., of Killoughram, co. Wexford.
Son of the late Lieut.-Col. Robert Phaire, by his 2nd wife; *b.* 18—; *s.* his half-brother Robert William Phaire, Esq., 1863; *m.* 18— Mary Anne, dau. of William Williams, Esq., and has issue. This family is descended from Col. Robert Phaire, Governor of Cork under Oliver Cromwell.—*Killoughram Forest, Enniscorthy, co. Wexford.*

PHAIRE, William, Esq., of Daphne House, co. Wexford.
Son of the late Robert William Phaire, Esq., of Killoughram Forest, co. Wexford; *b.* 18—; *s.* 1863. Is a Lieut. in the Indian Army.—*Daphne House, Enniscorthy, co. Wexford.*

PHAYRE, Rev. Richard, of West Raynham, Norfolk.
Son of the late Richard Phayre, Esq., of Shrewsbury; *b.* 1807; *m.* 1847 the Hon. Charlotte Laura, 2nd dau. of John, 2nd Lord Wodehouse. Educated at Trinity Coll., Dublin (B.A. 1830); is a Magistrate for Norfolk, and Rector of West Raynham.—*West Raynham Rectory, Rougham.*

PHELIPS, Charles, Esq., of Briggins Park, Herts.
Second son of the late Rev. Charles Phelips, of Piddletreuthide, Dorset, by Mary, dau. and heir of Thomas Blackmoore, Esq., of Briggins Park, Herts; *b.* 1794; *s.* 1824; *m.* 1820 Caroline Elizabeth, dau. of James Taylor, Esq., and has issue,
* Charles James, educated at Eton and Ch. Ch., Oxford; Barrister-at-Law; *b.* 1821.
Mr. Phelips, who was educated at Winchester and Trinity Hall, Cambridge (LL.B. 1818), is a J.P. and D.L. for Herts (High Sheriff 1828), and also for Essex (High Sheriff 1835), and Patron of 1 living.—*Briggins Park, Ware; Arthur's Club, s.w.*

PHELIPS, Richard, Esq., of Bayford, Somerset.
Second son of the late Rev. William Phelips, by Mary, dau. of the Rev. J. Messiter, and brother of W. Phelips, Esq., of Montacute (whom see); *b.* 1825; *m.* 1848 Charlotte Frances, dau. of Joseph Delafield, Esq. Educated at the Royal Military Coll., Woolwich; is a J.P. and D.L. for Somerset, and a Capt. on half-pay, Royal Artillery.—*Bayford Lodge, Wincanton; Army and Navy Club, s.w.*
748

PHELIPS, William, Esq., of Montacute, Somerset.
Eldest son of the late Rev. William Phelips, by Mary, dau. of the Rev. John Messiter; *b.* 1823; *s.* his uncle 1834; *m.* 1845 Ellen Harriet, dau. of Wm. Helyar, Esq., of Coker Court, Somerset, and has, with other issue,
* William Robert, *b.* 1846.
Mr. Phelips, who was educated at Harrow and Trinity Coll., Cambridge, is a J.P. and D.L. for Somerset, Lord of the Manor of Montacute, and Patron of 2 livings. —*Montacute House, Yeovil.*

PHELPS, William John, Esq., of Chestal, Gloucestershire.
Second but only surviving son of the late Rev. James Phelps, Rector of Brimpsfield-cum-Cranham and of Alderley, co. Gloucester, by Mary Anne, dau. of John Blagden Hale, Esq., of Alderley; *b.* 1813; *s.* his uncle John Delafield Phelps, Esq., 1842, and his brother James 1852. Educated at Oriel Coll., Oxford (B.A. 1835, M.A. 1838); called to the Bar at Lincoln's Inn 1839; is a Magistrate for co. Gloucester (High Sheriff 1860), and Lord of the Manor of Rangeworthy.—*Chestal, Dursley; Oxford and Cambridge Club, s.w.*

PHIBBS, Major Richard, of Coppall House, Lancashire, and Spotfield, co. Sligo.
Second son of the late John Phibbs, Esq., of Spotfield (who *d.* 1821, when High Sheriff of co. Sligo), by Anne, dau. of the Rev. Samuel Renshaw, Rector of Liverpool; *b.* 1810; *m.* 1836 Mary, dau. of Charles Tayleur, Esq., of Parkfield, co. Lancaster, and has, with other issue,
* John Ormsby, Capt. 3rd Hussars; *b.* 1840.
Major Phibbs, who is a Dep. Lieut. for co. Lancaster, and Major 4th Lancashire Militia, was formerly an Officer in the Army.—*Coppall House, Fazakerley, Liverpool; Spotfield, Collooney, co. Sligo; Conservative and Junior United Service Club, s.w.; 12, Rutland Gate, s.w.*

PHILIPPS, the Rev. Sir James Evans, Bart. (cr. 1621).
Second son of the late William Hollingworth Philipps, Esq., of Bristol, by Harriet, dau. of Anthony Fonblanque, Esq., Merchant, of London; *b.* 1793; *s.* his kinsman, Sir Godwin Philipps-Laugharne, as 11th Bart. 1857; *m.* 1822 Mary Anne, dau. of B. Bickley, Esq. Educated at Queen's Coll., Oxford (B.A. 1817, M.A. 1820); is Vicar of Osmington, Dorset. This family were formerly of Picton Castle, co. Pembroke.—*Osmington Vicarage, Weymouth.*
Heir, his son James Erasmus, M.A., of Ch. Ch., Oxford, Vicar of Warminster, Wilts; *b.* 1824; *m.* 1859 Mary Margaret, eldest dau. of the Hon. and Rev. Samuel Best, Rector of Abbotts Ann, Hants, and has, with other issue, * John Wynford, *b.* 1860.

PHILIPPS, Grismond, Esq., of Cwmgwilly, Carmarthenshire.
Eldest son of the late Grismond Philipps, Esq., of Cwmgwilly, Esq., of Thomas Warlow, Esq., of Castle Hall, and grandson of Thomas Philipps, Esq., of Poyston, co. Pembroke; *b.* 1821; *s.* 1850; *m.* 1854 Marianne, dau. of Thomas Bowen, Esq., formerly Capt. 10th Hussars, and has issue,
* Catharine Elizabeth.
Mr. Philipps, who was educated at King's Coll., London, is a J.P. and D.L. for co. Carmarthen, and was formerly Capt. 23rd Royal Welch Fusiliers.—*Cwmgwilly, Carmarthen; Army and Navy Club, s.w.*

PHILIPPS, Frederick Lewis Lloyd Lloyd-, Esq., of Penty Park, Pembrokeshire.
Eldest surviving son of the late Col. James Lloyd-Philipps (who *d.* 1837), by Winifred, dau. of John Thomas, Esq., of Llangryn, co. Merioneth; *b.* 1822;

s. his brother 1865; *m.* 1849 Elizabeth, dau. of John Walters Philipps, Esq., of Aberglasney, co. Carmarthen. Is a J.P. and D.L. for cos. Cardigan and Carmarthen. —*Penty Park, Haverfordwest.*

+PHILIPPS, the Rev. JAMES HENRY ALEX-ANDER, of Picton Castle, Pembrokeshire.
Son of the late Mr. Gwyther; *b.* 1815 ; *s.* his kinsman 1857, and assumed his name by Royal licence. Educated at Trinity Coll., Cambridge (B.A. 1837, M.A. 1840); is a Magistrate for co. Pembroke, Lord of the Manor of Picton, Vicar of St. Mary's, Haverford-west, Rural Dean, and Patron of 1 living; formerly Vicar of Madeley, co. Salop.—*Picton Castle, Haverfordwest.*

PHILIPPS, JOHN GEORGE, Esq., of Ystradwrallt, Carmarthenshire.
Eldest surviving son of the late John George Philipps, Esq., M.P., of Cwmgwilly, by Anne, dau. of John Ball, Esq.; *b.* 1783 ; *s.* 1818 ; *m.* 1808 Frances, dau. of Smith Hawford, Esq., of Portsea, Hants, and had, with other issue,

John George Hawford, J.P., late Capt. of the 61st Foot, *b.* 1809 ; *m.* 1845 Elizabeth, dau. of E. James, Esq., R.N., and *d.* 1864, leaving, with other surviving issue, *Vaughan Lloyd, *b.* 1848.

Mr. Philipps, who entered the Royal Navy in 1796, is a J.P. and D.L. for co. Carmarthen, and a retired Capt. R.N.—*Ystradwrallt, Carmarthen.*

+PHILIPPS, the late WILLIAM CHARLES ALLEN-, Esq., of St. Bride's Hill, Pembrokeshire.
Only son of the late Charles Allen-Philipps, Esq., of St. Bride's Hill, formerly High Sheriff of co. Pembroke (who assumed the name of Philipps on succeeding to this estate), by Cecilia, dau. of — Philipps, Esq., of Lampeter, co. Cardigan ; *b.* 1811 ; *d.* 1864. Was a J.P. and D.L. for co. Pembroke.—*St. Bride's Hill, Haverfordwest.*

PHILIPPS. (See *Lloyd-Philipps.*)

PHILIPPS. (See *Walters-Philipps.*)

PHILIPPS, of Williamston. (See *Scourfield.*)

PHILIPS, Sir GEORGE RICHARD, Bart., of Weston House, Warwickshire (cr. 1828).
Only son of the late Sir George Philips, Bart., M.P., of Weston House, by Sarah Anne, dau. of Nathaniel Philips, Esq., of Hollinghurst ; *b.* 1789 ; *s.* as 2nd Bart. 1847 ; *m.* 1819 the Hon. Sarah Georgiana, eldest dau. of Richard, 2nd Lord Waterpark. Educated at Eton ; is a J.P. and D.L. for co. Warwick (High Sheriff 1859), and a Magistrate for co. Worcester; was M.P. for Steyning 1820–32, for Kidderminster 1835–7, for Poole 1837–52.—*Weston House, Chipping Norton ; Athenæum and Reform Clubs, s.w.; 12, Hill Street, w.*

PHILIPS, FRANCIS, Esq., of Bank Hall, Lancashire, and of Lee Priory, Kent.
Eldest son of the late Francis Aspinall Philips, Esq., of Bank Hall (who was High Sheriff of co. Radnor 1852), by Jane, only dau. of William Jackson, Esq., of Liverpool; *b.* 1830 ; *s.* 1859; *m.* 1856 Caroline Mary, dau. of the Rev. Charles Kenrick Prescot, M.A., Rector of Stockport. Educated at Eton and Ch. Ch., Oxford (B.A. 1852, M.A. 1855); called to the Bar at the Inner Temple 1855 ; is a Magistrate for Kent. —*Bank Hall, Stockport ; Lee Priory, Wingham.*

Heir Pres., his brother George Henry (of Abbey Cwm Hir, near Rhayadr, Radnor-hire), M.A. of Ch., Oxford, and a J.P. and D.L. for co. Radnor (High Sheriff 1860); *b.* 1831 ; *m.* 1867 Anna Theophila, fifth dau. of the Rev. C. K. Prescot, Rector of Stockport.

PHILIPS, JOHN CAPEL, Esq., of the Heath House, Staffordshire.
Eldest son of the late John Burton Philips, Esq., of Heath House, by Joanna Freeman, dau. of Capel Cure, Esq., of Blake Hall, Essex; *b.* 1831 ; *s.* 1847 ; *m.* 1857 the Hon. Fanny Esther, 2nd dau. of Henry, 5th Viscount Ashbrook, and has issue a daughter. Mr. Philips is a J.P. and D.L. for co. Stafford.—*The Heath House, Cheadle.*

PHILIPS, JOHN WILLIAM, Esq., of Heybridge, Staffordshire.
Eldest son of the late Robert Philips, Esq., of Heybridge, by Lætitia, dau. of William Hibbert, Esq., of Hare Hill, co. Chester; *b.* 1827 ; *s.* 1853; *m.* 1st 1852 Adelaide Louisa, dau. of Edward Buller, Esq., of Dilborn Hall, co. Stafford; 2nd 1867 Olivia, dau. of the late William Dodsworth, M.A., and has, by the former, with other issue,

* William Morton, *b.* 1852.

Mr. Philips, who was educated at Edinburgh and the University of London (B.A. 1847), is a J.P. and D.L. for co. Stafford (High Sheriff 1861) : is a manufacturer at Tean, co. Stafford. This family was seated in Checkley, co. Stafford *temp.* Edward VI.; its head is John C. Philips, Esq., of The Heath House (whom see). —*Heybridge, Cheadle; Brooks's and Windham Clubs,s.w.*

PHILIPS, MARK, Esq., of Snitterfield and Welcombe, Warwickshire.
Elder son of the late Robert Philips, Esq., of The Park, Prestwich, and Snitterfield, co. Warwick, by Anne, dau. of Matthew Needham, Esq., of Nottingham ; *b.* 1800 ; *s.* 1844. Educated at Manchester New Coll., York, and Glasgow University; is in the Commission of the Peace for cos. Lancaster and Warwick, and a Dep.-Lieut. for co. Warwick (High Sheriff 1851); was M.P. for Manchester 1832–47.—*Welcombe and Snitterfield, Stratford-upon-Avon ; The Park, Prestwich, Manchester ; Brooks's, Athenæum, and Reform Clubs, s.w.*

Heir Pres., his brother Robert Needham (whom see).

PHILIPS, RICHARD GAILE, Esq., of Cashel, co. Tipperary.
Eldest son of the late Samuel Philips, Esq., by Caroline, dau. of Richard Long, Esq., of Longfield, near Cashel; *b.* 1825 ; *s.* 1846; *m.* 1847 Mary Elizabeth, dau. of Fitzmaurice Hunt, Esq., of Cappagh, co. Tipperary, and has with other issue,

* Samuel, *b.* 1849.

Mr. Philips is a Magistrate for co. Tipperary.—*Cashel, Tipperary.*

PHILIPS, ROBERT NEEDHAM, Esq., of The Park, Lancashire.
Younger son of the late Robert Philips, Esq., of The Park, by Anne, dau. of Matthew Needham, Esq., of Nottingham ; *b.* 1815 ; *m.* 1st 1845 Anna Maria, dau. of the late Joseph Brooks Yates, Esq., of West Dingle, Liverpool, who *d.* 1850; 2nd 1852 Mary Ellen, dau. of John Ashton Yates, Esq., and has issue.

* Caroline Marianne, and Anna Maria.

Mr. Philips, who was educated at Rugby and Manchester New Coll., is a J.P. and D.L. for co. Lancaster (High Sheriff 1857), a Dep.-Lieut. for co. Warwick, and a Merchant and Manufacturer; elected M.P. for Bury 1865.—*The Park, Manchester; Brooks's, Reform, and Athenæum Clubs, s.w.; 47, Berkeley Square, w.*

PHILLIMORE, the Right Hon. Sir ROBERT JOSEPH, Knt., D.C.L., of The Coppice, Oxon (cr. 1862).
Second son of the late Joseph Phillimore, Esq., D.C.L., M.P., of Shiplake House, Oxon, by Elizabeth, dau. of the Rev. Walter Fagot, Rector of Blithfield, brother of

William, 1st Lord Bagot; *b.* 1810; *m.* 1814 Charlotte, 3rd dau. of the late John Denison, Esq., M.P., of Ossington Hall, Notts, and has, with other issue,

* Walter, *b.* 1845.

Sir Robert, who was educated at Westminster and Ch. Ch., Oxford (B.A. 1831, M.A. 1834, D.C.L. 1838), and called to the Bar at the Middle Temple 1841, was M.P. for Tavistock 1853–7; appointed Queen's Advocate 1862, Judge of the Admiralty Court 1867, is Official Principal of the Arches Court of Canterbury, and Judge of the Admiralty of the Cinque Ports.—*The Coppice, Henley-on-Thames; Oxford and Cambridge Club,* s.w.; *5, Arlington Street,* s.w.

PHILLIMORE, the Rev. GEORGE.
Eldest son of the late William Phillimore, Esq. (of Deacon's Hill, Herts, who *d.* 1860), by Almeria, dau. of the late Godfrey Thornton, Esq., of Moggerhanger House, Beds; *b.* 1808; *m.* 1st 1832 Emily, dau. of the late T. H. Haworth, Esq., of Barham Wood, Herts (she *d.* 1837); 2nd 1841 Harriette Maria, dau. of the late William Willoughby Prescott, Esq., of Hendon, and has, with other issue,

* Henry John, *b.* 1845.

Mr. Phillimore, who was educated at Westminster and Ch. Ch., Oxford (B.A. 1829, M.A. 1831), is a Magistrate for Bucks, and Rector of Radnage.—*Radnage Rectory, Stokenchurch; Oxford and Cambridge Club,* s.w.

PHILLIMORE, EGERTON GREVILLE BAGOT, Esq., of Shiplake House, Berks.
Eldest son of the late John George Phillimore, Esq., Q.C., of Shiplake House (who was some time M.P. for Leominster), by Rosalind Margaret, dau. of the late Lord Justice Knight-Bruce; *b.* 1857; *s.* 1864. This is a younger branch of the Phillimores of Kendalls, Herts. —*Shiplake House, Henley-on-Thames.*

PHILLIMORE, WILLIAM BROUGH, Esq., of Kendalls Hall, Herts.
Only son of the late William Robert Phillimore, Esq., of Newberries, Herts, by Anna, dau. of W. West, Esq.; *b.* 1828; *s.* 1846; educated at Eton; is a Magistrate for Herts; was formerly a Capt. 6th Dragoon Guards and Grenadier Guards.—*Kendalls Hall, Elstree, Herts; Army and Navy, and Arthur's Clubs,* s.w.

PHILLIPPS, Sir THOMAS, Bart, of Middle Hill, Worcestershire (cr. 1821).
Only son of the late Thomas Phillipps, Esq., of Middle Hill (who was High Sheriff of co. Worcester in 1801, and *d.* 1818), by Hannah, dau. of James Walton, Esq., of Sowerby, co. York; *b.* 1792; *m.* 1st 1819 Harriet, 3rd dau. of Lieut.-General Sir T. Molyneux, Bart.; 2nd 1842 Elizabeth Harriet Anne, dau. and co-heir of the Rev William J. Mansell. Educated at Rugby and University Coll., Oxford (B.A. 1815, M.A. 1820); is a J.P. and D.L. for co. Worcester (High Sheriff 1825), and Patron of 1 living.—*Middle Hill, Broadway; Athenæum Club,* s.w.

PHILLIPPS, HENRY, Esq., of Sproughton, Suffolk.
Fourth son of the late Rev. John Phillipps, of Eaton House, co. Hereford, and Rector of Stoke Saint Milborough, co. Salop, by Anne, dau. of the late Charles Pye, Esq., of Wadley House, Berks; *b.* 1792; *m.* 1841 Lucy Burch, eldest dau. of Joseph B. Smyth, Esq., of Stoke Hall, Ipswich, and has, with other issue,

* Henry Burch Pye, *b.* 1843.

Mr. Phillipps, who was educated at Eton, is a J.P. and D.L. for Suffolk, a Magistrate for Ipswich, and Lord of the Manor of Sproughton; he was a Lieut.-Col. in the Army, and for many years a Capt. in the 3rd Light Dragoons. This family is descended from a younger

branch of the family of Phillipps of Picton Castle, co. Pembroke. Colonel Phillips is 19th in direct descent from Henry III., and 5th from Ann, 2nd daughter of the 'Patriot,' John Hampden.—*The Manor House, Sproughton, Ipswich; Junior United Service Club,* s.w.

+PHILLIPPS, HENRY CRANMER MARCH-, Esq., of Torquay, Devonshire.
Sixth son of the late Thomas March-Phillipps, Esq., of Garendon Park, co. Leicester, by Susan, dau. of — Lisle, Esq.; *b.* 1793. Educated at the R. Naval Coll.; is a Magistrate for Devon, and was formerly in the Royal Navy.—*Torquay, Devon.*

PHILLIPPS, JAMES, Esq., of Bryngwyn, Herefordshire.
Eldest son of the late James Phillipps, Esq., of Bryngwyn, by Lucy Mary Anne, eldest dau. of the late Lieut.-General Daniel Burr, of the Madras Army; *b.* 1827; *s.* 1853. Educated at Rugby; is a J.P. and D.L. for co. Hereford.—*Bryngwyn, Ross.*

PHILLIPPS - DE - LISLE, AMBROSE LISLE MARCH, Esq., of Garendon, and Grace Dieu, Leicestershire.
Eldest son of the late Charles March Phillipps, Esq., J.P. and D.L., of Garendon, High Sheriff in 1825, and formerly M.P. for co. Leicester, by Harriet, dau. of J. Ducarel, Esq., of Walford, Somerset; *b.* 1809; *s.* 1862; *m.* 1833 Laura Mary, eldest dau. and co-heir of the late Hon. Thomas Clifford, of Ugbrooke, Devon, and has, with other issue,

* Ambrose Charles, *b.* 1834; *m.* 1861 Frances Victoria, youngest dau. of the late Sir Richard Sutton, Bart., of Norwood Park, Notts, and has issue, * Everard, *b.* 1862.

Mr. Phillipps-de-Lisle, who was educated at Trinity Coll., Cambridge, is a J.P. and D.L. for co. Leicester (High Sheriff 1868), and Patron of 4 livings. This family are descended from FitzAzor and Jordanus de Insula, or De l'Isle, who received the grant of the lordship of Woodyton, in the Isle of Wight, from the Conqueror, in 1069.—*Garendon Park, Loughborough, and Grace Dieu Manor, Ashby-de-la-Zouch.*

PHILLIPS, Sir BENJAMIN TRAVELL, Knt. (cr. 1858).
Son of Stephen Howell Phillips, Esq., of Harroldstone, co. Pembroke, by Mary, dau. of John Tappen, Esq., of Forest Hill, Sydenham, Kent; *b.* 1804; *m.* 1833 Mary Sophie, dau. of Major James Marrie (she *d.* 1845). Is a Major-General Bengal Cavalry, retired; late Lieut. of Her Majesty's Royal Body Guard of Yeomen. —*United Service Club,* s.w.; *32, Regent Street,* w.

PHILLIPS, Sir BENJAMIN SAMUEL, Knt., of Mapleton, Kent (cr. 1866).
Fourth son of the late Samuel Phillips, Esq., by Hannah dau. of Solomon Jonas, Esq.; *b.* 1811; *m.* 1833 Rachel, only dau. of Samuel Henry Faudel, Esq., and has, with other issue,

* Samuel Henry, *b.* 1835.

Sir Benjamin, who is a J.P. and D.L. for Middlesex, a Magistrate for Kent, and an Alderman of London, was Sheriff of London 1859–60, Lord Mayor 1865–6.—*Mapleton, Westerham, Kent; Reform Club,* s.w.; *46, Portman Square,* w.

PHILLIPS, the Rev. FREDERICK PARR, of Stoke d'Abernon House, Surrey.
Eldest son of the late William Phillips, Esq., of Cavendish Square, London; *b.* 1818; *m.* 1845 Jane Grant, dau. of the late Sir James McGrigor, Bart., K.C.B., and has issue an only surviving son,

* Frederick, *b.* 1850; educated at Eton.

Mr. Phillips, who was educated at Winchester and

Ch. Ch., Oxford (B.A. 1840, M.A. 1844), is a Magistrate for Surrey, Lord of the Manor and Patron of Stoke d'Abernon.—*Stoke d'Abernon House, Cobham.*

PHILLIPS, JOHN FREDERICK LORT, Esq., of Lawrenny, Pembrokeshire.
Elder son of the late Richard Ilbert Lort Phillips, Esq. (who *d.* 1860), by Frederica, eldest dau. of the Baron de Rutzen, of Slebech Hall, co. Pembroke; *b.* 1854; *s.* his uncle, G. Lort Phillips, Esq., of Lawrenny, 1866. —*Lawrenny Park, Pembroke.*

Heir Pres., his brother.

PHILLIPS, JOHN, Esq., of Winsley Hall and Cause Castle, Shropshire.
Eldest son of the late General Robert Phillips, H.E.I.C.S., by Elizabeth, dau. of Edward Poole, Esq.; *b.* 1819; *s.* 1838; *m.* 1840 Mary Emily, eldest surviving dau. of J. B. Tipton, Esq., of Elms House, co. Lancaster, and has, with other issue,

* John, *b.* 1840.

Mr. Phillips is 7th in descent from Fabian Phillips, one of Queen Elizabeth's Judges of the Welsh Marches, who obtained a grant of arms 1579.—*Winsley Hall and Cause Castle, Shrewsbury.*

PHILLIPS, JOHN ROBERTS SPENCER-, Esq., of Riffhams Lodge, Essex.
Eldest son of the late Hugh Spencer, Esq. (who assumed the name of Phillips), by Bridget, eldest dau. of John Phillips, Esq., of Barwick-in-Helmet, co. York; *b.* 1788; *m.* 1811 Anna Maria, elder dau. of the late Sir John Tyrell, Bart., of Boreham House, Essex, and by her, who *d.* 1862, has, with other issue,

* John, a Barrister-at-Law, of the Inner Temple, *b.* 1813 ; is married, and has issue.

Mr. Phillips, who was educated at Brasenose Coll., Oxford, is a J.P. and D.L. for Essex; formerly Capt. Essex Militia.—*Riffhams Lodge, Danbury, Chelmsford.*

PHILLIPS, JOHN SHAWE, Esq., of Culham House, Oxon.
Eldest son of the late John Shawe Phillips, Esq., J.P. and D.L. of Culham House (who was High Sheriff of Oxon 1844), by Anna, dau. of the late Thomas Duffield, Esq., M.P., of Marcham Park, Berks (she *m.* 2nd 1861 the Rev. C. R. Powys); *b.* 1843; *s.* 1859; *m.* 1866 Maria Elizabeth, only dau. of Henry G. Greaves, Esq., and has issue,

* John Henley Shawe, *b.* 1867.

Mr. Phillips is a Magistrate for Berks, and Lord of the Manor of Blewbury, Berks.—*Culham House, Abingdon.*

PHILLIPS, JOHN SOUTH, Esq., of Barton, Suffolk.
Only son of the late John Phillips, Esq., by Mary Elizabeth, dau. of John South, Esq., of Huntingdon; *b.* 1825; *m.* 1849 Mary Anna Charlotte. 2nd dau. of John Henry Heigham, Esq., of Hunston Hall, Suffolk, and by her, who *d.* 1859, has issue,

* John William Heigham, *b.* 1851.

Mr. Phillips, who was educated at Bury St. Edmund's and Trinity Coll., Cambridge (B.A. 1848, M.A. 1852), is a Magistrate for Suffolk.—*Great Barton, Bury St. Edmund's.*

PHILLIPS, Capt. MICHAEL, of Glenview, otherwise Droghill, or Bagshawe, co. Cavan.
Eldest son of the late Thomas Phillips, Esq., by his 1st wife Anne, dau. of John Tandy, of Johnsbrook, co. Meath; *b.* 1807; *m.* 1832 Mary Anne, dau. of Heygate

Tench, Esq., of Ballyhaly House, co. Wexford, and has, with other issue,

* Thomas George Johnston Phillips, M.A., in Holy Orders, *b.* 1834; *m.* 1860 Charlotte Maria, dau. of Edward Lewis, Esq., J.P., of Violetstown House, co. Westmeath.

Mr. Phillips, who is a Magistrate for co. Cavan, descends from Sir Thomas Phillips, Knt., who settled in Ireland from Pembrokeshire *temp.* Elizabeth.—*Glenview, Belturbet, co. Cavan.*

+**PHILLIPS, WILLIAM,** Esq., of Whitson House, Monmouthshire.
Son of the late William Phillips, Esq., of Whitson House; *b.* 179–; *m.* 1st 182– Margaret, dau. of Thomas Rodie, Esq.; 2nd 184– Matilda, dau. of George Potter, Esq., Lieut. R.N., and has, with other issue,

* William, *b.* 1850.

Mr. Phillips is a J.P. and D.L. for co. Monmouth (High Sheriff 1845).—*Whitson House, Newport, Monmouthshire.*

PHILLIPS, WILLIAM PAGE THOMAS, Esq., of Hasketon and Burgh, Suffolk.
Only son of the late Benjamin Phillips, Esq., F.R.S., by Elizabeth, dau. and co-heiress of William Woods Page, Esq., of Woodbridge, Suffolk; *b.* 1833; *s.* his father in 1861, and uncle, Sir T. Phillips, in 1867; *m.* 1857 Clara Matilda, dau. of Henry Browning, Esq., of Grosvenor Street, and has, with other issue, a son,

* William Page, *b.* 1858.

Mr. Phillips, who was educated at Eton and Exeter Coll., Oxford (B.A. 1855, M.A. 1858); and called to the Bar at Lincoln's Inn 1857; is Lord of the Manor of Thistleton Hall, Suffolk. This family was formerly settled in Breconshire; it descended on the female side from Sir David Gam.—*Hasketon, Woodbridge; Union Club, s.w.; 77, Gloucester Place, w.*

PHILLIPS. (See *Mansel-Phillips, under Mansel, Bart.*)

PHILLIPSON. (See *Burton-Phillipson.*)

PHILLPOTTS, HENRY, Esq., of Longcroft, Devonshire.
Second son of the Rt. Rev. Henry Phillpotts, D.D., Lord Bishop of Exeter, by Deborah Mary, 5th dau. of William Surtees, Esq., of Seaton Burn, Newcastle-on-Tyne; *b.* 1809; *m.* 1837 Anne Elizabeth Waller, dau. of John Young, Esq., of Philpotstown, co. Meath, and has, with other issue,

* Henry Francis, *b.* 1840.

Mr. Phillpotts, who was educated at Winchester and Sandhurst Coll., is a Magistrate for Devon, and was formerly Capt. 29th Regt.—*Longcroft, Torquay.*

PHILLPOTTS, the Rev. THOMAS.
Only son of the late John Phillpotts, Esq., M.P., by Sarah, dau. of Thomas Chandler, Esq., of Ashcroft House, co. Gloucester: *b.* 1807; *s.* 1849; *m.* 1831 Mary Emma Penelope, only dau. of the late Ulysses Theophilus Hughes, Esq., of Grovesend, co. Glamorgan, and has, with other issue,

* John Hughes, *b.* 1841.

Mr. Phillpotts, who was educated at Eton and King's Coll., Cambridge (B.A. 1829, M.A. 1855); is a Magistrate for Cornwall, Vicar of St. Feock, and Chaplain to the Bishop of Exeter.—*Porthgwidden, St. Feock, Truro.*

PHIPPS, Lady.
Margaret Anne, dau. of the Ven. Archdeacon Bathurst; *m.* 1835 Col. the Hon. Sir Charles Beaumont Phipps, K.C.B., who was sometime Keeper of Her Majesty's Privy Purse, and Receiver-General of the Duchy of Cornwall, and who *d.* 1866, leaving, with other issue,

* Charles Edmund, Ensign and Lieut. Scots Fusilier

751

Guards, *b.* 1844—*Abergeldy-Mainse, Balmoral, N.B.; The Castle, Windsor.*

PHIPPS, the Hon. and Rev. Augustus Frederick.

Fourth son of Henry, 1st Earl of Mulgrave, by Sophia, dau. of Christopher Thompson Maling, Esq., of West Herrington, Durham, and brother of Constantine, 1st Marquis of Normanby; *b.* 1809 ; *m.* 1837 Lady Mary Elizabeth Emily, eldest dau. of the 5th Duke of Grafton, and has issue. Educated at Harrow and Trinity Coll., Cambridge (M.A. 1830) ; is a Magistrate for Suffolk ; Chaplain to the Queen, Rector of Euston, and Rural Dean.—*Euston Rectory, Thetford.*

PHIPPS, Charles Hare, Esq., of Cregg, co. Cork.

Eldest son of the late John Pedder Phipps, Esq., of Cregg, by Jane, dau. of John Hare, Esq., of The Deer Park, co. Tipperary ; *b.* 1841 ; *s.* 1862. Educated at Trinity Coll., Dublin ; descended from a common ancestor with the Marquis of Normanby.—*Cregg, Fermoy, co. Cork.*

PHIPPS, Charles Paul, Esq., of Dilton Court, Wiltshire.

Youngest son of the late Thomas Henry Hele Phipps, Esq., of Leighton, Wilts, by Mary, dau. of Richard Leckonby, Esq., of Eccleston and Hothersall Hall, co. Lancaster ; *b.* 1815 ; *s.* his uncle 1866 ; *m.* 1844 Emma Mary, dau. of M. Benson, Esq., of Liverpool, and grandau. of M. G. Benson, Esq., of Lutwyche Hall, co. Salop, and has, with other issue,

* Charles Nicholas Paul, *b.* 1845.

Mr. C. P. Phipps is a Magistrate for Wilts and Lord of the Manor of Dilton. This manor with the Dilton Estate originally formed part of the Hungerford property, and passed to the Phipps family in 1684.—*Dilton Court, Westbury, Wilts.*

PHIPPS, Col. Richard Leckonby, of Charlton, Somerset.

Third son of the late Thomas Henry Hele Phipps, Esq., of Leighton House, Wilts (who *d.* 1841), by Mary, only dau. of Richard Leckonby, Esq., of Great Eccleston, co. Lancaster ; *b.* 1804 ; *m.* 1842 Mary, dau. of —— Esq., and has issue,

* Mary.

Col. Phipps, who was educated at R. M. Academy, Woolwich, is a J.P. and D.L. for Somerset, and a Col. in the Army retired ; was formerly in the 68th Regt. This family is a branch of the Phipps, of Leighton House, Wilts (whom see).—*Charlton House, near Shepton Mallet, Somerset ; Junior United Service Club, s.w.*

PHIPPS, John Lewis, Esq., of Leighton, Wilts.

Eldest surviving son of the late Thomas Hele Phipps, Esq., of Leighton House (who was Chairman of Wilts Quarter Sessions, &c.), by Mary, dau. of Richard Leckonby, Esq., of Great Eccleston ; *b.* 1801 ; *s.* 1847 ; *m.* 1871 Mary, dau. of William Barney, Esq., and has with other issue,

* Richard Leckonby Hothersal, student of the Inner Temple ; *b.* 1839.

Mr. Phipps is a J.P. and D.L. for Wilts (High Sheriff 1864).—*Leighton House, Westbury.*

PHIPPS, Mrs., of Oaklands, co. Tipperary.

Anna, dau. of Major Smith, R.M., and sister of the late Lady Osborn, of Newtown Anner, co. Tipperary ; *m.* 18—Col. Pownoll Phipps, K.C., H.E.I.C.S., who was a Magistrate for Somerset, and who *d.* 1858, leaving issue, 2 sons and 1 dau.—*Oaklands, Clonmel.*

PHIPPS. (See under *Normanby, Marquis of.*)

752

PICKARD, Henry William, Esq., of Sturminster Marshall, Dorset.

Fourth and youngest son of the late Rev. George Pickard, of Bloxworth, Dorset, by Frances, dau. of the late Edward Payne, Esq., of Ealing House, Middlesex ; *b.* 1794 ; *m.* 1829 Elizabeth, dau. of J. Fullerton, Esq., of Thryberg Park, co. York, and has, with other issue,

* Henry Adair, M.A. of Ch. Ch., Oxford, in Holy Orders ; *b.* 1832.

Mr. Pickard, who was educated at Woolwich, and joined the Royal Artillery 1812, is a Magistrate for the W. Riding of Yorkshire.—*Sturminster Marshall, Wimborne.*

PICKARD. (See *Trenchard.*)

PICKARD-CAMBRIDGE. (See *Cambridge.*)

+**PICKERING, Leonard, Esq., of Wilcot, Oxon.**

Son of the late L. Pickering, Esq. ; *b.* 18—. Is a J.P. and D.L. for Oxon.—*Wilcot Grange, Charlbury.*

PICKERSGILL, William Cunliffe, Esq., of Blendon Hall, Kent.

Eldest son of John Pickersgill, Esq., of Netherne House, Surrey, by Sophia, youngest dau. of John Cunliffe, Esq., of Addingham. co. York ; *b.* 1811 ; *m.* 1835 Anita, dau. of George Washington Riggs, Esq., of Woodville, Baltimore, U.S., and has, with other issue, an only surviving son,

* William Cunliffe.‡ *b.* 1844 ; *m.* 1865 Sophia, 2nd dau. of Joseph Whitaker, Esq., of Palermo.

Mr. Pickersgill purchased this property in 1864 from the family of the Smiths.—*Blendon Hall, Bexley.*

PICKFORD, Rev. Francis, of Hagworthingham, Lincolnshire.

Only surviving son of the late Charles Pickford, Commander, R.N. (who *d.* 1841), by Mary, dau. of C. V. Mackinnon, Esq., and grandson of the late Sir Joseph Radcliffe, Bart., of Milnsbridge, co. York ; *b.* 1801 ; *m.* 1831 Sophia, dau. of Matthew Bancroft Lister, Esq., of Burwell Park, co. Lincoln, and has issue,

* Four daughters.

Mr. Pickford, who was educated at Queen's Coll., Cambridge (B.A. 1824, M.A. 1827). is a Magistrate for co. Lincoln, and Rector of Hagworthingham. This family is descended from one long settled at Althill, near Macclesfield.—*Hagworthingham Rectory, Spilsby.*

+**PICKFORD, James Hollins, Esq., of Brighton, Sussex.**

Son of the late J. Pickford, Esq. ; *b.* 18—; *m.* 1830 Anna Henwood, dau. of John Mills, Esq., of Brighton. Is a J.P. and D.L. for Sussex.—*Brighton, Sussex.*

+**PICKWICK, Major William, of Bathford Manor, Somersetshire.**

Son of the late W. Pickwick, Esq., of Bathford ; *b.* 1810. Is a Dep.-Lieut. for Somerset ; formerly a Major in the Army.—*Bathford Manor, Bath.*

Heir Pres., his nephew Capt. Charles Pickwick, of Pemblergh, near Bradford, Wilts, *b.* 18—.

PIDCOCK, Mrs., of Oakfield, Worcestershire.

Augusta Bramley, dau. of Col. Fraser, Aide-de-Camp to the Marquis Wellesley ; *m.* 1817 (as his 2nd wife) Henry Pidcock, Esq., J.P. and D.L. ; formerly in the E.I.C.S. (who *d.* 1862).—*Oakfield, Worcester.*

PIDGEON, William, Esq., of Athlone, co. Westmeath.

Eldest son of the late William Pidgeon, Esq., of Hermitage, co. Kildare, by Charlotte, dau. of William

‡ Died whilst these sheets were at press.

Grierson, Esq., of Lostown, co, Meath ; b. 1806 ; s. 1849 ; m. 1853 Ellen Fitzgerald, eldest dau. of Robert Smithwick, Esq., of Williamsfort, co. Limerick. Is a Magistrate for cos. Westmeath and Roscommon. —*Athlone, co. Westmeath ; 15, Upper Sackville Street, Dublin.*

PIERCE, FRANCIS ROCKCLIFFE, Esq., of West Asbby Manor, Lincolnshire.
Only child of the Rev. William Matthews Pierce, A.M., Incumbent of West Ashby. &c. by Elizabeth, only child of the late Rev. Francis Rockcliffe. LL.B., Rector of Fulletby, co. Lincoln ; b. 1828. Educated at Caius Coll., Cambridge (B.A. 1851) ; called to the Bar at Lincoln's Inn 1854 ; is a Magistrate for co. Lincoln, and Lord of the Manor of West Ashby ; formerly Capt. N. Lincoln Militia.—*The Manor House, West Ashby, Horncastle ; Junior United Service Club*, s.w.

PIERCE, JAMES PARKER, Esq.
Second son of the late George Pierce, Esq., of London, by Betsy, dau. of the late John Matthews, Esq., of Calne, Wilts ; b. 1794 ; m. 1826 Mary, younger dau. of the late John Timbrell, Esq., of London, and has, with other issue,
   * John Timbrell, of the Middle Temple, b. 1831 ; m. 1861 Mary, younger dau. of Henry Milward, Esq., of Redditch, co. Worcester (whom see).
Mr. Pierce is a Magistrate for Middlesex. This family was formerly settled in Monmouthshire. — *Clifton Lodge, The Grove, Highgate Road*, N.W.

PIERREPONT, the Hon. Mrs., of Evenley Hall, Northamptonshire.
Georgina, only dau. and heir of the late Herbert Gwynne Browne, Esq., of Evenley Hall ; m. 1st 180– Pryce Edwards, Esq., of Talgarth, co. Merioneth ; 2nd 1810 Col. the Hon. Philip Sydney Pierrepont (youngest son of Charles, 1st Earl of Manvers), who d. 1864.—*Evenley Hall, Brackley.*
   Heir Pres., her husband's kinsman Major-General George Campbell, a J.P. and D.L. for co. Northampton, formerly Col. R.A. ; b. 1800.

PIERREPONT, HENRY BENNET, Esq., of Ryhall, Rutlandshire.
Only surviving son of the late Rear-Admiral William Pierrepont, of Ryhall, by Maria, dau. of Elliott Salter, Esq., Post Capt., R.N. ; b. 1810 ; s. his uncle 1834 ; m. 1842 Elizabeth Fridzeweed. eldest dau. of Col. Joshua Wilson, of Roseville, co. Wexford. Is a Dep.-Lieut. for co. Rutland (High Sheriff 1845).—*Ryhall, Stamford ; Laywell House, Brixham, Torquay.*

PIERREPONT. (See under *Manvers, Earl of.*)

PIERS, Sir EUSTACE FITZMAURICE, Bart., of Tristernagh, co. Westmeath (cr. 1660).
Elder son of the late Sir Henry Samuel Piers, Bart., of Tristernagh Abbey. by Alice, dau. of J. T. Glindon, Esq., R.N. ; b. 1840 ; s. as 8th Bart. 1850.—*Tristernagh Abbey, Mullingar, co. Westmeath.*
   Heir Pres., his brother Pigott Samuel. b. 1842.

PIERSON, JAMES ALEXANDER, Esq., of The Guynd, Forfarshire.
Only son of the late James Pierson, Esq., of Cheltenham, by Margaret, 2nd dau. of John Ochterlony, Esq., of The Guynd ; b. 1800 ; s. his mother 1819 ; m. 1857 Elizabeth Townsend, 2nd dau. of James Murray Grant, Esq., of Glenmoriston, co. Inverness, and Moy, co. Moray. Educated at Winchester ; is a J.P. and Commissioner of Supply for co. Forfar.—*The Guynd, Arbroath, N.B.*

PIGGOTT, FRASER, Esq., of Fitzhall, Sussex.
Son of the late Simon Fraser Piggott, of Fitzhall, who assumed that name in lieu of his patronymic Cooke

on his marriage with Jane, eldest dau. of the late James Piggott, Esq., of Fitzhall ; b. 1834 ; s. 1866 ; m. 1852 Fanny Margaret, only child of George Bush, Esq., of St. Vincent's Priory, Clifton.—*Fitzhall, Petersfield ; 93, Ebury Street*, s.w.

PIGOT, Sir ROBERT, Bart., of Branches Park, Cambridgeshire (cr. 1764).
Eldest surviving son of the late General Sir George Pigot, Bart., by Mary Anne, dau of the Hon. John Monckton, of Finesbade ; b. 1801 ; s. 1841 ; m. 1st 1826 Mary, dau. of William Bamford, Esq. ; 2nd 1850 Emily Georgiana Elise, dau. of Samuel Yates Benyon, Esq., of Stetchworth Park, co. Cambridge. Educated at Eton and Trinity Coll , Cambridge ; is a Dep.-Lieut. for co. Stafford ; was M.P. for Bridgnorth 1832–53. —*Branches Park, Newmarket ; Carlton Club*, s.w.
   Heir, his son George, b. 1850.

PIGOT, the Right Hon. DAVID RICHARD.
Eldest son of the late David Pigot, Esq., M.D., of Kilworth, co. Cork ; b. 1805. Educated at Trinity Coll., Dublin (B.A. 1825, M.A. 1827) ; called to the Irish Bar 1826 ; was M.P. for Clonmel 1838–46 ; appointed Solicitor-General for Ireland 1839, Attorney-General 1840, a Bencher of King's Inns 1839, Chief Baron of Exchequer, Ireland, 1846 ; sworn a Member of the Privy Council in Ireland 1840.—8, *Merrion Square, Dublin.*

PIGOTT, Sir CHARLES ROBERT, Bart. (cr. 1808).
Eldest son of the late Sir Thomas Pigott, Bart., of Knapton, Queen's Co., by Georgiana Anne, dau. of William Brummel, Esq., of Wivenhoe, Essex ; b. 1835 ; s. as 3rd Bart. 1847 ; m. 1856 Mary Louisa, dau. of the late Capt. Hallowell Carew, of Beddington, Surrey. Was formerly Lieut. 90th Foot.
   Heir, his son Charles Berkeley, b. 1859.

PIGOTT, Sir GILLERY, Knt., of Sherfield Hill, Hants (cr. 1863).
Fourth son of the late Paynton Pigott-Stainsby-Conant. Esq., of Archer Lodge, Sherfield, Hants, by Lucy, 2nd dau. of Richard Drope Gough, Esq. ; b. 1813 ; m. 1836 Frances, only child of Thomas Drake, Esq., of Ashday, near Halifax, co. York. Called to the Bar at the Middle Temple 1839 ; appointed, 1856, a Serjeant-at-Law with patent of precedence, and Recorder of Hereford, 1859 ; one of the Judges of the Court of Exchequer 1863 ; was M.P. for Reading 1860–3.—*Sherfield Hill, Basingstoke ; Athenæum Club*, s.w. ; 7, *Bayswater Square*, w.

+**PIGOTT**, FRANCIS BERNARD, Esq., of Eagle Hill, co. Galway.
Eldest son of the late Capt. Henry Pigott. of Eagle Hill, by Margaret, dau. of the late Sir Scrope Bernard-Morland, Bart. ; b. 1800 ; s. 1865 ; m. 1st 1850 Lætitia Charlotte, eldest dau. of Thomas Tyringham Bernard. Esq., of Winchendon Priory, Bucks ; 2nd 1867 Octavia. dau. of the late James Raymond ..., ..., Esq. of West Nab, and widow of James Harrison Chelmely, Esq. Is a Magistrate for co. Galway.—*Eagle Hill, Loughrea.*

PIGOTT, GEORGE PEMBERTON, Esq., of Slevoy, co. Wexford.
Eldest son of the late William Pemberton Pigott, Esq., by Ellen, dau. of Henry Thomas Houghton, Esq., of Killmannock ; b. 1800 ; s. 1855 ; m. 1834 Mary, dau. of Elward Beatty, Esq., of Heathfield, co. Wexford, and has issue,
   * Edward Pemberton, Lieut. 44th Regt., b. 1836 ; m. 1859 Eliza Anne, dau. of Wm. Liphinstone Underwood, Esq.
Mr. Pigott is a Magistrate for co. Wexford, and a Capt.

in the Wexford Militia. This family was formerly Pemberton, but they assumed the name of Pigott.—*Slevoy Castle, Foulkes Mill, co. Wexford.*

PIGOTT, the Rev. WELLESLEY POLE.
Youngest son of the late Sir George Pigott, Bart., by Anabella, dau. of Chief Justice Kelly, of Kellyville, Queen's Co.; *b.* 1810 ; *m.* 1st 1845 Anna Maria, elder dau. of the late Vice-Admiral Lord H. Paulet, K.C.B. ; 2nd 1858 Fanny, dau. of Bernard Granville, Esq., of Wellesbourne, co. Warwick, and has with other issue,
  * Wellesley George, *b.* 1861.
Mr. Pigott, who was educated at Eton and Brasenose Coll., Oxford (B.A. 1836), and appointed Rector of Bemerton, &c. 1836, is a Magistrate for Wilts, and Chaplain to the Earl of Pembroke.—*Bemerton Rectory, Wilton.*

PIGOTT, WILLIAM, Esq., of Dullingham, Cambridgeshire.
Third son of the late Sir George Pigott, Bart., of Knapton, by Annabella, dau. of the Right Hon. Thomas Kelly, of Kellyville, Queen's Co.; *b.* 1804 ; *m.* 1st 1827 Harriet, only dau. and heir of the late Lieut.-General C. Jeaffreson, of Dullingham (she *d.* 1838) ; 2nd 1847 Charlotte Maria, widow of John, 1st Lord Keane, G.C.B., and has by the former,
  * Christopher William Robinson, Esq., *b.* 1836 ; *s.* his mother 1838 ; assumed the name of Jeaffreson by Royal licence in 1838 ; subsequently took the name of Robinson in pursuance of the will of his cousin the late William Henry Robinson, Esq., of Denston Hall, Suffolk..
Mr. Pigott, who was educated at Winchester and Trinity Coll., Cambridge (B.A. 1827), is a Dep.-Lieut. for co. Cambridge.—*Dullingham House, Newmarket.*

PIGOTT, WILLIAM, Esq., of Ryevale, co. Kildare.
Eldest son of the late Rev. Thomas Pigott, by Mary, dau. of Richard Croasdaile, Esq., of Rynn, Queen's Co. ; *b.* 1815 ; *m.* 1844 Lucy Henrietta, dau. of John Trench, Esq., of St. Catharine's, co. Kildare, and has issue,
  * Thomas, *b.* 1847.
Mr. Pigott, who was educated at Trinity Coll., Dublin (B.A. 1836), is a Magistrate for Queen's Co.—*Ryevale, Leixlip, co. Kildare.*

PIGOTT, WILLIAM HARVEY, Esq., of Doddershall, Bucks.
Eldest son of the late George Grenville Wandesford Pigott, Esq., J.P. and D.L., of Doddershall (who was formerly M.P. for St. Mawes), by Charlotte, dau. of William Lloyd, Esq., of Aston, co. Salop; *b.* 1848 ; *s.* 1865. —*Doddershall Park, Winslow, Bucks.*

PIGOTT. (See *Graham-Foster-Pigott*.)

PIGOTT. (See *Smyth-Pigott*.)

PIGOTT-CARLETON, FRANCIS PAYTON, Esq., of Archer Lodge, and Heckfield, Hants.
Eldest son of the late Francis Pigott-Stainsby Conant, Esq., J.P., of Archer Lodge and Heckfield Heath (who was M.P. for Reading), by Frances Phillips, dau. of General Sir Francis Wilson; *b.* 1837 ; *s.* 1864 ; *m.* 1864 the Hon. Henrietta Anne, eldest dau. of Guy, 3rd Lord Dorchester, when he assumed the name of Carleton, in lieu of those of Stainsby and Conant. Is Lord of the Manor of Sherfield, and a Lieut. in the Hants Yeomanry Cavalry.—*Archer Lodge, Sherfield, Reading ; Heckfield Heath, Winchfield, Hants ; Banbury, Oxon.*

PIGOTT-CORBET, the Rev. JOHN DRYDEN, of Edgmund and Sundorne, Shropshire.
Eldest son of the late Rev. John Dryden Pigott (who was many years Rector of Edgmund), by Fanny, dau.
751

of — Bevan, Esq. ; *b.* 1809. Educated at Westminster and Ch. Ch., Oxford (B.A. 1830) ; is Lord of the Manor, Rector, and Patron of Edgmund ; assumed the additional name of Corbet in 1866, on succeeding to the estate of Sundorne.—*Edgmund Rectory, Newport ; Sundorne Castle, Shrewsbury.*

PIKE-SCRIVENER, Mrs., of Sibton, Suffolk.
Dorothea, eldest dau. of the late Right Rev. Dr. John Fisher, Bishop of Salisbury, and grand-dau. and heir of the late John Freston Scrivener, Esq., of Sibton Abbey, Suffolk ; *m.* 1839 John Frederick Pike, Esq., who assumed the additional surname of Scrivener, and who *d.* 1866. Is Lady of the Manor of Sibton.—*Sibton Abbey, Yoxford ; 20, Bryanston Square, w.*

+PILGRIM, CHARLES, Esq., late of Gayton House, Northamptonshire.
Eldest son of the late Charles Pilgrim, Esq., of Southampton ; *b.* 17— ; is married, and has, with other issue,
  * Charles Henry, *b.* 179— ; *m.* 1821 Mary, only child of the late Charles Holford, Esq., of Hampstead, Middlesex, and has issue.
Mr. Pilgrim, who is a Magistrate for co. Northampton, is descended from an old Essex family.—*Axley, Buckingham.*

PILKINGTON, Sir LIONEL MILBORNE SWINNERTON, Bart., of Chevet, Yorkshire (cr. 1635).
Third son of the late Sir William Pilkington, Bart., of Chevet Park (who *d.* 1850), by Mary Milborne, dau. of Thomas Swinnerton, Esq., of Butterton, co. Stafford ; *b.* 1835 ; *s.* his brother as 11th Bart. 1855 ; *m.* 1857 Isabella Elizabeth Georgiana, dau. of the Rev. Charles Kinleside. Educated at the Charterhouse : is a Dep.-Lieut. for the W. Riding of Yorkshire (High Sheriff 1859).—*Chevet Park, Wakefield ; Butterton Hall, Newcastle-under-Lyne ; Wonastow Court, Monmouth ; Carlton Club, s.w.*
  Heir, his son Thomas Edward, *b.* 1857.

PILKINGTON, Lady, of Catsfield, Sussex.
Maria Elizabeth, only dau. of the late Right Hon. Sir Vicary Gibbs, Chief Justice of the Common Pleas, by Frances Cerjat Kenneth, dau. of the late Major William Mackenzie, and sister of Francis, late Lord Seaforth (*ext.*) ; *m.* 1808 Lieut.-General Sir A. Pilkington, K.C.B., who *d.* 1853.—*Catsfield Place, Battle.*

PILKINGTON, EDWARD WILLIAMS, Esq., of Chilgrove, Sussex.
Second son of the late Rev. Charles Pilkington, Canon of Chichester, by Harriet Elizabeth, dau. of the late William Williams, Esq. ; *b.* 1803 ; *m.* 1835 Louisa Frances, eldest dau. of the late Rev. W. S. Bayton, of Eastergate, Sussex, by whom he has, with other issue,
  * Edward, Lieut. R.N. ; *b.* 1840.
Mr. Pilkington is a Magistrate for Sussex, and a Capt. R.N.—*Chilgrove, Chichester.*

PILKINGTON, HENRY FOSTER, Esq., of Park-Lane Hall, Yorkshire.
Eldest son of the late Henry Pilkington, Esq., of Park Lane Hall, by Etheldred, 6th dau. of the Rev. Thomas Foster, M.A., of Ryhall, co. Rutland ; *b.* 1818 ; *s.* 1863 ; *m.* 1st 1848 Maria, dau. and heir of Jean Albert Guichard, Esq., and widow of Harris Dansford, Esq., M.D. (she *d.* 1865) ; 2nd 1866 Hannah Clark, 2nd dau. of William Fretwell Hoyle, Esq., of Perham House, co. York (whom see). Is a Magistrate for the Settlement of Lagos.—*Park-Lane Hall, Doncaster.*

PILKINGTON, HENRY MULOCK, Esq., Q.C., of Tore, co. Westmeath.
Eldest son of the late Henry Pilkington, Esq., J.P., of Tore, by Barbara, 4th dau. of the late Rev. John Langsl

b. 1813; *s.* 1865; *m.* 1855 Wilhelmina Charity, dau. of John Macdonnell. Esq., Medical Poor-Law Commissioner for Ireland. Educated at Trinity Coll., Dublin (B.A. 1836, M.A. 1839), and also M.A. *ad eundem* of Cambridge; called to the Irish Bar 1836; is a Magistrate for co. Westmeath. This family is a branch of the Pilkingtons of Rivington, co. Lancaster.—*Tore, Tyrrel's Pass, co. Westmeath; 35, Gardiner's Place, Dublin.*

PILKINGTON, JAMES, Esq., of Park-Place House, Lancashire.
Son of the late James Pilkington, Esq., of Blackburn; *b.* 1804; *m.* 1831 Mary Jane, only dau. of Capt. Skaife, and by her, who *d.* 1865, has, with other issue,
* Edward, *b.* 1842; *m.* 1867 Agatha Mary, 2nd dau. of the late Hon. Peter Constable-Maxwell.

Mr. Pilkington is a J.P. and D.L. for co. Lancaster, a Director of the Lancashire and Yorkshire Railway Company, and a Cotton-spinner and Merchant in Blackburn; he was M.P. for Blackburn 1847–65.—*Park-Place House, Blackburn; Swinethwaite Hall, Bedale, Yorkshire; Reform Club,* s.w.; *23, Cork Street,* w.

PILKINGTON, RICHARD, Esq., of Windle Hall, Lancashire.
Eldest son of the late William Pilkington, Esq., of Windle Hall, by Anne, dau. of Richard Hatton, Esq., of Parbold; *b.* 1795; *s.* 18—; *m.* 1838 Anne, dau. of Richard Evans, Esq., of Haydock, and has, with other issue,
* William, of Audley House, a Magistrate for co. Lancaster, *b.* 1839; *m.* 1867 Louisa, 4th dau. of the Rev. W. A. Slater, of Leamington.

Mr. Pilkington is a Magistrate for co. Lancaster. This family is a branch of the Pilkingtons of Rivington. —*Windle Hall, St. Helen's, Lancashire.*

PILKINGTON, WILLIAM, Esq., of Eccleston Hall, Lancashire.
Second son of the late William Pilkington, Esq., of Windle Hall, by Anne, dau. of Richard Hatton, Esq., of Parbold; *b.* 1800; *m.* 1824 Eliza Charlotte, only dau. of Lieut. Boyes, R.N., and has, with other issue,
* William, a Magistrate for co. Lancaster, *b.* 1827; *m.* 1854 Elizabeth, dau. of the late Lee Watson, Esq., of St. Helen's, and has issue.

Mr. Pilkington is a J.P. and D.L. for co. Lancaster. —*Eccleston Hall, Prescot; Sutton Grange, St. Helen's, Lancashire.*

PILKINGTON WILLIAM, Esq., of Wilpshire Grange, Lancashire.
Second son of the late James Pilkington, Esq., of Blackburn; *b.* 1807; *m.* 1853 Martha, dau. of Henry Shaw, Esq., of Buxton, co. Derby. Is a Magistrate for co. Lancaster.—*Wilpshire Grange, Blackburn.*

PILKINGTON, WILLIAM ORMEROD, Esq., of Preston, Lancashire.
Second son of the late John Pilkington, Esq., of Rivington, by Sarah, dau. of William Ormerod, Esq., of Foxstones, near Burnley; *b.* 1786; *m.* 1st 1823 Catharine, dau. of John Pilkington, Esq., of Bolton, co. Lancashire; 2nd 1861 Mary, dau. of John Stanton, of London, and has, with other issue,
* John Ormerod, *b.* 1854.

Mr. Pilkington is a Magistrate for co. Lancaster, and for the borough of Preston. This family is descended from the ancient Lords of Pilkington, and from Bishop Pilkington of Durham, the founder of Rivington School. —*The Willows, Ashton-upon-Ribble, near Preston.*

PIM, JONATHAN, Esq., of Greenbank, co. Dublin.
Eldest son of the late Thomas Pim, Esq., of Dublin, Merchant, by Mary, dau. of William Harvey, Esq., of Youghal; *b.* 1806; *m.* 1828 Susan, dau. of John Todhunter, Esq., of Dublin, Merchant (she *d.* 1868). Is a Merchant and Manufacturer in Dublin; elected M.P. for Dublin 1865.—*Greenbank, Monkstown, co. Dublin; 22, William Street, Dublin; 115, Jermyn Street,* w.

PINE, Sir BENJAMIN CHILLEY CAMPBELL, Knt. (cr. 1856).
Son of the late Benjamin C. Pine, Esq., of Tunbridge Wells; *b.* 1811; *m.* 1st 1841 Elizabeth, dau. of the late John Campbell, Esq. (she *d.* 1847); 2nd 1859 Margaretta Anne, only dau. of the late Col. John Simpson, of the Bengal Army. Educated at Trinity Coll., Cambridge (M.A. 1834); called to the Bar at Gray's Inn 1841; was Queen's Advocate at Sierra Leone 1850–4; appointed Governor of Western Australia 1868; has been Governor and Commander-in-Chief of the Gold Coast, Lieut.-Governor of St. Kitts, and Governor of the Leeward Islands.—*Oriental Club,* w

PINE-COFFIN, CHARLES JOHN SAMUEL, Esq., of East-Down House, Devon.
Only son of the late Rev. Charles Pine-Coffin, Rector of East Down, by Charlotte, dau. of Samuel Knight, Esq., of Milton Hall, co Cambridge; *b.* 1830; *m.* 1855 Margaret Juliana, youngest dau. of the late Rev. William Carwithen, D.D., Rector of Stoke Climsland, Cornwall, and has issue,
* Charles, *b.* 1857.

Mr. Pine-Coffin is Lord of the Manor of East Down.— *East-Down House, Barnstaple.*

PINE-COFFIN. (See *Coffin*.)

PINFOLD, Miss, of Walton Hall, Bucks.
Fanny Maria, only dau. of the late Rev. Charles John Pinfold, Rector of Bramshall, co. Stafford, by Anna Maria, dau. of the Rev. John Seagrave, Rector of Castle Ashby, co. Northampton; *s.* 1857. Is Lady of the Manor of Walton.—*Walton Hall, Bletchley.*

+ **PINNEY, FREDERICK WAKE, Esq., of Somerton, Somerset.**
Elder son of the late Charles Pinney, Esq., of Clifton (who was Mayor of Bristol 1830–1, and *d.* 1867), by Frances Mary, dau. of the late John Still, Esq., of Noyle, Wilts; *b.* 18—; is a Magistrate for Somerset (High Sheriff 18—).—*Somerton, Somerset.*

Heir Pres., his brother John Charles, *b.* 18—.

PINNEY, Col. WILLIAM, of Somerton Erleigh, Somerset.
Only son of the late John Frederick Pinney, Esq., of Somerton Erleigh, by Frances, only dau. of the late William Dickinson, Esq., M.P., of Kingweston, Somerset; *b.* 1806; *s.* 1845. Educated at Eton and Trinity Coll., Cambridge (B.A. 1828, M.A. 1833); is a J.P. and D.L. for Somerset, a Magistrate for Dorset and Devon, and Col. 2nd Somerset Militia; was formerly Capt. and Major W. Somerset Yeomanry; was M.P. for Lyme 1832–42, for E. Somerset 1847–52, and again for Lyme 1852–65.—*Somerton Erleigh, Somerton; United Service, Brooks's, Reform, Arthur's, and Travellers' Clubs,* s.w.; *30, Berkeley Square,* w.

PIPE-WOLFERSTAN. (See *Wolferstan*).

PITMAN, JAMES SAMUEL, Esq., ‡ of Dunchideock, Devon.
Eldest son of the late James Samuel Pitman, Esq., J.P. and D.L., of Dunchideock, by Catharine, eldest dau. of the late John Harris, Esq., of Mount Radford, Devon; *b.* 1806; *s.* 1848; *m.* 1850 Elizabeth, dau. of

the Rev. Nathaniel Cole, Vicar of South Brent (she d.
1852), and has issue,
* Elizabeth Katherine.
Mr. Pitman. who was educated at Eton and Exeter
Coll., Oxford, is a J.P. and D·L. for Devon (High
Sheriff 1856); he was formerly a Lieut. in the 1st Dragoons.—*Dunchideock House, Exeter.*

PITMAN, SAMUEL, Esq., of Oulton, Norfolk.
Eldest son of the late Rev. Samuel Pitman, of Oulton
Hall, by Barbara, dau. and sole heir of Coulson
Bell, Esq.; b. 1816; s. 1854; m. 1842 Elise, only dau.
and heir of the Rev. W. Salter, Rector of Cadeleigh,
Devon, and has, with other issue,
* Samuel Coulson Bell, b. 1843 ; educated at Eton.
Mr. Pitman, who was educated at Eton and Trinity
Coll., Cambridge, is a Magistrate for Norfolk and
Somerset, Lord of the Manor of Irmingland, and Capt.
W. Somerset Yeomanry Cavalry. — *Oulton Hall,
Aylsham; Bishop's Hull Manor, Taunton; Junior
Carlton Club,* s.w.

PITT. (See under *Rivers, Lord.*)

PIX, THOMAS SMITH, Esq., of Rye, Sussex.
Eldest son of the late Thomas Pix, Esq., of Peasmarsh,
Sussex, by Ann, dau. of the late Rev. Jeremiah Smith,
of Woodside, Peasmarsh; b. 1807; s. 1853. Educated
at Harrow; is a Magistrate for Sussex, and Lord of
the Manors of Ewhurst and Moat, Sussex; was formerly Lieut. 4th Dragoon Guards.—*Broomhill Cottage,
Rye; Junior United Service Club,* s.w,

+PLAISTOWE, JOHN, Esq., of Lee, Buckinghamshire.
Eldest son of the late J. Plaistowe, Esq., of Lee, by
Mary, dau. and heir of the late Henry Dering, Esq.,
of the same place; b. 18—; s. his mother 18—. Is
Lord of the Manor and Patron of Lee.—*Lee, Wendover.*

PLATT, JOHN, Esq., of Bryn-y-neuadd, Carnarvonshire.
Second son of the late Henry Platt, Esq. (who d. 1842),
by Sarah, dau. of Joseph Whitehead, Esq., of Saddleworth; b. 1817; m. 1842 Alice, dau. of Samuel Radcliffe, Esq., of Lower House, Oldham, and has, with
other issue,
* Henry, Capt. Royal Carnarvon Militia, a Magistrate for
co. Carnarvon; b. 1842 ; m. 1868 Eleanor, 2nd dau. of
Richard Sykes, Esq., of Edgeley House, co. Chester.
Mr. Platt, who is a J.P. and D.L. for co. Lancaster,
and a Magistrate for co. Carnarvon (High Sheriff 1863)
was elected M.P. for Oldham 1865.—*Bryn-y-neuadd,
Bangor; Werneth Park, Oldham; Reform Club,* s.w.

PLAYFAIR, Lady.
June, youngest dau. of the late William Dalgleish, Esq.,
of Scotscraig; m. 1820 Col. Sir Hugh Lyon Playfair,
LL.D., Provost of St. Andrew's, who d. 1861, leaving,
with other issue, * Frederick, b. 1830 ; m. 1855
Margaret, dau. of C. Farnie, Esq.—*St, Andrew's, N.B.*

PLAYNE, WILLIAM, Esq., of Longfords, Gloucestershire.
Eldest son of the late William Playne, Esq., of Longford House, and Avening, co. Gloucester, by his 1st
wife Catherine; b. 1805; m. 1836 Mary Anne, only
dau. of Joseph Ellis Viner, Esq., of Badgworth House,
co. Gloucester, and by her (who d. 1868) has, with
other issue,
Frederick Charles, Capt. Rifle Brigade (served in the Crimea
and in India 1854-8), b. 1837 ; m. 1862 Jane, dau. of W. F.
McLaren, Esq., of Canada, and d. 1865, leaving issue a dau.
* Mary Viner.
Mr. Playne is a Magistrate for. co. Gloucester.—*Longfords, Minchinhampton.*
750

PLEYDELL-BOUVERIE.
(See *Radnor, Earl of ;* and *Bouverie.*)

PLOWDEN, WILLIAM HENRY CHICHEL_ _ Esq.
Fifth, but eldest surviving, son of the] _ Richard
Chicheley Plowden, Esq., by Elizabeth Sophia, dau. of
George Augustus Prosser, Esq.; b. 1788; m. 1st 1818
Catharine, dau. of the late William Harding, Esq., of
Barasset, co. Warwick; 2nd 1830 Annette, dau. of the
late Edward Campbell, Esq., and by her, who d. 1863,
has, with other issue,
* William Henry, E. I. Civil Service; educated at Harrow
and Haileybury; b. 1832; m. 1862 Emily, dau. of M. T.
Bass, Esq., of Rangemore, co. Stafford, and has issue, * a
dau., b. 1864.
Mr. Plowden, who was educated at Westminster; is
F.R.S., a J.P. and D.L. for Middlesex, a Magistrate for
Hants, and a Commissioner of Lieutenancy for London;
he was in the H.E.I.C.S. 1806-35, a Director of the
East-India, Co. 1841-54, M.P. for Newport 1847-52.
—Residence: *Ewhurst Park, Basingstoke; Union and
Carlton Clubs,* s.w.

PLOWDEN, WILLIAM HENRY FRANCIS, Esq., of
Plowden Hall, Shropshire.
Eldest son of the late William Plowden, Esq., of Plowden, by Mary, dau. of Simon Winter, Esq.; b. 1802; s.
his uncle Edmund 1838 ; m. 1846 Barbara, eldest dau.
of Francis Cholmeley, Esq., of Brandsby Hall, co. York,
and by her, who d. 1857, has, with other issue,
* William Francis, b. 1853.
Mr. Plowden, who was educated at Stonyhurst Coll., is
Lord of the Manor of Plowden; was High Sheriff of co.
Salop 1848. This family have been settled at Plowden
since the 11th century.—*Plowden Hall, Bishop's Castle;
Maiden Erleigh, Reading; Union Club,* s.w.

PLUMER, HALL, Esq., of Canons, Middlesex.
Second but eldest surviving son of the late Thomas Hall
Plumer, Esq., and grandson of the late Sir Thomas
Plumer, some time Master of the Rolls; b. 1827; m.
1854 Louisa Alice Hudson, only dau. of the late Henry
Turnley, Esq., of Kensington, Middlesex, and has issue.
—*Canons Park, Edgware; Conservative Club,* s.w.; 23,
Talbot Square, Hyde Park, w.

PLUMMER, CHARLES SCOTT-, Esq., of Middlestead and Sunderland. Selkirkshire.
Only son of the late Charles Balfour Scott, Esq., of
Woll, co. Roxburgh, by Eliza, dau. of the Rev. Alexander Ker; b. 1821 ; s. 1839; m. 1857 Sophia, eldest dau.
of Joseph Goff, Esq., of Hale Park, Hants, and has,
with other issue,
* Charles Henry, b. 1859.
Mr. Scott-Plummer, who was educated at Oriel Coll.,
Oxford (B.A. 1842, M.A. 1845), and called to the Scottish Bar 1846, is a Magistrate for co. Roxburgh, and a
J.P. and D.L. for co. Selkirk ; he assumed the name of
Plummer in 1839, on succeeding to the entailed estates
of Middlestead and Sunderland Hall, when he relinquished the estate of Woll in favour of his uncle, Lieut.-
Col. John Scott. — *Sunderland Hall. Selkirk, N.B.;
Gordon Club,* s.w.

PLUMPTRE, CHARLES JOHN, Esq., of Fredville
House, and Fedding, Kent.
Only son of the late Rev. Charles Thomas Plumptre,
M.A.. Rector of Wicklamlbreux, Kent (who d. 1862),
by his 2nd wife, Elizabeth. dau. of John Wright, Esq.,
of Lenton Hall, Notts; b. 1835; s. his uncle John
Pemberton Plumptre, Esq., 1864; m. 1860 Fanny Augusta, dau. of the late Rev. Henry W. Plumptre, Rector
of Eastwood, and has, with other issue, an only son.
* John Charles, b. 1863.
Mr. Plumptre, who was educated at Harrow and University Coll., Oxford (B.A. 1858, M.A. 1863), is a

Magistrate for Kent, and Patron of 2 livings. This family was formerly seated in Notts.—*Fredville Park, Wingham, Kent.*

PLUMRIDGE, Lady, of Hopton Hall, Suffolk.
Maria, dau. of Col. Skinner, R.A.; *m.* 1849, as his 3rd wife, Admiral Sir James Hanway Plumridge, K.C.B., of Hopton Hall, sometime M.P. for Penryn, (who *d.* 1863) leaving, with other issue, * Preston, *b.* 1850.—*Hopton Hall, Lowestoft.*

PLUNKET, Lord (JOHN PLUNKET).—Cr. 1827.
Second, but eldest surviving, son of William Conyngham, 1st Lord (who was some time Lord Chancellor of Ireland, and who *d.* 1854), by Katharine, dau. of John McCausland, Esq., of Strabane; *b.* 1794; *s.* his brother 1866; *m.* 1824 Charlotte, dau. of the Right Hon. Charles Kendall Bushe. Educated at Trinity Coll., Dublin; called to the Irish Bar 1817; appointed a Q.C. 1834; formerly Assistant Barrister for co. Meath.—*Old Connaught, Bray, co. Wicklow.*
Heir, his son William Conyngham, in Holy Orders, *b.* 1828; *m.* 1863 Anne, only dau. of the late Sir Benjamin Lee Guinness, Bart., and has issue, * William Lee, *b.* 1864.

PLUNKETT.
(See under *Fingall, Earl of; Dunsany, Lord;* and *Louth, Lord.*)

POCHIN, Capt. RALPH GEORGE, of Braunstone House, Leicestershire.
Youngest son of the late George Pochin, Esq., of Barkby Hall, co. Leicester, by Elizabeth, 2nd dau. of Richard Norman, Esq., of Melton Mowbray, and brother of William A. Pochin, Esq. (whom see); *b.* 1829; *m.* 1855 Anna Jane, eldest dau. of the late Rev. George Winstanley, Rector of Glenfield, and sister of James B. Winstanley, Esq., of Braunstone, who bequeathed that estate to her in 1862, and has, with other issue,
* Ralph George, *b.* 1860.
Capt. Pochin, who is a Commander R.N., is Lord of the Manor of Braunstone and Patron of the Rectory of Glenfield.—*Braunstone House, Leicester.*

POCHIN, WILLIAM ANN, Esq., of Edmondthorpe Hall, Leicestershire.
Eldest son of the late George Pochin, Esq., of Barkby Hall, co. Leicester, by Elizabeth, 2nd dau. of Richard Norman, Esq., of Melton Mowbray, co. Leicester; *b.* 1820; *s.* 1831; *m.* 1857 Giuliana Maria Elizabeth, dau. of Robert A. C. Godwin-Austen, Esq., of Chilworth Manor, Surrey, and has issue,
* George William, *b.* 1843.
Mr. Pochin, who was educated at Rugby and Trinity Coll., Cambridge, is a J.P. and D.L. for co. Leicester (High Sheriff 1846), Lord of the Manor of Barkby, and Patron of 3 livings.—*Edmondthorpe Hall, Oakham; Oxford and Cambridge Club, s.w.*

POCKLINGTON, GEORGE HENRY, Esq., of Chelsworth, Suffolk.
Eldest son of the late Rev. Henry Sharpe Pocklington, of Stebbing, Essex (who *d.* 1842), by Amelia Georgina, dau. of Major-Gen. George Stracey Smythe, Governor of New Brunswick; *b.* 1833; *s.* his cousin, M. R. Pocklington, Esq., 1865; *m.* 1857 Agnes Eliza, only dau. of Robert A. C. Godwin-Austen, Esq., of Chilworth Manor, Surrey, and has issue,
* Harry Evelyn Stracey, *b.* 1858.
Capt. Pocklington was educated at Sandhurst; is Lord of the Manor of Chelsworth, and Capt. 18th Foot; has served in Burmah, the Crimea, and India. The property of Chelsworth came into the possession of the great grandfather of the present possessor in 1768, in right of his wife, Pleasance, dau. of John Pykarell, Esq., of Roydon, Norfolk, by bequest of her cousin, Robert

Pocklington, Esq., of Chelsworth.—*Chelsworth Hall, Bildestone, Suffolk; Army and Navy Club, s.w.*

POCKLINGTON, the Rev. ROGER, of Walesby, Notts.
Eldest son of the late Roger Pocklington, Esq., of Carlton House, Notts, by Jane, dau. of Sir James Campbell, of Inverneil and Ross, co. Argyll; *b.* 1802; *s.* 1847; *m.* 1st 1831 Mary, 2nd dau. of George W. Hutton, Esq., of Carlton-on-Trent, Notts (she *d.* 1864); 2nd 1866 Anne Amelia, 3rd dau. of the late Alexander Campbell, Esq., of Possil, co. Lanark, and Torosay, co. Argyll; he has by the former, with other issue,
* Roger, H.M.C.S., an Officer in the 1st Middlesex Engineer Volunteers; *b.* 1832.
Mr. Pocklington, who was educated at Eton and Exeter Coll., Oxford (B.A. 1825, M.A. 1829), is Vicar of Walesby, Notts, and Rector of Skegness, co. Lincoln.—*Walesby Vicarage, Ollerton, Notts; Oxford and Cambridge Club, s.w.*

POCKLINGTON-SENHOUSE. (See *Senhouse.*)

POCOCK, Sir GEORGE FRANCIS COVENTRY, Bart., of Hart, co. Durham (cr. 1821).
Elder son of the late Sir George Edward Pocock, Bart., of Hart, by Augusta Elinor, dau. of the Hon. Thomas William Coventry, of North-Cray Place, Kent; *b.* 1831; *s.* as 3rd Bart. 1866; *m.* 1856 Honora Harriet Alicia, dau. of the Rev. E. H. Ravenhill. Is a Lieut.-Col. in the Army, late of the 30th Regt.—*Residence: Horsham, Sussex.*
Heir Pres., his brother Alfred George Drake, *b.* 1838; *m.* 1st 1863 Mary, dau. of the late Charles Culverhouse, Esq. (*dir.* 1866); 2nd 1868 Caroline Wentworth, youngest dau. of Thomas Wickham, Esq., of Ham, Somerset.

POCOCK, Sir GEORGE BARTHOLOMEW, Knt. (cr. 1821).
Son of the late Mr. Thomas Pocock, by Anne, dau. of Mr. Bartholomew; *b.* 1779; *m.* 1820 Susan Barbara, 2nd dau. of Col. Kelly (she *d.* 1854). Was Standard bearer to the corps of Gentlemen-at-Arms to George IV.—1, York Street, Portman Square, w.

POCOCK, ISAAC JOHN INNES, Esq., of Bridge Lodge, Berks.
Eldest son of the late Isaac Pocock, Esq., of Ray Lodge, Maidenhead, Berks, by Louisa, dau. of Henry Hime, Esq.; *b.* 1819; *s.* 1835; *m.* 1850 Anna Louisa, dau. of Benjamin Currey, Esq., of Eltham Park, Kent. Educated at Eton and Merton Coll., Oxford (B.A. 1842); was called to the Bar at the Inner Temple 1817; is a Magistrate for Berks.—*Bridge Lodge, Maidenhead; Arthur's Club, s.w.*

+**POCOCK**, Mrs., of Puckrup Hall, Gloucestershire.
Mary, dau. of ——, Esq.; *m.* 18— John Innes Pocock, Esq., of Puckrup Hall, a Magistrate for cos. Gloucester and Worcester, who *d.* 1865.—*Puckrup Hall, Tewkesbury.*

PODE, JOHN DUKE, Esq., of Slade, Devon.
Eldest son of the late Thomas Julian Pode, Esq., of Plympton Earle (who *d.* 1862), by Anne Duke, youngest dau. of the late Rev. Duke Yonge, Vicar of Cornwood, Devon; *b.* 1832; *s.* his uncle, Captain William Pode, 1864; *m.* 1860 Augusta Boevey, youngest dau. of the late Rev. Charles Crawley, Vicar of Hartpury, co. Gloucester, and has, with other issue,
* Ernest Duke Yonge, *b.* 1862.
Mr. Pode, who was educated at Winchester and Exeter Coll., and New Coll., Oxford (B.A. 1853, M.A. 1857), was called to the Bar at the Inner Temple 1858. This family inherited Slade from the heiress of the Squirrells.—*Slade, Ivybridge.*

757

POË, the Hon. Mrs.
Elizabeth Mary, youngest dau. of the late Harriett Skeffington, 9th Viscountess Massereene, and Thomas Henry, 2nd Viscount Ferrard; m. 1854 William T. Poë, Esq., M.A., of Curraghmore, co. Tipperary, Barrister-at-Law.—Residence: *Glen Ban, Abbeyleix, Queen's Co.*

POË, ARTHUR, Esq., of Harley, co. Tipperary.
Eldest surviving son of the late James Purefoy Poë, Esq., of Harley Park (who *d.* 1851). by Catharine, only dau. of Arthur Adams, Esq., of Bengerstown, co. Meath; *b.* 1828; *s.* his brother Purefoy, 1860; *m.* 1858 Olivia Elizabeth, dau. of John Jacob, Esq., M.D., of Maryborough; has, with other issue,

* James, *b.* 1859.

Mr. Poë, who was educated at Trinity Coll., Dublin, is a Magistrate for cos. Kilkenny and Tipperary, and a Grand Juror for co. Tipperary.—*Harley Park, Callan.*

POER, GEORGE BERESFORD, Esq., of Belleville Park, co. Waterford.
Eldest son of the late Samuel Poer, Esq., of Ballyhane-East, by Anne Letitia, dau. of Sir George Browne, Bart., of Neale Park, co. Mayo; *b.* 1802 ; *s.* 1842 ; *m.* 1830 Elizabeth Grace, 3rd dau. of Edward Hoare Reeves, Esq., of Ballyglissane, co. Cork, and has, with other issue,

* Samuel Beresford, *b.* 1837.

Mr. Poer, who was educated at Trinity Coll., Dublin (B.A. 1822), is a Magistrate for co. Waterford (High Sheriff 1853).—*Belleville Park, Cappoquin, co. Waterford.*

POLAND, Sir WILLIAM HENRY, Knt. (cr. 1831).
Son of the late Peter Raymond Poland, Esq., of Highgate, Middlesex ; *b.* 1797 ; *m.* 1820 his cousin, Miss Sophia Poland, and by her, who *d.* 1863, has, with other issue,

* Richard Henry, *b.* 1821 ; *m.* 1845 Harriet, eldest dau. of John Allan, Esq., of Deptford, Kent.

Sir W. H. Poland, who is a Commissioner of Lieutenancy for London, was Sheriff of London and Middlesex 1830–1.—*Blackheath, Kent, s.e.*

POLE, Sir JOHN GEORGE REEVE DE-LA-, Bart., of Shute, Devon (cr. 1628).
Eldest son of the late Sir William Templer Pole, Bart., of Shute, by Sophia Anne, dau. of the late George Templer, Esq., of Shapwick House, Somerset ; *b.* 1808 ; *s.* as 8th Bart. 1847 (assumed the additional name of Reeve in 1823); *m.* 1st 1829 Margaretta, dau. of Henry Barton, Esq., of Saucethorpe Hall, co. Lincoln : 2nd 1818 Josephine Catherine Denise Carré, of Anse, Rhone, France. Educated at Winchester ; is a J.P. and D.L. for Devon, a Magistrate for Dorset and Somerset, and Patron of 2 livings.—*Shute, Axminster ; Junior United Service Club, s.w.*

Heir Pres., his brother William Edmund, M.A., of Ch. Ch., Oxford, Barrister-at-Law ; *b.* 1816 ; *m.* 1841 Margaret Victorious, 2nd dau. of the late Admiral the Hon. Sir John Talbot, G.C.B., and has, with other issue, * Edmund Reginald Talbot, *b.* 1844, educated at Winchester.

POLE, Sir PETER VAN NOTTEN-, Bart., of Todenham, Gloucestershire (cr. 1791).
Eldest son of the late Sir Peter Pole, Bart., of Todenham House, by Anna Guerherhnina, dau. of Richard Buller, Esq.; *b.* 1801 ; *s.* 1850 ; *m.* 1825 1st Louisa, dau. of 1st Earl of Limerick (she *d.* 1852); 2nd 1863 Louisa, dau. of the late S. Lands, Esq. Assumed the name of Van Notten 1853. Educated at Harrow and Brasenose Coll., Oxford (M.A. 1822) ; is a J.P. and D.L. for cos. Gloucester and Warwick (High Sheriff 1856).—*Todenham House, Moreton-in-Marsh ; Union and Conservative Clubs, s.w.*; 6, *Upper Harley Street, w.*

Heir, his son Cecil Charles, of Buryfields House, Burton-on-the-Water, co. Gloucester, a Magistrate for cos, Gloucester
758

and Warwick. *b.* 1829 ; *m.* 1861 Frances Anna, dau. of the Rev. Henry Rice, of Great Rissington, co. Gloucester, and has, with other issue, * Cecil Pery, *b.* 1863.

POLE, CHARLES RICHARD, Esq., of Wick Rissington, Gloucestershire.
Eldest son of the late Charles Van Notten-Pole. Esq. of Wick Rissington, by Felizarda Matilda, 2nd dau. of the late Richard Buller, Esq.; *b.* 1797 ; *s.* 1864 ; *m.* 1824 Anne Eliza, only dau. of the late Edward Rudge, Esq., of the Abbey, Evesham, co. Worcester, and has, with other issue,

* Charles Van Notten, a Major in the Army ; *b.* 1828.

Mr. Pole represents a younger branch of the family of Sir P. Pole, Bart., of Todenham.—*Wick Rissington, Stow-on-the-Wold.*

POLE. (See *Chandos Pole.*)

POLE-CAREW, WILLIAM HENRY, Esq., of Antony, Cornwall.
Eldest son of the late Right Hon. Reginald Pole-Carew, of Antony, by his 2nd wife the Hon. Caroline Anne, dau. of William Henry, 1st Lord Lyttelton; *b.* 1811 ; *s.* 1835 ; *m.* 1838 Frances Anne, dau. of John Buller, Esq., of Morval, and has, with other issue,

* Reginald, *b.* 1849.

Mr. Pole-Carew, who was educated at the Charterhouse and Oriel Coll., Oxford (B.A. 1832), is a J.P. and D.L. for Cornwall (High Sheriff 1854–5), and a Deputy Warden of the Stannaries ; was M.P. for East Cornwall from 1845–52.—*Antony, Devonport ; Carlton Club, s.w.*

POLEY. (See *Weller-Poley.*)

POLHILL - TURNER, Capt. FREDERICK CHARLES, of Howbury Hall, Beds.
Eldest son of the late Col. Frederick Polhill, M.P., of Howbury Hall, by Frances Margaretta, dau. of John Dukeyne, Esq., of Ragthorpe House, Notts; *b.* 1826 ; *s.* 1848 ; *m.* 1852 Emily Frances, dau. of Sir Henry Winston Barron, Bart., and has, with other issue,

* Frederick Edward Fiennes, *b.* 1858.

Mr. Polhill-Turner, who is a J.P. and D.L. for Beds (High Sheriff 1855), and Patron of 1 living, was formerly Capt. 6th Dragoon Guards ; he assumed the name and arms of Turner 1853, by Royal licence, under the will of his maternal grandmother Lady Page Turner.—*Howbury Hall, Bedford ; Army and Navy Club, s.w.*

POLLARD, GEORGE THOMAS, Esq., of Stannary Hall, and Handhill Hall, Yorkshire.
Eldest son of the late Lieut.-Col. George Pollard, Esq., J.P. and D.L. of Stannary Hall, by Charlotte, only child and heir of the Rev. Sir Thomas Horton, Bart., of Chadderton Hall, co. Lancaster, and of Handhill Hall, co. York ; *b.* 1809 ; *s.* 1866 ; *m.* 1835 Clara, dau. of James Royds, Esq., of Woodlands, near Northwich, co. Chester, and has issue.

* Three daughters.

Mr. Pollard is a Magistrate for the W. Riding of Yorkshire ; late Capt. 2nd W. Yorkshire Yeomanry Cavalry.—*Stannary Hall, Halifax ; Ashfield, Cheltenham ; Handhill Hall, Pontefract ; Union Club, s.w.*

POLLARD, GEORGE, Esq., of Boston Spa, Yorkshire.
Youngest son of the late William Pollard, Esq., of Scarr Hill, co. York, by Beatrix, dau. of Joshua North, Esq.; *b.* 1796 ; *m.* 1845 Harriet, 2nd dau. of the late Rev. Lamplugh Hird, M.A., Vicar of Paull and Prebendary of York ; is a J.P. and D.L. for the W. Riding of Yorkshire.—*Boston Spa, Tadcaster.*

POLLARD, JOSHUA, Esq., of Scarr Hill, Yorkshire.

Second but eldest surviving son of the late William Pollard, Esq., of Scarr Hill (who d. 1840), by Beatrix, dau. of Joshua North, Esq.; b. 1794; m. 1821 Jane, dau. of John Sturges, Esq., of Bowling Hall, near Bradford, and has an only surviving son,

* William, of Crow Trees, Bradford, a J.P. and D.L. for the W. Riding of Yorkshire; late Lieut. 17th Foot, now Capt. and Adjutant 4th W. York Militia; b. 1827; m. 1851 Jane, dau. of C. Bicknell, Esq., of Southam, co. Warwick, and has issue.

Mr. Pollard is a J.P. and D.L. for the W. Riding of Yorkshire.—*Scarr Hill, Bradford.*

POLLARD-URQUHART, WILLIAM, Esq., of Kinturk, co. Westmeath, and Craigston, Aberdeenshire.

Eldest son of the late William Dutton Pollard, Esq., of Kinturk, by Louisa Anne, dau. of Admiral the Hon. Sir Thomas Pakenham, of Coolure, co. Westmeath; b. 1815; s. 1839; m. 1846 Mary Isabella, dau. of William Urquhart, Esq., of Craigston (whose name he assumed), and has, with other issue,

* Walter William Dutton, b. 1847.

Mr. Pollard-Urquhart, who was educated at Harrow and Trinity Coll., Cambridge (B.A. 1838, M.A. 1843), kept terms at the Inner Temple, but was never called to the Bar; is a J.P. and D.L. for co. Westmeath (High Sheriff 1840), and a Magistrate for cos. Aberdeen and Banff; was M.P. for co. Westmeath 1852–7, re-elected 1859.— *Kinturk, Castle Pollard; Cra;gs'on Club, Turriff, N.B.; Arthur's and Athenæum Clubs, s.w.*

POLLEN, Sir RICHARD HUNGERFORD, Bart., of Rodbourne, Wilts.

Eldest son of the late Richard Pollen, Esq., of Rodbourne, who d. 1838, by Anne, dau. of the late Samuel Pepys Cockerell, Esq.; b. 1815; s. his uncle as 3rd Bart. 1863; m. 1845 Charlotte Elizabeth, dau. of the late John Godley, Esq., of Killigar, co. Leitrim (she d. 1860). Educated at Eton and Ch. Ch., Oxford (B.A. 1836); is a Magistrate for Wilts.—*Rodbourne, Chippenham; Carlton Club, s.w.*

Heir, his son Richard Hungerford, b. 1846.

POLLEN, Lady, of Redenham, Hants.

Charlotte Elizabeth, only dau. of the late Rev. John Craven, of Chilton House, Wilts, by Catherine, dau. of James Hughes, Esq., of Litcombe, Berks; m. 1819 Sir John Walter Pollen, Bart., of Redenham, J.P. and D.L., Col. S. Hants Militia, and formerly M.P. for Andover, who d. s. p. 1863.—*Redenham, Andover.*

POLLEN. (See *Boileau-Pollen.*)

POLLINGTON. (See under *Mexborough, Earl of.*)

POLLOCK, the Right Hon. Sir FREDERICK, Bart., P.C., F.R.S., F.S.A., &c. (cr. 1866).

Son of the late Mr. David Pollock, of London, and brother of General Sir G. Pollock, G.C.B., G.C.S.I., and of Sir David Pollock, Chief Justice of Bombay; b. 1783; m. 1st 1813 Frances dau. of F. Rivers, Esq., of Spring Gardens; 2nd 1834 Sarah Ann, dau. of Capt. Richard Langslow. Educated at St. Paul's School and Trinity Coll., Cambridge (B.A. 1806, as Senior Wrangler), elected Fellow of Trinity Coll. 1807 (M.A.1809); is a Magistrate for Middlesex; was called to the Bar at the Middle Temple 1807, and was made K.C. 1827; was Attorney-General 1834–5, and again in 1841–4; M.P. for Huntingdon 1831–44; Lord Chief Baron of the Exchequer 1844–66.— *Hatton House, Hounslow, Middlesex.*

Heir, his son William Frederick, Barrister-at-Law, and a Master of the Court of Exchequer; b. 1815; m. 1844 Julia, dau. of the Rev. Henry Creed, and has, with other issue,
* Frederick, B.A. of Trinity Coll., Cambridge, b. 1846.

POLLOCK, Sir GEORGE, G.C.B. (cr. 1842).

Son of the late Mr. David Pollock, of London, and brother of the Right Hon. Sir F. Pollock, Bart; b. 1786; m. 1st 1810 Frances Webbe, dau. of — Barclay, Esq., 2nd 1852 Henrietta, dau. of the late George Hyde Wollaston, Esq., and has by the former, with other issue,

* Frederick, b. 1812; m. 1861 Laura Caroline, only surviving dau. of the late Henry Seymour Montagu, Esq., of Westleton Grange, Suffolk, and has issue, * a son, b. 1864.

Sir G. Pollock is a General in the Indian Army, and a Magistrate for Surrey; late Director of the H.E.I.C.; commanded the Bengal Artillery in the Burmese war 1824–5, and the Army in Cabul in 1842; he became afterwards Envoy to the King of Oude, and a Member of the Supreme Council at Calcutta; has received the thanks of Parliament for his Indian services.— *The Common, Clapham, s.; United Service Club, s.w.*

POLLOCK, ARTHUR JOHN OSBORNE, Esq., of Oatlands and Newcastle, co. Meath.

Son of the late George Annesley Pollock, Esq., of Oatlands and Newcastle, by Louisa, dau. of Daniel McKay, Esq., of St. Stephen's Green, Dublin; b. 1846; s. 1867. Educated at Sandhurst Coll.; is Lieut. 21st Fusiliers. —*Oatlands, Navan; Newcastle, Kingscourt, Cavan.*

POLLOCK, JOHN OSBORNE GEORGE, Esq., of Mountainstown, co. Meath.

Eldest son of the late Arthur Hill Cornwallis Pollock, Esq., of Mountainstown, by Louisa, dau. of George Clark, Esq., of Westhatch, Middlesex; b. 1815; s. 1846; m. 1856 Maria Louisa, dau. of Henry Darley, Esq., of Dublin, and has, with other issue,

* Arthur Henry Taylor, b. 1858.

Mr. Pollock is a Magistrate for co. Meath (High Sheriff 1854.— *Mountainstown, Navan, co. Meath; Kildare Street Club, Dublin; Carlton Club, s.w.*

POLLOK, ALLAN, Esq., of Faside, Renfrewshire.

Eldest son of the late Allan Pollok, Esq., of Faside, by Jean, dau. of John Coats, Esq., of Philips Hill and Kilbride; b. 1815; s. 1853; m. 1839 Margaret, dau. of Arthur Pollok, Esq., of Lochliboside, and has, with other issue,

* John, b. 1850.

Mr. Pollok, who was educated at the University of Edinburgh, is a J.P. and D.L. for co. Renfrew, and a Magistrate for co. Argyll.—*Broom, Glasgow; Ronachan, Terbert, N.B.; Lismany, Ballinasloe.*

POLLOK. (See *Crawfurd-Pollok.*)

POLLOK-MORRIS, ALLAN, Esq., of Craig, Ayrshire.

Eldest son of the late William Pollok-Morris, Esq., of Craig (who assumed the additional name of Morris on succeeding his cousin in this estate), by Janet, only dau. of James Buchanan, Esq., of Dowanhill; b. 1836; s. 1862. Is a Magistrate for co. Ayr. The estate of Craig was purchased in 1780, by Capt. John Morris, an ancestor of the late owner. —*The Craig, Kilmarnock, N.B.*

Heir Pres., his brother Robert Morris, a Magistrate for co. Ayr. and Capt. Ayrshire Yeomanry; b. 1842; m. 1864 Agnes Tennent, eldest dau. of John Buchanan, Esq., and grand-dau. of James Buchanan, of Dowanhill, and has surviving issue, * William, b. 1867.

POLTIMORE, Lord (AUGUSTUS FREDERICK GEORGE WARWICK BAMPFYLDE).—Cr. 1831.

Only son of George, 1st Lord, by his 2nd wife Caroline, dau. of General Buller, of Pelynt and Lanreath, Cornwall; b. 1837; s. 1858; m. 1858 Florence Sara Wilhelmine, dau. of Richard Brinsley Sheridan, Esq., M.P., of Frampton Court, Dorset. Educated at Harrow and Ch. Ch., Oxford; is a J.P. and D.L. for Devon and

Somerset, Patron of 5 livings, and Major South Devon Yeomanry.— *Court Hall, North Molton; Poltimore, Exeter; Cattistock Lodge, Dorchester; Brooks's, Travellers,' and Boodle's Clubs*, s.w.

Heir, his son Coplestone Richard George Warwick, b. 1859.

POLWARTH, Lord (WALTER HUGH HEPBURN-SCOTT).—Cr. 1690.
Elder son of Henry Francis. 5th Lord, by Lady Georgiana, dau. of George Baillie, Esq., of Jerviswood and Mellerstain, and sister of Thomas, 10th Earl of Haddington; *b.* 1838; *s.* 1867; *m.* 1863 Lady Mary, eldest dau. of George, 5th Earl of Aberdeen. Is a Magistrate for co. Berwick.—*Mertoun House, St. Boswell's, Berwickshire.*

Heir, his son Walter George, Master of Polwarth; b. 1864.

POLWHELE, RICHARD GRAVES, Esq., of Polwhele, Cornwall.
Second but eldest surviving son of the late Rev. R. Polwhele, M.A., of Polwhele (the well-known historian of Devon and Cornwall), by his 2nd wife Mary, dau. of R. Tyrrell, Esq., of Starcross, Devon; *b.* 1794 ; *s.* 1838 ; *m.* 1829 Louisa Frances, only dau. of the late Rev. R. Gréville, of Wyastone Grove, co. Derby. Educated at Addiscombe Coll.; is a J.P. and D.L. for Cornwall, and a retired Lieut.-Col. of Madras Artillery.—*Polwhele House, Truro.*

Heir Pres., his brother Thomas, a Major-General Bengal Infantry, *b.* 1797 ; *m.* 1829 Edith. dau. of John James, Esq., and has, with other issue. * Thomas Roxburgh, M.A., a Magistrate for Cornwall, *b.* 1831 ; *m.* 1861 Fanny Carne, and has, with other issue, *Ernest, b.* 1862.

POMEROY (See under *Harberton, Viscount.*)

POMEROY-COLLEY, the Hon. GEORGE FRANCIS, of Leopardstown, and Ferney, co. Dublin.
Third son of John, 4th Viscount Harberton, by Esther, eldest dau. and heir of James Spencer, of Rathnangan, co. Kildare ; *b.* 1797 ; *m.* 1825 Frances, 3rd dau. of the late Very Rev. Dean Trench, and has, with other issue,

* Henry Fitz-George, *b.* 1827.

Mr. Pomeroy-Colley, who was educated at Westminster, is a Magistrate for co. Kildare, and a Commander R.N. retired; he assumed the additional name of Colley 1830.—*Ferney, Stillorgan, co. Dublin.*

PONSONBY, the Hon. ASHLEY GEORGE JOHN, of Hatherop, Gloucestershire.
Second son of William, 1st Lord de Mauley, by Lady Barbara Ashley, only dau. and heir of Anthony, 5th Earl of Shaftesbury ; *b.* 1831 ; *m.* 1857 the Hon. Louisa, dau. of Lord Henry Gordon, late Maid of Honour to the Queen, and has, with other issue,

* Claude Ashley Charles, *b.* 1859.

Mr. Ponsonby, who was educated at Eton and Trinity Coll., Cambridge, is a J.P. and D.L. for co. Gloucester : he was formerly Capt. Grenadier Guards, M.P. for Cirencester 1852-7 and 1859-65.—*Hatherop, Fairford; Brooks's, Travellers', and Army and Navy Clubs*, s.w.

PONSONBY, the Hon. and Rev. WILLIAM WALTER BRABAZON.
Fifth son of John Wilhelm, 4th Earl of Bessborough, by Lady Maria, 3rd dau. of John, 10th Earl of Westmoreland ; *b.* 1821 ; *m.* 1850 Lady Louisa, dau. of Edward Granville, 3rd Earl of St. Germain's. Educated at Harrow and Trinity Coll., Cambridge (M.A. 1843); appointed Rector of Great Canford 1846.—*Great Canford Rectory, Wimborne.*

760

PONSONBY, MILES, Esq., of Hale, Cumberland.
Eldest son of the late John Ponsonby. Esq., of Hale, by his cousin Dorothy, dau. of the late Miles Ponsonby, Esq., of Hale ; *b.* 1808 ; *s.* 1852 ; *m.* 1837 Barbara, dau. of the late Christopher Wilson, Esq., of Rigmaden, co. Westmoreland, and has, with other issue,

* Miles de Hale, *b.* 1841 ; *m.* 1866 Malvina, eldest dau. of George Williams, Esq., of Tasmania.

Mr. Ponsonby, who was educated at Shrewsbury, is a Magistrate for Cumberland. This family derive from an ancient and noble family in Picardy, in France, who came over with William I.—*Hale Hall, Beckermet, Cumberland.*

PONSONBY.
(See under *Bessborough, Earl of*, and *De Mauley, Lord.*)

PONSONBY, of Kilcooly. (See *Barker.*)

PONSONBY-PURDON. (See *Purdon.*)

POOLE, HEWITT, Esq., of Monkstown, co. Cork.
Eldest son of the late Thomas Poole, Esq., of Mayfield, near Bandon, co. Cork, by Joanna Meade, dau. of the late Rev. Horace Townsend, of Ross Carbery, co. Cork ; *b.* 1812 ; *m.* 1st 1836 Jane, dau. of the late Joseph Deane Freeman, Esq., of Castle Cor, co. Cork (she *d.* 1841) ; 2nd 1849 Lucia Anne, dau. of the late Richard Wills Gason, Esq., of Richmond, co. Tipperary, and has, with other issue,

* Hewitt Richard, *b.* 1853.

Mr. Poole is a Magistrate for co. Cork, and a Capt. South Cork Militia.—*Residence: Monkstown, Cork.*

+POOLE, Mrs., of Terrick Hall, Shropshire.
Elizabeth, only dau. of the late Richard Francklin, Esq., of Great Barford, Beds, and Gonalston, Notts ; *m.* 1829 Capt. William Halstead Poole, R.A., who is *dec.*—*Terrick Hall, Whitchurch.*

POOLE, the Rev. WILLIAM JAMES, of Aberffraw, Anglesey.
Eldest son of the late William Price Poole, Esq., of Beaumaris, by Maria Baynton, dau. of James Furness. Esq., of Clewer, Berks ; *b.* 1813 ; *s.* 1841. Educated at Jesus Coll., Oxford (B.A. 1835); is a J.P. and D.L. for co. Anglesey, and Rector of Aberffraw.—*Aberffraw Rectory, Anglesey.*

Heir Pres., his brother Henry Robert, *b.* 1825.

POOLER, the Rev. JAMES GALBRAITH, of Tyross, co. Armagh.
Only surviving son of the late Robert Pooler. Esq., of Tyross, by Frances, dau. of the late Samuel Reid, Esq., of Newry ; *b.* 1824 ; *s.* 1859 ; *m.* 1855 Angelica, dau. of the late Rev. Edward Leslie, D.D., Rector of Anahilt, co. Down, and grandson-dau. of Charles P. Leslie, Esq., of Castle Leslie, co Monaghan, and has, with other issue,

* Leslie, *b.* 1858.

Mr. Pooler, who was educated at Trinity Coll., Dublin (Sch. 1844, B.A. 1847), is Incumbent of Newtownards, co. Down, and Chaplain to the Marquis of Londonderry. This family is of great antiquity in co. Armagh.—*The Rectory, Newtownards, Downshire ; Tyross, Armagh.*

POOLEY, the Rev. JOHN HENRY, B.D.
Eldest son of the late Henry Pooley, Esq., of Kelvedon, Essex, by Sarah, dau. of James Strange, Esq., of Tottenham ; *b.* 1802 ; *m.* 1840 Sarah, dau. of Ralph Fletcher, Esq., of Bolton, and has, with other issue.

* Henry Fletcher, M.A., Barrister-at-Law ; *b.* 1841.

Mr. Pooley, who was educated at St. John's Coll., Cam-

bridge (B.A. 1825. M.A. 1828, B.D. 1839), and was Fellow of St. John's Coll. 1826–33; is Rector of Scotter, Prebendary of Lincoln, and Rural Dean, and a Magistrate for co. Lincoln.—*Scotter, Kirton-in-Lindsey.*

POORE, Sir EDWARD, Bart. (cr. 1795).

Only son of the late Sir Edward Poore, Bart., of Niton, Wilts, by Agnes, dau. of the late Sir John Marjoribanks, Bart., of Lees, co. Berwick; *b.* 1826; *s.* 1838; *m.* 1851 Frances Eliza, dau. of the Rev. Henry Riddell Moody. Was formerly Lieut. Scots Fusilier Guards. —*Salisbury, Wilts.*

Heir, his son Richard, *b.* 1858.

POORE, EDWARD DYKE, Esq., of Syrencot, Wiltshire.

Eldest son of the late Edward Dyke Poore, Esq., of Figheldean, by Maria, dau. of J. H. Pakenham, Esq., of Portman Sq., London; *b.* 1815; *s.* 1859; *m.* 1840 Frances, dau. of Rev. J. Williams, M.A., of Matherne, co. Monmouth, and has surviving issue,

* Two daughters.

Mr. Poore, who was educated at New Coll., Oxford (B.A. 1837), is a J.P. and D.L. for Wilts, Lord of the Manor of Figheldean, and a Commissioner of Income and Assessed Taxes. This family is descended from Philip, brother of Richard Poore (Bishop), founder of Salisbury Cathedral, A.D. 1220.—*Syrencot, Figheldean, Amesbury.*

+ **POPHAM, CHRISTOPHER WALLIS, Esq., of Trevarno, Cornwall.**

Son of the late Joseph Lamb Popham, Esq., of Trevarno, by Philippa, only child and heir of Christopher Wallis, Esq., and nephew of the late Admiral Sir Home Popham, K.C.B.; *b.* 1802; *m.* 1832 Harriet Elizabeth, dau. of the late Sir Vyall Vyvyan, Bart., and has, with other issue,

* Vyvyan Wallis, in Holy Orders, *b.* 1833; *m.* 1866 Catherine Helen, elder dau. of the late Rev. W. Gillboe, Vicar of Gwennap, Cornwall.

Mr. Popham is a J.P. and D.L. for Cornwall (High Sheriff 1831).—*Trevarno, Helston.*

POPHAM, of Bagborough. (See *Fenwick-Bisset.*)

POPHAM, FRANCIS WHITE-, Esq., of Wotton, Isle of Wight.

Only son of the late Rev. R. Walton White, by Mary, dau. and heir of John Popham, Esq., of Kitchill and Shanklin, Isle of Wight, whose name he assumed by Royal licence in 1853; *b.* 1829. Educated at Eton and University Coll., Oxford (B.A. 1855, M.A. 1856); is a Magistrate for Hants, Dep.-Lieut. for the Isle of Wight, and Patron of 2 livings.—*Wotton Lodge, Wotton Bridge, I. of Wight; Oxford and Cambridge Club, s.w.*

POPHAM, Mrs., of Ardchattan, Argyllshire.

Jane Elizabeth Mary, eldest dau. of the late Col. Alexander Campbell, of Ardchattan Priory, by Jane Meux, dau. and co-heir of Edward Meux Worsley, Esq., of Gatecombe Park, I. of Wight; *s.* her uncle, Col. T. D. Campbell 1846; *m.* 1841 Strachan Irving Popham, Esq., J.P. and D.L. for co. Argyll, son of the late Admiral Sir Home Popham (who *d.* 1861).—*Ardchattan Priory, Bonaw, Argyllshire.*

Heir Pres., her cousin the Rev. William C. C. Preston, son of the late Robert Clarke, Esq., of Comrie, and grandson of Anne, dau. of Patrick Campbell, Esq., of Ardchattan.

POPHAM, HARCOURT FRANCIS PAUNCEFOTE, Esq., of Stourfield, Hants.

Only surviving son of the late Admiral William Charnock Popham, J.P., of Stourfield House (who *d.* 1861), by Clara, dau. of Robert Pauncefote, Esq., of Preston Court, co. Gloucester; *b.* 1845; *s.* his brother 1861; *m.*

1866 Annie Kate, only child of the late Henry Gibson, Esq., of Greenhithe, Kent. Is Lord of the Manor of Stourfield.—*Stourfield, Christchurch, Hants.*

POPHAM. (See *Leyborne-Popham.*)

PORCH, THOMAS PORCH, Esq., of Edgarley, Somerset.

Eldest son of the late John Fry Reeves, Esq., of London, by Maria, dau. of Thomas Porch, Esq., of Wells, Somerset; *b.* 1808; *s.* 1859; *m.* 1830 Jane, only dau. of Edward Barber, Esq., of Barston Hall, co. Warwick, and has, with other issue,

* John Albert, *b.* 1833.

Mr. Porch, who was educated at the Charterhouse and Trinity Coll., Cambridge (B.A. 1829, M.A. 1836), is a Magistrate for Somerset.—*Edgarley, Glastonbury.*

PORCHER, Mrs., of Clyffe, Dorset, and Borough Green, Cambridgeshire.

Ellinor, dau. of Thomas Redhead, Esq., of Snare Hill, Norfolk; *m.* 1828 Charles Porcher, Esq., of Clyffe, J.P. and D.L. (High Sheriff of Dorset 1846), who *d.* 1863. Mrs. Porcher is Lady of the Manors of Borough Green, co. Cambridge, and Tincleton, Dorset, and Patron of the living of Borough Green. — *Clyffe, Dorchester, Dorset; Borough Green, Newmarket.*

PORCHESTER. (See under *Carnarvon, Earl of.*)

PORTAL, MELVILLE, Esq., of Laverstoke, Hants.

Eldest surviving son of the late John Portal, Esq., J.P. and D.L., of Laverstoke and Freefolk Priors, Hants, by Elizabeth, dau. of Henry Drummond, Esq., of The Grange, Hants; *b.* 1819; *s.* 1848; *m.* 1855 Lady Charlotte Mary, dau. of Gilbert, 2nd Earl of Minto, G.C.B., and has, with other issue,

* Melville Raymond, *b.* 1856.

Mr. Portal, who was educated at Harrow, and Ch. Ch., Oxford (B.A. 1842, M.A. 1844), and called to the Bar at Lincoln's Inn 1845, is a J.P. and D.L. for Hants (High Sheriff 1863), Lord of the Manor and Patron of Laverstoke, and Capt. N. Hants Yeomanry; he was M.P. for N. Hants 1849–57.—*Laverstoke House, Overton, Hants; Travellers' and Carlton Clubs, s.w.*

PORTAL, WYNDHAM SPENCER, Esq., of Malshanger, Hampshire.

Third son of the late John Portal, Esq., J.P. and D.L., of Laverstoke, Hants, by his 2nd wife Elizabeth, only dau. of the late Henry Drummond, Esq., of The Grange, near Alresford, Hants; *b.* 1822; *m.* 1849 Mary Jane, dau. of the late William Hicks-Beach, Esq., of Oakley Hall, Hants, and has, with other issue,

* William Wyndham, *b.* 1850.

Mr. W. Portal, who was educated at Harrow and the Royal Military Coll., Sandhurst, is a Magistrate for Hants; late Capt. in the Hampshire Yeomanry. —*Malshanger, near Basingstoke; Travellers' Club, s.w.; 3, Wilton Crescent, s.w.*

PORTARLINGTON, Earl of (HENRY JOHN REUBEN DAWSON-DAMER).—Cr. 1785.

Only son of the late Hon. Henry Dawson-Damer, Capt. R.N. (who *d.* 1841), by Eliza, dau. of Edmund Joshua Moriarty, Esq., Capt. R.N.; *b.* 1822; *s.* his grandfather as 3rd Earl 1845; *m.* 1847 Lady Alexandrina, dau. of Charles William, 3rd Marquis of Londonderry, K.G. Is a J.P. and D.L. for Queen's Co.; elected a Representative Peer for Ireland 1855.—*Emo Park, Queen's Co.; 44, Brook Street, w.*

Heir Pres., his cousin Lionel Seymour William, M.P. for Dorchester, a Dep.-Lieut. for Dorset, and Lieut. Queen's Own Dorsetshire Yeomanry Cavalry; late Capt. Scots Fusilier Guards (only son of the late Right Hon. George Lionel

Dawson-Damer, M.P., of Came House. Dorchester, by Mary Georgiana, dau. of the late Lord Hugh Seymour) ; *b.* 1842 ; *m.* 1855 the Hon. Harriet Lydia, dau. of Henry, 6th Lord Rokeby, and has, with other issue, * George Lionel Henry Seymour, *b.* 1858.

PORTEOUS, ALEXANDER, Esq., of Lauriston and Woodstone, Kincardineshire.

Eldest son of the late David Porteous, Esq., of Hawkshaw; co. Perth ; *b.* 1800 ; *m.* 1851 Helen, dau. of David Scott, Esq., of Brotherton, co. Kincardine, and has, with other issue,

* David Scott, *b.* 1852.

Mr. Porteous, who was educated at Edinburgh University, is a J.P. and D.L. for co. Kincardine.—*Lauriston Castle, Montrose, N.B. ; New Club, Edinburgh.*

PORTER, the Rev. JOHN GREY, of Kilskeery, co. Tyrone.

Eldest son of the late Right Rev. John Porter, D.D., Lord Bishop of Clogher, by Mary, only dau. of John Smith, Esq., of Haltersot ; *b.* 1789 ; *s.* 1819 ; *m.* 1816 Margaret Lavinia, eldest dau. of Thomas Lindsey, Esq., of Hollymount House, co. Mayo, and has issue,

* John Grey Vesey, of Belleisle, co. Fermanagh, a J.P. and D.L. for co. Fermanagh (High Sheriff 1849) ; *b.* 1818 ; *m.* 1863 Elizabeth Jane, younger dau. of Richard Hall, Esq., of Innismore Hall, co. Fermanagh.

Mr. Porter, who was educated at Harrow and Trinity Coll., Cambridge (LL.B. 1813), is a Magistrate for cos. Fermanagh and Tyrone, and Commissioner of Education in Ireland ; Rector of Kilskeery, co. Tyrone.—*Kilskeery, Ballinamallard, co. Tyrone; Sackville Street Club, Dublin ; Carlton Club, s.w.*

PORTER, Mrs., of Winslade House, Devon.

Rose Aylmer, youngest dau. of the late Sir Henry Russell, Bart. (formerly Chief Justice in Bengal), by his 2nd wife, Anne Barbara, dau. of Sir Charles Whitworth ; *m.* 1824 Henry Porter, Esq., of Winslade House (who *d.* 1859), leaving issue, * Henry Aylmer, a Magistrate for Devon, late Lieut. Royal Fusiliers ; *b.* 1826 ; *m.* 1861 Susanna, youngest dau. of the late Lieut.-Col. Faunt, and has, with other issue, * Henry, *b.* 1853. —*Winslade House, Exeter ; 41, Southernhay, Exeter.*

+PORTER, THOMAS, Esq., of Rockbeare, Devon.

Son of the late Thomas Porter, Esq., of Rockbeare Court, by Mary Lee his wife, who both *d.* 1857 ; *b.* 18—; *s.* 1857. Is Lord of the Manor of Rockbeare. —*Rockbeare Court, Exeter.*

PORTER, WILLIAM, Esq., of Hembury, Devon.

Youngest son of the late Right Rev. John Porter, D.D., Lord Bishop of Clogher, by Mary, dau. of J. Smith, Esq., of Cottishall, Norfolk ; *b.* 1802 ; *m.* 1830 Elizabeth Gibbs, dau. of the late Abraham Ludlow, Esq., of Heywood House, Wilts, and has issue. Mr. Porter, who was educated at Harrow and Trinity Coll., Cambridge, is a J.P. and D.L. for Devon, and served in the 6th Dragoon Guards.— *Hembury Fort, Honiton ; National Club, s.w.*

PORTLAND, Duke of (WILLIAM JOHN BENTINCK-SCOTT).—Cr. 1716.

Eldest son of William, 4th Duke, by Henrietta, dau. of General John Scott, of Balcomie, co. Fife ; *b.* 1800 ; *s.* 1854. Is a Dep.-Lieut. for Notts, and Patron of 12 livings ; was M.P. for Lynn 1824-6. This family is of Dutch extraction, and came over to England with William III.—*Welbeck, Worksop, Notts; Bolsover, Derby; Langwell, Caithness, N.B. ; 19, Cavendish Square, w.*

Heir Pres., his brother Lord Henry William, educated at Ch. Ch. Oxford ; a Family Trustee of the British Museum; and late M.P. for North Notts; *b.* 1804.

762

PORTMAN, Lord (EDWARD BERKELEY PORTMAN).—Cr. 1837.

Eldest son of the late Edward Berkeley Portman, Esq., M.P., of Bryanston and Orchard-Portman, by his 1st wife Lucy, dau. of the Rev. Thos. Whitby, of Cresswell, co. Stafford ; *b.* 1799 ; *m.* 1827 Lady Emma, dau. of Henry, 2nd Earl of Harewood (she *d.* 1865). Educated at Eton and Ch. Ch., Oxford (B.A. 1820) ; is a Magistrate for Middlesex and Somerset, a J.P. and D.L. for Dorset, and Chairman of Quarter Sessions, Patron of 14 livings, a Member of the Council of H.R.H. the Prince of Wales for the Duchies of Lancaster and Cornwall, Lord Warden of the Stannaries, and Master Forester of Dartmoor; late Lord-Lieutenant and Custos Rotulorum of Somerset ; was M.P. for Dorset 1823-32, for Marylebone 1832-3.—*Bryanston, Blandford ; University Club, s.w. ; 5, Prince's Gate, w.*

Heir, his son William Henry Berkeley, educated at Eton and Merton Coll., Oxford, a Magistrate for Dorset and Somerset, and Col.-Commandant W. Somerset Yeomanry, M.P. for Dorset, and late M.P. for Shaftesbury ; *b.* 1829 ; *m.* 1855 Mary Selina Charlotte, dau. of William Charles, Viscount Milton, and grand-dau. of John, 2nd Earl Fitzwilliam, and has, with other issue, * Edward William Berkeley, *b.* 1856.

PORTMAN, the Rev. FITZHARDING BERKELEY.

Youngest son of the late Edward Berkeley Portman, Esq., of Bryanston, Dorset, by Lucy, dau. of the Rev. Thomas Whitby, of Cresswell Hall, co. Stafford, and brother of Edward, 1st Lord Portman : *b.* 1811 ; *m.* 1840 Frances Anne, dau. of the Rev. W. N. Darnell, Rector of Stanhope, and has, with other issue,

* Reginald FitzHarding Berkeley, *b.* 1853.

Mr. Portman, who was educated at Eton and Ch. Ch., Oxford (B.A. 1831, M.A. 1834), and was Fellow of All Souls Coll., is Rector of Staple Fitzpaine and Orchard-Portman, and Rural Dean, and a Dep.-Lieut. for Somerset.—*Staple Fitzpaine, Taunton.*

PORTMAN, HENRY WILLIAM BERKELEY, Esq.

Second son of the late Edward Berkeley Portman, Esq., of Bryanston, Dorset, and Orchard-Portman, Somerset, by Lucy, dau. of the Rev. Thomas Whitby, of Cresswell Hall, co. Stafford, and Newland, Hants, and brother of Edward, 1st Lord Portman ; *b.* 1801 ; *m.* 1832 Harriet Emily Cavendish, 2nd dau. of Thomas L. Napier Sturt, Esq., and has, with other issue,

* Henry Fitzhardinge Berkeley, educated at the Charterhouse, and Magdalen Coll., Oxford; Rector of Tylle, Somerset ; *b.* 1838 ; *m.* 1866 Alice Elizabeth, youngest dau. of the late John Mainwaring Paine, Esq., of Farnham.

Major Portman, who was educated at Harrow and Trinity Coll., Cambridge, and entered the 7th Hussars in 1822, was formerly Major 6th Inniskilling Dragoons, and Lieut. Dorset Yeomanry Cavalry ; is a Magistrate for Dorset. — *Residence : Dean's Court, Wimborne ; Arthur's Club, s.w.*

PORTMAN, Capt. WYNDHAM BERKELEY, of Hare Park, Cambridgeshire.

Third son of the late Edward Berkeley Portman, Esq., of Bryanstone, Dorset, by Lucy, dau. of the Rev. Thomas Whitby, of Cresswell Hall, co. Stafford, and brother of Lord Portman ; *b.* 1804 ; *m.* 1829 Sarah, dau. of Thomas Thornhill, Esq., of Riddlesworth, Norfolk, and has, with other issue,

* Wyndham Berkeley, *b.* 1831 ; *m.* 1853 Emily, dau. of George Newton, Esq., of Croxton Park, co. Cambridge.

Mr. Portman was educated at the Royal Naval Coll., entered the Navy 1817, is a Magistrate for co. Cambridge, and a Commander R.N. retired.—*Hare Park, Dullingham, Newmarket.*

PORTSMOUTH, Earl of (ISAAC NEWTON WALLOP).—Cr. 1743.

Only son of Newton, 4th Earl, by his 2nd wife Lady Katharine, dau. of Hugh, 1st Earl Fortescue, K.G. ;

b. 1825; *s.* 1854; *m.* 1855 Lady Eveline Alicia, eldest dau. of Henry, 3rd Earl of Carnarvon. Educated at Rugby and Trinity Coll., Cambridge; is a Magistrate for Hants, a J.P. and D.L. for Devon, Hereditary Bailiff of Burley, and Patron of 8 livings.—*Hurstborne Park, Whitchurch, Hants; Engesford, Crediton; Boodle's Club, s.w.; 57, St. James's Street, s.w.*

Heir, his son Newton, Viscount Lymington, *b.* 1856.

POSTLE, WILLIAM, Esq., of Smallburgh, Norfolk.

Only son of the late John Postle, Esq., of Smallburgh Hall, by Sarah, dau. of the late Thomas Cockrell, Esq.; *b.* 1806; *m.* 1837 Elizabeth Postle, only child of the late John Seaman, Esq., of Felmingham Hall, Norfolk, and has, with other issue,

* John Seaman, *b.* 1847.

Mr. Postle is a J.P. and D.L. for Norfolk. Lord of the Manors of Catts Smallburgh and Felmingham Stubbs, and Patron of Felmingham.—*Smallburgh Hall, Norwich.*

POSTLETHWAITE, RICHARD BLOMLEY, Esq., of The Grange, Lancashire.

Eldest son of the late Rev. Thomas Postlethwaite, of Yealand Conyers, co. Lancaster, by Elizabeth, 2nd dau. of John Satterthwaite, of The Castle Park, Lancaster, and Rigmaden Park, co. Westmorland; *b.* 1806; *s.* 1819; *m.* 1841 Jemima Christina, youngest dau. of James Losh, Esq., of Jesmond House, Recorder of Newcastle-upon-Tyne. Educated at Shrewsbury; is a Magistrate for co. Lancaster.—*The Grange, Cartmel.*

POSTLETHWAITE, WILLIAM, Esq., of The Oaks, Cumberland.

Second surviving son of the late Robert Postlethwaite, Esq., J.P. and D.L., of The Oaks and Broughton-in-Furness (who *d.* 1859), by Agnes, dau. of William Lewthwaite, Esq., of Broadgate, Cumberland; *b.* 1829; *m.* 1859 Annie Camilla, eldest dau. of Sir Robert Brisco, Bart., of Crofton Hall, and has issue,

* Robert Hodgshon, *b.* 1862.

Mr. Postlethwaite is a Magistrate for Cumberland (High Sheriff 1865).—*The Oaks, Broughton-in-Furness.*

POTT, ARTHUR, Esq., of Bentham Hill, Kent.

Second son of the late Robert Pott, Esq., by Sarah, dau. of Hamilton Kirby, Esq., of Antigua, West Indies; *b.* 1793; *m.* 1817 Elizabeth, eldest dau. of the late William Gilpin, Esq., of East Sheen, Surrey; 2nd 1863 Frances Sarah, dau. of the late Robert William Brandling, Esq., of Low Gosforth, Northumberland, and widow of Col. Armytage, late Coldstream Guards, of Broom-hill Bank, Kent. Mr. Pott, who was educated at Eton, is a J.P. and D.L. for Surrey, Sussex, and Kent (High Sheriff 1840), and formerly a Merchant in London.—*Bentham Hill, Tunbridge Wells.*

POTT, GEORGE, Esq., of Todrig, Roxburghshire.

Eldest son of the late George Pott, Esq., of Todrig, by Barbara, eldest dau. of the late Walter Turnbull, Esq., of Firth; *b.* 1780; *s.* 1781; *m.* 1807 Katharine, dau. of the late David Reid, Esq., and has, with other issue,

* George, a Magistrate for co. Selkirk, *b.* 1811; *m.* 1810 Julia, dau. of the late Rev. Robert Sparke Hutchings.

Mr. Pott is a J.P. and D.L. for cos. Roxburgh and Selkirk, and a Convener for the latter county.—*Todrig and Borthwickshiels, Hawick, Roxburghshire, N.B.*

POTTER, CHARLES, Esq., of Earnsdale, Lancashire.

Eldest son of the late John Potter, Esq., of Darwen, co. Lancaster, by Sarah, dau. of the late James Greenway, Esq., of Darwen; *b.* 1802; *m.* 1828 Grace, 2nd

dau. of David Gordon, 2nd son of Sir Alexander Gordon, of Culvennan, and has issue,

* John Gerald, of Darwen, a Magistrate for co. Lancaster, *b.* 1829; *m.* 1851 Eliza Adelaide, dau. of the late James Chapman, Esq., Lieut. R.N., and has issue, * John Charles, *b.* 1853; educated at Eton.

Mr. Potter, who is a Magistrate for co. Lancaster, and was formerly a Manufacturer, is descended from John Potter, Esq., of Ardwick, who was a large proprietor in the same county.—*Earnsdale House, Over Darwen; Whalley Range, Manchester.*

POTTER, DANIEL, Esq., of Missenden, Bucks.

Son of the late Daniel Potter, Esq., of Collyhurst, co. Lancaster; *b.* 1816; *m.* 1840 Jane, dau. of the late Capt. William Bate, Governor of the Island of Ascension. Was formerly an East Indian and China Merchant.—*Missenden Abbey, Great Missenden, Bucks; Oriental Club, w.; City of London Club, e.c.*

POTTER, EDMUND, Esq., F.R.S., of Dinting Vale, Derbyshire, and Camfield, Herts.

Eldest son of the late James Potter, jun., Esq., of Manchester; *b.* 1802; *m.* 1829 Jessy, dau. of A. Crompton, Esq., of Lune Villa, Lancaster, and has issue. Is a J.P. and D.L. for co. Derby, and a Manufacturer at Glossop, Manchester; elected M.P. for Carlisle 1861; he purchased Camfield from the Dinsdales in 1866.—*Dinting Vale, Glossop; Camfield Place, Hatfield; Reform Club, s.w.; 22, Prince's Gardens, Kensington, w.*

POTTER, RICHARD, Esq., of Standish House, Gloucestershire.

Only son of the late Richard Potter, Esq., M.P., of Manchester, by Mary, only dau. of William Seddon, of Wigstone, co. Leicester; *b.* 1817; *m.* 1844 Lawrencina, only dau. of Lawrence Heyworth, Esq., M.P., of Yewtree, Liverpool. and has, with other surviving issue,

* Lawrencina, *m.* 1867 Robert D. Holt, Esq., of Liverpool.

Mr. Potter, who was educated at the University of London, and called to the Bar at the Middle Temple 1842, is a Magistrate for cos. Gloucester and Hereford, and a Merchant at Gloucester and Great Grimsby.—*Standish House, Stonehouse, Gloucestershire.*

POTTER, THOMAS BAYLEY, Esq., of Buile Hill, Lancashire.

Second son of the late Sir Thomas Potter, Knt., by Esther, dau. of Thomas Bayley, Esq., of Booth Hall, near Manchester; *b.* 1817; *m.* 1846 Mary, dau. of Samuel Ashton, Esq., and has, with other issue,

* Thomas Ashton, *b.* 1847.

Mr. Potter, who was educated at Rugby and the London University, is a J.P. and D.L. for Lancashire, and Magistrate for Manchester; elected M.P. for Rochdale 1861.—*Buile Hill, Pendleton, Manchester; Pitnacree, Strathtay, Perthshire; Reform Club, s.w.*

POTTER, WILLIAM ROBERTS CRAWFORD, Esq., of Gonvena, Cornwall.

Eldest son of the late Rev. I. wis Potter, M.A., by Maria M. Maurice, dau. of the late Rev. George Crawford, LL.D., Vicar-General of the Diocese of Ardagh; *b.* 1825; *m.* 1851 Susanna Vercoe, only dau. of Samuel Symons, Esq., and has issue.

* Samuel Symons, *b.* 1854.

Mr. Potter, who was educated at Trinity Coll., Dublin, is a Magistrate for Cornwall; was formerly in the 5th Fusiliers and 38th Regt.—*Gonvena House, Wadebridge.*

POTTINGER, Sir HENRY, Bart. (cr. 1839).

Younger, but only surviving, son of the late Right Hon. Sir Henry Pottinger, Bart., G.C.B. (who was Ambassador to China in 1841, Governor of Hong-Kong 1843-4, of the Cape 1846-8, and of Madras 1850-4.

and who d. 1856), by Henrietta, dau. of R. Cooke, Esq.; b. 1834; s. as 3rd Bart. 1865; m. 1863 Mary Adeline, eldest dau. of the Rev. E. H. Shipperdson, of Hermitage, co. Durham (she d. 1866). Educated at Merton Coll., Oxford (B.A. 1855); called to the Bar at the Inner Temple 1861.—10, King's Bench Walk, Temple, E.C.

POTTS, GEORGE EDWARD BAYLY, Esq., of Elm Grove, Devon.
Eldest son of the late George Potts, Esq., of Elm-Grove House (who was M.P. for Barnstaple 1859–63), by his 1st wife Louisa, dau. of Samuel Jeffery, Esq., R.N., of Sidmouth, Devon; b. 1834; s. 1863. Was formerly Lieut. 11th Hussars. — Elm-Grove House, Dawlish; Trafalgar House, Barnstaple.

POTTS, HENRY, Esq., of Glanrafon, Flintshire.
Eldest son of the late Henry Potts, Esq., of Glanrafon, by Anne, dau. of Samuel Taylor, Esq., of Moston, co. Lancaster; b. 1810; s. 1845; m. 1844 Cecilia Anne, dau. of Major Martin, and has with other issue,
   • Henry John, educated at Exeter Coll., Oxford; b. 1845.
Mr. Potts, who was educated at Shrewsbury and Magdalen Coll., Cambridge, is a Magistrate for cos. Denbigh and Flint (High Sheriff 1852).—Glanrafon, Mold; Conservative Club, s.w.

+POTTS, Major JOHN, of Benton Park, Northumberland.
Son of the late —Potts, Esq., of Benton Park; b. 18—; is married, and has, with other issue,
   • John, Capt. Northumberland Militia; b. 18—.
Mr. Potts is a Magistrate for Northumberland, Lord of the Manor of Benton, and Major Northumberland Militia.— Benton Park, Newcastle-on-Tyne; 30, St. James's Square, Notting Hill, w.

POTTS, WILLIAM TRUMPERANT, Esq., of Correen Castle, co. Galway.
Eldest son of the late John Trumperant Potts, Esq., of St. Mark's, co. Westmeath, by Catherine, dau. of the Rev. Michael Griffin, of Elphin; b. 18—; s. 1836. Educated at Trinity Coll., Dublin. This family is of Norman origin.—Correen Castle, Ballinasloe, co. Galway; Sackville Street Club, Dublin.
Heir Pres., his brother Harry Trumperant, a Magistrate for cos. Galway and Roscommon; b. 18—.

POULETT, Earl (WILLIAM HENRY POULETT).
—Cr. 1706.
Only surviving son of the late Vice-Admiral the Hon. George Poulett (who d. 1854), by Catherine, dau. of Sir George Dallas, Bart.; b. 1827; s. his uncle as 6th Earl, 1864; is married. Is Capt. 22nd Foot, and Patron of 7 livings. Descended from a common ancestor with the Marquis of Winchester. — Hinton House, Hinton St. George, Crewkerne; Waterloo, Cosham, Hants; Arthur's Club, s.w.; 3, Buckingham Gate, s.w.

POULETT-SCROPE. (See Scrope.)

+POULTER, JOHN SAYER, Esq.
Eldest son of the late Rev. Edmund Poulter, Prebendary of Winchester, by a dau. of the late Right Rev. Dr. R. North, Lord Bishop of Winchester; b. 1795. Educated at Winchester and New Coll., Oxford (B.C.L. 1817); called to the Bar at the Inner Temple 1819; was M.P. for Shaftesbury 1832–8.

POUNDEN, JOHN COLLEY, Esq., of Ballywalter, co. Wexford.
Eldest son of the late Rev. P. Pounden, by Elizabeth, dau. of the Rev. W. Dawson, of Clontibret, co. Monaghan; b. 1827; s. 1817; m. 1852 Britannia Catherine, [?]

only dau. of George Battersby, Esq., Q.C., and has, with other issue,
   • Patrick Colley, b. 1861.
Mr. Pounden, who was educated at Trinity Coll., Dublin (B.A. 1847), is a Magistrate for co. Wexford.—Ballywalter House, Clonevan, co. Wexford.

POUNDEN, LONSDALE, Esq., of Brownswood, co. Wexford.
Eldest son of the late John W. Pounden, Esq., of Brownswood, by Charlotte Emily, dau. of the late Patrick Bruce Boyd, Esq., of Verona, co. Dublin; b. 1800; m. 1839 Lady Jane, 2nd dau. of Francis, 10th Earl of Moray, and has issue,
   • A daughter.
Mr. Pounden, who was educated at Trinity Coll., Dublin, is a Magistrate for co. Wexford, a Dep.-Lieut. for the Tower Hamlets, and Capt. Inverness-shire Highland Light Infantry.—Brownswood House, Enniscorthy, co. Wexford; United Service Club, Dublin; Junior United Service Club, s.w.

POWELL, ALEXANDER PITTS ELLIOTT, Esq., of Hurdcott, Wilts.
Eldest son of the late Alexander Powell, Esq., M.P., of Hurdcott, by Joanna, dau. of the Right Rev. G. H. Law, D.D., Lord Bishop of Bath and Wells; b. 1809; s. 1847; m. 1839 Mary Elizabeth Vere Booth, dau. of Wiliam Tyndale, Esq., of Bathford, Somerset, and has, with other issue,
   • Alexander Francis, b. 1842.
Mr. Powell, who was educated at Exeter Coll., Oxford, is a J.P. and D.L. for Wilts, and Lord of the Manor of Hurdcott.—Hurdcott, Salisbury.

POWELL, CALEB, Esq., of Clonshavoy, co. Limerick.
Eldest son of the late Evre Burton Powell, Esq., of Clonshavoy, Barrister-at-Law, by Henrietta, dau. of John Magill, Esq., of Tollycairne, co. Down; b. 178—; s. 1800; m. 1838 Georgina Frances, 3rd dau. of the late George Waller, Esq., of Prior Park, co. Tipperary, and has, with other issue,
   • Eyre Burton, b. 1839.
Mr. Powell, who was educated at Trinity Coll., Dublin, and called to the Irish Bar 1817, is a Magistrate for co. Limerick (High Sheriff 1858); he was M.P. for co. Limerick 1841–7. This family was originally from Shropshire.—Clonshavoy, co. Limerick.

+POWELL, CHARLES, Esq., of Sutton, Shropshire.
Son of the late C. Powell, Esq., of Sutton; b. 178—; is married. Is a J.P. and D.L. for co. Salop, and Lord of the Manor of Sutton.—Sutton, Ludlow.

+POWELL, CHARLES, Esq., of Speldhurst, Kent.
Eldest surviving son of the late Baden Powell, Esq., of Langton, Kent, and brother of the late Rev. Baden Powell F.R.S.; b. 1798; s. his brother 1860. Is a Magistrate for Kent.—Speldhurst, Tunbridge Wells.

POWELL, FRANCIS SHARP, Esq., of Horton Hall, Yorkshire.
Son of the late Rev. Benjamin Powell, of Fellingham Lodge, Wigan, a Magistrate for co. Lancaster (who d. 1861), by Anne, dau. of the Rev. T. Wade; b. 1827; s. his uncle 1810; m. 1858 Annie, 2nd dau. of Matthew Gregson, Esq., of Toxteth Park, co. Lancaster. Educated at St. John's Coll., Cambridge (B.A. 1850, M.A. 1853); called to the Bar at the Inner Temple 1853, and goes the Northern Circuit; is a J.P. and D.L. for W. Riding of Yorkshire; was M.P. for Wigan

1857–9 ; elected M.P. for Cambridge 1863.—*Horton Old Hall, Bradford ; Oxford and Cambridge Club, s.w. ; Plowden Buildings, Temple, e.c. ; 1, Cambridge Square, w.*

POWELL, HENRY BUCKWORTH, Esq., of Wilverley Park, Hampshire.
Eldest son of the late Henry Weyland Powell, Esq., of Foxlease Park, Hants, (who *d.* 1840) by Eliza, his wife ; *b.* 1820. Is a Dep.-Lieut. for Berks ; was formerly an Officer in the Grenadier Guards. — *Wilverley Park, Lyndhurst ; Arthur's and Guards' Clubs, s.w.*

POWELL, HENRY FOLLIOTT, Esq., of Brandlesome Hall, Lancashire.
Eldest surviving son of the late Samuel Powell, Esq., of Brandlesome Hall, by Frances, dau. of Henry Richmond, Esq., of Bath, M.D. ; *b.* 1803 ; *s.* 1834 ; *m.* 1830 Catherine Vassall, dau. of George Burleigh, Esq., of Ceylon, and has issue. Mr. Powell was formerly Capt. Ceylon Rifle Regiment.—*Brandlesome Hall, Bury ; Union Club, s.w. ; Royal Victoria Yacht Club.*

+POWELL, JOHN, Esq., of Watton Mount, Brecknockshire.
Son of the late J. Powell, Esq., of Watton Mount ; *b.* 18—. Is a J.P. and D.L. for co. Brecon (High Sheriff 1840).—*Watton Mount, Brecon.*

POWELL, JOHN JOSEPH, Esq., Q.C.
Eldest son of the late Thomas Powell, Esq., of Gloucester ; *b.* 1816. Called to the Bar at the Middle Temple 1847 ; goes the Oxford Circuit ; appointed a Q.C. 1863, and Recorder of Wolverhampton 1864 ; was M.P. for Gloucester 1862–5. — *Reform Club, s.w. ; 9, King's Bench Walk, Temple, e.c.*

POWELL, NATHANAEL, Esq., of Buckhurst Hill, Essex.
Third son of the late James Powell, Esq., of Hackney, Middlesex, by Catharine, dau. of the Rev. Nathanael Cotton, of Thornby, co. Northampton ; *b.* 1814 ; *m.* 1838 Agnes, dau. of David Powell, Esq., of Loughton, Essex, and has, with other issue,
* Harry James, *b.* 1853.
Mr. Powell is a Magistrate for Essex.—*Buckhurst Hill, Woodford.*

POWELL, the Rev. SAMUEL HOPPER, of Sharow Lodge, Yorkshire.
Third son of the late Samuel Powell, Esq., of Upper Harley Street, London, by Frances, dau. of Henry Richmond, Esq., of Bath ; *b.* 1805 ; *m.* 1832 Louisa Burnaby, dau. of Capt. Pitt Burnaby Greene, R.N., and has, with other issue,
* Samuel Hopper, *b.* 1835 ; *m.* 1865 Frederica, youngest dau. of Richard Machrell Jaques, Esq. (whom see).
Mr. Powell, who was educated at Durham and Trinity Coll., Cambridge (B.A. 1829, M.A. 1831), and ordained 1830, is a Magistrate for the W. and N. Ridings of Yorkshire.—*Sharow Lodge, Ripon ; Union Club, s.w.*

+POWELL, THOMAS, Esq., of The Gaer, Monmouthshire.
Son of the late Thomas Powell, Esq., of The Gaer (who was a Magistrate for co. Monmouth, High Sheriff 1859) ; *b.* 1810 ; *s.* 1863.—*The Gaer, Newport, Monmouthshire.*

+POWELL, THOMAS, Esq., Gabalva, Glamorganshire.
Son of the late T. Powell, Esq., of Gabalva ; *b.* 1810. Is a J.P. and D.L. for co. Glamorgan.—*Gabalva, Cardiff*

+POWELL, THOMAS HENRY, Esq., of Hook, Pembrokeshire.
Son of the late Thomas Powell, Esq., of Hook : *b.* 18—. Was High Sheriff of co. Pembroke 1864.—*Hook, Pembrokeshire.*

+POWELL, THOMAS HARCOURT, Esq., of Drinkstone Park, Suffolk.
Eldest son of the late John Harcourt Powell, Esq., of Drinkstone Park, by a dau. of — Waddington, Esq. ; *b.* 1819 ; *s.* 1855. Educated at Eton ; is a Magistrate for Suffolk, Lord of the Manor of Drinkstone ; late Capt. Scots Fusilier Guards. — *Drinkstone Park, Woolpit, Suffolk ; Guards' Club, s.w.*
Heir Pres., his brother George, Capt. Indian Army ; *b.* 1830 ; served in India, and was present at the capture of Lucknow.

+POWELL, the Rev. THOMAS PROSSEE, of Dorstone, Herefordshire.
Son of the late T. Powell, Esq. ; *b.* 18—. Is a Dep.-Lieut. for co. Hereford, and Lord of the Manor of Dorstone.—*Dorstone, Hay.*

POWELL, WALTER RICE HOWELL, Esq., of Maesgwynne, Carmarthenshire.
Eldest son of the late Walter Rice Howell Powell, Esq., of Maesgwynne, by Mary, dau. of Joshua Powell, Esq., of Brislington ; *b.* 1819 ; *s.* 1834 ; *m.* 1st 1840 Emily Anne, 2nd dau. of Henry Skrine, Esq., of Stubbings, Berks (she *d.* 1846) ; 2nd 1851 Catherine Anne, 2nd dau. of Grismond Philipps, Esq., of Cwmgwilly, co. Carmarthen, and has issue,
* Caroline Mary.
Mr. Powell, who was educated at Ch. Ch., Oxford, is a J.P. and D.L. for cos. Pembroke and Carmarthen (High Sheriff 1849).—*Maesgwynne, Llanboidy.*

POWELL, WILLIAM, Esq., of Tickford, Bucks.
Third son of the late John Folliott Powell, Esq., by Frances, dau. of Charles Armett, Esq., of Toft Hall, co. Stafford ; *b.* 1805 ; *m.* 1833 Eliza, dau. of Thomas Miller, Esq., of Leicester, and has, with other issue,
* Thomas Folliott, Capt. 6th Foot ; *b.* 1834.
Mr. Powell is Lord of the Manor of Tickford Abbey, and a Solicitor at Newport Pagnell.—*Tickford Abbey, Newport Pagnell.*

POWELL, Col. WILLIAM THOMAS ROWLAND, of Nant-Eos, Cardiganshire.
Eldest son of the late Col. William Elward Powell, of Nant-Eos (Lord-Lieutenant of, and M.P. for, co. Cardigan), by his 1st wife Laura Edwina, dau. of James Sackville Tufton Phelp, Esq., of Coston House, co. Leicester ; *b.* 1815 ; *m.* 1859 Rosa Edwina, dau. and co-heir of William George Cherry, Esq., of Buckland, co. Hereford, and by her, who *d.* 1860, has issue,
* George Ernest John, *b.* 1842 ; educated at Eton.
Col. Powell, who was educated at Westminster, is a J.P. and D.L. for co. Cardigan, a Magistrate for co. Montgomery, Patron of 1 living, and Lieut.-Col. Royal Cardigan Militia ; he was M.P. for co. Cardigan 1859–65, and formerly Capt. 85th Foot.—*Nant-Eos, Aberystwith ; United Service Club, s.w.*

POWELL-RODNEY. (See *Rodney.*)

POWER, Sir JOHN, Bart., of Kilfane, co. Kilkenny (cr. 1836).
Eldest son of the late Sir John Power, Bart., of Kilfane, by Harriet, dau. of Gervase Parker Bushe, Esq., of Kilfane ; *b.* 1798 ; *s.* as 2nd Bart. 1844 ; *m.* 1855 Frances Elizabeth, dau. of William Blaney Wade, Esq. Educated at Trinity Coll., Cambridge ; is a J.P. and D.L. for co. Kilkenny.—*Kilfane, Thomastown, co. Kilkenny.*
Heir, his son Richard Crampton, *b.* 1853.

765

POWER, Sir JAMES, Bart., of Edermine, co. Wexford (cr. 1841).

Eldest son of the late Sir John Power, Bart., of Sampton, co. Wexford, by Mary, dau. of Thomas Brenan, Esq., of Wexford ; *b.* 1800 ; *s.* as 2nd Bart. 1855 ; *m.* 1843 Jane Anna Eliza, dau. of John Hyacinth Talbot, Esq., of Ballytrent, co. Wexford. Is a J.P. and D.L. for co. Wexford (High Sheriff 1851), and High Sheriff for the city of Dublin 1859 ; was M.P. for co. Wexford 1835-47, re-elected 1865.—*Edermine House, Enniscoorthy, co. Wexford ; 20, Harcourt Street, Dublin ; Stephen's-Green Club, Dublin.*

Heir, his son John; *b.* 1845.

POWER, Sir WILLIAM JAMES TYRONE, K.C.B., of Annaghmakerrig co. Monaghan (cr. 1865).

Son of the late Tyrone Power, Esq., by Anne, dau. of John Gilbert, Esq., of Newport, I. of Wight ; *b.* 1819 ; *m.* 1859 Martha, dau. of John Moorhead, Esq., J.P., of Leesborough House, co. Monaghan. Educated at Tonbridge School ; is Commissary-General-in-Chief of the Army. — *Annaghmakerrig, Newbliss, co. Monaghan ; Junior United Service Club,* s.w. ; *42, Cleveland Square,* w.

POWER, KINGSMILL MANLEY, Esq., of The Hill Court, Herefordshire.

Eldest son of the late Lieut.-General Sir Manley Power, K.C.B. and K.T.S., by his 2nd wife Anne, 3rd dau. of Lieut.-Col. Kingsmill Evans, of Lydart, co. Monmouth ; *b.* 1819 ; *s.* his maternal uncle, Kingsmill Evans, Esq., 1851 ; *m.* 1852 Anna Eliza Blanche, only surviving dau. of John Probyn, Esq., of Longhope, co. Gloucester, and has, with other issue,

* Manley Kingsmill Manley, *b.* 1853.

Mr. Power, who is a J.P. and D.L. for co. Hereford, was formerly Capt. 9th and 16th Lancers.—*The Hill Court, Ross ; Army and Navy Club,* s.w.

+POWER, MAURICE, Esq., of Ringacoltig, co. Cork.

Eldest son of the late Maurice Power, Esq., of Ringacoltig ; *b.* 1811 ; *m.* 1832 Mary, dau. of the Hon. B. Livingstone, Judge of the Supreme Court of America. Is a Magistrate for co. Cork ; was M.P. for co. Cork 1847-52.—*Ringacoltig, Queenstown, co. Cork.*

+POWER, NICHOLAS MAHON, Esq., of Faithlegg House, co. Waterford.

Son of the late Nicholas Power, Esq., of Ballinakill, co. Waterford, by Miss Rivers ; *b.* 1787 ; *m.* 1818 Catharine, dau. of — Mahon, Esq., of Dublin, and has issue,

* Patrick Mahon, High Sheriff of co. Waterford 1855 ; *b.* 1820 ; *m.* 1859 Olivia Jane, dau. of Anthony Francis Nugent, Esq., of Pallas, co. Galway (whom see).

Mr. Power, who is a J.P. and D.L. for co. Waterford was M.P. for co. Waterford 1847-59.—*Faithlegg House, Waterford.*

POWER. (See *De la Poer, of Gurteen.*)

POWER-LALOR, EDMUND JAMES, Esq., of Long Orchard, co. Tipperary.

Second son of the late Edmund Power. Esq., of Gurteen, co. Waterford, by Anastasia, dau. of John Lalor, Esq., of Cranagh and Long Orchard ; *b.* 1819 ; *s.* 1852 ; *m.* 1858 Mary Frances, eldest dau. of George Ryan, Esq., of Inch House, and has, with other issue,

* George Richard, *b.* 1864.

Mr. Power-Lalor, who was educated at Downside and Stonyhurst Colls., is a J.P. and D.L. for co. Tipperary (High Sheriff 1857), late Capt. 1st Dragoon Guards. — *Long Orchard, Templetuohy, co. Tipperary.*

766

POWERSCOURT, Viscount (MERVYN WINGFIELD).—Cr. 1743.

Eldest son of Richard, 6th Viscount (who was some time M.P. for Bath, by Lady Elizabeth Frances, eldest dau. of Robert, 3rd Earl of Roden (she *m.* 2nd 1846 Frederick, 4th Marquis of Londonderry) ; *b.* 1836 ; *s.* 1844 ; *m.* 1864 Lady Julia, eldest dau. of Thomas William, 2nd Earl of Leicester. Educated at Eton ; is a J.P. and D.L. for co. Wicklow, a Representative Peer for Ireland, late Lieut. 1st Life Guards.—*Powerscourt Castle, Enniskerry, co. Wicklow ; White's Club,* s.w.

Heir Pres., his brother Lewis Strange, *b.* 1842 ; *m.* 1868 Cecilia Emily Emma, dau. of the Rt. Hon. John Wilson FitzPatrick, M.P.

POWIS, Earl of (EDWARD JAMES HERBERT).— Cr. 1804.

Eldest son of Edward, 2nd Earl, by Lady Lucy, 3rd dau. of James, 3rd Duke of Montrose ; *b.* 1818 ; *s.* 1848. Educated at Eton and St. John's Coll., Cambridge (M.A. 1840) ; is a Magistrate for co. Hereford, a J.P. and D.L. for cos. Montgomery and Salop, Chairman of the Quarter Sessions for co. Montgomery, Patron of 14 livings, Lieut.-Col. S. Salop Yeomanry ; was M.P. for N. Salop 1843-8.—*Powis Castle, Welshpool, co. Montgomery ; Walcot Hall, Shrewsbury ; Carlton Club,* s.w. ; *45, Berkeley Square,* w.

Heir Pres., his brother the Right Hon. Percy Egerton, C.B., P.C. (of Eastbourne, Sussex), educated at Eton and Sandhurst, Col. in the Army, A.D.C. to the Queen, a Magistrate for co. Salop, M.P. for South Salop, and Treasurer of the Household ; *b.* 1822 ; *m.* 1860 Lady Mary Petty Fitzmaurice, only child of William Thomas. late Earl of Kerry, and has surviving issue, * George, *b.* 1862.

POWIS, Countess of.

Lucy, 3rd dau. of James, 3rd Duke of Montrose. by his 2nd wife Lady Caroline, eldest dau. of George, 4th Duke of Manchester ; *m.* 1818 Edward, 2nd Earl of Powis, K.G., who *d.* 1848.—45, *Berkeley Square,* w.

POWLETT, the Hon. AMIAS CHARLES ORDE-, of Thorney Hall, Yorkshire.

Youngest son of the late Hon. Thomas Powlett Orde-Powlett, by Letitia, dau. of the late Henry O'Brien, Esq., and brother of William Henry, 3rd Lord Bolton ; *b.* 1828 ; *m.* 1852 Anne Martha, dau. of Christopher Topham, Esq., of Middleham Hall, co. York, and has, with other issue,

* Amias Christopher Thomas, *b.* 1862.

Mr. Powlett is a J.P. and D.L. for the N. Riding of Yorkshire.—*Thorney Hall, Spennithorne, Bedale.*

POWLETT, the Hon. and Rev. THOMAS ORDE-.

Second surviving son of the late Hon. Thomas Powlett Orde-Powlett, by Letitia, dau. of the late Henry O'Brien, Esq., and brother of William Henry, 3rd Lord Bolton ; *b.* 1822 ; *m.* 1846 Elizabeth Jane, dau. of Marmaduke Wyvill, Esq., of Constable Burton, co. York, and has, with other issue,

* Thomas Charles, *b.* 1849.

Mr. Powlett was educated at Eton and Trinity Coll., Cambridge (M.A. 1843). and was appointed Rector of Wensley, co. York, 1850. *Wensley Rectory, Bedale.*

POWLETT. (See under *Bayning, Lord ; Bolton, Lord ; and Cleveland, Duke of.*)

POWLETT. (See *Orde-Powlett.*)

POWNALL, HENRY, Esq., of Spring Grove, Middlesex.

Eldest son of the late John Pownall. Esq., by Mary, dau. of B. Durkin, Esq. ; *b.* 1792 ; *m.* 1816 Amelia Sophia, dau. of William Waterhouse, Esq., and by her, who *d.* 1860, has, with other issue,

* John Fish, M.A., of Trinity Coll., Cambridge, a Magistrate

for Middlesex, and a Barrister-at-Law; *b.* 1817; *m.* 1851 Charlotte Sarah, eldest dau. of the Rev. Thomas Harrison, Incumbent of Nonington.

Mr. Pownall is a J.P. and D.L. for Middlesex, Chairman of the Middlesex Sessions, and a Knight of the Order of St. John of Jerusalem.—*Spring Grove, Hounslow; Carlton Club,* s.w.; 63, *Russell Square,* w.c.

POWYS, the Hon. HENRY WENTWORTH FEILDING, of Berwick House, Shropshire.
Second son of William Robert, late Viscount Feilding (who *d.* 1799), by Anne Catherine, dau. of the late Thomas Jelf Powys, Esq., of Berwick House, and brother of William, 7th Earl of Denbigh; *b.* 1798. Educated at Eton; assumed the name of Powis after his maternal grandfather 1832; is a J.P. and D.L. for Shropshire, Patron of 1 living, and Major South Shropshire Yeomanry.—*Berwick House, Shrewsbury.*

POWYS, the Hon. Mrs.
Penelope, dau. and co-heir of James Hatsell, Esq., and sole surviving representative of John Hatsell, Esq., of Warden Park, Bencher of the Inner Temple, and Chief Clerk of the House of Commons; *m.* 1809 the Hon. and Rev. Littleton Powys, Rector of Tichmarsh, who *d.* 1842, leaving issue, * Littleton, *b.* 1817, who in 1853 took by Royal licence the additional name of Hatsell. —43, *Sussex Gardens,* w.

+POWYS, THOMAS, Esq., of Westwood House, Staffordshire.
Eldest son of the late Edward Powys, Esq., of Westwood House, by M'ss Hodges; *b.* 179—; *m.* 183— Miss Birkett. Is a Magistrate for co. Stafford, and Lord of the Manor of Wetley Rocks; was formerly Capt. Coldstream Guards.—*Westwood House, Cheddleton, Leek.*

POWYS. (See under *Lilford, Lord.*)

POWYS-KECK, HENRY LEYCESTER, Esq., of Stoughton Grange, Leicestershire.
Eldest son of the late Major the Hon. Henry Littleton Powys-Keck, J.P. and D.L., of Stoughton Grange (who assumed the additional name of Keck in 1861), by his 1st wife Margaretta Matilda, 2nd dau. of John Bancho, Esq.; *b.* 1841; *s.* 1863; educated at Brasenose Coll., Oxford (B.A. 1864), is a J.P. and D.L. for co. Leicester, and Lieut. Leicestershire Yeomanry Cavalry. This family is a younger branch of that of Lord Lilford. —*Stoughton Grange, Leicester; National Club,* s.w.; 35, *Great Cumberland Place,* w.

Heir Pres., his brother Charles Horatio Gardiner, Lieut. 60th Rifles; *b.* 1843.

POWYS-LYBBE, PHILIP LYBBE, Esq., of Hardwicke House, Oxon.
Eldest son of the late Henry Philip Powys, Esq., Hardwicke House, by Julia, dau. of Sir Fitz-William Barrington, Bart., of Barrington Hall, Essex; *b.* 1818; *s.* 1859; *m.* 1854 Anne Phyllis, eldest dau. of the late Thomas Greenwood, Esq. Educated at Eton and Balliol Coll., Oxford (B.A. 1839, M.A. 1813), called to the Bar at the Inner Temple 1843, and went the Oxford Circuit; is a Magistrate for Oxon; was M.P. for Newport, I. of Wight, 1859-65; he assumed the additional name of Lybbe, by Royal licence, in 1863.—*Hardwicke House, Reading; St. Thomas, East Cowes, I of Wight; Broomfield House, Southgate, Middlesex; Oriental Club,* w.; 88, *St. James's Street,* s.w.

POYER. (See *Callen.*)

POYNDER, THOMAS HENRY ALLEN, Esq., of Hillmarton and Hartham, Wilts.
Eldest son of the late Thomas Poynder, Esq., of Hillmarton and Hartham, by Sarah Marianne, dau. of Allen Cooper, Esq., of the H.E.I.C.'s Service; *b.* 1814;

m. 1842 Mary Anne, dau. of Robert Edmeades, Esq. Educated at the Charterhouse and Brasenose Coll., Oxford (B.A. 1836, M.A. 1838), called to the Bar at Lincoln's Inn 1839; is a J.P. and D.L. for Middlesex and Wilts (High Sheriff 1865), a Commissioner of the Lieutenancy of London, and Lord of the Manor of Hillmarton.—*Hillmarton Manor, Calne; Hartham Park, Chippenham; University Club,* s.w.; 21, *Upper Brook Street,* w.

PRAED. (See *Tyringham.*)

PRATT, Sir THOMAS SIMSON, K.C.B. (cr. 1861).
Son of the late Capt. Pratt, by Anne, dau. of the late William Simson, Esq.; *b.* 1797; *m.* 1827 Frances Agnes, dau. of John S. Cooper, Esq., Comptroller-General of Stamps, Ireland, and has, with other issue,

  * Thomas Arthur Cooper, in Holy Orders, M.A. of St. Peter's Coll., Cambridge; *b.* 1829; *m.* 1865 Anne Margaret Catherine, eldest dau. of the late Thomas Gilbert, Esq., of Cotton Hall, co. Stafford.

Sir T. S. Pratt, who was educated at the University of St. Andrew's, is a Lieut.-General and Col. 37th Regt.; was formerly Adjutant-General at Madras.—*Camden Crescent, Bath; United Service Club,* s.w.

PRATT, EDWARD ROGER MURRAY, Esq., of Ryston Hall, Norfolk.
Eldest son of the late Rev. Jermyn Pratt, Esq., of Ryston Hall, by Mary Louisa, dau. of the late Right Rev. George Murray, Lord Bishop of Rochester; *b.* 1847; *s.* 1867. Educated at Eton and Trinity Coll., Cambridge; is a Magistrate for Norfolk, Lord of the Manor of Ryston, and Patron of 2 livings.—*Ryston Hall, Downham Market.*

PRATT, the Rev. JOSEPH.
Eldest son of the late Rev. Joseph Stephen Pratt, of St. Margaret's, Herts, by Frances Cecilia, dau. of Major Cowper, of Park House, Herts; *b.* 1784; *m.* 1811 Mary, dau. of Rev. John Boak, of Brockley, Somerset, and has, with other issue, a son,

  * Henry, Canon of Peterborough Cathedral, and Rector of Shepton Mallet, Somerset; *b.* 1814; *m.* 1844 Mary, dau. of the late Right Rev. George Davys, Bishop of Peterborough.

Mr. Pratt was educated at Queen's Coll., Cambridge (B.A. 1807, M.A. 1811); is a Magistrate for co. Northampton and the Liberty of Peterborough, and Rector of Paston.—*Paston Rectory, Peterborough.*

PRATT, MERVYN, Esq., of Cabra, co. Cavan; Enniscoe, co. Mayo; and Manor Pratt, co. Donegal.
Eldest son of the late Col. Joseph Pratt, of Cabra Castle, by his 1st wife, Jemima Roberta, dau. and heir of Sir Jas. Stratford Tynte, Bart.; *b.* 1807; *s.* 1863; *m.* 1834 Madaline Eglantine, only dau. and heir of the late Col. Jackson, of Enniscoe, and has, with other issue,

  * Joseph, *b.* 1842.

Mr. Pratt, who was educated at Trinity Coll., Dublin, and St. Mary's Hall, Oxford, is a Dep.-Lieut. for co. Mayo and a Magistrate for cos. Cavan, Meath, and Mayo. —*Cabra Castle, Kingscourt, co. Cavan; Enniscoe, Crossmolina, co. Mayo; Kildare Street Club, Dublin.*

PRATT, RICHARD CHARLES, Esq., of Kinsale, co. Cork.
Eldest son of the late James Pratt, Esq., of Kinsale, by Sarah, dau. of the late Benjamin Scott, Esq., of Coolmain, co. Cork; *b.* 1819; *s.* 1844; *m.* 1st 1850 Sarah, dau. of William Lewis, Esq., of Kinsale (she *d.* 1855); 2nd 1858 Mary Del Hoste, dau. of Lieut.-Col. Heyland, and has, with other issue,

Mr. Pratt, who is a Magistrate for co. Cork, was formerly Lieut. 95th Regt.—*Kinsale, co. Cork.*

PRATT, ROBERT, Esq., of Knockane, co. Cork.
Eldest son of the late Major Henry Pratt, of Sundawell, Cork, by Sarah, dau. of the late Richard Fitton, Esq., Barrister-at-Law, of Gawsworth, co. Cork; *b.* 1835; *s.* 1858; *m.* 1855 Anna Maria, dau. of the late Astin Cooper Chadwick, Esq., of Damerville, co. Tipperary, and has, with other issue,
 • Henry, *b.* 1857.
This family has been seated in co. Cork for more than 200 years.—*Knockane, Castlemartyr, co. Cork.*

PRATT, WALTER CAULFEILD, Esq., of Ovington House, Bucks.
Third son of the late Col. Pratt, of Cabra Castle. co. Cavan (who *d.* 1863), by his 1st wife Jemima, only dau. and heir of the late Sir James Stratford Tynte, Bart. ; *b.* 1820 ; *m.* 1852 the Hon. Catherine Cecilia, 6th dau. of George, 3rd Lord Boston, and has, with other issue,
 • Douglas Walter Caulfeild, *b.* 1853.
Mr. Pratt, who is a J.P. and D.L. for Bucks, and Lieut.-Col. Bucks Militia, was formerly Capt. 67th Regt. —*Ovington House, Aylesbury ; 10, Lansdown Crescent, Cheltenham; Army and Navy Club, s.w.*

PRATT. (See under *Camden, Marquis.*)

PRATT. (See *Tynte.*)

+ PRENTICE, HENRY LESLIE, Esq., of Caledon, co. Tyrone.
Son of the late H. Prentice, Esq. ; *b.* 18—. Is a J.P. and D.L. for co. Tyrone.—*Caledon, co. Tyrone.*

PRENTIS, WILLIAM TAYLOR, Esq., of Ightham, Kent.
Only son of George Prentis, Esq., by Mary, dau. and heir of the late William Taylor, Esq., of The Warren, Ightham; *b.* 1832. Educated at Rugby, is a Magistrate for Kent, and Lieut. W. Kent Yeomanry Cavalry ; was formerly Capt. Royal Scots Greys.—*The Warren, Ightham, Sevenoaks ; Army and Navy Club, s.w.*

PRESCOTT, Sir GEORGE RENDLESHAM, Bart., of Theobald's, Herts (cr. 1794).
Eldest son of the late Sir George William Prescott, Bart., of Theobald's, by his 2nd wife Eliza, youngest dau. of Henry Hillier, Esq., and nephew of Frederick, 4th Lord Rendlesham ; *b.* 1846 ; *s.* as 4th Bart. 1850. Educated at Eton.—*Theobald's, Cheshunt, Herts ; 17, Grafton Street,* w.
Heir Pres., his brother Charles William, *b.* 1848 ; educated at Rugby.

PRESCOTT, Sir HENRY, K.C.B. (cr. 1856).
Son of the late Admiral Isaac Prescott, by Mary, dau. of the late Rev. Richard Walter; *b.* 1783 ; *m.* 1815 Mary Anne Charlotte, dau. of the late Vice-Admiral D'Auvergne, Duc de Bouillon (she *d.* 1868). Is an Admiral of the Blue, and a Magistrate for Surrey ; late Governor of Newfoundland, and Admiral Superintendent at Portsmouth : was a Lord of the Admiralty 1846–53. —*Southampton, Hants ; United Service Club, s.w. ; 7, Leinster Terrace,* w.

PRESCOTT, JOHN, Esq., of Dalton, Lancashire.
Second son of the late William Budd Prescott, Esq., of Liverpool, by Jane, dau. of John Ravenhill, Esq., of Clapham Common, Surrey ; *b.* 1834 ; *s.* his cousin 1858 ; *m.* 1860 Frances, dau. of Robert Ledson, Esq., of Liverpool, and has, with other issue,
 • John Ravenhill, *b.* 1863.
Mr. Prescott, who was educated at Marlborough Coll. and Wadham Coll., Oxford (B.A. 1859, M.A. 1863), is a Magistrate for co. Lancaster.—*Dalton Grange, Ormskirk.*

768

PRESCOTT-DECIE, RICHARD, Esq., of Bockelton, Worcestershire.
Third son of the late Timothy Decie. Esq., of Douglas, co. Cork, by Catherine Hale, dau. of the late Sir George Beeston Prescott, Bart., of Theobald's Park, Herts ; *b.* 1838 ; *m.* 1860 Arabella, only dau. of the late William George Prescott, Esq., of Clarence, Roehampton, Surrey, and has, with other issue,
 • Francis Edward, *b.* 1861.
Mr. Prescott-Decie, who was educated at Woolwich Academy, was formerly Captain in the Royal Engineers, is Lord of the Manors of Bockelton and Hill, and Patron of 2 livings ; he assumed the name and arms of Prescott by Royal licence in 1867, his wife having succeeded to the family property on her brother's death.—*Bockelton Court, Tenbury ; Junior United Service Club, s.w.*

PRESCOTT, Mrs., of Roehampton, Surrey, and Bockleton, Worcestershire.
Arabella, only dau. of Edward Wolstenholme, Esq., of Newberry Hall, co. Kildare ; *m.* 1838 William George Prescott, Esq., of Rochampton, who was head of the firm of Prescott, Grote, & Co., Bankers, and who *d.* 1865, having had issue an only son, William Wolstenholme, *b.* 1845, *d.* 1865.—*Clarence, Roehampton, Surrey ; Bockleton, Tenbury.*

PRESS, GEORGE LATHAM, Esq., of Reymerstone Hall, Norfolk.
Second son of the late Rev. Edward Press, of Norwich, by Elizabeth, dau. and co-heir of Thomas Grigson Payne, Esq., of Hardingham, and also co-heiress of the Rev. William Grigson, of Reymerstone ; *b.* 1806. Is a Magistrate for Norfolk. This family was formerly of Hoxne, Suffolk, and intermarried with the old Suffolk family of Rivett, of Brockford.—*Reymerstone Hall, Hingham.*

PRESSLY, Sir CHARLES, K.C.B. (cr. 1866).
Son of the late Charles Pressly, Esq.. of Warminster, Wilts, by Annie, dau. of Robert Hooper, Esq., of Pewsey, Wilts ; *b.* 1794 ; *m.* 1825 Annie, dau. of George Thompson, Esq., of Andover, Hants ; was formerly Chairman of the Board of Inland Revenue.—*Fernhill, Farnboro'. Hants ; Reform Club, s.w.*

PRESTON, Sir HENRY LINDSAY, Bart.. of Kirkforthar, Fifeshire (cr. 1637).
Eldest surviving son of the late Sir Robert Preston, Bart., of Kirkforthar (who *d.* 1847), by Euphemia, dau. of John Preston, Esq., of Gorton ; *b.* 1789 ; *s.* his brother as 9th Bart. 1858. Is a Magistrate for co. Berwick, and a retired Capt. Royal Navy.—*Kirkforthar, Markinch, N.B.*

PRESTON, Sir JACOB HENRY, Bart. of Beeston Hall, Norfolk (cr. 1815).
Eldest son of the late Sir Thomas Preston. Bart.. of Beeston Hall, by Jane, dau. of the late Thomas Bagge, Esq. of Stradsett Hall Norfolk : *b.* 1812 ; *s.* as 2nd Bart. 1823 ; *m.* 1840 Amelia, dau. of the late William Willoughby Prescott, Esq., of Handon. Middlesex. Educated at Westminster and Trinity Coll.. Cambridge (B.A. 1833) ; is a J.P. and D.L. for Norfolk (High Sheriff 1847). Lord of the Manor of Beeston, and Patron of 2 livings.—*Beeston Hall, Norwich ; Oxford and Cambridge and Carlton Clubs. s.w.*
Heir, his son Henry Jacob, *b.* 1841.

PRESTON, Sir GEORGE, Knt. (cr. 1838).
Son of the late William Preston, Esq. of Dublin (Chief Commissioner of Courts of Appeal, Ireland), by the Hon. Frances Dorothea, dau. of John, 5th Lord Carbery ; *b.* 1810 ; *m.* 1832 Jane, dau. of Alexander

Montgomery, Esq., of Dublin. Was formerly Capt. 4th Royal Lancashire Light Infantry; has been High Sheriff of Dublin.—67, *Lower Gardiner Street, Dublin.*

PRESTON, the Hon. THOMAS, of Silverstream, co. Dublin.

Seventh son of Jenico, 12th Viscount Gormanston, by the Hon. Margaret, eldest dau. of Thomas Arthur, 2nd Viscount Southwell; *b.* 1817; *m.* 1843 Margaret, dau. of the late John Hamilton, Esq., of Sundrum, co. Ayr, and has, with other issue,

* Jenico John, Ensign Rifle Brigade; *b.* 1846.

Mr. Preston, who is a J.P. and D.L. for co. Dublin, a Magistrate for co. Meath, and a Commissioner of National Education, was Capt. Meath Militia 1852–6.—*Silverstream, Balbriggan, Dublin.*

PRESTON, ISAAC, Esq., of The Denes, Great Yarmouth, Norfolk.

Eldest son of the late Isaac Preston, Esq., of Great Yarmouth, J.P. and D.L. (who was Mayor of Great Yarmouth in 1816 and 1822), by Elizabeth, dau. of Samuel Tower, Esq.; *b.* 1798; *m.* 18— Mary, dau. of John Farr, Esq., of Cove Hall, Suffolk, and has issue two daughters. Mr. Preston, who is a Magistrate for Norfolk, and a Solicitor at Great Yarmouth, represents a family who have been settled in Yarmouth since the Commonwealth.—*The Denes, Gt. Yarmouth.*

PRESTON, the Rev. JOHN D'ARCY WARCOP, of Askham Bryan, Yorkshire.

Eldest son of the late Rev. John D'Arcy Preston, of Askham Bryan, by his 1st wife, Elizabeth, dau. of Peter Spence, Esq., of Kensington; *b.* 1825; *s.* 1867; *m.* 1858 Emily, dau. of the late Rev. J. Brownlow, and has, with other issue.

* D'Arcy Brownlow, *b.* 1864.

Mr. Preston, who was educated at Worcester Coll., Oxford (B.A. 1845, M.A. 1847), is Incumbent of Sandgate, Kent; late Assistant-Chaplain to the Forces.—*Askham Bryan, York; Residence: Sandgate, Folkestone.*

PRESTON, JOHN JOSEPH, Esq., of Bellinter, co. Meath.

Eldest son of the late Rev. Joseph Preston, of Bellinter, by Mary Jane, dau. of the late Godfrey Massey, Esq., of Ballywire, co. Tipperary; *b.* 1815; *s.* 1839; *m.* 1842 Sarah, dau. of the late Denis O'Meagher, Esq., of Kilmoyler, co. Tipperary, and has issue,

* Helen Marie.

Mr. Preston, who was educated at Trinity Coll., Dublin, represents a younger branch of the House of Gormanston.—*Bellinter, Navan, co. Meath.*

PRESTON, JOHN NORCLIFFE, Esq., of Flasby Hall, Yorkshire.

Second son of the late Cooper Preston, Esq., J.P. and D.L., of Flasby Hall, by Mary Jean, dau. of Col. Cathcart Taylor; *b.* 1827; *s.* 1860. Educated at Rugby, is a Magistrate for the W. Riding of Yorkshire, and a Commissioner of Income Tax; was formerly Capt. 3rd Light Dragoons.—*Flasby Hall, Gargrave; Army and Navy Club, s.w.*

PRESTON, JOHN WILBY, Esq., of Dalby Hall, Lincolnshire.

Only son of the late Rev. Stephen Preston, B.D., of Louth, by Harriet, dau. of Thomas Bennett Dobbs, Esq., of Seremby, co. Lincoln; *b.* 1836; *s.* 1840; *m.* 1859 Julia, dau. of the Rev. John Leonward Travers, of Mumby, co. Lincoln, and has, with other issue,

* John Wilby, *b.* 1859.

Mr. Preston, who was educated at Rugby and Wadham Coll., Oxford (B.A. 1858), is Lord of the Manor of Dalby, and Capt. 7th (Spilsby) Lincolnshire Rifle Volunteers.—*Dalby Hall, Spilsby.*

PRESTON, THOMAS HENRY, Esq., of Moreby, Yorkshire.

Eldest son of the late Henry Preston, Esq., of Moreby, by Maria Anne, eldest dau. of the late Joshua Crompton, Esq., of Esholt Hall, co. York; *b.* 1817; *m.* 1847 Georgina Louisa, 3rd dau. of the late Sir Guy Campbell, Bart., and has, with other issue,

* Henry Edward, *b.* 1857.

Mr. Preston, who was educated at Eton, is a J.P. and D.L. for the E. and a Magistrate for the W. Riding of co. York; Capt. 7th Hussars.—*Moreby Hall, York.*

PRESTON, WILLIAM, Esq., of Ellel Grange and Rock House, Lancashire.

Eldest son of the late Thomas Preston, Esq., of Pilling, by Mary, dau. of William Procter, Esq., of Paulton, co. Lancaster; *b.* 1804; *m.* 1829 Margaret, dau. of Thomas Gardner, Esq., of Pilling Hall, co. Lancaster, and has, with other issue, an only son,

* George Theophilus Robert, *b.* 1834; *m.* 1865 Helena Cornelia, eldest dau. of George Bagster Denton, Esq., of Liverpool.

Mr. Preston, who is a J.P. and D.L. for co. Lancaster (High Sheriff 1865), and a Magistrate and Alderman for the Borough of Liverpool, was Mayor of Liverpool 1858–9. The pedigree of this family is given in Baines' 'History' of Lancashire.'—*Ellel Grange, Lancaster; Rock House, West Derby, Liverpool; Reform Club, s.w.*

PRESTON, the Rev. WILLIAM STEPHENSON, of Warcop Hall, Westmoreland.

Eldest son of the late Rev. William Michael Stephenson Preston, by Margaret, only child and heir of Charles Moyes, Esq., of Lumbenney, co. Fife; *b.* 1821; *s.* 1842; *m.* 1859 Dorothy, 2nd dau. of the late Thomas Wood Wilson, Esq., of Gate Fulford, York, and has issue three daughters.

* Beatrice, Ethel, and Eve'ene.

Mr. Preston, who was educated at St. John's Coll., Oxford (B.A. 1845), is Lord of the Manor of Warcop, and Patron of that living.—*Warcop Hall, Penrith.*

PRESTON. (See under *Gormanston, Viscount.*)

PRETYMAN, the Rev. FREDERICK, B.D., of Great Carlton, Lincolnshire.

Eldest surviving son of the late Rev. George Thomas Pretyman, Chancellor of Lincoln Cathedral (who *d.* 1859), by Emily, dau. of the late Christopher T. Tower, Esq., of Weald Hall, Essex; *b.* 1819; *m.* 1858 Georgina Elizabeth, eldest dau. of Edward Knight, Esq., of Godmersham, Kent, and Chawton House, Hants, and by her, who *d.* 1864, has, with other issue,

* Ernest George, *b.* 1859.

Mr. Pretyman, who was educated at Winchester and at Balliol and Magdalen Colls., Oxford (B.A. 1841, M.A. 1844), is a Magistrate for co. Lincoln and Rector of Gt. Carlton; late Fellow of Magdalen Coll., Oxford. —*Great Carlton, Louth; Arthur's Club, s.w.*

PREVOST, the Ven. Sir GEORGE, Bart., of Stinchcombe, Gloucestershire (cr. 1805).

Only son of the late Lieut.-General Sir George Prevost, Bart. of Belmont, Hants (who was Governor-General of Canada 1811–15), by Catherine Anne, dau. of Major-General John Phipps, R.E.; *b.* 1804; *s.* as 2nd Bart. 1816; *m.* 1828 Jane, dau. of the late Isaac Lloyd Williams, Esq., of Cwmcynfelyn, co. Cardigan. Educated at Oriel Coll., Oxford (B.A. 1825, M.A. 1827); is Lord of the Manor, and Incumbent of Stinchcombe, Rural Dean of Dursley, Hon. Canon of Gloucester, Proctor in Convocation for Gloucester and Bristol, and Archdeacon of Gloucester.—*Stinchcombe, Dursley.*

Heir, his son George Phipps, B.A. of Balliol Coll., Oxford, and Capt. 23rd Regt.; *s.* 1841; *m.* 1861 Charlotte Arabella, eldest dau. of Sir Charles Anderson, Bart.

PRICE, Sir FREDERICK POTT, Bart., of Spring Grove, Surrey (cr. 1804).

Eldest surviving son of the late Sir Charles Price, Bart., of Spring Grove (who *d.* 1847). by Mary Anne, dau. of William King, Esq., of Westminster; *b.* 1806; *s.* his brother as 4th Bart. 1866; *m.* 1868 Rosina Mary, dau. of the late Richard Price. Esq.. of South Lambeth. Is a partner in the Bank of Sir C. Price and Co.

Heir Pres., his brother Arthur James, *b.* 1808 ; *m.* 1836 Mary, dau. of the late Richard Price, Esq., and has, with other issue, * Charles, *b.* 1841.

PRICE, Sir CHARLES DUTTON, Bart. (cr. 1815).

Eldest son of the late Sir Rose Price. Bart., of Trengwainton, Cornwall, by Elizabeth, dau. of Charles Lambart, Esq., of Beaupark, co. Meath.; *b.* 1800 ; *s.* as 2nd Bart. 1834.

Heir Pres., his nephew Rose Lambert (eldest son of the late Francis Price, Esq., who was formerly Capt. 19th Foot, and who *d.* 1863, by Catharine Henrietta, dau. of the late Henry Hewitt, Esq., of Cork), *b.* 1837.

PRICE, Lady, of Mongewell House, Oxon.

Mary Anne Elizabeth, only dau. of the late Rev. Robert Price, D.D. (who *d.* 1823), by his 2nd wife Mary Ann, dau. of the Rev. Thomas Saunderson, of Haslemere, Surrey, and grand-niece of the late Right Rev. Shute Barrington, D.D., Lord Bishop of Durham; *m.* 1823 her cousin, Sir Robert Price, Bart., of Foxley, co. Hereford, M.P., who *d.* 1857, when his title became ext.; is Lady of the Manor and Patron of Mongewell. —*Mongewell House, Wallingford.*

PRICE, DAVID ALBODY, Esq., of Oaklands, Carmarthenshire, and Llanddu, Breconshire.

Eldest surviving son of the late Walter Price, Esq.. (H.B.M.'s Consul at Tangiers), by Louisa, 2nd dau. of the late Robert Westfield Benjamin, Esq., of Dover, Kent ; *b.* 1836; *s.* his uncle, Admiral David Price, 1854; *m.* 1861 Gwladus, eldest dau. of the Rev. Evan Andrews, M.A., Rector of Llanfrothen, co. Merioneth, and has, with other issue,

* Walter Evan, *b.* 1862.

Mr. Price is a Magistrate for co. Brecon.—*Oaklands, Carmarthen ; Llanddu, Brecon.*

+PRICE, HUGH POWELL, Esq., of Castle Madoc, Brecknockshire.

Eldest son of the late Hugh Price, Esq., of Castle Madoc, by Sophia, dau. of the late Francis Brodie, Esq. ; *b.* 1822 ; *s.* 185–: is married, and has issue. Is a J.P. and D.L. for co. Brecon (on roll for High Sheriff 1869). —*Castle Madoc. Brecknock.*

PRICE, JAMES CHARLES, Esq., of Saintfield House, Downshire.

Eldest son of the late James Blackwood, Esq., of Strangford, co. Down, by Elizabeth Anne, only dau. and heir of the late Nicholas Price. Esq., of Saintfield House. and of Lady Sarah Pratt, dau. of John Jeffreys. 1st Earl Camden ; *b.* 1807 ; *s.* 1855 ; *m.* 1840 Anne Margaret, elder dau. of Major Patrick Savage, of Portaferry, co. Down, and has, with other issue,

* Nicholas Price, *b.* 1842.

Mr. Price, who has assumed the maiden name of his mother, by Royal licence, is a Magistrate for co. Down. —*Saintfield House, Down, Ireland.*

+PRICE, JOHN, Esq., of Llanbraiadr Hall, Denbighshire.

Son of the late — Price, Esq., of Llanbraiadr Hall ; *b.* 18—; is married, and has, with other issue,

* R. Wynne, dau. Capt. 15th Foot ; *b.* 18—; *m.* 1863 Laura FitzRoy, 2nd dau. of the late Samuel Cartwright, Esq., of Nizell's House, Kent.

Mr. Price is a J.P. and D.L. for co. Denbigh, and

770

Lord of the Manor of Llanbraiadr.—*Llanbraiadr Hall, Denbigh.*

PRICE, JOHN BULKELEY, Esq., of Plas Cadnant, co. Anglesea.

Son of the late Lloyd John Price, Esq. (who *d.* 1852), by his cousin Mary Jane, dau. of Bulkeley Price, Esq., of Withington ; *b.* 1851 ; *s.* his grandfather, the late John Price, Esq., J.P. and D.L., and formerly High Sheriff, 1854.—*Plas Cadnant, Menai Bridge, Anglesea.*

PRICE, LLEWELLYN LLOYD, Esq., of Glangwilly, Carmarthenshire.

Eldest son of the late John Lloyd Price, Esq., J.P. and D.L., of Glangwilly, by Sarah Anne, only dau. of Sparkes Martin Phelps. Esq., of Withybush, co. Pembroke ; *b.* 1840 ; *s.* 1862. Is a J.P. and D.L. for co. Carmarthen.—*Glangwilly, Carmarthen.*

Heir Pres., his brother John Lloyd, *b.* 1842.

PRICE, RICHARD JOHN LLOYD, Esq., of Rhiwlas, Merionethshire.

Eldest son of the late Richard John Price, Esq. (who *d.* 1842), by Charlotte, dau. of Edward Lloyd. Esq., of Rhagatt, co. Merioneth; *b.* 1844 ; *s.* his grandfather 1864. Educated at Eton and Ch. Ch., Oxford; is a Magistrate for co. Merioneth (High Sheriff 1868), Lord of the Manor of Penllyn, and Captain in the Merioneth Rifles.—*Rhiwlas, Bala, Merionethshire; Carlton, Boodle's, and Junior Carlton Clubs, s.w.; 8, Duke Street, St. James's, s.w.*

Heir Pres., his cousin H. H. H. Clough. Esq., Chief Constable of Merioneth, *b.* 1820 ; *m.* 1840 Emily, dau. of E. Johnes, Esq., of Cork, and has issue.

PRICE, THOMAS, Esq., of Heywood, Surrey.

Eldest son of the late Thomas Price, Esq., of Muswell Hill, Middlesex, by Harriet, dau. of George Carter, Esq.; *b.* 1797 ; *m.* 1826 Anna Maria. dau. of Richard Hickman, Esq., of Old Swinford. co. Worcester. Was High Sheriff of Surrey 1864.—*Heywood, Cobham ; 29, Upper Bedford Place, w.c.*

PRICE, WILLIAM., Esq., of Glantwrch, Glamorganshire.

Fourth son of the late Rev. Watkin Price. J.P., Rector of Cilybebyll, co. Glamorgan, by Dorothy, dau. of Thomas Penderel, Esq.. of Aberdulais ; *b.* 1802 ; *m.* 1845 Mary, eldest dau. of Elias Jenkins, Esq., of Kilvey House, and has issue.

* Jane Rogers and Dora Penderel.

Mr. Price, who was educated at Cowbridge. and became M.R.C.S. of England 1824, is a Magistrate for co. Brecon.—*Glantwrch, Swansea.*

PRICE, WALTER OWEN, Esq., of Castle Piggin, Carmarthenshire.

Second son of the late Jeremiah Price, Esq., of Glangwilly, co. Carmarthen (who *d.* 1819), by Jane, dau. of Daniel Lloyd, Esq., of Laques, in the same county ; *b.* 1805 ; *m.* 1833 Eleanor, only child of John Evans, Esq., of Glannantcety, co. Cardigan, and has, with other issue,

* Lloyd, *b.* 1834 ; *m.* 1856 Priscilla Willy, only child of James Lewes, Esq., of Cwmhŵr, co. Cardigan. and has, with other issue, * Meredydd Lewes Willy Lloyd, *b.* 1857.

Mr. Price, who was educated at Rugby, represents a family that has been resident at Glangwilly since 1586. —*Castle Piggin, Carmarthen.*

PRICE, WILLIAM PHILIP, of Tibberton Court, Gloucestershire.

Eldest son of the late Wm. Price, Esq., of Gloucester. by Frances, dau. of the late Philip George, Esq., of

Bristol; *b.* 1817; *m.* 1837 Frances Anne, dau. of the late John Chadborn, Esq., and has, with other issue,

* William Edwin, *b.* 1841.

Mr. Price, who is a J.P. and D.L. for Gloucester (High Sheriff 1849), was M.P. for Gloucester 1852–9, re-elected 1865.—*Tibberton Court, Gloucester ; Brooks's and Reform Clubs, s.w.*

PRICE. (See *Green-Price*.)

PRICHARD, the Rev. RICHARD, B.D., of Collenna, Glamorganshire.
Second but eldest surviving son of the late Rev. Richard Prichard, B.D., of Collenna and Landaff (who *d.* 1856), by Eleanor, dau. of Hopkin Llewellyn, Esq., of Margam, co. Glamorgan; *b.* 1811; *s.* his brother 1863; *m.* 1849 Elizabeth, dau. of George Pinchin, Esq., of Bath, Somerset, and has, with other issue,

* George Herbert, *b.* 1853.

Mr. Prichard, who was educated at Jesus College, Oxford (B.A. 1832. M.A. 1834, B.D. 1836), is Rector of Newbold-on-Stour, co. Worcester, and Rural Dean of Kineton South; was formerly Rector of Himley, and Incumbent of St. John's, Kidderminster. — *Collenna, Pontyprudd ; Newbold, Shipston-on-Stour.*

PRICHARD, RICHARD WILLIAMS, Esq., of Dinam, Anglesey.
Second but eldest surviving son of the late Rev. Richard Prichard, of Dinam, by Anne, dau. of John Higgon, Esq., of Tredary, co. Pembroke; *b.* 1798; *s.* 1850; *m.* 1834 Elizabeth, 3rd dau. of the Rev. Robert Housman, of Lancaster (who was a Magistrate for the county during forty years), and has, with other issue,

* Richard Williams, in Holy Orders, M.A. and late Scholar of St. John's, Cambridge, *b.* 1835.

Mr. Prichard is a J.P. and D.L. for co. Anglesey (High Sheriff 1853).—*Dinam, Anglesey ; Parkfield, Birkenhead.*

PRICHARD, of Tyllwyd, Cardiganshire.
(See *Jones-Parry*.)

+PRICKARD, THOMAS, Esq., of Dderw, Radnorshire.
Son of the late Thomas Prickard, Esq.; *b.* 18—; is married, and has issue,

* Thomas Charles, in Holy Orders, M.A., Rector of New Radnor; *b.* 1836; *m.* 1866 Emily Matilda, eldest dau. of the Rev. Augustus James Tharp, and grand-dau. of the late John Tharp, Esq., of Chippenham Park, co. Cambridge.

Mr. Prickard, who was educated at St. Mary's Hall, Oxford (B.A. 1824, M.A. 1832), is a J.P. and D.L. for co. Radnor.—*Dderw, Rhayader.*

PRICKETT, GEORGE, Esq., of Boreas Hill, Yorkshire.
Elder surviving son of the late M. T. Prickett, Esq., of Hull, by Anastasia, dau. of the Rev. John Armitstead, of Cranage Hall, Cheshire; *b.* 1820; *s.* 1861; *m.* 1854 Anna Maria, dau. of the late Sir Charles Dodsworth, Bart., of Thornton Hall, and Newland Park, co. York. Educated at Rugby; is a Magistrate for the E. Riding of co. York, and Major 5th W. Yorkshire Militia. —*Boreas Hill, Hull.*

PRICKETT, THOMAS, Esq., of Bridlington, Yorkshire.
Youngest son of the late Marmaduke Prickett, Esq., of Bridlington, by Elizabeth, dau. of Paul Prickett, Esq., of London; *b.* 1814; *s.* 1841; *m.* 1841 Elizabeth Ann, dau. of the late Rev. John Rollest'on, of Burton Joyce, Notts, and has issue. Is a J.P. and D.L. for the E. Riding of Yorkshire.—*The Avenue, Bridlington.*

PRIDEAUX, Sir EDMUND SAUNDERSON, Bart., of Netherton Hall, Devon (cr. 1622).
Younger but only surviving son of the late Sir John Wilmot Prideaux, Bart., of Netherton (who *d.* 1826), by Phœbe Anne, dau. of — Pridille, Esq.; *b.* 1793; *s.* his brother, the late Sir John Wilmot, as 9th Bart., 1833; *m.* 1st 1832 Frances Mary Anne, dau. of the Rev. William Edward FitzThomas, Esq., of Awliscombe, Devon; 2nd 1841 Caroline, dau. of the late Rev. James Bernard, Rector of Combe Flory, Somerset; 3rd 1842 Frances, dau. of the late Edmund Irton, Esq., of Irton Castle; 4th 1855 Louisa, dau. and co-heir of the late Robert Bodle, Esq., of Woolston Hall, Essex, and widow of George Watlington, Esq., of Caldecote House, Herts. Is a J.P. and D.L. for Devon. and Hon. Col. 1st Exeter and S. Devon Rifles; formerly Major 12th Foot.—*Netherton Hall, Honiton ; United Service Club, s.w.*

PRIDEAUX-BRUNE, CHARLES, Esq., of Prideaux Place, Cornwall.
Eldest son of the late Rev. Charles Prideaux-Brune, of Prideaux Place, by Frances, 4th dau. of Thomas Patten, Esq., of Bank Hall, co. Lancaster; *b.* 1798; *s.* 1833; *m.* 1820 Frances Mary, 2nd dau. of the late Edmund John Glynn, Esq., of Glynn, and has, with other issue,

* Charles Glynn, educated at Ch. Ch., Oxford; a J.P. and D.L. for Cornwall; *b.* 1821; *m.* 1846 the Hon. Ellen Jane, younger dau. of Robert, 1st Lord Carew.

Mr. Prideaux-Brune was High Sheriff of Cornwall 1834.—*Prideaux Place, Padstow ; 20, Charles Street, w.*

+PRIESTLEY, JOHN, Esq., of Hirdrefaig, Anglesea.
Son of the late W. Priestley, Esq., of Hirdrefaig; *b.* 18—; is a J.P. and D.L. for cos. Anglesea and Carnarvon.—*Hirdrefaig, Anglesea.*

PRIESTLEY, Mrs., of Boston House, Yorkshire.
Eliza, 2nd dau. of the late Ven. Archdeacon Paley: *m.* 1808 William Priestley, Esq., who was a J.P. and D.L. for the W. Riding of Yorkshire, and *d.* 1861.—*Boston House, Tadcaster.*

PRIESTLEY, SAMUEL OWEN, Esq., of Trefan, Carnarvonshire.
Son of the late S. Priestley, Esq., of Trefan; *b.* 18—. Is a J.P. and D.L. for co. Carnarvon.—*Trefan, Pwllheli.*

PRIME, ARTHUR, Esq., of Walberton, Sussex.
Eldest son of the late Richard Prime, Esq., J.P. and D.L., of Walberton (who was High Sheriff 1823 and M.P. for W. Sussex 1847–54) by Anne, dau. of the late James Shuttleworth, Esq., of Gawthorpe Hall, co. Lancaster: *b.* 1819; *s.* 1866; *m.* 1855 Matilda, dau. of the Rev. Robert Machell, of Beverley, co. York. Educated at Eton; is a Magistrate for Sussex; late of the 5th Dragoon Guards.—*Walberton House, Arundel.*

PRIME, CHARLES EDWARD, Esq., of Hitchin, Herts.
Second son of the late Richard Prime, Esq., M.P., of Walberton, Sussex (who *d.* 1866), by Anne, dau. of the late James Shuttleworth, Esq., of Gawthorpe Hall, co. Lancaster; *b.* 1821; *m.* 1st 1843 Eleanor Caroline, dau. of G. Wynne, Esq., of Dublin (she *d.* 1844); 2nd 1848 Elizabeth, dau. of James Donovan, Esq., of Buckham Hill, Sussex, and has surviving issue, two daus.,

Hannah Augusta and Amy Eleanor.

Mr. Prime is a Magistrate for Herts and Beds.—*The Hermitage, Hitchin.*

PRIMROSE, the Hon. BOUVERIE FRANCIS.
Second son of Archibald John, 4th Earl of Rosebery (by his 1st wife Harriet, dau. of the Hon. Bartholomew Bouverie); *b.* 1813; *m.* 1838 the Hon. Frederica Sophia,

5th dau. of Thomas, 1st Viscount Anson, and by her, who *d.* 1867, has, with other issue,

* Francis Archibald, *b.* 1843.

Mr. Primrose, who is Capt. Edinburgh Rifle Volunteers, and Secretary of Boards of Manufactures and Fisheries, Scotland, was formerly Receiver-General of the Post Office, Scotland.—*22, Moray Place, Edinburgh.*

PRIMROSE.   (See under *Rosebery, Earl of.*)

PRINGLE, Sir JOHN, Bart., of New Hall, Selkirkshire (cr. 1683).
Eldest son of the late Sir James Pringle, Bart., of New Hall, by Elizabeth, dau. of Norman Macleod, Esq., of Macleod; *b.* 1784; *s.* 1809; *m.* 1st 1809 Emilia Anne, dau. of General Norman Macleod, of .Macleod; 2nd 1831 Lady Elizabeth Maitland Campbell, dau. of John, 1st Marquis of Breadalbane.   Educated at Edinburgh; is a J.P. and D.L. for co. Berwick, and Vice-Lieutenant of co. Roxburgh; was formerly Capt. 12th Light Dragoons.—*New Hall, Selkirk, N.B.; Langton House, Dunse; Moness House, Aberfeldy;* 57, *Cleveland Square, w.*

PRINGLE, ALEXANDER, Esq., of Whytbank, Selkirkshire.
Only son of the late Alexander Pringle, Esq., M.P., of Whytbank (Clerk and Keeper of Registers of Sessions in Scotland), by Agnes Joanna, dau. of the late Sir William Dick, Bart., of Prestonfield; *b.* 1837; *s.* 1857. Educated at Edinburgh Academy and Trinity Coll. Cambridge (B.A. 1860, M.A. 1863); called to the Scottish Bar 1863; is a Magistrate for co. Selkirk, and Cornet Midlothian Yeomanry Cavalry.—*Whytbank and Yair, Selkirk, N.B.*

Heir Pres., his cousin William John, *b.* 1831.

PRINGLE, DAVID, Esq., of Wilton Lodge, Roxburghshire.
Fifth son of the late Alexander Pringle, Esq., M.P., of Whytbank, co. Selkirk, by Mary, dau. of Sir Alexander Dick, Bart., of Prestonfield; *b.* 1806 ; *m.* 1st 1835 Frances, dau. of Alexander Tod, Esq., of Alderston; 2nd 1858 Mary, only dau. and heir of James Anderson, Esq., of Wilton Lodge.   Is a Magistrate for co. Roxburgh; formerly in the Bengal Civil Service.—*Wilton Lodge, Hawick, N.B.; New Club, Edinburgh, N.B.*

PRINGLE, Lieut. JAMES THOMAS, of Torwoodlee, Selkirkshire.
Eldest son of the late Admiral James Pringle, of Torwoodlee (who was a J.P. and D.L. for co. Selkirk), by May, dau. of J. Frazer, Esq., of Invermay ; *b.* 1832 ; *s.* 1859 ; *m.* 1862 Ann Parminter, only child of the late Lieut.-Col. John Lewis Black, and has issue. Lieut. Pringle is a Magistrate for cos. Selkirk and Roxburgh, and a Lieut. R.N.   This family is said to be an off-shoot of the Pringles of Gala.—*Torwoodlee, Galashiels, N.B.*

PRINGLE, Mrs. DOUGLAS-, of The Haining, Selkirkshire.
Margaret Violet, dau. of the late Mark Pringle, Esq., M.P., of The Haining ; *s.* her brother, Robert Pringle, Esq., M.P., 1841 ; *m.* 1824 Archibald Douglas, Esq., of Edderstane, and has issue,

* Anne Elizabeth.

This family have represented Selkirkshire in Parliament for five generations.—*The Haining, Selkirk, N.B.*

PRINGLE, ROBERT KEITH, Esq., of Darleydale, Derbyshire.
Fourth son of the late Alexander Pringle. Esq., of Whytbank, co. Selkirk (who *d.* 1827), by Mary, dau. of Sir Alexander Dick, Bart., of Prestonfield. Midlothian ; *b.* 1802 ; *m.* 1848 Mary Jane, eldest dau. of

772

Lieut.-General George Moore, of H.M.'s Bombay Army, late Military Auditor-General at Bombay, and has, with other issue,

* Alexander, *b.* 1850.

Mr. Pringle, who was educated at the High School of Edinburgh and Haileybury Coll., is a Magistrate for co. Derby ; was formerly in the Bombay Civil Service, and Chief Secretary to the Government of Bombay.—*The Grove, Darleydale, Matlock.*

PRINGLE.   (See *Hughes.*)

PRINSEP, HENRY THOBY, Esq.
Fourth son of the late Alderman John Prinsep, of London, M.P., by Elizabeth, dau. of James Auriol, Esq., of Languedoc, France ; *b.* 1792 ; *m.* 1835 Sara, 3rd dau. of James Pattle, Esq., H.E.I.C.S., and has, with other issue,

* Henry Thoby, in the Bengal Civil Service ; *b.* 1837.

Mr. Prinsep, who was educated at Haileybury Coll., is a Dep. Lieut. for London, and a Member of the India Council, late a Dr. of the E.I.C., was formerly in the Bengal C.S.; was M.P. for Harwich March-May, 1851.—*Carlton Club, s.w.; Little Holland House, Kensington, w.*

PRIOR, Sir JAMES, Knt. (cr. 1858).
Son of the late Matthew Prior, Esq., of Lisburn, co. Antrim ; *b.* 1790 ; *m.* 1st 1817 Dorothea, widow of E. James, Esq.; 2nd 1847 Caroline, widow of Charles H. Watson, Esq.   Is Deputy Inspector-General of Hospitals and Fleets ; Author of ' Life of Burke,' &c.—*20, Norfolk Crescent, Hyde Park, w.*

PRIOR, CHARLES BUTLER, of Crossoge, co. Tipperary.
Eldest son of the Rev. John Prior, Rector of Kirklington, co. York, by his 2nd wife, Sarah Butler, dau. of the late Hon. Charles B. C. S. Wandesforde and of Lady Sarah, 4th dau. of Henry, 2nd Earl of Carrick ; *b.* 1840; *m.* 1866 Dora, eldest dau. of Richard Phillips, Esq., of Yaile House, co. Tipperary, and has, with other issue,

* A son, *b.* 1868.

Mr. Prior is a Magistrate for co. Tipperary.—*Crossoge, Thurles, co. Tipperary.*

PRIOR, the Rev. JOHN LAURENCE, of Lynby, Notts.
Only son of the late Andrew Redmond Prior, Esq., of Brighton, Sussex : by Catherine, youngest dau. of the late Sir John Call, Bart., of Whiteford House, Cornwall; *b.* 1821 ; *m.* 1847 Emma Catherine, dau. of the late Sir William Lawrence Young. Bart.. of Delaford and Bradenham House, Bucks : and has, with other issue,

* George Redmond, *b.* 1849.

Mr. Prior was educated at Exeter Coll., Oxford (B.A. 1842, M.A.1846); is a Magistrate for Essex and Notts, and Rector of Lyuby with Papplewick ; formerly Vicar of Maldon, Essex.—*Lynby Rectory, Nottingham.*

PRIOR, RICHARD CHANDLER ALEXANDER, Esq., M.D., of Halse House, Somerset.
Eldest son of the late Richard Hayward Alexander, Esq., of Corsham, Wilts, by Mary, eldest dau. of George Prior, Esq., of Halse House, Somerset ; *b.* 1809 ; *s.* 1859.   Educated at the Charterhouse and Wadham Coll., Oxford (B.A. 1830, M.D. 1836).   Is a Magistrate for Somerset, Fellow of the Royal Coll. of Physicians of London, and of the Linnæan and other Societies. Assumed the name of Prior under the will of his maternal uncle, Edward Prior.—*Halse House, Taunton : Union Club, s.w.;* 48, *York Terrace, Regent's Park, N.W.*

Heir Pres., his brother George, *b.* 1810 ; *m.* 1845 Elizabeth Maria, only dau. of John Baby Hasler, Esq., of Ca'ton Hall, Norfolk.

PRITCHARD, HENRY, Esq., of Trescawen, Anglesea.
Eldest surviving son of the late W. Pritchard, Esq., of Trescawen, by Ellen, dau. of W. Rowland, Esq., of Holyhead ; b. 1800 ; s. his brother 1855 ; m. 1837 Martha, dau. of J. Moulsdale, Esq., of Bryndyfryn, and has issue,

    • Henry, b. 1838.

Mr. Pritchard, who was educated at Shrewsbury and Jesus Coll., Oxford, is a J.P. and D.L. for Anglesea (High Sheriff 1829).—*Trescawen, Anglesea.*

PRITCHARD, JOHN, Esq., of Broseley, Shropshire.
Only surviving son of the late John Pritchard, Esq., Banker, of Bridgenorth (who d. 1861) ; b. 1797 ; m. 1847 Jane, dau. of George Osborn Gordon, Esq. Called to the Bar at Lincoln's Inn 1841 ; is a J.P. and D.L. for co. Salop, and a Banker at Bridgenorth ; has been M.P. for Bridgenorth since 1853.—*High Street, Broseley, Salop ; 89, Eaton Square, s.w.*

PRITCHARD. (See *Sergison.*)

PRITTIE, the Hon. GEORGE PONSONBY, of Oakville, co. Tipperary.
Second son of the late Hon. Francis Aldborough Prittie, of Corville, co. Tipperary, by his 2nd wife, Elizabeth, dau. of the late Right Hon. George Ponsonby, and next brother of Henry, 3rd Lord Dunalley ; b. 1809 ; m. 1841 Henrietta Hester, only dau. of the late Lieut.-Col. Gregory. Is Clerk of the Peace for co. Tipperary. —*Oakville, Clonmel.*

PRITTIE, FRANCIS WILLIAM, Esq., of The Lodge, Clonmel, co. Tipperary.
Elder surviving son of the late Hon. Francis Sadleir Prittie, of Clonmel, by his 1st wife Mary, only child of the Hon. Peter Roso, of Rose House, Georgetown, Demerara ; b. 1839 ; s. 1867. Was formerly Lieut. 97th Foot.—*The Lodge, Clonmel, co. Tipperary.*

    Heir Pres., his brother Edward, b. 1851.

PRITTIE. (See under *Dunalley, Lord.*)

PROBY. (See under *Carysfort, Earl of.*)

PROBY, the Hon. WILLIAM.
Younger surviving son of Granville Leveson, 3rd Earl of Carysfort, by Isabella, 2nd dau. of the Hon. Hugh Howard ; b. 1836 ; m. 1860 Charlotte Mary, eldest dau. of the Rev. R. B. Heathcote, Rector of Chingford, Essex. Educated at Eton and Trinity Coll., Cambridge (M.A. 1859), is a Magistrate for co. Wicklow (High Sheriff 1866), and Capt. Wicklow Militia Rifles.—*Glenart Castle, Arklow ; Kildare Street Club, Dublin.*

PROBYN, EDMUND, Esq., of Longhope Manor, Gloucestershire.
Eldest son of the late John Probyn, Esq., J.P. and D.L., of Longhope Manor (Capt. S. Gloucestershire Militia), by Anna, younger dau. of the late Thomas Lloyd, Esq., of Coldmore, co. Cardigan ; b. 1825 ; s. 1863 ; m. 1853 Charlotte Seymour, 2nd dau. of John Jones, Esq., of Derry Ormond, co. Cardigan. Mr. Probyn, who is a J.P. and D.L. for co. Gloucester, Lord of the Manor of Longhope, Patron of 2 livings, and Capt. Gloucestershire Yeomanry Cavalry, was formerly Lieut. 6th Dragoon Guards.—*Longhope Manor, Gloucester.*

PROCTOR-BEAUCHAMP, Sir THOMAS WILLIAM BROGRAVE, Bart., of Langley Park, Norfolk (cr. 1744).
Eldest son of the late Admiral Sir William Beauchamp-Proctor, Bart., J.P. and D.L., of Langley Park, by

Anne, dau. of Thomas Gregory, Esq. ; b. 1815 ; s. as 4th Bart. 1861 ; m. 1852 the Hon. Caroline Esther, dau. of Granville George, 2nd Lord Radstock. Is a J.P. and D.L. for Norfolk (on roll for High Sheriff 1869), Lord of the Manor of Langley, and Patron of 4 livings. The additional name of Proctor was assumed by the 1st Bart. under the will of his maternal uncle, George Proctor, Esq., of Langley.—*Langley Park, Norwich.*

    Heir, his son Reginald William, b. 1853.

PRODGERS, the Rev. EDWIN.
Eldest son of the late Rev. Edwin Prodgers (who was a J.P. for Herts and Surrey, and many years Rector of Ayot St. Peter), by Caroline, dau. and coheiress of John Blades, Esq., of Brockwell Hall, Surrey, (she d. 1863) ; b. 1833 ; s. 1861 ; m. 1864 Elizabeth Ellen, eldest dau. of Henry E. Surtees, Esq., M.P., of Dane End, Herts. Educated at Ch. Ch., Oxford (B.A. 1855) ; appointed Rector of Ayot St. Peter 1862 ; is a Magistrate for Herts, and Patron of 1 living.—*Ayot Bury, Welwyn, Herts ; Oxford and Cambridge Club, s.w.*

PRODGERS, HERBERT, Esq., of Kington House, Wiltshire.
Son of the late Rev. Edwin Prodgers, Rector of Ayot, Herts, by Caroline, dau. of John Blades, Esq., of Brockwell Hall ; b. 1835 ; m. 1860 Emily Sibella, eldest dau. of the Rev. Thomas Phillpotts, of Porthgwidden, Cornwall, and has, with other issue,

    • Cecil Herbert, b. 1861.

Mr. Prodgers, who was educated at Eton and Ch. Ch., Oxford, is a Magistrate for Wilts. This family is of Welsh origin, and formerly lived at Gwarnadee, co. Monmouth (see 'Cox's Monmouthshire').—*Kington House, Kington St. Michael, Chippenham ; Junior Carlton Club, s.w.*

PROPERT, JOHN LUMSDEN, Esq., of Blaenpistill, Cardiganshire.
Eldest son of the late John Propert, Esq., D.L., of Blaenpistill, by Julia Ann, dau. of Robert Ross, Esq., of Cork, (who was High Sheriff of co. Cardigan 1857) ; b. 1834 ; s. 1867 ; m. 1864 Mary Jessica, eldest dau. of W. S. P. Hughes, Esq., of Powick, co. Worcester. Is Lord of the Manor of Blaenpistill. —*Blaenpistill, Cardigan ; 6, New Cavendish Street, w.*

PROSSER, FRANCIS RICHARD WEGG-, Esq., of Belmont, Herefordshire.
Only son of the late Rev. Francis Haggitt, D.D., Rector of Nunclum Courtenay, Oxon. and Prebendary of Durham, by Lucy, 3rd dau. of William Parry, Esq., of King Street, co. Hereford ; b. 1824. Assumed the name of Wegg-Prosser on succeeding, in 1849, to the property of his uncle, the late Rev. Richard Prosser, D.D., of Belmont, Prebendary of Durham ; m. 1850 Lady Harriet Catharine, 2nd dau. of John, 2nd Earl Somers, and has, with other issue,

    • John Francis, b. 1854.

Mr. Wegg-Prosser, who was educated at Eton and Balliol Coll., Oxford (B.A. 1845), is a J.P. and D.L. for co. Hereford (High Sheriff 1855) ; he was M.P. for Herefordshire 1847-52.—*Belmont, Hereford ; Carlton Club, s.w. ; Stafford Club, s.w.*

+PROTHERO, Lieut.-Col. EDWARD, of Hooton Roberts, Yorkshire.
Son of the late E. Prothero, Esq., of Hooton Roberts ; b. 18—. Is a Dep. Lieut. for the W. Riding of Yorkshire, Lord of the Manor of Hooton Roberts, and Lieut.-Col. in the 3rd W. York Militia.—*Hooton Roberts, Doncaster.*

PROTHERO, the Rev. THOMAS, of Malpas Court, Monmouthshire.

Eldest son of the late Thomas Prothero, Esq., of Malpas Court (who was High Sheriff of co. Monmouth 1846), by Mary, dau. of John Collins, Esq., of Ingatestone, co. Hereford; *b.* 1811; *s.* 1854; *m.* 1837 Georgiana Mary, only dau. of the Rev. Matthew Marsh, Chancellor of Salisbury, and has, with other issue,

* Francis Thomas Egerton, educated at Eton and Balliol Coll., Oxford. *b.* 1837; *m.* 1864 Mary Frances Susanna, only dau. of the Rev. Francis Lewis, of St. Pierre, co. Monmouth.

Mr. Prothero, who was educated at the Charterhouse and Brasenose Coll., Oxford (B.A. 1834, M.A. 1837), is a J.P and D.L. for co. Monmouth, Patron of 1 living and Chaplain to the Queen; was formerly Chaplain in Ordinary to H.R.H. the late Prince Consort.—*Malpas Court, Newport, Monmouthshire.*

PROTHEROE, Mrs., of Dolewilim, Carmarthenshire.

Only child and heir of the late Evan Protheroe, Esq., J.P. and D.L., of Dolewilim, by Emma, dau. of Percival Hart, Esq., of Roxeth, Middlesex, and widow of David Garrick, Esq., of Hampton, Capt. 1st Dragoons; *m.* 1819 William Garrick Bridges Schaw, Capt. 46th Regt. (son of the late Lieut.-Col. F. B. Schaw, of Weston Park, Surrey), who took the name of Protheroe on his marriage, and who *d.* 1856, leaving, with other surviving issue,

* Edward Schaw, Surgeon-Major Royal Artillery, *b.* 1822; *m.* 1859 Ellen Augusta Cecilia, dau. of S. T. Beynon, Esq., of Trewern, co. Pembroke.

The family of Protheroe have been settled in Carmarthenshire for many centuries. The Schaws are of Scotch origin, being originally from Greenock, and related by marriage to the Cathcarts and other noble families.—*Dolewilim, St. Clear's.*

PROWER, JOHN ELTON MERVIN, Esq., of Purton House, Wilts.

Only son of the Rev. Canon Prower, by Susan, dau. and heir of the late John Coles, Esq., of Cadoxton, co. Glamorgan; *b.* 1811; *m.* 1844 Harriet, dau. of the late William Payn, Esq., of Kidwells, Berks, and has, with other surviving issue,

* John Elton, *b.* 1852.

Mr. Prower, who was educated at the Charterhouse, is a J.P. and D.L. for Wilts (High Sheriff 1862), and Major R. Wilts Militia; was formerly Capt. 67th Foot. —*Purton House, Swindon; Garrick Club, w.c.*

PRYCE, JOHN, Esq., of Penns Rocks, Sussex.

Third and only surviving son of the late Thomas Pryce, Esq., of Losden Hall, Beds (who *d.* 1831), by Elizabeth, dau. of — Mercer, Esq., of Hendon, Middlesex; *b.* 1799; *m.* 1838 Dora Isabella, dau. of Major-General Beatson, of Knowle, Sussex, and has, with other issue,

* Alexander, *b.* 1841.

Mr. Pryce, who is a Magistrate for Sussex, represents a family of Welsh extraction.—*Penns Rocks, Wilkyam, Tunbridge Wells.*

PRYCE, JOHN BRUCE-, Esq., of Duffryn, Glamorganshire.

Eldest son of the late John Knight, Esq., of Fairlinch, Devon, and Llanblethian, co. Glamorgan, by Margaret, dau. of William Bruce, Esq., of Llanblethian; *b.* 1784; *m.* 1st 1807 Sarah, dau. of the Rev. Hugh Williams Austin, of Barbados (she *d.* 1812); 2nd 1814 Alicia Grant, dau. of William Bushby, Esq., of Kirkmichael, co. Dumfries, and had, with other issue,

John Wyndham, *b.* 1809; *d.* 1868, having *m.* 1835 Marianne, dau. of Col. Cameron, of Swansea, and left, with other issue,
* Alan Cameron, *b.* 1836; *m.* 1858 Louisa, only child of the late Lieut.-Col. J. H. Slade.

Mr. Bruce-Pryce, who was educated at Sherborne
774

School and Exeter Coll., Oxford, is a J.P. and D.L. for cos. Brecon and Glamorgan (High Sheriff 1843), and Patron of 2 livings.—*Duffryn, Cardiff.*

PRYCE, Mrs., of Gunley, Montgomeryshire.

Eliza, only child and heir of John Williams, Esq.; *m.* 1856 the Rev. Richard Henry Mostyn Pryce, who *d. s. p.* 1859. Is Lady of the Manor of Gunley, which has been in the possession of the Pryce family for two centuries.—*Gunley Hall, Chirbury.*

PRYCE, ROBERT DAVIES, Esq., of Cyfronydd, Montgomeryshire.

Eldest son of the late Pryce Jones, Esq., of Cyfronydd, by Jane, dau. of the late John Davies, Esq., of Aberllefenny, co. Merioneth; *b.* 1820; *s.* 1858, when he assumed the surname of Pryce; *m.* 1849 Jane, dau. of St. John Chiverton Charlton, Esq., of Apley Castle, co. Salop, and has, with other issue,

* Athelstane Robert, *b.* 1850.

Mr. Pryce, who was educated at Rugby and St. John's Coll., Cambridge (B.A. 1842), and is a J.P. and D.L. for cos. Montgomery and Merioneth (High Sheriff 1848), Capt. Montgomeryshire Yeomanry.—*Cyfronydd, Welshpool, Montgomeryshire; Trefrifach, Machynlleth, Merionethshire; Oxford and Cambridge Club, s.w.*

PRYCE, of Pigeonsford. (See *Jordan.*)

PRYME, GEORGE, Esq., of Wistow, Hunts.

Eldest son of the late Christopher Pryme, Esq., of Cottingham, co. York (who *d.* 1781), by Alice, dau. of George Dinsdale, Esq., of Nappa Hall, co. York; *b.* 1781; *m.* 1813 Jane Townley, dau. of Thomas Thackeray, Esq., and has issue,

* Charles De la Pryme, M.A. of Trinity Coll., Cambridge; *b.* 1815.

Professor Pryme was educated at Trinity Coll., Cambridge (B.A. 1803, M.A. 1806), and was for some years Fellow of Trinity, called to the Bar at Lincoln's Inn 1806, and appointed the first Professor of Political Economy in the University of Cambridge 1828. is a Magistrate for Hunts; was M.P. for Cambridge 1832-41. The family of the De la Prymes is one of about eighty Protestant refugee families who migrated from France and the Netherlands to Yorkshire about 1628.—*Wistow, Huntingdon; Reform Club, s.w.*

PRYOR, ARTHUR, Esq., of Hylands, Essex.

Third son of the late Vickris Pryor, Esq., of Baldock, Herts, by Jane Ann, dau. of John Peacock, Esq., of London; *b.* 1816; *m.* 1841 Elizabeth Sophia, eldest dau. of Tomkyns Dew, Esq., of Whitney Court, co. Hereford, and has, with other issue,

* Arthur Vickris, *b.* 1846.

Mr. Pryor, who is a J.P. and D.L. for Essex (High Sheriff 1866), purchased Hylands of Mr. John Attwood in 1858.—*Hylands, Chelmsford.*

PRYOR, MARLBOROUGH, Esq., of Weston, Herts.

Eldest son of the late Thomas Marlborough Pryor, Esq., of Hampstead, Middlesex, by Hannah, dau. of the late Samuel Hoare, Esq., of Hampstead; *b.* 1807; *m.* 1837 Eleanor, dau. of the late William L. Rogers, Esq., of Hampstead. Is a Magistrate for Beds, Herts, and Middlesex, and for the city of Westminster. —*Weston, Stevenage.*

+PRYOR, MORRIS, Esq., of Baldock Manor and Clay Hall, Hertfordshire.

Second son of the late John Izard Pryor, Esq., of Clay Hall, Herts; *b.* 18—; *m.* 1838 Louisa Mary, youngest dau. of the late Edward F. Colston, Esq., of Filkins Hall, Oxon. Is a Magistrate for Herts and a Brewer at Baldock.—*The Manor House, Baldock, Herts; Clay Hall, Walkern, Stevenage.*

PRYOR, ROBERT, Esq., of High Elms, Herts.
Younger son of the late Thomas Marlborough Pryor, Esq., of Hampstead, Middlesex, by Hannah, dau. of the late Samuel Hoare, Esq., of Hampstead; b. 1812; m. 1844 Elizabeth Caroline, dau. of the late Wyrley Birch, Esq., of Wretham Hall, Norfolk, and has, with other issue,

• Marlborough Robert, b. 1848.

Mr. R. Pryor, who was educated at Trinity Coll., Cambridge (B.A. 1834, M.A. 1837), and called to the Bar at Lincoln's Inn 1837, is a Magistrate for Herts (High Sheriff 1868).—High Elms, Watford; Athenæum, and Oxford and Cambridge Clubs, s.w.

PRYOR, THOMAS, Esq., of Baldock, Herts.
Fourth son of the late Vickris Pryor, Esq., of Baldock, by Jane Anne, dau. of J. Peacock, Esq.; b. 1826; m. 1857 Mary Matilda Willoughby, dau. of Augustus Foster, Esq., of Warmwell House, Dorset. Educated at Eton and Ch. Ch., Oxford; is a Magistrate for Herts, and Lord of the Manor of Baldock.—The Elms, Baldock.

Heir Pres., his brother Felix, b. 1814; m. 1845 Helen Mary, dau. of the late Sir John Norton.

PRYSE, Sir PRYSE, Bart., of Gogerddan, Cardiganshire (cr. 1866).
Eldest son of the late Pryse Loveden (formerly Pryse), Esq., M.P., of Gogerddan, and of Buscot Park, Berks (who d. 1855), by Margaretta Jane, dau. of the late Walter Rice, Esq., of Llyn-y-brain, co. Carmarthen; b. 1837; m. 1859 Louisa Joan, youngest dau. of Capt. Lewes, of Llanlear, co. Cardigan. Is a J.P. and D.L. for co. Cardigan (High Sheriff 1861); resumed the original family name of Pryse by Royal licence in 1863.—Gogerddan, Aberystwith; Junior United Service and Brooks's Clubs, s.w.

Heir, his son Pryse, b. 1859.

PRYSE, EDWARD LEWIS, Esq., of Peithyll, Cardiganshire.
Second son of the late Pryse Pryse, Esq., M.P., of Gogerddan, co. Cardigan, by his 2nd wife Jane, dau. of Peter Cavallier, Esq., of Whitby; b. 1817; is Lord Lieutenant of co. Cardigan; elected M.P. for Cardigan 1857; was formerly Capt. 6th Dragoon Guards.—Peithyll, Aberystwith; Army and Navy Club, s.w.

PRYSE, JOHN PUGH VAUGHAN-, Esq., of Bwlchbychan, Cardiganshire.
Youngest son of the late Pryse Pryse, Esq., M.P., of Gogerddan, co. Cardigan, and of Buscot Park, Berks, by Jane, dau. of Peter Cavallier, Esq., of Whitby, co. York; b. 1818; m. 1st 1844 Mary Anne, 2nd dau. of John Walters Philips. Esq., of Aberglasney (she d. 1851, leaving one daughter); 2nd 1853 Decima Dorothea, youngest dau. of the late Walter Rice, Esq., of Llwyngbrain, co. Carmarthen, and has, with other issue,

• John Carbery Pugh, b. 1862.

Mr. Vaughan-Pryse is a J.P. and D.L. for co. Cardigan; he assumed the additional surname of Vaughan in 1866.—Bwlchbychan, Carmarthen.

PUDSEY. (See Aston-Pudsey.)

PUGET, JOHN, Esq., F.R.G.S., of Pointer's Grove, Herts.
Eldest son of the late John Hey Puget, Esq., of Pointer's Grove, by Isabella, dau. of F. Hawkins, Esq., a Judge in India; b. 1829; s. 1867; m. 1863 Florence Annie, 3rd dau. of Anselm de Arroyave, Esq., of Palace Gardens, Kensington. Educated at Trinity Coll., Cambridge (B.A. 1849, M.A. 1854); is Major 8th Hussars. —Pointer's Grove, Totteridge.

PUGH, CHARLES VAUGHAN, Esq., of Llanerchydol, Montgomeryshire.
Only son of the late David Pugh, Esq., M.P., of Llanerchydol, J.P. and D.L., by Anne, only dau. of Evan Vaughan, Esq., of Beguildy, co. Radnor (she d. 1863); b. 1818; s. 1862; m. 1849 Felicia Harriet, dau. of the late Capt. George Gosling, R.N. Educated at Eton; is a Dep. Lieut. for co. Montgomery, and Lord of the Manor of Llanerchydol; was formerly Capt. 90th Light Infantry.—Llanerchydol and Eynant, Welshpool; Junior United Service Club, s.w.; 10, Arlington Street, s.w.

Heir Pres., his sister Mary, m. 1856 Capt. J. S. Willes Johnson, R.N., M.P., who d. 1863, leaving issue, • three daughters.

PUGH, DAVID, Esq., of Manoravon, Carmarthenshire.
Eldest son of Col. Pugh, D.L., of Manoravon (formerly High Sheriff of co. Carmarthen), by Elizabeth, dau. of W. Beynon, Esq., of Trewern, co. Pembroke; b. 1806. Educated at Rugby and Balliol Coll., Oxford; called to the Bar at the Inner Temple 1837; is a Magistrate for co. Carmarthen, and a Dep. Lieut. for co. Cardigan; has been M.P. for co. Carmarthen since 1857.—Manoravon, Llandilo; Oxford and Cambridge Club, s.w.; 4, Paper Buildings, Temple, E.C.

PUGH. (See Bockett-Pugh, in Supplement.)

PULESTON, Sir RICHARD PRICE, Bart., of Emral, Flintshire (cr. 1813).
Eldest son of the late Sir Richard Puleston, Bart., of Emral (formerly Col. Royal Flintshire Militia, and Capt. Shropshire Militia), by his 1st wife Anne, dau. of Lieut.-General England; b. 1813; s. 1860; m. 1853 Catherine Judith, dau. of the late Richard Fountayne Wilson, Esq., of Melton Park, co. York. Is a Magistrate for co. Flint, and Patron of 2 livings; late Capt. 44th Foot.—Emral, Wrexham.

Heir Pres., his nephew Richard Puleston, Esq., b. 1848.

+PULESTON, the Rev. THEOPHILUS GRESLEY HENRY, of Worthenbury, Flintshire.
Second son of the late Sir Richard Puleston, Bart., of Emral, co. Flint, by his 2nd wife Elizabeth, dau. of John Shaw, Esq. (who d. 1847); b. 1823; m. 1849 Mary Christian Anne, dau. of the late Rev. W. S. Marvin, Vicar of Shrewsbury. Educated at Brasenose Coll., Oxford (B.A. 1845); is a Magistrate for co. Flint, and Rector of Worthenbury.—Worthenbury, Wrexham.

PULLEINE, JAMES, Esq., F.G.S., of Clifton Castle, Yorkshire.
Second but eldest surviving son of the late Henry Percy Pulleine, Esq., of Crake Hall, co. York, by Elizabeth, dau. of A. Askew, Esq., of Queen's Square, London; b. 1804; s. 1833; m. 1841 Annie Caroline, eldest dau. of Edward Marjoribanks, Esq., and has issue,

• Georgina Elizabeth.

Mr. Pulleine, who was educated at Trinity Coll., Cambridge (B.A. 1827, M.A. 1831), and called to the Bar at the Middle Temple 1832, is a J.P. and D.L. for the N. Riding of Yorkshire; was formerly Chairman of the North-Eastern Railway Company; and Chairman of Quarter Sessions for the N. Riding of Yorkshire. He inherited the Clifton Castle estate 1863, under the will of the late Timothy Hutton, Esq.—Clifton Castle, Bedale; Oxford and Cambridge Club, s.w.

PULLER, ARTHUR GILES GILES-, Esq., of Youngsbury, Herts.
Eldest son of the late Christopher William Giles-Puller, Esq., J.P. and D.L., of Youngsbury, late M.P. for Herts (who assumed the additional name of Giles in 1857), by Emily, youngest dau. of the late William Blake, Esq.; b. 1833; s. 1864. Educated at Eton and

Trinity Coll., Cambridge (B.A. 1855, M.A. 1859); called to the Bar at Lincoln's Inn 1861; is a Magistrate for Herts, Lord of the Manor of Youngsbury, and an Officer in the South Herts Yeomanry.—*Youngsbury, Ware; Athenæum and Arthur's Clubs, s.w.*

Heir Pres., his brother Charles, M.A., and Fellow of Trinity Coll., Cambridge, Vicar of Standon, Herts; *b.* 1834.

PULLING, Mr. Serjeant ALEXANDER, of Newark Park, Gloucestershire.

Eldest son of the late Capt. George C. Pulling, R.N., of St. Arvans, co. Monmouth, by Elizabeth, dau. of Robert Moser, Esq., and niece of Richard Crawshay, Esq., of Cyfarthfa, co. Glamorgan; *b.* 1813; *m.* 1855 Elizabeth, dau. of Luke Hopkinson, Esq., and niece of General Sir Charles Hopkinson, C.B., and has, with other issue,

* Alexander, *b.* 1857.

Mr. Serjeant Pulling, who was called to the Bar at the Inner Temple 1843, and became Serjeant-at-Law 1864. is a Magistrate for co. Gloucester. He purchased this property in 1867.—*Newark Park, Wotton-under-Edge; 3, Crown Office Row, Temple, E.C.*

PULTENEY, JOHN GRANVILLE BEAUMONT, Esq., of Northerwood, Hants.

Eldest son of the late John Apsley Pulteney, Esq., of Northerwood (formerly Capt. 12th Lancers), by Emily, 3rd dau. of C. T. Tower, Esq., of Weald Hall, Essex; *b.* 1836; *s.* 1856. Educated at Harrow; is Lord of the Manors of Old and New Lymington, and Pennington. —*Northerwood, Lyndhurst; 10, Rutland Gate, s.w.*

Heir Pres., his uncle the Rev. Richard Thomas Pulteney, of the Hargreaves, Stanstead, Essex (youngest son of the late John Pulteney, Esq., by Elizabeth Evelyn, dau. of the late Sir R. Sutton, Bart.); *b.* 1811; *m.* 1845 Emma, dau. of M. D. Dalison, Esq., of Hamptons, Kent. Educated at Trinity Coll., Oxford (B.A. 1833); appointed Rector of Ashley, co. Northampton, 1853.

PURCELL, JOHN MATHEW, Esq., of Burton, co. Cork.

Only son of the late John Mathew Purcell, Esq., J.P. and D.L., of Burton Park, by Anna Maria, dau. of M. K. Dempsey, Esq., of Kildare; *b.* 1852; *s.* 1853. Is a ward of the Court of Chancery.—*Burton Park, Churchtown, co. Cork.*

PURCELL, PETER VALENTINE, Esq., of Halverstown House, co. Kildare.

Eldest son of the late Peter Valentine Purcell, Esq., of Halverstown House (formerly Capt. 13th Light Dragoons), by Agnes Maria, 8th dau. of Sir John Hesketh Lethbridge, Bart.; *b.* 1859; *s.* 1864. This family, formerly settled in co. Waterford, is of Norman extraction.—*Halverstown House, Kilcullen, co. Kildare.*

PURCELL, PIERCE, Esq., of Dromore, co. Cork.

Eldest son of the late James Purcell, Esq., of Dromore, by Ellen, dau. of W. P. Williamson, Esq.; *b.* 1811; *s.* 1830; *m.* 1856 Alicia Ellen, 2nd dau. of the late Richard Wills Cason, Esq., J.P. and D.L., of Richmond, co. Tipperary, and has, with other issue,

* James Charles Henry, *b.* 1859.

Mr. Purcell is a Magistrate for co. Cork.—*Dromore, Mallow, co. Cork.*

PURCELL. (See *Williams-Purcell.*)

PURCELL-FITZGERALD. (See *Fitzgerald.*)

PURDON, GEORGE FREDERICK ROBERT PONSONBY-, Esq., of Tinerana, co. Clare.

Second but eldest surviving son of the late Simon George Purdon, Esq., of Tinerana, J.P. and D.L. (who was High Sheriff of co. Clare 1829, and *d.* 1862), by the Hon. Louisa Elizabeth Eleanor, dau. of the late Hon. and Right Rev. Richard Ponsonby, D.D., Bishop of Derry,

and sister of William, 4th Lord Ponsonby; *b.* 1840; *s.* his brother 1864; *m.* 1867 Anne, only dau. of the late Major-Gen. James Caulfeild, of Copsewood. co. Limerick. Is Lord of the Manor of Tinerana and Lieut. R.N. —*Tinerana, Killaloe, co. Clare.*

Heir Pres., his brother Richard Ponsonby, Lieut. R.N.; *b.* 1842.

+PURDON, GEORGE NUGENT, Esq., of Lisnabin, co. Westmeath.

Son of the late Edward Purdon, Esq., of Lisnabin; *b.* 18—; *m.* 1852 Elizabeth Anne, eldest dau. of Samuel Winter, Esq., of Augher, co. Meath. Is a Magistrate for co. Westmeath.—*Lisnabin, Killucan.*

PUREFOY. (See *Bagwell-Purefoy.*)

PURNELL, JOHN BRANSBY, Esq., of Stancombe Park, Gloucestershire.

Eldest son of the late Purnell Bransby Purnell, Esq., J.P. and D.L., of Stancombe Park (Chairman of Gloucester, Quarter Sessions), by Charlotte Anne, 3rd dau. of Nathaniel Clifford, Esq., of Frampton Court, co. Gloucester; *b.* 1820; *s.* 1866; educated at C. C. C., Oxford; is a J.P. and D.L. for co. Gloucester. Mr. Purnell is the lineal representative of the families of Purnell of Stinchcombe. co. Gloucester, and of Cooper and Bransby, both of Norfolk. The late Mr. Purnell assumed the surname of Purnell, in lieu of his patronymic Cooper, by Sign-Manual in 1805.—*Stancombe Park, Dursley.*

Heir Pres., his brother Col. William Paxton Purnell, C.D.; a Magistrate for co. Gloucester; Ensign of the Yeomen of the Guard; late Col. 90th Foot; *b.* 1821; *m.* 1st 1843 Emily, da. of John Agar, Esq., of Ballyhar, co. Kerry (she *d.* 1854); 2nd 1865 Elizabeth Susan, only dau. of the late Sir George Young, Bart., R.N., of Formosa Place, Berks.

PURNELL, the Rev. THOMAS, of Boddington Manor, Gloucestershire.

Only son of the late Robert John Purnell, Esq., J.P. and D.L., of Kingshill, by Mary Anne, only child of the Rev. Lewis Hughes, of Anglesea, niece and heir of Lieut.-Col. Purnell, of Kingshill; *b.* 1814; *s.* 1862; *m.* 1844 Ann, only dau. of the late Major Wilkinson, Madras Artillery, and has, with other issue,

* Robert Hughes Wilkinson, *b.* 1848.

Mr. Purnell, who was educated at New Inn Hall, Oxford (B.A. 1838), is a Magistrate for co. Gloucester. and Patron and Vicar of Staverton.—*Boddington Manor, Cheltenham.*

PURTON, THOMAS PARDOE, Esq., of Faintree, Shropshire.

Eldest son of the late William Purton, Esq., by Hester Maria, only child of Thomas Pardoe, Esq., of Faintree, and grandson of the late John Purton, Esq., of Eudon, co. Salop; *b.* 1801; *s.* 1855; *m.* 1831 Caroline Frances, 4th dau. of Lionel Lampet, Esq., and has. with other issue,

* William Cecil Pardoe, a Barrister-at-Law, of the Inner Temple, *b.* 1835; *m.* 1862 Frances Elizabeth, only dau. of John Browne Twist, Esq., of Stoke Prior, co. Worc.;

Mr. Purton, who was educated at Trinity Coll., Cambridge (B.A. 1826). is a Magistrate for co. Salop. —*Faintree Hall, Bridgnorth.*

PURVIS, ARTHUR, Esq., of Darsham, Suffolk.

Eldest son of the late Col. Charles Purvis, of Darsham, by Margaret Eleanor, dau. and co-heir of John Randall, Esq. (she *d.* 1859) ; *b.* 1813 ; *s.* 1859 ; *m.* 1847 Mary Jane, 2nd dau. of the late Lieut.-General Sir Alexander K. Clark-Kennedy, K.C.B., and has, with other issue,

* Arthur Kennedy, Ensign 87th Foot; *b.* 1848.

Mr. Purvis, who is a Magistrate for Suffolk, was formerly in the Madras Civil Service.—*Darsham, Saxmundham.*

PURVIS, GEORGE THOMAS MAITLAND, Esq., of Blackbrook, Hants.

Only son of the late George Purvis. Esq., J.P., of Blackbrook, by Renira Charlotte, dau. of David Maitland, Esq., of Gosport, Hants ; *b.* 1802 ; *m.* 1st 1828 Mary Jane, dau. of Admiral Sir F. W. Austen, K.C.B. (she *d.* 1836) ; 2nd 1838 Esther North, dau. of the Rev. William Harrison, Vicar of Fareham, Hants, and has by the former, with other issue,

    * George Thomas Maitland, Commander R.N.; *b.* 1829.

Mr. Purvis, is a Magistrate for Hants, and a Capt. R.N. —*Blackbrook Cottage, Fareham.*

PURVIS, Capt. RICHARD, of Bury Hall, Hants.

Only surviving son of the late Admiral John Brett Purvis, J.P. and D.L. of Bury Hall, by Renira Charlotte, eldest dau. of George Purvis, Esq., of Blackbrook House, Hants ; *b.* 1826 ; *s.* 1857 ; *m.* 1851 Georgiana Rachel, elder dau. of Major-General James Cock, of Hopton Hall, Suffolk, and has, with other issue,

    * Charles Hotham, *b.* 1852.

Capt. Purvis, who entered the Royal Navy in 1839, is a Magistrate for Hants, and a Post-Captain R.N.—*Bury Hall, Alverstoke ; United Service Club, s.w.*

PURVIS, the Rev. RICHARD FORTESCUE,‡ of Whitsbury, Hants.

Only surviving son of the late Admiral John Child Purvis, of Vicars Hill House, Hants, by Catharine, dau. of John Sowers, Esq., Clerk of the Cheque of H.M.'s Dockyard, Deptford ; *b.* 1789 ; *m.* 1824 Elizabeth Helen, dau. of the Rev. Thomas Baker, Rector of Rollesby, Norfolk, and has, with other issue,

    * Fortescue Richard, *b.* 1828 ; *m.* 1860 his cousin Louisa Harriet Eyre, dau. of George Matcham, Esq., of New House, Wilts, and grand-niece of Horatio, 1st Lord Nelson.

Mr. Purvis was educated at the Royal Naval Coll., Portsmouth, and Jesus Coll., Cambridge (First Class Law Tripos 1821; LL.B. 1825) ; is a Magistrate for Hants and Wilts, and Vicar of Whitsbury ; a retired Capt. of H.M.'s Indian Army, having medal and clasp for battles in Nepaul under Sir David Ochterlony in 1816–17.—*Whitsbury, Breamore, Hants.*

PUSEY, SIDNEY EDWARD BOUVERIE, Esq., of Pusey, Berks.

Only son of the late Philip Pusey, Esq., M.P., of Pusey, by Lady Emily Frances Theresa, 2nd dau. of Henry George, 2nd Earl of Carnarvon ; *b.* 1839 ; *s.* 1855. Educated at Eton and Ch. Ch., Oxford ; is a Magistrate for Berks, and Lord of the Manor of Pusey. This family is a younger branch of the Bouveries, Earls of Radnor ; the grandfather of the present owner assumed the additional name of Pusey, on succeeding to the Pusey estates, which have been held since the Saxon times by the tenure of a horn, still preserved at Pusey. —*Pusey, Farringdon.*

    Heiresses Pres., his sisters Edith, Lucy, and Clara.

PUTLAND, CHARLES, Esq., of Bray Head, co. Wicklow.

Eldest son of the late Charles Putland, Esq., of Bray Head (who *d.* 1859), by Constance, dau. of the Hon. George Massy ; *b.* 1813 ; *s.* 1859; *m.* 1st 1000 Charlotte, dau. of Capt. Christian, R.N. ; 2nd 1849 Georgina, dau. of the late Sir James C. Anderson, Bart., of Butetvant. co. Cork, and has by the former, with other issue,

    * George, *b.* 1841.

Mr. Putland is a Magistrate for co. Cork.—*Bray Head, co. Wicklow ; Kildare Street Club, Dublin.*

PUXLEY, HENRY LAVALLIN, Esq., of Llangan, Carmarthenshire, and Dunboy, co. Cork.

Second but eldest surviving son of the late John Lavallin Puxley, Esq., of Dunboy Castle (who *d.* 1837), by Frances Rosa Mary, dau. of the late Simon Whit-, Esq., of Glengariff; *b.* 1833 ; *s.* his brother Col. John Simous Lavallin Puxley, 1860 ; *m.* 1857 Katherine Ellen, dau. of the Rev. William Waller, of Castletown, co. Limerick (whom see), and has, with other issue,

    * John Lavallin, *b.* 1860.

Mr. Puxley, who was educated at Eton and Brasenose Coll., Oxford (B.A. 1855), is a Magistrate for co. Cork (High Sheriff 1865) and for co. Carmarthen (High Sheriff 1864), and Lord of the Manor of Llangan. —*Llangan, St. Clear's ; Dunboy Castle, Castletown, Berehaven, co. Cork.*

PYCROFT, Sir THOMAS, Knt. (cr. 1866).

Son of the late Mr. T. Pycroft ; *b.* 180–; educated at Haileybury Coll. ; is in the Madras Civil Service, and a Member of the Council of the Government of Madras; appointed Secretary to the Revenue and Judicial Departments at Madras 1828.—Residence : *Madras.*

PYE, HENRY JOHN, Esq., of Clifton Hall, Staffordshire.

Eldest son of the late Henry James Pye, Esq., M.P., of Farringdon, Berks, and Pinner. Middlesex (Poet Laureate), by his 2nd wife Martha, dau. of — Corbett, Esq.; *b.* 1802 ; *s.* 1833 ; *m.* 1825 Mary Anne. 3rd dau. of William Walker, Esq., of East Barnet, Herts, and has, with other issue,

    * Henry John, Rector of Clifton Campville, *b.* 1827 ; *m.* 1851 Emily Charlotte, dau. of the Right Rev. S. Wilberforce, D.D., Lord Bishop of Oxford.

Mr. Pye, who was educated at Magdalen Coll., Cambridge (B.A. 1823), is a J.P. and D.L. for co. Stafford (High Sheriff 1840), a Magistrate for co. Derby, Lord of the Manor of Clifton Campville, and Patron of 2 livings.—*Clifton Hall, Tamworth ; Pinner, Middlesex ; University and Oxford and Cambridge Clubs, s.w.*

PYE. (See *Alington-Pye.*)

+PYKE, JOHN, Esq., of Ford, Devonshire.

Eldest son of the late J. Pyke, Esq., of Ford ; *b.* 18—. Is a Magistrate for Devon.—*Ford, Bidcford.*

PYKE, JAMES NOTT, Esq., of Parracombe, Devon.

Younger son of the late Rev. John Pyke. Rector and Patron of Parracombe, by his 2nd wife Elizabeth, dau. of John Nott, Esq., of Bydown : *b.* 1845 ; *s.* 1868. Educated at Winchester and at Exeter Coll., Oxford (B.A. 1867) ; is Lord of the Manor and Patron of Parracombe.—*Parracombe, Barnstaple.*

PYKE-NOTT, JOHN NOTT, Esq., of Bydown and Parracombe, Devon.

Elder son of the late Rev. John Pyke. Rector and Patron of Parracombe, by his 2nd wife Elizabeth, dau. of John Nott, Esq., of Bydown ; *b.* 1841 ; *s.* 1868 ; *m.* 1867 Caroline Isabella, dau. of Frederick Ward, Esq., of Westmoreland, and has issue,

    * John Mosley, *b.* 1868.

Mr. Pyke-Nott, who was educated at Winchester and Exeter Coll., Oxford (B.A. 1863), is Lord of the Manor of Rowley, and an Officer in the R. N. Devon Yeomanry Cavalry.—*Bydown House, Swimbridge, Barnstaple, Devon.*

PYM, FRANCIS, Esq., of The Hasells, Beds.

Eldest son of the late Francis Leslie Pym, Esq., J.P. and D.L., of The Hasells, by Mary Jemima, dau. of the Rev. Henry Palmer, of Withcote, co. Leicester ; *b.* 1818 ; *s.* 1860. Is Lord of the Manors of Girtford, Beds, and Norton, Herts, and Patron of 3 livings.—*The Hasells, Biggleswade ; Radwell House, Baldock, Herts.*

    Heir Pres., his brother Henry Leslie, *b.* 1816.

    ‡ Died whilst these sheets were at press.

PYNE, Major JOHN, of East Charlton, Somerset.
Eldest son of the late Rev. Anthony Pyne, M.A., Rector
of Pitney and Kingweston, Somerset (who d. 1819), by
Catherine, dau. of Simon Wetherell, Esq.; b. 1795;
formerly Major in the Bengal army. This family have
held lands in Somerset since the reign of Richard II.
—East Charlton, Somerton ; East India United Service
Club, s.w.

Heir Pres., his brother William, in Holy Orders, M.A. of
Pembroke Coll., Oxford, and Rector of Sock Dennis, Somerset ; b. 1800 ; m. 1st 1825 Polyxena Ann, only dau. and heir
of the late Robert Michell, Esq.. of Langport, Somerset
(she d. 1864) ; 2nd 1867 Myra, widow of the Rev. C. C.
Luxmoore, Rector of Worplesden, Surrey ; and he has, by the
former, with other issue, * John Charles Edward, b. 1831.

PYRKE, DUNCOMBE, Esq., of Deane Hall,
Gloucestershire,
Eldest son of the late Joseph Pyrke, Esq., of Deane
Hall, by Eliza, dau. of Thomas Apperley, Esq., of Plas
Grunnow, North Wales ; b. 1809 ; s. 1851 ; m. 1833

Harriet, dau. of the Rev. W. Mairis, D.D., of West
Lavington, Wilts, and has, with other issue,
   * Duncombe, a J.P. and D.L. for co. Gloucester. b. 1836 ; m.
   1857 Susan, dau. of Thomas Evans, Esq.., M.D., of Gloucester, and has, with other issue, * Reginald Duncombe, b.
   1858.

Mr. Pyrke, who is a J.P. and D.L. for co. Gloucester,
and a Verderer of the Forest of Dean, was formerly in
the 10th Hussars.—Deane Hall, Newnham.

PYTCHES, THOMAS, Esq., of Melton, Suffolk.
Only son of the late Thomas Pytches, Esq., of Melton,
by Elizabeth Susanna, dau. of the late Richard Rout,
Esq., of Abbot's Hall, Stowmarket ; b. 1803 ; s. 1824 ;
m. 1841 Anne, only dau. of the late Rev. Thomas Carthew, of Woodbridge, and has, with other issue,
   * John Thomas, b. 1843.

Mr. Pytches, who was educated at Harrow and Caius
Coll., Cambridge (B.A. 1825), is a J.P. and D.L. for
Suffolk ; was formerly Major East Suffolk Militia.
—Melton, Woodbridge.

Q

QUANTOCK, Mrs., of Norton, Somerset.
Merelina, 2nd dau. of the late John Hartnoll Moore, Esq., R.N., of Cadeleigh Court, Devon, by Sophia, 2nd dau. of Thomas Woodforde, Esq., of Taunton, Somerset ; *m.* 1862 John Matthew Quantock, Esq., J.P., of Norton House (who was High Sheriff of Somerset 1847, and *d. s. p.* 1863). Mrs. Quantock is Lady of the Manor of Norton-sub-Hampden, and Lay-Rector of South Pethertou.—*Norton House, Ilminster.*

QUAYLE, MARK HILDESLEY, Esq., of Crogga, I. of Man.
Only son of the late Mark Hildesley Quayle, Esq., of Castletown, I. of Man, by Mary, eldest dau. of Senhouse Wilson, Esq., of Farm Hill, Douglas ; *b.* 1804 ; *m.* 1837 Mary Jane Hamilton, dau. of James Spedding, Esq., of Summergrove, Cumberland, and has, with other issue,

* John, *b.* 1840 ; *m.* 1864 Emily Catherine, eldest dau. of Edward Moore Gawne, Esq., of Kentraugh, Isle of Man.

Mr. Quayle, who was called to the Manks Bar 1825, and promoted to the Bench as Clerk of the Rolls of the Isle of Man 1847, is a Magistrate and Member of the Legislative and Executive Council of that island, and held the office of Deputy Governor.—*Crogga, Douglas.*

QUEENSBERRY, Marquis of (JOHN SHOLTO DOUGLAS).—Cr. 1682.
Eldest son of Archibald William, 7th Marquis, by Caroline Margaret, dau. of the late Lieut.-General Sir William Robert Clayton, Bart., of Harleyford, Bucks ; *b.* 1844 ; *s.* 1858 ; *m.* 1866 Sibyl, 2nd dau. of Alfred Montgomery, Esq. Educated at Magdalen Coll., Cambridge ; is a Dep.-Lieut. for co. Dumfries, and was formerly a Lieut. R.N.—*Glenstewart, Kinmount, co. Dumfries.*

Heir, his son Francis Archibald, Viscount Drumlanrig. *b.* 1867.

QUICKE, JOHN, Esq., of Newton House, Devon.
Eldest son of the late John Quicke, Esq., J.P. and D.L., of Newton House (who was High Sheriff of Devon 1833), by Frances Catharine, youngest dau. of Thomas Cumming, Esq. ; *b.* 1816 ; *s.* 1859 ; *m.* 1847 Mary Elizabeth, only dau. of the late Thomas Wentworth Gould, Esq., of Bathealton Court, Somerset. Educated at Eton and Trinity Coll., Cambridge, is a J.P. and D.L. for Devon (High Sheriff 1867), Lord of the Manors of Newton, and Stoke Pero, and Patron of 3 livings. This family have resided at Newton House since A.D. 1525.—*Newton House, Exeter ; Arthur's Club, s.w.*

Heir Pres, his brother Thomas, *b.* 1817.

QUIN, Lord GEORGE, of Quinsboro', co. Clare.
Second son of Thomas, 1st Marquis of Headfort, by Mary, dau. of George Quin. Esq., of Quinsborough, (whose name he has assumed); *b.* 1792; *m.* 1st 1814 Lady Georgiana Charlotte, dau. of George John, 2nd Earl Spencer (*d.* 1823) ; 2nd 1847 Louisa Mary Isabella, eldest dau. of the late Sir John Ramsden, Bart., and has by the former, with other issue, an only son,

* Richard Robert, a Capt. R.N. ; *b.* 1820 ; *m.* 1st 1852 Selina, eldest dau. of the late Rev. David Frederick Markham, Canon of Windsor ; 2nd 1868 Georgiana Olivia, only surviving dau. of the Hon. John Boyle.

Lord G. Quin, who was educated at Harrow, is a J.P. and D.L. for co. Cavan.—*Quinsborough, Sixmilebridge, co. Clare ; Kells, co. Cavan ; Travellers' Club, s.w.; 15, Belgrave Square, s.w.*

QUIN, WILLIAM, Esq., of Loughloher, co. Tipperary.
Eldest son of the late William Quin, Esq., of Loughloher (High Sheriff of co. Tipperary 1813), by Mary Jamima, dau. of J. Going, Esq., of Killough Hill ; *b.* 1800 ; *s.* 1836; *m.* 1832 Ellen, dau. of Brook Brazier. Esq., of Mitchell's Fort, and has, with other issue,

* William, Capt. Tipperary Artillery ; *b.* 1841.

Mr. Quin is a Magistrate for co. Tipperary.—*Loughloher Castle, Cahir, co. Tipperary.*

QUIN. (See under DUNRAVEN, Earl of.)

QUINN, PETER, Esq., of the Agency, co. Armagh.
Fourth son of the late John Quinn, Esq., of Newry, by Mary, dau. of the late Rev. William Campbell, Vicar of Newry ; *b.* 1814 ; *m.* 1835 Sarah Jane, dau. of the Rev. Josiah Erskine, Rector of Knockbride, co. Cavan. Is a Magistrate for cos. Armagh and Down ; formerly a Merchant at Newry ; elected M.P. for Newry 1859. —*The Agency, Newry ; Carlton Club, s.w.*

R

+RABAN, GEORGE, Esq., of Hatch Beauchamp, Somerset.
Eldest son of the late Col. William Raban, of Hatch Beauchamp, who was a J.P. and D.L. for Somerset; *b.* 18—. Is a Magistrate for Somerset.—*The Lodge, Hatch Beauchamp, Taunton.*

RABETT, REGINALD, Esq., of Bramfield, Suffolk.
Only son of the late Capt. George Rabett, R.N. (who *d.* 1858), by Lady Lucy Louisa Maria, sister of Edward, 3rd Earl of Winterton; *b.* 1842; *s.* his uncle, the Rev. Reginald Rabett, 1861. This family has been connected with Suffolk for upwards of 400 years.—*Bramfield Hall, Saxmundham.*

RADCLIFFE, Sir JOSEPH, Bart., of Rudding Park, Yorkshire (cr. 1813).
Only son of the late Rev. Josiah Pickford Radcliffe, by Mary, only dau. of Sir John Archibald Grant, Bart., of Monymusk; *b.* 1799; *s.* his grandfather as 2nd Bart. 1819; *m.* 1819 Jacobina Maria, dau. of the late Capt. John Macdonell, of Leake, co. Inverness (she *d.* 1868). Educated at Westminster; is Patron of 1 living; was High Sheriff of Yorkshire 1857; formerly a Major in the Army. This family descend from a common ancestor with the Radcliffes, Earls of Sussex (ext.).—*Rudding Park, Wetherby; Royton Hall, Oldham.*

Heir, his son Joseph Percival Pickford, of Caverswall Castle, near Cheadle, co. Stafford; educated at Catherine Hall, Cambridge; a Magistrate for co. Stafford; *b.* 1824; *m.* 1854 Katharine Mary Elizabeth, only surviving child of the late Sir Edward Doughty, Bart., of Tichborne Park, Hants, and grand-dau. of James Everard, 9th Lord Arundell of Wardour, and has, with other issue, *Joseph Edward, *b.* 1858.

RADCLIFFE, JOHN, Esq., of Moorfield, Lancashire.
Youngest surviving son of the late Samuel Radcliffe, Esq., of Lower House, Oldham, by Mary, dau. of Robert Buckley, Esq., of Saddleworth, co. York; *b.* 1825; *m.* 1st 1850 Sarah Sidebottom, eldest dau. of George Adshered, Esq., of Stanley, co. Chester (she *d.* 1856); 2nd 1859 Louisa, eldest dau. of Thomas Christy, Esq., of Broomfield, Essex, and has, with other issue,
* Edgar Christy, *b.* 1867.
Mr. Radcliffe is a Magistrate for co. Lancaster, a Merchant and Manufacturer at Oldham, Rochdale, and Manchester, and Joint Patron of St. Mary's, Balderstone.—*Moorfield, Withington, Manchester; Union Club, Manchester; Reform Club, s.w.*

+RADCLIFFE, JOSIAH, Esq., of Werneth Park, Lancashire.
Eldest son of Josiah Radcliffe, Esq.; *b.* 18—; *m.* 1866 Lucy Jane, 2nd dau. of John Platt, Esq., of Werneth Park. Is a Magistrate for co. Lancaster.—*Werneth Park, Oldham.*

RADCLIFFE, SAMUEL, Esq., of Werneth, Lancashire.
Son of the late Samuel Radcliffe, Esq., of Lower House; *b.* 1814; *m.* 1st 1846 Sarah, dau. of the late John Duncuft, Esq., M.P., of Westwood, Oldham (she *d.* 1857); 2nd 1861 Ann. dau. of the late John Thomas Cocker, Esq., of New Bank, Crompton (she *d.* 1864); 3rd 1865 Elizabeth, 3rd dau. of the late John Gartside, Esq., of

Ashton-under-Lyne. Is a Magistrate for co. Lancaster; purchased Werneth Park from the Lees family in 1845.—*Werneth Park, Oldham.*

RADCLIFFE, WALTER COPLESTON, Esq., of Warlegh, Devon.
Eldest son of the late Rev. Walter Radcliffe, of Warlegh, by Abby Emma, dau. of A. Franco, Esq., and sister of the late Sir Ralph Lopes, Bart., M.A., of Maristow, Devon; *b.* 1815; *s.* 1867; *m.* 1850 Hannah Charlotte, dau. of the Rev. Richard Ellicombe, Vicar of Alphington, Devon. This family has been seated in Devon since A.D. 1560.—*Warlegh, Plymouth.*

RADCLIFFE. (See *Delmé-Radcliffe.*)

RADCLYFFE, CHARLES JAMES, Esq., of Foxdenton, Lancashire, and Hyde, Dorset.
Eldest surviving son of the late Robert Radclyffe, Esq., of Foxdenton Hall and Hyde House (High Sheriff of Dorset), by Mary, dau. of the late Thomas Wilson-Patten, Esq., of Bank Hall, Warrington; *b.* 1804; *s.* 1854; *m.* 1835 Anna Maria, dau. of Robert Lillington, Esq., of Stockley, Dorset, and has, with other issue,
* Charles James, *b.* 1840.
Mr. Radclyffe, who was educated at the Royal Military Coll., Sandhurst, is a Magistrate for Dorset and co. Lancaster, and Patron of 2 livings; was formerly in the 5th Dragoon Guards.—*Foxdenton Hall, Oldham; Hyde Manor House, Wareham.*

RADFORD, ARTHUR, Esq., of Smalley, Derbyshire.
Only son of the late John Radford, Esq., J.P. and D.L., of Smalley, by Mary Buttle, dau. of James Dowker, Esq., of North Dalton, co. York; *b.* 1848; *s.* 1866.—*Smalley Hall, Derby.*

RADFORD, EDWARD, Esq., of Tansley, Derbyshire.
Sixth son of the late John Radford, Esq., of Smalley, co. Derby, by Theophila, dau. of Alexander Vaughan, Esq., of Rowdatch, co. Radnor; *b.* 1788; *m.* 1820 Eliza Diana, youngest dau. of Childers Wallbanke Childers, Esq., of Cantley, co. York, and has, with other issue,
* Childers Charles, of Darley Dale, near Matlock, Derbyshire, a Magistrate for co. Derby, and Lieut. Derbyshire Yeomanry Cavalry; *b.* 1828; *m.* 1855 Mary Elizabeth, eldest dau. of Major James Hurt, of Wirksworth. co. Derby.
Mr. Radford is a J.P. and D.L. for co. Derby.—*Tansley Wood, Matlock.*

RADNOR, Earl of (WILLIAM PLEYDELL-BOUVERIE).—Cr. 1765.
Eldest son of Jacob, 2nd Earl, by the Hon. Anne, dau. of Anthony, Lord Feversham; *b.* 1779; *s.* 1828; *m.* 1st 1800 Lady Katharine, dau. of Henry, late Earl of Lincoln; 2nd 1811 Judith Anne, dau. of the late Sir Henry Paulet St. John-Mildmay, Bart. (she *d.* 1851). 2nd title Viscount Folkestone. Is a J.P. and D.L. for Berks and Wilts, and Patron of 7 livings; was M.P. for Downton 1801-2, for Salisbury 1802-28. This family is of French Huguenot extraction.—*Coleshill House, Farringdon; Longford Castle, Salisbury; Reform Club, s.w.; 41, Wilton Crescent, s.w.*

Heir, his son Jacob, Viscount Folkestone, a J.P. and D.L. for Berks, a Magistrate for Wilts (High Sheriff 1810); *b.* 1815;

m. 1840 Lady Mary Augusta Frederica, 3rd dau. of James Walter, 1st Earl of Verulam, and has, with other issue, • William, *b.* 1841 ; *m.* 1866 Helen Matilda, only surviving dau. of the late Rev. H. Chaplin, of Ryhall, co. Rutland.

RADSTOCK, Lord (Granville Augustus William Waldegrave).—Cr. 1800.
Only son of Vice-Admiral Granville George, 2nd Lord, by Esther Caroline, dau. of the late John Puget, Esq., of Totteridge, Herts ; *b.* 1833 ; *s.* 1857 ; *m.* 1858 Susan Charlotte, dau. of John Hales Calcraft, Esq., of Rempstone Hall, Dorset. Educated at Harrow and Balliol Coll., Oxford (B.A. 1854, M.A. 1857) ; is Lieut.-Col. Commandant W. Middlesex Rifles, and represents a younger branch of the family of Earl Waldegrave.—30, *Bryanston Square,* w.
Heir, his son Granville George, *b.* 1859.

RADSTOCK, Dowager Lady.
Esther Caroline, dau. of the late John Puget, Esq., of Totteridge, Herts ; *m.* 1823 Granville George, 2nd Lord Radstock (who *d.* 1857).—26, *Portland Place,* w.

RAE, Sir William, Knt., C.B., M.D. (cr. 1858).
Son of the late Matthew Rae, Esq., of Park End, co. Dumfries ; *b.* 1786 ; *m.* 1st 1814 Mary, dau. of Robert Bell, Esq. ; 2nd 1831 Maria, dau. of General Lee. Educated at Edinburgh ; is a Magistrate for Devon and co. Dumfries, and Inspector-General of Hospitals and Fleets.—*Hornby Lodge, Newton Abbot.*

RAE, Edward, Esq., of Keel House, co. Kerry.
Eldest son of the late Giles Rae, Esq., of Keel House, by Deborah, dau. of John Langford, Esq., of Killorglin Castle, co. Kerry ; *b.* 1814 ; *s.* 1841. Is a Magistrate for co. Kerry. This family, formerly of co. Caithness, have been settled in Ireland for above 250 years.—*Keel House, Castlemaine, co. Kerry.*

RAE, Langford, Esq., of Mountain Lodge, co. Tipperary.
Third son of the late Giles Rae, Esq., of Keel House, co. Kerry, by Deborah, dau. of John Langford, Esq., of Killorglin Castle, co. Kerry ; *b.* 18—. Is a Magistrate for co. Tipperary, and an Associate of the Institution of Civil Engineers of Ireland ; late Lieut. 7th Lancashire Rifles.—*Mountain Lodge, Mitchelstown, co. Tipperary ; Keel House, Castlemaine, co. Kerry.*

+**RAEBURN, Henry, Esq., of St. Bernard's, Midlothian.**
Eldest son of the late Henry Raeburn, Esq., of St. Bernard's (who was a J.P. for Midlothian) ; *b.* 18— ; *s.* 1863. Is a Magistrate for Midlothian. — *Charlesfield House, Midcalder, Midlothian.*

RAFFLES, Thomas Stamford, Esq., of Edge Hill, Lancashire.
Eldest son of the late Thomas Raffles, D.D., of Edge Hill, by Mary Catherine, only dau. of James Hargreaves, Esq. ; *b.* 1818 ; *s.* 1863 ; *m.* 1849 Maria, elder dau. of the late Edward Cearns, Esq., junr. Educated at the London University (B.A. 1840) ; called to the Bar at the Inner Temple 1841 ; is a Magistrate for co. Lancaster, and a Police Magistrate at Liverpool.—*Edge Hill, Liverpool.*

RAGLAN, Lord (Richard Henry FitzRoy Somerset).—Cr. 1852.
Only surviving son of Fitz-Roy, 1st Lord (who was a son of Henry, 5th Duke of Beaufort, and a Field-Marshal in the Army, and commanded the British Forces in the Crimea 1854-5), by Lady Emily Harriet, dau. of William, 3rd Earl of Mornington ; *b.* 1817 ; *s.* 1855 ; *m.* 1856 Lady Georgiana, dau. of Henry, 4th Earl Beauchamp (she *d.* 1865). Is a J.P. and D.L. for co. Monmouth, and Capt. Gloucestershire Hussars ; formerly

in the Ceylon Civil Service ; was Secretary to the King of Hanover 1849-55. — *Cefntilla House, Usk, Monmouthshire ; White's and Carlton Clubs,* s.w.
Heir, his son George FitzRoy Henry, *b.* 1857.

RAGLAN, Dowager Lady.
Emily Harriet, 2nd dau. of William, 3rd Earl of Mornington, by Catharine Elizabeth, dau. of Admiral the Hon. John Forbes ; *m.* 1814 F.M. FitzRoy, 1st Lord Raglan, who *d.* in the Crimea 1855.—5, *Great Stanhope Street,* w.

RAIKES, Henry Cecil, Esq., of Llwynegriu Hall, Flintshire.
Eldest son of the late Henry Raikes, Esq., of Llwynegrin Hall, by Lucy Charlotte, dau. of the late Ven. Archdeacon Francis Wrangham ; *b.* 1838 ; *s.* 1863 ; *m.* 1861 Charlotte Blanche, 4th dau. of C. B. Trevor Roper, Esq., of Plas Teg, co. Flint, and has, with other issue,
• Henry St. John Digby, *b.* 1863.
Mr. Raikes, who was educated at Shrewsbury and Trinity Coll., Cambridge (B.A. 1860, M.A. 1863), was called to the Bar at the Middle Temple 1863, and is a J.P. and D.L. for co. Flint.—*Llwynegrin Hall, Mold ; University and Junior Carlton Clubs,* s.w. ; 33, *Gloucester Place,* w.

RAIKES, Stanley Napier, Esq., of Hill Ash House, Gloucestershire.
Youngest son of the late Rev. Robert Raikes, Vicar of Longhope, and of Old Sodbury, co. Gloucester, by Caroline, dau. of the Very Rev. John Probyn, of Longhope Manor, co. Gloucester, Dean of Llandaff ; *b.* 1824 ; *m.* 1858 Arabella Veronica, dau. of the late Rev. Charles Dighton, Vicar of Longhope, and widow of J. James, Esq. Major Raikes, who is a Magistrate for Gloucester, was formerly an Officer in the Indian army. —*Hill Ash House, Dymock, Gloucestershire.*

RAIKES, Robert, Esq., of East Dale, Yorkshire.
Second son of the late Robert Raikes, Esq., by Anne, dau. of Thomas Williamson, Esq., of Welton House ; *b.* 1801 ; *m.* 1827 Eleanor Catherine, eldest dau. of Rear-Admiral Puget, C.B. Is a J.P. and D.L. for the East Riding of Yorkshire, and a Magistrate for Kingston-upon-Hull ; was formerly an Alderman of Hull. —*East Dale House, Brough.*

RAIKES, Robert, Esq., of Treberfydd, Brecknockshire.
Eldest son of Thomas Raikes, Esq., J.P., late of Brafferds, co. York, by his 1st wife Elizabeth, dau. of Thomas Armstrong, Esq., of Castle Armstrong, Ireland ; *b.* 1819 ; *m.* 1841 Frances, dau. of the late Sir William E. Taunton, Knt., a Judge of the Court of King's Bench. Educated at Exeter Coll., Oxford (B.A. 1841, M.A. 1846) ; is a J.P. and D.L. for co. Brecon, of which he has been High Sheriff.—*Treberfydd, Brecon.*

RAINES, William, Esq., of Wyton, Yorkshire.
Eldest son of the late William Raines, Esq., by Fanny only dau. of Marmaduke Browne, Esq. ; *b.* 1808. Called to the Bar at Lincoln's Inn 1833 ; appointed Judge of the Hull and East Yorkshire County Courts 1847 ; is a Magistrate for the N. Riding, and a J.P. and D.L. for the East Riding of Yorkshire.—*Wyton Hall, Hull ; Athenæum Club,* s.w.

RAINSFORD-HANNAY, Frederick, Esq., of Kirkdale, Kirkcudbrightshire.
Son of the late Thomas Rainsford, Esq., of the 2nd Life Guards, by Jane, dau. of Sir Samuel Hannay, Bart., of Mochrum and Kirkdale (ext. 1841) ; *b.* 1810 ; *s.* his brother 1350 ; *m.* 1840 Rhoda, dau. of the late

781

Charles Johnston, Esq., formerly of the 21st Regt., and by her (who *d.* 1855) has, with other issue,

* Ramsay William, Lieut. R.A., *b.* 1844.

Mr. Rainsford-Hannay, who was educated at Edinburgh University, is a Magistrate for co. Kirkcudbright, and a retired Major Bengal Army.—*Kirkdale, Gatehouse, N.B.*

RAINY, GEORGE HAYGARTH, Esq., of Raasay, Inverness-shire.

Eldest son of the late George Rainy, Esq., of Raasay, (who was a J.P. and D.L. for co. Inverness), by Margaret Elizabeth, dau. of the Rev. George Haygarth; *b.* 1845; *s.* 1863. Is Lord of the Barony of Raasay.—*Raasay House, Broadford, N.B.*

RAIT, Major JAMES, of Anniston, Forfarshire.

Eldest son of the late John Rait, Esq., of Anniston, by Elizabeth, dau. of J. Guthrie. Esq., of Craigie, co. Forfar; *b.* 1805; *m.* 1838 Lady Clementina, 2nd dau. of David, 9th Earl of Airlie, and by her, who *d.* 1848, has, with other issue,

* Arthur John, Lieut. R.A. ; *b.* 1839.

Major Rait, who was educated at Eton, Edinburgh, and the University of St. Andrew's, is a J.P. and D.L., for Forfar, and a Major Forfarshire Militia; formerly Capt. 15th Hussars.—*Anniston House, Arbroath, N.B.*

RAM, the Rev. ABEL JOHN, of Clonattin, co. Wexford.

Eldest son of the late Abel John Ram, Esq., of Clonattin, by Frances Anne, dau. of John Port, Esq., of Ilam Hall, co. Stafford; *b.* 1804; *s.* 1823; *m.* 1833 Lady Jane Stopford, dau. of James George, 3rd Earl Courtown, and has, with other issue,

* George Stopford, in Holy Orders, M.A. of Wadham Coll., Oxford ; Incumbent of St. Ann's, Highgate ; *b.* 1838 ; *m.* 1866 the Hon. Charlotte Anne, 2nd dau. of Lucina, 13th Lord Inchiquin, and has issue, a dau.

Mr. Ram, who was educated at Oriel Coll., Oxford (B.A. 1826, M.A. 1830), represents a branch of the Rams of Ramsfort.—*Clonattin, Gorey, co. Wexford ; West Ham, Essex, x.*

RAM, Mrs., of Chilton House, Berks.

Eleanor Sarah, only dau. and heir of the late Jerome William Knapp, Esq., Barrister-at-Law, of Bedford Row, Middlesex, by Eleanor, dau. and heir of Edmund Robinson, Esq., of Plymouth ; *m.* 1816 Abel Ram, Esq., of Ramsfort, co. Wexford, who *d.* 1832, leaving, with other issue,

* Stephen Ram, Esq., of Ramsfort, co. Wexford (whom see).

Mrs. Ram is Patron of 2 livings, and Lady of the Manors of Bermondsey, Surrey, and of Chilton, Berks.—*Chilton House, Abingdon ; 3, Wilton Terrace, s.w.*

RAM, STEPHEN, Esq. of Ramsfort, co. Wexford.

Eldest son of the late Abel Ram, Esq., of Ramsfort, by Eleanor Sarah, dau. of Jerome Knapp, Esq. ; *b.* 1818 ; *s.* 1832 ; *m.* 1839 Mary Christian, dau. of the late James Casamaijor, Esq., and has, with other issue,

* Stephen James, Capt. Scots Fusilier Guards; *b.* 1840.

Mr. Ram, who was educated at Eton and Ch. Ch., Oxford, is a J.P. and D.L. for co. Wexford (High Sheriff 1840). This family settled in Ireland from Essex, *temp.* Queen Elizabeth.—*Ramsfort, Gorey ; Carlton Club, s.w.*

RAMONO, Sir JEAN EDOUARD, Knt. (cr. 1860).

Is first Puisne Judge of the Supreme Court of the Mauritius.

RAMSAY, GEORGE, Bart., of Bamff, Perthshire (cr. 1666).

Second son of the late Sir William Ramsay, Bart., of Bamff (who *d.* 1807), by Agnata Frances, dau. of John
782

Hilton Biscoe, Esq., of Hookwood, Surrey ; *b.* 1800 ; *s.* his brother as 9th Bart. 1859 ; *m.* 1830 Emily Eugenia, dau. of Henry Lennon, Esq. (late of the 49th Foot). Educated at Harrow and Trinity Coll. Cambridge (B.A. 1822); is descended from a common ancestor with the Earl of Dalhousie.—*Bamff House, Alyth, N.B.*

Heir, his son James Henry. M.A., of Ch. Ch., Oxford ; *b.* 1832 ; *m.* 1861 Elizabeth Mary Charlotte, eldest dau. of W. S. Kerr, Esq., of Chatto and Sunlaws, co. Roxburgh, and has issue, three daus.

RAMSAY, Sir ALEXANDER, Bart., of Balmain, Kincardineshire (cr. 1806).

Eldest son of the late Sir Alexander Ramsay, Bart., of Balmain, by Jane, dau. of Major Russell, of Blackhall, N.B.; *b.* 1813 ; *s.* as 3rd Bart. 1852 ; *m.* 1835 Ellen Matilda, dau. of the late John Entwisle, Esq., of Foxholes, co. Lancaster. Is a J.P. and D.L. for co. Kincardine, and a Magistrate for co. Forfar ; formerly Lieut. 85th Foot; was M.P. for Rochdale 1857-9. The 1st Bart. assumed the name of Ramsay in lieu of Burnett. — *Balmain, Fettercairn, N.D. ; Lansdowne, Cheltenham ; Union Club, s.w.*

Heir, his son Alexander Entwisle, a Magistrate for co. Kincardine ; *b.* 1837 ; *m.* 1864 Octavia, youngest dau. of Thomas Haigh, Esq., Elm Hall, near Liverpool.

RAMSAY, BEVILLE, Esq., of Croughton Park, Northamptonshire.

Second son of the late John Turner Ramsay, Esq., of Croughton Park, Tusmore, Oxon, by Philippa Maria, adopted dau. of William Fermor, Esq., of Tusmore, and Croughton ; *b.* 1833 ; *m.* 1858 Sarah Maria, dau. of Rev. Matthew Carrier Tompson, Patron and Rector of Woodstone, co. Northampton, and Vicar of Alderminster, co. Warwick, and has, with other issue,

* Edward Dryden, *b.* 1864.

Mr. Ramsay, who was educated at Sandhurst Coll., is a Magistrate for co. Northampton. and a Lieut. in the Oxfordshire Yeomanry ; he was formerly Capt. 62nd Regt. This family is of Scotch origin ; the grandfather of the present owner, William Ramsay, living at Inveresk, N.B.—*Croughton Park, Brackley ; Windham and Arthur's Clubs, s.w.*

RAMSAY, Major-General JAMES.

Third son of the late Lieut.-General the Hon. John Ramsay (4th son of George, 8th Earl of Dalhousie), by Mary. dau. of Philip Deisle, Esq.; *b.* 1808 ; *m.* 1840 Harriet Charlotte, dau. of the late William Robert Burlton Bennett, Esq., of the Bengal Civil Service, and has, with other issue,

* James Andrew, *b.* 1850.

Major-General Ramsay, who was educated at the Military Coll., Addiscombe, and appointed to the Indian Army 1824, was Commissary-General in Bengal 1852-8 ; became a Major-General 1859.—*Oriental Club, w. ; United Service Club, s.w. ; 1, Sussex Square, w.*

RAMSAY, JOHN, Esq., of Barra, Aberdeenshire.

Only son of the late John Ramsay. Esq. of Barra, by Susan, 3rd dau. of the late Alexander Innes. Esq., of Pitmedden, co. Aberdeen ; *b.* 1831 ; *s.* 1832 ; *m.* 1858 Leonora Sophia, only dau. of the Rev. Nathaniel Bond, of Creech Grange, Dorset, and by her, who *d.* 1867, has issue, a daughter. Educated at Eton and Trinity Coll., Cambridge (B.A. 1855, M.A. 1858); is a Dep. Lieut. for co. Banff, a J.P. and D.L. for co. Aberdeen, Capt. Royal Aberdeenshire Highlanders, and Major Aberdeen Rifle Volunteers. This family is a branch of the family of Innes, Bart. of Edingight.— *Barra, Aberdeen ; Barra Castle, Old Meldrum, N.B. ; New Club, Edinburgh, Guelloa and Junior Carlton Clubs, s.w.*

RAMSAY, JOHN, Esq., of Kildalton, Argyll-shire.

Youngest son of the late Robert Ramsay, Esq., of Stirling, by Elizabeth, dau. of William Stirling, Esq., of Craigforth, co. Stirling; *b.* 1814; *m.* 1857 Elizabeth, dau. of the late William Shields, Esq., of Lanchester, co. Durham (she *d.* 1864). Educated at the University of Glasgow, is a Magistrate for co. Lanark, a J.P. and D.L. for co. Argyll, and a Merchant at Glasgow; elected M.P. for Stirling 1868.—*Kildalton House, Greenock, N.B.*

RAMSAY, ROBERT BALFOUR WARDLAW-, Esq., of Whitehill, Midlothian.

Second son of the late Robert Wardlaw-Ramsay, Esq., of Whitehill, by Anne, 2nd dau. of Alexander, 6th Earl of Balcarres; *b.* 1815; *s.* 1837; *m.* 1841 Lady Louisa Jane, 3rd dau. of George, 8th Marquis of Tweeddale, K.T., and has, with other issue,

* Robert George, *b.* 1852.

Mr. Wardlaw-Ramsay, who was educated at Edinburgh and Haileybury Coll., is a J.P. and D.L. for Midlothian, was formerly in the H.E.I.Co.'s Civil Service, Bengal. —*Whitehill, Edinburgh; Tillicoultry, Clackmannan, N.B.*

RAMSAY, THOMAS BURNETT-, Esq., of Banchory Lodge, Kincardineshire.

Only son of the late Lieut.-Col. W. Burnett-Ramsay, of Banchory Lodge, by Anne. 2nd dau. of the late Duncan Davidson, Esq., of Inchmarlo, co. Kincardine; *b.* 1862; *s.* 1865. This family is descended paternally from a common ancestor with the Burnetts, Barts., of Leys, and maternally from the Ramsays of Balmain. —*Banchory Lodge, Banchory, N.B.*

Heir Pres., his eldest sister Frances.

RAMSAY. (See under *Dalhousie, Earl of.*)

RAMSAY-GIBSON-MAITLAND. (See *Maitland.*)

RAMSBOTHAM, JAMES, Esq., of Crowborough Warren, Sussex.

Eldest surviving son of the late Thomas Ramsbotham, Esq., of Todmorden, by Esther, dau. of James Openshaw, Esq., of Redvales, co. Lancaster; *b.* 1814; *s.* 1839; *m.* 1837 Jane, dau. of Joshua Fielden, Esq., of Todmorden, and has, with other issue,

* John, *b.* 1838; is married, and has issue.

Mr. Ramsbotham, who was educated at Shrewsbury and St. John's Coll., Cambridge, represents a family formerly seated at Centro Vale, Todmorden, and at Old Hall, Stand, co. Lancaster.—*Crowborough Warren, Tunbridge Wells.*

RAMSBOTTOM, JOHN RICHARD SNEYD, Esq., late of Woodside, Berks.

Eldest son of the late John Ramsbottom, Esq. (who was thirty-five years M.P. for Windsor), by Sophia Augusta, dau. of Major Pryor, of the 16th Light Dragoons; *b.* 1801; *m.* 1831 Laura Augusta, dau. of John Bronchley, Esq., of Maidstone, and of Wanlass How, Westmoreland, and has, with other issue,

* John Richard, Capt. 97th Regt.; *b.* 1837.

Mr. Ramsbottom, who was educated at Eton, and appointed to the 16th Lancers 1821, is a Dep.-Lieut. for Berks, and a Magistrate for Kent.—*Waterloo Crescent, Dover; Junior United Service Club, s.w.*

RAMSDEN, Sir JOHN WILLIAM, Bart., of Byrom Hall, Yorkshire (cr. 1689).

Eldest son of the late John Charles Ramsden, Esq., of Byrom Hall (sometime M.P. for Malton), by the Hon. Isabella, dau. of Thomas, 2nd Lord Dundas; *b.* 1831; *s.* his grandfather as 5th Bart. 1839; *m.* 1865 Lady Helen Gwendaline, dau. of Edward, 13th Duke of

Somerset. Educated at Eton and Trinity Coll., Cambridge (M.A. 1852); is a J.P. and D.L. for the W. Riding of Yorkshire (High Sheriff 1868), and Patron of 4 livings; was M.P. for Taunton 1853-7, for Hythe 1857-9, and for the W. Riding of Yorkshire 1859-65. Under Secretary for War 1857-8.—*Byrom Hall, Ferrybridge; Longley Hall, Huddersfield; Brooks's, Athenæum, and Travellers' Clubs, s.w.; 6, Upper Brook Street, w.*

Heir Pres., his uncle Henry James, of Oxton Hall, Tadcaster, 3rd son of the late Sir John Ramsden, Bart., of Byrom Hall, co. York, by the Hon. Louisa Susanna, youngest dau. and co-heir of Charles, 9th Viscount Irvine (*ext.*); educated at Harrow and at the Royal Military Coll., Woolwich; a J.P. and D.L. for the W. Riding of co. York, and late Capt. in the Army; *b.* 1799; *m.* 1829 the Hon. Frederica Selina, 8th dau. of Edward, 1st Lord Ellenborough, and has, with other issue, * John Charles Francis, late Capt. R.A.; *b.* 1838; *m.* 1863 Emma. youngest dau. of the Rev. Edward Duncombe, and widow of Ellis Gosling, Esq., of Busbridge Hall, Surrey, and has issue, a dau.

RAMSDEN, ROBERT JOHN, Esq., of Carlton Hall, Notts.

Eldest son of the late Robert Ramsden, Esq., J.P., of Carlton Hall (High Sheriff of Notts 1837), by Frances Matilda, 4th dau. of the late John P. Plumptre, Esq., of Fredville, Kent; *b.* 1817; *s.* 1865; *m.* 1844 Mary, dau. of the Rev. Henry Gipps, and has, with other issue,

* Robert Henry, Midshipman R.N.; *b.* 1845.

Mr. Ramsden, who was educated at Trinity Coll., Cambridge (B.A. 1841, M.A. 1844), is a Magistrate for Notts.—*Carlton Hall, Worksop.*

RAND, JOHN, Esq., of Wheatley, Yorkshire.

Eldest son of the late John Rand, Esq., of Bradford, co. York, by Mary, dau. of the late Samuel Swaine, Esq.; *b.* 1793; *m.* 1834 Eliza, dau. of George M'Turk, Esq., of South Cave, co. York. Is a J.P. and D.L. for the W. Riding of Yorkshire, and Mill-owner at Bradford.—*Wheatley Hill, Bradford.*

RAND, WILLIAM, Esq., of Baildon, Yorkshire.

Younger son of the late John Rand, Esq., of Bradford, co. York, by Mary, dau. of the late Samuel Swaine, Esq.; *b.* 1794. Is a Magistrate for the W. Riding of Yorkshire, and an Alderman and Magistrate for the borough of Bradford; was formerly twice Mayor of Bradford, and President of the Bradford Chamber of Commerce. —*Baildon House, Otley.*

RANDALL, ALEXANDER, Esq., of Foley House, Kent.

Son of the late Mr. James Randall, of Maidstone; *b.* 1797; *m.* 1st 1840 Mary, only dau. of Samuel Chambers, Esq., of Maidstone; 2nd 1849 Alicia, dau. of F. Ferguson, Esq., M.D., of Dublin. Is a J.P. and D.L. for Kent (High Sheriff 1860), and a Banker at Maidstone.—*Foley House, Maidstone.*

RANDOLPH, Admiral CHARLES GRENVILLE, of Great Comp, Kent.

Third son of the late Right Rev. John Randolph, D.D., Lord Bishop of London, by Jane, dau. of the late Thomas Lambarde, Esq., of Sevenoaks, Kent; *b.* 1793; *m.* 1829 Julia, dau. of Multon Lambarde, Esq., of Sevenoaks. Educated at Westminster and Ch. Ch., Oxford; is a Magistrate for Kent, and an Admiral in the Navy.—*Great Comp, Wrotham. Sevenoaks; United Service Club, s.w.*

RANDOLPH, the Rev. JOHN HONYWOOD, M.A., of Sanderstead, Surrey.‡

Second son of the late Right Rev. John Randolph, D.D., Bishop of London, by Jane, dau. of Thomas Lambarde, Esq., of Sevenoaks. Kent; *b.* 1791; *m.* 1814 Sarah, dau. of Richard Wilson. Esq., of Bildeston, Suffolk. Educated at Westminster and Ch. Ch., Oxford (B.A. 1812, M.A. 1815); is a Magistrate for Essex and co. Lincoln, Rector of Sanderstead, Prebendary of St.

‡ Died whilst these sheets were at press.

Paul's, Patron of St. Andrew's, Croydon, and Proctor in Convocation for the Archdeaconry of Surrey. He was formerly Preacher of Gray's Inn, Rector of Wainfleet, &c., and Chaplain to H.R.H. the Duke of Sussex. —*Sanderstead Rectory, Croydon; University Club*, s.w.

RANELAGH, Viscount (THOMAS HERON JONES). —Cr. 1628.
Only son of Thomas, 6th Viscount, by his 2nd wife Elizabeth Caroline, dau. of the late Sir Philip Stevens, Bart.; *b.* 1812; *s.* 1820. Is a Dep.-Lieut. for Middlesex, a Magistrate for Norfolk (High Sheriff 1868), Lord of Manor and Patron of Horsham St. Faith's, Norfolk, and Col. Commandant South Middlesex Rifles; was formerly Lieut. 1st Life Guards.—*Horsham, St. Faith, Norwich; Fulham, Middlesex*, s.w.; *Carlton Club*, s.w.; *7, New Burlington Street*, w.
Heir Pres., his cousin Alexander Montgomery (eldest son of the late Hon. Alexander Jones, who *d.* 1862, by Caroline, dau. of Thomas Palmer. Esq., of Hambledon, Hants), *b.* 1812; is M.A. of Trinity Coll., Cambridge.

RANFURLY, Earl of (THOMAS GRANVILLE HENRY STUART KNOX).—Cr. 1831.
Eldest son of Thomas, 3rd Earl, by Harriet, dau. of the late James Rimington, Esq., of Bromhead Hall, co. York; *b.* 1849; *s.* 1858; second title Viscount Northland. Educated at Eton; is Lord of the Manor of Dungannon.—*Dungannon Park, co. Tyrone.*
Heir Pres., his brother John Mark, *b.* 1856.

RANKIN, PATRICK, Esq., of Otter, Argyllshire.
Eldest son of the late Patrick Rankin, Esq., of Meikle Drumgray, by Elizabeth, dau. of Mathew Thomson, Esq., of Whiterig; *b.* 1790; *s.* 1808; *m.* 1818 Margaret, dau. of James Thomson, Esq., of Oakersdykes, and had issue,
    James Thomson, *b.* 1819; *m.*, and *d.* 1861, leaving issue,
        * Patrick, *b.* 185–.
Mr. Rankin is a Magistrate for co. Lanark, and Lord of the Baronies of Otter and Auchengray.—*Otter House, Kilfinan, Argyleshire.*

+RANT, THOMAS, Esq., of Chediston, Suffolk.
Son of the late Thomas Rant, Esq.; *b.* 1810; *m.* 1848 Mary, widow of George Parkyns, Esq., of Chediston Park (who *d. s. p.* 1851). Is a Magistrate for Suffolk, *jure uxoris* Lord of the Manor, and Patron of Chediston.—*Chediston Park, Halesworth.*

RAPER. (See *Lamplugh-Raper.*)

RASCH, FREDERICK CARNE, Esq., of Woodhill House, Essex.
Eldest son of the late John Peter Rasch, Esq., of Merton, Surrey (who *d.* 1846), by Louisa Mays Sophia, dau. of the Rev. John Leroux, of Belford, Suffolk; *b.* 1808; *m.* 1842 Catherine, dau. of James Edwards, Esq., of Harrow, and has issue,
    * Frederick Carne, educated at Eton and Trinity Coll., Cambridge, Cornet 6th Dragoon Guards; *b.* 1846.
Mr. Rasch, who was educated at Trinity Coll., Cambridge (B.A. 1830, M.A. 1834) and called to the Bar at Lincoln's Inn 1834, is a J.P. and D.L. for Essex. This family is of Danish extraction.—*Woodhill House, Danbury, Chelmsford; Oxford and Cambridge Club*, s.w.; *30, Cambridge Square*, w.; *10, New Square, Lincoln's Inn*, w.c.

RASHLEIGH, Sir COLMAN, Bart., of Prideaux, Cornwall (cr. 1831).
Only son of the late Sir John Colman Rashleigh, Bart., of Prideaux, by Harriett, dau. of the late Robert Williams, Esq., M.P., of Bridehead, Dorset; *b.* 1819; *s.* as 2nd Bart., 1847; *m.* 1845 Mary Anne, only dau. of Nicholas Kendall, Esq., M.P., of Pelyn, Cornwall, Educated at Eton and Trinity Coll., Cambridge; is a
784

J.P. and D.L. for Cornwall (High Sheriff 1851), a Special Deputy Warden of the Stannaries, Lieut.-Col. of the Royal Cornwall and Devon Miners' Artillery Militia, and Patron of 1 living.—*Prideaux, Par Station, Cornwall; Junior United Service Club*, s.w.
Heir, his son Colman Battie, *b.* 1846.

RASHLEIGH, WILLIAM, Esq., of Menabilly, Cornwall.
Eldest son of the late William Rashleigh, Esq., M.P., of Menabilly, by his 2nd wife Caroline, dau. of H. Hinxman, Esq., of Ivy Church, Wilts; *b.* 1817; *s.* 1855; *m.* 1843 the Hon. Catherine, eldest dau. of Robert Walter, 11th Lord Blantyre, and has issue,
    * Edith Frances.
Mr. Rashleigh, who is a J.P. and D.L. for Cornwall, Patron of 4 livings, and Lieut. Royal Cornwall Rangers Rifle Militia, was M.P. for E. Cornwall 1841–7.—*Menabilly, Par Station, Cornwall; Carlton Club*, s.w.; *31, Hill Street*, w.

RATCLIFF, Lady, of Wyddrington, Warwickshire.
Jane, dau. of George Pugh, Esq., of Coalport, co. Salop; *m.* 1829 Sir John Ratcliff, Knt., who was a Magistrate for Birmingham, of which place he was Mayor in 1857–9, and who *d.* 1864. The late Sir J. Ratcliff was knighted when Mayor of Birmingham on the Queen's visit in 1858.—*Wyddrington, Edgbaston, Birmingham.*
Heir Pres., her husband's brother Charles, F.S.A., of Downing Coll., Cambridge, Barrister-at-Law; *b.* 1824.

+RATHBONE, WILLIAM, Esq., of Greenbank, Lancashire.
Son of the late William Rathbone, Esq., J.P., of Greenbank; *b.* 18—; *s.* 1868. Is a Magistrate for co. Lancaster.—*Greenbank, Liverpool.*

RATTRAY, GRANTHAM YORKE RUNNYGULLION, Esq.
Only son of the late Admiral James Rattray (who *d.* 1862), by Emily, dau. of John Vivian, Esq., of Claverton, Somerset; *b.* 1834; *m.* 1863 Charlotte Anne, dau. of the Rev. H. H. Adcock, and has issue,
    * A son, *b.* 1864.
Mr. Rattray, who was educated at the Royal Naval Coll., Portsmouth, is a Lieut. R.N. This family was formerly of Drimmie and Corb, co. Perth.—*Brook, Newport, I. of Wight; 9, Hanover Terrace*, n.w.

RATTRAY. (See *Clerk-Rattray.*)

+RAVENHILL, JOHN, Esq., of Ashton, Wiltshire.
Eldest son of the late Rev. John Ravenhill, D.D., of Ashton Gifford; *b.* 18—; is married and has issue. Is a Magistrate for Somerset, a J.P. and D.L. for Wilts, Deputy Chairman of the Wilts Quarter Sessions, and Chairman of the Warminster Union. — *Ashton Gifford, Heytesbury.*

RAVENSCROFT, JOHN, Esq., of Lingdale House, Cheshire.
Eldest surviving son of the late William Ravenscroft, Esq., of Lingdale House, by Eleanor, dau. of W. Betteley, Esq.; *b.* 1820; *s.* 1850; *m.* 1851 Anne, dau. of R. Scholes, Esq., and has, with other issue,
    * John, *b.* 1856.
Mr. Ravenscroft, who is a Magistrate for co. Chester, represents a family which was formerly of Raven-Croft Hall, Cheshire. (See Ormerod's 'History of Cheshire.') —*Lingdale House, Oxton, Birkenhead.*

RAVENSWORTH, Lord (HENRY THOMAS LIDDELL).—Cr. 1821.

Eldest son of Thomas Henry, 1st Lord (of 2nd creation), by Maria Susanna, dau. of John Simpson, Esq., of Bradley, co, Durham; *b.* 1797; *s.* 1855; *m.* 1820 Isabella Horatio, dau. of the late Lord George Seymour (she *d.* 1856). Educated at Eton; is a Dep.-Lieut. for co. Durham, and a J.P. and D.L. for Northumberland, and Patron of 2 livings; was M.P. for Northumberland 1826-30, for N. Durham 1837-47, for Liverpool 1853-5.—*Eslington Park, Alnwick; Ravensworth Castle, Gateshead; Carlton Club, s.w. ; Percy's Cross, Fulham, s.w.*

Heir, his son Henry George, *b.* 1821 ; *m.* 1852 Mary Diana, dau. of Capt. Orlando Gunning Sutton, R.N. ; educated at Eton and Ch. Ch., Oxford ; is a J.P. and D.L. for co, Durham, and a Dep.-Lieut. for Northumberland, and Capt. Northumberland Yeomanry Cavalry ; has been M.P. for S. Northumberland since 1852.

RAWDON.

(See under *Cremorne, Dowager Lady,* and *Hastings, Marquis of.*)

RAWLINGS, HENRY PETER, Esq., of St. Edmund's, Cornwall.

Third son of the late Rev. William Rawlings, Vicar of Padstow, Cornwall, by Susanna, dau. of Peter Salmon, Esq., of Padstow; *b.* 1796. Is a Magistrate for Cornwall.—*St. Edmund's, Padstow.*

RAWLINGS, the Rev. JAMES.

Fourth son of the late Rev. William Rawlings, Vicar of Padstow, by Susanna, dau. of Peter Salmon, Esq., of Padstow; *b.* 1802 ; *m.* 1842 Elizabeth, dau. of Henry Pethick, Esq., M.D., of Park Cottage, Launceston, and has, with other issue,

* William Henry, *b.* 1844.

Mr. Rawlings, who was educated at Queen's Coll., Cambridge (B.A. 1826, M.A. 1829), is Rector and Joint Patron of St. Pinnock.—*St. Pinnock, Liskeard.*

RAWLINS, Lieut.-Col. HENRY WILLIAM, of Brean House, Somerset.

Eldest son of the Rev. H. W. Rawlins, M.A. of Fiddington, Somerset; *b.* 1820 ; *m.* 1845 Emma Matilda. dau. of Capt. Patton, R.N., of Bishop's-Hull House, Somerset, and has, with other issue,

* Henry de Courcy, *b.* 1851.

Col. Rawlins, who is a Magistrate for Somerset, represents a family of Welsh extraction.— *Brean House, Weston-super-Mare.*

RAWLINSON, Sir CHRISTOPHER, Knt. (cr. 1847).

Eldest surviving son of the late John Rawlinson, Esq., of Alresford. Hants; *b.* 1806 ; *m.* 1847 Georgina Maria, youngest dau. of the late Alexander Radclyffe Sidebottom, Esq. Educated at the Charterhouse and Trinity Coll., Cambridge (B.A. 1828, M.A. 1831); called to the Bar at the Middle Temple 1831 ; was Recorder of Prince of Wales Island 1847-50, Chief Justice of Madras 1850-9.

RAWLINSON, Sir HENRY CRESWICKE, K.C.B. (cr. 1856).

Son of the late Abraham Tyzack Rawlinson, Esq., of Chadlington, Oxon, by Eliza Eudocia Albinia, dau. and co-heir of Henry Creswicke, Esq., of Moreton, co. Gloucester (she *d.* 1863); *b.* 1810 ; *m.* 1862 Louisa, youngest dau. of the late Henry Seymour, Esq., of Knoyle, Wilts, and has, with other issue,

* Henry Seymour, *b.* 1864.

Sir Henry, who was educated at Ealing, is a retired Lieut.-Col. H.E.I.C.'s Service (Bombay), late Political Agent at Candahar, and Consul-General at Bagdad;

served in Persia and Affghanistan; discovered the interpretation of the ancient cuneiform inscriptions at Babylon and Nineveh; appointed an East-India Company Director 1856, a Member of Council for India 1858; Envoy Extraordinary to Persia, with the local rank of Major-General in that country, 1859 : was M.P. for Reigate in 1858; elected M.P. for Frome 1865.—*Atheneum Club, s.w.; 1, Hill Street, w.*

RAWLINSON, WILLIAM SAWREY, Esq., of Graythwaite and Duddon Hall, Lancashire.

Eldest son of the late John Job Rawlinson, Esq., J.P., of Graythwaite (who *d.* 1864), by Mary, eldest dau. of the Rev. John Romney, B.D., of Whitestock Hall, co. Lancaster; *b.* 1835 ; *s.* his maternal ancestor, the Rev. George Millers, M.A., in Duddon Hall estate, 1860 ; *m.* 1862 Elizabeth Mary, only dau. of the late Robert Brooke, Esq., of Bath, and has, with other issue,

* A son, *b.* 1863.

Mr. Rawlinson is a Magistrate for Cumberland, Lord of the Manor of Graythwaite, and Patron of 1 living; was formerly Major 6th Inniskilling Dragoons, and 12th Lancers.—*Graythwaite, Newton-in-Cartmel ; Duddon Hall, Broughton-in-Furness, Ulverstone.*

RAWLINSON. (See *Lindow.*)

RAWNSLEY, the Rev. EDWARD, of Raithby Hall, Lincolnshire.

Eldest son of the late Rev. T. H. Rawnsley, of Halton Holegate, by Sophia, dau. of Edward Walls, Esq., of Boothby Hall, co. Lincoln ; *b.* 1816; *m.* 1848 Mary, only child of John Jackson, Esq., of Hamburgh, and has, with other issue,

* Edward Preston, *b.* 1852.

Mr. Rawnsley, who was educated at Eton, and B.N.C. Coll., Oxford (B.A. 1838, M.A. 1840), is a Magistrate for co. Lincoln, was formerly Vicar of Hundleby, co. Lincoln.—*Raithby Hall, Spilsby; Oxford and Cambridge Club, s.w.*

RAWSON, CHRISTOPHER, Esq., late of The Hurst, Surrey.

Eldest son of Thomas Samuel Rawson, Esq., late of Bridgen Place, Bexley, Kent, by Sarah Colbeck, dau. of Richard Holdsworth, Esq., of West End, near Otley, co. York ; *b.* 1816; *m.* 1840 Ellen Frances, dau. of John Naylor Wright, Esq., of Beaumaris, Anglesey, and has issue,

* Christopher Wright, *b.* 1842.

Mr. Rawson is a Magistrate for Surrey, and of Yorkshire extraction.—Residence: *Canada.*

RAWSON, Miss, of Nidd Hall. Yorkshire.

Elizabeth, only surviving dau. of the late Benjamin Rawson, Esq., of Nidd Hall, by Elizabeth, only child of the late Thomas Plumbe. Esq., of Bolton, co. York; *s.* 1844. Is Lady of the Manor of Bradford, Yorkshire.—*Nidd Hall, Ripley; 4, Tilney Street, w.*

RAWSON, WILLIAM HENRY, Esq., of Haughend and Mill House, Yorkshire.

Eldest son of the late William Henry Rawson, Esq., of Haughend, by Mary, dau. of John Priestley, Esq., of Thorpe, Halifax ; *b.* 1812 ; *s.* 1865; *m.* 1847 Ellen Louisa, dau. of Amaziah Empson, Esq., of Spellow Hill, Knaresborough, and has, with other issue,

* William Henry, *b.* 1848.

Mr. Rawson is a J.P. and D.L. for the W. Riding of co. York.—*Haughend, Halifax.*

RAWSTORNE, LAWRENCE, Esq., of Penwortham, Lancashire.

Eldest son of the late Lawrence Rawstorne, Esq., J.P, and D.L. of Penwortham (High Sheriff of co. Lancaster

1817), by Margaret Elizabeth, dau. of Edward Ledward, Esq., of Everton; *b.* 1842; *s.* 1850. Educated at Eton and Ch. Ch., Oxford; is Lord of the Manor of Penwortham, and Patron of 2 livings.—*Penwortham Priory and Hutton Hall, Preston.*

RAYER, the Rev. WILLIAM, of Holcombe, Devon.

Son of the late William Rayer, Esq., of Tiverton, Devon; *b.* 1785; *m.* 1816 Jane, dau. of Sir Thomas Carew, Bart., and by her, who *d.* 1851, has issue,
  • William, *b.* 1820.

Mr. Rayer, who was educated at Trinity Coll., Oxford (B.A. 1807, M.A. 1810), is a Magistrate for Devon, Lord of the Manor of Holcombe Rogus, Rector of Tidcombe and Chevithorne, and Patron of 2 livings.—*Holcombe Court, Wellington; St. Athan, Cowbridge.*

RAYLEIGH, Lord (JOHN JAMES STRUTT).— Cr. 1821.

Only son of the late Col. Joseph Holden Strutt, of Terling Place, Essex (who was many years M.P. for Maldon), by Lady Charlotte Mary Gertrude, dau. of James, 1st Duke of Leinster (cr. Baroness Rayleigh); *b.* 1796; *s.* 1836; *m.* 1842 Clara Elizabeth Latouche, dau. of the late Capt. Vicars, R.E. Educated at Winchester and Trinity Coll., Oxford (B.A. 1818, M.A. 1821); is a J.P. and D.L. for Essex, Lord of the Manor of Terling, and Patron of 2 livings. — *Terling Place, Witham, Essex; Carlton and University Clubs, s.w.*
  Heir, his son John William, Fellow of Trinity Coll., Cambridge, and a J.P. and D.L. for Essex; *b.* 1842.

RAYMOND, the Rev. GREGORY, of Symondsbury, Dorset.

Eldest son of the late Rev. G. Syndercombe, by Elizabeth, dau. of John Fort, Esq.; *b.* 1781; *s.* 1804; assumed the name of Raymond 1805. Educated at Tiverton and Balliol Coll., Oxford (B.A. 1802, M.A. 1808); appointed Rector of Symondsbury 1806; is a J.P. and D.L. for Dorset, and Patron of 2 livings. —*Symondsbury Rectory, Bridport.*

RAYMOND, JAMES, Esq., of Hildersham Hall, Cambridgeshire.

Only surviving son of the late Rev. John Raymond, formerly Vicar of Wimbish, Essex, by Mary, dau. of William Archer, Esq., of Saffron Walden, Essex; *b.* 1797; *m.* 1st 1830 Mary Sophia, dau. of Col. Weston (Thudowbush), of Poslingford, Suffolk (she *d.* 1845); 2nd 1847 Anna, dau. of the late Swynfen Jervis, Esq., of Gordon Square, London. This family have held lands in Essex and Cambridgeshire for three centuries.—*Hildersham Hall, Cambridge.*

RAYMOND, the Rev. JOHN MAYNE ST. CLERE, of Belchamp Hall, Essex.

Eldest son of the late Samuel Milbank Raymond, Esq., J.P., of Belchamp Hall, by Sarah, dau. of the late Rev. William Cooke, Rector of Preston, Suffolk; *b.* 1814; *s.* 1863; *m.* 1857 Louisa Anne, dau. of the Rev. Charles Fisher, Rector of Ovington-cum-Tilbury, Essex, and has, with other issue,
  • Samuel John St. Clere, *b.* 1858.

Mr. Raymond, who was educated at Eton and University Coll., Durham (B.A. 1837, M.A. 1840), is Lord of the Manor of Belchamp Walte, Rector of Belchamp Otten, and Patron of 1 living, was formerly Vicar of Dinnington, Northumberland.—*Belchamp Hall, Sudbury.*

RAYMOND, of The Lee, Essex.

Caroline Louisa and Elizabeth Augusta, only surviving daus. of the late Lieut.-General Raymond, of The Lee, Littlebury (who *d.* 1830), by Anne, dau. and coheir of Alexander Forbes, Esq., and sisters of the late Ven.
786

William Forbes Raymond, Archdeacon of Northumberland; *s.* their brother 1860; are Ladies of the Manor and Patrons of the living of Strethall, Essex. The younger sister, Elizabeth Augusta, *m.* 1831 General Sir R. Lluellyn (who *d.* 1868).—*The Lee, Saffron Walden.*
  Heir Pres., their nephew William Inglis, Esq., Col. in the Army (elder son of the late Sir William Inglis, by Margaret Mary Anne, eldest dau. of the above Lieut.-General Raymond); *b.* 1823; *m.* 1860 Mary, dau. of the late Hector B. Monro, Esq., of Edmonsham, Dorset.

RAYMOND-BARKER, JOHN RAYMOND, Esq., of Fairford Park, Gloucestershire.

Eldest son of the late Daniel Raymond-Barker, Esq., of Fairford Park, by Sophia Ann, youngest dau. of John Ives, Esq., of Norfolk; *b.* 1801; *s.* 1827; *m.* 1st 1823 Harriott Ives, dau. of Wm. Bosanquet, Esq., of London (she *d.* 1830); 2nd 1841 Lady Catherine, youngest dau. of Thomas, 1st Earl Ducie, and has, with other issue,
  • Percy Fitzhardinge, a Magistrate for co. Gloucester; *b.* 1842.

Mr. Raymond-Barker, who was educated at Oriel Coll., Oxford, is a J.P. and D.L. for co. Gloucester (High Sheriff 1854).—*Fairford Park, Gloucester.*

RAYNSFORD, Major-Gen. HANBURY, ‡ of Henlow Grange, Beds.

Youngest, but only surviving, son of the late George Raynsford, Esq., of Henlow Grange, by Frances, dau. of — Edwards. Esq., and nephew of the late George Edwards, Esq., of Henlow Grange; *b.* 1785; *s.* his brother 1854; is a Major-Gen. in the Indian Army, and Lord of the Manor of Henlow Lanthony.—*Henlow Grange, Shefford.*
  Heir Pres., his kinsman, the Rev. Henry Addington, Rector of Langford, Beds; *m.* 1852 Matilda Frances, dau. of the late Thomas Alexander Raynsford, Esq. (she *d.* 1857).

READ, CLARE SEWELL, Esq., of Honingham, Norfolk.

Eldest son of the late Mr. George Read, of Barton Bendish Hall, Norfolk, by Sarah Anne, dau. of the late Mr. Clare Sewell, of Barton Bendish Hall; *b.* 1826; *m.* 1859 Sarah Maria, only dau. of the late James Watson, Esq., of Norwich (Sheriff of that city in 1848). Is a Magistrate for Norfolk; elected M.P. for E. Norfolk 1865. —*Honingham, Thorpe, Norwich; Farmers' Club, s.c.*

+**READ**, JOSEPH, Esq., of Uplands, Devon.

Son of the late J. Read, Esq.; *b.* 18—; *m.* 18— Elizabeth, eldest dau. of the late John Gill, Esq., of Bickham Park, Devon, and widow of William Smith, Esq. Is a Magistrate for Devon, and a Banker at Tavistock.—*Uplands, Tamerton, Plymouth; Heathfield, Hampstead, N.W.*

READ, WILLIAM HENRY RUDSTON-, Esq., of Hayton, Yorkshire.

Eldest son of the late Rev. Thomas Cutler Rudston-Read, by Louisa, 3rd dau. of the late Henry Cholmley, Esq., of Howsham and Whitby Abbey; *b.* 1808; *s.* 1858. Educated at Eton and Trinity Coll., Cambridge (B.A. 1831, M.A. 1834); called to the Bar at Lincoln's Inn 1834; is a Magistrate for the E. and W. Ridings of Yorkshire.—*Hayton, [...] Canton [...] s.w.*

READ, the Rev. THOMAS FREDERICK RUDSTON-.

Third son of the late Rev. Thomas Cutler Rudston-Read, of Frickley Hall, Doncaster, by Louisa, dau. of the late Henry Cholmley, Esq., of Howsham, York; *b.* 1811; *m.* 1815 Louisa Lucy, 2nd dau. of the late Hon. and Very Rev. Henry David Erskine, Dean of Ripon. Educated at Eton and University Coll., Oxford (B.A. 1832, M.A. 1833); is a Magistrate for co. Lincoln, and Rector of Wintringham.—*Wintringham, Brigg.*

  ‡ Died whilst these sheets were at press.

READ. (See *Crewe-Read*.)

READE, Sir GEORGE, Bart., of Shipton Court, Oxon (cr. 1660).

Only son of the late George Compton Reade, Esq. (who *d.* 1866), by Maria Jane, dau. of the late Sir Hungerford Hoskyns, Bart., of Harewood, co. Hereford.; *b.* 1812; *s.* his uncle, as 7th Bart., 1868. Is Lord of the Manor of Shipton, and Patron of 2 livings.—*Shipton Court, Chipping Norton.*

Heir Pres., his cousin John Edmund (only son of the late Thomas Reade, Esq., who *d.* 1837, by Catherine, dau. of Sir John Hill), *b.* 1804; *m.* 1847 his cousin Maria Louisa, elder dau. of the late George Compton Reade, Esq., and has issue a dau.

+ READE, EDWARD ANDERTON, Esq., C.B., of Ipsden Place, Berks.

Fifth son of the late John Reade, Esq., of Ipsden, by Anna Maria, eldest dau. of the late Major John Scott, M.P., and brother of W. B. Reade, Esq. (whom see); *b.* 1807; *m.* 1838 Eliza, dau. of Richard Burnard, Esq., of Crewkerne, Somerset, and has, with other issue,

    * Burnard, of the Indian Army; *b.* 1839.

Mr. Reade, who is a Magistrate for Berks and Oxon, was formerly in the Bengal Civil Service.—*Ipsden Place, Wallingford.*

READE, JOHN PAGE, Esq., of Crow Hall, Suffolk.

Second son of the late George Reade, Esq., of Crow Hall, by Eliza, dau. of the late George Swinton, Esq., of Swinton, co. Berwick; *b.* 1806; *s.* his brother 1826; *m.* 1829 Helen, younger dau. of the late Sir James Colquhoun, Bart., of. Luss, N.B. (she *d.* 1852); 2nd 1854 Lady Mary, 2nd dau. of Thomas, 2nd Earl of Ranfurly, and has issue by the former,

    * James Colquhoun Revell, Cornet 14th Hussars; *b.* 1840.

Mr. Reade, who was educated at Exeter Coll., Oxford (B.A. 1828), is a J.P. and D.L. for Suffolk (High Sheriff 1865), and Patron of the Rectory of Thorpe Abbotts. —*Crow Hall, Stutton, Ipswich;* 3, *Buckingham Gate,* s.w.

READE, FRANCIS EDWARD, Esq., of Holbrook, Suffolk.

Eldest surviving son of the late John Reade, Esq., of the Madras Civil Service (who was High Sheriff of Suffolk 1831, and *d.* 1843), by Elizabeth, dau. of the late General Gowdie, of the Madras Army; *b.* 1807; *m.* 1843 Henrietta Maria, eldest dau. of W. H. Belli, Esq., late of the B.C.S., and by her, who *d.* 1864, has, with other issue,

    * Charles Gowdie Belli, *b.* 1845.

Mr. Reade, who was educated at Chiswick and Haileybury Coll., and appointed to the Bengal Civil Service 1826, is a Magistrate for Suffolk.—*Holbrook House, Ipswich;* 1, *Queen's Terrace, Gore Road,* s.w.

READE, PHILIP, Esq., of the Wood Parks, co. Galway.

Eldest son of the late William Francis Reade, Esq., of The Wood Parks, and Wood Town, co. Meath, by Jane Peacock, only dau. of Edward Borr, Esq., of Newpark and Balindolon, co. Kildare; *b.* 1793; *s.* 1801; *m.* 1829 Grace, dau. of John Rutherfoord, Esq. of St. Donloughs, co. Dublin, and has, with other issue,

    * Philip William Villiers, *b.* 1839; *m.* 1862 Caroline, only dau, of Robert Dupré Alexander, Esq., and grand dau. of the late Sir Robert Alexander, Bart., and has issue, Florence Jane.

Mr. Reade, who was educated at Trinity Coll., Dublin (B.A. 1811, M.A. 1816), and called to the Irish Bar 1816, is a Magistrate for cos. Galway and Clare. —*The Wood Parks, Mountshannon, co. Galway; University Club,* s.w.

READE, WILLIAM BARRINGTON, Esq., of Ipsden and Dogmore End, Oxon.

Fourth but eldest surviving son of the late John Reade, Esq., of Ipsden House, Oxon, by Anna Maria, eldest dau. of the late Major Scott Waring, M.P. (she *d.* 1863); *b.* 1803; *s.* 1849; *m.* 1837 Elizabeth, only child of Capt. John Murray, R.N., of Ardbennie, co. Perth, and has, with other issue,

    * William Winwood, *b.* 1838.

Mr. Reade, who is a J.P. and D.L. for Oxon, was formerly Lieut. in the H.E.I.C.'s Cavalry.— *Ipsden House, Wallingford; Dogmore End, Henley-on-Thames.* Residence: 5, *Rock Houses, Tenby.*

READE. (See *Morris-Reade*.)

REAVELY, THOMAS, Esq., of Kinnersley Castle, Herefordshire.

Eldest son of Thomas Reavely, Esq., of Kenton, Northumberland, by Ann Wilson, dau. of Douglas Sands, Esq., of Killymuir, N.B.; *b.* 1829; *m.* 1850 Johanna M. Wilhelmina, only child of the late George Stiefvater, Esq., of Hamburgh, and has, with other issue

    * Thomas George Wood, *b.* 1852.

Mr. Reavely, is a J.P. and D.L. for co. Hereford (High Sheriff 1867). This family is of Northumberland origin, having settled at the Manor House of Reveley in that county A.D. 1403.—*Kinnersley Castle, Weobly.*

REAY; Lord (ERICK MACKAY).—Cr. 1628.

Only son of Alexander, 8th Lord, by Marian. widow of D. Ross, Esq.; *b.* 1813; *s.* 1863; formerly an Officer in the 28th Foot; represents an ancient Sutherlandshire clan.—*Windsor Terrace, Plymouth.*

Heir Pres., his kinsman Baron Mackay, of the Hague. Vice-President of the Council of the King of the Netherlands; *b.* 1806; *m.* 1837 Maria Catherine Fagel, and has issue, * Donald, *b.* 1839.

REBOW. (See *Gurdon-Rebow*.)

REDESDALE, Lord (JOHN THOMAS FREEMAN MITFORD).—Cr. 1802.

Only son of John, 1st Lord (who was Chancellor of Ireland, and Speaker of the House of Commons 1800-2), by Lady Frances, dau. of John, 2nd Earl of Egmont; *b.* 1805; *s.* 1830. Educated at Eton and New Coll., Oxford (B.A. 1825, M.A. 1828); is a Magistrate for co. Gloucester, Patron of 3 livings, a Speaker by Royal Commission, and Chairman of Committees of the House of Lords.—*Batsford, Moreton-in-the-Marsh; Birdhope Crais, Reedsdale, Northumberland; Compton Club,* s.w.; 6, *Park Place, St. James's,* s.w.

REDINGTON, CHRISTOPHER TALBOT, Esq., of Kilcornan House, co. Galway.

Eldest son of the late Sir Thomas Nicholas Redington, K.C.B., of Kilcornan (sometime M.P. for Dundalk, Under-Secretary of State for Ireland, and Secretary to the Board of Controls), by Anna Eliza Mary, eldest dau. of John Hyacinth Talbot, Esq., M.P. of Ballytrent, co. Wexford; *b.* 1847; *s.* 1862. Educated at Oscott Coll. and Ch. Ch., Oxford; is Lord of the Manor of Kilcornan —*Kilcornan House, Oranmore, co. Galway.*

+ REDINGTON, JOHN, Esq., of Dangan House, co. Galway.

Son of the late J. Redington, Esq.; is a J.P. and D.L. for co. Galway (High Sheriff 1861).—*Dangan House, Galway.*

REDMOND, JOHN HENRY O'BYRNE, Esq., of Killoughter, co. Wicklow.

Son of the late Henry Thompson Redmond, Esq., of Killoughter House (who was formerly Resident Magistrate for co. Wicklow), by Margaret, youngest dau. of

the late Jonathan Lynch, Esq.; *b.* 1825; *s.* 1861; *m.* 1849 Amelia, dau. of General Count Manley, and has, with other issue,

* Reginald, *b.* 1851.

Mr. Redmond, who is Chamberlain to Pope Pius IX., represents a branch of the ancient family of Redmond of Redmond's Hall (now called Loftus Hall) and of Killygown, co. Wexford.—*Killoughter House, Ashford.*

REDMOND, Mrs., of The Deeps, co. Wexford.
Margaret, dau. of Nicholas Archer, Esq., M.D.; *m.* 1827 John Edward Redmond, Esq., of The Deeps, who was a Magistrate and sometime M.P. for co. Wexford, and who *d.* 1865.—*The Deeps, Enniscorthy, co. Wexford ; 20, Molesworth Street, Dublin.*

REDMOND, PATRICK WALTER, Esq., of Pembroke House, co. Wexford.
Eldest son of the late John Redmond, Esq., of Somerton, co. Wexford, by Eliza, dau. of M. Sutton, Esq.; *b.* 1803; *m.* 1st 1822 Esther, dau. of the late J. Kearney, Esq., of Rocklands, co. Wexford ; 2nd 1850 Teresa, dau. of W. Parsons Hoey, Esq., of Dublin, and has, by the former, with other issue,

* John Patrick, Lieut.-Col. 61st Foot ; *b.* 1821; *m.* 1864 Roberta Elizabeth, eldest dau. of the late Edwin Leaf, Esq.

Mr. Redmond is a J.P. and D.L. for co. Wexford (High Sheriff 1845).—*Pembroke House, Dublin ; Union Club, s.w.*

REDMOND, GABRIEL JOHN WALSINGHAM, Esq., of Movilla, co. Wexford.
Son of the late John Walsingham Cooke Redmond, Esq., J.P., of Movilla, by Eleanor Fetherston-Haugh, dau. of the late J. Sweeny, Esq., of Clonakilty, co. Cork; *b.* 1850; *s.* 1862. Is head representative of the Redmond family, who went over to Ireland with the Earl of Pembroke, temp. Henry II. — *Movilla, Screen, co. Wexford ; Richmond Cottage, Monkstown, co. Dublin.*

REED, Sir THOMAS, K.C.B., of Ampfield House, Hants (cr. 1865).
Son of the late Thomas Reed, Esq., by Eliza, dau. of Col. Sir Francis James Buchanan ; *b.* 1796 ; *m.* 1835 Elizabeth Jane, dau. of John Clayton, Esq., of Enfield Old Park, Middlesex. Educated at the Royal Military Coll., Sandhurst; is a Lieut.-General in the Army; was formerly Aide-de-Camp to the Queen.—*Ampfield House, Romsey ; United Service Club, s.w.*

REED, STEPHEN, Esq., of Cragg, Northumberland.
Youngest son and devisee of John Reed, Esq., late of Acklington Park, Northumberland, by Diana, dau. of William Watson, Esq., of Newcastle-upon-Tyne; *b.* 1781; *s.* 1829; *m.* 1819 Isabella, dau. of John Barras, Esq., and has, with other issue,

* Charles John, of Newbiggin House, Northumberland, Major Northumberland Militia Artillery ; *b.* 1820.

Mr. Reed, who is a Solicitor in the Court of Chancery, and an Attorney in the Courts of Law at Westminster, was elected Coroner for Northumberland in 1815. —*Cragg, Bellingham, Northumberland ; Saville Place, Newcastle-on-Tyne.*

REED, Major WILLIAM, of Bedfont, Middlesex.
Only son of the late William Reed, Esq., of Bedfont, by Sarah, dau. of John Marshall, Esq., of Cambridge, and grandson of Samuel Marshall, Esq., of South Well Park, Suffolk; *b.* 1814; *s.* 1865; *m.* 1860 Celina Adelaide, youngest dau. of the late Robert Chester Cooper, Esq., J.P. and D.L. for Sussex, and has, with other issue,

* William Bernard, *b.* 1863.

Major Reed is a J.P. and D.L. for Middlesex, and
738

Major 1st R. E. Middlesex Militia ; late Capt. 6th Fo·
—*St. Mary's, Bedfont, Hounslow ; Army and Navy Clu·
s.w.*

+REES, GEORGE RICHARD GRAHAM, Esq., o
Penllwyn, Pembrokeshire.
Son of the late G. Rees, Esq. ; *b.* 18—. Is a Magistra:
for co. Pembroke (High Sheriff 1868).—*Penllwy,
Cowbridge.*

REES, JOHN HUGHES, Esq., of Killymaenllwyd
Carmarthenshire.
Eldest son of the late John Rees, Esq., J.P. and D.L.
of Killymaenllwyd, Lieut.-Col. of the Local Militia
by Anne Catherine, dau. of Elias Van-der-Horst, Esq.
of Carolina, American Consul at Bristol; *b.* 1806; *s.*
1843; *m.* 1832 Isabella, only child of Thomas Rutson,
Esq., of Colham, and has, with other issue,

* John Van-der-Horst, Lieut. 40th Foot ; *b.* 1834.

Mr. Rees is a J.P. and D.L. for co. Carmarthen. This
family is descended from Urien Rheged, Lord of Rheged.—*Killymaenllwyd, Llandly ; Colham, Middlesex.*

REES, WILLIAM, Esq., of Scoveston, Pembrokeshire.
Eldest son of the late James Rees, of Haverfordwest,
by Martha, dau. of Mr. Collins, of Marloes : *b.* 1799;
m. 1st 1822 Mary, dau. of David Evans, of Haverfordwest ; 2nd 1858 Mary, dau. of Thomas Dicker, Esq., of
Lewes, Sussex, and widow of Samuel Salter, Esq., of
Trowbridge, Wilts. Is a J.P. and D.L. for co. Pembroke (High Sheriff 1863), and an Alderman and Magistrate for Haverfordwest ; was Mayor of Haverfordwest
in 1840, and 1856—57 ; formerly a Solicitor at Haverfordwest.—*Scoveston, Haverfordwest.*

REES, WILLIAM, Esq., of Tonn, Carmarthenshire.
Third but eldest surviving son of the late David Rees.
Esq. (who *d.* 1831), by Sarah, dau. of Rice Rees, Esq.,
of Llaudovery ; *b.* 1808 ; *s.* his brother in 1816, and to
the estates of his maternal uncle, Rev. W. Jenkins
Rees, M.A., F.S.A., Rector of Cascob, co. Radnor 1855 ;
m. 1836 Fanny, co-heiress of G. Farmer, Esq., of Cardiff, and has, with other issue,

* George Arthur, *b.* 1843.

Mr. Rees is a Magistrate for co. Brecon.—*Tonn, Llandovery.*

REEVE, Sir THOMAS NEWBY, Knt.‡ (cr. 1868).
Second son of the late Charles Reeve, Esq., of Southall.
Middlesex ; *b.* 1792 ; *m.* 1816 Frances Anne, only dau.
of John Catling, Esq. (she *d.* 1868). Is a Magistrate for
Surrey ; has been Standard-bearer to the corps of Gentlemen-at-Arms; knighted at the Coronation of Queen
Victoria.—*Kew Road, Richmond, s.w.*

REEVE, JOHN, Esq., of Leadenham, Lincolnshire.
Eldest son of the late General John Reeve, J.P. and
D.L., of Leadenham, by Lady Susan Sherard, youngest
dau. of Philip, 6th Earl of Harborough (extra: · b. 1808;
s. 1864 ; *m.* 1st 1837, Frances Wilhelmina, eldest dau.
of Sir Glynne Earle Welby-Gregory, Bart., of Denton
Hall, co. Lincoln (she *d.* 1858) ; 2nd 1863 Edith Anne,
eldest dau. of the Hon. and Rev. Charles Dundas,
Rector of Epworth, co. Lincoln. Is a Magistrate for co.
Lincoln; late Lieut.-Col. Grenadier Guards.—*Leadenham House, Grantham ; Carlton, Guards', and United
Service Clubs, s.w.*
Heir Pres., his brother William, late Lieut.-Col. Coldstream
Guards ; *b.* 1827.

REEVE-DE-LA-POLE. (See *Pole.*)

‡ Died whilst these sheets were at press.

REEVES, EDWARD HOARE, Esq., of Castle Kevin, co. Cork.

Eldest son of the late Edward Hoare Reeves, Esq., J.P., of Castle Kevin, by Elizabeth Mary Maria, dau. of Lieut.-General Burke, of Prospect Villa, co. Cork; b. 1840; s. 1867. Is a Magistrate for co. Cork. — *Castle Kevin, Mallow, co. Cork.*

+ **REEVES**, FRANCIS, Esq., of Ballyglissane, co. Cork.

Eldest son of the late Edward Hoare Reeves, Esq., of Ballyglissane, by his 2nd wife Dorothy, dau. of the late John Carleton, Esq., and niece of the late Lord Castleton (*ext.*); b. 1805; s. 184—. Educated at Addiscombe Coll., is a Major in H.M.'s Indian Army. This family is a younger branch of the Reeveses, formerly of Vostersberg (whom see.)—*Ballyglissane, Rathcormac.*

REEVES, JAMES, Esq.,‡ of Danemore Park, Kent, and Godstone, Surrey.

Second son of the late W. J. Reeves, Esq., of Woburn Place, Russell Square, by Anne, dau. of the late John Pughe, Esq., of Montgomery; m. 1824 Jane Mary, 2nd dau. and co-heir of Henry Carington Bowles, Esq., F.S.A., of Myddelton House, Enfield (she d. 1863). Is a J.P. and D.L. for Essex.—*Danemore Park, Speldhurst, Kent.*

REEVES, ROBERT WILLIAM CARY, Esq., of Burrane, co. Clare.

Eldest son of the late William Maunsell Reeves, Esq., of Vostersberg, co. Cork, by Rose, eldest dau. of the late Rev. Robert Conway Dobbs (she d. 1863); b. 1837; s. 1857; m. 1866 Grace Dorothea, youngest dau. of Col. Crofton Moore Vandeleur, of Kilrush House, co. Clare, and has issue,

* Grace Wilhelmina.

Mr. Reeves, who was educated at Trinity Coll., Cambridge (LL.B. 1859), and called to the Bar at the Inner Temple 1862, is a Magistrate for co. Clare. —*Burrane, Knock, co. Clare ; Union Club, s.w.*

REEVES, THOMAS SOMERVILLE, Esq., of Tramore House, co. Cork.

Eldest son of the late Joseph Hoare Reeves, Esq., of Spring Valley, Cork, by his 1st wife Anna, dau. of Thomas Somerville, Esq., of Dawny Hills, co. Cork; b. 1787; s. 1832; m. 1814 Rebecca, dau. of the late Isaac Morgan, Esq., of Cork, and has, with other issue,

* Isaac Morgan, in Holy Orders, Rector of Myros, co. Cork ; b. 1822; m. 1857 Ann Maria Toke, dau. of the Rev. Henry Bourchier Wrey, Rector of Tawstock, Devon, and has issue, Helen Wrey, b. 1860.

Mr. Reeves, who was educated at Trinity Coll., Dublin, is a Magistrate for Cork (High Sheriff 1848), and a Harbour Commissioner of Cork. This family is a branch of that descended from Col. Reeves, who settled from Sussex, in Ireland (*temp.* Charles I.), and m. a daughter of Lord Clanmaleer.—*Tramore House, Cork.*

REID, Sir ALEXANDER, Bart. (cr. 1703).

Eldest son of the late Sir John Reid, 3rd Bart., of Barra, co. Aberdeen, by Barbara, dau. of Thomas Livingstone, Esq., M.D., of Dawny Hills, co. Aberdeen; b. 1798; s. his brother as 5th Bart. 1815; m. 1840 Dorothea Amelia Ferraro de Sampayo.

Heir Pres., his brother David, b. 1801.

REID, Sir JOHN RAE, Bart., of Ewell, Surrey (cr. 1823).

Elder son of the late Sir John Rae Reid, Bart., of Ewell Grove, by Maria Louisa, dau. of Richard Eaton, Esq., of Stetchworth Park, co. Cambridge; b. 1841;

s. as 3rd Bart. 1867; is Patron of 1 living and Lieut. 16th Regt.—*Ewell Grove, Epsom.*

Heir Pres., his brother Henry Rae, b. 1845.

REID, Sir JAMES JOHN, Knt. (cr. 1840).

Son of John Reid, Esq., Advocate of the Scottish Bar; b. 1800; m. 1843 Mary, dau. of the late Robert Theshie, Esq. A Member of the Scottish Bar, called in 1827; is a Member of the Supreme Council in the Ionian Islands, of which he has been Chief Justice.

+ **REID**, the late WILLIAM, Esq., of The Node, Herts.

Son of the late W. Reid, Esq.; b. 18—; m. 1840 Miss Campbell, and had, with other issue,

Hugh William, Lieut. Rifle Brigade ; b. 1841 ; d. 1865.

Mr. Reid was High Sheriff of Herts 1857, and a partner in Messrs. Reid and Co.'s Brewery.—*The Node, Codicote, Welwyn.*

REID. (See *Fenwick.*)

REILLY, JOHN TEMPLE, Esq., of Scarvagh House, Downshire.

Eldest son of the late John Lushington Reilly, Esq., of Scarvagh, by Louisa, dau. of Gustavus Hancock Temple, Esq., of Waterstown, co. Westmeath ; b. 1812; s. 18—; m. 1865 Elizabeth, dau. of the late James O'Hara, Esq., of Lenaboy, co. Galway, and grand-dau. of the late Archbishop of Tuam. Is a J.P. and D.L. for co. Down (High Sheriff 1854), and a Magistrate for co. Armagh.—*Scarvagh House, Loughbrickland.*

REILLY. (See *Adams-Reilly.*)

RELPH. (See *Greenhow-Relph.*)

REMINGTON, the Rev. REGINALD, of Aynsome, Lancashire.

Eldest son of the late Henry Remington, Esq., J.P., of Aynsome, by Mary, only child of George Ashburner, Esq.; b. 1827; s. 1866. Educated at Pembroke Coll., Oxford (B.A. 1851, M.A. 1855): is Curate of Downham, co. Lancaster.—*Aynsome, Newton-in-Cartmel : The Crow Trees, Melling, Lancaster ; Downham, Clitheroe.*

+ **REMINGTON**, the late REGINALD FREDERICK, Esq., of Elm Bank, Surrey.

Third son of the late Reginald Remington, Esq., of Crow Trees, co. Lancaster, by Catharine, youngest dau. of Thomas Machell, Esq., of Aynsome, co. Lancaster; b. 18—; d. 1866, having married, and left issue. He was a Magistrate for Surrey —*Elm Bank, Leatherhead.*

RENDLESHAM, Lord (FREDERICK WILLIAM BROOK THELLUSSON).—Cr. 1806.

Only son of Frederick, 4th Lord, by Elizabeth Charlotte, dau. of the late Sir George Beeston Prescott, Bart., and widow of James Duff, Esq.; b. 1840; s. 1852. Educated at Eton and Ch. Ch., Oxford: is a Magistrate for Suffolk, Lord of the Manors of Rendlesham, &c., Patron of 1 living, and Cornet Ayrshire Yeomanry Cavalry—*Rendlesham Hall, Woodbridge ; 3, Upper Belgrave Street, w.*

Heir Pres., his cousin Arthur John Bethell, a Magistrate for Suffolk, and Lieut.-Col. Suffolk Rifle Volunteers (eldest son of the late Hon. Arthur Thellusson, who d. 1873, by Caroline, dau. of the late Sir Christopher Bethell-Codrington, Bart.); b. 1826 ; m. 1853 Henrietta Frances Elizabeth, 2nd dau. of Frederick William Thomas Vernon-Wentworth, Esq., of Wentworth Castle, co. York and has, with other issue, *a son, b. 1863.

RENNIE, Sir JOHN, Knt., F.R.S. (cr. 1831).

Son of the late John Rennie, Esq., Civil Engineer (who d. 1821), by Martha, dau. of E. Mackintosh, Esq.; b. 1794 ; m. 1833 Selina, dau. of Charles Graves

Colleton, Esq., and grand-dau. of the late Right Hon.
R. Pole Carew. Is an eminent Architect.—7, *Lowndes
Square*, s.w.

RENNY-STRACHAN-CARNEGIE. (See *Carnegie*.)

RENNY-TAILYOUR, THOMAS, Esq., of Borrowfield, Forfarshire.
Third son of the late Alexander Renny-Tailyour, Esq.,
of Borrowfield, by Elizabeth Bannerman, eldest dau. of
the late Sir Alexander Ramsay, Bart., of Balmain;
b. 1812; *s.* 1849; *m.* 1847 Isabella Eliza, 2nd dau. of
the late Major A. Atkinson, of Lorbottle, Northumberland, and has, with other issue,
    • Henry Waugh, *b.* 1849.
Mr. Renny-Tailyour, who was educated at Addiscombe,
is a J.P. and D.L. for co. Forfar, Lieut.-Col. Forfarshire Rifle Volunteers, and a Major in full pay, was
formerly in the Bengal Engineers.—*Newmanswalls,
Montrose, N.B.*

RENTON. (See *Campbell-Renton*.)

REPINGTON. (See *À Court-Repington*.)

REPTON, GEORGE WILLIAM JOHN, Esq., of
Odell, Beds.
Only son of the late George Stanley Repton, Esq. (who
d. 1858), by Lady Elizabeth, eldest dau. of John, 1st
Earl of Eldon; *b.* 1818; *m.* 1848, Lady Jane, dau. of
Augustus Frederick, 3rd Duke of Leinster. Educated
at University Coll., Oxford; was M.P. for St. Alban's
1841–52; has been M.P. for Warwick since that time.
—*Odell, Bedford; Carlton Club, s.w.; 29, Curzon
Street, w.*

REVELEY, HUGH JOHN, Esq., of Bryn-y-gwin,
Merionethshire.
Only son of the late Hugh Reveley, Esq. (some time
Secretary to the Speaker of the House of Commons, and
afterwards Pursebearer to the Lord Chancellor in Ireland), by Jane, only dau. and heir of Robert Hartley
Owen, Esq., of Bryn-y-gwin; *b.* 1812; *s.* 1851; *m.*
1850 his cousin Jane, dau. of Algernon Reveley, Esq.,
of the Bengal Civil Service, and has issue,
    • Five daughters.
Mr. Reveley, who was educated at Wadham Coll., Oxford, is a J.P. and D.L. for co. Merioneth (High Sheriff
1859).—*Bryn-y-gwin, Dolgelly.*

REYNARD, EDWARD HORNER, Esq., of Sunderlandwick, and Hobgreen, Yorkshire.
Eldest son of the late Horner Reynard, Esq., of Sunderlandwick and Hobgreen, by Ursula, only dau. of
Edward Elwick, Esq., of Ainderby, co. York; *b.* 1809;
s. 1834; *m.* 1846 Elizabeth, dau. of Thomas Mason,
Esq., of Copt Hewick Hall, co. York, and has, with
other issue,
    • Frederick, *b.* 1848.
Mr. Reynard, who was educated at Harrow and Lincoln Coll., Oxford, is a J.P. and D.L. for the E. Riding
of Yorkshire, and Lord of the Manor of Sunderlandwick; was formerly Capt. Yorkshire Hussars.—*Sunderlandwick, Driffield; Oxford and Cambridge Club, s.w.*

REYNARDSON, CHARLES THOMAS SAMUEL
BIRCH-, Esq., of Holywell, Lincolnshire.
Eldest son of the late General Thomas Birch, who
assumed the additional name of Reynardson, on his
marriage with Etheldred Anne, eldest dau. and co-
heir of the late Jacob Reynardson, Esq., of Holywell;
b. 1810; *s.* his mother 1854; *m.* 1st 1836 Anne, eldest
dau. of the late Simon Yorke, Esq., of Erddig, near
Wrexham, N. Wales (she *d.* 1853) + and 1867 Victoria,
790

3rd dau. of the late George Dodwell, Esq., of Kevinafoi
co. Sligo; he has issue by the former,
    • Charles, *b.* 1846.
Mr. Birch-Reynardson is a Dep.-Lieut. for co. Linco,
(High Sheriff 1859), Lord of the Manor and Patron of
Holywell.—*Holywell, Stamford.*

REYNARDSON, Col. EDWARD BIRCH-, C.B
of Rushington Manor, Hants.
Third son of the late Gen. Thomas Birch, who assume
the additional name of Reynardson on his marriage wit
Etheldred Anne, eldest dau. and co-heir of the lat
Jacob Reynardson, Esq., of Holywell Hall, Stamford
co. Lincoln; *b.* 1812; *m.* 1849 Emily, 2nd dau. of tho
late Vere Fane, Esq., of Little Ponton Hall, co. Lincoln
and has, with other issue,
    • Sydney Louis, *b.* 1861.
Col. Edward Birch-Reynardson, who was educated at
the Royal Military Coll., Sandhurst, is a Magistrate for
Hants, Lord of the Manor of Rushington, and a Col. in
the Army; was formerly an Officer in the Grenadier
Guards.—*Rushington Manor, Eling, Southampton.*

REYNARDSON, HENRY BIRCH-, Esq., of
Adwell House, Oxon.
Fourth son of the late General Thomas Birch, who
assumed the name of Reynardson on his marriage with
Etheldred Anne, eldest dau. and co-heir of the late
Jacob Reynardson, Esq., of Holywell Hall, co. Lincoln
(see that family); *b.* 1814; *m.* 1847 Eleanor Dorothea,
youngest dau. of Henry S. Partridge, Esq., of Hockham
Hall, Norfolk, and has, with other issue,
    • William John, *b.* 1849.
Mr. Birch-Reynardson is a Magistrate for Oxon (High
Sheriff 1861).—*Adwell House, Tetsworth, Oxon.*

REYNELL, RICHARD WINTER, Esq., of Killynon,
co. Westmeath.
Eldest surviving son of the late Richard Reynell, Esq.,
of Killynon, by his cousin Harriette, dau. and co-heir
of Robert Reynell, Esq., of Edmondston, co. Westmeath; *b.* 1804; *s.* 1834; *m.* 1830 Frances Alexandrina, youngest dau. of James Saunderson, Esq., D.L.,
of Clover Hill, co. Cavan, and has, with other issue,
    • Richard, *b.* 1831.
Mr. Reynell, who was educated at Trinity Coll., Dublin,
is a Magistrate and Grand Juror for co. Westmeath
(High Sheriff 1839).—*Killynon, Killucan, co. Westmeath.*

REYNELL, SAMUEL AB HUR, Esq., of Arches-
town, co. Westmeath.
Second son of the late Richard Reynell, Esq., of
Killynon, by Harriett, dau. of Robert Reynell, Esq., of
Edmonton; *b.* 1814; *s.* 1834; *m.* 1836 Frances, dau.
of General Nugent, and has, with other issue,
    • Frances.
Mr. Reynell, who was educated at Trinity Coll., Dublin,
is a Magistrate for cos. Westmeath and Meath, and
Master of the Meath Foxhounds.—*Archestown, Delvin;
Sackville-Street Club, Dublin; Raleigh Club, s.w.*

REYNELL-PACK, Col. ARTHUR JOHN, C.B., of
Avisford, Sussex.
Eldest son of Major-General Sir Denis Pack, K.C.B.,
of Avisford, by Lady Elizabeth Louisa, youngest child
of George, 1st Marquis of Waterford, K.P.; *b.* 1817;
m. 1850 Frederica Katherine, 2nd dau. of Col. the Hon.
H. Hely-Hutchinson, by Harriet Wrightson, widow of
the Hon. F. Silvester North Douglas, and has issue. Educated at Eton and Geneva; is a Magistrate for Sussex,
Knight of the Legion of Honour, &c.; elected M.P. for
co. Carlow 1862; was formerly Lieut.-Col. 7th Royal
Fusiliers.—*Avisford, Walberton, Arundel; Army and
Navy Club, s.w.; 41, Hasley Street, w.*

REYNOLDS, Lady, of Penair, Cornwall.
Eliza Ann, 3rd dau. of M. Dick. Esq., of Pitkerro, co. Forfar ; *m.* 1832 Sir Barrington Reynolds, G.C.B., who was an Admiral in the Navy, and a J.P. and D.L. for Cornwall, and *d.* 1861.—*Penair, Truro.*

REYNOLDS, Charles Andrew, Esq., of Trevenson, Cornwall.
Eldest surviving son of the late William Reynolds, Esq., of Trevenson, by Philippa, dau. of J. Tellam. Esq.; *b.* 1813 ; *s.* 1844 ; *m.* 1841 Jane, 2nd dau. of J. Plomer, Esq., and has, with other issue,

* Charles William, *b.* 1844.

Mr. Reynolds, who was called to the Bar at the Middle Temple 1840, is a J.P. and D.L. for Cornwall.—*Trevenson, Redruth.*

REYNOLDS, John, Esq., of Adragoole, co. Galway.
Son of the late Henry Reynolds, Esq., by Margaret, dau. of Thomas Bulkeley, Esq., M.D., of Nenagh, co. Tipperary ; *b.* 1802 ; *m.* 1828 Anne, eldest dau. of Nicholas Furlong, Esq., of Dublin and Wexford, and has, with other issue,

* Henry Nicholas, Barrister-at-Law ; *b.* 1829.

Mr. Reynolds, who was elected Lord Mayor of Dublin 1850, and Senior Alderman of Dublin 1853, is a Magistrate for cos. Galway and Dublin, and for the city of Dublin ; was M.P. for Dublin 1847-52.—*Adragoole, Kiltormar, Ballinasloe, co. Galway; Marine Villa, Howth, co. Dublin ; 10, Fleet Street, Dublin.*

+REYNOLDS, Richard Anthony, Esq., of Paxton House, Hunts.
Eldest son of the late Richard Reynolds, Esq., of Paxton House ; *b.* 18—. Is a Magistrate for Hunts. —*Paxton House, St. Neot's.*

REYNOLDS, Vincent John, Esq., of Canonsgrove, Somerset.
Only son of the late Vincent Stuckey Reynolds, Esq., of Canonsgrove, by Marian, dau. of the late George Basevi, Esq., of Brighton ; *b.* 1825 ; *s.* 1843 ; *m.* 1859 Jessie, dau. of the Rev. Thomas Prowse Lethbridge, of Combe Flory, and grand-dau. of the late Sir T. B. Lethbridge, Bart., of Sandhill Park, and has issue. a dau. Mr. Reynolds, who was educated at Trinity Coll., Cambridge (B.A. 1847, M.A. 1851), and called to the Bar at Lincoln's Inn 1851, is a Magistrate for Somerset. This family descend from Thomas Reynolds, Esq., grandfather of the third and fourth Lords Ducie.—*Canonsgrove, Pitminster, Taunton; Junior Carlton Club, s.w.*

RHODES, the Rev. James Armitage, of Carlton, Yorkshire.
Eldest son of the late Peter Rhodes, Esq., of Leeds, by Elizabeth, dau. of James Armitage, Esq., of Farnley Hall, co. York, and brother of William Rhodes, Esq., of Bramhope (whom see), *b.* 1785 ; *m.* 1810 Mary, dau. of Alexander Turner, Esq., of Leeds. Educated at Queen's Coll., Cambridge (B.A. 1806, M.A. 1809); is a J.P. and D.L. for the W. Riding of Yorkshire, and a Chairman of Quarter Sessions.—*Carlton, Pontefract.*

RHODES, John William, Esq., of Hennerton, Oxfordshire.
Second son of the late Matthew Rhodes, Esq., of Leeds, by Mary, dau. of John Smith, Esq.; *b.* 1795; *m.* 1824 Sarah, dau. of Edward Brooke, Esq., of Chapel Allerton, near Leeds. Educated at Harrow ; is a Magistrate for the W. Riding of Yorkshire, and a Trustee of the Leeds Vicarage.—*Hennerton, Henley-on-Thames,*

RHODES, Mrs., of Teign Lawn, Devon.
Barbara, dau. of Charles Clay, Esq., of Rhyllon, St. Asaph ; *m.* 1817 Capt. John Henry Rhodes, R.N., of Teign Lawn, who *d.* 1864.—*Teign Lawn, Bishopsteignton, Teignmouth.*

RHODES, William, Esq., of Bramhope, Yorkshire.
Second son of the late Peter Rhodes, Esq., by Elizabeth, dau. of James Armitage, Esq., of Farnley Hall ; *b.* 1791; *m.* 1817 Anne, only child of Christopher Smith, Esq., of Bramhope, and has, with other issue,

* James, *b.* 1819.

Mr. Rhodes, who was educated at Woolwich, is a J.P. and D.L. for the W. Riding of Yorkshire ; and Capt. 19th Light Dragoons.—*Bramhope Hall, Otley ; 57, Brunswick Square, Brighton ; Windham Club, s.w.*

RHODES. (See *Darwin.*)

RIALL, Phineas, Esq., of Conna Hill, co. Wicklow.
Eldest son of the late Charles Riall, Esq., of Conna Hill, by Anne, 3rd dau. of the late John Roberts. Esq., of Old Conna Hill; *b.* 1803 ; *s.* 1857 ; *m.* 1834 Mary Anne, dau. of the late John Roe, Esq., and has, with other issue,

* Lewis John Roberts, *b.* 1838.

Mr. Riall, who was educated at Trinity Coll., Dublin, is a Magistrate for co. Dublin (High Sheriff 1863). —*Conna Hill, Bray, co. Wicklow.*

RIBBLESDALE, Lord (Thomas Lister).—Cr. 1797.
Eldest son of Thomas, 2nd Lord, by Adelaide, dau. of Thomas Lister, Esq., of Armitage Park, co. Stafford, and stepson of John, 1st Earl Russell, K.G. ; *b.* 1828; *s.* 1832; *m.* 1853 Emma, dau. of the late Col. William Mure, of Caldwell, co. Ayr. Educated at Eton and Ch. Ch., Oxford ; is a J.P. and D.L. for the W. Riding of Yorkshire, late Lieut. R. Horse Guards.—*Gisburne Park, Skipton ; 25, Eaton Place, s.w.*

Heir, his son Thomas, b. 1854.

RIBTON, Sir John Sheppey, Bart., of Woodbrook, co. Dublin (cr. 1759).
Elder son of the late Sir George Ribton, Bart., of Grove, co. Dublin, by his 2nd wife Jane, dau. and coheir of John Sheppey, Esq., of Rockfield, co. Dublin ; *b.* 1797 ; *s.* as 3rd Bart. 1807 ; *m.* 1st 1818 Mary Anne, only dau. and heir of Jeremiah Hayes, Esq., of Killurag, co. Limerick ; 2nd 1841 Emily Caroline, dau. of Thomas Quinan, Esq., and widow of Walter Hussey Hill, Esq. Was formerly in the Rifle Brigade ; was High Sheriff of co. Dublin 1824.—*Woodbrook, Bray, co. Dublin ; United Service Club, Dublin.*

Heir, his son George, b. 1812.

RICARDO, Henry David, Esq., of Gatcombe, Gloucestershire.
Eldest son of the late David Ricardo, Esq., M.P., of Gatcombe Park (who was a J.P. and D.L. for co. Gloucester, High Sheriff 1830), by Catherine, dau. of the late William Thomas St. Quintin, Esq., of Scampston, co. York ; *b.* 1833 ; *s.* 1864 ; *m.* 1858 Ellen, dau. of the Ven. Archdeacon Crawley, and has, with other issue,

* Henry George, *b.* 1860.

Mr. Ricardo is Lord of the Manor of Minchinhampton, and Patron of 4 livings.—*Gatcombe Park, Minchinhampton.*

RICARDO, Mortimer, Esq., of Mudiford, Hants.
Third son of the late David Ricardo, Esq., of Bromsberrow, co. Worcester, by Priscilla, dau. of Edward

Wilkinson, Esq.; b. 1807; m. 1836 Catherine, 4th dau. of the late General the Hon. Robert Meade. Is a Dep.-Lieut. for Oxon.—Bure Homage, Mudiford, Christchurch; 18, Portman Square, w.

RICARDO, OSMAN, Esq., of Bromsberrow, Worcestershire.

Eldest son of the late David Ricardo, Esq. (some time M.P. for Portarlington), by Priscilla, dau. of Edward Wilkinson, Esq.; b. 1795; m. 1817 Harriet, dau. of Robert Harvey Mallory, Esq., of Woodcote, co. Warwick. Educated at the Charterhouse and Trinity Coll., Cambridge (B.A. 1816); is a J.P. and D.L. for co. Worcester, a Magistrate for cos. Gloucester and Hereford; was M.P. for Worcester 1847–65.—Bromsberrow Place, Ledbury; Brooks's and Union Clubs, s.w.; 71, Eaton Place, s.w.

RICE, the Hon. and Rev. AUBREY RICHARD SPRING.

Fourth son of Thomas Spring, 1st Lord Monteagle, by his 1st wife Lady Theodosia, dau. of Edmond Henry, 1st Earl of Limerick; b. 1822; m. 1852 Anna Maria Jane, dau. of the late Paulet St. John Miklmay, Esq., of Hazlegrove House, Somerset. Educated at Trinity Coll., Cambridge (M.A. 1844); appointed Vicar of Netherbury 1852.—Netherbury Vicarage, Beaminster.

RICE, the Hon. CHARLES WILLIAM THOMAS SPRING.

Second son of Thomas Spring, 1st Lord Monteagle, by his 1st wife Lady Theodosia, dau. of Edmond Henry, 1st Earl of Limerick; b. 1819; m. 1855 Elizabeth Margaret, dau. of W. Marshall, Esq., M.P., of Patterdale Hall, Cumberland, and has, with other issue,

* Stephen Edward Spring, b. 1856.

Mr. Rice was educated at Trinity Coll., Cambridge (M.A. 1840), and appointed a Clerk in the Foreign Office 1839.—17, Eaton Place South, s.w.

RICE, the Hon. WILLIAM CECIL SPRING.

Fifth son of Thomas Spring, 1st Lord Monteagle, by his 1st wife Lady Theodosia, dau. of Edmond Henry, 1st Earl of Limerick; b. 1823. Educated at Trinity Coll., Cambridge (M.A. 1845); called to the Bar at Lincoln's Inn 1848; appointed Secretary to Lord Cranworth, as Vice-Chancellor, 1850, as Lord Justice of Appeal, Principal Secretary to the Lord Chancellor, 1853, Secretary to the Commissioners in Lunacy 1861, Registrar in Bankruptcy 1865.—165, New Bond Street, w.

RICE, DOMINICK, Esq., of Bushmount, co. Kerry.

Only child of the late John Colles Rice, Esq., of Ballymacquin Castledenesene, co. Kerry, by Elizabeth, eldest dau. of the late Muncton Villiers Carey, Esq., of Dromartin, co. Kerry, and widow of John Payne, Esq., of Tralee; b. 1786; s. 1788; m. 1807 Frances, 2nd dau. and only surviving child of the late Justice Griffin, Esq., of Lacca, co. Kerry, and grand-dau. of the late Francis Creaghe, Esq., of Ballybunion House, co. Kerry, and has, with other issue,

* Justice Dominick, a Magistrate for co. Kerry; b. 1813; m. 1850 Bidelia, only surviving child of the late John Greghe, gan, Esq., of the city of Cork, by whom he has, with other issue, * Dominick, b. 1851.

This family descend from Peter Rice, of Fort-del-ore, co. Kerry, who owned large possessions in the 16th century.—Bushmount, Tralee, co. Kerry.

RICE, EDWARD ROYD, Esq., of Dane Court, Kent.

Third, and only surviving son of the late Henry Rice, Esq., of Bramling, Kent, by Sarah, dau. and heir of — Sampson, Esq.; b. 1790; m. 1818 Elizabeth, dau. of

the late Edward Knight, Esq., of Godmersham Park, Kent, and has, with other issue,

* Edward Bridges, a Magistrate for Kent, and Capt. R.N.; b. 1819; m. 1864 Cecilia Caroline, 2nd dau. of the Rev. Wm. Vernon Harcourt, of Nuneham Park, Oxon.

Mr. Rice, who was educated at Worcester Coll., Oxford (B.A. 1813. M.A. 1815), is a J.P. and D.L. for Kent (High Sheriff 1830); formerly Capt. East Kent Yeomanry Cavalry; was M.P. for Dover 1837–57.—Dane Court, Sandwich; University Club, s.w.

RICE, GEORGE WATKIN, Esq., of Llwyn-y-Brain, Carmarthenshire.

Eldest, and only surviving son of the late Major Walter Rice, Esq., of Llwyn-y-Brain (which property he inherited from the family of Griffith), by Mary Anne, dau. of Herbert Evans, Esq., of Highmead, co. Cardigan, and cousin of E. Rice, Esq., of Dane Court (whom see); b. 1816; s. 1844. Educated at Winchester and Woolwich, is a J.P. and D.L. for cos. Carmarthen, Cardigan, and Brecon, and Lord of the Manor of Llwyn-y-Brain: late High Sheriff of co. Carmarthen; was formerly Adjutant and Capt. 23rd R. W. Fusiliers, and Major R. Carmarthen Militia.—Llwyn-y-Brain, Llandovery.

RICE, JOHN TALBOT, Esq., of Oddington, Gloucestershire.

Youngest son of the late Hon. and Very Rev. Edward Rice, D.D., Dean of Gloucester, by Charlotte, 2nd dau. of the late General Lascelles; b. 1819; m. 1st 1846 Clara Louisa, dau. of the late Sir John C. Reade, Bart. (she d. 1853); 2nd 1855 Elizabeth Lucy, dau. of Robert Boyd, Esq. Is a Magistrate for co. Gloucester. —Oddington, Stow-on-the-Wold; Ardington, Broadwell, Gloucestershire.

RICE.

(See under Dynevor, Lord, and Monteagle, Lord.)

RICH, Sir CHARLES HENRY STUART, Bart. (cr. 1791).

Only surviving son of the late Sir Charles Henry John Rich, Bart., by Harriet Theodosia, dau. of John Stuart Sullivan, Esq., M.C.S.; b. 1859; s. as 4th Bart. 1866. Is Patron of 1 living.—12, Nottingham Place, w.

Heir Pres., his uncle Frederick Dampier, Capt. R.N. (third son of the late Sir Charles Henry Rich, who d. 1857, by Frances Maria, youngest dau. of Sir John Lethbridge, Bart.): b. 1818; m. 1854 Jessie Catharine, 2nd dau. of Sir J. H. Lethbridge, Bart.

RICH, Sir HENRY, Bart. (cr. 1863).

Youngest son of the late Admiral Sir Thomas Rich, by Elizabeth, youngest dau. of the late General Burt; b. 1803; m. 1852 Julia, dau. of the late Rev. James Tomkinson, of Dorfold Hall, co. Chester. Educated at Trinity Coll., Cambridge (B.A. 1825); has been a Groom-in-Waiting; was a Lord of the Treasury 1846–52. M.P. for Knaresborough 1837–41, for Richmond 1846–61. —Brooks's and Athenaeum Clubs, s.w.; 16, Great Street, w.

RICH, JOHN SAMPSON, Esq., of Woodlands, co. Limerick.

Second son of the late Admiral Sir Thomas Rich, of Sunning, Berks, by Elizabeth, youngest dau. of the late General Burt, and brother of Sir Henry Rich, Bart. (whom see); b. 1789; m. 1821 Amelia, only child of Thomas Whitfield, Esq., of Congleton, co. Chester, and has, with other issue,

* Frederick Henry, Lieut.-Col. R.E.; b. 1824.

Mr. Rich, who was educated at Woolwich, was formerly a Capt. R.A.—Woodlands, Castle Connell.

+RICHARDES, ALEXANDER, Esq., of Penglais, Cardiganshire.

Eldest son of the late Roderick Eardley Richardes, Esq., of Penglais, by Anne Corbetta Hannah Maria, dau. of the late William E. Powell, Esq., of Nanteos, co. Cardigan; b. 18—; is married, and has issue,

* Alexander Eardley, b. 18—.

Mr. Richardes is Lord of the Manor of Penglais. —*Penglais, Aberystwith.*

RICHARDES, WILLIAM EARDLEY, Esq., of Bryneithen, co. Cardigan.

Third son of the late William Richardes, Esq., of Penglais, by Anna Arabella, dau. of Thomas Rivett, Esq., of Derby; b. 1795; m. 1827 Marian, dau. of Hugh Stephens, Esq., of Cascob, co. Radnor, and had, with other issue,

Charles James Haley, b. 1828 ; d. 1867.

Mr. Richardes, who was educated at Great Marlow and Woolwich, is a Magistrate for co. Cardigan, and Lieut. R.A., retired.—*Bryneithen, Aberystwith.*

RICHARDS, Sir Peter, K.C.B. (cr. 1865).

Son of the late P. Richards, Esq.; b. 178—. Entered the Royal Navy in 1798; is an Admiral R.N., retired. —38, *Wimpole Street*, w.

RICHARDS, Mrs., of Langford, Somerset.

Charlotte Emilie, dau. of Robert Sillery, Esq., of Charlton Lodge, Dover; m. 1855 Edward Griffith Richards, Esq., J.P., of Langford House, formerly Capt. 2nd Somerset Militia, and who d. 1863, leaving, with other issue, * Henry Sillery Griffith, b. 1858. —*Langford House, Bristol.*

RICHARDS, EDWARD MOORE, Esq., of Grange, co. Wexford.

Only surviving son of the late Goddard Hewetson Richards, Esq., by Dorothea, dau. of Edward Moore, Esq., of co. Tipperary; b. 1826; s. his brother 1860; m. 1851 Sarah Elizabeth, dau. of William Tisdall, Esq., of Prince Edward's, Virginia, U.S., and has issue,

* Adela.

Mr. Richards, who was a Civil Engineer, is Lord of the Manor of Grange.—*Grange, Kilanne, Enniscorthy.*

RICHARDS, EVAN MATTHEW, Esq., of Brook-lands, Glamorganshire.

Youngest son of the late Richard Richards, Esq., of Swansea, by Catharine, his wife; b. 1821. Is a J.P. and D.L. for co. Glamorgan; was Mayor of Swansea 1855–6 and 1862–3.—*Brooklands, Swansea; Reform Club*, s.w.

RICHARDS, the Right Hon. JOHN, of Sand-field, co. Clare.

Second son of the late John Nunn Richards, Esq., of Hermitage, co. Wexford, by Elizabeth, only dau. of Oliver Fitzgerald, Esq., of Ballycorlan, co. Galway; b. 1790; m. 1st 1812 Catherine, 2nd dau. of the late H. G. Mahon, Esq., of Dublin (she d. 1841); 2nd 1852 Christina, only dau. of the late Lieut.-Col. Christopher James O'Brien, of Ballinalacken Castle, co. Clare, and has, with other issue,

* John Henry, Barrister-at-Law, and Chairman of Sessions for co. Mayo; b. 1818.

Mr. Richards, who was educated at Trinity Coll., Dublin (M.A. 1813), called to the Bar 1811, appointed Solicitor-General for Ireland and Bencher of the King's Inns 1835, Attorney-General and Privy Councillor in Ireland 1836, was a Baron of the Irish Exchequer 1837–49, Chief Commissioner of the Encumbered Estates Court in Ireland; again in 1856 became Baron of Exchequer. This family was formerly seated in co. Wexford.—*Sandfield, Lahinch, co. Clare.*

RICHARDS, JOHN, Esq., of Mackmine Castle, co. Wexford.

Eldest son of the Rev. George Richards, Prebendary of Coolstuffe, co. Wexford, by Margaret Sophia, dau. of the late James Johnston, Esq., of Fir House, co. Dublin, and Corkerran, co. Monaghan; b. 1800; m. 1858 Harriet Martha, only dau. of the late Major Gledstanes, 68th Regt., and has, with other issue,

* George Gledstanes, Capt. Wexford Militia; b. 1839.

Mr. Richards, who was educated at Trinity Coll., Dublin (M.A. 1824), is a Magistrate for co. Wexford. —*Mackmine Castle, Enniscorthy, co. Wexford.*

RICHARDS, Mrs., of Mordon, Flintshire.

Margaret, dau. of the late Rees Davies, Esq., of the Court House, Merthyr Tydfil; m. 1840 Edward Lewis Richards, Esq., who d. 1863. The late Mr. Richards was a Magistrate for cos. Denbigh, Flint, &c., Judge of the County Courts of N.E. Wales, and Chairman of the Flintshire Quarter Sessions.—*Mordon House, Rhyl.*

RICHARDS, Mrs., of Ounavarra, co. Wexford.

Florence, dau. of the Rev. Henry Moore, Rector of Ferns, and grand-dau. of the Hon. Ponsonby Moore; m. 1852 (as his 2nd wife) Solomon Richards, Esq., of Ounavarra, who was a Magistrate for co. Wexford (High Sheriff 1855), and d. 1862. This family is a junior branch of the house of Solsborough.—*Ounavarra, Gorey, co. Wexford.*

RICHARDS, OWEN, Esq., of Bala, Merioneth-shire.

Youngest son of the late Mr. Owen Richards, of Arthach, co. Cardigan, by Susanna, dau. of the late William Lloyd, Esq., of Gwyddfrynian, co. Merioneth: b. 1813. Educated at Cardigan; is a Magistrate for co. Merioneth, Doctor of Medicine, Fellow of the Royal College of Surgeons of England, and Surgeon to the R. Merioneth Rifles.—*Bala, Merioneth.*

RICHARDS, RICHARD MEREDYTH, Esq., of Caerynwch, Merionethshire, and Cerrig Llwydion, Denbighshire.

Only son of the late Richard Richards, Esq., of Caerynwch (who was M.P. for co. Merioneth 1835–52, and many years a Master in Chancery), by Harriett, elder dau. and co-heir of Jonathan Dennett, Esq.; b. 1821; s. 1860; m. 1st 1845 Elizabeth Emma, dau. of William Bennett, Esq., of Farringdon House, Berks (she d. s. p. 1852); 2nd 1863 Louisa Janette Anne, only child of the late Edward Lloyd Edwards, Esq., of Cerrig-Llwydion, Denbighshire (and heiress to her grandmother, who d. 1866), and has, with other issue,

* Richard Edward Lloyd, b. 1865.

Mr. Richards, who was educated at Westminster and Merton Coll., Oxford (B.A. 1842, M.A. 1846), and called to the Bar at the Inner Temple 1845, is a J.P. and D.L. for co. Merioneth (High Sheriff 1865), and Chairman of Quarter Sessions for that County, and a Magistrate for co. Denbigh; he was formerly Lieut. Royal Merioneth Light Infantry Militia.—*Caerynwch, Dolgelly, Merionethshire; Cerrig-Llwydion, Denbigh; Carlton and United University Clubs, s.w.*

RICHARDS, SOLOMON, of Solsborough, co. Wexford.

Eldest son of the late Rev. Solomon Richards, of Solsborough, by Elizabeth, eldest dau. of Col. Thomas Bermingham Daly Henry Sewell, senior co-heir to the Barony of Athenry; b. 1810; s. 1866. Is a Lieut.-Col. in the Indian Army, and Commandant 51st N.I. This family is of very old standing in the co. Wexford. —*Solsborough, Enniscorthy, co. Wexford.*

RICHARDS, SOLOMON AUGUSTUS, Esq., of Arda-
mine, co. Wexford.
Eldest son of the late John Goddard Richards, Esq., of
Ardamine, by Anne Katherine, dau. of the late Hon.
Robert Ward, of Bangor, co. Down; b. 1828; s. 1846;
m. 1856 Sophia Mordaunt, dau. of the Rev. Bernard J.
Ward, and has, with other issue,

* Bernard John Goddard, b. 1857.

Mr. Richards, who was educated at Eton and Trinity
Coll., Oxford (B.A. 1850), is a Magistrate for co. Wex-
ford (High Sheriff 1854), late Capt. Wexford Militia.
—Ardamine, Gorey; Kildare Street Club, Dublin.

+RICHARDS, WILLIAM POWELL, Esq., of Llandaff Court, Glamorganshire.
Son of the late Edward Windsor Richards, Esq., by
Jane, dau. of Thomas Edwards, Esq., of Llandaff Hall,
co. Glamorgan; b. 1827; s. his uncle 1840; m. 1857
Mary Eleanor, dau. of Col. Ramsbottom, of Gibraltar,
and has issue,

* Edward Windsor, b. 1858.

Mr. Richards, who was educated at Woolwich, was
formerly Major R.A. His uncle took the name of
Edwards in lieu of Richards, under the will of his
maternal uncle, in 1826.—Llandaff Court, Cardiff.

+RICHARDS, WILLIAM HAGGATT, Esq., of
Stapleton House, Somersetshire.
Eldest son of the late William Haggatt Richards, Esq.,
of Stapleton House; b. 1825. Is a Magistrate for
Devon and Somerset.—Stapleton House, Martock.

Heir Pres., his brother John Whitehead, b. 1830; m. 1862
Mary Ann, only dau. of Robert Chaffey, Esq., of East Stoke
House, Somerset.

RICHARDSON, Sir JOHN STEWART, Bart., of
Pitfour Castle, Perthshire (cr. 1630).
Eldest son of the late James Richardson, Esq., of Pit-
four, by Elizabeth, dau. of the late James Stewart,
Esq., of Urrard, co. Perth; b. 1797; s. 1837; m. 1826
Mary, 3rd dau. of James Hay, Esq., of Collipriest,
Devon. Educated at Edinburgh University; called
to the Scottish Bar 1820; is a J.P. and D.L. for co.
Perth; appointed Secretary to the Order of the Thistle
1843.—Pitfour Castle, Perth, N.B.; Carlton Club, s.w.

Heir, his son James Thomas, late Capt. 78th Foot; b. 1840.

RICHARDSON, CHRISTOPHER, Esq., of Field
House, Yorkshire.
Eldest son of the late Christopher Richardson, Esq.,
J.P. and D.L., of Field House, by his 1st wife, Anne,
dau. of the late Joseph Barker, Esq.; b. 1807; s. 1866;
m. 1860 Marian Catherine, 2nd dau. of the late Barnard
Hague, Esq., of Kelfield Hall, co. York.. Educated at
Exeter Coll., Oxford (B.A. 1830); was called to the
Bar at Lincoln's Inn 1834.—Field House, Whitby; 4,
St. Leonard's, York.

RICHARDSON, CHRISTOPHER, Esq., of St.
Hilda's, Yorkshire.
Eldest son of the late John Richardson, Esq., by
Margaret, 4th dau. of Joseph Barker, Esq., by
b. 1807; m. 1855 Ann, dau. of the late Aaron Chapman,
Esq., M.P. Is a J.P. and D.L. for the N. Riding of co.
York.— St. Hilda's, Whitby.

RICHARDSON, HENRY THOMAS, Esq., of Aber-
Hirnant, Merionethshire.
Only surviving son of the late Henry Richardson, Esq.,
J.P. of Aber-Hirnant (High Sheriff of co. Merioneth
1851). By Caroline, dau. of the late Arthur Lemuel
Shuldham, Esq., of Dunmanway, co. Cork; b. 1826; s.
1861; m. 1856 Harriet Annie, 3rd dau. of the late

704

Rev. C. W. Davy, of Heathfield, Hants. Is a Magistrate
for co. Merioneth; was formerly Cornet and Lieut. in the
4th Dragoon Guards.—Aber-Hirnant, Bala.

RICHARDSON, HENRY MERVYN, Esq., of Rossfad, co. Fermanagh.
Only son of the late John Richardson, Esq., of Rossfad,
by Angel, dau. of Col. Mervyn Archdall, M.P., of Castle
Archdall, co. Fermanagh; b. 1808; s. 1841; m. 1834
Mary Jane, dau. of Charles Ovenden, Esq., and has,
with other issue,

* John Mervyn Archdall Carleton, Capt. Fermanagh Light
Infantry; b. 1836.

Mr. Richardson, who was educated at Armagh Coll.,
and Christ's Coll., Cambridge, is a Magistrate for co.
Tyrone, and a J.P. and D.L. for and Treasurer of co.
Fermanagh.—Rossfad, Ballycassidy, co. Fermanagh.

RICHARDSON, Capt. JOHN, of Poplar Vale,
co. Monaghan.
Son of the late Christopher Richardson, Esq.; b. 18—;
has been twice married, and has issue. Is a Magistrate
for co. Monaghan (High Sheriff 1845-6).—Poplar Vale,
Monaghan.

RICHARDSON, JOHN, Esq., of Lancrigg, Westmoreland.
Son of the late Sir John Richardson, C.B., of Lancrigg
(formerly Inspector of Haslar Hospital), by his 2nd
wife Mary, dau. of John Booth, Esq.; b. 1838; s. 1865.
Educated at Woolwich; is a Lieut. R.N.—Lancrigg,
Grasmere, Westmoreland.

RICHARDSON, JONATHAN, Esq., of Lambeg,
co. Antrim.
Eldest son of John Richardson, Esq., of Lisburn, by
Harriet, dau. of J. Green, Esq., of Clanroie; b. 1801;
m. 1828 Margaret, dau. and heir of Alexander Airth,
Esq., of Craigs, co. Dumfries, and has, with other issue,

* John, b. 1829; m. 1862 Emily Margaret, only dau. of the
late Rev. George M. Black. of Stranmillis, co. Antrim.

Mr. Richardson, who was educated at Lisburn and
Southgate, is a Magistrate for cos. Antrim and Down;
was M.P. for Lisburn 1857-63.—Lambeg, Lisburn.

RICHARDSON, JONATHAN JOSEPH, Esq., of Kircassock, Downshire.
Son of Joseph Richardson, Esq., of Lisburn, by Mary,
dau. of Joseph Strangman, Esq., of Waterford (city);
b. 1815; m. 1848 Eliza, dau. of J. Christy, Esq., of
Kircassock, co. Down. A Member of the Society of
Friends; is a Magistrate for cos. Antrim and Down;
was M.P. for Lisburn 1863-7.—Kircassock, Lurgan;
Reform Club, s.w.

RICHARDSON, of Rich Hill, co. Armagh.
Isabella and Louisa, daus. and co-heirs of the late
William Richardson, Esq., of Rich Hill (for many
years M.P. for co. Armagh), of whom Louisa m. in
1832 Edmund, eldest son of the late Sir Edmund
Bacon, Bart. (who d. 1852).—Rich Hill, Armagh.

RICHARDSON, Lieut.-Col. ROLAND, of Kirk-
lands, Roxburghshire.
Son of the late John Richardson, Esq., of Kirklands, by
Elizabeth, dau. of Lawrence Hill, Esq.; b. 1821; s.
1864. Is Lord of the Barony of Kirklands, and Lieut.-
Col. 19th Hussars.—Kirklands, Jedburgh, N.B.; Junior
United Service Club, s.w.

RICHARDSON, Capt. THOMAS, of Sutton
Hurst, Sussex.
Third son of the late Thomas Richardson, Esq., of
Warminghurst Park, Sussex, by Frances, younger dau.
of the late John Margesson, Esq., of Offington, Sussex;
b. 1791. Is a J.P. and D.L. for Sussex; late Capt.

20th Light Dragoons. Is heir pres. to his brother William W. Richardson, Esq., of Findon (whom see). —*Sutton Hurst, Barcombe, Lewes.*

RICHARDSON, Thomas, Esq., of Tyaquin, co. Galway.
Son of the late Ralph Richardson, Esq., of Springfield, co. Down, by Jane, dau. of John Johnstone, Esq., of Clare House, co. Tyrone; *b.* 1810; *m.* 1839 Alicia Catherine, dau. of Rev. N. Gosselin, Rector of Taughshinny, co. Loughford, and has, with other issue,
* Thomas Alexander, educated at the Royal Military Academy; a Lieut. R.A.; *b.* 1848.

Mr. Richardson is a Magistrate for co. Galway.—*Tyaquin, Monivea; Demesne, Waringstown, co. Down.*

RICHARDSON, Thomas Rumbold, Esq., of Somerset, co. Londonderry.
Only son of the late Henry Richardson, Esq., of Somerset, by Lady Emily Frances Kerr, youngest dau. of the late Lord Mark Kerr, and Charlotte (in her own right), Countess of Antrim; *b.* 1839; *s.* 1849; *m.* 1862 Edith, eldest dau. of the late Frederick Harford, Esq., of Down Place, Berks. Mr. Richardson, who was educated at Harrow and Ch. Ch., Oxford, is a J.P. and D.L. for co. Londonderry, and an Officer in the 1st Life Guards. —*Somerset, Coleraine, Ireland; Windham Club, s.w.*

+ **RICHARDSON, William Westbrooke, Esq., of Findon Place, Sussex.**
Eldest son of the late Thomas Richardson, Esq., of Warminghurst Park, Sussex, by Frances, younger dau. of the late John Margesson, Esq., of Offington, Sussex; *b.* 178—. Is a J.P. and D.L. for Sussex.—*Findon Place, Shoreham.*

RICHARDSON. (See *Bunbury.*)

RICHARDSON-ROBERTSON. (See *Robertson.*)

RICHARDSON-WORMLEY, Edward, Esq., of Riccall Hall, Yorkshire.
Only son of the late Toft Richardson, Esq., of Riccall Hall, by Jane, dau. of — Farrer, Esq., and widow of Christopher Wormley, Esq.; *b.* 1809; *s.* 1843; *m.* 1846 Isabel, 5th dau. of Sir Henry Boynton, Bart. Is a Magistrate for co. York; Lord of the Manor and Patron of Riccall, and Capt. 5th W. York Regt. of Militia. —*Riccall Hall, Selby; Junior United Service Club, s.w.*

RICHMOND, Duke of (Charles Henry Gordon-Lennox).—Cr. 1675.
Eldest son of Charles, 5th Duke of Richmond, K.G., by Lady Caroline Paget, dau. of Henry William, 1st Marquis of Anglesey; *b.* 1818; *s.* 1861; *m.* 1843 Frances Harriet, eldest dau. of Algernon Frederick Greville, Esq., of Hillingdon, Middlesex. Educated at Westminster and Ch. Ch., Oxford; is a Magistrate for Sussex, a Dep.-Lieut. for co. Banff, Chancellor of Aberdeen University, a Capt. in the Army unattached, and Patron of 4 livings; was President of the Poor-Law Board March–June, 1859; was sworn a Privy Councillor in 1859; he was formerly Lieut. Royal Horse Guards; M.P. for West Sussex 1841–61; appointed President of the Board of Trade 1867.—*Goodwood, Chichester; Gordon Castle, Fochabers, Banffshire; White's Club, s.w.; 49, Belgrave Square, s.w.*

Heir, his son Charles Henry, Earl of March; b. 1845; educated at Eton; Ensign and Lieut. Grenadier Guards.

RICHMOND-GALE-BRADDYLL.
(See *Braddyll.*)

RICKARDS, the Rev. Hely Hutchinson Keating, of Llandough, Glamorganshire.
Second surviving son of the late Richard Fowler Rickards, Esq., of Llantrissant, co. Glamorgan, by Charlotte, dau. of Isaac Hillier, Esq., of Holt, Wilts: *b.* 1812; *m.* 1840 Katherine Diana, dau. of the late Sir Robert Lynch-Blosse. Bart., of Gabalva, co. Glamorgan. Educated at Merton Coll., Oxford (B.A. 1835); is a Magistrate for co. Glamorgan, and Rector of Michaelstone, Llandough, &c.—*Llandough, Cardiff.*

RICKARDS, Robert Hillier, Esq.
Eldest son of the late Richard Fowler Rickards, Esq., of Llantrissant, co. Glamorgan, by Charlotte, dau. of Isaac Hillier, Esq., of Holt, Wilts; *b.* 1804; *s.* 1848; *m.* 1831 Caroline Octavia Knox, dau. of Andrew Knox, Esq., of Prehen, co. Londonderry, and had, with other issue,

Richard, *b.* 1832; *m.* 1861 Charlotte, youngest dau. of the Rev. George Salt, and *d.* 1865, leaving, with other issue,
* Robert Tayleur, *b.* 1862.

Mr. Rickards, who was called to the Bar at the Middle Temple 1835, is a J.P. and D.L. for co. Glamorgan. —*Caledonia Place, Clifton, Bristol.*

RICKETTS, Sir Cornwallis, Bart., of The Elms, Gloucestershire (cr. 1827).
Eldest son of the late Sir Robert Tristram Ricketts, Bart., of the Elms, by Rebecca, dau. of Richard Gumbleton, Esq., of Castle Richards, co. Waterford; *b.* 1803; *s.* as 2nd Bart. 1842; *m.* 1st 1834 Henrietta, dau. of Col. Tempest; 2nd 1852 Lady Caroline Augusta, dau. of Henry Pelham, 4th Duke of Newcastle. Educated at the Royal Naval Coll., Portsmouth; is a Magistrate for co. Leicester (High Sheriff 1851), and a Rear-Admiral retired.—*The Elms, Cheltenham; Beaumont Leys, Leicester; United Service Club, s.w.; 55, Grosvenor Place, s.w.*

Heir, his son Robert Tempest, b. 1836; m. 1861 Amelia Helen, eldest surviving dau. of J. Steuart, Esq., of Dalguise, co. Perth.

RICKETTS, Sir Henry, K.C.S.I. (cr. 1866).
Third son of the late George William Ricketts, Esq., by Letitia, dau. of Carew Mildmay, Esq., of Shawford, Hants; *b.* 1802; *m.* 1823 Jane, dau. of General George Carpenter, F.I.C.S. (she *d.* 1830). Educated at Winchester and Haileybury Coll.; entered the East-India Civil Service 1821, and retired in 1860; held several high offices in India; in 1858 and 1859 was a Member of the Council of the Governor-General.—*Onslow Hill Grove, Surbiton, Kingston-on-Thames; Oriental Club, w.*

RICKETTS, Mrs., of Dorton House, Bucks.
Caroline Sophia, only surviving child and heir of the late Col. Thomas Aubrey, M.P. (who *d.* 1814), by an American lady, and grand-dau. of the late Sir Thomas Aubrey, Bart., of Borstal, Bucks; *s.* her uncle, Sir Thomas Digby Aubrey, Bart. (*ext.*), 1858; *m.* 1814 Charles Spencer Ricketts, Esq., a Magistrate for Bucks. Is Lady of the Manors of Dorton Borstall, &c., and Patron of 1 living.—*Dorton House, Thame.*

+ **RICKETTS, Capt. George Crawford, of Combe, Herefordshire.**
Eldest son of the late Thomas Bourke Ricketts, Esq., of Combe House (who was a Magistrate for co. Radnor), by Harriett, younger dau. of the late Major-General William Loftus, M.P., Col. of the 2nd Dragoon Guards (she *d.* 1860); *b.* 1825; *s.* 1861. Was formerly an Officer in the Army.—*Combe House, Hereford.*

RICKETTS. (See under *Wilkinson, of Thopton House.*)

RICKFORD, Capt. THOMAS PARKER, of Hamilton House, Hants.

Only son of the late Thomas Rickford, Esq., of Reading, Berks; b. 1820; m. 1849 Frances Elizabeth Maria,
only child of Charles Wyndham, Esq., of Donhead
Hall, Wilts, and has, with other issue,

* Charles Wyndham Heathcote, b. 1850.

Capt. Rickford, who was formerly in the R. Welsh Fusiliers, was appointed Exon of the Guard 1851.—*Hamilton House, Southampton; Army and Navy Club, s.w.;
Colour Court, St. James's Palace, s.w.*

RIDDELL, Sir THOMAS MILLES, Bart., of Ardnamurchan and Sunart, Argyleshire (cr.
1778).

Eldest son of the late Sir James Milles Riddell, Bart.,
of Ardnamurchan and Sunart (who was a J.P. and D.L.
for co. Argyle, and formerly Lieut.-Col. Commandant
of the 1st Regt. of Argyle Local Militia), by Mary,
dau. of the late Sir Richard Brooke, Bart., of Norton
Priory, co. Chester; b. 1822; s. as 3rd Bart. 1861; m.
1851 Mary Anne, dau. of John Hodgson, Esq. Is a
J.P. and D.L. for co. Argyll, and a Magistrate for co.
Inverness—*Strontian, Fort William, Argyleshire.*

Heir Pres., his cousin Rodney Steuart, Lieut. 70th Foot (son
of the late Campbell D. Riddell, Esq., by Caroline, dau. of
the Hon. John Rodney, Esq.), b. 1841.

RIDDELL, Sir WALTER BUCHANAN, Bart., of
Hepple, Northumberland (cr. 1628).

Eldest son of the late Sir John Buchanan Riddell, Bart.,
M.P., by Lady Frances, dau. of Charles, 1st Earl of
Romney; b. 1810; s. as 10th Bart. 1819; m. 1859
Alicia, dau. of William Ripley, Esq. Educated at Eton
and Ch. Ch., Oxford (B.A. 1831, M.A. 1834); called
to the Bar at Lincoln's Inn 1834; is a Magistrate for
Kent, Northumberland, and co. Stafford; Recorder of
Maidstone, and Judge of the Staffordshire County
Courts.—*Hepple, Rothbury; 31, Prince's Gardens, w.;
13, Old Square, Lincoln's Inn, w.c.*

Heir Pres., his brother the Rev. John Charles Buchanan;
educated at Eton; M.A. of Ch. Ch., Oxford, and late Fellow
of All Souls' Coll.; Rector of Harrietsham, Kent, and
Proctor of the Clergy in Convocation; b. 1814; m. 1846
Frances Sophia, dau. of the late George James Cholmondeley, Esq., and has, with other issue, * John Walter,
b. 1849.

RIDDELL, Lady FRANCES.

Elder dau. of Charles, 1st Earl of Romney, by Lady
Frances Wyndham, younger dau. of Charles, 1st Earl
of Egremont (ext.); m. 1805 Sir John Buchanan Riddell, Bart. (who d. 1819).—*The Palace, Maidstone.*

RIDDELL, EDWARD, Esq., of Cheeseburn
Grange, Northumberland.

Eldest surviving son of the late Ralph Riddell, Esq.,
of Cheeseburn Grange, by Isabella, dau. of William
Salvin, Esq., of Croxdale, co. Durham, and widow of
Edward Horsley Widdrington Riddell, Esq.; b. 1804;
s. 1831. Educated at Ushaw Coll.; is a J.P. and D.L.
for Northumberland (High Sheriff 1842).—*Cheeseburn
Grange, Newcastle-on-Tyne; Windham Club, s.w.*

Heir Pres., his brother Frederick, of Leyburn Grove, co.
York; b. 1808.

RIDDELL, EDWARD WIDDRINGTON, Esq., of
Bootham House, Yorkshire.

Second son of the late Ralph Riddell, Esq., of Felton
Park and Swinburn Castle, co. Northumberland (see
that family), and Catharine, eldest dau. of the late Joseph
Blount, Esq., of Mapledurham House, Oxon; b. 1803;
m. 1850 the Hon. Catharine, eldest dau. of the late
Thomas Stapleton, Esq., of Carlton Hall, co. York, and
798

sister of Miles Thomas, 8th Lord Beaumont, and has,
with other issue,

* Edward Widdrington. of Pocklington. co. York; b. 1831;
  in Holy Orders of the Roman Catholic Church.

Mr. Riddell, who was educated at Stonyhurst Coll.,
was formerly an Officer 16th Hussars.—*Bootham House,
York.*

RIDDELL, GEORGE HUTTON-, Esq., of
Carlton-on-Trent, Notts.

Eldest son of the late George William Hutton, Esq. of
Carlton-on-Trent, by Frances, dau. of Bertram Mitford,
Esq., of Mitford; b. 1807; s. 1835; m. 1st 1855 Mary,
dau. of Walter Riddell, Esq., of Jedburgh, N.B. (whose
name he assumed); 2nd 1858 Hannah Elizabeth,
widow of J. O. Lambert, Esq.; 3rd 1862 Janetta Gonville, 4th dau. of Sir Edmund Gonville Bromhead, Bart.,
and has by the former, with other issue,

* George William, b. 1856.

Mr. Riddell, who is a Magistrate for Notts, descends
from Sir Richard Hutton, a Judge of the Common
Pleas (who d. 1638).—*Carlton-on-Trent, Newark, Notts;
Windham Club, s.w.*

RIDDELL, THOMAS, Esq., of Felton Park and
Swinburn Castle, Northumberland.

Eldest son of the late Ralph Riddell. Esq., of Felton
Park and Swinburn Castle, by Elizabeth, dau. of Joseph
Blount, Esq., of Mapledurham. Oxon; b. 1802; s. 1833;
m. 1st 1827 Mary, sister of the late Sir Robert George
Throckmorton, Bart. (she d. 1843): 2nd 1845 Laura
Anne, eldest dau. of the late Sir Thomas Joseph De
Trafford, Bart., and has, with other surviving issue,

* John Giffard, b. 1830; m. 1866 Victoria Henrietta. 5th dau.
  of the late Peter Purcell, Esq., of Halverstown, co. Kildare,
  and has issue, * a son, b. 1867.

Mr. Riddell, who was educated at Stonyhurst Coll., is
a J.P. and D.L. for Northumberland (High Sheriff
1836).—*Felton Park, Morpeth; Swinburn Castle, Chol-
lerton, Hexham.*

RIDDELL, Major-General WILLIAM, C.B., of
Camieston, Roxburghshire.

Eldest son of the late Thomas Riddell, Esq., the
younger, of Camieston, by Jane, dau. of Walter Ferrier,
Esq., of Somerford, co. Stirling; b. 1805; m. 1857
Margaret, dau. of Capt. John Wilkie, Bengal Army,
and has, with other surviving issue,

* William Carre, Ensign 103rd Royal Bombay Fusiliers; b.1847.

Major-General Riddell, who was educated at the University of Edinburgh, is a Magistrate for co. Roxburgh,
and a Major-General. Bengal Army, retired. — *The
Anchorage, Melrose, N.B.; United Service Club, Edinburgh.*

RIDDELL-CARRE. (See *Carre.*)

+RIDER, THOMAS, Esq., of Boughton Monchelsea, Kent.

Son of the late W. Rider. Esq.. and nephew of the late
Thomas Rider. Esq.. of Boughton Monchelsea (who
was M.P. for Kent 1831-?, for West Kent 1832-41);
b. 18—. Is a Magistrate for Kent —*Boughton Monchelsea, Staplehurst; Reform Club, s.w.*

RIDGWAY, ALEXANDER, Esq., of Sheplegh,
Devon.

Eldest son of the late Alexander Foxcroft Ridgway,
Esq., of Sheplegh, by Jane, dau. of the late John Grey.
Esq.; b. 1826; m. 1856 Sarah Ann, dau. of John
Joseph, Esq., of Bishton, and has, with other issue.

* Thomas Archer, b. 1864.

Mr. Ridgway is a Magistrate for Devon, Lord of the
Manor of Dallacombe Preston (otherwise Preston) and
Capt. 1st Devon Militia.—*Sh-, Segh. Blackaw-ton, S.
Devon; 5, Weymouth Street, w.*

+ RIDGWAY, EDWARD JOHN, Esq., of Rownall Hall, Staffordshire.

Son of the late E. Ridgway, Esq.; *b.* 18—; is married and has, with other issue,

* Henry Akroyd, of Woodlands, Halifax, *b.* 18—; *m.* 1867 Mary Gertrude, eldest dau. of Marcus Huish, Esq.

Mr. Ridgway is a Magistrate for co. Stafford.—*Rownall Hall, Hanley, Staffordshire.*

RIDGWAY, JOSEPH, Esq., of Wallsuches, Lancashire, and Fairlawn, Kent.

Eldest son of the late Thomas Ridgway, Esq., of Wallsuches, by Anne, dau. of Henry Stanley Gill, Esq., of Ormskirk; *b.* 1820; *s.* 1839; *m.* 1st 1843 Selina Harriet, dau. of the late Sir Francis Doyle, Bart.; 2nd 1865 the Hon. Georgiana Clementina, youngest dau. of the late Hon. Gen. Sir Charles Colville, G.C.B., and sister of Charles John, 11th Lord Colville of Culross; he has issue by the former, an only child,

* Cicely Marguerite Wilhelmina.

Mr. Ridgway, who was educated at Shrewsbury School, is a Magistrate for co. Lancaster and Kent, Lord of the Manors of Shiphorne and Puttenden, and Patron of one living. This family descend from the Ridegways of Torre, Devon.—*Fairlawn, Sevenoaks; Wallsuches, Bolton.*

RIDLEY, Sir MATTHEW WHITE, Bart., of Blagdon, Northumberland (cr. 1756).

Eldest son of the late Sir Matthew White Ridley, Bart., M.P., of Blagdon, by Laura, dau. of George Hawkins, Esq.; *b.* 1807; *s.* as 4th Bart. 1836; *m.* 1841 Cecilia Anne, eldest dau. of the late Lord Wensleydale (she *d.* 1815). Educated at Westminster and Ch. Ch., Oxford (B.A. 1828); is a J.P. and D.L. for Northumberland (High Sheriff 1841), Patron of 3 livings, and Lieut.-Col. Northumberland Yeomaury Cavalry; was elected M.P. for N. Northumberland 1859.—*Blagdon, Morpeth; Boodle's and Carlton Clubs, s.w.; 10, Carlton Terrace, s.w.*

Heir, his son Matthew White, a Magistrate for Northumberland; *b.* 1842.

RIDLEY, Major-Gen. CHARLES WILLIAM, C.B., of Fir Grove, Hampshire.

Second son of the late Sir Mathew White Ridley, Bart., of Blagdon, Northumberland, by Laura, dau. of George Hawkins, Esq.; *b.* 1812; *m.* 1845 Hon. Henrietta Araminta, dau. of Dominick, 1st Lord Oranmore, and has, with other issue,

* Henry Colborne Monck. *b.* 1848.

General Ridley, who was educated at Westminster, is a Major-General in the Army, late Commander of the Dublin Division; formerly in the Grenadier Guards. —*Fir Grove, Eversley, Winchfield.*

RIDLEY, GEORGE, Esq.

Youngest son of the late Sir Matthew White Ridley, Bart., of Blagdon, Northumberland, by Laura, dau. of George Hawkins, Esq.; *b.* 1818. Educated at Winchester and Ch. Ch., Oxford (B.A. 1841); was M.P. for Newcastle-on-Tyne 1856-60.—2, *Charles Street, w.*

RIDLEY, JOHN MATTHEW, Esq., of Walwick Hall, Northumberland.

Second son of the late John Ridley, Esq., of Park End, Northumberland (who *d.* 1865), by Bridget, youngest dau. of Matthew Atkinson, Esq., of Temple Sowerby, Westmoreland; *b.* 1820; *m.* 1844 Anna Maria, youngest dau. of Henry Hilton, Esq., of Sole Street, Kent, and has, with other issue,

* John Hilton, *b.* 1848.

Mr. Ridley, who was educated at Jesus Coll., Cambridge (B.A. 1843, M.A. 1846), and was called to the Bar at Lincoln's Inn 1846, is a Magistrate for Northumberland.—*Walwick Hall, Hexham; Oxford and Cambridge Club, s.w.*

RIDLEY, the Rev. NICHOLAS JAMES, of Hollington House, Hants.

Second son of the late Rev. Henry Colborne Ridley, Rector of Hambleden, Bucks, by Mary, dau. of James Farrer, Esq., of Ingleborough, co. York; *b.* 1821; *m.* 1845 Frances, dau. of John Touchet, Esq., and has issue. Educated at Ch. Ch., Oxford (B.A. 1841, M.A. 1845); appointed Perpetual Curate of Woolton Hill, East Woodhay, 1849. This family is a younger branch of that of Sir M. W. Ridley, Bart., and of the late Lord Colborne (ext.).—*Hollington House, Newbury; University Club, s.w.; 7, Cambridge Square, w.*

RIDLEY, THOMAS, Esq., of Park End, Northumberland.

Eldest son of the late John Ridley, Esq., of Park End, by Bridget, youngest dau. of Matthew Atkinson, Esq., of Temple Sowerby, Westmoreland; *b.* 1817; *s.* 1865; Is a Magistrate for Northumberland.—*Park End, Hexham.*

Heir Pres., his brother John Matthew (whom see).

RIDSDALE, the Rev. ROBERT.

Son of the late — Ridsdale, Esq.; *b.* 1791; *m.* 1826 Lady Audrey Harriet, dau. of the late Lord John Townshend, M.P., and sister of John, 4th Marquis Townshend, and has, with other issue,

* George John, in Holy Orders, M.A. of Magdalen Coll., Cambridge, and Vicar of South Creake, Norfolk; *b.* 1827; *m.* 1857 Mary, only dau. of John Stoveld, Esq., of Stedham Hall, Sussex.

Mr. Ridsdale, who was educated at Clare Coll., Cambridge (B.A. 1815, M.A. 1818), and appointed Rector of Knockin, co. Salop, 1826, Rector of Tillington 1854, and Prebendary of Chichester 1835, was Fellow of Clare Coll., Cambridge, 1816-26.—*Tillington Rectory, Petworth.*

RIGBY, JAMES, Esq., of Moss House, Lancashire.

Only surviving son of the late William Rigby, Esq., of Liverpool, by Alice, dau. of William Rigg, Esq., of Liverpool; *b.* 1805; *s.* 1829; *m.* 1844 Catherine, eldest dau. of Joseph Nead Walker, Esq., of Calderstone, co. Lancaster. Is a Dep.-Lieut. for co. Lancaster, and Capt. 1st Royal Lancashire Militia.—*Moss House, Liverpool.*

RIGG, Lieut.-Col. HUGH, of Crossrigg Hall, Westmoreland.

Third son of the late Rev. Hugh Rigg, by Maria, grand-dau. of Christopher Addison, Esq., of Wickerfield, Westmoreland; *b.* 1823; *s.* his great-uncle, Robert Addison, Esq., 1862; *m.* 1848 Margaret, dau. of Major-General Morden Carthew, and has, with other issue,

* Hugh Carthew, *b.* 1849.

Lieut.-Col. Rigg, who served under the East India Company and in H.M.'s Indian Army from 1840 to 1862, was High Sheriff of Westmoreland 1867.—*Crossrigg Hall, Marland, Penrith.*

RIGG, JAMES HOME, Esq., of Tarvit, Fifeshire.

Eldest son of the late Patrick Rigg, Esq. (who *d.* 1861) by Margaret, dau. of John Waugh Brougham, Esq., and grandson of the late James Home Rigg, Esq., of Tarvit House; *b.* 1845; his grandfather 1862.—*Tarvit House, Capar, Fifeshire.*

RIGG, JONATHAN, Esq., of Wrotham Hill, Kent.

Youngest son of the late Thomas Rigg, Esq., of Selside, Westmoreland, by Ann, dau. of John Mounsey, Esq., of Newbiggin, Cumberland; *b.* 1808; *m.* 1839 Mary

Darling, only dau. of the late William Thomas Goad, Esq., of Hackbridge House, Carshalton, Surrey, and by her, who d. 1852, has, with other issue,

   • William Thomas, b. 1840 ; m. 1861 Mary Selina, only child of the Ven. Owen Davys, Archdeacon of Northampton.

Mr. Rigg, who purchased this estate in 1847, is a Magistrate for Kent and Middlesex ; he was formerly a Merchant in Liverpool and London.—*Wrotham Hill Park, Sevenoaks ; Conservative Club*, s.w. ; 4, *Chester Place, Hyde Park Square*, w.

RIGGE, HENRY FLETCHER, Esq., of Wood Broughton, Lancashire.

Eldest son of the late Gray Rigge, Esq., of Wood Broughton, by Sarah, dau. of Edward Moore, Esq., of Stockwell, Surrey ; b. 1809 ; s. 1857 ; m. 1849 Rosetta Margaret, only dau. of the late James Machell, Esq., of Newbybridge, Windermere, and has, with other issue,

   • Gray, b. 1857.

Mr. Rigge, who was educated at the Charterhouse and C.C.C., Cambridge (B.A. 1831), is a J.P. and D.L. for co. Lancaster.—*Wood Broughton, Cartmel.*

+RIGGE, JOHN SANDERSON, Esq., of Belmont Castle, Essex.

Son of the late John Rigge, Esq., merchant, of London, b. 18—. Is a Magistrate for Essex, and an East India Merchant in the firm of Sanderson, Rigge, & Co.—*Belmont Castle, Gray's Thurrock, Tilbury, Essex ; 14, St. Helen's Place, Bishopsgate*, E.C.

+RILEY, WILLIAM FELIX, Esq., of Forest Hill, Berks.

Eldest son of the late William Felix Riley, Esq., J.P. and D.L., of Forest Hill, by Mary Sophia Harcourt, dau. of the late John Ramsbottom, Esq., M.P. ; b. 1823 ; s. 1863 ; is married, and has issue. Mr. Riley was formerly an Officer in the 52nd Foot.—*Forest Hill, Clewer, Windsor.*

+RIPLEY, HENRY WILLIAM, Esq., of Lightcliff, Yorkshire.

Only child of Edward Ripley, Esq., of Boling Lodge, near Bradford, by a dau. of — Smith, Esq., of Bradford ; b. 1814 ; m. 1836 Anne, dau. of J. Milligan, Esq., and niece of the late Robert Milligan, Esq., of Acacia, M.P., and has, with other issue,

   • Edward, b. 184- ; educated at Cheltenham Coll.

Mr. Ripley is a Magistrate for the Borough of Bradford, and a Manufacturer at Bradford, and President of the Bradford Chamber of Commerce 1862-3.—*Lightcliff, Halifax.*

RIPLEY, the Rev. WILLIAM NOTTIDGE, of Earlham Hall, Norfolk.

Son of the late W. Ripley, Esq. ; b. 182- ; is married, and has, with other issue,

   • A son b. 1861.

Mr. Ripley, who was educated at Caius Coll., Cambridge (B.A. 1818, M.A. 1851), is Incumbent of St. Giles's, Norwich.—*Earlham Hall, Norwich.*

RIPON, Bishop of, ROBERT BICKERSTETH, D.D.

Son of the late Rev. John Bickersteth, Rector of Sapcote, co. Leicester, by a dau. of George Lang, Esq., and nephew of Henry, 1st Lord Langdale (*crd.*) ; b. 1816 ; m. 1846 Elizabeth, dau. of Joseph Garde, Esq., of Cork. Educated at Queen's Coll., Cambridge (B.A. 1841, M.A. 1844) ; was Incumbent of St. John's, Clapham, Rector of St. Giles's, London, and Canon of Salisbury ; consecrated 1857 ; Patronage 52 livings. The see was erected by Act of Parliament in 1836. —*The Palace, Ripon ; National Club*, s.w.

RIPON. (See *De Grey, Earl.*)

RIPPON, Mrs., of Waterville, Northumberland.

Margaret, youngest dau. of the late John Fryer of Newcastle-on-Tyne ; m. 1818 George Rippon. Esq., of Waterville, who was a Magistrate for Northumberland. and formerly Capt. in the Tyne Yeomanry Hussars. and who d. s. p. 1864. The cradle of Queen Elizabeth is preserved at Waterville.—*Waterville, North Shields.*

RIPPON, VALENTINE, Esq., of Rogerley Hall, co. Durham.

Youngest son of the late Cuthbert Rippon. Esq., M.P., of Stanhope Castle, co. Durham, by Eleanor, dau. of the late Thomas Moxon, Esq., of Twickenham, Middlesex ; b. 1825 ; m. 1857 Sarah Anne, dau. of T. Drake, Esq., and niece of the late Charles Penrose, Esq., of Little Brickhill, Bucks, and has, with other issue,

   • Valentine Arthur, b. 1862.

Mr. Rippon is a Magistrate for co. Durham, and Lord of the Manor of Frosterley.—*Rogerley Hall, Frosterley, co. Durham.*

RISING, ROBERT, Esq., of Horsey Norfolk.

Only son of the late Robert Rising, Esq., of Horsey Hall, by Mary, dau. of Isaac Preston, Esq., of Great Yarmouth ; b. 1801 ; s. 1841 ; m. 1830 Elizabeth, dau. of Charles Compton Parish, Esq., of Hemesby, and has, with other issue,

   • Robert Arthur, late Lieut. 77th Regt. ; b. 1836.

Mr. Rising, who was educated at Pembroke Coll., Cambridge (Wrangler and B.A. 1824, M.A. 1827). and called to the Bar at Lincoln's Inn 1828, is a Magistrate for Norfolk, and a District Poor-law Auditor ; Lord of the Manor and Patron of Horsey ; was formerly Commissioner of Bankrupts for Yarmouth and Beccles. —*Horsey Hall, Gt. Yarmouth.*

RISLEY, the Rev. WILLIAM COTTON, of Deddington, Oxon.

Eldest son of the late Rev. John Risley, Rector of Thornton, Bucks, and Ashton-cum-Roade, co. Northampton, by Sarah Anne, only child of the late Rev. Charles Cotton, Rector of Heyford Warren and Newton Purcell, Oxon ; b. 1798 ; m. 1828 Susanna, only child of Robert Wells, Esq., and niece of the late John Barber, Esq., of Adderbury West, Oxon, and by her, who d. 1865, has, with other issue,

   • Holford Cotton, a Magistrate for Oxon ; b. 1831.

Mr. Risley, who was educated at Winchester and New Coll., Oxford (B.A. 1820. M.A. 1824). is a Magistrate for Oxon, and Patron of 1 living ; he was formerly Vicar of Deddington, and Rural Dean. This family was settled for several generations in Beds and Bucks. —*Deddington, Oxfordshire.*

RIVERS, Lord (HORACE PITT-RIVERS).—Cr. 1802.

Only surviving son of William Horace, 3rd Lord, by Frances, dau. of Col. Francis Hale Rigby, of Mistley Hall, Essex, and uncle of Henry Peter, 5th Lord ; b. 1814 ; s. his nephew 1867 ; m. 1815 Miss Eleanor Smart. Is Patron of 11 livings, was formerly Capt. in the R.H. Guards. The Pitts, Earls of Chatham, represented a junior branch of this family.—*Rushmore Lodge, Salisbury.*

RIVERS, SIR JAMES FRANCIS, Bart. (cr. 1624).

Eldest son of the late Rev. Sir Henry Rivers, Bart., of Chafford, Kent (who was Rector of Martyr Worthy, Hants), by Charlotte, dau. of Samuel Eales, Esq. ; b. 1822 ; s. as 10th Bart. 1851 ; m. 1st 1859 Sarah Elizabeth, dau. of George Gambier, Esq., of Canterbury (she d. 1865) ; 2nd 1867 Catherine, widow of R. D. Fastcott, Esq. Educated at Winchester ; was formerly an Officer in the Army.—Residence : *Beacon Hill, Bath.*

   Heir Pres., his brother Henry Chandos, b. 18--.

RIVETT-CARNAC. (See *Carnac*.)

RIVIS, THOMAS WILLIAM, Esq., of Newstead House, Yorkshire.
Eldest son of Matthew Rivis, Esq., by Mary, dau. of John Hall, Esq., of Wykeham ; *b.* 1813 ; *s.* his uncle, John Rivis, Esq., late an Alderman of Hull, 1844 ; *m.* 1842 Mary, dau. of William Preston, Esq., and has, with other issue,
  * John William, *b.* 1843.
Mr. Rivis is a Dep.-Lieut. for the E. Riding of Yorkshire.—*Newstead House, Malton.*

ROBARTES. (See *Agar-Robartes*.)

ROBARTS, ABRAHAM JOHN, Esq., of Lillingstone, Bucks.
Eldest son of the late Abraham George Robarts, Esq., Banker of London (who *d.* 1860), by Elizabeth Sarah, dau. of John Henry Smyth, Esq., of Heath Hall, co. York, and grandson of the late Abraham Wildey Robarts, Esq., M.P. (who *d.* 1858); *b.* 1838. Educated at Eton and Ch. Ch., Oxford (B.A. 1859); is a Magistrate for Bucks, and a Capt. Royal Bucks Yeomanry. —*Lillingstone Dayrell, Buckingham.*

ROBARTS, HENRY CHRISTOPHER, Esq.
Second but eldest surviving son of the late Abraham Wildey Robarts, Esq., sometime M.P. for Maidstone, who *d.* 1858, by Charlotte Anne, dau. of Edward Wilkinson, Esq., of Potterton Lodge, near Tadcaster, co. York; *b.* 1811 ; *m.* 18— Janet, dau. of the late Admiral Dundas. Is a Dep.-Lieut. for Buckinghamshire, and a Banker in London.—*Travellers' and Athenæum Clubs,* s.w.; 41, *Lowndes Square,* s.w.

ROBERTS, Sir RANDALL HOWLAND, Bart., of Roberts Cove, co. Cork (cr. 1809).
Only son of the late Sir Thomas Howland Roberts, Bart., of Roberts Cove (who was a Magistrate for co. Cork), by his 1st wife Eliza Caroline, dau. of John Maitland, Esq., of Eccles, co. Dumfries; *b.* 1837 ; *s.* as 4th Bart. 1864 ; *m.* 1858 Mary, dau. of the late Col. Turnbull, of the Bombay Artillery. Was formerly Lieut. 33rd Foot.
  Heir Pres., his brother Howland (eldest son of the late Sir T. H. Roberts, by his 2nd wife Anne, dau. of Capt. W. Langdon, R.N.), *b.* 1846.

ROBERTS, Sir ABRAHAM, K.C.B. (cr. 1865).
Son of the late Rev. John Roberts (who was a Magistrate for co. Waterford). by Anne, dau. of Abraham Sandys, Esq.; *b.* 1784 ; *m.* 1st 1820 Frances Isabella, dau. of the late Poyntz Ricketts, Esq., Bengal Civil Service ; 2nd 1830 Isabella, dau. of the late Abraham Bunbury, Esq., of co. Tipperary, and widow of Major Hamilton Maxwell, Bengal Army ; is a General in the Army, and Col. 101st Regt.—*Clifton, Bristol ; United Service Club,* s.w.

ROBERTS, Lady, of Hazeldine, Worcestershire.
Julia Maria, dau. of the Rev. Robert Raikes, Rector of Longhope, co. Gloucester ; *m.* 1838 Major-General Sir Henry Gee Roberts, K.C.B., who *d.* 1860, leaving, with other issue, * Frederic Boyd, *b.* 1841.—*Hazeldine House, Redmarley, Ledbury.*

ROBERTS, ARTHUR TROUGHTON, Esq., of Coeddû, Flintshire, and Glan-y-Menai, Anglesey.
Eldest son of the late Hugh Roberts, Esq., of Glan-y-Menai, Anglesey, by Anne, dau. of John Hughes, Esq., of Chester; *b.* 1819 ; *s* 1857; *m* 1849 Grace Rebecca

eldest dau. of Wm. Phillips, Esq., of Wiston House, co. Monmouth, and has, with other issue,
  * Arthur Phillips, *b.* 1851.
Mr. Roberts, who was educated at Rugby, is Clerk of the Peace for co. Flint, and a Dep.-Lieut. for co. Anglesey.—*Coeddû, Mold, Flintshire ; Glan-y-Menai, Anglesey ; Carlton Club,* s.w.

ROBERTS, ERASMUS CORYTON, Esq., of Treval, Cornwall.
Eldest son of the late John Coryton Roberts, Esq., J.P., of Treval, by Harriet, dau. of the Rev. Nicolas Dobree, Rector of St. Mary De Castro, Guernsey ; *b.* 1832 ; *s.* 1864 ; *m.* 1st 1859 Florence, dau. and co-heir of John Anderson, Esq., of Cox Lodge, Northumberland ; 2nd 1863 Emma, dau. of the late Pelham Dutton, Esq., of Sydney, and has issue by the former,
  * John Anderson Dobree, *b.* 1860.
Mr. Roberts, who was educated at Queen's Coll., Oxford (B.A. 1853, M.A. 1856), is a Magistrate for Cornwall.—*Treval, Torpoint ; Carvealc, Antony, Cornwall.*

ROBERTS, GABRIEL, Esq., of Cefnoch, Denbighshire.
Son of the late Ffoulke Roberts, Esq., of Llandyrnog, by Ellenor, dau. of the late Thomas Hughes, Esq., of Pentremawr, Llandyrnog ; *b.* 1786 ; *m.* 1819 Margaret, dau. of the late Gabriel Davies, Esq., of Bala. co. Merioneth, and by her, who *d.* 1864, has, with other issue, an only son,
  * Gabriel Lloyd, M.A. of St. John's Coll., Cambridge. Rector of Ryton, co. Salop, and a Magistrate for co. Denbigh; *b.* 1820; *m.* 1863 Mary Jane, eldest dau. of Henry Tayleur, Esq., of Brynyffrynon, co. Denbigh.
Mr. Roberts is a J.P. and D.L. for co. Denbigh, and Patron of 1 living.—*Plas Gwyn, Ruthin.*

ROBERTS, HUGH BEAVER, Esq., of Plas Llandoget, Denbighshire.
Second son of the late Hugh Roberts, Esq., of Glan-y-Menai, Anglesey, by Anne, dau. of John Hughes. Esq., of Chester ; *b.* 1820 ; *m.* 1848 Harriet, eldest dau. of James Wyatt, Esq., of Bryn-Gwynant, co. Carnarvon, and has, with other issue,
  * Hugh Stuart, *b.* 1851.
Mr. Roberts, who was educated at Rugby, is a Magistrate for cos. Carnarvon and Denbigh, and a J.P. and D.L. for co. Merioneth.—*Plas Llandoget. Harvest, Denbighshire ; Oriental Club,* w.; *Junior Carlton Club,* s.w.

ROBERTS, the Rev. JAMES CORRALL, of Witherley, co. Leicester.
Only son of the late Rev. James Roberts. Rector of Stoneleigh, co. Warwick, and subsequently Rector of Witherley ; *b.* 1795. Educated at Trinity Coll., Oxford (B.A. 1818, M.A. 1833); is a Magistrate for cos. Warwick and Leicester, and Rector and Patron of Witherley.—*Witherley, Atherstone.*

ROBERTS, MARTYN JOHN, Esq., F.R.S., of Pendarren House, Brecknockshire.
Eldest son of the late John Roberts. Esq., by Caroline, dau. of William Yalden, Esq., of Lovington, Hants; *b.* 1806 ; *m.* 1829 ; *m.* 1810 Anne Eliza, sister of Sir John Gordon, Bart., and has, with other issue,
  * William Scarlett, *b.* 1849.
Mr. Roberts, who was educated at Edinburgh University, is a J.P. and D.L. for Brecon.—*Pendarren House, Crickhowell.*

ROBERTS, Capt. RICHARD THOMAS, of Gadlys Uchaf, Glamorganshire.
Eldest son of the late James Lewis Roberts. Esq., of Gadlys Uchaf (who was a Magistrate for cos. Glamorgan and Brecon), by Mary, dau. of Thomas Thomas,

Esq., of Abernant Glyn Neath, co. Glamorgan; b. 1844; s. 1864. Educated at the Royal Military Academy, Woolwich; is a Magistrate for cos. Glamorgan and Brecon, and Capt. R. Glamorgan Infantry Militia; was formerly Lieut. R.A.—*Gadlys Uchaf, Aberdare.*

ROBERTS, Richard William, Esq., of Ardmore, co. Cork.
Eldest son of the late John Roberts, Esq., of Ardmore, by Anne, dau. of William Johnson, Esq.; b. 1828; m. 1856 Henrietta Sarah, eldest dau. of Robert Hedges Eyre White, Esq., of Raffeen House and Glengariffe Castle, co. Cork, and has, with other issue,
* John, b. 1857.
Mr. Roberts, who was educated at Trinity Coll., Dublin (B.A. 1863), is a Magistrate for co. Cork, and Lord of the Manor of Ardmore.—*Ardmore, Passage West.*

ROBERTS, the Rev. Samuel Wallis, B.D., of Trethill, Cornwall.
Eldest son of the late Rev. Dr. Bryan Roberts, LL.D., Rector of Drewsteignton, Devon, and St. John's, Cornwall, by Anne, eldest dau. and co-heir of the Rev. M. Wallis of Trethill; b. 1792; s. his mother 1836. Was Founder's Kin Fellow of Pembroke Coll., Oxford (B.A. 1813, M.A. 1814, B.D. 1830); is a Magistrate for Cornwall.—*Trethill, Sheviock, Devonport.*

ROBERTS, Thomas, Esq., of Hamilton House, Pembrokeshire.
Eldest son of the late William Roberts, Esq., of Milford, co. Pembroke, by Margaret, dau. of John Davies, Esq., of Newport; b. 1823; s. 1837; m. 1848 Jane, eldest dau. of John Ralph, Esq., of Beaumaris, and has, with other surviving issue,
* William Robert, b. 1856.
Mr. Roberts is a J.P. and D.L. for co. Pembroke.—*Hamilton House, Milford.*

ROBERTS, Thomas Lewis, Esq., of Dormstown, co. Meath.
Eldest son of the late Rev. John Roberts, by Anna Maria, dau. of David Thompson, Esq., of Oatlands, co. Meath; b. 1808; m. 1836 Anna Matilda, eldest dau. of Robert Richards, Esq., Assistant Barrister for co. Wexford, and has, with other issue,
* John Richards, b. 1838; m. 1868 Mathilde Barbara Eliza, eldest dau. of the late Capt. Richard Nugent Everard, of Randlestown House, co. Meath.
Mr. Roberts, who was educated at Trinity Coll., Dublin (B.A. 1829), is a Magistrate and a Grand Juror for co. Meath.—*Dormstown Castle, Navan, co. Meath; Hendré, Killiney, co. Dublin; University Club, Dublin.*

ROBERTS, Wightwick, Esq., of Trethill, Cornwall.
Third son of the late Rev. Dr. Bryan Roberts, Rector of Drew-steignton, Devon, and of St. John's, Cornwall, and brother of the Rev. S. W. Roberts (whom see), by Anne, eldest dau. and co-heir of the Rev. Mydhope Wallis, of Trethill; b. 18—. Is a Magistrate for co. Cornwall.—*Trethill, Sheviock, Devonport.*

ROBERTS. (See *Cramer-Roberts.*)

ROBERTS-WEST, James, Esq., of Alscot Park, Warwickshire.
Eldest son of the late James Roberts-West, Esq., of Alscot Park, by Anne, dau. and heiress of Joseph Roberts, Esq., of New-Combe House, co. Gloucester; b. 1811; s. 1838; m. 1814 Elizabeth, 3rd dau. of the late Joseph Moore Boultbee, Esq., and the Lady Elizabeth Boultbee, of Springfield House, co. Warwick, and has, with other issue,
* James, b. 1843.
Mr. Roberts-West, who was educated at Eton and
890

Caius Coll., Cambridge, is a J.P. and D.L. for co. Warwick (High Sheriff 1845), and a Magistrate for co. Gloucester.—*Alscot Park, Stratford-on-Avon; Oxford and Cambridge and Arthur's Clubs, s.w.*

ROBERTSON, Andrew, Esq., of Foveran, Aberdeenshire.
Eldest son of the late John Robertson, Esq., of Foveran, by Mary, dau. of David Steuart, Esq., of Dalguise, co. Perth; b. 1818; s. 1826. Mr. Robertson, who was educated at Rugby, is a J.P. and D.L. for co. Aberdeen, and was formerly in H.M.'s 14th Light Dragoons.—*Foveran House, Aberdeen; Conservative Club, s.w.*

ROBERTSON, Arthur John, Esq., of Inshes, Inverness-shire.
Eldest son of the late Masterton Robertson, Esq., of Inshes, by Mary, dau. of Charles Shearer, Esq.; b. 1805; m. 1st 1824 Marianne, only child of Richard Pattinson, Esq.; 2nd 1840 Charlotte Maria, dau. of Thomas Mathias Bearda Batard, Esq., and has, by the former, with other issue,
* Arthur Masterton, b. 1826; m. 1858 Sarah Louisa, eldest dau. and heiress of the late Col. James McAlpine, of Wyndsor, co. Mayo, late 15th Hussars, and by her, who d. 1863, has issue, * Arthur Masterton Macalpine, b. 1859.
Mr. Robertson is a J.P. and D.L. for co. Inverness.—*Inshes, Inverness, N.B.*

ROBERTSON, Charles, Esq., of Kindeace, Ross-shire.
Eldest son of the late William Robertson, Esq., of Kindeace and Green Yarde, by Mary, dau. of Alexander Chisholm, of Chisholm; b. 1790; s. 1844; m. 1816 Helen, 4th dau. of Patrick Cruikshank, Esq., of Stracathro, co. Forfar, and has, with other surviving issue,
* Charles, b. 1831.
Mr. Robertson, who is a J.P. and D.L. for cos. Ross and Cromarty, was formerly in the 78th and 96th Regts.; served in Java, including the action of Weltvreeden, in batteries before Cornelis, siege and capture of Jokajarta; noticed in despatches, wounded, and received silver war medal. This family is descended from the Robertson of Inshes, the 1st cadet of the Robertsons of Strowan, co. Perth.—*Kindeace, Invergordon, Ross-shire, N.B.; New Club, Edinburgh.*

ROBERTSON, David, Esq., of Ladykirk, Berwickshire.
Youngest son of the late Sir John Marjoribanks, Bart., M.P., of Lees, co. Berwick, by Alison, dau. of the late William Ramsay, Esq., of Barnton, Midlothian, N.B.; b. 1797; m. 1834 Mary Sarah, eldest dau. of the late Sir Thomas Haggerston, Bart., and grand-dau. of the late Wm. Robertson, Esq., of Ladykirk, whose name they assumed, and has surviving issue.
* Two daughters.
Mr. Robertson, who was educated at the University of Edinburgh, is Lord Lieutenant of co. Berwick; he was elected M.P. for that county 1859.—*Ladykirk, Berwick-on-Tweed, N.B.; Union and R. Yacht Clubs, s.w.*

ROBERTSON, David Souter, Esq., of Lawhead, Lanarkshire, and Whitehill, Linlithgowshire.
Grand-nephew of the late Thomas Robertson, Esq., of Whitehill and Lawhead; b. 1802; m. 1st 1835 Mary Jane, dau. of the late Rev. A. Farquhar (she d. 1845); 2nd 1847 Elizabeth, dau. of the late John Leith Ross, Esq., of Arnage, Dep.-Lieut. for co. Aberdeen, and has by the former, with other issue,
* Stewart, b. 1839; m. 1862 Ann, niece of John Hamilton, Esq., of Fairholm, Dep.-Lieut. for co. Lanark, and has, with other issue, * David, b. 1863.
Mr. Robertson, who was educated at Edinburgh, is a

Member of the Chartered Body of Accountants there, a J.P. and D.L. for cos. Lanark and Bute, and a Commissioner of Lieutenancy of the former county.—*Lawhead House, Carnwath, N.B. ; United Service Club, Edinburgh ; 10, Great Stuart Street, Edinburgh.*

ROBERTSON, EBEN WILLIAM, Esq., of Chilcote, Leicestershire.
Only surviving son of the late Francis Robertson, Esq., of Chilcote, by Laura, dau. of William Ross, Esq., of the Aldie family ; *b.* 1815 ; *s.* 1852 ; *m.* 1838 Isabella, youngest dau. of William M. Colegrave, Esq., of Downsells and Cann Hall, Essex, and Meer Hall, and Bracebridge, co. Lincoln, and has, with other issue,
* Francis William, *b.* 1849.
Mr. Robertson, who was educated at Worcester Coll., Oxford (B.A. 1837), and called to the Bar at Lincoln's Inn 1845, is a Magistrate for co. Derby, and a J.P. and D.L. for co. Leicester. This family descend from the Robertsons of Strowan, by the same line as the families of Inshes and Kindeace.—*Chilcote, Netherseal, Ashby-de-la-Zouche ; Athenæum and Conservative Clubs, s.w.*

ROBERTSON, HENRY, Esq., of Crogen, co. Merioneth.
Son of the late H. Robertson, Esq. ; *b.* 1816 ; *m.* 1846 Elizabeth, dau. of William Dean, Esq., of Shrewsbury. Educated at King's Coll., Aberdeen (M.A. 183-) ; is a Civil Engineer and Ironmaster ; was M.P. for Shrewsbury 1862-5.—*Crogen, Corwen ; Reform Club, s.w. ; 40, Euston Square, N.W.*

ROBERTSON, JAMES, Esq., of Woodend, Renfrewshire.
Eldest son of the late John Murray Robertson, Esq., of Peebles (who *d.* 1822), by Elizabeth, dau. of Robert Williamson, Esq., of Sanquhar, co. Dumfries ; *b.* 1803 ; *m.* 1832 Marian Corrie, dau. of William Lawson, Esq., of Drungans, co. Dumfries, and by her, who *d.* 1865, has, with other issue,
* John Murray, *b.* 1833 ; *m.* 1862 Catherine Jane, dau. of Archibald Nimmo, Esq., of Edinburgh.
Mr. Robertson, who was educated at Edinburgh, is a Magistrate for cos. Lanark and Renfrew ; was formerly a Banker at Glasgow, and Major 1st Lanarkshire Rifle Volunteers.—*Woodend House, Cathcart, Glasgow, N.B. ; New Club, Edinburgh ; Western Club, Glasgow ; Conservative Club, s.w. ; 13, King Street, St. James's, s.w.*

+ROBERTSON, Major JAMES, of Cray House, Perthshire.
Eldest son of the late Major James Robertson, of Cray House ; *b.* 18—; *s.* 184-. Is Lord of the Barony of Cray, and Major Perthshire Militia.—*Cray House, Blairgowrie, N.B.*

ROBERTSON, PATRICK FRANCIS, Esq., of Halton, Sussex.
Eldest son of the late Rev. Daniel Robertson. D.D., of St. Andrew's, N.B., by Isabella, dau. of the Rev. Alexander Small, D.D., of Kilconquhar, co. Fife ; *b.* 1807. Educated at the University of St. Andrew's ; is a Magistrate for Hastings and a Dep.-Lieut. for Sussex ; was M.P. for Hastings 1852-9, re-elected 1865 ; formerly a Merchant at Canton.—*Halton, Hastings ; Carlton and Conservative Clubs, s.w. ; 7, Pall Mall, s.w.*

ROBERTSON, ROBERT, Esq., of Auchlecks, co. Perth.
Eldest son of the late Robert Robertson, Esq., J.P. and D.L., of Auchlecks, by Bridget, eldest dau. of the late George Atkinson, Esq., of Temple Sowerby and Morland, co. Westmoreland ; *b.* 1816 ; *s.* 1869, *m.* 1848

Emily, eldest dau. of John Cay, Esq., of Edinburgh and has, with other issue,
* Robert John, *b.* 1851.
Mr. Robertson, who was educated at Eton and Ch. Ch. Oxford, is a Magistrate for co. Perth.—*Auchlecks, Blair Athole, N.B. ; Braddon Tor, Torquay ; New Club, Edinburgh.*

ROBERTSON, Capt. ROBERT EUSTACE, of Trininallan House, Stirlingshire.
Only son of the late Robert Robertson, Esq., of Trininallan House, by Alicia Catherine, eldest dau. of the Rev. Charles Eustace, of Robertstown, co. Kildare ; *b.* 1828 ; *s.* 1865 ; *m.* 1863 Lady Katharine, 4th dau. of William, late Earl of Dartmouth, and has issue,
* A son, *b.* 1867.
Mr. Robertson is a Magistrate for co. Stirling and Capt. 60th Rifles.—*Trininallan House, Stirling, N.B.*

ROBERTSON, Major-General ROBERT RICHARDSON, C.B., of Tulliebelton, Perthshire.
Youngest son of the late James Richardson, Esq., of Pitfour, by Elizabeth, dau. of James Stewart, Esq., of Urrard, co. Perth, and brother of Sir John Stewart Richardson, Bart., of Pitfour (whom see); *b.* 1809 ; *s.* to Tulliebelton, as heir of entail in right of his mother, 1850 ; *m.* 1850 the Hon. Martha, youngest dau. of John, 8th Lord Rollo (she *d.* 1857). Is a J.P. and D.L. for co. Perth, a Major-General in the Army, and Col. 3rd Dragoon Guards.—*Tulliebelton, Ballathie, Perth, N.B. ; Carlton and United Service Clubs, s.w.*

ROBERTSON, WILLIAM, Esq., of Auchinroath, Elginshire.
Eldest son of the late John Robertson, Esq., by Mary Anne, dau. of the late John Kemp, Esq., of Loudon, and grandson of the late William Robertson, Esq., of Auchinroath ; *b.* 1821 ; *s.* his grandfather 1857 ; *m.* 1st 1857 Elizabeth, only dau. of Capt. Henry D. Peers, of Everton House, Hants (she *d.* 1858); 2nd 1861 Jane Craufurd, eldest dau. of the Hon. Lord Ardmillan, of Ardmillan, (a Judge of Session), and has, with other issue,
* James Craufurd, *b.* 1866.
Mr. Robertson, who was educated at the University of Edinburgh, is a Magistrate for cos. Elgin and Banff.—*Auchinroath, Rothes, N.B.*

ROBERTSON, WILLIAM Esq., of Hazel Hill, Pembrokeshire.
Son of the late Robert Robertson, Esq., of Milford, co. Pembroke ; *b.* 1800. Is a J.P. and D.L. for co. Pembroke ; was formerly an extensive Merchant and Shipowner.—*Hazel Hill, Milford.*

ROBERTSON, WILLIAM, Esq., of Kinlochmoidart, Inverness-shire.
Eldest son of the late Lieut.-Col. David Robertson, of Kinlochmoidart, by Margaret MacDonald, dau. of Lieut.-Col. A. MacDonald, of the 72nd Regt.; *b.* 1802 ; *s.* 1844 ; *m.* 1828 Sarah Adams, dau. of James Beck, Esq., of Priors Hardwick, co. Warwick, and has, with other issue,
* William James, late Capt. 90th Foot ; *b.* 1829 ; *m.* 1857 Matilda Helen, dau. of Frederic Sydney Crawley, Esq.
Mr. Robertson, who was educated at the University of Edinburgh, and called to the Scottish Bar 1824, is a J.P. and D.L. for co. Inverness.—*Kinlochmoidart, Strontian, N.B. ; New Club, Edinburgh.*

RODERTSON. (See *Benholme, Lord.*)

ROBERTSON-GLASGOW, ROBERT BRUCE, Esq., of Montgreenan, Ayrshire.

Eldest son of the late Robert Robertson-Glasgow, Esq., J.P., of Montgreenan, by Mary Wilhelmina, dau. of John Campbell, Esq., of Stonefield, co. Argyll; b. 1842 ; s. 1860; m. 1867 Deborah Louisa Grace, 2nd dau. of the late Simon George Purdon, Esq., of Tinerana, co. Clare. Educated at Trinity Coll., Glenalmond, and the Royal Military Coll., Sandhurst; is Lieut. 74th Highlanders. This family is descended from the ancient family of Strowan, in Perthshire, and has possessed lands in Berwickshire considerably upwards of two centuries. —Montgreenan House, Kilwinning, Ayrshire.

Heir Pres., his brother John Campbell, Ensign 12th Foot; b. 1844.

ROBERTSON-ROSS, Lieut.-Colonel PATRICK, of Glenmoidart, Inverness-shire.

Second son of the late Hon. Lord Robertson (a distinguished Scottish Judge), by Mary Cameron, dau. of the Rev. Dr. Ross, of Kilmonivaig, co. Inverness ; b. 1828 ; s. his maternal uncle, the late Lieut.-General Hugh Ross, of Glenmoidart, 1865, when he assumed the additional surname of Ross by Royal licence; m. 1851 Amelia Ann, third dau. of the late Charles Maynard, Esq. (a branch of the Essex family of Maynard), and has, with other issue,

* Hugh Maynard, b. 1856.

Lieut.-Col. Robertson-Ross, who was educated at Edinburgh, is a Lieut.-Col. in the Army, late Major 25th Foot; served in the Kaffir war and through the Crimean campaign ; is a Knight of the Legion of Honour and of the Turkish Order of the Medjidie, and is maternally descended from the ' Camerons of Lochiel,' chiefs of the ' Clan Cameron.'—Glenmoidart, Bonaw, Inverness-shire ; Junior United Service Club, s.w.

ROBERTSON-WALKER, Mrs., of Gilgarran, Cumberland.

Katharine, dau. of the late John Mackenzie, Esq., J.P. (Sheriff of Lewis); m. 1856 (as his 2nd wife) James Robertson-Walker, Esq., Capt. R.N., a Magistrate for Cumberland, and High Sheriff 1841, who d. 1858.—Gilgarran, Whitehaven, Cumberland.

Heir Pres., her husband's nephew, James Robertson, Esq.

ROBINS, JOHN, Esq., of The Elms, Herts.

Son of the late Hugh Robins, Esq., of Sidmouth, Devon, by Susan, dau. of Stephen Stocker, Esq.; b. 1797 ; m. 1820 Ellen, dau. of Robert Mackay, Esq., of co. Antrim, and has issue,

* John William, educated at St. John's Coll., Oxford; b. 1821 ; m. 1846 Emily Mary, dau. of F. Newsam, Esq., of Stamford Hill, Middlesex.

Mr. Robins is a Magistrate for Herts and the Liberty of St. Alban's.—The Elms, Watford.

ROBINSON, the Rev. Sir GEORGE STAMP, Bart., of Cranford, Northamptonshire (cr. 1660).

Eldest son of the late Rev. William Villiers Robinson (who was Rector of Grafton Underwood, co. Northampton), by Anne, dau. of Sarah Brookbank, Esq. ; b. 1797 ; s. his uncle as 7th Bart. 1833 ; m. 1827 Emma, dau. of Robert Willis Duncowe, Esq., of Hayes, Middlesex. Educated at Winchester and New Coll., Oxford (B.A. 1819, M.A. 1824), is Hon. Canon of Peterborough and Patron of 2 livings; late Rector of Cranford.—Cranford Hall, Kettering.

Heir, his son John Bienowe, educated at Eton and Ch. Ch., Oxford; a Magistrate for co. Northampton; b. 1830 ; m. 1861 Winifred, eldest dau. of the Rev. Edward Stewart.

ROBINSON, Sir JOHN STEPHEN, Bart., of Rokeby Hall, co. Louth (cr. 1819).

Eldest son of the late Lieut.-Col. Sir Richard Robinson, Bart., of Rokeby Hall, by Lady Helena Eleanor Moore,
802

dau. of Stephen, 2nd Earl of Mountcashell ; b. 1816 ; s. as 3rd Bart. 1847 ; m. 1841 Sarah Blackett, dau. of Anthony Denny, Esq., of Tralee, Ireland. Is a Magistrate for co. Louth (High Sheriff 1849), and Lieut.-Col. Louth Militia ; was formerly Lieut. 60th Rifles. —Rokeby Hall, Dunleer, co. Louth.

Heir, his son Richard Collingwood, Lieut. 60th Rifles; b. 1842.

ROBINSON, Sir GEORGE ABERCROMBIE, Bart. (cr. 1823).

Eldest son of the late Sir George Best Robinson, Bart. (formerly superintendent of British trade in China), by Louisa, dau. of the late Major-General Douglas ; b. 1826 ; s. as 3rd Bart. 1855. Educated at the Royal Military Coll., Sandhurst, late Major 22nd Foot, was formerly Instructor of Musketry at Hythe.—Junior United Service Club, s.w.

Heir Pres., his twin brother Douglas, Major 72nd Foot; b. 1826 ; m. 1857 his cousin Matilda, dau. of the Rev. W. S. Robinson.

ROBINSON, Sir JAMES LUKIN, Bart. (cr. 1854).

Eldest son of the late Sir John Beverley Robinson, Bart. (who was many years Chief Justice in Upper Canada, and late President of the Court of Appeal), by Emma, dau. of C. Walker, Esq.; b. 1818 ; s. as 2nd Bart. 1863 ; m. 1845 Elizabeth, eldest dau. of John Arnold, Esq., formerly of Halsted, Kent.—Beverley House, Toronto, Upper Canada.

Heir, his son Henry, b. 1849.

ROBINSON, Sir HENRY, Knt., of Knapton House, Norfolk (cr. 1845).

Only son of the George Robinson, Esq., of Knapton House, by Hannah, eldest dau. of Henry Atkinson, Esq., of Bacton, Norfolk; b. 1805 ; m. 1842 Lucy, youngest dau. of the late W. D. Cooper Cooper, Esq., of Toddington Manor, Beds, and has, with other issue,

* Henry, b. 1851.

Sir Henry, who is a Dep.-Lieut. for Norfolk, was appointed 1840 Standard-bearer of, and in 1845 Lieut. Commanding, the Queen's Body-guard of Gentlemen-at-Arms.—Knapton House, North Walsham ; Conservative Club, s.w.

ROBINSON, Sir HERCULES GEORGE ROBERT, Knt. (cr. 1859).

Second son of the late Admiral Hercules Robinson (who d. 1864), by Frances Elizabeth, only dau. of Henry Widman Wood, Esq., of Rosmead, co. Westmeath ; b. 1824 ; m. 1846 the Hon. Nea Arthur Ada Rose d'Amour, 5th dau. of Arthur, 10th Viscount Valentia. Educated at the Royal Military Coll., Sandhurst ; formerly an Officer in 87th Royal Irish Fusiliers; was employed in various capacities in the Civil Service in Ireland till 1852 ; was appointed President of Montserrat 1854, Lieut.-Governor of St. Christopher's 1855, Governor of Hong Kong 1859, Governor of Ceylon 1865; is a Magistrate for co. Kildare. —Government House, Colombo, Ceylon ; St. James's and Arthur's Clubs, s.w.

ROBINSON, AUGUSTIN, Esq., of Lavant House, Sussex.

Son of the late A. Robinson, Esq.; b. 1815. Educated at Balliol Coll., Oxford (B.A. 1838); called to the Bar at Lincoln's Inn 1845; is a J.P. and D.L. for Middlesex.—Lavant House, Chichester.

ROBINSON, CHRISTOPHER WILLIAM, Esq., of Denston Hall, Suffolk.

Only son of William Pigott, Esq., J.P. and D.L., by Harriet, dau. and heir of Lieut.-General Christopher Jeaffreson, of Dullingham House, co. Cambridge ; b. 1836. Assumed the name of Jeaffreson in compliance

with the will of General Jeaffreson, of Dullingham House, and subsequently that of Robinson only in 1857, under the will of William Henry Robinson, Esq., of Denston (the last male of that family); is Lord of the Manor of Denston, and Patron of 2 livings. —*Denston Hall, Newmarket.*

+ ROBINSON, FREDERICK DARBY, Esq., of Ashmans, Suffolk.

Eldest son of Samuel Robinson, Esq., of Henstead and Mutford, Suffolk; *b.* 18—; purchased the above property from the family of the late Rev. R. R. Cooper Rede in 1867.—*Ashmans, Beccles.*

ROBINSON, FRANCIS EDWARD, Esq., of Woodbourne House, Berkshire.

Eldest son of the Rev. Francis Robinson, of Stonesfield, Oxon, by Sophia Elizabeth, dau. of the Rev. Edward Rowden, Vicar of Highworth, Wilts; *b.* 1833; *m.* 1st 1861 Henrietta, dau. of the Rev. Charles Barter, Rector of Sarsden, Oxon, (she *d.* 1863); 2nd 1867 Mary Caroline, dau. of the Rev. William J. Butler, Rector of Appleton, Berks, and has issue by the former,
* Grace.

Mr. Robinson, who was educated at Winchester and Exeter Coll., Oxford (B.A. 1853, M.A. 1856), is a Magistrate for Berks.— *Woodbourne House, Tubney, Abingdon.*

ROBINSON, the Rev. GEORGE, of Almorness, Kirkcudbrightshire.

Eldest son of the late William Rose Robinson, Esq., of Clermiston, Midlothian (who was Sheriff of co. Lanark), by Mary, second dau. of the late James Douglas, Esq., of Orchardton and Almorness; *b.* 1814; *s.* 1864; *m.* 1849 Jane Eleanor, only dau. of the late Boyd Miller, Esq., of Colliers Wood, Surrey, and has, with other issue,
* William Douglas, b. 1851.

Mr. Robinson, who was educated at Balliol Coll., Oxford (B.A. 1837, M.A. 1840), was formerly Rector of Bisley, Surrey.—*Almorness, Castle Douglas, N.B.*

ROBINSON, HENRY JEFFERY, Esq., of Port Stewart, co. Londonderry.

Eldest surviving son of the late Rev. William Robinson, Rector of Bo.evagh, co. Derry, and Precentor of Christ's Church, Dublin (2nd son of the late Rev. Sir John Robinson, Bart.), by the Hon. Susanna Sophia, eldest dau. of Henry, 4th Viscount Ashbrook; *b.* 1831; *m.* 1857 Agnes Strachan, 5th dau. of the Hon. John R. Partelow, Auditor-General of New Brunswick. Is a Magistrate for cos. Antrim and Londonderry; formerly Lieut. 76th Foot.—*The Castle, Port Stewart, Londonderry; Army and Navy Club, s.w.*

ROBINSON, JAMES, Esq., of Widmerpool, Notts.

Second son of the late James Robinson, Esq., of Widmerpool (who *d.* 1817), by Ann, dau. of Heneage Parker, Esq., of Mansfield Woodhouse, Notts; *b.* 1784; *s.* his brother 1863. Educated at St. Peter's Coll., Cambridge (B.A. 1804, M.A. 1811), is Lord of the Manor of Widmerpool, and Patron of 2 livings, and also of Broxholme, co. Lincoln.—*Widmerpool Hall, Nottingham.*

Heir Pres., his brother John; educated at Eton, Trinity Coll., Cambridge, and at Trinity Coll., Oxford (B.A. 1813), in Holy Orders, Rector of Widmerpool; *b.* 1790; *m.* 1st 1823 Arabella Savile, dau. of Francis Ferrand Foljambe, Esq., of Osberton, Notts; 2nd 1841 Martha Walker, eldest dau. of John Booth Freer, Esq., M.D., of Leicester, and has surviving issue, by the former, one dau., Arabella Martha, married to the Hon. Edmund G. Monckton.

ROBINSON, JOHN, Esq., of Lydd, Kent.
Eldest son of the late Gilbert Robinson, Esq., of Shinrone, King's Co., Ireland, by Mary, dau. of the late

Rev. John Goodwin, of Lydd, Kent; *b.* 1803; *s.* 1821; *m.* 1827 Elizabeth, dau. of Michael Russell, Esq., of Wimbledon; by whom (who *d.* 1861), he has, with other issue,
* Charles Gilbert, Lieut. Bengal Horse Artillery; b. 1835.

Mr. Robinson, who was educated at Sandhurst, is a Magistrate for Kent, and Major W. Kent Militia; formerly Lieut. 24th Foot.—*Lydd, New Romney; Stone House, Maidstone.*

ROBINSON, RANDOLPH, Esq., of Torquay, Devon.

Son of the late W. Tooke Robinson, Esq., of Walthamstow, Essex, by Isabella (who *d.* 1837), dau. of George Stralur, Esq.; *b.* 1813; *m.* 1st 1842 Caroline Ernle, only dau. of the late Ernlè Warriner, Esq., J.P. and D.L., of Conock Manor House, Wilts (she *d.* 1851); 2nd 1854 Diana Matilda, dau. of the Rev. J. S. M. Anderson, and has issue,
* Frances Maud.

Mr. Robinson, who was called to the Bar at Lincoln's Inn 1842, is a Magistrate for Devon.— *Residence: Torquay.*

ROBINSON, WILLIAM, Esq., of Summerhill, Worcestershire.

Younger son of the late John Robinson, Esq., of Dudley, by Elizabeth, dau. of John Wood, Esq., of Whiston, co. Salop; *b.* 1802; *m.* 1832 Harriet, dau. of John Johnson, Esq., of Leverington, co. Cambridge, and has, with other issue,
* Brooke, b. 1835.

Mr. Robinson, who was educated at Rugby, is a Dep.-Lieut. for co. Worcester.—*The Park, Cheltenham.*

ROBINSON, WILLIAM, Jun., 'Esq., of Reedley Bank, Lancashire.

Eldest son of William Robinson, Esq., of Settle, co. York, by Jane, dau. of John Peart, of Settle; *b.* 1823; *m.* 1857 Elizabeth, dau. of the Rev. John Taylor Allen, of Stradbrooke, and has, with other issue, a son,
* William Peart, b. 1861.

Mr. Robinson, who was educated at Oriel Coll., Oxford, is a Magistrate for co. Lancaster, and a Banker at Burnley. This family was formerly resident at Chatbourn, near Clitheroe.—*Reedley Bank, Burnley.*

ROBINSON, WILLIAM ROBINSON, Esq., of Silksworth Hall, co. Durham.

Eldest surviving son of the late Lieut.-Col. Thomas Robinson Grey, of Norton, co. Durham, by Elizabeth, dau. of Thomas Hogg, Esq., of Norton; *b.* 1804; *s.* 1834, and assumed the name and arms of Robinson; *m.* 1839 Sarah Dorothy, only dau. of William Grey, Esq., of Norton, and has, with other issue,
* William Grey, b. 1846.

Mr. Robinson, who was educated at Westminster, is a J.P. and D.L. for co. Durham. — *Silksworth Hall, Bishopwearmouth.*

ROBINSON. (See under *De Grey, Earl of.*)

ROBINSON. (See *Tyrgan-Robinson.*)

ROBINSON of Dullingham. (See under *Pigott.*)

ROBSON, THOMAS, Esq., of Holtby, Yorkshire.

Eldest son of the late Thomas Robson, Esq., of Holtby, by Ann, dau. of Christopher Pickering, Esq., of Crake Hall, co. York; *b.* 1784; *s.* 1797; *m.* 1806 Caroline, 2nd dau. of the late Sir William Young, Bart., and has, with other issue,
* Thomas William, in Holy Orders; b. 1807; m. 1842 Anne, eldest dau. of Michael Stewart, Esq.

Mr. Robson, who is a Dep.-Lieut. for the N. Riding of

Yorkshire, was formerly Lieut.-Col. N. York Militia. —*Holtby House, Catterick.*

ROBSON. (See *Brooke, of Gateforth House.*)

ROCH, GEORGE, Esq., of Woodbine Hill, co. Waterford.
Eldest son of the late George Butler Roch, Esq., J.P., of Woodbine Hill, by Jane, dau. of William Wilkinson, Esq., of Cork; *b.* 1819; *s.* 1859. This family, formerly of Tourin and Glynn, co. Waterford, descend from the ancient house of Roch, Viscount Fermoy, in the forfeited peerage of Ireland.— *Woodbine Hill, Youghal.*
Heir Pres., his brother Sampson, an Officer R.A.; *b.* 1829.

ROCH, WILLIAM FRANCIS, Esq., of Butter Hill, Pembrokeshire.
Second son of the late George Roch, Esq., J.P. and D.L., of Butter Hill (who was High Sheriff of co. Pembroke 1841), by Martha Jane, only dau. of the Rev. William Ford Protheroe, of Stone Hall, co. Pembroke; *b.* 1849; *s.* his brother 1858. Educated at Winchester; is a Midshipman R.N.—*Butter Hill, Haverfordwest.*
Heir Pres., his brother Thomas James, *b.* 1851.

+ROCH, NICHOLAS, Esq., of Paskeston, Pembrokeshire.
Eldest son of the late Nicholas Adamson Roch, Esq., J.P. and D.L., of Paskeston; *b.* 18—; *s.* 1866; is a Magistrate for co. Pembroke, and Lord of the Manor of Paskeston.—*Paskeston, Pembroke.*

ROCHE, Sir DAVID VANDELEUR, Bart., of Carass, co. Limerick (cr. 1838).
Elder son of the late Sir David Roche, Bart., of Carass, by his first wife Frances, dau. of Col. John Ormsby Vandeleur, of Maddenstown, co. Kildare; *b.* 1833; *s.* as 2nd Bart. 1865; *m.* 1867 the Hon. Isabella Susannah Adelaide, youngest dau. of Eyre, 3rd Lord Clarina. Is a Magistrate for co. Limerick (High Sheriff 1865). —*Carass, Croom, co. Limerick.*
Heir Pres., his brother Standish Deane O'Grady, *b.* 1845.

ROCHE, Col. EDMUND, of Ballymonis, co. Cork.
Second surviving son of the late Francis Roche, Esq., of Rochemount, co. Cork, by Esther, dau. of John Webb, Esq.; *b.* 1819; *m.* 1845 Anna Matilda, dau. of the Rev. Robert Austen, LL.D., of Hadwell, co. Cork; is a Magistrate for cos. Waterford and Cork, and Lieut.-Col. S. Cork Light Infantry Militia, late Col. in the Army.—*Ballymonis, Whitegate, co. Cork; United Service Club,* s.w.

ROCHE, JOHN WEBB, Esq., of Rochemount, co. Cork, and Tregunter Park, Brecknockshire.
Second but eldest surviving son of the late Francis Roche, Esq., of Rochemount (who *d.* 1826). by Esther, only dau. of the late John Webb, Esq., of Rosanna. co. Cork; *b.* 179—; *s.* his brother 1821; *m.* 1851 Eliza Anne, only dau. of William A. Maddocks, Esq., M.P. of Tremadoc, co. Carnarvon, and has, with other issue,
* Francis William Alexander, *b.* 1844.
Mr. Roche represents a younger branch of the family of Lord Fermoy.—*Rochemount, Whitegate, co. Cork; Tregunter Park, Bronllys, Brecknockshire.*

ROCHE. (See under *Fermoy, Lord.*)

ROCHESTER, Bishop of (the Rt. Rev. THOMAS LEGH CLAUGHTON, D.D.).
Eldest son of the late Thomas Claughton, Esq., M.P., of Havlock Lodge, co. Lancaster, by Maria, dau. of the late Thomas Peter Legh, Esq., of Lyme Park, co. Chester; *b.* 1808; *m.* 1842 the Hon. Julia Susannah, dau. of William, 10th Lord Ward, and sister of the Earl

of Dudley. Educated at Rugby and Trinity Coll., Oxford (B.A. 1831, M.A. 1834); was vicar of Kiddeminster 1841-67; Professor of Poetry in Oxford University 1852-57; consecrated 1867; Patron of 5 livings. — *Danbury Palace, Chelmsford; Athenæum Club,* s.w.

ROCHFORT, CHARLES GUSTAVUS, of Rochfort Bridge, co. Westmeath.
Son of the late Charles Rochfort, Esq., of Rochfort Lodge, co. Donegal, by Hannah Eliza, dau. of Joseph Pratt, Esq., of Cabra Castle, co. Cavan, and grandson of the late Col. Gustavus Rochfort, M.P., of Rochfort; *b.* 1837; *s.* 1843; is Capt. 20th Foot. He is the representative of the ancient family of Rochfort, formerly Earls of Belvedere. — *Rochfort Bridge, Bundoran, Ireland; Army and Navy Club,* s.w.

ROCHFORT, HORACE WILLIAM NOEL, Esq., of Clogrenane, co. Carlow.
Eldest son of the late John Staunton Rochfort, Esq., by Harriette, dau. of the late Sir Horace Mann, Bart. (ext.), of Linton Park, Kent; *b.* 1809; *s.* 1844; *m.* 1st 1837 Frances, dau. of the late Thomas P. Cosby, Esq., of Stradbally Hall, Queen's Co. (she *d.* 1840); 2nd 1845 the Hon. Charlotte, dau. of Samuel, 2nd Lord Bridport, and has, by the former, with other issue,
* John de Burgh, Lieut. R.H.A.; *b.* 1838; *m.* 1863 Filiare Charlotte, eldest dau. of the late Henry Hall, Esq., of Barton Abbey, Oxon.
Mr. Rochfort, who was educated at Eton and Trinity Coll., Cambridge (B.A. 1831), is a J.P. and D.L. for co. Carlow (High Sheriff 1833), and for Queen's Co. —*Clogrenane, Carlow; Carlton Club,* s.w.; 12, *Wimpole Street,* w.

ROCHFORT-BOYD, GEORGE AUGUSTUS, Esq., of Middleton Park, co. Westmeath.
Only child of the late Abraham Boyd, Esq., K.C., by Jane, Countess of Belvedere (dau. and heir of the Rev. James Mackay), relict and devisee of George Rochfort, last Earl of Belvedere; *b.* 1817; *s.* 1822 to his paternal estates, and in 1836 to the estates of the Earl of Belvedere, when he assumed, by Royal licence, the name of Rochfort; *m.* 1843 Sarah Jane, eldest dau. of George Woods, Esq., of Milverton Hall, co. Dublin, by Sarah, eldest dau. of Hans Hamilton, Esq., M.P., and has, with other issue,
* Rochfort Hamilton, Lieut. 15th Hussars, *b.* 1844.
Mr. Boyd, who was educated at Trinity Coll., Dublin, is a J.P. and D.L. for Westmeath (High Sheriff 1839). This family is descended from the Lords Boyd, subsequently Earls of Kilmarnock.—*Middleton Park, Castletown, co. Westmeath; Sackville Street Club, Dublin; Carlton Club,* s.w.

ROCKE, JOHN, Esq., of Clungunford, Shropshire.
Eldest son of the late Rev. John Rocke, of Clungunford House, by Anne, dau. of Thomas Beele, Esq., of Henlla House, co. Salop; *b.* 1817; *s.* 1849; *m.* 1853 Constance Anne, 2nd dau. of the late Sir Charles Cuyler, Bart., and has, with other issue,
* John Charles Leveson, *b.* 1855.
Mr. Rocke, who was educated at Harrow and Trinity Coll., Cambridge (B.A. 1839), is a J.P. and D.L. for co. Salop, Lord of the Manor and Patron of Clungunford, and Lieut. in the S. Salopian Yeomanry Cavalry. —*Clungunford House, Aston-on-Clun, Shropshire; Oxford and Cambridge Club,* s.w.

RODD, FRANCIS, Esq., of Trebartha, Cornwall.
Eldest son of the late Rev. Edward Rodd, D.D., of Trebartha, by Harriet, dau. of Charles Eashleigh, Esq., of Duporth, Cornwall; *b.* 1806; *s.* 1842; *m.* 1837

Mary, dau. of the Rev. Jonathan Stackhouse Rashleigh, and by her, who *d.* 1866, has, with other issue,
* Francis Rashleigh, a Magistrate for Cornwall, *b.* 1839.

Mr. Rodd, who was educated at Winchester and Trinity Coll., Cambridge (B.A. 1829), is a J.P. and D.L. for Cornwall (High Sheriff 1845), and Patron of 2 livings. —*Trebartha Hall, Launceston.*

RODDAM, Mrs., of Roddam, Northumberland.
Selina Henrietta, dau. of John Cotes, Esq., and Lady Maria Cotes, of Woodcote, co. Salop; *m.* 1849, as his 2nd wife, William Roddam, Esq., of Roddam (fourth son of the late Walter Spencer Stanhope, Esq., of Cannon Hall, co. York), who *d.* 1864, having *m.* 1st 1835 Charlotte, dau. of Henry Percy Pulleine, Esq., by whom, who *d.* 1837, he left issue,
* Charlotte Pulleine.

The late Mr. Roddam, who was a Commander R.N., and High Sheriff of Northumberland 1834, assumed the name of Roddam under the will of his kinsman, Admiral Roddam, 1820.—*Roddam, Alnwick.*

RODEN, Earl of (ROBERT JOCELYN, K.P., P.C.). —Cr. 1771.
Eldest son of Robert, 2nd Earl, by his 1st wife Frances, dau. of the Very Rev. Dean Bligh; *b.* 1788; *s.* 1820; *m.* 1st 1813 the Hon. Maria Frances, dau. of Thomas, 22nd Lord le Despencer; 2nd 1862 Clementina, dau. of Thomas Andrews, Esq., of Green Knowes, N.B., and widow of Capt. Reilly, of Scarva, co. Down. Educated at Harrow; is Custos Rotulorum of, co. Louth; and Patron of. 1 living; formerly Auditor of the Irish Exchequer; sits in the House of Peers as Lord Clanbrassil, U.K. (cr. 1821).—*Hyde Hall, Sawbridgeworth; Tollymore Park, Castlewellan, co. Louth; Un.t.d S.rvice Club, s.w.*

Heir, his grandson Robert, Viscount Jocelyn (eldest son of the late Robert, Vi-count Jocelyn, who *d.* 1854, by Lady Frances, dau. of Peter, 2nd Earl Cowner); *b.* 1846; educated at Eton and Trinity Coll., Cambridge.

RODGER, ROBERT, Esq., of Hadlow, Kent.
Eldest son of the late William Rodger, Esq., J.P., co. Lanark, by Agnes, dau. of — Robertson, Esq.; *b.* 1815; *m.* 1844 Sophia, eldest dau. of John Pickersgill, Esq., of Nitherne House, Surrey, and has, with other issue,
* Robert, educated at Balliol Coll., Oxford; *b.* 1847.

Mr. Rodger, who was educated at the University of Glasgow, purchased the estate of Hadlow Castle in 1859; he is a Magistrate for Kent (High Sheriff 1865), and for co. Lanark, and Lord of the Manors of Hadlow and Peckham, Kent.—*Hadlow Castl, Tunbridge; The Hollands, Lanark, N.B.; Carlton Club, s.w.*

RODICK, THOMAS, Esq., of Ash Meadow, Westmoreland.
Only surviving son of the late Thomas Rodick, Esq., J.P. and D.L., of Gaisacre, co. Lancaster, and of Beach Wood, co. Westmoreland (who *d.* 1855), by Judith, dau. of Robert Preston, Esq., of Lower House, West Derby, near Liverpool; *b.* 1823; *s.* his brother 1859; *m.* 1847 Margaret, dau. of Mr. Thomas Bainbridge, of Milnthorpe, Westmoreland, and has, with other issue,
* Thomas, *b.* 1849.

This family is of Scotch descent, as appears from the entry in the College of Arms, London.—*Ash Meadow, Milnthorpe.*

RODNEY, Lord (GEORGE BRIDGES HARLEY DENNETT RODNEY).—Cr. 1782.
Elder son of Robert Dennett, 6th Lord, by Sarah, 2nd dau. of the late John Singleton, Esq.; *b.* 1857; *s.* 1864. The 1st Peer was the celebrated Admiral Rodney, who was raised to the peerage for his victory over the French fleet.—*Berrington, Leominster.*

Heir Pres, his brother Robert William Henry, *b.* 1838.

RODNEY, Dowager Lady.
Charlotte Georgiana, dau. of the late Sir Charles Morgan, Bart., M.P., of Tredegar, co. Monmouth. by Mary Margaret, dau. of Capt. George Stoney, R.N.; *m.* 1819 George, 3rd Lord Rodney, who *d.* 1842.—*Old Alresford House, Alresford, Hants.*

RODNEY, the Hon. and Rev. HENRY.
Sixth son of George, 2nd Lord Rodney, by Anne, 2nd dau. of the Right Hon. Thomas Harley; *b.* 1790. Educated at Westminster and Trinity Coll., Cambridge (M.A. 1814); is a Magistrate for co. Hereford, Vicar of Eye, Prebendary of Hereford, and Rector of Llangattock. —*The Cloisters, Hereford; Eye Vicarage, Leominster.*

RODNEY, the Hon. WILLIAM POWELL-, of Llanvibangel Court, Monmouthshire.
Son of George, 2nd Lord Rodney, by Anne, dau. of the Right Hon. Thomas Harley (son of Edward, 3rd Earl of Oxford and Mortimer); *b.* 1794; *m.* 1824 Eliza Ann, youngest dau. of the late Thomas Brown, Esq., Member of the Supreme Council in India, and had, with other issue, an only son,

William Powell, a Magistrate for co. Monmouth; *b.* 1829; *m.* 1856 Diana Hotham, 2nd dau. of the late Sir J. W. Lubbock, Bart., and *d.* 1868, leaving, with other issue, * Harley, *b.* 1858.

Mr. Powell-Rodney, who was educated at Eton, is a J.P. and D.L. for co. Monmouth (High Sheriff 1860) and a Magistrate for co. Hereford; he was appointed in 1811 to the Bengal Civil Service, and afterwards held the situation of Secretary to the Comptrollers of Army Accounts at home until the amalgamation of that Department in 1835.—*Llanvibangel Court, Abergavenny.*

RODON, JOHN, Esq., of Newgrove, co. Meath.
Only son of John Rodon, Esq., of Newgrove, by Marianne, dau. of the late George Mackenzie, Esq.; *b.* 1816; *m.* 1846 Frances Alicia, dau. of the late James Fetherston, Esq., and has issue,
* George Seaforth, *b.* 1847.

Mr. Rodon, who was educated at Eton, is a Magistrate for cos. Meath and Westmeath, and late Capt. 16th Lancers. —*Newgrove, Kells, co. Meath; Conservative Club, s.w.*

RODWELL, WILLIAM, Esq., of Woodlands, Suffolk.
Son of the late Josiah Rodwell, Esq., by Elizabeth, dau. of John Medows Theobald, Esq., of Henley Hall; *b.* 1792; *m.* 1814 Elizabeth Anne, only child of Benjamin Hunter, Esq., of Glencarse, co. Perth, Barrister-at-Law of the Middle Temple, and has, with other issue,

* Benjamin Bridges Hunter, Q.C., of Ampton Hall, Bury St. Edmunds, Barrister-at-Law; educated at the Charterhouse, and M.A. of Trinity Coll., Cambridge, a Bencher of the Middle Temple, a Magistrate and Chairman of the Quarter Sessions for Suffolk, and Patron of 1 living; *b.* 1815; *m.* 1844 Mary, dau. of the late James Boggis, Esq., of Great Baddow Court, Essex (she *d.* 1862), and has issue.

Mr. Rodwell is a Magistrate for Suffolk, and a Banker at Ipswich.—*Woodlands, Halbrook, Ipswich.*

ROE, Lady, of Worthing, Sussex.
Mary, dau. of George Knowles, Esq., of Ensal. co. York; *m.* 1831 Sir Frederick Adair Roe, Bart., of Beach House, formerly Chief Magistrate at Bow Street, who *d.* 1866, when his title became ext.—*Beach House, Worthing.*

ROE, GEORGE CHARLES LIONEL, Esq., of Rocsborough, co. Tipperary.
Second but only surviving son of the late James Roe, Esq., M.P., of Roesborough, by Catharine, dau. of the late Richard Chadwick, Esq., of Perryville, co. Tipperary; *b.* 1827; *s.* 1844; *m.* 1848 Elizabeth Letitia,

youngest dau. of the Rev. Richard Mauleverer, Rector of Tipperary, and has, with other issue,
* Richard Mauleverer, b. 1854.
Mr. Roe was educated at the King's School, Sherborne, Dorset.—*Roesborough, Tipperary.*

ROE, the Rev. HENRY FARWELL, of Lesnewth, Cornwall.
Eldest son of Henry Richard Roe, Esq., J.P. and D.L., late of Gnaton Hall, Devon, by Anna Maria, dau. of the late Col. Farwell, of Totnes, Devon; *b.* 1827; *m.* 1855 Isabella, dau. of James B. Messenger, Esq., of Callington, Cornwall, and has surviving issue,
* Samuel Henry Farwell, b. 1856.
Mr. Roe, who was educated at Winchester and Lincoln Coll., Oxford (B.A. 1850, M.A. 1853), is a Magistrate for Cornwall, and Rector of Lesnewth.—*Lesnewth, Boscastle, Cornwall.*

ROE, Mrs., of Ballyconnell House, co. Cavan.
Mary, dau. of the late Major Samuel Noble, H.E.I.C.S., by Prudentia, dau. of Major Jerome Noble, of Broomfield, co. Dublin; *m.* 1829 George Roe, Esq., M.D., of Ballyconnell (who *d.* 1858), leaving issue,
* Samuel, M.B., Surgeon 92nd Highlanders ; b. 1830.
This family is of English descent.—*Ballyconnell House, co. Cavan.*

ROEBUCK, JOHN ARTHUR, Esq., Q.C., of Ashley Arnewood, Hants.
Son of the late E. G. Roebuck, Esq., of Madras, and grandson of Dr. Roebuck, of Carron, N.B.; *b.* 1803; *m.* 1834 Henrietta, dau. of the Rev. Thomas Falconer, of Bath, and Leighton Hall, co. Chester, and has issue,
* A daughter.
Mr. Roebuck, who was called to the Bar at the Inner Temple 1831, and went the Northern Circuit, is a Bencher of the Inner Temple; was M.P. for Bath 1833–7 and 1841–7; has been M.P. for Sheffield since 1849.—*Ashley Arnewood, Lymington ; Reform Club, s.w.;* 19, *Ashley Place, Pimlico, s.w.*

ROGERS, Sir FREDERIC, Bart., of Blachford, Devon (cr. 1699).
Eldest son of the late Sir Frederick Leman Rogers, Bart., of Blachford, by Sophia, dau. of Lieut.-Col. Charles Russell Deare, of the Bengal Artillery ; *b.* 1811; *s.* as 8th Bart. 1851 ; *m.* 1847 Georgiana Mary, dau. of Andrew Colvile, Esq., of Ochiltree, N.B. Educated at Eton and Oriel Coll., Oxford (B.A. 1832, M.A. 1835, B.C.L. 1838), and was afterwards Fellow of Oriel Coll. ; called to the Bar at Lincoln's Inn 1836 ; is Under-Secretary of State for the Colonies ; late a Commissioner of Colonial Land and Emigration.—*Blachford, Ivybridge; Athenæum Club, s.w.;* 18, *Radnor Place, Hyde Park, w.*
Heir Pres., his brother John Charles, b. 1818.

ROGERS, the Rev. EDWARD HENRY, of Rainscombe, Wilts.
Elder surviving son of the late Francis James Newman-Rogers, Esq., Q.C., Recorder of Exeter (who *d.* 1851), by Julia Eleanora, dau. of William Walter Yea, Esq., of Pyrland, Somerset ; *b.* 1827 ; *s.* his brother 1859. Educated at Eton and King's Coll., Cambridge (B.A. 1850, M.A. 1852) ; appointed Incumbent of Thames Ditton, Surrey, 1860.—*Rainscombe, Marlborough ; Vicarage, Thames Ditton ; Oriental Club, w.;* 39, *Montagu Square, w.*
Heir Pres., his brother Walter Lacy, b. 1831.

+ ROGERS, THOMAS, Esq., of Stagenhoe Park, Herts.
Eldest son of the late Henry Rogers, Esq., J.P., of Stagenhoe, Herts, by Mary, dau. of John Burcham,
806

Esq., of Coningsby, co. Lincoln ; *b.* 1816 ; *s.* 1865 : *m.* 1858 Gertrude Lewis, youngest dau. of the late Rev. Henry J. Hall, of King's Walden, Herts.—*Stagenhoe Park, Welwyn.*

ROGERS, JOHN, Esq., of Holt Hall, Norfolk.
Second son of the late Henry Rogers, Esq., of Stagenhoe Park, Herts, by Mary, dau. of John Burcham, Esq., of Coningsby, co. Lincoln; *b.* 1818: *m.* 1845, dau. of the late H. Francis, Esq., and has, with other issue,
* John Henry Burcham, b. 1854.
Mr. Rogers, who was educated at Eton and Trinity Coll., Cambridge (B.A. 1840, M.A. 1843), and was called to the Bar at Lincoln's Inn 1843, is a Magistrate for co. Lincoln, and a Commissioner of Income and Assessed Taxes. Mr. Rogers purchased this property of W. H. Pemberton, Esq., in 1862.—*Holt Hall, Cromer.*

ROGERS, the Rev. JOHN, of The Home, Salop, and Stanage Park, Radnorshire.
Eldest son of the late Rev. John Rogers, of The Home, by Marianne, dau. of J. Bodenham, Esq., of The Grove, co. Radnor ; *b.* 1817 ; *s.* his father 1856, and his cousin, Miss Harriet Rogers, in the estate of Stanage Park, 1866 ; *m.* 1851 Charlotte Victoria, dau. of the Rev. F. S. Newbold, D.D., and has, with other issue,
* Charles Coltman, . 1853.
Mr. Rogers, who was educated at Shrewsbury and St. John's Coll., Cambridge (B.A. 1838), is a Magistrate for cos. Hereford and Radnor, Lord of the Manor of Stanage, and Vicar of Aymestry.—*The Home, Wentnor, co. Salop; Stanage Park, Kington, Radnorshire; Aymestry Vicarage, Leominster ; University Club, s.w.*

ROGERS, JOHN EDWARDES, Esq., of Abermeirig Talsarn, Cardiganshire.
Only son of the late John Rogers, Esq., M.D., of Abermeirig, by Anne, dau. of the late Thomas Jones, Esq., of Llaniofaur, co. Cardigan; *b.* 1826 ; *s.* 1846. Educated at Wadham Coll., Oxford (B.A. 1849) ; is a Magistrate for co. Cardigan.—*Abermeirig Talsarn, Lampeter.*

ROGERS, JOHN JOPE, Esq., of Penrose, Cornwall.
Eldest son of the late Rev. John Rogers, of Penrose (some time Canon of Exeter), by Mary, dau. of the Rev. John Jope, of St. Cleer, Cornwall ; *b.* 1816 ; *s.* 1856 : *m.* 1844 Maria, eldest dau. of Wm. Hichens, Esq., of London, and has, with other issue,
* John Percivell, b. 1846.
Mr. Rogers, who was educated at Shrewsbury and Trinity Coll., Oxford (B.A. 1838, M.A. 1840), and called to the Bar at the Inner Temple 1842, is a J.P. and D.L. for Cornwall, and one of the Chairmen of Quarter Sessions ; he was M.P. for Helston 1859–65.—*Penrose, Helston ; Carlton Club, s.w.*

ROGERS, JOHN THORNTON, Esq., of River Hill, Kent.
Eldest son of the late John Rogers, Esq., F.R.S., of River Hill (a Magistrate for Kent), by Harriet, 2nd dau. of John Thornton, Esq., of Clapham ; *b.* 1834 ; *s.* 1867 ; *m.* 1862 Margaret, 2nd dau. of John Bagwell, Esq., of Marlfield, co. Tipperary and has issue.
* John Middleton, b. 1864.
Mr. Rogers, who was educated at Eton and Balliol Coll., Oxford, was formerly Capt. 33rd Foot.—*River Hill, Sevenoaks ; Army and Navy Club, s.w.*

ROGERS, THOMAS ENGLESBY, Esq., of Yarlington, Somersetshire.
Eldest son of the late Francis Rogers, Esq., J.P., of Yarlington Lodge, by Catharine Elizabeth, eldest dau.

of Benjamin Bickley, Esq., of Ettingshall Lodge, co. Stafford ; *b.* 1817 ; *s.* 1863 ; *m.* 1853 Elizabeth Hannah, dau. and heir of John Stanger, Esq., of Tydd St. Mary, co. Lincoln, and has issue. Mr. Rogers, who was educated at C.C.C., Oxford (B.A. 1838, M.A. 1841), and called to the Bar at Lincoln's Inn 1846, is a Magistrate for Somerset, and Lord of the Manor of Yarlington.—*Yarlington Lodge, Woolston, Wincanton; Oxford and Cambridge Club, s.w.*

ROGERS, THOMAS STEPHENS, Esq., of Kinnerton Court, Radnorshire.
Eldest surviving son of the late William Rogers, Esq., of Kington, by Ann, dau. of John Stephens, Esq., of Kinnerton Court; *b.* 1793 ; *s.* his brother, the Rev. John Rogers, 1840 ; *m.* 1816 Elizabeth Jane, dau. of Thomas Meredith, Esq., of Kington co. Radnor ; was admitted an Attorney in 1813, but has ceased to practise.—*Kinnerton Court, Radnor ;* Residence : *Kington, Herefordshire.*

Heir Pres., his nephew Charles Rogers Cope, Esq.. b. 1812 ; m. 1847 Sarah Ann, dau. of Edward Richards, Esq., of Birmingham, and has issue, * Charles, b. 185—.

+ ROGERS, WILLIAM KISSANE, Esq., late of Lota, co. Cork.
Eldest son of the late Michael Rogers, Esq., of Lota, co. Cork, by Elizabeth, dau. of William Kissane, Esq., of Stalaheen, co. Tipperary ; *b.* 1808 ; *s.* 1850 ; *m.* 1852 Harriet, only dau. of the late Rev. S. Serrell, and has, with other issue,
* Serrell Michael, b. 1855.
Mr. Rogers, who is a Magistrate for co. Cork (High Sheriff 1844), is of Dorset extraction.—*County Club, Cork.*

ROGERS. (See *Coxwell-Rogers.*)

ROKEBY, Lord (HENRY MONTAGU, K.C.B.).— Cr. 1777.
Fifth son of Matthew, 4th Lord (who *d.* 1831), by Elizabeth Charlotte, dau. and heir of Francis Charlton, Esq., and brother of Edward, 5th Lord ; *b.* 1798 ; *s.* 1847 ; *m.* 1826 Magdalen, dau. of the late Lieut.-Col. Thomas Huxley. Is a Dep.-Lieut. for Berks, a Lieut.-General in the Army, Col. 77th Foot, and Patron of 1 living.—*United Service Club, s.w. ;* 1, *Upper Berkeley Street, Portman Square, w.*

Heir Pres , his brother Spencer Dudley, of Wargrave Hill, Berks, formerly a Clerk in the Irish Office; b. 1807; m. 1st 1842 Anna Louisa, dau. of the 1-te Sir C. W. Flint, and widow of Joseph Jekyll. Esq., of Wargrave Hill, Berks (she d. 1863); 2nd 1868 Henrietta, 2nd dau. of Christopher Robert Pemberton Esq., of Newton, co. Cambridge.

ROKEBY, the Rev. HENRY RALPH, of Arthingworth Manor, Northamptonshire.
Second son of the late Rev. Langham Rokeby, of Arthingworth Manor, by Maria Isabella, dau. of Somerset Davies, Esq., of Wigmore Hall, co. Hereford ; *b.* 1788 ; *s.* 1844 ; *m.* 1st 1827 Caroline, dau. of the Rev. George Boulton ; 2nd 18— Harriet, dau. of Joseph Walley, Esq., and has issue,
* Henry Ralph, b. 1831.
Mr. Rokeby, who was educated at Downing Coll., Cambridge (B.A. 1830), and appointed Rector of Arthingworth 1831, is Lord of the Manor and Patron of Arthingworth ; he was formerly a Commander R.N.—*Arthingworth Manor, Northampton.*

ROKEWOOD-GAGE. (See *Gage.*)

ROLFE. (See *Boggis-Rolfe.*)

ROLFE. (See *Neville-Rolfe.*)

ROLLE, the Hon. MARK GEORGE KERR, of Stevenstone, Devon.
Second son of Charles Rodolph, 18th Lord Clinton, by Lady Elizabeth, 2nd dau. of William, 6th Marquis of Lothian; *b.* 1835 ; *m.* 1860 Lady Gertrude Douglas, 5th dau. of George Sholto, 17th Earl of Morton. Educated at Eton; assumed the name of Rolle after his uncle, John, late Lord Rolle, 1852 ; is a J.P. and D.L. for Devon (High Sheriff 1864), and Cornet N. Devon Yeomanry.—*Stevenstone, Torrington, Devon ; Carlton Club, s.w.*

ROLLE, Lady, of Bicton, Devon.
Louisa, younger dau. of Robert, 16th Lord Clinton, by Marianne, dau. of Rodolph Gaulis, of Lausanne (who was for many years Syndic of that town); *m.* 1822 John, 1st Lord Rolle (ext.), who *d.* 1842 ; is Lady of the Manor of Bicton, and Patron of 2 livings.—*Bicton, Budleigh Salterton ;* 18, *Upper Grosvenor Street, w.*

ROLLESTON, JAMES FFRANCK, Esq., of ffranckfort Castle, King's Co.
Eldest son of the late Charles Rolleston, Esq., of Silverhills, by Helena Maria, dau. of Richard Maunsell, Esq., of Quinsboro', co. Limerick; *b.* 1806 ; *s.* his uncle 1826 ; *m.* 1828 Georgiana Elizabeth, 2nd dau. of John Bland, Esq., of Blandsfort, Queen's Co., and has, with other issue,
* Charles ffrank, Capt. King's Co. Rifles; b. 1833.
Mr. Rolleston, who was educated at Trinity Coll., Dublin, is a J.P. and D.L. for King's Co. (High Sheriff 1831).—*ffranckfort Castle, Dunkerrin, Roscrea.*

ROLLESTON, the Rev. JOHN, of Burton-Joyce, Notts.
Youngest son of the late Christopher Rolleston, Esq., of Watnall Hall, Notts, by Anne, dau. of Capt. Nicholas, R.N.; *b.* 1787 ; *m.* 18— Elizabeth, dau. of the Rev. Philip Smith, and has, with other issue,
* Christopher, b. 18— ; m. 1834 Catharine, youngest dau. of the late William Leslie, Esq., of Warthill, co. Aberdeen.
Mr. Rolleston, who was educated at Ch. Ch., Oxford (B.A. 1809, M.A. 1815), is Vicar of Burton-Joyce.—*Burton-Joyce Vicarage, Nottingham.*

ROLLESTON, LANCELOT, Esq., of Watnall Hall, Notts.
Eldest surviving son of the late Lancelot Rolleston, Esq., M.P., of Watnall Hall (who was formerly Chairman of Notts Quarter Sessions), by his 2nd wife Eleanor Charlotte, only surviving dau. of Robert Fraser, Esq., of Torbreck, co. Inverness: *b.* 1847 ; *s.* 1862. Educated at Ch. Ch., Oxford; is Lord of the Manors of Watnall and Chaworth. Notts. and Teynton, co. Lincoln. This family is a branch of the old Staffordshire family of Rollestons of Rolleston.—*Watnall Hall, Nottingham.*

Heir Pres., his brother Robert Sidney, Midshipman, R.N.; b. 1849.

ROLLO, Lord (JOHN ROGERSON ROLLO).—Cr. 1651.
Only son of the late William, 9th Lord, by Elizabeth, dau. of Dr. Rogerson, of Dumfries, co. Dumfries ; *b.* 1835 ; *s.* 1852 ; *m.* 1857 Agnes Bruce, eldest dau. of Col. Trotter. Educated at Trinity Coll., Cambridge (M.A. 1856); is a Magistrate for co Perth, a Dep.-Lieut. for co. Dumfries, and a Representative Peer for Scotland.—*Duncrub Castle, Perth ; Dunecrieff, Moffat, Damfriesshire, N.B. ; Athenæum Club, s.w.*

Heir, his son William Charles Wordsworth, Master of Rollo ; b. 1860.

ROLLS, Major ALEXANDER, of Croft-y-Bwla, Monmouthshire.
Second son of the late John Rolls, Esq., of the Hendre, co. Monmouth, by Martha, only dau. and heir of Jacob

Barnett, Esq. (who d. 1837); b. 1818; m. 1839 Kate, 3rd dau. of the late Ambrose Steward, Esq., of Stoke Park, Suffolk. Major Rolls, who was educated at Harrow and the University of Göttingen, is a J.P. and D.L. for co. Monmouth, and was formerly Major in the 4th (R. Irish) Dragoon Guards; late Major R. Monmouthshire Militia.—*Croft-y-Bwla, Monmouth ; Army and Navy Club, s.w.*

ROLLS, JOHN ETHERINGTON WELCH, Esq., of The Hendre, Monmouthshire.
Eldest son of the late John Rolls, Esq., of The Hendre, by Martha, only dau. of Jacob Barnett, Esq.; b. 1807; s. 1837; m. 1833 Elizabeth Mary, 3rd dau. of Walter Long, Esq., of Preshaw, Hants, and has, with other issue,

* John Allan, educated at Eton; a J.P. and D.L. for co. Monmouth, and Lieut. Gloucestershire Hussars; b. 1837.

Mr. Rolls, who was educated at Ch. Ch., Oxford, is a J.P. and D.L. for co. Monmouth (High Sheriff 1842), and Patron of 1 living; he was formerly Capt. Royal Monmouth and Brecon Militia.—*The Hendre, Monmouth ; Royal Yacht Squadron, Cowes ; Carlton, Arthur's, and Boodle's Clubs, s.w.*

ROLT, Lady.
Anne, youngest dau. and co-heir of the late George Caswall, Esq., of Sackett Park, Herts; m. 1824 Lieut.-General Sir John Rolt, K.C.B., of Sacomb Park, Herts, who d. 1856, leaving, with other issue, * Henry George Holt, in Holy Orders; m. 1859 Fanny Paulet, only child of. Col. James Wood.—30, *Great Cumberland Place, w.*

ROLT, the Right Hon. Sir JOHN, Knt., P.C., of Ozleworth, Gloucestershire (cr. 1866).
Second son of the late James Rolt, Esq., of Calcutta, by Anne Braine, dau. of Richard and Margaret Hiorns, of Fairford, co. Gloucester; b. 1804; m. 1st 1826 Sarah, dau. of the late Mr. T. Bosworth; 2nd 1857 Elizabeth, dau. of the late Stephen Godson, Esq. (she d. 1864); he has by the former, with other issue,

* John, a Magistrate for co. Gloucester; b. 1834.

Sir John, who was called to the Bar at the Inner Temple 1837, and became a Queen's Counsel 1846, is a J.P. and D.L. for co. Gloucester; was M.P. for West Gloucestershire 1857–67; Attorney-General 1866–7; Lord Justice of Appeal 1867–8.—*Ozleworth Park, Wootton-under-Edge ; 52, Harley Street, w.*

ROLT, PETER, Esq.
Son of the late John David Rolt, Esq., of Deptford, Kent; b. 1798; m. 1820 Mary, eldest dau. of Thomas Brocklebank, Esq. of Deptford, Kent (she d. 1845). Is a J.P. and D.L. for Middlesex, and a Merchant at Deptford; was M.P. for Greenwich 1852–7.—*Gresham Club, e.c. ; 72, Cornhill, e.c. ; 15, Cork Street, w.*

ROMILLY, Lord, JOHN ROMILLY (cr. 1865).
Second son of the late Sir Samuel Romilly, by Anne, eldest dau. of Francis Garbett, Esq., of Knill Court, co. Hereford; b. 1802; m. 1833 Caroline, dau. of the late Rt. Rev. Dr. William Otter, Lord Bishop of Chichester (she d. 1856). Educated at Trinity Coll., Cambridge (B.A. 1823, M.A. 1826); called to the Bar at Gray's Inn 1827; is a Magistrate for co. Radnor, and Master of the Rolls; has been Solicitor and Attorney General; was M.P. for Bridport 1832–5 and 1846–7, and for Devonport 1847–52.—*Tandhurst, Dorking, Surrey ; Reform Club, s.w. ; 14, Hyde Park Terrace, w.*

Heir, his son William, Barrister-at-Law of Gray's Inn ; b. 1835 ; m. 1865 Emily Idonea Sophia, eldest dau. of Lieut.-Gen. Sir Gaspard Le-Marchant, and by her (who d. 1868) has issue, a son, b. 1866.
000

ROMILLY, EDWARD, Esq., of Porthkerry, Glamorganshire.
Third son of the late Sir Samuel Romilly, by Anne, eldest dau. of Francis Garbett, Esq., of Knill Court, co. Hereford, and younger brother of John, Lord Romilly; b. 1804; m. 1830 Sophia. dau. of Alexander Marcet, a J.P. and D.L. for co. Glamorgan; was M.P. for Ludlow 1833–4; appointed 1836 one of the Commissioners for Auditing Public Accounts, and was Chairman of the Board 1854–65.—*Porthkerry, Penmark, Cowbridge ; 14, Stratton Street, w.*

ROMILLY, Lieut.-Col. FREDERICK, of Barry, Glamorganshire.
Sixth and youngest son of the late Sir Samuel Romilly, by Anne, eldest dau. of Francis Garbett, Esq., of Knill Court, co. Hereford, and brother of John, Lord Romilly; b. 1810; m. 1848 Lady Elizabeth Amelia Jane, dau. of Gilbert, 2nd Earl of Minto, and has, with other issue,

* Samuel Henry, b. 1849.

Mr. Romilly, who entered the Army in 1826, is a J.P. and D.L. for co. Glamorgan, a Lieut.-Col. in the Army retired, and a Commissioner of the Board of Customs; was formerly an Officer in 90th and 79th Regiments, and S. F. Guards; was M.P. for Canterbury 1850–2.—*Barry, Cardiff, Glamorganshire.*

ROMILLY, HENRY, Esq., of Huntington Park, Herefordshire.
Fourth son of the late Sir Samuel Romilly, by Anne, eldest dau. of Francis Garbett, Esq., of Knill Court, co. Hereford; b. 1805; m. 1850 Rosa Gardiner. dau. of James Pemberton Morris, Esq., of Bolton, Pennsylvania, U.S.—*Huntington Park, Kington.*

ROMNEY, Earl of (CHARLES MARSHAM).—Cr. 1801.
Elder son of Charles, 2nd Earl, by his 1st wife Sophia. dau. of the late William Morton Pitt, Esq., of Kingston, Dorset; b. 1808; s. 1845; m. 1832 Lady Margaret Harriet, dau. of Charles William. 4th Duke of Buccleuch (she d. 1846). Is a J.P. and D.L. for Kent, Chairman of Kent Quarter Sessions, Lord of the Manors of Maidstone and Boxley, Patron of 2 livings, a Governor of the Charterhouse. and President of the Marine Society; was M.P. for W. Kent 1841–5.—*The Mote, Maidstone ; Carlton Club, s.w. ; 48, Green Street, w.*

Heir, his son Charles, Viscount Marsham, a Magistrate for Kent, b. 1841 ; m. 1866 Lady Frances Augusta Constance, youngest dau. of George, 2nd Marquis of Hastings, and has, with other issue, * Charles, b. 1864.

RONEY, Sir CUSACK PATRICK, Knt. (cr. 1858).
Son of the late Cusack Roney, Esq., M.D., of Dublin (who d. 1849); b. 1810; m. 1837 Elizabeth Anne, dau. of James Whitcombe, Esq. (she d. 1861). Educated at Trinity Coll., Dublin (B.A. 1829); has been Secretary to Grand Trunk Railway of Canada, Secretary to the Royal Literary Fund, the Eastern Counties Railway, and the Great Exhibition in 18[?]—[?] Court, G [?] s.w ; 60, Cleveland Square, w.

ROOKE, Sir HENRY WILLOUGHBY, K.C.H., C.B., of Pilstone, Monmouthshire (cr. 1855).
Eldest surviving son of the late Col. Charles Rooke, by Elizabeth, dau. of Ambrose Dawson, Esq., of Bilston Hall and Langcliff Hall, co. York; b. 1782; m. 1804 Selina Mary, dau. of Major Henry Rooke, and had, with other issue,

George Charles, of Bigswear, co. Gloucester, b. 1815 ; married, and d. 18—, leaving, with other issue. * Willoughby Sackvillelands (whom see).

Sir Henry, who was educated at Eton, is a Magistrate

for co. Monmouth, a J.P. and D.L. for Berks; and Major-General in the Army.—*Pilstone House, Monmouth; United Service Club*, s.w.

ROOKE, WILLIAM WOWEN, Esq., of Woodside, Hants.
Eldest son of the late William Rooke, Esq., of Woodside, by Mary Anne, dau. of the late Col. Burrard, of Lymington, Hants; *b.* 1804; *m.* 1838 Persis, dau. of the late John Allen, Esq., of Blackheath, Kent, and has, with other issue,
　　• Henry Douglas Rooke, Capt. 53rd Regt.; *b.* 1842.
Mr. Rooke, who was educated at Eton, is a Magistrate for Hants; he was formerly in the 2nd Life Guards, and Capt. 12th Foot.—*Woodside, Lymington.*

ROOKE, Lieut.-Col. WILLOUGHBY SANDILANDS, of Bigswear House, Gloucestershire.
Only son of the late George C. Rooke, Esq., of Bigswear, co. Gloucester, Capt. Scots Fusilier Guards, and grandson of Major-General Sir H. W. Rooke (whom see); *b.* 1837; *m.* 1864 Constance Lawson, youngest dau. of Henry Adams, Esq., and has issue,
　　• George Douglas Willoughby, *b.* 1867.
Lieut.-Col. Rooke, who was educated at Eton, was formerly Col. Scots Fusilier Guards.—*Bigswear House, Coleford; Guards' Club*, s.w.

ROOKER, the Rev. JAMES YATES, of Lower Gornal, Staffordshire.
Eldest son of the late Abel Rooker, Esq., of Darlaston, co. Stafford; *b.* 1820. Educated at St. Catherine's Coll., Cambridge (B.A. 1845); is a Magistrate for co. Stafford, and Incumbent of Lower Gornal.— *Lower Gornal, Dudley; County Club, Stafford.*

ROOPER, BONFOY, Esq., of Abbotts Ripton, Hunts.
Eldest son of the late John Bonfoy Rooper, Esq., M.P., of Abbotts Ripton, by Harriott, dau. of William Pott, Esq., of Gloucester Place, London; *b.* 1820; *s.* 1855. Educated at Eton; was formerly an Officer in the 34th Regt.—*Abbotts Ripton Hall, Huntingdon.*
　　Heir Pres., his brother Plumer Pott, in Holy Orders, B.A. of Brasenose Coll., Oxford, a Magistrate for Hunts, and Rector and Patron of Abbotts Ripton ; *b.* 1827 ; *m.* 1851 Georgiana, dau. of the late George Thornhill, Esq., M.P., of Diddington, Hunts.

ROOPER, GEORGE, Esq., of Nascott, Herts.
Third son of the late Rev. Thomas R. Rooper, of Wick Hill, Brighton, by Persis, dau. of Henry Pointer Standly Esq., of Paxton Hall, Hunts, and cousin of Bonfoy Rooper, Esq., of Abbotts Ripton (whom see); *b.* 1812; *m.* 1841 Mary, dau. of the late Peere Williams-Freeman, Esq., of Fawley Court, Oxon, and by her (who *d.* 1856) has, with other issue,
　　• Frederick, *b.* 184-.
Mr. Rooper, who was educated at St. John's Coll., Cambridge, is Lord of the Manor of Nascott.—*Nascott, Watford; Oxford and Cambridge Club*, s.w.

ROOPER, Lady.
Charlotte Lydia, dau. of the late Hon. and Rev. F. Pleydell Bouverie, by Elizabeth, dau. of the late Sir Richard Joseph Sullivan, Bart.; *m.* 1817 Sir Henry Roper, Kt., who was Chief Justice of Bombay 1839–47, and who *d.* 1863.

+ROPER, BLAYNEY TENISON, Esq., of Castle Mitchell, co. Kildare.
Youngest son of the late Hon. and Very Rev. Henry Roper, D.D., Dean of Clonmacnoise, by Mary, dau. of the Rev. Thomas Chamberlayne, *b.* 1810, *m.* 1848

Emily Jane, only dau. and heir of William Kilkpatrick, Esq., and has, with other issue,
　　• Blayney Tenison, *b.* 1853.
Mr. Roper, who is a Grand Juror for co. Kildare, and Lord of the Manor of Castle Mitchell, represents a younger branch of the family of Lord Teynham.—*Castle Mitchell, Kildare.*

+ROPER, the late ROPER STOTE DONNISON ROWE, Esq., of Sudbury Park, Yorkshire.
Eldest son of the late Robert Roper, Esq., of Sudbury Park, by a dau. of the late Rev. — Donnison, Vicar of Felskirk, co. York; *b.* 1814; *d.* 1867, having *m.* 18—Jemima Margaret, dau. of ——, Esq., and by her (who *d.* 1863) he had issue. Was a Magistrate for co. Durham and the N. Riding of Yorkshire.—*Sudbury Park, Richmond, Yorkshire.*

ROPER, WILLIAM, Esq., of Knockmaine, co. Roscommon.
Son of the late Edward Roper, Esq., of Hazlebrook, co. Roscommon, by Prudentia Noble, dau. of Henry Leslie Thompson, Esq., of Whitepark, co. Fermanagh; *b.* 1824; *m.* 1857 Georgina, dau. of M. Greene, Esq., of Monkstown, co. Dublin, and has, with other issue,
　　• Edward Ormsby, *b.* 1861.
Mr. Roper, who was educated at Trinity Coll., Dublin (B.A. 1844), and called to the Bar at Dublin 1846, is a Magistrate for Roscommon.—*Knockmaine, near Roscommon; 60, Upper Mount Street, Dublin.*

ROPER. (See under *Teynham, Lord.*)

ROPER. (See *Trevor-Roper.*)

ROPER-CURZON, the Hon. SIDNEY CAMPBELL HENRY.
Third surviving son of Henry Francis, 14th Lord Teynham, by Bridget, dau. and co-heiress of Thomas Hawkins, Esq., of Nash Court, Kent; *b.* 1810; *m.* 1837 Frances, dau. of R. Purves, Esq., of Sunbury Place, Middlesex, and has, with other issue,
　　• Edwin Purves, *b.* 1848.
Mr. Roper-Curzon, who is a Magistrate for Surrey, was formerly an Examiner in the Audit Office.—*Grove House, Tooting, Surrey.*

RORKE, JOHN, Esq., of Johnstown House, co. Meath.
Second son of the late John Rorke, Esq., of Tyrelstown House, co. Dublin, by Mary, eldest dau. of the late John Ball, Esq., of Eccles Street, Dublin; *b.* 1831; *m.* 1861 Nora, dau. of the late Patrick Forde, Esq., of Summer Hill, Cork, and has issue,
　　• John Patrick, *b.* 1867.
Mr. Rorke, who was educated at Clongowes Coll., is a Magistrate for co. Meath, and a Lieut. Royal Limerick Co. Militia.—*Johnstown House, Enfield, co. Meath; Stephens Green Club, Dublin.*

ROSE, Sir GEORGE, Knt., F.R.S. (cr. 1831).
Son of the late Mr. — Rose; *b.* 1791; *m.* 1821 Anne, dau. of the late Capt. Robert Pouncey (she *d.* 1855). Educated at Westminster and Trinity Coll., Cambridge (M.A. 1855); called to the Bar 1809; made a King's Counsel 1827; is a Master in Chancery, a Bencher of the Inner Temple, and a Judge of the Court of Review. —4, *Hyde Park Gardens*, w.

ROSE, Sir WILLIAM, K.C.B., of Leiston Old Abbey, Suffolk (cr. 1867).
Second surviving son of the late Right Hon. Sir George Henry Rose, G.C.H. (Minister at the Courts of Bavaria and Prussia), by Frances, dau. of Thomas Duncombe, Esq., of Duncombe Park, co. York, and brother of Lord

Strathnairn, G.C.B. ; *b.* 180– ; *m.* 1856 the Hon. Sophia Thellusson, 2nd dau. of John, 2nd Lord Rendlesham. Educated at St. John's Coll., Cambridge ; is a Dep.-Lieut. for Bucks, a Magistrate for Suffolk, and Deputy Clerk of the Parliaments.—*Leiston Old Abbey, Saxmundham ; Travellers' and White's Clubs*, s.w. ; 30, *Bruton Street*, w.

ROSE, Sir WILLIAM ANDERSON, Knt., F.R.G.S. (cr. 1867).

Second son of Arthur Rose, Esq., Merchant, of London, by Susannah, dau. of William Anderson, Esq. ; *b.* 1820 ; *m.* 1st 1851 Charlotte, widow of Thomas M. Flockton, Esq. ; 2nd 1858 Grace Charlotte, elder dau. of Capt. Winterton Snow, of the Madras Army. Educated at University Coll., London, is a Magistrate for Middlesex (Sheriff 1855–6), an Alderman of the City of London (Lord Mayor 1862–3), and Senior Major London Rifle Brigade ; was M.P. for Southampton 1862–5.—*Upper Tooting, Surrey ; Carlton Club*, s.w.

ROSE, the Rev. FRANCIS, D.D., of Baulking, Berks.

Second son of the late David Rose, Esq., of Ardclach, by Emilia, dau. of James Laing, Esq., of Boyndie, co. Banff, and Elizabeth Fraser, of Lovat, co. Inverness ; *b.* 1792 ; *s.* 1816 ; *m.* 1819 Ann Frances, dau. of John Josselyn, Esq., of Copdock Lodge, co. Suffolk. Educated at the University of Aberdeen (M.A. 1813, D.D. 1841) ; was Rector of Woughton, Bucks, and of Woalstone 1823–46 ; is a Magistrate for Bucks, a J.P. and D.L. for co. Northampton, and Rector of Baulking. —*Baulking Parsonage, Faringdon ; 2, Berners Street*, w.c.

ROSE, the Rev. HUGH FRANCIS, of Holme, Inverness-shire.

Elder surviving son of the late Sir John Rose, K.C.B., of Holme (who *d.* 1852), by Lillias, dau. of Col. James Fraser, of Culduthell, co. Inverness ; *b.* 1821 ; *s.* his brother 1867 ; *m.* 18— Isabella Baillie, dau. of — Grant, Esq., and has, with other issue,

   • Hugh Francis, *b.* 18—.

Mr. Rose, who was educated at C.C.C., Cambridge (B.A. 1843, M.A. 1847), is Rector of Homersfield and St. Cross, Suffolk. This family is a branch of the Roses of Kilravock.—*Holme, Croy, Inverness-shire ;* Residence: *St. Cross Rectory, Harleston.*

ROSE, Major JAMES, of Kilravock, Nairnshire.

Only surviving son of the late Hugh Rose, Esq., of Kilravock Castle, by his 2nd wife Catherine, dau. of — Mackintosh, Esq., of Farr ; *b.* 1820 ; *s.* his brother John Baillie 1854 ; *m.* 1850 Anna Maria, dau. of Major-General George H. Twemlow, of the Bengal Artillery, and by her, who *d.* 1867, has, with other issue,

   • Hugh, *b.* 1863.

Major Rose, who was educated at Edinburgh and Addiscombe Coll., is a J.P. and D.L. for co. Nairn, Lord of the Barony of Kilravock, and Patron of 1 living, and a Major in the Army.—*Kilravock Castle, Nairn, N.B.*

ROSE, Lieut.-Col. JOHN ROSE HOLDEN, of Wivelsfield, Sussex.

Eldest son of the late Hickman Leland Rose, Esq., of Clare, Ireland, formerly Capt. in the 3rd King's Own Dragoons, by Mary, dau. of the late Rev. John Rose Holden, Rector of Upminster, Essex ; *b.* 1812 ; *m.* 1834 Emilia, dau. of Major Jackson, C.B., and has issue,

   • Two daughters.

Lieut.-Col. Holden Rose, who was educated at Queen's Coll., Oxford, is a Magistrate for Sussex, a Commissioner of Lieutenancy for London, and a Lieut.-Col. in the Army, late of the 17th Lancers.—*The Ferns, Wivelsfield, Cuckfield ; United Service Club*, s.w,

810

ROSE, PHILIP, Esq., of Rayners, Bucks.

Son of the late William Rose, Esq., of High Wycombe, by Charlotte, dau. of William Baly, Esq. ; *b.* 1816 ; *m.* 1830 Margaret, dau. of Robert Ranking, Esq., and has with other issue,

   • Philip Frederick, *b.* 1832 ; *m.* 1866 Rose Annie, dau. of the late Rev. William Wollaston Pym, Rector of William Herts.

Mr. Rose, who is a Dep.-Lieut. for Middlesex, was appointed one of H.M.'s Treasurers of County Courts 1858. —*Rayners, High Wycombe ; Carlton and Conservative Clubs*, s.w. ; 59, *Rutland Gate*, s.w.

+ROSE, WILLIAM GEORGE, Esq., of Wolston Heath, Northamptonshire.

Eldest son of the late William Rose Rose, Esq., J.P. and D.L., of Harleston Park (formerly High Sheriff of co. Northampton), by Maria Isabella, 3rd dau. of the late Rev. George Strachan, D.D., Rector of Cranham, Essex ; *b.* 1813 ; *s.* 1861 ; *m.* 1841 Charlotte, dau. of the late E. B. Blackburn, Esq., Chief Justice of the Mauritius, and has, with other issue,

   • William, *b.* 184–.

Mr. Rose is a Magistrate for co. Northampton, and Lord of the Manor of Wolston. This family was formerly named Holden, but the name of Rose was assumed, by Royal licence, by the grandfather of the present owner.—*Wolston Heath, Rugby ; 15A, Hill Street*, w.

ROSE, WILLIAM SOMERSET, Esq., of Cransley, Northamptonshire.

Eldest surviving son of the late John Capel Rose, Esq., of Cransley, by Catherine, dau. of William Symons, Esq., of Bury St. Edmunds ; *b.* 1806 ; *s.* 1815 ; *m.* 1st 1832 Charlotte, dau. of the late Allen E. Young, Esq., of Orlingbury, who *d.* 1833 ; 2nd 1837 Frances Priscilla, dau. of the late Rev. Henry John Wollaston, Rector of Scotter, co. Lincoln, and has, with other issue,

   • William Robinson, *b.* 1837.

Mr. Rose, who was educated at Bedford and Brasenose Coll., Oxford. is a J.P. and D.L. for co. Northampton (High Sheriff 1867), Lord of the Manor of Cransley, and Patron of 1 living ; he is a cadet of the house of Rose of Kilravock.—*Cransley, Kettering.*

ROSEBERY, Earl of (ARCHIBALD PHILIP PRIMROSE).—Cr. 1703.

Eldest surviving son of Archibald, late Lord Dalmeny. who *d.* 1851, by Lady Catharine, only dau. of Philip Henry, 4th Earl Stanhope, and grandson of Archibald John, 4th Earl, K.T. ; *b.* 1847 ; *s.* his grandfather 1868. Educated at Eton and Ch. Ch., Oxford.—*Dalmeny Park, Queensferry, N.B. ; Rosebery, Edinburgh, N.B. ; Postwick Lodge, Norwich ;* 139, *Piccadilly*, w.

   Heir Pres., his brother Everard Henry, *b.* 1848.

ROSEHILL. (See under *Northesk, Earl of.*)

ROSEVEAR, WILLIAM SLOGGATT, Esq., of Boscastle, Cornwall.

Youngest son of the late John Rosevear, Esq., of Bristol, by Mary, only dau. of Thomas Rhodes, Esq., of Bristol ; *b.* 1820. Is a J.P. and D.L. for Cornwall. —*Boscastle, Camelford.*

ROSS, Sir CHARLES WILLIAM FREDERIC AUGUSTUS, Bart., of Balnagowan, Ross-shire (cr. 1668).

Eldest son of the late Lieut.-General Sir Charles Ross, Bart., of Balnagowan, by Lady Mary, dau. of William Robert, 2nd Duke of Leinster ; *b.* 1812 ; *s.* his part. 1814 ; *m.* 1st 1841 Elizabeth, dau. of the late Col. Robert Ross ; 2nd 1865 Rebecca Sophia. dau. of the late Henry Barnes. Esq. Educated at Eton and Ch. Ch., Oxford ; is a J.P. and D.L. for co. Ross, and a

Magistrate for cos. Cromarty and Lanark.—*Balma-gowan Castle, Tain, N.B. ; Bonnington, Lanark, N.B.*
Heir Pres., his cousin James Ross Farquharson, Esq., of Invercauld (whom see).

ROSS, Sir HEW DALRYMPLE, G.C.B., of Stonehouse, Cumberland (cr. 1855).
Son of the late Major Ross, of Balkail, co. Galloway, by Jane, dau. of John Buchan, Esq., of Letham, co. Haddington; *b.* 1779 ; *m.* 1816 Elizabeth Margaret, dau. of Richard Graham, Esq., of Stonehouse, co. Cumberland. Is a Field-Marshal in the Army; late Adjutant-General R.A.; formerly Lieut.-General of the Ordnance; served in the Peninsula, Netherlands, and France ; created a K.C.B. 1815.—*Stonehouse, Brampton; United Service Club, s.w. ; 34, Rutland Gate, w.*

ROSS, Sir THOMAS, Knt., of Dardistown Castle, co. Meath (cr. 1839).
Second son of the late Thomas Ross, Esq., of Rossfort, co. Cork, by Anne, dau. of John Attridge, Esq., of Greenmount, co. Cork ; *b.* 1797 ; *m.* 1835 Anna Maria, dau. of George French, Esq., Q.C., of Dublin, uncle of Lord De Freyne, and has, with other issue,
* Allen, *b.* 1845.
Sir T. Ross, who entered the Navy 1812, is a Capt. R.N. on half-pay ; was formerly Inspecting Commander of the Coast-guard in Ireland.—*Dardistown Castle, Drogheda, co. Meath.*

ROSS, Sir DAVID, Knt. (cr. 1864).
Eldest son of the late John Ross, Esq., of Perth, by Margaret, dau. of John Manson, Esq., of Perth ; *b.* 1802 ; is a Merchant at Perth ; was Lord Provost of Perth 1863–4.—*Fairmount Villa, Barnhill, Perth, N.B.*

ROSS, Lieut.-Col. GEORGE WILLIAM HOLMES, of Cromarty, Cromartyshire.
Son of the late Hugh Rose Ross, Esq., of Glastullich and Cromarty, by his 2nd wife Katharine, dau. of Duncan Munro, Esq., of Culcairn, co. Ross ; *b.* 1825 ; *s.* his mother 1852 ; *m.* 1849 Adelaide Lucy, dau. of Duncan Davidson, Esq., of Tulloch, co. Ross, and by her, who *d.* 1860, has, with other issue,
* Duncan Munro, *b.* 1851.
Col. Ross is a J.P. and D.L. and Convener of co. Cromarty, a Magistrate for co. Ross, Lieut.-Col. Commanding the Highland Rifle Militia, and Capt. Commanding the Cromarty Volunteer Artillery ; was formerly Lieut. 92nd Highlanders.—*Cromarty House, Cromarty, N.B. ; Army and Navy Club, s.w.*

ROSS, HORATIO, Esq., of Netherley, Kincardineshire.
Eldest son of the late Hercules Ross, Esq., of Rossie Castle, Montrose, by Henrietta, dau. of John Parish, Esq., of Neinstaden; *b.* 1801 ; *s.* 1817 ; *m.* 1833 Justine Henrietta, dau. of Colin Macrae, Esq., of Cornhill, co. Perth, and has, with other issue,
* Horatio, Bengal Civil Service; *b.* 1834 ; *m.* 1858 Caroline De Latour, dau. of the late Sir Theophilus St. George, Bart.
Mr. Ross, who was educated at Edinburgh, and entered the 14th Light Dragoons 1820, is a J.P. and D.L. for cos. Forfar and Kincardine; was M P for Aberdeen 1831–2, for Montrose, &c. 1832–4.—*Netherley, Stonehaven, N.B. ; Carlton Club, s.w.*

ROSS [OF BLADENSBURG], ROBERT SKEFFINGTON, Esq., of Carrig Bhan, Downshire.
Eldest son of the late David Ross [of Bladensburg], Esq., J.P. and D.L., of Carrig Bhan, by his 2nd wife, the Hon. Harriett Margaret, dau. of Thomas Henry, 2nd Viscount Ferrard, and the Viscountess Massareene; *b.* 1847 ; *s.* 1866. Educated at Exeter Coll., Oxford. —*Carrig Bhan, Rosstrevor, co. Down.*
Heir Pres., his brother John Foster George, b. 1848.

ROSS, WILLIAM, Esq., of Dailling, Argyll-shire.
Second son of the late Thomas Ross, Esq., by Margaret, 2nd dau. of William McDonald, Esq., of Cullicudden, co. Ross ; *b.* 1802 ; *m.* 1832 Elizabeth, 2nd dau. of Robert Anderson, Esq., of Glasgow. Is Proprietor of the Barony of Dailling, which he purchased in 1865 from Thomas Boyd, Esq.—*Dailling, Dunoon, N.B.*

ROSS.   (See *Robertson-Ross.*)

ROSS-KING.   (See *King.*)

ROSS-LEWIN, the Rev. GEORGE, of Ross Hill, co. Clare.
Eldest son of the late Major Henry Ross-Lewin, J.P., of Ross Hill, by Ann, dau. of Wm. Burnet, Esq., of Court; *b.* 1810 ; *m.* 1843 Grace, dau. of Henry Sargint, Esq., of Castleview, co. Tipperary, and has, with other issue,
* Henry Hastings, *b.* 1845.
Mr. Ross-Lewin, who was educated at St. Catharine's Hall, Cambridge (B.A. 1831, M.A. 1842), is a Magistrate for co. Clare; was formerly in the Royal Navy. —*Ross Hill, Kildysart, co. Clare.*

ROSSBOROUGH-COLCLOUGH.
(See *Colclough.*)

ROSSE, Earl of (LAWRENCE PARSONS).—Cr. 1806.
Eldest son of William, 3rd Earl, K.P., by Mary, dau. and co-heir of the late John Wilmer Field, Esq., of Heaton Hall, co. York ; *b.* 1840 ; *s.* 1867. Is a Magistrate for King's Co. (High Sheriff 1867).—*Birr Castle, Parsonstown, King's Co. ; Heaton Hall, Bradford, Yorkshire.*
Heir Pres., his brother Randal, b. 1848.

+ROSSETER, Mrs., of Iford Manor, Sussex.
Elizabeth Mary, dau. of Mr. Skelton, and niece and heir of the late Henry Hurly, Esq., of Iford Manor; *m.* 1847 the Rev. Robert Grafton Rosseter, M.A., of Ch. Ch., Oxford (only son of James M. Rosseter, Esq., of Kennington Place, Surrey), who *d.* 1861. Is Patron and Lady of the Manor of Iford.—*Iford Manor, Lewes.*

ROSSLYN, Earl of (FRANCIS ROBERT ST. CLAIR-ERSKINE).—Cr. 1801.
Eldest son of James Alexander, 3rd Earl, by Frances, dau. of Lieut.-General William Wemyss ; *b.* 1833 ; *s.* 1866 ; *m.* 1866 Blanche Adeliza, 2nd dau. of Henry Fitzroy, Esq., of Salcey Lawn, co. Northampton, and widow of the Hon. Charles Maynard. Educated at Eton and Merton Coll., Oxford (B.A. 1852, M.A. 1855) ; a J.P. and D.L. for co. Fife, and Lieut. 1st Fifeshire Mounted Rifles.—*Dysart House, Kircaldy, N.B.*

ROSSMORE, Lord (HENRY CAIRNS WESTENRA).—Cr. 1796.
Eldest son of the late Henry Robert, 3rd Lord, by his 2nd wife Julia Ellen Josephine, dau. of Henry Lloyd, Esq., of Farinrora, co. Tipperary; *b.* 1851 ; *s.* 1860. Educated at Eton ; is Lord of the Manor of Rossmore. —*Rossmore Park, Monaghan, Irela d.*
Heir Pres., his brother Derrick Warner William, b. 1853.

ROTHERAM, EDWARD, Esq., of Crossdrum, co. Meath.
Eldest son of the late George Rotheram, Esq., of Crossdrum, by Catharine Margaret, dau. of Henry Smith, Esq., of Baubeg, co. Meath ; *b.* 1816 ; *m.* 1855 Barbara, 3rd dau. of the late Sir Hugh Crofton, Bart., and has, with other issue,
* George Augustus, *b.* 1856.
Mr. Rotheram, who is a Magistrate for co. Meath, has been High Sheriff for cos. Meath and Cavan.—*Crossdrum, Oldcastle, co. Meath ; Royal Yacht Club, Kingstown ; Longford Terrace, Monkstown, Dublin.*

+ ROTHERAM, RICHARD KEVETT, Esq., of Coventry, Warwickshire.
Son of the late R. Rotheram, Esq.; b. 18—. Is a J.P. and D.L. for co. Warwick.—*Coventry.*

ROTHERAM, THOMAS, Esq., of Triermore, co. Meath.
Eldest son of the late Thomas Rotheram, Esq., J.P., of Triermore (formerly Lieut. 18th Foot), by Maria, dau. of the Rev. W. Cox; b. 1825; s. 1861. This family is of Yorkshire extraction. — *Triermore, Fordstown, co. Meath.*

ROTHERY, CHARLES WILLIAM, Esq., of Greta Hall, Cumberland.
Son of the late John Rothery, Esq., Merchant, of Leeds, by Mary Clayton, dau. of William Simpson, Esq., of Knaresborough; b. 1823; s. 1844. Educated at Edinburgh University. This family is traced back in the maternal line to the reign of Edward the Confessor, through Edward III.—*Greta Hall, Keswick; Littlethorp House, Ripon.*

ROTHES, Countess of (HENRIETTA ANDERSON MORSHEAD LESLIE).—Cr. 1427.
Only dau. of George, 14th Earl, who d. 1841, by Louisa, dau. of the late Col. Henry Anderson Morshead, of Widey Court, Devon; s. her brother as 16th Countess 1859; m. 1861 the Hon. George Waldegrave-Leslie; 2nd title Baroness Leslie. The Hon. Mr. Waldegrave-Leslie, who is a J.P. and D.L. for co. Fife. and Capt. Leslie Rifle Volunteers; elected M.P. for Hastings 1864; was formerly Secretary to the Speaker of the House of Commons.—*Leslie House, Fife;* 10, *Harley Street,* w.
Heir Pres., her Aunt Lady Mary Elizabeth Haworth.

ROTHSCHILD, Baron LIONEL NATHAN DE, of Gunnersbury Park, Middlesex.
Eldest son of the late Baron Meyer de Rothschild, by Hannah, dau. of Levi Barnet Cohen, Esq., of London, and brother to Sir A. de Rothschild, Bt. (whom see); b. 1808; m. 1836 Charlotte, dau. of Baron Chas. de Rothschild, and has, with other issue,
* Nathaniel Meyer, educated at Trinity Coll., Cambridge, a Commissioner of Lieutenancy for London; and M.P. for Aylesbury; b. 1840; m. 1867 Emma, dau. of Baron Charles de Rothschild, and has issue, * a son, b. 1868.
The Baron, who was educated at Göttingen, is a Magistrate for Middlesex, a Dep.-Lieut. for London, and a Partner in the firm of Rothschild & Co., Public Loan Contractors and Money Brokers: he is a Baron of the Austrian empire, and has been M.P. for London since 1847.—*Gunnersbury Park, Acton; Brooks's and Reform Clubs,* s.w.; 148, *Piccadilly,* w.

ROTHSCHILD, Baron MEYER AMSCHEL DE, of Mentmore, Bucks.
Fourth son of the late Baron Nathan Meyer de Rothschild, by Hannah dau. of Levi Barnet Cohen, Esq.; b. 1818; m. 1850 Juliana, dau. of the late Isaac Cohen, Esq. Is a J.P. and D.L. for Bucks, Lord of the Manor of Mentmore, and Patron of that living, and a Partner in the firm of Rothschild & Co., St. Swithin's Lane, City: he was elected M.P. for Hythe 1859 — *Mentmore, Buckingham; Brooks's Club,* s.w.; 148, *Piccadilly,* w.

ROTHSCHILD, Sir ANTHONY, Bart., of Aston Clinton, Bucks (cr. 1846).
Second son of the late Baron Nathan Meyer de Rothschild (who d. 1836), by Hannah, dau. of Levi Barnet Cohen, Esq., of London; b. 1810; m. 1840 Louisa, dau. of the late Abraham Montefiore, Esq. Is a J.P. and D.L. for Bucks (High Sheriff 1861), Lord of the Manor of Aston Clinton, and a Merchant and Banker in London.—*Aston Clinton, Tring;* 2, *Grosvenor Place Houses,* s.w.
Heir Pres., his nephew Nathaniel Meyer, M.P. (whom see above).
812

ROTHWELL, RICHARD RAINSHAW, Esq., of Sharples Hall, Lancashire.
Eldest son of the late Ralph Rothwell, Esq., of Ribbleton House, Preston, co. Lancaster, by Ellen, 2nd dau. of Robert Kellet, of Leyland; b. 1809; s. 1821; m. 1862 Martha Lydiard, widow of S. Wright, Esq. Educated at Brasenose Coll., Oxford (B.A. 1833, M.A. 1835); called to the Bar at the Inner Temple 1847; received the title of Count De Rothwell from Victor Emmanuel, King of Italy, in 1860, and that of Marquis De Rothwell from Charles III., Sovereign Prince of Monaco, in 1861; is Lord of 'Sharples,' joint Lord of the Manor of Much Hoole, and Patron of 1 living. —*Sharples Hall. Bolton-le-Moors;* 27, *Mornington Road, Regent's Park,* N.w.

ROTHWELL, THOMAS, Esq., of Rockfield, co. Meath.
Eldest son of the late Richard Rothwell, Esq., of Rockfield, by Elizabeth. only child of the Rev. Thomas Sutton, Rector of Kilshine, co. Meath; b. 1834; s. 1858; m. 1866 Louisa Catherine Hannah, eldest dau. of Mervyn Pratt, Esq., of Cabra Castle, co. Cavan. Educated at Magdalen Coll., Oxford (B.A. 1857); is a Magistrate for co. Meath (High Sheriff 1867), Lord of the Manor of Rockfield, and Lieut. Meath Militia. —*Rockfield House, Kells, co. Meath; Conservative Club,* s.w.; *Kildare Street Club, Dublin.*
Heir Pres., his brother John Sutton, Lieut. R.A.; b. 1841.

ROTHWELL.   (See *Fitzherbert.*)

ROUND, DANIEL GEORGE, Esq., of The Hange, Staffordshire.
Eldest son of the late John Round, Esq., of Daisy Bank, co. Stafford, by Phœbe, dau. of Isaac Caddick, Esq., of Wednesbury Oak, co. Stafford; b. 1820; s. 1846. Is a Magistrate for cos. Stafford and Worcester. This family was settled in Tipton, temp. Charles I., and have been for many years engaged in the iron trade in co. Stafford.—*The Hange, Tividale, Tipton; Portland House, Edgbaston, Birmingham; The Grove, Knowle, Warwickshire.*

ROUND, EDMUND, Esq., late of Springfield Lyons, Essex.
Youngest son of the late John Round. Esq., of Danbury Park, Essex, formerly High Steward of Colchester, M.P. for Ipswich and Maldon (who d. 1861). by Susan Constantia, eldest dau. of the late George Caswall, Esq., of Sacombe Park. Herts (she d. 1844); b. 1820; m. 1847 Louisa Caroline. dau. of the late Charles G. Parker, Esq., of Springfield Place. Essex. Educated at Harrow and Balliol Coll., Oxford (B.A. 1811, M.A. 1844); called to the Bar at the Inner Temple 1845; is a Magistrate for Essex, and a Member of the Parliamentary Bar; was formerly a Banker at Chelmsford. —1, *Harcourt Buildings, Temple,* e.c.

ROUND, JAMES, Esq., of Birch, Essex.
Eldest son of the late Rev. James Thomas Round, B.D., Rector of All Saints' Colchester (who d. 1861), by Louisa, dau. of the Rev. George Barlow, and nephew of the late Charles Gray Round. Esq., of Birch Hall; b. 1812; s. his uncle 1867. Educated at Eton and Ch. Ch., Oxford (B.A. 1861), called to the Bar at the Inner Temple 1868, a Magistrate for Essex, Lord of the Manor of Birch and Layer-de-lay Haye. Patron (in reversion) of 3 livings, and Capt. W. Essex Militia. Mr. Round is also the Proprietor of Colchester Castle. This family has been seated at Birch since the reign of George I.—*The Holly Trees, Colchester; University Club,* s.w.
Heir Pres., his brother Francis Richard, b. 1844; educated at Marlborough Coll. and Balliol Coll., Oxford.

ROUND, John, Esq., of Bergholt, Essex.
Eldest son of the late John Round, Esq., M.P., of Danbury Park, Essex (who d. 1860), by Susan Constantia, eldest dau. of the late George Caswall, Esq., of Sacomb Park, Herts ; b. 1816 ; m. 1853 Laura, youngest dau. of the late Horace Smith, Esq., and has, with other issue,
　　　• John Horace, b. 1854.
Mr. Round, who was educated at Harrow and Balliol Coll., Oxford (B.A. 1838, M.A. 1841), and called to the Bar at the Inner Temple 1843, is Lord of the Manor of West Bergholt ; he represents a younger branch of the Rounds of Birch (whom see).— West Bergholt Manor, Colchester ; 15, Brunswick Terrace, Brighton ; Carlton Club, s.w.

ROUND. Mrs. C., of Birch Hall, Essex.
Emma Sarah, dau. of Major G. Brock, of Colchester, Essex ; m. 1838 Charles Gray Round, Esq., of Birch Hall, who was a Magistrate for Essex and Chairman of Quarter Sessions ; formerly Recorder of Colchester and M.P. for N. Essex, who d. 1867.—Birch Hall, Colchester.

ROUND, Mrs. G., of East Hill, Essex.
Margaret, dau. of the late Major-General Borthwick, of the Royal Artillery ; m. 1824 George Round, Esq., of East Hill, elder son of the late George Round, Esq., of Colchester, and of Eliza Anne, dau. of the Ven. James Waller, D.D., Archdeacon of Colchester, who d. 1857 This family is a younger branch of the Rounds of Birch Hall.—East Hill, Colchester.

ROUNDELL, the Rev. Danson Richardson, of Gledstone, Yorkshire.
Third son of the late Rev. William Roundell, of Gledstone, by Mary, dau. of the Rev. Henry Richardson, M.A., of Thornton ; b. 1784 ; s. 1851 ; m. 1815 Hannah. eldest dau. of Sir William Foulis, Bart., of Ingleby Manor, co. York, and has, with other issue,
　　　• William, M.A. of Ch. Ch . Oxford ; b. 1817 ; m. 1864 Harriet Jane, youngest dau. of the late Francis Beynon Hacket, Esq., of Moor Hall, co. Warwick.
Mr. Roundell, who was educated at Harrow and Ch. Ch., Oxford (B.A. 1806, M.A. 1809), is a Magistrate for the E. Riding, a J.P. and D.L. for the N. and W. Ridings of co. York, and Patron of 2 livings.—Gledstone, Skipton-in-Craven.

ROUS, the Hon. Henry John.
Second son of John, 1st Earl of Stradbroke, by his 2nd wife Charlotte Maria, dau. of Abraham Whittaker, Esq., of Lyston House, co. Hereford ; b. 1795 ; m. 1836 Sophia, dau. of the late James Ramsay Cuthbert, Esq. Educated at Westminster ; is an Admiral R.N. ; was M.P. for Westminster 1841–6 ; was formerly A.D.C. to the Queen.—23, Grafton Street, w.

ROUS, the Hon. William Rufus, of Worstead, Norfolk.
Third son of John, 1st Earl of Stradbroke, by his 2nd wife Charlotte Maria, dau. of Abraham Whittaker, Esq., of Lyston House, co. Hereford ; b. 1796 ; m. 1822 Louisa, youngest dau. of the late James Hatch, Esq., of Claybury Hall, Essex, and has, with other issue,
　　　• William John, Capt. Scots Fusilier Guards ; b. 1833.
Mr. Rous, who was educated at the Royal Military Coll., Sandhurst, is a J.P. and D.L. for Norfolk, and Lord of the Manor of Worstead : late Capt. Coldstream Guards.—Worstead House, N. Walsham.

ROUS, Col. George Grey, of Courtyrala, Glamorganshire.
Eldest son of the late Thomas Bates Rous, Esq., of Courtyrala, by Charlotte, dau. of Sir Robert Salusbury, Bart., of Llanwern, co. Monmouth ; b. 1819 ; s 1850.

Educated at Eton ; is a J.P. and D.L. for co. Glamorgan (High Sheriff 1860) ; and Lieut.-Col. Grenadier Guards 1856.—Courtyrala, Cardiff ; Fern Hill. Pembrokeshire ; Guards' and Travellers' Clubs, s.w. ; 23, Bruton Street, w.

ROUS. (See under Stradbroke, Earl of.)

ROUSE-BOUGHTON. (See Boughton-Knight.)

ROWAN, Sir William, G.C.B. (cr. 1856).
Son of the late Robert Rowan Esq., of Garry, co. Antrim, by Mary, dau. of Hill Wilson, Esq., of Purdysburn, co. Down, and brother of the late Sir C. Rowan, K.C.B. ; b. 1789 ; m. 1811 Martha, dau. of the late John Spong, Esq., of Mill Hall, Maidstone, Kent ; a General in the Army and Col. 52nd Foot ; was Commander of the Forces in Canada 1849–55.—United Service Club, s.w.

ROWAN, the Rev. Robert Wilson, of Mount Davys, co. Antrim.
Only son of the late John Rowan, Esq., of Merville, by Eliza Honoria, dau. of Lieut.-Col. Alexander McManus, of Mount Davys, co. Antrim ; b. 1810 ; s. 1855 ; m. 1834 Anna, 2nd dau. of Joshua Minnitt, Esq., of Annabeg, co. Tipperary, and has issue,
　　　• John Joshua, b. 1838 ; m. 1866 Anna Townsend, eldest dau. of the late Major Gahan, Bengal Army.
Mr. Rowan, who was educated at Trinity Coll., Dublin (B.A. 1829), late J.P. for co. Down, succeeded his uncle as representative of McManus of Mount Davys, an Irish family originally resident in Leitrim or Fermanagh.—Mount Davys, Ballymena, co. Antrim.

ROWAN-LEGG, William, Esq., of Glynn Park, co. Antrim.
Eldest son of Edward Rowan, Esq., Commander R.N., by Elizabeth Maria, dau. of the late John Legg, Esq., of the Scotch Quarter, Carrickfergus, and nephew of Gen. Sir William Rowan, G.C.B. (whom see), and cousin to the Rev. Robert Wilson Rowan, of Mount Davys, co. Antrim (whom see) ; b. 1843 ; s. 1861 to the estates of his maternal uncle, John Legg, Esq., J.P., of Glynn Park, and assumed his name and arms by royal licence 1864. Educated at Trinity Coll., Dublin (B.A. 1863) ; High Sheriff for Carrickfergus 1868. The families of Rowan and Legg are very ancient in co. Antrim. — Glynn Park, Carrickfergus ; 6, High Street, Carrickfergus, co. Antrim.
Heir Pres., his brother, Edward Lutwidge Rowan. Esq., b. 1848.

ROWE, Sir Joshua. Knt., C.B., of Torpoint House. Cornwall (cr. 1832).
Son of the late Joshua Rowe, Esq., of Torpoint House, near Devonport ; b. 1799 ; m. 1823 Frances Ann. dau. of James Bate, Esq., of Exeter ; called to the Bar at the Inner Temple 1824 ; was Chief Justice of Jamaica and a Member of the Legislative Council there 1832–56.—Torpoint House, Devonport ; Windham Club, s.w. ; 10, Queen Anne Street, w.

ROWE, Lady.
Frances Elizabeth, youngest dau. of James Hamilton Story, Esq., LL.D., of Lockington, co. Cavan, and Bryanston Square. London ; m. 1856 Sir William Carpenter Rowe, Knt., Q.C., J.P. and D.L., Chief Justice of Ceylon, who d. 1859, leaving issue. • William Henry Pendarves, b. 1857.—17, Bryanston Square. w.

ROWE, John. Esq., of Ballycross, co. Wexford.
Only son of the late Ebenezer Rowe, Esq., by Elizabeth, dau. of Col. William Irvine, of Castle Irvine, co. Fermanagh ; b. 1807 ; m. 1837 Margaret Barbara. 4th dau. of Gabriel R. Redmond, Esq., and has, with other issue.
　　　• John Henry Reymond, b. 1844.
Mr. Rowe who was educated at Trinity Coll. Cam-

bridge, is a J.P. and D.L. for co. Wexford (High Sheriff 1858.—*Ballycross House, Wexford; Duffry Lodge, Bridgetown, co. Wexford; Sackville-Street Club, Dublin.*

ROWE. (See *Hussey*.)

ROWLAND, FRANCIS, Esq., of Kilboy, co. Cork.
Eldest son of the late Major Edward Rowland, of Kilboy, by Mary Eliza, dau. of Thomas Garde, Esq., of Ballinacurra, co. Cork; *b.* 1793; *s.* 1802; *m.* 1827 Clotilda, dau. of Henry P. Garde, Esq., of Garryduffe, co. Waterford, and has, with other issue, an only son,
* Francis Edward. *b.* 1837; *m.* 1863 Maria Elizabeth, dau. of the late Charles Eyre Coote, Esq.

Mr. Rowland, who was educated at Jesus Coll., Cambridge (B.A. 1816), is a Magistrate for co. Cork.—*Kilboy House, Cloyne, co. Cork.*

ROWLAND, JOHN HENRY, Esq., of Ffrwd Vale, Glamorganshire.
Eldest son of the late John Rowland, Esq., of Neath, by Sarah, dau. of Philip Henry Witton, Esq., of Birmingham; *b.* 1819; *m.* 1st 1847 Fanny, dau. of William Jevons, Esq., of Neath, who *d.* 1848; 2nd 1854 Emma, dau. of Christopher James, Esq., of Swansea. Is a Magistrate for co. Glamorgan.—*Ffrwd Vale, Neath.*

ROWLEY, Sir CHARLES ROBERT, Bart., of Tendring Hall, Suffolk (cr. 1786).
Fourth son of the late Sir William Rowley, Bart., of Tendring Hall, Suffolk, by Susannah Edith, dau. of the late Col. Sir Robert Harland, Bart. (*ext.*); *b.* 1800; *s.* as 4th Bart. 1857; *m.* 1830 the Hon. Maria Louisa, dau. of Joshua, 2nd Lord Huntingfield. Is a J.P. and D.L. for Suffolk, Lord of the Manor of Tendring Hall, and Patron of 4 livings; was formerly in the Grenadier Guards.—*Tendring Hall, Colchester.*
Heir, his son Joshua Thellusson, *b.* 1838.

ROWLEY, Sir CHARLES, Bart. (cr. 1836).
Eldest son of the late Admiral Sir Charles Rowley, Bart., by Elizabeth, dau. of Admiral Sir Richard King, Bart., &c.; *b.* 1801; *s.* as 2nd Bart. 1845; *m.* 1st 1822 Frances, dau. of the late John Evelyn, Esq., of Wooton, Surrey; 2nd 1843 Peroline, dau. of Mons. Marcowitz. Is a Dep.-Lieut. for Norfolk; was formerly Lieut.-Col. Coldstream Guards.—3, *Hanover Terrace, N.W.*
Heir, his son Charles Evelyn, Capt. R.N. retired, *b.* 1824; *m.* 1848 Grace Anna, dau. of J. W. Boughton-Leigh, Esq., of Brownsover Hall, co. Warwick.

ROWLEY, the Hon. RICHARD THOMAS, of Bodrhyddan, Flintshire.
Second son of Clotworthy, 1st Lord Langford, by Frances, only dau. of the Hon. Clotworthy Rowley; *b.* 1797; *m.* 1835 Charlotte, dau. of the late Lieut.-Col. Shipley, and has, with other issue,
* Guynydd, *b.* 1839.

Mr. Rowley, who is a J.P. and D.L. for co. Flint, and Col. R. Denbigh and Flintshire Militia, late Lieut. and Capt. Scots Fusilier Guards, was M.P. for Harwich 1860–65.—*Bodrhyddan, Rhyl; Guards' Club, S.W.;* 47, *Berkeley Square, W.*

ROWLEY, GEORGE FYDELL, Esq., of Morcott Hall, Rutlandshire.
Only child of George Dawson Rowley, Esq., of Brighton, by Caroline Frances, only child of the late Ven. Charles Lindsay, Archdeacon of Kildare, and grand-dau. of the Hon. and Right Rev. Charles Lindsay, D.D., Bishop of Kildare; *b.* 1851; *s.* his great-uncle S. R. Fydell, Esq., of Morcott 1868; educated at Eton. Is Lord of the Manor of Morcott.—*Morcott Hall, Uppingham.*
814

ROWLEY, HENRY, Esq., of Maperath, co. Meath.
Elder son of the late Thomas Taylor Rowley, Esq., of Maperath (formerly High Sheriff of co. Meath), by his 1st wife Eliza, dau. and co-heir of Paul Foster, Esq., M.P., of Buckwood, co. Tipperary; *b.* 1803; *s.* 1859; *m.* 1859 Mary, dau. of the Rev. Henry Lucas St. George. Educated at Trinity Coll., Dublin; is a Magistrate for co. Meath, and a Dep.-Lieut. for co. Monaghan.—*Maperath, Kells, co. Meath; Cordoolough, co. Monaghan.*
Heir Pres., his brother Standish Grady Rowley, Esq., of Sylvan Park, Kells, co. Meath; educated at Trinity Coll., Dublin; a Magistrate for co. Meath; *b.* 1834; *m.* 1861 Frances Macnaghten, eldest dau. of the Hon. John C. Erskine.

ROWLEY, JOSIAS, Esq., of Mount Campbell, co. Leitrim.
Eldest son of the late Rev. John Rowley, LL.D., Canon of Ch. Ch., Dublin, by Catharine, dau. of Joseph Clarke, Esq.; *b.* 1829; *s.* his uncle, Admiral Sir Josias Rowley, Bart. 1842. Is a J.P. and D.L. for co. Leitrim (High Sheriff 1851), and a Commander R.N. This family is descended from the Rowleys of Tendring Hall, Suffolk.—*Mount Campbell, near Drumsna, co. Leitrim; Junior United Service Club, S.W.*
Heir Pres., his brother William, *b.* 1833.

ROWLEY. (See under *Langford, Lord.*)

ROXBURGHE, Duke of (JAMES HENRY ROBERT INNES-KER, K.T.).—Cr. 1707.
Only son of James, 5th Duke, by his 2nd wife Harriet, dau. of Benjamin Charlewood, Esq.; *b.* 1816; *s.* 1823; *m.* 1836 Susanna Stephania, dau. of the late Major-General Sir James Charles Dalbaic, M.P., K.C.H. Educated at Eton; is a Dep.-Lieut. for co. Roxburgh; a Magistrate for cos. Berwick and Haddington, and Lieut.-General in the Queen's Body Guard of Scotland; sits in the House of Lords as Earl Innes, U.K. (cr. 1837).—*Floors Castle, Kelso, N.B.; Broxmouth Park, Dunbar, Haddingtonshire; Clarendon Hotel, W.*
Heir, his son James Henry Robert, Marquis of Bowmont, *b.* 1839; educated at Eton and Ch. Ch., Oxford.

ROXBY, THOMAS MAUDE, Esq., of Blackwood, Yorkshire.
Eldest son of the late Rev. Henry Roxby Roxby, LL.D., of Blackwood (sometime Vicar of St. Olave, London), by his 1st wife Jane, dau. of Thomas Meux, Esq.; *b.* 1830; *s.* 1861; *m.* 1861 Fanny Mary Ann, dau. of Thomas Warner, Esq., of the Abbey, Shrewsbury, and has, with other issue,
* Walter Anlomar Maude, *b.* 1862.

Mr. Roxby, who is Lord of the Manor of Blackwood, was formerly Capt. 55th Regt. The father of the present representative assumed the name of Roxby by Royal licence in 1837, in lieu of Maude, on succeeding to the estates of his maternal grandfather, Henry Roxby, Esq.—*Blackwood, North Duffield, Selby.*

ROY, FREDERICK LEWIS, Esq., of Nenthorn House, Berwickshire.
Eldest son of the late Frederick Lewis Roy, Esq., J.P., of Nenthorn, by his 1st wife Margaret Louisa, 2nd dau. of the late Charles Maitland-Makgill, Esq., of Rankeilour, co. Fife; *b.* 1836; *s.* 1868; *m.* 1868 Frances Georgiana, dau. of John Dudley Oliver, Esq., of Cherrymont, co. Wicklow. Is a Magistrate for co. Berwick.—*Nenthorn, Kelso, N.B.*

ROYDS, ALBERT HUDSON, Esq., of Falinge, Lancashire.
Eldest son of the late Clement Royds, Esq., by Jane, dau. of Charles Hudson, Esq., of Shaw Hill, co. York; *b.* 17 ; *m.* 1809 Susan Eliza, only child and heir of

Robert Nuttall, Esq., of Kempsey House, co. Worcester, and has, with other issue,

* Clement Robert Nuttall, *b.* 1841 ; *m.* 1867 Mary Alice Gibson, only child of the late John Halliwell Bewicke, Esq., of Pyke House, Littleborough, co. Lancaster.

Mr. Royds, who is a J.P. and D.L. for cos. Lancaster and Worcester (High Sheriff 1865), was formerly Capt. Lancashire Yeomanry.—*Brown Hill, Falinge, Rochdale ; Crown East Court, Worcester.*

ROYDS, the Rev. CHARLES SMITH, M.A., of Haughton, Staffordshire.
Fourth son of the late James Royds, Esq., (J.P. and D.L.), of Falinge, co Lancaster, by Mary, dau. of Charles Smith, Esq., of Summer Castle, co. Lancaster ; *b.* 1800 ; *m.* 1837 Mary Anne, eldest dau. of Francis Twemlow, Esq., of Betley Court, co. Stafford, and has, with other issue,

* Charles Twemlow, in Holy Orders ; educated at Rugby, B.A. of Christ's Coll., Cambridge, Rector of Heysham. co. Lancaster ; *b.* 1838 ; *m.* 1862 Louisa, 2nd dau. of William Hudson, Esq., of Ousecliffe, co. York, and has issue, * Francis Twemlow, *b.* 1863.

Mr. Royds, who was educated at Christ's Coll., Cambridge (B.A. 1822, M.A. 1825), is in the Commission of the Peace for co. Stafford ; Rector of Haughton, and Patron of 3 livings, and Prebendary of Lichfield Cathedral.—*Haughton Rectory, Stafford.*

ROYDS, HENRY, Esq., of Elm House, Wavertree, Lancashire.
Second son of the late Rev. Edward Royds, Rector of Brereton, co. Chester, by Mary, dau. of Thomas Molyneux, Esq., J.P., of Newsham House, co. Lancaster ; *b.* 1822 ; *m.* 1848 Margaret, dau. of Peter Bourne, Esq., of Hackinsall and Liverpool (who *d.* 1865), and has, with other issue,

* Henry Bourne, *b.* 1855.

Mr. Royds is a Magistrate for co. Lancaster, and a Merchant in Liverpool.—*Elm House, Wavertree, Liverpool ; Junior Carlton Club,* s.w.

ROYSE, THOMAS, Esq., of Ballinvirick, co. Limerick.
Eldest son of the late Robert Royse, Esq., of Ballinvirick, by Elizabeth, dau. of John Stack, Esq., of Ballyconry, co. Kerry ; *b.* 1797 ; *s.* 1859 ; *m.* 1832 Fanny, dau. of Henry Ross, Esq., of Castleview, and has issue,

* Four daughters.

Mr. Royse, who was educated at Trinity Coll., Dublin (B.A. 1827, M.A. 1832), is a Magistrate for co. Limerick.—*Ballinvirick, Askeaton, co. Limerick.*

ROYSTON. (See under *Hardwicke, Earl of.*)

RUCK-KEENE, the Rev. CHARLES EDMUND, of Swyncombe House, Oxon.
Second son of the late Benjamin Keene, Esq., of Weston Lodge, co. Cambridge, and Swyncombe House, by Mary, dau. of George Ruck, Esq., of Swyncombe, Oxon ; *b.* 1792 ; *s.* 1837 ; *m.* 1821 Rebecca Frances, 2nd dau. of the late Sir George Shiffner, Bart., and has, with other issue,

* Edmund, a Magistrate for Oxon, late Major 2nd Dragoon Guards ; *b.* 1822 ; *m.* 1861 Elizabeth Jane, eldest dau. of the late William Elmhirst, Esq., of West Ashby, co. Lincoln, and has, with other issue, * a son, *b.* 1866.

Mr. Ruck-Keene, who was educated at Eton and Ch. Ch., Oxford (B.A. 1815, M.A. 1819), and elected Fellow of All Soul's Coll., 1814, is a J.P. for Oxon and Cambridgeshire, and Patron of 1 living.—*Swyncombe House, Henley-on-Thames ; University Club,* s.w. ; *38, Charles Street, Berkeley Square,* w.

+RUDD, HENRY, Esq., of Kilbryde, Perthshire.
Son of the late — Rudd, Esq. ; *b.* 18— ; is married, and has, with other issue,

* Thomas, *b.* 18— ; *m.* 1863 Louisa Matilda, dau. of the Rev. Laurence Lockhart, of Milton Lockhart, co. Lanark.

Mr. Rudd is Lord of the Barony of Kilbryde.—*Kilbryde Castle, Dunblane, N.B.*

+RUDDLE, GEORGE, Esq., of Walton House, Gloucestershire.
Son of the late — Ruddle, Esq., of Walton House ; *b.* 18— ; *m.* 1863 Louisa, youngest dau. of the late Rev. Francis Laing, of the Mythe, Tewkesbury. Is a J.P. and D.L. for co. Gloucester, a Magistrate for co. Worcester, and Patron of 1 living.—*Walton House, and The Mythe, Tewkesbury.*

RUDGE, EDWARD CHARLES, Esq., of Evesham Abbey, Worcestershire.
Eldest son of the late Edward John Rudge, Esq., of Evesham Abbey (who was a J.P. and D.L. for co. Worcester), by Felizarda, 2nd dau. of Charles Van Nottenpole, Esq. ; *b.* 1828 ; *s.* 1861. Is a Dep.-Lieut. for co. Worcester (High Sheriff 1866), a Magistrate for co. Gloucester, and Lord of the Manor of Evesham.—*Abbey Manor House, Evesham ; 52, Upper Harley Street,* w.

RUDGE, SAMUEL NOUAILLE, Esq., of Threckingham, Lincolnshire.
Second son of the late Edward Rudge, Esq., of Abbey Manor, Evesham, co. Worcester, by Anne, dau. of Peter Nouaille, Esq., of Great Ness House, Sevenoaks, Kent ; *b.* 1801 ; *s.* 1834 ; *m.* 1842 Mary Magdalen, youngest dau. of the Rev. William Collins Colton, of Cheltenham, and has issue,

* Walter William Nouaille, *b.* 1842 ; *m.* 1862 Florence Caroline, youngest dau. of Edward Collins Woodbridge, Esq., of Porchester Square, Hyde Park, and has issue, * a son, *b.* 1867.

Mr. Rudge, who was educated at Caius Coll., Cambridge, and called to the Bar at Lincoln's Inn 1826, is a Dep.-Lieut. for co. Lincoln.—*Threckingham, Folkingham ; Braybrooke, Market Harboro' ; Cavendish Club,* w. ; *6, Harley Street,* w.

RUDSDELL, Sir JOSEPH, K.C.M.G. (cr. 1832).
Son of the late J. I. Rudsdell, Esq., of Morton, co. Lincoln ; *b.* 1789 ; *m.* 1833 Henrietta, only dau. of R. Duckle, Esq. (she *d.* 1864). Late Chief Secretary to the Governor of the Ionian Islands ; was formerly Lieut.-Col. Grenadier Guards ; served in Sicily, Spain, and Italy. — *Beckingham, Gainsborough ; United Service Club,* s.w.

RUDSTON-READ. (See *Read.*)

RUGGLES-BRISE. (See *Brise.*)

+RUMBALL, ARTHUR GRIFFIN, Esq., of Harpenden, Hertfordshire.
Eldest son of the late J. G. Rumball, Esq., of Harpenden Hall ; *b.* 18— ; *m.* 1862 Emma Elizabeth, only dau. of the late Harry Charrington, Esq., of Woolmer Green, Welwyn, Herts, and has, with other issue, * a son, *b.* 1863.—*Harpenden Hall, St. Alban's.*

RUMBOLD, Sir ARTHUR CARLOS HENRY, Bart. (cr. 1779).
Third but eldest surviving son of the late Sir William Rumbold, 3rd Bart., by the Hon. Henrietta Elizabeth, dau. of Thomas, 1st Lord Rancliffe ; *b.* 1820 ; *s.* his brother as 5th Bart. 1853 ; *m.* 1846 Antoinette, dau. of

the late Commandant de Kerven (she *d.* 1867). Educated at Sandhurst; is a Col. in the Turkish service, and President of Executive Council of the Virgin Islands; was formerly Capt. 70th Regt; late President of Council of Nevis.—*St. James's Club, s.w.*

Heir Pres., his brother Charles Hale, b. 1822.

RUMBOLD, CHARLES AUGUSTUS, Esq., late of Preston Candover, Hants.

Eldest son of the late Charles Edmund Rumbold, Esq., M.P., of Preston Candover, by Harriet, dau. of John Gardner, Esq., of Ashford, Kent; *b.* 1834; *s.* 1857; *m.* 1863 Agatha Ellen, 2nd dau. of George Woodroffe Franklyn, Esq., M.P., of Lovell Hill, Berks. Educated at Downing Coll., Cambridge; is Patron of 1 living. —*Chichester Terrace, Brighton.*

Heir Pres., his brother Thomas Henry, B.A. of Trinity Coll., Cambridge; b. 1835.

RUSH, ALFRED, Esq., of Farthinghoe Lodge, Northamptonshire.

Youngest son of the late George Rush, Esq., of Elsenham Hall, Essex, and Farthinghoe Lodge, co. Northampton, by Clarissa, dau. of Sir William Beaumaris Rush, of Wimbledon House, Surrey; *b.* 1818; *s.* his brother 1854; *m.* 1846 Mary Warkman, eldest dau. of Col. Joseph Anderson, C.B. and K.H., late commanding 50th Regt., and has, with other issue,

• Alfred George Anderson, *b.* 1851. .

Mr. Rush, who was educated at Sandhurst Coll., is a Magistrate for co. Northampton (High Sheriff 1864), and Patron of 1 living; was formerly Capt. 77th Regt. —*Farthinghoe Lodge, Brackley.*

RUSH, Mrs., of Elsenham Hall, Essex.

Clarissa, dau. of the late Sir William Beaumaris Rush, Bart., of Wimbledon House, Surrey; *m.* 18— her cousin George Rush, Esq., of Elsenham Hall, Essex. who *d.* 1848, leaving issue. Mrs. Rush is Lady of the Manor of Elsenham.—*Elsenham Hall, Bishop Stortford.*

+RUSHBROOKE, ROBERT FREDERICK BROWNLOW, Esq., of Rushbrooke Hall, Suffolk.

Eldest son of the late Col. Robert Rushbrooke, M.P., of Rushbrooke Hall, by Frances, natural dau. of the late Sir Charles Davers, Bart.; *b.* 1811; *s.* 1845; *m.* 1st 1844 Albinia Maria, 2nd dau. of Thomas Evans, Esq. (div. 1854); 2nd 1855 Violet Emily, 2nd dau. of John Alfred Tanner, Esq., of Hazlemere, Surrey (she *d.* 1858); 3rd 1860 Mary, dau. of — Ray, Esq., of the Suffolk Constabulary, and has issue by his 2nd wife,

ª A son, *b.* 1858.

Mr. Rushbrooke, who was formerly in the Scots Fusilier Guards, is Lord of the Manor of Rushbrooke, &c. —*Rushbrooke Hall, Bury St. Edmund's; Guards' Club, s.w.*

RUSHOUT, Sir CHARLES RUSHOUT, Bart., of Sezincote, Gloucestershire (cr. 1809).

Eldest son of the late Sir Charles Cockerell, Bart., of Sezincote (who was sometime M.P. for Evesham), by the Hon. Harriette, dau. of John, 1st Lord Northwick; *b.* 1809; *s.* as 2nd Bart. 1837; *m.* 1831 the Hon. Cecilia Olivia, dau. of Thomas, 3rd Lord Foley. Educated at Eton and Ch. Ch., Oxford; is a Dep.-Lieut. for co. Gloucester (High Sheriff 1856); assumed the name of Rushout instead of that of Cockerell in 1849.—*Sezincote, Stow-in-Weld.*

Heir, his son Charles Fitzgerald, Capt. Royal Horse Guards; b. 1840.

RUSHOUT. (See under *Northwick, Lord.*)

RUSSBOROUGH. (See under *Milltown, Earl of.*)

810

RUSSELL, the Right Hon. Earl (JOHN RUSSELL, K.G.).—Cr. 1861.

Third son of John, 6th Duke of Bedford, by his 1st wife Hon. Georgiana Elizabeth, dau. of George, 4th Viscount Torrington, and brother of Francis, 7th Duke; *b.* 1792; *m.* 1st 1835 Adelaide, dau. of Thomas Lister, Esq., of Armitage Park, co. Stafford (widow of Thomas, 2nd Lord Ribblesdale); 2nd 1841 Lady Frances Anna Maria, dau. of Gilbert, 2nd Earl of Minto. Educated at Sunbury, Westminster, and Edinburgh University; was Paymaster of the Forces 1830–4; Home Secretary of State 1835–9; Colonial Secretary 1839–41; First Lord of the Treasury, 1846–52; Foreign Secretary of State Dec. 1852—Feb. 1853; held a seat in the Cabinet without office Feb. 1853—June 1854; was President of Council June 1854—Jan. 1855; Colonial Secretary April—July 1855; appointed Secretary of State for Foreign Affairs 1859; was M.P. for Tavistock 1813–17 and 1818–19, for Hunts 1820–6, for Bandon Bridge 1826–30, for Devon 1831–2, for S. Devon 1832–5, for Stroud 1835–41, and for the City of London 1841–61. —*Ardsalla, Navan, co. Meath; Rodborough Manor, Stroud; Pembroke Lodge, Richmond Park; Reform Club, s.w.; 31, Chesham Place, s.w.*

Heir, his son John, Viscount Amberley, M.P. for Nottingham; b. 1842; m. 1864 the Hon. Katharine Louisa, dau. of Edward, 2nd Lord Stanley of Alderley, and has issue, • John Francis Stanley, b. 1865.

RUSSELL, Lord CHARLES JAMES FOX.

Sixth son of John, 6th Duke of Bedford, by his 2nd wife Georgiana, 5th dau. of Alexander, 4th Duke of Gordon; *b.* 1807; *m.* 1834 Isabella Clarissa, dau. of William Davies, Esq., of Penylan, co. Carmarthen, and has, with other issue,

• Henry Charles, *b.* 1842.

Lord Charles Russell, who was educated at Westminster, is a J.P. and D.L. for Beds, became Lieut.-Col. in the Army 1848; appointed Serjeant-at-Arms to the House of Commons same year; was M.P. for Beds 1832–47. —*The Palace, Westminster, s.w.*

RUSSELL, Lord EDWARD, C.B.

Fifth son of John, 6th Duke of Bedford, by his 2nd wife Georgiana, 5th dau. of Alexander, 4th Duke of Gordon; *b.* 1805; *m.* 1863 Mary Ann, eldest dau. of A. Taylor, Esq. Educated at Royal Navy Coll.; entered the Navy 1819; became an Admiral in 1867; is a Naval A.-D.-C. to Her Majesty; was M.P. for Tavistock 1841–7; Superintendent of Malta Dockyard 1858–64. —19, *Sussex Place, Regent's Park, n.w.*

RUSSELL, Lord FRANCIS JOHN.

Seventh son of John, 6th Duke of Bedford, by his 2nd wife, Georgiana, dau. of Alexander, 4th Duke of Gordon; *b.* 1808; *m.* 1844 Elizabeth, dau. of the Rev. Algernon Peyton. Is a Capt. R.N. retired.—3. *Haldin Place, s.w.*

RUSSELL, the Rev. Lord WRIOTHESLEY.

Fourth son of John, 6th Duke of Bedford, by his 2nd wife Georgiana, dau. of Alexander, 4th Duke of Gordon; *b.* 1804; *m.* 1829 Elizabeth Laura Henrietta, dau. of the late Lord Wm. Russell, and has, with other issue,

• Alfred John, *b.* 1825.

Lord W. Russell, who was educated at Trinity Coll., Cambridge (M.A. 1829), is Rector of Chenies, Canon of Windsor, and Chaplain to her Majesty.—*Chenies Rectory, Amersham, Bucks; The Cloisters, Windsor.*

RUSSELL, Lady FRANKLAND., of Thirkleby, Yorkshire, and Chequers, Bucks.

Louisa Anne, 3rd dau. of the late Right Rev. Lord George Murray, Lord Bishop of St. David's, by Ann Charlotte, dau. of Lieut.-General Francis Grant, and grand-dau. of John, 3rd Duke of Athole; *m.* 1815 Sir Robert Frankland, Bart., M.P., who assumed the name of Russell on inheriting the estate of Chequers Court

and *d.* 1849, leaving issue. Is Lady of the Manors of Ellesborough, Thirkleby, and Great and L'ttle Kimble, Bucks, and Patron of 1 living. — *Thirklsby Park, Thirsk; Chequers Court, Aylesbury.*

RUSSELL, Lady WILLIAM.

Elizabeth Anne, only dau. of the Hon. John Theophilus Rawdon; *m.* 1817 Major-General Lord George William Russell, G.C.B. (2nd son of John, 6th Duke of Bedford), who *d.* 1846, leaving issue.—2, *Audley Square,* w.

RUSSELL, Sir CHARLES, Bart., of Swallow-field Park, Berks (cr. 1812).

Eldest surviving son of the late Sir Henry Russell, Bart., of Swallowfield Park, by Maria Clotilde, dau. of Mons. Mottel de la Fontaine, Baron Fieffé; *b.* 1826; *s.* as 3rd Bart. 1852. Educated at Eton; is a J.P. and D.L. for Berks; and a Capt. and Lieut.-Col. Grenadier Guards; elected M.P. for Berks 1865. —*Swallowfield Park, Reading; Carlton and Guards' Clubs,* s.w.; 18, *S'. James's Place,* s.w.

Heir Pres., his brother George B.A., of Exeter Coll., Oxford, Recorder of Wokingham; *b.* 1828; *m.* 1857 Constantine, eldest dau. of the late Lord Arthur Lennox.

RUSSELL, Sir WILLIAM, Bart., C.B., of Charlton Park, Gloucestershire (cr. 1832).

Only son of the late Sir William Russell, Bart., of Charlton Park, by his 2nd wife Jane Eliza, eldest dau. of Major-General James Doddington Sherwood, of the H.E.I.Co.'s Service (she assumed the additional name of Prinn in 1841); *b.* 1822; *s.* as 2nd Bart. 1839; *m.* 1863 Margaret, only child of the late R. Wilson, Esq. Is a Magistrate for co. Gloucester, late Col. 14th Hussars; was M.P. for Dover 1857-9; elected M.P. for Norwich 1860.—*Charlton Park, Cheltenham; Arthur's, Travellers', and Army and Navy Clubs,* s.w.; 10, *James Street,* s.w.

Heir, his son William, *b.* 1865.

RUSSELL, ARTHUR JOHN EDWARD, Esq.

Second son of the late Lord George William Russell, G.C.B., by Elizabeth Anne, dau. of the late Hon. John Theophilus Rawdon; *b.* 1825; *m.* 1865 Laura, dau. of the Count de Peyronnet. Was formerly Private Secretary to Earl Russell; has been M.P. for Tavistock since 1857.—*Athenæum and Brooks's Clubs,* s.w.; 2, *Audley Square,* w.

RUSSELL, the Rev. CECIL.

Son of the Rev. Christopher Russell, Rector of Ballynakill, co. Galway, by Charlotte, dau. of the late Rev. Cecil Crampton, Rector of Headford, co. Galway; *b.* 1802; *m.* 1st 1835 Frances Elizabeth, dau. of the Rev. Roger Chambers, of Clover Hill, co. Sligo; 2nd 1842 Hon. Elizabeth Esther, only dau. of John, 4th Viscount Harberton, and has issue by the former,

* Christopher Josiah, Lieut., R.E.; *b.* 1829.

Mr. Russell, who was educated at Trinity Coll., Dublin (B.A. 1823, M.A. 1832), is Rector and Vicar of Drumcree, co. Westmeath; was formerly Rector of Clonfad-faran, co. Westmeath.—*Drumcree Rectory, Kilucan, co. Westmeath; University Club, Dublin.*

RUSSELL, CHAMPION, Esq., of Stubbers, Essex.

Eldest son of the late Champion Edward Branfill, Esq., J.P. and D.L., of Upminster Hall, Essex (w o *d.* 1841), by Anne Eliza, dau. of the Rev. Anthony Egerton Hammond, and brother of Capt. B. A. Branfill (whom see); *b.* 1820; assumed the name of Russell in 1820 on succeeding to the estates of the late Joseph Russell, Esq.; *m.* 1855 Emily Augusta, eldest dau. of the Rev. C. Way. and has, with other issue,

* Champion Branfill, *b.* 1860.

Mr. Russell, who was educated at Trinity Coll., Cam-

bridge, is a J.P. and D.L. for Essex (High Sheriff 1859), and Major W. Essex Militia.—*Stubbers, Romford.*

RUSSELL, FRANCIS CHARLES HASTINGS, Esq., of Oakley House, Beds.

Eldest son of the late Major-General Lord George William Russell, G.C.B. (who *d.* 1846), by Elizabeth Anne, only child of the late Hon. J. Theophilus Rawdon, and cousin and heir pres. to the Duke of Bedford; *b.* 1819; *m.* 1844 Lady Elizabeth, eldest dau. of George John, 5th Earl de la Warr, and has, with other issue,

* George William Francis Sackville, *b.* 1852.

Mr. Russell is a J.P. and D.L. for Beds. and Lieut.-Col. Beds Rifle Volunteers; late Major Beds Militia; was elected M.P. for Beds 1847; was formerly Capt. Scots Fusilier Guards. — *Oakley House, Bedford; Brooks's, Travellers', and Senior United Service Clubs,* s.w.; 82, *Eaton Square,* s.w.

RUSSELL, FRANCIS WILLIAM, Esq.

Eldest son of the late John N. Russell, Esq., Merchant, of Limerick, by Mary, eldest dau. of Alderman Thompson, of Cork; *b.* 1800; *m.* 1834 Fanny, youngest dau. of the late Thomas Clarke. Esq. Educated at Fermoy and at Trinity Coll., Dublin; called to the Irish Bar 1824; is a Merchant of Limerick and London; has been M.P. for Limerick since 1852. —*Limerick House, Limerick; Union Club,* s.w.; 9, *Lancaster Gate,* w.

RUSSELL, JAMES, Esq., of Aden, Aberdeenshire.

Second son of the late Alexander Russell, Esq., of Aden, by Margaret. dau. of James Cumine, Esq., of Kininmonth; *b.* 1797; *s.* 1831; *m.* 1832 Miss Caroline Lambton, of Aden, and by her, who *d.* 1864, has, with other issue,

* James George, *b.* 1836; *m.* 1858 Elizabeth Sophia, dau. of the late Sir William Lawrence Young, Bart., M.P.

Mr. Russell is a J.P. and D.L. for co. Aberdeen.—*Aden House, Mintlaw, N.B.; Carlton Club,* s.w.; 3, *Berkeley Square,* w.

+**RUSSELL, Mrs., of Ashford Hall, Salop.**

Harriet Elizabeth, dau. of the late — Smith, Esq.; *m.* 18— Major-Gen. Lechmere Coore Russell, C.B., of the H.E.I.C.S. (Bombay), who *d.* 1851, leaving issue,

* Katherine Elizabeth.—*Ashford Hall, Ludlow.*

RUSSELL, Miss, of Ashiestcel, Selkirkshire.

Helen Jane. elder dau. of the late General Sir James Russell, K.C.B., of Ashiesteel, by Katharine Mary, dau. of Sir James Hall, Bart., of Dunglass. and Lady Helen Douglas, dau. of the 4th Earl of Selkirk; *b.* 1837; *s.* 1859.—*Ashiesteel House, Ga'ashiels. N.B.*

Heir Pres., her only sister Katherine Anne. *b.* 1839; *m.* 1860 Laurence W. M. Lockhart. Esq., 92nd Highlanders, and has issue, one son and one daughter.

RUSSELL, ROBERT, Esq., of Newton House. Yorkshire.

Youngest, but only surviving son of the late Capt. Robert Russell. R.N. (who *d.* 1848). by Hester, dau. of the Right Hon. Stephen Lushington; *b.* 1848; *s.* his brother 1865. Educated at Eton; is Patron of 1 living.—*Newton House, Bedale.*

+**RUSSELL, THOMAS, Esq., of Wallington House, Staffordshire.**

Eldest son of the late John Russell, Esq., of Wallington House; *b.* 18—; *m.* 1860 Emily, 3rd dau. of William Harrison, Esq., of Norton Hall, co. Stafford. and of Eastland House. Leamington.—*Wallington House, Bloxwich, Walsall.*

RUSSELL, the late THOMAS ARTEMIDORUS, Esq., of Cheshunt Park, Herts.
Third, but last surviving son of the late Thomas Artemidorus Russell, Esq., by Elizabeth Oliveria, dau. of Oliver Cromwell, Esq., of Cheshunt Park (she d. 1849); b. 1810; s. 1858; d. 1863. This family descend in the direct female line from the Protector, Oliver Cromwell.—Cheshunt Park, Waltham Cross.
Heir Pres., his niece Avarilla Oliveria, m. 1840 the Rev. Paul Bush (whom see).

RUSSELL. (See under Bedford, Duke of, and De Clifford, Baroness.)

RUSSELL. (See Oldnall-Russell.)

RUSSELL. (See Pakington.)

RUSSELL. (See Watts-Russell.)

+RUST, GEORGE, Esq., of Cromwell House, Hunts.
Eldest son of the late James Rust, Esq., Banker, of Huntingdon, by Margaret, dau. of Lancelot Brown, Esq.; b. 1793; is married, and has issue. Educated at Brasenose Coll., Oxford (B.A. 1815, M.A. 1818); is a J.P. and D.L. for Hunts.—Cromwell House, Huntingdon.

RUST, JAMES, Esq., of Alconbury, Hunts.
Second son of the late James Rust, Esq., of Huntingdon, by Margaret, dau. of Lancelot Brown, Esq.; b. 1798; m. 1st 1829 Mary, only dau. of Lieut.-Col. Rowles; 2nd 1837 Mary Ann, eldest dau. of Col. Roberts. Educated at Rugby and University Coll., Oxford (B.A. 1819, M.A. 1822); elected Fellow 1823; called to the Bar at Lincoln's Inn 1825, but retired in 1836; a J.P. and D.L. for Hunts, and Chairman of the Quarter Sessions; was M.P. for Hunts 1855–9.—Alconbury House, Huntingdon; Athenæum Club, s.w.
Heir Pres., his nephew George John, b. 1831.

RUTHERFORD, GEORGE SHAW, Esq., M.D., of Cornastalk, co. Leitrim.
Son of the late James Rutherford, Esq., of Cornastalk, by Mary, dau. of William Shaw, Esq., of Clunie, co. Sligo; b. 1789; m. 1832 Elizabeth, 2nd dau. of John Tilden, Esq., of Ifield Court, Kent, and has issue.
* John James, b. 1841.
Mr. Rutherford, who is a Surgeon R.N., represents a Scottish family.—Cornastalk, co. Leitrim; 23, Devonshire Street, w.

RUTHERFURD, HENRY, Esq., of Fairnington, Roxburghshire.
Eldest son of the late Thomas Rutherfurd, Esq., of Fairnington, by Caroline Sanderson, dau. of William Ball, Esq.; b. 1831; s. 1863. Educated at Edinburgh University; called to the Bar at the Middle Temple 1855; is a Magistrate and Commissioner of Supply for co. Roxburgh.—Fairnington, Kelso, N.B.; Athenæum Club, s.w.; 3, Elm Court, Temple, e.c.

RUTHERFURD, WILLIAM OLIVER, Esq., of Edgerston, Roxburghshire.
Son of the late William Oliver, Esq., of Dinlabyre, and nephew of the late John Rutherfurd, Esq., whose name he assumed; b. 1781; s. his father in 1830, and his uncle in 1834; m. 1804 Agnes, dau. of Alexander Chatto, Esq., of Mainhouse, and by her (who d. 1859) has, with other issue,
* William Alexander, a Magistrate for co. Roxburgh; b. 1808; m. 1861 Margaret Jane, only dau. of the late Edward Young, Esq., and has, with other issue, * a son, b. 1863.
Mr. Oliver-Rutherfurd, who was educated at Eton and Edinburgh University, called to the Scottish Bar 1803
818

and appointed Sheriff of co. Roxburgh in 1807, is J.P. and D.L. for co. Roxburgh, and Convener of c Roxburgh.—Edgerston, Jedburgh, N.B.

RUTHVEN, Lord (WALTER JAMES HORE RUTHVEN).—Cr. 1651.
Eldest son of the late Hon. William Hore-Ruthv (who d. 1847); by Dells Honoria, dau. of Lieut.-Co Pierce Lowen, K.H.; b. 1838; s. as 8th Lord 185; is a J.P. and D.L. for cos. Perth and Hereford, an Capt. Rifle Brigade.—Freeland House, Bridge of Ear Perthshire, N.B.; Harperstown House, Taghmon, c Wexford; Brampton Bryan Park, Hereford; Carlt and Boodle's Clubs, s.w.
Heir Pres., his brother Charles Stewart, b. 1839.

RUTHVEN. (See Bermingham-Ruthven.)

RUTHVEN. (See Hore-Ruthven.)

RUTLAND, Duke of (CHARLES CECIL JOHN MANNERS, K.G.).—Cr. 1703.
Eldest son of John Henry, 5th Duke, by Lady Elizabeth, dau. of Frederick, 5th Earl of Carlisle; b. 1815; s. 1857. Educated at Eton and Trinity Coll., Cambridge (M.A. 1835); is Hon. Col. Leicestershire Militia, and Lord-Lieutenant of that county, and Patron of 26 livings; late Lord-Lieutenant of co. Lincoln; was M.P. for Stamford 1837–52, for N. Leicestershire 1852–7; was a Lord of the Bedchamber to the late Prince Consort 1843–6.—Belvoir Castle, Grantham; and Haddon Hall, Bakewell; Longshawe, Sheffield; Carlton Club, s.w.; Bute House, Campden Hill, w.
Heir Pres., his brother Lord John James Robert; educated at Eton, and M.A. of Trinity Coll., Cambridge; M.P. for N. Leicestershire; Chief Commissioner of Works and buildings, and M.P. for Newark and Colchester, and late Lieut. Leicestershire Militia; b. 1818; m. 1st 1851 Katharine Louisa Georgiana, dau. of the late Col. Marlay. C.B. (she d. 1854); 2nd 1862 Janette, dau. of Thomas Hughan, Esq., of Airds, co. Kirkcudbright, and has issue, by the former, * Henry John Brinsley, educated at Eton, b. 1852.

RUTSON, WILLIAM, Esq., of Newby Wiske, Yorkshire.
Only son of the late William Calton Rutson, Esq., of Newby Wiske, by Frances, dau. of Simon Wrather, Esq.; b. 1791; s. 1817; m. 1825 Charlotte Mary, dau. of William Ewart, Esq., and has, with other issue,
* John, a Magistrate for the N. Riding of co. York; b. 1829.
Mr. Rutson, who was educated at Trinity Coll., Cambridge (B.A. 1814, M.A. 1818), is a J.P. and D.L. for the N. Riding of co. York (High Sheriff 1850).—Newby Wiske, Thirsk; University Club, s.w.

RUTTLEDGE, DAVID, Esq., of Barbersfort, co. Galway
Eldest son of the late David Watson, Esq., by Elizabeth, dau. of Thomas Bragg, Esq., of Lyremont; b. 1811; s. his step-father 1833, and took the name of Ruttledge only; m. 1836 Eleanor, youngest dau. of John Knox, Esq., and has, with other issue,
* David, a Magistrate for co. Galway, and a Lieut. Galway Militia; b. 1838; m. 1861 [...] dau. of the late Edward Levi of Cregmoy, Kingstown, and has, with other issue, * David Knox, b. 1863.
Mr. Ruttledge, who was educated at the High Sch. Edinburgh, and Trinity Coll., Dublin (B.A. 1833, M.A. 1836), and called to the Irish Bar 1838, is a Magistrate for co. Galway, and for co. Mayo (High Sheriff 1850), and a Capt. South Mayo Militia.—Barbersfort, Esq., c. Galway; Hibernian United Service Club, Dublin; 3. Fitzwilliam Place, Dublin.

RUTTLEDGE, ROBERT, Esq., of Bloomfield, co. Mayo.
Eldest son of the late Rev. Francis Ruttledge, of Bloomfield (who, in 1819, assumed that name instead

of Lambert), by Margaret, dau. of the late Col. Henry Bruen, of Oak Park, co. Carlow ; *b.* 1823 ; *s.* 1854; *m.* 1850 Katharine, dau. of Peter Low, Esq., by Louisa, dau. of the late Sir Richard Butler, Bart., of Garry-hundon, and by her, who *d.* 1856, has issue,

* Thomas Henry Bruen, *b.* 1852.

Mr. Ruttledge, who is a J.P. and D.L. for co. Mayo (High Sheriff 1863-4), and Lieut.-Col. Commandant South Mayo Militia Rifles, was formerly an Officer in the 24th Foot.—*Bloomfield, Hollymount, co. Mayo.*

RUTZEN. (See *De Rutzen.*)

+RUXTON, Major GEORGE, of Rahanna House, co. Louth.
Son of the late G. Ruxton, Esq. ; *b.* 1805 ; *m.* 1832 Mary, dau. of ——, Esq., and by her (who *d.* 1866) has issue,

* George William, *b.* 1834 ; *m.* 1863 Arabella Anna, 2nd dau. of George Bomford, Esq., of Oakley Park, co. Meath.

Major Ruxton, who is a Magistrate for co. Louth (of which he has been High Sheriff), was formerly Major 34th Foot.—*Rahanna House, Ardee, co. Louth.*

RUXTON, JOHN HENRY HAY, Esq., of Broad Oak, Kent.
Eldest son of the late John Ruxton, Esq., of Broad Oak, by Anna Maria, dau. of Col. Patrick Hay, of Alderstone, N.B. ; *b.* 1818 ; *s.* 1828 ; *m.* 1843 Isabel Sarah, eldest dau. of William Hooper, Esq., and has, with other issue,

* Julian Henry Hay, Lieut. 15th Foot ; *b.* 1844.

Mr. Ruxton, who is a Dep.-Lieut. for Kent, was formerly Lieut. 4th Foot, and Capt. Kent Artillery; appointed Chief Constable of Kent 1857.—*Broad Oak, Staplehurst ; Army and Navy Club, s.w.*

RUXTON, WILLIAM, Esq., of Ardee House, co. Louth.
Eldest son of the late John Fitzherbert Ruxton, Esq., of Ardee House, by Anna Elizabeth, dau. of the late Nicholas Coddington, Esq., of Old Bridge, co. Meath ; *b.* 1823 ; *s.* 1826 ; *m.* 1854 Caroline Diana, youngest dau. of Charles Vernon, Esq., and has issue,

* A son, *b.* 1863.

Mr. Ruxton, who was educated at Oriel Coll., Oxford, is a J.P. and D.L. for co. Louth (High Sheriff 1848), and a Magistrate for co. Cavan.—*Ardee House, co. Louth; Sackville Street Club, Dublin ; Carlton Club, s.w.*

RYAN, the Right Hon. Sir EDWARD, Knt. (cr. 1826).
Son of the late W. Ryan, Esq. ; *b.* 1793; *m.* 1814 Louisa, dau. of the late William Whitmore, Esq., of Dudmaston, co. Salop (she *d.* 1866). Educated at Trinity Coll., Cambridge (B.A. 1814, M.A. 1817); called to the Bar at Lincoln's Inn 1817 ; is a Magistrate for Middlesex, a Civil Service Commissioner, and one of the Senate of the University of London; late Assistant-Comptroller of the Exchequer, and formerly Chief Justice at Calcutta.—*Athenæum Club, s.w.; Garden Lodge, Kensington, w.*

RYAN, DANIEL PHILIP, Esq., of Knocklyon, co. Dublin.
Son of the late John Philip Ryan, Esq., of Tipperary, by Honoria, dau. of Daniel Murphy, Esq., of Ballimore ; *b.* 1798 ; *m.* 1832 Elizabeth Mary, dau. of John Small, Esq., of Rutland Square, Dublin, and has issue four daughters. Mr. Ryan, who is a Magistrate for co. Dublin, succeeded 1828 to the estates of his uncle, the Ven. Dr. Ryan, Archdeacon of Lismore.—*Knocklyon, Templeogue, co. Dublin ; Friendly Brothers' Club, Dublin.*

RYAN, EDMOND FITZGERALD, Esq., of Limerick.
Eldest son of the late Michael Ryan, Esq., of Limerick, by Maria, dau. of William Fitzgerald, Esq., of Geraldine, co. Limerick ; *b.* 1819; *m.* 1st 1843 Christina Margaret, dau. of Martin Ryan, Esq., of Limerick ; 2nd 1850 Anna Maria, dau. of Owen Kieran, Esq., of Rath-brist House, co. Louth, and has issue,

* Edmond Kieran, *b.* 1857.

Mr. Ryan, who is a Magistrate for the city of Limerick and Resident Magistrate of Cork, was Mayor of Limerick 1846.—*Limerick.*

RYAN, GEORGE, Esq., of Inch, co. Tipperary.
Eldest surviving son of the late George Ryan, Esq., of Inch, by Mary Anne, dau. of Philip John Roche, Esq., of Newcastle, co. Limerick ; *b.* 1791 ; *s.* his brother Daniel 1830 ; *m.* 1839 Catherine Elizabeth, dau. of Capt. Edward Whyte, R.N., of Loughbrickland, co. Down, and has, with other issue,

* George Edward, *b.* 1844.

Mr. Ryan, who was educated at Oscott Coll., is a J.P. and D.L. for co. Tipperary (High Sheriff 1851).—*Inch House, Thurles, co. Tipperary.*

RYAN, WILLIAM, Esq., of Ballymackeogh, co. Tipperary.
Eldest son of the late William Ryan, Esq., of Bally-mackeogh, by Anne, dau. of the Rev. Dr. Pennefather, D.D., of Newport, co. Tipperary ; *b.* 1815 ; *s.* 1835 ; *m.* 1842 Jane, sister of Sir Edward Grogan, Bart., M.P., and has, with other issue,

* William Edward, *b.* 1851.

Mr. Ryan is a Magistrate for co. Tipperary.—*Bally-mackeogh, Newport, co. Tipperary.*

RYCROFT, Sir NELSON, Bart., of Calton, Yorkshire (cr. 1784).
Eldest son of the late Sir Richard Henry Charles Rycroft, Bart., by Charlotte Anne Josephine, dau. of William Tennant, Esq., of Little Aston Hall, co. Stafford, and niece of Charles, 1st Earl of Yarborough ; *b.* 1831 ; *s.* as 4th Bart. 1864 ; *m.* 1858 Juliana, dau. of Sir John Ogilvy, Bart., of Inverquharity, N.B. Educated at Eton ; is a Magistrate for Kent and Hants. The family name was originally Nelson. —*Residence: Kempshott Park, Basingstoke.*

Heir, his son Richard Nelson, *b.* 1859.

RYCROFT, CHARLES ALFRED WILLIAM, Esq., of Everlands, Kent.
Second son of the late Sir Richard Henry Charles Rycroft, Bart., of Calton, co. York (who *d.* 1864), by Charlotte Anne Josephine, dau. of William Tennant, Esq., of Little Aston Hall, co. Stafford ; *b.* 1838 ; is a Magistrate for Kent, and Capt. 33rd Kent Rifle Volunteers ; was formerly in the Royal Navy.—*Everlands, Sevenoaks; Arthur's Club, s.w.*

RYDER, the Hon. FREDERICK DUDLEY, of Ickleford, Herts.
Third son of Dudley, 1st Earl of Harrowby, K.G., by Lady Susan, dau. of Granville, 2nd Marquis of Stafford; *b.* 1806, *m.* 1842 Marian Charlotte Emily, only child of the late Thomas Cockayne, Esq., of Ickleford House, Herts (div. 1861), and has, with other issue,

* Hugh Cuthbert, *b.* 1843.

Mr. Ryder, who was educated at Eton and Trinity Coll., Cambridge (M.A. 1827), is a Magistrate for Beds, Herts, and co. Stafford; he was formerly a Clerk in the Foreign Office.—*Ickleford House, Herts.*

RYDER, the Hon. GRANVILLE DUDLEY, of West-brook Hay, Herts.
Second son of Dudley, 1st Earl of Harrowby, K.G., by Lady Susan, dau. of Granville, 2nd Marquis of Staf-

ford; *b.* 1799; *m.* 1825 Lady Georgiana Elizabeth, 3rd dau. of Henry Charles, 6th Duke of Beaufort, and has, with other issue,

> * Dudley Henry, a Magistrate for Herts and for St. Alban's, and Capt. 7th Herts Rifle Volunteers; *b.* 1830; *m.* 1857 Georg'ana Emily, 2nd dau. of John Hales and Lady Caroline, dau. of William, 5th Duke of Manchester, and has, with other issue, * Dudley Granville Richard, *b.* 1858.

Mr. Ryder, who was educated at Trinity Coll., Cambridge (M.A. 1825), entered the Navy 1813; is a J.P. and D.L. for Herts, a Magistrate for Bucks, Patron of 1 living, and a Commander R.N., retired; he was M.P. for Tiverton 1830–2, and for Herts 1841–7.—*Westbrook Hay, Hemel-Hempstead; Carlton Club, s.w.*

RYDER. (See under *Harrowby, Earl of.*)

+RYDER-IRTON, J. O., Esq., of Irton Hall, Cumberland.
Son of the late Mr. J. Ryder; *b.* 18—; *s.* to this estate on the death of Samuel Irton, Esq., M.P., 1866; *m.* 18— Mary, dau. of the Rev. S. Irton-Fell; assumed the additional name of Irton 1867.—*Irton Hall, Whitehaven.*

RYLANDS, JOHN, Esq., of Thelwall Grange, Cheshire.
Eldest son of the late John Rylands, Esq., of Bewsey House, Warrington, by Martha, dau. of the Rev. James Glazebrook, Vicar of Belton; *b.* 1815; *m.* 1842 Harriet, dau. of the Rev. James Jackson, of Green Hammerton. Is a Magistrate for co. Lancaster, and an Iron Master and Merchant at Warrington.—*Thelwall Grange, Warrington.*

RYLANDS, PETER, Esq., of Bewsey House, Lancashire.
Son of the late John Rylands, Esq., of Bewsey House, by Martha, dau. of the Rev. James Glazebrook, Vicar of Belton; *b.* 1820; *m.* 1861 Caroline, dau. of William Reynolds, Esq., of Warrington, and has, with other issue,

> * Louis Gordon, *b.* 1862.

Mr. Rylands is a Magistrate for co. Lancaster, and Merchant at Warrington (Mayor 1853–4), and a Director of the Manchester and Liverpool District Banking Company.—*Bewsey House, Warrington.*

RYND, CHRISTOPHER, Esq., of Mount Armstrong, co. Kildare.
Youngest son of the late James Rynd, Esq., of Ryndville (who *d.* 1814), by his 3rd wife Hester, dau. of Robert Fleetwood, Esq., of Parkstown; *b.* 1810; *m.* 1842 Helen Maria, only dau. of Peter Wolfe, Esq., of Blackhall, co. Kildare, and has, with other issue,

> * Robert Fleetwood, *b.* 1843.

Mr. Rynd was educated at Carlow and Trinity Coll., Dublin; is a Magistrate for co. Kildare.—*Mount Armstrong, Donadea, co. Kildare; Kildare Street Club, Dublin.*

+RYND, ROBERT FLEETWOOD, Esq., of Ryndville, co. Meath.
Eldest son of the late James Rynd, Esq., of Dublin (who *d.* 1814), by his 3rd wife Hester, dau. of Robert Fleetwood. Esq., of Parkstown, co. Meath; *b.* 1800; *m.* 183– Maria, sister of Francis Longworth Dames, Esq., of Greenhills, King's Co., and has, with other issue,

> * Robert, *b.* 18—.

Mr. Rynd is a Magistrate for co. Meath, and Lord of the Manor of Ryndville.—*Ryndville, Enfield, co. Meath.*

S

SABINE-PASLEY. (See *Pasley.*)

SACKVILLE-WEST, the Hon. MORTIMER, of Hartwell, Kent.
Third surviving son of George John, 5th Earl Dela-Warr, by Lady Elizabeth, 2nd dau. of John Frederick, 3rd Duke of Dorset; *b.* 1820; *m.* 1847 Fanny Charlotte, dau. of the late Major-General Dickson, C.B., of Been-ham, Berks. Is a Groom-in-Waiting to Her Majesty; has been a Gentleman-in-Waiting; and a Groom of Privy Chamber; formerly Capt. Grenadier Guards. —*Hartwell, Tunbridge Wells; 15, Chester Square, s.w.*

SACKVILLE-WEST.
(See under *Buckhurst, Baroness,* and *DelaWarr, Earl.*)

SADLEIR, THOMAS OWEN SANDERS. Esq., of Ballinderry and Castletown, co. Tipperary.
Only son of the late Thomas Sadleir, Esq., J.P., of Castletown (High Sheriff of co. Tipperary 1859-60), by Ellen, eldest dau. of Owen Sanders. Esq., of Bal-linderry, and of Largay, co. Cavan; *b.* 1835; *s.* 1863. Educated at Trinity Coll., Dublin; is Lord of the Manors of Ballinderry and Castletown. — *Ballinderry House and Cas letown, Borrisokane, co. Tipperary.*
Heirs Pres., his sisters.

SADLER, Sir THOMAS SEYMOUR, Knt. (cr. 1849.)
Son of the late Jonathan Sadler, Esq., of co. Tipperary, by Anne Alicia Seymour, only dau. of Capt. Charles Seymour Lynn, R.N.; *b.* 1809. Late Capt. in the Lei-cestershire Militia; was formerly Senior Exon of the Yeomen of the Guard.—*8, Regent Street, s.w.*

SADLER, JAMES HAYES, Esq., of Keynsham Bury, Gloucestershire.
Eldest son of the late Rev. James Hayes Sadler, of Keynham Bury; *b.* 1826; *s.* 1845; *m.* 1850 Sophia Jane, dau. of the late James Taylor, Esq., and has issue.—*Keynsham Bury, Cheltenham.*

SAFFORD, the Rev. JAMES CUTTING, of Met-tingham Castle, Suffolk.
Eldest son of the late Samuel Safford, Esq., of Met-tingham Castle, by Mary, dau. of John Cole, Esq., of Boyland Hall, Norfolk; *b.* 1799; *s.* 1824; *m.* 1825 Louisa, dau. of the Rev. James Chartres, Vicar of God-manchester and W. Haddon, and has, with other issue,
* William Chartres, in Holy Orders, educated at St, Paul's Schooi. M.A. of Corpus Coll. Cambridge, and a Magistrate for co. Chester; *b.* 1828; *m.* 1854 Mary. dau. of Philip Whiteway, Esq., of Grove House, Runcorn.
Mr. Safford, who was educated at Caius Coll., Cam-bridge (B.A. 1822), is a Magistrate for Suffolk, Per-petual Curate of Ilketshall St. Lawrence. Suffolk, Lord of the Manor of Mettingham Castle cum Bungay Soca, and Vicar and Patron of Mettingham. — *Mettingham Castle, Bungay.*

SAGAR, WILLIAM LISTER, Esq., of Southfield House, Lancashire.
Eldest son of the late William Sagar, Esq., of South-field House, by Hannah, dau. of John Cooper, Esq., of Blackrod; *b.* 1819; *s.* 1825; *m.* 1843 Frances Louisa, dau. of James Wilde, Esq., and has, with other issue.
* William Lister, *b.* 1848.
Mr. Sagar is a Magistrate for co. Lancaster, and Capt.

in the Lancashire Militia.—*Southfield House, Marsden, Burnley.*

SAGAR-MUSGRAVE, JOHN MUSGRAVE, Esq., of Sandford House, Yorkshire.
Eldest son of the late Richard Hartley Sagar, Esq., of Kirkstall Hall, by Margaret, dau. of John Musgrave, Esq., of Bramley; *b.* 1835; *s.* 1844; *m.* 1860 Clara Kate, only dau. of Robert Collinson Brooksbank, Esq., of Sydenham Hill, Kent, and has, with other issue,
* Abraham Musgrave, *b.* 1861.
Mr. Sagar-Musgrave, who is a Cornet 2nd W. Yorkshire Yeomanry Cavalry, assumed in 1863 the name and arms of Musgrave in addition to that of Sagar, under the will of his great uncle, Abraham Musgrave, Esq., of Bramley, co. York. — *Sandford House, Kirkstall, Leeds; Conservative Club, s.w.*

ST. ALBAN'S, Duke of (WILLIAM AMELIUS AU-BREY DE VERE BEAUCLERK).—Cr. 1684.
Only son of William, 9th Duke, by his 2nd wife Eliza-beth Katharine, dau. of General Gubbins (she re-mar-ried 1859 Viscount Falkland); *b.* 1840; *s.* 1849; *m.* 1867 Sybil Mary, eldest dau. of Lieut.-Gen. the Hon. Charles Grey. Educated at Eton and Trinity Coll., Cambridge; is a J.P. and D.L. for co. Lincoln, Heredi-tary Grand Falconer of England. Patron of 2 livings, and Registrar of the Court of Chancery.—*Redbourne Hall, Brigg; Bestwood Lodge, Nottingham; 4, Prince's Gate, s.w.*
*Heir Pres., his uncle Lord Frederick Charles Peter. Capt. R.N.; b. 1808; m. 1848 Jemima Eleanora. dau. of the late James Raymond Johnstone. Esq.. and has, with other issue, * William Nelthorpe, b. 1849.*

ST. ASAPH, Bishop of (the Rt. Rev. THOMAS VOWLER SHORT, D.D.).
Son of the late Ven. Archdeacon William Short, D.D., by Elizabeth, dau. of the Rev. T. Hodgkinson; *b.* 1790; *m.* 1833 Mary. dau. of the Rev. Charles Davies (widow of the Rev. J. J. Conybeare; she *d.* 1848). Educated at Westminster and Ch. Ch. Oxford (B.A. 1812. M.A. 1815); was successively Public Examiner 1820-4, Select Preacher 1823-30. and Rector of St. George's. Bloomsbury, 1834-41; consecrated Bishop of Sodor and Man 1841; translated 1846. Patron of 121 livings. —*The Palace, St. Asaph; Athenæum Club, s.w.*

ST. ASAPH. (See under *Ashburnham, Earl of.*)

ST. AUBYN, Sir EDWARD, Bart., of St. Michael's Mount, Cornwall (cr. 1866).
Eldest son of the late Edward St. Aubyn. Esq. of Stoke Damerel, Devon; *b.* 1799; *m.* 1828 Emma. 2nd dau. of the late Gen. William Knollys. Educated at Trinity Coll., Cambridge (B.A. 1822. M.A. 1826); is a Magis-trate for Devon.—*St. Michael's Mount, Marazion, Cornwall; United University Club, s.w.*
*Heir, his son John (of Pendrea, Penzance), educated at Eton, and M.A. of Trinity C.'11., Cambridge; a J.P. and D.L. for Cornwall. Deputy special Warden of the Stannaries. Major Royal Cornwall Rangers. and M.P. for W. Cornwall; b. 1829; m. 1856 Lady Elizabeth Clementina. 2nd dau. of John, 4th Marquis Townshend, and has, with other issue, * John Townshend, b. 1857.*

ST. AUBYN, the Rev. HENDER MOLES-WORTH-, of Clowance, Cornwall.
Second son of the late Rev. John Molesworth, Rector of St. Breock and St. Ervan. Cornwall, by his cousin Catherine, 2nd dau. of the late Sir John St. Aubyn, Bart., of St. Michael's Mount, Cornwall; *b.* 1798; *s.* his brother 1844; *m.* 1829 Helen Matilda Isabella, 5th dau. of the Rev. Timothy Napleton, late Rector of Powderham, Devon, and has, with other issue,

* Hender John Molesworth, a J.P. and D.L. for Cornwall, and Capt. Royal Miners' Artillery Militia; *b.* 1829; *m.* 1856 Kythe, 2nd dau. of Christopher Wallis Popham, Esq.

Mr. Molesworth-St. Aubyn, who was educated at Harrow and Exeter Coll., Oxford (B.A. 1821), is a Magistrate for Cornwall, and Patron of 1 living; was Rector of Redruth, Cornwall, 1822–33; he took the name of St. Aubyn in addition to that of Molesworth, by Royal licence, 1844.—*Clowance, Camborne.*

+ ST. AUBYN, LANGLEY, Esq., late of Alfoxton, Somersetshire.
Eldest son of the late St. Aubyn Gravenor, Esq., of Bristol, by Mary, only surviving dau. of Joseph Langley, Esq., of Great Farringdon, Berks; *b.* 1784; *s.* 1843; *m.* 1810 Frances, dau. of the Rev. Lawrence Heard Luxton, of Ash Priors, Somerset, and has, with other issue,

* Lancelot, *b.* 1811.

Mr. St. Aubyn, who was educated at Balliol Coll., Oxford (B.A. 1806, M.A. 1810), is a J.P. and D.L. for Somerset (High Sheriff 1850), and Patron of 1 living; he assumed the name of St. Aubyn in lieu of his patronymic Gravenor, in 1806, under the will of his great uncle the Rev. Lancelot St. Aubyn.

ST. BARBE, GEORGE FOSTER, Esq., of Lymington, Hants.
Second son of the late Charles St. Barbe, Esq., by Mary dau. of the Rev. Thomas Foster, of Tinwell, co. Rutland; *b.* 1808; *s.* 1849; *m.* 1st 1842 Henrietta Maria, dau. of Col. Cleaveland, R.H.A.; 2nd 1850 Caroline Mary Stewart, dau. of Alexander Reid, Esq., Lieut. R.A., and has, with other issue,

* Charles, *b.* 1853.

Mr. St. Barbe is Lieut. in the Lymington troop of Yeomanry Cavalry.—*Lymington, Hants.*

ST. CLAIR, WILLIAM HOME CHISHOLME, Esq., of Eyemouth, Berwickshire.
Eldest son of the late Hon. Charles St. Clair, J.P., of Eyemouth, by his 1st wife Isabella Jane, dau. of the late William Forman Home, Esq., of Wedderburn and Paxton; *b.* 1841; *s.* 1863. Is a Lieut. R.N., and represents a junior branch of the family of Lord Sinclair.—*Eyemouth, Ayton, Berwickshire.*

Heir Pres., his brother Matthew John, *b.* 1845.

ST. CLAIR, JAMES LOUIS, Esq., of Staverton Court, Gloucestershire.
Second son of Col. James Pattison St. Clair, of Felcourt Lodge, Surrey, by Charlotte, dau. of Michael Head, Esq., of Halifax, Nova Scotia; *b.* 1818; *s.* his uncle Capt. D. L. St. Clair, R.N. 1861; *m.* 1818 Juliet, dau. of George Crawshay, Esq., of Colney Hatch, Middlesex, and has, with other issue.

* James Lattuner Crawshay, *b.* 1849.

Mr. St. Clair, who was educated at Trinity Coll., Cambridge, is a Magistrate for co. Gloucester, Lord of the Manor of Staverton, and was formerly a Capt. in the Indian Army.—*Staverton Court, Cheltenham; Junior United Service Club, s.w.*

ST. CLAIR, Lieut.-Col. WILLIAM AUGUSTUS, of Felcourt Lodge, Surrey.
Eldest son of James Pattison St. Clair, Esq., of Felcourt Lodge, by his 1st wife Charlotte, dau. of Michael Head, Esq., of Halifax, Nova Scotia; *b.* 1810; *s.* 1867; *m.* 1846 Emma, dau. of George Crawshay, Esq., of Colney Hatch, Middlesex. Is Lieut.-Col. Indian Artillery, a Magistrate for Sussex, and Lieut.-Col. Sussex Militia Artillery.—*Felcourt Lodge, East Grinstead.*

ST. CLAIR.
(See under *Sinclair, Lord;* and *Rosslyn, Earl of.*)

ST. DAVID'S, Bishop of (the Rt. Rev. CONNOP THIRLWALL, D.D.).
Son of the late Rev. Thomas Thirlwall, Rector of Bowers Gifford, Essex; *b.* 1797. Educated at the Charterhouse and Trinity Coll. Cambridge (B.A. 1818, as Senior Optime and Senior Medallist; elected Fellow of Trinity 1819, M.A. 1821); called to the Bar at Lincoln's Inn 1823, but afterwards entered Holy Orders; was formerly one of the Examiners of the London University; consecrated 1840; is a Member of the Senate of the University of London; author of 'History of Greece.' Patronage 131 livings.—*The Palace, Abergwilli, Carmarthenshire; Athenæum Club, s.w.*

ST. GEORGE, Sir JOHN, Bart., of Woodsgift, co. Kilkenny (cr. 1766).
Son of the late Sir Theophilus John St. George, Bart., of Woodsgift (who *d.* 1857), by his 2nd wife Maria, eldest dau. of John Power, Esq., of Churchtown, co. Waterford; *b.* 1851; *s.* as 5th Bart. 1861. This family is descended from a common ancestor with the Lord St. George (*ext.*)—*Woodsgift, Carlingford, co. Kilkenny.*

Heir Pres., his brother Arthur, *b.* 1852.

ST. GEORGE, ARCHIBALD, Esq., of Camma, co. Roscommon.
Second son of the late Lieut.-Col. John St. George, of Birkenhead, co. Chester, by Frances. dau. of the late Archibald Campbell, Esq., M.D., of Stafford; *b.* 1813; *s.* his uncle, Archibald St. George, Esq., of Camma, 1863; *m.* 1862 his cousin, Kate, dau. of the late Archibald St. George, Esq., and has issue,

* Frances Millicent.

Mr. St. George, who was educated at Trinity Coll., Dublin, is a Magistrate for co. Roscommon. This family was formerly seated at Hatley St. George, co. Cambridge, for five centuries, and settled in Ireland in the reign of Elizabeth.—*Camma, Athlone.*

ST. GEORGE, CHRISTOPHER, Esq., of Tyrone House, co. Galway.
Eldest son of the late Arthur St. George. Esq., of Tyrone House, by Henrietta, dau. of the late Earl of Howth; *b.* 1811; *s.* 1811. Educated at Trinity Coll. Dublin (B.A. 1832); is a J.P. and D.L. for co. Galway; was M.P. for co. Galway 1847–52; claims the Barony of Athenry.—*Tyrone House, Galway; Union Club. s.w.*

Heir Pres., his brother Arthur, *b.* 181-.

ST. GEORGE, HERCULES LANGRISHE, Esq., of Bailef, co. Kilkenny.
Eldest son of the late Thomas Bligh St. George. Esq., of Bailef, by Hannah, 3rd dau. of the late Sir Hercules Langrishe, Bart.; *b.* 1810; *s.* his uncle Robert St. George, Esq., 1840; *m.* 1848 Margaret, dau. of Alexander Tayler, Esq., of co. Banff. N.B. Educated at Trinity Coll., Dublin; is a Magistrate for co. Kilkenny (High Sheriff 1818)—*Bailef, Johnstown, co. Kilkenny.*

ST. GEORGE, Major HOWARD JOHN, of Kilrush, co. Kilkenny.

Eldest son of the late Arthur St. George, Esq., of Kilrush, by Harriett, dau. of Theophilus Blakeney, Esq., of Abbert, co. Galway; *b.* 1813; *s.* 1853; *m.* 1843 Caroline, dau. of Col. George Grogan, of Seafield, co. Dublin, and has, with other issue,

 * Arthur George, *b.* 1849.

Mr. St. George, who was educated at Trinity Coll., Dublin, is a J.P. and D.L. for co. Kilkenny (High Sheriff 1858–9), and Major Kilkenny Militia; was formerly Lieut. 12th Royal Lancers.—*Kilrush House, Freshford, co. Kilkenny; Army and Navy Club*, s.w.

ST. GEORGE, JAMES CUFFE, Esq., of Sheane, co. Kildare.

Youngest surviving son of the late Sir Richard St. George, Bart., of Woodsgift, co. Kilkenny (who *d.* 1852), by Bridget, dau. of Theophilus Blakeney, Esq., of Abbert, co. Galway, Ireland; *b.* 1814; *m.* 1856 Jane Grey, only dau. of Capt. Arthur Loftus, R.N., and has issue,

 * Loftus, *b.* 1858.

Mr. St. George is a Magistrate for co. Kildare.—*Sheane, Rathangan, co. Kildare.*

+ST. GEORGE, THOMAS GORDON, Esq., of Wood Park, co. Armagh.

Eldest son of the late Acheson St. George, Esq., of Wood Park, by his 1st wife Eleanor, dau. of Robert Gordon, Esq., of Clonmel; *b.* 18—; *s.* 1855. Was formerly in the Indian Civil Service. This family descended from a common ancestor with Sir John St. George, Bart.—*Wood Park, Armagh, Ireland.*

ST. GEORGE. (See *Mansergh-St. George.*)

ST. GERMAN'S, Earl of (EDWARD GRANVILLE ELIOT, G.C.B., P.C., LL.D.).—Cr. 1815.

Eldest son of William, 2nd Earl, by his 1st wife Lady Georgiana, dau. of Granville, 1st Marquis of Stafford; *b.* 1798; *s.* 1845; *m.* 1824 Lady Jemima, dau. of Charles, 2nd Marquis Cornwallis (she *d.* 1856). Educated at Ch. Ch., Oxford; is a J.P. and D.L. for Cornwall, and Patron of 4 livings; was M.P. for Liskeard 1823–32, for E. Cornwall 1837–45; a Lord of the Treasury 1827–8; Envoy to Spain 1835; Chief-Secretary for Ireland 1841; Postmaster-General 1846; Lord Lieutenant of Ireland 1852–5; Lord Steward of the Household 1857–8, and 1859–65.—*Port Eliot, St. German's; 36, Dover Street*, w.

Heir, his son William Gordon Cornwallis, Lord Eliot, educated at Eton; M.P. for Devonport, Dep.-Lieut. for Cornwall, late Sec. of Legation at Rio de Janeiro; *b.* 1829.

ST. JOHN OF BLETSOE, Lord (Sr. ANDREW BEAUCHAMP ST. JOHN).—Cr. 1558.

Only son of St. Andrew, 13th Lord, by Louisa, dau. of the late Sir Charles William Rouse-Boughton, Bart.; *b.* 1811; *s.* 1817; *m.* 1838 Eleanor, dau. of the late Vice-Admiral Sir Richard Hussey Hussey, K.C.B., of Wood Walton, Hunts. Educated at Trinity Coll., Cambridge; is a J.P. and D.L. for Beds, and Patron of 6 livings; descended from a common ancestor with Viscount Bolingbroke. — *Melchbourne, Higham Ferrers; Carlton Club*, s.w.

Heir, his son St. Andrew, a J.P. and D.L. for Beds, *b.* 1840; *m.* 1866 Ellen Georgiana, youngest dau. of the late Edward Senior, Esq.

ST. JOHN. (See under *Bolingbroke, Viscount.*)

ST. LAWRENCE. (See under *Howth, Earl of.*)

ST. LEGER, Major JOHN, of Park Hill, Yorkshire.

Eldest son of the late Lieut.-General John Chester, of Ashtead, Surrey, by Sophia Elizabeth, dau. of the late

Charles Stuart, Esq.; *b.* 1823; *s.* his cousin Antony F. B. St. Leger, Esq., in 1862; *m.* 1858 Philippa, dau. of the late John Bonfoy Rooper, Esq., M.P., of Abbotts Ripton Hall, Hunts, and has, with other issue,

 * Arthur John Bonfoy, *b.* 1859.

Major St. Leger, who is a Magistrate for Norfolk and the W. Riding of Yorkshire, was formerly in the 53rd Foot. His grandfather, who was brother to the 1st Lord Bagot, assumed the name of Chester by Act of Parliament, and afterwards took the name of St. Leger, by Royal licence, under the will of his cousin.—*Park Hill, Rotherham, Yorkshire; Junior United Service and Travellers' Clubs*, s.w.

ST. LEGER. (See under *Doneraile, Viscount.*)

ST. LEONARDS, Lord (EDWARD BURTENSHAW SUGDEN, P.C., LL.D.).—Cr. 1852.

Second son of the late Mr. Richard Sugden, of Duke Street, St. James's; *b.* 1781; *m.* 1808 Winifred, dau. of John Knapp, Esq. (she *d.* 1861). Called to the Bar at Lincoln's Inn 1807; is High Steward of Kingston-on-Thames, a Trustee of the British Museum, a Bencher of Lincoln's Inn, and a Dep.-Lieut. for Sussex; practised for many years at the Chancery Bar; was M.P. for Weymouth 1826–30, for St. Mawes 1831–2, for Ripon 1837–41; Solicitor-General 1829–30, Lord Chancellor of Ireland 1834–5 and 1841–7; Lord Chancellor of England Feb.–Dec. 1852.—*Boyle Farm, Thames Ditton, Surrey; Carlton Club*, s.w.

Heir, his grandson Edward Burtenshaw (eldest son of the late Hon. Henry Sugden, who *d.* 1866, by Marianne, dau. of Lieut.-Col. Cookson); *b.* 1847; educated at Ch. Ch., Oxford.

+ST. LO, GEORGE LEWIS, Esq., of Marsh Court, Dorsetshire.

Son of the late — St. Lo, Esq., of Marsh Court; *b.* 1789; is married, and has issue,

 * Lewis.

Mr. St. Lo, who is a Magistrate for Dorset, and was formerly an Officer in the Army, represents a family of ancient Norman extraction.—*Marsh Court, Sherborne.*

ST. MAUR, Lord ALGERNON PERCY BANKS, of Burton Hall, Leicestershire.

Third son of Edward, 12th Duke of Somerset, by his 1st wife Lady Charlotte, dau. of Archibald, 9th Duke of Hamilton and Brandon; *b.* 1813; *m.* 1845 Horatia Isabella Harriet, 3rd dau. of J. Philip Morier, Esq., late Minister at Dresden, and has, with other issue,

 * Algernon, *b.* 1846.

Lord St. Maur, who was educated at Eton, was formerly Capt. Royal Horse Guards Blue.—*Burton Hall, Loughborough; White's Club*, s.w.; 1, *Park Lane*, w.

ST. MAUR, Lord ARCHIBALD HENRY ALGERNON, of Snibston, Leicestershire.

Second son of Edward, 12th Duke of Somerset, by his 1st wife Lady Charlotte, dau. of Archibald, 9th Duke of Hamilton and Brandon; *b.* 1810. Educated at Eton; is a J.P. and D.L. for co. Leicester (High Sheriff 1844).—*Snibston, Leicester.*

ST. MAUR. (See under *Somerset.*)

ST. PAUL, Sir HORACE, Bart., of Ewart Park, Northumberland (cr. 1813).

Only son of the late Sir Horace David Cholwell St. Paul, Bart., of St. Ninians, by the Hon. Anna Maria, dau. of John, Viscount Dudley and Ward; *b.* 1812; *s.* as 2nd Bart. 1840; *m.* 1867 Jane Eliza, dau. of George Annett Grey, Esq., of Millfield, Northumberland. Is a Dep.-Lieut. for Northumberland (High Sheriff 1841), and a Count of the Holy Roman Empire; was M.P. for E. Worcestershire 1837–41.—*Ewart Park, Wooler; Carlton Club*, s.w.

ST. QUINTIN, MATTHEW CHITTY DOWNES, Esq., of Scampston Hall, Yorkshire.
Second but eldest surviving son of the late William Thomas Darby, Esq., of Newtown House, Hants (who assumed the name of St. Quintin), by Arabella Bridget, dau. of the late General Thomas Calcraft; b. 1800; s. his brother 1859; m. 1850 Amy Elizabeth, 4th dau. of the late Henry Cherry, Esq., of Denford, Berks, by whom he has, with other issue,

* William Herbert, b. 1851.

Mr. St. Quintin, who was educated at Westminster, is Lord of the Manor of Scampston, Patron of 2 livings, and a Col. in the Army, retired. A Baronetcy conferred upon this family in 1641, became extinct in 1795.—Scampston Hall, York; Lowthorpe Lodge, Hull.

ST. QUINTIN, THOMAS, Esq., of Hatley Park, Cambridgeshire.
Eldest son of the late Thomas St. Quintin, Esq., of Hatley Park (who d. 1847), by Marianne, dau. of Col. Fisher, of Brentwood, Essex; b. 18·5; m. 1832 Louisa, 3rd dau. of the late William Thornton (afterwards Astell), Esq., of Everton House, Hunts, by whom he has, with other issue,

* Thomas Astell, educated at Eton, and R. Military Coll., Sandhurst: Lieut. 10th Hussars; b. 1841; m. 1868 the Hon. Eleanor Mary Frances, dau. of John, 3rd Lord Kilmaine, and widow of Major George Bagot.

Mr. St. Quintin is a J.P. and D.L. for co. Cambridge, Lord of the Manor and Patron of Hatley, and Vice-Chairman of the Quarter Sessions.—Hatley Park, Gamlingay, Cambridge.

ST. VINCENT, Viscount (CARNEGIE ROBERT JOHN JERVIS).—Cr. 1801.
Eldest son of the late Hon. William Jervis Jervis (who d. 1859), by Sophia, only child and heiress of George Narbonne Vincent, Esq.; b. 1825; s. his grandfather as 3rd Viscount 1859; m. 1848 Lucy Charlotte, youngest dau. of John Baskervyle Glegg, Esq., of Withington Hall, co. Chester. Educated at Eton; is a J.P. and D.L. for co. Stafford, and Patron of 2 livings.—Meaford Hall, Stone; Residence: Godmersham, Canterbury; Carlton and Arlington Clubs, s.w.

Heir, his son John Edward Leveson, b. 1850.

SALISBURY, Marquis of (ROBERT ARTHUR TALBOT GASCOIGNE-CECIL, P.C.).—Cr. 1789.
Eldest surviving son of James, 2nd Marquis, K.G., by his first wife, Frances Mary, dau. of Bamber Gascoigne, Esq.; b. 1830; s. 1868; m. 1857 Georgiana Caroline, dau. of the late Sir Edmund Henry Alderson. Educated at Eton and Ch. Ch., Oxford (B.A. 1850, M.A. 1852); is a Dep.-Lieut. for Middlesex; was M.P. for Stamford 1853–68; Secretary for State for India 1866–7.—Hatfield House, Herts; The Manor House, Cranborne, Dorset; Childwall Hall, Liverpool; Athenæum Club, s.w.; 1, Mansfield Street, w.

Heir, his son James Edward Hubert, Viscount Cranborne, b. 1861.

SALISBURY, Bishop of (the Rt. Rev. WALTER KERR HAMILTON, D.D.).
Eldest son of the late Ven. Archdeacon Hamilton, by Charity Greene, dau. of the late Sir Walter Farquhar, Bart.; b. 1808; m. 1845 Isabel Elizabeth, dau. of the late Very Rev. Francis Lear, Dean of Salisbury. Educated at Eton and Ch. Ch., Oxford (B.A. 1830, M.A. 1833); elected Fellow of Merton College 1831; became Vicar of St. Peter's, Oxford, 1837, Canon of Salisbury 1841, Precentor of Salisbury 1842; consecrated 1854; is Provincial Precentor of Canterbury. Patron of 51 livings.—The Palace, Salisbury; Athenæum Club, s.w.

824

SALISBURY, ENOCH ROBERT GIBBON, Esq., of Glan-Aber, Cheshire.
Son of Mr. Joseph Salisbury, of Naut. co. Flint, by Mary, dau. of Mr. Joseph Gibbon, of Whitehaven; b. 1819; m. 1842 Sarah, youngest dau. of the Rev. A. Jones, D.D., of Bangor, and has, with other issue,

* Philip Henry Bentham, b. 1855.

Mr. Salisbury, who was called to the Bar at the Inner Temple 1852, and went the N. Wales Circuit, was M.P. for Chester 1857–9, and has since practised at the Parliamentary Bar.—Glan-Aber, Chester; Reform Club, s.w.

+SALKELD, JOSEPH, Esq., of Penrith, Cumberland, and Ovoca, co. Wicklow.
Son of the late W. Salkeld, Esq.; b. 18—. Is a J.P. and D.L. for Cumberland and a Magistrate for cos. Westmoreland and Wicklow.—Penrith, Cumberland; Ovoca, Rathdrum, co. Wicklow.

SALKELD, THOMAS, Esq., of Holm Hill, Cumberland.
Son of the late J. Salkeld, Esq., of Holm Hill; b. 1810; m. 1st 1843 Mary, 3rd dau. of D. A. Carruthers, Esq., of Warmanbie (she d. 1844); 2nd 1847 Lucy, only dau. of the Rev. Edward Booth (she d. 1849); he has issue, by the former, an only daughter,

* Mary Fanny.

Mr. Salkeld, who is a J.P. and D.L. for Cumberland, a Magistrate for Westmoreland, Col. of Westmoreland Militia, and Col. of the Cumberland Artillery Volunteers, was formerly in the 11th Hussars.—Holm Hill, Carlisle; Carlton Club, s.w.

SALMON, HENRY THOMAS, Esq., of Gayton, Northamptonshire, and of Olveston, Gloucestershire.
Eldest son of the late Thomas Stokes Salmon, Esq., of Olveston, co. Gloucester, by Elizabeth Rosetta, dau. of the Rev. T. Carter, Vice-Provost of Eton College, Bucks; b. 1835; m. 1862 Gertrude Rose, only dau. of the Rev. J. Harwood Harrison, of Bugbrooke, co. Northampton, and has, with other issue,

* Henry Roope Pomeroy, b. 1865.

Mr. Salmon, who was educated at Magdalen Coll., Oxford (B.A. 1858, M.A. 1860), and called to the Bar at Lincoln's Inn 1862, is a Magistrate for co. Northampton, a Commissioner for the Lower Level of co. Gloucester, and a Lieut. in the Northamptonshire and Rutland Militia. This family claims to be lineally descended from Sir Thomas Salmon, Knt., temp. Richard I., and collaterally from John Salmon, Chancellor of England, temp. Edward II., and in the female line from the Pomeroys of Berry Pomeroy, Devon.—Gayton House, Northampton.

SALMON, WILLIAM, Esq., of Penllyne Court, Glamorganshire.
Only son of the late William Salmon, Esq., of Fettstree House, Suffolk, by Sarah, dau. of Denny Cole, Esq., of Sudbury Priory, Suffolk, ... elder dau. and co-heir of Harold Thomas Deere, Esq., J.P. and D.L., of Penllyne Court, and has surviving, with other issue,

* Thomas Deere educated at Eton, M.A. of Exeter Coll., Oxford, and of Lincoln's Inn, Barrister-at-Law; b. 1829.

Mr. Salmon is J.P. and D.L. for co. Glamorgan.—Penllyne Court, Cowbridge.

SALMOND, Lieut.-Col. JAMES, of Waterfoot, Cumberland.
Eldest son of the late Major-General James Salmond, by Louisa, dau. of David Scott, Esq., of Dunninald, N.B.; b. 1805; m. 1839 Emma Isabella, dau. of D'Ewes

Coke, Esq., of Brookhill Hall, co. Derby, and has, with other issue,

* Henry, R.N.; b. 1838.

Lieut.-Col. Salmond, who was educated at Rugby and Oriel Coll., Oxford (B.A. 1826), is a Magistrate for Cumberland. Westmoreland, Notts, and Derbyshire, and Lieut.-Col. Westmoreland and Cumberland Yeomanry; was formerly Capt. in the 2nd Dragoon Guards.—*Waterfoot, Penrith; Langton Hall, Alfreton, Derbyshire; Junior United Service Club, s.w.*

SALOMONS, David, Esq., of Broomhill, Kent.

Second son of the late Levy Salomons, Esq., by Matilda de Mitz, of Leyden; b. 1797; m. 1825 Jeanette, dau. of Solomon Cohen, Esq. Called to the Bar at Middle Temple 1849; is a J.P. and D L. for Kent, Sussex, and Middlesex, and an Alderman of the City of London; was Lord Mayor of London 1856, M.P. for Greenwich 1851-2, re-chosen 1859.—*Broomhill, Tunbridge Wells; Brooks's, Athenæum, and Reform Clubs, s.w.; 26, Great Cumberland Place, w.*

SALT, Thomas, Esq., of Weeping Cross, Staffordshire.

Eldest son of the late John Stevenson Salt, Esq., of Russell Square, London; b. 1802; m. 1829 Harriet Letitia, dau. of the Rev. James Hayes Petit, and has, with other issue,

* Thomas. educated at Rugby, and B.A. of Balliol Coll., Oxford, a J.P. and D.L. for co Stafford, and Capt. 2nd Stafford Militia. late M.P. for Stafford; b. 1830; m. 1861 Helen, youngest dau. of George Anderdon Esq., of Chiselhurst, Kent, and has, with other issue. * Thomas, b. 1863.

Mr. Salt, sen., is a Dep.-Lieut. for co. Stafford.—*Weeping Cross, Stafford.*

SALT, Titus, Esq., of Saltaire and Crow Nest, Yorkshire.

Eldest son of the late Daniel Salt, Esq., of Bradford, co. York, by Grace, dau. of Isaac Smithies, Esq., of The Manor House, Morley; b. 1803; m. 1831 Caroline, youngest dau. of George Whitlam, Esq., of Great Grimsby, and has, with other issue,

* William Henry. of Kirby Firth, co. Leicester; a Magistrate for co. Leicester and the W. Riding of Yorkshire; b. 1832; m. 1854 Emma Dove Octavinna, only child of John Dove Harris. Esq., of Ratcliffe Hall, co. Leicester, and has, with other issue, * shirley Harris, b. 1857.

Mr. Salt, who was educated at Wakefield, is a J.P. and D.L. for the W. Riding of Yorkshire, and for Bradford; was M.P. for Bradford 1859-61.—*Saltaire, Bradford; Crow Nest, Halifax.*

SALTMARSHE, Philip, Esq., of Saltmarshe, Yorkshire.

Eldest son of the late Philip Saltmarshe, Esq., J.P. and D.L., of Saltmarshe, by Harriet, dau. of Robert Denison, Esq., of Kilnwick Percy, co. York; b. 1827; s. 1846; m. 1852 Blanche, youngest dau. of Robert Denison, Esq., of Waplington Manor, and has, with other issue,

* Philip, b. 1853.

Mr. Saltmarshe is a J.P. and D.L. for the E. Riding of co. York, Patron of 1 living, and Capt. E. Yorkshire Rifle Volunteers; late Lieut. 8th Hussars.—*Saltmarshe, Howden.*

SALTOUN, Lord (Alexander Fraser).—Cr. 1445.

Eldest son of the late Hon. William Fraser (who d. 1845), by Elizabeth Graham, dau. of David Macdowall Grant, Esq., of Arndilly, co. Banff; b. 1820; s. his uncle as 17th Lord 1853; m. 1849 Charlotte, dau. of Thomas Browne Evans, Esq., of Tuddenham, Norfolk. Educated at the Royal Military Coll., Sandhurst; is a Dep.-Lieut. for co. Inverness; late Lieut.-Col. Royal Aberdeen Militia, and Major 28th Foot.—*Philorth,*

Fraserburgh, N.B.; Ness Castle, Inverness, N.B.; Carlton Club, s.w.; 9, Gr. at Stanhope Street, w.

Heir, his son Alexander William Frederick, b. 1851.

SALTOUN. (See Jones-Saltoun.)

SALUSBURY, the Rev. Sir Charles John, Bart., ‡ of Llanwern, Monmouthshire (cr. 1795).

Eldest surviving son of the late Sir Robert Salusbury, 1st Bart., of L'anwern (who d. 1817), by Catherine, dau. of Charles Vanne, Esq., of Llanwern; b. 1792; s. his brother as 3rd Bart. 1835. Educated at Eton and Trinity Hall, Cambridge (LL.B. 1815); is Rector of Llanwern, a Magistrate for co. Monmouth, and Patron of 3 livings.—*Llanwern Hous:, Caerleon.*

SALUSBURY, the Rev. George Augustus, of Brynbella, Flintshire.

Eldest surviving son of the late Sir John Salusbury Piozzi-Salusbury, of Brynbella, by Harriet Maria, dau. of E. Pemberton, Esq., of Ryton Grove, co. Salop; b. 1822; s. 1858; m. 1852 Fanny, 3rd dau. of Luke T. Crossley, Esq., of Olive Mount, Liverpool, and has issue,

. * Edward Pemberton, b. 1854.

Mr. Salusbury, who was educated at Magdalen Coll., Cambridge (S.C.L. 1849), and appointed Rector of Westbury, Salop, 1852, is Patron of 2 livings. This family, of Italian extraction, assumed the name of Salusbury after Hester, only child and heir of John Salusbury, Esq., of Bach-y-graig, widow, 1st of Henry Thrale, Esq., of Streatham Park, Surrey, and 2ndly of Gabriel Piozzi, Esq.—*Westbury Rectory, Shrewsbury; Brynbella, Flint.*

SALVIN, Francis Henry, Esq., of Sutton, Surrey.

Fifth son of the late William Thomas Salvin, Esq., of Croxdale Hall, co. Durham, by Anna Maria, eldest dau. of John Webbe, Esq., of Sutton Place, who assumed the additional name of Weston; b. 1817; s. his uncle, the late Thomas Mornington Weston, Esq., 1857. Educated at St. Lawrence's Coll., Ampleforth; late a Capt. W. York Rifles.—*Sutton Place, Guildford.*

SALVIN, Gerard John, Esq., of Croxdale, co. Durham.

Eldest son of the late William Thomas Salvin, Esq., of Croxdale, by Anna Maria, 2nd dau. of the late John Webbe Weston Esq., of Sutton Place, Surrey; b. 1801; s. 1842; m. 1834 Winifred, dau. of the late Henry Witham, Esq., of Larrington Hall, co. York, and has, with other issue,

* Henry Thomas Thornton, b. 1838.

Mr. Salvin, who was educated at Stonyhurst Coll., is a J.P. and D.L. for co. Durham, and Lord of the Manor of Croxdale.—*Croxdale Hall, Durham; Stafford Club, w.*

SALVIN, Marmaduke Charles, Esq., of Burn Hall, co. Durham, and Sarnesfield, Herefordshire.

Fourth son of the late William Thomas Salvin, Esq., of Croxdale Hall, co. Durham, by Anna Maria, 2nd dau. of John Webbe Weston. Esq., of Sutton Place, Surrey, and Sarnesfield Court, co. Hereford; b. 1812; m. 1845 Caroline, dau. of Sir Charles Wolseley, Bart., of Wolseley, co. Stafford, and has, with other issue,

* Bryan John, b. 1846.

Mr. Salvin, who was educated at St. Cuthbert's Coll., Ushaw, is a J.P. and D.L. for cos. Durham and Hereford.—*Burn Hall, Durham; Sarnesfield Court, Weob'.*

‡ Died whilst these sheets were at press.

SALWEY, Col. Henry, of Runnymede Park, Surrey.
Third son of the late Theophilus Richard Salwey, Esq., of The Lodge, near Ludlow, co. Salop, by Anna Maria, 2nd dau. and co-heir of Thomas Hill, Esq., of Court of Hill, near Ludlow, Salop; *b.* 1794; *m.* 1828 Eliza Philippa, dau. of John H. Holder, Esq., of Stanton Lacy, near Ludlow, and has, with other issue,
* Herbert Augustus, *b.* 1848.
Col. Salwey, who is a Magistrate for Surrey, and a Col. in the Army retired, was formerly in the Cold-stream Guards; he was M.P. for Ludlow 1837–41 and 1847–52.—*Runnymede Park, Egham; Reform Club, s.w.*

SALWEY, John, Esq., of Moor Park, Shrop-shire.
Only son of the late Richard Salwey, Esq., of Moor Park, by Isabella, 3rd dau. of Job Walker Baugh, Esq., of Ferney Hall, near Ludlow, Salop; *b.* 1798; *s.* 1825; *m.* 1843 Harriet Anne, eldest dau. of Thomas Bourke Ricketts, Esq., of Combe House, co. Hereford, and widow of Edward Salwey, Esq., of The Lodge. Was educated at Eton.—*Moor Park, Ludlow.*

+SALWEY, Mrs., of Elton Hall, Hereford-shire.
Harriet, eldest dau. of the late Thomas B. Ricketts, Esq., of Combe, co. Hereford; *m.* 1st 1838 Edward Salwey, Esq., of The Lodge, co. Salop, and Elton Hall, co. Hereford (who *d.* 1840); 2nd 1843 John Salwey, Esq., of Moor Park (whom see), and by her former marriage has issue, two daughters,
(1) Harriet; (2) Margaret Frances, *m.* 1862 her cousin Alfred Salwey, Esq.
Mrs. Salwey is Lady of the Manor of Elton. This family is a younger branch of the Salweys of Moor Park. —*Elton Hall, Ludlow.*

SAMBORNE, Samborne Stukely Palmer-, Esq., of Timsbury House, Somersetshire.
Eldest son of the late Samborne Stukely Palmer-Samborne, Esq., of Timsbury House, by Lucy Penelope, eldest dau. of the late Rev. Richard Lane, of Coffleet, Devon; *b.* 1827; *s.* 1865; *m.* 1860 Lucy, 2nd dau. of Francis Baring Short, Esq., of Bickham House, Devon, and has, with other issue,
* John Stukely, *b.* 1861.
Mr. Samborne was educated at Rugby and Exeter Coll., Oxford; his father assumed the additional name of Samborne, by Royal licence, in 1843. — *Timsbury House, Bath.*

SAMPSON, Charles Johns, Esq., of Tower House, Carnarvon.
Eldest son of the late Rev. Charles Sampson, Rector of Ripley, Yorkshire, and Llansannan, Denbighshire, by Mary Ann, dau. of Stephen Johns, Esq., of Trewince, Cornwall; *b.* 1796; *s.* 1806; *m.* 1839 Emily Jane, only child of the late Henry Wynn, Esq., of the house of Maesyneuodd, co. Merioneth, Capt. 23rd Foot, and has, with other issue,
* Desmond Henry Wynn, B.A. of Magdalen Coll., Oxford; *b.* 1842.
Mr. Sampson is a J.P. and D.L. for co. Carnarvon, and a Commissioner of Income, Land, and Assessed Taxes. —*Tower House, Carnarvon.*

SAMPSON, Edward, Esq., of Henbury, Gloucestershire.
Only son of the late Edward Sampson, Esq., of Henbury, by Joanna, the youngest dau. of the late George Daubeny, Esq., of Redland, near Bristol; *b.* 1810; *s.* 1848; *m.* 1839 Belinda, 4th dau. of the late Benjamin Way, Esq., of Denham Place, Bucks. Educated

826

at Balliol Coll., Oxford (B.A. 1832, M.A. 1834); is a J.P. and D.L. for co. Gloucester (High Sheriff 1867); was High Sheriff of Bristol 1847.—*Henbury, Bristol.*

+SAMPSON, Thomas, Esq., of Moor Hall, Sussex.
Son of the late — Sampson, Esq., of Moor Hall; *b.* 18—; *m.* 1863 Julia, youngest dau. of Victor de Méric, Esq., of Brook Street, London, and has, with other issue, * a son, *b.* 1865.—*Moor Hall, Ninfield, Battle.*

SAMUEL-GIBBON. (See *Gibbon.*)

SAMUELSON, Bernhard, Esq., of Bodicote Grange, Oxfordshire.
Son of Samuel Hermann Samuelson, Esq., of Petersburg, Virginia, U.S. (who *d.* 1863); *b.* 1820; *m.* 1844 Caroline, 5th dau. of Henry Blundell, Esq., J.P., of Kingston-upon-Hull, and has, with other issue,
* Herman, *b.* 1847; educated at Trinity Coll., Oxford.
Mr. Samuelson, who is an Ironmaster and Manufacturer, was M.P. for Banbury Feb.–April 1859, re-elected 1865. —*Bodicote Grange, Banbury; Reform Club, s.w.*

+SANCTUARY, Thomas, Esq., of Springfield, Sussex.
Son of the late Thomas Sanctuary, Esq.; *b.* 18—; is married, and has, with other issue,
* Thomas, in Holy Orders, M.A. of Exeter Coll., Oxford, Vicar of Powerstock, Dorset, Rector of North Poorton, and Archdeacon of Dorset; *b.* 1822; *m.* 1847 Isabella, 3rd dau. of the late Right Rev. Charles Lloyd, D.D., Lord Bishop of Oxford.
Mr. Sanctuary is a J.P. and D.L. for Sussex.—*Springfield, Horsham.*

SANDARS, George, Esq., late of Chesterford Park, Essex.
Son of the late Samuel Sandars, Esq., of Gainsborough, by Jane, dau. of John Marshall. Esq.; *b.* 1805; *m.* 1st 1829 Mary, dau. of George Neden, Esq., of Ardwick, Manchester; 2nd 1849 Arabella, dau. of John Walker, Esq., of Hyde Park, London, and has issue,
* Samuel, B.A. of Trinity Coll., Cambridge; *b.* 1837; *m.* 1863 Elizabeth Maria, eldest dau. of Francis William Russell, Esq., M.P.
Mr. Sandars, who is a J.P. and D.L. for the W. Riding of Yorkshire, and a Magistrate for Essex, was M.P. for Wakefield 1847–57.—*Carlton and Conservative Clubs, s.w.*; 27, *Sussex Square, w.*

SANDARS, Joseph, Esq.
Eldest son of the late Joseph Sandars. Esq., formerly of Taplow House, Bucks (who *d.* 1860); *b.* 1821; *m.* 1850 Lady Virginia, dau. of Thomas, 2nd Marquis of Headfort, K.P. Educated at Downing Coll., Cambridge; is a Dep.-Lieut. for Bucks; was M.P. for Yarmouth 1848–52.—*Arthur's and Carlton Clubs, s.w.*; 15, *Eaton Square, s.w.*

SANDBACH, the Rev. Gilbert.
Third surviving son of the late Samuel Sandbach, Esq., by Elizabeth, dau. of the Rev. Harry Robertson, D.D., of Kiltearn; *b.* 1817; *m.* 1846 Margaret, dau. of Archibald Maxwell, Esq. Educated at Eton and Brasenose Coll. Oxford (B.A. 1839, M.A. 1842); is a Magistrate for cos. Worcester and Hereford; was Rector of Upper Sapey 1846–59.

SANDBACH, Henry Robertson, Esq., of Hafodunos, Denbighshire.
Eldest surviving son of the late Samuel Sandbach, Esq., of Woodlands, by Elizabeth, dau. of the Rev. Harry Robertson, of Kiltearn, co. Ross; *b.* 1807; *s.* 1851; *m.* 1st 1832 Miss Margaret Roscoe (she *d.* 1852); 2nd 1855 Charlotte Elizabeth, dau. of Martin Williams,

Esq., of Bryngwyn, co. Montgomery, and has, with other issue,

* Samuel, b. 1856.

Mr. Sandbach, who was educated at Glasgow University, is a J.P. for co. Denbigh (High Sheriff 1855). —*Hafod:mos, Llanrwst; Athenæum Club*, s.w.

+ SANDBACH, WILLIAM ROBERTSON, Esq.
Second son of the late Samuel Sandbach, Esq., of Woodlands, co. Lancaster, by Elizabeth, dau. of the Rev. Henry Robertson, of Kiltearn, co. Ross; b. 180—; m. 18— Sara, Baroness Van Capellan. Is a J.P. and D.L. for co. Lancaster.—10, *Prince's Gate*, s.w.

SANDEMAN, DAVID GEORGE, Esq., of Kirkwood, Dumfriesshire.
Only son of the late David Sandeman, Esq., of Kirkwood, by Julia, dau. of Andrew Robertson, Esq., of Foveran, co. Aberdeen; b. 1844; s. 1852; m. 1866 Alice, 4th dau. of Col. Cockburn, of Bracondale, Norfolk. Educated at Rugby; is Patron of 1 living; late Cornet 16th Lancers.—*Kirkwood, Lockerbie, N.B.*

Heir Pres., his uncle Thomas Fraser, a Magistrate for co. Dumfries, and late t'ant. 73rd Regt.; b. 1807; m. 1844 Amelia, dau. of the late William Crawshay, Esq., of Caversham Park, Oxon, and has issue.

SANDERS, BENJAMIN LAWRENCE, Esq., of Street Court, Herefordshire.
Only surviving child of James Sanders, Esq., of Street Court, co. Hereford, by Charlotte, dau. of John Lawrence, Esq., of Whitford; b. 1830; m. 1860 Annie Sarah, only dau. of Francis Watt, Esq., of The Forelands, Bromsgrove, and Ottringham Grange, Holderness, co. York, and has, with other issue,

* Benjamin Watt, b. 1862.

Mr. Sanders, who was educated at Bromsgrove and Trinity Hall, Cambridge (S.C.L. 1853, LL.B. 1855), is a J.P. and D.L. for co. Worcester and Hereford. —*Street Court, Kingsland, Leominster.*

SANDERS, EDWARD ANDREW, Esq., of Stoke, Devon.
Eldest son of the late Edward Lloyd Sanders, Esq., of Stoke, by Isabella, dau. of the late Ven. John Andrew, Archdeacon of Barnstaple; b. 1813; s. 1839; m. 1848 Marianne, dau. of the Rev. James Ford, M.A., Prebendary of Exeter, and has, with other issue,

* Edward James, b. 1852.

Mr. Sanders, who was educated at Harrow and Wadham Coll., Oxford, is a Magistrate for Devon, a Banker at Exeter (of which city he has also been Mayor), and Capt. 1st Devon Yeomanry Cavalry.—*Stoke House, Exeter; Oxford and Cambridge Club*, s.w.

SANDERS, JOHN HARRY, Esq., of Cheshunt, Hertfordshire.
Third son of the late Thomas Sanders, Esq.; b. 1784; m. 1823 Susanna, 2nd dau. of John Jefferson, Esq., of Cheshunt, Herts. Mr. Sanders, who entered the Navy in 1799, is a Magistrate for Herts (High Sheriff 1835), and a Capt. R.N. retired.—*Waterlane House, Cheshunt.*

SANDERS, THOMAS, Esq., of Sanders Park, co. Cork.
Third but eldest surviving son of the late William Sanders, Esq., of Sanders Park (who d. 1820), by Eliza, dau. of Thomas Andrews, Esq., of Dublin; b. 1816; s. his brother 1860; m. 1861 Mary Charlotte, dau. of Richard Duckworth Dunn, Esq., of Surbiton, Surrey, and has, with other issue,

* Robert Massy Dawson, b. 1862.

Mr. Sanders, who was educated at Trinity Coll., Dublin (B.A. 1839, LL.D. 1845), and called to the Irish Bar 1842, is a Magistrate for cos. Cork and Limerick. —*Sanders Park, Charleville, co. Cork.*

SANDERS-BRADFIELD. (See *Bradfield.*)

SANDERSON, RICHARD BURDON BURDON-, Esq., of West Jesmond, Northumberland.
Son of the late Richard Burdon-Sanderson, Esq., J.P. and D.L. of West Jesmond, by Elizabeth, only dau. and heir of the late Sir James Sanderson, Bart., of West Jesmond (whose name he assumed); b. 1821; s. 1855; m. 1848 Isabella Mitchelson, dau. of the late James Alexander Haldane, Esq., of Edinburgh, is a Magistrate for Northumberland.—*West Jesmond, Newcastle-on-Tyne.*

SANDES, CHARLES, Esq., of Carrigafoyle, co. Kerry.
Eldest son of the late Charles Launcelot Sandes, Esq., of Indiaville, Queen's Co., by Mary, only sister of the late Sir Charles H. Coote, Bart., of Ballyfin; b. 1815; s. 1855; m. 1st 1842 Isabella Georgina, dau. of Ralph Carr, Esq., of Cocken Hall, co. Durham; 2nd 1856 Mildred, only child of the late Wm. Brown, Esq., of Springmount, co. Limerick, and has, with other issue,

* Launcelot Charles, b. 1846.

Mr. Sandes is a Magistrate for co. Kerry, and late Lieut. 89th Foot.—*Carrigafoyle Castle, Ballylongford, co. Kerry; Bayview, Clontarf, co. Dublin.*

SANDES, MAURICE FITZGERALD, Esq., of Oak Park, co. Kerry.
Sixth son of the late Thomas William Sandes, Esq., of Sallow Glen, co. Kerry, by Margaret, dau. of Francis Chute, Esq., of Chute Hall, in the same county; b. 1807; m. 1857 Ellen Louisa, dau. of Thomas Stratford Dennis, Esq., of Fortgranite, co. Wicklow. Educated at Trinity Coll., Dublin (B.A. 1829); called to the Irish Bar 1831; appointed Registrar of the Supreme Court of Calcutta 1848, and Administrator-General of Bengal 1850; is a Magistrate for co. Kerry. —*Oak Park, Tralee; University Club, Dublin.*

SANDES, WILLIAM, Esq., of Sallow Glen, co. Kerry.
Eldest son of the late Thomas William Sandes, Esq., of Sallow Glen, by Margaret, dau. of Francis Chute, Esq., of Chute Hall, co. Kerry; b. 1799; s. 1835; m. 1836 Rupertia, only dau. of the late Charles Higgs, Esq., of Charlton Kings, co. Gloucester. Educated at Trinity Coll., Dublin (B.A. 1825); was High Sheriff of co. Kerry 1828.—*Sallow Glen, Tarbert, co. Kerry; Charlton Kings, Cheltenham.*

Heir Pres., his brother Thomas, a J.P. and D.L. for co. Kerry; b. 180.; m. 1839 Elizabeth, dau. of Francis Bernard Chute, Esq., of Bahttany, co. Kerry.

SANDES, WILLIAM GOUGH, Esq., of Greenville, co. Kerry.
Youngest son of the late George Sandes. Esq., of Greenville, by Elizabeth, dau. of Fitzmaurice O'Connor. Esq., Major 16th Regt.; b. 1802; s. 1829; m. 1832 Margaret Elliott, 4th dau. of Francis William Bowyer, Esq. Is a Magistrate for co. Kerry.—*Greenville, Listowel, co. Kerry.*

SANDFORD, Sir FRANCIS RICHARD, LL.D. (cr. 1863).
Eldest son of the late Sir Daniel K. Sandford, D.C.L., M.P., sometime Professor of Greek in the University of Glasgow (who d. 1838), by Henrietta Cecilia, only dau. of John Charnock. Esq.; b. 1824; m. 1849 Margaret, dau. of Robert Findlay, Esq., of Boturich Castle, co. Dumbarton. Educated at Glasgow University (of which he is LL.D.) and at Balliol Coll., Oxford (B.A. 1846, M.A. 1858), where he was 1st Class in Classics; is Assistant-Secretary to the Committee of Privy Council on Education; was Secretary of the Great International Exhibition 1862.—5, *Gloucester Terrace*, w.

SANDFORD, Lady.

Henrietta Cecilia, only dau. of the late Robert Charnock, Esq.; *m.* 1823 Sir Daniel Keyte Sandford, M.P., who *d.* 1838.—*Wyndham, Isle of Bute, N.B.*

SANDFORD, George Montagu Warren, Esq., of Moulton Park, Northamptonshire.

Eldest son of the late George Peacocke, Esq., of Moulton Park, by Mary, dau. of Col. Durnford, and nephew and heir of the late General Sir M. W. Peacocke, of Reeves Hall, Essex; *b.* 1821 ; *m.* 1858 Augusta Mary, youngest dau. of Algernon Greville, Esq., and has issue. Educated at Eton and Magdalen Coll. Cambridge (B.A. 1845, M.A. 1817); called to the Bar at the Inner Temple 1846, but does not practise; is a J.P. and D.L. for Essex, and a Magistrate for Hants; assumed the name of Sandford in lieu of Peacocke, by Royal licence, 1866 ; was M.P. for Harwich 1852–3, for Maldon 1854–7, re-chosen 1859.—*Moulton-Park, Northampton; Reeves Hall, Mersea Island, Essex; Carlton Club,* s.w.; 33, *Hertford Street,* w.

SANDFORD, Humphrey, Esq., of The Isle, Shropshire.

Eldest son of the late Rev. Humphrey Sandford, of The Isle, by Frances, only child and heir of the Rev. George Holland, Rector of Hanwood, co. Salop; *b.* 1811 ; *s.* 1856 ; *m.* 1852 Anne Taylor, 5th dau. of Joseph Armitage, Esq., and has, with other issue,

   * Humphrey, *b.* 1856.

Mr. Sandford, who was educated at Shrewsbury and St. John's Coll., Cambridge (B.A. 1834, M.A. 1837), and called to the Bar at the Middle Temple 1827, is a Magistrate for co. Salop, and Patron of the livings of Eaton-under-Heywood, and of Edgton, co. Salop. This family is descended from Nicholas Sandford, of Calverhall, 3rd son of Nicholas, Lord of Sandford, Sheriff of Shropshire in 1386.—*The Isle, Shrewsbury.*

SANDFORD, Thomas George Wills-, Esq., of Wills Grove, and Castlerea, co. Roscommon.

Eldest son of the late William Robert Wills, Esq., of Wills Grove and Castlerea, by Mary Grey, elder dau. and co.-heir of the late Rev. William Sandford, brother of the last Lord Mount Sandford, whose name he assumed; *b.* 1817 ; *s.* his father 1859 ; *m.* 1842 Theodosia Eleanor, only dau. of Robert H. Blagden Hale, Esq., of Alderly Park, co. Gloucester, and by her, who *d.* 1857, has, with other issue,

   * William Robert, *b.* 1844.

Mr. Wills-Sandford, who was educated at Harrow and Ch. Ch., Oxford, is a J.P. and D.L. for co. Roscommon (High Sheriff 1843).—*Castlerea House, co. Roscommon; Kildare Street Club, Dublin; Carlton Club,* s.w.

SANDFORD, Thomas Hugh, Esq., of Sandford, Shropshire.

Eldest son of the late Thomas Hugh Sandford, Esq., of Sandford, by Lilias Ann, dau. of Thomas Kirkpatrick, Esq., of Whitchurch; *b.* 1820 ; *s.* 1826 ; *m.* 1st 1819 Alexina, dau. of the Hon. Charles Lindsay (she *d.* 1851); 2nd 1856 Sarah, dau. of William Halsted Poole, Esq., of Terrick Hall, co. Salop. Educated at Trinity Coll., Cambridge; is a J.P. and D.L. for co. Salop (High Sheriff 1866), a Magistrate for co. Chester, Lord of the Manor of Sandford, and Capt. in the North Salopian Yeomanry. This family is of great antiquity in co. Salop, 'Sandford Manor being one of those very few Shropshire estates which can be said to be held by the lineal male descendant of its earl est known Feoffee.' (See Eyton's ' Antiquities.')—*Sandford Hall, Prees, Shropshire; University Club,* s.w.
828

SANDHAM, Major Charles Freeman, of Rowdell House, Sussex.

Son of the late Wm. Sandham, Esq., of Midhurst, Sussex; *b.* 1782 ; *m.* 1812 Mar a, only dau. of Geo. Munro, Esq., of Charlton, Kent, and has, with other issue,

   * George, Col. R.A. ; *b.* 1813.

Major Sandham is J.P. and D.L. for Sussex, and a Major in the Artillery, retired.—*Rowdell House, Steyning ; United Service Club,* s.w.

SANDILANDS. (See under *Torphichen, Lord.*)

SANDON. (See under *Harrowby, Earl of.*)

SANDWICH, Earl of (John William Montagu, P.C.).—Cr. 1660.

Only son of George John. 6th Earl, by Lady Louisa Mary Ann, dau. of Armar. 1st Earl of Belmore ; *b.* 1811 ; *s.* 1818 ; *m.* 1st 1838 Lady Mary, dau. of Henry William, 1st Marquis of Anglesey, K.G. (she *d.* 1859); 2nd 1856 Lady Blanche, youngest dau. of Francis, 1st Earl of Ellesmere. Educated at Trinity Coll., Cambridge; is High Steward of Huntingdon, Lord-Lieut. of Hunts, Patron of 2 livings, and Col. Hunts Militia ; has been Capt. of the Gentlemen-at-Arms ; was Master of the Buckhounds 1858–9.—*Hinchinbrook House, Huntingdon ; Carlton and Travellers' Clubs,* s.w.; 46, *Grosvenor Square,* w.

   Heir, his son Edward George Henry, Viscount Hinchingbrook; educated at Eton ; a Magistrate for Hunts, and Lieut. and Capt. Grenadier Guards ; *b.* 1839.

SANDYS, Lord (Augustus Frederick Arthur Sandys).—Cr. 1802.

Eldest son of Arthur Marcus, 3rd Lord, by Louisa, youngest dau. of Joseph Blake, Esq., of London ; *b.* 1840 ; *s.* 1863. Is Lord of the Manor and Patron of Ombersley, and Lieut. 2nd Life Guards. This family is a younger branch of that of the Marquis of Downshire.—*Ombersley Court, Droitwich ;* 2, *Chesham Place,* s.w.

   Heir Pres., his brother Marcus Windsor George, *b.* 1849.

SANDYS, Lady Windsor-.

Mary Anne, eldest dau. of William Stephens Mereweather, Esq., of Grovefield, co. Gloucester ; *m.* 1835 the Rev. Sir Edwin Windsor-Sandys, who *d.* 1838.

SANDYS, Henry, Esq., of Dargle, co. Wicklow.

Only son of the late Robert Sandys, Esq., of Dargle. by Helena, dau. of Thomas Jervis White, Esq., of Dublin; *b.* 1828 ; *s.* 1848; *m.* 1861 Emily Alice, youngest dau. of Henry Darley, Esq., of Wingfield, co. Wicklow, and has issue,

   * Henry Jervis, *b.* 1863.

Mr. Sandys is a Magistrate for co. Wicklow.—*Dargle, Enniskerry, co. Wicklow.*

SANDYS, John Dalrymple, Esq., of Graythwaite Hall, Lancashire.

Second but eldest surviving son of the late Myles Sandys, Esq., of Graythwaite (who *d.* 1839), by Elizabeth, sister of North, 9th Earl of Stair; *s.* 1755 ; his brother 1855. Educated at Winchester ; is a Magistrate for co. Lancaster.—*Graythwaite Hall, Newton-in-Cartmel ;* 33, *Lansdowne Place, Leamington.*

   Heir, his nephew Thomas Myles, of the Bengal Military Service (son of the late Thomas Sandys, Esq., by Frances, dau. of Capt. Sanders, R.N., who *d.* 1856) ; *b.* 1837.

SANDYS-LUMSDAINE, the Rev. Edwin, of Lumsdaine, and Blanerne, Berwickshire, and Innergellie, Fifeshire.

Eldest son of the late Edwin H. Sandys, Esq., of Kingstone, Kent, by Helen, dau. of Edward Lord Chick, Esq.; *b.* 1785 ; *m.* 1816 Mary Lillias, dau. of the late William Lumsdaine, Esq. (who on her brother's death

s. to the family estates in Scotland), and by her, who *d.* 1864, has, with other issue,

* Francis Gordon, *b.* 1828 ; in Holy Orders. M. A. and late Student of Ch. Ch., Ox'ord ; *m.* 1857 Mary Alice. dau. of the late John Oattley E q., of Shabden Park, Surrey, and has, with other issue. * a son. *b.* 1864.

Mr. San.lys-Lumsdaine, who was educated at St. John's Coll., Oxford (B.A. 1807, M.A. 1808), is a Magistrate for cos. Berwick and Fife, and Rector of Upper Hardres-cum-Stelling, Kent.— *Upper Hardres Rectory, Canterbury ; Innergellic, Anstruther, F.feshire.*

SANFORD, EDWARD AYSHFORD, Esq., of Nynehead Court, Somerset.

Only son of the late William Ayshford Sanford, Esq., J.P., of Nynehead Court, by Mary, dau. of the Rev. E. Marshall ; *b.* 1794 ; *m.* 1st 1817 Henrietta, only surviving dau. of the late Sir William Langham, Bart. (she *d.* 1836) ; 2nd 1843 Lady Caroline Anna, dau. of Charles, 3rd Earl of Harrington (she *d.* 1853), and has, by the former, with other issue,

* William Ayshford, a J.P. and D.L. for Wilts. a Magi-trate for Devon a d Somerset and Capt. 13th ho merset Rifle Volunteers ; *b.* 1818 ; *m.* 1857 Sarah Ellen. dau. of Henry Seymour, Esq., Knoyle House. Wilts., and by her, who. *d.* 1867. has issue a son and four daughters.

Mr. Sanford, who was educated at Eton and Brasenose Coll., Oxford, is a J.P. and D.L. for Somerset (High Sheriff 1848), and a Magistrate for Devon and Middlesex ; was M.P. for Somerset 1830–2, and for W. Somerset 1833–41.— *Nynehead Court, Wellington ; Brooks's and Boodle's Clubs, s.w.*

SANFORD, HENRY AYSHFORD, Esq., of Waltham House, Essex.

Third son of Edward Ayshford Sanford, Esq., of Nynehead Court, Somerset, by his 1st wife Henrietta, only surviving dau. of the late Sir William Langham, Bart. ; *b.* 1822 ; *m.* 1859 Emily Catharine Anne, eldest dau. of the late Lord Granville, C. H. Somerset. Is a Magistrate for Somerset, and Major Royal Bucks Militia. — *Waltham House, Waltham Abbey.*

+SANKEY, Capt. JACOB HIRAM, R.N., of Coolmore, co. Tipperary.

Only surviving son of the late Matthew Villiers Sankey, Esq., of Coolmore, by Mary, dau. of — Elrington Esq.; *b.* 18 — ; *m.* 1844 M-lita Anne, only dau. of the late Capt. G. W. Hamilton, R.N. Is a Magistrate for co. Tipperary and a Commander R.N.— *Coolmore, Fethard.*

SANKEY, MATTHEW HENRY, Esq., of Lurganbrae, co. Fermanagh.

Second son of the late Matthew Sankey, Esq., of Clydaville, co. Cork, by Eleanor, dau. of the late Col. O'Hara of O'Harabrook, co. Antrim ; *b.* 1823 ; *m.* 1st 1850 Mary Charlotte, only dau. of the late Rev. William L. Roper (she *d.* 1851) ; 2nd 1853 Mehetabel, youngest dau. of the late John Roe, Esq., of Rockwell, co. Tipperary, and has issue,

* William Roper, *b.* 1851.

Mr. Sankey, who was educated at Trinity Coll., Dublin (B.A. 1815), is a Magistrate for co. Fermanagh.— *Lurganbrae, Brookborough, co. Fermanagh.*

SARGEAUNT, JAMES PRIMATT, Esq., of Tewkesbury Park, Gloucestershire.

Third son of the late Rev. John Sargeaunt, Rector of Stanwick, co. Northampton, by Sarah, dau. of R. Steed, Esq.; *b.* 1831 ; *m.* 1856 Fanny, dau. and heir of the Rev. Joseph Shapland, of Tewkesbury Park, and by her who *d.* 1868, has with other issue,

* James Shapland, *b.* 1858.

Mr. Sargeaunt, who was educated at the Charterhouse and Jesus Coll. Cambridge (B A 1853, M.A 1856), is a Magistrate for co. Gloucester, and Lieut. Commanding

1st Subdivision Gloucestershire Rifle Volunteers ; was formerly Inspector of Army Schools.— *Tewkesbury Park, Gloucestershire.*

SARGENT, Sir CHARLES, Knt. (cr. 1860).

Younger son of the late Wm. Sargent, Esq., by Sophia, dau. of the late George Arnold, Esq., of Halsted Place, Kent, and grandson of the late John Sargent, Esq., M.P., of Wool Lavington, Sussex ; *b.* 1821. Educated at King's Coll., London, and London University, and at Trinity Coll., Cambridge (B.A. 1843, M.A. 1846) ; called to the Bar at Lincoln's Inn 1848, and practised as an Equity Draftsman and Conveyancer ; is Judge of the High Court of Bombay ; late Chief Justice of the Ionian Islands.— *Bombay.*

SARSFIELD, DOMINICK RONAYN PATRICE, Esq., of Doughcloyne, co. Cork.

Only son of the late Thomas Ronayn Sarsfield, Esq., J.P. and D.L., of Doughcloyne (who was High Sheriff of co. Cork 1849), by Angelina, dau. of the Rev. William Stopford, Rector of Garrycloyne ; *b.* 1828 ; *s.* 1855 ; *m.* 1858 Mary Anne Elizabeth Helena, dau. of James De La Cour, Esq., of Mallow, co. Cork, and has, with other issue,

* Thomas Ronayn, *b.* 1862.

Mr. Sarsfield, who was educated at Trinity Coll., Dublin (B.A. 1851). is a Magistrate for co. Cork and Lord of the Manor of Doughcloyne ; late Capt. N. Cork Rifles. This family is descended from Thomas de Sarsfield, who was Chief Standard-Bearer to Henry II. on his landing in Ireland in 1172.— *Doughcloyne, Cork.*

SARTORIS, EDWARD JOHN, Esq., of Warnford, Hants.

Eldest son of the late Urban Sartoris, Esq., of Sceaux Park, near Paris (who *d.* 1832), by Matilda. dau. of the late Edward Rose Tunno, Esq., of Warnford Park ; *b.* 1817 ; *s.* his uncle 1863 ; *m.* 1842 Adelaide, elder dau. of the late Charles Kemble, Esq., and has, with other issue,

* Greville Edward, educated at Eton ; late Cornet 11th Hussars ; *b.* 1843.

Mr. Sartoris. who was educated at Trinity Coll., Cambridge, is a Magistrate for Hants. Lord of the Manor of Warnford, and Patron of 1 living.— *Warnford Park, Bp's. Waltham ; Brooks's Club, s.w. ; 9, Park Place., s.w.*

SARTORIS, FREDERICK URBAN, Esq., of Rushden Hall, Northamptonshire.

Second son of the late Urban Sartoris, Esq. of Sceaux Park, near Paris (who *d.* 1832) by Matilda, dau. of the late Edward Rose Tunno, Esq., of Warnford Park, Hants ; *b.* 1819 ; *m.* 1843 Mary, dau. of the Rev. Joseph Pratt. Rector of Faston, near Peterborough, and has, with other issue,

* Frederick Maitland, educated at Eton ; Attaché in the Diplomatic Service ; *b.* 1841.

Mr. Sartoris. who was educated at Paris and Trinity Coll., Cambridge. is a Magistrate for co. Northampton (High Sheriff 1856).— *Rushden Hall, Higham Ferrers ; Arthur's Club, s.w. ; 11 Green S uare, Westminster, s w*

SARTORIS, Mrs., of Linden Castle, co. Dublin.

Georgina, dau. of the late A. Lyster, Esq., of Stillorgan, co. Dublin ; *m.* 1851 Julius Alexander Sartoris, Esq., formerly Capt. 16th Lancers, who *d.* 1863, leaving issue,

* Three daughters.

Mrs. Sartoris is Lady of the Manor of Linden.— *Linden Castle, The Grove, Stillorgan, co. Dubl n.*

SARTORIUS, Sir GEORGE ROSE, K.C.B., of Henley House, Sussex (cr. 1841).

Eldest son of the late Col. Sartorius, formerly of the H.E.I.C.'s Service, by Anna, dau. of George Rose,

Esq.; *b.* 1790 ; *m.* 1839 Sophia, dau. of John Lamb, Esq., and has issue, late Naval A.D.C. to her Majesty, and formerly Chief in Command on the Irish station; has served on the Portuguese and North American coasts, and was present at Trafalgar; is Vice-Admiral of Portugal, Count of Penhafirme, Grand Cross of St. Bento d'Aviz, and K.T.S. in Portugal.—*Henley House, Frant, Tunbridge Wells ; United Service Club,* s.w.

SASSOON, JOSEPH, Esq., of Ashley Park, Surrey.
Eldest son of the late Sassoon David Sassoon, Esq., of Ashley Park, by Flora, dau. of S. R. Sassoon, Esq., of Bagdad; *b.* 1856 ; *s.* 1867. This family were formerly merchants in India.—*Ashley Park, Walton-on-Thames;* 17, *Cumberland Terrace,* N.W.
Heir Pres, his brother Alfred, *b.* 1859.

SAUMAREZ. (See under *De Saumarez, Lord.*)

+ SAUNDERS, the late FRANCIS DAVID, Esq., of Tymawr, Cardiganshire.
Son of the late — Saunders. Esq.; *b.* 1788; *d.* 1867. Was a J.P. and D.L. for co. Cardigan.—*Tynawr, Lampeter.*

SAUNDERS, ROBERT FRANCIS, Esq., of Saunders Grove, co. Wicklow.
Eldest son of the late Morley Saunders, Esq., of Saunders Grove, by Ellen Katherine dau. and heir of James Glascock, Esq., of Music Hall, co. Dublin; *b.* 1794; *s.* 1825 ; *m.* 1840 Elizabeth Martha, 3rd dau. of Lieut.-Col. Joseph Pratt, of Cabra Castle, co. Cavan, and has, with other issue,
* Robert Joseph Pratt, Lieut. R.A. ; *b.* 1841.
Mr. Saunders, who was educated at Trinity Coll., Dublin, is a J.P. and D.L. for co. Wicklow (High Sheriff 1822), and a Magistrate for co. Kildare ; was formerly Lieut. 68th Foot.—*Saunders Grove, Stratford-on-Slaney, co. Wicklow ; Loretto, Cheltenham.*

SAUNDERS, THOMAS BUSH, Esq., of Bradford Priory, Wilts.
Eldest son of the late Thomas Hosier Saunders, Esq., by Harriet, dau. of the late Thomas Bush, Esq., of Bradford, Wilts ; *b.* 1808; *m.* 1849 Maria Albers, only dau. of the late Frederick Hoffham Pedder, Esq., of Brompton, Middlesex, and has, with other issue,
* Frederick Thomas, *b.* 1853.
Mr. Saunders, who was educated at Warminster and Wadham Coll., Oxford (B.A. 1828, M.A. 1831), and called to the Bar at Lincoln's Inn 1831, is a Magistrate for Wilts.—*The Priory, Bradford-on-Avon ; Oxford and Cambridge Club,* s.w.

SAUNDERS, WILLIAM ALLEN FRANCIS, Esq., of Wennington Hall, Lancashire.
Only son of the late Richard Saunders, Esq., of Wennington Hall, by Anna Maria, dau. of the late John Leaper Newton, Esq., of Mickleover Hall, co. Derby ; *b.* 1818 ; *s.* 1851 ; *m.* 1841 Dorothy dau. of the late Josias Morley, Esq., of Marrick Park, co. York, and has, with other issue,
* Charles Morley, *b.* 1851.
Mr. Saunders, who was educated at Rugby and Trinity Coll , Oxford, is a J.P. and D.L. for co. Lancaster (High Sheriff 1862), and a Magistrate for Westmoreland and the W. Riding of Yorkshire.—*Wennington Hall, Lancaster.*

SAUNDERSON, LLEWELLYN TRAHERNE BASSETT, Esq., of Dromkeen House, co. Cavan.
Youngest son of the late Alexander Saunderson. Esq., of Castle Saunderson, co. Cavan (who *d.* 1857), by the

Hon. Sarah Juliana, eldest dau. of Henry, 6th Lord Farnham ; *b.* 1841 ; *s.* 1857 ; *m.* 1866 Lady Rachel Mary Scott, 3rd dau. of John Henry, 3rd Earl of Clonmell, and has issue,
* A dau., *b.* 1867.
Mr. Saunderson, who is a Magistrate for co. Cavan, Lord of the manor of Dromkeen, and Capt. Dublin Militia, was formerly in the 11th Hussars.—*Dromkeen House, Cavan, Ireland ; St. James's Club,* s.w.

SAUNDERSON, SOMERSET BASSET, Esq., of Castle Saunderson, co. Cavan.
Eldest surviving son of the late Col. Alexander Saunderson, J.P. and D.L., of Castle Saunderson (High Sheriff 1818, and some time M.P. for co. Cavan, who *d.* 1857), by the Hon. Sarah Juliana, eldest dau. of Henry, 6th Lord Farnham ; *b.* 1834 ; *s.* his brother 1860; *m.* 1864 Emily Mary, dau. of the late Edward Henry Cole, Esq., of Stoke Lyne, Oxon. Was formerly Lieut. 11th Hussars.— *Castle Saunderson, Belturbet.*
Heir Pres., his brother Edward James, a Magistrate and M.P.for co. Cavan (High Sheriff 1859) ; *b.* 1837 ; *m.* 1865 the Hon. Helena Emily, youngest dau. of Thomas, 3rd Lord Ventry, and has, with other issue, * a son, *b.* 1867.

SAURIN, MARK ANTHONY, Esq., of Orielton and Kilwendeg, Pembrokeshire.
Youngest son of the late Right Rev. James Saurin, Bishop of Dromore, by Elizabeth, dau. of Wm. Lyster, Esq. ; *b.* 1815 ; *m.* 1844 Margaretta Sutton, dau. of the Rev. John Jones, and niece of Morgan Jones, Esq., of Kilwendeg, and has, with other issue,
* Morgan James, Cornet 6th Dragoon Guards ; *b.* 1845.
Mr. Saurin, who was educated at Trinity Coll., Dublin, is a Magistrate for co. Pembroke (High Sheriff 1867), and Lord of the Manor of Orielton.—*Orielton, Pembroke ; Kilwendeg, Newcastle-Emlyn ; Union Club,* s.w.

SAVAGE, JOHN, Esq.,‡ of West Malling, Kent.
Eldest son of the late Benjamin Savage, Esq., by Elizabeth, dau. of the late James Dunn, Esq.; *b.* 1798 ; *m.* 1st 182- Elizabeth Miller, dau. of the late Thomas Patrickson, Esq. (she *d.* 1836) ; 2nd 1842 Sarah Charlotte, dau. of the late Baldwin Duppa Duppa, Esq., of Hollingbourne, Kent, and has issue,
* Two daughters.
Mr. Savage, who was educated at Emmanuel Coll., Cambridge (B.A. 1820, M.A. 1842), and called to the Bar at the Middle Temple 1821, is a J.P. and D.L. for Kent (High Sheriff 1857) ; he was formerly a Judge in India.—*St. Leonard's, West Malling, Maidstone ; University Club,* s.w.

SAVAGE, JOHN, Esq., of Tetbury, Gloucestershire.
Eldest son of the late Rev. John Savage, by Charlotte, dau. of Walter Wiltshire, Esq., of Shockerwick, Bathford, Somerset ; *b.* 1785 ; *s.* 1803 ; *m.* 1811 Rachel, dau. of the late Robert Claxton, Esq., of Bristol, and has issue,
* Francis, *b.* 1814; *m.* 1860 Caroline Bass, widow of W. J. Sharpe, Esq., of Aylesbury.
Mr. Savage is a Magistrate for co. Gloucester.—*Gorse-nour House, Bath , Tetbury, Gloucestershire.*

SAVAGE, the Rev. WILLIAM, M.A., of Tarrant Hinton, Dorset.
Second surviving son of John Savage, Esq., of Tetbury (whom see), by Rachel, dau. of Robert Claxton. Esq., of Bristol ; *b.* 1820 ; *m.* 1850 Anne Hunt, youngest dau. of the late Rev. Charles Holdsworth, of Stokenham, Devon. Educated at Queen's Coll., Oxford (B.A. 1842, M.A. 1845); is Curate of Tarrant Hinton; late Curate of Bishop's Canning.—*Tarrant Hinton, Blandford.*

‡ Died whilst these sheets were at press.

+ SAVERY, ALMERICUS BLAKENEY, Esq., late of Hardwick Lodge, Monmouthshire.
Eldest son of the late John Savery, Esq., of Butcombe Court, Somerset ; b. 18— ; is a Magistrate for co. Monmouth, late Capt. in the Monmouthshire Militia.

SAVILE, the Hon. and Rev. ARTHUR.
Sixth son of John, 3rd Earl of Mexborough, by Lady Anne, eldest dau. of Philip, 3rd Earl of Hardwicke; b. 1819 ; m. 1852 the Hon. Lucy Georgina, youngest dau. of Richard, 3rd Lord Braybrooke, and has, with other issue,
　　* Arthur Cornwallis, b. 1865.
Mr. Savile was educated at Eton and Trinity Coll., Cambridge (M.A. 1841) ; appointed Vicar of Ashby Magna, co. Leicester, 1847, Rector of Foulmire 1850, Rural Dean of the Deanery of Barton, co. Cambridge, 1867.—Foulmire Rectory, Royston.

SAVILE, the Hon. and Rev. PHILIP YORKE.
Third son of John, 3rd Earl of Mexborough, by Lady Anne, eldest dau. of Philip, 3rd Earl of Hardwicke ; b. 1814 ; m. 1842 Emily Mary, dau. of William Hale, Esq., of King's Walden, and has, with other issue,
　　* George, b. 1847.
Mr. Savile was educated at Eton and Trinity Coll., Cambridge (M.A. 1839), and appointed Rector of Methley 1841.—Methley Rectory, Leeds.

SAVILE, ALBANY BOURCHIER, Esq., late of Oaklands, Devon.
Eldest son of the late Albany Savile, Esq., of Oaklands, Devon, by Eleanora Elizabeth, dau. of the late Sir Bourchier Wrey, Bart. ; b. 1816 ; s. 1831 ; m. 1848 Elizabeth Anna, dau. of Sir Lawrence V. Palk, Bart. Educated at Eton ; is a Magistrate for Devon; formerly Cornet 7th Hussars.—Address : Down House, Redland, Bristol ; Arthur's and Junior United Service Clubs, s.w.

+ SAVILE, Capt. HENRY, of Rufford, Notts.
Natural son of John, 8th Earl of Scarborough ; b. 1810; s. 1856. Educated at Eton ; is a Dep.-Lieut. for Notts (High Sheriff 1861) ; was formerly Capt. Grenadier Guards.—Rufford Abbey, Ollerton ; Army and Navy Club, s.w.

SAVILE. (See under Mexborough, Earl of.)

SAVILL-ONLEY, ONLEY, Esq., of Stisted Hall, Essex.
Only son of the late Charles Harvey, Esq. (who assumed the names of Savill-Onley), by Sarah, dau. of John Haynes, Esq., of Twickenham : b. 1795; s. 1843; m. 1st 1818 his cousin Caroline Mary, dau. of John Harvey, Esq. ; 2nd 1851 Jane, eldest dau. of William Fox, Esq., of Chester Terrace, Regent's Park, and has by the former, with other issue,
　　* Charles, b. 1827.
Mr. Savill-Onley, who was educated at the Charterhouse and at Pembroke Coll. Cambridge (B.A. 1817), and called to the Bar at the Middle Temple 1821, is a J.P. and D.L. for Essex (High Sheriff 1849), and a Magistrate for Norfolk ; descended from a common ancestor with the Harveys of Bracoudale.—Stisted Hall, Braintree ; Carlton and University Clubs, s.w.

SAWBRIDGE, Mrs., of East Haddon, Northamptonshire.
Grace Julia, youngest dau. of Thomas Charles Bigge, Esq., of Benton House, Northumberland (who was High Sheriff of that county in 1771), by Jemima, dau. of William Ord, Esq., of Fenham, in the same county; m. 1st 1817 Thomas Christopher Glyn, Esq. who d. 1827; 2nd 1836 Henry Barne Sawbridge, Esq., of East Haddon, J.P. and D.L. for co. Northampton, Lord of the Manor and Patron of East Haddon, who d. s. p. 1851.—East Haddon House, Northampton.

SAWBRIDGE-ERLE-DRAX. (See Drax.)

SAWLE, Sir CHARLES BRUNE GRAVES., Bart., of Penrice, Cornwall (cr. 1836).
Only son of the late Sir Joseph Sawle Graves-Sawle, Bart., of Penrice, by his 1st wife Dorothea, dau. of the Rev. Charles Prideaux Brune, Esq., of Prideaux Place, Cornwall ; b. 1816 ; s. as 2nd Bart. 1865 ; m. 1846 Rose Caroline, dau. of the late David Rose Paynter, Esq., C.B., of Dale, co. Pembroke. Educated at Eton and Clare Hall, Cambridge (B.A. 1841) ; is a J.P. and D.L. for Cornwall, and Patron of 1 living; was M.P. for Bodmin 1852-6.—Penrice, St. Austell, Restormel, Cornwall ; Reform Club, s.w.
　　Heir, his son Francis Aylmer, b. 1849.

SAWYER, CHARLES, Esq., of Heywood Lodge, Berks.
Eldest son of the late John Sawyer, Esq., of Heywood Lodge, by Sarah, dau. of Anthony Dickins, Esq., of Cherington, co. Warwick ; b. 1787 ; s. 1845 ; m. 1812 Henrietta, eldest dau. of the late Sir George Bowyer, Bart., and by her, who d. 1864, has, with other issue,
　　* Charles, Col. Commandant 6th Dragoon Guards, and Lieut.-Col. in the Army ; b. 1813 ; m. 1840 Anna Maria, dau. of J. F. Timins, Esq.
Mr. Sawyer, who was educated at Eton and Ch. Ch., Oxford (B.A. 1808), is a J.P. and D.L. for Berks and High Steward of Maidenhead : he was formerly Lieut. 16th Light Dragoons, and Major 2nd Berks Local Militia.—Heywood Lodge, Maidenhead.

SAY, RICHARD HALL, Esq., of Oakley Court, Berks.
Eldest son of the late Richard Hall, Esq., by Harriet, dau. of Robert Say, Esq., of Downham, Norfolk, and nephew of the Rev. Henry Say, Rector of North Pickenham and Houghton, Norfolk ; b. 1827 ; s. 1855 ; m. 1857 Ellen, only child of Edward Evans, Esq., of Boveney Court, Bucks, and has, with other issue,
　　* Lionel Henry, b. 1859.
Mr. Hall-Say, who is a Magistrate for Norfolk and Berks (High Sheriff 1864), assumed the name and arms of Say under the will of his uncle.—Oakley Court, Windsor ; Swaffham, Norfolk ; Reform Club, s.w., Royal Thames Yacht Club, s.w.

SAYE AND SELE, Lord (FREDERICK TWISLETON - WYKEHAM - FIENNES, D.C.L.).—Cr. 1603.
Eldest son of the late Hon. and Rev. Dr. Thomas James Twisleton, by his 2nd wife Anna, dau. of Benjamin Ashe, Esq., and cousin of William, 12th Lord ; b. 1799; s. 1847 ; m. 1st 1827 the Hon. Emily, dau. of Richard, 4th Viscount Powerscourt ; 2nd 1857 the Hon. Caroline, dau. of Chandos, 1st Lord Leigh. Educated at Winchester and New Coll. Oxford (M.A. 1823, D.C.L. 1832) ; is a Magistrate for co. Hereford, Treasurer and Canon of Hereford Cathedral, Archdeacon of Hereford, and High Steward of Banbury.—Broughton Castle, Banbury ; The Close, Hereford ; Brooks's Club, s.w.
　　Heir, his son John Fiennes, educated at Harrow and Ch. Ch. Oxon, a J.P. and D.L. for co., a Magistrate for co. Warwick, and Capt. Oxfordshire Yeomanry ; b. 1830 ; m. 1856 Lady Augusta, 5th dau. of Thomas Robert, 16th Earl of Kinnoull, and has, with other issue, * Geoffrey Cecil, b. 1858.

SAYER, GEORGE, Esq., of Statenborough, Kent.
Son of the late Terry Sayer, Esq., of Sandwich, by Elizabeth, dau. of William Bell, Esq., of Guernsey ;

531

b, 1788; *m*. 1828 Roberta, dau. of Robert Curling, Esq., of Sandwich, Kent. and has issue, an only daughter,

* Roberta, *m*. 1850 John James Harvey, Esq.

Mr. Sayer is a Magistrate for Kent, and a Commander R.N., retired.—*Statenborough House, Sandwich.*

SAYER, GEORGE EDWARD, Esq., of Pett, Kent.
Only son of the late Rev. George Sayer, LL.B., of Pett; *b*. 1795. Is a J.P. and D.L. for Kent.—*Pett, Charing, Ashford, Kent.*

SAYERS. (See *Brydges-Sayers.*)

SCARBOROUGH, Earl of (RICHARD GEORGE LUMLEY).—Cr. 1690.
Only son of the late Frederick Lumley-Savile, Esq., of Tickhill Castle, co. York (who *d*. 1837), by Charlotte Mary, dau. of the late Bishop (Beresford) of Kilmore; *b*. 1813; *s*. his cousin as 9th Earl 1856; *m*. 1846 Frederica Mary Adeliza. dau. of the late Andrew Robert Drummond, Esq., of Cadlands, Hants. Educated at Eton; is a Dep.-Lieut. for the W. Riding of co. York, and Patron of 13 livings; was formerly in the 7th Hussars.—*Sandbeck Park, and Tickhill Castle, Rotherhem; Lumley Castle, Durham; Glentworth Manor, Linco'n; White's and Boodle's Clubs, s.w.*

Heir, his son Lyulph Richard Granby William, Viscount Lumley, *b*. 1850.

SCARBROUGH, JOHN LATOYSONERE, Esq., of Stafford House, Devonshire.
Eldest son of the late William Scarbrough, Esq., of Lyme Regis, Dorset, by Mary, dau. of William Shepheard, Esq., of Betty's Town House, co. Meath; *b*. 1805; *m*. 1844 Marian, only child of Admiral Impey, of Coly House, Devon, and has, with other issue,

* John, *b*. 1846.

Mr. Scarbrough, who was educated at Ch. Ch., Oxford, is a Magistrate for Devon and Dorset.—*Stafford House, Colyford, Devon.*

SCARISBRICK, Lady, of Scarisbrick, Lancashire.
Anne, eldest dau. of the late Thomas Eccleston, Esq., of Scarisbrick (who assumed the name of Scarisbrick), by Eleanora, elder dau. of the late Thomas Clifton, Esq., of Lytham, co. Lancaster; *s*. her brother 1860; *m*. 1807 Sir Thomas Windsor Hunloke, Bart., of Wingerworth, co. Derby (ext.), who *d*. 1816. Is Lady of the Manor of Scarisbrick; assumed her present name, by Royal licence, in 1860.—*Scarisbrick Hall, Ormskirk.*

SCARLETT, the Hon. Sir JAMES YORKE, K.C.B., of Bank Hall, Lancashire (cr. 1855).
Second son of James, 1st Lord Abinger, by Louisa Henrietta, dau. of Peter Campbell, Esq; *b*. 1799; *m*. 1835 Charlotte Anne, 2nd dau. and co-heir of the late Col. Hargreaves, of Bank Hall. Educated at Eton and Trinity Coll., Cambridge; is a Magistrate for co. Lancaster, a Lieut.-General in the Army, and Hon. Col. 40th Middlesex Volunteers (Gray's-Inn Rifle Rangers), and 3rd Lancashire Volunteer Battalion; Col. 5th Dragoon Guards; served in the Crimea 1854-6, in command of the Heavy Brigade, and subsequently Cavalry Division; appointed to command the Cavalry Brigade at Aldershot 1856; Commander-in-Chief of the South-Western District 1857; Adjutant-General to the Forces 1860; was M.P for Guildford 1837-41.—*Bank Hall, Burnley. Lancashire; Carlton, United Service, and University Clubs, s.w.; 25, Princes Terrace, s.w.*

SCARLETT, the Hon. PETER CAMPBELL, C.B.
Third son of James. 1st Lord Abinger, by Louisa Henrietta, dau. of Peter Campbell, Esq.; *b*. 1804; *m*. 1843

832

Frances Sophia Mostyn, dau. of E. Lomax, Esq. Educated at Eton; is a Dep.-Lieut. for Surrey; was successively Attaché at Constantinople, at Paris, and Rio Janeiro; Secretary of Legation at Florence 1844-55; appointed Envoy Extraordinary and Minister Plenipotentiary at Rio Janeiro 1855, at Florence 1858, at Mexico 1864.—*British Embassy, Mexico.*

SCARLETT, JAMES WILLIAMS, Esq., late of Copped Hall, Herts.
Only surviving son of the late Sir William A. Scarlett, Chief Justice of Jamaica (brother of James, 1st Lord Abinger), by Mary, dau. of Joseph Williams, Esq., of Jamaica; *b*. 1812; *m*. 1837 Anne Rhodes Williams, dau. of the late James Brown, Esq., of Harehills Grove, Leeds, and has, with other issue,

* William James, *b*. 1839.

Mr. Scarlett, who was educated at Eton and Trinity Coll., Cambridge (B.A. 1836), and called to the Bar at the Inner Temple 1838. is a Magistrate for Herts and for St. Alban's.—*Residence: Thryburgh, Rotherkam.*

SCARSDALE, Lord (ALFRED NATHANIEL HOLDEN CURZON).—Cr. 1761.
Second son of the late Hon. and Rev. Alfred Curzon (who was 2nd son of Nathaniel, 2nd Lord Scarsdale, and who *d*. 1860), by Sophia, dau. of the late Robert Holden, Esq., of Nuttall Temple, Notts; *b*. 1831; *s*. his uncle as 4th Lord 1856; *m*. 1856 Blanche, 2nd dau. of Joseph Pocklington-Senhouse, Esq., of Netherhall, Cumberland. Educated at Rugby and Merton Coll., Oxford (B.A. 1852, M.A. 1855); is in Holy Orders, and Patron of 4 livings; a Magistrate for co. Derby; Lord of the Manor of Kedleston.—*Kedleston Hall, Derby; Carlton and Arthur's Clubs, s.w.*

Heir, his son George Nathaniel, *b*. 1859.

SCHANK, HENRY ALEXANDER, Esq., of Castlerig, Fifeshire.
Eldest son of the late Alexander Schank, Esq., of Castlerig, by Harriett Georgina, dau. of Lieut.-Col. Henry Dundas Campbell; *b*. 1850; *s*. 1866. This family have possessed the lands of Castlerig and Gleniston since the time of Robert Bruce.—*Castlerig, Kinghorn, N.B.; 42, Wilton Crescent, s.w.*

SCHANK, JOHN MACKELLAR SKEENE GRIEVE, Esq., of Barton House, Devon.
Third but only surviving son of Admiral John Wight, by Margaret, dau. of Admiral John Schank, of Barton House, Dawlish; *b*. 1898; *m*. 1856 Mary, dau. of Henry Parish, Esq., and by her, who *d*. 1866, has, with other issue,

* Henry Alexander, *b*. 1856.

Mr. Schank assumed that name, by Royal sign-manual, in 1843, in lieu of his patronymic Wight.—*Barton House, Dawlish; Northumberland House, Teignmouth.*

SCHENLEY, EDWARD WYNDHAM HARRINGTON, Esq.
Second son of the late Major Schenley, F.A.; *b* 1799; *m*. 1st 1843 Jane Marie younger dau. of the late Sir William Templer Pole, Bart., of Shute, Devon (she *d*. 1837); 2nd 1850 Mary Elizabeth Croghan, of Pittsburgh, Pennsylvania. Educated at the Royal Military Coll., Marlow; was a Commissioner for the Repression of the Slave Trade; is a Magistrate for co. Bant'; was Acting-Judge at the Havannah 1835-40, and M.P. for Dartmouth May-July 1859; was formerly in the Army. —*Arthur's and Boodle's Clubs, s.w.; 14, Princes Gate, w.*

SCHNEIDER, HENRY WILLIAM, Esq., of Lightburn House, Lancashire.
Son of the late John Henry Powell Schneider, Esq., of Southgate, Middlesex (who *d*, 1861); *b*. 1817; *m* 1st

1842 Augusta, dau. of Richard Smith, Esq., of Poulton Manor, co. Chester (she *d.* 1862); 2nd 1864 Elizabeth, 2nd dau. of the Rev. Joseph Turner, M.A., Vicar of Lancaster. Is a Merchant, Shipowner, and Ironmaster; was M.P. for Norwich 1857-9; elected for Lancaster 1865, but unseated on petition 1866; late a Magistrate for co. Lancaster.—*Lightburn House, Ulverstone, Lancashire; Athenæum Club,* s.w.; 14, *Sussex Gardens,* w.

+ SCHOFIELD, WILLIAM WHITWORTH, Esq., of Buckley Hall, Lancashire.
Son of the late W. Schofield, Esq.; *b.* 18—; is married, and has issue. Is a Magistrate for co. Lancaster. —*Buckley Hall, Rochdale.*

SCHOLEFIELD, CLEMENT COTTERILL, Esq., of Edgbaston, Warwickshire.
Son of the late William Scholefield, Esq., M.P., of Birmingham (who was a J.P. and D.L. for Warwick), by Jane Matilda, dau. of J. Miller, Esq.; *b.* 1839; *s.* 1867.—*Edgbaston, Birmingham.*

SCHREIBER, CHARLES, Esq.
Eldest surviving son of the late Lieut.-Col. James Alfred Schreiber, of Melton, Suffolk (formerly of the 11th Light Dragoons and 6th Dragoon Guards) by Mary, dau. of Thomas Ware, Esq., of Woodfort, co. Cork; *b.* 1826; *m.* 1855 Lady Charlotte Elizabeth Bertie, dau. of Albemarle, 9th Earl of Lindsey, and widow of Sir J. J. Guest, Bart., M.P. Educated at Cheltenham and Trinity Coll., Cambridge (B.A. 1850, M.A. 1853); was Senior Chancellor's Medallist 1850, and Fellow of Trinity 1852-5; elected M.P. for Cheltenham 1865.—*Langham House,* w.; *Carlton and University Clubs,* s.w.

SCHREIBER, CHARLES ALFRED, Esq., of The Round Wood, Suffolk.
Second son of the late William Frederick Schreiber, Esq., of the Round Wood, by Frances Mary, dau. of the late William Shuldham, Esq., of Marlesford Hall, Suffolk; *b.* 1817; *s.* 1860; *m.* 1st 1845 Elizabeth Hester, dau. of the late Owen Hogan, Esq., of Auburn, co. Westmeath (she *d.* 1863); 2nd 1866 Rosa Alexandrina, dau. of John Robert Thomson, Esq., of Blackstones, Surrey; he has by the former, with other issue,

* William Frederick Duff, Ensign 73rd Regt.; *b.* 1847.

Mr. Schreiber, who is a Magistrate for Suffolk, was Capt. 34th Regt.—*The Round Wood, Ipswich.*

SCHREIBER, FREDERICK WILLIAM, Esq., of Melton, Suffolk.
Eldest son of the late William Frederick Schreiber Esq., of The Round Wood, Ipswich (who *d.* 1860), by Frances Mary, dau. of the late Wm. Shuldham, Esq., of Marlesford Hall, Suffolk; *b.* 1814; *m.* 1847 Matilda Robertina, only child of the late Robert Houghton, Esq., of Portland Place, by whom he has, with other issue,

* Frederick Ernest Lowther, *b.* 1849.

Mr. Schreiber, who served as an Officer (1832–48) in the Prussian Dragoon Guards, is a J.P. and D.L. for Suffolk, and Hon. Col. 2nd Battalion Suffolk Rifle Volunteers.—*Hill House, Melton, Woodbridge.*

SCHREIBER, the late JOHN CHARLES, Esq., of Henhurst, Kent.
Eldest son of the late William Schreiber, Esq., of Henhurst, by Mary, dau. of James Sewell, Esq., of Alton Hall, Suffolk; *b.* 1782, and *d.* 1863, having *m.* 1823 Amelia, dau. of the late Lieut.-General Sir J. Cameron, K.C.B. Was a Magistrate for Kent and Sussex.—*Henhurst, Woodchurch, Kent*

SCHREIBER, the Rev. JOHN EDWARD LEMUEL, of Barham, Suffolk.
Third son of the late William Frederick Schreiber, Esq., of the Round Wood, Suffolk (who *d.* 1860), by Frances Mary, dau. of the late William Shuldham, Esq., of Marlesford Hall, Suffolk; *b.* 1818; *m.* 1863 Lucy, eldest dau. of the late Charles Phillipps, Esq., of Clayton, Suffolk. Educated at Balliol Coll., Oxford (B.A. 1839, M.A. 1842); is a Magistrate for Suffolk, and Patron and Rector of Barham.—*Barham, Ipswich.*

+ SCHUSTER, LEO, Esq., of Roehampton, Surrey.
Son of the late L. Schuster, Esq.; *b.* 18—; is married, and has, with other issue,

* Samuel Leo, of Iver Park, Bucks; educated at Rugby; Capt. 3rd Surrey Militia; *b.* 18—; *m.* 1858 Lady Isabella, eldest dau. of Thomas John, 5th Earl of Orkney, and has issue.

Mr. Schuster is a Magistrate for Surrey, and a Merchant in London. This family is of German extraction.—*Roehampton,* s.w.

SCLATER, JAMES HENRY, Esq., of Newick, Sussex.
Eldest son of the late James Henry Sclater, Esq., J.P. and D.L., of Newick Park (High Sheriff in 1827), by Cecil, dau. of the late Francis Saunderson, Esq., of Castle Saunderson, co. Cavan; *b.* 1819; *s.* 1862; *m.* 1846 Louisa Catherine, 2nd dau. of Robert Fowler, Esq., of Rahinston, co. Meath, and has, with other issue,

* James Robert Charles, *b.* 1848.

Mr. Sclater, who was educated at Harrow and Oriel Coll., Oxford, is a J.P. and D.L. for Sussex, and Lord of the Manors of Warningore and Newick.—*Newick Park, Uckfield; Oxford and Cambridge Club,* s.w.

SCLATER, WILLIAM LUTLEY, Esq., of Hoddington House, Hants.
Eldest son of the late Rev. Bartholomew Lutley Sclater, M.A., by Elizabeth Rebecca, dau. of George Bristow, Esq., of Ashford, Middlesex; *b.* 1790; *m.* 1821 Anne Maria, youngest dau. of William Bowyer, Esq., of Bedford Row, London, and has, with other issue,

* George Sclater-Booth, Esq., educated at Winchester, M.A. of Balliol Coll., Oxford, a Barrister-at-Law of the Inner Temple, a Magistrate for Hants, M.P. for N. Hants, and Capt. Hants Yeomanry; Sec. to the Treasury, late Sec. to the Poor Law Board; assumed the additional name of Booth by Royal licence in 1857; *b.* 1826; *m.* 1857 Lydia Caroline only dau. of the late George Birch, Esq., of Clare Park, Hants, and has, with other issue, * George Limbrey, *b.* 1859.

Mr. Sclater, who was educated at Winchester and Brasenose Coll., Oxford (B.A. 1811, M.A. 1814), is a Magistrate for Hants, Chairman of Magistrates of the Basingstoke Division, and Chairman of the Board of Guardians in the Basingstoke Union.—*Hoddington House, Odiham.*

SCOBELL, EDWIN, Esq., of Goodameavy, Devon.
Eldest son of the late Joseph Scobell, Esq., of Goodameavy, by Jane, dau. of J. Cooper, Esq.; *b.* 1814; *s.* 1836; *m.* 1847 Georgianna, dau. of Admiral C. B. H. Ross, C.B., and has, with other issue,

* Edwin Charles, Capt. Royal Cornwall Rangers; *b.* 1848; *m.* 1863 Mary Anne Elizabeth, 2nd dau. of the late Robert John Peel, Esq., of Bartonmoor Trent.

Mr. Scobell, who is Lord of the Manor of Goodameavy, and was formerly Lieut. 62nd Regt., represents a branch of a family of Cornish extraction (see Scobell of Nancealverne).—*Goodameavy House, Roborough, Devon.*

SCOBELL, GEORGE TREWEEKE, Esq., of Kingwell, Somerset.
Second son of the late Peter Edward Scobell, Esq., M.D., by his 1st wife Hannah, only dau. of John King

3 H 833

ford, Esq., of Penzance, Cornwall; *b.* 1785; *m.* 1818 Hester, dau. of Charles Savage, Esq. Is a J.P. and D.L. for Somerset (High Sheriff 1863), and Capt. Royal Navy, retired; was M.P. for Bath 1851-7.—*Kingwell House, Bath ; Reform Club, s.w.*

+ SCOBELL, Col. HENRY SCALES, of Pershore, Worcestershire.
Son of the late H. Scobell, Esq.; *b.* 18— ; is married, and has issue. Is a J.P. and D.L. for co. Worcester, and Lieut.-Col. Worcestershire Rifle Volunteers.—*The Abbey, Pershore.*

SCOBELL, EDWARD, Esq., of Nancealverne, Cornwall.
Elder son of the late John Scobell, Esq., J.P. and D.L. of Nancealverne, by his 1st wife Susanna, dau. and heir of William Usticke, Esq., of Leha, St. Burian, Cornwall ; *b.* 1803 ; *s.* 1866 ; *m.* 1832 Frances Skey, 2nd dau. and co-heir of Richard Langford, Esq., of Montvale House, Somerset. Educated at Balliol Coll., Oxford (B.A. 1826) ; called to the Bar at the Middle Temple 1830 ; is a Magistrate for Cornwall and Somerset, and Lord of the Manor of Kingsbridge, Devon. —*Nancealverne, Penzance.*

Heir Pres., his brother George, b. 1805.

SCOONES, EDWARD, Esq., of Tunbridge, Kent.
Son of the late William Scoones, Esq., of Tunbridge, by Mary Ann, dau. of Thomas Dalton, Esq., of Parrock House, Gravesend ; *b.* 1794 ; *m.* 1833 Jane Esther, 3rd dau. of the late Henry Streatfeild, Esq., of Chiddingstone, Kent, and has, with other issue,

* Henry Dalton, late Capt. 49th Regt. ; *b.* 1834.

Mr. Scoones, who was educated at the R. Military Coll., is a Magistrate for Kent, and a Major in the Army, retired.—*Tunbridge, Kent ; United Service Club, s.w.*

SCOTLAND, Sir WALTER COLLEY HARMAN, Knt. (cr. 1861).
Eldest son of the late Thomas Scotland, Esq. (Registrar of the island of Antigua), by Sarah, youngest dau. of James Haverham, Esq. ; *b.* 1819 ; *m.* 1853 Sarah Anne, only surviving dau. of the late John Joseph Bygrave, Esq., and by her, who is deceased, has issue,

* Harriette Jessie.

Sir Walter, who was called to the Bar at the Middle Temple 1843, and went the Oxford Circuit, is Chief Justice at Madras.—*Residence : Madras.*

SCOTT, Sir WILLIAM, Bart., of Ancrum, Roxburghshire (cr. 1671).
Only son of the late Sir John Scott, Bart., of Ancrum, by Harriet, dau. of William Graham, Esq., of Gartmore, co. Stirling ; *b.* 1803 ; *s.* as 6th Bart. 1814 ; *m.* 1826 Elizabeth, dau. of David Anderson, Esq., of Balgay, co. Forfar. Educated at the Royal Military Coll., Sandhurst ; is a J.P. and D.L. for co. Roxburgh, and a Magistrate for co. Forfar ; formerly Lieut. 2nd Life Guards ; was M.P. for co. Roxburgh 1829-30 : rechosen 1859.— *Ancrum, Jedburgh, N.B. ; Balgay, Dundee ; Brooks's and Travellers' Clubs, s.w.*

Heir, his son William Monteath, a Magistrate for co. Forfar ; b. 1829 ; m. 1861 Amelia Murray, eldest dau. of General Sir Monteith Douglas, K.C.B., of Stonebyres, co. Lanark, and has issue, a son, b. 1863.

SCOTT, Sir EDWARD WILLIAM DOLMAN, Bart., of Great Barr, Staffordshire (cr. 1806).
Eldest son of the late Sir Francis Edward Scott, Bart., J.P. and D.L., of Great Barr, by Mildred Anne, dau. of Sir William Cradock-Hartopp, Bart. ; *b.* 1854 ; *s.* as 3rd and 4th Bart. 1863. Is Lord of the Manor of Hartington, and Patron of 1 living. Two distinct Baronetcies—viz., those of Bateman and Scott, both created

831

in 1806—meet in the present Bart.—*Great Barr Hall, Birmingham ; 97, Euston Square, s.w.*

Heir Pres., his brother Arthur Douglas, b. 1860.

SCOTT, Sir JAMES SIBBALD DAVID, BART. (cr. 1806).
Eldest son of the late Sir David Scott, Bart., K.H., by Caroline, dau. and co-heir of Benjamin Grindall, Esq. ; *b.* 1814 ; *s.* as 3rd Bart. 1851 ; *m.* 1844 Harriet Anne, dau. of Henry Shank, Esq., of Castlerig and Gleniston, co. Fife. Educated at Eton and Ch. Ch., Oxford (B.A. 1835) ; is a J.P. and D.L. for Sussex and Middlesex ; late Capt. Sussex Militia Artillery.—*Sillwood, Brighton ; Arthur's Club, s.w.; 30, Hyde Park Square, w.*

Heir, his son Michael David Sibbald, b. 1849.

SCOTT, Sir CLAUDE EDWARD, Bart., of Sundridge Park, Kent (cr. 1821).
Eldest son of the late Sir Samuel Scott, Bart., of Sundridge Park, by Anne, dau. of John Ommaney, Esq., of London ; *b.* 1804 ; *s.* as 3rd Bart. 1819 ; *m.* 1838 Mary, dau. of Theophilus Russell Buckworth, Esq., of Cockley Clay Hall, Norfolk (she *d.* 1844). Is a Banker in London.—*Sundridge Park, Bromley ; Union and Carlton Clubs, s.w. ; 29, Bruton Street, w.*

Heir, his son Claude Edward, b. 1840 ; m. 1861 Maria Selina, 2nd dau. of H. C. Burney, Esq., LL.D., Principal of the Military Training Coll., Richmond, Surrey.

SCOTT, Admiral Sir JAMES, K.C.B. (cr. 1862).
Eldest son of the late Thomas Scott, Esq., of Glenluce, N.B., by Elizabeth, dau. of John Smyth, Esq., of Newcastle-on-Tyne ; *b.* 1790 ; *m.* 1819 Caroline Anne, only dau. of the late Richard Donovan, Esq., and Caroline Elizabeth Yate, of Tibberton Court, co. Gloucester, and has, with other issue,

* Honywood Dobyn Yate, in Holy Orders, B.A. of Trinity Coll., Cambridge ; Rector of Tibberton ; b. 1821.

Sir J. Scott, who entered the Navy 1803, is an Admiral R.N., and Patron of Tibberton.—*United Service Club, s.w.*

SCOTT, Sir JOHN, K.C.B. (cr. 1865).
Only son of the late John F. Scott, Esq., by Mary. dau. of the late John Serjeant, Esq., of Whitehaven, Cumberland ; *b.* 1797 ; *m.* 1829 Alicia, dau. of the Rev. Henry Forster Mills. Educated at Westminster ; is a Lieut.-Gen. in the Army, and Col. of the 3rd Dragoon Guards ; was formerly A.D.C. to the Queen, Lieut.-Col. 4th Light Dragoons, and 9th Lancers.—*United Service Club, s.w. ; 1, Cromwell Road, w.*

SCOTT, Lord HENRY JOHN MONTAGU-DOUGLAS, of Beaulieu, Hampshire.
Second son of Walter Francis, 5th Duke of Buccleuch, K.G., by Lady Charlotte Anne, 3rd dau. of Thomas, 2nd Marquis of Bath ; *b.* 1832 ; *m.* 1865 the Hon. Cecily Susan, youngest dau. of John, 2nd Lord Wharncliffe, and has issue,

* John Walter Edward, b. 1868.

His Lordship, who was educated at Eton, is a Magistrate for Hants and Midlothian, Capt. Royal Midlothian Yeomanry Cavalry, late lieutenant commanding the Ettrick Rifle Volunteers ; was elected M.P. for co. Selkirk 1861.—*Beaulieu, Southampton ; 3, Tilney Street, w.*

SCOTT, the Hon. CHARLES GRANTHAM, of Baginton, Warwickshire.
Second son of Thomas, 2nd Earl of Clonmell, by Lady Henrietta Louisa Greville, 2nd dau. of George, 2nd Earl of Warwick ; *b.* 1818 ; *m.* 1843 Frances Mary, dau. of the late R. W. Grey, Esq., of Backworth, Northumberland, and has, with other issue.

* Beauchamp Henry John, b. 1847.

Mr. Scott, who was educated at Eton, is a J.P. and D.L. for co. Worcester, a Magistrate for co. Warwick. Lieut.-

Col. Scots Fusilier Guards (retired), and Lieut.-Col. 1st Warwickshire Rifle Volunteers.—*Baginton, Coventry; 79, Eaton Square, s.w.*

SCOTT, the Hon. FRANCIS, of Mertoun, Berwickshire.

Fifth son of Hugh, 4th Lord Polwarth, by Harriet, dau. of the late Hans-Moritz, Count Brühl von Martinskirchen; *b.* 1806; *m.* 1835 Julia Frances Laura, dau. of the Rev. Charles Boultbee (she *d.* 1868). Educated at Trinity Coll., Cambridge (B.A. 1827, M.A. 1832); called to the Bar at the Middle Temple 1832, and went the Northern Circuit; is a Magistrate for cos. Berwick and Roxburgh, and for Surrey; was M.P. for co. Roxburgh 1841–7, for co. Berwick 1847–59.—*Mertoun House, Berwick, N.B.; Sandhurst Grange, Ripley, Surrey; Carlton Club, s.w.*

SCOTT, the Hon. and Rev. WILLIAM HUGH.

Second son of Hugh, 4th Lord Polwarth, by Harriet, dau. of the late Hans-Moritz, Count Brühl von Martinskirchen, Saxon Minister in England; *b.* 1801; *m.* 1833 Eleanor Sophia, dau. of the late Rev. C. Baillie Hamilton. Educated at St. John's Coll., Cambridge (M.A. 1827); appointed Rector of Maiden Newton 1837, Prebendary of Salisbury 1848.—*Maiden Newton Rectory, Dorchester, Dorset.*

SCOTT, Lady JOHN DOUGLAS-MONTAGU-, of Cawston Lodge, Warwickshire.

Alicia Anne, elder dau. of the late John Spottiswoode, Esq., of Spottiswoode, co. Berwick, by Helen, dau. of Andrew Wauchope, Esq., of Niddrie Marischall, co. Midlothian; *m.* 1836 Lord John Douglas-Montagu-Scott (youngest son of Charles William, 4th Duke of Buccleuch), who *d. s. p.* 1860.—*Cawston Lodge, Dunchurch, Rugby.*

SCOTT, Lady, of Woodville, co. Dublin.

Mary, 2nd dau. of the late Joseph Davie-Bassett, Esq., of Umberleigh, Devon, by Mary, dau. of — Irwin, Esq., of Barnstaple, Devon; *m.* 18— Sir Hopton Stratford Scott, K.C.B., who was a General in the H.E.I.C.'s Service, and who *d.* 1860.—*Woodville House, Lucan, Ireland.*

+SCOTT, CARTERET GEORGE, Esq., of Malleny House, Midlothian.

Eldest surviving son of the late Francis Carteret Scott, Esq., of Malleny, by Charlotte Elizabeth, eldest dau. of the late Major-General George Cunningham; *b.* 1804; *m.* 1st 1830 Charlotte, dau. of the late Col. McDougall (she *d.* 1831); 2nd 1833 Emily, dau. of Admiral Francis Holmes Coffin, and has, with other issue,

   • Francis Cunningham, Capt. 42nd Highlanders, *b.* 1834.

Mr. Scott, who is a J.P. and D.L. for co. Edinburgh, was formerly Capt. H.E.I.C.'s Service.—*Malleny House, Edinburgh.*

+SCOTT, CHARLES CUNINGHAM, Esq., of Hawkhill, Ayrshire.

Son of the late Charles Scott, Esq.; *b.* 18—; is married, and has, with other issue,

   • John, *b.* 18—; *m.* 1864 Annie, eldest dau. of the late Robert Spalding, Esq., Kingston, Jamaica.

Mr. Scott is a Magistrate for co. Renfrew, and a merchant at Glasgow.—*Hawkhill, Ayr; Garvel Park, Greenock, N.B.*

SCOTT, the Rev. CHARLES THOMAS, of Shadingfield Hall, Suffolk.

Eldest son of the late Thomas C. Scott, Esq., of Shadingfield Hall, by Mary, 3rd dau. of Nicholas Ingate, Esq., of Shadingfield; *b.* 1810; *s.* 1855; *m.* 1843 Arabella, 2nd dau. of the late Rev. W. D. Thring, D.D., Rector of Sutton Veny, and Vicar of Fisherton

Delamere, Wilts, and has issue. Educated at St. John's Coll., Cambridge (B.A. 1834); is Rector of Shadingfield (1839), and Lord of the Manor of Francis, in that parish.—*Shadingfield Hall, Beccles.*

SCOTT, Col. EDWARD, of Maidstone, Kent.

Second son of the late Rev. Edward Scott, D.D., of Worton Hall, Isleworth, by Jennette, dau. of William Walker, Esq.; *b.* 1809; *m.* 1843 Elizabeth, only child of John Day, Esq., M.D., of Maidstone, and has issue. Educated at Chiswick; late Major 8th Hussars, Lieut.-Col. 3rd Batt. Kent Rifle Volunteers; was M.P. for Maidstone 1857–9.—*The Priory, Maidstone, Kent; Army and Navy, and Junior United Service Clubs, s.w.*

SCOTT, EDWARD DOLMAN, Esq., of Great Barr, Staffordshire.

Second son of the late Sir Edward Dolman Scott, Bart., of Great Barr, by Catharine Juliana, eldest dau. of the late Sir Hugh Bateman, Bart. (*ext.*), of Hartington Hall, co. Derby; *b.* 1826. Educated at Harrow and Oriel Coll., Oxford (M.A. 1848); is a Magistrate for cos. Stafford and Warwick, and Dep.-Lieut. for co. Stafford.—*Great Barr, Birmingham; Conservative Club, s.w.*

SCOTT, JAMES GEORGE, Esq., of Lovel Hill, Berks.

Eldest son of the late George Denniston Scott, Esq., J.P. and D.L. of Lovel Hill, by Frederica Harriet, dau. of — Broderip, Esq.; *b.* 1839; *s.* 1864. Entered the Army in 1857; is Capt. 83rd Foot.—*Woodside, Lovel Hill, Winkfield, Windsor.*

SCOTT, GEORGE JONATHAN, Esq., of Betton-le-Strange, Shropshire.

Son of G. Scott, Esq., of the 1st Dragoon Guards, by Anne, dau. of Edward Morse, Esq., of Drayton, Middlesex; *b.* 180—; *m.* 1840 Augusta Frances, dau. of William E. W. Wynne, Esq., of Peniarth, co. Merioneth, and has issue,

   • Sydney Louisa.

Mr. Scott, who was educated at Westminster and Ch. Ch., Oxford, is a Magistrate for co. Merioneth (High Sheriff 1844).—*Betton-le-Strange, Shrewsbury; Peniarthuchaf Tongie, Machynlleth, Merionethshire.*

+SCOTT, HENRY RICHARD, Esq., of Wood Hall, Yorkshire.

Second son of Sir John V. B. Johnstone, Bart., of Hackness Hall, co. York, by Louisa Augusta, dau. of the late Hon. and Most Rev. Dr. E. Vernon-Harcourt, Lord Archbishop of York; *b.* 1830; *s.* his maternal uncle in this estate, and assumed his name by Royal licence in 1860. Is a J.P. and D.L. for the E. Riding of Yorkshire, and Lord of the Manor of Wood Hall.—*Wood Hall, Wetherby.*

SCOTT, HERCULES, Esq., of Brotherton, Kincardineshire.

Only son of the late David Scott, Esq., of Brotherton, by Mary, dau. of the late William Selden, Esq., of Acres Barn, co. Lancaster; *b.* 1823; *s.* 1859; *m.* 1857 Anna, only surviving dau. of James Moon, Esq., of Hillside House, Liverpool, and has, with other issue,

   • Hercules James, *b.* 1860.

Mr. Scott, who was educated at Harrow and Haileybury Coll., is a J.P. and D.L. for co. Kincardine, and Lieut. Commanding 2nd Kincardine Artillery Volunteers; was formerly in the Bengal Civil Service.—*Brotherton House, Bervie, Fordoun, N.B.; E. India United Service Club, s.w.*

SCOTT, HUGH, Esq., of Gala, Selkirkshire.

Eldest son of the late John Scott, Esq., of Gala, by Madalen, dau. of Sir Archibald Hope, Bart., of Craig-

hall; *b.* 1822; *s.* 1840; *m.* 1857 Elizabeth Isabella, dau. of Capt. Johnstone-Gordon, of Craig, and has, with other issue,
  • John Henry Francis Kinnaird, *b.* 1859.

Mr. Scott, who is a J.P. and D.L. for co. Selkirk, was formerly Capt. in the 92nd Highlanders, and Major in the Dumfries, Roxburgh, and Selkirk Militia.—*Gala House, Galashiels, N.B.*.

SCOTT, Major JAMES FITZMAURICE, of Commieston, Kincardineshire.
Eldest son of the late William Fitzmaurice, Esq., of Spring Hill and Barrow, co. Limerick, who assumed the name of Scott on his marriage with Alicia, dau. and heir of James Scott, Esq., of Commieston; *b.* 1810; *s.* his mother 1815; *m.* 1837 Fanny, dau. and co-heir of the late Thomas Drinkwater, Esq., of Irwell House, co. Lancaster. Educated at Edinburgh; is a J.P. and D.L. for co. Kincardine, and Major in the Forfar and Kincardine Militia Artillery, was formerly Lieut. in the 6th Dragoon Guards.—*Commieston, Montrose, N.B.;* Residence: *Langley Park, Montrose, N.B.*

SCOTT, JAMES WINTER, Esq., of Rotherfield, Hants.
Eldest son of the late James Scott, Esq., M.P., of Rotherfield Park, by Martha, dau. of Thomas Bradbury Winter, Esq., of Shenley, Herts; *b.* 1799; *s.* 1854; *m.* 1828 Lucy, dau. of the late Rev. Sir Samuel Clarke Jervoise, Bart., and has, with other issue,
  • Arthur Jervoise, *b.* 1833.

Mr. Scott, who was educated at C.C.C., Oxford (B.A. 1822), is a J.P. and D.L. for Hants (High Sheriff 1864), Lord of the Manor and Patron of Rotherfield; was M.P. for North Hants 1835–7.— *Rotherfield Park, Alton; University Club, s.w.*

+SCOTT, JOSEPH, Esq., of Colney Hall, Norfolk.
Son of the late J. Scott, Esq.; *b.* 1800; *m.* 1828 Louisa Elizabeth, dau. of the late John William Tomlinson, Esq., and niece of the late Sir Charles Chad, Bart. (ext.), of Thursford Pinckney, Norfolk, and has, with other issue,
  • Joseph Stonehewer Scott-Chad, Esq., of Thursford Hall, near Thetford; educated at Harrow, M.A. of Trinity Coll., Cambridge, a Magistrate for Norfolk (High Sheriff 1863), and Patron of 2 livings; assumed the additional name of Chad by Royal licence in 1858, on succeeding to the property of his great-uncle Sir C. Chad, Bart.; *b.* 1829; *m.* 1856 Edith Elizabeth, youngest dau. of John J. Rawlinson, Esq., of Graythwaite, co. Lincoln, and has, with other issue,
    • Charles, *b.* 1857.

Mr. Scott is a J.P. and D.L. for Norfolk. Lord of the Manor and Patron of Colney. He purchased this property in 1838 from the Postles.—*Colney Hall, Norwich.*

SCOTT, MONTAGU DAVID, Esq., of Hove, Sussex.
Second son of the late Sir David Scott, Bart., K.H., M.P., by Caroline, dau. and co-heir of Benjamin Grindall, Esq.; *b.* 1818; *m.* 1848 Miss Margaret Briggs, of Oaklands, Herts, and has issue,
  • Mabel Montagu.

Mr. Scott, who was educated at University Coll., Oxford (B.A. 1840, M.A. 1844) and was called to the Bar at the Middle Temple 1840, is a J.P. and D.L. for Sussex, Middlesex, and Westminster, and a Magistrate for Brighton.—*Hove, Brighton; Carlton Club, s.w.*

SCOTT, Mrs., of The Red House, Staffordshire.
, Sarah, only dau. and heir of John Scott, Esq., J.P. and D.L., of The Red House (High Sheriff of co. Worcester 1830), by Sarah, dau. of John Kettle, Esq., of Birmingham; *m.* 1830 Robert Wellbeloved, Esq., Barrister-at-Law (who on his marriage assumed the surname of Scott), and who *d.* 1856, leaving, with other issue,
  • John Charles Addyes (of Butlinghope Manor, Pulverbatch, Staffordshire), M.A., of University Coll., London, and a
836

Magistrate for cos. Stafford and Worcester; *b.* 1830; *m.* 1863 Mahlah, eldest surviving dau. of Mr. Jesse Homer, of Birfield Cottage, co. Worcester.
Mr. Robert Scott was a Dep.-Lieut. for co. Worcester, a Magistrate for cos. Worcester and Stafford, and M.P. for Walsall 1841–7.—*The Red House, Great Barr, Staffordshire.*

SCOTT, ROBERT, Esq., of Raeburn and Lessudden, Roxburghshire.
Eldest surviving son of the late William Scott, Esq., of Raeburn, by Susan, dau. of Alexander Horsburgh, Esq., of Horsburgh, co. Peebles; *b.* 1817; *s.* 1856; *m.* 1861 Louisa, eldest dau. of William Campbell, Esq., of Ederline, Argyllshire, and has, with other issue,
  • Walter, *b.* 1866.

Mr. Scott was educated at Edinburgh University. This family is descended from a common ancestor with the Scotts of Harden.—*Lessudden House, St. Boswell's, N.B.*

+SCOTT, THOMAS, Esq., of Willsborough, co. Londonderry.
Eldest son of the late James Scott, Esq., of Willsborough, by Catharine, dau. of Dr. Leslie, Bishop of Limerick: *b.* 1783; *s.* 1820; *m.* 1st 1823 Hannah, widow of John Campbell, Esq., of Newtown, Limavady; 2nd 18— Anne, dau. of the Rev. Edward Lucas; 3rd 18— Catharine, dau. of the Rev. Thomas Richardson, of Somerset, co. Londonderry, and has, with other issue,
  • William, *b.* 183–.

Mr. Scott is a J.P. and D.L. for co. Londonderry. —*Willsborough, Eglinton, Londonderry.*

SCOTT, THOMAS EDWARD, Esq., of Swanthorpe, Hants.
Eldest son of the late Rev. Thomas Scott, of Carbrooke and Watton, by Sarah Anne, dau. of Capt. Turner, of the 33rd Foot; *b.* 1792; *m.* 1827 Mary, dau. of Col. Williamson, and has, with other issue,
  • Thomas James, *b.* 1828.

Mr. Scott is a J.P. and D.L. for Norfolk. This family was formerly seated at Carbrooke, in Norfolk.—*Swanthorpe, Croudall, Hants.*

SCOTT, WILLIAM, Esq., M.D., of Castletown Bawn, co. Tyrone.
Eldest son of John Scott, Esq., of Emarew, co. Fermanagh, by Martha, dau. of Adam Richey, Esq.; *b.* 1821; *m.* 1860 Anne Atkinson, dau. of the Rev. C. Crassie, A.M., Rector of Newtown Hamilton, co. Armagh, and has, with other surviving issue,
  Charles Edward, *b.* 1862.

Mr. Scott, who was educated in London, Edinburgh, and Dublin, is a Graduate of several Universities, and a Fellow of the Royal College of Physicians of Edinburgh 1845, and of the Royal College of Surgeons of England 1859, also of the King and Queen's College of Physicians, Ireland, 1860, and Vice-President of the Ulster Medical Society; is a Magistrate for co. Tyrone and for the town of Aughnacloy; was formerly in the Royal Tyrone Fusiliers. This family[‡] is descended from a common ancestor with the Duke of Buccleuch. —*Castletown Bawn, and Aughnacloy, co. Tyrone; Reform Club, s.w.*

SCOTT, WILLIAM, Esq., of Charlton Place, Kent.
Second son of the late George John Scott, Esq., of Betton Strange, co. Salop, by Anne, dau. of Wm. Morse, Esq., of Drayton, Middlesex; *b.* 1811; *m.* 1852 Selina,

[‡] Andrew Scott, the first of this branch who came to Ireland took a leading part at Edinburgh in the discussions of the times, and, owing to his zeal in the Covenanting cause, narrowly escaped with his life from the hands of Claverhouse, and settled in the county Tyrone.

dau. of the late Alexander Erskine, Esq., of Balhall, co. Forfar, and has, with other issue,

 * William Erskine Scott, b. 1853.

Mr. Scott, who is a Magistrate for Kent, and was formerly Capt. in the Carabineers, purchased this property in 1859 from the Mulcasters.—*Charlton Place, Bishopsbourne, Canterbury.*

SCOTT, WILLIAM, Esq., of Harescombe Court, Gloucestershire.

Son of the late W. Scott, Esq.; b. 1800; m. 1822 Jessy, eldest dau. of John William Freese, Esq., Col. Commandant of the Madras Artillery, and has, with other issue,

 * William, b. 1824; m. 185– Agnes Kate, dau. of — Hinxman, Esq.

Mr. Scott, who was formerly an Officer in the Madras Army, purchased this property in 1865.—*Harescombe Court, Stroud.*

SCOTT, WILLIAM HUGH, Esq., of Draycott House, Derbyshire.

Eldest son of the late William Scott, Esq., of Lessudden, co. Roxburgh, by Susan, dau. of Alex. Horsbrugh, Esq., of The Pirn, co. Peebles; b. 1822; s. his uncle 1859; m. 1863 Sarah, dau. of Alfred Fellows, Esq., of Beeston House, Notts, and has, with other issue,

 * Hugh, b. 1865.

Mr. Scott is a Magistrate for co. Derby. This family is a branch of the Scotts of Harden, represented by Lord Polwarth.—*Draycott House, Derby.*

+SCOTT, the late WILLIAM, Esq., of Empshott Grange, Hants.

Second son of the late James Scott, Esq., of Rotherfield, Hants, by Martha, dau. of the late Thomas B. Winter, Esq., of Shenley, Herts; b. 180–; d. 1864. —*Empshott Grange, Petersfield.*

SCOTT.

 (See under *Buccleuch, Duke of; Clonmell, Earl of; Eldon, Earl of;* and *Polwarth, Lord.*)

SCOTT, of Abbotsford. (See Hope-Scott.)

SCOTT-CHAD, of Thursford Hall.

 (See under *Scott, of Colney.*)

SCOTT-CHISHOLME. (See *Chisholme.*)

SCOTT-DOUGLAS. (See *Douglas.*)

SCOTT-MAKDOUGALL, Miss, of Makerstown, Roxburghshire.

Maria, eldest dau. of the late John Scott, Esq., of the H.E.I.C.S. (see *Scott of Gala*), by Isabella Monro; s. her cousin, Miss Hay-Makdougall, 1864. Is Lady of the Barony of Makerstown.—*Makerstown, Kelso, N.B.*

 Heir Pres., her sister.

SCOTT-KERR, WILLIAM, Esq., of Sunlaws and Chatto, Roxburghshire.

Only son of the late Robert Scott-Kerr, Esq., of Sunlaws and Chatto, by Elizabeth Bell, dau. of David Fyffe, of Drumgeith; b. 1807; s. 1831; m. 1st 1837 Hannah Charlotte, only dau. and heir of Henry Scott, Esq., and widow of Sir John James Douglas, Bart., of Springwood (she d. 1850); 2nd 1855 Frances Louisa, dau. of Robert Fennessy, Esq., of Belford, and has, with other issue,

 * Robert, b. 1859.

Mr. Scott-Kerr, who is a J.P. and D.L. for co. Roxburgh, is descended from the Scotts of Thirlestane, co. Roxburgh.—*Sunlaws, Kelso, N B*

SCOTT-MONCRIEFF, ROBERT, Esq., of Fossaway, Perthshire.

Eldest son of the late William Scott-Moncrieff, Esq., of Fossaway, by Elizabeth, dau. of Thomas Hogg, Esq., of Edinburgh; b. 1793; s. 1846; m. 1st 1826 Susan, dau. of Alexander Pringle, Esq., of Whytebank, co. Selkirk; 2nd 1851 Mary, dau. of Robert Hamilton, Esq., and has, with other issue,

 * William, in Holy Orders, M.A. of Trinity Coll., Cambridge; b. 1825; m. 1850 Hannah, youngest dau. of Robert Overton, Esq., of Leicester.

Mr. Scott-Moncrieff, who was called to the Scottish Bar 1819, is a Magistrate for cos. Edinburgh, Perth, and Kinross.—*Fossaway Lodge, Kinross, N.B.*

SCOTT-MURRAY, CHARLES ROBERT SCOTT, Esq., of Danesfield, and Hambleden, Bucks.

Eldest son of the late Charles Scott-Murray, Esq., of Danesfield, by Augusta Eliza, dau. of John Nixon, Esq.; b. 1818; s. 1837; m. 1846 the Hon. Amelia Charlotte, dau. of Thomas Alexander, 14th Lord Lovat, and has, with other issue,

 * Charles Aloysius, b. 1847.

Mr. Scott-Murray, who was educated at Eton and Ch. Ch., Oxford (B.A. 1841), is a J.P. and D.L. for Bucks (High Sheriff 1852), and Patron of 1 living; he was M.P. for Bucks 1841–5.—*Danesfield, Great Marlow; Hambleden House, Henley-on-Thames; 11, Cavendish Square, w.*

SCOTT-PLUMMER. (See *Plummer.*)

SCOTT-STONEHEWER, WILLIAM, Esq., of Old Shoreham, Sussex.

Only son of the late William Scott-Stonehewer, Esq., of Brighton, by Annabella, dau. of the late Ellis Hodgson, Esq., of Stapleton, co. York; b. 1830. Mr. Scott-Stonehewer, who was educated at Eton, is a Magistrate for Sussex. This family is of Yorkshire extraction.—*Adur Lodge, Old Shoreham, Sussex.*

SCOURFIELD, JOHN HENRY, Esq., of Williamston, Pembrokeshire.

Only son of the late Owen Philipps, Esq., of Williamston, by Ann Elizabeth, dau. of the late Henry Scourfield, Esq., of Roberton Hall, co. Pembroke; b. 1808; m. 1845 Augusta, dau. of the late John Lort Philipps, Esq., of Lawrenny Park, co. Pembroke, and has issue,

 * Owen Henry, b. 1847.

Mr. Scourfield, who was educated at Harrow and Oriel Coll., Oxford (B.A. 1828, M.A. 1832), is Lord-Lieutenant of Haverfordwest, a J.P. and D.L. for co. Pembroke (High Sheriff 1835), and Chairman of the Pembrokeshire Quarter Sessions: he has been M.P. for Haverfordwest since 1862. He assumed the surname of Scourfield, in lieu of his patronymic, by Royal licence, 1862.—*Williamston, Haverfordwest; University, Oxford and Cambridge, and Boodle's Clubs, s.w.*

SCRASE-DICKINS. (See *Dickins.*)

+SCRATTON, DANIEL, Esq., of Penenden Heath, Kent.

Son of the late Daniel Scratton, Esq., of Penenden Heath, and grandson of the late Robert Scratton, Esq., of Prittlewell Priory, Essex; b. 1815. Educated at Worcester Coll., Oxford (B.A. 1837); is a Magistrate for Kent.—*Penenden Heath, Maidstone.*

+SCRATTON, DANIEL ROBERT, Esq., of Prittlewell Priory, Essex.

Only son of the late John Baynton Scratton, Esq., of Prittlewell Priory, by Harriet, his wife, b. 1818; s.

                 887

183–; *m.* 1844 Maria, dau. of Mr. James Thornton. Is a J.P. and D.L. for Essex, and Lord of the Manor of Prittlewell.—*Prittlewell Priory, Rochford.*

SCRIVEN, Col. JOHN, of West Moulsey, Surrey.

Son of the late John Scriven, Esq., Serjeant-at-Law, by Mary, dau. of — Fitzgerald, Esq., of co. Kerry, Ireland; *b.* 1808; *m.* 1837 Selina, dau. of Henry Perkins, Esq., of Hanworth Park, Middlesex, and has, with other issue,

  * John Bagot, *b.* 1839.

Col. Scriven, who was educated at the Charterhouse and Emmanuel Coll., Cambridge, is a J.P. and D.L. for Middlesex, and Lieut.-Col. Commandant of the Royal South Middlesex Militia; was formerly in the 51st Foot.—*The Priory, West Moulsey,* s.w.; *United Service Club,* s.w.

SCRIVENER. (See *Pike-Scrivener.*)

SCROPE, GEORGE POULETT-, Esq., F.R.S., F.G.S., late of Castle Combe, Wilts.

Second son of the late J. Poulett-Thomson, Esq., of Roehampton, Surrey, by Charlotte, dau. of Dr. Jacob, of Salisbury, and brother of Charles, late Lord Sydenham (*ext.*); *b.* 1797; *m.* 1st 1821 Emma, dau. and heir of the late William Scrope, Esq., of Castle Combe, whose name he assumed (she *d.* 1866); 2nd 1867 Margaret Elizabeth, 3rd dau. of Thomas John Savage, Esq. Is a J.P. and D.L. for Wilts; was M.P. for Stroud 1833–67.—*Fairlawn, Cobham, Surrey; Athenæum and Reform Clubs,* s.w.

SCROPE, SIMON THOMAS, Esq., of Danby, Yorkshire.

Eldest son of the late Simon Thomas Scrope, Esq., of Danby Park, by Catherine Dorothy, dau. of Edward Meynell, Esq., of Kelvington and the Fryerage, near Yarm, co. York; *b.* 1790; *s.* 1839; *m.* 1821 Mary, eldest dau. of John Jones, Esq., of Llanarth and Treowen, co. Monmouth, and has, with other issue,

  * Simon Thomas, a J.P. and D.L. for the N. Riding of co. York; *b.* 1822; *m.* 1855 Emily Jane, 3rd dau. of Robert Berkeley, Esq., of Spetchley, and has, with other issue,
  * Simon, *b.* 1860.

Mr. Scrope, who was educated at Stonyhurst Coll., claims the ancient Earldom of Wilts, created 1397.‡—*Danby Park, Bedale; Cockerington, Louth, Lincolnshire.*

+SCRYMGEOUR-WEDDERBURN, FREDERICK LEWIS, Esq., of Wedderburn, Forfarshire, and Birkhill, Fifeshire.

Only son of the late Henry Scrymgeour-Wedderburn, Esq., of Wedderburn, by Mary Turner, eldest dau. of the late Capt. the Hon. F. L. Maitland, R.N., and granddau. of Charles, 6th Earl of Lauderdale; *b.* 1810; *s.* 1812; *m.* 1st 1839 the Hon. Helen, youngest dau. of the late Viscount Arbuthnot (she *d.* 1846); 2nd 1852 Selina Mary, 2nd dau. of the late Capt. Thomas Garth, R.N., of Haines Hill, Berks, and has, with other issue,

  * Frederick, *b.* 18—.

Mr. Scrymgeour-Wedderburn is a J.P. and D.L. for cos. Fife and Forfar, Hereditary Royal Standard-Bearer of Scotland, and Lord of the Baronies of Wedderburn and Birkhill.—*Birkhill, Cupar-Fife; Wedderburn, Dundee, N.B.*

  ‡ This claim is now (1868) before the House of Lords, and if established, Mr. Scrope will become Premier Earl in the Peerage of England.

SCRYMSOURE-FOTHRINGHAM, WALTER THOMAS JAMES, Esq., of Powrie and Fothringham, Forfarshire.

Only son of the late Thomas Frederick Scrymsoure-Fothringham, Esq., by Lady Charlotte, sister of James, 9th Earl of Southesk; *b.* 1802; *s.* 1864. Is lineal male representative and head of the family of Fothringham, who originally came from England, and have owned Powrie more than 400 years.—*Fothringham House, Forfar, N.B.*

  Heir Pres., his sister Marion.

SCUDAMORE, JOHN LUCY, Esq., of Kentchurch Court, Herefordshire.

Only son of the late John Scudamore, Esq., of Kentchurch Court, by Lucy, dau. of the late James Walwyn, Esq., M.P.; *b.* 1797; *s.* 1805; *m.* 1822 Sarah Laura, dau. of the late Sir Harford Jones-Brydges, Bart., and by her, who *d.* 1863, has issue,

  * Laura Adelaide, *m.* 1852 Major Fitzherbert Dacre, 2nd son of the Right Hon. Edward Lucas, of Castle Shane, co. Monaghan.

Mr. Scudamore, who is a J.P. and D.L. for co. Hereford, a Magistrate for co. Monmouth, and Patron of 1 living, was formerly a Lieut.-Col. in the Army.—*Kentchurch Court, Hereford; Athenæum Club,* s.w.

SCULLY, ROGER, Esq., of Dunally, co. Tipperary.

Fifth and only surviving son of the late William Scully, Esq., of Dunally, by Margaret, dau. of John Roe. Esq., of Bachelors' Hill, near Thurles, co. Tipperary; *b.* 18—. Is a Magistrate for co. Tipperary.—*Dunally, Cashel.*

SCULLY, VINCENT, Esq., Q.C., of Mantlehill, co. Tipperary.

Eldest son of the late Denys Scully, Esq., of Kilfeacle, co. Tipperary, and Merrion Square, Dublin, by Catherine, dau. of the late Vincent Eyre, Esq., of Highfield, co. Derby; *b.* 1810; *m.* 1841 Susanna, sister of Sir Edward Grogan, Bart., and has, with other issue,

  * Vincent, *b.* 1845.

Mr. Scully, who was educated at Oscot, Trinity Coll., Dublin, and Trinity Coll., Cambridge, and called to the Irish Bar 1833, appointed Q.C. 1849; was M.P. for co. Cork 1852–7 and 1859–65.—*Mantlehill, Golden, co. Tipperary;* 13. *Merrion Square South, Dublin: The Ferns, Grove End Road,* n.w; *Reform Club,* s.w.

SCURFIELD, GEORGE JOHN, Esq., of Hurworth House, co. Durham.

Second son of the late William Grey, Esq., of Norton, co. Durham, by Johanna, dau. and heir of the late William Scurfield, Esq., whose name he has assumed by Royal licence; *b.* 1809; *m.* 1839 Ann Alice, dau. of the Rev. Hopper Williamson, and has, with other issue,

  * George John, *b.* 1840.

Mr. Scurfield, who was educated at St. John's Coll., Cambridge (B.A. 1833, M.A. 1836), is a Magistrate for the N. Riding of Yorkshire and a J.P. and D.L. for co. Durham.—*Hurworth House, Darlington.*

SEAFIELD, Earl of (JOHN CHARLES GRANT OGILVIE).—*Cr.* 1701.

Second but eldest surviving son of Francis William, 6th Earl, by Mary Ann, dau. of John Charles Dunn, Esq., of Higham House, Surrey; *b.* 1815; *s.* 1853; 1850 the Hon. Caroline, dau. of Robert Walter, 11th Lord Blantyre. Sits in the House of Peers as Lord Strathspey, U.K. (cr. 1858); is a Dep.-Lieut. for cos. Inverness, Elgin, and Banff, and a Magistrate for co.

Aberdeen; was a Scotch representative Peer 1853-9.—*Castle Grant, Grantown; Balmacaan, Glen Urquhart, Inverness, N.B.; Cullen House, Banffshire; Carlton Club, s.w.*

Heir, his son Ian Charles, Viscount Reidhaven, b. 1851.

SEAFIELD, Dowager Countess of.
Louisa Emma, 2nd dau. of the late Robert George Maunsell, Esq., of Richmond Place, Limerick, by Mabella, dau. and co-heir of Standish Grady, Esq., of Elton, co. Limerick; *m.* 1st 1843 (as his 2nd wife) Francis William, 6th Earl of Seafield (who *d.* 1853); 2nd 1856 Major Godfrey William H. Massy, of Castlerea, co. Tipperary (who *d.* 1862); 3rd 1864 Lord Henry Loftus, son of John, 2nd Marquis of Ely. She has by her 2nd marriage, * Godfrey Lennox. Eyre, *b.* 1856.—*Grant Lodge, Elgin, N.B.; Almond's Hotel, 6, Clifford Street, w.*

SEAFORD, Lady.
Ann Louisa Emily, dau. of the late Admiral the Hon. Sir George C. Berkeley, G.C.B., by Lady Emily Lennox, sister of Charles, 4th Duke of Richmond; *m.* 1st 1807 Sir Thomas Masterman Hardy, Bart., who *d.* 1839; 2nd 1840 Charles, 1st Lord Seaford, who *d.* 1845.—*The Palace, Hampton Court, s.w.*

SEAHAM. (See under *Vane, Earl.*)

SEALE, Sir HENRY PAUL, Bart., of Mount Boone, Devon (cr. 1838).
Eldest son of the late Sir John Henry Seale, Bart., of Mount Boone (who was M.P. for Dartmouth 1832–44), by Pauline Elizabeth, dau. of the late Sir Paul Jodrell, Knt.; *b.* 1806; *s.* as 2nd Bart. 1844; *m.* 1840 Emily, dau. of the late Col. Isaac R. Hartman, of the Coldstream Guards, a Baron of the Kingdom of Denmark. Educated at Eton; is a J.P. and D.L. for Devon, Patron of 3 livings, and Major S. Devon Militia.—*Mount Boone and Norton House, Dartmouth.*

Heir, his son John Henry, b. 1843.

SEALE-HAYNE, CHARLES, Esq., of Fuge and Kingswear, Devon.
Only son of the late Charles Hayne Seale-Hayne, Esq., of Fuge House, by Louisa, dau. of Richard Jennings, Esq., of Ridge, Herts (she *m.* 2nd 1856 James Buller, Esq., of Whimple, whom see); *b.* 1833; *s.* 1842. Educated at Eton; called to the Bar at Lincoln's Inn, 1857; is a Magistrate for Devon, Capt. S. Devon Militia, and Lieut.-Colonel of the 2nd Administrative Brigade of Devon Volunteer Artillery. The late Mr. Seale-Hayne (who was 2nd son of Sir J. H. Seale, Bart.), inherited Fuge with other estates from his great-uncle Col. Hayne, of Fuge, whose name he assumed.—*Fuge House and Kingswear Castle, Dartmouth; Reform Club, s.w.; 3, Eaton Square, s.w.*

SEALY, HENRY NICHOLAS, Esq., of Nether Stowey, Somerset.
Third son of the late Edward Sealy, Esq., of Bridgewater, and Castle Hill House, Nether Stowey, by Mary, only surviving child of Jasper Tyley, Esq., of Somerton; *b.* 1783. Is a J.P. and D.L. for Somerset; author of a 'Treatise on Coins, Currency, and Banking.'—*Castle Hill House, Nether Stowey, Bridgwater.*

SEALY, JOHN LOVELL, Esq., of Bridgwater, Somerset.
Eldest son of John Sealy, Esq., of Bridgwater, by Emma, dau. of George Lovell, Esq., of Rookley House, Hants; *b.* 1820. Educated at Eton and Merton Coll., Oxford (B.A. 1841, M.A. 1844); is a Magistrate for Somerset, and a Banker at Bridgwater.—*Bridgwater, Somerset.*

SEALY. (See *Vidal.*)

SEATON, Lord (JAMES COLBORNE).—Cr. 1839.
Eldest son of John, 1st Lord (who was a Field-Marshal in the Army, G.C.B. and formerly Governor-General of Canada, and Lord High Commissioner of the Ionian Isles), by Elizabeth, dau. of the late Rev. James Yonge, of Puslinch, Devon, Rector of Newton Ferrars, Devon; *b.* 1820; *s.* 1863; *m.* 1851 the Hon. Charlotte, 2nd dau. of Ulysses, late Lord Downes (*ext.*) (she *d.* 1863). Educated at Sandhurst and Trinity Coll., Cambridge; is a Col. in the Army, and was formerly Military Secretary in Ireland.—*Beechwood, Plympton; Bert House, Athy, co. Kildare; United Service Club, s.w.; 11, Belgrave Street, s.w.*

Heir, his son John Reginald Upton, b. 1854.

SEATON, Sir THOMAS, K.C.B., of Bergholt, Suffolk (cr. 1858).
Son of John Fox Seaton, Esq., Merchant, of Pontefract, co. York, and of Clapham, Surrey; *b.* 1806; *m.* 1st 1838 Caroline, dau. of J. Corfield, Esq., of Taunton; 2nd 1858 Elizabeth, dau. of Joseph Harriman, Esq., of Tivoli, Cumberland. Is a Major-General Bengal Army, retired; late Col. 35th Bengal N.I.; served in Affghanistan 1840–2, and commanded an Infantry regiment in India 1857–8.—*Ackworth House, East Bergholt; Junior United Service Club, s.w.*

SEBRIGHT, Sir JOHN GAGE SAUNDERS, Bart., of Besford, Worcestershire (cr. 1626).
Eldest son of the late Sir Thomas Gage Saunders Sebright, Bart., of Besford Court (who was a J.P. and D.L. for Herts, High Sheriff 1853, and a Magistrate for St. Alban's), by his 1st wife Sarah Anne, dau. of Capt. Hoffman; R.N.; *b.* 1843; *s.* as 9th Bart. 1864; *m.* 1865 Olivia Amy Douglas, dau. of the Rt. Hon. J. W. Fitzpatrick. Educated at Ch. Ch., Oxford; is Lord of the Manor of Besford, and Patron of 2 livings.—*Beechwood House, Watford; Besford Court, Pershore; Windham Club, s.w.*

Heir Pres., his brother Edgar Reginald Saunders, b. 1854.

SEBRIGHT, Sir CHARLES, K.C.M.G. (cr. 1864).
Son of the late C. Sebright. Esq.; *b.* 18 —. Is British Consul at Cephalonia.—*Cephalonia, Ionian Islands.*

SEEL. (See *Molyneux-Seel.*)

SEELY, CHARLES, Esq., of Heighington, Lincolnshire.
Only son of the late Mr. Charles Seely, of Lincoln, by Anne, his wife (she *d.* 1863); *b.* 1803; *m.* 1831 Mary, dau. of Jonathan Hilton, Esq., of Newcastle-on-Tyne, and has, with other issue,

* Charles, of Brookhill Hall, near Alfreton, co. Derby; *b.* 1833; *m.* 1857 Emily, dau. of William Evans, Esq., and has, with other issue, * a son, *b.* 1861.

Mr. Seely, who is a Magistrate for Lincoln, and a J.P. and D.L. for co. Lincoln, was High Sheriff of Hants 1860; M.P. for Lincoln 1847–8, re-elected 1861.—*Brookhillington, Lincoln; Brooke House, I. of Wight; Reform Club, s.w.; 26, Prince's Gate, Hyde Park, w.*

SEFTON, Earl of (WILLIAM PHILIP MOLYNEUX).—Cr. 1771.
Eldest son of Charles William, 3rd Earl, by Mary Augusta, dau. of Robert Gregge Hopwood, Esq., of Hopwood Hall, co. Lancaster; *b.* 1835; *s.* 1855; *m.* 1866 Cecil Emily, 4th dau. of William George, 1st Lord Hylton. Educated at Eton; is Lord-Lieutenant and Custos Rotulorum of Lancashire, and Patron of 2 livings; sits in the House of Peers as Lord Molyneux,

U.K. (cr. 1831).—*Croxteth Hall, Liverpool; Boodle's Club, s.w.*

Heir, his son Charles William Hylton, Viscount Molyneux, *b.* 1867.

SEGRAVE, O'NEAL, Esq., of Cabra, co. Dublin.

Eldest son of the late Henry John Segrave, Esq., of Cabra, by Anna Frances, dau. of William Kellet, Esq., of Great Clonard, co. Wexford; *b.* 1819; *s.* 1843; *m.* 1848 Matilda, 3rd dau. of the late John Hyacinth Talbot, Esq., M.P., of Talbot Hall, co. Wexford. Educated at Stonyhurst; is a J.P. and D.L. for co. Dublin, late Lieut. 7th Dragoon Guards.—*Kiltynnon, Newtown Mt. Kennedy, co. Wicklow; Cabra, co. Dublin; Stephen's-Green Club, Dublin.*

Heir Pres., his brother Henry, late Capt. 12th Foot; *b.* 1823; *m.* 1850 Marr Elizabeth, dau. of Edward Francis Dehane, Esq., of Wolverhampton.

SELBY, CHARLES, Esq., of Yearle, Northumberland.

Eldest son of the late Thomas Selby, Esq., of Yearle, by Anne, dau. of Walter Rowland, Esq., of Berwick-on-Tweed; *b.* 1813; *s.* 1846; *m.* 1st 1846 Margaret, dau. of William Willoughby, Esq., of Berwick-on-Tweed; 2nd 1859 Julie Maria, dau. of the late Franz Horner, of Munich, Königlicher, Rath. Is a Magistrate for Northumberland.—*Yearle, Wooler.*

Heir Pres., his brother Leopold, *b.* 1817; *m.* 1840 Mary, dau. of William Reid, Esq., of Newcastle-on-Tyne, and has issue.

SELBY, GEORGE, Esq., of Shilbottle, Northumberland.

Second son of the late George Selby, Esq., of Twizel House and Beal, Northumberland, by Margaret, 2nd dau. of John Cook, Esq.; *b.* 1789; *m.* 1840 Mary Anne, eldest dau. of the late Rev. Charles Thomson, of Howick, Chaplain to Earl Grey, K.G. Mr. Selby, who was educated at Christ's Coll., Cambridge (B.A. 1820), is a Magistrate for Northumberland, and a Commander R.N.—*Belle Vue, Alnwick.*

SELBY, PRIDEAUX, Esq., of Paston, Northumberland.

Eldest son of the late Prideaux Selby, Esq., of Paston; *b.* 1810; *s.* 1839; *m.* 1840 Harriet Elizabeth, dau. of the late Admiral Sir William Beauchamp-Proctor, Bart., and has, with other issue,

 * Beauchamp, *b.* 1841.

Mr. Selby, who was educated at St. John's Coll., Cambridge (B.A. 1832, M.A. 1837), and called to the Bar at Gray's Inn 1843, is a J.P. and D.L. for Northumberland.—*Paston, Swansfield, Alnwick; Brooks's Club. s.w.;* 61, *Prince's Gate, s.w.*

SELBY, THOMAS, Esq., of Whitley, and Wimbish, Essex.

Only son of the late Rev. Charles Bridge Selby, by Anne, dau. of Thomas Davies, Esq., and granddau. of the late Thomas Selby, Esq., of Ightham Mote, Kent; *b.* 1807; *s.* 1820; *m.* 1858 Elizabeth, youngest dau. of Ralph Foster, Esq., of Holderness, co. York, and has, with other issue,

 * Walford Daking, educated at Tunbridge School; a Clerk in the Record Office; *b.* 1845.

Mr. Selby, who was educated at Tunbridge School, claims the dormant Viscountcy of Montagu (created 1554), as representative of George, 3rd son of the 1st Viscount. His great-grandfather assumed the name of Selby in lieu of Browne, by Royal licence, in 1783.—*Whitley, Halstead, Essex; Wimbish Hall, Saffron Walden, Ash Mount, Abbey Wood, s.k.*
810

SELBY, WALTER, Esq., of Biddlestone, Northumberland.

Elder son of the late Walter Selby, Esq., of Biddlestone, by Alicia, dau. of Thomas Swarbrick, Esq.; *b.* 1822; *s.* 1533; *m.* 1857 Laura Ann, dau. of Henry Tempest, Esq., and has, with other issue,

 * Walter Charles, *b.* 1858.

Mr. Selby, who was educated at St. Gregory's Coll., Downside, is a J.P. and D.L. for Northumberland (High Sheriff 1854).—*Biddlestone, Rothbury.*

SELBY. (See *Luard-Selby.*)

SELBY, of Twizell. (See *Antrobus.*)

SELBY-HELE, HENRY HORNE, Esq., of The Rocks, Sussex.

Eldest son of the late Rev. Selby Hele, of Grays Thurrock, Essex, by Sara Maria, dau. of John Leach Panter, Esq., of Fulham, Middlesex; *b.* 1840; *m.* 1863 Maria, only dau. of Thomas Mountstephen, Esq., of Almondsbury, co. Gloucester, and has issue,

 * Two daughters.

Mr. Selby-Hele was educated at King William's Coll., Isle of Man. This family, formerly of Devonshire, once enjoyed the title of Lord Hele.—*The Rocks, West Hoathly, East Grinstead.*

SELBY-LOWNDES. (See *Lowndes.*)

SELKIRK, Earl of (DUNBAR JAMES DOUGLAS). —Cr. 1646.

Only son of Thomas, 5th Earl, by Jean, dau. of the late James Wedderburn-Colville, Esq., of Ochiltree, co. Fife; *b.* 1809; *s.* 1820. Educated at Ch. Ch., Oxford (B.A. 1830); is Lord-Lieutenant of co. Kirkcudbright, and a Representative Peer for Scotland; was Keeper of the Great Seal of Scotland 1852 and 1858-9.—*St. Mary's, Kirkcudbright, N.B.; Athenæum, United Service, and Carlton Clubs, s.w.*

SELLAR. (See *Supplement.*)

SELSEY, Lady.

Anna Maria Louisa, 5th dau. of Frederick, 2nd Lord Boston, by Christina, only dau. of Paul Methuen, Esq., of Corsham House, Wilts; *m.* 1817 Henry John, 3rd Lord Selsey (ext.), who *d. s. p.* 1838.—71, *Chester Square, s.w.*

SELWIN, Sir JOHN THOMAS, Bart., of Down Hall, Essex (cr. 1748).

Fourth son of the late Sir James Ildeston, Bart., of Denton Park, co. York (who *d.* 1795), by Jane, dau. of J. Caygill, Esq., of Shaw House, co. York; *b.* 1785; *s.* his nephew, Sir Charles Henry Ildetson, Bart., as 6th Bart. 1861; *m.* 1825 Isabella, dau. of the late General John Leveson-Gower, of Bill Hill, Berks. Educated at Eton and St. John's Coll., Cambridge; is a Dep.-Lieut. for Essex, and Patron of 1 living. Sir John assumed in 1825 the name of Selwin on succeeding his brother Charles in the estates of the late Thomas Selwin, Esq., of Down Hall.—*Down Hall, Essex.*

Heir, his son Henry John Ildeston-Selwin, Esq., M.A. of St. John's Coll., Cambridge, a J.P. and D.L. for Essex, and M.P. for S. Essex; *b.* 1826; *m.* 1st 1850 the Hon. Sarah Elizabeth, eldest dau. of John, Lord Lyndhurst (*née s.* 1865); 2nd 1867 Eden, dau. of J. T. Thackrah, Esq., and widow of Sir Charles Ildetson, Bart., whose name he has assumed.

SELWYN, the Right Hon. Sir CHARLES JASPER, M.P., Q.C., P.C., of Richmond, Surrey (cr. 1867).

Youngest son of the late William Selwyn, Esq., Q.C., of Richmond, Surrey, by Latitia Frances, dau. of Thomas Kynaston, Esq., of Wytham, Essex; *b.* 1813; *m.* 1856 Hester, 5th dau. of J. G. Ravenshaw, Esq.,

formerly Chairman of the Hon. East India Company, and widow of T. Dowler, Esq., M.D. Educated at Eton and Trinity Coll., Cambridge (B.A. 1836, M.A. 1839, LL.D. 1862) ; called to the Bar at Lincoln's Inn 1840 ; appointed Commissary of the University of Cambridge 1855, Q.C. 1856, Solicitor-General 1867, Lord Justice of Appeal 1858 ; is a Dep.-Lieut. for Surrey and a Bencher of Lincoln's Inn : was M.P. for Cambridge University 1859–68 ; sworn a Member of the Privy Council 1868.—*Pagoda House, Richmond, Surrey ; Oxford and Cambridge, Athenæum, United University, Carlton and Union Clubs, s.w.; 37, Eaton Square, s.w. ; 6, Stone Buildings, Lincoln's Inn, w.c.*

SELWYN, the Rev. WILLIAM.

Eldest son of the late William Selwyn, Esq., Q.C., of Richmond, Surrey, by Lætitia Frances, dau. of Thomas Kynaston, Esq., of Witham, Essex; *b.* 1806 ; *m.* 1832 Juliana Elizabeth, eldest dau. of George Cooke, Esq., of Carr House, Doncaster. Educated at Eton and St. John's Coll., Cambridge (B.A. 1828, M.A. 1831) ; appointed Rector of Branstone, co. Leicester, 1831, Canon of Ely 1833, Lady Margaret's Professor of Divinity, Cambridge, 1855, Chaplain in Ordinary to Her Majesty 1859. This family was formerly settled at Matson, co. Gloucester.—*The College, Ely, Cambridgeshire ; Foxton, Royston ; Oxford and Cambridge Clubs, s.w.*

SELWYN, WILLIAM MARSHALL, Esq., of Bierley Hall, Yorkshire.

Third son of the late Rev. Edward Selwyn, Rector of Hemingford Abbotts, Hunts (who *d.* 1867), by Fanny, dau. of the late Rev. John Simons, Rector of St. Paul's Cray, Kent; *b.* 1825 ; *m.* 1851 Mary Anne, dau. of the late Col. Simons, and has issue.—*Bierley Hall, Bradford, Yorkshire.*

SEMPILL, Baroness (MARIA JANET SEMPILL). —Cr. 1489.

Elder dau. of Hugh, 14th Lord, by Maria, dau. of Charles Mellish, Esq., of Ragnal, Notts, and sister of Selkirk, 15th Lord ; *b.* 1795 ; *s.* 1835 ; *m.* 1836 Edward Candler, Esq., of Moreton Pinkney, a Dep.-Lieut. for co. Northampton, who, as well as the Baroness, assumed, by Royal licence, the name of Sempill only, in 1853. The family of Sempill were formerly Hereditary Sheriffs of their county, an office answering to that of Lord-Lieut. of the present day.—*Moreton-Pinkney Manor, Daventry.*

Heir Pres., her kinsman Sir William Forbes, Bart., of Craigievar (whom see).

SEMPILL, EDWARD, Esq., of Moreton-Pinkney.

Eldest surviving son of Henry Candler, Esq., by Mary, dau. and heir of William Ascough, Esq., of Kirby Mabzart, co. York, and grandson of William Candler, Esq., of Callan Castle, co. Kilkenny, and Ascough co. York ; *b.* 1803 ; *s.* his uncle, Sir Jonathan Cope, Bart., 1821, in the estate of Moreton-Pinkney ; *m.* 1836 Maria Janet, in her own right Baroness Sempill, and assumed by Royal sign manual the name and arms of Sempill only. Is a Dep.-Lieut. for co. Northampton. The family of Candler, of considerable antiquity in Norfolk and Suffolk, are of Saxon origin, and are maternally descended from the ancient family of Vavasour, now extinct in the male line.—*Moreton-Pinkney Manor, Northampton ; New Club, Edinburgh ; Carlton Club, s.w.*

SENHOUSE, JOSEPH POCKLINGTON-, Esq., of Netherhall, Cumberland.

Second son of the late Roger Pocklington, Esq., of Carlton House, Notts, by Jane, dau. of Sir James Campbell, Knt., of Inverneil and Ross, co. Argyll ; *b.* 1804 ; *s.* 1642, *m.* 1805 Elizabeth, eldest dau. of the late

Humphrey Senhouse, Esq., of Netherhall (whose name he assumed), and has, with other issue,

* Humphrey, *b.* 1843 ; educated at Eton.

Mr. Pocklington-Senhouse, who was educated at Eton and Exeter Coll., Oxford, is a Magistrate for Notts. and a J.P. and D.L. for Cumberland (High Sheriff 1846), and Patron of 1 living.—*Netherhall, Maryport ; Oxford and Cambridge Club, s.w.*

SENIOR, JAMES TREVOR, Esq., of Broughton, Bucks.

Eldest son of the late James Senior, Esq., of Broughton House, by Elizabeth, dau. of John Trevor, Esq., of Whitchurch, co. Salop ; *b.* 1804 ; *m.* 1837 Elizabeth, dau. of Stephen Grantham, Esq., of Sussex, and has, with other issue,

* James Trevor Lee, *b.* 1844.

Mr. Senior, who was educated at Eton, is a J.P. and D.L. for Bucks (High Sheriff 1843). This family is descended from a Roman duke, and maternally from an ancestor of the late Viscount Dungannon (ext.). —*Broughton House, Aylesbury.*

SENIOR, Mrs., of Glass Drummond, co. Down.

Adelaide, 3rd dau. of the late Jerningham Fitz-Henry, Esq., of Borough Hill, co. Wexford, by Mary, dau. of Thomas Colclough, Esq., of Ballyteigue Castle, co. Wexford ; *m.* 1828 Col. Henry Senior. 65th Regt., a Magistrate for co. Down, who *d. s. p.* 1861.—*Glass Drummond House, Kilkeel, co. Down.*

SENIOR. (See Huscy-Hunt.)

SERGISON, Capt. WARDEN, of Cuckfield Park, Sussex.

Only son of the late Warden George Sergison, Esq., J.P. and D.L., of Cuckfield Park (and grandson of the late Rev. William Saint Pritchard, who assumed the name of Sergison), by Editha, 3rd dau. of the late Sir Jacob H. Astley, Bart., and sister of Jacob, late Lord Hastings ; *b.* 1835 ; *s.* 1868 ; *m.* 1867 Emelia, youngest dau. of the late Sir William Gordon-Cumming, Bart., and has issue,

* Charles Warden, *b.* 1867.

Mr. Sergison, who was educated at Ch. Ch., Oxford, is Lord of the Manors of Cuckfield and Slaugham. Patron of 1 living, and Capt. 4th Hussars.—*Cuckfield Park, Butler's Green, Sussex ; Junior United Service Club, s.w.*

SERJEANTSON, GEORGE JOHN, Esq., of Hanlith Hall, Yorkshire.

Eldest surviving son of the late William Rookes Leedes Serjeantson, Esq., of Camp Hill and Hanlith Hall, by Elizabeth, dau. of Henry Dawkins, Esq., of Over Norton, Oxon ; *b.* 1800 ; *s.* 1840 ; *m.* 1835 Emma, dau. of Robert Chaloner, Esq., of Guisborough. Educated at Eton and Ch. Ch. Oxford (B.A. 1821); is a J.P. and D.L. for the N. and W. Ridings of Yorkshire, and a Dep.-Lieut. for the N. [...] Riding [...] *Camp Hill, Bedale ; Leeds's Club, s.w.*

SEROCOLD. (See Pearce-Serocold.)

SETON, Sir HENRY JOHN, Bart. (cr. 1646).

Eldest son of the late Sir Alexander Seton, Bart., of Abercorn, co. Linlithgow, by Lydia, dau. of the late Sir Charles William Blunt, Bart. ; *b.* 1796 ; *s.* as 5th Bart. 1810. Is a Groom-in-Waiting ; was formerly Capt. 5th Dragoons.—*Arthur's Club, s.w.*

*Heir Pres., his brother Charles Hay, late Capt. 5th Dragoons, b. 1797 ; m. 1829 Caroline, dau. of Walter Perry Hodges, Esq., and has issue, * Bruce Maxwell, b. 1836.*

SETON, Sir WILLIAM COOTE, Bart., of Pitmedden, Aberdeenshire (cr. 1684).
Only son of the late Major James Seton (who d. 1814),
by Frances, dau. of the late Capt. George Coote; b.
1808; s. his grandfather in 1819; m. 1834
Eliza Henrietta, dau. of the late Henry Lumsden, Esq.,
and widow of Capt. John Wilson. Educated at Edinburgh University; called to the Bar at Edinburgh
1830; is a J.P. and D.L. for co. Aberdeen.—*Pitmedden,
Udney, N.B.*
*Heir, his son James Lumsden, Capt. 102nd Royal Madras
Fusiliers, late Lieut. 1st Fusiliers; b. 1835.*

SETON, ALEXANDER, Esq., of Preston House,
Linlithgowshire.
Eldest son of the late Patrick Baron Seton, Esq., of
Preston, by Agnes, dau. of James Thompson, Esq.; b.
1806; s. 1838; m. 1st 1842 Mary, dau. of James Camp-
bell, Esq., of Dunmore (she d. 1847); 2nd 1848 Mary
Isabella, 4th dau. of Sir Wm. Baillie, Bart., of Polkem-
met, and by her, who d. 1864, has, with other issue,
  * Patrick Baron, b. 1849.
Mr. Seton, who was educated at Edinburgh, is a J.P.
and D.L. for co. Linlithgow.—*Preston House, Linlith-
gow, N.B.*

SETON, DAVID, Esq., of Mounie, Aberdeen-
shire.
Eldest surviving son of the late Alexander Seton, Esq.,
J.P. and D.L., of Mounie (who d. 1850), by Janet Skene,
dau. of the Rev. Skene Ogilvy, D.D., and grand-dau. of
George Seton, Esq., of Mounie; b. 1818; s. his brother
1852. Was formerly an Officer in the 93rd Highlanders, and 49th Foot. This family descended from
George, Lord Pittmedden, 2nd son of Sir Alexander
Seton, Bart.—*Mounie, Old Meldrum, N.B.; United
Service Club, Edinburgh; Junior United Service Club,
s.w.*
*Heir Pres., his brother George, a Major in the Army, formerly
of the R. Canadian Rifles; b. 1820; m. 18— Anne Lucy, only
surviving dau. of the late Baldwin Wake, Esq., and has issue.*

SETON, GEORGE, Esq.
Only son of the late George Seton, Esq., of the Indian
Country Service, by Margaret, dau. of James Hunter,
Esq., of Seaside, co. Perth; b. 1822; m. 1849 Sarah
Elizabeth, 2nd dau. of James Hunter, Esq., of Thurston,
and has, with other issue,
  * George, b. 1852.
Mr. Seton, who was educated at Edinburgh and Exeter
Coll., Oxford (B.A. 1845, M.A. 1848); called to the
Scottish Bar 1846, appointed Secretary to the Regis-
trar-General for Scotland 1854, and Superintendent of
Civil Service Examinations in Scotland 1862: is a Fel-
low and Member of Council of the Architectural Insti-
tute of Scotland, and a Fellow of the Society of Scottish
Antiquaries: he represents the family of Seton of Cari-
ston.—*Residence: St. Bennet's, Greenhill, Edinburgh.*

SETON, MILES CHARLES, Esq., of Treskerby,
Cornwall.
Eldest son of the late Col. William Carden Seton, C.B.;
b. 1800; m. 1st 1823 Ann, only child of J. Cooke, Esq.;
2nd 1841 the Hon. Mary Ursula, eldest dau. of William,
2nd Viscount Sidmouth, and has issue, by the former,
  * William Carden, Lieut. 82nd Foot; b. 1837.
Mr. Seton is the 27th in unbroken male descent from
Dougall, Lord Seton, in the Peerage of Scotland.—*Tres-
kerby, Camborne; Randolph House, Maida Hill, w.*

SETON-KARR, the Rev. JOHN, of Kippilaw,
Roxburghshire.
Eldest son of the late Andrew Seton-Karr, Esq., of Kip-
pilaw, by Alicia, dau. of William Rawlinson, Esq., of
Aucotts Hall, co. Lancaster; b. 1813; s. 1832; m. 1855
Anna, dau. of Archibald Douglas, Esq., of Glenfinart,

co. Argyll (she d. 1866). Educated at St. Mary's Hall,
Oxford (B.A. 1838), is a Magistrate for co. Gloucester,
and Vicar of Berkeley. This family descend from Andrew Ker, of Yair, a cadet of the house of Ferniehurst,
who changed his name to Karr.—*Kippilaw, Melrose,
N.B.; The Vicarage, Berkeley, Gloucestershire.*

SETON-STEUART. (See *Steuart.*)

SEVERN. (See *Cheesement-Severn.*)

SEVERNE, JOHN EDMUND, Esq., of Thenford,
Northamptonshire.
Eldest son of the late John Michael Severne, Esq., of
Thenford, by Anna Maria, dau. and co-heir of Edmund
M. Wigley, Esq., M.P., of Shakenhurst, co. Worcester,
and Ullesthorpe, co. Leicester; b. 1826; s. 1855; m.
1858 Florence Morgan, dau. of the Very Rev. Hugh
Tighe, Dean of Ardagh. Educated at Brasenose Coll.,
Oxford (B.A. 1848); is a J.P. and D.L. for cos.
Northampton (High Sheriff 1861) and Salop, and a
Magistrate for co. Montgomery; late Capt. 16th Light
Dragoons; elected M.P. for Ludlow 1865; served as
Deputy High Sheriff for his father in 1854 for co.
Montgomery. — *Thenford, Banbury; Wallop Hall,
Shrewsbury; Carlton and Army and Navy Clubs, s.w.*
*Heir Pres., his brother Arthur, in Holy Orders, M.A. of
Trinity Coll., Oxford, Rector of Thenford, late Rector of
Rock, co. Worcester; b. 1827.*

+SEVERNE, Mrs., of Poslingford Hall,
Suffolk.
Sarah Boddicott, dau. of the late John Yelloly, Esq., of
Cavendish Hall, Suffolk; m. 1861 (as 2nd wife) Samuel
Amy Severne, Esq., of Poslingford, J.P. and D.L. for
Suffolk, who d. 1865, having left by his 1st wife (Jean,
only dau. of the late Richard Dixon, Esq.) an only child,
  * Elizabeth Julia, m. 1860 Henry FitzWarren, 2nd son
  of the Very Rev. Lord Edward Chichester, and has issue,
  * a son, b. 1861. This family is a younger branch of the
Severnes of Thenford.—*Poslingford Hall, Clare, Suffolk.*

SEYMER, Mrs., of Handford, Dorset.
Isabella Helen, youngest dau. of the late William Webber, Esq., of Binfield Lodge, Berks; m. 1839 Henry
Ker Seymer, Esq., M.P., of Hanford, who was J.P.
and D.L. for Dorset, and d. 1864.—*Hanford, Blandford;
62, Eccleston Square, s.w.*

SEYMOUR.
(See under *Hertford, Marquis of,* and *Somerset, Duke of.*)

SEYMOUR, the Rev. Sir JOHN HOBART
CULME-, Bart., of Tothill, Devon (cr.
1809).
Eldest son of the late Admiral Sir Michael Seymour,
Bart., K.C.B., of Highmount, co. Limerick, by Jane,
dau. of the late James Hawker, Esq., Capt. R.N.; b.
1800; s. as 2nd Bart. 1834; m. 1st 1833 Elizabeth
dau. and co-heir of the Rev. Thomas Culme, of Tothill,
Devon (whose name he assumed 1841); 2nd 1844 Maria
Louisa, dau. of the late Charles Smith, Esq. Educated at
Winchester and Exeter Coll., Oxford; B.A. 1821, M.A.
1824); is a Prebendary of Gloucester, and Litany,
Rector of Northchurch, and Chaplain to the Queen.
—*Northchurch, Berkhampstead; Tothill, Plymouth.*
*Heir, his son Michael Culme, Capt. R.N.; b. 1836;
Mary Georgiana, eldest dau. of the Hon. Richard Watson,
of Rockingham Castle, co. Northampton.*

SEYMOUR, Sir GEORGE FRANCIS, G.C.B. (cr.
1831). (See under *Hertford, Marquis of.*)

SEYMOUR, the Right Hon. Sir GEORGE HA-
MILTON, G.C.B., G.C.H. (cr. 1836).
Eldest son of the late Lord George Seymour, by Isa-
bella, dau. of the Hon. and Rev. George Hamilton and

grandson of Francis, 1st Marquis of Hertford; *b.* 1797; *m.* 1831 the Hon. Gertrude, dau. of Henry Otway, 20th Lord Dacre. Educated at Merton Coll., Oxford (B.A. 1818, M.A. 1823); formerly Envoy Extraordinary and Minister Plenipotentiary at Vienna; previously Ambassador at St. Petersburg, and Minister at Florence, Brussels, and Lisbon.—10, *Grosvenor Crescent*, s.w.

SEYMOUR, Sir MICHAEL, G.C.B. (cr. 1855).
Second son of the late Admiral Sir Michael Seymour, Bart., by Jane, dau. of Capt. James Hawker, R.N.; *b.* 1802; *m.* 1829 Dora, dau. of the late Sir W. Knighton, Bart., and has issue,—
* Michael, *b.* 183–; *m.* 1863 Elizabeth Georgina Frederica, only dau. of Capt. W. H. Kennedy, R.N., and grand-dau. of the late Admiral the Hon. Sir Charles Paget.
Sir M. Seymour, who was educated at the Royal Naval Coll., is a Magistrate for Hants, and an Admiral of the Blue; late Naval Commander-in-Chief at Portsmouth, and formerly Commander-in-Chief on E. Indian Station, &c.; formerly Secretary and Registrar to the Order of the Bath; was M.P. for Devonport 1859–63.
—*Cadlington, Horndean; United Service Club*, s.w.

SEYMOUR, EDWARD WILLIAM, Esq., of Porthmawr, Brecknockshire.
Second son of the late Col. Francis Compton Seymour, by Mary his wife, grandson of Lord Francis Seymour, Dean of Wells, and great-grandson of Edward, 8th Duke of Somerset; *b.* 1791; *m.* 1st 1821 Charlotte Alice, dau. and co-heir of the late James Greene, Esq., of Turton Tower, co. Lancaster (she *d.* 1847); 2nd 1849 Elizabeth, eldest dau. of the late Rev. Charles Graham; 3rd 1863 Louisa Frances, youngest dau. of the late William Grant Macdowall, Esq., of Arndilly, co. Moray. Educated at the R. Naval Coll.; is a Magistrate for cos. Brecon and Monmouth, and a Commander R.N., retired.—*Porthmawr, Crickhowell.*

SEYMOUR, HENRY DANBY, Esq., of Knoyle, Wilts.
Eldest son of the late Henry Seymour, Esq., J.P. and D.L., of Northbrook, Devon, and of Knoyle (High Sheriff of Wilts in 1835), by Jane, dau. of Benjamin Hopkinson, Esq.; *b.* 1820; *s.* 1849. Educated at Eton and Ch. Ch., Oxford; is a J.P. and D.L. for Wilts, a Magistrate for Somerset, Patron of 1 living, and Lieut. Royal Wilts Yeomanry Cavalry; has been M.P. for Poole since 1850; was Joint Secretary to the Board of Control 1855–8. Represents a younger branch of the ducal house of Somerset.— *Knoyle, Hindon; Northbrook Lodge, Devon; Travellers' and Reform Clubs*, s.w.; 39, *Upper Grosvenor Street*, s.w.
Heir Pres. his brother Alfred, of East Knoyle, Wilts, and Norton Hall, Northamptonshire; educated at Ch. Ch., Oxford; a J.P. and D.L. for Wilts, late M.P. for Totnes; *b.* 1824; *m.* 1866 Isabella, 2nd dau. of Sir Baldwin Leighton, Bart., and widow of Beriah Botfield, Esq., M.P., of Norton Hall.

SEYMOUR, HENRY RICHMOND, Esq., of Crowood, Wilts.
Eldest son of the late J. R. Seymour, Esq., of Inholmes, Berks, by Mary Ann, eldest dau. and co-heir of General Read of Crowood; *b.* 1816; *s.* 1848. Educated at the Royal Military Coll., Sandhurst; is a J.P. and D.L. for Wilts, and a Magistrate for Berks; Major in the Royal Berkshire Yeomanry; was formerly Capt. 40th Regt. The family of Read was formerly of Wanborough, Wilts, and settled at Crowood about 1677.—*Crowood, Ramsbury, Wilts; Army and Navy Club*, s.w.
Heir Pres., his brother Charles Frederick, M.A. of University Coll., Oxford, Rector of Winchfield, Hants; *b.* 1818.

SEYMOUR, Mrs., of Barwick House, Norfolk.
Sophia Margaret, eldest dau. of the late Derick Hoste, Esq., of Barwick House, by Anne, dau. of the Rev. Dixon Hoste, of Titleshall, Norfolk; *s.* 1847; *m.* 1801 Rear-Admiral George Henry Seymour, C.B., a Magistrate for

Norfolk, M.P. for co. Antrim, and a Lord of the Admiralty, and has, with other issue,
* George Hoste, *b.* 1862.
Mrs. Seymour is Patron of 1 living.—*Barwick House, King's Lynn.*

SEYMOUR, THOMAS, Esq., of Ballymore, co. Galway.
Eldest son of the late Thomas Seymour, Esq., of Ballymore, by Jane, dau. of David Thompson, Esq., of Banagher, co. Down; *b.* 1794; *s.* 1821; *m.* 1822 Margaret Matilda, dau. of Walter Lawrence, Esq., of Belle Vue, co. Galway, and has, with other issue,
* Walter, *b.* 1825; *m.* 1859 Bellinda, only child of the Rev. A. A. Gordon, of Anerley Grove, Norwood, Surrey.
Mr. Seymour, who was educated at Trinity Coll., Dublin (B.A. 1815, M.A. 1832), and called to the Irish Bar 1819, is a Magistrate for co. Galway, was High Sheriff of King's Co. 1859.—*Ballymore Castle, Lawrencetown, co. Galway; Sackville Street and University Clubs, Dublin.*

SEYMOUR, WILLIAM DIGBY, Esq.
Son of William Seymour, Esq., of Gloucester Terrace, Hyde Park; *b.* 1805; *m.* 1833 Emily, dau. of the late Rev. Brackley C. Kennett, Rector of East Ilsley, Berks, and has issue,—Is a Merchant in London; was M.P. for Hull 1854–7.—61, *Lowndes Square*, s.w.

SEYMOUR, WILLIAM DIGBY, Esq., Q.C.
Son of the late Rev. Charles Seymour, Vicar of Kilronan, by Beata, dau. of Fergus Langley, Esq., of Knockanure, co. Tipperary; *b.* 1822; *m.* 1847 Emily, dau. of Joseph John Wright, Esq. Mr. Seymour, who was educated at Trinity Coll., Dublin (B.A. 1843), called to the Bar at the Middle Temple 1846, appointed Recorder of Newcastle-on-Tyne 1854, made a Q.C. 1861; was M.P. for Sunderland 1852–5; M.P. for Southampton 1859–65. He is cousin of Thomas Seymour, Esq., of Ballymore Castle, co. Galway, the head of an Irish branch of the ducal house of Seymour.—2, *Doctor Johnson's Buildings, Temple, E.C.; The Terrace, Putney.*

SEYS, WILLIAM ÆNEAS, Esq., of Tutshill House, Gloucestershire.
Eldest son of the late Rev. William Seys, M.A., of Tutshill House (who was Vicar of Trelleck, co. Monmouth, and *d.* 1842), by Anne, dau. of the late Rev. Edmund Rawlins, Rector of Dorsington, co. Gloucester; *b.* 1822; *m.* 1854 Maria Guilhermina Power, and has, surviving issue,
* Godfrey, *b.* 1859.
Mr. Seys is a Magistrate for cos. Gloucester and Monmouth.—*Tutshill House, Chepstow.*

SHADWELL, WILLIAM DREW LUCAS-, Esq., of Fairlight Hall, Sussex.
Eldest son of the late William Stent, Esq., of Fittleworth, Sussex, by Sarah, dau. of William Drew, Esq.; *b.* 1816; *m.* 1851 Florentia Margaret Frances, only child and heir of the Rev. Henry Wynch, Rector of Pett, Sussex, and has, with other issue,
* William, *b.* 1852.
Mr. Lucas-Shadwell, who was educated at Wadham Coll., Oxford, assumed the name of Lucas-Shadwell after his relative the late William Lucas Shadwell, Esq., of Hastings; he is a J.P. and D.L. for Sussex (High Sheriff 1854), and Capt. 2nd Sussex Volunteer Artillery.—*Fairlight Hall, Hastings.*

SHAFTESBURY, Earl of (ANTHONY ASHLEY COOPER, K.G.).—Cr. 1672.
Eldest son of Cropley, 6th Earl, by Lady Anne, dau. of George, 4th Duke of Marlborough; *b.* 1801; *s.* 1851; *m.* 1830 Lady Emily, dau. of Peter Leopold, 5th Earl Cowper. Educated at Harrow and Ch. Ch., Oxford

(B.A. 1822); is Lord-Lieutenant and Custos Rotulorum of Dorset, and Patron of 8 livings; was M.P. for Woodstock 1826-30, for Dorchester 1830-1, for co. Dorset 1831-46, and for Bath 1847-51.—*St. Giles's, Cranbourne; Carlton and Athenæum Clubs, s.w.*; 24, *Grosvenor Square, w.*

Heir, his son Anthony, Lord Ashley, educated at Rugby; a J.P. and D.L. for Dorset, and Lieut.-Col. Dorset Militia; late Lieut. Dorset Yeomanry Cavalry; and formerly in the Navy; M.P. for Hull 1857-9, and for Cricklade 1859-65; *b.* 1831; *m.* 1857 Lady Harriet, dau. of George Hamilton, 3rd Marquis of Donegal.

SHAFTO, the Rev. ARTHUR DUNCOMBE, of Brancepeth, co. Durham.

Youngest son of the late Robert Eden Duncombe Shafto, Esq., of Whitworth Park, co. Durham, by Catharine, 3rd dau. of Sir John Eden, Bart., of Windlestone; *b.* 1815; *m.* 1842 Dorothea, dau. of George Hutton Wilkinson, Esq., of Harperley Park, co. Durham, and by her, who *d.* 1866, has, with other issue,

* Edward, Lieut. R.A.; *b.* 1843.

Mr. Shafto, who was educated at University Coll., Durham, is a Magistrate for cos. Durham and Hunts, Rector of Brancepeth and Rural Dean, and Patron of 2 livings.—*Brancepeth Rectory, Durham.*

SHAFTO, ROBERT DUNCOMBE, Esq., of Whitworth Park, co. Durham.

Eldest son of the late Robert Eden Duncombe Shafto, Esq., M.P., of Whitworth Park, by Catharine, dau. of Sir John Eden. Bart., of Windlestone; *b.* 1806; *s.* 1848; *m.* 1838 Charlotte Rose, dau. of the late William Baring, Esq., and has, with other issue,

* Robert Charles, *b.* 1843.

Mr. Shafto, who is a J.P. and D.L. for co. Durham, a Magistrate for Wilts, and Patron of 3 livings, has been M.P. for North Durham since 1847.—*Whitworth Park, Ferryhill; Hampworth Lodge, Salisbury; Brooks's Club, s.w.; Cromwell Road, South Kensington, w.*

SHAFTO, WILLIAM HENRY, Esq., of Bavington Hall, Northumberland.

Elder son of the late Sir Cuthbert Shafto, of Bavington Hall (who was High Sheriff of Northumberland in 1795), by Mary, dau. of William Swinburne, Esq.; *b.* 1784; *s.* his younger brother 1866; *m.* 1831 Mary, widow of — Nield, Esq., and has issue,

* William Henry, *b.* 1834.

Mr. Shafto is Lord of the Manor of Bavington.—*Bavington Hall, Newcastle-on-Tyne.*

SHARP, THOMAS, Esq., of Houstoun, co. Linlithgow.

Eldest son of the late Norman Sharp, Esq., J.P. and D.L. of Houstoun, Major H.E.I.C.S., by Elizabeth Binning, 4th dau. of John Campbell, Esq., of Kiddalloig. co. Argyll; *b.* 1811; *s.* 1861. Mr. Sharp, who was educated at St. Andrew's University, is a J.P. and D.L. for co. Linlithgow, Lord of the Barony of Houstoun, and a Major in the County Militia.—*Houstoun House, Broxburn, N.B.; New Club, Edinburgh.*

Heir Pres. his brother John Campbell, Professor of Humanity at St. Andrews; *b.* 1819; *m.* 1855 Eliza, dau. of Andrew Douglas, Esq., of Lockerbie, co. Dumfries, and has issue,
* John Campbell, *b.* 1858.

SHAKERLEY, Sir CHARLES WATKIN, Bart., of Somerford, Cheshire (cr. 1838).

Only son of the late Sir Charles Peter Shakerley, Bart., of Somerford, by his 2nd wife Jessy, dau. of the late James Scott, Esq., of Rotherfield Park, Hants; *b.* 1833; *s.* 2nd Bart. 1857; *m.* 1858 Georgiana Harriott, dau. of George Holland Ackers. Esq., of Gt. Moreton Hall, co. Chester. Is a J.P. and D.L. for co. Chester (High Sheriff 1865), and Patron of 1 living.—*Somerford Park, Congleton; Boodle's Club, s.w.*

Heir, his son Walter Geoffrey, *b.* 1859.

SHAKERLEY, GEOFFREY JOSEPH, Esq., of Whatcroft, Cheshire.

Younger son of the late Charles Watkin John Shakerley, Esq., of Somerford Park. co. Chester, and Shakerley, co. Lancaster, by Dorothy, dau. of J. Moreland, Esq., of Chapplethwaite Hall. Westmoreland; *b.* 1800; *s.* 1834; *m.* 1827 Eleanor Maria, dau. of the Rev. James Webster, and has, with other issue,

* Geoffry Joseph, Capt. R.A.; *b.* 1832; *m.* 1867 Emma, 2nd dau. of the late Sir Richard P. Butler, Bart., of Ballin-Temple, co. Carlow.

Mr. Shakerley, who was educated at Westminster and Ch. Ch., Oxford (B.A. 1821), is a Magistrate for Cheshire, and is descended from a common ancestor with Sir C. W. Shakerley, Bart.—*Whatcroft, Davenham; Carlton Club, s.w.*

SHAND, CHARLES FARQUHAR, Esq., LL.D., &c., Chief Justice of Mauritius.

Son of the late Rev. James Shand, M.A., of Marykirk, co. Kincardine, by Margaret, sister of the late Robert Farquhar, Esq., of Newark, co. Renfrew; *b.* 1812; *m.* 1850 Margaret, dau. of the late Col. Lee Harvey, of Castle Semple, and has, with other issue,

* James Widdrington, *b.* 1853.

Mr. Shand, who was educated at the Universities of Aberdeen and Edinburgh. and on the Continent, was admitted an Advocate 1834; he was formerly Counsel for the Lords of the Treasury and Commissioners of Woods and Forests: appointed Chief Judge of the Mauritius 1860; late Capt. in the Edinburgh Volunteer Rifles.—*The Mauritius.*

SHAND, FRANCIS, Esq., of Woolton, Lancashire.

Eldest son of the late Charles Shand, of Rupert House, Everton, co. Lancaster, by Grace, eldest dau. of John Mitchell, Esq., of Maryton, near Montrose, N.B.; *b.* 1800; *m.* 1837 Lydia, eldest dau. of Sir William Bram, of Cedar Hill, Antigua, and Westwood, Hants, and has, with other issue,

* Francis, *b.* 1848.

Mr. Shand, who was educated at Rugby, is a Magistrate for co. Lancaster, and for Liverpool (Mayor 1856-7).—*Woolton Wood, Liverpool.*

SHANK, JAMES, Esq., of Laurencekirk, Kincardineshire.

Third son of Henry Shank, Esq., of Castlerig, co. Fife, by Anna Maria, eldest dau. of James Rivett-Carnac, Esq., of Rockcliff, Hants; *b.* 1818. Is a J.P. and D.L. for co. Kincardine.—*The Ville, Laurencekirk, N.B.*

SHANK. (See *Schank.*)

SHANNON, Earl of (RICHARD BOYLE).—Cr. 1756.

Eldest son of Henry, 3rd Earl, by Sarah, dau. of the late John Hyde, Esq., of Castle Hyde, co. Cork; *b.* 1809; *s.* 1842; *m.* 1832 Emily Henrietta, dau. of the late Lord George Seymour. Sits in the House of Lords as Lord Carleton, U.K. (cr. 1786): is a Magistrate for co. Cork, Patron of 4 livings, and Col. W. Cork Artillery: descended from a common ancestor with the Earl of Cork.—*Castle Martyr, co. Cork.*

Heir, his son Henry Bentinck, Viscount Boyle, *b.* 1833; *m.* 1st 1859 Lady Blanche Emma, dau. of Henry, 3rd Earl of Harewood (she *d.* 1867); 2nd 1868 Julia Charlotte, youngest dau. of the late Sir William Cradock-Hartopp, Bart.; he has, by the former, with other issue, * Richard Henry, *b.* 1860.

SHAPLAND, JOSEPH, Esq., of Cradley, Herefordshire.

Second son of the late Thomas Shapland, Esq., Banker, of Marshfield, co. Gloucester, by Anne, dau. of James

Hatherell, Esq.; *b.* 1815; *m.* 1st 1842 Susannah Hales, representative of the old family of Hill, of the Hill House; 2nd 1861 Sarah Louisa, dau. of George Brace, Esq., of Cavendish Square, London. Called to the Bar at the Middle Temple 1841, and went the Oxford Circuit.—*Hill House, Cradley, Great Malvern; Union Club, s.w.*

SHARLAND-CRUWYS. (See *Cruwys.*)

SHARMAN-CRAWFORD. (See *Crawford.*)

SHARP, ARCHIBALD, Esq., of Rothesay, Buteshire.
Youngest son of the late Robert Sharp, Esq., of Rothesay, by Janet, dau. of Daniel Duncan, Esq.; *b.* 1802; *s.* 1832; *m.* 1832 Maria, dau. of James Smith, Esq., of Liverpool, and has, with other issue,
* Robert, *b.* 1835.
Mr. Sharp is a J.P. and D.L. for co. Bute.—*Mountstuart Road, Rothesay, N.B.*

SHARP, WILLIAM, Esq., F.R.S., of Horton House, Warwickshire.
Eldest surviving son of the late Richard Sharp, by Mary, dau. of John Turton, Esq., of Gildersome; *b.* 1805; *m.* 1st 1833 Anne, dau. of Samuel Hailstone, Esq., F.S.A., of Bradford; 2nd 1836 Emma, dau. of the Rev. John Scott, M.A., Vicar of N. Ferriby, co. York, &c., and has, with other issue,
* John, M.A. of Queen's Coll., Oxford, in Orders (now in India); *b.* 1837.
Mr. Sharp, who was educated at Westminster, Guy's Hospital, and the University of Paris, is a Physician, formerly in practice at Bradford, Yorkshire. This family have long held land near Bradford, Horton Hall being their residence before 1545. — *Horton House, Rugby.*

+ **SHARP, WILLIAM LISTER,** Esq., of Morton House, Lincolnshire.
Son of the late W. Sharp, Esq., of Morton House; *b.* 18—; *m.* 1860 Martha, widow of the Rev. Herbert N. Beaver, Vicar of Grinley-on-the-Hill, Notts, and has issue. Mr. Sharp was formerly a Merchant.—*Morton House, Gainsborough.*

SHARP. (See *Jelf-Sharp.*)

SHARPE, WILLIAM JOHN, Esq., of Hoddam, Dumfriesshire.
Youngest and only surviving son of the late Charles Sharpe, Esq., of Hoddam (who assumed the name of Sharpe in lieu of Kirkpatrick, under the will of Matthew Sharpe, Esq., of Hoddam), by Eleanora, dau. of John Renton, Esq., of Lammerton, and of Lady Susan Montgomerie, dau. of Alexander, Earl of Eglinton; *b.* 1797; *s.* his brother 1858. Educated at the University of Edinburgh, admitted a Writer to the Signet 1820, is a Commissioner of Supply for co. Dumfries, and Patron of 1 living; was Secretary of the Royal Caledonian Hunt 1827–63.—*Hoddam Castle Knockhill, Ecclefechan, N.B.*

SHAW, Sir JOHN CHARLES KENWARD, Bart., of Kenward, Kent (cr. 1665).
Eldest son of the late Capt. Charles Shaw, R.N. (who *d.* 1829), by Frances Anne, dau. of the late Sir Henry Hawley, Bart., of Leybourne Grange, Kent; *b.* 1829; *s.* his uncle as 7th Bart. 1857; *m.* 1860 Maria, only dau. of the late Henry Sparkes, Esq. (she *d.* 1863). Educated at Eton and Merton Coll., Oxford; is a Magistrate for Kent; was Lieut. W. Kent Yeomanry Cavalry 1852–8.—*Kenward, Pembury, Tunbridge.*

Heir Pres., his twin-brother Charles John Kenward, Rector of Newington-next-Hythe, late Vicar of Dreusett, Kent; *b.* 1829; *m.* 1859 Julia Elizabeth, dau. of Capt. Bowyer, R.N.; and has, with other issue, • Charles John Motson, *b.* 1860.

SHAW, Sir JOHN, Bart., of Kilmarnock, Ayrshire (cr. 1813).
Eldest son of the late John Macfie, Esq., of Whitehall Place, London, by Margaret, sister of the late Sir James Shaw, Bart.; *b.* 1787; *s.* his uncle as 2nd Bart. 1843. Is Patron of 1 living. Exchanged his family name of Macfie for that of Shaw 1807. The 1st Bart. was Lord Mayor of London, and obtained the Baronetcy with remainder to his nephew.—*The Lodge, Kilmarnock, N.B.; 33, Sussex Gardens, w.*

SHAW, Sir ROBERT, Bart., of Bushy Park, co. Dublin (cr. 1821).
Eldest son of the late Sir Robert Shaw, Bart., of Dublin (many years M.P. for Dublin), by his 1st wife Maria, only dau. of A. Wilkinson, Esq., of Bushy Park; *b.* 1796; *s.* as 2nd Bart. 1849. Educated at Trinity Coll., Dublin (B.A. 1815, M.A. 1817); is a J.P. and D.L. for the city of Dublin; formerly Lieut.-Col. Queen's Own Dublin Militia. — *Bushy Park, Rathfarnham, Dublin; Carlton Club, s.w.*

Heir Pres., his brother the Right Hon. Frederick, of Kimmage House, near Rathfarnham, co. Dublin. Educated at Trinity Coll., Dublin, and at Brasenose Coll., Oxford (B.A. 1819, cr. Hon. LL.D. Dublin, 1838); called to the Irish Bar 1822; appointed Recorder of Dundalk 1826, Recorder of Dublin 1828, a Bencher of King's Inns 1829, sworn a Member of the Privy Council in Ireland 1852; was M.P. for Dublin 1830–2, for University of Dublin 1832–48; *b.* 1799; *m.* 1819 Thomasine Emily, youngest dau. of the late Hon. George Jocelyn, and grand-dau. of Robert, 1st Earl of Roden, and by her, who *d.* 1859, has, with other issue, • Robert, Lieut.-Col. Royal Dublin Militia; *b.* 1821; *m.* 1852 Kate, dau. of W. Burton, Esq., of Grove, co. Tipperary.

SHAW, Sir CHARLES, Knt. (cr. 1838).
Son of the late Charles Shaw, Esq., of Ayr, N.B.; *b.* 1795; *m.* 1841 Louisa Hannah, dau. of Major M. Curry. Educated at the University of St. Andrew's; is a Col. in the Portuguese Army, and Brigadier-General in the Spanish Service; Knight of Tower and Sword in Portugal, and San Fernando in Spain; formerly Lieut. 52nd and 90th Foot; has been Chief Commissioner of Police at Manchester and Bolton.—Residence: *Blagdon-on-Tyne, Durham.*

SHAW, BENTLEY, Esq., of Woodfield, Yorkshire.
Eldest son of the late William Shaw, Esq., of Woodfield House, by Anne, eldest dau. of the late Timothy Bentley, Esq., of Lockwood; *b.* 1816; *s.* 1840; *m.* 1842 Jane Elizabeth, only child and heir of the late John Lancaster, Esq., of Huddersfield, and has, with other issue.
* Robert Bentley, *b.* 1843.
Mr. Shaw is a Magistrate for the W. Riding of Yorkshire.—*Woodfield House, Huddersfield.*

SHAW, BERNARD ROBERT, Esq., of Monkstown Castle, co. Cork.
Eldest son of the late Bernard Shaw, Esq., of Monkstown Castle, by Jane, dau. of Michael Roberts Westropp, Esq., Merchant, of Cork; *b.* 1801; *s.* 1808; *m.* 1st 1822 Rebecca, dau. of Edward Reeves, Esq., of Ballyglissane; 2nd 1852 Eliza, dau. of James Finucane (Major), and one of the co-heirs of the late Andrew Finucane, Esq., of Ennistymon, co. Clare, and had, with other issue.
Bernard Robert, late Capt. 56th Regt., *b.* 1824; *d.* 18—, having married, and left, with other issue, an only son, • Bernard Robert, *b.* 1860.

Mr. Shaw, who was educated at Trinity Coll., Dublin, is a Magistrate for co. Cork, and Lord of the Manors of Belvelly and Ballydanielmore, co. Cork. This family is of Scotch extraction, and formed part of the Clan Chattan, and settled at an early period in Hampshire —*Monkstown Castle, near Cork.*

SHAW, JOHN RALPH, Esq., of Arrowe Park, Cheshire.

Second son of the late William Nicholson, Esq., of Chadkirk, co. Chester, by Hannah, 3rd dau. of William Roe, Esq., of Liverpool (she *m.* 2ndly Sir Duncan McDougall, K.S.F., and *d.* 1866); *b.* 1811; assumed, 1837, the name of Shaw, under the will of his uncle, John Shaw, Esq.; *m.* 1837 Fanny Harriet, 3rd dau. of the Rev. William C. Cruttenden, M.A., and has, with other issue,

* William Otho Nicholson, *b.* 1846.

Mr. Shaw, who was educated at Ch. Ch., Oxford, is a Magistrate for co. Chester (High Sheriff 1864), and formerly a Capt. 1st Royal Lancashire Militia.—*Arrowe Park, Woodchurch; Glencarron, Dingwall, Rosshire; Conservative Club, s.w.; 35, Queen's Gate, Kensington, s.w.*

+SHAW-HELLIER, THOMAS, Esq., of Rodbaston Hall, Staffordshire.

Son of the late T. Shaw-Hellier, Esq., of Woodhouse, co. Stafford; *b.* 18—; *m.* 18— Mary, dau. of — Bradney, Esq., and has, with other issue,

* Thomas Bradney, educated at Winchester, a Magistrate for co. Stafford; *b.* 1836.

Mr. Shaw-Hellier is a Magistrate for co. Stafford, and Lord of the Manor of Rodbaston.—*Rodbaston Hall, Penkridge, Staffordshire.*

SHAW-LEFEVRE. (See *Lefevre.*)

SHAW-STEWART. (See *Stewart.*)

SHAWE, RICHARD FLEETWOOD, Esq., of Brantingham, Yorkshire.

Eldest son of the late Richard Shawe, Esq., of Brantingham, by Emily, dau. of Henry Deffell, Esq., of London; *b.* 1804; *s.* 1816; *m.* 1832 Anna, eldest dau. of Col. Robert Bell. Educated at Harrow; is a Dep.-Lieut. for the E. Riding of Yorkshire; formerly Capt. 9th Lancers.—*Brantingham, Brough; Junior United Service Club, s.w.*

Heir Pres., his brother Nathaniel, *b.* 1807; *m.* 1841 Helen, dau. of Frederick Perkins, Esq.

SHAWE, Mrs., of Maple Hayes, Staffordshire.

Maria Mary, only dau. of the late Col. Edward Miles; *m.* as his 2nd wife 1837 Samuel Pole Shawe, Esq., a J.P. and D.L. of Maple Hayes (who was High Sheriff of co. Stafford 1855, and *d.* 1856). Mrs. Shawe is Lady of the Manor of Maple Hayes. This family was formerly of Hints Hall, co. Stafford, and of Cliff Hall, co. Warwick.—*Maple Hayes, Lichfield.*

Heir Pres. (under the entail), her step-son Henry Curliffe, *b.* 1840, m. 1848 Georgina Wilson, moldan of the late Rev. Sir William Nigel Gresley, Bart., of Nether-cale Hall, co. Leicester, and has, with other issue, * a son, *b.* 1864.

SHAWE-TAYLOR. (See *Taylor.*)

+SHEARLEY, the Rev. WILLIAM JAMES, of Mellefont Abbey, Somersetshire.

Son of the late W. Shearley, Esq.; *b.* 181—. Educated at St. Peter's Coll., Cambridge (B.A. 1840, M.A. 1843), is Perpetual Curate of Henton, Somerset.—*Mellefont Abbey, Wookey, Wells.*

SHEDDEN, Miss, of Morris Hill, Ayrshire.

Jessie Caldwell, only child of the late Alexander

816

Shedden, Esq., of Morris Hill, by his 1st wife Jessie, 2nd dau. of James Henderson, of Greenock; *s.* 1867. —*Morris Hill, Beith, N.B.*

SHEDDEN, ROSCOW COLE, Esq., of Millfield, I. of Wight.

Third son of the late George Shedden, Esq., of Spring Hill, East Cowes, by Mary, dau. of William Goodrich, Esq., of East Cowes; *b.* 1811; *m.* 1854 Charlotte Joanna, dau. of James Fitchett Burrell, Esq., of Belvoir House, Fareham, Hants, and has, with other issue,

* George, *b.* 1856.

Mr. Shedden, who was educated at Winchester, is a Magistrate for Hants.—*Millfield House, E. Cowes.*

SHEDDEN, WILLIAM GEORGE, Esq., of Spring Hill, Isle of Wight.

Eldest son of the late George Shedden, Esq., of Paulersbury Park, co. Northampton (who *d.* 1855), by Mary, elder dau. and co-heir of William Goodrich, Esq., of Spring Hill; *b.* 1803; *s.* his mother 1827; *m.* 1861 Caroline, youngest dau. of the late Admiral Sir Graham Eden Hamond, Bart., G.C.B. Educated at Winchester and at the University of Edinburgh; is a Magistrate for Hants, Lord of the Manors of Hardmead, Bucks, and Spring Hill, Isle of Wight, and Patron of 1 living. —*Spring Hill, East Cowes.*

SHEDDEN, WILLIAM LINDESAY, Esq., of Delawarr House, Hampshire.

Youngest son of the late Col. John Shedden, of Eastonton and Efford, Hants, and Pont-y-Pandy, co. Glamorgan, by Sophia, dau. of Matthew Lewis, Esq., Under Secretary of War, and co-heir (with her sister, Lady Lushington) of M. G. Lewis, Esq., M.P.; *b.* 1809; *m.* 1851 Martha Sophia, 2nd dau. of the late S. Meade Hobson, Esq., of Dublin, and Muckridge House, co. Cork, and has issue,

* Lewis William, *b.* 1853.

Mr. Shedden, who was educated at Harrow, is a Magistrate for Hants, and was formerly in the 17th Lancers. This family is a younger branch of the Sheddens, of Paulersbury.—*Pont-y-Pandy, Caerphilly, Swansea; Delawarr House, Lymington; Junior U.S. Club, s.w.*

SHEE, Sir GEORGE, Bart., of Dunmore House, co. Galway (cr. 1794).

Eldest and only surviving son of the late Sir George Shee, Bart., of Castlebar, co. Mayo, by Elizabeth Maria, dau. of James Crisp, Esq.; *b.* 1784; *s.* as 2nd Bart., 1825; *m.* 1st 1808 Jane, dau. of William Young, Esq., of Heston House, Herts (who *d.* 1832); 2nd 1841 Sarah, dau. of Henry Barrett, Esq., of Denton, Norfolk (she *d.* 1866). Is a J.P. and D.L. for co. Galway (High Sheriff 1828); formerly Minister at Berlin and Stutgardt; was Under-Secretary for Foreign Affairs 1830-5.—*Dunmore House, Galway; 38, Grosvenor Place, s.w.*

+SHEEPSHANKS, WILLIAM, Esq., of Rawdon Hill, Yorkshire.

Second son of the late Joseph Sheepshanks, Esq., Merchant, of Leeds, by Ann, dau. of R. Wilson, Esq., of Kendal; *b.* 179—; *s.* 1834; *m.* 1818 Sarah, dau. of Lucas Nicholson, Esq., of Leeds, and has, with other issue,

* Thomas, in Holy Orders, Incumbent of Bilton, near Harrogate; *b.* 1819; *m.* 1849 Margaret, dau. of N. Milner, Esq.

Mr. Sheepshanks is a Merchant and Manufacturer at Leeds, Lord of the Manor of Arthington, and Patron of 2 livings.—*Rawdon Hill, Otley; Arthington Hall, Harrogate.*

SHEFFIELD, Earl of (GEORGE AUGUSTUS FREDERICK CHARLES HOLROYD).—Cr. 1816.

Only son of John, 1st Earl, by his 3rd wife, Lady Ann

dau. of Frederick, 2nd Earl Guilford; b. 1802 ; s. 1821 ; m. 1825 Lady Harriet, dau. of Henry, 2nd Earl of Harewood. Educated at Eton; sits in the House of Lords as Lord Sheffield, U.K. (cr. 1802) ; is a J.P. and D.L. for Sussex, and Patron of 2 livings ; was a Lord in Waiting 1858-9.—*Sheffield Park, Uckfield ; Carlton Club, s.w. ; 20, Portland Place, w.*

Heir, his son Henry North, Viscount Pevensey ; educated at Eton ; is a J.P. and D.L. for Sussex ; late M.P. for E. Sussex ; formerly Attaché at Copenhagen ; b. 1832.

SHEFFIELD, Sir ROBERT, Bart., of Normanby, Lincolnshire (cr. 1755).
Eldest son of the late Sir Robert Sheffield, Bart., J.P. and D.L., by Julia Brigida, dau. of the late Sir John Newbolt, Knt., Chief Justice of Madras ; b. 1823 ; s. as 5th Bart. 1862 ; m. 1867 Priscilla Isabella Laura, 3rd dau. of the late Lieut.-Col. Henry Dumaresq, R.E. Educated at C. C. C., Oxford ; is a J.P. and D.L. for co. Lincoln, Lord of the Manor of Conesby, and Patron of Burton ; late Capt. R. Horse Guards. This family descend from a brother of the last Duke of Buckingham (cr. 1703) of this name.—*Normanby Hall, Brigg ; Carlton Club, s.w. ; 35, Portland Place, w.*

Heir Pres., his brother Henry Digby, b. 1830.

SHEFFIELD, the Rev. CHARLES.
Younger son of the late Rev. Sir Robert Sheffield, Bart., of Normanby, co. Lincoln (who d. 1815), by his 2nd wife Sarah Anne, dau. of the Rev. Brackley Kennett, D.D., of East Ilsley, Berks ; b. 1798 ; m. 1820 Lucy, dau. of Col. Smelt, Lieut.-Governor of Isle of Man, and by her (who d. 1857), has issue,

* Four daughters.

Mr. Sheffield, who was educated at Westminster and Ch. Ch., Oxford (B.A. 1820, M.A. 1824), is a Magistrate for Lindsey, Lincolnshire, Rector of Flixborough with Burton Stather, and Rural Dean. — *Flixborough Rectory, Brigg.*

SHEGOG, GEORGE ALEXANDER, Esq., of Munnilly, co. Monaghan.
Second and only surviving son of the late George Shegog, Esq., J.P., of Munnilly, by Margaret, dau. of John P. Hamilton, Esq.; b. 1835 ; s. his brother 1867. Was formerly in the 5th Fusiliers. This family descend from the Shegogs of Lubec, Lower Saxony, who came to Ireland in 1760.—*Munnilly, Clones, Ireland.*

SHEIL, Sir JUSTIN, K.C.B., of Kilmactalway, co. Dublin (cr. 1855).
Son of the late Edward Sheil, Esq., of Bellevue, Waterford, by Catherine, dau. of — MacCarthy, Esq., of Spring House, co. Tipperary, and brother of the late Right Hon. R. L. Sheil, M.P.; b. 1803 ; m. 1848 Mary Leonora, dau. of the late Chief Baron Stephen Woulfe, and has, with other issue,

* Edward, b. 1851.

Sir J. Sheil, who is a Major-General in the Indian Army, has been Envoy Extraordinary and Minister Plenipotentiary to Persia ; he purchased Kilmactalway (Castle Bagot) from the family of Mr. Moore-O'Ferrall 1866.—*Kilmactalway, Rathcoole, co. Dublin ; Athenæum and United Service Clubs s.w. ; 13, Eaton Place, s.w.*

SHEIL, JAMES, Esq., of Killymeal, co. Tyrone.
Eldest son of the late James Sheil, Esq., Q.C., of Killymeal House, by Jane, eldest dau. of the late Robert Hall, Esq., of Merton Hall, co. Tipperary ; b. 1829 ; s. 1853. Educated at Trinity Coll., Dublin (B.A. 1848) ; called to the Bar at Gray's Inn 1852. This family descend from ' Nial of the Nine Hostages,' and originally bore the family name of O'Sheil.—*Windham Club, s.w.; 9, King's Bench Walk, Temple, e.c.*

SHELDON, HENRY JAMES, Esq., of Brailes House, Warwickshire.
Second son of the late Edward Ralph Charles Sheldon, Esq., of Brailes (some time M.P. for S. Warwickshire), by Marcella, only child of Thomas Meredith Winstanley, Esq., of Lissen Hall, co. Dublin ; b. 1823 ; s. 1836 ; m. 1852 Alicia Mary, dau. of General Sir Evan Lloyd, by the Dowager Lady Trimlestown, and widow of W. Oakeley, Esq., of Oakeley, Salop. Educated at Trinity Coll., Cambridge (B.A. 1845) ; is a Magistrate for cos. Worcester and Warwick (High Sheriff 1860) ; was for several years an Officer in Warwickshire Yeomanry. This family is one of the oldest in Warwickshire.—*Brailes House, Shipston-on-Stour ; Arthur's and Pratt's Clubs, s.w.*

Heir Pres., his brother Edward Ralph Charles, b. 1828 ; m. 1855 Elizabeth, youngest dau. of Lieut.-General Loftus.

SHELLEY, Sir FREDERICK, Bart., of Maresfield Park, Sussex (cr. 1611).
Eldest surviving son of the late Sir John Shelley, Bart., of Maresfield Park (who d. 1852), by Frances, dau. of Thomas Winckley, Esq., of Brockholes, co. Lancaster ; b. 1809 ; s. as 8th Bart. 1867 ; m. 1845 Charlotte Martha, dau. of the late Rev. Henry Hippisley, Rector of Lambourne, Berks. Educated at Trinity Coll., Dublin ; is in Holy Orders, Rector of Beer Ferris, Devon ; is a claimant for the Barony of S deley.—*Maresfield Park, Uckfield ; Beer Ferris, Tavistock.*

Heir, his son John, b. 1848.

SHELLEY, Sir PERCY FLORENCE, Bart., of Castle Goring, Sussex (cr. 1806).
Eldest son of the late Percy Bysshe Shelley, Esq. (the eminent poet), by Mary, dau. of William Godwin, Esq., and Mary Woolstonecraft ; b. 1819 ; s. his grandfather as 3rd Bart. 1844 ; m. 1848 Jane, dau. of Thomas Gibson, Esq., and widow of the Hon. Charles Robert St. John. Is a J.P. and D.L. for Sussex (High Sheriff 1865) ; late Capt. Sussex Militia.—*Boscombe, Christchurch ; Reform Club, s.w.*

Heir Pres., his cousin Edward Shelley, Esq., of Avington (whom see).

SHELLEY, EDWARD, Esq., of Avington, Hants.
Eldest son of the late John Shelley, Esq., J.P. and D.L., of Avington House (who was High Sheriff of Hants 1853), by Elizabeth, dau. of Charles J. Bowen, Esq., of Kilna Court, Queen's Co.; b. 1827 ; s. 1866 ; m. 1866 Mary, dau. of the late Henry Mitchell Smyth, Esq., of Castle Widenham, co. Cork. Was formerly Capt. 10th Hussars, represents a younger branch of the Barts. of the same name.—*Avington House, Winchester.*

Heir Pres., his brother Charles. Capt. Scots Fusilier Guards ; b. 1837.

SHELLEY, the Misses, of Elcot House, Berks.
Hellen and Margaret, daus. of the late Sir Timothy Shelley, Bart., of Field Place, Sussex (who d. 1844), by Elizabeth, dau. of Charles Pilfold, Esq., of Effingham, Surrey, and sisters of the late eminent poet, P. Bysshe Shelley, Esq.; are Ladies of the Manor of Elcot. This family came from Normandy with the Conqueror, and have been seated in Sussex since the reign of Henry VIII.—*Elcot House, Kintbury, Hungerford, Berks.*

Heir Pres., her nephew Edward, son of John Shelley, Esq., who d. 1867, by Elizabeth, dau. of Charles Bowen, Esq., of Kilnacourt, Queen's Co.; b. 1827 ; m. 1866 Mary Smith, niece of Princess of Cahua and Lady Doceline.

SHEPHERD, ARTHUR, Esq., of Shaw-End, Westmoreland.
Eldest son of the late Henry Shepherd. Esq., of Shaw-End, by Mary Ann his wife (she d. 1863); b. 1825 ;

s. 1850; *m.* 1834 Janie, only dau. of the late James Bryans, Esq., of Belfield, Windermere, and has issue,
* Arthur, *b.* 1857.

Mr. Shepherd is a J.P. and D.L. for Westmoreland (High Sheriff 1865).—*Shaw-End, Kendal.*

SHEPHERD.   (See *Lowry-Corry.*)

SHEPPARD, FREDERICK, Esq., of Folkington, Sussex.

Youngest son of the late Thomas Sheppard, Esq., M.P., of Folkington, and of Hilton Verney and Shrewton, Wilts, by Sarah, dau. of Richard Down, Esq., of Colney Hatch, Middlesex; *b.* 1815; *s.* 1858.—*Folkington Place, Willingdon, Sussex.*

SHEPPARD, GEORGE WOOD, Esq., of Fromefield House, Somersetshire.

Second son of the late George Sheppard, Esq., of Fromefield House, by Mary Ann Stuart, dau. of Sir Thomas Byard, of Mount Tamar, Devon; *b.* 1808; *m.* 1834 Emma, dau. of I. T. Brown, Esq., H.E.I.C.S., of Winifred House, Bath, and has, with other issue,
* George Frederick, Bombay Civil Service ; *b.* 1835 ; *m.* 1861 Adeline Babington, dau. of the late Rev. B. W. Peite, of Hatfield, Herts, and has issue, * Philip Arthur Sneade, *b.* 1862.

Mr. Sheppard is a Magistrate for Somerset.—*Fromefield House, Frome.*

SHEPPARD, JOHN GEORGE, Esq., of Ashe High House, Suffolk.

Eldest son of the late John Wilson Sheppard, Esq., of Ashe High House (High Sheriff of Suffolk 1830), by Harriet, dau. and co-heir of Col. George Crump, of Alexton Hall, Leicester; *b.* 1824; *s.* 1830; *m.* 1846 Harriett Anna, 2nd dau. of the late Sir Thomas John Tyrwhitt-Jones, Bart. Educated at Harrow and Trinity Coll., Cambridge; is a J.P. and D.L. for Suffolk (High Sheriff 1859).—*Ashe High House, Wickham Market; Carlton and National Clubs, s.w.*

Heir Pres., his brother Henry Wilson, *b.* 1827 ; *m.* 1860 Louisa Sophia, 2nd dau. of the Very Rev. Edward Newenham Hoare, dean of Waterford.

SHEPPARD, WILLIAM HULBERT, Esq., of Keyford House, Somerset.

Eldest son of the late William Sheppard, Esq., of Styles Hill, by his 1st wife Susannah, dau. and co-heir of John Lewin, Esq., of the Manor of St. Katherine, Ruislip; *b.* 1791; *s.* 1814; *m.* 1818 Hannah, only child of William Pollett, Esq., of Great Bardfield, Essex, and has, with other issue,
* William, *b.* 1823 ; *m.* 1850 Emilie Lynes, 3rd dau. of J. H. Scrivenor, Esq., of Liverpool, and has issue, * Wm. Lewin, *b.* 1860.

Mr. Sheppard, who was educated at Winchester, is a Magistrate for Somerset, late Capt. in the North Somerset Yeomanry.—*Keyford House, Frome.*

SHERARD, Lord (PHILIP CASTELL SHERARD).—Cr. 1627.

Eldest son of the late Rev. Philip Castell Sherard, of Glatton, Hunts. by Sarah Haughton, dau. of Montague James, Esq., of Jamaica, & 3rd son of the 4th Earl of Harborough, as 9th Lord 1859 ; *m.* 1831 Anne, youngest dau. of Nathaniel Weeks, Esq., of Barbados. Is a Magistrate for Hunts (High Sheriff 1860).—*Glatton, Stilton; Union and Carlton Clubs, s.w.*
* *Heir Pres.,* his brother Simon Haughton, in Holy Orders, LL.B. of Christ's Coll., Cambridge ; *b.* 1806 ; *m.* 1843 Mary, dau. of the late Sir Simon Haughton Clarke, Bart., and has issue, * Castell, *b.* 1844.

SHERBORNE, Lord (JAMES HENRY LEGGE DUTTON).—Cr. 1784.

Eldest son of John, 2nd Lord, by the Hon. Mary Legge, dau. of the 2nd Lord Stawel (ext.) ; *b.* 180-; *s.* 1862 ; *m.* 1st 1826 Lady Elizabeth Howard, eldest dau. of

818

Thomas, 16th Earl of Suffolk (she *d.* 1845); 2nd 1857 Susan Elizabeth, eldest dau. and co-heir of James Block, Esq., of Charlton, Wilts. Educated at Eton; is a J.P. and D.L. for co. Gloucester, Lord of the Manors of Sherborne and Holybourne, Hants, and Patron of 2 livings. The grandfather of the present peer assumed, by Royal licence, the name of Dutton in lieu of Napper.—*Sherborne Lodge, Northleach; Bibury House, Fairford; 45, Grosvenor Square, w.*
Heir, his son Edward Lenox, *b.* 1831.

SHERBROOKE, HENRY, Esq., of Oxton, Notts.

Eldest son of the late Rev. Robert Lowe, Rector of Bingham, Notts, and Prebendary of Southwell, by Ellen, dau. of the Rev. Reginald Pyndar, of Madresfield, co. Worcester; *b.* 1810; took the name and arms of Sherbrooke on succeeding his cousin, W. Sherbrooke, Esq., of Oxton, 1847; *m.* 1840 Louisa, dau. of William Fane, Esq., of the Indian Civil Service, and has, with other issue,
* William, R.N.; *b.* 1844.

Mr. Sherbrooke, who was educated at Eton and Trinity Hall, Cambridge (B.A. 1832), is a J.P. and D.L. for Notts (High Sheriff 1859), a Dep. Chairman of Quarter Sessions, and Capt. S. Notts Yeomanry Cavalry.—*Oxton, Southwell; Boodle's Club, s.w.*

SHERER, Sir GEORGE MOYLE, K.S.I. (cr. 1866).

Third son of the late Rev. Joseph Sherer, of Godmersham and Westwell, Kent, by Margaret, dau. of Admiral Sir John Knight; *b.* 1800; *m.* 1827 Jane, dau. of the late Sir Joseph O'Halloran, G.C.B., General Bengal Army. Is a Major-General in the Army; was formerly Commandant 73rd Regt. Bengal Native Infantry, and A.D.C. to the Queen.—*21, Inverness Road, Bayswater, w.*

SHERIDAN, HENRY BRINSLEY, Esq.

Son of the late Garrett Sheridan, Esq., of co. Cavan, by Jane Juliana Darnley, dau. of the late Sir Richard Perrott, Bart.; *b.* 1820; *m.* 1851 Elizabeth Frances, dau. of the Rev. J. Wood, and has issue,
* A son, *b.* 1863.

Mr. Sheridan, who was called to the Bar at the Inner Temple 1856, is a Magistrate for Middlesex and Kent, and Capt. 6th Cinque Ports Artillery; has been M.P. for Dudley since 1857.—*St. Peter's, Isle of Thanet, Kent; 5, Essex Court, Temple, E.C.; 17, Westbourne Terrace, Hyde Park, w.*

SHERIDAN, RICHARD BRINSLEY, Esq., of Frampton Court, Dorset.

Eldest son of the late Thomas Sheridan, Esq. (who *d.* 1835), by Caroline Henrietta, 4th dau. of Col. Sir James and Lady Elizabeth Callender, of Craigforth and Ardkinglass, co. Stirling, and grandson of the late Rig'ht Hon. R. B. Sheridan, M.P.; *b.* 1806; *m.* 1835 Maria Maria, only child and heir of Lieut.-General Sir Colquhoun Grant, K.C.B., of Frampton Court, and has, with other issue,
* Richard Brinsley, *b.* 1838.

Mr. Sheridan, who is a J.P. and D.L. for Dorset (High Sheriff 1838, and Patron of 3 livings, has been M.P. for Dorchester since 1852; was M.P. for Shaftesbury 1845-52.—*Frampton Court, Dorchester, Dorset; Royal Yacht Society's Club, Cowes; White's, Brooks's, and Travellers' Clubs, s.w.; 48, Grosvenor Place, s.w.*

SHERIFFE, Mrs., of Henstead Hall, Suffolk.

Madeline, dau. of R. Oliver Massey, Esq., of Hill Street, London; *m.* 1851 Thomas Bowen Sheriffe, Esq., of Henstead Hall, who *d.* 1864, leaving, with other issue,
* Robert Thomas, *b.* 1860.

Mrs. Sheriffe is Lady of the Manor and Patron of Henstead.—*Henstead Hall, Wangford.*

+SHERRARD, JAMES COREY, Esq., of Kennersley Manor, Surrey.

Eldest son of William Sherrard, Esq., of Kilbogget, co. Dublin; *b.* 18—; *m.* 1846 Louisa, eldest dau. of Charles Hill Hall, Esq., of West Wickham, Kent. Is a Magistrate for Surrey. This family is descended from a common ancestor with Lord Sherard and with the Earls of Harborough (ext.).—*Kennersley Manor, Horley, Reigate.*

SHERRIFF, ALEXANDER CLUNES, Esq., of Perdiswell Hall, Worcestershire.

Son of the late Mr. A. Sherriff, Merchant, of Worcester; *b.* 1816; *m.* 1841 Mary, eldest dau. of Thomas Tattersall, Esq., of Armley, near Leeds. Is a Magistrate for the city of Worcester; Dep. Chairman of the Metropolitan District Railway; Director of the Metropolitan Railway, &c.; elected M.P. for Worcester 1865. —*Perdiswell Hall, Worcester ; 9, Queen's Square, s.w.*

SHERSTON, JOHN DAVIS, Esq., late of Stoberry Park, Somerset.

Eldest son of the late Peter Davis Sherston, Esq., of Stoberry Park, near Wells, Somerset (who *d.* 1836), by Juliana Frances Anne, dau. of Col. Yorke; *b.* 1829; *m.* 1851 Innes Eiza, dau. of Major Hamilton Maxwell, of Ardwell, co. Wigton, N.B., and has, with other issue,
   * Charles Davis, *b.* 1852.
Mr. Sherston, who is a Magistrate for co. Lincoln, was formerly Capt. 6th Dragoon Guards.—Residence: *Burnford House, Bramshaw, Lyndhurst ; Army and Navy Club, s.w.*

SHERWIN. (See *Gregory*.)

SHERWOOD, WILLIAM, Esq., of Rysome Garth, Yorkshire.

Only son of the late George Henry Sherwood, Esq., of Rysome Garth, by Margaret, dau. of Robert Bell, Esq., of Humbleton House, co. York; *b.* 1815; *s.* 1854; *m.* 1859 Mary Anne Charlotte, eldest dau. of the late Sir Henry Boynton, Bart., of Burton Agnes, co. York. Is Lord of the Manor of Rysome Garth.—*Rysome Garth, Patrington, Hull.*

SHIFFNER, the Rev. Sir GEORGE CROXTON, Bart., of Coombe Place, Sussex (cr. 1818).

Eldest son of the late Rev. Sir George Shiffner, Bart., of Coombe Place, Canon of Chichester, &c., by Elizabeth, dau. of the Rev. Croxton Johnson, of Wilmslow, co. Chester; *b.* 1819; *s.* as 4th Bart. 1863; *m.* 1854 Elizabeth, dau. and heir of the late John Greenall, Esq., of Myddleton Hall, co. Lancaster. Educated at Harrow and Ch. Ch., Oxford (B.A. 1842, M.A. 1846); is Lord of the Manor of Allington; Patron of 1 living; Rector of Hamsey, Sussex, and Rural Dean of Lewes.—*Coombe Place, and Hamsey Rectory, Lewes.*
   Heir, his son John, *b.* 1857.

SHIFFNER, THOMAS, Esq., of Westergate, Sussex.

Youngest son of the late Sir George Shiffner, Bart., M.P., of Coombe Place, Sussex, by Mary, only dau. and heir of the Sir John Bridger, Knt.; *b.* 1796; *m.* 1812 Mary, dau. of the late James Brown, Esq., of Harehills, co. York, and has issue,
   * Annie Mary Emily Charlotte.
Mr. Shiffner, who was educated at Westminster and Ch. Ch., Oxford (B.A. 1819, M.A. 1823), is a J.P. and D.L. for Sussex.—*Westergate, Arundel.*

SHIPLEY, CONWAY MORDAUNT, Esq., of Twyford, Hants.

Eldest son of the late Rev. Charles Shipley, by Charlotte, dau. of Orby Slopes, Esq., of West Woodhay,

Perks; *b.* 1824; *s.* 1834; *m.* 1863 Caroline Grace, 3rd dau. of Thomas Clements Parr, Esq., of Clifton, Bristol. Appointed to the Royal Navy 1828, became Lieut. 1845, and has since retired from the service.—*Twyford Moors, Winchester ; Army and Navy Club, s.w.*
   Heir Pres., his brother Reginald Yonge, C.B., Col. 7th Foot; *b.* 1828; *m.* 1856 Amy, dau. of Lea Birch, Esq., and has issue, four sons.

SHIPPERDSON, the Rev. EDMUND HECTOR, of Hermitage, co. Durham.

Eldest son of the late Walter Carles Hopper, Esq., of Belmont, and of Walworth, co. Durham, by Margaret, dau. of the late Ralph Shipperdson, Esq., of Pittington Hall-Garth, co. Durham; *b.* 1806; *s* his uncle 1855, when he assumed his name by Royal licence; *m.* 1838 Adeline, dau. of John Kerrich, Esq., of Harleston, and Geldeston Hall, Norfolk, and has, with other issue,
   * Thomas Henry, *b.* 1839.
Mr. Shipperdson, who was educated at Durham and Christ's Coll., Cambridge (B.A. 1829, M.A. 1832), is a Magistrate for co. Durham.—*Hermitage, Chester-le-Street ; Pittington Hall-Garth, and Murton-in-the-Whins, Durham.*

SHIPTON, the Rev. JOHN NOBLE.

Eldest son of the late Rev. John Shipton, D.D., Rector of Portishead, and Magistrate for Somerset, by Jane, dau. of John Noble, Esq., of Bristol; *b.* 1788; *m.* 1841 Mary, dau. of Samuel Simmons, Esq., of Newland, co. Gloucester. Educated at Balliol Coll., Oxford (B.A. 1809, M.A. 1811, B.D. 1818, D.D. 1811); admitted *ad eundem* at Cambridge 1858; is a Magistrate for Somerset, and Vicar of Othery.—*Othery, Bridgwater.*

SHIRLEY, EVELYN PHILIP, Esq., of Eatington, Warwickshire.

Eldest son of the late Evelyn John Shirley, Esq., M.P., of Eatington, by Eliza, only dau. and heir of Arthur Stanhope, Esq., cousin of the Earl of Chesterfield; *b.* 1812; *s.* 1856; *m.* 1842 Mary Clara Elizabeth, dau. of the late Sir Edmund Hungerford Lechmere, Bart., and has, with other issue,
   * Sewallis Evelyn, *b.* 1844 ; educated at Ch. Ch., Oxford.
Mr. Shirley, who was educated at Eton and Magdalen Coll., Oxford (B.A. 1834, M.A. 1837), is a J.P. and D.L. for co. Warwick (High Sheriff 1867), and co. Monaghan (High Sheriff 1837), and Patron of 1 living, was M.P. for co. Monaghan 1841-7, and for South Warwickshire 1853-65; Author of ' The Noble and Gentle Men of England,' ' Some Account of Deer and Deer Parks,' &c. This family, seated at Lower Eatington from the time of Edward the Confessor, descend from the 2nd marriage of Robert, 1st Earl Ferrers. —*Lower Eatington Park, Stratford-on-Avon ; Lough Fea, Carrickmacross, co. Monaghan ; National Club, s.w.*

SHIRLEY. (See under *Ferrers, Earl*.)

SHORE. (See *Nightingale*.)

SHORE, (See under *Teignmouth, Lord*.)

+SHORE, OFFLEY, Esq., of Clifton Hall, Derbyshire.

Younger son of the late Samuel Shore, Esq., of Norton Hall, co. Derby (J.P. and D.L. for that co. and High Sheriff 1832) by Harriet, dau. of Fitzwalter Foy, 1 sq., of Buckland Newton, Dorset; *b.* 1797; *m.* 1823 Mary only dau. of Charles White, Esq., of Lincoln, and has, with other issue,
   * Harington Offley, B.A. of Trinity Coll., Cambridge; *b.* 1833.
Mr. Shore is a Dep.-Lieut. for co. Derby.—*Clifton Hall, Ashbourne.*

+ SHORROCK, ECCLES, Esq., of Over Darwen, Lancashire.

Son of the late W. Shorrock, Esq.; b. 18—. Is a Magistrate for co. Lancaster, and a Merchant and Manufacturer at Blackburn.—*Low Hill House, Over Darwen, Blackburn.*

SHORT, FRANCIS BARING, Esq., of Bickham, Devon.

Second son of the late John Jeffery Short, Esq., of Bickham, by Charlotte, dau. of the late John Baring, Esq., of Mount Radford, Devon; b. 1800; s. 1818; m. 1833 Emily Jane, dau. of the Rev. Richard Lane, late of Coffleet, Devon, and has, with other issue,

* John Baring, b. 1836.

Mr. Short, who was educated at Eton, is a Magistrate for Devon, and was formerly in the Navy.—*Bickham House, Exeter.*

SHORT, JOHN HASSARD, Esq., of Edlington Grove, Lincolnshire.

Eldest surviving son of the late Richard Samuel Short, Esq., of Edlington Grove, by Mary Anne, dau. of John Kendall, Esq., of York; b. 1810; s. 1826; m. 1831 Margaret, 4th dau. of the late Lieut.-Col. Richard Elmhirst, of Ashby Grove, co. Lincoln, and has, with other issue,

* Edward Hassard, b. 1848.

Mr. Short, who was educated at the Charterhouse and Trinity Coll., Cambridge, is a J.P. and D.L. for co. Lincoln.—*Edlington Grove, Horncastle.*

SHORTLAND, WILLOUGHBY, Esq., of Courtland, Devonshire.

Eldest surviving son of the late Thomas George Shortland, Capt. R.N., of Lipson, near Plymouth, by Elizabeth, dau. of P. Tonkin, Esq., of Plymouth; b. 1804; m. 1843 Isabelle Kate, dau. of R. A. Fitzgerald, Esq., of Geraldine, co. Limerick. Educated at the Naval Coll., Portsmouth; is a Magistrate for Devon, and a Commander R.N., retired; was formerly Colonial Secretary, and then Governor of New Zealand, subsequently of Nevis, and Tobago.—*Courtland, Kingsbridge.*

SHORTRIDGE, RICHARD, Esq., of Cleadon Meadows, co. Durham.

Son of the late Richard Turner Shortridge, Esq., by Caroline, dau. of Robert Davison, Esq., of Stockton; b. 1793. Is a Magistrate for co. Durham.—*Cleadon Meadows, Sunderland.*

SHREWSBURY AND TALBOT, 18th Earl of (HENRY JOHN CHETWYND TALBOT, C.B., P.C.‡).—Cr. 1442.

Eldest son of Charles Chetwynd, 2nd Earl Talbot, by Frances Thomasine, dau. of Charles Lambert, Esq., of Beau Park, co. Meath; b. 1803; s. 1849 as 3rd Earl Talbot, and established his claim to the Earldom of Shrewsbury 1858; m. 1828 Lady Sarah, dau. of Henry, 2nd Marquis of Waterford. Is an Admiral, retired ; is Earl of Waterford and Wexford in Ireland (cr. 1846), Hereditary Lord High Steward of Ireland, and Premier Earl in the English and Irish Peerage; a J.P. and D.L. for co. Stafford, and Patron of 13 livings; was M.P. for Hertford 1830-2, Dublin 1832-3, for South Staffordshire 1837-49.—*Ingestre Hall, Stafford; Alton Towers, Cheadle: United Service and Carlton Clubs, s.w.; 36, Belgrave Square.*

Heir, his son Charles John, Viscount Ingestre; educated at Eton and Merton Coll., Oxford; is a Magistrate for Middlesex, a J.P. and D.L. for co. Stafford, and Major Staffordshire Yeomanry; late Lieut. 1st Life Guards; was M.P. for Stafford 1857-9, for N. Staffordshire 1859-65; elected M.P. for Stamford 1868; b. 1830; m. 1855 Theresa, dau. of the late Richard Howe Cockerell, Esq.

‡ Died whilst these sheets were at press.

350

SHRUBB, the Rev. CHARLES, of Vicar's Hill, Hants.

Eldest son of the late John Peyto Shrubb, Esq., of Merrest Wood and Stoke, Surrey, by Charlotte, dau. of George Elers, Esq., of Chelsea; b. 1790; s. 1846; m. 1833 Charlotte Aubrey, dau. of Thomas G. Bailiff, Capt. H.E.I.C.S., and has issue,

* Charles Peyto, b. 1837; m. 1859 Henrietta Caroline, dau. of the late Isaac Newton Wigney, Esq., formerly M.P. for Brighton.

Mr. Shrubb, who was educated at Exeter Coll., Oxford (B.A. 1811, M.A. 1813), is Vicar of Boldre, Hants, and Patron of that living. This family is maternally descended from the Royal line of the Plantagenets. —*Vicar's Hill, Boldre, Lymington.*

SHUCKBURGH, Sir FRANCIS, Bart., of Shuckburgh Park, Warwickshire (cr. 1660).

Eldest son of the late Sir Stukeley Shuckburgh, Bart., of Shuckburgh Park, by Miss C. Tydd; b. 1800; s. as 8th Bart. 1839; m. 1825 Anne Maria, Draycott, dau. of the late Peter Denys, Esq. (she d. 1846). Is a J.P. and D.L. for co. Warwick (High Sheriff 1844), and Patron of 1 living.—*Shuckburgh Park, Daventry.*

Heir, his son George Thomas Francis, a Magistrate for co. Warwick, late Major Scots Fusilier Guards; b. 1827.

SHUCKBURGH, the Rev. CHARLES BLENCOWE, of Bourton Hall, Warwickshire.

Son of the late Samuel Blencowe, Esq., of Marston St. Lawrence, co. Northampton (who assumed the name of Blencowe in lieu of Jackson, on succeeding his uncle, John Blencowe, Esq.), by his 2nd wife Elizabeth Gramer, dau. of the Rev. Thomas Biker, Vicar of Culworth, co. Northampton; b. 1793; m. 1830 Arabella Anne, dau. of John Jones, Esq., of Withington House, co. Gloucester. Educated at Wadham and Lincoln Colls., Oxford (B.A. 1815, M.A. 1818); is Lord of the Manor of Bourton, and Patron of 1 living; late Vicar of Marston St. Lawrence, co. Northampton ; he took the name of Shuckburgh under the will of John Shuckburgh, Esq., of Bourton. 1848. —*Bourton Hall, Rugby.*

Heir Pres., his brother George Blencowe, Esq., of Great Houghton, co. Northampton; b. 1795; m. 18— Charlotte, dau. of the late Rev. Francis Montgomery, of Milton House, co. Northampton.

SHULDHAM, EDMUND ANDERSON, Esq., of Dunmanway, co. Cork.

Eldest son of the late General Edmund William Shuldham, of Dunmanway, by Harriet Eliza Boner, dau. of Dr. Rundell, of Bath: b. 1826; s. 1852. Educated at Eton and Ch. Ch. Oxford (B.A. 1848, M.A. 1853), is a Magistrate for co. Cork. Capt. S. Cork Militia, and A.D.C. to the Lord-Lieutenant of Ireland.—*Dunmanway, co. Cork; University Club, s.w.*

Heir Pres., his brother Leopold Arthur Francis, b. 1828.

SHULDHAM, JOHN, Esq., of Moigh, co. Longford.

Eldest son of the late Molyneux William Shuldham, Esq., of Moigh, by Helen, dau. of Lieut.-Col. Macpurine, of Munst Prusse, co. Antrim; b. 1825; s. 1850. Educated at Trinity Coll., Cambridge; is a J.P. and D.L. for co. Longford (High Sheriff 1856). Is descended from the ancient family of the Shuldhams of Norfolk, and represents, in Ireland, the Longford branch.—*Ballymuiny (or Moigh House), Ballymahon, co. Longford; Kildare Street Club, Dublin; Junior United Service Club, s.w.*

Heir Pres., his brother Alexander, Capt. Londonderry Light Infantry; b. 1827; m. 1853 Letitia Mary, eldest dau. of the late George Knox, Esq., of Prehen, co. Londonderry.

+ SHULDHAM, Miss, of Marlesford, Suffolk.

Only surviving child of the late William Shuldham, Esq., of Marlesford Hall. Is Lady of the Manor of

Marlesford ; represents an old Suffolk family.—*Marlesford Hall, Wickham Market.*

Heir Pres., her cousin Frederick Schreiber, Esq.

SHUM-STOREY, GEORGE HENRY, Esq., of Arcot Hall, Northumberland.

Only son of the late Henry Shum-Storey, Esq., (whose father, George Shum, Esq., assumed the name of Storey on succeeding to the e-tate of Arcot, in right of his wife Ann, eldest dau. and co-heir of Robert Storey, Esq.), by Emma, dau. of Robert Chester Cooper, Esq., of Sussex ; *b.* 1841 ; *s.* 1861. Educated at Winchester and Queen's Coll., Oxford ; is Lord of the Manor of Arcot. —*Arcot Hall, Cramlington, Newcastle-on-Tyne.*

Heir Pres., his sister Emmeline Anne.

SHUTTLEWORTH, Sir JAMES PHILLIPS KAY-, Bart., of Gawthorpe, Lancashire (cr. 1850).

Son of the late Robert Kay, Esq. ; *b.* 1804 ; *m.* 1842 Janet, only dau. and heir of the late Robert Shuttleworth, Esq., of Gawthorpe Hall, whose name he assumed in addition to his own. Educated at Scotch and foreign Universities ; is a J.P. and D.L. for co. Lancaster (High Sheriff 1864) ; was formerly Secretary to the Committee of Privy Council for Education.—*Gawthorpe Hall, Burnley ; Athenæum Club, s.w. ; 38, Gloucester Square, w.*

Heir, his son Ughtred James, *b.* 1844.

+**SHUTTLEWORTH**, JOHN JOSEPH, Esq., of Hodsack Park, Notts.

Son of the late William George Shuttleworth, Esq., of Hodsack Park, by Ann, dau. of Edward Young, Esq., of Normanby ; *b.* 17— ; *s.* 183— ; *m.* 1829 Helen Catharine, dau. of the late Thurston Dale, Esq., of Ashbourne, and has issue.—*Hodsack Park, Worksop.*

SHUTTLEWORTH, JOHN SPENCER ASHTON, Esq., of Hathersage, Derbyshire.

Second son of the late Ashton Ashton Shuttleworth, Esq., of Hathersage, by Anne, dau. of Thomas Youle, Esq. ; *b.* 1838 ; *m.* 1st 1842 Maria, eldest dau. of the Rev. Henry Wright, of Mottram Hall, co. Chester ; 2nd 1845 Emily, eldest dau. of Bolton Peel, Esq., of Dosthill Lodge, co. Warwick, and has issue. Educated at Merton Coll., Oxford ; is a J.P. and D.L. for co. Derby.—*Hathersage Hall, Sheffield ; Oxford and Cambridge Club, s.w.*

SHUTTLEWORTH.   (See *Holden*.)

SHYNE-LAWLOR.   (See *Lawlor*.)

SIBTHORP, CONINGSBY CHARLES WALDO-, Esq., of Canwick, Lincolnshire.

Eldest son of the late Major Gervaise Tottenham Waldo-Sibthorp, M.P., of Canwick Hall, J.P. and D.L., by Louisa, 3rd dau. of the late Robert Cracroft (subsequently Amcotts), Esq., of Hackthorn, co. Lincoln ; *b.* 1846 ; *s.* 1861. Educated at Eton and Magdalen Coll. Oxford ; is Patron of 1 living. This family were early seated in Norfolk and at Sibthorpe, Notts.—*Canwick Hall, Lincoln ; Potterels, Hertford.*

Heir Pres., his brother Montagu Richard, educated at Harrow and Magdalen Coll., Oxford ; *b.* 1848.

SICKLEMORE, the Rev. GEORGE WILSON, of Nether Court, Kent.

Second son of the late John Sicklemore, Esq., of Wetheringsett, Suffolk (who *d.* 1857), by Anne, youngest dau. of Colonel Cony, of Walpole Hall, Norfolk ; *b.* 1803 ; *m.* 1833 Catherine, only child of Benjamin Bushell, Esq., of Cleve, Isle of Thanet, Kent, and has, with other issue,

* Benjamin, a Magistrate for Kent and Liberties of Cinque Ports; *b.* 1840 ; *m.* 1865 Louisa, youngest dau. of Joseph Carham, Esq., M.D., of Southwood.

Mr. Sicklemore, who was educated at Trinity Coll., Cambridge (B.A. 1825, M.A. 1828), is a Magistrate for Kent and Liberties of Cinque Ports, Vicar of St. Lawrence, Lord of the Manor of Nether Court, and Patron of 1 living; was formerly Rector of St. Alphage, and Vicar of St. Mary, Northgate, Canterbury. This family formerly represented Suffolk and Ipswich in Parliament. They were strong adherents of the House of Stuart, having suffered great privations and loss of property during the Commonwealth. One of the family remained with James II. until his death.—*Cleve Monkton and Nether Court, St. Lawrence, Isle of Thanet.*

SIDEBOTTOM, CHARLES JOHN, Esq., of Elm Bank, Worcestershire.

Third son of the late Radclyffe Sidebottom, Esq., of Middleton, co. Lancaster, Barrister-at-Law, by Anne, dau. and sole heir of Kingsford Venner, Esq., of Borenden, Kent, and grandson of the late Rev. Samuel Sidebottom, Rector of Middleton ; *b.* 1789 ; *m.* 1825 Mary Abigail, dau. of John Freeman, Esq., of Gaines, co. Hereford, and has, with other issue,

* Francis John, a Capt. in the Army ; *b.* 1826 ; *m.* 1860 Flora Jane, dau. of the late Right Hon. W. Y. Peel, of Baginton Hall, co. Warwick ; assumed the name of Venner 1861.

Mr. Sidebottom, who was called to the Bar at the Middle Temple 1818, is a Magistrate for cos. Hereford and Worcester.—*Elm Bank, Worcester.*

SIDEBOTTOM, WILLIAM, Esq., of Etherow, Cheshire.

Second son of the late James Sidebottom, Esq., of Hollingworth House, Mottram, co. Chester ; *b.* 1797 ; *m.* 1825 Agnes, dau. of the late Jonah Harrop, Esq., of Bardsley, Ashton-under-Lyne, and has issue.   Mr. Sidebottom is a Magistrate for cos. Derby, Chester, and Lancaster.—*Etherow House, Mottram.*

SIDMOUTH, Viscount (WILLIAM WELLS ADDINGTON).—Cr. 1805.

Eldest son of William Leonard, 2nd Viscount, by Mary, dau. of the Rev. John Young ; *b.* 1824 ; *s.* 1864 ; *m.* 1848 Georgiana Susan, dau. of the late Hon. and Very Rev. George Pellew, D.D., Dean of Norwich ; is a J.P. and D.L. for Devon and Somerset, and Lord of the Manor of Upp Ottery, Devon ; late Capt. South Devon Rifle Volunteers, and formerly a Lieut. R.N. ; was M.P. for Devizes 1852-4.—*Upp Ottery Manor, Honiton ; Early Court, Reading ; Carlton Club, s.w.*

Heir, his son Gerald Anthony, *b.* 1854.

SIDNEY, THOMAS, Esq., of Bowes Manor, Middlesex, and Esher Place, Surrey.

Third son of the late William Sidney, Esq., of Stafford ; *b.* 1805 ; *m.* 1st 1831 Sarah, eldest dau. of William Hall, Esq., of Ranton, co. Stafford (she *d.* 1857) ; 2nd 1860 Eleanor Mary Ward, late of Beaumont Chase, Uppingham, dau. of W. Ward, Esq., and has, with other issue,

* Thomas Stafford, *b.* 1863.

Mr. Sidney, who is a Magistrate for Middlesex and Westminster, a Dep.-Lieut. and Alderman of the city of London, and Patron of 1 living, was Sheriff of London and Middlesex 1844, Lord Mayor 1854, and M.P. for Stafford 1847-52 and 1860-65 ; he purchased Esher Place in 1864 from J. W. G. Spicer, Esq.—*Bowes Manor, Southgate, Middlesex ; Esher Place, Surrey.*

SIDNEY, WILLIAM HENRY MARLOW, Esq., F.G.H.S., of Cowpen, Northumberland.

Eldest surviving son of the late Marlow Sidney, Esq., of Cowpen House (who *d.* 1839), by his cousin Mary,

dau. of John Mangaar, Esq., of London; *b.* 1777; *s.* his brother 1859; *m.* 18.6 Anastatia, only dau. of John Steingenberger, Esq., of London, and has, with other issue,

* Henry. *b.* 1898; *m.* 18— Helen. 2nd·dau. of Capt. Henry W.ir. R.N., C.B., and widow of Edmund Fouthcote, Esq. (she *d. s. p.* 1859).

Mr. S:dney, who was educated at the Coll. of St. Gregory, is a Magistrate for No·thumberland, and Lord of the Manor of Cowpen.—*Cowpen House, Morpeth.*

SIDNEY. (See under *Di L'Isle, Lord.*)

SIER, the Rev. **Thomas,** of Ravensden. Beds.

Only surviving son of the late Thomas Sier, Esq., by Anne. dau. of Philip Matthews, Esq.; *b.* 1826. Educated at Queen's Coll., Oxford (B.A. 1846, D.C.L. 1853); calle t to the Bar at the Middle Temple 1847, and was for some time a Member of the Oxford Circuit; afterwards ordained; appointed Vicar of Ravensden, Beds, 1851, Minister of St. James's Chapel, London, 1859; is Patron of 2 livings.—*Ravensden Vicarage, B·d ord; Woodfields, Ludlow; Windham, Cavendish, and National Clubs,* s.w.

SILCHESTER, Lord. (See under *Longford, Earl of.*)

SILLAR, Zechariah, Esq., M.D., of Rainford Hall, Lancashire.

Only son of the late David Sillar. Esq., of Rainford Hall, by Margaret. dau. of Zechariah Gemmil, Esq., of Irvine, N.B.; *b.* 1796; *s.* 1833; *m.* 1816 Mary, eldest dau. of the Rev. William Cameron, of Kirknewton, and has, with other issue,

* David. *b.* 1820; *m.* 1854 Elizabeth, 3rd dau. of the late Henry Copeland, Esq., of Priors Wood, co. Lancaster.

Mr. Sillar, who was educated at Glasgow and the University of Edinburgh (M.D. 1816), is a Magistrate for co. Lancaster; he was formerly Physician to the Northern Hospital, Liverpool.—*Rainford Hall, St. Helen's; Lester Villa, Norwood,* s.

SILLIFANT, John Woollcombe, Esq., of Coombe, Devon.

Eldest son of the late John Sillifant, Esq., J.P. and D.L., of Coombe (who was High Sheriff of Devon 1848, and Chairman of Quarter Sessions), by Caroline, youngest dau. of the late John M. Woollcombe, Esq., of Ashbury. Devon; *b.* 1828; *s.* 1855; *m.* 1st 1850 Charlotte Caroline. dau. of — Mackay, Esq. (she *d.* 1859); 2nd 1864 Charlotte Louisa, only dau. of the late Col. James Johnstone Cochrane, of the Scots Fusilier Guards. Educated at Exeter Coll., Oxford (B A. 1848); is a Magistrate for Devon.—*Coombe, Coplestone, N. Devon.*

SILVERTOP, Henry Charles, Esq., of Minster Acres, Northumberland.

Eldest son of the late Henry Englefield, Esq., by Ca·harine, dau. of Henry Witham, Esq., of Lartington Hall, co. York; *b.* 1826; *s.* his great-uncle, and took the name of Silvertop, 1849; *m.* 1st 18.2 the Hon Eliza, dau. of Thomas, 3rd Lord Camo·s; 2nd 1842 Caroline, eldest dau. of Edmund J. Weld, Esq. of Lulworth Castle, Dorset, and has issue by the former,

* Henry Thomas, *b.* 1853.

Mr. Silvertop is a Magistrate for Durham, and a J.P. and D.L. for Northumberland (High Sheriff 1859).—*Minster Acres, Newcastle-on-Tyne; Brooks's and Windham Clubs,* s.w.; *Salford Club,* w.

SIM. Adam, Esq., of Coulter, Lanarkshire.

Eldest son of the late David Sim. Esq., of Coulter Mains, and of Glasgow, by Alison. dau. of John Stodart, Esq., Merchant, of Carnwath; *b.* 1805; *s.* 1831. Educated

852

---

at the University of Glasgow; is a Magistrate for co. Lanark, Proprietor of the Barony of Coulter, and a Fellow and Member of Council of the Society of Antiquaries of Scotland.—*Coulter Mains, Biggar, N.B.*

SIMCOE, the Rev. Henry Addington, of Wolford, Devonshire.

Third but only surviving. son of the late General John Graves Simcoe, of Wolford Lodge, by Elizabeth Posthuma, dau. of Col. Gwillim; *b.* 1800; *s.* 1850; *m.* 1st 1822 Anne, 2nd dau. of the late Rev. Edward Palmer, of Moseley, co. Worcester (she *d,* 1840); 2nd 1842 Emily, 2nd dau. of the late Rev. Horace Mann; he has by the former, with other issue,

* John Kennaway. Commander, R.N., *b.* 1825; *m.* 1867 Mary. 2nd dau. of Col. Basil Jackson, of Glewston Court, co. Hereford.

The Rev. H. A. Simcoe, who was educated at Eton and Wadham Coll., Oxford (B.A. 1821, M.A. 1830), is Incumbent of Egloskerry-cum-Tremaynie, Cornwall, Lord of the Manor of Dunkeswell. and Patron of that living. —*Wolford Lodge, Dunkeswell, Honiton; Residence: Penh:z:e, Launceston.*

SIMCOX, the Rev. Thomas Green, of Harborne House, Staffordshire.

Eldest son of the late Thomas Green Simcox, Esq. of Harborne House, by Hannah Maria, dau. of John Lea, Esq., of Kidde minster; *b.* 1810; *s.* 1828; *m.* 1838 Hannah Nicholson, dau. of the Rev. T. H. Kingdon, Rector of Pyworthy, Devon, and has, with other issue,

* Henry Kingdon, M.A. of Lincoln Coll., Oxford, and Curate of Honiton, Devon; *b.* 1839.

Mr. Simcox, who was educated at King Edward's School, Birmingham, and Wadham Coll., Oxford (B.A. 1831, M.A. 1836), was appointed Vicar of North Harborne 1838. This family has held the Manor of Harborne since 1788.—*Harborne House, Birmingham.*

SIMEON, Sir John, Bart., of Swainston, Isle of Wight (cr. 1815).

Eldest son of the late Sir Richard Godin Simeon, Bart., M.P. of Swainston, by Louisa Edith, dau. of the late Sir Fitzwilliam Barrington, Bart.; *b.* 1815; *s.* his 3rd Bart. 1854; *m.* 1st 1840 Jane Maria, only dau. of Sir Frederick F. Baker. Bart., of Loventor. Devon (she *d.* 1830); 2nd 1851 the Hon. Catherine Dorothea. dau. of the late General the Hon. Sir C. Colville. Educated at Ch. Ch., Oxford (B.A. 1837, M.A. 1840); is a Magistrate for Hants, a Dep. Lieut. for the Isle of Wight, and Ma·or 1st Batt. Isle of Wight Rifle Volunteers; was M.P. for the Isle of Wight 1847–51, re-elected 1855. —*Swainston, Newport, I. of Wight; Athenæum, and Oxford and Cambridge Clubs,* s.w.

Heir, his son John Stephen Barrington, *b.* 1850.

SIMKINSON. (See *King, of Staunton.*)

SIMMONS. (See *Carlyon-Simmons.*)

SIMONDS, William Barrow, Esq., of Abbotts-Barton, Hants.

Eldest son of the late William Simonds, Esq., of Ab lotts-Barton, by Helen, dau. of John Barrow, Esq., of Bristol; *b.* 1820; *m.* 1858 Ellen Lampard. dau. of Frederick Bowker, Esq., of Winchester. Educated at Merchant Taylors' School; is a Magistrate for Hants and the City of Winchester. Capt. Com. 1st Hants R.V., and Auditor to King's Coll., Cambridge; elected M.P. for Winchester, 1865.—*Abbotts-Barton, Winchester; Athenæum Club,* s.w.

SIMPSON, Sir James Young, Bart., M.D., D.C.L., of Strathavon, Linlithgowshire. (cr. 1866).

Seventh son of the late David Simpson, of Bathgate,

by Janet, dau. of John Jarvie, of Carmendean, N.B.; b. 1811; m. 1839 Jessie, dau. of Walter Grindlay, Esq., of Liverpool. Educated at Bathgate Academy and Edinburgh University (cr. Hon. D.C.L. Oxon 1866); was appointed Professor of Medicine and Midwifery in the University of Edinburgh 1840; elected President of the Edinburgh Royal Coll. of Physicians 1849; Accoucheur to the Queen for Scotland, Vice President of the Society of Antiquaries of Scotland, Honorary Professor of Antiquities to the Royal Scottish Academy. Knight of the Order of St. Olaf of Norway, Laureate of the Imperial Institute of France, &c., &c.—*Stra'havon Lodge, Trinity, Edinburgh; 52, Queen Street, Edinburgh, N.B.*

Heir, his son Walter Grindlay, b. 1843.

SIMPSON, Sir JAMES, G.C.B. ‡ (cr. 1855).
Son of the late David Simpson, Esq., of Teviotbank, N.B., by Mary, dau. of John Eliott, Esq., of Borthwickbrae, N.B.; b. 1792; m. 1839 Elizabeth. dau. of Sir Robert Dundas, Bart., of Beechwood, Midlothian (she d. 1840.) Educated at Edinburgh; is a General in the Army, and Col. of the 87th Foot; served in the Peninsula, and at Waterloo, and in the East Indies; was Chief of the Staff in the Crimea, March–June, and Commander-in-Chief in the Crimea, June–Nov. 1855.—*United Service Club, s.w.*

SIMPSON, the Rev. FRANCIS, of Foston, Yorkshire.
Eldest son of the late Rev. Francis Simpson, Vicar of Boynton, by Anne, dau. of the late Sir William Strickland, Bart., of Boynton, co. York; b. 1815; m. 1846 Fanny Salina, dau. of the late Josias Du Pré Alexander, Esq., M.P., and has, with other issue,
   * Francis Charles, b. 1847.
Mr. Simpson, who was educated at Queens' Coll., Cambridge (B.A. 1838, M.A. 1841), is a Magistrate for the E. Riding of co. York, Vicar of Boynton, and Rector of Foston.—*Foston Hall, York.*

+SIMPSON, HENRY BRIDGEMAN-, Esq., of Babworth, Notts.
Eldest son of the late Hon. John Bridgeman-Simpson, of Babworth, by his 2nd wife Grace, dau. of S. Estwicke, Esq.; b. 1795; m. 1830 Frances Emily, dau. of the late Henry Baring, Esq., cousin of Lord Ashburton. Educated at Eton; is a J.P. and D.L. for Notts (High Sheriff 1855), Lord of the Manor of Babworth, and Patron of 1 living. This family is a younger branch of that of the Earl of Bradford.—*Babworth, East Retford.*

Heir Pres., his brother John, b. 1800.

SIMPSON, JAMES ALFRED, Esq., of Branches Park, Suffolk.
Only son of the late James Simpson, Esq., J.P., of Branches Park, by Hannah dau. of William Harvey, Esq., of Salford, co. Lancaster, and niece of the late Joseph Brotherton, Esq., M.P. for Salford; b. 1853; s. 1859: is Lord of the Manor of Cowlinge.—*Foxhall Bank, Blackburn; Branches Park, Cowlinge, Newmarket.*

Heir Pres., his sister Emily.

+SIMPSON, JOHN, Esq., C.B., of Salthrop, Wilts.
Son of the late John Simpson, Esq., of Salthrop (who d. 1867); b. 1817. Entered the Army 1835, is a Lieut.-Col. in the Army, half-pay; was formerly Capt. 34th Foot.—*Salthrop Lodge, Wroughton, Swindon.*

SIMPSON, JOHN, Esq., of Castle Lodge, Yorkshire.
Only son of the late William Simpson, Esq., of Castle

‡ Died whilst these sheets were at press.

Lodge, by Elizabeth, dau. of John Howgate, Esq., of Knaresborough, co. York; b. 1793; s. 1825; m. 1827 Elizabeth, dau. and heir of Thomas Ward, Esq., of Dore House, and has, with other issue,
   * Wilfrid Hudleston, b. 1828.
Mr. Simpson, who was educated at Edinburgh University (M.D. 1821), is a Magistrate for the W. Riding of Yorkshire, and was formerly an Officer in the Yorkshire Hussars.—*Castle Lodge, Knaresborough; 21, Gloucester Place, w.*

SIMPSON, JOSEPH, Esq., of Radwell, Herts, and Longstowe, Cambridgeshire.
Eldest son of the late Richard Simpson, by Sophia, dau. of Joseph Phillips, Esq., of Stamford; b. 1824; m. 1858 Evelina, eldest dau. of Thomas Shaw Hellier, Esq., and has issue,
   * A son, b. 1859.
Mr. Simpson, who was educated at Trinity Coll., Cambridge (B.A. 1817), is a Magistrate for co. Cambridge, and for Herts.—*Radwell House, Baldock; Longstowe Hall, Caxton; Windham Club, s.w.*

+SIMPSON, JOSEPH, Esq., of Whitburn West, co. Durham.
Son of the late C. Simpson, Esq., of Whitburn; b. 17—. Is a Magistrate for co. Durham.—*Whitburn West House, Sunderland.*

SIMPSON, PIERCE, Esq., of Cloncorick, co. Leitrim.
Only son and heir of the late Edward Simpson, Esq., of Cloncorick Castle, by Jane, dau. of Matthew Nesbitt, Esq., of Derryvarn, co. Leitrim; b. 1814; s. 1828; m. 1847 Catherine Henrietta, dau. of the Rev. William Betty, of Knightstown, Queen's Co. and Rector of Castlecor and Oldcastle, co. Meath. Educated at Trinity Coll., Dublin; is a J.P. and D.L. for cos. Roscommon and Leitrim (High Sheriff 1836).—*Cloncorick Castle, Carrigallen, co. Leitrim; Gorteculan Lodge, Drumsna, co. Leitrim; Hibernian United Service Club, and 55, Upper Sackville Street, Dublin.*

SIMPSON, RICHARD, Esq., of Mellor, Cheshire.
Third son of the late John Simpson, Esq., of Hart Hill, co. Lancaster, by Elizabeth, dau. of Thomas Hawkley, Esq., of Nottingham; b. 1792; m. 1815 Jane, only dau. of Thomas Beard, Esq., of Gorton House, co. Lancaster, and has, with other issue,
   * Richard, b. 1817.
Mr. Simpson is a Magistrate for cos. Chester, Derby, Stafford, and for the Isle of Man.—*Mellor Lodge, Stockport; The Cliffe, Douglas, I. of Man; Union Club, s.w.*

+SIMPSON, ROBERT, Esq., of Cobairdy, Aberdeenshire.
Son of the late R. Simpson, Esq. of Cobairdy; b. 18—; is married, and has issue,
   * Patrick Brown, a Magistrate for cos. Aberdeen an1 Banff; b. 18—.
Mr. Simpson is a J.P. and D.L. for cos. Aberdeen and Banff, Lord of the Barony of Cobairdy, and Capt. 7th Aberdeenshire Rifle Volunteers.—*Cobairdy House, Huntly, N.B.*

+SIMPSON, THOMAS, Esq., of Hutton Hall, Lancashire.
Eldest son of the late James Simpson, Esq., of Hutton Hall; b. 18—; is married; and has, with other issue,
   * Albert, b. 185-; m. 1862 Sarah Ann, youngest dau. of the late John Jackson, Esq., of Oaken Clough, near Garstang, co. Lancaster.—*Hutton Hall, Preston.*

+ SIMPSON, the Rev. WILLIAM BRIDGEMAN, of Babworth, Notts.

Youngest son of the late Hon. John Bridgeman-Simpson, of Babworth Hall, by his 2nd wife Grace, dau. of S. Estwicke, Esq., and brother of Henry Bridgeman-Simpson Esq. (whom see); b. 1813; m. 1837 Lady Frances Laura, fourth dau. of Charles. 5th Earl Fitzwilliam. Educated at Trinity Coll., Cambridge (B.A. 1838, M.A. 1842); is a Magistrate for Notts, and Rector of Babworth.—*Babworth Rectory, Retford.*

SIMPSON. (See *Finch-Simpson.*)

SIMPSON. (See *Hicks.*)

+ SIMS, FRANK, Esq., of Hubbard's Hall, Essex.

Son of the late F. Sims, Esq., of Hubbard's Hall, by Mary, dau. of — Johnson, Esq.; b. 1806; s. 18—. Educated at Eton and Haileybury Coll.; was formerly in the H.E.I.C.'s Service.—*Hubbard's Hall, Harlow.*

Heir Pres., his sister.

SIMSON, GEORGE, Esq., of Pitcorthie, Fifeshire.

Eldest son of the late George Simson, Esq., M.P., of Pitcorthie, Brunton, and Letham, by Mary, dau. of James Ramsay, Esq.; b. 1796; s. 1848; m. 1822 Mary Ann, dau. of James Sutherland, Esq., and has, with other issue,

* George Sutherland, educated at Eton ; a Major in the Army, and a Magistrate for co. Fife ; b. 1823.

Mr. Simson, who was educated at Eton and Ch. Ch., Oxford, is a J.P. and D.L. for co. Fife. This family, originally of Falkland, have been long established in the co. of Fife, in which they have held lands from the commencement of the 15th century.—*Pitcorthie House, Colinsburgh, N.B.; Brunton, Markinch, Fife, N.B.; Arthur's Club, s.w.*

SINCLAIR, Lord (JAMES ST. CLAIR).—Cr: 1489.

Eldest son of Charles, 12th Lord, by his 1st wife Mary Agnes, dau. of the late James Chisholme, Esq., of Chisholme, co. Roxburgh; b. 1803; s. 1863; m. 1830 Jane, dau. of Archibald Little, Esq., of Shabden Park, Surrey. Educated at Winchester; is a Dep.-Lieut. for co. Berwick; was formerly Capt. Grenadier Guards.—*Herdmanston, Haddington; Nisbet House, Berwick, N.B.; Carlton Club, s.w.*

Heir, his son Charles William, Major in the Army, late Capt. 57th Foot; b. 1841.

SINCLAIR, Sir JOHN, Bart., of Barrock House, Caithness-shire (cr. 1631).

Eldest son of the late John Sinclair, Esq., by Anne, dau. of Thomas Longmire, Esq., of Penrith; b. 1794; s. his cousin as 7th Bart 1812; m. 1821 Margaret, dau. of John Learmonth, Esq., of Edinburgh. Is a J.P. and D.L. for and Convener of co. Caithness, and a Magistrate for co. Roxburgh; represents a junior branch of the family of the Earl of Caithness.—*Barrock House, Wick, N.B.*

*Heir, his son Alexander Young, Major Bombay Army, b. 1824 ; m. 1861 Margaret Crichton, dau. of the late James Alston, Esq., and has, with other issue, * John Rose George, b. 1864.*

SINCLAIR, Sir ROBERT CHARLES, D.b., of Stevenson, Haddingtonshire (cr. 1636).

Eldest son of Admiral Sir John Gordon Sinclair, Bart., J.P. and D.L., of Stevenson, by Anne, dau. of the Hon. Admiral Michael de Courcy (she d. 1857); b. 1820; s. as 9th Bart. 1863; m. 1851 Charlotte Anne, dau. of John Coote, Esq., late Lieut. 71st Foot. Is a Dep.-Lieut. for cos. Haddington and Caithness, and Patron of 1 living; late Capt. 38th Foot.—*Stevenson, Haddington, N.B.; United Service Club, s.w.*

SINCLAIR, Sir GEORGE, Bart., of Thurso Castle, Caithness-shire (cr. 1786).

Eldest son of the late Right Hon. Sir John Sinclair,

854

Bart., M.P., by Diana, dau. of Alexander, 1st Lord Macdonald; b. 1790; s. as 2nd Bart. 1835; m. 1816 Lady Katharine Camilla, 2nd dau. of William, Lord Huntingtower, and sister of Lionel. 6th Earl of Dysart (she d. 1863). Educated at Harrow, Edinburgh, and Göttingen; is a J.P. and D.L. for co. Caithness; was M.P. for co. Caithness 1811–20 and 1831–41.—*Thurso Castle, Caithness, N.B.; New Club, Edinburgh.*

*Heir, his son John George Tollemache, J.P. and D.L. for co. Caithness; b. 1825; m. 1853 Emma Elizabeth Herriot, dau. of Wm. Standish Standish, Esq., of Duxbury Park, co. Lancaster, and has, with other issue, * Clarence Granville, b. 1858.*

SINCLAIR, JAMES, Esq., of Forss, Caithness-shire.

Eldest son of the late James Sinclair, Esq., of Forss, by Johanna, dau. of George Mackay, Esq., of Bighouse; b. 1802; s. 1822; m. 1828 Jessie, eldest dau. of William Wemyss, Esq., of Southam, and has issue,

* James Major, R.A.; b. 1829.

Mr. Sinclair, who was educated at the High School and University of Edinburgh, and called to the Scottish Bar 1827, is a J.P. and D.L. for co. Caithness, and Commissioner of Supply.—*Forss, Thurso, N.B.*

SINCLAIR, the Ven. JOHN, Archdeacon of Middlesex.

Son of the late Right Hon. Sir John Sinclair, Bart., of Thurso Castle, co. Caithness, by the Hon. Diana, dau. of Alexander, 1st Lord Macdonald; b. 1797. Educated at Pembroke Coll., Oxford (B.A. 1819, M.A. 1822; appointed Chaplain of the late Bishop (Blomfield), of London, and Secretary of the National Society 1839; Vicar of Kensington 1842, Archdeacon of Middlesex 1843.—*University Club, s.w.; Vicarage, Kensington, w.*

SINCLAIR, WILLIAM, Esq., of Holy Hill, co. Tyrone, and Drumbeg, co. Donegal.

Eldest son of the late James Sinclair, Esq., J.P. and D.L., of Holy Hill, by Dorothea, dau. and heir of the Rev. Samuel Law; b. 1810; m. 1839 Sarah, dau. of James Cranborne Strode, Esq., and has, with other issue,

* James Montgomery (of Bonnyglen, co. Donegal), a Magistrate for co. Donegal; b. 1841; m. 1868 Mary Everina, younger dau. of Lieut.-Col. Barton, of The Waterfoot, co. Fermanagh.

Mr. Sinclair, who was educated at Trinity Coll., Dublin, is a Magistrate for co. Donegal (High Sheriff 1854).—*Holy Hill, Strathbane; Drumbeg, Donegal.*

SINCLAIR. WILLIAM THOMSON-, Esq., of Dunbeath Castle, Caithness-shire.

Second son of the late George Thomson. Esq., of Edinburgh, by Katherine, dau. of the late Capt. Miller, of the 50th Regt ; b. 18—; m. 1843 Barbara Madelina Gordon, eldest dau. of William Sinclair, Esq., of Freswick, and has issue,

* William Sinclair, b. 1844.

Mr. Thomson-Sinclair, who is a J.P. and D.L. for co. Caithness, has been Deputy Commissary-General to Her Majesty's forces since 1846.—Dunbeath Castle, Caithness, N.B.; 4, Addison Crescent, w.

SINCLAIR. (See under *Caithness, Earl of.*)

+ SINGLETON, EDWARD, Esq., of Collon, co. Louth.

Eldest son of the late Henry Singleton, Esq., of Collon, by a dau. of — Burke, Esq.; b. 179—; m. 1822 Maria, dau. of — Cecil, Esq., and by her, who d. 1867, has, with other issue,

* Edward Cecil, late Capt. 51st Foot; b. 1823; m. 1861 Jane Josephine, only surviving child of the late A. Norris, Esq., of Dunkettle House, co. Cork.

Mr. Singleton is a Magistrate for co. Louth.—*Collon, co. Louth ; 5, Dean Street, Park Lane, w.*

SINGLETON, HENRY CORBET-, Esq., of Aclare, co. Meath.

Eldest son of the late Francis Corbet, Esq., of Aclare (who assumed, by Royal licence, the name of Singleton, under the will of his great grand-uncle the Right Hon. Henry Singleton, Master of the Rolls in Ireland), by Frances, dau. of Joseph Deane, Esq., of Terrenure, co. Dublin, and widow of Anthony Cliffe, Esq., of Abbey Braney, co. Wexford ; *b.* 1806; *s.* 1825; *m.* 1833 Jane Perceval Compton, youngest dau. of the late General William Loftus, and has, with other issue,

* Henry Corbet, Capt. 30th Foot ; *b.* 1837.

Mr. Corbet-Singleton, who is a J.P. and D.L. for co. Meath (High Sheriff 1842), was formerly Lieut. 7th Dragoon Guards.—*Aclare, Drumconrath, co. Meath.*

SINGLETON, JOHN, Esq., of Quinville, co. Clare.

Eldest son of the late Edward Dalton Singleton, Esq., of Quinville, by Mary, dau. of Hugh Brady, Esq., of Limerick ; *b.* 1793 ; *s.* 1814 ; *m.* 1st 1819 Isabella Carew, only child and heir of Michael Creagh, Esq., of Laurentinum, co. Cork ; 2nd 1867 Emma, dau. of the Rev. Mathew Phillips, of Pembroke, and widow of Thomas Woodforde, Esq., of Taunton, and has by the former, with other issue,

* Michael Creagh, late Lieut. 16th Foot ; served under Lord Gough in the campaign on the Sutlej; *b.* 1820.

Mr. Singleton, who was educated at Trinity Coll., Oxford, is a Magistrate for co. Clare (High Sheriff 1825).—*Quinville Abbey, Ennis, co. Clare.*

SINGLETON, THOMAS CRAWFORD-, Esq., of Fort Singleton, co. Monaghan, and Auburn, co. Dublin.

Eldest son of the late Andrew Crawford, Esq., of Auburn, co. Dublin, by Isabella, dau. of Thomas Singleton, Esq., of Fort Singleton, whose name he assumed ; *b.* 1807 ; *s.* 1843. Educated at Trinity Coll., Dublin ; is a J.P. and D.L. for co. Monaghan ; was formerly a Lieut. in the Army.—*Fort Singleton, Emyvale, co. Monaghan.*

SITWELL, Sir GEORGE RERESBY, Bart., of Renishaw, Derbyshire. (cr. 1808).

Only son of the late Sir Sitwell Reresby Sitwell, Bart., of Renishaw, by Louisa Lucy, dau. of the Hon. Henry Hely Hutchinson, of Weston Hall, co. Northampton ; *b.* 1860 ; *s.* as 4th Bart. 1862. Is Lord of the Manor of Renishaw.—*Renishaw, Chesterfield.*

Heir Pres., his uncle George Frederick, Capt. 3rd Light Dragoons ; *b.* 1828 ; *m.* 1857 Cecilia Fanny, dau. of Henry Fitz Roy, Esq., of Salcey Lawn, co. Northampton, and has, with other issue, * Claude George Henry, *b.* 1858.

SITWELL, FRANCIS HENRY MASSY, Esq., of Barmoor and Yeavering, Northumberland.

Eldest son of the late William Hurt Sitwell, Esq., of Barmoor and Yeavering, by Sarah Honoria, dau. of Sisson Cooper, Esq., of Merrion Street, Dublin ; *b.* 1831 ; *s.* 1865. Is Lord of the Manor of Barmoor, and represents a younger branch of the Sitwells, Barts., of Renishaw.—*Barmoor Castle, and Yeavering, Berwick.*

Heir Pres., his brother Albert Hurt, *b.* 1834.

SITWELL, the Rev. HERVEY WILMOT-, of Stainsby House, Derbyshire.

Fourth son of the late Edward Sacheverell Wilmot-Sitwell, Esq., of Stainsby House (who *d.* 1836), by Lucy, only dau. of the late Sir William Wheler, Bart. ; *b.* 1794 ; *s.* his brother 1860 ; *m.* 1824 Sophia, dau. of

C. J. Wheler, Esq. Educated at Rugby and St. John's Coll., Cambridge (B.A. 1817) ; is Lord of the Manor of Morley, and Patron of 2 livings.—*Stainsby House, Derby.*

SITWELL, ROBERT SACHEVERELL, Esq., of Morley House, Derbyshire.

Fifth son of the late Edward Sacheverell Wilmot, Esq. of Stainsby House (who assumed the name of Sitwell), by Lucy, dau. and heir of Sir William Wheler, Bart. ; *b.* 1796 ; *m.* 1821 Charlotte Ann, dau. of Francis Bradshaw, Esq., of Barton, co. Derby, and has, with other issue,

* Robert Sacheverell Wilmot (of Horsley, near Derby), educated at Brasenose Coll., Oxford (B.A. 1845), called to the Bar at the Middle Temple 1849, and a Magistrate for co. Derby ; *b.* 1823 ; *m.* 1861 Mary Blanche, dau. of John Senior, Esq., and has, with other issue, * Edward Sacheverell Wilmot, *b.* 1862.

Mr. Sitwell was formerly Lieut. 29th Regt.—*Morley House, Derby.*

SITWELL, WILLOUGHBY HURT-, Esq., of Ferney Hall, Shropshire.

Only son of the late Francis Hurt-Sitwell, Esq., of Ferney Hall, by Harriet, dau. of Sir Joseph Hoare, Bart., of Annabelle, co. Cork ; *b.* 1827 ; *s.* 1835 ; *m.* 1st 1853 Harriet, only dau. of William Henry Harford, Esq. (she *d.* 1855) ; 2nd 1858 Eliza Harriet, only dau. of R. B. Phillipson, Esq., of Dunston House, co. Stafford, and has issue by the former,

* Willoughby Harford, *b.* 1855.

Mr. Hurt-Sitwell, who is a J.P. and D.L. for co. Hereford, Lieut. S. Salop Yeomanry Cavalry, and Master of the Ludlow Foxhounds, was High Sheriff for co. Salop 1858.—*Ferney Hall, Shrewsbury ; Arthur's Club, s.w.*

SKEFFINGTON. (See under *Massareene, Viscount.*)

SKELMERSDALE, Lord (EDWARD BOOTLE-WILBRAHAM).—Cr. 1828.

Only son of the late Hon. Richard Bootle-Wilbraham (who was the eldest son of Edward, 1st Lord), by Jessy dau. of Sir Richard Brooke, Bart. ; *b.* 1837 ; *s.* his grandfather as 2nd Lord 1843 ; *m.* 1860 Lady Alice, 2nd dau. of George, 4th Earl of Clarendon. Educated at Eton and Ch. Ch., Oxford ; is a J.P. and D.L. for co. Lancaster, Lord of the Manor of Skelmersdale. Patron of 1 living, and Capt. Duke of Lancaster's Yeomanry, appointed in Waiting 1866.—*Latham House, Ormskirk ; Carlton Club. s.w.*

Heir, his son Edward George, *b.* 1864.

SKENE, GEORGE, Esq., of Rubislaw, Aberdeenshire.

Eldest son of the late James Skene, Esq., D.L., of Rubislaw, by Jane, dau. of Sir William Forbes, Bart., of Pitsligo ; *b.* 1807 ; *s.* 1864 ; *m.* 1831 Georgina, dau. of the late Dr. Alexander Munro, of Craiglockhart, Midlothian, and by her, who *d.* 1868, has surviving issue.

* Three daughters.

Mr. Skene is an Advocate at the Scottish Bars, a Magistrate for co. Aberdeen, and Professor of Civil Law and the Law of Scotland at Glasgow.—*Rubislaw D.n. Aberdeen, N.B. ; University Club, Edinburgh ; 20, Melville Street, Edinburgh, N.B.*

SKENE, WILLIAM BAILLIE, Esq., of Hallyards, Fifeshire.

Only surviving son of the late Patrick George Skene, Esq., of Hallyards (who *d.* 1861), by Jessie, 4th dau. of the late D. J. Campbell, Esq., of Skerrington, co. Ayr, and niece of the late Sir W. Baillie, Bart., of Polkemmet, co. Linlithgow ; *b.* 1838 ; *s.* his brother 1866. Educated at Harrow and C. C. C. Oxford (B.A. 1860, M.A. 1862) ; Fellow of All Souls' Coll. 1861 ; called to the Bar at Lincoln's Inn 1863 ; is a Magis-

trate for cos. Fife and Kinross. This family appears on record as early as 1296, when Johan and Patrick de Skene did homage to Edward I. of England. Their lands were erected into a Barony in 1317 by Robert I. of Scotland. — *Pit'our House, Strathmin'o, Fife-hire ; New C'nb, Elin'nrgh ; St. Jam's' and New University Clubs, s.w. ; 32, Green S.reet, Grosvenor Square, w.*

SKENE. (See *Gordon-Cumming-Skene*.)

SKERRETT, JOHN LOCKE, Esq., of Athgoe, co. Dublin.
Eldest son of the late John Denne Skerrett, Esq., of Ballinduff Castle, co. Galway, by Lucy, eldest dau. of the late John Locke, Esq., of Athgoe ; *b*. 1811 ; *s*. 1833. Educated at Clongowes Wood College, co. Kildare, and at Trinity Coll., Dublin (B.A. 1832) ; called to the Irish Bar 1837 ; is a Dep.-Lieut. for co. Dublin (High Sheriff 1840). — *Athgoe Park, Rathcoo'e ; Ballinduff Castle, Headfort, co. Galway* ; 16, *Mountjoy Square, Dublin.*

Heir Pres., his brother Peter Richard, b. 181-.

SKERRETT, WILLIAM JOSEPH, Esq., of Finnavara House, co. Clare.
Son of the late William Skerrett, Esq., of Finnavara House ; *b*. 18— ; *m*. 1850 Annie, dan. of J. M'Mahon, Esq., and has issue. Is a Magistrate for co. Clare (High Sheriff 1842-3). — *Finnavara House, Burrin, co. Clare.*

SKILLICORNE, WILLIAM NASH, Esq., of Cheltenham, Gloucestershire.
Only son of the late Rev. Richard Skillicorne Skillicorne, M.A., of Salford Rectory, Oxon, by Anna Maria. dau. of William Ballinger, Esq., of Cheltenham ; *b*. 1807 ; *s*. 1834 ; *m*. 1856 Mary Ann, dau. of Edward Greenwood. Esq., of Shurdington, co. Gloucester, and has, with other issue,

* William Nash, *b.* 1861.

Mr. Skillicorne, who was educated at Worcester Coll., Oxford (B.A. 1830. M.A. 1833), is a J.P. and D.L. for co. Gloucester, Chairman of Cheltenham Bench of Magistrates, and Patron of 1 living. His father, whose name was Nash, took the name of Skillicorne under the will of his uncle. Wm. Skillicorne, Esq., of Cheltenham, in 1803. — *Queen's Parade, Cheltenham.*

SKINGLEY, Mrs., of Wake's Colne Hall, Essex.
Catharine, youngest dau. of the late James Woodward, Esq., of Feering, Essex ; *m*. 1829 Henry Skingley, Esq., of Wake's Colne Hall, who *d*. 1858, leaving, with other issue,

* Henry, educated at Rugby ; *b.* 1812 ; *m.* 1865 Annie Katherine, 2nd dau. of H. Turkis, Esq., of Sturmere, Es-ex.

This family own the Lordship of the Manor of Wake's Colne. — *Wake's Colne Hall, Holstead.*

SKINNER, ALLAN MACLEAN, Esq., Q.C., of Brocton Lodge, Staffordshire.
Fourth son of the late Lieut.-General John Skinner, by Ann. 2nd dau. of the late John Maclean, Esq. ; *b*. 1809 ; *m*. 1837 Caroline Emily. only dau. of the late Rev. John Harding, M.A., of Glamorgan, Glamorgan, Rector of Coity and of Coychurch, co. Glamorgan, and has, with other issue,

* John Edwin Hilary, of Lincoln's Inn, Barrister-at-Law ; *b.* 1839 ; *m.* 1864 Louisa Sarah 2nl dau. of the late John Clarke Chaplin, Esq., of Tunbridge, Kent.

Mr. Skinner, who was educated at Eton and Balliol Coll., Oxford (B.A. 1832), and called to the Bar at Lincoln's Inn 1834, was appointed a Q.C. in 1857, Judge of the South Staffordshire County Courts 1859. Recorder of Windsor 1852 ; he is a Magistrate for cos. Stafford and Worcester, and propri tor of the estate of Cronk Ould, I. of Man. — *Brocton Lodge, Stafford.*

856

+SKINNER, CHARLES BRUCE, Esq., of The Chauntry, Suffolk.
Eldest son of the late Russell Skinner, Esq., of the Bengal Civil Service ; *b*. 18— ; *m*. 1857 Harriette Catherine, youngest dau. of the late Lieut.-Col. J. C. Tudor, C.B., Indian Army, and has, with other issue,

* Charles, educated at Eton ; *b.* 1858.

Mr. Skinner, who is Lord of the Manor of Sproughton, and was formerly in the Indian Civil Service (Bengal), purchased the above property from Sir Fitzroy Kelly 1867. — *The Chauntry, Sproughton, Ipswich ; Eccleston Square, s.w.*

SKINNER, Capt. CORTLANDT GEORGE MACGREGOR,‡ of Carisbrooke, I. of Wight.
Eldest son of the late Capt. Cortlandt Skinner, of the 76th Foot (J.P. for cos. Down and Antrim), by Isabella, dau. of the late Capt. John Macartney, R.N. ; *b*. 1798 ; *m*. 1822 Christina, only surviving dau. of the late Robert Grant, Esq., of Wester Elchies, co. Moray, N.B., and has, with other issue,

* Cortlandt George Macgregor. Lieut. 35th Fort ; *b.* 1832 ; *m.* 1864 Caroline Mary Anne. only dau. of the late Edward Wilson, Esq., of Newcastle. co. Stafford.

Capt. Skinner, who was educated at the Royal Colleges of Marlow and Sandhurst. is a Magistrate for cos. Down, Hants, and the I. of Wight ; was formerly Capt. 1st Dragoon Guards. This family, long distinguished for its loyalty, has, for four generations, been in the service of the Crown, Army and Navy. — *Carisbrooke House, Newport, I. of Wight.*

SKINNER, Mrs., of Branwoods, Essex.
Charlotte Sophia. eldest dau. of Jacob Elton. Esq., of The Grove, Dedham, Essex ; *m*. 1827 Samuel James Skinner, Esq., of Branwoods, a J.P. and D.L. for Essex. who assumed the name of Skinner in lieu of his patronymic Longmore. and who *d*. 1866. — *Branwoods, Great Baddow, Chelmsford.*

SKIPPER, CHARLES, Esq., of Blake Hall, Essex.
Third son of the late Peter Skipper, Esq., J.P., of Hope House, Little Burstead, Essex, by Elizabeth, dau. of William Cooper, Esq., of Bentley Heath ; *b*. 1798 ; *m*. 1833 Elizabeth Rippen. only dau. of the late Wm. East, Esq., of Tooting, Surrey, and has, with other issue,

* Charles, *b.* 1834 ; *m.* 1855 Harriet, eldest dau. of Arthur B. White, Esq.

Mr Skipper is a Magistrate for Essex, Middlesex, and Westminster, a J.P. and D.L. for the Tower Hamlets. and a Commissioner of Lieutenancy for London. — *Great Blake Hall, Wenstead* ; 28, *Russell Square, w.c.*

SKIPTON, GEORGE, Esq., of Beechill, co. Londonderry.
Eldest son of Alexander Skipton (5th son of G. Kennedy Skipton, of Beechhill, a Dep.-Governor of co. Derry). by Elizabeth. dau. and heir of James M'Crea ; *b*. 1827 ; *s*. his maternal grandfather 1857 ; is a J.P. and D.L. for co. Derry (High Sheriff 1863) ; contested in 1859 the representation of the borough of Londonderry. Mr. Skipton (once a contributor assumed until 1900 in 1802 on succeeding his cousin in the Beechill estate) is seventh in descent from John Kennedy. of Cregher (of the house of Uchtrdure. N.B.). through his son H. Kennedy, a Commissioner of the Poll-tax for co. Derry

‡ His grandfather, Brigadier General Cortlandt Skinner. Speaker of the House of Representatives of New York, at the outbreak of the American Revolution, raised three battalions and took the field lost in the struggle his property, which had been a sacrifice of his father's marriage into the wealthy Dutch family of Cortlandt. That gentleman forfeited his paternal estates in Fifeshire. N.B., which he held as William Macgregor, he espousing the standard cause ; and having been wounded at Prestonpans, in 1745, sat and dianed, and went out to New York.

1697-8, and Sheriff of Derby at its memorable siege in 1688.—*Beechill, Londonderry.*

Heir Pres., his cousin Kennedy, *b.* 1849.

SKIPTON, GEORGE ALEXANDER KENNEDY, Esq., of Beechill, Londonderry.

Eldest son of the late Henry Stacy Skipton, Esq., of Beechill, by Elizabeth M'Causland, dau. of Charles Stewart, Esq.; *b.* 1849; *s.* 1854. The Skiptons of the co. Derry were settled in Ireland by Alexander, a 2nd son of the Huntingdon-Skiptons. He settled on the lands of Ballyshasky, where he erected the mansion of Skipton Hall in 1625; burnt down in the rebellion of 1642. a second house was built 1645, which was burnt by the besieging army in 1688, and the present house built 1725, when the name was changed to Beechill. —*Bee hill, Londonderry; Lansdowne Terrace, Cheltenham.*

Heir Pres., his brother Charles Stewart, *b.* 1851.

SKIPWITH, Sir PEYTON ESTOTEVILLE, Bart., of Prestwould, Leicestershire (cr. 1622).

Elder son of the late Sir Thomas George Skipwith, Bart., J P. and D L. of Prestwould, by his 2nd wife Jane, dau. of Hubert Butler Moore, Esq., of Shannon View, co. Galway; *b.* 1857; *s.* as 10th Bart. 1863. Is Patron of 2 livings—*Brooks's and Arthur's Clubs*, s.w.; 18, *Lowndes Square*, w.

Heir Pres., his brother Gray Hubert, *b.* 1860.

SKIPWORTH, GEORGE BORMAN, Esq., of Moortown House, Lincolnshire.

Only surviving son of the late George Skipworth, Esq., of Moortown House (who was High Sheriff of co. Lincoln 1855), by Amelia, dau. of Wm. Dixon, Esq., of Holton Park, co. Lincoln; *b.* 1820; *s.* 1860; *m.* 1846 Alice, dau. of the Rev. Charles Bigsby, of Newark Priory, Notts, and has, with other issue,

* Albert George Philip, *b.* 1844.

Mr. Skipworth, who was called to the Bar at the Middle Temple 1845, is a Dep.-Lieut. for co. Lincoln. He is Lord of the Manor and alternate Patron of South Kelsey.—*Moortown House, South K le y, Caistor.*

SKRIMSHIRE, EDWARD AUGUSTUS, Esq., of Stanground, Hunts.

Youngest son of the late Fenwick Skrimshire, Esq., M.D., of Peterborough, by Charlotte, dau. of James Cobb. Esq., of Kettering, co. Northampton; *b.* 1820; *m.* 1851 Charlotte, eldest dau. of Charles Bowman, Esq., of Greatford, co. Lincoln. Is a Magistrate for the Liberty of Peterborough. This family descend in a direct line from Sir Alexander Serimgeour, Knt., Standard-bearer to Sir William Wallace.—*Stanground, Peterborough.*

SKRINE, HENRY DUNCAN, Esq., of Warleigh Manor, Somerset.

Eldest son of the late Henry Skrine, Esq., of Warleigh Manor, and of Stubbings. Berks, by Caroline Anne. dau. of the Rev. Benjamin Spry. Canon of Salisbury, &c.; *b.* 1815; *s.* 1853; *m.* 1843 Susanna Caroline, dau. of William Mills, Esq., of Saxham Hall, Suffolk, and has, with other issue,

* Henry Mills, *b.* 1844.

Mr. Skrine, who was educated at Wadham Coll., Oxford (B.A. 1837, M.A. 1812). is a Magistrate for Somerset and Patron of 1 living.—*Warleigh Manor, Bath ; Athenæum Club*, s.w.

SLADE, Sir ALFRED FREDERICK ADOLPHUS, Bart., Maunsell Grange, Somerset (cr. 1831).

Eldest son of the late Sir Frederick William Slade, Bart., of Maunsell Grange, by Barbara Maria, dau. of

the late Charles Browne Mostyn, Esq., and sister of Lord Vaux of Harrowden; *b.* 1834 ; *s.* as 3rd Bart. 1863; *m.* 1830 Mary Constance. 2nd dau. of Wi lliam Cuthbert, Esq., of Beaufront Castle, Northumberland. Is Lord of the Manor of Maunsell, and Lieut. W. Somerset Yeomanry; late Capt. 100th Foot.—*Maunsell Grange, North Petherton, Somerset; Army and Navy Club*, s.w.

Heir, his son Cuthbert, *b.* 1863.

SLADE, Sir ADOLPHUS, K C.B. (cr. 1858).

Fifth son of the late General Sir John Slade, Bart., by his 1st wife Anna Eliza, dau. of J. Dawson, Esq.; *b.* 1807. Is a Rear-Admiral R.N., retired, and an Admiral in the Turkish service.—*Travellers' and United Service Clubs*. s.w.

SLADE-GULLY, WILLIAM ALGERNON, Esq., of Trevennen, Cornwall.

Eldest son of the late Rev. Samuel Thomas Slade-Gully, Rector of Berrynarbor, by Anne, dau. of W. Hunt-Grubbe, Esq., of Eastwell, Wilts; *b.* 1827; *s.* 1860. Educated at Eton and King's Coll., Cambridge (B.A. 1851, M.A. 1854), and called to the Bar at the Inner Temple 1855; is a Magistrate for Cornwall. and Lord of the Manor of Trevennen.—*Trevennen, Mevagissey ; University Club*, s.w.

SLADEN, JOSEPH, Esq., of Hartsbourne Manor, Herts, and Swanton Court, Kent.

Eldest son of the late Joseph Sladen. Esq., of Swanton Court, by Anne, 2nd dau. of William Mainwaring, Esq., of London ; *b.* 1837 ; *m.* 1833 his cousin Etheldred, 2nd dau. of the late John Baker Sladen, Esq., of Ripple Court, Kent, and has, with other issue,

* Joseph, a Magistrate in the N.W. Provinces of India ; *b.* 1836; *m.* 1863 Augusta St. John, dau. of Joseph St. John Tetts, Esq., of Wellbank, co. Chester, and has issue,
    * Joseph, *b.* 1867.

Mr. Sladen was educated at Winchester.—*Hartsbourne Manor, Bushey Heath, Watford ; Swanton Court, Dover.*

SLADEN, JOSEPH, Esq., of Ripple Court, Kent.

Only son of the late Joseph St. Barbe Sladen, Esq. (who *d.* 1847), by Elizabeth Sladen, dau. of Lawrence Banks, Esq., of Boys Hall, Kent; *b.* 1840; *s.* his grandfather 1860 ; *m.* 1864 Caroline Mary, 2nd dau. of Sampson T. W. French, Esq., of Cuskinny, co. Cork, and has, with other issue,

* Arthur French, *b.* 1866.

Mr. Sladen, who was educated at the Royal Military Academy, Woolwich, is a Lieut. in the Royal Artillery. —*Ripple Court, Ringwould, Dover ; Royal Yacht Squadron, Cowes.*

SLANEY. (See *Kenyon-Slaney.*)

SLATER, of Newick. (See *Sclater.*)

SLATER-HARRISON. (See *Harrison.*)

SLATOR. (See *Wilson-Slator.*)

SLEIGH, Lady, of Hanworth, Middlesex.

Eliza, dau. of Ma or-General C. S. Fagan, C.B.; *m.* 1831 General Sir James Wallace Sleigh, K.C.B., of Hanworth House, formerly Inspector-General of Cavalry, who *d.* 1865.—*Hanworth House, Hounslow.*

SLIGO, Marquis of (GEORGE JOHN BROWNE). —Cr. 1800.

Eldest son of Howe Peter, 2nd Marquis, by Lady Hester, eldest dau. of John Thomas. 13th Earl of Clanricarde; *b.* 1820; *s.* 1845; *m.* 1st 1847 the Hon. Louisa Ellen Augusta. dau. of Percy, 5th Viscount Strangford (she *d.* 1852); 2nd 1858 Julia, dau. of

Anthony Nugent, Esq., of Pallas, co. Galway (she *d.* 1859). Educated at Eton; is a Magistrate for co. Mayo, and Col. S. Mayo Militia; sits in the House of Lords as Lord Mounteagle, U.K. (cr. 1806). Is descended from a common ancestor with the Earl of Kenmare and Lords Kilmaine and Oranmore.—*Westport House, co. Mayo ; Travellers' Club,* s.w.

Heir Pres., his brother Lord John Thomas, a J.P. and D.L. for co. Mayo, and M.P. for co. Mayo ; late a Lieut. R.N. ; *b.* 1824.

SLIGO. (See *Smith-Sligo.*)

SLINGSBY, Sir CHARLES, Bart., of Scriven Hall, Yorkshire (cr. 1635).

Only son of the late Charles Slingsby, Esq., of Loftness Hill, by Emma Margaret, dau. of Thomas Atkinson, Esq., of Maple Hayes, and nephew of the late Sir Thomas Slingsby, Bart.; *b.* 1824 ; *s.* as 10th Bart. 1835. Is a J.P. and D.L. for the W. Riding of Yorkshire, and Patron of 2 livings; late Lieut. R. Horse Guards.—*Scriven Hall, Knaresborough ; Carlton Club,* s.w.

SLOANE-STANLEY, FRANCIS, Esq., of Tedworth Park, Wilts.

Third son of the Rev. George Sloane-Stanley, by Laura, 3rd dau. of the late William Webber, Esq., of Binfield Lodge, Berks, and grandson of the late William Sloane-Stanley, Esq., of Paultons, Hants ; *b.* 184–; *s.* his aunt, Mrs. Aeshtou-Smith, 1859 ; *m.* 1866 Charlotte Amy, youngest dau. of the Hon. John Rose, of Montreal, Canada, and has issue,

* A son, *b.* 1867.

Mr. Sloane-Stanley is descended in the female line from an elder brother of Sir Hans Sloane.—*Tedworth Park, Andover.*

+SLOANE-STANLEY, WILLIAM HANS, Esq., of Paultons, Hampshire.

Eldest son of the late William Sloane, Esq., M.P., of Paultons (who assumed the additional name of Stanley), by Lady Gertrude, dau. of the 5th Earl of Carlisle, K.G. ; *b.* 1807 ; *s.* 1860 ; *m.* 1833 Honoria, dau. of the late General Gubbins, of Stoneham, Hants, and sister of the Duchess of St. Alban's, and has, with other issue, an only son,

* William, *b.* 1840 ; *m.* 1866 Emilie Josephine, only dau. of Francis Edwards, Esq., of Pickerage, Bucks.

Mr. Sloane Stanley is a J.P. and D.L. for Hants (High Sheriff 1867).—*Paultons, Romsey.*

SMALL-KIER. (See *Kier.*)

+SLOCOCK, CHARLES, Esq., of Donnington, Berks.

Eldest son of the late Charles Slocock, Esq., Banker, of Newbury, Berks; *b.* 179–; is married, and has, with other issue,

* Charles Samuel, a Magistrate for Berks ; *b.* 18—.

Mr. Slocock is a Magistrate for Berks, and a Banker at Newbury.—*Donnington, Newbury.*

+SMALL, the Rev. HARRY ALEXANDER, LL.B., of Clifton Reynes, Bucks.

Son of the late — Small, Esq.; *b.* 1802. Educated at Downing Coll., Cambridge (B.A. 1825, M.A. 1829, LL.B. 1836) ; is a Magistrate for co. Northampton and Rector and Patron of Clifton Reynes.—*Clifton Reynes, Olney.*

SMALL, JAMES, Esq., of Dirnanean, Perthshire.

Eldest son of the late Patrick Small, Esq., of Dirnanean, by Amelia, dau. of Francis Rattray, Esq., of Kirkhillocks, co. Forfar; *b.* 1855 ; *s.* 1860 ; *m.* 1867 Janet, 2nd dau. of Sir Jervoise Clarke-Jervoise, Bart., M.P. of

Idsworth, Hants. Is a Magistrate for co. Perth, and Lord of the Barony of Dirnanean. This family have been in posses-ion of the lands of Dirnanean, and have succeeded in direct line from the 14th century —*Dirnanean, Pitlochrie, N.B. ; New Club, Edinburgh.*

SMART, Lady.

Frances Margaret, dau. of the Rev. C. S. Hope; *m.* 1832 Sir George Thomas Smart, Knt., who was Organist and Composer to the Chapel Royal, St. James's, and *d.* 1867.—12, *Bedford Square,* w.c.

SMART, Vice-Admiral Sir ROBERT, K.C.B., K.H.,‡ of Mainsforth, co. Durham (cr. 1865).

Third son of the late John Smart, Esq., of Trewhitt House, Northumberland (who *d.* 1828), by Dorothy, dau. and co-heir of Robert Lynn, Esq., of Mainsforth, and brother of W. L. Smart, Esq. (whom see) ; *b.* 1796 ; *m.* 1848 Elizabeth Isabella, only dau. of the late Benjamin Sharpe, Esq., Banker, of London, and has, with other issue,

* Robert William John, *b.* 1849.

Admiral Sir R. Smart, who entered the Royal Navy in 1810, became Capt. 1837, and a Rear-Admiral of the Red 1857 ; late Commander-in-Chief of the Mediterranean Fleet, with temporary rank as Vice-Admiral; was nominated a K.H. 1832, and created a Knight of the Red Eagle of Prussia same year. — Residence : *Rothbury House, Chiswick,* s.w.

SMART, the Rev. NEWTON, of Goudhurst, Kent.

Fourth son of the late John Smart, Esq., of Trewhitt House, Northumberland, by Dorothy, dau. and co-heir of Robert Lynn, Esq.; *b.* 1798 ; *m.* 1st 1822 Mary Susan, dau. and heir of the late Stephen Groombridge, Esq., of Goudhurst ; 2nd 1831 Frances Charlotte Josephine, dau. of Major-General De Berniere, and has, with other issue,

* Henry De Berniere, educated at Eton and Sandhurst, Lieut. 54th Regt.; *b.* 1843.

Mr. Smart, who was educated at University Coll., Oxford (B.A. 1821, M.A. 1824), is Rector of Wittersham, Rural Dean, Prebendary of Salisbury, and Chaplain to the Archbishop of Canterbury ; late Vicar of Alderbury, Wilts.—*Goudhurst, Cranbrook ; Residence : Wittersham Rectory, near Staplehurst, Kent.*

SMART, WILLIAM LYNN, Esq., of Trewhitt, Northumberland, and of Linden, Beds.

Eldest son of the late John Smart, Esq., J.P. and D.L., of Trewhitt House, by Dorothy, dau. and co-heir of Robert Lynn, Esq., of Mainsforth, co. Durham ; *b.* 1791 ; *s.* 1828 ; *m.* 1st 1828 Rosamond, dau. of John Longley, Esq., of Angley, Kent ; 2nd 1842 Charlotte, dau. of Hesse Gordon, Esq. Is a Magistrate for Northumberland, and a J.P. and D.L. for Beds (on the roll of High Sheriffs for 1866-7, but excused from serving) ; was formerly Capt. of the Coquetdale Yeomanry.—*Trewhitt House, Rothbury ; Linden Hall, Woburn, Beds.*

Heir Pres., his brother John Newton, *b.* 1794 ; *m.* 1823 Marl... [illegible] ... Vicar of Henlow, Beds, by Marianne, dau. and heir of Christopher Prichard, Esq. of Preston, and has, with other issue, * William Lynn, *b.* 1824.

+SMEDLEY, JOHN, Esq., of Riber Castle, Derbyshire.

Son of the late John Smedley, Esq., of Wirksworth, co. Derby ; *b.* 1802 ; *m.* 184– Caroline, dau. of Rev. — Marsden, of Derbyshire. Is a Manufacturer at Lea Bridge, near Matlock.—*Riber Castle, Matlock.*

‡ This gentleman had the honour of escorting the Princess Alexandra of Denmark to England in 1863, when Rear-Admiral Commander-in-Chief of the Channel Fleet.

SMETHURST, Augustus William, Esq., of Rookwood, Lancashire.

Third son of the late Richard Smethurst, Esq., of Chorley (who was a J.P. and D.L. for co. Lancaster), by Anne, dau. of James Mellor, Esq., of Chorley; *b.* 1830; *m.* 1866 Theresa Maria Willoughby, elder dau. of Major-Gen. George W. Osborne, of Hawford, co. Worcester. Is a Magistrate for co. Lancaster; late Capt 4th Lancashire Militia.—*Rookwood, Chorley; Reform Club, s.w.*

SMETHURST, Richard, Esq., of Chorley, Lancashire.

Eldest son of the late Richard Smethurst, Esq., D.L., of Chorley, by Anne, dau. of James Mellor, Esq., of Chorley; *b.* 1824; *s.* 1857; *m.* 1853 Emily Jane, dau. of the late Joseph Holdsworth, Esq., M.P., and has issue,

* Emily Maud Mary.

Mr. Smethurst is a J.P. and D.L. for co. Lancaster. —Residence: *Ellerbeck, Chorley; Reform Club, s.w.*

SMIJTH, Sir William Bowyer-, Bart., of Hill Hall, Essex (cr. 1661).

Eldest son of the late Sir Edward Bowyer-Smijth, Bart., of Hill Hall (who assumed the additional name of Bowyer by Royal licence in 1839), by Letitia Cicely, dau. of the late John Weyland, Esq., of Woodeaton, Oxon; *b.* 1814; *s.* as 11th Bart. 1850; *m.* 1839 Marianne Frances, dau. of the late Sir Henry Meux, Bart. Educated at Eton and Trinity Coll., Cambridge (B.A. 1835). Is a J.P. and D.L. for Essex, a Magistrate for Norfolk, and Patron of 5 livings; was M.P. for Essex 1852-7.—*Hill Hall, Harlow; The Hall, Attleburgh*; 1, *Regent Street, s.w.*

Heir, his son William, in the Diplomatic Service; *b.* 1840.

SMIJTH, Dowager Lady BOWYER-,‡ of Thorpe Lee, Surrey.

Letitia Cicely, dau. of the late John Weyland, Esq., of Woodeaton, Oxon; *m.* 1813 Sir Edward Bowyer-Smijth, Bart., of Hill Hall, who *d.* 1850.—*Thorpe Lee, Chertsey.*

SMIJTH-WINDHAM. (See *Windham.*)

SMITH, Sir William CUSACK-, Bart. (cr. 1799).

Eldest son of the late Sir Michael Cusack-Smith, Bart., of Newtown, King's Co., by Eliza, dau. of C. P. Moore, Esq.; *b.* 1822; *s.* as 4th Bart. 1859; was formerly an Officer in the Royal Wurtemburg Lancers.

Heir Pres., his cousin William Robert Cusack (eldest son of the late Right Hon. Thomas Berry Cusack-Smith, who *d.* 1866, by Louisa, dau. of the late James Hugh Smith-Barry, Esq., of Marbury Hall, co. Chester, and of Fouty, co. Cork); *b.* 1829; *m.* 1856 Mary Blanche, dau. of the late John Chisenhale, Esq., of Arley Hall, co. Lancaster.

SMITH, Sir Charles Cunliffe, Bart., of Suttons, Essex (cr. 1804).

Only son of the late Sir Charles Joshua Smith, Bart., of Suttons, by his 2nd wife Mary, dau. of William Gosling, Esq., of Roehampton, Surrey; *b.* 1827; *s.* as 3rd Bart. 1848; *m.* 1855 Agnes Frederica, dau. of Capel Cure, Esq., of Blake Hall, Essex. Educated at Eton and Trinity Coll., Cambridge. Is a J.P. and D.L. for Essex (High Sheriff 1852), and Patron of 1 living. —*Suttons, Romford.*

Heir, his son Drummond Cunliffe, *b.* 1861.

SMITH, Sir William, Bart., of Eardiston, Worcestershire (cr. 1809).

Eldest son of the late Sir Christopher Sydney Smith, Bart., of Eardiston. by Mary, dau. of the Rev. R. Foley; *b.* 1823; *s.* as 2nd Bart. 1859; *m.* 1843 Susan. dau. of Sir William G. Parker, Bart. Is a J.P. and

D.L. for co. Worcester; late Capt. Worcester Yeomanry Cavalry.—*Eardiston, Tenbury; Carlton Club, s.w.*

Heir, his son Christopher Sydney Winwood, *b.* 1846.

SMITH, Sir Lionel Eldred, Bart. (cr. 1868).

Eldest son of the late Lieut.-General Sir Lionel Smith, Bart., by Isabella Curwen, dau. of Edward Curwen, Pottinger, Esq., of Mount Pottinger, co. Down; *b.* 1833; *s.* as 2nd Bart. 1842; *m.* 1854 Fanny, dau. of Thomas Pottinger, Esq., of Mount Pottinger, co. Down. Educated at Eton; is a Capt. in the Army, late of the 71st Foot, and Adjutant 1st Derby Militia.—*Derby.*

Heir, his son Lionel Eldred Pottinger, *b.* 1857.

SMITH, Sir Andrew, K.C.B., M.D., F.R.S. (cr. 1858).

Son of the late Mr. Thomas Smith, of Heron Hall, co. Roxburgh, by Grace, dau. of Mr. J. Tait; *b.* 1797 ; *m.* 1840 Ellen, dau. of R. Phillips, Esq., of co. Wicklow (she *d.* 1854). Educated at Edinburgh, where he graduated 1819 ; is Honorary Fellow of the Faculty of Physicians and Surgeons of Glasgow of the College of Surgeons of Edinburgh, of the Medico-Chirurgical Society of Aberdeen, and M.D., *honoris causâ,* of Trinity Coll., Dublin ; author of 'Illustrations of the Zoology of South Africa,' 'Origin and History of the Bushmen,' &c. ; was Director-General of the Army Medical Department 1851-8.—*Athenæum Club, s.w.* ; 51, *Thurloe Square, s.w.*

SMITH, Sir Francis (cr. 1862).

Son of the late Francis Smith, Esq., Merchant of London; *b.* 1819 ; called to the Bar at the Middle Temple 1842 ; is Judge of the Supreme Court of Tasmania. —*Hobart Town, Tasmania.*

SMITH, Sir Henry, Knt. (cr. 1860).

Son of the late Henry Smith. Esq.; *b.* 1812 ; *m.* 1836 Mary, dau. of Robert Talbot. Esq., of Kingston, Canada. Is Speaker of the House of Representatives in Canada. —*Kingston, Canada West.*

SMITH, Sir John Mark Frederic, Knt., K.H. (cr. 1832).

Son of the late Major-General Sir J. F. Sigismund Smith. K.C.H., and brother of the late L. V. Vernon. Esq., of Ardington, M.P. for Berks : *b.* 1792 ; *m.* 1813 Harriet, dau. of T. Horne. Esq. Is a Lieut.-General in the Army, and Col. Commanding the Royal Engineers at Aldershot ; late Inspector of Railways ; served in Sicily 1807-12; was M.P. for Chatham 1852-3. and 1857-65. —*Auckland House, Dover ; United Service and Carlton Clubs, s.w.* ; 39, *Hyde Park Square, s.w.*

SMITH, Sir John William, K.C.B. (cr. 1844).

Eldest son of the late William Smith. Esq., of Luton. Beds, by Dinah, dau. of Mr. William Milledge, of Weymouth, Dorset ; *b.* 1806 ; *m.* 1837 Agnes Campbell, second dau. of the late Capt. Donald Macarthur. Royal Veteran Battalion, and has, with other issue,

* Arthur Maclean, *b.* 1856.

Sir William is Commissary-General-in-Chief of the British Army, retired.—*Junior United Service Club, s.w.*

SMITH, Sir Montague Edward, Knt. (cr. 1865).

Eldest son of the late Thomas Smith, Esq., of Bideford. Devon; *b.* 1809. Called to the Bar at the Middle Temple, 1835; appointed Queen's Counsel 1853, a Judge of Common Pleas 1865; was M.P. for Truro 1859-65. —*Athenæum, Carlton, and Windham Clubs, s.w.*; 119, *Park Street, w.*

SMITH, Sir Peter, C.B., K.C.M.G. (cr. 1860).

Son of the late P. Smith, Esq.; *b.* 18—. Was formerly

Chief Clerk of the Colonial Office, and Secretary and Registrar of the Order of St. Michael and St. George.—3, *Finchley New Road*, N.W.

SMITH, ABEL, Esq., of Woodhall, Herts.

Eldest son of the late Abel Smith, Esq., M.P., of Woodhall, by his 2nd wife Frances Ann, dau. of the late Sir Harry Calvert, Bart., and nephew of Robert, 1st Lord Carington; *b.* 1829; *s.* 1858; *m.* 1853 Lady Susan Emma, dau. of Henry Thomas, 3rd Earl of Chichester, and has issue,

* Abel, *b.* 1855.

Mr. Smith, who was educated at Harrow and Trinity Coll., Cambridge, is a Magistrate for Herts, and Patron of 7 livings; he was M.P. for Herts 1852–7, and 1859–65, re-elected 1866.—*Woodhall Park, Ware; Travellers' and Carlton Clubs*, S.W.; 35, *Chesham Place*, S.W.

SMITH, ABRAHAM, Esq., of Treasbear, Devon.

Eldest son of the late Abraham Smith, Esq., of Treasbear, by Jane, dau. of John Barnes, Esq., of East Anstey; *b.* 1811; *s.* 1858; *m.* 1842 Harriet Mary Collyns, dau. of the Rev. Charles Elliott Walkey, and has issue. Was formerly Capt. R. Devon Yeomanry Cavalry.—*Treasbear, Exeter.*

+SMITH, the Rev. ALFRED, of Old Park, Wilts.

Son of the late — Smith, Esq.; *b.* 1813: is married, and has issue. Educated at Queen's Coll, Oxford (B.A. 1835, M.A. 1839); is a Magistrate for Wilts; late Chaplain to the British Embassy at St. Petersburg.—*Old Park, Devizes.*

SMITH, ARCHIBALD, Esq., F.R.S., of Jordan Hill, Renfrewshire.

Eldest son of the late James Smith, Esq., F.R.S., of Jordan Hill, by Mary, dau. of Alexander Wilson, Esq.; *b.* 1813; *s.* 1867; *m.* 1853 Susan Emma, dau. of Vice-Chancellor Sir James Parker, of Rothley Temple, co. Leicester. Educated at Trinity Coll., Cambridge (B.A. 1836, M.A. 1839); called to the Bar at Lincoln's Inn 1841.—*Jordan Hill, Glasgow; River Bank, Putney*, S.W.; 3, *Stone Buildings*, W.C.

SMITH, AUGUSTUS, Esq., of Tresco, Cornwall.

Eldest son of the late James Smith, Esq., of Ashlyns, Herts, by his 2nd wife Isabella, dau. of Augustus Pechell, Esq.; *b.* 1804; *s.* 1813. Educated at Harrow and Ch.Ch., Oxford; is a Magistrate for Herts, Bucks, and Cornwall, and a Dep.-Lieut. for Herts, and Patron of 1 living; was M.P. for Truro 1857–65.—*Tresco Abbey, Isles of Scilly; Reform, Brooks's, and Athenæum Clubs*, S.W.

+SMITH, BENJAMIN LEIGH, Esq., of Mountfield, Sussex.

Elder son of the late Benjamin Smith, Esq. (who was a Magistrate for Sussex and for Hastings; M.P. for Sudbury 1835–7, and for Norwich 1838–47, and *d.* 1860); *b.* 1826.—*Mountfield, Robertsbridge.*

SMITH, BROOKE, Esq., of Stoke Bishop, Gloucestershire.

Only son of the late Brooke Smith, Esq., Solicitor, of Bristol (who *d.* 1825), by Hannah, dau. of John Edye, Esq., of Bristol; *b.* 1803; *m.* 1852 Maria, dau. of the late Abram T. Rawlinson, Esq., of Cuddington, Oxon, and has issue, an only dau., Eudocia Maria Brooke. Mr. Smith is a Magistrate for co. Gloucester; was formerly a Solicitor at Bristol. This family was formerly settled at Stratford-on-Avon.— *Stoke Hill Cottage, Stoke Bishop, Bristol.*

800

SMITH, CECIL, Esq., of Lydeard House, Somerset.

Only son of the late Rev. Cecil Robert Smith, M.A., of Lydeard House, by Mary Jane, dau. of Col. Warren; *b.* 1826; *s.* 1861; *m.* 1858 Amelia, dau. of Sir Peter Stafford Carey, Bailiff of Guernsey, and has, with other issue,

* Cecil, *b.* 1860.

Mr. Smith, who was educated at Trinity Coll., Cambridge (B.A. 1848), called to the Bar at the Inner Temple 1852, and went the Western Circuit, is a Magistrate for Somerset.—*Lydeard House, Bishop's Lydeard, Taunton; Oxford and Cambridge Club*, S.W.

+SMITH, CHARLES HENRY, Esq., of Gwernllwynwith, Glamorganshire.

Son of the late C. Smith, Esq., of Gwernllwynwith; *b.* 18—; *m.* 18— Emily, youngest dau. of the late Sir George William Leeds, Bart., of Croxton Park, co. Cambridge. Is a Magistrate for co. Glamorgan.—*Gwernllwynwith, Swansea.*

SMITH, CHARLES HERVEY, Esq., of Aspley, Beds.

Eldest son of the late Lieut.-Col. Charles Hervey Smith, of Aspley, by Frances, dau. of Shallot Dale, Esq., of Newcastle; *b.* 1813; *s.* 1857. Educated at Winchester and Exeter Coll., Oxford; is a Magistrate for Bedfordshire, and a Property-Tax Commissioner; was formerly Capt. Beds Light Infantry Militia.—*Aspley House, Woburn.*

Heir Pres., his brother Villiers Shallot Chernocke, M.A. of New Coll., Oxford, in Holy Orders; *b.* 1822; *m.* 1851 Caroline Constantia, youngest dau. of the late Benjamin Holloway, Esq., of Lee Place, Charlbury, Oxon.

SMITH, CHARLES WILMOT, Esq., of Ballynanty, co. Limerick.

Eldest son of the late John Wilmot Smith, Esq., of Ballynanty, by Mary, youngest dau. of Thomas Lloyd, Esq., of Beechmount, co. Limerick; *b.* 1816; *s.* 1830; *m.* 1851 Charlotte Anne, youngest dau. of the late Hon. Merrick Lindsey Peter Burrell, of Stoke Park, Suffolk, and has, with other issue,

* John Wilmot Crosbie, *b.* 1853.

Mr. Smith, who was educated at Eton and Trinity Coll., Dublin, is a Magistrate for cos. Limerick and Clare, and Lord of the Manor of Ballynanty.—*Ballynanty House, Bruff; Killuran Abbey, Broadford, co. Clare.*

SMITH, EAGLESFIELD BRADSHAW, Esq., of Blackwood, Dumfriesshire, and Eyam, Derbyshire.

Eldest son of the late Eaglesfield Smith, Esq., of Eyam, by Judith Elizabeth, dau. of the late General Sir Paulus Æmilus Irving, Bart., of Woodhouse and Robgill; *b.* 1814; *s.* 1839; *m.* 1838 Elizabeth Macdonald, dau. of the late Norman Lockhart, Esq., of Tarbrax, co. Lanark, and has, with other issue,

* Eaglesfield, M.A. and Fellow of Christ's Coll. Cambridge; *b.* 1841.

Mr. B. Smith is a Magistrate for co. Dumfries, where his grandfather bought property about the end of the last century.—*Blackwood House, Ecclefechan, N.B.*

SMITH, EDMUND, Esq., of Ferriby, Yorkshire.

Son of the late George Smith, Esq., M.P. (who was a brother of Robert, 1st Lord Carington), by Frances Mary, dau. of Sir John Parker Mosley, Bart., of Rolleston Hall, co. Stafford; *b.* 1809; *m.* 1836 Hester, dau. of the late Charles May Lushington, Esq., formerly Member of Council at Madras, and has issue,

* Two daughters.

Mr. Smith, who was educated at the Charterhouse and Haileybury Coll., is a J.P. and D.L. for the E. Riding

of Yorkshire, and a Magistrate for Hull; was formerly in the Madras Civil Service.—*Ferriby, Brough; Union Club, s.w.*

SMITH, Major EDWARD HEATHCOTE, of Sydling, Dorset.

Sixth son of the late Sir John Wyldbore Smith, Bart., of the Down House, Dorset, by Elizabeth Anne, dau. and co-heir of the Rev. James Marriott, D.C.L., of Horsmonden, Kent; *b.* 1813; *m.* 1839 Christina, dau. of William Mackintosh, Esq., of Geddes, N.B., and has, with other surviving issue,

   • William Henry Curtis, Lieut. 104th Bengal Fusiliers; *b.* 1841; *m.* 1867 Annie 2nd dan. of the Rev. A. Wilkinson, Incumbent of St. James's, Poole.

Major Smith is a Magistrate for Dorset, and a Major in the Army; late Capt. 76th Foot.—*Sydling House, and Heathcote Lodge, Dorchester, Dorset.*

SMITH, FERDINANDO DUDLEY LEA, Esq., of Halesowen Grange, Shropshire.

Eldest son of the late Ferdinando Smith, Esq., of Halesowen Grange, by his 2nd wife Elizabeth, 4th dau. of Michael Grazebrook, Esq., of Audnam; *b.* 1834; *s.* 1841; *m.* 1865 Amy Sophia, youngest dau. of the late James Heath Leigh, Esq., of Belmont Hall, co. Chester. Educated at Eton and Ch. Ch., Oxford; called to the Bar at the Inner Temple 1858; is a Magistrate for cos. Worcester and Stafford, a Dep.-Lieut. for co. Worcester (High Sheriff 1860), Capt. Queen's Own Worcestershire Yeomanry, and Major 1st Batt. Worcestershire Rifle Volunteers. — *Halesowen Grange, co. Salop; Junior Carlton and Oxford and Cambridge Clubs, s.w.*

   Heir Pres., his brother William Lea, *b.* 1836.

SMITH, FRANCIS, Esq., of Salt Hill, Sussex.

Eldest son of the late John Smith, Esq., of London, by Mary, dau. of J. Richardson, Esq., of Lisburn, Ireland; *b.* 1806; *m.* 1832 Mary, only dau. and heir of the late Z. Levin, Esq., of Salt Hill, and has issue,

   • Archibald Levin, educated at Trinity Coll., Cambridge, a Barrister-at-Law of the Inner Temple, *b.* 1836; *m.* 1867 Isabel, eldest dau. of John Charles Fletcher, Esq., of Dale Park, Sussex.

Mr. Smith, who is a Magistrate for Sussex, represents a family formerly seated at Balby, co. York.—*Salt Hill, Chichester.*

SMITH, FREDERICK, Esq., of Sandfield, Staffordshire.

Younger son of Richard Smith, Esq., late of The Priory, Dudley, by Elizabeth, dau. of S. Fereday, Esq., late of Ettingshall Park; *b.* 1824; educated at Rugby and St. John's Coll., Oxford, of which he is a Fellow (B.A. 1846, M.A. 1850); called to the Bar at Middle Temple 1846; is a Magistrate for cos. Stafford and Worcester, Capt. in the Queen's Own Worcestershire Yeomanry Cavalry, and late Capt. in the Staffordshire Rifle Volunteers.—*Sandfield Lodge, Wordsley, Kingswinford, Staffordshire; The Priory, Dudley.*

+**SMITH**, GEORGE PERCEVAL, Esq., of Lower Eaton, Herefordshire.

Son of the late G. Smith, Esq.; *b.* 18—. Is a J.P. and D.L. for co. Hereford.—*Lower Eaton, Hereford.*

SMITH, GEORGE ROBERT, Esq., of Selsdon, Surrey.

Eldest son of the late George Smith, Esq., of Selsdon, by Frances Mary, dau. of the late Sir John Parker Mosley, Bart., of Rolleston Hall, and nephew of Robert, 1st Lord Carington; *b.* 1793; *s.* 1836; *m.* 1818

Jane, eldest dau. of the late John Maberly, Esq., M.P., and has, with other issue,

   • Fernald Mosley, *b.* 183-; *m.* 1863 Lindsay Elizabeth, 2nd dau. of the late John Murray, Esq., of Toucha lan and Fochabers, N.B.

Mr. Smith, who was educated at Eton, is a J.P. and D.L. for Surrey (High Sheriff 1852); was M.P. for Midhurst 1830–2, for Wycombe 1839–41.—*Selsdon House, Croydon; Reform, Forres, N.B.; Travellers' and Brooks's Clubs, s.w.; 78, Eaton Square, s.w.*

SMITH, GEORGE THOMAS CLEATHER, Esq., of Hollymount, co. Donegal.

Second son of the late John Smith, Esq., of Devonport, by Charlotte, dau. of the late John Pridham, Esq., of Plymouth; *b.* 1815; *m.* 1849 Mary Anna, 5th dau. of the Rev. Joseph Welsh, Rector of Killaghtee, co. Donegal, and has, with other issue,

   • George, *b.* 185-.

Mr. Smith, who entered the Navy 1828, is a Magistrate for co. Donegal, and a Commander R.N.—*Hollymount, Rathmullen, co. Donegal.*

SMITH, GUSTAVUS THOMAS, Esq., of Goldicote House, Worcestershire.

Second son of the late George Smith, Esq., of Goldicote; *b.* 1809; *m.* 1832 Sarah Elizabeth, dau. of the late Rev. William Yates, Rector of Eccleston, co. Lancaster (she *d.* 1852); 2nd 1853 Caroline Sophia, 2nd dau. of the late Right Rev. George Murray, D.D., Lord Bishop of Rochester, and widow of Sr John Mordaunt, Bart. Educated at Eton and Brasenose Coll., Oxford; is a Magistrate for co. Warwick; late Capt. Warwickshire Yeomanry; was formerly Capt. 2nd Dragoon Guards.—*Goldicote House, Stratford-on-Avon.*

SMITH, HENRY, Esq., of Ellingham, Norfolk.

Eldest son of the late Col John Smith, of Ellingham, by Maria, dau. of James Lockhart, Esq., of Sherfield House, Hants; *b.* 1831; *s.* 1852; *m.* 1857 Amelia Harriet, dau. of Col. Greene, of Twickenham, Middlesex, and by her, who *d.* 1858, has, with other issue,

   • Henry, *b.* 1859.

Mr. Smith, who was educated at Rugby and Trinity Coll., Cambridge (B.A. 1856, M.A. 1859), and was called to the Bar at Lincoln's Inn 1859, is a Magistrate for Norfolk, and Lord of the Manor of Ellingham. —*Ellingham Hall, Bungay; 1, Cloisters, Temple, x.c.*

+**SMITH**, HENRY JEREMIAH, Esq., of Beabeg, co. Meath.

Eldest son of the late Henry Jeremiah Smith, Esq., D.L., of Beabeg, by his 1st wife Margaret, dau. of Henry Osborne, Esq., of Dardistown Castle, co. Meath; *b.* 1803; *s.* 1817; *m.* 1st 1828 Sarah Maria, dau. of Robert Harrison, Esq., of Preston, Kent; 2nd 1826 the Hon. Henrietta Priscilla, sister of Guy, 3rd Lord Dorchester, and has issue by the former,

   • Henry Jeremiah, *b.* 1838.

Mr. Smith was educated at Trinity Coll., Dublin. —*Beabeg, Drogheda, co. Meath.*

SMITH, the Rev. HENRY RICHARD SOMERS, of Little Bentley, Essex.

Son of the late H. Smith, Esq.; *b.* 179-; is married. Educated at Trinity Coll., Cambridge (B.A. 1819); is a Magistrate for Essex, Rector of Little Bentley, and Rural Dean.—*Little Bentley, Colchester.*

SMITH, JAMES, Esq., of Olrig, Caithness-shire.

Eldest son of the late James Smith, Esq., of Olrig, by Isabella, dau. of Alexander Ross, Esq.; *b.* 1832; *s.* 1853. Educated at the University of Aberdeen; is a J.P. and D.L. for co. Caithness.—*Olrig House, Castletown, Thurso, N.B.*

SMITH, JOHN ABEL, Esq.

Elder son of the late John Smith, Esq., of Dale Park, Sussex (who was M.P. for Bucks 1831–4), by Mary, dau. of Lieut.-Col. Tucker, and a cousin of Robert John, 2nd Lord Carington; *b.* 1802; *m.* 1827 Anne, dau. of Sir Samuel Clarke Jervoise, Bart., and widow of Ralph W. Grey, Esq., of Backworth House, Northumberland, and by her, who *d* 1858, has, with other issue,

 * Jervoise, educated at Eton and Trinity Coll., Cambridge ; M.P. for Falmouth ; *b.* 1828.

Mr. Smith. who was educated at Christ's Coll., Cambridge (B.A. 1824, M.A. 1827), is a Magistrate for Middlesex and Sussex, and an E.-India Proprietor; was M.P. for Midhurst 1830–1, for Chichester 1831–59; re-elected 1863.—*Reform Club,* s.w.; 37, *Chester Square,* s.w.

SMITH, JOHN BENJAMIN, Esq.

Son of the late Benjamin Smith, Esq.; *b.* 179–; *m.* 1824 Jemina, dau. of William Durning, Esq., of Liverpool. Is a Manchester Merchant, retired ; was President of the Anti-Corn-Law League, and of the Manchester Chamber of Commerce 1839–41. Is a Magistrate for co. Lancaster; has been M.P. for Stockport since 1852; was M.P. for Stirling 1847–52. —*King's Ride, Ascot, Sunning Hill, Berks ; Reform Club,* s.w. ; 105, *Westbourne Terrace,* w.

SMITH, the Rev. JOHN JAMES.

Fourth son of the late Joseph Smith, Esq., of Shortgrove, Essex, by Margaret, dau. of Joseph Cocks, Esq., of Castleditch, co. Hereford ; *b.* 1808 ; *m.* 1849 Agnes Maria, dau. of George Mitford, Esq., of Laugharne, co. Carmarthen. Educated at Caius Coll., Cambridge (B.A. 1828, M.A. 1831), is a Magistrate for Norfolk, and Vicar of Loddon ; he was formerly Fellow and Tutor of his College.—*Loddon, Norfolk.*

SMITH, JOHN WILLIAM, Esq., of Oundle, Northamptonshire.

Eldest son of the late John Smith, Esq., of Oundle, by Sarah Bridget Eliza, dau. of Thomas Smith, Esq., of The Chapter House, St. Paul's, London ; *b.* 1814 ; *m.* 1854 Elitha, dau. of the Rev. Charles Hume, Rector of St. Michael's, London, and has, with other issue,

 * John Hume, *b.* 1859.

Mr. Smith is a Magistrate for co. Northampton, and Lay Rector of Oundle.—*The Rectory, Oundle.*

SMITH, the Rev. JOHN WILLIAM.

Third son of William Grey, Esq., of Norton, co. Durham, by Joanna, dau. and heir of William Scurfield, Esq., of Crimdon House, Hartlepool; *b.* 1811 ; *s.* 1853, and assumed the name of Smith only ; *m.* 1859 Maria, 4th dau. of the late Lieut.-Col. Grey, of Norton, and has, with other issue,

 * William Anthony Grey, *b.* 1819.

Mr. Smith, who was educated at Durham and Jesus Coll., Cambridge (B.A. 1834, M.A. 1837), and appointed Rector of Dinsdale 1859, is a Magistrate for co. Durham and N. Riding of Yorkshire.—*Dinsdale Rectory, Darlington.*

SMITH, JOSEPH, Esq., of The Oaks, Surrey.

Son of the late Benjamin Smith, Esq., of Manchester ; *b.* 1801 ; *m.* 1831 Augusta, dau. of John Gilliat, Esq., of Clapham Common, Surrey, and has issue,

 * Frederick Gilliat, *b.* 1832 ; *m.* 1853 Jessie Annette, only surviving dau. of Thomas Drake Bainbridge, Esq., and has, with other issue, * Ernest Frederick Gilliat, *b.* 1858.

Mr. Smith is a Magistrate for Surrey, and Lord of the Manor of Woodmansterne.—*The Oaks, Carshalton, Epsom ; Reform Club,* s.w.

SMITH, MARTIN TUCKER, Esq.

Son of the late John Smith, Esq., M.P., of Dale Park, Sussex, and brother of John Abel Smith, Esq. (whom see); *b.* 1803 ; *m.* 1831 Louisa, dau. of the late Sir

Matthew White Ridley, Bart., M.P., and has, with other issue,

 * Martin Ridley, *b.* 1833 ; *m.* 1861 Emily Catherine, 2nd dau. of Henry Stuart. Esq., of Newton Stuart, N.B., and has issue. * a son, *b.* 1863.

Mr. Smith, who is a Magistrate for Bucks, a Commissioner of Lieutenancy for London, and late a Director of the East India Company, was M.P. for Midhurst 1831–2 ; has been M.P. for Wycombe since 1847. —*High Wycombe, Bucks ; Brooks's Club* s.w. ; 13, *Upper Belgrave Street,* s.w.

SMITH, NATHANIEL BOWDEN, Esq., of Brockenhurst, Hants.

Son of the late Robert Smith, Esq., of Brockenhurst, by Anne. dau. of the late Daniel Bowden, Esq.; *b.* 18—; *m.* 18— Emily Mary, dau. of the late John Richard Ripley, Esq., of London. Is a Magistrate for Hampshire.—*Brockenhurst Lodge, Lymington.*

+**SMITH, RICHARD, Esq., of Dudley Priory, Worcestershire.**

Son of the late R. Smith, Esq.; *b.* 18—. Is a J.P. and D.L. for co. Stafford, and a Magistrate for co. Worcester.—*The Priory, Dudley.*

SMITH, RICHARD BRYAN Esq., of Lydiate, Lancashire.

Only son of the late Bryan Smith, Esq., of Lydiate, by Mary, dau. of Philip Kewley, Esq. of Cleveland Square, Liverpool; *b.* 1793 ; *s.* 1831 ; *m.* 1824 Marianne, 2nd dau. of William Egerton Jeffreys, Esq., of Coton Hill, co. Salop, and has issue,

 * Mary Emma.

Mr. Smith, who is a J.P. and D.L. for co. Lancaster, a Fellow and one of the Society of Antiquaries, of the Royal Society of Literature of London, &c.; was formerly Hanoverian Consul for Liverpool. — *Lydiate Lodge, Ormskirk ;* Residence: *Villa Nova, Shrewsbury.*

SMITH, ROBERT, Esq., of Glanbrydan, Carmarthenshire.

Son of Robert Smith, Esq., of Craig Avon, co. Glamorgan, by Anne, dau. of John Jones, Esq., of Evan, co. Merioneth ; *b.* 18— ; *m.* 1862 Anna Mary, dau. of the Rev. John W. Cobb, of Norwich (she *d.* 1866). Is a Magistrate for co. Carmarthen.—*Glanbrydan, Llandilo.*

SMITH, ROBERT, Esq., of Goldings, Herts.

Second son of the late Abel Smith, Esq., of Woodhall Park, Herts (who *d.* 1859), by Frances Anne, 2nd dau. of the late General Sir H. Calvert, Bart.; *b.* 1833 ; *m.* 1859 Elizabeth, dau. of the late Henry John Adeane, Esq. of Babraham, co. Cambridge, and has issue. Is a Magistrate for Herts. This family is a younger branch of that of Lord Carington.—*Goldings, Hertford.*

SMITH, SAMUEL GEORGE, Esq., of Sacombe, Herts.

Eldest son of the late Samuel George Smith, Esq., M.P. of Sacombe Park, by Eugenia, 3rd dau. of the Rev. Robert Chatfield, LL.D., Vicar of Chertsey, co. Cambridge ; *b.* 1822 ; *s.* 1863. Educated at Rugby, and Trinity Coll., Cambridge (B.A. 1844, M.A. 1847); is a Magistrate for Herts; elected M.P. for Aylesbury 1859. —*Sacombe Park, Ware ;* 33, *Eaton Place,* s.w.

SMITH, SPENCER, Esq., of Brooklands, Hants.

Second son of the late Charles Smith, Esq., M.P., of Suttons, Essex, by Augusta, dau. of Joshua Smith, Esq., M.P., of Stoke Park, Wilts; *b.* 1806 ; *m.* 1835 Frances Ann, dau. of the late Admiral Sir Michael Seymour, Bart., K.C.B., and has, with other issue,

 * Drummond, M.A. of Balliol Coll., Oxford ; *b.* 1836.

Mr. Smith, who was educated at Harrow and Balliol Coll., Oxford (B.A. 1828, M.A. 1830), is a Deputy-Lieut.

for Essex, and a Magistrate for Hants; he was formerly Capt. West Essex Militia.—*Brooklands, Southampton; Athenæum Club, s.w.*

+SMITH, Stephen Henry, Esq., of Annesbrooke, co. Meath.
Eldest son of the late Henry Smith, Esq., J.P., of Annesbrooke, by his 1st wife Mary, dau. of — Osborne, Esq.; *b.* 1810; *s.* 1858; *m.* 1830 Georgina Barbara, only dau. of the late Col. Pelly, C.B., of the 16th Lancers. Is a Magistrate for co. Meath, and Lord of the Manor of Annesbrooke.—*Annesbrooke, Duleek.*

SMITH, the Rev. William, of Dry Drayton, Cambridgeshire.
Eldest surviving son of the late Rev. Samuel Smith, D.D., Dean of Ch. Ch., Oxford, and Prebendary of Durham (who *d.* 1841), by Anne, dau. of William Barnett, Esq., of Arcadia, Jamaica; *b.* 1812; *m.* 1851 Constance Margaret, dau. of William Rose Rose, Esq., of Wolston Heath, co. Warwick, and has, with other issue,
 • William Rose, *b.* 1852.
Mr. Smith, who was educated at Westminster and Ch. Ch., Oxford (B.A. 1835, M.A. 1839), is a Magistrate for co. Cambridge, Rector of Dry Drayton, and Patron of one living. This family claims descent from the family of Smith, *alias* Heriz, of Withcote, co. Leicester.—*Dry Drayton, Cambridge.*

SMITH, William Charles, Esq., of Shortgrove, Essex.
Eldest son of the late Joseph Smith, Esq., of Shortgrove, by Margaret, dau. and co-heir of Joseph Cocks, Esq., a younger brother of Charles, 1st Lord Somers; *b.* 1801; *s.* 1822; *m.* 1859 Mary, dau. of Sir Henry King. Educated at Harrow and St. John's Coll.; Cambridge (B.A. 1822, M.A. 1825): is a J.P. and D.L. for Essex (High Sheriff 1868).—*Shortgrove, Saffron Walden; Carlton and University Clubs, s.w.*

SMITH, William Johnson, Esq., of Greenhill, Dorset.
Third son of the late William Smith, Esq., of Smithborough and Orchard-vale, Ireland, by Elizabeth, 2nd dau. of the late John Johnson, Esq., and sister of the late Sir Edward Johnson, K.C.S., to whose estates he succeeded in 1862; *b.* 1813. Educated at the University of Edinburgh (M.D. 1812), and at the Universities of Paris, Bonn, and Heidelberg; is a Member of the Coll. of Physicians of London; was Physician to H.R.H. the late Duke of Cambridge.—*Greenhill, Weymouth.*

SMITH, William Leigh, Esq., of Crowham, Sussex.
Younger son of the late Benjamin Smith, Esq., M.P., and brother of Benjamin Leigh Smith, Esq., of Mountfield; *b.* 1833; *m.* 1858 Georgina, eldest dau. of the late Lionel Halliday, Esq., R.N.—*Crowham, Hastings.*

SMITH. (See under *Carington, Lord*, and *Lyveden, Lord.*)

SMITH, of Pax Hill. (See *Bouchard.*)

SMITH. (See *Duff, of Vaynol.*)

SMITH. (See *Peckham.*)

SMITH. (See *Taylor-Smith.*)

SMITH. (See *Thackwell, of Aghada.*)

SMITH-BARRY, Arthur Hugh, Esq., of Foaty, co. Cork, Cordangan, co. Tipperary, and Marbury, Cheshire.
Eldest son of the late James Hugh Smith-Barry, Esq., of Foaty Island, and of Marbury Hall, co. Chester, by Eliza, dau. of Shallcross Jacson, Esq., of Newton Bank, co. Chester; *b.* 1843; *s.* 1857. Educated at Eton and Ch. Ch., Oxford, is a Dep.-Lieut. for co. Cork, a Magistrate for co. Chester, and Lieut. in the Earl of Chester's Yeomanry Cavalry; elected M.P. for co. Cork 1867.—*Foaty Island, Cork; Cordangan, Cashel, co. Tipperary; Marbury Hall, Northwich; St. James's Club, s.w.; 26, Chesham Place, s.w.*

SMITH-BARRY, Mrs., of Marbury Hall, Cheshire.
Eliza, dau. of the late Shallcross Jacson, Esq., Capt. 3rd Light Dragoons, of Newton Bank, co. Chester, by Frances, eldest dau. of the Rev. Joseph Cook; *m.* 1841 James Hugh Smith-Barry, Esq., of Marbury Hall, and of Foaty Island, co. Cork (who *d.* 1857).—*Marbury Hall, Northwich.*

SMITH-BOSANQUET, Horace James, Esq., of Broxbournebury, Herts.
Son of the late Samuel George Smith, Esq., of Sacombe Park, Herts (who *d.* 1863), by Eugenia, dau. of the Rev. Robert Chatfield, LL.D., Vicar of Chatteris, co. Cambridge; *b.* 1824; *m.* 1858 Cecilia Jane Wentworth, only child and heir of the late George Jacob Bosanquet, Esq., of Broxbournebury. Is a Magistrate for Herts; assumed the additional surname of Bosanquet 1867.—*Broxbournebury, Hoddesden.*

SMITH-CUNINGHAME, William Cathcart, Esq., of Caprington, Ayrshire.
Eldest surviving son of the late John Smith, Esq., who assumed the name of Cuninghame, on his wife Anne, dau. of the late Sir William Dick, Bart., of Prestonville, N.B., succeeding her cousin, Sir William Cuninghame, Bart., at Caprington, 1829; *b.* 1814; *s.* his brother Thomas 1857; *m.* 1847 Maria, dau. of James Anstruther, Esq., and has, with other issue,
 • John Anstruther, *b.* 1852.
Mr. Smith-Cuninghame, who was educated at Haileybury Coll., was formerly in the Bengal Civil Service.—*Caprington Castle, Kilmarnock, N.B.*

SMITH-DE HERIZ, the Rev. Forbes, of Aston Botterell, Shropshire.
Eldest son of the late Robert Smith, Esq., of Crumlin, co. Dublin, by Eliza, dau. of Major-Gen. Col ins, E.I.C.S.; *b.* 1815; *m.* 1839 Sophia Mercy, dau. of the late Sir Frederick Fletcher Vane, Bart., of Hutton Hall, Cumberland, and has, with other issue,
 • Henry Vane, formerly a Midshipman, R.N.; *b.* 1841.
Mr. Smith-De Heriz, who was educated at Trinity Coll., Dublin (B.A. 1838), is a Magistrate for co. Salop, and Rector of Aston Botterell. He resumed, in 1865, the old family name of De Heriz in addition to that of Smith, which was originally resumed by the family temp. Henry VII —*Aston Botterell, Bridgnorth.*

SMITH-DORRIEN, Lieut.-Col. Robert Algernon, of Haresfoot, Herts.
Youngest son of the late James Smith, Esq., of Ashlyn Hall, Herts, by 2nd wife Mary Isabella, dau. of Augustus Pechell, Esq.; *b.* 1814; *m.* 1845 Mary Anne, dau. of the late Thomas Drever, Esq., and grand-dau. of the late Thomas Dorrien, Esq., of Haresfoot (whose name he assumed in 1845), and has, with other issue,
 • Thomas Algernon, Cornet 10th Hussars; *b.* 1846.
Lieut.-Col. Smith-Dorrien, who is a Magistrate for

Herts and the Liberty of St. Albans, and Lieut.-Col. Herts Militia, was formerly Capt. 3rd Light Dragoons and 16th Lancers.—*Harefscot, Great Berkhampstead.*

SMITH-MARRIOTT, Sir WILLIAM HENRY, Bart., of The Down House, Dorset (cr. 1774).

Eldest son of the late Rev. Sir William Marriott Smith-Marriott, Bart., of The Down House (who assumed the additional sur: ame of Marriott in 1811), by his 1st wife Julia Elizabeth, dau. of the late Thomas Law Hodges, Esq., of Hemsted Park, Kent; b. 1836; s. as 4th Bart. 1864; educated at Harrow and Balliol Coll., Oxford; is Patron of 3 livings.—*Sydling St. Nicholas, and The Down House, Blandford.*

Heir Pres., his brother John Bosworth, b. 1837; m. 1866 Julia Frances, dau. of Charles James Radclyffe, Esq., of Foxdenton, and Hyde House, Dorset, and has issue, a son, b. 1865.

SMITH-MARRIOTT, the Rev. HUGH FORBES, of Horsemonden, Kent.

Third son of the late Rev. Sir Wm. M. Smith-Marriott. Bart., of Sydling St. Nicholas, The Down House, Dorset, and of Horsemonden, by his 1st wife, Julia Elizabeth, dau. of the late Thomas Law Hodges, Esq., of Hemsted, Kent; b. 1840; s. his father in this property 1864; m. 1864 Frances Catharine Mary, 2nd dau. of Admiral the Hon. George Cavendish. Educated at Trinity Coll., Cambridge (B.A. 1862, M.A. 1865), is a Magistrate for Kent, Rector and Lord of the Manor and Patron of Horsemonden.—*Horsemonden, Staplehurst.*

SMITH-MASTERS, the Rev. ALLAN, of Camer, Kent.

Eldest son of the late William Cowburn, Esq., of Sydenham, Kent, by Catharine Rebecca, eldest dau. of Geo. Smith, Esq., of Camer; b. 1520; s. his uncle 1861; m. 1844 Rebe Mary, dau. of the Ven. James Randall, Archdeacon of Berks, and has, with other issue,

* William Allan, b. 1850.

Mr. Smith-Masters, who was educated at Winchester and Exeter Coll., Oxford (B.A 1842, M.A. 1815), is a Magistrate for Kent, Lord of the Manors of Luddesdown and Dolmer, and was formerly Vicar of Tidenham, co. Gloucester.—*Camer, Gravesend.*

SMITH-NEILL. (See *Neill.*)

SMITH-SLIGO, ARCHIBALD VINCENT, Esq., of Inzievar, Fifeshire.

Son of James Smith, Esq., of London, by Catharine, dau. of the late Lieut. Mackenzie; b. 1845; m. 1st 1846 Emily Jane, dau. of Herbert Foley, Esq., of Haverfordwest (who d. 1865); 2nd 1859 Margaret, dau. of George Sligo, Esq., of Seacliffe, widow of Major Sir W. C. Harris, Knt.—*Inzievar, Dunfermline, N.B.*

SMITHE, Mrs., of Staplefield, Sussex.

Lilla Rosalie, only child of the late Anthony Shepper Greene, Esq., of Malling Deanery, Lewes, Sussex; m. 1848 William Forster Smithe, Esq., of Staplefield Place, a Magistrate for Sussex (who d. 1898).—*Staplefield Place, Cuckfield; 13, Lansdowne Place, Brighton.*

SMITHETT, Sir LUKE, Knt. (cr. 1862).

Son of the late Luke Smithett, Esq.; b. 1800; m. 1827 Jane Dalrymple, dau. of the late Capt. Sir John Hamilton, R.N., and by her, who d. 1846, has, with other issue,

* Marcus Edmiston, Commander R.N.; b. 1829.

Sir Luke Smithett is a Magistrate for Dover, a Commissioner of Salvage under the Lord Warden of the Cinque Ports, a Knight of the Legion of Honour, &c., 604

was formerly Capt. in H.M.'S. Packet Service. —*Snargate Street, Dover; Royal Thames Yacht Club, 7, Albemarle Street, w.*

SMOLLETT, ALEXANDER, Esq., of Bonhill, Dumbartonshire.

Eldest son of the late Rear-Admiral John Roue: Smollett, of Bonhill, by his 2nd wife Elizabeth, 2nd dau. of the Hon. Patrick Boyle, of Shewalton, co. Ayr; b. 1881; s. 1812. Educated at the High School and University of Edinburgh; called to the Scottish Bar 1825; is a Member of the Faculty of Advocates, Edinburgh, and a Magistrate for said county. Convener of co. Dumbarton; was M.P. for co. Dumbarton 1841-59. —*Bonhill and Cameron House, Alexandria, Dumbartonshire; Carlton Club, s.w.*

Heir Pres., his brother Patrick Boyle. M.P. for co. Dumbarton; b. 1805; educated at Edinburgh and Haileybury Coll.; formerly of the H.E.I.C.'s Civil Service at Madras.

SMYLY, JOHN GEORGE, Esq., of Caums and Castlederg, co. Tyrone.

Eldest son of the late John George Smyly, Esq., Q.C., D.L., of Castlederg, by Eliza, dau. of the late Sir Andrew Ferguson, Bart., of the Farm, Londonderry; b. 1829; s. 1863. Educated at Winchester and Trinity Coll. Dublin (B.A. 1854). This family is of Scottish extraction, but settled in Ireland, in the neighbourhood of Strabane, in 1628. · Ca t'ederg. co. Tyrone; Kildare Street Club, Dublin; 23, Upper Merrion Street, Dublin.

Heir Pres., his brother Andrew Ferguson. (in Holy Orders) M.A., and Chaplain to the Earl of Caledon; b. 1831; m. 1856 Eliza, dau. of the Rev. Robert Alexander, of Blackheath, Kent.

SMYTH, Sir JOHN HENRY GREVILLE, Bart., of Ashton Court, Somerset (cr. 1859).

Only surviving son of the late Thomas Upton, Esq., of Ingmire Hall, Westmoreland, by Eliza, dau. of the late Benjamin Way, Esq., of Denham Place, Bucks; b. 1826; s. his grandmother, Mrs. Florence Upton. 1852, when he assumed the surname of Smyth, under the will of his great-uncle, Sir Hugh Smyth. Bart. Educated at Eton and Ch. Ch., Oxford; is a Magistrate for Somerset (High Sheriff 1865), and Patron of 1 living; elected High Sheriff 1858, but refused to serve. This family was twice raised to a Baronetcy, which has twice become extinct.—*Ashton Court, Bristol; Windham Club, s.w.*

Heirs Pres., his sisters Eliza Frances and Florence Anne. (See Cott ell-Dormer.)

SMYTH, Sir JOHN ROWLAND, K.C.B. (cr. 1867).

Son of the late J. Smyth. Esq.; b. 1803. Is a Major-Gen. in the Army, and Col. 6th Dragoon Guards; late commanding a division of the Madras Army.

SMYTH, the Hon. Col. LEICESTER, C.B., of Drumcree, co. Westmeath.

Youngest son of Richard, 1st Earl Howe, G.C.H., by his 1st wife Lady Harriet Georgiana, 2nd dau. of Robert, 6th Earl of Cardigan; b. 1829; m. 1856 Alicia Maria, elder dau. of the late R... Drumcree (whose name he has assumed). Educated at Eton; is a Col. in the Army, and Military Sec. at Dublin; late Major Rifle Brigade; was Assistant Military Sec. to Lord Raglan in the Crimea.—*Drumcree House, Killucan, co. Westmeath.*

SMYTH, the Hon. Mrs. MOORE-, of Ballynatray.

Charlotte Mary, only child of the late Richard Smyth. Esq., J P. and D.L., of Ballynatray, by the Hon. Harriet, dau. of Hayes, 2nd Viscount Doneraile; s. 1858; m. 1848 the Hon. Charles William Moore, 2nd son of the Earl of Mount Cashell, who has assumed the additional

name of Smyth (see *Moore-Smyth*), and has, with other issue,

* Richard Charles Moore, *b.* 1859.

This family have been seated at Ballynatray for upwards of two centuries.—*Ballynatray, Youghal.*

SMYTH, EDWARD SKEFFINGTON RANDALL, Esq., of Mount Henry, Queen's Co.

Only son of the late Henry Smyth, E-q., D.L., of Mount Henry and Torlicken, co. Longford, by Olivia, dau. of the Rev. Edward Lucas, of Cootehill; *b.* 1831; *s.* 1838; *m.* 1862 Gertrude, dau. of the Right Hon. J. W. Fitz-Patrick, and has issue,

* Charles Edward Skeffington Randall, *b.* 1864.

Mr. Smyth, who was educated at Cheltenham Coll. and Trinity Coll., Dublin, is a J.P. and D.L. for Queen's Co.; was formerly in the 28th Regt. This family are the lineal descendants of Dr. Edward Smyth, Bishop of Down and Connor, Chaplain to William III., whose ancestor, William Smyth, of Rossdale Abbey, co. York, settled in Ireland *temp.* Charles I.—*Mount Henry, Portarlington, Queen's Co.; Army and Navy Club, s.w.*

SMYTH, the Rev. HUGH BLAGG, of Houghton Regis, Beds.

Youngest son of Edward Smyth, Esq., of The Fence, Macclesfie'd, by Sarah, only dau. of the late Thomas Pickford, Esq., of Poynton, co. Chester; *b.* 1823; *m.* 1847 Jane Ewart, 2nd dau. of William Gott, Esq., of Wyther Grange, Leeds, and by her, who *d.* 1864, has, with other issue,

* Hugo William Nairne Scott, *b.* 1858.

Mr. Smyth, who was educated at Repton and Jesus Coll., Cambridge (B.A. 1845, M.A. 1849), appointed Vicar of Houghton Regis 1856, and was formerly Incumbent of Thornes, near Wakefield; is a Magistrate for Beds.—*Houghton Regis, Dunstable.*

SMYTH, Col. JOHN GEORGE, of Heath Hall, Yorkshire.

Eldest son of the late John Henry Smyth, Esq., M.P., of Heath Hall, by his 2nd wife Lady Elizabeth Anne, 3rd dau. of George Henry, 4th Duke of Grafton, K.G.; *b.* 1815; *s.* 1822; *m.* 1837 the Hon. Diana, dau. of Godfrey, 3rd Lord Macdonald, and has issue. Educated at Eton and Trinity Coll., Cambridge; is a J.P. and D.L. for the N. and W. Ridings of Yorkshire, and Col. of the 2nd West York Militia; was M.P. for York 1847-65.—*H ath Hall, Wakefield; Carlton Club, s.w.; 17; Lowndes Square, s.w.*

SMYTH, RALPH, Esq., of Newtown House, co. Louth.

Eldest son of the late Ralph Smyth, Esq., J.P., of Newtown House, by Anne, dau. of the Rev. Charles Crawford Vicar of St. Mary's, Drogheda; *b.* 1831; *s.* 1865; *m.* 1857 Mary Henrietta, dau. of Henry Smith, Esq., of Anneshrook, co. Meath. Is a Magistrate for co. Louth. This family descend from the Smyths of Barbaville, co. Westmeath.—*Newtown House, Drogheda.*

SMYTH, ROBERT, Esq., of Gaybrook, co. Westmeath.

Second son of the late Ralph Smyth, Esq., of Gaybrook, by his 2nd wife Hannah Maria, dau. of Sir Robert Staples, Bart; *b.* 1801; *s.* his brother 1827; *m.* 1830 Henrietta Frances, youngest dau. of the late Right Rev. Nathaniel Alexander, D.D., Lord Bishop of Meath, and has, with other issue,

* Ralph, late Capt. 17th Foot; *b.* 1831; *m.* 1861 the Hon. Selina Constance, 4th dau. of Vice-Admiral Lord Somerville.

Mr. Smyth, who was formerly Capt. 24th Regt., is a J.P. and D.L. for co. Westmeath (High Sheriff of co. Westmeath 1831, and of co. Antrim 1852). This family

was formerly of Rossdale Abbey, Yorkshire.—*Gaybrook, Mullingar, co. Westmeath; Kildare Street Club, Dublin.*

SMYTH, ROBERT RALPH, Esq., of Portlick Castle, co. Westmeath.

Eldest son of the late Robert Smyth, Esq., of Portlick Castle, by Frideswide, dau. of Thomas Ahmuty, Esq., of Bath; *b.* 1815; *s.* 1847; *m.* 1858 Sarah Maria, 2nd dau. of Montgomerie Martin, Esq. Educated at Trinity Coll., Dublin; is a Magistrate and a Grand Juror for co. Westmeath.—*Portlick Castle, Glasson, co. Westmeath.*

SMYTH, the Rev. THOMAS, of Ballynegall, co. Westmeath.

Eldest son of the late Thomas Hutchinson Smyth, Esq., of Benison Lodge. co. Westmeath. by Abigail, dau. of John Hamilton, Esq., of Ballyallolly. co. Down; *b.* 1796; *s.* 1830; *m.* 1832 Mary Anne, dau. of Adam T. Gibbons, Esq., and has, with other issue,

* Thomas James. B.A. of Trinity Coll., Dublin, and a Magistrate for co. Westmeath (High Sheriff 1858); *b.* 1833 *m.* 1864 Bessie, dau. of Edward Aukersl Jones, Esq., and has issue. * Thomas-Gibbon-Hawkesworth, *b.* 1855.

Mr. Smyth, who was educated at Trinity Coll., Dublin (B.A. 1817), is a Magistrate for co. Westmeath.—*Ballynegall, Mullingar, co. Westmeath.*

SMYTH, THOMAS JOHNSON, Esq., of Lisburn, co. Antrim.

Eldest son of the late Thomas Smyth. Esq., of Lisburn; *b.* 1790; *m.* 1812 Charlotte, dau. of E. Bruce, Esq., of Kilroot, co. Antrim, and has issue,

* Roger Johnson. late M.P. for Lisburn ; *b.* 1815.

Mr. Smyth, who was educated at Armagh and Trinity Coll., Dublin, is a Magistrate for co. Antrim, and Dep.-Lieu . for co. Down.—*Lisburn, Ireland.*

SMYTH, WARINGTON WILKINSON, Esq., F.R.S., of St. John's Lodge, Bucks.

Eldest son of the late Admiral William Henry Smyth, K.S.F. &c., of St. John's Lodge, by Ann, only dau. of Thomas Warington, Esq., of Naples; *b.* 1817; *s.* 1865; *m.* 1864 Anna Maria Antonia, 3rd dau. of Anthony Merrin Story Maskelyne, Esq., of Basset Down House, Wilts, and has issue,

* Herbert Warington, *b.* 1867.

Mr. Smyth, who was educated at Trinity Coll., Cambridge (B.A. 1839, M.A. 1844). is Chief Surveyor of Crown Mines. This family descend from the celebrated Capt. John Smith, Governor of Virginia *temp.* James I.—*St. John's Lodge, Aylesbury; Athenæum Club, s.w.; 13, Victoria Street, s.w.*

SMYTH, the Rev. WILLIAM, of South Elkington Hall, Lincolnshire.

Eldest son of the late Rev. Wm. Smyth (who *d.* 1837), by Susannah, dau. of Samuel Ray, Esq., of Worlingworth, Suffolk; *b.* 1791; *s.* 1825; *m.* 1829 Mary, dau. of Samuel Ray, Esq., of Tannington, Suffolk, and has, with other issue,

* William Henry, a Magistrate for co. Lincoln, and Chairman of Quarter Session; *b.* 1831; *m.* 1859 Sarah Ann, dau. of the late Rev. John Sargeaunt, Rector of Stanwick, co. Northampton.

Mr. Smyth, who was educated at Brasenose Coll. Oxford (B.A. 1813, M.A. 1816); is a Magistrate for co. Lincoln, Lord of the Manor of South Elkington. and Patron of 2 livings, was formerly Vicar of N. and S. Elkington.—*South Elkington Hall, Louth, Lincolnshire; Oxford and Cambridge Club, s.w.*

SMYTH, WILLIAM, Esq., of Little Houghton House, Northamptonshire.

Eldest son of the late William Tyler Smyth, Esq., of Little Houghton, co. Northampton, by Anne his wife;

b. 1808 ; *m.* 1844 Lucy Charlotte, 2nd dau. of the Hon. and Rev. R. B. Stopford, of Barton Seagrave. Educated at Wadham Coll., Oxford (B.A. 1832, M.A. 1836); called to the Bar at Lincoln's Inn 1840 ; is a J.P. and D.L. for co. Northampton (High Sheriff 1862), and Dep. Chairman of Quarter Sessions. This family is the second branch of the Smyths of Elkington, co. Lincoln. —*Little Houghton House, Northampton ; Oxford and Cambridge and Carlton Clubs, s.w.*

SMYTH, WILLIAM EDWARD, Esq., of Glananea, co. Westmeath.

Eldest son of the late Ralph Smyth, Esq., of Glananea, by Jane Alicia, dau. of T. W. Fitz-Gerald, Esq., of Dublin ; *b.* 1830 ; *s.* 1839. Educated at Harrow and Trinity Coll., Dublin (B.A. 1851) ; is a Magistrate for co. Westmeath. This family is a junior branch of the Smyths of Drumcree.— *Glananea, Drumcree, co. Westmeath ; Kildare Street Club, Dublin.*

SMYTH, WILLIAM HAMILTON, Esq., of Drum, Downshire.

Son of the late William Smyth, Esq., M.P., of Drumcree, by his 2nd wife Mary, dau. of H. Maxwell, Esq. ; *b.* 179–; *m.* 1821 Isabella Margaret, dau. of the late Henry Daniell, Esq., J.P. and D.L., of New Forest, co. Westmeath, and has, with other issue,

* William Maxwell, late Lieut. Westmeath Rifles ; *b.* 1826.

Mr. Smyth, who was educated at Trinity Coll., Dublin, is a Magistrate for co. Down.—*Drum, Belfast.*

SMYTH, WILLIAM NUGENT, Esq., of Royds Hall, Yorkshire.

Third son of the late Rev. W. St. John Smyth, of Ballymoney, co. Antrim ; *b.* 1831 ; *m.* 1863 Catherine Isabel, eldest dau. of the late Charles Hardy, Esq., of Odsall House, co. York, and Chilham Castle, Kent, and has issue, * Arthur Nugent, *b.* 1864.—*Royds Hall, Low Moor, Bradford.*

SMYTH-PIGOTT, JOHN HUGH WADHAM PIGOTT, Esq. of Brockley Court, Somerset.

Eldest son of the late John Hugh Smyth Pigott, Esq., by Ann, dau. of Wm. Provis, Esq., of Brockley Court ; *b.* 1819 ; *s.* 1823 ; *m.* 1857 Blanche Mary, 2nd dau. of Henry R. Arundell, Esq., and has, with other issue,

* Cecil Hugh, *b.* 1860.

Mr. Smyth-Pigott, who is a Magistrate for Somerset, and Patron of 3 livings, was formerly in the North Somerset Yeomanry Cavalry ; he was elected Commodore of the Royal Harwich Yacht Club 1845.—*Brockley Court and Brockley Hall, Bristol ; Villa Marina, Weston-super-Mare ; Royal Yacht Squadron, Cowes ; 7, Albemarle Street, w.*

SMYTH-TEMPLE. (See *Temple.*)

SMYTHE, Sir CHARLES FREDERICK, Bart., of Acton-Burnel, Shropshire (cr. 1660).

Eldest son of the late Sir Edward Joseph Smythe Bart., of Acton-Burnel, by Frances, dau. of the late Sir Edward Bellew, Bart. ; *b.* 1819 ; *s.* aa 7th Bart. 1856 ; *m.* 1855 the Hon. Maria, dau. of Thomas, 3rd Lord Camoys. Educated at St. Gregory's Coll., Downside ; is a J.P. and D.L. for Salop (High Sheriff 1867), and Patron of 1 living.— *Acton-Burnel, Shrewsbury ; Eshe Hall, Durham ; Wotton, Henly-in-Arden, Warwickshire.*

Heir Pres., his brother John Walter, *b.* 1827 ; *m.* 1861 Louisa, 2nd dau. of William Herbert, Esq., of Clytha, co. Monmouth.

SMYTHE, Hon. Mrs., of Linton, Yorkshire.

Eleanor Mary, 8th dau. of William, 17th Lord Stourton, by Catherine, dau of the late Thomas Weld, Esq.,

866

of Lulworth Castle, Dorset ; *m.* 1844 Richard Pete: Carrington Smythe, Esq., who *d.* 1853.—*Linton Spring Wetherby.*

SMYTHE, HENRY MATTHEW, Esq., of New Park, co. Roscommon.

Second son of the late Ralph Smythe, Esq., of Barbavilla, by Eliza, dau. and heir of Matthew Lyster, Esq., of New Park (High Sheriff 1778) ; *b.* 1810 ; *s.* 1845 ; *m.* 1855 Maria, 2nd dau. of the late Robert Coote, Esq., Capt. 18th Hussars, and has, with other issue,

* William Lyster, *b.* 1859.

Mr. Smythe, who was educated at Winchester and at New Coll., Oxford (B.A. 1834), is a Magistrate for co. Roscommon.—*New Park, Athlone, Ireland.*

SMYTHE, THOMAS, Esq., of Hilton, Shropshire.

Eldest son of the late John Groome Smythe, Esq., of Hilton, by Anne, youngest dau. of Thomas Parke, Esq., of Highfield House, co. Lancaster, and sister of the late Lord Wensleydale ; *b.* 1808 ; *s.* 1835 ; *m.* 1857 Mary, only surviving child of the late Admiral Deans, who *d.* 1862, leaving three daughters. Mr. Smythe, who was educated at Shrewsbury and Addiscombe Military Coll., is Lieut.-Col. Commanding 3rd Battalion Staffordshire Rifle Volunteers ; was formerly Lieut.-Col. Madras Engineers.—*Hilton, Bridgnorth ; East India Club, s.w.*

Heir Pres. (under entail), his brother George, Commander R.N. ; *b.* 1811 ; *m.* 1855 Georgiana, dau. of Dr. Allardyce, of Cheltenham.

SMYTHE, WILLIAM, Esq., of Methven, Perthshire.

Eldest surviving son of the late David Smythe, Esq., of Methven (one of the Senators of the College of Justice in Scotland), by his 2nd wife Amelia Euphemia, only dau. of Mungo Murray, Esq., of Lintrose ; *b.* 1803 ; *s.* his half-brother 1847 ; *m.* 1st 1838 Margaret, eldest dau. of James Walker, Esq., of Westminster ; 2nd 1849 Emily, dau. of the late General Sir John Oswald G.C B., of Dunnikier, and has, with other issue,

* David Murray, *b.* 1850.

Mr. Smythe, who was educated at Westminster and Ch. Ch., Oxford (B.A. 1826, M.A. 1828), was called to the Bar at Lincoln's Inn, 1829, and to the Scottish Bar 1836, is a J.P. and D.L. for and Convener of co. Perth ; was formerly Secretary to the Board of Supervision in Scotland.—*Methven Castle, Perth, N.B. ; Athenaeum Club, s.w.*

SMYTHE, WILLIAM BARLOW, Esq., of Barbavilla, co. Westmeath.

Eldest son of the late Ralph Smythe, Esq., of Barbavilla, by Eliza, dau. and heir of Matthew Lyster, Esq., of New Park ; *b.* 1809 ; *s.* 1815 ; *m.* 1837 Lady Emily, dau. of the late Earl of Rathdown (*ext.*). Educated at Winchester and C.C.C., Oxford (B.A. 1830), admitted *ad eundem* at Trinity Coll., Dublin ; is a J.P. and D.L. for co. Westmeath (High Sheriff 1832).—*Barbavilla House, Collinstown, co. Westmeath ; Sackville Street Club, Dublin ; National Club, s.w.*

Heir Pres., his brother Henry Matthew, of New Park, co. Roscommon (whom see).

SMYTHE. (See under *Strangford, Viscount.*)

SMYTHE-GARDINER. (See *Gardiner.*)

SMYTHIES, JOHN KINNERSLEY, Esq., of Lynch Court, Herefordshire.

Eldest son of the late Rev. John Robert Smythies, of Lynch Court ; *b.* 1808 ; *m.* 1835 Kezia, dau. of Thomas Brown, Esq. Educated at Rugby and Trinity Coll., Cambridge ; called to the Bar at the Inner Temple 1836.—*Lynch Court, Leominster ; 27, Kensington Park Gardens, w.*

SNADDON. (See *Laurie*.)

SNAGG, Sir WILLIAM, Knt. (cr. 1859).
Son of the late William Snagg, Esq., of St. Vincent, West Indies; b. 1806; m. 1st 1838 Ann, dau. of John Turner, Esq. (she d. 1861); 2nd 1865 Adeline, only child of C. H. Okey, Esq., Puisne Judge of Antigua. Called to the Bar at the Middle Temple 1829; is Chief Justice of Antigua and Montserrat; formerly Attorney-General of Grenada.—*Antigua, W. Indies.*

SNEYD, the Rev. JOHN, of Ashcombe Park, Staffordshire.
Second but eldest surviving son of the late William Sneyd, Esq., of Ashcombe Park (who was in the Commission of the Peace, and a Dep. Lieut. for co. Stafford), by Jane, only child of Simon Debank, Esq., of The Ashes; b. 1798; s. 1851; m. 1st 1822 Penelope, dau. of John Holley, Esq., of Aylsham; 2nd 1850 Mary, dau. of Charles Marsh Adams, Esq., of Shrewsbury, and has by the former, with other issue,

   • John William, a J.P. and D.L. for co. Stafford, Capt. King's Own Staffordshire Militia, late Capt. of the Leek Troop of Yeomanry Cavalry; b. 1822; m. 1860 Agnes Maria, eldest surviving dau. of the late Rev. Charles Evelin Cotton, of Etwall, co. Derby, and has issue, * Ralph De Tunstall, b. 1862.

Mr. Sneyd, who was educated at Brasenose Coll., Oxford (B.A. 1820, M.A. 1824), is a Magistrate for co. Stafford, Lord of the Manors of Bradnop and Basford, &c., and joint Patron of 2 livings; he was the first Rural Dean of Leek. This family has been seated in Staffordshire for upwards of five centuries.—*Ashcombe Park, Leek.*

+**SNEYD,** JOHN, Esq., of Huntley Hall, Staffordshire.
Only son of the late Rear-Admiral John Sneyd, of Huntley Hall, by his 1st wife Helen, 3rd dau. of Roger Swetenham, Esq., of Swetenham Booths, co. Chester; b. 1814; s. 1854. This family is a younger branch of the Sneyds of Keele Hall (whom see). — *Huntley Hall, Cheadle.*

SNEYD, RALPH, Esq., of Keele Hall, Staffordshire.
Eldest son of the late Walter Sneyd, Esq., of Keele Hall, by the Hon. Louisa, dau. of William, 1st Lord Bagot; b. 1793; s. 1829. Educated at Eton and Ch. Ch., Oxford; is a Dep.-Lieut. for co. Stafford (High Sheriff 1844); Lord of the Manors of Keele, Wolstanton, Tunstall, Burslem, Mow, &c., and Patron of 4 livings. This family have been settled in Staffordshire since temp. Henry III.—*Keele Hall, Newcastle-under-Lyne.*

   Heir Pres., his brother Walter, in Holy Orders, M.A. of Ch. Ch., Oxford; b. 1809; m. 1856 his cousin Henrietta, dau. of Richard Sneyd, Esq., and has, with other issue, * Ralph, b. 1863.

SNEYD-KYNNERSLEY. (See *Kynnersley*.)

SNOW, the Rev. GEORGE D'OYLY, of Langton Lodge, Dorset.
Eldest son of the late Rev. Thomas Snow, of Langton Lodge (Rector of St. Dunstan's, London, and afterwards of Newton Valence, Hants), by Maynard Eliza, dau. of the late Sir John D'Oyly, Bart., and grandson of George Snow, Esq., of Langton House, Dorset; b. 1818; s. 1867; m. 1850 Maria Jane, dau. of Robert Barlow, Esq., late of the Bengal Civil Service, and of Molybourne, Hants, and has, with other issue,

   • Thomas D'Oyly, b. 1858.

Mr. Snow, who was educated at Exeter Coll., Oxford (B.A. 1840), is Vicar of Hilton, Dorset, late Curate of Newton Valence, Hants.—*Langton Lodge, and Hilton Vicarage, Blandford.*

SNOW, THOMAS, Esq., of Franklyn, Devonshire.
Son of the late Thomas Snow, Esq., of Belmont, Exeter; b. 1791; m. 1817 Charlotte, dau. of William Maitland, Esq., and has, with other issue,

   • Thomas Maitland (a Banker at Exeter), b. 1817; m. 1851 Eliza, 2nd dau. of the late J. P. Nathan, Esq., of Trelawny, Jamaica.

Mr. Snow is a Dep.-Lieut. for co. Devon, and a Banker at Exeter.—*Franklyn, St. Thomas's, Exeter.*

SOAME, Sir CHARLES BUCKWORTH-HEARNE-, Bart., (cr. 1697).
Only surviving son of the late Sir Buckworth Buckworth-Hearne-Soame, Bart., of Heydon Hall, Essex, by Susan, dau. of Stephen Simperingham, Esq., of Cambridge; b. 179—; s. his brother at 8th Bart. 1860; m. 1830 Lydia, dau. of — Agger, Esq. The 5th and 6th Barts. respectively assumed the names of Hearne and Soame in addition to the family name of Buckworth.—*Parndon, Harlow.*

   Heir, his son John, b. 1832.

+**SOAMES,** CHARLES, Esq.
Son of the late C. Soames, Esq.; b. 18—; is married, and has, with other issue,

   • Stephen, b. 18—; m. 1863 Julia Constance, youngest surviving dau. of the late William Bennet Martin, Esq., of Worsborough, and has issue, * a son, b. 1865.

Mr. Soames is a Magistrate for Herts.—*Residence: Coles Park, Buntingford.*

SODOR AND MAN, Bishop of (the Hon. and Rt. Rev. HORATIO POWYS, D.D.).
Third son of Thomas, 2nd Lord Lilford, by Henrietta Maria, eldest dau. and co-heir of Robert Vernon Atherton, Esq., of Atherton Hall, co. Lancaster; b. 1805; m. 1833 Percy Gore, dau. of the late William Currie, Esq., of East Horsley, Surrey, and has, with other issue,

   • Percy William, M.A., b. 1838.

The Bishop, who was educated at Eton and St. John's Coll., Cambridge (M.A. 1826, D.D. 1854), was Rector of Warrington, co. Lancaster, 1831–54, and Rural Dean of Chester; Patron of 16 livings. Consecrated 1854. —*Bishop's Castle, Douglas, Isle of Man.*

SOLLY, EDWARD HARRISON, Esq., of West Heath, Cheshire.
Eldest son of Isaac Solly, Esq., of Enfield, Middlesex, by Marianne, dau. of Francis Houssemayne du Boulay, Esq., of Walthamstow, Essex; b. 1827; m. 1854 Lucy Charlotte, dau. of the Rev. George James Cornish, Vicar of Kenwyn, Cornwall, and has, with other issue,

   • George Edward, b. 1855.

Mr. Solly is a Magistrate for co. Chester, and Lieut. Earl of Chester's Yeomanry Cavalry. This family was formerly, for several centuries, resident at Great Fedding, in the parish of Ash, Kent.— *West Heath, Congleton.*

SOLLY, JAMES, Esq., of Tell-End Hall, Staffordshire.
Fifth son of the late Hollis Solly, Esq., of Seafield Lodge, Sussex, by Charlotte, dau. of John Harrison, Esq., of London; b. 1817; m. 1852 Caroline, 2nd dau. of Edward Fordham, Esq., of Odsey Grange, co. Cambridge, and has, with other issue,

   • James Raymond, b. 1853.

Mr. Solly is a Magistrate for co. Stafford.—*Tell-End Hall, Tipton.*

SOLLY, NATHANIEL NEAL, Esq.
Third son of the late Hollis Solly, Esq., of Seafield Lodge, Sussex, by Charlotte, dau. of John Harrison, Esq., of London; b. 1811; m. 1844 Martha, dau. of

John George Fordham. Esq., of The Priory, Royston, Herts, and has, with other issue,
* Leonard Hollis, b. 1853.
Mr. Solly is a Magistrate for co. Stafford.—Residence: *Moseley Hall, Bushbury, Wolverhampton.*

+SOLLY, WILLIAM HAMMOND, Esq., of Serge Hill, Herts.
Son of the late Samuel Reynolds Solly, Esq., F.R.S., J.P. and D.L., of Serge Hill; b. 1814; s. 1866; m. 1853 Catharine Elizabeth, eldest surviving dau. of the late Lieut.-General Sir Henry Goldfinch, K.C.B. Educated at Trinity Coll., Cambridge (B.A. 1837); is a Magistrate for Dorset, Herts, and the Liberty of St. Alban's.—*Serge Hill, Bedmont, Hemel Hempstead ; 10, Manchester Square, w.*

SOLLY-FLOOD. (See *Flood.*)

SOLTAU, GEORGE WILLIAM, Esq., of Little Efford, Devon.
Eldest son of the late George Soltau, Esq., of Little Efford, by Elizabeth Maria, dau. of William Symons, E-q.. of Chaddlewood. Devon: b. 1801; s. 1819; m. 1st 1823 Frances Goddard, 2nd dau. of the Rev. Thomas Culme. of Tothill, Plymouth (she d. 1860); 2nd 1862 Anne Catherine Emma, dau. of the late John Walmesley, Esq., of Ince Hall, Wigan; he has, by the former, with other issue,
* George William Culme Soltau-Symons. Esq.. of Chaddlewood, Plymston. Devon; educated at Winchester and Ch Ch., Oxford ; a J.P. and D.L. for Devon. Assumed by Royal licence, 184?. the surname of Symons, after his paternal great-uncle William Hales Symons. Esq.. of Chaddlewood. deceased ; b. 1831 ; m. 1859 the Hon. Adèle Isabella, 2nd dau. of Thomas William, 3rd Lord Graves, and has, with other issue, * George James, b. 1867.
Mr. Soltau is a J.P. and D.L. for Devon.—*Little Efford, Plymouth.*

SOLTAU, JOHN THOMAS, Esq., of Plympton St. Mary, Devon.
Second son of George William Soltau. Esq., of Little Efford, Devon, by Frances Goddard, dau. of the Rev. Thomas Culme, of Tothill, Devon ; b. 1832 ; m. 1860 Florence Lady Young, 2nd dau. of Erving Clarke, Esq., of Efford Manor. and widow of Sir William Norris Young, Bart.—*Plympton St. Mary, Devon.*

SOMERS, Earl (CHARLES SOMERS SOMERS-COCKS).— Cr. 1821.
Only son of John Somers, 2nd Earl, by Lady Caroline Harriet, 4th dau. of Philip, 3rd Earl of Hardwicke; b. 1819 ; s. 1852 ; m. 1850 Virginia, dau. of the late James Pattle. Esq., of the Indian Civil Service. Educated at Ch. Ch., Oxford (B.A. 1840); is a J.P. and D.L. for co. Hereford and for Surrey, and Patron of 7 livings ; was M.P. for Reigate 1841–52, a Lord in Waiting 1853–7.—*The Priory, Reigate ; Eastnor Castle, Ledbury; 33, Prince's Gate, w.*
Heir Pres. (to the Barony of Somers only), his cousin Charles Richard, in Holy Orders (eldest son of the late Hon. Philip James Cocks, who d. 1857, by Frances, dau. of Arthur Heelece, Esq.), educated at Eton, and M.A. of Ch. Ch., Oxford ; a Magistrate for co. Hereford, Vicar of Wolverley, co. Worcester, and of Neen Savage, co. Salop ; b. 1814.

SOMERS, Countess Dowager.
Caroline Harriet. 4th dau. of Philip, 3rd Earl of Hardwicke, by Lady Elizabeth Lindsay, 3rd dau. of James, 5th Earl of Balcarres ; m. 1815 John, 2nd Earl Somers, who d. 1852.—45, Grosvenor Place, s.w.

SOMERS, Countess Dowager.
Jane, dau. of the late James Cocks, Esq.; m. 1st 18— the Rev. George Waddington ; 2nd 1834 (as 2nd wife), John, 1st Earl Somers, who d. 1841.—28, *Norfolk Street, Hyde Park, w.*

SOMERS, JOHN RICHARD, Esq., of Tyrrellspass, co. Westmeath.
Eldest son of the late Richard Somers, Esq., of Tyrrellspass, by Anne Sarah, dau. of Thomas Fouace, Esq., of Tyrrellspass ; b. 1814 ; s. 1848 ; m. 1836 Maria Jane, 6th dau. of Samuel Handy, Esq., of Bracca Castle, co. Westmeath, and has, with other issue,
* Richard John, Capt. 11th Hussars ; b. 1838.
Mr. Somers is a Magistrate for co. Westmeath.—*Tyrrellspass, co. Westmeath.*

SOMERSET, Duke of (EDWARD ADOLPHUS SEYMOUR, P.C., K.G.).— Cr. 1547.
Eldest son of Edward Adolphus, 12th Duke, by his 1st wife Lady Charlotte, dau. of Archibald, 9th Duke of Hamilton; b. 1804 ; s. 1855 ; m. 1830 Jane Georgiana, dau. of the late Thomas Sheridan, Esq. Educated at Ch. Ch., Oxford ; is Lord Lieutenant and Custos Rotulorum of Devon, and Patron of 3 livings; was M.P. for Totnes 1834–55 ; a Lord of the Treasury 1835–9, Secretary to the Board of Control 1839–41, Chief Commissioner of Woods and Forests 1849–51, and of Public Works 1851–2 ; First Lord of the Admiralty 1859–66. was formerly a Commissioner of Lunacy. Is descended from a common ancestor with the Marquis of Hertford.—*Stover, Newton Abbot, Devon ; Bulstrode Park, Gerard's Cross, Bucks ; Maiden Bradley, Wilts ; Athenæum and Travellers' Clubs, s.w. ; 24, Dover Street, w.*
Heir. his son Edward Adolphus Ferdinand. Earl St. Maur, late Cornet 4th Dragoons, and formerly Cornet Wilts Yeomanry (called to the House of Peers in his father's Barony of Seymour, 1863) ; b. 1835.

SOMERSET, Dowager Duchess of.
Margaret, eldest dau. of the late Sir Michael Shaw-Stewart, Bart., M.P., of Greenock and Blackhall. co. Renfrew, by Catharine, youngest dau. of Sir William Maxwell, Bart.. of Sprinkell, co. Dumfries ; m. 1836 (as 2nd wife) Edward, 11th Duke of Somerset, who d. 1855.—*Somerset House, Park Lane, w.*

SOMERSET, Lady ARTHUR, of St. Mabyn, Cornwall.
Elizabeth, elder dau. of George Evelyn, 3rd Viscount Falmouth, by Elizabeth Anne. only dau. and heir of the late John Crewe, Esq., of Bolesworth Castle. co. Chester; m. 1808 Lord Arthur John Henry Somerset. who d. 1816. leaving. with other issue, * George Henry, in Holy Orders, M.A. of St. Mary Hall. Oxford, and Rector of St. Mabyn, Cornwall ; b. 1809 ; m. 1835 Philippa Elizabeth, dau. of the late Sir William Pratt Call, Bart., and has. with other issue, * Arthur William Henry, b. 1843.—*St. Mabyn, Bodmin.*

SOMERSET, the Hon. Mrs.
Frances, 2nd dau. of the late Hon. and Rev. John Evelyn Boscawen (who was second son of George Evelyn, 3rd Viscount Falmouth), by Catherine Elizabeth, dau. of Arthur Annesley. Esq.. of Bletchingdon Park. Oxon, and sister of Eve'yn, 6th Viscount Falmouth ; m. 1850 Arthur Edward Somerset. Esq. (son of Lord Arthur Somerset), who d. 1853.—*St. Leonard's, Sussex.*

SOMERSET, Col. ALFRED PLANTAGENET FREDERICK CHARLES, of Enfield, Middlesex.
Only son of the late Col. Lord John Thomas Henry Somerset (7th son of Henry, 5th Duke of Beaufort, K.G.), by the Lady Catherine Annesley, dau. of Arthur, 1st Earl of Mountmorris (extl.); b. 1820 ; s. 1852 ; m. 1857 Adelaide Harriet, youngest dau. of the late Vice-Admiral Sir G. R. Brooke Pechell, Bart., M.P. Is a J.P. and D.L. for Middlesex, a Magistrate for Westminster, a Commissioner of Metropolitan Roads. and

a Lieut.-Col. Central London Rifle Rangers; was formerly Capt. 13th Foot.—*Enfield Court, Middlesex*, N.E.; *Army and Navy Club*, s.w.

SOMERSET, Col. EDWARD ARTHUR, C.B.
Son of the late General Lord Robert Edward Henry Somerset, M.P. (son of Henry, 5th Duke of Beaufort). by the Hon. Louisa Augusta, youngest dau. of William 2nd Viscount Courtenay; *b.* 1817; *m.* 1849 Agatha, dau. of Sir William Miles, Bart., M.P., of Leigh Court, Somerset. Educated at Sandhurst: is a Magistrate for co. Monmouth; late Col. Commanding Rifle Brigade; was M.P. for co. Monmouth 1848–59; elected M.P. for co. Gloucester 1867; is Quartermaster-General of the Forces in Ireland.—*Carlton Club*, s.w.

SOMERSET, Col. POULETT GEORGE HENRY, C.B., of Heath Lodge, Surrey.
Youngest son of the late General Lord Charles Henry Somerset, by his 2nd wife Lady Mary, dau. of John, 4th Earl Poulett; *b.* 1822; *m.* 1847 Barbara Augusta Norah, dau. of the late John Mytton, Esq., of Halston, co. Salop, and has, with other issue,
* Vere Francis John, *b.* 1854.
Col. Somerset, who was educated at Eton and the Royal Military Coll., Sandhurst, is a J.P. and D.L. for co. Monmouth, late Col. Coldstream Guards; was elected M.P. for co. Monmouth 1859.—*Heath Lodge, Chertsey; Guards' Club*, s.w.; 6, *Stratford Place*, w.

SOMERSET.
(See under *Beaufort, Duke of*, and *Raglan, Lord*.)

SOMERTON. (See under *Normanton, Earl of*.)

SOMERVILLE, Lord (HUGH SOMERVILLE).—Cr. 1430.
Elder son of Kenelm, 17th Lord, by Frances Louisa, dau. of John Hayman, Esq.; *b.* 1839; *s.* 1864. Is a Lieut. Warwickshire Yeomanry Cavalry, and Patron of 1 living. This title, from the 8th to the 12th peer in succession, was never assumed; it was, however, confirmed by Parliament in 1723, to James, 13th Lord. —*The Pavilion, Melrose, N.B.; Arthur's Club*, s.w.
Heir Pres., his cousin Everard Wiliam (eldest son of the late Hon. and Rev. William Somerville, who *d.* 1857, by Charlotte, dau. of the late Rev. Walter Bagot, brother of the 1st Lord Bagot); *b.* 1839.

SOMERVILLE, JAMES CURTIS, Esq., of Dinder, Somerset.
Second but eldest surviving son of the late James Somerville-Fownes, Esq., of Dinder (who assumed the surname of Somerville only in 1831), by Frances, 2nd dau. of the late William Ilbert, Esq., of Bowringsleigh, Devon; *b.* 1807; *s.* 1848; *m.* 1846 Emily Periam, eldest dau. of the late Sir Alexander Hood, Bart., and has, with other issue,
* Arthur Fownes, *b.* 1850.
Mr. Somerville, who was educated at Trinity Hall, Cambridge (B.A. 1832, M.A. 1836), and called to the Bar at the Middle Temple 1840, is a J.P. and D.L. for Somerset (High Sheriff 1861).—*Dinder House, Wells; Oxford and Cambridge Club*, s.w.

SOMERVILLE, THOMAS, Esq., of The Prairie, co. Cork.
Eldest son of the late Philip Somerville, Esq., by Henrietta, dau. of Richard Townsend, Esq., of The Point; *b.* 1817; *s.* 1861; *m.* 1st 1853 Mary, dau. of the Rev. James Hingston; 2nd 1859 Millicent Harte, dau. of Michael Alleyn Becher, Esq., of Ballidurane, co. Cork, and has, with other issue,
* Thomas, *b.* 1862.
Mr. Somerville is a Magistrate for co. Cork, and Capt. South Cork Militia.—*The Prairie, Skull, co. Cork.*

SOMERVILLE, THOMAS, Esq., of Drishane, co. Cork.
Eldest son of the late Thomas T. Somerville, Esq., J.P. of Castle Haven and Drishane, by Elizabeth Becher, dau. of the late John Townsend, Esq., M.P., of Shepperton; *b.* 1797; *s.* 1811; *m.* 1822 Henrietta Augusta, dau. of the late Richard Boyle Townsend, Esq., of Castle Townsend, and has, with other issue,
* Thomas Henry, of Malmaison, near Castle Townsend; a Magistrate for co. Cork, and late Lieut.-Col. 3rd Bufs; *b.* 1824; *m.* 1857 Adelaide Eliza, dau. of the late Admiral Sir Josiah Coghill, Bart., and has, with other issue, * Thomas Cameron Fitzgerald, *b.* 186–.
Mr. Somerville, who was educated at University Coll., Oxford, is a J.P. and D.L. for co. Cork (High Sheriff 1863), and Chairman of the Skibbereen Board of Guardians.—*Drishane, Skibbereen, co. Cork.*

SOMERVILLE. (See under *Athlumney, Lord*.)

SOMES, JOSEPH, Esq., F.S.A., F.R.G.S.
Eldest son of the late Samuel Francis Somes, Esq., by Sarah, dau. of the late Daniel Hill, Esq., of London; *b.* 1819; *m.* 1865 Frances, youngest dau. of the late Charles Saxton, Esq. Is a Magistrate for Middlesex and Essex, a Dep.-Lieut. for London and Tower Hamlets, and a Shipowner at Blackwall; was M.P. for Hull 1859–65.—*Muswell Hill, Middlesex*, N.; *City Club*, E.C.

SONDES, Lord (GEORGE JOHN MILLES).—Cr. 1760.
Eldest surviving son of Lewis Thomas, 2nd Lord, by Mary Elizabeth, dau. of the late Richard Milles, Esq., of North Elmham Hall, Norfolk; *b.* 1794; *s.* his brother as 4th Lord 1836; *m.* 1823 Eleanor, dau. of the late Right Hon. Sir Edward Knatchbull, Bart. Is a J.P. and D.L. for Norfolk, High Steward of Gt. Yarmouth, and Patron of 3 livings. Descended from a common ancestor with Lord Monson; assumed, in 1830, the name of Milles in lieu of Watson.—*Elmham Hall, and Gatsley Hall, East Der ham; Lees Court, Faversham; Carlton Club*, s.w.; 32, *Grosvenor Square*, w.
Heir, his son George Watson, educated at Eton and Sandhurst, a J.P. and D.L. for Norfolk, a Magistrate for Kent; Lieut.-Col. E. Kent Yeomanry Cavalry, late Capt. Royal Horse Guards; *b.* 1824; *m.* 1859 Charlotte, dau. of Sir Henry J. Strawey, Bart., and has, with other issue, * George Edward, *b.* 1861.

SOTHERON-ESTCOURT. (See *Estcourt*.)

SOTHEBY, CHARLES WILLIAM HAMILTON, Esq., of Sewardstone, Essex.
Only son of the late Rear-Admiral Charles Sotheby, of Sewardstone, Essex (who *d.* 1854), by his first wife, the Hon. Jane, 2nd dau. of William, 7th Lord Belhaven; *b.* 1820; educated at Harrow; was formerly Capt. 60th Rifles.—*Sewardstone Manor House, High Beech, Waltham Abbey; Army and Navy, Brookes's and Travellers' Clubs*, s.w.
Heir Pres., his half-brother Frederick Edward, *b.* 1837.

SOUTHAMPTON, Lord (CHARLES FITZROY). —Cr. 1780.
Eldest son of George Ferdinand, 2nd Lord, by his 2nd wife Frances Isabella, dau. of the late Lord Robert Seymour; *b.* 1804; *s.* 1810; *m.* 1st 1826 Harriet, dau. of the late Hon. Henry FitzRoy Stanhope (she *d.* 1860); 2nd 1862 Ismenia Catharine FitzRoy, dau. of Walter Nugent, Esq., a Baron of the Austrian Empire. Is Lord Lieut. and Custos Rotulorum of co. Northampton, and Patron of 1 living. Descended from the 2nd Duke of Grafton.—*Whittlebury Lodge, Towcester; Carlton Club*, s.w.; 58, *Upper Grosvenor Street*, w.
Heir, his son Charles Henry, *b.* 1867.

SOUTHBY. (See *Hayward-Southby*.)

+**SOUTHBY,** EDMUND R., Esq., M.D., M.R.C.S., of Bulford, Wilts.
Son of the late Anthony Southby, Esq., M.D., of Bulford; *b.* 183–. Is Lord of the Manor of Bulford, and Patron of that living.—*Bulford Manor, Amesbury, Wilts.*

SOUTHESK, Earl of (JAMES CARNEGIE).—Cr. 1633.
Eldest son of the late Sir James Carnegie, Bart., by Charlotte, dau. of the Rev. Daniel Lysons, of Hempsted Court, co. Gloucester; *b.* 1827; *m.* 1st 1849 Lady Catharine Hamilton, dau. of Charles, 1st Earl of Gainsborough (she *d.* 1855); 2nd 1860 Lady Susan, eldest dau. of Alexander Edward, 6th Earl of Dunmore. Educated at Sandhurst; is a Dep.-Lieut. for co. Forfar; late Lord Lieutenant of co. Kincardine; formerly Lieut. Grenadier Guards. The 1st Earl of Southesk was elder brother to the 1st Earl of Northesk. This earldom, attainted in 1718, was restored in 1855, with the original precedence.—*Kinnaird Castle, Brechin, N.B.; Brooks's Club, s.w.*
Heir, his son Charles Noel, Lord Carnegie, b. 1854.

SOUTHWELL, Viscount (THOMAS ARTHUR JOSEPH SOUTHWELL).—cr. 1776.
Eldest son of the late Lieut.-Col. the Hon. Arthur Francis Southwell (who *d.* 1849), by Mary Jane Agnes, eldest dau. of the late Thomas Dillon, Esq., of Mt. Dillon, co. Dublin; *b.* 1836; *s.* his uncle as 4th Visct. 1860. Educated at St. Mary's Coll., Oscott. Is Lord of the Manor of Castle Matrix, Patron of 1 living, and a Lieut. Lancashire Yeomanry Hussars; late Lieut. 13th Light Dragoons.—*Castle Matrix, Rathkeale, co. Limerick; Hibernian United Service Club, Dublin; Windham Club, s.w.; Derby Lodge, Mortlake, s.w.*
Heir Pres., his brother Charles Francis, b. 1839.

SOWERBY, GEORGE, Esq., ‡ of Putteridge Bury, Herts, and Dalton Hall, Yorkshire.
Eldest surviving son of the late John Sowerby, Esq., of Putteridge Bury; *b.* 1794; *s.* his brother 1864; *m.* 1831 Ann, dau. of William Hutchinson, Esq., of Newsham, co. York, and has, with other issue,
• George, of Lilley House, Herts; *b.* 1832; *m.* 1863 Emily Isabella Jane, 3rd dau. of the late Robert Airey, Esq., of Newcastle-on-Tyne, and has, with other issue, • Thomas George, *b.* 1866.
Mr. Sowerby, who was educated at Harrow and Trinity Coll., Cambridge (B.A. 1816, M.A. 1819), and called to the Bar at Lincoln's Inn 1819, is a J.P. and D.L. for the N. Riding of Yorkshire, a Magistrate for cos. Beds, Herts, and Rutland, and Lord of the Manor of Dalton.—*Putteridge Bury, Luton; Dalton Hall, Greta Bridge.*

SOWLER, ROBERT SCARR, Esq., of Sawrey Knotts, Westmoreland.
Eldest son of the late Thomas Sowler, Esq., of Motley Bank, Bowdon, co. Chester, by Helen, dau. of John Slack, Esq., of Salford, co. Lancaster; *b.* 181.; *s.* 1857; *m.* 1849 Frances, youngest dau. of George Sowler, Esq., of London. Called to the Bar at the Middle Temple 1841; appointed Queen's Counsel of the co. Palatine of Lancaster 1858.—*Sawrey Knotts, Lake Windermere, Westmoreland; Clarkshill, Stand, Manchester; 2, Plowden Buildings, Temple, e.c.*

SPAIGHT, JAMES, Esq.
Second son of the late Francis Spaight, Esq., of Derry Castle, co. Tipperary (who *d.* 1861), by Agnes, eldest dau. of the late James Campbell Paterson, Esq., of Kilnish; *b.* 1820; *m.* 1850 Elizabeth, dau. of the late

John Eckford, Esq., H.E.I.Co's Service. Educated at Trinity Coll., Dublin; is a Merchant in Limerick, and a Magistrate for that city, of which he was Mayor in 1856; was M.P. for Limerick 1858–9.—*George Street, Limerick; Conservative Club, s.w.*

SPAIGHT, THOMAS, Esq., of Ardtagle, co. Clare.
Eldest son of the late William Spaight, Esq., of Ardtagle House, by Millicent, dau. of Thomas Studdert, Esq., of Bunratty Castle, co. Clare; *b.* 1785; *s.* 1800; *m.* 1837 Mary, dau. of the Rev. Robert Gabbett, of Castlelake. This family settled in Ireland *temp.* Charles I.—*Ardtagle House, Limerick.*

SPAIGHT, WILLIAM, Esq., of Derry, co. Tipperary.
Eldest son of the late Francis Spaight, Esq., of Derry Castle, by Agnes, sister of the MacIver Campbell, of Loch-Gair House, Inverary, co. Argyle; *b.* 1817; *s.* 1861; *m.* 1845 Anne, dau. of the late Marcus Paterson, Esq., of Sheperton, co. Clare, and has, with other issue,
• Francis Wyndham, *b.* 1847.
Mr. Spaight is a Magistrate for cos. Clare and Tipperary. This family is a branch of the Spaights of Corbally and Lodge, co. Clare.—*Derry Castle, Killaloe; Conservative Club, s.w.*

SPALDING, JOHN EDEN, Esq., of The Holme, and Shirmirs, Kirkcudbrightshire.
Only son of the late John Spalding, Esq., of The Holme, and Shirmirs, by Mary Anne, only dau. of the late Thomas Eden, Esq., brother of Lords Auckland and Henley (she *m.* 2nd Lord Brougham and Vaux): *b.* 1808; *s.* 1815; *m.* 1831 the Hon. Mary Wilhelmina, only dau. of John Henry, 1st Viscount Templetown, and has, with other surviving issue,
• Augustus Frederick Montagu, *b.* 1838.
Mr. Spalding, who is a Magistrate for the Stewartry of Kirkcudbright and Lord of the Manors of The Holme and Shirmirs, was formerly in the 9th Lancers and 2nd Life Guards.—*The Holme, New Galloway, N.B.; 12, Curzon Street, w.*

SPARKE, the Rev. JOHN HENRY, of Gunthorpe Hall, Norfolk.
Eldest son of the late Right Rev. Bowyer E. Sparke, D.D., Lord Bishop of Ely (who *d.* 1836), by Hester, dau. of S. Hobbs, Esq., of Homersfidge; *b.* 1794; *m.* 1825 Agnes, youngest sister of Jacob, late Lord Hastings, and has, with other issue,
• Edward Bowyer, a Magistrate for Norfolk, *b.* 1832.
Mr. Sparke, who was educated at Eton and Pembroke Coll., Cambridge (B.A. 1815, M.A. 1818), is a Magistrate for Norfolk and Isle of Ely, Rector and Lord of the Manor of Gunthorpe, and Patron of that living, Rector also of Leverington, and Canon of Ely.—*Gunthorpe Hall, Thetford; University Club, s.w.*

SPARKES, ARNDELL FRANCIS, Esq., of Bridgnorth, Salop.
Only son of the late Joseph Arndell Sparkes, Esq., of Pennyworlodd Hall, co. Brecon, by Elizabeth, dau. of Francis Best, Esq., of Worcester; *b.* 1803; *s.* 1824; *m.* 1831 Mary Anne, dau. of the late William W. Whitmore, Esq., of Dudmaston Hall, co. Salop, and has issue,
• Janetta Elizabeth; Eleanora, *m.* John Charles Lloyd, Esq.; Caroline Sophia, *m.* 1st Frederick Neville Isaac, Esq., 2nd John Watts, Esq.; Frances Marianne, *m.* Capt. Charles Walsham Maynard, R.H.A.; and Lucy Dorothea.
—*Bridgnorth, Salop.*

SPARKES, JOHN FREDERICK WINCKWORTH, Esq., of Gosden House, Surrey.

Son of the late John Sparkes, Esq., of Gosden House, by Emma, 3rd dau. of the late James More Molyneux, Esq., of Loseley Park, Surrey; b. 1838; s. 185–.—*Gosden House, Guilford.*

SPARLING, the Rev. JOHN.

Third son of William Sparling, Esq., of Petton Park, co. Salop, by Emma Elizabeth, dau. of John Walmesley, Esq., of Bath; b. 1815; m. 1843 Catherine Sybilla, dau. of the late Sir Thomas Joseph de Trafford, Bart., and has issue,

* Emma Florence, m. 1867 Ellis Brooke, eldest son of the late Ellis Watkin Cunliffe, Esq.

Mr. Sparling, who was educated at Oriel Coll., Oxford (B.A. 1837, M.A. 1814), and instituted Rector of Eccleston 1854, is a Magistrate for co. Lancaster.—*Eccleston, Chorley; Oxford and Cambridge Club, s.w.*

SPARLING, WILLIAM, Esq., of Petton, Shropshire.

Eldest son of the late John Sparling, Esq., of Petton Park, by Elizabeth, dau. of James Greenhow, Esq., of Beaumont, co. Lancaster; b. 1777; s. 1800; m. 1805 Emma Elizabeth, dau. of John Walmesley, Esq., of Ince Hall, co. Lancaster, and has, with other issue,

* William, a Magistrate for co. Salop; b. 1813.

Mr. Sparling, who was educated at Eton and Oriel Coll., Oxford, is a J.P. and D.L. for co. Salop (High Sheriff 1810), and Lord of the Manor of Petton, was formerly Lieut. 10th Hussars.—*Petton Park, Shrewsbury; University Club, s.w.; 20, Stratford Place, w.*

SPARROW, HENRY WEARE, Esq., of Gosfield, Essex.

Eldest son of the late James Goodeve Sparrow, Esq., of Gosfield Place, by his 2nd wife Dorothy, eldest dau. of the late Rev. Basil B. Beridge, of Algarkirk, co. Lincoln; b. 1819; s. 1838. Educated at Eton; is Lord of the Manor of Gosfield.—*Gosfield Place, Halstead.*

Heir Pres., his brother Basil, a J.P. and D.L. for Essex, and banker at Chelmsford, &c.; b. 1820; m. 1846 Julia, dau. of the late John Beriston, Esq., of Prittlewell Priory, Essex, and has, with other issue, * Basil James Harold, b. 1853.

SPARROW, JOHN FRANCIS, Esq., of Blackburn, Lancashire.

Eldest son of the late John Sparrow, Esq., J.P., of Blackburn, by his first wife, Elizabeth, dau. of Michael Fergus Kiernan, Esq.; b. 1839; s. 1868; m. 1861 Jennette Mary, youngest dau. of the late Nicholas Baskell, Esq., of Liverpool. Was formerly an Officer in the 23rd Royal Welsh Fusiliers.—*Blackburn, Lancashire.*

SPARROW, WILLIAM MANDER, Esq., of Penn, Staffordshire.

Eldest son of the late William Hanbury Sparrow, Esq., J.P. and D.L., of Penn, by his 1st wife, Caroline, dau. of Thomas Mander, Esq., of Edgbaston; b. 1811; s. 1867. Is a Magistrate for co. Stafford. and Lord of the Manor of Albrighton.—*Penn, Wolverhampton.*

Heir Pres., his brother Arthur, a Magistrate for co. Stafford; b. 1813.

+SPARROW, WILLIAM HENRY, Esq., of Habberley, Shropshire.

Son of the late William Sparrow, Esq.; b. 18—. Is Lord of the Manor of Habberley.—*Habberley, Shrewsbury.*

SPEARMAN, Sir ALEXANDER, Bart., of Hanwell, Middlesex (cr. 1840).

Eldest son of the late Alexander Young Spearman, Esq., by Agnes, dau. of James Morton, Esq., of Bonan Hill; b. 1793; m. 1826 Jane, dau. of Duncan Campbell, Esq., of Inveraw, co. Argyle. Is a Magistrate for Middlesex, and Comptroller-General of the National Debt; was Assistant-Secretary of the Treasury 1836–40.—*The Spring, Hanwell, Middlesex.*

Heir, his grandson Joseph Layton Elmes' only surviving issue of the late A. Y. Spearman, Esq., (who d. 1856), by his 1st wife Mary Anne Betha, dau. of the late Sir T. Bailey, Bart.; b. 1867.

SPEARMAN, HENRY CHARLES, Esq., of Thornley Hall, co. Durham.

Son of the late J. Spearman, Esq.; b. 1836; s. his uncle H. J. Spearman, Esq., who was a J.P. and D.L. for co. Durham, and formerly M.P. for Durham, 1863; late Capt. 66th Foot.—*Burn Hall and Thornley Hall, Durham.*

SPEDDING, JAMES, Esq., of Summergrove, Cumberland.

Eldest son of the late James Spedding, Esq., of Summergrove, by Elizabeth, dau. of Thomas Harrington, Esq., of Carlisle; b. 1779; m. 1808 Mary, dau. of Lawson D. Ballantine, Esq., of Crookdale Hall, and had issue,

* James, Capt. Westmoreland Militia; b. 1810; m. 1847 Emily, youngest dau. of the late Hon. William Frederick Wyndham, and d. 1851, leaving issue, * James Wyndham Harrington Percy, b. 1849.

Mr. Spedding, who was educated at Rugby, is a J.P. and D.L. for Cumberland; was formerly Capt. 1st Foot Guards, and Major R. Westmoreland Militia.—*Summergrove and Greta Bank, Whitehaven.*

SPEIR, ROBERT THOMAS NAPIER, Esq., of Burnbrae, Renfrewshire, and Culdees, Perthshire.

Eldest son of the late Robert Speir, Esq., of Culdees and Burnbrae, by Mary Milliken, dau. of Sir William Milliken Napier, Bart., of Milliken and Napier, co. Renfrew; b. 1841; s. 1853; m. 1868 the Hon. Emily, 3rd dau. of Robert Francis 2nd Lord Gifford. Educated at Eton and Ch. Ch., Oxford. Is a Magistrate for co. Renfrew.—*Burnbrae, Johnstone, N.B.; Culdees Castle, Auchterarder, N.B.*

Heir Pres., his sister Elizabeth Christian, m. 1867 Archibald Campbell Douglas, Esq., of Mains, co. Dumbarton (whom see).

SPEIR, THOMAS, Esq., of Blackstoun, Renfrewshire.

Only surviving son of the late Robert Speir, Esq., of Burnbrae, co. Renfrew (who d. 1841), by Isabella, dau. of John Robertson, Esq.; b. 1801. Is a J.P. and D.L. and Convener of co. Renfrew, and Lord of the Barony of Blackstoun. This family is a junior branch of that of Speir of Burnbrae and Culdees.—*Blackstoun House, Paisley, N.B.; Windham Club, s.w.*

Heir Pres., his nephew Robert Thomas Napier, Esq., of Burnbrae and Culdees (whom see).

SPEIRS, ALEXANDER GRAHAM, Esq., of Culcreuch, Stirlingshire.

Eldest son of the late Peter Speirs, Esq., of Culcreuch, by Martha Harriet, 2nd dau. of the late Robert Cunningham Graham, Esq., of Gartmore; b. 1793; s. 1829; m. 1828 Mary, 2nd dau. of William Murray, Esq., of Polmaise, N.B. Educated at Trinity Hall Military Coll., Marlow; is a J.P. and D.L. for and Convener of co. Stirling, a Magistrate for cos. Lanark, Dunbarton, Renfrew, and Perth, and Lord of the Barony of Culcreuch; formerly an Officer in the Army; was M.P. for Paisley 1835–6.—*Culcreuch, Fintry, by Glasgow, N.B.*

Heir of Entail, his niece Anne, b. 1855; m. 1858 Sir George Home, Bart., and has, with other issue, * James, b. 1861.

SPEIRS, ARCHIBALD ALEXANDER, Esq., of Elderslie, Renfrewshire.

Only son of the late Alexander Speirs, Esq., M.P., of Elderslie (who was Lord-Lieut. of co. Renfrew), by Eliza Stewart, eldest dau. of Thomas C. Hagart, Esq.,

of Bantaskine, near Falkirk; *b.* 1840; *s.* 1844; *m.* 1867 the Hon. Anne, eldest dau. of Jacob, Viscount Folkestone, and grand-dau. of William, 3rd Earl of Radnor. Educated at Eton; is a Magistrate for co. Renfrew. and Lord of the Barony of Elderslie; elected M.P. for co. Renfrew 1865.—*Elderslie House and Houston House, Paisley N.B.; Brooks's and Guards' Clubs*, s.w.; 10, *Eaton Place*, s.w.

Heir Pres., his sister Eliza.

SPEKE, WILLIAM, Esq., of Jordans, Somerset. Eldest son of the late William Speke, Esq., of Jordans, by his 1st wife Mary, dau. of B. Dickenson, Esq., of Tiverton, Devon; *b.* 1798; *s.* 1839; *m.* 1824 Georgina Elizabeth, dau. of William Hanning, Esq., of Dillington, Somerset. and has, with other issue,

* William, of Monks Park. Cor-ham. Wilts. a Magistrate for Wilts and Somerset; *b.* 1825; *m.* 1850 Eliza, eldest dau. of the Rev. Charles W. Ethelston (whom see).

Mr. Speke, who is a J.P. and D.L. for Somerset, Lord of the Manor of Ashill, and Patron of 2 livings, was formerly in the 14th Dragoons.—*Jordans Park, Ashill, Ilminster.*

SPENCER, Earl (JOHN POYNTZ SPENCER, K.G., P.C., LL.D.).—Cr. 1765. Eldest son of Frederick, 4th Earl. by his 1st wife Elizabeth Gorgiana. dau. of the late William Stephen Poyntz, Esq., M.P., of Cowdray Park, Sussex; *b.* 1835. *s.* 1857; *m.* 1858 Charlotte, dau. of the late Frederick Charles Seymour. Esq. Educated at Harrow and Trinity Coll., Cambridge (M.A. 1856); is a J.P. and D.L. for Northampton, Patron of 11 livings, and Major Northamptonshire Rifle Volunteers; appointed Groom of the Stole to H.R.H. the late Prince Consort 1859, and to H.R.H. the Prince of Wales 1862; cr. Hon. LL.D. Cambridge 1864; was M.P. for S. Northamptonshire April–Dec. 1867. — *Althorp, Northampton; Brooks's Club*, s.w.; 27, *St. James's Place*, s.w.

Heir Pres., his half-brother Charles Robert, *b.* 1857.

SPENCER, Dowager Countess. Adelaide Horatia Elizabeth, only dau. of the late Sir Horace Beauchamp Seymour, by his 1st wife Elizabeth Mallet, eldest dau. of Sir Lawrence Palk, Bart.; *m.* 1854 (as 2nd wife) Frederick, 4th Earl Spencer, who *d.* 1857.—*Hampton*, s.w.; 27, *St. James's Place*, s.w.

SPENCER, the Hon. Sir AUGUSTUS ALMERIC, K.C.B. (cr. 1865). Third son of Francis, 1st Lord Churchill, by Lady Frances, dau. of Augustus Henry, 3rd Duke of Grafton; *b.* 1807; *m.* 1836 Helen Maria, dau. of the late Lieut-General Sir Archibald Campbell, Bart., G.C.B., and has, with other issue,

* Augustus Campbell, *b.* 1832.

Sir Almeric Spencer, who entered the Army in 1825, is a Major-General in the Army, and Col. 96th Foot; late Lieut.-Col. 44th Foot; appointed Commander of the Western District 1865.—*United Service Club*, s.w.

SPENCER, the Hon. and Rev. CHARLES FREDERIC OCTAVIUS. Eighth son of Francis, 1st Lord Churchill, by Lady Frances, dau. of Augustus Henry, 3rd Duke of Grafton; *b.* 1824; *m.* 1847 Hester Eliza, dau. of the Rev. H. Fardell, and has. with other issue,

* Charles Francis Henry, *b.* 1848.

Mr. Spencer, who was educated at Clare Hall, Cambridge (M.A. 1817), is a Magistrate for Berks; was appointed Vicar of Cumnor 1819, and Vicar of Sutton 1861.—*Sutton Vicarage, Ely.*

SPENCER, the Hon. GEORGE AUGUSTUS. Second son of Francis Almeric, 1st Lord Churchill, qv Lady Frances, dau. of Augustus Henry, 3rd Duke of Grafton; *b.* 1804; *m.* 1834 Charlotte, only dau. of the

late Major-Gen. Munro, of Teaninich, co. Ross, and has, with other issue,

* Almeric Astley John, Lient. 52nd Foot; *b.* 1842.

Lieut.-Gen. Spencer, who was educated at Sandhurst, is a Dep-Lieut. for Oxon and a Lieut.-Gen. in the Army; late Lieut.-Col. 37th Foot, and Coldstream Guards.

SPENCER, the Hon. ROBERT CHARLES HENRY, of Combe, Oxon. Seventh son of Francis, 1st Lord Churchill, by Lady Frances, dau. of Augustus Henry, 3rd Duke of Grafton; *b.* 1817; *m.* 1845 Lady Louisa, only dau. of George, 6th Duke of Marlborough, and has, with other issue,

* Gerald Robert, *b.* 1853.

Mr. Spencer, who was educated at Woolwich, entered the Royal Artillery 1835, became Capt. 1846. and Col. 1854. is a Magistrate for Oxon. — *Combe, Woodstock, Oxon; United Service Club*, s.w.

SPENCER, the Hon. and Rev. WILLIAM HENRY. Fourth son of Francis, 1st Lord Churchill, by Lady Frances, dau. of Augustus Henry, 3rd Duke of Grafton; *b.* 1810; *m.* 1st 1838 Elizabeth Rose, dau. of T. Thornhill, of Woodleys, Oxon; 2nd 1852 Louisa Mercer, dau. of the late Sir William P. Call, Bart., and has by the former, with other i-sue,

* William Francis, Capt. 46th Regt.; *b.* 1878.

Mr. Spencer was educated at Westminster, Rugby, and Ch. Ch., Oxford (B.A. 1831, M.A. 1834); appointed Vicar of Urchfont, Wilts, 1839; Rector of Stoke Climsland 1850.—*Stoke Climsland Rectory, Callington.*

SPENCER, the Rev. CHARLES VERE, of Wheatfield, Oxfordshire. Eldest son of the late Rev. Frederick Charles Spencer, of Wheatfield, by Mary Anne, 2nd dau. of the late Sir Serope Bernard-Morland, Bart., of Nettleham, Bucks; *b.* 1827; *s.* 1831; *m.* 1852 Emma Frederica, only child of John R. A'Court Gray, Esq., and has, with other issue,

* Aubrey John, *b.* 1853.

Mr. Spencer, who was educated at Eton and Ch. Ch., Oxford (B.A. 1849, M.A. 1852), is a Magistrate for Oxon, Rector and Lord of the Manor of Wheatfield, and Patron of 1 living.—*Wheatfield, Tetsworth.*

SPENCER, HENRY, Esq., of Woodlands, Hampshire. Youngest son of Peter Shield, Esq., of Earsdon, Northumberland, by Harriot. 2nd dau. of Ralph Spencer. Esq., of Helmington Hall, co. Durham; *b.* 1818; *s.* his uncle the Rev. Robert Spencer, of Helmington Hall, whose name he assumed 1812; *m.* 1843 Jane Hamilla. youngest dau. of the late John Hamilton, Esq., of Sundrum. co. Ayr, and has, with other issue,

* Rudolph Hamilton, *b.* 1848.

Mr. Spencer is a J.P. and D.L. for co. Durham, and a Magistrate for Hants.—*Woodlands, Havant.*

SPENCER, JOHN TREVOR. Esq., of Edgemoor, Derbyshire. Only son of the late William Cavendish Spencer. Esq. (who *d.* 1850), by Patience Caroline, dau. of Col. Hanington, of the Bengal Army, and grandson of the late Rt. Rev. George Trevor Spencer, of Edgemoor, formerly Bishop of Madras; *b.* 1859; *s.* his grandfather 1866. Represents a younger branch of the Duke of Marlborough's family.—*Edgemoor, Buxton, Derbyshire; Wilton-on-the-Wolds, Loughborough.*

SPENCER. (See under *Churchill, Lord*, and *Marlborough, Duke of.*)

SPENCER-PHILLIPS, (*See Phillips.*)

SPENCER-STANHOPE, JOHN, Esq., F.R.S., of Cannon Hall, Yorkshire.

Eldest son of the late Walter Stanhope, Esq., M.P., of Cannon Hall and Horsforth Hall, co. York (who assumed the additional surname of Spencer), by Mary Winifred, dau. and heir of Thomas B. Pulleine, Esq., of Carlton Hall, co. York; b. 1787; s. 1821; m. 1822 Lady Elizabeth Wilhelmina, 3rd dau. of Thomas Wm., 1st Earl of Leicester, and has, with other issue.

* Walter Thomas William, J.P. and D.L. for the W. Riding of Yorkshire; b. 1827; m. 1856 Elizabeth Julia, dau. of Sir John Jacob Buxton, Bart., and has issue, * a son, b. 1863.

Mr. Spencer-Stanhope, who was educated at Westminster and Ch. Ch., Oxford, is a J.P. and D.L. for the W. Riding of Yorkshire, Lord of the Manor of Horsforth, and a Correspondent of the Imporial Institute of France. — *Cannon Hall and Horsforth Hall, Barnsley; Travellers' Club, s.w.*

SPENS, NATHANAEL, Esq., of Craigsanquhar, Fifeshire.

Elder son of the late Lieut. Col. James Spens, J.P. and D.L., of Craigsanquhar, by his 3rd wife Elizabeth Joanna, 2nd dau. of the late John Davidson, Esq., of Ravelrig, Midlothian; b. 1805; s. 1840; m. 1840 Janet Law, dau. of George Guild, Esq., and has, with other issue.

* Colin, Lieut. 42nd Highlanders; b. 1843.

Mr. Spens, who was educated at the University of Edinburgh, is a Magistrate for co. Fife.—*Craigsanquhar, Cupar-Fife, N.B.; 28, Walker Street, Edinburgh.*

SPERLING, ARTHUR, Esq., of Papworth St. Agnes, Cambridgeshire.

Eldest son of the late Rev. Harvey James Sperling, of Lattenbury Hill, Hunts, Rector of Papworth St. Agnes, co. Cambridge, by Anne, eldest dau. and heiress of John Macnab, Esq., of Newton, co. Perth; b. 1823; s. 1858; m. 1858 Adelaide Noel, dau. of the late Admiral Sir Henry Loraine Baker, Bart., C.B., of Dunstable House, Surrey, and has, with other issue.

* Arthur Harvey Baker, b. 1866.

Mr. Sperling, who was educated at Rugby and Trinity Coll., Cambridge (LL.B. 1849), and called to the Bar at Lincoln's Inn 1851, is a Magistrate for Hunts and for co. Cambridge, and Patron of 1 living. This family is a branch of the Sperlings of Dynes Hall, Essex.—*Papworth St. Agnes, and Lattenbury Hill, St. Ives; University Club, s.w.*

SPERLING, CHARLES BROGDEN, Esq., of Stanmore Manor, Middlesex.

Eldest son of the late Charles Robert Sperling, Esq., of Stanmore Manor, by Louisa, only dau. of Thomas Astle, Esq., of Gosfield Hall, Essex; b. 1825; s. 1863; m. 1852 Eliza Mary, dau. of Denne Denne, Esq., of Elbridge House, Kent, and has, with other issue,

* Charles Frederic Denne, b. 186–.

Mr. Sperling is a Magistrate for Essex. This family was formerly resident at Hargrave Lodge, Stanstead Mountfitchet, Essex.—*The Manor House, Great Stanmore, Middlesex; Castle Hedingham, Essex.*

SPERLING, HENRY GRACE WILSON, Esq., of Grovehurst, Kent.

Only son of the late Rev. Henry Grace Sperling, Rector of Papworth St. Agnes, Hunts, by Mary, dau. of the late Joseph Wilson, Esq., of Highbury Hill, Middlesex; b. 1821; m. 1st 1844 Anna Margaretta, eldest dau. of the Rev. C. D. Brereton, Rector of Little Massingham, Norfolk; 2nd 1851 Mary Maitland, eldest dau. of the late Henry Wilson, Esq., of Stow-langtoft Hall, Suffolk, and has issue,

* Henry Maitland, b. 1863.

Mr. Sperling, who was educated at Oriel Coll., Oxford,

is a Magistrate for Middlesex, Kent, and Sussex, and represents a younger branch of the Sperlings of Dynes Hall.—*Grovehurst, Pembury, Tunbridge Wells.*

SPERLING, HENRY JOHN, Esq., of Dynes Hall, Essex.

Only surviving son of the late John Sperling, Esq., of Dynes Hall, by Harriet, dau. of the Hon. William Rochfort, of Clontarf, Ireland; b. 1795; m. 1827 his cou-in Maria, 4th dau. of Henry Piper Sperling, Esq., of Norbury Park, Surrey. Is a J.P. and D.L. for Essex. This family are supposed to have sprung from Swedish Pomerania.—*Dynes Hall, Halstead.*

SPICER, JOHN WILLIAM GOOCH, Esq., of Spye Park, Wilts.

Eldest son of the late John William Spicer, Esq., D.L., of Esher Place, Sur ey (who d. 1862), by Hannah Maria Theresa, dau. of the late Philip Webb, Esq., of Milford House, Surrey (she d. 1863): b. 1817; m. 1845 Juliana, dau. of the late Rev. E lmund Probyn, of Long-hope, co. Gloucester, and has, with other issue,

John Edmund Philip, b. 1853.

Mr. Spicer, who was educated at Eton, is a J.P. and D.L. for Surrey, a Magistrate for Wilts, late Major 3rd Surrey Militia; forme.ly Capt. 9th Lancers and 3rd Dragoon Guards. — *Spye Park, Chippenham; B celle's and Army and Navy Clubs, s.w.; 35, Belgrave Square, s.w.*

+ SPINK, Lieut.-General JOHN, K.H., of Alton, Hampshire.

Son of the late — Spink, Esq.: b. 1788. Entered the Army in 1806; is a Magistrate for Hants; a Lieut.-General in the Army, and Col. 2nd Foot.—*Alton, Hants.*

SPITTY, THOMAS JENNER, Esq., of Billericay, Essex.

Only son of the late Thomas Spitty, Esq., by Mary, dau. of the late Rev. John Jenner, D D., of Bille.i:av; b. 1812; s. 1858. Educated at St. Peter's Coll., Cambridge; is a J.P. and D.L. for E-sex; appointed Capt. E. Essex Militia 1834, and in 1854 Major Commanding the Essex Rifles.—*Billericay, Brentwood.*

SPLATT, WILLIAM FRANCIS, Esq., of Flete, Devon.

Son of the late John Splatt, of Chudleigh, Devon; b. 1811; purchased this property in 1864 from the Bulteel family; m. 1840 Elizabeth Satterly, dau. of the late Joseph Pynsent. Esq., of North Bovey, Devon. Is a Magistrate for Devon, and Lord of the Manors of Holbeton and Ermington, was formerly a Merchant in Australia, and a Member of the Legislature Council, Victoria.—*Flete House, Holbeton.*

SPLATT. (See *Collins-Splatt.*)

SPODE, JOSIAH, Esq., of Hawkesyard Park, Staffordshire.

Only child of the late Josiah Spode, Esq., of Great Fenton, co. Stafford, by Mary, dau. of Robert Williamson, Esq., of Knypersley Hall and Longport, co. Stafford; b. 1823; s. 1829; m. 1848 Helen, dau. of William Heywood, Esq., of Broughton, co. Lancaster. Educated at Trinity Coll., Cambridge: is a J.P. and D.L. for co. Stafford (High Sheriff 1856), and a Magistrate for co. Anglesey.—*Hawkesyard Park, Rugeley.*

SPOFFORTH, ROBERT, Esq., of Thorpe, Yorkshire.

Son of the late Robert Spofforth, Esq., of East Thorpe, by Ann, his wife; b. 180–; m. 183– Sarah Ann, dau. of

S: 3

the late Capt. Jefferson. This family have been settled in Yorkshire for nearly three centuries.—*East Thorpe, Malton.*

SPOONER, the Rev. ISAAC.

Eldest son of the late Richard Spooner, Esq., J.P. and D.L., of Leamington, M.P. for N. Warwickshire (who *d.* 1864), by Charlotte, dau. of the late Very Rev. Dr. Nathan Wetherell, Dean of Hereford ; *b.* 1808 ; *m.* 1843 Eliza St. George, dau. of Lieut.-Gen. Ord, R.E. Educated at Clare Coll., Cambridge (B.A. 1831, M.A. 1834), is Vicar of Edgbaston, and Chaplain to Lord Calthorpe. —*Edgbaston Vicarage, Birmingham.*

SPOONER, ISAAC, Esq., of Wightwick, Staffordshire.

Eldest son of the late Isaac Spooner, Esq., of Witton, co. Warwick, by Elizabeth Lucy, dau. of the late John Tyler, Esq., of Redlands, co. Gloucester ; *b.* 1810 ; *m.* 1853 Charlotte Augusta, dau. of the late John Chatfield Tyler, Esq., of Kingswood, co. Gloucester, and has issue,

* Charles Herbert, *b.* 1855.

Mr. Spooner, who was educated at Winchester and Caius Coll., Cambridge (B.A. 1833, M.A. 1837), and called to the Bar at Lincoln's Inn, 1837, is a Magistrate for co. Stafford, and Stipendary Magistrate for South Staffordshire district. This family is an elder branch of the Spooners of Elmdon.—*Wightwick, Wolverhampton.*

SPOONER, WILLIAM, Esq., of Walton, Staffordshire.

Eldest son of the late Ven. William Spooner, Archdeacon of Coventry, and Rector of Elmdon, co. Warwick, by Anna Maria, dau. of Sir Lucius O'Brien, Bart., of Dromoland, co. Clare ; *b.* 1811 ; *m.* 1841 Jane Lydia, dau. of John Wilson, Esq., of Seacroft Hall, W. Riding, and Cliffe Hall, N. Riding, co. York, and has, with other issue,

* William Archibald, M.A. and Fellow of New Coll., Oxford ; *b.* 1845.

Mr. Spooner, who was educated at Oriel Coll., Oxford (B.A. 1832, M.A. 1834), and called to the Bar at Lincoln's Inn 1837, and went the Oxford Circuit, is a Magistrate for co. Stafford, and Judge of County Courts of N. Staffordshire. This family was formerly settled at Tamworth, co. Worcester, and subsequently at Homwood Hall, co. Warwick, and afterwards at Elmdon Hall, in the same county. The elder branch of the family has assumed the name of Lillingston (which see).—*Walton Lodge, Stafford; Oxford and Cambridge Club, s.w.*

SPOOR, HERBERT, Esq., of Whitburn, co. Durham.

Only son of the late Capt. Spoor, 25th Regt., D.L., of Whitburn, co. Durham, and of Warkworth, Northumberland ; *b.* 1857 ; *s.* 1860.—*Whitburn, Sunderland.*

Heir Pres., his only sister Ida Maria Graydon, *b.* 1859.

SPOTTISWOODE, Mrs., of Spottiswoode, Berwickshire.

Helen, second dau. of the late Andrew Wauchope, Esq., of Niddrie Marischall, Midlothian, by Alicia, dau. of William Baird, Esq., of Newbyth, co. Haddington ; *m.* 1809 John Spottiswoode, Esq., J.P. and D.L., of Spottiswoode, who *d.* 1866, leaving, with other surviving issue.

* Alicia Ann, widow of Lord John Douglas-Montagu-Scott (whom see).

Mrs. Spottiswoode is Lady of the Barony of Spottiswoode.—*Spottiswoode, Lauder, N.B.*

SPOTTISWOODE. (See *Farquhar-Spottiswoode.*)

SPRATT, HARMER DEVEREUX, Esq., of Pencil Hill, co. Cork.

Eldest son of the late Thomas Edward Spratt, Esq., of Pencil Hill, by Barbara dau. of Lieut.-Col. Foott, of Milfort, co. Cork ; *b.* 1820 ; *s.* 1833 ; *m.* 1849 Eliza Louisa, only dau. of Edward Townsend Warren, Esq., of Belleville, and grand-niece of the late Sir Augustus Warren, Bart. Educated at Trinity Coll., Dublin ; is Vice-Guardian of the Boyle Union and Vice-Chairman of Mallow Union.—*Pencil Hill, Mallow, co. Cork.*

Heir Pres., his brother Richard, *b.* 1822 ; *m.* 1854 Eliza Louisa, eldest dau. of Henry Baldwin Foott, Esq., of Carrigicunna Castle, co. Cork, and has, with other issue,
* Richard Henry, *b.* 1856.

SPRING-RICE. (See *Monteagle, Lord.*)

SPROSTON, the Rev. SAMUEL THOMAS, of Sproston Wood, Cheshire.

Great-nephew of the late Samuel Sproston, Esq. ; *b.* 1817 ; *s.* 1858 ; *m.* 1846 Frances Maria, dau. of the Rev. George Sproston, and has issue,

* Samuel, *b.* 1848.

Mr. Sproston, who was educated at Trinity Coll., Cambridge (B.A. 1840), was appointed Incumbent of Wednesfield Heath, Staffordshire, 1852.—*Sproston Wood, Wrenbury.*

SPROT, JAMES, Esq., of Spott House, Haddingtonshire.

Second son of the late John Sprot, Esq., of Clapham Common, by Mary, dau. of Benjamin Yule. Esq., of Edinburgh ; *b.* 1804 ; *m.* 1834 Mary, dau. of Richard Watt, Esq., of Bishop Burton. Educated at Trinity Coll., Cambridge ; is a J.P. and D.L. for co. Haddington, Lord of the Barony of Spott, and Patron of that living.—*Spott House, Spott, Dunbar, N.B. ; Conservative Club, s.w.*

SPROT, MARK, Esq., of Garnkirk, Lanarkshire.

Second son of the late Alexander Sprot, Esq. ; *b.* 1795 ; *m.* 1821 Harriet, dau. of the late Rev. Dr. Hill, Principal of St. Andrew's Coll., and by her, who *d.* 1865, has, with other issue,

* Mark, *b.* 182-.

Mr. Sprot, who was called to the Scottish Bar 1818, is a Magistrate for co. Lanark, and Lord of the Barony of Garnkirk.—*Garnkirk House, Moodiesburn, Glasgow, N.B.*

SPROT, MARK, Esq., of Riddell, Roxburghshire.

Eldest son of the late John Sprot, Esq., of Riddell, by Mary, dau. of Benjamin Yule, Esq. ; *b.* 1802 ; *s.* 1817 ; *m.* 1829 Elizabeth, dau. of John Shewoll, Esq., and has, with other issue,

* John, *b.* 1830.

Mr. Sprot, who was educated at Trinity Coll., Cambridge, is a J.P. and D.L. for co. Roxburgh, a Magistrate for co. Selkirk, and Lord of the Barony of Riddell. —*Riddell, Selkirk ; New Club, Edinburgh.*

SPRY, Sir SAMUEL THOMAS, Knt., of Tregolls, Cornwall (cr. 1840).

Son of the late Admiral Spry (formerly Davy) of Place House, Cornwall, by Anna Maria, sister and heir of Samuel Thomas, Esq., of Tregolls ; *b.* 1804. Educated at Exeter Coll., Oxford (B.A. 1826) ; is a J.P. and D.L. for Cornwall, and Patron of 1 living ; has been Lieut. of the Corps of Gentlemen-at-Arms, was M.P. for Bodmin 1832–41 and 1843–7.— *Tregolls, Truro ; Union and Windom Clubs, s.w. ; 8, Arlington Street, s.w.*

SPRY, RICHARD, Esq., of Guddra, Cornwall.

Younger son of the late Admiral Thomas Davy, of Place House, Cornwall (who assumed the name of Spry), by

Anna Maria, sister and heir of Samuel Thomas, Esq., of Tregolls, Cornwall, and brother of Sir S. T. Spry (whom see); *b.* 1806. Educated at Wadham Coll., Oxford (B.A. 1828, M.A. 1831); is a J.P. and D.L. for Cornwall.—*Cuddra, St. Austell.*

+ SPURGEON, ASTLEY COOPER, Esq., of Gressenhall, Norfolk.
Son of the late A. Spurgeon, Esq.; *m.* 18— a dau. of the Rev. Robert Norris, formerly Rector of Tatterford. Is a Magistrate for Norfolk, and Lord of the Manor of Gressenhall Parva.—*Gressenhall, E. Dereham.*

SPURWAY, the Rev. EDWARD BRIAN COMBE, of Heathfield, Somerset.
Youngest son of the late Capt. John Spurway, R.N., of Milverton, Somerset, by Frances, eldest dau. and co-heir of William Purlewent, Esq., of Shepton Mallet, Somerset; *b.* 1825; *m.* 1862 Harriet Mary, eldest dau. of Christopher Wallis Popham, Esq., of Trevarno, Cornwall, and has, with other issue,

* Edward Popham, *b.* 1863.

Mr. Spurway, who was educated at Trinity Coll., Cambridge (B.A. 1848, M.A. 1851), is Rector and Patron of Heathfield.—*Heathfield Rectory, Taunton.*

SPURWAY, JOHN PURLEWENT, Esq., of Spring Grove Park, Somerset.
Eldest son of the late Capt. John Spurway, R.N., of Spring Grove Park, by Frances, eldest dau. and heir of William Purlewent, Esq., of Shepton Mallet and Bath, Somerset; *b.* 1819; *s.* 1866; *m.* 1866 Fanny, dau. of the late William Stephens Dicken, Esq., Deputy Inspector-General of Bengal Medical Service, and has issue,
* Wyndham Byrt Purlewent, *b.* 1867.—*Spring Grove Park, Milverton.*

SQUIRE, WILLIAM, Esq., of Cheltenham, Gloucestershire.
Eldest son of William Walcot Squire, Esq., of Cheltenham, by Julia, eldest dau. of the late Thomas Alderson Cooke, Esq., of Peterborough; *b.* 1820; *m.* 1853 Emma, youngest dau. of the late John Perfect, Esq., of Pontefract, co. York, and has, with other issue,

* William Walcot, *b.* 1857.

Mr. Squire, who was educated at Eton, was formerly an Officer in the 3rd Dragoon Guards. This family is a younger branch of that of the Squires of Barton Place, Suffolk (whom see).—*8, Lansdown Villas, Cheltenham.*

SQUIRE, WILLIAM THOMAS, Esq., of Barton, Suffolk.
Son of the late Wright Thomas Squire, Esq., of Peterborough, by Mary, dau. of the Rev. John Burton Philipson; *b.* 1807; *s.* 1812; *m.* 1838 Anne, dau. of James Stewart, Esq., of Boston, U.S., and has, with other issue,

* Wright Thomas, Lieut. Bombay Army; *b.* 1840.

Mr. Squire, who was educated at Eton and Trinity Coll. Cambridge, was formerly Capt. 2nd Life Guards.—*Barton Place, Mildenhall ; Junior United Service Club, s.w.*

STACEY, the Rev. THOMAS, of Old Castle, Glamorganshire.
Third son of the late Mr. John Stacey, of Carmarthen, by Ann, dau. of Mr. Rice Williams, of Dryslwyn, co. Carmarthen; *b.* 1796; *m.* 1824 Mary Ann, dau. of John Richards, Esq., of Cardiff, and has, with other issue,

* John Thomas Cyril, in Holy Orders; *b.* 1828; *m.* 1860 Mary, only surviving dau. of T. W. Booker-Blakemore,

Esq., M.P., of The Leys, co. Hereford, and Velindra, co. Glamorgan.

Mr. Stacey, who was educated at Jesus Coll., Oxford (B.A. 1820, M.A. 1824), is a J.P. and D.L. for co. Glamorgan; Precentor and Honorary Canon of Llandaff Cathedral, and Rector of Coity; was formerly Vicar of Roath and Rector of Gelligaer.—*Old Castle, Bridgend.*

STACK, Sir MAURICE, K.C.B. (cr. 1867).
Second son of the late Rev. John Stack (Fellow of Trinity Coll., Dublin), by Eliza, dau. of the late Capt. Barker, R.N.; *b.* 1796; *m.* 1824 Cecilia, 2nd dau. of the late Hugh Spottiswoode, Esq., of the Madras Civil Service, and has issue,

* Charles Edward, Capt. 1st Bombay Lancers, *b.* 1826 ; *m.* 1867 Isabella Helen, eldest dau. of the late Thomas Grainger, Esq., of Craig Park, Midlothian.

Sir M. Stack is a Major-Gen. in the Bombay Army.—*Broomville, Tullow, co. Carlow ; United Service Club, s.w.*

STACK, NATHANIEL MASSEY, Esq., of Ballyconory, co. Kerry.
Third son of the late John Stack, Esq., of Ballyconory, by the Hon. Catherine Jane, younger dau. of Eyre, 1st Lord Clarina; *b.* 1811; *s.* his brother 1856 ; *m.* 1858 Catherine Jane, dau. of the late Richard FitzGerald, Esq., of the Castle, Listowel, co. Kerry, and has, with other issue,

* George FitzGerald, *b.* 1860.

Mr. Stack is a Magistrate for co. Kerry, Lord of the Manor of Ballyconory, and a Major-General in the Army; late Lieut.-Col. 71st Foot.—*Ballyconory, Lake Cara, co. Kerry ; United Service Club, s.w.*

STACPOOLE, RICHARD, Esq., of Eden Vale, co. Clare.
Son of the late Richard John Stacpoole, Esq., J.P. and D.L., of Eden Vale (who was High Sheriff of co. Clare 1827), by Jane, dau. of the late Andrew Stacpoole, Esq., of Ballyally, co. Clare; *b.* 1826 ; *s.* 1866. Educated at Trinity Coll., Dublin ; is a Magistrate for co. Clare (High Sheriff 1864).—*Eden Vale, Ennis, co. Clare.*

Heir Pres., his brother George William, *b.* 1828.

STACPOOLE, Capt. WILLIAM, of Ballyally, co. Clare.
Eldest son of the late Andrew Stacpoole, Esq., of Ballyally, by Diana, dau. of Daniel Finucane, Esq., of Stamer Park, Ennis ; *b.* 1830 ; *s.* 185–. Educated at Cheltenham Coll., and Trinity Coll., Dublin ; is a Magistrate for co. Clare and a Capt. in the Clare Militia; elected M.P. for Ennis 1860.—*Ballyally, Ennis, co. Clare ; Kildare Street Club, Dublin ; Union and Junior United Service Clubs, s.w.*

STAFFORD, Lord (HENRY VALENTINE STAFFORD-JERNINGHAM).—Cr. 1640.
Eldest son of George William, 8th Lord, by his 1st wife Frances, dau. of the late Edward Sulyarde, Esq., of Wetherden, Suffolk ; *b.* 1802 ; *s.* 1851; *m.* 1st 1829 Julia, dau. of the late Edward Charles Howard, Esq. (she *d.* 1856) ; 2nd 1859 Emma Eliza, 2nd dau. of Frederick Sewallis Gerard, Esq., of Aspull House, co. Lancaster. Is a J.P. and D.L. for Norfolk ; Lord of the Manor and Patron of Cossey ; was M.P. for Pontefract 1830–4. The title was forfeited in 1678, but the attainder was reversed in 1824.—*Cossey Park, Norwich ; Athenæum Club, s.w. ; 69, Eaton Place, s.w.*

Heir Pres., his nephew Augustus Frederick Fitzherbert, eldest son of the late Hon. Edward Jerningham, who *d.* 1849, by Marianne, dau. of the late John Smythe, Esq.); *b.* 1830.

STAFFORD. (See under *Sutherland, Duke of.*)

STAFFORD-JERNINGHAM. (See *Jerningham*.)

STAG. (See *Blake, of Twizel.*)

+STAINFORTHE, RICHARD TERRICKE, Esq., of Barton-le-Street, Yorkshire.
Son of the late R. Stainforthe, Esq.; *b.* 18—. Is a Dep.-Lieut. for the N. Riding of co. York.—*Barton-le-Street, Malton.*

STAINSBY-CONANT. (See *Pigott-Carleton*.)

STAIR, Earl of (JOHN HAMILTON DALRYMPLE, K.T.).—Cr. 1703.
Elder son of North Hamilton, 9th Earl, by his 1st wife, Margaret, dau. of the late James Penny, Esq., of Arrad, co. Lancaster; *b.* 1819; *s.* 1864; *m.* 1846 Louisa Jane Henrietta Emily de Franquetot, dau. of Augustin, late Duke de Coigny. Educated at Harrow; is a Dep.-Lieut. for co. Lanark, Lord-Lieutenant of co. Wigton, late Capt. 1st Wigton Artillery Volunteers; was M.P. for co. Wigton 1841–56, and formerly Capt. Scots Fusilier Guards; sits in the House of Lords as Lord Oxenfoord, U.K. (cr. 1841).—*Oxenfoord Castle, Edinburgh Lochinch, Stranraer, N.B.*

Heir, his son John Hew North Gustave Henry, Viscount Dalrymple; educated at Harrow; *b.* 1848.

STALLARD, the Rev. GEORGE, M.A.
Eldest son of the late George Stallard, Esq.; *b.* 1813; *m.* 1839 Anne Fane, only surviving dau. of John Taylor, Esq., M.D., of Bath, and has, with other issue,

* Arthur Gordon Bury, B.A. of Exeter Coll., Oxford, in Holy Orders; *b.* 1843.

Mr. Stallard, who was educated at St. John's Coll., Cambridge (B.A. 1843. M.A. 1847), is Incumbent of East Grafton, and a Diocesan Inspector of Schools; he was Vicar of St. Mary's, Marlborough, 1847–51.—*East Grafton, Marlborough.*

STAMER, the Rev. Sir LOVELACE TOMLINSON, Bart., of Beauchamp, co. Dublin (cr. 1809).
Eldest son of the late Sir Lovelace Stamer, Bart., of Beauchamp, by Caroline, only dau. of the late John Tomlinson, Esq., of Cliffville co. Stafford; *b.* 1829; *s.* as 3rd Bart. 1860; *m.* 1857 Ellen Isabel, only dau. of Joseph Deut, Esq., of Ribston Hall, co. York. Educated at Rugby and Trinity Coll., Cambridge (B.A. 1853, M.A. 1856). Rector of Stoke-on-Trent, and Rural Dean. This family is of Saxon origin, and possessed large estates in Essex.—*Cliffville, Stoke-on-Trent.*

Heir, his son Lovelace, *b.* 1859.

STAMFORD AND WARRINGTON, Earl of (GEORGE HARRY GREY).—Cr. 1628.
Only son of George Harry, Lord Grey, of Groby (who *d.* 1835), by Lady Katharine, dau. of Francis, 6th Earl of Wemyss, and grandson of George Harry, 6th Earl; *b.* 1827; *s.* his grandfather as 7th Earl 1845; *m.* 1st 1848 Elizabeth, dau. of Mr. John Billage; 2nd 1855 Katharine, dau. of the late Mr. Henry Cocks. Educated at Eton and Trinity Coll., Cambridge; is a Dep.-Lieut. for co. Stafford, and Patron of 8 livings; late Capt. Cheshire Yeomanry.—*Dunham Massey, Knutsford; Bradgate Park, Leicester; Enville Hall, Stourbridge; Carlton, Conservative, Travellers' and Boodle's Clubs, s.w.; 33, Hill Street, w.*

Heir Pres., his 2nd cousin Harry, in Holy Orders (eldest son of the late Rev. Harry Grey, who *d.* 1860, by his 1st wife Frances Elizabeth, dau. of Hugh Ellis, Esq., of Carnarvon); *b.* 1812; *m.* 1844 Miss Susan Gaydon.

876

STANCOMB, JOHN PERKINS, Esq., of The Prospect, Wilts.
Eldest son of the late John Stancomb, Esq., of The Prospect, by Mary, dau. of William Perkins, Esq., of Trowbridge; *b.* 1814; *s.* 1850; *m.* 1839 his cousin Margaret, dau. of the late William Stancomb, Esq., and has, with other issue,

* John Frederick, *b.* 1847.

Mr. Stancomb is a Magistrate for Wilts.—*The Prospect, Trowbridge.*

STANDISH, CHARLES HENRY LIONEL WIDDRINGTON, Esq., of Standish Hall, Lancashire.
Eldest son of the late Charles Standish, Esq., J.P. and D.L., of Standish Hall (formerly M.P. for Wigan), by Emma, dau. of M. de Mathiesen, of Paris; *b.* 1822; *s.* 1863; *m.* 1846 Sabina de Noailles, dau. of the Prince de Poix. Is a Dep.-Lieut. for co. Lancaster. The grandfather of the present owner, Thomas Strickland, Esq., of Sizergh, assumed the name of Standish.—*Standish Hall, Wigan.*

STANDISH, ROWLAND EDMOND WALTER PERY, Esq., of Farley Hill, Berks, and Scaleby, Cumberland.
Second son of the late Rowland Stephenson, Esq., of Farley Hill (who assumed the name of Standish in 1834, and *d.* 1843), by Lady Lucy Pery, dau. of Edmond, 1st Earl of Limerick; *b.* 1826; *s.* his brother 1845; *m.* 1850 Caroline, dau. of Samuel Clogstoun, Esq. Is a J.P. and D.L. for Cumberland and a Magistrate for Berks; was formerly in the 6th Foot.—*Scaleby Castle, Carlisle; Farley Hill, Reading.*

Heir Pres., his brother William Cecil Standish; *b.* 1821; *m.* 1855 Emma, dau. of William Robins, Esq., of Hagley House, Stourbridge, and has, with other issue, * William, *b.* 1858.

STANDISH, WILLIAM STANDISH CARR, Esq., of Duxbury Park, Lancashire, and of Cocken Hall, co. Durham.
Only son of the late William Standish Standish, Esq., of Cocken Hall and Duxbury Park (who was a Dep.-Lieut. for co. Lancaster, and High Sheriff 1846, and who assumed the name of Standish in lieu of Carr); *b.* 1835; *s.* 1856. Is in the Commission of the Peace for co. Lancaster; formerly in the 7th Hussars. Represents in the maternal line the family of Standish of Duxbury, and in the paternal line that of Carr of Cocken, co. Durham.—*Duxbury Park, Chorley.*

Heir Pres., his sister.

STANE, JOHN BRAMSTON, Esq., of Buckfield, Hants.
Only son of the late Rev. John Bramston, of Forest Hall, Essex (who assumed the name of Stane), by Maria, dau. of S. Newton, Esq., of St. Croix; *b.* 1803; *s.* 1857. Educated at Eton and Ch. Ch., Oxford; is a J.P. and D.L. for Essex. This family is a junior branch of the Bramstons of Skreens. *Buckfield, Sherfield, Basingstoke; Arthur's and Travellers' Clubs, s.w.; 19, Half Moon Street, w.*

STANFORD, Sir ROBERT, Knt. (cr. 1859).
Eldest son of the late Major Stanford, formerly of co. Mayo, by his 1st wife, a dau. of the late Robert Hopkin, Esq.; *b.* 1803; *m.* 1832 Mary, only dau. of the late Major-General Loudman, H.E.I.C.'s Service, and has issue. Sir R. Stanford, who was formerly Capt. Inniskilling Dragoons, served with distinction in India and Africa.

STANFORD, JOHN FREDERICK, Esq., F.R.S.
Only surviving son of the late Major Stanford, of Ballina-Stanford, co. Mayo (who was formerly an Officer in the 1st Life Guards), by his 2nd wife, Mary,

2nd dau. of William Gorton, Esq., of Windsor; b. 1815. Educated at Eton and Christ's Coll., Cambridge (B.A. 1838, M.A. 1842); called to the Bar at Lincoln's Inn 1844; is a Magistrate for Middlesex and a Dep.-Lieut. for Berks; was M.P. for Reading 1849–52. —*Foley House, Langham Place*, w.

STANFORD, of Preston Hall, Sussex. (See *Bennett*.)

STANHOPE, Earl (PHILIP HENRY STANHOPE, F.R.S., F.S.A., D.C.L., LL.D.).—Cr. 1718. Eldest son of Philip Henry, 4th Earl, by the Hon. Katharine, dau. of Robert, 1st Lord Carington; b. 1805; s. 1855; m. 1834 Emily Harriet, dau. of the late General Sir Edward Kerrison, Bart., M.P. Is a J.P. and D.L. for Kent, President of the Society of Antiquaries, a Trustee of the British Museum, and Patron of 1 living; Author of a 'History of England,' and other works; was M.P. for Hertford 1835–52; elected Lord Rector of Aberdeen 1858; cr. Hon. LL.D., Cambridge, 1834. Descended from a common ancestor with the Earls of Chesterfield and Harrington.—*Chevening, Sevenoaks; Athenæum, Carlton, and Travellers' Clubs*, s.w.; 3, *Grosvenor Place Houses*, s.w.

Heir, his son Arthur Philip. Viscount Mahon; educated at Harrow; is M.P. for Leominster, and Lieut. and Capt. Grenadier Guards; b. 1838.

STANHOPE, Sir EDWYN FRANCIS SCUDAMORE, Bart., of Holme Lacy, Herefordshire (cr. 1807). Only son of the late Admiral Sir Henry Elwyn Stanhope, Bart., of Stanwell, Middlesex, by Margaret, dau. of Francis Malbone, Esq., of Newport, Rhode Island; b 1793; s. as 2nd Bart. 1814; m. 1820 Mary, dau. of T. Dowell, Esq., of Parkers' Well, Devon (she d. 1859). Is a J.P. and D.L. for co. Hereford (High Sheriff 1843). Lord of the Manor of Holme Lacy, and Patron of 2 livings, and a Capt. R.N., retired.—*Holme Lacy, Hereford; United Service Club*, s.w.; 1, *Regent Street*, s.w.

Heir, his son Henry Elwyn Chandos, a J.P. and D.L. for co. Hereford; b. 1821; m. 1851 Dorothea, eldest dau. of Sir Adam Hay, Bart., of Haystonn, co. Peebles, and has, with other issue, * Edwyn Francis, b. 1854.

STANHOPE, the Rev. BERKELEY LIONEL SCUDAMORE. Third son of Sir Edwyn Stanhope, Bart., of Holme Lacy, by Mary, dau. of Thomas Dowell, Esq., of Parkers' Well, Devon; b. 1824; m. 1858 Caroline Sarah, eldest dau. of the late John Arkwright, Esq., of Hampton Court, co. Hereford. Educated at Balliol Coll., Oxford, and was sometime Fellow of All Souls Coll. (B.A. 1845, M.A. 1851); is a Magistrate for co. Hereford, and Rector of Byford; was formerly Vicar of Bosbury.—*Byford Rectory, Hereford*.

STANHOPE, JAMES BANKS, Esq., of Revesby Abbey, Lincolnshire. Only son of the late Col. the Hon. James Hamilton Stanhope, of Revesby Abbey, by Lady Frederica Louisa, eldest dau. of the 3rd Lord of Mansfield, and great-grandson of James, 1st Earl Stanhope; b. 1821; s. 1824. Educated at Westminster; is a J.P. and D.L. for co. Lincoln, and Patron of 1 living; has been M.P. for North Lincolnshire since 1851; was formerly Lieut. Rifle Brigade; is in remainder to the Earldom of Stanhope.—*Revesby Abbey, Boston; Carlton, Boodle's, and Travellers' Clubs*. s.w.

STANHOPE, Lieut.-General PHILIP SPENCER. Sixth son of the late Walter Spencer-Stanhope, Esq., of Cannon Hall, co. York, by Mary Winifred, sole dau. and heiress of Thomas Babington Pulleine, Esq., of Carlton Hall, co. York; b. 1799; m. 1865 Mary Catherine, widow

of Edward Rowland Strickland, Esq. (she d. 1875). Educated at Westminster and Sandhurst; appointed to the Grenadier Guards 1816; is a Lieut.-General in the Army, and Col. 13th Foot. This family is a distant branch of that of the Earl of Chesterfield.—*United Service, Boodle's, and Travellers' Clubs*, s.w.; 70, *Harley Street*, w.

STANHOPE. (See under *Chesterfield, Earl of*, and *Harrington, Earl of*.)

STANHOPE. (See *Roddam*.)

STANHOPE. (See *Spencer-Stanhope*.)

+STANHOPE-STOTT, GEORGE, Esq., of Eccleshill Hall, Yorkshire. Eldest son of the late George Stott, Esq., of Manchester, by Mary, dau. of Barton Stanhope, Esq.; b. 1795; m. 1st 1828 Anne, dau. of — Ford, Esq.; 2nd 1838 Mary, dau. of — Purtington, Esq., of Manchester, and has issue,

* Herbert, b. 1844.

Mr. Stanhope-Stott, who is a Col. in the Indian Army, retired, descends in the female line from a junior branch of the house of Chesterfield.—*Eccleshill Hall, Bradford*.

STANIER-BROADE, FRANCIS PHILIP, Esq., of Fenton Vivian, Staffordshire. Eldest son of the late Francis Stanier, Esq., of Madeley Manor, co. Stafford, by Mary Stanier, dau. of Thomas Sparrow Wilkinson, Esq., of Newcastle-under-Lyne; b. 1838; s. 1856; m. 1860 Caroline, dau. of General Justice, of Green Park, Bath, and has, with other issue,

* Frank Justice, b. 1862.

Mr. Stanier-Broade, who is a Magistrate for co. Stafford, Lord of the Manor of Fenton, and Capt. 3rd K. O. Staffordshire Militia, took the name of Broade in 1856, under the will of Philip Barnes Broade, Esq., of Fenton Vivian.—*Fenton Vivian, Stoke-on-Trent; Silverdale, Newcastle*.

+STANIFORTH, the Rev. THOMAS, of Storrs Hall, Westmoreland. Son of the late Thomas Staniforth, Esq.; b. 1810. Educated at Eton and Ch. Ch., Oxford (B.A. 1830, M.A. 1833); was Rector of Bolton-by-Bolland, co. York, 1831–59.—*Storrs Hall, Windermere*.

STANILAND, MEABURN, Esq., of Harrington Hall, Lincolnshire. Son of the late James Staniland, Esq., of Harrington Hall, co. Lincoln, by Amy, dau. of James Meaburn, Esq., of Boston; b. 1809; m. 1840 Emma, dau. of Robert William Stainbank, Esq., of Skirbeck, co. Lincoln. Is a Magistrate for co. Lincoln, Deputy Clerk of the Peace for co. Lincoln, a Solicitor in practice at Boston, and Patron of 1 living; was M.P. for Boston 1859–65, and 1866–7.—*Harrington Hall, Spilsby; Reform Club*, s.w.

STANLEY OF ALDERLEY, Lord (EDWARD JOHN STANLEY, P.C.).—Cr. 1839. Eldest son of John Thomas, 1st Lord, by Lady Maria Josepha, dau. of John, 1st Earl of Sheffield; b. 1802; s. 1850; m. 1826 the Hon. Henrietta Mary, dau. of Henry Augustus, 13th Viscount Dillon. Graduated B.A. 1823 at Ch. Ch., Oxford; is a J.P. and D.L. for Cheshire, and Patron of 2 livings; was M.P. for Hindon 1831–2, for North Cheshire 1832–48; Joint Secretary of the Treasury 1835–41, President of the Board of Trade 1855–8; Postmaster General 1830–66; has been Under-Secretary for Foreign Affairs and the Home Department; called to the Upper House

as Lord Eddisbury 1848.—*Alderley Park, Congleton ; Reform and Travellers' Clubs*; s.w. ; 40, *Dover Street*, w.

Heir, his son Henry Edward John, *b.* 1827 ; educated at Eton and Trinity Coll., Cambridge ; appointed Précis Writer in the Foreign Office 1845 ; Attaché at Constantinople 1851 ; was Secretary of Legation at Athens 1854–9.

STANLEY, the Hon. CHARLES JAMES FOX, of Loxley Park, Staffordshire.

Third son of Edward, 13th Earl of Derby, by his cousin Charlotte Margaret, dau. of the late Rev. Geoffrey Hornby ; *b.* 1808 ; *m.* 1836 Frances Augusta, dau. of the late General Sir Henry Frederick Campbell, K.C.B., and has, with other issue,

* Charles Edward, *b.* 1843.

Mr. Stanley, who was educated at Eton, is a Magistrate for co. Lancaster and for the N. Riding of co. York, and Col. Lancashire Militia ; was formerly Col. Grenadier Guards.—*Loxley Park, Uttoxeter.*

STANLEY, the Hon. FREDERICK ARTHUR.

Youngest son of Edward Geoffrey, 14th Earl of Derby, K.G., by the Hon. Emma Caroline, 2nd dau. of Edward, 1st Lord Skelmersdale ; *b.* 1841 ; *m.* 1864 Constance, eldest dau. of the 4th Earl of Clarendon, and has, with other issue,

* Edward George Villiers, *b.* 1865.

Mr. Stanley, who was educated at Eton, is a Magistrate for co. Lancaster, late Lieut. and Capt. Grenadier Guards; was elected M.P. for Preston 1865.—*Knowsley, Prescot ; Carlton Club*, s.w. ; 23, *St. James's Square*, s.w.

STANLEY, the Hon. HENRY THOMAS, of Stanley Hall, Lancashire.

Second son of Edward, 13th Earl of Derby, K.G., by his cousin Charlotte Margaret, 2nd dau. of the late Rev. Geoffrey Hornby, Rector of Winwick ; *b.* 1803 ; *m.* 1835 Ann, dau. of the late Richard Woolhouse, Esq., and has, with other issue,

* Edward Henry, *b.* 1838.

Mr. Stanley, who is a J.P. and D.L. for co. Lancaster, was M.P. for Preston 1832–7.—*Stanley Hall, Preston.*

STANLEY, the Hon. WILLIAM OWEN, of Penrhos, Anglesey.

Second son of John Thomas, 1st Lord Stanley of Alderley, by Lady Maria Josepha, eldest dau. of John, 1st Earl of Sheffield ; *b.* 1802 ; *m.* 1832 Ellen, dau. of the late Sir John Williams, Bart. Educated at Eton ; a J.P. and D.L. for Anglesey ; formerly Capt. Grenadier Guards ; was M.P. for Anglesey 1837–47, for Chester 1850–7 ; has been since then M.P. for Beaumaris.—*Penrhos, Holyhead, I. of Anglesey ; Travellers' Club*, s.w. ; 40, *Grosvenor Place*, s.w.

STANLEY, CHARLES, Esq., of Ronghan Park, co. Tyrone.

Fifth son of the late John Stanley, Esq., of Armagh, by Septima, dau. of Thomas Walker. Esq., of Richhill, co. Armagh ; *b.* 1817 ; *m.* 1847 Jane Charlotte, dau. of Joseph Trimble, Esq., of Ashfield Park, Clogher, co. Tyrone, and has issue, one daughter. Mr. Stanley, who was educated at Armagh Coll., is a Magistrate for cos. Tyrone and Armagh.—*Ronghan Park, Dungannon.*

STANLEY, EDWARD, Esq., of Crosshall, Lancashire.

Eldest son of the late James Stanley, Esq., of Crosshall, by Augusta, dau. of John Cornwall, Esq. ; *b.* 1789 ; *m.* 1819 Lady Mary, 2nd dau. of James, 8th Earl of Lauderdale, and has, with other issue,

* Edward James, *b.* 1836.

Mr. Stanley, who was educated at Trinity Coll., Cambridge (B.A. 1812), is a J.P. and D.L. for co. Lancaster. This family is a younger branch of that of the Earl of Derby.—*Crosshall, Ormskirk ; 14, Grosvenor Square*, w.

+ STANLEY, JAMES THOMAS, Esq., late . . . attiford House, Somerset.

Younger son of the late Capt. Bouteïn, by Mary Anne, only child and heir of the late Sir Edmond Stanley, M.P., Prime Serjeant of Ireland (whose name he assumed by Royal licence); *b.* 1821 ; *m.* 1853 Frances Susannah Caroline, 4th dau. of Charles Douglas Halford, Esq., of West Lodge, Bergholt, Suffolk. Educated at Eton ; is a Magistrate for Somerset, and Major 2nd Somerset Militia ; formerly Capt. 89th Foot ; is maternally descended from a younger branch of the family of the Earl of Derby, but which had been settled in Ireland since 1688.

STANLEY, SIDNEY, Esq., of Longstowe Hall, Cambridgeshire.

Son of the late William Wentworth, Esq., of Cambridge, by Mary Ann, dau. of George Newport, Esq., of London, and grand-nephew of Joseph Stanley, Esq., of Cambridge, whose name he assumed in 1856 ; *b.* 1828 ; *m.* 1859 Sarah, dau. of Edmond Foster, Esq., of Cambridge, and has, with other issue,

* Charles Wentworth, *b.* 1860.

Mr. Stanley, who was educated at C.C.C., Cambridge (B.A. 1850, M.A. 1853), is a Magistrate for co. Cambridge, Lord of the Manor of Longstowe, and Lieut. Hunts Yeomanry.—*Longstowe Hall, Caxton ; Union Club*, s.w.

STANLEY, WILLIAM, Esq., of Ponsonby Hall, Cumberland.

Eldest son of the late Edward Stanley, Esq., J.P. and D.L., of Ponsonby Hall (formerly M.P. for W. Cumberland), by Mary, dau. of William Douglas, Esq., a Judge in India ; *b.* 1829 ; *s.* 1863 ; *m.* 1859 Caroline, eldest dau. of Sir George Musgrave, Bart., of Edenhall, Cumberland, and has, with other issue,

* Edward, *b.* 1859.

Mr. Stanley, who was educated at Ch. Ch., Oxford, is a J.P. and D.L. for Cumberland, Lord of the Manors of Ponsonby, Birkby, Austhwaite, and Birker, and Patron of 2 livings. This family is descended from a common ancestor with the Earl of Derby, and the family estates at Delegarth have descended through an unbroken male succession for 500 years.—*Ponsonby Hall, Whitehaven.*

STANLEY. (See under *Derby, Earl of.*)

STANLEY, of Hooton. (See *Stanley-Errington.*)

STANLEY. (See *Sloane-Stanley.*)

STANLEY-ERRINGTON, Sir ROWLAND, Bart., of Sandhoe, Northumberland (cr. 1661).

Eldest surviving son of the late Sir Thomas Stanley-Massey-Stanley, Bart., of Hooton (who *d.* 1841), by Mary, dau. of Sir Carnaby Haggerston, Bart. ; *b.* 1809 ; *s.* his brother as 11th Bart. 1863 ; *m.* 1839 Julia, dau. of the late General Sir John Macdonald, K.C.B. (she *d.* 1860). Is a J.P. and D.L. for Northumberland ; assumed the name of Errington in 1826 under the will of Henry Errington, Esq., of Red Rice, Herts, and assumed his patronymic in 1863, on succeeding to the Baronetcy.—*Sandhoe House, Hexham ; Paddington Hall, Newton ; b. Stratford Place*, w.

Heir Prev., his brother John, *b.* 1810 ; *m.* 1841 Maria, only dau. of the Baron de Talleyrand.

STANNUS, ROBERT TREVOR, Esq., of Portarlington, Queen's Co.

Eldest surviving son of the late Thomas Stannus, Esq., of Portarlington and of Carlingford, co. Louth, by Catherine, dau. of Robert Hamilton, Esq., of Clonsilla, co. Dublin ; *b.* 1821 ; *s.* 1851 ; *m.* 1852 Caroline Sophia,

dau. of John Hamilton, Esq., LL.D. Is a Magistrate for Queen's Co., and a retired Capt. Bengal Army.—*Portarlington, Queen's Co.*

STANSFELD, GEORGE, Esq., of Settle, Yorkshire.

Eldest son of the late Robert Stansfeld, Esq., of Field House, co. York, eldest male representative of the ancient family of Stansfeld, or Stansfield, of Stansfield, in the parish of Halifax; *b.* 1803; *m.* 1834 Sarah, dau. of William Birkbeck, Esq., and has, with other issue,

* George, *b.* 1836; *m.* 1867 Hannah, dau. of John Foster, Esq., of Hornby Castle. co. York.

Mr. Stansfeld is a Magistrate for cos. York and Lancaster, a Barrister-at-Law, and Banker at Settle.—*Settle, Yorkshire.*

STANSFELD, HENRY WILLIAM, Esq., of Flockton Manor, Yorkshire.

Second son of the late William Stansfeld, Esq., of Flockton Manor (who *d.* 1835), by Margaret, dau. of James Milnes, Esq.; *b.* 1828; *m.* 1858 Anne Walker, younger dau. of the late George M'Kay Sutherland, Esq., of Aberarder; and has, with other issue,

* Logan Sutherland, *b.* 1859.

Mr. Stansfeld is a Magistrate for the W. Riding of Yorkshire.—*Flockton Manor, Wakefield.*

STANSFELD, JAMES, Esq., of Moorlands, Yorkshire.

Seventh son of the late David Stansfeld, Esq., of Leeds, by Sarah, dau. and heir of Thomas Wolrich, Esq., of Armley, co. York; *b.* 1792; *m.* 1817 Emma, dau. of the Rev. John Ralph, of Halifax, and has, with other issue,

* James, M.P. for Halifax, LL.B. of University Coll., London. a Barrister-at-Law of the Inner Temple, late Under Sec. of State for India, and formerly a Lord of the Admiralty; *b.* 1820; *m.* 1844 Caroline, dau. of the late W. H. Ashurst, Esq.

Mr. Stansfeld is a Magistrate for the W. Riding of Yorkshire, and Judge of the Yorkshire County Court.—*Moorlands, Halifax.*

STANSFELD, ROBERT, Esq., of Field House, Yorkshire.

Second son of the late Robert Stansfeld, Esq., of Field House; *b.* 1805; *m.* 1834 Hannah Louisa, dau. of the late L. F. C. Johnston, Esq., one of Her Majesty's Judges of the Island of Trinidad, and by her, who *d.* 1864, has, with other issue,

* Robert Johnston, Capt. 38th Foot; *b.* 1838.

Mr. Stansfeld is a Magistrate for the W. Riding of Yorkshire, and Major in the 6th West York Militia; late 19th Regt.—*Field House, Halifax; Junior United Service Club, s.w.*

STANSFELD, THOMAS WOLRYCHE, Esq., of Weetwood Grove, Yorkshire.

Eldest son of Hatton Hamer Stansfeld, Esq., by Elizabeth, dau. of Woodhouse Crompton, Esq., of Warwick, and cousin of T. W. Stansfeld, Esq., late of Burley Wood; *b.* 1822; *m.* 1851 Marian, eldest dau. of Edward Townsend, Esq., of Paxton Hill, Hunts (she *d.* 1861); 2nd 1863 Louisa Agnes, 2nd dau. of J. D. Chapman, Esq., of Highbury, and has, with other issue,

* Edward, *b.* 1852.

Mr. Stansfeld, who is a Merchant at Bradford, represents a younger branch of an ancient Yorkshire family.—*Weetwood Grove, Leeds.*

STANSFIELD. (See *Crompton-Stansfield.*)

STANTON, ALFRED JOHN, Esq., of The Thrupp, Gloucestershire.

Second son of William Henry Stanton, Esq., of The Thrupp, by Jane, dau. of Roger Smith, Esq., of The Manor House, Walworth, Surrey; *b.* 1825; *m.* 1st 1857 Anna, eldest dau. of the late John Alexander, Esq., of Newtownlimavady, Ireland (she *d.* 1858); 2nd 1862 Harriet Margaret, eldest dau. of H. H. Wilton, Esq., of Whitminster House, co. Gloucester, and has issue,

* Two daus.

Mr. Stanton is a Magistrate for co. Gloucester.—*The Thrupp, Stroud.*

STANTON, WILLIAM HENRY, Esq., of The Thrupp, Gloucestershire.

Son of the late William Stanton, Esq., of Stroud, by Ann, dau. of John Caruthers, Esq., of Holmains, N.B.; *b.* 1790; *m.* 1823 Jane, eldest dau. of the late Roger Smith, Esq., of The Manor House, Walworth, Surrey, and has, with other issue,

* William Henry, B.A. of Exeter Coll., Oxford; *b.* 1824; *m.* 1851 Mary, dau. of C. Lawrence, Esq., of Cirencester.

Mr. Stanton, who is a J.P. and D.L. for co. Gloucester, was M.P. for Stroud 1841-52.—*The Thrupp, Stroud.*

STAPLES, Sir NATHANIEL ALEXANDER, Bart., of Lissane, co. Tyrone (cr. 1628).

Son of the late Rev. John Molesworth Staples, Rector of Lissane and Moville, co. Tyrone (who *d.* 1858), by Annie, dau. of the late Most Rev. Nathaniel Alexander, D.D., Lord Bishop of Meath; and nephew of the late Sir Thomas Staples, Bart., Q.C.; *b.* 1817; *s.* his uncle as 8th Bart. 1865; *m.* 1846 Elizabeth, only dau. of Capt. James Head.—*Lissane, Cookstown, co. Tyrone.*

Heir, his son John Molesworth, *b.* 1848.

STAPLES, MOSES WILLIAM, Esq., of Broughton Gifford, Wilts.

Eldest son of the late Moses William Staples, Esq., of Broughton Gifford, by Frances, dau. of John Bates, Esq., Alderman, of London; *b.* 1786; *s.* 1802; *m.* 1811 Anne, dau. of the late Rev. William Frederick Browne, D.D., Prebendary of Wells, and had, with other issue,

Richard Thomas Staples-Browne, of Launton; *b.* 1814; *m.* 1843 Ann, dau. of Robert Brittie Bate, Esq. and *d.* 1855, leaving issue. * Frederick John, *b.* 1814; *m.* 1867 Mary Jane, only child of C. E. Molineux, Esq., of Ethal House, co. Salop.

Mr. Staples was educated at Westminster and Ch. Ch., Oxford.—*Broughton Gifford, Melksham; Norwood, S.*

STAPLETON, the Hon. and Rev. Sir FRANCIS JERVIS, Bart., of Greys Court, Oxon (cr. 1679).

Only surviving son of the late Sir Thomas Stapleton, Bart. (who was also Lord Le Despencer), by Elizabeth, dau. of Samuel Eliot, Esq., of Antigua; *b.* 1807; *s.* as 10th Bart. 1831; *m.* 1830 Margaret, dau. of the late Lieut.-General Sir George Airey, G.C.B. Educated at Harrow and Trinity Coll. Cambridge (M.A. 1828); is a Magistrate for Kent, and Rector of Mereworth, and Vicar of Tudeley, Kent.—*Greys Court, Henley-on-Thames; Mereworth Rectory, Maidstone.*

Heir, his son Francis George, Capt. Grenadier Guards, and A.D.C. to the Governor of Nova Scotia; *b.* 1831.

STAPLETON, the Hon. BRYAN JOHN, of Richmond, Yorkshire.

Sixth son of the late Thomas Stapleton, Esq., of Carlton Hall, co. York (who *d.* 1839), by his 2nd wife Henrietta Lavinia, 2nd dau. of the late Richard Fitzgerald Anster, Esq. (she *d.* 1858), and half-brother of Miles Thomas, 8th Lord Beaumont; *b.* 1831; *m.* 1857 Mary Helen Alicia, only dau. of the late John Thomas Dolman, Esq., M.D., of Souldern House, Oxon. and has, with other issue,

* Nicholas, *b.* 1861.

Mr. Stapleton, who was educated at Oscott Coll., is a

Dep.-Lieut. for the N. Riding of Yorkshire, and Capt. 4th West York Militia.—*The Grove, Richmond, Yorkshire;* Residence: *Glenmoor, Dursley, Gloucestershire.*

STAPLETON, the Hon. Mrs., of Ditton Hall, Lancashire.

Marr. only child of Bartholomew Bretherton, Esq., of Rainhill and Ditton, co. Lancaster, and of Lackham, Wilts., by Mary, dau. of John Atkin-on, Esq., of Appleby, co. Westmor-land ; *m.* 1st 1829 William Gerard, Esq., brother of Sir John Gerard, Bart., who *d.* 1844 ; 2nd 1848 the Hon. Gilbert Stapleton, of Richmond, co. York (brother of Miles, late Lord Beaumont), who *d.* 1836. Is Lady of the Manor of Lackham, &c.—*Ditton Hall, Warington ; Lackham, Chippenham.*

STAPLETON, JOHN, Esq., of Berwick Hill, Northumberland.

Fourth son of the late Thomas Stapleton, Esq., of Carlton Hall, co. York (who *d.* 1839), by his 1st wife Maria Juliana, dau. of the late Sir Robert Gerard, Bart., of Bryn, co. Lancaster ; *b.* 1816 ; *m.* 1860 Frances Dorothea. 2nd dau. of Edward Bolton King. Esq., of Charlshunt, co. Warwick. Called to the Bar at Lincoln's Inn 1840, and goes the Northern circuit ; elected for Berwick 1852, but unseated on petition ; re-chosen 1857.—*Berwick Hall, Northumberland ; Athenæum Club, s.w. ; 44, Queen's Gate Terrace, w.*

STAPLETON.
(See under *Le Despencer, Lord,* and *Beaumont, Lord.*)

STAPYLTON, HENRY MILES, Esq., of Myton Hall, Yorkshire.

Eldest son of the late Stapylton Stapylton, Esq., of Myton Hall, by his 2nd wife Margaret, dau. of Thomas Tomlinson, Esq., of York ; *b.* 1831 ; *s.* 1864 ; educated at Sandhurst ; is a J.P. and D.L. for the N. Riding of Yorkshire, and Lord of the Manor of Myton ; late Major 2nd Dragoon Guards. His grandfather assumed the name of Stapylton in lieu of Bree, in 1817, on succeeding to the estates of his uncle, Sir Martin Stapylton, Bart.—*Myton Hall, Boroughbridge ; Army and Navy and Reform Clubs, s.w. ; 6, Charles Street, w.*

Heir Pres., his brother Martin Bryan, *b.* 1832 ; *m.* 1860 Mary, dau. of John Brymes, Esq., of Ilsington House, Dorset, and has issue, two daughters.

STAPYLTON. (See *Chetwynd-Stapylton.*)

STAREY, BENJAMIN HELPS, Esq., of Milton Ernest, Bedfordshire.

Cn'y son of the late Benjamin Starey. Esq., of London. Merchant, by Elizabeth, dau. of James Helps, Esq., of Gloucester ; *b.* 1807 ; *m.* 1838 Anne, dau. of William Butterfield, Esq., of London, and has, with other issue,

   * Anne Blercbley, *m.* 1863 Richard William. son of the late George Drew, Esq., of Caterham and Streatham, Surrey.

Mr. Starey is a Magistrate for Middlesex and Beds (High Sheriff 1863).—*Milton Ernest, Bedford.*

STARK-CHRISTIE, JAMES HENRY ROBERTSON, Esq., of Teasses, Fifeshire.

Eldest son of the late Robert Stark-Christie. Esq., of Teasses, by Mary Butler, of Ballindean and Teasses, eldest dau. of the late James Stark, Esq., of Kingsdale, co. Fife ; *b.* 1830 ; *s.* his mother 1862 ; *m.* 1860 Marion Jane, youngest dau. of Archibald Young Howison, Esq., of Hyndford. co. Lanark, and has issue. Mr. Stark-Christie, who was educated at Trinity Coll., Cambridge (B.A. 1852. M.A. 1855), and called to the Bar at Edinburgh 1854, is a Magistrate for co. Fife. Mr. Stark-Christie's father, 5th son of the late James Christie, Esq., of Durie, assumed the additional surname of Stark in 1839.—*Teasses, Largo, N.B. ; New Club, Edinburgh.*

880

STARK-CHRISTIE, THOMAS, Esq., of Ballindean, Fifeshire.

Younger son of the late Robert Stark-Christie, Esq., of Teasses, co. Fife, by Mary Butler, of Ballindean and Teasses, eldest dau. of the late James Stark, Esq., of Kingsdale, co. Fife ; *b.* 1840 ; *s.* his mother 1862. Educated at Edinburgh ; was formerly in the 11th Hussars.—*Ballindean, Cupar, N.B.*

STARKE, JAMES, Esq., F.S.A., of Troqueer Holm, Kirkcudbrightshire.

Son of the late William Starke, Esq.; *b.* 1798 ; *m.* 1835 Hamilton, dau. of Major James Gibson, and by her (who *d.* 1859), has, with other issue,

   * James Gibson, M.A., Advocate at the Scottish Bar. a Magistrate for co. Kircudbright. and Lieut. 5th Kirkcudbright-shire R.V. ; *b.* 18.7 ; *m.* 1863 Amelia Charlotte, dau. of the Rev. Richard Rowland Bloxham, Rector of Harleston, co. Stafford, and grand-dau. of the late General Goldie, of Goldieleigh, co. Kirkcudbright.

Mr. Starke, who was called to the Scottish Bar 1824, is a Magistrate for cos. Dumfries and Kirkcudbright, and was formerly a Magistrate for Edinburgh ; was appointed Advocate-General of Ceylon 1839, a Judge of the Supreme Court of that Island 1840.—*Troqueer Holm, Dumfries, N.B. ; 34, Heriot Row, Edinburgh.*

STARKE, JAMES RAVENSCROFT, Esq., of Laugharne, Carmarthenshire.

Third surviving son of the late Lieut.-Col. Richard Isaac Starke, of Epsom, Surrey (who *d.* 1827), by Elizabeth, only dau. and heir of the late Col. Ravenscroft, of Laugharne Castle ; *b.* 1810 ; *s.* his mother 1848 ; *m.* 1838 Alicia, dau. of the Rev. James Ellard, Vicar of Kilfinane, and has, with other issue,

   * James Ravenscroft, *b.* 1849.

Mr. Starke is a Major in the County Militia.—*Laugharne Castle, Carmarthen.*

STARKEY, LEWIS RANDLE, Esq., of Spring Lodge, Yorkshire.

Eldest son of the late John Starkey, Esq., of Spring Lodge, by Sarah Anne, dau. of Joseph Armitage, Esq., of Milns-Bridge House, near Huddersfield ; *b.* 1836 ; *s.* 1856 ; *m.* 1858 Constance Margarette, dau. of the late Thomas Starkey, Esq., of Spring-Wood House, Huddersfield, and has, with other issue,

   * John Ralph, *b.* 1853.

Mr. Starkey, who was educated at Rugby and at the University of Berlin, is a J.P. and D.L. for the W. Riding of Yorkshire, and an Officer in the 2nd West Yorkshire Yeomanry Cavalry.—*Spring Lodge, Huddersfield ; Conservative Club, s.w.*

STARKEY, Major SAMUEL CROSS, of Wrenbury Hall, Cheshire.

Second son of the late John Cross Starkey, Esq., of Wrenbury Hall, by his 1st wife Susan, dau. of John Warren, Esq.; *b.* 1807 ; *s.* 1855 ; *m.* 1st 1839 Henrietta Suit, dau. of Col. Manson ; 2nd 1853 E'eanor, dau. of Charles Simpson, Esq., of Waterloo, Liverpool, and has, with other issue,

   * Arthur, *b.* 1841.

Major Starkey is a Magistrate for co. Chester, and a Major H.E.I.C.'s Service.—*Wrenbury Hall, Nantwich.*

STARKIE, JOHN PIERS CHAMBERLAIN, Esq., of Ashton Hall, Lancashire.

Second son of the late Le Gendre N. Starkie, Esq., M.P., of Huntroyd, co. Lancaster (who *d.* 1865), by Anne, dau. of A. Chamberlain, Esq., of Rilston, co. York ; *b.* 1830 ; *s.* 1865 ; *m.* 186- Anne Charlotte Amelia, dau. of Harington Hudson, Esq., of Bessingby, co. York, and has, with other issue,

   * Francis Chamberlain Legendre, *b.* 1863.

Mr. Starkie, who was educated at Eton and Trinity

Hall, Cambridge (LL.B. 1856), is a Magistrate for co. Lancaster, and Lord of the Manors of Ashton and Stodday.—*Ashton Hall, Lancaster; Oxford and Cambridge Club, s.w.*

STARKIE, LE GENDRE NICHOLAS, Esq., of Huntroyde, Lancashire.

Elder son of the late Le Gendre Nicholas Starkie, Esq., J.P. and D.L., of Huntroyde (who was formerly M.P. for Pontefract), by Ann, dau. of A. Chamberlain, Esq., of Rilston-in-Craven, co. York; *b.* 1828; *s.* 1865; *m.* 1867 Jemima Monica Mildred, 2nd dau. of the late Henry Tempest, Esq., of Newland Park, co. York. Educated at Trinity Coll., Cambridge (B.A. 1851, M.A. 1854); is a J.P. and D.L. for co. Lancaster (High Sheriff 1868), Patron of 2 livings, and Capt. 2nd Lancashire Militia; was M.P. for Clitheroe 1853–6. This family is a branch of the ancient house of Starkie of Stretton, co. Chester.—*Huntroyde, Burnley; Ashton Hall, Lancaster.*

Heir Pres., his brother John Piers Chamberlayne, *b.* 1830.

STAUNTON, the Rev. FRANCIS, of Staunton Hall, Notts.

Eldest surviving son of the late Rev. William Job Charlton Staunton, of Staunton Hall (who *d.* 1840), by Isabella, only dau. of the late Very Rev. G. Gordon, D.D., Dean of Lincoln; *b.* 1839; *s.* his brother 1866; *m.* 1867 Lucy Ada, only dau. of the Rev. Henry Spelman Marriott, Rector of Woolpit, Suffolk. Educated at Rugby and St. John's Coll., Cambridge (B.A. 1861); is Patron and Rector of Staunton with Flawborough.—*Staunton Hall, Elton, Nottingham.*

Heir Pres., his brother William Charlton, *b.* 1840.

STAUNTON, JOHN, Esq., of Longbridge, Warwickshire.

Eldest son of the late William Staunton, Esq., J.P. and D.L., of Longbridge, formerly Capt. 1st Life-Guards, by Elizabeth, eldest dau. of Osborne Standert, Esq., of London; *b.* 1799; *s.* 1848; *m.* 1833 Mary Anne, eldest dau. of the Rev. Thomas L. Snow, of Tidmington, co. Worcester, and has issue, two daughters. Mr. Staunton, who was educated at Rugby and Caius Coll., Cambridge, is a Magistrate for co. Warwick, and represents the eldest branch of the Stauntons or Stantons, who have held this property in direct male succession since the reign of Henry VI.—*Longbridge, Warwick.*

Heir Pres., his brother Thomas, *b.* 1807; *m.* 1833 Frances Maria, dau. of Samuel Barrett, Esq., of Bath, and has issue, * Thomas Tufnell, *b.* 1844.

STAUNTON. (See *Lynch-Staunton*.)

STAVELEY, Sir CHARLES WILLIAM DUNBAR, K.C.B. (cr. 1865).

Eldest son of the late Lieut.-Gen. William Staveley, C.B., by Sarah, dau. of Thomas Mather, Esq.; *b.* 1817; *m.* 1864 Susan Millicent, 2nd dau. of C. W. Minet, Esq., of Castle Hill, Dorset. Educated at the Naval and Military Academy, Edinburgh; entered the Army in 1835, is a Col. in the Army, and Lieut.-Col. 44th Foot; was Brigadier-Gen. commanding the troops in China in 1862–3; is a Brigadier-General commanding the Northern Division of the Bombay Army.—*Ahmedabad, Bombay; United Service Club, s.w.*

STAVELEY, the Misses, of Sleningford, Yorkshire.

Roseberry Mary and Martha Charlotte, only surviving children of the late Thomas Kitchingman Staveley, Esq., J.P., Capt. R.E., of Old Sleningford Hall (who was M.P. for Ripon 1833–4, and who *d.* 1860), by his 2nd wife Annie Elizabeth, only dau. of the late Staff-

Surgeon Burmester; *s.* their brother 1867. Are Ladies of the Manor of Newton, and Patrons of 1 living.—*Old Sleningford Hall, and North Stainley Hall, Ripon.*

STAWELL, Sir WILLIAM FOSTER, Knt. (cr. 1857).

Son of the late Jonas Stawell, Esq., of Old Court, co. Cork, by Anne Elizabeth, dau. of the late Right Rev. Dr. Foster, Lord Bishop of Kilmore; *b.* 1815; *m.* 1856 Mary Frances, dau. of the late W. P. Greene, Esq., R.N. Educated at Trinity Coll., Dublin; called to the Irish Bar 1839; appointed Attorney-General of Victoria, and a Member of the Executive Council there, 1851; Chief Justice of the Supreme Court of Victoria, 1856.—*Melbourne, Australia.*

STAWELL. (See *Alcock-Stawell*.)

STEEL, JOHN, Esq.,‡ of Derwent Bank, Cumberland.

Eldest son of the late Joseph Steel, Esq., of Cockermouth, by Dorothy, dau. of John Ponsonby, Esq., of Hale Hall, Cumberland; *b.* 1786; *m.* 1817 Frances, dau. of the Rev. Richard Coxe, of Bucklebury, Berks. Is a Magistrate for co. Cumberland; late a Solicitor at Cockermouth; has been M.P. for Cockermouth since 1854.—*Derwent Bank, Bridekirk, Cockermouth.*

+STEELE, Major MATTHEW FREDERICK, of Sutton, Surrey.

Son of the late M. Steele, Esq.; *b.* 1800; is married, and has, with other issue,

  * Frederick Samuel, Capt. in the Militia; *b.* 18—; *m.* 1860 Martha, eldest dau. of the late Sir Francis Blake, Bart., of Twizell Castle, Northumberland.

He was formerly a Major in the Army.—*Sutton Court, Epsom*

STEELE, the Rev. THOMAS JAMES, of Whepstead, Suffolk.

Eldest son of the late Capt. Steele, of the 25th Light Dragoons, by his 1st wife Sarah Anne, dau. of — Neale, Esq.; *b.* 1814; *m.* 1842 Agnes, dau. of Anthony Wright, Esq., of Alston, and has issue. Mr. Steele, who was educated at St. Bees Theological Coll., is a Magistrate for Suffolk, Rector and Patron of Whepstead, and Domestic Chaplain to the Earl of Tankerville.—*Whepstead Rectory, Bury St. Edmunds.*

+STEELE, Major-Gen. THOMAS MONTAGU, C.B., of Guilsborough Park, Northamptonshire.

Eldest son of the late Major-General Thomas Steele, of Guilsborough Park, by Lady Elizabeth Montagu, 2nd dau. of William, 5th Duke of Manchester; *b.* 1820; *s.* 1847; *m.* 1856 Isabella, dau. of — Fitzgerald, Esq., by whom (who *d.* 1858), he has issue. Educated at Eton and the Royal Military Coll., Sandhurst; is a Magistrate for co. Northampton, and a Major-Gen. in the Army; late Col. Coldstream Guards.—*Guilsborough Park, Northampton; 36, Chester Square, s.w.*

STEELE-GRAVES, Sir JOHN MAXWELL, Bart., of Mickleton, Gloucestershire (cr. 1668).

Eldest surviving son of the late Sir Richard Steele, Bart., of Hampstead, co. Dublin, by Frances, dau. of the late Edward, Count d'Alton, Lieut.-General in the Austrian Service; *b.* 1812; *s.* as 4th Bart. 1830; *m.* 1838 Elizabeth Anne,§ dau. and co-heir of the late John Graves, Esq., of Mickleton Manor, whose name he assumed in 1862. Educated at Brasenose Coll., Oxford (B.A. 1833); is a J.P. and D.L. for co. Gloucester (High Sheriff 1866), a Magistrate for co. War-

‡ Died whilst these sheets were at press.
§ Lady Steele-Graves succeeded her uncle in 1818, as heir of entail of her grandfather, the Rev. R. M. Graves, D.D.

wick and Worcester, and Major Royal North Gloucester Militia.—*Mickleton Manor, Chipping Campden ; Junior United Service and Oxford and Cambridge Clubs, s.w.*

Heir Pres. (to the estates), his dau. Frances Elizabeth.

+ STEERE, LEE STEERE, Esq., of Jayes, Surrey.
Eldest son of the late Lee Steere Witts, Esq., of Jayes (who in 1796 assumed the name of Steere only, in lieu of Witts), by Sarah, eldest dau. of Robert Harrison, Esq., of Ripley Surrey (she *d.* 1855); *b.* 1803 ; *s.* 1834; *m.* 1826 Anne, 2nd dau. of James Kearo Watson, Esq., of Hepple, co. York, by whom he has, with other issue,
   • Lee Steere, *b.* 1826 ; *m.* 1858 Mary, dau. of the Rev. — Hodgson, and has issue, • Lee Steere, *b.* 1859.
Mr. Lee Steere is a J.P. and D.L. for Surrey, and a Magistrate for Sussex.—*Jayes, Dorking.*

STENT. (See *Shadwell.*)

STEPHEN, Sir ALFRED, Knt. (cr. 1841).
Son of the late John Stephen, Esq., and cousin of Sir George Stephen and of the late Right Hon. Sir James Stephen; *b.* 1802; *m.* 1st 1824 Virginia, dau. of Matthew Consett, Esq. ; 2nd 1838 Eleanor, dau. of the Rev. Dr. Bedford. Called to the Bar at Lincoln's Inn 1823 ; was Chief Justice of New South Wales 1841–57 ; was previously Solicitor and Attorney-General of Tasmania. —*Sydney.*

STEPHEN, Sir GEORGE, Knt. (cr. 1838).
Youngest son of the late James Stephen, Esq., M.P., a Master in Chancery, by Ann, only child of Henry Stent, Esq., of Stoke Newington, Middlesex ; *b.* 1794 ; *m.* 1821 Henrietta, dau. of the Rev. W. Ravenscroft. Called to the Bar at Gray's Inn 1849, and went the Northern Circuit; has been in practice as a Barrister at Melbourne since 1851 ; is a Dep.-Lieut. for Bucks.—*St. Kilda, Melbourne, Victoria.*

STEPHENS, CECIL, Esq., of Foston, Yorkshire.
Eldest son of the late Arthur Stephens, Esq., J.P. and D.L., of Foston Hall, by Anna Maria, youngest surviving dau. of the late James Ward. Esq., of Willey Place, Farnham, and widow of John Haigh. Esq., of Whitwell Hall. co. York (she *m.* 3rd 1867 William Mott, Esq., of Wall, co. Stafford (whom see); *b.* 1847 ; *s.* 1865. —*Foston Hall, York ; 58, Rutland Gate, w.*

+ STEPHENS, EDWARD, Esq., of Trewornan, Cornwall.
Eldest son of the late Rev. Darell Stephens, Vicar of Maker; *b.* 1800. Is a J.P. and D.L. for Cornwall. —*Trewornan, Wadebridge.*

STEPHENS, the late HENRY LEWIS, Esq., of Tregenna Castle, Cornwall.
Son of the late Samuel Stephens, Esq., of Tregenna Castle, by Betty, only child and heir of Samuel Wallis, Esq., R.N.; *b.* 1810; *s.* 1834 ; *d.* 1867. Educated at Oriel Coll., Oxford (B.A. 1831); was a Magistrate for Cornwall (High Sheriff 1841).—*Tregenna Castle, Hayle.*

STEPHENS, JOHN, Esq., of Llananno, Radnorshire, and The Bank, Montgomeryshire.
Third and youngest son of the late Evan Stephens, Esq., of The Bank, Newtown (who *d.* 1833), by Mary, dau. of Edward Morgan, Esq., of Aberllechan Hall, co. Montgomery ; *b.* 1814 ; *s.* his brother Edward Morgan Stephens 1858 ; *m.* 1844 Hannah Rogers, dau. of James Stephens, Esq., of Llananno and Presteigne. Is a J.P. and D.L. for co. Radnor, and a Magistrate for co. Montgomery. This family have been settled in Radnorshire for many generations, being connected with the Stephenses of Kinnerton Court, and served the office of

High Sheriff in the 17th, 18th, and 19th centuries. —*Castle Vale, Llananno, Radnorshire ; The Bank, Newtown, Montgomeryshire.*

STEPHENS, WILLIAM, Esq., of Caversham Rise, Oxfordshire.
Eldest son of the late William Stephens, Esq., of Caversham Rise, by Ellen, his wife; *b.* 1820 ; *m.* 1851 Elizabeth Emma, 2nd dau. of the late Thomas Lyons Walcott, Esq., of Higham Court, co. Gloucester. Was formerly an Officer in the Army.—*Caversham Rise, Reading.*

STEPHENS. (See *Lyne-Stephens.*)

STEPHENSON, Sir ROWLAND MACDONALD (cr. 1856).
Son of the late Rowland Stephenson, Esq., by Mary Eliza, dau. of the late Edward Stephenson, Esq., of Farley Hill, Berks, and Scaleby Castle, Cumberland : *b.* 1808; *m.* 1840 Marianne, dau. of Lieut. Edward Hedersterdt, R.N. Educated at Harrow ; is a Civil Engineer, and Director of the East-India Railway Company; received the honour of knighthood for his services in introducing and carrying out railway communication in India.—*72, Lancaster Gate, w.*

STEPNEY. (See *Cowell-Stepney.*)

STERLING, Sir ANTHONY CONINGHAM, K.C.B. (cr. 1860).
Eldest son of the late Edward Sterling, Esq., by Hester, dau. of John Coningham, Esq., of Londonderry ; *b.* 1805; *m.* 1829 Charlotte, dau. of Major-General Joseph Baird (she *d.* 1863). Educated at Trinity Coll., Cambridge ; is a Col. in the Army; was formerly Brigade-Major Highland Brigade. Adjutant-General to the Highland Division in the Crimea, and afterwards Military Secretary to the Commander-in-Chief in India 1857–60.—*South Lodge, Knightsbridge, s.w.*

STEUART, Sir WILLIAM DRUMMOND, Bart., of Grantully, Perthshire (cr. 1683).
Eldest surviving son of the late Sir George Steuart, Bart., of Grantully, by Catharine, dau. of John Drummond, Esq., of Logie Almond, N.B. ; *b.* 1796 ; *s.* his brother as 7th Bart. 1838 ; *m.* 1830 Christina Mary, dau. of — Stewart, Esq. (she *d.* 1856). Is a J.P. and D.L. for co. Perth ; served in the 15th Hussars in the campaign of 1815 ; is a Knight of the Order of Christ of Italy and Portugal.—*Grantully Castle, Aberfeldy, N.B.; Murthly, Dunkeld. N.B.*

Heir, his son William George, a Major in the Army unattached, and V.C.; late Capt. 93rd Highlanders ; *b.* 1831.

STEUART, Sir HENRY JAMES SETON-, Bart., of Allanton, Lanarkshire, and Touch, Stirlingshire (cr. 1815).
Eldest son of the late Sir Reginald Macdonald Seton-Steuart, Bart., of Staffa, by Elizabeth, dau. and heir of Sir Henry Steuart, Bart., F.R.S., of Allanton (who was created a Baronet with remainder to his son-in-law); *b.* 1812 ; *s.* as 3rd Bart. 1838 ; *m.* 1852 Elizabeth, d. u. of Robert Montgomery, Esq., and grand-dau. of the late Sir James Montgomery, Bart., of Stanhope, Lord Chief Baron of Scotland; is a J.P. and D.L. for cos. Stirling and Lanark, and Hereditary Armour-bearer and Squire of the Royal Body in Scotland. The mother of the present Bart., who added the name of Seton to that of her own, on succeeding to the estate of Touch. *d.* 1866. —*Touch House, Stirling, N.B.; Allanton House, Motherwell, N.B.; New Club, Edinburgh, N.B.*

Heir Pres., his bro her Archibald, *b.* 1814 ; *m.* 1853 Katherine, dau. of R. Stein, Esq., and has, with other issue, • Alan Henry, *b.* 1856.

STEUART, ANDREW, Esq., of Auchlunkart, Banffshire.

Only son of Patrick Steuart, Esq. of Auchlunkart, by Rachel, dau. of the late Lachlan Gordon, Esq., of Park; *b.* 1822 ; *m.* 1847 Elizabeth Georgiana Graham, 3rd dau. of Col. T. Gordon, of Park, and has issue. Educated at Trinity Coll., Cambridge (B.A. 1844); entered at the Inner Temple 1851, but was not called to the Bar ; is a J.P. and D.L. for co. Banff, and a Magistrate for co. Aberdeen ; was M.P. for Cambridge 1857–62.—*Auchlunkart House, Keith, N.B.*

STEUART, DAVID, Esq., of Steuarthall, Stirlingshire.

Only son of the late Robert Steuart, Esq., of Steuarthall (who *d.* 1844), by Helen, dau. of Walter Buchanan, Esq.; *b.* 1830 ; *m.* 1861 Dorothy Emily, only dau. of the late Rev. John Cox, Rector of Fairstead, Essex, and has, with other issue,

* Robert John Archibald, *b.* 1863.

Mr. Steuart, who was formerly Capt. 34th Foot, represents a younger branch of the Shaw-Steuart family.—*Steuarthall, Stirling, N.B.; Herongate, Brentwood ; Army and Navy Club, s.w.*

STEUART, JOHN, Esq., of Dalguise, Perthshire.

Eldest son of the late Charles Steuart, Esq., of Dalguise, by his 2nd wife Amelia Anne, dau. of the late Lawrence Oliphant, Esq., of Gask, N.B.: *b.* 179–; *s.* 1821 ; *m.* 1829 the Hon. Janet Oliphant, eldest dau. of Alexander, 8th Lord Elibank, and has issue five daughters. Mr. Steuart, who was educated at Edinburgh, is a Barrister-at-Law, J.P. and D.L. for co. Perth, Lord of the Barony of Dalguise, and Master of the Supreme Court of the Cape of Good Hope.—*Dalguise, Dunkeld, N.B. ; Cape Town, South Africa.*

STEUART, Mrs., of Steuart's Lodge, co. Carlow.

Elizabeth Dawson, only dau. of the late William Duckett, Esq., of Duckett's Grove, co. Carlow ; *m.* 1820 William Richard Steuart, Esq., of Steuart's Lodge, who was a Magistrate for co. Carlow, and High Sheriff in 1821, and *d.* in 1852.—*Steuart's Lodge, Leighlin Bridge.*

Heiress Pres., her husband's sister Henrietta Maria ; *m.* 1813 the Rev. William Hickey.

STEUART, Major ROBERT, of Ballechin, Perthshire.

Eldest son of the late Hope Steuart, Esq., of Ballechin, by Louisa, 2nd dau. of James Morley, Esq., of Kempshott Park, Hants ; *b.* 1806 ; *s.* 1834. Is a Magistrate for co. Perth ; late Major E.I.C.S.—*Ballechin, Perth, N.B.*

Heir Pres., his brother James Charles, *b.* 1808.

STEUART. (See *Gow-Steuart.*)

STEUART-MENZIES. (See *Menzies.*)

STEUART-GROSETT-MUIRHEAD, ROBERT DALRYMPLE, Esq., of Bredisholm, Lanarkshire.

Only son of the late Robert Steuart, Esq., M.P., of Alderston, by Maria, 3rd dau. of the late Col. Dalrymple, C.B.; *b.* 1836 ; *s.* 1843 ; *m.* 1863 Emily Eliza. eldest dau. and co-heir of the late H. R. D'V. Grosett-Muirhead, Esq., of Bredisholm (whose name he assumed under the deed of entail), and by her, who *d.* 1864, has issue.

* Emily Gertrude Lilias.

Mr. Steuart-Grosett-Muirhead is Lieut. R. Horse Guards, late Lieut. 7th Hussars. The Muirheads have held Bredisholm and Lauchope for more than four centuries.—*Bredisholm, Baillieton, N.B.; St. James's Club, s.w.*

+**STEVENS, JOHN CURZON MOORE-, of Winscott House, Devon.**

Son of the late Ven. John Moore-Stevens, of Winscott House, Archdeacon of Exeter (who assumed the additional name of Stevens in 1832 under the will of his cousin, Mrs. Elizabeth Cleveland, of Tapley), by Anne Eleanor, dau. of the late Rev. W. Roberts, Vice-Provost of Eton Coll.; *b.* 1818 ; *s.* 1865; *m.* 1850 Elizabeth Anne, dau. of the Rev. Peter Johnson, Prebendary of Exeter, and has, with other issue,

* John Henry, *b.* 1852.

Mr. Stevens, who was educated at Winchester and Ch. Ch., Oxford (B.A. 1841, M.A. 1844), and called to the Bar at the Middle Temple 1844, is a Magistrate for Devon, and Patron of 1 living ; late Capt. R. Devon Mounted Rifles.—*Winscott House, Marland, Torrington.*

STEVENS, the Rev. THOMAS, of Bradfield, Berks.

Second but eldest surviving son of the late Rev. Henry Stevens, Rector of Bradfield, by Maria, dau. of William Tinney, Esq., of Salisbury ; *b.* 1809 ; *s.* 1842; *m.* 1st 1839 Caroline Octavia, dau. of George Tollet, Esq., of Betley Hall, co. Stafford (she *d. s. p.*); 2nd 1843 Susanna dau. of the Rev. Robert Marriott, of Cotesbach, co. Leicester, and has, with other issue,

* Henry, *b.* 1847.

Mr. Stevens, who was educated at Oriel Coll., Oxford (B.A. 1830, M.A. 1832), is a Magistrate for Berks and Oxon, Rector and Lord of the Manor of Bradfield, Patron of 1 living, and Founder and first Warden of St. Andrew's Coll., Bradfield ; he was formerly Assistant Poor-Law Commissioner. — *Bradfield Rectory, Reading.*

+**STEVENS, WILLIAM, Esq., of Hillfield, Hants.**

Son of the late Wm. Stevens, Esq., of Hillfield ; *b.* 18—; *m.* 184– Georgina, dau. of ——, Esq. (she *d.* 1863). Is a Magistrate for Berks.—*Hillfield, Yateley, Farnborough.*

STEVENSON, CHARLES BENJAMIN, Esq., of Hennor House, Herefordshire.

Only son of the late Charles Stevenson, Esq., R.M., of London (who *d.* 1830), by Caroline, youngest dau. of Major James Poole, of Ludlow, and Hennor House, *b.* 1820. Mr. Stevenson, who was educated at Eton and Heidelberg, is a J.P. and D.L. for co. Hereford, was formerly in the Worcester Militia. — *Hennor House, Leominster.*

+**STEVENSON, JOHN NEWCOMBE, Esq., of Hayne, Devon.**

Son of the late J. Stevenson, Esq., of Hayne ; *b.* 18—; *m.* 1st 1833 Anne Caroline, eldest dau. of the Rev. William Clack, Rector of Moreton and Woolborough. Devon ; 2nd 18— Georgina Lucy, dau. of ——, Esq. (she *d.* 1863); 3rd 1868 Fanny Lucia, youngest dau. of the late Robert Ayiward, Esq. Is a Magistrate for Devon, and Lieut.-Col. S. Devon Militia.—*Hayne, Exeter.*

STEVENSON, JAMES PEEL, Esq., of Uffington, Lincolnshire.

Eldest son of the late James Stevenson, Esq., of Uffington, by Elizabeth Anne, eldest dau. of Lawrence Peel, Esq.; *b.* 1808; *s.* 1853; *m.* 1855 Maria, dau. of Walter McKenzie, Esq., of Canada, and has, with other issue,

* Walter George Bellairs, *b.* 1858.

This family changed the name from Bellairs to Stevenson in 1811. *Uffington, Stamford.*

3 L 2   883

STEVENSON, ROBERT, Esq., of Ardkill, co. Londonderry.

Heir and successor of the late Robert Stevenson, Esq., of Ardkill; *b.* 1812; *s.* 1839; *m.* 1838 Jane, dau. of William Long, Esq., of Irvey, co. Londonderry, and has, with other issue,

* Robert, *b.* 1842.

Mr. Stevenson, who was educated at Londonderry, is a Magistrate for co. Tyrone.—*Ardkill, Londonderry.*

STEWARD, ANTHONY BENN, Esq., of Newton Manor, Cumberland.

Eldest son of the late John Steward, Esq., of Chapel House, Hensingham, by Margaret Cecilia. dau. of Anthony Benn, Esq., of Hensingham; *b.* 1805; *m.* 1842 Mary Anne, dau. of Milham Hartley, Esq., of Rose Hill. Is a J.P. for Cumberland (High Sheriff 1858). —*Newton Manor, Gosforth, Cumberland; Union Club, s.w.*

STEWARD, CHARLES, Esq., of Blundeston, Suffolk.

Third son of the late Timothy Steward, Esq., of Great Yarmouth, by Mary, dau. of John Fowler, Esq., of Yarmouth; *b.* 1798; *m.* 1827 Harriet, eldest dau. of the late Ambrose Harbord Steward, Esq., of Stoke Park, Suffolk, and has issue, a son,

* Charles John, in Holy Orders, B.A. of Trinity Coll., Cambridge; *b.* 1828.

Mr. Steward, who is a J.P. and D.L. for Suffolk, and a Magistrate for Norfolk, was formerly a Commander in the H.E.I.C.'s Service.—*Blundeston, Lowestoft.*

STEWARD, the Rev. HENRY, of Carlton, Norfolk.

Eldest son of the late Rev. John Henry Steward, J.P., of East Carlton, Vicar of Swardiston and Rector of Hethel; *b.* 1825; *s.* 1863. Educated at Corpus Christi Coll., Cambridge (B.A. 1847, M.A. 1850). Is Lord of the Manors of Peverells, in East Carlton, and of Saxlingham-Thorpe, Patron of 3 livings, and Curate of Swardiston.—*East Carlton, Norwich.*

STEWARD, RICHARD OLIVER FRANCIS, Esq., of Nottington House, Dorset.

Eldest son of the late Col. Richard Augustus Steward, M.P., of Nottington House (who was a J.P. and D.L. for Dorset), by Louisa Henrietta, only dau. of Edward Morgan, Esq., of Golden Grove, co. Flint; *b.* 1823; *s.* 1842; *m.* 1856 Olivia Elizabeth, 3rd dau. of Sir H. A. Johnson, Bart. Educated at Winchester Coll.; is a Magistrate for Dorset and a Lt.-Colonel in the Army. —*Nottington House, Dorchester, Dorset; Army and Navy and United Service Clubs, s.w.*

Heir Pres., his brother Frederick Gordon, *b.* 1826.

STEWART, Sir JAMES ANNESLEY, Bart., of Fort Stewart, co. Donegal (cr. 1623).

Only surviving son of the late Sir James Stewart, Bart., of Fort Stewart, by Susanna, dau. of Richard Chapel Whaley, Esq., of Whaley Abbey, co. Wicklow; *b.* 1795; *s.* as 7th Bart. 1827. Is Vice-Lieut. of co. Donegal. The 4th Baronet was created Earl of Blesinton but the title became extinct 1769.—*Fort Stewart, Ramelton.*

STEWART, Sir MICHAEL ROBERT SHAW-, Bart., of Blackhall, Renfrewshire (cr. 1667).

Eldest son of the late Sir Michael Shaw-Stewart, Bart., M.P., of Blackhall, by Eliza Mary, dau. of Robert Farquhar, Esq., of Newark, co. Renfrew; *b.* 1826; *s.* as 7th Bart. 1836; *m.* 1852 Lady Octavia, dau. of Richard, 2nd Marquis of Westminster, K.G. Educated at Ch. Ch., Oxford; is Vice-Lieutenant of co. Renfrew; was M.P. for co. Renfrew 1855-65, and formerly Lieut. 2nd Life Guards. Sir Michael represents the Stewarts of Black-
884

hall and Ardgowan, and the Shaws of Greenock.—*Blackhall and Duchall, Port Glasgow; Ardgowan, Greenock, N.B.; Carlton Club, s.w.; 42, Belgrave Square, s.w.*

Heir, his son Michael Hugh, *b.* 1854.

STEWART, Sir JOHN MARCUS, Bart., of Ballygawley, co. Tyrone (cr. 1803).

Eldest son of the late Sir Hugh Stewart, Bart., of Ballygawley, by Julia, dau. of Marcus M'Causland Gage, Esq., of Bellarena; *b.* 1830; *s.* as 3rd Bart. 1854; *m.* 1856 Annie Coote, dau. of the late George Powell Houghton, Esq., of Kilmanock, co. Wexford. Educated at Rugby; is a J.P. and D.L. for co. Tyrone (High Sheriff 1858); is Gentleman Usher and Master of the Ceremonies to the Lord Lieut. of Ireland; late Lieut. Inniskilling Dragoons; served in the Crimea 1855. —*Ballygawley House, co. Tyrone; Fincoul Lodge, Carrickmore, Omagh, co. Tyrone; Carlton Club, s.w.*

Heir, his son Hugh Houghton, *b.* 1858.

STEWART, Sir HOUSTON, G.C.B. (cr. 1865).

Third son of the late Sir Michael Shaw-Stewart, Bart., of Blackhall, co. Renfrew, by Catharine, dau. of the late Sir William Maxwell, Bart., of Springkell, co. Dumfries; *b.* 1791; *m.* 1819 Martha, dau. of Sir William Miller, Bart. Is a Magistrate for co. Perth and an Admiral in the Navy; late Commander-in-Chief at Devonport; has been a Lord of the Admiralty; served at Flushing and the siege of Acre, and was second in command in the Black Sea 1855; was M.P. for Greenwich in 1852.—*Guaton Hall, Yealampton, Devon.*

STEWART, ALEXANDER, Esq., of Ballyedmond, Downshire.

Son of the late Thomas Ludford Stewart, Esq., of Belfast, co. Antrim; *b.* 1801; *m.* 1830 Elizabeth, 2nd dau. of James Douglas, Esq. Is a Magistrate for co. Down. —*Ballyedmond, Rostrevor, Downshire.*

STEWART, ALEXANDER JOHN ROBERT, Esq., of Ards, co. Donegal.

Only son of the late Alexander Robert Stewart, Esq., of Ards, by Lady Caroline Anne, 3rd dau. of John Jeffreys, 1st Marquis Camden, K.G.; *b.* 1827; *s.* 1850; *m.* 1851 Lady Isabella Rebecca, 6th dau. of Hector John, 2nd Earl of Norbury, and has, with other issue,

* Alexander George John, *b.* 1852.

Mr. Stewart, who was educated at Trinity Coll., Cambridge, is a J.P. and D.L. for co. Down (High Sheriff 1861-2) and for co. Donegal (High Sheriff 1853). This family is a collateral branch of the Londonderry family. —*Chancellor House, Tunbridge Wells; Ards, Cashelmore, Letterkenny, co. Donegal; Lawn-town, Gilford, co. Down; Carlton and Traveller's Clubs, s.w.; Sackville Street Club, Dublin; 42, Upper Grosvenor Street, w.*

+**STEWART**, CHARLES A., Esq., of Auchnacone, Argyleshire.

Son of the late G. Stewart, Esq., and nephew of the late Miss Stewart, of Auchnacone (who *d.* 1863). Is Lord of the Barony of Auchnacone.—*Auchnacone House, Appin, Benaw, N.B.*

+**STEWART**, the Rev. EDWARD.

Eldest son of the late Hon. Edward Richard Stewart (6th son of John, 7th Earl of Galloway), by Lady Katharine Charteris, sister of Francis, 7th Earl of Wemyss; *b.* 1808; *m.* 1838 Louisa Anne, dau. of the late Charles John Herbert, Esq., of Muckross, co. Kerry, and has, with other surviving issue,

* Herbert, Lieut. and Adjutant 37th Regt., *b.* 1843.

Mr. Stewart, who was educated at Eton and Oriel Coll., Oxford (B.A. 1829, M.A. 1834), appointed Rector of Lainston 1850, and Vicar of Sparsholt, Hants, 1842, was M.P. for Wigton, &c., 1831-4.—*Sparsholt Vicarage, Winchester.*

STEWART, HENRY, Esq., of Corcam, co. Donegal.
Third son of the late Henry Stewart, Esq., of Tyrcallen, co. Donegal, by the Hon. Elizabeth, dau. of Edward, 2nd Lord Longford; *b.* 1799; *m.* 1st 1835 Lucy, eldest dau. of John Norris, Esq. (she *d.* 1854); 2nd 1856 Frances Isabella Anne, elder dau. of the late William Style, Capt. R.N., of Bicester House, Oxon, and had issue by the former, William Norris, *b.* 1836, and *d.* 1843. Mr. Stewart, who was educated at Belfast, represents a family who were formerly seated at Killymoon, co. Tyrone.—*Corcam, Stranorlar, co. Donegal.*

Heir Pres., his brother the Rev. Edward Michael, *b.* 1797; *m.* 1834 Jane, dau. of John Jeffrey, Esq., of Balsanock, N.B., and has, with other issue, * Henry William, in Holy Orders, *b.* 1835.

STEWART, HENRY, Esq., of St. Fort, Fifeshire.
Second son of the late Robert Stewart, Esq., of St. Fort, by Anne Stewart, dau. of Henry Balfour, Esq., of Denboy; *b.* 1796; *s.* 1836; *m.* 1837 Jane, dau. of James Fraser, Esq., of Culduthell, co. Inverness, and has, with other issue,
* Robert Balfour, *b.* 1838.

Mr. Stewart is a J.P. and D.L. for co. Fife. This family is representative of the Stewarts of Urrard, co. Perth.—*St. Fort, Newport, Fifeshire, N.B.; Carlton Club, s.w.*

STEWART, JAMES, Esq., of Cairnsmore, Kirkcudbrightshire.
Eldest son of the late Patrick Stewart, Esq., of Cairnsmore, by Lillias, dau. of Hugh Miller, Esq.; *b.* 1791; *s.* 1814; *m.* 1829 Elizabeth, only dau. of Gilbert Macleod, Esq., and has, with other issue,
* Colvin, *b.* 1830.

Mr. Stewart is a J.P. and D.L. for the Stewartry of Kirkcudbright, and a Magistrate for co. Wigton.—*Cairnsmore, Newton Stewart, N.B.*

STEWART, Capt. JAMES, of Lesmurdie, Banffshire.
Eldest son of the late Major-General Francis Stewart, of Lesmurdie, by Margaret, dau. of the late Sir James Grant, Bart.; *b.* 1797; *s.* 1824. Mr. Stewart is a J.P. and D.L. for co. Banff, and a Capt. in the Army, retired. This family is a branch of Stewart, Earl of Athol, and has been in possession of the estate of Lesmurdie for about 400 years.—*Lesmurdie, Elgin, N.B.*

+ **STEWART, JAMES ROBERT, Esq., of Gortleitragh, co. Dublin.**
Fifth son of the late Henry Stewart, Esq., Tyrcallen. co. Donegal, by the Hon. Eliza Pakenham, eldest dau. of Edward, 2nd Lord Longford; *b.* 1805; *m.* 1835 Martha Eleanor, dau. of the late Richard Benson Warren, Esq., and by her, who *d.* 1865, has, with other issue,
* Henry, in Holy Orders. *b.* 1836; *m.* 1861 Martha, dan. of the Rev. Edward M. Hamilton.

Is a Magistrate for the co. and a Dep.-Lieut. for the city of Dublin.—*Gortleiragh, Monkstown, co. Dublin;* 6, *Leinster Street, Dublin.*

STEWART, JOHN, Esq., late of Belladrum, Inverness-shire.
Only surviving son of the late Thomas Stewart, Esq., of Belladrum, by Anne, dau. of F. Gordon, Esq.; *b.* 1784; *m.* 1814 Jamesina, dau. of the late Capt. Simon Fraser, and widow of Col. W. Campbell, and has surviving issue, two daughters. Mr. Stewart, who is a J.P. and D.L. for co. Inverness, was M.P. for Beverley 1828–32. This family was formerly of Drumin, co. Banff.—2, *Queen Anne Street, w.*

STEWART, JOHN, Esq., of Loughveagh, co. Donegal.
Eldest son of the late Alexander Stewart, Esq., of Gartnafuaro, Ballquihidder, co. Perth, by Jane, dau. of James Buchanan, Esq., of Perthshire; *b.* 1800. Is a Magistrate for cos. Donegal and Tipperary. This family formerly held extensive possessions in Perthshire, which were forfeited in 1715.—*Loughveagh House, Letterkenny, co. Donegal; Royal W. Yacht Club, Dublin.*

STEWART, JOHN LEVESON DOUGLAS, Esq., of Nateby Hall, Lancashire.
Eldest son of the late John Stewart, Esq., of Nateby Hall, by Elizabeth, only dau. of the late Richard Thompson, Esq., of Nateby Hall; *b.* 1842; *s.* 1867. Is descended from Alexander, 6th Earl of Galloway.—*Nateby Hall, Garstang.*

STEWART, JOHN LORNE, Esq., of Coll and Knochrioch, Argyleshire.
Eldest son of the late Duncan Stewart. Esq., of Glenbuckie, by Margaret, dau. of Duncan Stewart, Esq., of Ardsheal; *b.* 1800; *m.* 1831 Mary Campbell, dau. of Archibald Campbell, Esq., and has, with other issue,
* Duncan, *b.* 1834; *m.* 1858 Ferooza Margaret, dau. of the Right Hon. Sir John M'Neill, G.C.B.

Mr. Stewart is a Magistrate for Perthshire, and a Dep.-Lieut. for co. Argyle. This family was formerly of Benmore, co. Perth.—*Stronvar House, Campbelltown; Brechaha Castle, Coll, Argyleshire; United Service Club, Edinburgh.*

STEWART, JOHN THOMAS HAMILL-, Esq., of Ballyatwood House, Downshire.
Only son of John Stewart, Esq. (late Deputy Remembrancer of the Court of Exchequer in Ireland), by Harriet Louisa, dau. and co-heir of the late Hans Mark Hamill, Esq., of Ballyatwood, and grandson of the late Rev. Henry Stewart, D.D.; *b.* 1819; *m.* 1846 Marion Elizabeth, dau. of Edward Hudson, Esq., of Loughbrickland, co. Down, and has, with other issue,
* John Donald, Ensign 11th Hussars; *b.* 1847.

Mr. Hamill-Stewart, who was educated at Trinity Coll., Dublin, is Lord of the Manor of Ballyatwood; he assumed the additional surname of Hamill by Royal licence in 1865.—Residence: *Fulwood Park, Cheltenham; Conservative Club, s.w.*

STEWART, JOHN VANDELEUR, Esq., of Rock Hill, co. Donegal.
Third son of the late Alexander Stewart. Esq., of Ards, by Lady Mary, 3rd dau. of Charles, 1st Marquis of Drogheda, K.P.; *b.* 1804; *m.* 1837 Helen, 4th dau. of Hector, 2nd Earl of Norbury, and has, with other issue,
* Alexander Charles Hector, High Sheriff of co. Donegal 1863–4, and Capt. 2nd Life Guards; *b.* 1838.

Mr. Stewart is a J.P. and D.L. for co. Donegal (High Sheriff 1838). This family is a junior branch of that of the Marquis of Londonderry.—*Rock Hill, Letterkenny; Carlton Club, s.w.;* 13, *Warwick Square, s.w.*

STEWART, MARK S., Esq., of Southwick, Kirkcudbrightshire.
Son of the late Robert Hathorn Stewart, Esq., of Physgill, by Isabella, dau. of the late Sir Stair Agnew, Bart., of Lochnaw, co. Wigtown; *b.* 1802; *m.* 1831 Janet, dau. of the late John Sprot, Esq., of London, and has, with other issue,
* Mark John, J.P.; *b.* 1833; educated at Winchester and Ch. Ch., Oxford (M.A. 1858), and called to the Bar at Inner Temple 1862; *m.* 1866 Marianne Susanna, only child of the late John Orde Ommanney, Esq.

Mr. Stewart, who is a J.P. and D.L. for the Stewartry of Kirkcudbright, is descended from a common ancestor with the Earl of Galloway.—*Southwick, Dumfries, N.B.; New Club, Edinburgh.*

855

STEWART, Mrs. ALSTON-, of Urrard, Perth-shire.

Frances Louisa, eldest dau. and co-heir of the late William Alston-Stewart, Esq., of Urrard, by Penelope Crichton, dau. of Col. Bishop ; *s.* 1842 ; *m.* 1850 Capt. Benjamin Hallowell Boxer (son of the late Rear-Admiral Edward Boxer, C.B.), and had, with other issue,

* William Edward Hallowell, *b.* 1852.

Mrs. Stewart is Lady of the Barony of Urrard.—*Urrard, Killecrankie, N.B.*

STEWART, ROBERT, Esq., of Ardvorlich, Perthshire.

Second but eldest surviving son of the late William Murray Stewart, Esq., of Ardvorlich, by Charlotte, eldest dau. of Major R. J. Debnam ; *b.* 1829 ; *s.* his brother 1857. Is Lord of the Barony of Ardvorlich.—*Ardvorlich, Crieff, N.B.*

Heir, his brother John, *b.* 1833.

STEWART, ROBERT HATHORN JOHNSTON-, Esq., of Physgill, Wigtownshire, and Straiton, Midlothian.

Eldest son of the late Stair Hathorn Stewart, Esq., J.P. and D.L. of Physgill, by his 1st wife Margaret, only dau. of the late Alexander Johnston, Esq., of Straiton, co. Linlithgow ; *b.* 1824 ; *s.* his uncle in the Straiton and Champfleurie estates 1842, and his father at Physgill 1865 ; *m.* 1st 1851 Eleanor Louisa, dau. of Archibald Douglas, Esq., of Glenfinart, co. Argyle ; 2nd 1856 Anne Murray, 2nd dau. of Sir William Maxwell, Bart., and has by the former, with other issue,

* Stair Hathorn, *b.* 1852.

Mr. Stewart, who was educated at Eton, is a J.P. and D.L. for Linlithgow, Midlothian, and co. Wigtown, Lord of the Barony of Straiton, and a Major in the Linlithgow Volunteer Rifles ; was formerly Capt. 13th Light Dragoons.—*Glasserton and Physgill, Whithorn, Wigtownshire, N.B. ; Straiton, Edinburgh ; Champfleurie, Linlithgow, N.B. ; New Club, Edinburgh.*

STEWART, THOMAS BLAKENEY-LYON-, Esq., of Whitegate House, co. Cork.

Fourth son of the late Henry Stewart, Esq., M.P., of Tycaller, co. Donegal, by Elizabeth, eldest dau. of Edward, 2nd Lord Longford ; *b.* 1802 ; *s.* 1854 ; *m.* 1855 Anne, 4th dau. of James Penrose, Esq., of Woodhill, co. Cork; assumed the additional names of Blakeney and Lyon in 1855, on succeeding to the Mount Blakeney estates. Educated at Trinity Coll., Dublin (A.M. 1832) ; is a Magistrate for co. Cork.— *Whitegate House, Cloyne, co. Cork ; National Club, s.w.*

Heir Pres., his brother James Robert, *b.* 1805 ; *m.* 1835 Martha Eleanor, dau. of Richard Benson Warren, Esq.

STEWART, WILLIAM, Esq., of Shambellie, Kirkcudbrightshire.

Eldest son of the late William Stewart, Esq., of Shambellie, by Bethia, dau. of Charles Donaldson, Esq., of Broughton ; *b.* 1815 ; *s.* 1814 ; *m.* 1845 Katherine, dau. of John Hardie, Esq., of Edinburgh, and has, with other issue,

* William, *b.* 1848.

Mr. Stewart, who was educated at Edinburgh University, is a J.P. and D.L. for the Stewartry of Kirkcudbright ; was formerly Major in the Galloway Militia.—*Shambellie, Dumfries, N.B.*

STEWART. (See under *Galloway, Earl of*, and *Londonderry, Marquis of*.)

STEWART. (See *Murray-Stewart*.)

STEWART-MURRAY. (See under *Athole, Duke of*.)

886

STEWART-MACKENZIE. (See *Mackenzie*.)

+STEWART-MENZIES, JOHN, Esq., of Chesthill, Perthshire.

Eldest son of the late Joseph Stewart, Esq., of Foss. co. Perth, by Elizabeth, dau. and heir of Alexander Menzies, Esq., of Chesthill ; *b.* 1804 ; *s.* 1835. Is a J.P. and D.L. for co. Perth, and Lord of the Barony of Chesthill.—*Chesthill House, Aberfeldy, N.B.*

STEWART-NICOLSON, MICHAEL HUGH, Esq., of Carnock, Stirlingshire.

Eldest son of Sir Michael Shaw-Stewart, Bart., of Blackhall (whom see), by Lady Octavia, dau. of Richard, 2nd Marquis of Westminster, K.G. ; *b.* 1854. Educated at Eton ; is Lord of the Barony of Carnock. The estate was left by Dame H. Nicolson, in 1711, to the heir of Ardgowan in perpetual succession, subject to the assumption of the name of Nicolson.—*Carnock, Stirling, N.B.*

Heir Pres., his brother Charles Robert, *b.* 1856.

STIEGLITZ. (See *Von Stieglitz*.)

+STILL, CHARLES STEWART, Esq., of Burgar, Isle of Orkney.

Son of the late C. Still, Esq., of Burgar ; *b.* 18—. Is a J.P. and D.L. for the Isle of Orkney.—*Burgar, Orkney, N.B.*

STILL, Capt. JOHN TRYON, of Castle Hill, Devonshire.

Son of the late Major Nathaniel Tryon Still, of Castle Hill, by Mary, dau. of Col. Richard Bingham, of Melcombe, Dorset ; *b.* 1820 ; *s.* 1862 ; *m.* 1845 Charlotte Mallock, dau. of Charles Bond, Esq., of Axminster, Devon, and has, with other issue,

* John Nathaniel, *b.* 1847.

Capt. Still, who was educated at the Royal Military Coll., Sandhurst, is a Magistrate for Devon ; late Capt. 34th and 30th Regts.—*Castle Hill, Axminster.*

STIRLING, Sir CHARLES ELPHINSTONE FLEMING, Bart., of Glorat, Stirlingshire (cr. 1666).

Third and only surviving son of the late Capt. George Stirling, by his 1st wife Anne, dau. of William Gray, Esq., of Oxgang, and grandson of the late Sir John Stirling, Bart., of Glorat ; *b.* 1832 ; *s.* his brother 1861 ; *m.* 1867 Anne Georgiana, eldest dau. of James Murray, Esq. Represents paternally the extinct Earls of Bothwell and Dunbar, and the Homes of Renton.—*Glorat House, Glasgow, N.B.*

STIRLING, Sir WALTER GEORGE, Bart., of Faskine, Lanarkshire (cr. 1800).

Only son of the late Sir Walter Stirling, Bart., of Faskine, by Susannah, dau. of George T. Goodenough, Esq., of Bordwood, Isle of Wight : *b.* 1802 ; *s.* as 2nd Bart., 1832 ; *m.* 1835 Lady Caroline Frances, dau. of John, 1st Earl of Strafford. Educated at Westminster and Ch. Ch., Oxford ; is a Magistrate for Kent.—*Faskine, Lanark, N.B. ; ... ; Barswood, Tunbridge Wells ; ... and ... Clubs, s.w.; 36, Portland Square, w.*

Heir, his son Walter George, Lieut. R.H.A., and Extra Groom in Waiting to Her Majesty ; *b.* 1839.

STIRLING, ANDREW, Esq., of Muiravonside, Stirlingshire.

Eldest son of the late Charles Stirling, Esq., J.P., of Muiravonside, by Charlotte Dorothea, only dau. of the late Vice-Admiral Charles Stirling, of Woburn Farm, Chertsey, Surrey ; *b.* 1829 ; *s.* 1867 ; *m.* 1861 Georgina Louisa, 2nd dau. of the late Sir Henry Martin Blackwood, Bart. Educated at Edinburgh Academy, is Lord of the Barony of Muiravonside.—*Muiravonside House, Linlithgow, N.B.*

STIRLING, CHARLES, Esq.

Eldest son of the late Vice-Admiral Charles Stirling, of Woburn Farm, Surrey, by Charlotte, 2nd dau. of the late Andrew Grote, Esq., of Blackheath; *b.* 1793; *m.* 1833 Mary Elizabeth, eldest dau. of the late Henry Harrison, Esq., of Heath Bank, near Stockport, and has, with other issue,

* Charles Henry, Commander R.N.; *b.* 1836; *m.* 1867 Lillie, 4th dau. of the late Rev. Henry Gray, of Oaklands, co. Gloucester, and niece of the 2nd Earl of Limerick.

Mr. Stirling, who was educated at the University of Glasgow, represents a younger branch of the Stirlings of Drumpellier.—Residence: *Buckridge House, Teignmouth.*

STIRLING, GILBERT, Esq., of Larbert.

(See under *Chalmer, of Larbert House.*)

STIRLING, Capt. JAMES, of Glentyan, Renfrewshire.

Fourth son of the late John Stirling, Esq., of Kippendavie, by Mary, dau. of William Graham, Esq., of Airth; *b.* 1789; *m.* 1st 1820 Mary, dau. of the late Day Hort Macdowall, Esq., of Castle Semple, co. Renfrew; 2nd 1844 Elizabeth, dau. of James Dundas, Esq., of Ochtertyre, and widow of William Macdowall, Esq., of Carruth, co. Renfrew. Is a J.P. and D.L. for Renfrew, a Magistrate for co. Perth, and a Capt. R.N., retired. This family is a cadet of the Stirlings of Keir.—*Glentyan, Johnstone, Paisley, N.B.*

STIRLING, JOHN, Esq., of Kippendavie, Perthshire.

Eldest son of the late Patrick Stirling, Esq., of Kippendavie, by Catherine Georgina, 2nd dau. of John Wedderburn, Esq., of Jamaica; *b.* 1811; *s.* 1816; *m.* 1839 Catherine Mary, only child of the Rev. John Wellings, and has, with other issue,

* Patrick, *b.* 1846.

Mr. Stirling is a Magistrate for co. Perth, and Lord of the Barony of Kippendavie.—*Kippendavie, Dunblane, N.B.; Carlton Club,* s.w.

STIRLING, JAMES, Esq., of Cosdale, Dumbartonshire.

Eldest son of the late William Stirling, Esq., of Cosdale, by Margaret Hamilton, dau. of James Ritchie, Esq., of Busbie; *b.* 1805. Educated at Edinburgh High School and University of Göttingen; is a J.P. and D.L. for co. Dumbarton; elected M.P. for co. Dumbarton 1865, but unseated on scrutiny.—*Cosdale, Dumbarton, N.B.; Reform Club,* s.w.

STIRLING, JOHN STIRLING, Esq., of Gargunnock, Stirlingshire.

Only son of the late Charles Stirling, Esq., of Gargunnock, by Christian, dau. of John Hamilton, Esq. of Sundrum, co. Ayr; *b.* 1832; *s.* 1839. Educated at the Royal Military Academy, Woolwich; is Lord of the Barony of Gargunnock, and a Capt. R.A. This family is a branch of the Stirlings of Keir.—*Gargunnock House, Stirling, N.B.; Army and Navy Club,* s.w.

STIRLING, Miss, of Drumpellier, Lanarkshire.

Agnes, dau. of the late Andrew Stirling, Esq., of Drumpellier (who *d.* 1823), by Anna, dau. of the late Sir Walter Stirling, Knt., Capt. R.N.; *s.* her brother, Walter Stirling, Esq., 1864. Her nephew, Thomas Mayne Stirling, Esq., holds the feudal superiority of the barony of Drumpellier, and is lineal male representative of the ancient family of the Stirlings of Cadder and Ochiltree.—*Drumpellier, Coatbridge, N.B.;* 18, *Curzon Street,* w.

+STIRLING, Mrs., of Holme Hill, Perthshire.

Christian, eldest dau. of the late David Erskine, Esq., of Flambagar, Bengal; *m.* 1844 James Stirling, Esq.,

of Holme Hill, a Magistrate for co. Perth, who *d.* 1866.—*Holme Hill, Dunblane, N.B.*

STIRLING, WILLIAM, Esq., of Tarduf, Stirlingshire.

Third son of the late William Stirling, Esq. (who *d.* 1862), by Elizabeth, dau. of Henry Barrett, Esq. of Cinnamon Hill, Jamaica, and is grandson of the late John Stirling, Esq., of Kippendavie, co. Perth; *b.* 1822; *m.* 1855 his cousin Mary Katherine, dau. of the late Sylvester Douglas Stirling, Esq., of Glenbervie, co. Stirling, and has, with other issue,

* William George Hay, *b.* 1861.

Mr. Stirling is a Magistrate for cos. Stirling and Lanark, and Col. 5th Lanark Rifle Volunteers.—*Tarduf, Linlithgow, N.B.*

STIRLING. (See *Graham-Stirling.*)

STIRLING-CRAWFURD. (See *Crawfurd.*)

STIRLING-MAXWELL, Sir WILLIAM, Bart., of Keir, Perthshire, and Pollok, Renfrewshire (cr. 1682).

Eldest son of the late Archibald Stirling, Esq., of Keir, by Elizabeth, 2nd dau. of the late Sir John Maxwell, Bart., of Pollock; *b.* 1818; *s.* 1850; *m.* 1865 Lady Anna Maria, 2nd dau. of David, 10th Earl of Leven and Melville. Educated at Trinity Coll., Cambridge (B.A. 1839, M.A. 1843); is Vice-Lieut. of co. Perth, Lord of the Barony of Keir, and Patron of 1 living: has been M.P. for co. Perth since 1852; author of ' Cloister Life of the Emperor Charles V.,' ' Annals of the Artists of Spain,' &c.—*Keir, Dunblane; Pollok, Glasgow. N.B.; Cawder House, Corrance, Dunblane, N.B.; Travellers', Athenæum, and Carlton Clubs,* s.w.; 128, *Park Street,* w.

Heir, his son John Maxwell, *b.* 1866.

STIRLING-STUART, Capt. JAMES, of Castlemilk, Lanarkshire.

Son of the late William Stirling, Esq., of Castlemilk, by his 2nd wife Anne Charlotte, dau. of Sir A. Gibson-Maitland, Bart., of Clifton Hall, and half-brother of W. S. Stirling-Crawfurd, Esq. (whom see); *b.* 1825; *m.* 1852 Harriet, dau. of the late Matthew Fortescue, Esq., and has, with other issue,

* William, *b.* 1854.

Mr. Stirling, who assumed the additional name of Stuart on succeeding to the estate of Castlemilk, is a Magistrate for co. Lanark, and was formerly Capt. King's Dragoon Guards.—*Castlemilk, Glasgow.*

STOBART, WILLIAM, Esq.

Eldest son of the late William Stobart, Esq., of Picktree, co. Durham (who *d.* 1830), by Barbara, dau. of the late William Hayton, Esq., of Sunderland; *b.* 1822; *m.* 1851 Sophia, dau. of General William Wylde, C.B., R.A. Educated at St. John's Coll., Oxford; is a Magistrate for co. Durham.—Residence: *Cot..... ....l, Pica.... House, Durham.*

STOBART, Mrs., of Etherley House, co. Durham.

Elizabeth Rachel Maurice, youngest dau. of the late Rev. Thomas Richards, Vicar of Icklesham, Sussex; *m.* 1855 Col. Henry Stobart, J.P. and D.L., of Etherley House, who *d.* 1866, leaving, with other issue, * Henry *b.* 1822.—*Etherley House, Bishop-Auckland.*

STOCK, OSBORNE, Esq., M.P.

Eldest son of the late Charles Stock, Esq., by Rebecca, dau. of William Rankin, Esq., of Layne, near Braintree, Essex; *b.* 1822; *m.* 1849 Juliana Priscilla, dau.

of the late Capt. Farmar. Is a Merchant in the City; elected M.P. for Carlow 1865.—*Reform Club, s.w.; 2, Harley Street, w.*

STOCKDALE, HENRY MINSHULL, Esq., of Mears Ashby Hall, Northamptonshire.
Third but second surviving son of the late Rev. William Stockdale, of Mears Ashby Hall. and Vicar of Mears Ashby, by Honor. dau. of the Rev. Godfrey Wolley, Vicar of Hutton Bushell. co. York; *b.* 1822; *s.* 1858; *m.* 1858 Sarah Emily, dau. of the Rev. Robert Hervey Knight, and has, with other issue,
    * Henry Minshull, *b.* 1861.
Mr. Stockdale, who was educated at Jesus Coll., Cambridge (B.A. 1845, M.A. 1848), and was called to the Bar at Lincoln's Inn 1848, is a Magistrate for co. Northampton, and Patron of 3 livings; he was Capt. Wellingborough Rifle Volunteers, and previously Capt. Northamptonshire Militia.—*Mears Ashby Hall, Northampton; University Club, s.w.*

STOCKENSTRÖM, Sir GYSBERT HENRY, Bart. (cr. 1840).
Eldest son of the late Sir Andries Stockenström, Bart. (who was formerly Lieut.-Governor of the Cape of Good Hope). by Elsabe Helena, dau. of Gysbert Henry Maasdorp, Esq., of the Cape of Good Hope; *b.* 1841; *s.* as 2nd Bart. 1864. Educated at King's Coll., London; late Ensign 61st Foot. This family is of Swedish extraction.—*Maastrōm, Bedford, Cape of Good Hope.*
    Heir Pres., his brother Andries. B.A. of London University. Barrister-at-Law of the Middle Temple; b. 1844; m. 1868 Maria Henrietta, eldest dau. of Andries J. Hartzenberg, Esq.

STODART. (See *Twedie-Stodart.*)

STOKES, FREDERICK TANFIELD, Esq., of Denmark Hill, co. Dublin.
Eldest son of the late James Stokes. Esq., of London, by Sarah, dau. of John Duff, Esq., of London; *b.* 1820; *m.* 1839 Rebecca, dau. of Richard Dore, Esq. Is a Magistrate for co. Dublin, and Chairman of the Rathmines Commission.—*Denmark Hill, Rathmines, co. Dublin.*

STOKES, GEORGE DAY, Esq., of Mounthawk, co. Kerry.
Eldest son of the late Oliver Stokes, Esq., of Tralee, co. Kerry, by Elizabeth, dau. of John Day, Esq., of Cork; *b.* 1802; *s.* 1844; *m.* 1826 Mary Anne, dau. and co-heir of Robert Barett, Esq., of Horstead Hall, Norfolk, and has, with other issue,
    * Henry Bowles George, late Capt. 17th Regt.; *b.* 1891.
Mr. Stokes, who was educated at Trinity Coll., Dublin (B.A. 1828, M.A. 1832), is a Magistrate for co. Kerry, and Treasurer of the county.—*Mounthawk, Tralee.*

STOKES, Mrs., of Lassenagh, co. Kerry.
Jane, youngest dau. of the late Col. Littlejohn, of the Bengal Army; *m.* 1829 Major-Gen. John Day Stokes. J.P., formerly British representative at the Court of Mysore, who *d. s. p.* 1863.—*Lassenagh, Tralee.*
    Heir Pres., her husband's nephew Oliver, b. 18—.

STONE, EDWARD GRESLEY, Esq., of Chambers Court, Worcestershire.
Son of the late John Stone, Esq., of Chambers Court, by Arabella, dau. of Capt. Edward Thorley, of Colchester, Essex; *b.* 1807; *s.* 1811; *m.* 1829 Susannah, dau. of the Rev. Henry Shepherd, D.D., Chaplain at Calcutta, and has, with other issue,
    * Edward Henry Montagu, in Holy Orders; educated at Rugby and Wadham Coll., Oxford; *b.* 1830; *m.* 1st 1855 Jane, dau. of the Rev. Henry Somers-Cocks (she *d.* 1857); 2nd 1863 Elizabeth, dau. of the Rev. Charles Hubert Parker, Rector of Great Comberton, co. Worcester.
Mr. Stone, who was educated at Winchester and Uni-
888

versity Coll., Oxford, is a Magistrate and Dep.-Lieut. for co. Worcester (High Sheriff 1847), and a Dep.-Lieut. for Essex.—*Chambers Court, Longdon, Tewkesbury.*

STONE, GEORGE, Esq.
Eldest son of the late Rev. George Stone, Rector of Hopton, Suffolk; *b.* 1789. Educated at Eton; entered the Royal Horse Guards as Cornet in 1806; was formerly an Officer in the Blues, and afterwards in the 7th Hussars, and served in the Peninsula; is a Magistrate for co. Northampton.—Residence : *Blisworth House, Northampton.*

STONE, HENRY, Esq., of Badbury, Wilts.
Eldest son of the late Baynton Stone, Esq., Lieut.-Col. 58th Foot, by Anne, only dau. of John Stone, Esq., of Badbury. Wilts; *b.* 1824; *m.* 1850 Katherine Mary, eldest dau. of the late Anthony George Biddulph. Esq., of Burton Park, Sussex. Was formerly in the 6th Inniskilling Dragoons.—*Badbury, Swindon; Army and Navy Club, s.w.; Stafford Club, w.*

+ STONE, JOHN SPENCER, Esq., of Collingswood, Staffordshire.
Eldest son of late — Stone, Esq., of Collingswood; *b.* 1813. Educated at Eton and Ch. Ch., Oxford.—*Collingswood, Burton-on-Trent.*

STONE, Mrs., of Streatley House, Berks.
Emily, only dau. of the late James Morrell. Esq., of Headington House, Oxon, by Jane, dau. of Theophilus Wharton, Esq., of Headington ; *m.* 1830 William Henry Stone, Esq., of Streatley House. who was a J.P. and D.L. for Oxon and for Berks (High Sheriff 1847), and who *d. s. p.* 1863. This family have been located in Berkshire for a century.—*Streatley House, Reading.*

STONE, WILLIAM HENRY, Esq., of Leigh Park, Hants.
Eldest son of the late William Stone, Esq., of Dulwich Hill, Surrey, by Mary, dau. of the late Thomas Platt. Esq., of Child's Hill, Hampstead; *b.* 1834; *m.* 1864 Milicent, 2nd dau. of Arthur Helps, Esq., of Vernon Hill, Hants, and has issue,
    * A son, *b.* 1866.
Mr. Stone, who was educated at Harrow and Trinity Coll., Cambridge (B.A. 1857, M.A. 1860), and elected Fellow of Trinity Coll. 1859, is a Magistrate for Surrey and Hants, Lord of the Manors of Havant and Flood, and Patron of 5 livings ; elected M.P. for Portsmouth 1865.—*Leigh Park, Havant; University Club, s.w.; Dulwich Hill, Surrey, s.*

STONE. (See under *Lowndes-Norton.*)

STONEHEWER. (See *Scott-Stonehewer.*)

STONESTREET. (See *Griffin-Stonestreet.*)

STONEY, THOMAS BUTLER, Esq., of Portland, co. Tipperary.
Eldest son of the late Richard Falkiner Stoney, Esq., of Portland. by Jane, 2nd dau. of the late James Butler, Esq., of Castlecrine, co. Clare, s. 1848; m. 1847 Sarah, eldest dau. and co-heir of Robert Fannin, Esq., of Dublin, and has, with other issue,
    * Thomas Bowes, *b.* 1843.
Mr. Stoney, who was educated at Trinity Coll., Dublin, is a Magistrate for cos. Galway and Tipperary (High Sheriff 1855), and was formerly in the 12th Regt.—*Portland, Roscrea, co. Tipperary.*

STONEY, THOMAS GEORGE, Esq., of Kyle, co. Tipperary.
Only son of the late George Stoney. Esq., of Arran Hill, co. Tipperary, by Mary Anne, dau. of William Smith, Esq., of Gurteen, co. Tipperary; *b.* 1808; *s.*

1810; *m.* 1829 Anna Henrietta, only dau. of the late Thomas Waller, of Finnoe, and has, with other issue,

* George Francis, Capt. Tipperary Militia; *b.* 1834.

Mr. Stoney, who was educated at Trinity Coll., Dublin, is a Magistrate for co. Tipperary, and Lord of the Manor of Kyle.—*Kyle Park, Borrisokane.*

STONHOUSE, Sir HENRY VANSITTART, Bart.
(cr. 1670).

Son of the late Sir Timothy Stonhouse, Bart., by Mary Diana, dau. of the Rev. George William Sturt, of Long Critchill, co. Dorset; *b.* 1827; *s.* as 11th Bart. 1866; *m.* 1851 Charlotte, dau. of the late John Beatty West, Esq., M.P. (she *d.* 1857). Was formerly an Officer in the 94th Regt. Two distinct baronetcies met in the person of the 6th Bart.

Heir, his son Reginald Charles, *b.* 1853.

STONHOUSE-VIGOR, Mrs.

Louisa Burt, dau. of the late J. Taylor-Gordon, Esq., M.D., by Eliza Barham, dau. of R. M. Hansard, Esq., of Miskin House, co. Glamorgan; *m.* 1833 the Rev. Henry Stonhouse-Vigor, grandson of the Rev. Sir James Stonhouse, Bart.; he *d.* 1838, leaving issue, * Alfred Henry Say, heir of entail to the family estates, B.A. of St. John's Coll., Cambridge, and a Barrister-at-Law of Lincoln's Inn; *b.* 1835; *m.* 1867 Gertrude, youngest dau. of William Bird, Esq., of Crouch Hall, Middlesex. —*Marine Parade, Eastbourne.*

STONOR, CHARLES JOSEPH, Esq., of Anderton Hall, Lancashire.

Only son of the late Hon. Charles Henry Stonor, of Anderton, by Sophia, dau. of the late John Cary, Esq., of Tor Abbey, Devon; *b.* 1837; *s.* 1840; *m.* 1865 Maude Mary, 3rd dau. of Charles Noel Welman, Esq., of Norton Manor, Somerset (whom see). Educated at St. Mary's Coll., Oscott; represents a younger branch of the family of Lord Camoys.—*Anderton Hall, Chorley; Stafford Club, w.*

STONOR. (See under *Camoys, Lord.*)

STOPFORD, Lady.

Lucy, youngest dau. of John Clay, Esq., of North Charlton, Northumberland; *m.* 1853 (as his 2nd wife) the Hon. Sir Montagu Stopford, K.C.B., fourth son of James George, 3rd Earl of Courtown, who was a Magistrate for co. Wexford, and an Admiral on the reserved half-pay list, and who *d.* 1864.

STOPFORD, the Hon. and Rev. HENRY SCOTT.

Third son of James George, 3rd Earl of Courtown, by Lady Mary, eldest dau. of Henry, 3rd Duke of Buccleuch; *b.* 1797; *m.* 1826 Annette, dau. of W. Browne, Esq., who *d.* 1842. Educated at Trinity Coll., Cambridge (M.A. 1819); appointed Rector of Clonmore and Archdeacon of Leighlin 1824, and Rector of Killeban 1826.—*Clonmore Rectory, Bolinglass, co. Carlow.*

STOPFORD, Capt. EDWARD, of Falconer's Hill, Northamptonshire.

Sixth son of the late Hon. and Rev. Richard Bruce Stopford, formerly Canon of Windsor, Prebendary of Hereford (who *d.* 1844), by the Hon. Eleanor, eldest dau. of Thomas, 1st Lord Lilford; *b.* 1809; *m.* 1840 Julia Maria, eldest dau. of the late Capt. William Wilbraham, R.N., and has, with other issue,

* Henry Edward, Lieut. 36th Regt.; *b.* 1841.

Mr. Stopford, who was educated at the R. Naval Coll., is a Magistrate for co. Northampton, and a Capt. R.N. This family is a branch of that of the Earl of Courtown. —*Falconer's Hill, Daventry; United Service Club, s.w.*

STOPFORD, WILLIAM BRUCE, Esq., of Drayton House, Northamptonshire.

Fourth son of the late Hon. and Rev. Richard Bruce Stopford, by Eleanor, dau. of Thomas, 1st Lord Lilford, and grandson of James, 2nd Earl of Courtown; *b.* 1806; *s.* 1813; *m.* 1837 Caroline Harriet, dau. of the late Hon. George Germain, and niece and heir of Charles, 5th Duke of Dorset (ext.), and has, with other issue,

* Sackville George, educated at Eton and Ch. Ch., Oxford; M.P. for N. Northamptonshire; *b.* 1840.

Mr. Stopford, who was educated at Woolwich, is a J.P. and D.L. for co. Northampton (High Sheriff 1850), and Patron of 3 livings; was formerly a Clerk in the Foreign Office.—*Drayton House, Thrapstone; Travellers' and Carlton Clubs, s.w.; 7, Grosvenor Gardens, s.w.*

STOPFORD. (See under *Courtown, Earl of.*)

STOPFORD-BLAIR, WILLIAM HENRY, Esq., of Penninghame House, Wigtonshire.

Eldest surviving son of the late Hon. Edward Stopford (son of James, 1st Earl of Courtown), who assumed the name of Blair on succeeding to the property of his brother-in-law, James Blair, Esq., M.P., of Penninghame, by Letitia, dau. of the late William Blacker, Esq., of Carrick Blacker; *b.* 178-; *m.* 1825 Mira Sophia, dau. of Lieut.-Col. Bull, C.B., and has, with other issue,

* Edward James, a J.P. and D.L. for co. Wigton, and late an Officer in the 13th Light Dragoons; *b.* 1826; *m.* 1854 Elizabeth Letitia Morgan, eldest dau. of the Very Rev. Hugh Usher Tighe, Dean of Ardagh.

Mr. Stopford-Blair, who is a Col. in the Army, was formerly in the Royal Artillery.—*Penninghame, Newton Stewart, N.B.; 4, Portman Square, w.*

STORER, ANTHONY MORRIS, Esq., of Purley Park, Berks.

Eldest son of the late Anthony Storer, Esq., of Purley, by Ann Katherine, dau. of Thomas Hill, Esq., of Shropshire; *b.* 1816; *m.* 1860 Cicely Barr, sixth dau. of the late Sir John Pollard Willoughby, Bart., and has issue a dau. Mr. Storer, who was educated at Eton, is a Magistrate for Berks. Lord of the Manor of Purley, and Major in the Oxfordshire Militia.—*Purley Park, Reading; Athenæum Club, s.w.*

+STORER, GEORGE, Esq., of Thoroton Hall, Notts.

Eldest son of the late George Storer, Esq., of Thoroton Hall; *b.* 18–; *m.* 1859 Harriet Anne, eldest dau. of M. Palmer, Esq., of Horncastle, and widow of Dr. Manson, of Spynie, N.B. Is Lord of the Manor of Thoroton.—*Thoroton Hall, Newark.*

STORER, the Rev. JOHN, of Combe Court, Surrey.

Eldest son of the late Rev. John Storer, M.A., Rector of Hawkesworth, Notts (who *d.* 1857), by his 1st wife Charlotte, dau. of the Rev. Charles Wylde; *b.* 1812; *m.* 1834 Margaret Amelia, eldest dau. of the Rev. Richard Tillard, of Street, and Ho..., Kent, and has with other issue.

* John, *b.* 1836.

Mr. Storer, who was educated at Trinity Hall, Cambridge (B.A. 1834, M.A. 1858), is a Magistrate for Notts, and Patron and late Rector of Hawkesworth, Notts. —*Combe Court, Godalming; Residence: Bath.*

STORKS, the Right Hon. Sir HENRY KNIGHT, G.C.B., G.C.M.G. (cr. 1857).

Eldest son of the late Mr. Serjeant Storks, Chief Justice of Ely and Recorder of Cambridge, by Mary Ann dau. and co-heir of the late Thomas Trundle, Esq.; *b.* 1811; *m.* 1841 Eliza Adelaide Maria, only child of the

Chevalier Giuseppe Nizzoli, of Milan, and by her, who *d.* 1848, has issue,
* Henry, *b.* 1842.

Sir H. K. Storks, who was educated at the Charterhouse, is a Major-General in the Army; was Secretary for Military Correspondence at the War Office 1857–9, and Lord High Commissioner of the Ionian Islands 1859–64; appointed Governor of Malta 1864; was Governor and Commander of the Forces at Jamaica 1866, and President of the Royal Commission of Inquiry into the disturbances in that Island; sworn of the Privy Council 1866; appointed Director-General of Supplies at the War Department 1867.—*United Service Club,* s.w. 11A *Albany,* w.

STORMONT. (See under *Mansfield, Earl of.*)

STORY, JAMES, Esq., of Ture, co. Cavan, and Errington, co. Tyrone.
Only son of the late James Hamilton Story, Esq., J.P., Barrister-at-Law, of Errington and of Loughinton, co. Cavan (High Sheriff of Cavan 1822), by Sarah Thorpe, only child of Henry Waymouth, Esq., of Bryanston Square, London; *b.* 1828; *s.* 1863. Mr. Story, who was educated at King's Coll., London, and Trinity Coll., Cambridge (B.A. 1851, M.A. 1853), and M.A. of Trinity Coll., Dublin, is a Magistrate for cos. Tyrone and Cavan (High Sheriff 1860), and was formerly Capt. co. Cavan Militia.—*Ture, Belturbet, co. Cavan; Errington, Kilskerry, Enniskillen, co. Tyrone; Carlton Club,* s.w.; 17, *Bryanston Square,* w.
Heir Pres., his sisters—Mary, and Frances, *m.* 1856 Sir W. Carpenter Rowe, Chief Justice, Ceylon, who *d.* 1859.

+**STORY,** JOHN BAINBRIDGE, Esq., of Lockington, Leicestershire.
Son of the late John Story, Esq., of Lockington Hall; *b.* 180–; is married, and has, with other issue,
* John Bainbridge (late of Sutton Field, Kegworth), educated at Eton, a Magistrate for co. Leicester; late of the 52nd Foot; *b.* 1832.

Mr. Story, who was educated at Eton, is a Magistrate for co. Leicester, Lord of the Manor and Patron of Lockington.—*Lockington Hall, Loughborough.*

STORY, JOSEPH, Esq., of Bingfield, co. Cavan.
Eldest son of the late Rev. Joseph Story, of Bingfield, by Louisa, dau. of the late Sir Peter Rivers, Bart.; *b.* 1837; *s.* 1838; *m.* 1852 Caroline Sophia Kenneth, dau. of Nevile Reid, Esq., of Runnymede, Berks, and has, with other issue,
* Robert, *b.* 1854.

Mr. Story, who was educated at Winchester and Trinity Coll., Dublin (B.A. 1859), and called to the Irish Bar 1841, is a Magistrate for co. Cavan (High Sheriff 1853). — *Bingfield, Crossdoney, co. Cavan; Sackville Street Club, Dublin.*

STOTHERT, WILLIAM, Esq., of Blaiket, Kirkcudbrightshire.
Eldest son of the late James Stothert, Esq., of Cargen, by Margaret, dau. of Thomas Cockburn, Esq., of Rochester, co. Berwick; *b.* 1791; *s.* 1812; *m.* 1815 Rebecca, dau. of the late Robert Monteith, Esq., of Rocksoles, and has, with other issue,
* James, *b.* 1817.

Mr. Stothert, who was educated at the University of Edinburgh, is a J.P. and D.L. for co. Kirkcudbright, and Lord of the Manor of Blaiket.—*Blaiket, Crocketford, Dumfries, N.B.; Cargen Lodge, Edinburgh.*

STOUGHTON, CHARLES WILLIAM, Esq., of Ballynoe, co. Kerry.
Younger son of the late Thomas Anthony Stoughton, Esq., of Ballyhorgan, co. Kerry, and Owlpen Park, co. Gloucester (who *d.* 1862), by Mary, dau. and heir of
890

the late Thomas Daunt, Esq., of Gortigrenane, co. Cork; *b.* 181–; *s.* his uncle 1849; *m.* 1855 Percy Georgina Laura, 2nd dau. of the late George Bagot Gosset, Esq., 4th Dragoon Guards, and has, with other issue,
* Charles Cecil Percy, *b.* 1856.

Mr. Stoughton, who was educated at Trinity Coll., Cambridge, is a Magistrate for co. Kerry, Dep.-Lieut. for co. Gloucester, and Lord of the Manor of Ballynoe.—*Ballynoe, Causeway, co. Kerry; Arthur's, Brooks's, and Union Clubs,* s.w.

+**STOUGHTON,** CLARKE, Esq., of Bawdeswell Hall, Norfolk.
Son of the late — Stoughton, Esq.; *b.* 18—. Is a Magistrate for Norfolk.—*Bawdeswell Hall, Thetford.*

STOUGHTON, Mrs., of Ballyhorgan, co. Kerry, Owlpen, Gloucestershire, and Gortigrenane, co. Cork.
Mary, dau. and heir of the late Thomas Daunt, Esq., of Owlpen Park and Gortigrenane, by Mary, dau. of George Baker, Esq., of Cork: *s.* her father 1803; *m.* 1815 Thomas Anthony Stoughton, Esq., of Ballyhorgan, J.P. and D.L. (who *d.* 1862), leaving, with other issue,
* Thomas Anthony, a J.P. and D.L. for cos. Gloucester, and a Magistrate for co. Kerry; *b.* 1818; *m.* 1862 Rose, youngest dau. of the late William Plunkett, Esq., Barrister-at-Law.

Mrs. Stoughton is Lady of the Manor of Owlpen, and Patron of 1 living. — *Owlpen Park, Dursley; Gortigrenane, Carrigaline, co. Cork; Ballyhorgan, Listowel.*

STOURTON, Lord (CHARLES STOURTON).—Cr. 1448.
Eldest son of William, 17th Lord, by Catharine, dau. of the late Thomas Weld, Esq., of Lulworth Castle, Dorset (sister of Cardinal Weld); *b.* 1802; *s.* 1846; *m.* 1825 the Hon. Mary Lucy, dau. of Charles, 6th Lord Clifford, of Chudleigh. Is a Dep.-Lieut. for the E. Riding of Yorkshire, and Patron of 1 living.—*Stourton, Knaresborough.*
Heir, his son Alfred Joseph, a Dep.-Lieut. for the W. Riding of co. York, late Lieut. Yorkshire Hussars; *b.* 1829; *m.* 1865 Mary Margaret, only child of M. E. Corbally, Esq., of Corbalton Hall (whom see), and has issue, *a* son, *b.* 1847.

STOURTON, HENRY, Esq., of Holme Hall, Yorkshire.
Only son of the late Hon. Philip Stourton, of Holme Hall, by Catharine, eldest dau. of the late Henry Howard, Esq., of Corby Castle, Cumberland; *b.* 1844; *s.* 1860. Educated at Stonyhurst Coll. and Ch. Ch., Oxford; is Lord of the Manor of Holme.—*Holme Hall, York.*
Heir Pres., his sisters.

STOURTON, the Hon. WILLIAM.
Third son of William, 17th Lord Stourton, by Catharine, dau. of Thomas Weld, Esq., of Lulworth Castle, Dorset; *b.* 1810; *m.* 1838 Catharine Alicia, dau. of Edmund Scully, Esq., of Bloomfield, co. Tipperary, and has, with other issue, * Marmaduke Lieut. 8th Foot; *b.* 1840.—*Residence; Bath*

STOVELD, JOHN, Esq., of Stedham Hall, Sussex.
Only son of the late John Stoveld, Esq., of Steyning, Sussex, by Jane, dau. of Charles Ockenden, Esq., of Wiston, Sussex; *b.* 1797; *m.* 1822 Mary, dau. of — and Phœbe Stoveld, of Kirdford, Sussex, and has issue an only child,
* Mary, *m.* 1852 the Rev. George John Ridsdale, M.A., Vicar of South Croake, Norfolk.

Mr. Stoveld is Lord of the Manor of Stedham; was formerly for many years a Banker at Petworth, Sussex. This family were formerly merchants at Steyning and elsewhere, and the present proprietor of Stedham Hall

was the first country banker who issued Bank of England notes in preference to his own.—*Stedham Hall, Midhurst.*

STOWEY, AUGUSTUS, Esq., of Kenbury, Devon.
Only son of the late Philip Stowey, Esq., of Kenbury ; by Martha, dau. of Joseph Hickman, Esq., of Herts ; *b.* 1800 ; *s.* 1846. Educated at Eton and Ch. Ch., Oxford (B.A. 1824) ; is a Magistrate for Devon (High Sheriff 1840).—*Kenbury, Exeter ; Oxford and Cambridge Club, s.w.*

STRACEY, Sir HENRY JOSIAS, Bart., of Rackheath Hall, Norfolk (cr. 1818).
Eldest son of the late Sir Josias Henry Stracey, Bart., of Rackheath Hall, by Diana, dau. of David Scott, Esq., of Dunniald, N.B. ; *b.* 1803 ; *s.* as 5th Bart. 1851 ; *m.* 1835 Charlotte, only dau. and heiress of George Denny, Esq., of The Paddock, Canterbury. Educated at Eton ; is a J.P. and D.L. for Norfolk, and Patron of 2 livings ; formerly Capt. 1st Dragoons ; was M.P. for E. Norfolk 1855-7, and for Gt. Yarmouth 1859-65.—*Rackheath Park, Norwich ; Carlton, Boodle's, and Arthur's Clubs, s.w.; 99, Eaton Place, s.w.*

Heir, his son Edward Henry Gervase, Capt. Norfolk Artillery Militia ; b. 1839.

STRACEY-CLITHEROW, EDWARD JOHN, Esq., of Boston House, Middlesex, and Sprowston, Norfolk.
Eldest son of the late John Stracey, Esq., of Sprowston, by Emma Elizabeth, dau. of the late C. Clitherow, Esq., of Bird's Place, Herts (she *d.* 1863), and grandson of the late Sir Edward Stracey, Bart., of Rackheath, Norfolk ; *b.* 1820 ; *m.* 1846 Harriot, 5th dau. of Edward Marjoribanks, Esq., of Greenlands, Bucks. Educated at Harrow ; is a Magistrate for Norfolk and co. Gloucester ; late Lieut.-Col. Scots Fusilier Guards ; assumed the additional name of Clitherow in 1865, under the will of the late J. Clitherow, Esq., of Boston House.—*Sprowston, Norwich ; Boston House, Brentford ; Guards' Club, s.w.*

Heir Pres., his brother William James, in Holy Orders, M.A. of Magdalen Coll., Oxford ; Vicar of Buxton, Norfolk ; b. 1821.

STRACHEY, Sir EDWARD, Bart., of Sutton Court, Somerset (cr. 1801).
Eldest son of the late Edward Strachey, Esq. (who *d.* 1832), by Julia, dau. of C.J. Kirkpatrick ; *b.* 1812 ; *s.* his uncle as 3rd Bart. 1858 ; *m.* 1st 1844 Elisabeth, dau. of the late Rev. W. Wilkieson, of Woodbury Hall, Beds ; 2nd 1857 Mary Isabella, dau. of John Addington Symonds, Esq., M.D., of Clifton. Is a J.P. and D.L. for Somerset (High Sheriff 1864).—*Sutton Court, Pensford, Bristol.*

Heir, his son Edward, b. 1858.

STRACHEY, RICHARD CHARLES, Esq., of Ashwick Grove, Somerset.
Eldest son of the late Richard Strachey, Esq., of Ashwick Grove (who was 3rd son of Sir Henry Strachey, 1st Bart.), by Anne Maria, dau. of Alexander Powell, Esq., of Hurdcott, Wilts ; *b.* 1835 ; *s.* 1856 ; *m.* 1857 Charlotte Lindsay, youngest surviving dau. of the late Ralph Burchard Hankin, Esq., of Bedford, and has, with other issue,

* Richard Sholto, *b.* 1859.

Mr. Strachey, who was educated at Eton and C. C. C., Cambridge, is a Magistrate for Somerset ; late an Officer in the N. Somerset Yeomanry. — *Ashwick Grove, Oakhill, Bath.*

STRADBROKE, Earl of (JOHN EDWARD CORNWALLIS ROUS).—Cr. 1821.
Eldest son of John, 1st Earl, by his 2nd wife Charlotte, dau. of the late Abraham Whittaker, Esq., of Lyston House, co. Hereford ; *b.* 1794 ; *s.* 1827 ; *m.* 1857 Augusta, dau. of Sir Christopher Musgrave, Bart., of Edenhall, Cumberland (widow of Col. Bonham). Educated at Westminster ; is Lord-Lieutenant and Custos Rotulorum of Suffolk, Vice-Admiral of that county, a Magistrate for cos. Waterford and Tipperary, and Patron of 8 livings ; late Col. Suffolk Militia. —*Henham Hall, Wangford ; Glenahirey Lodge, co. Waterford ; White's and Boodle's Clubs, w. ; 33, Belgrave Square, s.w.*

Heir, his son George Edward John Mowbray, Viscount Dunwich, b. 1862.

STRAFFORD, Earl of (GEORGE STEVENS BYNG, P.C., F.R.S.).—Cr. 1847.
Eldest son of John, 1st Earl, by his 1st wife Mary, dau. of Peter Mackenzie, Esq., of Twickenham ; *b.* 1806 ; *s.* 1860 ; *m.* 1st 1829 Lady Agnes, dau. of Henry William, 1st Marquis of Anglesea, K.G. (she *d.* 1846) ; 2nd 1848 the Hon. Harriet Elizabeth, dau. of Charles, 1st Lord Chesham. Educated at Sandhurst ; is a Dep.-Lieut. for Middlesex, and Col. 2nd Middlesex Militia ; formerly Capt. Rifle Brigade ; was M.P. for Milbourne Port 1830-1, for Chatham 1834, for Poole 1835-7, for Chatham 1837-52 ; summoned to the House of Peers as Baron Strafford 1853 ; has been a Lord of the Treasury, Comptroller and Treasurer of the Household, and Secretary to the Board of Control. —*Wrotham Park, Barnet ; Mount Lebanon, Twickenham, s.w. ; Boodle's, Brooks's, White's, and Travellers' Clubs, s.w. ; 5, St. James's Square, s.w.*

Heir, his son George Henry Charles, Viscount Enfield ; educated at Eton and Ch. Ch., Oxford, a Dep.-Lieut. for Middlesex, a Magistrate for Herts and St. Albans, and Lieut.-Col. Commandant Royal Middlesex Rifles ; M.P. for Middlesex, late Sec. to the Poorlaw Board, and formerly M.P. for Tavistock ; b. 1830 ; m. 1854 Lady Alice Harriet Frederica, dau. of Francis, 1st Earl of Ellesmere.

STRAKER, JOHN, Esq., of Tynemouth, Northumberland, and Willington House, Durham.
Youngest son of the late Joseph Straker, Esq., of Benwell House, Northumberland, by Ann, dau. of Henry Smith, Esq., of Loosing Hill, Durham ; *b.* 1815 ; *m.* 1846 Isabella, dau. of John Coppin, Esq., and has, with other issue,

* John Coppin, *b.* 1852.

Mr. Straker is a J.P. and D.L. for cos. Durham and Northumberland, and Lord of the Manors of Barradon, Wingates, and Stagshaw, Northumberland ; and of Bradley Hall, co. Durham.—*West House, Tynemouth ; Willington House, Durham.*

STRANGE. (See *Styleman Le Strange.*)

STRANGFORD, Viscount (PERCY ELLEN ALGERNON FREDERICK WILLIAM SYDNEY-SMYTHE).—Cr. 1628.
Third son of Percy Clinton Sydney, 6th Viscount, by Ellen, dau. of the late Sir Thomas Burke, Bart., and widow of Nicholas Browne, Esq., of Mount Harell, co. Galway ; *b.* 1825 ; *s.* his brother as 8th Viscount 1857 ; *m.* 1862 Emily Anne, youngest dau. of the late Admiral Sir Francis Beaufort, K.C.B. Educated at Harrow and Merton Coll., Oxford ; sits in the House of Lords as Lord Penshurst, U.K. (cr. 1825) ; is a Dep.-Lieut. for Kent ; late Oriental Secretary to the British Embassy at Constantinople. — *Westenhanger, Hythe, Kent ; Athenæum and St. James's Clubs, s.w. ; 58, Cumberland Street, w.*

STRANGWAYES. (See *Swainston Strangwayes.*)

STRANGWAYS, the Hon. Mrs.
Amelia, 3rd dau. of Edward Marjoribanks, Esq., by Georgiana, dau. of Francis Lautour, Esq.; m. 1844 the Hon. John George Charles Fox Strangways, youngest son of Henry Thomas, 2nd Earl of Ilchester, who d. 1859, leaving, with other issue, * Henry Edward, Earl of Ilchester (whom see).—39, Eaton Square, s.w.

+**STRANGWAYS, HENRY BULL, Esq., of Shapwick, Somerset.**
Son of the late Henry Bull Strangways, Esq., of Shapwick, by Sophia Anne, only child and heir of the late George Henry Templer, Esq., J.P. and D.L., of Shapwick; b. 18—; m. 1841 Harriet Ann, only dau. of the late William Lawrence, Esq., of the Greenway, co. Gloucester. Is a Magistrate for Somerset, and Lord of the Manor of Shapwick.—Shapwick, Glastonbury.

STRANGWAYS. (See under Ilchester, Earl of.)

STRANSHAM, Sir ANTHONY BLAXLAND, K.C.B. (cr. 1867).
Eldest surviving son of the late Lieut.-Colonel A. Stransham, by Mary, dau. of the late Thomas Bidwell, Esq., of Stanhoe, Norfolk; b. 1806; m. 1843 Eliza, dau. of Harvey Combe, Esq., late of Madras Civil Service. Educated at the Academy, Woolwich; is a Lieut.-General in the Army, and Col. 4th Division of R. Marine Light Infantry; was Inspector-General of Royal Marine Forces 1862-7.—Bruges, Belgium.

STRATFOLD-COLLETT. (See Collett.)

+**STRATFORD, HUGH STRATFORD, Esq., of Lugwardine, Herefordshire.**
Eldest son of the late Rev. Hugh Harmer Morgan, B.D., of Swindon, co. Gloucester (Canon of Hereford), by Helen Mary, dau. of William Beale, Esq., of Swindon; b. 18—. Is a Magistrate for co. Hereford; assumed the name of Stratford in lieu of his patronymic by Royal licence, 1842.—Residence: Hereford.

STRATFORD, JOHN WINGFIELD-, Esq., of Addington Place.
Eldest son of the late Hon. John Wingfield, who assumed the additional name of Stratford, by his 1st wife Frances, only child of Leonard Bartholomew, Esq., of Addington Place, Kent; b. 1810; s. 1850; m. 1844 Jane Elizabeth, 2nd dau. of General Sir John Wright Guise, Bart., and has, with other issue,
* Edward John, b. 1849.
Mr. Wingfield-Stratford, who was educated at Eton and Ch. Ch., Oxford, is a J.P. and D.L. for Kent, and Patron of 2 livings.—Addington Place, West Malling, Maidstone; Carlton Club, s.w.

STRATFORD. (See under Aldborough, Earl of.)

STRATFORD DE REDCLIFFE, Viscount (STRATFORD CANNING, G.C.B., P.C., D.C.L.) —Cr. 1852.
Third son of the late Stratford Canning, Esq., Merchant, of London, by Mehetabel, dau. of Robert Patrick, Esq., of Summerhill, co. Dublin, and cousin of the Right Hon. George Canning; b. 1788; m. 1st 1816 Harriet, dau. of the late Thomas Raikes, Esq., Merchant, of London, some time Governor of the Bank of England; 2nd 1825 Eliza Charlotte, dau. of James Alexander, Esq., of Summer Hill, Kent. Educated at Eton and King's Coll., Cambridge (M.A. 1813); entered the Diplomatic Service 1806; was sent in 1807 on a special mission to Copenhagen; has been Ambassador at several Foreign Courts, and at Constantinople 1842-58; was M.P. for old Sarum 1828-30, for Stockbridge
892

1831-2, for Lynn 1835-42.—Carlton Club, s.w.; 29 Grosvenor Square, w.
Heir, his son George Stratford, b. 1832; educated at Et and Trinity Coll, Cambridge (M.A. 1854).

STRATHALLAN, Viscount (WILLIAM HENRY DRUMMOND).—Cr. 1686.
Eldest son of William Henry, 5th Viscount, by Lady Amelia Sophia, dau. of John, 4th Duke of Atbole; b 1810; s. 1851; m. 1833 Christina Maria, dau. of the late Robert Baird, Esq., of Newbyth (she d. 1867) Educated at the Charterhouse; is a Representative Peer for Scotland, and a Dep.-Lieut. for co. Perth; was a Lord in Waiting 1858-9, re-appointed 1866. This title, forfeited in 1745, was restored in 1824.—Strathallan Castle, Auchterarder, N.B.; Carlton Club, s.w.
Heir, his son James David, Master of Strathallan, Capt. 90th Regt.; b. 1839; m. 1868 Ellen, 2nd dau. of Cuthbert B. Thornhill, Esq., C.S.I.

STRATHEDEN. (See under Campbell, Lord.)

STRATHMORE AND KINGHORN, Earl of (CLAUDE LYON-BOWES).—Cr. 1677.
Only surviving son of Thomas George, late Lord Glamis (who d. 1834), by Charlotte, dau. of Joseph Valentine Grinstead, Esq., and grandson of Thomas, 11th Earl; b. 1824; s. his brother as 13th Earl, 1865; m. 1853 Frances Dora, dau. of the late Oswald Smith, Esq., of Blendon Hall, Kent. Educated at Winchester. a Dep.-Lieut. for co. Forfar, and Capt. Forfar Yeomanry; late Lieut. 2nd Life Guards.— Glamis Castle, Forfar. N.B.; The Den, Bognor, Sussex; Carlton Club, s.w.; 33, Lowndes Square, s.w.
Heir, his son Claude George, Lord Glamis, b. 1855.

STRATHNAIRN, Lord (HUGH HENRY ROSE, G.C.B., G.C.S.I.).—Cr. 1866.
Third son of the late Right Hon. Sir George Henry Rose, G.C.H. (who d. 1855), by Frances, dau. of Thomas Duncombe, Esq., of Duncombe Park, co. York; b. 1803. Educated at Berlin; is a General in the Army, Col. 92nd Foot, and Commander of the Forces in India 1860-5.—Phœnix Lodge, Dublin; United Service Club, s.w.

STRATON, the Rev. GEORGE WILLIAM.
Second son of the late John Warde Straton, Esq., of Lisnawilly, co. Louth, by Lady Emily Jocelyn, dau. of Robert, 1st Earl of Roden; b. 1806; m. 1832 Elinor Katherine, eldest dau. of Richard Norman. Esq., and Lady Elizabeth Isabella Manners, dau. cf Charles, 4th Duke of Rutland, and has, with other issue,
* Norman, b. 1840.
Mr. Straton, who was educated at Rugby and C.C.C., Cambridge (B.A. 1829), was appointed Rector of Aylestone 1843. He is lineally descended from the Stratons of Straton, co. Perth.—Aylestone Rectory, Leicester; National Club, s.w.

+**STRATTON, GEORGE THOMAS, Esq., of Kirkside, Kincardineshire.**
Son of the late G. Stratton, Esq., or Kirkside; b. 18—. Is a J.P. and D.L, for co. Kincardine.—Kirkside, Montrose, N.B.

STRATTON, JOHN LOCKE, Esq., of Turweston House, Bucks.
Eldest son of the late John Stratton, Esq., of Turweston, by Maria Frances, dau. of John Bowor Jodrell, Esq., of Yeardsley; b. 1818; s. 1819; m. 1st 1845 Mary, dau. of John Horrocks, Esq.; 2nd 1855 Mary, 2nd dau. of William Willes, Esq., of Astrop House, co. Northampton, and has issue. Educated at Eton and Ch. Ch., Oxford; is a Magistrate for Bucks and co. Northampton, and Lord of the Manor of Turweston.—Turweston House, Brackley, Arthur's Club, s.w.

STRAUBENZEE. (See *Van-Straubenzee.*)

STREATFEILD, Capt. HENRY DORRIEN, of Chiddingstone, Kent.
Eldest son of the late Henry Streatfeild, Esq., of Chiddingstone, by Maria, dau. of the late Magens Dorrien Magens, Esq., of Hammerwood Lodge, Sussex, and widow of John Pepper, Esq., of Bigods, Essex; *b.* 1825; *m.* 1854 Marion Henrietta, youngest dau. of the late Oswald Smith, Esq., of Blendon Hall, Kent, and has, with other issue,
　• Henry, *b.* 1857.
Capt. Streatfeild, who was educated at Eton, is a Magistrate for Kent, and was formerly Capt. 1st Regt. Life Guards.—*Chiddingstone House, Penshurst ; White's and Carlton Clubs,* s.w.

STREATFEILD, RICHARD JAMES, Esq., of The Rocks, Sussex.
Only son of the late Richard Shuttleworth Streatfeild, Esq., J.P. and D.L., formerly High Sheriff of Sussex, by Charlotte Ann, dau. of the late James Brown, Esq., of Harehills, co. York; *b.* 1844; *m.* 1865 Mary Williams, eldest dau. of James Williams Scarlett, Esq., of Thryburgh Park (whom see). Is a Magistrate for Sussex, and a Lieut. 1st W. Yorkshire Yeomanry Cavalry. This family is a branch of the Streatfeilds of Chiddingstone, Kent.—*The Rocks, Uckfield.*

STREATFEILD, Mrs., of Charte's Edge, Kent.
Hannah, dau. of Joseph Fry, Esq., of Plashet, Essex, by Elizabeth, 3rd dau. of John Gurney, Esq., of Earlham, Norfolk ; *m.* 1832 William Champion Streatfeild, Esq., ultimately eldest surviving son of the Rev. Thomas Sreatfeild, of Charl's Edge, who *d.* 1852, leaving, with other issue,
　• Alexander Edward Champion, *b.* 1837 ; *m.* 1861 Helen, only surviving dau. of the late Capt. McNeill, of Colonsay, N.B., and has issue • a son, *b.* 1863.
This family descend from a common ancestor with the Streatfeilds of Chiddingstone.—*Charl's Edge, Westerham, Kent.*

STREET. (See *Wright.*)

STRETTON, Col. SEVERUS WILLIAM LYNAM, of Lenton Priory, Notts.
Second but eldest surviving son of the late William Stretton, Esq., of Lenton Priory, by Susanna, dau. of the late William Lynam, Esq., of Eakring, Notts; *b.* 1793; *s.* his brother, 1841 ; *m.* 1851 the Hon. Catherine Adela, youngest dau. of John Stapleton, 28th Lord Kingsale. Is a Magistrate for Southampton, and Lieut. Col. of the Hampshire Militia ; was formerly Lieut.-Col. 40th Regt.—*Lenton Priory, Nottingham ; Grosvenor Villa, Southampton ; United Service Club,* s.w.

STRETTON, Major WILLIAM RICHARD,‡ of Brynderwen, Monmonthshire.
Eldest son of the late William Thomas Stretton, Esq., of Twickenham, Middlesex (who *d.* 1814) by Marian, dau. of the Rev. Richard Glover, of Ilford, Essex ; *b.* 1806 ; *m.* 1st 1831 the Hon. Catherine Eliza Marianne, 4th dau. of George, 13th Viscount Hereford ; 2nd 1857 Julia Cecilia, dau. of the Rev. John Collinson, of Boldon, Northumberland. Educated at Harrow and Trinity Coll., Cambridge; is a Magistrate for cos. Monmouth, Brecon, and Radnor (High Sheriff 1835), and a Dep.-Lieut. for co. Monmouth ; was formerly in the 23rd Royal Welsh Fusiliers, and Major in the Brecknock Militia.—*Brynderwen, Usk.*

‡ Died whilst these sheets were at press.

STRICKLAND, CHARLES, Esq., of Loughglyn, co. Roscommon.
Eldest son of the late Jarrard Edward Strickland. Esq., of Loughglyn (who *d.* 1844), by Annie, dau. of Francis Cholmeley, Esq., of Brandsby Hall, co. York ; *b.* 1818 ; *m.* 1852 Maria Jane, dau. of the late Richard Farrell, Esq., Q.C., Judge of Her Majesty's Court of Insolvency in Ireland. Is a Magistrate for the cos. Roscommon and Mayo.—*Loughglyn House, Castlerea, co. Roscommon.*

STRICKLAND, HENRY EUSTATIUS, Esq., of Apperley, Gloucestershire.
Youngest son of the late Sir G. Strickland, Bart., of Boynton, co. York, by Elizabeth Lætitia, dau. of the late Sir Rowland Winn, Bart., of Nostell Priory, co. York; *b.* 1777; *m.* 1802 Mary, dau. of the Rev. Edmund Cartwright, D D., and by her, who *d.* 1858, has, with other issue,
　• John Henry, *b.* 1818.
Mr. Strickland is a Magistrate for co. Worcester.—*Apperley, Court, Deerhurst, Tewkesbury.*

STRICKLAND, WALTER, Esq., of Cokethorpe, Oxon.
Eldest son of the late Walter Strickland, Esq., of Flamborough, co. York, by his 1st wife Frances, 2nd dau. and co.-heir of Maximilian Western. Esq., of Cokethorpe Park ; *b.* 1804 ; *s.* his mother 1836 ; *m.* 1844 Katharine, 3rd. dau. of Thomas Thornhill, Esq., of Woodleys, Oxon. Educated at Harrow and Oriel Coll., Oxford; is a J.P. and D.L. for Oxfordshire (High Sheriff 1844), Lord of the Manors of Flamborough and Ducklington, and Patron of 1 living.—*Cokethorpe Park, Witney.*

STRICKLAND, WALTER, Esq., of Sizergh, Lancashire.
Eldest son of the late Thomas Strickland, by Ida, youngest dau. of the Baron de Finguerlin Bisahengen ; *b.* 1825; *s.* 1846. Educated at Oscott Coll. ; is a J.P. and D.L. for co. Lancaster.—*Sizergh House, Milnthorpe.*

STRICKLAND. (See *Cholmley.*)

+STRODE, GEORGE SIDNEY, Esq., of Newnham, Devon.
Only son of the late George Strode. Esq., J.P. and D.L., of Newnham Park (High Sheriff of Devon in 1839, by Dorothy Bird, dau. of William Symons, Esq., of Chuddlewood (she *d.* 1862); *b.* 1829 ; *s.* 1857 ; *m.* 1858 Mary Hutchings, 2nd dau. of Sir William Coles Medlycott, Bart., of Ven House, Somerset. Is a Magistrate for Devon, and Lord of the Manor of Newnham.—*Newnham Park, Plympton.*

STRODE, NATHANIEL WILLIAM JOHN, Esq., of Camden, Kent, and Candie, Stirlingshire.
Only son of the late Capt. Nathaniel Nugent Strode, an officer in the 16th Regt. of Foot (who *d.* 1804), by Caroline, dau. of Capt. Kirk, 47th Regt.; *b.* 1816. Represents a family of Somersetshire extraction.—*Camden Park, Chislehurst, Kent ; Candie House, Linlithgow, N.B. ; Conservative Club,* s.w. ; *The Albany.* w.

STRODE. (See *Chetham-Strode.*)

STRONG, CHARLES ISHAM, Esq., of Thorpe Hall, Northamptonshire.
Only son of the late Rev. William Strong, J.P., of Thorpe Hall, by his 3rd wife, Isabella Mary, dau. of the Rev. Charles E. Isham, Rector of Polebrook, co. Northampton ; *b.* 1838 ; *s.* 1866 ; *m.* 1864 Katharine

Anne, only dau. of the Rev. Percy William Powlett, Rector of Frankton, co. Warwick, and has issue,

* A daughter.

Mr. Strong is a Magistrate for the Liberty of Peterborough.—*Thorpe Hall, Peterborough.*

STRONG, GEORGE, Esq., M.D., of The Chase, Herefordshire.

Son of the late Rev. Robert Strong, Rector of Brampton Abbott, co. Hereford, by Sophia Margaretta Bean, grand-dau. of Governor Drake, of Madras; *s.* 1849; *m.* 1839 Charlotte, dau. of John Cooke, Esq., of The Chase, and has issue,

* Two daughters.

Mr. Strong, who was educated in Paris and Edinburgh, is a J.P. and D.L. for co. Hereford.—*The Chase, Ross.*

STRONG, LEONARD, Esq., of Camster, Caithness-shire.

Only son of the late Rev. Clement Strong, Rector of Gedney, co. Lincoln, by Catherine, dau. of Vincent Hilton Biscoe, Esq., of Hookwood Park, Surrey; *b.* 1833. Educated at New Coll., Oxford. This family was originally of Nether-Stronge, Somerset.—*Camster, Wick, N.B.; Hayes, Bromley, Kent; Oriental Club, w.; Junior United Service Club, s.w.*

STRONG-HUSSEY. (See *Hussey.*)

STRONGE, Sir JAMES MATTHEW, Bart., of Tynan Abbey, co. Armagh (cr. 1801).

Eldest son of the late Sir James Matthew Stronge, Bart.; J.P. and D.L., of Tynan Abbey, by Isabella, eldest dau. of the late Nicholson Calvert, Esq., of Hunsdon House, Herts; *b.* 1811; *s.* as 3rd Bart. 1864; *m.* 1836 Selina, eldest dau. of Andrew Savage Nugent, Esq. Is a J.P. and D.L. for co. Armagh, and Hon. Col. Royal Tyrone Fusiliers; elected M.P. for co. Armagh 1864; was formerly Lieut. 5th Dragoon Guards.—*Tynon Abbey, co. Armagh; Mulnaver, Drumquin, co. Tyrone; Carlton Club, s.w.*

Heir Pres., his brother John Calvert, *b.* 1833; *m.* 1848 Lady Zoe Margaret, dau. of the late Hon. Henry Caulfeild, and sister of James, 3rd Earl of Charlemont.

STRONGE, Capt. MAXWELL DU PRE, of Raheenduff, co. Wexford.

Fifth son of the late Sir James M. Stronge, Bart., of Tynan, co. Armagh (who *d.* 1864), by Isabella, eldest dau. of the late Nicholson Calvert, Esq., of Hunsdon, Herts; *b.* 1824; *m.* 1851 Jane Colclough, only dau. and heir of the late Joseph Fade Goff, Esq., of Raheenduff. Is Capt. and Adjutant of the Sligo Rifles; was formerly Capt.—*Raheenduff, Foulksmill, co. Wexford; Brunswick, Clonmel, co. Tipperary; Army and Navy Club, s.w.*

STROTHER, Mrs., of Eastfield, Northumberland.

Ann, dau. of William Maudorson, Esq., of Woolwich, Kent, by Ann, dau. of James Baxter, Esq., of London; *m.* 1831 Anthony Strother, Esq., of Eastfield Hall, who *d.* 1863, leaving, with other issue,

* James Baxter, in Holy Orders, educated at King's Coll., London; M.A. of Magdalen Hall, Oxford, and Rector of St. Mary Steps, Exeter; *b.* 1832; *m.* 1864 Louisa, 5th dau. of Charles Webb, Esq., of Clapham Common, Surrey, and has issue a dau.

Mrs. Strother is Lady of the Manor of Eastfield.—*Eastfield Hall, Warkworth, Northumberland.*

STRUTT, ANTHONY RADFORD, Esq., of Milford, Derbyshire.

Third son of the late George B. Strutt, Esq., of Belper, co. Derby, by Catharine, dau. of the late A. Radford, Esq., of Holbrook; *b.* 1791. Is a Manufacturer at Belper, and a J.P. and D.L. for co. Derby; represents a younger branch of the family of Lord Belper.—*Milford, Derby.*

STRUTT, GEORGE HENRY, Esq., of Bridgehill, Derbyshire.

Eldest son of the late Jedediah Strutt, Esq., of Belper, by his 1st wife Susanna, only dau. of Joshua Wright, Esq., of Clifton House, Rotherham, and cousin of Edward, 1st Lord Belper; *b.* 1826; *s.* 1854; *m.* 1849 Agnes, dau. of Edward Ashton, Esq., of Prescot, co. Lancaster, and has, with other issue,

* George Herbert, *b.* 1854.

Mr. Strutt, who was educated at Harrow, is a J.P. and D.L. for co. Derby.—*Bridgehill, Belper; Union Club, s.w.*

STRUTT. (See *Rayleigh, Lord,* and *Belper, Lord.*)

STUART, Sir SIMEON HENRY, Bart. (cr. 1660).

Eldest son of the late Sir Simeon Stuart, Bart., of Hartley Maudit, Hants, by Lady Frances Maria, dau. of John, 3rd Earl of Carhampton (*ext.*); *b.* 1790; *s.* as 5th Bart. 1816; *m.* 1815 Georgiana Frances, dau. of George Gun Cuninghame, Esq. (she *d.* 1810).—*Birch Green, Lindfield, Sussex.*

Heir, his son Simeon Henry, Capt. 7th Lancashire Militia, and late Lieut. Royal Canadian Rifles; *b.* 1823; *m.* 1st, 1845 Julia Maria, dau. of the Hon. James Cuthbert, of Berthier Manor, Canada; 2nd 1850 Katharine Henrietta, dau. of Major-General Worrall, of Clifton, and has, with other issue, * Simeon Henry Lechmere, *b.* 1864.

STUART, Sir CHARLES JAMES, Bart. (cr. 1840).

Eldest son of the late Sir James Stuart, Bart., LL.D. (who was a Judge in Canada), by Elizabeth, dau. of Alexander Robertson, Esq., of Faskally, co. Perth; *b.* 1824; *s.* as 2nd Bart. 1853. Educated at Eton and University Coll., Oxford (B.A. 1845).—*Oxford and Cambridge Club, s.w.*

Heir Pres., his brother Edward Andrew, Capt. 1st Foot; *b.* 1832.

STUART, Sir JOHN, Knt., of Loch Carron, Ross-shire (cr. 1853).

Second son of the late Dugald Stuart, Esq., of Ballachulish, co. Argyle; *b.* 1793; *m.* 1813 Jessie, dau. of Duncan Stewart, Esq., and has, with other issue.

* Dugald, *b.* 1817.

Sir J. Stuart, who was called to the Bar at Lincoln's Inn 1819, is a Vice-Chancellor and a Bencher of Lincoln's Inn; he was M.P. for Newark 1847–52, and for Bury St. Edmund's July–October 1852. This family is a branch of the Stuarts of Appin, descended from John, the last Stewart Lord Lorn, whose son Dugald acquired the lands of Appin in 1469.—*Loch Carron, Dingwall, Ross-shire; Carlton and Athenæum Clubs, s.w.; 3, Queen's Gate, w.*

STUART, Sir CHARLES SHEPHERD, K.C.B. (cr. 1859).

Son of the late William Stuart, Esq.; *b.* 1803; *m.* 1st 1833 Mary, dau. of the late Major-Gen. Willis, of the Bombay Army; 2nd 1861 Adelaide, dau. of Major J. Rāse Godfrey, of Northenhay House, and has issue. Entered the Indian Army (Bombay) 1819, became Col. 1855, and Major-General 1867.—*Rāse House, Leighton, Welshpool, Montgomeryshire.*

STUART, the Hon. ANDREW GODFREY, of Lisdhu and Crevenagh, co. Tyrone.

Second son of Andrew Thomas, 1st Earl of Castle Stuart; *b.* 1790; *m.* 1814 Sophia Isabella, eldest dau. of George Lennox Conyngham, Esq., of Spring Hall, co. Londonderry, and by her, who *d.* 1854, his other issue.

* George William Conyngham, Adjutant Royal Fermanagh Militia Rifles; *b.* 1830; *m.* 1854 Marianne, only child of

the late James Crutwell, Esq., and Widow of the Rev. Aaron Forster, of Milton Lodge, Wells.

Mr. Stuart is a J.P. and D.L. for co. Tyrone.—*Lisdhu, near Dungannon ; Crevenagh House, Armagh, co. Tyrone.*

STUART, Lady LOUISA, of Traquair, Peeblesshire.
Only surviving child of Charles, 7th Earl of Traquair (*ext.*), by Mary, dau. of George Ravenscroft, Esq., of Wickham, co. Lincoln ; *b.* 1776 ; *s.* her brother Charles, 8th and last. Earl, 1861 ; is Lady of the Manor and Barony of Traquair. This family is descended from the Scottish Royal House of Stuart.—*Traquair Castle, Innerleithen N.B.*

STUART, ALEXANDER, Esq., of Inchbreck, Kincardineshire, and Laithers, Aberdeenshire.
Eldest son of the late Alexander Stuart, Esq., of Inchbreck and Laithers, by Isabella, 2nd dau. of the late Capt. John Lawson, R.N. ; *b.* 1832 ; *s.* 1846 ; *m.* 1864 the Hon. Clementina, dau. of John, 9th Visct. Arbuthnot. Educated at Marischal Coll., Aberdeen (M.A. 1851) ; is a Magistrate for cos. Aberdeen and Kincardine. This family is of long standing in co. Kincardine.—*Laithers House, Turriff, N.B.*

STUART, ALEXANDER CHARLES, Esq., of Eaglescarnie, Haddingtonshire.
Eldest son of the late General the Hon. Sir Patrick Stuart, G.C.M.G., of Eaglescarnie (whe was 2nd son of Alexander, 10th Lord Blantyre), by Catherine Henrietta, dau. of the late Hon. John Rodney ; *b.* 1814 ; *s.* 1855 ; *m.* 1850 Hon. Elizabeth Frederica, dau. of Lord George Lennox (formerly a Maid of Honour to the Queen). Is a J.P. and D.L. for co. Haddington.—*Eaglescarnie, Haddington, N.B.*

Heir Pres., his brother George, *b.* 1825.

STUART, Major-General CHARLES, of Hubborne, Hants.
Only son of the late Capt. John Stuart, R.N., by Albinia, eldest dau. of the late Right Hon. John Sullivan, and grand-dau. of George, 3rd Earl of Buckinghamshire ; *b.* 1810 ; *m.* 1839 the Hon. Georgiana Gore, dau. of the late Vice-Admiral Sir John Gore, K.C.B. and G.C.H., formerly Maid of Honour to Queen Adelaide. Is a Magistrate for Hants, Vice-Lieut. of co. Bute, and a Major-General in the Army ; was formerly Military Secretary to the Governor-General of India.—*Hubborne Lodge, Christchurch ; United Service Club, s.w.*

STUART, CHARLES POLE, Esq., late of Langley Broom House, Bucks.
Second son of William Stuart, Esq., of Aldenham Abbey, Herts, by Henrietta Maria Sarah, eldest dau. of the late Admiral Sir Charles M. Pole, Bart., G.C.B. ; *b.* 1826 ; *m.* 1860 Anne, dau. of Robert Smyth, Esq., of Gaybrook, co. Westmeath, and has, with other issue,

* Robert Alexander, *b.* 1862.

Mr. Stuart, who was educated at St. John's Coll., Cambridge, is a Magistrate for Bucks. — *Oxford and Cambridge Club, s.w.*

STUART, the Rev. EDMUND LUTTRELL.
Fourth son of the late Hon. Archibald Stuart (2nd son of Francis, 8th Earl of Moray), by Cornelia, dau. of E. M. Pleydell, Esq., of Milbourne, St. Andrew's, Dorset ; *b.* 1798 ; *m.* 1834 Elizabeth, 2nd dau. of the late Rev. J. L. Jackson, Rector of Swanage, Dorset, and has, with other issue,

* Edmund Archibald, *b.* 1840.

Mr. Stuart, who was educated at Exeter Coll., Oxford (B.A. 1822), and was Rector of Winterbourne Houghton 1823–58, is in remainder to the Earldom of Moray.—*Blandford, Dorset ; National Club, s.w.*

+STUART, JOHN ALEXANDER, Esq., of Carnock, Stirlingshire.
Younger and only surviving son of the late Charles Stuart, Esq., M.D., of Dunearn, by Mary, dau. of John Erskine, Esq., of Carnock ; *b.* 1787 ; *m.* 1824 Margaret, dau. of J. Murray, Esq., and has, with other issue,

* Charles, *b.* 1825 ; *m.* 1851 Georgina, dau. of the Rev. J. Edgar.

Mr. Stuart, who is Lord of the Manor of Carnock, represents a collateral branch of the family of the Earl of Moray.—*Carnock House, Stirling, N.B.*

STUART, WILLIAM, Esq., of Aldenham Abbey, Herts.
Eldest son of the late Hon. William Stuart, D.D. (who was a son of John, 3rd Earl of Bute), by Sophia Margaret, dau. of Thomas Penn, Esq., of Stoke Park, Bucks ; *b.* 1798 ; *s.* 1822 ; *m.* 1st 1821 Henrietta Maria Sarah, eldest dau. of the late Admiral Sir Charles Morice Pole, Bart., G.C.B. (she *d.* 1853) ; 2nd 1854 Georgiana Adelaide, dau. of General Walker, of the Manor House, Bushey, Herts, and has by the former, with other issue,

* William, of Kempstone, Beds ; educated at Eton and St. John's Coll., Cambridge ; a Barrister-at-Law of the Inner Temple, a Magistrate for Herts and St. Alban's, a J.P. and D.L. for Beds, a Chairman of Quarter Sessions, Lieut.-Col. Beds Militia Light Infantry, and M.P. for Bedford ; *b.* 1825 ; *m.* 1859 Katharine, eldest dau. of John Armytage Nicholson, Esq., of Balrath, co. Meath, and has, with other issue, * a son, *b.* 1860.

Mr. Stuart, who was educated at St. John's Coll., Cambridge (M.A. 1820), is a J.P. and D.L. for Beds (High Sheriff 1846), and a Magistrate for Herts and St. Alban's ; was M.P. for Armagh 1820-6, for Beds 1830-4.—*Aldenham Abbey, Watford ; Carlton Club, s.w. ; 18, Hill Street, w.*

STUART, WILLIAM VILLIERS, Esq., of Castletown House, co. Kilkenny.
Second son of the late Lord Henry Stuart, by Gertrude Amelia, dau. of George, late Earl of Grandison, and brother of Lord Stuart de Decies (whom see) ; *b.* 1804 ; *m.* 1833 Catharine, only dau. of Michael Cox, Esq., and niece of Henry, 2nd Lord Dunalley, and has, with other issue,

* Henry John Richard, Lieut. 68th Foot ; *b.* 1837.

Mr. Stuart, who is a J.P. and D.L. for co. Waterford, and a Dep.-Lieut. for cos. Kilkenny and Tipperary, Lieut.-Col. Waterford Artillery Militia, and late Capt. 12th Lancers, was M.P. for co. Waterford 1835-47.—*Castletown, Carrick-on-Suir ; Reform Club, s.w.*

STUART.
(See under *Bute, Marquis of ; Moray, Earl of ; Castle-Stuart, Earl of ; Stuart de Decies, Lord ; Wharncliffe, Lord ;* and *Blantyre, Lord.*)

STUART. (See *Burnett-Stuart.*)

STUART. (See *Crichton-Stuart.*)

STUART. (See *Stirling-Stuart.*)

STUART DE DECIES, Lord (HENRY VILLIERS STUART, P.C.).—Cr. 1839.
Eldest son of the late Lord Henry Stuart, by Lady Gertrude Amelia, dau. of George, late Earl of Grandison (*ext.*), and grandson of John, 1st Marquis of Bute ; *b.* 1803 ; *m.* 1826 Madame Pfölt (she *d.* 1867). Is Lord-Lieutenant of co. Waterford, and Col. Waterford Artillery ; was M.P. for Waterford 1826-30, for Banbury 1830-1. Represents a younger branch of the family of the Marquis of Bute.—*Dromana, Cappoquin, co. Waterford ; Reform Club, s.w. ; 43, Albemarle Street, w.*

Heir, his son Henry Windsor, in Holy Orders, M.A. of University

versity Coll., London, and Vicar of Napton, co. Warwick;
b. 1827 ; *m.* 1863 Mary, 2nd dau. of the Ven. Ambrose
Power, Archdeacon of Lismore.

STUART DE ROTHESAY, Lady, of High-cliff, Hants.

Elizabeth Margaret, 3rd dau. of Philip, 3rd Earl of
Hardwicke, by Lady Elizabeth, 3rd dau. of James, 5th
Earl of Balcarres ; *d.* 1867, having *m.* 1816 Charles,
Lord Stuart de Rothesay (ext.), who *d.s.p.* 1845.—*High-cliff, Christchurch.*

STUART-MENTETH. (See *Menteth.*)

STUART-WORTLEY, the Right Hon. JAMES, of East Sheen, Surrey.

Third son of James Archibald, 1st Lord Wharncliffe,
by Lady Caroline, dau. of John, 1st Earl of Erne ; *b.*
1805 ; *m.* 1846 the Hon. Jane, dau. of Paul Beilby, 1st
Lord Wenlock, and has, with other issue,

* Archibald John, *b.* 1849.

Mr. Stuart-Wortley, who was called to the Bar at the
Inner Temple 1831, and was formerly of the Northern
Circuit, is a Dep.-Lieut. for London and Buteshire, a
Magistrate for Surrey, and a J.P. and D.L. for the W.
Riding of co. York ; was Solicitor-General to the late
Queen Dowager, Judge-Advocate-General 1845–6, Re-corder of London 1850–6, and Solicitor-General 1856–7 ;
M.P. for Halifax 1835–7, for co. Bute 1842–59 ; became
a Q.C. 1840, and Privy Councillor 1856.—*Wortley Lodge,
East Sheen, Surrey ; Carlton Club, s.w.*

STUART-WORTLEY, ARCHIBALD HENRY PLAN-TAGENET.

Only son of the late Hon. Charles Stuart-Wortley, by
Lady Emmeline Charlotte, dau. of John Henry, 5th
Duke of Rutland, and grandson of James Archibald, 1st
Lord Wharncliffe ; *b.* 1832 ; *m.* 1865 Augusta, young-est dau. of Robert Verschoyle, Esq. Is a Lieut.-Col.
in the Army, unattached ; served in the Crimea 1854–5 ;
was M.P. for Honiton 1857–9. — *Boodle's and Junior
United Service Clubs, s.w.*

STUART-WORTLEY.

(See under *Wharncliffe, Lord.*)

STUBBER, ROBERT HAMILTON STUBBER, Esq., of Moyne, Queen's Co.

Only son of the late Robert Hamilton-Stubber, Esq.,
J.P. and D.L., of Moyne (who assumed the additional
name of Stubber by Royal licence in 1824), by Olivia,
dau. of the Rev. Edward Lucas, and widow of H. Smyth,
Esq.; *b.* 1844 ; *s.* 1863. Is Lord of the Manor of Moyne.
— *Moyne, Durrow, Queen's Co. ; Kildare Street Club,
Dublin.*

STUBBS, WALTER, Esq., of Beckbury, Shrop-shire.

Eldest son of the late Walter Stubbs. Esq., of Beck-bury, by Harriet, dau. of William Hunt, Esq., of Strat-ford-on-Avon ; *b.* 1786 ; *s.* 1815 ; *m.* 1838 Elizabeth,
dau. of John Stanier, Esq., of Leaton, is a Magistrate
for co. Salop. This family was formerly settled in
Norfolk.—*Beckbury Hall, Shifnal.*

STUCKEY, VINCENT, Esq., of Hill House, So-mersetshire.

Second son of the Rev. William Wood, by Julia, eldest
dau. of the late Vincent Stuckey, Esq., of Hill House ;
b. 1829 ; *m.* 1865 Mary, eldest dau. of the late Rev.
Thomas Prowse Lethbridge, Rector of Combe Florey,
Somerset, and has issue,

* A dau.

Mr. Stuckey, who was educated at Eton and Trinity
Coll., Cambridge, is a Magistrate for Somerset, and
896

Capt. W. Somerset Yeomanry; he exchanged the name of
Wood for Stuckey by Royal licence, 1861.—*Hill House,
Langport, Somerset ; Carlton Club, s.w.*

STUCLEY, Sir GEORGE STUCLEY, Bart., of Hartland Abbey, Devon (cr. 1859).

Only son of the late Lewis William Buck, Esq., of
Morton House, Devon, and of Hartland Abbey, some
time M.P. for North Devon, by Anne, dau. of Thomas
Robbins, Esq., of Roundham, Berks ; *b.* 1812 ; *s.* 1858 ;
m. 1835 Lady Elisabeth O'Bryen, dau. of William, 2nd
Marquis of Thomond (ext.). Educated at Eton and
Ch. Ch., Oxford ; appointed Lieut.-Col. Commanding
Devon Artillery Militia 1849 ; formerly served in the
Royal Horse Guards ; is a J.P. and D.L. for Devon and
Cornwall (High Sheriff of Devon 1863), and Patron of
3 livings ; was M.P. for Barnstaple 1856–7, re-elected
1855 ; assumed, 1858, the surname of Stucley, as sole
male representative of that family.—*Hartland Abbey,
Bideford ; Carlton Club, s.w. ; 8, Eaton Square, s.w.*

Heir, his son William Stucley, educated at Eton ; Capt.
Grenadier Guards ; *b.* 1836.

STUDD, Major-General EDWARD, of Oxton, Devon.

Eldest son of the late Edward Studd, Esq., H.E.I.C.S.,
by Mary, only child of Christopher Bell, Esq., of Sax-mundham, Suffolk ; *b.* 1799 ; *m.* 1st 1821 Mary, dau. of
William Spurrier, Esq., of Albrighton Hall. co. Salop
(she *d.* 1853) ; 2nd 1855 Beatrice Emma, dau. of the
late Charlton Bayly, Esq., of Sidmouth, and has, with
other issue,

* Edward, *b.* 1856.

Major-General Studd is a J.P. and D.L. for Devon
(High Sheriff 1862), and a Major-General in the Army ;
formerly in Command of the 76th Regt.—*Oxton House,
Kenton, Exeter.*

STUDDERT, CHARLES FITZ-GERALD, Esq., of Newmarket House, co. Clare.

Third son of the late Charles Fitz-Gerald Studdert, Esq.,
of Newmarket House. by Maria, only dau. of the late
Robert Wogan. Esq., of Dublin ; *b.* 181– ; *m.* 1862 Eliza,
4th dau. of the late Charles Putland, Esq., of Bray
Head, co. Wicklow. Is a Magistrate for co. Clare ;
late Major 80th Regt.—*Newmarket House, Newmarket-on-Fergus, co. Clare.*

STUDDERT, GEORGE STUDDERT, Esq., of Crag-gane Tower, co. Clare.

Fourth son of the late Charles Fitz-Gerald Studdert.
Esq., of Newmarket House. co. Clare. by Maria, only
dau. of the late Robert Wogan, Esq., of Dublin ; *b.*
1823 ; *m.* 1858 Agnes, 2nd dau. of the late Rev.
Charles Waller, of Trinley, Suffolk, and has, with other
issue,

* Charles Fitzgerald, *b.* 1859.

Mr. Studdert is a Magistrate for Clare, and Capt. co.
Clare Militia.— *Craggane Tower, Killaloe, co. Clare.*

+STUDDERT, Admiral JOHN FITZ-GERALD, of Pella, co. Clare.

Fifth son of the late Thomas Studdert, Esq., of Bun-ratty Castle, co. Clare, by Anna, dau. of James Fitz-gerald. Esq., of Shepperton, Middlesex ; *b.* 1790 ; *m.*
1830 Anne, eldest dau. of the Rev. Richard Studdert
Welsh, of Newtown House. co. Limerick, and Vicar of
Kilfinaghty, co. Clare; and had, with other issue,

Thomas, Lieut. R.N.; *b.* 183–, and *d.* 1863.

Admiral Studdert, who was educated at the Royal
Naval Coll., and entered the Navy 1805, is a Magis-trate for co. Clare.—*Pella, Kilrush, co. Clare.*

+ STUDDERT, ROBERT WOGAN, Esq., of Cullane, co. Clare.

Eldest surviving son of the late Charles Studdert, Esq., of Cullane, by Maria, dau. of the late Robert Wogan. Esq., of Dublin; b. 18—. Is a Magistrate for co. Clare (High Sheriff 1864), and Lord of the Manor of Cullane.—*Cullane, Kilkishen, co. Clare.*

STUDDERT, THOMAS, Esq., of Bunratty, co. Clare.

Eldest son of the late Thomas Studdert, Esq., of Bunratty, by Anne, dau. of James Fitz-Gerald, Esq., of Shepperton; b. 1779; s. 1825; m. 181– Alicia, dau. of George Studdert, Esq., of Kilkishen, and has, with other surviving issue,

* George, b. 18—.

Mr. Studdert, who is a J.P. and D.L. for co. Clare (High Sheriff 1804), was formerly an officer in the Militia, and commanded a Corps of Cavalry in 1798. —*Bunratty Castle, co. Clare.*

STUDDERT, THOMAS, Esq., of Kilkishen, co. Clare.

Eldest son of the late George Studdert, Esq., of Kilkishen, by Hannah, dau. of John Blood, Esq., of Castle Fergus; b. 1781; s. 1830; m. 1807 Elusina, dau. of Robert Ashworth, Esq., of Merrion Square, Dublin, and has issue, an only surviving son.

* Robert Ashworth, b. 1817; m. 1849 Maria. dau. of the Rev. William Waller, of Castletown, co. Limerick, and has issue, Thomas, b. 1850.

Mr. Studdert, who was educated at Trinity Coll., Dublin (B.A. 1804), called to the Irish Bar 1806, was formerly Magistrate for co. Clare (High Sheriff 1809); he is Lord of the Manor of Kilkishen.—*Kilkishen House, Kilkishen, co. Clare.*

STUDDERT, WILLIAM STEELE, Esq., of Keeper View, co. Clare.

Third son of the late Charles Studdert, Esq., of Newmarket House, co. Clare, by Maria, dau. of the late Robert Wogan, Esq., of Dublin; b. 1821; m. 1854 Constance, 2nd dau. of Robert George Massy, Esq., and has, with other issue,

* Charles Henry Thompson, b. 1856.

Mr. Studdert is a Magistrate for co. Clare.—*Keeper View, O'Brien's Brid., e, co. Clare.*

STUDDY, HENRY, Esq., of Watton, Devon.

Eldest son of the late Henry Studdy, Esq., of Coombe House, Ipplepen, Devon, by Harriet, dau. of R. Bray, Esq., of Winchelsea, Sussex; b. 1820; s. his father 1835, and his uncle 1840; m. 1842 Eleanor Frances, eldest dau. of the Rev. Robert Holdsworth, Vicar of Brixham, Devon, and has, with other issue,

* Henry, Lieut. R.N.; b. 1843; m. 1867 Amelia Margaret Elizabeth, eldest dau. of Edward Cropper, Esq., of Swaylands, Kent.

Mr. Studdy, who was educated at Winchester and Downing Coll., Cambridge, is a Magistrate for Devon, Lord of the Manor of Watton, and Capt. S. Devon Militia.—*Watton Court, Stoke Gabriel, Torquay.*

STURGES-BOURNE. (See *Bourne.*)

STURGEON, CHARLES, Esq., late of Pond Head Lodge, Lyndhurst, Hants.

Only son of the late Charles Alexander Sturgeon, Esq., by Anne, only dau. and heir of George Smithwaite, Esq., of West Hall, Wakefield; b. 1799; m. 1st 1830 Harriet, dau. of Rev. Peter Geary; 2nd 1838 Louisa Sydney Jane, only dau. and eventually heir of Lieut.-Col. George Pinckney, late 11th Foot, and has issue,

* Charles Wentworth Dillon, of Creeting St. Mary, Suffolk;

Barrister-at-Law of the Inner Temple; b. 1841; m. 1864 Caroline Seymour, only dau. of the late Jonathan Sadler, Esq., and sister of Sir Seymour Sadler (whom see).

Mr. Sturgeon was called to the Bar at the Inner Temple 1830.—25, *Gloucester Place, w.*

STURT, Lieut.-Col. CHARLES NAPIER.

Younger son of the late Henry Charles Sturt, Esq., of Critchill, Dorset (who d. 1856), by Lady Charlotte Penelope, 3rd dau. of Robert, 6th Earl of Cardigan; b. 1832. Educated at Harrow; is a Magistrate for Dorset, and Lieut.-Col. Grenadier Guards; has been M.P. for Dorchester since 1856 —*Guards' and White's Clubs, s.w.; 61, St. James's Street, s.w.*

STURT, HENRY GERARD, Esq., of Critchill, Dorset.

Elder son of the late Henry Charles Sturt, Esq., J.P. and D.L., of Critchill (who was M.P. for Dorset 1835–46), by Lady Charlotte Penelope, 3rd dau. of Robert, 6th Earl of Cardigan; b. 1825; s. 1866; m. 1853 Lady Augusta, dau. of George Charles, 3rd Earl of Lucan, and has, with other issue,

* Henry, b. 1859.

Mr. Sturt, who was educated at Eton and Ch. Ch., Oxford, is a J.P. and D.L. for Dorset, and Patron of 7 livings; was M.P. for Dorchester 1847–56, and has been M.P. for Dorset since 1856 —*Critchill, Wimborne; Carlton and White's Clubs, s.w.; 25, Upper Brook Street, w.*

STYLE, SIR THOMAS CHARLES, Bart. (cr. 1627).

Eldest son of the late Sir Charles Style, Bart., by Camilla, dau. of James Whatman, Esq., of Vintners, Kent; b. 1797; s. his brother as 8th Bart. 1813; m. 1822 Isabella, dau. of the late Sir G. Cayley, Bart. Educated at the Royal Naval Academy, Gosport; is a J.P. and D.L. for co. Donegal; was M.P. for Scarborough 1837–41. This family was formerly of Wateringbury Place, Kent.—*Bath; Union Club, s.w.*

Heir Pres., his kinsman William Henry Marsham, of Glenmore, co. Donegal (eldest son of the late Capt. William Style, of Bicester House, Oxon, who d. 1868, by Louisa Charlotte, dau. of the Hon. Jacob Marsham); educated at Eton, and M.A. of Merton Coll., Oxford, a Magistrate for co. Monmouth and a J.P. and D.L. for co. Donegal (High Sheriff of co. Donegal 1866); b. 1826; m. 1848 the Hon. Rosamond Marian Morgan, eldest dau. of Charles, 1st Lord Tredegar, and has, with other issue, * William Charles Marsham, b. 1849.

STYLEMAN LE STRANGE, HAMON, Esq., of Hunstanton, Norfolk.

Eldest son of the late Henry Le Strange Styleman, Esq., J.P. and D.L., of Hunstanton (who assumed the additional surname of Le Strange in 1839), by Jamesina Joyce Ellen, dau. of John Stewart, Esq., late of Belladrum, co. Inverness; b. 1840; s. 1862; m. 1866 Emmeline, dau. of William Austin, Esq., of Boston, U.S. Educated at Eton and Ch. Ch., Oxford; is a J.P. and D.L. for Norfolk, Lord of the Manors of Hunstanton, Snettisham, Ringstead, &c., in the said co., and Patron of the livings of Hunstanton with Barrett-Ringstead, Great Ringstead, and Snettisham, entered the Diplomatic service 1864, and is now Attaché to H.M. Embassy at Paris. The family of Le Strange is of knightly dignity, and has been seated at Hunstanton since the Conquest.—*Hunstanton Hall, and Snettisham Hall, Lynn; St. James's Club, s.w.*

Heir Pres., his brother Charles, Lieut. R.N.; b. 1847.

SUART, Major WILLIAM SWAINSON, of Bowls, Essex.

Second son of the late Edward Suart, Esq., of Westbury-on-Trim, co. Gloucester, by Emma, dau. of the late William Hodgson, Esq., of Bowls; b. 1814; s. his maternal uncle John Hodgson, Esq., 1854; m. 1849

Elizabeth Murray, youngest dau. of Patrick Rose, Esq., of Banff, N.B., and has, with other issue,

* William Hodgson, b. 1850.

Major Suart, who was educated at the Royal Military Coll., Addiscombe, is a Magistrate for Essex, and an Officer in the Royal Bombay Corps of Engineers.—*Bowls, Chigwell; East-India United Service Club, s.w.*

SUCKLING, ROBERT, Esq., of Barsham, Suffolk.
Elder son of the late Rev. Robert A. Suckling, Incumbent of Bussage, co. Gloucester, by Anna Maria, dau. of the late John Yelloly, Esq., and grandson of the late Rev. Alfred I. Suckling: *b.* 1842; *s.* his grandfather 1856; educated at St. Edmond's Hall and Cuddesden Coll., Oxford; is Lord of the Manors and Patron of Barsham and Ship-Meadow.—*Barsham, Beccles.*

Heir Pres., his brother Thomas, *b.* 1844.

SUDELEY, Lord (SUDELEY CHARLES GEORGE HANBURY-TRACY).—Cr. 1838.
Eldest son of Thomas Charles, 2nd Lord, by Emma Elizabeth Alicia, dau. of the late George Hay Dawkins-Pennant, Esq., M.P., of Penrhyn Castle, co. Carnarvon; *b.* 1837; *s.* 1863. Is a Dep.-Lieut. for co. Montgomery, Lord of the Manor of Toddington, Patron of 5 livings, and late Capt. Grenadier Guards; descended from a common ancestor with Lord Bateman; his grandfather assumed the additional name of Tracy on his marriage with the Hon. Henrietta, only dau. of Henry, 8th and last Viscount Tracy (ext).—*Gregynog, Newtown, Montgomeryshire; Toddington, Winchcombe, Gloucestershire;* 1, *Eastern Terrace, Brighton; Reform Club,* s.w.; 35, *Dover Street,* w.

Heir Pres., his brother Charles Douglas Richard, Barrister-at-Law of Lincoln's Inn; M.P. for Montgomery, and late Lieut. R.N.; *b.* 1840; *m.* 1868 Ada Maria Katherine, only dau. of the Hon. Frederick Tollemache.

SUDLEY, Viscount. (See under *Arran, Earl of.*)

SUFFIELD, Lord (CHARLES HARBORD).—Cr. 1786.
Eldest surviving son of Edward, 3rd Lord, by his 2nd wife Emily Harriot, dau. of the late Evelyn Shirley, Esq., M.P., of Eatington Park, co. Warwick; *b.* 1830; *s.* his brother as 5th Lord 1853; *m.* 1854 Cecilia, dau. of the late Henry Baring, Esq., of Berkeley Square, London. Is a J.P. and D.L. for Norfolk, and Patron of 9 livings, and late Lieut. Lancashire Hussars; appointed Vice-Lieutenant of Norfolk 1862; is Lieut.-Col. 1st Batt. Norfolk Rifle Volunteers; was formerly Lieut. 7th Dragoons.—*Gunton Park, Norwich;* 11, *Berkeley Square,* w.

Heir, his son Charles, *b.* 1855.

SUFFIELD, Dowager Lady.
Emily Harriot, dau. of the late Evelyn Shirley, Esq., of Eatington Park, co. Warwick, by Phillis, dau. of Charlton Wollaston, Esq.; *m.* 1826 (as 2nd wife) Edward, 3rd Lord Suffield, who *d.* 1835. Lady Suffield is a Patron of 2 livings.—*Horstead Hall, Norwich.*

SUFFOLK AND BERKSHIRE, Earl of (CHARLES JOHN HOWARD).—Cr. 1603.
Eldest son of Thomas, 16th Earl, by the Hon. Elizabeth, eldest dau. of James, 1st Lord Sherborne; *b.* 1804; *s.* 1811; *m.* 1829 Isabella, dau. of the late Lord Henry Howard. Is a J.P. and D.L. for Wilts, and Capt. Wilts Yeomanry; was M.P. for Malmesbury 1832–41. Is descended from a common ancestor with the Duke of Norfolk and the Earls of Carlisle and Effingham.—*Charlton Park, Malmesbury;* 1, *George Street, Hanover Square,* w.

Heir, his son Henry Charles, Viscount Andover; educated at Eton; a Magistrate for Wilts, Capt. N. Gloucester Militia, and M.P. for Malmesbury; *b.* 1833.

898

SUGDEN, the Hon. and Rev. ARTHUR.
Third son of Edward Burtenshaw, 1st Lord St. Leonard's, by Winifred, only child of Mr. John Knapp; *b.* 1822; *m.* 1854 Annie Jane, 2nd dau. of the Rev. George Eaton. Educated at Trinity Coll., Dublin (B.A. 1851), appointed Rector of Newdigate 1852.—*Newdigate Rectory, Dorking.*

SUGDEN, the Hon. and Rev. FRANK.
Second son of Edward, 1st Lord St. Leonard's, by Winifred, only child of Mr. John Knapp; *b.* 1817; *m.* 1850 Henrietta, dau. of the late Philip Saltmarshe, Esq., of Saltmarshe, co. York, and has, with other issue,

* Frank, *b.* 1852.

Mr. Sugden was educated at Eton and Trinity Coll., Cambridge (B.A. 1838, M.A. 1841), appointed Vicar of Adlingfleet 1845, Vicar of Brignall 1855, and Vicar of Hale Magna 1859.—*Hale Magna Vicarage, Sleaford.*

SUGDEN. (See under *St. Leonard's, Lord.*)

SUIRDALE. (See under *Donoughmore, Earl of.*)

SULIVAN, Col. GEORGE AUGUSTUS FILMER.
Eldest son of the late George James Sulivan, Esq., of Wilmington, I. of Wight, by Mary Plomley, dau. of the Rev. S. Jenkins, of Locking, Somerset, and Stone, co. Gloucester; *b.* 1818; *s.* 1858; *m.* 1842 Emily Anne, only dau. of the late Richard Prime, Esq., of Walberton House, Sussex, and has, with other issue,

* George Digby Filmer, *b.* 1850.

Col. Sulivan was educated at St. Omer's Coll., was formerly in the R. Scots Greys, and 5th Royal Irish Lancers on their re-formation. This family claims direct descent from Oliol Ullum, King of Munster, in Ireland, A.D. 125; and to be the rightful O'Sulivan More.—*Junior United Service Club,* s.w.

SULIVAN, Miss, of Broom House, Middlesex.
Charlotte, youngest child of the late Right Hon. Lawrence Sulivan, by the Hon. Elizabeth Temple, younger dau. of Henry, 2nd Viscount Palmerston; *s.* her father 1866.—*Broom House, Fulham,* s.w.

SULLIVAN, Sir EDMUND ROBERT, Bart., of Ember Court, Surrey (cr. 1804).
Younger son of the late Admiral Sir Charles Sullivan, Bart., of Ember Court, Surrey; (who *d.* 1862), by Jean Anne, dau. of Robert Taylor, Esq., of Ember Court, Surrey; *b.* 1826; *s.* as 5th Bart. 1865; *m.* 1859 Mary, youngest dau. of H. W. Currie, Esq., of West Horsley, Surrey.—Residence: *Ryde, I. of Wight.*

SULLIVAN, EDWARD, Esq.
Eldest son of Edward Sullivan, Esq., of Raglan Road, Dublin, and formerly of Mallow, co. Cork; *b.* 1822; *m.* 1850 Bessie Josephine, dau. of the late Robert Bailey, Esq., of Cork. Educated at Trinity Coll., Dublin (B.A. 1841); called to the Irish Bar 1848; became a Q.C. 1858; appointed Serjeant-at-Law 1860, Law Adviser to the Crown in Ireland 1861; was Solicitor-General for Ireland 1865–6; elected M.P. for Mallow 1865.—*Reform Club,* s.w.; 32, *Fitzwilliam Place, Dublin.*

SULLIVAN, the Rev. FREDERICK.
Fourth son of the late Sir Richard Joseph Sullivan, Bart., by Mary, dau. of Thomas Lodge, Esq., of Leeds; *b.* 1797; *m.* 1st 1821 Arabella Jane, dau. of V. H Wilmot, Esq.; 2nd 1843 Emily, dau. of Levi Ames, Esq., and has, by the former, with other surviving issue,

* Francis William, a Magistrate for Beds and Herts, and a Capt. R.N.; *b.* 1831; *m.* 1861 Agnes, 2nd dau. of Rodney Bell, Esq., and has, with other issue. * Frederick, A. Iresh.

Mr. Sullivan, who was educated at Eton and Brasenose Coll., Oxford, is a Magistrate for Herts; appointed Vicar of Kimpton 1827.—*Kimpton Vicarage, Welwyn.*

SULLIVAN, the Rev. JAMES, of Chesterfield, co. Limerick.

Eldest son of the late James Sullivan, Esq., J.P., of Chesterfield, Major 83rd Foot, by Mary Ann, eldest dau. of the late Rev. William Ashe, Prebendary and Rector of Croagh, co. Limerick; b. 1818; s. 1850; m. 1856 Georgina Lucie, only dau. of George Annesley Owen, Esq., of Ramsgate, co. Wexford, and has, with other issue,

* Ponsonby Augustus Moore, b. 1857.

Mr. Sullivan, who was educated at Trinity Coll., Dublin (B.A. 1841), was formerly Incumbent of Kew, near Melbourne, Australia.—Chesterfield, Newcastle, co. Limerick; National Club, s.w.

SULLIVAN, JOHN JEREMIAH, Esq., of Curramore, co. Limerick.

Eldest son of the late J. Sullivan, Esq., of Curramore, by Melian, dau. of John Sullivan, Esq., of Tullilease House, co. Cork; b. 1825; s. 1825; m. 1st 1852 Isabel, dau. of the late Richard Harrison, Esq., of Wyton Hall, Yorkshire (she d. 1863); 2nd 1866 Caroline Harriet, only child of the late Rev. John Fletcher, Rector of Quidgeley, co. Gloucester, and has issue by the former,

* Herbert, b. 1852.

Mr. Sullivan, who was educated at Trinity Coll., Dublin (B.A. 1846), is a Magistrate for co. Limerick. This family claim descent from 'Oliol Ullum,' King of Munster in the second century of the Christian era.—Curramore, Dromcolloher; Warberry, Torquay.

SULLIVAN, MICHAEL, Esq., of Lacken Hall, co. Kilkenny.

Second son of the late William Sullivan, Esq., Merchant, of Kilkenny, and brother of Richard Sullivan, Esq., who was M.P. for Kilkenny 1832-6; b. 1809; m. 1864 Margaret Sabina, dau. of the late Thomas Cormac, Esq. Educated at Clongowes Coll.; was M.P. for Kilkenny 1847-65.—Lacken Hall, Kilkenny; 23, Cork Street, w.

+ SUMMERS, THOMAS, Esq., of Cradley, Herefordshire.

Son of the late T. Summers, Esq.; b. 18—. Is a Dep.-Lieut. for co. Hereford.—Cradley, Bromyard.

SUMNER, ARTHUR HOLME, Esq., of Hatchlands, Surrey.

Only son of the late William Holme Sumner, Esq., of Hatchlands, by Mary Barnard, eldest dau. of John B. Hankey, Esq., of Fetcham Park, Surrey; b. 1836; s. 1859; m. 1860 Georgina, dau. of the late Col. Thomas H. Kingscote, of Kingscote Park, co. Gloucester, and has issue, two daughters. Mr. Sumner, who was educated at Harrow, is Capt. 2nd Royal Surrey Militia.—Hatchlands, Guildford; Arthur's Club, s.w.

Heir Pres., his uncle Charles Vernon Holme, b. 1800; is married.

+ SUMNER, FRANCIS, Esq., of Glossop, Derbyshire.

Son of the late F. Sumner, Esq.; b. 18—. Is a J.P. and D.L. for co. Derby.—East View, Glossop.

SUMNER, RICHARD, Esq., of Puttenham Priory, Surrey.

Only son of the late Richard Sumner, Esq. (who d. 1798), by Susanna, sister of the late Admiral Lord Gambier; b. 1795; m. 1819 Francis Juditha, dau. of the late George Molyneux-Montgomerie, Esq., of Garboldisham Hall, Norfolk, and has, with other issue, an only son,

* Morton Cornish, b. 1825; m. 1st 1849 Penelope, only dau.

of Count Valsamachi, of Corfu and Cephalonia; 2nd 1867 Mary Douglas, eldest dau. of the late James Henry Frankland, Esq., of Kashing Park, Surrey.

Mr. Sumner, who was educated at Eton and Trinity Coll., Cambridge, is a J.P. and D.L. for Surrey (High Sheriff 1843).—Puttenham Priory, Guildford; Conservative Club, s.w.

SUNDERLAND, GEORGE HENRY CARLETON, Esq., of Swarthdale, Lancashire.

Youngest son of the late Rev. John Sunderland, of Little Croft (who d. 1837), by Anne, dau. of Edward King, Esq., of Askham, co. Lancaster; b. 1814; m. 1844 Margaret, dau. and co-heir of Lieut.-Col. Story, R.A., and has, with other issue,

* John William, R.N.; b. 1846.

Mr. Sunderland, who was educated at Shrewsbury, is a Dep.-Lieut. for co. Lancaster, and a Commander R.N., retired.—Swarthdale, Ulverstone.

SURMAN, JOHN, Esq., of Tredington House, Gloucestershire.

Eldest son of the late John Surman, Esq., of Tredington and Malvern, by Susanna, dau. of William Washer, Esq., of Seaford, Sussex; b. 1835; m. 1837 Elizabeth, dau. of John Hughes Goodlake, Esq., of Swindon Hall, co. Gloucester. Is a J.P. and D.L. for co. Gloucester, a Major in the Royal S. Gloucester Militia, and was formerly an Officer in the 58th Foot.—Tredington House, Tewkesbury.

SURMAN, JOHN SURMAN, Esq., of Swindon Hall, and Lay Court, Gloucestershire.

Eldest son of the late John Hughes Goodlake, Esq., of Swindon Hall (who d. 1821), by Elizabeth, only dau. of the late William Surman, Esq., of Lower Tooting, Surrey; b. 1809. Mr. Surman, who is Patron of the living of Swindon, assumed, under the will of his maternal great-uncle, John Surman, Esq., the surname and Arms of Surman.—Swindon Hall, Cheltenham; Lay Court, Westbury-on-Severn; Gloucestershire Club, Cheltenham.

Heir Pres., his brother the Rev. Thomas William Goodlake, M.A. of Pembroke Coll., Oxford, and Rector of Swindon; b. 1811; m. 1845 Mary, dau. of the Rev. William Price, Rector of Coln St. Denis, co. Gloucester, and has, with other issue, * Thomas Surman, b. 1847; Scholar of Balliol Coll., Oxford.

SURTEES, Lady, of Silkmore, Staffordshire.

Barbara Eliza, only dau. of the late Rev. W. Bosworth, of Charley Hall, co. Leicester (who d. 1834), by Eliza, dau. of William Smith, Esq., Banker, of Birmingham; m. 1859 (as 2nd wife) Sir Stephenson Villiers Surtees, Knt., of Silkmore House, formerly a Judge at Mauritius, and afterwards Chief Justice and also Judge of the Vice-Admiralty Court, who d. 1867.—Silkmore House, Stafford.

SURTEES, CHARLES FREVILLE, Esq., of Mainsforth Hall, co. Durham.

Youngest son of the late Robert Surtees, Esq., of Redworth Hall, co. Durham, by [...] dau. of Isaac Cookson, Esq., of Whitehill, co. Durham; b. 18—; m. 1855 Bertha, dau. of N. Snell Chauncy, Esq., late of Green End, Herts. Educated at Harrow; is a Dep.-Lieut. for co. Durham; was formerly Capt. 10th Hussars; elected M.P. for S. Durham 1865.—Mainsforth Hall, Bishop Auckland; Army and Navy and Junior Carlton Clubs, s.w.

SURTEES, HENRY EDWARD, Esq., of Redworth House, co. Durham, and Dane End, Herts.

Second but eldest surviving son of the late Robert Surtees, Esq., of Redworth House (who d. 1857), by Elizabeth, dau. of Isaac Cookson, Esq., of Whitehill; b.

3 M 2   899

1819; *s.* his brother 1863 ; *m.* 1843 Elizabeth Snell, only surviving ch'ld of the late Charles Snell Chauncy, Esq., of Dane End, Herts, and has issue three daughters. Mr. H. E. Surtees, who was educated at Harrow, is a Magistrate for Herts and co. Durdam, Chairman of the Ware Board of Guardians. and Major 2nd Herts Rifle Volunteers ; was elected M.P. for Herts 1864 ; he was formerly in the 10th Royal Hussars.—*Redworth House, Darlington ; Dane End House, Little Munden, Ware ; Army and Navy, Carlton, and Junior Carlton Clubs, s.w.*

SURTEES, HENRY GEORGE, Esq., of Dinsdale-on-Tees, co. Durham.
Eldest son of the late Rev. John Surtees, Canon of Bristol, by Mary Anne, sister of Sir John C. Hawkins, Bart., of Kelston, Somerset; *b.* 1812 ; *s.* 1830. Educated at Harrow and Brasenose Coll., Oxford (B.A. 1831); was High Sheriff of co. Durham 1862. This family were owners of Dinsdale in the time of the Norman Princes, and took local name—'Super Teysam,' Surteys, or Surtees—from the River Tees.—*Dinsdale-on-Tees, Darlington.*

Heir Pres., his brother Scott Frederic, in Holy Orders. B.A. of University Coll., Oxford, and Rector of Sprotborough, co. York ; *b.* 1814 ; *m.* 1840 Almeria, dau. of Philip Hamond, Esq., of Westacre, Norfolk.

SURTEES, Mrs., of Hamsterley, co. Durham.
Elizabeth Jane, dau. of Addison Fenwick, Esq., of Bishop Wearmouth ; *m.* 1841 Robert Smith Surtees, Esq., D.L. of Hamsterley Hall. High Sheriff of co. Durham 1856, who *d.* 1864, leaving, with other issue,

* Anthony, *b.* 1817.

This branch of the old family of Surtees has been for many generations located in co. Durham.—*Hamsterley Hall, Gateshead.*

SURTEES, VILLIERS, Esq., of Pigdon, Northumberland.
Eldest surviving son of the late Aubone Surtees, Esq., of Pigdon (some time Sheriff and Mayor of Newcastle-on-Tyne, and formerly an Officer in the 11th Light Dragoons), by Frances, dau. of Sir John Honywood, Bart. ; *b.* 18—; *s.* 1859. This family derives its name from the fact of having held large possessions on the banks of the Tees.—*Pigdon, Newcastle-on-Tyne.*

Heir Pres., his brother John Honywood.

SURTEES, WILLIAM EDWARD, Esq., D.C.L., of Seaton Carew, co. Durham.
Only son of the late Edward Surtees, Esq., of Seaton-burn, by Anne Catherine, sister of the late Walker Fernand, Esq., M.P., of Harden Grange, co. York ; *m.* 1853 Carolina, dau. of the Rev. Adolphus Pyke, of Haythorn Park, Essex, and widow of General Sir Stephen R. Chapman. Educated at Winchester and University Coll., Oxford (B.A. 1833, M.A. 1836, D.C.L. 1841): called to the Bar at Lincoln's Inn 1836 ; is a Magistrate for cos. Durham, Northumberland, and Somerset, and Dep.-Lieut. for co. Durham (High Sheriff 1866).—*Seaton Carew, West Hartlepool ; Tainfield House, Taunton ; Oxford and Cambridge Club, s.w.*

SUTCLIFFE, JOHN CROSLEY, Esq., of Lee, Yorkshire.
Eldest son of the late John Sutcliffe, Esq., of Lee, by Esther, eldest dau. of John Crossley, Esq., of Great House, near Todmorden ; *b.* 1813 ; *s.* 1818; *m.* 1839 Ann, dau. of Richard Potter, Esq., of Gisburne Park, co. York, and has, with other issue,

* John, *b.* 1841.

Mr. Sutcliffe, who is a J.P. and D.L. for W. Riding of Yorkshire, and a Magistrate for co. Lancaster; was for-

merly Capt. in the 3rd West York Light Infantry, and late Capt. in the 4th West York Rifle Volunteers.—*Lee, Hebden Bridge, Yorkshire.*

SUTHERLAND, Duke of (GEORGE GRANVILLE WM. LEVES N-GOWER, K.G.).—Cr. 1833.
Eldest son of George, 2nd Duke of Sutherland, K.G., by Lady Harriet Elizabeth Georgiana, dau. of George, 6th Earl of Carlisle, K.G. ; *b.* 1828 ; *s.* 1861 ; *m.* 1849 Anne, dau. of the late John Hay-Mackenzie, Esq., of Newhall and Cromartie (she was cr. Countess of Cromartie 1862). Is Lord-Lieutenant of co. Sutherland and Cromarty, and Patron of 15 livings; was M.P. for co. Sutherland 1852–61.—*Lilleshall, Newport, Salop ; Tarbat, Park Hill, Ross-shire ; Trentham Hall, Stoke-on-Trent ; Dunrobin, Golspie, and House of Tongue, Thurso, N.B. ; Stafford House, St. James's, s.w.*

Heir, his son Cromartie, Marquis of Stafford, *b.* 1851.

+SUTHERLAND, GEORGE, Esq., of Forse, Caithness-shire.
Eldest son of the late George Sutherland, Esq., of Forse ; *b.* 1825. Educated at Eton ; is a J.P. and D.L. for co. Caithness, and Lord of the Barony of Forse.—*Forse House, Thurso, Caithness-shire.*

Heir Pres., his brother Francis, educated at Eton ; late Capt. Scots Fusilier Guards; *b.* 1827.

+SUTHERLAND, JOHN WILLIAM, Esq., of Coombe, Surrey.
Son of the late John Sutherland, Esq.; is a J.P. and D.L. for Surrey.—*Coombe, Croydon.*

SUTHERLAND-GRÆME, ALEXANDER, Esq., of Græmeshall, co. Orkney.
Eldest son of the late William Sutherland, Esq. (who assumed in 1819 the additional name of Græme, on inheriting the estate of Græmeshall); *b.* 1810 ; *m.* 1841 Mary Ann, dau. of Robert Graham. Esq., of Cussington House, Somerset, and has, with other issue,

* Alexander Malcolm, R.N.; *b.* 1845.

Mr. Sutherland-Græme is Lord of the Barony of Græmeshall.—*Græmeshall, Orkney, N.B. ; Sudley Lodge, Bognor, Sussex.*

SUTHERLAND-WALKER, EVAN CHARLES, Esq., of Aberarder, Inverness-shire.
Eldest surviving son of the late George Mackay Sutherland, Esq., of Aberarder, by Elizabeth. dau. of John Walker, Esq., of Crow Nest, co. York, whose name he assumed ; *b.* 1835 ; *m.* 1859 Alice Sophia, dau. of Henry Tudor. Esq. and has, with other issue,

* William Tudor, *b.* 1862.

Mr. Sutherland-Walker is a Magistrate for the W. Riding of Yorkshire.—*Aberarder, Inverness ; Windham Club, s.w. ; 2, Grosvenor Crescent, s.w.*

SUTTIE, Sir GEORGE GRANT-, Bart., of Preston, Haddingtonshire (cr. 1702).
Eldest son of the late Sir James Grant-Suttie, Bart., of Preston, by Katharine Isabella, dau. of J. Hamilton, Esq. ; *b.* 1797 ; *s.* as 5th Bart. 1836 ; *m.* 1829 Lady Harriet, dau. of Francis, 7th Earl of Wemyss (she *d.* 1858). Is a J.P. and D.L. for co. Haddington, and a Magistrate for cos. Aberdeen and Berwick. The additional name of Grant was assumed by his father in 1818, under the will of his aunt Janet, Countess of Hyndford, on succeeding to the Preston estates.—*Preston Grange, Haddington, N.B. ; Carlton Club, s.w.*

Heir, his son James, a Magistrate for co. Haddington ; b.

1830; *m.* 1857 Lady Susan Harriet, dau. of James, 6th Duke of Roxburghe.

SUTTON, Sir JOHN, Bart, of Norwood Park, Notts (cr. 1772).

Eldest son of the late Sir Richard Sutton, Bart., of Norwood Park, by Mary Elizabeth, dau. of Benjamin Burton, Esq., of Burton Hall, co. Carlow ; *b.* 1820 ; *s.* as 3rd Bart. 1855 ; *m.* 1844 Emma Helena, dau. of Col. Sherlock, K.H., of Southwell (*d.*). Educated at Eton and Jesus Coll., Cambridge ; was High Sheriff of Notts 1867 ; is Lord of the Manors of Skeffington, Westminster, and Patron of 4 livings.—*Norwood Park, Southwell ; Stafford Club, w.*

Heir Pres., his brother Richard, of Skeffington Hall, Leicester, and Beuham Park, Newbury, Berks ; a Magistrate for co. Leicester (High Sheriff 1861), Lord of the Manor of Benham, Master of the Skeffington Hounds ; formerly an Officer in the Royal Navy, and late Lieut. Life Guards ; *b.* 1821 ; *m.* 1st 1845 Anna, dau. of the Rev. H. Hoosen (she *d.* 1849) ; 2nd 1851 Harriet Anne, dau. of W. F. Burton, Esq., and has, with other issue, * Richard Francis, *b.* 1853.

SUTTON, the Rev. AUGUSTUS, M.A.

Son of the late Sir Richard Sutton, Bart., of Norwood Park, Notts, by Mary Elizabeth, dau. of Benjamin Burton, Esq., of Burton Hall, co. Carlow ; *b.* 1825 ; *m.* 1851 Charlotte Robina, dau. of John Carter, Esq., of Northwold, and has, with other issue,

* Arthur Frederick, *b.* 1852.

Mr. Sutton, who was educated at Eton and University Coll., Oxford (B.A. 1847, M.A. 1852), is a Magistrate for Norfolk, and Rector of West Tofts.— *West Tofts, Brandon.*

SUTTON, JAMES, Esq., of Shardlow Hall, Derbyshire.

Eldest son of the late James Sutton, Esq., J.P. and D.L., of Shardlow Hall, by Sophia, dau. of the late Abraham Hoskins, Esq., of Newton Park, Derby ; *b.* 1837 ; *s.* 1868. Is Lord of the Manor of Shardlow, and Patron of that living.—*Shardlow Hall, Derby.*

SUTTON, JOHN MAULE, Esq., of Landshipping House, Pembrokeshire.

Only son of the late John Maule Sutton, Esq., of Greenwich, by Eliza, dau. of John Ely, Esq., of Dundee ; *b.* 1828 ; *s.* 1832 ; *m.* 1854 Maria Frances, only dau. of William Price, Esq., of Pengegin, co. Pembroke. Is a J.P. and D.L. for co. Pembroke, a Magistrate for Tenby, and a Fellow of the Royal College of Physicians of London, and of Ediuburgh.—*Landshipping, Pembroke ; Windham Club, s.w.*

SUTTON, JOHN STAPYLTON, Esq., of Elton Hall, co. Durham.

Eldest surviving son of the late George William Sutton, Esq., of Elton Hall, by Olivia, dau. of Henry Stapylton, Esq.; *b.* 1832 ; *s.* 1854 ; *m.* 1855 Sarah, dau. of John Charles Maynard, Esq., of Harsley Hall, co. York, and has, with other issue,

* George, *b.* 1856.

Mr. Sutton is Lord of the Manor of Elton and of Facely (in Cleveland), and Patron of 1 living.—*Elton Hall, Stockton-on-Tees.*

SUTTON, the Rev. ROBERT, of Scawby Hall, Lincolnshire.

Eldest son of the late Robert Nassau Sutton, Esq., by Mary Georgiana, dau. of John Manners Sutton, Esq., of Kelham, Notts ; *b.* 1813 ; *m.* 1847 Charlotte, only dau. of the late John Nelthorpe, Esq., of Ferriby, and sister

of the late Sir John Nelthorpe, Bart., of Scawby Hall (ext.), and has, with other issue,

* Robert Nassau, *b.* 1850.

Mr. Sutton, who was educated at Eton and Trinity Coll., Cambridge (B.A. 1835, M.A. 1838), is a Magistrate for co. Lincoln, and *jure uxoris* Lord of the Manor of Scawby, and Patron of 3 livings ; was Rector of Bilsthorpe, Notts, 1859–67.—*Scawby Hall, Brigg ; University Club, s.w.*

SUTTON, the Rev. ROBERT, late of Rossway, Bucks.

Son of the late Robert Sutton, Esq., J.P. and D.L., of Rossway (who *d.* 1864), by Harriet, dau. of William Ludlow, Esq., of Andover, Hants ; *b.* 1828 ; *m.* 1858 Lucy, dau. of the Right Rev. Dr. Gilbert, Lord Bishop of Chichester. Educated at Eton and Exeter Coll., Oxford (B.A. 1855, M.A. 1859) ; is Vicar of West Hampnett, Sussex, late Incumbent of St. Leonard's, Aston Clinton.—*West Hampnett Vicarage, Chichester.*

SUTTON. (See under *Manners, Lord,* and *Canterbury, Viscount.*)

SUTTON. (See *Manners-Sutton.*)

SWABEY, MAURICE, Esq., of Langley, Bucks.

Eldest son of the late Maurice Swabey, Esq., D.C.L., of Langley Marish, by Catherine, dau. of Robert Bird, Esq., of Barton-on-the-Heath, co. Warwick ; *b.* 1785 ; *s.* 1826 ; *m.* 1820 Frances, only dau. of Charles Clowes, Esq., of Delaford, Bucks, and by her, who *d.* 1859, has, with other issue,

* Maurice Charles Merttins, D.C.L., a Magistrate for Bucks ; *b.* 1821 ; *m.* 1856 Mary Katharine, eldest dau. of the late John Haggard, Esq., LL.D., Chancellor of Winchester.

Mr. Swabey, who was educated at Westminster and Ch. Ch., Oxford (B.A. 1807, M.A. 1810 , and called to the Bar at Lincoln's Inn 1810, is a J.P. and D.L. for Bucks and a Magistrate for Middlesex. — *Langley Marish, Slough ; University Club, s.w.*

+SWAFFIELD, ROBERT HASSELL OWEN, Esq., of West Down, Dorset.

Son of the late R. Swaffield, Esq. ; *b.* 18—. Is a J.P. and D.L. for Dorset (High Sheriff 1861).—*West Down Lodge, Wyke Regis.*

SWAINSON, the Rev. EDWARD CHRISTOPHER, of Wistanstow, Shropshire.

Elder son of the late Rev. Christopher Swainson, Rector of Wistanstow and Vicar of Clun, by Elizabeth, dau. of Thomas Low, Esq.; *b.* 1811 ; *s.* 1854 ; *m.* 1st 1833 Alice, dau. of Richard Miller, Esq. (who *d. s. p.*) ; 2nd 1840 Harriet, dau. of the Rev. John Rocke, of Clunguuford, and has, with other issue,

* John Grandorge, *b.* 1842 ; educated at Ch. Ch., Oxford.

Mr. Swainson, who was educated at Worcester Coll., Oxford (B.A. 1832, M.A. 1843), is Rector, Lord of the Manor, and Patron of Wistanstow — *Wistanstow, Shrewsbury.*

SWAINSON, JOHN, Esq., of Summerfield House, Lancashire.

Eldest son of the late John Swainson, Esq., of Halton Hall, co. Lancaster (who *d.* 1867), by Elizabeth Susannah, dau. of Edward Tatham, Esq., of Hipping Hall, co. Lancaster ; *b.* 1813 ; *s.* his uncle, Edward Tatham, Esq., 1863 ; *m.* 1841 Maria Pierce, dau. of the late John Lloyd, Esq., of Strangeways Hall, co. Lancaster, and has, with other issue, * Edward Tatham Swainson, *b.* 1844.—*Summerfield House, Kirkby Lonsdale.*

+SWAINSON, JOHN, Esq., of Elmswood, Lancashire.
Son of the late Anthony Swainson, Esq., by Mary, dau. of Thomas Clay; *b.* 1814; *m.* 1st Eliza, dau. of Edward Gibbon, Esq.; 2nd 1866 Agnes, youngest dau. of the late Richard Atkinson, Esq., of Town End, Kirkby Lonsdale. Is a Magistrate for co. Lancaster.—*Elmswood, Lancaster.*

SWAINSTON-STRANGWAYES, EDWARD, Esq., of Alne Hall, Yorkshire.
Only son of the late Edward Swainston-Strangwayes, Esq., D.L., of Alne Hall, by Eliza, dau. of John Hanning, Esq., of Whitelackington, Somerset; *b.* 1808; *s.* 1862; *m.* 1833 Ann Susanna, dau. of Henry Karn, Esq., of London, and has issue, an only surviving son,
   * John, *b.* 1836.
Mr. Swainston-Strangwayes, who was educated at Trinity Coll., Cambridge, represents a family formerly of Harlesey Castle, co. York, and of Strangwayes Hall, near Manchester.—*Alne Hall, Easingwold.*

SWALE, the Rev. HOGARTH JOHN, of Ingfield, Yorkshire.
Only son of the late John Swale, Esq., of Kendal, Westmoreland, by Ann, dau. of John Hogarth, Esq., of Kendal; *b.* 1810; *s.* 1812; *m.* 1st 1841 Mary, dau. of James Lambert, Esq., of London; 2nd 1851 Emily, dau. of W. Goter, Esq., of Hammersmith, Middlesex, and has, with other issue,
   * John Lambert, 4th Hussars; *b.* 1844.
Mr. Swale, who was educated at Queen's Coll., Oxford (B.A. 1832, M.A. 1836), is a Magistrate for co. Lancaster and W. Riding of Yorkshire, Joint Lord of Manor of Dargate, Kent; late British Embassy Chaplain at Paris. This family was formerly of Grassington, in Craven, and Swaledale.—*Ingfield, Settle ; National Club, s.w.*

SWAN, JOSEPH PERCIVAL, Esq., of Baldwinstown Castle, co. Wexford.
Eldest son of the late Percival Swan, Esq., of Baldwinstown Castle, by Penelope, dau. of Richard Waddy, Esq., of Kilmago, co. Wexford; *b.* 1818; *s.* 1834; *m.* 1841 Catherine Rhoda, 4th dau. of Benjamin Risky, Esq., of Ballynoe House, co. Carlow. Educated at Trinity Coll., Cambridge; is Capt. 3rd Middlesex Militia; a Baronetcy in this family became extinct in 1711.—*Baldwinstown Castle, Wexford ; Junior United Service and Conservative Clubs, s.w.*
   Heir Pres., his brother Richard Waddy, *b.* 1819; *m.* 1839 Barbara, only dau. of Sandham Symes, Esq., of Dublin.

SWANN, JOHN, Esq., of Askham, Yorkshire.
Son of the late Robert Swann, Esq., by Ursula, dau. of Robert Carr, Esq., of Horbury, co. York; *b.* 1794; *m.* 1830 Catherina Elizabeth, dau. of the late Col. William Thomlinson, 18th Foot, and has, with other issue,
   * Robert, *b.* 1832; *m.* 1859 Blanche Maria, 3rd dan. of Sir John V. B. Johnstone, Bart., and has, with other issue.
   * Edward John, *b.* 1863.
Mr. Swann is a Dep.-Lieut. for the W. Riding of Yorkshire.—*Askham Richard Hall, York.*

SWANN, WILLIAM BROWN, Esq., of Merrixton House, Pembrokeshire.
Eldest son of the late Charles Swann, Esq., J.P. and D.L., of Merrixton House, by Sarah, dau. of Robert Brock, Esq.; *b.* 18—; is a J.P. and D.L. for co. Pembroke, and a Magistrate for co. Carmarthen.—*Merrixton House, Narberth.*

SWANSTON, CLEMENT TUDWAY, Esq., of Holly House, Middlesex.
Only son of the late Clement Tudway Swanston, Esq., Q.C., of Holly House (who was a Magistrate for Middlesex), by Mary Jane, dau. of Lieut.-Col. Swann Hill;

b. 1831; *s.* 1863; *m.* 1861 the Hon. Anne, eldest dau. of John, Lord Romilly, and has, with other issue,
   * William Knight Bruce, *b.* 1864.
Mr. Swanston, who was educated at Trinity Coll., Cambridge (B.A. 1854, M.A. 1858). was called to the Bar at Lincoln's Inn 1856.—*Holly House, Twickenham, s.w.; Athenæum Club, s.w. ; 23, Old Square, Lincoln's Inn, w.c.*

SWEET, the Rev. GEORGE, of Broadleigh, Somerset.
Eldest son of the late Rev. Charles Barter Sweet, of Broadleigh, by Lucy, dau. of George Forest, Esq., of Alderbury House, Salisbury; *b.* 1815; *s.* 1862; *m.* 1859 Anne Emmeline, eldest dau. of the Rev. Samuel Thomas Slade-Gully, of Trevennen, Cornwall, and has, with other issue,
   * Charles Francis Long, *b.* 1860.
Mr. Sweet, who was educated at Tiverton and Balliol Coll., and afterwards at St. Mary's Hall Oxford (B.A. 1838, M.A. 1840), is Vicar and Patron of Sampford Arundell.—*Broadleigh, Sampford Arundell, Wellington.*

SWEETMAN, LAURENCE, Esq., of Ballymackesey, co. Wexford.
Eldest son of the late Michael Sweetman, Esq., of Newlawn, co. Wexford, by Eliza, only dau. of N. Fitzhenry, Esq., of Gubbins Town; *b.* 1791; *s.* 1839; *m.* 1820 Eliza, 2nd dau. of Farrel Kehoe, Esq., of Coolhull Castle, and has, with other issue,
   * Michael Kehoe, *b.* 1822; *m.* 1854 Maria. dau. of Edward Hay, Esq., of Ballinastraw, and niece of the late Lieut.-General Hay, of Ballinkeel Castle, co. Wexford.
Mr. Sweetman is a Magistrate for co. Wexford.—*Ballymackesey, Clonroche, Enniscorthy.*

SWEETMAN, MICHAEL JAMES, Esq., of Lamberton Park, Queen's Co.
Son of the late Michael Sweetman, Esq., of Longtown House, co. Kildare, by his 2nd wife. Margaret, dau. of J. Blackney, Esq., of Bally Ellen, co. Carlow; *b.* 1820 ; *m.* 1819 Mary Margaret. dau. and heiress of the late Michael Powell, Esq., of Fitzwilliam Square, Dublin, and has, with other issue,
   * John Michael, *b.* 1852.
Mr. Sweetman is a Magistrate for Queen's Co. (High Sheriff 1862).—*Lamberton Park, Maryborough.*

SWEETMAN, WALTER, Esq., of Annagh, co. Kilkenny.
Son of the late Walter Sweetman, Esq., of Annagh; *b.* 18—. Is a Magistrate for cos. Kilkenny and Wexford (has been High Sheriff of co. Kilkenny).—*Annagh, New Ross, co. Kilkenny.*

SWETENHAM, CLEMENT, Esq., of Somerford Booths, Cheshire.
Eldest son of the late Clement Swetenham, Esq., of Somerford Booths, by Eleanor, dau. of J. Buchanan, Esq.; *b.* 1819; *s.* 1852; *m.* 1852 Louisa Cecilia, Sophia, dau. of St. John C. Charlton, Esq., of Apley Castle, co. Salop, and has, with other issue.
   * Clement William, *b.* 1852.
Mr. Swetenham, who was educated at Rugby and Sandhurst Coll., and served in the Army 1837-49, is a Magistrate for co. Chester (High Sheriff 1860).—*Somerford Booths Hall, Congleton.*

SWETTENHAM, Mrs., of Swettenham, Cheshire.
Anna Maria, dau. of the late Col. Luke Alen, of Dublin; *m.* 1829 Thomas John Wyland Swettenham, Esq., who was a J.P., and D.L. for co. Chester, and *d. r. p.* 1841 ;

she is Lady of the Manor of Swettenham.—*Swettenham Hall, Congleton.*

Heir Pres., her nephew Michael, son of Sarah Eaton Swettenham, by Michael Warren, Esq., of Sandford's Court, co. Kilkenny.

SWIFT, RICHARD, Esq., of Herongate, Essex.
Son of the late Timothy Swift, Esq., by Susannah, dau. of J. Cary, Esq.; *b.* 1811; *m.* 1836 Kate, dau. of John O'Brien, Esq. Is a Magistrate for Middlesex, and a Merchant and wholesale Manufacturer in London; was Sheriff of London 1851–2; M.P. for co. Sligo 1852–7. —*St. Mary's, Herongate, Brentwood ; Westhill House, Wandsworth, s.w.*

SWINBURNE, Sir JOHN, Bart., of Capheaton, Northumberland (cr. 1660).
Elder son of the late Edward Swinburne, Esq., of Calgarth (who *d.* 1855), by Miss Anne Sutton, and grandson of the late Sir John Edward Swinburne, Bart.; *b.* 1831; *s.* his grandfather as 7th Bart. 1860; *m.* 1863 Emily Elizabeth, only dau. of Admiral Broadhead, R.N.; is a Magistrate for Northumberland (High Sheriff 1866), a Lieut. R.N., and Lord of the Manor of Capheaton. —*Capheaton and Edlingham, Newcastle-on-Tyne ; 9, Queen Square, s.w.*

Heir, his son John, *b.* 1867.

SWINBURNE, Admiral CHARLES HENRY, of East Dene, Isle of Wight.
Second son of the late Sir John Edward Swinburne, Bart., of Capheaton, Northumberland (who *d.* 1861), by Emilia Emma, dau. of Richard Henry Alexander Bennett, Esq., of Northcourt, Isle of Wight; *b.* 1798; *m.* 1836 Lady Jane Henrietta, dau. of George, 2nd Earl of Ashburnham, and has, with other issue,
   * Algernon Charles, educated at Eton and Balliol Coll., Oxford; *b.* 1838.

The Admiral, who was educated at the Royal Naval Coll., is a J.P. and D.L. for Hants and Oxon, and an Admiral reserved. — *Holmewood, Henley-on-Thames ; Travellers' Club, s.w.*

SWINBURNE, JAMES, Esq., of Marcus Lodge, Forfarshire.
Only surviving son of the late Lieut.-Gen. Thomas Robert Swinburne, of Marcus Lodge, and of Pontop Hall, co. Durham, by his 2nd wife, Helen, eldest dau. of the late James Aspinall, Esq., of Liverpool; *b.* 1830; *s.* 1864. Educated at the Scottish Naval and Military Academy, Edinburgh; is Proprietor of the Barony of Marcus and Muiry Hillocks, and Lieut.-Col. 4th Hussars; served in India 1857–64.—*Marcus Lodge, Forfar, N.B.; New Club, Edinburgh ; Army and Navy Club, s.w.*

Heir Pres., his half-brother Thomas, *b.* 18—.

SWINBURNE, THOMAS ANTHONY, Esq., of Pontop Hall, co. Durham.
Son of the late Lieut.-Gen. Thomas Robert Swinburne, of Pontop Hall, and of Marcus Lodge, co. Forfar, by his 1st wife Maria, 3rd dau. of the Rev. Anthony Coates; *b.* 1820; *s.* 1864; *m.* 1852 Mary Ann, dau. of the late Capt. Edward Fraser, Esq., of the Indian Army, and has, with other issue,
   * Thomas Robert, *b.* 1854.

Mr. Swinburne, who entered the Royal Navy in 1836, became a Lieut. 1846, and a Commander in 1861; he is Lord of the Manor of Pontop, and represents a younger branch of the Swinburnes, Barts., of Capheaton.—*Pontop Hall, Lanchester, co. Durham; Eilan Mona, Inverness-shire.*

SWINFEN-BROUN, Mrs., of Swinfen, Staffordshire.
Patience, dau. of the late John Williams, Esq., of Llanfair, co. Montgomery, by Patience, dau. of John Thomas,

Esq., of Rhosfawr, co. Montgomery ; *s.* her father-in-law 1854 ; *m.* 1st 1831 Henry John Swinfen, Esq. (who *d.* June 1854) ; only son of the late Samuel Swinfen, Esq. (who *d.* July 1854) ; 2nd 1861 Charles Wilson Broun, Esq., of Linburn, co. Dumbarton.— *Swinfen Hall, Lichfield.*

SWINTON, JOHN EDULFUS, Esq., of Swinton, Peebles-shire.
Eldest son of the late Robert Hepburne Swinton, Esq., by Juliana, dau. of the late J. Harker, Esq., of Springhall, co. York; *b.* 1831; *s.* 1852; *m.* 1863 Frances Jane, only dau. of Daniel Ainslie, Esq., of The Gart, Perthshire, and has issue,
   * John Edulf Blagrave, *b.* 1864.

Mr. Swinton, who was educated at Addiscombe Coll., is a Capt. in the Madras Army.—*Swinton, Peebles.*

SWINTON. (See *Campbell-Swinton.*)

+**SWINY, Mrs., of Tubberlumine, co. Wexford.**
Isabella, 2nd dau. of the late Lieut.-Col. Hugh Piper, formerly commanding the 38th Foot; *m.* 1857 Shapland Swiny, Esq., of Tubberlumine, who *d.* 1864.—*Tubberlumine, Clohamon, co. Wexford.*

SWIRE, SAMUEL, Esq., of Hartwith and Little-thorpe, Yorkshire.
Eldest son of the late Rev. John Swire, of Cononley, co. York, by Ann, dau. of William Robson, Esq.; *b.* 1819; *s.* 1860; *m.* 1st 1846 Elizabeth, dau. of James Kendle, Esq.; 2nd 1857 Gertrude Elizabeth, dau. of Charles Stanton, Esq., and has issue,
   * Elizabeth.

Mr. Swire, who was educated at University Coll., Oxford (B.A. 1842), is a Magistrate for the N. and W. Ridings of Yorkshire and for the Liberty of Ripon, and co-Patron of 1 living.—*Littlethorpe, Ripon.*

SYDENHAM, Rev. JOHN PHILIP, of Collumpton, Devonshire.
Eldest son of the late Rev. John Sydenham, of Collumpton, by Frances, dau. of John Crosse, Esq., of Knowle, Collumpton; *b.* 1803; *s.* 1828; *m.* 1st 1832 Sarah Dally, dau. of John Pugh, Esq., of Thorverton; 2nd 185– Mary Elizabeth, widow of the Rev. Edward Bartlett, and has, by the former, with other issue,
   * John George, *b.* 1836; *m.* 1863 Mary Hooper, dau. of the Rev. John Law, Vicar of Bradworthy, Devon.

Mr. Sydenham, who was educated at Exeter Coll., Oxford (B.A. 1825, M.A. 1829), is a Magistrate for Devon, and Rector of Willand, near Collumpton. This family was formerly of Sydenham, of North Petherton, Somerset, Robert de Sydenham, witness to a charter, sans date, of Hillary of Oswald. John de Sydenham, his son, of the same place, and of Mellbury, in Dorset, *d.* 9 Henry III. 1224. Is descended from Margaret, queen of Edward I., and Eleanor, queen of Henry III. (*Vide* 'Records of the College of Arms, London.') —Residence : *Collumpton, Devon.*

SYDNEY, Viscount (JOHN ROBERT TOWNSHEND, P.C.).—Cr. 1789.
Eldest son of John Thomas, 2nd Viscount, by his 2nd wife Lady Caroline, dau. of Robert, 1st Earl of Leitrim; *b.* 1805 ; *s.* 1831 ; *m.* 1832 Lady Emily Caroline, dau. of Henry William, 1st Marquis of Anglesey. Educated at Eton and St. John's Coll., Cambridge (M.A. 1824); is Lord-Lieutenant of Kent, Col. of Kent Artillery Militia, Patron of 2 livings, and Lieut.-Col. Commandant W. Kent Yeomanry; formerly a Groom and Lord in Waiting, and Capt. of the Yeomen of the Guard; Lord Chamberlain 1859–66. Is descended from a common ancestor with the Marquis Townshend.—*Matson Hall, Gloucester ; Frognal, Foots-cray ; Carlton and Travellers' Clubs, s.w. ; 3, Cleveland Square, s.w.*

SYER, the Rev. WILLIAM HENRY, of Kedington, Suffolk.

Youngest son of the late Rev. B. B. Syer, of Kedington (who d. 1844), by Elizabeth Maria, dau. of the late Rev. Temple Chevalier, of Aspal Hall, Suffolk; b. 1807; m. 1839 Elizabeth Mary, dau. of Samuel Croughton, Esq., of Clare, Suffolk, and has, with other issue,
* Barrington Blomfield, in Holy Orders, b. 1841.

Mr. Syer, who was educated at Jesus Coll., Cambridge (B.A. 1829), is Rector and Patron of Kedington.—*Kedington Rectory, Haverhill.*

SYKES, Sir FREDERICK HENRY, Bart. (cr.1781).

Eldest surviving son of the late Sir Francis William Sykes, Bart., of Basildon Park, Berks (who d. 1843), by Henrietta, dau. of Henry Villebois, Esq., of Marham, Norfolk; b. 1826; s. his brother, as 4th Bart., 1866. Was formerly Capt. 11th Hussars.—*Is nhurst, Mayfield, Sussex; Junior United Service and Army and Navy Clubs, s.w.*

Heir Pres., his brother Henry, late Capt. 1st Dragoons; b. 1828.

SYKES, Sir TATTON, Bart., of Sledmere, Yorkshire (cr. 1783).

Eldest son of the late Sir Tatton Sykes, Bart., of Sledmere (who was a Dep.-Lieut. for the E. Riding of co. York, and High Sheriff in 1828), by Mary Anne, dau. of Sir William Foulis, Bart.; b. 1826; s. 1863. Is a Dep.-Lieut. for the E. Riding of Yorkshire, and Patron of 4 livings.—*Sledmere House, Malton; Carlton Club, s.w.*

Heir Pres., his brother Christopher, educated at Trinity Coll., Cambridge; M.P. for Beverley, and a Dep.-Lieut. for the E. Riding of co. York; b. 1831.

SYKES, DANIEL, Esq., of Kirk Ella, Yorkshire.

Second surviving son of the late Nicholas Sykes, Esq., of Cottingham Hall, co. York; b. 179—; m. 1830 Catharine, youngest dau. of the late James Phillipps, Esq., of Bryngwyn, co. Hereford. Was formerly M.P. for Hull.—*Kirk Ella, Hull.*

SYKES, EDMUND, Esq., of Mansfield Woodhouse, Notts.

Eldest son of the late William Sykes, Esq., of Edgeley House, by Martha, dau. of John Townend, Esq. of Middleton, Leeds; b. 1784: m. 1823 Mary, dau. of Richard Townend, Esq., of Tottenham, Middlesex.—*Mansfield Woodhouse, Mansfield.*

SYKES, RICHARD, Esq., of Edgeley, Cheshire.

Second son of the late William Sykes. Esq., of Edgeley, by Martha, dau. of John Townend, Esq., of Middleton, Leeds; b. 1793; s. his father 1837; m. 1825 Jane, dau. of Thomas Hardcastle, Esq., of Bolton-le-Moors, and has with other issue,
* Edmund Howard, b. 1827; m. 1856 Frances Anne, dau. of George Peel. Esq., Brookfield House, co. Chester.

Mr. R. Sykes is a Magistrate for co. Chester.—*Edgeley House, Stockport.*

SYKES, RICHARD, Esq., of West-Ella, Yorkshire.

Only son of the late Rev. Richard Sykes, of West-Ella, by Mary, dau. of James Rowe, Esq., of Cheshire; b. 1783; s. 1833; is a Dep.-Lieut. for the E. Riding of co. York, Lord of the Manor of West-Ella, and Patron of 2 livings.—*West-Ella, Hull.*

Heir Pres., his cousin Joseph (son of the late Joseph Alfred Sykes, Esq., of Raywell, co. York, who d. 18.., by Charlotte, dau. of the Hon. Arthur Duncombe, of Kilnwick-Percy, co. York); b. 1861.

SYKES, Col. WILLIAM HENRY, M.P.

Son of the late Samuel Sykes, Esq., of Friezing Hall, co. York, by Elizabeth, dau. of Thomas Dench, Esq., of London; b. 1790; m. 1824 Elizabeth, youngest dau. of

William Hay, Esq., of Renistoun, N.B., and has, with other issue,
* Henry Peter. Capt. Bengal Light Cavalry; b. 182–; m. 1865 Mary Albina, eldest dau. of the Rev. Walter Bellairs, of Apsley Lodge, Oxon.

Col. Sykes, who joined the Bombay Army in 1804, was formerly Statistical Reporter to the Government at Bombay, and retired as Colonel 1833; he was an East India Director, and Chairman of that Company 1856–7; Lord Rector of Marischal Coll., Aberdeen, 1854–5, and has been M.P. for Aberdeen since 1857; is a Knight Commander of the Royal Prussian Order of the Red Eagle.—*Athenæum Club, s.w.; 47, Albion Street, w.*

+SYME, DAVID, Esq., of Warroch, Kinross-shire.

Son of the late D. Syme, Esq.; b. 18—. Is a J.P. and D.L., and Sheriff Substitute, for co. Kinross.—*Warroch, Kinross, N.B.*

SYMONDS, Sir THOMAS MATTHEW CHARLES, K.C.B. (cr. 1867).

Eldest son of the late Sir William Symonds, of The Refuge, Yarmouth, Isle of Wight (who d. 1856), by Elizabeth, dau. of Matthew Luscombe, Esq., F.R.S.; b. 1811; m. 1st 1846 Anna Maria, dau. of Captain Edmund Heywood, C.B.; 2nd 1856 Prestwood Mary, dau. of Capt. Thos. Wolrige, R.N. Educated at the Royal Naval Coll., Portsmouth; is a Vice-Admiral R.N.; was formerly Admiral-Superintendent of Devonport Dockyard.—*Torquay, Devon.*

SYMONDS, the Rev. SAMUEL.

Second son of the late Samuel Symonds, Esq., of Stratton House, Falmouth, by Jane, dau. of James Bolitho, Esq., of Constantine, Cornwall; b. 1792; m. 1812 Winifred, dau. of Henry Noye, Esq., of Budock, Falmouth. Educated at Clare Hall, Cambridge (B.A. 1815, M.A. 1819); is a Magistrate for Cornwall, and Rector of Phillleigh.—*Philleigh, Grampound.*

SYMONDS, Admiral THOMAS EDWARD,‡ of Yeovilton House, Hants.

Eldest son of the late Capt. Thomas Symonds. R.N. (who d. 1793), by his 2nd wife Elizabeth, dau. of Hugh Malet, Esq.; b. 1781; m. 1815 Lucinde, dau. of the late Lieut. Francis Joseph Touzi, of the French Navy, and by her, who d. 1864, has, with other issue,
* Thomas Edward, a Commander R.N.; b. 1817; m. 1848 Anne, only child of the late John George Schweitzer, Esq., of Southall, Middlesex, and widow of the Rev. S. Tindall.

Admiral Symonds, who entered the Royal Navy in 1795, became an Admiral on the retired list 1861.—*Yeovilton House, Milford, Lymington.*

SYMONDS, the Rev. THOMAS POWELL, of Pengethly, Herefordshire.

Only son of the late Rev. Joseph Symonds, Rector of Dinedor, co. Hereford, by Charlotte, dau. of — Bamford, Esq.; b. 1790; m. 1816 Eliza, dau. of A. H. Turner, Esq., and has issue,
* Thomas Powell, J.P. and D.L., ... Col. in the Hereford Militia; b. 1817; m. 1852 Anna, 3rd dau. of the Rev. ...., Rector of Littleton.

Mr. Symonds, who was educated at St. John's Coll., Cambridge (B.A. 1813, M.A. 1818), and ordained 1815, is a J.P. and D.L. for co. Hereford.—*Pengethly, Ross.*

SYMONS, THOMAS GEORGE, Esq., of Mynde Park, Herefordshire.

Eldest son of the late Thomas Hampton Symons, Esq., of Mynde Park, by Elizabeth, 2nd dau. of the Rev. Dr. Hannington, of Hampton Bishop, co. Hereford; b. 1818; s. 1831; m. 1st 1839 Mary Louisa, only child and heir

of Capt. Richard Harcourt Symons, of Lyme Regis, Dorset (she *d.* 1863); 2nd 1864 Mary Hayley, only surviving child of the late Rev. Thomas Edward Allen, and grand-dau. of the late Sir H. M. Farrington, Bart., and has, with other issue,

* Thomas Raymond, *b.* 1866.

Mr. Symons, who was educated at Harrow, is a J.P. and D.L. for co. Hereford, and Patron of 1 living; was formerly in the 4th Dragoon Guards. This family was formerly Raymond, and assumed the surname and arms of Symons in 1796.—*Mynde Park, Dewchurch, Hereford.*

SYMONS, WILLIAM, Esq., of Hatt, Cornwall. -

Eldest son of the late William Symons, Esq., of Hatt and Broadmoor, by Agnes, dau. of William Broadmore Penn, Esq., and great-grandson of the late William Symons, Esq., of Hatt, who was High Sheriff of Cornwall in 1735; *b.* 1818; *m.* 1842 Caroline, dau. of Wm. Courtis, Esq., of Plymouth, and has, with other issue,

*William Penn, Lieut. 24th Foot; *b.* 1843.

Mr. Symons, who is Recorder of Saltash, represents an ancient Norman family who came over with the Conqueror and returned to Normandy.—*Hatt, Saltash, Cornwall.*

SYMONS. (See *Soltau-Symons*, under *Soltau*.)

SYNDERCOMBE. (See *Raymond*.)

SYNAN, EDWARD JOHN, Esq., of Ashbourne, co. Limerick.

Youngest son of the late John Synan, Esq., by Eleanor, dau. of John Sheehy, Esq., formerly of Donoman Castle, co. Limerick; *b.* 1820. Educated at Glongowes Coll., and Trinity Coll., Dublin (B.A. 1842); called to the Irish Bar 1843; is a Magistrate for co. Limerick; elected M.P. for that county 1865.—*Ashbourne, Limerick; Reform Club,* s.w.

SYNGE, Sir EDWARD, Bart., of Leslee House, co. Cork (cr. 1801).

Eldest son of the late Sir Edward Synge, Bart., of Leslee House, by Mary Helena, dau. of Robert Welsh,

Esq., Barrister-at-Law; *b.* 1809; *s.* as 3rd Bart. 1843; *m.* 1st 1836 Margaret, dau. of Owen Sanders, Esq., of Newtown Sanders, co. Wicklow; 2nd 1846 Anne, dau. of Henry Irwin, Esq., of Streamstown, co. Sligo. Educated at Westminster and Trinity Coll., Dublin; is a Den.-Lieut. for co. Cork (High Sheriff 1844), and a Magistrate for King's Co.—*Leslee House, Bandonbridge, co. Cork;* 20, *St. George's Place,* s.w.

Heir Pres., his brother Noah Hill Neale, *b.* 1814.

SYNGE, FRANCIS, Esq., of Glanmore, co. Wicklow.

Eldest son of the late John Synge, Esq., of Glanmore, by Isabella, dau. of Alexander Hamilton, Esq., Q.C., of Rutland Square, Dublin; *b.* 1819; *m.* 1861 Editha Jane, only dau. of Robert Holt Truell, Esq., of Cionmanon, co. Wicklow, and has issue,

* Francis, *b.* 1862.

Mr. Synge, who was educated at Trinity Coll., Dublin, is a J.P. and D.L. for co. Wicklow.—*Glanmore Castle, Ashford, co. Wicklow.*

SYNGE, Mrs., of Weston Lodge, Somerset.

Mary Anne, dau. of the late John Paget, Esq., of Cranmore Hall and Newberry House, Somerset; *m.* 1819 Francis Hutchinson Synge, Esq. (2nd son of the late Sir Robert Synge, Bart.), a J.P. and D.L. for Somerset (who *d.* 1854).—*Weston Lodge, Weston-super-Mare.*

SYNGE-HUTCHINSON. (See *Hutchinson*.)

SYNNOT, MARCUS, Esq., of Ballymoyer, co. Armagh.

Eldest son of the late Marcus Synnot, Esq., of Ballymoyer, by Jane, dau. of T. Gibson, Esq., of Wood Lodge, co. Lincoln; *b.* 1816; *s.* 1855; *m.* 1844 Ann, eldest dau. of William Parker, Esq., of Hanthorpe House, co. Lincoln. Educated at Trinity Coll., Dublin (B.A. 1836); called to the Irish Bar 1840; is a J.P. and D.L. for co. Armagh (High Sheriff 1852).—*Ballymoyer House, Newtown Hamilton, co. Armagh; Sackville-Street Club,* Dublin.

Heir Pres., his brother Mark Seton, *b.* 1820; *m.* 1843 Ann Jane, dau. and co-heiress of the late Mark Synnot, Esq.

T

TAAFFE, Viscount (CHARLES RUDOLPH JOSEPH FRANCIS CLEMENT TAAFFE).—Cr. 1628.
Elder son of Louis, 9th Viscount, by Princess Amelia, dau. of Charles Augustus, late Prince of Bretzenheim Von Regenz; *b.* 1823; *s.* 1855. Is a Count of the Holy Roman Empire, and Chamberlain to the Emperor of Austria, Knight of Malta, and a Lieut.-Col. of Hussars in the Austrian Service, appointed Minister of Police and Military Affairs 1867.—*Elischal Castle, Bohemia.*

Heir Pres., his brother Edward, a Knight of St. John; *b.* 1833; *m.* 1860 Maria Francisca, Countess Ceaky, of Austria.

TAAFFE, EDMOND, Esq., of Woodfield, co. Mayo.
Eldest son of the late Henry Edmond Taaffe, Esq., of Woodfield, by Eleanor, only dau. of Edmond Lynch Athy, Esq., of Renville House, co. Galway; *b.* 1802; *s.* 1841; *m.* 1830 Bridget Louisa, dau. of Richard Ferrall, Esq., of Corkagh, co. Roscommon, and has issue,

* Henry Edmond Taaffe Ferrall, *b.* 1832; *m.* 1855 Alice, dau. of John Keogh, Esq.

Mr. Taaffe, who was educated at Trinity Coll., Dublin, is a Magistrate for co. Mayo; descends from a common ancestor with Viscount Taaffe.—*Woodfield, Swinford.*

TAAFFE, JOHN ROBERT, Esq., of Ardmulchan, co. Meath.
Only son of the late Robert Taaffe, Esq., of Ardmulchan, by Catharine Isabella, only dau. of the late Theobald MacKenna, Esq., of Dublin; *b.* 1829; *s.* 1854; *m.* 1857 Catalina Aliga, 3rd dau. of Patrick William Kelly, Esq., of Kingstown, co. Dublin, and has, with other issue,

* Robert Joseph, *b.* 1858.

Mr. Taaffe, who was educated at Stoneyhurst Coll., Lancashire, is a Magistrate for co. Meath. This family is a younger branch of that represented by Viscount Taaffe.—*Ardmulchan House, Navan.*

TAAFFE, MYLES, Esq., of Smarmore, co. Louth.
Eldest son of the late George Taaffe, Esq., of Smarmore Castle, by Elizabeth Anne, dau. of Randal McDonnell, Esq., of Fairfield, co. Dublin; *b.* 1823; *s.* 1848. Is a J.P. and D.L. for co. Louth (High Sheriff 1859). This family is a younger branch of that of Viscount Taaffe. —*Smarmore Castle, Ardree, co. Louth.*

Heir Pres., his brother John, *b.* 1828.

TABOR, JAMES, Esq., of Earl's Hall and Rochford Hall, Essex.
Fourth son of the late John English Tabor, Esq., of Bocking, Essex, by Elizabeth, dau. of James Clement, Esq., of Great Saling, Essex; *b.* 1799; *m.* 1831 Mary, dau. of Major Leach, and has, with other issue,

* James Albert Clement, educated at Eton and Trinity Coll., Cambridge, Barrister-at-Law of the Inner Temple; *b.* 1840; *m.* 1865 Catherine Agnes, 2nd dau. of Samuel Webb Savile, Esq., of Bocking, Essex.

Mr. Tabor is a J.P. and D.L. for Essex, and Lord of the Manors of Little Stambridge and Mucking Hall, Essex; he purchased the estate of Rochford Hall from the representatives of the late Earl of Mornington 1867. —*Earl's Hall, Prittlewell, Rochford; Reform Club, s.w.*
906.

TAILBY, WILLIAM WARD, Esq., of Skeffington Hall, Leicestershire.
Only son of the late William Tailby, Esq., of Humberstone, by Elizabeth, dau. of R. Stevens, Esq., of Hallaton; *b.* 1825; *s.* 1853; *m.* 1850 Mary, 2nd dau. of W. Taylor, Esq., of Humberstone. Educated at Trinity Coll. Cambridge (B.A. 1845, M.A. 1849); called to the Bar at Lincoln's Inn 1850; is a Magistrate for cos. Northampton and Leicester (High Sheriff 1856,), and Lord of the Manors of Skeffington and Welham.—*Skeffington Hall, Leicester; Carlton Club, s.w.*

TAILYOUR. (See *Renny-Tailyour.*)

TAIT, ALEXANDER DUNCAN, Esq., of Milrig, Ayrshire.
Eldest son of the late Admiral Tait, of Edinburgh, by Mary, dau. of Alexander Duncan, Esq., of Restalrig, N.B.; *b.* 1813; *s.* 1846; *m.* 1840 Marion. eldest dau. of John Sprot, Esq., and has, with other issue,

* James Alexander, Capt. 4th Dragoon Guards; *b.* 1841.

Mr. Tait, who entered the Army in 1830, is a J.P. and D.L. for co. Ayr, and late Capt. 4th Dragoon Guards. —*Milrig House, Galston, Kilmarnock, N.B.*

TALBOT, Sir CHARLES, K.C.B. (cr. 1862).
Second son of the late Very Rev. Charles Talbot, Dean of Salisbury, by Lady Elizabeth. dau. of Francis. 5th Duke of Somerset; *b.* 1801; *m.* 1838 Charlotte Georgiana, dau. of the late Hon. Sir William Ponsonby, K.C.B., and has, with other issue,

* Charles Walter, of Imokelly, co. Cork. Lieut. R.N., who has assumed the additional surname of Ponsonby; *b.* 1843; *m.* 1868 Constance Louisa, youngest dau. of F. D. Delme-Radcliffe, Esq., of Hitchin Priory, Herts.

Sir C. Talbot, who is an Admiral R.N., late Commander-in-Chief at the Nore, was formerly Commander-in-Chief on the Irish Station.—*United Service Club, s.w.*

TALBOT, the Hon. and Rev. ARTHUR CHETWYND.
Third son of Charles, 2nd Earl Talbot, by Frances Themasine, eldest dau. of Gustavus Lambart. Esq., of Beau Park, co. Meath, and brother of Henry, 18th Earl of Shrewsbury; *b.* 1805; *m.* 1st 1832 Harriet, dau. of the late Henry Charles Hervey-Aston, Esq. (she *d.* 1845); 2nd 1854 Mary Ann, dau. of the late John Masterman, Esq., of Hull, and has by the former, with other issue,

* Charles Arthur, *b.* 1834; married, and has issue.

Mr. Talbot, who was educated at Rugby and Ch. Ch . Oxford (B.A. 1826), and was afterwards Fellow of All Souls Coll., is a Magistrate for co. Stafford, and Rector of Ingestre.—*Ingestre, Stafford.*

TALBOT, the Hon. and Rev. EDWARD PLANTAGENET AIREY.
Sixth son of James, 3rd Lord Talbot de Malahide, by Anne Sarah, dau. of Samuel Rodbard, Esq., of Evercreech House, Somerset; *b.* 1818; *m.* 1850 Catharine Elinor, dau. and co-heir of the late Francis Richard Hoey, Esq., of Dunganstown, co. Wicklow. Entered the Army 1837, and became Capt. 34th Foot; afterwards graduated at Trinity Coll., Dublin, and was appointed (1852) Vicar of Evercreech.—*Evercreech Vicarage, Bath*

TALBOT, the Hon. and Very Rev. GEORGE.
Fifth son of James, 3rd Lord Talbot de Malahide, by
Anne Sarah, dau. of Samuel Rodbard, Esq., of Ever-
creech House, Somerset; *b.* 1816. Educated at Eton,
Balliol Coll., and St. Mary's Hall, Oxford (B.A. 1839,
M.A. 1841); appointed Vicar of Evercreech 1841, re-
signed 1843; appointed 1849 one of the Chamberlains
to Pope Pius IX.—*Il Vaticano, Rome.*

TALBOT, the Hon. and Rev. GEORGE GUSTAVUS
CHETWYND.
Fifth son of Charles, 2nd Earl Talbot, by Frances, dau.
of Gustavus Lambart, Esq., of Beau Park, co. Meath,
and brother of Henry, 18th Earl of Shrewsbury; *b.*
1810; *m.* 1842 Emily Sarah, dau. of Henry Elwes, Esq.,
of Colesbourn Park, co. Gloucester, and has, with other
issue,
    • George Canning, *b.* 1845.
Mr. Talbot, who was educated at Charterhouse and Ch.
Ch., Oxford (B.A. 1831, M.A. 1833), is a Magistrate
for co. Gloucester, Rector of Withington, and Chairman
of the Northleach Highway Board.—*Withington, Cheltenham.*

TALBOT, the Hon. GERALD CHETWYND.
Ninth son of Charles, 2nd Earl Talbot, by Frances,
dau. of Gustavus Lambart, Esq., of Beau Park, co.
Meath, and brother of Henry, 18th Earl of Shrewsbury;
b. 1819; *m.* 1840 Margaret, only child of Lieut. Mac-
Ray, and has, with other issue,
    • Charles Alexander, Lieut. 14th Hussars; *b.* 1842.
Mr. Talbot, who was educated at Charterhouse and
Harrow, and entered the Ceylon Civil Service 1838, is
Director-General of Military Stores in the Indian De-
partment; he was Private Secretary to Earl Canning,
Governor-General of India, 1851–8, and Private Secre-
tary to Lord Stanley, Secretary of State for India,
1858–9.—*Carlton Club, s.w.; Surbiton, s.w.*

TALBOT, the Hon. RICHARD GILBERT, of Ballinclea, co. Dublin.
Third son of James, 3rd Lord Talbot de Malahide, by
Anne Sarah, dau. of Samuel Rodbard, Esq., of Evercreech House, Somerset; *b.* 1814; *m.* 1847 Anne, dau.
of the late Ellis Cunliffe Lister Kay, Esq., of Manningham Hall, co. York, and has, with other issue,
    • Richard Gilbert, *b.* 1856.
Mr. Talbot, who was educated at Balliol Coll., Oxford,
is a J.P. and D.L. for co. Dublin.—*Ballinclea, Kingstown, co. Dublin; Brooks's Club, s.w.*

TALBOT, the Hon. WALTER CECIL, ‡ of Kiplin
Park, Yorkshire.
Second son of Henry, 18th Earl of Shrewsbury, by Lady
Sarah, eldest dau. of Henry, 2nd Marquis of Waterford;
b. 1834; *s.* his relative, Sarah, Countess of Tyr-
connel 1868. Educated at Royal Naval Coll.; entered
the Navy 1847, is a Capt. R.N.; was M.P. for co. Waterford 1859–65.—*Kiplin Park, Catterick; 32, St. James's
Place, s.w.*

TALBOT, the Hon. WELLINGTON PATRICK MAN-
VERS CHETWYND, of Honeybourne, Worces-
tershire.
Eighth son of Charles, 2nd Earl Talbot, by Frances
Thomasine, eldest dau. of Gustavus Lambart, Esq., of
Beau Park, co. Meath, and brother of Henry, 18th Earl
of Shrewsbury; *b.* 1817; *m.* 1860 Lady Emma Char-
lotte, only dau. of Edward, 14th Earl of Derby, and
has, with other issue,
    • Charles Stanley, *b.* 1862.
Mr. Talbot, who was educated at Eton and Sandhurst,

‡ This gentleman assumed by Royal licence, in June 1868, the
surname of Carpenter, in lieu of his patronymic.

and was formerly Capt. 7th Foot, was Comptroller of
the Household 1845–6; is a Magistrate for cos. Gloucester and Worcester, and Lieut.-Col. Staffordshire Militia; was appointed Serjeant-at-Arms in the House
of Lords 1858.—*Honeybourne, Evesham; 27, Chesham
Place, s.w.*

TALBOT, the Hon. WILLIAM LEOPOLD PORSENNA.
Seventh son of James, 3rd Lord Talbot de Malahide,
by Anne Sarah, dau. of Samuel Rodbard, Esq., of Evercreech House, Somerset; *b.* 1824; *m.* 1852 Mary Louisa,
2nd dau. of Anthony Lefroy, Esq., M.P. Is a Major
in the Army, unattached; was formerly Capt. 34th
Foot.—*Army and Navy Club, s.w.*

TALBOT, the Hon. and Rev. WILLIAM WHIT-
WORTH CHETWYND.
Sixth son of Charles, 2nd Earl Talbot, by Frances
Thomasine, eldest dau. of Gustavus Lambart, Esq., of
Beau Park, co. Meath, and brother of Henry, 18th Earl
of Shrewsbury; *b.* 1814; *m.* 1843 Eleanora Julia, dau.
of the Hon. William Coventry. Educated at the
Charterhouse and Ch. Ch., Oxford (B.A. 1834); is a
Magistrate for co. Worcester; was appointed Vicar of
Ombersley 1837, and Rector of Hatfield 1854.—*Hatfield
Rectory, Herts; Carlton Club, s.w.*

TALBOT, CHRISTOPHER RICE MANSEL, Esq., of
Margam, Glamorganshire.
Eldest son of the late Thomas Mansel Talbot, Esq., of
Margam, by Lady Mary Lucy, dau. of Henry Thomas,
2nd Earl of Ilchester; *b.* 1801; *m.* 1835 Lady Charlotte,
dau. of the late Earl of Glengall (ext.), and by her, who
d. 1846, has issue,
    • Theodore Mansel, M.A. of Ch. Ch., Oxford, a Magistrate
    for co. Gloucester; *b.* 1837.
Mr. Talbot, who was educated at Harrow and Oriel
Coll., Oxford (B.A. 1823); is Lord Lieutenant of co.
Glamorgan, and Patron of 5 livings; has been M.P. for
co. Glamorgan since 1830. This family is maternally
descended from the Earls of Shrewsbury.—*Margam,
Taibach; Travellers' Club, s.w.; 3, Cavendish Square, w.*

TALBOT, GEORGE, Esq., late of Honeybrooke,
Worcestershire.
Only son of the late George Talbot, Esq., of Green Hill,
by Hannah, dau. of Thomas Pemberton, Esq., of Kid-
derminster; *b.* 1792; *m.* 1818 Louisa, dau. of Thomas
Stokes, Esq., and has, with other issue,
    • Alfred, *b.* 1824; *m.* 1851 Hannah Helen, dau. of J. Chel-
    lingworth, Esq.
Mr. Talbot is a Magistrate for co. Stafford, and for the
borough of Kidderminster, and a J.P. and D.L. for co.
Worcester.—*Burley, Leeds.*

TALBOT, GEORGE, Esq., of Knockmullen, co.
Wexford.
Eldest son of the late James Talbot, Esq., of Knock-
mullen, by Mary, dau. of Edward Sutton, Esq., of Sum-
mer Hill; *b.* 18—; *m.* 18— Mary, dau. of Francis
O'Bierne, Esq., D.L., of Jamestown Lodge, co. Leitrim.
Is a Magistrate for co. Wexford, and a Stipendiary
Magistrate for co. Mayo; was formerly a Capt. in the
Army.—*Knockmullen, near Ross; Castlebar, co. Mayo.*

TALBOT, HENRY, Esq., of Oakland, Worcestershire.
Eldest son of the late Henry Talbot, Esq., of Oakland,
by Rosa, dau. of John Broom, Esq., of Spennells House,
near Stone; *b.* 1803; *s.* 1849; *m.* 1829 Caroline, dau.

of William Harding, Esq., of Aston, co. Warwick, and has issue an only child,

* Edith Caroline, m. 1858 William Mayne, Esq., of Rahagbey, co. Tyrone (whom see).

Mr. Talbot is a Magistrate for Kidderminster and co. Stafford, and a J.P. and D.L. for co. Worcester.—*Oakland, Kidderminster.*

TALBOT, HERVEY ARTHUR, Esq., of Aston Hall, Cheshire.

Second son of the Hon. and Rev. Arthur Chetwynd Talbot (whom see), by his 1st wife Harriet, dau. of the late Henry Charles Hervey-Aston, Esq.; *b.* 1838; *s.* his grand-uncle the late Sir Arthur Ingram Aston, G.C.B., 1859. Was formerly an Officer in the Army; served in India 1858-9.—*Aston Hall, Runcorn.*

TALBOT, JOHN GILBERT, Esq., of Falconhurst, Kent.

Eldest son of the late Hon. John Chetwynd Talbot, Q.C. (brother of Henry, 18th Earl of Shrewsbury), by Caroline Jane, dau. of James Archibald, 1st Lord Wharncliffe; *b.* 1835 ; *m.* 1860 the Hon. Meriel Sarah, eldest dau. of George, 4th Lord Lyttelton, and has, with other issue,

* George John, *b.* 1861.

Mr. Talbot, who was educated at the Charterhouse and Ch. Ch., Oxford (B.A. 1858, M.A. 1860), is a J.P. and D.L. for Kent, a Magistrate for Suss-x and Middlesex, and Chairman of W. Kent Quarter Sessions.—*Falconhurst, Eden Bridge, Kent ; Carlton and Travellers' Clubs,* s.w. ; 10, *Gt. George Street,* s.w.

TALBOT, JOHN HYACINTH, Esq.,‡ of Ballytrent, co. Wexford.

Second son of the late Matthew Talbot. Esq., of Castle Talbot, co. Wexford, by his 2nd wife Jane, only dau. of the late John D'Arcy. Esq , of Kiltulla, co. Galway ; *b.* 1793 ; *m.* 1st 1822 Anne Eliza, only dau. of the late Walter Redmond. Esq., of Bettyville, co. Wexford; 2nd 1851 Eliza, dau. of the late Sir John Power, Bart., of Roebuck House, co. Dublin, and has issue by the latter,

* John Hyacinth, *b.* 1851.

Mr. Talbot, who is a J.P. and D.L. for co. Wexford (High Sheriff 1855) ; was M.P. for New Ross 1832-41 and 1847-52.—*Ballytrent, Broadway, co. Wexford ; Castle Talbot, Blackwater, co. Wexford.*

TALBOT, JOHN REGINALD FRANCIS GEORGE, Esq., of Rhode Hill, Devon.

Eldest son of the late Admiral the Hon. Sir John Talbot, G.C.B., of Rhode Hill (who was 3rd son of Margaret, 1st Baroness Talbot de Malahide), by the Hon. Julia, dau. of James, 9th Lord Arundell of Wardour; *b.* 1826 ; *s.* 1851 ; *m.* 1858 Sarah Jane Mary, dau. of the late Rev. David Jones, Rector of Panteg, co. Monmouth, and has, with other issue,

* John Reginald Charles, *b.* 1861.

Mr. Talbot, who was educated at Prior Park Coll., Bath. is a Magistrate for Devon and Dorset, and Lord of the Manor of Uplyme.—*Rhode Hill, Lyme Regis ; Tulaghorne, Mullingar, co. Westmeath ; Athenæum Club,* s.w. ; *Stafford Club,* w.

TALBOT, Misses, of Temple Guiting, Gloucestershire.

Isabella and Jane Elizabeth, daus. of the late George Talbot, Esq., of Temple Guiting, by Charlotte Elizabeth, 4th dau. and co-heir of the Rev. Thomas Drake, D.D. ; *s.* 1836 ; descended from Sir Gilbert Talbot, of Grafton, 2nd son of John, 2nd Earl of Shrewsbury.—*Temple Guiting, Winchcombe ; 25, Curzon Street,* w.

‡ Died whilst these sheets were at press.

908

TALBOT, WILLIAM HAWKSHEAD, Esq., of Bagganley Hall, Lancashire.

Only son of the late James Talbot. Esq., of Bagganley Hall, by Ciceley, dau. of William Hawkshead, Esq., of Howbrook House, Heskin, co. Lancaster; *b.* 1813 ; *s.* 1863 ; *m.* 1846 Elizabeth, dau. of William Bretherton, Esq., of Leyland, co. Lancaster. Is a Magistrate for co. Lancaster.—*Bagganley Hall, Chorley ; Writington, Wigan ; The Parsonage, Southport.*

TALBOT, WILLIAM HENRY FOX-, Esq., of Lacock, Wilts.

Only son of the late William Davenport Talbot, Esq., of Lacock, by Lady Elizabeth Theresa, dau. of Henry, 2nd Earl of Ilchester ; *b.* 1800; *m.* 1832 Constance, youngest dau. of the late Francis Mundy, Esq., of Markeaton, co. Derby, and has, with other issue,

* Charles, *b.* 1842.

Mr. Fox-Talbot, who was educated at Harrow and Trinity Coll., Cambridge (B.A. 1821, M.A. 1825), is a J.P. and D.L. for Wilts, and was M.P. for Chippenham 1833-4.—*Lacock Abbey, Chippenham ; Athenæum Club,* s.w.

TALBOT, WILLIAM JOHN, Esq., of Mount Talbot, co. Roscommon.

Only son of the late John Talbot, Esq., of Mount Talbot (who was a J.P. and D.L. for co. Roscommon. and High Sheriff 1857), by his 2nd wife Gertrude Caroline, dau. of Lieut.-Col. Bivly, of Ballyarthur, co. Wicklow (she *m.* 2nd 1864 the Hon. Francis George Crofton) ; *b.* 1859 ; *s.* 1859. –*Mount Talbot House, Roscommon.*

Heir Pres., his cousin Lindsey Crosbie, *b.* 18—.

TALBOT. (See under *Shrewsbury, Earl of.*)

TALBOT-CROSBIE, WILLIAM, of Ardfert, co. Kerry.

Eldest son of the late Rev. John Talbot, of Ardfert (who assumed the name of Crosbie on inheriting this property under the will of his maternal uncle John, last Earl of Glandore), by Jane, dau. of Thomas Lloyd, Esq. ; *b.* 1818; *s.* 1818; *m.* 1st 1839 Susan Anne, 4th dau. of the late Hon. Merrick Lindsey P. Burrell; 2nd 1853 Emma. sister of the same (she *d.* 1865) ; he has, by the former, with other issue,

* John Talbot, *b.* 1843.

Mr. Talbot-Crosbie, who was educated at Trinity Coll., Dublin, is a J.P. and D.L. for co. Kerry (High Sheriff 1840), and Lord of the Manor and Barony of Ardfert. This family is a younger branch of the Talbots of Mount Talbot.—*Ardfert Abbey, co. Kerry, Ireland.*

TALBOT DE MALAHIDE, Lord (JAMES TALBOT, F.R.S., F.A.S., F.G.S.).—Cr. 1831.

Eldest son of James, 3rd Lord, by Ann Sarah, dau. and co-heir of Samuel Rodbard. Esq., of Evercreech House, Somerset : *b.* 1805 ; *s.* 1850 ; *m.* 1842 Maria, dau. of the late Patrick Murray, Esq., of Simprim. co. Forfar. N.B. Educated at Trinity Coll., Cambridge (B.A. 1847, M.A. 1830) ; sits in the House of Peers as Lord Talbot de Malahide, U.K. (cr. 1856), is a Magistrate for co. Dublin, a J.P. and D.L. for Somerset, President of the R. Irish Academy, President of the Royal Agricultural Society of Ireland. Vice-President of the Royal Dublin Society ; was M.P. for Athlone 1832-4 ; a Lord in Waiting 1863-6. Descended from a common ancestor with the Earl of Shrewsbury.—*Malahide Castle, Dublin ; Athenæum Club,* s.w.

Heir, his son Richard Wogan, educated at Eton ; Lieut. 9th Lancers ; *b.* 1846.

TANCRED, Sir THOMAS. Bart. (cr. 1662).

Eldest son of the late Sir Thomas Tancred, Bart., by Harriet Lucy, dau. of the Rev. Otley Crewe, of Manton,

co. Stafford; *b.* 1808 ; *s.* as 7th Bart. 1844; *m.* 1839 Jane, dau. of the late Prideaux John Selby, Esq., of Twizell House, Northumberland. Educated at Merton Coll., Oxford (B.A. 1830, M.A. 1833) ; was formerly a settler in New Zealand.

Heir, his son Thomas Selby, b. 1840; m. 1866 Mary Harriett, 2nd dau. of George Willoughby Hemans, Esq.

TANKERVILLE, Earl of (CHARLES BENNET, P.C.).—Cr. 1714.
Eldest son of Charles Augustus, 5th Earl, by Corisande, dau. of the Duc de Grammont; *b.* 1810 ; *s.* 1859 ; *m.* 1850 Lady Olivia, elder dau. of George, 6th Duke of Manchester. Educated at Harrow and Ch. Ch., Oxford (B.A. 1831). Is a J.P. and D.L. for Northumberland, Patron of 3 livings, and Lieut.-Col. 1st Battalion Northumberland Rifle Volunteers; was M.P. for N. Northumberland 1832-59 ; called to the House of Peers as Lord Ossulston 1859 ; appointed Capt. Hon. Corps of Gentlemen-at-Arms 1856, Lord Steward of the Household 1867.—*Chillingham Castle, Belford ; White's Club, s.w.; 19, Curzon Street, w.*

Heir, his son Charles, Lord Ossulston, b. 1850.

TANNER, JOHN VOWLER, Esq., of King's Nympton, Devon.
Elder son of the late James Tanner, Esq., J.P. and D.L. of King's Nympton by Elizabeth, dau. of the late John Vowler, Esq., of Parnacott, Devon; *b.* 1830 ; *s.* 1866. Educated at Caius Coll., Cambridge (B.A. 1854) ; a J.P. and D.L. for Devon, late Lieut. 6th Devon Mounted Rifles.—*King's Nympton Park, Chulmleigh.*

Heir Pres., his brother James Melluish, Ensign 6th Devon Mounted Rifles ; b. 1853.

+**TANNER**, WILLIAM, Esq., of Patcham, Sussex.
Son of the late W. Tanner, Esq. ; *b.* 18—. Is a Dep.-Lieut. for Sussex.—*Patcham, Brighton.*

TAPPS-GERVIS. (See *Gervis.*)

TARBAT. (See under *Cromartie, Countess of.*)

TARDY, the Rev. ELIAS.
Eldest son of the late James Tardy, Esq., of Mount Pleasant House, co. Dublin (who *d.* 1835). by Mary Anne, 2nd dau. of James Johnston, Esq., of Fir House, co. Dublin ; *b.* 1814 ; *m.* 1837 Sarah, 2nd dau. of Edmund Charles Cotterill, Esq., of The Grove, Essex, and has, with other issue,

* *James Francis Barham, b. 1841.*

Mr. Tardy, who was educated at Trinity Coll., Dublin (B.A. 1834), was appointed Vicar of Grinton, co. York, 1841, and Rector of Aughnamullen, co. Monaghan, 1850 ; he is a Magistrate for co. Monaghan.—*Aughnamullen Rectory, Ballibay, co. Monaghan.*

+**TARRATT**, JOSEPH, Esq., of Ford House, Staffordshire.
Eldest son of the late Joseph Tarratt, Esq., of Ford House ; *b.* 1796 ; is married, and has, with other issue,

* *Joseph, late of the 16th Lancers; b. 1831 ; m. 1860 Anne, 2nd dau. of the late Major-Gen. Waddington, C.B., of the Bombay Engineers.*

Mr. Tarratt is a Magistrate for co. Stafford.—*Ford House, Wolverhampton; Conservative Club, s.w.; 9, Halfmoon Street, w.*

TASSELL, ROBERT, Esq., of Ditton, Kent.
Third son of the late Robert Tassell, Esq., of Maidstone; *b.* 1784 ; *m.* 1808 Mary, dau. of John Watts, of Wye, Kent, and had issue, an only son,

Robert, educated at Eton, Barrister-at-Law ; *b.* 1819; *d.* 1852.
Mr. Tassell is a Magistrate for Kent.—*Ditton, Maidstone.*

TASWELL, GEORGE MORRIS, Esq., of St. Martin's, Kent.
Eldest surviving son of the late George Taswell, Esq., of Cheltenham, by Honora, dau. of Richard Dickes, Esq., of Dover; *b.* 1784 ; *m.* 1813 Anne, dau. of the Rev. George Gipps. Rector of Ringwould, Kent, and has, with other issue.

* *George, Vicar of Bekesbourne, Kent, b. 1821 ; m. 1855 Elizabeth Arabella, dau. of the late Rev. William Cheshyre.*

Mr. Taswell is a Magistrate for Kent, and Patron of 1 living.—*St. Martin's, Canterbury.*

TATCHELL-BULLEN, JOHN BULLEN, Esq., of Marshwood, Dorset.
Only son of the late John Tatchell-Bullen, Esq., J.P. and D.L. of Marshwood Manor (who assumed the additional surname of Tatchell), by his 2nd wife Ann, dau. of William Hoey, Esq., of Alnwick, Northumberland, and widow of Capt. Forster, R.N.; *b.* 1847 ; *s.* 1864. Is Lord of the Manor of Marshwood.—*Marshwood Manor, Bridport.*

Heir Pres., his uncle Charles. Capt. R.N., retired (son of the late William Fitzherbert Bullen. Esq., of Lavers ook House. Dorset, who d. 1852, by Mary, dau. of John Tatchell, Esq., of Stoke-sub-Handon, Somerset); b. 1811 ; m. 1848 Mary, eldest dau. of William Baker, Esq., of Langstone Court, co. Monmouth.

TATHAM, the Rev. ARTHUR, M.A.
Second son of the late Charles Heathcote Tatham, Esq. of London, by Harriet, dau. of William Williams, Esq.; *b.* 1808 ; *m.* 1853 Jemima Amabel, dau. of Francis Glanville, Esq., of Catchfrench, Cornwall, and has, with other issue,

* *Arthur Glanville, b. 1856.*

Mr. Tatham, who was educated at St. Paul's School, London, and Magdalen Coll., Cambridge (B.A. 1832, M.A. 1835), is a Magistrate for Cornwall. Rector of Boconnoc and Broadoak, Prebendary of Exeter Cathedral.—*Broadoak Rectory, Lostwithiel.*

TATHAM, THOMAS DANIEL FEARON, Esq., of Althorne Lodge, Essex.
Eldest son of the late Thomas James Tatham. Esq., of Althorne, Essex, by Sally, dau. of Devy Fearon. Esq., of Bedford Place, London ; *b.* 1791 ; *m.* 18— Barbara, dau. of the late Rev. J. Landon. Vicar of Aberford. co. York, and Aymostrey, co. Hereford. Is a J.P. and D.L. for Essex. This family is a branch of the Tathams of Summerfield, co. Lancaster.—*Althorne Lodge, Maldon ; 27, Bedford Place, w.c.*

TATHAM, of Summerfield House, and Hipping Hall, Lancashire. (See *Swainson.*)

TATLOCK, Miss, of Bramfield House, Suffolk.
Harriet Helen, dau. of the late Paul Tatlock. Esq. of London, by Helen, ... of ... of Upper Gower Street ; *s.* 1856. Is Lady of the Manor of Bramfield.—*Bramfield House, Saxmundham ; 41, Upper Gower Street, w.*

TATTON, THOMAS WILLIAM, Esq., of Wythenshawe, Cheshire.
Eldest son of the late Thomas William Tatton. Esq., of Wythenshawe (who assumed the surname of Egerton, in lieu of Egerton, on succeeding to Wythenshawe), by Emma, dau. of the late Hon. John Grey, younger son of Harry, 4th Earl of Stamford; *b.* 1816 ; *s.* 1827 ; *m.* 1843 Harriet Susan, eldest dau. of Robert Townley

909

Parker, Esq., of Cuerden Hall, co. Lancaster, and has, with other issue,
* Thomas Egerton, b. 1846.
Mr. Tatton, who was educated at Eton and Ch. Ch., Oxford, is a J.P. and D.L. for co. Chester (High Sheriff 1848), late Lieut.-Col. of the 3rd Battalion of Cheshire Rifle Volunteers. This family is descended from a common ancestor with that of Lord Egerton of Tatton. —*Wythenshawe, Northenden ; Arthur's Club*, s.w.

TAUBMAN. (See *Goldie-Taubman*.)

TAUNTON, Lord (HENRY LABOUCHERE, P.C.). —Cr. 1859.
Eldest son of the late Peter Cæsar Labouchere, Esq., of Hylands, Essex, by Dorothy Elizabeth, dau. of the late Sir Francis Baring, Bart. (she *d.* 1859); *b.* 1798 ; *m.* 1st 1840 Frances, dau. of the late Sir Thomas Baring, Bart. ; 2nd 1852 Lady Mary Matilda Georgiana, dau. of George, 6th Earl of Carlisle, K.G., and has issue three daughters. Educated at Winchester and Ch. Ch., Oxford (B.A. 1820) ; is a J.P. and D.L. for Essex and Somerset, and an Elder Brother of the Trinity House. Has been successively a Lord of the Admiralty (1832); Master of the Mint, and Vice-President of the Board of Trade (1835); President of the Board of Trade (1839) ; Secretary for Ireland (1846), and again President of the Board of Trade (1852) ; Colonial Secretary 1855–Feb. 1858 ; was M.P. for St. Michael's 1826–30, and for Taunton 1830–59.—*Quantock Lodge, near Bridgewater ; Reform Club*, s.w. ; 27, *Belgrave Square*, s.w.

TAUNTON, Lady, of Treberfydd, Brecon.
Maria, youngest dau. of the late Henry William Atkinson, Esq., Provost of the Company of Moneyers, Royal Mint ; *m.* 1814 Sir William Elias Taunton, Knt., a Judge of the Court of King's Bench, who *d.* 1835. —*Treberfydd, Brecon, S. Wales.*

TAUNTON, WILLIAM ELIAS, Esq., of Freeland Lodge, Oxon.
Eldest son of the late Sir William Elias Taunton, Knt., of Freeland Lodge (one of his late Majesty's Judges of the Court of King's Bench), by Maria, youngest dau. of the late Henry William Atkinson, Esq., Provost of the Company of Moneyers, Royal Mint ; *b.* 1818 ; *s.* 1835 ; *m.* 1848 Sarah Percival, youngest dau. of the late Percival Walsh, Esq., of Stanton Harcourt, Oxon, and has, with other issue,
* Ernest Hippisley, b. 1856.
Mr. Taunton, who was educated at Westminster and Trinity Coll., Cambridge (B.A. 1841, M.A. 1847), is a J.P. and D.L. for Oxon.—*Freeland Lodge, Eynsham ; British Service Club*, s.w.

TAWKE, ARTHUR, Esq., of Rochford, Essex.
Only son of the late Christian Tawke, Esq., of Rochford, by Rebecca, dau. of Daniel Gillman, Esq., of Chigwell, Essex ; *b.* 1817 ; *m.* 1st 1845 Hannah, dau. of Edward Smyth, Esq. ; 2nd 1852 Augusta Mary, dau. of Col. J. P. Hamilton, Scots Fusilier Guards, and has, by the former, with other issue,
* Arthur Christian, b. 1846.
Mr. Tawke, who was educated at Trinity Coll., Oxford (B.M. 1841, D.M. 1844), is a J.P. and D.L. for Essex, Major 3rd Administrative Battalion Essex Rifle Volunteers, and Capt. 7th Essex Rifle Volunteers.—*The Lawn, Rochford ; Carlton Club*, s.w.

TAWNEY, ARCHER ROBERT, Esq., of Wroxton, Oxon.
Son of the late Richard Tawney, Esq., of Dunchurch, co. Warwick (who *d.* 1832), by Eleanor, dau. of Thomas
910

Edkins, Esq., of Coleshill, co. Warwick ; *b.* 1818 ; *m.* 1853 Emma Harriet, youngest dau. of W. Parry Richards, Esq., of Park Crescent, London. Educated at Rugby and Merton Coll., Oxford (B.A. 1841, M.A. 1844) ; is a Dep.-Lieut. for Oxon.—*Wroxton, near Banbury.*

TAYLER, RICHARD, Esq., of Bedfont, Middlesex.
Only son of the late Richard Tayler, Esq., of Sunbury, Middlesex, by Elizabeth, dau. of the late Thomas Wood, Esq., of Littleton, Middlesex ; *b.* 1782 ; *s.* 1812 ; *m.* 1803 Martha, eldest dau. of the late Robert Gibbons, Esq., and has surviving issue,
* Robert Gibbons, b. 1809.
Mr. Tayler, who was educated at Harrow, is Lord of the Manor of Staines, and was formerly in the 10th Light Dragoons.—*Bedfont, Hounslow.*

TAYLER, WILLIAM JAMES, Esq., of Glenbarry, Banffshire.
Eldest son of the late Major Alexander Francis Tayler, of Rothiemay House, co. Banff, by Lady Jane Duff, dau. of Alexander, 3rd Earl of Fife ; *b.* 1810 ; *s.* 1854 ; *m.* 1864 Georgina Lucy, dau. of the late Admiral Norwich Duff, and has issue,
* A dau., b. 1868.
Mr. Tayler, who was educated at Trinity Coll., Cambridge (B.A. 1830, M.A. 1835), and called to the Bar at the Inner Temple 1838, is a J.P. and D.L. for cos. Banff and Elgin.—*Rothiemay House, Huntly, N.B.*

+TAYLEUR, JOHN, Esq., of Market Drayton, Shropshire.
Eldest son of the late Rev. Charles Tayleur (who *d.* 1847), by Frances, youngest dau. of the Rev. Richard Lane, of Coffleet, Devon ; *b.* 1840. Is a Magistrate for co. Salop. This family is a younger branch of the Tayleurs of Buntingsdale Hall (whom see).—*The Fields, Market Drayton.*

TAYLEUR, WILLIAM, Esq., of Buntingsdale Hall, Shropshire.
Eldest son of the late John Tayleur, Esq., of Buntingsdale (who was a J.P. and D.L. for co. Salop) ; *b.* 179–. Was High Sheriff of co. Salop 1827, and M.P. for Bridgewater 1833–4.—*Buntingsdale Hall, Market Drayton.*

TAYLOR, Sir CHARLES, Bart., of Hollycombe, Sussex (cr. 1827).
Eldest son of the late Sir Charles William Taylor, Bart., M.P., by Charlotte, dau. of the late John Paulett Thompson, Esq., of Rochampton, Surrey ; *b.* 1817 ; *s.* as 2nd Bart. 1857 ; *m.* 1867 Anne Augusta, widow of J. Rose, Esq. Educated at Eton ; is a Magistrate for Hants, Somerset, and Sussex, and Lord of the Manor of Liss, Hants.—*Forest Lodge, near Liphook ; Carlton Club*, s.w., *and Garrick Club*, w.c. ; 28, *Park Crescent*, N.W.

TAYLOR, General Sir HENRY GEORGE ANDREW, K.C.B. (cr. 1862).
Son of the late James Taylor, Esq., of Lavender Hill, Clapham, Surrey ; *b.* 1783 ; *m.* 1812 Eliza, dau. of Capt. Thomas Maughan. Is a General in the Madras Army (which he entered in 1798) and Col. 23rd Madras Native Infantry.—*United Service Club*, s.w. ; *Oriental Club*, w. ; 3, *Clarendon Place, Hyde Park*, w.

TAYLOR, Sir ALEXANDER, Knt., M.D., F.R.S.E. (cr. 1865).
Son of the late William Taylor, Esq., of Alton, N.B., by Jane, dau. of G. Morison, Esq. ; *b.* 18— ; *m.* 1840

Julia, dau. of the late Rev. Robert Hare, Rector of Hurstmonceaux, Sussex. Was Staff-Surgeon to the English Auxiliary Force in Spain, and afterwards President of a Board for the granting of pensions to wounded officers and men.—Residence: *Pau, Basses Pyrénées, France.*

TAYLOR, EDWARD CLOUGH-, Esq. of Kirkham Abbey, Yorkshire.

Eldest son of the late Edward Clough, Esq., of Kirkham (who assumed the name of Taylor in 1802), by Emma Georgina Bentley, dau. of Wm. Badcock, Esq., of Bath; *b.* 1822; *s.* 1851; *m.* 1848 Sophia Mary, eldest dau. of the late Rev. Thomas Harrison, of Firby, co. York, and has, with other issue,

* Edward Harrison Clough, *b.* 1849.

Mr. Taylor, who was educated at Harrow and Trinity Coll., Cambridge (B.A. 1845, M.A. 1848), is a Magistrate for the N. Riding of Yorkshire, and a J.P. and D.L. for the E. Riding.—*Kirkham Abbey, York; Brooks's Club,* s.w.

TAYLOR, GEORGE, Esq., of Kirktonhill, Kincardineshire.

Son of the late G. Taylor, Esq.; *b.* 18—. Is a J.P. and D.L. for co. Kincardine.—*Kirktonhill House, Montrose, N.B.*

+TAYLOR, HERBERT, Esq., of Uttoxeter, Staffordshire.

Son of the late H. Taylor, Esq.; *b.* 18—. Is a Dep.-Lieut. for co. Stafford.—*Uttoxeter House, Uttoxeter, Staffordshire.*

TAYLOR, HERBERT EDWARD, Esq., of Roselands, Kent.

Eldest son of the late Edward Taylor, Esq., of Bifrons, Kent, by Louisa, dau. of the Rev. Charles Beckingham, of Bourne Place, Kent; *b.* 1807; *s.* 1843; *m.* 1838 Harriot, 5th dau. of the late George John Legh, Esq., of High Legh, co. Chester, and has, with other issue,

* Herbert, *b.* 1846.

Mr. Taylor, who was educated at Eton, was formerly Capt. 85th Foot.—*Roselands, Walmer; Travellers' Club,* s.w.

TAYLOR, HUGH, Esq., of Chipchase Castle, Northumberland.

Son of the late John Taylor, Esq., of Shilbottle, Northumberland, by Margaret, dau. of J. Darling, Esq., of Ford, in the same county; *b.* 1817; *m.* 1842 Mary, dau. of the late Thomas Taylor, Esq., of Cramlington Hall, Northumberland, and by her, who *d.* 1852, has, with other issue,

* Thomas, *b.* 1849.

Mr. Taylor, who is a Magistrate for Middlesex and Northumberland, and an extensive coal and shipowner, was M.P. for Tynemouth 1852-3 and 1859-61.—*Chipchase Castle, Hexham.*

TAYLOR, JAMES, Esq., of Todmorden Hall, Lancashire.

Eldest son of the late James Joseph Hague Taylor, Esq., of Whitworth, by Ann, only child and heir of Anthony Crossley. Esq., of Todmorden Hall; *b.* 1802; *s.* 1810; *m.* 1st 1831 Betty, 2nd dau. of James Maden, Esq., of Greenhouse, co. Lancaster; 2nd 1851 Mary Anne, dau. of John Jones, Esq., and by her, who *d.* 1864, has, with other issue,

* Arnold Dawes, *b.* 1852.

Mr. Taylor is a Magistrate for Berks, for co. Lancaster, and the W. Riding of Yorkshire.—*Todmorden Hall, Lancashire; Culverlands, Reading.*

TAYLOR, JAMES ARTHUR, Esq., of Strensham Court, Worcestershire.

Eldest son of the late James Taylor, Esq., of Strensham Court, by his 1st wife Louisa, 2nd dau. and co-heir of the late Samuel Skeye, Esq., of Spring Grove, co. Worcester; *b.* 1817; *s.* 1832; *m.* 1843 Maria Theresa, dau. of the late George Rush, Esq., of Elsenham Hall, Essex, and has, with other issue,

* Arthur James, *b.* 1858.

Mr. Taylor, who was educated at Winchester and Trinity Coll., Cambridge, is a J.P. and D.L. for co. Worcester, Lord of the Manors of Strensham, Yardley, Bishops Itchington and Dowles, and Patron of 3 livings; was M.P. for E. Worcestershire 1841-7.—*Strensham Court, near Tewkesbury; Carlton Club,* s.w.

+TAYLOR, JEREMIAH, Esq., of Prestbury, Gloucestershire.

Eldest son of the late J. Taylor, Esq., of The Grange, co. Worcester; *b.* 17—; *m.* 18— Sophia, dau. of the late John Barton, Esq., of Swinton, co. Lancaster; is a Magistrate for co. Worcester, a Lieut.-Gen. in the Army, and Col. of the 59th Foot.—*Prestbury Lodge, Cheltenham.*

TAYLOR, the late JOHN, Esq., of Bashall Hall, Yorkshire, and Moreton Hall, Lancashire.

Only son of the late John Taylor, Esq., of Accrington, co. Lancaster (who *d.* 1808), by Anne, dau. of James Fort, Esq., of Altham; *b.* 1802; *s.* 1828 to the estates of his uncle, James Taylor, of Moreton and Bashall Hall, and *d.* 1867. Educated at Rugby and Trinity Hall, Cambridge; was a Magistrate for Lancashire and the W. Riding.—*Bashall Hall, Clitheroe; Moreton Hall and Whalley Abbey, Whalley.*

TAYLOR, JOHN BAGSHAW, Esq., of Radcliffe-on-Trent, Notts.

Eldest son of the late William Taylor, Esq., of Radcliffe-on-Trent, by Juliana, dau. of Benjamin Bagshaw, Esq., of Mansfield; *b.* 1811; *s.* 1857; *m.* 1854 Anna Maria, eldest dau. of the late H. C. Dakeyne. Esq., of Hamilton Terrace, London, and has, with other issue,

* John Montague Wood, *b.* 1856.

Mr. Taylor, who was educated at Christ's Coll., Cambridge, is a Magistrate for Notts (High Sheriff 1868), and was formerly Capt. R. Notts Militia.—*Radcliffe-on-Trent, Nottingham.*

TAYLOR, JOHN EDWARD, Esq., of Cranbrooke, co. Fermanagh.

Third son of the late James Taylor. Esq., by Eliza, dau. of Abraham Browne, Esq., of Aghadoey, co. Londonderry; *b.* 1800; *m.* 1st 1826 Elizabeth, dau. of Robert Wilson, Esq., of Belfast; 2nd 1843 Letitia Elizabeth, youngest dau. of the late John Kearney, Esq. Is a Magistrate for cos. Tyrone and Fermanagh.—*Cranbrooke, Fivemiletown, Ireland.*

TAYLOR, JOHN ODDIN, Esq., of Hardingham, Norfolk.

Eldest son of the late John Taylor, Esq., of Thuxton, Norfolk, by Elizabeth, only child of James Barnard, Esq.; *b.* 1805; *s.* 1855; *m.* 1834 Elizabeth, dau. of John S. Brewer, Esq., of Norwich, and has, with other issue,

* John Odin Howard, *b.* 1857; *m.* 1864 Louisa Barret Minshull, dau. of Richard Minshull Jones, Esq., of London.

Mr. Taylor is a Dep.-Lieut. for Norfolk, Patron of 1 living, and an Alderman of Norwich, of which city he was Mayor 1861-2.—*St. Giles, Norwich; Hardingham Grove, Attleburgh.*

TAYLOR, PETER ALFRED, Esq.

Eldest son of the late Peter Alfred Taylor, Esq., of London, by Catharine, dau. of the late George Courtauld,

tauld, Esq., of Braintree, Essex; *b.* 1819; *m.* 1842 Clementia, dau. of John Doughty, Esq., of Brockdish, Norfolk. Was elected M.P. for the borough of Leicester in 1862.—*Aubrey Hous', Notting Hill,* w.; *Reform Club, s.w.*

TAYLOR, PIERCE GILBERT EDWARD, Esq., of West Ogwell House, Devonshire.
Eldest son of the late Major-General Thomas William Taylor, C.B., of West Ogwell House, by Anne Harvey, dau. of John Petrie, Esq., M.P., of Gatton Park, Surrey; *b* 1810; *s* 1852: *m.* 1st 1837 Sophie Amaranthe, dau. of Col. Shaw, Bengal Army, (she *d.* 1863); 2nd 1865 Anna Maria Elizabeth, dau. of the late Hon. John E. Elliot; he has by the former, with other issue,

* Pierce Thomas Henry (Royal Artillery in India), *b.* 1843.

Mr. Taylor, who was educated at Eton, entered the Bengal Civil Service in 1828. is Lord of the Manor of East and West Ogwell, and Patron of 2 livings.—*West Ogwell House, Newton Abbots.*

TAYLOR, Lieut.-General PRINGLE, K.H., of Pennington House, Hants.
Eldest surviving son of the late William Taylor, Esq., Chief Justice of Jamaica, by Eliza, dau. of Col. Philip Van Cortlandt, of the Manor of Cortlandt; *b.* 1796; *m.* 1827 Adelaide Frances, eldest dau. of Col. John Shedden, of Efford, Hants; and has, with other issue,

* Cortlandt, *b.* 1828.

General Taylor entered the Army as Cornet 22nd Dragoons 1811, became a Major-General 1857. This family, formerly of Shadoxhurst, Kent, enjoyed a Baronetcy created 1664 (ext. 1720).—*Pennington House, Lymington; United Service Club, s.w.*

TAYLOR, ROBERT JOHN, Esq., of Burnham Manor, Lincolnshire.
Eldest son of the late John Taylor. Esq., of Burnham Manor, by Jane, dau. of the late John Swale, Esq., of Croom House, co. York; *b.* 1824; *s.* 1856: *m.* 1860 Isabelle, dau. of W. N. de Pledge, Esq., of Kingston-on-the-Hill, co. York, and has issue,

* Robert John, *b.* 1867.

Mr. Taylor is a J.P. and D.L. for co. Lincoln, Lord of the Manor of Burnham, and a Major R. N. Lincoln Regt. of Militia.—*Burnham Manor, Barton-on-Humber.*

TAYLOR, SAMUEL, Esq., of Eccleston Hall, Lancashire.
Eldest son of the late Col. Samuel Taylor, of Moston, co. Lancaster, by Hannah, dau. of William Hutchinson, Esq., of Bury, co. Lancaster; *b.* 1801; *s.* 1820; *m.* 1825 Mary Anne, dau. of the Rev. John Still, Prebendary of Sarum, and has issue,

* Samuel, a Magistrate for cos Lancaster and Westmoreland; *b.* 1826; *m.* 1878 Maria, dau. of the Rev. Isten Fell, of Ambleside, and has issue. two sons and a daughter.

Mr. Taylor, who was educated at St. Mary's Hall, Oxford, is a Magistrate for cos. Westmoreland and Lancaster, Lord of the Manor of Eccleston, and Patron of 1 living. This family has resided at Moston near Manchester and possessed property there since the fourteenth century. The grandfather of the present proprietor was a Merchant in Manchester.—*Eccleston Hall, Prescot; Ilbotsholme, Windermere.*

TAYLOR, THOMAS, Esq., of Aston House, Oxon.
Eldest son of the late James Taylor, Esq., of Wigan, co. Lancaster, by Mary, dau. of John Hopwood, Esq., of Wigan; *b.* 1815; *m.* 1857 Sara Helen, dau. of Thomas Biggs, Esq., of London, and has surviving issue three daughters. Mr. Taylor, who is a Magistrate for co. Lancaster, and for Wigan, is Lord of the Manor of

912

Aston Rowant, was High Sheriff of Oxon 1863.—*Aston House, Tetsworth; The Limes, Wigan.*

TAYLOR, THOMAS, Esq., of Dunkerron, co. Kerry.
Eldest son of the late Joseph Taylor, Esq., of Dunkerron who was a Magistrate for co. Kerry, by Anne, only dau. of William Duckett Esq., Solicitor, of Clonmel; *b.* 18—; *s.* 1830. Is Lord of the Manor of Dunkerron.—*Dunkerron Castle, Kenmare, co. Kerry.*
Heir Pres., his brother William Duckett.

+TAYLOR, THOMAS LOMBE, Esq., of Starston, Norfolk.
Eldest son of the late Thomas Taylor, Esq., of Starston, by a dau. of — Lombe, Esq.; *b.* 18—. Is a Magistrate for Norfolk, and Lord of the Manor of Pressingham.—*Starston, Harleston.*

TAYLOR, WALTER TAYLOR NEWTON SHAWE-, Esq., of Castle Taylor, co. Galway.
Only son of the late Francis Manley Shawe-Taylor, Esq., of Castle Taylor (who was a J.P. for co. Galway, and Capt. Coldstream Guards), by Albinia Hester, dau. of Lieut.-General Sir John Taylor, K.C.B.; *b.* 1832; *s.* 1863; *m.* 1864 Elizabeth, dau. of Dudley Persse, Esq., of Roxborough, co. Galway, and has issue,

* John, *b.* 1866.

Mr. Taylor is a Magistrate for co. Galway. The additional name of Taylor was assumed by the father of the present owner.—*Castle Taylor, Ardrahan, co. Galway; Kildare Street Club, Dublin.*

TAYLOR, WILLIAM FRANCIS, Esq., of Moseley Hall, Worcestershire.
Second surviving son of the late James Taylor, Esq., of Moseley Hall and Strensham Court, by Anne Elizabeth, dau. of Walter Michael Moseley, Esq., of Buildwas, co. Salop; *b.* 1830; *s.* 1852; *m.* 1863 Augusta Charlotte, dau. of Samuel Steward, Esq., of Connaught Square, Hyde Park, and has, with other issue,

* George William, *b.* 1864.

Mr. Taylor, who was educated at Eton and Trinity Coll., Cambridge (B.A. 1852), is a Magistrate for co. Worcester.—*Moseley Hall, and Moor Green, Birmingham; Oxford and Cambridge Club, s.w.*

TAYLOR. (See *Cavendish.*)

TAYLOR. (See *Watson-Taylor.*)

+TAYLOR-DOMVILLE, MASCIE DOMVILLE, Esq., of Lymm Hall, Cheshire.
Eldest son of the late Rev. Mascie Domville Taylor, M.A., of Lymm Hall, co. Salop, and of Lington, co. York, by his 1st wife, Diana, dau. of John Houghton, Esq.; *b.* 1815; *s.* 1845; is Lord of the Manor of Lymm. Was formerly an Officer in the Army.—*Lymm Hall, Warrington.*
Heir Pres., his brother Thomas John, *b.* 1817.

+TAYLOR-SMITH, EDWARD, Esq., of Calpike Hall, co. Durham.
Eldest surviving son of the late Edward Taylor, Esq., by Anne, dau. of George Garry. Esq., of Newby, in co. Durham; *b.* 1803; *m.* 1829 Ann, dau. of Isaac Nicholson, Esq., of Penrith, and has, with other issue,

* George Garry, *b.* 1838; *m.* 1862 Clare, youngest dau. of the late James Holdforth, Esq., of Burley, co. York.

Mr. Taylor-Smith, who is Lord of the Manor of Calpike, assumed the additional name of Smith in 1842, on succeeding to the Calpike estate.—*Calpike Hall, Durham.*

TAYLOUR, ROBERT, Esq., of Corbal Lis, co. Meath.
Eldest son of the late J. S. Taylour, Esq., of Corbal Lis, by Ellen, dau. of Richard Bridge, Esq., of co. Lancaster; *b.* 1818; *s.* 1848. Educated at Trinity Coll., Dublin (B.A. 1844, LL.D. 1859); called to the Irish Bar 1844; is a Magistrate for cos. Meath and Waterford; was High Sheriff of Drogheda 1866.—*Corbal Lis, Laytown, Drogheda; Friendly Brothers' Club, Sackville Street, Dublin.*

TAYLOUR, THOMAS EDWARD, Esq., of Ardgillan Castle, co. Dublin.
Eldest son of the late Hon. and Rev. Henry Edward Taylour, by Marianne, dau. of the Hon. Henry Richard St. Leger, and cousin of Thomas, 2nd Marquis of Headfort; *b.* 1812; *m.* 1862 Louisa Harrington, 2nd dau. of the Hon. and Rev. Francis Tollemache, and has, with other issue,

* Edward Richard, *b.* 1863.

Mr. Taylour, who was educated at Eton, is a J.P. and D.L. for co. Dublin, and a Lieut.-Col. unattached; formerly Capt. Dragoon Guards; has been M.P. for co. Dublin since 1841; was a Lord of the Treasury 1858–9; appointed Sec. to the Treasury 1866.—*Ardgillan Castle, Balbriggan, co. Dublin; Dowerton, Navan, co. Meath; Carlton Club, s.w.; 99, Eaton Square, s.w.*

TAYLOUR. (See under *Headfort,, Marquis of.*)

+TEBBITT, Mrs., of Charmondean, Sussex.
Mary, widow of Mr. Tebbitt, of London; *s.* 1867 on the death of her sister, Mrs. Thwaytes, widow of Mr. Thwaytes, of Fenchurch Street, who *d.* 1834. —*Charmondean, Worthing.*

TEIGNMOUTH, Lord (CHARLES JOHN SHORE, LL.D., D.C.L., F.R.S.).—Cr. 1797.
Eldest son of John, 1st Lord, by Charlotte, dau. of James Cornish, Esq., of Teignmouth, and grandson of Thomas Shaw, Esq., of Melton, Suffolk; *b.* 1796; *s.* 1834; *m.* 1838 Caroline, dau. of the late William Browne, Esq., of Tallantire Hall, Cumberland. Educated at Trinity Coll., Cambridge (M.A. 1816, LL.D. 1835, Hon. D.C.L. Oxford); is a Magistrate for Middlesex, and a J.P. and D.L. for the N. Riding of Yorkshire; was M.P. for Marylebone 1838–41. This family was seated in Derbyshire for several generations. —*Langton Hall, Northallerton; University Club, s.w.*

Heir, his son Charles John, educated at Harrow; Major N. York Rifle Volunteers, late Capt. Scots Fusilier Guards; *b.* 1840.

TELEKI, the Hon. Countess, of Eywood, Herefordshire.
Jane Frances Harley, only dau. of Henry, 1st Lord Langdale (ext.), by Jane Elizabeth, eldest dau. of Edward, 5th Earl of Oxford (ext.); *m.* 1857 Alexander John Joseph Count Teleki de Szek, Count of the Holy Roman Empire.—*Eywood, Kington.*

TEMPEST, Sir CHARLES HENRY, Bart., of Heaton, Lancashire (cr. 1866).
Eldest son of the late Henry Tempest, Esq., by Jemima, dau. of the late Sir Thomas Joseph De Trafford, Bart., of Trafford Park, Manchester; *b.* 1854; *m.* 1862 Cecilia Elizabeth Tichborne, dau. of J H. Washington Hibbert, Esq., of Bilton Grange, co. Warwick; (*sto d.* 1865). Educated at Stonyhurst Coll., is a J.P. and D.L. for co. Lancaster and for the W. Riding of co. York, and Lord of the Manor of Heaton.—*Heaton, Bolton; 29, Albemarle Street, s.w.*

Heir, his son Henry Arthur Joseph (of Broughton Hall, Yorkshire, and Coleby Hall, co. Lincoln), *b.* 1863.

TEMPEST, THOMAS RICHARD PLUMBE, Esq., of Tong Hall, Yorkshire.
Only son of the late Col. John Tempest, of Tong (who assumed the name of Tempest in lieu of Plumbe in 1824), by Sarah, 2nd dau. of the late Rev. William Plumbe, of Aughton; *b.* 18—; *s.* 1858. Is a J.P. and D.L. for co. Lancaster and the W. Riding of co. York, Lord of the Manor and Patron of Tong, and Major Duke of York's Own Rifle Corps.—*Tong Hall, Leeds.*

Heirs Pres., his sisters Catharine and Sarah.

TEMPEST, WILFRID FRANCIS, Esq., of Ackworth Grange, Yorkshire.
Fourth son of the late Joseph Francis Tempest, Esq., by Frances, eldest dau. of John Hercy, Esq., of Cruchfield House, Berks.; *b.* 1846; *s.* his brother 1865; *m.* 1868 Agnes Mary, dau. of Thomas Aloysius Perry, Esq., of Avon Dasset, co. Warwick. Educated at Stonyhurst; descended from a common ancestor with Sir Charles H. Tempest, Bart.—*Ackworth Grange, Pontefract.*

TEMPEST. (See under *Vane, Earl.*)

TEMPLE, Sir GRENVILLE LOUIS JOHN, Bart., (cr. 1612).
Eldest son of the late Sir Grenville Leofric Temple, Bart., Lieut. R.N., by Marie Aron von Bristen, dau. of the Financial Minister for Transylvania; *b.* 1858; *s.* as 12th Bart. 1860; is head of the noble house of Temple, of which Lord Palmerston represented a branch.

Heir Pres., his uncle Algar Bowdoin (son of the late Sir Grenville Temple, Bart., who *d.* 1847, by Mary, dau. of George Baring, Esq.), Lieut. in the Bengal Army, and Adjutant Kemaoon Battalion; *b.* 1823; *m.* 1858 Mary, dau. of the late Capt. Frederick Knowles.

TEMPLE, Sir RICHARD, K.C.S.I. (cr. 1868).
Son of the late Temple, Esq.; *b.* 18—; entered the Bengal Civil Service 1846; appointed Finance Minister of India, and a Member of the council of the Governor-General of India 1868; was formerly Chief Commissioner of the Central Provinces.

TEMPLE, FREDERIC JAMES HENRY SMYTH-, Esq., of Wrathay, Westmoreland.
Only son of the late Wm. G. H. Smyth, Esq., of Temple Corran, co. Antrim, by Eliza, youngest dau. of the late Admiral Ahns, of Chichester; *b.* 1801; *m.* 1st 1822 Susanna, eldest dau. of the late Rev. Thomas Ramshay, of Brampton, Cumberland; 2nd 1850 Agnes, eldest dau. of Mr. H. Kitchin, and has issue,

* Thomas Ramshay, *b.* 1823; educated at Eton, the University of Bonn, and Trinity Coll., Cambridge (B.A. 1848, M.A. 1851); called to the Bar at Lincoln's Inn 1851.

Mr. Smyth-Temple, who was educated at Shrewsbury, assumed the latter name in 1835, under a settlement made by his father's half-brother, Frederic James Temple, Esq.—*Wrathay, Kendal; Portland Club, w.; 15, Chapel Street, w.*

TEMPLE, RICHARD, Esq., of The Nash, Worcestershire.
Eldest son of the late John Temple, Esq., of The Nash, by Elizabeth, dau. of Capt. Richard Beger, R.N., of Cornwall; *b.* 1809; *s.* 1831; *m.* 1st 1834 Louisa Anne, dau. of James Rivett-Carnac, Esq. (she *d.* 1837); 2nd 1840 Penelope, only child of the Rev. Alexander Luders, Rector of Woolstone, co. Gloucester, and has, by the former, with other issue,

* Richard, F.I.C.S., *b.* 1836; *m.* 1848 Charlotte Fraser, dau. of Benjamin Martindale, Esq., and by her, who *d.* 1854, has, with other issue, *Richard Carnac, b.* 1858.

Mr. Temple, who was educated at Eton and Balliol Coll., Oxford, is a J.P. and D.L. for co. Worcester; he was formerly Capt. Queen's Own Worcestershire Yeomanry Cavalry.—*The Nash, Kempsey, Worcester.*

TEMPLE, WILLIAM, Esq., of Bishopstrow, Wilts.

Only son of the late William Temple, Esq., of Bishopstrow, by his 3rd w'fe Sarah, dau. of the late Thomas Gaisford, Esq., of Westbury; *b*. 1781; *s*. 1781; *m*. 1831 Fanny, dau. of the Rev. T. Stonhouse Vigor, and has, with other issue,

   • George, a Magistrate for Wilts; *b*. 1834; *m*. 1861 Sarah Amelia Lucy, dau. of John Lane, Esq., of Leyton Grange, Essex, and of King's Bromley, co. Stafford, and has issue,
    • a son, *b*. 1863.

Mr. Temple is a J.P. and D.L. for Wilts (High Sheriff 1833) and F.L.S.—*Bishopstrow House, Warminster*.

TEMPLE. (See under *Buckingham, Duke of*.)

TEMPLE. (See *Harris-Temple*.)

TEMPLEMORE, Lord (HENRY SPENCER CHICHESTER).—Cr. 1831.

Eldest son of Arthur, 1st Lord, by Lady Augusta, dau. of Henry William, 1st Marquis of Anglesey, K.G.; *b*. 1821; *s*. 1837; *m*. 1842 Laura Caroline, dau. of the late Hon. Sir Arthur Paget. Educated at Eton and Ch. Ch., Oxford; is a J.P. and D.L. for co. Wexford; late Capt. Sussex Militia, and formerly Cornet 1st Life Guards.—*Dunbrody Park, Arthurstown, co. Wexford; Carlton and Travellers' Clubs, s.w.*

   Heir, his son Arthur Henry, *b*. 1854.

TEMPLER, JAMES GEORGE JOHN, Esq., of Lindridge, Devon.

Only son of the late Rev. James A. Templer, by Anne, dau. of J. Finch Mason, Esq., of Aldenham Lodge, Herts; *b*. 1829; *m*. 1854 Frances Elizabeth, dau. of Joseph Mortimer, Esq., and has, with other issue,

   • John George Edmund, *b*. 1855.

Mr. Templer, who was educated at Eton and Ch. Ch., Oxford (B.A. 1852, M.A. 1864). is a Magistrate for Devon; Capt. Royal 1st Devon Yeomanry; and Major Commandant Devon Rifle Volunteers.—*Lindridge, Teignmouth; Oriental Club, w.*

TEMPLER, the Rev. JOHN, of Knowles, Devon.

Second son of the late James Templer, Esq., of Stover, Devon; *b*. 1788; *s*. his brother 1843; *m*. 1818 Elizabeth, dau. of Joseph Sunter, Esq., of Ashburton, Devon, and has, with other issue,

   • Reginald William, *b*. 1826; *m*. 1854 Emily Laurentia, dau. of Laurence Gwynne, Esq., D.C.L.

Mr. Templer, who was educated at Exeter Coll., Oxford (B.A. 1809, M.A. 1818), was appointed Rector of Teigngrace, Devon, 1832. This family was formerly of Stover, now the property of the Duke of Somerset. —*Knowles, Newton Abbot.*

TEMPLER, Mrs., of Stoke, Devon.

Anne, dau. of the late George Davey, Esq., of Exmouth, Devon; *m*. 18— John Line Templer, Esq., of Stoke, a Magistrate for Devon, and Major S. Devon Militia, who *d*. 1865, leaving, with other issue, one surviving son. This family is a younger branch of the Templers of Knowles (whom see).—*Stoke, Devonport.*

TEMPLETOWN, Viscount (GEORGE FREDERICK UPTON).—Cr. 1806.

Second but eldest surviving son of John Henry, 1st Viscount (who *d*. 1846), by Lady Mary, dau. of John, 5th Earl of Sandwich; *b*. 1802; *s*. his brother 1863; *m*. 1850 Susan, dau. of Sir Alexander Woodford, K.C.B. Educated at Eton; is a Lieut.-Gen. in the Army, late Lieut.-Col. Coldstream Guards; was M.P. for co. Antrim 1859-63; elected a Representative Peer for Ireland 1866.—*Castle Upton, Templepatrick, co. Antrim; Guards' Club, s.w.; 27, George Street, Hanover Square, w.*

   Heir Pres, his brother Arthur, educated at the Royal Military

Coll., Sandhurst; a Lieut.-General in the Army, late Lieut.-Col. Coldstream Guards; *b*. 1807; *m*. 1866 Elizabeth Frederica, eldest dau. of Joseph, 3rd Lord Wallscourt.

TENCH, SAMUEL EDWARD, Esq., of Ballyhaly House, co. Wexford.

Eldest son of the late Samuel Tench, Esq., of Ballyhaly, by his 1st wife Mary, dau. of Edward Rogers Cookman, Esq., of Monart House, co. Wexford; *b*. 1845; *s*. 1859. This family settled at Mullenderry, co. Wexford, *temp*. Oliver Cromwell, descend from an old Norman house. —*Ballyhaly, Kilmore, co. Wexford*.

   Heir, his half-brother Charles Heygate, *b*. 1856.

TENISON, EDWARD KING, Esq., of Kilronan Castle, co. Roscommon.

Second son of the late Lieut.-Col. Thomas Tenison. M.P., of Kilronan, by his 1st wife Lady Frances Anne, dau. of Edward, 1st Earl of Kingston :–*b*. 1805; *s*. his brother 1843; *m*. 1838 Lady Louisa Mary Anne, eldest dau. of Thomas William, 1st Earl of Lichfield, and has issue,

   • Louisa Frances Mary.

Mr. Tenison, who was educated at Trinity Coll., Cambridge (B.A. 1826. M.A. 1842), appointed in 1840 Lord Lieutenant and Custos Rotulorum co. Leitrim, and transferred in 1856 to co. Roscommon, is a Magistrate for cos. Leitrim and Sligo, and has been High Sheriff of both those counties; formerly Capt. in the 14th Light Dragoons; was M.P. for co. Leitrim 1847-52.—*Kilronan Castle, Carrick-on-Shannon; Kildare Street Club, Dublin; Brooks's and Travellers' Clubs, s.w.*

TENISON, THOMAS JOSEPH, Esq., of Port Nelligan, co. Armagh.

Only son of the late Rev. Joseph Tenison, J.P., by Mary, dau. of the Rev. Martyn Lucius O'Brien, D.D.: *b*. 1805; *m*. 1831 Margaret, eldest dau. of the late Alexander Cross, Esq., and Margaret Coote, dau. of John Bond, Esq., of Bondville, and by her, who *d*. 1861, has issue surviving,

   • William Cross O'Brien, educated at Trinity Coll., Dublin Capt. 75th Armagh Light Infantry; *b*. 1856.

Mr. Tenison, who was educated at Trinity Coll., Dublin, is a Barrister-at-Law (called 1832), North-East Circuit, a Grand Juror and Magistrate for co. Armagh, and a Member of several literary and other societies.—*Port Nelligan, Tynan, co. Armagh.*

TENNANT, CHARLES, Esq., of the Glen, Peeblesshire.

Son of John Tennant, Esq., of St. Rollox, near Glasgow; *b*. 1823; *m*. 1849 Emma, dau. of Richard Winsloe, Esq., of Mount Nebo, Taunton, Somerset, and has, with other issue,

   • Edward Priaulx, *b*. 1855.

Mr. Tennant is a J.P. and D.L. for co. Peebles.—*The Glen, Traquair, N.B.; Brooks's and Reform Clubs, s.w.*

TENNANT, CHARLES RICHARD, Esq., of Needwood House, Staffordshire.

Only son of the late Charles Edmund Tennant, Esq., of Needwood House (who was a Commander R.N., and a J.P. and D.L. for co. Stafford), by his 1st wife Sophia Ann, eldest dau. of Richard Temple, Esq., of the Nash, co. Worcester; *b*. 1851; *s*. 1862. The family of Tennant (or Tennent) were formerly seated in Craven, co. York.—*Needwood House, Burton-on-Trent.*

   Heir Pres, his uncle George Tennant, Esq., of The Lindes, co. Worcester, Major 82th Foot, retired (2nd son of the late Wm. Tennant, Esq., of Little Aston Hall, co. Stafford, by the Hon. Maria Charlotte, 4th dau. of Lord Yarborough); *b*. 1811.

TENNANT, JOHN ROBERT, Esq., of Kildwick, Yorkshire.

Only son of the late John Tennant, Esq., J.P., of Chapel House, near Skipton, co. York (who assumed the name

of Tennant only, in lieu of Tennant-Stansfield, under the will of his uncle), by Rebecca, dau. of the Rev. J. F. Wilson, M.A.. Vicar of Otley, co. York; b. 1815; s. 1830; m. 1839 his cousin Frances Mary. dau. of Matthew Wilson, Esq., of Eshton Hall, co. York; is a J.P. and D.L. for the W. Riding of Yorkshire.—*Kildwick Hall, Skipton.*

TENNENT, Sir JAMES EMERSON-, Bart., of Tempo Manor, co. Fermanagh, cr. 1867.
Son of William Emerson, Esq., of Belfast, by Sarah, dau. of William Arbuthnot, Esq., of Rockvale, co. Down; b. 1804; m. 1831 Letitia, dau. of William Tennent, Esq., of Tempo Manor (whose name he assumed by Royal licence). Has the degree of LL.D. of Cambridge, and of Trinity Coll., Dublin; is a Magistrate for co. Fermanagh, and has been Dep.-Lieut. for Fermanagh and Sligo. He has been Secretary to the India Board, the Poor-Law Board, and the Board of Trade, and Lieut.-Governor of Ceylon. He was M.P. for Belfast 1833-7, 1838-41. and 1842-5, and for Lisburn 1852; Author of a 'History of Modern Greece,' and various works on Ceylon.—*Tempo Manor, co. Fermanagh; 66, Warwick Square, s.w.*

Heir, his son William William, a J.P. and D.L. for co. Fermanagh; b. 1835.

TENNENT, the late HUGH, Esq., of Wellpark, Lanarkshire, and Errol, Perthshire.
Son of the late H. Tennent, Esq.; b. 1800, and d. 1864, having married Miss Christian Mary, who d. 1863. He was a Magistrate for co. Lanark.—*Wellpark, Glasgow; Errol, Perth, N.B.*

TENNENT, Mrs. HAMILTON-, of Pynnacles, Middlesex.
Helen Howorth, only dau. of the late General Samuel Graham, of Stirling Castle, N.B., by Jane, dau. of the late James Ferrier, Esq., of Edinburgh; m. 1836 Colonel Hamilton-Tennent, of Pynnacles and Overton (who d. s. p. 1866). The late Colonel Tennent assumed the name of Tennent in lieu of his patronymic Tovey, on succeeding by will to his cousin James Tennent, of Pynnacles, Poole, and Overton, in 1832.—*Pynnacles, Great Stanmore; Stranraer Place, Maida Vale, w.*

TENNENT, ROBERT JAMES, Esq., of Rush Park, co. Antrim.
Only son of the late Dr. Tennent, of Belfast, by Eliza, only dau. of James Macrone, Esq., M.D.; b. 1803; m. 1830 Eliza, dau. of the late John McCracken, Esq., of Belfast (she d. 1850). Educated at Trinity Coll., Dublin; called to the Irish Bar 1833, and also to the English Bar at Lincoln's Inn 1838; is a J.P. and D.L. for co. Antrim, and a Magistrate for co. Down; was M.P. for Belfast 1847-52.—*Rush Park, Whitehouse, Belfast; Athenæum Club, s.w.*

TENNYSON-D'EYNCOURT, GEORGE HILDE- YARD, Esq., C.M.G., of Bayons Manor, Lincolnshire.
Eldest son of the late Right Hon. Charles Tennyson-d'Eyncourt, of Bayons Manor (who assumed the additional name of d'Eyncourt by Royal licence, in 1835), by Frances Mary, only child of the Rev. John Hutton, of Morton Hall, co. Lincoln; b. 1809; s. 1861. Educated at Westminster and Trinity Coll., Cambridge; is a J.P. and D.L. for co. Lincoln, Lord of the Manors of Bayons, Tealby, Morton, and Hemswell, and Patron of 2 livings; was formerly in the Civil Service in the Ionian Islands, and is a Companion of the Order of St. Michael and St. George; is a co-heir of the Earls of Scarsdale and Barons d'Eyncourt of Sutton. *Bayons*

Manor and Usselby Hall, Market Rasen; Reform Club, s.w.

Heir Pres., his brother Edwin Clayton, Admiral R.N.; b. 1813; m. 1859 Lady Henrietta, youngest dau. of Henry, 4th Duke of Newcastle, K.G., and has issue a daughter.

TENNYSON-D'EYNCOURT, LOUIS CHARLES, Esq., of Hadley House, Middlesex.
Third son of the late Right Hon. Charles Tennyson-d'Eyncourt, of Bayons Manor, co. Lincoln (who d. 1861), by Frances Mary, only dau. of the Rev. John Hutton, of Morton, co. Lincoln; b. 1814; m. 1852 Sophia, dau. of the late John Ashton Yates, Esq., M.P., of Dingle Head, near Liverpool, and has, with other issue,

* Edmund Charles, b. 1855.

Mr. L. Tennyson-d'Eyncourt, who was educated at Westminster and King's Coll., London, and was called to the Bar at the Inner Temple 1840, was in 1851 appointed a Police Magistrate for the Metropolis.—*Hadley House, Monken Hadley, Barnet; Reform Club, s.w.*

TENTERDEN, Lord (JOHN HENRY ABBOTT).— Cr. 1827.
Elder son of Charles, 1st Lord (who was for many years Chief Justice of the Common Pleas), by Mary, dau. of John Lagier Lamotte, Esq., of Grotto House, Berks; b. 1796; s. 1832. Educated at Winchester and at Balliol Coll., Oxford (B.A. 1818. M.A. 1821). —*Hendon Place, Middlesex; Carlton Club, s.w.; Garrick Club, w.c.; 12, Wilton Street, s.w.*

Heir Pres., his nephew Charles Stuart Aubrey; educated at Eton; a Clerk in the Foreign Office (son of the late Hon. Charles Abbott, who d. 1858, by Emily Frances, dau. of the late Rear-Admiral Lord George Stuart); b. 1834; m. 1859 Penelope Mary Gertrude, dau. of Col. John Rowland Smyth, C.B., and has, with other issue, • a son, b. 1865.

TEULON, JOHN, Esq., of Bandon, co. Cork.
Eldest son of the late John Teulon, Esq., of Cork, by Mary, eldest dau. of the Rev. G. Wood, late of Bandon, co. Cork; b. 1782; s. 1827; m. 18— Katharine Morris, eldest dau. of George Beamish, Esq., late of Cloghen House, co. Cork, and has, with other issue,

* George Beamish, educated at Trinity Coll., Dublin; a Magistrate for co. Cork; b. 1815.

Mr. Teulon, who was educated at Trinity Coll., Dublin, is a Magistrate for co. Cork. This family is of Huguenot extraction.—*Bandon, Cork.*

TEW, EDWARD, Esq., of Crofton Hall, York- shire.
Eldest son of the late Thomas Wm. Tew, Esq.. of Doncaster. by Catherine, dau. of the late John Jackson. Esq., of Fairburn, co. York; b. 1798; s. 1832; m. 1827 Sarah Susanna, dau. of Martin Hind, Esq., of Newton Green, Leeds, and by her, who d. 1865, has, with other issue,

* Thomas William. of Carleton, co. York; a Magistrate for the W. Riding of Yorkshire; b. 1828.

Mr. Tew, who is a J.P. and D.L. for the W. Riding of Yorkshire, and a Banker at Wakefield and Pontefract, was formerly Capt. 1st W. York Yeomanry Cavalry. —*Crofton Hall, Wakefield.*

TEWART, Capt. JOHN EDWARD, of Glanton and Swinhoe, Northumberland.
Eldest son of the late William Tewart. Esq.. J.P., of Glanton and Swinhoe, by Eliza, dau. of the late Edward Tewart, Esq., of Southgate Park, Middlesex, and Coupland Castle, Northumberland; b. 1832; s. 1846. Educated at Rugby, is a Capt. of the 6th Royals.—*Glanton Hall and Swinhoe House, London wch.*

Heir Pres., his brother William Lawson, b. 1838.

TEYNHAM, Lord (GEORGE HENRY ROPER-CUR- ZON).—Cr. 1616.
Eldest surviving son of Henry Francis, 14th Lord (who d. 1842), by his 1st wife Bridget, eldest dau. of Thomas Hawkins, Esq., of Nash Court, Kent; b. 1798; s. his

3 N 2   915

brother as 16th Lord 1842; *m.* 1822 Eliza Joynes. Educated at Westminster and Woolwich; was formerly Lieut. Royal Artillery.—*West Barnet, Herts ; 10, Shaftesbury Crescent, s.w.*

*Heir, his son Henry George, an Examiner in the Audit Office ; b. 1824; m. 1869 Harriet Anne Lovell, 5th dau. of the late Rev. Thomas Heathcote, of Shaw-Hill House, Wilts, and has, with other issue, * a son, b. 1867.*

THACKERAY, Miss, of Old Windsor, Berks.
Mary Ann Elizabeth, only dau. of the late Rev. George Thackeray, D.D., Provost of King's Coll., Cambridge, by Mary Ann, eldest dau. of the late Alexander Cottin, Esq., of Cheverells, Herts ; *s.* 1850.—*The Grove, Old Windsor ; 27, Portman Square, w.*

THACKWELL, Lady, of Aghada Hall, co. Cork.
Maria Audriah, eldest dau. of the late Francis Roche, Esq., of Rochemount, co. Cork, by Esther, only dau. of the late John Webb, Esq., of Rosanna, co. Cork ; *m.* 1825 Sir Joseph Thackwell, G.C.B., of Aghada Hall, who *d.* 1859, leaving, with other issue, Edward Joseph (of Norman's Land, Dymock, co. Gloucester), Barrister-at-Law, late Capt. 50th Regt.; *b.* 1827 ; *m.* 1851 Charlotte Price. dau. and co.-heir of the late Capt. Lucas, Bengal Army, and has, with other issue, * Joseph Edward Lucas, *b.* 1853, who inherits, under his grandfather's will, the estate of Conneragh, co. Waterford.—*Aghada Hall, Cloyne, co. Cork.*

THACKWELL, JOHN CAM, Esq., of Wilton Place, Gloucestershire.
Eldest son of the late John Thackwell, Esq., J.P. and D.L., of Wilton Place, by Winifred, dau. of J. Seabright, Esq., of Lea, co. Worcester, and brother of the late Lieut.-General Sir Joseph Thackwell, G.C.B.; *b.* 1807 ; *s.* 1829 ; *m.* 1842 Charlotte Eleanor, eldest dau. of the late Rev. John Hugh Polson, Prebendary of Exeter, and has, with other issue,

* John, *b.* 1844.

Mr. Thackwell is a J.P. and D.L. for co. Gloucester, and a Magistrate for co. Worcester.—*Wilton Place, Dymock, Gloucestershire ; Birts Morton Court, and Rye Court, Ledbury.*

THARP, JOSEPH SIDNEY, Esq., of Chippenham Park, Cambridgeshire.
Eldest son of the late John Tharp, Esq., of Chippenham Park (formerly of the Royal Horse Guards Blue). by Anna Maria, dau. of Charles Philips, Esq., of Ruxley, Surrey ; *b.* 1797 ; *s.* 1851 ; *m.* 1st 1825 Anna Maria. dau. of the late Major-General George Gent, of Moyns Park, Essex (she *d.* 1845) ; 2nd 1852 Laura, 4th dau. of the late Sir John Trollope, Bart., and has issue by the former,

* John Manners Gordon, *b.* 1826.

Mr. Tharp, who was educated at Eton, is a J.P. and D.L. for co. Cambridge, Lord of the Manors of Chippenham, Snailwell, and Badlingham, and Patron of 2 livings; he was formerly in the Coldstream Guards.—*Chippenham Park, Newmarket.*

+**THEAKSTONE, ROBERT, Esq., of Seaforth, Lancashire.**
Son of the late Mr. Robert Theakstone, of Seaforth ; *b.* 17—; is a Magistrate for co. Lancaster, and a Merchant at Liverpool.—*Studley Lodge, Seaforth, Liverpool.*

THELLUSSON, the Hon. Mrs., of Casins, Suffolk.
Caroline Anna Maria, dau. of the late Sir Christopher Bethell-Codrington, Bart., of Dodington Park, co. Gloucester, by the Hon. Caroline, dau. of Thomas, 2nd Lord Foley ; *m.* 1826 the Hon. Arthur Thellusson, who

916

d. 1858, leaving, with other issue, * Arthur John Bethell, (see *Rendlesham*).—*Casins House, Woodbridge.*

THELLUSSON, CHARLES SABINE AUGUSTUS, Esq., of Brodsworth, Yorkshire.
Eldest son of the late Charles Thellusson, Esq., of Brodsworth, by Mary, dau. of George Grant, Esq., of Ingoldisthorpe; *b.* 1822 ; *s.* 1856 ; *m.* 1850 Georgiana. dau. of W. Theobald, Esq., of Stockwell, Surrey, and has, with other issue,

* Peter, *b.* 1850.

Mr. Thellusson, who is a Dep.-Lieut. for the W. Riding of Yorkshire (High Sheriff 1866), Lord of the Manor of Brodsworth and Patron of 1 living, was formerly Capt. 12th Lancers.—*Brodsworth Hall, Doncaster; Army and Navy Club, s.w.*

THELLUSSON. (See under *Rendlesham, Lord.*)

THESIGER. (See under *Chelmsford, Lord.*)

THEXTON, Mrs., of Ashton House, Westmoreland.
Isabella, only dau. and heir of the Rev. John Hudson, Vicar of Kendal; *m.* 1841 John Yeats Thexton, Esq., of Ashton House, J.P. and D.L., who *d.* 1859, leaving, with other issue,

* Edward Yeats, *b.* 1847.

Mrs. Thexton is Lady of the Manor of Ashton.—*Ashton House, Milnethorpe.*

THICKNESSE, the Rev. FRANCIS HENRY, of Beech Hill, Lancashire.
Second son of the Rev. William E. Coldwell, Prebendary of Lichfield, Rector of Stafford, by Mary, dau. of E. Norman, Esq., of Mistley, Essex; *b.* 1829 ; *m.* 1855 Anne, only surviving child and heir of the late Ralph A. Thicknesse, Esq., M.P., of Beech Hill, and has, with other issue,

* Ralph, *b.* 1856.

Mr. Thicknesse, who was educated at Eton and Brasenose Coll., Oxford (B.A. 1851), is Honorary Canon of Manchester, Vicar of Deane, and Rural Dean of Bolton : he assumed the name of Thicknesse in 1859.—*Beech Hill, Wigan ; Deane Vicarage, Bolton.*

THICKNESSE. (See under *Audley, Lord.*)

THISTLETHWAYTE, THOMAS, Esq., of Southwick, Hants.
Eldest son of the late Thomas Thistlethwayte, Esq., of Southwick, by his 1st wife Mary Anne, dau. of John Guiton, Esq., of Wickham, Hants ; *b.* 1809 ; *s.* 1850 ; *m.* 1850 Elizabeth Catharine, dau. of the late Lieut.-Gen. the Hon. Sir Hercules Pakenham, K.C.B., and has, with other issue,

* Alexander Edward, *b.* 1854.

Mr. Thistlethwayte, who was educated at Eton and Ch. Ch., Oxford, is Lord of the Manor of Southwick, and represents an old Yorkshire family.—*Southwick Park, Fareham.*

THOMAS, Sir GODFREY VIGNOLES, Bart., of Chingford, Essex (cr. 1694).
Eldest son of the late Sir Godfrey John Thomas, Bart., by Emily, eldest dau. of William Chambers, Esq., of Hafod, co. Cardigan; *b.* 1856 ; *s.* 1861. This family was formerly of Wenvoe Castle, co. Glamorgan.—*Tho Plâs, Chingford, Essex.*

Heir Pres., his brother Edmund Herbert, b. 1861.

THOMAS, Sir GEORGE SIDNEY MEADE, Bart. (cr. 1766).
Eldest surviving son of the late Sir William Sidney Thomas, Bart., by his 1st wife Thomasin, dau. of Capt.

Henry Haynes, R.N.; *b.* 1847; *s.* as 6th Bart. 1867. —*The Grange, Great Malvern.*

Heir Pres., his brother Frederick Louis Charles, *b.* 1853.

THOMAS, Sir JOHN, Knt. (cr. 1859).

Son of the late L. Thomas, Esq., of Barbados; *b.* 1797; *m.* 1832 Susan, dau. of the late Samuel Hinds, Esq., M.D. Is a member of the executive council at Barbados, and late Speaker of the Legislative Assembly there. —*Barbados, W. Indies.*

THOMAS, EDWARD DAVID, Esq., of Welfield House, Brecknockshire.

Eldest son of the late David Thomas, Esq., of Welfield, by Catherine, eldest dau. of William Jones, Esq., of Ystrad Walter, co. Carmarthen; *b.* 1808; *s.* his father 1830, and his mother in 1841; *m.* 1837 Arabella Emma, younger dau. and co-heir of John S. Gowland, Esq., of Cagebrook, Hereford, and has, with other issue,

  • Edward David, educated at Rugby, and B.A. of University Coll., Oxford; a Magistrate for co. Radnor; *b.* 1839.

Mr. Thomas, who was educated at Shrewsbury and Wadham Coll., Oxford (B.A. 1829, M.A. 1832), is a J.P. and D.L. for cos. Brecon and Radnor (High Sheriff 1843), and Patron of 1 living.—*Welfield House, Builth.*

THOMAS, FRANCIS HENRY, Esq., of Bewell, Herefordshire.

Only son of the late Francis Baladon Thomas, Esq., of Hereford, by Mary, dau. of the Rev. H. Davies; *b.* 1788; *m.* 1812 Elizabeth, dau. of Mr. Heming, and by her, who *d.* 1864, has, with other surviving issue,.

  • Thomas, *b.* 1814.

Mr. Thomas, who was educated at Balliol Coll., Oxford (B.A. 1809, M.A. 1813), is a J.P. and D.L. for co. Hereford (High Sheriff 1826).—*Bewell House, Hereford.*

THOMAS, Mrs. GEORGE, of Ystrad Mynach, Glamorganshire.

Eliza, dau. of William Crawshay, Esq., of Cyfartha Castle, co. Glamorgan, and Caversham Park, Oxon; *m.* 1832 the Rev. George Thomas, who *d.* 1860, leaving issue, • George William Griffith, educated at Ch. Ch., Oxford; *b.* 1843; *m.* 1864 Ellen, youngest dau. of R. W. Kennard, Esq., M.P., and has issue, • a son, *b.* 1865.—*Ystrad Mynach, Cardiff.*

+**THOMAS, GEORGE FREEMAN, Esq., of Ratton, Sussex.**

Eldest son of the late Freeman Thomas, Esq., of Yapton and Ratton, by Amelia, dau. of Col. Frederick; *b.* 1837; *s.* 1858. Educated at Eton; is Lord of the Manor of Ratton.—*Ratton, Willingdon, Sussex.*

Heir Pres., his brother Frederick Freeman, a Magistrate for Sussex, and Capt. Sussex Rifle Volunteers; *b.* 1838; *m.* 1863 Mabel, 3rd dau. of the Hon. Henry Bouverie William Brand, of Glynde, Sussex, and has issue two daughters.

THOMAS, Mrs. HENRY, of Llwynmadoc, Breconshire, and Pencerrig, Radnorshire.

Clara, only child and heir of Thomas Thomas, Esq., of Pencerrig, co. Radnor, and of Llanbradac, co. Glamorgan (who *d.* 1859), by his 2nd wife Bridget, dau. and heir of Marmaduke Gwynne, Esq., of Llanelwydd, co. Radnor, and Garth, co. Brecon; *m.* 1835 Henry Thomas, Esq., J.P. and D.L., of Llwynmadoc and Pencerrig, who was Chairman of Quarter Sessions for co. Glamorgan, and who *d.* 1863, leaving surviving issue,

  • Clara.

Mrs. Thomas is Patron of the living of Builth, Breconshire. This family have been settled at Llwynmadoc upwards of 600 years.—*Llwynmadoc, Builth, Breconshire; Pencerrig, Radnor.*

THOMAS, HONORATUS LEIGH, Esq., of Bryn Elwy, Flintshire.

Eldest son of the late John Thomas, Esq., of St. Asaph, by Annie, dau. of Samuel Boydell, Esq., of The Manor, Hawarden, co. Flint; *b.* 1798; *s.* 1821; *m.* 1835 Sophia Boydell, 4th dau. of Honoratus Leigh Thomas, Esq., F.R.S., and has issue,

  Charles Whiteman, Capt. 21st Hussars; *b.* 1840; *d.* 1847, having *m.* 1866 Isabella, 2nd dau. of the late Thomas Mather, of Glyn Abbot, Holywell.

Mr. Thomas, who was educated at Bangor, is a J.P. and D.L. for co. Flint, and a Magistrate for co. Denbigh; was formerly Commander in the H.E.I.C's Maritime Service.—*Bryn Elwy, St. Asaph.*

+**THOMAS, JOHN EVAN, Esq., of Penishapentre, Brecon.**

Son of the late J. Thomas, Esq.; *b.* 18—; is a Magistrate for co. Brecon (High Sheriff 1868).—*Penishapentre, Brecon.*

THOMAS, JOHN LEWES, Esq., of Caeglas, Carmarthenshire.

Eldest son of the late James Thomas, Esq., by Catherine, dau. of Thomas Taylor, Esq.; *b.* 1818; *m.* 1849 Frances Mary, dau. of William H. Thomas, Esq. Is a Magistrate for co. Carmarthen.—*Caeglas, Llandilo.*

THOMAS, REES GORING, Esq., of Gelly-Wernen, Carmarthenshire.

Eldest son of the late Rees Goring Thomas, Esq., J.P. and D.L., of Gelly-Wernen, by Caroline, dau. of William Esdaile, Esq., and sister of Edward J. Esdaile, Esq., of Terhill House (whom see); *b.* 1824; *s.* 1863; *m.* 1861 Emily, dau. of the late Richard J. Nevill, Esq., of Llangennech, co. Carmarthen, and has, with other issue,

  • A son, *b.* 1864.

Mr. Thomas, who was educated at Eton and Ch. Ch., Oxford (B.A. 1847, M.A. 1850), is a Magistrate for co. Carmarthen, and Patron of 3 livings; late Lieut. Royal Carmarthenshire Rifles.—*Gelly-Wernen, Llanelly; Firey Side, Kidwelly, Carmarthenshire; Union Club, s.w.*

THOMAS, RICE WILLIAM, Esq., of Coedhelen, Carnarvonshire.

Eldest son of the late Rev. Rice Robert Hughes, of Jesus Coll., Oxford, Rector of Newborough, co. Anglesey, by Charlotte, dau. of the late Very Rev. John Warren, Dean of Bangor; *b.* 1841; *s.* his maternal great-grandfather, Rice Thomas, Esq., of Coedhelen, in 1853, when he assumed the name of Thomas. Educated at Eton and Ch. Ch., Oxford. The father of this gentleman was younger brother of William Bulkeley Hughes, Esq., of Plâs-Coch (whom see).—*Coedhelen, Carnarvon.*

Heir Pres., his brother Lloyd Warren George, *b.* 1848.

THOMAS, RICHARD, Esq., of The Court House, Glamorganshire.

Eldest son of the late William Thomas, Esq., of The Court House, by Jane, eldest dau. and heir of the late Samuel Rees, Esq., of The Werfa, Aberdare, and The Court House; *b.* 1823; *s.* 1857 Lousit Jane of Thomas Thomas, Esq., of Lechwen, Llavdisan, co. Glamorgan. This family is nearly related to the Lewises of the Van, Caerphilly, and of Gwaelod-y-Garth, co. Glamorgan. —*The Court House, Merthyr Tydvil.*

Heir Pres., his brother William, *b.* 1825; *m.* 1859 Mary, dau. of Daniel Thomas, Esq., of Merthyr Tydvil.

THOMAS, THOMAS EDWARD, Esq.,‡ of Glanmor, Glamorganshire.

Youngest son of the late Iltid Thomas, Esq., of Hill House, co. Glamorgan, by Mabel, only dau. and heir of Robert Neilson, Esq., of Corsock, Galloway, N.B.; *b.* 1782; *m.* 1811 Mary Anne, dau. and heir of the late

Thomas Wilkins (afterwards Morgan), Esq., of Easton in Gordano, Somerset, and has issue,

* Iltid, B.A. of Oriel Coll., Oxford, and a Magistrate for co. Glamorgan; b. 1812; m. 1st 1836 Isabella Mary, dau. of the late William Foreman, Esq., of Penydarran, co. Glamorgan (she d. 1846); 2nd 1867 Mary Dulcibella. youngest dau. of Thomas Eden, Esq., of The Brym, co. Glamorgan.

Mr. Thomas is a J.P. and D.L. for co. Glamorgan (High Sheriff 1826).—*Glanmor, Swansea; Windham Club, s.w.*

THOMAS, the Rev. WILLIAM.

Youngest son of the late David Thomas, Esq., of Trehowell, co. Pembroke, by Jane, dau. of the Rev. Howell Howell, of Kilhernie, co. Carmarthen; b. 1792; m. 1818 Frances, dau. of William Waldegrave, Esq., of Castor, co. Northampton. Educated at Jesus Coll., Cambridge (B.A. 1815, M.A. 1829); is a Magistrate for Cornwall, and Vicar of Sithney.—*Sithney, Helston.*

+THOMAS, WILLIAM, Esq., of Bryn Merlyn, Flintshire.

Eldest son of the late William Thomas, Esq., of Bryn Merlyn; b. 18—; m. 1845 Jane Henrietta, youngest dau. of the late Matthew Stephens, Esq., of Nannerch Hall, co. Flint.—*Bryn Merlyn, Holywell.*

THOMAS. (See *Le Marchant-Thomas.*)

THOMAS. (See *Treherne.*)

THOMLINSON-GRANT, Mrs., of The Hill, Cumberland.

Mary, only surviving child of the late Sir James Robert Grant, Knt., C.B., J.P. and D.L., of The Hill, Inspector-General of Army Hospitals, by Frances, dau. of Henry Birkett, Esq., of Etterby Lodge, Cumberland; *s.* 1864, when she assumed the name of Grant under her father's will; m. 1839 Joseph Thomlinson, Esq., by whom, who d. 1843, she has, with other issue,

* Grant, Lieut. 92nd Highlanders; b. 1841.

This family is descended from James Grant, of Auchernack, Strathspey, Chief of the Clan Allan, a junior branch of the Grants of Grant.—*The Hill, Carlisle.*

THOMOND, Marchioness of.

Ann, sister of the late Sir Charles W. Flint; m. 1st 1824 Rear-Admiral Francis William Fane (d. 1844); 2nd 1847 (as 3rd wife) James, 3rd Marquis of Thomond (ext.), who d. 1855.—*Bath.*

THOMPSON, Sir THOMAS RAIKES, Bart. (cr. 1806).

Elder son of the late Admiral Sir Thomas Raikes Trigge Thompson, Bart., by Gertrude, dau. of the Rev. Robert Napier Raikes, Vicar of Longhope, co. Gloucester; b. 1852; s. as 3rd Bart. 1865.—10, *Lansdowne Terrace, Cheltenham.*

Heir Pres., his brother Edward, b. 1853.

THOMPSON, the Rev. Sir HENRY, Bart. (cr. 1797).

Third and only surviving son of the late Vice-Admiral Sir Charles Thompson, Bart. (who d. 1799), by Jane, dau. of R. Selby, Esq., of Bonnington, N.B.; b. 1796; s. his brother as 3rd Bart. 1826; m. 1st 1828 Hannah Jean, dau. of the late Hon. Sir George Grey, Bart. K.C.B.; 2nd 1835 Emily Frances Anne, dau. of Ralph Leeke, Esq., of Longford Hall, co. Salop. Educated at Harrow and Oriel Coll., Oxford (B.A. 1819, M.A. 1822); is Rector of Frant, Prebendary of Chichester, Rural Dean and Proctor in Convocation for the Archdeaconry of Lewes, and Patron of 1 living.—*Frant Rectory, Tunbridge Wells; National and Athenæum Clubs, s.w.*

THOMPSON, Sir HENRY, Kt. (cr. 1867).

Son of the late Henry Thompson, Esq., of Framlingham, Suffolk, by Susanna, dau. of Samuel Medley, Esq.,

918

b. 1820; m. 1851 Kate Fanny, dau. of George Loder, Esq., of Bath. Educated at University College, London. Is Surgeon Extraordinary to H.M. Leopold II., King of the Belgians, Surgeon to and Professor of Clinical Surgery in University College Hospital, &c.—*Garrick Club, w.c.; 35, Wimpole Street, w.*

THOMPSON, ANDREW GREEN-, Esq., of Bridekirk, Cumberland.

Eldest son of the late Andrew Green, Esq., of Cockermouth, by Ester, dau. of H. Thompson, Esq., of Cheltenham; b. 1820; m. 1849 Alexandrina, dau. of John Berry, Esq., of Glasgow, and has, with other issue,

* Andrew, b. 1852.

Mr. Green-Thompson, who was educated at the Royal Military Coll. Sandhurst, is a J.P. and D.L. for Cumberland, and Lord of the Manor of Whinfell; elected M.P. for Cockermouth 1868; was formerly Major 46th Regt. He took the surname of Thompson on succeeding his maternal uncle, Henry Thompson, Esq. in 1855. —*Bridekirk, Cockermouth; United Service Club, s.w.*

THOMPSON, DAVID, Esq., of Clonskeagh, co. Dublin.

Eldest son of the late George Thompson. Esq., of Clonskeagh, by his 1st wife Eleanor, dau. of Allan Wade, Esq., of Bachelor's Lodge, co. Meath; b. 1798; s. 1800. Educated at Trinity Coll., Dublin (M.A. and LL.D. 1862); called to the Bar at Dublin 1822; is a Magistrate for co. Dublin and for King's Co. This family is descended from a common ancestor with the Thompsons of Clonfin.—*Clonskeagh, Dublin; Kildare Street and University Clubs, Dublin; 95, Lower Leeson Street, Dublin.*

Heir Pres., his brother Thomas Higginbotham, b. 1808; m. 1836 Martha, dau. of the late Thomas Wallace, Esq., Q.C., of Belfield, Donnybrook, and has, with other issue, * Robert Wade, b. 1845.

THOMPSON, GEORGE, Esq., of Pitmedden, Aberdeenshire.

Son of the late A. Thompson, Esq., of Madras, by Anne, dau. of G. Stephens, Esq.; b. 1804; m. 1830 Christiana, dau. of the Rev. Dr. Kidd. Educated at Marischal Coll. Aberdeen; is a Magistrate for co. Aberdeen, and a Merchant and Shipowner of Aberdeen, of which town he has also been Provost; was M.P. for Aberdeen 1852-7.—*Aberdeen; Pitmedden House. Dyce, N.B.; Reform Club, s.w.*

THOMPSON, Lieut.-Col. GEORGE HAMILTON, of Kirk Hamilton Hall, and Barlow, Yorkshire.

Eldest son of the late Joseph Thompson Esq., of Barlow, by Mary, dau. of Henry Walker, Esq., of Whitley; b. 1805; s. 1809; m. 1831 Anne, eldest dau. of the late Col. Arthur Maister, of Wood Hall, co. of York, and has, with other issue,

* George Arthur, educated at Harrow, b. 1845.

Mr. Thompson, who was educated at Eton, is a Deputy Lieut. for the E. Riding, and a Magistrate for the W. Riding of Yorkshire, Lieut.-Col. E. York Militia. Lord of the Manor of Kirk Hammerton and Barlow, and Patron of the living of Barlow, &c.; formerly in the 1st Dragoon Guards.—*Kirk Hammerton Hall, York.*

THOMPSON, HENRY STEPHEN, Esq., of Kirby Hall, Yorkshire.

Eldest son of the late Richard John Thompson. Esq. of Kirby Hall, by Elizabeth, dau. of John Turton, Esq., of Sugnall Hall, co. Stafford; b. 1809; s. 1855; m. 1813 Elizabeth Anne, dau. of the late Sir John Coul. Bart., and has, with other issue,

* Henry Meysey, b. 1844.

Mr. Thompson, who was educated at Trinity Coll., Cambridge (B.A. 1831), is a J.P. and D.L. for the N. and W. Ridings of Yorkshire (High Sheriff 1856) and

Chairman of the N. Eastern Railway Company; he was M.P. for Whitby 1859-65.—*Kirby Hall, York; Travellers' Club, s.w.*

THOMPSON, JOHN, Esq., of Clonfin, co. Longford.

Son of the late Major William Thompson, J.P., of Clonfin; *b.* 1795; *m.* 1826 Catherine, dau. of Robert Blackall, Esq., of Colamber Manor, co. Longford, and has, with other issue,

* John, formerly an Officer in the Army, *b.* 1841; *m.* 1861 Emily, eldest dau. of the Rev. J. Fox, of Kinawley, co. Fermanagh.

Mr. Thompson, who was educated at Trinity Coll., Dublin, is a J.P. and D.L. for co. Longford (High Sheriff 1820).—*Clonfin, Granard, co. Longford.*

THOMPSON, LEONARD, Esq., of Sheriff-Hutton Park, Yorkshire.

Eldest son of the late George Lowther Thompson, Esq., of Sheriff-Hutton, by Mary Anne, dau. of the Rev. Edward Waldron; *b.* 1806; *s.* 1841; *m.* 1831 Lady Mary, 2nd dau. of Charles William, 5th Earl Fitzwilliam. Educated at Eton and Trinity Coll., Cambridge (B.A. 1829); is a J.P. and D.L. for the N. and E. Ridings of Yorkshire, and a Magistrate for Hunts. —*Sheriff-Hutton Park, York.*

THOMPSON, MATTHEW, Esq., of Kirkby Stephen, Westmoreland.

Only son of the late Richard Thompson, Esq., of Kirkby Stephen, by Mary, eldest dau. of the late William Elyetson, Esq., of Scarsykes, Ravenstonedale; *b.* 1815; *s.* 1834; *m.* 1845 Mary, only dau. of Wm. Dawson, Esq., of Garshill, Ravenstonedale, and has issue,

* Mary.

Mr. Thomson, who was educated at Eton, is a J.P. and D.L. for Westmoreland (High Sheriff 1864).—*Kirkby Stephen, Westmoreland.*

THOMPSON, MATTHEW WILLIAM, Esq., of Guiseley, Yorkshire.

Eldest son of the late Matthew Thompson, Esq., J.P. and D.L., of Manningham Lodge, co. York, by Elizabeth Sarah, dau. of the Rev. William Atkinson, of Thorp Arch; *b.* 1820; *m.* 1843 his cousin Mary Ann, dau. and heir of the late Benjamin Thompson, Esq., J.P., of Park Gate, Guiseley, and has, with other issue,

* Pelle, *b.* 1844.

Mr. Thompson, who was educated at Trinity Coll., Cambridge (B.A. 1843, M.A. 1846), and called to the Bar at the Inner Temple 1846, is an Alderman of Bradford (Mayor 1863); Capt. 25th W. Riding Rifle Volunteers; elected M.P. for Bradford 1867.—*Park Gate, Guiseley, Bradford; 18, Kent Terrace, N.W.*

THOMPSON, RICHARD, Esq., of Stansty, Denbighshire.

Son of the late John Thompson, Esq., of Stansty, by Margaret, dau. of the late Richard Bullock, Esq.; *b.* 1799; *s.* 1852; *m.* 1827 Ellen, only dau. of the late Hugh Bourke, Esq., of London, and has, with other issue,

* John James, *b.* 1828.

Mr. Thompson, who was educated at Ushaw Coll., is a Magistrate for co. Denbigh.—*Stansty Hall, Wrexham.*

THOMPSON, the Hon. MRS., of Prior Park, Somersetshire.

Charlotte Margaret, 4th dau. of the late Sir Gerard Noel-Noel, Bart., M.P., of Exton Park, co. Rutland, and sister of Charles, 1st Earl of Gainsborough; *m.* 1st 1813 Thomas Welman, Esq., of Poundisford Park, Somerset, who *d.* 1829; 2nd 1839 Thomas Thompson, Esq., who *d.* 1865. *Prior Park, Bath.*

THOMPSON, Lieut.-General THOMAS PERRONET, F.R.S.

Eldest son of the late Thomas Thompson, Esq., Banker of Hull, and M.P. for Midhurst, and of his wife, grand-dau. of the Rev. Vincent Perronet, Vicar of Shoreham, Kent; *b.* 1783; *m.* 1811 Anne Elizabeth, dau. of the Rev. T. Barker. Educated at Queens' Coll., Cambridge (B.A. 1802, M.A. 1806); is a Lieut.-General unattached. Was Editor of the 'Westminster Review' 1830-6; was M.P. for Hull 1835-7, and for Bradford 1847-52 and 1857-9.—*Elliot Vale, Blackheath.*

THOMPSON, WILLIAM, Esq., of Clements, Essex.

Eldest son of William Thompson, Esq., by Sarah, dau. of the late John Kynaston, Esq., of Poole, Dorset; *b.* 1822; *s.* his uncle, John Scrafton Thompson, Esq. 1839; *m.* 1847 Sarah, only dau. of Robert Slade, Esq., J.P., and has, with other surviving issue,

* John Stanley, *b.* 1855.

Mr. Thompson is a Magistrate for Essex.—*Clements, Ilford, Essex; Melcombe Regis, Weymouth.*

+THOMPSON, the Rev. WILLIAM HAMILTON, of Beaumont, co. Cork.

Son of the late — Thompson, Esq.; *b.* 1812; *m.* 1846 Anne Jane Margaret, youngest dau. and eventual heir of the late William Beamish, Esq., of Beaumont, co. Cork, and has, with other issue,

* Charles Chetwode, *b.* 1850.

Mr. Thompson, who was educated at Trinity Coll., Dublin (B.A. 1835), is a Magistrate for co. Rutland, and Rector of Stoke Dry.—*Stoke Dry Rectory, Uppingham; Beaumont House, Cork.*

THOMPSON. (See Bullock.)

THOMPSON-CORBETT. (See Corbett.)

THOMSON, Sir WILLIAM, LL.D., F.R.S. (cr. 1866).

Son of the late James Thomson, Esq., LL.D., Professor of Mathematics in Glasgow University, by Margaret, dau. of William Gardiner, Esq.; *b.* 1824; *m.* 1852 Margaret, dau. of Walter Crum, Esq., of Thornliebank, N.B. Educated at Glasgow University and St. Peter's Coll., Cambridge; is Professor of Natural Philosophy in the University of Glasgow; late Fellow of St. Peter's Coll., Cambridge.—*The College, Glasgow, N.B.*

THOMSON, ALEXANDER, Esq.,‡ of Banchory, Aberdeenshire.

Eldest son of the late Andrew Thomson, Esq., of Banchory, by Helen, dau. of Robert Hamilton, LL.D., Professor of Mathematics in the University of Aberdeen; *b.* 1798; *s.* 1896; *m.* 1825 Jessy, dau. of Alexander Fraser, Esq., Lord Provost of Aberdeen. Educated at Marischal Coll., Aberdeen, and Edinburgh University (M.A. 1816); called to the Scottish Bar 1822; is F.R.S.E., F.A.S., Scotland, &c. &c.; was Vice-President of the British Association 1859; is a J.P. and D.L. for cos. Aberdeen and Kincardine; convener of co. Aberdeen 1857.—*Banchory House, Aberdeen, N.B.*

THOMSON, JOHN, Esq., of Low Wood, co. Antrim.

Second son of the late John Thomson, Esq., of Castleton, co. Antrim, by Anne, dau. of Walter Wilson, Esq., of Croglin, co. Dumfries; *b.* 1798; *m.* 1825 Elizabeth Grace, dau. of Cortland Macgregor, Esq. Is a Magistrate for cos. Antrim and Down, and a Banker at Belfast. This family, from Argyllshire, settled near Belfast, A.D. 1645, and intermarried A.D. 1782 with the Legges, of Malone House.—*Low Wood, Belfast.*

THOMSON, ROBERT CUNNINGHAM, Esq., of Castleton, co. Antrim.

Eldest son of the late Robert Thomson, Esq. of Castleton (who was a Magistrate for co. Antrim), by Alicia, dau. of the late Cuningham Greg, Esq., of Ballymenock, co. Down; b. 1833; s. 1862; m. 1865 Elize, eldest dau. of W. T. B. Lyons, Esq., of Old Park, co. Antrim. Was formerly Capt. in the 2nd Queen's Royals.—*Castleton, Belfast; Army and Navy Club*, s.w.

THOMSON, Lieut.-Col. ROBERT THOMAS, of Broomford Manor, Devonshire.

Eldest son of the late Robert Thomson, Esq., of Camphill, co. Renfrew, by Mary, dau. of Thomas White, Esq., of The Close, Lichfield; b. 1831; s. 1833; m. 1857 Fanny Julia, dau. of Gen. Sir H. Ferguson-Davie, Bart., of Creedy Park, Devon, and has, with other issue,

• Henry Noel, b. 1858.

Lieut.-Col. Thomson, who was educated at Eton, is a Magistrate for Devon, Patron of Jacobstowe, and Lieut.-Col. 1st Devon Militia; was formerly Major King's Dragoon Guards. — *Broomford Manor, Jacobstowe, Exbourne, Devon; Army and Navy Club*, s.w.

THOMSON, WILLIAM, Esq., of Balgowan, Perthshire.

Second son of the late John Thomson, Esq., of Gogar Burn, Midlothian, by Mary, dau. of James Maitland, Esq.; b. 1812; m. 1845 Margaret Cunninghame, youngest dau. of Major Campbell, of Walton Park, co. Kirkcudbright, and has, with other issue,

• Maitland, b. 1847.

Mr. Thomson is a J.P. and D.L. for co. Perth.—*Balgowan, Perth, N.B.*

THOMSON. (See *Anstruther-Thomson*.)

THOMSON-SINCLAIR. (See *Sinclair*.)

THOREN, the Baron de (OSCAR JOSEPH DE SATGÉ), of St. Anne's Hill, Worcestershire.

Second son of the late Baron de Thoren, of Thoren and Prades (Pyr. Or.), France, by Françoise, dau. of the Vicomte de St. Jean, of Ille (Pyr.-Orientales), France; b. 1804; s. 1849; m. 1836 Millicent, dau. of William Ellis Wall, Esq., of Worcester and Gt. Malvern, and has, with other issue,

• Oscar William, educated at Harrow and Ch. Ch., Oxford; Lieut. 45th Regt.; b. 1837.

The Baron, who was educated at the École Militaire de Cavalerie, Saumur, France, and is a Knight of the Legion of Honour, was formerly an Officer in 2nd Dragoons (French Army); he became a naturalised British subject by Act of Parliament 1836. This family is of French and Spanish extraction, and has been seated at Thoren upwards of 550 years.—*St. Anne's Hill, Malvern; Thoren, Villefranche (Pyr. Or.), France.*

THORN, Lady.

Amelia Eleanor, dau. of the late Charles Worthington, Esq., of Bath; m. 1831 Lieut.-General Sir Nathaniel Thorn, K.C.B. (who d. 1857).—7, *St. James's Square, Bath.*

THORNEWILL, EDWARD JOHN, Esq., of Dove Cliff, Staffordshire.

Son of the late Edward Thornewill, Esq., D.L., of Dove Cliff, by Mary, dau. of the late Rev John Batteridge Pearson, Rector of Croxall, co. Derby; b. 1836; s. 1836. Educated at Harrow and Trinity Coll., Cambridge. —*Dove Cliff, Burton on Trent.*

920

THORNEYCROFT, THOMAS, Esq., of Tettenhall, Staffordshire, and Hadly, Shropshire.

Only son of the late George Benjamin Thorneycroft, Esq., of Hadly Park, by Eleanor, dau. of Mr. T. Page; b. 1822; s. 1851; m. 1847 Jane, dau. of A. Whitelaw, Esq., and has, with other issue,

• George Benjamin, b. 1849.

Mr. Thorneycroft is a J.P. and D.L. for co. Stafford (High Sheriff 1864), a Magistrate for co. Salop, and Major Queen's Own Royal Staffordshire Yeomanry Cavalry. This family was formerly seated at Thorneycroft Hall, co. Chester.—*Hadly Park, Wellington; Tettenhall Wood, Wolverhampton; Conservative Club*, s.w.

THORNHILL, CHARLES EDWARD, Esq., of Woodleys, Oxon.

Eldest son of the late Thomas Thornhill, Esq., of Woodleys, by Elizabeth, dau. of Anthony Bacon, Esq., Aberaman, S. Wales; b. 1817; m. 1850 Ellen, dau. of Major George Fraser. Educated at Rugby and Ch. Ch., Oxford (B.A. 1839, M.A. 1842); called to the Bar at Lincoln's Inn 1842; is a Magistrate for Oxon, and Vice-Chairman of Quarter Sessions.—*Woodleys, Woodstock; Oriental Club*, w.

THORNHILL, GEORGE, Esq., of Diddington, Hunts.

Eldest son of the late George Thornhill, Esq., M.P., of Diddington, by Charlotte Matilda, dau. and heir of the Rev. Charles Green, of Offord Darcy, Hunts; b. 1811; s. 1852; m. 1845 Elizabeth Mary, dau. of Robert Wilkinson, Esq., and has, with other issue,

• George, b. 1849.

Mr. Thornhill, who was educated at Eton, is a J.P. and D.L. for Hunts, and Patron of 2 livings. This family is a branch of the Thornhills of Stanton Fixby and Riddlesworth (whom see).—*Diddington, Buckden.*

THORNHILL, THOMAS, Esq., of Riddlesworth, Norfolk.

Son of the late Thomas Thornhill, Esq., of Riddlesworth and Fixby; b. 1801; s. 1811; m. 1830 Martha Mary Anne, eldest dau. of the late H. S. Waddington, Esq., M.P., of Cavenham Hall, Suffolk, and has, with other issue,

• Thomas, a Magistrate for Norfolk; b. 1837; m. 1843 Katharine Edith Isabella, only child of Richard Hodgson, Esq., M.P., of Carham, Northumberland, and has issue, • Thomas Compton, b. 1863.

Mr. Thornhill is a Magistrate for Norfolk and a Depy.-Lieut. for Suffolk (High Sheriff 1860). Lord of the Manor of Riddlesworth, and Patron of 3 livings.—*Riddlesworth Hall, E. Harling.*

THORNHILL, WILLIAM POLE, Esq., of Stanton, Derbyshire.

Second but only surviving son of the late Henry Bache Thornhill, Esq., by Helen, eldest dau. of Charles Bache, Esq., of Liverpool; b. 1806; s. his grandfather 1854; m. 1828 Isabella, only dau. and heir of Philip Gell, Esq., of Hopton Court, co. Derby. Educated at Eton and Corpus Christi Coll., Oxford; is a J.P. and D.L. for co. Derby (High Sheriff 1856), was M.P. for N. Derbyshire 1853-65. — *Stanton, Bakewell; Brookes's, Boodle's, Arthur's, and University Clubs*, s.w.; 44, Eaton Square, s.w.

Heir Pres., his uncle William Thornhill, Esq., of New Park, Hants, formerly Col. 7th Hussars; b. 1806.

THORNHILL. (See *Clarke-Thornhill*.)

+THORNLEY, THOMAS, Esq., of Oaklands, Cheshire.

Eldest son of the late Thomas Thornley, Esq., of Liverpool, Merchant and Manufacturer (who was M.P. for

Wolverhampton 1835–59); *b.* 18—; *s.* 1864. Is a Magistrate for co. Chester, and a Merchant and Manufacturer at Manchester.—*Oaklands, Godley, Manchester.*

THORNTON, CHARLES EDMUND, Esq., of Kirkland Hall, and Beaumont Cote, Lancashire.
Only surviving son of William Thomas Thornton, Esq., of Caton, co. Lancaster (whom see), by Hannah Isabella Cornelia, eldest dau. of Col. John Cornelius Craigie Halkett, of Lahill and Dumbarnie, co. Fife; *b.* 1825; *m.* 1862 Eliza Amanda, eldest surviving dau. of the late Lieut.-Col. Stephen Williams, of the 56th Bengal N.I., and relict of William Campbell Deans Campbell, Esq., of Corraith House, co. Ayr, and has issue,

  • Cornelia Amanda Augusta, and Edmund William Tankerville, *b.* 1866.

Major-Thornton, who was educated at the Royal Military Coll., Sandhurst, is a Major in the Army, late Staff Officer of Pensioners; was formerly in the Royal Fusiliers; descends from the Butlers of Kirkland, through his grandmother, Mrs. Thornton, of Whittington Hall, co. Lancaster, dau. of Archdeacon Butler, of Bentham and Whittington.—*Kirkland Hall, Garstang ; Beaumont Cote, Bolton-le-Sands ; 6, Victoria Park, Dover.*

THORNTON, the late GEORGE SMITH, Esq., of Marden Hill, Herts.
Son of the late Claude George Thornton, Esq., of Marden Hill (who was High Sheriff of Herts 1838), by Frances Ann, 2nd dau. of the late Samuel Smith, Esq., M.P., of Woodhall Park, Herts ; *b.* 1808 ; *s.* 1866. He was a Magistrate for Herts, and *d.* 1867.—*Marden Hill, Tewin Water, Hatfield.*

THORNTON, the Rev. FRANCIS VANSITTART.
Third son of John Thornton, Esq., of Clapham (who *d.* 1861), by Eliza, dau. of Edward Parry, Esq.; *b.* 1816 ; *m.* 1847 Mary Louisa, dau. of the late Rev. Horace G. Cholmondely, and has, with other issue,

  • Francis Cholmondely, *b.* 1849.

Mr. Thornton was educated at Rugby and Trinity Coll., Cambridge (M.A. 1842), and appointed Rector of Chilton Candover 1848.—*Chilton Candover Rectory, Micheldever Station.*

THORNTON, the Rev. GEORGE.
Eldest surviving son of the late Stephen Thornton, Esq., of Moggerhanger, Beds, by Mary, dau. of the late Thos. Littledale Esq.; *b.* 1833. Educated at Westminster and Trinity Coll. Cambridge (B.A. 1825, M.A. 1830). Appointed Vicar of Sharnbrook 1844.—*Sharnbrook, Bedford ; University Club,* s.w.

THORNTON, HARRY, Esq., of Goldington, Beds.
Fifth son of the late Stephen Thornton, Esq., of Moggerhanger House, Beds, by Mary, dau. of Thomas Littledale, Esq., of Rotterdam; *b.* 1812 ; *m.* 1842 Caroline Margaret, eldest dau. of the late John Christie, Esq., and has, with other issue,

  • Harry Godfrey, *b.* 1845.

Mr. Thornton is a Magistrate for Beds and a J.P. and D.L. for Bucks.—*Goldington Bury, Bedford.*

+THORNTON, Mrs., of Kempstone Grange, Beds.
Mary, dau. of the late Thomas Littledale, Esq., of Rotterdam, by Anne Elizabeth, dau. of Charles Allan, Esq., of Beverley, and sister of the late Henry Littledale, Esq., of Kempstone Grange; *s.* her brother 1866 ; *m.* 179– Stephen Thornton, Esq., of Moggerhanger House, Beds, who is *dec.*—*Kempstone Grange, Bedford.*

THORNTON, PERROTT MEE, Esq., of Grenville, co. Cavan.
Eldest son of the late Perrott Thornton, Esq., of Grenville, by Elizabeth, dau. of John Mee, Esq., of Armagh ; *b.* 1781 ; *s.* 1802 ; *m.* 1811 Ellen, dau. of George Cochrane, Esq., of Dromard, and has issue,

  • Perrott Tristram, late Capt. 12th E. Suffolk Regt.; *b.* 1814.

Mr. Thornton, who was educated at Harrow and Trinity Coll., Dublin (B.A. 1804), is a Magistrate for co. Cavan (High Sheriff 1812).—*Grenville, Ardlogher, Belturbet.*

THORNTON, REGINALD, Esq., of Frome Whitfield, Dorsetshire.
Fourth son of the late John Thornton, Esq., of Clapham, Surrey, by Eliza, dau. of Edward Parry, Esq.; *b.* 1821 ; *m.* 1846 Louisa Frances, elder dau. of Sir Henry Lushington, Bart., and has, with other issue,

  • Reginald Douglas, *b.* 1852.

Mr. Thornton, who was educated at Rugby and Trinity Coll. Cambridge, is a Magistrate for Dorset, and Joint Patron of two livings; was formerly in the Indian Civil Service.—*Frome Whitfield, Dorchester.*

THORNTON, SAMUEL, Esq., of The Elms, Birmingham, Warwickshire.
Eldest son of the late Mr. James Thornton, of Birmingham (who *d.* 1846), by Catherine, dau. of Samuel Cox, Esq., of Walsall ; *b.* 1804 ; *m.* 1830 Deborah, dau. of John Cary, Esq., of Monkspath Hall, co. Warwick, and has issue, one son,

  • Falkland Samuel, educated at Trinity Coll. Cambridge (B.A. 1862) ; *b.* 1841 ; *m.* 1866 Emma. only ch ld of Rob rt Rawlinson, Esq., C.E., of Boltons, West B ompton.

Mr. Thornton is a Magistrate for co. Warwick and for Birmingham. — *The Elms, Camp Hill, Birmingham ; Reform Club,* s.w.

THORNTON, the Rev. THOMAS COOKE, of Brockhall, Northamptonshire.
Eldest son of the late Thomas Reeve Thornton, Esq., J.P. and D.L., of Brockhall (formerly High Sheriff of co. Northampton), by Susannah, dau. and heir of Peter John Fremeaux, Esq., of Kingsthorpe ; *b.* 1801 ; *s.* 1862. Educated at Clare Coll., Cambridge (B.A. 1822, M.A. 1825); is Lord of the Manors of Newnham and Hannington. Patron of 3 livings.—*Brockhall, Weedon ; University Club,* s.w.

  Ecar Prct., his brother the Rev. William Thornton, of Kingsthorpe House, Northampton ; educated at Harr w M.A. of C.C.C., Cambridge, and formerly Vicar of Isca and ; b. 1806 ; *s.* his mother 1862; *m.* 18–– Anne Gertrude Frances, dau. of the late General Sir William Anson, Bart., K.C.B., and has, with other issue, • Thomas William, *b.* 1830.

THORNTON, Col. WILLIAM, of Moggerhanger, Beds.
Fourth surviving son of the late Stephen Thornton, Esq., of Moggerhanger House, by Mary, dau. of Thomas Littledale, Esq., of Rotterdam ; *b.* 1802 ; *m.* 1826 Frances Beth, dau. of Thomas Vigne, Esq., of Woodford, Essex. Educated at Westminster; is a Magistrate for Beds and a Col. in the Army ; was formerly in the Grenadier Guards.—*St. John's, Moggerhanger, St. Neots ; Guards' and United Service Clubs,* s.w.

THORNTON, WILLIAM THOMAS, Esq., of Caton, Lancashire.
Only surviving son of the late Edmund Thornton, Esq., of Whittington Hall, co. Lancashire, by Jane, dau. of Ven. Thomas Butler, Rector of Bentham and Whittington, co. Lancashire, Archdeacon of Chester; *b.* 1799 ; *s.* 1821 ; *m.* 1824 Hannah Isabella Cornelia,

dau. of Col. John Cornelius Craigie-Halkett, of Lahill, and Dumbarnie, co. Fife, and has had, with other issue,

* Charles Edmund Thornton, Major in the Army; *b.* 1825; *m.* 1862 Eliza Amanda, dau. of the late Lieut.-Col. Stephen Williams, of the 26th Bengal N.I.

Mr. Thornton, who was educated at Rugby, was formerly Receiver-General of Her Majesty's Inland Revenue. This family has held property at Skerton, Whittington, and Caton, Lancashire, for several centuries.—*Caton, Lancaster;* Residence: *Edinburgh.*

THORNTON. (See *Astell.*)

THORNTON-DUESBERY. (See *Duesbery.*)

THORNTON-WOODHOUSE. (See *Woodhouse.*)

THORNYCROFT, the Rev. JOHN, of Thorny-croft Hall, Cheshire.

Second but only surviving son of the late Rev. Charles Mytton, of Eccleston (who assumed the name of Thornycroft), by Henrietta, dau. of the Hon. John Grey, and grand-dau. of Harry, 4th Earl of Stamford; *b.* 1809; *s.* 1840; *m.* 1848 Charlotte Blanche, 2nd dau. of John Beaumonte Swete, Esq., formerly of Oxton, Devon, by whom he has, with other issue,

* Charles Edward, *b.* 1849.

Mr. Thornycroft, who was educated at the Charterhouse and Brasenose Coll., Oxford (B.A. 1831, M.A. 1834), is a Magistrate for co. Chester. — *Thornycroft Hall, Congleton.*

THOROLD, Sir JOHN HENRY, Bart., of Syston Park, Lincolnshire (cr. 1642).

Eldest son of the late Sir John Charles Thorold, Bart., of Syston Park, by Elizabeth Frances, dau. of Col. Hildyard; *b.* 1842; *s.* as 12th Bart. 1866. Educated at Eton; is a J.P. and D.L. for co. Lincoln, and Patron of 4 livings; late Lieut. 17th Foot; elected M.P. for Grantham 1865. — *Syston Park, Grantham; Carlton Club,* s.w.

Heir Pres., his brother Montague George, *b.* 1844.

THOROLD, CECIL, Esq., of Boothby, Lincolnshire.

Third son of the late Sir John Charles Thorold, Bart., of Marston, co. Lincoln, by Elizabeth, dau. of the late Col. Thomas Blackborne Thornton Hildyard, of Flintham, Notts; *b.* 1847; *s.* to this property under the bequest of the late John Litchford, Esq., in 1862. Educated at Eton; is Patron and Lord of the Manor of Boothby Pagnell, and Lieut. 1st Life Guards.—*Boothby Hall, Grantham.*

THOROLD, CHARLES, Esq., of Welbam, Notts.

Second but eldest surviving son of the late Samuel Thorold, Esq., by Charlotte Laurance, eldest dau. of the late Robert Mower, Esq., of the Woodseats, co. Derby; *b.* 1821; *m.* 1845 Mary Bettina Georgina, 7th dau. of the late Col. Kirke, of Markham, Notts, and has, with other issue,

* Charles Edmund de More, *b.* 1848.

Mr. Thorold is a Magistrate for Notts.—*Welham, Retford.*

THOROLD, HENRY, Esq., of Cuxwold, Lincolnshire.

Eldest son of the late Henry Thorold, Esq., of Cuxwold, by Mary, eldest dau. of the Rev. John Skynner, Rector of Easton, co. Northampton; *b.* 1793; *s.* 1803; *m.* 1830 Maria Antonia, only dau. of the late Rear-Admiral Mansel, of Charlton, co. Gloucester, and has, with other issue,

* William, a Magistrate for co. Lincoln; *b.* 1840.

Mr. Thorold, who was educated at Winchester and St. John's Coll., Cambridge, is a J.P. and D.L. for co.

922

Lincoln, and Lord of the Manor and Patron of Cuxwold. — *Ravendale, Lincoln; Cuxwold Hall, Caistor; Boodle's and Arthur's Clubs,* s.w.

THOROLD, ALEXANDER WILLIAM THOROLD GRANT-, Esq., of Weelsby, Lincolnshire.

Eldest son of the late Alexander Grant, Esq., by Helen, dau. of the Rev. William Thorold, of Weelsby House; *b.* 1820; *s.* his uncle Richard Thorold, Esq., 1864, when he assumed the name of Thorold; *m.* 1863 Anna Hamilton, 3rd dau. of the late Admiral Sir James Stirling, and has issue,

* Two daughters.

Mr. Grant-Thorold is a Magistrate for co. Lincoln, and Lord of the Manor of Weelsby. — *Weelsby House, Gt. Grimsby; Conservative Club,* s.w.

THORNTON-HILDYARD. (See *Hildyard.*)

THORP, the Rev. CHARLES.

Eldest son of the late Ven. Charles Thorp, D.D., Archdeacon of Durham and Rector of Ryton (who *d.* 1862), by his 2nd wife Mary, 2nd dan. of E. Robinson, Esq., of Thorp Green, co. York; *b.* 1825; *m.* 1857 Isabella Frances, only surviving child of the late Andrew Robert Fenwick, Esq., of Whitten and East Thriston, Northumberland. Educated at the University Coll., Oxford (B.A. 1849, M.A. 1850); is a Magistrate for co. Durham, and Vicar of Ellingnam.—*Ellingham Vicarage, Alnwick.*

THOYTS, MORTIMER GEORGE, Esq., of Sulhamstead, Berks.

Only son of the late William Thoyts, Esq., of Sulhamstead, by Jane, dau. of Abraham Newman, Esq., of Brook House, Essex; *b.* 1804; *s.* 1817; *m.* 1st 1828 Emma, 3rd dau. of Thomas Bacon, Esq., of Padworth House, Berks (she *d.* 1846); 2nd 1848 Catherine, dau. of Robert Sherson, Esq., of Fetcham, Surrey, and widow of Major Smith (she *d.* 1852), and has issue by the former,

* William Richard Mortimer, *b.* 1828; *m.* 1856 Annabella, dau. of the late Sir Richard Puleston, Bart., of Emral, co. Flint.

Mr. Thoyts, who was educated at Winchester and Ch. Ch., Oxford (B.A. 1827) is a J.P. and D.L. for Berks (High Sheriff 1839). — *Sulhamstead House, Reading; Conservative Club,* s.w.

THREIPLAND, Sir PATRICK MURRAY-, Bart., of Fingask, Perthshire (cr. 1687).

Eldest son of the late Sir Patrick Murray Threipland, Bart., of Fingask, by Jessy Murray, dau. of William Scott Kerr, Esq., of Chatto, co. Roxburgh; *b.* 1800; *s.* as 4th Bart. 1847. Educated at Edinburgh and Paris; is a J.P. and D.L., and Commissioner of Supply for cos. Perth and Caithness; was formerly Major of the Perth Militia. This title, attainted in 1715, was restored in 1826.—*Fingask Castle, Perth; Toftingall House, Caithness, N.B.*

THRESHER, of Bentley, Hants. (See *Gass.*)

THRING, the Rev. JOHN GALE DALTON, of Alford House, Somerset.

Only son of the late John Thring, J.P. and D.L., of Alford House, by Elizabeth, dau. of William Everett, Esq., of Heytesbury, Wilts; *b.* 1784; *s.* 1850; *m.* 1811 Sarah, 2nd dau. of the late Rev. John Jenkyns, Vicar of Evercreech and Prebendary of Wells, and has with other issue,

* Theodore, a Magistrate for Somerset; *b.* 1816; *m.* 1852 Julia Jane, 4th dau. of William Mills, Esq., of Saxham Hall, Suffolk.

Mr. Thring, who was educated at Winchester and St.

John's Coll., Cambridge (B.C.L. 1806), is a J.P. and D.C.L. for Somerset, and Patron of 1 living.—*Alford House, Castle Cary; Oxford and Cambridge Club, s.w.*

THROCKMORTON, Sir NICHOLAS WILLIAM, Bart., of Coughton Court, Warwickshire (cr. 1642).

Eldest surviving son of the late Sir Robert George Throckmorton, Bart., J.P. of Coughton Court, by Elizabeth, dau. of the late Sir John Acton, Bart., of Aldenham Park, co. Salop; *b.* 1838; *s.* 1862. Is a J.P. and D.L. for Berks and co. Warwick, Lord of the Manors of Coughton, Buckland, and Weston Underwood, Bucks, and Patron of 2 livings.—*Coughton Court, Alcester; Buckland House, Farringdon; Weston Underwood, Olney, Brooks's and St. James's Clubs, s.w.*

Heir Pres., his brother Richard Charles Acton, Capt. 87th Foot; *b.* 1839; *m.* 1866 Frances, only dau. of the late Major John Arthur Moore, E.I.S., and has issue, * a son, *b.* 1867.

THRUPP, JOSEPH WILLIAM, Esq., of Merrow, Surrey.

Son of the late Joseph Thrupp, Esq., by Mary, dau. of James Pillow, Esq., of Bransil, co. Hereford; *b.* 1799; *m.* 1826 Ruth Louisa, eldest dau. of Thomas John Burgoyne, Esq., and has issue,

* Joseph Francis, in Holy Orders, M.A. of Trinity Coll., Cambridge; educated at Winchester, and late Fellow of Trinity Coll., Cambridge; Vicar of Barrington, co. Cambridge; *b.* 1827; *m.* 1853 Elizabeth Bligh, dau. of the Rev. J. D. Glennie.

Mr. Thrupp is a Magistrate for Middlesex.—*Merrow House, Guildford; 50, Upper Brook Street, w.*

THRUSTON, CHARLES FREDERICK, Esq., of Talgarth Hall, Merionethshire.

Eldest son of the late Charles Thomas Thruston, Esq., Capt. R.N., of Pennal Tower, co. Merioneth, by his 1st wife Frances, dau. of Lewis Edwards, Esq., of Talgarth Hall; *b.* 1824; *s.* 1845; *m.* 1848 Mary, dau. of the late Capt. Josiah Nisbet, R.N., and has, with other issue,

* Charles Nisbet, *b.* 1854.

Mr. Thruston, who was educated at Rugby, is a J.P. and D.L. for co. Merioneth (High Sheriff 1860), and a Magistrate for co. Montgomery; was formerly in the 90th Foot.—*Talgarth Hall, Pennal, Machynlleth.*

THRUSTON, CLEMENT ARTHUR, Esq., of Pennal Tower, Merionethshire.

Second surviving son of the late Capt. Charles Thos. Thruston, R.N., of Pennal Tower, and formerly of Talgarth, in the same co. (who *d.* 1858), by his second wife, Eliza, dau. of the late Admiral Sotheby; *m.* 1861 Constance Sophia Margaret, youngest dau. of the late Major-General Lechmere C. Russell, C.B., of Ashford Hall, co. Salop, and has, with other issue,

* Edmund Heathcote, *b.* 1863.

Mr. Thruston, who was educated at Rugby and University Coll., Oxford (B.A. 1860), is a Magistrate for co. Merioneth, and Lieut. Montgomeryshire Yeomanry Cavalry.—*Pennal Tower, Machynlleth, N. Wales.*

THUNDER, MICHAEL, Esq., of Lagore, co. Meath.

Eldest son of the late Patrick Thunder, Esq., of Lagore, by Elizabeth, eldest dau. of the late John Taaffe, Esq., of Smarmore Castle, co. Louth; *b.* 1804; *s.* 1829; *m.* 1834 Charlotte Mary, only dau. of Lieut.-Col. Dalton, Bengal Army, and has, with other issue,

* Patrick, *b.* 1835.

Mr. Thunder, who was educated at Stonyhurst Coll., is a J.P. and D.L. for co. Meath (High Sheriff 1850), and a Magistrate for co. Dublin.—*Lagore, Dunshaughlin, co Meath; Edely, co Dublin.*

THURLOW, Lord (EDWARD THOMAS HOVELL-THURLOW).—Cr. 1792.

Eldest son of Edward Thomas, 3rd Lord, by Sarah, dau. of Peter Hodgson, Esq.; *b.* 1837; *s.* 1857. Is a J.P. and D.L. for Suffolk, and Patron of 1 living. The 1st Peer was Lord Chancellor 1778–92.—*Ashfield Lodge, Ixworth.*

Heir Pres., his brother Thomas John, 2nd Sec. in H.M.'s Diplomatic Service, late Attaché to the Embassy at Vienna, and formerly Private Secretary to the Viceroy of India; *b.* 1838; *m.* 1864 Lady Elma, eldest dau. of James, 8th Earl of Elgin, and has issue, * a son, *b.* 1867.

THURLOW, the Rev. THOMAS, of Baynard's Park, Surrey.

Second son of the Right Rev. Thomas Thurlow, D.D., formerly Lord Bishop of Durham, by Anne, dau. of William Brere, Esq., of Lymington, Hants; *b.* 1788; *m.* 1811 Mary Frances, 3rd dau. of the late Hon. Thomas Lyon, of Hetton Castle, co. Durham, and has, with other issue,

* Thomas Lyon, M.A. of Trinity Coll., Cambridge, *b.* 181–.

Mr. Thurlow, who was educated at St. John's Coll., Cambridge (B.A. 1811, M.A. 1816), is a Magistrate for Surrey and Suffolk, Prothonotary of the Common Pleas for the co. Palatine of Durham, and formerly Rector of Boxford, Suffolk.—*Baynard's Park, Guildford.*

THURSBY, the Rev. WILLIAM, of Ormerod House, Lancashire.

Second son of the late John Harvey Thursby, Esq., of Abington Abbey, co. Northampton (who *d.* 1838), by Emma, dau. of the late William Pigott, Esq., J.P., of Doddershall, Bucks; *b.* 1795; *m.* 1824 Eleanor Mary, eldest dau. of the late John Hargreaves, Esq., and of Charlotte Anne, his wife, heiress of Ormerod, and has, with other issue,

* John Hardy, a Magistrate for co. Lancaster; late Lieut. 94th Light Infantry, Major of the 7th Royal Lancaster Rifles; *b.* 1826; *m.* 1860 Clara, youngest dau. of the late Col. Williams, R.E., niece of the Hon. Mr. Justice Williams (she *d.* 1867).

Mr. Thursby, who was educated at Oriel Coll., Oxford (B.A. 1818, M.A. 1820), is a Magistrate for co. Lancaster, and Incumbent of St John's, Worsthorne; late Vicar of All Saints, Northampton, and of Hardingstone; was Domestic Chaplain to his late R.H. the Duke of Cambridge.—*Ormerod House, Burnley.*

THURSBY-PELHAM, the Rev. HENRY, of Cound Hall, Salop.

Only son of the late Rev. George Augustus Thursby, Rector of Abington, co. Northampton, by Frances, eldest dau. of H. Cressett Pelham, Esq., and sister and co-heir of the late John Cressett Pelham, Esq., M.P.; *b.* 1801; *s.* 1852; *m.* 1827 Mary Elizabeth, 6th dau. of the late Thomas Papillon, Esq., of Acrise, Kent, and has, with other issue,

* Walter, *b.* 1830; *m.* 1863 Emily Fitzgerald, eldest dau. of the Hon. James Butler, and has issue, * a son, *b.* 1867.

Mr. Thursby-Pelham was educated at Oriel Coll. Oxford (B.A. 1824), ordained 1827, is Rector and Patron of Cound. This family are descended in the male line from the Thursbys of Abington, co. Northampton.—*Cound Hall, Shrewsbury.*

THWAITES, Sir JOHN, Knt. (cr. 1865).

Son of the late Mr. Christopher Thwaites, of Teddy Gill Hall, Westmorland, by Hannah, dau. of John Smith, Esq.; *b.* 1815; *m.* 1st 1836 Harriott, dau. of William Bardwell, Esq.; 2nd 1861 Eliza, dau. of Daniel Woodruffe, Esq., and widow of R. Carrington, Esq., M.D. Is a J.P. and D.L. for Middlesex, and Chairman of the Metropolitan Board of Works.—*Meaburn House, Putney, s.w., 6, Spring Gardens, s.w.*

743

THYNNE, Lord CHARLES.

Seventh son of Thomas, 2nd Marquis of Bath, by the Hon. Isabella, dau. of George, 4th Viscount Torrington; *b.* 1813 ; *m.* 1837 Harriet Frances, dau. of the late Hon. and Rev. Richard Bagot, D.D., Lord Bishop of Bath and Wells, and has, with other issue,

* Frederick Charles, *b.* 1838.

Lord C. Thynne was educated at Harrow and Ch. Ch., Oxford (B.A. 1834, M.A. 1837) ; was formerly Rector of Longbridge and Kingston Deverill, Wilts, and Canon of Canterbury.—*Malvern Wells, Worcester.*

THYNNE, Lord EDWARD.

Sixth son of Thomas, 2nd Marquis of Bath, by the Hon. Isabella, dau. of George, 4th Viscount Torrington ; *b.* 1807 ; *m.* 1st 1830 Elizabeth, dau. of the late William Mellish, Esq. ; 2nd 1853 Cecilia Anne Mary, dau. of the late Charles Arthur Gore, Esq. Educated at the Charterhouse and Oriel Coll., Oxford (B.A. 1828) ; is Cornet Wilts Yeomanry Cavalry ; was M.P. for Weobley 1831-2, and for Frome 1859-65. —29, *Wilton Crescent, s.w.*

THYNNE, Lord HENRY FREDERICK.

Younger son of Henry Frederick, 3rd Marquis of Bath, by Harriet, 2nd dau. of Alexander, 1st Lord Ashburton; *b.* 1832 ; *m.* 1858 Lady Ulrica Frederica Jane St. Maur, 2nd dau. of Edward Adolphus, 12th Duke of Somerset, and has, with other issue,

* Henry Frederick Botteville, *b.* 1860.

Lord Henry, who was educated at Eton and Ch. Ch., Oxford, is a Magistrate for Somerset, a J.P. and D.L., for Wilts, and Capt. R. Wilts Yeomanry Cavalry ; elected M.P. for S. Wilts 1859.—*Carlton, White's, and Boodle's Clubs, s.w.* ; 83, *Portland Place, w.*

THYNNE, the Rev. Lord JOHN, of Hawnes, Beds.

Second surviving son of Thomas, 2nd Marquis of Bath, by the Hon. Isabella, dau. of George, 4th Viscount Torrington; *b.* 1798 ; *m.* 1824 Anne Constanta, dau. of the Rev. Claudius Cobbe Beresford, and by her (who *d.* 1866) has, with other issue,

* Francis John, a J.P. and D.L. for Beds ; *b.* 1830 ; *m.* 1864 Edith Marcia Caroline, eldest dau. of Richard Brinsley Sheridan, Esq., M.P., and has, with other issue, * Devil Glauville Carteret, *b.* 1867.

Lord J. Thynne, who was educated at Eton and St. John's Coll., Cambridge (M.A. 1819, D.D. 18-8), appointed Rector of Blackwall 1823, and Prebendary of Westminster ; is Sub-Dean of Westminster, a Magistrate for Somerset, and Patron of 3 livings. —*Hawnes Park, Bedford ; Cloisters, Westminster, s.w.*

THYNNE. (See under *Bath, Marquis of.*)

TIBBITS, JOHN BONHASE, Esq., of Barton Seagrave, Northamptonshire.

Fourth son of Col. Thomas Philip Maunsell, of Thorpe Malsor, co. Northampton (whom see), by the Hon. Caroline Elizabeth, dau. of the late Hon. William Cockayne, and sister of the last Viscount Cullen (ext.) ; *b.* 1820 ; *m.* 1858 Mary Isabella Viscountess Head. Educated at Eton ; assumed the name of Tibbits in lieu of Maunsell by Royal licence in 1858, is a Magistrate for co. Northampton, Lord of the Manor of Barton Seagrave, and Patron of 1 living ; was formerly Capt. 12th Lancers. — *Barton Seagrave, Kettering ; Army and Navy Club, s.w.* ; 44, *Bryanstone Square, w.*

924

TICHBORNE, Sir HENRY ALFRED JOSEPH DOUGHTY-, Bart.,‡ of Tichborne, Hants, and Upton House, Dorset (cr. 1620).

Only surviving son of the late Sir Alfred Joseph Doughty-Tichborne, Bart., of Tichborne Park, by Hon. Teresa, eldest dau. of Henry Benedict, 11th Lord Arundell of Wardour ; *b.* (posthumous), and *s.* as 12th Bart. 1866 ; is Lord of the Manor of Tichborne, and Patron of 1 living.—*Tichborne Park, Alresford ; Upton House, Poole.*

TIGHE, the Very Rev. HUGH USSHER, Dean of Londonderry.

Second but only surviving son of the late Robert Hearne Tighe, Esq., of Mitchelstown, co. Westmeath, by Catherine, only child of Col. Hugh Morgan, of Cottlestown, co. Sligo; *b.* 1802 ; *m.* 1828 Anne Florence, dau. of John MacClintock, Esq., M.P., of Drumcar, and has surviving issue, two daughters. Dean Tighe, who was educated at Eton and Corpus Christi Coll., Oxford (B.A. 1822, M.A. 1826, D.D. 1844), is Dean of Derry ; was formerly Dean of the Chapel Royal, Dublin, and of Ardagh. — *Deanery House, Londonderry ; Kildare Street Club, Dublin.*

TIGHE, ST. LAWRANCE ROBERT MORGAN, Esq., of the Grove, co. Cork.

Eldest and only surviving child of the late Robert Morgan Tighe, Esq., of Mitchelstown, co. Westmeath, by Frances Elizabeth, youngest dau. and eventual co-heir of the late Hon. and Right Rev. Thomas St. Lawrance, Lord Bishop of Cork and Ross ; *b.* 1838 ; *s.* 1853. Educated at Trinity Coll., Dublin. This family were amongst the first Protestant settlers in Ireland, and Mr. Tighe is 18th in direct descent from Edward III.— *The Grove, Passage West, co. Cork ; Kildare Street Club, Dublin.*

TIGHE, the Right Hon. WILLIAM FREDERICK FOWNES, of Woodstock, co. Kilkenny.

Eldest son of the late William Tighe, Esq., M.P., of Woodstock, by Marianne, dau. and co-heir of the late Daniel Gahan, Esq., M.P., of Coolquill, co. Tipperary ; *b.* 1794 ; *s.* 1816 ; *m.* 1825 Lady Louisa Madelina, 5th dau. of Charles, 4th Duke of Richmond. Educated at Eton and Emmanuel Coll., Cambridge ; is a Magistrate for cos. Wexford, Westmeath, and Carlow, and Lord-Lieutenant and Custos Rotulorum of co. Kilkenny, and Col. of the Kilkenny Militia ; was High Sheriff of co. Kilkenny 1823, of co. Carlow 1849 ; sworn a Privy Councillor in 1846. — *Woodstock, Inistioge, co. Kilkenny.*

Heir Pres., his brother Daniel, of Rossana, near Ashford, co. Wicklow, educated at Eton ; a J.P. and D.L. for co. Wicklow (High Sheriff 1827), and formerly an officer in the Grenadier Guards ; *b.* 1790 ; *s.* 1846 ; *m.* 1825 the Hon. Frances, 3rd dau. of the late Hon. Sir F. Cotton, Bart., of Mote Park, co. Roscommon, and sister of Lord Combermere, and has, with other issue, * Frederick Edward, Lieut.-Commandant Kilkenny Militia, formerly an officer in the 82nd Foot ; *b.* 1826 ; *m.* 1848 Lady Kathleen Louisa Georgiana, dau. of John William, 4th Earl of Bessborough (she *d.* 1863).

TILGHMAN-HUSKISSON. (See *Huskisson.*)

TILLARD, PHILIP, Esq., of Stukeley, Hunts.

Eldest son of the late Rev. Richard Tillard, of Sandy End House, Kent, by Margaret, 3rd dau. of the late Rev. William Smelt, and niece of Philip, 6th Earl of Chesterfield ; *b.* 1811 ; *s.* 1830 ; *m.* 1834 Julia, dau. of John Thomas Baumgartner, Esq., of Godmanchester ; is a J.P. and D.L. for Hunts.—*Stukeley, Huntingdon.*

‡ The succession to this title is disputed by a person claiming to be Roger, son of the 10th Bart., who is said to have been lost at sea in 1854.

TILSON. (See *Chowne*.)

TILSON-MARSH, the Rev. WILLIAM NATHANIEL, of Brickendon, Herts, and Stretham, Cambridgeshire.

Only son of the late Rev. William Marsh, D.D., Honorary Canon of Worcester, and Rector of Beddington, Surrey, by Maria Chowne, dau. of the late John Tilson, Esq., J.P. and D.L. of Watlington Park, Oxon; *b.* 1815; *m.* 1850 Selina Rosa, dau. of the late George Gould Morgan, Esq., M.P. Educated at Oriel Coll., Oxford (B.A. 1838, M.A. 1841); appointed Vicar of Dunston, co. Lincoln, 1846, and Incumbent of St. Leonard's 1857; is Patron of 1 living.—*Marina, St. Leonard's-on-Sea; Brickendon Priory Manor, Great Berkhampstead, Herts; Stretham Manor, Ely; National, and Oxford and Cambridge Clubs, s.w.*

TIMINS, the Rev. DOUGLAS CARTWRIGHT, of Hilfield, Herts.

Only son of the late Douglas Thompson Timins, Esq., H.E.I.C.S. (who *d.* 1840), by Mary Anne, dau. of Fryer Todd, Esq.; *b.* 1839; *s.* his uncle William Raikes Timins, Esq., of Hilfield, 1866; *m.* 1863 Eliza Henrietta, dau. of Adam Keir, Esq., M.D., late H.E.I.C.S., of Avonholm, Kent. Educated at Oriel Coll, Oxford (B.A. 1864, M.A. 1865), is a Member of several Scientific Societies, and was formerly Curate of Seaford. This family, descended from the Marquises de Thémines, is of French Huguenot extraction.—*Hilfield, Watford; Union Club, Oxford.*

Heir Pres., his uncle, the Rev. John Henry Timins, M.A. of Trinity Coll., Cambridge, Vicar of Malling, Kent; *b.* 1815.

TIMSON, the Rev. EDWARD, of Tatchbury Mount, Hants.

Eldest son of the late Henry Thomas Timson, Esq., of Tatchbury Mount, by Susanna, dau. of Samuel Plumbe, Esq., of Tooting, Surrey (who was twice Lord Mayor of London); *b.* 1797; *s.* 1848; *m.* 1830 Margaret Angelina, dau. of James Greene, Esq., of Clayton Hall and Turton, co. Lancaster, and has, with other issue,

* Henry, educated at Harrow; late Captain in the 5th Dragoons; *b.* 1835.

Mr. Timson was educated at Eton and Trinity Coll. Oxford, where he graduated B.A. in 1819, and proceeded M.A. in 1823.—*Tatchbury Mount, Eling, Southampton; Conservative Club, s.w.*

TINDAL, ACTON, Esq., of The Manor House, Aylesbury, Bucks.

Eldest son of the late Thomas Tindal, Esq., of Aylesbury, many years Clerk of the Peace and Treasurer of Bucks, by Anne, dau. of Acton Chaplin, Esq., also Clerk of the Peace and Treasurer of the said county, and nephew of the late Right Hon. Sir Nicolas Tindal, Chief Justice of the Common Pleas; *b.* 1811; *m.* 1846 Henrietta Euphemia, only surviving child of the late Rev. John Harrison, of Ramsey, Essex, and Vicar of Dinton, Bucks, and has, with other issue,

* Nicolas, *b.* 1848.

Mr. Tindal who was educated at the Charterhouse, is a Magistrate and Clerk of the Peace for Bucks, and Lord of the Manor of Aylesbury.—*The Manor House, Aylesbury.*

TINDAL, Capt. LOUIS SYMONDS, of Hanningfield, Essex.

Second but eldest surviving son of the late Right Hon. Sir Nicholas C. Tindal, Chief Justice of the Court of Common Pleas (who *d.* 1846), by Merelina, youngest dau. of Capt. Thomas Symonds, R.N.; *b.* 1811; *m.*

1853 Miss Henrietta Maria O'Donnel Whyte, and has, with other issue,

* Nicolas Charles, *b.* 1857.

Mr. Tindal, who is a Capt. R.N., represents a family settled in Devon in 1655, and afterwards at Coval Hall, Chelmsford. — *Hanningfield, Chelmsford; Chase Lodge, Enfield, Middlesex.*

+TINLING, CHARLES HENRY, Esq., of Ashwell, Herts.

Eldest son of the late William Tinling, Esq., of Southampton, and nephew of Lady Chelmsford; *b.* 18—; *m.* 1st 1857 Mary Susan, only surviving dau. and co-heiress of the late Michael Leheup, Esq., of Hessett, Suffolk, and Ashwell, Herts (she *d.* 1857); 2nd 1860 Eliza, 2nd dau. of the late W. H. Conolly, Esq., R.M.—*Ashwell, Baldock.*

TINNE, JOHN ABRAHAM, Esq., of Aigburth, Lancashire.

Eldest son of the late Philip F. Tinne, Esq., by Anna, dau. of the late William Rose, Esq., of Montcoffer, co. Banff; *b.* 1807; *m.* 1833 Margaret, dau. of Samuel Sandbach, Esq., and has, with other issue,

* Philip Frederic, *b.* 1836; *m.* 1862 Alice Ann, only dau. of the late Charles Hopley, Esq., and has issue * Alice.

Mr. Tinne, who is a J.P. and D.L. for co. Lancaster, was formerly a Merchant at Liverpool. This family is of Dutch extraction.—*Briarley, Aigburth, Liverpool.*

TIPPING, GARTSIDE GARTSIDE, Esq., of Rossferry, co. Fermanagh.

Eldest son of the late Thomas Tipping, Esq., of Davenport Hall, co. Chester (who *d.* 1846), by Anna, dau. of Robert Hibbert, Esq., of Birtles Hall, co. Chester, and Chalfont Park, Bucks (she *d.* 1863); *b.* 1810; *m.* 1844 Jane Margaret, elder dau. of Robert Fowler, Esq., of Rahinstown, co. Meath, and Jane, sister of John, 3rd Earl of Erne, and by her (who *d.* 1857) has, with other issue,

* Henry Thomas, Lieut. R.N., *b.* 1848.

Mr. Tipping, who was educated at Rugby, is a Magistrate for co. Fermanagh, and Lord of the Manor of Bolton-le-Moors. This family was settled near Blackburn and Preston, co. Lancaster, *temp.* Edward III. —*Rossferry House, Lisnaskea, co. Fermanagh; Sackville Street Club, Dublin.*

TIPPING, WILLIAM, Esq., of Brasted, Kent.

Only child of John Tipping, Esq., of Liverpool; *b.* 1816; *m.* 1846 Maria, dau. of Benjamin Walker, Esq., of Leeds, co. York, and has, with other issue,

* John Walker, *b.* 1849.

Mr. Tipping is a Magistrate for Kent, co. Lancaster, and the W. Riding of Yorkshire. — *Brasted Park, Sevenoaks; Bank Hall, Clithero.*

TIPPINGE, EDMUND JOSEPH, Esq.

Third son of the late Thomas Tippinge, Esq (who *d.* 1846), by Anna, dau. of Robert Hibbert, Esq., of Birtles Hall, co. Chester; *b.* 1815. Educated at Shrewsbury, is a Magistrate for co. Chester, and Major 6th Cheshire Rifle Volunteers.—Residence: *The Grand Hall, Congleton, Cheshire; Conservative Club, s.w.*

Heir Pres., his brother Alfred, educated at Shrewsbury and the R. Military Coll., Sandhurst; joint Lord of the Manor of Bolton-le-Moors; formerly Lieut.-Col. Grenadier Guards; *m.* 1861 Flora Louisa, 2nd dau. of the late Rev. Nicolson Calvert, of Quentin Castle, co. Down, and has issue two daughters.

TIPPINGE, the Rev. FRANCIS GARTSIDE, of Llwyn Onn Hall, Denbighshire.

Fifth son of the late Thomas Tippinge, Esq., by Anna, eldest dau. of Robert Hibbert, Esq., of Birtles, co. Chester; *b.* 1821; *m.* 1846 Marion, dau. of Joseph

925

Dobinson, Esq., of Egham Lodge, Surrey, and has, with other issue,
* Leonard, b. 1849.
Mr. Tippinge, who was educated at Rugby and Brasenose Coll., Oxford B.A. 1843, M.A. 1846), is a Magistrate for co. Denbigh.—*Llwyn Onn Hall, Wrexham.*

+TIREMAN, GEORGE WILLIAM, Esq., of Lofthouse Hall, Yorkshire.
Son of the late — Tireman, Esq.; b. 18—. Is a Dep.-Lieut. for the N. and W. Ridings of co. York.—*Lofthouse Hall, Redcar.*

TISDALL, CHALRES NEWBURGH, Esq., of Clifford, co. Cork.
Son of the late John Tisdall, Esq., by Alicia Maria C., dau. of Arthur Robert Newburgh, Esq., of Ballyhaise Castle, co. Cavan; b. 1821; m. 1st 1848 Lucy, only dau. of Alexander Elliott, Esq. (she d. 1849); 2nd 1858 Matilda Maria, 2nd dau. of the late Major Carter, and has by the former, with other issue,
* Charles Elliott. b. 1848.
Mr. Tisdall is a Magistrate for co. Cork. This family was formerly seated in co. Louth.—*Clifford, Castletownroche, co. Cork.*

TISDALL, JOHN, Esq., of Charlesfort, co. Meath.
Eldest son of the late Charles Arthur Tisdall, Esq., of Charlesfort, by Elizabeth, dau. of John Vernon, Esq., of Clontarf Castle, co. Dublin; b. 1815; s. 1835; m. 1837 Isabella, dau. of the late Hon. George Knox, D.C.L., and has, with other issue,
* Charles Arthur, Capt. 18th Hussars, b. 1838.
Mr. Tisdall, who was educated at Trinity Coll., Dublin (B.A. 1835), is a Magistrate for co. Meath.—*Charlesfort, Navan, co. Meath ; Sackville Street Club, Dublin.*

TITE, WILLIAM, Esq., F.R.S.
Son of the late Arthur Tite, Esq., Merchant, of London; b. 1800; m. 1832 Emily, 5th dau. of John Curtis, Esq., of Herny Hill, Surrey. Educated at Hackney; is a Magistrate for Middlesex and Somerset, and a Dep.-Lieut. for London; has been M.P. for Bath since 1855.—*Reform Club, s.w.; 42, Lowndes Square, s.w.*

+TITTLE, JOHN MOORE, Esq., of Portstewart, co. Londonderry.
Son of the late John Tittle, Esq.; b. 1791; is married, and has issue,
* John Moore, b. 1825 ; entered the Army 1841, and was formerly an Officer in the late West-Indian Regt. of Foot.
Mr. Tittle is a Magistrate for co. Londonderry, and for Coleraine, and a Capt. in the Army, unattached.—*Portstewart, co. Londonderry.*

TOBIN, Sir THOMAS, Knt., F.R.S.N.A., F.S.A., of Ballincollig, co. Cork (cr. 1855).
Eldest son of the late Thomas Tobin, Esq., of Liverpool, by Olivia, dau. of Thomas Garforth, Esq., of Steeton, co. York; b. 1807; m. 1835 Catherine, dau. of the late Lister Ellis, Esq., of Crofthead, Cumberland. Is a J.P. and D.L. for the county and city of Cork, President of the Cork Athenæum, and a Member of several literary societies.—*Ballincollig, Cork.*

TOBIN, JAMES ASPINALL, Esq., of Eastham, Cheshire.
Fourth son of the late Thomas Tobin, Esq., of Liverpool, by Esther, dau. of J. Watson, Esq., of Preston, co. Lancaster; b. 1818; m. 1842 Olivia Maria, dau. of Lister Ellis, Esq., of Crofthead, Cumberland, and has, with other issue,
* Frank, b. 1849.
Mr. Tobin, who was educated at Rugby, is a Magistrate for co. Lancaster, and a Merchant at Liverpool.—*Eastham, Chester ; Conservative Club, s.w.*

TOD, of Drygrange. (See *Leith, Sir G. H., Bart.*)

TODD. (See *Wilson-Todd.*)

TOKE, JOHN LESLIE, Esq., of Godinton, Kent.
Eldest son of the late Rev. Nicholas Toke, of Godinton, by Emma, 2nd dau. of the late Right Rev. John Leslie, D.D., Lord Bishop of Elphin; b. 1839; s. 1866; m. 1864 Agnes Elletson, youngest dau. of the late Patrick Robertson Reid, Esq., of Spring Hall, co. Lanark, and by her, who d. 1865, has issue,
* Francis Nicholas John, b. 1865.
Mr. Toke is a Magistrate for Kent, late Capt. 2nd Foot, and was formerly Capt. 96th Foot.—*Godinton, Ashford.*

TOLER. (See under *Norbury, Earl of.*)

TOLL, HENRY LIMBREY, Esq., of Street and Perridge, Devon.
Only son of the late Henry Limbrey Toll, Esq., J.P. and D.L., of Perridge and Street, by Ann, dau. of Walter Vavasour, Esq., of Heath, co. York; b. 1828; s. 1846; m. 1855 Louisa Frances, only dau. of Capt. W. B. Burne, Exeter, and has, with other issue,
* Henry Limbrey, b. 1855.
Mr. Toll, who was educated at the Royal Military Coll., Sandhurst, is a Magistrate for Devon, and was formerly an Officer in the Army.—*Street, Dartmouth ; Perridge House, Exeter.*

TOLLEMACHE, the Hon. FERDRICK JAMES.
Fifth son of William, late Lord Huntingtower, by Catherine Rebecca, dau. of Francis Gray, Esq., of Lehena, co. Cork, and brother of Lionel, 8th Earl of Dysart; b. 1801; m. 1st 1831 Sarah, dau. of Robert Bomford Esq., of Rahinstown, co. Meath; 2nd 1847 Isabella, dau. of Gordon Forbes, Esq. (she d. 1859). Educated at Harrow; was M.P. for Grantham 1826-30, 1857-52, and 1857-65.—*Ham House, Richmond, Surrey ; Athenæum Club, s.w.*

TOLLEMACHE, the Hon. and Rev. HUGH FRANCIS.
Fourth son of William, late Lord Huntingtower, by Catherine Rebecca, dau. of Francis Gray, Esq., and brother of Lionel, 8th Earl of Dysart; b. 1802; m. 1824 Matilda, dau. of Joseph Hume, Esq., and has, with other issue,
* Ralph William Lyonel, in Holy Orders. M.A. of St. Peter's Coll., Cambridge; a Magistrate for co. Lincoln, and Rector of South Witham, co. Lincoln; b. 1826; m. 18—— Caroline, dau. of the late Hon. Felix Thomas Tollemache, and has issue.
Mr. Tollemache was educated at Harrow and St. Peter's Coll., Cambridge (B.A. 1831), and appointed Rector of Harrington 1831.—*Harrington Rectory, Northampton.*

TOLLEMACHE, JOHN, Esq., of Helmingham, Suffolk, and Peckforton, Cheshire.
Son of the late Admiral John Richard Delap Tollemache, of Helmingham and Peckforton, by Lady Elizabeth, dau. of John, 3rd Earl of Aldborough, and grandson of Lionel, 4th Earl of Dysart; b. 1805; m. 1st 1826 Georgiana, dau. of Thomas Best, Esq.; 2nd 1850 Minnie, dau. of James Duff, Esq., step-dau. of Frederick, 4th Lord Rendlesham, and has by the former, with other issue,
* Wilbraham Frederick, a Magistrate for co. Chester ; b. 1832 ; m. 1858 Lady Emma Georgiana, dau. of Randolph, 9th Earl of Galloway, and has, with other issue, * a son, b. 1865.
Mr. Tollemache, who is a J.P. and D.L. for co. Chester, and Lord of the Manors of Helmingham, Peckforton, &c., and Patron of 5 livings, has been M.P. for S.

Cheshire since 1841.—*Helmingham Hall, Ipswich; Peckforton Castle, Nantwich; Carlton, Arthur's, and National Clubs, s.w.; 8, St. James's Square, s.w.*

TOLLEMACHE, WILBRAHAM SPENCER, Esq., of Dorfold Hall, Cheshire.

Second son of the late Admiral John Richard Delap-Tollemache, by Lady Elizabeth Stratford, dau. of John, 3rd Earl of Aldborough, and Brother of John Tollemache, Esq., of Helmingham and Peckforton (whom see); *b.* 1807; *m.* 1844 Anne, eldest dau. and heir of the late Rev. James Tomlinson, of Dorfold Hall, and has issue. Mr. Tollemache, who was educated at Westminster, is a J.P. and D.L. for Cheshire (High Sheriff 1865), and (*jure uxoris*) Lord of the Manor of Dorfold; he was formerly in the Rifle Brigade and the Coldstream Guards.—*Dorfold Hall, Nantwich.*

TOLLEMACHE. (See under *Dysart, Earl of.*)

TOLLET. (See *Wicksted.*)

TOMBS, Sir HENRY, K.C.B. (cr. 1868).

Son of the late — Tombs, Esq.; *b.* 1820. Is a Major-Gen. in the Army, late of the Royal (Bengal) Artillery. —*United Service Club, s.w.*

TOMKINS, GEORGE, Esq., late of Grey Thorn, co. Dublin.

Only son of the late Major Samuel Tomkins, Esq., of Grey Thorn, by his 2nd wife Jane Bunbury, 3rd dau. of the late Rev. B. Arthur, of Seafield, Dublin; *b.* 1815; *s.* 1824; *m.* 1842 Catherine Jane, eldest dau. of Major Richard Young, J.P., of Coolkeiragh House, Londonderry. Is a Magistrate for cos. Limerick and Londonderry.—*Residence: Dublin.*

TOMKINSON, Lieut.-Col. EDWARD, of Reaseheath, Cheshire.

Eldest son of the late Rev. Henry Tomkinson, of Reaseheath, by Harriet Sophia, dau. of the late Shakespeare Phillips, Esq., and grandson of the late Henry Tomkinson, Esq., of Dorfold; *b.* 1825. Entered the Army as Cornet 8th Hussars 1843, became Lieut.-Col. unattached 1857; served in the Crimea 1854–5.— *Reaseheath, Nantwich; United Service and Army and Navy Clubs, s.w.*

TOMKINSON, Lieut.-Col. WILLIAM, of Willington Hall, Cheshire.

Fourth son of the late Henry Tomkinson, Esq., of Dorfold Hall, co. Chester, by Anne, dau. of John Darlington, Esq., of Aston, co. Chester; *b.* 1790; *m.* 1836 Susan, dau. of the late Thomas Tarleton, Esq., of Bolesworth Castle, co. Chester, and has issue.

 • William, a Magistrate for co. Chester. *b.* 1839; *m.* 1866 Sarah, 2nd surviving dau. of the late Dudley North, Esq., of Rougham, Norfolk.

Lieut.-Col. Tomkinson, who is a J.P. and D.L. for co. Chester, Lord of the Manor of Willington, and a Lieut.-Col. in the Army, served in the Peninsular 1809–14, and at Waterloo.—*Willington Hall, Kelsall, Chester; United Service Club, s.w.*

TOMLIN, ROBERT SACKETT, Esq.,‡ of Dane Court, Kent.

Eldest son of the late Robert Tomlin, Esq., of North Down, Thanet, by Sarah, dau. and heir of Richard Sackett, Esq., of Dane Court, Thanet; *b.* 1790; *s.* 1817 to the estates in Thanet, and to Fotheringhay Castle estate in 1833; *m.* 1817 Elizabeth Ann, dau. of John Bankes, Esq., of Otley Park, co. York, and by her, who *d.* 1868, has, with other issue,

 • Robert Tomlin, *b.* 1820.

Mr. Tomlin, who is a J.P. and D.L. for co. Northamp-

ton, and a Magistrate for Peterborough, has been twice nominated High Sheriff of co. Northampton.—*Dane Court, Thanet, Kent; West Gate House, Peterborough; Runwell Hall, Somerset; Cal.donian Hotel, w.*

TOMLINE, GEORGE, Esq., of Riby Grove, Lincolnshire, and Orwell Park, Suffolk.

Son of the late William E. Tomline, Esq., M.P., by Frances, only dau. of the late John Amley, Esq., of Ford Hall, co. Salop, and grandson of the late Bishop (Tomline) of Winchester, who assumed the name of Tomline in 1803, under the will of the late Marmaduke Tomline, Esq., of Riby Grove; *b.* 1812. Educated at Eton; is a Magistrate for Suffolk (High Sheriff 1838), a J.P. and D.L. for co. Lincoln (High Sheriff 1852), Patron of 2 livings, and Col. Lincoln Militia; was M.P. for Sudbury 1840–1, for Shrewsbury 1841–7; re-elected 1852.—*Riby Grove, Gt. Grimsby; Orwell Park, and Kesgrave Hall, Woodbridge; Bacton Hall, Stowmarket; Carlton, Travellers', and Boodle's Clubs, s.w.; 1, Carlton Terrace, s.w.*

+TOMPSON, EDWARD, Esq., of Iver Heath, Bucks.

Son of the late E. Tompson, Esq., of Uxbridge; *b.* 1800; was admitted a Solicitor 1829.—*Dromenagh, Iver Heath, Uxbridge; 4, Stone Buildings, Lincoln's Inn, w.c.*

TOMPSON, GEORGE EDWARD, Esq., of Boxted, Essex.

Eldest son of the late Edward Tompson, Esq., of Gt. Yarmouth, Norfolk, by Elizabeth Mary, dau. of the late James Fisher, Esq., of Broweston Hall, Suffolk; *b.* 1816; *s.* 1826; *m.* 1st 1840 Caroline, eldest dau. of Francis Smythies, Esq., of Colchester (she *d.* 1844); 2nd 1847 Eliza, youngest dau. of the late J. H. Nunn, Esq., of Nether Hall, Bradfield, Essex, and has, with other issue,

 • Herbert Edward, *b.* 1848.

Mr. Tompson, who was educated at Eton and Trinity Coll., Cambridge, is a Magistrate for Essex.—*Boxted House, Colchester; Cavendish Club, w.*

TOMPSON, HENRY KETT, Esq., of Witchingham, Norfolk.

Second son of the late Charles Tompson, Esq., of Witchingham, by Juliana, 2nd dau. of Thomas Kett, Esq., of Seething Hall, Norfolk; *b.* 1813; *s.* 1851; *m.* 1843 Margaret Amelia, 2nd dau. of the late Rear-Admiral the Hon. Frederick Paul Irby, C.B. Educated at Harrow and Trinity Coll., Cambridge (B.A. 1845); is a Magistrate for Norfolk.—*Witchingham Hall, Norwich.*

TOMPSON-DELMAR, FREDERICK ORLANDO, Esq., of Ruislip Park, Middlesex.

Youngest son of the late Col. William Tompson, of Booth Hall, by Mary, dau. of Joseph Hopkins, Physician in Ordinary to the Duke of Kent; *b.* 1811; *m.* 1842 Maria, widow of Col. Delmar, of the Netherlands; assumed the additional surname of Delmar 1865. —*Ruislip Park, ... w.*

TONGE, Capt. AUGUSTUS HENRY, of Highway, Wilts.

Fifth, but eldest surviving son of the late William Norris Tonge, Esq., of Highway, and of Alvestoa, co. Gloucester, by Mary Ann, only child of the late Rev. John Bryan, of West Charlton, Somerset; *b.* 1818; *s.* his brother 1867; *m.* 1852 Charlotte Augusta, 2nd dau. of the late Hon. and Very Rev. George Pellew, Dean of Norwich, and by her, who *d.* 1865, has, with other issue,

 • Francis Henry, *b.* 1855.

Mr. Tonge is a Capt. R.N.—*Highway, Calne; Lymington, Hants; Army and Navy Club, s.w.*

TONGE, Mrs., of Starborough Castle, Surrey.
Margaret Mary, dau. of the late Jacob George Bryam, Esq., J.P., of Chatham, Kent; *m.* 1833 John Tonge, Esq., of Starborough Castle, a Magistrate for Surrey, who *d.* 1858, leaving, with other issue, an only son,
* William John, *b.* 1838; *m.* 1861 Anna Penelope, eldest dau. of George Bird, Esq., of Bayshill Mansion, Cheltenham.
Mrs. Tonge is Lady of the Manor of Starborough. This family is a branch of the Tonges of Highway, Wilts.—*Starborough Castle, Lingfield, Godstone.*

TOOKE. (See *Chevall-Tooke*).

TOOTAL, EDWARD, Esq., of Weaste, Lancashire.
Youngest son of the late Thomas Tootal, Esq., of Cheret, co. York, by Eleanor Minethorpe, of Pigburn, co. York; *b.* 1799; *m.* 1828 Margaret, 2nd dau. of James Kennedy, Esq. Is a J.P. and D.L. for co. Lancaster.—*The Weaste, Eccles, Manchester; Athenæum Club,* s.w.

TOOTH, ROBERT, Esq., of Swift's Park, Kent.
Eldest son of the late Robert Tooth, Esq., J.P., of Cranbrook, Kent, by his 1st wife Mary Anne, dau. of John Reader, Esq., of Ashford, Kent; *b.* 1821; *s.* 1867. Is a Magistrate for Kent, and Lord of the Manor of Widehurst, in that county.—*Swift's Park, Cranbrook.*

TOPHAM, Sir WILLIAM, Knt. (cr. 1858).
Eldest son of the late Lupton Topham, Esq., of Middleham, co. York, by Mary, only dau. and heir of Edward Clough, Esq., of Acomb, co. York; *b.* 1810; *m.* 1854 Lady Mary, 5th dau. of William, 4th Duke of Portland. Is a Col. in the Army, and Lieut. of H.M.'s Hon. Corps of Gentlemen-at-Arms.—*Caldbergh, Middleham, Yorkshire; Noirmont, Weybridge; Conservative and Junior Carlton Clubs,* s.w.; *St. James's Palace,* s.w.

TOPHAM, CHRISTOPHER, Esq., of Middleham, Yorkshire.
Eldest son of the late Christopher Topham, Esq., of Middleham, by Jenny, dau. and co-heir of Mark Bulmer, Esq., of Middleham; *b.* 1797; *s.* 1832; *m.* 1831 Anne, only child and heir of the late John Dixon, Esq., of Middleham, and has issue,
* Annie Martha, *m.* 1852 the Hon. Amias Charles Orde Powlett, brother of William Henry, 3rd Lord Bolton, and has, with other issue, * Amias Christopher Thomas, *b.* 1862.
This family was formerly of Caldbergh in Coverdale, co. York.—*Middleham Hall, Bedale.*

TOPP, the Misses, of Whitton Hall, Shropshire.
Agatha Cecile and Isabella Christine, daus. and co-heirs of the late Rev. John Topp, of Whitton Hall, co. Salop, by Maria, dau. of William Harley, Esq., of Shrewsbury; *s.* 1836; are Ladies of the Manor of Whitton. The family of Topp originally from Wilts, have been seated at Whitton since 1594.—*Whitton Hall, Westbury, Shrewsbury.*

TORKINGTON, Capt. LAURENCE JOHN, of Great Stukeley, Hunts.
Eldest son of the late James Torkington, Esq., of Great Stukeley, by Elizabeth, dau. of Charles Bourchier, Esq., of Sandridge, Herts; *b.* 1809; *s.* 1828; *m.* 1839 Mary Anne, dau. of Lieut.-Col. Walker, R.A., and has issue,
* John, *b.* 1840.
Mr. Torkington, who was educated at the Charterhouse and Clare Hall, Cambridge, is a Magistrate for Hunts,
928

and was formerly Capt. 4th Light Dragoons.—*Gt. Stukeley, Huntingdon; Junior United Service Club,* s.w.

TORPHICHEN, Lord (ROBERT SANDILANDS). —Cr. 1564.
Eldest son of James, 10th Lord, by Margaret Douglas, 2nd dau. of the late John Stirling, Esq., of Kippendavie, N.B.; *b.* 1807; *s.* 1862; *m.* 1865 Helen, youngest dau. of the late Thomas Maitland, Esq., M.P., of Dundrennan, co. Kirkcudbright. Is a Magistrate for Midlothian, Lord of the Barony and Honor of Calder, and Patron of 2 livings; was formerly Capt. Scots Fusilier Guards.—*Calder House, Edinburgh; Preceptory, West Lothian, N.B.; Junior United Service and Brooks's Clubs,* s.w.
Heir Pres., his nephew James Walter (son of the late Hon. and Rev. John Sandilands, Rector of Coston, co. Leicester, who *d.* 1865, by Helen, 2nd dau. of the late James Hope, Esq., W.S., of Edinburgh), Ensign Rifle Brigade; *b.* 1846.

+TORR, the Rev. THOMAS JOSEPH, of Dummer House, Hants.
Son of the late — Torr, Esq.; *b.* 1834. Educated at Trinity Coll., Cambridge (B.A. 1855); is Rector of Bisley, Surrey, and Lord of the Manor of Dummer, which estate he purchased from S. Terry, Esq., in 1864. —*Dummer House, Basingstoke; Bisley Rectory, Bagshot.*

+TORRE, JAMES WHITWELL, Esq., of Snydale Hall, Yorkshire.
Eldest son of the late James Torre, Esq., by Rose Ellen, dau. of Edward Whitwell, Esq., and grandson of the late James Torre, Esq., of Snydale; *b.* 1805; *s.* his grandfather 1816; *m.* 1830 Jane Helena, eldest dau. of Major-General Beatson, of Henley, Sussex (she *d.* 1866). Is Lord of the Manor of Snydale.—*Snydale Hall, Normanton.*

TORRENS, Lady.
Maria Jane, youngest dau. of the late General Murray, of Glenalla, co. Donegal, and sister of Major-General Freeman Murray, late Governor of Bermuda; *m.* 1832 Major-General Sir Arthur Wellesley Torrens, K.C.B., who *d.* 1855.—*Hampton Court Palace,* s.w.

TORRENS, ROBERT, Esq.
Second son of the late Venerable John Torrens, D.D., Archdeacon of Dublin, by Mary, dau. of S. Ball, Esq., of Grouse Hall, co. Donegal; *b.* 1810. Educated at Haileybury College; is Capt. Essex Yeomanry Cavalry; was formerly in the Bengal Civil Service; elected M.P. for Carrickfergus 1869.—*Rowde Green House, Staines; Carlton Club* s.w.; 19, *Piccadilly,* s.w.

TORRENS, WILLIAM TORRENS McCULLAGH-, Esq.
Eldest son of the late James McCullagh, Esq., of Greenfield, co. Dublin, by Jane, dau. of Andrew Torrens, Esq.; *b.* 1813; *m.* 1836 Margaret Henrietta, dau. of John Gray, Esq., of Clanmorris, co. Mayo, and has issue. Educated at Trinity Coll., Dublin (B.A. 1833, LL.B. 1856), called to the Irish Bar 1836, formerly an Assistant Commissioner of the Poor Law Inquiry; was M.P. for Dundalk 1848–52; for Great Yarmouth in 1857; elected for Finsbury 1865. Author of ' The Life of the Right Hon. R. L. Sheil.' 'Life of Sir James Graham,' &c.—*Brooks's and Reform Clubs* s.w.; 49, *St. George's Road,* s.w.

TORRINGTON, Viscount (GEORGE BYNG, D.C.L.).—Cr. 1721.
Eldest son of George, 6th Viscount, by his 2nd wife Frances, dau. of the late Sir Robert Barlow, G.C.B.; *b.* 1812; *s.* 1831; *m.* 1833 Mary Anne, dau. of the late Sir John Dugdale Astley, Bart. Is a J.P. and D.L. for

Kent, Lieut.-Col. West Kent Militia, and a Lord-in-Waiting; was Governor of Ceylon 1847–50; descended from a common ancestor with the Earl of Strafford. —*Yotes Court, Maidstone*; 4, *Warwick Square, s.w.*

Heir Pres., his nephew George Stanley, Lieut. Rifle Brigade (eldest son of the late Hon. Major Robert Barlow Palmer Byng, who *d.* 1857, by Elizabeth, dau. of Col. Gwatkin, of the Bengal Army); *b.* 1841.

TOTTENHAM, ABRAHAM LOFTUS, Esq., of Glenade, co. Leitrim.

Eldest son of the late Loftus Anthony Tottenham, Esq., of Glenade, by Elizabeth Charlotte, only child of the late Hon. Abraham Creighton, only child of the late S r Francis Hopkins, Bart.; *b.* 1819; *s.* 1860; *m.* 1851 Constance Marion, dau. of the late Isaac Newton Wigney, Esq., M.P., of Brighton, and has, with other issue,

• Beresford Loftus. *b.* 1855.

Mr. Tottenham, who was educated at Trinity Coll., Dublin, is a Magistrate for co. Leitrim (High Sheriff 1847).—*Glenade, Manor Hamilton, co. Leitrim.*

TOTTENHAM, ARTHUR LOFTUS, Esq., of Glenfarne Hall, co. Leitrim.

Eldest son of the late Nicholas Loftus Tottenham, Esq., of Glenfarne Hall, by Anna Maria, elder dau. of the late S r Francis Hopkins, Bart.; *b.* 1838; *s.* 1851; *m.* 1859 Mary Ann, dau. of the late George Addenbroke Gore, Esq., of Barrowmount, Gore's Bridge, co. Kilkenny, and has, with other issue,

• Charles Gore, *b.* 1861.

Mr. Tottenham, who was educated at Eton, is a J.P. and D.L. for co. Leitrim (High Sheriff 1866), and a Magistrate for cos. Cavan and Fermanagh; late Capt. Rifle Brigade.—*Glenfarne Hall, Enniskillen, co. Leitrim; Junior United Service and Junior Carlton Clubs, s.w.; Kildare Street Club, Dublin.*

TOTTENHAM, CHARLES, Esq., of Ballycurry, co. Wicklow.

Eldest son of the late Charles Tottenham, Esq., of Ballycurry, by Catharine, eldest son of the late Sir Robert Wigram, Bart.; *b.* 1807; *s.* 1843; *m.* 1833 Isabella Catharine, youngest dau. of the late Lieut.-General Sir George Airey, G.C.B., and by her, who *d.* 1863, has, with other issue,

• Charles George, Capt. and Lieut.-Col. Scots Fusilier Guards, and M.P. for New Ross; *b.* 1835; *m.* 1859 Catharine Elizabeth, dau. of the Hon. and Rev. Sir Francis Stapleton, Bart., and has issue.

Mr. Tottenham, who was educated at Trinity Coll., Cambridge, is a J.P. and D.L. for co. Wexford, and a Magistrate for cos. Kilkenny and Wicklow; was High Sheriff of co. Wexford 1848, and of co. Wicklow 1847; M.P. for New Ross 1831–2 and 1856–63.—*Ballycurry, Ashford, co. Wicklow; University Club, s.w.*

TOTTENHAM, Lieut.-Col. CHARLES JOHN, of Woodstock, co. Wicklow.

Eldest son of the late Right Rev. Lord Robert Ponsonby Tottenham, D.D., Lord Bishop of Clogher, by the Hon. Alicia, dau. of Cornwallis 1st Viscount Hawarden, and grandson of Charles, 1st Marquis of Ely, K.P.; *b.* 1808; *s.* 1850; *m.* 1839 the Hon. Isabella Jane, eldest dau. of Cornwallis, 2nd Viscount Hawarden, and has, with other issue,

• Charles Robert Worsley, *b.* 1845.

Lieut.-Col. Tottenham, who was educated at the Charterhouse and Balliol Coll., Oxford (B.A. 1830), is a Magistrate for cos. Wicklow, Wexford, Tyrone, and Denbigh, and a J.P. and D.L. for co. Merioneth (was High Sheriff for co. Merioneth 1853, for co. Wicklow 1859, and for co. Denbigh 1861), and Lieut.-Col. Commanding the Denbighshire Yeomanry Cavalry, and Royal Merioneth Militia, formerly Capt. Mad Life

Guards.—*Plâs Berwyn, Llangollen, N. Wales; Woodstock, Newtown Mt. Kennedy; Tottenham Green, Taghmon, co. Wexford; White's and Carlton Clubs, s.w.*

TOTTENHAM, Mrs., of Rochfort, co. Westmeath.

Anna Maria, elder and only surviving dau. of the late Sir Francis Hopkins, 1st Bart., M.P., of Athboy, co. Meath, by Eleanor, dau. of the late Skeffington Thompson, Esq., of Rathnally, in the same county; *s.* her bro her, the late Sir Francis Hopkins, 2nd Bart., 1860; *m.* 1835 Nicholas Loftus Tottenham, Esq., of Glenfarne, co. Leitrim, who *d.* 1851, leaving, with other issue,

• Arthur Loftus.

(See *Tottenham of Glenfarne.*) The family of Hopkins are descended from Dr. Ezekiel Hopkins, Bishop of Derry temp. James II.—*Rochfort Park, Mullingar.*

TOTTENHAM, the Rev. ROBERT LOFTUS.

Second son of the Right Hon. and Right Rev. Lord Robert P. Tottenham, D.D., Bishop of Clogher (son of Charles, 1st Marquis of Ely), by the Hon. Alicia, 3rd dau. of Cornwallis, 1st Viscount Hawarden; *b.* 1809; *m.* 1833 Anne, dau. of Wm. Anketel, Esq., of Anketel Grove, co. Monaghan, and has, with other issue,

• Robert Loftus, Capt. R.A.; *b.* 1834; *m.* 1864 Mary Anne Kate, dau. of the late Henry Wise Harvey, Esq.

Mr. Tottenham, who was educated at Eton and St. John's Coll., Cambridge (B.A. 1833, M.A. 1840), was appointed Rector of Donaghmoine 1842, and Surrogate of Clogher diocese 1840.—*Donaghmoine, Carrickmacross.*

TOTTIE, JOHN WILLIAM, Esq., of Coniston Hall, Yorkshire.

Only son of the late Thomas William Tottie, Esq., of Leeds, by Jenny Braithwaite, only child of John Dunn, Esq., of St. Lawrence Jewry, London. and widow of Peter Garforth, Esq., of Coniston Cold; *b.* 1811; *m.* 1859 Frances Catharine, dau. and heir of the late James Braithwaite Garforth, Esq., of Coniston Cold, and has, with other issue,

• James Braithwaite Garforth, *b.* 1860.

Mr. Tottie, who was called to the Bar at the Middle Temple 1850, is a Magistrate for the W. Riding of Yorkshire.—*Coniston Hall, Bell Busk, Leeds; Windham Club, s.w.*

TOULMIN, HENRY HEYMAN, Esq., of Childwick, Herts.

Son of the late Joseph Toulmin, Esq., by Maria, dau. of Capt. Sampson, of the late H.E.I.C.'s Service; *b.* 1807; *m.* 1833 Jemima Brodie, dau. of Alexander Berjer, Esq., by whom he has

• Henry Joseph, a Magistrate for Herts. and Capt. Herts Yeomanry; late of the 10th Light Dragoons; *b.* 1834; *m.* 1861 Emma Louisa, dau. of Philip Wroughton, Esq., of Woolley Park, Berks.

Mr. Toulmin is a Magistrate for Herts (High Sheriff 1866), and for the Liberty of St. Alban's.—*Childwick Bury, St. Alban's.*

+TOULSON, JOHN PARKER, Esq., of Skipwith, Yorkshire.

Elder son of the late John Toulson Parker, Esq., of Skipwith, by Esther, dau. of John Arthur Worsop, Esq.; *b.* 1805. Is Lord of the Manor of Skipwith; has assumed the name of Toulson.—*Skipwith, Selby.*

Heir Pres., his brother the Rev. Richard Parker, M.A. of C.C.C., Cambridge, Rector of Well, and a Magistrate for co. Lincoln; *b.* 1814.

TOURNAY, Miss, of Brockhull, Kent.

Mary, eldest dau. of the Rev. William Tournay, Rector of Denton, Kent (who *d.* 1827), by Philadelphia, dau. of John Stevenson, Esq., of Teddington, Middlesex; *s.* her brother 1857. The family of Tournay acquired

3 o   629

this estate in marriage with the heir of the Brockhulls, who frequently served as High Sheriffs of and M.P.'s for Kent.—*Brockhull, Hythe.*

Heir Pres., her nephew Henry Tournay Allen, Esq. (elder son of her sister Frances Anne, by the Rev. John Henry Allen, Rector of Mappowder, co. Dorset), *b.* 1842.

TOWER, CHRISTOPHER, Esq., of Weald Hall, Essex, and Huntsmore Park, Bucks.

Eldest son of the late Christopher Thomas Tower, Esq., J.P. and D.L., of Weald Hall (High Sheriff of Essex 1840), by Harriet, 2nd dau. of the late Sir Thomas Beauchamp-Proctor, Bart., of Langley Park, Norfolk; *b.* 1804; *s.* 1867; *m.* 1836 Lady Sophia Frances, eldest dau. of John, 1st Earl Brownlow, and has, with other issue,

  • Christopher John Hume, a Magistrate for Essex; *b.* 1841 ; *m.* 1865 Mary, 2nd dau. of the late Rev. Delves Broughton, of Broughton Hall, co. Stafford (she *d.* 1865).

Mr. Tower, who was educated at Harrow and Oriel Coll., Oxford, is a J.P. and D.L. for Essex and Bucks, a Magistrate for Beds and Middlesex, and Patron of 1 living; Lieut.-Col. West Essex Militia; formerly Capt. 7th Hussars; was M.P. for Bucks 1845-7.— *Weald Hall, Brentwood ; Huntsmore Park, Iver, Uxbridge.*

+**TOWER, HARVEY,** Esq., of Braughing, Herts.

Only son of the late Rev. William Tower, by Maria, dau. and co-heir of the late Admiral Sir Eliab Harvey, G.C.B., of Rolls Park, Essex; *b.* 1831. Is a Magistrate for Herts, and a Lieut.-Col. Coldstream Guards. —*Braughing, Ware, Herts ; Guards' Club, s.w.*

TOWER, the Rev. **ROBERT BEAUCHAMP.**

Third son of the late Christopher Thomas Tower, Esq., of Weald Hall, Essex, by Harriet, dau. of the late Sir Thomas Beauchamp-Proctor, Bart. of Langley Park, Norfolk ; *b.* 1815 ; *m.* 1844 Josephine Rose, youngest dau. of the Rev. Samuel Smith, D.D. Educated at Eton and Durham University (B.A. 1837, M.A. 1841); is a Magistrate for Essex, and Rector of Moreton. —*Moreton Rectory, Ongar.*

TOWER. (See *Baker.*)

TOWNELEY, Col. CHARLES, F.R.S., F.S.A., F.A.S., of Towneley, Lancashire.

Elder son of the late Peregrine Edward Towneley, Esq., of Towneley, by Charlotte Theresa, dau. of the late Robert Drummond Esq., of Cadlands, Hants ; *b.* 1803 ; *s.* 1846 ; *m.* 1836 Lady Caroline Harriet, 5th dau. of William Philip, 2nd Earl of Sefton, and has issue 3 daughters. Col. Towneley, who was educated at St. Mary's Coll., Oscott, is a J.P. and D.L.for co. Lancaster (High Sheriff 1857), Hon. Col. 5th R. Lancashire Militia, a Magistrate for the W. Riding of Yorkshire, and a Trustee of the British Museum; was M.P. for Sligo 1848, and 1852-3.— *Towneley, Burnley ; Brooks's, White's, and Athenæum Clubs, s.w. ; 12, Charles Street, w.*

Heir Pres., his brother John, educated at Oscott Coll. ; a Dep.-Lieut. for co. Lancaster, Lieut.-Col. 5th Royal Lancashire Militia, and late M.P. for Beverley ; *b.* 1806 ; *m.* 1840 Lucy, youngest dau. of the late Sir Henry Joseph Tichborne, Bart., and has, with other issue, • Richard, educated at Ch. Ch., Oxford, *b.* 1849.

TOWNLEY, CHARLES WATSON, Esq., of Fulbourn, Cambridgeshire.

Eldest son of the late Richard Greaves Townley Esq., M.P., of Fulbourn, by Cecil, dau. of the late Sir C. Watson, Bart.; *b.* 1823 ; *s.* 1855 ; *m.* 1861 Georgiana, dau. of Maximilian D. D. Dalison, Esq., of Hampton, Kent, and has, with other issue,

  • Richard Greaves, *b.* 1863.

Mr. Townley, who was educated at Eton and Trinity Coll., Cambridge, is a J.P. and D.L. for co. Cambridge, and a Magistrate for the Isle of Ely and for Norfolk. —*Fulbourn, Cambridge ; Beaupré Hall, Wisbeach.*

930

TOWNSEND, the Rev. **CHARLES** GLOU · GRETTON, of Berwick Place, Essex.

Only son of the late Richard Townsend, Esq., of C shall, Essex, by Mary Johnson, dau. of the la, Gretton. Esq., D.L., of Springfield, and cousin late A. Johnson, Esq., of Berwick Place ; *b.* 1848 ; *m.* 1845 Elizabeth Mary, dau. of the late John Ward, Esq., of Hatfield Peverel, Essex, and has, wide other issue,

  • William Johnson Howard, *b.* 1849.

Mr. Townsend, who was educated at Clare Coll., Cambridge (B.A. 1841. M.A. 1849), is a Magistrate for Essex.—*Berwick Place, Hatfield Peverel, Chelmsford ; University Club, s.w.*

TOWNSEND, the Rev. **HENRY,** of Honington Hall, Warwickshire.

Second but eldest surviving son of the late Gore Townsend, Esq. of Honington Hall (who was a Magistrate for co. Warwick), by Lady Elizabeth, 2nd dau. of Other Lewis, 4th Earl of Plymouth; *b.* 1783; *s.* 1826; *m.* 1811 Catherine Anne, 2nd dau. of Augustus Pechell, Esq., and grand-dau. of the late Sir Paul Pechell, Bart. (she *d.* 1867). Educated at Rugby and Magd. Coll., Oxford (B.A. 1805, M.A. 1808); appointed Rector of Ilmington 1807. but resigned 1831 ; is a Magistrate for cos. Warwick and Worcester, Lord of the Manor of Honington, and Patron of that living. This is a branch of the ancient family of Townesend, or Townshend, who settled in Ireland *temp.* Charles I. —*Honington Hall, Shipston-on-Stour.*

Heir Pres., his nephew Frederick (son of his brother, the late Rev. Edward James Townsend, by Mary, only dau. of ... Hambrough, Esq., of Marchwood, Hants) ; *b.* 18 ... ; 1843 Mary Elizabeth, only child of the late Rev. ... Butler, Vicar of St. John's, Kilkenny (grand-son of the late John Butler, and great-grandson of Humphrey, 2nd Viscount Lanesborough).

TOWNSEND, HORATIO PAYNE-, Esq., of Derry, co. Cork, and Edstaston, Salop.

Eldest son of the late Rev. Chambre Corker Townsend of Derry, by his 1st wife Frances Vere. dau. of Edward Stuart, Esq. ; *b.* 1825 ; *s.* 1852 ; *m.* 1855 Mary Susanna, dau. and co-heir of the late Lieut.-Col. Thomas Cox Kirby, and has issue,

  • Charlotte Frances, and Mary Stewart.

Mr. Payne-Townsend, who was educated at Trinity Coll., Dublin, and called to the Bar at Lincoln's Inn, 18 ... is a Magistrate for co. Cork. He assumed the additional surname of Payne, in 18 ... , under the will of Horatio Payne, Esq., of Elsinston. —*Derry, Ross Carbery, Cork ; Edstaston House, Wem, Salop ; Union Club ...*

TOWNSEND, JOHN CREWE CHETWOOD, Esq., of Woodside, co. Cork.

Eldest son of the late Horatio Townsend, Esq., J.P. and D.L., of Woodside (who was High Sheriff of co. Cork 1840), by his 2nd wife Henrietta Maria ... youngest dau. of the Rev. J. Chetwood. of Glanmire, co. Cork; *b.* 1824 ; *s.* 1864. Is Capt. N. Cork R. .. This family sprung from a common ancestor ... Townshends of Norfolk.—*Woodside, Glanmire, co. Cork.*

Heir Pres., his brother Horatio Hamilton, *b.* 1830 ; *m.* Elizabeth, dau. of N. Webb Ware, Esq., of Woodfort, co. Cork.

TOWNSEND, JOSEPH, Esq., of Alveston, Warwickshire.

Seventh son of the late Gore Townsend, Esq., J.P. of Honington Hall, co. Warwick, by Lady Elizabeth, dau. of Other Lewis, 4th Earl of Plymouth ; *b.* 17 ...; *m.* 1825 Louisa, sister of Robert John, 16th Lord Willoughby de Broke, and has, with other issue,

  • Charles John, *b.* 1848.

Mr. Townsend, who was educated at the Royal Aca

Woolwich, and was formerly in the Royal Engineers, is a J.P. and D.L. for co. Warwick, and Lord of the Manor of Alveston.—*Alveston Hall, Stratford-on-Avon.*

TOWNSEND, ROBERT LAWRENCE, Esq., of Steanbridge House, Gloucestershire.
Eldest son of the late Rev. Dr. Robert Lawrence Townsend, Rector of Bishop's Cleeve, by Anne, dau. of M. Wallbank, Esq., of Malmesbury, Wilts; *b.* 1794; *s.* 1830; *m.* 1834 Elizabeth Netherton, dau. of W. Williams, Esq., and by her, who *d.* 1867, has issue,
  * Robert, *b.* 1836.
Mr. Townsend, who was educated at Winchester, is a Magistrate for co. Gloucester; is a Lieut. in the Army. His father assumed the present name on inheriting an estate devised to him by Charles Townsend, Esq., of Lyttleton.—*Steanbr.dge House, Stroud.*

TOWNSEND, the Rev. MAURICE FITZGERALD STEPHEN, of Castle Townsend, co. Cork.
Second son of the late Richard Boyle Townsend, Esq., of Castle Townsend, by Harriet, dau. of John Newenham, Esq., of Maryborough, co. Cork; *b.* 1790; *s.* his brother 1845; *m.* 1826 Alice Elizabeth, only dau. of Henry Shute, Esq., and heir of her maternal uncle Henry Stephens, Esq., of Chavenage House, Gloucester, and has, with other issue,
  * Henry John, *b.* 1827.
Mr. Townsend, who was educated at Westminster and Ch. Ch., Oxford (B.A. 1812, M.A. 1815). and appointed Rector of Thornbury 1823, is a J.P. and D.L. for co. Gloucester.—*Castle Townsend, Cork; Thornbury Rectory, Gloucestershire; Conservative Club, s.w.*

TOWNSEND, the Rev. WILLIAM LAWRENCE, of Bishop's Cleeve, Gloucestershire.
Second son of the late Rev. Robert L. Townsend, D.D., of Bishop's Cleeve, by Anne, dau. of M. Wallbank, Esq., of Malmesbury, Wilts; *b.* 1798; *s.* 1830; *m.* 1835 Ann, dau. of Henry Ricketts, Esq., of Brislington, Somerset. Educated at Bristol and Worcester Coll., Oxford (B.A. 1821, M.A. 1823); is a Magistrate for co. Gloucester, and Rector and Patron of Bishop's Cleeve.—*Bishop's Cleeve, Cheltenham.*

TOWNSEND-FARQUHAR. (See *Farquhar.*)

TOWNSHEND, Marquis (JOHN VILLIERS STUART TOWNSHEND).—Cr. 1787.
Eldest but only surviving son of John, 4th Marquis, by Elizabeth June, dau. of Lord G. Stuart; *b.* 1831; *s.* 1863; *m.* 1865 Lady Anne Elizabeth Clementina, eldest dau. of James, 5th Earl of Fife. Educated at Eton; is a Magistrate for Norfolk, a J.P. and D.L. for Herts, Patron of 2 livings, and Lieut. Staffordshire Militia; was a Clerk in the Foreign Office 1850-4, M.P. for Tamworth 1856-63.—*Rainham Hall, Fakenham; Ball's Park, Hertford; The Castle, Tamworth; United Service and Brooks's Clubs, s.w.; 6, Stratford Place, w.*
  Heir, his son John James Dudley Stuart, Viscount Raynham, b. 1866.

TOWNSHEND, Lady JAMES, of Yarrow House, Norfolk.
Elizabeth, dau. of P. Wallis, Esq.; *m.* 1st 1813 Lord James Townshend (who *d.* 1842); 2nd 1844 Capt. W. H. Henderson, C.B., R.N.—*Yarrow House, Bintree, Reepham.*

TOWNSHEND, the Rev. CHAUNCY HARE.‡
Only surviving son of the late Hare Townshend, Esq., formerly of Busbridge Hall, Surrey, by Charlotte, dau. of Sir James Lake, Bart.; *b.* 1800; is married. Educated at Trinity Hall, Cambridge (B.A. 1821, M.A.

1824); is Lord of the Manor and Patron of Walpole St. Andrew, and Lord of the Manor of Walpole St. Peter, near Lynn; Patron of a moiety of West Walton, and Lord of the Manor of Coleraine in that parish.—21, *Norfolk Street, Park Lane, w.*

TOWNSHEND, HENRY DIVE, Esq., of Trevallyn, Denbighshire.
Eldest surviving son of the late John Stanislaus Townshend, Esq., of Trevallyn (who *d.* 1826), by Dorothea, only child of Thomas Gladwin, Esq., of Stubbing, co. Derby; *b.* 1795; *s.* his brother 1861. Is a Lieut.. General in the Army, and Col. 25th Foot.—*Trevallyn, Wrexham.*
  Heir Pres., his brother George, b. 1798.

TOWNSHEND, JOHN HANDCOCK, Esq., of Myross Wood, co. Cork.
Eldest son of the late Richard Townshend, Esq., of Myross Wood, by Helena, dau. of the late Very Rev. Thomas Trench, Dean of Kildare; *b.* 1829; *s.* his grandfather 1852; *m.* 1853 Katherine Emma, 2nd dau. of the Rev. William Tower, of How Hatch, Essex, and has, with other issue,
  * Richard Harvey, *b.* 1854.
Mr. Townshend is a Magistrate for co. Cork.—*Myross Wood, Leap, co. Cork.*

TOWNSHEND, LEE PORCHER, Esq., of Wincham Hall, Cheshire.
Eldest son of the late Elward Venables Townshend, Esq., of Wincham Hall, by Cornelia Anne, dau. of Josias Du Pré, Esq., of Wilton Park, Bucks; *b.* 1804; *s.* 1845; *m.* 1832 Emma Johanna, dau. of Birkenhead Glegg, Esq., of Backford Hall, co. Chester, and has, with other issue,
  * Edward, late Capt. 5th Fusiliers; *b.* 1833; *m.* 1867 Alicia Jane, dau. of Thomas Poor, Esq., of Grappenhall Heyes, co. Chester.
Mr. Townshend, who was educated at Rugby and the Royal Military Coll., Sandhurst, is a J.P. and D.L. and Chairman of the Quarter Sessions for co. Chester, and Major Earl of Chester's Yeomanry; formerly Major 49th Foot.—*Wincham Hall, Knutsford.*

TOWNSHEND. (See under *Townshend, Marquis of,* and *Sydney, Viscount.*)

TRACY. (See under *Sudeley, Lord.*)

TRACY. (See *Hanbury-Tracy.*)

TRAFFORD, EDWARD WILLIAM, Esq., of Wroxham Hall, Norfolk.
Third and youngest son of the late Sigismund Trafford, Esq., of Wroxham, by Margaret, eldest dau. and co-heir of James Crowe, Esq., of Lakenham, near Norwich; *b.* 1809; *s.* 1842; *m.* 1st 1831 Louisa, dau. of Thomas Thistlethwaite, Esq., of Southwick's Park, Hants; 2nd 1840 Marnine, dau. of M. Antoine Lecvinach, of Saumur, Anjou, and has, with other issue,
  * William Henry, a Magistrate for Norfolk (High Sheriff 1845); *b.* 1835.
Mr. Trafford, who was educated at the Charterhouse and Trinity Coll., Cambridge, is a Magistrate for Norfolk, Lord of the Manor and Patron of Wroxham. —*Wroxham Hall, Norwich.*

TRAFFORD, Mrs., of Panthoel, Carmarthenshire.
Maria, dau. of the late John Le Marchant, Esq., of Melrose, Guernsey, by Mary, dau. of Robert P. Le Marchant, Esq., of Guernsey; *m.* 1844 Major General Thomas Samuel Trafford, of Panthoel, and formerly of

Swithamley Park, co. Stafford (who *d.* 1857) leaving, with other issue, * Edward Le Marchant, Ensign 5th Foot, *b.* 1845.—*Panthoel, Carmarthen.*

TRAFFORD, GEORGE, Esq., of Oughtrington Hall, Cheshire.

Eldest son of the late Richard Leigh Trafford, Esq., D.L., of Oughtrington Hall (who was a Judge of the Warwickshire County Court), by Eliza Frances, dau. of Thomas Tarleton, Esq., of Bolesworth Castle, Cheshire; *b.* 1833 ; *s.* 1864. Educated at Rugby. This family is descended from William Wylme, of Oughtrington, living there *temp.* Henry III. The heiress of the Wylmes married one of the Leighs of West Hall, High Leigh, co. Chester, and the late Mr. Trafford's father took the name and arms of Trafford, in pursuance of the will of Richard Trafford, Esq., his maternal uncle. —*Oughtrington Hall, Lymm, Warrington.*

TRAFFORD. (See *De Trafford.*)

+ TRAGETT, the Rev. THOMAS HEATHCOTE, of Awbridge Danes, Hampshire.

Eldest son of the late — Tragett, Esq.; *b.* 1797 ; *m.* 182- Mary, dau. of — Heathcote, Esq., and had, with other issue,

Thomas Heathcote, educated at Rugby ; *b.* 1830 ; killed in N. Zealand 1863.

Mr. Tragett, who was educated at C. C. C., Oxford (B.A. 1819, M.A. 1822), is a Magistrate for Hants ; was formerly Curate of Christ Church, Coventry (1832–13), Vicar of Timsbury, Hants (1843–53). —*Awbridge Danes, Romsey, Hants.*

TRAHERNE, GEORGE MONTGOMERY, Esq., of St. Hilary, Glamorganshire.

Elder son of the late Rev. George Traherne, M.A., Vicar of St. Hilary, and Rector of St George's, co. Glamorgan, by Elin, dau. of the late John Gilbert Royds, Esq., of Greenhill, co. Lancaster ; *b.* 1836 ; *m.* 1860 Harriet, dau. of the late Jonathan Beever, Esq. Educated at Brasenose Coll., Oxford (B.A. 1849, M.A. 1852). Is a Magistrate for co. Glamorgan.—*St. Hilary, Cowbridge.*

Heir Pres., his brother Llewellyn Edmund, late 60th Rifles. *b.* 1832 ; *m.* 186– Miss ——, and has issue, a son, *b.* 1867.

TRAHERNE, JOHN POPKIN, Esq., of Coytrehen, Glamorganshire.

Eldest surviving son of the late Morgan Popkin, Traherne, Esq., J.P. and D.L., of Coytrehen (High Sheriff of co. Glamorgan 1812), by Elizabeth Margaret, dau. of R. F. Rickards, Esq., of Llantrissant ; *b.* 1826 ; *s.* 1859 ; *m.* 1852 Arabella Diana, dau. of John Richards, Esq., of Plasnewydd, co. Glamorgan. Educated at the Royal Military Coll., Sandhurst ; is a J.P. and D.L. for co. Glamorgan (High Sheriff 1863) and Major R. Glamorgan Militia; was formerly in the 39th Foot.—*Coytrehen, Bridgend ; Junior United Service Club,* s.w.

Heir Pres., his brother Arthur, *b.* 1828 ; *m.* 1861 Harriet Margaret Anne, dau. of the late Rear-Admiral Head Hanway Christian.

TRAHERNE, Mrs., of Coedriglan, Glamorganshire.

Charlotte Louisa, 3rd dau. of the late Thomas Mansel Talbot, Esq., of Margam and Penrice Castle, co. Glamorgan, by Lady Mary Lucy, dau. of the 2nd Earl of Ilchester ; *m.* 1830 the Rev. John Montgomery Traherne, of Coedriglan, J.P. and D.L. for co. Glamorgan, and sometime Chancellor of Llandaff Cathedral, who *d. s. p.* 1860.—*Coedriglan House, Cardiff.*

Heir Pres., her husband's nephew George Montgomery Traherne, Esq., of St. Hilary (whom see).
952

TRAILL, GEORGE, Esq., of Castle Hill, Caithness-shire.

Son of the late James Traill, Esq., of Ratter, N.B. ; *b.* 1788. Called to the Scottish Bar 1811, is a J.P. and D.L. for co. Orkney, and Vice-Lieutenant of co. Caithness, which he has represented in Parliament since 1841 ; was M.P. for Shetland and Orkney 1830–4.— *Castle Hill, Caithness, N.B. ; Trefness and Gramont, I. of Orkney, N.B. ; Brooks's and Reform Clubs,* s.w. ; *Stevens's Hotel, Bond Street,* w.

TRAILL, THOMAS, Esq., of Holland, I. of Orkney.

Eldest son of the late George Traill, Esq., of Holland, by Mary, dau. of Wm. Swan, Esq., of Ayr ; *b.* 1822 ; *s.* 1840; *m.* 1846 Margaret, 2nd dau. of Robert Menzies, Esq., of Perth, and has issue,

* George, *b.* 1847.

Mr. Traill, who was educated at Edinburgh University, is a Magistrate for co. Orkney. This family, originally from co. Fife, have held property in Orkney since 1560.—*Holland, Kirkwall, N.B.*

TRAILL, THOMAS, Esq., of Westove, Orkney.

Eldest son of the late Rev. Walter Traill ; *b.* 1790 ; *m.* 1814 Anne, dau. of Patrick Fotheringham, Esq., of Kirkwall, and had issue,

John Heddle, *b.* 1816 ; *m.* 1841 Eliza Dunbar, dau. of Robert Heddle, Esq., of Melsetter, and *d.* 1847, leaving issue, * Henry William, *b.* 1843.

Mr. Traill, who was educated at Wadham Coll., Oxford, is a Magistrate for co. Orkney, and was formerly in the 21st Foot.—*Westove, Kirkwall, N.B.*

TRAILL, WILLIAM, Esq., M.D., of Woodwick, Orkney.

Eldest son of the late William Traill, Esq., of Woodwick, by his 1st wife, Harriet, dau. of the late Charles Sarle, Esq., of Kirkwall ; *b.* 1818 ; *s.* 1858 ; *m.* 1847 his cousin Emma, dau. of the late James Harvey, Esq., of Bath, and has, with other issue,

* John, *b.* 1851.

Mr. Traill, who was educated at Edinburgh University, is a Magistrate for co. Orkney. This family is a branch of the Traills of Holland, and have held property in Orkney nearly 300 years.—*Woodwick, Kirkwall, N.B. ; 144, North Street, St. Andrew's, N.B.*

TRAILL-BURROUGHS. (See *Burroughs.*)

TRANT, JOHN, Esq., of Dovea, co. Tipperary.

Eldest son of the late John Frederick Trant, Esq., of Dovea, by Caroline, dau. of Francis Brooke, Esq., of Colebrooke, co. Fermanagh; *b.* 1819 ; *s.* 1858 ; *m.* 1842 Sarah Sophia, 2nd dau. of Sir Henry Cardeu, Bart., of Templemore, and has, with other issue,

* FitzGibbon, *b.* 1849.

Mr. Trant is a J.P. and D.L. for co. Tipperary (High Sheriff 1847–8).—*Dovea, Thurles ; Carlton Club,* s.w.

TRAPPES, THOMAS BYRNAND, Esq., of Stanley House, Lancashire.

Eldest son of the late Robert Trappes, Esq., of Stanley House, by Mary, dau. of Henry Fielding, Esq., of Myerscough, co. Lancaster; *b.* 1832; *s.* 1863; *m.* 1866 Helen, dau. of Thomas Lomax, Esq., of Preston, and has issue,

* A daughter.

Mr. Trappes, who was educated at Stonyhurst Coll., is a Magistrate for cos. Lancaster and the W. Riding of Yorkshire, and Capt. Lancashire Militia. This family descend from Sir Francis Trappes Byrnand, of Nidd, co. York, *temp.* James I.—*Stanley House, Clitheroe.*

TRAVERS, Sir WILLIAM HENRY ST. LAWRENCE CLARKE-, Bart. (cr. 1804).

Eldest son of the late General Sir William Clarke, Bart., by Margaret, dau. of Thomas Prendergast, Esq., of Dublin; *b.* 1801; *s.* as 2nd Bart. 1808; *m.* 1827 Elizabeth Barbara, dau. of John Moore Travers, Esq., of Clifton, co. Cork, whose surname he assumed in 1853. Is a J.P. and D.L. for co. Cork.—*Rossmore, co. Cork; 3, Queen's Gardens, w.*

Heir, his son John Moore Travers, late Capt. 17th Regt.; *b.* 1834.

TRAVERS, Capt. ROBERT OTHO, of Great Baddow, Essex.

Eldest son of the late Thomas Otho Travers, Esq., of Leemount, co. Cork, by Mary, dau. of Charles Henry Leslie, Esq., of Wilton, co. Cork, *b.* 1819; *m.* 1856 Louisa Elizabeth, dau. of the late Thomas Joseph Turner, Esq., of Little Olivers, Stanway, Essex, and has, with other issue,

• Mordaunt Thomas Otho. *b.* 1858.

Capt. Travers, who entered the army in 1837, is a Magistrate for Essex, and Capt. and Adjutant West Essex Militia; he was formerly Capt. 1st Dragoon Guards. This family is descended from Laurentius Travers, of Natesby, co. Lancaster, who settled in Ireland A.D. 1599.—*Pitt Place, Great Baddow, Chelmsford; Army and Navy Club, s.w.*

TREACY, JOHN, Esq., of Tenikilly, Queen's Co.

Eldest son of the late John Treacy, Esq., of Tenikilly, by Mary, dau. of Kyran Delany, Esq., of Tenikilly; *b.* 1800; *s.* 1827; *m.* 1838 Mary, dau. of James Madden, Esq., of Sligo, and has, with other issue,

• John, *b.* 1838.

Mr. Treacy is a Magistrate for Queen's Co.—*Tenikilly, Mountrath, Queen's Co.*

TREBY, Miss, of Goodamoor, Devon.

Blanche Jemima, dau. of the late Paul Treby Ourry, Esq., M.P., of Goodamoor (who assumed his maternal name of Treby), by Lætitia Anne, dau. of the late Sir William Trelawny, 8th Bart., and grand-dau. of Capt. Paul Henry Ourry, R.N., who married Charity, coheiress of the Treby family; *s.* her brother, 1867. —*Goodamoor, Plympton.*

TREEBY, JOHN WRIGHT, Esq., of High Cliff, Dorset.

Eldest son of the late James Treeby, Esq.; *b.* 1809; *m.* 1st 1835 Mary, 2nd dau. of the late Richard Cockburn, Esq.; 2nd 1847 Elizabeth, only dau. of the late James Lambert, Esq., R.N. Is a J.P. and D.L. for Middlesex, and a Merchant in London; was M.P. for Lyme Regis 1865-8.—*High Cliff, Lyme Regis; Conservative Club, s.w.; 121, Westbourne Terrace, w.*

TREDCROFT, EDWARD, Esq., of Horsham, Sussex.

Eldest son of the late Henry Tredcroft, Esq., of Warnham Court, Sussex, by Mary, eldest dau. of Robert H. Crowe, Esq., and widow of James Eversfield, Esq.; *b.* 1828; *s.* 1844; *m.* 1850 Theodosia, eldest dau. of Edward Bligh, Esq., and has, with other issue,

• Henry, *b.* 1853.

Mr. Tredcroft, who was educated at Eton, is a Dep.-Lieut. for Sussex; was formerly in the 4th Light Dragoons.—*Horsham Manor, Sussex.*

TREDEGAR, Lord (CHARLES MORGAN ROBINSON MORGAN, D.C.L.).—Cr. 1859.

E'dest son of the late Sir Charles Gould-Morgan, Bart., M.P., of Tredegar, by Mary Margaret, dau. of Capt. George Stoney, R.N.; *b.* 1793; *m.* 1827 Rosamond, dau. and heir of General Godfrey Basil Mundy, of Ruperra Castle, co. Glamorgan. Educated at Ch. Ch., Oxford; is Lord Lieut. of co. Brecon (High Sheriff 1850), a J.P. and D.L. for co. Monmouth, and Patron of 4 livings; was M.P. for Brecon 1830-2 and 1835-47. —*Tredegar Park, Newport, Monmouthshire; Ruperra Castle, Cardiff; Mansion House, Brecknock; Carlton Club, s.w.; 39, Portman Square, w.*

Heir, his son Godfrey Charles. J.P. and D.L. for cos. Brecon and Monmouth. Major Royal Gloucestershire Yeomanry Hussars. M.P. for Brecon, and late Capt. 17th Light Dragoons; *b.* 1830.

TREDENNICK, JOHN ARNOLD, Esq., of Camlin, co. Donegal.

Eldest son of the late Galbraith Tredennick, Esq., of Camlin, by Anne, dau. of George Nesbitt, Esq., of Woodhill, co. Donegal; *b.* 1795; *s.* 1817; *m.* 1819 Elizabeth, dau. of Joseph Johnston, Esq., of Summer Hill, co. Donegal. Educated at Trinity Coll., Dublin; is a Magistrate for cos. Donegal, Roscommon, and Fermanagh (High Sheriff 1821).—*Camlin, Ballyshannon.*

Heir Pres., his brother George Nesbitt, *b.* 1796; *m.* 1827 Lydia, 6th dau. of the late Most Rev. William Magee, D.D., Archbishop of Dublin.

TREFFRY, the Rev. EDWARD JOHN, of Place, Cornwall.

Eldest son of Edward Wilcocks, Esq., by Jane Treffry, dau. of Thomas Dormer, Esq., co-heir with her cousin, Joseph Th mas Treffry, Esq., *b.* 1809; *s.* his cousin, and assumed the name of Treffry 1850; *m.* 1855 Anne, only dau. of Charles Steel, Esq., and has, with other issue,

• Charles Ebenezer, of Magdalen Coll., Cambridge. 1st Lieut. in the Royal Miners' Artillery; *b.* 1842; *m.* 1866 Udney Blakeley, elder dau. of the Baron von Bretton.

Mr. Treffry, who was educated at Exeter and Lincoln Colls., Oxford (B.A. 1832, M.A. 1842), is a Magistrate for Cornwall, and Patron of 1 living.—*Place, Fowey.*

TREFUSIS. (See under *Clinton, Lord*.)

TREGONWELL, JOHN, Esq., of Cranbourne Lodge, and Anderson, Dorsetshire.

Second but eldest surviving son of the late Lewis Dimoke Grosvenor Tregonwell, Esq., of Cranbourne Lodge (who *d.* 1832), by Henrietta, 2nd dau. of the late Henry William Portman, Esq., of Bryanston, Dorset; *b.* 1811; *s.* his brother 1859; *m.* 1836 Rachael, dau. of the Rev. Robert Lowth, and has issue three daughters. Mr. Tregonwell, who was educated at Eton and Ch. Ch., Oxford, is Lord of the Manor and Patron of Anderson.—*Cranbourne Lodge, Dorset; Bournemouth, Hants; Windham Club, s.w.*

TREHERNE, Mrs., of Gate House, Sussex.

Louisa Frances, dau. and heir of John Apsley Dalrymple, Esq., of Gate House; *m.* 1835 Morgan Thomas, Esq., a Magistrate for Sussex, a Dep.-Lieut. for Surrey, and some time M.P. for Coventry, who resumed the ancient family name of Treherne 1866, and *d.* 1867, having, with other issue, • Morgan Dalrymple, Capt. West Kent Militia. *b.* 1858.—*Gate House, Rye....*

TRELAWNY, Sir JOHN SALUSBURY, Bart., of Trelawne, Cornwall (cr. 1628).

Eldest son of the late Sir William L. Salusbury Trelawny, Bart., M.P., of Harewood (formerly Lord Lieutenant of Cornwall), by Patience Christian, dau. of John Phillipps Carpenter, Esq., of Mount Tavy, Devon; *b.* 1816; *s.* as 9th Bart. 1856; *m.* 1842 Harriet Jane, dau. of the late John Hearle Tremayne, Esq., M.P., of Heligan, Cornwall. Educated at Westminster and Trinity Coll., Cambridge (B.A. 1839); called to the Bar at Lincoln's Inn 1841; is a J.P. and D.L. for Cornwall, late Capt. Commanding 2nd Cornwall Rifles;

953

was M.P. for Tavistock 1843–52 and 1857–65.—*Trelawne, Liskeard; Reform Club, s.w.; 17, Prince's Terrace, s.w.*

Heir, his son William Lewis Salusbury, a J.P. and D.L. for Cornwall, b. 1844.

TRELAWNY, CHARLES, Esq., of Coldrenick, Cornwall.

Eldest son of the late Edward Trelawny, Esq., of Coldrenick, by Jane, dau. of Thomas Woollcombe, Esq., of Trolsworthy, Devon; b. 1799; s. 1807. Educated at Winchester and Oriel Coll., Oxford; was High Sheriff of Cornwall in 1822.—*Coldrenick, Liskeard.*

TRELAWNY, the Rev. CHARLES TRELAWNY COLLINS-, of Ham, Devonshire.

Son of the late George Collins, Esq., by Mary, only dau. and heir of the late Samuel Pollexfen Trelawny, Esq., of Ham (whose name he assumed 1838); b. 1793; s. his mother 1837; m. 1831 Elizabeth Ayliffe, youngest dau. of Edward Boodle, Esq., of London. Educated at Balliol Coll., Oxford (B.A. 1815, M.A. 1818); was Fellow of Balliol Coll. 1818–25; Rector of Timsbury, Somerset, 1825–41. Is maternally descended from a common ancestor with the Trelawnys, Baronets of Trelawne.—*Ham House, Plymouth.*

TRELAWNY, HARRY BRERETON-, Esq., of Shotwick, Cheshire.

Eldest son of the late Col. Charles Trelawny, of Shotwick (who assumed the name of Brereton under the will of Owen Salusbury Brereton, Esq.), by Maria, sister of the late Sir Christopher Hawkins, Bart.; b. 1792; s. 1820; m. 1821 Caroline, dau. of Capt. Monk, R.N., and has, with other surviving issue,

* Horace Dormer, late Lieut. Royal Horse Guards; b. 1824; m. 1858 the Hon. Maria Katharine, dau. of John, 1st Lord Ormathwaite, and has issue.

Mr. Brereton-Trelawny, who was educated at Eton, is a Dep.-Lieut. for co. Chester, and Lord of the Manor of Shotwick. This family is descended from a common ancestor with the Trelawnys, Barts., of Trelawne, co. Cornwall.—*Saughall, Shotwick, Chester; 30, Hertford Street, w.*

TRELAWNY, HARRY REGINALD SALUSBURY, Esq., of Harewood, Cornwall.

Second surviving son of the late Sir William Lewis Salusbury Trelawny, Bart., M.P., of Harewood (some time Lord Lieut. of Cornwall), by Patience Christian, dau. of John Phillipps Carpenter, Esq., of Mount Tavy, co. Devon; b. 1826; m. 1853 Juliana, eldest dau. of Arthur Kelly, Esq., of Kelly, Devon, and has, with other issue,

* Harry, b. 1858.

Mr. Trelawny, who was educated at the Royal Military Coll., Sandhurst, is a J.P. and D.L. for Cornwall, and Major R. Cornwall Rangers Militia; was formerly Lieut. 6th Dragoons.—*Harewood, Tavistock; Army and Navy Club, s.w.*

TREMAYNE, Lieut.-Col. ARTHUR, of Carclew, Cornwall.

Second son of the late John Hearle Tremayne, Esq., of Heligan, Cornwall (who d. 1851), by Caroline Matilda, dau. of the late Sir W. Lemon, Bart.; b. 1827; s. his uncle, Sir C. Lemon, Bart., in the estate of Carclew 1868; m. 1858 Lady Frances Margaret, 2nd dau. of John, 3rd Earl of Donoughmore, and by her, who d. 1866, has, with other issue,

* William Francis, b. 1862.

Col. Tremayne, who was educated at Eton and Ch. Ch., Oxford, is a Dep.-Lieut. for Cornwall, and a Lieut.-Col. in the Army, retired; he was formerly in the 13th Hussars.—*Carclew, Penryn; Army and Navy and Boodle's Clubs, s.w.*

904

TREMAYNE, JOHN, Esq., of Heligan, Cornwall.

Eldest son of the late John Hearle Tremayne, Esq., M.P., of Heligan, by Caroline Matilda, dau. of the late Sir William Lemon, Bart. (ext.), of Carclew, Cornwall; b. 1825; m. 1860 the Hon. Mary Charlotte Martha, eldest dau. of Charles, 2nd Lord Vivian, and has surviving issue,

* Three daughters.

Mr. Tremayne, who was educated at Eton and Ch. Ch., Oxford (B.A. 1847), is a J.P. and D.L. for Cornwall (High Sheriff 1859), a Magistrate for Devon, Lord of the Manor of Heligan, and Patron of 2 livings—*Heligan, St. Austel; Sydenham, Lew Down, Devon; Carlton and Arthur's Clubs, s.w.*

TRENCH, the Hon. ROBERT LE POER.

Son of Richard, 2nd Earl of Clancarty, by Henrietta, dau. of the late Right Hon. John Staples; b. 1809; m. 1847 Catharine Maria, dau. of John Thompson, Esq., of Clonfin, co. Longford, and has issue,

* Richard, b. 1851.

Mr. Trench is a Magistrate for cos. Galway and Roscommon, and a Commander R.N., retired.—*Ballinasloe, co. Galway.*

TRENCH, CHARLES O'HARA, Esq., of Clonfert House, co. Galway.

Eldest surviving son of the late John Eyre Trench, Esq., of Clonfert House (who d. 1864), by Grace, 3rd dau. of the late Rev. John Burdett, Rector of Rynagh and Galleen, King's Co., and of Ballygarth, co. Meath; b. 1846; s. his brother 1867. Is Ensign 14th Foot, and represents a younger branch of the family of the Earl of Clancarty.—*Clonfert House, Eyre Court, co. Galway.*

TRENCH, HENRY, Esq., of Cangort, King's Co.

Second son of the late William Trench. Esq., of Cangort (who d. 1849), by Sarah Elizabeth Frances Henrietta Ricarda, only dau. of the late Hon. Robert Moore, of Ballintubber, Queen's Co.; b. 1807; m. 1836 the Hon. Georgiana Amelia Mary, dau. of Benjamin, 1st Lord Bloomfield, and has, with other issue,

* Henry Bloomfield, b. 1840.

Mr. Trench, who was educated at Eton and Edinburgh University, is a Magistrate for co. Tipperary and King's Co. (High Sheriff 1842).—*Cangort Park, Roscrea.*

TRENCH, HENRY, Esq., of Glenmalyre, Queen's Co.

Third, out eldest surviving son of the Very Rev. Thomas Trench, Dean of Kildare (who d. 1834), by Mary, eldest dau. of the late Walter Weldon, Esq., M.P., of Rahenderry; b. 1806; m. 1838 Elizabeth, dau. of Charles L. Sandes, Esq., and has, with other issue,

* Thomas Sandes, b. 1840.

Mr. Trench, who was educated at Trinity Coll., Dublin, is a Magistrate for King's Co. and Queen's Co., and represents a collateral branch of the family of Lord Ashtown.—*Glenmalyre, Ballybrittas, Queen's Co.*

TRENCH, JOHN ALFRED, Esq., of Cerbane, co. Galway.

Eldest son of the late Rev. Frederick Fitz-John Trench, Rector of Carlow (who d. 1859), by Elizabeth, eldest dau. of John Maconchy, Esq., of Edenmore, co. Dublin; b. 1839; m. 1866 Fanetta, dau. of Wilbraham Taylor, Esq., of Hadley Hurst, Barnet, Herts. Educated at Trinity Coll., Dublin; is Lord of the Manor of Naballmore, and represents a younger branch of the family of Lord Ashtown.—Address: *St. Catharine's Park, Leixlip, co. Kildare.*

Heir Pres., his brother William Wallace, b. 1840; m. 1864 Elizabeth French, eldest dau. of the late Thomas Allin, Esq., of Avoncore, Middleton, co. Cork.

TRENCH, the Misses, of Heywood, Queen's Co.
Mary Elizabeth Sarah, Anne, and Elizabeth, daus. of the late Michael Frederick Trench, Esq., of Heywood, by Anne Helena, only dau. and heir of Patrick Stewart, Esq.; *s.* their brother, the late Lieut.-General Sir Frederick William Trench, K.C.H., M.P., 1859. Are descended from a common ancestor with the Earl of Clancarty and Lord Ashtown.—*Heywood, Ballynakil, Queen's Co.; 47, Grosvenor Street,* w.

TRENCH, Mrs., of Cloona Castle, co. Mayo.
Anne, dau. and heir of the late James Cuff Gildea, Esq., of Cloona Castle; *m.* 1856 the Rev. John Edmund Trench, Rector of Kenmare, co. Kerry, who *d.* 1860, leaving, with other issue,
* Frederick John Arthur, *b.* 1857.
This family are a branch of the noble house of Ashtown.—*Cloona Castle, Hollymount, co. Mayo.*

TRENCH, Philip Charles, Esq., late of Botley Grange, Hampshire.
Youngest son of the late Richard Trench, Esq., of Botley, Barrister-at-law, by Melesina, dau. of Rev. Philip Chenevix, and widow of Col. Rich. St. George; *b.* 1809; *s.* 1860; *m.* 1846 Ellen Maria, dau. of Thos. Turner, Esq., E.I.C.S., and has, with other issue,
* Philip Francis, *b.* 1849.
Mr. Trench, who was educated at Harrow and Haileybury Coll., is a Magistrate for Hampshire, and was formerly in the Bengal Civil Service.—*Residence : Botley, Southampton ; Oriental Club,* s.w.

TRENCH, William Steuart, Esq., of Cardtown, Queen's Co.
Fourth son of the late Very Rev. Thomas Trench, Dean of Kildare, by Maria, dau. of Stuart Weldon, Esq., of Kilmorony, Queen's Co.; *b.* 1809; *m.* 1833 Elizabeth, dau. of John Sealy Townsend, Esq., late Master in Chancery, and has, with other issue,
* Thomas Weldon, *b.* 1834.
Mr. Trench, who was educated at Armagh and Trinity Coll., Dublin (B.A. 1833), is a Magistrate for Queen's Co., and for cos. Monaghan and Kerry.—*Essex Castle, Carrickmacross, co. Monaghan ; Caraiown, Mountrath, Queen's Co. ; Kildare Street Club, Dublin.*

TRENCH.
(See under *Ashtown,* Lord, and *Clancarty,* Earl *of.*)

TRENCH. (See *Cooke-Trench.*)

TRENCH. (See *Le Poer Trench.*)

TRENCH-GASCOIGNE. (See *Gascoigne.*)

TRENCHARD, John Trenchard, Esq., of Greenhill House, Dorset.
Third son of the late Rev. George Pickard, Rector of Warmwell-cum-Poxwell, Dorset, by Frances, eldest dau. of the late Edward Payne, Esq., of Ealing House, Middlesex; *b.* 1792; assumed the name of Trenchard only, in 1840, under the will of his grand-uncle, on succeeding to the Poxwell and Ringstead estates, Dorset; *m.* 1821 Maria, eldest dau. of the late George Tennant, Esq., of Cadoxton Lodge, co. Glamorgan (she *d.s.p.* 1861). Educated at Winchester and New Coll., Oxford (S.C.L. 1812, D.C.L. 1822); called to the Bar at Doctors' Commons 1822, and was enrolled of the College of Advocates; is a J.P. and D.L. for Dorset, and Patron of 1 living.—*Greenhill House, Weymouth ; University Club,* s.w.

TRENCHARD. (See *Ashfordby-Trenchard.*)

TREVANION, Hugh Charles, Esq.
Only son of John Charles Bettesworth-Trevanion, Esq. (late of Carhayes Castle, Cornwall), by Charlotte, youngest dau. of Charles Brereton-Trelawny, Esq.; *b.* 1828; *m.* 1858 Frances, only surviving sister of Thomas George, 12th Earl of Strathmore, and has issue,
* Hugh Arundell, *b.* 1859.
This family were seated at Carhayes, Cornwall, *temp.* Edward III.—*Arthur's and Boodle's Clubs,* s.w.

TREVELYAN, Sir Walter Calverley, Bart., of Nettlecomb Court, Somerset (cr. 1661).
Eldest son of the late Sir John Trevelyan, Bart., of Nettlecomb Court, by Maria, dau. of the late Sir Thomas Spencer Wilson, Bart., of Charlton House, Kent; *b.* 1797; *s.* as 6th Bart. 1846; *m.* 1st 1835 Pauline, dau. of the Rev. Dr. Jermyn; 2nd 1867 Laura, youngest dau. of the late Capell Lofft, Esq., of Troston Hall, Suffolk. Educated at Harrow and University Coll., Oxford (B.A. 1818, M.A. 1822); is a J.P. and D.L. for Somerset and Northumberland (High Sheriff 1850), and Patron of 3 livings.—*Nettlecomb Court, Taunton ; Wallington, Newcastle-on-Tyne ; Athenæum Club,* s.w.
Heir Pres., his brother Arthur, *b.* 1802 ; *m.* 1835 Elizabeth, dau. of — Mackay, Esq.

TREVELYAN, Sir Charles Edward, K.C.B. (cr. 1848).
Fourth son of the late Venerable Archdeacon Trevelyan, and grandson of the late Sir John Trevelyan, Bart.; *b.* 1807; *m.* 1834 Hannah, dau. of Zachary Macaulay, Esq., and has, with other issue,
* George Otto (of Chirton, Northumberland), educated at Harrow ; M.A. of Trinity Coll., Cambridge ; a Dep.-Lieut. for Northumberland, and M.P. for Tynemouth ; *b.* 1848.
Educated at the Charterhouse and East-India Coll., Haileybury ; formerly in the H.E.I.C.'s Civil Service ; was Assistant Secretary to the Treasury 1812–59 ; Governor of Madras 1859–60, and a Member of the Council of the Governor-General of India 1862–5. —8, *Grosvenor Crescent,* s.w.

TREVELYAN, Thornton Roger, Esq., of Netherwitton, Northumberland.
Son of the late Thornton Raleigh Trevelyan, Esq. (who *d.* 1845), by Dorothy, dau. of — Henderson, Esq., and grandson of the late Raleigh Trevelyan, Esq., of Netherwitton ; *b.* 1843 ; *s.* his grandfather 1865 ; *m.* 1864 Duntée Wilkinson, dau. of the late J. W. Fraser, Esq. Is descended from a common ancestor with Sir W. Trevelyan, Bart.—*Netherwitton, Morpeth.*

TREVELYAN, the Rev. William Pitt, of Wolverton, Bucks.
Youngest son of the late Ven. George Trevelyan, Archdeacon of Taunton, by Harriet, dau. of the late Sir Richard Neave, Bart., of Dagnam, Essex ; *b.* 1812 ; *m.* 1852 Maria, 3rd dau. of the Hon. Philip Pleydell-Bouverie, of Brymore House, Somerset, and has, with other issue,
* William Bouverie, *b.* 1853.
Mr. Trevelyan, who was educated at Eton and Worcester College, Oxford (M.A.), is a Magistrate for co. Northampton, Vicar of Wolverton, and Rector of Calverton, Bucks.—*Wolverton Vicarage, Stony Stratford ; Oxford and Cambridge Club,* s.w.

+**TREVELYAN, Willoughby John, Esq.,** of Goldsithney, Cornwall.
Elder son of the late John Trevelyan, Esq. (who *d.* 1852), by Jane Caroline, dau. of the late Rev. J. W. Astley, Rector of Quennington, co. Gloucester ; *b.* 1838 ; is a Magistrate for Cornwall.—*Goldsithney, Marazion.*
935

TREVOR, the Misses, of Tingrith, Beds.
Mary, Elizabeth Jane, and Catherine, dans. and coheiresses of the late Robert Trevor. Esq., of Tingrith House, by Mary. dau. of the late Rev. Edmond Williamson. Rector of Milbrook, Beds ; s. their father in 1834. Are Ladies of the Manors of Tingrith and Little Hampden.—*Tingrith House, Woburn.*

TREVOR (RICE-). (See under *Dynevor, Lord.*)

TREVOR. (See *Hill-Trevor.*)

TREVOR-ROPER, CHARLES BLAYNEY, Esq., of Plâs Têg, Flintshire.
Eldest son of the late Cadwallader Blayney Trevor-Roper, Esq., of Plâs Têg (who assumed the name of Trevor), by his 1st wife Elizabeth Anne, dau. of Henry Revely. Esq. ; b. 1799 ; s. 1832 ; m. 1821 Mary, only dau. of Samuel Knight. Esq., and has, with other issue,
   a Charles James, M.A. of St. John's Coll., Oxford, a J.P. and D.L. for co. Flint and Major Flintshire Militia; b. 1823; m. 1854 Lucy Anne, dau. of Samuel Aldersey, Esq., of Aldersey Hall, co. Chester.
Mr. Trevor-Roper, who is a J.P. and D.L. for co. Flint (High Sheriff 1835), represents a younger branch of the families of Dacre and Teynham.—*Plâs Têg, Mold.*

TRIMBLE. (See *Brackenbridge.*)

TRIMLESTON, Lord (THOMAS BARNEWALL).—Cr. 1461.
Only son of John Thomas, 15th Lord, by Maria Teresa, dau. of Richard Kirwan, Esq., of Cregg Castle, co. Galway ; b. 1796 ; s. 1839 ; m. 1836 Randalina, dau. of the late Philip Roche, Esq., and grand-dau. of Randall, 13th Lord Dunsany. Is a J.P. and D.L. for co. Dublin.—*Turvey House, Dublin ; Athenæum, Union, and Windham Clubs,* s.w. ; 24, *Park Lane,* w.

TRIPP, the Rev. HENRY, of Esgair Evon, Montgomeryshire.
Eldest son of the late Rev. Charles Tripp, D.D., of Esgair Evon, Rector of Silverton, Devon, by Frances, dau. of Brigad er-General William Owen ; b. 1816 ; s. 1865 ; m. 1857 Anne, dau. of the Rev. George James Gould, Incumbent of Mariansleigh, Devon, and has, with other issue,
   a Owen Howard, b. 1862.
Mr. Tripp, who was educated at Worcester Coll.. Oxford (B.A. 1839, M.A. 1841), is Rector of Winford, Somerset, and Patron of 1 living.—*Esgair Evon, Llanbrynmair ; Winford Rectory, Bristol.*

TRIST, JOHN FINCHER, Esq., of Carnegan, Cornwall.
Eldest son of the late Thomas Trist, Esq., of Carnegan, Capt. Bengal Army, by Frances, dau. of the late John Grose, Esq., of Bloomfield House, near Bath ; b. 1822 ; s. 1849 ; m. 1848 Jane Warren, eldest dau. and co-heir of Rear-Admiral Devonshire, and has, with other issue,
   a Richard Fincher Warren, b. 1849.
Mr. Trist, who was educated at the King's School, Sherborne. is a J.P. and D.L. for Cornwall, and Capt. R. Cornwall Rangers Militia; was formerly Lieut. 41st Regt. Madras Army.—*Carnegan, Fowey ; 2, Lansdowne Place, Plymouth.*

TROLLOPE, the Ven. EDWARD, M.A., F.S.A.
Son of the late Sir John Trollope, Bart., by Anne, dau. of Henry Thorold, Esq., of Cuxwold, co. Lincoln ; b. 1817 ; m. 1846 Grace, dau. of Sir J. H. Palmer, Bart., of Carlton Park, co. Northampton. Educated at Eton and Ch. Ch., Oxford (B.A. 1840) ; is a Magistrate for co. Lincoln, Rector of Leasingham, Prebendary of Lincoln, and Archdeacon of Stow.—*Leasingham Rectory, Sleaford.*

936

TROLLOPE. (See under *Kesteven, Lord.*)

TROTTER, ROBERT ARCHIBALD, Esq., of Bush, Midlothian.
Son of the late Archibald Trotter, Esq., J.P., of Bush (formerly in the Bengal Civil Service), by Laura Maria, 2nd dau. of Thomas Chase, Esq., E.I.C.S.; b. 1814; s. 1868. Is a Magistrate for Midlothian.—*Bush, Penny-cuick, Edinburgh.*

TROTTER, JOHN, Esq., of Dyrham, Herts.
Only son of the late John Trotter, Esq., of Dyrham Park, by Felicity, dau. of Capt. Swinton, R.N., of Swinton, co. Berwick ; b. 1808 ; s. 1833 ; m. 1833 the Hon. Charlotte Amelia, dau. of Thomas Henry, 1st Lord Ravensworth. Educated at Harrow ; is a Magistrate for Middlesex, Westminster, Herts, and the Liberty of St. Alban's ; late Capt. 2nd Life Guards. This family was formerly of Glencorse, near Edinburgh.—*Dyrham Park, Barnet ; Travellers' Club,* s.w. ; 13, *Connaught Place,* w.

TROTTER, Miss, of Horton, Surrey.
Elizabeth, only surviving dau. of the late James Trotter, Esq., of Horton, Surrey, and Cattleshiell, co. Berwick, by Elizabeth, dau. of James Meyrick, Esq., and sister of the late John Trotter, Esq., M.P., of Horton ; is Lady of the Manor of Horton. This family is of Scottish extraction.—*Horton, Epsom.*

TROTTER, RICHARD, Esq., of Morton, Midlothian.
Second but eldest surviving son of the late Lieut.-General Alexander Trotter, of Morton, by Margaret Catherine, dau. of Richard Fisher, Esq., of Loretto, Midlothian ; b. 1797 ; s. 1838 ; m. 1836 Mary, dau. of the late General Sir John Oswald, G.C.B., of Dunnikier, co. Fife, and has, with other issue,
   a Henry, Lieut. and Capt. Grenadier Guards; b. 1841; m. 1866 the Hon. Eva, eldest dau. of Robert, 2nd Lord Gifford, and has issue a dau.
Mr. Trotter, who was educated at Edinburgh University, is a J.P. and D.L. for. and Convener of, co. Midlothian.—*Morton Hall, Liberton, N.B. ; Charter Hall, Dunse, Berwickshire.*

TROTTER, Lieut.-Col. ROBERT KNOX, of Ballindean, Perthshire.
Eldest son of the late William Trotter, Esq., of Ballindean, by St. Clair Stewart, dau. of Robert Knox, Esq.; b. 1832 ; m. 1833 the Hon. Mary, eldest dau. of John, 8th Lord Rollo, and has, with other issue,
   a William, b. 1834.
Lieut.-Col. Trotter is a J.P. and D.L. for co. Perth, a Lieut.-Col. in the Army. and Sub-Inspector of Militia.—*Ballindean, Inchture, N.B.*

TROTTER. (See *Bermingham-Ruthven.*)

TROUBRIDGE, Sir THOMAS HERBERT COCHRANE, Bart. (cr. 1799).
Elder son of the late Sir Thomas C.. Vincent Hope Cochrane Troubridge, Bart., C.B., by Louisa Jane, dau. of Daniel Gurney, Esq., and grand-dau. of William, 15th Earl of Erroll; b. 1860; s. as 4th Bart. 1867. This family are traditionally sprung from the ancient family of Trowbridge, of Trowbridge, Devon.—17, *Queen's Gate, Kensington,* w.
   Heir Pres., his brother Ernest Charles, b. 1862.

TROYTE, CHARLES ARTHUR WILLIAMS, Esq., of Huntsham, Devon.
Eldest son of the late Arthur Henry Dyke-Acland, Esq., of Huntsham (who assumed the name of Troyte on succeeding to the Huntsham estate), by Frances, dau. of Robert Williams, Esq., M.P., of Bridehead,

Dorset, and grandson of Sir T. Dyke Acland, Bart.; *b.* 1842; *s.* 1857; *m.* 1864 Katharine Mary. eldest dau. of John Walrond Walrond, Esq., of Bradfield, Devon (whom see), and has, with other issue,
* Arthur Acland. *b.* 1865.

Mr. Troyte, who was educated at St. Peter's Coll., Radley, Berks, and Trinity Hall. Cambridge. is a Magistrate for Devon, Lord of the Manor, and Patron of Huntsham, and Cornet 1st Devon Yeomanry Cavalry. —*Huntsham Court, Bampton.*

TROYTE-BULLOCK. (See *Bullock of North Coker.*)

TRUELL, ROBERT HOLT, Esq., of Clonmannon, co. Wicklow.

Eldest son of the late Rev. Robert Truell, D.D., of Clonmannon, by Editha, only dau. and heir of Edward Jones, Esq., of Dublin; *b.* 1797; *s.* 1830; *m.* 1824 Phœbe, 4th dau. of the Rev. George Vesey, D.D., of Derrabard House, co. Tyrone. and has, with other issue,
* Robert. *b.* 1826; *m.* 1858 Frances Emily. 4th dau. of the Rev. William Knox. Rector and Vicar of Clonleigh, Lifford, co. Donegal. and has issue. two daughters.

Mr. Truell, who was educated at Trinity Coll., Dublin (B.A. 1820), is a J.P. and D.L. for co. Wicklow (High Sheriff 1824.—*Clonmannon. Ashford, co. Wicklow; University Club, Dublin; 15. Fitzwilliam Square, Dublin.*

TRUEMAN, CHARLES, Esq.

Son of Joseph Trueman, Esq., of Walthamstow, Essex. by Mary, dau. of Thomas Daniell. Esq.; *b.* 1814; *m.* 1837 Emma Maria, dau. of W. Parkinson, Esq., of Studham Grove. Herts. Is a Merchant in London; was M.P. for Helston 1857-9.—*Walthamstow Lodge, Essex; Welwyn, Herts.*

TRURO, Lord (CHARLES ROBERT CLAUDE WILDE).—Cr. 1850.

Elder son of Thomas, 1st Lord (who was Lord Chancellor 1850-2), by his 1st wife Mary, dau. of William Wildman, Esq. (widow of William Devaynes, Esq.); *b.* 1816; *s.* 1855; *m.* 1858 Lucy, dau. of Robert Ray, Esq. Educated at the Charterhouse; called to the Bar at the Inner Temple 1842; is a J.P. and D.L. for Middlesex, Lieut.-Col. 4th Middlesex Rifle Volunteers, Capt. Commandant 1st Middlesex Light Horse Volunteers, and Lieut.-Col. 3rd Middlesex Artillery Volunteers; formerly Clerk of Assize on the Oxford Circuit.—*Reform Club, s.w.; 29, Dover Street, w.*

Heir Pres.. his brother Thomas Montagne Carrington. educated at the Charterhouse. and M.A. of Trinity Coll., Cambridge; a Barrister-at-Law of the Inner Temple, and a Commissioner of Bankruptcy; *b.* 1618; *m.* 1843 Emily. dau. of Charles Chapman, Esq., and has issue, * Thomas Montague Morison, *b.* 1856.

TRYE, the Rev. CHARLES BRANDON, of Leckhampton, Gloucestershire.

Second but eldest surviving son of the late Charles Brandon Trye, Esq., of Leckhampton Court. by Mary, dau. of the late Rev. Samuel Lysons, Rector of Rodmarton, co. Gloucester; *b.* 1806; *m.* 1832 Jane Riland, dau. of Edward Pickard. Esq. of Aston, co. Warwick, and has, with other issue,
* Henry Norwood (of Ursucan House. and Weston-sub). M.A. of Pembroke Coll., Oxford; *b.* 1825; *m.* 1865 Mary Elizabeth. only child of Richard Roberts Jee, Esq., of Hartshill, co. Warwick, and has issue, * Charles Brandon, *b.* 1867.

Mr. Trye, who was educated at Brasenose Coll., Oxford (B.A. 1829, M.A. 1832), is a Magistrate for co. Gloucester. Lord of the Manor and Patron of Leckhampton. —*Leckhampton Court, Cheltenham.*

TRYON, RICHARD, Esq., of Loddington Hall, Leicestershire.

Youngest son of Thomas Tryon, Esq., of Bulwick Park, co. Northampton, by Anne, dau. of the late Sir John Trollope, Bart., of Casewick. co. Lincoln; *b.* 1837;

m. 1867 Jane Anna Lucy, eldest dau. of the late Lieut.-Gen. W. A. Johnson, of Witham, co. Lincoln. and widow of John William Cheney Ewart, Esq., of Loddington Hall. Educated at Harrow; was formerly Capt. Rifle Brigade.—*Loddington Hall, Leicester.*

TRYON, THOMAS, Esq., of Bulwick, Northamptonshire.

Eldest son of the late Thomas Tryon, Esq., of Bulwick, by Harriet, dau. of the late Very Rev. Dr. Brereton, Dean of Lichfield; *b.* 1802; *s.* 1825; *m.* 1827 Anne, dau. of the late Sir John Trollope, Bart., of Casewick, co. Lincoln, and has. with other issue,
* Thomas, Lieut.-Col. 7th Royal Fusiliers; *b.* 1830.

Mr. Tryon, who was educated at Westminster and Ch. Ch., Oxford. is a J.P. and D.L. for co. Northampton (High Sheriff 1833), Lord of the Manors of Bulwick and Harringworth, and Patron of 1 living.—*Bulwick Park, Wansford, Northamptonshire; Boodle's Club, s.w.*

TUAM, Bishop of (the Hon. and Right Rev. CHARLES BRODERICK BERNARD, D.D.).

Second son of James, 2nd Earl of Bandon, by Mary Susan Albinia. dau. of the late Hon. and Most Rev. Charles Brodrick, Archbishop of Cashel: *b.* 1811; *m.* 1843 Jane Grace, dau. of the late Percy Evans-Freke, Esq., and sister of George, 7th Lord Carbery, and has, with other issue,
* Percy Brodrick, educated at Eton and Oriel Coll., Oxford; a Magistrate for co. Cork. and Capt. S Cork Light Infantry Militia; *b.* 1844.

The Bishop, who was educated at Balliol Coll., Oxford (B.A. 1832, M.A. 1834. D.D. 1866), was Rector and Prebendary of Kilbrogan. co. Cork, 1842-66; consecrated 1866; Patron of 95 livings.—*The Palace, Tuam, co. Galway.*

TUCHET. (See under *Audley, Lord.*)

TUCK, Mrs. GILBERT, of Strumpshaw, Norfolk.

Lydia Anne, eldest dau. of the late Robert G'lbert, Esq., of Thorpe, Norwich; *m.* 1825 Thomas Gilbert Tuck, Esq., of Strumpshaw Hall, J.P. and D.L. who *d.* 1862. Is Lady of the Manor of Brundall.—*Strumpshaw Hall, Blofield, Norfolk.*

Heir Pres.. her brother the Rev. Clement Gilbert. M.A., late Vicar of Hemsby. Norfolk; *b.* 1822; *m.* 1858 Agnes Katharine. dau. of the Rev. Thomas Henry Copeman, of Hemsby Vicarage. and has, with other issue, * Thomas Cecil Clement, *b.* 1855.

TUCKER, CHARLES, Esq., of Coryton, Devon.

Second but eldest surviving son of the late Rev. Marwood Tucker, many years Vicar of Harpford. and Rector of Venn-Ottery. Devon. by Charlotte Jane. dau. of William Foulkes. Esq., formerly of Medland, Devon; *b.* 1799; *s.* 1850 Hermana Drewe. dau. of the late Edward Wright Bond, Esq., of Wookey House, Somerset; is Lord of the Manor of Kilmington. This family have been seated at Coryton above two centuries, and Members of it were High Sheriffs of Devon in 1726 and 1763.—*Coryton Park. Kilmington, Axminster.*

Heir Pres.. his brother, the Rev. Marwood Tucker. M.A. of Balliol Coll., Oxford. and Rector of Widworthy. Devon; *b.* 1801, *m.* 1841 Anne (mother dau. of Thomas of Light. Esq.. (she *d.* 1860); 2nd 1842 Frances. dau. of John Short. Esq., and has by the former, with other issue, * Edmund Beauchamp (whom see).

TUCKER, EDMUND BEAUCHAMP, Esq., of Trevince, Cornwall.

Eldest son of the Rev. Marwood Tucker, M.A., of Balliol Coll., Oxon, and Rector of Widworthy, Devon. by Anne Cranmer, dau. of Edmund Nagle, Esq.; *b.* 1833; *m.* 1856 Maria Sadleir. dau. of Burton Persse, Esq., of Moyode Castle, co. Galway, and has issue.
* Matilda.

Mr. Tucker, who was educated at Winchester, is a

Magistrate for Cornwall; he was formerly in the Army, and represents (jointly with his aunt, Mrs. James Ford) the ancient family of Beauchamp of Trevinee. —*Trevince, Truro; Junior United Service Club*, s.w.

TUCKER, HENRY, Esq., of Bourton, Berks.
Sixth son of the late William Tucker, Esq., of Bourton; *b.* 1803; *m.* 1833 Elizabeth, dau. of Thomas Parker, Esq., of Snarestone; is a Magistrate for Berks, and a Merchant in London.—*Bourton House, Shrivenham; 30, Gresham Street*, E.C.

TUCKER, the Rev. HENRY TIPPETTS, of Angersleigh, Somerset.
Second son of the late Rev. George Tucker, Rector of Musbury and Uplyme. Devon, by Elizabeth Symes Warmington, heiress of Henry Gardener Tippetts, Esq., of Barnstaple; *b.* 1799; *m.* 1825 Charlotte, dau. of the late Rev. William Michell, of Cotleigh, Devon. Educated at St. John's Coll., Oxford (B.A. 1820, M.A. 1823); is a Magistrate for Devon, and Rector and Patron of Angersleigh; was Rector of Uplyme 1824-42.—*Leigh Court, Angersleigh, Wellington.*

TUCKER, Vice-Admiral JOHN JERVIS, R.N., of Trematon, Cornwall.
Eldest surviving son of the late Benjamin Tucker, Esq., J.P., of Trematon (who *d.* 1829), by his 1st wife Jane, dau. of the Rev. John Lyne. of Liskeard; *b.* 1802; *s.* his brother 1861; *m.* 1831 Sabina Anne. eldest dau. of Vice-Admiral James Young, and has, with other issue,
   • Jervis, Capt. R.A.; *b.* 1833.
Admiral Tucker, who entered the Royal Navy in 1816, is a Magistrate for Cornwall.—*Trematon Castle, Saltash.*

TUCKER, JOSEPH, Esq., of Pavenham, Beds.
Eldest son of the late William Tucker, Esq., of Bourton, Berks; *b.* 179—; *m.* 1841 Maria, dau. of Thomas Peacock, Esq., by whom he has an only child,
   • Mary.
Mr. Tucker, who is a Magistrate for Beds (High Sheriff 1861), and Patron of 1 living, was formerly a Merchant in London.—*Pavenham Bury, Bedford.*

TUCKER-EDWARDES, Mrs., of Sealyham, Pembrokeshire.
Anna Martha, dau. of John George Philipps, Esq., M.P., of Cwmgwilly, co. Carmarthen; *m.* 1807 William Tucker-Edwardes, Esq., J.P. and D.L. for co. Pembroke (High Sheriff 1829). and Major R. Pembroke Militia, who *d.* 1858, leaving issue,
   • John Owen, *b.* 1808; *m.* 1840 Anna Jane, dau. of W. Jones, Esq., of Heathfield, co. Pembroke.
The Tuckers have resided at Sealyham for upwards of 400 years. The Edwardes's are descendants of Tudor Trevor.—*Sealyham, Haverfordwest.*

TUCKEY, CHARLES HENRY, Esq., of Carlow.
Son of the late Rev. Dr. Tuckey, by Elizabeth. dau. of John Lloyd, Esq., of Lloydsborough, Templemore; *b.* 1795; *m.* 1841 Ellen, dau. of Davys Tuckey, Esq., of Cork, and has issue,
   • Charles, B.A. of Trinity Coll., Dublin, and Ensign 87th Foot; *b.* 1841.
Mr. Tuckey is a Magistrate for Queen's Co., and for cos. Carlow, Kildare, Kilkenny, Wicklow, and Wexford; appointed resident Magistrate at Carlow 1837; late Inspector of the Constabulary of Kilkenny.—*Carlow.*

TUDOR, GEORGE SINGLETON, Esq., of Lapley, Staffordshire.
Eldest son of the late William Tudor, Esq., of Merridale, co. Stafford, by Mary Ann, dau. of George Singleton, Esq., of Wolverhampton; *b.* 1827; *m.* 1849

938

Mary, dau. of David Jones Bache, Esq., of Wolverhampton, and has, with other issue,
   • George William Henry, *b.* 1859.
Mr. Tudor is a Magistrate for co. Stafford and Captain Commandant 5th Staffordshire Rifle Volunteers.—*Park House, Lapley, Penkridge.*

TUDWAY, CHARLES CLEMENT, Esq., of The Cedars, and Stobery Park, Somerset.
Only surviving son of the late Robert Charles Tudway, Esq., of The Cedars (who was some time M.P. for Wells), by Maria Catherine, eldest dau. of Sir William Miles, Bart., of Leigh Court, Somerset; *b.* 1846; *s.* 1855. Educated at Harrow; is Capt. Wells Yeomanry Cavalry.—*The Cedars, and Stobery Park, Wells.*
   Heir Pres., his uncle,Henry, M.A. of Trinity Coll., Oxford, in Holy Orders; *b.* 1826; *m.* 1856 Mary, dau. of John Phipps, Esq., of Leighton House, Wilts.

TUFNELL, JOHN JOLLIFFE, Esq., of Langleys, Essex.
Eldest son of the late John Jolliffe Tufnell, Esq., J.P. and D.L., of Langleys (who was High Sheriff of Essex in 1823), by Catherine Dorothy, eldest dau. of Sir Michael Pilkington, Bart., of Chevet, co. York; *b.* 1805; *s.* 1864; *m.* 1st 1830 Caroline Mary, 2nd dau. of the late Christopher T. Tower, Esq., of Weald Hall, Essex (she *d.* 1841); 2nd 1853 Eleanor Margaret, 6th dau. of the late Right Rev. Dr. George Murray, Lord Bishop of Rochester, and has by the former, with other issue,
   • Arthur Jolliffe, a Magistrate for Essex, and Capt. 61st Foot; *b.* 1833.
Mr. Tufnell, who was educated at Harrow and Oriel Coll., Oxford, is a J.P. and D.L. for Essex, Lord of the Manor of Gt. Waltham, and Patron of 2 livings. —*Langleys,Gt.Waltham,Chelmsford; Arthur's Club,* s.w.

TUFNELL, WILLIAM MICHAEL, Esq., of Hatfield Place, Essex.
Second son of the late John Jolliffe Tufnell, Esq., of Langleys, by Catherine Dorothy, eldest dau. of the late Sir Michael Pilkington, Bart., of Chevet Hall, co. York; *b.* 1816; *m.* 1841 Eliza Isabella, eldest dau. of Sir John T. Tyrell, Bart., of Boreham House, Essex, and has, with other issue,
   • John Lionel, educated at Harrow; Lieut. Rifle Brigade; *b.* 1842.
Mr. Tufnell, who was educated at Winchester, is a J.P. and D.L. for Essex a Banker at Chelmsford, and Lieut.-Col. Commandant Essex Volunteers; he purchased this property from the late Rev. W. Walford in 1848.—*Hatfield Place, Chelmsford; Carlton Club,* s.w.

TUFTON, Sir RICHARD, Bart., of Appleby. Westmorland, and Hothfield, Kent (cr. 1851).
Natural son of the late Earl of Thanet (whose estates he inherited by will), by a foreign lady; *b.* 1813; *m.* 1843 Adelaide Amelia Lacour. Is a Dep.-Lieut. for Kent (High Sheriff 1859), and Patron of 10 livings; was naturalized in 1849, when he assumed the name of Tufton.—*Skipton Castle, Yorkshire; The Castle, Appleby; Hothfield Place, Ashford.*
   Heir, his son Henry Jacques, educated at Ch. Ch., Oxford; a Magistrate for Kent; *b.* 1844.

TUITE, Sir MARK ANTHONY HENRY, Bart., of Lislievoolin, co. Westmeath (cr. 1622).
Eldest son of the late Sir George Tuite, Bart., of Lislievoolin, by Janet, widow of Major Thomas Woodall, 12th Regt.; *b.* 1808; *s.* as 10th Bart., 1841; *m.* 1854 Charlotte. dau. of R. H. Levinge, Esq., of Levington Park, co. Westmeath. Educated at Trinity Coll., Dublin; formerly Capt. 19th Foot.—*Lislievoolin, Mullingar, co. Westmeath.*
   Heir Pres., his brother Hugh Manley, Major General Royal

Artillery; b. 1811; m. 1854 Fanny, dau. of Dr. Williams, late of the 68th Regt., and has, with other issue, *Morgan Harry Paulet, b. 1861.

TUITE, HUGH MORGAN, Esq., of Sonna, co. Westmeath.

Eldest surviving son of the late Hugh Tuite, Esq., of Sonna, by Sarah Elizabeth, dau. of the late Lieut.-Col. D. Chenevix, of Corcagh; b. 1794; s. 1843; m. 1st 1826 Mary, dau. of Maurice Nugent O'Connor, Esq., of Mount Pleasant, King's Co. (she d. 1863); 2nd 1863 Hester M., dau. of J. Hagan, Esq., of Antrim; he has by the former, an only son,

     * Joseph. of Cullen. Mullingar, co. Westmeath; a Magistrate for co. Westmeath (High Sheriff 1868), and late an Officer in the 15th Regt.; b. 1828; m. 1st 1852 Ellen Mary, dau. of the Rev. Charles Fox Chawner, Rector of Bletchingley. Surrey (she d. 1863); 2nd 1868 Ellen, youngest dau. of the late J. B. Boothby, Esq., of Twyford Abbey, Middlesex; he has by the former, with other issue, * Henry Maurice, b. 1857.

Mr. Tuite, who was educated at Ch. Ch., Oxford, is a J.P. and D.L. for co. Westmeath (High Sheriff 1822), and a Magistrate for co. Longford (High Sheriff 1837); he was M.P. for co. Westmeath 1826–30 and 1841–7. —*Sonna, Mullingar, co. Westmeath; Kildare Street Club, Dublin; Brooks's and Reform Clubs, s.w.*

TULL, RICHARD, Esq., of Crookham, Berks.

Eldest son of the late Richard Tull, Esq., of Crookham House, by Mary, dau. of Thomas May, Esq.; b. 1801; s. 1822; m. 1834 Sarah, dau. of John Sancton, Esq., of Hornsey, Middlesex, and has, with other issue,

     * Albert Richard, b. 1835.

Mr. Tull is a J.P. and D.L. for Berks.—*Crookham House, Newbury.*

TULLIBARDINE. (See under *Athole, Duke of.*)

TULLOCH, Lady.

Emma Louisa, dau. of the late Sir William Hyde Pearson, Knt., M.D., F.R.S. (who d. 1848), by Elizabeth Jane, dau. of Thomas Francis Jennings, Esq., of Park Hill, near Doncaster, co. York; m. 1844 Major-General Sir Alexander Murray Tulloch, K.C.B., who d. 1864.

TUNNARD, the Rev. JOHN, of Frampton House, Lincolnshire.

Eldest son of the late Charles Keightley Tunnard, Esq., J.P., of Frampton House, by Charlotte, youngest dau. of Bartholomew Claypon, Esq., of Boston; b. 1814; s. 1837; m. 1843 Martha Copland, dau. of Charles Tawney, Esq., and has, with other issue,

     * Charles Thomas, educated at Eton, b. 1843; m. 1866 Georgina, 3rd dau. of Conolly Norman, Esq., of Crosthwaite Park, co. Dublin.

Mr. Tunnard, who was educated at Eton and Exeter Coll., Oxford (B.A. 1837, M.A. 1819), is a Magistrate for co. Lincoln, and Patron and Vicar of Frampton. —*Frampton House, Boston.*

TUNNICLIFFE, HENRY COTTON, Esq., of Yarlet, Staffordshire.

Eldest son of the late John Tunnicliffe, Esq., of Yarlet, by Sarah, dau. of Thomas Sockett, Esq., of Wellington, co. Salop; b. 1821; s. 1858; m. 1841 Anne Jane, dau. of the Rev. Edward Freeman Parsons, of Whitley, co. Chester, and has, with other issue,

     * George Henry, b. 1860.

Mr. Tunnicliffe is Lord of the Manor of Yarlet, and a Merchant at and Magistrate for Liverpool.—*Yarlet, Stafford; Wavertree, Liverpool; Conservative Club, s.w.*

TUNNO, of Warnford Park. (See *Sartoris, Edward, Esq.*)

TUPPER, FERDINAND BROCK, Esq , of Guernsey.

Eldest surviving son of the late John E. Tupper, Esq., by Elizabeth, dau. of John Brock, Esq., of Guernsey,

and sister of the late Major-General Sir Isaac Brock, K.B.; b. 1795; m. 1834 Marianne eldest dau. of the late General Dennis Herbert. Mr. Tupper, who was educated at Harrow, is a member of a family which has been seated in Guernsey since 1592.—*Guernsey.*

TUPPER, MARTIN FARQUHAR, Esq., D.C.L., F.R.S., of Albury, Surrey.

Eldest son of the late Martin Tupper, Esq., of Guernsey, by Ellin Devis, dau. of Robert Marris, Esq., of co. Lincoln; b. 1610; s. 1844; m. 1835 Isabella, only dau. of A. W. Devis, Esq., late of Calcutta, and has, with other issue,

     * Martin Charles Selwyn, b. 1841.

Mr. Tupper, who was educated at the Charterhouse and Ch. Ch., Oxford (B.A. 1832, M.A. 1845, D.C.L. 1847), and was called to the Bar at Lincoln's Inn 1835, is descended from a Lutheran ancestor exiled from France in 1549, by Charles V.—*Albury, Guildford ; Furze Hill, Brighton.*

TURBERVILL, Capt. THOMAS PICTON, of Ewenny Abbey, Glamorganshire.

Eldest son of the late Capt. Thomas Warlow, R.E., and grandson of the late John Warlow, Esq., of Haverfordwest, and of Catherine, dau. of Thomas Picton, Esq., of Poyston, Rudbaxton, co. Pembroke; b. 1827; m. 1857 Lucy Eliza, only dau. of the late Lieut.-Col. Henry Connop, of Birdhurst, Croydon, of the 93rd Highlanders. Educated at the Academy, Woolwich; is a Magistrate for co. Glamorgan, Lord of the Manor of Ewenny, Patron of 2 livings, and a Capt. R.A.; he assumed the name of Turbervill by Royal licence 1867, in lieu of Warlow, on succeeding to the estates of his cousin, the late Miss Elizabeth Margaret Turbervill of Ewenny. —*Ewenny Abbey, Bridgend; Junior United Service Club, s.w.*

TURBETT, JAMES EXHAM PUREFOY, Esq., of Owenstown, co. Dublin, and Kilmackshane, co. Galway.

Only child of the late Robert Turbett, Esq., of Greenmount, by Mary, dau. of Capt. James Purefoy, of Woodfield, co. Galway; b. 1790; m. 1822 Sophia, eldest dau. of the late Hon. and Rev. George Gore, D.D., Dean of Killala, and has, with other issue,

     * Robert Exham, b. 1828; m. 1858 Lucy, 3rd dau. of Capt. Benjamin Lefroy, J.P., of Cardenton House, co. Kildare.

This family is identical with that of the Turbutts of Derbyshire.—*Owenstown House, Dundrum, co. Dublin.*

TURBUTT, GLADWIN, Esq., of Ogston, Derbyshire.

Only son of the late William Turbutt, Esq., of Ogston, and of Arnold Grove, Notts, by Anne, dau. of General Gladwin, of Stubbin Court, co. Derby; b. 1823; s. 1836; m. 1850 Ellen, youngest dau. of the late Baldwin Duppa Duppa, Esq., of Hollingbourne House, Kent, and has, with other issue,

     * William Gladwin, b. 1853.

Mr. Turbutt, who was educated at Ch. Ch., Oxford (B.A. 1846), and afterwards a student of the Inner Temple, is a J.P. and D.L. for co. Derby (High Sheriff 1858), and Lord of the Manor of Ogston and of half the Manors of Shirland and Stratton, and Patron of 2 livings.—*Ogston Hall, Alfreton; University Club, s.w.*

TURING, Sir ROBERT FRASER, Bart., of Foveran, Aberdeenshire (cr. 1638).

Eldest son of the late Sir James Henry Turing, Bart., of Foveran, by Antoinette, dau. of the late Sir Alexander Ferrier, K.H.; b. 1827; s. as 4th Bart. 1860; m. 1853 Catherine Georgiana, 2nd dau. of Walter S. Davidson, Esq., of Lowndes Square, London. Is British Consul at Rotterdam. This title, dormant for

many years, was resumed 1792.— *British Consulate, Rotterdam.*

Heir, his son James Walter, b. 1862.

TURNBULL, JOHN, Esq., of Abbey St. Bathan's, Berwickshire.
Eldest son of the late George Turnbull, Esq., of Abbey St. Bathan's, by Grace, dau. of James Brunton, Esq.; *b.* 1820; *s.* 1855. Educated at the High School and University of Edinburgh; became a Writer to the Signet in 1841; is a J.P. and D.L. for co. Berwick, and a Capt. in the Royal Midlothian Yeomanry Cavalry.— *Abbey St. Bathan's, Dunse, N.B.;* 49, *George Square, Edinburgh; Caledonian United Service Club, Edinburgh.*

TURNER, Sir EDWARD HENRY PAGE-, Bart., of Battlesden Park, Beds (cr. 1733).
Only son of the late Sir Edward George Thomas Page-Turner, Bart., of Battlesden Park, by Miss Williams, of Southampton - *b.* 1823; *s.* as 6th Bart. 1846. Educated at Ch. Ch., Oxford (B.A. 1844); is a Magistrate for Beds, and Patron of 7 livings. The 3rd Bart. assumed the name of Page on succeeding to the property of Sir G. Page, Bart.—*Battlesden Park, Dunstable; Conservative Club, s.w.;* 18, *Wilton Place, s.w.*

Heir Pres., his cousin Sir Henry Edward Leigh Dryden, Bart. (whom see).

TURNER, Sir WILLIAM WEST, K.C.S.I. (cr. 1867).
Son of the late W. Turner, Esq.; *b.* 1823. Is a Colonel in the Army, late of the 27th Regt.; some time Brigadier commanding the second column of the Bundlecund Field Force.

TURNER, Lady.
Louisa; dau. of E. Jones, Esq.; *m.* 1823 the Rt. Hon. Sir George James Turner, Knt., Judge of Appeal in Chancery, who *d.* 1867, leaving, with other issue, • George Richard, in Holy Orders, M.A. of Caius Coll., Cambridge, and Rector of New Radnor: *b.* 1824; *m.* 1857 Emily Murray, youngest dau. of the late John Edwards, Esq., of Ness Strange, co. Salop.—*Moult, Kingsbridge, Devon;* 23, *Park Crescent, N.W.*

TURNER, Lady, of Menie, Aberdeenshire.
Margaret, dau. of the late John Ramsay, Esq., of Barra, co. Aberdeen (who *d.* 1832), by Susan, 3rd dau. of the late Alexander Innes, Esq., of Pitmedden, co. Aberdeen; *m.* 1822 Lieut.-Gen. Sir George Turner, K.C.B., of Menie, who *d.* 1864, leaving surviving issue, Helen an1 Rubina.—*Menie, Belhelvie, N.B.*

TURNER, ANGUS, Esq., of Glentyre, Perthshire.
Son of the late John Turner, Esq., of Greenfield, co. Dumbarton, by Christina, dau. of James Morrison, Esq., of co. Argyle; *b.* 1800; *m.* 1830 Mary, dau. of Robert Græme, Esq., of Garvock, co. Perth (whom see), and has issue two daughters,
• Jane Anne Aytoun, *m.* 1857 R. R. Bewley Caton, Esq. (late Royals), only son of R. R. Caton, Esq., of Binbrook and Bishop Norton, co. Lincoln; and Mary Helena de Jersey, *m.* 1863 Capt. Luke Edward O'Connor, of the 8-th Regt.
Mr. Turner, who was educated at Glasgow University, is a Commissioner of Supply, and a Magistrate for cos. Perth and Lanark; appointed Legal Assessor and Town Clerk of Glasgow 1859.—*Pitcairns House, Bridge of Earn;* 14, *Woodside Terrace, Glasgow; Conservative Club, s.w.*

TURNER, CHARLES, Esq., of Ferriby, Yorkshire.
Son of the late Ralph Turner, Esq., of Kingston-on-Hull, by Rachel, dau. of Horner Reynard, Esq., of Sunder Lindwick, co. York; *b.* 1803; *m.* 1843 Anne,
940

dau. of C. Whitaker, Esq., of Melton Hill, co. York, and has, with other issue,
• Charles William, *b.* 184-.
Mr. Turner, who is a J.P. and D.L. for co. Lancaster, and a Magistrate for Liverpool and a Merchant in that city, was M.P. for Liverpool 1852-3; elected M.P. for South Lancashire 1861.—*Dingle Head. Liverpool; Ferriby, Yorkshire; Union and Carlton Clubs, s.w.*

TURNER, the Rev. CHARLES MICHAEL, of Aldford, Cheshire.
Eldest son of the late Lieut.-General Turner, Col. 19th Regt., by Harriet, dau. of the Very Rev. George Stevenson, LL.D., Dean of Kilfenora. Ireland; *b.* 1810; *m.* 1844 Louisa, dau. of Thomas W. Tatton, Esq., of Wythenshawe. co. Chester, and has, with other issue,
• Frederic Mansel, *b.* 1846.
Mr. Turner, who was educated at Caius Coll., Cambridge (B.A. 1837), is a Magistrate for Essex, and Rector of Aldford.—*Aldford Rectory, Chester.*

+**TURNER, HENRY EDWARD, Esq., of Rook's Nest, Surrey.**
Only surviving son of the late Charles Hampden Turner, Esq., of Rook's Nest (who *d.* 1842). by Henrietta, youngest dau. of the late Matthew Wilson, Esq., of Eshton. Hall, co. York; *b.* 1840; *s.* his brother 1866. Is a Magistrate for Surrey, and Patron of 1 living.—*Rook's Nest, Tandridge, Godstone.*

+**TURNER, JOHN JAMES, Esq., of Pentreheylin, Montgomeryshire.**
Son of the late — Turner, Esq., of Pentreheylin; *b.* 18—; is married, and has issue. Is a J.P. and D.L. for co. Montgomery.—*Pentreheylin, Oswestry.*

TURNER, Mrs., of Little Oliver's, Essex.
Jane, dau. of John Bawtree, Esq., of Abberton. Essex; *m.* 1820 Thomas Joseph Turner, Esq., of Little Oliver's, a J.P. and D.L. for Essex, and formerly Capt. H.E.I.C.S., who *d.* 1866, leaving issue, two daughters. —*Little Oliver's, Stanway, Colchester.*

TURNER, Mrs., of Pendlebury House, Lancashire.
Sarah, dau. of R. G. Blackmore, Esq., of Manchester; *m.* 1823 James Aspinall Turner, Esq., of Pendlebury House, who was a J.P. and D.L. for co. Lancaster. and some time M.P. for Manchester. and who *d.* 1867, leaving issue.—*Pendlebury House, Manchester.*

TURNER. (See *Tollhill Turner.*)

TURNER-FARLEY, THOMAS MACNAGHTEN, Esq., of Marnhull, Dorset.
Second, but eldest surviving. son of the late Thomas Jacob Turner, Esq., of Worthy Park. Hants, by Eliza Rachel Lowe, only dau. of Colonel McComb'e. LR., Commander 14th Regt., and grandson of the late Jacob Turner, Esq., of Park Hall, co. Worcester, by Ann. only dau. of Thomas Farley, Esq., of Horwick, co. Worcester; *b.* 1859. Educated at Eton; assumed the additional name of Farley, by Royal license, 1867; was formerly Lieut. 3rd Hussars.—*Marnhull, Blandford, Dorset; Junior United Service Club, s.w.*

TURNLY, ROBERT ALEXANDER, Esq., of Drumnasole, co. Antrim.
Eldest son of the late Francis Turnly, Esq., of Drumnasole. by Dorothea Emelia. dau. of Col. John Rochfort, of Clogrenane, co. Carlow; *b.* 1805; *s.* 1845. Educated at Trinity Coll., Dublin. This family settled in Ireland *temp.* Oliver Cromwell.—*Drumnasole, Glenarm, co. Antrim.*

Heir Pres., his brother John, B.A. of Trinity Coll., Dublin.

and a Magistrate and Grand Juror for co. Antrim; *b.* 1819; *m.* 1850 Charlotte Emily, dau. of Edward Litton, Esq., Q.C.

TURNOR, CHRISTOPHER, Esq., of Stoke Rochford, Lincolnshire.

Second son of the late Edmund Turnor, Esq., of Stoke Rochford and Panton House, by his 2nd wife Dorothea, dau. of Lieut.-Col. Tucker; *b.* 1809; *s.* 1829; *m.* 1837 Lady Caroline, dau. of William, 10th Earl of Winchilsea, and has, with other issue,

* Edmund (of Panton Hall, Wragby), educated at Rugby and Ch. Ch., Oxford; a Magistrate for co. Lincoln, and M.P. for Grantham; *b.* 1838; *m.* 1866 Lady Mary Katherine, eldest dau. of Charles, 19th Marquis of Huntly.

Mr. Turnor, who was educated at Eton and Trinity Coll., Cambridge, is a J.P. and D.L. for co. Lincoln (High Sheriff 1833), and Lord of the Manor of Binbrook, and Patron of 5 livings; was M.P. for S. Lincolnshire 1841–7.—*Stoke Rochford, Grantham; Carlton and National Clubs*, s.w.; 34, *Chesham Place*, s.w.

TURNOUR. (See under *Winterton, Earl of.*)

TURTON, Capt. EDMUND HENRY, of Upsall, Yorkshire.

Eldest son of the late Edmund Turton, Esq., M.P., of Upsall, by Marianne, only child and heir of the late Robert Bell Livesey, Esq., of Kildale; *b.* 1825; *s.* 1857; *m.* 1856 Lady Cecilia Mary, eldest dau. of Joseph, 4th Earl of Miltown, and has, with other issue,

* Edmund Russborough, *b.* 1857.

Mr. Turton, who was educated at Eton, is a J.P. and D.L. for the N. Riding of Yorkshire; late Capt. 3rd Dragoon Guards.—*Upsall, near Thirsk; Larpool Hall and Ugthorpe Lodge, Whitby; Reform and Army and Navy Clubs*, s.w.

TURTON, Capt. FRANCIS WILLIAM, R.N., of Lea House, Staffordshire.

Eldest son of the late Rev. Henry Turton, Vicar of Betley, co. Stafford, by Harriet Elizabeth, eldest dau. of the late Francis Hickin Northen, Esq., of Lea House; *b.* 1830; *s.* his maternal grandfather 1861; *m.* 1856 Sophy, eldest dau. of the late F. Curwen Smith. Esq., of Frognal Hall, Hampstead, and has, with other issue,

* Francis Montagu, *b.* 1863.

Mr. Turton, who was appointed to the Royal Navy in 1863, is a Commander R.N. This family was formerly of Sugnall, co. Stafford.—*Lea House, Eccleshall; Junior Unit.d Service Club*, s.w.

+**TURVILLE, FRANCIS CHARLES FORTESCUE, Esq., of Bosworth Hall, Leicestershire.**

Eldest son of the late George Fortescue Turville, Esq., of Bosworth Hall, by Henrietta, dau. of Baron von der Lancken, of Galenbeck, Mecklenburg-Schwerin; *b.* 1831; *s.* 1859; was formerly Capt. Oxford Militia. —*Bosworth Hall, Rugby.*

TUTHILL. (See *Cooper.*)

TWEED, the Rev. JOSEPH BARTHORP, of Capel, Suffolk.

Eldest son of the late Rev. Joseph Tweed, Rector and Patron of Capel, by Caroline Frances, dau. of Robert Barthorp, Esq., of Hollesley, Suffolk; *b.* 1831 : *s.* 1867 ; *m.* 1860 Sarah Anne, dau. of Thomas Vallance, Esq., of Sittingbourne, Kent. Educated at C.C.C., Cambridge (B.A. 1856); is Rector and Patron of Capel-cum-Wenham. This family is of ancient Scottish extraction.—*Capel Rectory, Ipswich.*

TWEEDDALE, Marquis of (GEORGE HAY, K.T., K.C.B.)—Cr. 1694.

Eldest son of George, 7th Marquis, by Lady Hannah Charlotte, dau. of James, 7th Earl of Lauderdale; *b.*

1787; *s.* 1804; *m.* 1816 Lady Susan, dau. of William, 5th Duke of Manchester. Is a General in the Army, Col. 2nd Life Guards; late Col. 42nd Foot; Lord-Lieutenant of co. Haddington, a Magistrate for co. Berwick and Fife, and Gold-Stick in Waiting to the Queen; was Governor and Commander-in-Chief at Madras 1841–6.—*Yester House, Haddington, N.B.; United Service and Junior United Service Clubs*, s.w.

Heir, his son Arthur Hay, Viscount Walden, a Col. in the Army, late Lieut.-Col. 17th Lancers; *b.* 1824; *m.* 1857 Helena Eleonore Charlotte Auguste, only child of the late Count Adolphe Auguste Frederic of Kielmansegge.

TWEEDIE, JAMES, Esq., of Quarter and Rachan, Peeblesshire.

Eldest son of the late Thomas Tweedie, Esq., of Quarter and Rachan, Physician-General H.E.I.C.'s service, by Benjamina, dau. of Charles Mackay, Esq.; *b.* 1831; *s.* 1855; *m.* 1863 Emma Charlotte, 2nd dau. of David Cunliffe, Esq., E.I.C.S., and has, with other issue,

* A son, *b.* 1864.

Mr. Tweedie was educated at Edinburgh University, entered the Army 1851, and retired as Lieut. 1855; he is Magistrate for co. Peebles, and Lord of the Baronies of Rachan, Kingsdores, and Manner. *Rachan House, Hall Manor, Biggar, N.B.; United Service Club, Edinburgh.*

TWEEDIE, Capt. MICHAEL, of Rawlinson, Kent.

Fourth son of the late Alexander Tweedie, Esq., of Quarter, co. Peebles, by Anne, dau. of Michael Carmichael, Esq., of East End, co. Lanark; *b.* 1794; *m.* 1826 Frances, dau. of Richard Walter Forbes, Esq., of Rawlinson, and has, with other issue,

* Alexander Forbes, Solicitor, *b.* 1826; *m.* 1859 Alice, dau. of Robert Bell, Esq., of Gower Street, London, and has issue.

Capt. Tweedie, who was educated at Edinburgh and the Military Colleges of Marlow and Woolwich, is a Magistrate for Kent, and a retired Officer in the Royal Artillery.—*Rawlinson, Rolvenden, Staplehurst.*

TWEEDIE-STODART, GEORGE, Esq., of Oliver, Peeblesshire.

Eldest son of the late Thomas Stodart, Esq. (who *d.* 1820), by Christian, dau. of Thomas Tweedie, Esq., of Oliver; *b.* 1799; *s.* his uncle Laurence Tweedie, Esq., of Oliver, whose name he assumed. 1837; *m.* 1833 Mary, dau. of Alexander Paul, Esq., of Birmingham, and has, with other issue,

* Thomas, *b.* 1838.

Mr. Tweedie-Stodart, who was educated at Edinburgh, and admitted a Writer to Her Majesty's Signet in 1821, is a Magistrate for co. Peebles. The family of the Tweedies has been in possession of Oliver for several centuries. — *Oliver, Crook, Biggar, N.B.; 16, Abercromby Place, Edinburgh.*

TWEMLOW, THOMAS, Esq., of Peatswood, Staffordshire.

Eldest son of the late Thomas Twemlow, Esq. of Sandbach, co. Chester by his Cool wife Mary Ann, and coheir of the Rev. Joseph Wood, Vicar of Prestbury; *b.* 1782; *s.* 1801; *m.* 1808 Harriet Frances, youngest dau. of the late Edward Townshend, Esq., of Wincham, co. Chester. Educated at Brasenose Coll., Oxford; is a J.P. and D.L. for cos. Salop and Stafford (High Sheriff 1830).—*Peatswood, Market Drayton.*

Heir Pres., his nephew Thomas Fletcher Twemlow, Esq., of Betley Court, Crewe, co. Stafford (eldest son of the late Francis Twemlow, Esq., who *d.* 1865, by Elizabeth, 2nd dau. of the late Sir Thomas Fletcher, Bart., of Betley Court); educated at Rugby, and M.A. of Ch. Ch. Oxford; a Barrister-at-Law of Lincoln's Inn, a J.P. and D.L. for co. Stafford and a Magistrate for co. Chester, and Deputy-Chairman of the Staffordshire Quarter Sessions; *b.* 1816; *m.* 1849 Eliza Anne, dau. of William Paynter, Esq., of Richmond, Surrey.

TWISDEN, the Misses, of Bradbourn, Kent.
Daughters of the late Capt. Twisden, R.N., of Brad-
bourn. Are Ladies of the Manors of Brooke and East
Malling, and lay impropriators of the great tithes of
East Malling; descended from a common ancestor
with the Baronets of the same name.—*Bradbourn
Park, Larkfield, Maidstone; 60, Russell Square, w.c.*
*Heir Pres., their youngest and only surviving brother Thomas
Edward, a Solicitor in London, b. 1818.*

TWISLETON, the Hon. EDWARD TURNER BʸD.
Youngest son of the late Hon. and Rev. Thomas James
Twisleton, D.D., Archdeacon of Colombo (who d. 1824)
by his 2nd wife Anna, dau. of Benjamin Ashe, Esq.;
and brother of Frederick, 13th Lord Saye and Sele; b.
1809; m. 1852 Ellen, dau. of E. Dwight, Esq. (she d.
1862). Educated at Winchester and Trinity and Balliol Colls, Oxford (B.A. 1829, M.A. 1834); called to
the Bar at the Inner Temple 1835; appointed Assistant
Commissioner of Poor Laws in England in 1839; Commissioner of Inquiry into the Poor Laws of Scotland in
1843. He was Chief Commissioner of Poor Laws in
Ireland from 1845 to 1849; Oxford University Commissioner in 1855; Public Schools Commissioner in
1861, and has been Civil Service Commissioner since
1862.—3, *Rutland Gate, s.w.*

TWISLETON. (See under *Saye and Sele, Lord.*)

TWISS, Sir TRAVERS, Knt., D.C.L. (cr. 1867).
Son of the late Rev. Robert Twiss, LL.D.; b. 1810.
Educated at University Coll., Oxford (B.A. 1830, M.A.
1832, D.C.L. 1841); called to the Bar at Lincoln's Inn
1840; appointed Commissary General of the diocese of
Canterbury 1849, Vicar-General of the Archbishop of
Canterbury 1852, and Chancellor of the diocese of Lon-
don 1858, Q.C. 1858; was Queen's Advocate 1867-8.
—*Athenæum Club, s.w.; 19, Park Lane, w.*

TWISS, GEORGE, Esq., of Birdhill House, co.
Tipperary.
Eldest son of the late Robert Twiss, Esq., of Cordal,
co. Kerry (who was High Sheriff of co. Kerry 1802-3),
by Elizabeth, 2nd dau. of Robert Atkins, Esq., of Firville, Cork; b. 1809; s. 1851. Is a Grand Juror for
co. Tipperary.—*Birdhill House, Birdhill co. Tipperary.*
*Heir Pres., his brother Hastings, M.D., b. 1817; m. 1855
Sarah, dau. and co-heir of Capt. Stourton, H.E.I.C.S.*

+TWIST, JOHN BROWNE, Esq., of Stoke House,
Warwickshire.
Son of the late J. Twist, Esq., of Stoke House; b. 18--
is married, and has issue an only dau., * Frances Elizabeth, m. 1863 William Cecil Pardoe, only son of Thomas
Pardoe Pardoe, Esq., of Faintree Hall, co. Salop (whom
see).—*Stoke House, Coventry.*

TWOPENY, EDWARD, Esq., of Woodstock,
Kent.
Eldest son of the late Edward Soan Twopeny, Esq., of
Rochester, by Susannah, dau. of David Jones, Esq.; b.
1794; s. his uncle William Twopeny, Esq., 1826; m.
1st 1822 Elizabeth, youngest dau. of the late George
Smith, Esq., of Camer, Kent; 2nd 1855 Elizabeth
Tucker, 2nd dau. of Henry William Brooke, Esq., of
Walmer, and has, with other issue,
    * Edward, in Holy Orders, b. 1827; m. 1857 Caroline Eliza-
    beth, dau. of the Rev. Charles Parkin, Vicar of Lenham,
    Kent, and has issue. * Edward Maxwell, b. 1860.
Mr. Twopeny is a Magistrate for Kent.—*Woodstock
House, Sittingbourne.*

TWYSDEN, Sir WILLIAM, Bart. (cr. 1611).
Eldest son of the late Sir William Jervis Twysden,
Bart., of Roydon Hall, Kent, by Frances, dau. of Alexander Wynch, Esq., Governor of Madras; b. 1788; s. as
8th Bart, 1834; m. 1831 Eliza, dau. of the late Walter
942

May, Esq., of Hadlow, Kent, and widow of the Rev.
John Bosanquet Polhill (she d. 1863). This family
were formerly seated in Kent.
    Heir Pres., his nephew Louis (son of the late John Twysden,
    Esq., who d. 1863, by his 1st wife Miss Cecilia Bazalgette),
    b. 1831.

TYLDEN, Lady.
Mary, elder dau. of the late Rev. George Dinely
Goodere; m. 1st Capt. J. H. Baldwin; 2nd 1851 Bri-
gadier-General William Burton Tylden, who d. 1854.
—*Egerton House, Charing, Maidstone; 56, Buckingham
Place, Brighton.*

TYLDEN, the Rev. WILLIAM, of Milstead
Manor, Kent.
Elder son of the late Major William Burton Tylden,
R.E., by Lecilina, eldest dau. of the late William Bald-
win, Esq., of Stede Hill, Kent; b. 1818; s. his uncle
Sir J. M. Tylden, Knt. 1866. Educated at Balliol
Coll., Oxford (B.A. 1841, M.A. 1844), is Lord of the
Manor of Milstead, and Incumbent and Patron of
Stanford, Kent.—*Milstead Manor, Sittingbourne; Stan-
ford, Hythe, Kent.*

TYLDEN-PATTENSON, WILLIAM HODGES,
Esq., of Ibornden, Kent.
Eldest son of the late Lieut.-Col Cooke Tylden-Pattenson, of Ibornden, by his 1st wife Anne Rebecca, eldest
dau. of the late Thomas Law Hodges, Esq., of Hemsted,
Kent; b. 1822; s. 1858; m. 1854 Eliza Matilda, only
child of the Rev. James Boys, Rector of Biddenden, and
has, with other issue,
    * William Boys, b. 1855.
Mr. Tylden-Pattenson, who is a Magistrate for Kent,
was formerly Capt. 25th Regt. The Rev. Richard
Cooke-Tylden, Rector of Frinsted and Milsted, Kent,
assumed the name of Pattenson in 1799, on succeeding
to the Ibornden estate.—*Ibornden and Dashmunden,
Staplehurst.*

TYLECOTE, the Rev. THOMAS, of Marston-
Moretaine, Bedfordshire.
Eldest son of the late Samuel Tylecote, Esq., of Tamworth (who d. 1844), by Frances, dau. of Walter Lyon,
Esq., of Tamworth; b. 1799; m. 1842 Elizabeth, dau.
of the late Joseph Fereday, Esq., and has, with other
issue,
    * Thomas Beauford, b. 1842.
Mr. Tylecote, who was Fellow of St. John's Coll., Cambridge (B.A. 1821, M.A. 1824, B.D. 1850), is a Magistrate for Beds, Rector of Marston-Moretaine, Rural Dean
and Hon. Canon of Ely Cathedral.—*The Rectory, Marston-Moretaine, Ampthill.*

TYLER, Sir JAMES, Knt. (cr. 1851).
Son of the late William Watt Tyler, Esq.; b. 1816. Is
a J.P. and D.L. for Middlesex; late Lieut. of Corps of
Gentlemen-at-Arms.—*Pine House, Holloway, N.*

TYLER, CHARLES HENRY, Esq., of Linsted
Lodge, Kent.
Son of the late C. Tyler, Esq.; b. 18—; is a Dep.-
Lieut. for Kent.—*Linsted Lodge, Sittingbourne.*

+TYLER, GEORGE HENRY, Esq., of Cottrell,
Glamorganshire.
Eldest son of the late Vice-Admiral Sir George Tyler,
K.H., M.P., of Cottrell, by Harriet Margaret, dau. of
the late Right Hon. John Sullivan, of Ritchings Park,
Bucks; b. 1823; s. 1862. Is a Lieut.-Col. in the
Army, and late Capt. 13th Foot: served with distinc-
tion in the Crimea and in India.—*Cottrell, Cardiff.*

TYLER, GWINNETT, Esq., of Mount Gernos, Cardiganshire.

Second surviving son of the late Vice-Admiral Sir George Tyler, K.H., of Cottrell, co. Glamorgan, by Harriet Margaret, dau. of the late Right Hon. John Sullivan, of Ritchings Park, Bucks; *b.* 1828; *m.* 1852 Judith, only dau. of the late Major Parry, of Mount Gernos, co. Cardigan, and has, with other issue,

* Gwinnett George, *b.* 1853.

Mr. Tyler, who is a J.P. and D.L. for co. Cardigan and a Magistrate for co. Carmarthen, was formerly Lieut. R.N.—*Mount Gernos, Newcastle Emlyn; 12, Worcester Terrace, Clifton, Bristol; Raleigh Club, s.w.*

TYLER, HENRY, Esq., of Newtonlimavady, co. Londonderry.

Eldest son of the late Henry Huey, Esq. (who assumed the additional name of Tyler on succeeding to the property of his grandfather George Tyler, Esq., of Newton-limavady, in 1793), by Helen, dau. of Archibald Mac-larty, Esq., of Greenock; *b.* 1813; *s.* 1834; *m.* 1845 Jane, dau. of David Cather, Esq., J.P., and has, with other issue,

* George, *b.* 1852.

Mr. Tyler, who was educated at Addiscombe, is a Magistrate for co. Londonderry, and was formerly in the Madras Artillery.—*Newtonlimavady, co. Londonderry.*

TYLER, the Rev. ROPER TREVOR, M.A.

Second son of the late Admiral Sir Charles Tyler, G.C.B., of Cottrell, co. Glamorgan (who *d.* 1836), by Margaret, dau. of A. Leach, Esq., of Corston, co. Pembroke; *b.* 1801; *m.* 1838 Isabel, dau. of J. Bruce Pryce, Esq., of Duffryn, co. Glamorgan, and has, with other issue,

* Trevor Bruce, *b.* 1841.

Mr. Tyler, who was educated at Westminster and University Coll., Oxford (B.A. 1823, M.A. 1827), is a Magistrate for co. Glamorgan, Rural Dean, and Perpetual Curate of Monachlogddû, co. Pembroke, and Rector of Llantrithyd; was formerly Domestic Chaplain to His Majesty King William IV. when Duke of Clarence. —*Llantrithyd Rectory, Cowbridge.*

TYLER, ST. VINCENT, Esq., of Wisteston Court, Herefordshire.

Son of the late Vice-Admiral Sir George Tyler, K.H., of Cottrell, co. Glamorgan, by Harriet Margaret, dau. of the late Right Hon. John Sullivan; *b.* 1834; *m.* 1862 Emma Maud, dau. of John Lewis Phipps, Esq, of Leighton, Wilts; *s.* to this property 1863, under the will of the late Mrs. Gwinnett. Is a Magistrate for co. Hereford, and Lord of the Manor of Wisteston.—*Wisteston Court, Marden, Hereford; Windham Club, s.w.*

TYNDALE. (See *Biscoe*.)

TYNDALL, ROBERT, Esq., of Oaklands, co. Wexford.

Eldest son of the late Robert Tyndall, Esq., of Oaklands (formerly of Ballow Park, co. Dublin), by Eliza dau. of the Rev. William Bolton; *b.* 1800; *s.* 1834; *m.* 1833 Grace Sophia, only dau. of the Rev. T. Harman, of Palace, co. Wexford, and has, with other issue,

* Robert, *b.* 1837.

Mr. Tyndall, who is a Magistrate for cos. Wexford and Kilkenny (High Sheriff 1849).—*Oaklands, New Ross, co. Wexford; Milltown, co. Kilkenny.*

TYNDALL, THOMAS ONESIPHORUS, Esq., of The Fort, Gloucestershire.

Only son of the late Thomas Tyndall, Esq., of The Fort, by Mary Sybella, dau. of Jeremiah Hill, Esq., of Bristol; *b.* 1814; *s.* 1841; *m.* 1844 Caroline Lucy, 2nd dau. of the late Sir Charles A. Elton, Bart., of Clevedon

Court, Somerset, and has issue six daughters. Mr. Tyndall was educated at Eton and Ch. Ch., Oxford. Of this family was Tyndale, the Protestant martyr.—*The Fort, Bristol.*

TYNTE, Col. CHARLES JOHN KEMEYS-, F.R.S. of Halswell House, Somerset.

Only son of the late Col. Charles K. Kemeys-Tynte, M.P., of Halswell House; *b.* 1800; *s.* 1860; *m.* 1st 1821 Elizabeth, dau. and co-heir of the late Thomas Swinnerton, Esq., of Butterton Hall, co. Stafford; 2nd 1841 Vincentia, dau. of the late Wallop Brabazon, Esq., of Rath House, co. Louth, and has, by the former, with other issue,

* Charles Kemeys, of Cefn-Mably, co. Glamorgan, educated at Eton; a J.P. and D.L. for cos. Monmouth and Somerset, a Magistrate for co. Glamorgan, Hon. Col. 1st Somerset Militia, and Alternate Patron of 1 living; formerly Capt. 11th Hussars and Grenadier Guards; *b.* 1822; *m.* 1848 Mary, eldest dau. of the late Rev. George Frome, of Punck-noll, by Mary, 2nd dau. of Edmund Merton-Pleydell, Esq., and by her, who *d.* 1864, has, with other issue, * Halswell, *b.* 1852.

Col. Kemeys-Tynte, who was educated at Eton, is a J.P. and D.L. for cos. Gl morgan, Monmouth, and Somerset, Provincial Grandmaster of Freemasons in Monmouthshire, Lord of the Manor of Halswell, and Patron of 6 livings, and late Col. Loyal Glamorgan Militia; was M.P. for West Somerset 1832-7, and for Bridgewater 1847-65. Is senior co-heir to the Barony of Wharton.—*Halswell House, Bridgewater; Cefn-Mably. Cardiff; Burleigh Hall, Loughborough; Llanellan House, Abergavenny; United Service, Boodle's, Brooks's and Travellers' Clubs, s.w.*

TYNTE, JOSEPH, Esq., of Tynte Park, co. Wicklow.

Second son of Joseph Pratt, Esq., of Cabra Castle, co. Cavan, by Jemima, only dau. and heir of Sir James Stratford Tynte, Bart.; *b.* 1815; *m.* 1840 Geraldine, 2nd dau. of the late William R. Hopkyns Northey, Esq. of Oving House, Bucks, and has, with other issue,

* Fortescue, *b.* 1841.

Mr. Tynte is a J.P. and D.L. for cos. Wicklow, Cork, and Kilkenny.—*Tynte Park, Dunlavin, co. Wicklow; Tynte Lodge, Leitrim; The Hall, Cheltenham; Kildare Street Club, Dublin.*

TYRELL, Sir JOHN TYSSEN, Bart., of Boreham House, Essex (cr. 1809).

Elder and only surviving son of the late Sir John Tyrell, Bart., of Boreham House, by Sarah, dau. of William Tyssen, Esq., of Waltham House, Herts; *b.* 1795, *s.* as 2nd Bart. 1852; *m.* 1819 Eliza, dau. of the late Sir Thomas Pilkington, Bart. (crd.), and has issue three daughters. Sir J. T. Tyrell, who was educated at Winchester and Trinity Coll. Cambridge, is a J.P. and D.L. for Essex, Lord of the Manor of Boreham, and Patron of 2 livings; formerly Col. W. Essex Militia; was M.P. for Essex 1830-1, for N. Essex 1855-57. —*Boreham House, Chelmsford; Carlton Club, s.w.*

TYRELL, CHARLES, Esq., of Gipping and Plashwood, Suffolk.

Son of the late Rev. Charles Tyrell, Vicar of Thurston, Suffolk, and cousin of the late Edmund Tyrell, Esq., of Gipping Hall (who was High Sheriff of Suffolk 1774); *b.* 1776; *m.* 1st 1802 Elizabeth, only child and heir of the late Richard Ray, Esq., of Denbow, [...]; 2nd 1828 Maryanne, dau. of John Matthews, Esq., and widow of Thomas William Cooke, Esq., of Braxted Hall, Suffolk (she *d.* 1855), and has by his 1st wife, with other issue,

* Charles, educated at Emmanuel Coll., Cambridge; J.P. and D.L. for Suffolk; *b.* 1803.

Mr. Tyrell, who was educated at Emmanuel Coll., Cambridge (B.A. 1797), is a J.P. and D.L. for Suffolk (High Sheriff 1815), and Lord of the Manors of Gip-

ping, Polestead, Cotton, &c., and Patron of 2 livings; he was M.P. for Suffolk 1823-2, for West Suffolk 1833-4, and formerly served in the W. Suffolk Militia and Suffolk Volunteers. He is descended from a common ancestor with Sir J. Tyrell, Bart.; and his ancestors have resided at Gipping Hall, Suffolk, above 300 years.—*Plashwood, Haughley, Stowmarket.*

TYRINGHAM, WILLIAM BLACKWELL, Esq., of Tyringham, Bucks.

Eldest son of the late James Blackwell Praed, Esq., M.P., of Tyringham, by Sophia, dau. of the late Charles Chaplin, Esq., of Blankney, co. Lincoln; *b.* 18—; *s.* 1837; *m.* 1865 Fanny Adela, dau. of Col. W. Wilby, 4th Regt., and has issue a dau. Mr. Tyringham, who was educated at Eton and Ch. Ch., Oxford; is a J.P. and D.L. for Bucks (High Sheriff 1860), and Lord of the Manor of Tyringham; he assumed the name of Tyringham in 1859.—*Tyringham, Newport Pagnell; Trevethoe, Hayle, Cornwall; Carlton Club, s.w.*

TYRONE. (See under *Waterford, Marquis of.*)

+TYRRELL, JOHN, Esq., of St. Leonard's, Devonshire.

Son of the late John Tyrrell, Esq., of Clonmel, cc. Kildare; *b.* 1788; *m.* 1st 1822 Mary Anne, only child of J. Mackintosh, Esq., of Exeter; 2nd 1838 Diana Mary, 2nd dau. of the late Rev. James Wild, of Blunsdon House, Wilts; 3rd 1849 Lucy Clynes, eldest dau. of the late W. N. Robertson, Esq., of Lythe Hall, near Whitby, co. York (she *d.* 1854); 4th 1857 Georgina, dau. of the late T. Dains, Esq., of St Malo, and widow of E. W. Nias, Esq., of Providence, U.S.; he has, with other issue, by his 1st wife,

* John. *b.* 1824; *m.* 1849 Marianna Louisa, 3rd dau. of William Wingfield Yates, Esq., of Salcombe Hill House, Devon.

Mr. Tyrrell, who was called to the Bar at Lincoln's Inn 1813, is a Magistrate for Devon, and Judge of the County Courts in North and East Devon.—*St. Leonard's, Exeter; New Court, Topsham, Devon.*

TYRWHITT, Sir HENRY THOMAS, BART., of Stanley Hall, Shropshire (cr. 1808).

Eldest son of the late Sir Thomas John Tyrwhitt-Jones, Bart., of Stanley Hall, by Elizabeth Walwyn, dau. of John Macnamara, Esq., of St. Kitts, West Indies; *b.* 1824; *s.* as 3rd Bart. 1839; *m.* 1853 Emma Harriet, dau. of the late Hon. and Rev. Robert Wilson (she is heiress presumptive to the Barony of Berners). Is a Magistrate for co. Salop and for Norfolk; formerly Lieut. Rifle Brigade.—*Stanley Hall, Bridgnorth.*

Heir, his son Harry, *b.* 1854.

TYRWHITT-DRAKE. (See *Drake.*)

+TYSSEN, CHARLES AMHURST DANIEL, Esq., of Northwonld Lodge, Norfolk.

Second son of the late William George Daniel Esq., of Foley House, Kent (who assumed the additional name of Tyssen by Royal licence, and *d.* 1838), by Amelia. dau. of John Amhurst, Esq., of Rochester, and uncle of W. A. Tyssen-Amhurst, Esq., of Diddlington (whom see); *b.* 1804. Is a Magistrate for Norfolk; formerly a Capt. in the Army.—*Northwald Lodge, Brandon.*

Heir Pres., his brother John Robert. *b.* 1805; *m.* 1825 Harriet Caroline, dau. of Charles Hopkinson. Esq., of Cadogan Place, and has, with other issue, * Ridley, *b.* 1841.

+TYSSEN, FRANCIS SAMUEL DANIEL, Esq., of Sandgate, Kent.

Youngest son of the late W. G. Daniel Tyssen. Esq., of Westbrook House, D.L. (formerly High Sheriff of Kent, who *d.* 1838; by Mary, dau. of — Tyssen, Esq.; *b.* 1813; *m.* 1843 Eliza Julia, eldest dau. of the late Vice-Chancellor, Sir James Lewis Knight Bruce; is a Magistrate for Kent; was formerly an Officer in the 4th Dragoon Guards.—*Castle House, Sandgate, Kent.*

TYSSEN-AMHURST, WILLIAM AMHURST, Esq., of Diddlington, Norfolk.

Eldest son of the late William George Tyssen Tyssen-Amhurst, Esq., of Hackney, and of Foulden Hall, Norfolk, (who assumed the name of Tyssen-Amhurst in 1852, by Mary. eldest dau. of Andrew Fountaine, Esq., of Narford Hall, Norfolk; *b.* 1835; *s.* 1855; *m.* 1856 Margaret Susan, only dau. of Admiral Robert Mitford, of Hunmanby Hall, co. York, and has issue four daughters. Mr. Tyssen-Amhurst, who was educated at Eton and Ch. Ch., Oxford, is a Magistrate for Middlesex, Westminster and Norfolk (High Sheriff 1866). —*Diddlington Park, Brandon, Norfolk; The Manor House, Hackney, Middlesex.*

TYTLER, JAMES STUART Esq., of Woodhouselee, Midlothian.

Eldest surviving son of the late James Tytler, Esq., of Woodhouselee (2nd son of Alexander Fraser-Tytler, Lord Woodhouselee), by Elizabeth. dau. of Maurice Carmichael, Esq., of Eastend, co. Lanark: *b.* 1820; *s.* 1862; *m.* 1850 Mary Elizabeth, only child of Alexander Blair, Esq., who *d.* 1857, leaving, with other issue,

* James William, *b.* 1854.

Mr. Tytler is a Magistrate for co. Midlothian.—*Woodhouselee, Roslin, N.B.; New Club, Edinburgh.*

TYTLER. (See *Fraser-Tytler.*)

U

UFFINGTON. (See under *Craven, Earl of*.)

UNETT, WILLIAM, Esq., late of Venwood, Herefordshire.

Only surviving son of the late Henry Unett, Esq., of Freens Court, Marden Court (who *d.* 1807), by Jane, dau. of William Lingen, Esq.; *b.* 1795; *m.* 1822 Elizabeth Selina, youngest dau. of John Kennedy, Esq., of Cultra, co. Down, and has issue,

* Thomasine Elizabeth, *m.* 1848 John Price Williams, Esq., Barrister-at-Law, of Shrewsbury.

Mr. Unett, who is a J.P. and D.L. for co. Hereford, was formerly in the 43rd Regiment, and Capt. Herefordshire Militia.

UNETT, of Freen's Court, Herefordshire.

Henry Unett, Esq., of Freen's Court, *d.* 1854, having *m.* Mary, dau. of Sandys Lechmere, Esq., of Fown Hope, co. Hereford, who *d.* 1867, leaving issue five daughters co-heirs: Mary Jane, *m.* Edward Wakefield, Esq.; Charlotte, *m.* Lieut.-Col. Charles Pratt Kennedy; Ursula Milborough, *m.* Thomas Edward Davies; Elizabeth Frances Letitia, *m.* George Unett; and Sarah Blanche Lingen.—*Freen's Court, Hereford.*

UNIACKE, Mrs., of Ballyre, co. Cork.

Esther, dau. of Percy Scott Smyth, Esq., of Headborough, co. Waterford; *m.* 1835 Crofton Uniacke, Esq., of Ballyre, who *d. s. p.* 1864.—*Ballyre, Killeagh, co. Cork.*

UNIACKE, NORMAN JAMES BIGGS, Esq., of Mount Uniacke, co. Cork.

Eldest son of the late Norman Uniacke, Esq., of Mount Uniacke, by Eleanor, dau. of George Lax, Esq., of Wells, Somerset, and grandson of the late James Fitz-Gerald Uniacke, Esq., of Mount Uniacke; *b.* 1823; *s.* 1861; *m.* 1844 Mary Elizabeth, dau. of the late Col. Drinkwater Bethune, of Balfour, co. Fife, and by her (who *d.* 1863) has, with other issue,

* Norman Compton Fitz-Gerald, *b.* 1848.

Mr. Uniacke, who was formerly Lieut. Denbigh Yeomanry Cavalry, descends from the Ducal House of Leinster.—*Mount Uniacke, Killeagh, co. Cork.*

UNSWORTH. (See *Molyneux-Sorl.*)

UNTHANK, CLEMENT WILLIAM, Esq., of Intwood Hall, Norfolk.

Youngest son of the late William Unthank, Esq., of Heigham (who *d.* 1837), by Anne, dau. of John May, Esq., of Southwold, Suffolk; *b.* 1804; *s.* Mrs. Gooch 1856 in the Stone family estates of Bedingham Hall; *s.* his father-in-law 1860; *m.* 1835 Mary Anne, dau. and heir of the late Joseph Salisbury Muskett, Esq., of Intwood Hall, and has, with other issue,

* Clement William Joseph, *b.* 1847.

Mr. Unthank is a J.P. and D.L. for Norfolk, Lord of the Manor of Bedingham, and Patron of Intwood.—*Intwood Hall, Norwich;* 18, *Queen's Gate Gardens,* w.

UPCHER, HENRY RAMEY, Esq., of Sheringham Hall, Norfolk.

Eldest son of the late Abbot Upcher, Esq., of Sheringham Hall, by the Hon. Charlotte, eldest dau. of Henry, Lord Berners, *b.* 1010, *s.* 1819, *m.* 1888 Caroline,

dau. of Joseph Morris, Esq., of Ampthill House, Bedfordshire, and has, with other issue,

* Henry Morris, *b.* 1839.

Mr. Upcher, who was educated at Harrow and Trinity Coll., Cambridge (B.A. 1832, M.A. 1835), is a J.P. and D.L. for co. Norfolk.—*Sheringham Hall, Cromer.*

UPPLEBY, GEORGE CHARLES, Esq., of Barrow Hall, Lincolnshire.

Only son of the late Rev. George Uppleby, Vicar of Barton-on-Humber, by Mary, dau. of William Fox, Esq., of Girsby, co. Lincoln; *b.* 1819; *s.* his uncle 1853; *m.* 1852 Emily, dau. of the Rev. Wm. Worsley, of Braytoft, co. Lincoln, and has, with other issue,

* Charles Gylby Oliver, *b.* 1853.

Mr. Uppleby, who was educated at Shrewsbury and Magdalen Coll., Cambridge (B.A. 1840, M.A. 1843), and was called to the Bar at Lincoln's Inn 1844, is a J.P. and D.L. for co. Lincoln (High Sheriff 1863), Patron of the living of Barton-on-Humber, and Major 1st Batt. Lincoln Rifle Volunteers.—*Barrow Hall, Ulceby; Oxford and Cambridge Club,* s.w.

UPPLEBY, LEADBETTER, Esq., of Wootton House, Lincolnshire.

Eldest son of the late John Uppleby, Esq., of Wootton House, by Kitty, only surviving dau. and heir of Roger Leadbetter, Esq., of Glandford Brigg; *b.* 1799; *s.* 1839; *m.* 1847 Eliza Roberta, dau. of Admiral Sir Robert Barrie, K.C.B., of Swarthdale, co. Lancaster, and has issue,

* John, *b.* 1855.

Mr. Uppleby, who was educated at Eton, is a J.P. and D.L. for co. Lincoln; late Major R. N. Lincoln Militia. —*Wootton House, Barrow-on-Humber; Ardrishaig, Argyllshire, N.B.; Junior United Service Club,* s.w.

UPTON, LEWIS, Esq., of Glyde Court, co. Louth.

Second surviving son of the late Rev. Shuckburgh Whitney Upton, Rector of Kilmoon, co. Meath who *d.* 1807), by Margaret, dau. of Lewis F. Irwin, Esq., of Tanragee, co. Sligo; *b.* 1805; *s.* his brother 1824; *m.* 1844 Isabella Sophia Georgina, only child of Henry William Fielde, Esq., of Netherfield House, Herts (who *d.* 1865). Is a Magistrate for co. Louth (High Sheriff 1846); a Captain in the Army, retired : was formerly in the 4th Light Dragoons and 9th Lancers.—*Glyde Court, Carlingford; Stanstedbury, Ware, Herts; Junior United Service Club,* s.w.

Heir Pres., his brother Arthur Shuckburgh, *b.* 1807.

UPTON, Miss, of Ingmire Hall, Westmoreland-Eliza Frances, eldest dau. of the late Thomas Upton, Esq., of Ingmire Hall (who *d.* 1843), by Eliza, dau. of Benjamin Way, Esq., of Denham Place, Bucks, and sister of Sir J. H. Greville Smyth, Bart (whom see); *s.* 1853. This family was settled in Cornwall before the Norman Conquest.—*Ingmire, Hall, Kendal.*

UPTON. (See under *Templetown, Viscount*.)

UPTON. (See *Smyth, Sir J. H. G., Bart*.)

UPTON GLEDSTANES. (See *Gledstanes*.)

UPWOOD, the Rev. THOMAS THOROGOOD, M.A.,‡ of Lovell's Hall, Norfolk.

Only son of the late Thomas Upwood, Esq., of Lovell's Hall, by Anne, dau. of Joseph Hare, Esq., of Coombe Grove, Bath; b. 1794; m. 1822 Jane, dau. of the late William Stevens, Esq., of Aldermaston, Berks, and by her (who d. 1858), has issue, seven daughters. Mr. Upwood, who was educated at Clare Hall and Pembroke Coll., Cambridge (B.A. 1817, M.A. 1820), late Fellow of Clare Coll., is a Magistrate for Norfolk, Vicar of Terrington St. Clement, and Lord of the Manor of Lovell's Hall, late Rector of Clenchwarton, Norfolk. —Lovell's Hall, Terrington St. Clement, Lynn.

URQUHART, BEAUCHAMP COLCLOUGH, Esq., of Meldrum and Byth, Aberdeenshire.

Eldest surviving son of the late Beauchamp Colclough Urquhart, Esq., J.P. and D.L., of Meldrum and Byth, by Anne Jane Fitz-Simmons, dau. of the late Patrick Fitz-Simons, Esq., of Streamstown, co. Westmeath; b. 1830; s. 1861; m. 1856 Isabella Forbes, dau. of General Sir Hugh Fraser, K.C.B., of Braelangwell, co. Ross, and has, with other issue,

* Beauchamp Colclough, b. 1860.

Mr. Urquhart is head of the clan Urquhart, who were heritable Sheriffs of Cromarty from the time of Edward I. till 1745.—Old Meldrum and Byth, Turriff, N.B.

URQUHART, DAVID, Esq.

Only surviving son of the late David Urquhart, Esq., of Cromarty, N.B.; b. 1805; m. 1854 Harriett, younger sister of Lord Clermont. Educated at St. John's Coll., Oxford; appointed to the Diplomatic Service 1825, and was formerly Secretary of the Embassy at Constantinople; was M.P. for Stafford 1847-52.

URQUHART. (See Pollard-Urquhart.)

USBORNE, THOMAS HENRY, Esq., of Mardley-Bury Manor, Herts.

Only son of the late Thomas Usborne, Esq., of Sewardstone, Essex, by Rebecca, dau. of George Price, of Walworth Grove; b. 1810; s. 1845; m. 1st 1831 Emma, youngest dau. of Thomas Starling Benson, Esq., of North Cray Place, Kent; 2nd 184- Isabel Jane, eldest dau. of Rear-Admiral Thomas Henderson, of Dawlish, who d. s. p.; he has issue by the former,

* Thomas Starling, late 7th Dragoon Guards; b. 1834.

Mr. Usborne, who was educated at Eton and Göttingen, is the author of a 'New Guide to the Levant, Egypt, Syria, &c.;' 'The Jesuits, their Rise and Progress,' &c. This family descends from Osbertus de Henghurst A.D. 1405.—Great St. Dennis, Staplehurst, Kent; Mardley-Bury Manor, Therfield, Herts; National Club, s.w.; 30, Onslow Square, s.w.; 4, Percy Terrace, Hereford Square, South Kensington, s.w.

‡ Died whilst these sheets were at press.

USSHER, CHRISTOPHER, Esq., of Eastwell, co. Galway.

Eldest son of the late John Ussher. Esq., of Eastwell, by Mary, dau. of the late Capt. Ussher, of Canada; b. 1834; s. 1855. Educated at Trinity Coll., Dublin. Is descended from a common ancestor with the Usshers of Landscape (whom see).—Eastwell, Kilrickle, co. Galway, Kildare Street Club, Dublin.

USSHER, RICHARD, Esq., of Landscape, co. Wexford.

Eldest surviving son of the late John Ussher, Esq., of Landscape (who d. 1844), by Lucy, dau. of the Rev. William Glascott, of Pilltown, co. Wexford; b. 18..; s. his brother John 1863; m. 1859 Charlotte, dau. of the Rev. James Metge, and has issue,

* Lucy Cassandra.

This family formerly bore the name of Neville, but this branch took the name of Usher (or Ussher) from the office of Usher of Black Rod, held at Dublin temp. King John.—Landscape, New Ross.

USSHER, RICHARD JOHN, Esq., of Cappagh, co. Wexford.

Only son of the late Richard Kelly Ussher, Esq., of Cappagh, by his 2nd wife Isabella, dau. of Col. Jasper Grant; b. 1841; s. 1854. Educated at Trinity Coll., Dublin. This family claim the 'King-maker,' Guy, Earl of Warwick, as an ancestor.—Cappagh, Cappoquin.

USTICKE. (See Nowdl-Usticke.)

UTHWATT, the Rev. WILLIAM ANDREWES, of Maids Moreton, and Great Linford, Bucks.

Second but eldest surviving son of the late Rev. Henry Uthwatt-Uthwatt, of Great Linford (who d. 1812), by Judith, dau. of — Yates, Esq.; b. 1822; m. 1853 Mary, 2nd dau. and co-heir of the late Rev. James Long Long, Rector of Maids Moreton, and has issue,

* Mary Henrietta Turner Hutton Andrewes Andrewes.

Mr. Uthwatt, who was educated at St. John's Coll., Cambridge (M.A. 1815), is a Magistrate for Bucks, Rector of Maids Moreton and Vicar of Stowe, Lord of the Manors of Maids Moreton and Great Linford, and Patron of those livings, and Joint Patron of the Chapelry of Gowcott, Bucks.—Maids Moreton House, Buckingham; Great Linford Place, Newport Pagnell.

UTTERMARE, THOMAS BAMPFIELD, Esq., of Langport, Somerset.

Only son of the late Robert Uttermare, Esq., of Langport, by Harriet, dau. of Robert Michell, Esq., of Langport and Polyxena, only child of Elias Bampfield, of Knowle St. Giles', Somerset; b. 1801; s. 1824; m. 1859 Elizabeth, 2nd dau. of Daniel Terry, Esq., of Bath. Educated at St. Peter's, Cambridge (B.A. 182..) is a Magistrate for Somerset, and Lord of the Manor of Hatch Beauchamp. This family were formerly of Curry Mallet, where they were lessees under Sir Anthony Poulet in the 39th year of Elizabeth (1597). —Langport, Somerset.

UXBRIDGE. (See under Anglesey, Marquis of.)

V

VADE-WALPOLE, RICHARD HENRY, Esq., of Freethorpe, Norfolk.

Only surviving son of the late Rev. Ashton Vade (who was Chaplain to H.R.H. George, Prince of Wales), by Mary Rachael, dau. and heir of the Hon. Richard Walpole, M.P., whose name he assumed; *b.* 1800; *m.* 1834 Harriet, dau. of the late Thomas Duncombe, Esq., and niece of Charles, 1st Lord Feversham. Is a Dep.-Lieut. for Norfolk.—*Freethorpe, Acle, Norfolk; Hardwick Grange, Shrewsbury; Travellers' and Boodle's Clubs,* **s.w.**; 38, *Upper Brook Street,* **w.**

VAIZEY, GEORGE DE HORNE, Esq., of Star Style, Essex.

Second son of the late John Vaizey, J.P., of Star Style (who *d.* 1831), by Sarah, youngest dau. of the late George de Horne, Esq., of Stanway Hall, Essex; *b.* 1800; *m.* 1826 Mary, dau. of the Rev. John Savill, of Colchester, and has, with other issue,

* John Savill, Barrister-at-Law; *b.* 1827.

Mr. Vaizey is a Magistrate for Essex.—*Star Style, Halstead.*

VAIZEY, JOHN ROBERT, Esq., of Attwoods, Essex.

Only son of the late John Vaizey, Esq., of Attwoods, and Gray's Inn, by Ann, dau. of Robert Bousefield, Esq., of London, and nephew of G. de Horne Vaizey, Esq. (wnom see); *b.* 1839 ; *s.* 1865 Alice, eldest dau. of Edward Hornor, Esq. Educated at Trinity Coll., Cambridge (LL.B. 1863); called to the Bar at the Inner Temple 1863. Is a Magistrate for Essex.—*The Howe, Halstead, Essex; Attwood's, Halstead; Reform Club,* **s.w.**

VALE, MARTINDALE, Esq., of Mathon Court, Worcestershire.

Son of the late William Vale, Esq., R.N., of Mathon Court, by Catherine, dau. of Thomas Ridgley, Esq.; *b.* 1826. Educated at Trinity Hall, Cambridge (B.A. 1853); called to the Bar at Lincoln's Inn 1856; is a J.P. and D.L. for co. Worcester, and Captain Worcester Militia.—*Mathon Court, Malvern.*

VALE, the Rev. WILLIAM SCARLETT, of Mathon Lodge, Worcestershire.

Eldest son of the late William Vale, Esq., R.N., of Mathon Lodge, by Catherine, dau. of Thomas Ridgley, Esq.; *b.* 1820; *m.* 1858 Charlotte, only child of the late Major Croxton, of the Bengal Artillery, and has, with other issue,

* William Croxton, *b.* 1859.

Mr. Vale, who was educated at Worcester Coll., Oxford (B.A. 1843, M.A. 1845). is a Magistrate for cos. Worcester and Hereford.—*Mathon Lodge, Malvern; Conservative Club,* **s.w.**

VALENTIA, Viscount (ARTHUR ANNESLEY).—Cr. 1622.

Only son of the late Hon. Arthur Annesley (who *d.* 1844). by Flora Mary, dau. of Lieut.-Col. James Macdonald; *b.* 1813; *s.* his grandfather as 11th Viscount 1863. Is Lord of the Manor of Bletchingdon, Cornet 10th Hussars, and Patron of 1 living. Descended from a common ancestor with Earl Annesley.—*Bletchingdon Park, Oxford.*

Heir Pres., his uncle Algernon Sydney Arthur Annesley, Capt. Oxfordshire Militia; *b.* 1829 ; *m.* 1864 Helen Sydney, elder dau. of the late Griffith Richards, Esq., and has issue,
* Arthur Sydney Evelyn, *b.* 1865.

VALIANT-CUMMING, Mrs., of Logie, Morayshire.

Emily Frances, 2nd and only surviving-dau. of the late Alexander Cumming, Esq., of Logie (who *d.* 1840), by Louisa Wynne, dau. of General Martin White; *m.* 1858 Lockhart Mure Valiant, Esq., who took her name (son of the late Sir Thomas Valiant, K.C.B. and K.H.), and by him (who *d.* 1866) has issue,

* Leslie Marianne.

Capt. Valiant-Cumming, who was formerly Capt. 1st Bombay Lancers, served in the Caubul Campaign. and was at the siege of Ghuznee and at the taking of Mooltan.—*Logie, Forres, N.B.*

VALLENTIN, JAMES, Esq., of Walthamstow, Essex.

Second son of the late James Vallentin, Esq., of London, by Mary, dau. of John Grimble, Esq., of London ; *b.* 1814 ; *m.* 1st 1838 Susannah Hartley, dau. of John Workman, Esq., of Hackney (she *d.* 1862); 2nd 1863 Anna Maria, dau. of the Rev. John Cox, M.A., of Walgrave, co. Northampton, and has, by the former, with other issue,

* James Rose, *b.* 1847.

Mr. Vallentin is Lord of the Rectory Manor of Walthamstow, and a Merchant in the City. This family descend from Robert de Vallentin, Seigneur d'Eschepy, France, living 1328.—*Rectory Manor, Walthamstow.*

VALLETORT. (See under *Mount-Edgcumbe, Earl of.*)

+**VALPY,** Capt. ROBERT HARRIS, of Euborne, Berks.

Only son of Capt. Anthony Blagrave Valpy. R.N., by Annie, dau. of the late Robert Harris, Esq., Banker of Reading ; *b.* 1820 ; *m.* 1850 Miss Faller-Mitland, and has issue. Is a J.P. and D.L. for Berks.—*Euborne Lodge, Newbury.*

VANCE, JOHN, Esq.

Eldest son of the late Andrew Vance, Esq., of Rutland Square. Dublin ; *b.* 1805 ; *m.* 1846 Anne Eliza, dau. of Henry Dresser, Esq., of Farnborough Lodge, Kent. Graduated M.A. at Trinity Coll., Dublin; is a Merchant in the Irish and Colonial Trade, and a Dep.-Lieut. tor the W. Riding of Yorkshire ; was M.P. for Dublin 1852–65 ; elected M.P. for Armagh 1867.—18. *Rutland Square, Dublin ; Carlton and Windham Clubs,* **s.w.**

VANDERBYL, PHILIP, Esq.

Fourth son of the late Hon. P. V. Vanderbyl, of the Cape of Good Hope, by Johanna Isabella, dau. of Alexander J. Van Breda, Esq.; *b.* 1827 ; *m.* 1858 Sara, only child of James Alexander, Esq., of Porchester Terrace, London. Educated at the University of Edinburgh, where he obtained the gold medal ; is Member of the Royal College of Physicians, London ; retired from the Medical profession in 1858, and is now an Australian Merchant and Banker; elected M.P. for Bridgewater 1866.—*Reform Club,* **s.w.**; 51, *Porchester Terrace,* **w.**

VANDELEUR, Col. CROFTON MOORE, of Kilrush House, co. Clare.

Eldest son of the late Right. Hon. John Ormsby Vandeleur, of Kilrush, by Lady Frances, dau. of Charles, 1st Marquis of Drogheda, K.P.; *b.* 1809; *m.* 1832 Lady Grace Toler, 2nd dau. of Hector John, 2nd Earl of Norbury, and has, with other issue,

* Hector Stewart, Capt. Rifle Brigade; *b.* 1836 ; *m.* 1867 Charlotte, eldest dau. of Wm. O, Foster, Esq., of Stourton Castle. co. Stafford.

Col. Vandeleur, who was educated at Harrow and Trinity Coll., Cambridge, is a J.P. and D.L. for co. Clare (High Sheriff 1832), and Col. Clare Militia; elected M.P. for co. Clare 1859.—*Kilrush House, co. Clare ; Carlton Club,* s.w.

VANDERMEULEN, the Rev. FREDERICK, of Thorley, Herts.

Eldest son of the late Frederick Vandermeulen, Esq., J.P., of Bishop's Stortford, Herts (who *d.* 1851), by Rachel, dau. of William Thompson, Esq., of Sydney Place, Bath ; *b.* 1812 ; *m.* 1838 Georgina, dau. of Samuel Baldwin Harrison, Esq., of Her Majesty's Customs, and has, with other issue,

* Frederick Samuel, Lieut. R.N. ; *b.* 1840.

Mr. Vandermeulen, who was educated at Trinity Coll., Cambridge (B.A. 1834, M.A. 1837), is a Magistrate for Herts, and Rector of Thorley, Lord of the Manor of Inges, Herts, and Patron of 1 living ; Rector of Bow-cum-Broadnymet, Devon. This family is of Dutch extraction.—*Thorley Rectory, Bishop's Stortford.*

VANDERSTEGEN, WILLIAM HENRY, Esq., of Cane End, Oxfordshire.

Eldest son of the late William Vanderstegen, Esq., of Cane End, by his 2nd wife Elizabeth Grace, dau. of Charles Kirby, Esq., of Bath ; *b.* 1808 ; *s.* 1831 ; *m.* 1852 Ellen, dau. of Richard Denny, Esq., of Berg Apton, Norfolk, and has, with other issue,

* Henry Brigham Douglas, *b.* 1853.

Mr. Vanderstegen, who was educated at Eton and Brasenose Coll., Oxford (B.A. 1830, M.A. 1833), is a J.P. and D.L. for Oxfordshire (High Sheriff 1843). This family is Dutch, and settled in England *temp.* William III.—*Cane End House, Caversham, Reading.*

VAN DE WEYER, Madame, of New Lodge, Berks.

Elizabeth, only child of Joshua Bates, Esq., of Sheen House, Surrey, and Winkfield Place, Berks, by Lucretia Augusta, dau. of Samuel Sturgis, Esq., of Boston, U.S.; *m.* 1839 His Excellency Sylvain Van de Weyer, Envoy Extraordinary and Minister Plenipotentiary of the King of the Belgians at St. James's, and has, with other issue, * Victor William Bates, educated at Eton ; a Magistrate for Berks, Capt. Berks Militia, and an Officer Berks Yeomanry and Volunteers; *b.* 1839.—*New Lodge, Windsor Forest, Berks ; 21, Arlington Street,* s.w.

VANE, Earl (GEORGE HENRY ROBERT CHARLES VANE-TEMPEST).—Cr. 1823.

Second son of Charles William, 3rd Marquis of Londonderry, K.G., &c., by his 2nd wife Frances Ann, dau. of the late Sir Henry Vane-Tempest, Bart.; *b.* 1821 ; *s.* 1854 ; *m.* 1846 Mary Cornelia, only dau. of Sir John Edwards, Bart. Educated at Eton and Balliol Coll., Oxford (B.A. 1845); is a Magistrate for co. Merioneth, and a Dep.-Lieut. for cos. Durham and Montgomery, and Patron of 1 living ; Col. N. Durham Militia, and Lieut.-Col. Commandant 2nd Durham Artillery Volunteers; late Lieut. 1st Life Guards ; was M.P. for N. Durham 1847-51.—*Seaham Hall, Sunderland; Wynyard Park, Stockton-on-Tees, Garron Tower, Larne, co.*

948

Antrim ; *Plâs Machynlleth, Montgomery ; Carlton Club,* s.w. ; *Holdernesse House, Park Lane,* w.

Heir, his son Charles Stewart, Viscount Seaham, *b.* 1852.

VANE, Sir HENRY RALPH, Bart., of Hutton Hall, Cumberland (cr. 1786).

Eldest son of the late Sir Francis Vane, Bart., of Hutton Hall, by Diana Olivia, dau. of Charles George Beauclerk, Esq., of St. Leonard's Lodge, Horsham, Sussex ; *b.* 1830 ; *s.* as 4th Bart. 1842. Educated at Ch. Ch., Oxford ; is a J.P. and D.L. for Cumberland (High Sheriff 1856), Patron of 1 living, and Capt. Westmoreland and Cumberland Yeomanry.—*Hutton Hall, near Penrith ; Armathwaite Hall, Cockermouth ; Arthur's Club,* s.w. ; 64, Wellington Road, St. John's Wood, N.W.

Heir Pres., his uncle Frederick Henry, *b.* 1807 ; *m.* 1859 Rosa, dau. of John Moore, Esq., of Prospect Hill, Galway, and has issue, * Francis Patrick, *b.* 1861.

VANE, HENRY MORGAN, Esq., of Sutton Basset, Northamptonshire.

Elder son of the late John Henry Vane, Esq., who was younger son of Morgan Vane, Esq., by Eliza, youngest dau. of John Nicholson, Esq., of Glandford Bridge, and great-grandson of the Hon. Morgan Vane, of Billy Hall, Notts ; *b.* 1808 ; *s.* 1849 ; *m.* 1853 Louisa, youngest dau. and co-heir of the Rev. Richard Farrer, Rector of Ashley, co. Northampton, and has, with other issue,

* Henry de Vere, *b.* 1854.

Mr. Vane, who was called to the Bar at the Inner Temple 1843, and appointed Secretary to the Charity Commission 1853, is a Dep.-Lieut. for co. Durham; he descends from a cadet of the ducal house of Cleveland.—*Reform Club,* s.w. ; 74, *Eaton Place,* s.w.

VANE, the Rev. JOHN, of Burrington, Somersetshire.

A natural son of the late Duke of Cleveland: *b.* 1792. Educated at Westminster and Trinity Coll. Cambridge (B.A. 1814), and at Magdalen Coll., Cambridge (M.A. 1817); is a Dep.-Lieut. for Somerset, Rector of Wrington with Burrington, and Chaplain in Ordinary to the Queen; was formerly Fellow of Magdalen Coll., Cambridge, Deputy-Clerk of the Closet to the Queen, Chaplain to the House of Commons, Preacher of the Rolls, &c.—*The Parsonage, Burrington, Bristol; Brooks's, Oxford and Cambridge, and Reform Clubs,* s.w. ; 39, *Cambridge Street, Hyde Park,* w.

VANE, MORGAN, Esq.

Only son of the late Rev. Robert Morgan Vane, of Lowick, co. Northampton (who *d.* 1842), by Sarah, dau. of Joseph Telson, Esq., of Bradley, Cumberland, who was elder son of Morgan Vane, of Billy, Notts, Comptroller of the Stamp-Office, and grandson of the Hon. Morgan Vane, younger son of Christopher, Lord Barnard ; *b.* 1833 ; *m.* 1865 Alice Elizabeth, 2nd dau. of Henry William Booth, Esq., and niece of Sir William Gooch, Bart. Educated at Shrewsbury and Ch. Ch. Oxford ; Lieut. Huntingdon Rifles ; is in remainder to the Barony of Barnard, one of the inferior titles of the Duke of Cleveland.—*Villas, &c., Leamington.*

VANE.

(See under *Cleveland, Duke of,* and *Londonderry, Marquis of.*)

VANNECK. (See under *Huntingfield, Lord.*)

VAN NOTTEN-POLE. (See *Pole.*)

VANS-AGNEW, ROBERT, Esq., of Barnbarroch, Wigtownshire.

Eldest son of the late Col. Patrick Vans-Agnew, of Barnbarroch and of Sheuchan, co. Wigtown, by Catharina, dau. of D. Fraser, Esq.; *b.* 1817 ; *s.* 1842 ; *m.* 1841

Mary Elizabeth. 2nd dau. of the late Sir David Hunter Blair, Bart., and has, with other issue,

　　• Patrick Alexander, b. 1856.

Mr. Vans-Agnew, who was educated at Eton, is a J.P. and D.L. for co. Wigtown, and represents in the male line the old family of Vans (or Vans-de-Vallibus) of Barnbarroch, and in the female line the Agnews of Sheuchan.—*Barnbarroch, Wigtown, N.B. ; Park House, Stranraer, N.B.*

VANSITTART, COLERAINE ROBERT, Esq., of Shottesbrook Park, Berks. ·

Only son of the late Arthur Vansittart, Esq., of Shottesbrook Park, by Diana, dau. of the late Sir John Crosbie, K.H., of Watergate, Sussex ; b. 1833 ; s. 1859. Is Lord of the Manor of Shottesbrook, and Patron of that living ; was formerly Capt. 11th Hussars ; is head and representative of the family of Vansittart.—*Shottesbrook Park, Maidenhead ; Foots Cray, Bromley, Kent.*

　　Heir Pres., his uncle Robert (of Chuffs, Maidenhead). a Magistrate for Berks ; late Lieut.-Col. Coldstream Guards ; b. 1808 ; m. 1835 Harriet Elizabeth, dau. of the late John Willis-Fleming, Esq., of Stoneham Park, Hants.

VANSITTART, GEORGE HENRY, Esq., of Bisham Abbey, Berks.

Eldest son of the late General George Henry Vansittart, of Bisham Abbey, by Ann Mary, dau. of Thomas Copson, Esq. ; b. 1823 ; m. 1851 Catherine Elizabeth, dau. of John Steuart Menzies, Esq., of Culdares, co. Perth. Educated at Eton and Balliol Coll., Oxford ; is a J.P. and D.L. for Berks, a Magistrate for Bucks, and Patron of 1 living ; was M.P. for Berks 1847–59 ; represents a younger branch of the Vansittarts of Shottesbrook.—*Bisham Abbey, Maidenhead ; Carlton Club, s.w.*

　　Heir Pres., his brother Augustus Arthur, b. 1824 ; m. 1857 the Hon. Rachel, eldest dau. of George, 4th Lord Boston.

VANSITTART, WILLIAM, Esq.

Third son of the late Col. Arthur Vansittart, of Shottesbrook Park, Berks, by Caroline, dau. of William, 1st Lord Auckland ; b. 1813 ; m. 1st 1839 Emily, dau. of Col. R. Anstruther, of Bengal Cavalry ; 2nd 1847 Henrietta, eldest dau. of the late Ambrose Humphrys, Esq. (she d. 1852) ; 3rd 1866 Melanie, youngest dau. of the late Sir Richard Jenkins, G.C.B. Educated at Eton and Haileybury ; was M.P. for Windsor 1857–65 ; late in the H.E.I.C.'s Civil Service.—*Carlton and Conservative Clubs, s.w. ; 27, Dover Street, w.*

VANSITTART, of Kirkleatham. (See *Newcomen.*)

VANSITTART-NEALE. (See *Neale.*)

VAN-STRAUBENZEE, Sir CHARLES THOMAS, K.C.B. (cr. 1858).

Second son of the late Thomas Van-Straubenzee, Esq., of Spennithorne, co. York, Major Royal Artillery, by Maria, dau. of Henry Bowen, Esq., and brother of Major Van-Straubenzee, of Spennithorne (whom see); b. 1812 ; m. 1841 Charlotte, youngest dau. of General John Luther Richardson. Is a Major-General in the Army (which he entered 1839) ; is Col. 39th Foot, late Col. 47th Foot, and formerly Lieut.-Col. 3rd Foot ; made a K.C.B. for his services as Commander of the Forces before Canton.—*United Service Club, s.w.*

VAN - STRAUBENZEE, Major HENRY, of Spennithorne Hall.

Eldest son of the late Major Thomas Van-Straubenzee, R.A., by Maria, dau. of Major Bowen ; b. 1810 ; s. his grand-uncle 1824 ; m. 1832 the Hon. Henrietta, dau. of John, 1st Lord Wrottesley, and has, with other issue,

　　• Turner, Lieut. R.H.A. ; b. 1838.

Major Van-Straubenzee, who is a J.P. and D.L. for the N. Riding of Yorkshire, a Dep.-Lieut. for the W.

Riding, Major 14th Light Dragoons, and Major 2nd West York Light Infantry Militia, descends from a Capt. in the Dutch Guards who came to England with William III.—*Spennithorne Hall, Bedale.*

VAUGHAN, the Rev. CHARLES JOHN, D.D.

Second son of the late Rev. Edward Thomas Vaughan, Vicar of St. Martin's, Leicester, by Agnes, dau. of John Pares, Esq., of Hopwell Hall, co. Derby ; b. 1816 ; m. 1850 Catherine Maria, dau. of the late Right Rev. Edward Stanley, D.D., Lord Bishop of Norwich. Educated at Rugby and Trinity Coll., Cambridge (B.A. 1838, M.A. 1841, D.D. 1845) ; was Fellow of his College, and afterwards Vicar of St. Martin's, Leicester, 1841–4 ; Head Master of Harrow School 1844–59 ; is Vicar of Doncaster, Chaplain in Ordinary to the Queen, and Chancellor of York Cathedral.—*The Vicarage, Doncaster ; Athenæum Club, s.w.*

VAUGHAN, GEORGE MONTGOMERY, Esq., of Quilly, Downshire.

Eldest son of the late George Vaughan, Esq., of Quilly, by Mary, dau. of G. Tyrrell, Esq., of co. Westmeath ; b. 1825 ; m. 1850 Frances St. Laurence, dau. of the late General the Hon. Arthur Grove Annesley, and has, with other issue,

　　• George Henry, b. 1854.

Mr. Vaughan was educated at Trinity Coll., Dublin (B.A. 1847). The family, of Welsh extraction, went over to Ireland in 1661.—*Quilly House, Dromore, co. Down ; 6, Palmerston Villas, Rathmines, co. Dublin.*

VAUGHAN, HERBERT, Esq., of Brynog and Green Grove, Cardiganshire.

Son of the late Lieut.-Col. Edward Vaughan (who was a Magistrate for co. Cardigan, and formerly Lieut.-Col. 98th Regt. ; b. 1833 ; s. 1855 ; m. 1862 Julia Radclyffe Paten, only child of the Rev. Lewis C. Davies, of Ynyshir, co. Cardigan, and grand-dau. of the late Robert Radclyffe, Esq., of Foxdenton Hall. co. Lancaster, and has issue 4 children. Is a J.P. and D.L. for co. Cardigan (High Sheriff 1862), late Capt. 65th Foot. This family is a younger branch of that of the Earl of Lisburne.—*Green Grove, Brynog, Leinjeter.*

VAUGHAN, the Rev. HUGH, of Llansaintfraid, Radnorshire.

Eldest son of the late Hugh Vaughan, Esq., D.L., of Llwynmadock (who was High Sheriff of co. Radnor 1826, and d. 1851), by Hannah, dau. of Lewis Lewis, Esq., of Builth, co. Brecon; b. 1802. Educated at Jesus Coll. Oxford (B.A. 1825, M.A. 1828); is a Magistrate for co. Radnor, and Vicar of Llansaintfraid-in-Elvel.—*Llansaintfraid, Builth.*

VAUGHAN, JAMES, Esq., F.R.G.S., of Builth, Breconshire.

Youngest son of the late Hugh Vaughan, Esq., of Llwynmadock (who d. 1851), by Hannah, dau. of Lewis Lewis, Esq., of Builth, co. Brecon; b. 1818. Is a Magistrate for cos. Brecon and Radnor; was formerly in the Bombay Medical Service.—*Llwynmadock, Llansaintfraid-in-Elvel, Builth ; East India United Service Club, s.w.*

VAUGHAN, Mrs., of Llangoedmore, Cardiganshire.

Sara, only dau. of the Ven. Archdeacon Millingchamp, of Llangoedmore, co. Cardigan; m. 1826 Capt. Herbert Vaughan (afterwards Lieut.-Col. Commanding H.M.'s 90th Light Infantry, a J.P. and D.L. for co. Cardigan), who d. 1862, leaving, with other issue,

　　• John, a Magistrate for co. Cardigan; b. 1830.

This family is a younger branch of that of the Earl of Lisburne.—*Llangoedmore, Cardigan,*

+VAUGHAN, John, Esq., of Nannau, Merionethshire.

Eldest son of the late John Vaughan, Esq., of the Madras Civil Service (who *d.* 1812), by Catherine Maitland, dau. of John Babington, Esq.; *b.* 1820; *s.* his grandfather, John Vaughan, Esq., 185—; *m.* 1863 Eleanor Anne, youngest dau. of the late Edward Owen, Esq., of Garthynghared, co. Merioneth, and has issue,

    † A son, *b.* 1865.

Mr. Vaughan, who is a J.P. and D.L. for co. Merioneth and Patron of 2 livings, represents a younger branch of the Vaughans of Hengwrt.—*Nannau Park, Dolgelley.*

VAUGHAN, Lieut.-Col. JOHN FRANCIS, of Court-Field, Herefordshire.

Eldest son of the late William Vaughan, Esq., J.P. and D.L., of Court-Field, by his 1st wife Teresa, dau. of the late Thomas Weld, Esq., of Lulworth Castle, Dorset; *b.* 1808; *s.* 1861; *m.* 1st 1830 Eliza Louisa, dau. of the late John Rolls, Esq., of The Hendre, co. Monmouth; 2nd 1860 Mary Charlotte, only dau. of the late Joseph Weld, Esq., of Lulworth, and has issue by the former,

    * Herbert Alfred, *b.* 1832.

Lieut.-Col. Vaughan, who was educated at Stonyhurst and St. Acheul, is a Dep.-Lieut. for co. Monmouth, and a Magistrate for cos. Gloucester, Hereford, Monmouth, and Mayo.—*Court-Field, Ross; Union Club, s.w.*

+VAUGHAN, JOHN WILLIAMS, Esq., of Velin Newydd, Brecknockshire.

Son of the late J. Vaughan, Esq., of Velin Newydd; *b.* 18—. Is a J.P. and D.L. for cos. Brecon and Radnor. —*Velin Newydd, Brecon.*

VAUGHAN, ROBERT CHAMBRE, Esq., of Burlton Hall, Shropshire.

Only child of the late Capt. Thomas Vaughan, of Burlton Hall, by Lowry Nanney, dau. of William Wynn, Esq., of Maes-y-neuadd, co. Merioneth; *b.* 1796; *s.* 1804; *m.* 1828 Anna, 3rd dau. of the Hon. Edward Massy, and has, with other issue,

    * John Nanney Chambre, of Woodgate, co. Salop, *b.* 1830; *m.* 1855 Catherine Masey, eldest dau. of Thomas Dickin, Esq., of Loppington House, co. Salop.

Mr. Vaughan was educated at Rugby and Brasenose Coll., Oxford (B.A. 1818). This family, formerly of Plâs Thomas, is descended from the celebrated Tudor Trevor.—*Burlton Hall, Shrewsbury.*

VAUGHAN. (See under *Lisburne, Earl of.*)

VAUGHAN. (See *Edwards-Vaughan.*)

VAUGHAN. (See *Gwynne-Vaughan.*)

VAUGHAN. (See *Lloyd-Vaughan.*)

VAUGHAN, OF RHUG. (See *Wynn, Hon. C. P.*)

VAUGHAN-JENKINS. (See *Jenkins.*)

VAUGHAN-PRYSE. (See *Pryse.*)

VAUGHTON, ROBERT DYMOCK, Esq.

Eldest son of the late Robert Darwin Vaughton, Esq., of Doddington, Salop, by Mary Anne, only dau. of the late Edward Dymock, Esq., of Penley Hall, co. Flint; *b.* 1827; *s.* 1855; *m.* 1858 Emily, dau. of J. M. Boultbee, Esq., and Lady Elizabeth Boultbee, of Springfield, co. Warwick. Is a Magistrate for co. Warwick, and a Capt. 1st Warwick Militia; was formerly Capt. 90th Foot. This family were formerly of Ashfurlong, co. Warwick, and of Doddington, co. Salop.—*Residence: Warwick; Junior United Service Club, s.w.*

    Heir Pres., his brother Theophilus, Capt. R.M.; *b.* 1829.

VAUX OF HARROWDEN, Lord (GEORGE MOSTYN).—Cr. 1523.

Only son of the late Charles Browne Mostyn, Esq., of Kiddington, Oxon (who *d.* 1821), by Mary Lucinda, dau. of the late George Butler, Esq.; *b.* 1804; *m.* 1828 Caroline, dau. of the late Col. Arthur Vansittart, of Shottesbrook Park, Berks. Is a Magistrate for cos. Mayo, Westmeath, and Surrey. This peerage was in abeyance 1663-1838.—*Rosmeade, Delvin, co. Westmeath; Brooks's Club, s.w.; Stafford Club, w.*

    Heir, his son George Charles, educated at Oscott, Capt. 3rd Surrey Militia; *b.* 1830; *m.* 1859 Mary, 2nd dau. of the late Right Rev. Dr. James Henry Monk, Lord Bishop of Gloucester and Bristol, and has, with other issue, * Hubert George Charles, *b.* 1860.

VAVASOUR, Sir EDWARD, Bart., of Hazelwood, Yorkshire (cr. 1791).

Eldest son of the late Hon. Sir Edward Marmaduke Vavasour, Bart. (who was a younger son of Charles Philip, 16th Lord Stourton, and who assumed the name of Vavasour on succeeding to the Hazelwood estates), by Marcia Bridget, dau. of the late James Lane-Fox, Esq., of Bramham Park, co. York; *b.* 1815; *s.* as 2nd Bart. 1847. Is Patron of 1 living.—*Hazelwood Castle, Tadcaster.*

    Heir Pres., his nephew William Edward (eldest son of the late William Vavasour, Esq., who *d.* 1860, by the Hon. Mary Constantia, dau. of Hugh Charles, 7th Lord Clifford (she *m.* 2nd 1865 Mr. M. D. Kavanagh); *b.* 1846.

VAVASOUR, Sir HENRY MERVYN, Bart., of Spaldington Hall, Yorkshire (cr. 1801).

Eldest son of the late Sir Henry Maghull Mervin Vavasour, Bart., of Spaldington Hall, by Anne, dau. of William Vavasour, Esq., LL.D., of Dublin; *b.* 1814; *s.* as 3rd Bart. 1838; *m.* 1853 the Hon. Louisa Anne Neville, dau. of Richard, 3rd Lord Braybrooke. Is a Magistrate for the E. Riding of co. York; late Major E. York Militia. Is descended maternally from the ancient family of Vavasour, of Spaldington and Hazelwood, whose Baronetcy became extinct in 1826, and is senior Baronet of the United Kingdom.—*Spaldington Hall, Howden.*

VAVASOUR, Mrs., of Fosse Cottage, Gloucestershire.

Caroline Susan, 2nd dau. of the late Lieut.-General Sir Henry Mervin Vavasour, Bart., of Spaldington; *m.* 1841 William Thomas Vavasour, Esq., who was a J.P. for co. Gloucester, and *d.s.p.* 1863. Her husband's family was a younger branch of the Vavasours of Spaldington.—*Fosse Cottage, Stow-on-the-Wold.*

VAWDREY, the Rev. DANIEL.

Eldest son of the late Daniel Vawdrey, Esq., of Tutsham, co. Chester (who *d.* 1814), by Anne, dau. of Benjamin Wyatt, Esq., of Lime Grove, co. Caernarvon; *b.* 1808; *m.* 1812 Christiana Anne, only dau. of Robert Pownall Hadfield, Esq., of Winnington, co. Chester, and has issue,

    * Lewis Pownall, *b.* 1846.

Mr. Vawdrey was educated at Brasenose Coll., Oxford (B.A. 1830, M.A. 1832); is Rector of North Darley. —*North Darley Rectory, Matlock.*

VEALE, JAMES HARRIS, Esq., of Passaford, Devon.

Eldest son of the late James Veale, Esq., of Passaford, and grandson of William Mallet, Esq., of Ash House, Iddesleigh, Devon (who assumed the name of Veale under the will of his uncle, James Veale, Esq., of Passaford); *b.* 1800; *s.* 1816; *m.* 1830 Emily, eldest dau. of the late Henry Nevile, clerk, Rector of Cottesmore, co.

Rutland. Educated at Catharine Hall, Cambridge, and has, with other issue,
* Henry Mallet, *b.* 1831.
Mr. Veale is a J.P. and D.L. for Devon.—*Passaford, Hatherleigh.*

+ VEALE, the Rev. WILLIAM, of Trevelian, Cornwall.
Only son of the late William Veale, Esq., of Trevelian, by Mary, dau. of Alexander Penrose Cumming, Esq.; *b.* 1783; *m.* 18— Miss Mary (she is *dec.*). Educated at Winchester and New Coll., Oxford (B.A. 1806, M.A. 1810).—*Trevelian, Gulval, Penzance.*

VEASEY, DAVID, Esq., of Castle Hill, Hunts.
Third son of the late David Veasey, Esq., Banker, of Huntingdon; *b.* 1791; *m.* 1817 Elizabeth, eldest dau. of the late Ingram Chapman, Esq., of Whitby, co. York, and has, with other issue,
* Francis Gerald, educated at Harrow, and M.A. of Trinity Coll., Cambridge; Rector of All Saints and St. John's, Huntingdon; *b.* 1832.
Mr. Veasey is a J.P. and D.L. for Hunts.—*Castle Hill House, Huntingdon; Union Club, s.w.*

VEITCH, JAMES, Esq., of Eliock, Dumfriesshire.
Eldest son of the late Henry Veitch, Esq., of Eliock, by Zepherina, dau. of Thomas Loughnan, Esq., of Madeira; *b.* 1799; *s.* 1838; *m.* 1831 Hannah Charlotte, dau. of the late James Hay, Esq., of Hopes. Educated at Edinburgh; called to the Scottish Bar 1821; appointed Sheriff Substitute of co. Lanark 1833, a J.P. and D.L. for co. Dumfries 1829.—*Eliock House, Sanquhar, N.B.*
Heir Pres., his nephew Henry, in Holy Orders,(son of the Rev. William Douglas Veitch, by Eleanor, dau. of Lieut.-Col. Rait); *b.* 1833.

VENABLES, the Rev. RICHARD LISTER, of Clyro, Radnorshire, and of Llysdinam, Breconshire.
Eldest son of the late Ven. Richard Venables, of Llysdinam, co. Brecon (some time Archdeacon of Carmarthen), by Sophia, youngest dau. of George Lister, Esq., of Girsby, co. Lincoln; *b.* 1809; *m.* 1st 1834 Mary Augusta Dalrymple, dau. of General Poltoratzky, of Russia, and widow of Francis J. Adam, Esq. (she *d.* 1865); 2nd 1867 Agnes Minna, youngest dau. of the late Henry Shepherd Pearson, Esq. Educated at the Charterhouse and Emmanuel Coll., Cambridge (B.A. 1831, M.A. 1835); is a J.P. and D.L. for co. Radnor, a Magistrate for co. Hereford, Chairman of the Radnorshire Quarter Sessions, and Vicar of Clyro.—*Clyro, Hay; Oxford and Cambridge Club, s.w.*

VENABLES, ROWLAND JONES, Esq.,‡ of Oakhurst, Shropshire.
Eldest son of the late Rev. Joseph Venables, by Mary, dau. of Edward Rowland, Esq., of Garthen Lodge, near Ruabon, co. Denbigh; *b.* 1812; *m.* 1837 Harriet, dau. of Edgar Corrie, Esq., of Arlington Manor, near Newbury. Is a Magistrate for cos. Salop and Denbigh, and Lieut. N. Salop Yeomanry Cavalry.—*Oakhurst, Oswestry; Carlton Club, s.w.*

VENABLES, THOMAS ALFRED, Esq., of Woodhill, Shropshire.
Fourth but eldest surviving son of the late Lazarus Jones Venables, Esq., of Woodhill, by Alice, dau. of Thomas Jolley, Esq., of Liverpool; *b.* 1816; *s.* his brother 1858.—*Woodhill, Oswestry.*
Heir Pres., his brother William, *b.* 1818; *m.* 1859 Augusta Mary, dau. of John Adams, Esq., of Holyland, co. Pembroke, and has issue, a son, *b.* 1863.

‡ Died whilst these sheets were at press.

VENABLES. (See *Chambers-Venables.*)

VENABLES-VERNON. (See *Vernon.*)

VENN, EDWARD BEAUMONT, Esq., of Freston, Suffolk.
Only son of the late Edward Venn, Esq., of Camberwell, Surrey, by Charlotte Ann, dau. of William Gambier, Esq., of Camberwell; *b.* 1781; *s.* 1830; *m.* 1806 Harriet, dau. of Francis Green, Esq., of Dorking, Surrey, and has, with other issue,
* Gerard Noel, *b.* 1809; *m.* 1858 Emma Gerrard, dau. of George Mayhew, E.-q., of Ipswich, and has issue.
Mr. Venn, who was educated at Ipswich School, is a J.P. and D.L. for Suffolk, and Lord of the Manor of Cotton Hempnalls.—*Freston Lodge, Ipswich.*

VENNER. (See under *Sidebottom, of Elm Bank.*)

VENTRY, Lord (DAYROLLES BLAKENEY DE MOLEYNS).—Cr. 1800.
Eldest son of Thomas Townsend Aremberg, 3rd Lord, by Elizabeth Theodora, dau. of Sir John Blake Blake, Bart.; *b.* 1828; *s.* 1868; *m.* 1860 Harriet Elizabeth, eldest dau. of Andrew Wauchope, Esq., of Niddrie Marischal, Midlothian. Is Lieut.-Col. Kerry Militia.—*Burnham House, Kerry.*
Heir, his son Frederick, *b.* 1861.

VERE, JOHN, Esq., of Carlton House, Notts.
Eldest son of the late Peter Vere, Esq., of Grosvenor Place, London, by Elizabeth, only dau. of John Egginton, Esq.; *b.* 1797. Educated at C.C.C., Oxford (B.A. 1819, M.A. 1823); is a Magistrate for Notts (High Sheriff 1847).—*Carlton House, Newark; University Club, s.w.*
Heir Pres., his brother James, *b.* 1800.

VERE. (See *Hope-Vere.*)

VEREKER, the Hon. JOHN PRENDERGAST.
Second son of John Prendergast, 3rd Viscount Gort, by the Hon. Maria, dau. of Standish, 1st Viscount Guillamore; *b.* 1822; *m.* 1858 Louisa, only child of George Medlicott, Esq., and grand-dau. of the late Arthur Magan, Esq., of Clonearl, King's Co., and niece of the late Baroness Castlecoote, and has, with other issue,
* George Medlicott, *b.* 1860.
Mr. Vereker, who was educated at Trinity Coll., Dublin (B.A. 1843), and called to the Irish Bar in 1847, was Lord Mayor of Dublin 1863-4.—*16, Merrion Square, South, Dublin.*

VEREKER. (See under *Gort, Viscount.*)

VERNER, Sir WILLIAM, Bart., of Verner's Bridge, co. Armagh (cr. 1846).
Eldest son of the late James Verner, Esq., of Verner's Bridge, by Jane, dau. of the Rev. Henry Clarke, of Ancasummery, co. Armagh; *b.* 1782; *s.* 1849 Harriet, dau. of the Hon. Col. Edward Winefield. Is a J.P. and D.L. for cos. Tyrone, Monaghan, and Armagh (of which cos. he has been High Sheriff), and a Lieut.-Col. in the Army retired, served in 7th Hussars in the Peninsular war; has been M.P. for co. Armagh since 1832.—*Inniskmagh, co. Tyrone; Verner's Bridge, Moy, co. Antrim; Carlton and Junior United Service Clubs, s.w.; 86, Eaton Square, s.w.*
Heir, his son William (of Churchhill, Verner's Bridge, co. Armagh), a J.P. and D.L. for co. Tyrone (High Sheriff 1847), a Magistrate for co. Armagh (High Sheriff 1848); late Lieut. and Capt. Coldstream Guards; *b.* 1822; *m.* 1859 Mary Frances Hester, dau. of the late Lieut.-General the Hon. Sir Hercules Pakenham, K.C.B., and has, with other issue, * William Edward Hercules, *b.* 1859.

+ VERNER, EDWARD WINGFIELD, Esq.
Second son of Sir William Verner, Bart., M.P., of Verner's Bridge, co. Armagh, by Harriet, dau. of the Hon. Col. Edward Wingfield; *b.* 1830; *m.* 1864 Selina Florence, dau. of Thomas V. Nugent, Esq., and has issue.
   * A son, *b.* 1865.
Mr. Verner was educated at Eton and Ch. Ch., Oxford, and elected M.P. for Lisburn 1863.—*Cork Abbey, Bray, co. Dublin ; Junior United Service and Carlton Clubs,* s.w.; 86, *Eaton Square,* s.w.

VERNER, Capt. THOMAS, of Lilliput, co. Antrim.
Third son of the late Lieut.-Col. Verner, and brother of Lieut.-Col. W. Verner, of Belfast, co. Antrim (whom see); *b.* 1811. Is a J.P. and D.L. for cos. Antrim and Down, and Capt. of the Queen's Royal Antrim Rifles.—*Lilliput, Belfast ; Carlton Club,* s.w.

VERNER, Lieut.-Col. WILLIAM, of Steephill Castle, Isle of Wight, and Belfast, co. Antrim.
Second son of the late Lieut.-Col. James Verner, M.P., of Churchill, co. Armagh (who was brother of Sir William Verner, Bart., M.P.), by Elizabeth, dau. of Sir Edward May, Bart., of Mayfield, co. Waterford, and sister of Anna Marchioness of Donegal; *b.* 1809 ; *m.* 1st 1833 his cousin Charlotte Elizabeth, dau. of the Rev. Edward May, of Westbrook, co. Down (she *d.* 1861); 2nd 1867 Charlotte Jane, dau. of the late John Fleming, Esq., M.P., of Stoneham Park, Hants, and widow of Albert John Hambrough, Esq., J.P. and D.L., of Steephill Castle, Isle of Wight. Educated at Eton and Trinity Coll., Dublin (B.A. 1837); is a Magistrate for and Treasurer of co. Antrim, and Lieut.-Col. Commandant Antrim Artillery. This family were formerly of Auchentennie, N.B.—*Steephill Castle, Ventnor, Isle of Wight ; Belfast, co. Antrim ; Carlton and Junior Carlton Clubs,* s.w.

VERNEY, Sir HARRY, Bart., of Claydon, Bucks (cr. 1818).
Eldest son of the late General Sir Harry Calvert, Bart., G.C.B., of Claydon, by Caroline, dau. of Thomas Hammersley, Esq., of London; *b.* 1801; *s.* as 2nd Bart. 1826; *m.* 1st 1835 Eliza, dau. of Admiral Sir George Johnstone-Hope, K.C.B.; 2nd 1858 Frances Parthenope dau. of William Edward Nightingale, Esq., of Embly Park, Hants. Educated at Harrow and the Military Coll., Marlow; is a J.P. and D.L. for Bucks, Patron of 4 livings, and a Major in the Army, retired; was formerly attached to the Mission in Würtemberg, and in Grenadier Guards, and Major Bucks Militia; was M.P. for Buckingham 1832–41, for Bedford 1847–52, re-chosen for Buckingham 1857, 1859, and 1865. He assumed the name of Verney in lieu of Calvert 1827.—*Claydon House, Winslow ; Travellers' and United Service Clubs,* s.w.; 32, *South Street,* w.
   Heir, his son Edmund Hope, a J.P. and D.L. for Bucks, and a Commander R.N.; *b.* 1838; *m.* 1868 Margaret Maria, eldest dau. of the late Sir John Hay Williams, Bart.

VERNEY. (See under *Willoughby de Broke, Lord.*)

VERNON, Lord (AUGUSTUS HENRY VERNON).—Cr. 1762.
Elder son of George John, 5th Lord (who assumed the name of Warren in lieu of Vernon 1837), by his 1st wife Isabella Catharine, dau. of the late Cuthbert Ellison, Esq., of Hepburn Hall, co. Durham; *b.* 1829 ; *s.* 1866; *m.* 1851 Lady Harriet, 3rd dau. of Thomas William, 1st Earl of Lichfield. Is a J.P. and D.L. for cos. Derby and Stafford, a Dep.-Lieut. for co. Chester, and Patron of 4 livings; Capt.-Commandant 2nd Derbyshire Rifles, and late Lieut. Scots Fusilier Guards.—*Sudbury Hall, Derby ; Poynton Ha'l, Stockport,*
962

Cheshire ; Widdrington Castle, Morpeth ; Travellers' and Brooks's Clubs, s.w.; 5, *Upper Belgrave Street,* s.w.
   Heir, his son George William Henry, *b.* 1854.

VERNON, the Hon. and Rev. COURTENAY JOHN.
Third son of Robert, 1st Lord Lyveden, by Emma Mary, dau. of John, late Earl of Upper Ossory (ext.); *b.* 1828; *m.* 1856 Alice Gertrude, dau. of the Rev. Maurice Fitzgerald Stephens Townsend, and has, with other issue,
   * Courtenay Robert Percy, *b.* 1857.
Mr. Vernon, who was educated at Eton and Trinity Coll., Cambridge, is a Magistrate for co. Northampton, and Rector of Grafton Underwood.—*Grafton Underwood Rectory, Kettering.*

VERNON, the Hon. GOWRAN CHARLES.
Second son of Robert, 1st Lord Lyveden, by Emma Mary, dau. and co-heir of John, 2nd and last Earl of Upper Ossory (ext.); *b.* 1825 ; *m.* 1857 Caroline, dau. of the late John Nicholas Fazakerley, Esq., M.P., of Burwood, Surrey, and has issue. Educated at Eton and Trinity Coll., Cambridge; is a Barrister-at-law of the Midland Circuit; appointed Recorder of Lincoln 1859.—37, *Montague Square,* w.; 11, *King's Bench Walk, Temple,* E.C.

VERNON, the Hon. and Rev. JOHN VENABLES.
Third son of Henry, 3rd Lord Vernon, by his 2nd wife Alice Lucy, dau. of Sir John Whitford, Bart.; *b.* 1798; *m.* 1st 1830 Frances Barbara, 2nd dau. of Thomas Duncombe, Esq., of Copgrove, co. York (she *d.* 1848); 2nd 1853 Caroline, dau. of the late Hon. General Edward Paget, G.C.B. Educated at Westminster and Ch. Ch., Oxford (B.A. 1819, M.A. 1822); appointed Rector of Kirkby 1829, of Nuthall 1837.—*Nuthall Rectory, Nottingham.*

VERNON, the Hon. WILLIAM JOHN BORLASE-WARREN-VENABLES-.
Younger son of George John, 5th Lord Vernon, by Isabella Caroline, dau. of Cuthbert Ellison, Esq., M.P. for Newcastle; *b.* 1834; *m.* 1855 Agnes Lucy, dau. of Sir John Peter Boileau, Bart. Educated at Eton; is a J.P. and D.L. for co. Stafford; late Lieut. Staffordshire Militia. Assumed the names of Borlase-Warren 1856.—35, *Rutland Gate,* w.

VERNON, GRANVILLE HARCOURT-, Esq., of Grove Hall, Notts.
Sixth son of the late Hon. and Most Rev. Dr. Edward Vernon-Harcourt, Lord Archbishop of York, by Lady Anne, sister of George, 1st Duke of Sutherland, K.G.; *b.* 1792; *m.* 1st 1814 Frances Julia, dau. and heir of the late Anthony Hardolph Eyre, Esq., of Grove Hall (she *d.* 1844); 2nd 1855 Pyne Jessie, eldest dau. of Henry Otway, 22nd Lord Dacre, and has by the former, with other issue,
   * Evelyn Hardolph, in Holy Orders, S.C.L. of University Coll., Oxford, and Rector of Cotgrave, Notts; *b.* 1821; *m.* 1849 Jane Catherine, dau. of Edward St. John Mildmay, Esq., and has, with other issue. †James H. Evelyn, *b.* 1868.
Mr. Harcourt-Vernon, who was educated at Ch. Ch., Oxford (B.A. 1814, M.A. 1816), is a J.P. and D.L. for Notts, Chancellor of the Province of York, and Patron of 3 livings; was M.P. for E. Retford 1831–47.—*Grove Hall, Retford ; 5, Belgrave Square,* s.w.

VERNON, HARRY FOLEY, Esq., of Hanbury Hall, Worcestershire.
Younger son of the late Thomas T. Vernon, Esq., of Hanbury Hall (who *d.* 1838), by Anna Lætitia, dau. of J. H. Foley, Esq., of Ridgeway, co. Pembroke; *b.* 1834; * his brother 1859; *m.* 1861 Lady Georgina Sophia

Baillie Hamilton, dau. of George, 10th Earl of Haddington, by whom he has, with other issue,
* Bowater George Hamilton, b. 1865.

Mr. Vernon, who was educated at Harrow and Magdalen Coll., Oxford (B.A. 1858, M.A. 1860), is a J.P. and D.L. for co. Worcester; Lieut. Queen's Own Worcestershire Yeomanry Cavalry, and Major 18th Worcestershire Volunteer Rifles. Elected M.P. for E. Worcestershire 1861.—*Hanbury Hall, Droitwich; Oxford and Cambridge, and Brooks's Clubs, s.w.; 48, Prince's Gardens, Kensington, w.*

VERNON, HENRY CHARLES, Esq., of Hilton Park, Staffordshire.
Eldest son of the late General Henry Charles Edward Vernon, C.B., of Hilton Park, by Maria, 4th dau. of the late George John Cooke, Esq., of Harefield Park, Middlesex; b. 1805; s. 1861; m. 1828 Catherine, youngest dau. of Richard Rice Williams, Esq., of Hendredenny, co. Glamorgan, and has, with other issue,
* Augustus Leveson (of Dean's Field, Brewood, Stafford), a Magistrate for co. Stafford; b. 1836; m. 1864 Selina Anne, younger dau. of Walter F. Giffard, Esq., of Chillington, co. Stafford.

Mr. Vernon is a J.P. and D.L. for Stafford (High Sheriff 1867), and Lord of the Manor of Hilton.—*Hilton Park, Wolverhampton; United Service Club, s.w.*

VERNON, JOHN EDWARD, Esq., of Erne Hill, co. Cavan.
Only son of the late Rev. John Fane Vernon, of Aubawn, co. Cavan, by Frances, dau. of the late Right Rev. John Kearney, D.D., Lord Bishop of Ossory; b. 1816; s. 1843; m. 1846 Harriet, dau. of the late Right Rev. John Leslie, D.D., Bishop of Kilmore; 2nd 1857 Maria Esther, elder dau. of the Hon. George Francis Colley, of Ferney, co. Dublin, and has by the former, with other issue,
* John Fane, b. 1849.

Mr. Vernon, who was educated at Trinity Coll., Dublin (B.A. 1839, M.A. 1842), is a J.P. and D.L. for co. Cavan (High Sheriff 1864), and a Magistrate for cos. Dublin and Wicklow.—*Erne Hill, Belturbet, co. Cavan; Kildare Street Club, Dublin; Athenæum Club, s.w.*

VERNON, JOHN EDWARD VENABLES, Esq., of Clontarf Castle, co. Dublin.
Second son of the late George Vernon, Esq., of Clontarf Castle (who d. 1822), by Henrietta, Maria, dau. of Wilson Gale Braddyll, Esq., of Conishead Priory, Lancaster; b. 1813; s. his brother 1833; m. 1st 1836 Louisa Catherine, only dau. of C. P. Bowles, Esq., of Park Lane, London; 2nd 1856 the Hon. Rosa Gertrude Harriet, dau. of James Lord Dunsandle (she d. 1859), and has by the former, with other issue,
* Edward, b. 1838.

Mr. Vernon is a J.P. and D.L. for co. Dublin.—*Clontarf Castle, Dublin; Carlton Club, s.w.*

VERNON, Mrs., of Ardington House, Berks.
Emily, dau. of the late William St. Leger Douglas, Esq.; m. 1825 Capt. Leicester Viney Vernon, R.E., of Ardington House, M.P. for Berks (who d. 1860). The late Capt. Vernon took the name of Vernon by Royal licence in 1849, on succeeding to the estates of Robert Vernon, Esq., who presented his collection of modern paintings to the nation.—*Ardington House, Wantage.*

VERNON, WILLIAM FREDERICK, Esq., of Harefield Park, Middlesex.
Second son of the late General Henry C. E. Vernon, C.B., of Hilton Park, co. Stafford (who d. 1861), by Maria, 4th dau. of the late George John Cooke, Esq., of Harefield Park; b. 1807; s. his maternal uncle 1810; m. 1841 Elizabeth, 2nd dau. of the late James Shuttleworth, Esq., of Barton, co. Lancaster (who d. s. p. 1650).

Mr. Vernon, who was educated at Harrow, is a Dep. Lieut. for Middlesex; late Capt. 68th Foot.—*Harefield Park, Uxbridge; Junior United Service Club, s.w.*
Heir Pres., his brother George Augustus, a J.P. and D.L. for co. Stafford, Lieut.-Col. in the Army, and Provincial Grand Master of Freemasons for Staffordshire; b. 1811; m. 1842 Louisa Jane Frances, dau. of Admiral Bertie Cator, R.N., and has, with other surviving issue, * Bertie Wentworth, Sub-Lieut. R.N., b. 1846.

VERNON-HARCOURT. (See *Harcourt.*)

VERNON-SMITH. (See under *Lyveden, Lord.*)

VERNON-HARCOURT, the Rev. CHARLES GRANVILLE, of Rothbury, Northumberland.
Eighth son of the late Hon. and Most Rev. Edward Harcourt, D.C.L., Lord Archbishop of York, by Lady Anne, 3rd dau. of Granville, 1st Marquis of Stafford, K.G.; b. 1798. Is a Magistrate for Northumberland, Rector of Rothbury, and Prebendary of Carlisle.—*Rothbury, Morpeth.*

VERNON-WENTWORTH, FREDERICK WILLIAM THOMAS, Esq., of Wentworth Castle, Yorkshire.
Second son of the late Henry Vernon, Esq., of Hilton, by his 2nd wife Margaret, dau. of Thomas Fisher, Esq., of Acton, Middlesex; b. 1795; s. 1814; m. 1826 Lady Augusta Brudenell-Bruce, 2nd dau. of Charles, 1st Marquis of Ailesbury, K.T., and has with other issue,
* Thomas Frederick Charles, of Stoke Park, near Towcester, and Dall-Pitlochrie, co. Perth; educated at Eton, and M.A. of Trinity Coll., Cambridge; a Magistrate for the W. Riding of Yorkshire and for Bucks, and late M.P. for Aylesbury; b. 1831; m. 1859 Lady Harriet Augusta, dau. of Ulrick John, 1st Marquis of Clanricarde, K.P., and has issue, * a son, b. 1866.

Mr. Vernon-Wentworth, who was educated at Ch. Ch., Oxford, is a J.P. and D.L. for Yorkshire (High Sheriff 1841), and Patron of 2 livings. He assumed the latter name in compliance with the will of his father's cousin, the sister of the last Earl of Strafford (ext.), who d. 1802.—*Wentworth Castle, Barnsley; Aldborough Lodge, Suffolk; 11, Connaught Place, w.*

VERULAM, Earl of (JAMES WALTER GRIMSTON).—Cr. 1815.
Eldest son of James Walter, 1st Earl, by Lady Charlotte, dau. of Charles, 1st Earl of Liverpool; b. 1809; s. 1845; m. 1844 Elizabeth Jeanna, dau. of Major Richard Weyland, of Woodeaton, Oxon. Educated at Harrow and Ch. Ch., Oxford (B.A. 1830); is Lord-Lieutenant and Custos Rot. of Herts; Chairman of the Herts Quarter Sessions, and Patron of 6 livings; late Lieut.-Col. S. Herts Yeomanry; was M.P. for Herts 1832-45, a Lord in Waiting Feb.-Dec. 1852 and 1858-9.—*Gorhambury, St. Alban's; Carlton Club, s.w.; 42, Grosvenor Square, w.*
Heir, his son James Walter, Viscount Grimston, educated at Harrow; b. 1852.

VESEY, JOHN THOMAS, Esq., of Knapton, Queen's Co.
Eldest son of the late Hon. and Rev. Arthur Vesey, by Sydney, dau. of Edward Johnstone, Esq.; b. 1815; s. 1832. Represents a younger branch of the family of Viscount De Vesci.—*Knapton, Abbeyleix, Queen's Co.*
Heir Pres., his brother Arthur George, Lieut.-Col. 46th Foot; b. 1818; is married, and has issue.

VESEY, SAMUEL, Esq., of Derrybard, co. Tyrone.
Eldest son of the late Rev. Dr. Vesey, of Dublin, by Barbara, dau. of Samuel Taylor, Esq., of Grange, co. Dublin; b. 1795; s. 1800; m. 1816 Waller, dau. of the ...

- late Right Rev. Dr. Kearney, Lord Bishop of Ossory, and has, with other issue,

* George Waller, Paymaster 3rd Dragoon Guards ; b. 1821.

Mr. Vesey is a J.P. and D.L. for co. Tyrone (High Sheriff 1826).—*Derryhard House, Omagh, co. Tyrone; Sackville Street Club, Dublin.*

VESEY.   (See *Colthurst-Vesey.*)

VESEY.   (See under *De Vesci, Viscount.*)

VESEY.   (See *Foster-Vesey-Fitz Gerald.*)

VIDAL, EDWARD URCH, Esq., of Cornborough, Devonshire.
Only son of the late Edward Sealy, Esq., J.P., of Friarn House, Bridgewater (who *d.* 1864), by Elizabeth, dau. of the Rev. W. Lewis, of Cannington, Somerset ; *b.* 1816 ; *m.* 1842 Emma Harriet, dau. of Walpole Eyre, Esq., of Weybridge, and has, with other issue,

* Edward Sealy, *b.* 1848.

Mr. Vidal, who was educated at Westminster and Ch. Ch., Oxford (B.A. 1837, M.A. 1841), called to the Bar at the Middle Temple 1841, and went the Western Circuit, is a Magistrate for Somerset and Devon. The surname of Vidal was assumed by Mr. Sealy under the will of R. S. Vidal, Esq., who *d.* in 1841.—*Cornborough, Bideford.*

VIGNOLES, the Very Rev. CHARLES, D.D., of Cornahir, co. Westmeath.
Eldest son of the late Rev. John Vignoles, of Cornahir (who was formerly a Major 39th Foot), by Anna Honora, dau. of the Rev. Dr. Low; *b.* 1788; *m.* 1811 Elizabeth, dau. of Thomas Durell, Esq., of Southampton, and had, with other issue,

John, *b.* 1812 ; *m.* 1841 Eleanor, dau. of Thomas Featherston Haugh, Esq., of Bracklyn, co. Westmeath, and *d.* 1843, leaving issue, * Charles Howard, *b.* 1842.

Mr. Vignoles, who was educated at Trinity Coll., Dublin (B.A. 1809, M.A. 1812), is Dean of Ossory, Rector of Aghavoe, and of St. Patrick's, Kilkenny.—*Cornahir, Tyrrelspass ; The Deanery, Kilkenny.*

VIGOR.   (See *Stonhouse-Vigor.*)

+**VIGORS, FERDINAND, Esq., of Old Leighton, co. Carlow.**
Natural son of the late Nicholas Aylward Vigors, Esq., D.C.L., who was a Dep.-Lieut. for co. Carlow, and sometime M.P. for that county; *b.* 18—; *m.* 1847 Emma, only dau. of Jean Antoine Branchu, of Geneva.—*Old Leighton, co. Carlow.*

+**VIGORS, HENRY RUDKIN, Esq., of Erindale, co. Carlow.**
Only son of the late Thomas Tench Vigors, Esq., of Erindale, who was a J.P. and D.L. for co. Carlow (High Sheriff, 1842–3), by Jane, dau. of Gilbert P. Rudkin, Esq., of Wells, co. Carlow (she remarried 1852 P. M. Murphy, Esq., Q.C.), *b.* 1833, *s.* 1849. Was formerly Capt. 10th Foot.—*Erindale, Carlow.*

VIGORS, JOHN CLIFFE, Esq., of Burgage, co. Carlow.
Eldest surviving son of the late Rev. Thomas Mercer Vigors, of Burgage, by Anne, dau. of the Rev. John Cliffe, of New Ross; *b.* 1815 ; *s.* 1850. Educated at Trinity Coll., Dublin (B.A. 1836); is a Magistrate for co. Carlow, and Major Carlow Militia.—*Burgage, Leighlin Bridge, co. Carlow.*

Heir Pres., his nephew Thomas Mercer (only child of the late Bartholomew Urban Vigors, Esq., who *d.* 1854, by Charlotte, dau. of Lieut.-Col. John Bruce), *b.* 1853,
954

VILLEBOIS, HENRY, Esq., of Marham, Norfolk.
Only son of the late Henry Villebois, Esq., of Marham; *b.* 1807 ; *s.* 1847 ; *m.* 1831 Maria, elder dau. of the late Thomas Philip Bagge, Esq., of Stradsett Hall, Norfolk. Is a J.P. and D.L. for Norfolk (High Sheriff 1849), Lord of the Manor of Marham, and Patron of 1 living.—*Marham House, Downham ; ,23, Belgrave Square, s.w.*

Heir Pres., his sister Maria, Viscountess Glentworth ; she *m.* Col. Baillie, of the Royal Horse Guards.

VILLIERS, the Right Hon. CHARLES PELHAM.
Third son of the late Hon. George Villiers, by the Hon. Theresa Parker, dau. of John, 1st Lord Boringdon, and brother of George, 4th Earl of Clarendon, K.G.; *b.* 1802. Educated at St. John's Coll., Cambridge (B.A. 1824, M.A. 1827); called to the Bar at Lincoln's Inn 1827 ; is a J.P. and D.L. for Herts ; has been M.P. for Wolverhampton since 1835 ; formerly an Examiner in the Court of Chancery, and a Poor-Law Commissioner; was Judge-Advocate General 1852; President of the Poor-Law Board 1859–66.—*Athenæum, Reform, and Travellers' Clubs, s.w. ; 39, Sloane Street, s.w.*

VILLIERS, the Hon. FREDERICK WILLIAM CHILD-, of Sulby, Northamptonshire.
Third son of George, 5th Earl of Jersey, by Lady Sarah, eldest dau. of John, 10th Earl of Westmoreland; *b.* 1815 ; *m.* 1812 Lady Elizabeth, dau. of Renaud, 8th Earl of Athlone (ext.). Educated at Eton ; is a Magistrate for cos. Leicester and Middlesex ; a J.P. and D.L. and Chairman of Quarter Sessions for co. Northampton; formerly a Capt. in the Army ; late Lieut.-Col. Middlesex Militia ; was M.P. for Weymouth 1847–52.—*Sulby Hall, Welford ; 38, Berkeley Square, w.*

VILLIERS, the Hon. Mrs. EDWARD.
Elizabeth Charlotte, 5th dau. of Thomas Henry, 1st Lord Ravensworth, by Maria, dau. of John Simpson, Esq., of Bradley, co. Durham; *m.* 1835 the Hon. Edward Ernest Villiers (who *d.* 1843).—*Grove Mill House, Watford.*

VILLIERS.
(See under *Clarendon, Earl of,* and *Jersey, Earl of.*)

VINCENT, Sir FRANCIS, Bart., of Stoke d'Abernon, Surrey, and Debden, Essex (cr. 1620).
Eldest son of the late Sir Francis Vincent, Bart., of Stoke d'Abernon, Surrey, and Debden Hall, Essex, by Jane, dau. of the Hon. Edward Bouverie ; *b.* 1803 ; *s.* as 10th Bart. 1809 ; *m.* 1824 Augusta Elizabeth, dau. of the Hon. Charles Herbert. Is a Dep.-Lieut. for Essex, and Patron of 1 living ; was M.P. for St. Alban's 1832–4.—*8, Berkeley Street, w.*

Heir Pres., his cousin the Rev. Frederick Vincent (whom see).

VINCENT, the Rev. FREDERICK.
Second son of the late Henry Dormer Vincent, Esq., by Isabella, dau. of the Hon. Felton Henry, and grandson of the late Sir F. Vincent, Bart.; *b.* 1798; *m.* 1st 1826 Louisa, dau. and co-heir of J. Norris, Esq., of Hughenden, Bucks; 2nd 1844 Maria Copley, dau. of Robert H. Young, Esq., and has, with other issue,

* William, in Holy Orders, *b.* 1854 ; *m.* 1860 Lady Margaret, dau. of Henry David, 12th Earl of Buchan.

Mr. Vincent, who was educated at Brasenose Coll., Oxford (B.A. 1819), is a Magistrate for Bucks ; was appointed Rector of Slinfold, Sussex, 1844 ; late Vicar of Hughenden, Bucks.—*Slinfold Rectory, Horsham.*

VINCENT, Mrs., of Lily Hill, Berks.
Elizabeth Anne, dau. of the late Col. George Callander, of Craigfo~th and Ardkinlas, N.B., by Elizabeth Cromp-ton, eldest dau. of the Hon. Henry Erskine; *m.* 1830 Henry William Vincent, Esq., of Lily Hill, a Dep.-Lieut. for Berks, who *d.* 1865, leaving issue two daughters, Susan, and Harriet, *m.* 1860 Capt. Camp-bell, of Ardpatrick, co. Argyll (whom see).—*Lily Hill, Bracknell.*

+VINCENT, the Very Rev. JAMES VINCENT, Dean of Bangor.
Son of the late J. Vincent, Esq.; *b.* 1793. Educated at Jesus Coll., Oxford (B.A. 1815, M.A. 1818); is a J.P. and D.L. for co. Carnarvon; Rector of Llanfairfecha, and Dean of Bangor.—*The Deanery, Bangor.*

VINCENT, WILLIAM CLARKE, Esq., of Boston Lodge, Yorkshire.
Elder son of the late William Read Vincent, Esq., of Boston Lodge (who was a Capt. in the 3rd West York Militia), by Sarah, elder dau. and co-heir of the late John Clarke, Esq., of Boston Lodge and Wakefield; *b.* 1828; *s.* 1862. This family migrated from Ireland to Yorkshire towards the end of last century.—*Boston Lodge, Tadcaster.*

Heir Pres., his brother John, a Capt. in the Military Train; *b.* 1830; *m.* 1862 Anne, dau. of the Rev. J. Linton, of He-mingford House, Huntingdon, and has issue, * William Henry Hutchinson, *b.* 1863.

+VINER, JOSEPH ELLIS-, Esq., of Badge-worth House, Gloucestershire.
Son of the late Daniel Ellis, Esq., of Badgeworth, by Mary, dau. of — Viner, Esq.; *b.* 1785; *m.* 1814 Anne, dau. of Capt. John Twysden, of The Rock, Tiverton, Devon, and has, with other issue,

* Alfred William, educated at University Coll., Oxford (B.A. 1845); *b.* 1823.

Mr. Ellis-Viner, who assumed the latter name in com-pliance with the will of his uncle, William Viner, Esq., of Badgeworth, is a Magistrate for co. Gloucester, and Patron and Lord of the Manor of Badgeworth.—*Badge-worth House, Gloucester.*

VIPAN, JOHN, Esq., of Sutton, Cambridgeshire.
Eldest son of the late Joseph Vipan, Esq., of Sutton, by Ann, dau. of John Maylin, Esq., of Sutton; Isle of Ely; *b.* 1794; *s.* 1840; *m.* 1819 Mary, dau. of Benja-min Vipan, Esq., of Mepal, Isle of Ely, and has, with other issue,

* John Maylin, of Stilbington, near Wansford, educated at Eton; a Magistrate for Hunts and Liberty of Peterborough; *b.* 1824; *m.* 1845 Harriet, dau. of Simon Goodman, Esq.

Mr. Vipan, who is a J.P. and D.L. for the Isle of Ely, was High Sheriff of cos. Cambridge and Hunts 1850.—*Sutton, Ely.*

VIVEASH. (See *Baskerville.*)

VIVIAN, Lord (CHARLES CRESPIGNY VIVIAN) — Cr. 1841.
Eldest son of Richard Hussey, 1st Lord, by his 1st wife Eliza, dau. of Philip Champion de Crespigny, Esq.; *b.* 1808; *s.* 1842; *m.* 1st 1833 Arabella, dau. of the Rev. J. Scott; 2nd 1841 Mary Elizabeth, dau. of J. Panton, Esq. Is a J.P. and D.L. for Anglesey, and Lord-Lieu-tenant of Cornwall; late Major 10th Dragoons; was M.P. for Bodmin 1835-42.—*Glynn, Bodmin; Plas Gwyn, Anglesey; Brooks's and United Service Clubs,* s.w.; 17, *Queen's Gate Terrace,* s.w.

Heir, his son Hussey Crespigny, educated at Eton; a Magis-trate for Cornwall, and a Clerk in the Foreign Office; *b.* 1834.

VIVIAN, Dowager Lady.
Letitia, dau. of the Rev. James Agnew Webster; *m.* 1833 (as 2nd wife) Richard Hussey, 1st Lord Vivian (who *d.* 1842).—8, *Wilton Crescent,* s.w.

VIVIAN, Sir ROBERT JOHN HUSSEY, K.C.B. (cr. 1857).
Natural son of Richard Hussey, 1st Lord Vivian; *b.* 1802; *m.* 1846 Emma, widow of Capt. Gordon, of the Madras Army. Is a Major-General in the Madras Army, of which he was Adjutant-General 1849-54; was formerly Lieut.-Col. 1st European Regt.; appointed a Member of the Council for India 1858; was a Direc-tor of the East India Company 1855-8.—*United Ser-vice Club,* s.w.; *Cambridge Lodge, Kingston Vale,* s.w.

VIVIAN, the Hon. JOHN CRANCH WALKER, of -. Park, Cornwall.
Second son of Richard Hussey, 1st Lord Vivian, by his 1st wife Eliza, dau. of Philip Champion de Crespigny, Esq.; *b.* 1818; *m.* 1st 1841 Louisa, only dau. of the late Henry Woodgate, Esq. (she *d.* 1855); 2nd 1861 Florence, dau. of the late Major Rowley, of the Bom-bay Cavalry, and has issue,

* Sybil Agnes and Violet Jane Henrietta.

Mr. Vivian is a J.P. and D.L. for Cornwall; was for-merly Capt. 11th Hussars; was M.P. for Penryn and Falmouth 1841-7, for Bodmin 1857-9; elected M.P. for Truro 1865.—*Park, Truro; Arthur's Club,* s.w.; 14, *Belgrave Square,* s.w.

VIVIAN, ARTHUR PENDARVES, Esq., of Glana-fon, Glamorganshire.
Third son of the late John H. Vivian, Esq., M.P., of Singleton, co. Glamorgan (who *d.* 1855), by Sarah, dau. of the late Arthur Jones, Esq., of The Priory, Reigate; *b.* 1834; *m.* 1867 Lady Augusta Emily, eldest dau. of Edwin, 3rd Earl of Dunraven. Educated at Eton and Trinity Coll., Cambridge; is a J.P. and D.L. for co. Gla-morgan, and Major Glamorganshire Volunteers.—*Glana-afon, Taibach; Brooks's and St. James's Clubs,* s.w.

VIVIAN, EDWARD, Esq., of Torquay. Devon.
Youngest son of the late Rev. Richard Vivian, J.P., Rector of Bushey, Herts, by Mary Catherine, dau. of E. J. Emmett, Esq., of Dalton's, St. Alban's; *b.* 1808; *m.* 1836 Emma Catherine, dau. of the late Rev. Henry Johnson, and sister of the Very Rev. the Dean of Wells (she is deceased), and has issue.

* Richard Henry Danzey Vivian, Lieut. R.A.; *b.* 1837; *m.* 1866 Mary Frances, dau. of the late Thomas Joseph Fitz-gerald, Esq., of Ballina Park, co. Waterford.

Mr. Vivian, who was educated at Exeter Coll., Oxford (B.A. 1828), is a Magistrate for Devon, and Major Devon Volunteer Artillery; he represents a younger branch of Lord Vivian's family.—*Woodfield, Torquay.*

VIVIAN, GEORGE, Esq., of Claverton, Somerset.
Eldest son of the late John Vivian, Esq., of Claverton Manor, by Mary Anne, dau. of the late Samuel Edwards, Esq., of Cotham, Bristol; *b.* 1800; *s.* 1828; *m.* 1841 Elizabeth Anne, eldest dau. of the late Ralph William Grey, Esq., of Backworth, Northumberland, and has, with other issue,

* Ralph, Lieut. Scots Fusilier Guards; *b.* 1845.

Mr. Vivian, who was educated at Eton and Ch. Ch., Oxford, is a Dep.-Lieut. for Somerset, and Lord of the Manor and Patron of Claverton.—*Claverton Manor, Bath;* 11, *Upper Grosvenor Street,* s.w.

VIVIAN, HENRY HUSSEY, Esq., of Park Wern, Glamorganshire.
Eldest son of the late John Henry Vivian, Esq., M.P., of Singleton, co. Glamorgan, by Sarah, eldest dau. of Arthur Jones, Esq.; *b.* 1821; *s.* 1855; *m.* 1st 1847 Jessie Dalrymple, dau. of the late Ambrose Goddard

Esq., M.P., of The Lawn, Swindon, Wilts; 2nd 1853 Caroline Elizabeth, dau. of Sir Montague J. Cholmeley, Bart., M.P. (she d. 1868); he has issue, by the former,

* Ernest Ambrose, b. 1848.

Mr. Vivian, who was educated at Eton and Trinity Coll., Cambridge, is a J.P. and D.L. for co. Glamorgan, and Patron of 1 living; has been M.P. for co. Glamorgan since 1857; was M.P. for Truro 1852-7.—*Park Wern, Swansea; Reform, Arthur's, Athenæum, Boodle's, and Brooks's Clubs, s.w.; 6, Upper Belgrave Street, w.*

+ VIVIAN, JOHN ENNIS, Esq., of Tregwithan, Cornwall.

Son of the late John Vivian, Esq., of Tregwithan; b. 1794. Called to the Bar at the Middle Temple 1819; is a J.P. and D.L. for Cornwall, a Special Deputy Warden of the Stannaries, and Lord of the Manor of Tregwithan; he was M.P. for Truro 1834-57.—*Tregwithan, Truro.*

VIVIAN, the Rev. JOHN VIVIAN, of Pencalenick, Cornwall.

Eldest son of the late John Vivian, Esq., of Pencalenick, by Cordelia, dau. of Thomas Grylls, Esq., of Bosahan, near Helstone; b. 1818; m. 1846 Harriette Maria, dau. and co-heir of William Robinson Hill, Esq., of Carwythenack, Helstone, and has, with other issue,

. * John William Harold, b. 1851.

Mr. Vivian, who was educated at Harrow and Trinity Coll., Cambridge (B.A. 1841, M.A. 1844), and appointed Rector of Cardynham 1845, descends from John, brother of Thomas Vivian, Prior of Bodmin. — *Pencalenick, Truro; Cardynham Rectory, Bodmin.*

VIVIAN, Mrs., of Singleton, Glamorganshire.

Sarah, eldest dau. of the late Arthur Jones, Esq., of Reigate Priory, Surrey; m. 1816 John Henry Vivian, Esq., F.R.S., of Singleton, who was many years M.P. for Swansea, and d. 1855, leaving, with other issue,

* Henry Hussey (whom see).

Mrs. Vivian is Lady of the Manor of Singleton.—*Singleton, Swansea.*

+ VIVIAN, QUINTUS, Esq., of Wellingborough, Northamptonshire.

Son of the late John Vivian, Esq., of Claverton Manor, Somerset; b. 180-; is married, and has issue. Is a Magistrate for co. Northampton, and Lord of the Manor and Patron of Wellingborough.—*Manor House, Wellingborough; 15, Hyde Park Square, w.*

VIVIAN, WILLIAM GRAHAM, Esq.

Second son of the late John Henry Vivian, Esq., F.R.S., of Singleton, many years M.P. for Swansea (who d. 1855), by Sarah, eldest dau. of Arthur Jones, Esq.; b. 1827. Is a J.P. and D.L. for co. Glamorgan (High Sheriff 1866).—*Residence: Singleton, Swansea.*

VON STIEGLITZ, CHARLES AUGUSTUS, of Knockbarragh Park, Downshire.

Youngest son of the late Henry, Baron von Stieglitz, of Lewis Hill, co. Armagh, by Charlotte, dau. of John Atkinson, Esq., of Will Mount, co. Armagh; b. 1819; m. 1844 Sophia Louisa, dau. of Joseph William Belcher, Esq., of Evora, Richmond, grand-dau. of the late Thomas Austin, Esq., of Waterfall, co. Cork, and niece of the late General Austin, of Bath. Is a Magistrate for co. Down.—*Knockbarragh Park, Rosstrevor.*

VON STIEGLITZ, The Baroness, of The Glen, co. Armagh.

Hester Anna, dau. of the late George Blacker, Esq., of Carrick-Blacker, co. Armagh, by Anne, dau. of Capt.
956

Sloane; m. 1859 Frederick Lüdwig, Baron von Stieglitz, of The Glen, who was formerly a Member of the Legislative Council of Tasmania, and who d. 1866. The family of the late Baron, originally of Saxony, was ennobled by Rudolph II. in 1583; its last patent, conferred by the Emperor Joseph II., dates from 1765. —*The Glen, Newry, Ireland.*

VON STIEGLITZ, JOHN, Esq., of Altmore Lodge, co. Tyrone.

Third son of the late Henry, Baron von Stieglitz, of Lewis Hill, co. Armagh, by Charlotte, dau. of John Atkinson, Esq., of Will Mount, co. Armagh; b. 1809; m. 1836 Emma, dau. of Henry Lewis Cowie, Esq., of Russell Square, London; is a Magistrate for co. Tyrone; was formerly resident in Australia, and a Magistrate there.—*Altmore Lodge, Dungannon, co. Tyrone.*

VON STIEGLITZ, ROBERT WILLIAM, Esq., of Mucklagb, King's Co.

Fifth son of the late Henry, Baron von Stieglitz, of Lewis Hill, co. Armagh, by Charlotte, dau. of John Atkinson, Esq., of Will Mount, co. Armagh; b. 1816; m. 1845 Marcella, dau. of Joseph William Belcher, Esq., of Evora, Richmond, grand-dau. of the late Thomas Austin, Esq., of Waterfall, co. Cork, and niece of the late General Austin, of Bath, and has issue,

* Four daughters.

Mr. Von Stieglitz is a Magistrate for King's Co. —*Mucklagh, Tullamore, King's Co.*

VOWLER, JOHN, Esq., of Parnacott, Devon.

Eldest son of the late John Vowler, Esq., of Parnacott, by Ann, dau. of John Bound, Esq., of Sheepwash; b. 1787; s. 1830; m. 1817 Harriet, dau. of Samuel Nicholson, Esq., and has, with other issue,

* John Nicholas (of Leawood, near Bridestow), a Magistrate for Devon; b. 1818; m. 1850 Mary Northcott, 2nd dau. of the Rev. Henry Addington Simcoe, of Penheale, Cornwall, and has issue.

Mr. Vowler is a J.P. and D.L. for Devon and Cornwall. —*Parnacott, Holsworthy.*

+ VYE, NATHANIEL, Esq., of Ilfracombe, Devon.

Son of the late N. Vye, Esq.; b. 18—. Is a J.P. and D.L. for Devon.—*Ilfracombe, Devon.*

VYNER, HENRY FREDERICK CLARE, Esq., of Newby Hall, Yorkshire.

Eldest son of the late Henry Vyner, Esq., J.P. and D.L. of Newby Hall, by Lady Mary Gertrude, dau. of Thomas Philip, 2nd Earl De Grey; b. 1836; s. 1861. Educated at Eton; is a Magistrate for the N. Riding of co. York, and Lord of the Manor of Newby.—*Newby Hall, Ripon; 7A, Mansfield Street, w.*

Heir Pres., his brother Reginald Arthur, educated at Eton; a Magistrate for the N. Riding of co. York, Cornet York Yeomanry Cavalry, and late M.P. for Ripon; formerly a Clerk in the Foreign Office; b. 1842.

VYNER, ROBERT, Esq., of Gautby, Lincolnshire.

Eldest son of the late Robert Vyner, Esq., of Gautby, by Lady Theodosia, dau. of John, 1st Earl of Ashburnham; b. 1796; s. 1810. Educated at Eton; is Lord of the Manors of Gautby and Withern, and Patron of 2 livings; was High Sheriff of co. Lincoln in 1814. —*Gautby Hall, Horncastle; 67, Portland Place, w.*

Heir Pres., his nephew Henry Frederick Clare Vyner, Esq. of Newby Hall (whom see).

VYSE. (See *Howard-Vyse*.)

VYVYAN, Sir RICHARD RAWLINSON, Bart., of Trelowarren, Cornwall (cr. 1644).

Eldest son of the late Sir Vyell Vyvyan, Bart., of Trelowarren, by Mary, dau. of the late Thomas Hutton

Rawlinson, Esq., of Lancaster; *b.* 1800; *s.* as 8th Bart. 1820. Educated at Harrow; is a J.P. and D.L. for Cornwall (High Sheriff 1840), Lord of the Manor of Trelowarren, and Patron of 1 living; was M.P. for Okehampton 1831-2, for Bristol 1835-7, for Helstone 1841-57.—*Trelowarren, Helstone; Athenæum and Carlton Clubs, s.w.*

> *Heir Pres.,* his brother Vyell Francis, in Holy Orders, M.A. of Trinity Coll., Cambridge; a Magistrate for Cornwall, and Rector of Withiel; *b.* 1801; *m.* 1825 Anne, dau. of the late John Vickeris Taylor, Esq., and has. with other issue, *Vyell Donnithorne (in Holy Orders), B.A. of St. John's Coll., Cambridge; Rector of Winterbourne-Monkton, Dorset; *b.* 1826; *m.* 185– Louisa Mary Froderica, dau. of Richard Bourchier, Esq., of Brook Lodge, Dorset.

+**VYVYAN**, RICHARD HENRY STACKHOUSE, Esq., of Trewan, Cornwall.

Eldest son of the late Col. Richard Vyvyan, J.P. and D.L., of Trewan; *b.* 18—. Is a Magistrate for Cornwall; represents a younger branch of the Vyvyans of Trelowarren.—*Trewan, St. Columb.*

VYVYAN-ROBINSON, PHILIP, Esq., of Nansloe, Cornwall.

Second son of the late Rev. Richard Vyvyan, Vicar of Lamerton and South Sydenham, Devon, by Anna, dau. of — Down, Esq., of Burrough; *b.* 1777; *s.* 1818, and added the name of Robinson to that of Vyvyan on the death of his kinsman, the Rev. William Robinson; *m.* 1818 Mary Elizabeth, dau. of Henry Hance, Esq., and has, with other issue,

> * Philip, in Holy Orders, Rector of Llandewednack and Ruan Major, Cornwall; *b.* 1820; *m.* 1st 1851 Augusta Baker, dau. of Hugh Norris, Esq., of Taunton (she *d.* 1859); 2nd 1862 Elizabeth Maria, 3rd dau. of the late Joseph Vivian, Esq., of Roseworthy, Cornwall.

Mr. Vyvyan-Robinson, who is a J.P. and D.L. for Cornwall, was formerly in the 69th Regt. (in which he served at Waterloo) and the 88th Regt.—*Nansloe,* ‡ *Helstone.*

---

‡ This property is held on the tenure of providing H.R.H. the Prince of Wales with a boat and nets whenever he chooses to fish in the Loe Pool, near Helstone.

W

WADDELL, WILLIAM, Esq., of Easter Moffat, Lanarkshire.
Younger son of the late George Waddell, Esq., by Janet, dau. of Robert Waddell, Esq.; *b.* 1791; *s.* his uncle, William Waddell, Esq., 1806; *m.* 1829 Margaret, eldest dau. of Archibald Campbell, Esq., of Melfort, co. Argyll, and has, with other issue,
    • William, *b.* 1831.
Mr. Waddell is a J.P. and D L. for co. Lanark, and a Writer to the Signet in Edinburgh.—*Moffat House, Airdrie, N.B. ; United Service Club, Edinburgh ; 20, Royal Circus, Edinburgh, N.B.*

WADDILOVE, GEORGE MARMADUKE DARLEY, Esq., of Woodborne, Northumberland.
Eldest son of the late Rev. William James Darley Waddilove, of Beacon Grange (who *d.* 1859), by Elizabeth Anne, dau. of the late Sir James Graham, Bart., of Netherby ; *b.* 1823 ; *m.* 1862 June, 2nd dau. of the Rev. Edmund Bucknall-Estcourt, Rector of Eckington, co. Derby (she *d.* 1865). Is a Magistrate for Northumberland, and Lord of the Manor of Woodhorne ; formerly Major in the Bengal Army.—*Address : Brunton House, Hexham ; East India United Service Club, s.w.*
Heir Pres., his brother Charles, Capt. R.N.; *b.* 182-.

WADDINGHAM, JOHN, Esq., of Guiting Grange, Gloucestershire.
Eldest son of the late Thomas Waddingham, Esq., by Ann, dau. of Mark Husband, Esq. ; *b.* 1799 ; *m.* 1837 Margaret, dau. of James Wilkinson, Esq., and has, with other issue,
    • John, *b.* 1838.
Mr. Waddingham is a Magistrate for co. Gloucester (High Sheriff 1861), and Lord of the Manor of Guiting Grange ; he purchased this property from the Wynniatts in 1847.—*Guiting Grange, Winchcombe.*

WADDINGTON, HARRY SPENCER, Esq., of Cavenham Hall, Suffolk.
Eldest son of the late Harry Spencer Waddington, Esq., J.P. and D.L., of Cavenham Hall (High Sheriff of Suffolk, and formerly M.P. for W. Suffolk), by Mary Anne, dau. of the late Richard Slater Milnes, Esq., of Fryston Hall, co. York ; *b.* 1816 ; *s.* 1861 ; *m.* 1852 Caroline, dau. of the late Sir William Beauchamp-Proctor, Bart., and has, with other issue,
    • Spencer Beauchamp, *b.* 1854.
Mr. Waddington, who was educated at Eton, is a Magistrate for Suffolk, and Impropriator of the Rectory of Cavenham ; was formerly in the Rifle Brigade.—*Cavenham Hall, Mildenhall ; Army and Navy Club, s.w.*

WADDINGTON, JOHN, Esq., of Langrish House, Hampshire.
Eldest son of the late John Dorsey Waddington, Esq., J.P., of Langrish House, by Emma Phillippa, dau. of the late Thomas Grove, Esq., of Ferne House, Wilts ; *b.* 1808 ; *s.* 1863. Educated at Harrow ; is a Magistrate for Hants ; was formerly Capt. 6th Dragoons.—*Langrish House, Petersfield.*
Heir Pres, his brother George Grove, *b.* 1810.

+**WADDINGTON, the late JOHN THOMAS, Esq., of Twyford Lodge, Hants.**
Younger son of the late Dr. Waddington, Prebendary of Ely ; *b.* 1796 ; *d.* 1863, leaving a widow, who in-
herits the property for life, with ultimate remainder to her husband's nephew, Mr. Powell. Mr. Waddington was a J.P. and D.L. for Hants.—*Twyford Lodge, Winchester.*

WADDY, JOHN, Esq., of Clougheast, co. Wexford.
Eldest son of the late Richard Waddy, Esq., M.D., of Clougheast Castle, by Sophia, dau. of the late John Green, Esq., of Maidstone, Kent ; *b.* 1807 ; *s.* 1828 ; *m.* 1840 Elizabeth Dorothy, dau. of S. Boxwell. Esq., of Linziestown. Educated at Trinity Coll., Dublin (B.A. 1831, M.A. 1834, M.B. 1835, M.D. 1856· LL.D. 1865); is a Magistrate for co. Wexford. This family is descended from a cavalry officer in the army led to Ireland by Cromwell 1649.—*Clougheast Castle, Churchtown, co. Wexford.*

WADE, CHARLES JOSEPH, Esq., of Stonelands, Devon.
Youngest son of the late Charles Wade, Esq., of Drewood, co. Stafford, by Mary, dau. of Joseph Cholmondeley, Esq., of Penkridge, co. Stafford ; *b.* 1816 ; *m.* 1844 Emily, dau. of Robert Colmer, Esq., of Lincoln's Inn, and Yoxford, Suffolk. Called to the Bar at the Inner Temple 1847 ; is a Magistrate for Devon.—*Stonelands, Bovey Tracey.*

+**WADE, GEORGE, Esq., of Sarratt Hall, Herts.**
Son of the late G. Wade, Esq.; *b.* 181- ; *m.* 1st 1848 Lady Frances, dau. of William, 6th Marquis of Lothian (she *d.* 1863) ; 2nd 1863 Elizabeth Emma, dau. of Mr. Ladkin, of Lutterworth, co. Leicester, and has issue a dau. Mr. Wade is Lord of the Manor of Sarratt.—*Great Sarratt Hall, Rickmansworth.*

WADE, THOMAS, Esq., of Carrowmore, co. Galway.
Eldest son of the late Samuel Wade, Esq., of Carrowmore, by Catherine, dau. of James Davies, Esq., of The Castle and Manor of Aughrim, co. Galway ; *b.* 1788 ; *s.* 1826 ; *m.* 1813 Dorothea, youngest dau. of the late Gustavus H. Rochfort, Esq., M.P., of Rochfort, co. Westmeath, and had, with other issue,
    Samuel, *b.* 1814 ; *m.* 1847 Eliza, dau. of Burton Persse, Esq., of Moyode Castle, co. Galway, and *d.* 1862, leaving, with other issue, • Robert Rochfort, *b.* 184-.
This family was formerly seated at Glastonbury, Somerset, and subsequently in co. Westmeath, and in King's Co.—*Carrowmore House, Aughram, co. Galway.*

WADE, the Rev. WILLIAM SEROCOLD.
Son of the late Rev. William Wade, B.D., Rector of Lilley, Herts, by Margaret, youngest dau. and co-heir of the Rev. Walter Serocold, of Cherry Hinton, co. Cambridge ; *b.* 1801 ; *m.* 1st 1844 Elizabeth Mary, dau. of the late J. S Story, Esq., of St. Alban's ; 2nd 1863 Isabella, 2nd dau. of the late Rev. Thomas Pugh, of Flamstead, Herts, and has, with other issue, by the former,
    • Arthur Gregory, *b.* 1849 ; educated at Eton.
Mr. Wade, who was educated at Harrow and St. John's Coll., Cambridge (B.A. 1824, M.A. 1827), is a Magistrate for Herts and the Liberty of St. Alban's, and Vicar of Redbourn.—*The Poplars, Redbourn, St. Alban's.*

WADE, ROBERT CRAVEN, Esq., of Clonebraney, co. Meath.

Eldest son of the late William Blaney Wade, Esq., J.P. and D.L., of Clonebraney, by Frances, elder dau. of Sir John Craven Carden, 1st Bart., of Templemore, co. Tipperary; *b.* 1800; *s.* 1861. Is a Magistrate for co. Meath.—*Clonebraney, Crossakiel, co. Meath.*

WADE-GERY, WILLIAM HUGH, Esq., of Bushmead Priory, Beds.

Eldest son of the late Rev. Hugh Wade-Gery, of Bushmead Priory, by Hester, dau. of William Gery, Esq., of Bushmead Priory; *b.* 1794; *s.* 1832; *m.* 1829 Anne, dau. of John Milnes, Esq., of Beckingham, and has, with other issue,

* William, *b.* 1832.

Mr. Wade-Gery, who was educated at Emmanuel Coll., Cambridge (B.A. 1817, M.A. 1821), is a Magistrate for Beds and Hunts.—*Bushmead Priory, Eton Socon.*

WAGNER, GEORGE HENRY MALCOLM, Esq.

Eldest son of the late Melchior Henry Wagner, Esq., by Ann Elizabeth, dau. of the Rev. H. Michell, Vicar of Brighthelmston; *b.* 1786; *m.* 1814 Anne, dau. of John Penfold, of Annington, Sussex, late of Hurstmonceux Place, and has issue an only surviving son,

* John Henry, of Hemingfold, near Battle, a Magistrate for Sussex; late Lieut. 5th Fusiliers; *b.* 1821; *m.* 1851 Margaret, widow of the Rev. W. Mossop, and has, with other issue, * Malcolm, *b.* 1856.

Mr. Wagner is a J.P. and D.L. for Sussex (High Sheriff 1838).—*Marina, St. Leonard's-on-Sea.*

WAGNER, THOMAS RICHARD PRYCE, Esq., of Manarcifed, Cardiganshire.

Only son of the late John Wagner, Esq., of Penalltcifort, by Martha, dau. of F. Martin, Esq., of Cranley, Surrey; *b.* 1800; *s.* his great uncle, Sir Thomas Pryce, Bart., of Cardigan, 1808; *m.* 1828 Rosalind, dau. of Wm. Martin, Esq., of Brompton. Is a J.P. and D.L. for co. Cardigan; late Capt. R. Cardigan Militia. This family is descended in the female line from the Pryces of Newtown Hall, Montgomeryshire, Sir Thomas Pryce of Cardigan being the last baronet, at whose decease the baronetcy became extinct.—*Manarcifed, Cardigan.*

WAINMAN, WILLIAM BRADLEY, Esq., of Carr Head, Yorkshire.

Only son of the late Richard Bradley Wainman, Esq., of Carr Head, by Amelia Theresa, dau. of Capt. Edward Hall Campbell, R.N., of Whitley Hall, Northumberland, and widow of Sir W. E. Amcotts, Bart., of Kettlethorpe Park, co. Lincoln; *b.* 1812; *s.* 1842; *m.* 1836 Maria, dau. of Lieut.-Col. G. Hotham, and has issue,

* Mary Amelia (*m.* 1862 John Hall, Esq., eldest son of James Hall, Esq., of Scarbro', co. York), and Edith.

Mr. Wainman, who was educated at Eton, is a J.P. and D.L. for the W. Riding of Yorkshire.—*Carr Head, Cross Hills, West Yorkshire; Carlton Club, s.w.*

WAIT, WILLIAM SAVAGE, Esq., of Woodborough, Somerset.

Eldest surviving son of the late Daniel Wait, Esq., of Belluton, Somerset, by Anne Purnell, dau. of Charles Savage, Esq., of Midsomer Norton, Somerset; *b.* 1808; *s.* his maternal great-uncle John Purnell, Esq., 1839; *m.* 1848 Caroline, youngest dau. of Langley St. Albyn, Esq., of Alfoxton, Somerset, and has surviving issue,

* Five daughters.

Mr. Wait is a Magistrate for Somerset.—*Woodborough, Bath.*

WAITHMAN, JOSEPH, Esq., of Wray House, Lancashire.

Second son of William Waithman, Esq., of Westville, Yealand Conyers (whom see), by Eleanor, only dau. of

John Armistead, Esq., of Leeds; *b.* 1831; *m.* 1854 Elizabeth, youngest dau. of William Sharp, Esq., of Linden Hall, co. Lancaster, and has, with other issue,

* Hubert Waithman de Lindeth, *b.* 1859.

Mr. Waithman is a Magistrate for cos. Lancaster and York, and Lieut. 6th W. York Militia.—*Wray House, Lancaster.*

WAITHMAN, ROBERT WILLIAM, Esq., of Moyne, co. Galway, and Bentham House, Lancashire.

Eldest son of William Waithman, Esq., of Westville, co. Lancaster (whom see), by Eleanor, only dau. of John Armistead, Esq.; *b.* 1828; *m.* 1851 Millicent, 3rd dau. of William Sharp, Esq., of Linden Hall, co. Lancaster, and has, with other issue,

* William Sharp, *b.* 1853.

Mr. Waithman is a J.P. and D.L. for the W. Riding of co. York, a Magistrate for co. Lancaster, and Lord of the Manors of Mewith, Burton-in-Lonsdale, and Ingleton. —*Moyne, Ballyglunin; Bentham House, Lancaster.*

WAITHMAN, WILLIAM, Esq., of Westville, Lancashire.

Eldest son of the late Joseph Waithman, Esq., of Westville, and of Yealand Conyers, by Grace, dau. of John Spence, Esq., of Birstwith, co. York; *b.* 1799; *s.* 1836; *m.* 1825 Eleanor, only dau. of John Armistead, Esq., of Leeds, and has, with other issue, * Robert William (whom see above).—*Westville, Yealand Conyers, Lancaster; Reform Club, s.w.*

WAKE, Sir HEREWALD, Bart., of Courteen Hall, Northamptonshire (cr. 1621).

Eldest son of the late Sir William Wake, Bart., of Courteen Hall, by Margaret Anne, dau. of Henry Fricker, Esq.; *b.* 1852; *s.* as 12th Bart. 1865. Educated at Eton; is Lord of the Manor of Courteen Hall, and also of Nazing, and of Waltham Abbey, Essex. —*Courteen Hall, Northampton.*

Heir Pres., his brother Archibald James, *b.* 1856.

+**WAKE, GEORGE ANTHONY, Esq., of Tatchbury Manor, Hants.**

Eldest son of the late Anthony D. Wake, Esq., of Tatchbury Manor, by a dau. of ⸺ Heathcote, Esq.; *b.* 1819; *s.* 1857. Is Lord of the Manor of Tatchbury, and a Solicitor. Descended from a common ancestor with Sir W. Wake, Bart., of Courteen Manor.—*Tatchbury Manor, Southampton.*

Heir Pres., his brother Heathcote Allen, in Holy Orders; M.A. of University Coll., Oxford; *b.* 1821; is married.

WAKEFIELD, WILLIAM HENRY, Esq., of Sedgwick House and Prizet, Westmoreland.

Only son of the late John Wakefield, Esq., of Sedgwick House (who was a Magistrate for co. Westmoreland, and High Sheriff in 1855), by Fanny, dau. of Dr. MacArthur, of Glasgow; *b.* 1828; *s.* 1866; *m.* 1851 Augusta, dau. of John Haggarty, Esq., late United States Consul at Liverpool, and has, with other issue,

* John, *b.* 1857.

Mr. Wakefield is a J.P. and D.L. for Westmoreland. —*Sedgwick House, and Prizet, Kendal.*

WAKELY, JOHN, Esq., of Ballyburly, King's Co.

Eldest son of the late James Wakely, Esq., of Dublin, by Elizabeth, dau. of George Heron, Esq., of Dublin; *b.* 1820; *s.* his cousin 1817; *m.* 1855 Mary Catherine, dau. of the late Rev. Richard George, of Kentstown, co. Meath, and has, with other issue,

* John, *b.* 1861.

Mr. Wakely, who was educated at Trinity Coll., Dublin (B.A. 1843, M.A. 1846), is a J.P. and D.L. for King's

Co. (High Sheriff 1853), Lord of the Manor and Patron of Ballyburly.—*Ballyburly, Edenderry, King's Co.; Kildare Street Club, Dublin.*

WAKEMAN, Sir OFFLEY, Bart., of Perdiswell Hall, Worcestershire (cr. 1828).

Eldest son of the late Sir Offley Penbury Wakeman, Bart., of Perdiswell Hall, by Mary, dau. of Thomas Adlington, Esq., of Bradenham, Norfolk; *b.* 1850; *s.* as 3rd Bart. 1858. Educated at Eton; is Lord of the Manor of Perdiswell, and Patron of 1 living.—*Perdiswell Hall, Worcester; Hinton Hall, Shrewsbury.*

Heir Pres., his brother Henry Offley, *b.* 1852.

WAKEMAN, THOMAS, Esq.,‡ of The Graig, Monmouthshire.

Only son of the late Charles Wakeman, Esq., by Anne, dau. of Thomas Davis, Esq., of Chepstow; *b.* 1788. Is a Magistrate for co. Monmouth.—*The Graig, Monmouth.*

WALCOT, the Rev. CHARLES, of Bitterley, Salop.

Eldest son of the late Rev. John Walcot, of Bitterley Court, by Sarah, sister of the late Sir John Dashwood, Bart., of West Wycombe, Bucks; *b.* 1794; *s.* 1834; *m.* 1st 1818 Anne, eldest dau. of Major William Walcot, of Ferry Park, co. Dublin; 2nd 1827 Charlotte, eldest dau. of John Molyneux, Esq., of Ludlow; 3rd 1851 Mary Anne, eldest dau. of the Rev. John Rocke, of Clungunford House, co. Salop; he has, by his 1st wife, with other issue,

    * John, in Holy Orders, B.A. of Lincoln Coll., Oxford. and Rector of Ribbesford, co. Worcester; *b.* 1820; *m.* 1844 Mary Sophia, dau. of Sir Thomas Phillipps, Bart., of Middle Hill, co. Worcester, and by her, who *d.* 1858, has, with other issue, *Owen Charles Bampfylde Dashwood, *b.* 1846.

Mr. Walcot, who was educated at Westminster and Trinity Coll., Oxford (B.A. 1817, M.A. 1826), is a Magistrate for co. Salop, and Lord of the Manor, Rector, and Patron of Bitterley. — *Bitterley Court, Ludlow.*

WALCOT, Admiral JOHN EDWARD, of Winkton House, Hants.

Eldest son of the late Edmund Walcot, Esq., of Winkton, by Catharine, dau. of John Lyons, Esq.; *b.* 1790; *s.* 1847; *m.* 1819 Charlotte Anne, dau. of Col. John Nelley, of the Bengal Artillery, and by her (who *d.* 1863) has, with other issue,

    * Mackenzie Edward Charles, M.A. of Exeter Coll., Oxford. F.S.A., Precentor and Prebendary of Chichester; *b.* 1822; *m.* 1852 Rose Anne, dau. of Major Frederick Brownlow, 73rd Highlanders, and niece of Charles, 1st Lord Lurgan.

Admiral Walcot, who is a J.P. and D.L. for Hants. and an Admiral on the reserved list, was elected M.P. for Christchurch, 1852. — *Winkton House, Ringwood; Woodland Villa, Bath; United Service Club, s.w.*

WALDEGRAVE, Earl (WILLIAM FREDERICK WALDEGRAVE).—Cr. 1729.

Elder son of William Frederick, late Viscount Chewton (who *d.* 1854), by Fanny, only dau. of the late Capt. John Bastard, R.N., of Sharpham, Devon; *b.* 1851; *s.* his grandfather as 9th Earl 1859. Educated at Eton. —37, *Wilton Crescent, s.w.*

Heir Pres., his brother Henry Noel, *b.* 1854.

WALDEGRAVE, the Countess of, Hastings, Sussex.

Sarah, dau. of the late Rev. William Whitear, Prebendary of Chichester; *m.* 1st 1817 Edward Milward,

Esq., of Hastings; 2nd 1846, William, 8th Earl Waldegrave, a Vice-Admiral in the Navy, who *d.* 1859.—*The Mansion, Hastings.*

WALDEGRAVE.
(See under *Radstock, Lord,* and *Carlisle, Bishop of.*)

WALDEGRAVE-LESLIE. (See under *Rothes.*)

WALDEN. (See under *Tweeddale, Marquis of.*)

WALDIE-GRIFFITH.
(See under *Griffith, Sir R. J., Bart.*)

WALDO, EDMUND WALDO MEADE, Esq., of Stonewall Park and Hever Castle, Kent.

Eldest son of the late Edmund Wakefield Meade Waldo, Esq., J.P. and D.L., of Stonewall Park and Hever Castle, by Harriet Bloomfield, dau. of the late Col. Gustavus Rochfort, M.P., of Rochfort, co. Westmeath (she *d.* 1838); *b.* 1829; *s.* 1858; *m.* 1854 Harriette Ellen, dau. of Henry Owens Becher, Esq., of Aughadown, co. Cork, and has, with other issue,

    * Edmund Gustavus Bloomfield, *b.* 1855.

Mr. Waldo, who was educated at Rugby, is a Magistrate for Kent, Lord of the Manor and Patron of Hever Brocas; was formerly an Officer in the 1st Life Guards. This family first settled in England after the revocation of the Edict of Nantes.— *Stonewall Park, Chiddingstone, Edenbridge.*

WALDO-SIBTHORP. (See *Sibthorp.*)

+WALDRON, EDWARD FRANCIS, Esq., of Lismoyle House, co. Leitrim.

Son of the late Francis Waldron, Esq., of Lismoyle (a Magistrate for cos. Leitrim and Roscommon), by Mary Anne, dau. of the late Joseph Caddy, Esq.; *b.* 1837; *s.* 1858. Is a Magistrate for cos. Leitrim and Roscommon, and Lord of the Manor of Lismoyle.—*Lismoyle House, Drumsna, co. Leitrim.*

WALDRON, LAURENCE, Esq., of Ballybrack, co. Dublin.

Eldest and only surviving son of the late Patrick Waldron, Esq., Merchant, of Dublin, by Mary, dau. of John Shinnor, of Doneraile, co. Cork, and nephew and heir of the late Laurence Waldron, Esq., of Landscape, co. Dublin; *b.* 1811; *m.* 1842 Anne, dau. of Francis White, Esq., M.D., and has, with other issue,

    * Patrick John, *b.* 1850.

Mr. Waldron, who was called to the Irish Bar 1840, is a Commissioner of National Education in Ireland, a J.P. and D.L. for co. Tipperary (High Sheriff 1868), and a Magistrate for co. Dublin; was High Sheriff of co. Louth 1860, and appointed High Sheriff of co. Kilkenny 1862-3, but declined to serve; re-appointed 1867; was M.P. for co. Tipperary 1857-65.—*Ballybrack, Killiney, Dublin; Helen Park, Killenaule, co. Tipperary; Ballagh mistress, co. Mayo; as Isaac's, s., West Dublin, Reform Club, s.w., Stephen's Club, &.*

WALDY, THOMAS WILLIAM, Esq., of Egglescliffe, co. Durham.

Third son of the late John Waldy, Esq., of Egglescliffe, by Margaret, only child of Richard Garmonsway, Esq. of Bourdon, co. Durham; *b.* 1801; *s.* 1812; *m.* 1st 1828 Jane, only child and heir of Robert Scott, Esq., of York (she *d.* 1851); 2nd 1854 Ellen, only dau. of Henry Thomas Faber, Esq.; 3rd 1849 Emily Margaret, dau. of Rowland Webster, Esq.; he has issue by his 2nd wife,

    * Edward Garmonsway, a Magistrate for the W. Riding of

York, late Capt. 76th Foot ; *b.* 1835 ; *m.* 1868 Cecily Jane, elder dau. of the late Rev. John Garvey, Vicar of Hough-on-the-Hill, co. Lincoln.

Mr. Waldy is a J.P. and D.L. for co. Durham and the N. Riding of Yorkshire.—*Egglescliffe, Yarm.*

WALDY, WILLIAM THOMAS, Esq., of Howdens, Devonshire.

Fifth son of the Rev. Richard Waldy, M.A., of Haughton-le-Skerne and Longnewton, co. Durham (whom see), by Isabella, dau. of the Rev. William Greenwood, B.D., and grand-niece of John, Earl St. Vincent; *b.* 1833; *m.* 1862 Emily, dau. of the late William Bradshaw, Esq., of Homerton, Middlesex, and has, with other issue,

* Lionel St. Clair, *b.* 1863.

Mr. Waldy, who is a Magistrate for Devon, was formerly Capt. 43rd Regt.; served in the Crimea and the Indian Mutiny.—*Howdens, Tiverton.*

WALE, Mrs., of Shelford, Cambridgeshire.

Henrietta, dau. of the late Right Rev. Richard Whately, Archbishop of Dublin, by Mary, dau. of William Pope, Esq.; *m.* 1848 Charles Brent Wale, Esq., of Shelford, J.P. and D.L., and Auditor of Poor Law Accounts for co. Cambridge, who *d.* 1864, leaving, with other issue,

* Charles, *b.* 1853.

This family is descended from Sir Thomas Wale, who was created Knight of the Garter A.D. 1340.—*Little Shelford, Cambridge.*

WALE, Lieut.-Col. ROBERT GREGORY, of Little Shelford, Cambridgeshire.

Third son of the late General Sir Charles Wale, K.C.B., of Little Shelford (who *d.* 1843), by his 3rd wife Henrietta, 3rd dau. of the Rev. Thomas Brent, of Croscombe, Somerset; *b.* 1820; purchased property of his eldest brother the Rev. Alexander Malcolm Wale, 1850 ; *m.* 1849 Fanny, only child and heir of the late Sir E. West, Chief Justice of Bombay, and has issue six daughters. Lieut.-Col. Wale, who was educated at the Royal Military Coll., Sandhurst, is a J.P. and D.L. for co. Cambridge, and Lieut.-Col. of the Cambridgeshire Militia; late Capt. 33rd Regt. Infantry.—*Little Shelford, Cambridge; Army and Navy Club, s.w.*

WALES, H.R.H. Prince of.

(See *Cornwall, Duke of,* and under *The Queen.*)

WALES, the Rev. WILLIAM, Chancellor of Peterborough.

Eldest son of the late John Wales, Capt. H.E.I.C.S., by Maria Catherine, 3rd dau. of Marcus Dixon, Esq., of Barwell Court, Middlesex; *b.* 1804; *m.* 1st 1836 Frances, 7th dau. of Lancelot Haslope, Esq., of Highbury, Middlesex ; 2nd 1859 the Hon. Louisa Diana, 3rd dau. of Francis George, 1st Lord Churchill. Educated at Catharine Coll., Cambridge (B.A. 1827, M.A. 1833), is a Magistrate for co. Rutland, Rector of Uppingham, and Chancellor and Hon. Canon of Peterborough.—*The Rectory, Uppingham.*

WALFORD, CHARLES, Esq., of Foxborough, Suffolk.

Younger son of the late Rev. William Walford, by Diana, dau. of Randall Burroughes, Esq., of Manor House, Long-Stratton, Norfolk, and brother of the Rev. Ellis Walford (whom see); is a Magistrate for Suffolk. This family descend from a common ancestor with the Walfords, formerly of Boreham, and of Hatfield, Essex.—*Foxborough Hall, Woodbridge.*

WALFORD, the Rev. ELLIS, of Dallinghoo, Suffolk.

Eldest surviving son of the late Rev. William Walford, by Diana, dau. of the Rev. Randall Burroughes, of Manor House, Long-Stratton, Norfolk; *b.* 1803; *m.*

1st 1832 Henrietta Hall, dau. of James Colvin, Esq., of The Grove, Little Bealings, Suffolk; 2nd 1842 Frances Matilda, dau. of the Rev. E. R. Brown, Rector of Kelsale, Suffolk, and has, with other issue,

* Henry Alexander, Capt. 20th Hussars ; *b.* 1836.

Mr. Walford, who was educated at Corpus Christi Coll., Cambridge (B.A. 1825, M.A. 1828), is Rector of Dallinghoo and Bucklesham, Rural Dean of Wilford, and Patron of 2 livings. Mr. Walford descends in a direct line from King Edward III.—*Dallinghoo, Wickham Market.*

WALFORD, JOHN HENSHAW NICHSON, Esq., of Roden House, Salop.

Eldest son of the late John Henshaw Walford, Esq., J.P., of Roden House, by Mary, only surviving child of Jonathan Nichson, Esq., of Wem; *b.* 1836; *s.* 1865; *m.* 1862 Mary, only child of William Staley, Esq., of Thistlemount, Rossendale, co. Lancaster, and has, with other issue,

* John, *b.* 1863.

Mr. Walford, who was educated at Ch. Ch., Oxford, is a Magistrate for co. Hereford, and Patron of 1 living. Descended from a common ancestor with the Walfords of Essex and Suffolk. This family originally came from Walford, near Ross, co. Hereford.—*Roden House, Wem, co. Salop; Trego, Ross, Herefordshire.*

WALFORD, Mrs., late of Hatfield Place, Essex.

Mary Anne, eldest surviving dau. of the late Rev. Henry Hutton (some time Rector of Beaumont, Essex), by Elizabeth Royal, eldest dau. and co-heir of the late Sir William Pepperell, Bart.; ‡ *m.* 1822 the Rev. William Walford, M.A., of Hatfield Place, near Witham, Essex, formerly Rector of St. Runwald's, Colchester, who *d.* 1855, leaving, with other issue, * Edward, educated at the Charterhouse, and M.A. and late Scholar of Balliol Coll., Oxford; *b.* 1823; *m.* 1st 1847 Mary Holmes, younger dau. of the late John Gray, Esq., of Clifton (she *d.* 1851); 2nd 1852 Julia Christina, 4th dau. of the late Admiral the Hon. Sir John Talbot, G.C.B., of Rhode Hill, Devon, and has issue.—*Address: Oxford.*

WALFORD, ROBERT CROOK, Esq., of Hillingdon, Middlesex.

Eldest son of the late Thomas Witts Walford, Esq., of Hillingdon, by Rachel, dau. of Robert Crook, Esq.; *b.* 1809; *m.* 1840 Mary, dau. of Nathaniel Rumsey, Esq., and has issue an only dau.,

* Emily Mary.

Mr. Walford is a J.P. and D.L. for Middlesex, and descended from a family who settled at Walford, co. Hereford, in the 14th century.—*The Lodge, Hillingdon, Uxbridge.*

WALFORD-GOSNALL, JOHN DESBOROUGH, Esq., of Bentley, Suffolk.

Only son of the late Desborough Walford, Esq., of St. Matthew's, Ipswich (who *d.* 185.), by Harriet, dau. of the late John Gosnall, Esq., of Bentley Hall, and grandson of the late Rev. William Walford, of Boreham House and Hatfield Place, Essex; *b.* 1822; *s.* his grandfather in 1857; assumed the additional name of Gosnall 1847; *m.* 185. Harriet, younger dau. of the late Charles Pearson, Esq., of Great Yarmouth, Capt. R.N., and has, with other issue,

* John Desborough Pearson, *b.* 1858.

Mr. Walford-Gosnall, who was educated at Lincoln

‡ This gentleman, one of the richest and most influential subjects in America, having lost his large fortune on account of his fealty to George III., came to England on the outbreak of the American revolution, and was raised, in 1774, to a baronetcy, which became extinct on his death without male issue, in 1816

Coll., Oxford, is 1st Lieut. Norfolk Artillery Volunteers. The Gosnall family, formerly seated at Otley Hall, near Woodbridge, suffered much for their loyalty to Charles I. They were also seated for some years at Lawford Hall, near Manningtree, Essex, and afterwards for nearly half a century at Bentley Hall, near Ipswich. The name was originally spelt Gosnold.—*Park Cottage, Bentley, Ipswich.*

WALKER, Sir GEORGE FERDINAND RADZIVIL, Bart., of Castleton, Glamorganshire (cr. 1835).
Eldest son of the late General Sir George Townshend Walker, Bart., G.C.B., of Castleton (who was formerly Lieut.-Governor of Chelsea Hospital), by Helen, dau. of Alexander Caldcleugh, Esq., of The Manor House, Croydon, Surrey; *b.* 1825; *s.* as 2nd Bart. 1842; *m.* 1854 the Hon. Fanny Henrietta, 3rd dau. of Charles, 1st Lord Tredegar. Educated at Sandhurst; is a J.P. and D.L. for co. Monmouth; was formerly Capt. Coldstream Guards. This family is descended from Sir Edward Walker, Knt., Chancellor to Queen Katherine, Consort of Charles II.—*Castleton, Cardiff; Army and Navy Club,* s.w.

Heir, his son George Ferdinand, b. 1855.

WALKER, Sir BALDWIN WAKE, Bart., of Oakley House, Suffolk, K.C.B. (cr. 1856).
Eldest son of the late John Walker, Esq., by Frances his wife, niece of the late Sir William Wake, Bart., of Courteen Hall, co. Northampton; *b.* 1802; *m.* 1834 Mary Catherine Sinclair, dau. of Capt. John Worth, R.N., of Duren, co. Caithness. Is a Vice-Admiral R.N.: was formerly an Admiral in the Turkish Service, and Surveyor-General of the Navy; appointed to the Command of the South African Station 1862; Commander-in-Chief at the Nore 1866.— *Oakley House, Scole, Suffolk; United Service Club,* s.w.

Heir, his son Baldwin Wake, b. 1846.

WALKER, Sir EDWARD SAMUEL, Knt., of Berry Hill, Notts (cr. 1841).
Third son of the late Joseph Walker, Esq., of Eastwood House, Rotherham, co. York, and of Aston Hall, co. Derby, by Elizabeth, dau. of the late S. Need, Esq., of Nottingham; *b.* 1799; *m.* 1st 1842 Frances Valentine, dau. of George Stevens, Esq. (died *d.* 1864); 2nd 1866 Mary Elizabeth, 2nd dau. of Capt. Hallowes, R.N., of Glapwell Hall, co. Derby, and has issue, by the former,

• Edward William, *b.* 1844.

Sir E. Walker, who was educated at Rugby and St. John's Coll., Cambridge (LL.B. 1821), is a Magistrate for Notts (High Sheriff 1866), for the co. and city of Chester, and a Dep.-Lieut. for co. Flint; has been twice Mayor of Chester.—*Berry Hill, Mansfield; Union Club,* s.w.

+WALKER, ARTHUR ABNEY, Esq., of Blythe, Notts, and Clifton House, Yorkshire.
Only surviving son of the late Hall Walker, Esq., J.P. and D.L., of Clifton House (who *d.* 1860), by Elizabeth, only dau. of the late Edward Abney, Esq., of King's Newton, co. Derby; *b.* 1820; *s.* his brother 1866. Is Lord of the Manor o Blythe.—*Blythe Hall, Bawtry; Clifton House, Rotherham.*

WALKER, CHARLES ARTHUR, Esq., of Tykillen, co. Wexford.
Eldest son of the late Thomas Walker, Esq., of Tykillen, Master of Chancery in Ireland, by Maria, dau. of William Acton, Esq., of West Aston, co. Wicklow; *b.* 1 9 ; *l.* 1837; *m.* 1837 Eleanor, dau. of Joseph Leigh, Esq., of

Rosegarland, co. Wexford, and of Tinnykilly, co. Wicklow, and has, with other issue,

• Thomas Joseph, Lieut. 1st Royal Dragoons ; *b.* 1838.

Mr. Walker, who was educated at Trinity Coll., Dublin, is a Magistrate for and Vice-Lieut. of co. Wexford; was M.P. for Wexford 1830-43.—*Tykillen, Enniscorthy, co. Wexford; Reform Club,* s.w.

WALKER, Col. CHARLES PYNDAR BEAUCHAMP, C.B., of Redland, Gloucestershire.
Eldest son of the late Charles Ludlow Walker, Esq., J.P. and D.L., of Redland, by Mary Anne, dau. of Reginald Pyndar, Esq.; *b.* 1817; *s.* 1856; *m.* 1845 Georgiana, dau. of Richard Armstrong, Esq. Educated at Eton; entered the Army 1836, became a Col. in the Army 1860; was formerly in the 2nd Dragoon Guards. —*Redland, Bristol.*

WALKER, Major-General EDWARD WALTER FORESTIER, C.B., of Bushey Manor, Herts.
Eldest son of the late General F. Walker, K.C.H., R.A., by Annabella, dau. of Edward Cane, Esq., of Donnybrook, co. Dublin; *b.* 1812; *s.* 1857; *m.* 1st 1843 Lady Jane Grant, only dau. of Francis William, 6th Earl of Seafield (she *d.* 1861); 2nd, 1862, Lady Juliana Caroline Frances Knox, dau. of Thomas, 2nd Earl of Ranfurly, and has, with other issue,

Frederick William Edward Forestier, Lieut. and Capt. Scots Fusilier Guards ; *b.* 1844.

Major-General Walker, who entered the Army 1827, became a Major-General 1859; he was appointed to command the North British District 1861.—*Manor House, Bushey, Watford; United Service Club,* s.w.; 16, *Charlotte Square, Edinburgh.*

WALKER, HENRY BACHELER, Esq., of The Gables, New Romney, Kent.
Eldest surviving son of the late John Walker, Esq., of New Romney, by Harriet, dau. of Edward Dering, Esq., of Ashford, Kent; *b.* 1809; *m.* 1841 Anna Maria, dau. of Samuel Giles, Esq., of Ivychurch, Kent, and by her (who *d.* 1852) has, with other issue,

• Edward Bacheler, *b.* 1852.

Mr. Walker, who was elected Mayor of New Romney 1848, 1852, 1856, 1859, 1862, 1864, and 1866, is a Magistrate for Kent and the borough of New Romney. This family, of Scandinavian origin, have been located in various places in Kent for several centuries.—*The Gables, New Romney, Folkestone.*

WALKER, GEORGE GUSTAVUS, Esq., of Crawfordton, Dumfriesshire.
Eldest son of the late John Walker, Esq., of Crawfordton, by Jessy, dau. of J. Johnston, Esq.; *b.* 1831; *m.* 1856 Anne Murray, dau. of Admiral J. G. Lennock, and has issue. Educated at Rugby and Balliol Coll., Oxford (B.A. 1851, M.A. 1855); is a Magistrate for co. Kirkcudbright, and Major in the Scottish Borderers Militia; elected M.P. for co. Dumfries 1865.—*Crawfordton, Dumfries; Conservative Club, Monkgate ; Conservative Club,* s.w.

WALKER, JAMES, Esq., of Dalry, co. Midlothian.
Eldest son of the late James Walker, Esq., of Dalry, J.P. and D.L., by his 1st wife Lilias, dau. of R. Mackenzie, Esq., of Scotsburn, Ross-shire; *b.* 1850; *s.* 1856; *m.* 1859 the Hon. Anna, 5th dau. of Barry John, 3rd Viscount Avonmore, and has issue,

• Two daughters.

Mr. Walker, who was called to the Scotch Bar in 1853, is a Magistrate for co. Midlothian.—*Dalry House, Edinburgh.*

WALKER, JAMES, Esq., of Sand Hutton, York-shire.

Only son of the late James Walker, Esq., of Beverley, by Jane, only dau. and heir of John Porter, Esq., of Hull; b. 1803; s. 1829; m. 1st 1829 Mary, 4th dau. of Robert Denison, Esq., of Kilnwick Percy, co. York; 2nd 1833 Maria dau. of the Rev. Robert Stephen Thompson, of Bilbrough, co. York, and has, by the former, with other issue,

* James Robert, educated at Rugby, and B.A. of Ch. Ch., Oxford; a J.P. and D.L. for the N. Riding of Yorkshire, Lieut. Yorkshire Yeomanry Hussars, and M.P. for Beverley; b. 1829; m. 1863 Louisa Marlborough, 3rd dau. of Sir John Heron Maxwell, Bart., and has, with other issue,
    * James Heron, b. 1865.

Mr. Walker, who was educated at Rugby and Trinity Coll., Oxford (B.A. 1824), is a J.P. and D.L. for the E. and N. Ridings of Yorkshire (High Sheriff 1846), and Patron of 1 living.—Sand Hutton, York; The Hall, Beverley; University Club, S.W.

+WALKER, JOHN, Esq., of Lochtreig, Inver-ness-shire.

Second son of the late John Walker, Esq., of Craw-fordton, co. Dumfries, by Jessy, dau. of J. Johnston, Esq., and brother of Major G. G. Walker (whom see); b. 1834. Is a J.P. and D.L. for co. Inverness.—Loch-treig, Inverness, N.B.

WALKER, the Rev. JOHN THOMAS.

Eldest son of the late Rev. John Walker, Rector of Cottered, Herts, by Sophia Mary, dau. of the Rev. Thomas Sisson, of Wallington, Herts; b. 1816; m. 1856 Augusta, 2nd dau. of Charles Soames, Esq., of Coles Park, Herts. Educated at Caius Coll., Cambridge (B.A. 1838, M.A. 1841); called to the Bar at Lincoln's Inn 1842; entered Holy Orders 1846; is a Magistrate for Essex, and Rector of Ashdon.—Ashdon Rectory, Linton, Cambridgeshire; University Club, S.W.

WALKER, JONATHAN WALKER METCALFE, Esq., of Hawk Hills, Yorkshire.

Son of the late Jonathan Walker, Esq., of Hawk Hills; b. 18—; m. 1860 Emily Laura, younger dau. of the late Thomas Vardon, Esq. Is a Magistrate for the W. Riding of Yorkshire, late an Officer in the 7th Dragoon Guards. This family is a branch of the Walkers of Blythe Hall and Berry Hill (whom see).—Hawk Hills, Easingwold; Army and Navy Club, S.W.

+WALKER, JOSEPH NEED, Esq., of Calder-stone, Lancashire.

Son of the late J. Walker, Esq.; b. 1809. Is a Dep.-Lieut. for co. Lancaster.—Calderstone, Liverpool.

WALKER, OLIVER ORMEROD, Esq., of Chesham, Lancashire.

Eldest son of the late William Walker, Esq., of Bury, co. Lancaster, by Mary, dau. of William Ormerod, Esq., of Foxstones, near Burnley; b. 1794; m. 1st 1826 Mary, dau. of Thomas Haslam, Esq., of Chesham; 2nd 1831 Helen Elizabeth, dau. of T. T. Garston, Esq., of Chester, and has, with other issue,

* Oliver Ormerod (of Gorsey Brow, Bury), a Magistrate for co. Lancaster; b. 1834; m. 1866 Jane, dau. of Thomas Harrison, Esq., of Singleton Park, Westmoreland.

Mr. Walker is a J.P. and D.L. for co. Lancaster. —Chesham, Bury.

+WALKER, SAMUEL, Esq., of The Grange, Leicestershire.

Eldest son of the late William Kenworthy Walker, Esq., of The Grange, Mayor of Leicester, by Rachel, 2nd dau. of Samuel Walker, Esq., of Lascelles Hall, co. York; b. 18—; s. 1861; m. 1840 Elizabeth, 2nd dau. of the late Hon. Sir Robert Le Poer Trench, K.C.B. —The Grange, Leicester.

+WALKER, SAMUEL, Esq., of Doveridge, Derbyshire.

Son of the late S. Walker, Esq.; b. 18—. Is a Dep.-Lieut. for the W. Riding of co. York.—Doveridge, Uttoxeter.

WALKER, THOMAS, Esq., of Berkswell, War-wickshire.

Eldest son of the late John Walker, Esq., of Wishaw Hall, co. Warwick (who d. 1848), by Charlotte, dau. of William Bannister, Esq., of Great Chatwell, co. Stafford; b. 1817; m. 1840 Ruth, dau. of John Eades, Esq., of The Delph, Brierly Hill, co. Stafford, and has, with other issue,

* Thomas Eades, b. 1843.

Mr. Walker, who was educated at Harrow and Ch. Ch., Oxford, is a Magistrate for cos. Stafford and Warwick, Lord of the Manors of Studley, Berkswell, Middleton, &c., and Patron of 3 livings. He purchased Berkswell Hall of Sir J. Eardley Wilmot, Bart., in 1859.—Berks-well Hall, Coventry.

WALKER, THOMAS, Esq., of The Woodlands, Yorkshire.

Second son of the late William Walker, Esq., of Wilsick, co. York, by Margaret, dau. of Samuel Walker, Esq., of Masborough; b. 1808; m. 1841 Anna, dau. of John Stephenson Ferguson, Esq., of Ballysinnon, co. Antrim. Educated at Trinity Hall, Cambridge (B.A. 1830, M.A. 1833); is a J.P. and D.L. for the W. Riding of York-shire, a Magistrate for Doncaster, and a Capt. 1st W. Yorkshire Yeomanry Cavalry.—The Woodlands, Doncaster; Oxford and Cambridge Club, S.W.

WALKER, TYRWHITT, Esq., of Bossington, Hants.

Third son of the late Capt. Walker (of the 26th Ca-meronians), by Martha Sophia, dau. of John Tyrwhitt, Esq., of Pentre Park; b. 1818; m. 1853 Frances Eliza-beth Ann, dau. of the late James Ewing, Esq., of Down House, Richmond, Surrey. Is a Magistrate for Hants; was formerly in the Inniskilling Dragoons.—Bossington House, Stockbridge; Conservative Club, S.W.

WALKER, WILLIAM, Esq., of Bolling Hall, co. York.

Son of the late William Walker, Esq., of Almondbury (who d. 1842), by Lydia, dau. of J. Dup11ey, Esq., of London; b. 1802; m. 1829 Kezia Wesley, dau. of the Rev. John Stamp, of Woodhouse Grove, co. York, and has, with other issue,

* William (of Red Hall, Shadwell, co. York), a Magistrate for the W. Riding of co. York and Capt. W. York Rifles; b. 1834; m. 1868 Louisa Elizabeth, youngest dau. of the late Henry M. Bingham Kelly, Esq., of Larrane, co. Galway, and niece of Denis, 3rd Lord Clanmorris, and has, with other issue, * William St. George, b. 1858.

Mr. Walker is a Magistrate for the W. Riding of York-shire, and a Merchant at Bradford.—Bolling Hall, Brad-ford; Clayton Grange, Huddersfield.

WALKER, WILLIAM, Esq., of Wilsick, York-shire.

Eldest son of the late William Walker, Esq., Barrister-at-law, of Wilsick, by Margaret, dau. of Samuel Walker, Esq., of Masborough, co. York; b. 1807; s. 1830; m. 1848 Alice, dau. of the late Hugh Parker, Esq., of Tickhill, co. York. Educated at Trinity Coll., Cam-bridge (B.A. 1829, M.A. 1832); called to the Bar at Lincoln's Inn 1834, and went the Northern Circuit; is a J.P. and D.L. for the W. Riding of Yorkshire, and late a Judge of the Yorkshire County Courts.—Wilsick, Doncaster.

Heir Pres., his brother Thomas, of The Woodlands, co. Don-caster (whom see).

WALKER, WILLIAM DERING, Esq., of Honey-child Manor, Kent.

Youngest son of the late John Walker, of New Romney, by Harriet, youngest dau. of the late Edward Dering, Esq., of Ashford, Kent; *b.* 1811; *m.* 1838 Catherine, dau. of Nicholas Green, Esq., of Lydd, Kent, and has, with other issue, an only son,

* John Dering, *b.* 1847.

Mr. Walker is a Magistrate for Kent, and for the town and port of New Romney; was Mayor of New Romney 1867.—*Honeychild Manor, New Romney, Folkestone.*

WALKER, WILLIAM STUART, Esq., of Bowland, Midlothian.

Eldest son of the late Brigadier-General Alexander Walker, of Bowland, by Barbara, dau. of Sir James Montgomery, Bart., of Stanhope; *b.* 1813; *s.* 1831; *m.* 1836 Eliza, dau. of William Loch, Esq., H.E.I.C.'s Civil Service, and has, with other issue,

* William Campbell, M.A. of Trinity Coll., Oxford, a Magistrate for cos. Edinburgh and Selkirk, and M.P.C. of Canterbury, New Zealand; *b.* 1838.

Mr. Walker, who was educated at St. Mary's Hall, Oxford (B.A. 1835), called to the Bar at Edinburgh 1840, and appointed Secretary to the Scotch Poor Law Board 1852, is a J.P. and D.L. for cos. Edinburgh and Selkirk. This family is descended from the Walkers of St. Fort, co. Fife.]—*Bowland, Stow, N.B.; Carlton Club, s.w.*

WALKER.   (See *Sutherland-Walker.*)

WALKER.   (See *Robertson-Walker.*)

WALKER-ARNOTT, GEORGE ARNOTT, Esq., of Arlary, Kinross-shire.

Eldest son of the late David Walker-Arnott, Esq., of Arlary, by Emilia, dau. of Capt. John Stewart, of Stenton; *b.* 1799; *s.* 1823; *m.* 1831 Mary Hay, dau. of Arthur Barclay, Esq., of Glendy, co. Perth, and has, with other issue,

* David, *b.* 1832.

Mr. Walker-Arnott, who was educated at Edinburgh (M.A. 1818, LL.D. Aberdeen 1837), called to the Scottish Bar 1821, and appointed Regius Professor of Botany, University of Glasgow, 1845, is a J.P. and D.L. for co. Kinross, and a Magistrate for co. Fife. —*Arlary, Milnathort, Kinross-shire, N.B.; Victoria Terrace, Dowanhill, Glasgow.*

WALKER-DRUMMOND.   (See *Drummond.*)

WALKER-HENEAGE, GEORGE HENEAGE, Esq., of Compton Basset, Wilts.

Eldest son of the late Rev. George Wyld, of Speen, Berks, by Mary, dau. of the late General Calcraft; *b.* 1799; *m.* 1824 Harriet, eldest dau. of the late William Webber, Esq., of Binfield Lodge, Berks, and has, with other issue,

* Clement, Major 8th Hussars, V.C.; *b.* 1833; *m.* 1863 Henrietta Letitia Victoria, 3rd dau. of the late J. H. Vivian, Esq., of Singleton, co. Glamorgan.

Mr. Walker-Heneage, who was educated at Westminster and Ch. Ch., Oxford, is a J.P. and D.L. for Wilts, and Patron of 5 livings; was M.P. for Devizes 1838-57. He assumed the names of Walker-Heneage by Royal licence in 1818, on inheriting the property of his maternal grand-uncle, John Walker-Heneage, Esq.—*Compton Basset, Calne; Carlton and Travellers' Clubs, s.w.*

WALKEY, the Rev. CHARLES ELLIOTT, of Clyst St. Laurence, Devonshire.

Elder and only surviving son of the late Benjamin Walkey, Esq., of Exeter, by Mary, only child of Joseph

Elliott, Esq.; *b.* 1780; *m.* 1803 Elizabeth, 2nd dau. of Charles Collyns, Esq., Banker, of Exeter, and has, with other issue,

* Charles Collyns, M.A. of Worcester Coll., Oxford; *b.* 1804; *m.* 1832 Milborough Ann, only dau. of the Rev. John Huyshe, of Clysthydon, Devon, and has, with other issue,
* Charles John Elliott, M.A. of Lincoln Coll., Oxford, and Vicar of Llantrissent, co. Monmouth; *b.* 1853; *m.* 1851 Louisa Whitmore, 4th dau. of J. H. Whitmore-Jones, Esq., of Chastleton, Oxon.

Mr. Walkey, who was educated at Balliol Coll., Oxford (B.A. 1802), was appointed Rector of Clyst St. Laurence in 1804, and represents a family of ancient Cornish extraction.—*Clyst St. Laurence, near Collumpton, Devon.*

WALKEY, JOSEPH ELLIOTT COLLYNS, Esq., of Poll House, Devonshire.

Youngest son of the Rev. Charles Elliott Walkey, Rector of Clyst St. Laurence, by Elizabeth, dau. of Charles Collyns, Esq., Banker, of Exeter; *b.* 1817; *m.* 1846 Catherine, dau. of Pitman Jones, Esq., of St. Loyes, Devon, and has issue. Mr. Walkey is a Magistrate for Devon.—*Poll House, Ide, Exeter.*

WALL, the Rev. CHARLES JOSEPH.

Only surviving son of the late Rev. D. H. Wall, Rector of Clonmel, Ireland, by Caroline, dau. of Joseph Hardy, Esq., of Benvardine, co. Antrim; *b.* 1824; *m.* 1852 Caroline, dau. of Thomas Bramall, Esq., of Tamworth. Educated at Winchester and St. Peter's Coll., Cambridge (B.A. 1848, M.A. 1851). Is a Magistrate for the E. Riding of Yorkshire, Rural Dean of Hedon, and Rector of Sproatley.—*Sproatley Rectory, Hull.*

+WALL, the Rev. FREDERICK SANDYS, of Bradley Wood, Devon.

Son of the late — Wall, Esq.; *b.* 1795; is married, and has issue,

* A daughter.

Mr. Wall, who was educated at Winchester and New Coll., Oxford (B.C.L. 1817), is a Magistrate for Devon. —*Bradley Wood, Newton Bushel.*

WALL, GEORGE ALFRED ELLISS, Esq., of King's Worthy Park, Hants.

Third but only surviving son of the late Samuel Wall, Esq., of King's Worthy Park, by Mary, dau. of — Elliss, Esq.; *b.* 1825; *m.* 1852 Katharine, 7th dau. of the late Rev. Sir Henry Rivers, Bart., some time Rector of Martyr Worthy, and has issue,

* Katharine Georgiana.

Mr. Wall is a Magistrate for Hants.—*King's Worthy Park, Winchester; Romney Abbey, Hertford.*

WALLACE, Sir WILLIAM THOMAS FRANCIS AGNEW-, Bart., of Lochryan, Wigtownshire (cr. 1669).

Eldest son of the late General Sir John Alexander Agnew-Wallace, Bart., K.C.B., &c., of Lochryan, by Jannette, dau. of William Rodger, Esq.; *b.* 1830; *s.* at 8th Bart. 1857. Educated at Sandhurst and Trinity Coll., Cambridge; is a Magistrate for co. Wigtown, entered the Army in 1847, became Capt. and Lieut.-Col. Grenadier Guards 1859, and retired 1860. This family is that of which the renowned Sir William Wallace was a younger son.—*Lochryan House, Stranraer, N.B.; Guards' Club, s.w.*

Heir Pres., his brother Robert Agnew, b. 1834; m. 1859 Jane, dau. of John Bell, Esq., of Enterkine, co. Ayr, and has issue.

WALLACE, Sir ROBERT, K.C.S.I. (cr. 1866).

Second son of the late Col. R. C. Wallace, Esq., by Henrietta, dau. of Major Ellis; *b.* 1816; *m.* 1840 Corbetta, dau. of Joseph Loyd, Esq., and niece of the late Sir John Owen, Bart. Educated at Addiscombe; en-

‡ See Douglas's 'Baronage.'

tered the Indian Army as Ensign 18th Bombay N.I. 1833; is a Lieut.-Col. Bombay Staff Corps; late Resident at Baroda; formerly Political Agent at Mahee.—16, *Rue St. Ferdinand, Aux St. Turnes, Paris.*

WALLACE, ALBANY, Esq., of Worthing, Sussex.
Fifth son of the late John Wallace, Esq., of Sidcup, Kent, by Elizabeth, only dau. of R. French, Esq., of Frenchland, N.B.; *b.* 1788; *s.* his brother 1846. This family is descended from a common ancestor with the late Lord Wallace.—*Worthing, Sussex.*

Heir. Pres., his brother Robert Clarke, K.H., Col. in the Army, and late Major King's Dragoon Guards; *b.* 1789; *m.* 1814 Henrietta, dau. of Major Ellis, of Abbeyfeal, co. Cork.

WALLACE, THOMAS JAMES, Esq., of Bally Courcy, co. Wexford.
Eldest son of the late William James Wallace, Esq., of Bally Courcy, by Mary, dau. of Anthony Hawkins, Esq., Clerk of the Peace, Wexford; *b.* 1834; *s.* 1858. Is an Engineer in Russia.—*Bally Courcy, Enniscorthy.*

Heir Pres., his brother John Thornhill, *b.* 1836.

WALLACE. (See *Hope-Wallace.*)

WALLACE-LEGGE. (See *Legge.*)

WALLER, Sir EDMUND ARTHUR, Bart., of Newport, co. Tipperary (cr. 1780).
Eldest son of the late Sir Edmund Waller, Bart., of Newport, by his 2nd wife Rebecca, dau. of Arthur Guinness, Esq., of Beaumont, co. Dublin; *b.* 1846; *s.* as 5th Bart. 1851. Educated at Lansing Coll. and Eton; is Ensign 84th Foot. This family was long seated in cos. Dublin and Tipperary.—*47, Brunswick Road, Brighton.*

WALLER, Sir THOMAS WATHEN, Bart. (cr. 1815).
Eldest son of the late Sir Jonathan Wathen Waller, Bart. (who assumed the name of Waller in lieu of Phipps), by Elizabeth, dau. of Thomas Slack, Esq., of Braywick Lodge, Berks; *b.* 1805; *s.* as 2nd Bart. 1853; *m.* 1836 Catharine, dau. of the Rev. Henry Wise, of Offchurch, co. Warwick (she *d.* 1861). Was formerly Attaché and Secretary of Legation at Brussels and other foreign Courts; retired from the diplomatic service 1858.—16, *Eaton Square, s.w.*

Heir, his son Thomas, *b.* 1837.

WALLER, EDWARD, Esq., of Finnoe House, co. Tipperary.
Eldest son of the late Thomas Maunsell Waller, Esq., J.P., of Finnoe House, by Margaret, only dau. of John Vereker, Esq.; *b.* 1803; *s.* 1843; *m.* 1829 Mary, only dau. of the late Henry Crosslé, Esq., of Annahoe, co. Tyrone. Educated at Trinity Coll., Dublin (B.A. 1826); called to the Bar at Dublin 1830: is a Magistrate for cos. Tipperary and Tyrone.—*Finnoe House, Borrisokane; Lisderry, near Aughnacloy, co. Tyrone.*

+WALLER, HARRY EDMUND, Esq., of Farmington, Gloucestershire.
Eldest son of the late Rev. Harry Waller, Rector of Farmington, by Mary, dau. of the Rev. John Dolphin; *b.* 1804; *s.* 1824; *m.* 1826 Caroline, dau. of John Larking, Esq., of Clare Hall, Kent, and has issue,

* Edmund, a Magistrate for co. Gloucester; *b.* 1828; *m.* 1858 Lucy, dau. of the late Henry Elwes, Esq., of Colesbourne Park, co. Gloucester.

Mr. Waller is a J.P. and D.L. for co. Gloucester, and Patron of 1 living.—*Farmington Lodge, Northleach.*

WALLER, JAMES NOBLE, Esq., of Allenstown, co. Meath.
Third son of the late Rev. Mungo Henry Waller, of Allenstown, by Maria, dau. of the late Archbishop (Newcome) of Armagh; *b.* 1800; *m.* 1838 Julia, eldest dau. of Charles Arthur Tisdale, Esq., of Charlesfort, co. Meath, and has, with other issue,

* William Newcome, *b.* 1839.

Mr. Waller, who was educated at Trinity Coll., Dublin, is a J.P. and D.L. for co. Meath (High Sheriff 1846).—*Allenstown, Navan, co. Meath.*

WALLER, the Rev. JOHN THOMAS, of Castletown, co. Limerick.
Second son of the late Rev. William Waller, J.P., of Castletown, by Maria, 2nd dau. of James O'Grady, Esq., of Limerick, and niece of Standish, 1st Viscount Guillamore; *b.* 1827; *s.* 1863; *m.* 1855 Fanny, only dau. of John Lavallin Puxley, Esq., of Dunboy, co. Cork, and has, with other issue,

* William, *b.* 1857.

Mr. Waller, who was educated at Trinity Coll., Dublin (B.A. 1851, M.A. 1857), is Rector of Kilcornan, co. Limerick.—*Castletown, Pallas Kenry, co. Limerick.*

WALLER, WILLIAM THOMAS, Esq., of Prior Park, co. Tipperary.
Third son of the late George Waller, Esq., of Prior Park, by Elizabeth, dau. of George Studdart, Esq.; *b.* 1811; *s.* 1833; *m.* 1834 Eliza Augusta, dau. of the Rev. Dr. Guinness, and has, with other issue,

* George Arthur, *b.* 1835; *m.* 1865 Sarah Harriett, dau. of Grey Atkinson, Esq., of Cangort, King's Co.

Mr. Waller, who was educated at Eton and Trinity Coll., Dublin, is a Magistrate for co. Tipperary.—*Prior Park, Nenagh, co. Tipperary.*

WALLINGTON, CHARLES ARTHUR GRANARD, Esq.
Eldest son of the late Rev. Charles Wallington, Rector of Hawkeswell, Essex, by Frances Russell, dau. of Hamlyn Harris, Esq.; *b.* 1785; *s.* 1843. Is a J.P. and D.L. for co. Warwick, and Lieut.-General in the Bengal Presidency.—*Leamington ; Oriental Club, w.*

WALLINGTON, JOHN, Esq., of Dursley, Gloucestershire.
Second son of the late Edward Wallington, Esq., of Dursley; *b.* 1797; *m.* 1820 Anne, dau. of Edward Sheppard, Esq., late of The Ridge, Uley, co. Gloucester, and has issue,

* John Williams, a Magistrate for cos. Gloucester and Wilts, late Capt. 4th Light Dragoons; Lieut.-Col. of the Royal N. Gloucester Militia; *b.* 1822; *m.* 1852 Henrietta Maria, dau. of the late William Beach, Esq., of Oakley Hall, Hants, and Keevil House, Wilts, and has, with other issue. * John Arthur Beach, *b.* 1853.

Mr. Wallington is a Magistrate for co. Gloucester.—Residence, *Keevil House, Trowbridge, Wilts.*

WALLIS, Sir PROVO WILLIAM PARRY, K.C.B., of Funtington, Sussex (cr. 1860).
Only son of Provo Featherstone Wallis, Esq., of Halifax, Nova Scotia, by Elizabeth, eldest dau. of Major William Lawlor; *b.* 1791; *m.* 1st 1817 Juliana, 2nd dau. of the Ven. Archdeacon Massey; 2nd 1849 Jemima Mary Gwyn, eldest surviving dau. of the late General Sir Robert Wilson. Entered the Navy 1804; appointed A.D.C. to the Queen in 1847; became an Admiral of

the Blue 1863 ; was Commander-in-Chief in South America 1857–58.—*Funtington House, Chichester ; United Service Club,* s.w.

WALLIS, ALFRED ARTHUR, Esq., of Healing, Lincolnshire.
Youngest son of the late Lieut.-General Loft, M.P., of Cainby Hall, co. Lincoln (who *d.* 1842) by Elizabeth, 2nd dau. of the late Gilbert Farr, Esq., of Healing and Caistor (under whose wi l he assumed, in 1837, the name of Wallis) ; *b.* 1816 ; *m.* 1848 Gloriana Margret'a, only dau. of the late Capt. James Sanders, R.N., C.B., and has, with other issue,
  * Gilbert Farr, *b.* 1854.
Mr. Wallis is joint Lord of the Manor and alternate Patron of Healing.—*Healing, Ulceby.*

WALLIS, JOHN RICHARD SMYTH, Esq., of Drishane, co. Cork.
Eldest son of the late Lieut.-Col. Henry Wallis, J.P. and D.L. of Drishane Castle, by Ellen, dau. of Grice Smyth, Esq., of Ballinatray ; *b.* 1810 ; *s.* 1862 ; *m.* 1853 Octavia, natural dau. of Digby, 7th Lord Middleton, of Wollaton Hall, Notts, and has surviving issue,
  * Henry Aubrey Beaumont, *b.* 1861.
Mr. Wallis, who was educated at Trinity Coll., Dublin, is a Magistrate for co. Cork (High Sheriff 1857).—*Drishane Castle, Millstreet, co. Cork.*

WALLIS, ROBERT, Esq., of Old Ridley, Northumberland.
Second son of the late Thomas Wallis, Esq., of Old Ridley, by Ann, dau. of Joseph Smith, Esq. ; *b.* 1810 ; *s.* his brother 1853 ; *m.* 1862 Mary, eldest dau. of Mr. Webster. of Weston, and niece of Francis Sikes, Esq., of The Chauntry House, Newark. Educated at University Coll., London ; is a Magistrate for co. Durham. —*Old Ridley, Gateshead.*

WALLOP. (See under *Portsmouth, Earl of.*)

+**WALLS, the Rev. RICHARD GEORGE, of Boothby Hall, Lincolnshire.**
Eldest son of the late Joseph Walls, M.A., of Boothby Hall (who was Incumbent of Welton-in-the-Marsh and Boothby) ; *b.* 1818 ; *s.* 1857. Educated at Brasenose Coll., Oxford (B.A. 1841, M.A. 1844) ; is a Magistrate for co. Lincoln, and Rector and Patron of Gt. Steeping.—*Boothby Hall, Spilsby.*

WALLSCOURT, Lord (ERROLL AUGUSTUS BLAKE).—Cr. 1800.
Third but only surviving son of Joseph Henry. 3rd Lord, by Elizabeth, dau. of the late William Lock. Esq., of Norbury Park, Surrey ; *b.* 1841 ; *s.* 1849. Educated at Eton ; late Lieut. and Capt. Coldstream Guards. — *Ardfry House, near Galway ; 5, Montagu Square,* w.
  Heir Pres., his uncle Henry James, late Lieut. co. Galway Militia (youngest but only surviving son of the late Lieut.-Col. Henry James Blake, who was brother of Joseph, 1st Lord Wallscourt, and *d.* 1811, by Anne, dau. of John French, Esq.) ; *b.* 1805 ; *m.* 1859 Anne, widow of Lieut.-Col. Swayne (who *d.* 1867).

WALMESLEY, RICHARD, Esq.
Fourth son of the late John Walmesley, Esq., of The Hall of Ince, co. Lancaster, by his 2nd wife Ellen, dau. of the late Richard Godolphin Long, Esq., M.P., of Rood Ashton, Wilts ; *b.* 1816. Is a Magistrate for Wilts.— Residence: *Standerwick Court, near Frome, Somerset.*

WALMESLEY, WILLIAM, Esq., of The Hall of Ince, Lancashire.
Eldest son of the late John Walmesley, Esq., of The Hall of Ince, by his 1st wife Hannah, dau. of Christo-

966

pher Couron, Esq., of Cork ; *b.* 1800 ; *s.* 1867 ; represents a branch of the Walmesleys of Sholey and Westwood.— *The Hall of Ince, Wigan.*
  Heir Pres. his brother Christopher, *b.* 1808.

WALMESLEY, WILLIAM GERARD, Esq., of Westwood House, Lancashire.
Eldest surviving son of the late Charles Walmesley, Esq., of Westwood House, by Elizabeth, only child of John Jeffreys, Esq., of the Inner Temple, London ; *b.* 1808 ; *s.* 1833 ; *m.* 1838 Caroline, dau. of the late Sir Thos. De Trafford, Bart., and has, with other issue,
  * William Gerard, Lieut. 17th Lancers ; *b.* 1841.
Mr. Walmesley, who was educated at Stonyhurst, is a Magistrate for co. Lancaster.—*Westwood House, Wigan.*

WALMSLEY, Sir JOSHUA, Knt., of Wolverton Park, Hants (cr. 1840).
Son of the late John Walmsley, Esq., by Elizabeth, dau. of — Perry, Esq. ; *b.* 1794 ; *m.* 1815 Adeline, dau. of H. Mullineux, Esq., and has issue. Educated at Holt Hill ; is a Magistrate for Lancashire and for Lancaster ; late a Merchant and Mayor of Liverpool; was M.P. for Leicester 1847–8 and 1852–7 ; for Bolton 1849–52.—*Snibston, near Leicester ; Brunswick Street, Liverpool ; Wolverton Park, Kingsclere ; Reform Club,* s.w.

WALPOLE, Sir ROBERT, K.C.B. (cr. 1859).
Third son of the late Thomas Walpole. Esq., of Stagbury, Surrey, by Lady Margaret. 8th dau. of John, 2nd Earl of Egmont, and cousin of Horatio, Earl of Orford; *b.* 1808 ; *m.* 1846 Gertrude, youngest dau. of the late General Ford, and has issue. Sir R. Walpole is Major-General in the Army, late Commander of the Forces in Chatham district. and formerly Commandant of the Garrison at Gibraltar; was formerly Col. Rifle Brigade; served with distinction during the Indian Mutiny. —*United Service Club,* s.w.

WALPOLE, the Hon. FREDERICK, F.S.A., F.G.S., &c., of Rainthorpe, Norfolk.
Third son of Horatio, 3rd Earl of Orford. by Mary, dau. of the late William Augustus Fawkner. Esq. ; *b.* 1822; *m.* 1852 Laura Sophia Frances, dau. of Francis Walpole. Esq., and has, with other issue,
  * Robert Horace Walpole, *b.* 1854.
Mr. Walpole is a Magistrate for Norfolk. a Commander R.N. retired. and Major W. Norfolk Militia. —*Rainthorpe Hall. Long Stratton ; Travellers' and Athenæum Clubs,* s.w.; 65, *Eaton Square,* s.w.

WALPOLE, REGINALD ROBERT. Esq.
Eldest son of the late Rev. Robert Walpole, Rector of Christ Church. Marylebone, by Caroline, dau. of Sir John Hyde. formerly Chief Justice of Calcutta ; *b.* 1817 ; *m.* 1st 1849 Anne Eliza, dau. of John Heaton, Esq., of Plas-Heaton, co. Denbigh ; 2nd 1856 Caroline, dau. of the Rev. G. Anthony, of Grendon Rectory, co. Leicester, and widow of William Watts. Esq., of Hanslope Park, Bucks. Educated at Caius Coll., Cambridge (B.A. 1842, M.A. 1846) ; called to the Bar at Lincoln's Inn 1846, and was formerly Reader on the Law of Real Property to the Hon. Society of Gray's Inn; is a Magistrate for Bucks and co. Northampton. —*Hanslope Lodge, Stony Stratford ; United University Club,* s.w.

WALPOLE, the Right Hon. SPENCER HORATIO, Q.C., of Ealing, Middlesex.
Second son of the late Thomas Walpole. Esq., of Stagbury Park. Surrey. by Lady Margaret. 8th dau. of John, 2nd Earl of Egmont ; *b.* 1806 ; *m.* 1835 Isabella,

dau. of the late Right Hon. Spencer Percival, M.P., and has, with other issue,

* Spencer, Inspector of Fisheries; *b.* 1839; *m.* 1867 Marian, youngest dau. of Sir John Digby Murray, Bart.

Mr. Walpole, who was educated at Eton and Trinity Coll., Cambridge (B.A. 1828), and called to the Bar at Lincoln's Inn 1831, was late a Commissioner of Ecclesiastical Estates; he was Secretary of State for the Home Department in 1852, 1858-9, and 1866-7; M.P. for Midhurst 1846-56, and has been M.P. for the University of Cambridge since 1856. — *Ealing, Middlesex; Carlton Club, s.w.*; 109, *Eaton Square, s.w.*

WALPOLE, the Rev. THOMAS, of Stagbury, Surrey.
Eldest son of the late Thomas Walpole, Esq., of Stagbury Park, by Lady Margaret Perceval, dau. of John, 2nd Earl of Egmont; *b.* 1805; *m.* 1833 Margaret Harriet Isabella, eldest dau. of the late Col. Henry Hugh Mitchell, and of Lady Harriet Somerset, and has, with other issue,

* Henry Spencer, *b.* 1837.

Mr. Walpole was educated at Eton and Balliol Coll., Oxford (B.A. 1826, M.A. 1829), and appointed Rector of Alverstoke 1847.—*Stagbury Park, Epsom; Alverstoke Rectory, Gosport.*

WALPOLE. (See under *Orford, Earl of.*)

WALPOLE. (See *Vade-Walpole.*)

WALROND, BETHELL, Esq., of Dulford House, Devon.
Second and only surviving son of the late Joseph Lyons Walrond, Esq., of Dulford, by Caroline, dau. of Edward Codrington, Esq.; *b.* 1802; *s.* his brother 1819; *m.* 1829 Lady Janet, only dau. of Henry, 2nd Earl of Rosslyn, G.C.B., and has, with other issue,

* Henry, educated at Ch. Ch., Oxford; *b.* 1841.

Mr. Walrond, who is a J.P. and D.L. for Devon, was formerly an Officer in the Army, and was M.P. for Sudbury and Saltash 1826-32. He is a co-heir of the Barony of Welles (1854), and a Spanish ‡ Marquis and Count, and a Grandee of the first class. — *Dulford House, Collumpton.*

WALROND, JOHN WALROND, Esq., of Bradfield, Devon.
Eldest son of the late Benjamin Bowdon Dickinson, Esq., of Knightshayes, Devon (who took the name of Walrond in 1845), by Frances, dau. and co-heir of William Henry Walrond, Esq., of Bradfield; *b.* 1818; *s.* 1851; *m.* 1845 the Hon. Frances Caroline, dau. of Samuel, 2nd Lord Bridport, and has, with other issue,

* William Hood, *b.* 1849.

Mr. Walrond is a J.P. and D.L. for Devon, and a Magistrate for Somerset; elected M.P. for Tiverton 1865. This family have been settled at Bradfield since the reign of King John.—*Bradfield, Collumpton; Carlton Club, s.w.*; 12, *Warwick Street, s.w.*

WALSH, Sir JOHN ALLEN JOHNSON-, Bart., of Ballykilcavan, Queen's Co. (cr. 1775).
Only son of the late Rev. Sir Hunt Henry Johnson-Walsh, Bart., of Ballykilcavan, by his 1st wife, Frances, dau. of William Thomas Monsell, Esq., of Tervoe, co. Limerick; *b.* 1829; *s.* as 4th Bart. 1855; *m.* 1859 Henrietta Anne, dau. of the Rev. Matthew Forde, of Seaforde, co. Down. Is a J.P. and D.L. for Queen's

‡ The Spanish honours were conferred by Philip IV. of Spain, August 5th, 1653, on Colonel Humphrey Walrond, a zealous adherent of Charles I., and afterwards Governor and President of Barbados.

Co. (High Sheriff 1854-5); late Capt. Queen's Co. Rifles.—*Ballykilcavan, Stradbally.*
Heir, his son Hunt Henry Allen, b. 1864.

WALSH, JOHN, Esq., of Fanningstown, co. Kilkenny.
Eldest son of the late Thomas Walsh, Esq., of Fanningstown, by Barbara, only dau. of the late Cornelius O'Meagher, Esq., of Orchardtown, co. Tipperary; *b.* 1799; *s.* 1827; *m.* 1836 Elizabeth, youngest dau. of the late Richard Power, Esq., J.P., of Bollendeart, co. Waterford. Educated at St. John's Co l., Waterford; is a Magistrate for cos. Kilkenny, Tipperary, and Waterford. — *Fanningstown, near Pilltown, co. Kilkenny.*

WALSH, the Right Hon. JOHN EDWARD.
Only son of the late Rev. Robert Walsh, LL.D., by Anne Eliza, dau. of John Bayly, Esq.; *b.* 1816; *m.* 1841 Blair Belinda, dau. of Gordon MacNeill, Esq. Educated at Trinity Coll., Dublin (B.A. 1837, M.A. 1840, LL.D. 1845); called to the Bar at Dublin, 1839; appointed a Q.C. 1857: Attorney-General for Ireland, July 1866; Master of the Rolls in Ireland, Dec. 1866; sworn a Privy Councillor for that kingdom 1866; was M.P. for Dublin University, July-Dec. 1866. — 14. *Merrion Square South, Dublin; University Club, Dublin; Carlton Club, s.w.*

+ WALSH, the Rev. WILLIAM, of Great Tey, Essex.
Son of the late William Walsh, Esq., of Dublin; *b.* 1816; is married. Educated at St. John's Coll., Cambridge (B.A. 1839, M.A. 1842); is a Magistrate for Essex, Rector and Patron of Great Tey.—*Great Tey, Kelvedon.*

+ WALSH, WILLIAM, Esq., of Stedalt, co. Meath.
Son of the late W. Walsh, Esq., of Stedalt, by a dau. of — O'Farrell, Esq.; *b.* 180-. Is a Magistrate for co. Meath, and Lord of the Manor of Stedalt.—*Stedalt, Balbriggan, co. Meath.*

WALSH [BENN-.]
(See under *Ormathwaite, Lord.*)

WALSHAM, Sir JOHN JAMES, Bart., of Knill Court, Herefordshire (cr. 1831).
Only son of the late Col. Garbett Walsham, of Knill Court (who *d.* 1819), by Anna Maria, only dau. and heir of Hugh Hughes, Esq., of Redwryn, in Anglesea; *b.* 1806; *m.* 1826 Frances, dau. of Matthew Bell, Esq., of Woolsington, Northumberland (she *d.* 1857). Educated at Eton and on the Continent. Is a J.P. and D.L. for cos. Hereford and Radnor, Patron of 1 living, and a Governor of Bury School: was formerly a Commissioner of Charities and Major Herefordshire Militia; Assistant Poor-Law Commissioner 1835-47, and a Poor Law Inspector 1847-68.—*Knill Court, Kington, Herefordshire; Windham Club, s.w.*

Heir, his son John, M.A. of Trinity Coll. Cambridge, a Diplomatist, late in Lanarkshire, ... at Madrid ... 1867 Florence, only dau. of the Hon. Peter Campbell Scarlett, C.B., of Parkhurst, Surrey.

WALSINGHAM, Lord (THOMAS DE GREY).—Cr. 1780.
Eldest son of Thomas, 4th Lord, by Elizabeth, dau. of the late Right Rev. Dr. Brownlow North, Lord Bishop of Winchester; *b.* 1804; *s.* 1839; *m.* 1st 1842 Augusta Louisa, dau. of the late Sir R. Frankland-Russell, Bart.; 2nd 1847 the Hon. Emily Elizabeth, dau. of John, 2nd Lord Rendlesham. Called to the Bar at Lincoln's Inn 1827; is a J.P. and D.L. for Suffolk and Norfolk; Lord of the Manors of Merton, &c., and Patron of 3

livings. — *Merton Hall, Thetford; Carlton Club, s.w.; 23, Arlington Street, s.w.*

Heir, his son Thomas, educated at Eton, and M.A. of Trinity Coll., Cambridge; a J.P. and D.L. for Norfolk, and M.P. for W. Norfolk; *b.* 1843.

WALTER, JOHN, Esq., of Bearwood, Berks.
Eldest son of the late John Walter, Esq., M.P., of Bearwood, by Mary, dau. of Henry Smithe, Esq., of Eastling, Kent; *b.* 1818; *s.* 1847; *m.* 1st 1842 Emily Frances, dau. of Major Henry Court, of Castlemans, Berks (she *d.* 1858); 2nd 1861 Flora, 3rd dau. of the late James Monro Macnabb, Esq., of Highfield Park, Hants, and has by the former, with other issue,

    * John Balston, *b.* 1844.

Mr. Walter, who was educated at Eton and Exeter Coll., Oxford (B.A. 1840, M.A. 1843), and called to the Bar at Lincoln's Inn 1847, is a J.P. and D.L. for London and Berks, a Magistrate for Middlesex, and Patron of 2 livings; he was M.P. for Nottingham 1847–59, for Berks 1859–65. — *Bearwood, near Reading; Reform Club, s.w.; City Club, e.c.; 40, Upper Grosvenor Street, w.*

WALTER, RALPH, Esq.
Third son of the late Robert Walters, Esq., of Newcastle-on-Tyne, by Isabella, dau. of William Clayton, Esq., of Newcastle-on-Tyne; *b.* 1801; *m.* 1st 1824 Elizabeth, dau. of Robert Hole, Esq., of Stickwick House, Devon; 2nd 1858 Elizabeth, only child of the Rev. Thomas Stone, D.D., Rector of Wootton Rivers, Wilts. Educated at the University of Durham; called to the Bar at the Middle Temple 1854; is a Magistrate for Middlesex; was M.P. for Beverley May–August, 1859. *51, Eaton Square, s.w.*

+WALTERS, WILLIAM, Esq., of Haverfordwest, Pembrokeshire.
Son of the late — Walters, Esq.; *b.* 18—. Is a J.P. and D.L. for co. Pembroke (High Sheriff 1866).—*Haverfordwest, co. Pembroke.*

WALTERS-PHILIPPS, JOHN, Esq., of Aberglasney, Carmarthenshire.
Only son of the late Abel Griffiths Walters, Esq., of Perthygeraint, co. Cardigan, by Bridget, dau. of the late Thomas Philipps, Esq., of Pembroke; *b.* 1787; *s.* his maternal uncle 1824, when he assumed the name of Philipps; *m.* 1817 Ann, dau. of Thomas Bowen, Esq., of Waun Ifor, co. Cardigan, and by her (who is deceased) had issue, three daughters,

    * Bridget Jane. *m.* Cecil A. Harries, Esq., of Llanwnwas, co. Pembroke (whom see); Mary Ann, *m.* John Pugh Pryse, Esq., of Bwlchbychar, co. Cardigan (whom see), and is deceased, leaving issue one daughter, Mary Ann Emily Jane; and Elizabeth Frances, *m.* Frederick Louis Lloyd Philipps, Esq., of Pentrepark, co. Pembroke (whom see).

Mr. Walters-Philipps is a Magistrate for cos. Pembroke and Carmarthen (High Sheriff 1841), and a Dep.-Lieut. for co. Cardigan.—*Aberglasney, Carmarthen.*

WALTON, ELLIS ANDERSON STEPHENS, Esq., of Haverhill Hamlet, Essex.
Eldest son of the late Major Charles Walton, of the 4th Light Dragoons, by Mary Ann, eldest dau. of Ellys Anderson Stephens, Esq., of Bower Hall, Steeple Bumpstead, Essex; *b.* 1820; *s.* 1811; *m.* 1850 Mary Louisa, only dau. of William Henry Layton, Esq., of Baythorne Grove, Essex, and has, with other issue,

    * Bendysho William Ellys, *b.* 1855.

Mr. Walton is a Magistrate for Suffolk and for Essex, and Paymaster of the West Essex Militia, when embodied.—*Haverhill Hamlet, Newmarket.*

WALWYN, RICHARD HENRY, Esq.
Only son of the late Rev. Richard Walwyn, by Caroline, dau. of the Hon. and Very Rev. Henry Roper, of

968

Clones, Ireland; *b.* 1804; *m.* 1837 Laura Elizabeth Sanders, dau. of Charles Sanders, Esq., of Exeter, and has, with other issue,

    * James Harford, *b.* 1838.

Mr. Walwyn, who was educated at Oriel Coll., Oxford (B.A. 1823, M.A. 1825), was formerly an Officer in the Army. This family, formerly of Longworth, co. Hereford, represented the city and co. of Hereford at various times, from 1338 to 1763.—*Clifton, Bristol.*

WANKLYN, EDWARD, Esq., of Fulmer, Bucks.
Fourth son of the late William Wanklyn, Esq., by Sarah, dau. of John Bradshaw, Esq., of Manchester; *b.* 1806; *m.* 1839 Mary Jane, 2nd dau. of John Bradshaw, Esq., of Weaste House, co. Lancaster. Educated at Brasenose Coll., Oxford (B.A. 1829); called to the Bar at Lincoln's Inn 1834; is a Magistrate for Bucks.—*Fulmer Place, Slough.*

WARBURTON, RICHARD, Esq., of Garryhinch, King's Co.
Eldest son of the late Richard Warburton, Esq., J.P. and D.L., of Garryhinch (who was High Sheriff of King's Co. 1845, and of Queen's Co. 1849, and formerly an Officer in the Army), by Mary Ellinor, dau. of Lieut.-Col. Kelly, of Millgrove, King's Co.; *b.* 1846; *s.* 1862. Is a Magistrate for Queen's Co. — *Garryhinch, Portarlington, Ireland.*

Heir Pres., his brother Dutton, *b.* 1662.

WARBURTON, ROWLAND EYLES EGERTON-, Esq., of Arley Hall, Cheshire.
Eldest son of the late Rev. Rowland Egerton, by Emma, dau. of James Croxton, Esq., of Norley Bank, co. Chester; *b.* 1804; *s.* by will to the estates of his great uncle Sir Peter Warburton, Bart., and assumed the name of Warburton by Royal licence 1813; *m.* 1831 Mary, eldest dau. of the late Sir Richard Brooke Bart., of Norton Priory, and has, with other issue,

    * Piers, B.A. of Ch. Ch., Oxford, a Magistrate for co. Chester; *b.* 1839.

Mr. Egerton-Warburton, who was educated at Eton and C.C.C. Oxford, is a J.P. and D.L. for co. Chester (High Sheriff 1833), and Patron of 1 living. — *Arley Hall, Northwich; Carlton Club, s.w.*

WARD, the Hon. HUMBLE DUDLEY.
Second son of William Humble, 10th Lord Ward, by Amelia, dau. of William Gooch Pillans, Esq., of Bracondale, Norfolk, and brother of William, 1st Earl of Dudley; *b.* 1821; *m.* 1843 Eleanor Louisa, 3rd dau. of Thomas Hawkes, Esq., M.P., and has, with other issue,

    * William Humble Dudley, *b.* 1849.

Mr. Ward, who was educated at Harrow, is a Dep.-Lieut. for co. Stafford; late Capt. Staffordshire Yeomanry Cavalry.—*Himley, Dudley; 4, Queen's Gate Terrace, w.*

WARD, the Hon. and Rev. HENRY.
Youngest son of the late Hon. Edward Ward (who *d.* 1812), by Lady Arabella, youngest dau. of William, 1st Earl of Glandore, and brother of Edward, 3rd Viscount Bangor; *b.* 1795; *m.* 1833 Anne, eldest dau. of the Rev. Henry Mahon, of Killigshy, King's Co., and has, with other issue,

    * Crosbie, *b.* 1833; *m.* 1857 Marcia, 7th dau. of James Townsend, Esq., of Canterbury, New Zealand.

Mr. Ward, who was educated at Trinity Coll., Dublin, (B.A. 1818), is Rector of Killinchy.—*Killinchy Rectory, co. Down.*

WARD, EDWARD FOOTE, Esq., of Salhouse, Norfolk.
Only son of the late Richard Ward, Esq., J.P. and D.L., of Salhouse Hall, by Elizabeth, 3rd dau. of the late Vice-Admiral Sir Edward James Foote, K.C.B.; *b.* 1848; *s.* 1868.—*Salhouse Hall, Norwich.*

WARD, HENRY, Esq., of Oaklands, Stafford-shire.
Eldest son of the late William Ward, Esq., of Wolver-hampton, by Anne, dau. of John Barnett, Esq., of Comberton, near Kidderminster; b. 1828; s. 1849; m. 1855 Jane, dau. of the late John Bagnall, Esq., of West Bromwich, co. Stafford. Is a J.P. and D.L. for co. Stafford.—*Oaklands, Wolverhampton.*

WARD, MICHAEL FOSTER, Esq., F.R.A.S. and F.M.S., of Ogbourne St. Andrew, and Draycot Foliat, Wilts.
Eldest son of the late Thomas Rawdon Ward, Esq., J.P., of Obourne St. Andrew and Draycot Foliat (Lieut.-Col. Wilts Yeomanry Cavalry), by Ann, dau. and heir of Thomas Clark, Esq., of Greenham, Berks; b. 1826; s. 1863; m. 1854 Helen Christina, dau. of the late Robert Clerk-Rattray, Esq., of Craighall-Rattray, co. Perth, and has, with other issue,
* Thomas Rawdon Rattray, b. 1861.

Mr. Ward, who was educated at Eton, is a Magistrate for Wilts, and Lieut.-Col. N. Wilts Rifles; was formerly a Captain in the 90th Light Infantry.—*Draycot Foliat, Swindon; Ogbourne St. Andrew, Marlborough; Castle House, Calne; Army and Navy and Junior Carlton Clubs, s.w.*

WARD, NEVILLE, Esq., late of Taplow Court, Buckinghamshire.
Younger son of the late John Ward, Esq., M.P., of Holwood, Kent, by Jane Frances, eldest dau. of the late Robert Lambert, Esq., of Elland Hall, co. York; b. 1815; m. 1839 Florentine Louisa, youngest dau. of the late Col. Houlton, of Farley Castle, Somerset, and has, with other issue,
* Ellis Houlton, b. 1840.

Mr. Ward is a Magistrate for Kent and Sussex.—Residence: *Calverley Park, Tunbridge Wells.*

WARD, OWEN FLORANCE LOUIS, Esq., of Willey, Surrey.
Only surviving son of the late James Ward, Esq., of Willey, by Elizabeth, dau. of Thomas Smith, Esq., of Shalden, Hants; b. 1823; s. 1855; m. 1847 Annie Alice, dau. of Major Harvey Welman, late 57th Regt., and has, with other issue,
* James, b. 1848.

Mr. Ward, who was educated at the Royal Military Coll., Sandhurst, was formerly Capt. 11th Regt. This family was originally seated in Cheshire.—*Willey Place, Farnham.*

WARD, ROBERT EDWARD, Esq., of Bangor, Downshire.
Only son of the late Michael Edward Ward, Esq., of Bangor Castle, by Lady Matilda, 6th dau. of Robert, 1st Marquis of Londonderry, K.G.; b. 1819; s. 1840; m. 1857 Harriette, dau. of the Hon. and Rev. Henry Ward, and has issue,
* Matilda Catherine.

Mr. Ward, who was educated at Harrow and Ch. Ch., Oxford, is a J.P. and D.L. for co. Down (High Sheriff 1841-2); was formerly in the 10th Royal Hussars. —*Bangor Castle, co. Down; Travellers' Club, s.w.*

WARD, THOMAS JOHNSON, Esq., of Fern Park, Gloucestershire.
Only child of the late Alfred Ward, Esq., of Olveston, co. Gloucester, by Martha Ward, dau. of the late Thomas Johnson, Esq., of Elberton, in the same co.; b. 1827; s. 1849; m. 1849 Ellen Isabella, youngest dau. of John Bush, Esq., of Beach Bilton, co. Gloucester, and has, with other issue,
* Alfred Thomas Johnson, b. 1852.

Mr. Ward is a Magistrate for co. Gloucester. This family were resident at Elberton for above 100 years. —*Fern Park, Olveston, Bristol.*

WARD, WILLIAM GEORGE, Esq., of Northwood, I. of Wight.
Eldest son of the late William Ward, Esq., M.P., by Emily, dau. of Harvey Christian Combe, Esq., M.P.; b. 1812; s. his uncle 1849; m. 1845 Frances Mary, youngest dau. of the late Rev. John Wingfield, D.D., and has, with other issue,
* Edmund Granville, b. 1853.

Mr. Ward, who was educated at Winchester and Ch. Ch., Oxford, was afterwards Fellow of Balliol Coll. (B.A. 1834, M.A. 1837).—*Northwood Park, Cowes; Old Hall, Ware; 21, Hamilton Terrace, N.W.*

WARD.
(See under *Bangor, Viscount,* and *Dudley, Earl of.*)

WARD-BOUGHTON-LEIGH.
(See *Leigh, of Brownsover Hall.*)

WARDE, Admiral CHARLES, K.H., of Squerries, Kent.
Second son of the late General George Warde, of Wood-land Castle, co. Glamorgan, by Charlotte, dau. of the late Right Rev. Spencer Madan, D.D., Lord Bishop of Peterborough; b. 1786; s. 1861 his cousin, the late Charles Warde, Esq.; m. 1824 Marina, eldest dau. of the late Arthur William Gregory, Esq., and has, with other issue,
* George, a Magistrate for Kent, late Capt. 51st Foot, and Lieut.-Col. Commanding the London Rifle Brigade; b. 1827; m. 1862 the Lady Harriet North, dau. of Francis, 6th Earl of Guildford.

Admiral Warde is a J.P. and D.L. for co. Glamorgan, and a Magistrate for Kent.—*Squerries Court, Wester-ham, Sevenoaks; Preswylfa, Neath; United Service Club, s.w.*

WARDE, HENRY CHARLES LLOYD, Esq., of Clopton House, Warwickshire.
Eldest son of the late Charles Thomas Warde, Esq., J.P. and D.L., of Clopton House (who was High Sheriff of co. Warwick 1846), by Marianne, eldest dau. of the late John Bennet Lawes, Esq., of Rothamsted, Herts; b. 184-; s. 1865. This family was formerly of Barford, co. Warwick, and Bickleslly, Norfolk.—*Clopton House, Stratford-on-Avon; Arghery House, co. Leitrim, Ireland.*

WARDE, ST. ANDREW, Esq., of Hooton Pagnell, Yorkshire.
Eldest son of the late St. Andrew Warde, Esq., of Hooton Pagnell, by Mary Anne, dau. of Anthony Cooke, Esq., of Owston, co. York; b. 1780; s. 1822; m. 1800 Maria Josepha, dau. and co-heir of Stanhope Harvey, Esq., of Womersley, co. York, and has, with other issue,
* William, in Holy Orders, b. 1802.

Mr. Warde is a J.P. and D.L. for the W. Riding of Yorkshire.—*Hooton Pagnell Hall, Doncaster.*

WARDEN, Col. ROBERT, of Blackcraig, Lin-lithgowshire.
Eldest son of the late Robert Warden, Esq., of Park Hill, co. Stirling, by Helen, dau. of Sir Archibald Dunbar, Bart., of Duffus; b. 1822. Entered the Army as Ensign 19th Foot 1841, and served in the Crimean campaign; is a Col in the Army, Lieut.-Col. 19th Foot, Knight of the Legion of Honour, and a Knight of the

969

Order of Medjidie.—*Binny Cottage, Uphall, N.B.* ; 3, *Randolph Cliff, Edinburgh ; United Service Club,* s.w.

WARDLAW, Sir ARCHIBALD, Bart. (cr. 1631).
Only surviving son of the late Sir William Wardlaw, Bart., by Elizabeth, dau. of George Anderson, Esq., of Carlungie, N.B. ; *b.* 1796 ; *s.* his brother Sir Alexander, as 14th Bart., 1863. This family were formerly of Pitreavie, co. Fife.—Residence : *Chessels Court, Canongate, Edinburgh.*
Heir Pres., his cousin.

WARDLAW, Mrs., of Belmaduthy, Ross-shire.
Jane, only dau. of the late Sir Colin Mackenzie, Bart., of Kilcoy, co. Ross, by Isabella, 2nd dau. of Ewen Cameron, Esq., of Glenevis, co. Inverness ; *m.* 1853 Major James Wardlaw (son of the late Lieut.-General Wardlaw, Colonel of H.M. 55th Regt., by the Hon. Anne, youngest dau. of Gerard, 1st Viscount Lake, G.C.B.), who *d.* 1867, leaving, with other issue, * John Colin, *b.* 1856.—*Belmaduthy House, Munlochy, Ross-shire, N.B.*

WARDLAW, Capt. JOHN.
Son of the late Lieut.-General Wardlaw. Col. of H.M.'s 55th Regt., by the Hon. Anne, youngest dau. of Gerard, 1st Vi-count Lake, G.C.B. ; *b.* 1826 ; *m.* 1854 Lady Horatia Elizabeth, 2nd dau. of John James, 6th Earl Waldegrave, and widow of J. Webbe Weston, E-q. Educated at Winchester and the Royal Military Academy ; is a Dep.-Lieut. for Essex, and one of H.M.'s Royal Body Guard of Scottish Archers ; late Exon of the Royal Body Guard of Yeomen of the Guard, and Capt. King's Own Light Infantry Militia ; formerly Lieut. Bengal Infantry.—*Langford Grove, Maldon ; Carlton and Junior United Service Clubs,* s.w. ; 37, *Prince's Gate,* w.

WARDLAW-RAMSAY. (See *Ramsay.*)

WARDROP, WILLIAM MACFARLANE, Esq., of Bridgehouse, Linlithgowshire.
Youngest son of the late John Wardrop, Esq., of Edinburgh, by Barbara, dau. of the late William Macfarlane, Esq., W.S., of Edinburgh ; *b.* 1823 ; *m.* 1852 Helen, 2nd dau. of the late William Doune Gillon, Esq., M.P., of Wallhouse, co. Linlithgow, and has, with other issue,
* William, *b.* 1855.
Mr. Wardrop, who is a J.P. and D.L. for co. Linlithgow, was formerly Lieut. 10th Royal Hussars.—*Bridgehouse, Bathgate, N.B.*

WARE, CHARLES NATHANIEL, Esq., of Poslingford, Suffolk, and Hendon, Middlesex.
Third son of the late Capt. John Cumberlege, H.E.I.C.S., by Anne, dau. of the late Samuel Ware, Esq., of Highgate, Middlesex ; *b.* 1800 ; *s.* in 1860 to the Suffolk and Middlesex estates of his maternal uncle, Samuel Ware, Esq., of Hendon Hall, whose name and arms he assumed in 1862 ; *m.* 1830 Caroline, eldest dau. of the late Richard Heaton, Esq., of Leamington, co. Warwick, and has, with other issue,
* Charles, in Holy Orders, B.A. of Trinity Coll., Cambridge, Vicar of Astwood, Bucks ; *b.* 1832 ; *m.* 1866 Elizabeth Anne, dau. and heir of Mrs. Montgomerie Williams, of Crawley Grange, Bucks.
Mr. Ware is Lord of the Manor of Poslingford.—*Hendon Hall, Middlesex,* N.W. ; *Poslingford Hall, Clare, Suffolk.*

+**WARE, THOMAS, Esq., of Woodfort, co. Cork.**
Son of the late Thomas Ware, Esq., of Woodfort, by Mary, dau. of William Beamish, Esq., of Wilsgrove, co. Cork ; *b.* 178-. Is a Magistrate for co. Cork.—*Woodfort, Mallow, co. Cork.*
970

WARING, CHARLES, Esq.
Third son of John Waring, Esq., by Mary Fletcher, dau. of William Fletcher, Esq., of Chesterfield ; *b.* 18—. Is a Chevalier of the Order of Leopold of Belgium ; Member of the firm of Waring Brothers, Contractors of Public Works ; elected M.P. for Poole 1865.—*Reform Club,* s.w. ; 5, *Victoria Street,* s.w.

WARING, THOMAS, Esq., of Waringstown, Down-shire.
Eldest son of the late Major Henry Waring, of Waringstown, by Frances Grace, 4th dau. of the Very Rev. Holt Waring, Dean of Dromore ; *b.* 1828 ; *s.* 1866 ; *m.* 1858 Esther, 3rd dau. of Ross T. Smyth, Esq., of Ardmore, co. Londonderry. Educated at Trinity Coll., Dublin ; called to the Irish Bar 1852 ; is a Magistrate for co. Down, and Capt. R. South Down Militia.—*Waringstown House, Lurgan ; Kildare Street Club, Dublin ; Junior United Service Club,* s.w.
Heir Pres., his brother Holt, Capt. 88th Connaught Rangers, *b.* 1834 ; *m.* 1862 Margaret, dau. of the late Robert McClintock, Esq., of Dunmore, co. Donegal.

WARING, WILLIAM, Esq., of Woodlands, Kent.
Eldest surviving son of the late Thomas Waring, Esq., of Chelsfield, Kent, by Sarah, dau. and heir of John Fuller, Esq., of Hewitts, Kent ; *b.* 1818 ; *s.* his mother 1842 ; *m.* 1843 Mary Wall, dau. of the late John Tasker, Esq., of Dartford, Kent, and has, with other issue,
* William Fuller, *b.* 1846.
Mr. Waring is a Magistrate for Kent, and Lord of the Manor of Hewitts and Chelsfield.—*Woodlands, Chelsfield, Bromley.*

WARING-MAXWELL. (See *Maxwell.*)

WARLOW. (See *Turbervill.*)

WARNER, EDWARD, Esq., of Higham Hall, Essex.
Eldest son of the late Edward Warner, Esq., of Walthamstow, Essex, by Mary, dau. of George Pearson, Esq., of Jamaica ; *b.* 1818 ; *m.* 1848 Maria, dau. of Thomas Carr, Esq., of New Ross, co. Wexford, and widow of J. Hibbitts, Esq., and has, with other issue,
* Thomas Courtenay Theydon, *b.* 1857.
Mr. Warner, who was educated at Wadham Coll., Oxford (B.A. 1840, M.A. 1844), and called to the Bar at Lincoln's Inn, 1830, is a J.P. and D.L. for Essex, and Patron of 2 livings ; he was M.P. for Norwich 1852-7, re-elected 1860.—*Higham Hall, Woodford ; Reform Club,* s.w. ; 12, *Brunswick Terrace, Brighton ;* 49, *Grosvenor Place,* s.w.

WARNER, EDWARD, Esq., of Quorndon Hall, Leicestershire.
Second son of the late Thomas Warner, Esq., of The Elms, Loughborough, by Harriet, dau. of John Handley, Esq., of Loughborough ; *b.* 1804 ; *s.* 1841 ; *m.* 1848 Marianne, dau. of the late Rev. J. W. R. Boyer, Rector of Swepstone-cum-Snar.-ton, and has, with other issue,
* John Henry Boyer, *b.* 1849.
Mr. Warner, who is a Magistrate for co. Leicester, purchased this estate from Sir John Sutton, Bart., in 1855.—*Quorndon Hall, Loughborough.*

WARNER, PATRICK, Esq., of Ardeer, Ayrshire.
Eldest son of the late Patrick Warner, Esq., of Ardeer, by Lucy Campbell, eldest dau. of Capt. Joseph Pearce, R.N. ; *b.* 1810 ; *s.* 1851 ; *m.* 1861 Matilda Louisa, dau. of the Rev. T. J. Theobald, Rector of Nunney, Somerset, and has issue,
* A dau., *b.* 1866.
Mr. Warner was educated at Trinity Hall, Cambridge.—*Ardeer House, Irvine, N.B.*

WARNER. (See Lee-Warner.)

WARNER-BROMLEY. (See Bromley.)

WARRAND, ROBERT, Esq., of Westhorpe, Notts.
Eldest son of the late Thomas Warrand, Esq., of Westhorpe, by Catherine, dau. of Gen. Munro, of Teaninich, co. Ross; b. 1798; s. 1836; m. 1830 Sarah Sophia, eldest dau. and co-heir of the Rev. Wm. Clay, of Westhorpe, and has, with other issue,
* Robert, Major Bengal Engineers; b. 1831.
Mr. Warrand, who was formerly Major in the 22nd Dragoons, is a J.P. and D.L. for Notts.—Westhorpe, Southwell; United Service Club, s.w.

+WARRE, Col. HENRY JAMES, C.B., of West Buckland, Somerset.
Only surviving son of the late Gen. Sir William Warre, Knt. (who d. 1853), by Selina, youngest dau. of Christopher Thomas Maling, Esq., of West Dirrington, co. Durham, and nephew of H. Warre, Esq., of Bindon House (whom see); b. 1819; m. 1855 Charlotte Emily, dau. of the late Robert Lukin, Esq., and widow of William Pitt Adams, Esq., Charge d'Affaires to Peru. Col. Warre, who was educated at Sandhurst Coll., is a Col. in the Army and Lieut.-Col. 57th Foot, which he commanded in the Crimea, in India, and New Zealand; he descends from a common ancestor with the Warres of Hestercombe.—West Buckland, Wellington; United Service Club, s.w.

WARRE, HENRY, Esq., of Bindon, Somerset.
Fifth son of the late James Warre, Esq., of Oporto, and of Hendon Place, Middlesex, by Eleanor, dau. of Thomas Greg, Esq., of Belfast, and cousin of the late John Ashley Warre, Esq., M.P.; b. 1795; m. 1832 Mary Caroline Maria, 3rd dau. of the late Nicolson Calvert, Esq., M.P., of Furneaux Pelham, and Hunsdon House, Herts, and has, with other issue,
* Francis, educated at Eton, and B.A. of Balliol Coll., Oxford; Vicar of Bere Regis, Dorset; b. 1838.
Mr. Warre is a Magistrate for Somerset; he is of a younger branch of the Warres of Hestercombe, who descend from Roger Warre, who d. A.D. 1617.—Bindon House, Wellington.

+WARRE, JOHN HENRY, Esq., of Cheddon, Somerset, and West Cliffe, Kent.
Eldest son of the late John Ashley Warre, Esq., J.P. and D.L. of West Cliffe (formerly M.P. for Taunton, &c.), by Florence Catherine, dau. of Richard Magenis, Esq., of Warrington, co. Down; b. 1825; s. 1860. Educated at Rugby and Ch. Ch., Oxford (B.A. 1847); is a Magistrate for Kent, and Patron of 2 livings. —West Cliffe House, Ramsgate; Travellers' and University Clubs, s.w.; 54 Lowndes Square, s.w.
Heir Pres., his brother Arthur, a Commander R.N.; b. 1827; m. 1860 Laura Frances, eldest dau. of the late Edward Joshua Cooper, Esq., of Markree Castle, co. Sligo, and has issue, * three daughters.

WARRE, Miss, of Hestercombe, Somerset.
Elizabeth Maria Tyndale, only surviving child and heir of the late John Tyndale (afterwards Warre), Esq., of Hestercombe, by Elizabeth, only child and heir of Joseph Farell, Esq., and grand-dau. of the late Sir Francis Warre, Bart., of Hestercombe; s. 1819. Is Lady of the Manors of West Monkton and Overton. This estate has been in the possession of the Warres since the reign of Henry III.—Hestercombe, Taunton.

WARREN, Sir AUGUSTUS RIVERSDALE, Bart., of Warren's Court, co. Cork (cr. 1784).
Eldest son of the late Sir John Borlase Warren, Bart., J.P., of Warren's Court, by Mary, dau. of the late Rev.

Robert Warren; b. 1833; s. as 5th Bart. 1863; m. 1864 Georgina, eldest dau. of the Rev. John Blennerhassett, Rector of Ryme, Dorset. Is a Magistrate for co. Cork (High Sheriff 1857), and Lieut.-Col. S Cork Militia; late Major 20th Foot.—Warren's Court, Lissardagh, co. Cork; Sillerdane Lodge, co. Kerry; Athenæum Club, s.w.
Heir, his son Augustus Riversdale John Blennerhassett, b. 1865.

WARREN, EDWARD LEWIS, Esq., of Lodge Park, co. Kilkenny.
Only son of the late Pooley Abel Warren, Esq., of Lodge Park, by Jessey Anne, dau. of Thomas Bryan, Esq.; b. 1830; s. 1834; m. 1857 Marianne Emilie, dau. of the late Col. Charles Garraway, H.E.I.C.'s Service, and has, with other issue,
* Edward George Shuldham, b. 1860.
Mr. Warren, who was educated at Eton and Trinity Coll., Dublin, is a J.P. and D.L. for co. Kilkenny (High Sheriff 1861).—Lodge Park, Freshford, co. Kilkenny.

WARREN, JOSEPH LOXDALE, Esq., of The Towers, Market Drayton, Staffordshire.
Son of the late Joseph Loxdale Warren, Esq., of Market Drayton, by Martha, dau. of Jacob Turner. Esq., of the Court House, Norton-Fitzwarren, Somerset; b. 1798; m. 1830 Mary Anne, only child of Richard Warren, Esq., of Ardwick, Manchester, and heir of his uncle Joseph Lycett, Esq., of Summer Hill, Birmingham, and has, with other issue,
* Joseph Loxdale, Barrister-at-Law of Lincoln's Inn; b. 1830; m. 1862 Annette, dau. of Capt. Forshaw, R.N.
Mr. Warren, who was educated at Rugby, is a Magistrate for co. Stafford and Lord of the Manor of Alcaston and Henley, co. Salop. This family descend from the Warrens of Poynton, co. Chester.—The Towers, Market Drayton; Alcaston, Church Stretton.

WARREN, RICHARD PELHAM, Esq., of Worting, Hants.
Eldest son of the late Pelham Warren, Esq., M.D., of Worting, by Penelope, dau. of the Very Rev. W. D. Shipley, Dean of St. Asaph; b. 1816. Educated at Westminster and Trinity Coll., Cambridge (B.A. 1838. M.A. 1844), is a Magistrate for co. Flint (High Sheriff 1868), and Capt. in the Flintshire Rifles.—Worting House, Basingstoke; Carlton and National Clubs, s.w.
Heir Pres., his brother Arthur Frederick, Major Rifle Brigade; b. 1830.

WARREN, ROBERT, Esq. of Killiney, co. Dublin.
Eldest son of the late Robert Warren, Esq. of Dublin, by Barbara, dau. of Joseph Swan, Esq., of Tombrean, co. Wicklow; b. 1787; s. 1814; m. 1819 Alicia, dau. of Athanasius Cusack. Esq., of Laragh, co. Kildare, and has, with other issue, * Robert, a Barrister-at-Law, and a Magistrate for co. Dublin; b. 1820; m. 1846 Anne Elizabeth, dau. of the late Cadwallader Waddy, Esq., M.D., of Ballymore, co. Wexford.—Killiney Castle, Dalkey, co. Dublin.

WARREN, the Right Hon. ROBERT RICHARD.
Only son of Henry Warren, Esq., by Catherine, dau. of the Rev. William Stewart; b. 1817; m. 1846 Mary, dau. of Charles Perry, Esq. Educated at Trinity Coll., Dublin (B.A. 1838, M.A. 1860); called to the Irish Bar 1839, Q.C. 1858, Bencher of King's Inn 1865; appointed Solicitor-General for Ireland March 1867. Attorney-General August 1867; elected M.P. for Dublin University 1867.—Kildare Street and University Clubs, Dublin; 12, Fitzwilliam Square, Dublin; Westminster Palace Hotel, s.w.

971

WARREN, SAMUEL, Esq., Q.C., D.C.L., F.R.S., Master in Lunacy.

Eldest son of the late Rev. Samuel Warren, LL.D., Rector of All Souls, Manchester (who d. 1862), by Ann, dau. of the late Richard Williams, Esq., of Gresford, co. Denbigh; b. 1807; m. 1831 Eliza, only child of the late James Ballenger, Esq., of Woodford, Essex, and has, with other issue,

* Samuel Lilckendey, M.A. and Fellow of Wadham Coll., Oxford, in Holy Orders; b. 1835.

Mr. Warren, who was educated at Edinburgh University, and called to the Bar at the Inner Temple 1837, was appointed a Queen's Counsel 1851, Recorder of Hull 1852, and Master in Lunacy in 1859; cr. Hon. D.C.L. Oxon, 1853; was M.P. for Midhurst 1856-9. —Carlton Club, s.w.; 16, Manchester Square, w.; 45, Lincoln's Inn Fields, w.c.

WARREN.

(See under De Tabley, Lord, and Vernon, Lord.)

WARRENDER, Sir GEORGE, Bart., of Bruntsfield, Midlothian (cr. 1715).

Only son of the late Sir John Warrender, Bart., of Bruntsfield, by his 1st wife Lady Juliana Jane, dau. of James, 8th Earl of Lauderdale; b. 1825; s. as 6th Bart. 1867; m. 1854 Helen, dau. of Sir Hugh Hume Campbell, Bart., of Marchmont. Is a J.P. and D.L. for co. Haddington; late Capt. Grenadier Guards. — Bruntsfield House, Edinburgh; Lochend, Dunbar, N.B.; 53, Eaton Place, s.w.

Heir, his son John, b. 1859.

WARRINGTON-CAREW. (See Carew.)

WARRY, GEORGE, Esq., of Shapwick, Somerset.

Second son of the late George Warry, Esq., of West Coker, Somerset, by Catherine, 2nd dau. of Elias Taylor, Esq., of Houndstone House, Somerset; b. 1795; s. his maternal uncle, the Rev. Elias Taylor, 1827; m. 1830 Isabella, 4th dau. of the late William Deedes, Esq., of Sandling Park, Kent, and has, with other issue,

* George Deedes, M.A., Barrister-at-Law of Lincoln's Inn, a Magistrate for Somerset; b. 1831; m. 1860 Catherine Emily, 2nd dau. of the late John C. Warren, Esq., of Taunton, and has, with other issue, * George Taylor, b. 1861.

Mr. Warry, who was educated at Winchester and Trinity Coll., Oxford (B.A. 1817, M.A. 1821), called to the Bar at Lincoln's Inn 1822, and practised at the Chancery Bar, and on the Western Circuit, is a Magistrate for Somerset.—Shapwick House, Glastonbury.

WARTER, the Rev. JOHN WOOD, B.D., of Cruckmeole, Shropshire.

Eldest son of the late Henry de Grey Warter, Esq., J.P. and D.L., of Cruckmeole, by Emma Sarah, dau. of W. Wood, Esq.; b. 1806; s. 1853; m. 1834 Edith May, dau. of the late Robert Southey, Esq., LL.D., and has, with other issue,

* Henry de Grey, a Magistrate for co. Salop, and a Capt. R.A.; b. 1841.

Mr. Warter, who was educated at Ch. Ch., Oxford (B.A. 1827, M.A. 1834, B.D. 1845), is Vicar of West Tarring and Lord of the Manor of Cruckmeole.—Cruckmeole, Shrewsbury; West Tarring Vicarage, Worthing.

WARTER-MEREDITH. (See Meredith.)

WARTON, Mrs., of Kensdale, Kent.

Lucy, second surviving dau. of the late William Perkins, Esq., Commander R.N., of Willesborough Court, Kent; m. 1843 Charles Warton, Esq., J.P. and D.L. of Kensdale, who d. 1863. The family of Warton purchased Kensdale in 1850.—Kensdale, Faversham.

WARWICK AND BROOKE, Earl of (GEORGE GUY GREVILLE).—Cr. 1746.

Only child of Henry Richard, 3rd Earl, by Lady Sarah Elizabeth, dau. of John, 2nd Earl of Mexborough; b. 1818; s. 1853; m. 1852 Lady Anne, dau. of Francis 8th Lord Elcho. Educated at St. John's Coll., Oxford (M.A. 1839); is a J.P. and D.L. for co. Warwick, Patron of 4 livings, and Lieut.-Col. Warwickshire Yeomanry; was M.P. for S. Warwickshire 1845-53.—The Castle, Warwick; Carlton and Travellers' Clubs, s.w.; Stable-yard, St. James's, s.w.

Heir, his son Francis Richard Charles Guy, Lord Brooke, b. 1853.

WASON, PETER RIGBY, Esq., of Corwar, Ayrshire.

Second son of the late James Wason, Esq., of Bristol, by Catherine, only dau. of Peter Rigby, Esq., Mayor of Liverpool; b. 1798; m. 1843 Euphemia, dau. of Mr. M'Tier, and has, with other issue,

* Rigby, educated at Westminster School; Cornet King's Dragoon Guards; b. 1844.

Mr. Wason, who was called to the Bar at the Middle Temple 1824, is a Magistrate for co. Ayr; he was M.P. for Ipswich 1830-7 and 1841-7.—Corwar, Girvan, N.B.; Reform Club, s.w.

WATERFORD, Marquis of (JOHN HENRY DE-LA-POER-BERESFORD).—Cr. 1789.

Eldest son of John, 4th Marquis, by Christiana, dau. of the late Col. Charles Powell Leslie, of Glasslough Castle, co. Monaghan; b. 1844; s. 1866. Educated at Eton; is Patron of 1 living, and Lieut. and Capt. 1st Life Guards; was M.P. for co. Waterford 1865-6; sits in the House of Peers as Lord Tyrone, U.K. (cr. 1786). —Curraghmore, Portlaw, co. Waterford; Kildare Street and Sackville Street Clubs, Dublin; White's Club, s.w.; 30, Charles Street, s.w.

Heir Pres., his brother Lord Charles William, Lieut. R.N.; b. 1846.

WATERFORD, Dowager Marchioness of, of Ford Castle, Northumberland, and Highcliffe, Hants.

Louisa, 2nd dau. of the late Lord Stuart de Rothesay, by Lady Elizabeth Margaret Yorke, 3rd dau. of Philip, Earl of Hardwicke, and grand-dau. of the Earl of Balcarres; m. 1842 Henry, 3rd Marquis of Waterford, whose mother inherited Ford Castle from her grandfather, John, late Lord Delaval, and who d. 1859. Lord Stuart de Rothesay represented a younger branch of the House of Bute.—Ford Castle, Coldstream; Highcliffe, Christchurch, Hants.

WATERHOUSE, JOHN, Esq., F.R.S., F.R.A.S., F.R.G.S., of Wellhead, Yorkshire.

Eldest son of the late John Waterhouse, Esq., of Wellhead, by Grace Elizabeth, dau. of John Rawson, Esq., of Stonyroyd, Halifax; b. 1806; s. 1847. Is a J.P. and D.L. for the W. Riding of Yorkshire. This family have resided near Halifax for five centuries.—Wellhead, Halifax; Athenæum Club, s.w.

Heir Pres., his brother Samuel, of Hope Hall, Halifax, J.P. and D.L. for the W. Riding of Yorkshire, M.P. for Pontefract, and Major 2nd W. York Yeomanry Cavalry; b. 1815; m. 1840 Charlotte Lydia, dau. of Henry Lees Edwards, Esq.

WATERLOW, Sir SYDNEY HEDLEY, Knt. (cr. 1867).

Fourth son of James Waterlow, Esq., of Huntingdon Lodge, Surrey, by Mary, dau. of the late Wm. Crakell, Esq.; b. 1822; m. 1845 Anna Maria, dau. of the late Wm. Hickson, Esq., of Fairseat, Westham, Kent. Is an Alderman for London, for the ward of Langbourn,

and a Magistrate for Middlesex; was Sheriff of London and Middlesex 1866-7.—*Fairseat House, Highgate, N.; Carpenter's Hall, London Wall, E.C.*

WATERPARK, Lord (HENRY ANSON CAVENDISH).—Cr. 1792.
Only son of Henry Manners, 3rd Lord, by the Hon. Elizabeth Jane, Lady of the Bedchamber to the Queen, youngest dau. of Thomas, 1st Viscount Anson, and sister of Thomas, 1st Earl of Lichfield; *b.* 1839; *s.* 1863. Educated at Harrow; is a J.P. and D.L. for co. Derby, & Magistrate for co. Stafford, and Lieut. Queen's Own Royal Staffordshire Yeomanry Cavalry; was formerly a Clerk in the Foreign Office.—*Doveridge Hall, Derby; Brooks's Club, S.W.*

Heir Pres., his uncle, the Hon. Richard Cavendish, of Thornton Hall, Bucks (whom see).

WATERS, THOMAS, Esq., of Sarnau, Carmarthenshire.
Second but eldest surviving son of the late Thomas Waters, Esq., by Julia, dau. of — Ormond, Esq., of Trynewydd, co. Pembroke; *b.* 1810. Educated at Queen's Coll., Oxford; a Magistrate for co. Carmarthen. —*Sarnau, Carmarthen; Penally, Pembroke.*

Heir Pres., his brother Edward, M.D., Fellow of the Royal Coll. of Physicians, Edinburgh; m. 1847 Georgina Maria Isabella, dau. of the Hon. and Rev. Lorenzo Hely-Hutchinson.

WATERTON, EDMUND, Esq., F.S.A., of Walton, Yorkshire.
Only son of the late Charles Waterton, Esq., of Walton Hall, author of 'Wanderings in South America,' and 'Essays on Natural History,' by Anne, 2nd dau. of Charles Edmondstone, Esq., of Cardross Park, N.B.; *b.* 1830; *s.* 1865; *m.* 1862 Josephine Margaret Alicia, 2nd dau. of Sir John Ennis, Bart., of Ballinahown, co. Westmeath, and has, with other issue,

* Edmund Charles, *b.* 1863.

Mr. Waterton is a J.P. and D.L. for the W. Riding of Yorkshire, Lord of the Manor of Walton, a Knight of St. John, and of the Order of Christ of Rome, and Chamberlain to Pius IX.—*Walton Hall, Wakefield.*

WATKIN, the Rev. EDWARD.
Eldest son of the late Rev. George Watkin, by Frances, dau. of George Thompson, Esq., of Northampton; *b.* 1788; *m.* 1812 Anna Maria, dau. of Wastel Briscoe Cliffe, Esq., of Bromwich. Educated at Rugby and Lincoln Coll., Oxford (B.A. 1811, M.A. 1814); is a Magistrate for co. Northampton, Vicar of St. Giles's, Northampton, and Rector of Cogenhoe.—*Cogenhoe Rectory, Northampton.*

WATKIN, EDWARD WILLIAM, Esq., of Northenden, Cheshire.
Eldest son of the late Absolom Watkin, Esq., of Rose Hill, Northenden (who was a Magistrate for co. Lancaster); *b.* 1819; *m.* 1846 Mary Briggs, dau. of the late William Mellor, Esq., of Oldham. Is a Magistrate for co. Chester and Lancaster, and a Director of the Oxford, Worcester, and Wolverhampton Railway; formerly a Merchant in Manchester; was M.P. for Gt. Yarmouth 1857-58; elected M.P. for Stockport 1864. —*Northenden, Stockport; Moatfield, Timperley, Manchester; Reform Club, S.W.*

WATKINS, CHARLES FITZGERALD, Esq., of Badby House, Northamptonshire.
Only child of the late Charles William Watkins, Esq., of Badby House (who was a Capt. in the Northampton Militia, and formerly Lieut. 38th Foot), by Mary Mitchell, youngest dau. of the late Richard John Uniacke, Esq., Judge of the Supreme Court in British America;

b. 1852; *s.* 1858. This family trace their descent, through the Rushworths and D'Anverses, from William of Wykeham.—*Badby House, Daventry.*

WATKINS, JOHN GREGORY, Esq., of Woodfield, Worcestershire.
Eldest son of the late John Watkins, Esq., of Woodfield, by Mary, dau. of Robert Bourne, Esq., cf Shrawley Court, co. Worcester; *b.* 1803; *s.* 1837; *m.* 1834 Elizabeth Randle, only dau. of John Parker, Esq., of Balsall Heath, co. Worcester, and by her (who *d.* 1866) has, with other issue,

* John Gregory, educated at Eton and Ch. Ch., Oxford, and a Member of Lincoln's Inn; *b.* 1837.

Mr. Watkins is a J.P. and D.L. for co. Worcester (High Sheriff 1850).—*Woodfield, Droitwich.*

WATKINS, the late Col. LLOYD VAUGHAN, of Pennoyre, Brecknockshire.
Only son of the late Rev. Thomas Watkins, F.A.S., of Pennoyre, by Susanna Eleonora, dau. of Richard Vaughan, Esq.; *b.* 1802; *s.* 1829; *d.* 1865, having *m.* 1st 1833 Sophia Louisa Henrietta. 3rd dau. of the late Sir George Pocock, Bart.; 2nd 1852 Eliza Luther. dau. of the late John Taylor-Gordon, Esq., and widow of Brigadier-General Hughes, C.B. (she *d.* 1856). Was Lord-Lieut. and Custos Rotulorum for co. Brecon, &c., and many years M.P. for Brecknock.—*Pennoyre and Rhosferic, Brecknock; Broadway, Carmarthen.*

WATLING, the Rev. HENRY FAIRCHILD, of The Fron, Denbighshire.
Second son of the Rev. Charles Henry Watling, Rector of Tredington, by Emily, 2nd dau. of Thomas Porter, Esq., of Liverpool; *b.* 1843; *s.* his uncle, Admiral J. W. Watling, of The Fron, 1867. Educated at Shrewsbury, and Lincoln Coll., Oxford. This family were formerly seated in North Devon.—*The Fron Llanrwst.*

Heir Pres., his brother John Wyatt, Lieut. 45th Rect.; b. 1840; m. 1867 Mary, dau. of Major Reynolds, 45th Regt.

WATLINGTON, JOHN WATLINGTON PERRY-, Esq., of Moor Hall, Essex.
Only son of the late Thomas Perry, Esq., of Moor Hall, by Maria Jane, dau. of the late George Watlington, Esq., of Caldecote House, Herts (whose name he assumed); *b.* 1823; *s.* 1833; *m.* 1849 Margaret Emily, 3rd. dau. of the Rev. Charles Wicksted-Ethelston, of Wicksted Hall, co. Chester, and Uplyme Rectory, Devon. Educated at Harrow and Trinity Coll. Cambridge (B.A. 1845, M.A. 1849); is a J.P. and D.L. for Essex (High Sheriff 1855), a Magistrate for Herts. and Major Essex Yeomanry Cavalry; was M.P. for S. Essex 1859-65.—*Moor Hall, Harlow; Carlton Club, S.W.*

WATSON, Sir CHARLES, Bart. (cr. 1760).
Eldest son of the late Sir Charles Wager Watson, Bart., of Wratting Park, co. Cambridge, by Jemima Charlotte, dau. of Charles Garth Colleton, Esq., of Haines Hill, Berks; *b.* 1828; *s.* as 4th Bart. 1852; *m.* 1854 Georgiana, dau. of the Rev. Robert Tredcroft. Was formerly Lieut. 71st Foot.—*Army and Navy Club, S.W.*

Heir Pres., his brother Wager Joseph, b. 1847.

WATSON, Sir THOMAS, Bart., M.D., F.R.S. (cr. 1866).
Eldest son of the late Joseph Watson, Esq., of Thorpe-le-Soken, Essex, by Mary, dau. of Thomas Catton, Esq., of West Dereham, Norfolk; *b.* 1792; *m.* 1825 Sarah, dau. of Edward Jones, Esq., of Brackley, co. Northampton. Educated at St. John's Coll., Cambridge (B.A. 1815, M.A. 1818, M.D. 1825); is President of the Royal College of Physicians and Physician Extra-

ordinary to the Queen.—*University Club*, s.w.; 16, *Henrietta Street, Cavendish Square*, w.

Heir, his son Arthur Townley, *b.* 1830; *m.* 1861 Rosamond, dau. of Charles Poulett Rushworth, Esq.

WATSON, Lady.
Mary, youngest dau. of the late Anthony Hollest, Esq., of Midhurst, Sussex; *m.* 1831 (as his 2nd wife) the Hon. Sir William Henry Watson, who was appointed a Baron of the Exchequer 1856, and *d.* 1860, leaving, with other issue, * John William, *b.* 1833; *m.* 1859 Margaret Goodman, eldest dau. of the late P. B. Fitzpatrick, Esq., of Fitzleet House, Bognor, Sussex.—*Residence*: *Midhurst, Sussex.*

WATSON, Lady, of Brunchetts, Berks.
Anna Rosetta, 4th dau. of the late William Thoyts, Esq., of Sulhampstead, Berks, by Jane, dau. of Abraham Newman, Esq., of Brook House, Essex; *m.* 1st Major-General Sir H. Watson, C.B. (who *d.* 1851); 2nd 1853 the Rev. Edwin J. Parker, B.D. (whom see). —*Brunchetts, Waltham St. Lawrence, Reading.*

WATSON, George Lewis, Esq., of Rockingham Castle, Northamptonshire.
Eldest son of the late Hon. Richard Watson, J.P. and D.L., of Rockingham Castle (sometime M.P. for Canterbury), by Lavinia Jane, dau. of Lord George Quin, and grand-dau. of Thomas. 1st Marquis of Headfort; *b.* 1841; *s.* 1852; *m.* 1867 Laura Maria, dau. of the Rev. Sir John Hubert Culme-Seymour, Bart. Mr. Watson, who was educated at Eton, is a Magistrate for co. Northampton, Lord of the Manor of Rockingham. Patron of 4 livings, and late Lieut. 1st Life Guards; he represents a younger branch of the family of Lord Sondes.—*Rockingham Castle, Northamptonshire.*

Heir Pres., his brother Edward Spencer, *b.* 1843.

WATSON, the Rev. Henry Lacon, of Sharnford Rectory, Leicestershire.
Eldest son of the Rev. Fisher Watson (late Vicar of Lancing, Sussex), by Louisa Sarah, dau. of Sir Edmund Lacon, Bart.; *b.* 1823; *m.* 1st 1851 Maria, dau. of the late Sir William Burnett, K.C.B.; 2nd 1857 Ellen Charlotte, dau. of the Rev. H. K. Richardson, Rector of Leire, co. Leicester, and has, with other issue,

* Edmund Henry Lacon, *b.* 1865.

Mr. Watson was educated at Caius Coll., Cambridge (B.A. 1846, M.A. 1849), is a Magistrate for co. Leicester, Rector of Sharnford, and one of the Diocesan Inspectors of Schools. This family was formerly settled in Gt. Yarmouth, and held for three generations the office of Receiver-General.—*Sharnford Rectory, Hinckley.*

WATSON, John Lecky, Esq., of Kilconner, co. Carlow.
Eldest son of the late John Watson, Esq., of Kilconner, by Elizabeth, eldest dau. of the late John Lecky, Esq., of Kilnock and Ballykealy; *b.* 1803; *s.* 1815; *m.* 1836 Sarah Louisa, eldest dau. of the late Thomas Henry Watson, Esq., of Lumclone, co. Carlow. Is a Magistrate for co. Carlow (High Sheriff 1860). This family settled in Ireland from Cumberland in 1641.—*Kilconner House, Fenagh, co. Carlow.*

WATSON, William Hugh, Esq., of The Den, Perthshire.
Son of the late Hugh Watson, Esq., of Keillor, co. Forfar (who *d.* 1865), by Margaret, dau. of the late James Rose, Esq., of Geddes, and heir male of Kilravock, co. Nairn; *b.* 1828; *s.* his mother 1866.—*The Den, Perth, N.B.*

WATSON, Richard Huxham, Esq., of Dorsley, Devonshire.
Only son of the late Richard Watson, Esq., of Dorsley, by Maria, dau. of Samuel Huxham, Esq., of Cholwell; *b.* 1826; *s.* 1848; *m.* 1864 Jane, dau. of William Webber, Esq., of Totnes, Devon, and has issue,

* Eleanor, *b.* 1864.

Mr. Watson, who was educated at Glasgow and Edinburgh University, is a Magistrate for Devon.—*Dorsley, Totnes.*

WATSON, Richard Luther, of Calgarth Park, Westmoreland.
Eldest son of the late Charles Luther Watson, Esq., Lieut.-Col. 3rd Dragoon Guards, and grandson of the late Rt. Rev. Richard Watson, D.D., of Calgarth, Lord Bishop of Llandaff; *b.* 1811; *s.* his grandfather 1831; *m.* 1842 Louisa Anne, only dau. of the late Rev. Francis Hawkins Cole, of Marazion, and has issue,

* Louisa (*m.* 1864 Lieut.-Col. C. E. Watson), Elizabeth, Margaret, and Rose.

Mr. Watson, who was educated at Woolwich, is a J.P. and D.L. for Westmoreland (High Sheriff 1857), and served in the Rifle Brigade 1831–42.—*Colgarth Park, Windermere; Junior United Service Club*, s.w.; 36, *Harley Street*, w.

WATSON, Samuel Henry, Esq., of Lumclone, co. Carlow.
Eldest son of the late Thomas Henry Watson, Esq., of Lumclone, by Anne. dau. of D. Walker, Esq., of Dublin; *b.* 1823; *s.* 1853; *m.* 1854 Sarah Sempill, dau. of the Rev. S. T. Roberts, LL.D., and has, with other issue,

* Henry Forbes Montague, *b.* 1856.

Mr. Watson, who was educated at Trinity Coll., Dublin (B.A. 1846), represents a younger branch of the Watsons of Kilconner.—*Lumclone, Fenagh.*

WATSON, Thomas Wright, Esq., of Kilmanahan Castle, co. Waterford.
Eldest son of the late William George Watson. Esq., of Chigwell, Essex, by Harriet, dau. of Hugh Atkins, Esq., of Russell Square, London; *b.* 1826; *m.* 1854 Claudine Marion, 5th dau. of the late John Gore. Esq., of Harts, Woodford, Essex; is a Magistrate for co. Waterford; appointed High Sheriff of co. Waterford 1855–6, and again in 1858. but declined to serve. —*Kilmanahan Castle, Clonmel.*

WATSON. (See *Rutledge*.)

WATSON-DOUGLAS.
(See under *Morton, Earl of.*)

WATSON-FARSYDE. (See *Farsyde*.)

WATSON-TAYLOR, Emilius, Esq., of Headington, Oxfordshire.
Youngest son of the late George Watson-Taylor, D.C.L., Esq., M P., of Erlstoke Park, Wilts (who *d.* 1841), by Anna Susanna, only dau. of the late Sir John Taylor, Bart., of Lyssons, Jamaica; *b.* 1819. Educated at Trinity Coll., Cambridge (B.A. 1844, M.A. 1847); purchased this property in 1858.—*Manor House, Headington, Oxford; Carlton Club*, s.w.

WATSON-TAYLOR, Simon, Esq., of Erlstoke, Wilts.
Eldest son of the late George Watson-Taylor, Esq., M.P., of Erlstoke, by Anna Susanna, eldest dau. of the late Sir John Taylor, Bart.; *b.* 1811; *s.* his mother 1853; *m.* 1843 Lady Hannah Charlotte Hay. 2nd dau.

of George, 8th Marquis of Tweeddale, K.T., and has, with other issue,

* George Simon Arthur, b. 1850.

Mr. Watson-Taylor, who was educated at Ch. Ch., Oxford, is a J.P. and D.L. for Wilts (High Sheriff 1855), and was M.P. for Devizes 1857-9.—*Erlestoke Park, Westbury; Erchfont Manor, Devizes; Boodle's Club, s.w.; 41, Grosvenor Square, w.*

+WATT, FRANCIS, Esq., of Bishop Burton, Yorkshire, and The Forelands, Worcestershire.
Son of the late F. Watt, Esq.; b. 1814. Educated at Eton; is a J.P. and D.L. for co. Worcester and the E. Riding of co. York (High Sheriff 1865); was formerly Capt. 3rd Dragoon Guards.—*Bishop Burton, Beverley; The Forelands, Bromsgrove; Carlton Club, s.w.*

+WATT, JAMES WATT GIBSON, Esq., of Doldowlod, Radnorshire.
Son of the late — Watt, Esq.; b. 18—. Is a J.P. and D.L. for co. Radnor, and a Magistrate for co. Hereford.—*Doldowlod, Rhayader; Carlton Club, s.w.*

WATTS, Sir JAMES, Knt., of Abney Hall, Cheshire (cr. 1857).
Youngest son of the late John Watts, Esq., of Burnage, near Manchester, by Elizabeth his wife; b. 1805; m. 1834 Margaret Anne, dau. of Nathaniel Buckley, Esq., of Carr Hill, Saddleworth, co. York, and has, with other issue,

* James, b. 1845.

Sir J. Watts, who is a Merchant at Manchester, is a Magistrate for co. Chester and for Manchester, of which he was Mayor 1857-8.—*Abney Hall, Cheadle; Portland Street, Manchester.*

WATTS, EDWARD HANSLOPE, Esq., of Hanslope, Bucks.
Only son of the late William Watts, Esq., of Hanslope, by Caroline, dau. of the late Rev. Frederic Apthorp (she m. 2nd Reginald R. Walpole, Esq., whom see); b. 1845; s. 1853; m. 1868 Sophia Edith, 3rd dau. of Richard Wm. Selby-Lowndes, Esq., of Bletchley, Bucks. Is Lord of the Manors of Hanslope and Castlethorpe.—*Hanslope Park, Stony Stratford.*

Heirs Pres., his two sisters, Caroline Florentia and Frederica Anne Fanny.

WATTS, JOHN JAMES, Esq., of Hawkesdale, Cumberland.
Eldest son of the late John Nicolson Watts, Esq., of Hawkesdale, by Anne Pitt, dau. of James Dodson, Esq., of Reading Hill, Berks; b. 1893; s. 1815; m. 18— Eliza Mary, dau. of — Selby, Esq., and by her (who d. 1858) has issue, * Mary.—*Hawkesdale Hall, Carlisle, Cumberland.*

WATTS, Mrs., of Langton Grange, co. Durham.
Elizabeth, 2nd dau. of John Robinson Foulis, Esq., of Heslerton and Buckton, by Decima Hester Beatrice, eldest dau. of the late Sir Christopher Sykes, Bart., of Sledmere, co. York; m. 1830 (as his 2nd wife) Vice-Admiral George Edward Watts, R.N., C.B., who d. 1859.—*Langton Grange, Darlington.*

+WATTS, RICHARD, Esq., of Clifton, Cumberland.
Son of the late R. Watts, Esq.; b. 18—. Is a J.P. and D.L. for Cumberland.—*Clifton House, Workington.*

+WATTS, WILLIAM JOHN, Esq., of Forde House, Devonshire.
Son of the late — Watts, Esq., of Forde House; b. 18—; is married, and has issue. Is a Magistrate for Devon, and a Banker at Exeter.—*Forde House, Newton Abbot.*

WATTS-RUSSELL, JESSE, Esq., of Ilam, Staffordshire, and Biggin, Northamptonshire.
Eldest son of the late Jesse Russell, Esq., of Newarth, co. Stafford, by Elizabeth, dau. of Thomas Noble, Esq., of Boroughbridge, co. York; b. 1786; m. 1st 1811 Mary, only child of the late David Pike Watts, Esq., of Portland Place, London; 2nd 1843 Maria Ellen, youngest dau. of the late Peter Henry Barker, Esq., of Norfolk; 3rd 1862 Martha, youngest dau. of the late Mr. J. Leech, of Wexford. By his 1st wife he has, with other issue,

: * Jesse David (of Biggin Grange, Oundle). B.A. of Ch. Ch., Oxford, a Magistrate for co. Northampton, a Magistrate for co. Stafford, and late M.P. for N. Staffordshire; b. 1812; m. 1845 Mary Neville, dau. of J. Smith Wright, Esq., of Rempstone Hall, Notts.

Mr. Watts-Russell, who was educated at Worcester Coll., Oxford (B.A. 1808, M.A. 1811, D.C.L. 1819), is a Magistrate for cos. Derby, Northampton, and Stafford (High Sheriff 1819).—*Ilam Hall, Ashbourne; Biggin House, Oundle.*

WAUCHOPE, ANDREW, Esq., of Niddrie Marischall, Midlothian.
Eldest son of the late William Wauchope, Esq., of Niddrie Marischall, by Elizabeth, dau. of Robert Baird, Esq., of Newbyth, N.B.; b. 1818; m. 1840 Frances Mary, dau. of Henry Lloyd, Esq., of Farrenroy, co. Tipperary, and by her (who d. 1858) has, with other issue,

William John, b. 1841.

Mr. Wauchope, who was educated at Harrow, is a J.P. and D.L. for co. Midlothian, and was formerly in the Army.—*Niddrie Marischall, Liberton, N.B.; New Club, Edinburgh, N.B.*

WAUCHOPE. (See Don-Wauchope.)

WAUD, EDWARD, Esq., of Mauston Hall and Chester Court, Yorkshire.
Second son of the late Samuel Wilkes Waud, Esq., of Chester Court, by Ellen, only dau. of Brian Hodgson, Esq., of Crakemarsh, co. Stafford; b. 1806; m. 1833 Mary Dorothy, eldest dau. of Thomas Sayle, Esq., of Wentbridge, and has, with other issue,

• Edward Wilkes, educated at Eton and Trinity Coll., Cambridge, a Magistrate for the W. Riding of York shire; b. 1834; m. 1859 the Hon. Elizabeth, eldest dau. of William, 2nd Lord Heytesbury, and has, with other issue, * Edward William, b. 1864.

Mr. Waud, who was educated at Eton, is a J.P. and D.L. for the W. Riding of Yorkshire, Lieut.-Col. 1st W. York Artillery Volunteers, and Major 4th W. York Militia.—*Mauston Hall, Leeds; Chester Court, Selby; United Service Club, s.w.*

WAUGH, Sir ANDREW SCOTT, Knt. (cr. 1860).
Eldest son of the late Gen. Gilbert Waugh, by Charlotte, dau. of Gen. Walsh, and grandson of Col. Gilbert Waugh, of Gracemount, Mid'othian; b. 1810; m. 1844 Josephine, dau. of Dr. W. Graham, of Edinburgh (she d. 1866). Educated at the High School of Edinburgh, and at Addiscombe; entered the Bengal Engineers 1827, and retired as Major-Gen. 1861; was appointed Surveyor-General of India and Superintendent of the Trigonometrical Survey 1843, and a Commissioner for Lieutenancy for London 1863. – *Athenæum Club, s.w.; 7, Petersham Terrace, Queen's Gate, w.*

WAWN, Mrs., of Boldon, co. Durham.

Mary, dau. of William Matherson, Esq.; *m.* (as his 2nd wife) John Twizell Wawn, Esq., a Magistrate for co. Durham, and some time M.P. for S. Shields (who *d.* 1859).—*Boldon, South Shields.*

WAY, ALBERT, Esq., F.S.A., of Wonham Manor, Surrey.

Son of the late Rev. Lewis Way, of Stanstead Park, Sussex (who *d.* 1840), by Mary, dau. of the Rev. Herman Drewe, Rector of Combraleigh, Devon ; *b.* 1805 ; *m.* 1844 the Hon. Emmeline, youngest dau. of John Thomas, 1st Lord Stanley of Alderley, and has issue,

   * Mary Alithea.

Mr. Way, who was educated at Trinity Coll., Cambridge (B.A. 1829, M.A. 1834), is a J.P. and D.L. for Surrey.—*Wonham Manor, Reigate; Athenæum Club, s.w.*

WAY, ARTHUR EDWIN, Esq., of Ashton, Somerset.

Youngest son of the late Benjamin Way, Esq., of Denham Place, Bucks (who *d.* 1834), by Mary, dau. of Thomas Smyth, Esq., of Stapleton, co. Gloucester, and sister of the late Sir John Smyth, Bart., of Ashton Court, Somerset ; *b.* 1813 ; *m.* 1849 Harriet Elizabeth, eldest dau. of the late Henry Butterworth, Esq., of Henbury Court, co. Gloucester, and has, with other issue,

   * Arthur, *b.* 1850.

Mr. Way was educated at Eton and Ch. Ch., Oxford, and was M.P. for Bath 1859-65.—*Ashton Lodge, Bristol; Windham Club, s.w.*

+**WAY, BENJAMIN,** Esq., of Denham Place, Bucks.

Eldest son of the late Benjamin Way, Esq., of Denham Place, by Susan, dau. of — Burrell, Esq. ; *b.* 1803 ; *s.* 1859 ; *m.* 1865 Isabel, 2nd dau. of the Rev. Henry Hugh Way, of Alderbourne, Bucks (whom see). This family were originally seated in Somerset, and afterwards in Devonshire.—*Denham Place, Uxbridge.*

WAY, the Rev. CHARLES JOHN, of Spaynes Hall, Essex.

Second but eldest surviving son of the late Gregory Lewis Way, Esq., of Spencer Farm, Essex, by Ann Frances, only dau. of the Rev. William Paxton. Rector of Taplow, Bucks ; *b.* 1796 ; *s.* his brother 1868. Educated at Trinity Coll., Cambridge (B.A. 1819, M.A. 1822); is Vicar of Boreham, Essex ; represents a younger branch of the Ways of Denham Place, Bucks (whom see).—*Spaynes Hall, Great Yeldham, Halstead ; Boreham Vicarage, Chelmsford.*

WAY, the Rev. HENRY HUGH, of Alderbourne Manor, Bucks.

Second son of the late Benjamin Way, Esq., of Denham Place, Bucks (who *d.* 1834), by Mary, dau. of Thomas Smyth, Esq., of Heath House, co. Gloucester, and uncle of Benj. Way, Esq. (whom see); *b.* 1808 ; *s.* his mother 1860 ; *m.* 1835 Emmeline, dau. of Thomas Daniel, Esq., of Henbury, co. Gloucester, and has, with other issue,

   * John Hugh, in Holy Orders, B.A. of Oriel Coll., Oxford, Vicar of Henbury; *b.* 1841; *m.* 1861 Caroline, dau. of the late Admiral Sir W. Edward Parry, and niece of Lord Stanley of Alderley.

Mr. Way, who was educated at Eton and Merton Coll., Oxford (B.A. 1829), is a Magistrate for Bucks, and Lord of the Manor of Alderbourne; was formerly Vicar of Henbury, co. Gloucester. This family was originally of Somersetshire. Wm. Way had a confirmation of arms from Robert Cooke, Clarenceux, 1574, and at the close of the 17th century Lewis Way married the heiress of the Hills, of Denham Place, Bucks, at

976

which place they have resided since that time.—*Alderbourne Manor, Gerrard's Cross, Bucks; Oxford and Cambridge Club, s.w.*

WAY, LEWIS JOHN, Esq., of Spencer Grange, Great Yeldham, Essex.

Eldest son of the late Rev. Lewis Way, of Spencer Grange, by Caroline Elizabeth, dau. of the late John Leech, Esq.; *b.* 1817 ; *s.* 1835 ; *m.* 1860 Mary Isabella, dau. of Holroyd Fitzwilliam, 3rd son of Benjamin Way, Esq., of Denham Place, Bucks, and has, with other issue,

   * Gregory Lewis Holroyd, *b.* 1863.

Mr. Way, who was educated at Eton and Magdalen Coll., Cambridge (B.A. 1843, M.A. 1846), is a Magistrate for Essex; was Capt. West Essex Militia 1852–59. This family is a younger branch of the Ways of Denham (whom see).—*Spencer Grange, Great Yeldham, Halstead.*

WAYNE, the Rev. WILLIAM HENRY, M.A., of Quorndon House, Derbyshire, and of Aberartro, Merionethshire.

Only son of the late William Henry Wayne, Esq., of Quorndon House, formerly Major of Militia (who *d.* 1856), by Anne, dau. of Bryan Salmon. Esq. ; *b.* 1803 ; *m.* 1829 Jane, dau. of the late Samuel Frederick Milford, Esq., J.P. and D.L. of Exeter, Devon, and has, with other issue,

   * William Henry, in Holy Orders, B.A. of Trinity Coll., Cambridge; *b.* 1832 ; *m.* 1856 Eliza, dau. of the late Capt. H. Foskett, of the 14th Light Dragoons, and has issue.

Mr. Wayne, who was educated at St. Peter's Coll., Cambridge (B.A. 1825), is Vicar of Wenlock, Chaplain to the 6th Company Shropshire Rifle Volunteers, and Patron of 2 livings.—*Aberartro, Barmouth ; Quorndon House, Derby ; The Vicarage, Much-Wenlock.*

WAYTE, the Rev. WILLIAM, of Bushton, Wilts.

Eldest son of the late William Wayte, Esq., F.R.A.S., J.P., of Bushton and Highlands, by Eliza, dau. of John Finniss, Esq., Chief Police Magistrate of Mauritius ; *b.* 1829 ; *s.* 1860 ; *m.* 1863 Mary Antoinette, eldest dau. of the Rev. Jonathan H. Lovett Cameron, Vicar of Shoreham, Kent. Educated at Eton and King's Coll., Cambridge (B.A. 1853, M.A. 1856). This family has been settled in Wilts since *temp.* Henry III., and has owned the estate of Bushton since 1695.—*Bushton, Wotton Bassett ; Eton College, Windsor ; New University Club, s.w.*

   Heir Pres., his brother George Hodgson, in Holy Orders, late Fellow of King's Coll., Cambridge ; *b.* 1832 ; *m.* 1863 Annie, youngest dau. of the late Sir Joseph Paxton.

WEARE, the Rev. THOMAS WILLIAM, of Hampton House, Herefordshire.

Eldest son of the late Col. Thomas Weare, K.H., and A.D.C. to the Queen, of Hampton House, by Ann, dau. of John Fugh, Esq., of The Gaer, co. Radnor ; *b.* 1813 ; *s.* 1850 ; *m.* 1st 1853 Louisa Emma Mary, dau. of Henry Fynes Clinton, Esq., of Welwyn, Herts : 2nd 1866 Henrietta Maria, dau. of Capt. W. R. Majendie, and grand-dau. of the late Bp (Majendie) of Bangor, and has by the former, with other issue,

   * Edwin Thomas Clinton, *b.* 1859.

Mr. Weare, who was educated at Westminster and Ch. Ch., Oxford (B.A. 1836, M.A. 1838), and ordained in 1839, is a Magistrate for co. Hereford, Rector of Isfield, Sussex, and Fellow of the Royal Astronomical Society ; he was formerly Second Master of Westminster, from 1841 to 1861. This family has been connected with Herefordshire since the reign of Q. Elizabeth, title-deeds of which date are still in their possession. The name is derived from Weare, near Axbridge, Somerset, and from Weare-Giffard, Devon, at which latter place the arms are still found in stone and in wood carving of the

date of King Henry VI. (see Gwillim's Heraldry, under 'Crozier.') — *Hampton House, near Hereford; United University Club*, s.w.

WEBB, Sir HENRY, Bart. (cr. 1644).
Eldest son of the late Sir Thomas Webb, Bart., of Old-stock, Wilts, by the Hon. Charlotte Frances, dau. of Charles, 12th Viscount Dillon; *b.* 1806; *s.* as 7th Bart. 1823. Represents an ancient Roman Catholic family long seated at Oldstock, Wilts.—*Reform Club*, s.w.

WEBB, JAMES NAPIER, Esq., of Knocktoran House, co. Limerick.
Eldest son of the late Daniel James Webb, Esq., of Woodville, co. Tipperary, by the Hon. Anne Wilhelmina, dau. of Charles Stanley, 1st Viscount Monck, of Charle-ville, co. Wicklow (she *d.* 1859); *b.* 1813; *s.* 1850; *m.* 1st 1841 the Hon. Anne, dau. of Charles, 3rd Viscount Monck (she *d.* 1853); 2nd 1855 Anna Thomasine, dau. of Joseph Gubbins, Esq., late of Kilrush, co. Limerick. Educated at Winchester and Trinity Coll., Dublin (B.A. 1835, M.A. 1838); is a Magistrate for cos. Limerick and Tipperary.—*Knocktoran House, Knocklong, co. Limerick.*

Heir Pres., his brother Charles Daniel Henry (of Woodville, Templemore), a Magistrate for co. Tipperary; *b.* 1825; *s.* 1850; *m.* 1856 Elizabeth Lacy, eldest dau. of the Rev. Lloyd Apjohn, of Bally-Brood Rectory, and Linfield, co. Limerick, and has, with other issue, • Daniel James Napier, *b.* 1857.

+WEBB, JOHN HENSON, Esq., of The Hough, Staffordshire.
Son of the late John Webb, Esq., of the Hough; *b.* 18—; is a J.P. and D.L. for co. Stafford.—*The Hough, Stafford.*

WEBB, JOHN McDONNELL, Esq., of The Hill, co. Cork.
Eldest son of the late Rev. John Webb, LL.D. (who *d.* 1842), by Johanna Waggett, only dau. of the late Par-ker Dunscombe, Esq.; *b.* 1829; *m.* 1862 his cousin, Cornelia Martha, eldest dau. of the late Lieut.-Col. Burne, and widow of Lieut. William Haslett, 13th Foot. Educated at Trinity Coll., Dublin; is a Magis-trate for co. Cork; was formerly Capt. 4th Royal Irish Dragoons, with which regiment he served in the Crimea. This family have been settled in Cork for upwards of two centuries.—*The Hill, Douglas, Cork.*

Heir Pres., his brother Randal Thomas, *b.* 185—; *m.* 1865, Mary Hunter, only dau. of Robert Dirom, Esq., and grand-dau. of the late Lieut.-General Dirom.

WEBB, RICHARD, Esq., of Donnington Hall, Herefordshire.
Only child of the late Francis Webb, Esq., of Donning-ton Hall, by his cousin Anne, dau. of William Webb, Esq.; *b.* 1795; *s.* 1806; *m.* 1816 Frances, 3rd dau. of the Rev. John George Hannington, D.D., Prebendary of Hereford, and has, with other issue, an only son,

• Richard Frederick, M.A. of Ch. Ch., Oxford, a Dep.-Lieut. for co. Hereford, and Capt. Hereford Militia; *b.* 1821; *m.* 1857 the Hon. Isabella Catherine, youngest dau. of Frede-rick, 13th Lord Saye and Sele, and has, with other issue, • a son, *b.* 1863.

Mr. Webb, who was educated at Eton and Oriel Coll., Oxford, is a J.P. and D.L. for co. Hereford, a Magis-trate for cos. Gloucester and Worcester (High Sheriff 1835), and Lord of the Manor and Patron of Donning-ton.—*Donnington Hall, Ledbury.*

WEBB, the Rev. RICHARD FRANCIS, of Caheragh House, co. Cork.
Eldest son of the late Rev. Richard Webb (who *d.* 1836), by Eliza, dau. of Francis Browne, Esq., of Kinsale; *b.* 1791; *m.* 1818 Mary, dau. of the Rev. Samuel

Beamish, of Mount Beamish, co. Cork, and has, with other issue,

• Richard, *b.* 1819; *m.* 1855 Annie, dau. of Augustus Warren, Esq., and has, with other issue, • Richard Francis, *b.* 1858.

Mr. Webb, who was educated at Trinity Coll., Dublin, is Rector of Dunderrow, and was formerly Rector of Caheragh.—*Dunderrow Rectory, Kinsale.*

WEBB, ROBERT WILLIAM, Esq., of Milford House, Surrey.
Eldest son of the late Col. Robert Smith Webb, J.P., of Milford House, by Harriet, dau. of William Currie, Esq., of East Horsley, Surrey; *b.* 1830; *s.* 1868. Is a Magistrate for Surrey; late Lieut. 37th Foot.—*Milford House, Godalming.*

WEBB, THEODORE VINCENT, Esq., of Gt. Grans-don, Hunts.
Only surviving son of the late Rev. William Webb, D.D., of Gt. Gransdon, Master of Clare Coll., Cam-bridge, by Anne, only child of the late Rev. T. V. Gould, Rector of Fornham, Suffolk; *b.* 1820; *s.* 1856; *m.* 1858 Martha Sophia, dau. of Mr. George Marshall, of Alconbury, Hunts. Educated at Clare Coll., Cam-bridge (B.A. 1841, M.A. 1844); is a Magistrate for co. Cambridge, and Lord of the Manor of Rippington.—*Great Gransdon, Caxton.*

WEBB, THOMAS, Esq., of Berrow, Worcester-shire.
Eldest son of the late Thomas Webb, Esq., J.P. and D.L., of Berrow, by Anne, dau. of John Thackwell, Esq., of Rye Court, co. Worcester; *b.* 1812; *s.* 1837; *m.* 1st 1847 Anne Elizabeth, dau. of the Rev. Bulkeley Williams, of Beaumaris, Anglesey (she *d.* 1854); 2nd 1858 Ellen Jane, 2nd dau. of the late Thomas Hampton Symons, Esq., of Mynde Park, co. Hereford, and has by the former, with other issue,

• Thomas Bulkeley Knight, Ensign 4th Foot; *b.* 1848.

Mr. Webb, who is a J.P. and D.L. for cos. Hereford and Worcester, and Lieut.-Col. Worcestershire Militia, was formerly Capt. 90th Foot.—*The Berrow, Ledbury.*

+WEBB, THOMAS, Esq., of The Longlands, Worcestershire.
Son of the late Thomas Webb, Esq.; *b.* 18—; is married, and has, with other issue,

• Charles (of Dennis Hall, Stourbridge), *b.* 18—; *m.* 1863, Maria Louisa, youngest dau. of the late Mr. Wm. Hall.

Mr. Webb, who is a Magistrate for co. Stafford and Worcester, descends from a common ancestor with the Webbs of The Berrow.—*The Longlands, Stourbridge; The Platts, Amblecote, Staffordshire.*

WEBB, THOMAS, Esq., of Smallwood Manor, Staffordshire.
Eldest son of the late John Webb, Esq., of Burton-under-Needwood, co. Stafford, by Frances, dau. of John Blurton, Esq., of Woodford, co. Stafford; *b.* 1817; *m.* 1843 Lucinda, dau. of John Baden, Esq., of Elhaston Lodge, co. Derby, and has, with other issue,

• Thomas Henry, *b.* 1851.

Mr. Webb is a J.P. and D.L. for cos. Derby and Staf-ford, a Manufacturer at Tutbury, Burton-on-Trent, Lord of the Manor of Smallwood, and Patron of 1 living.—*Smallwood Manor, Uttoxeter.*

WEBB, WILLIAM FREDERICK, Esq., of New-stead, Notts.
Eldest son of the late Frederick Webb, Esq., of West-wick, co. Durham, by Mary, dau. of R. Shell, Esq.; &

1829; *s.* 1847; *m.* 1857 Emilia Jane, dau. of Thomas M. Goodlake, Esq., of Wadley House, Berks, and has, with other issue,

* Algernon Frederick, *b.* 1865.

Mr. Webb, who was educated at Eton, is a J.P. and D.L. for the N. Riding of Yorkshire, a Magistrate for Notts (High Sheriff 1865), and Capt. Sherwood Rangers Yeomanry Cavalry; was formerly Lieut. 17th Lancers. —*Newstead Abbey, Nottingham; Cowton, Northallerton; Raskelfe, Easingwold; Brooks's, Boodle's, and Army and Navy Clubs, s.w.*

WEBB. (See *Peploe.*)

+WEBB-BOWEN, CHARLES WHEELER TOWN-SEND, Esq., of Camrose, Pembrokeshire.
Eldest son of the late Hugh Webb, Esq. (who assumed the name of Bowen on succeeding to the estates of Camrose), by his 2nd wife Emma, dau. of Thomas Ince, Esq., of Cheshire; *b.* 1797; *s.* 1833. Is a Magistrate for co. Pembroke (High Sheriff 1837).—*Camrose, Haverfordwest.*

WEBBER, CHARLES HENRY, Esq., of Buckland House, Devon.
Son of the late General Henry Webber, of Buckland, H.E.I.C.S., and grandson of Philip Rogers Incledon-Webber, Esq., by Mary, co-heir of Lewis Incledon, Esq.; *b.* 1810; *m.* 1832 Henrietta, youngest dau. of the late Charles Chichester, Esq., of Hall, Devon, by whom he has, with other issue,

* Edward Chichester Incledon. *b.* 1837; *m.* 1867 Georgina Chisholm, 3rd dau. of Major W. Gabbett Beare, of Holland House, Kingsgate, I. of Thanet.

Mr. Webber is a Magistrate for Devon, and Lord of the Manors of Buckland and Croyde.—*Buckland House, Braunton, Barnstaple.*

+WEBBER, CHARLES PHILLIP, Esq., of Carrowcullen, co. Sligo.
Eldest son of the late Charles Tankerville Webber, Esq., of Carrowcullen, by Lady Adelaide Charlotte, younger dau. of George, 3rd Earl of Kingston; *b.* 1826; *s.* 1854; *m.* 1868 Letitia Marian, eldest dau. of James Johnston, Esq., of Magheremena Castle, co. Fermanagh. Educated at Trinity Coll., Cambridge (B.A. 1855); is a J.P. and D.L. for co. Sligo.—*Carrowcullen, Skreen, co. Sligo.*

+WEBBER, WILLIAM DOWNES, Esq., of Leckfield, co. Sligo, and Kellyville, Queen's Co.
Eldest son of the late Rev. Thomas Webber, by Frances, dau. of the late Rev. Thomas Kelly, of Kellyville; *b.* 1835. Is a Magistrate for Queen's Co.—*Leckfield, co. Sligo; Kellyville, Athy, Queen's Co.*

WEBLEY-PARRY, DAVID KEDGWIN WILLIAM, Esq., of Noyadd-Trefawr, Cardiganshire.
Eldest son of the late William Henry Webley-Parry, Esq., of Noyadd-Trefawr, by Catherine Anghared, youngest dau. of Robert Adamson, Esq., of Pembroke; *b.* 1848; *s.* 1855; *m.* 1861 Nina Katherine, 2nd dau. of the Comte Demetrius de Palatiuo, of Corfu. Is a Magistrate for co. Cardigan, and was formerly in the Royal Navy.—*Noyadd-Trefawr, Cardigan.*

WEBSTER, Sir AUGUSTUS FREDERICK, Bart. (cr. 1703).
Eldest surviving son of the late Sir Godfrey Vassal Webster, 5th Bart., of Battle Abbey, Sussex (who *d.* 1836), by Charlotte, dau. of Robert Adamson, Esq., of co. Westmeath; *b.* 1819; *s.* his brother as 7th Bart., 1853; *m.* 1862 Amelia Sophia, 2nd dau. of Charles F. A. Prosser, Esq., of Hastings. Is a Magistrate for Sussex, Patron of 1 living, and a Commander R.N. re-978

tired. This family was formerly seated at Battle Abbey, Sussex.—*Army and Navy Club, s.w.*
Heir, his son Augustus Frederick Walpole Edward, b. 1864.

+WEBSTER, CHRISTOPHER MALING, Esq., of Pallion Hall, co. Durham.
Son of the late C. Webster, Esq.; *b.* 18—. Is a J.P. and D.L. for co. Durham.—*Pallion Hall, Sunderland.*

WEBSTER, FRANK DAVENPORT BULLOCK-, Esq., of Binfield Court, Berks.
Third son of the late Edward Webster Bullock-Webster, Esq., D.L., of Hendon, Middlesex (who assumed the name of Webster on the death of his uncle), by Mary, only dau. of Samuel Purkis, Esq.; *b.* 1821; *m.* 1856 Anne Jane, younger dau. of Charles Morgan, Esq., of Fairford, co. Gloucester. Called to the Bar at the Middle Temple 1847, but has not practised.—*Binfield Court, Bracknell; Conservative Club, s.w.*

WEDDERBURN, Sir DAVID, Bart., of Inveresk, Midlothian (cr. 1803).
Eldest surviving son of the late Sir John Wedderburn, Bart., of Inveresk, by Henrietta Louisa. dau. of William Milburn, Esq., of Bombay; *b.* 1835; *s.* 1862. Educated at Edinburgh and Trinity Coll., Cambridge (B.A. 1858); called to the Bar at Edinburgh 1861; is a Magistrate for Midlothian and Capt. Midlothian Yeomanry Cavalry. This family was formerly attached to the fortunes of the Stuart family; in 1745 the title was attainted, and Sir John Wedderburn executed. His son, however, still continued to assume the title until it was again conferred in 1803.—*Inveresk Lodge, Musselburgh, N.B.; New Club, Edinburgh.*
Heir Pres., his brother William, of the Bombay Civil Service, *b.* 1838.

WEDDERBURN. (See *Scrymgeour-Wedderburn.*)

WEDDERBURN-COLVILLE.
(See *Colville, Sir J. W., Knt., of Ochiltree.*)

WEEDEN, WILLIAM DAVISON, Esq., of Hall Court, Sussex.
Only surviving son of the late Thomas Weeden. Esq., of Hall Court, by Ann, dau. of William Saxby, Esq., of London (she *d.* 1855); *b.* 1830; *s.* 1862; *m.* 1856 Julia Jemima, only surviving dau. of Geo. Barraclough, Esq., of Streatham Hill, and has. with other issue,
* William George Barraclough. *b.* 1857.

Mr. Weeden, who was educated at Camberwell Collegiate School, was formerly Lieut. Royal Sussex Militia.—*Hall Court, Rye, Hurst Green; 10, Angel Terrace, Brixton Road, Surrey.*

+WEEKES, FREDERICK, Esq., of Coalwood, Sussex.
Second son of the late Hampton Weekes, Esq.. M.D., of Hampton Lodge, Hurstpierpoint, by Sarah, dau. of the late Wm. Borrer, Esq., of Pakyns Manor, Sussex; *b.* 1812; *m.* 1847 Elizabeth, dau. of William Marshall. Esq., of Hurstpierpoint, by whom he has issue.
* Two daughters.

Mr. Weekes is Lord of the Manor of Bolney.—*Coalwood Park, Bolney, Cuckfield.*

WEEKES, GEORGE, Esq., of Carey Hall, Sussex.
Third son of the late Hampton Weekes. Esq.. of Hampton Lodge, Hurstpierpoint. by Sarah, dau. of the late William Borrer, Esq., of Pakyns Manor, Sussex; *b.* 1817; *m.* 1846 Lucy Anne, dau. of the late William Boxall, Esq., of Cowfold, Sussex, and has issue.
* Julia Georgina.

Mr. Weekes is a Commissioner of Taxes, a Dep.-Lieut. for Sussex, and a Fellow of the Royal Coll. of Surgeons of London. This family, formerly De Wykes, Wyke,

or Wike, held knight's fees and lands by Serjeanty, in Kent and Devon, 1166; they descend from a common ancestor with the Weekeses of Devon, and through their grandmother, the heiress of Hampton, from Carey, Lord Hunsdon.—*Carey Hall, Hurstpierpoint; Militia and Yeomanry Club*, s.w.

WEEKES, RICHARD, Esq., of Hampton, Sussex.
Eldest son of the late Hampton Weekes, Esq., M.D., of Hampton, by Sarah, dau. of the late William Borrer, Esq., of Pakyns Manor, Sussex; *b.* 1808; *s.* 1855; *m.* 1st 1832 Anne, dau. and heir of Richard Locke, Esq., of Brighton (she *d.* 1833); 2nd 1836 Martha, dau. and co-heir of the late William Carlile, Esq., of Bolton, co. Lancaster, and by her, who *d.* 1867, has issue,

* William Hampton Carlile, *b.* 1837; *m.* 1860 Julia, dau. of William Vidler Langridge, Esq., of Lewes, and has, with other issue, * Philip Hampton Carlile, *b.* 1862.

Mr. Weekes was educated at Edinburgh University. This family were seated in Devonshire and Kent in 1166, and they still retain landed estates at Wittersham, in the latter county.—*Hampton Lodge, Hurstpierpoint; Long House, Cowfold, Sussex.*

WEGG-PROSSER. (See *Prosser*.)

+**WEELEY, JOHN,** Esq., of Weeley, Essex.
Eldest son of the late Samuel Weeley, Esq., of Weeley Hall; *b.* 18—. Is Lord of the Manor of Weeley. This family have held property at Weeley since 1639, when the estate was purchased from the D'Arcies by William Weeley, Esq., of London, ancestor of the present owner.—*Weeley Hall, Colchester.*

WEGUELIN, THOMAS MATTHIAS, of Goldings, Herts.
Youngest son of the late William A. Weguelin, Esq., of Weymouth Street, London, by Charlotte, dau. of J. Willmott, Esq.; *b.* 1809; *m.* 1st 1837 Charlotte, dau. of the late A. H. Poulett-Thomson, Esq., of Roehampton, Surrey; 2nd 1844 Catharine, dau. of Charles Hammersley, Esq. Is a Magistrate for Surrey, a Russia Merchant in London, and a Director of the Bank of England, of which he has been also Governor; was M.P. for Southampton 1857-9; elected M.P. for Wolverhampton 1861.—*Goldings, Hertford: Residence: Billingbear Park, Wokingham, Berks; Reform and Union Clubs*, s.w.; *23, Eaton Square*, s.w.

WEIR, CHARLES SIMS, Esq., of The Weir, Lanarkshire.
Second son of the late John Weir, Esq., of The Weir, by Mary, dau. of John Sims, Esq., of Walthamstow, Essex; *b.* 1819; *s.* his brother 1845. Educated at Trinity Coll., Cambridge (B.A. 1841, M.A. 1844); called to the Bar at Lincoln's Inn 1844; is a Director of the Royal Caledonian Asylum. This family held baronies and vast possessions in land in co. Lanark for many centuries.—*Lanark, N.B.*

+**WEIR, THOMAS DURHAM,** Esq., of Boghead, Midlothian.
Son of the late T. Weir, Esq., of Boghead House; *b.* 18—. Is a J.P. and D.L. for co. Linlithgow.—*Boghead House, Bathgate, N.B.*

+**WELBANK, ROBERT,** Esq., of Tandridge, Surrey.
Son of the late Robert Welbank, Esq., of Tandridge Priory, by Sarah his wife; *b.* 1810. Is a J.P. and D.L. for Surrey; was formerly a Capt. in the Army.—*Tandridge Priory, Godstone.*

+**WELBY, Rev. JOHN EARLE,** of Stroxton, Lincolnshire.
Youngest son of the late Sir Wm. Earle Welby, Bart., of Denton, co. Lincoln, by his 2nd wife Katharine, dau. of J. Cope, Esq., of Spondon, co. Derby, and widow of Thomas Williamson, Esq., of Allington Hall, co. Lincoln; *b.* 1786; *m.* 1819 Felicia Eliza, only dau. of the Rev. G. Hole, of Chumleigh, Devon, and grand-dau. of the Rt. Rev. Dr. George Horne, Lord Bishop of Norwich, and has, with other issue,

* George Earle, in Holy Orders, J.P. for co. Lincoln, and Rector of Barrowby, Grantham; *b.* 1821; *m.* 1859 Augusta, only child of the Rev. W. Woodall, of Branston, co. Lincoln.

Mr. Welby, who was educated at Eton and Emmanuel Coll., Cambridge (B.A. 1811, M.A. 1814), is a Magistrate for co. Lincoln; was Rector of Harston, co. Leicester, 1816-67.—*Stroxton, Grantham.*

WELBY-GREGORY, Sir GLYNNE EARLE, Bart., of Denton Hall, Lincolnshire (cr. 1801).
Eldest son of the late Sir William Earle Welby, Bart., M.P., of Denton Hall, by Wilhelmina, dau. of William Spry, Esq., Governor of Barbados; *b.* 1806; *s.* as 3rd Bart. 1852; *m.* 1828 Frances, dau. of the late Sir Montague Cholmeley, Bart. Educated at Rugby and Oriel Coll., Oxford; assumed the name of Gregory in 1861; is a J.P. and D.L. for cos. Lincoln and Leicester (High Sheriff for co. Lincoln 1860); was M.P. for Grantham 1830-57; formerly Lieut.-Col. R. S. Lincoln Militia.—*Denton Hall, Grantham; Carlton Club*, s.w.; *8, Upper Belgrave Street*, s.w.

Heir, his son William Earle (of Newton House, Folkingham), educated at Eton, and B.A. of Ch. Ch., Oxford, a J.P. and D.L. for co. Lincoln, Capt. Commandant and Lincolnshire Rifle Volunteers and M.P. for S. Lincoln-hire, late M.P. for Grantham; *b.* 1829; *m.* 1863 the Hon. Victoria Alexandrina, only dau. of the late Hon. Charles Stuart Wortley, and has, with other issue, * Victor Albert William, *b.* 1864.

WELCH, GEORGE ASSER WHITE, Esq., of Arle House, Gloucestershire.
Eldest son of the late John Gregory Welch, Esq., of Arle House, and of North Shoebury and Southchurch, Essex, by Frances Asser, dau. of Thomas White, Esq., of Alstone; *b.* 1800; *s.* 1854; *m.* 1828 Anne Catherine Gardiner, dau. and heir of the late Lieut.-Col. Manuooch, and niece of the late Vice-Admiral Sir Edward Brace, K.C.B., and has, with other issue,

* George Asser White, Commander R.N.; *b.* 1829; *m.* 1861 Mary Catherine, youngest dau. of the late Major England, and niece of Gen. Sir Richard England, G.C.B.

Mr. Welch, who was educated at Magdalen Coll., Oxford, is a J.P. and D.L. for Essex, and a Magistrate for co. Gloucester.—*Arle House, Cheltenham; North Shoebury, Southchurch, Southend.*

WELCH, Mrs., of Yaxley, Suffolk.
Henrietta, dau. and heir of Gilbert Francis Yaxley Leake, Esq., of Yaxley Hall, who was grandson of the eldest dau. of the last Earl of Sussex of Sutton, co. Derby; *m.* 1810 Patrick Robert Welch, Esq., of Yaxley, who *d.* 1867. Is Lady of the Manor of Yaxley.—*Yaxley Hall, Eye; Eye, w.; Bird, w. d.,* s.w.

WELD, CHARLES, Esq., of Chidiock, Dorset.
Eldest son of the late Humphrey Weld, Esq., of Chidiock House (who was brother of the late Joseph Weld, Esq., of Lulworth Castle), by the Hon. Christina Maria, 2nd dau. of Charles, 7th Lord Clifford of Chudleigh; *b.* 1812; *s.* 1852; *m.* 1851 Mary, dau. of Thomas Davison-Bland, Esq., of Kippax Park, co. York. Educated at Stonyhurst Coll.; called to the Bar at Lincoln's Inn 1838; is a Magistrate for Dorset, and Lord of the Manor of Chidiock.—*Chidiock House, Bridport; Stafford Club*, w.

Heir Pres., his brother Frederick, *b.* 1823; *m.* 185- a dau. of Ambrose Phillips De Lisle, Esq., of Garendon Park, co. Leicester, and has issue.

WELD, JOHN, Esq., of Leagram, Lancashire.
Eldest son of the late George Weld, Esq., J.P. and D.L., of Leagram, by Maria Maryetta, dau. of the late John Searle, Esq., of London; *b.* 1813; *s.* 1866; *m.* 1846 Eleanor, dau. of Nicholas Selby, Esq., of Acton, Middlesex, and has issue. Mr. Weld is a J.P. and D.L. for co. Lancaster.—*Leagram Hall, Preston.*

WELD, EDWARD JOSEPH, Esq., of Lulworth, Dorset.
Eldest son of the late Joseph Weld, Esq., J.P. and D.L., of Lulworth, by the Hon. Elizabeth Charlotte, dau. of Charles Philip, 16th Lord Stourton; *b.* 1806; *s.* 1863; *m.* 1838 Ellen Caroline, dau. of Sir Bourchier Palk Wrey, Bart., and by her, who *d.* 1866, has, with other issue,

   * Reginald Joseph, *b.* 1842.

Mr. Weld is a J.P. and D.L. for Dorset, a Magistrate for Hants, Lord of the Manor of Lulworth, and Patron of that living. This family bought Lulworth of the Earl of Suffolk in 1641.—*Lulworth Castle, Wareham.*

WELD-BLUNDELL, THOMAS, Esq., of Ince Blundell, Lancashire.
Second son of the late Joseph Weld, Esq., of Lulworth Castle, Dorset, by the Hon. Elizabeth Charlotte, dau. of Charles Philip, 16th Lord Stourton; *b.* 1808; *s.* 1836 by will to the estate of the late Charles Robert Blundell, Esq., whose name he assumed; *m.* 1839 Teresa Mary, dau. of the late William Michael Thomas John Vaughan, Esq., of Courtfield, co. Monmouth, and has, with other issue,

   * Charles Joseph, *b.* 1844 ; educated at Ch. Ch., Oxford.

Mr. Weld-Blundell, who was educated at Stonyhurst Coll., is a J.P. and D.L. for co. Lancaster (High Sheriff 1852).—*Ince Blundell Hall, Great Crosby, Liverpool; Stafford Club, w.*

WELDON, Sir ANTHONY CROSDILL, Bart., of Rahinderry and Kilmorony, Queen's Co. (cr. 1723).
Eldest son of the late Sir Anthony Weldon, Bart., of Rahinderry, by Harriet, dau. of Col. Thomas Hockley, of Her Majesty's Army (Line); *b.* 1827; *s.* as 5th Bart. 1858; *m.* 1862 Lizzie Caroline Thomasina, eldest surviving dau. of the late Lieut.-Col. Arthur Kennedy. Is a J.P. and D.L. for Queen's Co., a Magistrate for co. Kildare, and Patron of 1 living; was formerly in the Madras Artillery. The 1st Bart.'s name was Bardett, but the title was conferred with remainder to a nephew and his descendants.—*Rahinderry and Kilmorony, Athy, Queen's Co.; Hibernian United Service Club, Dublin; Oriental Club, s.w.*

Heir, his son Anthony Arthur, *b.* 1863.

WELFITT, the late Mrs., of Manby Hall, Lincolnshire.
Judith, dau. of the late James A. Calvert, Esq., of Louth, by Catherine Sophia, dau. of J. Raymond, Esq.; *d.* 1865, having *m.* 1814, as his 2nd wife, William Teale Welfitt, Esq., J.P., of Manby Hall, who *d.* 1801, leaving surviving issue two daughters. The late Mr. Welfitt was Lord of the Manor of Manby.—*Manby Hall, Louth, Lincolnshire.*

WELFITT, SAMUEL JAMES, Esq., of Farforth House, Lincolnshire.
Eldest son of the late Rev. Samuel Welfitt, of Louth Park House, by Maria, dau. of James Mason, Esq., of Keddington, and nephew of the late W. T. Welfitt, Esq., of Manby Hall, co. Lincoln; *b.* 1820; *s.* 1857; *m.* 1856 Elizabeth, dau. of Samuel Robson, Esq., of Louth, co. Lincoln. This family were formerly resi-

dent at North Cockerington Hall, whence they removed to Manby Hall.—*Farforth House, Louth, Lincolnshire.*

WELFITT, SAMUEL WILLIAM, Esq., of Langwith Lodge, Notts.
Eldest son of the late John Need, Esq., of Blidworth, Notts, by Mary, dau. of the Rev. William Welfitt, D.D., whose name he has assumed; *b.* 1806; *m.* 1837 Lætitia Mary, dau. of Major-General Hall. Educated at Rugby and Trinity Coll., Oxford; is a J.P. and D.L. for Notts (High Sheriff 1856), and Major Sherwood Rangers Yeomanry; late Capt. 17th Lancers.—*Langwith Lodge, Mansfield.*

WELLER-FOLEY, JOHN GEORGE, Esq., of Boxted, Suffolk.
Eldest son of the late George Weller-Poley, Esq., of Boxted, by Helen Sophia, dau. of James Fisher, Esq., Browston Hall, Suffolk; *b.* 1812; *s.* 1849; *m.* 1847 Diana, dau. of Thomas Hallifax, Esq., of Chadacre Hall, Suffolk, and has, with other issue,

   * John George, *b.* 1849.

Mr. Weller-Poley is a J.P. and D.L. for Suffolk (High Sheriff 1857), Lord of the Manor of Boxted, and Capt. Long Melford Troop of Suffolk Yeomanry Cavalry.—*Boxted Hall, Bury St. Edmund's; Arthur's Club, s.w.*

WELLESLEY, Lady VICTORIA CATHERINE MARY POLE-TYLNEY-LONG-, of Bolney, Sussex.
Only dau. of William, 4th Earl of Mornington (who *d.* 1857), by his 1st wife Catherine, eldest dau. and heir of the late Sir James Tylney-Long, Bart., of Draycot House, Wilts, Tylney Hall, Hants, and Wanstead House, Essex, and sister of William Arthur, 5th Earl (who *d.* 1863); *b.* 1818; is maternally representative of the Earls Tylney (*ext.*) and of the Longs of Draycot, an ancient Wiltshire family; purchased this property from the Hon. Sir F. W. Grey, K.C.B., in 1864.—*Bolney Lodge, Cuckfield.*

WELLESLEY, Lady CHARLES, of Conholt, Hants.
Augusta Sophia Anne, only child of the late Right Hon. Henry Manvers Pierrepont, of Conholt, by Lady Sophia, dau. of Henry, 1st Marquis of Exeter; *s.* 1851; *m.* 1844 Lieut.-Col. Lord Charles Wellesley (younger son of Arthur, 1st Duke of Wellington. K.G.), who *d.* 1858, leaving issue. * Henry (*Heir Pres.,* also to the Dukedom of Wellington), *b.* 1846.—*Conholt Park, Andover; 7, John Street, Berkeley Square, w.*

WELLESLEY.
(See under *Wellington, Duke of,* and *Cowley, Earl.*)

WELLINGTON, Duke of (ARTHUR RICHARD WELLESLEY, K.G., P.C.).—Cr. 1814.
Elder son of Arthur, 1st Duke, by the Hon. Katharine, 3rd dau. of Edward Michael, 2nd Lord Longford; *b.* 1807; *s.* as 2nd Duke of Wellington 1852, and as 6th Earl of Mornington 1863; *m.* 1839 Lady Elizabeth, dau. of George, 8th Marquis of Tweeddale, K.T. Educated at Eton and Trinity Coll., Cambridge; is Prince of Waterloo in the Netherlands, Duke of Ciudad Rodrigo, and a Grandee of 1st class in Spain; Duke of Vittoria, Marquis of Torres Vedras, and Count of Vimiera in Portugal; is Lord-Lieut. of Middlesex, a Magistrate for Norfolk, and Patron of 5 livings; sworn a Privy Councillor 1853; was M.P. for Aldeborough 1830-1, and for Norwich 1837-52; Master of the Horse 1853-8; late a Lieut.-General in the A[rmy]. The 1st Duke (celebrated for his victories in India and Spain, and at Waterloo), who was Premier 1828-30, and Commander-in-Chief 1842-52, was a younger son

of Garrett, 1st Earl of Mornington, and brother of the late Marquis Wellesley and Henry, 1st Lord Cowley. The family name was originally Colley, and that of Wesley or Wellesley was obtained by marriage with the heiress of a branch of that family, settled in co. Meath in the 18th century.—*Stratfieldsaye, Winchfield, Hants; Hilborough Hall, Swaffham; United Service, White's, and Carlton Clubs, s.w.; Apsley House, 149, Piccadilly, w.*

Heir Pres., his nephew Henry (elder son of his brother, the late Lord Charles Wellesley, who *d.* 1858, by Augusta Sophia Anne, only dau. of the late Right Hon. Henry Manvers Pierrepont), *b.* 1846; educated at Eton and Ch. Ch., Oxford.

WELLS, Sir MORDAUNT LAWSON, Knt. (cr. 1858).
Second son of the late Samuel Wells, Esq., Barrister-at-Law, by Jane, dau. of J. Fairey, Esq., of Huntingdon; *b.* 1817; *m.* 1840 Charlotte Mary, 3rd dau. of Thomas Gresham, Esq., of Burnley Dunn, co. York, and by her, who *d.* 1860, has, with other issue, an only son,

* Eudo George Gresham; educated at Merton Coll., Oxford; *b.* 1841; *m.* 1865 Agatha, only dau. of John Henry Benbow, of Kempsford, co. Gloucester.

Sir M. L. Wells, who was called to the Bar at the Middle Temple 1841, and went the Norfolk Circuit, became a Serjeant-at-Law 1855, appointed Recorder of Bedford 1856, was a Judge at Calcutta 1858–68.—*Union Club, s.w.; 107, Victoria Street, s.w.*

+WELLS, Lady ELIZABETH, of Huntercombe, Bucks.
Youngest dau. of John Joshua, 1st Earl of Carysfort, by his 2nd wife Elizabeth, 3rd dau. of the late Right Hon. George Grenville; *m.* 1816 Capt. William Wells, R.N., of Holmewood House, Hants, who *d.* 1826, leaving, with other issue,

* William (whom see).

Lady Elizabeth Wells is Lady of the Manor of Huntercombe.—*Huntercombe House, Burnham, Maidenhead.*

+WELLS, CHARLES COOKE, Esq., of Tenby, Pembrokeshire.
Son of the late Charles Wells, Esq.; *b.* 18—. Is a J.P. and D.L. for co. Pembroke.—*Tenby, Pembrokeshire.*

WELLS, JOHN, Esq., of Booth-Ferry, Yorkshire.
Fifth son of the late Peter Wells, Esq., of Kingston-on-Hull, by Elizabeth, dau. of William Hill, of Tibshelf, co. Derby; *b.* 1815; *m.* 1st 1845 Louisa Anne, dau. and only surviving child of the late William Wells, Esq., Jun., of Airmyn Hall, near Goole (she *d.* 1848); 2nd 1863 Eliza Augusta, youngest dau. of James Marley, Esq., of Greenstreet, East Ham, Essex, and has issue, by the former,

* Louisa Anne and Fanny Seymour.

Mr. Wells is a Magistrate for the W. Riding of Yorkshire, Chairman of the Goole Poor-Law Union, late Capt. 28th W. York Rifle Volunteer Corps.—*Booth-Ferry House, Howden, Yorkshire.*

WELLS, WILLIAM, Esq., of Holmewood, Hunts.
Eldest son of the late Capt. William Wells, R.N., of Holmewood, by Lady Elizabeth, dau. of John Joshua, 1st Earl of Carysfort; *b.* 1818; *s.* 1826; *m.* 1854 Lady Louisa, dau. of Francis, 8th Earl of Wemyss. Educated at Harrow and Balliol Coll., Oxford (B.A. 1839, M.A. 1842); is a J.P. and D.L. for Hunts and Kent; was M.P. for Beverley 1851–6, and formerly an Officer in the 1st Life Guards.—*Holmewood, Stilton; Redleaf, Penshurst; White's and Brooks's Clubs, s.w.; 22, Bruton Street, w.*

Heir Pres., his brother Grenville Granville, a Magistrate for Bucks and Hants, *b.* 1824.

WELLS-DYMOKE, EDMUND LIONEL, Esq., of West Molesey, Surrey.
Only surviving son of the late Dymoke Wells, Esq., of Grebby Hall and Kexby, by Anne, dau. and co-heiress of T. Waterhouse, Esq., of Beckingham, Notts; *b.* 1814; *m.* 1st 1840 Mary Ann, dau. of Thomas Gulliver, Esq., of Stapleton Castle; 2nd 1864 Laura de Blair, dau. of Thomas Jefferson, Esq., of Gloucester Square, and has issue. Mr. Wells-Dymoke, who was educated at Westminster and Queen's Coll., Cambridge, and called to the Bar at Middle Temple 1838, is Lord of the Manor of Grebby, late Capt. Royal Cumberland Militia; he assumed the name of Dymoke by Royal licence 1856. This family was formerly of Grebby Hall, co. Lincoln, and Willingham, co. Lincoln. — *Grebby Hall, Spilsby; The Grange, West Molesey; Junior United Service Club, s.w.; 28, Montagu Square, w.*

WELLWOOD-MONCRIEFF. -(See *Moncrieff.*)

WELMAN, CHARLES NOEL, Esq., of Norton Manor, Somerset.
Only son of the late Thomas Welman, Esq., of Norton Manor, by the Hon. Charlotte Noel, dau. of the late Sir Gerard Noel-Noel, Bart., and the late Baroness Barham; *b.* 1814; *s.* 1824; *m.* 1835 Anne Eliza, eldest dau. of Cornelius Henry Bolton, Esq., of Faithlegg, co. Waterford, and has, with other issue,

* Charles Cesar, late Lieut. 49th Foot, *b.* 1840; *m.* 1862 Eugenia Mary, youngest dau. of the late Hon. Charles Henry Stemor, of Holmwood, Oxon, and has, with other issue, * a son, *b.* 1865.

Mr. Welman, who was educated at Edinburgh University, is a J.P. and D.L. for Somerset, a Magistrate for Devon, Lord of the Manor of Norton Fitzwarren, and Capt. Somerset Yeomanry Cavalry.—*Norton Manor, Taunton; Athenæum Club, s.w.*

WELSH, the Rev. WILLIAM, of Mossfennan, Peeblesshire.
Son of the late Alexander Welsh. Esq. (who *d.* 1824), by Mary, dau. of Alexander Tweedie. Esq.; *b.* 1820; *s.* his uncle, Robert Welsh, Esq., of Mossfennan, 1855; *m.* 1854 Christina, dau. of the Rev. Thomas Guthrie, D.D., of Edinburgh. Mr. Welsh, who was educated at the High School and University of Edinburgh, is Lord of the Barony of Mossfennan, and Minister of the Free Church of Broughton. This family have held the estate of Mossfennan for upwards of a century.—*Mossfennan House, Rachan Mill, Biggar, N.B.*

WELSTEAD, GEORGE RICHARDS, Esq. of Stonely, Hunts.
Eldest son of the late Marion Welstead. Esq., of Stonely, by Susannah, dau. of James Osborne, Esq., of St. Ives, Hunts; *b.* 1805; *s.* 1856; *m.* 1846 Sarah Greaves, dau. of Richard Gibbeson, Esq. Educated at Emmanuel Coll., Cambridge; is a Magistrate for Hunts.—*Stonely Hall, Kimbolton; Kempsey, Worcester.*

WELSTED, RICHARD, Esq., of Ballywalter, co. Cork.
Eldest son of the late John Welsted, Esq., of Ballywalter, by Bridget, dau. of John Hawkes, Esq., of Suirmount; *b.* 1806; *s.* 1833; *m.* 1835 Honoria Sarah, dau. of George Sandes, Esq. Educated at Trinity Coll., Dublin (B.A. 1827); is a Magistrate for co. Cork. This family has held the estate since the time of O. Cromwell. — *Ballywalter, Castletownroche, co. Cork.*

WELWOOD. (See *Maconochie-Welwood.*)

WEMYS, Capt. JOHN OTWAY, of Danesfort, co. Kilkenny.
Only son of the late Col. Henry Wemys, J.P. and D.L., of Danesfort (formerly High Sheriff of co. Kilkenny),

981

by Lady Elizabeth, dau. of Otway, 1st Earl of Desart; b. 1826; s. 1860. Is a Mag'strate for co. Kilkenny, and Capt. 3rd Buffs; late Capt. 71st Highlanders. This family are descended f.om a common ancestor with the Earl of Wemyss.—*Dancsfort, Kilkenny.*

WEMYSS AND MARCH, Earl of (FRANCIS WEMYSS-CHARTERIS-DOUGLAS).—Cr. 1633.

Eldest son of Francis, 7th Earl, by Margaret, dau. of Walter Campbell, Esq.; b. 1796; s. 1853; m. 1817 Lady Louisa, dau. of Richard, 2nd Earl of Lucan. Sits in the House of Peers as Lord Wenyss, U.K. (cr. 1821); is Lord Lieutenant of co. Peebles, Vice-Lieutenant of co. Had lington, a Magistrate for cos. Berwick and Perth, a J.P. and D.L for Midlothian, and Lieut.-General of the Royal Archers of Scotland; Lord of the Manor and Patron of Stanway.—*Amisfield and Gosford, Haddington, N.B.; Ni dpath Castle, Perth, N.B.; Stanway. Moreton-in-the-Marsh; Echo Castle, Perth; Carlton Club, s.w.*

Heir, his son Francis, Lord Elcho, educated at Eton, and B.A. of Ch. Ch., Oxford, a Dep.-Lieut. for co. Ha idington. Lieut.-Col. London Scottish Volunteers, and late a Lord of the Treasury; M.P. for co. Haddington, and formerly M.P. for E. Gloucestershire; b. 1818; m. 1843 Lady Anne Frederica, dau. of Thomas William, 1st Earl of Lichfield, and has, with other issue, *Francis*, b. 1844.

WEMYSS, Sir JOHN, Bart., of Bogie, co. Fife (cr. 1704).

Son of the late John Wemyss; Esq., of Kirkcaldy, N.B. Is a Merchant at. Berhampore, Bengal; was served heir-male to his kinsman, Sir James, late Bart., 1858. —*Berhampore, Bengal, India.*

WEMYSS, JAMES, Esq., of Wemyss, Fifeshire.

Eldest son of the late James Balfour Wemyss, Esq., of Wemyss, who was Col. of the Fifeshire Militia, by Mary, dau. of Henry Manley, Esq., of Manley, Devon; b. 1798; s. 1827; m. 1827 Susan, dau. of the late David Gillespie, Esq., of Mountquhanie, co. Fife, and has, with other issue,

* James Balfour, a Magistrate for co. Fife; b. 1828.

Mr. Wemyss, who is a J.P. and D.L. for co. Fife, and a Major Fifeshire Militia, was formerly a Capt. in the Army; he is descended from a common ancestor with the Earl of Wemyss.—*Wemyss Hall, Cupar, N.B.*

WEMYSS, Mrs. ERSKINE-, of Wemyss Castle, Fifeshire.

Millicent Ann Mary, younger dau. of the Hon. John Kennedy Erskine and Lady Augusta Fitz-Clarence; m. 1855 James Hay Erskine-Wemyss, Esq., M.P., of Wemyss Castle, who was Lord-Lieut. of co. Fife, and who d. 1864, leaving, with other issue,

* Randolph Gordon, b. 1858.

This family derives from that of Macduff Maormhon. of Fife, in the reign of Malcolm Caenmore.—*Wemyss Castle, Kirkcaldy, N.B.; Torrie House, Dunfermline, N.B.; 66, Prince's Gate, s.w.*

WENLOCK, Lord (BEILBY RICHARD LAWLEY).—Cr. 1839.

Eldest son of Beilby, 1st Lord (who was a brother of the late Sir F. Lawley, Bart., but assumed the name of Thompson only), by the Hon. Caroline. dau. of Richard, 2nd Lord Braybrooke; b. 1818; s. 1852; m. 1846 Lady Elizabeth, dau. of Richard, 2nd Marquis of Westminster. Educated at Eton, is a Magistrate for the N. Riding, Lord Lieutenant of the E. Riding of co. York, Lord of the Manor of Riccall, Patron of 5 livings, and Capt. Yorkshire Hussars; was M.P. for Pontefract 1851-2. —*Escrick Park, York; Canwell Hall, Tamworth; Bourton Cottage, Wenlock; Travellers' Club, s.w.*

Heir, his son Beilby, b. 1849.
982

WENMAN, Baroness (SOPHIA ELIZABETH WYKEHAM).—Cr. 1834.

Only dau. of the late William Richard Wykeham. Esq., of Swalcliffe, Oxon (who d. 1830), by his 1st wife Elizabeth. dau. of William Marsh, Esq., and niece of Philip, 6th and last Viscount Wenman (ext. 1800). who was many years M.P. for Oxon; b. 1790. Is Lady of the Manors of Thame, Swalcliffe, and Haddenham. —*Swalcliffe, Tetsworth; Thame Park, Oxon.*

WENMAN, the Rev. WILLIAM, of Rowlstone, Herefordshire.

Eldest son of the late William Wenman, Esq., of Codsall, co. Stafford, by Mary Anne, dau. of Richard Emery, Esq., of Lichfield; b. 1804; s. 1857. Educated at Trinity Hall, Cambridge (S.C.L. 1831. B.C.L. 1833); is a Magistrate for co. Hereford, and Vicar of Rowlstone with Llancilloe.—*Rowlstone Court, Hereford.*

WENSLEYDALE, Lady.

Cecilia, dau. of Samuel F. Barlow, Esq., m. 1817 James Parke, Lord Wensleydale, formerly a Justice of the King's Bench and a Baron of the Exchequer, who d. 1868, when his title became ext.—*Residence: Ampthill Park, Beds; 122, Park Street, w.*

WENTWORTH, Lord (RALPH GORDON NOEL NOEL-MILBANKE).—Cr. 1529.

Only surviving son of William, 1st Earl of Lovelace, by the Hon. Augusta Ada, only dau. of George Gordon, 6th Lord Byron; b. 1839; s. his brother as 12th Lord 1862. Is styled by courtesy Viscount Ockham. This barony was in abeyance 1815-56.—*East Horsley, Ripley; 86, St. James's Street, s.w.*

+WENTWORTH, GODFREY HAWESWORTH, Esq., of Wolley Park, Yorkshire.

Eldest son of the late Godfrey Wentworth. Esq., J.P. and D.L., of Wolley Park (who was High Sheriff of Yorkshire 1862), by Anne, dau. of the late Walter Fawkes, Esq., of Farnley Hall, co. York. and grandson of the late G. W. Armytage, Esq., who assumed the name of Wentworth; b. 1824; s. 1865. Is Patron of 1 living; represents the ancient family of Wentworth, of Wentworth Woodhouse, from which Earl Fitzwilliam maternally descends.—*Wolley Park, Wakefield.*

WENTWORTH. (See *Vernon-Wentworth.*)

WESLEY, Lieut.-General Sir SAMUEL ROBERT, K.C.B. (cr. 1862).

Eldest son of the late Robert Wesley. Esq., of Mount Crozier, co. Cork, by Ellen, dau. of J. Butt. Esq., of Lismore Castle, co. Limerick; b. 1791; m. 1835 Mary, dau. of the Rev. Robert Butt, Rector of Stranorlar. Appointed Capt. Royal Marine Artillery 1837, became Colonel and Deputy Adjutant-General R.M. 1834, Major-General 1857, and Lieut.-General 1862.—*United Service Club, s.w.; 28, Grislon Road, Old Brompton, s.w.*

WEST, Sir AUGUSTUS, Knt., M.D. (cr. 1849).

Son of the late A. West, Esq.; b. 1788. Has been Deputy-Inspector-General of Army Hospitals, and Physician to the King of Portugal; served in Hanover, Sweden, and Peninsula.—*Rue de la Paix, Paris.*

WEST, FRANCIS GEORGE, Esq., of Horham, Essex.

Only son of the late Rev. George West, Rector of St. next-Guildford. Surrey, by Sarah, only dau. of Francis Creuzé, Esq. of Howfield House, Kent; b. 1805; s. 1853; m. 1830 Frances, youngest dau. of

late James Green, Esq., of Farnham, Surrey, and has, with other issue, an only surviving son,
* George, in Holy Orders. M.A. of Magdalen Hall., Oxford, and Curate of Ryton, Northumberland; *b.* 1823; *m.* 1861 Mary Ann Thorp, youngest dau. of William Dickson, Esq., of Alnwick, and Alnmouth, Northumberland, and has, with other issue, * Franci· George, *b.* 1864.

Mr. West, who was called to the Bar at Lincoln's Inn 1850, is a J.P. and D.L. for Essex; and Lord of the Manor of Thaxted.—*Horham Hall, Thaxted, Essex.*

WEST, FREDERICK MYDDELTON, Esq., of Ruthin Castle, Denbighshire.
Eldest son of the late Frederick Richard West, Esq., J.P. and D.L., M.P., of Ruthin Castle, by his 2nd wife Theresa, dau. of the late Capt. J. C. Whitby, R.N., of Newlands, Hants; *b.* 1830; *s.* 1862. Educated at Eton; is a Magistrate for co. Denbigh, and late Capt. Denbighshire Yeomanry Cavalry; was formerly in the 7th Hussars and 3rd Regt.—*Ruthin Castle, Denbigh.*

Heir Pres., his brother William Cornwallis, a J.P. and D.L. for co. Denbigh; *b.* 1833.

+ **WEST**, Mrs., of Newlands, Hants.
Theresa, dau. of the late Capt. J. C. Whitby, R.N., of Newlands; *m.* 1827 (as his 2nd wife) Frederick Richard West, Esq., of Ruthin Castle, co. Denbigh, who *d.* 1862, leaving, with other issue, *Frederick Myddelton (whom see), *b.* 1830.—*Newlands, Milford, Lymington.*

WEST. (See under *De-la-Warr, Earl.*)

WEST. (See *Roberts-West.*)

WEST. (See *Sackville-West.*)

WESTBURY, Lord (RICHARD BETHELL, D.C.L.). —Cr. 1861.
Son of the late Richard Bethell, Esq., M.D., of Bristol; *b.* 1800; *m.* 1825 Eleanor Mary, dau. of the late Robert Abraham, Esq. (she *d.* 1863). Educated at Wadham Coll., Oxford (B.A. 1818, M.A. 1820); called to the Bar at the Middle Temple 1823 ; is a Governor of the Charterhouse, and a Trustee of the British and Hunterian Museums; formerly Vice-Chancellor of the co. Palatine of Lancaster, and Standing Counsel to the University of Oxford; made Queen's Counsel 1839 ; was M.P. for Aylesbury 1851-9, and for Wolverhampton 1859-61 ; Solicitor-General 1852-6, Attorney-General 1856-8 and 1859-61, Lord Chancellor of Great Britain 1861-5. His Lordship is descended from the ancient Welsh family of Ap Ithel.—*Residence : Hinton St. George, Somerset; Celli Pistoja, Italy ; 75, Lancaster Gate, w.*

Heir, his son Richard Augustus, *b.* 1830 ; *m.* 1851 Mary-Florence, youngest dau. of the Rev. Alexander Fownes Luttrell, Rector of East Quantoxhead, Somerset, and has issue, *Richard Luttrell Pilkington, *b.* 1852.

WESTBY, EDWARD PERCEVAL, Esq., of Roebuck, co. Dublin, and Riltallyowen, co. Clare.
Eldest son of the late Nicholas Westby, Esq., by the Hon. Emily Susan Laura, eldest dau. of William, 1st Lord Radstock ; *b.* 1828 ; *s.* 1860 ; *m.* 1st 1852 Elizabeth Mary, dau. of the late Right Hon. Francis Blackburne, of Rathfarnham Castle, co. Dublin (she *d.* 1863); 2nd 1864 Susan Elizabeth, eldest dau. of John Davis Garde, Esq., and has by the former, with other issue,
* William Francis Perceval, *b.* 1854.

Mr. Westby, who was educated at Corpus Christi Coll., Oxford, is a Magistrate for cos. Dublin and Clare (High Sheriff 1854).—*Roebuck Castle, Dundrum, co. Dublin; Riltallyowen, co. Clare; Kildare Street Club, Dublin.*

WESTBY, JOCELYN TATE FAZAKERLEY-, Esq., of Mowbreck Hall, Lancashire.
Eldest son of the late George Westby, Esq., of Mowbreck, by Mary, eldest dau. of Major John Tate ; *b.*

1831 ; *s.* 1842 ; *m.* 1863 Matilda Harriet, eldest dau. of the late Henry Hawarden Fazakerley, Esq., of Gillibrand Hall and Fazakerley House, co. Lancaster, whose name he assumed. Educated at Eton ; is a J.P. and D.L. for co. Lancaster, was formerly in the 2nd Dragoons and Scots Greys.—*Mowbreck Hall, Kirkham; Junior United Service Club, s.w.*

Heir Pres., his brother Ashley George, late Lieut. 8th Foot ; *b.* 1835.

WESTBY, WILLIAM JONES, Esq., of High Park, co. Wicklow.
Eldest son of the late Edward Westby, Esq., of High Park, by Phœbe, dau. of Richard Palmer, Esq., of Glannacurragh Castle, King's Co.; *b.* 1802; *s.* 1838; *m.* 1828 Catharine, 2nd dau. of Col. Grogan, and has, with other issue,
* William Henry Jones, Lieut. 66th Foot ; *b.* 1831.

Mr. Westby, who was educated at Trinity Coll., Dublin (B.A. 1823, M.A. 1830), is a J.P. and D.L. for cos. Carlow and Wicklow (High Sheriff 1827).—*High Park, Baltinglass, co. Wicklow; United Service Club, Dublin.*

+ **WESTCAR**, HENRY, Esq., of Burwood, Surrey.
Only son of the late Henry Westcar, Esq., by Elizabeth, dau. of — Weatherstone, Esq.; *b.* 1798; *m.* 1827 Emma, 2nd dau. of William Leaf, Esq., of Peckham, Surrey, and has, with other issue,
* Henry Emerson, Lieut. R. Horse Guards ; *b.* 1839.

Mr. Westcar, who was educated at Eton and Exeter Coll., Oxford (B.A. 1820, M.A. 1826), is a Magistrate for Surrey.—*Burwood, Walton-on-Thames.*

WESTENRA, the Hon. JOHN CRAVEN, of Sharavogne, King's Co.
Fourth son of William, 2nd Lord Rossmore, by Mary Anne, 2nd dau. of Charles Walsh, Esq., of Walsh Park, co. Tipperary; *b.* 1798; *m.* 1st 1834 Eleanor Mary dau. of the late William Joliffe, Esq., of Merstham, Surrey, widow of Sir Gilbert East (she *d.* 1838); 2nd 1842 Anne, dau. of the late Louis Charles Dautuz. Esq., and has surviving issue, an only child,
* Mary Anne Wilmot, *m.* 1867 Lord Hastings (see *Hastingdon*).

Mr. Westenra, who is a Dep.-Lieut. for King's Co. (High Sheriff 1863), late Lieut.-Col. Scots Fusilier Guards, was M.P. for King's Co. 1857-52.—*Sharavogue, Parsonstown, King's Co.; Reform Club, s.w.*

WESTENRA. (See under *Rossmore, Lord.*)

WESTERN, Sir THOMAS BURCH, Bart., of Felix Hall, Essex, and Tattingstone, Suffolk (cr. 1864).
Eldest son of the late Rear-Admiral Thomas Western, K.T.S., by Mary, dau. of Thomas Burch, Esq., of Bermuda, West Indies ; *b.* 1795 ; *m.* 1819 Margaret Lætitia, dau. of William Bushby, Esq., of Kirkmichael, co. Dumfries. Educated at Trinity Coll., Cambridge (B.A. 1818, M.A. 1824); is a J.P. and D.L. for Suffolk and Essex (High Sheriff 1850), and Gentleman of the Privy Chamber ; elected M.P. for N. Essex 1830.— *Residence : Felix Hall and Rivenhall Place, Kelvedon, Essex : Brooks's and University Clubs, s.w.*

Heir, his son Thomas Sutton, a J.P. and D.L. for Essex and Suffolk, late M.P. for Maldon ; *b.* 1821 ; *m.* 1848 Giulietta Romana, dau. of Sir Edward Manningham-Buller, Bart., M.P., of Dilhorne Hall, co. Stafford, and by her, who *d.* 1850, has issue, *Thomas Charles Callis, *b.* 1850.

WESTERN, CHARLES MAXIMILIAN THOMAS, Esq.
Eldest son of the late Lieut.-Col. Charles Maximilian Thomas Western (who *d.* 1849), by Harriet, dau. of Christopher Clarke, Esq., of Twickenham, King's Co.; *b.* 1824; *m.* 1850 Harriet, dau. of William Balfour, Esq., of Trenaby. Educated at Edinburgh University.

This family is the senior branch of the Westerns of Felix Hall and Rivenhall Place, Essex.—33, *Marlborough Buildings, Bath.*

WESTHEAD, Joshua Proctor BROWN-, Esq., of Lea Castle, Worcestershire.

Eldest son of the late Edward Westhead, Esq., of Manchester, by Anne, dau. of Joshua Brown, Esq., of Dothill, Salop; *b.* 1807; *s.* 1833; *m.* 1828 Betsy, dau. of George Royle Chappell, Esq., and has, with other issue,

- George Edward, Lieut.-Col. in the Army; *b.* 1829.

Mr. Brown-Westhead is a J.P. and D.L. for co. Worcester, and a Magistrate for co. Stafford; was M.P. for Knaresborough 1847–53, and for York 1857–65. He assumed in 1850 the name of his maternal uncle, John Brown, Esq., High Sheriff of co. Worcester.—*Lea Castle, Wolverley; Brooks's and Reform Clubs,* s.w.

WESTHEAD, Thomas Chappell BROWN-, Esq., of Highfield House, Staffordshire.

Youngest son of Joshua Proctor Brown-Westhead, Esq., M.P. for York, of Lea Castle (whom see above), by Betsy, dau. of George Royle Chappell, Esq.; *b.* 1837; *m.* 1860 Marian, 4th dau. of George Fourdrinier, Esq., of Stoke-on-Trent, and has issue,

- George Marion York, *b.* 1861.

Mr. Brown-Westhead is a Magistrate for co. Stafford and a Major 1st Battalion Stafford Rifle Volunteers; he was formerly Lieut. Worcestershire Militia.—*Cauldon Place, Stoke-on-Trent; Highfield House, Barlastone, Staffordshire; Volunteer Service Club,* s.w.

WESTMEATH, Marquis of (George Thomas John Nugent).—Cr. 1822.

Eldest son of George Frederick, 7th Earl of Westmeath, by his 1st wife Marianne, dau. of James St. John Jeffreys, Esq., of Blarney Castle, co. Cork; *b.* 1785; *s.* as Earl 1814; *m.* 1st 1812 Lady Emily Anne, dau. of James, 1st Marquis of Salisbury (she *d.* 1858); 2nd 1858 Miss Maria Jarvis (div. 1862); 3rd 1864 Elizabeth Charlotte, 2nd dau. of the late David Verner, Esq. Educated at Rugby; is Lord Lieutenant and Custos Rotulorum of co. Westmeath, a Magistrate for co. Roscommon, and a Representative Peer for Ireland; late Col. Westmeath Militia.—*Castletown, Delvin, Westmeath; United Service Club,* s.w.; 39, *Devonshire Place,* w.

Heir Pres. (to the Earldom only), his cousin Anthony Nugent, Esq., of Pallas (whom see).

WESTMINSTER, Marquis of (Richard Grosvenor, K.G., P.C.).—Cr. 1831.

Eldest son of Robert, 1st Marquis, by Lady Eleanor, dau. of Thomas, 1st Earl of Wilton; *b.* 1795; *s.* 1845; *m.* 1819 Lady Elizabeth Mary, dau. of George Granville, 1st Duke of Sutherland. Educated at Westminster; is a Magistrate for Dorset, Flint, and Wilts, and Patron of 11 livings; late Lord Lieutenant and Custos Rotulorum of co. Chester; was M.P. for Chester 1818–30, and South Cheshire 1830–34; Lord Steward of the Household 1850–2.—*Eaton Hall, Chester; Motcombe House, Shaftesbury; Calveley Hall, Nantwich; Fonthill Gifford, Hindon;* 33, *Upper Grosvenor Street,* w.

Heir, his son Hugh Lupus, Earl Grosvenor, educated at Eton and Balliol Coll., Oxford; a Magistrate for co. Chester, Lieut.-Col. Commandant Queen's Westminster Rifle Volunteers, Capt. Cheshire Yeomanry, and M.P. for Chester; *b.* 1825; *m.* 1852 Lady Constance Gertrude, dau. of George Granville, 2nd Duke of Sutherland, and has issue, • Victor Alexander, Viscount Belgrave, *b.* 1853.

WESTMORLAND, Earl of (Francis William Henry Fane).—Cr. 1624.

Eldest son of John, 11th Earl, by Lady Priscilla Anne, dau. of William, 3rd Earl of Mornington; *b.* 1825; *s.* 1859; *m.* 1857 Lady Adelaide Ida, 2nd dau. of Richard, 1st Earl Howe. Is a Magistrate for co. Northampton, Patron of 2 livings, and Lieut.-Col. Coldstream G[illegible]. This family is descended from a common [illegible] the Duke of Cleveland.—*Apthorpe, Wansford; G[illegible] Club,* s.w.; 54, *Green Street,* w.

Heir, his son Anthony Mildmay Julian, Lord Burghersh, *b.* 1859.

+WESTON, Major Charles Samuel, of Morvich, Sutherlandshire.

Son of the late C. Weston, Esq., of Morvich; [illegible] Is a J.P. and D.L. for co. Sutherland, and [illegible] Sutherlandshire Rifle Volunteers; late Capt. [illegible] Native Infantry.—*Morvich, Golspie, N.B.*

WESTON, Henry Macgregor, Esq., of West Horsley Place, Surrey.

Eldest son of the late Henry Weston, Esq., of West Horsley Place, by Frances Harriet, dau. of A[illegible] Hubbard la Fargue, Esq., of Husband's Bosworth, Leicester; *b.* 1853; *s.* 1863. Is Lord of the Manor of West Horsley; represents an old Surrey family.—*West Horsley Place, Ripley, Surrey.*

Heir Pres., his brother Charles Edward, *b.* 18[illegible].

WESTON, William Henry Purcell, Esq., of Wolveton, Dorset.

Eldest son of the late Roper Weston, Esq., by Elizabeth, dau. and heir of John Purcell, Esq., of K[illegible] Cork; *b.* 1829; *m.* 1857 Alda Gertrude, dau. of Sir John Hesketh Lethbridge, Bart., of Sandhill Park, Somerset. Educated at St. John's Coll., Cambridge (B.A. 1850, M.A. 1854); is representative of the [illegible] Earl of Portland of a former creation. This family was seated in co. Stafford *temp.* Henry II.—[illegible] *Dorchester, Dorset; Conservative Club,* s.w.

WESTON. (See *Monington-Weston.*)

WESTPHAL, Sir George Augustus, Knt. (cr. 1824).

Son of the late George Westphal, Esq., by Mary, dau. of — McGrigor, Esq.; *b.* 1785; *m.* 1st 1817 Alicia, dau. of Charles Stuart, Esq. (widow of William Chambers, Esq.); 2nd 1847 Mary Ann, dau. of John R[illegible], Esq. (widow of George Addenbrooke Gore, Esq.). Is a Magistrate for Sussex, and an Admiral reserved; served at Trafalgar.—*Brunswick Square, Brighton; United Service Club,* s.w.

WESTROPP, Henry, Esq., of Green Park, co. Limerick.

Only son of the late Henry Westropp, Esq., of Richmond, co. Limerick, by Elinor Winthrop, dau. of the late William Jones, Esq., of Cork; *b.* 1811. Educated at Harrow and Trinity Coll., Dublin (B.A. 1831); is a Magistrate for co. Limerick; was M.P. for Bridgwater 1865–6.—*Green Park, Bruff; Union Club,* s.w.

WESTROPP, John, Esq., of Attyflin, co. Limerick.

Eldest son of the late John Westropp, Esq., of Attyflin, by Anna, eldest dau. of the late James Ness, Esq., of Osgodbie House, co. York; *b.* 1814; *m.* 1st 1836 Georgina Wilhelmina, youngest dau. of Col. Stamer, of Carnelly, co. Clare; 2nd 1856 Charlotte Louisa, eldest dau. of the late Lieut.-Gen. Sir Thomas Whitehead, K.C.B., of Uplands Hall, co. Lancaster, and has, by the former, with other issue,

- John Thomas, *b.* 1837; *m.* 1859 Margaret, youngest dau. of the late Thomas Robert Wilson France, Esq., of Rawcliffe Hall, co. Lancaster.

Mr. Westropp is a Magistrate for cos. Limerick and Clare, and the head of a family which has been seated in co. Limerick since the reign of John.—*Attyflin Park, Patrickswell, co. Limerick; Cornmoley, co. Clare; Ballylegan, co. Cork.*

+ WESTROPP, WALTER M., Esq., of Charlefort, co. Wexford.
Son of the late Walter Westropp, Esq., of Charlefort;
b. 18—; m. 1859 Laura Felicia Susan, youngest dau.
of Sir William Clay, Bart. Educated at Trinity Coll.,
Dublin; is Lord of the Manor of Charlefort.—Charlefort, co. Wexford.

WETENHALL, CECIL ALGERNON SALISBURY,
Esq., of Hatton Hall, Northamptonshire.
Only child of the late Col. Wetenhall, of Durham, by
Agnes Margaret, 4th dau. of the late Peter Wettenhall,
Esq., of Rushton, co. Chester; b. 1846; s. his maternal
aunt, Mrs. Ridgway, of Ridgmont, Lancashire, and
Hatton Hall, Northampton 1864. Mr. Wetenhall re-
presents a branch of the Wettenhalls of Wettenhall,
Rushton Hankelow, and Bostock, Cheshire.—Hatton
Hall, Wellingborough.

WETHERALL, Sir GEORGE AUGUSTUS, G.C.B.,
K.H.‡ (cr. 1856).
Eldest son of the late General Sir Frederick Wetherall,
by his 1st wife Elizabeth, dau. of George Mytton, Esq.;
b. 1788; m. 1812 Frances Diana, dau. of the late Capt.
Denton, H.E.I.C.'s Service (she d. 1867). Educated at
Winchester and the Royal Military Coll., Farnham; is
a General in the Army, Col. of the 84th Foot, and late
Adjutant-General at the Horse Guards; formerly Lieut.-
Col. 1st Foot; appointed Governor of the Royal Mili-
tary Coll., Sandhurst, 1866.—Royal Military College,
Sandhurst, Bagshot.

WETHERALL, Sir EDWARD ROBERT, K.C.S.I.,
C.B., K.L.H. (cr. 1867).
Youngest son of the late General Sir George Wetherall,
G.C.B., by Frances, dau. of the late Capt. Denton,
H.E.I.C.S.; b. 1819; m. 1847 Katharine, dau. of the
late John Durie, Esq., of Astley Hall, co. Lancaster.
Educated at the Royal Naval and Military School,
Edinburgh, and R.M. Coll., Sandhurst; is a Col. in
the Army, Deputy Quartermaster-Gen. of the Forces,
A.D.C. to the Queen; was formerly an Assistant
Quartermaster-Gen. of the Army in the Crimea, and
Chief of the Staff of the Central India Field Force.
—Astley Hall, Tyldesley, Lancashire; United Service
Club, s.w.; 112, Belgrave Road, s.w.

WETHERED, THOMAS OWEN, Esq., of Seymour
Court, Bucks.
Eldest son of the late Owen Wetherod, Esq., J.P., of
Remnantz, by Anne, dau. of the late Rev. Giles Ilsworth
Peel, of Basildon Grotto, Berks; b. 1832; s. 1862; m.
1856 Edith Grace, only dau. of the Rev. Hart Ethelston, and has issue three daughters. Mr. Wethered was
educated at Eton and Ch. Ch., Oxford. This family
are seated at Remnantz, which is in the possession
of the widow of Mr. O. Wethered for life.—Seymour,
Court, and Remnantz, Gt. Marlow.

Heir Pres., his brother Owen Peel, b. 1836; m. 1863 Frances
Alice, dau. of George T. Ellison, Esq., of Upper Seymour
Street, London, and has issue two sons and a daughter.

+ WETHERELL, RICHARD, Esq., of Frant,
Sussex.
Son of the late Richard Wetherell, Esq., and nephew of
the late Sir Charles Wetherell, M.P.; m. 1852 Edith
Lee, dau. of — Tebitt, Esq., of Park Farm, Hawkhurst,
Kent, and has issue an only son,
   * Robert William May, Lieut. and Adjutant 16th Regt.; b.
    1844; m. 1864 Emily Louisa, dau. of William Annand, Esq.,
    of Nova Scotia.
Mr. Wetherell is a Magistrate for Sussex, and Capt.
Sussex Artillery Militia.—Frant, Tunbridge Wells.

Died whilst these sheets were at press.

WEYLAND, JOHN, Esq., of Woodeaton, Oxon,
and Woodrising, Norfolk.
Eldest son of the late Major Richard Weyland. J.P.
and D.L. and M.P., of Woodeaton and Woodrising (who
was High Sheriff of Oxon 1832), by Charlotte, dau. of
Charles Gordon, Esq., of Cluny Castle, co. Aberdeen,
and widow of Sir John Lowther Johnstone, Bart., of
Westerhall; b. 1821; s. 1864; m. 1850 Lady Catherine,
dau. of Ulick John, 1st Marquis of Clanricarde, K.P.,
and has, with other issue,
   * John, b. 1855.
Mr. Weyland, who was educated at Eton and Ch. Ch.,
Oxford, is a J.P. and D.L. for Oxon, Lord of the
Manors of Woodrising and Woodeaton, and Patron of
3 livings.— Woodeaton, Oxford; Woodrising Hall,
Shipdham.

WEYMOUTH. (See under Bath, Marquis of.)

+ WHALEY, THOMAS, Esq., of Orrell Mount,
Lancashire.
Son of the late Thomas Whaley, Esq., of Winterbourne;
b. 18—; is a Magistrate for co. Lancaster and a Manufacturer at Wigan.—Orrell Mount, Wigan.

WHALLEY, Sir SAMUEL ST. SWITHIN BURDEN
(cr. 1827).
Son of the late S. Whalley, Esq., of Widdington Hall,
co. Warwick; b. 1800; m. 1st 1830 Amelia, dau. of
Samuel Webb Smith, Esq. (she d. 1835); 2nd 1853 the
Hon. Harriet Rose, dau. of the late Francis Trench.
Esq., and sister of Frederick Mason, 2nd Lord Ashtown.
Educated at Clare Coll., Cambridge (B.A. 1822, M.A.
1825); was M.P. for Marylebone 1833-8. Is descended
from a common ancestor with the Whalleys of Plas
Madog.—17, Rue de la Madeleine, Paris.

WHALLEY, GEORGE HAMMOND, Esq.
Eldest son of the late James Whalley, Esq., of Glou-
cester, by Elizabeth, dau. of Richard Morse, Esq., of
Blakeney, co. Gloucester; b. 1813; s. 1841; m. 1846
Anne Wakeford, dau. of Richard Attree, Esq., and has,
with other issue,
   * George Hampden, b. 1851.
Mr. Whalley, who was educated at University Coll.,
London, called to the Bar at Gray's Inn 1839, appointed
Assistant Tithe Commissioner 1839, and Examiner of
Private Bills in Parliament 1817, is a J.P. and D.L.
for co. Denbigh, and a Magistrate for co. Montgomery;
was High Sheriff of co. Carnarvon 1852; formerly
Capt. Denbighshire Yeomanry Cavalry; was M.P. for
Peterborough in 1852 and 1855-7; re-elected 1859.
—Residence: Plas Madog, Ruabon, N. Wales; Reform
Club, s.w.; 4, St. James' Place, s.w.

WHALLEY-SMYTHE-GARDINER.
(See Gardiner.)

WHARNCLIFFE, Lord (EDWARD MONTAGU
GRANVILLE STUART-WORTLEY).—Cr. 1826.
Eldest son of John, 2nd Lord, by Lady Georgiana
Elizabeth, dau. of Dudley, 1st Earl of Harrowby; b.
1827; s. 1855; m. 1855 Lady Susan Charlotte, dau. of
Henry, 3rd Earl of Harewood. Is a Magistrate for the
W. Riding of Yorkshire and co. Forfar, and Patron of
3 livings; formerly Capt. Grenadier Guards; repre-
sents a branch of the Bute family.— Worthy Hall,
Sheffield; Simonstone, Wensleydale; Balcaskie Castle,
Meade, Forfarshire, N.B.; White's, Guards, and Tra-
vellers' Clubs, s.w.; Wharncliffe House, Curzon Street, w.

Heir Pres., his brother Francis Dudley, of Overton House,
near Wakefield, a Magistrate for the W. Riding of co.
York, and a Barrister-at-Law of the Inner Temple; b.
1829; m. 1855 Maria Elizabeth, dau. of the late William
Bennet Martin, Esq., of Worsbrough Hall, co. York, and
has, with other issue, * Francis John, b. 1856.

WHARTON, JOHN THOMAS, Esq., of Skelton Castle, and Gilling Wood, Yorkshire.

Eldest son of the late Rev. William Wharton, Vicar of Gilling (who *d.* 1842), by the Hon. Charlotte, dau. of Thomas, 1st Lord Dundas; *b.* 1809; *s.* his uncle 1843; *m.* 1854 Charlotte, dau. of Henry W. Yooman, Esq., and Lady Margaret Yeoman, of Woodlands, and has issue,
* William Henry Anthony, *b.* 1859.

Mr. Wharton, who was educated at the Charterhouse and Trinity Coll., Cambridge (M.A. 1830), is a J.P. and D.L. for N. Riding of Yorkshire.—*Skelton Castle, Redcar; Oxford and Cambridge Club,* s.w.

WHARTON, WILLIAM LLOYD, Esq., of Dryburn, co. Durham.

Eldest son of the late Rev. Robert Wharton, Chancellor of Lincoln, by Sar.h, dau. of the Rev. John Whaley, Rector of Huggate, co. York; *b.* 1789; *m.* 1818 Frances, dau. of the Rev. H. Jacob, of The Close, Salisbury. Educated at Eton and Pembroke Coll., Cambridge (B.A. 1813), M.A. 1816); called to the Bar at Lincoln's Inn 1820; is a Magistrate for co. Durham (High Sheriff 1836).—*Dryburn, Durham,.*

Heir Pres., his brother John, a Magistrate for the N. Riding of co. York; *b.* 1793; *m.* 1832 Mary, 2nd dau. of Rev. H. Jacob, of Salisbury, and has, with other issue, * John Lloyd, *b.* 1837.

WHARTON-DUFF. (See *Duff.*)

WHATLEY, the Rev. HENRY LAWSON, of Aston Ingham, Herefordshire.

Fifth son of the late Rev. Charles Whatley, Rector of Aston Ingham, by Margaretta Elizabeth Anne, dau. of Frances Lawson, Esq., of Wimbledon House, Surrey; *b.* 1801; *s.* 1835; *m.* 1833 Anne, dau. of Rev. Joseph Higgins, Rector of Eastnor, and has, with other issue,
* Joseph Higgins, *b.* 1834; Solicitor, of Great Malvern.

Mr. Whatley, who was educated at Pembroke Coll., Oxford (B.A. 1823); is a Magistrate for co. Hereford; and Rector and Patron of Aston Ingham.—*Aston Ingham, La, Herefordshire.*

WHATLEY, the Rev. HENRY LAWSON, Jun., of Peopleton, Worcestershire.

Second son of the Rev. Henry Lawson, of Aston Ingham, co. Hereford (whom see), by Anne, dau. of the late Rev. Joseph Higgins; *b.* 1837; *m.* 1864 Isabella Margaret, 4th dau. of the late Benjamin Hooke, Esq., of Norton Hall, co. Worcester, and has issue, *Florence Isabella. Mr. Whatley, who was educated at University Coll., Durham (B.A. 1863), is Rector of North Piddle, co. Worcester.—*Peopleton, Pershore.*

WHATMAN, JAMES, Esq., F.R.S., of Vinters, Kent.

Eldest son of the late James Whatman, Esq., of Vinters, by Eliza Susanna, dau. of Samuel Richard Gaussen, Esq., M.P. of Brookman's Park, Herts; *b.* 1813; *s.* 1843; *m.* 1850 Louisa Isabella, dau. of the late Charles Ross, Esq., and has surviving issue five daughters. Mr. Whatman, who was educated at Eton and Ch Ch., Oxford (B.A. 1834, M.A. 1838), is a J.P. and D.L. for Kent, and a Commissioner of Lieutenancy for London; late Capt. W. Kent Militia; was M.P. for Maidstone 1852, for West Kent 1857-9, re-elected for Maidstone 1865—*Vinters, Maidstone; St. James's and Reform Clubs,* s.w.; 6, *Carlton Gardens,* s.w.

WHEATLEY-BALME. (See *Balme.*)

+**WHEATLEY**, Lieut.-Col. WILLIAM, of Erith, Kent.

Eldest son of the late Col. Wheatley, of the R. Glamorgan Militia, by Martha his wife (she *d.* 1862); *b.* 1822. Educated at Eton; entered the Army in 1830;
986

is a Magistrate for Kent; was formerly Lieut.-Col. Scots Fusilier Guards (retired 1859).—*Erith, Dartford; Guards' Club,* s.w.

WHEATSTONE, Sir CHARLES, F.R.S. (cr. 1868).

Son of the late Mr. C. Wheatstone, of Gloucester; *b.* 1802. Appointed Professor of Experimental Philosophy in King's Coll., London, 1834; was one of the Jurors of the Paris Universal Exhibition 1855; an Associate of the Ordnance Select Committee at Woolwich during the Crimean War 1855-9; has received the degrees of D.C.L. and LL.D. from the Universities of Oxford and Cambridge; knighted for his discoveries in connection with the electric telegraph; is a Corresponding Member of the Institute of France, and a Knight of the Legion of Honour; has been Vice-President of the Royal Society.—19. *Park Crescent, Regent's Park,* n.w.

WHEBLE, JAMES JOSEPH, Esq., of Bulmershe, Berks.

Eldest son of the late James Wheble, Esq., of Woodley Lodge, Berks (who *d.* 1840), by his 2nd wife Mary, dau. of Timothy O'Brien, Esq., of Kilcor; *b.* 1818; *m.* 1850 Lady Catherine Elizabeth, 2nd dau. of Thomas, 3rd Earl of Howth, K.P., and has, with other issue,
* James St. Lawrence, *b.* 1853.

Mr. Wheble, who was educated at St. Mary's Coll., Oscott, is a J.P. and D.L. for Berks (High Sheriff 1855); late Capt. Berks Militia.—*Bulmershe Court, Reading; Stafford Club,* w.; *Reform Club,* s.w.

+**WHEELER**, EDWARD, Esq., of The Rocks, co. Kilkenny.

Son of the late E. Wheeler, Esq., of The Rocks; *b.* 18—; *m.* 1860 Josephine, dau. of Dr. Helsham. of Park Place, London. Is a Magistrate for co. Kilkenny.—*The Rocks, Kilkenny, Ireland.*

WHEELER, EDWARD VINCENT, Esq., of Kyrewood, Worcestershire.

Eldest son of the late Vincent Wood Wheeler, Esq., of Newnham Court, co. Worcester, by Frances, dau. of James Graham, Esq., of Ludlow; *b.* 1831; *s.* 1853; *m.* 1854 Marianne, dau. of the Rev. James Vashon, of Salworp, co. Worcester, and has, with other issue,
* Edward Vincent Vashon, *b.* 1854.

Mr. Wheeler, who was educated at Rugby and Trinity Coll., Cambridge, is a Magistrate for co. Salop, and a J.P. and D.L. for co. Worcester (High Sheriff 1857). —*Kyrewood House, and Newnham Court, Tenbury.*

WHEELER, the Rev. GEORGE DOMVILE, of Barcheston, Warwickshire.

Only son of the late Rev. G. Wheeler, by Margaret, sister of the late Sir Compton Domvile, Bart., M.P., of Santry House, &c., co. Dublin; *b.* 1815; *s.* 1838; *m.* 1st 1843 Charlotte Emily, dau. and eventually co-heir of the late Admiral C. P. Boteler Bateman (she *d.* 1851); 2nd 1857 Sarah Anne, dau. of John Chetwynd, Esq., late Capt. 52nd Light Infantry, and A.D.C. to Sir John Moore at Corunna, and has, with other issue,
* George Domvile Chetwynd, *b.* 1843.

Mr. Wheeler, who was educated at Oriel and Wadham Colls., Oxford (B.A. 1837. M.A. 1839), is a Magistrate for cos. Warwick, Gloucester, and Worcester, Patron of 1 living, and Rector of Barcheston.—*Wolford Vicarage, Shipston-on-Stour.*

WHEELEY, JOHN GRIFFITHS, Esq., of The Pentre, Monmouthshire.

Eldest son of the late Robert Wheeley, Esq. of The Pentre, by Anne, dau. of the Rev. — Jenkins, Rector of Llanofoist; *b.* 1833; *s.* 1855; educated at Cheltenham Coll., is a Magistrate for co. Monmouth. and Capt. Monmouthshire Militia. *The Pentre &c.*

WHELAN, WM. CURTEIS, Esq., of Heronden, Kent.

Only son of the late William Whelan, Esq., Banker, of Heronden Hall, by Elizabeth Bradley Jane, only dau. and heir of Cornelius Neap, Esq., of London; b. 1817; s. 1851; m. 1851 Katherine Frances, eldest dau. of James R. Planché, Esq., of Her Majesty's College of Arms, London, and has issue,

* William Hugh Curteis, b. 1853.

Mr. Whelan, who was called to the Bar at Lincoln's Inn 1842, represents a family of Irish origin.—*Heronden Hall, Tenterden.*

WHELER, Sir TREVOR, Bart., of Leamington, Warwickshire (cr. 1660).

Eldest son of the late Sir Trevor Wheler, Bart., by Harriet, dau. of Richard Beresford, Esq., of Ashbourne, co. Derby; b. 1792; s. as 9th Bart. 1830; m. 1st 1817 Lucy, dau. of George Dandridge, Esq., of The Commandery, Worcester; 2nd 1865 Frances, 2nd dau. of the late Rev. William Carus-Wilson, and widow of the Rev. Jocelyn Willey, of Camblesforth Hall, co. York. Educated at Rugby and Royal Military Coll., Marlow; is a Magistrate for cos. Warwick and Devon; late Lieut.-Col. Commandant N. Devon Yeomanry Cavalry, and a Major in the Army unattached; was formerly Major 5th Dragoon Guards.—*Limerick House, Leamington; Camblesforth Hall, Selby, Yorkshire; Cross, Torrington; United Service Club, s.w.*

Heir Pres., his brother Francis, Major-General Bengal Army; b. 1801; m. 1st 1827 Caroline, dau. of the Rev. C. Palmer; 2nd 1834 Elizabeth, dau. of the late William Bishop, Esq.

WHELER, the Rev. CHARLES, of Ledstone, Yorkshire, and Otterden, Kent.

Son of the late Granville William Hastings Medhurst, Esq., of Kippax Hall, co. York, by Sarah, dau. of — Jenyns, Esq.; b. 1794; s. 1843 his cousin Granville Hastings Wheler, Esq., whose name he assumed; m. 1831 Anne, eldest dau. of the late Rev. James Landon, Vicar of Aberford, co. York, and has, with other issue,

* Charles, educated at Eton, and M.A. of Ch. Ch., Oxford; a Magistrate for the W. Riding of Yorkshire, and Lieut. Royal E. Kent Mounted Rifles; b. 1834.

Mr. Wheler, who was educated at C.C.C., Oxford (B.A. 1817, M.A. 1821), is Patron of 4 livings, and of 1 alternate.—*Ledstone Hall, Normanton; Otterden Place, Sittingbourne; Oxford and Cambridge Club, s.w.*

WHICHCOTE, Sir THOMAS, Bart., of Aswarby Hall, Lincolnshire (cr. 1660).

Eldest son of the late Sir Thomas Whichcote, Bart., of Aswarby Hall, by Lady Sophia Sherard, dau. of Philip, 5th Earl of Harborough (ext.); b. 1813; s. as 7th Bart. 1829; m. 1st 1839 Marianne, dau. of Henry Beckett, Esq.; 2nd 1856 Isabella Elizabeth, dau. of the late Sir Henry C. Montgomery, Bart. Is a Dep.-Lieut. for co. Lincoln, Lord of the Manors of Harpswell and Hempswell, &c., Patron of 4 livings, and Major S. Lincolnshire Militia.—*Aswarby Hall, Folkingham; Carlton Club, s.w.*

Heir Pres., his brother George. b. 1817; m. 1866 Louisa Day, 3rd dau. of the late Thos. William Clagett, Esq., of Fetcham.

WHICHCOTE, the Rev. CHRISTOPHER.

Eighth son of the late Sir Thomas Whichcote, Bart., of Aswarby Hall (who d. 1828), by Diana, dau. of Edmund Turnor, Esq., of Stoke Rochford, co. Lincoln; b. 1806; m. 1832 Harriet, only dau. of Thomas Tryon, Esq., of Bulwick Park, co. Northampton. Educated at St. John's Coll., Cambridge (B.A. 1828, M.A. 1831); is a Magistrate for co. Lincoln.—*Aswarby Rectory, Folkingham; National Club, s.w.*

WHIELDON, the Rev. EDWARD, of Hales Hall, Staffordshire.

Eldest son of the late Rev. Edward Whieldon, of Hales Hall, by Mary, dau. of John Bill, Esq., of Farley Hall; b. 1824; s. 1859; m. 1864 Mary Harriet, eldest dau. of the late Rev. William Sandford, of Newport, co. Salop. Educated at Shrewsbury and St. John's Coll., Cambridge (B.A. 1847, M.A. 1850); is Incumbent of Croxden and Bradley-le-Moors.—*Hales Hall, Cheadle.*

WHIELDON, GEORGE, Esq., of Wyke Hall, Dorset.

Eldest son of the late George Whieldon, Esq., of The Grove, Hants, and Springfield House, co. Warwick, (High Sheriff of co. Warwick 1847), by Mary, dau. of Richard Brettell, Esq., of Finstall House, co. Worcester; b. 1817; m. 1847 Anne, widow of James Mortimer, Esq., of Wyke Hall, Dorset, and Ferry Hill, co. Aberdeen (she d. 1861). Educated at Winchester and Trinity Coll., Oxford; is a J.P. and D.L. for Dorset (High Sheriff 1863).—*Wyke Hall, Gillingham, Dorset.*

WHIGHAM, JAMES, Esq., of Margreig, Kirkcudbrightshire.

Fourth son of the late Robert Whigham, Esq., of Halliday Hill, co. Dumfries, by Elizabeth, dau. of the late Robert Kennedy, Esq., of Knocknalling, co. Kirkcudbright; b. 1808; m. 1847 Emma, dau. of the late Laurence Brock-Hollinshead, Esq., of Highfield, co. Lancaster, and has, with other issue,

* Laurence Robert, b. 1848.

Mr. Whigham, who was educated at Edinburgh, and is a Member of the Council of the University, was called to the Bar at Lincoln's Inn 1832; he is a Magistrate for Bucks, and Judge of the County Courts in Circuit No. 37, and was formerly a Barrister of the Northern Circuit.—*Margreig, Irongray, Kirkcudbrightshire, N.B.; 4, Craven Terrace, Ealing, Middlesex, w.*

WHINYATES, Major-Gen. FREDERICK WILLIAM, of Walton, Cumberland.

Son of the late Major Thomas Whinyates, of Abbotsleigh, Devon, by Catherine, 6th dau. of the late Admiral Sir Thomas Frankland, Bart., and brother of the late Gen. Sir E. C. Whinyates, K.C.B.; b. 1793; s. his brother 1865; m. 1830 Sarah Marianne, dau. of the late Charles Whalley, Esq., of Stow-on-the-Wold, and has, with other issue,

* Frederick Thomas, Capt. R.H.A.; b. 1833.

Major-Gen. Whinyates was educated at the Royal Military Academy, Woolwich; is a Major-Gen. in the Army; he was formerly Col. R.E. This family was settled in Chelbaston, co. Derby, A.D. 1581, and afterwards in Peterborough, co. Northampton, and in the South of Devon.—*Walton, Carlisle; Dorset Villa, Cheltenham; United Service Club, s.w.*

WHIPPY, Mrs., of Lee Place, Oxon.

Fine Susanna 2nd dau. of Benjamin Holloway, Esq., of Lee Place; m. 1828 Benjamin John Whippy, Esq., a J.P. and D.L. for Oxon (High Sheriff 1855), and Major Oxfordshire Yeomanry Cavalry, who d. 1868. — *Lee Place, Enstone.*

WHITACRE, JOHN, Esq., of Woodhouse, Yorkshire.

Only son of the late John Whitacre, Esq., of Woodhouse, by Ann, 3rd dau. of the late Samuel Walker, Esq., of Masborough, near Rotherham, co. York; b. 1786. Is a Dep.-Lieut. for the W. Riding of Yorkshire.—*Woodhouse, Huddersfield.*

WHITAKER, the Rev. CHARLES, of Symonstone, Lancashire.

Eldest son of the late Charles Whitaker, Esq., of Symonstone, by Eliza, dau. of the late Samuel Horrocks, Esq., M.P., of Lark Hill, co. Lancaster; *b.* 1815; *s.* 1843. Educated at Brasenose Coll., Oxford (B.A. 1840); is Lord of the Manor of Symonstone.—*Symonstone Hall, Padiham, Lancashire.*

Heir Pres., his sister Eliza, *m.* 1849 the Rev. Thomas M. Raven.

WHITAKER, the Rev. GEORGE AYTON, of Knoddishall, Suffolk.

Second surviving son of the late Rev. Thomas Whitaker, M.A., of Mendham, Norfolk, by Jane, dau. of John Ayton, Esq., D.L., of Earl Soham Lodge, Suffolk; *b.* 1806; *m.* 1830 Anna Maria, 2nd dau. of the late Thomas Farr, Esq., of Beccles, Suffolk, and has, with other issue,

  * George Ayton, in Holy Orders, M.A. of Trinity Coll., Cambridge. and Rector of Henstead, Suffolk ; *b.* 1833 ; *m.* 1859 Mary Henrietta, only dau. of Edward Farrer Acton, Esq., J.P. and D.L., of Gatacre Park, co. Salop.

Mr. Whitaker, who was educated at Emmanuel Coll., Cambridge (B.A. 1830, M.A. 1841), is a Magistrate for Suffolk, Rector and Patron of Knoddishall and Rural Dean.—*Knoddishall Rectory, Saxmundham.*

WHITAKER, JAMES, Esq., of Hampton Hall, Salop.

Second son of the late James Whitaker, Esq., of Broadclough, co. Lancaster (who *d.* 1855), by Harriet, dau. of John Ormerod, Esq., of Bankside, near Bacup; *b.* 1831 ; *m.* 1863 Elizabeth, 2nd dau. of Lieut.-Col. Every Clayton, of Rowley, co. Lancaster, and has issue,

  * Two daughters.

Mr. Whitaker is a Magistrate for co. Salop.—*Hampton Hall, Worthen, Shrewsbury.*

WHITAKER, JOHN, Esq., of Broadclough, Lancashire.

Eldest son of the late James Whitaker, Esq., of Broadclough, by Harriet, youngest dau. of John Ormerod, Esq., of Bankside; *b.* 1829 ; *s.* 1855; *m.* 1858 Elizabeth Ann, dau. of Robert Munn, Esq., of Heath Hill, and has, with other issue,

  * James, *b.* 1863.

Mr. Whitaker, who is a Magistrate for co. Lancaster, represents a family first settled at Broadclough about A.D. 1500.—*Broadclough, Bacup.*

WHITAKER, JOHN, Esq., of Caldewell, Worcestershire.

Eldest son of the late Thomas Whitaker, Esq., of Caldewell, by Mary, dau. of John Hunt, Esq., of Naunton Beauchamp; *b.* 1805; *s.* 1833. Is a Magistrate for co. Worcester. This family were formerly seated in Cheshire.—*Caldewell, Kempsey.*

Heir Pres., his brother George, *b.* 1810.

WHITAKER, THOMAS HOLDEN, Esq., F.S.A., of The Holme, Lancashire.

Only son of the late Rev. Thomas Thoresby Whitaker, of The Holme, by Jane, eldest dau. of James Hordern, Esq., of Wolverhampton; *b.* 1814 ; *s.* 1834 ; *m.* 1st 1848 Mary, dau. of James B. Garforth, Esq., of Coniston, co. York; 2nd 1851 Margaret Nowell, youngest dau. of the Rev. J. Robinson, of Netherside, Craven, and has issue,

  Mary Charlotte.

Mr. Whitaker, who was educated at the Charterhouse and Exeter Coll., Oxford (B.A. 1836), is a J.P. and D.L. for co. Lancaster, and a Magistrate for the W. Riding of Yorkshire.—*The Holme, Burnley ; Athenæum Club, s.w.*

988

WHITAKER, WILLIAM WILLIAMSON, Esq., of Breckamore, Yorkshire.

Eldest son of the late Charles Whitaker, Esq., of Melton Hill, by Rachel, dau. of Horner Reynard, Esq., of Sunderlandwick ; *b.* 1813 ; *m.* 1834 Elizabeth, dau. of the late Marmaduke Hodgson, Esq., of Breckamore, co. York, and has, with other issue,

  * Marmaduke William, B.A. of Trinity Hall, Cambridge, and a Barrister-at-Law of the Inner Temple ; *b.* 1837 ; *m.* 1862 Gertrude Mary, dau. of Basil Thomas Woodd. Esq.. M.P., of Conyngham Hall, near Knaresborough, co. York.

Mr. Whitaker is a Magistrate for the E., W., and N. Ridings of co. York, and for the Liberty of Ripon. —*Breckamore, Ripon.*

WHITBREAD, the Rev. EDMUND SALTER, of Strumpshaw, Norfolk.

Third son of the late Jacob Whitbread, Esq., of Loudham Park, Suffolk; by his second wife Eleanor, dau. of J. Salter, Esq.; *b.* 1805; *m.* 1829 Charlotte Matilda, dau. of John Josselyn, Esq., of Sproughton, Suffolk ; and has, with other issue,

  * Edmund Jacob, *b.* 1835 ; *m.* 1863 Adelaide Thornton, dau. of Major-Gen. George Freeman Murray.

Mr. Whitbread, who was educated at Trinity Hall, Cambridge (B.A. 1828, M.A. 1832), is a Magistrate for Norfolk, and a Rector and Patron of Strumpshaw and Braydeston. This family is descended from a common ancestor with the Whitbreads of Bedfordshire (whom see).—*Strumpshaw Rectory, Burlingham, Norwich.*

WHITBREAD, Capt. JACOB WILLIAM CAREY, of Loudham Park, Suffolk.

Eldest son of the late Jacob Whitbread, Esq., of Loudham Park, Suffolk ; by his second wife Louisa, dau. of Samuel Mitchell, Esq., of Croft West, Cornwall, and who was Lord High Admiral of the Portugueso Navy; *b.* 1820 ; *s.* 1858 ; *m.* 1858 Ellen Belfield, 3rd dau. of Christopher Farwell, Esq., of Totnes, Devon, and has, with other issue,

  * Howard, Capt. East Suffolk Artillery Militia, and a Capt. in the Army ; *b.* 1843 ; *m.* 1864 Louisa, elder dau. of the late S. Fyson, Esq.

Capt. Whitbread is Lord of the Manors of Ufford and Loudham. This family are the elder branch of the Whitbreads of Southill.—*Loudham Park, Woodbridge ; United Service Institution, Whitehall, s.w.*

WHITBREAD, SAMUEL CHARLES, Esq., of Southill and Cardington, Bedfordshire.

Eldest surviving son of the late Samuel Whitbread, Esq., M.P., of Cardington and Southill (who *d.* 1815). by Lady Elizabeth, dau. of Charles, 1st Earl Grey, K.G.; *b.* 1796; *s.* his brother 1867 ; *m.* 1st 1824 the Hon. Juliana, 2nd dau. of Henry Otway, 22nd Lord Dacre (she *d.* 1858) ; 2nd 1868 Lady Mary, 3rd dau. of William Charles, 4th Earl of Albemarle, and widow of Henry Frederick Stephenson, Esq.; he has by the former, with other issue,

  * Samuel, educated at Eton and Trinity Coll., Cambridge, a J.P. and D.L. for Beds. M.P. for Bedford, and a Lord of the Admiralty ; *b.* 1830 ; *m.* 1855 Lady Isabella, dau. of Henry Thomas, and Earl of Chichester, and has issue, a son, *b.* 1867.

Mr. Whitbread, who was educated at Eton and St. John's Coll., Cambridge, is a J.P. and D.L. for Beds (High Sheriff 1831) and Patron of 5 livings ; was formerly M.P. for Middlesex. This family have been seated in Bedfordshire for two centuries.—*Southill, Biggleswade ; Cardington, Bedford ; Brooks's Club, s.w.*

WHITBY, Capt. THOMAS EDWARD, of Creswell Hall, Staffordshire.

Only son of the late George Whitby, Esq., of Creswell Hall, by Emmeretta, dau. of Edward Ratcliff, Esq., of Wood Hall, Wormingford, Essex ; *b.* 1823 ; *s.* 1852 ; *m.* 1855 Sophia Jane, only dau. of George Garrow, Esq.,

of the Madras Civil Service. widow of Lieut.-Col. Schonswar, and has, with other issue,

  * Edward Garrow, b. 1857.

Capt. Whitby, who was educated at Shrewsbury and Trinity Coll., Cambridge, and was formerly Capt. 3rd Dragoon Guards, is a J.P. and D.L. for co. Stafford, Lord of the Manors of Creswell and Tillington, and Patron of 1 living.—*Creswell Hall, Stafford ; Army and Navy Club,* s.w.

WHITE, Sir Thomas Woollaston, Bart., of Wallingwells, Notts (cr. 1802).

Eldest son of the late Sir Thomas Woollaston White, Bart., of Wallingwells, by Elizabeth, dau. of Thomas Blagg, Esq., of Tuxford, Notts ; *b.* 1801 ; *s.* as 2nd Bart. 1817 ; *m.* 1st 1824 Georgina, dau. of G. Ramsay, Esq., of Barnton, near Edinburgh ; 2nd 1827 Mary Euphemia, dau. of William Ramsay, Esq., of Edinburgh. Educated at Rugby ; is a J.P. and D.L. for Notts (High Sheriff 1839) ; was formerly Cornet 16th Lancers, 3rd Light Dragoons, and 10th Hussars ; late Lieut.-Col. of Notts Militia and Sherwood Rangers Yeomanry Cavalry. —*Wallingwells, Worksop.*

  Heir, his son Thomas Woollaston, Major 16th Lancers ; *b.* 1838.

WHITE, the Hon. Charles William.

Second surviving son of Henry, 1st Lord Annaly, by Ellen, eldest dau. of the late William S. Dempster, Esq. ; *b.* 1839. Educated at Trinity Coll., Dublin ; is a Capt. Scots Fusilier Guards ; elected M.P. for co. Tipperary 1866.—*Woodlands, Clonsilla, co. Dublin ; Guards' Club,* s.w. ; 7, *Minera Street, Chester Square,* s.w.

+WHITE, Algernon Holt, Esq., of Clement's Hall, Essex.

Only son of the late Thomas Holt White, Esq., of Clement's Hall, by Louisa, dau. of John Rashleigh, Esq., of Penquite, Cornwall (she *d.* 1860) ; *b.* 1808 ; *m.* 1838 Emma Louisa, only dau. of the late Thomas Harrison, Esq., of Streatham Park, Surrey, and has, with other issue,

  * Thomas Holt, b. 1842.

Mr. White is a Magistrate for Essex.—*Clement's Hall, Rochford.*

WHITE, George, Esq., of Keildra, co. Leitrim.

Eldest surviving son of the late William White, Esq., by Isabella, dau. of the Rev. Henry Paget Baillie ; *b.* 1828 ; *m.* 1851 Mary, dau. of Henry Hill, Esq., late of Ruislip Park, Middlesex, and has issue,

  * William Henry, b. 1855.

Mr. White is a J.P. and D.L. for co. Leitrim (High Sheriff 1861).—*Residence: Kilmore, Artane, co. Dublin.*

+WHITE, Henry William, Esq., of Monar and Lentran, Ross-shire.

Son of the late — White, Esq., of Lentran ; *b.* 18—. Is a J.P. and D.L. for co. Inverness and a Magistrate for co. Ross.—*Lentran House, Inverness, N.B.*

WHITE, James, Esq.

Second son of William White, Esq., of Tulse Hill, Surrey ; *b.* 1809 ; *m.* 1833 Mary, eldest dau. of Addison Lind, Esq., of Jamaica. Is a Merchant largely engaged in the China trade ; formerly an Alderman of London ; was M.P. for Plymouth 1857-9 ; elected M.P. for Brighton 1861—11, *Chichester Terrace, Brighton ; Reform Club,* s.w. ; 2, *Queen's Gate, Hyde Park,* w.

WHITE, the Rev. William, of Chevington, Suffolk.

Eldest son of the late Rev. John White, of Chevington, by Mary, dau. of the Rev. Thomas Image, of Whepstead ; *b.* 1829 ; *s.* 1852 ; *m.* 1855 Caroline Machinell

dau. of John Rawlins, Esq., of Handsworth, and has, with other issue,

  * John, b. 1857.

Mr. White, who was educated at Caius Coll., Cambridge (B.A. 1851, M.A. 1854), is Rector and Patron of Chevington.—*Chevington Rectory, Bury St. Edmund's.*

+WHITE, the late John, Esq., of Park Hall, Derbyshire.

Son of the late — White, Esq., of Park Hall ; *b.* 1790 ; *d.* 1866. Was a J.P. and D.L. for co. Derby.—*Park Hall, Hayfield, Stockport.*

+WHITE, John, Esq., of Drummelzier, Peebles-shire.

Son of the late — White, Esq., of Drummelzier ; *b.* 18—. Is a J.P. and D.L. for co. Peebles.—*Drummelzier, Biggar, N.B.*

WHITE, John, Esq., of Belmont, co. Limerick.

Youngest son of the late Jasper White, Esq., of Limerick, by Helen, dau. of Jasper Creagh, Esq., of Limerick ; *b.* 1793 ; *m.* 1835 Eleanor Mary, dau. of Richard Irwin, Esq., and has, with other issue,

  * Jasper John, b. 1839.

Mr. White, who was educated at Oscott Coll., is a Magistrate for co. Limerick (High Sheriff 1856), and was formerly Col. in the Royal Kingston Militia.—*Belmont, Castle Connell, co. Limerick ; Nantenan, Rathkeale, co. Limerick.*

WHITE, Joseph, Esq., of Bredfield, Suffolk.

Eldest son of the late Joseph White. Esq., of Sutton Hall, co. Chester, by Susan, dau. of Robert Pretyman, Esq., of Stoke, near Ipswich ; *b.* 1818 ; *m.* 1855 Emily, dau. of R. H. Lachlan, Esq., of Gloucester Gardens, Hyde Park, and has, with other issue,

  * Joseph, b. 1859.

Mr. White who was educated at Rugby and Trinity Hall, Cambridge, is a Magistrate for Suffolk.—*Bredfield House, Woodbridge.*

WHITE, Capt. Laurence Esmonde, of Newlands, co. Wexford.

Second son of the late Laurence Esmonde White. Esq., of Scarnagh, co. Wexford, by Jane, dau. of Thomas Plunkett, Esq., of Portmarnock, co. Dublin ; *b.* 1809 ; *m.* 1841 Fanny, only dau. of Richard Tayler, Esq., of Bedford, and has, with other issue,

  * Raymonde Esmonde, Lieut. 27th Inniskillings ; b. 1842.

Capt. White is a Magistrate for cos. Wexford and Carlow, late Capt. 84th Foot.—*Newlands, Ballycarney, Ferns.*

WHITE, Matthew Esmonde, Esq., M.B., of Killoughter, co. Wicklow.

Eldest son of the late Laurence Esmonde White, Esq., of Scarnagh, co. Wexford, by Jane, dau. of Thomas Plunkett, Esq., of Portmarnock House, co. Dublin ; *b.* 1801 ; *s.* 1845 ; *m.* 1832 Catharine, eldest dau. and co-heir of Thomas Byrne, Esq., of Killoughter, co. Wicklow, and has, with other issue,

  * Esmonde Thomas, b. 1834.

Mr. White, who was educated at Trinity Coll., Dublin (B.A. 1822, M.A. 1827; M.B. 1827), is a Magistrate for co. Carlow.—*Killoughter, Ballynakinch.*

WHITE, Mrs., of Upperwood House, Yorkshire.

Jane, only surviving daughter of the late Jasper Robson, Esq., of Idle, co. York, and formerly of Northumberland ; *m.* 1830 John White, Esq., of Upperwood House, by whom, who *d.* 1860, she has, with other surviving issue, *Arthur Robson, b.* 1840.—*Residence: Charlton House, Bellingham.*

WHITE, Mrs., of Charlton House, Dorset.
Margaret, dau. of Jacob Hagen (Baron von Iseltein), of Surrey; *m.* 1809 Samuel White, Esq., of Charlton House, who *d.* 1867, leaving issue.—*Charlton House, Blandford; Farncombe, Godalming.*

WHITE, ROBERT HEDGES EYRE, Esq., of Glengarriffe, co. Cork.
Eldest son of the late Col. Simon White (who was brother of Richard, 1st Earl of Bantry), by Sarah, dau. of Richard Newenham, Esq., of Maryborough; *b.* 1809; *s.* in 1840 to the Tipperary estates of R. Hedges Eyre, Esq., of Macroom Castle; *m.* 1834 Charlotte, only child and heir of Thomas Donnan, Esq., of Raffeen House, co. Cork, and has, with other issue,
  • Robert Hedges Eyre, a Magistrate for co. Cork, *b.* 1836; *m.* 1860 Minnie D'Esterre, youngest dau. of the late John Roberts, Esq., of Ardmore.
Mr. White was formerly Capt. in the Rifle Brigade.—*Raffeen House, and Glengarriffe Castle, Cork.*

+WHITE, ROBERT OWEN, Esq., of Swanscombe, Kent.
Eldest son of the late John Bazeley White, Esq., of Swanscombe; *b.* 18—. Is a Magistrate for Kent.—*Swanscombe, Gravesend.*

WHITE, Mrs. SAMUEL, of Killakee, co. Dublin.
Anne Salisbury, dau. of the late George Rothe, Esq., of Mount Rothe, co. Kilkenny, by Anne Salisbury Jephson, of Carrick House, Carrick-on-Snir; *m.* 1821 Samuel White, Esq., of Killakee (brother of Lord Annaly), who was M.P. for co. Leitrim 1824-47, and *d.* 1854.—*Killakee House, Rathfarnham, co. Dublin.*

WHITE, THOMAS, Esq., of Peppard's Castle, co. Wexford.
Only surviving son of the late Henry White, Esq., of Peppard's Castle (who was an Officer 5th Foot), by Catharine, dau. of the late Thomas Whelan, Esq., of Newstown House, co. Carlow; *b.* 1820; *s.* 1855; *m.* 1851 Barbara Jane, dau. of the late Thomas Battersby, Esq., of Newcastle House, co. Meath, and has, with other issue,
  • Henry James, *b.* 1852.
Mr. White, who was educated at Trinity Coll., Dublin, is a Magistrate for co. Wexford.—*Peppard's Castle, Clonevan, co. Wexford.*

WHITE, THOMAS GEORGE GRAHAM, Esq., of Wethersfield and Berechurch, Essex.
Eldest son of the late Thomas White, Esq., J.P. and D.L., of Wethersfield and Berechurch (High Sheriff of Essex 1854), by Charlotte, only dau. and heir of the late Sir George Henry Smyth, Bart., M.P., of Berechurch Hall; *b.* 1834; *s.* 1861. Is a Magistrate for Essex, Lord of the Manor of Wethersfield, late Lieut. 12th Essex Rifle Volunteers. — *The Manor House, Wethersfield, Braintree; Berechurch Hall, Colchester.*

WHITE, WILLIAM LOGAN, Esq., of Kellerslain, Midlothian.
Eldest son of the late John White, Esq., by Elizabeth, dau. of John Logan, Esq., H.E.I.C.S.; *b.* 1793; *m.* 1st 1819 Margaret, eldest dau. of the late Sir Alexander Charles Gibson-Maitland, Bart., of Clifton Hall (she *d.* 1840); 2nd 1844 Jane, youngest dau. of the late Sir James Foulis, Bart., of Colinton, and by her, who *d.* 1858, he has, with other issue,
  • James Maitland, *b.* 1848.
Mr. White, who was educated at Edinburgh University, and called to the Scottish Bar in 1816, is a Magistrate and Commissioner of Supply for co. Midlothian.—*Kellerslain House, Edinburgh.*
990

WHITE, the Rev. WILLIAM SPRANGER, of The Brae, Roxburghshire.
Son of the late W. A. Armstrong White, Esq., of Castor, co. Northampton, by Sarah, dau. of George Newman, Esq., Consul from H.I.M. the Empress Catherine of Russia; *b.* 1809; *m.* 1850 the Hon. Louise Madeline Campbell, eldest dau. of John, 1st Lord Campbell. Educated at Westminster and Trinity Coll., Cambridge (B.A. 1832, M.A. 1835), is Rector of Potter Hanworth; late Vicar of Chaddesley Corbett, and Incumbent of the Episcopal Chapel at Jedburgh.—*The Brae, Jedburgh, N.B.; Potter Hanworth Rectory, Lincoln.*

WHITE. (See under *Annaly, Lord.*)

WHITE. (See *Corrance.*)

WHITE. (See *Jervis-White-Jervis.*)

WHITE. (See *Popham.*)

WHITE-HEDGES. (See under *Bantry, Earl of.*)

WHITEHEAD, Major FREDERICK GEORGE.
Only son of the late Lieut.-General Sir Thomas Whitehead, K.C.B., &c., of Uplands Hall, by Charlotte, dau. of the late James Ness, Esq., of Osgodrie, co. York; *m.* 1851 Frances Elizabeth, dau. of Thomas Fitzgerald, Esq., J.P. and D.L., of Ballina Park, co. Waterford, and has, with other issue,
  • Gerald George, *b.* 1856.
Major Whitehead, who was educated at Eton, and was formerly Capt. 7th Fusiliers and 42nd Highlanders, is Major Essex Rifles Militia, and Lieut.-Col. Commanding North Middlesex Rifle Volunteers.—*Uplands Hall, Preston; Army and Navy, Senior United Service, Conservative, and Junior Carlton Clubs, s.w.; 25, Clifton Gardens, Maida Hill, w.*

WHITEHEAD, GEORGE, Esq., of Riccall, Yorkshire.
Third and only surviving son of the late Matthias Whitehead, Esq., of Park House, Selby, co. York (who *d.* 1848), by Eliza, dau. of John Audus, Esq., of Selby, co. York; *b.* 1833; *m.* 1863 Mary Jane, only dau. of the late Right Hon. Matthew Talbot Baines, M.P., of Lancaster, and has, with other issue,
  • James Audus, *b.* 1864.
Mr. Whitehead, who was educated at St. Peter's Coll., Cambridge (B.A. 1858, M.A. 1861), is a Magistrate for the E. and W. Ridings of Yorkshire, and Cornet Yorkshire Hussars.—*Riccall Hall, Escrick.*

WHITEHEAD, JAMES HEYWOOD, Esq., of Southside, Yorkshire.
Second son of the late William Whitehead, Esq., of Saddleworth, co. York, by Sarah, dau. of James Heywood, Esq., of Little Lever; *b.* 1810. Is a Magistrate for co. Lancaster and the W. Riding of Yorkshire.—*Southside, Saddleworth.*

WHITEHEAD, JOHN, Esq., of Barnjet, Kent.
Eldest surviving son of the late Charles Whitehead, Esq., of Ash Place, Kent, by Mary, dau. of John Miller, Esq., of Ewell, in the same county; *b.* 1793; *m.* 1st 182- Miss Martha Piper, of Conghurst Place, Hawkhurst, Kent; 2nd 1833 Mary, eldest dau. of Thomas Milles, Esq., and has, with other issue,
  • Charles (of St. Helen's), educated at Turbridge, a Magistrate for Kent, and Capt. Queen's Own, West Kent Yeo. Cav.; *b.* 1834; *m.* 1863 Catherine Lætitia, dau. of Richard Ellison Philip Ralston, Esq., of Thornhills, Maidstone, Kent (whom *m.e.*).
Mr. Whitehead is a Magistrate for Kent, and Lord of the Manor of Barnjet.—*Barnjet, Ferrying, Maidstone.*

+ WHITEHEAD, JOSEPH WOOD, Esq , of Alder Grange, Lancashire.-

Eldest son of the late Walter Whitehead, Esq., by Elizabeth, dau. of the late John Buckley, Esq.; *b.* 18—. Is a Magistrate for co. Lancaster, and a Merchant and Manufacturer at Manchester.—*Alder Grange, Rawtenstall, Manchester.*

WHITEHEAD, RALPH RADCLIFFE, Esq., of Amberley Court, Gloucestershire.

Eldest son of the late William Whitehead, Esq., of Saddleworth, co. York, by Sarah, dau. of James Heywood, Esq., of Little Lever, a descendant of Oliver Heywood; *b.* 1808; *m.* 1838 Rebecca, dau. of Edward Hudson, Esq., of Chalford. Is a Magistrate for co. Gloucester, and Patron of 2 livings.—*Amberley Court, Stroud ; National Club, s.w.*

WHITELOCK, the Rev. RICHARD.

Eldest son of the late Rev. Richard Hutchins Whitelock, M.A., by Frances, dau. of Thomas James Storer, Esq., and grand-dau. of John, 1st Lord Carysfort; *b.* 1803 ; *m.* 1830 Mary, dau. of John Elliott, Esq., of Rochdale. Educated at Lincoln Coll., Oxford (B.A. 1826, M.A. 1829); is a Magistrate for co. Lancaster and the W. Riding of Yorkshire.—*The Vicarage, Saddleworth.*

WHITEMAN, JOHN CLARMONT, Esq., of Theydon Grove, Essex.

Only surviving son of the late Andrew Whiteman, Esq., of Grenada, by Martha, dau. of James Edward Smith, Esq., of Lechlade, co. Gloucester; *b.* 1797 ; *m.* 1823 Sarah, dau. of the late Francis Horsley, Esq., of Gaston House, Little Hallingbury, Essex, and has surviving issue four daughters. Mr. Whiteman, who was formerly a Commander in the E.I.C.S., and a Director of the H.E.I.C. is a J.P. and D.L. for Essex (High Sheriff 1846), and a Magistrate for Middlesex.—*Theydon Grove, Epping ; Carlton Club, s.w.*

WHITESIDE, the Right Hon. JAMES, Q.C

Son of the late Rev. William Whiteside; *b.* 1806; *m.* 1833 Mary, dau. of the late William Napier, Esq. Educated at Trinity Coll., Dublin (B.A. 1827); called to the Iri-h Bar 1830 ; was Solicitor-General for Ireland March-Dec. 1852, Attorney-General for Ireland 1858-9; M.P. for Enniskillen 1851-8, and for the University of Dublin 1858-66 : appointed Chief Justice of the Queen's Bench (Ireland) 1866.—2, *Mountjoy Square, Dublin ; University Club, Dublin ; Carlton and Athenæum Clubs, s.w.*

WHITEWAY, PHILIP, Esq., of Runcorn, Cheshire.

Son of the late John Whiteway, Esq., of Kingsteignton, Devon, by Elizabeth, dau. of John Luscombe, Esq.; *b.* 1791; *m.* 1821 Anne, dau. of Robert Cheshyre, Esq., of Weston, Cheshire, and has, with other issue,

    • Robert Cheshyre *b.* 1524.

Mr. Whiteway is a Magistrate for co. Chester.—*Grove House, Runcorn.*

WHITFIELD, the Rev. GEORGE THOMAS, of Pudleston, Herefordshire.

Second son of the late Richard Whitfield, Esq., of St. Thomas's Hospital, London, by Frances Fountain, dau. of Thomas Wade, Esq.; *b.* 1808 ; *m.* 1833 Fanny, dau. of Philip Roberts Wilson, Esq., M.D., of Barnet, Herts (she *d.* 1864). Educated at Merchant Taylors' School and St. John's Coll., Oxford (B.A. 1831, M.A. 1835); is Rector of Pudleston-cum-While.—*Pudleston Rectory, Leominster.*

WHITGREAVE, FRANCIS, Esq., of Burton Manor, Staffordshire.

Second son of the late George Thomas Whitgreave, Esq., of Moseley Court, co. Stafford, by his 1st wife, Amelia, dau. of the late Benjamin Hodges, Esq., of Lambeth, Surrey; *b.* 1819 ; *m.* 1853 Teresa, 7th dau. of the late Sir Edward Mostyn, Bart., of Talacre, co. Flint, and has, with other issue,

    • Robert, *b.* 1855.

Mr. Whitgreave is a J.P. and D.L. for co. Stafford. —*Burton Manor, Stafford.*

WHITGREAVE, HENRY BENJAMIN GEORGE, Esq., of Moseley Court, Staffordshire.

Eldest son of the late George Thomas Whitgreave, Esq., J.P. and D.L., of Moseley Court (High Sheriff of co. Stafford 1837), by his 1st wife Amelia, dau. of Benjamin Hodges, Esq., of London (she *d.* 1848); *b.* 1816 ; *m.* 1st 1841 Henrietta Maria, youngest dau. of the late Hon. Thomas Edward Clifford (she *d.* 1852); 2nd 1858 Mary, dau. of the late Walter Selby, Esq., of Biddleston, Northumberland, and has, by the former, with other issue,

    • Henry George Hugh, *b.* 1842.

Mr. Whitgreave is a J.P. and D.L. for co. Stafford, and Lord of the Manor of Moseley. This family were settled at Whitgreave, co. Stafford. in the reign of King John. His ancestor, Mr. Whitgreave, sheltered Charles II. at Moseley Court after the battle of Worcester. —*Moseley Court, Wolverhampton.*

WHITLA, GEORGE ALEXANDER, Esq., of Lismoyne, co. Antrim.

Only surviving son of the late James Whitla, Esq., J.P., of Golrana, co. Antrim, by Catharine, dau. of the late Alexander Gunning, Esq.; *b.* 1818 ; *s.* 1862 ; *m.* 1858 Isabella Frances, dau. of the late Rev. John Hammond, Rector of Priston, Somerset, and has, with other issue,

    • James Alexander, *b.* 1859.

Mr. Whitla is a Magistrate for co. Antrim and Capt. R. Antrim Rifles.—*Lismoyne, Dunmurry, co. Antrim ; Ulster Club, Belfast.*

WHITLE, ROBERT, Esq., of Halton Hall, Lancashire.

Eldest son of the late Robert Whitle. Esq., of Whalley Abbey, co. Lancaster (who *d.* 1853), Capt. in 59th Foot, by Ann, dau. of Matthew Shaw, Esq., of Manchester; *b.* 1829 ; *m.* 1st 1859 Elizabeth, dau. of the late Lieut.-General Hutchesson, H.A. (she *d.* 1859), 2nd 1867 Eleanor, dau. of James Schofield, Esq., of Heybrook, and has, with other issue,

    • John William, *b.* 1863.

Mr. Whitle is a Magistrate for co. Lancaster, and a Major 1st Duke of Lancaster's Own Militia, also Major 5th Lancashire Rifle Volunteers ; Lord of the Manor of Halton, and Joint Lord of Little Bentley, Essex ; late in the 91st Argyllshire Highlanders.—*Halton Hall, Lancaster ; Junior United Service Club, s.w.*

WHITMORE, CHARLES SHAPLAND, Esq., Q.C., of Lower Slaughter, Gloucestershire.

Eldest surviving son of the late Gen. Sir George Whitmore, K.C.H., of Lower Slaughter, by Cornelia, eldest dau. of George Ainslie, Esq.; *b.* 1805 ; *m.* 1862 ; *m.* 1844 Katharine Elizabeth, eldest dau. of the late Lieut.-Col. Robert J. Browurigg, and sister of Sir Robert W. C. Brownrigg, Bart., and has, with other issue,

    • Charles Algernon, *b.* 1851.

Mr. Whitmore, who was educated at Rugby and Trinity Coll., Cambridge (B.A. 1827, M.A. 1830), and called to the Bar at Inner Temple 1830, became Q.C. and Bencher of the Inner Temple in 1855; is a Magistrate for

co. Gloucester, Recorder of Gloucester, and Lord of the Manor of Lower Slaughter. This family is a branch of the ancient family of Whitmores of Apley, and has been settled at Lower Slaughter for nearly 300 years. — *Manor House, Lower Slaughter, Stow, Gloucestershire; Travellers' and Oxford and Cambridge Clubs*, s.w.; *57, Rutland Gate, Hyde Park*, w.

WHITMORE, the Rev. FRANCIS HENRY WOLRYCHE-, of Dudmaston, Shropshire.
Eldest son of the late Rev. Francis Laing, of The Mythe co. Gloucester, by Mary Dorothea, dau. of William Whitmore, Esq., of Dudmaston, and nephew of the late William Wolryche-Whitmore, Esq.,of Dudmaston Hall; *b.* 1820; *s.* his uncle 1858; *m.* 1845 Isabella, dau. of Capt. Henry Bazely, R.N., and has, with other issue,
   • Francis Alexander. *b.* 1845.
Mr. Whitmore, who was educated at Wadham Coll., Oxford (B.A. 1843, M.A. 1845), is a Magistrate for co. Salop, and Rector of Quatt-Malvern, co. Salop, Lord of the Manors of Quatt and Lebotwood, co. Salop, and Patron of 2 livings; was formerly Incumbent of Forthampton, co. Gloucester; he assumed the name of Wolryche-Whitmore by Royal licence 1861.—*Dudmaston Hall, Bridgnorth ; University Club*, s.w.

WHITMORE, the Rev. GEORGE, of Stockton, Shropshire.
Second son of the late Thomas Whitmore, Esq., of Apley, co. Salop, by Catherine, only dau. aud heir of Thomas Thomason, Esq., of York; *b.* 1812; *m.* 1848 Sarah, 3rd dau. of the late John Deacon, Esq., of Mabledon, Kent, and has, with other issue,
   • Algernon George Bernard. *b.* 1849.
Mr. Whitmore, who was educated at Ch. Ch., Oxford B.A. 1834, M.A. 1836), is a Magistrate for co. Salop, and Rector of Stockton; was formerly Rector of Kemberton and Vicar of Sutton Maddock. This family is a younger branch of the Whitmores of Apley and Dudmaston.—*Stockton Rectory, Shiffnal ; Oxford and Cambridge Club*, s.w.

WHITMORE, HENRY, Esq., of Colebrooke Dale, Shropshire.
Third son of the late Thomas Whitmore, Esq.. M.P., of Apley Park, co. Salop, by Catherine, dau. of Thomas Thomason, Esq., of York ; *b.* 1814 ; *m.* 1852 Adelaide Anna, dau. and co.-heir of the late Francis Darby, Esq., of Colebrooke Dale, Salop. Educated at Ch. Ch., Oxford; is a Dep.-Lieut. for co. Salop; was a Lord of the Treasury and Keeper of the Privy Seal to H.R.H. the Prince of Wales 1858–9; reappointed a Lord of the Treasury 1866; has been M.P. for Bridgnorth since 1852.—*Sunniside, Colebrooke Dale, Wellington ; Carlton and Oxford and Cambridge Clubs*, s.w.; 68, *Eaton Place*, s.w.

WHITMORE, Capt. THOMAS CHARLES DOUGLAS, of Apley Park, Salop.
Eldest son of the late Thomas Charlton Whitmore, Esq., M.P., of Apley (who was High Sheriff of co. Salop 1863), by Lady Louisa Anne, eldest dau. of Charles, 5th Marquis of Queensberry ; *b.* 1839 ; *s.* 1865. Is Patron of 6 livings, and Capt. R. Horse Guards.—*Apley Park, Shiffnal.*

WHITMORE, WILLIAM, Esq., of Beckenham, Kent.
Eldest son of the late William Whitmore, Esq., J.P., of West Wickham, Kent, by Elizabeth, dau. of Monagu Booth, Esq., of Upton, Devon ; *b.* 1797 ; *m.* 1st 1830 Charlotte, dau. of George Norman, Esq., of Bromley Common, Kent (she *d.* 1855); 2nd 1866 Frances Maria, dau. of Francis Hollis Brandram, of Rosemount, St. Leonard's-on-Sea, and widow of the Rev. Aretas Akers.

of Malling Abbey, Kent. Is a Magistrate for Kent, and represents a younger branch of the Whitmores of Apley, co. Salop.—*Beckenham, Kent.*

WHITMORE-JONES, WILLIAM, Esq., of Chastleton, Oxon.
Second son of the late John Henry Whitmore, Esq., of Chastleton (who assumed the name of Jones in 1829, on inheriting that property), by Dorothy, dau. of Col. Thomas Clutton, of Pensax Court. co. Worcester, and Kinnersley Castle, co. Hereford; *b.* 1826 ; *s.* his brother 1857. Is a Magistrate for Oxon; represents a younger branch of the Whitmores of Apley, co. Salop. —*Chastleton House, Moreton-in-Marsh.*
   Heir Pres., his brother Walter Thomas, *b.* 1831.

WHITNEY, THOMAS ANNESLEY, Esq., of Merton, co. Wexford.
Only surviving son of the late Thomas Whitney. Esq., of Merton, by his cousin Alethea, dau. of Thomas Whitney, of Bush Park, co. Wexford ; *b.* 1794 ; *s.* 1831 ; *m.* 1825 Julia, dau. of Luke Gaven, Esq., of Dublin, and by her, who *d.* 1863, has surviving issue,
   • Alice Julia, *m.* 1848 the Rev. Arthur Eden; and Amelia Sarah, *m.* 1859 Henry Alexander Hewetson, Esq.
Mr. Whitney is a Magistrate for co. Wexford.—*Merton, Enniscorthy, co. Wexford.*

WHITSHED, Sir St. VINCENT KEENE HAWKINS-, Bart., of Killincarrick, co. Wicklow (cr. 1834).
Only son of the late Admiral Sir James Hawkins-Whitshed, Bart. (who assumed the name of Whitshed), by Sophia Henrietta, dau. of Capt. John Albert Bentinck, R.N.; *b.* 1801; *s.* as 2nd Bart. 1849; *m.* 1832 the Hon. Elizabeth, dau. of David Montagu, 2nd Lord Erskine. Educated at Ch. Ch., Oxford (B.A. 1824). —*Killincarrick, Greystones.*
   Heir, his son St. Vincent Bentinck, a Magistrate for co. Wicklow (High Sheriff 1867); *b.* 1837 ; *m.* 1868 Alice. youngest dau. of the Hon. and Rev. John Handcock, and has issue, Elizabeth-Alice-Frances.

WHITTAKER, CHARLES GUSTAVUS, Esq., of Barming, Kent.
Eldest son of the late Thomas Whittaker. Esq., of Barming ; *b.* 1792 ; *s.* 1819 ; *m.* 1818 Camilla, dau. of M. Andrus, Esq., of Longfield, Kent, and has, with other issue,
   • Charles. *b.* 1819.
Mr. Whittaker, who was educated at Westminster, is a Magistrate for Kent, and Lord of the Manors of the Temple, Strood, and Buckland.—*Barming, Maidstone.*

WHITTAKER, Major JOHN ABRAHAM, of Newcastle Court, Radnorshire.
Eldest son of the late John Whittaker, Esq., of Newcastle Court, by Mary, dau. of the late Francis Garbett. Esq., of Knill Court. co. Hereford ; *b.* 1802 ; *s.* 1843. Educated at Harrow ; is a J.P. and D.L. for co. Radnor (High Sheriff 1844); was formerly Capt. 78th Foot, and Major Radnor Militia.—*Newcastle Court, Prestcign ; United Service, Carlton, and Windham Clubs*, s.w.; 18, *Berkeley Square*, w.

WHITTELL, Mrs., of Helmsley Lodge and Weston Hall, Yorkshire.
Phebe, dau. of the late Capt. Anthony Lefroy, 65th Regt.; *m.* 1831 Joshua Francis Whittell, Esq., of Helmsley Lodge and Weston Hall, a Magistrate for the E. Riding of Yorkshire, who *d* 1867, leaving surviving issue four daughters. — *Helmsley Lodge and Weston Hall, York.*

WHITTER, WILLIAM, Esq., of Ashurst, Sussex.
Only son of the late William Whitter, Esq., of Midhurst, Sussex; *b.* 1783; *m.* 1st 1812 Fanny, dau. of
William Bayly, Esq., of Warminster, Wilts; 2nd 1855
Caroline, dau. of the late General John Burgoyne, and
widow of Henry Thomas Parker, Esq., 9th Lancers, and
has by the former, with other issue,
　* William Wood, a Magistrate for Sussex, and late an Officer
　76th Foot; *b.* 1815; *m.* 1861 Emily, dau. of the late —
　Detmar, Esq.
Mr. Whitter is a J.P. and D.L. for Sussex.—*Ashurst,
Dorking ; Residence: Worthing, Sussex.*

+WHITTING, WILLIAM, Esq., of Thorney
　Abbey, Cambridgeshire.
Son of the late W. Whitting, Esq.; *b.* 18—. Is a Dep.
Lieut. for co. Cambridge. —*Thorney Abbey, I. of Ely,
Cambridgeshire.*

WHITTUCK, JOSEPH WHITTUCK, Esq., of Hanham Hall, Gloucestershire.
Fifth son of the late Samuel Whittuck, Esq., J.P. and
D.L., of Hanham Hall (who was High Sheriff of co.
Gloucester 1844), by his 1st wife Anne, dau. of the late
James Hooper, Esq., of Montague House, Bath ; *b.*
1813 ; *s.* 1849 ; *m.* 1840 Emily Rosa, youngest dau. of
the late Michael Hughes, Esq., of Sherdley House, co.
Lancaster, and has, with other issue,
　* Samuel Henry Pemberton, late Cornet 8th Hussars; *b.* 1843.
Mr. Whittuck is a J.P. and D.L. for co. Gloucester, and
a Magistrate for Somerset.—*Hanham Hall, Bitton,
Bristol ; Royal Crescent, Bath.*

WHITTY, JOHN IRWINE, Esq., D.C.L., LL.D.,
　F.R.G.S., of Ricketstown Hall, co. Carlow.
Eldest son of the late Rev. John Whitty, M.A., Prebendary of Killenellick, &c., by Hannah Augusta, dau. of
Edward Bridges-Sayers, Esq., M.D., of Crognachree, co.
Cork ; *b.* 1823 ; *s.* 1855 to the estates of his uncle
General Irwine Whitty ; *m.* 1857 Betnie Eliza Massy,
only dau. of Robert Butler, Esq., of Beech Mount, co.
Tipperary, and has, with other issue,
　* Robert Charles Irwine, *b.* 1858; and * John Edward, *b.*
　1859.
Mr. Whitty, who was educated at Trinity Coll., Dublin (B.A. 1846, M.A., LL.B., and LL.D. 1852), and in
1849 obtained a diploma as Civil and Mining Engineer
from Dublin University, was appointed in 1858 Agent
to H.M.'s Government for the Ordnance Surveys ; created Hon. D.C.L. Oxon 1861.—*Ricketstown Hall. Rathvilly, on Car'ow ; Providence Court, Ballickmoyler, Queen's
Co. ; Residence: Maritzburg, Natal.*

WHITWORTH, BENJAMIN, Esq., of Irwell
　House, Lancashire.
Fifth son of the late Nicholas Whitworth, Esq., of
Drogheda, by Sarah, dau. of John Barrett, Esq., of Manchester ; *b.* 1816 ; *m.* 1843 Jane, dau. of the late Thomas
Walker, Esq., of Salford, and has, with other issue,
　* Thomas, *b.* 1844 ; *m.* 1867 Elizabeth, elder dau. of Robert
　Shaw, Esq., of Colne, co. Lancaster.
Mr. Whitworth, who is a Magistrate for co. Lancaster,
and a Merchant at Manchester, was elected M.P. for
Drogheda 1865.—*Irwell House, Prestwich, Manchester ;
Reform Club, s.w.*

WHITWORTH, WILLIAM CHETWODE, Esq., of
　Earls Barton, Northamptonshire.
Eldest son of the late William Brudenell Whitworth,
Esq., of Earls Barton Hall, by Caroline Louisa, 2nd
dau. of William Povntz Mason Owsley, Esq., of Blastow, co. Leicester : *b.* 1858 ; *s.* 1861. Is Lord of the
Manor of Earls Barton.—*Earls Barton Hall, Northampton.*
　*Heir Pres., his brother George Lee, *b.* 1961.*

WHYTE, Col. JOHN JAMES, of Newtown Manor,
　and Glencar, co. Leitrim.
Eldest son of the late James Whyte, Esq., of Pilton
House, Devon, by Frances Honoria, dau. of the Right
Hon. John Beresford ; *b.* 1808 ; *s.* 1852; *m.* 1842 Marianne Jessie, dau. of Charles Dieudonné de Montenach,
of Fribourg, and has, with other issue,
　* Charles Cecil Beresford, *b.* 1845.
Col. Whyte, who was educated at Harrow and Sandhurst, is a J.P. and D.L. for co. Leitrim (High Sheriff
1854), a Magistrate for Sligo, and a Col. 1st Dragoon
Guards on half-pay ; was formerly in the 7th Hussars.
—*Newtown Manor (co. Leitrim), Sligo, Ireland; Glencar
Lodge, Manor-Hamilton, co. Leitrim; Kildare Street
Club, Dublin ; Arthur's Club, s.w.*

WHYTE, JOHN JOSEPH, Esq., of Loughbrick
　land, Downshire.
Eldest son of the late Capt. Nicholas Charles Whyte,
R.N., J.P. and D.L., of Loughbrickland, by Mary Louisa,
dau. of the late Thomas Segrave, Esq., of Dublin ; *b.*
1826 ; *s.* 1845 ; *m.* 1st 1855 Ellen Mary, dau. of Thomas
L. Kelly, Esq., of Dublin (she *d.* 1857); 2nd 1862
Caroline Letitia, dau. of George Ryan, Esq., of Inch
House, co. Tipperary, and has, with other issue,
　* John Nicholas, *b.* 1864.
Mr. Whyte, who was educated at Oscott Coll., is a J.P.
and D.L. for co. Down (High Sheriff 1862). This family,
originally Saxon, has been settled in Ireland since the
reign of Henry II.—*Loughbrickland, Downshire ; 33,
Gardiner's Place, Dublin.*

WHYTE-MELVILLE, JOHN, Esq., of Ben
　nochy and Strathkinness, Fifeshire.
Second son of the late John Whyte-Melville, Esq., of
Bennochy and Strathkinness, by Elizabeth, dau. of Archibald M'Gilchrist, Esq., of North Bar, co. Renfrew ;
b. 1797 ; *s.* his brother 1818 ; *m.* 1819 Lady Catherine
Anne Sarah Osborne, youngest dau. of Francis, 5th
Duke of Leeds, and has, with other issue.
　* George John, educated at Eton ; late Lieut. and Capt. Cold
　stream Guards; *b.* 1821; *m.* 1847 the Hon. Charlotte, dau.
　of William, 1st Lord Bateman, and has issue, Ellsabeth
　Florence.
Mr. Whyte-Melville, who was educated at Trinity Coll.,
Cambridge, is a J.P. and D.L. for, and Convener of, co.
Fife, and Capt. of the St. Andrew's Troop Fife Mounted
Rifle Volunteers; was formerly in the 9th Lancers,
and afterwards Major R. Fifeshire Yeomanry Cavalry.
—*Mount Melville, St. Andrew's, N.B. ; White's Club, s.w.*

WHYTEHEAD, HENRY YATES, Esq., M.D., of
　Crayke, Yorkshire.
Eldest son of the late Rev. Henry Robert Whytehead,
A.M., of Thormanby. co. York, by Hannah Diana, dau.
of the Rev. Thomas Bowman, Rector of Crayke, and
Vicar of Hessle, co. York : *b.* 1804 ; *s.* his uncle 1829 ;
m. 1833 Ann Mary, dau. of B. N. Wilson, Esq., and
has, with other issue,
　* Robert Yates, *b.* 1846.
Mr. Whytehead is a Magistrate for the North Riding
of Yorkshire, and for co. Durham.—*Crayke, Easingwold.*

WICKENS, JOHN, Esq., of Chilgrove, Sussex.
Second son of the late James Stephens Wickens Esq.,
of Mortimer Street, London, by Ann Goodenough, dau.
of John Hayter. Esq., of Winterborne Stoke, Wilts ; *b.*
1815 ; *m.* 1845 Harriet Frances, dau. of William Davy,
Esq., of Cowley House, co. Gloucester, and has, with
other issue,
　* William Henry, *b.* 1846.
Mr. Wickens, who was educated at Eton and Balliol
Coll., Oxford (B.A. 1836, M.A. 1839), and was called
to the Bar at Lincoln's Inn 1810, purchased this pro-

perty from the Pilkingtons 1864.—*Chilgrove, Chichester; Oxford and Cambridge Club, s.w.; 46, Gloucester Square, w.; 7, Stone Buildings, Lincoln's Inn, w.c.*

WICKHAM, the Rev. EDMUND DAWE, of Cheam Park, Surrey.
Fourth son of the late James Anthony Wickham, Esq., of Frome, Somerset, by Marianne, dau. of Hill Dawe, Esq., of Bridgwater; *b.* 1810; *m.* 1836 Emma, only child of the late Archdale Palmer, Esq., of Cheam Park, and has, with other issue,
   * Reginald Whalley, *b.* 1851.
Mr. Wickham, who was educated at Winchester and Balliol Coll., Oxford (B.A. 1831, M.A. 1833), is Incumbent of Holmwood, Surrey.—*Cheam Park, Epsom; Holmwood Parsonage, Dorking.*

WICKHAM, the Rev. HILL DAWE, of Horsington, Somerset.
Third son of the late James Anthony Wickham, Esq., of Frome (who *d.* 1854), by Marianne, dau. and heir of Hill Dawe, Esq., of Bridgwater, and brother of J. W. D. T. Wickham, Esq. (whom see); *b.* 1807; *m.* 1839 Jessie, only child of Hay Clephane, Esq., of Bath, and has, with other issue,
   * James Douglas Clephane, M.A. of Exeter Coll., Oxford, Rector of Cucklington, Somerset; *b.* 1840.
Mr. Wickham, who was educated at Exeter Coll., Oxford (B.A. 1828, M.A. 1831), is Rector of Horsington, and Patron of that living. He is the 7th of his family who have in succession held this Rectory since 1686.—*Horsington Rectory, Wincanton.*

WICKHAM, JAMES WHALLEY DAWE THOMAS, Esq., of Frome, Somerset.
Eldest son of the late James Anthony Wickham, Esq., of Frome (who was a Lieut.-Col. N. Somersetshire Yeomanry Cavalry), by Marianne, dau. and heir of Hill Dawe, Esq., of Bridgwater; *b.* 1802; *s.* 1854; *m.* 1834 Lucy Matilda, dau. of William Leader, Esq. Mr. Wickham is a Magistrate for Somerset, and Capt. Commandant 13th Somerset Rifle Volunteers, and represents a younger branch of the Wickhams of Horsington.—*North Hill House, Frome.*

WICKHAM, LAMPLUGH WICKHAM, Esq., of Low Moor House, Yorkshire.
Second, but eldest surviving son of the late Rev. Lamplugh Hird, Prebendary of York, and Rector of Paull, by Sarah Elizabeth, dau. of R. Hird, Esq., of Rudston, co. York; *b.* 1807; *m.* 1st 1835 Fanny, dau. of William Hale, Esq., of Acomb co. York; 2nd 1848 Mary, dau. of George Stone, Esq., of Blisworth Hall, co. Northampton, and has, with other issue,
   * William Wickham, a Magistrate for the W. Riding of Yorkshire; *b.* 1836.
Mr. Wickham is a J.P. and D.L. for the West Riding of Yorkshire, and an extensive Ironmaster.—*Low Moor House, Bradford; Chesnut Grove, Tadcaster.*

WICKLOW, Earl of (WILLIAM HOWARD, K.P.).—Cr. 1793.
Eldest son of William, 3rd Earl, by Eleanor, dau. of the late Hon. Francis Caulfeild; *b.* 1788; *s.* 1818; *m.* 1816 Lady Cecil Frances, dau. of John James, 1st Marquis of Abercorn (she *d.* 1860). Educated at St. John's Coll., Cambridge; is a Representative Peer for Ireland; Lord Lieut. and Custos Rotulorum of co. Wicklow; late Col. Wicklow Militia; represents a branch of the family of the Duke of Norfolk.—*Shelton Abbey, Arklow, co. Wicklow; Castle Forward, co. Donegal; 2, Cavendish Square, w.*
   Heir Pres., his nephew Charles Arnold, Lieut. 9th Hussars (son of the late Hon. and Rev. Francis Howard, who *d.* 1857, by his 2nd wife Sarah, dau. of Charles Hamilton, Esq., of Hamwood, co. Meath); *b.* 1839.
994

WICKSTED, CHARLES, Esq., of Betley Hall, Staffordshire.
Eldest son of the late George Tollet, Esq., J.P. and D.L., of Betley Hall, by Frances, dau. of William Joliffe, Esq., of Sulcoats; *b.* 1796; *s.* 1814, when he assumed the name of Wicksted; *m.* 1834 Mary Charlotte, youngest dau. and co-heir of Edmund Meysey Wigley, Esq., and has, with other issue,
   * George Edmund, *b.* 1836.
Mr. Wicksted, who is a Magistrate for co. Salop, was High Sheriff of co. Chester in 1822; he is Lord of the Manor and Patron of Betley.—*Betley Hall, Newcastle-under-Lyne; Shakenhurst, Bewdley.*

WIDDRINGTON, Capt. SHALLCROSS FITZHERBERT, of Newton, and Hauxley, Northumberland.
Third son of the late Shallcross Jacson, Capt. 3rd Light Dragoons, by Frances, eldest dau. of the Rev. Joseph Cook; *b.* 18—; assumed the name of Widrington in compliance with his uncle's will in 1856; *m.* 1864 Cecilia, eldest dau. of Edward J. Gregge-Hopwood, Esq., of Hopwood Hall, co. Lancaster, and has issue, *a dau.
Mr. Widdrington, who was educated at Rugby, is a Magistrate for cos. Chester and Northumberland, and Capt. in the Earl of Chester's Yeomanry.—*Newton Hall, Acklington; Newton Bank, Preston Brook, Cheshire.*

+WIGAN, EDMUND, Esq., of Lapley, Staffordshire.
Son of the late — Wigan, Esq.; *b.* 18—. Is a Dep.-Lieut. for co. Stafford.—*Lapley, Penkridge.*

WIGGETT, the Rev. JAMES SAMUEL, of Allanbay, Berks.
Eldest son of the late Rev. James Wiggett (some time Rector of Crudwell, Hankerton, Wilts), by Frances, only child of Samuel Lyde, Esq., of Bath, and brother of W. L. Wiggett-Chute, Esq., of The Vyne, Hants (whom see); *b.* 1797; *s.* 1838; *m.* 1834 Marianne, eldest dau. of Allan Thompson, Esq., of Cheltenham, and has, with other issue,
   * James Allan, *b.* 1831; *m.* 1862 Caroline Frederica, dau. of the late Gen. D'Oyly, Col. 33rd Foot; has issue two daughters.
Mr. Wiggett was educated at Winchester and Exeter Coll., Oxford (B.A. 1820, M.A. 1827).—*Allanbay, Binfie'd, Bracknell; Oxford and Cambridge Club, s.w.*

WIGHT, ALBERT, Esq., of Braboeuf Manor, Surrey.
Eldest surviving son of the late Arthur Wight, Esq., of Braboeuf Manor (Major 23rd Regt. B.N.I.), by Jane, dau. of the late James More Molyneux, Esq., of Loseley Park, Surrey; *b.* 1812; *s.* his brother 1855. This family was formerly of Wimbledon, Surrey.—*Braboeuf Manor, Guildford.*

WIGHT, Mrs., of Ormiston, Haddingtonshire.
Louisa Mary Catharine, youngest dau. and co-heir of the late Thomas Boycott, Esq., of Rudge Hall, co. Salop, by Jane, dau. of Thomas Tarleton, Esq., of Bolesworth Castle, co. Chester; *m.* 1841 Andrew Wight, Esq., of Ormiston, N.B., who *d.* 1858, leaving issue * Cathcart Boycott, *b.* 1849. This family is of Braboeuf, Surrey.—*Ormiston, East Lothian, N.B.*

WIGHT. (See Schank.)

WIGHTMAN, Lady.
Charlotte Mary, dau. of the late James Baird, Esq., of Laswade, Midlothian; *m.* 1819 Sir William Wightman, one of the Justices of the Court of Queen's Bench, who was Knighted in 1841, and who *d.* 1863.—*St. John's Bank, Hampton Court, s.w.; 73, St. George's Road, s.w.*

WIGHTMAN. (See *Weightman, of Burbage.*)

WIGHTMAN, JAMES SETON, Esq., of Courance, Dumfriesshire.

Only son of the late John Wightman, Esq., of Courance, by Margaret, dau. of James Seton, Esq., and sister of Adam Seaton, Merchant, of Glasgow ; *b.* 1800 ; *s.* 1831; *m.* 1843 Cordelia Caroline, dau. of James Cullen, Esq., of Edinburgh, and has, with other issue,

   * John Seton, *b.* 1846.

Mr. Wightman, who was educated at Edinburgh Coll., is a Magistrate for co. Dumfries, and Proprietor of Courance, Holehouse, and Lammonbie. — *Courance, Lockerby ; 7, Darnaway Street, Edinburgh.*

WIGHTWICK, Mrs., of Bloxwich, Staffordshire.

Dorothea, 3rd dau. of Richard Fryer, Esq., M.P., of the Wergs, co. Stafford ; *m.* 1829 Stubbs Wightwick, Esq., J.P. and D.L. for cos. Stafford and Gloucester (only surviving son of the late Thomas Devey Wightwick Esq., of Bloxwich), who *d.* 1858.—*Bloxwich, Walsall.*

WIGRAM, LOFTUS TOTTENHAM, Esq., Q.C.

Son of the late Sir Robert Wigram, Bart., by his 2nd wife Eleanor, youngest dau. of John Watts, Esq., and uncle to Sir R. Fitzwygram, Bart.; *b.* 1803 ; *m.* 1849 Lady Katharine, dau. of Thomas, 5th Earl of Selkirk (she *d.* 1863).. Educated at Trinity Coll., Cambridge (B A. 1825, M.A. 1828) ; is a Barrister-at-Law (called 1828) ; was M.P. for the University of Cambridge 1850–9.—*Athenæum Club, s.w. ; 43, Berkeley Square, w.*

WIGRAM, MONEY, Esq., of Moor Place, Herts.

Eldest son of the late Sir Robert Wigram, Bart., of Walthamstow, Essex, by his 2nd wife Eleanor, youngest dau. of John Watts, Esq., of Southampton ; *b.* 1790; *m.* 1822 Mary, dau. of the late Charles Hampden Turner, Esq., of Rook's Nest, Goodstone, Surrey, and has, with other issue,

   * Money, *b.* 1823 ; *m.* 1858 Anne, dan. of the late William Whittaker Maitland, Esq., of Loughton Hall, Essex, and has issue.

Mr. Wigram was formerly a Merchant and Shipowner in London.—*Moor Place, Much Hadham, Ware.*

WIGSELL, ATWOOD DALTON, Esq., of Sanderstead Court, and Purley House, Surrey.

Eldest son of the late Rev. Atwood Wigsell Wigsell, of Sanderstead ; *b.* 18—. Is Lord of the Manor and Patron of Sanderstead, Warlingham, and Chilsham.—*Sanderstead Court and Purley House, Croydon.*

WIGSTON, Admiral JAMES, of Bitterne Hill, Hampshire.

Second son of the late John Wigston, Esq., of Trent Park, Herts, by Mary, dau. of the late Sir James Winter Lake, Bart., and sister of the late Admiral Sir Willoughby T. Lake, K.C.B.; *b.* 1792 ; *m.* 1833 Mary Theodora, only dau. of the late Major-Gen. Sir John Chalmers, K.C.B., of the Madras Army, and has, with other issue,

   * William Francis Chalmers, Ensign 60th Rifles ; *b.* 1846.

Admiral Wigston, who was educated at Harrow, and entered the Navy in 1804, is a Magistrate for Hampshire, and an Admiral R.N. This family is descended from the Wigstons, who lived at Wigston Magna, co. Leicester, as early as the reign of Henry VI.—*Bitterne Hill, South Stoneham, Southampton.*

WILBERFORCE, the Right Rev. SAMUEL, D.D., of Lavington House, Sussex.

Third son of the late William Wilberforce, Esq., M.P., of Markington Grange, co. York, by Barbara Anna, dau. of Isaac Spooner, Esq., of Elmdon Hall, co. War-

wick; *b.* 1805 ; *m.* 1828 Emily, dau. of the late Rev. J. Sargent, of Lavington, and has, with other issue,

   * Reginald Garton, a Magistrate for Sussex, and Lieut. 2gr 1 Foot ; *b.* 1838 ; *m.* 1867 Anna Maria, 3rd dau. of the Hon. Richard Denman.

Dr. Wilberforce is Lord Bishop of Oxford (see *Oxford, Bishop of.*) — *Lavington House, Petworth ; Cuddesden Palace, Wheatley ; Athenæum Club, s.w.*

WILBERFORCE, WILLIAM, Esq., of Ingerthorpe Grange, Markington, Yorkshire.

Eldest son of the late William Wilberforce, Esq., of Markington Grange (who was many years M.P. for co. York), by Barbara Anne, dau. of the late Isaac Spooner, Esq., of Elmdon Hall, co. Warwick ; *b.* 1798 ; *s.* 1833 ; *m.* 1820 Mary Frances, dau. of the Rev. John Owen, M.A., and has issue,

   * William, Barrister-at-Law of Lincoln's Inn, *b.* 1821 ; *m.* 1849 Rosa, dau. of W. Jones, Esq., and has, with other issue,
   * William Basil, *b.* 1850.

Mr. Wilberforce, who was educated at Trinity Coll., Cambridge, and called to the Bar at the Middle Temple 1825, is a Magistrate for Middlesex and the W. Riding of Yorkshire, and Patron of 1 living. This family was formerly of Wilberfoss, co. York.—*Markington Grange, Ripley ; St. Ives Place, Maidenhead.*

WILBRAHAM, Col. the Hon. EDWARD BOOTLE.

Younger son of Edward, 1st Lord Skelmersdale, by Mary Elizabeth, dau. of the Rev. Edward Taylor, of Bifrons, Kent ; *b.* 1807 ; *m.* 1831 Emily, 4th dau. of James Ramsbottom, Esq., and has, with other issue,

   * Arthur, *b.* 1842.

Col. Wilbraham, who was educated at Eton, is a Magistrate for co. Lancaster, and Hon. Col. 6th Lancashire Militia, was formerly Capt. and Lieut.-Col. Coldstream Guards.—*Lathom, Ormskirk ; Guards' Club, s.w.*

WILBRAHAM, FRANCIS HENRY RANDLE, Esq., of Cresswellshawe, Cheshire.

Fourth son of the late Randle Wilbraham, Esq., of Rode Hall, co. Chester, by Sibylla, dau. of Philip Egerton, Esq., of Oulton ; *b.* 1819 ; *m.* 1858 Elizabeth Mary, dau. of John Barnard, Esq., of Ham Common. Educated at Peterhouse, Cambridge (B.A. 1845); called to the Bar at Lincoln's Inn 1848 ; is a Magistrate for co. Chester.—*Cresswellshawe, Alsager, Cheshire.*

WILBRAHAM, GEORGE FORTESCUE, Esq., of Delamere House, Cheshire.

Eldest son of the late George Wilbraham, Esq., of Delamere House (who was M.P. for Cheshire 1852–41), by Lady Anne, dau. of Hugh, 1st Earl Fortescue, K.G.; *b.* 1815 ; *s.* 1852. Educated at Harrow and Trinity Coll., Cambridge (B.A. 1838); called to the Bar at the Inner Temple 1843 ; is a Magistrate for co. Chester (High Sheriff 1858).—*Delamere House, Northwich ; Reform Club, s.w. ; 1, Verulam Buildings, Gray's Inn, w.c.*

Heir Pres., his brother Roger William, *b.* 1817 ; *m.* 1850 Louisa, 3rd dau. of Robert Gosling, Esq., of Botley's Park, Surrey.

WILBRAHAM, HUGH, Esq., of Boathaven, co. Mayo.

Youngest son of the late George Wilbraham, Esq., M.P., of Delamere House, co. Chester, by Lady Anne, dau. of Hugh, 1st Earl Fortescue, and youngest brother of G. F. Wilbraham, Esq., of Delamere House (whom see); *b.* 1847 ; *m.* 1868 Lady Marianne, youngest dau. of Howe Peter, 2nd Marquis of Sligo. Educated at Rugby and Trinity Coll., Cambridge ; is a Magistrate for co. Mayo.—*Boathaven Lodge, Westport, co. Mayo.*

WILBRAHAM, RANDLE, Esq., of Rode, Cheshire.

Eldest son of the late Randle Wilbraham, Esq., of Rode Hall (who was a brother of Henry, 1st Lord Skelmersdale), by his 1st wife, Lætitia, only child of the Rev.

Edward Rudd, Rector of Haughton-le-Skerne, co. Durham ; *b.* 1801 ; *s.* 1861 ; *m.* 1833 Sibella, dau. of William Egerton, Esq., of Gresford Lodge, co. Denbigh. Educated at Westminster and Ch. Ch., Oxford ; is a J.P. and D.L. for co. Chester. Represents a younger branch of an ancient Cheshire family, being 16th in direct male descent from Richard de Willurgham, High Sheriff in 1259.—*Rode Hall, Lawton, Cheshire.*

Heir Pres., his brother the Rev. Charles Philip Wilbraham, M.A. of St. Peter's Coll., Cambridge, Vicar of Audley, co. Stafford ; *b.* 1810.

WILBRAHAM. (See under *Skelmersdale, Lord.*)

WILCOCKS. (See *Treffry.*)

WILD, RICHARD, Esq., of Eldon Lodge, Lancashire.

Eldest son of the late Thomas Wild, Esq., of Broad Oak, co. Lancaster, by Mary, dau. of Richard Hamer, Esq., of Shuttleworth ; *b.* 1808 ; *m.* 1838 Mary, dau. of James Scholes, Esq., of Newton Heath, co. Lancaster, and has, with other issue,

* Scholes, *b.* 1839.

Mr. Wild is a Magistrate for co. Lancaster.—*Eldon Lodge, Birkdale Park, Southport.*

WILD, SAMUEL BAGNALL, Esq., of Costock, Notts.

Eldest surviving son of the late Rev. William Quinton Wild, of Costock, by Susannah, dau. of John Bagnall, Esq. ; *b.* 1791 ; *m.* 1813 his cousin Elizabeth, dau. and heir of Wade Bagnall, Esq., of Manchester. Is a Magistrate for Notts (High Sheriff 1854), and maternally descended from Sir Henry Bagnall, Bart., High Marshall of Ireland *temp.* Elizabeth.—*Manor House, Costock, Loughborough.*

WILDE, the Right Hon. Sir JAMES PLAISTED (cr. 1860).

Son of Edward Archer Wilde, Esq., by Marianne, dau. of William Norris, Esq., and nephew of the late Lord Chancellor Truro ; *b.* 1816 ; *m.* 1860 Lady Mary, youngest dau. of William, 3rd Earl of Radnor. Educated at Winchester and Trinity Coll., Cambridge (B.A. 1838, M.A. 1842) ; called to the Bar at the Inner Temple 1839, and went the Northern Circuit ; became a Q.C. 1855 ; appointed a Baron of the Exchequer 1860 ; transferred to the Court of Probate and Divorce 1863 ; sworn a Member of the Privy Council 1864.—*Mayfield, Shooter's Hill, Kent, s.e.* ; 2, *Grafton Street, w.*

WILDE, Sir WILLIAM ROBERT WILLS, Knt. (cr. 1864).

Youngest son of Dr. Thomas Wilde, of Castlerea, co. Roscommon, by Emily, dau. of — Fynn, Esq., of Ballynagillon, co. Mayo ; *b.* 1815 ; *m.* 1851 Jane Francesca Speranza, youngest dau. of Charles Elgee, Esq., and grand-dau. of the Ven. Archdeacon Elgee, of Wexford, and has, with other issue,

* William Charles Kingsbury, *b.* 1852.

Sir Wm. Wilde, who was educated at Trinity Coll., Dublin, is Surgeon Oculist in ordinary to Her Majesty in Ireland, a Member of the Royal Irish Academy, and of several foreign learned societies. This family were originally of Durham, but settled in Ireland about 150 years ago.—*Moytaura, Cong, co. Galway* ; 1, *Merrion-Square, Dublin.*

WILDE, the Rev. ALBERT SYDNEY.

Youngest son of the late Sir John Wilde (Chief Justice at the Cape of Good Hope), by Jane Elizabeth, dau. of J. Moore, Esq., and nephew of Thomas, 1st Lord Truro ; *b.* 1826 ; *m.* 1851 Laura Isabella, dau. of W. J. Coltman, Esq., of Naburn Hall, co. York. Educated at

Trinity Coll., Cambridge (B.A. 1849, M.A. 1857) ; appointed Rector of Greatford 1850, of Louth 1859.—*The Rectory, Louth, Lincolnshire.*

WILDE, SAMUEL JOHN, Esq., of Hadley, Middlesex.

Eldest son of the late Samuel Francis Thomas Wilde, Esq., J.P. of Hadley, by his 1st wife Maria Matilda, youngest dau. of John Rowland, Esq. (she *d.* 1821) ; *b.* 1820 ; *s.* 1862 ; *m.* 1852 Georgina, dau. of Edward Martineau, Esq.—*Hadley, Barnet.*

WILDE. (See under *Truro, Lord.*)

WILDER, FREDERICK, Esq., of Purley and Sulham, Berks.

Eldest son of the late Rev. Henry Watson Wilder, of Purley and Sulham, Berks, by Augusta, sister of the late Sir Charles Joshua Smith, Bart., of Suttons, Essex ; *b.* 1832 ; *s.* 1836 ; *m.* 1861 Sarah Fox. 2nd dau. of the late Sir Benjamin Hawes, K.C.B., Under Secretary of State for War. Educated at New Coll., Oxford (B.A. 1854) ; is a Magistrate for Berks, and Patron of 1 living.—*Purley Hall and Sulham House, Reading.*

Heir Pres., his brother Henry Beaufoy, in Holy Orders ; *b.* 1834 ; *m.* 1856 Augusta, dau. of the late Langham Christie, Esq., of Preston Deanery, co. Northampton, and has issue 2 sons and 1 dau.

WILDER, the Rev. JOHN, of Sulham, Berks.

Second son of the late John Wilder, Esq., of Purley Hall and Sulham (who *d.* 1834), by Harriet, dau. of the Rev. Edwards Beadon. Rector of North Stoneham, Hants ; *b.* 1801 ; *m.* 1st 1831 Mary, dau. of the Rev. Gilbert Heathcote, Archdeacon of Winchester, and grand-dau. of the late Sir Thomas Heathcote, Bart (she *d.* 1856) ; 2nd 1866 Mary Hood, dau. of the Rev. George Deane, Rector of Bighton, Hants. Educated at Eton and King's Coll. Cambridge (B.A. 1824, M.A. 1828), is Rector of Sulham, Rural Dean of Reading, and Fellow of Eton College. — *Sulham, near Reading ; Eton College, Windsor.*

WILKES, the Rev. ROBERT, of Lofts, Essex.

Only son of the late Rev. Robert Fiske, Rector of Wendon Lofts and Vicar of Elmdon. &c., by Mary Ann, dau. of John Fiske, Esq., of Saffron Walden ; *b.* 1818 ; *s.* 1838 to the estates of his cousin John Wilkes, Esq., of Lofts Hall (whose name he assumed) ; *m.* 1842 Emily-Lettice, eldest dau. of the Rev. Robert Roberts, Vicar of Haverhill, Suffolk, and has, with other issue,

* John, *b.* 1848.

Mr. Wilkes, who was educated at St. John's Coll. Cambridge (B.A. 1840. M.A. 1843), is Patron and Lord of the Manors of Wendon Lofts. Elmdon, and Great Chishull.—*Lofts Hall, Wendon Lofts, Saffron Walden.*

+WILKIE, ARCHIBALD, Esq., of Ormiston, Edinburghshire.

Eldest son of the late — Wilkie, Esq., of Ormiston ; *b.* 18—. Is a Magistrate for Midlothian, and Lord of the Barony of Ormiston.—*Ormiston, Edinburgh.*

WILKIE, EDWARD CHARLES HALES, Esq., of Ellington House, Kent.

Only son of the late Col. Fletcher Wilkie, by Elizabeth, 2nd dau. of the late Sir John Hales, Bart. ; *b.* 1809 ; *m.* 1834 Mary, only dau. of the late Thomas Wood, Esq., of Chislett Court, Kent, and has, with other issue,

* Hales, Major 29th Regt. ; *b.* 1842 ; *m.* 1861 Eleanor, dau. of the late W. Walker, Esq., of Summerfield, co. Chester, and has issue. * Edward Ormerod Hales, *b.* 1852.

Mr. Wilkie, who was educated at Winchester, is a J.P. and D.L. for Kent ; he was formerly in the 1st Dragoon Guards.—*Ellington House, Ramsgate.*

+ WILKIE, JOHN, Esq., of Foulden House, Berwickshire.
Son of the late J. Wilkie, Esq., of Foulden House; *b.* 18—; *m.* 1865 Henrietta Eleanor, 2nd dau. of Thomas Bruce, Esq., of Arnot, co. Kinross. Is a J.P. and D.L. for co. Berwick, and Lord of the Barony of Foulden. —*Foulden House, Berwick, N.B.*

WILKINS, the Ven. GEORGE, D.D., Archdeacon of Nottingham.
Third son of the late William Wilkins, Esq., of Newnham, co. Cambridge; *b.* 1785; *m.* 1812 Amelia Auriol, dau. of the Very Rev. E. Drummond Hay, D.D., and niece of Thomas, 8th Earl of Kinnoull. Educated at Bury St. Edmund's and Caius Coll., Cambridge (B.A. 1807, M.A. 1810, B.D. and D.D. 1824); late Vicar of St. Mary's, Nottingham; appointed Prebendary of Southwell 1823, Archdeacon of Nottingham 1832, Canon of Southwell 1844.—*Residence House, Southwell.*

WILKINS, THOMAS, Esq., of Ringstead, Northamptonshire.
Eldest son of the late Thomas Wilkins, Esq., of Stanwick, co. Northampton, by Mary, dau. of the Rev. Richard Haighton, Rector of Long Stow and Croxton, co. Cambridge; *b.* 1786; *s.* 1813; *m.* 1st 1814 Elizabeth, heir of the Rev. Thomas Sheepshanks, Rector of Wimpole, co. Cambridge; 2nd 1849 Augusta Sophia, dau. of James Dyson, Esq., of Bedford (she *d.* 1865). Is a J.P. and D.L. for co. Northampton, and a Magistrate for Hunts and co. Warwick.—*Ringstead, Thrapstone; Pelham Villa, Leamington; Coombe Fishacre, Newton Abbot.*
Heir, his grandson Richard Haighton, b. 1851.

WILKINSON, Sir JOHN GARDNER, Knt., D.C.L., F.R.S., of Brynfield, Glamorganshire (cr. 1839).
Son of the late Rev. John Wilkinson, of Hardendale, co. Westmoreland, F.S.A., by Mary Anne, dau. of the Rev. Richard Gardner, and great-great grand-dau. of Sir Salathiel Lovell, of Harleston, co. Northampton; *b.* 1797; *m.* 1856 Caroline Catharine, eldest dau. of Henry Lucas, Esq., of Uplands, co. Glamorgan. Educated at Harrow and Exeter Coll., Oxford; is author of several works on Egyptian Antiquities; knighted for his contributions to Archæological Literature. — *Brynfield House, Gower, Reynoldston, Glamorganshire; Athenæum Club, s.w.*

WILKINSON, ANTHONY, Esq., of Hulam (formerly Coxhoe Hall), co. Durham.
Eldest son of the late Anthony Wilkinson, Esq., of Coxhoe Hall, J.P. and D.L. (who was High Sheriff of co. Durham 1837), by Mary Ann, dau. of — Hall, Esq.; *b.* 1838; *s.* 1851. Educated at Ch. Ch., Oxford; is a J.P. and D.L. for co. Durham (High Sheriff 1868), Lord of the Manors of Hulam and Sheraton, co. Durham, and Clennell, Northumberland. — *Sheraton, Ferryhill; Hulam, Castle Eden; Arthur's and Brooks's Clubs, s.w.*
Heir Pres., his brother Clennell, Lieut. 12th Lancers, b. 1841.

WILKINSON, the Rev. CHRISTOPHER WILLIAM, of Ingmanthorpe Hall, Yorkshire.
Second but only surviving son of the late Edward Wilkinson, Esq., of Potterton, co. York, by Ann, dau. of Nicolas Pearse, Esq., of Woodford, Essex; *b.* 1796; *m.* 1834 Louisa Ann, dau. of Brice Pearse, Esq., of Monkham, Woodford, Essex, and has, with other issue,
* Christopher Brice, late Capt. 65th Foot; *b.* 1835.
Mr. Wilkinson, who was educated at Eton and St. John's Coll., Cambridge (B.A. 1819), was formerly Vicar of Bardsley, Yorkshire.—*Ingmanthorpe Hall, Wetherby; Bilton Hall, York; Boodle's Club, c.w.*

WILKINSON, the Rev. GEORGE HOWARD, of Oswald House, co. Durham.
Eldest son of the late George Wilkinson, Esq., of Oswald House, by his 1st wife Mary, dau. of John Howard Esq., of Ripon; *b.* 1833; *s.* 1856; *m.* 1857 Caroline Charlotte, dau. of Lieut.-Col. Des-Vœux. Educated at Oriel Coll., Oxford (B.A. 1852, M.A. 1855): appointed Incumbent of St. Peter's, Great Windmill Street, London 1867; late Incumbent of St. Andrews, Auckland, co. Durham. Mr. Wilkinson represents a branch of the Wilkinsons of Brancepeth, who are descended from the Wilkinsons of Coxhoe.—*Oswald House, Durham.*

WILKINSON, the Rev. GEORGE PEARSON, of Harperley Park, co. Durham.
Eldest son of the late George Hutton Wilkinson, Esq., D.L., of Harperley Park, some time Recorder of Newcastle-on-Tyne (who *d.* 1859), by his 1st wife Elizabeth Jane, only child of George Pearson, Esq., of Harperley Park; *b.* 1823; *m.* 1849 Frances Vernon, only child of the late William Mills, Esq., R.N., of Helme Park, co. Durham, and has issue,
* Two daughters.
Mr. Wilkinson, who was educated at Harrow and University Coll., Durham (B.A. 1845, M.A. 1846), and called to the Bar at the Middle Temple 1848, is a Magistrate for co. Durham. He entered Holy Orders 1857, and was appointed Incumbent of Thornley St. Bartholomew's, co. Durham 1858.—*Harperley Park, Darlington.*

WILKINSON, GEORGE YELDHAM, Esq., of Tapton House, Derbyshire.
Youngest son of the late Gilbert Ricketts, Esq., of Madras, by Harriet Worsley, dau. of Admiral Sir R. Rodney Bligh, K.C.B., of Belle Vue, Southampton; *b.* 1810; *s.* the late Isaac Wilkinson, Esq., whose name he assumed, 1831; *m.* 1830 Emily, dau. of the late John Michael Malouek, Esq., of Liverpool (Prussian Consul), and has, with other issue,
* George Lawrence Ricketts, who has assumed, by Royal licence, the surname of Ricketts, in lieu of his patronymic; *b.* 1831; *m.* 1865 Clarissa, younger dau. of the late John Harding, Esq., of Henbury, co. Gloucester.
Mr. Wilkinson, who was educated at Worcester Coll., Oxford, is a Dep.-Lieut. for co. Derby, and Lord of the Manor of Tapton; he is also nephew of the late Sir R. Tristram Ricketts, Bart.—*Tapton House, Chesterfield.*

WILKINSON, HENRY COX, Esq., of White Webbs Park, Middlesex.
Only surviving son of the late Henry Wilkinson, Esq., of White Webbs Park, by Jane, only dau. of Samuel Cox, Esq., of Bath; *b.* 1811; *s.* 1855; *m.* 1861 Louisa, youngest dau. of the late Major Waller. Educated at Trinity Coll., Cambridge; is a Magistrate for Herts. This property was purchased by his grandfather, Abraham Wilkinson, Esq., in 1788.—*White Webbs Park, Enfield; Athenæum and Conservative Clubs, s.w.*
Heirs Pres., his sisters Mary Elizabeth and Jane Caroline.

WILKINSON, HOOPER JOHN, Esq., of Walsham Hall, Suffolk.
Eldest son of the late George Wilkinson, Esq., of Walsham Hall; *b.* 1800; *s.* 1857; *m.* 1822 Anne, only dau. of Robert Howlett, Esq., of the Rookery, Yoxford, Suffolk, and has, with other issue,
* Hooper John, *b.* 1822.
Mr. Wilkinson, who was educated at Trinity Coll., Cambridge, is a Magistrate for Suffolk.—*Walsham Hall, Bury St. Edmund's.*

WILKINSON, ISAAC HERBERT, Esq., of Upper Hare Park, Cambridgeshire.
Third son of the late Robert Wilkinson, Esq., by Catherine, dau. of the late John Peter Allix, Esq., of Swaffham

897

ham House, Newmarket; b. 1818; m. 1839 Margaret Anne, only child of John Petrie Keble, Esq., Lieut.-Col. H.E.I.C.'s Service. Educated at Eton and Downing Coll., Cambridge (B.A. 1845, M.A. 1848); is a J.P. and D.L. for co. Cambridge.—Upper Hare Park, Newmarket.

WILKINSON, the Rev. JOHN.
Eldest son of the late Major Wilkinson, by Harriet, dau. of Lieut.-Col. W. C. Frome; b. 1816; m. 1844 Jean, dau. of R. P. Prat, Esq., and has, with other issue,

   * Henry Fazakerley, b. 1845.

Mr. Wilkinson, who was educated at Merton Coll., Oxon (B.A. 1838, M.A. 1848), appointed Rector of Broughton Giffard, Wilts, 1848, Prebendary of Sarum Cathedral 1863 ; he is a Magistrate for Wilts.—Broughton Giffard, Melksham.

WILKINSON, the Rev. JOHN JAMES.
Eldest son of the Rev. George Wilkinson, B.D., Rector of Whicham, Cumberland, by Elizabeth, dau. of James Ralph, Esq., of Sebergham, Cumberland; b. 1818; m. 1850 Gertrude Blanche, only dau. of W. H. Walpole, Esq. Educated at Queen's Coll., Oxford (B.A. 1842, M.A. 1845); appointed Rector of Lanteglos and Advent 1852 ; is a Magistrate for Cornwall.—Lanteglos Rectory, Camelford.

WILKINSON, the Rev. PERCIVAL SPEARMAN, of Mount Oswald, co. Durham.
Third son of the late Thomas Wilkinson, Esq., of Coxhoe Hall, by Hannah Elizabeth, dau. and co-heir of Robert Spearman, Esq., of Oldacres. co. Durham; b. 1792; m. 1817 Sophia, dau. of Capt. Anstruther, and has, with other issue,

   * Percival Spearman, a Magistrate for co. Durham ; b. 181—; m. 1860 Adela Julia Kirkby, eldest dau. of Kirkby Fenton, Esq., of Caldecot Hall, co. Warwick, and has, with other issue, * a son, b. 1865.

Mr. Wilkinson was educated at Eton and St. John's Coll., Cambridge (B.A. 1815, M.A. 1818), and entered Holy Orders 1817.—Mount Oswald, Durham.

WILKINSON, RICHARD SEPTIMUS, Esq., of Corby Birkholme, Lincolnshire.
Youngest son of the late Josiah Wilkinson. Esq., (who was youngest son of William Wilkinson, Esq., of Morra Hill, Bampton, Westmoreland), by Martha, dau. of Joseph Hinde, Esq., of Whitehaven; b. 18—. Is a Dep.-Lieut. for co. Lincoln. This family is an offshoot of the Wilkinsons of Bampton, Westmoreland.—Corby Birkholme, Grantham ; Conservative Club, s.w.

WILKINSON, ROBERT HINDLEY, Esq., of Chesfield Lodge, Herts.
Eldest son of the late Robert Wilkinson. Esq., of Montagu Square, by Catherine, dau. of the late J. P. Allix. Esq., of Swaffham House, co. Cambridge; b. 1811; m. 1858 ; m. 1852 Caroline, only dau. of Lieut.-Gen. Vicomte Obert, by Margaret, sister of Edward Parkyns, Esq., of Chesfield, by whom he has,

   * Edward Obert Hindley, b. 1857.

Mr Wilkinson, who was educated at Eton and King's Coll., Cambridge (B.A. 1832, M.A. 1836), is a Magistrate for Beds and Herts, and Hon. Lieut.-Col. Beds Militia.—Chesfield Lodge, Stevenage; Carlton Club, s.w.

WILKINSON, THOMAS CLIFTON, Esq., of Winterbourne, and Newall Hall, Yorkshire.
Only son of the late Thomas Wilkinson, Esq., of Winterbourne Hall, by Anne, dau. and heir of Thomas Clifton, Esq., of Newall Hall, co. York; b. 1815; s. 1691 ; m. 1849 the Hon. Julia Jemima, 2nd dau. of the

998

late Hon. Henry Butler, and sister of Henry, 13th Viscount Mountgarrett, and has, with other issue,

   * Thomas Clifton, Ensign 72nd Foot; b. 1844.

Mr. Wilkinson, who was educated at the University Coll., Oxford, is a Magistrate for the W. Riding of Yorkshire.—Winterbourne Hall, Skipton-in-Craven ; Newall Hall, Otley.

WILKINSON, THOMAS HUTTON, Esq., of Walsham-le-Willows, Suffolk.
Eldest son of the late Thomas Wilkinson, Esq., of Stokesley House, co. York, by Jane, dau. of — Hutton Esq., of Hurworth, co. Durham ; b. 1790. Educated at Harrow; is a J.P. and D.L. for Suffolk; was formerly Capt. in the H.E.I.C.'s Service.—West House, Walsham-le-Willows, Ixworth.

WILLCOCKS, St. GEORGE LAWRENCE, Esq., of Brookend, co. Tyrone.
Eldest son of the late George Willcocks, Esq., of Coal Island, co. Tyrone, by Isabella. dau. of the Rev. Charles Caulfeild ; b. 1820 ; s. 1854. Educated at Dungannon ; is a Magistrate for co. Tyrone. This family is a branch of the family of Willcocks, of Tottenham High Cross, Middlesex, but has been settled in Ireland for two centuries.—Brookend, Ardboe, Stewartstown, co. Tyrone.

   Heir Pres., his brother James Caulfeild. B.A. of Trinity Coll., Dublin, curate of Ballintemple, co. Mayo; b. 1822.

WILLES, Sir JAMES SHAW, Knt. (cr. 1855).
Eldest son of the late James Willes. Esq.. M.D.. of Cork, by Elizabeth Aldworth, dau. of J. Shaw, Esq., of Belmont ; b. 1814 ; m. 1856 Helen. dau. of the late Thomas Jennings, Esq., of Cork. Educated at Trinity Coll., Dublin (B.A. 1836); called to the Bar at the Inner Temple 1840; appointed a Judge of Common Pleas 1855.—Otterspool, Watford; Judges' Chambers, E.C.

+WILLES, CHARLES THOMAS, Esq., of Kingsutton, Oxon.
Fourth son of the late Rev. William Shippen Willes. Rector of Preston Bissett. Bucks, by his 2nd wife Margaret, only dau. and heir of John Williams. Esq.. of Punthowell. co. Carmarthen. and brother of the late J. Willes, Esq., of Astrop House, co. Northampton ; b. 1848 ; is a Magistrate for co. Northampton, and Lord of the Manor of Kingsutton.—Manor House, Kingsutton, Banbury.

+WILLES, GEORGE SHIPPEN, Esq., of Hungerford Park, and Clifton Lodge, Berks.
Eldest son of the late Major George Willes, of Hungerford Park, Berks, by his 1st wife Charlotte, 2nd dau. of the late Henry Cooke, Esq., of Chilton Lodge ; b. 18—; s. 1862; m. 1868 Susan Emily, 2nd dau. of Thomas Tyrwhitt Drake, Esq., of Shardeloes, Bucks. Is a Magistrate for Berks. This family is a younger branch of the Willeses of Astrop House, co. Northampton (whom see).—Hungerford Park, and Clifton Lodge, Hungerford.

WILLES, Mrs., of Goodrest, Berks.
Emily, 3rd dau. of the late Rev. J. Stonhouse : m. 1819 Edward Willes, Esq.. of Newbold Comyn, co. Warwick. and Goodrest, Shinfield (who d. 1847), leaving. with other issue, * Edward. b. 1820.—Goodrest, Shinfield, Reading.

+WILLES, WILLIAM, Esq., of Astrop House, Northamptonshire.
Eldest son of the late Rev. William Shippen Willes, of Astrop Hall, by Margaret, dau. and heir of John Williams, Esq ; b. 1802 ; s. 1822 ; m. 1831 Sophia,

dau. of the late William Ralph Cartwright, Esq., M.P., of Aynhoe, and has, with other issue,

     * John, b. 1836.

Mr. Willes is a J.P. and D.L. for co. Northampton (High Sheriff 1837), Lord of the Manor of Astrop, and Patron of 2 livings.—*Astrop House, Brackley.*

WILLETT. (See *Cleveland.*)

WILLEY. (See *Wheler, Sir T., Bart.*)

WILLIAM-BROWNE. (See *Browne.*)

+**WILLIAMES, JOHN BUCKLEY, Esq., of Pennant, Montgomeryshire.**
Son of the late J. Williames, Esq., of Pennant; *b.* 18—; is married, and has issue,

     * John Buckley, a J.P. and D.L. for co. Montgomery; b. 18—.

Mr. Williames is a Magistrate for co. Montgomery, and Lord of the Manor of Pennant.—*Pennant, Berriew, Montgomeryshire.*

WILLIAMS, Sir HUGH, Bart., of Bodelwyddan, Flintshire (cr. 1798).
Eldest surviving son of the late Sir John Williams, Bart., of Bodelwyddan (who *d.* 1830), by Margaret, dau. and heir of Hugh Williams, Esq., of Tyfry, co. Anglesey; *b.* 1802; *s.* his brother as 3rd Bart. 1859; *m.* 1843 Henrietta Charlotte, only dau. of the late Sir Watkin Wynn, Bart.; is Patron of 1 living; was High Sheriff of co. Denbigh 1862—*Bodelwyddan, St. Asaph.*

     Heir, his son William Grenville, b. 1844.

WILLIAMS, the Rev. Sir ERASMUS HENRY GRIFFIES-, Bart., of Llwyn-y-Wormwood Park, Carmarthenshire (cr. 1815).
Second but eldest surviving son of the late Sir George Griffies-Williams, Bart. (who assumed the additional name of Williams in compliance with the will of David Williams, Esq., of St. Peter, co. Carmarthen), by Anna Margaret, dau. of Herbert Evans, Esq.; *b.* 1797; *s.* as 2nd Bart. 1843; *m.* 1819 Caroline, only dau. of Henry Griffiths, Esq. (she *d.* 1867). Educated at Eton and St. John's Coll., Cambridge (B.A. 1818, M.A. 1824), is a Magistrate for Berks, Brecon, Carmarthen, Pembroke, and Wilts; Chancellor of St. David's, Rector of Rushall, Wilts, and Patron of 1 living; late Rector of St. Peter's, Marlborough.—*Llwyn-y-Wormwood Park, Llandovery, S. Wales ; Chancellor Manor, St. David's, Haverfordwest ; Norton House, Tenby.*

     Heir Pres., his brother Watkin Elias, a Gen. in the Indian Army ; b. 1799.

WILLIAMS, Sir WILLIAM FENWICK, Bart., K.C.B., of Kars (cr. 1856).
Only surviving son of the late Thomas Williams, Esq., of Nova Scotia; *b.* 1800. Educated at Woolwich; is a Lieut.-Gen. in the Army, late Lieut.-Governor of Nova Scotia, and formerly Col.-Commandant R.A.; served in Turkey, Persia, and Ceylon; appointed Commander of Woolwich Garrison 1856; Commander of the Artillery in Canada 1859; was M.P. for Calne 1856-9; received the baronetage for his defence of Kars in 1855. —*Army and Navy Club, s.w.*

WILLIAMS, Sir WILLIAM, Bart., of Tregullow, Cornwall (cr. 1866).
Youngest son of the late John Williams, Esq., of Scorier, Cornwall, by Catherine, dau. of Martyn Harvey, Esq., of Killifreth; *b.* 1791; *m.* 1826 Caroline, dau. of the late Richard Eales, Esq., of Easton, Devon. Is a J.P. and D.L. for Cornwall, and a Dep.-Warden for the Stannaries; was High Sheriff of Cornwall 1851. —*Tregullow, Scorier, Cornwall ; Ilcanton Court, Dur-*

staple; *Carlton and Windham Clubs*, s.w.; 42, *Brook Street*, w.

     Heir, his son Frederick Martin (of Goonvrea, Perran-ar-Worthal, Cornwall), educated at Winchester; a J.P. and D.L. for Cornwall, and M.P. for Truro; b. 1830; m. 1858 Mary Christian, dau. of the Rev. Robert Vanbergh Law, Rector of Christian Malford, Wilts, and grand-dau. of the late Bishop of Bath and Wells, and has, with other issue,
     * William Robert, b. 1860.

WILLIAMS, the Right Hon. Sir EDWARD VAUGHAN, Knt., P.C. (cr. 1847).
Son of the late Mr. Serjeant Williams, by Mary, dau. of Charles Clarke, Esq., of Forebridge, co. Stafford; *b.* 1797; *m.* 1826 June Margaret, dau. of the Rev. Walter Bagot, Rector of Blithfield, co. Stafford. Educated at Westminster and Trinity Coll., Cambridge; called to the Bar at Lincoln's Inn 1823; was a Judge of Common Pleas 1847-65; sworn a Member of the Privy Council 1865.—*Tanhurst, Dorking ; 1, Park Street, Westminster, s.w.*

WILLIAMS, Lady SARAH ELIZABETH, of Rhianva, Carnarvonshire.
Eldest dau. of William, 1st Earl Amherst, by his 1st wife Sarah, dau. and co.-heir of Andrew, 2nd and last Lord Archer, and widow of Other, 5th Earl of Plymouth; *m.* 1842 Sir John Hay Williams, Bart., M.P., of Edwinsford, who *d.* 1859.—*Rhianva, Bangor ; 23, Portman Square, w.*

WILLIAMS, Lady MARY, of Clovelly Court, Devon.
Fourth dau. of Hugh, 1st Earl Fortescue, by Hester, dau. of the Right Hon. George Grenville; *m.* 1823 Sir James Hamlyn Williams, Bart., who *d.* 1861. The late Bart. was a Dep.-Lieut. for Devon, High Sheriff of co. Carmarthen 1848, M.P. for co. Carmarthen 1820-1 and 1835-7, and Patron of 1 living.—*Clovelly Court, Bideford.*

WILLIAMS, ABRAHAM JONES, Esq., of Gelliwig, Carnarvonshire.
Fifth son of the late David Williams, Esq., of Saethon, co. Carnarvon; *b.* 1820; *m.* 1853 Sarah Elizabeth Margaret, dau. of the late Lieut.-Gen. Sir Love Parry Jones Parry, of Madryn Park, co. Carnarvon. Educated at University Coll., London: graduated as an M.D.; is a Magistrate for co. Merioneth, and a Dep.-Lieut. for co. Carnarvon (High Sheriff 1867).—*Gelliwig Hall, Pwllheli.*

+**WILLIAMS, CHARLES HENRY, Esq., of Roath Court, Glamorganshire.**
Son of the late C. Williams, Esq., of Roath Court; *b.* 18—; *m.* 1865 Millicent Frances, youngest dau. of Robert Herring, Esq., of Cromer, Norfolk, and has issue,

     * A son, b. 1866.

Mr. Williams is a J.P. and D.L. for co. Glamorgan, and a Magistrate for co. Monmouth.—*Roath Court, Cardiff.*

WILLIAMS, DAVID, Esq., of Deudraeth Castle, Merionethshire.
Third but eldest surviving son of the late David Williams, Esq., of Saethon, co. Carnarvon; *b.* 1800; *m.* 1841 Anne Louisa Loveday, only dau. of William Williams, Esq., of Peniarthuchaf, co. Merioneth, Barrister-at-Law, and has, with other issue,

     * William Edward Wynn, b. 1842.

Mr. Williams, who was educated at Chester, is a J.P. and D.L. for cos. Merioneth and Carnarvon (High Sheriff of Merioneth 1861, and of Carnarvon 1862). —*Deudraeth Castle, Tremadoc ; Reform Club, s.w.*

WILLIAMS, the Rev. DAVID.
Eldest son of the late Rev. David Williams (who was a Magistrate for Brecon), by Elizabeth, dau. of T. Williams, Esq., of Aberbrane; b. 1801; s. 1824; m. 1835 Elizabeth, dau. of J. Powell, Esq., of Penbryn, co. Brecon. Educated at Winchester and New Coll., Oxford (S.C.L. 1820, B.C.L. 1825); was appointed Rector of Alton Barnes 1835, and a Magistrate for Brecon 1824.—*Alton Barnes Rectory, Pewsey, Wilts; University Club, s.w.*

+ **WILLIAMS, the Rev. DAVID.**
Son of the late — Williams; b. 18—; m. 1800 Mary, 2nd dau. of the late Richard Janion Nevill, Esq., of Llangennech Park. Educated at St. David's Coll., Lampeter (B.D. 1855); is a Magistrate for co. Carmarthen; appointed Rector of Llanedy, and Professor of Welsh at St. David's Coll., 1854.—*The Rectory, Llanedy, Llanel'y.*

WILLIAMS, EDWARD WILMOT, Esq., of Herringstone House, Dorset.
Eldest son of the late James Wilmot Williams, Esq., of Herringston House, by Elizabeth Anne, 2nd dau. of R. Magenis, Esq., of co. Down, Ireland; b. 1826; s. 1853; m. 1862 the Hon. Sophia, dau. of Standish, 2nd Viscount Guillamore, and has, with other issue,

* Berkeley Cole Wilmot, b. 1865.

Mr. Williams, who was educated at Trinity Coll., Dublin (B.A. 1846), is a J.P. and D.L. for co. Dorset, and Lord of the Manor of Herringstone, and was formerly in the Bengal Cavalry.—*Herringstone House, Dorchester, Dorset; Carlton Club, s.w.*

WILLIAMS, EVAN, Esq., of Duffryn Frwd, Glamorganshire.
Eldest son of the late Henry Williams, Esq., of Duffryn Frwd, J.P. and D.L. for co. Glamorgan; b. 1800; s. 1847; m. 1834 Charlotte, 3rd dau. of William Thomas, Esq., J.P. and D.L., of Cefnllogell, co. Monmouth, and has, with other issue, an only son,

* Evan Thomas, b. 1841; m. 1863 Laura Rose, dau. of the late H. William Atkinson, Esq., 7th Dragoon Guards, and has issue, * Evan Ivor, b. 1866.

Mr. Williams is a J.P. and D.L. for co. Glamorgan (High Sheriff 1857). This family have been settled at Duffryn Frwd for several centuries.—*Duffryn Frwd, Cardiff.*

WILLIAMS, FRANCIS EDWARD, Esq., of Malvern Hall, Warwickshire.
Second son of the late John Williams, Esq., of Pitmaston, co. Worcester, by Dorothy, youngest dau. of the Rev. Henry Wigley, of Pensham House, co. Worcester; b. 1804; s. 1853; m. 1838 Ann, 3rd dau. and co.-heir of Henry Greswolde, Esq., of Malvern Hall, co. Warwick, and has, with other issue,

* Wigley Greswolde, a Magistrate for co. Warwick; b. 1839.

Mr. Williams, who is a Magistrate for cos. Hereford and Worcester, was on the roll of High Sheriffs for co. Worcester 1855-8, but excused the office on the ground of ill-health.—*Malvern Hall, Solihull; Pitmaston and Doddenham, Worcestershire.*

+ **WILLIAMS, GEORGE, Esq., of Scorrier, Cornwall.**
Younger son of the late Michael Williams, Esq., M.P., of Caerhayes, Cornwall, by Elizabeth, dau. of the late Richard Eales, Esq., of Eastdon, Devon; b. 1827; m. 1859 Charlotte Mary, dau. of Stephen Davey, Esq., of Bochym. Is a Magistrate for Cornwall.—*Scorrier, Truro.*

1000

WILLIAMS, GEORGE GRIFFITHS, Esq., of Rhoscellan, Cardiganshire.
Eldest son of the late Matthew Davies Williams, Esq., of Cwmcynfelin, J.P. and D.L., by Susanna, eldest dau. and heir of Simon Griffiths, Esq., of Cwmrhaidr, co. Montgomery: b. 1832; s. 1860. Educated at Trinity Coll., Oxford (B.A. 1854, M.A. 1857), is a J.P. and D.L. for co. Cardigan, and Patron of the living of Llangorwen. This family were formerly of Cwmcynfelin, in the same county.—*Rhoscellan, Aberystwith; Oxford and Cambridge Club, s.w.*

WILLIAMS, the Rev. HENRY BAYLEY, of Pantafon, Carnarvonshire.
Only son of the late Rev. P. Bayley Williams, J.P. and D.L., by Hannah, dau. of Henry Jones, Esq., of Llanrwst; b. 1805; s. 1836; m. 1829 Mary Anne, only child of the Rev. John Davids, of Coppy Hall, co. Stafford, and has, with other issue,

* John Bayley, Capt. Carnarvon Militia, b. 1833.

Mr. Williams, who was educated at Jesus Coll., Oxford (B.A. 1828), is a Magistrate for co. Carnarvon.—*Pantafon, Carnarvon; Aldridge, Walsall.*

WILLIAMS, HENRY MICHAEL, Esq., of Williamston, co. Kildare.
Eldest son of the late Michael Williams, Esq., J.P., of Williamston, by Martha, dau. of Andrew Armstrong, Esq., of Kilclare, King's Co.; b. 1838; s. 1863 Mary, eldest dau. of Francis Falkner, Esq., of Kingstown, co. Dublin, and has issue,

* Three daughters.

Mr. Williams is descended from a common ancestor with the Welsh Baronets of the same name.—*Williamston, Carbury, co. Kildare.*

WILLIAMS, HERBERT, Esq., of Stinsford, Dorset.
Younger son of the late William Williams, Esq., M.P., of Castle Hill, Dorset, by Anne, eldest dau. of John Rashleigh, Esq., of Penquite, Cornwall; b. 1807; m. 1832 Martha Maria Finden, only dau. of George Emery, Esq., of Banwell Grange, Somerset. Educated at Eton; is a J.P. and D.L. for Dorset, and Lieut. Queen's Own Regt. of Yeomanry. This family is a branch of the Williamses of Herringston.—*Stinsford, Dorchester, Dorset; Union Club, s.w.*

WILLIAMS, the Rev. HUGH.
Eldest son of the late George Williams, Esq., of East Williamston, co. Pembroke, by Mary his wife, dau. of George Williams Esq., of Daisylock, same co.; b. 1795; m. 1825 Mary, eldest dau. of the late Rev. W. J. Thomas, Incumbent of Caerau, co. Glamorgan, and has, with other issue,

* Hugh, educated at Marlborough Coll., LL.B. of St. John's Coll., Cambridge, Curate of Boswell, co. Stafford; b. 1823; m. 1863 Henrietta Mary, eldest dau. of William Fell, Esq., of The Close, Lichfield.

Mr. Williams, who was educated at Jesus Coll., Oxford (B.A. 1816, M.A. 1819), ordained Deacon 1818, Priest 1819, appointed Vicar of Bassaleg 1855; and Chancellor of the diocese of Llandaff 1815, is a Magistrate for co. Monmouth.—*Bassaleg Vicarage, Newport, Monmouthshire.*

+ **WILLIAM, the Rev. JAMES, of Tring Park, Bucks.**
Son of the late — Williams, Esq.; b. 18—; is married, and has issue. Is a Magistrate for Bucks.—*Tring Park, Tring, Bucks.*

WILLIAMS, JOHN, Esq., of Boones, Kent.
Eldest son of the late John Williams, Esq., of Boones, by Mary, elder dau. of the late John Seager, Esq., of Greenwich; b. 1800; s. 1831; m. 1840 Mary Stone-

feld, only dan. of Robert Alexander Gray, Esq., of Camberwell, J.P. for Surrey, and has, with other issue,

* John Aubrey, Lieut. 60th Rifles ; b. 1845.

Mr. Williams is a Magistrate for Kent.—*Boones, Edenbridge, Kent ; Junior Carlton Club, s.w. ; 98, Eaton Square, s.w.*

WILLIAMS, JOHN, Esq., of Treffos, Anglesey.
Eldest son of the late Rev. John Williams, of Treffos, by Eleanor, dau. of the Rev. James Vincent, of Bangor ; b. 1784; s. 1826; m. 1808 Elizabeth Jane Winter, 2nd dau. of Capt. William Goddard, R.N., and has, with other issue,

* Thomas Norris, in Holy Orders. M.A. of Merton Coll., Oxford, a J.P. and D.L. for co. Carnarvon, and Rector of Aber, near Bangor ; b. 1809 ; m. 1840 Mary Elizabeth, 3rd dau. of the Rev. Richard Howard, D.D., Rector of Beaumaris.

Mr. Williams, who was educated at Eton and Jesus Coll., Oxford, and called to the Bar at Lincoln's Inn 1809, is a J.P. and D.L. for Anglesey, a Magistrate for cos Carnarvon and Chester, and for Chester city ; Chairman of the Anglesey Quarter Sessions ; and Lieut.-Col. of the Anglesey Militia.—*Treffos, Llansadwrn, Anglesey, Wales ; Old Bank, Cheshire.*

+WILLIAMS, the Rev. JOHN, of Plâs Newydd, Merionethshire.
Son of the late Roger Williams, Esq., by Elizabeth, dau. of William Williams, Esq., of Llangynhaval ; b. 1812 ; m. 1836 Elizabeth, dau. of — Jones, Esq., and has, with other issue,

* John, b. 1839.

Mr. Williams, who was educated at Jesus Coll., Oxford (B.A. 1835, M.A. 1838), was formerly Rector of Llanymowddwy.—*Plâs Newydd, Llangollen.*

WILLIAMS, JOHN MICHAEL, Esq., of Caerhayes, Cornwall.
Eldest son of the late Michael Williams, Esq., M.P., of Gnaton and Caerhayes, by Elizabeth, dau. of the late Richard Eales, Esq., of Eastdon, Devon ; b 1813 ; s. 1858 ; m. 1852 Elizabeth Maria, eldest dau. of Stephen Davey, Esq., of Redruth, and has, with other issue,

* Michael, b. 1857.

Mr. Williams is a Dep.-Lieut. for Cornwall (High Sheriff 1865), and a Dep.-Warden of the Stannaries. —*Caerhayes Castle, Grampound ; Gnaton Hall, Devon.*

WILLIAMS, Major JOHN VINCENT HAWKESLEY.
Younger son of John Williams, Esq., of Treffos (whom see), by Elizabeth Jane Winter, dau. of Capt. William Goddard, R.N. ; b. 1817 ; m. 1842 Phœbe, dau. of the Rev. Richard Howard, D.D., Rector of Beaumaris, and has issue. Is a J.P. and D.L. for co. Carnarvon, and Major Carnarvon Militia.—Residence: *Bangor, N. Wales.*

WILLIAMS, JOSEPH WILLIAM, Esq., of Handsworth, Staffordshire.
Youngest son of the late Walks Williams, Esq., of Wednesbury Oak, co. Stafford (who d. 1867), by Mary, dau. of Joseph Moss, Esq., M.D. ; b. 1832. Is a Magistrate for co. Stafford.—*Handsworth Birmingham.*

WILLIAMS, JOSIAH DORE, Esq., of White Riding, Essex.
Youngest son of the late Thomas Williams, Esq., of Cowley Grove, near Uxbridge ; b. 1816 ; m. 1839 Emma Mary, eldest dau. of the late Rev. Henry Budd, Rector of White Riding, Essex. Mr. Williams, who is a Magistrate for Essex, purchased the property 1841.—*The Grange, White Riding, Harlow.*

+WILLIAMS, LEWIS, Esq., of Vronwnion, Merionethshire.
Son of the late Mr. Williams ; is a Magistrate for co. Merioneth (High Sheriff 1834), and a Capt. Merioneth Rifle Volunteers.—*Vronwnion, Dolgelley.*

WILLIAMS, MICHAEL HENRY, Esq., of Tredrea, Cornwall.
Second surviving son of the late Michael Williams, Esq., M.P., of Scorrier and Caerhayes, Cornwall, by Elizabeth, dau. of the late Richard Eales, Esq., of Eastdon, Devon ; b. 1824 ; m. 1853 Catherine Anne, eldest dau. of Richard Almack, Esq., of Melford, Suffolk, and has surviving issue,

* Three daughters.

Mr. Williams, who was educated at Harrow, is a Magistrate for Cornwall.—*Tredrea, Truro.*

WILLIAMS, MONTAGUE, Esq., of Woolland, Dorset.
Eldest son of the late Charles Montague Williams, Esq., Banker, of London, by Anna Maria. eldest dau. of the late Sir Samuel Scott, Bart., of Sundridge Park, Kent ; b. 1826 ; s. 1830 ; m. 1857 Sophia Elizabeth, eldest dau. of the Rev. L. Foot, Rector of Long Bredy, Dorset, and has, with other issue,

* Montague Scott, b. 1858.

Mr. Williams, who was educated at Harrow and Exeter Coll., Oxford (B.A. 1847, M.A. 1848), is a Magistrate for Dorset, Lord of the Manor and Patron of the Chapelry of Woolland, and a Lieut. in the 10th Dorset Rifle Volunteers. This family is a younger branch of the ancient Dorset family of Williams of Herringstone. —*Woolland House, Blandford ; University Club, s.w.*

WILLIAMS, MORGAN STUART, Esq., of Aberpergwm, Glamorganshire.
Eldest surviving son of the late William Williams, Esq., of Aberpergwm, by Matilda, only dau. and heir of Col. Smith, of Castella, co. Glamorgan : b. 1846 : s. his brother 1863. Is Patron of 1 living. This family descends from a long line of ancestors who held princely rule in parts of S. Wales.—*Aberpergwm, Neath.*

Heir Pres., his brother George Williams, b. 1850.

WILLIAMS, Mrs., of Crawley Grange, Bucks.
Elizabeth Margaret Montgomery, dau. of the late William Boswell, Esq., Advocate, and Sheriff of co. Berwick, by Elizabeth, youngest dau. of the late James Boswell, Esq., of Auchenleck, co. Ayr ; s. her father 1855 ; m. 1838 John Williams. Esq., of the Bombay Civil Service (who d. 1852). and has a daughter,

* Elizabeth Anne, m. 1860 the Rev. Charles Cumberlege, Vicar of Astwood, who, upon the death of his granduncle, Samuel Ware, Esq., of Hendon, took the name of Ware.

Mrs. Williams is Lady of the Manor of Astwood, Bucks. —*Crawley Grange, Newport Pagnell.*

WILLIAMS, PENRY, Esq., of Penpont, Brecknockshire.
Eldest son of the late Penry Williams, Esq., of Penpont (formerly Lord-Lieutenant of co. Brecon), by Maria, dau. of Samuel Yeats, Esq., of Monksmill, co. Gloucester ; b. 1807 ; s. 1817 ; m. 1832 Anne, dau. of Thomas Downes, Esq., of Hereford, and has, with other issue,

* Penry Boleyn, b. 1838.

Mr. Williams, who was educated at Westminster and Ch. Ch., Oxford (B.A. 1830), is a J.P. and D.L. for co. Brecon (High Sheriff 1848), and Chairman of the Brecon Quarter Sessions. *Penpont, Brecon.*

1001

+ WILLIAMS, PHILIP, Esq., of Aberbaiden, Monmouthshire.
Eldest son of the late — Williams, Esq.; *b.* 18—; *s.* his uncle 18—; is married, and has, with other issue,
* Sydney, educated at Cambridge, *b.* 1843.
Mr. Williams is a Magistrate for co. Monmouth, and a Banker at Abergavenny.—*Aberbaiden, Abergavenny.*

WILLIAMS, PHILIP ADDISON, Esq., of Harborow, Worcestershire.
Eldest son of the late Walter Williams, Esq., of Wednesbury Oak, co. Stafford, by Mary, dau. of Joseph Moss, Esq., M.D.; *b.* 1830; *s.* 1867; *m.* 1863 Mary, dau. of John Meire, Esq., of Brockton, co. Salop, and has, with other issue, * Walter, *b.* 1865.—*Harborow, Birmingham; Wednesbury Oak, Tipton.*

WILLIAMS, PHILIP HENRY, Esq., of Stoke House, Shropshire.
Youngest son of the late Penry Williams, Esq., of Penpont, co. Brecon, by Maria, dau. of Samuel Yents, Esq., of Monksmill, co. Gloucester; *b.* 1812; *m.* 1837 Charlotte Hamilton Seymour, youngest dau. of the late Capt. Francis E. Seymour, R.N.; and has, with other issue,
* Philip Seymour, *b.* 1842.
Mr. Williams, who was educated at Westminster and Ch. Ch., Oxford (B.A. 1834), is a J.P. and D.L. for cos. Brecon and Worcester, and a Magistrate for co. Salop. —*Stoke House, Burford, Tenbury.*

WILLIAMS, REGINALD FREKE, Esq., of Appuldercombe, I. of Wight.
Second son of the late Robert Wynne Williams, Esq., J.P., of Appuldercombe, by his 1st wife Marianne, dau. of Nathaniel Aked, Esq.; *b.* 1835; *s.* 1862; *m.* 1863 Charlotte Elizabeth, eldest dau. of Charles Rawson, Esq., of Wasdale Hall, Cumberland, and has issue,
♪ Gaynor Rudyerd, *b.* 1864.
Mr. Williams, who was educated at Highgate Grammar School and on the Continent, is Lord of the Manor of Appuldercombe.—*Appuldercombe, Newport, I. of Wight; Arthur's and Reform Clubs, s.w.*

WILLIAMS, RICHARD EDMUND, Esq., of Pentre-Mawr, Denbighshire.
Eldest son of the late Rev. Edmund Williams, J.P., of Pentre-Mawr (formerly Vicar of Llangerniew), by Susannah, 2nd dau. of John Price, Esq.; *b.* 1830; *s.* 1860; late Capt. 17th Regt. This family has been resident in this parish since 1603.—*Pentre-Mawr, Denbigh.*

WILLIAMS, RICHARD LLOYD-, Esq., of Bod Gwilym, Denbighshire.
Eldest son of the late Richard Lloyd-Williams, Esq., M.D., of Denbigh, by Mary, dau. of Richard Heaton, Esq., of Plâs Heaton, co. Denbigh; *b.* 1829; *s.* 1862; *m.* 1859 Jane Catherine, dau. of the Rev. John Jones, M.A., Rector of St. George, and has, with other issue,
* Roderic, *b.* 1861.
Mr. Lloyd-Williams, who was educated at Cheltenham Coll., is a Magistrate for co. Denbigh. This family has been seated at Hafodwyryd, near Llanrwst, co. Carnarvon, since *temp.* Elizabeth, and founded and endowed alms-houses in the year 1728, for the support of ten poor persons at Penmachno, in which parish the estate is situated.—*Bod Gwilym, Denbigh.*

WILLIAMS, ROBERT, Esq., of Bridehead, Dorset.
Only son of the late Robert Williams, Esq., of Bridehead, by Frances, youngest dau. of the late John Turner, Esq., of Putney; *b.* 1811; *s.* 1847; *m.* 1847 Mary Anne, dau. of the late Rev. J. W. Cunningham, Vicar of Harrow (she *d.* 1859); 2nd 1859 Lady Emily Maria,
1002

dau. of John Thornton, 11th Earl of Leven, and has, with other issue,
* Robert, educated at Eton and Ch. Ch., Oxford; *b.* 1848.
Mr. Williams, who was educated at Oriel Coll., Oxford (B.A. 1832, M.A. 1836), is a J.P. and D.L. for Dorset (High Sheriff 1855), Patron of 1 living, and a Banker in London and Dorchester; was J.P. for Dorchester 1835–41.—*Bridehead, Dorchester, Dorset; Grantham House, Putney H:ath, s.w.*

WILLIAMS, the Rev. St. GEORGE ARMSTRONG, M.A., of Plashen, Carnarvonshire.
Eldest son of the late Rev. Eliezer Williams, M.A., Vicar of Lampeter and Llansawel, and Prebendary of St. David's, by Jane Amelia Nugent, eldest dau. of Col. St. George Armstrong, of Annaduff House, Drumsna, co. Leitrim; *b.* 1805; *s.* 1820; *m.* 1827 Anne, only child of Thomas Jones, Esq., of Castellmai, co. Carnarvon, and has, with other issue,
* St. George Armstrong, educated at Rossall Hall and Jesus Coll., Oxford; *b.* 1833.
Mr. Williams, who was educated at Lampeter and Jesus Coll., Oxford (B.A. 1827, M.A. 1831), appointed Vicar of Pwllheli 1841, and Rector of Llangybi-cum-Llanarmon 1849, is a J.P. and D.L. for co. Carnarvon.—*Plashen, Pwllheli, N. Wales.*

WILLIAMS, THOMAS, Esq., of Warfield, Berks.
Only son of the late Robert Williams, Esq., of Warfield, by Jane, dau. of Thomas Cunningham, Esq., Lieut. R.N. (descended from the Cunninghams, Earls of Glencairn); *b.* 1796; *s.* 1803; *m.* 1st 1817 Mary Frances, 2nd dau. of John Paul Berthon, Esq., of the Register Office, Court of Chancery; 2nd 1833 Catherine, 2nd dau. of Edward Codd, Esq., of Kingston, Jamaica, and has by the former, with other issue,
* William Thomas, Lieut.-Col. Madras Army (32nd Regt.); *b.* 1817; *m.* 1842 Catherine, dau. of Lieut.-Col. Wilson, 32nd Regt. Madras, and has issue.
Mr. Williams, who was educated at Eton, and was formerly a Magistrate for co. Northampton (High Sheriff 1825), represents a younger branch of Williams of Herringstone.—*Warfield Lodge, Bracknell.*

WILLIAMS, the Very Rev. THOMAS, Dean of Llandaff.
Eldest son of the late Robert Williams. Esq., of Aberbran, co. Brecon, by Annabella, dau. of William Garnons, Esq., of Trelough, co. Hereford; *b.* 1801; *m.* 1828 Elizabeth, dau. of the late Venerable Richard Davies. Archdeacon of Brecon, and has, with other issue,
* Garnons, in Holy Orders, B.A. of Oriel Coll., Oxford, a Magistrate for cos. Radnor and Brecon; *b.* 1829; *m.* 1854 Catharine Frances, 2nd dau. of Fenton Hort, Esq., and has, with other issue, * Arthur Garnons, *b.* 1854.
Mr. Williams, who was educated at Shrewsbury and Oriel Coll., Oxford (B.A. 1823, M.A. 1826), appointed Archdeacon of Llandaff 1843, and Dean of Landaff 1857, is a Magistrate for cos. Monmouth and Brecon, and was formerly Rector of Llanvapley, co. Monmouth. —*Llandaff, Cardiff.*

WILLIAMS, THOMAS HUMFFREY, Esq., of Llwyn, Merionethshire.
Eldest son of Griffith Williams, Esq., by Mary, dau. of the late Thomas Hartley, Esq., J.P. and D.L. for co. Merioneth; *b.* 1836; *s.* his uncle, Robert Nanney Hartley, Esq., 1860. Educated at Jesus Coll., Oxford; is a Magistrate for co. Merioneth, and a Commissioner of the Turnpike Trust.—*Llwyn, Dolgelley.*
Heir Pres., his brother Robert Nanney Williams, *b.* 1840.

WILLIAMS, Col. THOMAS PEERS, of Temple House, Bucks.
Eldest son of the late Owen Williams, Esq., M.P., of Temple House, by Margaret, eldest dau. of the Rev. Edward Hughes, of Kinmel Park, co. Denbigh, and

sister of William, 1st Lord Dinorben; *b* 1795; *s.* 1832; *m.* 1835 Emily, youngest dau. of Anthony Bacon, Esq., of Benham Park, Berks, and has, with other issue,

  * Owen Lewis Cope, Capt. Royal Horse Guards; *b.* 1836.

Col. Williams, who was educated at Westminster and Ch. Ch., Oxford, is a J.P. and D.L. for Bucks. Berks, and Anglesey, Patron of 1 living, and Lieut.-Col. Commandant Royal Anglesey Militia; has been M.P. for Marlow since 1820.—*Temple House, Gt. Marlow; Craig-y-Don, Anglesey; Carlton Club, s.w.; 41, Berkeley Square, w.*

WILLIAMS, Trevor Samuel ADDAMS-, Esq., of The Garth, Monmouthshire.

Fourth son of the late William Addams-Williams, Esq., of Llangibby Castle, co. Monmouth (who *d.* 1824), by Caroline, dau. of Henry Marsh, Esq., of London; *b.* 1793; *m.* 1816 Eliza, dau. of the Rev. John Thomas, M.A., Vicar of Caerleon, co. Monmouth, and has, with other issue,

  * Henry John Trevor, *b.* 1820.

Mr. Addams-Williams is a Magistrate for co. Monmouth.—*The Garth, Caerleon.*

WILLIAMS, William ADDAMS-, Esq., of Llangibby Castle, Monmouthshire.

Only son of the late William Addams-Williams, Esq., J.P. and D.L., of Llangibby Castle (who was M.P. for co. Monmouth 1831–40), by Anna Louisa, eldest dau. of the late Rev. Iltyd Nicholl, D.D., of the Ham, co. Glamorgan; *b.* 1820; *s.* 1861; *m.* 1850 Catharine, eldest dau. of Thomas Cook, Esq., of Goytre House, co. Monmouth, and has, with other issue,

  * Rowland, *b.* 1851.

Mr. Williams, who was educated at King's Coll., London, is a Magistrate for co. Monmouth, Lord of the Manors of Tregrwg and Llangeview, and Patron of 3 livings. The name of Williams was assumed by the great-grandfather of the present owner, on his marriage with Ellen, eldest dau. and heir of Sir John Williams, of Llangibby.—*Llangibby Castle, Newport, Monmouthshire; Pembroke Road, Clifton, Bristol.*

WILLIAMS. See (*Brown of Rathbone.*)

WILLIAMS. (See *Drummond-Williams.*)

WILLIAMS. (See *Hanbury-Williams.*)

WILLIAMS. (See *Jones-Williams.*)

WILLIAMS-BULKELEY. (See *Bulkeley.*)

WILIAMS-ELLIS. (See *Clough of Plâs Clough.*)

WILLIAMS-FREEMAN. (See *Freeman.*)

WILLIAMS-PURCELL, John Ignatius, Esq., of Pentre-Mawr, Denbighshire.

Second son of the late Rev. Edmund Williams, of Pentre-Mawr, by Susannah, 2nd dau. of John Price, Esq., of Llanrhaiadr Hall, Denbigh; *b.* 1832; *s.* 1860; *m.* 1862 Annie, only child of Major Frederick Penn East, of Montreal, Canada, and has issue,

  * Annie Corse-Purcell.

Mr. Williams-Purcell is a Magistrate for co. Denbigh, and a Capt. Royal Denbigh Militia; was formerly in the Rifle Brigade; served throughout the Crimean campaign. This family has been resident in Llandyrnog since 1603.—*Pentre-Mawr, Llandyrnog, Denbigh, N.W.; Raleigh Club, w.*

WILLIAMS-WYNN. (See *Wynn.*)

WILLIAMSON, Sir Hedworth, Bart., of Whitburn Hall, co. Durham (cr. 1642).

Eldest son of the late Sir Hedworth Williamson, Bart., of Whitburn Hall (who was a Dep.-Lieut. for co. Durham, and formerly M.P. for Sunderland, by the Hon. Anne Elizabeth, dau. of Thomas Henry, 1st Lord Ravensworth; *b.* 1827; *s.* 1861; *m.* 1853 the Hon. Elizabeth, dau. of Henry Thomas, 2nd Lord Ravensworth. Educated at Eton and Ch. Ch., Oxford; is a J.P. and D.L. for co. Durham, Patron of 1 living, and 1 Capt. Commandant 1st Durham Volunteer Artillery; late Attaché to the British Embassy at St. Petersburg; elected M.P. for N. Durham 1864.—*Whitburn Hall, Monkswearmouth; Boodle's and Travellers' Clubs, s.w.*

  – *Heir, his son* Hedworth, *b.* 1867.

WILLIAMSON, David Robertson, Esq., of Lawers, Perthshire.

Only son of the late Charles A. Williamson, Esq., of Balgray, co. Dumfries, by Catherine Harriet, dau. of Thomas Bayard Clarke, Esq.; *b.* 1830; *s.* 1852; *m.* 1853 the Hon. Selina Maria, dau. of Charles, 1st Lord Tredegar, and has isssue,

  * Charles David Robertson, *b.* 1853.

Mr. Williamson, who was educated at the Royal Military College, Sandhurst, is a Magistrate for co. Perth, and was formerly in the Coldstream Guards.—*Lawers House, Crieff, N.B.*

WILLIAMSON, the Rev. Robert Hopper, of Hurworth, co. Durham.

Eldest son of the late Rev. Robert Hopper Williamson, Rector of Hurworth, by Ann, only dau. of the Rev. Dr. Williamson, Rector of Whickham, youngest son of Sir William Williamson, Bart., whose name he assumed, and grandson of the late Robert Hopper Williamson, Esq., of Whickham, co. Durham (Chancellor of the co. Palatine and Recorder of Newcastle-on-Tyne); *b.* 1813; *s.* 1865. Educated at Caius Coll., Cambridge (B.A. 1835, M.A. 1838); is Patron and Rector of Hurworth. —*Hurworth Rectory, Darlington.*

  Heir Pres., his brother William Williamson, late Lieut.-Col. 85th Regt., *b.* 1857; *m.* 1849 Margaret, dau. of Wm. Robinson, Esq., of Silksworth, co. Durham.

WILLIAMSON, Miss, of Kempston Manor, Beds.

Annie, only child of the late Rev. Edmond Roland Williamson, of Kempston Manor, Rector of Campton, Beds, by Charlotte, dau. of the late John Guy, Esq., of Hampton Wick, Middlesex; *s.* 1861; is Lady of the Manor of Kempston. The family of the Williamsons were settled at Husband Crawley, Beds, as far back as 1680.—*Kempston Manor, Bedford.*

WILLIAMSON. (See *Ker-Williamson.*)

WILLINGTON, Francis, Esq., of Tamworth, Warwickshire.

Only son of the late Thomas Willington, Esq., of Tamworth; *b.* 1800; *m.* 1825 Jane Anne, youngest dau. of the late Henry J. Pye, Esq., M.P., Poet-Laureate, and has, with other issue,

  * Francis Pye, in Holy Orders, M.A. of St. John's Coll., Cambridge, Vicar of Rudham, Norfolk; *b.* 1826.

Mr. Willington is descended from the knightly family of Willington, of Willington, co. Derby, whose ancestors were summoned to Parliament *temp.* Edward III.—Residence: *Tamworth.*

WILLINGTON, JAMES WALDYVE, Esq., of Castle Willington, co Tipperary.

Eldest son of the late John Willington, Esq., of Castle Willington (who was a Barrister-at-Law, and a Magistrate for co. Tipperary), by Alicia, 2nd dau. of John Willington, Esq., of Killoskehane Castle, co. Tipperary; *b.* 1846; *s.* 1861; descended from an ancient family formerly seated in Devon.—*Castle Willington, Nenagh.*

Heir Pres., his brother John Ormsby, *b.* 1847.

+**WILLINGTON, JOHN,** Esq., of Killoskehane, co. Tipperary.

Eldest son of the late John Willington, Esq., of Killoskehane, by Sarah, dau. of Christopher Ormsby, Esq., of Dublin; *b.* 1805; *s.* 1835. Is a Magistrate for co. Tipperary. This family is a younger branch of the ancient house of Wellington of Harley, co. Warwick. —*Killoskehane Castle, Templemore, co. Tipperary.*

WILLIS, DANIEL, Esq., of Halsnead, Lancashire.

Eldest surviving son of the late Richard Willis, Esq., of Halsnead (who *d.* 1837), by Cicely, only dau. of Joseph Feilden, Esq., of Witton Park, co. Lancaster; *b.* 1790; *s.* his brother 1863; *m.* 1833 Georgiana Amelia, dau. of Sir Wm. Feilden, Bart., and has, with other issue,

* Henry Rodolph de Auyers, Capt. 92nd Highlanders; *b.* 1834; *m.* 1862 Alice, dau. of the Rev. Robert Hornby, of Lythwood Hall, co. Salop.

Mr. Willis, who is Lord of the Manor of Whiston, descends from the family of the De Auyers, or Dauyel, who accompanied William the Conqueror into England, and the name of its head is to be found inscribed on the Roll of Battle Abbey.—*Halsnead Park, Pr. scot;*

WILLIS, JOHN WALPOLE, Esq., of Wick House, Worcestershire.

Second son of the late William Willis, Esq., Capt. 13th Light Dragoons, by Mary, dau. of the late Robert Hamilton Smyth, Esq., of Lismore, Ireland; *b.* 1793 ; *m.* 1st 1824 Lady Mary Isabella, eldest dau. of Thomas, late Earl of Strathmore (which marriage was dissolved 1833); 2nd 1836 Ann Susannah Kent, dau of the late Col. Thomas Henry Bund, of Wick House, co. Worcester, by whom he has, with other issue,

* John William Willis-Bund, *b.* 1843; assumed the surname and Arms of Bund under his grandfather's will; was educated at Eton and Caius Coll., Cambridge (B.A. 1865).

Mr. Willis, who was educated at the Charterhouse and Trinity Hall, Cambridge, called to the Bar at Gray's Inn, 1816, and practised in the Court of Chancery till 1827, has been a Colonial Judge in the Supreme Courts of Upper Canada, British Guiana, and N. S. Wales, and was the first Resident Judge of Victoria; he is a J.P. and D.L. for co. Worcester.—*Wick House, Worcester.*

WILLIS-FLEMING.

(See under *Fleming, of Stoncham Park.*)

WILLOCK, JOHN, Esq., of St. Bees, Cumberland.

Fourth son of the late Matthew Willock, Esq., by Olivia, dau. of Capt. C. Mainwaring, R.N., of Devon; *b.* 1786; *m.* 1819 Sarah, dau. of Anthony Dickinson, Esq., of Coolderton. Educated at the Grammar School, St. Bees; is a J.P. and D.L. for Cumberland; was formerly in the Army, and served in the Peninsula.—*St. Bees, Whitehaven.*

WILLOUGHBY, Sir JOHN CHRISTOPHER, Bart., of Baldon House, Oxon (cr. 1794).

Only surviving son of the late Sir John Pollard Willoughby, Bart., by his 2nd wife Maria Elizabeth, dau. of Thomas Hawkes, Esq.; *b.* 1859; *s.* as 5th Bart. 1866.—*Baldon House, Oxford ; Berwick Lodge, Bristol ; Fulmer Grove, Slough ; 18, Westbourne Terrace, s.w.*
1004

WILLOUGHBY, the Hon. and Rev. **CHARLES JAMES.**

Third son of Henry Willoughby, Esq., of Birdsall, co. York (who *d.* 1849), by Charlotte, eldest dau. of the Ven. John Eyre, Archdeacon of Nottingham, and brother of Henry, 8th Lord Middleton ; *b.* 1822 ; *m.* 1845 Charlotte, dau. of the late Henry John Hyde Seymour, Esq., of Wells, Somerset, and has, with other issue,

* Hugh St. Maur, *b.* 1849.

Mr. Willoughby, who was educated at Rugby and Trinity Coll., Cambridge (B.A. 1843, M.A. 1858), was appointed Rector of Wollaton and Cossal, Notts, 1846. —*Wollaton Rectory, Nottingham.*

WILLOUGHBY, the Hon. and Rev. **PERCIVAL GEORGE.**

Youngest son of the late Henry Willoughby, Esq., of Birdsall, co. York, by Charlotte, eldest dau. of the Rev. John Eyre, Archdeacon of Nottingham, and brother of Henry, 8th Lord Middleton ; *b.* 1827 ; *m.* 1852 Sophia, dau. of E. B. Beaumont, Esq., of Woodhall, near Barnsley and has, with other issue,

* Herbert Percival, *b.* 1853.

Mr. Willoughby was educated at Rugby and Trinity Coll., Cambridge (B.A. 1849) ; appointed Vicar of Carlton and Stapleford 1851, Rector of Saundby with North Wheatley 1858. —*Saundby Rectory, Gainsborough.*

WILLOUGHBY. (See *Middleton, Lord.*)

WILLOUGHBY DE BROKE, Lord (HENRY VERNEY).—Cr. 1492.

Eldest son of Robert John, 9th Lord, by Georgiana Jane, dau. of Major-General Thomas William Taylor, of Ogwell House, Devon ; *b.* 1844 ; *s.* 1862 ; *m.* 1867 Geraldine, eldest dau. of James H. Smith-Barry, of Marbury Hall, co. Chester. Educated at Eton and Ch. Ch., Oxford ; is a Dep.-Lieut. for co. Warwick, Lord of the Manor of Compton Verney. Patron of 9 livings, and Capt. 4th Warwickshire Rifle Volunteers. This family was formerly named Barnard, but the late Peer assumed by Royal licence the surname of Verney in 1853, on succeeding to the title of his maternal uncle Henry Peyto, 15th Lord, in right of his mother.—*Compton Verney, Warwick.*

Heir Pres., his brother Walter Robert, *b.* 1846 ; educated at Ch. Ch., Oxford.

WILLOUGHBY DE BROKE, Dowager Lady.

Margaret, dau. of the late Sir John Williams, Bart., of Bodelwyddan, co. Flint, by Margaret, dau. and heir of Hugh Williams, Esq., of Tyfry, co. Anglesey; *m.* 1829 Henry, 8th Lord Willoughby de Broke, who *d.* 1852. Is Patron of 1 living.—*Plas Newyd, Llanfair, Anglesea ; 21, Hill Street, w.*

WILLOUGHBY DE ERESBY, Lord (ALBERIC DRUMMOND-WILLOUGHBY).—Cr. 1295.

Only surviving son of Peter Robert, 20th Lord, by Clementina Sarah, dau. of James, Lord Perth (ext.); *b.* 1821 ; *s.* 1865. Is Joint Hereditary Great Chamberlain of England, a J.P. and D.L. for co. Lincoln, and Patron of 14 livings. This Barony was in abeyance 1778-80.—*Grimsthorpe, Bourne ; Gwydir Castle, Llanrwst, Carnarvonshire ; Drummond Castle, Perth, N.B. ; Cara Lodge, Twickenham, s.w.*

Heir Pres., his sister Clementina Elizabeth, Dowager Lady Aveland, *b.* 1809.

WILLS, the Rev. **JOHN.**

Eldest son of the late Rev. John Wills, by Flora Anne, dau. of Richard Nossiter Burnard, Esq., of Crewkerne ; *b.* 1812 ; *m.* 1836 Jane Ruscombe, 2nd dau. of Henry Coles, Esq. of Petherton Park, and has issue.

* Charles Henry, late of the 26th Cameronians ; *b.* 1838.

Mr. Wills, who was educated at Wadham Coll., Oxford

(B.A. 1832), is a Magistrate for Dorset, and Rector of South Perrott.—*South Perrott, Crewkerne.*

WILLS-SANDFORD. (See *Sandford.*)

WILLSHIRE, Sir ARTHUR REGINALD THOMAS, Bart., of Hill House, Berks (cr. 1840).
Eldest son of the late Lieut.-General Sir Thomas Willshire, Bart., G.C.B., of Hill House, by Annette Letitia, dau. of Capt. George Berkeley Maxwell, R.N.; *b.* 1850; *s.* as 2nd Bart., 1862.—*Hill House, Windsor.*

Heir Pres., his brother Earnest Maxwell, *b.* 1856.

WILLSON, JOHN, Esq., of High Wray, Lancashire, and Roundhay, Yorkshire.
Son of the late Anthony Willson, Esq., of High Wray, by Mary, dau. of Michael Barrow, Esq., of Troutbeck, Westmoreland, and niece of the Rev. Anthony Barrow, Vicar of Lindale, co. Lancaster; *b.* 1800; *m.* 1824 Margaret, dau. of John Atkinson, Esq., of Kendal, by whom he has, with other issue,

* John Joseph, *b.* 1836 ; *m.* 1861 Emily, dau. of John Hilliard, Esq., of New York, and has issue, Michael Anthony Hilliard, *b.* 1864.

Mr. Willson is a Magistrate for Leeds, of which Borough he was Mayor in 1854. This family was originally of Langdale, in Grasmere, Westmoreland.—*High Wray, Hawkshead; Roundhay, Leeds.*

WILLSON, MILDMAY, Esq., of Rauceby Hall, Lincolnshire.
Eldest son of the late Anthony Willson, Esq., J.P. and D.L., of Rauceby Hall (who was formerly M.P. for S. Lincolnshire, and who assumed the name. of Willson in lieu of his patronymic Peacock), by Mary Eliza Caroline, 2nd dau. of the late Edward Fane, of Fulbeck, co. Lincoln; *b.* 1847; *s.* 1866.—*Rauceby Hall, Sleaford.*

WILLYAMS (formerly WYLLYAMS), ARTHUR CHAMPION PHILLIPS, Esq., of Truro, Cornwall.
Youngest son of Humphrey Willyams, Esq., of Carnanton, Cornwall, by Ellen Frances, dau. of General Neynoe, of Castle Neynoe, co. Sligo; *b.* 1837; *m.* 1861 Charlotte Elizabeth, 2nd dau. of the Rev. Harry Longueville-Jones, of Ty-Maen, co. Glamorgan, H.M.'s Inspector of Schools, and has issue,

* Humphrey John, *b.* 1863.

Mr. Willyams, who was educated at Rugby and New Coll., Oxford, is a Magistrate for Cornwall, a Banker at Truro, and Capt. 12th Company of Duke of Cornwall's Rifle Volunteers.—*Truro, Cornwall; Reform and Volunteer Service Clubs, s.w.*

WILLYAMS, HUMPHRY, Esq., of Carnanton, Cornwall.
Son of the late James Willyams, Esq., of Carnanton, by Anne, dau. of William Champion. Esq., of Wormleigh, co. Gloucester; *b.* 1791 ; *s.* 1828 ; *m.* 1822 Ellen Frances, dau. of General Edward Brydges Neynoe, of Castle Neynoe, and has, with other issue,

* Edward William brydges, (of Nans-keval, near St. Columb, Cornwall,) educated at Eton and Merton Coll., Oxford ; a J.P. and D.L. for Cornwall, Major 16th Duke of Cornwall's Rifle Volunteers, and late M.P. for Truro; *b.* 1834 ; *m.* 1856 Jane, youngest dau. of Sir Trevor Wheler, Bart.

Mr. Willyams, who is a J.P. and D.L. for Cornwall, and a Deputy Warden of the Stannaries, was M.P. for Truro 1848-52, and formerly Major R. Cornwall Miners Militia.—*Carnanton, St. Columb; Reform Club, s.w.*

WILMOT, Sir HENRY SACHEVEREL, Bart., of Chaddesden Hall, Derbyshire (cr. 1759).
Eldest son of the late Sir Robert Wilmot, Bart. of Chaddesden Hall, by Lucy, eldest dau. of the late Robert Grimston, Esq., of Neswick Hall, co. York; *b.* 1800; *s.* as 4th Bart. 1842 ; *m.* 1826 Maria, eldest dau. of the late Edward Miller Mundy, Esq.. of Shipey Hall, near Derby (she *d.* 1865). Educated at Rugby; is a J.P. and D.L. for co. Derby (High Sheriff 1852), a Magistrate for Notts, Patron of 2 livings, and a Commander R.N. retired. This family is an elder branch of the Wilmots of Osmaston, and the Eardley-Wilmots of Berkswell.—*Chaddesden Hall, Derby; Junior United Service Club, s.w.*

Heir, his son Henry, V.C., a Magistrate for co. Derby, late Major Rifle Brigade; *b.* 1831 ; *m.* 1862 Charlotte Cecilia, 2nd dau. of the Rev. Edmund Pare.

WILMOT, Sir ROBERT EDWARD, Bart., of Osmaston Hall, Derbyshire (cr. 1772).
Eldest son of the late Right Hon. Sir Robert John Wilmot, Bart., of Osmaston Hall (who assumed the additional name of Horton), by Anne, dau. of the late Eusebius Horton, Esq., of Catton, co. Derby; *b.* 1808; *s.* as 4th Bart. 1841 ; *m.* 1842 Margaret, dau. of the late Rev. Andrew Kersteman, and widow of Robert Algeo, Esq. Educated at Eton and Ch. Ch., Oxford ; is Patron of 2 livings; was High Sheriff of co. Derby 1846.—*Osmaston Hall, Derby ; Travellers' Club, s.w.*

Heir Pres., his brother George Lewis Wilmot-Horton, M.A. of Trinity Coll., Cambridge, Rector of Garrioldisham, Norfolk; *b.* 1811 ; *m.* 1849 Frances Angusta, youngest dau. of Henry Pitches Boyce, Esq.

WILMOT, Sir JOHN EARDLEY-, Bart. (cr. 1820).
Eldest son of the late Sir John Eardley Eardley-Wilmot, Bart., M.P., of Berkswell Hall, co. Warwick (who was formerly Governor of Van Diemen's Land), by his 1st wife Elizabeth Emma. dau. of Caleb Hillier Parry, Esq., M.D., of Bath; *b.* 1810; *s.* as 2nd Bart. 1847 ; *m.* 1839 Eliza Martha, dau. of Sir Robert Williams Bulkeley, Bart., M.P. Educated at Winchester and Balliol Coll., Oxford (B.A. 1831): called to the Bar at Lincoln's Inn 1842; is a J.P. and D.L. for co. Warwick, Recorder of Warwick, and Judge of the Middlesex County Courts.—*Oxford and Cambridge Club, s.w ; 3, Elvaston Place, Queen's Gate, s.w.*

Heir, his son William Assheton, Lieut. 5th Foot; *b.* 1841.

+**WILMOT**, Gen. EARDLEY NICHOLAS, of Malvern, Worcestershire.
Second son of the late Sir Robert Wilmot, Bart.. by his 2nd wife, Marianne dau. of Charles Howard, Esq., of Pipe Grange, co. Stafford; *b.* 1809 ; *m.* 1855 Emily Elizabeth, 2nd dau. of the late Thomas Whinnore, Esq., of Apley, co. Salop. Entered the Army in 1819; is a Magistrate for co. Hereford, and a Gen. in the Army.—*Rose Bank, Malvern.*

WILMOT, EDMUND, Esq., of Milford, Derbyshire.
Youngest son of the late Sir Robert Wilmot. Bart., of Chaddesden, by Lucy, dau. of Robert Grimston, Esq., of Neswick, co. York : *b.* 1809 : *m.* 1848 Anne, youngest dau. of the late Francis Hurt, Esq., of Alderwasley, co. Derby, and has, with other issue,

* Francis Edmund, *b.* 1849.

Mr. Wilmot, who is a J.P. and D.L. for co. Derby and a Magistrate for Notts, was formerly in the Bengal Civil Service.—*Milford House, Derby.*

WILMOT, Mrs., of Buxton, Derbyshire.
Emma Elizabeth, 2nd dau. of the late Sir Francis Sacheverell Darwin, Knt.; *m.* 1841 (as his 2nd wife) Edward Wollett Wilmot, Esq., of Buxton, who was a Magistrate for co. Derby, and who *d.* 1864, leaving issue, five sons and two daughters. *Manor House, Buxton.*

WILMOT, FRANCIS SACHEVEREL, Esq., late of Newton Solney, Derbyshire.
Third son of the late Edward Sacheverel Wilmot, Esq., by Anne, only dau. of Dr. Chambers, of Stretton; b. 1806. Educated at St. John's Coll., Cambridge (B.A. 1829); represents a younger branch of the Wilmots, Baronets, of Chaddesden.

WILMOT-CHETWODE. (See Chetwode.)

WILMOTT-SITWELL. (See Sitwell.)

WILSHERE, CHARLES WILLES, Esq., of The Frythe, Herts.
Only surviving son of the late Thomas Wilshere, Esq., of Hitchin (who d. 1832), by Lora, dau. of Charles Beaumont, Esq.; b. 1814; s. his brother, William Wilshere, Esq., 1867; m. 1840 Elizabeth Marie, dau. of William M. Farmer, Esq., of Nonsuch Park, Surrey (formerly M.P. for Huntingdon), and has issue, four daus. Mr. Wilshere, who was educated at Trinity Coll., Cambridge, is a Magistrate for Herts. The family has been settled in Herts since the time of Edward III. —The Frythe, Welwyn; Oxford and Cambridge Club, s.w.

WILSON, Sir THOMAS MARYON, Bart., of Searles, Sussex, and Charlton, Kent (cr. 1660).
Eldest son of the late Sir Thomas Maryon Wilson, Bart. of Searles, by Elizabeth, dau. of James Smith, Esq., Capt. R.N; b. 1800; s. as 8th Bart. 1821. Educated at St. John's Coll., Cambridge (M.A. 1823); is a J.P. and D.L. for Kent (High Sheriff 1828), a Magistrate for Sussex and Surrey, and Col. W. Kent Militia; Lord of the Manor of Hampstead, and Patron of 4 livings. —Charlton House, Blackheath, s.e.; Searles, Uckfield; Carlton, United, Service, University, and Junior United Service Clubs, s.w.
　　Heir Pres., his brother John (of Fitzjohns, Great Canfield, Dunmow), a J.P. and D.L. for Essex; b. 1802; m. 1825 Charlotte Julia, dau. of George Wade, Esq., of Dunmow, Essex, and has issue.

WILSON, Sir ARCHDALE, Bart., G.C.B. (cr. 1857).
Third son of the late Rev. George Wilson, Rector of Didlington, by Anna Maria, dau. of the Rev. Charles Millard, and cousin of Henry, 2nd Lord Berners; b. 1803; m. 1842 Ellen, dau. of the late Col. Warren Hastings Frith, Bengal Artillery. Educated at Norwich, is a Magistrate for Norfolk, Col. Bengal Artillery and Major-General Bengal Army; was in command at the siege and capture of Delhi 1857.—Oriental Club, s.w.; 22, Park Crescent, w.
　　Heir Pres., his nephew Rowland Knyvet (2nd son of the late Rear-Admiral George Knyvet Wilson, who d. 1866, by Agnes Mary, youngest dau. of the late Rev. William Yonge, Vicar of Swaffham, Norfolk), b. 1840; educated at Eton and King's Coll., Cambridge (B.A. 1862).

WILSON, Sir JOHN MORILLYON, Knt., C.B.‡ (cr. 1838).
Son of the late Rev. John Wilson, Rector of Whitchurch, co. York; b. 1783; m. 1824 Amelia Elizabeth Bridgman, dau. of Col. John Houlton (she d. 1864). Is a Col. in the Army, and Major and Military Commandant of Chelsea Hospital; late Gentleman Usher of the Privy Chamber to Queen Adelaide; was formerly in the 1st Foot; served in Canada, the Peninsula and West Indies.—Royal Hospital, Chelsea, s.w.

WILSON, CHARLES MONCK, Esq., of Cahirconlish, co. Limerick.
Second but only surviving son of the late Thomas Maunsell Wilson, Esq., of Cahirconlish, by the Hon.

Isabella, dau. of Charles, 1st Viscount Monck, of Charleville, co. Wicklow; b. 1830; s. 1850; m. 1860 Alice Maria, dau. of the Rev. Hugh Edward Prior, Rector of Clonmel, and has issue,
　　* Thomas Hugh, b. 1861.
Mr. Wilson, who is a Magistrate for co. Limerick, was formerly in the 14th Foot.—Cahirconlish House, co. Limerick; Kildare Street Club, Dublin; Volunteer Service Club, s.w.

WILSON, EDWARD, Esq., of Rigmaden, Westmoreland.
Eldest son of the late Christopher Wilson, Esq., of Rigmaden, by Catherine, dau. of James Wilson, Esq., of Kendal, Westmoreland; b. 1797; s. 1845; m. 1830 Anne Clementina, only dau. of the late Lieut-General Sir Thomas Sidney Beckwith, K.C.B. Educated at Jesus Coll., Cambridge (B.A. 1820); is a J.P. and D.L. for Westmoreland (High Sheriff 1849).—Rigmaden Park, Kirkby-Lonsdale; Conservative Club, s.w.

WILSON, FRANCIS SILLERY, Esq., of Proudstown House, co. Meath.
Only son of the late Whitton William Wilson, Esq., of Proudstown House, by Jane, dau. of Francis Sillery, Esq., of Dunroo Nobber; b. 1826; s. 1832; m. 1860 Rachelle, dau. of Wm. North, Esq., of Black Hall Street, Dublin. This family has been seated in co. Meath since 1725.—Proudstown House, Tara, co. Meath.

WILSON, FULLER MAITLAND, Esq., of Stowlangtoft Hall, Suffolk.
Eldest son of the late Henry Wilson, Esq., J.P. and D.L., of Stowlangtoft (who was High Sheriff of Suffolk 1845), by his first wife Mary Fuller, eldest dau. of the late Ebenezer Fuller Maitland, Esq., of Park Place, Berks; b. 1825; s. 1867; m. 1852 Agnes Caroline, 2nd dau. of Vice-Chancellor Sir R. T. Kindersley, and has issue. Educated at Eton and Ch. Ch., Oxford (B.A. 1847, M.A. 1850); is a Magistrate for Suffolk, Lord of the Manor of Stowlangtoft. Patron of 4 livings, and Major W. Suffolk Militia.—Stowlangtoft Hall, Bury St. Edmund's.

WILSON, GEORGE EDWARD, Esq., of Dallam Tower, Westmoreland.
Eldest son of the late George Wilson, Esq., of Heath Hall, Wakefield, co. York, by Sarah, dau. of Daniel Wilson, Esq., of Dallam Tower; b. 1814; s. 1853; m. 1842 Gertrude Mary, dau. of the late Wm. Hulton, Esq., of Hulton, co. Lancaster, and has, with other issue,
　　* George Crowle, b. 1846.
Mr. Wilson, who was educated at Eton and Trinity Coll., Cambridge, is a J.P. and D.L. for Westmoreland (High Sheriff 1849-50), and a Magistrate for co. Lancaster; was formerly Capt. Westmoreland and Cumberland Yeomanry.—Dallam Tower, Milnthorp.

WILSON, GEORGE HOLT, Esq., of Redgrave, Suffolk, and Billingford, Norfolk.
Only son of the late George St. Vincent Wilson, Esq., of Redgrave Hall, by Louisa Matilda, dau. of the Rev. John Surtees, Prebendary of Bristol; b. 1841; s. 1850; m. 1865 Lucy Caroline, eldest dau. of William E. James, Esq., of Barrock Park, Cumberland, and has issue,
　　* A son, b. 1867.
Mr. Wilson, who was educated at Eton, is Lord of the Manors of Billingford and Thorpe Parva, and Patron of the livings of Redgrave and Billingford.—Redgrave Hall, Botesdale

+ WILSON, HENRY JOHN, Esq., of Sherwood, Notts.

Son of the late William Wilson, Esq., of Sherwood Hall, by his first wife; b. 18 —; s. 1866; m. 1859 Charlotte, dau. of Charles Cowan, Esq., of Valleyfield, Midlothian.—*Sherwood Hall, Mansfield, Notts.*

WILSON, the Rev. JAMES ALLEN, of Brinkcliffe Tower, Yorkshire.

Eldest son of the late James Wilson, Esq., of Brinkcliffe Tower, by Elizabeth, eldest dau. of the Rev. Jonathan Alderson, Rector of Harthill, co. York; b. 1827; s. 1867; m. 1860 Catharine, younger dau. of Henry Rennington, Esq., of Aynsome, co. Lancaster, and has issue two daughters. Mr. Wilson, who was educated at Trinity Coll., Cambridge (B.A. 1851, M.A. 1854); is Rector of Bolton-by-Bolland, co. York. The ancestors of this very ancient family resided at Broomhead from the time of Edward I.—*Brinkcliffe Tower, Sheffield; The Rectory, Bolton-by-Bolland, Clitheroe.*

WILSON, the Rev. JOHN, of Wigtoft, Lincolnshire.

Only son of the late Rev. John Wilson, Vicar and Patron of Donington, co. Lincoln (who d. 1850), by Hannah Charlotte, dau. of the Rev. John Smith, D.D., Rector of Nantwich, co. Chester; b. ˙1804; m. 1829 Frances, dau. of Richard Gleed, Esq., of Donington, co. Lincoln, but has no issue. Mr. Wilson, who was educated at St. Catharine's Coll., Cambridge (B.A. 1827, M.A. 1830), is a Magistrate and Senior Chairman for the Quarter Sessions for the Division of Holland and a Magistrate for the Division of Lindsey and Kesteven, co. Lincoln; is Impropriator and Patron of Donington, also Vicar of Wigtoft, with Quadring; formerly Vicar of Deeping, St. James's, co. Lincoln. This family was formerly of Alkertree and Uldale in Cumberland.—*The Vicarage, Wigtoft, Spalding; Cavendish Club, w.; Clergy Club, s.w.*

WILSON, JOHN, Esq., of Seacroft, Yorkshire.

Younger son of the late John Wilson, Esq., of Seacroft and of Cliffe Hall, in the N. Riding, by Martha, dau. of Richard Bassett, Esq., of Glentworth, co. Lincoln; b. 1808; s. 1836; m. 1846 Anna Maria Isabella, dau. of Roderick Macleod, Esq., of Cadboll, Ross-shire, and has, with other issue,

* Roderick John, b. 1847.

Mr. Wilson, who was educated at Rugby and Trinity Coll., Cambridge (B.A. 1830, M.A. 1838), is a J.P. and D.L. for the W. Riding of Yorkshire, and Lord of the Manors of Seacroft and Manston Ansthorpe; he was formerly Capt. 2nd W. York Militia. This family is a younger branch of the Wilsons of Cliffe (whom see).—*Seacroft Hall, Leeds; Oxford and Cambridge Club, s.w.*

WILSON, JOHN, Esq., of The Howe, Westmoreland.

Eldest son of the late Judge Wilson, of The Howe, by Mary Anne, dau. of the late Mr. Serjeant Adair: b. 1789; s. 1795; m. 1817 Dorothy, dau. of Charles Gibson, Esq., of Quernmore Park, co. Lancaster, and has, with other issue,

* John, b. 1818.

Mr. Wilson is a J.P. and D.L. for Westmoreland (High Sheriff 1854), and an Admiral R.N. retired.—*The Howe, Windermere; United Service Club, s.w.*

WILSON, JOHN GERALD, Esq., of Cliffe, Yorkshire.

Eldest son of the late Richard Bassett Wilson, Esq., J.P. and D.L., of Cliffe, by Anne, dau. of William Fitzgerald, Esq., of Adelphi, co. Clare, Ireland; b. 1841; s 1867. This family was founded by John Wilson, of

Camphall, Leeds, who established himself at Cliffe in the 18th century.—*Cliffe, Darlington.*

WILSON, JOSEPH HENRY, Esq., of Whiteley Hill, Berks.

Eldest son of the late Joseph Wilson, Esq., of Lower Worton, Oxon, by Emma, dau. of Christopher Aplin, Esq.; b. 1820; m. 1845 Henrica, eldest surviving dau. of Wm. Haigh, Esq., of Furzedown, and has issue,

* Frances Henrica.

Mr. Wilson, who was educated at Ex. Coll., Oxford, and called to the Bar at the Middle Temple 1845, is a Magistrate for Oxon and Devon.—*Whiteley Hill, Reading.*

WILSON, MATHEW, Esq., of Eshton Hall, and Kildwick, Yorkshire.

Eldest son of the late Mathew Wilson, Esq., of Eshton, by Margaret Clive (his first cousin), only dau. of Mathew Wilson, Esq., of Eshton Hall; b. 1802; s. 1854; m. 1826 Sophia Louisa Emerson, dau. of Sir Wharton Amcotts, Bart., of Kettlethorpe, co. Lincoln, and by her, who d. 1833, has issue,

* Mathew Wharton, of Ablington, near Fairford, a Magistrate for co. Gloucester; b. 1827; m. 1850 Grariana Mary, dau. of Admiral Richard Thomas, of Stonehouse, and has, with other issue, * Mathew Amcotts, b. 1853.

Mr. Wilson, who was educated at Harrow and Brasenose Coll., Oxford (B.A. 1824), is a J.P. and D.L. for co. Lancaster and for the W. Riding of co. York. Lord of the Manors of Eshton, North Bierley, Cleckheaton, and Scholes, and Patron of 2 livings; he was M.P. for Clitheroe 1841-2 and 1847-53.—*Eshton Hall, Gargrave; Athenæum Club, s.w.*

WILSON, Mrs., of The Chase, Norfolk.

Jane, youngest dau. of Lionel Self, Esq., of King's Lynn; m. 1827 Philip Wilson, Esq., of The Chase, who d. 1866, leaving issue three daughters. Mr. Wilson represented a younger branch of the family of Lord Berners.—*The Chase, King's Lynn.*

WILSON, SAMUEL, Esq., of Beckenham, Kent.

Son of John Wilson, Esq., of Stenson, co. Derby, by Elizabeth, heir of James Wyght, Esq., Merchant, of London; b. 1792; m. 1813 Jemima, dau. of Richard Lea, Esq., of Beckenham, Kent, an Alderman of London, and has, with other issue,

* Cornelius Lea (of The Cedars, Beckenham), a Magistrate for Kent; b. 1815; m. 1842 Mary Ann, dau. and heir of Isaac Wilcox. Esq. of Pembury, Kent, and has, with other issue, * Cornelius Wilcox, b. 1844.

Mr. Wilson is an Alderman and Commissioner of Lieutenantcy for London, a Magistrate for Surrey, Sussex, Kent, Essex, Middlesex. London, and Westminster and Col. of the R. London Militia; he was Sheriff of London and Middlesex 1833, Lord Mayor 1838.—*Beckenham, Bromley; New Barracks, Finsbury, e.c.*

WILSON, Mrs., of Farm Hill, Isle of Man.

Eliza, dau. of Samuel Thomson, Esq., of Heywood House, Douglas, I. of Man; m. 1819 Senhouse Wilson, Esq., of Farm Hill, who d. 1864, leaving issue,

* Senhouse Heywood, b. 1834.

The late Mr. Wilson who was called to the Manx Bar in 1835, was High Bailiff, or Chief Magistrate, of Douglas, Isle of Man, and formerly a Member of the House of Keys, and afterwards High Bailiff.—*Farm Hill and Sydney Mount, Douglas, I. of Man.*

WILSON, THOMAS, Esq., of Shotley Hall, Northumberland.

Eldest surviving son of the late John Wilson, Esq., of Shotley Hall, and of Nent Hall, Cumberland, by Mary, dau. of John Bownas, Esq.; b. 1800; m. 1868 Elizabeth, youngest dau. of the late Sir Samuel Cunard, Bart. Is a J.P. and D.L. for Cumberland, a Magistrate for co. Durham, and Patron of 1 living.—*Shotley Hall, Gateshead*

+WILSON, THOMAS FRANCIS, Esq., of Althorne Hall, Essex.
Eldest son of the late Alderman Wilson, of London; b 18—. Is a Dep.-Lieut. for Essex.—*Althorne House, Maldon.*

WILSON, WILLIAM, Esq., of High Park, Westmoreland.
Second son of the late Christopher Wilson, Esq., of Rigmaden Park, by Catherine, dau. of James Wilson, Esq., J.P., of Kendal; b. 1810; m. 1843 Maria Lætitia, dau. of Richard Parrott Hulme, Esq., of Maisonnette, Devon, and has, with other issue,
   • Christopher Wyndham, b. 1844.
Mr. Wilson, who was educated at Haileybury Coll., is a J.P. and D.L. for co. Westmoreland (High Sheriff 1863), and was formerly in the Indian Civil Service. —*High Park, Kendal.*

+WILSON, WILLIAM HENRY BOWEN JORDAN, Esq., of Knowle Hall, Warwickshire.
Son of the late Rev. William Wilson, of Knowle Hall, by Miss Jordan, of South Wales; b. 180—; m. 1831 Louisa, youngest dau. of the late Richard Le Hunte, Esq., of Artramon, co. Wexford, and by her, who d. 1864, has, with other issue,
   • William, b. 1834.
Mr. Wilson, who is a Magistrate for co. Warwick, and a Dep.-Lieut. for co. Pembroke, was High Sheriff of co. Carmarthen 1837, and formerly Capt. 3rd Dragoon Guards.—*Knowle Hall, Warwick.*

WILSON. (See under *Berners, Lord.*)

WILSON. (See *Carus-Wilson.*) .

WILSON. (See *Parkinson.*)

WILSON (FOUNTAYNE-). (See *Montagu.*)

WILSON-PATTEN, the Right Hon. JOHN, of Bank Hall, Lancashire.
Son of the late Col. Thomas Wilson-Patten, M.P., of Bank Hall (who assumed the additional name of Wilson in 1800), by Elizabeth, eldest dau. of Nathan Hyde, Esq., of Ardwicke, co. Lancaster; b. 1802; s. 1827; m. 1828 Anna Maria, dau. and co-heir of the late Peter Patten-Bold, Esq., of Bold, co. Lancaster, and by her, who d. 1846, has, with other issue,
   • Eustace John, Capt. 1st Life Guards; b. 1836; m. 1863 Emily Constantia, eldest dau. of the late Rev. Lord John Thynne, and has issue, a daughter.
Colonel Wilson-Patten, who was educated at Eton and Magdalen Coll., Oxford, is a J.P. and D.L. for co. Lancaster, and Col. 3rd Lancashire Militia; he was appointed an A.D.C. to the Queen 1856; was M.P. for Lancashire 1830-1, and has sat for N. Lancashire since 1832; was Chairman of the Committee of the House of Commons 1852-3, appointed Chancell'or of the Duchy of Lancaster, and sworn a Member of the Privy Council 1867.—*Bank Hall, Warrington ; Light Oaks, Cheadle; Carlton, United Service, and Travellers' Clubs, S.W.; 24, Hill Street, w.*

WILSON-SLATOR, GEORGE WARNER, Esq., of Belle Ville, co. Meath.
Only son of the late Henry Bevan Wilson-Slator, Esq., J.P., of Belle Ville (High Sheriff of co. Cavan 1852, and of co. Longford 1853), by Annabella, only dau. and heir of John Hinds, Esq., of Mulhussey Castle, co. Meath; b. 1825; s. 1857. Is a Magistrate for cos. Meath and Longford. The additional name of Slator was assumed by Royal licence in 1852, by the father of the present representative, on succeeding to his

maternal estates in co. Longford.—*Belle Ville, Dunshaughlin, co. Meath; White Hill, Edgeworth Town, co. Longford.*

WILSON-TODD, WILLIAM HENRY, Esq., of Tranby Park, Yorkshire.
Third son of the late Joshua Wilson, Esq., by Frances Maria, dau. of — Robinson, Esq.; b. 1828; m. 1855 Jane Maria Rutherford, only child and heiress of the late John Todd, Esq., of Halnaby Hall and Tranby Park, co. York (whose name he assumed), and has issue. Mr. Wilson-Todd, who is *jure uxoris* Lord of the Manor of Tranby, was formerly Capt. 39th Regt.— *Tranby Park, Hull ; Halnaby Hall, Darlington.*

WILTON, Earl of (THOMAS EGERTON, P.C., G.C.H., D.C.L.).—Cr. 1801.
Second son of Robert Grosvenor, 1st Marquis of Westminster, by Lady Eleanor, dau. of Thomas, 1st Earl of Wilton (so cr. with remainder to his daughter's younger children); b. 1799; s. 1814; m. 1st 1821 Lady Mary Margaret, dau. of Edward, 12th Earl of Derby (she d. 1858); 2nd 1863 Susan Isabella, only child of the late Major Elton Smith (Madras Army), of Ilminster, Somerset. Educated at Westminster; is a Dep.-Lieut. for co. Lancaster, Patron of 4 livings, and Col. Queen's Own Light Infantry and of the Tower Hamlets Militia; was formerly Lord Steward of the Household.—*Egerton Lodge, Melton Mowbray; Heaton Hall, Manchester, Carlton Club, s.w.; 7, Grosvenor Square, w.*
   Heir, his son Arthur Edward Holland Grey, Viscount Grey de Wilton, educated at Eton; late M.P. for Weymouth; late Lieut. 1st Life Guards, and formerly Lieut. Duke of Lancaster's Yeomanry Hussars; b. 1833; m. 1858 Lady Elizabeth Charlotte Louisa, eldest dau. of William, 2nd Earl of Craven.

WILTON, HENRY HOOPER, Esq., of Whitminster, Gloucestershire.
Second and only surviving son of the late Henry Wilton, Esq., of Gloucester (who d. 1822), by Margaret, 2nd dau. of the late Wm. Fryer. Esq.; b. 1795; m. 1827 Harriet, dau. of the late Rev. John Jones, Vicar of Foy, co. Hereford, and has, with other issue,
   • Charles Turner, M.A. of Exeter Coll., Oxford, Vicar of Foy, co. Hereford; b. 1832; m. 1860 Millicent Mary, dau. of the Rev. H. Mirehouse, of Easton-in-Gordano.
Mr. Wilton is a Magistrate for co. Gloucester.—*Whitminster House, Stonehouse, Gloucestershire.*

WINCHESTER, Marquis of (JOHN PAULET). —Cr. 1551.
Eldest son of Charles Ingoldsby, 13th Marquis, by Anne, dau. of John Andrews, Esq., of Shotney Hall, Northumberland; b. 1801; s. 1843; m. 1855 the Hon. Mary, dau. of Henry, 6th Lord Rokeby. Educated at Eton: is Lord-Lieutenant and Custos Rotulorum of Hants, Vice-Admiral of Dorset, and Col. N. Hants Militia; late Lieut.-Col. 10th Hussars. This family, who formerly enjoyed the Dukedom of Bolton, descend from a common ancestor with Earl Poulett. — *St. Mary's, Amport, Andover; Curbio... ...ha... Frome, Bristol, s w*
   Heir, his son Augustus John Henry Beaumont, Earl of Wiltshire, b. 1858.

WINCHESTER, Bishop of (the Right Rev. CHARLES RICHARD SUMNER, D.D.).
Third son of the late Rev. Robert Sumner, Vicar of Kenilworth and Stoneleigh (who d. 1802), by Harriet, dau. of William Bird, Esq., Merchant of London, and brother of the late Archbishop of Canterbury; b. 1790; m. 1816 Jane, dau. of J. P. Maunoir, Esq., b. 1830, and has issue. The Bishop, who was educated at Eton and Trinity Coll., Cambridge (B.A. 1811, M.A. 1815), is Provincial Subdean of Canterbury, Prelate of

1008

the Order of the Garter, and Patron of 80 livings; he was consecrated Bishop of Llandaff 1826; translated 1827.—*The Castle, Farnham; Athenæum Club*, s.w.; 19, *St. James's Square*, s.w.

WINCHILSEA AND NOTTINGHAM, Earl of (GEORGE JAMES FINCH-HATTON).— Cr. 1628.

Eldest son of George William, 10th Earl, by his 1st wife Lady Georgiana Charlotte, dau. of James, 3rd Duke of Montrose; *b*. 1815; *s*. 1858; *m*. 1846 Lady Constance Henrietta, dau. of Henry, 2nd Marquis of Anglesey. Educated at Eton and Ch. Ch., Oxford (B.A. 1835); is a Magistrate for co. Northampton, Lord of the Royal Manor of Wye, and Patron of 3 livings; was M.P. for N. Northamptonshire 1837–41. Is descended from a common ancestor with the Earl of Aylesford.—*Eastwell Park, Ashford; Kirby Hall, Northampton.; Carlton Club*, s.w.

Heir, his son George William Heneage, Viscount Maidstone, *b*. 1852.

WINCHILSEA, Dowager Countess of, of Haverholme, Lincolnshire.

Fanny Margaretta, dau. of Edward Royd Rice, Esq., M.P., of Dane Court, Kent, by Elizabeth, dau. of Edward Knight, Esq., of Godmersham Park, Kent; *m*. 1849 (as 3rd wife) George William, 9th Earl of Winchilsea, who *d*. 1858, leaving, with other issue,
* Murray Edward Gordon, *b*. 1851; educated at Eton.
The Countess is Patron of 3 livings.—*Haverholme Priory, Sleaford.*

WINDHAM, Sir CHARLES ASHE, K.C.B. (cr. 1865).

Fifth son of the late Vice-Admiral Windham, of Felbrigge, Norfolk (who assumed the name of Windham in lieu of Lukin), by Anne, dau. of Peter Thellusson, Esq., of Plaistow, Essex, and great-nephew of the late Right Hon. William Windham, M.P.; *b*. 1810; *m*. 1st 1849 Marianne Catherine Emily, dau. of the late Admiral Sir John Poo Beresford, Bart., K.C.B. (she *d*. 1865); 2nd 1866 Charlotte Jane, eldest dau. of the late Rev. Henry Des Vœux; he has by the former, with other issue,
* William, *b*. 1850.
Sir C. A. Windham, who was educated at Sandhurst, is a Lieut.-Gen. in the Army, Col. 46th Foot, and Commander in British North America; was Quartermaster-General 4th Division of the British Army in the Crimen 1854; held a command in India 1857–8; was M P. for E. Norfolk 1857–9.—*Travellers' and United Service Clubs*, s.w.; 60, *St. George's Square*, s.w.

WINDHAM, Capt. JOHN HENRY, of Cromer, Norfolk.

Eldest son of the late Vice-Admiral William Windham, of Felbrigge Hall, Norfolk, by Anne, dau. of Peter Thellusson, Esq.; *b*. 1809. Educated at the Royal Naval Coll., Portsmouth; is a Magistrate for Norfolk, and a Capt. R.N. retired; was Inspecting Commander of the Coast Guard 1843–8. — *The Cliff, Cromer, 19, Camden Cottages, Camden New Town*, N w; *United Service Club*, s.w.

WINDHAM, Mrs., of Hanworth, Norfolk.

Miss Agnes Anne Willoughby, *m*. 1861 William Frederick Windham, Esq., of Hanworth (and formerly of Felbrigg Hall, Norfolk), who *d*. 1866, leaving issue a son, *b*. 1864.—*Hanworth Hall, Aylsham.*

+WINDHAM, WILLIAM GEORGE SMIJTH-, Esq., of Wawne, Yorkshire.

Eldest son of the late Joseph Smijth-Windham, Esq., of Wawne, by Katharine, dau. of John Trotter, Esq.,

of Dyrham Park, Herts; *b*. 1825; *s*. 1858. Educated at Downing Coll., Cambridge (B.A. 1853, M.A. 1856); is a Dep.-Lieut. for the E. Riding of Yorkshire. *Wawne, Beverly.*

WINDSOR, Baroness, of Hewell Grange, Worcestershire (HARRIET WINDSOR-CLIVE). —Cr. 1592.

Daughter of Other Hickman, 5th Earl of Plymouth (*ext*.), by Sarah, dau. of Andrew, last Lord Archer (*ext*.); *b*. 1797; *m*. 1819 the Hon. Robert Henry Clive (son of Edward, 1st Earl of Powis), who *d*. 1854. Is Patron of 3 livings. This Barony was in abeyance 1833–55.—*Hewell Grange, Bromsgrove; 53, Grosvenor Street*, w.

Heir, her Grandson Robert George (son of the late Robert Windsor-Clive, Esq., M.P., who *d*. 1859, by Lady Mary, youngest dau. of George, 2nd Earl of Bradford), *b*. 1857.

WINDSOR-CLIVE, the Hon. GEORGE HERBERT.

Second son of Harriet, Baroness Windsor, by the late Hon. Robert Henry Clive; *b*. 1835. Educated at Eton; entered the Army 1852, became Lieut. 52nd Foot 1854, Capt. 1859; is a Dep.-Lieut. for co Worcester, and Lieut. and Capt. Coldstream Guards 1860; elected M.P. for Ludlow in 1860.—*Oakley Park, Ludlow; 53, Grosvenor Street*, w.

WING, WILLIAM, Esq., of Market Overton, Rutland.

Eldest son of the late Rev. William Wing, M.A., Rector of Stibbington, Hunts (who *d*. 1867), by Anne, dau. of the late William Margetts, Esq., of Huntingdon; *b*. 1825; *s*. 1859 to the estate of his cousin the Rev. John Hinman, M.A., of Market Overton; *m*. 1st 1854 Jane, dau. of the Rev. Kingsman Foster, M.A., Rector of Dowsby, co. Lincoln (who *d*. 1860); 2nd 1861 Julia Augusta, youngest dau. of the late John Baker Sladen, Esq., of Ripple Court, Kent, and has, with other issue,
* William Hinman, *b*. 1859.
Mr. Wing is a Magistrate for Rutland (High Sheriff 1866).—*Market Overton, Oakham.*

WINGATE, Major Sir GEORGE, K.C.S.I., of Crofton House, Hampshire (cr. 1866).

Second son of the late Andrew Wingate, Esq., of Glasgow, by Margaret, dau. of the late Alex. Miller, Esq.; *b* 1812; *m*. 1843 Agnes, dau. of the late John Muir, Esq., of Glasgow, and has, with other issue,
* George Miller, *b*. 1858.
Sir G. Wingate, who was educated at Addiscombe, and entered the Army in 1829, was for many years employed in organising the Revenue Surveys of the Presidency; he is a Magistrate for Hampshire, and a Major in the Bombay Engineers, retired; created K.C.S.I. for his services in India.—*Crofton House, Fareham; East India United Service Club*, s.w.

WINGFIELD, Sir CHARLES JOHN, K.C.S.I. (cr. 1866).

Fifth son of the late William Wingfield Baker, Esq., of Orsett Hall, Essex, by Elizabeth, dau. of William Mills, Esq., of Bisterne, Hants; *b*. 1820. Educated at Westminster; formerly a Member of the Bengal Civil Service; was Chief Commissioner of Oude 1859–66. —*Arthur's Club*, s.w.

WINGFIELD, the Hon. and Rev. WILLIAM.

Fourth son of Richard, 4th Viscount Powerscourt, by his 2nd wife Isabella, dau. of the late Right Hon. William Brownlow; *b*. 1799 ; *m*. 1830 Elizabeth, dau.

of the Rev. Thomas Kelly, of Kellyville, Queen's Co., and by her, who *d.* 1856, has, with other issue,

   * Richard Thomas, *b.* 1835 ; *m.* 1864 Isabella, dau. of the Rev. Edward Guille, of Jersey.

Mr. Wingfield was educated at Eton and Brasenose Coll., Oxford (B.A. 1822), and entered (as an A.B. *ad eundem*) Trinity College, Dublin, and appointed Vicar of Abbey Leix 1836.—*Abbey Leix, Queen's Co., Ireland.*

WINGFIELD, CHARLES GEORGE, Esq., of Onslow Hall, Shropshire.
Eldest son of the late Rev. Charles Wingfield, of The Gro, co. Montgomery, formerly Rector of Llanllwchaiarn (who *d.* 1851), by Emma, dau. of the late Richard Jenkins, Esq.; *b.* 1833 ; *s.* his uncle John Wingfield, Esq., 1862 ; *m.* 1865 Jane Mary Anne, only dau. of Clopton Wingfield, Esq., of the Rhysnant, co. Montgomery. Is a Magistrate for co. Salop.—*Onslow Hall, Shrewsbury.*

WINGFIELD, JOHN MUXLOE, Esq., of Tickencote, Rutland.
Eldest son of the late John Wingfield, Esq., of Tickencote, by Mary Anne, dau. of Edward Muxloe, Esq., of Pickwell, co. Leicester; *b.* 1790 ; *s.* 1841 ; *m.* 1819 Catherine Anne Harriet, only dau. of Harry Lancelot Lee, Esq., of Coton Hall, Salop, and by her, who *d.* 1863, has, with other issue,

   * John Harry Lee (of Market Overton, Oakham), a Magistrate for co. Rutland ; *b.* 1821 ; *m.* 1861 Elizabeth Anne, eldest dau. of Maurice Johnson, Esq., and has issue.

Mr. Wingfield, who was educated at Harrow and St. John's Coll., Cambridge (B.A. 1812, M.A. 1815), and called to the Bar at the Middle Temple 1815, is a J.P. and D.L. for co. Rutland (High Sheriff 1828), and Chairman of the Quarter Sessions, Lord of the Manor of Tickencote, and Patron of 3 livings.—*Tickencote Hall, Stamford.*

WINGFIELD. (See under *Powerscourt, Lord.*)

WINGFIELD-BAKER, RICHARD, Esq., of Orsett Hall, Essex.
Third son of the late William Wingfield-Baker, Esq., of Orsett Hall, by Lady Charlotte Maria, sister of Edward, 2nd Earl Digby; *b.* 1802 ; *m.* 1837 Margaret Maria, sister of Sir John Hanmer, Bart., and has, with other issue,

   * Digby Hanmer Richard, Capt. R. Horse Guards; *b.* 1838 ; *m.* 1857 Louise Gabrielle, dau. of Mons. A. St. Marie, of Bordeaux, France.

Mr. Wingfield-Baker, who was educated at Rugby and Ch. Ch., Oxford, and called to the Bar at the Inner Temple 1827, is a J.P. and D.L. and Chairman of Quarter Sessions for Essex (High Sheriff 1867); was M.P. for S. Essex 1857-9.—*Orsett Hall, Romford ; Boodle's, University, and Oxford and Cambridge Clubs, s.w. ; 2, Lowndes Square, s.w.*

WINGFIELD-DIGBY. (See *Digby.*)

WINGFIELD-STRATFORD. (See *Stratford.*)

+**WINGROVE, RICHARD FOWNES, Esq., of Langley, Hampshire.**
Son of the late R. Wingrove, Esq., of London ; *b.* 18—; *m.* 182- Mary Anne, dau. of — Bond, Esq., and by her, who *d.* 1860, has, with other issue, an only son,

   * Drummond Bond, *b.* 182- ; is married, and has, with other issue, * a son, *b.* 1861.

Mr. Wingrove, who is a Magistrate for Hants, was formerly a Merchant in London.—*Langley, Eling, Southampton.*
1010

WINN, the Hon. ROWLAND.
Second surviving son of the late Hon. George Winn (who *d.* 1827), by Elizabeth Mary, eldest dau. of the late Lewis Majendie, Esq., of Castle Hedingham, Essex (who *d.* 1863), and brother of Charles, 3rd Lord Headley ; *b.* 1816 ; *m.* 1854 Margaretta Stephana, dau. of the late George Walker, Esq., of Gestingthorpe Hall, Essex, and has, with other issue, * Rowland George Allanson, *b.* 1855.—*Glenbeigh, Kerry ; 63, Chester Square, s.w.*

WINN, CHARLES, Esq., of Nostell, Yorkshire.
Younger but only surviving son of the late John Williamson, Esq., by Esther Sabina, elder dau. of the late Sir Rowland Winn, 5th Bart., of Nostell, and heir of her brother, Sir Rowland Winn, 6th Bart., who *d.* 1805 ; *b.* 1791; *s.* his brother 1818, and assumed the name of Winn; *m.* 1819 Priscilla, dau. of the late Sir William Strickland, Bart., of Boynton, co. York, and has, with other issue,

   * Rowland (of Appleby, near Brigg, co. Lincoln), a Magistrate for that co. and for the E. and W. Ridings of Yorkshire, and High Sheriff of co. Lincoln 1858 ; *b.* 1820 ; *m.* 1854 Harriet Maria Amelia, 2nd dau. of the late Lieut.-Col. Dumaresq, and niece of the Earl of Lanesborough, and has, with other issue, * a son, *b.* 1858.

Mr. Winn, who was educated at Eton and St. John's Coll., Cambridge (B.A. 1823), is a J.P. and D.L. for the W. Riding of Yorkshire, Lord of the Manor and Patron of Nostell; was High Sheriff of co. Lincoln 1828. This family is (maternally) descended from a common ancestor with Lord Headley.—*Nostell Priory, Wakefield.*

WINN. (See under *Headley, Lord.*)

WINNINGTON, Sir THOMAS EDWARD, Bart., of Stanford, Worcestershire (cr. 1755).
Eldest son of the late Sir Thomas Edward Winnington, Bart., of Stanford Court, by Joanna, dau. of the late John Taylor, Esq., of Mosely Hall, co. Worcester ; *b.* 1811; *s.* as 4th Bart. 1839 ; *m.* 1842 Anne Helena, eldest dau. of the late Sir Compton Domville, Bart. Educated at Eton and Ch. Ch., Oxford (B.A. 1836); is a Magistrate for co. Hereford, and a J.P. and D.L. for co. Worcester (High Sheriff 1851), and Patron of 4 livings; was M.P. for Bewdley 1837-47 ; re-elected 1852. This family was formerly resident at Winnington Hall, co. Chester, and its head married the heiress of Salwey, co. Worcester, *temp.* Charles II.—*Stanford Court, Worcester ; Athenæum and Travellers' Clubs, s.w. ; 16, Suffolk Street, s.w.*

   Heir, his son Thomas Edward, *b.* 1848.

WINNINGTON, Capt. HENRY JEFFREYS.
Son of the late Sir Edward Winnington, Bart., by Anne, dau. of Thomas, 1st Lord Foley, and brother of the late Sir Thomas Edward Winnington, Bart. M.P. ; *b.* 1794. Is a Magistrate for co. Worcester, and Capt. half-pay 39th Foot ; was M.P. for W. Worcestershire 1833-41.—8. *Petersham Terrace, South Kensington ; Windham Club, s.w.*

WINSTANLEY, WILLIAM, Esq., of Chaigeley Manor, Lancashire.
Eldest son of the late William Winstanley, Esq., M.D., of Manchester, by Elizabeth, dau. of Samuel Hardman, Esq., also of Manchester; *b.* 1810 ; *m.* 1843 Charlotte Lavinia, elder dau. of the late Alfred Lowe, Esq., of Highfield House, Notts, and has, with other issue.

   * William Alfred, *b.* 1852.

Mr. Winstanley is a Magistrate for co. Lancaster. This family was formerly residing at Cuerden, near Leyland, co. Lancaster.—*Chaigeley Manor, Clitheroe.*

WINSTANLEY, of Braunston. (See *Pochin*.)

+WINTER, SAMUEL, Esq., of Agher, co. Meath.
Eldest son of the late John Pratt Winter, Esq., of
Agher, by Anne, dau. of Capt. Arthur Gore, of the
H.E.I.C.'s Service; *b.* 1796; *m.* 1826 Lucy, dau. of
James Sanderson, Esq., of Cloan Hill, co. Cavan, and
has, with other issue,

* James Saunderson, Capt. Royal Meath Militia, *b.* 183–.

Mr. Winter, who was educated at Trinity Coll., Dublin,
is a J.P. and D.L. for co. Meath.—*Agher, Summerhill.*

WINTERBOTHAM, HENRY SELFE PAGE, Esq.
Second son of Lindsey Winterbotham, Esq., of Stroud,
Banker, by Sarah Anne Seefe, dau. of the Rev. Henry
Page; *b.* 1837. Educated at Amersham Grammar
School and University Coll., London; called to the Bar
at Lincoln's Inn 1860; elected M.P. for Stroud 1867.
—*Stroud, Gloucestershire ; 7, New Square, Lincoln's Inn,
w.c.*

WINTERTON, Earl of (EDWARD TURNOUR).—
Cr. 1766.
Elder son of Edward, 3rd Earl, by Lucy Louis, dau. of
John Heys, Esq.; *b.* 1810; *s.* 1833; *m.* 1832 Maria,
dau. of the late Sir Peter Pole, Bart. Is a J.P. and
D.L. for Sussex, Patron of 1 living, and Capt. 6th
Sussex Rifle Volunteers; late Capt. Sussex Militia.
—*Shillinglee Park, Petworth.*

*Heir, his son Edward, Viscount Turnour, educated at Eton ;
Lieut. 6th Sussex Rifle Volunteers ; b.* 1837.

WISE, HENRY CHRISTOPHER, Esq., of Woodcote,
Warwickshire.
Eldest son of the late Rev. Henry Wise, of the Priory,
Warwick (who *d.* 1850), by Charlotte Mary, dau. of
Sir Stanier Porteu; *b.* 1806; *m.* 1st 1828 Harriet, dau.
of the late Sir Gray Skipwith, Bart., of Prestwold, co.
Leicester (she *d.* 1858); 2nd 1863 Jane Harriet,
youngest dau. of the late Sir Edward Cromwell Dis-
browe, G.C.B., and has, with other issue,

* George, *b.* 1830.

Mr. Wise, who was educated at Oriel Coll., Oxford
(B.A. 1830), is a J.P. and D.L. for co. Warwick, Lord
of the Manor and Patron of Woodcote; elected M.P.
for S. Warwickshire 1865.—*Woodcote, Warwick ; Carlton Club, s.w.*

WISE, JOHN AYSHFORD, Esq., of Clayton Hall,
Staffordshire.
Eldest son of the late Ayshford Wise, Esq., M.P., of
Wonwell Court, Devon, by Mary, dau. of Thomas
Whitby, Esq., of Cresswell Hall ; *b.* 1810 ; *s.* 1847 ;
m. 1st 1837 Mary Lovatt, dau. of Hugh Booth, Esq., of
Stoke-upon-Trent (she *d.* 1844); 2nd 1848 Anna, dau.
of the late Rev. Lewis Way, of Stanstead Park, Sussex,
and has, with other issue,

* Lewis Lovatt, Ensign 8th Foot ; *b.* 1844.

Mr. Wise, who is a J.P. and D.L. for Devon and co.
Stafford (High Sheriff 1852), has been M.P. for Stafford
since 1862.—*Clayton Hall, Newcastle-under-Lyne ; Reform Club, s.w.*

WISE, Mrs., of Shrublands, Warwickshire.
Elizabeth, dau. of William Staunton, Esq., of Long-
bridge, co. Warwick, by Elizabeth, dau. of Osborne
Standert, Esq.; *m.* 1834 Matthew Wise, Esq., D.L., of
Shrublands, who *d.* 1864, leaving, with other issue,

* Charles John, *b.* 1834 ; *m.* 1859 Louisa Caroline, youngest
   dau. of Richard Malone Sneyd, Esq., and has issue. * Louisa
   Elizabeth.

Mr. Wise is Lay Rector and Patron of the living of
Leam.—*Shrublands, Leamington.*

WISEMAN, Sir WILLIAM SALTONSTALL, Bart.,
K.C.B. (cr. 1628).
Eldest son of the late Sir William Saltonstall Wiseman,
Bart., by Cathrine, dau. of the late Right Hon. Sir
James Mackintosh, M.P.; *b.* 1814 ; *s.* as 8th Bart.
1845; *m.* 1840 Charlotte, dau. of Admiral Charles
William Paterson. Educated at Harrow and Royal
Naval Coll. ; is a J.P. and D.L. for Middlesex, and a
Capt. R.N. ; appointed Vice-President of the Ordnance
Select Committee 1859 ; served in New Zealand 1863–4.
This family was formerly seated in Essex.—*Marysfort
Lodge, Hillingdon End, Middlesex ; United Service Club,
s.w.; 88, Belgrave Road, s.w.*

Heir, his son William, b. 1846.

WITHAM, Lady, of Higham, Suffolk.
Jane, dau. of John Hoy, Esq., of Lower House, Suffolk,
by Sarah, dau. of William Davey, Esq. ; *m.* 1829 Sir
Charles Witham, R.N. (3rd son of William Witham,
Esq., of Gray's Inn, and descended from a common
ancestor with the Withams of Cliffe and Lartington),
who was knighted 1830, and *d.* 1853, leaving issue.
—*Higham, Stoke-by-Nayland ; 28, Clifton Road East,
n.w.*

WITHAM, ROBERT MAXWELL, Esq., of Kirkconnell, Kirkcudbrightshire.
Eldest son of the late William Witham, Esq., of Gray's
Inn, by Elizabeth, dau. of James Brooks, Esq., and
great-grandson of William Witham, Esq., of Cliffe, co.
York ; *b.* 1819; *m.* 1844 his cousin, Dorothy Mary,
only dau. of James Maxwell, Esq., of Kirkconnell, by
Dorothy, dau. of the said William Witham, Esq., by
whom he has, with other issue,

* James Kirkconnell, *b.* 1848.

Mr. Witham, who was educated at Oscott Coll., is a J.P.
and D.L. for the Stewartry of Kirkcudbright, a Magistrate for co. Dumfries, and Lord of the Barony of
Kirkconnell.—*Kirkconnell, New Abbey, Dumfries, N.B.*

WITHAM, the Rev. THOMAS, of Lartington
Hall, Yorkshire.
Only surviving son of the late Henry Thornton Maire
Witham (formerly Silvertop), Esq., of Minster Acres,
by Elizabeth, dau. of the late William Witham, Esq.,
of Cliffe Hall, co. York ; *b.* 1806 ; *s.* his brother George
1847. Educated at Stonyhurst Coll. ; is a Magistrate
for co. Durham, and in Holy Orders of the Church of
Rome.—*Lartington Hall, Barnard Castle.*

*Heir Pres., his nephew Henry Silvertop, Esq., of Minster
Acres (whom see).*

WITHER. (See *Bigg-Wither*.)

WITHINGTON, Capt. GEORGE RICHARD.
Only son of the late George Withington, Esq., of Park-
field, Didsbury, near Manchester (who *d.* 1865), by
Marianne, dau. of Richard Alsop, Esq., of Litchford
Hall, Blackley, near Manchester; *b.* 1829 ; *m.* 1854
Maria, dau. of the late Rev. John Swire, of Conouley,
co. York, and has surviving issue,

* Henry Swire ; *b.* 1857.

Capt. Withington, who was educated at Shrewsbury
and Trinity Hall, Cambridge (LL.B. 1854), is a Magistrate for co. Lancaster; was formerly Capt. York
Militia.—*Residence : Torquay, Devon.*

WITHINGTON, THOMAS ELLAMES, Esq., of
Culcheth Hall, Lancashire.
Eldest son of the late Thomas Ellames Withington,
Esq., of Culcheth Hall, by Anne, youngest dau. of
Edward Griffin, Esq., of Liverpool; *b.* 1831 ; *s.* 1852;
m. 1857 Cecilia Jane, eldest dau. of the late Rev. Ed-
ward Cardwell, D.D., Principal of St. Alban Hall, Ox-
ford, and has, with other issue,

* Thomas Ellames, *b.* 1858.

Mr. Withington, who was educated at Winchester and Merton Coll., Oxford, is a Magistrate for co. Lancaster, Lord of the Manor of Culcheth, and Cornet Lancashire Hussar Yeomanry Cavalry; late Capt. 3rd Duke of Lancaster's Own Regt. of Militia. — *Culcheth Hall, Warrington.*

+WITTS, the Rev. EDWARD FRANCIS, of Upper Slaughter, Gloucestershire.
Son of the late E. Witts, Esq.; *b.* 1815; *m.* 1854 Mary, dau. of W. T. Vavasour, Esq., of Lower Slaughter Manor. Educated at Magdalen Hall, Oxford (B.A. 1838, M.A. 1842); is a J.P. and D.L. for co. Gloucester, a Magistrate for co. Worcester, Lord of the Manor and Rector and Patron of Upper Slaughter.—*Upper Slaughter Rectory, Stow-on-the-Wold.*

WODDROP, WILLIAM ALLAN-, Esq., of Garvald, Peeblesshire, and Dalmarnock, Lanarkshire.
Eldest son of the late John Allan-Woddrop, Esq., of Garvald and Elsrickle (who assumed the name of Allan on succeeding to the estates of the late John Allan, Esq., of Elsrickle), by Marion, dau. and heir of Robert Hunter, Esq., of Kirkland, co. Ayr; *b.* 1829; *s.* 1845; *m.* 1856 Harriette Selina, dau. of the Rev. John Isaac Beresford, of Macbie Hill, co. Peebles. Educated at Harrow; is a Magistrate for co. Lanark, and Lord of the Barony of Garvald; was formerly Lieut. Scots Greys. This family, which has possessed the lands of Dalmarnock for upwards of three centuries, represents in the female line the Hamiltons of Aikenhead and Holmhead.— *Garvald House, Dolphinton, Edinburgh ; Dalmarnock House, Glasgow, N.B.; New Club, Edinburgh ; Army and Navy Club, s.w.*

WODEHOUSE, Sir PHILIP EDMOND, K.C.B., of Bracondale, Norfolk (cr. 1862).
Eldest son of the late Edmond Wodehouse, Esq., M.P., of Sennow Lodge, Norfolk (who *d.* 1855), by Lucy, dau. of the late Rev. Philip Wodehouse, M.A., a Prebendary of Norwich; *b.* 1811; *m.* 1833 Catherine Mary, eldest dau. of F. J. Templar, Esq., and by her, who *d.* 1866, has, with other issue,
   * Edmond Robert, educated at Eton and Balliol Coll., Oxford ; *b.* 1835.

Sir P. E. Wodehouse. who was educated at Eton. is a J.P. and D.L. for Norfolk; appointed Governor of British Guiana 1854, and Cape of Good Hope 1862; was formerly in the Civil Service at Ceylon. Is descended from a brother of John, 1st Lord Wodehouse. —*Government House, Cape Town, South Africa ; Travellers' Club, s.w.*

WODEHOUSE, the HON. BERKELEY.
Third son of John, 2nd Lord Wodehouse, by Charlotte Laura, only dau. and heir of John Norris, Esq., of Wilton Park, Norfolk; *b.* 1806; *m.* 1837 Fanny, only dau. of Alexander Holmes, Esq., of Curragh, co. Kildare, and has, with other issue,
   * Armine, *b.* 1840.
Mr. Wodehouse, who was educated at the Royal Military Coll., Sandhurst, entered the Army as Ensign 1824, became Major 8th Hussars 1840, and retired 1844, is Dep.-Lieut. for Norfolk, Col. East Norfolk Militia, and Consul at Zante ; formerly Major 8th Hussars.—*Residence : Zante, Ionian Islands.*

WODEHOUSE, the Hon. EDWARD THORNTON-, of Whitton, Norfolk.
Second son of John, 2nd Lord Wodehouse, by Charlotte Laura, only dau. and heir of John Norris, Esq., of Wilton Park, Norfolk; *b.* 1802; *m.* 1838 Diana,
1012

dau. of the late Col. Thornton, of Falconer's Hall, co. York (whose name he has assumed), and has, with other issue,
   * Albert, Lieut. R.A. ; *b.* 1840.
Mr. Thornton-Wodehouse is a J.P. and D.L. for Norfolk, and Vice-Admiral R.N., on the reserved list. —*Witton, Norwich.*

WODEHOUSE, the Hon. Mrs., of Loddon, Norfolk.
Emily, youngest dau. of the late Sir Thomas Beauchamp-Proctor, Bart., of Langley Park, Norfolk, by Mary, dau. of Robert Palmer, Esq., of Sunning, Berks; *m.* 1815 the Hon. and Rev. Armine Wodehouse, who *d.* 1853.—*Loddon, Norwich.*

WODEHOUSE, the Hon. and Rev. WILLIAM.
Fourth son of John, 1st Lord Wodehouse, by Sophia, only child of the Hon. Charles Berkeley, of Bruton Abbey, Somerset; *b.* 1782; *m.* 1807, Mary, dau. of the late Thomas Hussey, Esq., of Galtrim, Ireland, by Lady Mary Walpole, dau. of Horatio, Earl of Orford, and by her, who *d.* 1865, has, with other issue,
   * George, Capt. R.N.; *b.* 1810; *m.* 1848 Eleanor Charlotte, dau. of Andrew Mortimer Drummond, Esq.
Mr. Wodehouse, who was educated at Harrow and Ch. Ch., Oxford, and was afterwards Fellow of All Souls (B.A. 1805, M.A. 1811), and appointed Rector of Hingham 1811, is a Rural Dean in the diocese of Norwich, and a J.P. and D.L. for Norfolk.—*Hingham Rectory, Attleburgh ; 10, Green Street, Grosvenor Square, w.*

WODEHOUSE, the Rev. CHARLES NOURSE.
Youngest son of the late Rev. Philip Wodehouse, M.A., Prebendary of Norwich, by Apollonia, dau. and co-heir of John Nourse, Esq., of Wood Eaton, Oxon; *b.* 1790; *m.* 1821 Lady Dulcibella Jane, dau. of William, 15th Earl of Erroll, and has, with other issue,
   * Charles, *b.* 1822.
Mr. Wodehouse, who was educated at Harrow and Trinity Coll., Cambridge (B.A. 1813, M.A. 1817), is a J.P. and D.L. for Norfolk; late Perpetual Curate of St. Margaret's, Lynn, and Canon of Norwich, which benefices he resigned in 1859. This is a younger branch of the family of the Earl of Kimberley.—*Residence : Lowestoft, Suffolk.*

WODEHOUSE, WILLIAM HERBERT, Esq., of Woolmer's Park, Herts.
Only surviving son of the late Chappel Wodehouse, Esq., of Eastville, co. Lincoln, by Amelia, dau. of Sir Charles Oakeley, Bart.; *b.* 1815; *m.* 1833 ; *m.* 1838 Helena Sarah Charlotte, eldest dau. and co-heir of Sir Charles Oakeley, 2nd Bart., and has, with other issue,
   * Chappel Oakeley, *b.* 1842.
Mr. Wodehouse, who was educated at Eton and Ch. Ch., Oxford (B.A. 1837), is a J.P. and D.L. for Herts, and a Magistrate for co. Stafford. This family are lineal descendants of the ancient family of De la Wodehouse; they settled at Woolmer's, Wolverton, Stafford, A.D. 111 .... —*Woolmer's Park, Hertford ; Athenæum Club, s.w.; 44, Dover Street, w.*

WODEHOUSE. (See under *Kimberley, Earl of.*)

WOLCOTT, of Knowle, Devonshire.
Elizabeth (*m.* 1830 the Rev. Francis Goddard, Vicar of Hilmarton, Wilts) and Mary (*m.* 1843 James S. Lang, Esq., who *d.* 1857), daus. of the late John Wolcott, Esq., of Knowle (who *d.* 1820), by Elizabeth, dau. of Zachariah Lang, Esq., of Broad Clyst, Devon ; *s.* their brother, John Marwood Wolcott, Esq., 1861. Are conjointly Ladies of the Manor of Knowle.—*Knowle House, Salcombe, Salmouth.*

WOLFE, GEORGE, Esq., of Bishop Land, co. Kildare.

Eldest son of the late Major James Wolfe, of Black Hall, co. Kildare, by Elizabeth, dau. of the late Samuel Walker, Esq., of Sligo; *b.* 1815; *s.* 1840; *m.* 1852 Elizabeth Henrietta, dau. of Henry M. Ball, Esq., of Tipperkevin, co. Kildare, and has, with other issue,
* Richard, *b.* 1855.
Mr. Wolfe, who was educated at Dublin, is a Magistrate for cos. Wicklow and Kildare. This family descends from General James Wolfe, the hero of Quebec; also from Arthur Wolfe, Lord Kilwarden, Chief Justice, killed in the Irish Rebellion 1802.—*Bishop Land, Naas, co. Kildare ; 42, Upper Sackville Street, Dublin.*

WOLFE, THOMAS BIRCH-, Esq., of Wood Hall, Essex.

Only surviving son of the late Rev. Richard Birch, Rector of Widdington and Bradwell-juxta-Mare, Essex (who *d.* 1820), by Elizabeth, sister of the late Rev. Sir Henry Bate Dudley, Bart., of Willingham House, co. Cambridge; *b.* 1801; *m.* 1831 Eliza Vernon, formerly of Turin; assumed the name of Wolfe on succeeding to the estates of the late John Wolfe, Esq., on the death of his brother the Rev. William Birch-Wolfe, 1864.—*Wood Hall, Arkesden, Bishop Stortford.*

Heir Pres., his kinsman John Lewis Wolfe, Esq., *b.* 180-.

WOLFERSTAN, FRANCIS STAFFORD PIPE-, Esq., of Statfold Hall, Staffordshire.

Eldest son of the late Stanley Pipe-Wolferstan, Esq., of Statfold Hall, by his first wife, Elizabeth, eldest dau. of the late Swynfen Jervis, Esq., of Kensington; *b.* 1826; *s.* 1867; *m.* 1859 Sarah Maria Hill, dau. of William Hallows Belli, Esq., and has, with other issue,
* Egerton Stanley, *b.* 1861.
Mr. Pipe-Wolferstan, who was educated at Eton and Balliol Coll., Oxford (B.A. 1849), and called to the Bar at the Inner Temple 1857, is a Magistrate for co. Stafford. This family was originally from Wolverstone, near Ipswich, Suffolk, but has been settled at Statfold since early in the reign of Elizabeth, when that estate was acquired by the marriage of Humphrey Wolferstan, Esq., with the dau. of John Stanley, Esq., of Grove, Notts.—*Statfold Hall, Tamworth.*

WOLFF, Sir HENRY DRUMMOND, K.C.M.G. (cr. 1862).

Eldest son of the late Rev. Joseph Wolff, D.D., Vicar of Isle Brewers, Somerset, by Lady Georgiana Mary, dau. of Horatio, 2nd Earl of Orford; *b.* 1830; *m.* 1852 Adeline, dau. of the late Sbolto Douglas, Esq., and has, with other issue,
* Henry Horace, *b.* 1857.
Sir H. D. Wolff, who was educated at Rugby, entered the Foreign Office in 1846, was attached to the Legation at Florence, and to Lord Westmoreland's Special Mission to Belgium in 1856; was Private Secretary to the Earl of Malmesbury and Sir Edward Bulwer-Lytton, Secretaries of State for the Foreign and Colonial Departments; appointed Secretary to the Government of the Ionian Islands in 1859.—*Boscombe Tower, Bournemouth.; Athenæum, Carlton, St. James's, and Garrick Clubs, s.w.; 15, Rutland Gate, s.w.*

WOLLASTON, Major FREDERICK, K.J.J., of Shenton Hall, Leicestershire.

Eldest son of the late Rev. Henry John Wollaston, Rector of Scotter, co. Lincoln (who *d.* 1833), by Louisa, dau. of William Symons, Esq., of Bury St. Edmund's; *b.* 1804; *s.* his uncle, Col. Frederick William Wollaston, J.P. and D.L., 1849; *m.* 1850 Josette Eliza Jane, only dau. of Admiral Sir Alexander Dundas Arbuthnott, K C B, and has, with other issue,
* Frederick Eustace Arbuthnott, *b.* 1853.

Major Wollaston, who was formerly Major Inniskilling Dragoons, is a J.P. and D.L. for co. Leicester (High Sheriff 1853), and Lord of the Manor of Shenton.—*Shenton Hall, Nuneaton ; Junior United Service Club, s.w.*

+WOLLASTON, FREDERICK LUARD, Esq., of Shirley, Hampshire.

Eldest son of the late George Hyde Wollaston, Esq., of Clapham, Surrey (who *d.* 1841), by Mary Anne, dau. of William Luard, Esq.; *b.* 180-; *m.* 1834 Diana Harriet, 2nd dau. of the late John Sperling, Esq., of Dynes Hall, Essex (she *d.* 1862). Was called to the Bar at the Middle Temple 1832. Is descended from a common ancestor with the Wollastons of Shenton Hall.—*Tremona, Shirley, Southampton.*

+WOLLEN, JOSEPH, Esq., of Wedmore, Somersetshire.

Son of the late Joseph Wollen, Esq., of Wedmore ; *b.* 18—. Is a Magistrate for Somerset.—*Wedmore House, Weston-super-Mare.*

WOLLEY, the Rev. JOHN FRANCIS THOMAS, of Allen Hill, Derbyshire.

Fourth son of the late Charles Hurt, Esq., of Wirksworth, co. Derby, by Susanna, dau. of Sir Richard Arkwright, of Willersley ; *b.* 1796; *m.* 1822 Mary, eldest dau. of Adam Wolley, Esq., of Matlock, and by her, who *d.* 1844, has, with other issue, an only surviving son,
* Charles, *b.* 1826 ; *m.* 1850 Frances Lucy, dau. of the Rev. Felly Parker, and has, with other issue, * Francis, *b.* 1855.
Mr. Wolley, who was educated at Rugby and St. John's Coll., Cambridge (B.A. 1819, M.A. 1822), and appointed Vicar of Beeston 1822, took the name of Wolley in 1827, under the will of his father-in-law.—*Residence : Beeston, Nottingham.*

WOLRIGE.   (See *Gordon-Wolrige.*)

WOLRYCHE-WHITMORE.   (See *Whitmore.*)

WOLSELEY, Sir CHARLES MICHAEL, Bart., of Wolseley, Staffordshire (cr. 1628).

Eldest surviving son of the late Sir Charles Wolseley, Bart. of Wolseley, by Mary Anne, eldest dau. of the late Nicholas Selby, Esq., of Acton House, Middlesex; *b.* 1846; *s.* as 9th Bart. 1854. Educated at Ch. Ch. Oxford; is Lord of the Manor of Wolseley. This family was settled in co. Stafford in the 15th century.—*Wolseley Hall, Rugeley.*

Heir Pres., his brother Edward Talbot, *b.* 1848.

WOLSELEY, Sir JOHN RICHARD, Bart., of Mount Wolseley, co. Carlow (cr. 1744).

Eldest son of the late Sir Clement Wolseley, Bart., of Mount Wolseley, by Alice Elizabeth, dau. of the late Peter Van Homrigh, Esq., M.P.; *b.* 1834 ; *s.* as 6th Bart., 1857 ; *m.* 1859 Frances Annabella, youngest dau. of the late Arthur Blennerhassett, Esq., M.P., of Ballyseedy, co. Kerry. Is a J.P. and D.L. for co. Carlow (High Sheriff 1861), and a Magistrate for co. Wexford ; was formerly Lieut. 18th Royal Irish Regt.—*Mount Wolseley, Tullow.*

Heir Pres., his brother Clement James, *b.* 1847.

WOLSELEY, Dowager Lady.

Alice Elizabeth, dau. of the late Peter Van Homrigh, Esq., M.P.; *m.* 1833 Sir Clement Wolseley, Bart., who *d.* 1857.—*The Cottage, Hanwell, w.*

WOLSTENHOLME, EDWARD PARKER, Esq., of Dumbarton Manor, Kent.
Eldest son of the late Edward Breton-Wolstenholme, Esq., of Holly Hill, Sussex (who d. 1862), by Arabella Catherine, dau. of the late Hon. Edward Ward, and sister of Edward, 3rd Viscount Bangor; b. 1824. Educated at Trinity Coll., Cambridge (B.A. 1847, M.A. 1850); called to the Bar at Lincoln's Inn 1850. The grandfather of the present owner, whose name was Breton, assumed the name of Wolstenholme in 1806. —Dumbarton Manor, Reculver, Kent; 2, Stone Buildings, Lincoln's Inn, w.c.

WOMBWELL, Sir GEORGE ORBY, Bart., of Newburgh Park, Yorkshire (cr. 1788).
Eldest son of the late Sir George Wombwell, Bart., of Wombwell, co. York, by Georgiana, dau. of the late Thomas Orby Hunter, Esq., of Croyland, co. Lincoln; b. 1832; s. as 4th Bart. 1855; m. 1861 Lady Julia Sarah Alice, dau. of George, 6th Earl of Jersey. Is a Magistrate for the N. and W. Ridings of Yorkshire (High Sheriff 1861), and Lieut. in the Yorkshire Hussars; was formerly Lieut. 17th Lancers.—Newburgh Park, Easingwold; Carlton and White's Clubs, s.w.; 15, George Street, Hanover Square.
Heir, his son George, b. 1865.

WOMBWELL, HENRY HERBERT, Esq., of Wombwell, Yorkshire.
Third son of the late Sir George Wombwell, Bart., of Wombwell and Newburgh Park, Easingwold, Yorkshire (who d. 1855), by Georgina Mary, youngest dau. of the late Orby Hunter, Esq., of Croyland Abbey, co. Lincoln; b. 1840. Educated at Harrow; is Lord of the Manor of Wombwell, and Lieut. Royal Horse Guards; formerly in the 7th (Queen's Own) Hussars.—Wombwell, Barnsley; 13, Hill Street, Berkeley Square, s.w.

WOOD, Sir MATTHEW, Bart., of Rivenhall Place, Essex (cr. 1837).
Only son of the late Sir Francis Wood, Bart., of Rivenhall Place, by Louisa Mary, eldest dau. of Robert Studholme Hodgson, Esq., of Appleshaw, Hants; b. 1857; s. as 4th Bart. 1868.—Rivenhall Place, Witham.
Heir Pres., his uncle Charles (fourth son of the late Rev. Sir John Page Wood, Bart., who d. 1866, by Emma Carolina, youngest dau. of Admiral Sampson Mitchell, of Crofts West, Cornwall); b. 1836; m. 1864 Minna, dau. of the late Thomas White, Esq., of Berechurch Hall, Essex.

WOOD, Sir DAVID EDWARD, K.C.B. (cr. 1859).
Fourth son of the late Col. Thomas Wood, of Littleton House, near Staines, by Lady Caroline, dau. of Henry, 1st Marquis of Londonderry, K.G.; b. 1812; m. 1861 the Hon. Maria Isabella, eldest dau. of Henry Thomas, 2nd Lord Ravensworth. Educated at the Royal Military Academy, Woolwich; is a Major-Gen. in the Army, retired, late Col. R.E.; served in India and the Crimea. —Park Lodge, Sunningdale, Berks; Carlton and United Service Clubs, s.w.

WOOD, the Right Hon. Sir WILLIAM PAGE, Knt., F.R.S., LL.D., D.C.L. (cr. 1851).
Second son of the late Alderman Sir Matthew Wood, Bart., by Maria, dau. of John Page, Esq., of Woolbridge, Suffolk, and brother of the late Rev. Sir John P. Wood, Bart.; b. 1801; m. 1830 Charlotte, only dau. of Edward Moor, Esq., of Great Bealings, Suffolk. Educated at Winchester and Trinity Coll., Cambridge (B.A. 1824, M.A. 1827, LL.D. 1865); elected Fellow of his College 1825; called to the Bar at Lincoln's Inn 1827; was M.P. for Oxford 1847-53, Vice-Chancellor of co. Palatine of Lancaster 1849-51, and Solicitor-General 1851-2; appointed a Vice-Chancellor 1853; a Judge of Appeal in Chancery 1868; sworn a Member of the Privy Council 1868.—Reform Club, s.w; 31, Great George Street, s.w

WOOD, Sir WILLIAM, K.C.B. (cr. 1865).
Son of the late W. Wood, Esq.; b. 1782; m. 1823 Charlotte Elizabeth dau. of Capt. Edward Dix, R.N.; is a General in the Army, and Col. 14th Foot; was formerly Col. 3rd West India Regt.—Mountswood, Taunton; United Service Club, s.w.

WOOD, Lady.
Elizabeth Rachel, dau. of the late William Newton, Esq., of Elvedon Hall, Suffolk; m. 1st 1833 Sir Mark Wood, Bart. (ext.), who d. 1837; 2nd 1845 Charles Cox, Esq.—19, Lowndes Square, s.w.

WOOD, CHARLES ALEXANDER, Esq., of Glasbury, Breconshire.
Third son of the late Col. Thomas Wood, M.P., of Littleton (who d. 1861), by Lady Caroline, dau. of Robert, 1st Marquis of Londonderry, K.G.; b. 1810; m. 1838 Sophia, dau. of the late John Studholme Brownrigg, Esq., M.P., and has, with other issue,
      * Edward Alexander, Capt. 10th Hussars; b. 1841.
Mr. Wood is a Magistrate for Middlesex and co. Brecon. —The Lodge, Glasbury, Brecon; 25, Chesham Place, s.w.

WOOD, EDWARD, Esq., of Newbold Revel, Warwickshire.
Third son of the late Enoch Wood, Esq., of Burslem; b. 1796; m. 1st 1831 Sarah, dau. of Thomas Slater, Esq., of Manchester (she d. 1843); 2nd 1845 Elizabeth, dau. of James Scholfield, Esq., of Middleton, near Manchester, and has issue,
      * Edward Herbert, b. 1847.
Mr. Wood is a Magistrate for cos. Stafford and Warwick.—Newbold Revel, Rugby; Port Hill, Burslem, Staffordshire.

+ WOOD, Lieut.-Col. EDWARD ROBERT, of Stout Hall, Glamorganshire.
Son of the late — Wood, Esq.; b. 1818; m. 1843 Mary Catherine, dau. and heir of the late Col. John Nicholas Lucas, of Stout Hall. Is a Magistrate for cos. Carmarthen and Glamorgan, Lieut.-Col. Glamorganshire Militia, and late of the 12th Lancers.—Stout Hall, Swansea.

WOOD, EDWARD ATKYNS, Esq., of Osmington, Dorsetshire.
Only surviving son of the late Rev. Robert Serrell Wood, by Caroline, dau. of Edward Atkyns Bray, Esq., of Tavistock, and grandson of the late Robert Serrell Wood, Esq., of Osmington House; b. 1810; m. 1st 1834 Frances, dau. of Col. Hervey Smith, of Aspley House, Beds; 2nd 1859 Anna, dau. of Rev. J. Grasett, Rector of Elwin Loach, co. Hereford. Educated at the Charterhouse; is a Magistrate for Dorset, and Major in the Dorset Militia.—Osmington House, Weymouth.

WOOD, FREDERICK HENRY, Esq., of Hollin Hall, and Copmanthorpe, Yorkshire.
Eldest son of the late Henry Richard Wood, Esq., of Hollin Hall, by Anne Eliza, dau. of John Eckerstall, Esq., of Claverton House, near Bath; b. 1811; s. 1841; m. 1st 1840 Charlotte Augusta, eldest dau. of the late John Rothery, Esq., of Leeds (she d. 1861); 2nd 1865 Sarah Catherine Isabella, only child of the late Capt. W. Hay, C.B.; he has by the former, with other issue,
      * Albert Charles, Lieut. 8th Hussars; b. 1841.
Mr. Wood, who was educated at Magdalen Coll., Cambridge, is a J.P. and D.L. for the W. Riding of Yorkshire, and Lord of the Manor of Copmanthorpe; late Major in the Yorkshire Hussars.—Hollin Hall, Ripon.

WOOD, GEORGE, Esq., of Largo, Fifeshire; Testcombe, Hants; and Feltwell, Norfolk.
Only son of the late Major-General Sir George Wood, K.C.B., of Ottershaw, Surrey, and Frances Vic, 2nd

dau. of the late John Remington, Esq., D.L., of Barton End House, co. Gloucester ; b. 1814 ; s. his cousin Sir Mark Wood, Bart., 1837 ; m. 1847 Alexandrina Williamson, dau. of the late — Angus McLeod, Esq., of Edinburgh, and has, with other issue,

 • Andrew George, b. 1854.

Mr. Wood, who was educated at Eton, and was formerly an Officer in the Life Guards, is head of the family and Chief of Largo. The family descent from Sir Andrew Wood, of Largo, the gallant Admiral of Scotland, 1480–1520.—Testcombe Cottage, Stockbridge, Hants ; Feltwell Lodge, Brandon ; Thames Yacht Club ; 13, Queen's Gate Terrace, w.

WOOD, GEORGE, Esq., of Calverley Hall, Yorkshire.

Second son of the late William Wood, Esq., of Upper House, Bradford, co. York, by Harriette, dau. of Lepton Dobson, Esq. ; b. 1825 ; educated at Rugby and University Coll., Oxford ; called to the Bar at the Inner Temple 1852 ; is a Magistrate for the W. Riding of co. York, and Lieut.-Col. 1st W. Riding Administrative Brigade Volunteer Artillery.—Calverley Hall, Leeds ; Oxford and Cambridge Club, s.w.

WOOD, HERBERT HOWORTH, Esq., of The White House, Herefordshire.

Only son of the late William Seward Wood, Esq., of The White House ; by Mary Anne, only dau. of Jonathan Hardwick, Esq., of Lulham, co. Hereford ; b. 1834 ; s. 1862 ; m. 1867 Alice Wyatt, youngest dau. of Samuel Carrington, Esq., of Pittville Lawn, Cheltenham. Educated at St. John's Coll., Oxford (B.A. 1858) ; is a J.P. and D.L. for co. Hereford, and Lord of the Manor of Jenkin ap Richard or Newton.—The White House, Hereford.

WOOD, ISAAC MORETON, Esq., of Newton Hall, Cheshire.

Son of the late Ven. Isaac Wood, of Newton Hall, Archdeacon of Chester, by Mary, dau. of John Nugent, Esq., of Clay Hill, Epsom, Surrey, and niece of the Right Hon. Edmund Burke ; b. 1825 ; s. 1865. Is Patron of 1 living.—Newton Hall, Middlewich.

WOOD, JAMES, Esq., of Woodville, co. Sligo.

Eldest son of the late James Wood, Esq., of Woodville, by Judith, dau. of William Coristine, Esq., of Sligo ; b. 1797 ; s. 1814 ; m. 1st 1833 Rhoda, dau. of Sir Edmund Nugent, of Airfield, co. Dublin : 2nd 1842 Anne, dau. of A. Martin, Esq., of Cleveragh, co. Sligo, and has issue,

 • William Gregory, b. 1847.

Mr. Wood, who was educated at Exeter Coll., Oxford, is a Magistrate for co. Sligo (High Sheriff 1826), and Capt. Sligo Rifles.—Woodville, Sligo.

+WOOD, the Rev. JAMES AYTTON, of Pentre Court, Monmouthshire.

Son of the late J. Wood, Esq. : b. 179– ; m. 18— Mary, elder dau. and heir of the late Rev. Henry Morice, Vicar of Ashwell, Herts. Educated at St. John's Coll. Oxford (B.A. 1815, M.A., 1823), was formerly Curate of Revelsby, co. Lincoln.—Pentre Court, Llanwenarth, Abergavenny.

WOOD, JOHN, Esq., of Arden, Cheshire.

Eldest son of the late John Wood, Esq., of Thorncliffe Hall, Cheshire, by Hannah, dau. of Thomas Hadfield, Esq., of Simmondley Hall, co. Derby ; b. 1815 ; s. 1833. Is a Magistrate for cos. Chester and Derby.—Arden, Bredbury, Stockport.

WOOD, JOHN, Esq., of Martock, Somerset.

Youngest son of the late William Cole Wood, Esq., of Martock, by Sophia Anne, dau. of the Rev. William

Horsey, of Coat-Martock, Somerset ; b. 1802 ; m. 1832 Mary Anne, eldest dau. of the Rev. T. B. Coleman, Rector of Church Stretton, co. Salop, and has, with other issue,

 • William Cole Pendarves, a Barrister-at-Law of Lincoln's Inn ; b. 1841.

Mr. Wood, who was educated at Trinity Coll., Cambridge (B.A. 1823), and called to the Bar at the Middle Temple 1847, is a Magistrate for Somerset and Dorset. —Ashfield, Martock, Ilminster.

WOOD, JOHN, Esq., of Thedden Grange, Hants.

Son of the late William Wood, Esq., of Bradford, co. York ; b. 1790 ; m. 1833 Annie Elizabeth, eldest dau. of the late John Hardy, Esq., of Dunstall Hall, co. Stafford, and has, with other issue,

 • John Gathorne, b. 1839 ; m. 1st 1862 Susan Mary, only dau. of E. Pennefather, Esq., of Rathsalla, co. Wicklow (she d. 1864) ; 2nd 1866 the Hon. Mary Anne, eldest dau. of James, 4th Viscount Lifford.

Mr. Wood is a J.P. and D.L. for the W. Riding of co. York, a Magistrate for Hants (High Sheriff 1848), and Patron of 1 living.—Thedden Grange, Alton.

WOOD, JOHN ANDREW, Esq., of Woodcot, Haddingtonshire.

Second son of the late Alexander Wood, Esq., of Woodcot (who was formerly a Judge of the Supreme Court of Scotland, and who d. 1864), by Jane, dau. of John Anderson, Esq., of Inchyra, co. Perth ; b. 1819 ; s. by settlement on the death of his mother 1866. Educated at Edinburgh ; called to the Scottish Bar 1843. —Woodcot Park, Blacksheils, Edinburgh ; New Club, Edinburgh ; 7, South East Circus Place, Edinburgh, N.B.

WOOD, JOSEPH CARTER, Esq., of Marden, Surrey.

Eldest son of the late Joseph Wood, Esq., late of Manadon Park, Devon, by Mary, dau. of Thomas Carter, Esq., J.P., of Swaffham, Norfolk ; b. 1793 ; m. 1829 Julia, dau. of the late Rev. Thomas Robert Wrench, Rector of St. Michael's, Cornhill, and has, with other issue, an only son,

 • Joseph, b. 1832 ; m. 1856 Edith Mary, dau. of the late Lieut.-Col. Sir Samuel Edmund Riggs Falkiner, Bart.

Mr. Wood was educated at Ealing.—Marden Park, Godstone ; Union Club, s.w.

+WOOD, NICHOLAS PRICE, Esq., of Bignall Hill, Staffordshire.

Son of the late John Wood, Esq., of Brownhills, co. Stafford, by Mary, dau. of John Baddeley, Esq. ; b. 1811 ; m. 1844 Agnes, dau. of the Rev. Nathan Hubbersty, of Wirksworth, co. Derby. Is a Magistrate for cos. Derby and Stafford.—Bignall Hill, Burslem ; Wirksworth, Derby.

+WOOD, the Rev. RICHARD, of Woodhall Park, Yorkshire.

Eldest son of the late Rev. Richard Wood, M.A., of Woodhall Park (many years Vicar of Irchester and Wollaston, co. Northampton ; b. 1832 ; s. 1868. Educated at the University of Durham (B.A. 1856) ; is Vicar of Irchester and Wollaston, and Patron of these livings, was Incumbent of Askrigg, co. York, 1865–8.—Woodhall Park, Bedale.

WOOD, Lieut.-General THOMAS, of Littleton, Middlesex.

Eldest son of the late Col. Thomas Wood, M.P., of Littleton, by Lady Caroline, dau. of Robert, 1st Marquis of Londonderry, K.G. ; b. 1804 ; s. 1861 ; m. 1848 Francis, dau. of the late Col. John Henry Smyth, M.P., of Heath Hall, co. York, and has, with other issue,

 • Thomas, b. 1853.

General Wood, who was educated at Harrow and Vienna, is a Magistrate for Middlesex, Brecon, cos. Hereford, Radnor, and Surrey, Lord of the Manors of Littleton, Middleham, and Glasbury, Patron of 1 living, a Lieut.-Gen. in the Army, and Col. 84th Foot, late Col. Grenadier Guards; was M.P. for Middlesex 1837–47.—*Littleton, Chertsey; The Lodge, Brecon; Guards' and White's Clubs, s.w.*

WOOD, WESTERN, Esq., of North Cray, Kent.
Eldest son of the late Western Wood, Esq. (who was a Magistrate for Kent, M.P. for the city of London, and *d.* 1863), by Sarah Letitia, dau. of John Morris, Esq.; *b.* 1835 ; *m.* 1861 Lucy Elizabeth, eldest dau. of Frederick Orme Darvall, Esq., Registrar-General of Queensland.—*North Cray Place, Bexley.*

WOOD, WILLIAM, Esq., of Monkhill, Yorkshire.
Youngest son of the late James Wood, Esq., of Pontefract, by Mary, dau. of John Bland, Esq.; *b.* 1816 ; *m.* 1st 1840 Caroline, dau. of John Hussey, Esq., of Wilton, Wilts; 2nd 1855 Jane Elizabeth, dau. of Joseph Coley, Esq., of London, and has by the former, with other issue,

• James William, *b.* 1841.

Mr. Wood, who is a Magistrate for the W. Riding of Yorkshire, was M.P. for Pontefract 1857-9.—*Monkhill House, Pontefract.*

WOOD, WILLIAM EDWARD COLLINS-, Esq., of Keithick, Perthshire.
Eldest son of the late Edward Collins, Esq., of Frowlesworth, co. Leicester (Capt. in the 21st Light Dragoons), by Margaret his wife, only dau. of William Wood, Esq., of Perth, who assumed the name of Wood, by the will of his maternal grand-uncle, James Wood, Esq., of Keithick; *b.* 1811 ; *m.* 1840 Anne Wallace, dau. of the late Lieut.-Col. Goodwin Colquitt, C.B., Grenadier Guards, and has, with other issue,

• Edward, *b.* 1841.

Mr. Collins-Wood, who was educated at Magdalen Coll., Oxford, is a J.P. and D.L. for co. Perth.—*Keithick, Cupar Angus, N.B.*

WOOD, WILLIAM MARK, Esq., of Bishop's Hall, Essex.
Eldest son of the late William Joseph Lockwood, Esq., of Dews Hall, Lambourne, Essex, by Rachel, dau. of the late Sir Mark Wood, Bart., of Gatton Park, Surrey ; *b.* 1817 ; *s.* 1854 ; *m.* 1846 Amelia Jane, youngest dau. of the late Sir Robert Williams, Bart., and has, with other issue,

• Amelius Richard Mark, *b.* 1847.

Mr. Wood, who was educated at Eton, is a Magistrate for co. Monmouth and a Dep.-Lieut. for Essex, and Lord of the Manor of Dews Hall; late Col. Coldstream Guards; assumed the name of Wood under the will of his maternal uncle, Sir Mark Wood, Bart., 1857. —*Bishop's Hall, Romford; Guards', Arthur's, and Boodle's Clubs, s.w.; b. Audley Square, w.*

WOOD, WILLIAM RAYNER, Esq., of Singleton Lodge, Lancashire.
Only son of the late George William Wood, Esq., M.P. of Singleton Lodge, by Sarah, dau. of Joseph Oates, Esq., of Weetwood Hall, near Leeds ; *b.* 1811 ; *s.* 1843 ; *m.* 1841 Sarah Jane, dau. of James M'Connel, Esq., of Manchester, and by her, who *d.* 1867, has issue,

• George William Rayner, *b.* 1851.

Mr. Wood, who was educated at Manchester Coll., York, is a J.P. and D.L. for co. Lancaster.—*Singleton Lodge, Manchester; Athenæum Club, s.w.*
1010

WOOD, WILLIAM STUCKEY, Esq., of Charlton Musgrove, Somerset.
Eldest son of the Rev. William Wood, by Julia, eldest dau. of the late Vincent Stuckey, Esq., of Hill House, Langport, Somerset; *b.* 1829 ; *m.* 1852 Mary, eldest dau. of Richard Armit, Esq., of Monkstown, co. Dublin, and has, with other issue,

• Vincent Armit, *b.* 1853.

Mr. Wood, who is a Magistrate for Somerset, was formerly in the 7th Dragoon Guards.—*Charlton Musgrove, Wincanton.*

+ WOOD, WILLOUGHBY, Esq., of Thoresby, Lincolnshire, and Hollybank, Staffordshire.
Eldest son of the late Charles Thorold Wood, Esq., of Thoresby, by Jane, only dau. of the late Sir John Thorold, Bart.; *b.* 1814 ; *m.* 1845 Mary, dau. of John Clervaux Chaytor, Esq., of Spenhithorne Hall, co. York, and has, with other issue,

• Willoughby, *b.* 1850.

Mr. Wood is a Magistrate for co. Stafford, and Lord of the Manor of South Thoresby.—*Thoresby, Alford ; Hollybank, Needwood Forest, Burton-on-Trent.*

WOOD. (See under Halifax, Viscount.)

WOOD-CRASTER. (See Craster.)

WOOD. (See Grove.)

WOOD. (See Stuckey.)

WOODALL, JOHN, Esq., of Scarborough, Yorkshire.
Eldest son of the late John Woodall, Esq., of Scarborough, by Ann, dau. of John Dowker, Esq., of Salton, co. York; *b.* 1801 ; *s.* 1334 ; *m.* 1830 Mary Eleanor, dau. of the Rev. William Woodall, Rector of Branston and Waltham, co. Leicester, and has, with other issue,

• John Woodall, M.A., F.G.S. ; *b.* 1831.

Mr. Woodall is a J.P. and D.L. for the N. Riding of co. York, a Magistrate for the E. Riding, and Patron of 1 living.—*Scarborough, Yorkshire; Carlton Club, s.w.*

+ WOODARD, Rev. NATHANIEL, of Henfield, Sussex.
Son of the late N. Woodard, Esq.; *b.* 1810 ; is married, and has, with other issue,

• Mortimer Neville, an Officer in the 88th Regt. (Connaught Rangers); *b.* 1840 ; *m.* 1863 Catherine dau. of Paul Wilmot, Esq., barrister-at-Law, of the Middle Temple, and of Cliff House, near Bideford, Devon.

Mr. Woodard, who was educated at Magdalen Hall, Oxford (B.A. 1840), is Provost of St. Nicholas Coll., Shoreham.—*Henfield, Hurstpierpoint; St. Nicholas Coll., Shoreham.*

WOODCOCK, HENRY, Esq., of Bank House, Lancashire.
Third son of the late Thomas Woodcock, Esq., of Bank House, by Elizabeth, dau. and heir of Thomas Holme, Esq.; *b.* 1814 ; *m.* 1st 1840 Jane, dau. of Thomas Lechmere Marriott, Esq., of Dolgelley ; 2nd 1864 Emily Susan, dau. of Thomas Ridgway Bridson, Esq., of Walsuches, near Bolton-le-Moors, and has, with other issue,

• Thomas Holme, *b.* 1846.

Mr. Woodcock, who was educated at Wadham Coll., Oxford, is a Magistrate for co. Lancaster. This family has been settled at Newburgh, near Ormskirk, since 1605, married the heiress of a branch of the Spencers in 1738, and the heiress of Holme in 1799.—*Bank House, Wigan*

WOODCOCK, Henry Cleever, Esq., of Rearsby, Leicestershire.

Only son of the late John William Woodcock, Esq., of Syston, co. Leicester, by Johanna, dau. of George Williamson, Esq., of Gaddesby, co. Leicester; *b.* 1817; *m.* 1840 Agnes, dau. of Christopher Williamson, Esq., of Gaddesby, and has, with other issue,

• John William Graham, *b.* 1841.

Mr. Woodcock is a Magistrate for co. Leicester. —*Rearsby House, Leicester.*

WOODD, BASIL GEORGE, Esq., of Hillfield, Middlesex.

Fourth son of the late George B. Woodd, Esq., of Richmond, Surrey, by Gertrude, dau. of George Ballard, Esq., of Leatherhead, Surrey; *b.* 1781; *m.* 1814 Mary, only dau. of the Rev. Robert Mitton, and by her, who *d.* 1864, has, with other issue,

• Basil Thomas, of Conyngham Hall, near Knaresborough, M.A. of Trinity Coll., Cambridge, a Barrister-at-Law of the Inner Temple, a Magistrate for the N. Riding, and a J.P. and D.L. for the W. Riding of co. York, and M.P. for Knaresborough; *b.* 1815; *m.* 1837 Charlotte Mary, eldest dau. of the Rev. J. Dampier, of Colinshays, Somerset, and has, with other issue, • Basil Kilvington, in Holy Orders, *b.* 1842; *m.* 1867 Esther Harriett, 2nd dau. of the Rev. Edmund Hollond, of Benhall Lodge, Suffolk.

This family were formerly of Shine Wood, co. Salop, and suffered severely in the cause of Charles I.—*Hillfield, Hampstead ; 108, New Bond Street; w.*

WOODFORD, Sir ALEXANDER, G.C.B., G.C.M.G. (cr. 1852).

Son of the late Lieut.-Col. John Woodford, by Lady Susan, dau. of George, 3rd Duke of Gordon (widow of John, 9th Earl of Westmorland); *b.* 1782; *m.* 1815 Charlotte Mary Ann, dau. of Charles Henry Fraser, Esq., and has issue,

• John William Gordon, *b.* 182– ; *m.* 1865 Marian Elizabeth, eldest dau. of Richard Arabin, Esq.

Sir A. Woodford is a Field Marshal in the Army, and Lieut.-Governor of Chelsea Hospital, late Col. Scots Fusilier Guards; was formerly Aide-de-Camp to George IV.; has been Lieut.-Governor of Malta, Commander of the Forces in the Ionian Islands, and Governor of Gibraltar.—*Royal Hospital, Chelsea,* s.w.

WOODFORD, Sir JOHN GEORGE, K.C.B., K.C.H. (cr. 1832).

Son of the late Lieut.-Col. John Woodford, by Lady Susan, dau. of George, 3rd Duke of Gordon (widow of John, 9th Earl of Westmorland); *b.* 1785. A General in the Army, retired; served in the Peninsula and at Waterloo ; was formerly Ensign 1st Regt. of Foot, and afterwards served in the Grenadier Guards. —*United Service Club,* s.w.

+ WOODFORDE, GEORGE AUGUSTUS, Esq., of Ansford House, Somersetshire.

Only surviving son of the late William Woodforde, Esq., of Ansford House, by Anne, only surviving child of George Dukes, Esq., of Galhampton, Somerset; *b.* 1801; *s.* his brother 1856 ; *m.* 1832 Harriet Mary, dau. of the late Rev. William Loir, Rector of Ditcheat, Somerset, and has, with other issue, • Charles Neville, *b.* 183–.—*Ansford House, Castle Cary, Somerset.*

+ WOODHAM, the Rev. THOMAS FIELDER, of Farley Chamberlayne, Hampshire.

Eldest son of the late Thomas Woodham, Esq., of Winchester and Sandown (who *d.* 1858), by Elizabeth, dau. of — Fielder, Esq. (she *d.* 1851); *b.* 1804; *m.* 183– Martha Eliza, dau. of ——, Esq., and by her, who *d.* 1857, has, with other issue,

• Martha Eliza, *m.* Edward Waddilove, Esq.

Mr. Woodham, who was educated at Worcester Coll.,

Oxford (B.A. 1826), is a Magistrate for Hants, and Rector, Lord of the Manor, and Patron of Farley Chamberlayne; was formerly Rector of Walcot, Somerset, of Brancaster, Norfolk, and of St. Peter's, Winchester.—*Farley Chamberlayne, Romsey.*

+ WOODHAM, WILLIAM NASH, Esq., of Shepreth, Cambridgeshire.

Son of the late W. Woodham, Esq. ; *b.* 18—; is married, and has, with other issue,

• William, *b.* 18— ; *m.* 1860 Sophia, only dau. of William Clifton, Esq., of Lynn.

Mr. Woodham is a Magistrate for co. Cambridge. —*Shepreth, Royston.*

WOODHOUSE, JOHN ODINS, Esq., K.C.J.J., of Portadown, co. Armagh.

Eldest son of Curran Woodhouse, Esq., late Deputy-Governor and J.P., co. Armagh, by Mary, dau. of Dr. James Hall, of Parkrow, Dromore, co. Down ; *b.* 1804 ; *m.* 1834 Mary Burleigh, 2nd dau. of Thomas Lethem, Esq., and has, with other issue,

• John Odins, *b.* 1842.

Mr. Woodhouse is a Magistrate for cos. Armagh, Donegal, Down, and Louth. This family descend from a branch of the Wodehouses of Norfolk. who settled in Ireland *temp.* James I.—*Portadown, co. Armagh ; Kerryheel, Ramelton, co. Donegal ; Omeath Park, Newry, co. Louth.*

WOODHOUSE, Miss, of Irnham, Lincolnshire.

Isabel Hervey, only child and heir of the late William Hervey Woodhouse, Esq., J.P. and D.L., of Irnham Hall (who *d.* 1859), by Sarah Ellen, dau. of William Cole, Esq., of Birkenhead, co. Chester (she *m.* 2nd 1868 Alexander, eldest son of Alexander Crowe, Esq., of Woodcote Grove, Epsom; *s.* 1859. This estate was acquired by purchase from the brother of the late Lord Clifford, to whom it had descended through the Arundells, from the now extinct family of Conquest.—*Irnham Hall, Colsterworth.*

WOODHOUSE, SAMUEL, Esq., of Norley Hall, Cheshire.

Eldest son of the late Samuel Woodhouse, Esq., of Norley Hall, by Martha, dau. of Lewis Anthony Gordon, Esq., of London; *b.* 1821 ; *s.* 1834 ; *m.* 1844 Eliza, dau. of Henry Thornton Mostyn, Esq., M.D., late 47th Foot, and has, with other issue,

• Samuel Henry, *b.* 1848 ; educated at Eton and University Coll., Oxford.

Mr. Woodhouse is a Magistrate for co. Chester. —*Norley Hall, Frodsham.*

WOODS, GEORGE, Esq., of Milverton, co. Dublin.

Only son of the late John Woods, Esq., of Winter Lodge, co. Dublin, by Hannah, dau. and co-heir of Joshua Warren, Esq., of Galtrim, co. Meath ; *b.* 1786 ; *s.* 1826 ; *m.* 1812 Studia, ... dau. of Hans Hamilton, Esq., M.P., of Abbotstown, co. Dublin, and by her, who *d.* 1829, has, with other issue,

• Hans Hamilton Woods, Esq., of Whitestown House, Balbriggan, co. Dublin), educated at Trinity Coll., Dublin ; a J.P. and D.L. for co. Dublin (High Sheriff 1854), and a Magistrate for co. Meath (High Sheriff 1861), *b.* 1814 ; *m.* 1810 Louisa Catherine, dau. of the Rev. and Rev. Edward Taylor, and has, with other issue, • George John, *b.* 1842.

Mr. G. Woods, who was educated at the University of Glasgow, is a Magistrate for co. Dublin (High Sheriff 1821–2), and Patron of 1 living.—*Milverton Hall, Skerries, co. Dublin ; Winter Lodge, Balbriggan, co. Dublin ; Sackville Street Club, Dublin.*

WOODS, the Rev. GEORGE HENRY, of Shop-wyke House, Sussex.

Eldest son of the late Benjamin Woods, Esq., by Lucy, dau. of the Rev. Henry White, Rector of Fytield, Hants; b. 1802; s. his aunt 1848; m. 1841 Catherine, dau. of the late Rev. George Bethell, Fellow of Eton Coll. and Rector of Worplesdon, Surrey. Mr. Woods, who was educated at Wadham Coll., Oxford (B.A. 1825), M.A. 1828), is Lord of the Manor of Shopwyke Eagle. —Shopwyke House, Chichester; United University Club.

WOODS, HENRY, Esq., of Gillibrand Hall, Lancashire.

Only son of the late William Woods, Esq., of Wigan (who d. 1841), by Elizabeth, dau. of Jonathan Marsden, Esq.; b. 1822; m. 1st 1854 Hannah, only child of the late Charles Hindley, Esq., M.P., of Portland House, Ashton-under-Lyne (she d. 1857); 2nd 1864 Henrietta Emma, 5th dau. of the Right Rev. Ashhurst. T. Gilbert, D.D., Lord Bishop of Chichester; he has surviving issue, by the former,

* William, b. 1855.

Mr. Woods, who is a J.P. and D.L. for co. Lancaster, has been M.P. for Wigan since 1857.— Gillibrand Hall, Wigan; Warnford Park, Bishop's Waltham; Brooks's and Reform Clubs; s.w.; 21, Hyde Park Gardens, w.

WOODS, WILLIAM LEYLAND, Esq., of Chilgrove, Sussex.

Son of the late John Woods, Esq., of Chilgrove, by Mary, dau. of William Guy, Esq., of Chichester; b. 1802; m. 1836 Mary Anne, dau. of George Fort, Esq., of Alderbury, Wilts, and has, with other issue,

* John William, b. 1837.

Mr. Woods, who was educated at Winchester and St. John's Coll., Oxford (B.A. 1825, M.A. 1828), is a Magistrate for Sussex (High Sheriff 1864).—Chilgrove, Chichester.

WOODWARD, HENRY THOMAS, Esq., of Drum-barrow, co. Meath.

Second but eldest surviving son of the late Henry Woodward, Esq., of Drumbarrow (who d. 1838), by Sarah Catherine, dau. of the late Robert Wade, Esq., of Clonabraney, co. Meath; b. 1812; s. his brother 1864; m. 1835 Esther, 2nd dau. of the late Henry Thomas Woodward, Esq., of Park, Borey Tracey, Devon, and has, with other issue, * Henry Robert, b. 1842; m. 1862 Charlotte Susan, 3rd dau. of the Rev. Joseph Mays, and has, with other issue, Henry Joseph, b. 1864.—Drumbarrow, Kells, co. Meath.

+WOODWARD, JAMES PALMER, Esq., of The Hyde, Worcestershire.

Son of the late — Woodward, Esq.; b. 1800. Is a J.P. and D.L. for co. Worcester; formerly in the Madras Army; retired as Major 1846.— The Hyde, Upton-on-Severn.

WOODWARD, ROBERT, Esq., of Arley Castle, Worcestershire.

Second son of the late William Woodward, Esq., of Birlingham, by Mary, dau. of Robert Smith, Esq., of Crowle, co. Worcester; b. 1801; s. to the family estate at Birlingham, co. Worcester, in 1843; m. 1839 Mary, youngest dau. of William Hall, Esq., of Royals Court, Ripple, and has, with other issue,

* Robert, b. 1840.

Mr. Woodward, who is a Magistrate for cos. Stafford and Worcester, was formerly a Merchant in Liverpool. —Arley Castle, Bewdley; the Manor House, Birlingham, Pershore.

1018

WOODYEARE, the Rev. JOHN FOUNTAIN WOODYEARE, of Crookhill, Yorkshire.

Eldest son of the late Fountain John Elwin, by Frances, dau. of John Woodyeare, Esq., of Crookhill, co. York (whose name he assumed by Royal license in 1812); b. 1839; s. 1844; m. 1843 Mary Jane, dau. of the late William Phillips, Esq., and by her, who d. 1866, has, with other issue,

* Richard Elwin, b. 1853.

Mr. Woodyeare was educated at the Charterhouse and Ch. Coll., Cambridge (B.A. 1830).— Crookhill, Rotherham.

WOOLLCOMBE, the Rev. GEORGE LEY, of Hemerdon, Devon.

Eldest son of the late Admiral George Woollcombe, J.P., of Hemerdon, by Mary Elizabeth, 2nd dau. of George Ley, Esq., of Cockington, Devon: b. 1828; s. 1865; m. 1859 Edith, youngest dau. of H. Lamle, Esq., of Truro. Educated at Balliol Coll., Oxford (B.A. 1851, M.A. 1854); is Rector of Sennen, Cornwall, late Incumbent of Brinton, Devon. This family have been resident in the parish of Plympton St. Mary, Devon, since the time of Henry VII.—Hemerdon, Plympton.

+WOOLCOMBE, JOHN MORTH, Esq., of Ashbury, Devonshire.

Eldest son of the late Samuel Morth Woolcombe, Esq., of Ashbury, by Anne Eleanor, dau. of the late Sir Thomas Louis, Bart.; b. 1800. Is a J.P. and D.L. for co. Devon, and Patron of 1 living. This family is a younger branch of the Woolcombes of Hemerdon. —Ashbury, Okehampton.

WOOLRYCH, HUMPHRY WILLIAM Esq., (Serjeant-at-law), of Croxley, Herts.

Only son of the late Humphry Cornewall Woolrych, Esq., of Croxley, by Elizabeth, dau. of William Bentley, Esq., of London; b. 1795; m. 1817 Penelope, dau. of Francis Bradford, Esq., of Westwood, Herts, and has, with other issue,

* Humphrey Fitzroy, in Holy Orders, M.A. of London University; Curate of Hucking, Kent: b. 1823; m. 1862 Mary Katherine, dau. of Joseph Heapey Watson, Esq., Solicitor, of Oldbury, co. Stafford, and has issue.

Mr. Woolrych, who was called to the Bar at Lincoln's Inn 1821, and went the Western and subsequently the Home Circuit, is a Serjeant-at-Law, and a Magistrate for Herts and for the Liberty of St. Alban's.— Croxley, Rickmansworth.

WORCESTER, Bishop of (the Right Rev. HENRY PHILPOTT, D.D.)

Youngest son of the late Richard Philpott, Esq., of Chichester, by Jane, dau. of Richard Price, Esq.; b. 1807; m. 1846 Mary Jane Doria, dau. of the Marquis Spineto. Educated at St. Catherine's Coll., Cambridge (B.A. 1829, M.A. 1832, D.D. 1845); was Fellow, Tutor, and Master of his College, Consort of Norwich, and Chaplain to H.R.H. the late Prince Consort; consecrated 1861; Patron of 91 livings.—Hartlebury Castle, Kidderminster; Athenæum Club, s.w.

WORCESTER. (See under Beaufort, Duke of.)

WORDSWORTH, the Rev. JOHN, of Sockbridge, Westmoreland.

Elder son of the late William Wordsworth, Esq., of Rydal (Poet Laureate), by Mary, dau. of the late John Hutchinson, Esq., of Penrith; b. 1802; m. 1st 1830 Isabella, dau. of Henry Curwen, Esq., of Workington Hall, Cumberland; 2nd 18— Helen, dau. of Donald

Ross, Esq., of Edinburgh; 3rd 1856, Marianne, dau. of Luke Dolan, Esq., and has, with other surviving issue,

* William, B.A., of Balliol Coll., Oxford ; b. 1835.

Mr. Wordsworth, who was educated at Winchester and New Coll., Oxford (B.A. 1826, M.A. 1830), is Rector of Brigham and Plumbland, Cumberland.—*Plumbland Rectory, Carlisle.*

WORDSWORTH, WILLIAM, Esq., of St. Ann's Hill, Cumberland.

Younger son of the late William Wordsworth, Esq., of Rydal and of Sockbridge, Westmoreland (Poet Laureate), who d. 1850, by Mary, dau. of the late John Hutchinson, Esq., of Penrith; b. 1810; m. 1847 Fanny Eliza, dau. of the late Reginald Graham, Esq., and has, with other issue,

* Reginald Graham, b. 1852.

Mr. Wordsworth, who was educated at the Charterhouse and the University of Heidelberg, is a Magistrate for Cumberland, and was appointed, 1842, upon the resignation of his father, Distributor of Stamps for Cumberland, Westmoreland, and part of Lancashire. —*St. Ann's Hill, Carlisle.*

WORKMAN, HENRY, Esq., of Charlton House, Worcestershire.

Son of the late — Workman, Esq.; b. 179—; m. 1837 Elizabeth, dau. of James Wyley, Esq., of Langdon, co. Stafford (she d. s. p. 1847). Is a Magistrate for the borough of Evesham, and cos. Warwick and Gloucester, a J.P. and D.L. for co. Worcester, a Solicitor at Evesham, and Lord of the Manor of Charlton.—*Charlton House, Pershore.*

Heir Pres., his brother Benjamin (of Hampton House, Great Hampton, Evesham), a Magistrate for Evesham and cos. Worcester and Gloucester ; b. 179–.

WORKMAN-McNAGHTEN. (See *McNaghten.*)

WORLEY, Mrs., of New Barnes, Herts.

Isabella Charlotte, youngest dau. of the late Joseph Timperon, Esq., by Anne, dau. of the Rev. J. Keyt, D.D.; m. 1842 Henry Thomas Worley, Esq., of Dromenah Lodge, Iver, a Magistrate for Bucks and Herts (who d. 1855). Mrs. Worley is Patron of 1 Incumbency. —*Dromenagh Lodge, New Barnes, St. Alban's.*

+WORLLEDGE, JOHN, Esq., of Chevington, Suffolk.

Eldest son of the late John Worlledge, Esq., of Chevington (who was a Magistrate for Suffolk); b. 1809; s. 1862; m. 184- Mary, dau. of the Rev. John Wastell, of Risby, Bury St. Edmund's (she d. 1863). Educated at Trinity Coll., Cambridge (B.A. 1831, M.A. 1834); called to the Bar at the Middle Temple 1838, and went the Norfolk Circuit ; is a Magistrate for Suffolk, and Judge of the County Court.—*Ruffins House, Chevington, Bury St. Edmund's ; Hill House, Ipswich.*

WORMALD, FRANK, Esq., of Potterton Hall, Yorkshire.

Son of the late F. Wormald, Esq.; b. 1816; is married, and has issue,

* Fanny, m. 1865 Col. Valentine Baker, 10th Hussars.

Mr. Wormald, who was educated at Trinity Coll., Cambridge (B.A. 1831, M.A. 1834), is a Magistrate for the W. R. of co. York (High Sheriff 18 --).—*Potterton Hall, Aberford, Yorkshire.*

WORMLEY. (See *Richardson-Wormley.*)

WORSHIP, FRANCIS, Esq., of Great Yarmouth, Norfolk.

Eldest son of the late Harry Verelst Worship, Esq., of Yarmouth, by Sarah Turner, dau. of Thomas Dade,

Esq., of Hedenham, Suffolk; b. 1801. Is a Dep.-Lieut. for Norfolk, and a Magistrate for Yarmouth (Mayor 1857). This family has been settled in Yarmouth since the reign of James I.—*The Quay, Great Yarmouth.*

Heir Pres., his brother William, a Magistrate for Yarmouth, and Mayor 1859 and 1867 ; b. 1811 ; m. 1862 Rebecca, dau. of Richard Glasspoole, Esq., of Ormsby, St. Michael, Norfolk, J.P. for Norfolk, and has issue, * 3 children.

WORSLEY, Sir WILLIAM, Bart., of Hovingham, Yorkshire (cr. 1838).

Eldest surviving son of the late Rev. George Worsley, Rector of Staregrave, co. York, by Anne, dau. of Sir Thomas Cayley, Bart.; b. 1792; m. 1827 Sarah Philadelphia, dau. of the late Sir George Cayley, Bart., of Brompton, co. York. Is a J.P. and D.L. for the N. Riding of Yorkshire. This family were formerly seated at Worsley, co. Lancaster.—*Hovingham Hall, York.*

Heir, his son William Cayley, J.P. and D.L. for the N. Riding of co. York ; b. 1828 ; m. 1854 Harriet Philadelphia, dau. of Marcus Worsley, Esq.

WORSLEY, the Rev. JOHN HENRY.

Third, but eldest surviving son of the late Rev. James Worsley, of Billingham, Isle of Wight, by Sophia, dau. of Sir John Pinhorn, Knt., of Ringwood House, Isle of Wight; b. 1814; m. 1842 Catherine, dau. of Robert Wharton Myddleton, Esq., of Grinkle Park, co. York, and Old Park, co. Durham, and has no issue. Mr. Worsley, who was educated at Magdalen Coll., Oxford (B.A. 1836, M.A. 1838), is a Magistrate for Oxon, and Incumbent of Leafield, with Wychwood. This family is descended from Sir Elias de Workesley, Lord of the Manor of Workesley at the time of the Norman Conquest.—*Leafield Parsonage, Witney.*

+WORSLEY, PHILIP JOHN, Esq., of Brislington, Somersetshire.

Son of the late W. Worsley, Esq.; b. 18—; m. 1861 Anna, dau. of Thomas Taylor Lombe, Esq., of Starston Hall, Norfolk.—*Brislington, Bristol.*

WORSLEY. (See *Pennyman.*)

WORSLEY. (See *Carrill-Worsley.*)

WORTH, JOHN FRANCIS, Esq., of Worth, Devon.

Eldest son of the late John Worth, Esq., of Worth, by Jane Mary, dau. of Matthew Lee, Esq., of Ebford House, Devon; b. 1802; s. 1823; m. 1st 1821 Lucy, dau. of Henry Blagdon Worth, Esq. (she d. 1859); 2nd 1862 Isabella, dau. of the late Rev. Richard Adney, and widow of Walter Hitchcock, Esq., and has, with other issue,

* Reginald, b. 1831.

Mr. Worth, who was educated at Eton and New Coll., Oxford, is a J.P. and D.L. for Devon, Lord of the Manor and Patron of Washfield ; was formerly Major 1st Devon Royal Yeomanry, and Capt. 1st Devon Artillery. This family have been seated at Worth since the 13th century.—*Worth House, Washfield, Tiverton ; Wyddon..re, Vira. hoad.*

WORTHAM, BISCOE HILL, Esq., of Knesworth House, Cambridgeshire.

Eldest son of the late James Wortham, Esq., and nephew of the late Hale Wortham, Esq., of Royston ; b. 18—. Is a J.P. and D.L. for co. Cambridge, Lord of the Manor of Knesworth and Shepreth, &c., and Patron of Shepreth.—*Knesworth House, Royston.*

WORTHINGTON, EDWARD, Esq., of Sandiway, Cheshire.

Fourth son of the late William Henry Worthington, Esq., J.P. of Sandiway Bank, an Officer in the Hon.

Guards (Blue), by Margaretta, dau. of Daniel Seaman, Esq.; *b*. 1806; *s*. 1847; *m*. 1847 Maria, dau. of Christopher Temple, Esq., Q.C., and has issue,

* Margaretta Lucy.

This family, a branch of the ancient house of Worthington of Worthington. were settled at an early period in co. Lancaster, and afterwards at Ashton Hayes, co. Chester.—*Sandiway Bank, Northwich.*

WORTHINGTON, JONATHAN YORKE, Esq., of Llancaiach, Glamorganshire.
Eldest son of the late Jonathan Worthington, Esq., of Moorhall, co. Worcester, by Anne Maria, dau. of John Barnett, Esq., of Stourport; *b*. 1827; *s*. 1860; *m*. 1860 Henrietta Charlotte, dau. of Valentine Bryan, Esq., of co. Galway. Educated at Marlborough and Addiscombe Colls.; is a Capt. R.A. This family is of the ancient house of Worthington of Worthington, in the hundred of Leyland, co. Lancaster.—*Llancaiach, Caerphilly, Swansea; Junior United Service Club, s.w.*

WORTHINGTON, NATHAN, Esq., of Hollinwood, Lancashire.
Eldest son of the late John Worthington, Esq., of Hollinwood, by Sarah, dau. of the late John Duncuft, Esq., of Hathershaw, near Oldham; *b*. 1814; *s*. 1850. Is a J.P. and D.L. for co. Lancaster, and a Magistrate for the W. Riding of Yorkshire and for Oldham.—*Hollinwood, Manchester; Union Club, Manchester; Conservative Club, s.w.*

Heir Pres., his brother George Henry, a Magistrate for co. Lancaster; *b*. 1819.

WORTHINGTON, WILLIAM, Esq., of The Brockhurst, Cheshire.
Eldest son of the late William Worthington, Esq., of Liftwich, co. Chester, by Anne, dau. of Joseph Fletcher, Esq., of Norton, in the same co.; *b*. 1789; *s*. 1808; *m*. 1817 Mary, dau. of John Lindop, Esq., of Marton Hall, and has, with other issue,

* William, *b*. 1819.

Mr. Worthington, who was educated at Brasenose Coll., Oxford, is a Magistrate for co. Chester.—*The Brockhurst, Northwich.*

WORTHINGTON, WILLIAM, Esq., of Newton Park, Derbyshire.
Eldest son of the late William Worthington, Esq., of Burton-on-Trent; *b*. 1800; *m*. 1824 Mary Ann, 2nd dau. of Francis Calvert, Esq., of Houndhill, co. Derby, and has, with other issue,

* William Henry, *b*. 1826; *m*. 1858 Alice Elizabeth, eldest dau. of John Craig, Esq., of Horsehead House, co. Cork.

Mr. Worthington is a Magistrate for cos. Derby and Stafford. This family is of Leicestershire extraction.—*Newton Park, Burton-on-Trent.*

WORTHINGTON-WRIGHT, WILLIAM WRIGHT, Esq., of Flixton, Lancashire.
Eldest son of the late Samuel Worthington, Esq., by Mary, dau. of William Lee, Esq., of Flixton; *b*. 1805; *s*. 1847 to the estates of his maternal uncle, Ralph Wright, Esq., whose name he assumed; *m*. 1852 Margaret Amelia, dau. of Thos. Lee, Esq., and has issue,

* Samuel, *b*. 1859.

Mr. Worthington-Wright, who is a Magistrate for co. Lancaster, was formerly a Merchant in Liverpool.—*Flixton House, Manchester.*

WORTLEY. (See *Stuart-Wortley*.)

WORTLEY. (See under *Wharncliffe, Lord*.)
1020

WOULFE, Capt. STEPHEN ROLAND.
Only son of the late Right Hon. Stephen Woulfe, M.P., of Tiermaclane, co. Clare, Ireland, Chief Baron of the Exchequer, Ireland, by Mary Frances, dau. of Roger Hamill, Esq., of Dowth, co. Dublin; *b*. 1822; *m*. 1853 the Hon. Isabella Letitia, dau. of Thomas, 2nd Lord Graves. Late Capt. Huntingdon Militia; was formerly an Officer in the 7th Fusiliers. This family is of Danish origin, and settled in Ireland *temp.* Henry II.—*Brooks's Club, s.w.*

WRANGHAM, WALTER FRANCIS, Esq., of The Rocks, Gloucestershire.
Eldest son of the late Digby Cayley Wrangham, Esq., Q.C., J.P., and D.L., of The Rocks, by Amelia, dau. of Walter Fawkes, Esq., of Farnley Hall, co. York; *b*. 1829; *s*. 1863. Educated at Eton and Exeter Coll., Oxford; called to the Bar at Lincoln's Inn 1859. —*The Rocks, Marshfield, Bath; Oxford and Cambridge, and Junior Carlton Clubs, s.w.*

Heir Pres., his brother Digby Strangeways, in Holy Orders, M.A. of St. John's Coll., Oxford, a Magistrate for the E. Riding of co. York, and Vicar of South Cave, co. York; *b*. 1833.

WRAXALL, Sir HORATIO HENRY, Bart. (cr. 1813).
Second son of the late Charles Edward Wraxall, R.A. (who *d*. 1849), by Ellen Cecilia, dau. of J. Madden, Esq.; *b*. 1833; *s*. his brother as 4th Bart. 1865; *m*. 1855 Miss Laura Hammond. Sir John de Wraxall represented Somerset and Dorset in Parliament *temp.* Edward I.—8, *West Hill Grove, Wandsworth, S.*

Heir Pres., his brother Morville Nathaniel, *b*. 1858; *m*. 1860 Miss Susannah Claringbold, of Ireland, and has issue four children.

WRAY, WILLIAM, Esq., of Oak Park, co. Donegal.
Eldest son of the late William Wray, Esq., of Castle Wray, co. Donegal, by Anne Jane, dau. of John Johnston, Esq., of Brook Hill, co. Leitrim; *b*. 1818; *s*. 1843; *m*. 1850 Anna, dau. of the late Capt. Robert Johnston, 67th Foot (J.P. and D.L. for co. Leitrim), and has, with other issue,

* William Cecil, *b*. 1851.

Mr. Wray is a Magistrate for co. Donegal (High Sheriff 1851). This family was formerly seated at Glentworth, co. Lincoln.—*Oak Park, Ballymalecl, co. Donegal.*

WREN, Major THOMAS, of Lenwood, Devon.
Fourth son of the late Robert Wren, Esq., of Bideford, by Sarah, dau. of J. B. Greening, Esq.; *b*. 1781; *m*. 1820 Delitia Montagu, dau. of Admiral Baston, of Burrough, and has, with other issue,

* Adderley Barton, a Magistrate for Devon, *b*. 1821; educated at St. John's Coll., Cambridge (B.A. 1843.)

Major Wren, who is a J.P. and D.L. for Devon, was formerly Major Madras Army.—*Lenwood, Northam, Bideford.*

WREN ROSKYNE. (See under *Hockyns, Bart.*)

WRENCH, the Rev. FREDERICK, of Stowting, Kent.
Eldest surviving son of the late John George Wrench, Esq., by Mary, dau. of John Buxton, Esq., of Ewel Hall, Essex; *b*. 1807; *m*. 1855 Eliza Marr, dau. of Capt. John L. Stringer, of Effoll Lodge, Ettingham, Surrey; and has, with other issue, an only son.

* Frederick, *b*. 1849.

Mr. Wrench, who was educated at Trinity Coll., Oxford (B.A. 1830, M.A. 1834), is a Magistrate for Kent, Rector and Patron of Stowting.—*Stowting, Hythe.*

WREY, Sir BOURCHIER PALK, Bart., D.C.L., of Tawstock Court, Devon (cr. 1628).

Eldest son of the late Sir Bourchier Wrey, Bart., D.C.L., of Tawstock Court, by his 1st wife Anne, dau. of the late Sir Robert Palk, Bart., of Haldon House, Devon; b. 1788; s. 1826; m. 1st 1818 Ellen, widow of — Riddle, Esq.; 2nd 1843 Eliza, dau. of — Coles, Esq. Called to the Bar at Lincoln's Inn 1815; is a J.P. and D.L. for Devon, Lord of the Manors of Tawstock, &c., Patron of 2 livings, and co-heir to the Earldom of Bath and the Barony of Fitzwarren. —*Tawstock Court, Barnstaple; Holne Chace, Ashburton.*

Heir Pres., his brother Robert Bourchier, (of Warecliffe House, Lyme Regis, Devon), educated at Exeter Coll., Oxford; b. 1790; m. 1821 Mary Anne, dau. of Capt. James, R.N., of Exeter.

WREY, Mrs., of Thorntoun House, Ayrshire.

Sarah, eldest surviving dau. of the late Lieut.-Col. John Cuninghame, of Thorntoun, by Sarah, only dau. of Major John Peebles, late of the 42nd Foot, by Anna, dau. of Charles Hamilton, Esq., of Craighlaw, co. Wigton; s. her sister 1861; m. 1848 George Bourchier Wrey, Esq., of North Devon, who d. 1854, leaving issue, * George Edward Bourchier, b. 1851. —*Thorntoun House, Kilmarnock, N.B.*

WREY, the Rev. HENRY BOURCHIER.

Third son of the late Sir Bourchier Wrey, Bart., of Tawstock Court, by his 2nd wife Anne, dau. of John Osborne, Esq., of Alderley, co. Gloucester; b. 1797; m. 1827 Ellen Maria, dau. of Nicholas Roundell Toke, Esq., and by her, who d. 1864, has, with other issue,

* Henry Bourchier Toke, (of Holne Park, near Ashburton, Devon), B.A. of Trinity Coll., Oxford: a Magistrate for Devon, and ultimately *Heir Pres.* to the Baronetcy of Wrey; b. 1829; m. 1854 the Hon. Marianne Sarah, only child of Philip Castell, 9th Lord Sherard, and has issue, * Robert, b. 1855.

Mr. Wrey, who was educated at Eton and Balliol Coll., Oxford (B.A. 1818, M.A. 1820), is a Magistrate for Devon and Rector of Tawstock.—*Tawstock Rectory, Barnstaple.*

WRIGHT, CHARLES BOOTH ELMSALL, Esq., of Bolton Hall, Yorkshire.

Eldest son of the late Charles Swaine Wright, Esq., by Mary Ellen de Cardonnel, dau. of Colonel Elmsall, of Woodlands, near Doncaster; b. 1848. Was educated at Eton and Trinity Coll., Cambridge; is Lord of the Manor of Bolton by Bolland, Craven, and of Sinnington, near Pickering, N.R.; he purchased Bolton Hall from the family of the Littledales 1866. —*Bolton Hall, Clitheroe.*

Heir Pres., his brother Marmaduke Godfrey, b. 1850.

WRIGHT, CHARLES MICHAEL, Esq., of Downings, co. Kildare.

Eldest son of David Wright, Esq., J.P., of Emma Vale, co. Wicklow, by Eleanor, youngest dau. of the late Charles Bury, Esq., of Downings; b. 1830; s. his uncle, Michael Bury, Esq. 1850; m. 1856 Margaret, 3rd dau. of the late John Aylmer, Esq., of Courtown, co. Kildare. Is a Magistrate for co. Kildare.—*Downings, Naas, co. Kildare.*

WRIGHT, EDMUND, Esq., of Halston, Shropshire.

Son of the late Edmund Wright, Esq., of Halston, and of Mauldeth Hall, co. Lancaster; b. 1812; s. 1852; m. 1844 Helen, eldest dau. of the late Sir David Moncreiffe, Bart., of Moncreiffe, co. Perth, and has, with other surviving issue,

* Charles Henry, b. 1851.

Mr. Wright is a Magistrate for co. Salop (High Sheriff 1857), and Captain N. Salop Yeomanry Cavalry. His father purchased Halston of John Mytton, Esq., in 1847.—*Ha'ston Hall, Oswestry.*

WRIGHT, EDWARD ABBOTT, Esq., of Castle Park, Cheshire.

Only son of the late Joseph Wright, Esq., of Oldham, by Betsy, eldest dau. of John Lees, Esq., of the same place; b. 1808; m. 1836 Mary, 2nd dau. of Henry Berry, Esq., of Golden Square, Westminster, and has surviving issue,

* Four daughters, of whom, the eldest, Mary Berry, m. 1866 Frederick Poynton Weaver, Esq., M.D., of Frodsham.

Mr. Wright is a Magistrate for co. Lancaster and for the borough of Oldham.—*Castle Park, Frodsham.*

WRIGHT, EDWARD CARRINGTON, Esq., of Kelvedon Hall, Essex.

Only son of the late Edward Wright, Esq. (who d. 1853), by Barbara Magdalen, dau. of John Peter Bruno Bowdon, Esq., of Southgate House, and Beightonfields Priory, co. Derby, and nephew of the late John Francis Wright, Esq., of Kelvedon Hall; b. 1850; s. his uncle 1865. Is Lord of the Manor of Kelvedon. This family have been seated at Kelvedon Hall for upwards of three centuries, and they have always adhered to the Roman Catholic religion.—*Kelvedon Hall, Brentwood.*

WRIGHT, ELIZABETH ISABELLA, of Gola House, co. Monaghan.

Only surviving child of the late William Cairns Wright, Esq., by his 2nd wife Elizabeth, dau. of the Rev. M. Draffen, D.D., Rector of Garton, co. Donegal; s. 1816; m. 1811 James Wood, Esq., Lieut. 18th Foot, who assumed the name of Wright, and d. in 1837, leaving, with other issue,

* William Henry Edward, in Holy Orders. M.A. of Trinity Coll., Dublin; b. 1815; m. 1852 Jane Elizabeth, only dau. of N. Stewart, Esq., of Shellfield, co. Donegal, and has issue.

This family inherits the Gola property from Capt. James Wright, of Cromwell's army, to whom the Gola and other estates were granted in 1651.—*Gola House, Scot's Town, co. Monaghan.*

WRIGHT, FRANCIS, Esq., of Osmaston Manor, Derbyshire.

Second but elder surviving son of the late John Wright, Esq., of Lenton Hall, Notts, by Elizabeth, dau. of Francis Beresford, Esq., of Ashbourne, co. Derby; b. 1806; s. 1840; m. 1830 Selina, dau. of the late Sir Henry FitzHerbert, Bart., of Tissington Hall, co. Derby, and has, with other issue,

* John, of Yeldersley, near Derby, a Magistrate for co. Derby; b. 1831; m. 1st 1859 Emily Sophia, dau. of the Rev. Henry Western Plumtre (who d. 1860); 2nd 1861 Florence Mary, dau. of Edward Boyd Rice, Esq., of Dane Court, Kent.

Mr. Wright is a J.P. and D.L. for co. Derby and for Stafford and Notts (High Sheriff 1842), Lord of the Manors of Osmaston and Ashbourne, and Patron of 7 livings.—*Osmaston Manor, Derby.*

WRIGHT, FRANCIS BERESFORD, Esq., of Butterley Park, Derbyshire.

Third son of Francis Wright, Esq., of Osmaston Manor, co. Derby (whom see), by Selina, eldest dau. of Sir Henry FitzHerbert, Bart., of Tissington Hall, co. Derby; b. 1837; m. 1862 Adeline Frances Henrietta, eldest dau. of Col. FitzHerbert, of Somersal Herbert, co. Derby, and has, with other issue,

* Arthur FitzHerbert, b. 1865.

Mr. Wright, who was educated at Trinity Coll., Cambridge (B.A. 1859, M.A. 1862), is a Magistrate for co. Derby, and co-Trustee of five livings.—*Aiderwar Hall, Butterley, Heanor, Derbyshire.*

WRIGHT, ICHABOD CHARLES, Esq., of Mapperley, Notts.

Eldest son of the late Ichabod Wright, Esq., of Mapperley (sometime Col. Notts Militia), by Harriet Maria, dau. of Benjamin Day, Esq., of Norwich; b. 1795; s. 1862; m. 1825 the Hon. Theodosia, eldest dau. of Thomas, 1st Lord Denman, and has, with other issue,

* Charles Ichabod (of Stapleford Hall, Notts), Lieut.-Col. Robin Hood Rifle Volunteers; b. 1828; m. 1852 Blanche, eldest dau. of Henry C. Bingham, Esq., of Wartnaby Hall, co. Leicester, and has, with other issue, * Ichabod Denman, b. 1853.

Mr. Wright was educated at Eton and Ch. Ch., Oxford (B.A. 1817, M.A. 1820), and was formerly Fellow of Magdalen Coll. This family is descended from John Wright, Esq., Capt. in General Whalley's Horse, and subsequently in Col. Hutchinson's Infantry, on the side of the Parliament.—Mapperley Hall, and Ratcliffe Lodge, Nottingham.

WRIGHT, JAMES FREDERICK D'ARLEY, Esq., of Mottram Hall, Cheshire.

Third son of the late Captain John Street, R.A., by Catherine, 2nd dau. of Sir Henry Jardine, of Harwood, N.B.; b. 1827; m. 1857 Julia Catherine, youngest dau. and co-heir (with her sisters) of the late Rev. Henry Wright, B.A., of Mottram Hall, and has issue,

* Julia Mary Catherine.

Mr. Wright, who was educated at the R.M. Academy, Woolwich, is Lord of the Manor of Mottram, and was formerly Capt. in the Royal Artillery; he assumed the surname of Wright by Royal licence 1865, under the will of the Rev. H. Wright.—Mottram Hall, Mottram St. Andrew, Prestbury; Junior United Service Club, s.w.

WRIGHT, JOHN, Esq., of Dudwick, Norfolk.

Son of the late John Wright, Esq., of Dudwick House ; b. 1794; m. 1816 Anne, dau. of Truman Harford, Esq., of Chew Magna, Somerset (she d. 1861). Is a Magistrate for Norfolk, Lord of the Manor of Brampton-cum-Membris, and Founder of a Reformatory in Norfolk.—Dudwick House, Buxton, Aylsham.

WRIGHT, JOHN, Esq., of Hatfield Priory, Essex.

Eldest son of the late John Wright, Esq., of Wickham Place, Essex, by Mary, dau. of the late Sir John Tyrell, Bart., of Boreham House, Essex; b. 1821 ; s. 1851 his grandfather Peter Laurl, Esq. (who took the name and arms of Wright only by Royal licence 1796, under the will of his grandfather, John Wright, Esq., of Hatfield Priory); m. 1852 Emilia, dau. of the late William Plunkett, Esq., Deputy Chairman of the Board of Inland Revenue. Educated at Winchester and the Charterhouse; is a J.P. and D.L. for Essex, and Patron of 1 living; was formerly Capt. W. Essex Militia. This family is of French extraction, and settled in England A.D. 1674.— Hatfield Priory, Chelmsford ; Carlton Club, s.w.; 6, Chapel Street, Grosvenor Square, w.

+WRIGHT, JOHN, Esq., of Hulland, Derbyshire.

Son of the late J. Wright, Esq.; b. 1800.   Is a J.P. and D.L. for co. Derby.—Hulland Hall, Yeldersley, Ashbourne.

WRIGHT, the late JOHN SMITH, Esq., of Rempstone Hall, Leicester.

Second son of the late Thomas Wright, Esq., of Nottingham, by Mary, dau. of J. Smith, Esq., of Nottingham; b. 1773; m. 1st 1811 Lydia, only dau. of E. Gray, Esq., of Harringay (she d. 1820); 2nd 1822 Caroline, dau. of J. Stovin, Esq., of Whitgift Hall, co. York, and widow of Sir S. Sitwell, Bart. (she d. 1860). Was a J.P. and D.L. for Notts (High Sheriff 1815), and Capt. Notts Militia   He d. 1854, leaving issue,

- 1622

Kythe Caroline, m. 1829 Sir F. Mackenzie, Bart., of Gairloch ; Lydia Rachel. m. 1842 Egerton Legh, Esq., of High Leigh, co. Chester (whom see) ; and Mary Neville, m. 1835 David, eldest son of J. Watts-Russell, Esq., of Ilam Hall.—Rempstone Hall, Lough-borough.

WRIGHT, Mrs., of Bilham House, Yorkshire.

Mary Ellen de Cardonnel, eldest dau. of the late Col. J. E. G. Elmsall, of Woodlands, co. York; m. 1845 Charles Swayne Wright, Esq., of Owston Park, co. York, a Magistrate for the W. Riding (who d. 1859), leaving, with other issue, * Charles Booth Elmsall, b. 1848.—Bilham House, Doncaster.

WRIGHT, the Rev. RICHARD ROBERT.

Third and only surviving son of the late John Wright, Esq., of Compsey, co. Tipperary, by Mary Wharton Silleto ; b. 1808 ; m. 1st 1830 Mary, dau. of A. Leigh, Esq., of Abbey Leix, Queen's Co.; 2nd 1837 Eleanor Louisa, dau. of the late Capt. E. Maxwell (49th Foot). Educated at Trinity Coll., Dublin (B.A. 1830, M.A. 1839); is a Magistrate for Cornwall, and Rector of Marhamchurch.—Marhamchurch, Stratton.

WRIGHT, ROBERT FRANCIS, Esq., of Hinton Blewett, Somersetshire.

Eldest son of the late Francis Bowcher Wright, Esq., of Hinton Blewett, by Augusta Rebecca Anne, only dau. of the Rev. John Hoskyns (Abrahall), Rector of Compton Martin, Somerset; b. 1798 ; s. 1840 ; m. 1826 Sophia Matilda, dau. of the Rev. William Bingham, late Rector of Cameley, Somerset, and Melbury Bubb, Dorset, and only surviving sister of Richard Hippisley Bingham, Esq., of Bingham's Melcombe, Dorset, and has, with other issue,

* Augustus Robert Bingham, in Holy Orders, M.A. of Queen's Coll., Oxford, Vicar of Stebbing, Essex; b. 1828.

Mr. Wright is Lord of the Manor of Hinton Blewett. This family is of Yorkshire origin, a branch of which settled in Somersetshire 200 years ago.—Hinton Blewett House, Temple Cloud, Bristol.

WRIGHT, the Rev. WILLIAM, of Brattleby Hall, Lincolnshire.

Eldest son of the late Edward Wright, Esq., of Brattleby Hall ; b. 1807 ; s. 1863 ; m. 1842 Esther, 2nd dau. of the late Rev. Henry Ingilby, of Ripley, co. York, and niece of the late Sir I. Ingilby, Bart., and has issue. Educated at Pembroke Coll., Cambridge (B.A. 1830, M.A. 1837); is a Magistrate for co. Lincoln, and Lord of the Manor of Brattleby; was formerly Rector of Ulceby, co. Lincoln.—Brattleby Hall, Lincoln.

WRIGHT. (See Lawson, Bart.)

WRIGHT. (See Worthington-Wright.)

WRIGHT-BIDDULPH, ANTHONY JOHN, Esq., of Burton Park, Sussex.

Only son of the late Anthony G. Wright, Esq., of Burton Park (who assumed the name of Biddulph on succeeding to the estates of the late John Biddulph, Esq., of Biddulph), by [...] of the late Sam a Scrope, Esq., of Danby Hall, co. York; b. 1830 ; s. 1847 ; m. 1854 Sarah Anne, dau. of J. Downes, Esq., R.A.; is a Magistrate for Sussex. This family is a branch of the Wrights of Kelvedon, Essex.—Burton Park, Petworth ; Necton Hall, Fakenham ; Arthur's Club, s.w.

WRIGHTSON, RICHARD HEBER, Esq., of Warmsworth, Yorkshire.

Third son of the late William Wrightson, Esq., M.P., of Cusworth, co. York (who was High Sheriff of Yorkshire in 1819), by his 2nd wife Henrietta, dau. and co-heir of Richard Heber, Esq., of Marton, co. York ; A

1800; *m.* 1832 the Hon. Elizabeth Augusta de Grey, eldest dau. of Thomas, 4th Lord Walsingham; called to the Bar at Lincoln's Inn 1825; is a Magistrate for the W. Riding of Yorkshire.—*Warmsworth, Doncaster.*

WRIGHTSON, WILLIAM BATTIE, Esq., of Cusworth, Yorkshire.
Eldest son of the late William Wrightson, Esq., of Cusworth, by Henrietta, dau. of Richard Heber, Esq., of Marton, co. York; *b.* 1789; *m.* 1821 Georgiana, dau. of the late Inigo Thomas, Esq., of Ratton, Sussex. Educated at Winchester and Trinity Coll., Cambridge; called to the Bar at Lincoln's Inn, 1815; is a J.P. and D.L. for the W. Riding of Yorkshire, and Patron of 4 livings; was M.P. for E. Retford 1826–7, for Hull 1830–2, and for Northallerton 1835–65.—*Cusworth, Doncaster; Brooks's and Boodle's Clubs, s.w.; Oriental Club, w.; 22, Upper Brook Street, w.*

+**WRIGLEY, JAMES HARDY,** Esq., of Southport, Lancashire.
A younger son of the late James Wrigley, Esq., of Ashmeadow, Bury, co. Lancaster; *b.* 1810. Is a J.P. and D.L. for co. Lancaster, and Patron of 1 living.—*Southport, Lancashire.*

WRIGLEY, THOMAS, Esq., of Timberhurst, Lancashire.
Eldest son of the late James Wrigley, Esq., of Ashmeadow, Bury, by Mary, dau. of Dennis Grundy, Esq., of Bury; *b.* 1808; *s.* 1842; *m.* 1830 Hannah, dau. of Edmund Grundy, Esq., of Park Hill, Bury, and has, with other issue,

* Edwin Grundy, *b.* 1832; *m.* 1856 Mary Jessie, dau. of Edmund Potter, Esq., M.P., of Dinting Vale, co. Derby.

Mr. Wrigley is a Magistrate for co. Lancaster, and a Merchant and Manufacturer near Bury.—*Timberhurst, Bury; Wansfell, Windermere; Reform Club, s.w.*

WRIXON-BECHER. (See *Becher.*)

WROTTESLEY, Lord (ARTHUR WROTTESLEY). —Cr. 1838.
Eldest son of John, 2nd Lord, by Sophia Elizabeth, dau. of the late Thomas Giffard, Esq., of Chillington, co. Stafford; *b.* 1824; *s.* 1867; *m.* 1861 the Hon. Augusta, dau. of Albert, 1st Lord Londesborough. Educated at Rugby and Ch. Ch., Oxford (B.A. 1846); is a J.P. and D.L. for co. Stafford, and Patron of 2 livings; Major 2nd Staffordshire Militia, late Lieut.-Col. 4th Staffordshire R.V.—*Wrottesley, Wolverhampton; 18, Chapel Street, w.*
Heir, his son William, *b.* 1863.

WROTTESLEY, the Hon. EDWARD BENNET.
Youngest son of John, 1st Lord Wrottesley, by Lady Caroline, dau. of Charles, 4th Earl of Tankerville; *b.* 1811; *m.* 1846 Ellen Charlotte, 3rd dau. of George Rush, Esq., of Elsenham Hall, Essex, and has, with other issue,

* Alfred Edward, *b.* 1855.

Mr. Wrottesley, who was educated at Westminster, is a Dep.-Lieut. for co. Stafford.—*White Lodge, Putney, s.w.; Oxford and Cambridge Club, s.w.*

WROUGHTON, GEORGE WROUGHTON, Esq., of Wilcot, Wilts.
Eldest son of the late Admiral Sir George Montagu, by Charlotte, dau. and heir of George Wroughton, Esq., whose name he assumed by Royal licence; *b.* 1788. Is a Magistrate for Wilts (High Sheriff 1822), and Patron of 1 living: represents a branch of the ducal house of Manchester.—*Stowell Lodge, Wilcot, Marlborough*

Heir Pres., his brother John William, Vice-Admiral R.N.; *b.* 1790; *m.* 1840 Isabella Elizabeth, 5th dau. of Charles E. Beauclerk, Esq., by whom he has, with other issue, * George Edward, Ensign 84th Foot, *b.* 1841.

WROUGHTON, PHILIP, Esq., of Woolley Park, Berks.
Eldest son of the late Philip Wroughton, Esq., of Woolley Park (who was a Magistrate for Berks. a J.P. and D.L. for Bucks, and High Sheriff 1857), by Blanche, dau. of the late John Norris, Esq., of Hughenden House, Bucks; *b.* 1846; *s.* 1862. Educated at Harrow and Ch. Ch., Oxford; is a Magistrate for Berks.—*Woolley Park, Wantage.*
Heir Pres, his brother Edward Norris, *b.* 1847.

WYATT, Sir MATTHEW, Knt. (cr. 1848).
Son of the late — Wyatt, Esq.; *b.* 18—; *m.* 18— Mary Anne, dau. of ——, Esq. (she *d.* 1862). Late Lieut. of the Corps of Gentlemen-at-Arms.—*Union Club, s.w.; 5, Hyde Park Square, w.*

+**WYATT, Rev. CHARLES FRANCIS,** of Broughton, Oxfordshire.
Son of the late — Wyatt, Esq., by Mary, dau. of — Walford, Esq., of Sibford, Oxon; *b.* 1795; *m.* 1819 Mary, dau. of — Walford, Esq., of Sibford, and has, with other issue,

* Charles Francis, educated at Eton, M.A. of Ch. Ch., Oxford; *b.* 1820.

Mr. Wyatt, who was educated at Jesus Coll., Cambridge (B.A. 1818, M.A. 1821), is a Magistrate for Oxon. and Rector, Lord of the Manor, and Patron of Broughton.—*Broughton, Banbury.*

WYATT, HARVEY, Esq., of Barton-under-Needwood, Staffordshire.
Eldest son of the late Robert Harvey Wyatt, Esq., of Barton-under-Needwood, by Harriet, dau. of Samuel Wyatt, Esq., of Burton-on-Trent; *b.* 1798; *m.* 1823 Jemima, dau. of the late Edward Holland, Esq., of Barton-under-Needwood, and has, with other issue,

* Arthur Harvey, in Holy Orders, *b.* 1827; *m.* 1852 Emma, dau. of the late Edward White, Esq., of Great Marlborough Street, London.

This family is descended from Sir Thomas Wyatt, the poet and statesman (*temp.* Henry VIII).—*Barton-under-Needwood, Burton-on-Trent;* Residence: *Acton Hill, Stafford.*

WYATT, HUGH, Esq., of Cissbury and Court Wick, Sussex.
Eldest son of the late Hugh Wyatt, Esq., D.L. of Cissbury and Court Wick, by Frances, dau. of the late John Ingram, Esq., of Steyning, Sussex; *b.* 1813; *s.* 1864; *m.* 1855 Sarah Jane Emily, dau. of Vice-Admiral Hargood, of Worthing. Educated at Trinity Hall, Cambridge, of which he was a Fellow (LL.D. 1841), and called to the Bar at the Inner Temple 1857, is a Magistrate for Sussex, Recorder of Seaford, and Lord of the Manors of Wick and Sheepcomb.—*Cissbury, Worthing; Oxford and Cambridge Club, s.w.; 18, Clifford Square, Hyde Park.*

Heir Pres., his brother John Ingram Pendrell, M.A. of Trinity Coll., Cambridge, Perpetual Curate of Hawkey, Hants; *b.* 1817; *m.* 1856 Harriet, dau. of John W. Tipping, Esq., of Sandhurst, Berks, and has issue, two sons and two daughters.

WYATT, JAMES, Esq., F.G.S., of Bryn Gwynant, Carnarvonshire.
Son of the late Benjamin Wyatt, Esq., of Lime Grove, Bangor, by Sarah, dau. of William Ford, Esq., lineally descended from the Wyatts of Blorde Green, Staffordshire, *temp.* Henry III.; *b.* 1795; *m.* 1821 Anne Jane,

1023

youngest dau. of John Ainsworth, Esq., of Preston, co. Lancaster, and has, with other issue,

* James Henry, a Major in the Army, and C.B.; *b.* 1825; *m.* 1857 Jane Forbes, eldest dau. of William Hogarth, Esq., of Aberdeen.

Mr. Wyatt is a J.P. and D.L. for co. Carnarvon. This family descends from the Wyats of Weeford, co. Stafford, who settled there at the time of the execution of Sir Thomas Wyat, in the reign of Philip and Mary. —*Bryn Gwynant, Beddgelert, Carnarvon.*

WYATT, RICHARD, Esq., of Hill House, Gloucestershire.

Fourth son of the late Henry Wyatt, sen.; *b.* 1818. Educated at Corpus Christi Coll., Cambridge (B.A. 1840); called to the Bar at Lincoln's Inn 1842; is a J.P. and D.L. for co. Gloucester.—*Hill House, Stroud.*

+WYATT, THOMAS HENRY, Esq., of Weston Corbet, Hampshire.

Eldest son of the late — Wyatt, Esq., of Barton-under-Needwood, co. Stafford, and nephew of Harvey Wyatt, Esq. (whom see); *b.* 18—. This family is descended from Sir Thomas Wyat, the statesman and poet of the Tudor age.—*Weston Corbet, Odiham.*

Heir Pres., his brother Matthew, *b.* 18—.

WYATT-EDGELL. (See *Edgell.*)

WYBERGH, WILLIAM, Esq., of Isell Hall, Cumberland, and Clifton Westmoreland.

Eldest son of the late Thomas Wybergh, Esq., of Isell Hall and Clifton Hall (sometime Clerk of the Peace for the W. Riding of Yorkshire), by Isabella, dau. of John Hartley, Esq. (she *d.* 1827), and elder brother of Sir Wilfrid Lawson, Bart.; *b.* 1787; *s.* 1827. Is a Magistrate for Cumberland.—*Isell Hall, Cockermouth; Clifton Hall, Penrith.*

Heir Pres., his brother John, a Magistrate for Cumberland, *b.* 1789.

WYBERGH. (See *Lawson, Bart.*)

WYKE, Sir CHARLES LENNOX, K.C.B. (cr. 1860).

Third son of the late George Wyke, Esq., of Robbleston, co. Pembroke, by Charlotte, dau. of the late F. Meyrick, Esq.; *b.* 1815. Is H.M.'s Envoy Extraordinary and Minister Plenipotentiary in Denmark; was formerly Lieut. Royal Fusiliers, and afterwards Capt. on the Staff of the late King of Hanover; appointed Consul-General in America 1852; raised to the rank of Chargé d'Affaires in 1854; has been Minister Plenipotentiary at Mexico and Hanover.—*Athenæum Club, s.w.; British Embassy, Copenhagen.*

WYKEHAM, PHILIP THOMAS HERBERT, Esq., of Tythrop House, Oxon.

Elder son of the late Philip Thomas Wykeham, Esq., of Tythrop House, by his 1st wife Hester Louisa, dau. of the late Fiennes Trotman, Esq., of Syston Court, co. Gloucester; *b.* 1807; *s.* 1832. Educated at Eton and Oriel Coll., Oxford; is a Magistrate for Bucks and Oxon (High Sheriff 1857), and Capt. late Oxfordshire Rifle Volunteers; formerly Capt. 7th Hussars and Oxfordshire Yeomanry Cavalry. Of this family was William of Wykeham, Bishop of Winchester, and Founder of New Coll., Oxford.—*Tythrop House, Thame; Conservative Club, s.w.*

Heir Pres., his brother Aubrey Wenman, educated at Eton, and B.A. of Trinity Coll., Oxford; *b.* 1809; *m.* 1837 Georgiana, dau. of the late Sir James Musgrave, Bart., of Barnsley Park, co. Gloucester, and has, with other issue,
* Wenman Aubrey, Lieut. Oxfordshire Militia, *b.* 1838.

WYKEHAM. (See under *Wenman, Lady.*)

WYKEHAM MARTIN. (See *Martin.*)

WYLD, JAMES, Esq., D.C.L.

Son of the late James Wyld; *b.* 1812; *m.* 1838 Ann, only child of John Hester, Esq. Is a Geographer to the Queen; Knight and Knight-Commander of 14 European Orders; J.P. and D.L. for Middlesex and Westminster; was M.P. for Bodruin 1847–52. re-elected 1857.—*Reform Club, s.w.; 18, Gloucester Road, N.W.*

WYLD. (See *Walker-Heneage.*)

+WYLDE, JOHN CHARLES, Esq., of Southwell, Notts.

Eldest son of the late Lieut.-Col. William Wylde, J.P. and D.L., of Southwell (an officer in the Notts Militia), by Elizabeth, dau. and heir of the Rev. John Edwards; *b.* 180—; *s.* 1846. Is in the Commission of the Peace for Notts, and a Property and Income Tax Commissioner.—*Southwell, Notts.*

WYLDE-BROWNE. (See *Browne.*)

+WYLIE, —, Esq., of Hunsdon House, Herts.

Son of the late — Wylie, Esq.; *b.* 181–. Purchased this estate from the Calvert family in 1861. He was formerly a Merchant in India.—*Hunsdon House, Ware.*

WYLLIE, Sir WILLIAM, K.C.B. (cr. 1865).

Third son of the late John Wyllie, Esq., by Elisabeth, dau of William Brown, Esq.; *b.* 1802; *m.* 1831 Amelia, youngest dau. of the late Richards Hutt, Esq., of Appley, I. of Wight; is a Lieut.-General in the Army, and Colonel 109th Foot; served in the Indian Army 1819–59; was Assistant Adjutant-Gen. during the campaign in Scinde, Beloochistan, and Affghanistan 1838–44; and afterwards Dep. Adjutant-General of the Army. —*E. India United Service Club, s.w.; 38, Lansdowne Crescent, Kensington, w.*

WYMER, Sir GEORGE PETRE, K.C.B. (cr. 1857).

Son of the late George Wymer, Esq., of Reepham, Norfolk, by Elizabeth, eldest dau. of Col. Yarlie; *b.* 1788; *m.* 1833 Emily, dau. of C. F. Crespigny, Esq.; entered the Bengal Army 1804; became Lieut.-General 1855, and Col. 107th Foot 1862: served in Lord Lake's campaigns of 1805; joined the Army of the Indus in 1838; appointed A.D.C. to Her Majesty in 1842 for services in Afghanistan; made K.C.B. in 1857 for services in India.— *St. John's Lodge, Ryde; Junior United Service Club, s.w.*

WYNDHAM, the Hon. PERCY SCAWEN, of Cockermouth Castle, Cumberland.

Second surviving son of George, 1st Lord Leconfield, by Mary Frances, dau. of the late Rev. William Blunt, of Crabbetts, Sussex; *b.* 1835; *s.* his uncle 1860; *m.* 1860 Madeline, dau. of the late Major-General Sir Grey Campbell, Bart., and has, with other issue,

* George, *b.* 1863.

Mr. Wyndham, who was educated at Eton, is a Magistrate for Cumberland and Sussex, and Col. 6th Sussex Rifle Volunteers, elected M.P. for W. Cumb. sami 1860; was formerly Lieut. Coldstr. am Guards.—*The Castle, Cockermouth; Carlton Club s.w.; 44, Belgrave Square, s.w.*

WYNDHAM, CHARLES HENRY, Esq., of Wans House, Wilts.

Youngest son of the late William Wyndham, Esq., of Dinton, Wilts, by Letitia, dau. of Alexander Popham, Esq.; *b.* 1816; *m.* 1848 Eleonora Anne Julia, eldest dau. of the Rev. James Andrew Hunt Grubbe, and has issue four daughters. Mr. Wyndham is a J.P. and D.L. for Wilts.— *Wans House, Chippenham*

+ WYNDHAM, GEORGE HUGH, Esq., of Rogate, Sussex.

Eldest son of Col. Charles Wyndham, M.P., of Rogate Lodge, by the Hon. Elizabeth Anne, 3rd dau. of Hugh, 4th Lord Polwarth; *b.* 183–; *s.* 1866; *m.* 1863 Elizabeth Sophia, 2nd dau. of the late Hon. and Rev. William Hugh Scott, Rector of Maiden Newton, Dorset, and has issue,

* A son, *b.* 1864.

Mr. Wyndham is 2nd Secretary to H.M.'s Embassy at Berlin.—*Rogate Lodge, Midhurst.*

WYNDHAM, HENRY, Esq., of Roundhill, Somerset.

Second son of the late George Wyndham, Esq., by Elizabeth, dau. of George Dominicus, Esq., of East Farleigh, Kent; *b.* 1810; *m.* 1857 Agnes 3rd dau. of the late William Heald Ludlow-Bruges, Esq., of Seend, Wilts, and has, with other issue,

* Henry Heathcote, *b.* 1858.

This family is descended from a common ancestor with the Earls of Egremont (ext.).—*Roundhill Grange, Wincanton; Sandridge, Chippenham.*

WYNDHAM, JOHN EVELEIGH, Esq., of Sock Dennis, Somerset.

Only child of the late Rev. John Heathcote Wyndham, Rector of Corton, by Dorothy, only dau. of the late Rev. John Eveleigh, D.D., Provost of Oriel Coll., Oxford; *b.* 1814; *m.* 1841 Elizabeth, eldest dau. of Lieut.-Col. Fitzgerald, of Maperton, Somerset, and of Turlo Park, co. Mayo, and has, with other issue,

* Thomas Heathcote Gerald, educated at Eton, and M.A. of Oriel Coll., Oxford; *b.* 1842.

Mr. Wyndham, who was educated at Oriel Coll., Oxford (B.A. 1836, M.A. 1840), is a Magistrate for Somerset, and represents a younger branch of the Wyndhams of Dinton.—*Sock Dennis, Yeovil.*

WYNDHAM, JOHN HENRY CAMPBELL-, Esq., of Salisbury, Wilts, and Corhampton, Hants.

Eldest son of the late John Campbell, Esq., M.P., of Dunoon. co. Argyll, by Caroline Frances, only dau. of the late Henry Penruddock Wyndham, Esq., M.P., of The College, Salisbury; *b.* 1798; *s.* his uncle the late Wadham Wyndham, Esq., 1844, when he assumed the name of Wyndham; *m.* 1839 Urania Mary Anne, dau. of the late Lieut.-Col. Kington. Educated at Eton; is a J.P. and D.L. for Hants, and a Magistrate for Wilts (High Sheriff 1848); was M.P. for Salisbury 1843–7.—*The College, Salisbury; Corhampton. Bishop's Waltham; Boodle's, Arthur's, and Carlton Clubs, s.w.*

Heir Pres., his sister Julia Anne, m. 18— Stephen Edward Thornton, Esq., who *d.* 1857.

WYNDHAM, WILLIAM, Esq., of Dinton, Wilts.

Eldest son of the late William Wyndham, Esq., J.P. and D.L., of Dinton (who was M.P. for S. Wilts 1852–9), by Ellen, eldest dau. of the Rev. Samuel Heathcote, of Bramshaw Hill, Hants; *b.* 1834; *s.* 1862; *m.* 1867 Frances Ann, dau. of the Rev. James Charles Stafford. Educated at Harrow and Trinity Coll., Cambridge (B.A. 1856); is a J.P. and D.L. for Wilts, and Patron of 1 living.—*Dinton House, Salisbury.*

Heir Pres., his brother Edmund, B.A. of Magdalen Coll., Oxford, and a barrister-at-law of Lincoln's Inn; *b.* 1835; *m.* 1866 Augusta Margaret, 3rd surviving dau. of the Rev. William Moore Harrison, Rector of Clayhanger, Devon.

WYNDHAM.

(See under *Dunraven, Earl of,* and *Leconfield, Lord.*)

WYNFORD, Lord (WILLIAM SAMUEL BEST). —Cr. 1829.

Eldest son of William Draper, 1st Lord (who was Lord Chief Justice of the Common Pleas 1824–9), by Mary Anne, dau. of the late Jerome Knapp, Esq.; *b.* 1798; *s.* 1845; *m.* 1821 Jane, dau. of William Thoyts, Esq., of Sulhampstead Park, Berks. Educated at Eton and Brasenose Coll., Oxford; is a Magistrate for Dorset, and Patron of 1 living; was M.P. for St. Michael's 1831–2.—*Wynford Eagle, Maiden Newton; Carlton Club, s.w.; 7, Park Place, St. James's, s.w.*

Heir, his son William Draper Mortimer, a Magistrate for Dorset, and late Capt. Rifle Brigade; *b.* 1826; *m.* 1857 Caroline, dau. of Evan Baillie, Esq., and Lady Georgina Baillie, of Dochfour, co. Inverness.

WYNN, Sir WATKIN WILLIAMS-, Bart., of Wynnstay, Denbighshire (cr. 1688).

Eldest son of the late Sir Watkin Williams-Wynn, Bart., M.P., of Wynnstay, by Lady Henrietta, dau. of Edward, 1st Earl of Powis; *b.* 1820; *s.* 1840; *m.* 1852 Marie Emily, dau. of the late Right Hon. Sir Henry Watkin Williams-Wynn, K.C.B. Educated at Westminster and Magdalen Coll., Cambridge (M.A. 1842); is a J.P. and D.L. for cos. Denbigh, Salop, Merioneth, and Montgomery, High Steward of the Manorial Court of Denbigh, and Patron of 7 livings; has been M.P. for W. Denbigh since 1841; is Lieut.-Col. of the Montgomeryshire Yeomanry; was formerly Lieut. 1st Life Guards. This family have been seated in North Wales time out of mind. The name of Wynn was assumed by Sir Watkin Williams (great-grandfather of the present Baronet) in 1740, on inheriting the Wynnstay estates.—*Wynnstay, Ruabon; Llanvorda Hall. Oswestry; Carlton Club, s.w.; 18, St. James's Square. s.w.*

Heir Pres., his nephew Edward Watkin, of Cefn. co. Denbigh (eldest son of the late Col. Herbert Watkin Williams-Wynn, M.P., who *d.* 1862, by Anna, eldest dau. and heir of the late Edward Lloyd, Esq., of Cefn), *b.* 1857.

WYNN, the Hon. CHARLES HENRY, of Rhug, Merionethshire.

Third but 2nd surviving son of Spencer Bulkeley, 3rd Lord Newborough, by Frances, dau. of the Rev. Robert de Winton; *b.* 1847; *s.* to the property of Rhug under the will of his kinsman, the late Sir Robert Williams-Vaughan, Bart. (ext.), 1859.—*Rhug, Corwen.*

WYNN, CHARLES WATKIN WILLIAMS-, Esq., of Pentrego, Montgomeryshire.

Only surviving son of the late Right Hon. Charles Watkin Williams-Wynn, M.P., of Pentrego, by Mary, eldest dau. of the late Sir Forster Cunliffe, Bart.; *b.* 1822; *s.* 1850; *m.* 1853 the Lady Annora Charlotte, younger dau. of Charles, 2nd Earl Manvers, and has, with other issue,

* Arthur Watkin, *b.* 1856.

Mr. Wynn, who was educated at Westminster and Ch. Ch., Oxford (B.A. 1843, M.A. 1845), and called to the Bar at Lincoln's Inn 1846, is a J.P. and D.L. for co. Montgomery and Capt. Montgomery Yeomanry Cavalry; he was elected M.P. for co. Montgomery 1862. —*Pentrego, Machford, Montgomeryshire. Chalten and Travellers' Clubs, s.w.; 2, Lower Berkeley Street, w.*

WYNN, HENRY BERTIE WATKIN WILLIAMS-, Esq., of Howbery Park, Oxfordshire.

Third son of the late Right Hon. Sir Henry Watkin Williams-Wynn, G.C.B., by the Hon. Hester, 4th dau. of Robert, 1st Lord Carington; *b.* 1820; *s.* 1856; *m.* 1818 Marion, dau. of the late Major-General Sir James Limond, C.B. Educated at Rugby; is a J.P. and D.L. for co. Denbigh, and a Magistrate for co. Salop.—*Howbery Park, Wallingford; Carlton Club, s.w.; 50, South Audley Street, w.*

WYNN, Mrs. WILLIAMS-, of Cefn, Denbigh-shire.

Anna, eldest dau. and heir of the late Edward Lloyd, Esq., of Cefn, by Lætitia, dau. of William Pritchard, Esq., of Trescawen; *s.* 1848; *m.* 1855 Col. Herbert Watkin Williams-Wynn, M.P. (2nd son of the late Sir Watkin Williams-Wynn, Bart., of Wynnstay), who *d.* 1862, leaving, with other issue,

* Edward Watkin (who is also *Heir Pres.* to the Baronetcy of his uncle, Sir W. Williams-Wynn, Bart.), *b.* 1857.

Mrs. Williams-Wynn is Lady of the Manor of Cefn, and Patron of 1 living.—*Cefn, St. Asaph.*

WYNN. (See under *Newborough, Lord.*)

WYNN-NANNEY. (See *Nanney.*)

WYNNE, BROWNLOW WYNNE, Esq., of Gar-thewin, Denbighshire.

Only son of George Cumming, Esq., M.D., of Chester, by Lucy Margaret, dau. of the late Philip Yorke, Esq., of Erthig and Dyffryn Aled; *b.* 1815. Assumed the name of Wynne on succeeding to the estate of Garthe-win, under the will of his maternal kinsman, Robert William Wynne, Esq.; *m.* 1836 Mary Anne, dau. of John Waring, Esq. Mr. Wynne, who was educated at Rugby, and was called to the Bar at the Middle Temple 1841, is a Magistrate for co. Denbigh (High Sheriff 1846).—*Garthewin, Abergele.*

WYNNE, the Rev. JOHN, of Warnford, Hants.

Eldest son of the late Rev. John Wynne, of Warnford; *b.* 1795; is married, and has, with other issue,

* John, M.A. of St. Mary Hall, Oxford, in Holy Orders; *b.* 1830.

Mr. Wynne, who was educated at Queen's Coll., Oxford (B.A. 1817, M.A. 1822), is Rector and Patron of Warnford.—*Warnford Rectory, Bishops Waltham.*

WYNNE, JOHN HENRY COLE, Esq., of Ardagh-owen, Sligo.

Eldest son of the late Owen Wynne, Esq., of Ardagh-owen, by Susan, eldest dau. of Samuel Thompson, Esq., of Liverpool; *b.* 1830; *m.* 1861 Georgina, eldest dau. of Edmund L'Estrange, Esq., and Lady Harriet L'Estrange (she *d.* 1864). Mr. Wynne, who was edu-cated at St. John's Coll., Oxford, is a Magistrate for co. Sligo.—*Ardaghowen, Sligo.*

Heir Pres., his brother Charles Bradstreet, late Capt. in H.M.'s 90th Regt., served throughout the Crimea, &c.; *b.* 1831; *m.* 1860 Emily, eldest dau. of Sir Robert Gore-Booth, Bart., M.P., of Lissadell, co. Sligo, and has, with other issue,
* Owen Robert Graham, *b.* 1862.

WYNNE, JOHN LLOYD, Esq., of Coed Coch, Denbighshire.

Eldest son of the late John Lloyd Wynne, Esq., J.P. and D.L., of Coed Coch (formerly High Sheriff of co. Flint), by Mary, eldest dau. and co-heir of John Holland, Esq., of Teyrdon, co. Denbigh; *b.* 1807; *s.* 1862; *m.* 1833 Mary Anne Frances, dau. of the Rev. John Heggan, and has, with other issue,

* Henry John Lloyd, late Capt. 2nd Life Guards; *b.* 1834.

Mr. Wynne is a J.P. and D.L. for co. Denbigh (High Sheriff 1864-5).— *Coed Coch, Abergele;* 7, *Eaton Place,* s.w.

WYNNE, OWEN, Esq., of Haslewood, co. Sligo.

Elder son of the late Right Hon. John Arthur Wynne, M.P., of Haslewood (formerly Under Sec. for Ireland), by Lady Anne, dau. of James, 2nd Marquis of Or-monde; *b.* 1843; *s.* 1865. This family is of Welsh extraction.—*Haslewood, Sligo, Ireland.*

Heir Pres., his brother James, *b.* 1847

1026

+WYNNE, the late THOMAS HANMER, Esq., of Nerquis Hall, Flintshire.

Son of the late Thomas Lloyd Fletcher, Esq., of Nast-gwaelod, co. Flint; *b.* 1818; *s.* his uncle, the Rev. Lloyd Wynne, 1864, when he assumed, under the will of his maternal great uncle, the Rev. Maurice Wynne, LL.D., the surname of Wynne; *d.* 1867. He was a Dep.-Lieut. for co. Flint (High Sheriff 1867).—*Nerquis Hall, Mold.*

WYNNE, WILLIAM WATKIN EDWARD, Esq., of Peniarth, Merionethshire.

Eldest son of the late William Wynne, Esq., of Peni-arth, by Elizabeth, dau. of the Rev. Philip Puleston, D.D., of Pickhill Hall, co. Denbigh; *b.* 1801; *s.* 1834; *m.* 1839 Mary, 2nd dau. and co-heir of the late Robert Aglionby Slaney, Esq., M.P., of Walford Manor, and Hatton Grange, co. Salop, and by her (who *d.* 1866) has, with other issue,

* William Robert Manrice, educated at Eton; a J.P. and D.L. for co. Merioneth, M.P. for that county, late Ensign and Lieut. Scots Fusilier Guards; *b.* 1840.

Mr. Wynne, who was educated at Westminster and Jesus Coll., Oxford, is a Magistrate for co. Salop, and a J.P. and D.L. for co. Merioneth (High Sheriff 1867); was M.P. for that co. 1852-65.—*Peniarth, Towyn;* Carlton and University Clubs, s.w.

+WYNNE-FINCH, CHARLES, Esq., of Voelas, Denbighshire.

Eldest son of the late Charles Wynne Griffith Wynne, Esq., J.P. and D.L., of Voelas (who assumed the name of Wynne in lieu of Finch), by Sarah, dau. of the Rev. Henry Hildyard, of Stokesley, co. York; *b.* 1815; *s.* 1865; *m.* 1st 1840 Laura Susan, dau. of the late Richard Pollen, Esq., of Rodbourne, Wilts (she *d.* 1851); 2nd 1863 Jamesina Joyce Ellen, dau. of John Stewart, Esq., and widow of Henry Styleman-L'Estrange, Esq., of Hunstanton Hall, Norfolk; he has by the former, with other issue,

* Charles Arthur, Capt. Scots Fusilier Guards; *b.* 1841.

Mr. Wynne, who was educated at Eton and Ch. Ch., Oxford (B.A. 1836), is a J.P. and D.L. for co. Car-narvon, and Patron of 3 livings; was M.P. for Carnar-von 1859-65.—*Voelas, Denbigh; N. Wales; Cefnamlwch, Pwllheli, Carnarvonshire;* 39, *Portman Square,* w.

WYNNIATT, REGINALD, Esq., of Dymock Grange, Gloucestershire.

Eldest son of the late Rev. Reginald Wynniatt, of Guiting Park, co. Gloucester (who *d.* 1860), by Cathe-rine, dau. of Francis William Thomas Brydges, Esq., of Tibberton Court, co. Hereford; *b.* 1813; *s.* his uncle, Thomas Wynniatt, Esq., of Stanton and Dymock. Educated at Harrow and University Coll., Oxford (B.A. 1835); is a Magistrate for co. Gloucester, and Lord of the Manors of Little Dymock and Gamage Hall. This family have been settled at Dymock Grange since [......]—*Dymock Grange, Gloucester; Broadway, Worcestershire,* s.w.

Heir Pres., his brother Thomas William, of Stanton, near Broadway, a Magistrate for co. Gloucester; *b.* 1815.

WYSE, NAPOLEON ALFRED BONAPARTE, Esq., of The Manor of St. John, co. Waterford.

Eldest son of the late Right Hon. Sir Thomas Wyse, K.C.B., of the Manor of St. John (sometime M.P. for co. Tipperary, &c., and British Minister at Athens), by Letitia, dau. of the late Lucien Bonaparte, Prince of Canino; *b.* 1822; *s.* 1862. Educated at Oscott Coll., and in France; is a Magistrate for co. and city of Waterford, and Lord of the Manor of St. John

—*Manor of St. John, Waterford; Ballincourty, Dungarvan. co. Waterford; Palazzo Bonaparte, Viterbo, Italy.*
Heir Pres., his brother William Bonaparte, Capt. Waterford Militia; *b.* 1826.

WYVILL, MARMADUKE, Esq.,‡ of Constable Burton, Yorkshire.
Eldest son of the late Rev. Christopher Wyvill, of Constable Burton, by Sarah, dau. of J. Codling, Esq.;

‡ Mr. Wyvill claims the barony of Scrope of Masham, which was in abeyance between his family and that of the late William Danby, Esq., of Swinton Park, who *d. s. p.* in 1834.

b. 1791; *s.* 1821; *m.* 1813 Rachel, dau. of the late Richard Slater Milnes, Esq., of Fryston, co. York, and by her (who *d.* 1856) has, with other issue,

* Marmaduke (of Denton Park. co. York), B.A. of Trinity Coll., Cambridge, a J.P. and D.L. for the N. Riding of co. York. Patron of 1 living, and M.P. for Richmond; *b.* 1815; *m.* 1845 Laura, dau. of the late Sir Charles Ibbetson, Bart., of Denton Park, co. York, and has issue.

Mr. Wyvill, who was educated at Eton and Trinity Coll., Cambridge, is a J.P. and D.L. for the N. Riding of Yorkshire, and Patron of 2 livings; was M.P. for York 1820–30.—*Constable Burton, Bedale.*

X, Y

XIMENES, Lady, of Bear Ash, Berks.
Mary Eliza, dau. of the late Admiral Evans; *m.* 1816 Lieut.-General Sir David Ximenes, K.C.H., who *d.* 1848, leaving issue.—*Bear Ash, Maidenhead.*

YALDWYN, WILLIAM, Esq., of Blackdown, Sussex.
Eldest son of the late William Henry Yaldwyn, Esq., J.P. and D.L., of Blackdown (who was High Sheriff of Sussex 1842), by Henrietta Mary, dau. of Henry Bowles, Esq., of Cuckfield, Sussex; *b.* 1835; *s.* 1866. The title of 'Esquire' was granted to John Yaldwyn, of Blackdown, by Patent Royal, at the beginning of the 14th century.—*Blackdown, Lurgashall, Petworth.*

YALE, WILLIAM CORBET, Esq., of Plas-yn-Yale, Denbighshire.
Eldest son of the late Rev. John Parry Jones-Parry, Rector of Edern, co. Carnarvon, by Margaret, dau. of William McIvor, Esq., and nephew of the late Lieut.-Col. William Parry-Yale, of Plas-yn-Yale; *b.* 1825; *s.* his uncle 1867. Called to the Bar at the Inner Temple 1851; assumed the name of Yale by Royal licence 1867.—*Plas-yn-Yale, Corwen, Denbighshire.*

Heir Pres., his brother John, b. 1827.

YAPP, RICHARD, Esq., of Cradley, Herefordshire.
Eldest son of the late Richard Yapp, Esq., of Cradley, by Susannah, dau. of John Archer, Esq.; *b.* 1797; *s.* 1853; *m.* 1833 Mary, dau. of Alexander Pope, Esq., of Worcester, and by her (who *d.* 1864) has, with other issue,

* George Bailey, *b.* 1840.

Mr. Yapp is a J.P. and D.L. for co. Hereford (High Sheriff 1859-60), a Magistrate for co. and city of Worcester, and Lord of the Manor of Cradley.—*The Halesend, Cradley, Gt. Malvern.*

YARBOROUGH, Earl of (CHARLES ANDERSON-PELHAM).—Cr. 1837.
Eldest son of the late Charles Anderson Worsley, 2nd Earl, by the Hon. Maria Adelaide, dau. of Cornwallis, 2nd Viscount Hawarden; *b.* 1835; *s.* 1862; *m.* 1858 Lady Victoria Alexandrina, dau. of William, 2nd Earl of Listowel. Educated at Eton; is a J.P. and D.L. for co. Lincoln, High Steward of Great Grimsby, Lord of the Manors of Brocklesby, &c., Patron of 17 livings, and Capt. North Lincoln Militia; was M.P. for Grimsby 1857-62.—*Brocklesby Park, Ulceby; Manby Hall, Brigg; Brooks's and Boodle's Clubs, S.W.; 17, Arlington Street, S.W.*

Heir, his son Charles Alfred Worsley, Lord Worsley, *b.* 1859.

YARBOROUGH. (See Cooke-Yarborough.)

YARBURGH, GEORGE JOHN, Esq., of Heslington, Yorkshire.
Eldest son of the late George Lloyd, Esq., J.P. and D.L., of Stockton Hall (formerly Capt. 2nd Royal Lancashire Militia), by Alicia Maria, only dau. of the late John Greame, Esq., of Sewerby House, co. York; *b.* 1811; *s.* 1863; *m.* 1840 Mary Antonia, 3rd dau. of the late Samuel Cheetham Hilton, Esq., of Pennington Hall, co. Lancaster, and by her (who *d.* 1867) has issue,

* Mary Elizabeth, *m.* Geo. W. Paterson, 2nd son of the late Mr.

1028

R. Bateson, of Belvoir Park, Belfast, and has issue; and Susan Ann, *m.* Chas. Lethbridge, Esq., of Charge Lodge, Somerset, and has issue.

Mr. Yarburgh, who was educated at Rugby and Trinity Coll., Cambridge, and was called to the Bar at the Middle Temple 1840, is a Magistrate for the E. and W. Ridings of Yorkshire, and Lord of the Manor of Heslington. He assumed the name of Yarburgh in 1857, under the will of his maternal ancestor, the late Charles Yarburgh, Esq.—*Heslington Hall, York; University Club, S.W.*

YARDLEY, Sir WILLIAM, Knt., of Hadlow, Kent (cr. 1847).
Son of the late Edward Yardley, Esq., of Shrewsbury; *b.* 1810; *m.* 1847 Amelia, dau. of the late James Wilkin, Esq., and has issue. Educated at Shrewsbury; called to the Bar at the Middle Temple 1837; is a Dep.-Lieut. for co. Pembroke, and a Magistrate for Bucks and Kent; was a Puisne Judge at Bombay 1847-52, and Chief Justice there 1852-7.—*Hadlow Park, Tunbridge; Reform Club, S.W.*

YARKER, HENRY JOHN FORSTER, Esq., of Leyburn Hall, Yorkshire.
Third but eldest surviving son of the late Rev. Luke Yarker, of Leyburn Hall (who *d.* 1819), by Mary Beata, only dau. and heir of the Rev. Henry South, Rector of Much Dew, Hereford: *b.* 1839; *s.* his brother 1849. Educated at Durham School; is Lord of the Manor of Leyburn. This family has been settled at Leyburn since A.D. 1500.—*Leyburn Hall, Bedale.*

Heir Pres., his brother Charles Braddyll, *b.* 1841.

YATES, the Rev. EDMUND TELFER, M.A., of Burgh Hall, Norfolk.
Eldest son of the late Rev. Richard Yates, D.D., forty years Chaplain of Chelsea Hospital, and Rector of Ashen, Essex, by Ann, dau. of Patrick Telfer, Esq., of Jamaica; *b.* 1811; *m.* 1836 Mary Sophia Pollexfen, 2nd dau. of the Rev. W. F. Baylay, M.A., Canon of Canterbury, and has, with other issue,

* Frederick Hugh, *b.* 1846.

Mr. Yates, who was educated at the Charterhouse and Oriel Coll., Oxford (B.A. 1834, M.A. 1836), is a Magistrate for Norfolk, Vicar of Aylsham, and Rural Dean.—*Burgh Hall, Aylsham.*

YATES, JOSEPH ST. JOHN, Esq., of Wellbank, Cheshire.
Eldest son of the late Joseph Yates, Esq., of Peel, otherwise Wilderspool [...] by [...] Thomas Ainsworth, [...] of Pridge H [...] castor; *b.* 1808; *m.* 1842 Emily Augusta, dau. of D. Scott, Esq., of Brotherton, co. Kincardine, N.B., and has, with other issue,

* Joseph Maghull, educated at Trinity Coll., Cambridge; *b.* 1844.

Mr. Yates, who was educated at the Charterhouse and Ch. Ch., Oxford, called to the Bar at the Inner Temple 1835, is Judge of the Cheshire County Courts, and Deputy-Steward of the Manor and Forest of Macclesfield; formerly a Commissioner of Bankrupts for the Manchester district, and a Revising Barrister; is a Magistrate for cos. Chester, Derby, and Lancaster, and for Stockport.—*Wellbank, Stretton.*

YATES, WILLIAM HOLT, Esq., of Wickersley, Yorkshire.

Only son of the late William Yates, Esq., of Wickersley, by Elizabeth, dau. of Edward Thomas Titcomb, Esq., of London ; *b*. 1802 ; *s*. 1856 ; *m*. 1837 Amelia Mary, eldest dau. of William Maxwell, Esq., of Wilton Crescent, London. Educated at Edinburgh University and St. John's Coll., Cambridge (M.D. 1826) ; is a Member of the Royal Coll. of Physicians ; was formerly in practice as a Physician in London ; retired from practice in 1846. This family have been in possession of Wickersley from the time of the Reformation.—*Wickersley Hall, Rotherham ; 5, Sumner Terrace, Onslow Square, s.w.*

YATMAN, WILLIAM HAMILTON, Esq., of Wellesbourne, Warwickshire.

Second surviving son of the late William Yatman, Esq., by Ellen, dau. of John Mitchell, Esq. ; *b*. 1819 ; *m*. 1851 Elizabeth Tower, 3rd dau. of the late Rev. G. T. Pretyman, Chancellor of Lincoln, and Prebendary of Winchester, and has issue,

* William Frederic Hamilton, *b*. 1853.

Mr. Yatman, who was educated at Winchester and Caius Coll., Cambridge (B.A. 1841, M.A. 1845), and called to the Bar at the Inner Temple 1844, is a Magistrate for cos. Gloucester and Warwick.—*Wellesbourne, Warwick ; Highgrove, Tetbury ; University Club, s.w.*

YEA, of Pyrland Hall, Somerset.

Eleanora-Anne-Heckstetter, Charlotte-Mary (*m*. 1846 Cholmeley Charles William Dering, Esq., of Ayot St. Lawrence, Herts, brother of Sir Edward Dering, Bart.), and Julia-Eliza (*m*. 1844 the Rev. Henry Thompson), daus. and co-heirs of the late Sir William Walter Yea, Bart., of Pyrland Hall (who *d*. 1862), by Anne Heckstetter, youngest dau. of David Robert Michel, Esq., of Dewlish, Dorset ; *s*. their uncle, Sir Henry Lacy Yea, Bart. (ext.) 1864.—*Pyrland Hall, Taunton.*

YEATMAN, HARRY FARR, Esq., of Chalbury Lodge, Dorset.

Eldest son of the late Harry Farr Yeatman, Esq., of Manston House, Dorset (who *d*. 1852), by Emma, only dau. and heir of Harry Biggs, Esq., of Stockton House, Wilts, and grandson of the late Rev. Harry Farr Yeatman, LL.D., of Stock House, Dorset ; *b*. 1839 ; *s*. his grandfather 1861. Educated at the Royal Naval Coll.; is a Lieut. R.N., and Patron of 1 living. This family was first located in Dorset *temp.* Henry VI.—*Chalbury Lodge, Weymouth.*

Heir Pres., his brother Arthur Godolphin, Lieut. R.A.; *b*. 1843.

YEATMAN, MARWOOD SHUTTLEWORTH, Esq., of Stock House, Dorset.

Second son of the late Rev. Harry Farr Yeatman, LL.B., of Stock House (who *d*. 1861), by Sarah, only dau. and heir of James H. Wolcott, Esq.; *b*. 1826. Is a Magistrate for Dorset, and Capt. Queen's Own Dorset Yeomanry Cavalry.—*Stock House, Sherborne.*

YELVERTON, the Hon. WILLIAM HENRY, of Whitland Abbey, Carmarthenshire.

Second son of William Charles, 2nd Viscount Avonmore, by Mary, eldest dau. of John Read, Esq., of East Cams, Hants ; *b*. 1791 ; *m*. 1826 Elizabeth Lucy, dau. of the late John Morgan, Esq., of Furness. co. Carmarthen, and has, with other issue,

* William Henry Morgan, *b*. 1840.

Mr. Yelverton is a Magistrate for co. Pembroke, and a J.P. and D.L. for co. Carmarthen (High Sheriff 1831); was M.P. for co. Carmarthen 1832–1.—*Whitland Abbey, Carmarthen.*

YELVERTON, Rear-Admiral HASTINGS REGINALD, C.B.

Son of the late John Joseph Henry, Esq., of Straffan, co. Kildare, by Lady Emily Elizabeth Fitz-Gerald, dau. of William Robert, 2nd Duke of Leinster ; *b*. 1808 ; *m*. 1845 Barbara, Baroness Grey de Ruthyn, widow of George, 2nd Marquis of Hastings, who *d*. 1858. Assumed the name of Yelverton on his marriage ; entered the Royal Navy 1823 ; is a Magistrate for Hants, a Rear-Admiral R.N., late a Naval A.D.C. to the Queen, and some time Commander of the Channel Squadron. —*United Service Club, s.w.; 9, William Street, s.w.*

YELVERTON, Mrs., of Belle Isle, co. Tipperary,

Louisa, dau. of Guy Lenox Prendergast, Esq. ; *m*. 1857 the Hon. George Frederick William Yelverton, who was a Magistrate for cos. Mayo and Tipperary, formerly Capt. 64th Foot, and *d*. *s*. *p*. 1860.—*Belle Isle, Munster Harbour, co. Tipperary ; Hazelrock, co. Mayo.*

YELVERTON. (See under *Avonmore, Viscount*.)

YEO, WILLIAM ARUNDELL, Esq., of Fremington, Devonshire.

Eldest son of the late William Arundell Yeo, Esq., J.P., of Fremington (who was High Sheriff of Devon 1850); *b*. 1835 ; *s*. 1862. Is Lord of the Manor of Fremington. This family have been seated in N. Devon for upwards of two centuries.—*Fremington, Barnstaple ; Dinham House, St. Minver, Cornwall ; Essex Court, Temple, E.C.*

YEOMAN, HENRY WALKER, Esq., of Woodlands, Yorkshire.

Eldest son of the late Henry Walker Yeoman, Esq., of Woodlands, by Anne, 2nd dau. of General John Hale, of Plantation, near Guisborough; *b*. 1789 ; *m*. 1816 Lady Margaret Bruce, eldest dau. of Lawrence, 1st Earl of Zetland, and by her (who *d*. 1860) has, with other issue,

* Henry Walker, *b*. 1816.

Mr. Yeoman, who was educated at Harrow and Trinity Coll., Cambridge (B.A. 1813, M.A. 1817), is a J.P. and D.L. for the N. Riding of Yorkshire.—*Woodlands, Whitby.*

YERBURY, JOHN WILLIAM, Esq., of Belcomb, Wilts.

Eldest son of the late John William Yerbury, Esq., of Belcomb (Lieut.-Col. 3rd Light Dragoons), by Emma, 2nd dau. of the late Thomas Webb, Esq., of The Terrow, co. Worcester, and niece of the late Lieut.-General Sir Joseph Thackwell, G.C.B.; *b*. 1847 ; *s*. 1858. This family have possessed Belcomb since the early part of the 17th century.—*Belcomb Brook, Bradford-on-Avon.*

YONGE, the Rev. JOHN, of Puslinch, Devon.

Eldest son of the late Rev. James Yonge, of Puslinch, by Anne, dau. of the Rev. Edmund Granger, Rector of Sowton, Devon ; *b*. 1788 ; *s*. 1799 ; *m*. 1812 Althea Henrietta, dau. of the Rev. T. Bere, and Caroline Anne Garstin, widow of Samuel Cotherne, Esq., of Lyndhurst, Hants, and has issue an only surviving son,

* Duke, in Holy Orders, M.A. of Exeter Coll., Oxford ; *b*. 1824 ; *m*. 1862 Charlotte Cordelia, 2nd dau. of .... Julian Todd, Esq., of Plympton, Devon, and has, with other issue, * John, *b*. 1864.

Mr. Yonge, who was educated at Winchester and University Coll., Oxford (B.A. 1812), and appointed Rector of Newton Ferrers 1813, is Lord of the Manor of Puslinch, and Patron of 1 living. This family is lineally descended, through the heiresses of De Poeslynche, Mohun, and Upton, from Sir John De Poeslynche, of Puslinch, living in 1299.—*Puslinch, Yealmpton, Devon; Newton Ferrers Rectory, by Bridge, Devon.*

YONGE, JULIAN BARGUS, Esq., of Otterbourne, Hampshire.
Only son of the late William Crawley Yonge, Esq., J.P., of Otterbourne, of the 52nd Light Infantry, by Frances Mary, dau. of the late Rev. Thomas Bargus, Vicar of Barkway, Herts; b. 1830; m. 1858 Emma Frances, dau. of late Lieut.-Col. Edward Walter, E.I.C.S., and has, with other issue,

* Francis Arthur, b. 1861.

Mr. Yonge, who was educated at Eton and Balliol Coll., Oxford (B.A. 1851, M.A. 1856), is a Magistrate for Hants; he was formerly Lieut. in the Rifle Brigade. This family is a younger branch of the Yonges of Puslinch, Devon.—Otterbourne, Winchester.

YONGE, the Rev. VERNON GEORGE, of Charnes Hall, Staffordshire.
Eldest surviving son of the late Weston Yonge, Esq., of Charnes Hall, by Mary, dau. of N. Bond, Esq., of co. Carmarthen, South Wales; b. 1823; s. 1849; m. 1848 Frances, dau. of N. Cave, Esq., of Barbados, West Indies, and has, with other issue,

* Weston Edward Vernon, b. 1849.

Mr. Yonge, who was educated at St. John's Coll., Cambridge (B.A. 1845), ordained 1846, and appointed Incumbent of Doddington, co. Chester, 1863, was formerly Curate of Broughton, co. Stafford, and of Lyde and Ullingswick, co. Hereford; late Curate of Bolas Magna, co. Salop. This family trace their pedigree direct from Reginald of Chavernes, who was 'Dominus de Chavernes' A.D. 1100-50.—Charnes Hall, Eccleshall.

YORK, Archbishop of (the Right Hon. and Most Rev. WILLIAM THOMSON, D.D., P.C.).
Son of John Thomson, Esq., J.P., of Whitehaven, Cumberland; b. 1819; m. 1855 Zoë, dau. of J. H. Skene, Esq. Educated at Queen's Coll., Oxford (B.A. 1840, M.A. 1845); was successively Fellow and Tutor of his Coll., Rector of All Souls, Langham Place, Provost of Queen's Coll., Oxford, and Preacher of Lincoln's Inn; consecrated Bishop of Gloucester and Bristol 1861, translated to York 1862; is Patron of 120 livings. —Bishopthorpe Palace, York; Athenæum Club, s.w.

YORK, Capt. EDWARD, of Wighill, Yorkshire.
Only son of the late Richard York, Esq., of Wighill, by Lady Mary Anne, dau. of Edward, 1st Earl of Harewood; b. 1802; s. 1843; m. 1835 Penelope Beatrice, dau. of the Rev. C. Sykes, Rector of Roos, co. York, and has, with other issue,

* Edward Christopher, b. 1842.

Capt. York, who was educated at Ch. Ch., Oxford (B.A. 1824), is a J.P. and D.L. for the W. Riding of Yorkshire; was formerly Capt. Yorkshire Hussars. —Wighill Park, Tadcaster.

YORKE, Sir CHARLES, G.C.B. (cr. 1856).
Son of the late Col. Yorke, Lieut. of the Tower of London, by Juliana, dau. of John Dodd, Esq., of Swallowfield, Berks; b. 1791. Is a General in the Army, Col. Commandant Rifle Brigade, late Col. 33rd Foot; was formerly Military Secretary at the Horse Guards.—United Service Club, s.w.; 19, South Street, w.

YORKE, the Hon. ELIOT THOMAS.
Third son of the late Admiral the Hon. Sir Joseph Sydney Yorke, K.C.B., by Elizabeth Yorke, dau. of James Rattray, Esq., of Atherstone, and brother of Charles Philip, 4th Earl of Hardwicke; b. 1805; m. 1833 Emily Ann Melicent, dau. of Emilius Henry Delmé Radcliffe, Esq., Hitchen Priory, Herts. Educated at Harrow, and St. John's Coll., Cambridge (M.A. 1827); is a Barrister-at-Law (called 1832), retired; a Magistrate for co. Cambridge, and Chairman
1030

of the Cambridgeshire Quarter Sessions; was M.P. for Cambridgeshire 1834-65.—Carlton Club, s.w.; 15, Park Street, w.

YORKE, the Hon. and Rev. GRANTHAM MUNTON.
Fourth son of the late Admiral the Hon. Sir Joseph Sydney Yorke, K.C.B., by Elizabeth Weake, dau. of James Rattray, Esq., of Atherstone, and brother of Charles Philip, 4th Earl of Hardwicke; b. 1809; m. 1830 Marian Emily, dau. of Sir Henry Conyngham Montgomery, Bart., and has, with other issue,

* Joseph Augustus, Barrister-at-Law, of the Inner Temple; b. 1831.

Mr. York, who was educated at Eton and Queen's Coll., Cambridge, and appointed Rector of St. Philip's, Birmingham, 1844, is Prebendary of Lichfield and Rural Dean of 'Birmingham. — St. Philip's Rectory, Birmingham.

YORKE, the Hon. and Ven. HENRY REGINALD, Archdeacon of Huntingdon.
Second son of the late Admiral the Hon. Sir Joseph Sydney York, K.C.B., by Elizabeth Weake, dau. of James Rattray, Esq., of Atherstone, and brother of Charles Philip. 4th Earl of Hardwicke; b. 1803; m. 1833 Flora Elizabeth, dau. of the late General Sir Alexander Campbell, Bart., K.C.B., and by her (who d. 1852) has, with other issue,

* Philip Sidney, b. 1834.

Archdeacon Yorke, who was educated at Harrow and St. John's Coll., Cambridge (M.A. 1828), is a Magistrate for Cambridge; he was appointed Rector of Wimpole 1832, Archdeacon of Huntingdon 1856' and Canon of Ely 1859.—Wimpole Rectory, Arrington.

YORKE, JOHN, Esq., of Bewerley Hall, Yorkshire.
Eldest son of the late John Yorke, Esq., J.P. and D.L., of Bewerley Hall (formerly High Sheriff of co. York), by Mary, dau. of the late Ichabod Wright, Esq., of Mapperley Hall, Notts; b. 1827; s. 1857; m. 1859 Alice, dau. of James Simpson, Esq., of West Cliffe. Is a Magistrate for the W. Riding of Yorkshire, and Lord of the Manors of Bewerley, Appletrunick, and Ramsgill, in that county.—Bewerley Hall, Ripon.

YORKE, JOSEPH, Esq., of Forthampton Court, Gloucestershire.
Eldest son of the late Joseph Yorke, Esq. (who was a grandson of Philip, 1st Earl of Hardwicke), by Catherine, dau. of James Cocks, Esq., of London; b. 1807; s. 1830; m. 1834 Frances Antonia, dau. of the late Right Hon. Reginald Pole Carew, and has issue,

* John Reginald, educated at Eton and Balliol Coll., Oxford; a Dep.-Lieut. for co. Worcester, and M.P. for Tewkesbury; b. 1836; m. 1st 1862 Augusta Emme ine, younget dau. of Lieut.-General Sir Thomas Monteath Douglas, K.C.B., of Stonebyres, co. Lanark (she d. 1863); 2nd 1868 Sophie Mathilde, 2nd dau. of the late Baron Vincent de Tuil de Serooskerken, and has issue, by the former, * Augustus, b. 1863.

Mr. Yorke, who was educated at Eton and St. John's Coll., Cambridge, is a J.P. and D.L. for co. Worcester, a Magistrate for co. Gloucester (High Sheriff 1844), and Patron of 1 living.—Forthampton Court, Tewkesbury; Oxford and Cambridge Club, s.w.

YORKE, PEIRCE WYNNE, Esq., of Dyffryn Aled, Denbighshire.
Only son of the late Peirce Wynne Yorke, Esq., of Dyffryn Aled, by Elizabeth, dau. of the late Sir William Bulkeley-Hughes, Knt., of Plas-Coch, Anglesey; b. 1826; s. 1837; m. 1854 Lucy Penelope, eldest dau. of Sir Trevor Wheler, Bart. Educated at Eton; is a J.P. and D.L. for co. Denbigh (High Sheriff 1853).—Dyffryn Aled, Abergele.

+ YORKE, SIMON, Esq., of Erthig, Denbighshire.

Eldest son of the late Simon Yorke, Esq., M.P., of Erthig, by Margaret, dau. of John Holland, Esq., of Teyrdan, co. Denbigh; *b.* 1810; *s.* 1834; *m.* 1846 Victoria Mary Louisa, dau. of Lieut.-General the Hon. Sir Edward Cust, and has, with other issue,

* Philip, *b.* 1848.

Mr. Yorke is a J.P. and D.L. for co. Denbigh (High Sheriff 1848).—*Erthig, Wrexham.*

YORKE, THOMAS EDWARD, Esq., of Halton Place, Yorkshire.

Second son of the late John Yorke, Esq., of Bewerley Hall, co. York, by Mary, eldest dau. of the late Ichabod Wright, Esq., of Mapperley Hall, Notts; *b.* 1832; *m.* 1863 Augusta Margaret, eldest dau. of the Hon. and Rev. John Baillie, Rector of Elsdon, and Canon of York, and has, with other issue,

* A son, *b.* 1867.

Mr. Yorke, who was educated at Eton and St. John's Coll., Cambridge (B.A. 1853), is a Magistrate for the W. Riding of Yorkshire. — *Halton Place, Hellifield, Skipton.*

YORKE, WILLIAM LOCKWOOD, Esq., of Thrapston, Northamptonshire.

Eldest son of the late John Yorke, Esq., J.P. and D.L., of Thrapston (Vice-Chairman of the Quarter Sessions for co. Northampton), by his 1st wife Ellinor, only dau. of the Rev. William Lockwood Maydwell, of Thrapston; *b.* 1827; *s.* 1862. This family descend from a common ancestor with the Earl of Hardwicke.—*Thrapston House, Northamptonshire.*

YORKE. (See under *Hardwicke, Earl of.*)

YORKE. (See *Dallas-Yorke.*)

YORSTOUN. (See *Carthew-Yorstoun.*)

YOUNG, Sir CHARLES LAWRENCE, Bart., of Marlow Park, Bucks (cr. 1769).

. Third but only surviving son of the late Sir William Lawrence Young, Bart., of Marlow Park, who was some time M.P. for Bucks, and *d.* 1842) by Caroline, dau. of John Norris, Esq., of Hugheenden, Bucks; *b.* 1839; *s.* his brother as 7th Bart. 1854; *m.* 1863 Mary Florence, youngest dau. of Henry Heyman Toulmin, Esq., of Childwickbury, Herts. Educated at New Coll., Oxford (B.A. 1863); called to the Bar at the Inner Temple 1865—86, *Inverness Terrace,* w.; 8, *Mitre Court Chambers, Temple,* E.C.

Heir, his son William Lawrence, *b.* 1864.

YOUNG, Sir GEORGE, Bart., of Formosa, Berks (cr. 1813).

Eldest son of the late Sir George Young, Bart., of Formosa, by Susan, dau. of the late William Mackworth Praed, Esq., Serjeant-at-Law, of Bitton, Teignmouth, Devon; *b.* 1837; *s.* as 3rd Bart. 1848. Educated at Eton and Trinity Coll., Cambridge (B.A. 1860, M.A. 1863); called to the Bar at Lincoln's Inn 1864; is Fellow of Trinity Coll.—*Formosa Cottage, Maidenhead;* 0, *Plowden Buildings, Temple,* E.C.

Heir Pres., his brother Edward Mallet, *b.* 1839.

YOUNG, the Right Hon. Sir JOHN, Bart., K.C.B., G.C.M.G., of Baillieborough, co. Cavan (cr. 1821).

Eldest son of the late Lieut.-Col. Sir William Young, Bart., of Baillieborough, by Lucy, dau. of Lieut.-Col. Charles Frederick; *b.* 1807; *s.* 1848; *m.* 1855 Adelaide Annabella, dau. of Edward Tuite Dalton, Esq. Educated at Eton and C. C. C., Oxford (B.A. 1829); is a

Barrister-at-Law; is a J.P. and D.L. for co. Cavan; was M.P. for co. Cavan 1831–55; has been successively a Lord of the Treasury 1841, Secretary of the Treasury 1844, and Chief Secretary for Ireland 1852–5. Lord High Commissioner of the Ionian Islands 1855–9, Governor of New South Wales 1861–7.—*Baillieborough Castle, co. Cavan.*

Heir Pres., his nephew Thomas Muston Need (only son of the late Thomas Young, Esq., of the H.E.I.C.'s Service, who *d.* 1846, by Mary Jane, dau. of W. P. Muston, Esq.), *b.* posthumous 1847.

YOUNG, Sir CHARLES GEORGE, Knt., F.S.A., D.C.L. (cr. 1842).

Son of the late J. Young, Esq., M.D., of Lambeth, Surrey; *b.* 1795; *m.* 1854 Frances Susannah, youngest dau. of the Rev. Samuel Lovick Cooper (widow of Frederick Tyrrell, Esq.). Educated at the Charterhouse; is Garter King of Arms.—*Heralds' College,* E.C.; 9, *Prince's Terrace, Hyde Park,* w.

YOUNG, Sir HENRY EDWARD FOX, Knt., C.B. (cr. 1847).

Third son of the late Lieut.-Col. Sir Aretas William Young, some time Governor of Prince Edward's Isle, by Mary, dau. of the late John Cox. Esq., of Coolcliffe, co. Wexford; *b.* 1810; *m.* 1848 Augusta Sophia, dau. of Charles Marryat, Esq. Was Governor of Tasmania 1854–61; late Lieut.-Governor of the Cape of Good Hope and South Australia; was formerly a Judge at St. Lucia.—77, *Kensington Gardens Square,* w.

YOUNG, Lady.

Florence, 2nd dau. of Erving Clark, Esq., of Efford Manor (whom see), by Anne Lætitia, 3rd dau. of Paul Treby Treby, Esq., of Goodamoor and Plympton, Devon; *m.* 1st 1854, Sir William Norris Young, Bart., of the 23rd Royal Welsh Fusiliers, who fell at the Alma, September, 1854; 2nd 1860 John Soltau, Esq., of Little Efford, Devon.—*Efford Manor, Plymouth.*

YOUNG, ADOLPHUS WILLIAM, Esq., of Hare Hatch, Berks.

Son of the late John Adolphus Young, Esq., of Hare Hatch (who *d.* 1862), by Frances, dau. of William Henry Haggard, Esq., of Bradenham Hall, Norfolk; *b.* 1814; *m.* 1st 1837 Anne Eliza, dau. of E. Smith, Esq., of Woodford, Essex; 2nd 1847 Jane, dau. of Charles Throsby, Esq., of Throsby Park, N.S. Wales, and has, with other surviving issue,

* Charles Throsby, *b.* 1852.

Mr. Young, who is a J.P. and D.L. for Berks, was formerly High Sheriff of New South Wales, and represented Port Phillip in the Legislative Council of that Colony; he was M.P. for Great Yarmouth 1857–9, and for Helston 1865–6.—*Hare Hatch House, Twyford; Reform Club,* s.w.

+ YOUNG, ALLEN ALLICOCKE, Esq., of Orlingbury, Northamptonshire.

Son of the late Allen Edward Young, Esq., of Orlingbury, by Amelia, dau. of Thomas Neate, Esq.; *b.* 1838; *m.* 1862 Eliza, dau. of the [....] Young [....] and has, with other issue,

* Allen Allicocke, late Lieut. 33rd Foot; *b.* 1834.

Mr. Young, who was educated at Magdalen Coll. Cambridge (B.A. 1830, M.A. 1833), is a J.P. and D.L. for co. Northampton (High Sheriff 1846).—*Orlingbury, Willingborough.*

YOUNG, ANDREW KNIGHT, Esq., of Monaghan.

Eldest son of the late Andrew Young, Esq., J.P., and Capt. in the Irish Volunteers, by Elizabeth, dau. of Andrew Knight, Esq., of Cockimmun; *b.* 1804; *s.* 1848; *m.* 1829 Martha Augusta, dau. of the late Thomas

1031

Walshe, Esq., of Lower Dominick Street, Dublin, and has, with other issue,

* Thomas Andrew, Lieut. Royal Tyrone Fusiliers; *b.* 1831.

Mr. Young, who was educated at Dublin and Edinburgh, of which latter University he is an M.D., is a Magistrate for co. Monaghan; a Licentiate, Member, and Fellow of the R. C. of Surgeons in Ireland, and Surgeon and Physician to the county of Monaghan Infirmary. This family is of Scottish extraction. — *The Terrace, Monaghan, Ireland.*

YOUNG, ARTHUR JOHN, Esq., of Bradfield, Suffolk.

Son of the late Rev. Arthur Young, of Bradfield Hall; *b.* 1826; *s.* 1852; *m.* 1855 Sarah, only dau. of William de St. Croix, Esq., of Windsor. Is a Magistrate for Suffolk.—*Bradfield Hall, Bury St. Edmund's.*

YOUNG, CHARLES BARING, Esq., of Oakhill, Herts.

Second son of the late Sir Samuel Young, Bart., of Formosa, Berks, by Emily, dau. of Charles Baring, Esq., of Larkbear, near Exeter; *b.* 1801; *m.* 1843 Elizabeth, dau. of the late Stephen Winthrop, Esq., M.D., of Little Bounds, Tunbridge, Kent, and has, with other issue,

* Charles Edward Baring, *b.* 1850.

Mr. Young is a Merchant in London. — *Oakhill, East Barnet ; 4, Hyde Park Terrace, w.*

YOUNG, the Rev. EDWARD NEWTON, of Quainton, Bucks.

Second son of the late Rev. John Young, by Mary, dau. of Col. Wood, of the H.E.I.C.'s Service; *b.* 1795; *m.* 1829 Anne Catherine, dau. of William Travis, Esq., M.D., of Scarborough (she *d.* 1859). Educated at Rugby, Charterhouse, and Ch. Ch., Oxford (B.A. 1819); appointed Rector of Quainton 1822; is a Magistrate for Bucks.—*Quainton, Winslow ; Herne Bay, Canterbury.*

YOUNG, GEORGE, Esq., of Silverknowe, Midlothian.

Eldest son of the late Alexander Young, Esq., of Rosefield, co. Kirkcudbright, by Marian, dau. of William Corson, Esq.; *b.* 1819 ; *m.* 1847 Janet, dau. of George Graham Bell, Esq., of Cravie, co. Aberdeen. Educated at Edinburgh; called to the Scottish Bar 1840; is a Magistrate for co. Dumfries and the city of Edinburgh; elected M.P. for Wigton 1865 ; was Solicitor-General for Scotland 1862-6, and formerly Sheriff of co. Inverness, and subsequently of co. Haddington and Berwick. — *Silverknowe, Edinburgh, N.B.; 47, Murray Place, Edinburgh ; Reform Club, s.w.*

YOUNG, GEORGE, Esq., of Culdaff House, co. Donegal.

Eldest son of the late Robert Young, Esq., of Culdaff House, by Marcia, dau. of the late George Nesbitt, Esq., of Woodhill, co. Donegal; *b.* 1792; *s.* 1823 ; *m.* 1832 Mary Anne, dau. of the late John Ffolliott, Esq., of Hollybrook, co. Sligo, and has issue,

* Robert George, *b.* 1834 ; *m.* 1858 Letitia, dau. of the late Rev. Robert Staveley, of Limerick, and has, with other issue, * George Lawrence, *b.* 1859.

Mr. Young is a J.P. and D.L. for co. Donegal.—*Culdaff House, Carndonagh, co. Donegal.*

YOUNG, GEORGE AUGUSTUS, Esq., of Westbere, Kent.

Fourth son of the late Sir William Lawrence Young, Bart., of Marlow Park, Bucks (who *d.* 1821), by Anna Louisa, dau. of the late William Tufnell, Esq., of Langleys, Essex; *b.* 1822; *m.* 1848 Isabella Marianne, dau. of the Rev. George Moore, Canon of Canterbury. Is a Magistrate for Bucks and Kent ; was formerly in the 8th Foot, and Royal Canadian Rifles.—*Westbere, Surrey, Canterbury ; Junior United Service Club, s.w.*

1032

+ YOUNG, GEORGE FREDERICK, Esq., of Oakfield Lodge, Surrey.

Eldest son of the late Vice-Admiral William Young, by Ann Spencer his wife; *b.* 1790; *m.* 1814 Mary, youngest dau. of the late John Abbot, Esq., of Canterbury, and has issue. Is a Magistrate for Middlesex, and a Deputy-Lieut. for the Tower Hamlets ; a Shipowner and a Merchant in the City; was M.P. for Tynemouth 1831-8, for Scarborough 1851-2.—*Oakfield Lodge, Reigate ; Gresham and City Club.*

YOUNG, HARRY, Esq., of Cleish, Kinross-shire.

Eldest son of the late William Young, Esq., by Johnston, dau. of Alexander Cuningham, Esq., of Edinburgh ; *b.* 1816 ; *s.* his uncle 1840 ; *m.* 1844 Mary, dau. of Laurence Johnston, Esq., of Sands Kincardine, co. Perth. Educated at Eton and University of Edinburgh; is a Magistrate, Vice-Lieut., and Convener of co. Kinross.— *Cleish Castle, Kinross, N.B. ; Caledonian United Service Club, Edinburgh.*

Heir Pres., his brother Alexander, M.D.; *b.* 1817.

YOUNG, the Rev. HENRY TUFNELL, of Mallard's Court, Oxon.

Eldest surviving son of the late Sir William Lawrence Young, Bart. (who *d.* 1824), by Anna Louisa, dau. of the late J. Jolliffe Tufnell, Esq., of Langleys, Essex; *b.* 1810; *m.* 1st 1841 Josephine Isabella, dau. of J. Savill, Esq. ; 2nd 1854 Sarah Anne, only dau. of the late Rev. Thomas Leigh, Rector of Wickham-Bishops, Essex (she *d.* 1859) ; 3rd 1862 Emma, dau. of the late Philip Hills, Esq., of Colne Park, Essex, and has, with other issue,

* Henry Savill, a Barrister-at-Law, educated at Brasenose Coll., Oxford ; *b.* 1843.

Mr. Young, who was educated at Balliol Coll., Oxford (B.A. 1832, M.A. 1856), is a Magistrate for Bucks and Essex ; was formerly Vicar of Mundon, Essex. This family is descended from Sir John de Yonne, and takes its name from one of the departments of France. 'Yonne' having become Anglicised into 'Young.' — *Mallard's Court, Stokenchurch, Oxon ; Junior Carlton Club, s.w.*

YOUNG, JAMES, Esq., of Harristown, co. Roscommon.

Only son of the late Owen Young, Esq., of Harristown, by his 2nd wife Marianne, dau. of James Atkinson, Esq., of Rathangan ; *b.* 1834 ; *s.* 1843 ; *m.* 1864 Grace Elizabeth, dau. of the Hon. Waller O'Grady, of Castlegarde, co. Limerick, and has, with other issue,

* Owen Waller O'Grady, *b.* 1864.

Mr. Young, who was educated at Trinity Coll., Dublin (B.A. 1856), is a Magistrate for co. Roscommon.— *Harristown, Castlerea, co. Roscommon.*

YOUNG, JAMES, Esq., of Kingerby, Lincolnshire.

Eldest son of the late James Young, Esq., of Kingerby, by Mary, dau. and co-heir of Thomas Martin, Esq., of Harley Place, Marylebone; *b.* 1803 ; *s.* 1834. Is Lord of the Manor of Kingerby, and Patron of that living.— *Kingerby Hall, Market Rasen.*

Heir Pres., his brother Thomas Arthur, *b.* 1845.

YOUNG, JOHN, Esq., of Galgorm, co. Antrim.

Eldest son of the late William Young, M.P., Esq., of Galgorm, by Anne, dau. of Wm. Gihon, Esq., of Ballyhead, Ballymena ; *b.* 1827 ; *s.* 1854 ; *m.* 1855 Grace, dau. of Patrick Savage, Esq., and has, with other issue,

* William Robert, *b.* 1856.

Mr. Young, who was educated at Trinity Coll., Dublin (B.A. 1848), is a J.P. and D.L. for co. Antrim (High Sheriff 1863).— *Galgorm Castle, Ballymena, co. Antrim ; Sackville Street Club, Dublin.*

YOUNG, JOHN, Esq., of Stanwick, Northamptonshire.

Eldest son of the late Rev. John Young, Rector of Thorpe Malsor, co. Northampton, by Mary, dau. of Col. John Wood, of Madras; *b.* 1792; *m.* 1839 Ann Mary, dau. of George Ranking, Esq., of Cavendish Square, London. Mr. Young, who was educated at the Charterhouse, Haileybury Coll., and Trinity Hall, Cambridge (B.C.L. 1838), and was called to the Bar at the Middle Temple 1825, is a Magistrate for co. Northampton. —*Stanwick, Higham Ferrers.*

YOUNG, Lieut.-Col. JOHN SMITH, of Ness House, Inverness-shire.

Second son of the late E. Young, Esq., by Margaret Fraser, dau. of D. Smith, Esq., and niece of Alexander, 15th Lord Saltoun; *b.* 1796; *m.* 1st 1834 Frances, dau. of C. Treasure, Esq.; 2nd 1854 Jane Ogilvy, dau. of the late Patrick Grant, Esq., of Corrimony, Inverness-shire, and has by the former, with other issue,

* Donald Smith, in the Madras Army; *b.* 1836.

This family represents the ancient family of the Youngs of Auldbar in Forfarshire.—*Ness House, Inverness, N.B.; Junior Carlton Club,* s.w.

YOUNG, JOSEPH, Esq., of Hartford House, Northumberland.

Son of the late J. Young, Esq., of Hartford House; *b.* 1800; is married, and has, with other issue, an only son,

* William Joseph (of Ryhope House, near Sunderland), *b.* 1830 ; *m.* 1864 Mary Frances, eldest dau. of C. M. Webster, Esq., of Pallion Hall, co. Durham (whom see).

Mr. Young is a Magistrate for Northumberland, and Lord of the Manor of Hartford.—*Hartford House, Morpeth.*

YOUNG, RICHARD, Esq., of Wisbech, Cambridgeshire.

Eldest son of the late Mr. John Young, by Mary, dau. of Mr. John Spikings, of Tydd St. Giles's; *b.* 1809; *m.* 1834 Harriet Emma, dau. of Mr. John Pear, of Tydd St. Mary. Is a Magistrate for co. Cambridge, a Merchant and Shipowner, and Lieut. Wisbech Volunteer Corps; elected M.P. for co. Cambridge 1865; has been five times Mayor of Wisbech.—*Osborne House, Wisbech; City Club,* E.C.; *Reform Club,* s.w.

YOUNG, RICHARD JAMES CALDWELL, Esq., of Coolkeiragh, co. Londonderry.

Son of the late Alexander Thomas Young, Esq., J.P., of Coolkeiragh (who *d.* 1851), by Frances Mary, dau. of the Rev. James Johnston, of Coal Island, co. Tyrone; *b.* 1845; *s.* his grandfather 1858. This family are of Scottish extraction.—*Coolkeiragh, Muff, co. Londonderry.*

Heir Pres., his brother Alexander, *b.* 1847.

YOUNG, WILLIAM HENRY, of The Oaks, Cumberland.

Only son of the late Rev. William Young, Rector of Aller, Somerset (who *d.* 1857), by Sarah Susannah, youngest and only surviving child of the late William Blamire, Esq., of Thackwood, Cumberland; *b.* 1832; *s.* his mother 1866.—*The Oaks, Dalston, Carlisle;* Residence: *Crowcombe, Taunton.*

YOUNG-HERRIES. (See *Herries.*)

YOUNGHUSBAND, JOSEPH, Esq.

Eldest son of the late William Younghusband, Esq., of Floraville, Cumberland, by Hannah, dau. of Isaac Salkeld, Esq.; *b.* 1804; *s.* 1845; *m.* 1844 Harriet Louisiana, dau. of John Oldham, Esq., of Pernambuco, and has issue,

* William, *b.* 1845.

Mr. Younghusband is a J.P. and D.L. for co. Cumberland, and a Magistrate for co. Chester.—*Oakville, Birkenhead.*

YUILLE, ANDREW BUCHANAN, Esq., of Darleith House, Dumbartonshire.

Eldest son of the late George Yuille, Esq., of Carlross Park, co. Dumbarton (who *d.* 1819), by Matilda, dau. of Andrew Buchanan, Esq., of Ardinconal, co. Dumbarton; *b.* 1806; *s.* his uncle 1827; *m.* 1834 Margaret Murdoch, eldest dau. of John Buchanan, Esq., of Edinburgh, formerly of Catter, co. Stirling. Educated at the University of Glasgow; is a Magistrate for co. Dumbarton.—*Darleith House, Cardross, N.B.; Western Club, Glasgow.*

Heir Pres., his brother Archibald Buchanan, *b.* 1812 ; *m.* 1857 Janet Ritchie, dau. of H. Buchanan, Esq., of Glasgow.

YULE, Sir GEORGE UDNY, C.B., K.C.S.I. (cr. 1866).

Son of the late G. Yule, Esq.; *b.* 1812. Educated at Haileybury; entered the Bengal Civil Service 1830, as Assistant Under Magistrate and Collector at Dinagpore; is Resident at Hyderabad; late a Member of Council at Calcutta.—*Hyderabad, Bengal.*

YULE, Major-General PATRICK.

Son of the late James Yule, Esq., J.P., of Gibslees (of the family of Leyhouses, co. Haddington, which merged about 140 years ago in an adjoining estate‡), by Alison, dau. of Patrick Dudgeon, Esq., of East Craig; *b.* 1792; *m.* 1858 the Hon. Anne Louisa, only dau. of William Samuel, 2nd Lord Wynford. Entered the Royal Engineers 1811; became a Major-General 1857. This family is descended maternally from John Rose, of Cullies, and Rarichies, co. Ross, and Margaret, dau. of John Udny, of that Ilk.—26, *Inverleith Row, Edinburgh; Junior United Service Club,* s.w.

‡ See Nesbit's 'Heraldry.'

Z

ZETLAND, Earl of (THOMAS DUNDAS).—Cr. 1838.

Eldest son of Lawrence, 1st Earl, by Harriet, dau. of General John Hale; *b.* 1795; *s.* 1839; *m.* 1823 Sophia Jane, dau. of Sir Hedworth Williamson, Bart. (she *d.* 1865). Educated at Harrow and Trinity Coll., Cambridge (M.A. 1815); is Lord-Lieut. and Custos Rotulorum of the N. Riding of Yorkshire, Patron of 2 livings, and Grand Master of the Freemasons of England; was M.P. for Richmond 1818–30, for York 1830–4, and for Richmond 1835–9.—*Aske Hall, Richmond, Yorkshire; Upleatham, Guisborough; Kerse House, Falkirk, N.B.; Reform Club,* s.w.; *19, Arlington Street,* s.w.

Heir Pres., his nephew Lawrence (son of the late Hon. John Charles Dundas, of Wood Hall, Wetherby, co. York, who *d.* 1866, by Margaret Matilda, eldest dau. of James Talbot, Esq., of Maryville, co. Wexford), *b.* 1844.

ZOUCHE, Baroness (HARRIET ANNE CURZON).—Cr. 1308.

Elder dau. of Cecil Bisshopp, 12th Lord, by Harriet Ann, dau. of William Southwell, Esq., uncle to Lord de Clifford; *b.* 1787; *s.* (the abeyance being terminated in her favour) 1829; *m.* 1808 the Hon. Robert Curzon, J.P. and D.L., formerly M.P. for Clitheroe, who *d.* 1863. Is Patron of 2 livings. This barony was in abeyance 1625–1815.—*Parham Park, Petworth.*

Heir, her son Robert (of Hagley Hall near Rugeley, co. Stafford), educated at the Charterhouse and Ch. Ch., Oxford; a Dep.-Lieut. for Sussex and co. Stafford, Knight of the Turkish Order of the Nishan, and the Persian Order of the Lion and Sun; late Joint Commissioner at the Conference of Erzeroum, and Private Secretary to Lord Stratford de Redcliffe; *b.* 1810; *m.* 1850 Emily Julia, dau. of the late Right Hon. Sir Robert Wilmot-Horton, Bart., and by her (who *d.* 1866) has, with other issue, * Robert Nathaniel Cecil George, *b.* 1851.

SUPPLEMENT.

The following Names have been received too late for insertion in their proper place.

A

AINSLIE, GEORGE COMBE, Esq., of Woll, Roxburghshire.
Son of the late Archibald Ainslie, Esq., of East Lothian (who *d.* 1855), by Mary, dau. of — Peaston, Esq.; *b.* 1800; *m.* 1858 Christina Scott Gourlay, dau. of James Todd, Esq., of Dirleton, East Lothian. Mr. Ainslie, who was educated at Edinburgh, purchased the above property from the family of the Scotts in 1862.—*Woll, Ashkirk, Hawick, N.B.*

+ANDERSON, GEORGE, Esq., of Woodhouse, Dumfriesshire.
Son of the late George Anderson, Esq.; *b.* 1800. Educated at the University of Aberdeen; was formerly Surgeon in H.M.'s Forces, and is now Staff-Surgeon Major.—*Woodhouse, Ecclefechan, N.B.; United Service Club, Edinburgh.*

+ANDERSON, GEORGE, Esq., of Little Harle Tower, Northumberland.
Son of the late Thomas Anderson, Esq., of Little Harle Tower (J.P. and D.L. for, and formerly High Sheriff of, Northumberland), by Mary, dau of — Simson, Esq., of St. Petersburg; *b.* 1825; *s.* 1864. Is a Magistrate for co. Northumberland. This family were formerly of Jesmond House, in the same county, and originally came from Sutherlandshire.—*Little Harle Tower, Newcastle-on-Tyne.*

ANSTEY, THOMAS CHISHOLM, Esq.
Second son of the late Thomas Anstey, Esq., of Anstey Barton, Tasmania, by Mary, dau. of — Chisholm, Esq.; *b.* 1816; *m.* 1839 Harriet, 2nd dau. of the late J. E. Strickland, Esq., of Loughlin House, co. Roscommon, and has issue. Educated at University Coll., London; called to the Bar at the Middle Temple 1839; was M.P. for Youghal 1847-52; Attorney-General at Hong-Kong 1854-8.—2, *Wonden Buildings, Temple, &c.*

ARKWRIGHT, ARTHUR WILLIAM, Esq., of Broughton Astley, Leicestershire.
Youngest son of the late Rev. Joseph Arkwright, of Mark Hall, Essex, by Anne, dau. of Sir Robert Wigram, Bart.; *b.* 1831. Is a J.P. and D.L. for co. Leicester.—*Broughton Astley, Lutterworth.*

ASHBY, SHUCKBURGH, Esq., of Quenby Hall, Leicestershire.
Eldest son of the late William Ashby Ashby, Esq., of Quenby Hall (who assumed the name of Ashby in lieu

of Latham), by Mary, dau. of — Miller, Esq.; *b.* 179-; *s.* 185—. Is Lord of the Manor of Hungerton, and alternate Patron of that living.—*Quenby Hall, Hungerton, Leicester.*

Heir Pres., his twin brother, William, *b.* 179-.

AYLMER, MICHAEL VALENTINE, Esq., of Derry co. Tipperary.
Eldest son of the late Gerald Aylmer, Esq., of Heathfield, co. Dublin, by Catherine, dau. of P. Lambert, Esq., of Carnagh, co. Wexford; *b.* 1812; *s.* 1837; *m.* 1841 Marianne, dau. and sole heir of the late W. Conolly, Esq., of Dublin, and has, with other issue,
  • Gerald Joseph, *b.* 1849.
Mr. Aylmer, who was educated at Ampleforth and Stonyhurst Colls., and at Ch. Ch., Oxford (B.A. 1834), is head and lineal representative of this ancient family, which was formerly of Lyons, co. Kildare.—*Derry, Rathcabbin, co. Tipperary.*

B

+BAGEHOT, THOMAS WATSON, Esq., of Herd's Hill, Somersetshire.
Son of the late W. Bagehot, Esq., of Herd's Hill; *b.* 17—; is married, and has, with other issue,
  • Walter (M.A. of London University, a Magistrate for Somerset, and an unsuccessful candidate for bridge water 1846; *b.* 182-.
Mr. Bagehot is a Magistrate for Somerset.—*Herd's Hill Langport, Taunton.*

+BAILWARD, JOHN, Esq., of Horsington Manor, Somerset.
Son of the late Thomas Bailward, Esq., J.P. and D.L. of Horsington Manor . . . . Somerset and Lord of the Manor of Horsington.—*Horsington Manor, Wincanton.*

+BARNEBY, WILLIAM, Esq., of Clater Park, Herefordshire.
Eldest son of the late William Barneby, Esq., of Clater Park (who was many years a Magistrate for co. Hereford, and High Sheriff in 1849), by Mary, 2nd dau. of the late Richard Barneby, Esq., of Worcester; *b.* 1845; *s.* 1856. Educated at Eton. Is descended from a common ancestor with the Barnebys of Brockhampton (whom see).—*Clater Park, Lauton, Bromyard.*

1035

BARNETT, CHARLES GEORGE, Esq., of Sunningdale, Berks.
Son of G. H. Barnett, Esq., of Glympton Park, Oxon, by Elizabeth, dau. of Stratford Canning, Esq.; *b.* 1818; *m.* 1847 Marianne Jane St. John, dau. of Edward St. John Mildmay, Esq., and has, with other issue,
* Charles Edward, *b.* 1848.
Mr. Barnett is a Magistrate for Berks, and a Banker in London.—*King's Beeches, Sunningdale, Bagshot; White's Club, s.w.*

+ BARROW, JOHN JAMES, Esq., of Ringwood Hall, Derbyshire.
Eldest son of the late Richard Barrow, Esq., of Ringwood Hall, and nephew of W. H. Barrow, Esq., M.P. (whom see); *b.* 1825; *s.* 1865; *m.* 1867 Dorothea Mary, eldest dau. of the Rev. James Deans, Vicar of Exminster. Is a J.P. and D.L. for co. Derby.—*Ringwood Hall, Chesterfield.*

BEATSON-BELL, ANDREW, Esq., of Glenfarg, Perthshire, and Kilduncan, Fifeshire.
Only surviving son of the late John Beatson-Bell, Esq., of Glenfarg and Kilduncan (a J.P. for cos. Perth and Fife), by Ann, elder dau. of the late Charles Young, Esq., of Leith; *b.* 1831; *s.* 1868; *m.* 1865 Mary, dau. of the late Nicholas Dodd, Esq., of Bellshield, Northumberland, and has, with other issue,
* John, *b.* 1866.
Mr. Beatson-Bell, who was educated at the Edinburgh Academy, and the Universities of Edinburgh and Glasgow, was called to the Scottish Bar in 1854, and is a Sheriff-Substitute for co. Fife. The additional name of Beatson was assumed by the father of the present owner in 1840, on succeeding to the estates of his maternal uncle, Thomas Beatson, Esq., of Glenfarg.—*Glenfarg, Bridge of Earn, N.B.; Cuttlehill House, Inverleithing, N.B.; University Club, Edinburgh.*

+ BEAUMONT, GEORGE, Esq., of East Bridgford, Notts.
Son of the late G. Beaumont, Esq.; *b.* 18—; *m.* 1860 Emma, 4th dau. of the Rev. Charles Heycock, of Pytchley, co. Northampton (whom see).—*Old Hall, East Bridgford, Nottingham.*

+ BEEVOR, the Rev. EDWARD RIGBY, of Hevingham, Norfolk.
Son of the late Rev. Augustus Beevor, Rector of Burgh-Apton, Norfolk (who *d.* 1818); *b.* 1802. Educated at C. C. C., Cambridge (B.A. 1823); is Rector and Patron of Hevingham, and descended from a common ancestor with the Baronet of the same name.—*Hevingham Rectory, Norwich.*

+ BEEVOR, HENRY, Esq., of Blythe Hall, Notts.
Son of the late Rev. Thomas Beevor, M.A., of Newark, Notts; *b.* 18—. Is a Magistrate for Notts.—*Blythe, Retford.*

BELL, HENRY, Esq., of Tynemouth, Northumberland.
Youngest son of the late Thomas Bell, Esq., of Newcastle-on-Tyne; *b.* 18—. Is a Magistrate for Northumberland, and a Merchant and Manufacturer at Newcastle-on-Tyne.—*Residence: Tynemouth.*

BISCOE, the Rev. FREDERICK, M.A.
Fourth son of the late Vincent H. Biscoe, Esq., of Hookwood, Surrey; *b.* 1808. Educated at Westminster and Ch. Ch., Oxford (B.A. 1830, M.A. 1832); is a Magistrate for co. Gloucester, and Vicar of Turkdean.—*The Vicarage, Turkdean, Northleach, Gloucestershire.*
1036

+ BISCOE, the Rev. ROBERT, M.A.
Son of the late W. Biscoe, Esq.; *b.* 1800. Educated at Ch. Ch., Oxford (B.A. 1823, M.A. 1825); is a Magistrate for co. Hereford, and Rector of Whitbourne.—*Whitbourne Rectory, Worcester.*

BLACKWELL, the late EARDLEY JOHN, Esq., of Ampney Park, Gloucestershire.
Eldest son of the late George Graham Blackwell, Esq., of Ampney Park, by Elizabeth Emma, eldest dau. of the late Sir John Eardley Eardley-Wilmot, Bart., of Berkswell Hall, co. Warwick; *b.* 1832; *s.* 1838; and *d.* 1866, having *m.* 1858 Marie, dau. of Thomas Svec, Esq., of Vaage, Norway, and had issue two daughters. Mr. Blackwell was educated at Rugby and Trinity Coll., Cambridge, and was Lord of the Manor of Ampney-Crucis.—*Ampney Park, Cirencester.*

BLAND, the Rev. MILES, D.D., F.R.S., F.S.A., &c., of Lilley, Hertfordshire.
Eldest and only surviving son of the late Thomas Bland, Esq.; *b.* 1786; *m.* 1st 1823 Ann, dau. of Thomas Templeman, Esq., of Convngham House, Ramsgate; 2nd 1836 Emma, dau. of Claud Russell, Esq., of Binfield, Berks, and formerly Member of the Council at Madras (she *d.* 1867). He has, by the former, with other issue,
* Miles, *b.* 1828.
Dr. Bland, who was educated at St. John's Coll., Cambridge (B.A. 1808, M.A. 1811, B.D. 1818, D.D. 1826), is a Magistrate for Beds and Herts, a Prebendary of Wells, and Rector of Lilley; he was formerly Fellow and Tutor of St. John's Coll.—*Lilley, near Luton; 5, Royal Crescent, Ramsgate.*

+ BLAND, the Ven. NATHANIEL, of Beaufort, co. Kerry.
Eldest son of the late — Bland, Esq.; *m.* Ann, dau. of the late Capt. Edward Fuller (who *d.s.p.*). Educated at Trinity Coll., Dublin; is Archdeacon of Aghadoe and Rector of Knockane.—*Beaufort, near Killarney.*

BLUETT, PETER FREDERICK, Esq., late of Holcombe Court, Devon.
Son of the late William Bluett, Esq., of Cornwall (who *d.* 1811), by Elizabeth Maria, dau. of Charles Clarke, Esq., of Bayford, Somerset; *b.* 1800; *s.* his uncle, Peter Bluett, Esq., 1834; is married and has issue. This family acquired the Holcombe Court estate in the 15th century, through marriage with a co-heiress of the Chiseldens; it was, however, sold in 1858.—*Residence: South Wembury, Plymouth.*

BOCKETT-PUGH, HENRY PUGH, Esq., of Tunbridge Wells, Kent.
Second son of the Rev. Benjamin Bradney Bockett, M.A., of Epsom, Surrey, by Fanny S. Bickett, dau. of William Bramwell, Esq., of London; *b.* 1838; *m.* 1867 Margaret, dau. of Edward Mant Miller, Esq., of Clifton, Bristol, and has issue.
* Margaret Fanny, *b.* 1867.
Mr. Bockett-Pugh, who was educated at Abingdon Grammar School, assumed the additional surname of Pugh under the will of his aunt, Mrs. Sarah Pugh, late of Southborough and Tunbridge Wells, 1868. This family were formerly of Shinfield, Berks.—*Vale Royal, Tunbridge Wells.*

+ BOLDERO, Mrs., of Lower Beding, Sussex.
Margaret, dau. of the late William Christian, Esq., of Heddesden, Herts; *m.* 18— Henry Boldero, Esq., J.P., of Lower Beding, and has issue an only child,
* Margaret, *m.* 1868 Walter Bartttelot, Esq., M.P., of Stopham, Sussex (whom see).
Mrs. Boldero is Lady of the Manor of Lower Beding. The family of Boldero have been long connected with Sussex.—*North Lodge, Lower Beding, Horsham.*

BORTHWICK. (See *Brown-Borthwick.*)

BROWN-BORTHWICK, Mrs., of Hope Park, Midlothian.

Grace, only surviving dau. of the late John Borthwick, Esq., of Crookston, and Borthwick Castle, Midlothian, by Ann, dau. of the late Robert Dundas, Esq., of Arniston, Midlothian, and sister of John Borthwick, Esq., of Crookston (whom see); *m.* 1868 the Rev. Robert Brown, of St. Mary's Hall, Oxford, Curate of Quebec Chapel, London, and formerly Lieut. E. York Militia, who assumed on his marriage the additional name of Borthwick.—96, *Park Street, Grosvenor Square*, w.

+BUTLER, GEORGE, Esq., of Woolstone, Berkshire.

Eldest son of the late John Butler, Esq., of Kisby House, Inkpen, Berks; *b.* 18—; *m.* 18— Mary, dau. of — Cooper, Esq. (she is *dec.*). Is a Magistrate for Berks.—*Woolstone, Faringdon.*

C

CANDLISH, JOHN, Esq., M.P.

Son of the late Mr. J. Candlish; *b.* 1816; *m.* 1845 Elizabeth, dau. of Robert Candlish, Esq., of Bishopwearmouth, co. Durham. Is a Magistrate and Alderman for the Borough of Sunderland; elected M.P. for Sunderland 1866.—*Park Place East, Sunderland.*

+CANE, EDWARD, Esq., of St. Wolstan's, co. Kildare.

Son of the late E. Cane, Esq., of St. Wolstan's; *b.* 1810. Is a Magistrate for co. Kildare (of which he has been High Sheriff).—*St. Wolstan's, Celbridge, co. Kildare*; *Carlton and Travellers' Clubs*, s.w.

CANE, the Rev. THOMAS COATS, of Brakenhurst House, Notts.

Son of the late Rev. Robert Cane, of Southwell, Notts, by Kitty Cowart, dau. of John Coats, Esq., of Gainsborough, co. Lincoln; *b.* 1800; *m.* 1826 Mary, dau. of John Brettle, Esq., and has, with other issue,

  • John Brettle (in Holy Orders), M.A. of St. John's Coll., Cambridge, and Rector of Weston, Notts; *b.* 1828; *m.* 1863 Alicia Ealing, eldest dau. of the Rev. C. Boileau, Rector of Tattingstone, Suffolk.

Mr. Cane, who was educated at St. John's Coll., Cambridge (B.A. 1823, M.A. 1826), appointed Incumbent of Kirklington 1858, and of Hallonghton 1840, is a Magistrate for Notts.—*Brakenhurst House, Southwell.*

CAREW, CHARLES HALLOWELL-, Esq., late of Beddington Park, Surrey.

Eldest son of the late Admiral Sir Benjamin Hallowell-Carew, G.C.B. (who assumed the additional name of Carew), by Mary, dau. of the late Capt. John Englefield, R.N.; *b.* 1804; *s.* 1834; *m.* 1828 Mary, dau. of the late Capt. Sir Murray Maxwell, R.N., C.B. Is Patron of 1 living; a Capt. R.N.; assumed the additional surname of Carew in 1828, on inheriting the estates of the late Mrs. Carew.

CARPENTER. (See *Talbot, the Hon. Walter Cecil.*)

CARTER, SAMUEL, Esq., of Quarry Hill, Sussex.

Eldest son of the late Samuel Carter, Esq., of Coventry; *b.* 1805; *m.* 1833 Maria, dau. of Francis Ronalds, Esq. Admitted a Solicitor 1827; elected M.P. for Coventry 1868; was formerly Solicitor to the London and North-Western Railway Company, and to the Midland Railway Company.—*Quarry Hill, Battle; Reform Club*, s.w.; 13, *Cleveland Square, Hyde Park*, w.

CASTLE, ROBERT, Esq., of Cleeve Court, Somerset.

Eldest son of the late Thomas Castle, Esq., of Bristol, by Mary, dau. of William Morgan, Esq.; *b.* 1807; *m.* 1834 Augusta, dau. of Philip Protheroe, Esq., of Cote House, co. Gloucester; 2nd 1840 Mary, dau. of Thomas Fox, Esq., of Lewisham, Kent, and has issue by the former,

  • Thomas, *b.* 1835; *m.* 1860 Fanny, dau. of Charles Johnson, Esq., of Silverlands, co. Chester.

Mr. Castle is a Magistrate for Somerset and for the city and co. of Bristol, and Lord of the Manor of Yatton. This family originally came from Devonshire, and some members of it are mentioned amongst Prince's 'Worthies of Devon' in 1605.—*Cleeve Court, Yatton, Bristol.*

+CHALONER, CHARLES, Esq., of Aigburth Hall, Lancashire.

Eldest son of the late Charles Chaloner, Esq., of Liverpool; *b.* 18—. Is a Magistrate for co. Lancaster, and a Merchant at Liverpool. This family is traditionally descended from a common ancestor with the Chaloners of Guisborough (whom see).—*Aigburth Hall, Garston, Liverpool.*

+CHAMBERLAYNE, JOSEPH CHAMBERLAYNE, Esq., of Maugersbury, Gloucestershire.

Eldest son of the late John Hawksley Ackerley, Esq., Barrister-at-Law, by Elizabeth, dau. of the late Rev. John Chamberlayne, of Maugersbury House; *b.* 1792; inherited this property in 1831 from his maternal uncle, Edmund John Chamberlayne, Esq., whose name he assumed; *m.* 1825 Henrietta Catherine, dau. of the Rev. Guy Fairfax, and has had issue four daughters. Mr. Chamberlayne, who entered the Army in 1809, became Lieut. R.A. 1812, and retired on half-pay in 1826; is Lord of the Manor of Maugersbury, and Patron of the living of Charlton Abbotts.—*Maugersbury House, Stow-on-the-Wold.*

CHARLTON, the Rev. WILLIAM HENRY.

Eldest son of the late Rev. William Henry Charlton, of Nottingham Terrace, Regent's Park, by Harriet, dau. of Robert Masters, Esq., of Prospect House, Bath; *b.* 1814; *m.* 1843 Sarah, dau. of T. H. Jackson, Esq., of Stamford, and has, with other issue,

  • William Henry, *b.* 1852.

Mr. Charlton was educated at Westminster and Trinity Coll., Cambridge (B.A. 1837, M.A. 1841); is a Magistrate for co. Northampton, and Rector of Easton.—*Easton Rectory, Stamford.*

CHILDE, the Rev. EDWARD GEORGE, of Kinlet, Shropshire.

Third son of William Lacon Childe, Esq., of Kinlet Hall and of Kyre Park, co. Worcester (whom see) by Harriet, dau. of the late William Cludde, Esq., of Orleton; *b.* 1818; *m.* 1862 Frances Christina, dau. of Sir Baldwin Leighton, Bart., of Loton. Educated at Harrow and Trinity Coll., Cambridge (B.A. 1841, M.A. 1846); is a Magistrate for co. Salop, Vicar of Kinlet and of Cleobury Mortimer, and hereditary in to the Kyre estates. —*Kinlet Vicarage, Bewdley; University Club*, s.w.

CLARKE, THOMAS EDWARD, Esq., of Tremlet Hill, Somersetshire.

Eldest son of the late Thomas Edward Clarke (the 4th), of Tremlet Hill, and Charl. Somerset, by Frances Southwood, only dau. of the late Capt. Tristram Whitter, R.N., of Collumpton, Devon; *b.* 1819; *s.* 1840; *m.* 1846 Georgina, dau. of ——, Esq., and has, with other issue,

  • Thomas Edward, *b.* 1841.

Mr. Clarke, who was educated at Winchester Coll., and was called to the Bar at the Middle Temple 1848, is a Magistrate for Devon and Somerset, and Lord of the Manor of Greenham in Ashbrittle; late Capt. of the Wellington Troop of W. Somerset Yeomanry Cavalry. This family have been seated at Tremlet Hill since 1696.—*Tremlet Hill and Apsley House, Ashbrittle, Wellington.*

CLARKE, the Rev. WILLIAM HENRY, of Cold Higham, Northamptonshire.
Son of the late William Clarke, Esq., of Milland House, Trotton, Sussex; b. 1791; m. 18— Elizabeth, 2nd dau. of the late Rev. Thomas Welch, Vicar of Pattishall, and has issue an only dau., m. to the Rev. C. S. Bowles, of Great Malvern. Mr. Clarke, who was educated at Exeter Coll., Oxford (B.A. 1814. M.A. 1817), is a Magistrate for co. Northampton, and Rector of Cold Higham.—*Cold Higham, Towcester.*

COATS, THOMAS, Esq., of Ferguslie and Maxwellton, Renfrewshire.
Fourth son of the late James Coats, Esq., Merchant, of Paisley, co. Renfrew; b. 1809; m. 1840 Margaret, dau. of Thomas Glen, Esq., of Paisley. Is a Magistrate for co. Renfrew, Proprietor of the Estates of Ferguslie and Maxwellton (the former of which was acquired by him in 1845, and the latter in 1868), and a Merchant at Paisley.—*Ferguslie House, and Maxwellton, Paisley, N.B.*

+ COLE, GEORGE BEAUCHAMP, Esq., of Twickenham, Middlesex.
Second but eldest surviving son of the late Stephen Thomas Cole, Esq., of Twickenham, and of Stoke Lynn, Oxon, by Lady Elizabeth Henrietta, 2nd dau. of Edward, 12th Earl of Derby; b. 18—; m. 18— Julia, dau. of Colonel Espinasse. Is a Dep.-Lieut. for Middlesex. —*Twickenham, s.w.*

+ COLEMAN, EDWARD JOHN, of Stoke Park, Bucks.
Son of Edward Coleman, Esq., Accountant, of London; b. 1820; m. 1850 Gertrude, dau. of — Welch, Esq., but has no issue. Mr. Coleman, who is an Accountant in the City, in the firm of Coleman, Turquand, Youngs, & Co., is Lord of the Manor of Stoke Poges; he purchased this property from Lord Taunton in 1848. —*Stoke Park, Slough;* 13, *Tokenhouse-yard, Lothbury, e.c.*

+ COLES, General ROBERT BARTLETT, of Glencot, Somersetshire.
Son of the late R. Coles, Esq.; b. 1785. Is a J.P. and D.L. for co. Somerset, a General in the Army, and Col. 65th Foot.—*Glencot, Wells.*

COOPER, the Rev. WILLIAM W., of West Rasen, Lincolnshire.
Eldest son of the late Rev. William Cooper, of West Rasen, by Anne, dau. of the late Rev. Marmaduke Alington, of Swinhope, co. Lincoln; b. 1823; m. 1856 Marion Frances, dau. of the late Lawrence W. Brown, Esq., of London, and has, with other issue,
  * William Lawrence.
Mr. Cooper, who was educated at Eton and St. John's Coll., Cambridge (B.A. 1846. M.A. 1849), is a Magistrate for co. Lincoln. This family descended from Joan, daughter of Sir Oliver Cromwell, of Hinchingbrook, uncle of the Protector.—*West Rasen, Market Rasen.*

COOPER, Rev. THOMAS LOVICK, of Empingham, Rutlandshire.
Fourth son of the late Rev. Samuel Lovick Cooper, Patron and Rector of Ingoldesthorpe, Norfolk, by Sarah Leman,

dau. and heir of Thomas Rede, Esq., of Letheringham Abbey, Suffolk; b. 1801; m. 1st 1821 Emily Mary Swinfen, only dau. of Sir Thos. Durrant, Bart. (she d. 1838); 2nd 1841 Harriette, eldest dau. of Jacob Ricardo, Esq., and has, by the latter, with other issue, an only surviving child,
  * Sophie Gertrude Paston.
Mr. Cooper, who was educated at Magdalen Coll., Cambridge (B.A. 1824, M.A. 1826), is Rector and Patron of Mablethorpe, and Rector of Empingham, co. Rutland; was formerly Rector and Patron of Ingoldesthorpe, Norfolk, and Rector of Hawkshead. Mr. Cooper is a younger brother of the 2nd Bart. Sir A. Paston Cooper. —*Empingham, Stamford; Mablethorpe, Alford.*

+ COPPINGER, THOMAS STEPHEN, Esq., of Leemount, co. Cork.
Eldest son of the late Stephen Coppinger, Esq., of Leemount, Barrister-at-Law, by Juliana, dau. of J. Walsh, Esq., of Cork; b. 1845; s. 1861. This family is of great antiquity in co. Cork.—*Leemount, Coachford.*

+ COXE, FRANCIS LOVELOCK, Esq., of Edington, Berkshire.
Eldest son of the late Rev. Charles Benjamin Coxe, Rector of Avington and E. Shefford, Berks. by Mary, dau. of — Butler, Esq.; b. 18—; m. 18— Emma, dau. of — Compton, Esq. Is a Magistrate for Berks, and Lord of the Manor of Edington.—*Edington, Hungerford.*

CROSS, THOMAS, Esq., of Mortfield, Lancashire, and Ruddington Hall, Notts.
Eldest son of the late James Cross, Esq., of Mortfield, Solicitor and Banker, by Margaret, dau. of Thomas Kay, Esq., Gentleman, of Manchester; b. 1805; s. 1850; m. 1st 1842 Ellen Thompson Mann, dau. of Joseph Mann, Esq., of Liverpool; 2nd 1851 Anne, dau. of Paul Jean Baptist Chappe De Louval, of Manchester, and has by the former, with other issue,
  * James Percival, b. 1843.
Mr. Cross is a Magistrate for cos. Lancaster and Cumberland, and a Banker. &c., at Bolton.—*Ruddington Hall, Nottingham; Mortfield, Bolton-le-Moors.*

D

DARNELL, the Rev. WILLIAM, of Bamburgh Glebe, Northumberland.
Eldest son of the late Rev. Wm. N. Darnell, B.D., Rector of Stanhope, co. Durham, by Elizabeth, dau. of Rev. William Bowe, M.A., of Scorton, co. York; b. 1816; m. 1844 Frances, eldest dau. of the late Ven. Charles Thorp, D.D., Archdeacon and Canon of Durham, and has, with other issue,
  * William Nicholas, Lieut. 54th Regt.; b. 1848.
Mr. Darnell, who was educated at Winchester and C.C.C., Oxford (B.A. 1838, M.A. 1843), is a Magistrate for Northumberland, and Patron of 1 living, Vicar of Bamburgh, and Chaplain to .... &c.—*Bamburgh Glebe, Belford; Conservative Club, s.w.*

DASHWOOD, FREDERICK LOFTUS, Esq.
Third son of the late Sir George Dashwood, Bart., of Kirtlington Park, by Marianne Sarah, eldest dau. of Sir William Rowley, Bart.; b. 1824. Is a Magistrate for Oxon; was formerly Capt. 16th Lancers.—*Kirtlington, Oxford; Army and Navy Club, s.w.*

+ DAUBENY, EDMUND JOSEPH, Esq., of Cleve House, Somerset.
Third son of the late Rev. Andrew Daubeny, Rector of Publow, Somerset, by Elizabeth, dau. of the late George Daubeny, Esq., of Redland, co. Gloucester; b. 1813;

called to the Bar at the Middle Temple Inn 1838; is a Magistrate for Somerset.—*Cleve House, Yatton, Bristol.*

+DAUNCEY, PHILIP, Esq., of Little Horwood, Bucks.

Eldest son of the late Mr. Serjeant Dauncey, of Little Horwood; *b.* 18—; *m.* 18— a dau. of the late John William Spicer, Esq., of Esher Place, Surrey (she *d.* 185-), and has issue,

* Philip Sicklemore, Capt. 77th Foot; *b.* 1837; is married and has issue.

Mr. Dauncey is a Magistrate for Bucks and lay Impropriator of Little Horwood.—*Little Horwood, Winslow.*

+DAVIDSON, THOMAS, Esq., of Drumley, Ayrshire.

Son of the late T. Davidson, Esq., of Drumley; *b.* 18—. Is a Magistrate for co. Ayr, and represents the family of Sir William Davidson, of Curriehill, N.B., who was executed at Carlisle for high treason in 1715.—*Drumley, Ayr, N.B.*

+DAVIES, JAMES, Esq., of The Garth, Monmouthshire.

Eldest son of the late James Davies, Esq., of The Garth; *b.* 18—; *m.* 1850 Mary, eldest dau. of F. C. Hanbury Williams, Esq., of Coldbrook Park, co. Monmouth (from whom he is divorced), and has, with other issue,

* James, *b.* 18—.

Mr. Davies is a Magistrate for co. Monmouth, and a Capt. in the Monmouth Militia.—*The Garth, Monmouth.*

DAVIES, THOMAS, Esq., of Neuadd, Brecon.

Eldest son of the late David Davies, Esq., of Glamonney, Crickhowell, by Rebecca, dau. of Thomas Cunville, Esq., of Llangattock; *b.* 1799; *m.* 1827 Maria Selina, dau. of the late Sir Christopher Willoughby, Bart., of Baldon House, Oxon, and Berwick Lodge, co. Gloucester. Educated at Winchester; is a Magistrate for cos. Radnor, Monmouth, and Brecon (High Sheriff 1856), and a Dep.-Lieut. for cos. Brecon and Radnor; was formerly Agent to the Duke of Beaufort and other large landowners. This family is of ancient Welsh origin.—*Neuadd, Crickhowell; Windham Club, s.w.*

Heir Pres., his brother Edward, *b.* 1811; *m.* 1844 Elizabeth, dau. of Thomas Gratrex, Esq., of Herbert Hall, Crickhowell, co. Brecon, and has issue, * three sons and one daughter.

DE HAVILLAND, JOHN, Esq., of Langford-Budville, Somerset.

Son of the late John Havilland, Esq., of Langford-Budville, by Mary Wright, dau. and heir of William Louis von Sonnentag, Capt. in the French Army; *b.* 1826. Educated at St. Petersburg; is Member of the Inner Temple, and of the College of Arms, London. This family claims to be of Guernsey extraction.—*Langford Court, Wellington, Somerset; Reform Club, s.w.; 5, King's Bench Walk, E.C.*

DELANE, JOHN THADDEUS, Esq., of Ascot, Berks.

Son of the late William Frederick Augustus Delane, Esq., of Eaton Place, London, Treasurer of the County Courts of Kent (who *d.* 1858); *b.* 1817. Educated at Magdalen Hall, Oxford (B.A. 1840, M.A. 1846); called to the Bar at the Middle Temple 1847; is a Dep.-Lieut. for Berks.—*Ascot Heath, Staines; Athenæum and Reform Clubs, s.w.; 16, Serjeants' Inn, E.C.*

+DOBEDÉ, JOHN, Esq., of Exning Hall, Suffolk.

Son of the late T. Dobedé, Esq.; *b.* 179-; *m.* 18— Elizabeth, dau. of —— Esq., and by her (who *d.* 1860) has issue,

* Henry Frederick, *b.* 18 ; *m.* 1860 Louisa Frederika,

youngest dau. of the late Richard J. Eaton, Esq., of Stetchworth Park, co. Cambridge.

Mr. Dobedé is a J.P. and D.L. for co. Cambridge, and a Magistrate for Suffolk. This family is of foreign extraction.—*Exning Hall, Newmarket.*

+DODGSON, RICHARD BARTON, Esq., of Beardwood, Lancashire.

Son of the late R. Dodgson. Esq.; *b.* 18—; *m.* 1857 Jane, 2nd dau. of James Cross, Esq., of Gringley-on-the-Hill, Notts. Is a Magistrate for co. Lancaster. —*Beardwood, Blackburn.*

DOVETON, FREDERICK BRICKDALE, Esq.

Eldest son of the late Rev. John Frederick Doveton, J.P. and D.L., Rector of Mells-cum-Leigh, Somerset, and Vicar of Betchworth, Surrey, by Elizabeth, dau. of the late Rev. Dr. Crossman, Prebendary of Wells, and Rector of West Monkton, Somerset; *b.* 1805; *m.* 1834 Harriet Eliza, dau. of the late Major W. Pilkington, of Tore, co. Westmeath, and has, with other issue,

* Frederick Bazett, *b.* 1841; *m.* 1867 Annie, dau. of William Douglas, Esq., late of the Madras C.S.

Mr. Doveton is a Magistrate for Somerset, late Capt. R. Madras Fusiliers. This family, formerly of Dufton, are of Cumberland extraction.—*Residence: Woodville, Taunton.*

DOVETON, the Rev. JOHN BAZETT, of Burnett, Somerset.

Second son of the late Rev. John Frederick Doveton, Rector of Mells-cum-Leigh, Somerset, and Vicar of Betchworth, Surrey, by Elizabeth, dau. of the late Rev. Dr. Crossman, Prebendary of Wells, and brother of F. B. Doveton, Esq., of Woodville (whom see); *b.* 1807. Educated at Downing Coll., Cambridge (B.A. 1831, M.A. 1834); is Rector of Burnett.—*Burnett Rectory, Bristol.*

DUCKWORTH, RUSSELL, Esq., of Murtrey Hill, Somerset.

Second surviving son of William Duckworth, Esq., of Orchard Leigh Park, Somerset, by Hester Emily, dau. of Robert Philips, Esq., of Prestwich, co. Lancaster; *b.* 1830; *m.* 1863 Jeannette, dau. of Rev. Henry Clutterbuck, of Buckland Dinham, and has, with other issue,

* William Henry, *b.* 1867.

Mr. Duckworth, who was educated at Eton and Trinity Coll., Cambridge (B.A. 1857), and called to the Bar at Lincoln's Inn 1856, is a Magistrate for Somerset. —*Murtrey Hill, Frome.*

E

EARLE, HARDMAN, Esq., of Allerton, Lancashire.

Only surviving son of the late Thomas Earle, Esq., of Spekelands, co. Lancaster, by Mary, dau of Thomas Earle, Esq., of Liverpool; *b.* 1792; *m.* 1819. Mary dau. of the late William Langton, Esq., of Kirkham, co. Lancaster, and has, with other issue,

* Thomas, *b.* 1820; *m.* 1854 Emily, 2nd dau. of William Fletcher, Esq., of Liverpool, and has, with other issue,
* Henry, *b.* 1854.

Mr. Earle is a Magistrate for co. Lancaster, and a Merchant at Liverpool. This family has been settled in Liverpool since 1688. John Earle, Esq., was Mayor of that borough in 1709.—*Allerton Tower, Woolton, Liverpool.*

1039

-+EASTWOOD, JAMES, Esq., of Castletown, co. Armagh.
Eldest son of the late Charles Eastwood, Esq., of Castletown, by Elizabeth, dau. of Thomas Cavan, Esq., of Belfast; b. 1795; m. 1831 Louisa, dau. of the late James Dawson, Esq., of Fork Hill, co. Armagh. Is a J.P. and D.L. for co. Armagh.—Castletown, Dundalk.

+EDGE, JAMES THOMAS, Esq., of Strelly, Notts.
Eldest son of Major James Hurt, by Mary Margaret, dau. of the late Thomas Webbe Edge, Esq., of Strelly Hall; b. 1824; s. his uncle, Thomas Webbe Edge, Esq., 1844, whose name he assumed, by Royal licence, in 1848; m. 1st 1856 Julia Frances, 4th dau. of Samuel Trehawke Kekewich, Esq., M.P., of Peamore, Devon (she d. 1856); 2nd 1866 Emily Mary, youngest dau. of the late Robert Holden, Esq., of Nuttall Temple, Notts; he has issue by the former,
    * Thomas Lewis Kekewich, b. 1856.
Mr. Edge is a Magistrate for Notts, and Lord of the Manor and Patron of Strelly.—Strelly Hall, Nottingham.

EDGE, JOHN HENRY, Esq., of Clonbrock, co. Carlow.
Only surviving son of the late John Dallas Edge, Esq., Barrister-at-Law (who d. 1842), by Anne, dau. of T. Mansell, Esq.; b. 1841; s. his grandfather, the late John Edge, Esq., of Clonbrock, 1856.—Clonbrock, Orettyard, co. Carlow.

EDMANDS, CHARLES HENRY, Esq., late of Sutton Grange, Surrey.
Son of the late Thomas Edmands, Esq., by Anne, dau. of the late Richard Panting, Esq., of the Red House, Eldersfield, co. Worcester; b. 1822; m. 1st 1849 Arabella Rose, youngest dau. of the late Charles Ross, Esq., of Tain, Ross-shire (she d. 1859); 2nd 1868 Ellen Jane, dau. of Richard Dawes, Esq.; he has by the former, with other issue, * Charles Adolf, b. 1853. —Sudbury Hall, Sudbury, Middlesex, N.W.

EDMONDSON, JOHN, Esq., of Gresgarth Hall, Lancashire.
Eldest son of the late Thomas Edmondson, Esq., of Gresgarth Hall, by Mary Jane, dau. of John Brown, Esq., Merchant, of Lancaster; b. 1799; s. 1834; m. 1828 Margaret Elizabeth, dau. of John Dodson, Esq., of Lancaster, and has, with other issue,
    * Thomas Gresgarth, M.A. of Brasenose Coll., Oxford, and a Magistrate for co. Lancaster; b. 1835.
Mr. Edmondson is a J.P. and D.L. for co. Lancaster, and Lord of the Manor of Caton, co. Lancaster. His father was the first large worsted spinner in the kingdom. —Gresgarth Hall, Caton, Lancaster.

EDWARDS, CHARLES, Esq., of Wrington, Somerset.
Youngest son of the late Thomas Lyddon Edwards, Esq., of Brislington, Somerset, by Peggy, dau. of William Ball, Esq., of Donniford; b. 1819; m. 1847 Rachel, only child of Samuel Lund Fry, Esq., of Axbridge, Somerset, and has, with other issue,
    * Charles Lund Fry, b. 1849.
Mr. Edwards is a Magistrate for Somerset.—The Grove, Wrington, Somerset.

F

+FENTON, KIRBY, Esq., of Caldecot Hall, Warwickshire.
Son of the late — Fenton, Esq., of Caldecot Hall; b. 18—; is married, and has, with other issue,
    * William Kirkby, B.A. of Trinity Coll., Cambridge; b. 1834.
1040

Mr. Fenton is a Magistrate for co. Leicester, and Lord of the Manor and Patron of Caldecott.—Caldecott Hall, Nuneaton.

+FISHER, the Rev. GEORGE HUTCHINS, of Bentley Hall, Staffordshire.
Son of the late — Fisher, Esq., of Walsall; b. 1818. Educated at Christ's Coll., Cambridge (B.A. 1831, M.A. 1834); is a Magistrate for co. Stafford, and Incumbent of Willenhall, co. Stafford.—Bentley Hall, Walsall.

+FISHER, ROGER HORMAN-, Esq., of Freshford, Somerset.
Son of the late Roger Staples Fisher, Esq., of Freshford, who assumed the name of Horman on his marriage with Elizabeth, only child and heir of the late John Horman, Esq., of Pentonville; b. 1820; s. 1866. Educated at the Charterhouse and Ch. Ch., Oxford; called to the Bar at the Middle Temple 1845.—Freshford, Bath.

+FISHER, WILLIAM, Esq., of Maesfron, Montgomeryshire.
Son of the late W. Fisher, Esq., of Maesfron : b. 18—. Is a Magistrate for Montgomery (High Sheriff 1868). —Maesfron, Montgomery.

G

GELDART, the Rev. RICHARD JOHN, D.D.
Son of the late Rev. John Geldart: b. 1796. Educated at St. Catherine Hall. Cambridge (B.A. 1809, M.A. 1812, D.D. 1842) : is a Magistrate for co. Northampton, and Rector of Little Billing.—Little Billing Rectory, Northampton.

GLANVILLE, the Rev. EDWARD FANSHAWE.
Third son of the late Francis Glanville, Esq., of Catchfrench, Cornwall, by Elizabeth, dau. of Robert Fanshawe, Esq., R.N., Commissioner of Plymouth Dockyard; b. 1807; m. 1835 Mary Anne, dau. of the late Sir Scrope Bernard Morland, Bart., of Nether Winchendon, Bucks, and widow of the Rev. Frederick Charles Spencer, of Wheatfield, Oxon. Educated at Exeter Coll., Oxford (B.A. 1828, M.A. 1830), of which he was Fellow 1830-5 ; is a Magistrate for Oxfordshire ; was formerly Rector of Wheatfield, Oxon.—Clevedon House, Oxford.

GOLDSON, CHARLES BROWNE, Esq., of Blo' Norton, Norfolk.
Second son of the late James Goldson, Esq., of East Dereham, by Margaret, dau. of the late Rev. Charles Browne, Rector of Blo' Norton, and nephew of the late Rev. Charles Bowman Browne, of Blo' Norton: b. 1824; s. his uncle 1863. Educated at Caius Coll., Cambridge (B.A. 1857, M.A. 1860): is Lord of the Manor and Patron of Blo' Norton.—Blo' Norton Hall, East Harling, N. of B.

GOODENOUGH, the Rev. ROBERT WILLIAM.
Eldest son of the late Rev. R. P. Goodenough, by Cecilia, dau. of the Most Rev. W. Markham, D.D., Lord Archbishop of York, and grandson of the Right Rev. Samuel Goodenough, D.D., Lord Bishop of Carlisle; b. 1809; m. 1836 Elizabeth Anne, dau. of the late Anthony Litdesdale, Esq., and has issue.
    * Osborne Hall, Capt. R.A.: b. 1838.
Mr. Goodenough, who was educated at Westminster, and was Student of Ch. Ch., Oxford (B.A. 1830, M.A. 1832), is a Magistrate for Northumberland, and Vicar of Whittingham.—Whittingham Vicarage, Alnwick

H

HARRISON, JONATHAN STABLES, Esq., of Brandesburton Hall, Yorkshire.

Eldest son of the late Jonathan Harrison, Esq., of Scarboro', co. York, by Bessie, dau. of Seth Stables, Esq., of Pocklington ; *b.* 1818 ; *s.* 1867 ; *m.* 1851 Eliza Jane, dau. of Matthias Whitehead, Esq., of Park House, Selby, co. York, and has, with other issue,

• James Jonathan, *b.* 1857.

Mr. Harrison is a Dep.-Lieut. for the E. Riding of Yorkshire.—*Brandesburton Hall, Beverley.*

HARTLEY, JOHN, Esq., of The Oaks, Wheaton-Aston, and Prestwood, Staffordshire.

Second son of the late John Hartley, Esq., of Harborne, co. Stafford, by Margaret, dau. of J. Stevenson, Esq., of Douglas, Isle of Man; *b.* 1813 ; *m.* 1839 Emma, second surviving dau. of the late G. B. Thorneycroft, Esq., of Hadley Park, co. Salop, and Chapel House, co. Stafford, through whom he acquired the Wheaton-Aston property, and by whom he has, with other issue,

• George Thompson, *b.* 1844 ; educated at Harrow ; Cornet Queen's Own Royal Staffordshire Yeomanry Cavalry.

Mr. Hartley is a J.P. and D.L. for co. Stafford, and on the roll for High Sheriff (1869). This family was formerly of Hunslet, co. York, and migrated into Staffordshire at the commencement of the present century.—*The Oaks, Wolverhampton; Burlington Hotel, w.*

+**HEATHCOTE**, ROBERT, Esq., of Lobthorpe, Lincolnshire.

Only son of the late — Heathcote, Esq., by a French lady who remarried a German Baron, and cousin of Lord Aveland ; *b.* 1840. Educated in Germany and Trinity Coll., Cambridge (B.A. 1863); is Lord of the Manor of Lobthorpe.—*Lobthorpe, North Witham, Grantham.*

HEYCOCK, the Rev. CHARLES, of Pytchley, Northamptonshire.

Second son of the late John Heycock, Esq., of East Norton, co. Leicester, by Susanna, 2nd dau. of Tobias Hippisley, Esq., of Hambleton, co. Rutland, and uncle of Charles Heycock, Esq. (whom see) ; *b.* 1794; *s.* his cousin Henry Hensman, Esq., in this estate, 1854 ; *m.* 1831 Catharine, only child of Francis Bessill, Esq., of Knipton, co. Leicester, and has, with other issue, an only son,

• Charles Hensman, Lieut. 75th Foot ; *b.* 1841 ; *m.* 1865 Mary Jane, 2nd dau. of W. W. Chard, Esq., of Mount Tamar, near Plymouth.

Mr. Heycock, who was educated at St. John's Coll., Cambridge (B.A. 1816, M.A. 1823), is a Magistrate for co. Northampton ; was formerly Rector of Withcote and Incumbent of Owston, co. Leicester, and Surrogate.—*Pytchley House, Kettering.*

HEYCOCK, FREDERICK, Esq., of Braunston Manor, Rutlandshire.

Youngest son of the late John Heycock, Esq., of East Norton, co. Leicester, by Susanna, 2nd dau. of T. Hippisley, Esq., of Hambleton Manor, co. Rutland, and brother of the Rev. Charles Heycock (whom see) ; *b.* 1811 ; *m.* 1812 Mary, only child of E. Heywood, Esq., of Brampton, Hunts, and Bourn, co. Cambridge, and has, with other issue, • Alfred Heywood, *b.* 1841.—*Braunston Manor, Oakham.*

HOLLAND, WILLIAM RICHARD, Esq., of Barton-under-Needwood, Staffordshire.

Eldest son of the late Richard Holland, Esq., of Barton-under-Needwood, and Ashbourne, by Anne, dau. of the late John Smith, Esq., of Adbaston Hall, co. Stafford ; *b.* 1835 ; *s.* 1866 ; *m.* 1864 Sarah Martha, dau. of Samuel Healing, Esq., J.P., of Tewkesbury, co. Glou-

cester. Represents the ancient family of Holland, of Barton-under-Needwood (a branch of the Lancashire family), descended from Richard de Holland de Barton, to whom, in 7th Edward 2nd (1314), Thomas, Earl of Lancaster and Leicester, made extensive grants in Needwood Forest, the charter of which is recorded in the Augmentation Office.—*Ashbourne, Derby; Barton-under-Needwood, Burton-upon-Trent.*

HUBBARD, WILLIAM EGERTON, Esq., of Leonardslee, Sussex.

Youngest son of the late John Hubbard, Esq., of Stratford Grove, Essex, by Marianne, dau. of the late John Morgan, Esq., and brother of J. G. Hubbard, Esq., M.P. (whom see); *b.* 1812; *m.* 1835 Louisa Ellen, dau. of William Baldock, Esq., of Cowling, Kent, and has, with other issue, •

• William Egerton, *b.* 1844.

Mr. Hubbard is a Magistrate for Sussex.—*Leonardslee, Lower Beeding, Horsham; Athenæum Club, s.w.*

HULL, the Rev. JOHN.

Second son of the late John Hull, Esq., M.D., of Manchester, by Sarah, dau. of William Winstanley, Esq., of Woodcock Hall ; *b.* 1802; *m.* 1833 Lucy Brooke, dau. of Robert Bevan, Esq., of Rougham Rookery, and has, with other issue,

• Charles William, in Holy Orders, B.A. of Queen's Coll., Oxford; *b.* 1841.

Mr. Hull, who was educated at Brasenose Coll., Oxford (B.A. 1823, M.A. 1826), is Examining Chaplain to the Bishop of Manchester, Hon. Canon of the Cathedral, and Rector of Eaglescliffe, co. Durham ; was formerly Vicar of Poulton-le-Fylde. This family was formerly located at Poulton-le-Fylde. — *Eaglescliffe Rectory, Yarm.*

J

JERVIS, ERNEST SCOTT, Esq., of Eyford Park, Gloucestershire.

Youngest son of the late Col. George Ritso Jervis, of the Bombay Engineers (who *d.* 1851), by Harriet, dau. of Joseph George Brett, Esq., of Grove House, Brompton; *b.* 1838. Educated at Eton; entered the Army 1856, and served in the 106th Foot throughout the Persian War and Indian Mutiny; retired 1867.—*Eyford Park, Bourton-on-the-Water, Moreton-in-the-Marsh . E.I.U. Service Club, s.w. ; 42, Chester Square, s.w.*

JERVIS, GEORGE FREDERICK ROBINSON, Esq., of Croxton, Staffordshire.

Eldest son of the late Col. George Ritso Jervis, of the Bombay Engineers, by Harriet, dau. of Joseph George Brett, Esq., of Grove House, Brompton, Middlesex ; *b.* 1831 ; *s.* 1851 ; *m.* 1855 Léonie, youngest dau. of the Baron de Rosen, of Rakamois, Esthonia, Russia, and has, with other issue,

• Edward, *b.* 1862.

Mr. Jervis, who was educated at Eton and Exeter Coll., Oxford, and called to the Bar at the Middle Temple 1860, was formerly an officer in the Indian Army.—*Croxton, Eccleshall ; United University and E. I. U. Service Clubs, s.w.*

JOHNSON, JOHN HENRY, Esq., of St. Osyth's Priory, Essex.

Eldest son of the late John Johnson, Esq., of St. Osyth's Priory, by Anne, dau. of the late Wm. Haward, Esq. (who *d.* 1868); *b.* 1826 ; *s.* 1867. Is a Merchant in London, and Lord of the Manors of Ramsden Barrington, and of Fremnalls, Essex. He purchased this

5 A   1 (1)

property from the representatives of the Nassau family in 1863.—*St. Osyth's Priory, Colchester*; 16, *Mark Lane*, E.C.; 29, *Portland Place*, W.

K

KETTLEWELL, the Rev. SAMUEL, of Armley Grange, Yorkshire.

Son of the late Rev. William Kettlewell, of Kirkheaton, co. York, by Mary, dau. of Samuel Midgley, Esq., of Cookridge Hall, co. York; *b.* 1822; *m.* 1855 Anne Elizabeth, dau. of the late Samuel Eyres, Esq., of Armley, and has, with other issue,

　　* Henry William, *b.* 1857.

Mr. Kettlewell, who was educated at University Coll., Durham (M.A. 1862), is Incumbent of St. Mark's, Woodhouse, near Leeds.—*Armley Grange, Leeds.*

L

LEE, JOHN, Esq., of Woolley Firs, Berks.

Eldest son of the late Henry Pincke Lee, Esq., of Woolley Firs, by Matilda, dau. of Stanlake Batson, Esq., of Winkfield Place, Berks; *b.* 1812; *s.* 1826; *m.* 1864 Fanny, dau. of the Rev. Robert Ward, M.A., Rector of Santon Downham, Norfolk. Educated at Sandhurst Coll.; was formerly Capt. 34th Regt. This family are traditionally descended from the Lees, Earls of Lichfield, and have been seated at Woolley Green for more than two centuries.—*Woolley Firs, Maidenhead; Junior United Service Club, s.w.*

Heir Pres., his brother Stanlake (in Holy Orders), B.A., of Queen's Coll., Oxford, Rector of Broughton, near Stockbridge, Hants; *b.* 1817; *m.* 1841 Elizabeth, dau. of James Payn, Esq., of Kidwells Park, Maidenhead, and has issue three sons.

+LEESON-MARSHALL, RICHARD JOHN, Esq., of Shannon Vale, co. Kerry.

Third son of Robert Leeson, Esq., by Elizabeth, only surviving dau. and heir of the late Ralph Marshall, Esq., of Shannon Vale, whose name he has assumed; *b.* 1828; *m.* 1858 Zeena, dau. of the Ven. Ambrose Power, Archdeacon of Lismore. Is a Magistrate for co. Kerry.—*Shannon Vale, Tralee, co. Kerry.*

LISTER, JOHN, Esq., of Shibden Hall, Yorkshire.

Eldest son of the late John Lister, Esq., of Shibden Hall, by Louisa Ann, only dau. of Major Charles Grant, of the island of St. Vincent; *b.* 1847; *s.* 1868. Educated at Winchester and Brasenose Coll., Oxford; was admitted a Student of the Inner Temple 1868. This family has been resident at Shibden Hall since A.D. 1613, and traces its descent from Richard Lister, who purchased lands at Hipperholme, in the vicinity of Shibden Hall, *temp.* Henry VII. — *Shibden Hall, Halifax.*

Heir Pres., his brother Charles Edmond, of Caius Coll., Cambridge; *b.* 1849.

LOWTHER, WILLIAM, Esq.

Second surviving son of the late Hon. Col. Henry Cecil Lowther, M.P., of Barley Thorpe, Rutland (who *d.* 1867), by Lady Lucy Eleanor, eldest dau. of Philip, 5th Earl of Harborough; *b.* 1821; *m.* 1853 the Hon. Charlotte Alice, dau. of Lord Wensleydale. Was Attaché to Legation at Berlin 1841–52, Secretary to Legation at Naples 1862–58, Secretary to Legation at St. Petersburgh in 1858, Secretary of Legation at Berlin 1859–61, when he was made Secretary of Embassy; was appointed
1042

Minister Plenipotentiary to the Argentine Republic 1867; elected M.P. for Westmoreland 1868.—*Carlton and Travellers' Clubs, s.w.*; 122, *Park Street*, W.

LYLE, JOHN, Esq., of Bonython, Cornwall.

Youngest son of the late Richard Lyle, Esq., of Bonython (who *d.* 1829),by Grace, dau. of Thomas Peters, Esq.; *b.* 1799; *s.* his brother Joseph 1863; *m.* 1825 Mary Elizabeth, only dau. of the late Capt. Francis Storey, R.N., and niece of James Storey, Esq., of Crumlington Hall, Northumberland, and has, with other issue, an only son,

　　* Joseph, *b.* 1837; educated at Trinity Coll., Cambridge.

Mr. Lyle is Lord of the Manor of Bonython; also of the Trannack Estate in Sithney, and the Trenoweth Estate at the Lizard Point.—*Bonython, Helston.*

M

McCOMBIE, WILLIAM, Esq., of Tillyfour, Aberdeenshire.

Second son of the late Charles McCombie, Esq., of Tillyfour, by Anne, dau. of John Black, Esq., of Ardlaw; *b.* 1805. Educated at Aberdeen Coll.; is a Magistrate for co. Aberdeen, and President of the Chamber of Agriculture and Scottish Farmers' Club.—*Tillyfour, Whitehouse, near Aberdeen, N.B.; Douglas Hotel, Edinburgh.*

MEEK, Lady.

Mary Anne, dau. of Dr. Grant; *m.* 1853 (as 2nd wife) Sir James Meek, C.B., who *d.* 1856.—*Ilfracombe, Devon.*

P

PALMER, the Rev. GEORGE THOMAS.

Second son of the late George Palmer, Esq., of Boyne House, Kent, by Elizabeth, dau. of John Eede, Esq.; *b.* 1802; *m.* 1841 Clarissa Maria, younger dau. and co-heir of the Rev. Trefusis Lovell, Rector of St. Luke, Middlesex, and formerly Archdeacon of Derry, Ireland (last male representative of the ancient family of the Lovells, of Skelton, co. York), and has issue,

　　* Clarissa Georgiana, and Henrietta Maria.

Mr. Palmer was educated at the Charter House and Brasenose Coll., Oxford (B.A. 1824, M.A. 1827, in which latter year he was called to the Bar and practised till 1835, when he was ordained.—*United University Club, s.w.*; 53, *Lowndes Square, s.w.*

PALMER, the Rev. JAMES NELSON, of Breamore, Hants.

Son of the late Rev. James Nelson Palmer, of Breamore, by Elizabeth, dau. of the late Robert Mushet, Esq., of the Royal Mint; *b.* 1832; *s.* 1864; educated at Eton and St. John's Coll., Oxford (B.A. 1856, M.A. 1857); late Rector and Patron of the Donative Advowson of Breamore; was formerly Curate of Shipston-on-Stour.—*Breamore, Salisbury.*

S

+SALMOND, DUNCAN, Esq., of Rothesay, Buteshire.

Son of the late D. Salmond, Esq.; *b.* 18—. Is a J.P. and D.L. for co. Bute.—*Rothesay, Buteshire.*

+SELLAR, JOHN AUGUSTUS, Esq., of Ardtornish, Argyllshire.

Eldest son of the late Patrick Sellar, Esq., of Ardtornish; *b.* 18—; *s.* 1851. Is a Magistrate for co. Argyll, and Lord of the Barony of Ardtornish.—*Ardtornish, Oban. N.B.*

CORRIGENDA.

ALEXANDER, the Rev. John, of Carne : his wife Mary *d.* 1868.

ANNALY : Lady Annaly *d.* May 12, 1866.

ASHFORDBY-TRENCHARD, J., Esq., has a son *b.* 1868.

BALDWIN, W. J. A., Esq., of Dalton-in-Furness : add to address—*Militia and Yeomanry, and Gryphon Clubs,* s.w.

BARING, the Hon. and Rev. Frederick, *d.* June 1868.

BEVAN, G. P., Esq. : add to address—*Junior Athenæum Club,* w.

BIDWELL, Leonard Shelton, Esq., of Thetford, Norfolk, *d.* May 1868, aged 86.

BLACKETT, William Fenwick, Esq., *d.* June 1868.

BOOTH, George, Esq., of Lara, co. Wicklow : his wife Georgiana *d.* May 1868, aged 29.

BRIGSTOCKE, William Owen, Esq., of Gellydwyll : Emmeline his wife *d.* June 1868.

BROADMEAD, Thomas Palfrey, Esq., has a son *b.* 1868.

BROADWOOD, Thomas, Esq., of Holmbush, Sussex. This property was sold in 1866 to — Vans Agnew, Esq., a Merchant in London.

BROWNLOW, Earl : his Lordship *m.* June 1868 Lady Adelaide, dau. of Henry John, 18th Earl of Shrewsbury.

CAVENDISH, Lord Edward, has a son *b.* May 1868.

CHERRY, Benjamin, Esq. : his eldest son, the Rev. Benjamin Newman Cherry, *m.* June 1868 Rosa Georgina, younger dau. of Edward Pomeroy Barrett Lennard, Esq., of St. Leonard's, Perth, West Australia.

COLQUHOUN, William C., Esq., of Clathick, *m.* June 1868 Charlotte Emily Julian, 2nd dau. of the Rev. Leonard Shafto Orde, of Weetwood, Northumberland.

EBURY, Lord : The Hon. Robert Wellesley Grosvenor has a son *b.* June 1868.

FENWICK, James T., Esq., of Longframlington, *d.* June 1868.

KINNERSLEY, Edward, Esq., of Binfield Manor, *d.* June 1868.

LEIGH, J. WARD-BROUGHTON-, Esq., of Brownsover Hall, *d.* June 1868.

LILLIE, Sir John Scott, C.B., *d.* June 1868.

LLOYD, E. P., Esq., of Glansevin, *d.* June 1868.

LONGUEVILLE, T. L., Esq., of Penylan : his eldest son Thomas *m.* June 1868 Mary Frances, only dau. of the late Alexander Robertson, Esq., of Balgownie Lodge, co. Aberdeen.

LOWTHER, Sir J. H., Bart., *d.* June 1868.

MILLS, J., Esq., of Bisterne : his eldest son John *m.* June 1868 Louisa Frances, eldest dau. of Thomas Entwisle, Esq., of Wolhayes, Hants.

OWEN, Major William Mostyn, of Woodhouse, *d.* June 1868, aged 62.

RIDDELL, Lady Frances, *d.* June 1868.

RICHARDS, John, Esq., of Macmine : his eldest son George Gledstanes, Capt. Wexford Militia, *m.* June 1868 Marian, 2nd dau. of the late Loftus A. Bryan, Esq., of Upton, co. Wexford.

ST. AUBYN, the Rev. H. MOLESWORTH- : his eldest son Hender John *d.* June 1868.

SILY, Sir S. E., *d.* June 1868.

INDEX OF NAMES

ARRANGED UNDER THE SEVERAL COUNTIES.

Charley, of Seymour Hill
Cuppage, of Mount Edwards
Dalway, of Bella Hill
Dalway, of Belmont
Davison, of Belfast
De la Cherois-Crommelin, of Rockport
Dickey, of Cullybackey
Dickey, of Hollybrooke House
Dobbs, of Castle Dobbs
Douglas, of Dervoch
Ferguson, of Belfast
Fullerton, of Ballintoy
Fulton, of Braidujle
Gage, of Ballinacree
Gage, of Rathlin Island
Gibson, of Belfast
Gray, of Graymount
Haliday, of Charnmoney
Hannay, of Ballylough
Hartwell, of Glenmona
Hassard, of Parkmore
Heyland, of Glendarragh
Higginson, of Brook Hill
Higginson, of Brooklyn
Higginson, of Lisburn
Hutchinson, of Ballymoney
Hutchinson, of Stranocum House
Jopes, of Moneyglass
Lanyon, of White Abbey
Lecky, of Bushmills
Lee, of Aheghill
Legge, of Malone House
Leslie, of Leslie Hill
Leslie, of Seaport
Lyons, of Old Park
Macartney, of Lissanour
Macclintock, of Millmount
McDonnell, of Kilmore
McGarel, of Maghramorne House
McGilldowny, of Clare Park
McNeile, of Parkmount
Montgomery, of Bentarden
Montgomery, of Birch Hall
Moore, of Ballidivity
Moore, of Moore Fort
O'Hara, of Crebilly
O'Hara, of O'Hara Brook
O'Rorke, of Ballybollan
Ottley, of Landmore House
Owens, of Holestone
Pakenham, of Langford Lodge
Patrick, of Ducminning
Richardson, of Lambeg
Rowan, of Mount Davys
Rowan-Glegg, of Glynn Park
Smyth, of Lisburn
Tennent, of Rush Park
Thomson, of Castleton
Thomson, of Low Wood
Turnly, of Drumnasole
Verner, of Belfast
Verner, of Lilliput
Whitla, of Lismoyne
Young, of Glengormu Castle

ARGYLLSHIRE.

Argyll, Duke of
Breadalbane, Earl of
Morton, Earl of
Colonsay, Lord
Campbell, Sir Alexander, Bart.
Campbell, Sir Donald, Bart.
Campbell, Sir J. W., Bart.
Campbell, Sir L. H. D., Bart.

Orde, Sir J. P., Bart.
Riddell, Sir T. M., Bart.
Anderson, of Cromall Lodge
Callander, of Ardkinglas
Campbell, of Ardpatrick House
Campbell, of Aros
Campbell, of Auchindarroch
Campbell, of Ballimore
Campbell, of Balliveolan
Campbell, of Ballochyle
Campbell, of Barbreck House
Campbell, of Barcaldine
Campbell, of Craignish and Jura
Campbell, of Drimnamuckloch
Campbell, of Dunmore
Campbell, of Glendaruel
Campbell, of Inverneil
Campbell, of Killerry
Campbell, of Lochnell
Campbell, of Ormidale
Campbell, of Ormsary
Campbell, of Sonachan
Campbell, of South Hall
Campbell, of Stonefield
Campbell, of Strachur and Ardgartan
Compton, of Tarloisk
Dalgliesh, of Ardnamurchan
Douglas, of Glenfinart
Eddington, of Glencreggan
Ewing, of Lismore Lodge
Finlay, of Castle Toward
Fletcher, of Dunan's House
Forbes, of Kingairloch
Forsyth, of Glengorm
Fraser, of Skipness Castle
Gascoigne, of Craignish Castle
Gow-Steuart, of Colonsay
Graham-Campbell, of Shirvan
Greenhill-Gardyne, of Glenforsa
Guthrie, of Duart
Hall, of Killean
Hunter, of Halton
Laidlay, of Drumore
Lamont, of Knockdow
Lamont, of Lamont
Macalister, of Glenbarr and Cour
Macdonald, of Inchkenneth
Macdonald, of Sanda
Macdonald-Moreton, of Largie Castle
McDougall, of Dunolly Castle
McDougall, of Gallanach
Macfie, of Airds
McIver, of Asknish
Mackay, of Bighouse
Maclachlan, of Maclachlan
Maghaine, of Lochbuy
Maclaverty, of Keill
Maclean, of Ardgour
Maclean, of Pennycross
MacNeale, of Ugadale
MacNeill, of Canna
McNeill, of Carskey
Macquarie, of Jarvisfield
Malcolm, of Calitonmar and Poltalloch
Moir, of Milton
Morrison, of Islay
Pender, of Minard
Polock, of Ronachan
Popham, of Ardchattan
Ramsay, of Kildalton
Rankin, of Otter
Ross, of Dailing
Sellar, of Ardtornish
Stewart, of Auchnacone
Stewart, of Coll and Knochrioch
Uppleby, of Airdlishug

ARMAGH CO.

Armagh, Archbishop of
Charlemont, Earl of
Gosford, Earl of
Lurgan, Lord
Macartney, Sir J., Bart.
Molyneux, Sir C., Bart.
Stronge, Sir J. M., Bart.
Verner, Sir Wm., Bart.
Alexander, of Acton
Alexander, of Forkhill
Armstrong, of Killylea
Atkinson, of Crowbill
Blacker, of Carrick Blacker
Blacker, of Elm Park
Bond, of Bondville
Bond, of The Argory and Drumsill
Brush, of Benburb House
Caulfeild, of Hockley
Chambré, of Hawthorn Hill
Close, of Drumbanagher
Cope, of Loughgall Manor
Cross, of Dartan
De Salis, of Tanderagee
Dobbin, of Armagh
Dobbin, of The Mall
Douglas, of Mountain Lodge
Eastwood, of Castletown
Foxall, of Killeavy Castle
Garland, of Drummilly
Harden, of Harry brook
Harris, of Ashfort
Hutchinson, of Ballyrath
Kirk, of Annevale
M'Clintock, of Fellowes Hall
Molesworth, of Fairlawn
Obré, of Chantilew
Pooler, of Tyross
Quinn, of The Agency
Richardson, of Rich Hill
St. George, of Wood Park
Synnot, of Ballymoyer House
Tenison, of Port Nelligan
Verner, of Churchhill
Von Stieglitz, of The Glen
Woodhouse, of Portadown

AYRSHIRE.

Ailsa, Marquis of
Bute, Marquis of
Hastings, Marquis of
Eglinton, Earl of
Glasgow, Earl of
Orkney, Earl of
Barclay, Sir D. W., Bart.
Blair, Sir E. H., Bart.
Blane, Sir H. S., Bart.
Cathcart, Sir J. A., Bart.
Cuninghame, Sir T. M., Bart.
Dalrymple, Sir H. H., Bart.
Fairlie, Sir W. J. C., Bart.
Fergusson, Sir J., Bart.
Menteith, Sir J. Stuart-, Bart.
Shaw, Sir John, Bart.
Alexander, of Ballochmyle
Alexander, of Boyd-stone
Baird, of Cambusdoon
Bell, of Enterkine
Blackburn, of Ivonholm
Blair, of Blair
Boswell, of Auchinleck
Boyd, of Orchard and Law Castle
Boyle, of Shewalton
Brisbane, of Brisbane
Brown, of Waterhaughs

Burnett, of Gadgirth
Campbell, of Auchmannoch
Campbell, of Barquharrie
Campbell, of Craigie
Campbell, of Fairfield House
Campbell, of Skerrington
Campbell, of Treesbanks and Cess-
    nock
Carmichael, of Mansfield
Cathcart, of Auchendrane House
Cathcart, of Craigengillan
Cathcart, of Genoch and Knockdolian
Cooper, of Failford and Smithstone
Craufuird, of Grange
Craufurd, of Ardmillan
Craufurd, of Auchenames
Cuninghame, of Lainshaw
Cuninghame, of Logan
Dunlop, of Dunlop
Fairlie, of Coodham
Fairlie, of Holmes
Forsayth, of Failzerton
Gray-Farquhar, of Gilmilnscroft
Hamilton, of Cairn Hill
Hamilton, of Hullerhist
Hamilton, of Sundrum
Hamilton-Campbell, of Nether Place
Houison-Craufurd, of Craufurdland
Hughes-Onslow, of Balkissoch
Hunter, late of Bounyton
Hunter, of Hunterston
Kennedy, of Dalquharran Castle and
    Dunure
Kennedy, of Kirkmichael
M'Adam, of Ballochmorrie
M'Alester, of Kennox House
McKerrell, of Hill House
Macredie, of Perceton
Mure, of Caldwell
Neill, of Barnweill and Swindbridge-
    muir
Oswald, of Auchincruive
Patrick, of Woodside and Ladyland
Pollok-Morris, of Craig
Robertson-Glasgow, of Montgreenan
Scott, of Hawkhill
Shedden, of Morris Hill
Smith-Cuninghame, of Caprington
Tait, of Milrig House
Warner, of Ardeer
Weson, of Corwar
Wrey, of Thorntoun House

BANFFSHIRE.

Fife, Earl of
Seafield, Earl of
Abercromby, Sir G. S., Bart.
Dunbar, Sir Wm., Bart.
Gordon, Sir R. G., Bart.
Innes, Sir J. M., Bart.
Bruce, of Logie
Duff, of Glasshaugh
Duff, of Haddo
Garden-Campbell, of Troup
Gordon, of Cairnfield
Gordon-Duff, of Park and Drummuir
Grant, of Arndilly
Harvey, of Carnousie
Leslie, of Kininvie
Steuart, of Auchlunkart House
Stewart, of Lesmurdie
Tayler, of Glenburry

BEDFORDSHIRE.

Bedford, Duke of
Dynevor, Lord

Ongley, Lord
St. John, Lord
Lucas, Baroness
Burgoyne, Sir J. M., Bart.
Osborn, Sir G. R., Bart.
Payne, Sir C., Dart.
Payne, Sir C. G., Bart.
Turner, Sir E. H. Page-, Bart.
Adey, of The Cell
Alington, of Little Barford
Alston, of Odell Castle
Barnard, of Kempston Hoo
Barnard, of Cople House
Barnett, of Stratton Park
Brandreth, of Houghton Hall
Brooks, of Flitwick Manor
Chalk, of Wilden Manor
Cooper, of Toddington Manor
Coventry-Campion, of Westoning
Crawley, of Stockwood
Cust, of Cockayne Hatley
Dawes, of Moggerhanger House
De Lautour, of Hexton House
Edwards, of Arlesey Bury
Foster, of Brickhill
Foster, of Sandy Place
Gambier, of Sharnbrook
Gibbard, of Sharnbrook House
Gilpin, of Hockliffe Grange
Green, of Felmersham Grange
Harter, of Cranfield Court
Harvey, of Ickwellbury
Higgins, of Turvey Abbey
Higgins, of Turvey House
Higgins, of Picts Hill
Higgins, of Rosewood
Inglis, of Milton Bryant
Leigh, of Looton Hoo Park
Lindsell, of Fairfield
Littledale, of Kempston Grange
Moore, of Maulden Cottage
Mountain, of Blunham
Musgrave, of Sh llington Manor
Orlebar, of Crawley House
Orlebar, of Hinwick House
Osborn, of Campton Manor
Paddon, of Thralcsend
Palmer, of Clifton Lodge
Pearse, of Harlington
Pearson, of Tempsford Hall
Peel, of Sandy Lodge
Polhill-Turner, of Howbury Hall
Pym, of The Hazells
Reynsford, of Henlow Grange
Repton, of Odell
Russell, of Oakley House
Sier, of Ravensden
Smart, of Linden Hall
Smith, of Aspley House
Smyth, of Houghton Regis
Starey, of Milton Ernest
Stuart, of Kempston
Thornton, of Kempston
Thornton, of Goldington
Thornton, of Moggerhanger
Thynne, of Hawnes Park
Trevor, of Tingrith House
Tucker, of Pavenham Bury
Tylecote, of Marston-Moretaine
Wade-Gery, of Bushmead Priory
Whitbread, of Southill and Cardington
Williamson, of Kempston Manor

BERKSHIRE.

Her Majesty the Queen
Donegal, Marquis of

Downshire, Marquis of
Abingdon, Earl of
Carnarvon, Earl of
Craven, Earl of
Radnor, Earl of
Barrington, Viscount
Annaly, Lord
Braybrooke, Lord
Gardner, Lord
Ormathwaite, Lord
Bowyer, Sir G., Bart.
Conroy, Sir E., Bart.
East, Sir G. A. G., Bart.
Gooch, Sir D., Bart.
Hayter, Sir W. G., Bart.
Hunter, Sir C. S. P., Bart.
Martin, Sir W. F., Bart.
Morshead, Sir W. C., Bart.
Russell, Sir Charles, Bart.
Throckmorton, Sir N. W., Bart.
Willshire, Sir A. R. T., Bart.
Young, Sir G., Bart.
Aldworth, of West Hagbourne
Allfrey, of Wokefield Park
Arbuthnot, of Coworth House
Austen-Leigh, of Scarletts
Barker, of Stanlake Park
Barnett, of Sunningdale
Barrett, of Milton House
Beale, of Warfield Grove
Beauchamp, of Beech Hall
Bennett, of Faringdon House
Benyon, of Englefield House
Best, of Donnington Castle
Blagrave, of Calcot Park
Blandy-Jenkins, of Kinston Bagpuize
Blane, of Folie'on Park
Blyth, of Woolhampton House
Boldero, of Hurst Grove
Bosanquet, of Benham Park
Bowles, of Milton Hill
Breedon, of Delabere House
Bridges, of Holly Spring
Bulkeley, of Clewer Lodge
Bulkeley, of Linden Hall
Bunbury, of Marlston House
Bunny, of Spleen Hill
Burr, of Aldermaston Court
Butler, of Kirby House
Butler, of Woodstone
Campbell, of Buscot Park
Caswall, of Elm Grove
Cathcart, of Ascot Lodge
Chatteris, of Sandleford Priory
Cherry, of Den end House
Cherry, of Denford
Cobham, of Shinfield Manor
Cobham, of Leighton Park
Collins, of Betterton House
Coney, of Braywick Grove
Court, of Castlemans
Coxe, of Edington
Croft, of Grayshars Lodge
Crowdy, of Chieveley
Crutchley, of Sunning Hill Park
Currie, of Adbury House
Delane, of Ascot
Dickson, of Beenham
Duffield, of Marcham Park
Dundas, of Barton Court
Dunn, of Inglewood
Elliott, of Hurley Manor
Eykyn, of The Willows
Eyre, of Shaw House
Eyre, of Welford Park
Eyston, of East Hendred House
Ferard, of Ascot Place

Fitzgerald, of The Firs, Binfield
Floyd, of Frilsham Manor
Forbes, of Selwood Park
Forbes, of Winkfield Place
Foster, of Clewer Manor
Fywke, of Midgham House
Franklyn, of Lovel Hill
Fuller-Maitland, of Wargrave
Garth, of Haines Hill
Gataker, of White Knights
Gibbard, of Sharnbrook
Gibson. of Sandhurst Lodge
Gilliat, of Fern Hill
Golding, of Maiden Erleigh
Goodlake, of Wadley and Letcombe
  Regis
Green, of Midgham House
Grenfell, of Ray Lodge
Grey, of Lynwood
Griffith, of Padworth House
Grimshawe, of Aspley Guise
Harford, of Down Place
Hargreaves, of Arborfield Hall
Hargreaves, of Silwood
Hartley, of Bucklebury
Hay, of Harewood Lodge
Hayward-Southby, of Carswell
Hedges, of Wallingford Castle
Hercy, of Cruchfield House
Hibbert, of Braywick
Higgins, of Rosewood
Hilliard, of Little Wittenham
Hippesley, of Lamborne Place
Honywood, of Chilton Lodge
Hopkins, of Tidmarsh House
Hopkins, of Pangbourne Lodge
Howard, of Yattendon
Howard-Vyse, of Old Windsor
Hughes, of Donnington Priory
Hunter, of Beech Hill
Jekyll, of Wargrave
Johnson, of King's Mead
King, of Warfield Hall
Kinnersley, of Binfield Manor
Lee, of Ditton House
Lee, of Woolley Firs
Lenthall, of Bessels Leigh
Leveson-Gower, of Bill Hill
Leycester, of White Place
Loyd-Lindsay, of Lockinge
Martin-Atkins, of Kingston-Lisle
Martin-Atkins, of Farley Castle
Matthews, of Donnington House
Merry, of Highlands
Monck, of Coley Park
Montagu, of Wargrave Hall
Morland, of Sheepstead House
Morland, of West Ilsley
Morrison, of Basildon Park
Mount, of Wasing Place
Mowbray, of Warrennes Wood
Norris, of Sutton Courtney
Oliver, of Circourt
Palmer, of Canon Hill
Palmer, of Holme Park
Parker, of Brunchetts
Phillimore, of Shiplake House
Pocock, of Bridge Lodge
Pusey, of Pusey
Rain, of Chilton House
Ramsbottom, late of Woodside
Reade, of Ipsden Place
Riley, of Forest Hill
Robinson, of Woodbourne House
Rose, of Baulking
Sawyer, of Heywood Lodge
Ray, of Oakley Court
1048

Scott, of Lovel Hill
Shelley, of Elcot House
Siocock, of Donnington
Standish, of Farley Hill
Stevens, of Bradfield
Stone, of Streatley House
Storer, of Purley Park
Sutton, of Benham Park
Taylor, of Culverlands
Thackeray, of The Grove
Thoyts, of Sulhamstead House
Tucker, of Bourton House
Tull, of Crookham House
Valpy, of Emborne Lodge
Van de Weyer, of New Lodge
Vansittart, of Bisham Abbey
Vansittart, of Chuff
Vansittart, of Shottesbrooke Park
Vernon, of Ardington House
Vincent, of Lily Hill
Walter, of Bearwood
Watson, of Brunchetts
Webster, of Binfield Court
Wheble, of Bulmershe Court
Wiggett, of Allanbay
Wilder, of Purley and Sulham
Willes, of Goodrest
Willes, of Hungerford Park and Clif-
  ton Lodge
Williams, of Warfield Lodge
Wilson, of Whiteley Hall
Wroughton, of Woolley Park
Ximenes, of Bear Ash
Young, of Hare Hatch

BERWICKSHIRE.

Glasgow, Earl of
Haddington, Earl of
Home, Earl of
Lauderdale, Earl of
Polwarth, Lord
Sinclair, Lord
Boswall, Sir G. A. F. Houston-, Bart.
Campbell, Sir H. Hume-, Bart.
Home, Sir G., Bart.
Marjoribanks, Sir J., Bart.
Pringle, Sir J., Bart.
Baillie-Hamilton, of Rambleton Law
Balfour, of Newton Don
Bonar, late of Kimmerghame
Brown, of Longformacus
Campbell-Renton, of Lamberton and
  Mordington
Campbell-Swinton, of Kimmerghame
Cathcart, of Caldra
Collingwood, of Cornhill House
Cosens, of Peelwalls
Cosens-Weir, of Bogangreen
Fairholme, of Chapel-on-Leader
Fergusson-Home, of Bassendean
Fordyce-Buchanan, of Kelloe
Forsyth-Brown, of Whitsome-Newton
Greig, of Eccles
Haig, of Bemersyde
Hay, of Dunse Castle
Hodgson, of Carham
Home, of Broomhouse
Hood, of Kames
Hood, of Stoneridge
Hume, of Ninewells
Hunter, of Antons Hill
Innes, of Ayton Castle
L'Amy, of Netherbyres
Miller, of Manderston
Milne-Holme, of Milne Graden

Robertson, of Ladykirk
Roy, of Nenthorn
St. Clair, of Eyemouth
Sandys-Lumsdaine, of Lumsdaine and
  Blanerne
Scott, of Mertoun House
Spottiswoode, of Spottiswoode
Trotter, of Charter Hall
Turnbull, of Abbey St. Bathan's
Wilkie, of Foulden House

BRECKNOCKSHIRE.

Beaufort, Duke of
Camden, Marquis
Hereford, Viscount
Tredegar, Lord
Bailey, Sir J. R., Bart.
Hamilton, Sir E. A., Bart.
Bold, of Llanfihangel-Tal-y-Llyn
Davies, of Court-y-Gollen
Davies, of Neuadd
Devereux, of Middlewood
De Winton, of Priory Hill
De Winton, of Maesderwen
De Winton, of Tymawr
Dickinson, of Glan-onddu
Evans, of Brecon
Fredericks, of Abermellte
Fuller-Maitland, of Garth
Holford, of Buckland
Hotchkis, of Llanwysk
Jones, of Glyn Pedr
Jones-Williams, of Coity Mawr
Lloyd, of Aberllech
Lloyd, of Dinas
Marryat, of Maesydderwen
Maund, of Tymawr
Mayberry, of Brecon
Miles, of Llangattock
Morgan, of Bolgold
Pearce, of Ferwdgrech
Powell, of Walton Mount
Price, of Castle Madoc
Price, of Llanddu
Raikes, of Treberfydd
Roberts, of Pendarren House
Roche, of Trecunter Park
Seymour, of Porthmawr
Taunton, of Treberfydd
Thomas, of Llwynmadoc
Thomas, of Penrhapentre
Thomas, of Welfield House
Vaughan, of Builth
Vaughan, of Velin Newydd
Venables, of Llysdinam
Watkins, of Pennoyre
Williams, of Penpont
Wood, of Glasbury

BUCKINGHAMSHIRE.

Buccleuch and Queensberry, Duke of
Buckingham and Chandos, Duke of
Boston, Lord
Carington, Lord
Chesham, Lord
Chetwode, Sir J. N. L., Bart.
Clayton, Sir W. R., Bart.
Dashwood, Sir E. H., Bart.
Duncombe, Sir P. D. P., Bart.
Foulis, Sir Henry, Bart.
Fremantle, Sir T. F., Bart.
Morland, Sir F. B., Bart.
Palmer, Sir C. J., Bart.

Rothschild, Sir A., Bart.
Throckmorton, Sir N. W., Bart.
Verney, Sir H., Bart.
Willoughby, Sir J. C.. Bart.
Young, Sir C. L., Bart.
Acton, of Fernacres
Allen, of The Vache
Barlow, of Taplow
Barrington, of Westbury Manor
Bartlett, of Peverel Court
Baylis, of Hedgerley
Baynes, of Adstock
Bent, late of Wexham Lodge
Bernard, of Winchendon Priory
Blount, of Orchihill
Boteler-Casberd, of Taplow
Boultbee, of Iver Grove
Bracebridge, of Chetwode Priory
Bramley-More, of Langley Lodge
Cameron, of Hampden House
Carrington, of Great Missenden
Carson, of Spinfield
Cavendish, of Thornton Hall
Chambers. of Oakley
Chester, of Chicheley Hall
Chetwode, of Chilton House
Christie-Miller, of Britwell House
Clayton, of Hedgerley Park
Clowes, of Delaford Park
Cocks, of Thames Bank
Coleman, of Stoke Park
Collett, of Hale House
Connell, of the Lilies
Crewe, of Loakes Hill
Darby, of Stoke Court
Dauncy, of Little Harwood
Dayrell, of Lillingston Dayrell
De Broc, of Aston Clinton
D'Israeli, of Hughenden Manor
Drake, of Castle Thorp
Drake, of Shardeloes
Drummond, of Denham
Drummond. of Tile House
Duncan, of Bradwell House
Du Pré, of Wilton Park
Eyre, of Padbury
Farrell, of Woughton
Farrer, of Brayfield
Fitzgerald, of Shalstone House
Fortescue, of Dropmore House
Fuller, of Hyde House and German's
Goodall, of Dinton Hall
Graves, of Bradenham House
Gregory, of Castle Hill
Grenfell, of Taplow
Grote, of Wexham Park
Gyll, of Wyrardisbury House
Hall, of Datchet
Hanbury, of Hitcham
Hanmer, of Rushmere Lodge
Hanmer. of Stockgrove
Harcourt, of Ankerwyke
Hargreaves, of Hall Barn Park
Harvey, of Langley Park
Hibbert, of Chalfont Lodge
Hibbert, of Chalfont Park
Higginson, of Great Marlow
Hoare, of Wavendon Hall
Howard-Vyse, of Stoke Place
Hoyle, of Kames
Hubbard, of Addington Manor
Irby, of Taplow Grange
Jenney, of Drayton Lodge
Knapp, of Little Linford
Lambert, of Denham Court
Lee, of Hartwell House
Levy, of Woughton Green

Lovett, of Liscombe House
Lowndes, of Bletchley
Lowndes, of Broughton
Lowndes, of Chesham Bury
Lowndes, of North Crawley
Lowndes, of Whaddon Hall
Lowndes, of Winslow House
Mackenzie, of Fawley Court
Marjoribanks, of Greenlands
Martyn, of Ludgershall
Meeking, of Richings Park
Miller, of Britwell House
Morgan, of Biddlesden Park
Needham, of Datchet House
Newman, of Brands House.
Noble, of Berry Hill
Parkinson, of Cholesbury
Partridge, of Horsenden House
Pigott, of Doddershall
Pinfold, of Walton Hall
Plaistowe, of Lee
Potter, of Missenden Abbey
Fowell, of Tickford Abbey
Pratt, of Ovington House
Rickets, of Dorton House
Robarts, of Lillingstone
Rose, of Rayners
Rothschild, of Mentmore
Russell, of Chequers
Schuster, of Iver Park
Scott-Murray, of Danesfield nd
    Hambleden
Senior, of Broughton House
Small, of Clifton Reynes
Smyth, of St. John's Lodge
Stratton, of Turweston House
Stuart, late of Langley Broom House
Sutton, late of Rossway
Swabey, of Langley Marish
Tindal, of Aylesbury
Tompson, of Iver
Tower, of Huntsmore Park
Trevelyan, of Wolverton
Tyringham, of Tyringham
Uthwatt, of Maids Moreton House
    and Great Linford Place
Wanklyn, of Fulmer Place
Ward, late of Taplow Court
Watts, of Hanslope Park
Way, of Alderbourne
Way, of Denham Place
Wells, of Huntercombe House
Wetherad, of Seymour Court
Williams, of Crawley Grange
Williams, of Temple House
Williams, of Tring Park
Young, of Quainton

BUTESHIRE.

Hamilton, Duke of
Bute, Marquis of
Fullarton, of Kilmichael
Hoyle, of Eames Castle
Jamieson, of Rothesay
Miller, of Millburn
Muir, of Foley House
Salmond, of Rothesay
Sandford, of Wyndham
Sharp, of Rothesay

CAITHNESS-SHIRE.

Portland, Duke of
Caithness, Earl of
Duffus, Lord

Anstruther, Sir R., Bart.
Dunbar, Sir G. S., Bart.
Sinclair, Sir J., Bart.
Sinclair, Sir George. Bart.
Threipland, Sir P. M., Bart.
Bentley-Innes, of Thrumster
Guthrie, of Scots Calder
Henderson, of Stempster
Horne, of Stirkoke
Macdonald, of Sandside House
Macleay, of Keiss Castle
Sinclair, of Dunbeath Castle
Sinclair, of Forss
Smith, of Olrig House
Strong, of Camster
Sutherland, of Forse
Traill, of Castle Hill

CAMBRIDGESHIRE.

Leeds, Duke of
De la Warr, Earl
Hardwicke, Earl of
Ely, Bishop of
K, Lord
Pigot, Sir Robert, Bart.
Peyton, Sir A. W., Bart.
Adeane, of Babraham
Allix, of Swaffham House
Astell, of Woodbury Hall
Ball, of Burwell
Bamford, of Impington Hall
Bateson, of Horseheath Lodge
Baumgartner, of Milton House
Bendyshe, of Barrington Hall
Bennet, of Cheveley
Benyon, of Stetchworth Park
Brady, of Ely
Calvert, of Childerley Hall
Camps, of Wilburton
Cheere, of Papworth Hall
Cropley, of Egremont House
Dayrell, of Shudy Camps Park
De Fréville, of Hinxton
Eaton, of Stetchworth Park
Foster, of Brooklands
Frost, of Wratting Park
Fryer, of Chatteris
Fryer, of Moulton Paddocks
Gardner, of Chatteris
Gardner, of Fordham Abbey
Godfrey, of Kennett
Goodwin, of Gildersham
Graham-Foster-Pigott, of Abington
    Pigotts
Hailstone, of Anglesey Abbey
Hall, of Ely
Hall, of Weston Colville
Hamond, of Pampisford Hall
Haviland, of Ditton Hall
Haynes, of Grove House
Herbert, of The Caldrees
Hicks, of Wentworth Teagle
Hoblun, of Bartlow
Huddleston, of Sawston Hall
Huddleston, of Upwell Hall
Jenyns, of Bottisham Hall
King, of Madingly
Macaulay, of Ardingcaple House
Manners, of Cheveley Park
Martin, of Littleport
Mortlock, of Abington
Newton, of Croxton Park
Newton, of The Downs
Page, of Ely
Pearce-Serocold, of Cherry hinton
1019

Pell, of Wilburton Manor
Pemberton, of Newton
Pemberton, of Trumpington
Perkins, of Thriplow
Pigott, of Dullingham House
Porcher, of Borough Green
Portman, of Hare Park
Raymond, of Hildersham Hall
St. Quintin, of Hatley Park
Simpson, of Longstowe Hall
Smith, of Dry Drayton
Sperling, of Papworth St. Agnes
Stanley, of Longstowe Hall
Tharp, of Chippenham Park
Tilson-Marsh, of Stretham Manor
Townley, of Fulbourn
Vipan, of Sutton
Wale, of Little Shelford
Whitting, of Thorney Abbey
Wilkinson, of Upper Hare Park
Woodham, of Shepreth
Wortham, of Keesworth House
Young, of Wisbech

CARDIGANSHIRE.

Lisburne, Earl of
Vaughan, Viscount
Lloyd, Sir T. D., Bart.
Pryse, Sir P., Bart.
Bonsall, of Fronfraith
Bonsall, of Glanrheidol
Boultbee, of Noyadd
Bowen, of Troedyrawr
Brigstocke, of Blaenpant
Buck, of Stradmore
Chambers, of Hafod
Davies, of Castle Green
Davies, of Tyglyn Aeron
Durham, of Aberystwith
Fitzwilliams, of Adpar
Gwynne, of Monachty
Gwynne, of Rhydygorse and Lanlery
Harford, of Peterwell
Hughes, of Alltwyd
Jeffreys, of Glan Dyfi Caslte
Jones, of Aberystwyth
Jones, of Derry Ormond
Jones, of Glandenys
Jones, of Gwynfryn
Jones, of Penylan
Jones-Parry, of Tyllwyd
Jordan, of Pigeonsford
Lewes, of Llanllear
Lewis, of Gwasrod
Lloyd, of Coedmore
Lloyd-Phillips, of Mabwys
Loxdale, of Castle Hill
Powell, of Nant-Eos
Propert, of Blaenpistil
Pryse, of Bwlchbychan
Pryse, of Peithyll
Richardes, of Bryneithen
Rishardes, of l'englais
Rogers, of Abermeirig Talsarn
Saunders, of Tymawr
Tyler, of Mount Gernos
Vaughan, of Green Grove and Bryncg
Vaughan, of Llangoedmore
Wagner, of Manareifed
Webley-Parry, of Noyadd Trefawr
Williams, of Rhoscellan

CARLOW CO.

Beasborough, Earl of
Burton, Sir O. W. C., Bart.
1050

Butler, Sir T. P., Bert.
Paul, Sir R. J., Bart.
Wolseley, Sir J. R., Bart.
Alcock, of Ballynoe
Alexander, of Milford House
Bagenal, of Bennekerry
Blackney, of Bally Ellen
Brady, of Myshall
Browne, of Browne's Hill
Bruen, of Oak Park
Bunbury, of Moyle
Burton, of Burton Hall
Butler, of Spring Hill
Cogan, of Rahill
Duckett, of Duckett's Grove
Duckett, of Russelstown Park
Edge, of Clonbrock
Eustace, of Castlemore
Eustace, of Newstown
Faulkner, of Castletown
Fizmaurice, of Carlow
Garrett, of Janeville
Hamilton, of Rathoe House
Kavanagh, of Borris House
K Eogh, of Kilbride
Lecky, of Ballykealey
Lecky, of Lenham
M'Clintock-Bunbury, of Lisnavagh
Moreton, of Eastwood
Newton, of Dunleckuey
Pack-Beresford, of Fenagh
Rochfort, of Clogrenane
Steuart, of Steuart's Lodge
Tuckey, of Carlow
Vigors, of Burgage
Vigors, of Erindale
Vigors, of Old Leighton
Watson, of Kilconner
Watson, of Lumclone
Whitty, of Ricketstown Hall

CARMARTHENSHIRE.

Cawdor, Earl of
St. David's, Bishop of
Dynevor, Lord
Drummond, Sir J. W. Williams-, Bart.
Hamilton, Sir J. J., Bart.
Mansell, Sir J. B. W., Bart.
Williams, Sir E. B. Griffies-, Bart.
Abadam, of Middleton Hall
Arengo-Cross, of Abermarlais Park
Bishop, of Dollgarreg
Brigstocke, of Gellydywell
Brigstocke, of Robert's Rest
Campbell-Davys, of Neuadd-fawr
Cowell Stepney, of Llanelly House
Davies, of Pentre
Davies, of Upland
Davies-Lloyd, of Blaendyffryn
Du Buisson, of Glynhir
Edwardes, of Rhydygors
Foley, of Aberniarlais
Green, of Court Henry
Gulston, of Llwyn-y-berllan
Gwynne, late of Glanbrane Park
Gwynne-Vaughan, of Cynghordy
Horton, of Ystrad
Jennings, of Gellydeg
Johnes, of Dolancothy
Jones, of Blacnos
Jones, of Gurney
Jones, of Llanmiloe
Jones, of Ystrad
Jones, of Pantglas
Jones, of Vellindra

Laugharne, of Laugharne
Lawrance, of Bank House
Lewes, of Llysnewydd
Lewis, of Gwinfe
Lewis, of Stradey
Lloyd, of Brunant
Lloyd, of Dan-yr-alt
Lloyd, of Glansevrin
Lloyd, of Laques
Mansel, of Coedgain
Morris, of Carmarthen
Nevill, of Westfa
Peel, of Taliaris Park
Philipps, of Ystradwrallt
Philipps, of Cwmgwilly
Powell, of Maesgwynne
Price, of Castle Piggin
Price, of Glangwilly
Price, of Oaklands
Protherne, of Dolewilim
Pugh, of Manoravon
Puxley, of Llangan
Rees, of Killymaenllwyd
Rees, of Toun
Rice, of Llwyn-y-Brain
Smith, of Glanbrydan
Starke, of Laugharne Castle
Thomas, of Caeglas
Thomas, of Gelly-Wernen
Trafford, of Panthoel
Walters-Philips, of Aberglasney
Waters, of Sarnau
Watkins, of Broadway
Yelverton, of Whitland Abbey

CARNARVONSHIRE.

Bangor, Bishop of
Mostyn, Lord
Newborough, Lord
Penrhyn, Lord
Willoughby D'Eresby, Lord
Burgh, of Cae Henar
Clough, of Glasfryn
Darbishire, of Pen dyffryn
Duff-Assheton-Smith, of Vaynol
Edwards, of Benarth
Edwards, of Nanhoron
Ellis, of Glasfryn
Ellis-Lloyd, of Tralwyn
Holland, of Plas-yn-Penrhyn
Huddart, of Brynkir
Jones, of Deganway
Jones-Parry, of Aberdinant
Jones-Parry, of Madryn
Lenthall, of Maynan Hall
Mealy, of Perfeddgoed
Millar, of Penrhos
Morgan, of Hengwrtucha
Nanney, of Gwynfryn
Owen, of Llanystyn
Owen, of Ymwlch
Parry, of Trefan
Platt, of Bryngwenrallt
Priestly, of Trefan
Sampson, of Tower House
Thomas, of Coedhelen
Williams, of Gellieg
Williams, of Plantation
Williams, of Plashen
Williams, of Rhianva
Wyatt, of Bryn Gwynant
Wynne-Finch, of Cefnamlwch

CAVAN CO.

Headfort, Marquis of

Bruce, of Garlet and Kilbagie
Bruce, of Kennet
Dickson, of Greenfield
Johnstone, of Alva
Moir, of Hillfoot
Orr, of Harviestoun Castle
Ramsay, of Tillicoultry

CLARE CO.

Dunboyne, Lord
Inchiquin, Lord
Annaly, Lord
Fitzgerald, Sir A., Bart.
Massy, Sir H., Bart.
O'Loghlen, Sir C. M., Bart.
Armstrong, of Larch Hill
Armstrong, of Lismoher
Arthur, of Glanomera
Ashworth, late of Craggan Tower
Ball, of Fort Fergus
Bentley, of Hurlston
Blood, of Brickhill
Brown, of Clonboy
Burton, of Carrigaholt Castle
Butler, of Ballyline
Butler, of Bonmahon
Butler, of Castle Crine
Calcutt, of St. Catharine's
Carroll, of Merville
Cox, of Mount Pleasant
Creagh, of Dangan
Creagh, of Mount Elva
Crowe, of Cahircalla
Crowe, of Dromore
Fitzgerald, of Adelphi
Foster-Vesey-Fitzgerald, of Moyriesk
Furnell, of Heathermount
Gabbett, of Castle Lake
Going, of Violet Hill
Gore, of Tyredagh Castle
Henn, of Paradise
Keane, of Beech Park
Kelly, of Cahircon
Macadam, of Blackwater
Macdonnell, of New Hall and Liscrona
Macmahon, of Knockane
Macnamara, of Ayle
Macnamara, of Ennistymon
Mahon, late of Mahonburgh
Mayne, of Killaloe
Molony, of Kiltanon House
Moore, of Springfield
O'Brien, of Ballinalackin
O'Brien, of Birchfield
O'Brien, of Cruthos Woods
O'Callaghan, of Ballinahinch
O'Callaghan, of Maryfort
O'Donnell, of Trugh
O'Gorman, of Bellevue
Purdon, of Tinerana
Quin, of Quinshon'
Reeves, of Barrane
Richards, of Sandfield
Ross-Lewin, of Ross Hill
Singleton, of Quinville Abbey
Skerret, of Finnavara House
Spaight, of Ardtagle
Stackpoole, of Ballyally
Stackpoole, of Eden Vale
Studdert, of Bunratty Castle
Studdert, of Craggano Tower
Studdert, of Cullane
Studdert, of Killishen House
Studdert, of Kooper View
1052

Studdert, of Newmarket House
Studdert, of Pella
Vandeleur, of Kilrush House
Westby, of Riltallyowen
Westropp, of Clonmoney

CORK CO.

Bandon, Earl of
Bantry, Earl of
Cork, Earl of
Egmont, Earl of
Kingston, Earl of
Listowel, Earl of
Mountcashell, Earl of
Norbury, Earl of
Shannon, Earl of
Doneraile, Viscount
Midleton, Viscount
Cork, Bishop of
Carbery, Lord
Fermoy, Lord
Abercromby, Sir G. S., Bart.
Becher, Sir H. Wrixon-, Bart.
Brooke, Sir W. De Capell-, Bart.
Chatterton, Sir J. C., Bart.
Chinnery, Sir N., Bart.
Colthurst, Sir G. C., Bart.
Cotter, Sir J. L., Bart.
Fitzgerald, Sir G. R. D., Bart.
Hoare, Sir E., Bart.
Norreys, Sir C. D. O. Jephson-, Bart.
Roberts, Sir R. H., Bart.
Synge, Sir E., Bart.
Warren, Sir A. R., Bart.
Adams, of Jamesbrook
Adams, of Kilbree
Alcock-Stawell, of Kilbrittain
Alcock-Stawell, of Lisnegar
Aldworth, of Newmarket
Aldworth, of Rockmill
Allen, of Lisconville
Annesley, of Annes Grove
Arnott, of Fir Hill
Atkin, of Atkinville
Atkin, of Leadington
Atkins, of Waterpark
Atkins-Going, of Firville
Austen, of Hadwell Lodge
Bagwell, of East Grove
Bainbridge, of Frankfield
Baldwin, of Clohina
Barrett, of Carriganess Castle
Barry, of Castle Cor
Barry, of Barryclough
Barry, of Fota Island
Barry, of Glandore House
Barry, of Kilbolane Castle
Barry, of Lemlara House
Barry, of Lota Lodge
Beamish, of Ann Mount
Beamish, of Beaumont House
Beamish, of Belmont
Beamish, of Bntchley
Beamish, of Grenville House
Beamish, of Kilmalooda House
Beamish, of Mount Beamish
Beamish-Bernard, of Palace Anne
Becher, of Hollybrook
Becher, of Lakelands
Benson, of Montenotte
Bernard, of Coolmain Castle
Bernard, of The Farm
Blackburne, of Renny
Boland, of Pembrook
Bowen, of Bowenscourt

Bowles, of Ahern
Braddell, of Montdeligo
Brasier, of Ballyellis
Brasier-Creagh, of Creagh Castle
Brereton, of Queenstown
Broderick, of Leemount
Browne, of Coolcower House
Bruce, of Miltown Castle
Brydges-Sayers, of Croghacres
Bunbury, of Wood Hill
Burgh, of Kilfinnan Castle
Burke, of Prospect Villa
Callaghan, of Cork
Carbery, of Green Park
Carey, of Carey's Villa
Carleton, of Delgany
Carleton, of Greenfield
Carmichael, of Riverstown House
Clanchy, of Charleville
Clerke, of Mamore House
Colt, of Carhue
Colthurst, of Dripsey Castle
Conner, of Manch House
Cooke-Collis, of Castle Cooke and Fermoy
Coppinger, of Barryscourt and Ballyvolane
Coppinger, of Leemount
Coppinger, of Midleton
Courtenay, of Ballyedmond
Cramer, of Ballindinisk
Cramer, of Rathmore
Creagh, of Ballyandrew
Crofts, of Cloheen House
Crofts, of Yelvetstown
Crooke, of Derreen
Daunt, of Fahalea
Daunt, of Kilcascan
Daunt, of Newborough
Daunt, of Sheveron
Daunt, of Tracton Abbey
Drewe, of Brooke Lodge and Heathfield Towers
Dring, of Rock Grove
Dunscombe, of King William's Town
Dunscombe, of Mount Desart
Evans, of Carker
Fagan, of Feltrim
Foott, of Carrigacunna Castle
Forsayth, of The Mardyke
Frankland, of Assagrove
Franks, of Carrig Park
French, of Clackinty
French, of Marino
Frewen, of Innishannon
Garde, of Ballincurra
Gibbings, of Gibbingsgrove
Gibbings, of Curraghglass and Woolville
Gillman, of Enniskeen
Gillman, of Milane
Gillman, of Oakmount
Gillman, of The Retreat
Glasgow, of Old Court
Gollock, of Forest
Grant, of Kilmurry
Gumbleton, of Glanatore
Hanning, of Kircrone
Harding, of Firville
Harrison, of Castle Harrison
Hayman, of South Abbey
Heard, of Palacetown
Hennessy, of Ballindeasig
Herrick, of Bellmount
Herrick, of Shippool
Hill, of Graig
Hoare, of Carrigohane

Hobson, of Muckridge
Hodder, of Ballea Castle
Hodder, of Fountainstown
Hull, of Lemcon Manor
Hungerford, of Cahirmore
Hungerford, of The Island
Hutchins, of Ardnagashel
Hyde, of Creg
Jackson, of Ahanesk
Johnson, of Rockenham
Johnson, of Woodlands
Jones, of Lisselan
Knoles, of Oatlands
Lamb, of Kilcoleman Park
Lawton, of Cape View
Leader, of Mount Leader
Leader, of Dromagh Castle
Leahy, of Woodlawn
Leahy, of Shanakiel
Leahy-Arthur, of Hyde Park
Leycester, of East View
Little, of Knockadoo
Lloyd, of Buttevant Castle
Longfield, of Castle Mary
Longfield, of Longueville
Longfield, of Waterloo
Lucas, of Rathealy
Lyons, of Cork
McCarthy, of Currymount
McCarthy, of Rathduane
McKenny, of Ardmore
Maguire, of Armdanagh
Mansergh, of Lisnegar
Mansergh, of Macroney Castle
Mansergh, of Rocksavage
Massy, of Mount Massy
Meade, of Ballintober
Moore-Hodder, of Hoddersfield
Morgan, of Bridestown
Morris, of Dunkathal
Morrogh, of Old Court
Murphy, of Clifton
Murphy, of Ring Mahon Castle
Murphy, of Lauriston
Nagle, of Clogher House
Nason, of Newton
Nettles, of Nettleville
Newenham, of Coolmore
Newenham, of Maryborough Park
Newman, of Dromore
Newman, of Monkstown
Newport, of Kilboy
Notter, of Lissacaha
O'Donovan, of Lissard
O'Donovan, of Montpellier
O'Grady, of Aghamarta Castle
O'Leary, of Coomlagane
O'Leary, of Newton House
Parker, of Bellevue
Penrose, of Shandangan
Penrose, of Wood Hill
Penrose-Fitzgerald, of Corkbeg
Perrier, of Lota
Phipps, of Cregg
Poole, of Monkstown
Power, of Ringacoltig
Pratt, of Kinsale
Pratt, of Knockane
Purcell, of Burton Park
Purcell, of Dromore
Puxley, of Dunboy Castle
Reeves, of Ballyglissane
Reeves, of Castle Kevin
Reeves, of Tramore House
Roberts, of Ardmore
Roche, of Ballymorris
Roche, of Rochemount

Rogers, late of Lota
Rowlan, of Kilboy House
St. Lawrence, of The Grove
Sanders, of Sanders Park
Sarsfield, of Doughcloyne
Shaw, of Monkstown Castle
Shuldham, of Dunmanway
Smith-Barry, of Fowty Island
Somerville, of Drishane
Somerville, of Malmaison
Somerville, of The Prairie
Spratt, of Pencil Hill
Stewart, of Whitegate House
Stoughton, of Gortigrenane
Talbot-Ponsonby, of Imokelly
Teulon, of Bandon
Thackwell, of Aghada Hall
Thompson, of Beaumont
Tighe, of The Grove
Tisdall, of Clifford
Tobin, of Ballincollig
Townsend (Payne-), of Derry
Townsend, of Castle Townshend
Townsend, of Woodside
Townshend, of Myross Wood
Uniacke, of Ballyre
Uniacke, of Mount Uniacke
Wallis, of Drishane Castle
Ware, of Woodfort
Webb, of Caheragh House
Webb, of The Hill
Welsted, of Ballywalter
Westropp, of Ballylegan
White, of Glengarriffe Castle
White-Hedges, of Macroom Castle

CORNWALL.

Mount-Edgcumbe, Earl of
St. German's, Earl of
Exmouth, Viscount
Falmouth, Viscount
Vivian, Lord
Call, Sir W. G. M., Bart.
Onslow, Sir Henry, Bart.
Rashleigh, Sir Colman, Bart.
St. Aubyn, Sir E., Bart.
Sawle, Sir C. B. Graves-, Bart.
Trelawny, Sir J. S., Bart.
Vyvyan, Sir R. R., Bart.
Williams, Sir W., Bart.
Agar-Robartes, of Lanhydrock
Archer, of Trelask
Basset, of Tehidy Park
Bennett, of Tresillian House
Bevan, of Boskenna
Boger, of Wolsdon
Bolitho, of Penalverne and Kenegie
Bolitho, of Trewidden
Borlase, of Castle Horneck and Pen-
    deen
Braddon, of Treglith
Bray, of Langford Hall
Buller, of Morval
Buller, of Pelynt
Campbell, of Werrington
Carlyon, of Tregrehan
Carlyon, of Trevré
Carlyon-Simmons, of Trevella
Carnsew, of Flexbury Hall
Carus-Wilson, of Mount Charles
Cocks, of Treverbyn Vean
Coham, of Trevedoe Manor
Collins, of Trewardale
Collins, of Truthan and Newton Ferrers
Coode, of Moor Cottage, St. Austell

Coryton, of Pentillie Castle
Coryton, of St. Mellion
Coulson, late of Kenegie
Cregoe, of Trewithian
Curgenven, of Tretawn
Davey, of Bochym House
Davey, of Redruth
Edwards, of Trematon
Enys, of Enys
Fortescue, of Boconnoc
Foster, of Castle
Fox, of Grove Hill
Fox, of Pengerrick
Gilbert, of Bodmin Priory
Gilbert, of Trelissick
Glanville, of Catchfrench
Glencross, of Luxstowe
Gregor, of Trewarthenick
Gurney, of Bude
Hext, of Tredithy
Hext, of Trenarren
Hiliyar, of Torr House
Horndon, of Penerdar
Horsford, of Bosvathick
Hosken, of Ellenglaze House
Howell, of Ethy
Kempe, of Crugsillack
Kendall, of Pelyn
Kingdon, of Stamford Hill
Lakes, of Trevarrick
Le Grice, of Trereife House
Lethbridge, of Tregeare House
Ley, of Jetwells
Lyle, of Bonython
Lyne, of Tywardreath
Magor, of Penventon and Lamellen
Marshall, of Treworgy
Maskell, of Bude Castle
Mathew, of Pennyteuny
Mayow, of Bray
Messenger, of Heath House
Michell, of Bodmin
Molesworth, of Pencarrow
Mudge, of South Pill
Norway, of Lawn Cliff
Paynter, of Boskenna
Peard, of Penquite
Peel, of Trenant Park
Perry, of Perranporth
Peter, of Chyverton
Peter, of Ravanlanyhern
Peter-Roblyn, of Colquite
Pole Carew, of Antony
Polwhele, of Polwhele
Popham, of Tretarrae
Potter, of Gonvena
Prideaux-Brune, of Prideaux Place
Rashleigh, of Menabilly
Rawlings, of St. Ermund's
Reynolds, of Penair
Reynolds, of Trevenson
Roberts, of Trethill
Roberts, of Treval
Rodd, of ...
Roe, of ...
Rogers, of Penrose
Rosevear, of Roseacle
Rowe, of Turpoint House
St. Aubyn, of Clowance
St. Aubyn, of St. Michael's Mount
St. Aubyn, of Perdina
Scobell, of Nancealverne
Seton, of Trewkerby
Slade-Gully, of Trevennen
Smith, of Tresco Abbey
Somerset, of St. Mabyn
Spry, of Cuddra

1003

Spry, of Tregolls
Stephens, of Tregenna Castle
Stephens, of Trewornan
Symons, of Hatt
Treffry, of Place
Trelawny, of Coldrenick
Trelawny, of Harewood
Tremayne, of Carclew
Tremayne, of Heligan
Trevelyan, of Goldsithney
Trist, of Carnegan
Tucker, of Trematon Castle
Tucker, of Trevince
Tyringham, of Trevethoe
Veale, of Trevelian
Vivian, of Park
Vivian, of Pencalenick
Vivian, of Tregwithan
Vyvyan, of Trewan
Vyvyan-Robinson, of Nansloe
Williams, of Caerhayes Castle
Williams, of Goonvrea
Williams, of Scorrier
Williams, of Tredrea
Willyams, of Carnanton
Willyams, of Nanskeval
Willyams, of Truro

CROMARTYSHIRE.

Mackenzie, of Newhall House
Macleod, of Cadboll
Munro, of Poyntzfield House
Ross, of Cromarty

CUMBERLAND.

Carlisle, Earl of
Lonsdale, Earl of
Carlisle, Bishop of
Muncaster, Lord
Brougham, Lord
Ormathwaite, Lord
Brisco, Sir R., Bart.
Fletcher, Sir H., Bart.
Graham, Sir R. J. S., Bart.
Graham, Sir F. U., Bart.
Lawson, Sir W., Bart.
Musgrave, Sir Geo., Bart.
Vane, Sir H. R., Bart.
Ainsworth, of The Flosh
Allison, of Scaleby Hall
Askew, of Glenridding
Ballantine-Dykes, of Dovenby Hall
Barnes, of Bunker's Hill
Barwis, of Langrigg Hall
Brocklebank, of Greenlands
Browne, of Tallantyre Hall
Burrow, of Carleton Hall
Christian, of Ewanrigg Hall
Coulson, of Stonehouse
Cowper, of Carleton Hall
Curwen, of The Oaks
Curwen, of Wokington Hall
Dacre, of Kirklinton Hall
Dawson, of Ponsonby Hall
Deane, of Keekle Grove
Dickinson, of Red How and Haver-
   croft
Dixon, of Holme Eden
Dixon, of The Knells
Dixon, of Seaton Carew
Dixon, of Rheda
Dodgson, of Lanercost Abbey
Fairclough, of The Rooklands
1054

Fawcett, of Petterill Bank
Fenton, of Castlerigg
Ferguson, of Carlisle
Ferguson, of Morton
Fetuerstonhaugh, of The College
Fetherstonhaugu, of Staffield Hall
Friend, of Harbut Lodge
Gillbanks, of Whitefield House
Graham, of Edmond Castle
Harris, of Greysouthen
Harrison, of Winscales
Hartley, of Gillfoot
Hartley, of Rosehill
Hasell, of Dalemain
Hodgson, of Houghton House
Hodgson, of Newby Grange
Hoskins, of Higham
Howard, of Corby
Howard, of Greystoke
Howard, of Naworth Castle
Hudleston, of Hutton John
Irwin, of Calder Abbey and Justus-
   town
James, of Barrock Park
James, of Clarghyll Hall
Johnson, of Walton House
Lamplugh-Raper, of Lamplugh Hall
Leathes, of Dalehead Hall
Lewthwaite, of Broadgate
Lindow, of Cleator
Lord, of Inglewood Bank
Maclean, of Lazonby Hall
Marshall, of Keswick
Moore, of Whitehall
Mounsey, of Castletown
Mulcaster, of Laversdale
Musgrave, of Wasdale Hall
Oliphant-Ferguson, of Broadfield and
   Burgh
Ossalinski, of Musgrave Hall
Parker, of Skirwith Abbey
Percy, of Eskrigg
Ponsonby, of Hale Hall
Postlethwaite, of The Oaks
Robertson-Walker, of Gilgarran
Ross, of Stonehouse
Rothery, of Greta Hall
Ryder-Irton, of Irton Hall
Salkeld, of Holme Hill
Salkeld, of Penrith
Salmond, of Waterfoot
Senhouse, of Netherhall
Spedding, of Summergrove
Stanley, of Ponsonby Hall
Steel, of Derwent Bank
Steward, of Newton Manor
Tomlinson-Grant, of The Hill
Thompson, of Bridekirk
Watts, of Clifton House
Watts, of Hawkesdale Hall
Whinyates, of Walton
Willock, of St. Bees
Wordsworth, of St. Ann's Hill
Wybergh, of Isell Hall
Wyndham, of Cockermouth Castle
Young, of The Oaks

DENBIGHSHIRE.

Bagot, Lord
Mostyn, Lord
Brooke, Sir R., Bart.
Cunlifle, Sir R. A., Bart.
Wynn, Sir W. W., Bart.
Atcherley, of The Fïrythe
Bamford-Hesketh, of Gwyrch Castle

Barnes, of The Quinta
Chambres, of Llys Meirchion
Clough, of Plas Clough
Cooke, of Colommendy
Dod, of Llannerch Park
Edwardes, of Denbigh
ffoulkes, of Eriviatt
Fitzhugh, of Plâs Power
Freme, late of Pengwern Hall
Griffith, of Garn
Griffith, of Trevalyn Hall
Hanmer, of Bodnor Hall
Hardcastle, of Pen-y-lan
Heaton, of Plâs Heaton
Hill-Trevor, of Brynkinalt
Hinde, of Plâs Madog
Hope, of Marchwiel Hall
Hughes, of Kinmel Park
Hughes, of Ystrad
Hunter, of Mount Alyn
Jesse, of Llanbedr Hall
Jones, of Cefn Coch
Jones, of Llanorchrugog Hall
Jones-Bateman, of Pentre Mawr
Jones-Parry, of Llwyn Onn
Modocks, of Glanywern and Vron Iw
Mainwaring, of Galltfaenan
Marshall, of Pen-y-Gardden
Maurice, of Ruthin
Meredith, of Pentrebychan
Mostyn, of Llewenog
Myddelton, of Gwaenynog
Myddelton-Biddulph, of Chirk Castle
Owen, of Efenechtyd
Panton, of Plas Fron
Peck, of Cornish Hall
Peters, of Park Poslyn
Price, of Llanbrainadr Hall
Richards, of Cerrig Llwydion
Roberts, of Cefnoch
Roberts, of Plas Llandoget
Sandbach, of Hafodunos
Thompson, of Stansty Hall
Tippinge, of Llwyn Onn Hall
Tottenham, of Plâs Berwyn
Townshend, of Trevallyn
Watling, of The Fron
West, of Ruthin Castle
Williams, of Bod Gwilym
Williams-Purcell, of Pentre Mawr
Wynn, of Cefn
Wynne, of Coed Coch
Wynne, of Garthewin
Wynne-Finch, of Voelas
Yale, of Plâs-yn-Yale
Yorke, of Dyffryn Aled
Yorke, of Erthig.

DERBYSHIRE.

Devonshire, Duke of
Portland, Duke of
Rutland, Duke of
Harrington, Earl of
Howe, Earl
Hardinge, Viscount
Belper, Lord
Byron, Lord
Denman, Lord
Howard, Lord
Scarsdale, Lord
Vernon, Lord
Waterpark, Lord
Berney, Sir H., Bart.
Wilkinson, Sir R., Bart.
Blunt, Sir H. S., Bart.

Burdet, Sir R., Bart.
Cave, Sir M. C. B., Bart.
Crewe, Sir J. H., Bart.
Des Vœux, Sir H. W., Bart.
Every, Sir J. F., Bart.
Fitz-Herbert, Sir Wm., Bart.
Sitwell, Sir G. R., Bart.
Wilmot, Sir H. S., Bart.
Wilmot, Sir R. E., Bart.
Abney, of Measham Hall
Allcard, of Burton Closes
Arkwright, of Sutton Scarsdale
Arkwright, of Willersley
Arkwright, of Wirksworth
Bagshawe, of Ford Hall
Bagshawe, of The Oaks and Wormhill Hall
Bainbrigge, of Hill House
Baker, of Doveridge-wood House
Balguy, of Duffield Park
Barker, of East Lodge
Barrow, of Ringwood Hall
Barrow of Sydnope Hall
Bateman, of Derby
Bateman, of Hartington Hall
Bateman, of Middleton Hall and Lomberdale House
Beaumont, of Barrow Hall
Bent, of Ashbourne Hall
Bigsby-Chamberlin, of Sutton Bonnington
Bowdon, of Southgate House
Bradshaw of Barton Hall
Briscoe, of Melbourne Hall
Bristowe, of Twyford Hall
Broadhurst, of Foston
Buckstone, of Bradbourne
Cammell, of Norton Hall
Cantrell, of King's Newton
Carleill, of Longstone Hall
Cavendish, of Ashford Hall
Chandos-Pole, of Radborne Hall
Chandos-Pole-Gell, of Barton Fields
Clarke, of Matlock
Coke, of Brookhill
Coke, of Langton Hall
Coke, of Longford Hall
Colvile, of Lullington Hall
Cotton, of Etwall Hall
Cox, of Brailsford Hall
Crewe, of Repton Abbey
Crompton, of The Lilies
Dale, of Ashbourne Manor
Darwin of Fern
De Rodes, of Barlborough Hall
Dishrowe, of Walton Hall
Dury, of Bonsall
Evans, of Allestree Hall
Evans, of Darley Abbey
Ffytche, of Risley Hall
Fitzherbert, of Norbury Manor
Frank, of Ashborne
Gisborne, of Holme Hall
Gisborne, of Walton Hall
Goodwin, of Hinchley Wood
Goodwin, of Wigwell Grange
Greaves, of Ford Hall
Greaves, of Wirksworth
Gresley, of Barton-un-ler-Needwood
Hallowes, of Glapwell Hall
Harrison, of Snelston Park
Holden, of Aston Hall
Howard, of Glossop Hall
Huish, of Heanor
Hull, of The Knowle
Hunloke, of Wingerworth
Hunter, of Kilburne

Hurt, of Alderwasley
Jessop, of Butterley Hall
Jodrell, of Shallcross Hall
Johnson, of The Callow
Kingdon, of Hulland
Leacroft, of Matlock Bath
Leslie, of Hassop Hall
Lowe, of Locko
Lowndes, of Palterton
Maynard, of Chesterfield
Meynell, of Meynell Langley
Milnes, of Stubbing Edge
Mosley, of Burnaston House
Mundy, of Markeaton
Mundy, of Shipley Hall
Nesfield, of Castle Hill
Newdigate, of Derwent Hall
Newton, of Mickleover Manor
Newton, of Oilersett Hall
Nightingale, of Lea Hurst
Palmer-Morewood, of Alfreton
Pares, of Hopwell Hall
Peach, of Langley
Pegge-Burnell, of Beauchieff Abbey
Potter, of Dinting Vale
Pringle, of Darley Dale
Radford, of Smalley Hall
Radford, of Tansley Wood
Scott, of Draycott House
Shore, of Clifton Hall
Shuttleworth, of Hathersage Hall
Sitwell, of Horsley
Sitwell, of Morley House
Sitwell, of Stainsby House
Smedley, of Riber Castle
Smith, of Eyam
Spencer, of Edgemoor
Strutt, of Bridgehill
Strutt, of Milford
Sumner, of Glossop
Sutton, of Shardlow Hall
Thornhill, of Stanton
Turbutt, of Ogston Hall
Walker, of Doveridge
Wayne, of Quorndon House
White, of Park Hall
Wilkinson, of Tapton House
Wilmot, of Buxton
Wilmot, of Milford House
Wilmot, late of Newton Solney
Wolley, of Allen Hill
Worthington, of Newton Park
Wright, of Butterley Park
Wright, of Hulland Hall
Wright, of Osmaston Manor
Wright, of Yeldersley

DEVONSHIRE.

Bedford, Duke of
Buckinghamshire, Earl of
Devon, Earl of
Fortescue, Earl
Morley, Earl of
Mount-Edgcumbe, Earl of
Portsmouth, Earl of
Chetwynd, Viscount
Sidmouth, Viscount
Exeter, Bishop of
Churston, Lord
Clifford of Chudleigh, Lord
Clinton, Lord
Cranstoun, Lord
Graves, Lord
Kingsale, Lord

Lisle, Lord
Poltimore, Lord
Rolle, Lady
Seaton, Lord
Sinclair, Lord
Acland, Sir T. D., Bart.
Baker, Sir G., Bart.
Carew, Sir W. P., Bart.
Chichester, Sir A. P. B. Bart.
Chichester, Sir Arthur, Bart.
Davie, Sir H. R. F., Bart.
Drake, Sir T. T., Bart.
Duckworth, Sir J. T. B., Bart.
Duntze, Sir J. L., Bart.
Elton, Sir E. M., Bart.
Floyd, Sir J., Bart.
Fraser, Sir W. A., Bart.
Kennaway, Sir J., Bart.
Lopes, Sir M., Bart.
Louis, Sir J., Bart.
Newman, Sir L., Bart.
Northcote, Sir S. H., Bart.
Palk, Sir L., Bart.
Pole, Sir J. G. Reeve-de-la, Bart.
Prideaux, Sir E. S., Bart.
Rogers, Sir F., Bart.
Seale, Sir H. P., Bart.
Seymour, Sir J. H. C., Bart.
Stuckley, Sir G. S., Bart.
Williams, Sir W., Bart.
Wrey, Sir B. P., Bart.
Adair, of Colhays
Adams, of Bowdon
Adams, of Temple Hill
Aldridge, of Hillary House
Allen, of Coleridge House
Amery, of Druid House
Ames, of Clevelands
Amory, of Bolham
Arthur, of Atherington
Arundell, of Lifton
Bailey, of Lee Abbey
Baring-Gould, of Lew Trenchard
Barnes, of Great Durvard
Basset, of Watermouth
Bastard, of Kitley and Buckland
Bayley, of Cotford House
Beckett, of The Knoll
Belfield, of Primley Hall
Bellew, of Stockleigh Court
Bentinck, of Indio
Bere, of Morebath
Bere, of Timewell House
Beste, of Abbotsham Court
Bethune, of Chulmleigh
Bewes, of Beaumont House
Bidgood, of Rockbeare Court
Bliss, of Northcombe Hall
Bluett, late of Holcombe Court
Boles, of Byll Court
Bowring, of Claremont
Bowring, of Larkbear House
Braddon, of Blackford House
Bewnrick, of Coom
Brown, of Larton Hill
Buck, of Moreton House
Buckingham, of Doddiscombsleigh
Buller, of Downes
Buller, of Erle Hall
Buller, of Pound
Buller, of Strete Ralegh
Bultcel, of Fardle
Bury, of Denton House
Butland, of Diptford Court
Byne of Sattreleigh House
Calmady, of Langdon Court
Carew, of Collipriest

Carew, of Marley House
Carlyon, of Greenway
Carpenter-Garnier, of Mount Tavy
Carter, late of Rockview House
Cartwright, of Mont-le-Grand and Brimley House
Cary, of Follaton
Cary, of Torre Abbey
Cave, of Sidbury Manor
Champernowne, of Dartington
Chard, of Mount Tamar
Chichester, of Hall
Chichester, of Stokelake House
Chichester-Nagle, of Calverleigh
Clark, of Efford Manor
Clarke, of Bridwell
Clarke, of Buckland Tout Saints and Moorlands
Clayfield, of Dowrich House
Cleveland, of Tapeley Park
Coffin, of Portledge House
Coham, of Coham and Dunsland
Coham, of Compton Hartley
Coham, of Upcott-Avenel
Coleridge, of Heaths Court
Coleridge, of Ottery Manor
Coleridge, of Salston and Beaumont
Collier, of Grimston
Collins, of Wonham House
Collins-Splat, of Brixton House
Comyns, of Wood
Cornish, of Black Hall
Cornish, of Salcombe Hall
Cornish, of Salcombe House
Cottrell, of Dundridge
Cruwys, of Cruwys Morchard
Cutler, of Sidmouth
Daniel, of Stoodleigh
Davy, of Ashtown
Dayman, of Mambury
Deane, of Webbery House
Divett, of Bovey Tracey
Divett, of Bystock
Drake, of Ipplepen House
Drewe, of The Grange
Drury, of Knightstone
Durant, of Sharpham
Eales, of Eastdon
Edgcumbe, of Edgcumbe
Edwards, of Churchstanton
Edwards, of Ludbrooke
Elliot, of Burley House
Fane, of Clovelly Court
Fenton, of Liddicombe
Fleming, of Bigadon
Fortescue, of Fallapit
Fortescue, of Weston
Froude, of Dartington
Fulford, of Fulford
Furneaux, of Swilly House
Fursdon, of Fursdon
Furse, of Halsdon House
Gard, of Rougemont House
Garratt, of Bishop's Court
Gifford, of Cliff-End House
Gill, of Bickham Park
Gill, of Brooklands
Gill, of Venn
Goldsmid, of Honiton
Gordon, of Wiscombe Park
Grant, of Hillersdon House
Grylls, of Polsloe Park
Guille, of Cross
Hallett, of Stedcombe House
Hames, of Charford
Hamilton, of Fairfield Lodge
Hamilton, of The Retreat
1056

Hamlyn, of Leawood
Harding, of Hallsannery
Harding, of Upcott
Harris, of Haine
Harris, of Radford
Harris, of Yealmpton
Hawker, of Rock
Heathcote, of Raleigh
Henn-Gennys, of Whitleigh Hall
Hippesley, of Shobrooke
Hoare, of Luscombe
Hogg, of Berry Head House
Holdsworth, of Widdicombe House
Hole, of Beam
Hole, of Bovey Tracey Park
Hole, of Colliepriest Cottage
Hole, of Ebberly
Hole, of Georgeham
Hole, of North Tawton
Holley, of Oaklands
Honywood, of Woodhayes
Hotchkys, of Blatchborough
Hutton, of Filleigh
Huyshe, of Sand
Ilbert, of Horsewell House and Bowringsleigh
Ingle, of Sandford Orleigh
Ireland, of Dowrich House
Jeremy, of Lea Combe House
Johnson, of Winkleigh Court
Karslake, of Meshaw
Keats, of Porthill
Kekewich, of Peamore
Kelly, of Kelly
Kevill, of Sherford
Kingdon, of South Molton
Knight, of Cloakham House
Lee, of Balsdon
Lee, of Orleigh Court
Lewis, of Membland Hall
Ley, of Trehill
Ley, of Woodlands
Lindsay, of Deer Park
Llewellyn, of Buckland Filleigh
Lockwood, of Barcombe
Lousada, of Peak House
Luscombe, of Combe Royal
Luxmore, of Witherdon
Luxmore, of Kerslake
M'Alester, of Loup Villa
Maconchy, of Cadwell House
Mallet, of Ash
Mallock, of Cockington Court
Mallock, of Mount Hill
Manning, of Bratton Clovelly
Marker, of Grantlands
Marshall, of Barnstaple
Marshall, of Blagdon
Matthews, of Lukesland and Coombe
Melhuish, of Court Barn
Melhuish, of Green Mount
Mellor, of Otterhead
Meynell, of Brent Moor
Michell, of Holwell
Miles, of Dixfield
Milford, of Coaver
Mogridge, of Arcot House
Molesworth, of Tetcott
Molesworth, of Northdown
Monro, of Ingsdon
Morris, of Fishleigh
Morshead, of Widey Court
Mudge, of Sydney
Murray, of Hoopern House
Nation, of Rockbeare House
New, of Craddock House
Northcote, of Buckerell

Northcote, of Oakfield House
Northmore, of Cleeve House
Nowell-Usticke, of Ford Park
Oldham, of Strawbridge
Parker, of Delamore
Parker, of Whiteway
Parlby, of Manadon
Parr, of Stonelands
Patteson, of Feniton Court
Peek, of Hazelwood Park
Peters, of Harefield House
Phillipps, of Torquay
Phillpotts, of Longcroft
Pine-Coffin, of East-Down House
Pitman, of Dunchideock House
Pode, of Slade
Porter, of Hembury Fort
Porter, of Rockbeare Court
Porter, of Winslade House
Potts, of Elm-grove and Trafalgar House
Pyke, of Ford
Pyke, of Bydown and Parracombe
Quicke, of Newton House
Radcliffe, of Warlegh
Rayer, of Holcombe Court
Read, of Uplands
Rhodes, of Teign Lawn
Ridgway, of Sheplegh
Robinson, of Torquay
Rolle, of Bicton
Rolle, of Stevenstone
Sanders, of Stoke House
Savile, late of Oaklands
Scarbrough, of Stafford House
Schank, of Barton House and Northumberland House
Sclater, of Goodameavy
Seale-Hayne, of Fuge House and Kingswear Castle
Short, of Bickham
Shortland, of Courtland
Sillifant, of Coombe
Simcoe, of Wolford
Smith, of Trea-bear
Snow, of Franklyn
Soltau, of Little Efford
Soltau, of Plympton St. Mary
Soltau-Symons, of Chaddlewood
Splatt, of Flete House
Stevens, of Winscott
Stevenson, of Havno
Still, of Castle Hill
Stowey, of Kenbury
Strode, of Newnham Park
Studd, of Oxton House
Studdy, of Watton Court
Sydenham, of Collumpton
Talbot, of Rhode Hill
Tanner, of King's Nympton Park
Taylor, of West Ogwell House
Templer, of Knowles
Templer, of Lindridge
Templer, of ....
Thomson, of Bownafield
Toll, of Street and Perridge
Trebe, of Godamoor
Trelawny, of Ham
Tremayne, of Sydenham
Tr yte, of Huntsham Court
Tucker, of Coryton Court
Tyrrell, of St. Leonard's
Veale, of Passaford
Vidal, of Cornborough
Vivian, of Torquay
Vowler, of Leawood
Vowler, of Parracott

Vye, of Ilfracombe
Wade, of Stonelands
Waldy, of Howdens
Walkey, of Clyst St. Laurence
Walkey, of Poll House
Wall, of Bradley Wood
Walrond, of Dulford House
Walrond, of Bradfield
Watson, of Dorsley
Watts, of Ford House
Webber, of Buckland House
Williams, of Clovelly Court
Williams, of Gnaton Hall
Wolcott, of Knowle House
Woolcombe, of Ashbury
Woolcombe, of Hemerdon
Worth, of Worth
Wren, of Lenwood
Wrey, of Holne Park
Wrey, of Warecliffe House
Yeo, of Fremington
Yonge, of Puslinch

DONEGAL CO.

Conyngham, Marquis of
Donegall, Marquis of
Lifford, Viscount
Wicklow, Earl of
Bateson, Sir R. H., Bart.
Hayes, Sir S. H., Bart.
Montgomery, Sir H. C., Bart.
Stewart, Sir J. A., Bart.
Adair, of Glenveagh
Alexander, of Ahilly
Barton, of Greenfort House
Batt, of Rathmullan
Beers, of Leslie Hill
Boyd, of Ballymacool
Brooke, of Lough-Esk Castle
Cary, of White Castle
Chambers, of Fox Hall
Charley, of Island of Aranmore
Cochrane, of Crogan House
Cochrane, of Edenmore House
Delap, of Monellan
Grove, of Castle Grove
Hamilton, of Brown Hall
Hamilton, of St. Ernans
Hart, of Glen Alla
Hart, of Kilderry
Harvey, of Main Hall
Harvey, of Mintiaghs
Heard, of Killybegs
Hill, of Gweedore
Humfrey, of Cavanacor
Knox, of Clonleigh
M'Clintock, of Dunmore
Mansfield, of Ardrummon House and Castle Wray
Montgomery, of Convoy
Murray-Stewart, of Killybegs
Olphert, of Ballyconnell
Pratt, of Manor Pratt
Sinclair, of Bonnyglen
Sinclair, of Drumbeg
Smith, of Hollymount
Stewart, of Ards
Stewart, of Corean
Stewart, of Loughveagh House
Stewart, of Rock Hill
Style, of Glenmore
Tredennick, of Camlin
Woodhouse, of Kerryheel
Wray, of Oak Park
Young, of Culdaff House

DORSETSHIRE.

Westminster, Marquis of
Eldon, Earl of
Ilchester, Earl of
Shaftesbury, Earl of
Digby, Lord
Poltimore, Lord
Portman, Lord
Rivers, Lord
Wynford, Lord
Baker, Sir E. B., Bart.
Glyn, Sir R. G., Bart.
Guest, Sir I. B., Bart.
Lethbridge, Sir J. H., Bart.
Nepean, Sir M. H., Bart.
Oglander, Sir H., Bart.
Smith-Marriott, Sir Wm. H., Bart.
Tichborne, Sir H., Bart.
Adye, of Merly House
Allford, of Folke House
Astell, of Puddlehinton
Austen, of Ensbury House
Bankes, of Kingston Lucy and Studland Manor
Bastard, of Charlton Marshall
Batten, of Upcerne
Benthall, of Sherborne
Bingham, of Bingham's Melcombe
Bond, of Creech Grange
Bond, of Holme
Bond of Tyneham
Boucher, of Thornhill House
Bourchier, of Brook Lodge
Bourne, of Roseville
Bower, of Iwerne Minster
Bower, of Fontmell Parva
Bragge, of Sadborow
Bridge, of Puddletrenthide
Brodie, of Swanage
Brouncker, of Boveridge
Brymer, of Islington
Butts of Melplaish
Calcraft, of Rempstone Hall
Cambridge, of Bloxworth House
Castleman, of Chettle Manor
Churchill, of Alderholt Park
Clapcott, of Keynstone
Clayton, of Bradford Abbas
Coventry, of Henbury House and The Knoll
Cox, of Chedington
Cree, of Over Moigne
Cutler, of Sherborne Abbey
Dale, of Glanville's Wootton
Dawson-Damer, of Came House
Digby, of Sherborne Castle
Digby, of Studland
Dillon-Trenchard, of Lytchett House
Drax, of Charborough Park
Eliot, of Radipole
Eliot, of Weymouth
Evans, of Forde Abbey
Farquharson, of Castle Hill
Farquharson, of Langton House
Farrer, of Binegar
Fellowes, of Kingston House
Ferris, of Corscombe
Floyer, of West Stafford
Foster, of Warmwell
Frampton, of Moreton
Fyler, of Heffleton
Garland, of Stone Cottage
Gollop, of Strode House and Bowood
Goodden, of Nether Compton
Goodden, of Over Compton
Goodden, of Upway House

Gordon, of Leweston
Grant-Dalton, of Parkstone
Greathed, of Uddens House
Gundry, of Bridport
Gundry, of The Hyde
Hambro, of Milton Abbey
Hanham, of Manston House
Hawkins, of Lewell Lodge
Hounsell, of Wyke Court
Hussey, of Bredy
Hussey, of Marnhull
Hutton, of Pimperne
Jenkins, of Witherstone
Kindersley, of Syward Lodge
Lambert, of Knowle
Lillington, of Childhay
Littlehales, of Buckshaw House
Loveridge, of Paradise House
Luttrell, of Wootton Fitz Paine
Malet, of Fontmell Parva
Manning, of Portland Castle
Mansel, of Langton Lodge
Mansel, of Smedmore
Mansel, of Pucknoll
Michel, of Dewlish
Michel, of Whatcombe House
Middleton, of Bradford Peverell
Monro, of Edmondsham
Okeden, of Turnworth House
Pardoe, of Witherstone
Parke, of Henbury
Pearce, of Dorchester
Pickard, of Sturminster Marshall
Porcher, of Clyffe
Radclyffe, of Hyde House
Raymond, of Symondsbury
St. Lo, of Marsh Court
Savage, of Tarrant Henton
Seymer, of Hanford
Sheridan, of Frampton Court
Smith, of Greenhill
Smith, of Sydling House
Snow, of Langton Lodge
Steward, of Nottington House
Sturt, of Critchill
Swaffield, of West Down Lodge
Tatchell-Bullen, of Marshwood
Thompson, of Melcombe Regis
Thornton, of Frome Whitfield
Treeby, of High Cliff
Tregonwell, of Anderson and Cranbourne Place
Trenchard, of Greenhill House
Turner-Farley, of Marnhull
Weld, of Chidiock House
Weld, of Lulworth Castle
Weston, of Woiveton
Whieldon, of Wyke Hall
White, of Charlton House
Williams, of Bridehead
Williams, of Herringston House
Williams, of Stinsford
Williams, of West Hall House
Wood, of Ormiston
Yeatman, of Chilbury Lodge
Yeatman, of Stock House

DOWNSHIRE.

Donegall, Marquis of
Downshire, Marquis of
Londonderry, Marquis of
Annesley, Earl of
Kilmorey, Earl of
Bangor, Viscount
Bangor, Viscountess

3 Y

1057

Down, Connor, and Dromore, Bishop of
De Ros, Lord
Dufferin and Clandeboye, Lord
Bateson, Sir T., Bart.
Alexander, of Lessane
Annesley, of Ardilla
Annesley, of Oakley
Barron, of Kinghill House
Batt, of Purdysburn
Beauclerc, of King's Castle
Beauclerk, of Ardglass Castle
Binney, of Bangor Glebe
Blair, of Wheatfield
Blakiston-Houston, of Orangefield and Roddens
Bowen, of Banbridge
Bradshaw, of Milecross
Brady, of Newry
Browne, of Janeville
Charretie, of Gilford
Cleland, of Rath-Gael House
Cleland, of Rubane House and Tobar Mhuire
Cleland, of Stormont Castle
Coates, of Eastwood
Coates, of Glentoran
Corry, of Abbey Yard
Craig-Laurie, of Myra Castle
Crawford, of Crawfordsburn
De la Cherois, of Donaghadee
De la Cherois, of Ballywilliam
De la Cherois-Crommelin, of Carrowdore Castle
Dolling, of Edenmore
Douglass, of Grace Hall
Dunbar, of Woburn
Forde, of Seaforde
Gordon, of Florida
Gregg, of Ballymenoch
Hall, of Narrow Water
Hamilton, of Killyleagh Castle
Harrison, of Nerton Hall
Higginson, of Carnalea
Innes, of Dromantine
Jaffé, of Craigdarragh
Jocelyn, of Bryansford
Johnston, of Ballywillwill
Johnston, of Holly Park
Kennedy, of Cultra
Keown, of Ballydugan
Ker, of Montalto
Ker, of Portavo
Leslie, of Ballyward
Leslie, of Donaghadee
McClure, of Belmont
Maxwell, of Finnebrogue
Meade, of Burrenwood
Meredyth, of Hollymount
Montgomery, of Ballykeel House
Montgomery, of Tyrella
Mulholland, of Craigavad
Mulholland, of Spring Vale
Mussenden, of Larchfield
Nicholson, of Ballow
Nugent, of Portaferry
Nugent, of Strangford
Perceval-Maxwell, of Groomsport
Price, of Saintfield House
Reilly, of Scarvagh House
Richardson, of Kircassock
Ross, of Bladensburgh
Senior, of Glass-Drummond House
Smyth, of Drum
Stewart, of Ballyedmond
Stewart, of Ballyntwood House
Vaughan, of Quilly

1058

Von Stieglitz, of Knockbarragh Park
Ward, of Bangor Castle
Waring, of Waringstown House
Whyte, of Loughbrickland

DUBLIN CO.

Dublin, Archbishop of
Charlemont, Earl of
Meath, Earl of
Milltown, Earl of
Howth, Earl of
Gough, Viscount
Annaly, Lord
Cloncurry, Lord
Talbot de Malahide, Lord
Trimleston, Lord
Borough, Sir E. R. Bart.
Bradstreet, Sir J. V., Bart.
Corrigan, Sir D. J., Bart.
De Beauvoir, Sir J. E. B., Bart.
Domville, Sir C. C. W., Bart.
Guinness, Sir A. E., Bart.
Harty, Sir R., Bart.
Kennedy, Sir C. E. B., Bart.
Lighton, Sir C. R., Bart.
Marsh, Sir H., Bart.
Ribton, Sir J. S., Bart.
Shaw, Sir Robt., Bart.
Stamer, Sir L. T., Bart.
Armit, of Newtown Park
Armstrong, of Greenfield
Birch, of Dromartin Castle
Blackburne, of Rathfarnham Castle
Brady, of Hazelbrook
Brenan, of Kingston Lodge and Kilternan
Brooke, of Summerton
Brooke, of Taney-Hill House
Butler, of Frescati Lodge
Butler, of Belvedere House
Butler, of Walshestown
Caldbeck, of Moyle Park
Cobbe, of Newbridge House
Colclough, of Newpack
Colthurst-Vesey, of Lucan House
Coppinger, of Monkstown Castle
Cruise, of Drynan
Cuppage, of Clare Grove
Cusack, of Abbeville House
Cusack, of Bohomer
Dodwell, of Shankhill House
Evans, of Cromlech
Evans, of Portrane
Finlay, of Corkagh House
Fitzgerald, of Kilmarnock
FitzSimon, of Glencullen
Fortescue, of Belvedere
Gernon, of Dublin
Gerrard, of Batchelor's Hall
Golding, of Giasmere
Guinness, of Deepwell
Guinness, of Stillorgan
Hamilton, of Abbotstown
Hamilton, of Balbriggan
Hamilton, of Hampton Hall
Hartley, of Beech Park
Hatchell, of Fortfield House
Hughes, of The Grove
Hussey, of Westown House
Hutchinson, of Senfield
Hutton, of Elm Park
James, of Clarinda Park
Jessop, of Marlfield
Kennedy, of Belgard Castle
Kingsmill, of Hermitage Park

Kirkpatrick, of Coolmine House
La Touche, of Marlay
Layard, of Riversdale
Leigh, of Thorn Hill
Lentaigne, of Tallaght
Lewis, of Haddington House
Lewis, of Seatown
Lindesay, of Greenville
Lindsay, of Glasnevin
Little, of Cliff Castle
Loftus, of Bulcummin and Oldtown
Lombard, of South Hill
Lyster, of Stillorgan Park
Macartney, of Lowther Lodge
Macfarlane, of Huntstown House
M'Gregor, of Belvedere
Madden, of Inch House
Malpas, of Rochestown
Massy, of Clareville
Meekins, of Glasthule
O'Brien, of Beulah House
O'Byrne, of Cabinteely
O'Connor, of Rockfield House
O'Dwyer, of Orlagh
O'Grady, of Monkstown House
Perrin, of Sea Park
Pim, of Greenbank
Pomeroy-Colley, of Leopardstown and Fernie
Preston, of Silverstream
Reynolds, of Marine Villa
Roberts, of Hendré
Ryan, of Knocklyon
Sandes, of Bayview
Sartoris, of Linden Castle
Scott, of Woodville
Segrave, of Cabra
Shaw, of Kimmage House
Sheil, of Kilmactalway
Singleton, of Auburn
Skerrett, of Athgoe Park
Stewart, of Gartlerrogh
Stokes, of Denmark Hill
Talbot, of Ballinclea
Taylour, of Ardgillan Castle
Thompson, of Clonskeagh
Tomkins, late of Grey Thorn
Turbett, of Owenstown
Vernon, of Clontarf Castle
Waldron, of Ballybrack
Warren, of Killiney Castle
Westby, of Roebuck Castle
White, of Killkee House
Woods, of Milverton
Woods, of Whitestown House

DUMBARTONSHIRE.

Argyll, Duke of
Argyll, Dowager Duchess of
Campbell, Sir G., Bart.
Colquhoun, Sir James, Bart.
Alexander, of Cowden
Bontine, of Ardoch
Buchanan, of Ardoch House
Buchanan, of Auchinterlie
Buchanan, of Shandon
Cabbell, of Dunard
Campbell, of Colgrain
Campbell, of Tullichewan
Colquhoun, of Camstradden
Daglish, of Kilmardinny
Dennistoun-Brown, of Balloch
Douglas, of Mains
Dunlop, of Drumhead
Ewing, of Strathleven

Findlay, of Boturich
Geils, of Dumbuck
Geils, of Geilston
Hamilton, of Barnes and Cochno
Hamilton of Spittal
Hutchinson, of Rockend
Murray-Gartshore, of Gartshore
Smollett, of Bonhill and Cameron House
Stirling, of Cosdale
Yuille, of Darleith House

DUMFRIESSHIRE.

Buccleuch and Queensberry, Duke of
Queensberry, Marquis of
Mansfield, Earl of
Rollo, Lord
Grierson, Sir A. W., Bart.
Jardine, Sir Wm., Bart.
Johnstone, Sir F. J. W., Bart.
Maxwell, Sir J. H., Bart.
Pasley, Sir T. S., Bart.
Anderson, of Woodhouse
Baird, of Closeburn Hall
Butler-Johnstone, of Auchin Castle
Carruthers of Dormont
Carruthers, of Warmanbie
Carthew-Yorstoun, of East Tinwald
Colvin, of Craigielands
Connell, of Conheath
Copland, of Colliston
Corstorphine, of Broadchapel
Dirom, of Mount Annan
Douglas, of Lockerbie
Dunlop, of Corsock
Dury, of New Abbey
Fergusson, of Craigdarroch
Fogo, of Kirtleton
Gilchrist-Clark, of Speddoch
Gladstone, of Capenoch
Graham, of Mossknow
Hope-Johnstone, of Annandale
Hunter-Arundell, of Barjarg
Irving, of Bonshaw Tower
Jardine, of Castlemilk
Jardine, of Granton
Jardine, of Lanrick Castle
Johnston, of Carnsalloch
Johnston, of Cowhill
Johnstone, of Galabank
Laurie, of Maxwelton
Maculpine-Leny, of Dalswinton
Macconnel, of Rolgill Tower
Macdonald, of Rammerscales
Macrae, late of Holmains
Maitland, of Eccles
Malcolm, of Burnfoot
Maxwell, of Broomholme
Maxwell, of Milnhead
Maxwell, of Portrack
Maxwell, of Terraughtie
Murray, of Murraythwaite
Ogilvy, of The Cove
Paterson, of Nunfield and Brockelhurst
Sandeman, of Kirkwood
Sharpe, of Hoddam
Smith, of Blackwood
Veitch, of Eliock House
Walker, of Crawfordton
Wightman, of Courance
Witham, of Kirkconnell

DURHAM CO.

Cleveland, Duke of
Northumberland, Duke of

Durham, Earl of
Scarborough, Earl of
Vane, Earl
Boyne, Viscount
Durham, Bishop of
Ravensworth, Lord
Clavering, Sir W. A., Bart.
Constable, Sir T. A. C., Bart.
Eden, Sir Wm., Bart.
Hardinge, Sir H. C., Bart.
Pocock, Sir G. F. C., Bart.
Williamson, Sir H., Bart.
Alder, of Horncliffe
Allan, of Blackwell Hall
Annandale, of Shotley Grove
Aylmer, of Walworth Castle
Baker, of Elemore Hall
Beckwith, of Trimdon and Silksworth House
Bell, of Hanwick Hall
Bewicke, of Urpath Lodge
Bigge, of Stanhope
Blenkinsopp, of Hoppyland Castle
Bowes, of Streatlam Castle
Bramwell, of Enfield House
Bramwell, of Hardwick Hall
Briggs, of Hylton Castle
Brown, of Jarrow Hall
Bulmer, of Saltwell Hall
Burdon, of Castle Eden
Carr, of Bishop Wearmouth
Chaytor, of Witton Castle
Colling, of Red Hall
Cookson, of Neasham Hall
Cowen, of Stella Hall
Eden, of Beamish Park
Elliott, of Elvet Hill
Ellison, of Hebburn Hall
Ettrick, of High Barnes
Fawcett, of North Bailey
Fenwick, of Southill
Fenwicke, of Longframlington and Pagebank
Fowler, of Preston Hall
Greenwell, of Broomshields
Greenwell, of Greenwell Ford
Gregson, of Murton and Burdon
Grey, of Norton and Crimdon House
Hammond, of Over Dinsdale Hall
Hay, of Cresswell House
Headlam, of Gilmonby Hall
Headlam, of Whorlton Hall
Henderson, of Leazes House
Hildyard, of Horsley
Hodgson, of Bishop Auckland
Hogg, of Norton House
Horn, of Bishop Wearmouth
Hutchinson, of Whitton House
Hutt, of Gibside Hall
Hutton, of Houghton Hall
Ingham, of Westoe
Johnson, of Aykley Heads
Jackson, of Greatham Hall
Johnson, of The Deanery
Kearney, of the Ford
Lambton, of Biddick Hall
Lambton, of Murton House
Laycock, of Lintz Hall
Lipscombe, of Staindrop
Milbank, of Carbury House
Park, of Elwick Hall
Penreth, of Usworth House
Pease, of Brinkburn
Pease, of Pierremont and Stanhope Castle
Pease, of Southend
Pease, of Woodlands

Pemberton, of Barnes and Hawthorn Tower
Rippon, of Rogerley Hall
Robinson, of Silksworth Hall
Salvin, of Burn Hall
Salvin, of Croxdale Hall
Scurfield, of Hurworth House
Shafto, of Brancepeth
Shafto, of Witworth Park
Shipperdson, of Hermitage, Pittington Hall-Garth, and Burton
Shortridge, of Cleadon Meadows
Simpson, of Whitburn West House
Smart, of Mainsforth
Spearman, of Thornley Hall and Burn Hall
Spoor, of Whitburn
Standish, of Cocken Hall
Stobart, of Etherley
Straker, of Willington House
Surtees, of Dinsdale-on-Tees
Surtees, of Hamsterley Hall
Surtees, of Mainsforth Hall
Surtees, of Redworth House
Surtees, of Seaton Carew
Sutton, of Elton Hall
Swinburne, of Pontop Hall
Taylor-Smith, of Calpike Hall
Waldy, of Egglescliffe
Watts, of Langton Grange
Wawn, of Boldon
Webster, of Pallion Hall
Wharton, of Dryburn
Wilkinson, of Hulam (formerly Coxhoe Hall)
Wilkinson, of Harperley Park
Wilkinson, of Mount Oswald
Wilkinson, of Oswald House
Williamson, of Hurdworth
Wilson-Todd, of Halnaby Hall

EDINBURGH CO.

Buccleugh and Queensberry, Duke of
Dalhousie, Marquis of
Lothian, Marquis of
Morton, Earl of
Rosebery, Earl of
Stair, Earl of
Melville, Viscount
Dunfermline, Lord
Elphinstone, Lord
Sempill, Baroness
Torphichen, Lord
Arbuthnot, Sir R. K., Bart.
Baird, Sir D., Bart.
Baird, Sir J. G., Bart.
Carmichael, Sir W. H. Gibson-, Bart.
Clerk, Sir J., Bart.
Craig, Sir W. G., Bart.
Cunynghame, Sir W. H. D., Bart.
Don-Wauchope, Sir J., Bart.
Drummond, Sir J. W., Williams, Bart.
Dundas, Sir D., Bart.
Forrest, Sir John, Bart.
Foulis, Sir J. L., Bart.
Hope, Sir A., Bart.
Maitland, Sir A. C. R. G., Bart.
Nicolson, Sir A. B., Bart.
Warrender, Sir G., Bart.
Wedderburn, Sir D., Bart.
Arbuthnot, of Mavisbank House
Bonar, of Easter Warriston
Borthwick, of Crookston
Borthwick, of Springwood Park

Brown, of Ashley
Brown, of New Hall
Brown, of Park
Brown-Borthwick, of Hope Park
Barness, of Burncrae House
Callander, of Preston House
Campbell, of Edinburgh
Christie-Miller, of Craigentinny
Colt, of Inveresk House
Cowan, of Linburn House
Cowan, of Valleyfield
Cox, of Kinellan
Dalrymple, of Hailes
Deas, of Pittendreech
Dundas, of Arniston
Durham, of Polton
Gibsone, of Pentland
Gilmour, of Craigmillar
Halkett-Craigie-Inglis, of Cramond
Hare, of Calder Hall
Hepburn-Mitchelson, late of Middleton
Hog, of Dun Edin
Home, of Whitfield
Hope-Vere, of Craigie Hall
Inglis, of Glencorse
Inglis, of Loganbank
Inglis, of Red Hall and Auchendinny
Inglis, of Torsonce
Johnston, of Kirkhill House
Johnston-Stewart, of Straiton
Lauder, of The Grange House
Lawson, of Halheriot
Learmonth, of Dean
Macdonell, of Glengarry
Macfie, of Dreghorn
Mackenzie, late of Belmont
McLaren, of Newington House
M'Neill, of Granton
Maconochie - Wellwood, of Meadowbank
Maxwell, of Middlebie and Glenair
Melville, of Hanley
Miller, of Craigentinny
Milne, of Inveresk
Mitchell, of Stow
Monro, of Craiglockhart
Morison, of Johnsburn
Raeburn, of St. Bernards
Ramsay, of Whitehill
Scott, of Malleny House
Stewart, of Straiton
Trotter, of the Bush
Trotter, of Morton Hall
Tytler, of Woodhouselee
Walker, of Bowland
Walker, of Dalry
Wauchope, of Niddrie Marischall
Weir, of Boghead House
White, of Kellerstain
Wilkie, of Ormiston
Young, of Silverknowe

ELGIN OR MORAYSHIRE.

Fife, Earl of
Moray, Earl of
Seafield, Earl of
Calder, Sir H. R., Bart.
Cumming, Sir W. G. Gordon-, Bart.
Dunbar, Sir A., Bart.
Grant, Sir G. M., Bart.
Brander, of Rock House
Brodie, of Brodie
Brodie, of Lethen House
Brodie-Innes, of Milton Brodie

Brown, of Dunkinty
Cumming-Bruce, of Roseisle
Duff, of Milton Duff
Duff, of Orton
Dunbar, of Pitgaveny
Dunbar, of Sea Park
Ferguson, of Muirton
Forteath, of Newton House
Fraser-Tytler, of Burdsyards
Grant, of Kincorth
Grant, of Main
Grant-Peterkin, of Invererne and Grange
Macdonald, of Clonranald
Macleod, of Dalvey
Robertson, of Auchinroath
Valiant-Cumming, of Logie

ESSEX.

Rochester, Bishop of
Braybrooke, Lord
Petre, Lord
Rayleigh, Lord
Abdy, Sir T. N., Bart.
Affleck, Sir R., Bart.
De Crespigny, Sir C. W. C., Bart.
Henniker, Sir B. P., Bart.
Lennard, Sir T. B., Bart.
Neave, Sir R. D., Bart.
Pechell, Sir G. S. Brooke-, Bart.
Pelly, Sir H. C., Bart.
Selwin, Sir J. T., Bart.
Smijth, Sir W. Bowyer-, Bart.
Smith, Sir C. C., Bart.
Thomas, Sir G. V., Bart.
Tyrell, Sir J. T., Bart.
Vincent, Sir F., Bart.
Western, Sir T. B., Bart.
Wood, Sir M., Bart.
Alexander, of the Auberries
Arabin, of High Beach
Arkwright, of Mark Hall
Arkwright, of Rundells
Ashley, of Copt Hall
Bagshaw, of Dovercourt
Barclay, of Leyton
Barclay, of Walthamstow
Baring, of Langham Hall
Barnard, of Little Barfield
Battiscombe, of Hacton Hall
Bawtree, of Abberton
Bennet, of Tollesbury Lodge
Bingley, of Higham Lodge
Blencowe, of Thoby Priory
Bramston, of Skreens
Brandreth, late of St. Osyth
Branfill, of Upminster Hall
Brett, of Wakes Colne
Brewster, of Greenstead Hall
Brewster, of Ashford Lodge
Brise, of Spains Hall
Brocket, of Spains Hall
Brunwin, of Park House
Budworth, of Greensted Hall
Bullen, of Great Baddow
Bullock, of Faulkbourne Hall
Burges, of East Ham
Burmester, of Little Oakley
Byng, of Quendon Hall
Byron, of Langford
Capel, of Little Blake Hall
Capper, of Upton
Cardinal, of Tendring Manor
Carrington, of Bocking Deanery
Carwardine, of Colne Priory

Chafy, of Bowes House
Chamberlayne, of Stanstead
Chambers, of Croft House
Chamier, late of Waltham Hall
Chisenhale-Marsh. of Gaynes and Marsden Ash
Colgrave, of Downsell Hall
Coope, of Rochetts
Corsellis, of Wyvenhoe Hall
Cotton, of Leytonstone
Courtauld, of Gosfield Hall
Cox, of Harwood Hall and Herongate
Croll, of Harold's-Wood Hall
Crosse, of Berwick House
Cure, of Blake Hall
Daubuz, of Leyton
Davies, of Sewardstone
Davis, of Cranbrooke Park
De Horne, of Stanway Hall
Disney, of The Hyde
Du Cane, of Braxted Park
Earle, of High Ongar
Eden, of Messing
Edenborough, of Thrift Hall
English, of Warley House
Errington, of Lexden Park
Ewart, of Dedham
Fane, of Priors
Fanshawe, of Dengey Hall
Fanshawe, of Parsloes
Farman, of Layer Marney Tower
Fisher, of Ovington
Fortescue, of Dudbrooke House
Formby, of Dedham
Fry, of Woodford
Fuller-Maitland, of Stansted
Garland, of Michaelstowe Hall
Gayton, of Saffron Walden
Gent, of Moyns Park
Gepp, of High Easter
Glyn, of Darrington House
Gosling, of Hassobury
Graham, of Great Bromley
Green, of Colchester
Griffin-Stonestreet, of Stondon Hall
Gurdon-Rebow, of Wyvenhoe
Hamilton, of The Firs
Hamilton, of Holyfield Hall
Hamilton, of The Mount, and of Clingford
Hanbury, of Holfield Grange and Hone Batch
Hanson, of Chigwell
Harrison, of Copford Hall
Harrison, of Olivers
Haselfoot, of Boreham Manor
Hawkins, of Alresford Hall
Heathcote, of Chingford
Helme, of Hornchurch
Hills, of Colne Park
Hirst, of Great Ropers
Horton, of The Cot
Honywood, of Marks Hall
Hornor, of The Howe
Houblon, of Copersale
Houlton, of Hallingbury Place
Jesse, of Maisonette
Jessopp, of Waltham Abbey
Johnson, of St. Osyth's Priory
Judd, of Rickling
Kelso, of Red Park
Kemble, of Runwell Hall
Kirby, late of St. Osyth's Priory
Knox, of Runwell
Kortwright, of Furze Hall
Lampet, of Great Bardfield

Laurie, of Laurietown
Leigh, of Goldhanger
Lescher, of Boyles Court
Lloyd, of Rolls Park
Lowndes, of Barrington Hall
Luard, of Witham Lodge
Mackintosh, of Marshalls
Maitland, of Loughton
Majendie, of Hedingham Castle
Malthus, of Hadstock Place
Marsden, of Colne House
Marsden, of Great Oakley
Marsh, of Gaynes Park
Martin-Leake, of Thorpe Hall
Mashiter, of Priests
Mathew, Pentloe Hall
Maynard, of Easton Lodge
Mechi, of Tiptree Hall
Meyer, of Stondon House
Mildmay, of Bishop's Hall
Newall, of Forest Hall
Newman, of Nelmes
Nichols, of Lawford Hall
Norman, of Mistley Place
Nunn, of Bromley Hall
Palmer, of Nazing Park
Papillon, of Lexden Manor
Pardoe, of Leyton
Parker, of Woodham Mortimer
Pelly, of Plashet House
Pelly, of Upminster
Pemberton-Barnes, of Havering-atte-Bower
Penrose, of Dedham
Petre, of Shenfield Place
Phillips, of Riffhams Lodge
Powell, of Buckhurst Hill
Pryor, of Hylands
Pulteney, of The Hargreaves
Rasch, of Woodhill House
Raymond, of Belchamp Hall
Raymond, of The Lee
Rigge, of Belmont Castle
Round, of Bergholt
Round, of Birch
Round, of Birch Hall
Round, of East Hill
Round, late of Springfield Lyons
Rush, of Elsenham Hall
Russell, of Stubbers
Sandars, late of Chesterford Park
Sanford, of Waltham House
Savill-Onley, of Stisted Hall
Scratton, of Prittlewell Priory
Selby, of Whitley and Wimbish Hall
Sims, of Hubbard's Hall
Skingley, of Wake's Colne Hall
Skinner, of Braxwoods
Skipper, of Great Blake Hall
Smith, of Little Bentley
Smith, of Shortgrove
Sotheby, of Sewardstone
Sparrow, of Gosfield Price
Spurling, of Dynes Hall
Spitty, of Billericay
Stane, of Forest Hall
Suart, of Bowles
Swift, of Herongate
Tabor, of Earl's Hall and Rochford Hall
Tatham, of Althorne
Tawke, of Rochford
Thompson, of Clements
Tindal, of Hanningfield
Tompson, of Boxted House
Tower, of Weald Hall
Townsend, of Berwick Place

Travers, of Great Baddow
Tufnell, of Hatfield Place
Tufnell, of Langleys
Turner, of Little Oliver's
Vaizey, of Attwoods
Vaizey, of Star Style
Vallentin, of Walthamstow
Walford, late of Hatfield Place
Walsh, of Great Tey
Walton, of Haverhill Hamlet
Warner, of Higham Hall
Watlington, of Moor Hall
Way, of Spaynes Hall
Way, of Spencer Grange
Weeley, of Weeley
Welch, of North Shoebury
West, of Horham Hall
White, of Clement's Hall
White, of Withersfield Manor and Berechurch Hall
Whiteman, of Theydon Grove
Wilkes, of Lofts Hall
Williams, of White Riding
Wilson, of Althorne Hall
Wilson, of Great Canfield
Wingfield-Baker, of Orset Hall
Wolfe, of Wood Hall
Wood, of Bishop's Hall
Wright, of Hatfield Priory
Wright, of Kelveden Hall

FERMANAGH CO.

Ely, Marquis of
Belmore, Earl of
Enniskillen, Earl of
Erne, Earl of
Lanesborough, Earl of
Brooke, Sir V. A., Bart.
Tennent, Sir J. Emerson-, Bart.
Archdall, of Castle Archdall and Riversdale
Atthill, of Ardvarney
Barton, of Clonelly
Barton, of The Waterfoot
Bloomfield, of Castle Caldwell
Brackenridge, of Lisbeake
Brady, of Johnstown
Butler, of Innes-Rath
Dane, of Killyhevlin
D'Arcy-Irvine, of Castle Irvine and Rosaclare Lodge
Graham, of Drumgoon
Haire, of Armagh Manor
Hassard, of Gardenhill
Hassard, of Skea
Irvine, of Green Hill
Irvine, of Killadeas
Irwin, of Derrygore
Johnstone, of Magheremena Castle
Johnstone, of Snow Hill
Loudrum, of Machen cross
L'Estrange-Carleton, of Market Hill
Madden, of Manor Waterhouse
Madden, of Rosslea Manor
Maguire, of Gortoral
Porter, of Belleisle
Richardson, of Rossfad
Sankey, of Lurganbrae
Taylor, of Cranbrooke
Tipping, of Rossferry House

FIFESHIRE.

Elgin and Kincardine, Earl of
Fife, Earl of

Glasgow, Earl of
Kellie, Earl of
Moray, Earl of
Morton, Earl of
Rosslyn, Earl of
Rothes, Countess of
Alexander, Sir W. J., Bart.
Anstruther, Sir R., Bart.
Baxter, Sir D., Bart.
Bethune, Sir J. T. L., Bart.
Erskine, Sir T., Bart.
Gibb, Sir G. D., Bart.
Halkett, Sir P. A., Bart.
Murray, Sir R., Bart.
Preston, Sir H. L., Bart.
Wemys, Sir J., Bart.
Anderson, of Kingask
Anstruther-Thomson, of Charleton
Aytoun, of Inchdairnie
Babington, of Luscar House
Baird, of Elie
Balfour, of Balbirnie
Balfour, of Fernie Castle
Barclay, of Keavil House
Bean-Gourlay, of Kincraig
Beatson, of Rossend
Beatson-Bell, of Kilduncan
Berry, of Tayfield
Bethune, of Belho
Bethune, of Nydie
Campbell, of Edenwood
Cartwright, of Ladybank
Cathcart, of Pitcairlie
Cheape, of Strathtyrum and Wellfield
Christie, of Durie
Colvile, of Craigflower
Corstorphine, of Pittowie
Dalgleish, of Dura
Dalgleish, of Woodburne
Dalyell, of Lingo
Davidson, of Bogie
Dougall, of Scott's Craig
Drinkwater-Bethune, of Balfour
Drysdale, of Pitteuchar
Durham, of Largo
Erskine, of Kinnedder
Fergusson, of Raith
Gillespie, of Mountquhanie
Hannay, of King-muir
Hannay-Cunningham, of Pittarthie
Hastie, of Carnock
Hay, of Mortun
Heriot, of Ramornie
Hope, of Rankeillour
Hunt, of Pittencrieff
Kinnear, of Kinnear
Lindsay, of Balcarras and Leuchars
Lindsay, of Straiton
Low, of Clatton
Lumisdaine, of Lathallan
Lundin, of Auchtermairnie
Macnab of Wchward, of Garvock
Made, Blackwad, of Pitravie
Maitland, of Rossie House
Maitland-Makgill-Crichton, of Rankeilour-Makgill
Meldrum, of Kincaple
Mercer-Henderson, of Fordell
Monypenny, of Pitmilly
Morison, of Naughton
Moubray, of Cockairny
Moubray, of Otterston
Murray, of Ayton
Oswald, of Dunnikier
Pagan, of Clayton
Rigg, of Tarvit House

Sandys-Lumsdaine, of Innergellie
Scrymgeour-Wedderburn, of Birkhill
Schank, of Castlerig
Simson, of Pitcorthie House
Skene, of Hallyards and Pitlour
Smith-Sligo, of Inzievar
Spens, of Craigsanquhar
Stark-Christie, of Ballindean
Stark-Christie, of Teasses
Stewart, of St. Fort
Wemyss, of Wemyss Castle and Torrie House
Wemyss, of Wemyss Hall
Whyte-Melville, of Bennochy and Strathkinness
Wood, of Largo

FLINTSHIRE.

Feilding, Viscount
Denbigh, Earl of
Kenyon, Lord
Mostyn, Lord
Glynne, Sir S. R., Bart.
Hanmer, Sir J., Bart.
Mostyn, Sir P., Bart.
Puleston, Sir R. P., Bart.
Williams, Sir H., Bart.
Atcherley, of Cymman
Bankes, of Soughton Hall
Browne, of Bronwylfa
Buddicom, of Penbedw Hall
Churton, of Mörannedd
Clough, of Llwyn Offa
Conwy, of Bodrhyddan
Cooke, of Gwysaney
Cotton, of Knolton Hall
Dixon, of Nant
Dundas, of Aston Hall
Dymock, of Penley Hall
Echlin, of Bronington
Eyton, of Leeswood
Frost, of Meadowslea
Godsal, of Iscoed Park
Grosvenor, of Halkyn Castle
Howard, of Broughton Hall
Jones, of Wepre Hall
Jones, of Heartsheath
Lloyd, of Cilcen Hall and Nannerch
Morgan, of Golden Grove
Peel, of Bryn-y-Tys
Pennant, of Bodfari
Potts, of Glanrafon
Puleston, of Worthenbury
Raikes, of Llwynegrin Hall
Richards, of Mordon House
Roberts, of Coeddû
Rowley, of Bodrhyddan
Salusbury, of Brynbella
Thomas, of Bryn Elwy
Thomas, of Bryn Merlyn
Trevor-Roper, of Plâs Teg Park
Wynne, of Norquis Hall

FORFARSHIRE.

Airlie, Earl of
Dalhousie, Earl of
Fife, Earl of
Northesk, Earl of
Southesk, Earl of
Strathmore, Earl of
Panholme, Lord
Wharncliffe, Lord
Beresford, Sir G. De la Poer, Bart.
1062

Lyell, Sir C., Bart.
Munro, Sir Thomas, Bart.
Ochterlony, Sir C. M., Bart.
Ogilvy, Sir John, Bart.
Arbuthnot, of Marykirk
Bairnsfather, of Dunbarrow
Balfour-Ogilvy, of Tannadice
Baxter, of Ashcliff
Blair-Imrie, of Lunan
Bruce-Gardyne, of Middleton House
Campbell, of Stracathro House
Carnegie, of Tarrie
Carnegy, of Lour and Turin
Chalmers, of Aldbar
Clayhills, of Invergowrie
Clayhills-Henderson, of Carlingwell
Constable, of Wallace Craigie
Cruikshank, of Langley Park
Dempster, of Dunnichen
Dick, of Pitkerro
Duncan, of The Vine
Fraser, of Hospitalfield
Fyffe, of Broughty Ferry
Geekie, of Baldowrie
Gordon-Hallyburton, of Hallyburton Lodge
Graham, of Duntroon
Grant, of Craigo
Greenhill-Gardyne, of Finhaven
Guthrie, of Craigie
Guthrie, of Guthrie Castle
Haig, of Glen Ogil House
Haig, of Maulsden
Hay, of Letham
Hunter, of Blackness
Johnston, of Heathfield House
Kennedy-Erskine, of Dun
Kinloch, of Glenisla House
Kinloch, of Kilrie
Laird, of Strathmartine
L'Amy, of Dunkenny
Lindsay-Carnegie, of Kimblethmont
Lyon, of Glenogil
Macdonald, of Rossie Castle
Maule, of Maulesden
Meason, of Lindertis
Milne, of Woodhill
Mudie, of Pitmuies
Ogilvy, of Clova
Ogilvy, of Inshewan
Ogilvy, of Ruthven House
Pierson, of The Guynd
Rait, of Anniston House
Renny-Tailyour, of Borrowfield
Scrymgeour-Wedderburn, of Wedderburn
Scrymsour-Fetheringham, of Powrie and Fotheringham
Swinburne, of Marcus Lodge

GALWAY CO.

Clanricarde, Marquis of
Clancarty, Earl of
Gough, Viscount
Tuam, Bishop of
Ashtown, Lord
Clanmorris, Lord
Clonbrock, Lord
Dunsandle and Clanconal, Lord
Ffrench, Lord
Oranmore and Browne, Lord
Wallscourt, Lord
Bellew-Grattan, Sir H. C., Bart.
Blake, Sir T. E., Bart.
Burke, Sir T. J., Bart.

Guinness, Sir A. E., Bart.
Mahon, Sir W. V., Bart.
Shee, Sir G., Bart.
Alexander, of Maryville
Athy, of Renville
Bagot, of Ballymoe
Bagot, of Augbrane Castle
Bermingham-Ruthven, of Hearnesbrooke
Blake, of Ballyglunin
Blake, of Corofin
Blake, of Cregg Castle
Blake, of Frenchfort
Blake, of Furbough
Blake, of Gortnamona
Blake, late of Merlin
Blake, of Rathville
Blake, of Renvyle
Blake, of Toomnenaun
Blakeney, of Abbert
Bodkin, of Anuagh
Bodkin, of Kilcloony
Bodkin, of Roseberry
Browne, of Greenville
Browne, of Kilskeagh
Browne, of Mount Hazell
Browne, of Mount Kelly
Browne, late of Moyne
Burke, of Ballydugan
Burke, of Drum Park
Burke, of Knocknagur
Burke, of Ower
Burke, of St. Cleran's
Burke, of Slatefield
Butler, of Cregg and Greenfield
Butler, of Thorn Park
Butson, of Clonfert and Knocknagreena
Chevers, of Killyan
Clerke, of Fort Brown
Close, of Derrymacloughney Castle
Comyn, of Killeen Farm
Comyn, of Woodstock
Concanon, of Waterloo
Daly, of Castle Daly
Daly, of Cooliney
Daly, of Prospect Hill
Daly, of Raford
D'Arcy, of Castle Park
D'Arcy, of New Forest
Dickson, of South Hill
Dolphin, of Corr
Dolphin, of Turoe
Donelan, of Killiswood
Donelan, of Killagh
Donelan, of Sylane and St. Peter's Well
Eyre, of Eyrecourt Castle
Eyre, of Eyreville
ffrench, of Ballanamore
Forster, of Forster Park and Hermitage
Foster, of Ashfield
Foster-Vesey-Fitzgerald, of Glantreague
French, of Monivae Castle
Graham, of Ballinakill
Gregory, of Coole Park
Hall, of Knockbrack Lodge
Jameson, of Windfield
Joyce, of Merview
Joyce, of Rahoane Park
Kelly, of Castle Kelly
Kelly, of Mucklin
Kenney, of Ballyforan House
Kenney, of Kilclogher
Kingsmill, of Corrandoo

Kirwan, of Bawnmore
Kirwan, of Bluidwell
Kirwan, of Castle Hacket
Kirwan, of Barnaderg
Kirwan, late of Moyne
Lambert, of Aggard
Lambert, of Castle Lambert
Lambert, of Waterdale House
Lawrence, of Lisreaghan
Le Poer Trench, of Mount Pleasant
Longworth, of Oatfield
Lopdell, of Raheen Park
Lynch, of Barna
Lynch, of Duras and Renmore
Lynch-Staunton, of Clydagh
Maclachlan, of Earl's Island and Knocknakerna
Mansergh-St. George, of Headfort
Martin, of Ross
Maunsell, of Fort Eyre
Moore, of Shannon Grove
Morris, of Well Park
Nugent, of Cranna
Nugent, of Pallas
O'Ferrall, of Dalyston
O'Flahertie, of Lemonfield
O'Flaherty, of Knockbane
O'Kelly, of Gallagh Castle
O'Rorke, of Clonbern
Persse, of Moyode Castle
Persse, of Roxborough
Pigott, of Eagle Hill
Pollok, of Lismany
Potts, of Correen Castle
Reade, of The Wood Parks
Redington, of Dangan House
Redington, of Kilcornan House
Reynolds, of Adragoole
Richardson, of Tyaquin
Ruttledge, of Barbersfort
St. George, of Tyrone House
Seymour, of Ballymore Castle
Taylor, of Castle Taylor
Trench, of Cerbane
Trench, of Clonfert House
Turbett, of Kilmackshane
Ussher, of Eastwell
Wade, of Carrowmore
Waithman, of Moyne
Wilde, of Moyteura

GLAMORGANSHIRE.

Bute, Marquis of
Tredegar, Lord
Dunraven, Countess of
Llandaff, Bishop of
Morris. Sir J. A., Bart.
Walker, Sir G. F. R., Bart.
Bailey, of Aberaman
Basset, of Beaupré
Bassett, of Bonvilstone House
Deumel, of Talcgan House
Benson, of Fairy Hill
Biddulph, of Dderwen
Booker, of Velindra House
Bruce, of Duffryn
Bruce, of St. Nicholas
Cameron, of Murton House
Clark, of Tal-y-garn
Coffin, of Llandaff
Crawshay, of Cyfarthfa
David, of Radyr Court
Dillwyn, of Hendrefoilan
Dillwyn-Llewellyn, of Penllergare
Eaton, of Brynymôr

Edwardes, of Gileston Manor
Edwards-Vaughan, of Rheola
Entwistle, of Llanblethian
Evans, of Eaglesbush
Fothergill, of Hensol Castle
Franklen, of Clementstone
Gibbon, of Trecastle and Newton House
Gilbertson, of Pontardawe
Gough, of Yniscedwin
Gould, of Frampton
Grant, of The Groll
Grenfell, of Maesteg House
Gronow, of Ash Hall
Gwyn, of Dyffryn
Hewett, of Tyr-Mab-Ellis
Homfray, of Penllyne Castle
Jenkins, of Walterstone
Jenner, of Llanblethian
Jenner, of Wenvoe Castle
Jones of Fonmou Castle
Jones, of Heathfield
Knight, of Tythegston
Lee, of Dynas Powis
Lewis, of Green Meadow
Lewis, of The Heath and New House
Lindsay of Woodlands
Llewellin, of Hendrescythan
Llewellyn, of Baglan Hall
Llewellyn, of Owrt Colman
Lloyd, of Plâs-Cil-y-Belyll
Lucas, of Uplands
Lynh-Blosse, of New Castle House
Morgan, of St. Helen's
Morris, of Sketty
Mundy, of Plâs Newydd
Nicholl, of Merhyr Mawr
Nicholl, of The Ham
Nicholl-Carne, of Dinnlands and St. Donat's Castle
Nicholl-Carne, of Nash Manor
Paddon, of Norton Lodge
Penrice, of Kilvrough
Powell, of Gabalva
Price, of Glantwrch
Prichard, of Collenna
Pryce, of Duffryn
Richards, of Brooklands
Richards, of Llandaff Court
Rickards, of Llandough
Roberts, of Gadlys Uchaf
Romilly, of Barry
Romilly, of Porthkerry
Rous, of Courtyrala
Rowland, of Fîrwd Vale
Salmon, of Penllyne Castle
Smith, of Gwernllwynwith
Stacey, of Old Castle
Talbot, of Margam
Thomas, of Glanmor
Thomas, of Ystrad Mynach
Thomas, of The Court House
Traherne, of Coedriglan
Traherne, of Coytrehen
Traherne, of St. Hilary
Turbervill, of Ewenny Abbey
Tyler, of Cottrell
Tynte, of Cefn Mably
Vivian, of Glanafon
Vivian, of Park Wern
Vivian, of Singleton
Wilkinson, of Brynfield
Williams, of Aberpergwm
Williams, of Duffryn Frwd
Williams, of Roath Court
Wood, of Stout Hall
Worthington, of Llancaiach

GLOUCESTERSHIRE.

Beaufort, Duke of
Bathurst, Earl
Ducie, Earl
Dunraven, Countess of
Ellenborough, Earl of
Gainsborough, Earl of
Wemyss and March, Earl of
Sydney, Viscount
Gloucester and Bristol, Bishop of
De Mauley, Lord
De Saumarez, Lord
Fitzhardinge, Lord
Northwick, Lord
Redesdale, Lord
Sherborne, Lord
Sudeley, Lord
Beach, Sir M. E. Hicks-, Bart.
Boevey, Sir T. H. Crawley-, Bart.
Campbell, Sir James. Bart.
Codrington, Sir G. W. H., Bart.
Codrington, Sir W. R.. Bart.
Cuyler, Sir C. H. J., Bart.
Darell, Sir W. L., Bart.
East, Sir J. B., Bart.
Goldsmid, Sir F. H., Bart.
Guise, Sir W. V., Bart.
Jenkinson, Sir G. S., Bart.
Key, Sir K. G., Bart.
Musgrave, Sir W. A., Bart.
Owen, Sir H. O., Bart.
Pole, Sir P. Van-Notten-, Bart.
Prevost, Sir George, Bart.
Ricketts, Sir C., Bart.
Rushout, Sir C. R.. Bart.
Russell, Sir Wm., Bart.
Steele-Graves, Sir J. M., Bart.
Willoughby, Sir J. C.. Bart.
Ackers, of Prinknash Park
Adey, of Wotton-under-Edge
Agg. of Hewletts
Baillie, of Dunstbourne
Baillie, of Stoke Park
Baker, of Hardwicke Court
Baker, of Hasfield Court
Barnard, of Notcliffe House and Whitfield Court
Barnard, of Prestbury
Barnett, of Cheltenham
Bathurst, of Lydney Park
Belfield, of Malmains
Bengough, of The Ridge
Berkeley, of Overbury Court
Blackwell, of Ampney Park
Blagdon, of Boddington
Blathwayt, of Dyrham Park
Bourne, of Weston Subedge
Brookes, of Elmstree
Browne, of Salperton Park
Browne, of Stout's Hill
Buchanan, of North Cote
Burland, of New Court
Campbell, of Frilings
Capel, of Painswick Grove
Castle, of Stapleton
Cave, of Cleve Hill
Chamberlayne, of Maugersbury
Clifford, of Frampton Court
Clutterbuck, of Newark Park
Colquitt-Craven, of Brockhampton Park
Corbett-Holland, of Admington Hall
Cornwall, of Ashcroft House
Coxwell-Rogers, of Dowdeswell Court and Ablington Manor
Crawshay, of Oaklands Park

Crego-Colmore, of Moor End
Cripps, of Cirencester
Cromie, of Wicombe Park
Croome, of Cerney House
Crowdy, of Cheltenham
Crowther, of Somerville-Ashton
Dalton, of Dunkirk Manor
Daniel, of Longford
Daubeney, of Alston Lodge
Daubeney, of Ampney Crucis and Siddington
Daubeney, of Cote and Norton House
Davis, of Wellclose
Davy, of Tracy Park
Dent, of Sudeley Castle
De Paravicini, of Avening
De Winton, of Wallsworth Hall
Dhuleep Singh, of Hatherop
Dickenson, of Siston Court
Dighton, of Oak House
Dorington, of Lypiatt Park
Drummond, of Boyce Court
Edwards, of The Hayes
Ellison, of Elmestree
Elwes, of Colesborne
Estcourt, of Estcourt
Fenton, of Norton Hall
Foll, of Beckford Hall
Follet, of Cherington
Forbes, of Angeston Grange
Fortescue, of Cheltenham
Fortescue - Brickdale, of Birchamp House
Fox, of Frampton-Cotterell
Frampton, late of Barnwood Court
Francillon, of Blenheim House
Fullerton, of Sheethonger Manor
Gael, of Charlton Kings
Gardner, of Hadley House
Garrard, of Clopton House
George, of Cherrington
Goold, of Newnham and Haglon House
Gordon-Canning, of Hartpury
Gore-Langton, of Clifton Court
Graham-Clarke, of Frocester Manor
Grey, of The Parklands
Haines, of Duntsborne
Hale, of Alderley
Hallewell, of Beanchamps
Hallewell, of Stratford House
Hardwicke, of The Grange
Harford of Cheltenham
Harford, of Frenchay
Harford, of Stoke Park and Blaize Castle
Hartland, of The Oaklands
Hartley, of Lyegrove House
Hayward, of Nympsfield House
Hayward, of Quedgeley House
Hill, of Heath House
Hillhouse, of Clifton
Holford, of Weston Bird
Hopkinson, of Edgeworth Manor
Hopton, of Kemerton
Howard, of Thornbury Castle
Hunt, of Bowden Hall
Huntley, of Boxwell Court
Hutchinson, of Cowley Manor
Hyett, of Painswick House
Jervis, of Eyford Park
Jenner-Fust, of Hill Court
Jones, of Nass House
Kingscote, of Kingscote
Knox, of St. Leonard's Court
Lawrence, of Sandywell Park
Leigh, of Woodchester Park

1064

Leighton, of Bafford House
Lindow, of Gawcomb
Lippincott, of Over Court
Lloyd, of Flaxley Grange
Lorsey, of Chariton Kings
Lucy, of Claremont House
Lysons, of Hempsted Court
Machen, of Eastbach Court
Maclaine, of Kington House
Marklove, of Lullingworth House and Woburn Hall
Marling, of Norton Court
Marling, of Stanley Park
Marling, of Stonehouse Court
Master, of Knole and Cirencester Abbey
Miles, of Kingsweston House
Mills, of Miserdine
Millward, of Lechlade Manor
Mirehouse, of Hambrook Grove
Moreton, of Tortworth Old Court
Morse, of Ashmead House
Nash, of Old Sodbury
Newman, of Thornbury Park
Niblett, of Haresfield Court
Noel, of Clanna Falls
Onslow, of Oxenhall
Ormerod, of Sedbury Park
Palmer, of Hanham
Parr, of Bredon Old Hall
Parry, of Highman Court
Paul, of High Grove
Peach, of Tockington
Peel, of Aylesmore House
Peters, of Easington
Phelps, of Chestal
Playne, of Longford House
Pocock, of Puckrup Hall
Pole, of Buryfields House
Pole, of Wick Rissington
Ponsonby, of Hatherop
Potter, of Standish House
Price, of Tibberton Court
Probyn, of Longhope Manor
Pulling, of Newark Park
Purnell, of Bodlington Manor
Purnell, of Stancombe Park
Pyrke, of Deane Hall
Raikes, of Hill Ash House
Raymond-Barker, of Fairford Park
Ricardo, of Gatcombe Park
Rice, of Oddington
Rolt, of Ozleworth
Rooke, of Bigsweir House
Ruddle, of Walton House
Sadler, of Keynsham Bury
St. Clair, of Staverton Court
Sampson, of Henbury
Sargeaunt, of Tewkesbury Park
Saunders, of Loretto
Savage, of Tetbury
Scott, of Harescomb Court
Sevre, of Turshill House
Skillicorne, of Cheltenham
Smith, of Stoke Bishop
Squire, of Cheltenham
Stanton, of The Thrupp
Stoughton, of Owlpen Park
Strickland, of Apperley Court
Surman, of Swindon Hall and Lay Court
Surman, of Tredington
Talbot, of Temple Guiting
Taylor, of Prestbury
Thackwell, of Wilton Place
Townsend, of Bishop's Cleeve
Townsend, of Stcanbridge House

Trye, of Leckhampton Court
Tyndall, of The Fort
Vavasour, of Fosse Cottage
Viner, of Badgeworth
Waddingham, of Guiting Grange
Walker, of Redland
Waller, of Farmington Lodge
Wallington, of Dursley
Ward, of Fern Park
Welch, of Arle House
Whitehead, of Amberley Court
Whitmore, of Lower Slaughter
Whittuck, of Hanham Hall
Wilson, of Aldington
Wilton, of Whitminster
Witts, of Upper Slaughter
Wrangham, of The Rocks
Wyatt, of Hill House
Wynniatt, of Dymock Grange
Yorke, of Forthampton Court

GUERNSEY.

Carey, of Candie
Cockburn, of Elm House
Collings, of St. James's
De Havilland, of Havilland Hall
Hoskins, of York Place
Mansell, of Guernsey
Tupper, of Guernsey

HADDINGTONSHIRE.

Tweeddale, Marquis of
Dalhousie, Earl of
Haddington, Earl of
Hopetoun, Earl of
Lauderdale, Earl of
Wemyss and March, Earl of
Blantyre, Lord
Sinclair, Lord
Baird, Sir D., Bart.
Dalrymple, Sir H. H., Bart.
Hall, Sir J., Bart.
Hepburn, Sir T. B., Bart.
Lauder, Sir J. Dick-, Bart.
Kinloch, Sir D., Bart.
Sinclair, Sir R. C., Bart.
Suttie, Sir G. Grant-, Bart.
Warrender, Sir G. Bart.
Aitchison, of Alderson
Aitchison, of Drummore
Anderson, of St. Germain's
Balfour, of Whittinghame
Blantyre, of Lennoxlore
Brown, of Johnstowaburn
Cadell, of Cockenzie
Fletcher, of Salton Hall
Hamilton [Nisbet-], of Biel
Hay, of Belton
Hay, of Hayes
Hope, of Luffness
Houstoun, of Clerkintown
Laidlaw, of Seacliff
Newton, of Newton Hall
Sprot, of Spott House
Stuart, of Eaglescarnie
Wight, of Ormiston
Wood, of Woolvet Park

HAMPSHIRE.

Buccleuch and Queensberry, Duke of
Wellington, Duke of

Winchester, Marquis of
Waterford, Dowager Marchioness of
Carnarvon, Earl of
Hardwicke, Earl of
Malmesbury, Earl of
Normanton, Earl of
Northesk, Earl of
Portsmouth, Earl of
Eversley, Viscount
Palmerston, Viscountess
Winchester, Bishop of
Ashburton, Lord
Bolton, Lord
Calthorpe, Lord
Hylton, Lord
Dorchester, Lord
Ashburton, Dowager Lady
Stuart de Rothesay, Lady
Burrard, Sir Charles, Bart.
Burrard, Sir George, Bart.
Carnac, Sir J. Rivett-, Bart.
Cope, the Rev. Sir. W. H., Bart.
Cunynghame, Sir D. T., Bart.
Curtis, Sir Lucius, Bart.
Gardiner, Sir J. B. W. S., Bart.
Gervis, Sir G. E. M. T., Bart.
Goldsmid, Sir F. H., Bart.
Heathcote, Sir Wm., Bart.
Jervoise, Sir J. C., Bart.
Knighton, Sir W. W., Bart.
Macdonald, Sir A. K., Bart.
Mildmay, Sir H. B. P. St. John, Bart.
Miller, Sir C. J. H., Bart.
Paulet, Sir H. C., Bart.
Rycroft, Sir N., Bart.
Tichborne, Sir H. A. J. D , Bart.
Acland, of Langdown Lawn
Agar, of Milford Lodge
Aitchison, of Shrub's Hill
Arundell, of Candover House
Atherley, of Northbrook House
Baring, of Norman's Court
Beach, of Oakley Hall
Beardmore, of Uplands
Beauclerk, of Winchfield House
Bell, of Selborne
Berners, of Midanbury
Best, of Red Rice
Best, of Standen House
Beste, of Botleigh Grange
Bigg-Wither, of Manydown and
    Tangier Park
Bingham, of Heathfield Lodge
Birch. of Clare Park
Bishop, of Bramdean House
Blunt, of Kemshott Park
Blunt, of Wallop House
Bourne, of Testwood House
Brace, of Catisfield Lodge
Bradshaw, of Abshot House
Brander, of Somerford Grange
Breton, of the Polygon
Brewer, of Garlogs
Brice, of Puckham House
Burningham, of Froyle House
Burton-Phillipson, of Bramshaw
    House
Butler, of Bradshott
Butler, of Dowland House
Butler, of Empshott House
Butler, late of La Court
Byam, of Westwood
Carpenter-Garnier, of Rookesbury
Carter, of Adhurst St. Mary's
Carter, of Little Green
Castleman, of Beech House
Castleman, of St. Ives House

Cavan, of Middleton House
Chamberlayne, of Cranbury Park
    and Weston Grove
Chawner, of Newton Manor
Cheales, of Northend House
Cholmondeley, of Holly Hill
Chute, of The Vyne
Clinton, of Ashley Clinton
Codrington, of Dean House
Cole, of Holybourn Lodge
Coles, of Ditcham Park
Coles, of Middleton House
Collier, of Wickham
Colt, of Rownhams
Compton, of Minstead Manor
Coventry, of Burgate House
Crabbe, of Glen Eyre
Cunningham, of Bury House
Currie, of Minley Manor
Curzon, of East Dean
Dampier, of Twyford House
Davison, of Warblington House
Delme, of Cams Park
Deverell, of Purbrook Park
Dewar, of Doles
Dodson, of Mewsey
Drummond, of Cadlands
Drummond, of Eaglehurst
Drummond, of Redenham
Dutton, of Hinton House
Dutton, of Timsbury Manor
Ellis-Jervoise, of Herriard Park
Erle, of Bramshott Grange
Esdaile, of Burley Manor
Etwall, of Longstock Down
Everett. of Clanville
Eyre, of Warrens
Fane, of Avon Tyrrell
Farr, of Ilford House
Fitz-Gerald, of North Hall
Fitz-Roy, of Frogmore Park
Fleming, of Stoneham Park and Chil-
    worth Manor
Forbes, of Bordeigh House
Forbes, of Merry Oak
Freeman, of Pylewell
Freeston, late of Totton
Gale, of Kitnocks
Gale, of Upham House
Giles, of Bentley
Goff, of Hale Park
Goodlad, of Hill Place
Grame, of Highfield
Greenwood, of Broadhanger
Greenwood, of Brookwood Park
Haggard, of Bournemouth
Hall, of Fleetlands House
Hargreaves, of Cuffnells
Harrisson, of Bittern
Hawker, of Ashford House
Hawley, of West-Green House
Heathcote, of Bramshaw
Heasson, of Orington Park
Higgins, of Hambledon
Hirst, of The Down Grange
Hobart, of Langdown House
Holloway, of Marchwood
Hornby, of Upham House
Hornby, of The Hook
Houghton, of Armsworth House
Howard, of Hazelby
Humphery, of Penton Lodge
Humphrys, of Elm Lodge
Iremonger, of Wherwell Priory
Ives, of Bentworth Hall
James, of Dunhill
Jenkyns, of Botley Hill

Jodrell, of Merchistoun Hall
King, of Preston Candover
Kingsmill, of Sydmonton Court
Knapton, of Boldre and Rope Hill
Knight, of Chawton House
Laing, of Hordle House
Le Blanc, of Blackbrook House
Lee, of Kingsgate House
Lefroy, of Itchel House
Legge, of Mareland and Bramdean
Lempriere, of Pelham
Lewis, of Westbury House
Linzee, of Jermyns
Lockhart, of Sherfield English
Long, of Belmore House
Long, of Preshaw House
Loring, of Southwick and Boarhunt
Maberly, of Hawkley Hurst
Macnabb, of Highfield
Macnaghten, of Bittern Manor
Maine, of Bighton Wood
Malcolm, of Beechwood
Marsh, of Ramridge
Martin, of Bittern Lodge
Marx, of Arle-Bury
Massy, of Hazelhurst
Michel, of St. Ives
Mill, of Mottisfont Abbey
Miller, of Anstey Manor
Mills, of Bisterne
Mitford, of Exbury
Moody, of Stoneham
Morant, of Brokenhurst Park
Morant, of Ringwood Manor
Mundy, of Holly Bank
Munro, of Fritham
Naghten, of Blighmont
Napier, of Oaklands
Newcombe, of Aldershott
Nicholson, of Basing Park
Nightingale, of Embley Park
Onslow, of Ropley
Palmer, of Breamore
Palmer, of Selborne
Parkhouse, of Eastfield
Payne, of Bordean House
Pigott, of Sherfield Hill
Pigott-Carleton, of Archer Lodge and
    Heckfield Heath
Pollen, of Redenham
Popham, of Stourfield House
Portal, of Laverstoke
Portal, of Malshanger House
Powell, of Wilverley Park
Pulteney, of Northerwood
Purvis, of Blackbrook House
Purvis, of Bury Hall
Purvis, of Whitsbury
Read, of Amptield House
Reynardson, of Rushington Manor
Ricardo, of Mudiford
Rickford, of Hamilton House
Ridley, of Fir Grove
Ridley, of Holmpton House
Roebuck, of Ashley Arnewood
Rooke, of Woodside
Rumbold, late of Preston Candover
St. Barbe, of Lymington
Sartoris, of Warnford Park
Sclater, of Hoddington House
Scott, of Beaulieu
Scott, of Empshott Grange
Scott, of Rotherfield Park
Scott, of Swanthorpe
Sheldon, of Delawarr House
Shelley, of Avington House
Shipley, of Twyford

1065

Shrubb, of Vicars Hill
Simonds, of Abbotts-Barton
Sloane-Stanley, of Paultons
Smith, of Brockenhurst
Smith, of Brooklands
Spencer, of Woodlands
Spink, of Alton
Stane, of Buckfield
Stevens, of Hillfield
Stone, of Leigh Park
Stuart, of Hubborne
Sturgeon, late of Pond Head Lodge
Symonds, of Yeovilton House
Taylor, of Pennington House
Thistlethwayte, of Southwick Park
Timson, of Tatchbury
Torr, of Dummer House
Tragett, of Awbridge Danes
Trench, late of Botley Grange
Waddington, of Langrish House
Waddington, of Twyford Lodge
Wake, of Tatchbury
Walcot, of Winkton House
Walker, of Bossington House
Wall, of King's Worthy Park
Walmsley, of Wolverton Park
Warren, of Worting
Wellesley, of Conholt Park
West, of Newlands
Wigston, of Bitterne Hall
Willis-Fleming, of South Stoneham
Wingate, of Crofton House
Wingrove, of Langley
Wollaston, of Shirley
Wood, of Testcombe
Wood, of Thedden Grange
Woodham, of Farley Chamberlayne
Woods, of Warnford Park
Wyatt, of Weston Corbet
Wyndham, of Corhampton
Wynne, of Warnford
Yonge, of Otterbourne

HEREFORDSHIRE.

Meath, Earl of
Somers, Earl
Hereford, Bishop of
Oxford and Mortimer, Countess of
Bateman, Lord
Northwick, Lord
Rodney, Lord
Cockburn, Sir E. C., Bart.
Cornewall, Sir Velters, Bart.
Cotterell, Sir G. H., Bart.
Stanhope, Sir E. F. S., Bart.
Walsham, Sir. J. J., Bart.
Allaway, of Marstone
Allen, of The Moor
Arkwright, of Hampton Court
Arkwright, of Peaconbe
Armitage, of Dadnor
Ashton, of Hatfield Court
Aynsley, of Underdown
Bailey, of Easton Court
Barneby, of Bredenbury Court
Barneby, of Clater Park
Barneby-Lutley, of Brockhampton
Biddulph, of Ledbury Park
Bird, of Drybridge House
Blissett, of Letton
Blount, of Orleton
Bodenham, of Rotherwas Park
Boughton-Knight, of Downton Castle
Bridges, of Cainham
Bridgman, of Weston under-Penyard
1066

Bright, of Colwall
Browne, of Hall Court
Burmester, of Weston Lodge
Caldwell, of Leominster
Capper, of Lyston Court
Capper, of Northgate
Chadwick, of Pudleston Court
Cheese, of Castle Weir
Cherry, of Buckland
Clive, of Perrystone Court
Clive, of Whitfield
Clowes, of Burton Court
Coke, of Lemore
Collins, of Cubberley House
Collins, of Wythall Walford
Colvin, of Leintwardine
Cox, of Broxwood Court
Davenport, of Foxley
Davies, of Croft Castle
Davies, of Moor Court
Devereux, of Highwood
Dew, of Whitney Court
Downs, of The Friars
Dunne, of Bircher Hall
Eckley, of Credenhill Court
Evans, of Burton Court
Evans, of The Byletts
Evans, of Kingsland
Evans, of Sufton Court
Evans, of Eyton Hall
Feilden, of Dulas Court
Ferguson, of Yatton
Foley, of Stoke Edith
Freeman, of Gaines
Graham, of Stoke Edith
Griffiths, of New Court
Griffiths, of The Weir
Hamilton, of Kingsland
Harrison, of Kynaston
Hastings, of Titley Court
Hereford, of Sufton Court
Heygate, of Buckland
Heywood, of Hope End
Higgins, of Bosbury House
Higgins, of West Bank
Higginson, of Saltmarsh Castle
Hopton, of Cannon Frome Court
Hutchinson, of Hagley Park
Hutchinson, of Longworth House
Ingham, of Sugwas Court
Jay, of Derndale
Jay, of Litley Court
Jones, of Langstone Court
King, of Staunton Park
Lane, of Ryelands
Langdale of Eywood
Lechmere, of Fownhope Court
Lee, of Vowchurch
Lee-Warner, of Tibberton Court
Lewis, of Yatton Court
Lingwood, of Lyston House
Lloyd, of Huntingdon Court
Lowther, of Tarwaesione
Martin, of The Upper Hall
Martin, of Old Colwall
Meyrick, of Goderich Court
Mildmay, of Gayton
Miles, of Underdown
Money-Kyrle, of Homme House
Monington-Weston, of Sarnesfield
Myddleton-Biddulph, of Burghill
Mynors, of Llanwarne
Mynors, of Treago
Partridge, of Bishops Wood
Partridge, of Hazelhurst
Partridge, of Wyelands
Pateshall, of Hereford

Pearce, of Llangarron Court
Peploe, of Garnstone
Peyton, of Barton Colwall
Phillipps, of Bryngwyn
Powell, of Dorstone
Power, of The Hill Court
Prosser, of Belmont
Reaveley, of Kinnersley Castle
Ricketts, of Coombe
Romilly, of Huntington Park
Salvin, of Sarnesfield Court
Salwey, of Elton Hall
Sanders, of Cheslunt
Sanders, of Street Court
Scudamore, of Kentchurch Court
Shapland, of Cradley
Smith, of Lower Eaton
Smythies, of Lynch Court
Stevenson, of Hennor House
Stratford, of Lugwardine
Stronge, of The Chase
Summers, of Cradley
Symons, of Mynde Park
Symons, of Pengethly
Teleki, of Eywood
Thomas, of Bewell House
Tyler, of Wisteston Court
Unett, of Freen's Court
Unett, late of Venwood
Vaughan, of Court Field
Walford, of Trego
Weare, of Hampton House
Webb, of Donnington Hall
Wenman, of Rowlstone Court
Whatley, of Aston Ingham
Whitfield, of Pudleston
Wood, of The Whitehouse
Yapp, of The Halesend

HERTFORDSHIRE.

Salisbury, Marquis of
Townshend, Marquis
Brownlow, Earl
Clarendon, Earl of
Cowper, Earl
Essex, Earl of
Roden, Earl of
Rosebery, Earl of
Verulam, Earl of
Alford, Viscountess
Palmerston, Viscountess
Dacre, Lord
Ebury, Lord
Lucas, Baroness
Lytton, Lord
Clarke, Sir P. H., Bart.
Cooper, Sir A. P., Bart.
Lushington, Sir H., Bart.
Meux, Sir H., Bart.
Prescott, Sir G. B., Bart.
Sebright, Sir J. S., Bart.
Acworth, of The Hook
Adams, of Throcking
Alington, of Letchworth
Allen, of Hormead Bury
Ames, of The Hyde
Ames, of St. Ibbs
Arden, of Rickmansworth
Ashfordby-Trenchard, of Nyn Park
Bagnall, of Newberries Park
Baker, of Bayfordbury
Barnes, of Tring Park
Barnes, of Chorley Wood
Bashford, of Barvins
Beldam, of Royston

Bentley, of Woodgreen
Bevan, of Trent Park
Blake, of Danesbury
Bland, of Lilley
Block, of Greenhill Grove
Blomfield, of Stevenage
Booth, of Netherfield House
Bosanquet, of Osidge
Branton-Day, of Micklefield Green and Sarratt Hall
Brassey, of Green Hall
Bright, of Stocks House
Broun, of Amwell
Burgess, of Sarratt Hall
Butt, of Corney Bury
Caldecott, of Pishiobury
Caledon, of Tittenhanger Park
Campbell, of Bennington Park
Campbell, of Little Grove
Capel, of Kites House
Carew, of Carpenders Park
Carnegie, of Eastbury
Carr, of Barrowpoint Hill
Cass, of Monken Hadley
Cavendish, of Ayott St. Lawrence
Chapman, of High Cross
Cherry, of Brickendon Grange
Chetwynd-Stapleton, of Shenley Lodge
Church, of Woodside
Clinton, of Carlsbury Park
Clutterbuck, of Watford House
Copeland, of Russell Farm
Crawley, of Thorley Lodge
Culling-Hanbury, of Bedwell Park
Currie, late of Tewin Water
Daniell, of Little Berkhamstead
Dawson, of Albury Hall
Delme-Radcliffe, of Hitchin Priory
Dering, of Lockleys
Dickinson, of Abbots Hill
Dimsdale, of Essenden Place
Dukinfield, of Little Munden
Eaton, of Tyttenhanger Park
Eden, of Bovingdon House
Ellis, of Ponsbourne Park
Ellis, of Wyddial Hall
Faber, of Northaw House
Fairbairn, of Brambridge House
Fanshaw, of Debrow House
Finch, of Berkhampstead Castle
Finch, of Redheath
Fordham, of Royston Priory
Franks, of Dacre Lodge
Franks, of Woodhill
Frere, of Twyford House
Gape, of St. Alban's
Garrard, of Lamer Park
Gaussen, of Brookman's Park
Gee, of Abbot's Langley
Gibbs, of Aldenham
Goff, of Barton Grange
Gosselin, of Ware Priory
Greg, of Coles Park
Greville, of North Mymns Place
Hudden, of Rossway
Hale, of King's Walden
Halsey, of Gaddesden Park
Hamilton, of Kensworth
Hamilton, of Northaw
Hanbury, of Belmont
Hanbury, of Poles
Haworth, of Balham Wood
Hayward, of Loudwater
Heale, of Highfield
Heathcote, of Shephalbury
Heneage, of Stag's End

Herne, of Bushey Grange
Hibbert, of Munden House
Hoblyn, of White Barns
Hodgson, of Gilston Park
Hodgson, of Sparrow House
Horne, of Epping House
Hughes, of Caldicot Lodge
Hughes, of Offley Place
Kinder, of Sandridge Bury
King, of Wigan Hall
Lawes, of Rothamsted Manor
Lee, of Totteridge Park
Le Marchant, of New Lodge
Long, of East Barnet
Longman, of Shendish
Loyd, of Langleybury
Lushington, of Merry Hill
Lydekker, of Harpenden Lodge
McGeachy, of Shenley Hill
Macnamara, of Caddington Hall
Marjoribanks, of Bushy Grove
Marten, of Marshalls Wick
Mason, of Aldenham Lodge
Mayo, of Cheshunt
Meetkerke, of Julians
Mellish, of Hamels Park
Mills, of Tolmers
Moore, of Woodcock Hill
Moore-Halsey, of Gt. Gaddesden
Myers, of Porters
Napier, of Oaklands
Newcome, of Shenley
O'Brien, of Butler's Green
Oddie, of Co nie
Parker, of Ware Park
Phelips, of Briggins Park
Phillimore, of Kendall's Hall
Potter, of Camfield
Prime, of The Hermitage
Pryor, of Baldock Hall and Clay Hall
Pryor, of High Elms
Pryor, of Weston
Puget, of Pointer's Grove
Puller, of Youngsbury
Pym, of Radwell House
Reid, of The Node
Robins, of The Elms
Rogers, of Stagenhoe Park
Rooper, of Nascott
Rumball, of Harpenden
Russell, of Cheshunt Park
Ryder, of Ickleford House
Ryder, of Westbrook Hay
Scarlett, late of Copped Hall
Simpson, of Radwell House
Sladen, of Harestourne Manor
Smith, of Goldings
Smith, of Sacombe Park
Smith, of Woodhall Park
Smith-Bosanquet, of Broxbournebury
Smith-Dorrien, of Harestont
Solly, of Serge Hill
Sowerby, of Loley House
Sowerby, of Putteridge Bury
Stuart, of Aldenham Abbey
Surtees, of Dane End
Thornton, of Marden Hill
Tilson-Marsh, of Brickenden Priory
Timins, of Hilfield
Tinling, of Ashwell
Toulmin, of Childwick Bury
Tower, of Braughing
Trotter, of Dyrham Park
Upton, of Stan-steadbury
Usborne, of Mardley-Bury
Vandermeulen, of Thorley
Villiers, of Grove Mill House

Wade, of Great Sarratt Hall
Walker, of Bushey Manor
Weguelin, of Goldings
Wigram, of Moor Place
Wilkinson, of Chessfield Lodge
Wilshere, of The Fryth
Wodehouse, of Woolmer's Park
Woolrych, of Croxley
Worley, of New Barnes
Wylie, of Hunsdon House
Young, of Oakhill

HUNTINGDONSHIRE.

Manchester, Duke of
Huntly, Marquis of
Carysfort, Earl of
Sandwich, Earl of
Sherard, Lord
Booth, Sir W., Bart.
Ansley, of St. Ives
Baumgartner, of Godmanchester
Bevan, of Godmanchester
Duberly, of Gaynes Hall
Duncombe, of Waresley Park and Tetworth Hall
Fellowes, of Ramsey Abbey
Foley, of Wistow Manor
Heathcote, of Connington Castle
Heathcote, of Connington Rectory
Hopkinson, of Great Gidding
Humbley, of Eynesbury
Hussey, of Upwood
Linton, of Stirtloe
Onslow, of Staughton House
Pryme, of Wistow
Reynolds, of Paxton House
Rooper, of Abbotts Ripton
Rust, of Alconbury House
Rust, of Cromwell House
Skrimshire, of Stanground
Sperling, of Lattenbury Hill
Thornhill, of Diddington
Tillard, of Great Stukeley
Torkington, of Great Stukeley
Veasey, of Castle Hill House
Vipan, of Stibbington
Webb, of Great Gransden
Wells, of Helmewood
Welstead, of Stonely Hall

INVERNESS-SHIRE.

Dunmore, Earl of
Seafield, Earl of
Moray, Earl of
Abinger, Lord
Lovat, Lord
Macdonald, Lord
Saltoun, Lord
Grant, Sir G. M., Bart.
Marjoribanks, Sir D. C., Bart.
Orde, Sir J. P., Bart.
Ainslie, of Muirton House
Baillie, of Culduthell and Dochfour
Baillie, of Leys
Baird, of Knoydart
Biscoe, of Newton
Cameron, of Inveraliort
Cameron, of Lochiel and Achnacarry
Chisholm, of Lachlass Castle
Congreve, of Flichity
Davidson, of Cantray
Ellice, of Glengarry and Glenquoich
Forbes, of Culloden House

1067

Fraser, of Eilean Aigas
Fraser, of Kilbokie
Fraser, of Balnain, Farraline, and Dunchea
Fraser, of Reelick
Fraser-Tytler, of Aldourie and Balnain
Grant, of Glenmoriston
Grant, of Rothiemurchus
Hodgson, of Polmalie
Horsman, of Alvie
Inglis, of Kingsmills
Macdonnell, of Morar
Mackinnon, of Corry House
Mackintosh, of Balnespick
Mackintosh, of Daviot
Mackintosh, of Farr
Mackintosh, of Holme
Mackintosh, of Mackintosh
Mackintosh, of Raigmore
Macleod, of Macleod
Macpherson, of Belleville
Macpherson, of Cluny
Macqueen, of Airds
Malkin, of Corrybrough
Merry, of Belladrum
Ogilvy, of Corrimony
Rainy, of Raasay House
Robertson, of Inshes
Robertson, of Kinlochmoidart
Robertson-Ross, of Glenmoidart
Rose, of Holme
Stewart, late of Belladrum
Sutherland-Walker, of Aberader
Swinburne, of Eilan Mona
Walker, of Lochtreig
White, of Lentran
Young, of New House

JERSEY.

Budgen, of Beaulieu
Lempriere, of Rozel

KENT.

Camden, Marquis
Conyngham, Marquis of
Abergavenny, Earl of
Amherst, Earl
Aylesford, Earl of
Clanwilliam, Earl
Cowper, Earl
Darnley, Earl of
De la Warr, Earl
Guildford, Earl of
Norbury, Earl of
Romney, Earl of
Stanhope, Earl
Winchilsea, Earl of
Falmouth, Viscount
Hardinge, Viscount
Holmesdale, Viscount
Strangford, Viscount
Sydney, Viscount
Torrington, Viscount
Buckhurst, Baroness
Cranworth, Lord
De l'Isle and Dudley, Lord
Fitzwalter, Lord
Harris, Lord
Monson, Lord
Sondes, Lord
Carmichael, Sir J. R., Bart.
Croft, Sir J. T., Bart.

Curtis, Sir Wm., Bart.
Dering, Sir E. C., Bart.
Dyke, Sir P. H., Bart.
Fagge, Sir J., Bart.
Filmer, Sir E., Bart.
Geary, Sir W. R. P., Bart.
Hampson, Sir G. F., Bart.
Hawley, Sir J. H., Bart.
Herschel, Sir J. F. W., Bart.
Honywood, Sir C. J., Bart.
James, Sir W. C., Bart.
King, Sir R. D., Bart.
Knatchbull, Sir H. E., Bart.
Lecock, Sir Chas., Bart.
Lubbock, Sir J., Bart.
Montefiore, Sir M., Bart.
Musgrove, Sir J., Bart.
Oxenden, Sir H. C., Bart.
Scott, Sir C. E., Bart.
Shaw, Sir J. C. K., Bart.
Tufton, Sir R., Bart.
Wilson, Sir T. M., Bart.
Adams, of Elmers
Akers, of Malling Abbey
Alexander, of Stonehouse
Angerstein, of Woodlands
Arbuckle, of Charlton
Arbuthnot, of Bridgen Place
Armytage, of Broomhill
Atkins, of Halstead Place
Austen, of Kippington
Baillie-Hamilton, of Blackheath
Baily, of Hall Place
Baines, of Yalding
Baldwin, of Stede Hill
Balston, of Springfield
Bannerman, of Hunton Court
Baring, of Ash Grove
Barne, of May Place
Barrett, of Court Lodge
Baskcomb, of Chiselhurst Manor
Beare, of Holland House
Beattie, of Summerhill
Bell, of Bourne Park
Berens, of Kevington
Berens, of Sidcup
Beresford-Hope, of Bedgebury Park
Best, late of Chilston Park and Wierton
Best, of Park House
Betts, of Preston Hall
Billington, of Kennington
Blackburne-Maze, of Southborough
Bland, of Hartlip Place
Bligh, of Enbrook
Bockett Pugh, of Tunbridge Wells
Boteler, of Eastry
Boys, of The Oaks
Bradford, of Franks
Bramah, of Davington Priory
Brent, of Barton
Brockman, of Beachborough and Gore Court
Brome, of Malling House
Browell, of West-Cliff House
Burra, of Ashford
Burton, of Dunstall Priory
Busk, of Culverdens
Butler-Clarke-Southwell-Wandesforde of Ulcombe Place
Byng, of Shipbourne Lodge
Carnac, of Chandos Place
Carter, of Kennington Hall
Cator, of Beckenham
Chafy, of Canterbury
Chapman, of St. Paul's-Cray Hill
Cheeses of Aylesford

Child, of Bromley
Christy, of Apperfield
Clarke, of Kingsdown House
Claston, of Combe Bank
Cobbett, of Skeynes
Colquhoun, of Chartwell
Cook, of Roydon Hall
Cotton, of Quex
Cox, of Fordwich House
Crofts, of Dumpton House
Crupper, of Swaylands
Curteis, of Rowden Place and Wissenden
D'Aeth, of Knowlton Court
Dalison, of Hamptons
Dalison, of Stanley Grange
Darell, of Calehill
Darwin, of Down
Dashwood, of Hall Place and Halcot
Davies, late of Eaton House
Davies, of Withersdane
Deacon, of Mabledon
Deedes, of Sandling Park
Delaune-Faunce, of Sharsted
Delmar, of Elmstone Court
Denne, of Hythe
Denne, of Lydd
Dent, of Bickley Park
Dering, of Barham Court
Dering, of Finchden
Dering, of Trosley
Douglas, of Chilston Park
Drax, of Olentigh
Du Boulay, of Sandgate
Duppa, of Hollingbourne House
Dyke, of Glover's Green
Edmeades, of Nurstead Court
Elers, of Oldbury
Ellis, of Tankerton Tower
Farnall, of Lee Manor
Faulkner, of The Philippines
Faussett, of Heppington
Field, of Ashurst Park
Field, of Dornden
Fleet, of Sutton-at-Hone
Fletcher, of Kenward
Foley, of Ersham House
Fortescue, of Beckenham
Garrett, of Uplown House
Gipps, of Howletts
Glendiving, of Ash Grove
Godfrey, of Brook-street Hoath
Goldsmid, of Somerhill
Gordon, of Knockwood
Gosselin, of Mount Ospringe
Gossett, of Litham House
Gow-Stewart, of Fowler's Park
Grant, of Fowlers
Grevis-James, of Ightham Court
Groves, of Charing Meat
Hales, of Hales Place
Hamilton, of Brockland
Hammond, of St. Alban's Court
Hardy, of Chilham Castle
Hardy, of Hemsted Park
Harris-Temple, of Norton
Harvey, of Cowden
Harvey, of Walmer
Herries, of St. Julian's
Hilton, of Bramling House
Hilton, of Preston House
Hilton, of Sarre Court
Hoare, of Staplehurst
Hughes-Hallet, of Higham
Hunt, of Willesborough
Hussey, of Scotney Castle and Finch cox

Hyde, of Syndale
Isacke, of North Foreland
Jervis, of Fairhill
Jenkins, of Lyminge
Jones, of Hayle Place
Kingsford, of Littlebourne
Kirkpatrick, of Monk's Horton
Knatchbull, of Provender
Knatchbull-Hugessen, of Smeeth Paddock
Knight, of Godmersham Park
Lade, of Nash Court and Brenley House
Lambarde, of Beechmont
Laming, of Birchington Place
Lancaster-Lucas, of Wateringbury House
Larking, of Lee
Law, late of Ellington House
Lee, of Holborough
Legge, of Keston
Lennard, of Wickham Court
Lewin, of The Hollies
Long, of Bromley Hill
Lonsdale, of Sandgate
Loyd, of Lillesden
Luard-Selby, of Ightham Mote
Lushington, of Norton Court
Lushington, of Park House
Mackay, of Petham House
Mackinnon, of Acrise Park and Belvidere
Marsham, of Hayle
Martin, of Chislehurst
Martin, of Leeds Castle
Mildmay, of Otford House
Mildmay, of Shoreham Place
Molyneux, of Earl's Court
Monins, of Ringwould
Montresor, of Denne Hill
Monypenny, of Hadlow
Monypenny, of Hythe
Monypenny, of Maytham
Moore, of Frittenden House
Moore, of Tunstall
Moore, of Wierton
Morland, of The Court Lodge
Morrice, of Bettshanger
Mount, of Canterbury
Munn, of Throwley House
Neame, of Harbledown
Norman, of Bromley
Norwood, of Ashford
Oakden, of Ladham House
Oxenden, of Eastwell
Paterson, of Leesons
Paxton, of Sydenham
Pemberton, of Torry Hill
Pemberton, of Wrinsted Court
Perkins, of Chipstead Place
Petley, of Riverhead
Philips, of Lee Priory
Phillips, of Mapleton
Pickersgill, of Blendon Hall
Plumptre, of Fredville House and Pedding
Pott, of Bentham Hill
Powell, of Speldhurst
Prentis, of Ightham Warren
Randall, of Foley House
Randolph, of Great Comp
Reeves, of Danemore Park
Rice, of Dane Court
Rider, of Boughton Monchelsea
Ridgway, of Fairlawn
Rigg, of Wrotham Park
Robinson, of Lydd

Rodger, of Hadlow Castle
Rogers, of River Hill
Ruxton, of Broad Oak
Rycroft, of Everlands
Sackville-West, of Hartwell
Salomons, of Broomhill
Savage, of St. Leonard's
Sayer, of Pett
Sayer, of Statenborough
Schreiber, of Henhurst
Scoones, of Tonbridge
Scott, of Charlton Place
Scott, of Maidstone Priory
Scratton, of Penenden Heath
Sicklemore, of Cleve and Nether Court
Sladen, of Ripple Court
Sladen, of Swanton Court
Smart, of Goudhurst
Smith-Marriott, of Horsemonden
Smith Masters, of Camer
Sperling, of Grovehurst
Stratford, of Addington Place
Streatfield, of Chart's Edge
Streatfield, of Chiddingstone House
Strode, of Camden Park
Talbot, of Falconhurst
Tassell, of Ditton
Taswell, of St. Martin's
Taylor, of Roselands
Tipping, of Brasted Park
Toke, of Godinton
Tomlin, of Dane Court
Tooth, of Swift's Park
Tournay, of Brockhull
Tweedie, of Rawlinson
Twisden, of Bradbourn Park
Twopeny, of Woodstock House
Tylden, of Egerton House
Tylden, of Milstead Manor
Tylden-Pattenson, of Ibornden
Tyler, of Linsted Lodge
Tyssen, of Sandgate
Usborne, of Staplehurst
Vansittart, of Foot's Cray
Waldo, of Stonewall Park and Hever Castle
Walker, of New Romney
Walker, of Honeychild Manor
Warde, of Squerries Court
Waring, of Woodlands
Warre, of West Cliffe House
Warton, of Kemsdale
Wells, of Redleaf
Whatman, of Vinters
Wheatley, of Erith
Whelan, of Heronden Hall
Wheler, of Otterden Place
White, of Swanscombe
Whitehead, of Barnjet
Whitehead, of St. Helen's
Whitmore, of Beckenham
Whittaker, of Barming
Wilkie, of Ellington House
Williams, of Boones
Wilson, of Beckenham
Wolstenholme, of Dumbarton Manor
Wood, of North Cray
Wrench, of Stowting
Yardley, of Hadlow Park
Young, of Westbere

KERRY CO.

Kenmare, Earl of
Headley, Lord

Ventry, Lord
Blennerhassett, Sir R., Bart.
Denny, Sir Edward, Bart.
Godfrey, Sir V. D., Bart.
Blacker, of Tullahennel
Bland, of Derryquin Castle
Blennerhassett, of Ballyseedy House
Butler, of Waterville
Chute, of Chute Hall and Blennerville
Chute, of Leabrook
Collis, of Fort William
Collis, of Lismore
Collis, of Tieraclea
Coxon, of Flesk Priory
Cronin-Coltsmann, of Flesk Castle
Crosbie, of Ballyheigue Castle
Day, of Beaufort
Day, late of Beaufort
Day, of Edenburne House
Dennis, of Dromin
Denny, of Tralee
Eagar, of Killorglin
Fitzgerald, of Glanleam
Fitzmaurice, of Duagh House
Fosbery, of Blennerville
Fuller, of Glashnacree
Gun, of Ratoo and Ballybunion
Herbert, of Muckross
Hewson, of Inch
Hewson, of Ennismore
Hickie, of Kilelton House
hickson, of Fermoyle
Hickson, of Redcliffe
Hilliard, of Tralee
Hurley, of Bridge House
Hussey, of The Grove and Farannikella
Hussey, of Edenburn
Hyde, of Hollywood
Lawlor, of Grenagh
Leeson-Marshall, of Shannon Vale
Leslie, of Tarbert
McGillicuddy, of The Reeks
McGillicuddy, of Tralee
Mahony, of Castlequin
Mahony, of Cullina
Mahony, of Dromore Castle
Mahony, of Innuloe Castle
Mahony, of Gunsborough
Mayberry, of Riverside
O'Connell, of Ballynabloun
O'Connell, of Darrynane Abbey
O'Connell, of Grena
O'Connell, of Lakeview
O'Connor, of Ballyclamesil
O'Donoghue (The), or the Glens
Orpen, of Ardtully
Orpen, of Killaha Castle
Rae, of Keel House
Rice, of Bushmount
Sandes, of Carrigafoyle Castle
Sandes, of Greenville
Sandes, of Oak Park
Sandes, of Sallow Glen
Stack, of Ballyconry
Stokes, of Lassenagh
Stokes, of Mounthawk
Stoughton, of Ballyhorgan
Stoughton, of Ballynoe
Talbot-Crosbie, of Ardfert Abbey
Taylor, of Dunkerron Castle

KILDARE CO.

Leinster, Duke of

Drogheda, Marquis of
Kildare, Marquis of
Aldborough, Earl of
Clonmell, Earl of
Harberton, Viscount
Cloncurry, Lord
Aylmer, Sir G. G., Bart.
Borrowes, Sir E. D., Bart.
Echlin, Sir F. H., Bart.
Hort, Sir J. W., Bart.
Archbold, of Davidstown
Aylmer, of Courtown
Aylmer, of Painstown
Barton, of Straffan
Beauman, of Furness
Blacker, of Castle Martin
Bonham, of Ballintaggart
Bor, of Ballindolan
Borrowes, of Gilltown
Burdett, of Ballymany
Burgh, of Donore House
Cane, of St. Wolstan's
Carroll, of Moone Abbey
Cassidy, of Monasterevan
Cogan, of Athgarrett
Cole-Hamilton, of Ballitore House
Conolly, of Castletown
Cooke-Trench, of Millicent
Cramer-Roberts, of Sallymount
Dalyell, of Ticknevin
De Burgh, of Old Town
De Robeck, of Gowran Grange
Eustace, of Ballymore Eustace
Evans, of Ballitore House
Fitzgerald, of Geraldine
Gannon, of Lara
Henchy, of Stonebrook
Henry, of Lodge Park
Hort, of Hortland
La Touche, of Harristown
Lefroy, of Cardington House
Lewis, of Kilcullen
Lynch, of Whiteleas
McDonnell, of Donforth
Mansfield, of Morristown Lattin
Maunsell, of Oakley Park
Medlicott, of Dunmurry
Moore, of Moorefield
O'Ferrall, of Balyna
O'Ferrall, of Kildangan
O'Kelly, of Barrettstown
Palmer, of Rahan
Figott, of Ryevale
Purcell, of Halverstown House
Rapar, of Castle Mitchell
Rynd, of Mount Armstrong
St. George, of Sheune
Williams, of Williamston
Wolfe, of Bishop Land
Wright, of Downings

KILKENNY CO.

Ormonde, Marquis of
Bessborough, Earl of
Carrick, Earl of
Desart, Earl of
Ashbrook, Viscount
Clifden, Viscount
De Montmorency, Viscount
Mountgarret, Viscount
Ossory, Ferns, and Leighlin, Bishop of
Blunden, Sir J., Bart.
Cuffe, Sir C. F. W. D., Bart.
Langrishe, Sir J., Bart.
1070

Meredyth, Sir E. H. J., Bart.
Power, Sir John, Bart.
St. George, Sir J., Bart.
Aylward, of Shankhill Castle
Bolger, of Ballinabarna
Bookey, of Doninga
Briscoe, of Harristown
Bryan, of Jenkinstown
Butler, of Castle Comer
Butler, of Freshford
Butler, of Kilmurry
Cahill, of Ballyconra House
Conn, of Mount Ida
Connellan, of Coolmore
De Montmorency, of Castlemorres
Dillon, of Ballyquin House
Eyre, of Uppercourt
Flood, of Farmley
Flood, of New House
Flood, of Paulstown Castle
Golding, of Gowran Castle
Graves, of Rosbercon Castle
Green, late of Greenville
Hamilton, of Inistioge
Harman, of Ballycarron
Izod, of Chapel Izod
Jones, of Mullanabro'
Kearney, of Blanchville
Kirwan, of Castlecomer
Langton, of Danganmore
Meredyth, of Norelands
Milford, of Upper Court
Moore, of Ballyhale
Morris-Reade, of Rossenarra
Neville, of Borrismore House
St. George, of Bailef
St. George, of Kilrush House
Stuart, of Castletown House
Sullivan, of Lacken Hall
Sweetman, of Annagh
Tighe, of Woodstock
Tyndall, of Milltown
Walsh, of Fanningstown
Warren, of Lodge Park
Wemys, of Danesfort
Wheeler, of The Rocks

KINCARDINESHIRE.

Kintore, Earl of
Arbuthnott, Viscount
Craigstoun, Lord
Nairne, Baroness
Gladstone, Sir Thos., Bart.
Ramsay, Sir Alex., Bart.
Arbuthnot, of Hatton
Baird, of Ury House
Barclay-Allardice, late of Allardice
Burnett, of Monboddo
Carnegie, of Redhall
Davidson, of Inchmarlo
Douglas, of Tilquhillie
Duff, of Fetteresso
Farquhar, of Hallgreen
Grant, of Ecclesgrieg
Grieg, of Harviestoun
Hepburn, of Rickarton
Innes, of Cowie and Raemoir
Keith, of Easter Muchalls
Kinloch, of Altries
Kinloch, of Kair
McInroy, of The Burn
Nicol, of Bandentoy
Nicol, of Fawsyde
Nicolson, of Glenbervie
Orr, of Bridgeton

Porteous, of Lauriston Castle
Ramsay, of Banchory Lodge
Ross, of Netherley
Scott, of Brotherton
Scott, of Commieston
Shank, of Laurencekirk
Stratton, of Kirkside
Stuart, of Inchbreck
Taylor, of Kirktonhill House

KING'S CO.

Charleville, Earl of
Rosse, Earl of
Bloomfield, Lord
Digby, Lord
Armstrong, Sir E. F. Bart.
Armstrong, of Bal-Iver
Armstrong, of Claremont
Armstrong, of Gallen Priory
Armstrong, of Killclare
Atkinson, of Cangort
Bagot, of Ard
Bagot, of Kilcoursey House
Bennett, of Grange
Bennett, of Thomastown House
Berr d, of Castle Bernard
Bidculph, of Fortal
Bruce, of Tullimore
Burdett, of Hunstanton
Cassidy, of Killyon
Clarke, of Portarlington
Dames, of Greenhill
Darby, of Leap Castle
Drought, of Lettybrook
Drought, of Whigsborough
Fletcher, of Garr
Fox, of Annaghmore
Fox, of Kilcoursey
Gamble, of Killooly Hall
Garden, of River Lyons
Garvey, of Thornvale and Parsonstown
Hackett, of Moore Park
Hennessy, of Ballmacmoy House
Hutchinson, of Golden Grove
Joly, of Clonbologue
Kemmis, of Purrow
King, of Ballylin
Lloyd, of Glester
Lloyd-Vaughan, of Golden Grove and Mount Heaton
Lucas, of Mount Lucas
Magan, of Cloncarl
Morris, of Mount Pleasant
Palmer, of Ballinlough
Rolleston, of Franckfort Castle
Trench, of Cangort Park
Von Stieglitz, of Mucklagh
Wakely, of Ballyburly
Warburton, of Garrhinch
Westenra, of Charavogue

KINROSS-SHIRE.

Menerieff, Sir H. W., Bart.
Adam, of Blair Adam
Bruce, of Arnot
Coventry, of Shanwell
Maitland, of Whirlield
Syme, of Warroch
Walker-Arnott, of Arlary
Young, of Cleish Castle

KIRKCUDBRIGHTSHIRE.

Galloway, Earl of
Selkirk, Earl of
Gordon, Sir Wm., Bart.
Maxwell, Sir W., Bart.
Miller, Sir T. MacDonald, Bart.
Barbour, of Barley
Barbour, of Dalshangan
Caird, of Cassencary
Clarke-Kennedy, of Knockgrey
Craig-Laurie, of Redcastle
Cuninghame, of Duchrae
Fergusson, of Orroland
Gordon, of Balmaghie House
Gordon, of Campbelton
Gordon, of Culvennan
Gordon, of Kenmure
Hall, of Mollance
Hannay, of Rusko
Heron, of Heron and Kirouchtree
Herries, of Spottes
Hughan, of Airds
Hyslop, of Lotus
Johnston, of Dornal
Lawrie, of Woodhall
McCulloch, of Ardwall
Mackie, of Auchencairn
Mackie, of Ernespie
Maitland, of Dundrennan
Maitland-Kirwan, of Gelston Castle
Maxwell, of Carruchan
Maxwell, of Glenlee
Maxwell, of Munches
Maxwell, of Terregles
Murray-Stewart, of Broughton
Pagan, of Curriestanes
Robinson, of Almorness
Rainsford-Hannay, of Kirkdale
Spalding, of The Holme and Shirmirs
Starke, of Troqueer Holm
Stewart, of Cairnsmore
Stewart, of Shambellie
Stewart, of Southwick
Stothert, of Blaiket
Whigham, of Margreig
Witham, of Kirkconnell

LANARKSHIRE.

Hamilton, Duke of
Breadalbane, Earl of
Eglinton and Winton, Earl of
Haddington, Earl of
Stair, Earl of
Belhaven, Lord
Blantyre, Lord
Alison, Sir A., Bart.
Anstruther, Sir W. C., Bart.
Colebrooke, Sir T. E., Bart.
Lockhart, Sir N. M., Bart.
Maxwell, Sir H. B., Bart.
Steuart, Sir H. J. Seton-, Bart.
Stirling, Sir W. G. Bart.
Aikman, of The Ross and Broomelton
Alexander, of Airdrie and Rosolloch
Austruther-Thomson, of Carntyne
Baillie, of Culter-Allers
Baillie-Cochrane, of Lamington
Baird, of Lochwood
Bannatyne, of Millheugh
Bertram, of Kersewell
Campbell, of Possil
Carmichael, of Eastend

Carrick-Buchanan, of Drumpellier
Chancellor, of Shieldhill
Christie, of Bedlay and Petershill
Colquhoun, of Killermont and Gaddesden
Colt, of Gartsherrie
Crawford, of Milton
Dennistoun, of Golf Hill
Dickson, of Hartree and Kilbucho
Douglas, of Stonebyres and Rosehall
Downie, of Appin House
Dunlop, of Craigton
Dunlop, of Clyde
Dunlop, of Gairbraid and Lambhill
Edmondstoune - Cranstoun, of Corehouse
Findlay, of Easterhill
Gerard, of Rochsoles
Gordon, of Aikenhead House
Gordon, of Harperfield
Græme, of Well Hall
Graham - Barns, of Limekills and Kirkhills
Graham-Stirling, of Milngavie
Hamilton, of Broomhill
Hamilton, of Dalzell
Hamilton, of Fairholme
Hamilton, of Raploch
Harington, of Crutherland
Hope-Vere, of Blackwood
Hozier, of Newlands and Barrowfield
Lockhart, of Castlehill
Lockhart, of Cleghorn
Lockhart, of Wicketshaw and Milton Lockhart
M'Call, of Daldowie
Mackenzie, of Dolphinton
McKirdy, of Birkwood
Maclae, of Caithkin
Macqueen, of Hardington House
Mitchell, of Carwood
Monteith, of Carstairs
Nisbett, of Cairnhill
Robertson, of Lawhead
Sim, of Coulter
Sprot, of Garnkirk House
Steurt-Grosett-Muirhead, of Bredisholm
Stirling, of Drumpellier
Stirling-Stuart, of Castlemilk
Tennent, of Wellpark
Waddell, of Easter Moffat
Weir, of The Weir
Woddrop, of Dalmarnock

LANCASHIRE.

Hamilton and Brandon, Duke of
Crawford and Balcarres, Earl of
Derby, Earl of
Ellesmere, Earl of
Sefton, Earl of
Wilton, Earl of
Manchester, Bishop of
Skelmersdale, Lord
Birch, Sir T. B., Bart.
Brown, Sir W. R., Bart.
De Hoghton, Sir H., Bart.
De Trafford, Sir Humphrey, Bart.
Feilden, Sir W. H., Bart.
Fitzgerald, Sir G. R. Dalton-, Bart.
Gerard, Sir R. T., Bart.
Hesketh, Sir T. G. F., Bart.
Heywood, Sir T. P., Bart.
Shuttleworth, Sir J. P. Kay-, Bart.
Tempest, Sir C. H., Bart.

Ackers, of Bickershaw Hall
Addison, of Preston
Ainslie, of Grizedale
Ainslie, of Hall Garth
Ainsworth, of Buckbarrow
Ainsworth, of Smithills Hall
Alison, of Park Hall
Alison, of Woolton Heys
An!erton, of Euxton Hall
Andrew, of Apsley House
Andrews, of Rirington Hall
Archibald, of Rusland Hall
Armitage, of Hope Hall
Arrowsmith, of The Ferns
Ashton, of Middleton
Ashton, of Woodlands
Ashworth, of Turton
Askew, of Conishead Priory
Aspinall, of Standen Hall
Assheton, of Downham Hall
Atkinson, of Cockerham
Atkinson, of Claremont
Baldwin, of Dalton
Baldwin, of Leyland
Bankes, of Winstanley Hall
Barclay, of Wavertree Lodge
Bardsley, of The Orchard. Greenheys
Barnes, of Limefield and Farnworth
Beatt, of Lymm Hall
Beshall, of Lostock Hall
Baynes, of Claremont Hall
Bazley, of Hayesleigh
Bell, of Melling Hall
Bent, of Wennington
Bentley, of Birch House
Beswicke, of Pike House
Bigland, of Bigland Hall
Birley, of Bartle Hall
Birley, of Carr Hill
Birley, of Clifton Hall
Birley, of Highfield
Birley, of The Larches
Birley, of Kirkham
Birley, of Millbanke
Birley, of Pendleton
Blackburne, of Hale Hall
Blacklock, of Hopefield
Blair, of Mill-Hill House
Blundell, of Crock Hall
Blundell, of Crosby Hall
Blundell, of Deysbrook
Bolden, of Hyning
Bolden, of Springfield Hall
Bolling, of Darcy-Lever Hall
Boulton, of Aught en
Bourne, of Heckin-all Hall
Bourne, of Neasham Hall
Bourne, of Stalmine Hall
Bradley, of Slyne House
Braithwaithe, of Steek Park
Bromley-Moore, of Aiglurth
Brancker, of Greenfield
Brickson, of Southport
Brighton, of the Ash
Brighton, of the Ash
Brockhous, of Claughton Hall
Brownell, of Aigburth
Buckley, of Ardwick
Butler, of Litherland
Butler-Bowdon, of Pleasington Hall
Callender, of Ashburne House
Calrow, of Walton Lodge
Cardwell, of Ellerbeck Hall
Carill-Worsley, of Platt Hall
Catterall, of Preston
Chadwick, of Healey
Chadwick, of High Bank

Chaloner, of Aigburth Hall
Chambers, of Waterloo
Chambers-Venables, of Everton
Cheetham, of Eastwood
Clarke, of Summer Hill and The Laund
Clayton, of Adlington Hall
Clifton, of Clifton and Lytham
Clowes, of Broughton Old Hall
Collinge, of Kinnerton Lodge
Cooper, of The Oaks
Coulthart, of Croft House
Crook, of Oakfield
Cross, of Gidlow House
Cross, of Mortfield
Cross, of Red Scar
Crosse, of Shaw Hill
Crossley, of Scaitcliffe
Cunliffe, of Myerscough Hall
Curwen, of Belle Grange
Dauntsey, of Agecroft Hall
Dawes, of Westrooke Bolton
Dawson, of Aldcliffe Hall
Dearden, of Rochdale Manor
De Trafford, of Croston Hall
Diesonson, of Wrightington
Dickson, of Abbot's Reading
Dodgson, of Beardwood
Drinkwater, of Irwell House
Dugdale, of Witton
Dugdale, of Ivy Bank
Duncuft, of Westwood House
Earle, of Allerton
Eccles, of Spring Mount
Eccles, of Well Field
Eckersley, of Standish Hall
Edmondston, of Gresgarth Hall
Edwards-Moss, of Roby Hall
Entwisle, of Foxholes
Entwisle, of Rusholme
Evans, of Haydock Grange
Evans, of The Heyes
Every-Clayton, of Rowley
Fell, of Flan How
Fell, of Ulverston
Fenton, of Bamford Hall
Fenton, of Crimble Hall
Fenton, of Clegg Hall
Fenwick, of Burrow Hall
Fernley, of Clairville
ffarington, of Worden
ffeilden, of Hoghton Bank
ffeilden, of Witton Park
Fielden, of Dob Royd
Fildes, of Crumpsall
Fitz-Gerald, of Pendleton
Ford, of Ellel Hall
Formby, of Formby Hall
Fort, of Read Hall
Foster, of The Whins
Foster, of Hornby Castle
Gale, of Bardsey Hall
Gamble, of Windleburst
Gardner, of Chaseley Hall
Gardner, of Pilling
Garnett, of Bleasdale Tower and Quernmore Park
Garnett, of Wyreside
Gerard, of Aspull House
Gidlow, of Arley Hall
Gillow, of Leighton
Gladstone, of Court Hey
Graham. of Langley House
Gray, of Darcey Lever
Gray, of Wheatfield
Greenall, of Grappenhall
Greenall, of Walton Hall

1072

Greene, of Slyne
Gregge-Hopwood, of Hopwood
Gregson, of Caton
Gregson, of Moorlands
Grimshawe, of Tottington Hall
Grundy, of Westenholme Hall
Hannay, of Springfield
Hardcastle, of Firwood
Hargreaves, of Broadoak
Harrison, of The Lund
Harrison, of Samlesbury Hall
Harter, of Oak End
Heald, of Parrs Wood
Helsby, late of Brook House
Hesketh, of Rufford Old Hall
Heywood, of Norris Green
Heyworth, of Yewtree
Hibbert, of Urmston Grange
Hindle, of Woodfold Park
Hodgson, of South-Hill House
Holden, of Reedly House and Palace House
Hollinshead, late of Hollinshead Hall
Holt, of Stubbylee
Hopwood, of Rockcliffe
Hornby, of Dalton Hall
Hornby, of Druid's Cross
Hornby, of Raikes Hall
Hornby, of Knowsley
Hornby, of Ribby Hall
Hornby, of Sandown
Horrocks, of Merlewood
Horsfall, of Larkfield
Horsfall, of Milbank House
Hughes, of Sherdley Hall
Hulton, of Ashton
Hulton, of Hulton Park
Hulton, of Hurst Grange
Hulton-Harrop, of Bardsley
Jacson, of Barton
Jeffery, of Woolton Hall
Jones, of Lark Hill
Kelsall, of Deeplish Hall
Kemp, of Beechwood
Kershaw, of Lathom
Little, of Salem House
Lomax, of Clayton Hall
Machell, of Hollow Oak
Maclure, of Fallowfield
Marshall, of Monk Coniston
Marshall, of Penwortham Hall
Marton, of Capernway
Mayson, of Fallowfield
Melly, of Liverpool
Midgley-Munro, of Edge Hill
Milne, of Crompton Hall
Molesworth, of Spotland
Molyneux-Seel, of Huyton Hey
Munn, of Heath Hill
Munn, of Newchurch
Musgrave, of West Tower
Newsham, of Preston
Nevess, of Daresbulen Hall
Nuttall, of Thurland Castle
Openshaw, of Heaton Grove
Ormerod, of Edgeside
Ormerod, of Tyldesley House
Ormrod, of Halliwell Hall
Park, of Ollerton Park
Parker, of Alkincoats
Parker, of Charnock Hall
Parker, of Cuerden
Peddler, late of Whinfield
Peel, of Accrington House
Peel, of Peel Fold
Peel, of Singleton Brook
Peel, of Bwmion Park

Pemberton, of Hindley Hall
Pender, of Crumpsall House
Pendlebury, of Heaton Mersey
Pennington, of Hindley Lodge
Petre, of Dunkenhalgh
Petre, of Samlesbury
Phibbs, of Coppull House
Philips, of Bank Hall
Philips, of The Park
Pilkington, of Audley House
Pilkington, of Eccleston Hall
Pilkington, of Park-Place House
Pilkington, of Preston
Pilkington, of Wilpshire Grange
Pilkington, of Windle Hall
Platt, of Werneth Park
Postlethwaite, of The Grange
Potter, of Buile Hill
Potter, of Darwen
Potter, of Earnsdale
Powell, of Brandlesome Hall
Prescott, of Dalton
Preston, of Ellel Grange and Rock House
Radcliffe, of Moorfield
Radcliffe, of Werneth Park
Radclyffe, of Foxdenton Hall
Raffles, of Edge Hill
Rathbone, of Greenbank
Rawlinson, of Duddon Hall and Graythwaite
Rawstorne, of Penwortham Priory
Remington, of Aynsome and The Crow-trees
Ridgway, of Wallsuches
Rigby, of Moss House
Rigge, of Wood Broughton
Robinson, of Reedley Bank
Rothwell, of Sharples Hall
Royds, of Elm House
Royds, of Falinge
Rylands, of Bewsey House
Sagar, of Southfield House
Sandys, of Graythwaite Hall
Saunders, of Wennington Hall
Scarisbrick, of Scarisbrick Hall
Scarlett, of Bank Hall
Schofield, of Buckley Hall
Schneider, of Ligg'nturn House
Shand, of Woolton Wood
Shorrock, of Over Darwen
Sillar, of Rainford Hall
Simpson, of Hutton Hall
Smithurst, of Cuerley
Smethurst, of Rockwood
Smith, of Ludiate
Sowler, of Clark-hill
Sparrow, of Blackburn
Standish, of Duxbury Park
Standish, of Standish Hall
Stanley, of Cross-hall
Stanley, of Simleys Hall
Stapleton, of Carleton Hall
Starkie, of Ashton
Starkie, of Huntroyde
Stewart, of Nateby Hall
Stonor, of Anderton Hall
Strickland, of Sizergh House
Sunderland, of Swartbank
Swainson, of Linsewood
Swainson, of Summerfield House
Talbot, of Baggauley Hall
Taylor, of Eccleston Hall
Taylor, of Todmorden Hall
Taylor, of Moreton Hall and W. Abbey
Threakstone, of Scarforth

Thicknesse, of Beech Hill
Thursby, of Ormerod House
Tootal, of The Weaste
Thornton, of Kirkland and Beaumont Cote
Thornton, of Caton
Tinne, of Aigburth
Towneley, of Towneley
Trappes, of Stanley House
Turner, of Pendlebury House
Waithman, of Bentham House
Waithman, of Westville
Waithman, of Wray House
Walker, of Calderstone
Walker, of Chesham
Walmesley, of The Hall of Ince
Walmesley, of Westwood House
Weld, of Leaghram Hall
Weld-Blundell, of Ince Blundell
Westby, of Mowbreck Hall
Whaley, of Orrell Mount
Whitaker, of Broadclough
Whitaker, of The Holme
Whitaker, of Symonstone Hall
Whitehead, of Alder Grange
Whitle, of Halton Hall
Whitworth, of Irwell House
Wilde, of Eldon Lodge
Willis, of Halsnead Park
Willson, of High Wray
Wilson-Patten, of Bank Hall
Winstanley, of Chaigeley Manor
Withington, of Culcheth Hall
Wood, of Singleton Lodge
Woodcock, of Bank House, Wigan
Woods, of Gillibrand Hall
Worthington, of Hollingwood
Worthington-Wright, of Flixton House
Wrigley, of Southport
Wrigley, of Timberhurst

LEICESTERSHIRE.

Rutland, Duke of
Hastings, Marquis of
Bessborough, Earl of
Chesterfield, Earl of
Denbigh, Earl of
Ferrers, Earl
Harborough, Countess of
Harrington, Earl of
Lanesborough, Earl of
Stamford, Earl of
Wilton, Earl of
Curzon, Viscount
Berners, Lord
Braye, Baroness
De Clifford, Baroness
Beaumont, Sir G. H., Bart.
Cave, Sir M. O. B., Bart.
Dixie, Sir A. B. C., Bart.
Fowke, Sir F. T., Bart.
Greisley, Sir T., Bart.
Halford, Sir H., Bart.
Hazlerigg, Sir A. G., Bart.
Hewett, Sir G. J. R., Bart.
Heygate, Sir F. W., Bart.
Palmer, Sir A. R., Bart.
Ricketts, Sir C., Bart.
Skipwith, Sir P. E., Bart.
Adnutt, of Caddeby
Aikman, of New Parks
Arkwright, of Broughton Abbey
Arkwright, of Normanton Turville
Ashby, of Quenby Hall
Babington, of Rothley Temple

Beasley, of Harston
Bellairs, of Stockerston
Bewicke, of Hallaton Hall
Biggs, of Highfield House
Bingham, of Wartnaby Hall
Bosworth, of Charley
Braithley, of Stackley
Brook, of Enderby Hall
Brookes, of Croft Hall
Browne, of Higham Hall
Burnaby, of Baggrave Hall
Cheney, of Gaddesby Hall
Coleman, of Evington Hall
Cope, of Osbaston Hall
Cradock, of Knighton
Cradock, of Quorn Court
Craven, of Craven Lodge
Creswell, of Ravenston
Crosland, of Burbage House
Curzon, of Breedon-on-the-Hill
Dashwood, of Stanford Park
Dawson, of Launde Abbey
Dicey, of Claybrook Hall
Dumaresque, of Surkland Hall
Ellis, of The Newarke
Emerson, of Ulverscroft
Eyre, of Lindley Hall
Farnham, of Quorndon House
Fellows, of Bitteswell House
Fisher, of Cossington
Fosbrooke, of Ravenstone Hall
Freer, of The Coplow
Frewen, of Cold-Overton Hall
Goodchild, of The Grange
Goulton-Constable, of Cotesbach
Harris, of Ratcliffe-on-the-Wreake
Hartopp, of Dalby Hall
Hastings, of Willesley
Haymes, of Great Glenn
Hazlehurst, of Misterton Hall
Herrick, of Beaumanor
Heycock, of East-Norton Manor
Heygate, of Maplewell Grange
Hinrich, of Hallaton Manor
Hole, of Quorn Lodge
Hoskins, of Blaby
Hunt, of Kibworth Hall
Jacomb-Hood, of Bardon Park
Jee, of Peckleton Hall
Johnson, of Ulverscroft
King, of Stretton Hall
Knight, of Glen-Parva Manor
Lakin, of Gilmorton
Lynes, of Tooley Park
Martin, of Anstey Pastures
Martin, of Whatton House
Middleton, of Loughborough
Moore, of Appleby Hall
Moreton, of Lindridge House
Morrice, of Catthorpe Towers
Mowbray, of Grangewood House
Nevill, of Nevill Holt
Noble, of Danett's Hill
Norman, of Headly Manwood
Ord, of Langton Hall
Owsley, of Blaston
Packe, of Prestwold Hall
Paget, of Thorpe Satchville
Paget, of Humberstone
Palmer, of Withcote Hall
Pares, of Ulverscroft
Perkins, of Orton Hall
Phillipps-de-Lisle, of Garendon and Grace-Dieu Manor
Pochin, of Braunston House
Pochin, of Edmonthorpe Hall
Powys-Keck, of Stoughton Grange

Roberts, of Witherley
Robertson, of Chilcote
Salt, of Kirby Firth
St. Maur, of Burton Hall
St. Maur, of Snibston
Smith, of Leesthorpe Hall
Story, of Lockington
Story, of Sutton Field
Sutton, of Skeffington Hall
Tailby, of Skeffington Hall
Tryon, of Loddington Hall
Turrille, of Bosworth Hall
Tynte, of Burleigh Hall
Walker, of The Grange
Warner, of Quorndon Hall
Wollaston, of Shenton Hall
Woodcock, of Rearsby
Wright, of Rempstone Hall

LEITRIM CO.

Leitrim, Earl of
Crofton, Sir M. G., Bart.
Birchall, of Blackrock House
Crofton, of Lakefield
Cullen, of Glenade
Dickson, of Dungarberry and Tullaghan
Godley, of Killigar
Gore, of Derrycarne
Jones, of Drumard
Lestrange, of Tynte Lodge
Montgomery, of Bellavel
O'Beirne, of Jamestown Lodge
O'Brien, of Rockfield
O'Reilly, of The Heath House
Palmer, of Shriff
Peyton, of Castle Carrow
Peyton, of Driney House
Peyton, of Loughseur
Rowley, of Mount Campbell
Rutherford, of Cornastalk
Simpson, of Clooonrick Castle and Gortcoulou Lodge
Tottenham, of Glenade
Tottenham, of Glenfarne Hall
Waldron, of Lismoyle House
Warde, of Anzbery House
White, of Keiblra
Whyte, of Newtown Manor and Glencar

LIMERICK CO.

Charleville, Earl of
Devon, Earl of
Dunraven, Earl of
Limerick, Earl of
Gort, Viscount
Guillamore, Viscount
Limerick, Bishop of
Glarina, Lord
Cloncurry, Lord
Massy, Lord
Monteagle, Lord
Muskerry, Lord
Barrington, Sir W. H., Bart.
De Burgho, Sir R. B., Bart.
De Vere, Sir V. E., Bart.
Roche, Sir D. V., Bart.
Adams, of Ahavagurrah
Apjohn, of Linfield
Bloomerhassett, of Riddlestown Park
Boucher, of Biggotstown
Bourke, of Thornfields

3 z   1043

Seely, of Heighington
Sharp, of Morton House
Short, of Edlington Grove
Sibthorp, of Canwick Hall
Skipworth, of Moorton House
Smyth, of South-Elkington Hall
Stanhope, of Revesby Abbey
Staniland, of Harrington Hall
Stevenson, of Uffington
Sutton, of Scawby Hall
Taylor, of Burnham Manor
Tennyson-D'Eyncourt, of Bayons Manor and Usselby Hall
Thorold, of Boothby Hall
Thorold, of Cuxwold
Thorold, of Weelsby House
Tomline, of Riby Hall
Tunnard, of Frampton House
Turnor, of Panton Hall
Turnor, of Stoke Rochford
Uppleby, of Barrow Hall
Uppleby, of Wootton House
Vyner, of Gautby Hall
Wallis, of Healing
Walls, of Boothby Hall
Welby, of Stroxton
Welby-Gregory, of Newton House
Welfitt, of Farforth House
Welfitt, of Manby Hall
Wilkinson, of Corby Birkholme
Willson, of Rauceby Hall
Wilson, of Wigtoft
Winn, of Appleby
Wood, of Thoresby
Woodhouse, of Irnham Hall
Wright, of Brattleby Hall
Young, of Kingerby

LINLITHGOWSHIRE.

Buchan, Earl of
Hopetoun, Earl of
Roseberry, Earl of
Baillie, Sir W., Bart.
Dalyell, Sir R. A. O., Bart.
Simpson, Sir J. Y., Bart.
Blair, of Avontoun
Cadell, of Grange
Dawson, of Bonnytoun
Dundas, late of Duddingston
Dundas, of Dundas Castle
Falconar, late of Carlowrie
Fenton-Livingstone, of Bedlormio
Gillon, of Wallhouse
Hamilton, of Cathlaw
Hog, of Newliston and Kellie
Hope, of Bridge Castle
Hope, of Carriden
Innes, of Bangour
Johnston-Stewart, of Champfleurie
Livingstone, of Bedlormie
McLagan, of Pumpherston
Marjoribanks, of Balbardie
Pender, of Middleton Hall
Robertson, of Whitehill
Seton, of Preston House
Shairp, of Houston
Warden, of Blackeraig
Wardrop, of Bridgehouse

LONDONDERRY CO.

Derry and Raphoe, Bishop of
Garvagh, Lord
Bruce, Sir H. H., Bart.

Adams, of Ballydevit
Alexander, of Newtonlimavady
Baird, of Boom Hall
Beresford, of Learmount Park and Ashbrook
Blacker, of Glenkeen
Boyd, of Dunduan House
Browne, of Comber House
Bruce, of Ballyscullion House
Clark, of Largantogher
Conyngham, of Spring Hill
Cromie, of Cromore
Dawson, of Moyola Park
De Blaquiere, of Arkdill
Dolling, of Tamlaght O'Crilly
Gaussen, of Lakeview House
Giveen, of Rock Castle
Greer, of Spring Vale
Heygate, of Bellarena
Hill, of Bellaghy Castle
Hunter, of Straidarran
Knox, of Prehen
Kyle, of Laurel Hill
Lyle, of The Oaks
Lyle, of Portstewart House
Macausland, of Woodbank
MacCausland, of Drenagh
M'Clintock, of Hampstead Hall
M'Cormick, of Lisahawley House
Macky, of Almont
Marshall, or St. John's
Miller, of Moneymore
Murray, of Caw House
Nicholson, of Roe Park
Norman, of Glengollan
Ogilby, of Ardnargle
Ogilby, of Kilcatten
Ogilby, of Pellipar
Olpherts, of Milburn
Richardson, of Somerset
Robinson, of Port Stewart
Scott, of Willsborough
Skipton, of Beech Hill
Stevenson, of Ardkill
Tittle, of Portstewart
Tyler, of Newtonlimavady
Young, of Coolkeiragh

LONGFORD CO.

Granard, Earl of
Longford, Earl of
Annaly Lord
Fetherston, Sir T. J., Bart.
Ball, of Abbeylara
Blackall, of Colamber Manor
Bond, of Farra
Cordner, of Derramore and Mullogh
Dopping-Hepenstal, of Derrycassen
Edgeworth, of Edgeworthstown
Edgeworth, of Kilshrewly
Fox, of Fox Hall
Fox, of New Park
Hamlewk, of Cole Hill
Hinds, of New Grove
Jessop, of Doory Hill
King-Harman, of Newcastle
Lefroy, of Carrickglass
M'Cann, of Lismoy House
Mahonehy, of Rathmore
Newcomen, of Clonahard
Nugent, of Killasowna
O'Ferrall, of Lizard
O'Reilly, of Clonamber
Shuldham, of Moigh House
Thompson, of Clonfin
Wilson-Slater, of Whitehill

LOUTH CO.

Roden, Earl of
Massareene and Ferrard, Viscount
Netterville, Viscountess
Bellew, Lord
Clermont, Lord
Louth, Lord
Bellingham, Sir A. E., Bart.
Robinson, Sir J. S., Bart.
Armitage, of Coole
Balfour, of Townley Hall
Bigger, of Falmore Hall
Chester, of Cartown
Craven, of Richardstown
D'Arcy, of Carlingford
Dunlop, of Monasterboice
Fitzgerald, of Fane Valley
Fortescue, of Stephenstown
Foster, of Castlering
Garstin, of Bragganstown
Haig, of Dundalk
Hatch, of Ardee Castle
Jocelyn, of Dundalk
Lee-Norman, of Corballis
M'Clintock, of Drumcar
MacNeill, of Mount Pleasant
Marlay, of Bawn
Montgomery, of Beaulieu
Moore, of Nootka Lodge
O'Reilly, of Knock Abbey
O'Reilly-Dease, of Dee Farm
Pentland, of Black Hall
Ruxton, of Ardee House
Ruxton, of Rahanna House
Singleton, of Collon
Smyth, of Newtown House
Taaffe, of Smarmore Castle
Upton, of Glyde Court
Woodhouse, of Omeath Park

MAN, ISLE OF.

Bacon, of Seafield and Staward
Callister, of Thornton
Christian, of Milntown
Drinkwater, of Kirby
Eddington, of Share Valley
Farrant, of Ballamoar
Gawne, of Kentraugh
Goldie-Taubman, of The Nunnery
Quayle, of Crogga
Simpson, of The Cliffe
Wilson, of Farm Hill

MAYO CO.

Sligo, Marquis of
Arran, Earl of
Lucan, Earl of
Mayo, Earl of
Avonmore, Viscount
Clanmorris, Lord
Kilmaine, Lord
Oranmore and Browne, Lord
Lynch-Blosse, Sir R., Bart.
O'Donell, Sir R. A., Bart.
O'Malley, Sir W., Bart.
Palmer, Sir W. H. R., Bart.
Bingham, of Bingham Castle
Blacker, of Claremount
Blake, of Billinafad
Blake, of Towerhill
Bourke, of Carrowkeel
Bourke, of Curraghleagh

Brabazon, of Brabazon Park
Browne, of Browne Hall
Browne, of Grahan
Browne, of Raheens
Carter, of Erris
Clive, of Ballicroy
Costello, of Edmundstown
Coyne, of Altramont Villa
Coyne, of Kiltane Abbey
Crean, of Ballonvilla
D'Arcy, of Fisher Hill
Elwood, of Strandhill Park
Fitzgerald, of Turlough Park
French, of French Grove
Gardiner, of Farm Hill
Garvey, of Murrisk Abbey
Gilbert, of Clooncormack
Gore, of Belleek Manor
Higgins, of Glen Corrib
Howley, of Belleek Castle
Jackson, of Carramore
Jordan, of Rossleven Castle
Kearney, of Ballyvary
Kelley, of The Skerdaghs
Kenny, of Ballinrobe
Knox, of Castle Rea
Knox, of Ballinrobe
Knox, of Mount Falcon
Knox, of Netley Park
Knox, of Rappa Castle
Lambert, of Brookhill
Lewin, of Cloghans House
Lindsay-Bucknall, of Turin Castle
Lindsey, of Hollymount
Lynch, of Ballycurrin Castle
Lynch, of Clogher
Lynch, of Partree House
Macdonnell, of Doo Castle
Moore, of Ballinrobe
Moore, of Moore Hall
Mudge, of Glenrossera
O'Malley, of Newcastle
Orme, of Owenmore
Ormsby, of Ballinamore
Paget, of Knockglass
Palmer, of Invermore
Palmer, of Summerhill
Pratt, of Enniscoe
Ruttledge, of Bloomfield
Taaffe, of Woodfield
Talbot, of Castlebar
Trench, of Cloona Castle
Waldron, of Lung
Wilbraham, of Boatharen Lodge
Yelverton, of Hazelrock

MEATH CO.

Conyngham, Marquis
Headfort, Marquis of
Darnley, Earl of
Fingall, Earl of
Boyne, Viscount
Gormanston, Viscount
Netterville, Viscount
Meath, Bishop of
Athlumney, Lord
Dunsany, Lord
Langford, Lord
Barnewall, Sir R. A. J., Bart.
De Bathe, Sir W. P., Bart.
Dillon, Sir John, Bart.
Meredyth, Sir H., Bart.
Barker, of Stirling
Barnewall, of Bloomsberry
Bligh, of Brittas
1076

Bolton, of Bective Lodge
Bomford, of Ferrans and Gallow
Bomford, of Oakley Park
Boylan, of Hilltown
Brabazon, of Mornington House
Brodigan, of Pilton House
Burrowes, of Dangan Castle
Butler, of Priest-town
Butler. of Staffordstown
Caddell, of Harbourston
Caldwell, of New Grange
Chaloner, of Kingsfort
Charlton, of Curraghtown
Coddington, of Oldbridge
Corbally, of Corbalton Hall
Cusack, of Cussington
De Rinzi, of Trim
Despard, of Rathmolyon House
Drake, of Rathvale
Drake, of Rorristown
Farrell, of Moynalty
Farrell, of Archerstown
Fitzgerald, of Baltinoran
Fitzherbert, of Black Castle
Fowler, of Rahinston House
Garnett, of Summerseat
Gernon, of Athcarne Castle
Gerrard, of Boyne Hill
Gradw... , of Dowth Hall
Gradwell, of Flatten Hall.
Grainger, of Cauceston
Hamilton, of Ballinacoll .
Hamilton, of Hamwood
Hamilton, of Vessington
Hopkins, of Gravel Mount
Hussey, of Galtrim and Rathkenny
Kelly, of Seneschalstown House
Lambart, of Beau Parc
Langan, of Bellewston House
McCann, of Staleen House
M'Evoy, of Balramino
MacEvoy, of Tobertinan
M'Veagh, of Drewstown
Metge, of Athlumley
Moore, of Tara House
Murphy, of Kilcairne
Nangle, of Kildalkey
Naper, of Loughcrew
Nicholson, of Balrath
O'Reilly, of Baltrasna
Osborne, of Rosnaree
Osborne, of Smithstown
Pepper, of Ballygarth
Pollock, of Mountainstown
Pollock, of Oatlands and Newcastle
Preston, of Bellinter
Roberts, of Dormstown Castle
Rodon, of Newgrove
Rorke, of Johnstown House
Ross, of Dardistown Castle
Rotherham, of Crossdrum
Rotherham, of Tricmore
Rothwell, of Rockfield
Rowley, of Maperath
Rowley, of Sylvan Park
Rynd, of Ryndville
Singleton, of Aclare
Smith, of Anneshrooke
Smith, of Beabeg
Taaffe, of Ardmulchan House
Taylour, of Corbal Lis
Taylour, of Dowerton
Thunder, of Lagore
Tisdall, of Charlesfort
Wade, of Clonebraney
Waller, of Allenstown
Walsh, of Bitslah

Wilson, of Proudstown House
Wilson-Slator, of Belle Ville
Winter, of Agher
Woodward, of Drumbarrow

MERIONETHSHIRE.

Vane, Earl
Buckley, of Plâs Dinas Mawddwy
Corbet, of Ynysymaengwyn
Edwards, of Dolserau
Greaves, of Plâs Weunydd
Green, of Dolgelly
Hartley, of Llwyn
Lloyd, of Blaenglyn
Lloyd, of Nannau
Lloyd, of Rhagatt
Nanney, of Maes-y-Neuadd
Price, of Rhiwlas
Reveley, of Bryn-y-gwin
Richards, of Bala
Richards, of Caerynwch
Richardson, of Aber Hirnant
Robertson, of Crogen
Scott, of Peniarthuchaf Tongie
Thruston, of Pennal Tower
Thruston, of Talgarth Hall
Vaughan, of Nanney
Wayne, of Aberartro
Williams, of Deudraeth Castle
Williams, of Llwyn
Williams, of Plâs Newydd
Williams, of Vronwnion
Wynn, of Rhug
Wynne, of Peniarth

MIDDLESEX.

Northumberland, Duke of
Jersey, Earl of
Mansfield, Earl of
Lucan, Earl of
Strafford, Earl of
Cadogan, Earl
Enfield, Viscount
Ranelagh, Viscount
London, Bishop of
Dufferin, Lord
Holland, Lady
Tenterden, Lord
Clay, Sir Wm., Bart.
Gibbons, Sir J., Bart.
Lawrence, Sir J. J. T., Bart.
Pollock, Sir F., Bart.
Spearman, Sir A. Y., Bart.
Wiseman, Sir W. S., Bart.
Arden, of Sunbury Park
Bashford, of Norwood House
Baxendale, of Woodside
Bodkin, of Highgate
Bosanquet, of Osidwood
Beaumont et Clay more
Bruce, of Rivermead
Burdett-Coutts, of Holly Lodge
Burlton, of Oaklands
Busk, of Ford's Grove
Butler, of Cazenoves
Byles, of Harefield
Cadogan, of Wembley
Cave, of Belmont
Chapman, of Harringay
Clarke, of Swakeleys
Clayton, of Enfield Old Park
Cole, of Twickenham
Cooper, of Finchley Manor

Cox, of Hilliugdon House
Cox, of Boat Mount
Croll, of Southwood
Deane, of Eastcot House
De Burgh, of West-Drayton Manor
De Salis, of Hillingdon Place
Donnithorne, of Colne Lodge
Douglas-Willan, of Twyford Abbey
Drake, of Breakspears
Eyre, of St. John's Wood
Fane-de-Salis, of Dawley Court
Flood, of Hendon
Ford, of Enfield
Fuller, of Pinner Grove
Glossop, of Silver Hall
Glyn, of Stanmore Park
Gostling, of Whitton Park
Gray, of Wembley Park
Greville, of Hillingdon
Gunter, of Earles Court
Gyll, of Yeoveney Hall
Haggard, of Twickenham
Hawkins, of Canteloes
Hilliard, of Cowley House
Hoare, of Child's Hill
Hoare, of Mill Hill
Hoare, of Hampstead
Holland, of Holland House
Hollond, of Stanmore Hall
Kelk, of Bentley Priory
Kennard, of Woodlands
Lindsay, of Shepperton Manor
Mackinnon, of Bittacy House
Mackintosh, of Twickenham
Martin, of Rose Hill
Meyer, of Forty Hall
Miller, of Mariemont
Mills, of Hillingdon Place
Mitchison, of Sunbury Manor
Moorat, of Bush-Hill Park
Morley, of Stamford Hill
Neave, of Oak Hill
Otway, of Teddington Place
Paterson, of Poyle House
Peel, of Marble Hill
Penton, of Pentonville
Percival, of Bridgefoot House
Perkins, of Hanworth Park
Plumer, of Canons Park
Pownall, of Spring Grove
Reed, of Bedfont
Rothschild, of Gunnersbury Park
Sidney, of Iowes Manor
Sleigh, of Hanworth House
Somerset, of Enfield Court
Sperling, of Stanmore Manor
Stracey-Clitherow, of Boston House
Sullivan, of Broom House
Swanston, of Holly House
Tayler, of Bedfont
Tennent, of Pynnacles
Tennyson d'Eyncourt, of Hadley House
Tompson-Dolmar, of Ruislip Park
Vernon, of Harefield Park
Walford, of Hillingdon
Walpole, of Ealing
Ware, of Hendon Hall
Wilde, of Hadley
Wilkinson, of White Webbs Park
Wood, of Littleton
Woodd, of Hillfield

MIDLOTHIAN.
(See Edinburgh.)

MONAGHAN CO.

Dartrey, Earl of
Blayney, Lord
Rossmore, Lord
Cremorne, Lady
Forster, Sir Geo., Bart.
Adams, of Loughbawn
Anketell, of Anketell Grove
Bennie, of Farmoyle House
Cole, of Brandrum
Coote, of Brandrum House
Evatt, of Mount Louise
Forster, of Ballynure
French, of Ballybay House
Hamilton, of Cornacassa
Hope, of Castle Blayney
Johnston, of Fort Johnston
Johnstone, of Cassaugh Moune
Kane, of Drumreaske
Leslie, of Ballybay
Leslie, of Glasslough
Lewis, of Clanamully
Lewis, of Raconnell
Lucas, of Castle Shane
McClure, of Ballylech House
Madden, of Hilton Park
Mayne, of Glynch House
Morant, of Shirley House
Murr'-Ker, of Newbliss House
Power, of Arraghmakerrig
Richardson, of Poplar Vale
Rowley, of Cordoolough
Shegog, of Munnilly
Shirley, of Lough Fea
Singleton, of Fort Singleton
Trench, of Essex Castle
Wright, of Gola House
Young, of Monaghan

MONMOUTHSHIRE.

Beaufort, Duke of
Llanover, Lady
Tredegar, Lord
Mackworth, Sir A. W. J., Bart.
Salusbury, Sir C. J., Bart.
Bailey, of Maindiff
Bailey of Nant-y-glo
Bateman, of Bartholey House
Berrington, of Pant-y-Goitre
Bevan, of Llanellan
Bosanquet, of Dinastow
Brewer, of Danygreig
Brown, of Hardwick House
Byrde, of Goytrey House
Carruthers, of the Goudra
Cave, of Hilston Park
Clay, of Piercefield Park
Clifford, of Llantilio
Curre, of Itton Court
Davies, of The Garth
Dowling, of Llantarnam Abbey
Falconer, of Usk
Finch, of Blaenavon
Greatorex, of King's Hill
Greenfield, of Brynderwen
Greenhow-Relph, of Beech Hill
Hamilton, of Hilston Park
Hanbury, of Pontypool
Hanbury-Williams, of Colebrook
Hanbury-Williams, of Nantcor
Harding, of Rockfield
Harford, of Sirhonry
Hawkins, of Tredunnock
Herbert, of Llanarth

Herbert, of Clytha
Hill, of The Knoll
Hollis, of Shirenewton House
Homfray, of Glen Usk
James, of Lansoar
Kennard, of Crumlin Hall
Landor, of Llanthony Abbey
Lewis, of St. Pierre
Little, of Llanrair Grange
M'Donnell, of Plâs Newydd
Manning, of Coldbrook Park
Mitchell, of Llanfrechfa Grange
Moggridge, of Woodfield
Morgan, of Ruperra Castle
Morgan, of The Friars
Nicholl, of Court Blethin
Overton, of Ty Mawr
Phillips, of Whitson House
Powell, of The Gaer
Prothero, of Malpas Court
Rodney, of Llanvihangel Court
Rolls, of Croft-y-Bwla
Rolls, of the Hendre
Rooke, of Pilstone House
Savery, of Hardwick Lodge
Stretton, of Brynderwen
Tynte, of Llanellan
Wakeman, of The Graig
Wheeley, of The Pentre
Williams, of Aberbaiden
Williams, of The Garth
Williams, of Llangibby Castle
Wood, of Pentre Court

MONTGOMERYSHIRE.

Powis, Earl of
Vane, Earl
Sudeley, Lord
Conroy, Sir Edward, Bart.
Adams, of Plâs Lyssyn
Browne, of Mellington Hall
Crewe-Read, of Llandinam Hall
Curling, of Macsmawr Hall
Davies, of Peniarth
Davies, of Brynglas
Dugdale, of Llwyn
Edwards, of Greenfields
Fisher, of Maesfren
Gold, of Garthmyl Hall
Hanbury-Tracy, of Gregynog
Herbert, of Glan Hafren
Heyward, of Cresswood
Hind, of Clochfaen
Humffreys, of Llwyn
Johnson, of Monksfield
Jones, of Rhicwport
Jones, of Plâs Trdhelig
Jones-Saltoun, of Tron Fraith
Leighton, of Bansley
Lomax, of Bodfach
Long, of Dolforgan
Maurice, of Bodynfoel
Morris, of Bertie Lloyd
Mytton, of Garth
Naylor, of Leighton Hall
Owen, of Bettws Hall
Owen, of Broadway
Perrott, of Bronhydden
Pryce, of Cyfronydd
Pryce, of Guntley
Pugh, of Llanerchydol
Stephens, of Newtown
Tripp, of Esgair Evon
Turner, of Pentrehwilin
Williames, of Pennaut
Wynn, of Pentrego

MORAYSHIRE (see *Elgin*).

NAIRNSHIRE.

Cawdor, Earl of
Dunbar, Sir J. A., Bart.
Dougal, of Glenferness
Mackintosh, of Geddes House
Murray, of Househill
Rose, Kilravock Castle

NORFOLK.

Cornwall, H.R.H. Duke of
Wellington, Duke of
Cholmondeley, Marquis of
Lothian, Marquis of
Townshend, Marquis
Albemarle, Earl of
Kimberley, Earl of
Leicester, Earl of
Orford, Earl of
Rosebery, Earl of
Ranelagh, Viscount
Norwich, Bishop of
Ashburton, Lord
Bayning, Dowager Lady
Berners, Lord
Hastings, Lord
Sondes, Lord
Stafford, Lord
Suffield, Lord
Bacon, Sir H. H., Bart.
Bagge, Sir W., Bart.
Bedingfeld, Sir H. G. P., Bart.
Beevor, Sir T. B., Bart.
Berney, Sir H., Bart.
Boileau, Sir J. P., Bart.
Buxton, Sir R. J., Bart.
Buxton, Sir T. F., Bart.
Durrant, Sir H. J., Bart.
ffolkes, Sir W. H., Bart.
Foster, Sir Wm., Bart.
Hare, Sir T., Bart.
Hoste, Sir W. L. G., Bart.
Jodrell, Sir E. R., Bart.
Jones, Sir W., Bart.
Kemp, Sir W. R., Bart.
Lacon, Sir E. H. K., Bart.
Nugent, Sir G. E., Bart.
Preston, Sir J. H., Bart.
Proctor-Beauchamp, Sir T. W. B., Bart.
Stracey, Sir H. J., Bart.
Adlington, of Holme-Hale Hall
Angerstein, of Weeting Hall
Applewhaite, of Pickenham Hall
Atthill, of Brandiston Hall
Aufrère, of Faulsham
Back, of Hethersett Hall
Bagge, of Gaywood Hall
Baring, of Cromer
Barnwell, of Mileham
Barton, of Threxton House
Bayning, of Honingham Hall
Bedingfeld, of Ditchingham Hall
Beevor, of Hingham
Beevor, of Hevingham
Bellairs, of Mulbarton Lodge
Bentinck, of Terrington St. Clement
Berney, of Moreton and Hockering
Bidwell, of Thetford
Birch, of Wretham
Birch, of Wretham Hall
Birkbeck, of Stoke Holy-Cross

Birkbeck, of Thorpe
Blake, of Horstead
Blake-Humphrey, of Wroxham
Blofield, of Hoveton House
Blomefield, of Necton Hall
Blyth, of Burnham Westgate
Boycott, of Burgh St. Peter's
Bradfield, of Stoke Ferry
Bramhall, of Terrington St. John
Brereton, of Brinton
Browne, of Elsing Hall
Buckworth, of Cockley-Cley Hall
Bullock, of Shipdham
Bulwer, of Heydon Hall
Bulwer, of Quebec
Burroughes, of Burfield Hall
Burroughes, of Burlingham Hall and Coltishall
Burroughes, of Lingwood
Burroughes, of Stratton St. Mary
Buxton, of Catton Hall
Buxton, of Northrepps Hall
Cabbell, of Cromer Hall
Calthrop, of Stanhoe Hall
Cann, of Cavick
Cator, of Woodbastwick Hall
Coke, of Holkham
Coldham, of Anmer Hall
Collison, of East Bilney
Collyer, of Hackford Hall
Coop, of Morley
Copeman, of Hemsby Hall
Cowper, late of Sandringham Hall
Cozens-Hardy, of Letheringsett
Crabbe, of Merton
Crawshay, of Scole Lodge
Cubitt, of Catfield Hall
Cubitt, of Honing Hall
Currie, of Tilney
Curteis, of Scole
Custance, of Weston House
Davy, of Ingoldsthorpe and Kilverstone
De Grey, of Watton
Denny, of Burgh Ampton
Dewing, of Carbrooke Hall
Dolphin, of Swafield Hall
Donne, of Mattishall Hall
Dugmore, of Swaffham
Eden, of Gillingham Hall
Edwards, of Ashhill Rectory
Edwards, of Hardingham Hall
Edwards, of White Hall
Elwes, of Congham House
Elwin, of Thorp
Ensor, of Rollesby Hall
Evans, of North Tuddenham
Everard, of Congham
Fellowes, of Haverland Hall
Fellowes, of Shottisham Park
Fitz-Roy, of Kempstone
Fitz-Roy, of Stratton-Strawless
Foster, of Scratby Hall
Fountaine, of Narford Hall
France, of Brockdish
Frank, of Earlham Hall
Freeman, of Ashwicken
Frere, of Roydon Hall
Fryer, of Crowe Hall
Gay, of New Hall
Gay, of Thurning Hall
Gilbert, of Braydeston
Gilbert, of Cantley
Gilbert, of Chedgrave
Goldson, of Illo' Norton
Graver-Browne, of Morley Hall
Green, of Wroxham

Grigson, of Broomlay and Winburgh
Gunn, of Irstead
Gurdon, of Letton
Gurney, late of Catton
Gurney, of Keswick Hall
Gurney, of North Runcton
Gurney, of Thorpe
Gwyn, of Baron's Hall
Gwyn, of Tasburgh
Haggard, of Bradenham
Hamond, of Westacre
Hardy, of Hillborough
Hare, of Docking Hall
Harvey, of Bracondale and Mousehold House
Havers, of Thelton Hall
Hemsworth, of Rocklands
Hemsworth, of Shropham Hall
Hicks, late of Watton
Hill, of Gresenhall Hall
Hogg, of Thornham Hall
Hollway, of Stanhoe
Holmes, of Brockdish Hall
Holmes, of Brooke Hall
Holmes, of Gawdy Hall
Holmes, of Scole House
Hopper, of Starston
Houchen, of Wereham Hall
Howard, of Castle-Rising
Howes, of Morningthorpe Manor
Howman, of Bexwell
Hulton, of Islington Hall
Hume, of Burnley Hall
Irby, of Boyland Hall
Ives, of Colton
Jarvis, of Middleton Tower
Jary, of Burlingham
Jermy, of Stanfield Hall
Jex-Blake, of Swanton Abbott
Jodrell, of Bayfield Hall
Kemp, of Coltishall Manor
Keppel, of Lexham Hall
Kerrich, of Geldeston Hall
Kerrison, of Brome Hall
Kerslake, of Barmer House
Kett, of Brooke House
Ketton, of Felbrigg Hall
Knight, of Framlingham Hall
Lee-Warner, of Walsingham Abbey
Lely, of Framingham Hall
Loftus, of Bracon Lodge
Lombe, of Belaugh Hall
Long, of Dunston Hall
Lodge, of Spixworth Park
Lucas, of Filby House
Lyne-Stephens, of Lyneford Hall
Marcon, of Wallington Hall
Margitson, of Ditchingham House
Marsham, of Stratton-Strawless
Marsham, of Hayes' Hall
Marsham, of Rippon Hall
Marsham, of Saxlingham
Metcalfe, of ————
Micklethwaite, of ————
Mills, of ————
Molyneux-Montgomery, of Garboldisham Hall
Morse-Boycott, of Senowe
Mott, of Barningham Hall
Muskett, of Clippesby House
Neville-Rolfe, of Heacham Hall
Newcome, of Hockwold
Norris, of Woodnorton
North, of Rougham
Palmer, of Caston
Parker, of Swannington Hall
Partridge, of Caston

Partridge, of Hockham Hall
Patteson, of Thorpe
Penrice, of Great Yarmouth
Petre, of Westwick Hall
Phayre, of West Raynham
Pitman, of Oulton Hull
Postle, of Smallburgh
Pratt, of Ryston Hall
Press, of Reymerstone
Preston, of Great Yarmouth
Read, of Honingham
Ripley, of Earlham Hall
Rising, of Horsey
Robinson, of Knapton House
Rogers, of Holt Hall
Rous, of Worsted House
Scott, of Colney Hall
Scott-Chad, of Thursford Hall
Seymour of Barwick House
Smith, of Ellingham Hall
Sparke, of Gunthorpe Hall
Spurgeon, of Gressenhall
Steward, of East Carlton
Stoughton, of Bawdeswell Hall
Stracey, of Sprowston Hall
Styleman-le-Strange, of Hunstanton
Suffield, of Horstead Hall
Taylor, of Hardingham
Taylor, of Starston
Thornhill, of Riddlesworth
Tompson, of Witchingham Hall
Townley, of Beaupré Hall
Townshend, of Yarrow Hou~
Trafford, of Wroxham Hall
Tuck, of Strumpshaw Hall
Tyssen, of Northwould Lodge
Tyssen-Amhurst, of Didlington
Unthank, of Intwood Hall
Upcher, of Sheringham Hall
Upwood, of Lovell's Hall
Vade-Walpole, of Freethorpe
Villebois, of Marham House
Walpole, of Rainthorpe Hall
Ward, of Salhouse Hall
Weyland, of Woodrising Hall
Whitbread, of Strumpshaw
Wilson, of Billingford
Wilson, of The Chase
Windham, of Cromer
Windham, of Hanworth
Wodehouse, of Bracondale
Wodehouse, of Loddon
Wodehouse, of Witton
Wood. of Fletwell
Worship, of Great Yarmouth
Wright, of Buxton
Yates, of Burgh Hall

NORTHAMPTONSHIRE.

Buccleuch and Queensberry, Duke of
Grafton, Duke of
Northampton, Marquis of
Hood, Viscount
Cardigan, Earl of
Fitzwilliam, Earl
Spencer, Earl
Westmoreland, Earl of
Winchilsea, Earl of
Peterborough, Bishop of
Carbery, Lord
Henley, Lord
Kesteven, Lord
Lilford, Lord
Lyveden, Lord
Overstone, Lord

Penrhyn, Lord
Semphill, Baroness
Southampton, Lord
Brooke, Sir W. de Capel-, Bart.
Brown, Sir W. R., Bart.
Dryden, Sir E. H. L., Bart.
Gunning, Sir H. J., Bart.
Isham, Sir C. E., Bart.
Knightley, Sir R., Bart.
Langham, Sir J. H., Bart.
Palmer, Sir G., Bart.
Robinson, Sir G. S., Bart.
Wake, Sir H., Bart.
Arbuthnot, of Woodford House
Ashby, of Naseby
Bateman, of Guilsborough
Beasley, of Chapel Brampton
Bevan, of Flore House and Brixworth Hall
Bishop, of Upton
Blencowe, of Marston House.
Booth, of Glendon Hall
Bouverie, of Delapré Abbey
Burton, of Daventry
Capron, of Stoke Doyle
Cartwright, of Aynhoe
Cartwright, of Edgcote
Cartwright, of Eydon Hall
Cartwright, of Flore House
Christie, of Preston Deanery
Clarke, of Cold Higham
Clarke, of Welton Place
Clarke-Thornhill, of Rushton
Cole, of Paston Hall
Cust, of Arthingworth
Dolben, of Finedon Hall
Duthy, of Sudborough
Elewes, of Billing Hall
Farquhar, of Brackley House
Fitzroy, of Salcey Lawn
Fitzwilliam, of Alwalton
Fitzwilliam, of Milton Park
Gay, of Biddlesden Park
Gordon, of Woodstone
Grant, of Lichborough
Gulston, of Knuston Hall
Gunnell, of Woodford and Addington
Harpur, of Burton Hall
Harrison, of Bugbrooke
Heycock, of Pytchley
Hill, of Wollaston Hall
Holden-Hambrough, of Fipewell Hall
Holdich-Hungerford, of Dingley Park and Maidwell
Holroyd, of Hatton Hall
Howard-Vyse, of Boughton
Hunt, of Wadenhoe
Hutchinson, of Weston
Isham, of Landport
Istead, of Ecton
Ives, of Bradden House
Jackson, of Duddington
Maunsell, of Sprutt~n House
Mansel, of Cosgrove Hall
Martin, of Chacombe Priory
Maunsell, of Rothwell
Maunsell, of Thorpe Malsor
Monckton, of Fineshade Abbey
Montgomery, of Milton House
Nethercote, of Moulton Grange
Novile, of Wolcot
O'Brien, of Blatherwycke Park
Payne, of Pitsford
Pell, of Haslebeech
Pemberton, late of Milton
Perry, of Cottingham House
Pierrepont, of Evenley Hall

Pilgrim, late of Gayton House
Ramsay, of Croughton Park
Rokeby, of Arthingworth
Rose, of Cransley
Rose, of Wolston Heath
Rush, of Farthinghoe Lodge
Salmon, of Gayton House
Sandford, of Moulton Park
Sartoris, of Rushden Hall
Sawbridge, of East Haddon
Sempill, of Moreton Pinkney Manor
Severne, of Thenford
Shuckburgh, of Great Houghton
Smith, of Oundle
Smyth, of Little Houghton House
Steele, of Guilsborough Park
Stockdale, of Mears Ashby Hall
Stopford, of Drayton House
Stopford, of Falconer's Hill
Strong, of Thorpe Hall
Thornton, of Brockhall
Tibbets, of Barton Seagrave
Tryon, of Bulwick Park
Vane, of Sutton Bassett
Vernon-Wentworth, of Stoke Park
Villiers, of Sulby Hall
Vivian, of Wellingborough
Watkins, of Badby House
Watson, of Rockingham Castle
Watts-Russell, of Biggin House
Watts-Russell, of Biggin Grange
Wetenhall, of Hatton Hall
Whitworth, of Earls Barton Hall
Wilkins, of Ringstead
Willes of Astrop House
Yorke of Thrapston House
Young, of Orlingbury
Young, of Stanwick

NORTHUMBERLAND.

Northumberland, Duke of
Waterford, Marchioness of
Grey, Earl
Tankerville, Earl of
Decies, Lord
Hastings, Lord
Ravensworth, Lord
Redesdale, Lord
Vernon, Lord
Blackett, Sir E., Bart.
Grey, Sir G. Bart.
Haggerston, Sir J. de M. Bart.
Monck, Sir C. M. L. Bart
Riddle, Sir W. B. Bart
Ridley, Sir M. W., Bart.
St. Paul, Sir H. Bart.
Stanley-Errington, Sir R., Bart.
Swinburne, Sir J. Bart.
Allgood, of Nunwich
Ames, of Linden
Anderson, of Little H~ ~
Anstruther, of Larriton House
Armstrong, of Leswick
Askew, of Pallinsburn
Atkinson, of Angerton
Atkinson, of Larbottle
Atkinson, of Newton House
Baker-Cresswell, of Cresswell
Bates, of Milbourne Hall
Beaumont, of Bywell
Bell, of Tynemouth
Bell, of Woolsington
Bewicke, of Close House
Bigge, of Long Horsley
Bigge, of Ovingham House

1079

Blackett, of Newton Hall
Blackett, of Wylam Oakwood
Blackett-Ord, of Whitefield Hall
Blake, of Twizel Castle, and Tilmouth Park
Blanshard, of Jesmond Dene Hall
Blenkinsopp, of Humbleton Hall
Bosanquet, of Rock
Brown, of Unthank Hall
Bullock, of St. Leonard's
Burdon, of Brockalee House
Burdon, of Hartford House
Burrell, of Broomepark
Carr, of Hedgeley
Cay, late of Charlton Hall
Charlton, of Hesleyside
Clark, of Belford Hall
Clavering, of Callaly Castle
Clutterbuck, of Warkworth
Collingwood, of Dissington Hall
Collingwood, of Glanton Pyke
Collingwood, of Lilburn Tower and Chirton House
Cookson, of Benwell Tower and Elington
Cookson, of Meldon Park
Coppin, of North Shields
Coulson, of Blenkinsopp Castle
Craster, of Craster Tower and Bolton House
Crossman, of Cheswick House
Culley, of Coupland Castle
Culley, of Fowberry Tower
Cust, of Stagshaw House
Cuthbert, of Beaufront Castle
Darnell, of Bamburgh Globe
Davison, of Swarland Park
Dent, of Shortflatt Tower
Errington, of High Warden
Fearnley, of Iletton
FitzClarence, of Etal
Forster, late of Adderstone
Gillum, late of Middleton Hall
Gray, of East Bolton
Gregson, of Lowlynn
Grey, of Chipchase Castle
Grey, of Dilston
Grey, of Milfield
Grey, of Styford
Hodgson, of Morris Hall
Hodgson-Cadogan, of Brinkbourne Priory
Hodgson-Hinde of Stelling Hall
Hope - Wallace, of Featherstone Castle
Hughes, of Middleton Hall
Ilderton, of Ilderton
Ilderton, of Tosson
James, of Ottorburn Tower
Lamb, of West Denton
Lawson, of Longhirst
Laycock, of Low Gosforth and Winlaton
Leather, of Middleton Hall
Leyland, of Haggerston Castle
Linskill, of Morwick Hall
Lisle, of Dalton
Mason, of Whitfield
Mitford, of Mitford Castle
Mulcaster, of Benwell Park
Mulcaster, of Buthal
Ogle, of Eglingham Hall
Ogle, of Kirkley Hall
Orde, of Nunnykirk
Orde, of Weetwood and Shoreston
Potts, of Benton Hall
Reed, of Cragg
1080

Reed, of Newbiggin House
Riddell, of Cheseburn Grange
Riddell, of Felton Park and Swinburn
Ridley, of Park End
Ridley, of Walwick Hall
Rippon, of Waterville
Roddam, of Roddam
Sanderson, of West Jesmond
Selby, of Biddleston
Selby, of Paston
Selby, of Shilbottle
Selby, of Yearle
Shafto, of Barington Hall
Shum-Storey, of Arcot Hall
Sidney, of Cowpen House
Silvertop, of Minster Acres
Sitwell, of Barmoor and Yeavering
Smart, of Terwhitt House
Stapleton, of Berwick Hill
Straker, of Tynemouth
Strother, of Eastfield Hall
Surtees, of Pigdon
Taylor, of Chipchase Castle
Tewart, of Glanton and Swinhoe
Trevelyan, of Chirton
Trevelyan, of Netherwitton
Vernon-Harcourt, of Ruthbury
Waddilove, of Woodhorne
Wallis, of Old Ridley
Widdrington, of Newton Hall and Hauxley
Wilson, of Shotley Hall
Young, of Hartford House

NOTTINGHAMSHIRE.

Newcastle, Duke of
Portland, Duke of
Chesterfield, Earl of
Manvers, Earl
Carnarvon, Dowager Countess of
Galway, Viscount
Belper, Lord
Foley, Lord
Middleton, Lord
Bromley, Sir H., Bart.
Clifton, Sir R. J., Bart.
Parkyns, Sir T. G. A., Bart.
Sutton, Sir John, Bart.
White, Sir T. W., Bart.
Adams, of Lenton Firs
Allison, of Billy
Barrow, of Southwell
Beaumont, of East Bridgford
Becher, of Hill House
Beevor, of Blythe
Birkin, of Aspley Hall
Boddam, of Kirklington Hall
Bristowe, of Beesthorpe Hall
Burnaby, of Langford Hall
Burnside, of Gedling Hall
Cane, of Brakenhurst House
Charlton, of Chilwell
Clay, of Burgage Hill
Clifton, of Barton Lodge
Coke, of Trusley and Debdale Hall
Coke, of Kirby
Cook, of Beesthorpe Hall
Cross, of Ruddington Hall
Darwin, of Elston Hall
Davies, late of Chilwell Hall
Davis, of Rocklaverston Hall
Denison, of Ossington Hall
Doidsley, of Skegby Hall
Edge, of Strelley

Eyre, of Rampton
Fillingham, of Syerston
Fitzherbert, of Nettleworth
Foljambe, of Aldwarke
Foljambe, of Osberton
Francklin, of Gonalston
Girardot, of Carcolston
Godfrey, of Balderton
Gregory, of Bramcote
Hacker, of East Bridgford
Hall, of Park Hall
Hall, of Whatton Manor
Handley, of Muskham Grange
Handley, of North Gate
Herringham, of Hawksworth
Hildyard, of Flintham
Hodgkinson, of Winthorpe Hall
Holcombe, of Sherwood Lodge
Holden, of Nuttall Temple
Hole, of Caunton Manor
Hotham, of Scraftworth
Hudson, of Trowell
Huntsman, of West Retford
Ingilby, of Kettlethorpe
Kelham, of Bleasby Hall
Kirke, of Merfield Hall
Low, of Highfield House
Machin, of Gateford Hill
Manners-Sutton, of Kelham Hall
Marsland, of Beckingham
Martin, of Colston Bassett
Martin, of East Bridgford
Mason, of Morton Hall
Mellish, of Hodsock Priory
Milner, of West Retford
Milward, of Thurgarton
Monckton, of Southwell Manor
Musters, of Annesley Park and Colwick Hall
Need, of Blidworth
Need, of Mansfield Woodhouse
Needham, late of Lenton House
Nevile, of Thorney Hall and Wiseton Hall
Nevile, of Stubton
Norton, of Elton Manor
Padley, of Bulwell Hall
Paget, of Ruddington Grange
Parkyns, of Woodborough Hall
Pegge-Barnell, of Winkburn Hall
Pelham-Clinton, of Ramby Hall
Pocklington, of Walesby
Prior, of Lynby
Ramsden, of Carlton Hall
Riddell, of Carlton-on-Trent
Robinson, of Widmerpool Hall
Rolleston, of Burton Joyce
Rolleston, of Watnall Hall
Savile, of Rufford Abbey
Sherbrooke, of Oxton
Shuttleworth, of Hodsock Park
Simpson, of Babworth
Steinth[...] of S[...]
Storer, of Thoresby Hall
Stretton, of Lenton Priory
Sykes, of Mansfield Woodhouse
Taylor, of Radcliffe-on-Trent
Thorold, of William
Vere, of Carlton House
Vernon, of Grove Hall
Walker, of Berry Hill
Walker, of Blythe Hall
Warrand, of Westhorpe
Webb, of Newstead Abbey
Wellfitt, of Langwith Lodge
Wild, of Costock Hall
Wilson, of Sherwood Hall

Wright, of Mapperley Hall
Wright, of Stapleford Park
Wylde, of Southwell

ORKNEY AND SHETLAND.

Baikie, of Tankerness
Balfour, of Balfour and Trenabie
Bell of Lunna
Bruce, of Sumburgh
Burroughs, of Rolfsay
Dundas, of Papdale
Heddle, of Melsetter
Still, of Burgar
Sutherland-Græme, of Græmeshall
Traill, of Holland
Traill, of Tretness and Gramont
Traill, of Westove
Traill, of Woodwick

OXFORDSHIRE.

Marlborough, Duke of
Abingdon, Earl of
Ducie, Earl of
Effingham, Earl of
Jersey, Earl of
Macclesfield, Earl of
Dillon, Viscount
Valentia, Viscount
Oxford, Bishop of
Camoys, Lord
Churchill, Lord
Dynevor, Lord
Leigh, Lord
Saye and Sele, Lord
Brodie, Sir B. C., Bart.
Dashwood, Sir H. W., Bart.
Reade, Sir G., Bart.
Stapleton, Sir F. J., Bart.
Willoughby, Sir J. C., Bart.
Ashurst, of Waterstock
Atkins-Bowyer, of Steeple Aston
Barnett, of Glympton Park
Baskerville, of Crowsley Park
Bazley, of Eynsham Hall
Beresford, of Elsfield
Bertie, of Weston-on-the-Green
Biscoe, of Holton Park
Blackstone, late of Howberry
Blount, of Mapledurham House
Boulton, of Great Tew House
Bowles, of North Aston
Brown, of Kingston Blount
Brown, of Kingston Grove
Carter, of Watlington Park
Clarke, of Chesterton Lodge
Coker, of Bicester House
Corsellis, of Benson
Cottrell-Dormer, of Rousham
Crawley, of Littlemore
Crawshay, of Caversham Park
Cripps, of Partmoor
Croke, of Studley Priory
Davis, of Swerford Park
Dawkins, of Over-Norton
Dewar, of Cotmore House
Dolman, of Souldern House
Duff, of Woodcote
Evans, of Dean
Fane, of Wormsley
Forbes, of Whitchurch
Fowler, of Walliscote House
Franks, of Ibstone House

Gammié-Maitland, of Shottover House
Gardiner, of Coombe Lodge
Gaskell, of Kiddington Hall
Glen, of Stratton Audley
Goddard, of Adderbury House
Greenaway, of Barrington Grove
Guest, of Sandford Park
Hall, of Barton Abbey and Dunstew
Hamersley, of Pyrton Manor
Harcourt, of Nuneham
Harrison, of Shelswell Park
Henley, of Waterperry
Hibbert, of Bucknell
Hippisley, of Cote House
Hodges, of Bolney Court
Knollys, of Blount's Court
Lane, of Badgemore
Lowndes-Norton, of Brightwell Park
Marsham, of Caversfield
Montague, of Caversham Hill
Morrell, of Headington House
Muirhead, of Haseley Court
Neate, of Alvescote
Newell-Birch, of Henley Park
Norris, of Swalcliffe Park
North, of Wroxton Abbey
Phillimore, of The Coppice
Phillips, of Culham House
Pickering, of Wilcote Grange
Powys-Lyble, of Hardwicke
Price, of Mongewell House
Reade, of Dogmore End
Reynardson, of Ardwell Hull
Rhodes, of Hennerton
Risley, of Deddington
Ruck-Keene, of Swyncombe House
Samuelson, of Bodicote Grange
Spencer, of Coombe
Spencer, of Wheatfield
Staples-Browne, of Launton
Stephens, of Caversham Rise
Strickland, of Cokethorpe Park
Style, of Bicester House
Taunton, of Freeland Lodge
Tawney, of Wroxton
Taylor, of Aston House
Thornhill, of Woodleys
Vanderstegen, of Cane End House
Watson-Taylor, of Headington
Weyland, of Woodeaton
Whippy, of Leo Place
Whitmore-Jones, of Chastleton
Wyatt, of Broughton
Wykeham, of Tythrop House
Wynn, of Howbery Park
Young, of Mallard's Court

PEEBLESSHIRE.

Wemyss, Earl of
Elibank, Lord
Carmichael, the Rev. Sir W. H. G., Bart.
Fergusson, Sir W., Bart.
Hay, Sir R., Bart.
Montgomery, Sir G. G., Bart.
Nasmyth, Sir J. M., Bart.
Beresford, of Machichill
Brown, of Carlops
Chambers, of Glenmoriston
Erskine, of Venlaw
Forbes, of Medwyn
Forrester, of Barns
Giles, of Kailzie
Horsburgh, of Horsburgh

Kennedy, of Romanno
Ker-Williamson, of Cardrona
Mackenzie, of Portmore
Mackintosh, of Lamancha
Macneill, of Borthlands
Murray, of Callands
Murray, of Cringletie
Stuart, of Traquair Castle
Swinton, of Swinton
Tennant, of The Glen
Tweedie, of Quarter and Rachan
Tweedie-Stodart, of Oliver
Welsh, of Mossfennan
White, of Drummelzier
Willes, of Kingsutton
Woddrop, of Garvald

PEMBROKESHIRE.

Cawdor, Earl of
Lloyd, Sir T. D., Bart.
Owen, Sir H. O., Bart.
Ackland, of Boulston House
Adams, of Hollyland
Allen, of Bicton
Allen, of Cresselly
Allen, of Dunston Grove
Allen, of Kilrhue
Arden, of Portrane
Barham, of Trecwn
Beynon, of Trewern
Biddulph, of Amroth Castle
Bowen, of Llwyngwair
Buckby, of Begelly
Callen, of The Grove
Carew, of Carew Castle
Charlton-Meyrick, of Bush
Child, of Begelly House
Colby, of Fynone
Crompton, of Llanstinan House
Davies, of Clareston
Davies, of Trewarren
De Rutzen, of Slebech Hall
Dunn, of Elm Grove
Dunn, of Welston
Foley, of Ridgeway
Fortune, of Leweston
Gower, of Glandovan and Clynderwen
Greville, of Castle Hall
Harford, of Charleston Grange
Harries, of Cwmdig
Harries, of Hilton
Harries, of Llanunwas
Harries, of Priskilly
Harries, of Travaccoon
James, of Pantsaison
Jones, of Bolton Hill
Jones, of Laneych
Jordan, of Ashdale
Leach, of Corston
Leach, of Ivy Tower
Lewis, of Cygnas
Lewis, of Henllan
Llewellin, of Tregwynt
Lloyd-Philipps, of Dale Castle
Massy, of Cottesmore
Mathias, of Lamphey
Owen, of Hermon's Hill
Peel, of Stone Hall
Peel, of Demant
Philipps, of Penty Park
Philipps, of St. Bride's Hill
Philipps, of Picton Castle
Philipps, of Lawrenny
Powell, of Hook

1081

Reed, of Penllwyn
Rees, of Scoveston
Roberts, of Hamilton House
Robertson. of Hazel Hill
Roch, of Butter Hill
Roch, of Paskeston
Rous, of Fern Hill
Saurin, of Orielton and Kilwendeg
Scourfield, of Williamston
Sutton, of Landshipping
Swann, of Merrixton House
Tucker-Edwardes, of Sealyham
Walters, of Haverfordwest
Webb-Bowen, of Camrose
Wells, of Tenby

PERTHSHIRE.

Athole, Duke of
Breadalbane, Earl of
Camperdown, Earl of
Dundonald, Earl of
Kinnoull, Earl of
Mansfield, Earl of
Moray, Earl of
Wemyss and March, Earl of
Strathallan, Viscount
Abercromby, Lord
Elibank, Lord
Gray, Baroness
Kinnaird, Lord
Rollo, Lord
Ruthven, Lord
Willoughby d'Eresby, Lord
Nairne, Baroness
Campbell, Sir James, Bart.
Cunynghame, Sir D. T., Bart.
Dundas, Sir D., Bart.
Forbes, Sir W. S., Bart.
Macgregor, Sir M., Bart.
Mackenzie, Sir A. M., Bart.
Menzies, Sir R., Bart.
Moncreiffe, Sir T., Bart.
Murray, Sir P. K., Bart.
Pringle, Sir J., Bart.
Ramsay, Sir George, Bart.
Richardson, Sir J. S., Bart.
Steuart, Sir W. D., Bart.
Stirling-Maxwell, Sir W., Bart.
Threipland, Sir P. M., Bart.
Allen, late of Errol Park
Allen, of Inchmartine
Anderson, of Bleaton
Ayton, of Ashintully
Ballingall, of Altamont
Beatson-Bell, of Glenfarg
Beveridge-Duncan, of Damside
Binning-Home, of Argaty
Bontine, of Gartmore
Brown, of Lochton
Brown-Morison. of West Errol and
    Coupar Grange
Butter, of Faskally
Campbell, of Inverarloch
Campbell, of Monzie Castle
Carnegie, of Stronvar
Chalmers, of Glenricht
Clayhills-Henderson, of Hallyards
Clerk-Rattray, of Craighall
Colquhoun, of Clathick
Constable, of Balmyle
Constable. of Cully
Craigie, of Glendoick
Cuninghame, of Balgownie
Dalgleish, of Westgrange
1082

Dick, of Tullymet
Douglas, of Killiechassie
Drummond, of Blair Drummond
Drummond, of Balquhandie
Drummond, of Megginch Castle
Drummond-Moray, of Abercairny
Erskine, of Cardross
Finlay, of Deanston House
Gallwey, of Blair Castle
Garden-Campbell, of Glenlyon
Græme, of Garvock and Kippen
Græme, of Inchbrakie and Aberuth-
    ven
Græme-Oliphant, of Gask
Graham, of Leitchtown
Graham-Stirling, of Strowan
Grant, of Kilgraston
Greig, of Glencarse
Grove, of Kincardine Castle
Haig, of Blairhill
Hamilton, of Leny
Hay, of Leys
Hay, of Seggieden
Hay-Drummond, of Cromlix and In-
    nerpeffray
Hepburn, of Colquhalzie
Hore-Ruthven, of Freeland House
Hunter, of Seaside
Jelf-Sharp, of Kincarrathie
Johnston, of Sands
Johnston, of Kincardine Castle
Keir, of Kinmonth and Kindrogan
Kinloch, of Kinloch
Lawson, of Ballo
Lindsay, of Early Bank
Lowson, of Balthayock
Maccallum, of Braco
McDonald, of Dun Alastair
Macdonald, of St. Martin's and Glen-
    shee Lodge
Macnaghten, of Invertrosachs
Macpherson, of Blairgowrie House
Maxtone-Graham, of Cultoquhey
Menzies, of Rannoch Lodge
Menzies, of Meggernie Castle
Milu, of Murie
Monteath, of Broich
Murdoch, of Gartincaber
Murray, of Croftinloan
Murray, of Lintrose
Murray Graham, of Murrayshall and
    Bertha Park
Nairne, of Dunsinnane
Ogilvy, of Loyal
Oliphant, of Condie and Newtown
Paterson, of Carpow
Paterson, of Castle Huntly
Patton, of The Cairnies
Robertson, of Auchleeks
Robertson, of Gray House
Robertson, of Tullichetton
Rudd, of Kilbryde
Scott-Moncrieff, of Fossoway
Small, of Dinanoun
Smythe, of Methven Castle
Speir, of Culdees Castle
Steuart, of Ballechin
Steuart, of Dalguise
Stewart, of Ardvorlich
Stewart, of Urrard
Stewart-Menzies, of Chesthill
Stirling, of Holme Hill
Stirling, of Kippendavie
Tennent, of Errol
Thomson, of Balgowan
Trotter, of Ballindeen House
Turner, of Glentyre

Vernon-Wentworth, of Dall-Tirloch-
    rie
Watson, of The Den
Williamson. of Lawers
Wood, of Keithick

QUEEN'S CO.

Portarlington, Earl of
Ashbrook, Viscount
De Vesci, Viscount
Congleto, Lord
Coote, Sir C. H., Bart.
Crosbie, S. W. R., Bart.
O'Brien, Sir P., Bart.
Walsh, Sir J. A. Johnson-, Bart.
Weldon, Sir A. C., Bart.
Adair, of Bellegrove
Alloway, of The Derries
Betty, of Knightstown
Bland, of Blandsfort
Bowen, of Courtwood
Brownlow, of Knapton House
Butler, of Lamberton Park
Carden, of Knightstown
Cassan, of Sheffield House
Caulfield, of Raheenduff
Chetwode, of Woodbrook
Cooper, of Cooper Hill
Coote, of Huntington
Crosby, of Stradbally Hall
Dease, of Rath House
Delaney, of Castlewood
Despard, of Donore
Donville, of Heywood House
Dunne, of Ballymanus and Corbally
Dunne, of Brittas
FitzPatrick, of Lisduff and Granston
Hamilton, of Roundwood
Hawkesworth, of Forest
Howard-Brooke, of Roskelton
Kemmis, of Sheen
Lalor, of Tenakill
Lyons, of Mywanna
Maillard, of Huntington
Marsh, of Springmount
Marum, of Abarney
Smyth, of Mount Henry
Stannus, of Portarlington
Stubber, of Moyne
Sweetman, of Lamberton Park
Tracy, of Temikilly
Trench, of Cangorm
Trench, of Glenmalyre
Trench, of Heywood
Vesey, of Knapton
Webber, of Kellyville
Whitty, of Providence Court

RADNORSHIRE.

Romilly, Lord
Brydges, Sir H. J. J., Bart.
Lewis, Sir G. F., Bart.
Allen, of Oakfield
Baskerville, of Clyro
Brydges, of Boultibrooke
Busk, of Glenalder
Cheesement-Severn, of Penybont Hall
    and Devanner Park
Coates, of Whitton
De Winton, of Maeshwch Castle
Evans, of Llwynbarried House
Green-Price, of North Manor
Greenwood, of Aberuant

Haig, of Pen Ithon
Higgins, of Cwm Llanyre
James, of Womaston
Lewis-Lloyd, of Nantgwilt
Lingen, of Penlanolen
Miles, of Downfield House
Mynors, of Barland
Mynors, of Evancoyd
Otway, of Cwm Elan
Philips, of Abbey Cwm Hir
Prickard, of Dderw
Rogers, of Kinnerton Court
Rogers, of Stanage Park
Stephens, of Llananno
Thomas, of Pencerrig
Vaughan, of Llansaintfraid
Venables, of Clyro
Watt, of Doldowlod
Whittaker, of Newcastle Court

RENFREWSHIRE.

Abercorn, Marquis of
Eglinton, Earl of
Glasgow, Earl of
Blantyre, Lord
Crawfurd-Pollok, Sir H., Bart.
Napier, Sir R. J. M., Bart.
Stewart, Sir M. R. Shaw-, Bart.
Stirling-Maxwell, Sir W., Bart.
Alexander, of South Barr
Baine, of Greenock
Brown, of Underwook Park
Campbell, of Blytheswood
Coats, of Ferguslie of Maxwellton
Crum, of Thornliebank
Cuninghame, of Craigends and Walk-
ingshaw
Darroch, of Gourock
Dennistoun, of Dennistoun
Gilmour, of Eaglesham
Graham-Maxwell, of Williamswood
Greig, of Muirshiel
Harvey, of Castle Semple
Houstoun, of Johnstone Castle
Lowndes, of Arthurlie
Macdowall, of Garthland
Macfie, of Langhouse
Maxwell, of Dargavel
Napier, of Merchiston House
Pollok, of Faside
Robertson, of Woodend
Smith, of Jordan Hill
Speir, of Blackstoun
Speir, of Burnbrae
Speirs, of Elderslie House
Stirling, of Glentyan

ROSCOMMON CO.

Dillon, Viscount
Lorton, Viscount
Castlemaine, Lord
Crofton, Lord
De Freyne, Lord
Burke, Sir J. L., Bart.
Conroy, Sir E., Bart.
King, Sir G., Bart.
Bagot, of Carranure House
Bailey, of Rookwood
Balfe, of South Park
Browne, of Newton
Caulfeild, of Donamon
Devenish, of Mount Pleasant

Devenish, of Rush Hill
Dillon, of Johnstown House
Dillon, of Mount Dillon
Drought, of Cargins
Duckworth, of Mount Erris
Fallon, of Ballina House
Flanagan, of Drumdoe
French, of Cloonyquin
French, of Lough Erritt
Goff, of Oakport
Grace, of Mantua House
Grehan, of Mount Plunkett
Irwin, of Rathmile
Kelly, of Castle Park
Kirkwood, of Cloongoonagh
Kirkwood, of Woodbrooke
Lawder, of Aughamore
Lloyd, of Croghan
Lyster, of Lysterfield
Mahon, of Strokestown
Mitchell, of Castlestrange
Mulloy, of Hughestown
O'Conor, of Dundermot
O'Conor, of Elphin House
O'Conor, of Milton
O'Conor, of Mount Druid
O'Conor, Don, The, of Belanagre and
Clonalis
Pakenham-Mahon, of Strokestown
Roper, of Knocknaine
St. George, of Camma
Sandford, of Castlerea House and
Wills Grove
Smythe, of New Park
Strickland, of Loughglyn House
Talbot, of Mount Talbot
Tenison, of Kilronan Castle
Young, of Harristown

ROSS-SHIRE.

Sutherland, Duke of
Ashburton, Lord
Middleton, Lord
Mackenzie, Sir K. S., Bart.
Mackenzie, Sir W., Bart.
Mackenzie, Sir J. J. R., Bart.
Mackenzie, Sir E., Bart.
Matheson, Sir J., Bart.
Munro, Sir Chas., Bart.
Ross, Sir C. W. F. A., Bart.
Baillie, of Redcastle
Cameron, of Dingwall
Davidson, of Tulloch
Fletcher, of Rosehaugh
Forbes, of Ferrintosh
Fowler, of Reddery
Gillanders, of Highfield
Gillanders, of Newmore
Holmes, of Menar
Mackenzie, of Allangrange
Mackenzie, of Corryvoulzie and Ord
Mackenzie, of Findon
Mackenzie, of Flowerburn
Macleod, of Iyergordon
Mackenzie, of Kilcoy
Matheson, of Ardross
Moiro, of Allan
Munro, of Teaninich
Murray, of Geanies
Robertson, of Kindeace
Stewart-Mackenzie, of Seaforth
Stuart, of Loch Carrow
Wardlaw, of Belmaduthy
White, of Monar and Lemran

ROXBURGHSHIRE.

Roxburghe, Duke of
Lothian, Marquis of
Haddington, Earl of
Minto, Earl of
Campbell, Lord
Dickson, Sir A. C. T., Bart.
Douglas, Sir G. H. S., Bart.
Eliott, Sir W. F. A., Bart.
Fairfax, Sir W. G. H., Bart.
Scott, Sir Wm., Bart.
Leith, Sir G. H., Bart.
Ainslie, of Woll
Baker, of Langlee House
Binning-Home, of Softlaw
Black, of Priory Bank
Blair-Maconochie, of Gattonside
Brewster, of Allerly
Carre, of Cavers Carre
Chisholme, of Stirches
Clark, of Langhaugh
Cleghorn, of Weens
Douglas, of Cavers
Elliot, of Harwood and Clinton
Elliot, of Wolfelee
Erskine, of Drylurgh Abbey
Hope-Scott, of Abbotsford
Lockhart, of Bothwickbrae
Maxwell, of Teviotbank
Murray, of Wooplaw
Ogilvie, of Chesters
Paton, of Crailing
Pott, of Todrig
Pringle, of Wilton Lodge
Richardson, of Kirklands
Riddell, of Camieston
Rutherfurd, of Edgerston
Rutherford, of Fairnington
Scott, of Raeburn and Lessudden
Scott-Kerr, of Sunlaws and Chatto
Scott-Makdougall of Makerstown
Seton-Karr, of Kippilaw
Sprot, of Riddell
Waldie, of Hendersyde House
White, of The Brae

RUTLANDSHIRE.

Rutland, Duke of
Exeter, Marquis of
Gainsborough, Earl of
Aveland, Lord
Baker, of Cottesmore
Belgrave, of Preston Hall
Conant, of London
Cooper, of Empingham
Eaton, of Tolethorpe Hall
Evans-Freke, of Bisbrooke
Fazakerley, of Ketton
Finch, of Pucks Hd
Fludyer, of Ayston House
Gilford, of North Luffenham
Grantham, of Ketton Grange
Handley, of Clipsham Hall
Heathcote, of North Luffenham
Heycock, of Braunston Manor
Hotchkin, of Luffenham
Hunt, of Ketton House
Lowther, of Barley Thorpe Hall
Lucas, of Edithweston Hall
Noel, of Exton Park
O'Brien, of Tixover
Pierrepont, of Ryhall
Rowley, of Moycott Hall

Wing, of Market Overton
Wingfield, of Tickencote Hall

SELKIRKSHIRE.

Buccleugh and Queensberry, Duke of
Selkirk, Earl of
Elibank, Lord
Napier, Lord
Polwarth, Lord
Murray, Sir J., Bart.
Pringle, Sir John, Bart.
Ballantyne, of Holylee
Currie, of Linthill
Johnstone, of The Hangingshaw
Napier, of Broadmeadows
Plummer, of Middlestead and of Sunderland Hall
Pringle, of The Haining
Pringle, of Torwoodlee
Pringle, of Whytbunk
Russell, of Ashiesteel
Scott, of Gala

SHETLAND.
(See *Orkney and Shetland*.)

SHROPSHIRE.

Sutherland, Duke of
Bradford, Earl of
Kilmorey, Earl of
Powis, Earl of
Boyne, Viscount
Hill, Viscount
Berwick, Lord
Forester, Lord
Kenyon, Lord
Wenlock, Lord
Windsor, Baroness
Acton, Sir J. E. E. D., Bart.
Boughton, Sir C. H. Rouse-, Bart.
Corbet, Sir V. R., Bart.
Curtis, Sir Wm.. Bart.
Edwardes, Sir H. H., Bart.
Harnage, Sir H. G., Bart.
Leighton, Sir B., Bart.
Milman, Sir W., Bart.
Smythe, Sir C. F., Bart.
Tyrwhitt, Sir H. T.. Bart.
Wakeman, Sir O., Bart.
Acton, of Gatacre Park
Acton [Stackhouse-], of Acton Scott
Adams, of Chadwell Court
Atcherley, of Marton
Awdrey, of Worthen
Bather, of The Day House
Baxter, of Sibdon Castle
Beale, of Heath House
Benson, of Lutwyche Hall
Beringion, of Mote Hall
Betton, of Overton House
Borough, of Chetwynd Park and Edgmund House
Boultbee, of Great Chatwell
Bowen, of Coton Hall
Bridgeman, of Knockin
Bright, of Totterton Hall
Brooke, of Haughton Hall
Broughton, of Tunstall Hall
Broughton, of Holbeach Lodge
Browne, of The Woodlands
Buchanan, of Hale's Hall
1084

Bulkeley-Owen, of Tedsmore Hall
Burton, of Atcham
Burton, of Ford House
Burton, of Longner Hall
Carew, of Pentrepant
Cavendish, of Chyknell
Charlton, of Apley-Castle
Cheney, of Badger Hall
Child, of Kinlet
Childe-Pemberton, of Millichope
Cholmondeley, of Condover Park
Clement, of Shrewsbury
Clive, of Styche
Cludde, of Orleton
Coghlan, of Marrington Hall
Corbet, of Adderley Hall
Corbet of College Hill
Corbett, late of Longnor Hall
Cornewall, of Delbury Hall
Cotes, of Woodcote and Pychford
Creswell, of Sidbury
Cureton, of Brook House
Cust, of Ellesmere House
Davenport, of Davenport
Davies, of Marrington Hall
Dickin, of Loppington House
Drury, of Pontesbury.
Edwards, of Ness Strange
Ethelston, of Hinton Hall
Eyton, of Eyton and Walford Manor
Fereday, of Tuck Hill
Freme, of Wrentnall House
Galton, of Warley Tor
Gardner, of Leighton Hall
Garnett-Botfield, of Decker Hill
Gaskell, of Wenlock Abbey
Gatacre, of Gatacre Hall
Gore, of Porkington
Griffin, of Brand Hall
Harries, of Cruckton Hall
Haywood, of Kemsey Manor
Herbert, of Orleton
Heywood, of Cloverley
Hill, of Court of Hill
Hill, of Prees Hall
Hill, of Peplow Hall
Hinchcliffe, of Mucklestone
Holyoak, of Neachley Hall
Hope-Edwards, of Netley Hall
Hornby, of Lythwood Hall
Horsfall, of Kilhendre
Howard, of Longdon and Hinstock
Hudson, of Cheswardine
Hulton-Harrop, of Gatten
H mt. of Boreatton
Jebb, of The Lyth
Jeffreys, of Wem
Jenkins, of Charlton Hill
Jenkins, of Bicton Hall
Johnson, of Belmont House
Jones, of Ruckley Grange and Shackerley Hall
Justice, of Hinstock Hall
Kenrick, of Woore
Kent, of Dinham Hall
Kenyon, of Pradoe
Kenyon-Slaney, of Hatton Grange
Kinchant, of Llanvairwaterdine and Bettws
Kinchant, of Park Hall
Knight, of Henley Hall
Lechmere, of Ludford
Leeke, of Longford Hall
Legge, of Caynton
Lloyd, of Aston Hall
Lloyd, of Leaton Knolls
Lloyd, of Monkmoor

Lloyd, of Shawbury
Longueville, of Petylan
Lovett, of Belmont and Etnal
Lovett, of Fern Hill Hall
Lowe, of Court of Hill
Lyster, of Rowton Castle
Mainwaring, of Oteley Park
More, of Linley Hall
Morrall, of Plâs Yolyn and Plâs Warren
Morris, of Oxon
Morris, of The Hurst
Moseley, of Buildwas
Mytton, of Cleobury North
Mytton, of Shipton Hall
Oakeley, of Oakeley
Oakeley, of Roveries Hall
Owen, of Woodhouse
Pardoe, of Nash-Court
Pardoe, of Stanton Lacy
Payne-Townsend, of Edstaston House
Percy, of Hodnet Hall
Phillips, of Winsley Hall and Cause Castle
Pigott-Corbett, of Elgmund and Sundorne
Plowden, of Plowden .
Poole, of Terrick Hall
Powell, of Sutton
Powys, of Berwick House
Pritchard, of Broseley
Purton, of Faintree Hall
Rocke, of Clungunford House
Rogers, of The Home
Russell, of Ashford Hall
Salwey, of Moor Park
Sandford, of The Isle
Sandford, of Sandford Hall
Scott, of Betton-le-Strange
Sitwell, of Ferney Hall
Smith, of Halesowen Grange
Smith-De Heriz- of Aston Botterell
Smythe, of Hilton
Sparkes, of Bridgenorth
Sparling, of Petton Park
Sparrow, of Habberley
Stubbs, of Beckbury Hall
Swainson, of Winstanstow
Tayleur, of Buntings hale
Tayleur, of Market Drayton
Thorneycroft, of Hadly Park
Thursby-Pelham, of Cound Hall
Topp, of Whitton Hall
Vaughan, of Burlton Hall
Venables, of Oakhurst
Venables, of Woodhill
Walcot, of Bitterley Court
Walford, of Roden House
Warter, of Cruckmeole
Whitaker, of Hampton Hall
Whitmore, of Apley Park
Whitmore, of Cold nick Dale
Whitmore, of Ludford
Whitmore, of Stockton
Williams, of Stoke House
Wingfield, of Onslow Hall
Wolterston- of Statfold Hall
Wright, of Halston Hall
Wynn, of Llanvorda Hall

SLIGO CO.

Sligo, Marquis of
Mountmorres, Viscount
Booth, Sir R. Gore-, Bart.
Crofton, Sir Malby, Bart.

Armstrong, of Chaffpoole
Brinkley, of Fortland
Cogan, of Lisconny House
Cooper, of Markree Castle
Dodwell, of Glenmore
Duke, of Kincraevin
Duke, of New Park
ffolliott, of Hollybrook
Gethin, of Ballindoon
Griffith, of Port Royal and Castle Neyno
Houstoun, of Dhulough
Irwin, of Tanragee
Keogh, of Anghry
King, of Ballygrehane
Leyborne-Popham, of Kevinsfort
Lynch, of Rathtarmon
MacDermot, of Coolavin
Martin, of Bloomfield
Meredith, of Cloonmahon
O'Connor, of Cairnsfoot
O'Hara, of Annaghmore and Cooper's Hill
Olpherts, of Carrowmore
Olpherts, of Mountshannon
Orme, of Enniscrone
Parke, of Dunally
Perceval, of Temple House
Phibbs, of Spotfield
Webber, of Carrowcullen
Webber, of Lockfield
Wood, of Woodville
Wynne, of Ardaghowen
Wynne, of Haslewood

SOMERSETSHIRE.

Carnarvon, Earl of
Cavan, Earl of
Cork, Earl of
Egremont, Countess of
Lovelace, Earl of
Poulett, Earl
Auckland, Lord
Bridport, Lord
Clifford of Chudleigh, Lord
Poltimore, Lord
Portman, Lord
Talbot de Malahide, Lord
Taunton, Lord
Acland, Sir T. D., Bart.
Acland, Sir P. P. Fuller-Palmer-, Bart.
Davis, Sir J. F., Bart.
Elton, Sir A. H., Bart.
Hood, Sir A. B. P., Bart.
Lethbridge, Sir J. H., Bart.
Medlycott, Sir W. C., Bart.
Miles, Sir W., Bart.
Slade, Sir A. F. A., Bart.
Smyth, Sir J. H. G., Bart.
Strachey, Sir Edward, Bart.
Trevelyan, Sir W. C., Bart.
Adair, of Heatherton Park
Addington, of Langford Court
Adlam, of Chew Magna
Allen, of Bathampton
Allen, of Lyngford
Anderdon, of West Pennard
Anderdon, of Henlade House
Bagehot, of Herds Hill
Bailward, of Horsington
Baker, of West Hay
Band, of Wookey House
Barton, of Holbrook House
Batten, of Hollands

Batten, of Thorn Faulcon
Beckett, of Ringwell House
Bennett, of Cadbury House
Bennett, of Sparkford Hall
Bethell, of Springfield House
Blagrave, of Barrow Court
Blandford, of Weston Bampfylde
Blommart, of Willett House
Bouverie, of Brymore
Brigstocke, of Birdcombe Court
Broadmead, of Olands
Broderip, of Cossington Manor
Brooke, of Hinton Abbey
Ballock, of North Coker
Burrowes, of Bourton Court
Bythesea, of The Hill, Freshford
Capel, of Bulland
Carew, of Crowcombe
Castle, of Cleeve Court
Chetham-Strode, of Southill House
Clarke, of Avishays
Clarke, of Tremlet Hall
Clerk, of Burford
Clerk, of Westholme
Coles, of Glencot
Combe, of Earnshill
Conolly, of Midford Castle
Daubeny, of Norton House
Daubeny, of Clere House
Dawe, of Ditcheat House
De Havilland, of Langford-Budville
Dickinson, of Berkeley House
Dickinson, of Kingweston
Dodington, of Horsington House
Doveton, of Burnett
Drummond, of St. Catherine's Court
Duckworth, of Murtrey
Duckworth, of Orchard Leigh
Edgell, of East Hill
Edgell, of Standerwick Court
Edwards, of Wrington
Eastment, of Drayton
Egremont, of Orchard Wyndham
Elton, of Whitestaunton
Emery, of Banwell Grange
Ernst, of Westcombe House
Esdaile, of Cothelstone and Terhill House
Evered, of Hill House and Stone House
Falconer, of Bath
Fane, of Brympton
Fenwick-Bisset, of Bagborough
Finzel, of Frankfürt Hall
Fisher, of Freshford
FitzGerald, of Maperton
Foster-Melliar, of Milton Lodge
Freeman, of Somerleaze
Fryer, of Burnham
Fussell, of The Chantry
Galton, of Loxton Manor
Gibbs, of Tyntesfield
Giles, of Woolley
Glossop, of Inwood
Goodford, of Chilton Cantelo
Gore, of Barrow Court
Gore-Langton, of Newton Park and Hatch Beauchamp
Graham, of Cossington
Grant-Dalton, of Shanks House
Greenhill, of Knowle Hall
Halliday, of Chapel Cleeve
Hamilton, of Fyne Court
Harbin, of Newton
Harford, of Barley Wood
Hedley, of Silbrook
Helyar, of Croke Court

Helyar, of Poundsford Lodge
Henley, of Leigh House
Herbert, of Tetton House
Hippisley, of Ston-Easton
Hobhouse, of Hadspen House
Hood, of Wootton
Horner, of Mells Park
Hoskins, of Hinton St. George
Hoskins, of Haselbury Plucknett
Hoskins, of North Perrott
Ireland, of Brislington Hall
Jarrett, of Camerton Court
Jenkins, of Coombe Grove
Joliffe, of Ammerdown Park
Jones, of Hinton Charterhouse
Jones, of Kelston Park
Kinglake, of Wilton House
Kinglake, of Monkton
Kinglake, of Weston-super-Mare
Kington, of Charlton House
Knatchbull, of Babington House
Knyfton, of Uphill
Lambert, of Misterton
Law, of Banwell
Lawson, of Pitminster
Lean, of Ridge
Lee, of Dillington House
Leir, of Ditcheat
Lethbridge, of Easthrooke House
Llewellin, of Oakfield
Locke, of Northmoor
Lopes, of East Hill
Lord, of Farmborough
Luttrell, of Badgworth Court
Luttrell, of Dunster Castle
Luttrell, of East Quantoxhead
Luttrell, of Kilve Court
Luttrell, of Woodlands
Manley, of Buckland
Marsh, of Nethersole
Mattock, of Angersleigh
Meade-King, of Walford House
Messeter, of Barwick House
Metford, of Flook House
Mildmay, of Hazlegrove
Miles, of Ham Green
Mirehouse, of St. George's Hill
Mogg, of Farrington Manor
Montagu, of Bath
Moody, of Kingsdon
Mordaunt, of Flax Bourton
Moysey, of Bathealton Court
Munbee, of Weston-super-Mare
March, of Cranwells
Murchison, of Bathford
Mynors, of Keynsham
Naish, of Ston-Easton and Hardington Park
Napier, of Pennard Cottage
Napier, of Pennard House
Napier, of Woodlands
Neville-Grenville, of Butleigh Court
Newton, of Barr... George
Norman, of Claverham
Northcote, of Somerset Court
Notley, of Combe Sydenham
Page, late of Holebrook
Paget, of Cranmore and Newberry Court
Patton, of Bishop's Hall and Stoke Court
Perfect, of Woolstone House
Perkins, of Kingston Grange
Phelips, of Rayland lodge
Phelips, of Montacute House
Phipps, of Charlton
Pickwick, of Bathford Manor
Pinney, of Somerton

Pinney, of Somerton Erleigh
Porch, of Edgarley
Prior, of Halse House
Pyne, of East Charlton
Quantock, of Norton House
Raban, of Hatch Beauchamp
Rawlins, of Brean House
Reynolds, of Canonsgrove
Richards, of Langford House
Richards, of Stapleton House
Rogers, of Yarlington
St. Aubyn, late of Alfoxton
Samborne, of Timsbury
Sanford, of Nynehead Court
Scobell, of Kingwell
Sealy, of Bridgewater
Sealy, of Nether Stowey
Shearley, of Mellefont Abbey
Sheppard, of Fromefield House
Sheppard, of Keyford House
Sherston, late of Stoberry
Skrine, of Warleigh Manor
Smith, of Lydeard House
Smyth-Pigott, of Brockley Court
Somerville, of Dinder House
Speke, of Jordans
Spurway, of Heathfield
Spurway, of Spring Grove Park
Stanley, late of Lattiford House
Strachey, of Ashwick Grove
Strangways, of Shapwick
Stuckey, of Hill House
Surtees, of Tainfield House
Sweet, of Broadleigh
Synge, of Weston Lodge
Thompson, of Prior Park
Thring, of Alford House
Tomlin, of Rumwell Hall
Tucker, of Angersleigh
Tudway, of The Cedars and Stoberry Park
Tynte, of Halsewell House
Uttermare, of Langport
Vane, of Burrington
Vivian, of Claverton
Wait, of Woodborough
Walcot, of Woodland Villa
Warre, of Bindon
Warre, of West Buckland
Warre, of Hestercombe
Warre, of Cheddon
Warry, of Shapwick House
Way, of Ashton Lodge
Welman, of Norton Manor
Wickham, of Frome
Wickham, of Horsington
Wollen, of Wedmore
Wood, of Martock
Wood, of Charlton Musgrove
Woodforde, of Ansforde House
Worsley, of Brislington
Worth, of Wytchanger
Wright, of Hinton Blewett
Wyndham, of Rownhill Grange
Wyndham, of Sock Denis
Yea, of Pyland Hall

SOUTHAMPTON, CO. OF.
(See *Hants*.)

STAFFORDSHIRE.

Sutherland, Duke of
Anglesey, Marquis of
Townshend, Marquis

Dartmouth, Earl of
Dudley, Earl of
Ferrers, Earl
Granville, Earl
Harrowby, Earl of
Lichfield, Earl of
Shrewsbury, Earl of
Stamford and Warrington, Earl of
St. Vincent, Viscount
Lichfield, Bishop of
Bagot, Lord
Hatherton, Lord
Stafford, Lord
Wenlock, Lord
Wrottesley, Lord
Alleyne, Sir R. A., Bart.
Boughey, Sir T. F. Fenton-, Bart.
Broughton, Sir H. D., Bart.
Buller, Sir E. Manningham-, Bart.
Chetwode, Sir J. N. L., Bart.
Crewe, Sir J. H., Bart.
Mosley, Sir Oswald, Bart.
Parker, Sir W. B., Bart.
Peel, Sir Robert, Bart.
Pilkington, Sir L. M. S., Bart.
Scott, Sir E. W. D., Bart.
Wolseley, Sir C. M., Bart.
A'Court-Repington, of Amington Hall
Adderley, of Barlaston and Coton Halls
Allen, of Longcroft
Allen, of Woodhead Hall
Annesley, of Arley Castle
Amphlett, of Clent
Arden, of Longcrofts
Aston-Pudsey, of Seisdon Hall
Bagnall, of Charlemont Hall
Bagot, of Elford House
Barker, of Albrighton Hall
Barker, of The Birches
Bass, of Rangemoor
Bateman, of Biddulph Grange and Knypersley
Beech, of The Shawe
Belcombe, of The Brooms
Bennitt, of Priory House
Bennitt, of Ashwood House
Beresford-Hope, of Beresford Hall
Best, of Bilston
Birch, of Armitage Lodge
Bishop, of Shelton Hall
Bishop, of The Mount
Boothby, of The New Lodge
Bostock, of Cliff Park
Bott, of Coton Hall
Bourne, of Hilderstone Hall
Boycott, of Rudge Hall
Briscoe, of Elmhurst Hall
Brocklehurst, of Swithamley Park
Bromley-Davenport, of Wootton Hall
Brownfield, of Chatterley House
Buckworth, of Norbury
Burne, of Loynton Hall
Butler, of Pendeford Hall and Barton Hall
Campbell, of Woodseat
Cartwright, of The Leasowes
Chadwick, of Maresyn Ridware
Chance, of Brown's Green
Chawner, of The Abnalls
Chetwynd, of Brocton Hall
Chetwynd, of Longdon Hall
Child, of Stallington Hall
Clarke, of Brown's Green
Clay, of Stapenhill House
Cochrane, of Heath House
Congreve, of Congreve
Copeland, of Cliffe Bank Lodge

Coyney, of Weston Coyney
Curzon, of Hagley Hall
Davenport, of Newport House and Maer
Davenport, of Westwood Hall
Dawson, of Barrow Hill
Duncombe, of Calwich
Dyott, of Freeford Hall
Dyott, of Knowle Lodge
Eld, of Seighford Hall
Elwell, of Quarry House
Fisher, of Bentley Hall
Fitzherbert, of Swynnerton Park
Fletcher, of Lawneswood House
Floyer, of Hints Hall
Forster, of Lysways Hall
Fryer, of The Wergs
Gaunt, of Rudyard Vale
Giffard, of Chillington
Gisborne, of Yoxal Lodge
Grazebrooke, of Audnam
Griffin, of Pell Wall House
Hall, of Holly Bush
Harding, of Old Springs
Hardy, of Dunstall Hall
Hartley, of Wheaton-Aston and Prestwood
Harvey, of Blurton House
Haslope, of Chesterton Hall
Haywood, of Brownhills
Heathcote, of Apedale and Longton Hall
Hickin, of Audmore House
Hill, of Dunstall
Holland, of Barton-under-Needwood
Holland, of Stowe House
Hordern, of Oxley Manor
Horsfall, of Bellamour Hall
Horton, of The Hogue
Hussey, of Wyrley Grove
Inge, of Thorpe Constantine
Inge, of Wittington Hurst
Jackson, of Hammerwich
Jervis, of Darlaston Hall
Jervis, of Croxton
Jesson, of Oakwood
Killick, of Walton Hall
Kinnersley, of Binfield Manor
Kynnersley, of Loxley Park
Lane, of King's Bromley Manor
Lee, of Redcliffe
Levett, of Milford Hall
Levett, of Packington Hall
Levett, of Wichnor Park
Loch, of Tittensor
Lyon, of Silver Hill
Mainwaring, of Whitmor Hall
Manley, of Manley Hall
Marsh-Caldwell, of Linley Wood
Masefield, of Stone
Mathews, of Kingswinford
Meigh, of Ash Hall
Meynell, of Hoar Cross
Moncktton, of Somerford Hall
Monckton, of Stretton Hall
Morris, of Wood-Eaton
Mosley, of East Lodge
Mott, of Wall
Neville, of Haselour Hall
Nowdigate, of Byrkley Lodge
Okeover, of Okeover Hall
Parker-Jervis, of Caverswell
Perry, of Tettenhall
Philips, of The Heath House
Philips, of Heybridge
Powys, of Westwood House
Pye, of Clifton Hall

Radcliffe, of Caverswall Castle
Ridgway, of Rownall Hall
Round, of The Hange
Rooker, of Lower Gornal
Royds, of Haughton
Russell, of Wallington House
Salt, of Weeping Cross
Scott, of Great Barr
Scott, of The Red House
Scott, of Ratlinghope Manor
Shaw-Hellier, of Rodbaston Hall
Shawe, of Maple Hayes
Simcox, of Harborne House
Skinner, of Brockton Lodge
Smith, of Sandfield Lodge
Sneyd, of Ashcombe Park
Sneyd, of Huntley Hall
Sneyd, of Keele Hall
Solly, of Toll-End Hall
Sparrow, of Penn
Spode, of Hawkesyard Park
Spooner, of Walton
Spooner, of Wightwick
Stainer-Broade, of Fenton Vivian
Stanley, of Loxley Park
Stewart, of Wigginton Lodge
Stone, of Collingwood
Surtees, of Silkmore
Swinfen-Broun, of Swinfen Hall
Tarratt, of Ford House
Taylor, of Uttoxeter
Tennant, of Needwood House
Thornewill, of Dove Cliffe
Thorneycroft, of Tettenhall Wood
Tudor, of Lapley
Tunnicliffe, of Yarlet
Turton, of Lea House
Twemlow, of Betley Court
Twemlow, of Peatswood
Vernon, of Hilton Park
Ward, of Oaklands
Warren, of The Towers, Market
    Drayton
Watts-Russell, of Ilam
Webb, of The Hough
Webb, of Smallwood Manor
Westhead, of Highfield House
Whieldon, of Hales Hall
Whitby, of Creswell Hall
Whitgreave, of Burton Manor
Whitgreave, of Moseley Court
Wicksted, of Betley Hall
Wigan, of Lapley
Wightwick, of Bloxwich
Williams, of Handsworth
Williams, of Wednesbury Oak
Wilson-Patten, of Light Oaks
Wise, of Clayton Hall
Wolferstan, of Statfold Hall
Wood, of Bignall Hill
Wood, of Hollybank
Wyatt, of Barton-under-Needwood
Yonge, of Charnes Hall

STIRLINGSHIRE.

Montrose, Duke of
Dunmore, Earl of
Zetland, Earl of
Abercromby, Lord
Bruce, Sir W. C., Bart.
Edmondstone, Sir A., Bart.
Steuart, Sir R. J. Seton-, Bart.
Stirling, Sir C. E. F., Bart.
Alexander, of Westerton
Bain, of Livelands

Blackburne, of Killearn
Buchanan, of Craigend Castle
Buchanan-Kincaid, of Carbeth
Cadell, of Avoncrook
Callandar, of Craigforth
Campbell, of Boquhan House
Chalmer, of Larbert House
Cooper, of Ballindalloch
Cuninghame, of Throsk
Dundas, of Carron Hall
Dundas, of Ochtertyre
Ewing, of Arngomery
Fenton-Livingstone, of Westquarter
Forbes, of Callendar House
Graham, of Airth
Graham, of Craigallian
Graham, of Meiklewood
Graham-Stirling, of Craigbarnet
Hagart, of Bantaskine
Hamilton, of Bardowie
Hanbury-Kincaid-Lennox, of Lennox
    Castle
Lowis, of Plean
McCallum, of Reddoch
McFarlane, of Ballencleroch
Macfarlane, of Thornhill
McGrigor, of Cairnoch
Moir, of Leckie
Monro, of Auchenbowie
Murray, of Polmaise
Robertson, of Trininallan House
Speirs, of Culcreuch
Steuart, of Steuarthall
Stewart-Nicolson, of Carnock
Stirling, of Gargunnock
Stirling, of Muiravonside
Stirling, of Tarduf
Strode, of Candie
Stuart, of Carnock

SUFFOLK.

Grafton, Duke of
Hamilton and Brandon, Duke of
Bristol, Marquis of
Hertford, Marquis of
Ashburnham, Earl of
Cadogan, Earl
Gosford, Earl of
Guilford, Earl of
Stradbroke, Earl of
Henniker, Lord
Huntingfield, Lord
Rendlesham, Lord
Thurlow, Lord
Walsingham, Lord
Adair, Sir R. S., Bart.
Affleck, Sir R., Bart.
Blake, Sir H. C., Bart.
Blois, Sir J. R., Bart.
Broke-Middleton, Sir G. N., Bart.
Bunbury, Sir C. J. F., Bart.
Crossley, Sir F., Bart.
Fludyer, Sir Samuel, Bart.
Gage, Sir E. R., Bart.
Gooch, Sir E. S., Bart.
Hughes, Sir E., Bart.
Kerrison, Sir E. C., Bart.
Parker, Sir Wm., Bart.
Rowley, Sir C. R., Bart.
Walker, Sir B. W., Bart.
Western, Sir T. B., Bart.
Alderson, of Wetherden
Alston, of Pennington
Anderson, of Felsham
Anstruther, of Hintlesham Hall

Arcedeckne, of Glevering Hall
Austin, of Brandeston Hall
Barclay, of Higham
Barker, of Clare Priory
Barlow, of Hasketon
Barnardiston, of The Ryes
Barne, of Sotterley Hall and Grey
    Friars
Bassett, of Nether Hall
Beale, of Brettenham Park
Bence, of Kentwell Hall
Bence, of Thorington Hall
Bennet, of Rougham Hall
Benyon, of Culford Hall
Berners, of Woolverston Park
Betts, of Wortham Hall
Bevan, of Plumpton House
Bingham, late of Woodbridge Abbey
Blacker, of Toft-Monks House
Blake, of Thurston House
Bliss, of Brandon Park
Boldero, of White House
Borrett, of Cransford Hall
Bridgman, of Coney Weston Hall
Bromley, of Badmondisfield Hall
Brooke, of Brooke House
Brooke, of Sibton Park
Brooke, of Ufford Place
Brown, of Tostock Place and Brent
    Eleigh Hall
Burrell, of Stoke Park
Carthew, of Nettlestead
Carthew, of Woodbridge Abbey
Casborne, of New House
Chevallier, of Aspall
Chevallier, of The Grove
Clissold, of Wrentham
Cobbold, of Holywells
Cocksedge, of Drinkstone House
Collett, of Beightwell
Colvile, of Baylham
Colvin, of Little Bealings
Cooke, of Semere and Polestead
Cooper, of Syleham Hall
Corrance, of Parham Hall
Crawford, of Haughley Park
Cubitt, of Fritton House
Cullum, of Hardwick House
Dashwood, of Wherstel Park
Dawson, of Groton House
De Medewe, of Witnesham Hall and
    Great Bealings
Dhuleep Singh, of Elveden
Dobede, of Exning Hall
Doughty, of Theberton Hall
Doughty, of Woodbridge
Drury, of Claydon
Edgar, of Red House Park
Edge, of Nedging Hall
Elwes, of Stoke College
Fitz-Gerald, of Boulge Hall
Fitz-Gerald, of Wherstead
Fonnereau, of Christ Church Park
Forbes, of Little Glemham
Fowler, of Gipping Hall
Garden, of Redisham Hall
Garnham, of Bushall Vale
Garrett, of Alde House
Gibbs, of Ickingham Hall
Gorton, of Kirlingham
Gurdon, of Assington
Gurdon, of Rerham Court
Gurdon, of Grundisburgh
Gwilt, of Icklingham
Halford, of West Lexige
Halifax, of Chelsecre Hall
Halifax, of Wyken Hall

Hardcastle, of Nether Hall
Heigham, of Hunston Hall
Heigham, of Wetherden
Hemsworth, of Bacton
Hill, of Buxhall
Hollond, of Benhall Lodge
Homfray, of Stradishall
Hoy, of Stoke Priory
Huddleston, of Little Haugh Norton
Ireland, of Owsden Hall
Johnston, of Holton
Johnston, of Yoxford Grove
Josselin, of St. Edmund's Hill
Kerrison, of Birkfield Lodge
Knox, of Hadleigh
Leathes, of Herringfleet Hall
Leathes, of Normanstone
Leman, of Brampton Hall
Lillingston, of Southwold Lodge
Lofft, of Troston Hall
Long, of Hurts Hall
Lowry-Corry, of Edwardston Hall
Mannock, of Gifford's Hall
Martin, of Hemmingstone Hall
Mathew, of Lanyer House
Mayd, of Withersfield
Metcalfe, of Hawstead House
Mills, of Stutton
Mills, of Saxham Hall
Milner-Gibson, of Theberton House
Moseley, of Glemham House
Mure, of Herringswell
Murray, of Eriswell Lodge
Newton, of Elveden Hall
Oakes, of Nowton Court
Ord, of Fornham House
Orde, of Hopton House
Owen, of Heveningham
Packe, of Melton Lodge
Parker, of Clopton Hall
Pettiward, of Finborough Park
Phillipps, of Sproughton
Phillips, of Great Barton
Phillips, of Haskeeton and Burgh
Pike-Scrivener, of Sibton Abbey
Plumridge, of Hopton Hall
Pocklington, of Chelsworth
Powell, of Drinkstone Park
Purvis, of Darsham
Pytches, of Melton
Rabett, of Bramfield Hall
Rant, of Chediston Park
Reade, of Crow Hall
Reade, of Holbrook House
Robinson, of Ashmans
Robinson, of Denston Hall
Robinson, of Dullingham House
Rodwell, of Ampton Hall
Rodwell, of Woodlands
Rose, of Leiston Abbey
Rushbrooke, of Rushbrooke Hall
Safford, of Mettingham Castle
Schreiber, of Barham
Schreiber, of Melton
Schreiber, of The Round Wood
Scott, of Shadingfield Hall
Seaton, of Ackworth House
Severne, of Peslingford Hall
Sheppard, of Ash High-House
Sheriffe, of Henstead Hall
Shuldham, of Marlesford Hall
Simpson, of Branches Park
Skinner, of The Chauntry
Squire, of Barton Place
Steele, of Wepstead
Steward, of Blundeston
Suckling, of Barsham

Syer, of Kedington
Tatlock, of Bramfield House
Thellusson, of Casius House
Tollemache, of Helmingham
Tomline, of Orwell Kesgrave and Bacton
Tweed, of Capel
Tyrell, of Gipping and Plashwood
Venn, of Freston Lodge
Vernon-Wentworth, of Aldborough Lodge
Waddington, of Cavenham Hall
Walford, of Dallingham
Walford, of Foxborough Hall
Walford-Gosnall, of Bentley
Ware, of Poslingford Hall
Welch, of Yaxley Hall
Weller-Pooley, of Broxted Hall
Whitaker, of Knoddishall
Whitbread, of Londham Park
White, of Bredfield House
White, of Chevington
Wilkinson, of Walsham Hall
Wilkinson, of Walsham-le-Willows
Wilson, of Redgrave Hall
Wilson, of Stowlangtoft Hall
Witham, of Higham
Worlledge, of Chevington
Young, of Bradfield Hall

SURREY.

Canterbury, Archbishop of
Buccleugh and Queensberry, Duke of
Devonshire, Duke of
Somerset, Duke of
Cottenham, Earl of
Egmont, Earl of
Eldon, Earl of
Leven and Melville, Earl of
Lovelace, Earl of
Onslow, Earl
Somers, Earl
Downe, Viscount
Lifford, Viscount
Sidmouth, Viscount
Templetown, Viscount
Winchester, Bishop of
Abinger, Lord
Ashburton, Lord
Grantley, Lord
Hylton, Lord
Lovaine, Lord
Monson, Lord
Abdy, Sir W., Bart.
Antrobus, Sir E., Bart.
Baker, Sir H. W., Bart.
Baynes, Sir W. J. W., Bart.
Clark, Sir James, Bart.
Clayton, Sir W. R., Bart.
Cockburn, Rt. Hon. Sir A. J. E., Bart.
Colebrooke, Sir T. E., Bart.
Dundas, Sir J. R., Bart.
Farquhar, Sir W. R., Bart.
Frederick, Sir Richard, Bart.
Gabriel, Sir T., Bart.
Glyn, the Rev. Sir G. L., Bart.
Le Marchant, Sir D., Bart.
Magnay, Sir W., Bart.
Price, Sir F. P., Bart.
Reid, Sir J. R., Bart.
Sullivan, Sir E. R., Bart.
Vincent, Sir F., Bart
Adams, of Thorpe
Alcock, of Kingswood Warren

Austen, of Shalford House
Bainbridge, of Down Hall and Barrow Hedges
Baines, of East Moulsey
Barclay, of Bury Hill
Barclay, of Eastwick Park
Barnard, of Ham
Bateman, of Moor Park
Bathurst, of Hyams
Beaumont, of Buckland Court
Beckford, of Buxley Lodge
Bennett, of Thorpe Place
Best, of Eastburr House
Beynon, of Carshalton Lodge
Beynon, of Chelsham
Boileau-Pollen, of Little Bookham
Bovill, of Worplesdon
Bradshaw, of Knowle
Bray, of Shere
Bridges, of Beddington House
Brigstocke, of Cooper's Hill Cottage
Briscoe, of Fox Hills
Driscoe, of Nutfield
Broadwood, of Lyne
Brooks, of Woodcote Park
Brown, of Crouch Oak
Bruce, of Roehampton Priory
Burdett, of Shrubhurst
Buxton, of Fox Warren
Byron, of Coulsdon Court
Calvert, of Ockley Court
Carew, of Beddington Park
Carew-Gibson, of Bradstone Brook
Carter, of Epsom Grove
Cattley, late of Shalden Park
Cavendish, of Lyne Grove
Challoner, of Portnall Park
Chandler, of Witley
Chester, of Poyle Park
Cleasby, of The Legers
Cohen, of Asgill House
Cole, of Childown
Collyer-Bristow, of Beddington Place
Combe, of Cobham Park
Cook, of Knowle
Cooper, of Pain's Hill
Cornwell, of Elstead
Coussmaker, of Westwood
Crawford, late of Mickleham Hall
Crompton-Stansfield, of Frimley Park
Cubitt, of Denbies
Currey, of Erlwood
Currie, of West Horseley
Daniell, late of Esher
Davis, of Angiesea House
Donnithorne, of Trevellis
Drake, of Oatlands
Duffield, of Sunning Hill
Edcell, of Milton Place
Edmunds, late of Sutton Grange
Ellesmere, of Burwood House
Evelyn, of Wotton
Farmer, of Nonsuch Park
Farquhar, of Sunnyside
Fazakerley, of Burwood House
Foss, of Frensham House
Fuller, of Frensham Hill
Fyler, of Woodlands
Gardiner, of Melbourne Lodge
Garland, of Woodcote Grove
Garth, of Morden Hall
Glyn, of Banstead Place
Godman, of Park Hatch
Godwin-Austen, of Chilworth Manor
Gosling, of Botley's Park
Gosling, of Busbridge Hall
Goulburn, of Betchworth House

Grissell, of Norbury Park
Grote, of Ridgeway
Gurney, of Carshalton
Gurney, of Nutfield Hall
Hackblock, of Brockham Warren
Hall, of Sutton
Halsey, of Henley Park
Hamond, of Heling House
Hankey, of Fetcham Park
Hare, of Tetworth
Heath, of Anstie Grange
Heathcote, of Durdans Park
Holland, of St. Anne's Hill
Hollings, of The Watchetts
Hope, of Deepdene
Howard, of Ashstead Park
Hutton, of Putney Park
Kemmis, of Croham Hurst
Kershaw, of Streatham Manor
Key, of Streatham
King, of Brooklands
Labouchere, late of Broome Hall
Lambert, of Banstead
Lambert, of Woodmansterne
Langdale, of Garston House
Lawes, of Kingston Hall
Lee, of Windlesham Court
Legge, of Holmwood Lodge
Leveson-Gower, of Titsey Park and Hookwood
Long, of Hampton Lodge
Longman, of Farnborough Hill
Lowe, of Caterham
Loyd, of Monk's Orchard
Lyall, of Hedley House
Lyon, of Woking
Mackinnon, of Ormely Lodge
Mangles, of Pendell Court
Mangles, of Woodbridge
Marshall, of Broadwater
Master, of Barrow Green
Meller, of Broadlands
Miller, of Colliers Wood
Molesworth, of Cobham Lodge
Moore, of Brook Farm
More-Molyneux, of Losely Park
Mortimer, of Wigmore House
Mostyn, of Red Hill
Mount, of Poynters
Moultrie, of St. Austin's
Nicholson, of Waverley Abbey
Northey, of Woodcote House
Onslow, of Dansborough House
Onslow, of Stoke Park
Onslow, of Send Grove House
Palliser, of Wimbledon
Parbury, of Caterham Manor
Parratt, of Effingham House
Paynter, of Camborne House, Richmond
Penrhyn, of East Sheen
Phillips, of Stoke d'Abernon House
Prescott, of Rochampton
Price, of Heywood
Randolph, of Sanderstead
Rawson, late of The Hurst
Reeves, of Godstone
Remington, of Elm Bank
Roper-Curzon, of Grove House
St. Clair, of Felcourt Lodge
Salvin, of Sutton Place
Salwey, of Runnymede Park
Sassoon, of Ashley Park
Schuster, of Rochampton
Scriven, of West Moulsey Priory
Selwyn, of Pagoda House
Sherrard, of Kennersley Manor

Sidney, of Esher Place
Smith, of Thorpe Lee
Smith, of Selsdon House
Smith, of The Oaks
Somerset, of Heath Lodge
Sparkes, of Gosden House
Steele, of Sutton
Steere, of Jayes
Storer, of Combe Court
Stuart-Wortley, of Sheen House
Sumner, of Hatchlands
Sumner, of Puttenham Priory
Sutherland, of Coombe
Thrupp, of Merrow House
Thurlew, of Baynard's Park
Tollemache, of Ham House
Tonge, of Starborough Castle
Trotter, of Horton
Tupper, of Albury
Turner, of Rook's Nest
Walpole, of Stagbury Park
Ward, of Willey Place
Way, of Wonham Manor
Webb, of Milford House
Welbank, of Tandridge Priory
Wells-Dymoke, of West Molesey
Westear, of Burwood
Weston, of West-Horseley Place
Wickham, of Cheam Place
Wight, of Braboeuf Manor
Wigsell, of Sanderstead and Purley House
Williams, of Tanhurst
Wood, of Marden Park
Young, of Oakfield Lodge

SUSSEX.

Cleveland, Duke of
Devonshire, Duke of
Norfolk, Duke of
Richmond, Duke of
Bristol, Marquis of
Bath, Dowager Marchioness of
Ashburnham, Earl of
Chichester, Earl of
De la Warr, Earl
Egmont, Earl of
March, Earl of
Sheffield, Earl of
Winterton, Earl of
Waldegrave, Dowager Countess
Gage, Viscount
Chichester, Bishop of
Oxford, Bishop of
Buckhurst, Baroness
Colchester, Lord
Leconfield, Lord
Zouche, Baroness
Ashburnham, Sir A., Bart.
Blunt, Sir C. W., Bart.
Borrell, Sir Percy, Bart.
Dyke, Sir J., Bart.
Goring, Sir C., Bart.
Hamilton, Sir C. J. J., Bart.
Lamb, Sir A., Bart.
Lampson, Sir C. M., Bart.
Milbanke, Sir J. R., Bart.
Shelley, Sir F., Bart.
Shelley, Sir P. F., Bart.
Shiffner, Sir G. C., Bart.
Taylor, Sir Chas., Bart.
Wilson, Sir T. M., Bart.
Adamson, of Rushton Park
Aldridge, of St. Leonard's Forest
Archdall-Gratwicke, of Ham Place

Ashburnham, of Broomham
Ashburnham, of Shernfold Park
Austen, of Aldwick
Barchard, of Horsted Place
Baring, of Oakwood
Barttelot, of Bramblehurst
Barttelot, of Stopham House
Bayton, of Whyke
Benett, of Preston Place
Berkeley, of Old Park
Bigg, of The Hyde
Bishopp, of Northiam
Blaauw, of Beechland
Blaker, of Preston
Blencowe, of The Hooke
Bligh, of Rotherfield Hall
Blunt, of Crabbett
Boldero, of Lower Beding
Borrer, of Barrow Hill and Cowfield
Borrer, of Pakyns Manor
Borrer, of Pickwell
Borrer, of Portslade Manor
Bouchard, of Pax Hill Park
Boucher, of Heatherden House
Boxall, of Avery House
Brabazon, of Oaklands
Brandreth, of Worthing
Bray, of Darwell Bank
Bridger, of Buckingham House
Briscoe, of Bohemia House
Broadwood, of Buchan Hill
Broadwood, of Holmsbush
Brodie, of The Gore
Brodie, of Uckfield
Brooke-Pechell, of Castle Goring
Buckle, of Norton House
Buckner, of Wyke House
Burrell, of Ockenden House
Cabbell, of Aldwick
Campion, of Danny Park
Carew-Gibson, of Sandgate Lodge
Carnegie, of Fairoak
Carr-Lloyd, of Lancing Manor
Carter, of Quarry Hill
Chamberlain, of Bexhill
Chevall-Tooke, of Hurston Clays
Child, of Bouvelles Court
Cobden, of Dunford
Combe, of Oaklands
Courthorpe, of Whiligh
Crake, of Highlands
Cripps, of Novington
Crofts, of Somting Abbotts
Crosbie, of Northlands
Currie, of Haseldean
Curteis, of Leasham House
Curteis, of Windmill Hill and Pease-marsh Place
D'Albiac, of The Shelleys
Darby, of Markly
Davies, of Danehurst
Davis, of Heathfield Lodge
Day, of Uckfield House
Deekins, of Coolhurst
Dixon, of Stansted Park
Dodson, of Hurstpierpoint
Donovan, of Framfield Place
Dunn, of Wardleton
Egerton, of Mountfield Court
Elwood, of Clayton Priory
Evans, of Lyminster House
Eversfield, of Denne Park
Fawcett, of Brighton
Fetherstonhaugh, of Up Park
Fitzgerald, of Seaford Lodge
Fitzgerald, of Holbrook
Fitzhugh, of Street

4 A   1082

Massy, of Kingswell House
Massy-Dawson, of Ballinacourty
Meagher, of Ballinderry
Minchin, of Rathclough
Minnitt, of Anaghbeg
Moore, of Barne
Moore, of Mooresfort
Osborne, of Newtown-Anner
Otway, of Castle Otway
Pennefather, of Lakefield
Pennefather, of Ballylauigan
Perry, of Woodroof
Philips, of Cashel
Phipps, of Oaklands
Poë, of Harley Park
Power-Lalor, of Long Orchard
Prior, of Crossoge
Prittie, of Clonmel
Prittie, of Oakville
Quin, of Loughloher Castle
Rae, of Mountain Lodge
Roe, of Roesborough
Ryan, of Ballymackeogh
Ryan, of Inch
Sadleir, of Ballinderry House and Castletown
Sankey, of Coolmore
Scully, of Dunally
Scully, of Mantlehill
Smith-Barry, of Cordangan
Spaight, of Derry Castle
Stoney, of Kyle Park
Stoney, of Portland
Trant, of Doven
Twiss, of Birdhill House
Waldron, of Helen Park
Waller, of Finnoe House
Waller, of Prior Park
Webb, of Woodville
Willington, of Castle Willington
Willington, of Killoskchane Castle
Yelverton, of Belle Isle

TYRONE CO.

Abercorn, Marquis of
Belmore, Earl of
Caledon, Earl of
Castle-Stuart, Earl of
Charlemont, Earl of
Clanwilliam, Earl of
Ranfurly, Earl of
Hamilton, Sir J. J., Bart.
M'Mahon, Sir B. B., Bart.
Staples, Sir N. A., Bart.
Stewart, Sir J. M., Bart.
Adams, of Shinan House
Archdall, of Kilskerry
Auchinleck, of Castle Lodge and Mullans
Auchinleck, of Crevenagh
Blacker, of Lisnahauna
Brackenridge, of Ashfield Park
Brooke, of Dungannon
Browne, of Aughentaine
Burges, of Parkanaur
Caulfeild, of Drumcairne
Cole-Hamilton, of Beltrim
Eccles, of Ecclesville
Echlin, of Kirlish
Evans, of Gortmerron
Ferrall, of Augher Castle
Galbraith, of Clanabogan
Gervais, of Cecil
Gledstanes, of Fardross
Greer, of The Grange

Greer, of Rhonehill
Greer, of Tullylagan
Hutton, of Grange Foyle
Irvine, of Springhill House
Knox, of Dungannon Park
Knox, of Urney Park
Lindesay, of Loughry
Lindsey, of Gortavale
Litton, of Altmore
Lowry, of Drumreagh
Lowry, of Pomeroy House
Lowry, of Rockdale House
Macartney, of The Palace, Clogher
Macfarlane, of Fallagh Erin
Mann, of Dunmoyle and Corvey Lodge
Mayne, of Rahaghey
Montgomery, of Crilly House
Montgomery-Moore, of Garvey House
Moutray, of Favour Royal
Ogilby, of Altnachree
Porter, of Kilsherry
Prentice, of Caledon
Scott, of Castletown Bawn
Sheil, of Killymeal House
Sinclair, of Holy Hill
Smyly, of Caums and Castlederg
Stanley, of Roughan Park
Story, of Errington
Stronge, of Mulnavar
Stuart, of Crevengh House and Lisdhu
Vesey, of Derrybard
Von Stieglitz, of Altmore Lodge
Willcocks, of Brookend

WARWICKSHIRE.

Hertford, Marquis of
Townshend, Marquis
Aylesford, Earl of
Bradford, Earl of
Craven, Earl of
Warwick, Earl
Feilding, Viscount
Lifford, Viscount
Calthorpe, Lord
Dormer, Lord
Leigh, Lord
Willoughby de Broke, Lord
Biddulph, Sir T. W., Bart.
Chetwynd, Sir George, Bart.
Hamilton, Sir F. N. C., Bart.
Hartopp, Sir J. W. Cradock-, Bart.
Mordaunt, Sir Chas., Bart.
Parker, Sir H., Bart.
Philips, Sir G. R., Bart.
Shuckburgh, Sir F., Bart.
Smythe, Sir C. F., Bart.
Throckmorton, Sir N. W., Bart.
Wheler, Sir T., Bart.
Adams, of Anstey Hall
Adderley, of Fillongley Hall
Adderley, of Hams Hall
Allfrey, of Hemingford House
Alston, of Elmdon Hall
Amherst, of Fieldgate House
Arbuthnott, of Shenton
Arkwright, of Hatton House
Ashton, of Cliff Hall
Astley, of Ansley Park
Aston, of Rowington Hall
Attye, of Ingon Grange
Bagot, of Pipe Hayes Hall
Bedford, of Sutton Coldfield
Beech, of Brandon Lodge
Bickmore, of Berkswell Hall

Boultbee, of Salford
Boultbee, of Springfield
Bracebridge, of Atherstone Hall
Bracebridge, of Moreville Hall
Brackenridge, of Ashfield Park
Braddyll, of Leamington
Bromley-Davenport, of Baginton Hall
Bucknill, of Hillmorton House
Butler, of Coton House
Caldecott, of Holbrook Grange
Caldecott, of Rugby
Cartwright, of Preston Bagot
Chamberlayne, of Stoney Thorpe
Colmore, of Ashfurlong
Colville, of Barton House
Cooper, late of Weddington Castle
Corbet, of Riversdale
Cox, of Dosthill House
Crowdy, of Billesley Hall
De Bary, of Weston Hall
Dickins, of Cherrington
Digby, of Blythe Hall
Digby, of Meriden Hall
Dilke-Fetherston, of Maxstoke Castle
Dugdale, of Merevale
Dugdale, of Wroxhall Abbey
Fenton, of Caldecot Hall
Ferrers, of Baddesley Clinton
Fetherston, of Packwood House
Finch, of Diddington Hall
Freer, of Stratford-upon-Avon
Galton, of Claverdon Leys
Galton, of Leamington
Granville, of Brooklands
Granville, of Wellesbourne Hall
Greaves, of Avonside
Greaves, of The Cliff
Gregory, of Styrechale
Grisewood, of Daylesford House
Hacket, of Moor Hall
Harding, of Baraset
Harding, of Copeley Lodge
Harpur, of Chilvers Coton
Hibbert, of Bilton Grange
Holbech, of Farnborough Hall
Horsman, of Ashby St. Leger's
Hoskyns, late of Wroxhall Abbey
Huband, of Ipsley
Jarret, of Sherborne
Jee, of Hartshill
Jenkinson, of Alveston
Keighley-Peach, of Idlicote House
Kendall, of Austrey
King, of Chadshunt
Kittermaster, of Meriden
Landor, of Ipsley Court
Landor, of Tachbrooke
Landor, of Whitnash
Leathes, of Lillington
Leigh, of Brownsover
Leigh, of Newbold-on-Avon
Lloyd, late of Spark Hill
Lowry, of Charlecote Park
Martin, of Leamington Priors
Miller, of Radway Grange
Mordaunt, of Goldicote House
Muntz, of Edstone Hall
Muntz, of Umberslade Hall
Musgrave, of Clarendon
Neale, of Allesley Park
Newdegate, of Arbury
Newton, of Barrells Park
Noel, of Moxhull Park
Okeover, of Oldbury Hall
Parker-Jervis, of Aston Hall
Peel, of Hampton-in-Arden
Pennington, of Thickthorn

4 A 2

1091

Percy-Bertie, of Guys Cliffe
Perkins, of Sutton Coldfield
Perry, of Bitham House
Petre, of Whitley
Philips, of Welcombe and Snitter-field
Ratcliff, of Wyddrington
Roberts-West, of Alscot Park
Rotherham, of Coventry
Scholefield, of Birmingham
Scott, of Baginton
Scott, of Mertoun
Scott, of Cawston Lodge
Sharp, of Horton House
Sheldon, of Brailes House
Shirley, of Lower Eatingdon Park
Shuckburgh, of Bourton Hall
Staunton, of Longbridge
Thornton, of The Elms
Townsend, of Alveston
Townsend, of Honington Hall
Twist, of Stoke House
Walker, of Berkswell
Warde, of Clopton House
Wheeler, of Barcheston
Williams, of Malvern Hall
Willington, of Tamworth
Wilson, of Knowle Hall
Wise, of Woodcote
Wise, of Shrublands
Wood, of Newbold Revel
Yatman, of Wellesbourne

WATERFORD CO.

Devonshire, Duke of
Waterford, Marquis of
Huntingdon, Earl of
Cashel, Bishop of
Carew, Lord
Stuart de Decies, Lord
Carew, Dowager Lady
Barron, Sir W. H., Bart.
Humble, Sir J. N., Bart.
Keane, Sir J. H., Bart.
Musgrave, Sir Richard, Bart.
Paul, Sir R. J., Bart.
Anderson, of Grace Dieu
Bagge, of Ardmore House
Barron, of Carrig Barron
Barron, of Glenview
Barry, of Mocollop
Beresford, of Woodhouse
Blake, of Waterford
Bloomfield, of Newpark
Bolton, of Brook Lodge
Bolton, of Mount Bolton
Bosanquet, of Knockane Lodge and Kilnagemogue
Bushe, of Glencairn Abbey
Carew, of Ballinamona
Christmas, of Whitfield
Congreve, of Mount Congreve
Croker, of Lissinny Castle
Davis, of Ballynaclode
De la Poer, of Gurteen
Esmonde, of Pembrokestown
FitzGerald, of Little Island
Fitzgerald, of Ballina Park
Fortescue, of Summerville
Gerde, of Garryduffe
Gumbleton, of Fortwilliam
Hartford, of Suirville Glebe
Hassard, of Glenville
Lloyd, of Straneally Castle
Meagher, of Waterford

Medlicott, of Rockets Castle
Moore, of Ballynatray
Morris, of Rockenham
Mulcahy, of Ballymakee
Odell, of Carriglea
O'Keefe, of Ballinacourty
O'Shee, of Gardenmorris
Palliser, of Comragh
Perceval-Maxwell, of Moore Hill
Poer, of Belleville Park
Power, of Faithlegg House
Roch, of Woodbine Hall
Smyth, of Ballynatray
Thackwell, of Conneragh
Watson, of Kilmanahan Castle
Wyse, of Manor of St. John

WESTMEATH CO.

Westmeath, Marquis of
Longford, Earl of
Castlemaine, Lord
Kilmaine, Lord
Vaux of Harrowden, Lord
Chapman, Sir B. J. Bart.
Ennis, Sir J., Bart.
Grogan, Sir E., Bart.
Levinge, Sir R. G. A., Bart.
Nugent, Sir E., Bart.
Nugent, Sir P., Bart.
Piers, Sir E. F., Bart.
Tuite, Sir M. A. H., Bart.
Adams-Reilly, of Belmont
Battersby, of Lough Bane
Batty, of Ballyhealy
Bond, of Fairy Hall
Briscoe, of Rivendale
Briscoe, of Grangemore
Caulfeild, of Bloomfield
Chaigneau, of Benown
Chapman, of Southill
Conolly, of Coola
Cooke, of Cookesborough
Cooke, of Retreat
Cooper, of Dunboden
Daniel, of Auburn
Daniel, of New Forest
D'Arcy, of Hyde Park
Dawson, of Nohaville
Dease, of Turbotston
De Blaquiere, of Port Lemon
Devenish-Mears, of Mears Court
Evans, of Lough Park
Fetherstonhaugh, of Bulrath
Fetherstonhaugh, of Bracklyn Castle
Fetherstonhaugh, of Carrick
Fetherstonhaugh, of Grouse Lodge
Fetherstonhaugh, of Rockview
Gore-Brown, of Court Devenish
Greville, of Clonyn
Griffith, of Gortmore
Handcock, of Creaghduff
Harris-Temple, of Waterstown
Hornidge, of Calverstown
Huband, of Athlone
Kelly, of Lanestown
L'Estrange, of Cartronganny
Levinge, of Levington Park
Longworth, of Glynwood
Lyons, of Ledestown
Magill, of Lyttleton
Marlay, of Belvedere
Nugent, of Clonlost
Palmer, of Streamstown
Parnell, of Annerill House
Pidgeon, of Athlone

Pilkington, of Tore
Pollard-Urquhart, of Kanturk
Purdon, of Lisnabin
Reynell, of Archestown
Reynell, of Killynon
Rochfort, of Rochfort Lodge
Rochfort-Boyd, of Middleton Park
Smyth, of Ballynegall
Smyth, of Drumcree House
Smyth, of Gaybrook
Smyth, of Glananea
Smyth, of Portlick Castle
Smythe, of Barbavilla House
Somers, of Tyrellspass
Talbot, of Tullagherne
Tottenham, of Rochfort House
Trye, of Creggan House
Tuite, of Culleen
Tuite, of Sonna
Vignoles, of Cornahir

WESTMORELAND.

Devonshire, Duke of
Bective, Earl of
Lonsdale, Earl of
Brougham, Lord
Tufton, Sir R., Bart.
Addison, of The Friary
Airey, of Holme Park
Argles, of Eversley
Atkinson, of Burton House
Atkinson, of Morland Hall
Balme, of Loughrigg
Bellas, of Bongate
Bliss, of Sleddale Forest
Brccks, of Eden Gate
Burn, of Orton Hall
Carew, late of Foxghyll
Carus-Wilson, of Casterton Hall
Chamley, of Warcop House
Crackanthorpe, of Newbiggin Hall
Curwen, of Belle Isle
Davy, of Lesketh How
Fleming, of Rayrigg and Belfield
Fletcher, of Waterhead
Gandy, of Heaves
Gibson, of Whelprigg
Greene, of Whittington Hall
Harrison, of Scale How and Bellevue
Hill, of Castle Bank
Holt, of Red Bank
Hopes, of Brampton Crofts
Hutchinson, of Broad Oaks
Hutton, of Beetham House
Le Fleming, of Rhydal Hall
Marshall, of Patterdale Hall
Moore, of Grimeshill
Preston, of Warcop Hall
Richardson, of Lanerigg
Rigg, of Crossrigg Hall
Roshek, of Ash Meadow
Shepherd, of Shaw End
Sowler, of Sawrey Knotts
Staniforth, of Storrs Hall
Taylor, of Ibbotsholme
Temple, of Wrathay
Thexton, of Ashton House
Thompson, of Kirkby Stephen
Upton, of Ingmire Hall
Wakefield, of Sedgwick House and Prizett
Watson, of Calgarth Park
Wilson, of Dallam Tower
Wilson, of High Park
Wilson, of Rigmaden Park

Wilson, of The Howe
Wordsworth, of Sockbridge
Wybergh, of Clifton Hall

WEXFORD CO.

Ely, Marquis of
Courtown, Earl of
Carew, Lord
Ruthven, Lord
Templemore, Lord
Esmonde, Sir T., Bart.
Jervis, Sir H. M. J. W., Bart.
Palliser, Sir H. P., Bart.
Power, Sir James, Bart.
Alcock, of Wilton
Alexander, of Carne
Archer, of Ballysseskin
Beatty, of Borodale
Beauman, of Hyde Park
Blacker, of Woodbrook
Bolton, of The Island
Boyd, of Roslare House
Boyse, of Bannow House
Braddell, of Coolmelagh and Chellows Park
Bruen, of Coolbawn
Bryan, of Upton House
Budgen, of Ballindoney
Byrne, of Rosemount
Cliffe, of Belle Vue
Clifford, of Castle Annesley
Colclough, of Tintern Abbey
Cookman, of Monart and Curracloe
Cornock, of Cromwellsfort
Cox, of Cooleliffe
Deane, of Berkeley Forest
Deane-Drake, of Stokestown
De Rienzi, of Clobemon Hall
Devereux, of Ballyrankin
Devereux, of Rocklands
Donovan, of Ballymore
Doyne, of Wells
Farmar, of Bloomfield
Farmar, of Clohass
Flood, of Slaney Lodge
George, of Cahore House
Giffard, of Kilcorrall
Gifford, of Ballysop
Glascott, of Alderton
Glascott, of Killowen
Glascott, of Valentia
Goff, of Horetown House
Graves, of New Ross
Guinness, of Parkanmesley
Hall-Dare, of Newtownbarry
Harman, of Palace
Harvey, of Bargy Castle
Harvey, of Killane Castle
Harvey, of Kyle
Hatton, of Belmont House
Herney, of Killiane
Hill, of St. John's
Hore, of Pole Hore
Hore-Ruthven, of Harperston
Howlin, of Ballyharren
Hughes, of Ely House
Keane, of Castletown House
King, of Barrystown
Knox, of Kilmannock
Lambert, of Carnagh
Le Hunte, of Artramount
Le Hunte, of Knockalier
Leigh, of Rosegarland
Leigh, of Slan House
Magan, of Marlfield

Maher, of Ballinkeele
Morgan, of Ardcandrisk
Nunn, of St. Margaret's
Nunn, of Silverspring
Phaire, of Daphne House
Phaire, of Killoughram
Pigott, of Slevoy
Pounden, of Ballywater
Pounden, of Brownswood
Ram, of Clonattin
Ram, of Ramsfort
Redmond, of The Deeps
Redmond, of Movilla
Redmond, of Pembroke House
Richards, of Ardamine
Richards, of Grange
Richards, of Mackmine Castle
Richards, of Ounavarra
Richards, of Solsborough
Rowe, of Ballycross and Duffry
Stronge, of Balneenduff
Swan, of Baldwinstown Castle
Sweetman, of Ballymackesey
Swiny, of Tubberlumine
Talbot, of Ballytrent
Talbot, of Knockmullen
Tench, of Ballybaly House
Tottenham, of Tottenham Green
Tyndall, of Oaklands
Ussher, of Cappagh
Ussher, of Landscape
Waddy, of Clougheast Castle
Walker, of Tykillen
Wallace, of Bally Courcy
Westropp, of Charlefort
White, of Newlands
White, of Peppards Castle
Whitney, of Merton

WICKLOW CO.

Downshire, Marquis of
Londonderry, Marquis of
Aldborough, Earl of
Carysfort, Earl of
Fitzwilliam, Earl
Meath, Earl of
Milltown, Earl of
Wicklow, Earl of
Monck, Viscount
Powerscourt, Viscount
Plunket, Lord
Hodson, Sir G. F. J., Bart.
Howard, Sir R., Bart.
Hutchinson, Sir E. S., Bart.
Whitshed, Sir V. K. Hawkins-, Bart.
Acton, of West Aston
Barton, of Glendalough House
Bayly, of Ballyarthur
Booth, of Laragh
Braddell, of Ballingate
Byrne, of Cronroy Byrne
Carroll, of Ashford
Carroll, of Ballymure
Cogan, of Tinode
Crampton, of St. Valerie
Dennis, of Barnderry House
Dennis, of Eadstown
Dennis, of Fort Granite
Dick, of Humewood
Dickson, of Ballyfree
Domville, of Thornhill
Drought, of Glencarrig
Eccles, of Cronroe
Edwards, of Old Court
Fenton, of Ballinclea

Grattan, of Tinnehinch
Grogan, of Slaney Park
Gun-Cunningham, of Mount Kennedy
Heighington, of Denard
Hoey, of Hoey Field
Howard-Brooke, of Castle Howard
Jackson, of Novarra
Kemmis, of Ballinacor
Keogh, of Bushy Park
La Touche, of Bellevue
Lawson, of Clontra
Lindesay, of Glenview
Moore, of Kilbride Manor
Nuttall, of Tiltour
O'Grady, of Plattenstown
Oliver, of Cherrymount
O'Reilly-Dease, of Ravenswell
Parnell, of Avondale
Pennefather, of Rathsalla
Putland, of Bray Head
Redmond, of Killoughter
Riall, of Conna Hill
Salkeld, of Ovoca
Sandys, of Dargle
Saunders, of Saunders Grove
Seg-ave, of Kiltynon
Synge, of Glanmore Castle
Tighe, of Rossana
Tottenham, of Ballycurry
Tottenham, of Woodstock
Truell, of Tynte Park
Westby, of High Park
White, of Killoughter
Her Majesty the Queen

WIGHT, ISLE OF.

Her Majesty the Queen
Heytesbury, Lord
Clifford, Sir A. W. J., Bart.
Gordon, Sir H. P., Bart.
Hamond, Sir A. S., Bart.
Oglander, Sir H., Bart.
Simeon, Sir John, Bart.
Stirling, Sir W. G., Bart.
Atherley, of Southampton
Batten, of Fairlee
Bell, of Norris Castle
Brigstocke, of Stone Pitts
Cheeke, of Old Park
Cochrane, of Carr-Abbey House
Cruser, of Westhill
Danbar, of Buckingham Villa
Dawes, of Wydeombe and Sea
Duff, of Wilburg-a-Leek
Elers-Napier, of West Hill
Farnal, of Boldnor
Harington, of Woodyate
Glynn, of Fairy Hill
Hinxman, of Sea Court
Hughes, of Westhill Terrace
Kinnard, of Sea View
Kerr, of West Cliff
Legard, of Cowes
Le Marchant, of Sea View
Martins, of Wootton
Popham, of Wootton
Sheldon, of Mansel House
Sheldon, of Spring Hill
Skinner, of Carsbrooke
Swinburne, of East Dene
Vernon, of Steephill Castle
Ward, of Northwood Park
Williams, of Appuldurcombe
Wymer, of St. John's Lodge

WIGTOWNSHIRE.

Galloway, Earl of
Stair, Earl of
Agnew, Sir A., Bart.
Dalrymple, Sir H. H., Bart.
Dunbar, Sir William, Bart.
Hay, Sir A. G., Bart.
Hay, Sir J. C. D., Bart.
Maxwell, Sir W., Bart.
Wallace, Sir W. T. F. A., Bart.
Boyd, of Merton Hall
Carrick-Moore, of Corswall
Hamilton, of Craighlaw
M'Douall, of Logan
M'Micking, of Miltonise
Maitland, of Freugh
Ommanney-McTaggart, of Ardwell House
Stewart, of Glasserton and Physgill
Stopford-Blair, of Penninghame
Vans-Agnew, of Barnbarrach and Park House

WILTSHIRE.

Ailesbury, Marquis of
Bath, Marquis of
Lansdowne, Marquis of
Westminster, Marquis of
Cowley, Earl of
Malmesbury, Earl of
Nelson, Earl
Pembroke, Earl of
Radnor, Earl of
Suffolk, Earl of
Bolingbroke, Viscount
Salisbury, Bishop
Arundell of Wardour, Lord
Broughton, Lord
Churchill, Lord
Heytesbury, Lord
Methuen, Lord
Rivers, Lord
Antrobus, Sir E., Bart,
Astley, Sir F. D., Bart.
Bathurst, Sir F. H. Hervey-, Bart.
Beach, Sir M. E. Hicks-, Bart.
Burdett, Sir R., Bart.
Hoare, Sir H. A., Bart.
Hulse, Sir E., Bart.
Lopes, Sir M., Bart.
Malet, Sir A., Bart.
Neeld, Sir John, Bart.
Pollen, Sir R. H., Bart.
Alexander, of Westrop House
Ashe, of Langley House
Ashfordby-Trenchard, of Stanton Park
Awdry, of Notton House
Awdry, of Seend
Barton, of Corsley House
Baskerville, of Woolley House
Beach, of Keevil
Benett, of Pythouse
Bevan, of Fosbury
Biggs, of Stockton
Bridger, of Chantry House
Bristow, of Boxmoore Park
Browne, of Monkton-Farleigh
Buckley, of New Hall
Bush, of Fairwood
Caillard, of Wingfield House
Caldwell, of Lackham House
Calley, of Burderop Park
1091

Clark, of Bellefield
Clutterbuck, of Hardenhuish
Codrington, of Wroughton
Colston, of Roundway Park
Cresswell, of Pinkney Park
Crowdy, of Badbury Wick
Dickinson, of Ashton House
Du Boulay, of Donhead Hall
Duke, of Lake House
Ellis-Jervois, of Britford
Everett, of Greenhill House
Everett, of Biddesden House
Everett, of Harnham Cliff
Ewart, of Broadleas
Fane-de-Salis, of Teffont Manor
Foster, of Holt Manor
Fowle, of Durrington House
Fuller, of Neston Park
Gladstone, of Bowden Park
Goddard, of Clyffe Pypard Manor
Goddard, of The Lawn
Goldney, of Beechfield House
Gordon, of Wincombe Park
Gordon, of Kemble House
Graves, of Charlton House
Grove, of Fern House
Grubbe, of Potterne
Hall, of Blacklands Park
Heathcote, of Rollestone
Heathcote, of Shaw Hill
Houlton, of Farley Castle
Hunt-Grubbe, of Eastwell
Hussey, of Salisbury and Highworth
Johnson, of Brouncker's Court
Johnson, of Hannington Hall
Knatchbull, of Choklerton Lodge
Leir, of Jaggard's House
Leyborne-Popham, of Littlecote
Locke, of Chicklade House
Lock, of Cleve House
Locke, of Rowde Forde
Long, of Rood Ashton
Lopes, of Sandridge Park
Lovell, of Cole Park
Lowndes, of Castle Combe
Lowther, of Orcheston St. George
Luce, of Malmesbury
Ludlow, of Heywood House
Ludlow-Bruges, of Seend
Lysley, of Pewsham
Marklove, of Ogbourne St. George
Matcham, of New House
Mayne, of Teffont
Merewether, of Bowden Hill
Miles, of Burton Hill
Miles, of Danvsey House
Morrison, of Fonthill House
Mullings, of Eastcourt
Nelson, of Landford House
Nisbet, of Southbroome House
Olivier, of Potterne Manor
Paxton, of Cholderton
Penruddocke, of Compton Park
Perry-Keene, of Ninety House
Phipps, of Dilton Court
Phipps, of Leighton
Poore, of Screnodt
Powell, of Hurdcott
Poynder, of Hilmarton and Hartham
Prodgers, of Kington House
Prower, of Purton House
Ravenhill, of Ashton Gifford
Rogers, of Rainscombe
Saunders, of Bradford-on-Avon
Scrope, late of Castle Combe
Seymour, of Crowood
Seymour, of Knoyle

Seymour, of East Knoyle
Simpson, of Salthrop Lodge
Sloane-Stanley, of Tedworth Park
Smith, of Old Park
Southby, of Bulford
Speke, of Monk's Park
Spicer, of Spye Park
Stancomb, of The Prospect
Staples, of Broughton Gifford
Stone, of Badbury
Talbot, of Lacock Abbey
Temple, of Bishopstrow House
Tonge, of Highway
Troyte-Bullock, of Sedge Hill
Walker-Heneage, of Compton Bassett
Ward, of Ogbourne St. Andrew and Draycot Foliat
Watson-Taylor, of -Erlestoke Park and Erchfont Manor
Wayte, of Bushton
Wroughton, of Wilcot
Wyndham, of The College
Wyndham, of Dinton
Wyndham, of Wans House
Yerbury, of Belcomb Brook

WORCESTERSHIRE.

Beauchamp, Earl
Coventry, Earl of
Dudley, Earl of
Howe, Earl
Stamford, Earl of
Southwell, Viscount
Worcester, Bishop of
Foley, Lord
Lyttelton, Lord
Sandys, Lord
Windsor, Baroness
Blount, Sir E., Bart.
Boughton, Sir C. H. Rouse-, Bart.
Fitzwygram, Sir Robert, Bart.
Lambert, Sir H. E. F., Bart.
Lechmere, Sir E. A. H., Bart.
Pakington, Rt. Hon. Sir J. T., Bart.
Phillipps, Sir Thos., Bart.
Sebright, Sir J. G. S., Bart.
Smith, Sir Wm., Bart.
Wakeman, Sir O., Bart.
Winnington, Sir T. E., Bart.
Acton, of Wolverton
Allsopp, of Hindlip Hall
Amery, of Park House
Amphlett, of Wychbold Hall
Baker, of Sandbourne
Barrows, of Hagley
Bartleet, of The Shrubbery, Redditch
Bearcroft, of Mere Hall
Bennitt, of Stourton Hall
Berington, of Little-Malvern Court
Berkeley, of Spetchley Park
Best, of Blakebrook House
Blayney, of Evesham Lodge
Brettell, of Tin-tail House
Britten, of Kenswick
Browne, of Eastham
Candler, of Malvern Link
Chance, of Malvern
Childe, of Kyre House
Clutton-Brock, of Pensax Court
Collier, of Bockley
Collis, of Stourbridge
Colville, of Kempsey House
Contor, of Draycott House

Cookes, of Woodhampton
Coventry, of Earl's Croome Court
Coxwell, of South Bank
Curtler, of Beveré House
Dowdeswell, of The Down House
Dowdeswell, of Pull Court
Essington, of Ribbesford House
Eyston, of Overbury
Fetherstonhaugh, of Hopton Court
Flood, of Woollas Hall
Foley, of Prestwood
Foster, of Stourton Castle
Galton, of Hadsor House
Galton, of Shelsley Grange
Gresley, of High Park
Haden, of Dixon's Green
Haigh, of St. John's
Hancocks, of Blakeshall Hall
Hancocks, of Wolverley Court
Hastings, of Barbourne House
Haywood, of Sillins
Heaton, of Bryn-Issa
Hemming, of Bentley Manor
Hemming, of Spring Grove
Hickman, of Old Swinford House
Holland, of Cropthorne
Holland, of Dumbleton
Homfray, of Broadwaters
Hooke, of Norton Hall
Hornyold, of Blackmore and Hanley
Hudson, of Vandyke House
Johnson, of Bricklehampton Hall
Knight, of Wolverley House
Kynnersley, of Moor Green
Lane, of Moundsley Hall
Laslet, of Aberton Hall
Lea, of Astley Hall
Ledsam, of Northfield
Littlewood, of Clent House
Lloyd, of Showel Green
Lord, of Elmley Park
McKerrell, of Barrassie House
Marriott, of Avonbank
Martin, of Ham Court
Martin, of Overbury Court
Milward, of Redditch
Moillet, of Aberley Hall
Moore, of Townend House
Moxon, of Farncombe
Mynors, of Weatheroak
Nash, of Martley
Noel, of Bell Hall
Noel, of Bradford House
Norbury, of Sherridge
Oldnall-Russell, of Sion House
Padmore, of Henwick Hall
Pakington, of Kent's Green
Pidcock, of Oakfield
Prescott-Decie, of Bockelton
Ricardo, of Bromsberrow Place
Roberts, of Hazeldine House
Robinson, of Summerhill
Royds, of Crown East Court
Rudge, of Evesham Abbey
Scobell, of Pershore
Sherriff, of Perdiswell Hall
Sidebottom, of Elm Bank
Smith, of Dudley Priory
Smith, of Goldicote House
Stone, of Chambers Court
Talbot, of Honeybourne
Talbot, late of Honeybrooke
Talbot, of Oakland
Taylor, of Moseley Hall
Taylor, of Strensham Court
Temple, of The Nash
Tennant, of The Eades

Thackwell, of Birts-Morton Court and Rye Court
Thoren, Baron de, of St. Anne's Hill
Vale, of Mathon
Vale, of Mathon Lodge
Vernon, of Hanbury Hall
Watkins, of Woodfield
Watt, of The Forelands
Webb, of The Berrow
Webb, of The Longlands
Westhead, of Lea Castle
Whatley, of Peopleton
Wheeler, of Kyrewood and Newnham Court
Whitaker, of Caldewell
Williams, of Harborow
Willis, of Wick House
Wilmot, of Malvern
Woodward, of Arley Castle
Woodward, of The Hyde
Workman, of Charlton and Great Hampton

YORKSHIRE.

York, Archbishop of
Devonshire, Duke of
Leeds, Duchess of
Ailesbury, Marquis of
Normanby, Marquis of
Carlisle, Earl of
Cathcart, Earl
De Grey and Ripon, Earl
Effingham, Earl of
Fitzwilliam, Earl
Harewood, Earl of
Mexborough, Earl of
Rosse, Earl of
Scarborough, Earl of
Zetland, Earl of
Downe, Viscount
Falkland, Viscount
Halifax, Viscount
Ripon, Bishop of
Beaumont, Lord
Bolton, Lord
Conyers, Lord
De l'Isle and Dudley, Lord
Feversham, Lord
Grantley, Lord
Hawke, Lord
Herries of Terregles, Lord
Hotham, Lord
Howden, Lord
Londesborough, Lord
Macdonald, Lord
Middleton, Lord
Muncaster, Lord
Ribblesdale, Lord
Stourton, Lord
Teignmouth, Lord
Wenlock, Lord
Wharncliffe, Lord
Armytage, Sir G., Bart.
Beckett, Sir T., Bart.
Boynton, Sir H., Bart.
Cayley, Sir D., Bart.
Chaytor, Sir W. R. C., Bart.
Cholmley, Sir G., Bart.
Constable, Sir T. A., Clifford-, Bart.
Cooke, Sir W. R. C., Bart.
Copley, Sir J. W., Bart.
Crossley, Sir Francis, Bart.
Denys, Sir G. W., Bart.
Dodsworth, Sir C. E., Bart.
Edwards, Sir H., Bart.

Gallwey, Sir W. P., Bart.
Graham, Sir R. H., Bart.
Ingilby, Sir H. J., Bart.
Johnstone, Sir J. V. B., Bart.
Lawson, Sir J., Bart.
Legard, Sir C., Bart.
Lister-Kaye, Sir J. L., Bart.
Lowther, Sir J. H., Bart.
Milbanke-Huskisson, Sir J. R., Bart.
Milner, Sir W. M., Bart.
Pilkington, Sir L. M. S., Bart.
Radcliffe, Sir Joseph, Bart.
Ramsden, Sir J. W., Bart.
Rycroft, Sir N., Bart.
Slingsby, Sir C., Bart.
Sykes, Sir T., Bart.
Tempest, Sir C. R., Bart.
Tufton, Sir R., Bart.
Vavasour, Sir E., Bart.
Vavasour, Sir H. M., Bart.
Wombwell, Sir G. O., Bart.
Worsley, Sir Wm., Bart.
Addison, of Bolton House
Addison, of Manningham
Agar, of Brockfield
Akenhead, of Otterington Hall
Akroyd, of Bank Field
Alcock, of Aireville
Aldam, of Frickley Hall
Allott, of Hague Hall
Amcotts-Ingilby, of Broxholme
Armistead, of Roundhay
Armitage, of Birkby Grange
Armitage, of Milnsbridge House
Armstrong, of Holgate Lodge
Athorp, of Dinnington
Atkinson-Jowett, of Clock House
Audus, of Park House
Bagnall, of Sneaton Castle
Baines, of Bell Hall
Baines, of Headingley Lodge
Baker, of Adel Manor
Balme, of Cote Wall
Barnard, of Cave Castle
Barstow, of Garrow Hill
Barton, of Stapleton Park
Battye, of Skelton Hall and Crosland Manor
Bayley, of Castle Dyke
Beaumont, of Bretton Hall
Beaumont, of Darfield
Beaumont, of Whitley Beaumont
Beckett, of Kirkstall
Beecroft, of Kirkstall Abbey
Bell, of Thirsk Hall
Belt, of Bossall Hall
Bent, of Baildon House
Bentley, of Finningley Park and West House
Benyon, of Gledhow Lodge
Beresford-Peirse, of Bedale Hall
Beswick, of Gristhorpe
Bethell, of Rise and Watton Abbey
Beverly, of Scarborough
Bewicke, of Coulby Manor
Birkbeck, of Anley
Birkbeck, of Settle
Bolland, of Kirby Fleetham Hall
Bostile, of Ravenfield Park
Bower, of Broxholme
Bower, of Elmcrofts
Bower, of Firby Hall
Bower, of Welham
Briggs, of Birstwith Hall
Briggs, of Halifax
Brigham, of Higham
Broadley, of Kirk Ella

1085

Broadley-Harrison, of Welton
Broadrick, of Hamphall Stubbs
Brook, of Meltham Hall
Brooke, of Armitage Bridge
Brooke, of Gateforth House
Brooksbank, of Colton Lodge
Brooksbank, of Healough Hall
Brown, of Arncliffe Hall
Brown, of Endcliffe Hall
Brown, of Leeds
Brown, of Rossington
Brown, of Sedbury Park
Brown, of Woodthorpe Hall
Buck, of Denholme
Buckley, of Saddleworth
Burton, of Cherry Burton
Burton-Peters, of Hotham Hall
Busfield, of Upwood
Butler, of Burley
Cadman, of Underwood House and Mile-Hill House
Cadman, of Spring Bank House
Cadman, of Westbourne House
Calverley, of Oulton Hall
Carpenter, of Kiplin Park
Carrol, of Woodhouse and Tolston Lodge
Carter, of Theakstone Hall
Cator, of Wentbridge House
Cayley, of Wydale House
Chaloner, of Longhull Hall
Chambers, of Clough House
Chapman, of Charlecotes
Chapman, of Low Stakesby Hall
Chapman, of Whitby
Charlesworth, of Hatfield Hall and Chapelthorpe Hall
Chaytor, of Spennithorne
Childers, of Cantley Hall
Cholmeley, of Bradsby Hall
Christian, of Fysche Hall
Clapham, of Burley Grange
Clarke, of Knedlington Manor
Clarke-Thornhill, of Fixby Hall
Clough, of Clifton House and Newbald Hall
Colling, of Guisborough
Collins, of Foleyfote
Collins, of Kirkman Bank
Coltman, of Naburn Hall
Constable, of Otley Manor
Cooke, of Alverley Grange
Cooke, of Owston
Cooke-Yarborough, of Campsmount
Coore, of Scruton Hall
Coulthurst, of Gargrave
Cradock, of Hartforth
Crawhall, of Nun Monkton
Creyke, of Rawcliffe
Croft, of Aldborough Hall and Hutton Buscel
Croft, of Stillington Hall
Crompton, of Azerley Hall and Sion Hill
Crompton, of Carlton-in-Snaith
Crompton, of Wood End
Crompton-Stansfield, of Esholt Hall
Cropper, of Thornton Fields
Crosland, of Gledholt
Crossley, of Manor Heath
Dalton, of Sleningford Park
Darley, of Aldby Park and Spaunton Lodge
Darley, of Burton Field
Darling-Barker, of Linthorpe
Darwin, of Kirskill Hall
Davenport, late of Monks Hill

Davison-Bland, of Kippax Park
Dawnay, of Beningbrough Hall
Dawson, of Marshfield and Langcliffe Hall
Dawson, of Osgodby Hall
Dawson, of Royds Hall and Weston House
Dawson-Duffield, of Coverham
Denison, of Grimthorpe
Denison, of Meanwood Park
Dent, of Ribston Hall
Dixon, of Heaton Royds
Dixon, of Page Hall
Dixon, of Pledwick House
Dodsworth, of Thornton Watlass
Drax, of Ellerton Abbey
Duesbury, of Beverley and Gransmoor Lodge
Dugdale, of Crathorne
Duncombe, of Kilnwick Percy and Sutton Hall
Duncombe, of Westerdale
Dunn, of Allerton Hall
Dyneley, of Bramhope Manor
Eastwood, of Eastwood and Stony Royd
Eckersley, of Carlton
Edwards, of Fixby Hall
Egremont, of Reedness
Ellis, of Highfield House
Elmhirst, of Elm House
Elmhirst, of Ouslethwaite Hall
Elmhirst, of Elmhirst
Elmsall, of Woodlands
Elsley, of Mill Mount and Patrick Brompton
Elwon, of Cleveland House
Estcourt, of Darrington Hall
Fairbairn, of Woodsley House
Fairfax, of Gilling Castle
Fairfax, of Newton Kyme
Farrer, of Green Hammerton Hall
Farror, of Ingleborough
Farsyde, of Fylingdales
Fawcett, of Broadfield
Fawkes, of Farnley Hall
Fenton, of Underbank Hall
Ferrand, of St. Ives and Harden Grange
Foljambe, of Acomb
Forster, of Warfeside
Foster, of Northowram Hall
Foster, of Lawkland Hall
Foster, of Wadsworth Banks
Foster, of Heptonstall Slack
Frank, of Campsall
Fullerton, of Thrybergh Park
Gale, of Hawxwell Hall
Gardner, of Skelton
Garland, of Netherwood Hall
Gascoigne, of Parlington Park
Gaskell, of Lupsett Hall
Gaskell, of Thornes House
Geldart, of Kirk-Deighton
Gibbs, of The Yews
Gott, of Wether and Armley House
Graburn, of Tickton Grange
Greaves, of Thurgoland
Greenwood, of Dewsbury Moor
Greenwood, of Swarcliffe Hall
Grimston, of Etton House
Grimston, of Grimston Garth
Grimston, of Neswick
Gunter, of Wetherby Grange
Hatfeuden, of Waplington Manor
Hague, of Drighlington
Hague, of The Crow Nest

Hailstone, of Horton Hall
Hall, of Scorborough Hall
Hall, of Woolfreton House
Hamerton, of Hellifield Peel
Hanson, late of Osmanthorpe
Harcourt, of Swinton Park
Hardy, of Odsall House
Harpin, of Birks House
Harris, of Heaton Hall
Harrison, of Benningholme Hall
Harrison, of Brandesburton Hall
Harrison, of Devonshire House
Harrison, of Sinderby
Harvey, of Finningley Hall
Hatfield, of Skellow Grange
Haworth, of Fort Hall
Haworth, of Hull-Bank House
Haynes, of Thimbleby Lodge
Hemsworth, of Monk Fryston Hall
Hepworth, of Ackworth Lodge
Heywood, of Aketon
Hildyard, of Hutton Bonville
Hildyard, of Winestead Hall
Hill, of Thornton Dale
Hinchliffe, of Stoodley Lodge
Hincks, of Breckenbrough
Hodgson, of Highthorne
Hodgson, of Snydale Hall
Holden, of Oakworth House
Holdforth, of Caley Hall
Holdsworth, of Sandal Hall
Hollings, of Wheatley Hall
Holme, of Paull Holme
Hood, of Pepper Hall
Hopwood, of Bracewell
Horsfall, of Calverley Hall
Horsfall, of Hawksworth
Horsfall, of Hornby Grange
Howton, of Howroyde
Hounsfield, of High Hazles
Hoyle, of Ferham House and Hooton Levet Hall
Hubback, of Smeaton
Hudson, late of Newby Park
Hudson, of Bessingby Hall
Hudson, of Rudd Hall
Hustler, of Acklam Hall
Hutchinson, of Brotton
Hutchinson, of Startforth
Hutton, of Aldborough Hall and Marske
Hutton, of Sowber
Ingham, of Blake Hall
Ingham, of Marton House
Jackson, of Normanby Hall
Jaques, of Easby Abbey
Jeffcock, of High Hazles
Johnstone-Scott, of Wood Hall
Jones, of Badsworth Hall
Kay, of Farfield Hall
Kearsley, of Highfield
Kettlewell, of Armley
Lane-Fox, of Bramham Park
Lane-Fox, of Bran House
Langdale, of Houghton Park
Lascelles, of Sion Hill
Lawley, of Hutton Hall
Lawson, of Aldborough Manor
Leatham, of Whitley Park
Leatham, of Hemsworth Hall
Leather, of Leventhorpe Hall
Lee, of Grove Hall
Lee-Mainwaring, of Knutsborough Abbey
Lees, of Delph Lodge
Lister, of Barnsby Hall
Lister, of Manningham Hall

Lister, of Ousefleet Grange
Lister, of Shibden Hall
Littledale, late of Bolton Hall
Lloyd, of Cowesby Hall
Lloyd, of Sewerby House
Lockley, of Baildon Lodge
Lonsdale, of Thorleby House
Lowther, of Bawtry Hall
Maister, of Skeffling
Manley, of Caley Hall
Markham, of Becca Hall
Marshall, of Cookridge Hall
Marshall, of Headingley House
Marshall, of Heslerton Hall
Marshall, of Weetwood Hall
Marten, of Beverley
Martin-Edmunds, of Worsborough
Marwood, of Busby Hall
Maude, of Knowsthorpe House
Maynard, of Harlsey Hall
Medhurst, of Kippax Hall
Meynell, of The Fryerage and Kilvington Hall
Meynell-Ingram, of Temple Newsome
Michell, of Forcett Park
Micklethwait, of Ardsley
Micklethwait, of Thornhill Hall
Middleton, late of Linton Spring
Middleton, of Stockeld Park and Myddelton Lodge
Milbank, of Thorp Perrow and Barningham Park
Milbank, of Newsham
Miles, of Firbeck Hall
Miller, of Wadsley House
Milligan, of Acacia House
Milner, of Aldwarke Hall
Mitford, of Hunmanby Hall
Monson, of Kirby-under-Dale
Montagu, of Melton Park
Moorhouse, of Carr House
Morley, of Marrick Park
Morrison, of Malham Tarn
Morritt, of Rokeby Park
Murgatroyd, of Bankfield
Nevile, of Skelbrooke Park
Newcomen, of Kirkleatham Hall
Nicholson, of Roundhay Park
Norcliffe, of Langton Hall
Norton, of Kettlethorpe Hall
Norton, of Nortonthorpe Hall
Oakley, of Oswaldkirk Hall
O'Callaghan, of Cookridge Hall
Onslow, of Risby Park
O'Reilly, of Scarborough
Overend, of Sharrow Head
Oxley, of Ripon
Paget, of Welton
Paley, of Bishopton Grange
Paley, of Langcliffe
Palmes, of Naburn Hall
Parker, of Browsholme Hall
Parker, of Barrington Hall
Parker, of Street-thorpe
Parker-Toulson, of Skipwith
Pease, of Hesslewood
Pease, of Hutton Low Cross
Peel, of Ackworth Park
Peel, of Knowlmere Manor
Pennyman, of Ormesby Hall
Pilkington, of Park-Lane Hall
Pilkington, of Swinethorpe Hall
Pollard, of Boston Spa
Pollard, of Crow Trees
Pollard, of Scarr Hill
Pollard, of Flannery Hall and Handsbill Hall

Powell, of Horton Hall
Powell, of Sharrow Lodge
Powlett, of Thorney Hall
Preston, of Askham Bryan
Preston, of Flasby Hall
Preston, of Moreby Hall
Prickett, of Boreas Hill
Prickett, of Bridlington
Priestley, of Boston House
Prothero, of Hooton Roberts
Pulleine, of Clifton Castle
Raikes, of East-Dale House
Raines, of Wyton Hall
Ramsden, of Oxton Hall
Rand, of Baildon
Rand, of Wheatley Hill
Rawson, of Haughend and Mill House
Rawson, of Nidd Hall
Read, of Hayton
Reynard, of Sunderlandwick and Hobgreen
Rhodes, of Bramhope Hall
Rhodes, of Carlton
Richardson, of Field House
Richardson, of St. Hilda's
Richardson-Wormley, of Ricall Hall
Riddell, of Bootham House
Ripley, of Lightcliffe
Rivis, of Newstead House
Robson, of Holtby House
Roper, of Sudbury Park
Rothery, of Littlethorpe House
Roundell, of Gledstone
Roxby, of Blackwood
Russell, of Newtown House
Russell, of Thirkelby Park
Rutson, of Newby Wiske
Sagar-Musgrave, of Sandford House
St. Leger, of Park Hill
St. Quintin, of Scampston Hall
Salt, of Saltaire and Crow Nest
Saltmarshe, of Saltmarshe
Scott, of Wood Hall
Scrope, of Danby Park
Selwyn, of Bierley Hall
Serjeantson, of Hanlith Hall and Camp Hill
Shaw, of Woodfield House
Shawe, of Brantingham
Sheepshanks, of Rawdon Hill
Sherwood, of Rysome Garth
Simpson, of Castle Lodge
Simpson, of Foston Hall
Smith, of Ferriby
Smyth, of Heath Hall
Smyth, of Royds Hall
Smythe, of Linton Spring
Sowerby, of Dalton Hall
Spencer-Stanhope, of Cannon Hall and Horsforth Hall
Spofforth, of East Thorpe
Stainforthe, of Barton-le-Street
Stanhope-Stott, of Eccleshill Hall
Stansfeld, of Field House
Stansfeld, of Flockton Manor
Stansfeld, of Moorlands
Stansfeld, of Settle
Stansfeld, of Weetwood Grove
Stapleton, of The Grove
Stapylton, of Myton Hall
Starkey, of Spring Lodge
Staveley, of Old Sleningford
Stephens of Foston Hall
Stourton, of Holme Hall
Sutcliffe, of Lee
Swainston-Strangewayes, of Alne Hall

Swale, of Ingfield
Swann, of Askham Richard
Swire, of Hartwith and Littlethorpe
Sykes, of Kirk Ella
Sykes, of West Ella
Talbot [now Carpenter], of Kiplin Park
Taylor, of Bashall Hall
Taylor, of Kirkham Abbey
Tempest, of Ackworth Grange
Tempest, of Broughton Hall
Tempest, of Tong Hall
Tennant, of Kildwick Hall
Tew, of Crofton Hall
Thellusson, of Brodsworth
Thompson, of Guiseley
Thompson, of Kirby Hall
Thompson, of Kirk Hammerton Hall and Barlow
Thompson, of Sheriff-Hutton Park
Tireman, of Lofthouse Hall
Topham, of Caldbergh
Topham, of Middleham Hall
Torre, of Snydale Hall
Tottie, of Coniston Hall
Turner, of Ferriby
Turton, of Upsall, Larpool Hall, and Ugthorpe Lodge
Van Straubenzee, of Spennithorne
Vernon-Wentworth, of Wentworth Castle
Vincent, of Boston Lodge
Vyner, of Newby Hall
Wainman, of Carr Head
Walker, of Bolling Hall
Walker, of Hawk Hills
Walker, of Sand Hutton
Walker, of The Woodlands
Walker, of Wilsick
Warde, of Hooton Pagnel
Waterhouse, of Hope Hall
Waterhouse, of Wellhead
Waterton, of Walton Hall
Watt, of Bishop Burton
Waud, of Manston Hall and Chester Court
Welch, of Cowton and Raskelfe
Wells, of Booth-Ferry House
Wentworth, of Woolley Park
Wharton, of Skelton Castle and Gilling Wood
Wheler, of Ledstone Hall
Whitacre, of Woodhouse
Whitaker, of Breckamore
White, of Upperwood House
Whitehead, of Rievall Hall
Whitehead, of Southside
Whittell, of Helmsley Lodge and Weston Hall
Whytehead, of Crayke
Wickham, of Low Moor Hall
Wilkinson, of Bilton Hall
Wilberde ... ... at a Grange
Wilkinson, of Ingmanthorpe Hall
Wilkinson, of Winterburne and Newall Hall
Wilson, of Roundhay
Wilson, of Brankcliffe Tower
Wilson, of Cliffe
Wilson, of Eshton Hall and Kildwick
Wilson, of Seacroft Hall
Wilson-Todd, of Tranby and Halnaby Hall
Windham, of Wayne
Winn, of Nostell Priory
Witham, of Lartington Hall
Wombwell, of Wandwell

1091

WS - #0038 - 250121 - C0 - 229/152/58 - PB - 9781527791848 - Gloss Lamination